DATE

**Time-Saver
Standards
for
Architectural
Design Data**

Other McGraw-Hill Handbooks of Interest

Time-Saver Standards for Architectural Design Data

JOHN HANCOCK CALLENDER
Editor-in-Chief

Sixth Edition

McGraw-Hill Book Company

New York   St. Louis   San Francisco   Auckland
Bogotá   Hamburg   Johannesburg   London
Madrid   Mexico   Montreal   New Delhi
Panama   Paris   São Paulo   Singapore
Sydney   Tokyo   Toronto

Library of Congress Cataloging in Publication Data
Main entry under title:

Time-saver standards for architectural design data.
Includes index.
1. Building—Handbooks, manuals, etc.
I. Callender, John Hancock.
TH151.T55   1982   721'.021   81–23612
                                        AACR2

ISBN 0-07-009663-5

234567890   KPKP   89876543

The editors for this book were Patricia Allen-Browne and
Ruth L. Weine and the production supervisor was Paul A. Malchow.
It was set in Technica by The Kingsport Press.

Printed and bound by The Kingsport Press.

Contents

Contents

Contributors

Ronald Allwork, AIA *Architect*

James Arkin, AIA *Consultant, Architectural Woodwork Institute*

Louis A. Bello *Vice President, Syska & Hennessy, Inc., Consulting Engineers*

William Blackwell *Architectural Consultant*

Byron C. Bloomfield, AIA *Executive Director, Modular Building Standards Association*

John Hancock Callender *Professor of Architecture, Pratt Institute*

L. T. Chandler *Architect*

Ray E. Cumrine, AIA *Ketchum and Sharp, Architects*

William Demarest *Director, Plastics in Building, Chemical Manufacturers Association*

Albert G. H. Dietz *Professor of Building Engineering, Department of Architecture, Massachusetts Institute of Technology*

Richard DiMonda *American Hospital Association*

Richard J. Genova *Principal, Severud-Perrone-Szegezdy-Sturm, Consulting Engineers*

Burdett Green *Executive Vice President, Fine Hardwoods Association*

Alfred Greenberg, P. E. *Environmental Consultant*

Bernard F. Greene *Lighting Consultant*

Noyce L. Griffin, E. E. *Division of Hospital and Medical Facilities, Public Health Service*

Rita Harrold *Director Design Lighting, Lamp Commercial Division, Westinghouse Electric Corporation*

Arthur Hockman *National Bureau of Standards, U.S. Department of Commerce*

Seymour Howard *Professor of Architecture, Pratt Institute*

George R. Jerus, P. E. *Vice President, Meyer, Strong and Jones, Mechanical and Electrical Engineers*

Rudard A. Jones, AIA *Small Homes Council, University of Illinois*

W. H. Kapple, AIA *Architectural Consultant*

E. S. Kopecki *Committee of Stainless Steel Producers, American Iron and Steel Institute*

Wayne F. Koppes, FAIA *Architectural Consultant*

Y. S. Lee *Professor of Structural Design, School of Architecture, Pratt Institute; Associate, Severud-Perrone-Szegezdy-Sturm, Consulting Engineers*

William J. LeMessurier, P. E. *Wm. LeMessurier Associates*

F. M. Lescher, AIA *Architectural Consultant*

Henry L. Logan *Vice President in Charge of Research, Holophane Company, Inc.*

Hendrik P. Maas, AIA *Architect*

Stanley McCandless *Professor of Lighting, Yale University; Research and Development, Century Lighting, Inc.*

William J. McGuinness *McGuinness and Duncan, Consulting Engineers*

M. B. Mantooth *Chief Electrical Engineer, Office of Architecture and Engineering, U.S. Public Health Service*

John G. Mascioni, P. E. *Associate Professor of Structural Design, School of Architecture, Pratt Institute*

William T. Meyer *Architect; Associate, Building Systems Development, San Francisco*

Hans J. Milton FRAIA, *Center for Building Technology, National Bureau of Standards*

Robert B. Newman *Bolt, Beranek and Newman, Consultants in Acoustics*

Aladar Olgyay *Architect*

Victor Olgyay *Research Associate and Associate Professor, Princeton University*

Philip P. Page, Jr. *Goldreich, Page & Thropp, Consulting Engineers*

Sterling M. Palm, AIA *Architect*

Robert Paul *Director of Engineering, Baylor University Medical Center*

Peter Paulus *Director, Research and Development, Standard Products Company*

Robert E. Rapp *Regional Engineer, American Institute of Steel Construction, Inc.*

Contributors

Albert R. Rienstra *Architectural Consultant*

Jack M. Roehm, P. E. *Director of Technical Services, Architectural Aluminum Manufacturers Association*

Daniel Schwartzman, FAIA *Architect*

Elwyn E. Seelye *Seelye, Stevenson, Value and Knecht, Consulting Engineers*

R. W. Sexton *Architectural Consultant*

Sydney M. Shelov, AIA *Professor, School of Architecture, Pratt Institute*

Laurance Shuman *Consulting Engineer*

Mel Sprinkle, P. E. *Sprinkle and Associates, Consulting Acoustical-Audio Engineers*

Jule Robert von Sternberg, AIA *Architect*

Syska & Hennessy, Inc. *Consulting Engineers*

Howard P. Vermilya, AIA *Architect*

Donald J. Vild, P. E.

Frederick F. Wangaard *Associate Professor of Forest Products, Yale University*

Gerald R. Weissman *Director, Coatings Department, Foster D. Snell, Inc.*

Organizations

Acoustical and Insulating Materials Association

Aluminum Association

American Concrete Institute (ACI)

American Gas Association (AGA)

American Hardboard Association

American Hospital Association

American Institute of Steel Construction, Inc. (AISC)

American Institute of Timber Construction

American Insurance Association

American Iron and Steel Institute (AISI)

American National Standards Institute (ANSI)

American Plywood Association

American Society of Architectural Hardware Consultants

American Society of Heating, Refrigerating and Air Conditioning Engineers (ASHRAE)

American Society of Mechanical Engineers (ASME)

American Society for Testing and Materials (ASTM)

Architectural Aluminum Manufacturers Association (AAMA)

Architectural Woodwork Institute (AWI)

Asphalt Roofing Manufacturers Association

Brick Institute of America

Builders Hardware Manufacturers Association (BHMA)

Building Research Advisory Board (BRAB)

Building Research Institute (BRI)

Civil Defense, U.S. Office of (OCD)

Construction Specifications Institute (CSI)

Contracting Plasterers' and Lathers' International Association

Copper Development Association (CDA)

Fine Hardwoods Association

Flat Glass Manufacturers Association (FGMA)

Forest Products Laboratory (FPL), U.S. Department of Agriculture

Gypsum Association

Hardwood Plywood Institute

Housing and Urban Development (HUD), U.S. Department of

Illuminating Engineering Society (IES)

Institute of Boiler and Radiator Manufacturers

Institute of Electrical and Electronics Engineers, Inc.

Insulation Board Institute

International Cut Stone Contractors and Quarrymen's Association

Maple Flooring Manufacturers Association

Chemical Manufacturers Association

Marble Institute of America, Inc.

National Association of Architectural Metal Manufacturers (NAAMM)

National Association of Store Fixture Manufacturers

National Bureau of Standards (NBS), U.S. Department of Commerce

National Concrete Masonry Association (NCMA)

National Electrical Manufacturers Association (NEMA)

National Fire Protection Association (NFPA)

National Forest Products Association

National Oak Flooring Manufacturers Association

National Paint, Varnish and Lacquer Association, Inc.

National Particle Board Association

Organizations

National Terrazzo and Mosaic Association, Inc.

National Warm Air Heating and Air Conditioning Association

National Woodwork Manufacturers Association (NWMA)

New York City Housing Authority

Porcelain Enamel Institute (PEI)

Portland Cement Association (PCA)

Precast Concrete Institute (PCI)

Public Health Service (PHS), U.S. Department of Health and Human Services

Sheet Metal Contractors' National Association

Steel Door Institute

Steel Joist Institute (SJI)

Steel Window Institute

Tile Council of America

Underwriters Laboratories (UL)

Vermiculite Institute

Wood and Synthetic Flooring Institute

Preface to the Sixth Edition

In preparing the sixth edition of "Time-Saver Standards" the editor faced the usual flood of revisions and updatings, but also a new problem—what to do about the metric system. In 1975 the federal government committed the United States to conversion to the metric system, but the conversion was made voluntary and no dates were mentioned. Compliance in general has been spotty and slow, especially in the building industry. The environmental control fields have moved toward metrication more swiftly than other parts of the industry. Most of these disciplines are either already fully metricated or are in the state of transition where the conventional units are followed by metric units in parentheses. On the other hand, the structural design field appears so far to be ignoring the whole subject.

The editor decided to follow the current practices in the building industry, making no effort to push ahead or to hold back the transition to metric. The proper function of "Time-Saver Standards" has always been to supply building designers with useful and needed information. It seems inevitable that before the next edition of TSS can be prepared, the use of metric will have greatly increased and the need for metric conversion assistance will be recognized. We have therefore added a whole new section to the sixth edition devoted entirely to this subject. This new section, Part 5, contains the authoritative standard ANSI/ASTM E 621-78, "Metric (SI) Units in Building Design and Construction," which is followed by nine pages of conversion factors and, most useful of all, thirty-seven pages of conversion tables. The editor believes that this section will be invaluable to building designers in the coming years.

It should be noted that the metric system here referred to is not the one that most of us learned, to some extent, some time ago. The modern metric system, known universally as SI (Système International), differs in many respects from the old metric system—some familiar terms have been eliminated and many strange new terms have appeared. The editor recommends careful study of the opening pages of Part 5 to all readers, whether or not they have any immediate need to use metric.

JOHN HANCOCK CALLENDER

Preface to the Fifth Edition

Now and again we hear it said that building has not changed significantly since the age of the pyramids. Anyone who subscribes to this view should be given the task of trying to keep "Time-Saver Standards" up to date. Society's needs and aspirations are constantly changing, making new demands on buildings; functional requirements change and new building types appear; building materials proliferate and new building techniques come into use, without displacing the old. The result is a constant increase in the amount of technical data needed by building designers.

Since the fourth edition, with its 1300 pages, was already cumbersome to use, it was apparent that the considerably enlarged fifth edition would have to be published in two volumes. The division was made not arbitrarily but along a natural cleavage line. The material in the fourth edition concerning building types was removed and made the nucleus of a new book called "Time-Saver Standards for Building Types." The remaining material, expanded as necessary, is the present volume, now titled "Time-Saver Standards for Architectural Design Data," fifth edition. Thus there are now two TSS books which are closely related but are, in fact, separate and independent books.

It is my hope that this new edition of TSS and its companion volume will prove to be of even greater service to building designers than its predecessors have been.

JOHN HANCOCK CALLENDER

Preface to the Fourth Edition

"Time-Saver Standards" began in the pages of the *American Architect* in the middle 1930s. When that magazine was later merged with the *Architectural Record,* "Time-Saver Standards" was continued and soon became one of the most useful and popular features of the *Record.* In 1946 the TSS sheets which had been published up to that time were first issued in book form. In 1950 and again in 1954 the book was reissued with the addition of the pages which had been published in the *Record* since the previous edition.

This fourth edition of "Time-Saver Standards" has been completely revised and greatly expanded. Not only have the TSS sheets published in the *Architectural Record* since 1954 been included but also a great deal of material never previously published. Many obsolete pages from the earlier editions have been eliminated and most of the other pages have been revised and updated.

"Time-Saver Standards" is intended primarily to meet the needs of those who design buildings. It will also be found to be almost equally useful to draftsmen, contractors, superintendents, maintenance engineers, and students—to all, in fact, who design, construct, or maintain buildings.

The editor takes this opportunity to thank the scores of specialists, many of them recognized authorities in their fields, who have contributed their expertise to this edition of "Time-Saver Standards."

JOHN HANCOCK CALLENDER

1

Basic Data

Although no standards have been established for the drawing scales used on building plans that employ customary units of measurement (feet and inches), long practice has resulted in a considerable degree of standardization. Two series of scales are in general use:

1. "Architectural scale," expressed in inches or fractions of an inch which equal one foot (e.g., ¼ in. = 1 ft).
2. "Engineers' scale," expressed in inches equal to decimal multiples of feet (e.g., 1 in. = 40 ft).

Metric scales are expressed in ratios of the size of the drawn object to that of the actual object (e.g., 1:50, where 1 meter on the drawing represents 50 meters in the building). To assist in the transition to metric scales, Table 1 shows the customary foot-inch scales with their corresponding ratios and their usual applications.

DRAWING SCALES FOR METRIC BUILDINGS

A standard has been established for the use of drawing scales for metric buildings: ASTM E 713-80 "Scales for Metric Building Drawings." The recommended scales are based on the numbers 1, 2, and 5 (e.g., 1:10, 1:20, 1:50, 1:100, 1:200, etc.). This results in a reduction in the number of scales used in the traditional system (from 18 to 10) and should result in a saving in drafting time. It should be noted that many of the preferred metric scales differ only marginally (by 4 per cent) from traditional foot-inch ratios, so that the visual appreciation of the drawings is not altered drastically.

The following is from ASTM Standard E 713-80:

1. Scope

This standard specifies recommended scales for architectural, building product, and building drawings using metric (SI) units of measurement, and measured with scale instruments graduated in millimeters. Preferred scales are listed for various types of drawings.

2. Presentation of scales

General—A scale should be stated on every drawing. The scale may be indicated as a ratio prefixed by the word "scale," for example, "SCALE 1:100." Alternatively, a graphic (drawn) scale may be shown as a reference scale.

Single Scale—Where only one scale is used on a drawing sheet, the scale should preferably be indicated in or near the title block.

Multiple Scales—Where two or more scales are used on the same drawing sheet in order to provide different levels of detail, each scale should be clearly indicated, preferably below each particular title. A notation "SCALES AS SHOWN" should also be indicated in or near the title block.

Scale Enlargement or Reduction—Where it is likely that a drawing may be reproduced at a reproduction ratio other than the scale shown, it is recommended that a graphic (drawn) reference scale (as shown in Fig. 1) be added to provide a visual indication of the amount of enlargement or reduction. It is also recommended that prints enlarged or reduced in size be stamped to indicate that they are no longer to scale, for example, "REPRODUCTION NOT TO SCALE RATIOS SHOWN."

Dimensions Not to Scale—Where it is necessary to indicate that a dimension on a scale drawing is not to scale, the abbreviation "NTS" (not to scale) should be added.

3. Choice of Scale

Careful consideration should be given to the choice of suitable scales in metric building drawings. The following factors influence that choice:

The need to communicate both accurately and adequately the information necessary to carry out the intentions of the design,

The need to achieve economy of effort and time in the preparation and interpretation of drawings,

The character and size of the drawn subject (for example, house plans are generally drawn to a larger scale than plans for commercial buildings),

The desirability of keeping the drawing sheets for a project to one size, and

The characteristics and capabilities of reproductive and microfilming facilities used.

4. Scale Ratios

Scales for use with metric (SI) drawings are expressed as ratios only.

A scale of 1:100, for example, indicates that every dimension on the drawing is 100 times as large in production or construction; 1 mm on the drawing represents 100 mm, 10 mm represents 1000 mm (1 m), etc.

Table 1. Customary (foot-inch) scales, corresponding ratios, and usual applications

Scale	Ratio	Application
Full size	1:1	Details
Half size	1:2	Details
3″ = 1'-0″	1:4	Details
2″ = 1'-0″	1:6	Details
1½″ = 1'-0″	1:8	Details
1″ = 1'-0″	1:12	Details
¾″ = 1'-0″	1:16	Details
½″ = 1'-0″	1:24	Details
⅜″ = 1'-0″	1:32	Details
¼″ = 1'-0″	1:48	Plans, elevations, sections
⅛″ = 1'-0″	1:96	Plans, elevations, sections
¹⁄₁₆″ = 1'0″	1:192	Plans, elevations, plot plans
¹⁄₃₂″ = 1'0″	1:384	Site plans
1″ = 40'	1:480	Site plans
1″ = 50'	1:600	Site plans
1″ = 80'	1:960	Site plans block plans
1″ = 100'	1:1200	Site plans block plans
1″ = 160'	1:1920	Block plans
1″ = 200'	1:2400	Block plans

Adapted from a paper by Hans J. Milton, Center for Building Technology, National Bureau of Standards.

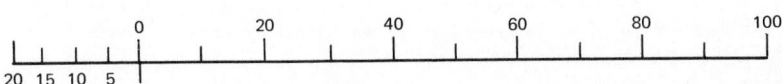

Fig. 1. Example of a graphic (drawn) reference scale for drawings likely to be reproduced at a different scale ratio

Table 2. Preferred Scales Recommended for use with Different Types of Metric Building Drawings

Phase	Type of drawing	Scale ratio	Remarks
Preliminary design	Sketch and preliminary drawings	——	Scales will vary, but it is recommended that preference be given to scale ratios used at the working drawing stage.
	Area location plan	——	Scales will vary according to reference maps used.
	Block (Locality) plan	1:2000 1:1000	
Working drawings	Site plans	1:1000 1:500 1:200	Use larger scales where details of services are to be shown on site plans.
	General location drawings (Plans, sections, elevations)	1:200 1:100 1:50	
	Component drawings (component schedules)	1:100 1:50 1:20	1:50 is the preferred ratio for schedules.
	Assembly (manufacturing) drawings	1:20 1:10 1:5	
	Component detail drawings	1:10 1:5 1:1	The scale of 1:2 has been deleted from the series because it is seldom used.

5. Drawing Types

For the purpose of classifying suitable scale ratios, the following drawing types are identified:

Area Location Plan, showing the general geographic location of a project.

Block (Locality) Plan, locating the site within the surrounding district.

Site Plans, locating the building and site works in relation to the site. On larger scale site plans (for example, 1:200) service networks may also be shown.

General Location Drawings, showing plans, sections, and elevations of the building or major building parts with an indication of the key reference dimensions for setting out, locating of rooms and spaces, and positioning of assemblies.

Component Drawings, also applicable to schedules, showing the range of specific components or assemblies to be used in a project, or the detailed location of components or assemblies in complex situations.

Assembly (Manufacturing) Drawings, providing information on components or assemblies, for shop manufacture.

Component Detail Drawings, showing the interface of two or more components or assemblies for construction purposes, or providing precise information on com- ponents and assemblies for shop manufacture.

6. Preferred Scales

The preferred scales recommended for various drawing types are shown in Table 2.

If a larger or smaller scale is needed for applications not listed in Table 2, the recommended range may be extended in either direction by the use of ratios in which the denominator or numerator is a product of the numbers 1, 2, or 5, and a power of 10 (1×10^n; 2×10^n; and; 5×10^n), for example, 1:10 000, 1:20 000, and 1:50 000.

7. Exaggerated Scales

In some applications, such as section drawings of drains, sewers, earthworks, or steelwork, it is desirable to use different scales for the horizontal and the vertical plane to facilitate the interpretation of drawings. In general, this involves the use of an exaggerated vertical scale to show the difference in levels or details.

Where exaggerated scales are used, both scale factors should be shown below each particular title or adjacent to the drawing, for example, "HORIZONTAL SCALE 1:100, VERTICAL SCALE 1:20."

8. Grid Paper

With the application of reference grids, such as in metric dimensional (modular) coordination based on the 100-mm module, the use of preprinted grid drawing paper is an obvious aid to drafting and provides an inbuilt reference scale during the drafting process.

Where grids are used, it is recommended that grid intervals of 10 mm, 5 mm, or 2 mm be chosen to complement the preferred scales indicated in Table 2.

A direct representation of the 100-mm basic module is achieved by the following combinations of grid paper and scale ratios:

10-mm grid—modular at a scale ratio of 1:10

5-mm grid—modular at a scale ratio of 1:20

2-mm grid—modular at a scale ratio of 1:50

Grids should preferably be printed in a nonreproducing type of ink.

9. Metric Drafting Scales

Metric scale instruments for use in drafting (hand scales or machine scales) will be the subject of separate standards.

The information on this page is from ANSI Y14.1-1975, "Drawing Sheet Size and Format," reproduced with the permission of the publisher, the American Society of Mechanical Engineers. The standard covers engineering drawings only and does not apply to architectural and building drawings.

Standard sheet and margin sizes are shown in Table 1. For comparison, international (ISO) sheet sizes which are close to U.S. sizes are shown in Table 2. With the margins shown in Table 1 the net drawing sizes are well within international sheet sizes; thus reproductions, whether by contact printing or microfilm projection, can be made on either standard size sheet.

The title block should be located in the lower right corner of the drawing. Title block sizes and layouts are shown in Fig. 1. Content of the title block is as follows:

A. Name and address of the company or design activity whose FSCM (code identification) number and drawing number appear in those blocks.

B. Drawing title.

C. Drawing number. Revision block optional.

D. Information relative to the preparation of the drawing, such as name and dates of drafter, checker, approving official, issue date, and contract number.

E. and F. Approval by authorities where different from the source preparing

Table 1. Standard drawing sheet sizes

Note: All dimensions are in inches. 1 in. = 25.4 mm

	Flat Sizes[1]					Roll Sizes[2]				
Size Designation	Width (Vertical)	Length (Horizontal)	Margin		Size Designation	Width (Vertical)	Length (Horizontal)		Margin[3]	
			Horizontal	Vertical			Min	Max	Horizontal	Vertical
A (Horiz)	8.5	11.0	0.38	0.25	G	11.0	22.5	90.0	0.38	0.50
A (Vert)	11.0	8.5	0.25	0.38	H	28.0	44.0	143.0	0.50	0.50
B	11.0	17.0	0.38	0.62	J	34.0	55.0	176.0	0.50	0.50
C	17.0	22.0	0.75	0.50	K	40.0	55.0	143.0	0.50	0.50
D	22.0	34.0	0.50	1.00						
E	34.0	44.0	1.00	0.50						
F	28.0	40.0	0.50	0.50						

Table 2. International and U.S. drawing size comparison

International Designation	Width		Length		Nearest USA Size	
	Millimeter	Inch	Millimeter	Inch	Letter	Inch
A0	841	33.11	1189	46.81	E	34.0 x 44.0
A1	594	23.39	841	33.11	D	22.0 x 34.0
A2	420	16.54	594	23.39	C	17.0 x 22.0
A3	297	11.69	420	16.54	B	11.0 x 17.0
A4	210	8.27	297	11.69	A	8.5 x 11.0

the drawing. Where not required for this purpose these blocks may be absorbed into block 4 or used for other purposes.

G. Predominant scale of the drawing.

H. FSCM code identification number.

J. Letter designation of drawing size.

K. Weight of the item, where required.

L. Sheet number.

Revision block should be located in the upper right corner of the drawing and extended downward as required. Revision block sizes and layouts are shown in Fig. 2.

Parts or materials list should be located at the lower right corner of the drawing just above the title block. No standard sizes have been established.

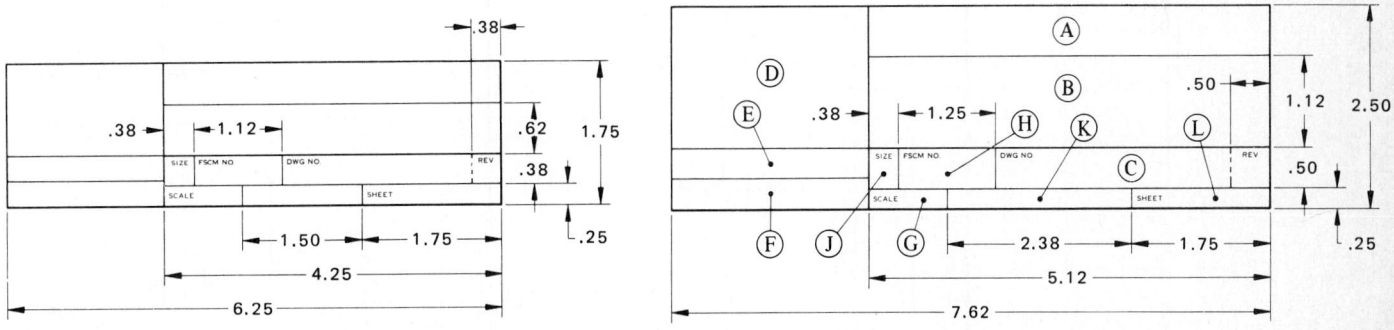

NOTE: All dimensions are in inches. 1 inch = 25.4 mm.

Fig. 1a. Title block for sheet sizes A, B, C, and G

Fig. 1b. Title block for sheet sizes D, E, F, H, J, and K

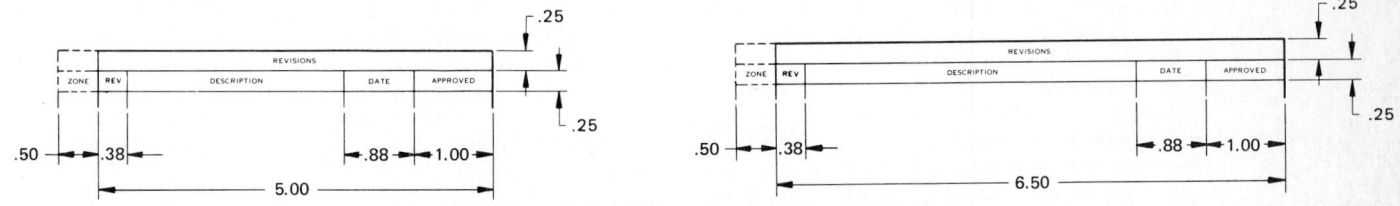

NOTE: All dimensions are in inches. 1 inch = 25.4 mm.

Fig. 2a. Revision block for sheet sizes A, B, C, and G

Fig. 2b. Revision block for sheet sizes D, E, F, H, J, and K

From ANSI Y14.2M-1979, "Line Conventions and Lettering," with the permission of the publisher, the American Society of Mechanical Engineers.

Note: This standard covers engineering drawings only. It does not pertain to architectural or building drawings. This standard includes the recognition of the requirements for photographic reduction and reproduction, incuding microfilm, as well as the conventional methods of reproduction.

Line Widths

Two widths of lines are recommended for use on drawings as shown in Fig. 1. There should be a distinct contrast between the two widths of lines. The ratios of line thicknesses should be approximately two-to-one. Thick-line widths of approximately 0.7 mm or 0.032 inch and thin-line widths of 0.35 mm or 0.016 inch are recommended. The actual width of each line is governed by the size and style of the drawing, and the smallest size to which it is to be reduced. All lines of the same type should be uniform throughout the drawing. Lines should be clean-cut, opaque, uniform, and properly spaced for legible reproduction by all commonly used methods, including microfilm. Spacing between parallel lines of no less than 1.5 mm (0.06 in) normally meets reproduction requirements

Lettering

Lettering on drawings must be legible and suitable for easy and rapid execution. These requirements are met in the recommended single-stroke gothic characters shown in Fig. 2. Opaque and well spaced lettering is required for microfilm-reproduction. Either vertical or inclined lettering is permissible, but the same style of lettering should be used throughout a drawing. The preferred slope for inclined letters is 2 in 5 or approximately 68 degrees with the horizontal. Upper-case letters should be used for all lettering on drawings unless lower-case letters are required to conform with other established standards, equipment nomenclature, or marking.

Letters in words should be spaced so that the background areas between the letters are approximately equal, and words are to be clearly separated by a space equal to the height of the lettering. For legible reproduction a space between letters of at least 1.5mm (0.06 in) is recommended. The space between two numerals having a decimal point between them is to be a minimum of two thirds the height of the lettering. Sentences should be separated horizontally by a space equal to twice the height of the lettering. The vertical space between lines of lettering should be no more than the height of the lettering, and no less than half the height of the lettering.

Notes should be placed horizontally on drawings and separated vertically by spaces at least equal to double the height of the character size used, to maintain the identity of each note.

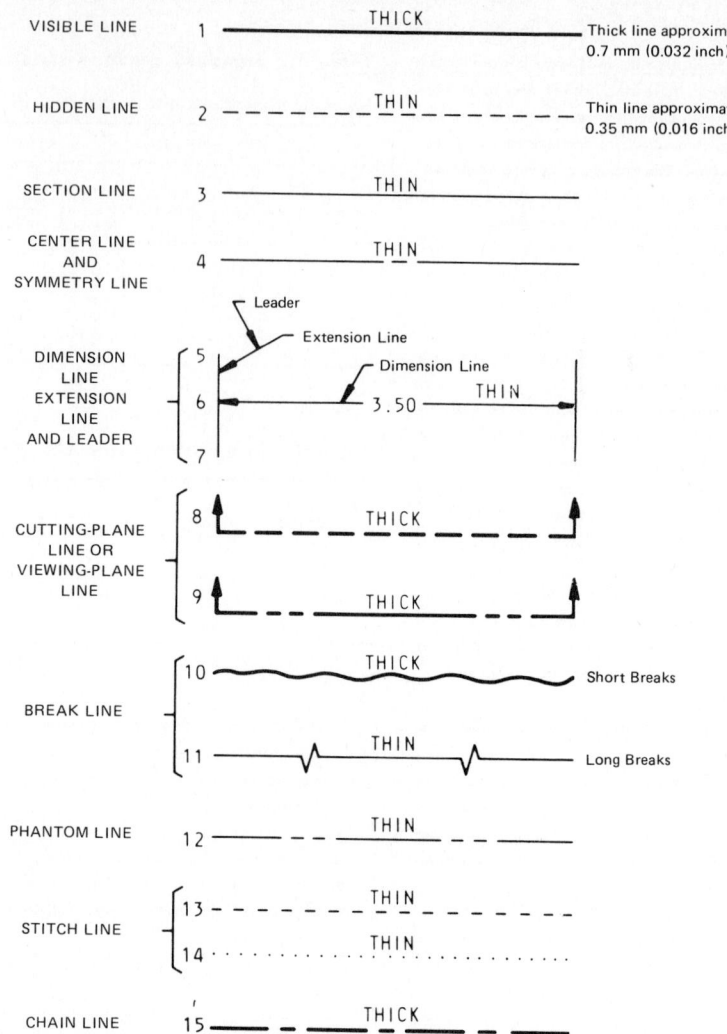

The metric line widths agree with ISO/DIS/128 (June 1977) and are not a soft metric conversion of the inch value.

These approximate line widths are intended to differentiate between THICK and THIN lines and are not values for control of acceptance or rejection of the drawings.

Fig. 1. Width and type of lines

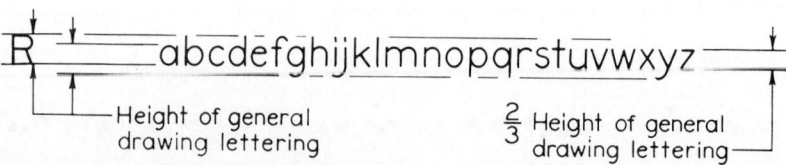

Fig. 2. Vertical single-stroke gothic lettering

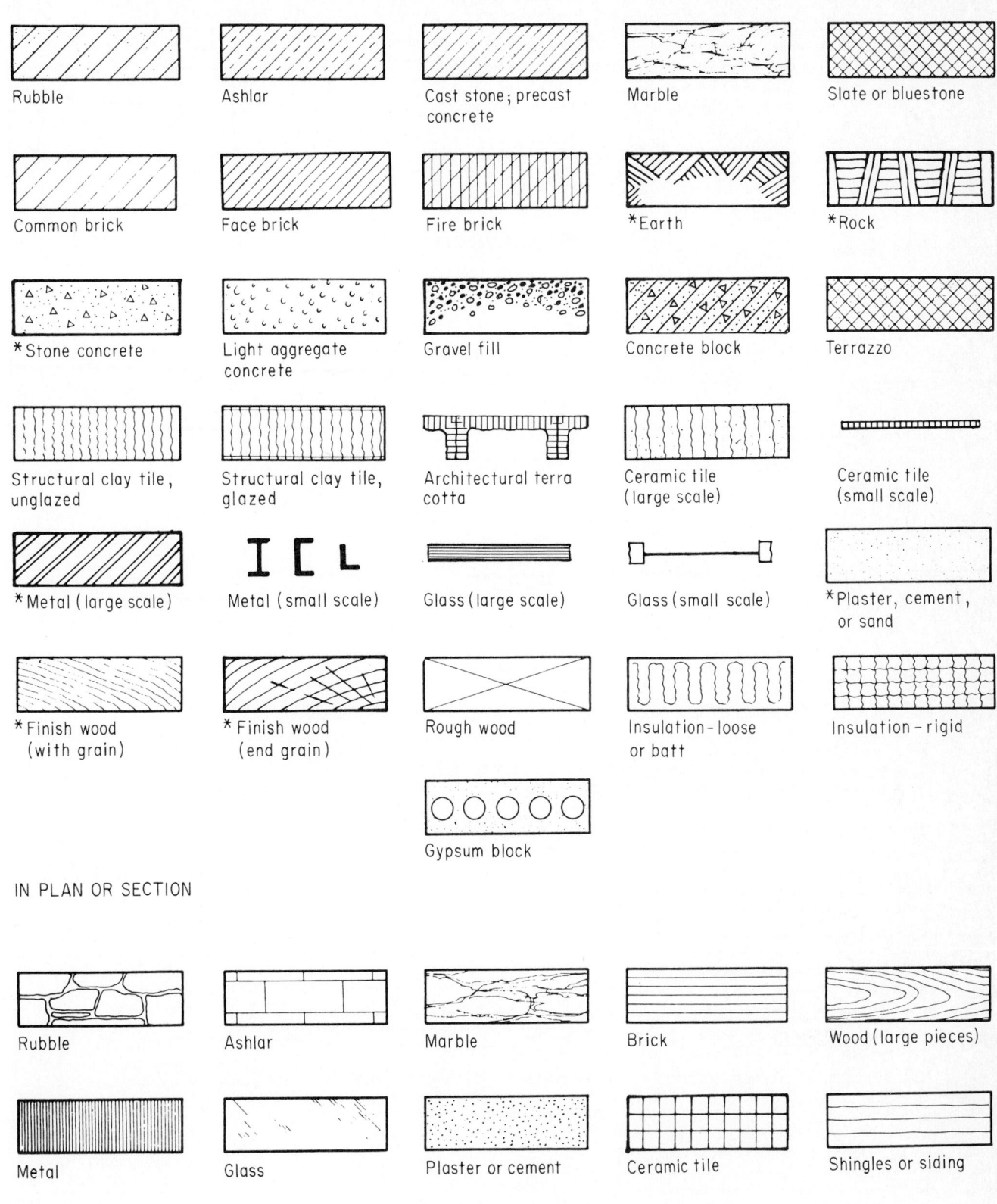

IN PLAN OR SECTION

IN ELEVATION

GRAPHIC SYMBOLS

Graphic symbols shown above are for use on drawings in plan or section and in elevation. Symbols marked with an asterisk are American National Standards (ANSI Y14.2M-1979). All others are recommended symbols that should be incorporated in a legend on each drawing when applicable. Specific kinds of metal, stone, and the like should not be indicated since they are the province of the specification.

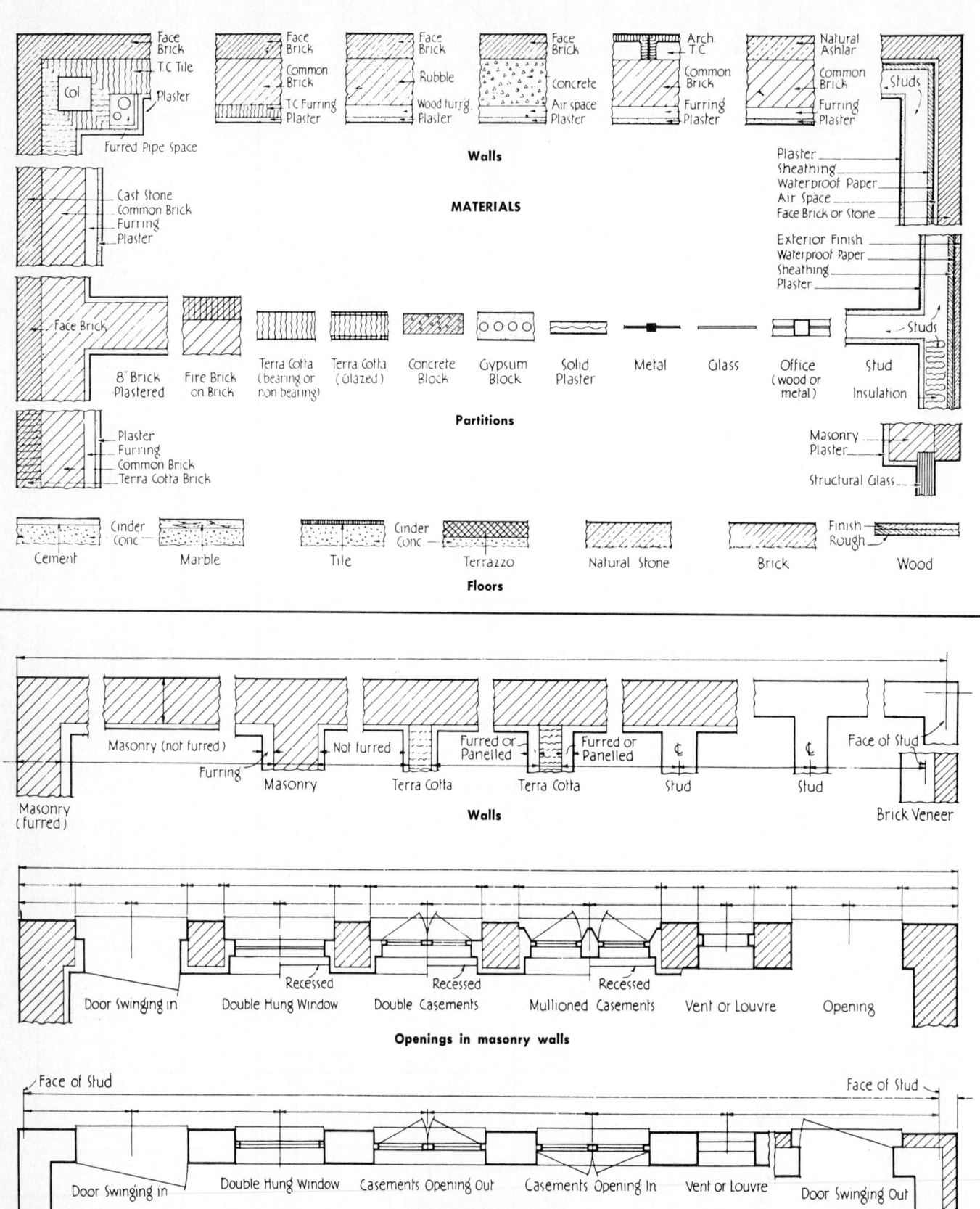

Walls

MATERIALS

Partitions

Floors

Walls

Openings in masonry walls

Openings in frame walls

DIMENSIONS

Graphic symbols shown on this and the following four pages have been extracted from American National Standards Z32.2.3–1949 (reaffirmed 1953), Z32.2.4–1949 (reaffirmed 1953), and Y32.4–1955, with the permission of the publisher, The American Society of Mechanical Engineers. Designations of the relevant publications are also given at the bottom of each page.

AIR CONDITIONING

Brine Return

Brine Supply

Circulating Chilled or Hot-Water Flow

Circulating Chilled or Hot-Water Return

Condenser Water Flow

Condenser Water Return

Drain

Humidification Line

Make-Up Water

Refrigerant Discharge

Refrigerant Liquid

Refrigerant Suction

HEATING

Air-Relief Line

Boiler Blow Off

Compressed Air

Condensate or Vacuum Pump Discharge

Feedwater Pump Discharge

Fuel-Oil Flow

Fuel-Oil Return

Fuel-Oil Tank Vent

High-Pressure Return

High-Pressure Steam

Hot-Water Heating Return

Hot-Water Heating Supply

Low-Pressure Return

Low-Pressure Steam

Make-Up Water

Medium-Pressure Return

Medium-Pressure Steam

PLUMBING

Acid Waste

Cold Water

Compressed Air

Drinking-Water Flow

Drinking-Water Return

Fire Line

Gas

Hot Water

Hot-Water Return

Soil, Waste or Leader (Above Grade)

Soil, Waste or Leader (Below Grade)

Vacuum Cleaning

Vent

PNEUMATIC TUBES

Tube Runs

SPRINKLERS

Branch and Head

Drain

Main Supplies

Air Eliminator		Access Door		
Anchor		Adjustable Blank Off		
Expansion Joint		Adjustable Plaque		
Hanger or Support				
Heat Exchanger		Automatic Dampers		
Heat Transfer Surface, Plan (Indicate type such as convector)		Canvas Connections		
Pump (Indicate type such as vacuum)		Deflecting Damper		
Strainer				
Tank (Designate type)		Direction of Flow		
Thermometer		Duct (1st figure, side shown; 2nd side not shown)		
Thermostat		Duct Section (Exhaust or Return)		
Trap, Boiler Return		Duct Section (Supply)		
Trap, Blast Thermostatic		Exhaust Inlet Ceiling (Indicate type)		
Trap, Float		Exhaust Inlet Wall (Indicate type)		
Trap, Float and Thermostatic		Fan and Motor with Belt Guard		
Trap, Thermostatic				
Unit Heater (Centrifugal fan), Plan		Inclined Drop in Respect to Air Flow		
Unit Heater (Propeller), Plan		Inclined Rise in Respect to Air Flow		
Unit Ventilator, Plan		Intake Louvers on Screen		
Valve, Check		Louver Opening		
Valve, Diaphragm		Supply Outlet Ceiling (Indicate type)		
Valve, Gate				
Valve, Globe		Supply Outlet Wall (Indicate type)		
Valve, Lock and Shield				
Valve, Motor Operated		Vanes		
Valve, Reducing Pressure				
Valve, Relief (Either pressure or vacuum)		Volume Damper		
Vent Point				

From ANSI Z32.2.4—1949 (reaffirmed 1953)

Capillary Tube		Motor-Compressor, Enclosed Crankcase, Rotary, Direct Connected	
Compressor			
Compressor, Enclosed, Crankcase, Rotary, Belted		Motor-Compressor, Sealed Crankcase, Reciprocating	
Compressor, Open Crankcase, Reciprocating, Belted		Motor-Compressor, Sealed Crankcase, Rotary	
Compressor, Open Crankcase, Reciprocating, Direct Drive		Pressurestat	
Condenser, Air Cooled, Finned, Forced Air		Pressure Switch	
Condenser, Air Cooled, Finned, Static		Pressure Switch With High Pressure Cut-Out	
Condenser, Water Cooled, Concentric Tube in a Tube		Receiver, Horizontal	
Condenser, Water Cooled, Shell and Coil		Receiver, Vertical	
Condenser, Water Cooled, Shell and Tube		Scale Trap	
Condensing Unit, Air Cooled		Spray Pond	
Condensing Unit, Water Cooled		Thermal Bulb	
Cooling Tower		Thermostat (Remote bulb)	
Dryer		Valve, Automatic Expansion	
Evaporative Condenser		Valve, Compressor Suction Pressure Limiting, Throttling Type (Compressor Side)	
Evaporator, Circular, Ceiling Type, Finned			
Evaporator, Manifolded, Bare Tube, Gravity Air		Valve, Constant Pressure, Suction	
Evaporator, Manifolded, Finned, Forced Air		Valve, Evaporator Pressure Regulating, Snap Action	
Evaporator, Manifolded, Finned, Gravity Air		Valve, Evaporator Pressure Regulating, Thermostatic Throttling Type	
Evaporator, Plate Coils, Headered or Manifold		Valve, Evaporator Pressure Regulating, Throttling Type (Evaporator side)	
Filter, Line			
Filter & Strainer, Line		Valve, Hand Expansion	
Finned Type Cooling Unit, Natural Convection		Valve, Magnetic Stop	
Forced Convection Cooling Unit		Valve, Snap Action	
Gauge		Valve, Suction Vapor Regulating	
High Side Float		Valve, Thermo Suction	
Immersion Cooling Unit		Valve, Thermostatic Expansion	
Low Side Float		Valve, Water	
Motor-Compressor, Enclosed Crankcase, Reciprocating, Direct Connected		Vibration Absorber, Line	

GRAPHIC SYMBOLS – 6
Plumbing

FIXTURES AND EQUIPMENT

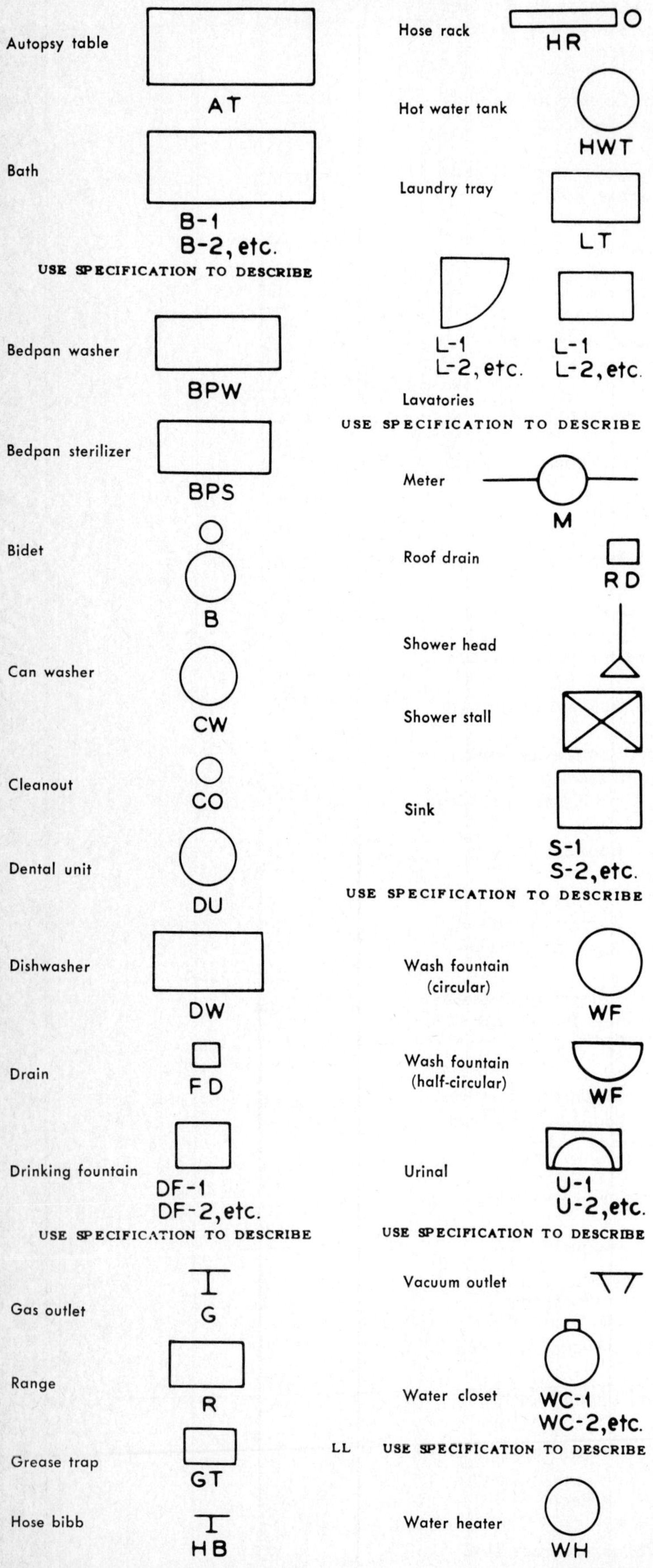

Fixture	Symbol
Autopsy table	AT
Bath	B-1 B-2, etc. USE SPECIFICATION TO DESCRIBE
Bedpan washer	BPW
Bedpan sterilizer	BPS
Bidet	B
Can washer	CW
Cleanout	CO
Dental unit	DU
Dishwasher	DW
Drain	FD
Drinking fountain	DF-1 DF-2, etc. USE SPECIFICATION TO DESCRIBE
Gas outlet	G
Range	R
Grease trap	GT
Hose bibb	HB

Fixture	Symbol
Hose rack	HR
Hot water tank	HWT
Laundry tray	LT
Lavatories	L-1 L-2, etc. L-1 L-2, etc. USE SPECIFICATION TO DESCRIBE
Meter	M
Roof drain	RD
Shower head	
Shower stall	
Sink	S-1 S-2, etc. USE SPECIFICATION TO DESCRIBE
Wash fountain (circular)	WF
Wash fountain (half-circular)	WF
Urinal	U-1 U-2, etc. USE SPECIFICATION TO DESCRIBE
Vacuum outlet	
Water closet	WC-1 WC-2, etc. LL USE SPECIFICATION TO DESCRIBE
Water heater	WH

PIPE FITTINGS AND VALVES

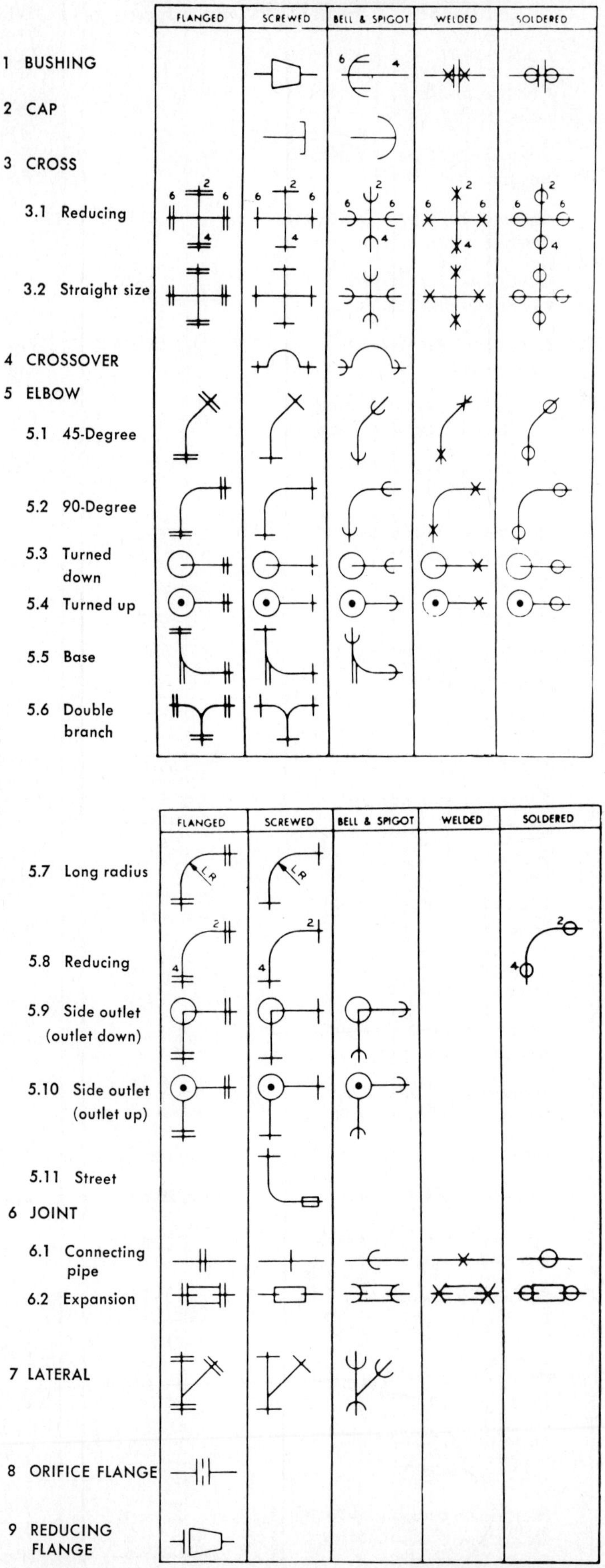

	FLANGED	SCREWED	BELL & SPIGOT	WELDED	SOLDERED
1 BUSHING					
2 CAP					
3 CROSS					
3.1 Reducing					
3.2 Straight size					
4 CROSSOVER					
5 ELBOW					
5.1 45-Degree					
5.2 90-Degree					
5.3 Turned down					
5.4 Turned up					
5.5 Base					
5.6 Double branch					

	FLANGED	SCREWED	BELL & SPIGOT	WELDED	SOLDERED
5.7 Long radius					
5.8 Reducing					
5.9 Side outlet (outlet down)					
5.10 Side outlet (outlet up)					
5.11 Street					
6 JOINT					
6.1 Connecting pipe					
6.2 Expansion					
7 LATERAL					
8 ORIFICE FLANGE					
9 REDUCING FLANGE					

From ANSI Y32.4–1955

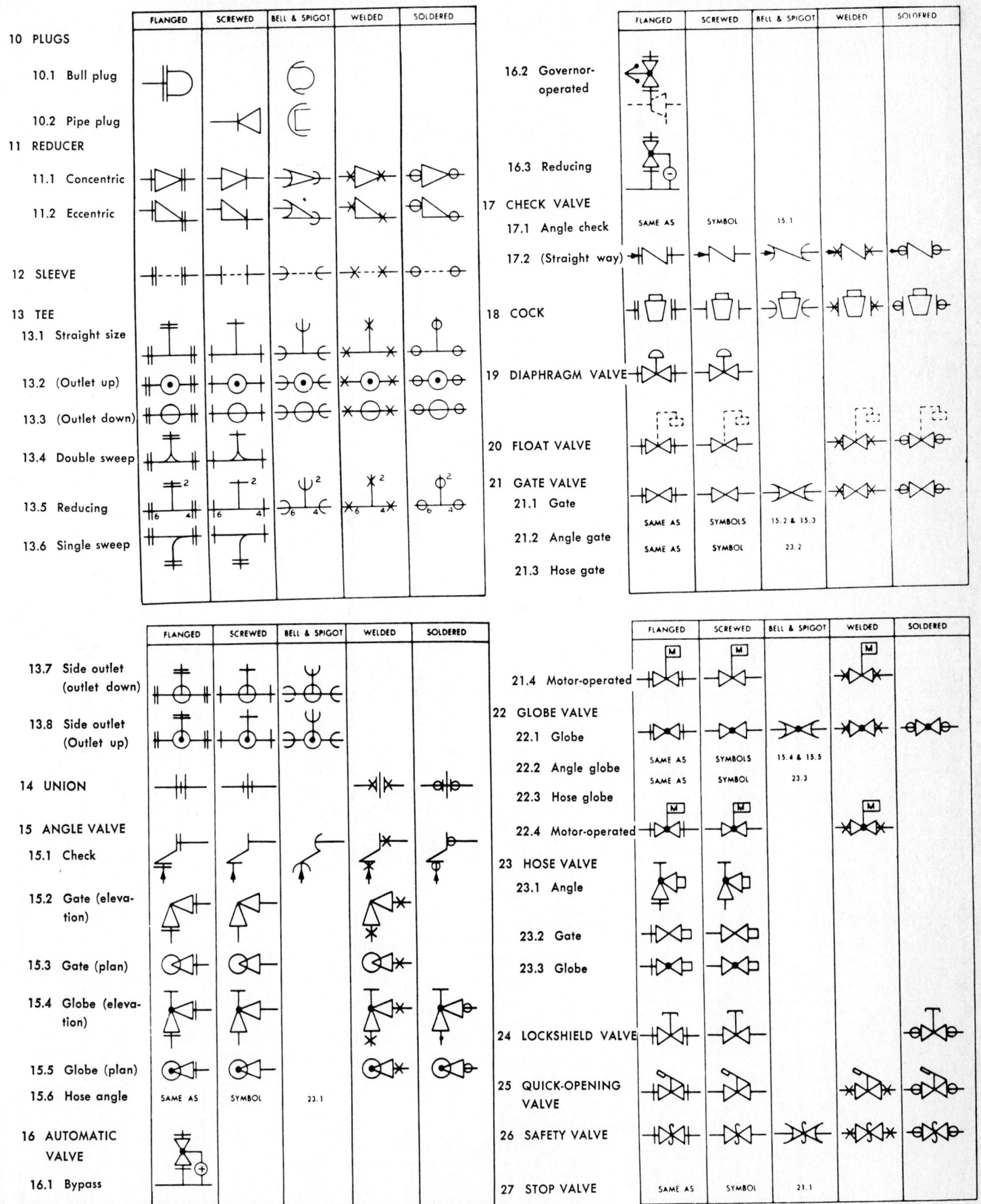

PIPE FITTINGS AND VALVES

From ANSI Y32.4—1955

The graphic symbols on these pages have been taken from *American National Standard Graphic Symbols for Electrical Wiring and Layout Diagrams Used in Architecture and Building Construction, ANSI Y32.9–1972*, with the permission of the publisher, the Institute of Electrical and Electronics Engineers.

LIGHTING OUTLETS

Ceiling	Wall	
◯	─◯	Surface or pendant incandescent fixture
ⓡ	─ⓡ	Recessed incandescent fixture
▭◯		Surface or pendant fluorescent fixture
▭ⓡ		Recessed individual fluorescent fixture
▭◯▭		Surface or pendant continuous fluorescent
ⓡ▭▭		Recessed continuous-row fluorescent fixture
├─┼─┤		Bare-lamp fluorescent strip
ⓧ	─ⓧ	Surface or pendant exit light
ⓡⓧ	─ⓡⓧ	Recessed exit light
Ⓑ	─Ⓑ	Blanked outlet
Ⓙ	─Ⓙ	Junction box
Ⓛ	─Ⓛ	Outlet controlled by low-voltage switching when relay is installed in outlet box

SIGNALING SYSTEM OUTLETS INSTITUTIONAL, COMMERICAL, AND INDUSTRIAL OCCUPANCIES

Use numbers in or adjacent to symbol to identify various items in the system; explain in schedule on drawing.

─Ⓘ	Nurse call system devices
─◇Ⓘ	Paging system devices
─▭Ⓘ	Fire alarm system devices
─◈Ⓘ	Staff register system devices
─⬡Ⓘ	Electric clock system devices
◀Ⓘ	Public telephone system devices
◁Ⓘ	Private telephone system devices
─⬠Ⓘ	Watchman system devices
─⬠Ⓘ	Sound systems
─⬡Ⓘ	Other signal system devices

RECEPTACLE OUTLETS

Where receptacles are to be of the ungrounded type, the notation UNG should be used at the outlet location. Similarly, where weatherproof, explosion proof, or other specific types are required, use uppercase subscript letters to indicate them.

─⊖	Single receptacle outlet
─⊜	Double receptacle outlet
─⊕	Triplex receptacle outlet
─⊞	Quadruplex receptacle outlet
─⊖	Duplex receptacle outlet—split wired
─⊜	Triplex receptacle outlet—split wired
─△*	Single special-purpose receptacle outlet*
─△*	Duplex special-purpose receptacle outlet*
═⊖ᵣ	Range outlet
─◐_DW	Special-purpose connection or provision for connection. Use subscript letters to indicate function (DW—dishwasher; CD— clothes dryer, etc.)
⊕ X″	Multioutlet assembly (Extend arrows to limit of installation; use appropriate symbol to indicate type of outlet; indicate spacing of outlets in inches.)
─Ⓒ	Clock hanger receptacle
─Ⓕ	Fan hanger receptacle
▣	Floor single receptacle outlet
◪	Floor duplex receptacle outlet
◭*	Floor special-purpose outlet*
◀	Floor telephone outlet— public
◁	Floor telephone outlet— private

Underfloor duct and junction box for triple, double, or single duct system as indicated by the number of parallel lines

Cellular floor header duct

| ⊖◀◁ | Example of the use of several floor outlet symbols to identify a two, three, or more gang floor outlet |

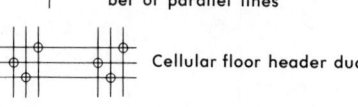

Example of use of various symbols to identify location of different types of services in underfloor duct or cellular floor systems

Use numeral or letter within the symbol or as a subscript keyed to explanation in the drawing list of symbols to indicate the type of receptacle or usage.

SIGNALING SYSTEM OUTLETS RESIDENTIAL OCCUPANCIES

⊡	Pushbutton
◺	Buzzer
◿	Bell
◿▭	Combination bell-buzzer
CH	Chime
◇	Annunciator
D	Electric door opener
M	Maid's signal plug
▢	Interconnection box
BT	Bell-ringing transformer
▶	Outside telephone
▷	Interconnecting telephone
R	Radio outlet
TV	Television outlet

SWITCH OUTLETS

S	Single-pole switch
S₂	Double-pole switch
S₃	Three-way switch
S₄	Four-way switch
Sₖ	Key-operated switch
Sₚ	Switch and pilot lamp
Sₗ	Switch for low-voltage switching system
Sₗₘ	Master switch for low-voltage switching system
─⊖S	Switch and single receptacle
─⊜S	Switch and double receptacle
S_D	Door switch
S_T	Time switch
S_CB	Circuit breaker switch
S_MC	Momentary contact switch or pushbutton for other than signaling system
Ⓢ	Ceiling pull switch

BUS DUCTS AND WIREWAYS

T T T	Trolley duct*
B B B	Busway (service, feeder, or plug-in)*
BP BP BP	Cable trough ladder or channel*
W W W	Wireway*

* *Identify by notation or schedule.*

REMOTE CONTROL STATIONS FOR MOTORS OR OTHER EQUIPMENT

(oval)	Pushbutton station
F	Float switch—mechanical
L	Limit switch—mechanical
P	Pneumatic switch—mechanical
	Electric eye—beam source
	Electric eye—relay
—T	Thermostat

ELECTRICAL DISTRIBUTION OR LIGHTING SYSTEM, AERIAL

○	Pole*
	Pole with street light*
△	Transformer*
———	Primary circuit*
- - - - -	Secondary circuit*
	Pole with down guy and anchor
	Head guy
	Sidewalk guy
	Service weather head*
	Switch, manual*

* *Identify by notation or schedule.*

PANELBOARDS, SWITCHBOARDS, AND RELATED EQUIPMENT

	Flush-mounted panelboard and cabinet*
	Surface-mounted panelboard and cabinet*
	Switchboard power control center, unit substations* – should be drawn to scale
TC	Flush-mounted terminal cabinet* (In small-scale drawings the TC may be indicated alongside the symbol)
TC	Surface-mounted terminal cabinet* (In small-scale drawings the TC may be indicated alongside the symbol)
	Pull box (identify in relation to wiring system section and size)
MC	Motor or other power controller*
	Externally operated disconnection switch*
	Combination controller and disconnection means*

* *Identify by notation or schedule.*

CIRCUITING

———————	Wiring concealed in ceiling or wall
—·—·—·—·	Wiring concealed in floor
- - - - - - -	Wiring exposed

   Note: Use heavyweight line to identify service and feeders. Indicate empty conduit by notation CO (conduit only)

Branch circuit home run to panelboard. Number of arrows indicates number of circuits. (A numeral at each arrow may be used to identify circuit number.)

   Note: Any circuit without further identification indicates two-wire circuit. For a greater number of wires, indicate with cross lines, e.g.: —///— *3 wires;* —////— *4 wires, etc.*

Unless indicated otherwise, the wire size of the circuit is the minimum size required by the specification.

Identify different functions of wiring system, e.g., signaling system by notation or other means.

—CO—	Empty raceway (conduit only)
——○	Wiring turned up
——●	Wiring turned down

ELECTRIC DISTRIBUTION OR LIGHTING SYSTEM, UNDERGROUND

M	Manhole*
H	Handhole*
TM	Transformer manhole or vault*
TP	Transformer pad*
- - - -	Underground direct burial cable (Indicate type, size, and number of conductors by notation or schedule)
- - -→	Underground duct line (Indicate type, size, and number of ducts by cross-section identification of each run by notation or schedule. Indicate type, size, and number of conductors by notation or schedule)
	Street light standard fed from underground circuit*

* *Identify by notation or schedule.*

OTHER GRAPHIC SYMBOLS USED IN ELECTRICAL DRAWINGS

The following symbols, which are commonly used in making electrical system layouts on drawings, are from *American National Standard Graphic Symbols for Electrical Diagrams*, ANSI Y32. 2.

MOT	Electric motor	WH	Electric watthour meter		Single-throw knife switch
GEN	Electric generator	CB	Circuit element, e.g., circuit breaker		Double-throw knife switch
	Power transformer		Circuit breaker		Ground
	Pothead (cable termination)		Fusible element		Battery

By HANS J. MILTON, F.R.A.I.A., *Center for Building Technology, National Bureau of Standards*

ABBREVIATIONS FOR USE ON BUILDING DRAWINGS

This section gives abbreviations for words or terms other than units of measurement used in building and associated activities (Part 1) and organizational acronyms relevant to the construction industry (Part 2).

Abbreviations have been selected from American National Standard ANSI Y1.1-1972, "Abbreviations for Use on Drawings and in Text," published by the American Society for Mechanical Engineers [ASME]. Where necessary, they have been supplemented by additional abbreviations commonly used in building design and construction. Also, where other forms of abbreviation have traditionally been used in building drawings, they are shown in parentheses. Abbreviations for use in drawings are shown, those for use in text have been omitted. While the ANSI/ASME standard lists an extensive range of abbreviations from all fields of activity, it does not promote their use, except when their meaning is unequivocally clear. The standard instructs: *When in doubt, spell out.*

Symbols, signs, or abbreviations for U.S. customary [inch-pound] units of measurement are shown in a separate list (Part 3). Correct letter symbols should be used in preference to capitalized abbreviations.

PART 1 ABBREVIATIONS FOR WORDS OR TERMS IN BUILDING

Capitalized abbreviations, without periods, are recommended for use on building drawings. Abbreviations shown in parentheses are forms that have been widely used in building drawings and associated technical documents.

A

Above	ABV
Acoustic	ACST
Acrylonitrile butadiene styrene	ABS
Actual	ACTL (ACT)
Adapter	ADPTR
Addendum, addition(al)	ADD
Adhesive	ADH
Adjacent	ADJ
Aggregate	AGGR
Air condition(ed)	AIR COND (A/C)
Alarm	ALM
Alignment	ALIGN
Allowance	ALLOW
Alloy	ALY
Alternate	ALTN (ALT)
Alternating current	AC
Aluminum (Chem. symbol: Al)	AL
American Wire Gage	AWG
Amperage (current)	A
Angle (structural)	L
Apartment	APT
Appendix	APPX
Approved	APVD (APPD)
Approximate	APPROX
Architecture, architectural	ARCH
Arc weld	ARCW
Artificial	ARTF (ART)
Asbestos	ASB
Asphalt	ASPH
Asphalt roof shingles	ASPHRS
Assembly	ASSY
Assistant	ASST
Association	ASSN
Automatic	AUTO
Automatic data processing	ADP
Avenue	AVE
Average	AVG
Awning	AWN

B

Balcony	BALC
Basement	BSMT
Base plate	BP (BPL)
Bathroom	B
Bathtub	BT
Beam	BM
Bearing	BRG
Bedroom	BR
Bell and spigot	B&S
Below	BLW
Benchmark	BM
Between	BETW (BET)
Bill of material	B/M
Birmingham Wire Gage	BWG
Black	BLK, BK
Blower	BLO
Blue	BLU, BL
Blueprint	BP
Board	BD
Boiler	BLR
Both sides	BS
Bottom	BOT
Boundary	BDY
Brass	BRS
Brick	BRK
Bridge, bridging	BRDG
Brinell hardness	BH
Bronze	BRZ
Brown	BRN, BR
Brown & Sharpe Wire Gage	B&S
Building	BLDG
Building Energy Performance Standards	BEPS
Building line	BL
Built-in	BLTIN (BI)

C

Cabinet	CAB
Cadmium plate(d)	CDPL
Cantilever	CANTIL
Capacity	CAP
Carpet	CARP
Cast iron	CI
Cast-iron pipe	CIP
Catalog	CAT
Caulking	CLKG
Ceiling	CLG
Cellulose acetate butyrate	CAB
Cement	CEM
Center	CTR
Centerline	CL
Center of gravity	CG
Center to center	C TO C
Ceramic	CER
Ceramic tile	CT
Change order	CO
Check valve	CV
Chilled drinking water	CDW
Chilled water	CHW
Chromium plate(d)	CRPL
Circle	CIR
Circuit	CKT
Circuit breaker	CB
Circular	CIRC
Circumference	CRCMF (CIRC)
Clay pipe	CP
Cleanout	CO
Clear	CLR
Clearance	CL
Closet	CLO
Coarse	CRS
Coated	CTD
Coefficient	COEF
Cold drawn	CD
Cold rolled	CR
Cold water	CW
Collector	COLL
Column	COL
Combination, combine(d)	COMB

Commercial qual-		
ity	CQ	
Common	COM	
Company	CO	
Composition	COMP	
Compressive	COMP	
Compressor	CPRSR (COMPR)	
Computer	CMPTR	
Concealed	CNCL	
Concentrated	CONC	
Concrete	CONC (CONCR)	
Conduit	CND	
Connect, connector	CONN	
Construction	CONSTR (CONST)	
Construction joint	CJ	
Continue, continu-		
ous	CONT	
Contract, contrac-		
tor	CONTR	
Cooling	CLG	
Cool room	CLRM	
Copper (Chem.		
symbol: Cu)	COP	
Cork	CK	
Corporation	CORP	
Corrugate(d)	CORR	
Countersink	CSK	
Critical path		
method	CPM	
Cross section	XSECT	
Cubic	CU	
Curve(d)	CRV	

D

Dampproofing	DP
Datum	DAT
Day (Intl. sym-	
bol: d)	D (DY)
Dead load	DL
Degree (Intl. sym-	
bol: °)	DEG
Delineation	DEL
Department(al)	DEPT
Design(ed)	DSGN
Detail	DET
Dew point	DP
Diagonal	DIAG
Diagram	DIAG
Diameter (Sym-	
bol: φ)	DIA
Dimension	DIM
Dimensional coor-	
dination	DC
Direct current	DC
Dishwasher	DW
Ditto	DO
Divide, division	DIV
Domestic	DOM
Door	DR
Door closer	DCL
Door stop	DST
Double	DBL
Double-hung (win-	
dow)	DH

Double-strength	
(glass)	DS
Down	DN
Downspout	DS
Dozen	DOZ
Drain	DR
Dressed (lumber)	DRS
Dressed and	
matched	D&M
Dry-bulb	
[temperature]	DB
Duplicate	DUP

E

Each	EA
East	E
Electric, electrical	ELEC (EL)
Elevation	EL
Elevator	ELEV
Enamel	ENAM
Engineer	ENGR
Engineering	ENGRG
Entrance	ENTR (ENT)
Epoxy, epoxide	EP
Equal	EQL (EQ)
Equipment	EQPT (EQUIP)
Equivalent direct	
radiation	EDR
Estimate(d)	EST
Excavate	EXC
Exhaust	EXH
Existing	EXIST
Expansion joint	EXP JT (EJ)
Exposed	EXP
Exterior	EXT
Extinguisher	EXT
Extra heavy	XHVY
Extra strong	XSTR
Extrude(d)	EXTD

F

Fabricate	FAB
Federal specifica-	
tion	FS
Fiberboard	FBRBD
Fiberglass-rein-	
forced plastics	FRP
Figure	FIG
Finish	FNSH (FIN)
Finished floor level	FFL
Fire door	FDR
Fire hydrant	FHY
Fireproof	FPRF (FP)
Fireproof door	FPDR
Fitted	FTD
Fitting	FTG
Fixture	FXTR (FIX)
Flange	FLG
Flashing	FL
Flat	FL
Flexible	FLEX
Floor	FL
Floor drain	FD

Flooring	FLG (FLRG)
Fluorescent	FLUOR
Fluorinated ethyl-	
ene propylene	FEP
Folding	FLDG
For example	EG
Footing	FTG
Foundation	FDN
Four-way	4WAY
Freezing point	FP
Full size	FS
Furnish(ed), furni-	
ture	FURN

G

Gage (gauge)	GA
Galvanize(d)	GALV
Galvanized iron	GALVI (GI)
Garage	GAR
Gas metal arc	
[welding]	GMA
Gasoline	GAS
Girder	G
Glass	GL
Glazed wall tile	GWT
Government(al)	GOVT
Grade	GR
Gravel	GVL
Grease trap	GT
Green	GRN, G
Ground	GRD
Gypsum	GYP
Gypsum wallboard	GWB

H

Half-hard	1/2H
Half-round	1/2R
Handrail	HNDRL
Hard	HD (H)
Hardware	HDW
Head(ed)	HD
Header	HDR
Heater	HTR
Heating, ventilat-	
ing, and air con-	
ditioning	HVAC
Heavy	HVY
Height	HGT (HT)
Hexagon(al)	HEX
High performance	HP
High point	HPT
High pressure	HP
High tensile	
strength	HTS
High tension	HT
Highway	HWY
Hinge(d)	HNG
Hollow	HOL
Hollow metal	HM
Hollow metal door	HMDR
Horizontal	HORIZ (HOR)
Horizontal sliding	
[window]	HS

Hospital	HOSP	Left hand	LH	Mixture	MXT
Hot-rolled	HR	Length	LG	Model	MOD
Hot water	HW	Length over all	LOA	Modification, mod-	
House	HSE	Level	LVL	ify	MOD
Humidity	HMD (HUM)	Library	LBRY (LIB)	Molding	MLDG
Hydraulic	HYDR (HYD)	License(d)	LIC	Month	MO
		Light	LT	Motor	MOT
I		Light switch	LTSW	Motor generator	MG
		Lightweight con-		Mounting	MTG
Illuminate, illumi-		crete	LWC	Movement	MVT
nation	ILLUM	Limited	LTD	Multiple	MULT
Illustrate	ILLUS	Linear, lineal	LIN		
Impact Noise Rat-		Linoleum	LINO		
ing	INR	Lintel	LNTL	**N**	
Impregnate	IMPRG (IMPG)	Liquid	LIQ		
Incinerator	INCIN	Live load	LL	National	NATL
Include(d), inclu-		Local	LCL	*National Electrical*	
sive	INCL	Logarithm	LOG	*Code*	NEC
Incorporated	INC	Long	L	Natural	NAT
Industrial	INDL (IND)	Louvered door	LVD	Necessary	NEC
Infinite, infinity		Low frequency	LF	Negative (—)	NEG
(Intl. symbol: ∞)	INF	Low pressure	LP	Nickel-plate(d)	NP
Information	INFO	Lumber	LBR	No change	NC
Inlet	INL			Noise frequency	NF
Inside diameter,		**M**		Noise-reduction	
internal diame-				coefficient	NRC
ter	ID	Main	MN	Nominal	NOM
Install(ed), installa-		Maintenance	MAINT	Nonslip tread	NST
tion	INSTL	Malleable iron	MI	Nonstandard	NONSTD
Institute	INST	Manager	MGR	North	N
Intercommunication	INTERCOM	Manhole	MH	Not available	NA
Interior	INTR (INT)	Manual	MNL (MAN)	Not to scale	NTS
International	INTL	Manufacturing	MFG	Number (#)	NO
International Sys-		Mark	MK	Nylon	NYL
tem of Units	SI	Masonry	MSNRY		
Iron [comb. form]		Masonry opening	MO		
(Chem. symbol:		Master bedroom	MBR		
Fe)	I	Master switch	MSW	**O**	
Iron pipe size	IPS	Mastic	MSTC		
Issue, issued	ISS	Material	MATL	Obscure	OB
		Material list	ML	Obsolete	OBS
J		Maximum	MAX	Octagon(al)	OCT
		Mechanical	MECH	Office	OFCE (OFF)
Joint	JT	Medium	MDM (MED)	Oil tank	OTK
Joist	J	Melamine formal-		On center	OC
Junction	JCT	dehyde	MF	One-way	1/W
Junction box	JB	Melting point	MP	Open-end(ed)	OE
Junior	JR	Member	MBR	Opening	OPNG
		Membrane	MEMB	Open web steel	
K		Memorandum	MEMO	joist	OWSJ
		Metal	MET	Opposite	OPP
Kiln-dried	KD	Metal lath	ML	Optional	OPTL
Knock down	KD	Metal lath and		Organic	ORG
		plaster	MLP	Origin, original	ORIG
L		Metal partition	METP	Otherwise speci-	
		Meter (instrument)	MET	fied	OS
Laboratory	LAB	Mezzanine	MEZZ	Outlet, output,	
Lacquer	LAQ	Microfilm	MF	outside	OUT
Laminate	LAM	Military	MIL	Outside diameter	OD
Large	LGE	Military standard	MIL-STD	Over	OV
Latitude	LAT	Minimum	MIN	Overall	OA
Lavatory	LAV	Minimum Property		Overhead	OVHD
Layout	LYT (LAY)	Standards	MPS	Oversize	OVS
Leather	LTHR	Mirror	MIR	Oxygen *(Chem.*	
Left	L	Miscellaneous	MISC	*symbol: O)*	OXY
		Mixing	MXG		

P

Page	P
Paint	PNT
Painted	PTD
Pair	PR
Panel	PNL
Panic bolt	PANB
Paragraph	PARA (PAR)
Parallel	PRL (PAR)
Parkway	PKWY
Part	PT
Partition	PTN
Passenger	PASS
Passive	PSIV
Patent	PAT
Pedestal	PED
Penny (nails, etc.)	D
Percent (%)	PCT
Perforate(d)	PERF
Permanent	PERM
Perpendicular	PERP
Phase	PH
Photograph	PHOTO
Piece	PC
Piling	PLG
Pipeline	PPLN
Place	PL
Plane	PLN
Plaster	PL
Plate	PL
Plated	PLD
Plate glass	PLGL
Plumbing	PLMB
Plywood	PLYWD
Pneumatic	PNEU
Point	PT
Pole	P
Polish	POL
Polycarbonate	PC
Polyester	POLYEST
Polyethylene, polythene	POLTHN (PE)
Polymethyl methacrylate (acrylic)	PMMA
Polypropylene	PP
Polystyrene	PS
Polytetrafluoroethylene	PTFE
Polyvinyl acetate	PVA
Polyvinyl chloride	PVC
Polyvinyl fluoride	PVF
Porcelain	PORC
Portable	PORT
Positive (+)	POS
Post office	PO
Power	PWR
Power and lighting	P&L
Precast	PRCST
Prefabricated	PREFAB
Preferred	PFD
Preferred Noise Criteria	PNC
Preformed	PREFMD
Preliminary	PRELIM
Preparation, prepare	PREP

Pressed metal	PRSD MET
Printed	PTD
Priority	PRI
Private automatic branch exchange	PABX
Private automatic exchange	PAX
Product, production	PROD
Product standard	PS
Program	PRGM
Project	PROJ
Property	PROP
Property line	PL
Provision(al)	PROV
Public address	PA
Publication	PUBN (PUB)
Pump	PMP
Push button	PB

Q

Quality	QUAL
Quality control	QC
Quantity	QTY
Quarry-tile floor	QTF
Quarter	QTR
Quarter-hard	1/4H
Quarter-round	1/4R

R

Radiation	RADN
Radiator	RDTR (RAD)
Radius	RAD (R)
Railroad	RR
Ready	RDY
Received	RCVD (RECD)
Receptacle	RCPT (RECP)
Recess	REC
Recreation room	REC RM
Rectangle, rectangular	RECT
Red	RED, R
Redrawn	REDWN
Reduction	RDCN
Refer, reference	REF
Reflective insulation	RI
Refractory	RFRC (REFR)
Refrigerate, refrigerator	REFR
Register	RGTR (REG)
Regular	RGLR (REG)
Reinforce	REINF
Reinforced concrete	RC
Reinforcing steel	RST
Relative	REL
Relative humidity	RH
Remove	RMV (REM)
Remove and replace	R&R
Repair	RPR (REP)

Replace	REPL
Reproduce, reproduction	REPRO
Required	REQD
Requisition	REQN (REQ)
Research and development	R&D
Return	RTN (RET)
Reverse	RVS
Review, revise, revision	REV
Right hand	RH
Right-of-way	R/W
Road	RD
Rockwell hardness	RH
Roof	RF
Roofing	RFG
Room	RM
Rough	RGH
Round	RND (RD)
Rubber	RBR
Rubber tile floor	RTF
Rustproof	RSTPF

S

Safety		SAF
Salt-glazed structural facing units		SGSFU
Sanitary		SAN
Schedule	SCHED	(SCH)
Schematic		SCHEM
Screen door		SCD
Sea level		SL
Seamless		SMLS
Section	SECT	(SEC)
Select		SEL
Self-closing	SELF	CL
Separate		SEP
Serial, series		SER
Service	SVCE	(SERV)
Sewage, sewer		SEW
Shear plate		SP
Sheet, sheeting		SH
Shield, shielding		SHLD
Shielded metal arc [welding]		SMA
Shipment		SHPT
Shower		SH
Shower and toilet		SH&T
Shower drain		SD
Side [comb. form]		S
Siding		SDG
Similar		SIM
Single		SGL
Single-phase		1PH
Single-pole switch	SP	SW
Single-strength (glass)		SS
Single weight		SW
Sink		SK
Sketch		SK
Skylight	SLT	(SKY)

Slide, sliding	SL	Surfaced or		Tread	TRD
Sliding door	SLD	dressed two		Treatment	TRTMT
Sliding glass door	SGD	sides	S2S	Trigonometric, tri-	
Slope	SL	Survey	SURV	gonometry	TRIG
Small	SM	Suspend(ed)	SUSP	Triple	TPL
Smokeless	SMKLS	Suspended acous-		Triple-pole switch	3P SW
Smooth-face	SF	tical-tile ceiling	SATC	Truss	TR
Soft	S	Suspension	SPNSN	Tubing	TBG (TUB)
Soil pipe	SP	Swing(ing) door	SWGD	Tunnel	TUN
Soil stack	SSK	Switch	SW	Two-phase	2PH
Solid	SOL	Switchboard	SWBD	Two-pole	DP
Solvent	SLVT	Symmetrical	SYMM (SYM)	Two-way	2WAY
Soundproof	SNDPRF	Synthetic	SYNTH (SYN)	Typewriter	TW
Sound-transmission		System	SYS	Typical	TYP
class	STC				
South	S	**T**		**U**	
Spare, spare part	SP				
Speaker	SPKR			Ultimate	ULT
Special	SPCL (SPL)	Tabulate	TAB	Ultraviolet	UV
Special-purpose	SP	Tangent	TAN	Under	UND
Specification	SPEC	Tarpaulin	TARP	Underground	UGND
Specific gravity	SP GR (SG)	Technical	TECH	Underside	U/S
Speed	SP	Technical report	TR	Undersize	US
Spiral	SPL	Tee, T-bar (struc-		Unfinished	UNF
Spot-weld(ed)	SW	tural)	T	Unified coarse	
Sprinkler	SPR	Telephone	TEL	thread	UNC
Square	SQ	Teletype	TT	Unified fine thread	UNF
Stack	STK	Television	TV	Uniform	UNIF
Stage	STG	Temperature	TEMP	Uniform Building	
Stainless steel	SST	Temporary	TEMP	Code	UBC
Stairway	STWY	Tensile	TNSL	Uniformly distrib-	
Standard	STD	Terra-cotta	TC	uted load	UDL
Standby	STBY	Terrazzo	TER	United States	US
Standpipe	SP	That is	IE	United States	
Station, stationary	STA	Thermocouple	TC	Gage	USG
Steam	ST	Thermostat	THERMO	Untreated	UNTRD
Steel	STL	Thick	THK	Upper	UPR
Stock	STK	Thread	THD	Upper and lower	U&L
Stone	STN	Three-conductor	3/C	Urea formalde-	
Storage	STOR (STG)	Three-phase	3PH	hyde	UF
Storeroom	STRM	Three-way	3WAY	Urinal	UR
Storm water	STW	Three-wire	3W		
Straight	STR	Through	THRU	**V**	
Street	ST	Tile floor	TF		
Strength	STR	Time [comb. form]	T	Vacant	VAC
Structural	STRL (STR)	Time delay	TD	Vacuum	VAC
Structural clay fac-		Time switch	TS	Valve	V
ing tile	SCFT	Toilet	T	Vapor seal(ed)	VS
Structural clay tile	SCT	Toilet-paper holder	TH	Variable, variance,	
Structure	STRUCT	Tolerance	TOL	variation	VAR
Subsoil drain	SSD	Tongue and groove	T&G	Varnish	VARN
Substitute	SUBST (SUB)	Top and bottom	T&B	Vent pipe	VP
Superintendent	SUPT	Top chord	TC	Vent stack	VS
Supersede	SUPSD	Top-hinged (win-		Ventilate, ventila-	
Supervise	SUPV	dow)	TH	tor	VENT
Supplement	SUPPL	Topping	TOPG	Versus	VS
Supply	SPLY (SUP)	Total	TOT	Vertical	VERT
Surface	SURF (SUR)	Total live load	TLLD	Vertical pivot	
Surfaced or		Total load	TLD	(window)	VP
dressed four		Towel rack, rail or		Vertical sliding (win-	
sides	S4S	rod	TR	dow)	VS
Surfaced or		Training	TNG	Vibrate, vibration	VIB
dressed one side	S1S	Transformer	XFMR (TRANS)	Vinyl asbestos tile	VAT
Surfaced or		Transom	TR	Vitreous	VIT
dressed one side		Transparent	TRANS	Vitrified clay	VC
and one edge	S1S1E	Transverse	TRANSV	Void	VD

Voltage	V	Water heater	WH	Wiring	WRG		
Voltage regulator	VR	Waterproof	WTRPRF (WP)	With [comb. form]	W/		
Volume	VOL	Wavelength	WL	Withdrawn	W/D		
		Weatherproof (in-		Without	W/O		
		sulation)	WP	Wood	WD		
W		Weather stripping	WS	Wood door	WD (WDR)		
		Week	WK	Wood panel	WDP		
Wall	W	Weight	WT	Workshop	WKS		
Wallboard	WBD	Welded	WLD	Wrought iron	WI		
Wardrobe	WRB	West	W				
Warehouse	WHSE	Wet bulb	WB	**Y**			
Washroom	WR	White	WHT, W				
Waste	W	Width	WD	Year (Intl. symbol:			
Waste pipe	WP	Window	WDO	a)	YR		
Waste stack	WS	Wire [comb. form]	W	Yellow	YEL, Y		
Water closet	WC	Wire gage	WG	Yield point	YP		
Water cooler	WCR	Wire mesh	WM	Yield strength	YS		

PART 2 ORGANIZATIONAL ACRONYMS

To conserve space in drawings or text, the names of organizations are commonly shown in the form of an acronym, that is, by an abbreviation formed of the initial letter or letters of the individual words in the name. Acronyms are shown in capital letters.

The following list contains acronyms of major U.S. organizations and selected international organizations of relevance to building or building standards.

A

Acoustical Society of America	ASA
Air-Conditioning and Refrigeration Institute	ARI
Aluminum Association	AA
American Association of State Highway and Transportation Officials	AASHTO
American Concrete Institute	ACI
American Gas Association	AGA
American Hospital Association	AHA
American Institute of Architects	AIA
American Institute of Steel Construction	AISC
American Institute of Timber Construction	AITC
American Insurance Association	AIA
American Iron and Steel Institute	AISI
American National Metric Council	ANMC
American National Standards Institute	ANSI
American Plywood Association	APA
American Society of Civil Engineers	ASCE
American Society for Engineering Education	ASEE
American Society of Heating, Refrigerating, and Air-Conditioning Engineers	ASHRAE
American Society of Mechanical Engineers	ASME
American Society for Testing and Materials	ASTM
American Welding Society	AWS
Architectural Aluminum Manufacturers Association	AAMA
Architectural Woodwork Institute	AWI
Associated General Contractors of America	AGC

B

Brick Institute of America	BIA
Building Officials and Code Administrators International, Inc.	BOCA

C

Construction Specifications Institute	CSI
Copper Development Association	CDA

D

Defense, U.S. Department of	DOD

E

Energy, U.S. Department of	DOE
Environmental Protection Agency	EPA

F

Federal Construction Council	FCC
Federal Housing Administration	FHA
Federal Highway Administration	FHWA
Forest Products Laboratory	FPL

G

General Conference on Weights and Measures	CGPM
General Services Administration	GSA

H

Housing and Urban Development, U.S. Department of	HUD

I

Illuminating Engineering Society of North America	IES
Institute of Electrical and Electronics Engineers	IEEE

International Conference of Building Officials | ICBO
International Organization for Standardization | ISO

N

National Academy of Sciences | NAS
National Association of Architectural Metal Manu-
facturers | NAAMM
National Association of Home Builders | NAHB
National Bureau of Standards | NBS
National Conference of States on Building Codes
and Standards | NCSBCS
National Electrical Manufactuers Association | NEMA
National Fire Protection Association | NFPA
National Forest Products Association | NFPA
National Institute of Building Sciences | NIBS
National Paint and Coatings Association | NPCA
National Research Council (National Academy of
Sciences) | NRC
National Roofing Contractors Association | NRCA
National Safety Council | NSC
National Science Foundation | NSF
National Woodwork Manufacturers Association | NWMA

O

Occupational Safety and Health Administration | OSHA

P

Portland Cement Association | PCA
Prestressed Concrete Institute | PCI
Public Health Service | PHS

S

Society of Automotive Engineers | SAE
Southern Building Code Congress International,
Inc. | SBIC
Steel Joist Institute | SJI

T

Tile Council of America | TCA

U

Underwriters Laboratories, Inc. | UL
U.S. Geological Survey | USGS
U.S. Metric Board | USMB

V

Veterans Administration | VA

PREFERRED LETTER SYMBOLS, SIGNS, AND ABBREVIATIONS FOR U.S. CUSTOMARY UNITS AND EXAMPLES OF INCORRECT OR DEPRECATED FORMS

Unlike metric (SI) units, which have only one recognized letter symbol for worldwide use, U.S. customary units, also referred to as inch-pound units, have utilized a variety of symbols, signs, or abbreviations, many of which are incorrect or deprecated. Symbols should never be pluralized.

Recognized letter symbols are listed in ANSI/IEEE Std 260-1978, "Letter Symbols for Units of Measurement." These are preferred and should be used wherever practicable. Abbreviations listed in column 3 of Table 1 are supplementary and may be used as alternatives where no superscripts are available or no ambiguity can arise. Symbols marked with an asterisk (*) are internationally agreed, and may differ from traditional usage in the United States. Abbreviations shown in parentheses should be avoided and replaced with the preferred letter symbols or signs shown in column 2.

Capitalized letter representations are shown for use on drawings, and for use in systems with limited character sets, such as computer printouts. In each case the first version is preferred where more than one representation is shown. Additional information is contained in American National Standard ANSI X3.50-1976, "Representations for U.S. Customary, SI, and Other Units to Be Used in Systems with Limited Character Sets."

Deprecated forms are those that have misleading units or unnecessary punctuation. They are shown in column 6.

TABLE 1.

Unit name written out	Preferred letter symbol or sign	Abbreviation	Capitalized letter symbol or abbreviation		Incorrect or deprecated forms
			Drawings	Computing	
Length					
inch; inches	in, "		IN	IN	In, ins
foot; feet	ft, '		FT	FT	Ft, ft.
yard; yards	yd		YD	YD	Yd, yds
mil [0.001 in]	mil				
mile (statute)	mi		MI	MI	Mi, M, m
Area					
square inch	in^2	sq in	IN^2, SQ IN	IN2, SIN	SI, si
square foot	ft^2	sq ft	FT^2, SQ FT	FT2, SFT	SF, sf
square yard	yd^2	sq yd	YD^2, SQ YD	YD2, SYD	SY, sy
acre	acr		ACR	ACR	ac, A
square mile	mi^2	sq mi	MI^2, SQ MI	MI2, SMI	
Volume					
cubic inch	in^3	cu in	IN^3, CU IN	IN3, CIN	CI, ci
cubic foot	ft^3	cu ft	FT^3, CU FT	FT3, CFT	CF, cf
cubic yard	yd^3	cu yd	YD^3, CUYD	YD3, CYD	CY
board-foot	bf		BF	BF	bdf, Bf
Capacity (Liquid Vol.)					
fluid ounce (U.S.)	fl oz		FL OZ	FLZ	Fl Oz, oz
pint (U.S.)	pt		PT	PT	Pt
quart (U.S.)	qt		QT	QT	
gallon, gallons (U.S.)	gal		GAL	GAL	Gal, gals
Mass (Weight)					
grain	gr		GR	GR	Gr, g
ounce (avoirdupois)	oz		OZ	OZ	Oz
pound, pounds	lb		LB	LB	lbs, p
hundredweight	cwt		CWT	CWT	
ton (U.S.) [2000 lb]	ton		TON	TON	tn, T, t
Time					
second	s*	(sec)	S	S, SEC	Sec
minute	min	min	MIN	MIN	Min, m
hour, hours	h*	(hr)	H	H, HR	hrs
day	d		D	D	dy

Internationally agreed units.

TABLE 1 (Cont.).

Unit name written out	Preferred letter symbol or sign	Abbreviation	Capitalized letter symbol or abbreviation		Incorrect or deprecated forms
			Drawings	Computing	
week	wk		WK	WK	Wk
month	mo		MO	MO	Mo
year [annum]	a*	yr	A	A, YR	Yr, ann
Plane Angle					
degree (of arc)	°	deg	°	°, DEG	Deg
minute (of arc)	'	(min)	'	', MNT	Min
second (of arc)	"	(sec)	"	", SEC	Sec
Temperature					
degree Fahrenheit	°F	deg F	°F	°F, DEGF	F
Force					
pound-force	lbf		LBF	LBF	lb, Lbf
kip [1000 lbf]	kip		KIP	KIP	Kip
ton-force [2000 lbf]	tonf		TONF	TONF	ton, Tonf
Energy					
British thermal unit	Btu		BTU	BTU	btu
therm [100 000 Btu]	thm		THM	THM	Th, th, Thm
Power					
horsepower	hp		HP	HP	Hp
Electrical Units					
ampere	A*	(amp)	A	A	Amp, amp
hertz [*replaces:* cycle per second]	Hz*	(c/s)	HZ	HZ	hz
kilowatt	kW*		KW	KW	Kw, kw
kilowatt hour	kWh		KWH	KWH	kwh, KWh
Acoustics					
decibel	dB		DB	DB	db, Db
Illumination Units					
footcandle	fc		FC	FC	Fc, ftc
footlambert	fL		FL	FL	fl, Fl
lumen per watt	lm/W*	(1pw)	LM/W	LM/W	lm/w, Lpw

EXAMPLES OF COMPOSITE FORMS OF U.S. CUSTOMARY UNITS

It has been common practice in the United States to use abbreviations for composite units of measurement, generally based on the initials of constituent units. Some of the composite units are shown below, and preferred letter symbols and capitalized letter symbols are given, as well as traditionally used abbreviations. It is internationally agreed practice to use the virgule or slash (/) as indication of division in lieu of the word "per," and to use the raised dot as multiplier between units that are products of constituent units. In computer representations, the multiplier dot is shown on the line.

TABLE 2.

Compound unit name written out	Preferred letter symbol or sign	Abbreviations	Capitalized letter symbol or abbreviation	
			Drawings	Computing
feet per second	ft/s	fps, FPS	FT/S	FT/S
feet per minute	ft/min	fpm, FPM	FT/MIN	FT/MIN
miles per hour	mi/h	mph, MPH	MI/H	MI/H
revolution per second	r/s*	(rev/s, REV/S) rps, RPS	R/S	R/S
revolution per minute	r/min	rpm, RPM	R/MIN	R/MIN
gallon per minute	gal/min	gpm, GPM	GAL/MIN	GAL/MIN
gallon per day	gal/d	gpd, GPD	GAL/D	GAL/D
cubic feet per minute	ft³/min	cfm, CFM	FT3/MIN	FT3/MIN
cubic feet per hour	ft³/h	cfh, CFH	FT³/H	FT3/H
cubic feet per day	ft³/d	cfd, CFD	FT³/D	FT3/D
pounds per [lineal] foot	lb/ft	plf, PLF	LB/FT	LB/FT
pounds per square foot (mass per unit area)	lb/ft²	psf†, PSF†	LB/FT²	LB/FT2
pounds per cubic foot	lb/ft³	pcf, PCF	LB/FT³	LB/FT3
foot pound-force	ft·lbf		FT·LBF	FT.LBF
pound-force foot	lbf·ft		LBF·FT	LBF.FT
pound-force per square inch	lbf/in²	psi, PSI	LBF/IN²	LBF/IN2
pound-force per square foot (force per unit area)	lbf/ft²	psf†, PSF†	LBF/FT²	LBF/FT2
kip per square inch	kip/in²	ksi, KSI	KIP/IN²	KIP/IN2
ton-force per square foot	ton/ft²	tsf, TSF	TON/FT²	TON/FT2
Btu per second	Btu/s		BTU/S	BTU/S
Btu per hour	Btu/h		BTU/H	BTU/H
Btu per day	Btu/d		BTU/D	BTU/D
horsepower-hour	hp·h	hph, HPH	HP·H	HP.H

* *Internationally agreed units.*
† *A clear distinction should be made between units based on pounds-mass and units based on pounds-force.*

Dimensions of adults

The dimensions and clearances shown for the average adult (Fig. 2.) represent minimum requirements for use in planning building layouts and furnishings. If possible, clearances should be increased to allow comfortable accommodations for persons larger than average. The height of tabletops shown on the next page is 29 in (740 mm); some authorities prefer 30 in (760 mm); metric preference is 750 mm.

Since doorways and passageways must normally be dimensioned to permit the movement of furniture, they should seldom be designed merely on the needs of the average adult. (See *Time-Saver Standards for Building Types* for furniture sizes.)

Dimensions of children

Children do not have the same physical proportions as adults, especially during their early years, and their heights vary greatly, but their space requirements can be approximated from the following table and from Fig. 1. (For heights of children's furniture and equipment, see section on "Schools" in *Time-Saver Standards for Building Types*.)

Average height of children

Age	Height in	Height mm	Age	Height in	Height mm
5	44	1120	11	56	1420
6	46	1170	12	58	1470
7	48	1220	13	60	1525
8	50	1270	14	62	1575
9	52	1320	15	64	1625
10	54	1370	16	66	1675

Metric conversions are to nearest 5 mm
References: Ernest Irving Freese, The Geometry of the Human Figure, *American Architect;* William W. Caudill, Space for Teaching *Bulletin of Texas Agricultural and Mechanical College.*

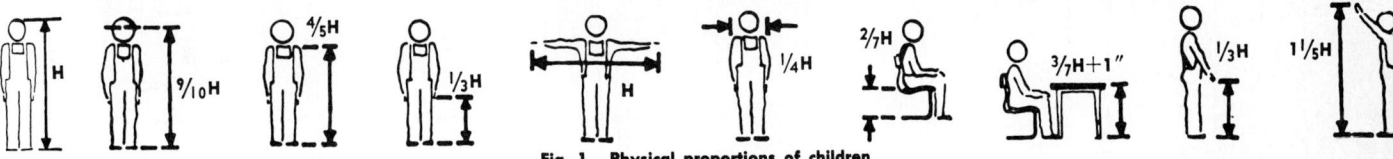

Fig. 1. Physical proportions of children

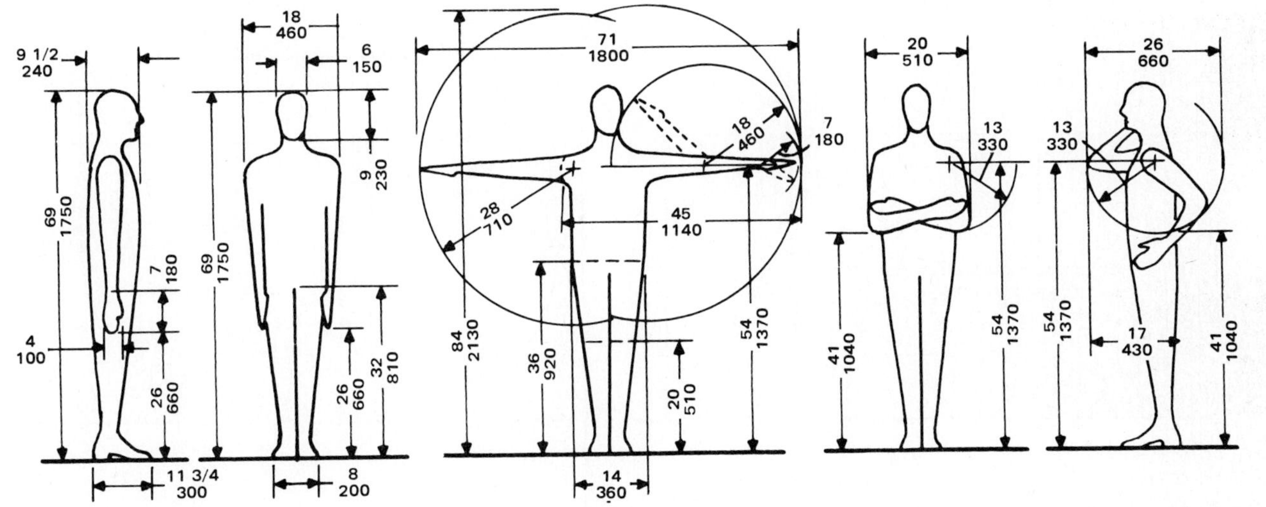

All figures reproduced to scale of 3/8″ = 1′ – 0″ (1:32)

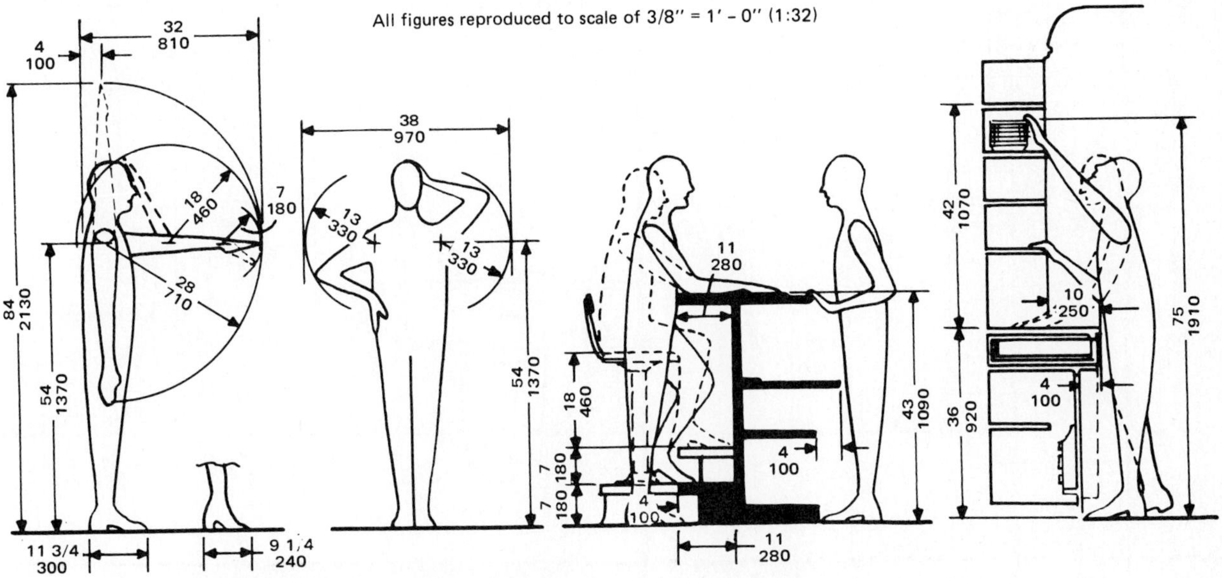

Fig. 2. **Dimensions and clearances for adults**

(Note: Upper figures are inches, lower figures are millimeters. Conversions are to nearest 10 mm.)

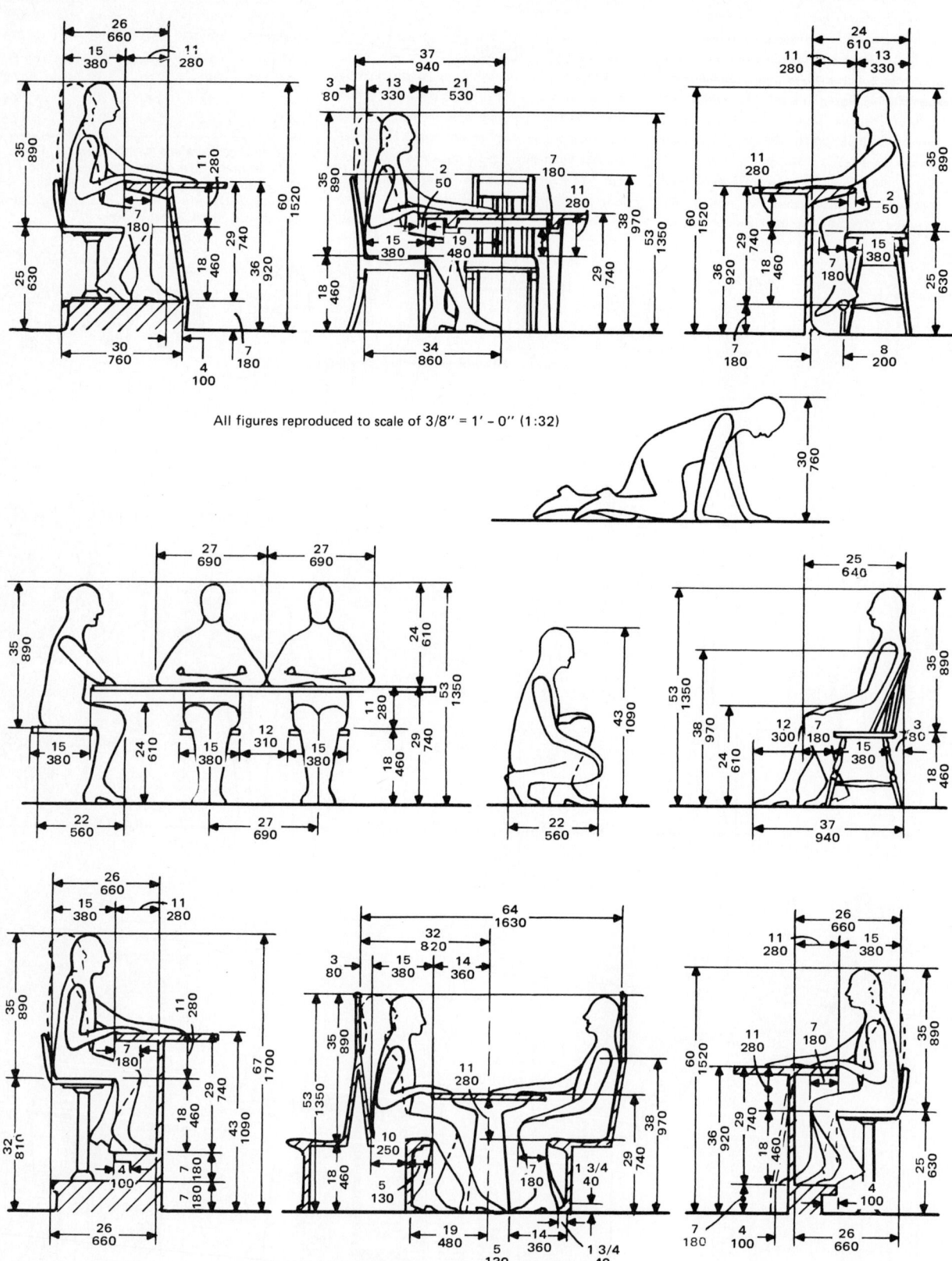

All figures reproduced to scale of 3/8″ = 1′ – 0″ (1:32)

Fig. 2. Dimensions and clearances for adults

(Note: Upper figures are inches, lower figures are millimeters. Conversions are to nearest 10 mm.)

The tables of equivalents on pages 1-32 and 1-33 were compiled by Hans J. Milton, Center for Building Technology, National Bureau of Standards. Exact equivalents are shown in boldface type. Fractions are rounded to four significant digits and shown with exponential notation (negative indices) where appropriate. For further information on conversion to metric (SI) units see Part 5 of this book.

MEASURES OF WEIGHT

Weights
(The grain is the same in all systems)

Avoirdupois Weight

16 drams	= 437.5 grains	= 1 ounce
16 ounces	= 7000 grains	= 1 pound
100 pounds		= 1 cental
2000 pounds		= 1 short ton
2240 pounds		= 1 long ton
1 std. lime bbl., small		= 180 lb. net
1 std. lime bbl., large		= 280 lb. net

Also (in Great Britain):

14 pounds	= 1 stone
2 stone = 28 lb.	= 1 quarter
4 quarters = 112 lb.	= 1 hundred-weight (cwt.)
20 hundredweight	= 1 long ton

Troy Weight

24 grains	= 1 penny-weight (dwt.)
20 pennyweights = 480 grains	= 1 ounce
12 ounces = 5760 grains	= 1 pound

1 **Assay Ton** = 29,167 milligrams, or as many milligrams as there are troy ounces in a ton of 2000 lb. avoirdupois. Consequently, the number of milligrams of precious metal yielded by an assay ton of ore gives directly the number of troy ounces that would be obtained from a ton of 2000 lb. avoirdupois

Apothecaries' Weight

20 grains	= 1 scruple ℈
3 scruples = 60 grains	= 1 dram ʒ
8 drams	= 1 ounce ℥
12 ounces = 5760 grains	= 1 pound

LINEAR MEASURE

Measures of Length

12 inches	= 1 foot
3 feet	= 1 yard
5½ yards = 16½ feet	= 1 rod, pole or perch
40 poles = 220 yards	= 1 furlong
8 furlongs = 1760 yards = 5280 feet	= 1 mile
3 miles	= 1 league
4 inches	= 1 hand
9 inches	= 1 span

Nautical Units

6080.20 feet	= 1 nautical mile
6 feet	= 1 fathom
120 fathoms	= 1 cable length
1 nautical mile per hr.	= 1 knot

Surveyor's or Gunter's Measure

7.92 inches	= 1 link
100 links = 66 ft. = 4 rods	= 1 chain
80 chains	= 1 mile
33⅓ inches	= 1 vara (Texas)

MEASURES OF AREA

144 square inches	= 1 square foot
9 square feet	= 1 square yard
30¼ square yards	= 1 square rod, pole or perch
160 square rods = 10 square chains = 43,560 sq. ft. = 5645 sq. varas (Texas) = 4 roods	= 1 acre
640 acres = 1 square mile	= 1 section of U.S. Govt. surveyed land

VOLUMETRIC MEASURE

Measures of Volume

1728 cubic inches	= 1 cubic foot
27 cubic feet	= 1 cubic yard
1 cord of wood	= 128 cu. ft.
1 perch of masonry	= 16½ to 25 cu. ft.

Liquid or Fluid Measure

4 gills	= 1 pint
2 pints	= 1 quart
4 quarts	= 1 gallon
7.4805 gallons	= 1 cubic foot

(There is no standard liquid barrel; by trade custom, 1 bbl. of petroleum oil, unrefined = 42 gal.)

Dry Measure

2 pints	= 1 quart
8 quarts	= 1 peck
4 pecks	= 1 bushel

1 std. bbl. for fruits and vegetables = 7056 cu. in. or 105 dry quarts, struck measure

Board Measure

1 board foot = $\begin{cases} 144 \text{ cu. in.} = \text{volume} \\ \text{of board 1 ft. sq. and} \\ 1 \text{ in. thick.} \end{cases}$

No. of board feet in a log = $[\frac{1}{4}(d-4)]^2 L$, where d = diam. of log (usually taken inside the bark at small end), in., and L = length of log, ft. The 4 in. deducted are an allowance for slab. This rule is variously known as the Doyle, Conn. River, St. Croix, Thurber, Moore and Beeman, and the Scribner rule.

LENGTH EQUIVALENTS

	Inches	Feet	Yards	Chains	Miles	Millimeters	Meters	Kilometers
Inches	1	0.083 33	0.027 78	0.001 263	1.578×10^{-5}	25.4	0.0254	2.54×10^{-5}
Feet	12	1	0.3333	0.015 15	1.894×10^{-4}	304.8	0.3048	3.048×10^{-4}
Yards	36	3	1	0.045 45	5.682×10^{-4}	914.4	0.9144	9.144×10^{-4}
Chains	792	66	22	1	0.0125	20 116.8	20.1168	0.020 117
Miles	63 360	5280	1760	80	1	1 609 344	1609.344	1.609 344
Millimeters	0.039 37	0.003 281	0.001 094	4.971×10^{-5}	6.214×10^{-7}	1	0.001	0.000 001
Meters	39.3701	3.280 8	1.0936	0.049 710	6.214×10^{-4}	1000	1	0.001
Kilometers	39 370	3280.84	1093.61	49.7097	0.621 37	1 000 000	1000	1

AREA EQUIVALENTS

	Square inches	Square feet	Square yards	Square rods	Square Chains	Acres	Square miles	Square meters	Hectares*
Square inches	1	0.006 944	7.716×10^{-4}	2.834×10^{-6}				6.452×10^{-4}	
Square feet	144	1	0.1111	0.003 673	2.296×10^{-4}	2.296×10^{-5}	3.587×10^{-8}	0.092 903	9.290×10^{-6}
Square yards	1296	9	1	0.033 058	0.002 066	2.066×10^{-4}	3.228×10^{-7}	0.836 127	8.361×10^{-5}
Square rods	39 204	272.25	30.25	1	0.0625	0.006 25	9.766×10^{-6}	25.2929	0.002 529
Square chains	627 264	4356	484	16	1	0.1	1.562×10^{-4}	404.6856	0.040 469
Acres	6 272 640	43 560	4840	160	10	1	0.001 562	4046.856	0.404 686
Square miles	——	27 878 400	3 097 600	102 400	6400	640	1	2 589 988	258.9988
Square meters	1550.00	10.7639	1.1960	0.039 537	0.002 471	2.471×10^{-4}	3.861×10^{-7}	1	0.0001
Hectares*	——	107 639	11 959.9	395.3686	24.7105	2.4711	0.003 861	10 000	1

1 hectare = 10 000 square meters (m²) = 0.01 square kilometer (km²)

VOLUME AND CAPACITY EQUIVALENTS

	Cubic inches	Cubic feet	Cubic yards	U.S. Fluid ounces	U.S. Quart (liquid)	U.S. Gallon (liquid)	U.S. Gallon (dry)	Liter	Cubic meter
Cubic inches	1	5.787×10^{-4}	2.143×10^{-5}	0.554 113	0.017 316	0.004 239	0.003 720	0.016 387	1.639×10^{-5}
Cubic feet	1728	1	0.037 037	957.506	29.922	7.4805	6.4285	28.3168	0.028 317
Cubic yards	46 656	27	1	25 852.7	807.896	201.974	173.57	764.555	0.764 555
U.S. Fl. oz.	1.8047	0.001 044	3.868×10^{-5}	1	0.031 25	0.007 812	0.006 714	0.029 574	2.957×10^{-5}
U.S. Quart (liq)	57.75	0.033 42	0.001 238	32	1	0.25	0.214 84	0.946 352	9.464×10^{-4}
U.S. Gallon (liq)	231	0.133 68	0.004 951	128	4	1	0.859 37	3.785 412	0.003 785
U.S. Gallon (dry)	268.8	0.1556	0.005 761	148.95	4.6546	1.1636	1	4.404 884	0.004 404
U.S. Bushel	2150.4	1.244 46	0.046 091	1191.57	37.237	9.3092	8	35.2391	0.035 239
Liter	61.024	0.035 31	0.001 308	33.814	1.0567	0.264 17	0.227 02	1	0.001
Cubic meter	61 024	35.3147	1.307 95	33 814	1056.67	264.172	227.021	1000	1

MASS (WEIGHT) EQUIVALENTS

	Grains	Ounces [Avoirdup.]	Ounces [Troy]	Pounds [Avoirdup.]	Pounds [Troy]	Short tons [2000 lb]	Long tons [2240 lb]	Kilograms	Metric tons
Grains	1	0.002 286	0.002 083	1.429×10^{-4}	1.736×10^{-4}	7.143×10^{-8}	6.378×10^{-8}	6.378×10^{-5}	6.480×10^{-8}
Ounces [Avoirdupois]	437.5	1	1.097 14	0.0625	0.075 95	3.125×10^{-5}	2.790×10^{-5}	0.028 35	2.835×10^{-5}
Ounces [Troy]	480	0.911 458	1	0.068 57	0.083 33	3.429×10^{-5}	3.061×10^{-5}	0.031 10	3.110×10^{-5}
Pounds (lb) [Avoirdupois]	7000	16	14.5833	1	1.215 28	0.0005	4.464×10^{-4}	0.453 59	4.546×10^{-4}
Pounds [Troy]	5760	13.1674	12	0.822 86	1	4.114×10^{-4}	3.673×10^{-4}	0.373 24	3.732×10^{-4}
Short Tons [2000 lb]	14 000 000	32 000	29 166.7	2000	2430.55	1	0.892 86	907.185	0.907 18
Long Tons [2240 lb]	15 680 000	35 840	32 666.7	2240	2722.22	1.12	1	1016.05	1.016 05
Kilograms	15 432.4	35.274	32.151	2.2046	2.6792	0.001 102	9.842×10^{-4}	1	0.001
Metric tons	15 432 358	35 273.96	32 150.8	2204.623	2679.23	1.102 311	0.984 207	1000	1

DECIMAL EQUIVALENTS OF FRACTIONS OF AN INCH

$\frac{1}{64}'' = 0.015\ 625$	$\frac{17}{64}'' = 0.265\ 625$	$\frac{33}{64}'' = 0.515\ 625$	$\frac{49}{64}'' = 0.765\ 625$
$\frac{1}{32}'' = 0.031\ 25$	$\frac{9}{32}'' = 0.281\ 25$	$\frac{17}{32}'' = 0.531\ 25$	$\frac{25}{32}'' = 0.781\ 25$
$\frac{3}{64}'' = 0.046\ 875$	$\frac{19}{64}'' = 0.396\ 875$	$\frac{35}{64}'' = 0.546\ 875$	$\frac{51}{64}'' = 0.796\ 875$
$\frac{1}{16}'' = 0.062\ 5$	$\frac{5}{16}'' = 0.312\ 5$	$\frac{9}{16}'' = 0.562\ 5$	$\frac{13}{16}'' = 0.812\ 5$
$\frac{5}{64}'' = 0.078\ 125$	$\frac{21}{64}'' = 0.328\ 125$	$\frac{37}{64}'' = 0.578\ 125$	$\frac{53}{64}'' = 0.828\ 125$
$\frac{3}{32}'' = 0.093\ 75$	$\frac{11}{32}'' = 0.343\ 75$	$\frac{19}{32}'' = 0.593\ 75$	$\frac{27}{32}'' = 0.843\ 75$
$\frac{7}{64}'' = 0.109\ 375$	$\frac{23}{64}'' = 0.359\ 375$	$\frac{39}{64}'' = 0.609\ 375$	$\frac{55}{64}'' = 0.859\ 375$
$\frac{1}{8}'' = 0.125$	$\frac{3}{8}'' = 0.375$	$\frac{5}{8}'' = 0.625$	$\frac{7}{8}'' = 0.875$
$\frac{9}{64}'' = 0.140\ 625$	$\frac{25}{64}'' = 0.390\ 625$	$\frac{41}{64}'' = 0.640\ 625$	$\frac{57}{64}'' = 0.890\ 625$
$\frac{5}{32}'' = 0.156\ 25$	$\frac{13}{32}'' = 0.406\ 25$	$\frac{21}{32}'' = 0.656\ 25$	$\frac{29}{32}'' = 0.906\ 25$
$\frac{11}{64}'' = 0.171\ 875$	$\frac{27}{64}'' = 0.421\ 875$	$\frac{43}{64}'' = 0.671\ 875$	$\frac{59}{64}'' = 0.921\ 875$
$\frac{3}{16}'' = 0.187\ 5$	$\frac{7}{16}'' = 0.437\ 5$	$\frac{11}{16}'' = 0.687\ 5$	$\frac{15}{16}'' = 0.937\ 5$
$\frac{13}{64}'' = 0.203\ 125$	$\frac{29}{64}'' = 0.453\ 125$	$\frac{45}{64}'' = 0.703\ 125$	$\frac{61}{64}'' = 0.953\ 125$
$\frac{7}{32}'' = 0.218\ 75$	$\frac{15}{32}'' = 0.468\ 75$	$\frac{23}{32}'' = 0.718\ 75$	$\frac{31}{32}'' = 0.968\ 75$
$\frac{15}{64}'' = 0.234\ 375$	$\frac{31}{64}'' = 0.484\ 375$	$\frac{47}{64}'' = 0.734\ 375$	$\frac{63}{64}'' = 0.984\ 375$
$\frac{1}{4}'' = 0.250$	$\frac{1}{2}'' = 0.500$	$\frac{3}{4}'' = 0.750$	$1'' = 1.000$

Inches to decimals of a foot

CONVERSION OF INCHES AND COMMON FRACTIONS TO DECIMALS OF A FOOT

Conversions have been given to six decimal places. Boldface values are exact. Factors may be rounded to the appropriate degree of precision required, for example, to three decimal places.

Common fractions	0	1"	2"	3"	4"	5"	6"	7"	8"	9"	10"	11"
0	—	0.083 333	0.166 667	**0.250**	0.333 333	0.416 667	**0.500**	0.583 333	0.666 667	**0.750**	0.833 333	0.916 667
1/16	0.005 208	0.088 542	**0.171 875**	0.255 208	0.338 542	**0.421 875**	0.505 208	0.588 542	**0.671 875**	0.755 208	0.838 542	**0.921 875**
1/8	0.010 417	**0.093 75**	0.177 083	0.260 417	**0.343 75**	0.427 083	0.510 417	**0.593 75**	0.677 083	0.760 412	**0.843 75**	0.927 083
3/16	**0.015 625**	0.098 958	0.182 292	**0.265 625**	0.348 958	0.432 292	**0.515 625**	0.598 958	0.682 292	**0.765 625**	0.848 958	0.932 292
1/4	0.020 833	0.104 167	**0.187 5**	0.270 833	0.354 167	**0.437 5**	0.520 833	0.604 167	**0.687 5**	0.770 833	0.854 167	**0.937 5**
5/16	0.026 042	**0.109 375**	0.192 708	0.276 042	**0.359 375**	0.442 708	0.526 042	**0.609 375**	0.692 708	0.776 042	**0.859 375**	0.942 708
3/8	**0.031 25**	0.114 583	0.197 917	**0.281 25**	0.364 583	0.447 917	**0.531 25**	0.614 583	0.697 917	**0.781 25**	0.864 583	0.947 917
7/16	0.036 458	0.119 792	**0.203 125**	0.286 458	0.369 792	**0.453 125**	0.536 458	0.619 792	**0.703 125**	0.786 458	0.869 792	**0.953 125**
1/2	0.041 667	**0.125**	0.208 333	0.291 667	**0.375**	0.458 333	0.541 667	**0.625**	0.708 333	0.791 667	**0.875**	0.958 333
9/16	**0.046 875**	0.130 208	0.213 542	**0.296 875**	0.380 208	0.463 542	**0.546 875**	0.630 208	0.713 542	**0.796 875**	0.880 208	0.963 542
5/8	0.052 083	0.135 417	**0.218 75**	0.302 083	0.385 417	**0.468 75**	0.552 083	0.635 417	**0.718 75**	0.802 083	0.885 417	**0.968 75**
11/16	0.057 292	**0.140 625**	0.223 958	0.307 292	**0.390 625**	0.473 958	0.557 292	**0.640 625**	0.723 958	0.807 292	**0.890 625**	0.973 958
3/4	**0.062 5**	0.145 833	0.229 167	**0.312 5**	0.395 833	0.479 167	**0.562 5**	0.645 833	0.729 167	**0.812 5**	0.895 833	0.979 167
13/16	0.067 708	0.151 042	**0.234 375**	0.317 708	0.401 042	**0.484 375**	0.567 708	0.651 042	**0.734 375**	0.817 708	0.901 042	**0.984 375**
7/8	0.072 917	**0.156 25**	0.239 583	0.322 917	**0.406 25**	0.489 583	0.572 917	**0.656 25**	0.739 583	0.822 917	**0.906 25**	0.989 583
15/16	**0.078 125**	0.161 458	0.244 792	**0.328 125**	0.411 458	0.494 792	**0.578 125**	0.661 458	0.744 792	**0.828 125**	0.911 458	0.994 792

Inches

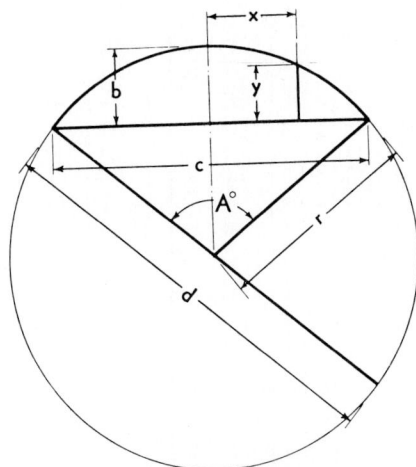

Functions of π with Logarithmic Equivalents

$\pi = 3.14159265,\ \log = 0.4971499$

$\dfrac{1}{\pi} = 0.3183099,\ \log = \overline{1}.5028501$

$\pi^2 = 9.8696044,\ \log = 0.9942997$

$\dfrac{1}{\pi^2} = 0.1013212,\ \log = \overline{1}.0057003$

$\sqrt{\pi} = 1.7724539,\ \log = 0.2485749$

$\sqrt{\dfrac{1}{\pi}} = 0.5641896,\ \log = \overline{1}.7514251$

$\dfrac{\pi}{180} = 0.0174533,\ \log = \overline{2}.2418774$

$\dfrac{180}{\pi} = 57.2957795,\ \log = 1.7581226$

PROPERTIES OF THE CIRCLE

Circumference = C
= d π = d $\times$ 3.1416
= 2 π r = 2 $\times$ r $\times$ 3.1416

Diameter = d
= C $\div$ 3.1416
= C $\times$ 0.31831

Diameter of Circle, having circumference equal to periphery of square
= side of square $\times$ 1.27324

Side of Square, having periphery equal to circumference of circle
= $\dfrac{d\pi}{4}$ = d $\times$ 0.7854

Diameter of Circle, circumscribed about square
= side of square $\times$ 1.41421

Side of Square, inscribed in circle
= d $\times$ 0.70711

Arc, $\quad$ a = $\dfrac{\pi r A^\circ}{180}$ = 0.017453 r A$^\circ$

Angle, A$^\circ$ = $\dfrac{180^\circ a}{\pi r}$ = 57.29578 $\dfrac{a}{r}$

Radius, r = $\dfrac{4 b^2 + c^2}{8 b}$

Diameter, d = $\dfrac{4 b^2 + c^2}{4 b}$

Chord, c = $2\sqrt{2 b r - b^2}$ = 2 r sin $\dfrac{A^\circ}{2}$

Rise, Trigonometric Calculations
$\quad$ b = $\dfrac{c}{2}$ tan $\dfrac{A^\circ}{4}$ = 2 r sin^2 $\dfrac{A^\circ}{4}$

Rise, Algebraic Calculations
$\quad$ b = r + y − $\sqrt{r^2 - x^2}$
$\quad$ b = r − $\frac{1}{2}\sqrt{4 r^2 - c^2}$
$\quad$ x = $\sqrt{r^2 - (r + y - b)^2}$
$\quad$ y = b − r + $\sqrt{r^2 - x^2}$

TABLE 1—AREAS OF CIRCLES IN SQUARE FEET—Diameter in Feet and Inches

Feet	Inches											
	0	1	2	3	4	5	6	7	8	9	10	11
0	.0000	.0055	.0218	.0491	.0873	.1364	.1963	.2673	.3491	.4418	.5454	.6600
1	.7854	.9218	1.069	1.227	1.396	1.576	1.767	1.969	2.182	2.405	2.640	2.885
2	3.142	3.409	3.687	3.976	4.276	4.587	4.909	5.241	5.585	5.940	6.305	6.681
3	7.069	7.467	7.876	8.296	8.727	9.168	9.621	10.08	10.56	11.04	11.54	12.05
4	12.57	13.10	13.64	14.19	14.75	15.32	15.90	16.50	17.10	17.72	18.35	18.99
5	19.63	20.29	20.97	21.65	22.34	23.04	23.76	24.48	25.22	25.97	26.73	27.49
6	28.27	29.07	29.87	30.68	31.50	32.34	33.18	34.04	34.91	35.78	36.67	37.57
7	38.48	39.41	40.34	41.28	42.24	43.20	44.18	45.17	46.16	47.17	48.19	49.22
8	50.27	51.32	52.38	53.46	54.54	55.64	56.75	57.86	58.99	60.13	61.28	62.44
9	63.62	64.80	66.00	67.20	68.42	69.64	70.88	72.13	73.39	74.66	75.94	77.24
10	78.54	79.85	81.18	82.52	83.86	85.22	86.59	87.97	89.36	90.76	92.18	93.60
11	95.03	96.48	97.93	99.40	100.9	102.4	103.9	105.4	106.9	108.4	110.0	111.5
12	113.1	114.7	116.3	117.9	119.5	121.1	122.7	124.4	126.0	127.7	129.4	131.0
13	132.7	134.4	136.2	137.9	139.6	141.4	143.1	144.9	146.7	148.5	150.3	152.1
14	153.9	155.8	157.6	159.5	161.4	163.2	165.1	167.0	168.9	170.9	172.8	174.8

If given diameter is not found in this table, reduce diameter to feet and decimals of a foot by aid of the following auxiliary table, and then find area from Table 4.

TABLE 2—Conversion from Inches and Fractions of an Inch to Decimals of a Foot

Inches	1	2	3	4	5	6	7	8	9	10	11
Feet........	.0833	.1667	.2500	.3333	.4167	.5000	.5833	.6667	.7500	.8333	.9167

Inches......	1/8	1/4	3/8	1/2	5/8	3/4	7/8				
Feet........	.0104	.0208	.0313	.0417	.0521	.0625	.0729				

Example. 5 ft. 7⅜ in. = 5.0 + 0.5833 + 0.0313 = 5.6146 ft.

NOTE 1
HOW TO FIND CIRCUMFERENCES (from Table 3)
This table gives the product of π times any number D from 1 to 10; that is, it is a table of multiples of π. (D = diameter.)
Moving the decimal point **one** place in column D is equivalent to moving it **one** place in the body of the table.

$\qquad$ Circumference = π $\times$ diam. = 3.141593 $\times$ diam.
Conversely,
$\qquad$ Diameter = $\dfrac{1}{\pi}$ $\times$ circumf. = 0.31831 $\times$ circumf.

Examples:

Diameter given; Circumference sought:
$\qquad$ Diameter = 3.57 feet. Find 3.5 in left hand column, read right to column 7 and find 11.22 feet = circumference.

Circumference given; Diameter sought:
$\qquad$ Circumference = 20.17 feet. Find 20.17 in body of table, read left and find 6.4, note 20.17 is in column 2, which add = 6.4 + .02 = 6.42 = diameter.

NOTE 2
HOW TO FIND AREAS (from Table 4)
Moving the decimal point **one** place in column D is equivalent to moving it **two** places in the body of the table. (D = diameter.)

$\qquad$ Area of circle = $\dfrac{\pi}{4}$ $\times$ (diam.^{2}) = 0.785398 $\times$ (diam.^{2})

Conversely,
$\qquad$ Diam. = $\sqrt{\dfrac{4}{\pi}}$ $\times$ $\sqrt{\text{area}}$ = 1.128379 $\times$ $\sqrt{\text{area}}$

Examples:

Diameter given; Area sought:
$\qquad$ Diameter = 12.3 feet. Move decimal one point left = 1.23. Find 1.2 in left column, read right to column 3, find area of 1.23 = 1.188. Move decimal two points right = 118.8 sq. ft. = area.

Area given; Diameter sought:
$\qquad$ Area = 4927 sq. in. Move decimal two points left = 49.27. Find 49.27 in column 2, which add = 7.9 + .02 = 7.92. Move decimal one point right = 79.2 inches = diameter.

Properties of the circle

TABLE 3—CIRCUMFERENCES BY HUNDREDTHS. SEE NOTE 1

D	0	1	2	3	4	5	6	7	8	9
1.0	3.142	3.173	3.204	3.236	3.267	3.299	3.330	3.362	3.393	3.424
.1	3.456	3.487	3.519	3.550	3.581	3.613	3.644	3.676	3.707	3.738
.2	3.770	3.801	3.833	3.864	3.896	3.927	3.958	3.990	4.021	4.053
.3	4.084	4.115	4.147	4.178	4.210	4.241	4.273	4.304	4.335	4.367
.4	4.398	4.430	4.461	4.492	4.524	4.555	5.587	4.618	4.650	4.681
1.5	4.712	4.744	4.775	4.807	4.838	4.869	4.901	4.932	4.964	4.995
.6	5.027	5.058	5.089	5.121	5.152	5.184	5.215	5.246	5.278	5.309
.7	5.341	5.372	5.404	5.435	5.466	5.498	5.529	5.561	5.592	5.623
.8	5.655	5.686	5.718	5.749	5.781	5.812	5.843	5.875	5.906	5.938
.9	5.969	6.000	6.032	6.063	6.095	6.126	6.158	6.189	6.220	6.252
2.0	6.283	6.315	6.346	6.377	6.409	6.440	6.472	6.503	6.535	6.566
.1	6.597	6.629	6.660	6.692	6.723	6.754	6.786	6.817	6.849	6.880
.2	6.912	6.943	6.974	7.006	7.037	7.069	7.100	7.131	7.163	7.194
.3	7.226	7.257	7.288	7.320	7.351	7.383	7.414	7.446	7.477	7.508
.4	7.540	7.571	7.603	7.634	7.665	7.697	7.728	7.760	7.791	7.823
2.5	7.854	7.885	7.917	7.948	7.980	8.011	8.042	8.074	8.105	8.137
.6	8.168	8.200	8.231	8.262	8.294	8.325	8.357	8.388	8.419	8.451
.7	8.482	8.514	8.545	8.577	8.608	8.639	8.671	8.702	8.734	8.765
.8	8.796	8.828	8.859	8.891	8.922	8.954	8.985	9.016	9.048	9.079
.9	9.111	9.142	9.173	9.205	9.236	9.268	9.299	9.331	9.362	9.393
3.0	9.425	9.456	9.488	9.519	9.550	9.582	9.613	9.645	9.676	9.708
.1	9.739	9.770	9.802	9.833	9.865	9.896	9.927	9.959	9.990	10.022
.2	10.05	10.08	10.12	10.15	10.18	10.21	10.24	10.27	10.30	10.34
.3	10.37	10.40	10.43	10.46	14.49	10.52	10.56	10.59	10.62	10.65
.4	10.68	10.71	10.74	10.78	10.81	10.84	10.87	10.90	10.93	10.96
3.5	11.00	11.03	11.06	11.09	11.12	11.15	11.18	11.22	11.25	11.28
.6	11.31	11.34	11.37	11.40	11.44	11.47	11.50	11.53	11.56	11.59
.7	11.62	11.66	11.69	11.72	11.75	11.78	11.81	11.84	11.88	11.91
.8	11.94	11.97	12.00	12.03	12.06	12.10	12.13	12.16	12.19	12.22
.9	12.25	12.28	12.32	12.35	12.38	12.41	12.44	12.47	12.50	12.53
4.0	12.57	12.60	12.63	12.66	12.69	12.72	12.75	12.79	12.82	12.85
.1	12.88	12.91	12.94	12.97	13.01	13.04	13.07	13.10	13.13	13.16
.2	13.19	13.23	13.26	13.29	13.32	13.35	13.38	13.41	13.45	13.48
.3	13.51	13.54	13.57	13.60	13.63	13.67	13.70	13.73	13.76	13.79
.4	13.82	13.85	13.89	13.92	13.95	13.98	14.01	14.04	14.07	14.11
4.5	14.14	14.17	14.20	14.23	14.26	14.29	14.33	14.36	14.39	14.42
.6	14.45	14.48	14.51	14.44	14.58	14.61	14.64	14.67	14.70	14.73
.7	14.77	14.80	14.83	14.86	14.89	14.92	14.95	14.99	15.02	15.05
.8	15.08	15.11	15.14	15.17	15.21	15.24	15.27	15.30	15.33	15.36
.9	15.39	15.43	15.46	15.49	15.52	15.52	15.58	15.61	15.65	15.68
5.0	15.71	15.74	15.77	15.80	15.83	15.87	15.90	15.93	15.96	15.99
.1	16.02	16.05	16.08	16.12	16.15	16.18	16.21	16.24	16.27	16.30
.2	16.34	16.37	16.40	16.43	16.46	16.49	16.52	16.56	16.59	16.62
.3	16.65	16.68	16.71	16.74	16.78	16.81	16.84	16.87	16.90	16.93
.4	16.96	17.00	17.03	17.06	17.09	17.12	17.15	17.18	17.22	17.25
5.5	17.28	17.31	17.34	17.37	17.40	17.44	17.47	17.50	17.53	17.56
.6	17.59	17.62	17.66	17.69	17.72	17.75	17.78	17.81	17.84	17.88
.7	17.91	17.94	17.97	18.00	18.03	18.06	18.10	18.13	18.16	18.19
.8	18.22	18.25	18.28	18.32	18.35	18.38	18.41	18.44	18.47	18.50
.9	18.54	18.57	18.60	18.63	18.66	18.69	18.72	18.76	18.79	18.82
6.0	18.85	18.88	18.91	18.94	18.98	19.01	19.04	19.07	19.10	19.13
.1	19.16	19.20	19.23	19.26	19.29	19.32	19.35	19.38	19.42	19.45
.2	19.48	19.51	19.54	19.57	19.60	19.63	19.67	19.70	19.73	19.76
.3	19.79	19.82	19.85	19.89	19.92	19.95	19.98	20.01	20.04	20.07
.4	20.11	20.14	20.17	20.20	20.23	20.26	20.29	20.33	20.36	20.39
6.5	20.42	20.45	20.48	20.51	20.55	20.58	20.61	20.64	20.67	20.70
.6	20.73	20.77	20.80	20.83	20.86	20.89	20.92	20.95	20.99	21.02
.7	21.05	21.08	21.11	21.14	21.17	21.21	21.24	21.27	21.30	21.33
.8	21.36	21.39	21.43	21.46	21.49	21.52	21.55	21.58	21.61	21.65
.9	21.68	21.71	21.74	21.77	21.80	21.83	21.87	21.90	21.93	21.96
7.0	21.99	22.02	22.05	22.09	22.12	22.15	22.18	22.21	22.24	22.27
.1	22.31	22.34	22.37	22.40	22.43	22.46	22.49	22.53	22.56	22.59
.2	22.62	22.65	22.68	22.71	22.75	22.78	22.81	22.84	22.87	22.90
.3	22.93	22.97	23.00	23.03	23.06	23.09	23.12	23.15	23.18	23.22
.4	23.25	23.28	23.31	23.34	23.37	23.40	23.44	23.47	23.50	23.53
7.5	23.56	23.59	23.62	23.66	23.69	23.72	23.75	23.78	23.81	23.84
.6	23.88	23.91	23.94	23.97	24.00	24.03	24.06	24.10	24.13	24.16
.7	24.19	24.22	24.25	24.28	24.32	24.35	24.38	24.41	24.44	24.47
.8	24.50	24.54	24.57	24.60	24.63	24.66	24.69	24.72	24.76	24.79
.9	24.82	24.85	24.88	24.91	24.94	24.98	25.01	25.04	25.07	25.10
8.0	25.13	25.16	25.20	25.23	25.26	25.29	25.32	25.35	25.38	25.42
.1	25.45	25.48	25.51	24.54	25.57	25.60	25.64	25.67	25.70	25.73
.2	25.76	25.79	25.82	25.86	25.89	25.92	25.95	25.98	26.01	26.04
.3	26.08	26.11	26.14	26.17	26.20	26.23	26.26	26.30	26.33	26.36
.4	26.39	26.42	26.45	26.48	26.52	26.55	26.58	26.61	26.64	26.67
8.5	26.70	26.73	26.77	26.80	26.83	26.86	26.89	26.92	26.95	26.99
.6	27.02	27.05	27.08	27.11	27.14	27.17	27.21	27.24	27.27	27.30
.7	27.33	27.36	27.39	27.43	27.46	27.49	27.52	27.55	27.58	27.61
.8	27.65	27.68	27.71	27.74	27.77	27.80	27.83	27.87	27.90	27.93
.9	27.96	27.99	28.02	28.05	28.09	28.12	28.15	28.18	28.21	28.24
9.0	28.27	28.31	28.34	28.37	28.40	28.43	28.46	28.49	28.53	28.56
.1	28.59	28.62	28.65	28.68	28.71	28.75	28.78	28.81	28.84	28.87
.2	28.90	28.93	28.97	29.00	29.03	29.06	29.09	29.12	29.15	29.19
.3	29.22	29.25	29.28	29.31	29.34	29.37	29.41	29.44	29.47	29.50
.4	29.53	29.56	29.59	29.63	29.66	29.69	20.72	29.75	29.78	29.81
9.5	29.85	29.88	29.91	29.94	29.97	30.00	30.03	30.07	30.10	30.13
.6	30.16	30.19	30.22	30.25	30.28	30.32	30.35	30.38	30.41	30.44
.7	30.47	30.50	30.54	30.57	30.60	30.63	30.66	30.69	30.72	30.76
.8	30.79	30.82	30.85	30.88	30.91	30.94	30.98	31.01	31.04	31.07
.9	31.10	31.13	31.16	31.20	31.23	31.26	31.29	31.32	31.35	31.38

TABLE 4—AREAS BY HUNDREDTHS. SEE NOTE 2

D	0	1	2	3	4	5	6	7	8	9
1.0	0.785	0.801	0.817	0.833	0.849	0.866	0.882	0.899	0.916	0.933
.1	0.950	0.968	0.985	1.003	1.021	1.039	1.057	1.075	1.094	1.112
.2	1.131	1.150	1.169	1.188	1.208	1.227	1.247	1.267	1.287	1.307
.3	1.327	1.348	1.368	1.389	1.410	1.431	1.453	1.474	1.496	1.517
.4	1.539	1.561	1.584	1.606	1.629	1.651	1.674	1.697	1.720	1.744
1.5	1.767	1.791	1.815	1.839	1.863	1.887	1.911	1.936	1.961	1.986
.6	2.011	2.036	2.061	2.087	2.112	2.138	2.164	2.190	2.217	2.243
.7	2.270	2.297	2.324	2.351	2.378	2.405	2.433	2.461	2.488	2.516
.8	2.545	2.573	2.602	2.630	2.659	2.688	2.717	2.746	2.776	2.806
.9	2.835	2.865	2.895	2.926	2.956	2.986	3.017	3.048	3.079	3.110
2.0	3.142	3.173	3.205	3.237	3.269	3.301	3.333	3.365	3.398	3.431
.1	3.464	3.497	3.530	3.563	3.597	3.631	3.664	3.698	3.733	3.767
.2	3.801	3.836	3.871	3.906	3.941	3.976	4.011	4.047	4.083	4.119
.3	4.155	4.191	4.227	4.264	4.301	4.337	4.374	4.412	4.449	4.486
.4	4.524	4.562	4.600	4.638	4.676	4.714	4.753	4.792	4.831	4.870
2.5	4.909	4.948	4.988	5.027	5.067	5.107	5.147	5.187	5.228	5.269
.6	5.309	5.350	5.391	5.433	5.474	5.515	5.557	5.599	5.641	5.683
.7	5.726	5.768	5.811	5.853	5.896	5.940	5.983	6.026	6.070	6.114
.8	6.158	6.202	6.246	6.290	6.335	6.379	6.424	6.469	6.514	6.560
.9	6.605	6.651	6.697	6.743	6.789	6.835	6.881	6.928	6.975	7.022
3.0	7.069	7.116	7.163	7.211	7.258	7.306	7.354	7.402	7.451	7.499
.1	7.548	7.596	7.645	7.694	7.744	7.793	7.843	7.892	7.942	7.992
.2	8.042	8.093	8.143	8.194	8.245	8.296	8.347	8.398	8.450	8.501
.3	8.553	8.605	8.657	8.709	8.762	8.814	8.867	8.920	8.973	9.026
.4	9.079	9.133	9.186	9.240	9.294	9.348	9.402	9.457	9.511	9.566
3.5	9.621	9.676	9.731	9.787	9.842	9.898	9.954	10.01	10.07	10.12
.6	10.18	10.24	10.29	10.35	10.41	10.46	10.52	10.58	10.64	10.69
.7	10.75	10.81	10.87	10.93	10.99	11.04	11.10	11.16	11.22	11.28
.8	11.34	11.40	11.46	11.52	11.58	11.64	11.70	11.76	11.82	11.88
.9	11.95	12.01	12.07	12.13	12.19	12.25	12.32	12.38	12.44	12.50
4.0	12.57	12.63	12.69	12.76	12.82	12.88	12.95	13.01	13.07	13.14
.1	13.20	13.27	13.33	13.40	13.46	13.53	13.59	13.66	13.72	13.79
.2	13.85	13.92	13.99	14.05	14.12	14.19	14.25	14.32	14.39	14.45
.3	14.52	14.59	14.66	14.73	14.79	14.86	14.93	15.00	15.07	15.14
.4	15.21	15.27	15.34	15.41	15.48	15.55	15.62	15.69	15.76	15.83
4.5	15.90	15.98	16.05	16.12	16.19	16.26	16.33	16.40	16.47	16.55
.6	16.62	16.69	16.76	16.84	16.91	16.98	17.06	17.13	17.20	17.28
.7	17.35	17.42	17.50	17.57	17.65	17.72	17.80	17.87	17.95	18.02
.8	18.10	18.17	18.25	18.32	18.40	18.47	18.55	18.63	18.70	18.78
.9	18.86	18.93	19.01	19.09	19.17	19.24	19.32	19.40	19.48	19.56
5.0	19.63	19.71	19.79	19.87	19.95	20.03	20.11	20.19	20.27	20.35
.1	20.43	20.51	20.59	20.67	20.75	20.83	20.91	20.99	21.07	21.16
.2	21.24	21.32	21.40	21.48	21.57	21.65	21.73	21.81	21.90	21.98
.3	22.06	22.15	22.23	22.31	22.40	22.48	22.56	22.65	22.73	22.82
.4	22.90	22.99	23.07	23.16	23.24	23.33	23.41	23.50	23.59	23.67
5.5	23.76	23.84	23.93	24.02	24.11	24.19	24.28	24.37	24.45	24.54
.6	24.63	24.72	24.81	24.89	24.98	25.07	25.16	25.25	25.34	25.43
.7	25.52	25.61	25.70	25.79	25.88	25.97	26.06	26.15	26.24	26.33
.8	26.42	26.51	26.60	26.69	26.79	26.88	26.97	27.06	27.15	27.25
.9	27.34	27.43	27.53	27.62	27.71	27.81	27.90	27.99	28.09	28.18
6.0	28.27	28.37	28.46	28.56	28.65	28.75	28.84	28.94	29.03	29.13
.1	29.22	29.32	29.42	29.51	29.61	29.71	29.80	29.90	30.00	30.09
.2	30.19	30.29	30.39	30.48	30.58	30.68	30.78	30.88	30.97	31.07
.3	31.17	31.27	31.37	31.47	31.57	31.67	31.77	31.87	31.97	32.07
.4	32.17	32.27	32.37	32.47	32.57	32.67	32.78	32.88	32.98	33.08
6.5	33.18	33.29	33.39	33.49	33.59	33.70	33.80	33.90	34.00	34.11
.6	34.21	34.32	34.42	34.52	34.63	34.73	34.84	34.94	35.05	35.15
.7	35.26	35.36	35.47	35.57	35.68	35.78	35.89	36.00	36.10	36.21
.8	36.32	36.42	36.53	36.64	36.75	36.85	36.96	37.07	37.18	37.28
.9	37.39	37.50	37.61	37.72	37.83	37.94	38.05	38.16	38.26	38.37
7.0	38.48	38.59	38.70	38.82	38.93	39.04	39.15	39.26	39.37	39.48
.1	39.59	39.70	39.82	39.93	40.04	40.15	40.26	40.38	40.49	40.60
.2	40.72	40.83	40.94	41.06	41.17	41.28	41.40	41.51	41.62	41.74
.3	41.85	41.97	42.08	42.20	42.31	42.43	42.54	42.66	42.78	42.89
.4	43.01	43.12	43.24	43.36	43.47	43.59	43.71	43.83	43.94	44.06
7.5	44.18	44.30	44.41	44.53	44.65	44.77	44.89	45.01	45.13	45.25
.6	45.36	45.48	45.60	45.72	45.84	45.96	46.08	46.20	46.32	46.45
.7	46.57	46.69	46.81	46.93	47.05	47.17	47.29	47.42	47.54	47.66
.8	47.78	47.91	48.03	48.15	48.27	48.40	48.52	48.65	48.77	48.89
.9	49.02	49.14	49.27	49.39	49.51	49.64	49.76	49.89	50.01	50.14
8.0	50.27	50.39	50.52	50.64	50.77	50.90	51.02	51.15	51.28	51.40
.1	51.53	51.66	51.78	51.91	52.04	52.17	52.30	52.42	52.55	52.68
.2	52.81	52.94	53.07	53.20	53.33	53.46	53.59	53.72	53.85	53.98
.3	54.11	54.24	54.37	54.50	54.63	54.76	54.89	55.02	55.15	55.29
.4	55.42	55.55	55.68	55.81	55.95	56.08	56.21	56.35	56.48	56.61
8.5	56.75	56.88	57.01	57.15	57.28	57.41	57.55	57.68	57.82	57.95
.6	58.09	58.22	58.36	58.49	58.63	58.77	58.90	59.04	59.17	59.31
.7	59.45	59.58	59.72	59.86	59.99	60.13	60.27	60.41	60.55	60.68
.8	60.82	60.96	61.10	61.24	61.38	61.51	61.65	61.79	61.93	62.07
.9	62.21	62.35	62.49	62.63	62.77	62.91	63.05	63.19	63.33	63.48
9.0	63.62	63.76	63.90	64.04	64.18	64.33	64.47	64.61	64.75	64.90
.1	65.04	65.18	65.33	65.47	65.61	65.76	65.90	66.04	66.19	66.33
.2	66.48	66.62	66.77	66.91	67.06	67.20	67.35	67.49	67.64	67.78
.3	67.93	68.08	68.22	68.37	68.51	68.66	68.81	68.96	69.10	69.25
.4	69.40	69.55	69.69	69.84	69.99	70.14	70.29	70.44	70.58	70.73
9.5	70.88	71.03	71.18	71.33	71.48	71.63	71.78	71.93	72.08	72.23
.6	72.38	72.53	72.68	72.84	72.99	73.14	73.29	73.44	73.59	73.75
.7	73.90	74.05	74.20	74.36	74.51	74.66	74.82	74.97	75.12	75.28
.8	75.43	75.58	75.74	75.89	76.05	76.20	76.36	76.51	76.67	76.82
.9	76.98	77.13	77.29	77.44	77.60	77.76	77.91	78.07	78.23	78.38

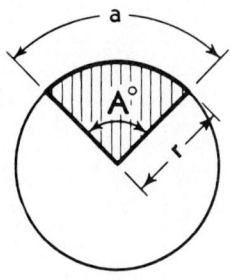

FIG. 1

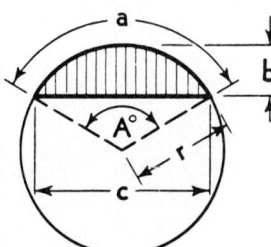

FIG. 2

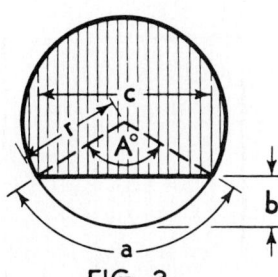

FIG. 3

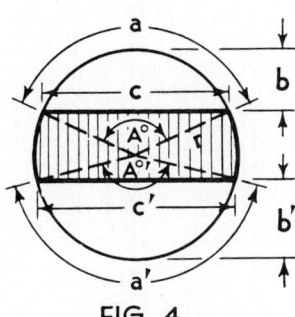

FIG. 4

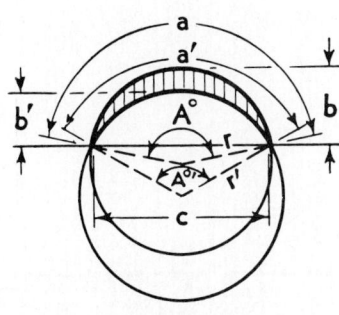

FIG. 5

Nomenclature—

$$A° = \text{Angle in degrees} = \frac{180° \, a}{\pi \, r}$$

$$a = \text{Arc} = 0.017453 \, r \, A°$$

$$b = \text{Rise} = 2 \, r \sin^2 \frac{A°}{4}$$

$$c = \text{Chord} = 2 \, r \sin \frac{A°}{2}$$

$$d = \text{Diameter} = 2 \, r = \frac{4 \, b^2 + c^2}{4 \, b}$$

$$\pi = 3.1416$$

$$r = \text{Radius} = \frac{d}{2} = \frac{4 \, b^2 + c^2}{8 \, b}$$

$$S = \text{Area} = \frac{\pi \, d^2}{4} = 0.7854 \, d^2$$

AREA OF CIRCULAR SECTOR—Figure 1

$$\text{Area} = \frac{a \, r}{2} = \frac{S \, A°}{360}$$

AREA OF CIRCULAR SEGMENT—Figure 2
(Less than half circle)

$$\text{Area} = \frac{a \, r - c \, (r - b)}{2} = \frac{S A°}{360} - \frac{c \, (r - b)}{2}$$

AREA OF CIRCULAR SEGMENT—Figure 3
(Greater than half circle)

$$\text{Area} = S - \left[\frac{a \, r - c \, (r - b)}{2} \right] = S - \left[\frac{S \, A°}{360} - \frac{c \, (r - b)}{2} \right]$$

AREA OF CIRCULAR ZONE—Figure 4

$$\text{Area} = S - \left[\frac{a \, r - c \, (r - b)}{2} + \frac{a^1 \, r - c^1 \, (r - b^1)}{2} \right]$$

$$= S - \left[\frac{S \, A°}{360} - \frac{c \, (r - b)}{2} + \frac{S A^{°1}}{360} - \frac{c^1 \, (r - b^1)}{2} \right]$$

AREA OF CIRCULAR LUNE—Figure 5

$$\text{Area} = \left[\frac{a \, r - c \, (r - b)}{2} \right] - \left[\frac{a^1 \, r^1 - c \, (r^1 - b^1)}{2} \right]$$

$$= \left[\frac{S A°}{360} - \frac{c(r - b)}{2} \right] - \left[\frac{S^1 A^{°1}}{360} - \frac{c \, (r^1 - b^1)}{2} \right]$$

AREA OF CIRCULAR SEGMENT—From Table 5
(Using Rise and Chord)

Area = c × b × coefficient.
Example: chord, c = 3.52; rise, b = 1.49

$$\frac{b}{c} = \frac{1.49}{3.52} = 0.4233$$

coefficient of 0.4233 = 0.7542
3.52 × 1.49 × 0.7542 = 3.9556 = area of segment

AREA OF CIRCULAR SEGMENT—From Table 6
(Using Rise and Diameter)

Area = d^2 × coefficient
Example: diameter, d = $5\frac{3}{32}$; rise, b = $2\frac{7}{16}$

$$5\tfrac{3}{32} = 5.09375; \quad 2\tfrac{7}{16} = 2.4375$$

$$\frac{b}{d} = \frac{2.4375}{5.09375} = 0.478528$$

Interpolation:
Coefficient for 0.479 = 0.371705
0.478 = 0.370706
.001 = 0.000999

.478528
.478000
.000528 × 528
0.000527

Coefficient + 0.370706
for 0.478528 = 0.371233

5.09375 × 5.09375 × 0.371233 = 9.6321 = area of segment

Circular sections

AREAS OF CIRCULAR SEGMENTS

Table 5. For ratios of rise and chord

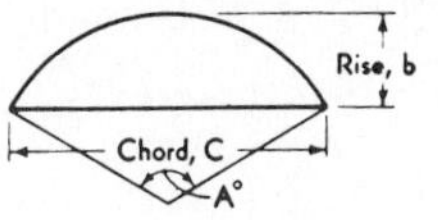

Area = C x b x Coefficient

A°	Coeff.-cient	b/C	A°	Coeffi-cient	b/C	A°	Coeffi-cient	b/C	A°	Coeffi-cient	b/C
1	.6667	.0022	16	.6674	.0350	31	.6691	.0681	46	.6722	.1017
2	.6667	.0044	17	.6674	.0372	32	.6693	.0703	47	.6724	.1040
3	.6667	.0066	18	.6675	.0394	33	.6694	.0725	48	.6727	.1063
4	.6667	.0087	19	.6676	.0416	34	.6696	.0747	49	.6729	.1086
5	.6667	.0109	20	.6677	.0437	35	.6698	.0770	50	.6732	.1109
6	.6667	.0131				36	.6700	.0792			
7	.6668	.0153	21	.6678	.0459	37	.6702	.0814	51	.6734	.1131
8	.6668	.0175	22	.6679	.0481	38	.6704	.0837	52	.6737	.1154
9	.6669	.0197	23	.6680	.0504	39	.6706	.0859	53	.6740	.1177
10	.6670	.0218	24	.6681	.0526	40	.6708	.0882	54	.6743	.1200
			25	.6682	.0548				55	.6746	.1224
11	.6670	.0240	26	.6684	.0570	41	.6710	.0904	56	.6749	.1247
12	.6671	.0262	27	.6685	.0592	42	.6712	.0927	57	.6752	.1270
13	.6672	.0284	28	.6687	.0614	43	.6714	.0949	58	.6755	.1293
14	.6672	.0306	29	.6688	.0636	44	.6717	.0972	59	.6758	.1316
15	.6673	.0328	30	.6690	.0658	45	.6719	.0995	60	.6761	.1340

A°	Coeffi-cient	b/C	A°	Coeffi-cient	b/C	A°	Coeffii cient	b/C	A°	Coeffi-cient	b/C
61	.6764	.1363	91	.6895	.2097	121	.7100	.2916	151	.7408	.3871
62	.6768	.1387	92	.6901	.2122	122	.7109	.2945	152	.7421	.3906
63	.6771	.1410	93	.6906	.2148	123	.7117	.2975	153	.7434	.3942
64	.6775	.1434	94	.6912	.2174	124	.7126	.3004	154	.7447	.3977
65	.6779	.1457	95	.6918	.2200	125	.7134	.3034	155	.7460	.4013
66	.6782	.1481	96	.6924	.2226	126	.7143	.3064	156	.7473	.4049
67	.6786	.1505	97	.6930	.2252	127	.7152	.3094	157	.7486	.4085
68	.6790	.1529	98	.6936	.2279	128	.7161	.3124	158	.7500	.4122
69	.6794	.1553	99	.6942	.2305	129	.7170	.3155	159	.7514	.4159
70	.6797	.1577	100	.6948	.2332	130	.7180	.3185	160	.7528	.4196
71	.6801	.1601	101	.6954	.2358	131	.7189	.3216	161	.7542	.4233
72	.6805	.1625	102	.6961	.2385	132	.7199	.3247	162	.7557	.4270
73	.6809	.1649	103	.6967	.2412	133	.7209	.3278	163	.7571	.4308
74	.6814	.1673	104	.6974	.2439	134	.7219	.3309	164	.7586	.4346
75	.6818	.1697	105	.6980	.2466	135	.7229	.3341	165	.7601	.4385
76	.6822	.1722	106	.6987	.2493	136	.7239	.3373	166	.7616	.4424
77	.6826	.1746	107	.6994	.2520	137	.7249	.3404	167	.7632	.4463
78	.6831	.1771	108	.7001	.2548	138	.7260	.3436	168	.7648	.4502
79	.6835	.1795	109	.7008	.2575	139	.7270	.3469	169	.7664	.4542
80	.6840	.1820	110	.7015	.2603	140	.7281	.3501	170	.7680	.4582
81	.6844	.1845	111	.7022	.2631	141	.7292	.3534	171	.7696	.4622
82	.6849	.1869	112	.7030	.2659	142	.7303	.3567	172	.7712	.4663
83	.6854	.1894	113	.7037	.2687	143	.7314	.3600	173	.7729	.4704
84	.6859	.1919	114	.7045	.2715	144	.7325	.3633	174	.7746	.4745
85	.6854	.1944	115	.7052	.2743	145	.7336	.3666	175	.7763	.4787
86	.6869	.1970	116	.7060	.2772	146	.7348	.3700	176	.7781	.4828
87	.6874	.1995	117	.7068	.2800	147	.7360	.3734	177	.7799	.4871
88	.6879	.2020	118	.7076	.2829	148	.7372	.3768	178	.7817	.4914
89	.6884	.2046	119	.7084	.2858	149	.7384	.3802	179	.7835	.4957
90	.6890	.2071	120	.7092	.2887	150	.7396	.3837	180	.7854	.5000

AREAS OF CIRCULAR SEGMENTS

Table 6. For ratios of rise and diameter

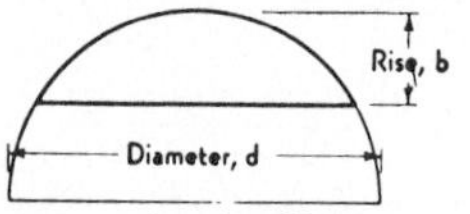

Area = d² x Coefficient

b/d	Coeffi-cient	b/d	Coeffi-cient	b/d	Coeffi-cient	b/d	Coeffi-cient	b/d	Coeffi-cient
.001	.000042	.046	.012971	.091	.035586	.136	.064074	.181	.096904
.002	.000119	.047	.013393	.092	.036162	.137	.064761	.182	.097675
.003	.000219	.048	.013818	.093	.036742	.138	.065449	.183	.098447
.004	.000337	.049	.014248	.094	.037324	.139	.066140	.184	.099221
.005	.000471	.050	.014681	.095	.037909	.140	.066833	.185	.099997
.006	.000619			.096	.038497			.186	.100774
.007	.000779	.051	.015119	.097	.039087	.141	.067528	.187	.101553
.008	.000952	.052	.015561	.098	.039681	.142	.068225	.188	.102334
.009	.001135	.053	.016008	.099	.040277	.143	.068924	.189	.103116
.010	.001329	.054	.016458	.100	.040875	.144	.069626	.190	.103900
		.055	.016912			.145	.070329		
.011	.001533	.056	.017369	.101	.041477	.146	.071034	.191	.104686
.012	.001746	.057	.017831	.102	.042081	.147	.071741	.192	.105472
.013	.001969	.058	.018297	.103	.042687	.148	.072450	.193	.106261
.014	.002199	.059	.018766	.104	.043296	.149	.073162	.194	.107051
.015	.002438	.060	.019239	.105	.043908	.150	.073875	.195	.107843
.016	.002685			.106	.044523			.196	.108636
.017	.002940	.061	.019716	.107	.045140	.151	.074590	.197	.109431
.018	.003202	.062	.020197	.108	.045759	.152	.075307	.198	.110227
.019	.003472	.063	.020681	.109	.046381	.153	.076026	.199	.111025
.020	.003749	.064	.021168	.110	.047006	.154	.076747	.200	.111824
		.065	.021660			.155	.077470		
.021	.004032	.066	.022155	.111	.047633	.156	.078194	.201	.112625
.022	.004322	.067	.022653	.112	.048262	.157	.078921	.202	.113427
.023	.004619	.068	.023155	.113	.048894	.158	.079650	.203	.114231
.024	.004922	.069	.023660	.114	.049529	.159	.080380	.204	.115036
.025	.005231	.070	.024168	.115	.050165	.160	.081112	.205	.115842
.026	.005546			.116	.050805			.206	.116651
.027	.005867	.071	.024680	.117	.051446	.161	.081847	.207	.117460
.028	.006194	.072	.025196	.118	.052090	.162	.082582	.208	.118271
.029	.006527	.073	.025714	.119	.052737	.163	.083320	.209	.119084
.030	.006866	.074	.026236	.120	.053385	.164	.084060	.210	.119898
		.075	.026761			.165	.084801		
.031	.007209	.076	.027290	.121	.054037	.166	.085545	.211	.120713
.032	.007559	.077	.027821	.122	.054690	.167	.086290	.212	.121530
.033	.007913	.078	.028356	.123	.055346	.168	.087037	.213	.122348
.034	.008273	.079	.028894	.124	.056004	.169	.087785	.214	.123167
.035	.008638	.080	.029435	.125	.056664	.170	.088536	.215	.123988
.036	.009008			.126	.057327			.216	.124811
.037	.009383	.081	.029979	.127	.057991	.171	.089288	.217	.125634
.038	.009764	.082	.030526	.128	.058658	.172	.090042	.218	.126459
.039	.010148	.083	.031077	.129	.059328	.173	.090797	.219	.127286
.040	.010538	.084	.031630	.130	.059999	.174	.091555	.220	.128114
		.085	.032186			.175	.092314		
.041	.010932	.086	.032746	.131	.060673	.176	.093074	.221	.128943
.042	.011331	.087	.033308	.132	.061349	.177	.093837	.222	.129773
.043	.011734	.088	.033873	.133	.062027	.178	.094601	.223	.130605
.044	.012142	.089	.034441	.134	.062707	.179	.095367	.224	.131438
.045	.012555	.090	.035012	.135	.063389	.180	.096135	.225	.132273

b/d	Coeffi-cient	b/d	Coeffi-cient	b/d	Coeffi-cient	b/d	Coeffi-cient	b/d	Coeffi-cient
.226	.133109	.281	.180918	.336	.231689	.391	.284569	.446	.338804
.227	.133946	.282	.181818	.337	.232634	.392	.285545	.447	.339799
.228	.134784	.283	.182718	.338	.233580	.393	.286521	.448	.340793
.229	.135624	.284	.183619	.339	.234526	.394	.287499	.449	.341788
.230	.136465	.285	.184522	.340	.235473	.395	.288476	.450	.342783
		.286	.185425			.396	.289454		
.231	.137307	.287	.186329	.341	.236421	.397	.290432	.451	.343778
.232	.138151	.288	.187235	.342	.237369	.398	.291411	.452	.344773
.233	.138996	.289	.188141	.343	.238319	.399	.292390	.453	.345768
.234	.139842	.290	.189048	.344	.239268	.400	.293370	.454	.346764
.235	.140689			.345	.240219			.455	.347760
.236	.141538	.291	.189956	.346	.241170	.401	.294350	.456	.348756
.237	.142388	.292	.190865	.347	.242122	.402	.295330	.457	.349752
.238	.143239	.293	.191774	.348	.243074	.403	.296311	.458	.350749
.239	.144091	.294	.192685	.349	.244027	.404	.297292	.459	.351745
.240	.144945	.295	.193597	.350	.244980	.405	.298274	.460	.352742
		.296	.194509			.406	.299256		
.241	.145800	.297	.195423	.351	.245935	.407	.300238	.461	.353739
.242	.146656	.298	.196337	.352	.246890	.408	.301221	.462	.354736
.243	.147513	.299	.197252	.353	.247845	.409	.302204	.463	.355733
.244	.148371	.300	.198168	.354	.248801	.410	.303187	.464	.356730
.245	.149231			.355	.249758			.465	.357728
.246	.150091	.301	.199085	.356	.250715	.411	.304171	.466	.358725
.247	.150953	.302	.200003	.357	.251673	.412	.305156	.467	.359723
.248	.151816	.303	.200922	.358	.252632	.413	.306140	.468	.360721
.249	.152681	.304	.201841	.359	.253591	.414	.307125	.469	.361719
.250	.153546	.305	.202762	.360	.254551	.415	.308110	.470	.362717
		.306	.203683			.416	.309096		
.251	.154413	.307	.204605	.361	.255511	.417	.310082	.471	.363715
.252	.155281	.308	.205528	.362	.256472	.418	.311068	.472	.364714
.253	.156149	.309	.206452	.363	.257433	.419	.312055	.473	.365712
.254	.157019	.310	.207376	.364	.258395	.420	.313042	.474	.366711
.255	.157891			.365	.259358			.475	.367710
.256	.158763	.311	.208302	.366	.260321	.421	.314029	.476	.368708
.257	159636	.312	.209228	.367	.261285	.422	.315017	.477	.369707
.258	.160511	.313	.210155	.368	.262249	.423	.316005	.478	.370706
.259	.161386	.314	.211083	.369	.263214	.424	.316993	.479	.371705
.260	.162263	.315	.212011	.370	.264179	.425	.317981	.480	.372704
		.316	.212941			.426	.318970		
.261	.163141	.317	.213871	.371	.265145	.427	.319959	.481	.373704
.262	.164020	.318	.214802	.372	.266111	.428	.320949	.482	.374703
.263	.164900	.319	.215734	.373	.267078	.429	.321938	.483	.375702
.264	.165781	.320	.216666	.374	.268046	.430	.322928	.484	.376702
.265	.166663			.375	.269014			.485	.377701
.266	.167546	.321	.217600	.376	.269982	.431	.323919	.486	.378701
.267	.168431	.322	.218534	.377	.270951	.432	.324909	.487	.379701
.268	.169316	.323	.219469	.378	.271921	.433	.325900	.488	.380700
.269	.170202	.324	.220404	.379	.272891	.434	.326891	.489	.381700
.270	.171090	.325	.221341	.380	.273861	.435	.327883	.490	.382700
		.326	.222278			.436	.328874		
.271	.171978	.327	.223216	.381	.274832	.437	.329866	.491	.383700
.272	.172868	.328	.224154	.382	.275804	.438	.330858	.492	.384699
.273	.173758	.329	.225094	.383	.276776	.439	.331851	.493	.385699
.274	.174650	.330	.226034	.384	.277748	.440	.332843	.494	.386699
.275	.175542			.385	.278721			.495	.387699
.276	.176436	.331	.226974	.386	.279695	.441	.333836	.496	.388699
.277	.177330	.332	.227916	.387	.280669	.442	.334829	.497	.389699
.278	.178226	.333	.228858	.388	.281643	.443	.335823	.498	.390699
.279	.179122	.334	.229801	.389	.282618	.444	.336816	.499	.391699
.280	.180020	.335	.230745	.390	.283593	.445	.337810	.500	.392699

FORM		METHOD OF FINDING AREAS
TRIANGLE		Base × ½ perpendicular height. $\sqrt{s(s-a)(s-b)(s-c)}$, s = ½ sum of the three sides a, b, c.
TRAPEZIUM		Sum of area of the two triangles
TRAPEZOID		½ sum of parallel sides × perpendicular height.
PARALLELOGRAM		Base × perpendicular height.
REG. POLYGON		½ sum of sides × inside radius.
CIRCLE		πr^2 = 0.78540 × diam^2. = 0.07958 × circumference^2
SECTOR OF A CIRCLE		$\dfrac{\pi r^2 A°}{360}$ = 0.0087266 $r^2 A°$, = arc × ½ radius
SEGMENT OF A CIRCLE		$\dfrac{r^2}{2}\left(\dfrac{\pi A°}{180} - \sin A°\right)$
CIRCLE of same area as a square		Diameter = side × 1.12838
SQUARE of same area as a circle		Side = diameter × 0.88623
ELLIPSE		Long diameter × short diameter × 0.78540
PARABOLA		Base × ⅔ perpendicular height.
IRREGULAR PLANE SURFACE		Divide any plane surface A, B, C, D, along a line a - b into an even number, n, of parallel and sufficiently small strips d, whose ordinates are h_1, h_2, h_3, h_4, h_5, ... h_{n-1}, h_n, h_{n+1}, and considering contours between three ordinates as parabolic curves, then for section A B C D,

$$\text{Area} = \frac{d}{3}\left[h_1 + h_{n+1} + 4(h_2 + h_4 + h_6 ...... + h_n) + 2(h_3 + h_5 + h_7 ...... + h_{n-1})\right]$$

or, approximately, Area = sum of ordinates × width d.

METHOD OF FINDING SURFACES AND VOLUMES OF SOLIDS

SHAPE	FORMULAE	SHAPE	FORMULAE

S = lateral or convex surface   **V** = volume

Parallelopiped

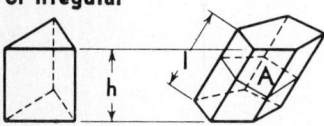

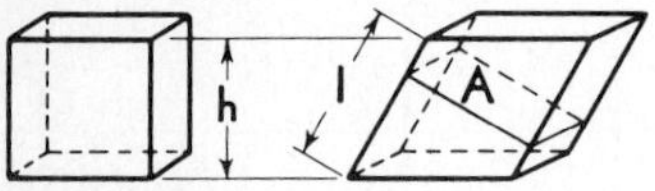

S = perimeter, P, perp. to sides × lat. length l :   **Pl** :

V = area of base, B, × perpendicular height, h :   **B h**.

V = area of section, A, perp. to sides, × lat. length l :   **Al**.

Prism right, or oblique, regular or irregular

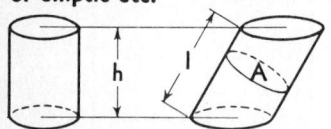

S = perimeter, P, perp. to sides × lat. length l :   **Pl** :

V = area of base, B, × perpendicular height, h :   **B h**.

V = area of section, A, perp. to sides, × lat. length l :   **Al**.

Cylinder, right or oblique, circular or elliptic etc.

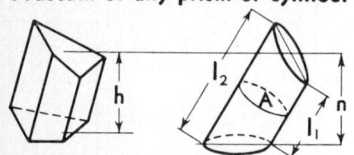

S = perimeter of base, P, × perp. height, h: **Ph**. S_l= perimeter, P_1, perp., × lat. length, l : P_1 **l**.

V = area of base, B, × perp. height, h:**Bh. V**=area of section, A, perp. to sides × lat. length l:**Al**.

Frustum of any prism or cylinder

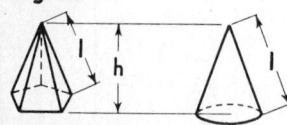

V = area of base, B, × perpendicular distance h, from base to centre of gravity of opposite face: **B h**. for cylinder, ½ **A** ($l_1 + l_2$)

Pyramid or Cone, right and regular

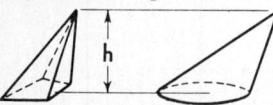

S = perimeter of base, P, × ½ slant height l : ½ **Pl**.

V = area of base, B × ⅓ perpendicular ht., h : ⅓ **Bh**.

Pyramid or Cone, right or oblique, regular or irregular

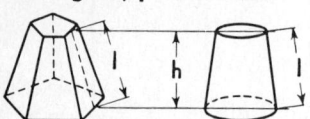

V = area of base, B, × ⅓ perp. height, h : ⅓ **Bh**.

V = ⅓ vol. of prism or cylinder of same base & perp. height.

V = ½ vol. of hemisphere of same base and perp. height.

Frustum of pyramid or cone, right and regular, parallel ends

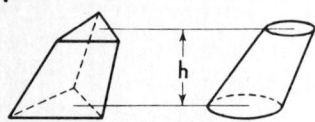

S = (sum of perimeter of base, P, and top, p) × ½ slant height l : ½l (P+p).

V = (sum of areas of base, B, and top, b+sq. root of their products) × ⅓ perp. height, h : ⅓ h (B+b+√B̄b̄).

Frustum of any pyramid or cone, parallel ends

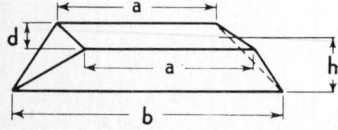

V = (sum of areas of base, B, and top, b, +sq. root of their products) × ⅓ perpendicular height, h : ⅓ h (B+b+√B̄b̄).

Wedge, parallelogram face

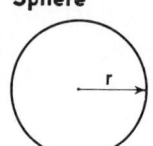

V = ⅙ (sum of three edges, a b a, × perpendicular height, h, × perpendicular width, d) : ⅙ d h (2 a+b)

S = lateral or convex surface   **V** = volume

Sphere

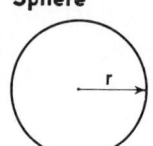

S = $4 \pi r^2 = \pi d^2$ = 3.14159265 d^2.

V = $\frac{4}{3} \pi r^3 = \frac{1}{6}\pi d^3$ = 0.52359878 d^3.

Spherical Sector

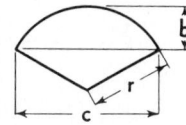

S = ½ π r (4b + c).

V = ⅔ πr^2 b.

Spherical Segment

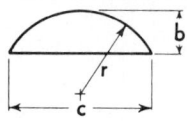

S = $2 \pi r b = \frac{1}{4}\pi (4b^2 + c^2)$.

V = $\frac{1}{3}\pi b^2 (3r - b) = \frac{1}{24}\pi b (3c^2 + 4b^2)$.

Spherical Zone

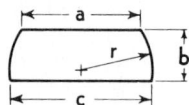

S = 2 π r b.

V = $\frac{1}{24} \pi b (3a^2 + 3c^2 + 4b^2)$.

Circular Ring

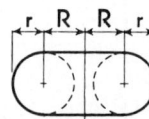

S = $4 \pi^2 R r$.

V = $2 \pi^2 R r^2$.

Ungula of right, regular cylinder

1. Base = segment, bab.   **2.** Base = half circle

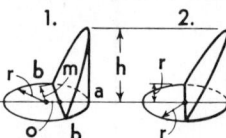

S = (2rm – o × arc, bab) $\frac{h}{r-o}$.   **S** = 2 r h.

V = (⅔m^3 – o × area, bab) $\frac{h}{r-o}$.   **V** = ⅔ r^2h.

1. Base = segment, cac.   **2.** Base = circle

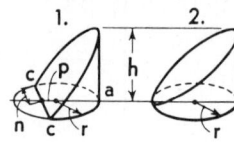

S = (2 r n + p × arc, cac) $\frac{h}{r+p}$.   **S** = π r h.

V = (⅔ n^3 + p × area, cac) $\frac{h}{r+p}$.   **V** = ½ $r^2 \pi$ h.

Ellipsoid

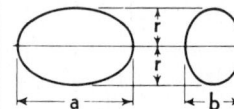

V = ⅓ π r a b.

Paraboloid

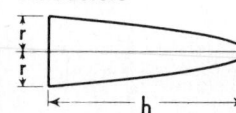

V = ½ π r^2 h.

Ratio of corresponding volume of a Cone, Paraboloid, Sphere & Cylinder of equal height: ⅓, ½, ⅔, 1.

RIGHT-ANGLED TRIANGLES

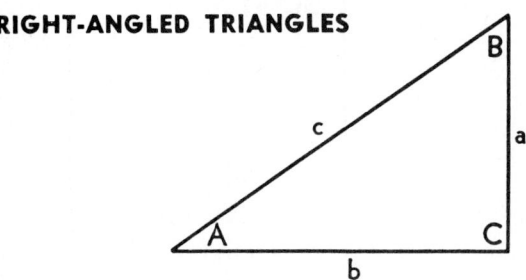

Given	Sought	Formulae
a, c	A, B, b	$\sin A = \dfrac{a}{c}$, $\cos B = \dfrac{a}{c}$, $b = \sqrt{c^2 - a^2}$
	Area	Area $= \dfrac{a}{2}\sqrt{c^2-a^2}$
a, b	A, B, c	$\tan A = \dfrac{a}{b}$, $\tan B = \dfrac{b}{a}$, $c = \sqrt{a^2 + b^2}$
	Area	Area $= \dfrac{a\,b}{2}$
A, a	B, b, c	$B = 90° - A$, $b = a \cot A$, $c = \dfrac{a}{\sin A}$
	Area	Area $= \dfrac{a^2 \cot A}{2}$
A, b	B, a, c	$B = 90° - A$, $a = b \tan A$, $c = \dfrac{b}{\cos A}$
	Area	Area $= \dfrac{b^2 \tan A}{2}$
A, c	B, a, b	$B = 90° - A$, $a = c \sin A$, $b = c \cos A$
	Area	Area $= \dfrac{c^2 \sin A \cos A}{2}$ or $\dfrac{c^2 \sin 2A}{4}$

OBLIQUE-ANGLED TRIANGLES

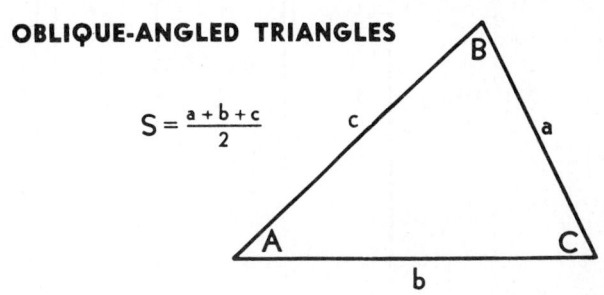

$$S = \frac{a+b+c}{2}$$

Given	Sought	Formulae
a, b, c	A	$\sin \tfrac{1}{2} A = \sqrt{\dfrac{(s-b)(s-c)}{bc}}$, $\cos \tfrac{1}{2} A = \sqrt{\dfrac{s(s-a)}{bc}}$, $\tan \tfrac{1}{2} A = \sqrt{\dfrac{(s-b)(s-c)}{s(s-a)}}$
	B	$\sin \tfrac{1}{2} B = \sqrt{\dfrac{(s-a)(s-c)}{ac}}$, $\cos \tfrac{1}{2} B = \sqrt{\dfrac{s(s-b)}{ac}}$, $\tan \tfrac{1}{2} B = \sqrt{\dfrac{(s-a)(s-c)}{s(s-b)}}$
	C	$\sin \tfrac{1}{2} C = \sqrt{\dfrac{(s-a)(s-b)}{ab}}$, $\cos \tfrac{1}{2} C = \sqrt{\dfrac{s(s-c)}{ab}}$, $\tan \tfrac{1}{2} C = \sqrt{\dfrac{(s-a)(s-b)}{s(s-c)}}$
	Area	Area $= \sqrt{s(s-a)(s-b)(s-c)}$
a, A, B	b, c	$b = \dfrac{a \sin B}{\sin A}$ $c = \dfrac{a \sin C}{\sin A} = \dfrac{a \sin(A+B)}{\sin A}$
	Area	Area $= \tfrac{1}{2} ab \sin C = \dfrac{a^2 \sin B \sin C}{2 \sin A}$
a, b, A	B	$\sin B = \dfrac{b \sin A}{a}$
	c	$c = \dfrac{a \sin C}{\sin A} = \dfrac{b \sin C}{\sin B} = \sqrt{a^2 + b^2 - 2ab \cos C}$
	Area	Area $= \tfrac{1}{2} ab \sin C$
a, b, C	A	$\tan A = \dfrac{a \sin C}{b - a \cos C}$, $\tan \tfrac{1}{2}(A-B) = \dfrac{a-b}{a+b} \cot \tfrac{1}{2} C$
	c	$c = \sqrt{a^2 + b^2 - 2ab \cos C} = \dfrac{a \sin C}{\sin A}$
	Area	Area $= \tfrac{1}{2} ab \sin C$

$a^2 = b^2 + c^2 - 2bc \cos A$, $b^2 = a^2 + c^2 - 2ac \cos B$ $c^2 = a^2 + b^2 - 2ab \cos C$

SINES

Degrees	0′	10′	20′	30′	40′	50′	60′	Cosines
0	0.00000	0.00291	0.00582	0.00873	0.01164	0.01454	0.01745	89
1	0.01745	0.02036	0.02327	0.02618	0.02908	0.03199	0.03490	88
2	0.03490	0.03781	0.04071	0.04362	0.04653	0.04943	0.05234	87
3	0.05234	0.05524	0.05814	0.06105	0.06395	0.06685	0.06976	86
4	0.06976	0.07266	0.07556	0.07846	0.08136	0.08426	0.08716	85
5	0.08716	0.09005	0.09295	0.09585	0.09874	0.10164	0.10453	84
6	0.10453	0.10742	0.11031	0.11320	0.11609	0.11898	0.12187	83
7	0.12187	0.12476	0.12764	0.13053	0.13341	0.13629	0.13917	82
8	0.13917	0.14205	0.14493	0.14781	0.15069	0.15356	0.15643	81
9	0.15643	0.15931	0.16218	0.16505	0.16792	0.17078	0.17365	80
10	0.17365	0.17651	0.17937	0.18224	0.18509	0.18795	0.19081	79
11	0.19081	0.19366	0.19652	0.19937	0.20222	0.20507	0.20791	78
12	0.20791	0.21076	0.21360	0.21644	0.21928	0.22212	0.22495	77
13	0.22495	0.22778	0.23062	0.23345	0.23627	0.23910	0.24192	76
14	0.24192	0.24474	0.24756	0.25038	0.25320	0.25601	0.25882	75
15	0.25882	0.26163	0.26443	0.26724	0.27004	0.27284	0.27564	74
16	0.27564	0.27843	0.28123	0.28402	0.28680	0.28959	0.29237	73
17	0.29237	0.29515	0.29793	0.30071	0.30348	0.30625	0.30902	72
18	0.30902	0.31178	0.31454	0.31730	0.32006	0.32282	0.32557	71
19	0.32557	0.32832	0.33106	0.33381	0.33655	0.33929	0.34202	70
20	0.34202	0.34475	0.34748	0.35021	0.35293	0.35565	0.35837	69
21	0.35837	0.36108	0.36379	0.36650	0.36921	0.37191	0.37461	68
22	0.37461	0.37730	0.37999	0.38268	0.38537	0.38805	0.39073	67
23	0.39073	0.39341	0.39608	0.39875	0.40142	0.40408	0.40674	66
24	0.40674	0.40939	0.41204	0.41469	0.41734	0.41998	0.42262	65
25	0.42262	0.42525	0.42788	0.43051	0.43313	0.43575	0.43837	64
26	0.43837	0.44098	0.44359	0.44620	0.44880	0.45140	0.45399	63
27	0.45399	0.45658	0.45917	0.46175	0.46433	0.46690	0.46947	62
28	0.46947	0.47204	0.47460	0.47716	0.47971	0.48226	0.48481	61
29	0.48481	0.48735	0.48989	0.49242	0.49495	0.49748	0.50000	60
30	0.50000	0.50252	0.50503	0.50754	0.51004	0.51254	0.51504	59
31	0.51504	0.51753	0.52002	0.52250	0.52498	0.52745	0.52992	58
32	0.52992	0.53238	0.53484	0.53730	0.53975	0.54220	0.54464	57
33	0.54464	0.54708	0.54951	0.55194	0.55436	0.55678	0.55919	56
34	0.55919	0.56160	0.56401	0.56641	0.56880	0.57119	0.57358	55
35	0.57358	0.57596	0.57833	0.58070	0.58307	0.58543	0.58779	54
36	0.58779	0.59014	0.59248	0.59482	0.59716	0.59949	0.60182	53
37	0.60182	0.60414	0.60645	0.60876	0.61107	0.61337	0.61566	52
38	0.61566	0.61795	0.62024	0.62251	0.62479	0.62706	0.62932	51
39	0.62932	0.63158	0.63383	0.63608	0.63832	0.64056	0.64279	50
40	0.64279	0.64501	0.64723	0.64945	0.65166	0.65386	0.65606	49
41	0.65606	0.65825	0.66044	0.66262	0.66480	0.66697	0.66913	48
42	0.66913	0.67129	0.67344	0.67559	0.67773	0.67987	0.68200	47
43	0.68200	0.68412	0.68624	0.68835	0.69046	0.69256	0.69466	46
44	0.69466	0.69675	0.69883	0.70091	0.70298	0.70505	0.70711	45
	60′	50′	40′	30′	20′	10′	0′	Degrees

Sines · COSINES

COSINES

Degrees	0′	10′	20′	30′	40′	50′	60′	Sines
0	1.00000	1.00000	0.99998	0.99996	0.99993	0.99989	0.99985	89
1	0.99985	0.99979	0.99973	0.99966	0.99958	0.99949	0.99939	88
2	0.99939	0.99929	0.99917	0.99905	0.99892	0.99878	0.99863	87
3	0.99863	0.99847	0.99831	0.99813	0.99795	0.99776	0.99756	86
4	0.99756	0.99736	0.99714	0.99692	0.99668	0.99644	0.99619	85
5	0.99619	0.99594	0.99567	0.99540	0.99511	0.99482	0.99452	84
6	0.99452	0.99421	0.99390	0.99357	0.99324	0.99290	0.99255	83
7	0.99255	0.99219	0.99182	0.99144	0.99106	0.99067	0.99027	82
8	0.99027	0.98986	0.98944	0.98902	0.98858	0.98814	0.98769	81
9	0.98769	0.98723	0.98676	0.98629	0.98580	0.98531	0.98481	80
10	0.98481	0.98430	0.98378	0.98325	0.98272	0.98218	0.98163	79
11	0.98163	0.98107	0.98050	0.97992	0.97934	0.97875	0.97815	78
12	0.97815	0.97754	0.97692	0.97630	0.97566	0.97502	0.97437	77
13	0.97437	0.97371	0.97304	0.97237	0.97169	0.97100	0.97030	76
14	0.97030	0.96959	0.96887	0.96815	0.96742	0.96667	0.96593	75
15	0.96593	0.96517	0.96440	0.96363	0.96285	0.96206	0.96126	74
16	0.96126	0.96046	0.95964	0.95882	0.95799	0.95715	0.95630	73
17	0.95630	0.95545	0.95459	0.95372	0.95284	0.95195	0.95106	72
18	0.95106	0.95015	0.94924	0.94832	0.94740	0.94646	0.94552	71
19	0.94552	0.94457	0.94361	0.94264	0.94167	0.94068	0.93969	70
20	0.93969	0.93869	0.93769	0.93667	0.93565	0.93462	0.93358	69
21	0.93358	0.93253	0.93148	0.93042	0.92935	0.92827	0.92718	68
22	0.92718	0.92609	0.92499	0.92388	0.92276	0.92164	0.92050	67
23	0.92050	0.91936	0.91822	0.91706	0.91590	0.91472	0.91355	66
24	0.91355	0.91236	0.91116	0.90996	0.90875	0.90753	0.90631	65
25	0.90631	0.90507	0.90383	0.90259	0.90133	0.90007	0.89879	64
26	0.89879	0.89752	0.89623	0.89493	0.89363	0.89232	0.89101	63
27	0.89101	0.88968	0.88835	0.88701	0.88566	0.88431	0.88295	62
28	0.88295	0.88158	0.88020	0.87882	0.87743	0.87603	0.87462	61
29	0.87462	0.87321	0.87178	0.87036	0.86892	0.86748	0.86603	60
30	0.86603	0.86457	0.86310	0.86163	0.86015	0.85866	0.85717	59
31	0.85717	0.85567	0.85416	0.85264	0.85112	0.84959	0.84805	58
32	0.84805	0.84650	0.84495	0.84339	0.84182	0.84025	0.83867	57
33	0.83867	0.83708	0.83549	0.83389	0.83228	0.83066	0.82904	56
34	0.82904	0.82741	0.82577	0.82413	0.82248	0.82082	0.81915	55
35	0.81915	0.81748	0.81580	0.81412	0.81242	0.81072	0.80902	54
36	0.80902	0.80730	0.80558	0.80386	0.80212	0.80038	0.79864	53
37	0.79864	0.79688	0.79512	0.79335	0.79158	0.78980	0.78801	52
38	0.78801	0.78622	0.78442	0.78261	0.78079	0.77897	0.77715	51
39	0.77715	0.77531	0.77347	0.77162	0.76977	0.76791	0.76604	50
40	0.76604	0.76417	0.76229	0.76041	0.75851	0.75661	0.75471	49
41	0.75471	0.75280	0.75088	0.74896	0.74703	0.74509	0.74314	48
42	0.74314	0.74120	0.73924	0.73728	0.73531	0.73333	0.73135	47
43	0.73135	0.72937	0.72737	0.72537	0.72337	0.72136	0.71934	46
44	0.71934	0.71732	0.71529	0.71325	0.71121	0.70916	0.70711	45
	60′	50′	40′	30′	20′	10′	0′	Degrees

Cosines · SINES

Trigonometric functions

Degrees	TANGENTS 0′	10′	20′	30′	40′	50′	60′	Cotangents
0	0.00000	0.00291	0.00582	0.00873	0.01164	0.01455	0.01746	89
1	0.01746	0.02036	0.02328	0.02619	0.02910	0.03201	0.03492	88
2	0.03492	0.03783	0.04075	0.04366	0.04658	0.04949	0.05241	87
3	0.05241	0.05533	0.05824	0.06116	0.06408	0.06700	0.06993	86
4	0.06993	0.07285	0.07578	0.07870	0.08163	0.08456	0.08749	85
5	0.08749	0.09042	0.09335	0.09629	0.09923	0.10216	0.10510	84
6	0.10510	0.10805	0.11099	0.11394	0.11688	0.11983	0.12278	83
7	0.12278	0.12574	0.12869	0.13165	0.13461	0.13758	0.14054	82
8	0.14054	0.14351	0.14648	0.14945	0.15243	0.15540	0.15838	81
9	0.15838	0.16137	0.16435	0.16734	0.17033	0.17333	0.17633	80
10	0.17633	0.17933	0.18233	0.18534	0.18835	0.19136	0.19438	79
11	0.19438	0.19740	0.20042	0.20345	0.20648	0.20952	0.21256	78
12	0.21256	0.21560	0.21864	0.22169	0.22475	0.22781	0.23087	77
13	0.23087	0.23393	0.23700	0.24008	0.24316	0.24624	0.24933	76
14	0.24933	0.25242	0.25552	0.25862	0.26172	0.26483	0.26795	75
15	0.26795	0.27107	0.27419	0.27732	0.28046	0.28360	0.28675	74
16	0.28675	0.28990	0.29305	0.29621	0.29938	0.30255	0.30573	73
17	0.30573	0.30891	0.31210	0.31530	0.31850	0.32171	0.32492	72
18	0.32492	0.32814	0.33136	0.33460	0.33783	0.34108	0.34433	71
19	0.34433	0.34758	0.35085	0.35412	0.35740	0.36068	0.36397	70
20	0.36397	0.36727	0.37057	0.37388	0.37720	0.38053	0.38386	69
21	0.38386	0.38721	0.39055	0.39391	0.39727	0.40065	0.40403	68
22	0.40403	0.40741	0.41081	0.41421	0.41763	0.42105	0.42447	67
23	0.42447	0.42791	0.43136	0.43481	0.43828	0.44175	0.44523	66
24	0.44523	0.44872	0.45222	0.45573	0.45924	0.46277	0.46631	65
25	0.46631	0.46985	0.47341	0.47698	0.48055	0.48414	0.48773	64
26	0.48773	0.49134	0.49495	0.49858	0.50222	0.50587	0.50953	63
27	0.50953	0.51320	0.51688	0.52057	0.52427	0.52798	0.53171	62
28	0.53171	0.53545	0.53920	0.54296	0.54674	0.55051	0.55431	61
29	0.55431	0.55812	0.56194	0.56577	0.56962	0.57348	0.57735	60
30	0.57735	0.58124	0.58513	0.58905	0.59297	0.59691	0.60086	59
31	0.60086	0.60483	0.60881	0.61280	0.61681	0.62083	0.62487	58
32	0.62487	0.62892	0.63299	0.63707	0.64117	0.64528	0.64941	57
33	0.64941	0.65355	0.65771	0.66189	0.66608	0.67028	0.67451	56
34	0.67451	0.67875	0.68301	0.68728	0.69157	0.69588	0.70021	55
35	0.70021	0.70455	0.70891	0.71329	0.71769	0.72211	0.72654	54
36	0.72654	0.73100	0.73547	0.73996	0.74447	0.74900	0.75355	53
37	0.75355	0.75812	0.76272	0.76733	0.77196	0.77661	0.78129	52
38	0.78129	0.78598	0.79070	0.79544	0.80020	0.80498	0.80978	51
39	0.80978	0.81461	0.81946	0.82434	0.82923	0.83415	0.83910	50
40	0.83910	0.84407	0.84906	0.85408	0.85912	0.86419	0.86929	49
41	0.86929	0.87441	0.87955	0.88473	0.88992	0.89515	0.90040	48
42	0.90040	0.90569	0.91099	0.91633	0.92170	0.92709	0.93252	47
43	0.93252	0.93797	0.94345	0.94896	0.95451	0.96008	0,96569	46
44	0.96569	0.97133	0.97700	0.98270	0.98843	0.99420	1.00000	45
Tangents	60′	50′	40′	30′	20′	10′	0′	Degrees
	COTANGENTS							

Degrees	COTANGENTS 0′	10′	20′	30′	40′	50′	60′	Tangents
0	∞	343.77371	171.88540	114.58865	85.93979	68.75009	57.28996	89
1	57.28996	49.10388	42.96408	38.18846	34.36777	31.24158	28.63625	88
2	28.63625	26.43160	24.54176	22.90377	21.47040	20.20555	19.08114	87
3	19.08114	18.07498	17.16934	16.34986	15.60478	14.92442	14.30067	86
4	14.30067	13.72674	13.19688	12.70621	12.25051	11.82617	11.43005	85
5	11.43005	11.05943	10.71191	10.38540	10.07803	9.78817	9.51436	84
6	9.51436	9.25530	9.00983	8.77689	8.55555	8.34496	8.14435	83
7	8.14435	7.95302	7.77035	7.59575	7.42871	7.26873	7.11537	82
8	7.11537	6.96823	6.82694	6.69116	6.56055	6.43484	6.31375	81
9	6.31375	6.19703	6.08444	5.97576	5.87080	5.76937	5.67128	80
10	5.67128	5.57638	5.48451	5.39552	5.30928	5.22566	5.14455	79
11	5.14455	5.06584	4.98940	4.91516	4.84300	4.77286	4.70463	78
12	4.70463	4.63825	4.57363	4.51071	4.44942	4.38969	4.33148	77
13	4.33148	4.27471	4.21933	4.16530	4.11256	4.06107	4.01078	76
14	4.01078	3.96165	3.91364	3.86671	3.82083	3.77595	3.73205	75
15	3.73205	3.68909	3.64705	3.60588	3.56557	3.52609	3.48741	74
16	3.48741	3.44951	3.41236	3.37594	3.34023	3.30521	3.27085	73
17	3.27085	3.23714	3.20406	3.17159	3.13972	3.10842	3.07768	72
18	3.07768	3.04749	3.01783	2.98869	2.96004	2.93189	2.90421	71
19	2.90421	2.87700	2.85023	2.82391	2.79802	2.77254	2.74748	70
20	2.74748	2.72281	2.69853	2.67462	2.65109	2.62791	2.60509	69
21	2.60509	2.58261	2.56046	2.53865	2.51715	2.49597	2.47509	68
22	2.47509	2.45451	2.43422	2.41421	2.39449	2.37504	2.35585	67
23	2.35585	2.33693	2.31826	2.29984	2.28167	2.26374	2.24604	66
24	2.24604	2.22857	2.21132	2.19430	2.17749	2.16090	2.14451	65
25	2.14451	2.12832	2.11233	2.09654	2.08094	2.06553	2.05030	64
26	2.05030	2.03526	2.02039	2.00569	1.99116	1.97680	1.96261	63
27	1.96261	1.94858	1.93470	1.92098	1.90741	1.89400	1.88073	62
28	1.88073	1.86760	1.85462	1.84177	1.82907	1.81649	1.80405	61
29	1.80405	1.79174	1.77955	1.76749	1.75556	1.74375	1.73205	60
30	1.73205	1.72047	1.70901	1.69766	1.68643	1.67530	1.66428	59
31	1.66428	1.65337	1.64256	1.63185	1.62125	1.61074	1.60033	58
32	1.60033	1.59002	1.57981	1.56969	1.55966	1.54972	1.53987	57
33	1.53987	1.53010	1.52043	1.51084	1.50133	1.49190	1.48256	56
34	1.48256	1.47330	1.46411	1.45501	1.44598	1.43703	1.42815	55
35	1.42815	1.41934	1.41061	1.40195	1.39336	1.38484	1.37638	54
36	1.37638	1.36800	1.35968	1.35142	1.34323	1.33511	1.32704	53
37	1.32704	1.31904	1.31110	1.30323	1.29541	1.28764	1.27994	52
38	1.27994	1.27230	1.26471	1.25717	1.24969	1.24227	1.23490	51
39	1.23490	1.22758	1.22031	1.21310	1.20593	1.19882	1.19175	50
40	1.19175	1.18474	1.17777	1.17085	1.16398	1.15715	1.15037	49
41	1.15037	1.14363	1.13694	1.13029	1.12369	1.11713	1.11061	48
42	1.11061	1.10414	1.09770	1.09131	1.08496	1.07864	1.07237	47
43	1.07237	1.06613	1.05994	1.05378	1.04766	1.04158	1.03553	46
44	1.03553	1.02952	1.02355	1.01761	1.01170	1.00583	1.00000	45
Cotangents	60′	50′	40′	30′	20′	10′	0	Degrees
	TANGENTS							

Degrees	SECANTS 0′	10′	20′	30′	40′	50′	60′	Cosecants
0	1.00000	1.00000	1.00002	1.00004	1.00007	1.00011	1.00015	89
1	1.00015	1.00021	1.00027	1.00034	1.00042	1.00051	1.00061	88
2	1.00061	1.00072	1.00083	1.00095	1.00108	1.00122	1.00137	87
3	1.00137	1.00153	1.00169	1.00187	1.00205	1.00224	1.00244	86
4	1.00244	1.00265	1.00287	1.00309	1.00333	1.00357	1.00382	85
5	1.00382	1.00408	1.00435	1.00463	1.00491	1.00521	1.00551	84
6	1.00551	1.00582	1.00614	1.00647	1.00681	1.00715	1.00751	83
7	1.00751	1.00787	1.00825	1.00863	1.00902	1.00942	1.00983	82
8	1.00983	1.01024	1.01067	1.01111	1.01155	1.01200	1.01247	81
9	1.01247	1.01294	1.01342	1.01391	1.01440	1.01491	1.01543	80
10	1.01543	1.01595	1.01649	1.01703	1.01758	1.01815	1.01872	79
11	1.01872	1.01930	1.01989	1.02049	1.02110	1.02171	1.02234	78
12	1.02234	1.02298	1.02362	1.02428	1.02494	1.02562	1.02630	77
13	1.02630	1.02700	1.02770	1.02842	1.02914	1.02987	1.03061	76
14	1.03061	1.03137	1.03213	1.03290	1.03368	0.03447	1.03528	75
15	1.03528	1.03609	1.03691	1.03774	1.03858	1.03944	1.04030	74
16	1.04030	1.04117	1.04206	1.04295	1.04385	1.04477	1.04569	73
17	1.04569	1.04663	1.04757	1.04853	1.04950	1.05047	1.05146	72
18	1.05146	1.05246	1.05347	1.05449	1.05552	1.05657	1.05762	71
19	1.05762	1.05869	1.05976	1.06085	1.06195	1.06306	1.06418	70
20	1.06418	1.06531	1.06645	1.06761	1.06878	1.06995	1.07115	69
21	1.07115	1.07235	1.07356	1.07479	1.07602	1.07727	1.07853	68
22	1.07853	1.07981	1.08109	1.08239	1.08370	1.08503	1.08636	67
23	1.08636	1.08771	1.08907	1.09044	1.09183	1.09323	1.09464	66
24	1.09464	1.09606	1.09750	1.09895	1.10041	1.10189	1.10338	65
25	1.10338	1.10488	1.10640	1.10793	1.10947	1.11103	1.11260	64
26	1.11260	1.11419	1.11579	1.11740	1.11903	1.12067	1.12233	63
27	1.12233	1.12400	1.12568	1.12738	1.12910	1.13083	1.13257	62
28	1.13257	1.13433	1.13610	1.13789	1.13970	1.14152	1.14335	61
29	1.14335	1.14521	1.14707	1.14896	1.15085	1.15277	1.15470	60
30	1.15470	1.15665	1.15861	1.16059	1.16259	1.16460	1.16663	59
31	1.16663	1.16868	1.17075	1.17283	1.17493	1.17704	1.17918	58
32	1.17918	1.18133	1.18350	1.18569	1.18790	1.19012	1.19236	57
33	1.19236	1.19463	1.19691	1.19920	1.20152	1.20386	1.20622	56
34	1.20622	1.20859	1.21099	1.21341	1.21584	1.21830	1.22077	55
35	1.22077	1.22327	1.22579	1.22833	1.23089	1.23347	1.23607	54
36	1.23607	1.23869	1.24134	1.24400	1.24669	1.24940	1.25214	53
37	1.25214	1.25489	1.25767	1.26047	1.26330	1.26615	1.26902	52
38	1.26902	1.27191	1.27483	1.27778	1.28075	1.28374	1.28676	51
39	1.28676	1.28980	1.29287	1.29597	1.29909	1.30223	1.30541	50
40	1.30541	1.30861	1.31183	1.31509	1.31837	1.32168	1.32501	49
41	1.32501	1.32838	1.33177	1.33519	1.33864	1.34212	1.34563	48
42	1.34563	1.34917	1.35274	1.35634	1.35997	1.36363	1.36733	47
43	1.36733	1.37105	1.37481	1.37860	1.38242	1.38628	1.39016	46
44	1.39016	1.39409	1.39804	1.40203	1.40606	1.41012	1.41421	45
Secants	60′	50′	40′	30′	20′	10′	0′	Degrees
	COSECANTS							

Degrees	COSECANTS 0′	10′	20′	30′	40′	50′	60′	Secants
0	∞	343.77516	171.88831	114.59301	85.94561	68.75736	57.29869	89
1	57.29869	49.11406	42.97571	38.20155	34.38232	31.25758	28.65371	88
2	28.65371	26.45051	24.56212	22.92559	21.49368	20.23028	19.10732	87
3	19.10732	18.10262	17.19843	16.38041	15.63679	14.95788	14.33559	86
4	14.33559	13.76312	13.23472	12.74550	12.29125	11.86837	11.47371	85
5	11.47371	11.10455	10.75849	10.43343	10.12752	9.83912	9.56677	84
6	9.56677	9.30917	9.06515	8.83367	8.61379	8.40466	8.20551	83
7	8.20551	8.01565	7.83443	7.66130	7.49571	7.33719	7.18530	82
8	7.18530	7.03962	6.89979	6.76547	6.63633	6.51208	6.39245	81
9	6.39245	6.27719	6.16607	6.05886	5.95536	5.85539	5.75877	80
10	5.75877	5.66533	5.57493	5.48740	5.40263	5.32049	5.24084	79
11	5.24084	5.16359	5.08863	5.01585	4.94517	4.87649	4.80973	78
12	4.80973	4.74482	4.68167	4.62023	4.56041	4.50216	4.44541	77
13	4.44541	4.39012	4.33622	4.28366	4.23239	4.18238	4.13357	76
14	4.13357	4.08591	4.03938	3.99393	3.94952	3.90613	3.86370	75
15	3.86370	3.82223	3.78166	3.74198	3.70315	3.66515	3.62796	74
16	3.62796	3.59154	3.55587	3.52094	3.48671	3.45317	3.42030	73
17	3.42030	3.38808	3.35649	3.32551	3.29512	3.26531	3.23607	72
18	3.23607	3.20737	3.17920	3.15155	3.12440	3.09774	3.07155	71
19	3.07155	3.04584	3.02057	2.99574	2.97135	2.94737	2.92380	70
20	2.92380	2.90063	2.87785	2.85545	2.83342	2.81175	2.79043	69
21	2.79043	2.76945	2.74881	2.72850	2.70851	2.68884	2.66947	68
22	2.66947	2.65040	2.63162	2.61313	2.59491	2.57698	2.55930	67
23	2.55930	2.54190	2.52474	2.50784	2.49119	2.47477	2.45859	66
24	2.45859	2.44264	2.42692	2.41142	2.39614	2.38107	2.36620	65
25	2.36620	2.35154	2.33708	2.32282	2.30875	2.29487	2.28117	64
26	2.28117	2.26766	2.25432	2.24116	2.22817	2.21535	2.20269	63
27	2.20269	2.19019	2.17786	2.16568	2.15366	2.14178	2.13005	62
28	2.13005	2.11847	2.10704	2.09574	2.08458	2.07356	2.06267	61
29	2.06267	2.05191	2.04128	2.03077	2.02039	2.01014	2.00000	60
30	2.00000	1.98998	1.98008	1.97029	1.96062	1.95106	1.94160	59
31	1.94160	1.93226	1.92302	1.91388	1.90485	1.89591	1.88709	58
32	1.88708	1.87834	1.86970	1.86116	1.85271	1.84435	1.83608	57
33	1.83608	1.82790	1.81981	1.81180	1.80388	1.79604	1.78829	56
34	1.78829	1.78062	1.77303	1.76552	1.75808	1.75073	1.74345	55
35	1.74345	1.73624	1.72911	1.72205	1.71506	1.70815	1.70130	54
36	1.70130	1.69452	1.68782	1.68117	1.67460	1.66809	1.66164	53
37	1.66164	1.65526	1.64894	1.64268	1.63648	1.63035	1.62427	52
38	1.62427	1.61825	1.61229	1.60639	1.60054	1.59475	1.58902	51
39	1.58902	1.58333	1.57771	1.57213	1.56661	1.56114	1.55572	50
40	1.55572	1.55036	1.54504	1.53977	1.53455	1.52938	1.52425	49
41	1.52425	1.51918	1.51415	1.50916	1.50422	1.49933	1.49448	48
42	1.49448	1.48967	1.48491	1.48019	1.47551	1.47087	1.46628	47
43	1.46628	1.46173	1.45721	1.45274	1.44831	1.44391	1.43956	46
44	1.43956	1.43524	1.43096	1.42672	1.42251	1.41835	1.41421	45
Cosecants	60′	50′	40′	30′	20′	10′	0′	Degrees
	SECANTS							

By SEYMOUR HOWARD, *Architect*
Associate Professor, Pratt Institute

The forms most suitable for the solution of many structural problems require facility in drawing and using curves. Many good designs have never been carried out because information has not been readily available on curve characteristics and methods for laying them out. These and subsequent sheets will provide such information, not only on the familiar curves, but also on curves used for geodesic lines on surfaces and for thin shells.

Simple, direct methods exist for drawing some curves. Most, however, require the setting of points by calculation or by geometrical construction. Great care must be taken in connecting the points to obtain a "fair" curve.

A fair curve is one in which there are no local undesired irregularities. The easiest way to judge fairness is to look along the curve as nearly as possible in the plane of the curve.

When a large number of similar curves must be drawn it is economical to use special machines.

Plastic or wooden templates are available in many types for joining points in a smooth curve. Sets of railroad curves are arcs of circles of varying radii and different arc lengths. Copenhagen ship curves are based on the most usual curves found in hull design. Small circle and ellipse templates are often an aid in drafting. Parabolic templates would be a great help for making structural analysis drawings. The usual French curves can be manipulated to join points by smooth curves, but they must be used carefully when they do not fit the curve exactly.

For drawing curves which do not lend themselves to simple mathematical analysis, the best method is to use wood splines or battens, held in position by lead weights called ducks.

It is not always necessary or desirable that a curve be one for which a simple equation can be written. The curves which determine the shape of a ship's hull, for example, are developed by eye on the basis of experiment and past experience.

Curves developed purely by drawing should be drawn on a material unaffected by changes in temperature or humidity, or the temperature and humidity should be kept constant in the drawing room. Marble slabs are sometimes used. If paper must be used, check points or grid lines can be marked for subsequent verification.

Such curves can be reproduced by measuring offsets from a baseline or preferably from the nearest gridline. Once a table of offsets has been made the curve can be redrawn easily at any time and at any scale.

Remarks on Curves Included

Each curve on the following sheets is accurately drawn, and its most characteristic relationships are shown. In architectural design and layout, direct geometrical methods of constructing the curve and finding tangents, etc. are the most useful and are shown where possible. For use in checking points and for engineering calculations the formulas may be more useful.

The *standard form* of the equation of a curve is one based on rectangular Cartesian coördinates in which the y ordinates are given as a function of the x intercepts. It is the form most often used in the building field.

The *parametric* equation is also based on rectangular coordinates but both the y ordinates and the x intercepts are expressed in terms of a third variable. (Such as $x = a \cos t$; $y = b \sin t$.)

The *polar equation* of a curve gives points as measured along a line from a central point or pole. The distance from the pole is expressed as a function of the angle between the base line and the line along which the distance is measured. Curves such as spirals are best given in this form.

In field layout the polar equation can be used to find points on a curve by chaining out from a centrally located transit, measuring off angles from a base line.

Tangents and normals to a curve at various points are necessary in order to work out neatly the intersections of straight lines or curves with the particular curve under consideration. The tangent and normal at any point on a curved structure such as an arch or a shell also give the directions along which forces should be resolved in order to analyze their effect on the structure most easily.

If the centers of curvature for all points on a curve are plotted, a new curve will be generated called the *evolute*, which is useful in visualizing the curvature of the curve. In engineering analysis the curvature of a deflection curve is the link by which deflection and bending moment (and therefore shear and loading) can be related.

From the evolute the original curve can be generated as indicated in Fig. 2.

Lengths of curves are given where convenient expressions exist. For practical drafting room use the length can be found most quickly by measuring along the curve with a strip of paper. By ticking off points as this is done the work can be done accurately and can be checked. For other purposes, such as determining lengths of cables for cutting, the exact formulas must be used, with allowance for stretch due to loading and temperature.

The *moment of inertia* of a curve

can be useful for long-barrel thin-shell structures in which the cross section of the shell (basically only a curved line) corresponds to the cross section of a beam.

The *areas* under certain curves and their centroids or centers of gravity are given and can be used for calculating the cubages and surfaces of parts of a building. They may also be useful in calculation of deflection (the moment-area method).

Conic Sections

Curves formed by the intersection of a plane with a right circular cone are all of the class called *conic sections*. The relationship between the plane, the cone and the conic section can be seen by the construction in Fig. 1.

A right circular cone is shown with vertex at V, cut by the plane of a conic. The plane is tangent at F to a sphere which lies wholly inside of the cone and which is tangent to the cone along a circle (like a latitude circle on the earth). The center of this tangent circle is at M; the center of the sphere is at C. The centerline of the cone lies on the line VNMC, in

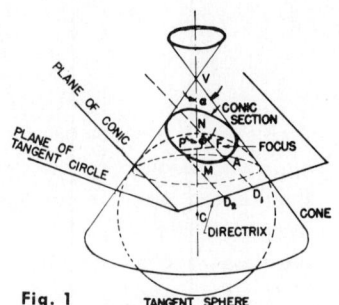

Fig. 1

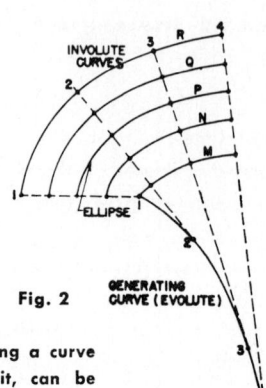

Fig. 2

Right: The use of an evolute curve in generating a curve such as an ellipse, and curves parallel to it, can be visualized by imagining a flexible, elastic ruler starting at point 1 on curve R and lying along the evolute curve. As it springs away from the evolute, its straight portion would be 2-2, 3-3, 4-4, etc. In this sketch only curve P is a true ellipse; other curves are parallel

Left: Basic relationships of a conic section. See also Sheet 19

which N is the intersection of the centerline or axis of the conic section with the centerline of the cone.

In all conic sections (ellipse, parabola, hyperbola) the focus is the point of tangency between the plane of the conic and the tangent sphere; and the directrix is the line of intersection of the plane of the conic with the plane of the tangent circle.

If α is the angle which the axis of the cone makes with the side of the cone and ϕ is the angle which the

plane of the conic makes with the axis of the cone.

$$\frac{PF}{PD_2} = \frac{\cos \phi}{\cos \alpha}$$

This is called the eccentricity of the conic.

Note that the same shape of curve can be generated on cones of different slope (α) by varying the angle of the plane of the conic (ϕ). For the same shape of curve only $\dfrac{\cos \phi}{\cos \alpha}$ must have the same value.

PARABOLA

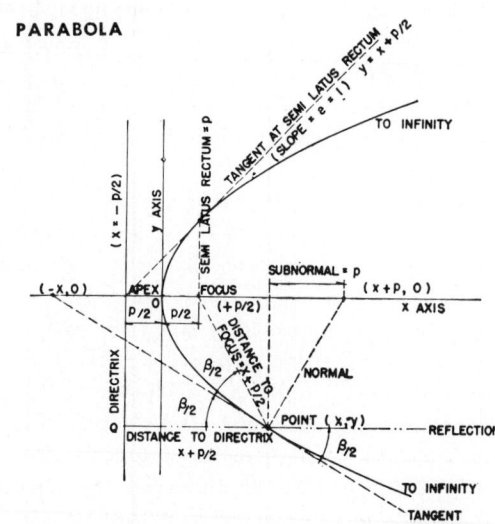

Definition:

$$\frac{\text{Distance from any point to focus}}{\text{Distance from point to directrix}} = \frac{PF}{PQ} = 1 = \text{eccentricity (e)}$$

Equation (standard form): $y^2 = 2px$

Note from characteristics of tangent, that a line from the focus (a ray of light, for example) to any point on the parabola will be reflected parallel to the axis of the parabola

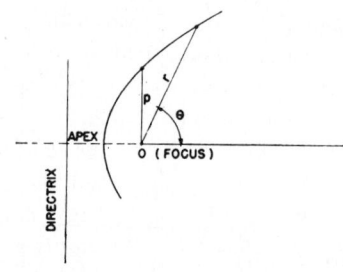

Equation (polar form, pole at focus): $r = \dfrac{p}{1 - \cos \phi}$

METHODS OF DRAWING A PARABOLA

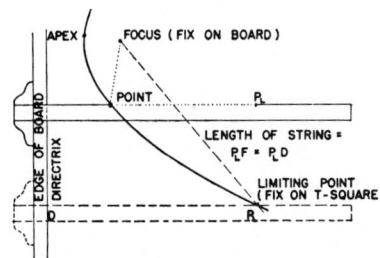

STRING METHOD

Above: attach a string (length equal to distance from limiting point on parabola to the focus) to the edge of the T-square and to the focus; hold string taut against T-square with a pencil and slide T-square.

Below: the parabola also can be constructed by knowing the heights of ordinates expressed as a ratio of the apex height (in this sketch 100.0). All parabolas have the same shape, differing only in scale. These relations hold true no matter what the ratio of height to width, provided the apex is included.

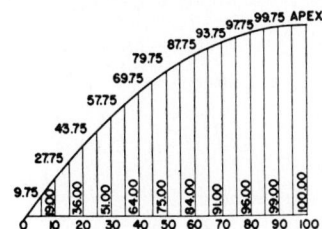

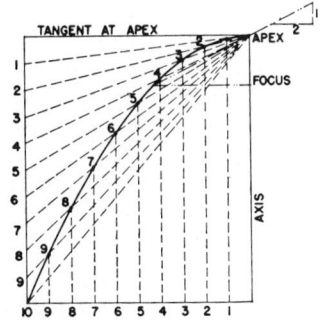

PARALLELOGRAM METHOD

To draw a parabola knowing apex, axis and one point: divide distance from point to axis in any number of equal parts; divide distance from point to the tangent through the apex into the same number of parts; draw lines parallel to the axis through points in the first line; draw lines from points in second line to apex; intersections of corresponding lines are points on the curve. To find focus, draw line through apex with slope = 1/2; from intersection with parabola drop perpendicular to axis

LENGTHS OF ARCS

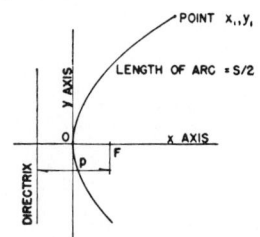

Length of arc from origin to point x_1, y_1

$$\frac{S}{2} = \frac{y_1}{2p} \sqrt{y_1^2 + p^2}$$

$$+ \frac{p}{2} \log_e \left[\frac{y_1 + \sqrt{y_1^2 + p^2}}{p} \right]$$

Length of parabola

Let $\dfrac{H}{L} = n$

Exact formula:

$$S = 2L \left\{ \sqrt{n^2 + \frac{1}{16}} + \frac{1}{16n} \left[\log_e \left(n + \sqrt{n^2 + \frac{1}{16}} \right) + \log_e 4 \right] \right\}$$

Approximate formula:

$S = L \left(1 + \dfrac{8}{3} n^2 \right)$, sufficiently accurate for construction purposes up to $n = 1/8$

AREAS AND CENTROIDS

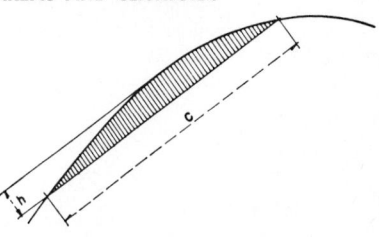

Area (A) of any segment $= \frac{2}{3} ch$

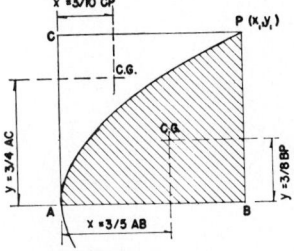

Area of half segment (APB) $= 2/3 \, AB \times BP$

Area of spandrel (ACP) $= 1/3 \, AC \times CP$

CENTERS OF CURVATURE

Radius of curvature: $R = \dfrac{(p + 2x)^{3/2}}{\sqrt{p}}$

Equation of evolute: $y^2 = \dfrac{8}{27p} (x - p)^3$
(curve of centers of curvature)

To find center of curvature C_4 for a point P_4, draw a line through P_4 parallel to x axis; set off $P_4Q_4 = 2P_4F$ and draw perpendicular through Q_4; draw normal P_4N_4 to P_4 by setting off subnormal $M_4N_4 = p$, and extend to meet perpendicular from Q_4 at C_4.

Radius of curvature at apex, $P_1C_1 = p$; $(P_1F = p/2 = FC_1)$
Center of curvature can also be found by same procedure as shown for ellipse and hyperbola: P_4N_4; N_4Q; QC_4 (see Evolute of Ellipse, Sheet 5).

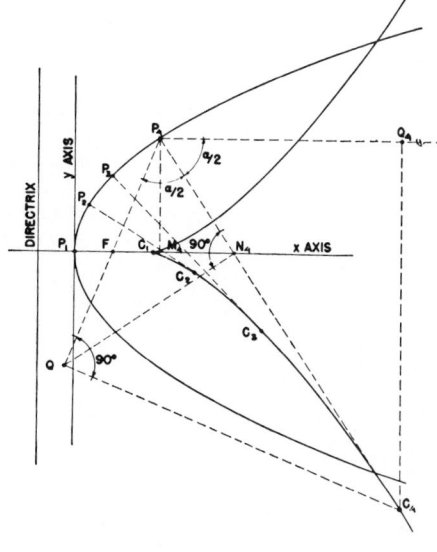

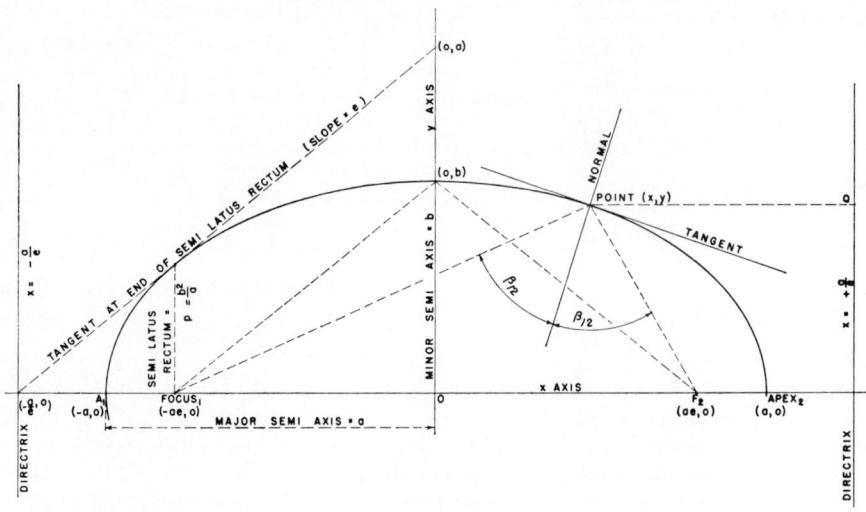

Note from characteristics of tangent (see diagram) that a line from a focus (a ray, for example) will be reflected by the ellipse and will pass through the other focus.

STANDARD FORM

$$\frac{x^2}{a^2} + \frac{y^2}{b^2} = 1$$

(b always less than a, except for circle when a = b)

Definition 1: $\dfrac{\text{Distance of Any Point to Focus}}{\text{Distance of Point to Directrix}} = \dfrac{PF}{PQ} = \text{Constant} = \text{Eccentricity (e)} = \sqrt{1 - \dfrac{b^2}{a^2}} = \text{Less Than 1}$

Definition II: Distance of Any Point to Focus_1 + Distance from Point to $\text{Focus}_2 = PF_1 + PF_2 = \text{Constant} = 2a$

See Sheet 20 for Conjugate Diameters, Sheet 34 for Parallelogram Method.

To Draw: (String Method) Find foci by swinging arc = a from end of minor semi axis; insert pins at foci and at end of minor semi axis; tie string around three pins; replace pin on minor axis by pencil; slide pencil against string, keeping string taut. The larger the ellipse, the better this method is (smallest practical size, major axis = 12 in (305 mm). It can easily be used for full size layout. For smaller ellipses, use method based on parametric equation.

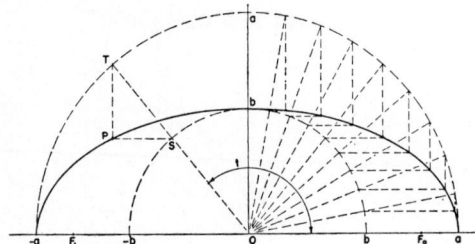

PARAMETRIC FORM

$$x = a \cos t$$
$$y = b \sin t$$

To Draw: Draw one circle with radius = a and one with radius = b, centers at O; from O draw any straight line, intersecting circle of radius b at S and circle of radius a at T; draw line through S parallel to x axis and a line through T parallel to y axis; the intersection of these lines is a point on the ellipse. Angle t is called the eccentric angle of point P (see Sheet 37).

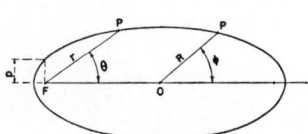

POLAR FORM

Pole at focus: $r = \dfrac{P}{1 - e \cos \theta}$

Pole at intersection of axes:

$$R^2 = \frac{a^2 b^2}{a^2 \sin^2 \phi + b^2 \cos^2 \phi}$$

$$P = \frac{b^2}{a} \text{ (semi-latus rectum)}$$

For the circle these equations become

$$r = R = a = b$$

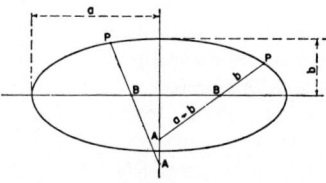

TRAMMEL METHOD

Make a stick (or piece of paper) of length PA = a; mark off PB = b, slide point A along minor axis and point B along major axis, point P will describe ellipse

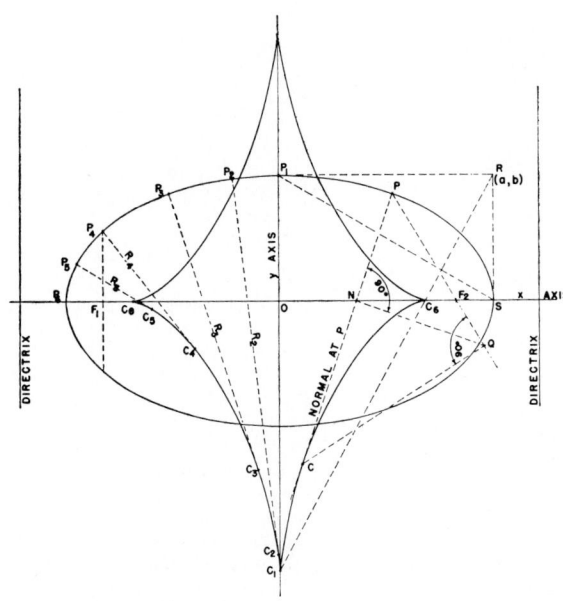

EVOLUTE OF ELLIPSE

The evolute can be used to visualize the curvature of the ellipse and to aid in constructing a curve parallel to the ellipse. (For example the intrados and extrados of an arch of uniform thickness whose centerline is an ellipse.) Such curves, called parallels to the ellipse, are not ellipses.

To find center of curvature for any point P: draw normal through P; from intersection N with major axis, erect perpendicular intersecting PF_2 extended at Q; from Q erect perpendicular to PQ intersecting normal PN extended at C. C is center of curvature, CP is radius of curvature.

Radius of Curvature

$$R = a^2 b^2 \left(\frac{x^2}{a^4} + \frac{y^2}{b^4}\right)^{3/2} \text{ for any point x, y on the ellipse}$$

To find points C_1 and C_6 on the evolute (see right hand half of curve): from point R drop perpendicular to line P_1 S; this cuts major axis at C_6, minor axis extended at C_1.

$$\text{Radius } C_6 P_6 = \frac{b^2}{a} = p \qquad \text{Radius } C_1 P_1 = \frac{a^2}{b}$$

Equation of Evolute (Standard form)

$$a^{2/3} x^{2/3} + b^{2/3} y^{2/3} = (a^2 - b^2)^{2/3}$$

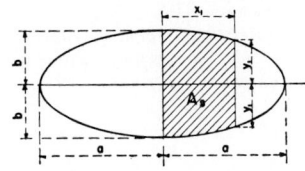

LENGTH OF ELLIPSE

Total Length

$$L = \pi \left[a + b\right] \left[1 + \frac{1}{4}\left(\frac{a-b}{a+b}\right)^2 + \frac{1}{64}\left(\frac{a-b}{a+b}\right)^4 + \frac{1}{256}\left(\frac{a-b}{a+b}\right)^6 + \ldots\right]$$

For lengths of arcs of ellipse, see the following publications: Smithsonian Mathematical Formulas and Tables of Elliptic Functions (Smithsonian Publ. No. 2672) Smithsonian Elliptic Functions Tables (Smithsonian Publication No. 3863).

AREAS

Total area bounded by ellipse = $A = \pi a b$

Area of segment bounded by ellipse, axis and line x = x_1 (as shaded) $A_s = x_1 y_1 + ab \text{ arc sin } \dfrac{x_1}{a}$

Note that these equations hold true for a circle, when $a = b = r$ and the eccentricity is zero.

ORDINATES of Quadrant of Circle.

To find corresponding ordinates of quadrant of an ellipse, multiply each ordinate as figured for circle by the ratio $\dfrac{b}{a}$. This process is called a *dilatation*.

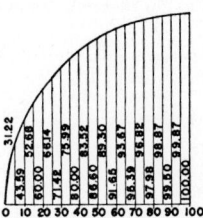

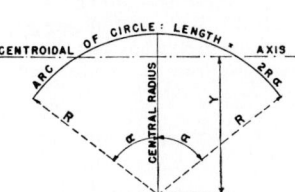

CENTROIDAL AXIS

For an arc of a circle the distance of the centroidal axis (normal to the central radius) from the center of the circle is:

$$Y = \frac{R \sin \alpha}{\alpha} \quad (\alpha \text{ in radians})$$

The "moment of inertia" of this arc about the centroid =

$$I = R^3 \left[\alpha + \frac{1}{2} \sin 2\alpha - \frac{2 \sin^2 \alpha}{\alpha}\right]$$

α in radians

Unfortunately there is no simple equation for finding the centroidal axis for an arc of an ellipse.

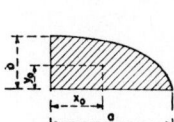

CENTROID

("Center of Gravity") of quadrant bounded by ellipse and two semi axes $\left(\text{Area} = \dfrac{\pi a b}{4}\right)$

$$x_0 = \frac{4}{3\pi} a = 0.4244 a$$

$$y_0 = \frac{4}{3\pi} b = 0.4244 b$$

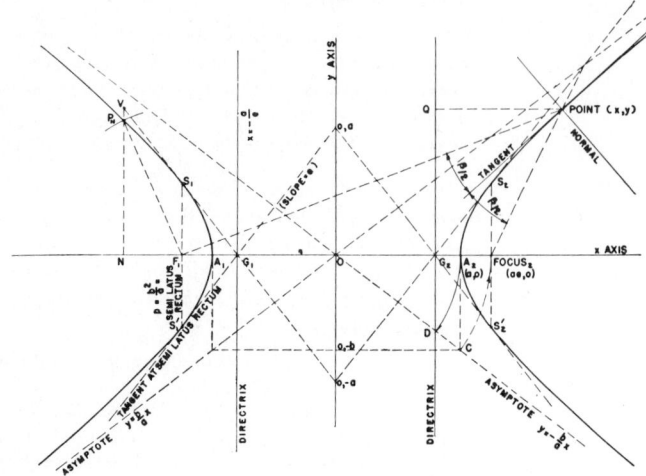

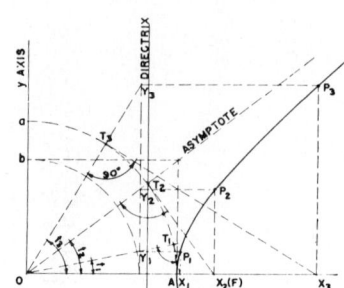

STANDARD FORM

$$\frac{x^2}{a^2} - \frac{y^2}{b^2} = 1 \quad \text{Asymptotes (tangents at infinity)}$$

$$\begin{cases} \dfrac{x}{a} - \dfrac{y}{b} = 0 \\[2mm] \dfrac{x}{a} + \dfrac{y}{b} = 0 \end{cases}$$

Note that b may be greater than a; in that case the curve is flatter. When a = b, asymptotes are at right angles to each other (called a rectangular hyperbola).

Definition I: $\dfrac{\text{Distance of any Point to Focus}}{\text{Distance of Point to Directrix}} =$

$\dfrac{PF}{PQ} = \text{Constant} = \text{Eccentricity (e)} = \sqrt{1 + \dfrac{b^2}{a}} = \text{Greater Than 1}$

Definition II: Distance of Any Point to Focus$_1$ — Distance of Point to Focus$_2$ = PF$_1$ — PF$_2$ = Constant = 2a

To Draw: Given a and b, draw asymptotes. Apex is at a or — a on x axis. Find directrix by swinging arc = Oa to intersect asymptote at D (see lower right quadrant). Find focus by swinging arc OC to intersect x axis at F (OC = $\sqrt{a^2 + b^2}$ = ae). Erect perpendicular through F. From points O, a and O, — a, draw lines through G$_1$ and G$_2$ and intersecting perpendiculars through F$_1$ and F$_2$ at S$_1$, S$'_1$, S$_2$, S$'_2$. To find any point on hyperbola (P$_n$, upper left quadrant), erect perpendicular at N to intersect G$_1$ S$_1$ at V. From F$_1$ swing an arc = NV to intersect NV at P$_n$. See also Sheet 33 for other methods.

PARAMETRIC FORM

$x = a \sec t = \dfrac{a}{\cos t}$

$y = b \tan t$

(only one quadrant shown)

To Draw: Draw circles with radii = a and = b, centers O. From O draw any line, intersecting circle of radius a at T. From T erect perpendicular (tangent to circle) intersecting x axis at X. From intersection of circle of radius b with x axis, erect perpendicular intersecting OT at Y. Through Y draw line parallel to x axis, which will intersect a line parallel to y axis drawn through X at P. P is a point on the hyperbola.

Note that tangent to circle of radius a at intersection with asymptote passes through focus.

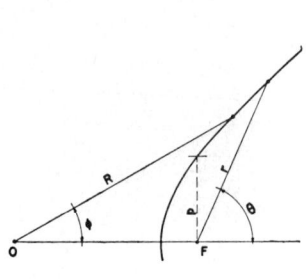

POLAR FORM

Pole at focus

$r = \dfrac{P}{1 - e \cos \theta}$

Pole at center O

$R^2 = \dfrac{a^2 b^2}{b^2 \cos^2 \phi - a^2 \sin^2 \phi}$

AREA

$A = ab \log_e \left(\dfrac{x}{a} + \dfrac{y}{b} \right) \qquad = ab \sinh^{-1} \dfrac{y}{b}$

$= ab \cosh^{-1} \dfrac{x}{a} \qquad = ab \tanh^{-1} \dfrac{ay}{bx}$

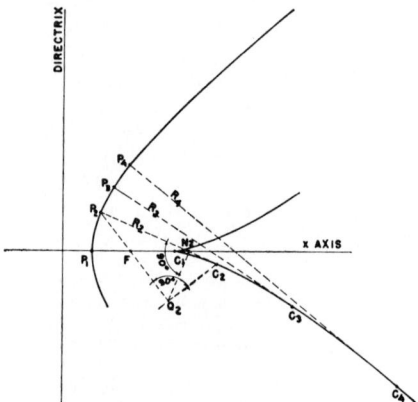

EVOLUTE OF HYPERBOLA

(For part of one quadrant)

Radius of Curvature

$R = a^2 b^2 \left(\dfrac{x^2}{a^4} + \dfrac{y^2}{b^4} \right)^{3/2}$ For any point

x, y on the hyperbola.

At apex (P$_1$), Radius C$_1$ P$_1$ = $\dfrac{b^2}{a}$ = p

Equation of Evolute

Standard form: $a^{2/3} x^{2/3} + b^{2/3} y^{2/3} = (a^2 + b^2)^{2/3}$

Center of curvature of hyperbola can be found by same procedure as shown for ellipse.

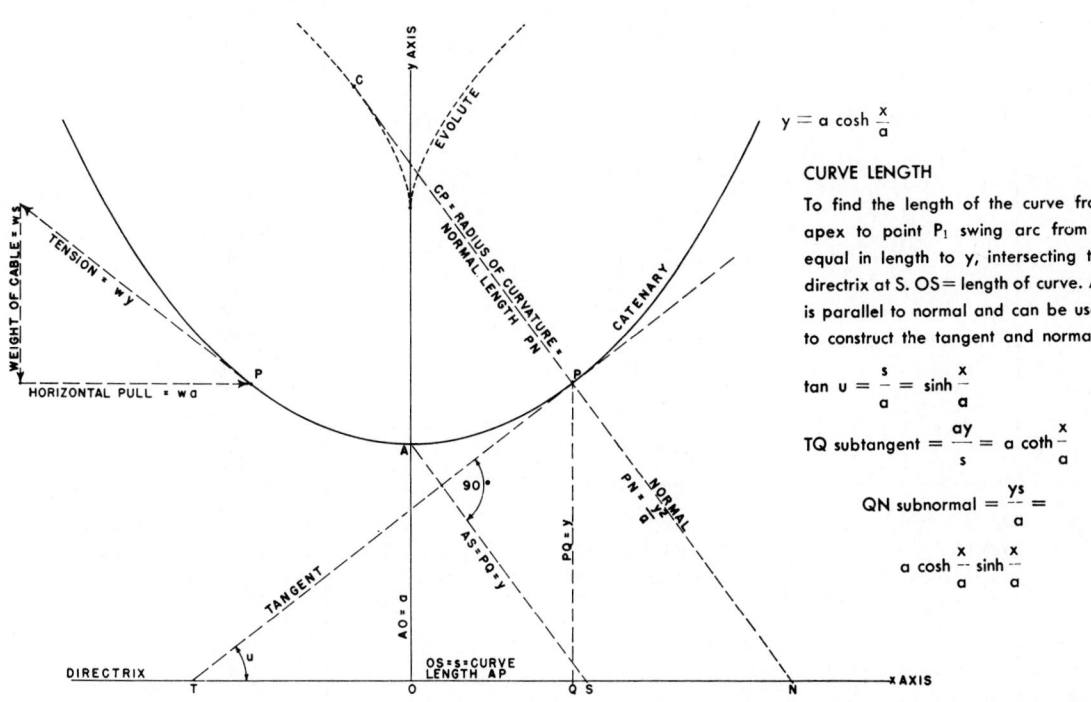

$$y = a \cosh \frac{x}{a}$$

CURVE LENGTH

To find the length of the curve from apex to point P_1 swing arc from A equal in length to y, intersecting the directrix at S. OS = length of curve. AS is parallel to normal and can be used to construct the tangent and normal.

$$\tan u = \frac{s}{a} = \sinh \frac{x}{a}$$

$$TQ \text{ subtangent} = \frac{ay}{s} = a \coth \frac{x}{a}$$

$$QN \text{ subnormal} = \frac{ys}{a} =$$

$$a \cosh \frac{x}{a} \sinh \frac{x}{a}$$

DEFINITION

The catenary is the curve described by a perfectly flexible cord of uniform weight, hanging freely between two supports. All catenaries have the same shape and differ only in scale (size). The measure of this scale is the parameter "a," which is the distance from the apex to the directrix.

The relationship between the tension at any point in the cable and the horizontal and vertical components is shown above. w = weight of cable per unit of length.

Upside down, the catenary is also the curve of the pressure line of an arch of uniform cross section, loaded only by its own weight. When the catenary is reversed, what is tension in the cable becomes compression in the arch.

METHODS OF DRAWING: THE CATENARY AS THE ROULETTE OF A PARABOLA

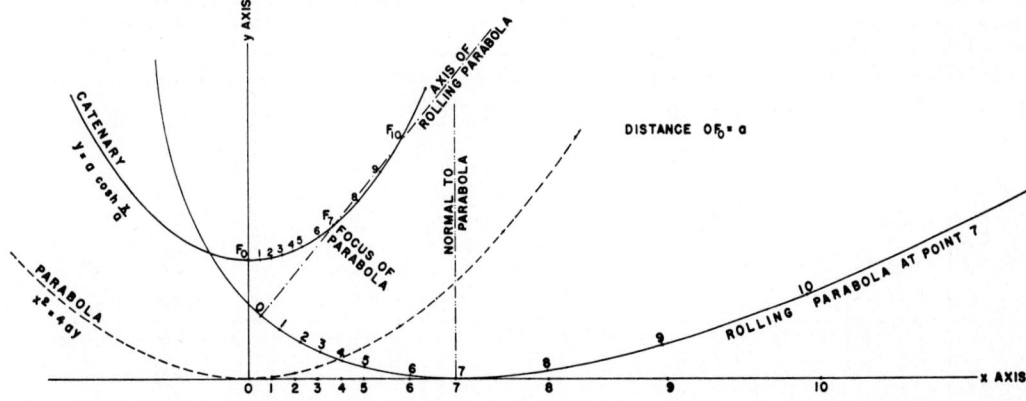

The catenary may be drawn by calculating points for the equation $y = a \cosh \frac{x}{a}$ and joining points, or it can be generated directly by rolling a parabola along the directrix. In either case the parameter "a," must be determined. As this is a trial and error procedure, the values of a in terms of SAG/SPAN ratios have been calculated and can be found directly from the graph on sheet 9. Having determined "a," the catenary can be drawn directly by first drawing a parabola with a parameter of 4a (2p in the notation on parabolas, Sheet 2–3), shown here as the parabola $x^2 = 4ay$. The parabola is then rolled along the x axis as shown above and its focus will describe the desired catenary.

This is known as a roulette curve (cycloids are the most well known roulettes). The only practical difficulty consists in preventing the rolling curve from slipping as it is rolled. The curve which is to be rolled (in this case the parabola) should be drawn on a piece of tracing paper. Make a hole in the paper at the point whose locus is sought (in this case the focus). Draw the curve (in this case the x axis) along which the curve is to be rolled on another piece of paper. Mark points along the length of the parabola and draw normal (and/or tangent) at each point. Mark points at the same distances measured along the straight line and draw normal at each point. Roll the parabola along the straight line, matching points and lining up normals (and/or tangents) at each point. Mark through the hole the corresponding point of the roulette (in this case the catenary).

PROBLEMS OF THE CATENARY FALL INTO THREE GENERAL CASES:

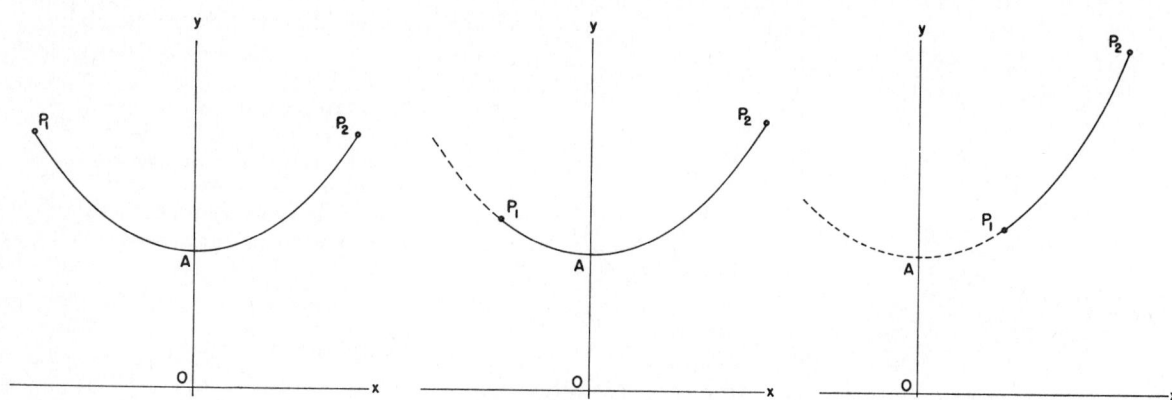

CASE 1: BOTH SUPPORTS AT SAME LEVEL   CASE II: SUPPORTS AT DIFFERENT LEVELS, LOW POINT IN BETWEEN   CASE III: SUPPORTS AT DIFFERENT LEVELS, NO LOW POINT BETWEEN

1. If locations of P_1, P_2 and A are known, the SAG/SPAN ratio can be calculated and the parameter "a" found from curve on sheet 9.

2. If only the locations of P_1 and P_2 are known, some additional information must be available. This may be:

a. The length of the curve between P_1 and P_2. With this it is possible to find "a" by trial and error graphically, remembering that the shape of the catenary is fixed and that the problem is one of scale. Over a catenary curve which has been accurately drawn, establish points P_1 and P_2 to some scale. The angle between the line which joins them and the y or x axis will be fixed. Measure the distance from P_1 to P_2 along the curve to this same scale. If this distance is less than the given distance, the points P_1 and P_2 must be moved higher (keeping their relative positions the same). (If greater, the points must be slid down the curve.) The correct scale for the new position must be worked out, the length along the curve measured according to the new curve and so on. When the scale is correct, measure the distance from A to O using this scale, and you will have the correct "a." This procedure can also be done algebraically, solving $S = a \sinh \dfrac{x}{a}$ by trial and error for each of the two distances P_1 A and P_2 A.

b. The tension in the cable and the weight per unit of length. Since $y = \dfrac{\text{tension}}{\text{unit weight}}$, the distance from P_1 or P_2 to the x axis can be found, and by adjusting the scale and drawing over an accurate curve, the apex A can be found and the parameter "a" calculated.

NOTES

TABLES OF HYPERBOLIC FUNCTIONS CAN BE FOUND:

1. "Smithsonian Mathematical Tables: Hyperbolic Functions," Pub. No. 1871, Gov. Printing Office, 1909, gives values to 5 decimal places
  for x = 0.0001 to x = 0.1000
  for x = 0.001 to x = 3.000
  and for x = 3.00 to x = 6.00

2. "Tables of Circular and Hyperbolic Sines and Cosines for Radian Arguments," published as a WPA project, New York, 1939, gives values to 9 decimal places
  for x = 0.0001 to x = 1.9999
  and for x = 2.0 to x = 10.00

CATENARY AS ROULETTE OF PARABOLA

The demonstration of the catenary as the roulette of a parabola was first made by James Clerk Maxwell, "Theory of Rolling Curves," Transactions Royal Soc. Edin., Vol. XVI, Part 5 (1849), republished in "Scientific Papers of James Clerk Maxwell," edited by W. D. Niven, Dover Pub., New York, 1952.

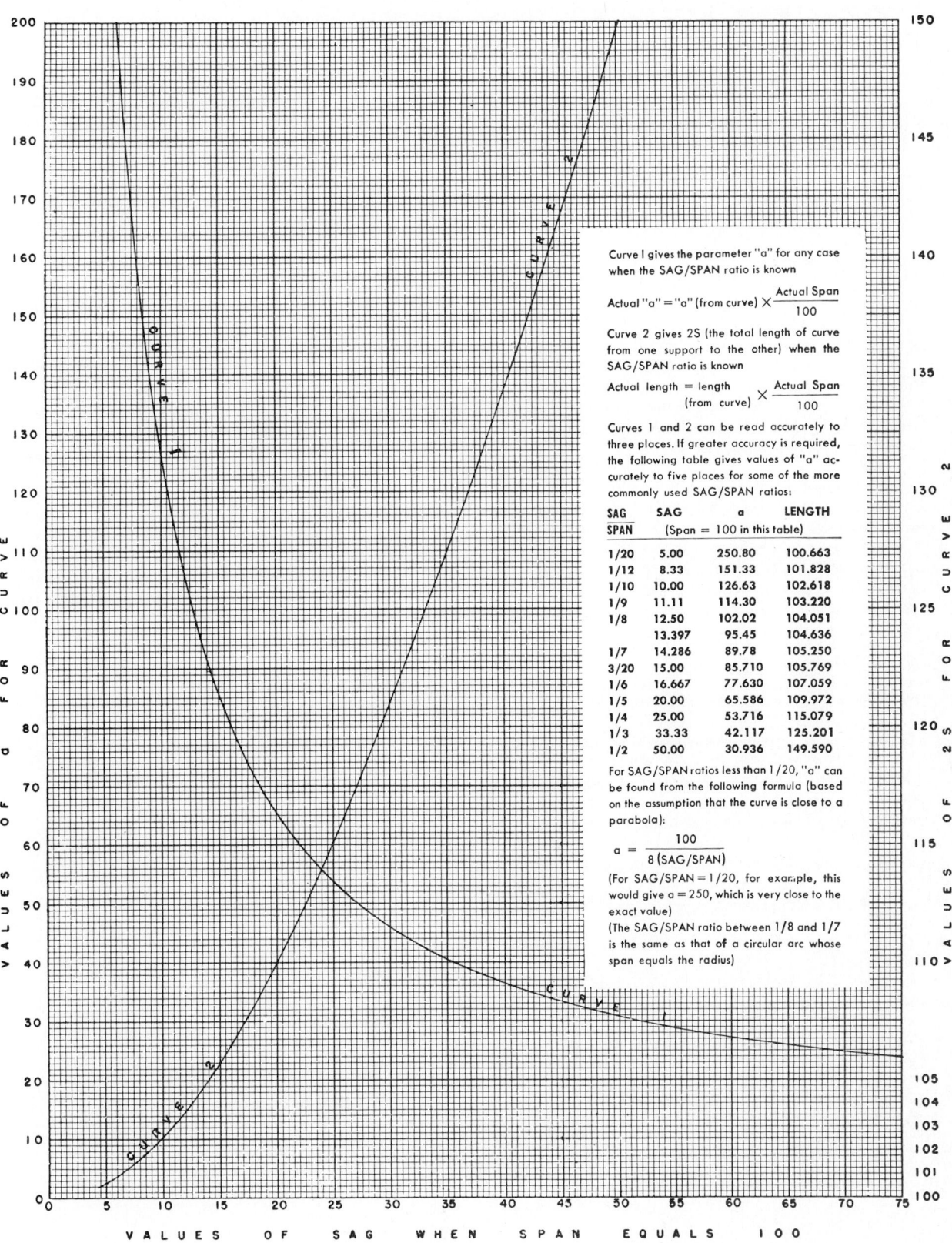

Curve I gives the parameter "a" for any case when the SAG/SPAN ratio is known

$$\text{Actual "a"} = \text{"a" (from curve)} \times \frac{\text{Actual Span}}{100}$$

Curve 2 gives 2S (the total length of curve from one support to the other) when the SAG/SPAN ratio is known

$$\text{Actual length} = \text{length (from curve)} \times \frac{\text{Actual Span}}{100}$$

Curves 1 and 2 can be read accurately to three places. If greater accuracy is required, the following table gives values of "a" accurately to five places for some of the more commonly used SAG/SPAN ratios:

$\frac{\text{SAG}}{\text{SPAN}}$	SAG (Span = 100 in this table)	a	LENGTH
1/20	5.00	250.80	100.663
1/12	8.33	151.33	101.828
1/10	10.00	126.63	102.618
1/9	11.11	114.30	103.220
1/8	12.50	102.02	104.051
	13.397	95.45	104.636
1/7	14.286	89.78	105.250
3/20	15.00	85.710	105.769
1/6	16.667	77.630	107.059
1/5	20.00	65.586	109.972
1/4	25.00	53.716	115.079
1/3	33.33	42.117	125.201
1/2	50.00	30.936	149.590

For SAG/SPAN ratios less than 1/20, "a" can be found from the following formula (based on the assumption that the curve is close to a parabola):

$$a = \frac{100}{8\,(\text{SAG/SPAN})}$$

(For SAG/SPAN = 1/20, for example, this would give a = 250, which is very close to the exact value)

(The SAG/SPAN ratio between 1/8 and 1/7 is the same as that of a circular arc whose span equals the radius)

VALUES OF SAG WHEN SPAN EQUALS 100

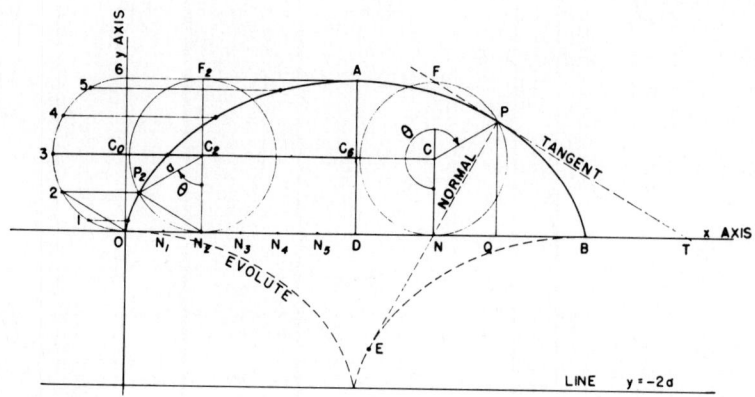

DEFINITION

The locus of a point P on the circumference of a circle which rolls along a straight line without slipping is called a cycloid. It has been used as a cross section of concrete shells.

PARAMETRIC EQUATION (most convenient)

$$x = a(\theta - \sin\theta)$$
$$y = a(1 - \cos\theta) \qquad (\theta \text{ in radians})$$

STANDARD FORM

$$x = a \text{ arc cos}\left(\frac{a-y}{a}\right) - \sqrt{2ay - y^2}$$

METHODS OF DRAWING

1. Draw directly as a roulette (see definition, sheet 7) by rolling a circle of radius "a" along x axis. Take care that circle does not slip.

2. On y axis draw generating circle, radius = a, center at C_0 ($C_0O = a$). Divide half circumference into whole number of arcs (here 6). On x axis lay off the lengths of these arcs ON_1, N_1N_2, N_2N_3, etc., by measuring directly or by measuring $OD = \pi a$ and dividing into same number of parts. Draw a horizontal line through C and project points N_1, N_2, etc.

up to find successive positions of center of circle. At each center draw the radius vector, where θ is the corresponding multiple of

$$\frac{180°}{\text{number of arcs}} \quad (C_2P_2 = a,\ \theta_2 = 2 \times \frac{180}{6} = 60°$$

for example). P_2 also lies on a horizontal line through point 2 on the generating circle as shown in initial position.

3. Proceed as directed in method 2, as far as measuring arc lengths along x axis. Then through points 1, 2, 3, etc. on circle in initial

position, draw horizontal lines. Measure on each line the corresponding length of arc and the corresponding point on the cycloid will be found. (For example, to find P_2, measure 2, $P_2 = ON_2$.)

4. Proceed as directed in method 2, as far as measuring arc lengths along x axis. To find P_2 shown, describe arc of radius 0, 2 from center N_2 and intersect horizontal line drawn through 2. Note that P_2N_2 is the normal to point P_2 and is half the length of the radius of curvature at P_2.

TANGENT to any point P passes through F at top of generating circle in corresponding position. Subtangent $QT = a\dfrac{(1-\cos\theta)^2}{\sin\theta}$

NORMAL to any point P passes through N at bottom of generating circle. Normal $PN = \sqrt{2ay}$. Subnormal $QN = a\sin\theta$.

LENGTH OF CURVE for one arch = 8a. Centroid of this length is $\dfrac{4a}{3}$ above x axis.

LENGTH OF AN ARC of curve $AP = 2 \times PF$ (length of arc $BP = 4a - 2\ PF$)

AREA UNDER ONE ARCH = $3\pi a^2$. Centroid of this area is $\dfrac{5a}{6}$ above x axis.

RADIUS OF CURVATURE = EP = twice length of normal $PN = 2\sqrt{2ay}$.

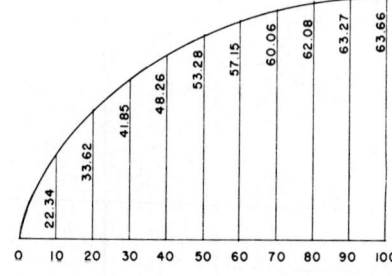

ORDINATES OF A CYCLOID expressed in terms of a half length of 100.

$$x = \frac{100}{\pi}(\theta - \sin\theta)$$

$$y = \frac{100}{\pi}(1 - \cos\theta)$$

$$\frac{100}{\pi} = 31.831$$

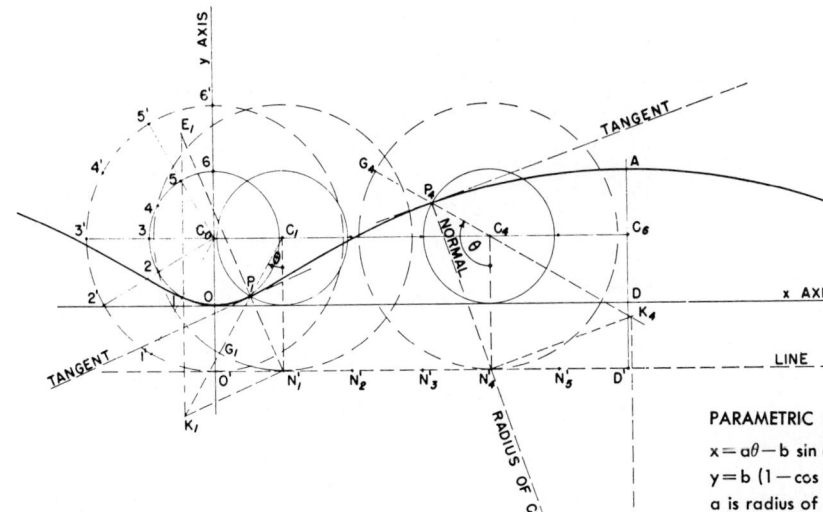

PARAMETRIC EQUATION

$x = a\theta - b \sin \theta$ (θ in radians)

$y = b (1 - \cos \theta)$

a is radius of rolling circle = CG

b is distance from center of circle to point = CP

NORMAL to any point P passes through N′ at bottom of generating circle.

TANGENT is found as perpendicular to normal at P

RADIUS OF CURVATURE = PE. Point E is found as follows. Erect perpendicular to normal at N′. Extend radius line PC to intersect perpendicular at K. Draw vertical line through K to intersect PN′ extended at E. E is center of curvature and PE is radius of curvature.

Equation:

$$PE = R = \frac{[a^2 - 2ab \cos \theta + b^2]^{3}/_2}{2a^2 - ab(\cos \theta + 2) + b^2}$$

At point 0, $\theta = 0$ and

$$R = \frac{(a - b)^3}{2a^2 - 3ab + b^2}$$

At point A, $\theta = 180° = \pi$ and

$$R = \frac{(a + b)^3}{2a^2 - ab + b^2}$$

EVOLUTE for the prolate trochoid is in two parts, one on each side of the curve. The normal which makes the smallest angle with the x axis passes through the point of contraflexure and is asymptotic to each portion of the evolute.

DEFINITION

The locus of a point P on the radius of a circle which rolls along a straight line without slipping is called a trochoid. If P lies inside the circle it is a prolate trochoid shown here. If outside, a curtate trochoid. The curtate trochoid curve has little possibility of use in the building field. The prolate trochoid has potentialities as a section for corrugated concrete shells (see Structural Forms—Reinforced Concrete). It is also used (upside down from position shown) as the curve of ocean waves for ship analysis, with a height (DA) equal to 20 times length (OB) and a length equal to length of ship.

METHODS OF DRAWING

The same methods as described for drawing a cycloid may be used. Note that the distance OB on the x axis is equal to $2\pi a$ and the height AD = 2b. Lengths of arcs must be measured on the circumference of the outer circle, heights from the inner circle.

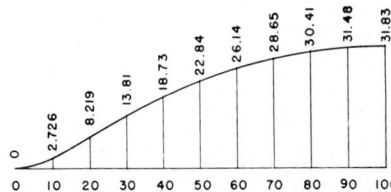

ORDINATES FOR A TROCHOID in which $a = 2b$, expressed in terms of a half-length of 100. This might be used as the cross-section of a shell roof.

$$x = \frac{50}{\pi} (2\theta - \sin \theta)$$

$$y = \frac{50}{\pi} (1 - \cos \theta)$$

$$\left[\frac{50}{\pi} = 15.915 \right]$$

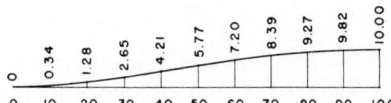

ORDINATES FOR A TROCHOID whose height is $\frac{1}{20}$ of its length, expressed in terms of a half-length of 100. This is the standard ocean wave, but upside down, i.e. the "0" ordinate is the crest, the "10" ordinate the hollow of the wave.

$$x = 5 \left(\frac{20}{\pi} \theta - \sin \theta \right) \qquad \left[\frac{20}{\pi} = 6.366 \right]$$

$$y = 5 (1 - \cos \theta)$$

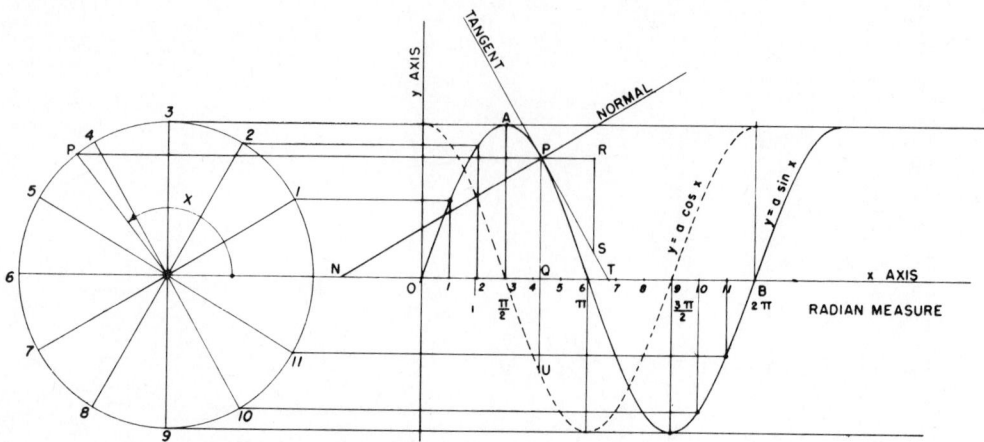

DEFINITION

The Sine Curve represents the vertical projection of a point P, moving with uniform velocity on the circumference of a circle, plotted against angular displacement. If a is the radius of the circle and b is the angular velocity of the point P on its circumference, and t is time; then x = bt and y = a cos bt. The amplitude = a and the period = 2π or 360° = OB.

In building work this curve has been used as the centerline of the cross section of corrugated concrete shells (see Structural Forms—Reinforced Concrete). It is also the elevation of a so-called spiral (helical) stair. And it is the projection of geodesic lines on a cylinder, such as plan projections of lamella arches.

EQUATION

y = a sin x

METHODS OF DRAWING

1. Draw the generating circle with radius a and divide circumference into a whole number of parts (here 12). Lay off the distance OB on the x axis and divide into the same number of parts. Erect a perpendicular at each point of division of the x axis. Draw horizontal lines through the corresponding points on the circumference of the circle and the intersections will be points on the curve. Note that distance

OB = 2π radians and that 57°18′ = one radian. To find the point at which x = 1 radian, divide OB into 2π or 6.283 parts and locate 1 cn this scale.

2. Calculate and plot points using table of sines.

TANGENT

The slope of the tangent at any point = a cos x. The curve y = a cos x has been drawn and has exactly the same shape but is displaced π/2 radians or 90° to the left. To draw the tangent at P, draw a horizontal line through P and measure PR = 1 radian. Draw a vertical line through P intersecting x axis at Q and extend to intersect cosine curve at U. Draw a vertical line RS through R of length RS = QU. The line PS is tangent to the sine curve at P, and can be extended to cut x axis at T.

NORMAL is drawn as perpendicular to tangent.

AREA under one arch (from origin to π or 180°) = 2a. Centroid of this area is $\frac{\pi a}{8}$ above x axis.

RADIUS OF CURVATURE $R = \frac{(1+a^2\cos^2 x)^{3/2}}{a \sin x}$. At apex A, $R = \frac{1}{a}$

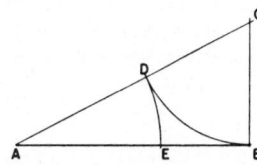

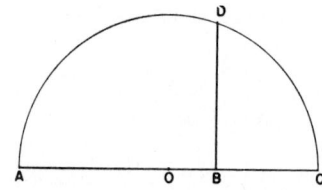

GOLDEN SECTION

Used by Greek artists and architects and often revived in theories of proportion. Basis of Modular of Le Corbusier, using 2 m 26 (or 7 ft 5 in.) or 1 m 13 (or 3 ft 8½ in.) as starting points for his two series. If a line AB is divided so that $\frac{AB}{AE} = \frac{AE}{EB}$ it is in golden section. Or if g is ratio such that AE = gEB,

$g^2 = g+1$ or $g - \frac{1}{g} = 1$ and $g = \frac{\sqrt{5}+1}{2} = 1.6180$

To find graphically, erect perpendicular $CB = \frac{AB}{2}$ and swing arc CD = CB. Then swing arc AD to cut AB at E.

The angle which the diagonal of a rectangle whose sides are in the ratio g:1 makes with the short side = arc tan 1.618 = 58° 17′.

GEOMETRICAL MEAN

General case of which golden section is a particular case. To find distance BD which is geometrical mean or mean proportional between AB and BC, divide AC in half at O and with O as center and radius equal to AO = OC, draw semicircle. Draw perpendicular at B to intersect circle at D

Then $BD^2 = AB \times BC$ or $\frac{AB}{BD} = \frac{BD}{BC}$

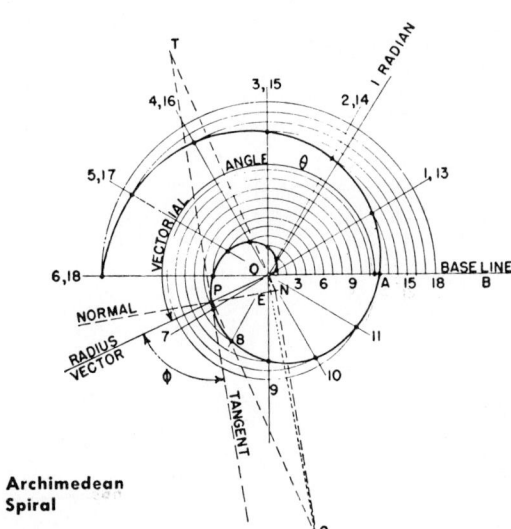

**Archimedean
Spiral**

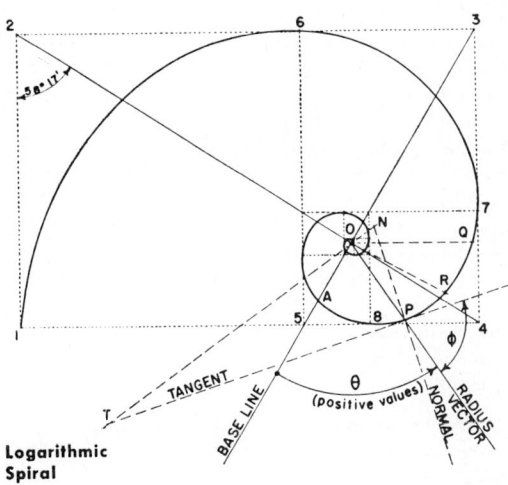

**Logarithmic
Spiral**

ARCHIMEDEAN SPIRAL

The locus of a point P which moves with uniform linear velocity along a line OP as OP revolves with uniform angular velocity about O is called a Spiral of Archimedes.

EQUATION:

$r = a\theta$ (θ in radians)

METHOD OF DRAWING (only positive values of θ are shown) Draw baseline OB. Measure off $OA = 2\pi a$. Divide OA into whole number of parts (here 12). Through O draw radial lines at equal spaces corresponding to the same number of parts (here $\frac{360}{12} = 30°$ or $\frac{2\pi}{12} = \frac{\pi}{6}$ radians). With O as center, draw arcs of circles with radii = O1, O2, O3 etc. Where each radius intersects corresponding radial line is a point on the spiral. Note that successive values of r are in arithmetical progression. To measure a, draw radial line at 1 radian (57° 18'), where $r = a$.

NORMAL

Through O draw $ON = a$ perpendicular to radius vector OP. PN is normal. TANGENT is drawn at right angles to normal at P. Note that the angle Φ between radius vector and tangent is the angle whose tangent $= \frac{r}{a}$ and that this angle is constantly increasing as θ increases.

RADIUS OF CURVATURE

Through N draw NQ parallel to tangent.

Through P draw PQ at right angles to radius vector. Line OQ cuts PN at E. E is center of curvature to spiral at P. Radius of curvature

$$R = \frac{(r^2 + a^2)^{\frac{3}{2}}}{r^2 + 2a^2}$$

LENGTH OF ARC = OP

$$\frac{a}{2}\left[\theta\sqrt{1 + \theta^2} + \log_e (\theta + \sqrt{1 + \theta^2}\right]$$

LOGARITHMIC (EQUIANGULAR) SPIRAL

The curve that cuts the radius vector at a constant angle Φ is called an Equiangular Spiral. If successive values of the vectorial angle θ are in arithmetical progression, the corresponding values of the radius vector are in geometric progression.

EQUATION

$r = ae^{m\theta}$ or $\log_e \frac{r}{a} = m\theta$

$m = \cot \Phi$ and $a = r = OA$ (when $\theta = 0°$)

METHODS OF DRAWING

In general, draw radial lines from pole O for equal increments of θ, calculate corresponding values of r and measure on each radial line. If r is calculated for large increments of θ and the points plotted, intermediate points can be found as follows: If OP and OQ are any two radii and if OR is a radius bisecting angle POQ, then OR is the mean proportional between OQ and OP (see sheet 12 for drawing method).

NORMAL

Through O draw $ON = rm = r \cot \Phi$ perpendicular to radius vector OP. PN is normal. TANGENT is drawn at right angles to normal at P and intersects ON extended at T.

RADIUS OF CURVATURE

$R = PN = r\sqrt{1 + m^2} = r \csc \Phi$.

Center of curvature is at N. Evolute is an identical spiral whose axis is inclined $\left[\frac{\pi}{2} - \frac{\log_e m}{m}\right]$ to axis of given spiral.

LENGTH OF SPIRAL from O to p = $r \sec \Phi = PT$

AREA swept by radius (from $r = O$ to $r = OP$) = $\frac{r^2}{4m}$ = ½ triangle OPT

The golden section spiral shown here is one whose radius vectors, separated by 90°, are in the golden section ratio. It is extensively discussed in theories of proportion. It can be drawn geometrically, without calculation. Here the rectangle 1234 is shown whose sides are in the golden section ratio. If a square (here 1265) is cut off, a similar rectangle (3456) is left, turned through 90°. This process can be continued indefinitely. Note the value of the diagonals in drawing the rectangles correctly. The diagonals cross at right angles at the pole O and are the axes of the equiangular spiral for which $\Phi = 73°$ (approx.) The corners of the squares (1, 6, 7, 8 etc.) are points on the spiral. The spiral crosses outside of the rectangle at these points.

ANALYTIC DESCRIPTION

Surfaces and skew curves can be described by a greater variety of analytical systems than curves which exist in only one plane. In architectural and related work we do not need all of these and will limit the descriptions to three types: 1. Triaxial Cartesian coordinates (a point is fixed by its projected distance on x, y and z axes); 2. Cylindrical coordinates (a point is fixed by a plane normal to a z axis and by its radius vector from a pole on this axis); and 3. Spherical coordinates (the familiar latitude and longitude or meridian lines). The purposes in analyzing a surface are:

a) to be able to recreate the surface;
b) to know its area and the volume enclosed;
c) to discover the stresses acting in the surface;
d) to discover the manner in which the surface will reflect light, heat, sound.

METHODS OF STUDY

Models are the best, and should be made as large as practicable. Wire and string can be used; sheet materials (cardboard, plastic) can be bent into the shape of developable surfaces, or can be cut to represent planes cutting the surface and put together like an egg-crate. Soft white pine can be carved in the solid and its surface studied. A solution of soap and glycerine* can be used to make minimal surfaces or membranes between wire boundary curves. From the models the surfaces can be transferred to paper, showing the traces of the surface as it is cut by a system of planes. Once drawn, the best method of construction in the field can be worked out. Usually a table of offsets should be prepared.

SKEW CURVE

A **skew curve** (also called a space curve or a twisted curve) is one which does not lie entirely in one plane. (See dwg.) The tangent line at any point defines the direction of the curve at that point. The normals to the tangent define the normal plane. The osculating

Soap solution recommended: Dissolve 10 grams of dry sodium oleate in 500 grams of distilled water. Mix 15 cubic parts of this solution with 11 cubic parts of glycerine. Alternatively, buy a prepared solution.

plane makes a right angle with the normal plane, contains the tangent and is the plane in which the curve most closely lies at the given point. The curve will pass through the osculating plane at a regular or ordinary point. The principal normal is the intersection of the osculating and normal planes. The radius of curvature (R) is found on this principal normal. The ratio $\frac{1}{R}$ is called the first curvature. The third orthogonal line of reference at the point is called the binormal and its plane the rectifying plane. The angular rate of change of the binormal as a point moves along the curve is called the torsion or second curvature.

SURFACES

At any regular (i.e. not singular) point on a surface there will exist a **tangent plane**. If the surface is cut by any variable plane, the tangent to the curve of intersection at the given point will always lie in this tangent plane. For a cup-shaped region of a surface this tangent plane will be entirely on one side of the surface; for a saddle-shaped region it will cut the surface. (See dwg.)

At right angles to the tangent plane an infinity of normal planes can be drawn. Each of these cuts the surface in a curve called a normal section; each of these sections has a radius of curvature at the given point. One of these radii will have a minimum value R_1 and another a maximum R_2. The normal planes in which these two radii lie are called the **principal normal planes** and they are at right angles to each other. The tangents to the principal normal sections are called the **principal directions.** For a cup-shaped region of a surface the centers of both radii will lie on the same side of the surface, (See dwg.), and will have the same sign. Such a point is called an elliptic point and the curvature of the surface is called positive. For a saddle-shaped region the center of one radius will lie on one side, and the center of the other on the opposite side of the surface; and the radii will have opposite signs. Such a point is called a hyperbolic point and the curvature is called negative. Parabolic points also exist; at these the maximum radius of curvature is infinite.

On a surface can be traced a **line of curvature,** which lies along one of the principal directions of each of a sequence of points.

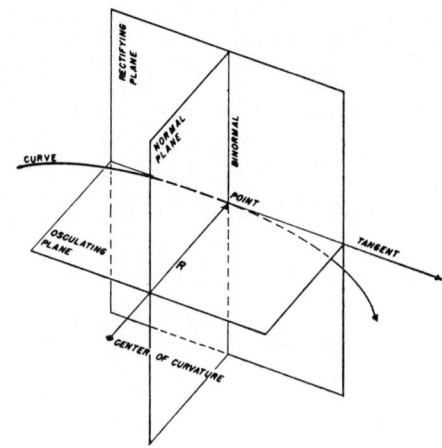

Skew Curve

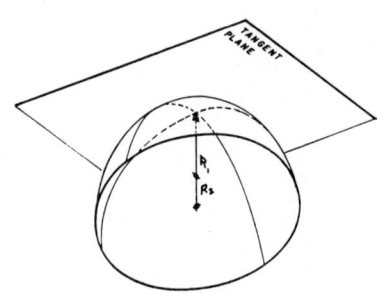

Surface of Positive Curvature

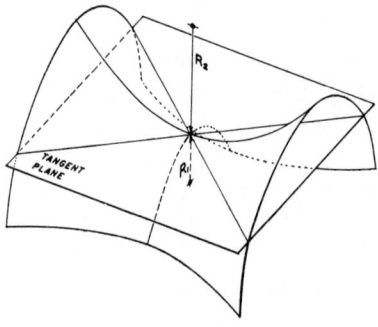

Surface of Negative Curvature

Through each point there will regularly be two such lines of curvature, which are at right angles to each other. On any surface of revolution the lines of curvature are the meridians (intersection with the surface of a plane containing the axis) and the circles of latitude. On any developable surface the rulings constitute one family of lines of curvature.

The **mean (or average) curvature** of a surface at a given point is the arithmetic mean of the two principal curvatures: $\frac{1}{2}\left(\frac{1}{R_1} + \frac{1}{R_2}\right)$. It is always zero for a minimal surface.

The **Gaussian curvature** (also called the total curvature) of a surface at a given point is the product of the two principal curvatures: $\frac{1}{R_1 R_2}$. It is positive at elliptic (cup-shaped) points, negative at hyperbolic (saddle-shaped) points, and zero at parabolic points. When a surface is bent, its Gaussian curvature does not change. This fact can be used to determine whether one surface can be formed or developed into another.

The **Dupin indicatrix** at a point is found by plotting, on the tangent plane, in the direction of every normal section, a distance from the point equal to the square root of the radius of curvature corresponding to that section. The indicatrix is always a conic section (including the degenerate conics). At an elliptic **point** (cup-shaped or synclastic region) the Dupin indicatrix is an ellipse. When both radii of curvature are equal, the ellipse becomes a circle and the point is called an **umbilic**. The umbilics are therefore singular points and have no principal directions. At a **hyperbolic point** the indicatrix is a hyperbola for all the radii of curvature on one side of the surface and the conjugate hyperbola for all the radii on the other side. The asymptotes of the hyperbolas give the **asymptotic directions**. The **asymptotic lines** consist of the family of curves which follow the asymptotic directions for every hyperbolic point and form a net over a negative surface. At a **parabolic point** one of the radii of curvature usually becomes infinite (and the corresponding curvature vanishes) and the Dupin indicatrix becomes a pair of straight lines.

On a surface on which some regions are negative, some positive, the locus of points separating the two regions traces a curve called the **parabolic curve** of the surface.

A **ruled surface** is generated by a straight line (called a generator of the surface) which moves continuously in some predetermined manner with respect to a curve or curves (called the directrix) and/or a point.

A **developable surface** is always a ruled surface, and the tangent plane to the surface at any point as the point moves along a given ruling lies in one plane throughout the length of the ruling. Cones and cylinders are typical. In general any surface generated by the tangents to a skew curve is a developable surface (called the tangential developable of the curve.) The Gaussian curvature of a developable surface is everywhere zero (as is that of a plane) and all its points are parabolic.

For all **other ruled surfaces** (which are not developable) the tangent plane at any point as the point moves along a given ruling turns through two right angles as it moves from infinity at one end to infinity at the other. The point at which the tangent has moved through only one right angle is called the **center point**. The locus of center points for the surface is called the **line of striction**.

Doubly ruled surfaces have two distinct families of rulings or straight lines on them. Only two such surfaces exist: the hyperbolic paraboloid and the hyperboloid of one sheet. The rulings are the asymptotic lines of the surfaces. The Gaussian curvature is everywhere negative and all the points are hyperbolic.

A **conoid** is generated by a straight line which, remaining parallel to a given plane, moves along a straight line (which is not parallel to the plane) and along some other geometrical figure. The hyperbolic paraboloid is thus a conoid as are the helicoids. The surface commonly referred to as a conoid in construction is Pluecker's conoid or cylindroid, generated by a straight line which moves along a straight line and an ellipse (or circle).

A **surface of revolution** is generated by rotating a curve about an axis. Typical are: the right circular cone and cylinder; the spheroids; the paraboloid of revolution; the hyperboloids of revolution, of one sheet and of two sheets; the unduloids (generated by rotating the roulette of any conic curve.) The two centers of curvature at any point on a surface of revolution are: 1) In the meridian plane, the center of curvature of the curve whose rotation generates the surface; and 2) The intersection with the axis of revolution of the line normal to the surface.

A **geodesic curve** is the shortest distance, measured on the surface, between two points on the surface. For any developable surface it can be found by drawing a straight line on the surface when developed out onto a plane and then bending the plane back onto the surface. Through any point on a surface there exists in general an infinite number of geodesic curves, going out from it in every direction and joining it to every other point on the surface. On a sphere all the geodesics are great circles. On a cylinder all the geodesics are helices (including meridian lines which are helices of infinite pitch and latitude circles which are helices of zero pitch). On a surface of revolution all the meridians are geodesics, but the other geodesics cannot be found so simply. The circles of latitude are generally not geodesics.

A **minimal surface** is the surface of smallest area among all the surfaces bounded by a given closed curve or curves. It is created automatically by the membrane formed when a wire model of the boundary curve(s) is dipped into a soap solution. Except for the plane, a minimal surface is saddle-shaped (anticlastic) at all points; all points are therefore hyperbolic. The Gaussian curvature is everywhere negative. The mean curvature vanishes for every point; i.e.

$$\frac{1}{2}\left(\frac{1}{R_1} + \frac{1}{R_2}\right) = 0.$$

In other words the least radii of curvature at any point are equal in magnitude and on opposite sides of the surface. The Dupin indicatrix for every point is an equilateral hyperbola and the asymptotic lines form an orthogonal net over the entire surface.

Surfaces and skew curves

Reflection. Analysis of the reflective properties of surfaces can always be made by knowing the point source of energy (heat, light, sound) and the tangent plane at all points on the surface. Rays can be drawn to each point on the surface and the reflected ray found by the law: angle of reflection equals angle of incidence. It is more revealing to find the image of the source on the opposite side of the surface and then, using this as a center, to draw concentric circles or rays. In general a concave surface will concentrate rays, a convex surface will scatter them.

Structural. In general a curved surface will carry the external forces acting on it by direct stresses only, provided the supports can furnish the required vertical and horizontal reactions and provided the boundaries or edges are properly stiffened. Bending stresses may be set up near the boundaries, near the supports and at points of application of concentrated loads. Bending stresses

may be set up where the curvature of the surface changes rapidly and especially at "knuckles" or sharp ridges. These bending stresses can be taken care of by thickening the shell or adding stiffening rings or ribs to the shell.

A surface of double curvature will be stiffer and deform less under load than one of single curvature, but generally it will be more expensive to calculate and to construct. While any imaginable three-dimensional surface can be drawn and built, whether it is susceptible of simple mathematical analysis or not, the description of a surface by relatively simple equations enables the engineer to make a more accurate estimate of the stresses to be expected. The mathematical surface should be taken at the centerline of the thickness of the shell or skin.

The usual procedure is first to analyze the so-called membrane stresses. These are all direct stresses and are found by analyzing

a typical region of the surface on the assumption that it has no boundaries. The disturbances set up by the existence of boundaries are taken care of by separate calculations. So-called line loads are applied to the edges. The stresses set up by these are added to the membrane stresses and the net stress calculated. (This is similar to the methods of analyzing continuous frames.)

As in the case of all statically indeterminate structures, curved shells (or stressed skin constructions generally) must be drawn accurately and completely dimensioned before they can be calculated. It is essential that the preliminary guess of shape and dimension be made on the basis of the maximum amount of experience, since the loads to be carried may consist largely of the weight of the structure itself. Simple, rough calculation methods should be used in the early stages until the lightest, thinnest and stiffest combination is found. Then more detailed calculations can be made.

	SINGLE CURVATURE DEVELOPABLE	DOUBLE CURVATURE NOT DEVELOPABLE				
		Negative Curvature (Saddle-Shaped)				Positive Curvature (Cup-Shaped)
RULINGS	All Ruled Singly	Ruled Singly	Ruled Doubly (Only Two Exist)		Unruled	All Unruled
NAMES of Some Surfaces	Cones; Cylinders; Tangential Developables of Space Curves	Conoids; Right Circular Helicoid	Hyperbolic Paraboloid	Hyperboloid of One Sheet	Hyperboloid of Two Sheets; Elliptic Paraboloid; Catenoid; Pseudosphere; Inner Half of Torus; Parts of Unduloids; General Helicoid	Sphere; Spheroid; Ellipsoid; Outer Half of Torus; Parts of Unduloids
SURFACES OF REVOLUTION	Cone and Circular Cylinder Only	None	None	May Be	May Be	May Be
MINIMAL SURFACES Mean Curvature = 0 Gaussian Curvature Always Negative	None	May Be (Right Circular Helicoid, for example)	None	None	May Be. Usually Fall in This Group	None
MEAN CURVATURE $\frac{1}{2}\left(\frac{1}{R_1}+\frac{1}{R_2}\right)$	+	+, 0, −	+, 0, −	+, 0, −	+, 0, −	+. Sphere Is Only Surface (Without a Boundary) of Constant Positive Mean Curvature
GAUSSIAN CURVATURE $\frac{1}{R_1 R_2}$	0	−	−	−	−. A few Surfaces Such as Pseudosphere Exist With Constant Negative Curvature	+. Sphere Is Only Surface (Without a Boundary) Of Constant Positive Curvature

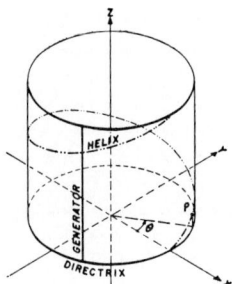

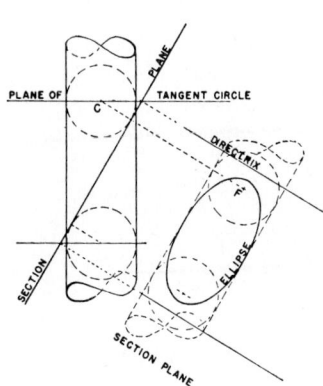

A cylinder is generated by a straight line element (the generator or generatrix) which moves along a plane curve (the directrix) parallel to an axis which is not in the plane of the curve. When the axis makes a right angle with the plane of the curve, the surface is called a right cylinder. For design purposes we can always arrange the cylinder to be right.

Any curve can be used for the directrix. If a conic is used, the cylinders are quadric surfaces and all sections are also conics. Only quadric cylinders are shown here, but other forms such as a catenary cylinder may be preferable for structural reasons.

The **right circular cylinder** is the surface
$$x^2 + y^2 = r^2;\ z = z$$
or, in cylindrical coordinates: $r = r,\ z = z$
$$x = r\cos\Theta;\ y = r\sin\Theta;\ z = z$$
[The elliptical cylinder, not shown, would have similar equations derived from those of the ellipse, (see sheet 4 on curves).]

The geodesics on the right circular cylinder are all circular helices and the most useful form of their equation is:
$$x = r\cos\Theta;\ y = r\sin\Theta;\ z = k\Theta$$

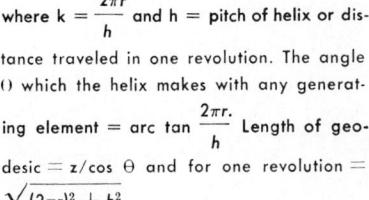

where $k = \dfrac{2\pi r}{h}$ and h = pitch of helix or distance traveled in one revolution. The angle Θ which the helix makes with any generating element $= \arctan\dfrac{2\pi r}{h}$. Length of geodesic $= z/\cos\Theta$ and for one revolution $= \sqrt{(2\pi r)^2 + h^2}$

The projection of the circular helix on the xz or yz planes (i.e. "side elevation") is always a sine curve (see sheet 12 on curves).

The lamellas or elements of a lamella roof (see sheet 41, Structural Design—Wood) trace helices on the surface of a cylindrical roof. The drawing of the parabolic cylinder explains this.

Any **section of a circular cylinder** is an ellipse. The foci of the ellipse are the projections on the section plane of the centers of the spheres tangent to the cylinder and to the plane. They are also the points of tangency of these spheres and the section plane. The directrix of the ellipse is the intersection of the section plane with the plane of the circle of tangency of the sphere.

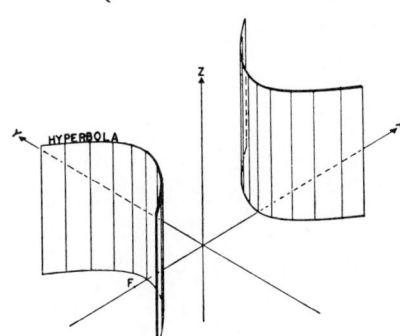

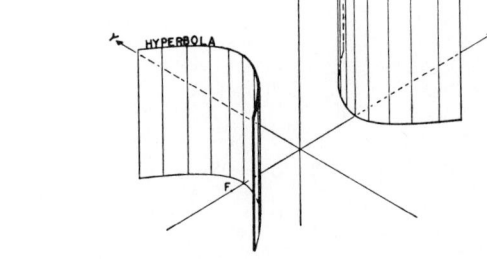

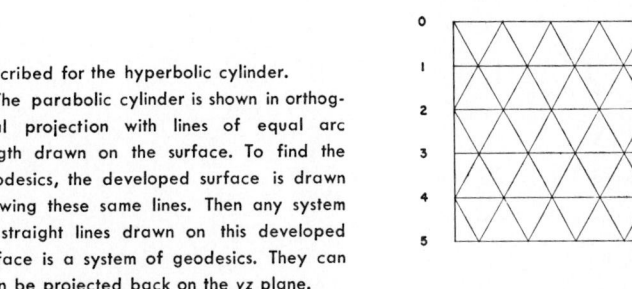

The **hyperbolic cylinder** is the surface

$$\frac{x^2}{a^2} - \frac{y^2}{b^2} = 1;\ z = z$$

All sections are conics and are most easily drawn by projecting a few points and using Pascal's method.

The **parabolic cylinder** (coordinates as shown) is the surface
$$x^2 = -2\,py;\ z = z$$
Sections are all conics and are drawn as

described for the hyperbolic cylinder.

The parabolic cylinder is shown in orthogonal projection with lines of equal arc length drawn on the surface. To find the geodesics, the developed surface is drawn showing these same lines. Then any system of straight lines drawn on this developed surface is a system of geodesics. They can then be projected back on the yz plane.

This method of drawing geodesics can be used for any developable surface. In the case of cylinders the geodesics are all helices or portions of helices. (See sheet 18 for possible regular patterns.)

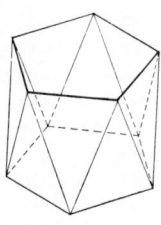

Prisms or anti-prisms offer convenient approximations to cylinders or may be chosen for their own shape. Any regular polygon can be used for the two bases; for the anti-prisms the two bases are twisted so that the vertices of one are above the mid points of the sides of the other.

(For areas, surfaces and volumes of cylinders, prisms, and anti-prisms see Mathematics—Areas and Solids.)

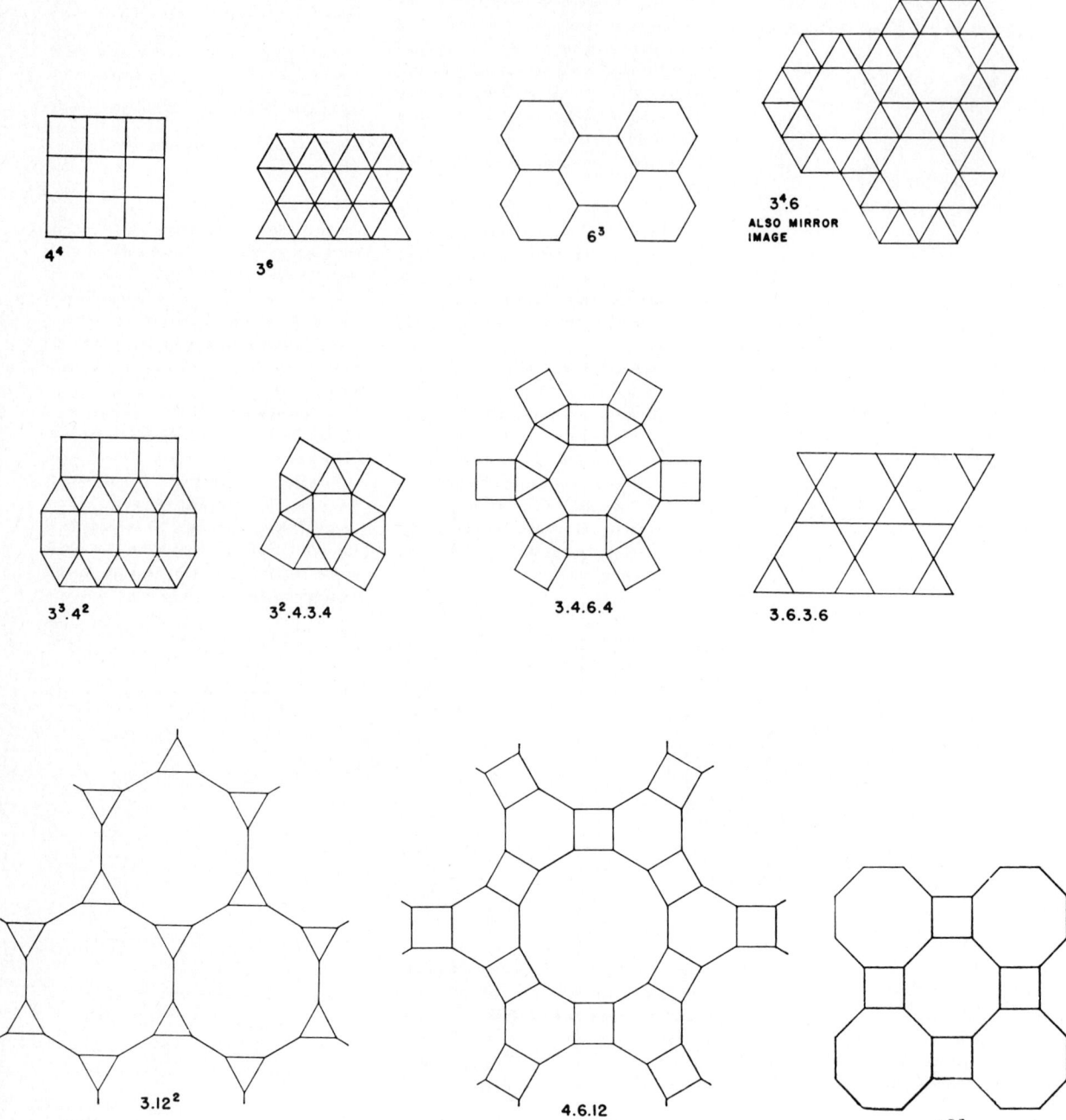

4^4

3^6

6^3

$3^4.6$
ALSO MIRROR
IMAGE

$3^3.4^2$

$3^2.4.3.4$

$3.4.6.4$

$3.6.3.6$

3.12^2

$4.6.12$

4.8^2

REGULAR AND SEMI-REGULAR PATTERNS

The division of a plane into regular polygons is often necessary for structural or decorative reasons. There are only three regular tessellations (patterns) in which all the polygons are identical. There are only eight semi-regular tessellations in which all the polygons are regular but not identical; all the sides are of equal length. One of the semi-regular tessellations has two forms which are mirror-images of each other. All vertices are congruent. The notation is based on the vertex figure of each tessellation. The polygons are listed by the number of sides as they are found in sequence around a vertex. These tessellations are related not only to the plane but to every surface which is developable and which can therefore be drawn without distortion on a plane. The sides of the polygons will, of course, all be geodesics. Not every tessellation can be used for every surface; it will be necessary to experiment to find which will fit and which will be most suited to the structural or esthetic purpose. Any polygon used structurally must be held rigid, either by division into triangles or by provision of a continuous membrane.

If every point on a plane curve is joined by a straight line to a point not in the plane of the curve, a cone is generated. Each straight line is called an element (or generator) of the cone; the curve is called the directrix. Since there is an infinity of possible plane curves, there is an infinity of possible cones. Every cone is a developable surface.

It helps in constructing a cone to know that every section of the surface is a curve of the same general type or degree as the directrix curve. All sections parallel to the plane of the directrix curve are curves which are parallel to the directrix curve (i.e. they are of the same shape, but larger or smaller.)

This fact is of value in drawing perspectives, since perspective projection consists essentially in drawing sections of a cone. Every second degree curve (conic section) drawn in perspective will therefore be a second degree curve. And every third degree curve will be some third degree curve; every transcendental curve (trig. functions, etc.) will be a transcendental curve.

The second degree or quadric cone is the one most used. Such a cone will be generated by using an ellipse, parabola or hyperbola as the directrix. These do not constitute different cones, in the way different cylinders are generated (see Sheet 17) but all generate cones of the general type:

$$\frac{x^2}{a^2} + \frac{y^2}{b^2} = \frac{z^2}{c^2}$$

Or, where $k = \tan \alpha = \dfrac{a}{c}$ and $l = \tan \beta = \dfrac{b}{c}$

$$\frac{x^2}{k^2} + \frac{y^2}{l^2} = z^2$$

See drawing of the general elliptic cone on Sheet 20.

All sections of this cone parallel to a tangent plane of the cone are parabolas; all sections which cut only one nappe or sheet (surface on one side of the vertex) are ellipses,

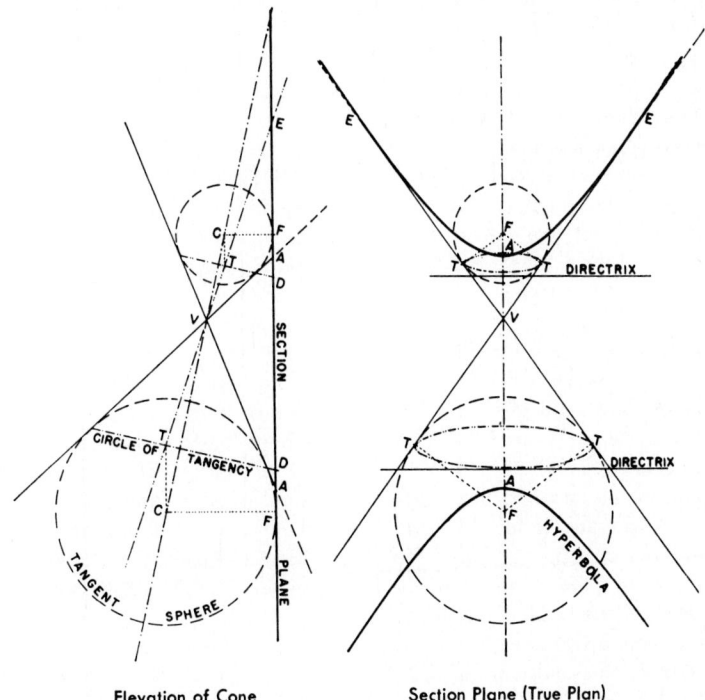

Elevation of Cone | Section Plane (True Plan)

Section of a Right Circular Cone By a Plane Which Cuts Both Nappes

(See also Sheet 20 for text)

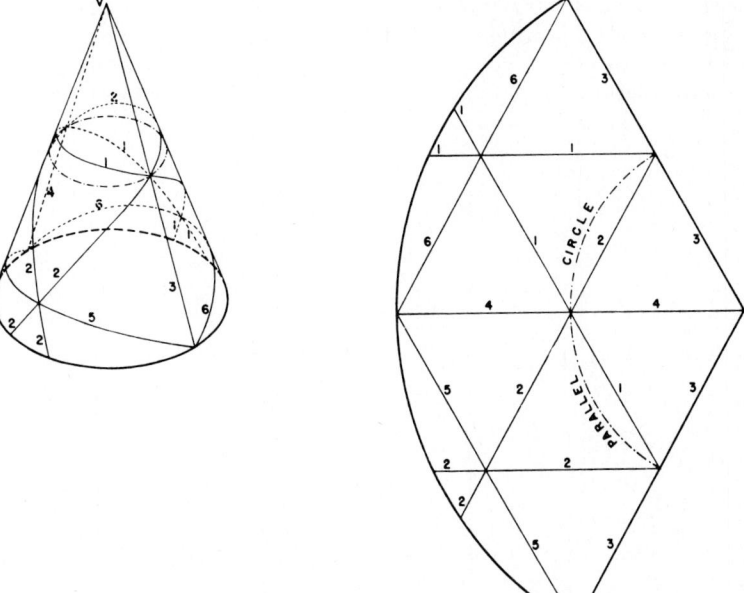

Isometric Projection of a Right Circular Cone and Its Development, Showing Geodesics

(See also Sheets 20, 21 for text)

the circle being a special case; and all sections which cut both nappes are hyperbolas.

It often happens that a pair of conjugate diameters of an ellipse are known, but not the major and minor axes. In the figure below (which shows the same ellipse as used for the generator of the general elliptic cone shown) the conjugate diameters Q_1CQ_2 and P_1CP_2 are known along the isometric axes. (Q_1CQ_2 and P_1CP_2 are defined as conjugate diameters if the tangents at Q_1 and Q_2 are parallel to P_1CP_2 and if the tangents at P_1 and P_2 are parallel to Q_1CQ_2.)

To find the major and minor axes, draw P_1A perpendicular to CQ_1. Make $P_1B_1 = P_1B_2 = CQ_1$ The line bisecting the angle B_1CB_2 is the major axis D_1CD_2. The minor axis is the line E_1CE_2 at right angles. Then find F, the midpoint of CB_2. Join P_1 to F, cutting CD at G and CE at H. The distance P_1G equals the semi-minor axis CE and P_1H equals the semi-major axis CD.

In the case of the isometric projection of a circle, the conjugate diameters are the 30 degree axes and the major and minor axes are along vertical and horizontal lines. Knowing P on the 30 degree axis, the line corresponding to PF can be drawn directly at 45 degrees.

The cone most often used, because it is the simplest, is the right circular cone, in which the directrix is a circle and the vertex is on the straight line which is perpendicular to the plane of the circle and which passes through the center of the circle. The equations of the right circular cone simplify from those of the elliptic cone to:

$$x^2 + y^2 = k^2z^2$$

and, in cylindrical coordinates:

$$r = kz$$

and in spherical coordinates, where ϕ is the co-latitude:

$$\phi = \text{constant} = \alpha.$$

The properties of the sections of the right circular cone are discussed on Sheet 2 of this series and also are the same as mentioned above under the general elliptic cone. In order to show clearly how the foci and directrices of the conic sections can be found geometrically, the diagram on Sheet 19 has been drawn showing a plane which cuts both nappes; the section is therefore an hyperbola. (The ellipses and parabolas are found in a similar fashion. See also the similar construction for the section of a cylinder, which gives an ellipse, on Sheet 17.)

Draw the two spheres which are tangent to the cone and to the section plane. Find the intersection of the plane of the circle of tangency with the section plane. This line is the directrix of the hyperbola. The point of tangency of the sphere with the section plane is the focus. It is also the projection of the center of the sphere. With the directrices and the foci established, follow one of the procedures of Sheet 6 for drawing the hyperbola.

Note that the traces of the sides of the cone as projected can be located by drawing on the elevation a line through the center of the sphere parallel to the section plane. The point T where this intersects the circle of tangency is a point on the trace. The line joining this point to the vertex is the edge desired. The point E is the intersection of this edge with the section plane.

The most useful way to draw a right circular cone so that it can be drawn in any projection, including perspective, is to utilize spheres which are tangent to the inside of the surface of the cone. The spheres are circles in any projection and the cone is always tangent.

To develop the surface of a right circular cone, draw an arc of a circle with the vertex as center and an element (straight line on the side) as radius. Measure off on this arc a length equal to circumference of the base circle. Join end points to vertex. (See drawing, Sheet 19.)

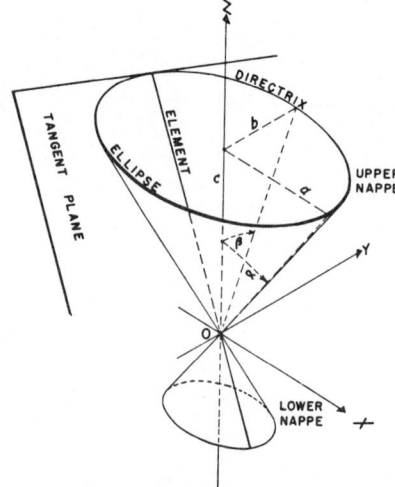

General Elliptic Cone (Isometric Projection)

(See also text on Sheet 19)

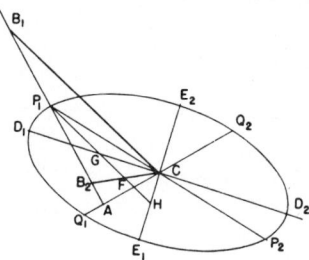

Conjugate Diameters of An Ellipse

General definition of Conjugate Diameters (true for all conic sections): A and B are conjugate diameters if both are lines through the center and if B bisects all the chords parallel to A, and if A bisects all the chords parallel to B.

Geodesics can always be found by drawing straight lines on this developed surface when flat. One triangular net of geodesics which might be used structurally is shown. The development, of course, gives the true area of any portion of the surface.

The lines of curvature on a right circular cone are the straight elements (or meridians), lines 3 and 4 on the drawing on Sheet 19, and the parallel (or latitude) circles, only one of which is shown here as a dot-dash line.

Note that the parallel circles are not geodesics, although the elements are. The parallel circles show as arcs on the development.

The conical helix (not shown) is the space curve which lies on the surface of the right circular cone and which makes a constant angle with each parallel or latitude circle. Its plan projection is a logarithmic spiral (see Sheet 13). It is not a geodesic line.

To develop any arbitrary conical surface (see drawing): Given the plan and elevaton, divide the length of the directrix curve into any convenient number of parts by a series of points, here 16. Draw the straight line elements joining each of these points to the vertex. Starting with number one, find the true length of each element, by setting V'V as the true height of the vertex and V'1 as the true plan projection. The hypotenuse V.1 is the true length. For the development, from the vertex draw a line V1; then swing an arc of length V2 from V, and from 1 swing an arc of the true arc length 1.2; where these intersect is the developed position of 2. Continue in this way until all the elements are drawn. Then draw a smooth curve through all the numbered points. It will be noted that the accuracy of this method depends on the number of elements used, since the chord lengths are used as arc lengths in the development.

The elements are also lines of curvature; the other lines of curvature are found by drawing arcs on the development with the vertex as center. One such line is shown here as a dotted line. These can then be transferred to the plan and elevations or other projections. These lines of curvature are helpful when using rolls to bend a flat plate into a cone; the axes of the rollers can be inclined, and the lines of curvature which are at right angles to the elements must form closed curves.

Pyramids are surfaces generated by joining every point on a polygon to a point not in the plane of the polygon. They may be used to approximate cones or for their own sake.

For areas and volumes of pyramids and cones see Mathematics—Areas and Solids.

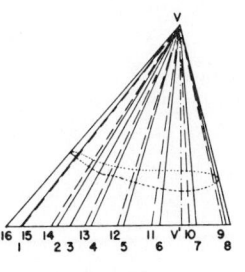

Elevation

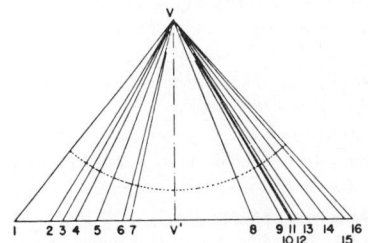

True Lengths of Elements

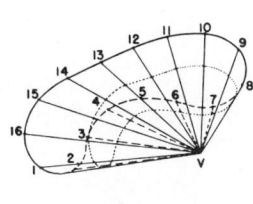

Plan

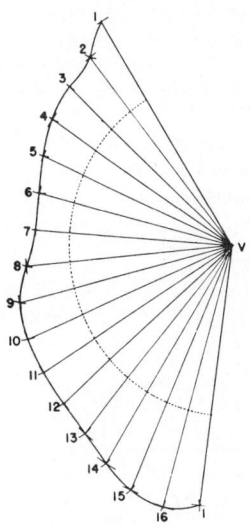

Development

Development of an Arbitrary Cone

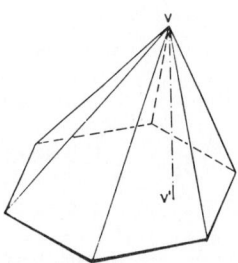

An Oblique Regular Hexagonal Pyramid

DEFINITION

Every point on the sphere is equidistant from a fixed point called the center. It is the only surface for which this is true. It is also the surface of revolution generated by the rotation of a circle about a diameter. Every section of a sphere is a circle. When the section plane contains the center, the circle is called a great circle or geodesic and has the same radius as the sphere; otherwise the section will be a "little circle" and may have any radius less than that of the sphere and more than zero. Longitude circles (or meridians) on the earth are all great circles; and latitude circles except the equator are little circles.

Every point on a sphere is an umbilical point; i.e. there is no principal direction and no line of curvature (see Sheets 14 and 15). Every geodesic line is a portion of a great circle. The mean curvature is everywhere constant and positive (equaling 1/R); the sphere is the only closed surface (without a boundary) for which this is true. The Gaussian curvature is also everywhere constant and positive (equaling $1/R^2$); and again it is the only closed surface for which this is true.

Of all closed surfaces the sphere contains the maximum possible volume for a given amount of surface.

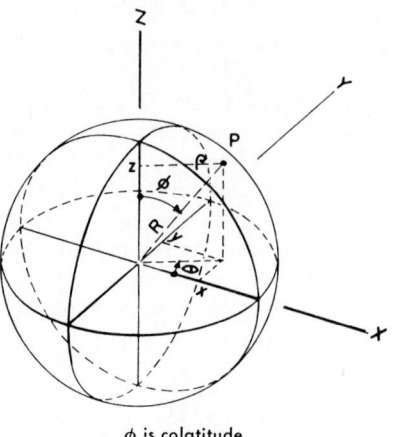

ϕ is colatitude

Equations:

In rectangular coordinates:

$$x^2 + y^2 + z^2 = R^2$$

In cylindrical coordinates:

$$z^2 = R^2 - \rho^2$$

$$[\text{where } x = \rho \cos \Theta$$
$$\text{and } y = \rho \sin \Theta]$$

In spherical coordinates:

$$r = R$$

$$[\text{where } x = R \sin \phi \cos \Theta$$
$$y = R \sin \phi \sin \Theta$$
$$z = R \cos \phi]$$

The area of the sphere $= 4\pi \ R^2 =$ lateral area of circumscribed cylinder.

The volume enclosed $= \frac{4}{3}\pi \ R^3 = \frac{2}{3}$ volume of circumscribed cylinder.

A lune (sometimes called a gore) is the surface between two great circles passing through the same pair of poles. A spherical wedge is the volume between the planes of these two great circles and the lune.

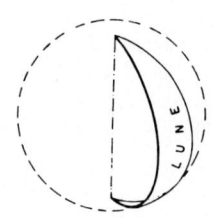

A zone is the surface between any two parallel section planes. The volume is called a segment and equals

$$\frac{1}{6}\pi h \ (3\rho_1{}^2 + 3\rho_2{}^2 + h^2)$$

where h = distance between two planes and ρ_1 and ρ_2 are radii of section circles. Area $= hR2\pi$

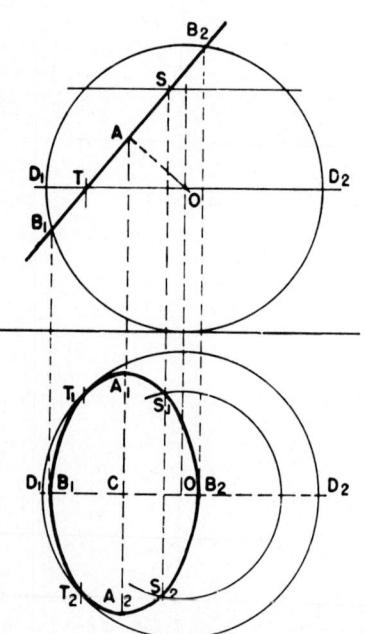

To draw the plan projection of the section of a sphere by any plane normal to the elevation, given the elevation: (Unless the section plane is parallel to that of the plane, the section will be projected as an ellipse.)

1. Draw AO normal to B_1B_2. Draw D_1OD_2 parallel to the plan.

2. Draw the plan below. Project B_1 and B_2 onto D_1OD_2 in the plan. The line joining B_1B_2 is the minor axis. Project A as a line normal to D_1OD_2 on the plan. This lies on the major axis and in plan $A_1C = CA_2 =$ true radius of the little circle, which can be measured as AB from the elevation.

3. With these two axes given, an ellipse can now be drawn by any of the methods shown on Sheet 4. T_1 and T_2 are the points of tangency of the ellipse with the plan. If desired, other points such as S_1 and S_2 can be found by drawing a line through S on the elevation parallel to the plan. The length of this line is the diameter of the little circle through S. Draw this circle on the plan and project S down to S_1 and S_2.

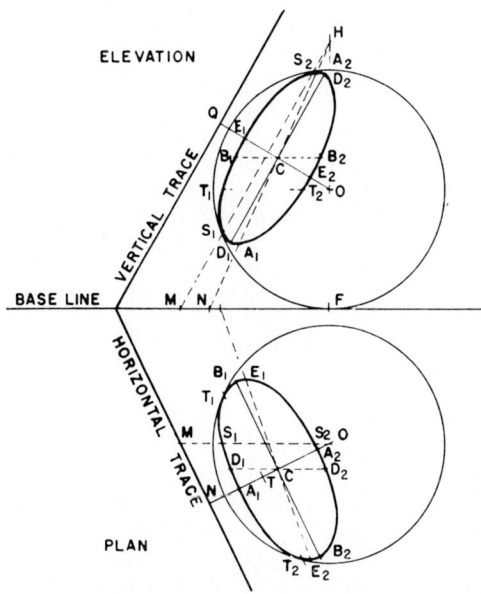

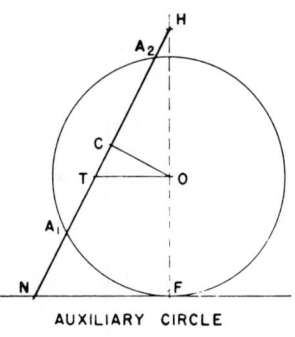

AUXILIARY CIRCLE

To draw the *plan and elevation projections of the section of a sphere cut by any plane, given the horizontal and vertical traces of the plane on the plan and elevation. (The Base Line is the plane of the plan as seen in elevation and the plane of the elevation as seen in plan.)*

1. On the plan, draw ON normal to the horizontal trace. This line represents a plane cutting the sphere in a great circle and cutting the section plane in a straight line. Draw OM parallel to the elevation plane. Project N and M up to the Base Line.

2. Draw MH parallel to the vertical trace, H being the point above O. H is the true height above O of the line NO in the plan. Connect NH; this is the vertical trace of the line NO.

3. Draw an auxiliary circle in line with the elevation. This is to be the true elevation of the plane through NO; the section plane appearing as the line NH. Set FH = FH and NF = true plan length = NO measured on the plan. Join NH: this cuts the circle at A_1 and A_2. Draw OC normal to A_1A_2. C is the center of the little circle which is the required section of the sphere, and is the center of the ellipses in plan and elevation which are the projections of this little circle.

4. Project C back onto NH on the elevation and the plan. The axes of the ellipse in plan lie along NO and a line through C parallel to the horizontal trace. The axes

of the ellipse in elevation lie along CQ, normal to the vertical trace and a line through C parallel to the vertical trace.

5. From the auxiliary circle, project A_1 and A_2 onto NH in elevation. These are points on the ellipse in elevation. Project them down to the plan; they are the ends of the minor axis of the ellipse in plan. Draw a line through C parallel to the horizontal trace and measure $CB_1 = CB_2$, equal to the diameter of the little circle, which can be measured from the auxiliary circle as A_1C. B_1 and B_2 are the ends of the major axis of the ellipse in plan. The ellipse can be completed by any convenient method (see Sheet 4). To verify the points of tangency T_1 and T_2, draw OT on the auxiliary circle. Transfer the distance OT onto the plan and draw T_1TT_2 parallel to the horizontal trace.

6. From the plan ellipse the elevation ellipse can be drawn. On the plan, draw a line through C parallel to the Base Line, cutting the plan ellipse at D_1 and D_2. This is the plan projection of the major axis of the ellipse in elevation. Draw a line through C in the elevation, parallel to the vertical trace and project D_1 and D_2 up onto it. These are the ends of the major axis. The length $CD_1 = CD_2$ (in elevation) = CB_1 = CB_2 (in plan) and is equal to the true diameter of the little circle. This is the plan projection of the minor axis of the ellipse in elevation. Project E_1 and E_2 up to the elevation; these are the ends of the minor axis. Draw the ellipse. The points of tangency S_1 and S_2 can be checked by projecting S_1 and S_2 on OM up from the plan to the elevation.

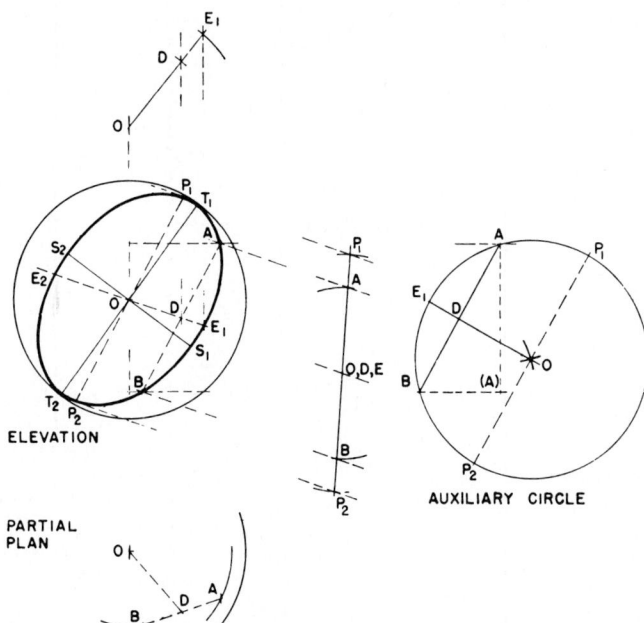

ELEVATION

PARTIAL PLAN

AUXILIARY CIRCLE

Given any two points, A and B, on the elevation of a sphere, to draw the projection of the geodesic (arc of great circle) through them. (This projection will be typically an ellipse.)

1. Draw the chord AB on the elevation. Join the center O to the midpoint D of the chord AB. Draw a line through O parallel to AB. These two lines through O lie on perpendicular diameters of the great circle and therefore lie on conjugate diameters of the ellipse.

2. Draw part of the plan below, showing the portions of the arcs of the little circles on which A and B lie. Project down A and B.

3. From the elevation project horizontal lines through A and B. On one of these lines measure B (A) equal to the true plan length AB. Erect a perpendicular on (A) to A. The hypotenuse of this right triangle is the true length of the chord AB. Draw the circle, of the same radius as the sphere, through A and B. Draw the diameter EDO normal to the chord AB and draw the diameter P_1OP_2 at right angles. (This auxiliary circle is the true plan or elevation of the great circle and gives the true angular length of the geodesic AEB.)

4. With proportional dividers or by measuring along oblique lines, as shown here, find the projected points P_1, P_2 and E on the elevation.

5. OP_1 and OE on the elevation are now conjugate semi-diameters of the ellipse. Use method of Sheet 20 to find the major axis T_1OT_2 and the minor axis S_1OS_2 and draw the ellipse. T_1 and T_2 are of course the points of tangency between the circle and the ellipse, the length of the major axis always being the diameter of the circle.

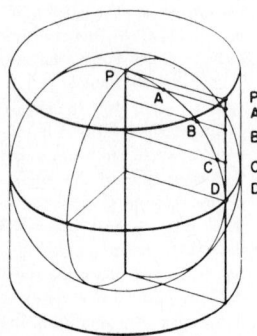

MAPPINGS OF THE SPHERE

Since the sphere cannot be developed onto a plane, many methods of studying it in various projections or mappings have been devised. The construction of spherical domes, particularly the newly developed "geodesic dome," is facilitated by understanding some of these.

A. Cylindrical projection

This is an "area-preserving" mapping of the sphere onto a cylinder. Each point on the sphere is projected onto the circumscribed cylinder along the normals to the cylinder. The area (zone) on the sphere cut off by any two parallel planes, normal to the axis of the cylinder, will be equal to the corresponding area cut off on the cylinder.

The great circles which have the axis of the cylinder as a diameter (i.e. longitude lines) become straight lines; the latitude circles are mapped as straight lines. All geodesics except the longitude lines and the equator are mapped as curves. The whole sphere is mapped onto a plane rectangular area, $2\pi R$ wide and $2R$ high.

B. Mercator's Projection

Like the cylindrical projection, this shows all meridian and latitude lines as straight lines, forming an orthogonal network. The longitude lines are equally spaced, proportionately to the degree of longitude; the latitude lines are spaced further and further apart as the latitude angle increases. On the map $x = R\Theta$; $y = R \log_e (\sec \psi + \tan \psi)$ where Θ is longitude and ψ latitude. This projection was developed for navigation: to map rhumb lines or loxodromes as straight lines. The rhumb line is a curve on the sphere which cuts all meridians at the same angle; it is the path taken by a ship whose course is fixed on a constant bearing with respect to true north. The whole sphere is mapped on a plane strip $2\pi R$ wide and of infinite height (although it is only the last fraction of a latitude degree which goes to infinity). Angles are preserved. The only geodesics which become straight lines are the longitude lines and the equator.

C. Stereographic projection

All points on the sphere are projected onto a plane which is tangent to the sphere, by rays from the pole which is diametrically opposite the point of tangency. All circles, geodesics and little circles, on the sphere are preserved as circles on the mapping. The arc of a geodesic is shown here as a dotted line. The radii of the projected circles are generally not the same as the circles on the sphere; the geodesics which pass through the pole are mapped as straight lines (which can be considered as circles whose radii are infinite). The angles between lines on the sphere are preserved on the mapping. Areas and distances are increasingly distorted as the mapping goes outward. However, the ratios of distances in any small area are approximately correct, and the stereographic projection can therefore be called a "conformal" mapping. The whole sphere is mapped onto the whole infinite plane once.

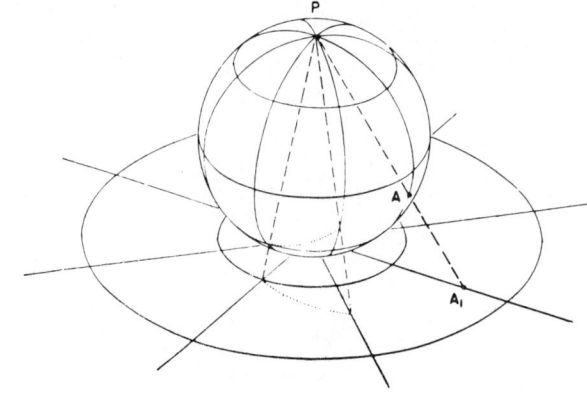

D. Central projection (sometimes called gnomonic projection)

If a sphere is projected from its center onto a tangent plane, all geodesics become straight lines. A geodesic is shown here as a dotted line. Such a projection is called a geodesic map, because all the geodesics on one surface, i.e. the sphere, are geodesics on the other, i.e. the plane. Angles are not preserved, nor are areas. The whole sphere is mapped twice onto the infinite plane; in other words each half of the sphere covers the plane once.

Both stereographic and central projections may be useful in studying geodesic domes. The plane of projection can be moved about at will to show different portions with a minimum of distortion.

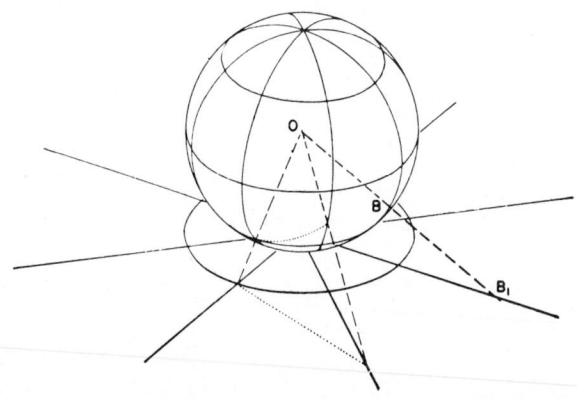

Since the sphere is curved in two directions and cannot be developed, many methods have been used to build domes of this shape. These may be grouped under the headings of radial domes and geodesic domes.

1. Radial Domes. This is the most commonly used method and is based on the image of latitude and longitude circles. Curved ribs are built along the longitude circles, radiating from the top, with or without transverse ribs on the latitude lines. The lune or gore spaces between the ribs are filled with thinner vaulting or paneling. If the lune (see Sheet 22) is thought of as the unit, this method is adaptable for prefabrication; domes have been built with a minimum of formwork by first erecting two diametrically opposite lunes, forming an arch against which the others can be constructed. The only difficulty is to join the many ribs which converge at the top; this is solved by introducing a compression ring. The ring may be closed or open.

If the radial dome is constructed as a triangulated network, with one side of each triangle lying on a latitude line, this system has the inconvenience of presenting ever diminishing triangles as the latitude circles become smaller toward the top. The lamella dome is built on this principle, with the latitude ribs replaced by a membrane or by simple struts.

Essentially similar is the method of building by zones (see Sheet 22), particularly adapted to small vaults. All the stones in one zone can be cut alike, but those in the next higher zone must be different. If the blocks follow along some kind of a helical line, as in an igloo, every block would have to be different to make an accurate sphere.

2. Geodesic Domes. The so-called spherical geodesic dome consists of a network of framing members which make a more or less uniform pattern over the whole surface, particularly the truncated icosahedron and the snub dodecahedron. (See drawings of polyhedra, Sheet 26.) It could be built with curved members which would lie along geodesic curves and thus be a portion of a true sphere, but is usually built as a polyhedron with straight members which form the chords of geodesic arcs. The perimeter of the dome at the bottom usually presents an irregular, ragged line.

If one attempts to cover a sphere with such a network, certain basic principles must be observed. Since the triangle is the simplest polygon and also the only one which is rigid in itself, the network will usually consist of triangles. These form larger configurations, depending on how many triangles meet at a point or vertex.

If six equilateral triangles meet on a plane surface, they form a regular hexagon. This is impossible on a sphere because the sum of the angles must be less than 360° around the vertex. On the sphere, therefore, all the members cannot be of the same length and the hexagons formed cannot be regular. Even if the pattern is made up of irregular hexagons, no matter how distorted, it is impossible to cover a complete sphere with them. A minimum of 12 pentagons must be introduced in order to satisfy Euler's formula.

Euler's formula states that, in any convex polyhedron, the number of faces (F), the number of vertices (V) and the number of edges (E) are related:

$$F + V - 2 = E$$

This formula can be used to check a dome which is not a complete sphere by considering the open bottom as a single face or non-plane polygon, the number of whose sides equals the number of members along the perimeter of the framework of the dome.

The basic possibilities and limitations of this type of framework are given by studying all the regular and semi-regular polyhedra and their duals, remembering that polygonal faces can be subdivided. Their number is quite limited.

There are only five regular polyhedra, all of whose edges are the same length and all of whose faces are regular, identical polygons. Called the Platonic polyhedra, they can have a sphere inscribed within them touching each face in its center, or have a sphere circumscribed about them, passing through each vertex. These points of tangency or vertices are the only regular systems of points which are equidistant from each other on the surface of a sphere.

There are the 13 semi-regular polyhedra, called Archimedean. All edges are the same length and every face is a regular polygon, but all the faces are not identical. The vertices are all congruent (identical) but not regular (the angles between pairs of edges are not all the same). These polyhedra can have a sphere circumscribed about them, passing through each vertex. Prisms and anti-prisms (see sheet 17 for drawings) also meet these conditions if the top and bottom polygons are regular and if the sides are squares in the case of the prisms and equilateral triangles in the case of the anti-prisms.

There are also the 13 duals of the Archimedean polyhedra. A polyhedron P_2 is the dual of polyhedron P_1 if the faces of P_2 correspond to the vertices of P_1. Thus, the octahedron is the dual of the cube, the icosahedron is the dual of the dodecahedron. The number of vertices and the number of faces are interchanged; the number of edges remains constant. The vertices of the Archimedean duals do not fall on a sphere, but a sphere tangent to every face at its center can be inscribed within each dual. Every face is identical but is not a regular polygon. Every vertex is regular but all vertices are not identical. (The duals of the prisms are called dipyramids, made of two pyramids placed base to base. The faces are all isosceles triangles. The duals of the antiprisms are called trapezohedra. The faces are kites, or quadrilaterals with adjacent pairs of sides of equal length.)

In order to keep strut lengths as short as possible and avoid buckling, and in order to provide complete triangulation for rigidity, the polygons forming the polyhedra can be subdivided into triangles, and all triangles can be further subdivided. If the members thus added are the same length as the others, the added vertex will not be on the sphere; if the added vertex is held on the sphere, the added members will have to be of a different length. Continuous membranes, plane or warped, may also be used to provide rigidity.

See Sheets 26 and 27 following for diagrams and schedules of the polyhedra. The index number lists the number of faces of the polygons meeting at a vertex (see sheet 18 for similar index numbering system). For the Archimedean duals the index number of the corresponding semi-regular polygon is used with the prefix V.

Drawings of the Polyhedra, shown in plan, with name of each and number of faces, vertices, and edges of each. (Cube not shown.)

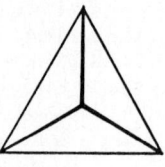

Tetrahedron
F	V	E
4	4	6

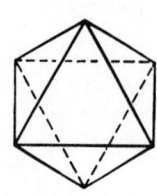

Octahedron
F	V	E
8	6	12

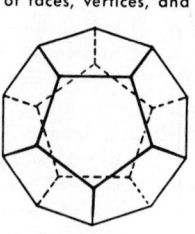

Dodecahedron
F	V	E
12	20	30

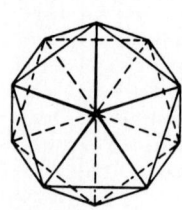

Icosahedron
F	V	E
20	12	30

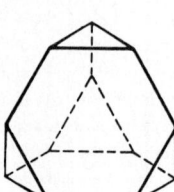

Truncated Tetrahedron
F_3	F_4	V	E
4	4	12	18

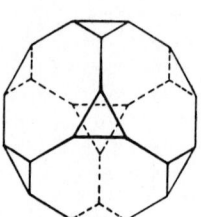

Truncated Cube
F_3	F_8	V	E
8	6	24	36

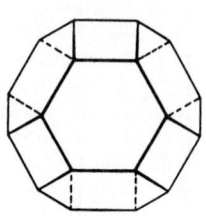

Truncated Octahedron
F_4	F_6	V	E
6	8	24	36

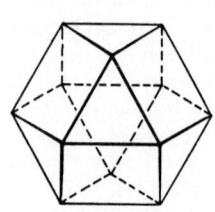

Cuboctahedron
F_3	F_4	V	E
8	6	12	24

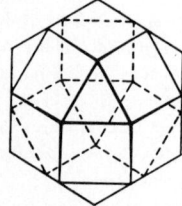

Rhombicuboctahedron
F_3	F_4	V	E
8	18	24	48

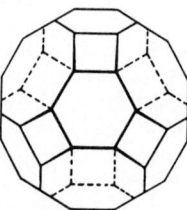

Truncated Cuboctahedron
F_4	F_6	F_8	V	E
12	8	6	48	72

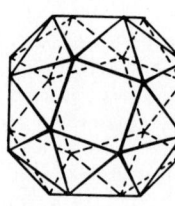

Snub Cube
F_3	F_4	V	E
32	6	24	60

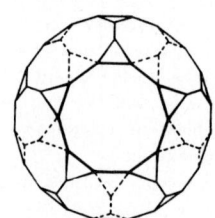

Truncated Dodecahedron
F_3	F_{10}	V	E
20	12	60	90

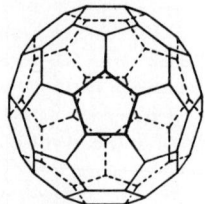

Truncated Icosahedron
F_5	F_6	V	E
12	20	60	90

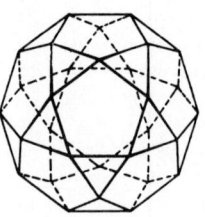

Icosidodecahedron
F_3	F_5	V	E
20	12	30	60

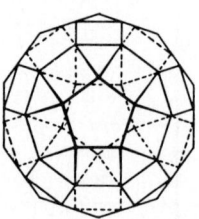

Rhombicosidodecahedron
F_3	F_4	F_5	V	E
20	30	12	60	120

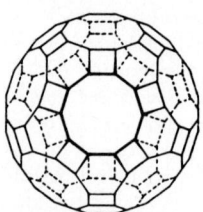

Truncated Icosidodecahedron
F_4	F_6	F_{10}	V	E
30	20	12	120	180

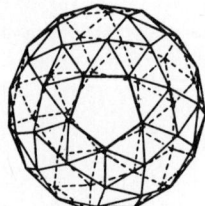

Snub Dodecahedron
F_3	F_5	V	E
80	12	60	150

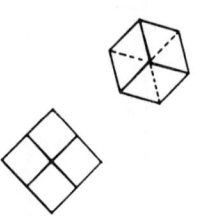

Plans

Rhombic Dodecahedron
F	V	E
12	14	24

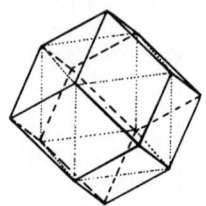

Projection

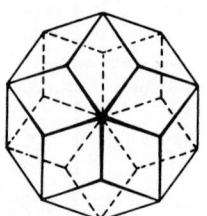

Rhombic Triacontahedron
F	V	E
30	32	60

Notes:
1. Only two of the Archimedean duals are shown. The rhombic dodecahedron is drawn in an oblique or axonometric projection, as well as in two plan views. Note it is a cube (shown in fine dotted line) with a square pyramid added to each face. The others can be drawn from the corresponding Archimedean polyhedron: (a) Draw plan with vertex in center; (b) Draw on plan the perpendicular bisector of each edge which meets at vertex; (c) Extend all bisectors until they intersect; they form irregular polygonal face of the dual.
2. For making models, polygons can be drawn on a flat sheet, with some edges of each polygon in common with adjacent polygons, making a continuous strip called a net.

INDEX NO.	DUALS OF SEMI-REGULAR POLYHEDRA	E/r	DIHEDRAL ANGLE	FACE ANGLES	R/r
V.3.6²	Triakis Tetrahedron	3.127 / 1.876	129° 32'	112° 53' / 33° 33½'	1.2222
V.3.8²	Triakis Octahedron	2.083 / 1.219	147° 21'	117° 14' / 31° 23'	1.0858
V.4.6²	Tetrakis Hexahedron	1.491	143° 8'	83° 37' / 48° 11½'	1.1111
V.(3.4)²	Rhombic Dodecahedron (Octahedral Granatohedron)	1.118 / 1.225	120°	109° 28' / 70° 32'	1.3333
V.3.4³	Trapezoidal Icositetrahedron	0.887 / 0.686	138° 7'	115° 16' / 81° 34½'	1.1464
V.4.6.8	Hexakis Octahedron	1.070 / 0.878 / 0.656	155° 5'	87° 12' / 55° 1½' / 37° 46½'	1.0488
V.3⁴.4	Pentagonal Icositetrahedron (Two Enantiomorphs)	0.727 / 0.513	136° 20'	114° 48½' / 80° 46'	1.1602
V.3.10²	Triakis Icosahedron	1.254 / 0.778	160° 36'	119° 3' / 30° 28½'	1.0302
V.5.6²	Pentakis Dodecahedron	0.780 / 0.692	156° 43'	68° 36' / 55° 42'	1.0425
V.(3.5)²	Rhombic Triacontahedron (Icosahedral Granatohedron)	0.727	144°	116° 34' / 63° 26'	1.1056
V.3.4.5.4	Trapezoidal Hexecontahedron	0.584 / 0.379	154° 8'	118° 16' / 86° 59' / 67° 46'	1.0530
V.4.6.10	Hexakis Icosahedron	0.689 / 0.586 / 0.373	164° 54'	89° 0' / 58° 14' / 32° 46'	1.0174
V.3⁴5	Pentagonal Hexecontahedron (Two Enantiomorphs)	0.500 / 0.286	153° 10'	118° 8' / 67° 28'	1.0574

NOTES:

e = length of edge of regular and semi-regular polyhedra. θ = angle subtended by edge at center (for regular and semi-regular polyhedra). R = Radius of circumscribed sphere (regular + semi-regular polyhedra). r = radius of inscribed sphere (regular polyhedra and duals of semi-regular polyhedra). E = length of edges of duals of semi-regular polyhedra. R/r: This ratio, when given for the Archimedean duals, is the ratio of the radius of the circumscribed sphere of the corresponding Archimedean polyhedron to the radius of the sphere inscribed within the dual. Enantiomorph means form of opposite hand (in drawing, change broken lines to solid and solid lines to broken). There are only five possible ways of filling up three dimensional spaces with only one type of regular or Archimedean polyhedra and their duals = cubes; triangular prisms; hexagonal prisms; truncated octahedra; rhombic dodecahedra. There are three additional ways, using more than one type = tetrahedra + octahedra; tetrahedra + truncated tetrahedra; octahedra = cuboctahedra.

INDEX NO.	REGULAR POLYHEDRA	e/R	DIHEDRAL ANGLE	θ	R/r
3³	Tetrahedron	1.633	70° 32'	109° 28'	3.00
4³	Cube	1.155	90°	70° 32'	1.732
3⁴	Octahedron	1.414	109° 28'	90°	1.732
5³	Dodecahedron	0.714	116° 34'	41° 49'	1.258
3⁵	Icosahedron	1.051	138° 11'	63° 26'	1.258

INDEX NO.	SEMI-REGULAR POLYHEDRA	e/R	DIHEDRAL ANGLES		θ
			Faces	Angles	
3.6²	Truncated Tetrahedron	0.853	6-6 / 6-3	70° 32' / 109° 28'	50° 28'
3.8²	Truncated Cube	0.562	8-8 / 8-3	90° / 125° 16'	32° 39'
4.6²	Truncated Octahedron (Tetrakaidecahedron)	0.6325	6-4 / 6-6	125° 16' / 109° 28'	36° 52'
(3.4)²	Cuboctahedron	1.00		125° 16'	60°
3.4³	Rhombicuboctahedron	0.715	4-4 / 3-4	135° / 144° 44'	41° 53'
4.6.8	Truncated Cuboctahedron	0.431	8-4 / 8-6 / 6-4	135° 16' / 125° 16' / 144° 44'	24° 55'
3⁴.4	Snub Cube (Two Enantiomorphs)	0.744	4-3 / 3-3	142° 59' / 153° 14'	43° 40'
3.10²	Truncated Dodecahedron	0.337	10-10 / 10-3	116° 34' / 142° 37'	19° 24'
5.6²	Truncated Icosahedron	0.4035	6-6 / 6-5	138° 11' / 142° 37'	23° 17'
(3.5)²	Icosidodecahedron (Triacontagon)	0.618		142° 37'	36°
3.4.5.4	Rhombicosidodecahedron	0.448	5-4 / 3-4	148° 17' / 159° 6'	25° 52'
4.6.10	Truncated Icosidodecahedron	0.263	10-4 / 10-6 / 6-4	148° 17' / 142° 37' / 159° 6'	15° 6'
3⁴.5	Snub Dodecahedron (Two Enantiomorphs)	0.464	5-3 / 3-3	152° 56' / 164° 10'	26° 50'

References: Cundy and Rollett, Mathematical Models (Oxford, 1951); Matila C. Ghyka, Esthetique des Proportions (Gallimard, 1927).

Geodesic domes

The most perfect development of the geodesic dome has been made by R. Buckminster Fuller. Combining the tetrahedron and the sphere, it is derived from his concept of "energetic geometry." Of all regular convex polyhedra the tetrahedron encloses the minimum of space with the maximum of surface, and is the stiffest form against external and tangential pressures. The sphere encloses the maximum of space with a minimum of surface and is the strongest form against internal or radial pressures.

In the Fuller dome a space-frame, built up of elongated tetrahedra, is given the overall shape of a sphere. The basic unit is rhombus or diamond shaped in plan, triangular in elevation.

The unit may be built of struts or, in the type being manufactured by the Kaiser Aluminum Co., of a bent sheet, stiffened by edge flanges and with one strut across the short axis.

The tetrahedral units are combined to form a complete framework by joining six units together. Assuming the diagonal members to be fastened already to the short axis and long axis members, a six-way fastener is required at the vertices of the short axes. As the units are combined to cover the whole sphere, there will be a minimum of 12 cases where five instead of six units come together. (See sheet 25 for explanation.)

The framework is dimensioned so that

TETRAHEDRON UNITS

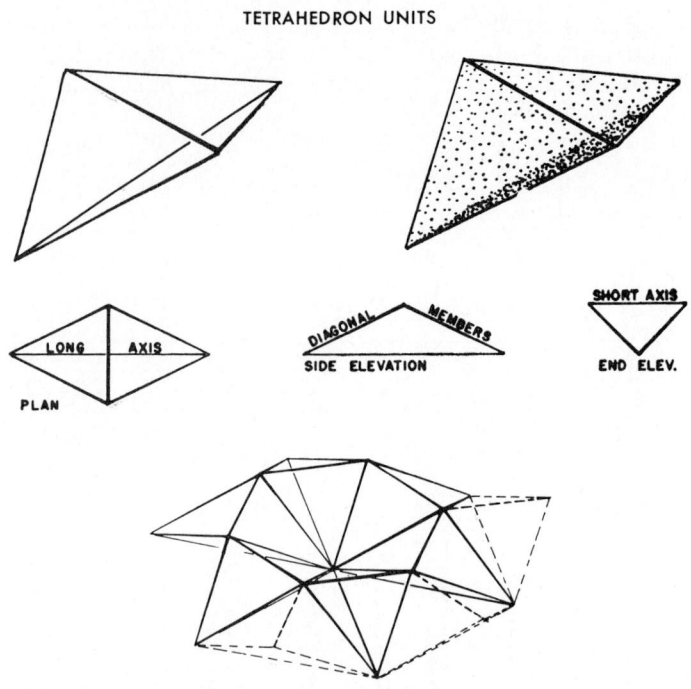

The structures designed according to the information in this article are covered by United States Patent No. 2,682,235 and Canadian Patent No. 512,422 granted to R. Buckminster Fuller. They include any building framework designed with an overall pattern of three-way great circle gridding.

all the long axis vertices of the tetrahedra lie on a sphere. The struts forming the long axes thus lie along chords of geodesic arcs. The other struts are placed to lie outside the surface of the sphere and are dimensioned to give the depth of

frame considered necessary for stiffness. (In the aluminum dome manufactured by Kaiser this depth is 12 in (305 mm) and is used for their standard dome with a sphere radius of 80 ft (24.4 m). See Sheet 35 of Structural Design—Steel.)

The method of subdividing the surface of the sphere to find the correct position of these long axis vertices is as follows:

1. Divide the surface of the sphere into 20 equilateral spherical triangles. Graphically this can most easily be done by starting with icosahedron (see Sheets 26 and 27) and joining the vertices by geodesic arcs instead of by straight lines. All the angles of the equilateral triangle are 72^0; the sides are 63^0 $26'$ $5.47''$ or 1.107147 radians. This is a spherical icosahedron and is the maximum number of equilateral triangles into which a sphere can be divided. Usually only five of these equilateral triangles would be used, making a dome that is one-quarter of a sphere, with a $\frac{rise}{span}$ ratio of about $\frac{1}{3}$. The method of division can be carried out

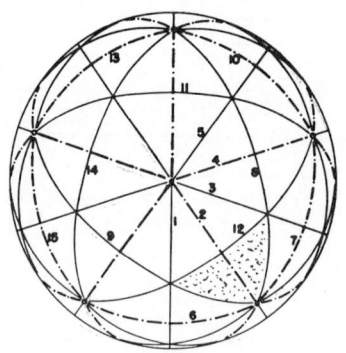

PLAN
Plan of opposite side is identical, but rotated through 36^0

ELEVATION
Elevation from other side is identical, but turned upside down

Shaded area is typical spherical isosceles triangle, as analyzed on the following page and as shown on Sheet 9 of Structural Forms—Steel.

over the whole surface of a sphere, however, and will be described in this way.

2. Draw the medians of each of these triangles, dividing each side in half. This is the same as extending the sides of all triangles to form 15 complete great cir-

cles. These lines will be the only complete symmetrically spaced, great circles on the sphere, no matter how much further it is subdivided. (In the diagrams the icosahedral division is shown with a dot-dash line, the medians and other subdivisions with a full line.)

3. The medians divide each equilateral triangle into six identical spherical right triangles, with the angles 90°, 60° and 36.° On the complete sphere there are 6 x 20 or 120 of these right triangles.

4. Pair off the 120 right triangles into 60 isosceles triangles. The apex angle is 72°, the two base angles are each 60°.

The lengths of the two equal sides are 37° 22' 38.5'' (0.652358 radians); the length of the base 41° 48' 37.1'' (0.729727658 radians). The altitude is 31° 43' 2.7'' (0.553574 radians) or half the side of the original equilateral triangle.

5. The 60 identical spherical isosceles triangles are further subdivided by using the

base as the measuring line. The base is divided into any even number of equal arcs, called the "frequency" and referred to by the Greek letter nu ν. From each point of division a great circle arc is projected out at 90° to the base across the triangle until it intersects the other side. The simplest cases in order are:

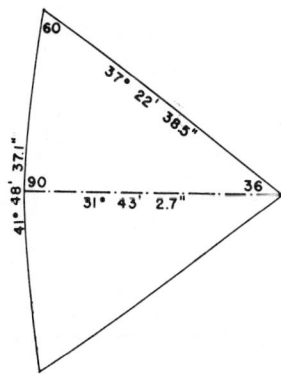

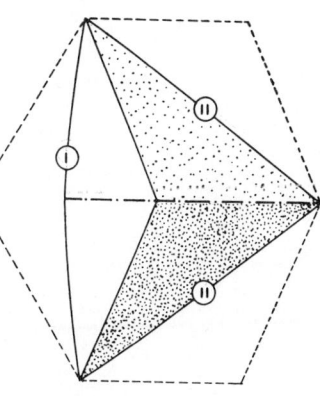

6. The minimum number of divisions or the smallest "frequency" is 2. For $\nu = 2$, the only arc projected is the altitude of the isosceles triangle itself. The lengths of the long axes of the tetrahedra or diamonds (marked as I and II) are the lengths of the sides of the triangle. The dimensions are given on sheet 30. In the plan of the basic isosceles triangle we now have three "half" diamonds, the other halves being provided by the neighboring triangles (shown here dashed). The diagonal struts

and the short axis struts are above or outside of the sphere. There are a total

of 3/2 x 60 = 90 diamonds for a complete sphere.

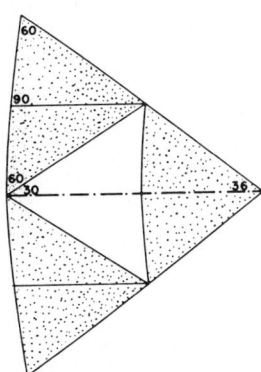

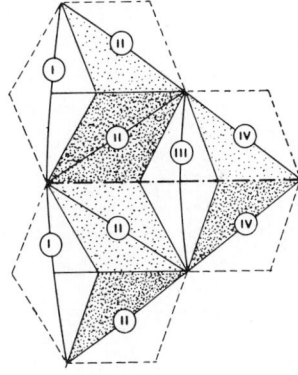

7. For a "frequency" of 4 ($\nu = 4$), the base is divided into four equal arcs. Three arcs at 90° to the base are projected into the triangle from the points of division; and two additional arcs are projected at 60° to the base from the second or center point of division. All calculations can be performed on the basis of the formulas for spherical right triangles (see Sheet 39 for the list of these formulas). These 60° lines divide the large isosceles triangle into four smaller, non-identical isosceles triangles of three sizes. The sides of

these triangles are the long axis diagonals of the tetrahedra or diamonds. They are marked I, II, III and IV and the lengths are tabulated on Sheet 30. We now have four types of diamond and a total of three

complete and six half diamonds within the plan of the basic isosceles triangle. Thus there are 6 x 60 = 360 diamonds in the complete sphere.

8. For a "frequency" of 6 ($\nu = 6$), the base is divided into six equal arcs. Five arcs at 90° to the base are projected into the triangle from the points of division; and two additional arcs are projected at 60° to the base from both the second and fourth points of division. These 60° lines divide the basic isosceles triangle into nine smaller isosceles triangles of five sizes. The sides of these triangles are the long axis diagonals of the tetrahedra or diamonds. They are marked I, II, III, IV, V and VI; the lengths are tabulated below.

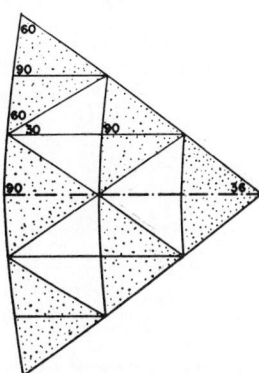

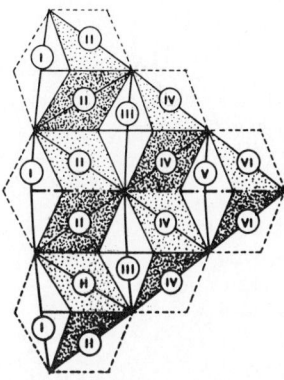

We now have six types of diamonds and a total of nine complete and nine half diamonds in the plan of the basis isosceles

triangle. Thus there are 13½ x 60 = 810 diamonds on the complete sphere.

Geodesic domes

9. This procedure can be continued without limit. In every case:

a) The number of smaller isosceles triangles into which the basic isosceles triangle is divided is $\left(\dfrac{v}{2}\right)^2$.

b) The number of types of tetrahedra or diamonds is equal to the frequency number v (number of divisions of the base).

c) The number of tetrahedra or diamonds in one of the basic isosceles triangles is $\dfrac{3}{2}\left(\dfrac{v}{2}\right)^2$. Since there are 60 basic isosceles triangles, the number of tetrahedra to a complete sphere is $90\left(\dfrac{v}{2}\right)^2$.

The following table gives the lengths of the long axes of the tetrahedra for different frequencies. The lengths are measured as geodesic arcs along the surface of the sphere.

	Frequency v or number of divisions of base	2	4	6	8	10	12
	Number of types of tetrahedra	2	4	6	8	10	12
	Number of tetrahedra to complete sphere $90\left(\dfrac{v}{2}\right)^2$	90	360	810	1440	2250	3240
LENGTHS OF LONG AXIS DIAGONALS IN DEGREES AND RADIANS — To convert to linear measure, multiply length in radians by radius of sphere	I	41° 48′ 37.12″ 0.729728	20° 54′ 18.56″ 0.364864	13° 56′ 12.4″ 0.243243	10° 27′ 9.3″ 0.182432	8° 21′ 43.4″ 0.145946	6° 58′ 6.2″ 0.121621
	II	37° 22′ 38.5″ 0.652358	20° 15′ 8.4″ 0.353470	13° 44′ 11.4″ 0.239747	10° 22′ 1.4″ 0.180939	8° 19′ 4.8″ 0.145176	6° 56′ 34.2″ 0.121175
	III		19° 56′ 1″ 0.347908	13° 37′ 59.2″ 0.237943	10° 19′ 17.8″ 0.180146	8° 17′ 39.4″ 0.144762	6° 55′ 43.9″ 0.120932
	IV		17° 7′ 30.1″ 0.298888	12° 39′ 33.5″ 0.220947	9° 53′ 7″ 0.172531	8° 3′ 51.7″ 0.140750	6° 47′ 37.2″ 0.118572
	V			12° 51′ 22.8″ 0.224385	9° 58′ 0.5″ 0.173954	8° 6′ 17.4″ 0.141456	6° 48′ 59.6″ 0.118971
	VI			10° 58′ 53.6″ 0.191664	9° 3′ 23.8″ 0.158068	7° 36′ 18.5″ 0.132735	6° 30′ 57″ 0.113723
	VII				9° 27′ 51.9″ 0.165185	7° 49′ 23.5″ 0.136540	6° 38′ 40.3″ 0.115969
	VIII				8° 4′ 6.3″ 0.140820	7° 0′ 58″ 0.122454	6° 8′ 36.5″ 0.107224
	IX					7° 28′ 57.6″ 0.130597	6° 25′ 41.4″ 0.112193
	X					6° 22′ 25.5″ 0.111243	5° 42′ 54.6″ 0.099748
	XI						6° 11′ 11″ 0.107973
	XII						5° 15′ 59″ 0.091916

The hyperbolic paraboloid, a quadric surface, is shown here in isometric and orthogonal projection. It is a doubly curved surface and therefore not developable. However, since it is ruled surface, it can easily be formed or molded in a framework of straight members.

It can be generated in two ways:

1. A generating parabola (AOA in diagrams) is moved along another directrix parabola (BOB) in such a way that the successive positions of the plane of AOA are always parallel and the successive positions of the line AA are always parallel.

2. As a ruled surface: Given two straight lines (here 5'5' and 5 5) lying in a horizontal plane, two vertical planes containing these straight lines. Move one of these lines, say 5'5', called the generator, along the other (5 5), called the directrix, in such a way that its successive positions are always skew but always parallel to its initial position. Thus no plane can contain any two positions of the line 5'5'. These successive positions are the straight lines of one family, sometimes called a regulus. The other family is found by sliding the other straight line 5 5 along the line 5'5'.

The equation, with axes as shown:

$$\frac{x^2}{a} - \frac{y^2}{b^2} = \frac{z}{c}$$

(See below for the equations referred to the asymptotes as axes.)

All sections containing the z axis are parabolas. As such a section is rotated about the z axis, from one principal plane (the xz) to the other (the yz), the parabolas become wider and wider, but all with their centers of curvature above the xy plane, until at the sections containing 5 5 or 5'5', the parabola becomes a straight line; as rotation continues, the parabolas have their centers of curvature below the xy plane, and become narrower until the section plane reaches the yz plane. All sections parallel to any given plane containing the z axis are identical parabolas (or a straight line).

Every section parallel to the xy plane is a hyperbola. The lines 5'5' and 5 5 are the asymptotes of all of these hyperbolas. Every section above the xy plane will be a hyperbola with its axis parallel to the x axis; every section below the xy plane has its axis parallel to the y axis. The hyperbolas at the same distance above and below the xy plane (i.e. when z = +d or −d) are conjugate. On the xy plane the hyperbola becomes the pair of straight lines 5'5' and 5 5.

Every section which is not parallel to a plane containing the z axis is also a hyperbola (or a straight line). There are no elliptical or circular sections.

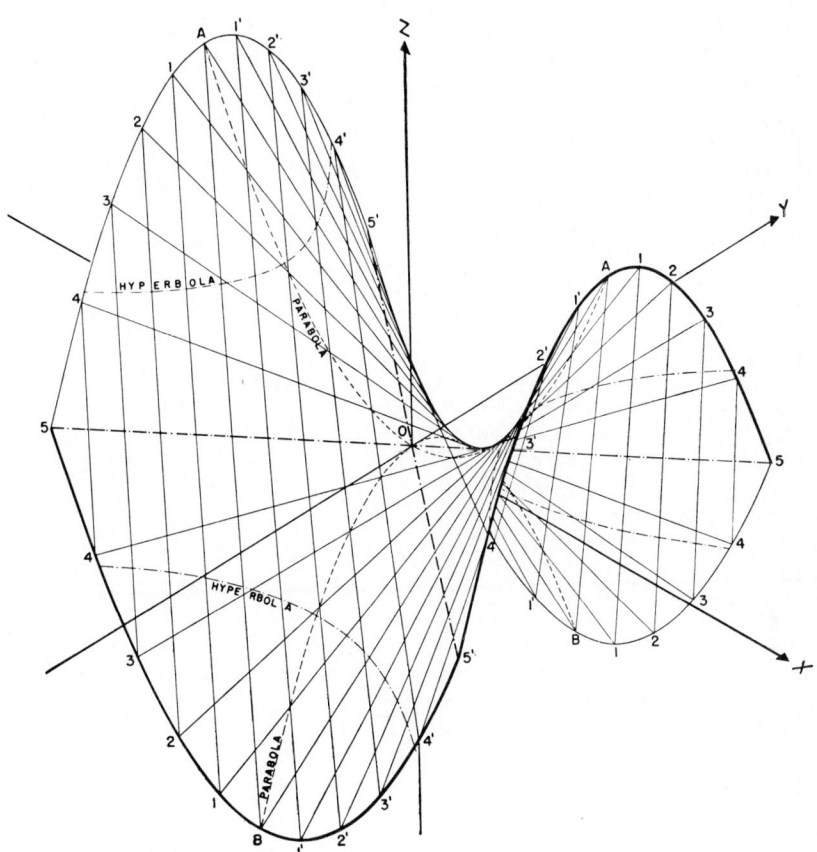

Isometric Projection

X Z-Plane

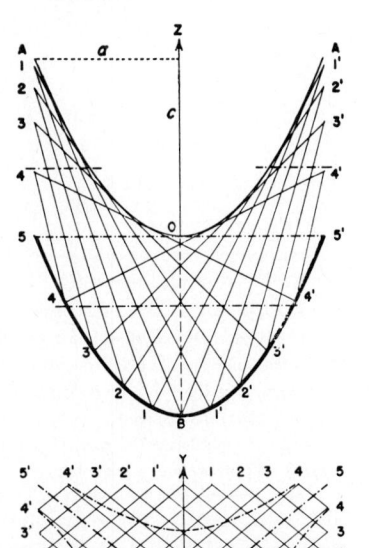

Plan

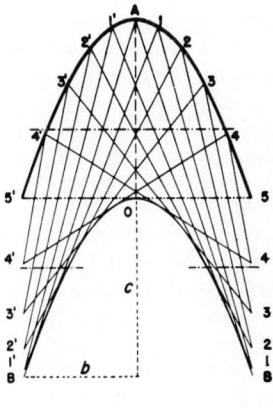

Y Z-Plane

Hyperbolic paraboloid

Every contour or visible edge in axonometric or orthogonal projection is a parabola.

A plane can be passed through any two straight lines of different families or reguli; no plane can be passed through two straight lines of the same family. Through any point on the surface pass only two straight lines, one from each family. The tangent plane at that point is defined by these two straight lines.

Note that the plan projection consists of two families of parallel lines, forming a network of identical rhombuses. When $a = b$, the rhombus becomes a square. Note also that, although the angle between two straight lines of different families is constant in plan, it varies on the surface. (Therefore the hyperbolic paraboloid cannot be a minimal surface, since two such straight lines are the asymptotic lines at the point. On a minimal surface asymptotic lines must meet everywhere at right angles.) The lines of curvature bisect the angles between the straight lines on the surface.

TO DRAW: Given the rectangular plan with the parabolas 5'A5, 5A5', 5'B5 and 5B5' as the sides, divide each side into the same number of spaces (here 10) and draw the diagonal straight lines connecting corresponding points. These are the plan projections of the straight line generators of the surface. See Sheet 31.

The numbered points can be used to construct the parabolas, in elevation, in isometric or other projection, following the method of Sheet 31. These points are equidistant from the xz or yz planes; they are not equidistant along the true length of the parabolas.

Draw the elevations (projections on the xz and yz planes) by establishing the height c of A above the xy plane and the equal height c of B below the xy plane. Join the corresponding points on the parabolas with straight lines. With the numbering system shown, for example, each point such as 2 is joined by two straight lines to the two nearest points also numbered 2, the point such as 2' is joined to the nearest points numbered 2'. These straight lines will generate the surface.

In elevation the straight lines are tangents to the contour parabola AOA; this parabola is identical to the parabola 5B5'. In axonometric projection (here an isometric) the contour is also always a parabola, which can be drawn from the straight line tangents.

Warped Parallelogram

Axonometric projection

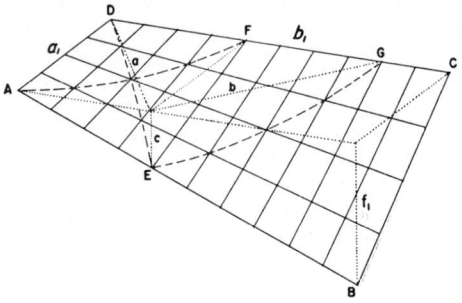

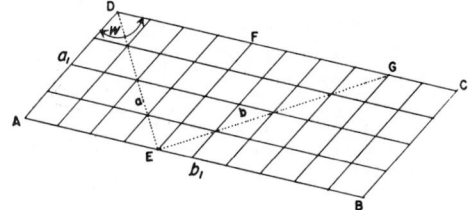

Plan

The hyperbolic paraboloid as a warped parallelogram. A surface which is a parallelogram in plan can be set so that three corners (here A, C and D) are all in one plane (here horizontal), and the fourth corner (B) is not in the plane (here lowered). Divide the sides into equal spaces and join the pairs of opposite sides by straight lines. The surface will be a portion of a hyperbolic paraboloid.

Comparing this with the diagrams on Sheet 31, the lines AD and DC correspond to the lines 05 and 05'. The parabola DE corresponds to the parabola OB. The parabolas AF and EG correspond to the parabola AOA as it slides down OB; and their tangents are horizontal at the intersections with DE.

In writing the equation, the edges AD (length a_1) and DC (length b_1) are usually taken as axes, with the angle w between them. The equation is

$$k \; x_1 \; y_1 \; \sin \; w = z \quad \text{Where}$$

$$k = \frac{f}{a_1 b_1 \sin w}$$

Note that, since $c = \frac{a_1}{b_1} f_1$,

$$k = \frac{c}{a_1^2 \sin w}$$

This therefore corresponds to the equation $x_1 y_1 = a_1^2 \frac{z}{c}$ (see below). The area of the plan projection of the parallelogram is $a_1 b_1 \sin w$.

When the edges of the parallelogram, corresponding to the principal asymptotes of the hyperbolic paraboloid, are taken as the axes, care must be used to compare the constants used in the two types of equation. The difference is basically the same as that between the equation of a hyperbola referred to its center line and that referred to its asymptotes. (When $z = c$, the section of the hyperbolic paraboloid is the hyperbola whose parameters are a and b.)

For the hyperbola, the two cases are:

1. The equilateral hyperbola (corresponding to rectangular hyperbolic paraboloid). In standard form, referred to x and y axes:

$$x^2 - y^2 = a^2 \text{ or } \frac{x^2}{a^2} - \frac{y^2}{a^2} = 1$$

Axes rotated through 45° to x_1 and y_1:

$$x_1 y_1 = a_1^2,$$

where

$$a_1 = \frac{a}{\sqrt{2}}$$

2. The general hyperbola. In standard form, referred to x and y axes:

$$\frac{x^2}{a^2} - \frac{y^2}{b^2} = 1$$

Axes changed from rectangular to oblique and rotated to x_1 and y_1

$$x_1 y_1 = a^2_1$$

where

$$a_1 = \sqrt{\frac{a^2 + b^2}{2}}$$

Or, if w = angle between x_1 and y_1,

$$x_1 y_1 \sin w = \frac{ab}{2}$$

All equations referred to the asymptotes as axes can be checked by the fact that the area of the parallelogram made by the x_1 and y_1, coordinates of any point on a hyperbola is constant. This is shown shaded on the diagrams.

The values of the functions of the angle w are:

$$\tan \frac{w}{2} = \frac{b}{a} \qquad\qquad \tan w = \frac{2ab}{a^2 - b^2}$$

$$\sin \frac{w}{2} = \frac{b}{\sqrt{a^2 + b^2}} \qquad \sin w = \frac{2ab}{a^2 + b^2}$$

$$\cos \frac{w}{2} = \frac{a}{\sqrt{a^2 + b^2}} \qquad \cos w = \frac{a^2 - b^2}{a^2 + b^2}$$

The drawing of hyperbolas may be simplified by using one of these two methods instead of those shown on Sheet 6.

1. Secant or chord method. Given the two asymptotes as shown and any point P_1 (which may be the apex). Draw any secant line through P_1, cutting the asymptotes at A and B. Measure BP_2 equal to AP_1. P_2 is a point on the hyperbola. This process can be continued, using more lines through P_1 or through P_2.

2. Parallelogram method. Given the apex A_1 and the apex A_2 and one point P. Draw the axis through A_1 A_2. Draw PN perpendicular to the axis. Draw PB parallel to the axes and of length A_2N. Divide PB into any number of equal spaces (here four); divide PN into the same number of equal spaces. From A_1, draw lines to the points on PN; from A_2, draw lines to the points on PB. The intersections of corresponding lines are points on the hyperbola. (This is basically the same method as that shown on Sheet 3 for drawing the parabola.)

Two Cases For Hyperbola

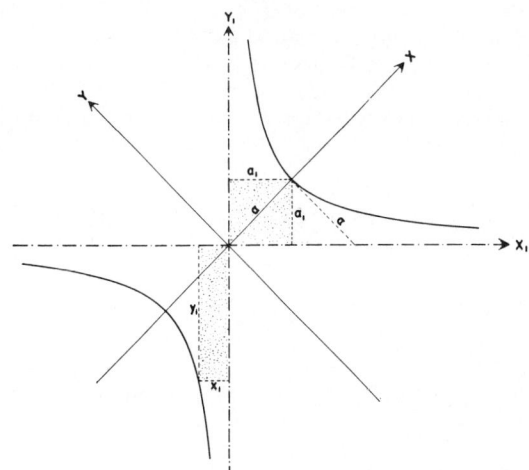

1

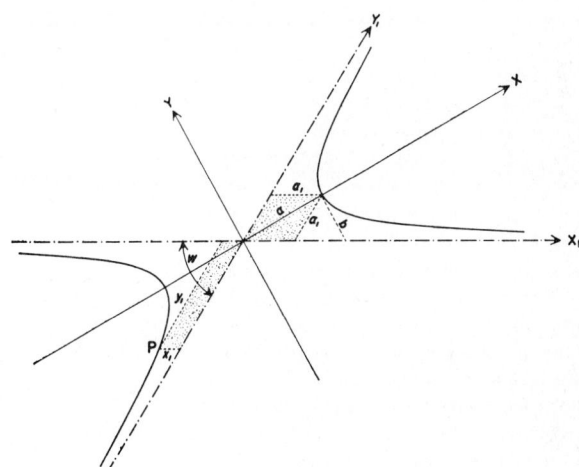

2

Drawing of Hyperbolas

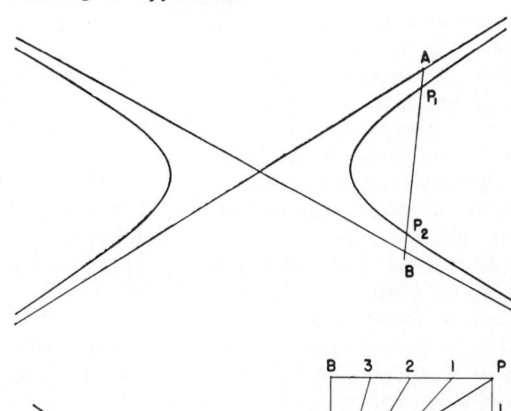

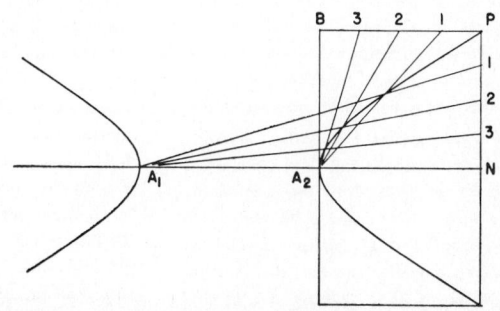

The ellipsoid, shown here in isometric projection, is one of the quadric surfaces and is generated by rotating a variable ellipse about an axis. It has three principal sections, shown here as the sections by the xy, xz and yz planes.

Its equation:

$$\frac{x^2}{a^2} + \frac{y^2}{b^2} + \frac{z^2}{c^2} = 1$$

where a = OA in the diagram,
b = OB
c = OC

Every section is an ellipse (or a circle; for the circular sections, see construction right). When b = a, the ellipsoid becomes the surface of revolution called an oblate spheroid (Dutch cheese shape); when b = c, it is a prolate spheroid (watermelon shape), also a surface of revolution. When a = b = c, it is, of course, a sphere. The volume is $\frac{4}{3}\pi\,a\,b\,c$. There is no simple formula for the area.

To draw in projection, first draw the projections of the ellipses on the three principal planes. The axes will be conjugate diameters (see Sheet 20) and the ellipses can be constructed from them. Then, second, draw the ellipse which is the projected or contour edge of the ellipsoid; (a) find its points of tangency T_1 and T_2 with the ellipse on the xy plane by simply drawing any two parallel chords (see separate diagram below giving general method of finding points of tangency); (b) construct the auxiliary ellipse (one quarter of which is shown) which is the section of the ellipsoid by the vertical plane through the z axis normal to the plane of projection; draw a chord DD normal to the plane of projection, find M the midpoint, draw OM extended to V_1; this is the point on the contour ellipse corresponding to the vertical plane through the z axis; (c) project V_1 back onto the isometric projection and mark V_2 at the same distance on the opposite side of O; (d) V_1V_2 and T_1T_2 are conjugate diameters of the contour ellipse; use method of Sheet 20 or parallelogram method to complete ellipse; (e) check points of tangency between contour ellipse and ellipse of xz plane by drawing a chord parallel to the y axis, finding its midpoint and extending to cut the ellipse at the point of tangency; repeat procedure for ellipse of yz plane, using a chord parallel to x axis.

Parallelogram method of drawing ellipse. This is often easier than other methods, particularly in projections. Given two diameters D_1D_2 and D_3D_4, draw the surrounding parallelogram. Divide one of the sides into any number of equal spaces; divide the intersecting diameter into the same number of equal spaces. From D_2 draw rays through

the points on the diameter; from D_1 draw rays through the points on the side. The points of intersection of the rays lie on the ellipse. The same construction can be used with any two conjugate diameters. (This is basically the same construction as shown on Sheet 3 for the parabola; in the case of the parabola, D_2 is at infinity and the rays from it through the points on the chord D_3D_4 are all parallel).

To find the points of tangency between an ellipse and the tangents to it drawn from any external point: From P draw any two lines cutting the ellipse at A B C D. Draw CB and DA extended to meet at Q. Draw the diagonals of the quadrilateral ABCD, intersecting at R. Draw QR, cutting the ellipse at T_1 and T_2, which are the required points of tangency. When P is at infinity, AB and CD become parallel chords and the line QR bisects both of them.

Construction of Ellipsoid: Lamellas. Ellipsoids have been built as domes on the

lamella principle, using a radial distribution of points of intersection of the lamellas along latitude lines, similar to the lamella construction of a spherical dome. This means that every lamella in a half ellipse is different; there is no repetition along a given latitude line such as there is on a sphere.

Circular Sections. Another method, which might simplify construction, is based on the fact that on every ellipsoid there are two families of parallel circles which are sections of the ellipsoid. Looking at the isometric drawing of the ellipsoid, imagine the plane yz rotated about the mean axis. The minor semi-axis of the ellipse which is OC in the vertical position will increase continuously until the plane is coincident with the xy plane, when this semi-axis will become equal to OA. Somewhere between these two values, this semi-axis will have the value equal to OB and the section would therefore be a circle.

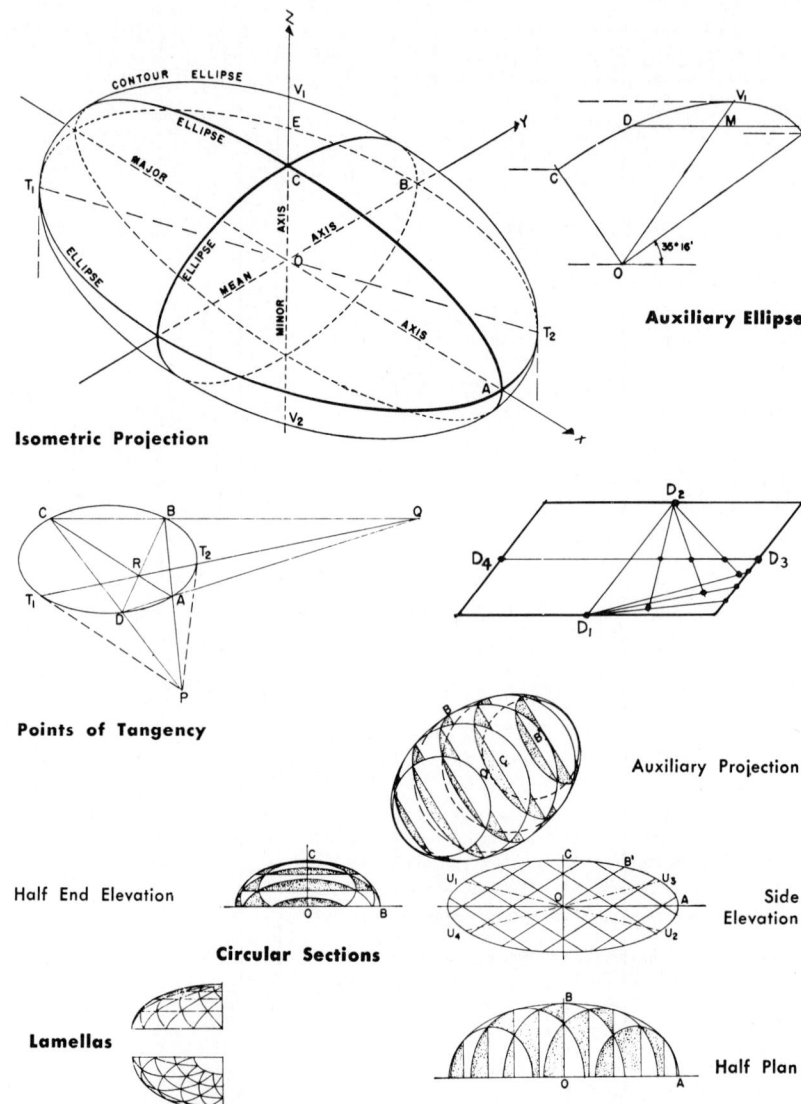

Isometric Projection

Auxiliary Ellipse

Points of Tangency

Half End Elevation

Circular Sections

Lamellas

Auxiliary Projection

Side Elevation

Half Plan

Given an ellipsoid, to find the two families of circles which are its sections.

Draw the side elevation of the ellipsoid, showing an ellipse with semi-axes OA and OC. Swing an arc OB of length equal to half the mean axis to intersect the ellipse at B'. All the circular sections of one family will be parallel to this radius vector; the other family will be symmetrical, making the same angle with the base on the opposite side of the minor axis.

On the side elevation the lines U_1OU_2 and U_3OU_4 are the conjugate diameters of the two principal circular sections (shown here as straight lines passing through O). Each bisects every chord of the family. The four points U are the umbilical points of the ellipsoid.

Lines of curvature on the ellipsoid are the traces of the intersection of the ellipsoid with the hyperboloids of one and two sheets which are confocal with the ellipsoid. At the umbilical points the curvature is the same for all normal sections. A drawing can be found in Hilbert "Geometry and The Imagination," p. 189.

The principal sections of the ellipsoid are lines of curvature and are also the only closed geodesic curves on the ellipsoid. All other geodesics are not closed curves and are very difficult to work out in detail. Every geodesic passing through one umbilical point passes through the umbilical point diametrically opposite, but not symmetrically. One set of geodesic curves is shown in Hilbert on p. 223.

Elliptic Paraboloid

The elliptic paraboloid, shown here in isometric projection, is one of the quadric surfaces and is generated by rotating a variable parabola about an axis.

Its equation (with the axis as shown)

$$\frac{x^2}{a^2} + \frac{y^2}{b^2} = \frac{c-z}{c}$$

The sections of the surface by any plane parallel to the z axis is a parabola. The two principal sections are the xz and yz planes. All other sections are ellipses. The section by the xy plane is an ellipse with semi-major axis equal to the constant a (OA in the diagram) and semi-minor axis equal to constant b (OB in the diagram). This ellipse is drawn here as the bottom of the paraboloid, although the surface actually continues to infinity. When a equals b, it is a paraboloid of revolution, and its equation may also be written in cylindrical coordinates as:

$$\frac{r^2}{a^2} = \frac{c-z}{c}$$

Volume = ½ (area of base) (altitude)

To draw in projection, first draw the projections of the paraboloids on the xz and yz planes. These will also be parabolas in projection. Second, draw the projection of the ellipse on the xy plane. Third, on z axis, measure CW equal to OC. W is the vertex of an elliptic cone which is tangent to the paraboloid at every point around the ellipse in the xy plane. Fourth, draw tangents WT_1 and WT_2 to the ellipse (see method of finding exact points of tangency above), and draw T_1T_2. Fifth, find M the midpoint of T_1T_2, which will be on the vertical line OW, and find V the midpoint of MW. Sixth, with MV as vertical axis and T_1MT_2 as base, draw a parabola. This is the parabola which is the contour or visible edge of the paraboloid in projection. To check the point of tangency between the contour parabola and the parabola in the xz plane, draw a chord of the xz parabola parallel to the y axis; find the midpoint of the chord and draw a line parallel to the z axis through it; the point where this line cuts the parabola is the required point of tangency. The point of tangency between the contour parabola and the parabola in the yz plane is found in the same way, using a chord parallel to the x axis.

All sections parallel to a plane containing the z axis are identical parabolas; i.e. they are all the same size. All sections normal to a plane containing the z axis are ellipses of the same proportions; i.e. the major axis is always equal to $\frac{a}{b}$ times the minor axis.

To find the circular sections: On every elliptic paraboloid there are two families of parallel circles which are sections of the surface (this is similar to the general ellipsoid, see sheet 34. Given the elliptic paraboloid $\frac{x^2}{a^2} + \frac{y^2}{b^2} = \frac{z}{c}$, draw the projections on the yz and xz planes as shown. Draw OB of length b along the y axis and draw BN at right angles at B. Swing an arc OA of length a to intersect BN at A. Draw AO extended to cut the parabola at P. OP is the trace of one of the circular sections. It is shown in projection, as an ellipse, on the xz plane.

The planes of all the other circular sections of this family will be parallel to OP. The other family is symmetrical on the opposite side of the z axis.

To find the umbilical point U, find M the midpoint of OP. Draw a line through M parallel to the z axis. This line is the conjugate diameter (i.e. passes through the mid-points) of all the chords parallel to OP. It cuts the parabola at U. Every elliptic paraboloid has only two umbilical points. In the case of the paraboloid of revolution, the two families of circular sections coincide (as parallels of "latitude") and the two umbilici coincide at the vertex O.

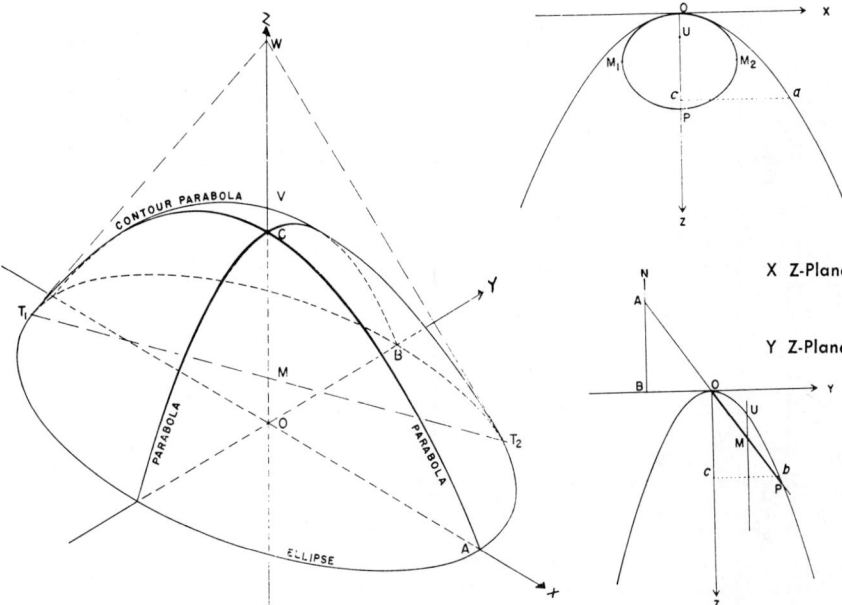

Isometric Projection

Circular Sections

Another quadric surface, the hyperboloid of one sheet (or of one nappe) is shown here in isometric and orthogonal projections. It is one of the only two possible doubly ruled curved surfaces; the other is the hyperbolic paraboloid. It is easily constructed from straight members. It can be generated in several ways:

1. As a ruled surface: A straight line (such as 3'12) is moved so that it touches at all times three given, non-intersecting straight lines (such as 3'18, 4'19 and 5'20), no two of which are in the same plane and which are not all parallel to any one plane. The three given straight lines are all members of one family or regulus; the successive position of the line 3' 12 generate the other family (such as 4' 13, 5' 14, 6' 15, etc.).

2. By the rotation of a variable hyperbola about its conjugate axis (here the z axis), with its apex always in contact with an ellipse (the throat ellipse) which is in a plane normal to this axis. When the throat ellipse is a circle, the hyperbola does not vary and the surface is a hyperboloid of revolution of one sheet.

3. By the translation of a variable (but always similar) ellipse with its plane always normal to a straight line through its center (here the z axis) and with the extremities of its axes on two fixed hyperbolas (here the sections of the xz and yz planes) whose planes are perpendicular and whose conjugate axis is this straight line.

The equation (axes as shown): $\dfrac{x^2}{a^2} + \dfrac{y^2}{b^2} - \dfrac{z^2}{c^2} = 1$

(The equation of the asymptotic cone, shown here in section as a dotted line, is $\dfrac{x^2}{a^2} + \dfrac{y^2}{b^2} - \dfrac{z^2}{c^2} = 0$)

All sections containing the z axis are hyperbolas. The xz and yz hyperbolas are principal sections. All sections parallel to any given plane containing the z axis are hyperbolas whose asymptotes are the projections on this section plane of the parallel section of the asymptotic cone containing the z axis. Such vertical sections which cut the throat ellipse will have the axes of the hyperbolas in the xy plane; sections which do not, will have their axes parallel to the z axis. The vertical section which is tangent to the throat ellipse will consist of the pair of straight lines passing through the point of tangency. (The dotted lines shown on the xz and yz planes are projections of these.) Portions of the hyperboloid as cut off by two parallel planes, both parallel to the z axis, have been used for shell roofs, such as the Hippodrome at Madrid by Torroja.

All sections parallel to the xy plane are similar ellipses.

All other sections are conics, including circles, ellipses, parabolas and hyperbolas. Circular sections are shown on Sheet 38. The contour edge of the "inside" will be an ellipse, of the "outside" a hyperbola.

The nature of such curves can be determined for each case by a simple test (see diagram). Given a curve such as ACB. Draw the chord AB and the tangents AO and BO. Find the midpoint M of AB. Draw OM, cutting the curve at C. If C lies at the midpoint of OM (such as C_2) the curve is a parabola; if C is closer to M (such as C_1) it is an ellipse; if closer to O (such as C_3) a hyperbola.

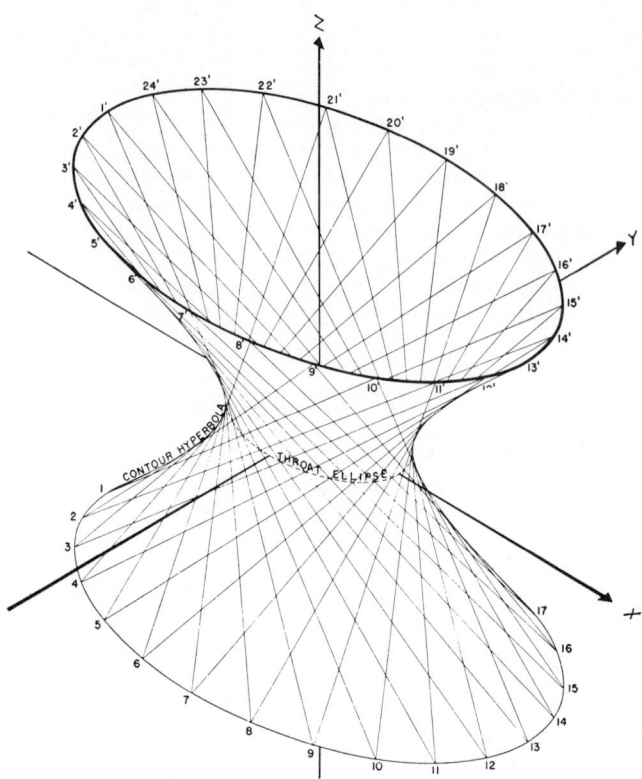

Isometric Projection

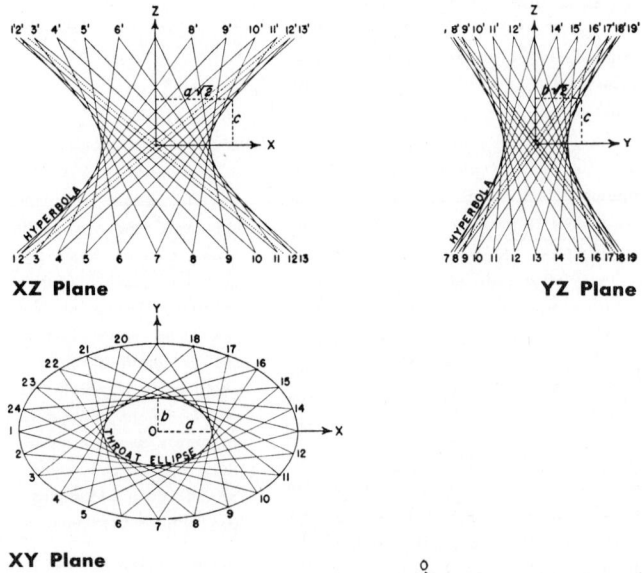

XZ Plane

YZ Plane

XY Plane

Test Diagram

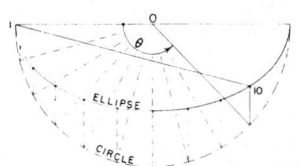

As in the case of the hyperbolic paraboloid, two straight lines, and only two, one from each family, pass through every point on the surface. These two define the tangent plane at that point.

The hyperboloid of one sheet is not a minimal surface. The minimal surface connecting two circular sections (corresponding to the top and bottom ellipses shown in drawing of the hyperboloid) is a catenoid; the edges which are hyperbolas for the hyperboloid are catenaries for the catenoid.

To Draw:

Given the two principal hyperbolas, draw them on the xz and yz planes. Draw the plan, showing the upper (and lower) and throat ellipses. In plan, from a point (such as 1') on the upper ellipse, draw the two tangents to the throat ellipse. These are the plan projections of the two straight lines, one from each family, passing through point 1'.

To find the angular distance (in plan) between this point 1' and the two points where the straight lines touch the lower

ellipse (here numbered 10 and 16) we use the eccentric angle of points on the ellipse. See diagram, where θ is the eccentric angle, in this case 135°. Dividing this into a convenient number of parts, here 9, we find the corresponding points on the ellipse whose eccentric angles all have a constant difference, (here 15°). It is then easy to draw the rulings on the surface, in elevation or projection.

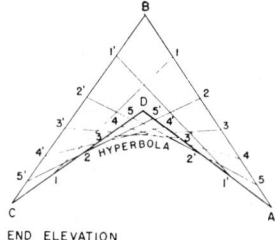

END ELEVATION

The hyperboloid of one sheet as a warped quadrilateral

Given the quadrilateral in space ABCD, shown in plan, side and end elevations, to draw a hyperboloid of one sheet passing through these four lines and one point P. P has been chosen here on the plane of symmetry passing through BD and the midpoint of AC and also on a line between this midpoint and the midpoint M of BD, closer to M.

Draw the auxiliary projection which makes DC appear as a point, locate P and draw DP extended to intersect AB at 2. Project this point 2 back onto side elevation and plan. Draw 2'P 2' symmetrically on the plan, project the points 2' back onto the side elevation and onto the auxiliary projection. (If this is done correctly, the line 2' P 2 on the side elevation will be found to be parallel to BD).

On the auxiliary projection we now have three skew lines (CD, 2'P 2' and AB) of one family (N') and line AD and CB of the other family (N). To find other lines of N family, draw rays through D on the auxiliary projection to intersect lines 2'2' and AB at various points. Project these points back onto the side elevation and plan. The rulings on the surface can now be drawn and the end elevation completed.

The contour edge DPB in elevation must here be an ellipse, while the contour in end elevation is a hyperbola. Note that if P were chosen as closer to the midpoint of AC than to M, the contour edge DPB of the

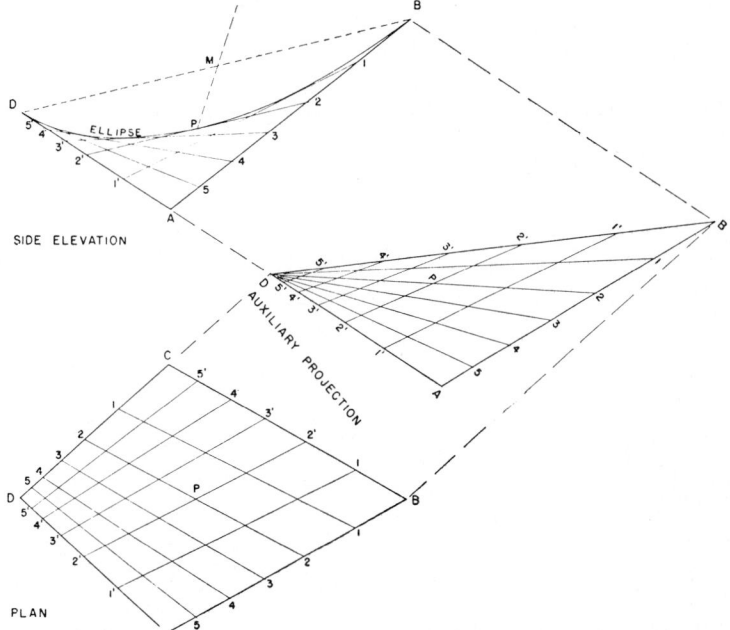

SIDE ELEVATION

AUXILIARY PROJECTION

PLAN

side elevation would become a hyperbola and the contour edge of the end variation would become an ellipse.

The warped quadrilateral as a hyperbolic paraboloid

If P is chosen at the midpoint between the midpoint of AC and M, the surface would be a hyperbolic paraboloid. This would be evident on the auxiliary projection, where all the lines of the N' family

(5'5, 4'4', etc.) would be found to be parallel (satisfying one condition for the hyperbolic paraboloid). Also the points in plan would be found to be evenly spaced along each side. In this case the Z axis of the hyperbolic paraboloid would be parallel to the line PM; the xy plane can be found from the rulings which would appear normal to the line PM in side elevation.

SUMMARY OF SYSTEMS OF DOUBLE RULINGS

Given, in Space;	Two Families of Rulings Will Generate;
Two Parabolas or three Straight lines, non-intersecting but parallel to one plane	a Hyperbolic Paraboloid
Two Circles or two Ellipses or one Hyperbola and one Ellipse or three general Straight Lines	a Hyperboloid of One Sheet
Two Hyperbolas or one Hyperbola and one Parabola or two Straight Lines, non-intersecting or a general Quadrilateral	a Hyperbolic Paraboloid or a Hyperboloid of One Sheet

Hyperboloids

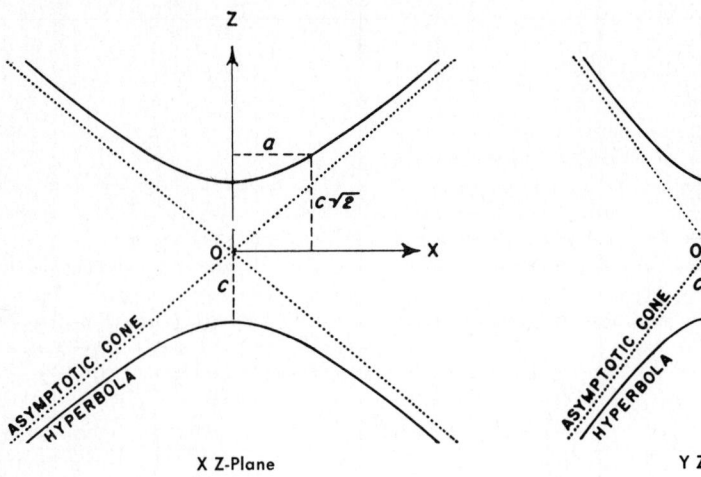

X Z-Plane

Y Z-Plane

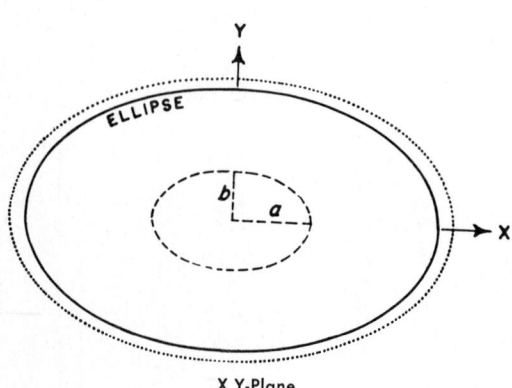

X Y-Plane

Hyperboloid of Two Sheets

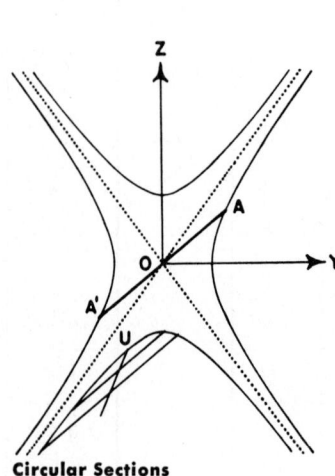

Circular Sections

One of the nine quadric surfaces, the hyperboloid of two sheets (or two nappes) is shown here in orthogonal projections. It consists of two cup-shaped surfaces facing each other across the xy plane, each extending into infinity on its own side. The curvature is always positive and there are no straight lines on the surface.

The equation: $\dfrac{z^2}{c^2} - \dfrac{x^2}{a^2} - \dfrac{y^2}{b^2} = 1$

All sections parallel to the xy plane are similar ellipses (except for the region between $z = c$ and $z = -c$). All sections parallel to any given plane containing the z axis are hyperbolas whose asymptotes are the projection on this section plane of the parallel section of the asymptotic cone containing the z axis. All other sections are also conics, in general of the

same type as corresponding sections of the asymptotic cone.

Circular Sections of the Elliptic Cone and of the Hyperboloids of One and Two Sheets

As for the ellipsoid and the elliptic paraboloid, there exist circular sections of these three surfaces. (See sheet 34 on the ellipsoid for more discussion.)

To find the circular sections, we make use of the hyperboloid of one sheet. The equations of the three surfaces are as given above in describing each type.

Draw the section by the yz plane, showing all three surfaces. The section of the asymptotic cone is drawn as a dotted line, the other two by solid lines. Note that the z axis is the axis of the cone and of the hyperboloid of two sheets, but is the con-

jugate axis of the hyperbola which is the section of the hyperboloid of one sheet.

From O swing an arc of length equal to a, intersecting the hyperboloid of one sheet at A and A'. This line is in the plane of a circular section of the hyperboloid of one sheet. All planes parallel to this will cut all three surfaces in circles. There is also a symmetrical system of planes making the same angle with the xy plane, but tilted from upper left to lower right.

There are no umbilics on the cone or the hyperboloid of one sheet.

To find the umbilics on the hyperboloid of two sheets, draw on the yz section any two chords parallel to the plane of circular sections (as shown), to find their midpoints, join them by a line which cuts the hyperbola at U. The other three umbilics are symmetrically arranged about O.

In order to calculate in detail any spherical dome or any astronomical information, such as sun angles and insolation, we must use the formulas of spherical trigonometry.

SPHERICAL TRIANGLE

In the diagram, ABC is a spherical triangle. The letters A, B, and C refer to the *angles* at the vertices (measured in degrees or radians). Angle A, for example, is the angle between the tangents to the sides b and c at the vertex. Angle A is also the dihedral angle between the plane containing the side b and the center O and the plane containing the side c and the center O. The letters a, b, and c refer to the three *sides* and are measured in degrees or radians. Each side is a portion or arc of a great circle, and its length is sometimes referred to as the central angle. The side b, for example, is the angle AOC. Both OA and OC are radii of the sphere.

Unlike plane triangles, the *sum of the angles* is not the same for all spherical triangles. It is always greater than 180° and less than 540°:

$$180° \text{ (or } \pi) < \Sigma (A + B + C) < 540° (3\pi)$$

The amount by which the sum of the angles exceeds 180° (or π) is called the *spherical excess*:

$$E = \Sigma (A + B + C) - 180° \text{ (or } \pi)$$

E can be used to find the area of a spherical triangle:

$$\frac{\text{Area of spherical triangle}}{\text{Area of sphere } [4\pi P^2]} = \frac{E°}{720°}$$
$$= \frac{E \text{ (in radians)}}{4\pi}$$

Thus,

Area of spherical triangle $= E_{(\text{radians})} R^2$

A *steradian* is the solid angle subtended by the portion of a sphere whose area $= R^2$. (The area of a spherical polygon can be found in the same manner. If N is the number of sides of the polygon, the spherical excess

$$E° = \Sigma (A + B + C + D \ldots + X_N)$$
$$- (N-2) \, 180°$$

E° can be substituted in the formula given above for the spherical triangle.) The sum of the sides is always less than 360°:

$$\Sigma (a + b + c) < 360° \text{ (or } 2\pi)$$

The sides and the angles are related by the following formulas:

Law of cosines:

$\cos a = \cos b \cos c + \sin b \sin c \cos A$
$\cos b = \cos a \cos c + \sin a \sin c \cos B$
$\cos c = \cos a \cos b + \sin a \sin b \cos C$
$\cos A = -\cos B \cos C + \sin B \sin C \cos a$
$\cos B = -\cos A \cos C + \sin A \sin C \cos b$
$\cos C = -\cos A \cos B + \sin A \sin B \cos c$

Law of sines:

$$\frac{\sin A}{\sin a} = \frac{\sin B}{\sin b} = \frac{\sin C}{\sin c}$$

Haversine formula:

$\text{hav } a = \text{hav } (b - c) + \sin b \sin c \text{ hav } A$
$\text{hav } b = \text{hav } (a - c) + \sin a \sin c \text{ hav } B$
$\text{hav } c = \text{hav } (a - b) + \sin a \sin b \text{ hav } C$

The haversine of any angle θ is defined as

$$\text{hav } \theta = \frac{1 - \cos \theta}{2}$$

Haversine is an abbreviation for half versed sine.

Half-angle formula:

$$\tan \frac{A}{2} = \frac{f}{\sin (s - a)}$$

$$\tan \frac{B}{2} = \frac{f}{\sin (s - b)}$$

$$\tan \frac{C}{2} = \frac{f}{\sin (s - c)}$$

in which

$$s = \frac{a + b + c}{2}$$

and

$$f = \sqrt{\frac{\sin (s - a) \sin (s - b) \sin (s - c)}{\sin s}}$$

Half-side formula:

$$\tan \frac{a}{2} = F \cos (S - A)$$

$$\tan \frac{b}{2} = F \cos (S - B)$$

$$\tan \frac{c}{2} = F \cos (S - C)$$

in which

$$S = \frac{A + B + C}{2}$$

and

$$F = \sqrt{\frac{- \cos S}{\cos (S - A) \cos (S - B) \cos (S - C)}}$$

The significance of f and F in the half-angle and half-side formulas is found in the inscribed and circumscribed circles of the spherical triangle: the tangent of the radius of the inscribed circle $= f$; the tangent of the radius of the circumscribed circle $= F$. These radii are arcs of great circles and are measured from their respective centers, which are the poles of the corresponding circles. The inscribed and circumscribed circles are always little circles.

SPHERICAL RIGHT TRIANGLE

If one (or more) of the angles of a spherical triangle is a right angle, the triangle is a spherical right triangle. The diagram shows two spherical right triangles: ABC and $a_2 b_2 c_2$, with C equal to a right angle.

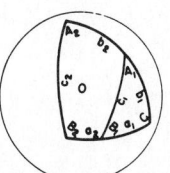

Spherical triangle

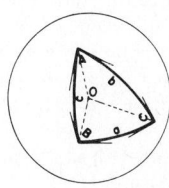

Spherical right triangle

The formulas can be simplified as follows:

$\sin a = \sin A \sin c$
$\sin b = \sin B \sin c$
$\sin a = \cot B \tan b$
$\sin b = \cot A \tan a$
$\cos c = \cos a \cos b$
$\cos c = \cot A \cot B$
$\cos A = \sin B \cos a$
$\cos B = \sin A \cos b$
$\cos A = \tan b \cot c$
$\cos B = \tan a \cot c$

If B is also a right angle, then b and c are both right angles and A = a. Conversely, if b = c = 90°, then B = C = 90° and A = a; if A = B = C = 90°, then a = b = c = 90°, and conversely.

REFERENCES FOR COMPLETE SERIES

1. *Practical Geometry* by David Allen Low, Longmans Green, 1912.
2. *Mechanical Engineers' Handbook* by Lionel S. Marks — section "Mathematics" by E. V. Huntington (McGraw Hill, 1941).
3. *The Mathematics of Engineering* by Ralph E. Root (Bailliere, Tindall and Cox, 1927).
4. *Elements of the Differential and Integral Calculus* by Granville, Smith and Longley (Ginn 1941).
5. *Geometry and the Imagination* by D. Hilbert and S. Cohn-Vossen (Chelsea, 1952).
6. *Mathematical Models* by H. Martyn Cundy and A. R. Rollett (Oxford 1951).
7. *The Geometry of Repeating Design* by A. Day Bradley (Columbia, 1933).
8. *Elementary Crystallography* by M. J. Buerger (Wiley, 1956).
9. *Engineering Graphics* by John T. Rule and Earle F. Watts (McGraw-Hill, 1951).
10. *Technical Descriptive Geometry* by B. Leighton Williams (McGraw-Hill, 1957).
11. *What is Mathematics?* by Richard Courant and Herbert Robbins (Oxford, 1941).
12. *Solid Analytical Geometry and Determinants* by Arnold Dresden (Wiley, 1930).

By STERLING M. PALM, *Architect*

THE handling of curved and double curved surfaces has long been commonplace in the shipbuilding, automotive and airplane industries. Although such surfaces have not appeared so frequently in architectural design, they are becoming more and more apparent in contemporary design. It is not the intent of the present discussion to go into the method of such surface delineation, but a brief statement of the basic principle provides a good starting point.

A curved surface, to be a smooth surface, without humps or depressions, must be so formed that a section through the surface will be projected as a "smooth" regular curve in that plane. A curve to be "smooth" must be such that the rate of curvature, or radius, at any point does not change too rapidly with respect to the rate of curvature at any adjacent point. All conics meet this requirement and, in general, any curve that is pleasing to the eye will usually be found to be a "conic" of some type, or a combination of conics. Thus a review of the characteristics of the conics is essential to the study of surfaces.

The study of these curves also provides a valuable tool for the delineation of curves of any type and has a number of practical applications in architectural or engineering work.

A "conic" may be defined as any curve formed by the intersection of a plane with a right circular cone. Referring to Fig. 1, it is evident that an infinite variety of curves is possible, dependent on the slope of the sides of the cone, the slope of the cutting

plane, and the relation between the cutting plane and the axis of the cone.

All of the conics described by planes *A* to *D* in Fig. 1 are familiar curves, susceptible of simple mathematical description and analysis.

Although the mathematics of the conics forms an interesting study, no space will be devoted to it here. We are primarily interested in an understanding of the conditions differentiating one curve from another, and in a practical application of the principles involved. Fortunately these principles are extremely simple and entirely general in nature. To anyone familiar with the procedure it should no longer be necessary to refer to a handbook to refresh one's memory as to the method of constructing a parabola or hyperbola; for these, together with an ellipse or even a circle, can all be constructed by the same simple process.

In the latter part of this discussion I will, for the benefit of those interested, develop a proof of the method about to be described. However, for those who just wish something for ready reference, it will only be necessary to follow the procedure outlined in Figs. 3 to 7 inclusive. Fig. 2 is introductory, but shows clearly the entire procedure necessary for the determination of any one point on the curve, developed to greater length in Fig. 3.

It can be shown that every conic or second-degree curve can be determined, given any one of the following five sets of conditions:

Case I. One point and two point-slopes (direction of tangent).

Case II. Three points and one point-slope.

Case III. Five points.

Case IV. Two points and a point-slope-curvature.

Case V. A point-slope and a point-slope-curvature.

Cases IV and V will not be discussed as their treatment would require more space than warranted. Fig. 5 illustrates the method of determining a sixth point on a conic given five points (Case III). In practice it generally will be found that one or two tangents are known, together with one or two points of tangency and with an additional point or points on the curve available, so that Cases I and II above will

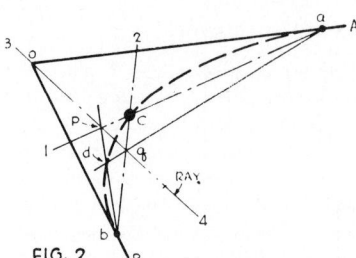

FIG. 2

be found to be those most generally useful. These cases are illustrated in Figs. 3 and 4.

Referring to Fig. 2, we have two tangents, *OA* and *OB*, with two points of tangency, *a* and *b*. Point *a* on the tangent *OA* and point *b* on the tangent *OB* constitute two point-slopes. These are, in themselves, insufficient to determine a curve. If, however, we are given an additional point, such as point *c*, it will be seen that we have the previously listed first set of conditions, namely, "one point and two point-slopes."

In order to find any other point on the curve the procedure is as follows: Draw a line through *a* and *c* prolonged to intersect *OB* at *1*, and a line through *b* and *c* prolonged to intersect *OA* at *2*. Now through *O* draw any line, *3–4*, known as a "ray," or in later reference, a "Pascal line." Designate as *p* the intersection of this ray with line *a–1* and as *q* the intersection of the ray with line *b–2*. Draw lines through *a* and *q* and through *b* and *p*. These lines extended will intersect in a point, *d*, which is the point sought lying on the curve. Additional points on the curve are found by repeating the above process, after which the points are connected with a smooth curve by means of a french curve, ship curve or spline.

Fig. 3 illustrates merely an expansion of the above principle so as to determine a number of points on the curve. Fig. 4 illustrates the application of the method by the second set of conditions, namely three points (*P*, *A* and *B*) and one point-slope (point of tangency *T* on the tangent *XY*).

It will at times be found necessary to draw a tangent to a given curve at a given point. Figs. 6 and 7 illustrate the application of the foregoing principle, in reverse, in determining such tangents.

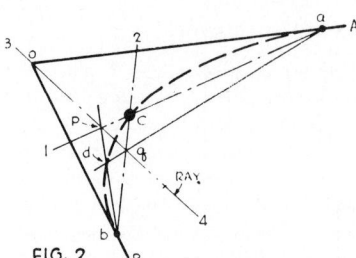

FIG. 1

PLANE "A"
(⊥ TO AXIS) -
CIRCLE

PLANE "B" (CUTS BOTH
SIDES OF CONE) - ELLIPSE

PLANE "E" (ANY INTER-
MEDIATE PLANE) -
CONIC OF INTER-
MEDIATE TYPE

BASE OF
RIGHT
CIRCULAR
CONE

PLANE "C" (PARALLEL TO
ELEMENT OF CONE) - PARABOLA
PLANE "D" (PARALLEL TO AXIS) -
HYPERBOLA

AXIS
APEX
"O"

Fig. 3. TO CONSTRUCT A SECOND-DEGREE CURVE THROUGH A CONTROL POINT D AND TANGENT TO LINES OA AND OB AT POINTS A AND B:

1. Draw line BE through D and line AF through D.
2. Divide DF into any number of spaces, e.g. four. This gives points G_1, G_2, and G_3.
3. Draw BG_1, BG_2, and BG_3.
4. Draw OG_1, OG_2, and OG_3, intersecting BE at H_1, H_2, and H_3.
5. From A, draw AH_1, AH_2, and AH_3, extended to intersect BG_1, BG_2, and BG_3, respectively, at points P_1, P_2, and P_3, which are points on required curve.
6. Additional points P_4, P_5, and P_6 are found likewise.
7. Curve fitted to these points is the required curve.

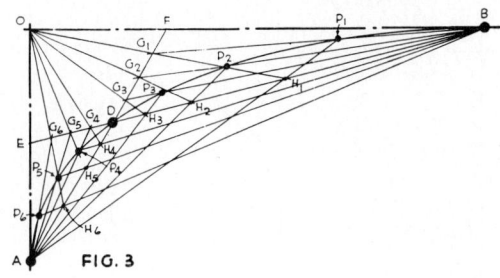

FIG. 3

Fig. 4. TO CONSTRUCT A SECOND-DEGREE CURVE TANGENT TO LINE XY AT POINT T; GIVEN THREE OTHER POINTS ON THE CURVE, P, A, AND B:

1. Draw lines BT and PA extended to intersect at point 1.
2. Draw lines PB and TA, intersecting at point 2.
3. Draw a line through points 1 and 2, extending to intersect tangent XY at point O.
4. Draw line OP, which will be tangent to the required curve.
5. Having two tangents, OT and OP, two points of tangency, T and P, and a control point, A or B (whichever is more convenient), proceed as in Fig. 3 to find additional points on the curve.

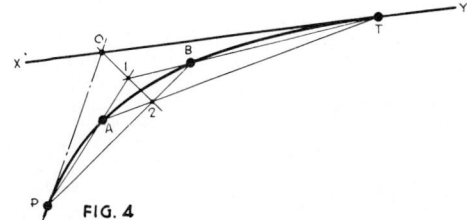

FIG. 4

Fig. 5. TO FIND A SIXTH POINT WHEN FIVE POINTS (1, 2, 3, 4, AND 5) ARE GIVEN:

1. Draw lines 1–3 and 2–4, calling intersection point o.
2. Draw lines 2–5 and 1–5.
3. Draw any "ray," AB, through point o, cutting line 2–5 at p and line 1–5 at q.
4. Draw lines through 3 and p and through 4 and q, intersecting at point 6, which will be an additional point on the curve.
5. Repeat procedure with different rays to find other points.

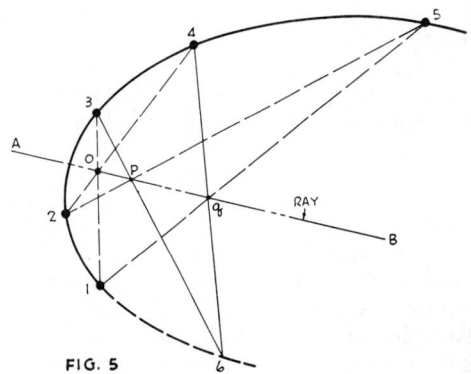

FIG. 5

Fig. 6. TO CONSTRUCT A TANGENT:

(Given, second-degree curve OB, tangent to CO and CB at points O and B, respectively; tangent to be constructed at any point, P.)

1. Select any two points, M and N, on curve OB.
2. Draw PN and BM, intersecting at point D.
3. Draw PS and BN extended to intersect PS at point E.
4. Draw a line through intersections D and E, extending it to intersect tangent BC at point R.
5. Draw a line through P and R, which will be required tangent.

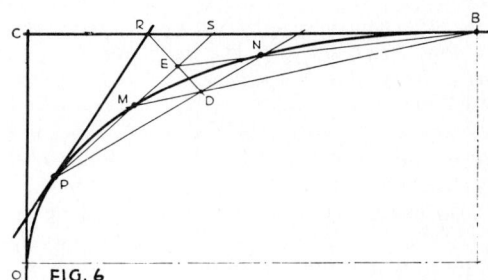

FIG. 6

Fig. 7. TO CONSTRUCT A TANGENT:

(Given, second-degree curve HJ; tangents to be constructed at any two points, P and T.)

1. Select any three points, A, B, and C, located conveniently between points P and T.
2. From P, draw lines PA, PB, and PC.
3. From point T, draw TA, TB, and TC.
4. Extend PA and TC to intersect at E.
5. Extend TB to intersect PE at G.
6. Call intersection of lines TA and PC, point D, and intersection of lines TA and PB, point F.
7. Draw lines DE and FG, extended to intersect at R.
8. Lines RP and RT are required tangents at points P and T.

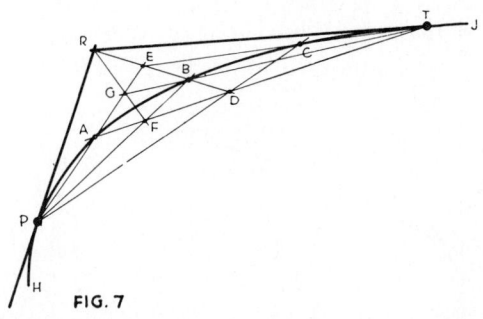

FIG. 7

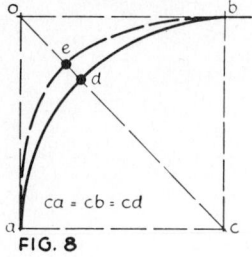

FIG. 8

$ca = cb = cd$

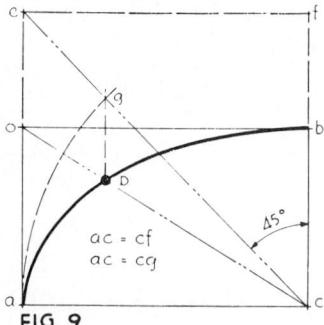

FIG. 9

$ac = cf$
$ac = cg$

45°

Following the procedure previously outlined and using the conditions stated, it will be found that an accurate ellipse will result.

A parabola, hyperbola or other conic will be determined similarly when there is given, in addition to the point-slopes, a control point which is known to lie on the curve in question. Mathematically, the slope of the tangents can be determined once the equation of the parabola or hyperbola is known. In a great number of cases however the tangents will be given, so that it will be possible to construct these curves without recourse to mathematics.

PRACTICAL APPLICATIONS

There are many practical applications of the foregoing principles, among which might be included the following examples. In all, it should be noted that the process consists of determining two points of tangency on their respective tangents (i.e., two point-slopes) together with a control point. Following this, the method outlined in Figs. 2 and 3 is followed to determine points along the curve.

Possibly one of the most useful applications consists of transforming a curve, carefully determined by freehand methods, into a definite geometric figure which can be duplicated, enlarged or otherwise utilized. Such a curve thus becomes definitely tied down. Fig. 10 might represent a profile, a section of a surface or possibly a roadway.

The usual method of duplicating this curve would be to determine, by trial, a series of radii describing sections of the curve, or possibly a system of offsets from a traverse line might be established. Both of these methods or others of a similar nature are tedious, inaccurate, and crude as compared with the simple and direct method of conics. This principle, as applied to the case at hand, would consist of splitting the curve up into convenient sections, such as ab, bc and cd of Fig. 10. Tangents would then be determined at points a, b,

Referring again to Fig. 2, it should be noted that the point c, which was selected somewhat at random in this case, is of particular importance, in that, with two point-slopes oa and ob given, the character of the curve will vary considerably depending on the location of the point c, known as the "control" or "shoulder" point. The extent to which the control or shoulder point influences the shape of the conic is illustrated in Fig. 8, in which, with two equal tangents, $ob = oa$, the control point d is so taken that $cd = cb = ca$. The resulting curve in this case will be, as expected, an arc of a circle.

If point e were to be used as a control point, the resulting curve would be a parabola or other conic, depending on the exact location of point e.

In Fig. 9, the control point D is determined by projecting down to diagonal oc from the intersection of circular arc ag with diagonal ec. With D as a control point, tangents ob and oa and points of tangency b and a, a quarter ellipse would be anticipated.

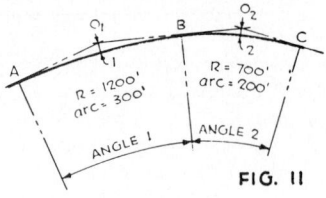

FIG. 11

$R = 1200'$
arc = 300'

$R = 700'$
arc = 200'

ANGLE 1   ANGLE 2

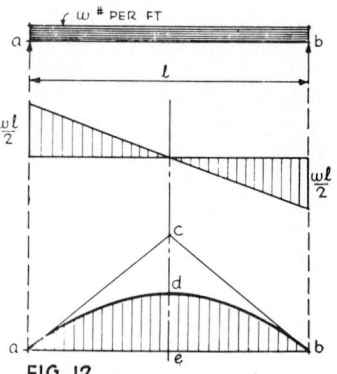

FIG. 12

w # PER FT

l

$\frac{wl}{2}$ $\frac{wl}{2}$

c and d and control points in each section, such as k_1, k_2, and k_3. The curve is now definitely tied down and can be reproduced exactly. Some points on the curve should be checked by the method described in Fig. 3, and if discrepancies appear it will undoubtedly be apparent that the freehand curve was not smooth at the point in question.

A similar application is illustrated in Fig. 11, which represents a street line consisting of two circular arcs AB and BC of radii such that the centers are inaccessible or off the drawing. The arc lengths being given, the central angles, 1 and 2, can easily be determined and consequently the tangents for both sections can be plotted. The distances $O_1 1$ and $O_2 2$ may then be computed, being in each case equal to R times exsec of half the angle. We would then have established for each section the two tangents and control point, after which points on the curve would be determined as previously described.

Fig. 12 illustrates the application of the principle to the construction of a moment diagram, such as might be required for use in the design of a plate girder. The bending moment curve for the portion of a beam subject to uniform loading can be described as a portion of a parabola. Inasmuch as the shear diagram gives the slope of the parabola representing the moment diagram at any point along the span, the slope at the two supports a and b are each equal to

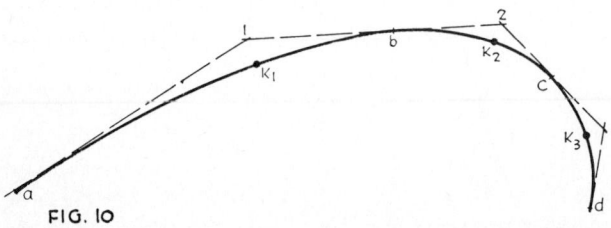

FIG. 10

one-half of *wl*. The ordinate *ce* is thus equal to *wl*² divided by 4, while the ordinate *de* is half of this or *wl*² divided by 8. With w and l given, it is necessary only to plot, at some convenient scale, the two tangents *ac* and *bc* and the ordinate *de* locating the control point *d*, after which additional points on the curve are determined, as before. This method will, in a great number of cases, be found considerably simpler than the usual method of determining points by figuring moments at various points along the span.

Always bearing in mind that the two tangents and a control point fix definitely the shape of the curve, the principle outlined can be put to use in solving problems such as the intersection of surfaces of all types, vaulting and vault ribs, graphs and diagrams, or in fact any problem involving curves or curved surfaces. The examples just given have all fallen under the previously cited Case I, involving two tangents and a control point. It will be found in practice that these conditions are usually present or can be established. Where this is not possible it will only then be necessary to fall back upon one of the other applications, Cases II and III as illustrated in Figs. 4 and 5 respectively.

BASIC THEORY

It will possibly be of interest to some readers to follow the development of the relationship upon which the foregoing is based. This relationship, known as the "Pascal Theorem," is diagrammed in Fig. 13, and may be stated as follows: "If the extremities of any hexagram inscribed in a conic are numbered in consecutive order 1 to 6 as shown in the sketch, the intersection of the opposite pairs of sides *1–3* and *2–4*, *4–6* and *1–5*, and intersection of the diagonals *2–5* and *3–6* will always lie in a straight line, known as a 'Pascal line'." Thus the intersections *o*, *p* and *q* lie on a "Pascal line" *ab*.

A "hexagram" may be briefly described as a six-pointed star, and in Fig. 13 is clearly visible as such when the sides *3–5* and *2–6* (dotted) are drawn. The term "hexagram" is, however, possible of much broader application: the figure need not be regular in shape, nor is the curve in which the hexagram is inscribed limited, except in one respect — it must be a conic.

In Fig. 14, the same relationship is again indicated, the nomenclature of Fig. 13 being retained; the hexagram in this case being irregular in form and inscribed in an ellipse. In both Figs. 13 and 14, lines *1–3* and *2–4* intersect at *o*, lines *1–5* and *4–6* intersect at *q* and lines *2–5* and *3–6* intersect at *p*. From the "Pascal theorem" above stated, points *o*, *p* and *q* will always lie in a straight line known as a Pascal line.

Earlier in this article we stated as Case III the condition that five points on a conic curve were sufficient to determine the curve, or stated otherwise: five points on a conic are sufficient to establish a sixth point, also on the conic. A comparison of Fig. 14 with Fig. 5 will show that the procedure outlined in Fig. 5 is derived directly from the relationship shown in Fig. 14, the only difference being that in Fig. 5, with five points given, the Pascal line passed through the point *o* at random determines the two other intersection points *p* and *q*, which immediately determine the location of the sixth point as shown.

It will be observed that as the position of the fifth point varies the sixth will also vary, but the ensuing curve will be the same. Referring again to Fig. 5 it will be noticed that if point *3* is moved, but always remains between points *2* and *4*, the intersection *o* will lie on the inside of the curve. If point *3* is moved, however, until it lies between points *1* and *2* the intersection of lines *2–4* and *1–3* will lie outside the curve. If now we assume that point *2* is rotated clockwise until it coincides with point *4*, and point *3* is rotated counterclockwise until it coincides with point *1*, indicating the combined points *2–4* and *1–3*, as in Fig. 15, it will be seen that the lines joining points *1* and *3* and points *2* and *4* must be tangents to the curve at the combined points *1–3* and *2–4* respectively. As before, the intersection of these two lines will be indicated as point *o*.

It was previously indicated that the fifth point was not restricted as to position as long as it remained on the conic. Assume point *5*, in Fig. 15, to be intermediate between the combined points *1–3* and *2–4*. With this arrangement we would now have established the first set of conditions mentioned earlier: "One point and two point-slopes."

Proceeding as in Fig. 5, we draw

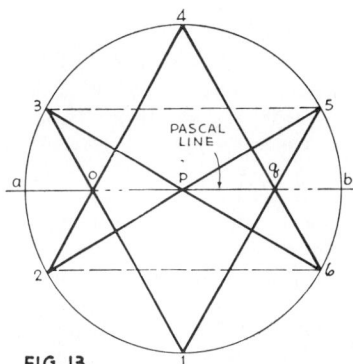

FIG. 13

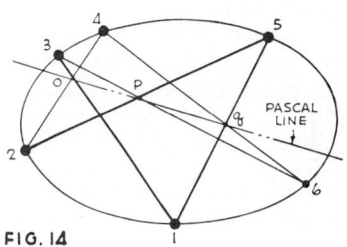

FIG. 14

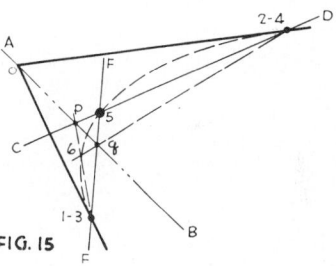

FIG. 15

lines *CD* through points *2* and *5* and *EF* through points *1* and *5*. If we then pass a Pascal line *AB* at random through point *A* and call the intersection of this line with line *CD* (or *2–5*) the point *p* as before, and also the intersection with line *EF* (or *1–5*) the point *q*, we will then have retained the same relationship of lines and points in both cases. Continuing as in Fig. 5, we will draw lines through points *3* and *p* and through *4* and *q* intersecting at point *6*, which is the point sought. If we now compare Fig. 15 with Fig. 2, it will be seen that the procedure is the same as previously outlined.

Also, since the procedure followed in Figs. 5 and 15 was identical it is apparent that the method is general as to Cases I and III. A study of Fig. 4 will show that the procedure in Case II is likewise similar.

By WILLIAM BLACKWELL

Geometry in architecture, sometimes boldly expressed and sometimes artfully concealed, is a part of the common core of knowledge and understanding which the architect uses to enclose space for human needs—one of his instruments, one of the tools, to be used in organizing and planning and decorating and integrating spaces so they can be built and understood and used. This study of some of the formal, basic series of geometric shapes which the architect uses, or may use, takes as its structure the unchanging relationship between the area and the perimeter of each shape.

Some shapes enclose an area with more or less perimeter than others, and this is a characteristic of the shape which can easily be expressed mathematically.

For example, the area enclosed by each unit of perimeter of a square is equal to the length of a side divided by four. The larger the square, the greater will be the area enclosed per unit of perimeter—the area/perimeter value. The same thing is true of a circle where the area enclosed per unit of circumference is equal to the diameter divided by four; and so the larger the circle, the greater will be the area/perimeter value. It is true also of any other shape that the larger it is the larger will be the area/perimeter value.

Because of this scale effect, because the area/perimeter value of all shapes changes with size in the same way, they have always the same relationship one to the other with respect to their area enclosure properties. For any given area then, the area/perimeter value of one shape can be expressed relative to the area/perimeter value of another shape.

Because a circle encloses a given area with less perimeter than any other closed shape, its area/perimeter value will always be greater—and so it is used here to express the relative area enclosure properties of other plane shapes. The area/perimeter value of a square, for instance, will always be 88.6 per cent of the area/perimeter value of a circle with the same area. This value is the area/perimeter factor, a comparison of the area enclosure properties of a square to those of a circle. Similar values can be found for other shapes, regular or irregular, by using the equation:

$$A_f = \frac{2\sqrt{\pi a}}{p} \times 100 \text{ or } \frac{354.5\sqrt{A}}{p}$$

Once the area/perimeter factor has been found for a shape, the process can be reversed and the area/perimeter factor used to find the actual area or perimeter of a shape if one or the other is known, providing a useful numerical relationship between the two similar to the 'k' and 'f' factors sometimes employed in handbooks to simplify calculations.

If the area is known, the perimeter can be found using the equation in this way:

$$p = \frac{2\sqrt{\pi A}}{A_f/100} \text{ or } \frac{354.5\sqrt{A}}{A_f}$$

If the perimeter is known, the area can be found by the equation:

$$A = \frac{1}{4\pi}\left[\frac{A_f}{100} \times p\right]^2 \text{ or } .0796\left[\frac{A_f}{100} \times p\right]^2$$

For circles, squares or rectangles finding the area or perimeter isn't a very serious problem but in the case of many sided polygons, ellipses or irregular shapes, the area/perimeter factor can be useful.

The reciprocal of the area/perimeter factor can also be used to express the difference in the area enclosure properties of a shape and a circle. A square has a perimeter/area value of 1.128 (100/88.6) compared to a circle of 1, which is to say that a square has 12.8 per cent more perimeter than a circle with the same area.

It might be emphasized, too, that although the area/perimeter factor is independent of "the scale effect" and is an unchanging factor regardless of the size of the shape, it is nonetheless an expression of the relative area enclosure properties of shapes for a given area. A large square might have an actual area/perimeter value twice that of a small circle. The usefulness of the factor lies then only in comparing the area enclosure properties of shapes for a given area.

The chart below illustrates the relative area enclosure properties of four related series of geometric shapes. They are arranged from bottom to top according to their area/perimeter factors, from 0 to 100 per cent, and from left to right according to the number of sides in the shape, from one to infinity.

In outline form and starting with the square are also shown some rectangles of different proportion to illustrate the change that occurs in the area enclosure properties of rectangles as the length-to-width ratio changes.

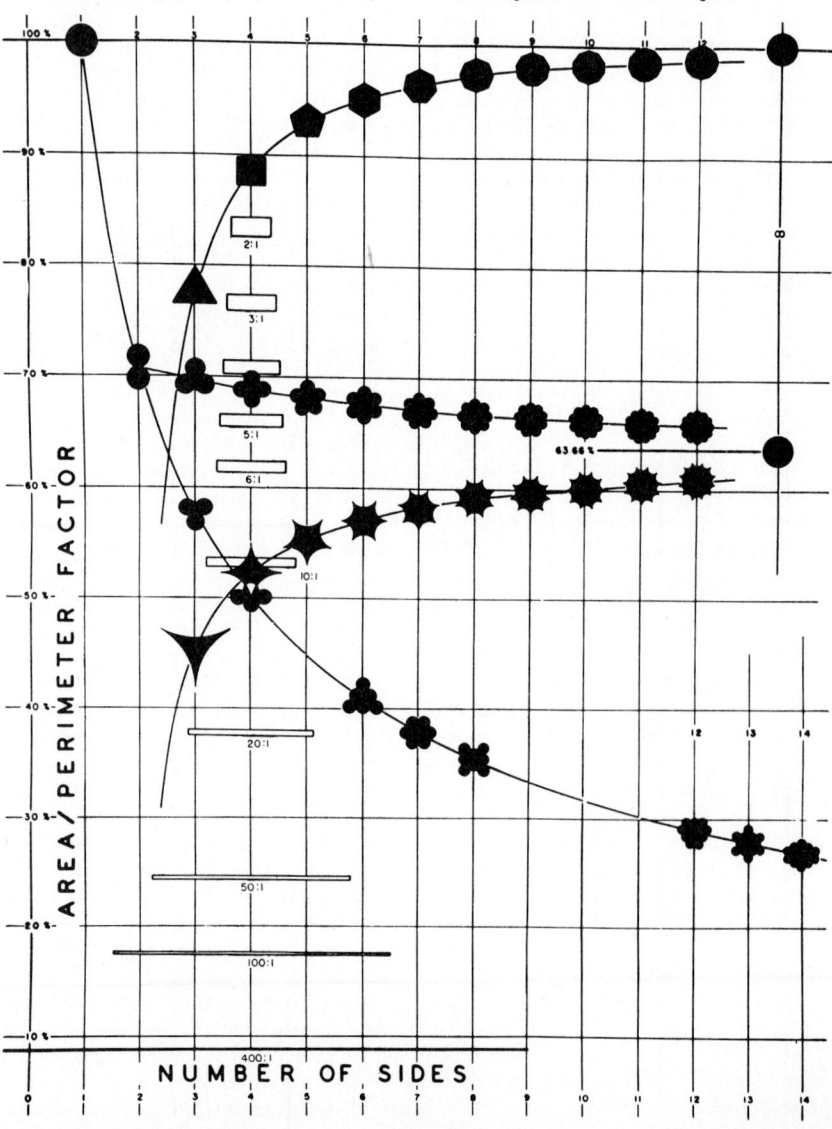

AREA/PERIMETER FACTOR

NUMBER OF SIDES

The shapes on the chart all have the same area, so the difference in apparent size, as between one shape and another, can be seen.

The Regular Polygons

First of the four series of shapes shown in black on the chart is the regular straight-sided polygon series—the triangle, square, pentagon, etc. It begins, theoretically, with a straight line. Having two sides, a perimeter equal to twice its length but zero area, a straight line has an area/perimeter factor of 0 per cent. The first solid equilateral shape is the equilateral triangle (77.7 per cent), then a square (88.6 per cent), the five-sided pentagon (93 per cent) and so on—gradually approaching a circle (100 per cent) as the number of sides increases to infinity. Area/perimeter factors for some of the polygons in this series are given in the table below. The latter shapes in this series are extremely compact, with polygons of 13 sides or more having area/perimeter factors within 1 per cent of the area/perimeter factor of a circle.

In a limited sense, area/perimeter factors are a kind of efficiency factor, reflecting the degree of proximity of a shape to the area enclosure properties of a circle—as for instance, when a circular structure is divided into a number of straight sides for ease of fabrication.

Concave-Convex Series:

Under the regular polygons are two complementary series of shapes, seldom used, but still familiar to architects as the shapes of brightly colored rose windows and vertically lined, fluted columns. These are the concave and convex aspects of the straight-sided polygons. Actually, which is which depends on whether the point of view is from the outside or the inside but the upper curve, the "rose" shapes, are taken to be the convex series and the lower curve, the "fluted" shapes, the concave.

Of the shapes in these two series, the most interesting is the three-sided concave shape formed by the interior arcs of three mutually tangent circles. It might be called a "triarc." This shape has an area/perimeter factor of 45.2 per cent, the lowest of the regular geometric shapes. Although actually having the same area, it appears larger than any other shape on the chart. The circle and the "triarc" represent two extremes in area enclosure—the one with minimum and the other with maximum perimeter for a given area in a regular shape. Because of this difference (a 55 per cent difference in area/perimeter factors) and because of their opposite curvature, the two together form a very strong contrast in shape.

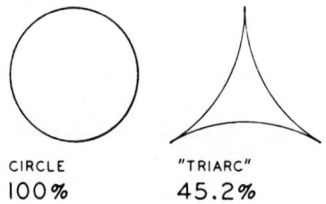

CIRCLE 100%   "TRIARC" 45.2%

As the number of arcs in the circumference of both the concave and convex shapes increases, they converge on what appears to be a circle. Theoretically, it is a circle with its circumference made up of a very large number of very small arcs. With the area of each shape the same as it is on the chart, the arcs in the circumference become smaller as more are added. Finally, they are no longer apparent—the shape appears to be a circle. The actual circumference, greatly enlarged, would appear to be a line of semi-circles, like a series of arches, turned outward for the convex shapes, inward for the concave:

Because of the small arcs, the circumference is 1.57 times longer than the circumference would be without them. The area/perimeter factor of the shape then is 1:1.57 or 63.66 per cent.

The Area/Perimeter Factor For Any Number of Separate Identical Shapes:

Beginning with one circle at the upper left-hand corner of the chart is a curve showing the area/perimeter factor for various groups containing different numbers of circles. The groups shown were arrived at by starting with one, two or three circles at the center and proceeding outward, adding circles in the vacant pockets of each concentric ring. The same number of circles might, however, have been arranged in any other manner or even randomly placed and still have the same area/perimeter factor. Providing they all are of the same size, only the number of circles considered determines the area/perimeter factor.

The area/perimeter factor of any number of separate circles of the same size is equal to the area/perimeter factor of one circle (100 per cent) divided by the square root of the number of circles considered. And, it happens that this is true of other shapes: the area/perimeter factor of any number of separate, identical shapes taken as a whole is equal to the area/perimeter factor of one of the shapes divided by the square root of the number of shapes. One square has an area/perimeter factor of 88.6 per cent; nine squares, 29.5 per cent (88.6/3). A single leaf on a tree might have an area/perimeter factor of say 50 per cent, but if all the leaves are counted they would as a whole have an area/perimeter factor of very nearly zero.

The curve showing the area/perimeter factor for groups containing a different number of circles, then, illustrates what happens to the area/perimeter factor of any shape when it is divided into a number of separate identical shapes.

ONE SQUARE 88.62%   NINE SQUARES 29.54%

Instead of being arranged in their more compact form as they are on the chart, the same number of circles might have been arranged in a ring, adjacent to one another and equidistant from the center, as illustrated on the next page.

Lines between the centers (or the points of tangency) of adjacent circles form the regular straight-sided polygon series—the pentagon

REGULAR POLYGON SERIES:

No. of Sides	Area/Perimeter Factor	No. of Sides	Area/Perimeter Factor
3	77.756%	20	99.587
4	88.623	24	99.714
5	92.995	25	99.736
6	95.231	27	99.774
8	97.368	30	99.817
9	97.931	32	99.839
10	98.330	36	99.872
12	98.846	40	99.897
15	99.264	45	99.920
16	99.354	48	99.929
18	99.490	50	99.934

in the illustration. The exterior perimeter of the whole form is the convex aspect of the polygon and the interior perimeter of the circles the concave. The circles themselves, the regular polygon and its concave and convex aspects make up the four series of shapes shown in black on the chart.

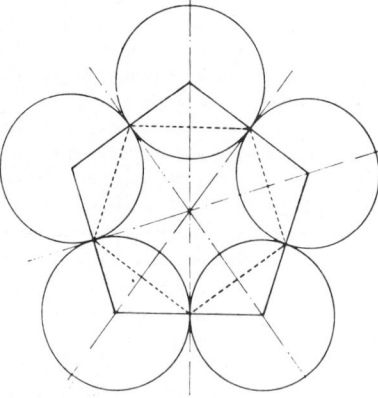

Rectangles:

In outline form, and starting with the square in the regular polygon series are some rectangles, the shapes most frequently used by architects because of the ease with which they accommodate most needs for enclosed space. The area/perimeter factor of a rectangle is determined simply by the length-to-width ratio, the proportion. A square (1:1) has the highest factor, 88.6 per cent, and the farther the rectangle deviates from the square in proportion, the lower will be its area/perimeter factor. As the length becomes very great with respect to the width, the "width" disappears, leaving a straight line with an area/perimeter factor of 0 per cent. It is possible then for a rectangle, depending on its proportion, to have any area/perimeter factor from 0 to 88.6 per cent.

The greatest difference in the area/perimeter factors of two closed shapes is, of course, 100 per cent—reached between a straight line and a circle and approached between a circle and a very long rectangle. There is one example of this contrast, used architecturally to a softer degree, in the chapel Saarinen designed for M.I.T. Here one enters the dimly-lighted, circular brick chapel through a lightly enclosed rectangular passageway. Between the high area/perimeter factor of the circle and the lower factor of the rectangular entry, there is a difference of about 25 per cent. Looking at the chart and the range of shapes normally used architecturally, this is a very considerable difference.

Room shapes, for instance, are normally nearly square in plan, with length-to-width ratios from 1:1 to about 1½:1; seldom greater than 2:1. The difference in the area/perimeter

factor of a square room and one with a relatively high length-to-width ratio of 2:1 is only about 5 per cent.

Building shapes, especially low buildings, cover virtually the whole range of rectangles, from squares to the mile-long production line enclosures of the Second World War. "L" and "T" and other arrangements are equivalent to relatively long rectangles. Because they have lower area/perimeter factors (more perimeter) they have also a higher degree of light and openness and flexibility in the arrangement and rearrangement of the internal spaces than the more compact shapes.

On the other hand, economy of exterior perimeter is an important consideration in almost every building, too, because of material and labor saving, maintenance costs, and reduction in heating and cooling loads. It is particularly important in multistory buildings where the outside wall surface is very large compared to the roof area. These buildings tend to have more compact shapes, with the perimeter reduced just to the point where if it were reduced further the spaces within would be adversely affected. To give one example, the glass-enclosed rectangles of Lever House have a length-to-width ratio of about 3:1 and an area/perimeter factor of 77.5 per cent. A square plan (88.6 per cent) might have been more economical in terms of the perimeter but would not have the same degree of light and openness and planning flexibility (and interest, too) that the rectangular shape has with some additional perimeter.

As a matter of interest, the "golden section" (1.62:1) has an area/perimeter factor of 86.12 per cent, 2½ per cent less than a square. The area/perimeter factor for other rectangles can be found by using the equation

$$A_f = \frac{\sqrt{\pi l/w}}{1 + l/w} \times 100$$

or taken directly from the curve below.

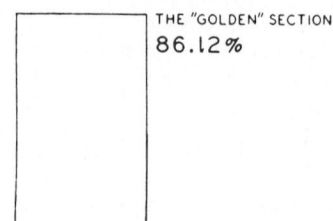

THE "GOLDEN" SECTION
86.12%

Ellipses:

On the same graph with the rectangle curve is another curve showing the area/perimeter factor for ellipses of different proportion. In the same manner as the rectangles, ellipses have lower and lower area/perimeter factors the further they deviate from a circle in proportion. It happens that for proportions less than about 5.75:1 ellipses have higher area/perimeter factors than rectangles of the same proportion but for proportions greater than 5.75:1 rectangles have the higher factors. With a length-to-width ratio of 5.75:1, both have an area/perimeter factor of 62.98 per cent.

When the major and minor axis of an ellipse are known, the area can be found using the equation, πab. The circumference can then be found by taking the approximate area/perimeter factor from the curve and using the basic equation:

$$p = \frac{2\sqrt{\pi A}}{A_f/100}$$

This will be as accurate as the area/perimeter factor can be read from the curve, plotted from tabulated values of elliptic integrals.

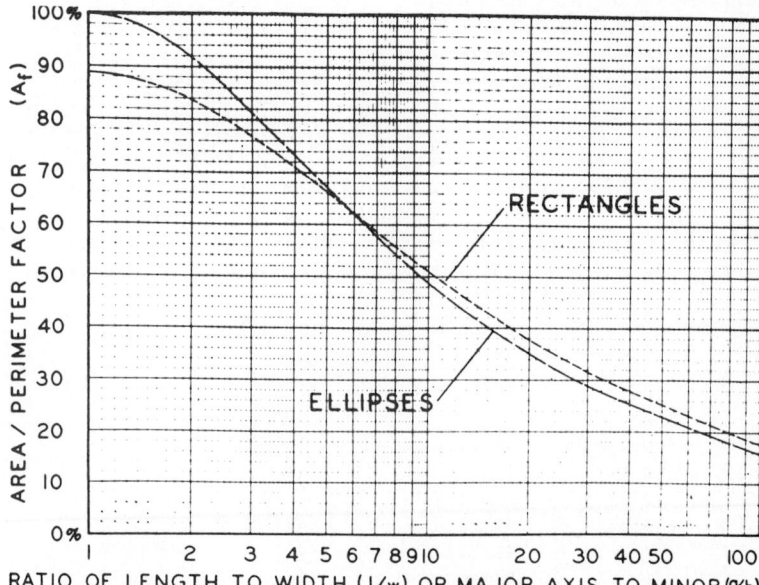

RECTANGLES

ELLIPSES

RATIO OF LENGTH TO WIDTH (l/w) OR MAJOR AXIS TO MINOR (a/b)

By HENDRIK P. MAAS, *AIA*

SHORT CUTS TO SOLAR ANGLES

With the increasing use of larger glass areas and more emphasis generally on solar orientation, it is increasingly important for an architect to have in his files information on the sun's position as it varies from season to season and from hour to hour. Only with that information can he solve problems of sunlight and shade.

The purpose of this presentation is to simplify the architect's calculations. While the determination of the sun's position at any given time has involved the author in some fairly complicated exercises in navigational mathematics, the data here given should leave little for the reader to do, except, of course, to apply the data to his own design. This involves only some graphic projection of a routine nature. For the designer who demands hairline accuracy the necessary formulas are appended. But a navigator's accuracy could hardly ever be required

for a building problem; the charts and tables on succeeding pages should eliminate the mathematics for all normal purposes of architects.

The scope of the data is for selected hours between sunrise and sunset, at each fifth parallel of latitude from 70° North to 70° South, for the critical dates of December 22, March 21, September 23, and June 22. These dates give, of course, the extreme and the mean conditions for sun angles. For the latitudes of the United States (see map), diagrams illustrating the sun's angles are given with the tables on sheets 4 and 5. The diagrams are really horizontal projections of the sun's paths, as illustrated a bit more graphically in the sketch at the top of sheet 2. For other latitudes the data only is given in the tables on sheet 6.

The diagrams and tables may be used directly for the latitudes given; for intermediate latitudes the answer is readily obtained by interpolation between the figures given,

for the desired hour, for the nearest latitudes above and below.

SOLAR ANGLES MADE EASY

The position of the sun with respect to any point on the earth's surface is defined by the angle of *azimuth* and the angle of *altitude*. These angles, of course, are determined by the latitude, the date, and the hour.

The *azimuth* is simply the angle measured horizontally from the North meridian. For morning hours it is measured in an Easterly direction; for afternoon hours, Westerly.

The *altitude* is the angle, measured vertically, between the sun and the horizontal plane of the horizon. These angles are illustrated in the sketch above. It should be noted that the North meridian is the true North, not the magnetic North. The dia-

LATITUDES IN THE UNITED STATES

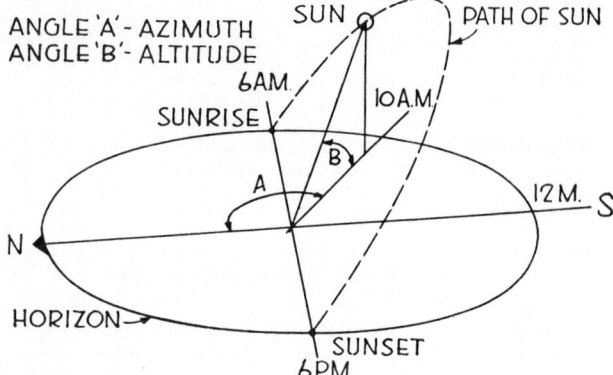

ANGLE 'A'- AZIMUTH
ANGLE 'B'- ALTITUDE

FORMULAS FOR DETERMINING AZIMUTH AND ALTITUDE

For those who may have a special need of knowing accurately the *azimuth* and *altitude* for a particular date or hour not given in the tables the following formlas and information are given:

I $\sin h = \sin L \sin d + \cos L \cos d \cos t$

II $\sin Z = \sin t \cos d \sec h$

III $\cos t = -\tan L \tan d$ (when $h = 0°$)

IV $\cos Z = \sin d \sec L$ (when $h = 0°$)

V $\cos t = \dfrac{\sin h - \sin L \sin d}{\cos L \cos d}$

in which:

L = latitude

d = declination; i.e., the angle between a line connecting the centers of the sun and earth and the plane of the equator.

t = time of day expressed in degrees. Since there are 24 hours and also 360 degrees in one revolution of the earth, 1 hour = 15°, 1 minute = 15' and 1 second = 15". This angle is always measured from the noon position of the sun, therefore noon = 0°, 10 A.M. = 30°, 4 P.M. = 60°, etc.

Z = azimuth

h = altitude

grams with the actual data, sheets 4 and 5, represent the path of the sun for the given date and the given latitude, as shown in plan. The elliptical curve represents the horizontal projection of the path of the sun. The heavier lines are the horizontal projections of the angles of altitude for each line of azimuth shown. The angles of azimuth and altitude for various hours are tabulated below the diagrams. The earliest and latest hours are those of sunrise and sunset, to the nearest ten minutes.

The diagrams and tables may be applied to southern latitudes simply by transposing the summer and winter dates and the fall and spring dates.

How to use the tables

To illustrate the procedure for using the tables we will determine, graphically, the condition of sunlight on a simple one-room structure with a roof overhang, choosing, just for instance, the hour of 11 A.M. on June 22, and the latitude of 42° (Chicago). We shall locate the line of the shadow cast by the roof overhang.

For the calculation, the plan of the structure is drawn in the normal manner. Next the North line is drawn on the sheet, just as in any plot plan. This North lines gives us the starting point for the graphic solution of the problem.

Now we refer to the diagrams and tables (sheet 3) to find azimuth and altitude angles for the given condition. Here comes the interpolation. Azimuth of 40°, 11 A.M., summer, is 138°. For 45°, same time, 145°30'. By simple interpolation, we get an azimuth for 42° of 141°. In the same manner the altitude for 42°N, 11 A.M., summer, is found to be 67°30'.

Now, on the plan at any convenient point,

we draw the line A-B, 141° East of the North position indicated on the plan.

Parallel to A-B, a ray line is drawn on the plan, through the point we are interested in, the point C' at the juncture of the wall and the roof. Now we project this point on line A-B and thus get a starting point for drawing an elevation (or as much of an elevation as is necessary) of the building on A-B. On this elevation the critical point we are locating is point C.

Next we add the altitude to the calculation, by drawing, through point C, a line at 67°30' from A-B. This line crosses A-B at point P, which gives us another projection point. Projecting this back to the plan we locate P_1 on the ray line R_4. At this point we have located the shadow line on the terrace—it will run along the terrace through P_1 parallel to the roof line.

We can continue, if we like, to get other shadow lines, until we can outline the shadow of the building all around, and even learn where the sun will strike the floor inside (through the window). To carry on, we project point P_1 down to a section below, to the terrace level at P_2. Now from C_2 to P_2 we get still another angle, which is measured and found to be 80°30'. This angle, it will be seen, has been found graphically; it is the direct elevation of the angle at which the sunlight at this particular time casts shadows around our particular building.

Using this new angle, 80°30', we can carry the projection process backwards from section to plan, and so outline the shadow of the building.

Note: See also sheet 11 in section on "Daylighting" and sheets 38–40 in section on "Heating, Ventilating, and Air Conditioning."

Declination of the sun varies for each day of the year from approximately 23°27' North to 23°27' South. When the declination is North, it is considered plus (+), when South, minus (−). The precise declination as it varies for each year can be found in the American Nautical Almanac issued annually by the U.S. Naval Observatory, Washington, D.C., and may be purchased from the Superintendent of Documents, Washington 25, D.C. For convenience a table of declinations for each seventh day of the year, simplified to the nearest 5' is included (below). Intermediate declinations may be interpolated with reasonable results. The reader is cautioned to remember that when the declination is South it carries a minus (−) sign in which case, in the above formulas, the sin and tan will have a negative value, while the cos will have a plus value.

When h = 0°0' it is the hour of sunrise or sunset. Example: Find AZIMUTH and ALTITUDE of sun at 2 P.M., May 15, at Latitude 42° N.

L = 42°

d = +18°40' (interpolated between +19°25' and +17°40' from Table of Declinations)

t = 30°

Computations by slide rule

From I $\sin h = \sin 42° \sin 18°40' + \cos 42°$
$\cos 18°40' \cos 30°$
$= .670 \times .320 + .745 \times .950$
$\times .865$
$= .215 + .612 = .827$
$h = 56°$

From II $\sin Z = \sin 30° \cos 18°40' \sec 56°$
$= .500 \times .950 \times 1.79$
$Z = 59°$ or $121°$

Since Z is measured from the North meridian, by inspection the proper answer is 121° to the West.

The hour of sunrise (or sunset) and its AZIMUTH may be found from III and IV. Local sun time* may be found from V.

The noon ALTITUDE of the sun may be quickly found for any latitude and any declination by the following additional formulas.

1. $h = 90° - (L - d)$ when L is greater than d

2. $h = 90° - (d - L)$ when d is greater than L (L and d same name)

3. $h = 90° - (L + d)$
(L and d contrary name)

Sun time is the hour of day as determined by the position of the sun with relation to its noon meridian. Since standard time (clock time) is based on the sun time at the center of each hourly time zone, sun time may vary as much as ½ hour from standard time depending on the locality.

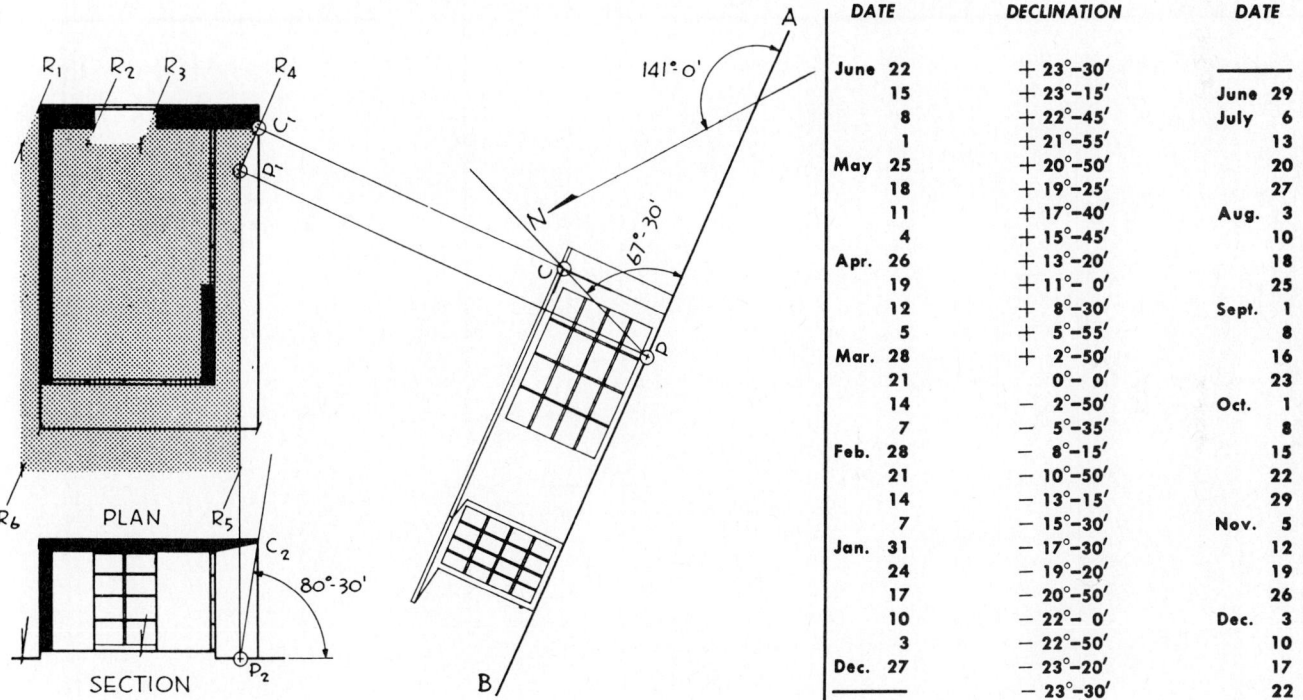

Declination of the Sun—to Nearest 5'

DATE	DECLINATION	DATE
June 22	+ 23°–30'	
15	+ 23°–15'	June 29
8	+ 22°–45'	July 6
1	+ 21°–55'	13
May 25	+ 20°–50'	20
18	+ 19°–25'	27
11	+ 17°–40'	Aug. 3
4	+ 15°–45'	10
Apr. 26	+ 13°–20'	18
19	+ 11°– 0'	25
12	+ 8°–30'	Sept. 1
5	+ 5°–55'	8
Mar. 28	+ 2°–50'	16
21	0°– 0'	23
14	− 2°–50'	Oct. 1
7	− 5°–35'	8
Feb. 28	− 8°–15'	15
21	− 10°–50'	22
14	− 13°–15'	29
7	− 15°–30'	Nov. 5
Jan. 31	− 17°–30'	12
24	− 19°–20'	19
17	− 20°–50'	26
10	− 22°– 0'	Dec. 3
3	− 22°–50'	10
Dec. 27	− 23°–20'	17
	− 23°–30'	22

DIAGRAMS OF AZIMUTH AND ALTITUDE OF THE SUN

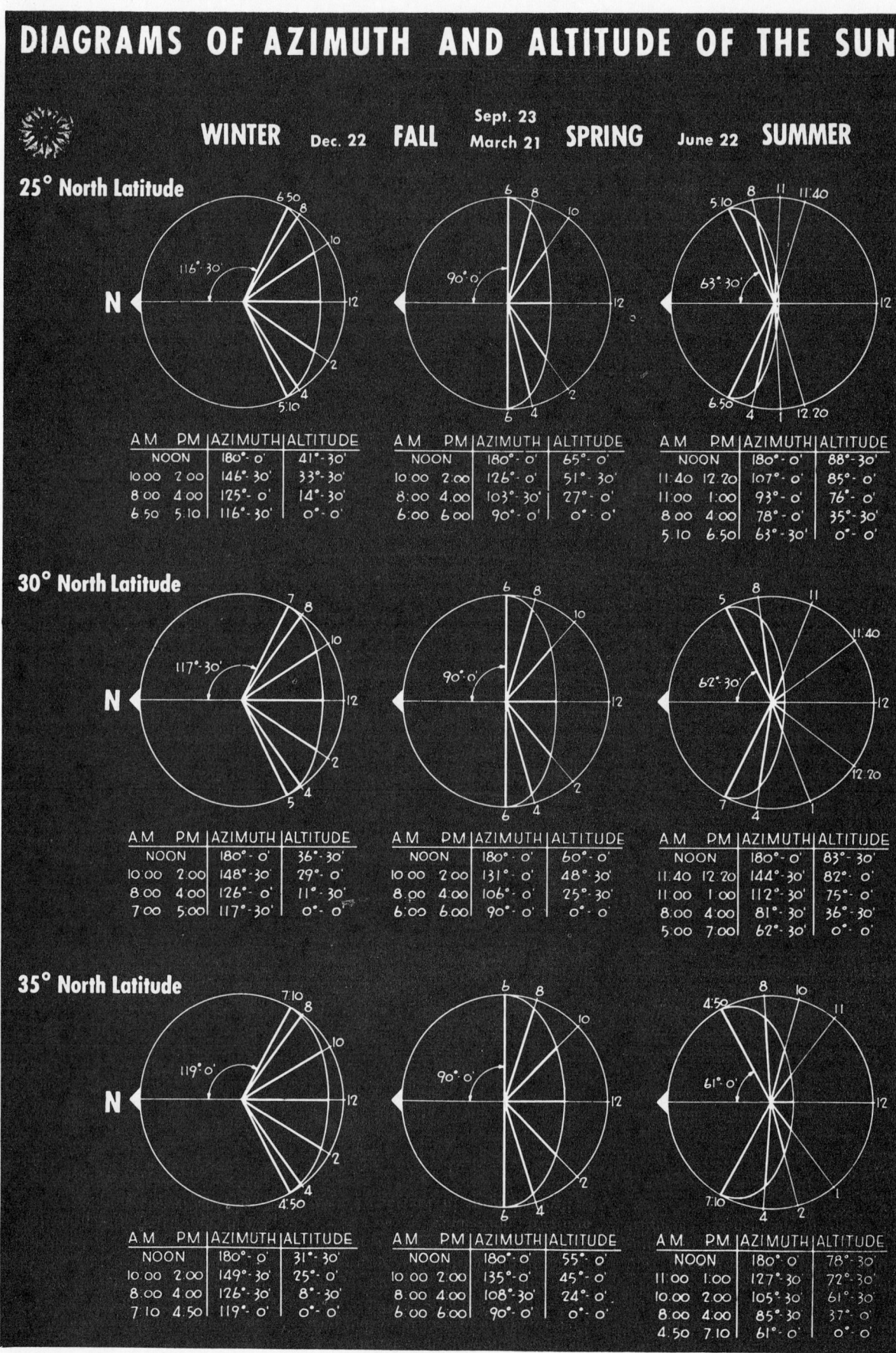

WINTER Dec. 22 **FALL** Sept. 23 March 21 **SPRING** June 22 **SUMMER**

25° North Latitude

A.M.	P.M.	AZIMUTH	ALTITUDE
NOON		180°· 0'	41°· 30'
10:00	2:00	146°· 30'	33°· 30'
8:00	4:00	125°· 0'	14°· 30'
6:50	5:10	116°· 30'	0°· 0'

A.M.	P.M.	AZIMUTH	ALTITUDE
NOON		180°· 0'	65°· 0'
10:00	2:00	126°· 0'	51°· 30'
8:00	4:00	103°· 30'	27°· 0'
6:00	6:00	90°· 0'	0°· 0'

A.M.	P.M.	AZIMUTH	ALTITUDE
NOON		180°· 0'	88°· 30'
11:40	12:20	107°· 0'	85°· 0'
11:00	1:00	93°· 0'	76°· 0'
8:00	4:00	78°· 0'	35°· 30'
5:10	6:50	63°· 30'	0°· 0'

30° North Latitude

A.M.	P.M.	AZIMUTH	ALTITUDE
NOON		180°· 0'	36°· 30'
10:00	2:00	148°· 30'	29°· 0'
8:00	4:00	126°· 0'	11°· 30'
7:00	5:00	117°· 30'	0°· 0'

A.M.	P.M.	AZIMUTH	ALTITUDE
NOON		180°· 0'	60°· 0'
10:00	2:00	131°· 0'	48°· 30'
8:00	4:00	106°· 0'	25°· 30'
6:00	6:00	90°· 0'	0°· 0'

A.M.	P.M.	AZIMUTH	ALTITUDE
NOON		180°· 0'	83°· 30'
11:40	12:20	144°· 30'	82°· 0'
11:00	1:00	112°· 30'	75°· 0'
8:00	4:00	81°· 30'	36°· 30'
5:00	7:00	62°· 30'	0°· 0'

35° North Latitude

A.M.	P.M.	AZIMUTH	ALTITUDE
NOON		180°· 0'	31°· 30'
10:00	2:00	149°· 30'	25°· 0'
8:00	4:00	126°· 30'	8°· 30'
7:10	4:50	119°· 0'	0°· 0'

A.M.	P.M.	AZIMUTH	ALTITUDE
NOON		180°· 0'	55°· 0'
10:00	2:00	135°· 0'	45°· 0'
8:00	4:00	108°· 30'	24°· 0'
6:00	6:00	90°· 0'	0°· 0'

A.M.	P.M.	AZIMUTH	ALTITUDE
NOON		180°· 0'	78°· 30'
11:00	1:00	127°· 30'	72°· 0'
10:00	2:00	105°· 30'	61°· 30'
8:00	4:00	85°· 30'	37°· 0'
4:50	7:10	61°· 0'	0°· 0'

DIAGRAMS OF AZIMUTH AND ALTITUDE OF THE SUN

WINTER Dec. 22 **FALL** Sept. 23 / March 21 **SPRING** June 22 **SUMMER**

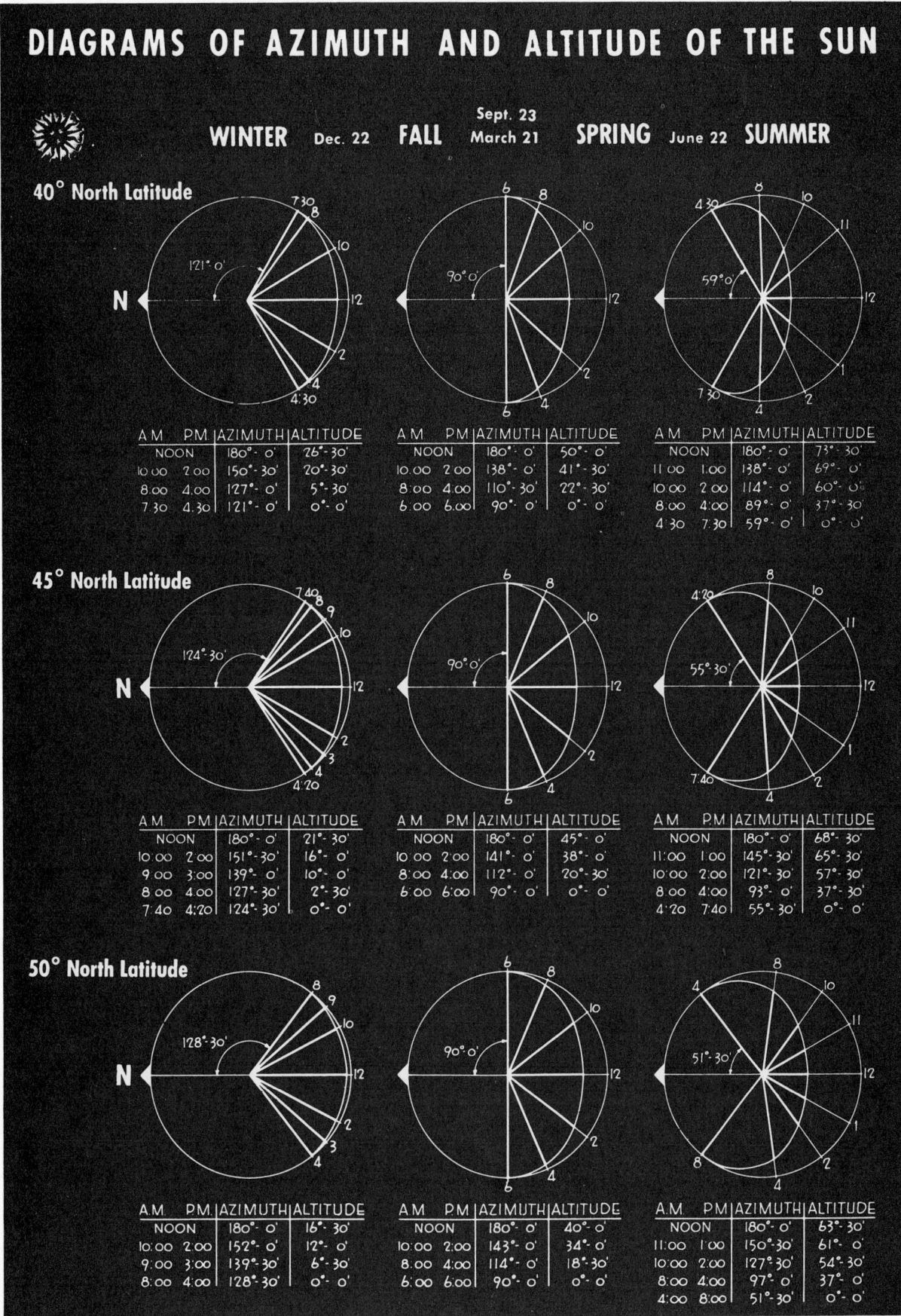

40° North Latitude

A.M.	P.M.	AZIMUTH	ALTITUDE
NOON		180°- 0'	26°- 30'
10:00	2:00	150°- 30'	20°- 0'
8:00	4:00	127°- 0'	5°- 30'
7:30	4:30	121°- 0'	0°- 0'

A.M.	P.M.	AZIMUTH	ALTITUDE
NOON		180°- 0'	50°- 0'
10:00	2:00	138°- 0'	41°- 30'
8:00	4:00	110°- 30'	22°- 30'
6:00	6:00	90°- 0'	0°- 0'

A.M.	P.M.	AZIMUTH	ALTITUDE
NOON		180°- 0'	73°- 30'
11:00	1:00	138°- 0'	69°- 0'
10:00	2:00	114°- 0'	60°- 0'
8:00	4:00	89°- 0'	37°- 30'
4:30	7:30	59°- 0'	0°- 0'

45° North Latitude

A.M.	P.M.	AZIMUTH	ALTITUDE
NOON		180°- 0'	21°- 30'
10:00	2:00	151°- 30'	16°- 0'
9:00	3:00	139°- 0'	10°- 0'
8:00	4:00	127°- 30'	2°- 30'
7:40	4:20	124°- 30'	0°- 0'

A.M.	P.M.	AZIMUTH	ALTITUDE
NOON		180°- 0'	45°- 0'
10:00	2:00	141°- 0'	38°- 0'
8:00	4:00	112°- 0'	20°- 30'
6:00	6:00	90°- 0'	0°- 0'

A.M.	P.M.	AZIMUTH	ALTITUDE
NOON		180°- 0'	68°- 30'
11:00	1:00	145°- 30'	65°- 30'
10:00	2:00	121°- 30'	57°- 30'
8:00	4:00	93°- 0'	37°- 30'
4:20	7:40	55°- 30'	0°- 0'

50° North Latitude

A.M.	P.M.	AZIMUTH	ALTITUDE
NOON		180°- 0'	16°- 30'
10:00	2:00	152°- 0'	12°- 0'
9:00	3:00	139°- 30'	6°- 30'
8:00	4:00	128°- 30'	0°- 0'

A.M.	P.M.	AZIMUTH	ALTITUDE
NOON		180°- 0'	40°- 0'
10:00	2:00	143°- 0'	34°- 0'
8:00	4:00	114°- 0'	18°- 30'
6:00	6:00	90°- 0'	0°- 0'

A.M.	P.M.	AZIMUTH	ALTITUDE
NOON		180°- 0'	63°- 30'
11:00	1:00	150°- 30'	61°- 0'
10:00	2:00	127°- 30'	54°- 30'
8:00	4:00	97°- 0'	37°- 0'
4:00	8:00	51°- 30'	0°- 0'

TABLE OF AZIMUTH AND ALTITUDE OF THE SUN
From Latitude 0° to 20° N. and 55° N. to 70° N.

	Dec. 22 WINTER			FALL Sept. 23 Mar. 21 SPRING			June 22 SUMMER		
	A.M.–P.M.	Azi.	Alt.	A.M.–P.M.	Azi.	Alt.	A.M.–P.M.	Azi.	Alt.
0°	Noon	180°–0'	66°–30'	Noon	90°–0'	90°–0'	Noon	0°–0'	66°–30'
	10–2	131°–0'	52°–30'	10–2	90°–0'	60°–0'	10–2	49°–0'	52°–30'
	8–4	116°–30'	27°–30'	8–4	90°–0'	30°–0'	8–4	63°–30'	27°–30'
	6–6	113°–30'	0°–0'	6–6	90°–0'	0°–0'	6–6	66°–30'	0°–0'
5° N.	Noon	180°–0'	61°–30'	Noon	180°–0'	85°–0'	Noon	0°–0'	71°–30'
	10–2	135°–30'	49°–0'	10–2	98°–30'	59°–30'	10–2	54°–30'	55°–30'
	8–4	119°–0'	25°–0'	8–4	93°–0'	30°–0'	8–4	66°–0'	29°–30'
	6:10–5:50	114°–0'	0°–0'	6–6	90°–0'	0°–0'	5:50–6:10	66°–30'	0°–0'
10° N.	Noon	180°–0'	56°–30'	Noon	180°–0'	80°–0'	Noon	0°–0'	76°–30'
	10–2	139°–0'	45°–30'	11–1	123°–0'	72°–0'	11–1	45°–0'	70°–30'
	8–4	120°–30'	22°–30'	10–2	106°–30'	58°–30'	10–2	61°–0'	58°–30'
	6:20–5:40	114°–0'	0°–0'	8–4	95°–30'	29°–30'	8–4	68°–30'	31°–30'
				6–6	90°–0'	0°–0'	5:40–6:20	66°–0'	0°–0'
15° N.	Noon	180°–0'	51°–30'	Noon	180°–0'	75°–0'	Noon	0°–0'	81°–30'
	10–2	142°–0'	41°–30'	11–1	134°–0'	69°–0'	11–1	56°–30'	73°–30'
	8–4	122°–30'	20°–0'	10–2	114°–0'	57°–0'	10–2	68°–30'	60°–30'
	6:30–5:30	114°–30'	0°–0'	8–4	98°–30'	29°–0'	8–4	71°–30'	33°–0'
				6–6	90°–0'	0°–0'	5:30–6:30	65°–30'	0°–0'
20° N.	Noon	180°–0'	46°–30'	Noon	180°–0'	70°–0'	Noon	0°–0'	86°–30'
	10–2	144°–30'	37°–30'	11–1	142°–0'	65°–0'	11:40–12:20	52°–0'	84°–0'
	8–4	124°–0'	17°–0'	10–2	120°–30'	54°–30'	11–1	73°–0'	75°–30'
	6:40–5:20	115°–0'	0°–0'	8–4	101°–0'	28°–0'	8–4	74°–30'	34°–30'
				6–6	90°–0'	0°–0'	5:20–6:40	65°–0'	0°–0'
55° N.	Noon	180°–0'	11°–30'	Noon	180°–0'	35°–0'	Noon	180°–0'	58°–30'
	10–2	152°–30'	7°–30'	10–2	145°–0'	30°–0'	11–1	154°–30'	56°–30'
	9–3	139°–30'	3°–0'	8–4	115°–30'	16°–30'	10–2	132°–30'	51°–30'
	8:30–3:30	134°–30'	0°–0'	6–6	90°–0'	0°–0'	8–4	100°–30'	36°–0'
							3:30–8:30	45°–30'	0°–0'
60° N.	Noon	180°–0'	6°–30'	Noon	180°–0'	30°–0'	Noon	180°–0'	53°–30'
	11:20–12:40	171°–0'	6°–0'	10–2	146°–30'	29°–30'	10–2	137°–0'	48°–0'
	10–2	153°–0'	3°–0'	8–4	116°–30'	14°–30'	8–4	104°–0'	35°–0'
	9:10–2:50	143°–0'	0°–0'	6–6	90°–0'	0°–0'	6–6	77°–30'	20°–0'
							2:50–9:10	37°–0'	0°–0'
65° N.	Noon	180°–0'	1°–30'	Noon	180°–0'	25°–0'	Noon	180°–0'	48°–30'
	10:30–1:30	162°–0'	0°–0'	10–2	147°–30'	21°–30'	10–2	140°–0'	44°–0'
				8–4	117°–30'	12°–0'	8–4	107°–30'	33°–30'
				6–6	90°–0'	0°–0'	6–6	79°–30'	21°–0'
							1:30–10:30	14°–30'	0°–0'
70° N. Sun does not rise from about Nov. 22nd to Jan. 21st				Noon	180°–0'	20°–0'	Noon	180°–0'	43°–30'
				10–2	148°–30'	17°–0'	10–2	143°–0'	40°–30'
				8–4	118°–30'	10°–0'	8–4	110°–30'	36°–0'
				6–6	90°–0'	0°–0'	6–6	81°–30'	22°–0'
							4–8	54°–30'	12°–30'
							Midnite	0°–0'	3°–30'

By HANS J. MILTON, FRAIA, *Technical Consultant and Chairman, ASTM Committee E-6.62, Coordination of Dimensions for Building Materials and Systems.*

Incorporating material from the Fifth Edition, prepared by BYRON BLOOMFIELD, AIA, formerly Executive Director, Modular Building Standards Association.

BACKGROUND

Any building, when completed, represents an entity made up of thousands of individual components that have been "coordinated"—or fitted together—on site. In historical buildings, individual components were generally custom made and fitted by master craftsmen, and the total range of building materials was small. With the advent of industrialization, new materials, systems (such as electrical or mechanical services), and assembly techniques were introduced. Today, buildings are composed of manufactured products that come from a wide variety of sources, are often unrelated in dimensions, and which are then assembled by skilled or semiskilled workers. Concrete is used extensively for structural and fire-protection purposes and has the advantage that it can be cast to predetermined dimensions and shapes. All buildings are now based on prototype drawings and details, which have to be clearly understood by all parties and which form the basis for building approval at the local government level.

It is against this background that a technique for the systematic selection of preferred dimensions for buildings and related sizes of components became a necessity in order to improve the economy of all phases of design, production, and construction. The technique for dimensional rationaliztion and coordination of dimensions now in worldwide use in building is *modular coordination.*

MODULAR COORDINATION IN THE UNITED STATES

Modular coordination originated in the United States during the 1920s and 1930s, and is largely credited to the pioneering work of the American industrialist Albert Farwell Bemis (1870–1936), who outlined comprehensive principles for dimensional coordination based on a cubical modular method of design using a 4-in module as fundamental unit.[1] The concept provided for an all-inclusive basis to "precoordinate" the dimensions of structural components, building materials, and installed equipment, founded on "modular lines as a design matrix" and standard grids with a 4-in. interval for the referencing of building plans and assembly details. Bemis' ideas, both profound and simple, have given impetus to the notion of prefabrication, which removes activity from the building site to the factory where better quality control and volume production are possible.

In 1938, the heirs of Mr. Bemis founded the Modular Service Association as a nonprofit corporation to assist the building industry in developing dimensional coordination. The industry effort led to a standards development project (A62) in the American Standards Association, the forerunner of ANSI, with the American Institute of Architects and The Producers' Council as joint sponsors. ASA Project A62 led to the development and adoption of a series of national standards between 1945 and 1947, and in 1968 and 1971.[2] These documents are all based on the 4-in module, which is represented by the symbol M, and they still provide sound references on the concepts of modular coordination. In 1974, the responsibility for the development of standards on dimensional coordination was transferred to the American Society for Testing and Materials (ASTM), and a new Subcommittee, E-6.62, was formed to continue the work in both U.S. customary (foot-inch) units and metric (SI) units.

In January 1977, ANSI/ASTM E 577-76, "Standard for Dimensional Coordination of Rectilinear Building Parts and Systems,"[3] was published. Though largely based on earlier work, it introduced a novel concept of assigning the symbol U—for unit dimension—to the 100-mm module in metric units and the 4-in. module in customary units. While this simplifies "modular" preferences, their actual dimensions would differ in metric and nonmetric units, due to the 1.6 per cent difference between 4 in. [101.6 mm] and 100 mm. This could lead to difficulties during a transition to metric measurement; therefore, the standard is now subject to review and reissue in separate "companion" standards.

INTERNATIONAL MODULAR COORDINATION

Modular coordination efforts in Europe began in the 1940s, and were based on a 100-mm (10-cm) module right from the beginning, except in Germany, where an octametric module of 125 mm was initially proposed. By 1954, 10 countries had adopted the basic module of 100 mm, and cooperative efforts increased first under the auspices of the European Productivity Agency and, later, the International Organization for Standardization (ISO). A number of international standards on the subject have been issued by ISO since 1973,[4] and, except for the United States, the 100-mm basic module is now accepted throughout the metric building world. All countries that have changed from nonmetric to metric dimensions in recent years have made a simultaneous switch to the metric building module. Due to the similarity of building techniques, Canadian precedent is of most interest to the U.S., and National Standard of Canada CAN3-A31.M-75, "Series of Standards for Metric Dimensional Coordination,"[5] gives well-presented guidance on the principles and practical application of controlling and coordinating dimensions.

A comprehensive list of international and national standards from over 50 countries on dimensional coordination, modular coordination, tolerances, and joints in building was issued by the National Bureau of Standards as NBS Special Publication 595.[6] The document illustrates the widespread adoption of modular principles and the 100-mm building module around the world.

The significant difference between metric and customary modular coordination arises from the choice of module: In metric units, all modular dimensions are immediately visible as they have two zeros (00) as last digits in the numerical value; moreover, the multiplier, or multimodule, is the number in front of the two zeros, so that a designer can see at the outset whether a dimension is highly divisible (such as 4800 mm), or a prime number multiple, (such as 4700 mm). In customary units, the multiplier is generally concealed because of the use of two measurement units, feet and inches. For example, it is not immediately apparent that 10'-8" represents 32 modules or is a whole multiple of 16 in., while a metric dimension of 3200 mm would give this information directly. An additional advantage of the 100-mm module is that the square with sides of one module is exactly one hundredth of a square meter (0.01 m^2) making estimating and cost calculations much easier, compared with the customary square module (16 in.²), which equals one ninth of a square foot and one eighty-first of a square yard. The metric cubic module has a volume of exactly one thousandth of a cubic meter (0.001 m^3), or one liter (1 L), thus facilitating all volumetric calculations in modular buildings.

OBJECTIVES OF MODULAR COORDINATION

The principal aim of modular coordination is to achieve dimensional compatibility between building dimensions, spans, or spaces and the sizes of components and equipment, by using related modular dimensions for both. This reduces the need for "special" sizes, minimizes the need for field cutting, and simplifies practices in the drafting office and in estimating. An industry-wide system of coordinated sizes gives the designer more "interchangeable" alternatives for horizontal and vertical building elements.

MODULAR COORDINATION – 2
Theory

A comparison of conventional (uncoordinated) building components and a coordinated range of components is shown in Figs. 1 and 2.

As the U.S. building and construction industry has not as yet formulated a position on metric conversion, most examples in this section have been chosen to reflect traditional U.S. practices.

BASIC PRINCIPLES OF MODULAR COORDINATION

The basis of the modular method in component sizing is dimensioning from *joint-centerline to joint-centerline*, using multiples of the standard module of 4 in. (or 100 mm). Therefore, the modular size of a component is an "ideal size" which takes into account half a joint thickness all round—the actual size is generally smaller. The joint thickness is computed to allow for manufacturing deviations and installation clearances so that there is neither a need to cut materials nor an excessive clearance to be filled up or covered over.

Figure 3 shows the basic sizing of a component and the concepts of a minimum and maximum acceptable joint thickness to accommodate positive and negative deviations in manufacturing, and indicates limits (minimum and maximum dimensions). Different components have different joint thickness requirements, but for all modular products one-half the minimum joint thickness at any edge must provide an adequate clearance for installation.

The joint-centerline to joint-centerline principle is illustrated for a modular masonry unit (Fig. 4), which also indicates how the actual size of a modular component is determined—in this case the joint thickness is 3/8 in. Note the undersizing of the component on all faces by the thickness of the half-joints.

The method of combining modular components is illustrated in Fig. 5., showing a door frame assembly located within different surrounds. Note that the outside dimensions of the frame assembly are important, not the size of the door itself.

The method applies to all modular components, assemblies of components, building parts (elements or systems), and dimensions of building spaces.

COORDINATING PLANES AND LINES

Modular coordination uses a three-dimensional (orthogonal) modular space grid in which the grid lines are one module apart, as shown in Fig. 6, parallel, and mutually perpendicular to each other. The space grid can also be considered as a three-dimensional system of horizontal and vertical reference planes, one module apart. Various conventions have been used to designate the coordinates, so that any point on the grid can be referenced in relation to a datum, or zero datum point. ANSI A62.8-1971, "American Standard Numerical Designation of Modular Grid Coordinates," provides a systematic numerical shorthand for the location of reference planes, lines, and

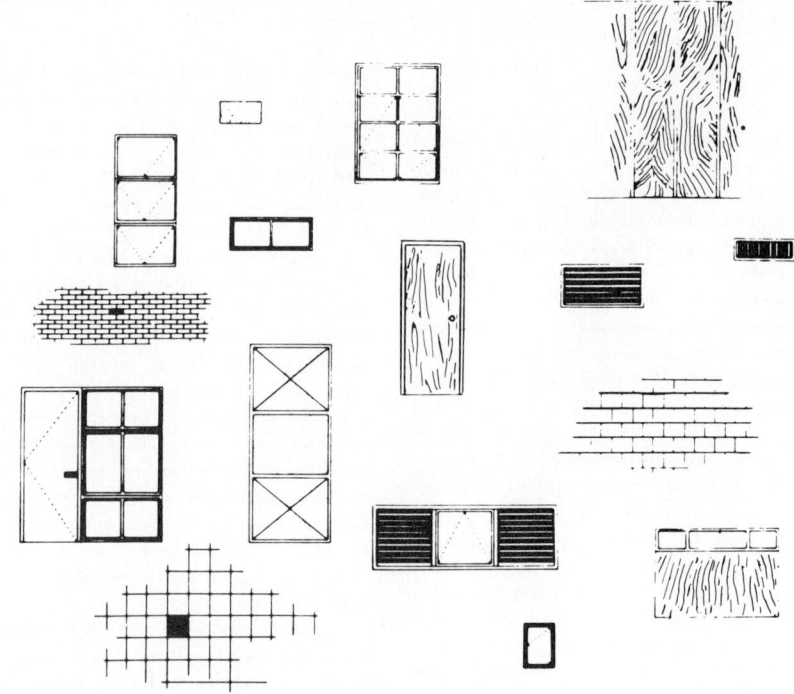

Fig. 1.   Conventional components of a specific building

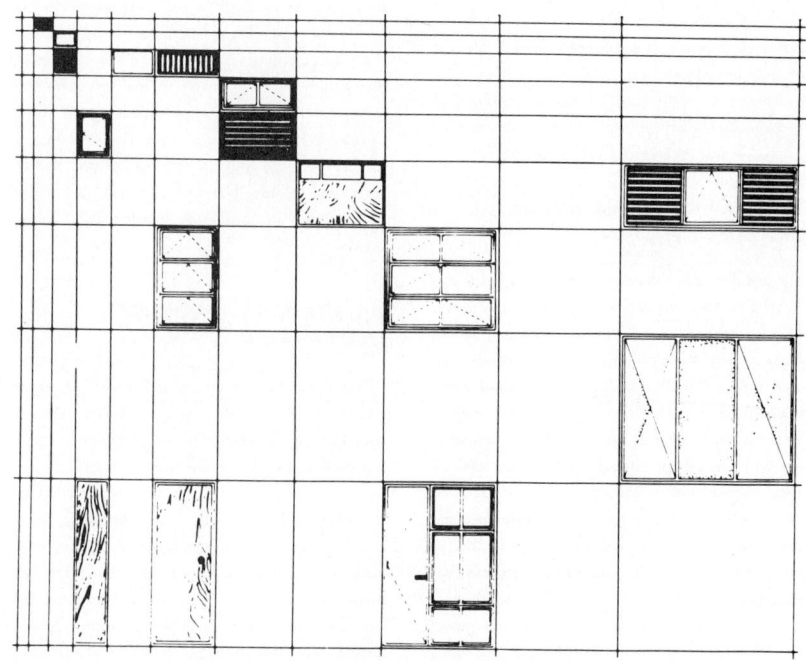

Fig. 2.   Coordinated range of components

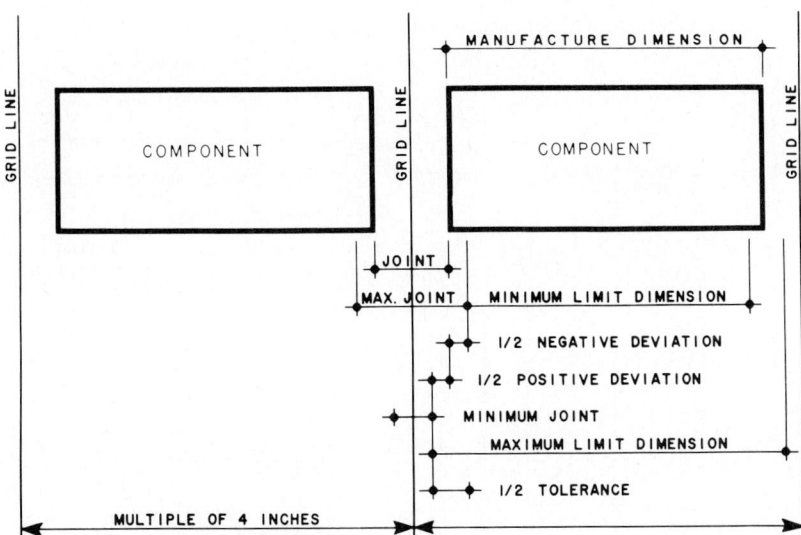

Fig. 3. Basis for sizing a component

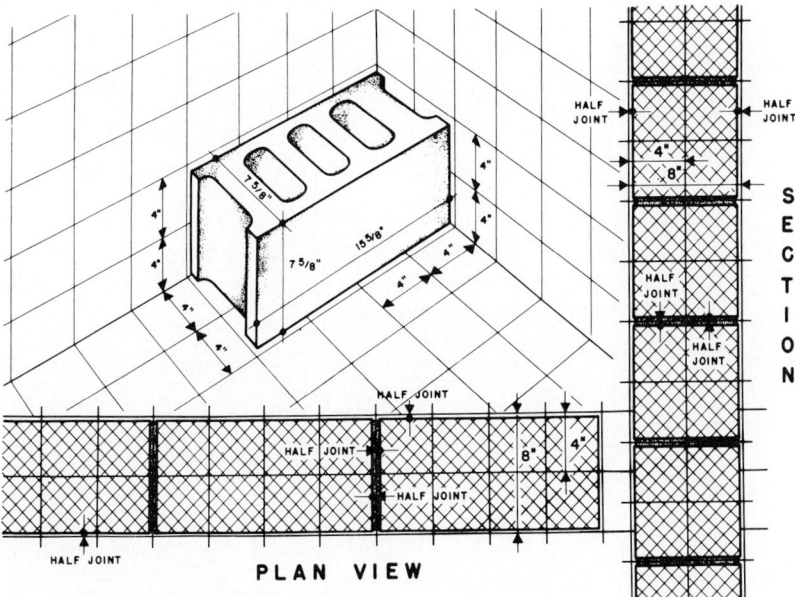

Fig. 4. Example of a modular unit

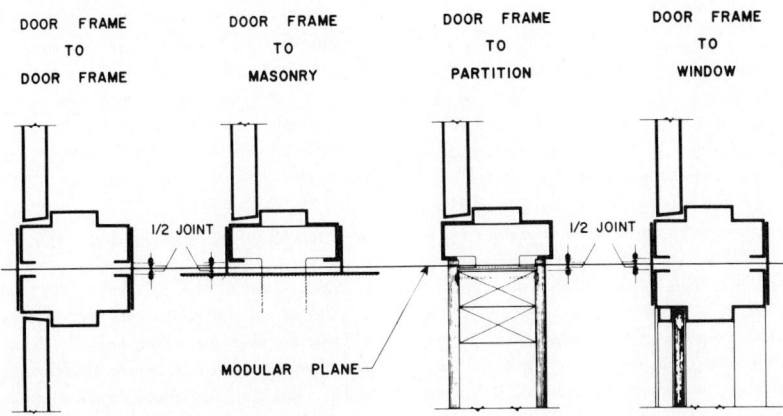

Fig. 5. Combining modular components

MODULAR COORDINATION – 4
Application to building systems

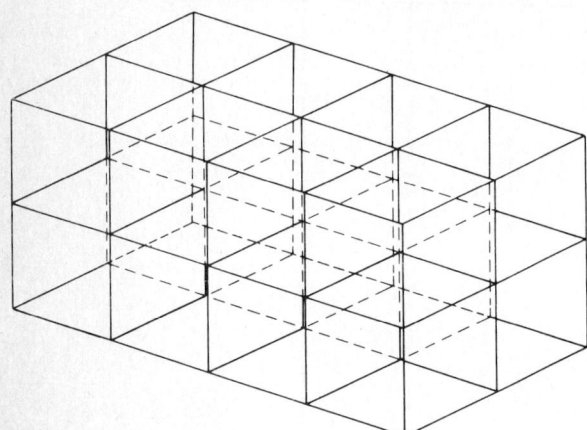

Fig. 6. The modular space grid

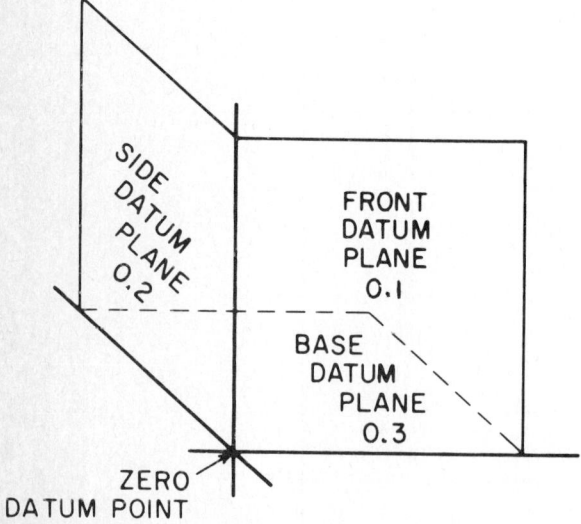

Fig. 7. Position of the coordinate datum planes and their numerical designation

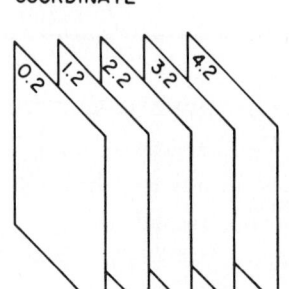

DATUM COORDINATE

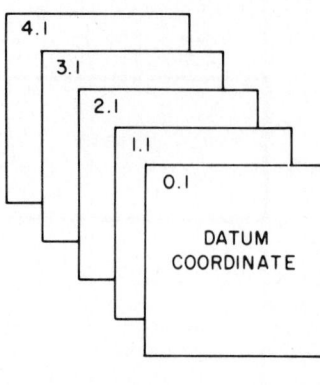

DATUM COORDINATE

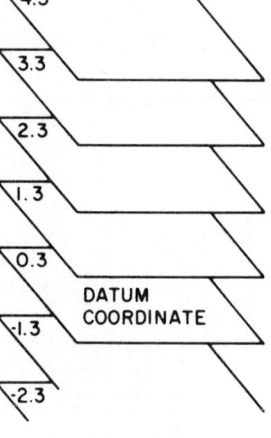

DATUM COORDINATE

Fig. 8. Numerical designation of coordinates

points in relation to a zero datum point, as shown in Fig. 7. All coordinate planes parallel to a datum plane are identified by the same number following the decimal point as that which identifies the datum plane in the particular direction. All coordinate planes parallel to 0.1 are identified by the suffix .1; all planes parallel to 0.2 by suffix .2; and all planes parallel to 0.3 by the suffix .3. The distance from the datum plane, in multiples of the basic module, is indicated by the number in front of the decimal point. For example, coordinate plane 2.1 is parallel to datum plane 0.1 at a distance of two basic modules. The designation 24.2 indicates a coordinate parallel to datum coordinate 0.2 at a distance of 24 basic modules.

Positive numbers are used as follows:

1. In the .1 series, from the front datum plane toward the back

2. In the .2 series, from the side datum plane on the left toward the right
3. In the .3 series, from the base datum plane upward

For any locations in opposite directions from the zero datum, negative numbers are used. However, with an appropriate choice of zero datum point, this would be rare. A graphic representation of the coordinate numbering system is shown in Fig. 8.

The referencing of building parts and components by coordinates is useful in plan formulation, detailing, and, especially, in computer applications. When noting the position of a component, its relation to the 0.1 coordinate series is noted first, the 0.2 series next, and the 0.3 series last. When all three dimensions are specified, the coordinate series need not be shown, since the sequence does so automatically. Thus, a no-

tation 34–38, 8–16, and 21–24 indicates that a component lies between 34.1 and 38.1, between 8.2 and 16.2, and between 21.3 and 24.3. The notation 34/8/21 to designate the coordinate datum point, and the notation of component size 4M/8M/3M would have conveyed the same information. The datum point for a component is established at its lower left-front corner as placed in the building. In the change to metric modular dimensions, this method of numerical designation has the advantage that the numerical designations can be converted directly to millimeters by adding two zeros. For example, a datum point 34/8/21 is located 3400 mm toward the back of the zero datum.

APPLICATION TO BUILDING SYSTEMS

Coordination in the horizontal plane of a building can be related to the surfaces of structural elements, called *boundary lines,* or to the centerlines of structural elements, called *axial lines.* The establishment of modular preferences reduces the variety of multiples of the basic module used in a project.

For large spans or spaces, a larger module called the *systems module* (SM) has been established, equal to 60 modules (1SM = 60M = 20 ft in customary units, and 1SM = 60M = 6000 mm in metric units). Preferred coordinating dimensions for the horizontal plane and building components are 30M, 20M, 15M, 12M, 10M, 6M, 5M, 4M, 3M, and 2M, all of which are subunits of 60M.

Coordination in the vertical plane of a building can be related to controlling reference lines at the floor plane, ceiling plane, or roof plane. In addition, window and door head and window sill lines form an intermediate controlling plane in many buildings. Figure 9 shows the application of preferred vertical dimensions. The values given in ANSI A62.7-1969, "American National Standard Basis for the Vertical Dimensioning of Coordinated Building Components and Systems," and ANSI/ASTM E 577-76[3] differ, inasmuch as the former favors 4M and 2M increments while the latter prefers 3M increments and values more in line with ISO recommendations. The list of preferred dimensions provides both series, with common values emphasized, but wherever possible compatible preferences should be used.

Where structural or economic factors prevent adherence to coordinated dimensions, a second preference would be to select a whole multiple of the basic module not included in the schedule in Fig. 9's legend. Where this is not possible, the designer should handle the nonconforming dimensions as an uncoordinated neutral zone; for example, in a single-story building without suspended ceiling it may not be economically feasible for the horizontal structure thickness of the roof to be a coordinated dimension. In such an instance, the choice is between a preferred dimension for the story height (A) or the ceiling height (B).

ON-SITE TOLERANCES

For practical on-site layout, the accuracy in positioning elements and coordinates is dependent upon measuring instruments and practices. Laser levels can reduce inaccuracies, but the range of tolerances indicated in Table 1 should be used in accuracy calculations.

MODULAR DRAFTING

To complement modular principles, modular drafting techniques have been developed for use by the architectural drafter as well as the manufacturer.

There is little gain in having building components manufactured in modular sizes if modular methods are not used in the design

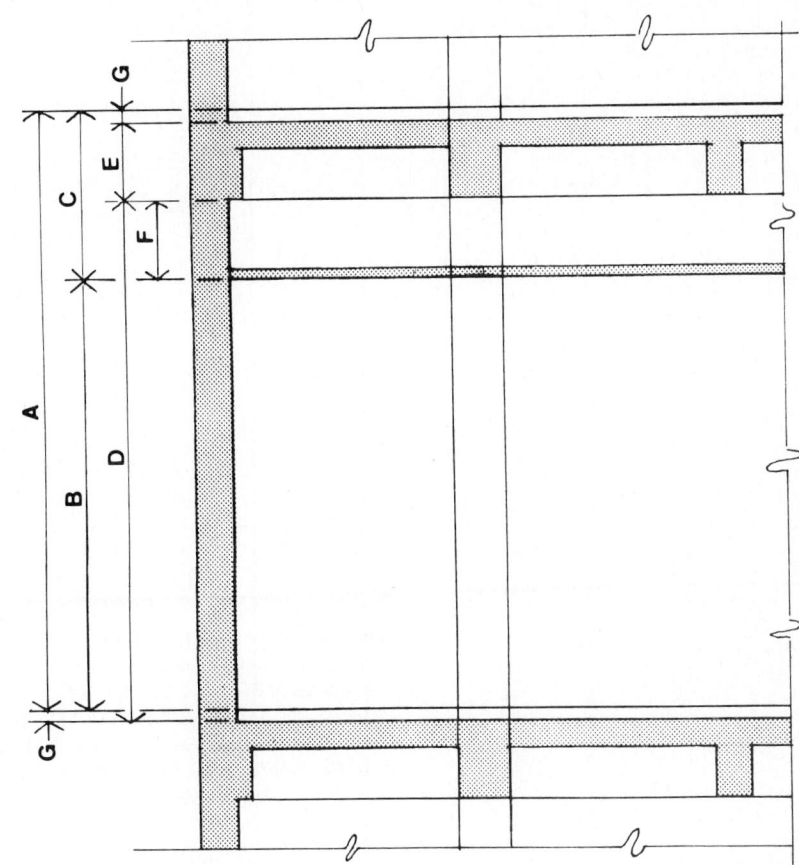

Fig. 9. Application of preferred dimensions

Vertical building element	Preferred modular dimensions
A Story height	28M, 32M, *36M*, 40M, *48M*
	27M, 30M, 33M, *36M*, 39M, 42M, 45M, *48M*
B Ceiling height	20M, *24M*, 28M, 32M, *36M*
	24M, 27M, 30M, 33M, *36M*
C Floor-ceiling thickness thickness	4M, 8M, *12M*
	3M, 6M, 9M, *12M*
D Structural column height (Clear structure height)	20M to 48M in 2M increments
E Horizontal structure thickness (Structural floor thickness)	2M, 4M, 6M, 8M
	Multiple of M when greater than 3M
F Ceiling space dimension	*2M, 4M, 6M, 8M*
	2M, 3M, 4M, 6M, 9M
G Floor finish thickness	**No preferred thickness**

Table 1. Range of tolerances for on-site layout of coordinates

Spacing of coordinates	Acceptable tolerance
1M to 20M	+ ³⁄₆₄ in. (1 mm)
	− 0
Over 20M to 60M (1 SM)	+ ⁵⁄₆₄ in. (2 mm)
	− 0
Over 1 SM to 3 SM	+ ⅛ in. (3 mm)
	− 0
Over 3 SM (180M)	+ $\sqrt{\text{no. of SMs}} \times$ ⅛ in. (3 mm)
	− 0

The grid interval is one basic module (4 in. or 100 mm), horizontally or vertically throughout the structure. It should be shown on all drawings requiring dimensional reference points.

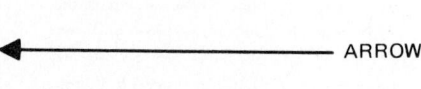

To be used exclusively for modular dimensions related to grid lines. (An open 45-degree arrow is used internationally.)

Fig. 10. Modular drafting conventions

Note: Use of the same type of arrow for modular dimensions and for notes results in some confusion. This can be avoided by the use of the international standard open arrow with 45-degree sides for modular dimensions and a narrow solid arrow for notes.

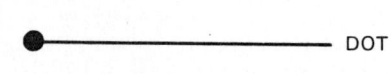

To be used for dimensional reference to points other than grid lines. Use only where essential to the clarity of a drawing.

and detailing of buildings. Fortunately, modular drafting conventions are few and simple and require no extra effort to put into practice.

The three basic conventions include the grid, the arrowhead, and the dot (Fig. 10). The grids provide imaginary reference planes extending through the structure in a three-dimensional eggcrate fashion, 4 in. (100 mm) on center in all directions. When drafting, the architect actually draws certain grid lines on large-scale drawings to provide key dimensional reference planes (or controlling planes), such as the location of foundation lines, floor lines, and door or window heads and jambs. A larger multiple of the 4-in. (100-mm) module, called a multimodule, may be used as a planning grid and shown on certain plans.

The arrowhead is used for all dimensions that originate or terminate on a modular grid line. In the U.S., a solid arrow has been commonly used, while an open arrow is used in international practice. Dots are used on all dimensions that are off the grid and nonmodular.

Two observations can be made: (1) If only dots were used on a drawing, it would not differ from any "premodular" architectural drawing, and (2) the fewer the number of dots and the greater the number of arrowheads, the greater the simplicity of the structure and the fewer the joining problems. Theoretically, if only arrowheads were shown, the architect would enjoy the ultimate in drafting simplicity and the building would benefit from the ultimate in construction simplicity.

The use of standardized drafting conventions throughout the dimensioning of all plans, elevations, and details reduces the need for fractional dimensions and the corresponding possibility of errors in the addition or subtraction of series of dimensions involving such fractions. The drawings are simpler to prepare and simpler to use, resulting in savings during all stages: preliminaries, working drawings, details, shop drawings, checking, estimating, field layout, and supervision.

Modular masonry units

Let us consider, for example, the use of modular dimensioning in the assembly of *un-*its to comprise a building element in masonry construction. Figure 11 shows the relative positions of the masonry *units* to the grid lines in *plan* and *section*. The actual units would not, of course, appear in the final plan, nor would the grid lines. Notice that the arrowheads identify the locations of the grid planes. The final plan expression is shown in Fig. 12, and further illustrates the use of the drafting conventions.

The use of dots and arrows quickly reveals that the column centerlines are not on grid planes, although the distances between columns are indeed multiples of 4 in. Jointing conditions around the windows will be further defined as the architect develops his larger-scale window details. One of the chief virtues of this procedure is that it permits significant details to be worked out before their relationships are made final in working drawings.

From the preliminaries, it is possible to determine the critical jointing conditions. The room dimensions and wall thicknesses will determine the location of grid references. Starting with the intersection of the principal horizontal and vertical grids, the detail

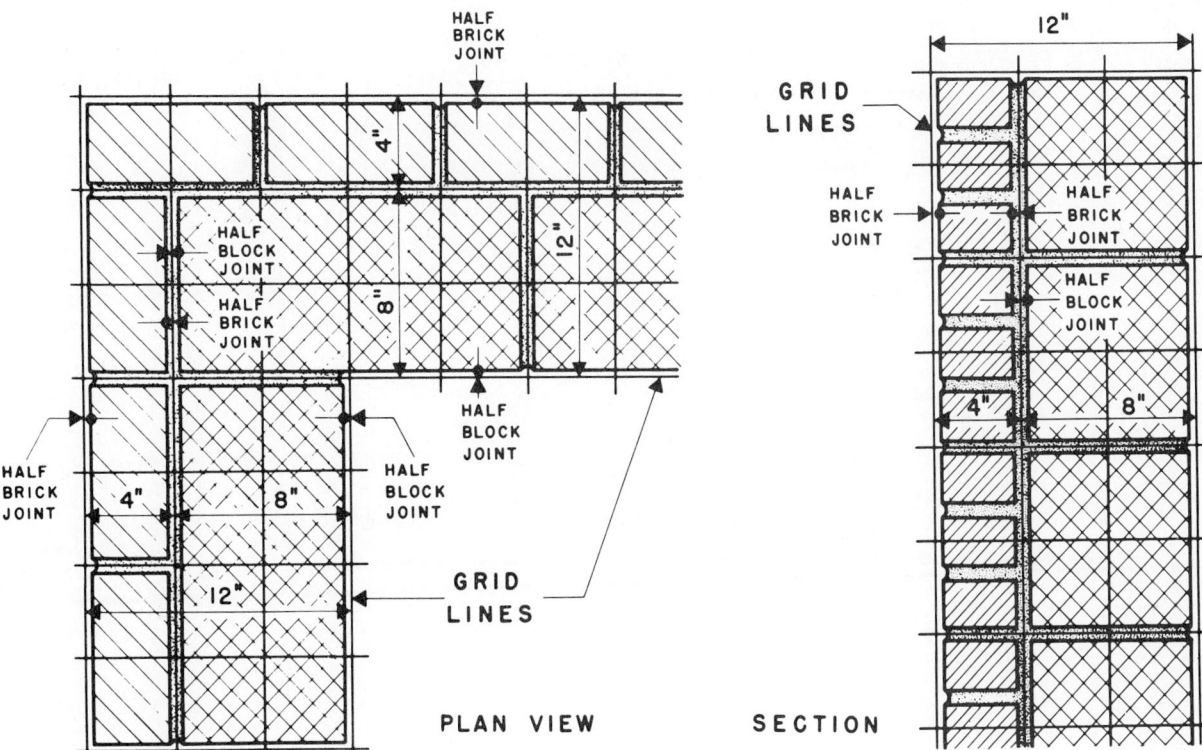

Fig. 11. Expression of modular grid in plan and section

PLAN VIEW   SECTION

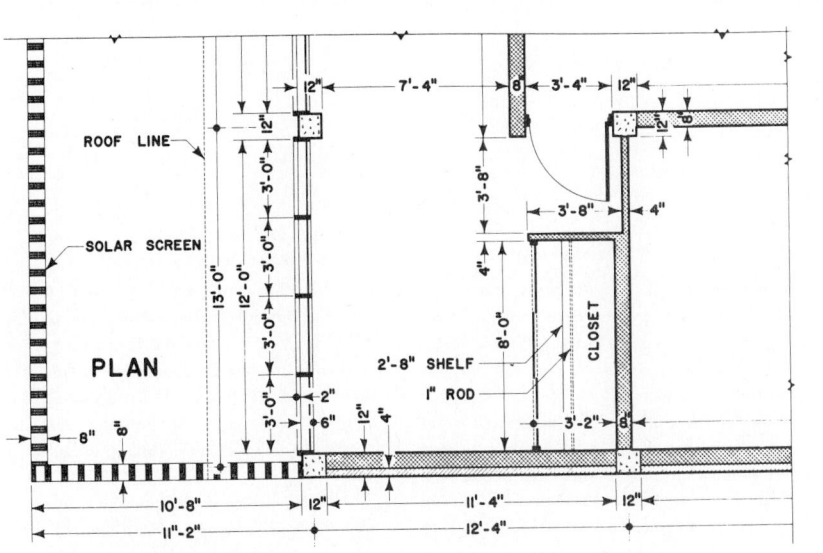

Fig. 12. Dimensioned masonry plan

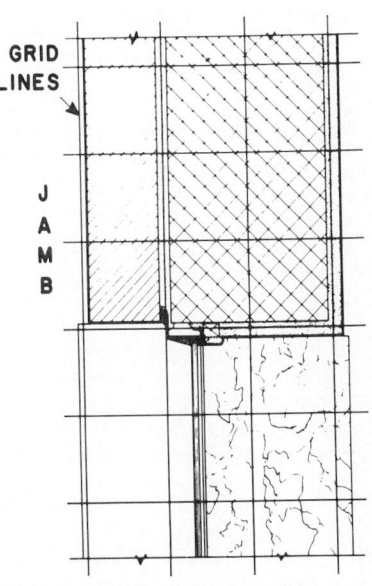

Fig. 13. Modular window detail

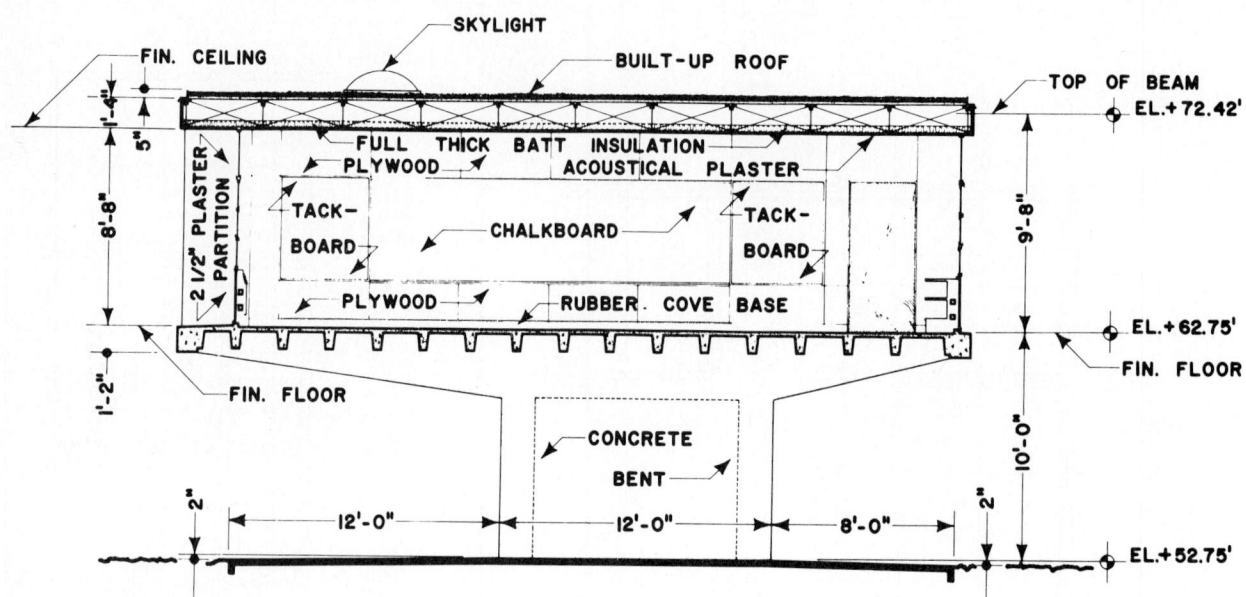

Fig. 14.   Cross section of a modular building

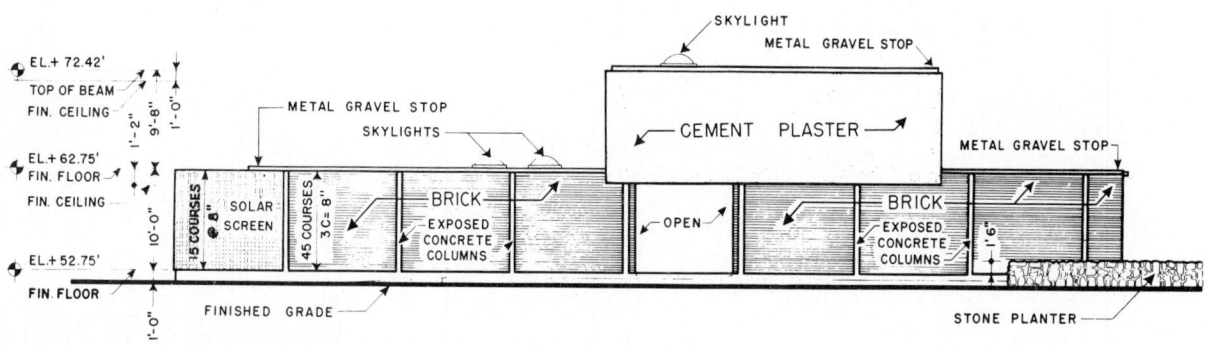

Fig. 15.   Exterior elevation of a modular building

can then be rapidly worked out in freehand or drafted in final form. All that remains is to correlate plan and detail by simply showing on the plan the location of the same reference grid lines used in the large detail. The development of such a detail is shown in Fig. 13.

The application of dimensions to full cross sections is shown in Fig. 14. Note that many of the dimensions and dimensional reference points correspond to the elevation shown in Fig. 15. In both cases, the dimensional reference points identified by arrowheads can be easily located on the large-scale details and also serve as reference planes for structural drawings. Figure 16 shows the evolution of a large-scale detail from its relationship in cross section. To start the detail study, the intersection of the floor grid plane and the principal foundation grid plane was marked off. From this point, it was then possible to relate, downward, the floor-slab thickness, insulation, gravel fill, and top of footing. From the outside foundation grid plane the foundation thickness and sill-width dimensions were then established. Although it is optional, the complete 4-in. grid, horizontally and vertically, is shown on the working-drawing detail.

The brick-veneer construction shown in Fig. 17 is an example of the choices available in delineating modular construction. In

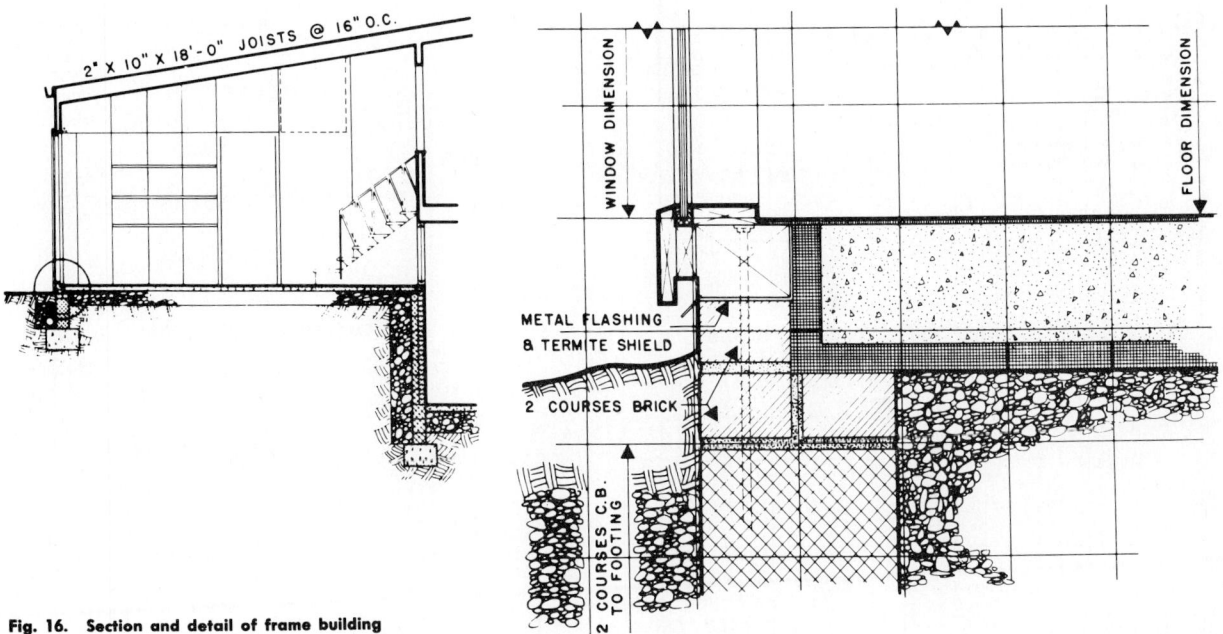

Fig. 16. Section and detail of frame building

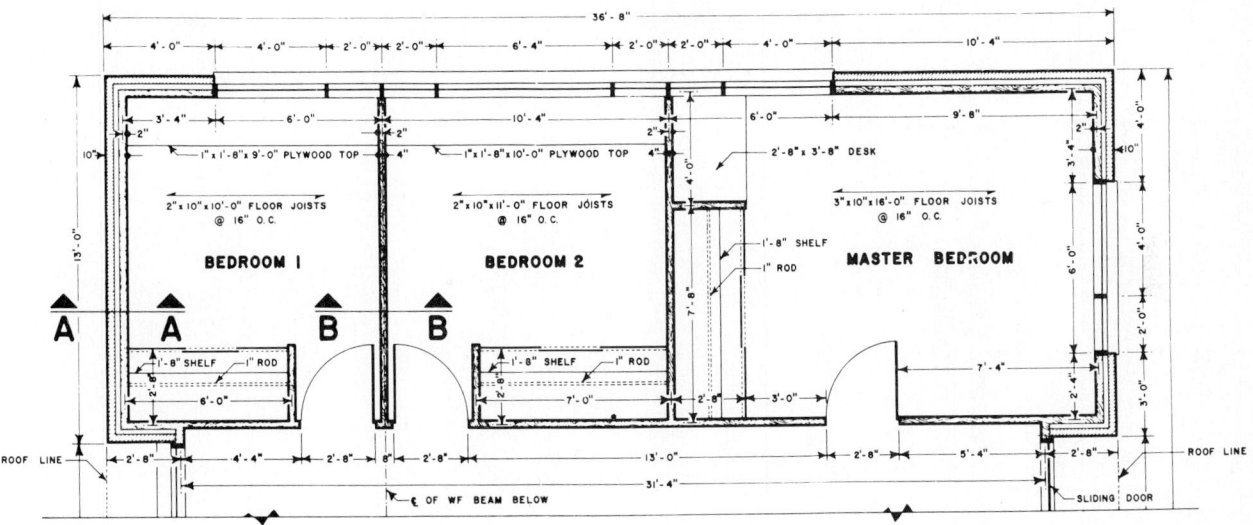

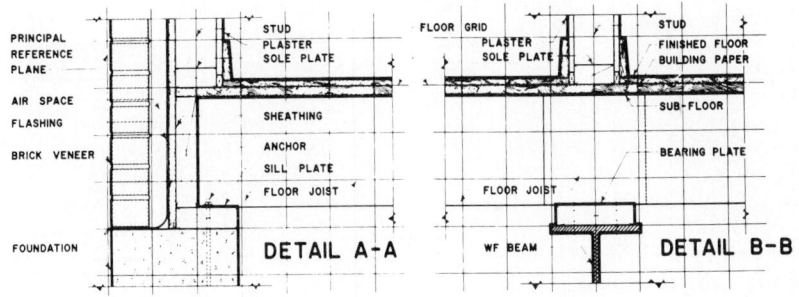

Fig. 17. Plan and details of brick-veneer construction

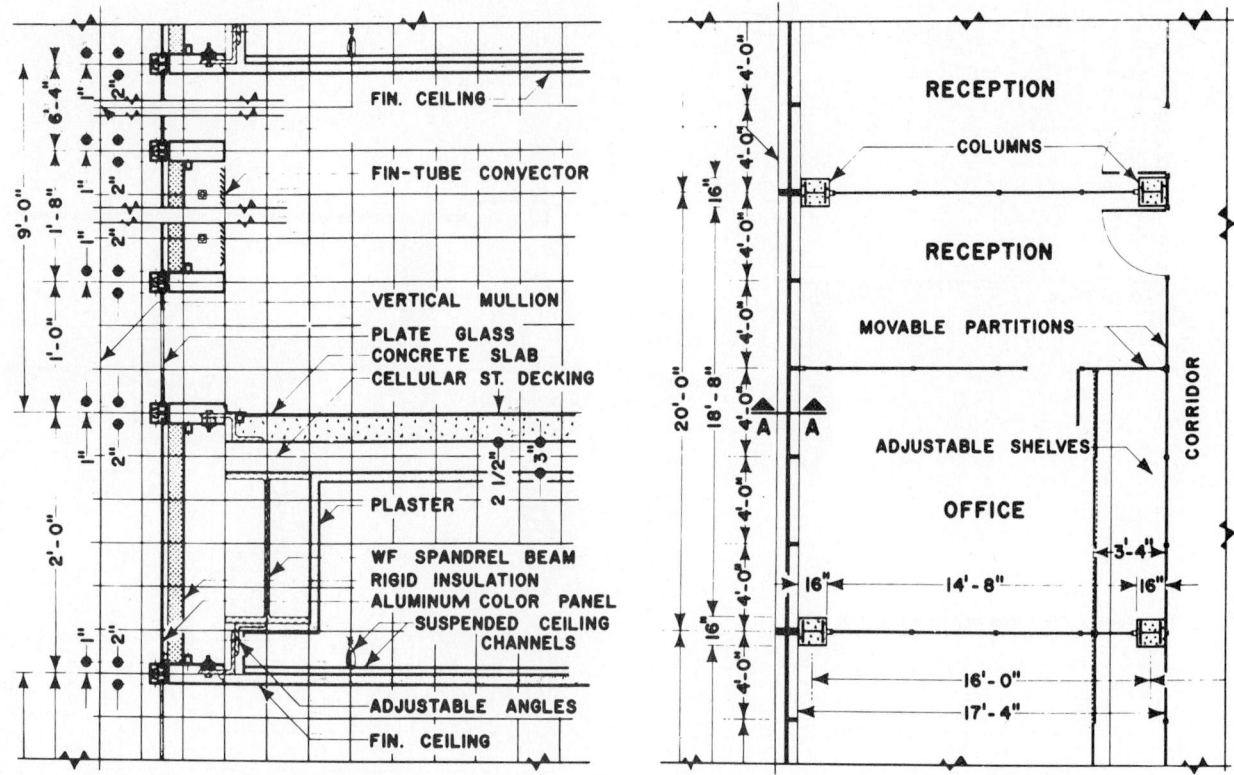

Fig. 18. Plan and detail of modular curtain wall

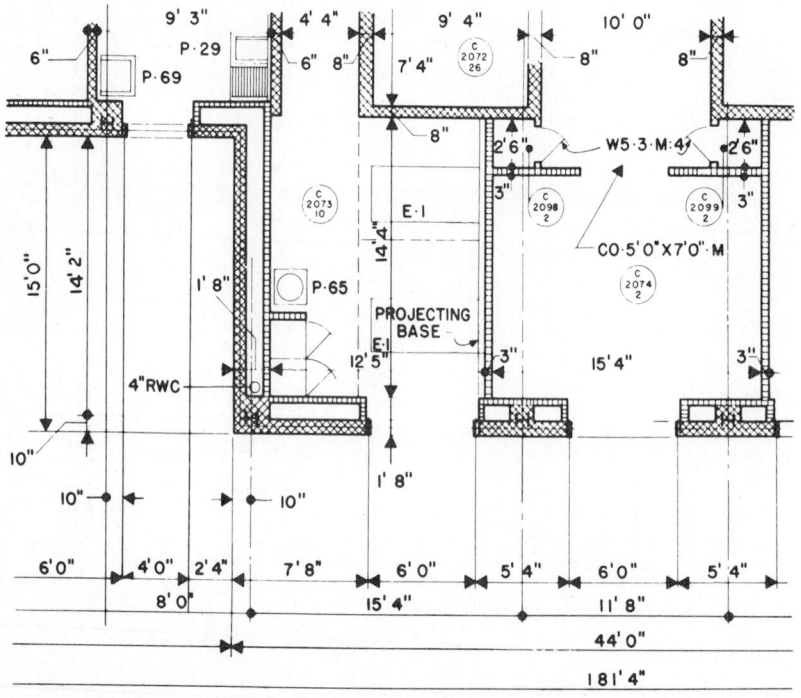

Fig. 19. Dimensioning of skeleton-frame construction

general, typical wood-frame construction is most efficiently planned when the stud framing members are centered *between* grid lines. Then both the sheathing and the interior finish materials can be efficiently installed in multiples of 4 in. In masonry veneer, however, the 10-in. total wall thickness requires further consideration of the best location of grid lines. Either the studs or the masonry may be centered between grid lines. Construction efficiency would not necessarily be affected by either choice; the over-all masonry, gypsum board, and sheathing dimensions would still remain multiples of 4 in. However, the drawings themselves are simplified by making the outside reference planes conform to the masonry placement and using centerline notations for all wood-frame interior partitions, as shown in Fig. 17.

Another decision that must be made by the architect is the method of construction. Notice that in detail A-A of Fig. 17 the *floor grid* does not coincide with an 8-in. increment of masonry. Door heads, window heads, and eave details must all be considered in establishing the first course of brick. Depending on these details, it might be better to provide an offset in the poured foundation to permit the alignment of the floor grid with a horizontal brick joint. Again, the detail is generated by establishing the principal grids and then determining the desired construction method.

Panelized construction usually results in simpler dimensional relationships than other types of construction. Modular drafting is particularly appropriate for panelized construction because it permits easy and continuous checking for the most efficient use of standard production items.

For purposes of illustration and study, detail A-A of Fig. 18 includes the complete modular grid. Also, all sash-extrusion sizes have been shown, although under normal conditions the principal grids, plus a typical mullion size, would be adequate. From the plan and detail drawings, the structural engineer can easily establish the proper steel sizes, plan location, and elevations. (See also Fig. 19.)

In general, modular coordination is a dimensional reference system that encourages simplified construction details and takes advantage of the inherent dimensional qualities of modular building materials and components. It applies to any type of construction in which the plan and structural elements are geometric in character.

Freedom of design is not undesirably affected by the use of modular coordination.

Both designing and preparation of drawings on a modular basis follow closely the conventional methods; the only important difference is the helpful discipline of a 4-in. grid. The small size of the grid and the possibility of integrating nonmodular-sized items permit as infinite a variety of plan and elevation solutions as the more traditional practices.

Planning on a modular system can be divided into five steps:

1. Preliminary drawings
2. Selection of over-all dimensions
3. Identification of significant details
4. Development of modular details
5. Correlation of details on working drawings.

Preliminary plans are developed from the schematics prepared for presentation to the client and for cost estimates. The grid placement, discussed on the preceding pages, should be carefully studied at this stage. The 4-in. grid may be used for these plans, but more often a large layout module using some multiple of 4 in., say 4 ft 8 in., is employed. Grid lines are not usually shown at the small scale of these drawings.

Over-all dimensions for the entire structure, wall lengths, opening widths and heights, partition locations, and the like should all be planned in multiples of 4 in. to ensure agreement of plans with grid, and to eliminate unnecessary details.

Significant details should be chosen for development into working drawings; duplications should be avoided. Similar sills, heads, jambs, and other details that fall on corresponding grid openings need only be shown once.

Modular details are then chosen from standards or catalogs, or if these do not satisfy the problem, are individually developed.

Correlation of details with working drawings is accomplished by the use of appropriate symbols to key the detail to plans and sections.

Modular architectural plans are most successful if the structural drawings are also modular. Simplified checking results when all shop drawings are submitted on the basis of modular drafting. These considerations are often included in the engineering contract and in the appropriate paragraphs of the bidding documents. Most contractors in the United States have already built at least one modular project, and thus are familiar with the dimensioning system and its use in construction layouts. Some architects include notes on the dimensioning conventions on the first sheet of their drawings.

Prepared notes can be purchased from the Stanpat Company, Port Washington, New York.

REFERENCES

1. Albert Farwell Bemis and John Burchard II: *The Evolving House: Volume III, Rational Design,* The Technology Press, Cambridge; 1936

2. American National Standards Institute (ANSI): A62 Series, issued by ANSI, 1430 Broadway, New York, NY 10018:

ANSI (ASA) A62.1—1957	American Standard Basis for the Coordination of Dimensions of Building Materials and Equipment, 2 ed.
ANSI (ASA) A62.2—1945	American Standard Basis for the Coordination of Masonry
ANSI (ASA) A62.3—1946	American Standard Sizes of Clay and Concrete Modular Masonry Units
ANSI (ASA) A62.4—1947	American Standard Sizes of Clay Flue Linings
ANSI (USAS) A62.5—1968	USA Standard Basis for the Horizontal Dimensioning of Coordinated Building Components and Systems
ANSI A62.6—1969	American National Standard Classification for Properties and

ANSI A62.7—1969 Performances of Coordinated Building Components and Systems

ANSI A62.8—1971 American National Standard Basis for the Vertical Dimensioning of Coordinated Building Components and Systems

American National Standard Numerical Designation of Modular Grid Coordinates

3. American Society for Testing and Materials (ASTM): 1916 Race Street, Philadelphia, PA 19103:

ANSI/ASTM E 577—76 Standard for Dimensional Coordination of Rectilinear Building Parts and Systems

4. International Standards issued by the International Organization for Standardization (ISO), Geneva, Switzerland:

ISO 1006—1973 Modular Coordination—Basic Module

ISO 1040—1973 Modular Coordination—Multimodules for Horizontal Coordinating Dimensions

ISO 1789—1973 Modular Coordination—Story Heights and Room Heights for Residential Buildings

ISO 1971—1973 Modular Coordination—Vocabulary (English and French)

ISO 2776—1974 Modular Coordination—Coordinating Sizes for Doorsets: External and Internal

ISO 2777—1974 Modular Coordination—Coordinating Sizes for Rigid Flat Sheet Boards Used in Building

ISO 2848—1974 Modular Coordination—Principles and Rules

ISO 3881—1977 Building Construction—Modular Coordination—Stairs and Stair Openings: Coordinating Dimensions

5. Canadian National Standards, A31 Series, issued by the Canadian Standards Association (CSA), Rexdale, Ontario, Canada:

CAN3-A31.M-75 Series of Standards for Metric Dimensional Coordination

Part 1: Glossary of Terms for Metric Dimensional Coordination in Building

Part 2: Principles and Rules for Dimensional Coordination in Buildings

Part 3: Controlling Dimensions in Building

Part 4: Recommended Metric Coordinating Dimensions for the Sizing of Building Components

Part 5: A Guide to the Establishment of Tolerances for Metric Dimensional Coordination in Building

6. National Bureau of Standards (NBS), U.S. Department of Commerce: NBS Special Publication 595, "International and National Standards on Dimensional Coordination, Modular Coordination, Tolerances and Joints in Building," October 1980. Available through Superintendent of Documents, U.S. Government Printing Office, Washington, DC 20402 ($5.00)

By WILLIAM T. MEYER, Architect; Associate, Building Systems Development, San Francisco

Industrialized building systems have now been developed to the point where their existence should be recognized by architects and viewed as additional factors to be considered when developing a building design for a client, particularly in the area of housing or schools. Quite often the architect will find that definite potential for reducing construction time and cost and increasing building flexibility may be obtained without any significant design limitations if an industrialized building system is selected for constructing the building he is designing.

An architect who is unfamiliar with industrialized building systems but wishes to consider the possibility of their use for his project is likely to ask, "How do I determine whether or not a building system is right for my client's project, and if it is, which ones are available, and how do I select the best one?" The following discussion responds to these questions for one building type: housing. It will attempt to describe the range of generic options currently available in terms of building systems for housing and it will outline approaches which may be taken to procure such systems for use in housing projects. The basic principles and concepts outlined for procuring building systems for housing projects are similar to those for other building types such as schools and industrial facilities. A complete description of such approaches for each different building type, however, is beyond the scope of this article.

Before embarking on a description of industrialized building systems and their problems and potentials, it is necessary to present a few definitions so that later misunderstandings and misconceptions may be minimized.

A system, for the purposes of this discussion, is defined as "a set of parts with holistic potential." In other words, a set of parts organized to act as a whole (see Fig. 1). The parts of any system may be tangible or intangible, hardware or software, products or policies.

A special kind of system which is of particular interest to this analysis is a *generating system*[1] This type of system may be defined as a set of parts which may be combined in a variety of different ways to create a variety of different wholes (see Fig. 2).

When the term "building system" is used, it usually means a *generating system for building*, or, in other words, a set of building parts which may be combined or assembled in a variety of different ways to create a variety of different building configurations.

Any generating system for building should have as its objective the achievement of a maximum number of configurations with a minimum number of parts. The measure of effectiveness of any generating system is the ratio of the number of parts to the number of possible configurations.

Finally, the term "industrialized" is defined, for the purposes of this discussion, as "fabricated by machines and/or highly organized production-line labor." An *industrialized building system*, therefore, may be defined as a set of building parts which are mass produced and which may be assembled in a wide variety of configurations.

TYPES OF SYSTEMS

In this analysis, building systems for housing will be generally described and classified according to the following categories: material, component interchangeability, housing type, structure type, fabrication location, and standardization approach. The latter categories will be used for the

[1] This term was, to this writer's knowledge, first used by Christopher Alexander in a paper he wrote for Inland Steel Products Company entitled Systems Generating Systems.

greater part of this discussion because they provide the most definitive description of the present state of the art. The other categories will, however, be briefly noted here for the reader's information.

The basic *materials* from which housing systems are currently constructed do not differ significantly from materials used in conventional construction. They include the following: reinforced concrete—including lightweight concrete, prestressed concrete, chemically stressed concrete, and spray-applied concrete; wood—including both lumber and plywood; metals—primarily steel and aluminum; plastics—generally fiber-glass reinforced; and composite materials, usually in the form of sandwich panels with cores of paper-honeycomb or polyurethane foam and facings of plywood, sheet metal, gypsum, or plastic.

There are two types of building system in terms of *component interchangeability*; closed and open. Closed building systems are those which are made up of subsystems and components which cannot be interchanged with the subsystems of another building system without modification. Open building systems may utilize a wide range of subsystems on the market and offer much greater opportunity for component interchangeability.

The housing types provided by building systems are those common to all of the housing industry: single-family detached, single-family attached (row house), low-rise apartments (up to three stories), and high-rise apartments (above three stories with, at the time of this writing, a thirty-story maximum).

There are generally three *structure* types used in building systems for housing: box systems, i.e., volumetric room-size modules; structural frame systems; and bearing panel systems.

Box systems are available in a range of materials and can usually be procured either as basic shells or as partially or

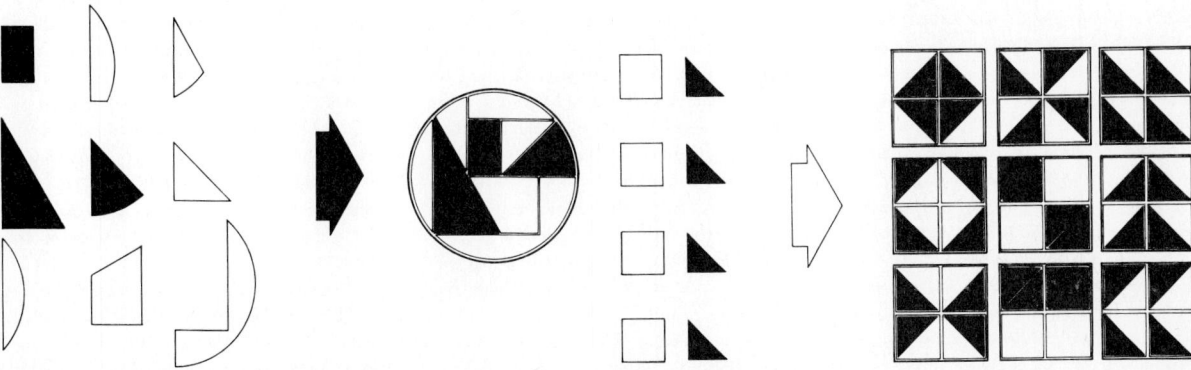

Fig. 1.   A system is a set of parts which creates a whole

Fig. 2.   A generating system is a set of parts which creates a number of different wholes

fully completed packages with integrated mechanical and electrical subsystems. The structural element is a three-dimensional space-enclosing unit, usually fabricated at an off-site location. There are, however, a few systems which utilize on-site three-dimensional casting techniques. Transportation constraints usually restrict their width to between 12 and 14 ft maximum, and their weight is restricted by the capacity of standard erection equipment to between 10 and 30 tons. This type of structure can provide a surprising variety of building configurations suitable for a wide range of site conditions.

Box systems, or "modulars," as they are popularly referred to, have two basic structural variations: (1) the boxes are either load bearing and stacked one on top of the other in a number of different ways or (2) they are nonstructural and inserted into a structural frame in order to create a complete building.

Structural frame systems usually consist of premanufactured columns and beams with either structural or nonstructural in-fill panels and planks. Generally, the materials employed are structural steel or precast reinforced concrete. Frame systems, when compared with box or panel systems, usually have more potential for flexibility and variety in terms of dwelling unit planning and design. Such systems, however, are almost always economically feasible solely for high-rise structures usually six stories or more.

Bearing panel systems differ from frame systems in terms of vertical and horizontal structural elements. Vertical structural components are wall panels instead of columns and horizontal spanning components are floor panels instead of beams. Frame structures are composed of linear, essentially one-dimensional structural elements; panel systems are composed of two-dimensional or planar elements; and box systems are made up of three-dimensional or volumetric structural elements.

Panel systems are made of a variety of materials including wood framing, reinforced concrete, and sandwich panels. Systems are available using panel construction for all housing types from single-family detached to high-rise. Panel systems for one-story housing are usually of wood or sandwich construction. At the other end of the scale, reinforced concrete is invariably used in panel systems for high-rise housing.

In terms of low- and high-rise *bearing panel* systems, two basic variations may be observed. In one variation (see Fig. 3), bearing panels, when assembled for a typical apartment building, act as facade walls and corridor walls with horizontal spans running perpendicular to the corridor. In the other case (see Fig. 4), bearing panels act as party or demising walls with horizontal spans running parallel to the corridor.

Some systems are composed of very large wall panels comprising one whole side of a dwelling. These systems are assembled very quickly but are somewhat inflexible in terms of site and dwelling unit planning. Other systems made up of small panels offer much more flexibility and can accommodate many more varying site conditions.

Besides those which may be classed neatly into the categories of structure described above, there are some building systems for housing which have structural systems comprising a combination of these categories. For example, some manufacturers of low-rise housing systems manufacture a *box* structure for the kitchen and bathroom spaces and use *panels* to enclose the remaining living spaces of the dwelling unit. Others, as mentioned earlier, fabricate box structures which are inserted into structural frames to create high-rise housing.

A variety of fabrication processes are used in available panel systems. Wall and floor panels are made in off-site factories, on-site factories and, in some cases, they are fabricated in place.

Building systems for housing utilize one or more of the following *fabrication locations* in the creation and assembly of the structure and enclosure elements of the system: off site, on site, and in place in the building.

The first fabrication location approach which will be described is off-site fabrication and assembly. The purpose of this technique is to reduce the amount of on-site construction time by performing a large amount of fabrication, assembly, and finishing of components in an off-site factory. Examples of this type of construction are "stackable" and "plug-in" volumetric box-type housing systems and "sectionalized" homes. Potential savings with this approach lie in the reduction of on-site assembly time and in the inherent advantages of factory production, i.e., lower wage scales of factory (versus site) labor; greater use of machines and assembly lines, resulting in faster and more accurate production of components; and weather-protected working areas, resulting in constant year-round production. Disadvantages encountered using this approach to fabrication lie in the high initial investment needed for factory facilities and fabrication equipment; restrictions imposed by transportation from factory to site (dimensional limitations resulting in planning and design inflexibilities); high shipping costs, resulting in a limited economical distribution radius; and damage to joints and finishes incurred during loading, shipping, and erection.

The next general fabrication location method which is widely used is off-site fabrication with on-site assembly. The general purpose of this method is, as before, to reduce on-site construction time. Building components are, in this case, fabricated in an off-site factory with the major amount of assembly still performed on site. Examples of this type of construction are sandwich-panel systems for single-family detached housing and precast reinforced concrete bearing-panel or structural-frame systems for low- and high-rise housing. When compared with the previous category, this fabrication process will generally result in an increase in planning and design flexibility and a reduction in the transportation cost per unit (resulting in a larger economical distribution radius) while maintaining the inherent advantages of factory fabrication. However, the greatly increased number of parts which have to be field assembled in this process results in a greater number of jointing conditions to resolve, greater exposure to changing weather conditions, and wider use of expensive on-site labor.

A third major approach is on-site fabrication and assembly. The fabrication of components in this case takes place on the building site but away from the final position of the components in the building. Examples of this type of construction are systems using mobile casting machines or on-site assembly lines. As before, the primary purpose of housing systems in this category is to reduce on-site construction time. By comparison with the two previous processes, the characteristics of components fabricated with on-site techniques are much the same. Volumetric modules and bearing-panel systems are, for example, fabricated in on-site as well as off-site factories. Besides the innate benefits of factory fabrication, certain other advantages are realized with on-site prefabrication when compared with off-site prefabrication. For example, manufacturing facilities on site are usually much smaller and less complex than most off-site factories; thus the investment needed for equipment and facilities is generally somewhat lower than usual. Also, since all work is performed on site, the restrictions and extra costs of transportation are eliminated. A couple of potential disadvantages are inherent in this type of fabrication, however. Extra space must be available on the building site for manufacturing facilities, and higher-cost on-site labor is generally required.

The last approach to be discussed here is in-place fabrication. This process is characterized by *new* ways of fabricating components in place in the building in order to reduce on-site construction time. Examples of such systems are reinforced concrete bearing-wall construction for high-rise buildings fabricated in situ by using special steel "tunnel" forms, and reinforced concrete housing units fabricated by spraying concrete onto steel frame and mesh forms. In comparison with the other prefabrication techniques, use of in-place fabrication methods reduces jointing problems, eliminates transportation, and does away with the need for space on site for manufacturing facilities. As in the previous category, however, the high-cost on-site labor may prevent significant savings from being gained using this type of fabrication.

The *standardization approaches* used in the industry are of two types: custom prefabricating or standardized prefabricating. If a manufacturer custom prefabricates, he usually has standardized connection details *only* while maintaining the flexibility of modifying the components he produces to tailor-fit each particular building project. This approach fails to recognize the principles and advantages of the generating system concept and usually requires a large project size in order to reach any economy in production. Most of the concrete panel systems developed in Europe take this approach.

Standardized prefabricating involves producing a standard set of parts with few if any variations. Manufacturers taking this

approach will be able to take orders for much smaller projects. Such an approach, however, may or may not be based on a generating system concept. Some standardized prefabrication approaches result simply in standard dwelling plans which have very limited potential for varied building configurations. Many of the producers of box structures take this rather limited approach. While the principle is fundamental to all, few if any of the industrialized housing system manufacturers have actually developed generating systems in the formal sense of the word, although some of the recently developed panel systems for low-rise housing are beginning to incorporate the concept more clearly into their production.

The range of services offered by producers of industrialized housing systems varies widely. The most limited set of services generally offered is the manufacture of a set of coordinated components for part of the building and delivery to the site with no erection services provided— only a set of written directions to guide the assembly of the components, and perhaps a field supervisor. This is contrasted with the other extreme which is represented by manufacturers of coordinated building components who offer to provide, and sometimes insist upon providing, services for nothing less than construction of the com-

plete building and often the site work as well. In this case, the producer acts also as a general contractor.

There is another service at the "complete building" end of the scale of services which often occurs but which will only occasionally be of interest to architects; it is mentioned here simply to present a more complete description of the industry. There are a few industrialized housing producers who act as real estate developers, and, with an in-house architectural design staff, they manufacture almost entirely for their own account. Depending on the project and the degree of responsibility which they can assume, however, these manufacturers will sometimes be interested in negotiating for a project for which they will *not* be the developer and/or owner. If such a manufacturer becomes involved in a project, the need for outside architectural services is minimized.

The proportion of the total building which an industrialized housing system may represent varies considerably from producer to producer. Some manufacturers, for example, will provide no more than a package of preassembled outside-wall and partition panels along with precut floor joists representing perhaps 25 per cent of the cost of constructing the building. Others will, on the other hand, provide a set of coordinated and prefabricated building components which go together to provide for everything but foundations. The variations between manufacturers in terms of what building elements are provided and what percentage of the complete building

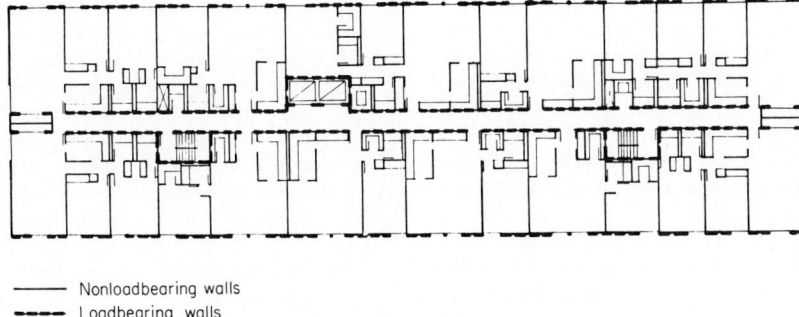

——— Nonloadbearing walls
- - - - Loadbearing walls

Fig. 3. Apartment building with loadbearing walls parallel to corridor

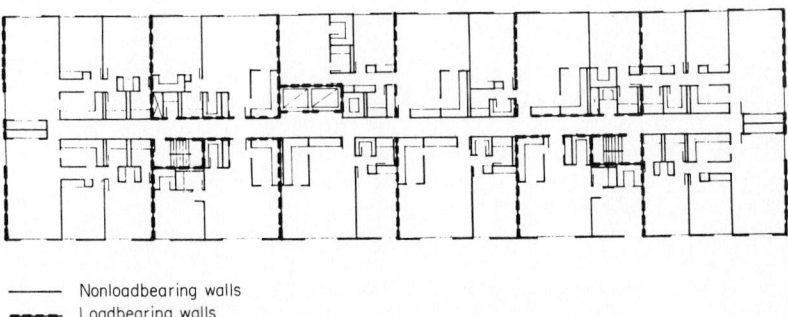

——— Nonloadbearing walls
- - - - Loadbearing walls

Fig. 4. Apartment building with loadbearing walls perpendicular to corridor

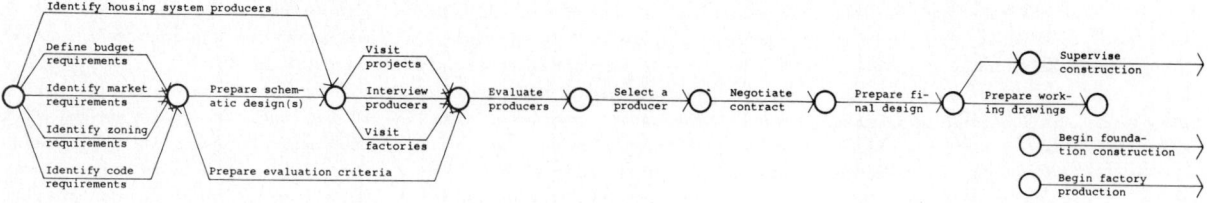

Fig. 5. Sole-source contract approach to selection of a housing system producer

their system represents is almost infinite. The situation is such that virtually no two manufacturers offer the same range of components. This results in some procurement complexities which require special considerations. These considerations will be discussed in the following section of this analysis.

PROCUREMENT APPROACHES

There are a variety of ways in which industrialized housing technologies may be incorporated into a housing project. These approaches are of two basic types and are similar to the means which are used to obtain the services of a general contractor. With his client, the architect may (1) evaluate the range of available housing systems and, based on that evaluation, award a *sole-source* contract, or (2) the architect may prepare a set of contract documents to award a contract on the basis of a *competitive bid.*

If the sole-source approach is used, the architect will become involved in a number of activities both before and after the contract award (see Fig. 5). Initially, the architect must identify the industrialized housing producers who are in a position to supply components to the geographic area in which the project is to be constructed. There are a variety of consultants and directories which are available to help him or her in this identification effort. Next, the architect must determine his or her client's budget restrictions, the market requirements, the building code and zoning requirements, and the site conditions. This set of requirements

will serve as the criteria which may be used to evaluate the industrialized housing producers he or she has identified. These requirements may also, of course, be used to guide the preparation of a schematic design of the project. After developing a set of project requirements and a schematic design, he or she should interview each producer, visit projects which have been built with the producer's system, and visit the manufacturing facilities of each producer. During these interviews and field trips, he or she should scrutinize, among other things, the general cost and time of construction using the producer's system, the producer's knowledge and expertise, his or her financial strength, the quality control of this technology both in the plant and at the site, and the amount of work which will remain to be done to complete the project beyond the scope of the producer's products and services. The architect should then compare the characteristics and capabilities of each producer with the list of project requirements (budget, market, code, and site) which he or she has compiled and determine which producer would be best for his or her client's project. Once such a selection has been made, a contract may be negotiated. As in conventional construction contracts, either a fixed-price contract or a cost-plus-fixed-fee contract may be used. The latter, however, may perhaps be more beneficial to the architect's client, especially if combined with some sort of incentive clause which allows the producer to share in any project cost savings below a prescribed cost level.

Once a contract has been negotiated and signed, and depending on the amount of design work the system producer has al-

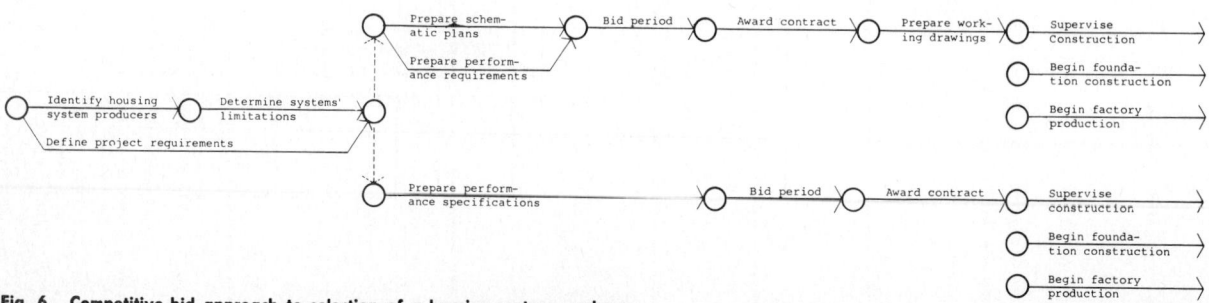

Fig. 6. Competitive-bid approach to selection of a housing system producer

ready done, the architect should then continue with the design of the project in cooperation with the selected housing system producer. In other words, the architect should work with the producer to make sure that the designs he or she develops incorporate the best features and greatest economies of the producer's technology. In most cases, working drawings using an industrialized housing system should be greatly simplified, as most of the connection and joint details have already been worked out by the system producer. In many cases, the time required for the architect's services will be substantially reduced.

Once a design has been developed and working drawings finished, fabrication of the building's foundations and shell may begin concurrently. Use of an industrialized building system will, in many cases, result in a significant reduction in construction time when compared with conventional construction methods. This, coupled with a reduction in design and working drawing time, usually results in savings to the client both in terms of earlier rental revenues (if the property is being built for rental) and less interest on interim financing.

If, on the other hand, a *competitive bid* procurement approach is used, the role and activities of the architect are somewhat different from those described below (see Fig. 6). In this case, the architect must still identify, as described earlier, housing system producers potentially available for his client's projects. The architect should then interview each producer to determine the design and performance limits which are characteristic of each system. Such limitations might be a maximum horizontal span limit, a limit on the number of stories, a required planning dimensional module, etc. Once those limitations have been deter-

mined, the architect may proceed in one of two general directions. He or she may prepare a set of contract documents which either include a design layout of a building or which do *not*. In the first case, the architect should prepare a schematic design of the building which could be built with any of the systems he had originally analyzed. The drawings should be quite generalized and should not delineate joint details or specific materials, as these would be determined by the system eventually selected in the bidding process. The specifications developed by the architect would have to be nonspecific in terms of actual materials; i.e., they would have to be performance-oriented, specifying levels of quality rather than specific solutions. Drawings and specifications prepared in this manner would facilitate competitive bidding by a variety of different housing system technologies representing a variety of different structural approaches, materials, finishes, etc. In other words, based on schematic drawings and performance-oriented specifications, manufacturers of bearing-wall systems, box systems, and frame systems (and also, for that matter, a general contractor representing conventional construction methods) could compete with each other for a project by bidding on a common set of bid documents.

Once a low bidder is identified and the contract awarded, the architect may proceed with completing the working drawings by using the joint and connection details supplied by the producer. Or, depending on the way the procurement is organized, the producer might complete the working drawings with the architect reviewing and approving them, in the same way that normal shop drawings are prepared by a manufacturer and approved by the architect.

In the competitive bid procurement ap-

proach where *no* building layout is prepared by the architect, the following activities are likely to occur. During the process of identifying housing system producers, the architect may find that most of the system producers which are likely candidates for the client's project have "turnkey" capability. In other words, they have the capability of designing as well as constructing a project and provide the greatest economies to an owner when doing so. In this case, the architect for the client may find the range of his or her services limited. The principal responsibility may become that of preparing contract documents which define the project requirements on a performance basis and which facilitate the procurement of a turnkey bid price for his client's project. No drawings would be prepared by the architect for the client. Rather, each turnkey bidder would have his or her own architect for the design of his bid proposal. Once the winning bidder had been selected, the client's architect would act as a contract administrator for the client to make sure that the designs and construction produced were in conformance with the contract documents and the client's best interests.

In each of the above cases, there are a wide range of variations. Each housing system manufacturer is different from his and her competitors in terms of quality and configuration of his product and the range of items and services which are provided. Likewise, each building project has a different requirement and may require a different set of activities and, quite often, a different fee arrangement for the architect. This discussion has been presented primarily to provide a frame of reference—a point of departure—for the architect who wishes to consider using a building system for his or her next project.

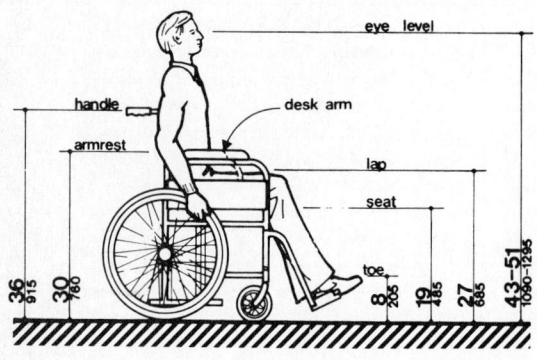

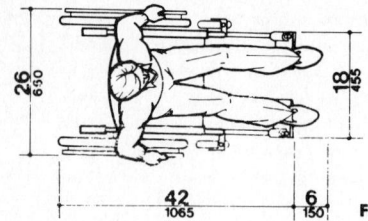

Fig. 1. Wheelchair dimensions

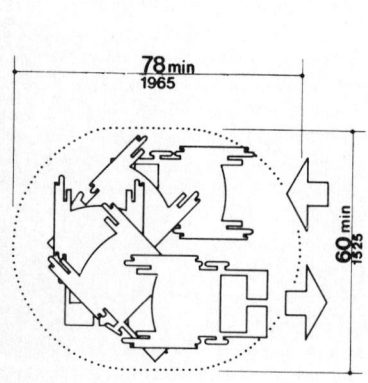

Fig. 2. Space needed for smooth U-turn

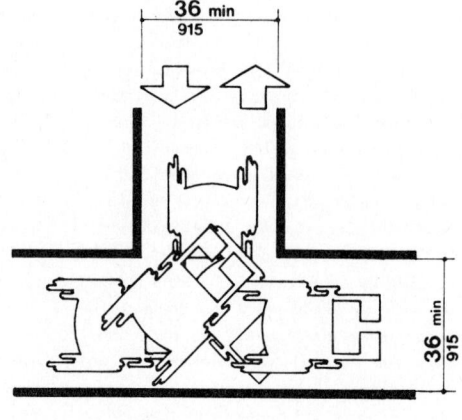

Fig. 3. T-shaped space for 180-degree turns

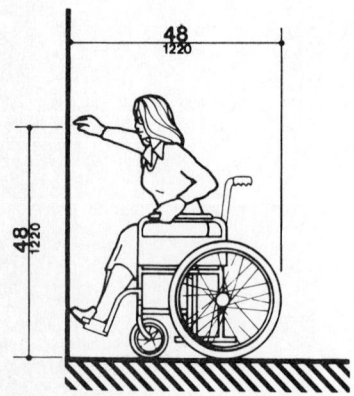

Fig. 4. Forward reach limits

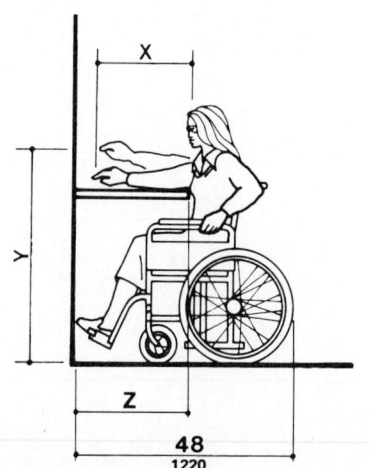

NOTE: X shall be ≤ 25 in (635 mm); Z shall be ≥ X. When X < 20 in (510 mm), then Y shall be 48 in (1220 mm) maximum. When X is 20 to 25 in (510 to 635 mm), then Y shall be 44 in (1120 mm) maximum.

The following material has been reproduced with permission from "American National Standard Specifications for Making Buildings and Facilities Accessible to and Usable by Physically Handicapped People," ANSI A117.1-1980.

Note: All dimensions in the following text are given in inches followed by millimeters in parentheses. In the figures, dimensions are given in inches above the line and in millimeters below the line. Dimensions for short distances are shown on extensions of the dimension line. Boundary of the clear floor space required is shown in dotted lines.

Wheelchair dimensions and clearances

Basic wheelchair dimensions are shown in Fig. 1. The minimum clear floor space required for one wheelchair is 30 by 48 in (760 by 1220 mm). Minimum clear passage width for one wheelchair is 36 in (915 mm), for two wheelchairs 60 in (1525 mm). Minimum diameter required for a 180-degree turn is 60 in (1525 mm); a more comfortable turn can be made in a space 60 by 78 in (1525 by 1965 mm) as shown in Fig. 2. A T-intersection of two 36-in (915-mm) wide corridors will also permit a 180-degree turn as shown in Fig. 3. Dimensions for maximum front and side reach are shown in Figs. 4 and 5.

Floor surfaces

Floor surfaces including walks, ramps, stairs, and curb ramps shall be stable, firm, and relatively nonslip under all weather conditions. Changes in level up to ¼ in (6 mm) may be without edge treatment. Changes in level between ¼ and ½ in (6 and 13 mm) shall be beveled with a slope no greater than 1:2. Changes in level greater than ½ in (13 mm) shall be accomplished by means of a ramp as defined below. Carpet, if used, shall be securely attached and have a firm pad or no pad. Maximum pile height shall be ½ in (13 mm). Exposed edges shall be fastened to floor surface and have trim along the entire length. Gratings located in walking surfaces shall have spaces no greater than ½ in (13 mm) in one direction. They should be placed with the long dimension perpendicular to the dominant direction of travel.

Parking spaces

Parking spaces for disabled people shall be located as close as possible to an accessible entrance to the building, and shall be designated by a sign (Fig. 6) which cannot be obscured by parked cars. Minimum dimensions of parking space and access aisle are shown in Fig. 7. Access aisle may be

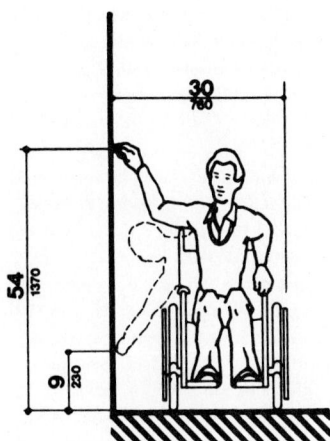

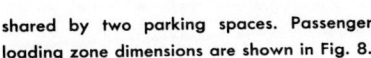

Fig. 5. Side reach limits

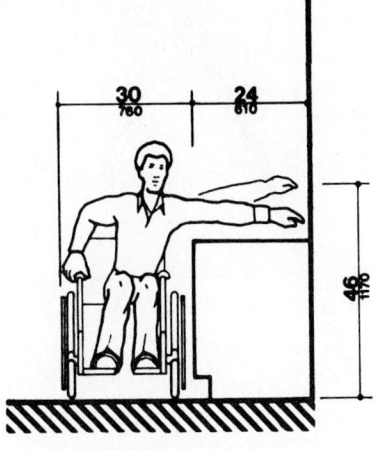

Fig. 6. International symbol of accessibility

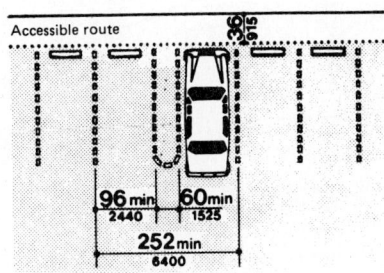

Fig. 7. Parking space and access aisle

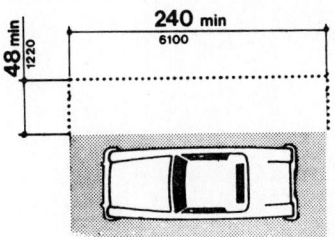

Fig. 8. Passenger loading zone and access aisle

shared by two parking spaces. Passenger loading zone dimensions are shown in Fig. 8.

Curb ramps

Minimum width for curb ramps is 36 in (915 mm) except that diagonal or corner ramps shall be at least 48 in (1220 mm) wide. Slope shall not exceed 1:10. If the ramp occurs where pedestrians must walk across it, flared sides shall be provided with slopes not greater than 1:10.

Ramps

The least possible slope shall be used for any ramp. The maximum slope shall be 1:12 and the maximum rise for any run shall be 30 in (760 mm). Minimum clear width of any ramp shall be 36 in (915 mm). Level landings not less than 60 in (1525 mm) long are required at the top and bottom of each run. If a ramp changes direction at a landing, the minimum landing size shall be 60 by 60 in (1525 by 1525 mm). Any ramp with a rise greater than 6 in (250 mm) must have handrails on both sides. Where the ramp makes a 90- or 180-degree turn, the inside rail shall be continuous. If not continuous, handrails shall extend 12 in (305 mm) beyond the top and bottom of the ramp, and shall be level (Fig. 9). The clear space between the handrail and a wall shall be 1½ in (38 mm). Ramp and landing edges must be protected to keep people from slipping off. This can be done by means of a curb (Fig. 9), or by using handrails supported by closely spaced balusters or a solid wall. Outdoor ramps, landings, and walks must be pitched for drainage but the cross slope shall not exceed 1:50.

Stairs

Treads shall be no less than 11 in (280 mm) wide, measured from riser to riser. Nos-

ings shall project no more than 1½ in (38 mm) and the radius of curvature at the leading edge shall be no greater than 1½ in (38 mm). Risers shall be sloped or the under side of the nosing shall have an angle not less than 60 degrees from the horizontal, as shown in Fig. 10. Handrails are required on both sides of all stairs. Where the stair makes a 90- or 180-degree turn the inside handrail shall be continuous. Where handrails are not continuous they shall extend at least 12 in. (305 mm) beyond the top riser and at least 12 in (305 mm) plus the width of one tread beyond the bottom riser. At the top the extension shall be level; at the bottom the handrail shall continue its

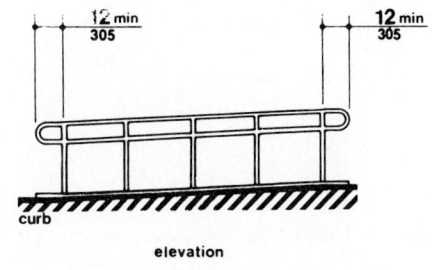

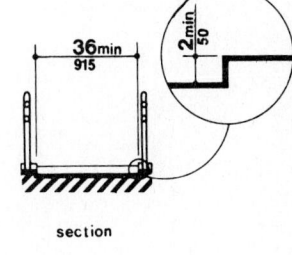

Fig. 9. Ramp handrails and curb

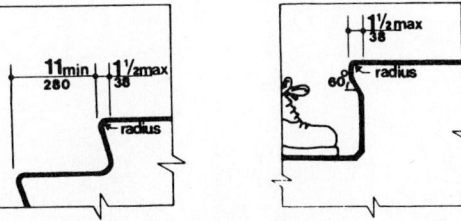

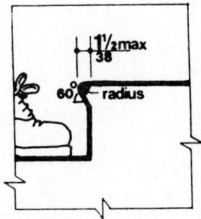

Fig. 10. Stair tread, riser, and nosing details

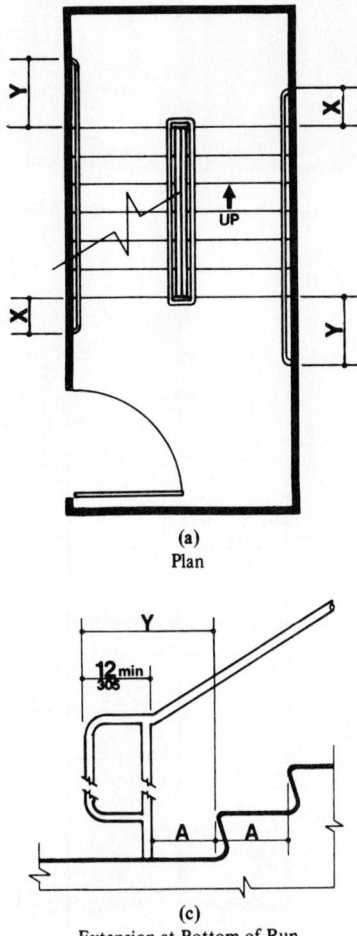

(a)
Plan

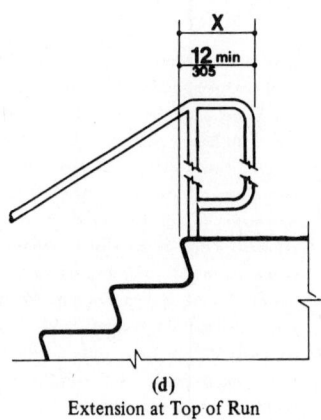

(c)
Extension at Bottom of Run

Fig. 11. Stair handrail details

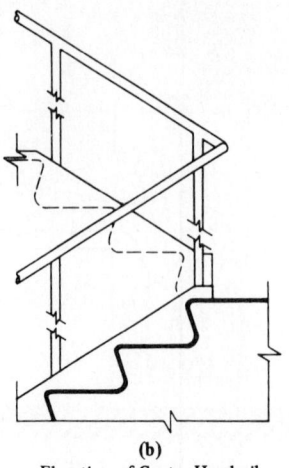

(b)
Elevation of Center Handrail

(d)
Extension at Top of Run

slope for the width of one tread beyond the bottom riser and then become level (Fig. 11). Clear space between handrail and wall shall be 1½ in (38 mm).

Elevators

Elevators shall comply with American National Standard Safety Code for Elevators, Dumbwaiters, Escalators, and Moving Walks, ANSI A17.1-1978 and A17.1a-1979. Elevator operations shall be automatic and self-leveling within a tolerance of ½ in (13 mm). Figure 12 shows the location of signals, signs, and devices required at elevator entrances. Call buttons shall be at least ¾ in (19 mm) in the smallest dimension. A visual and audible signal shall announce the arrival of the car and indicate whether it is going up or down. Floor designation signs shall be provided on both jambs of each elevator entrance; numerals shall be 2 in (50 mm) high and shall be raised or indented.

The floor area of elevator cars shall provide space for wheelchair users to enter the car, maneuver within reach of the controls, and exit from the car. Dimensions shown in Fig. 13 are acceptable. Car control panels may be located on the front wall of the car on either side of a center opening door, or on the side wall of the car near a side opening door. The centerline of the highest controls shall not be more than 54 in (1370 mm) and the lowest not less than 35 in (890 mm) above the floor. Design of an acceptable control panel is shown in Fig. 14. Designations (numerals, letters, and symbols) at the side of the control buttons shall be raised or indented. A visual and audible car position indicator shall be provided above the control panel or over the door.

Doors

Doorways shall have a minimum clear opening of 32 in (815 mm) with the door open 90 degrees, measured between the face of the door and the stop. Doorways more than 24 in (610 mm) deep must be 36 in (915 mm) wide. Maneuvering space required at manually operated doors varies with the direction of approach and the hinging of the door, as illustrated in Fig. 15. The minimum space between two hinged doors in series shall be 48 in (1220 mm) plus the width of any door swinging into the space. Maximum height of thresholds shall be ½ in (13 mm) except that ¾ in (19 mm) height is permitted for exterior sliding doors. Thresholds shall be beveled with a slope not greater than 1:2. Door latch handles shall be easy to grasp and operate with one hand; lever type handles are acceptable. The maximum force required for opening a door shall be 8.5 lbf (37.8 N)

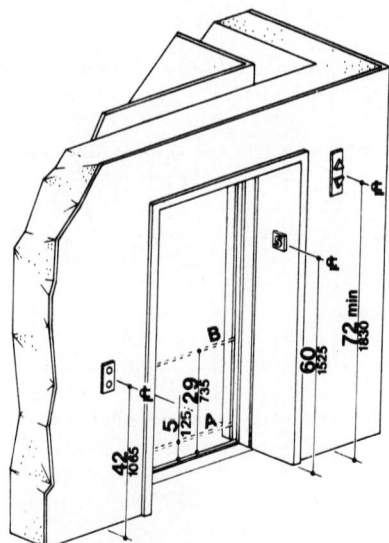

Fig. 12. Elevator entrance details. The automatic door reopening device is activated if an object passes through either line A or line B.

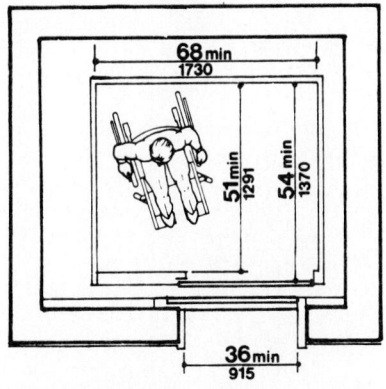

Fig. 13. Elevator car dimensions. Elevator cars with a minimum width of 54 in (1370 mm) are allowed for elevators with capacities of less than 2000 lb. A center-opening door application may necessitate increasing the 68-in (1730-mm) dimension.

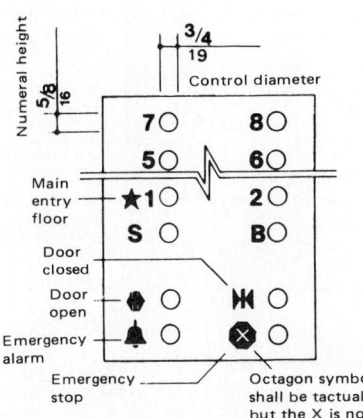

Fig. 14. Elevator car control panel

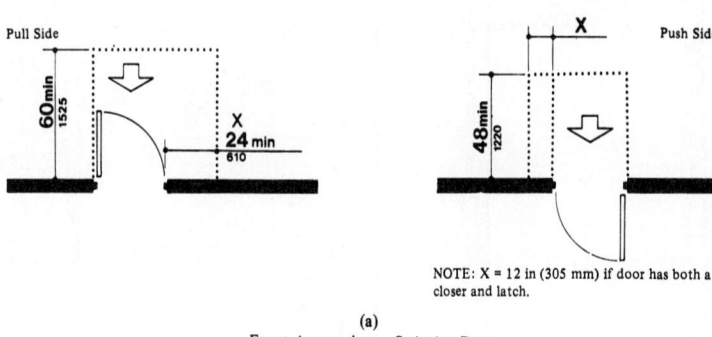

NOTE: X = 12 in (305 mm) if door has both a closer and latch.

(a)
Front Approaches – Swinging Doors

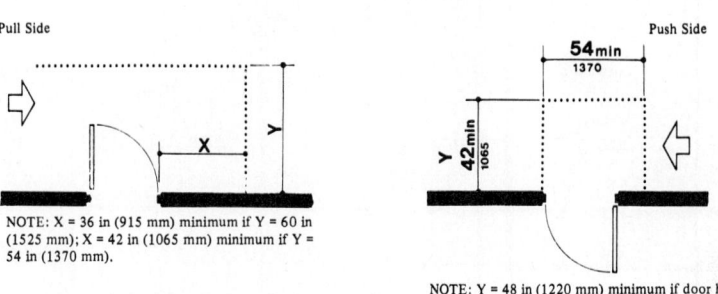

NOTE: X = 36 in (915 mm) minimum if Y = 60 in (1525 mm); X = 42 in (1065 mm) minimum if Y = 54 in (1370 mm).

NOTE: Y = 48 in (1220 mm) minimum if door has both a latch and closer.

(b)
Hinge Side Approaches – Swinging Doors

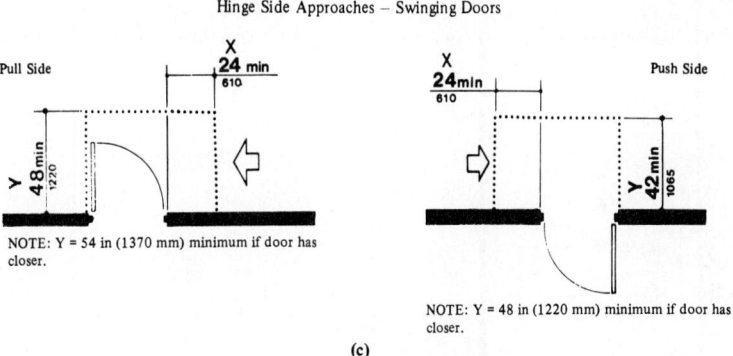

NOTE: Y = 54 in (1370 mm) minimum if door has closer.

NOTE: Y = 48 in (1220 mm) minimum if door has closer.

(c)
Latch Side Approaches – Swinging Doors

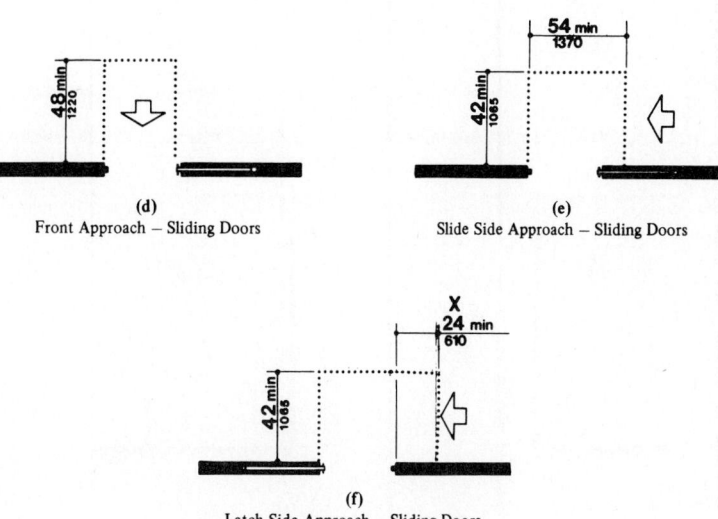

(d)
Front Approach – Sliding Doors

(e)
Slide Side Approach – Sliding Doors

(f)
Latch Side Approach – Sliding Doors

Fig. 15. Maneuvering clearances at doors

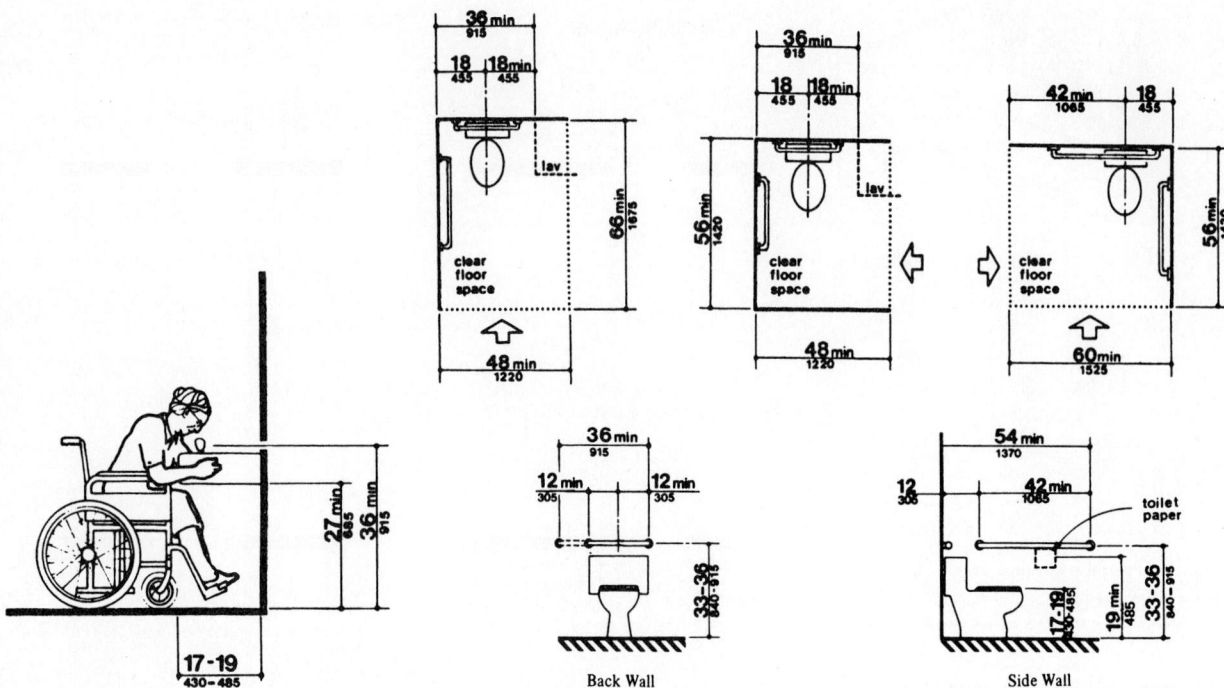

Fig. 16. Drinking fountain, cantilevered type

Fig. 17. Clear floor spaces and grab bars at toilets

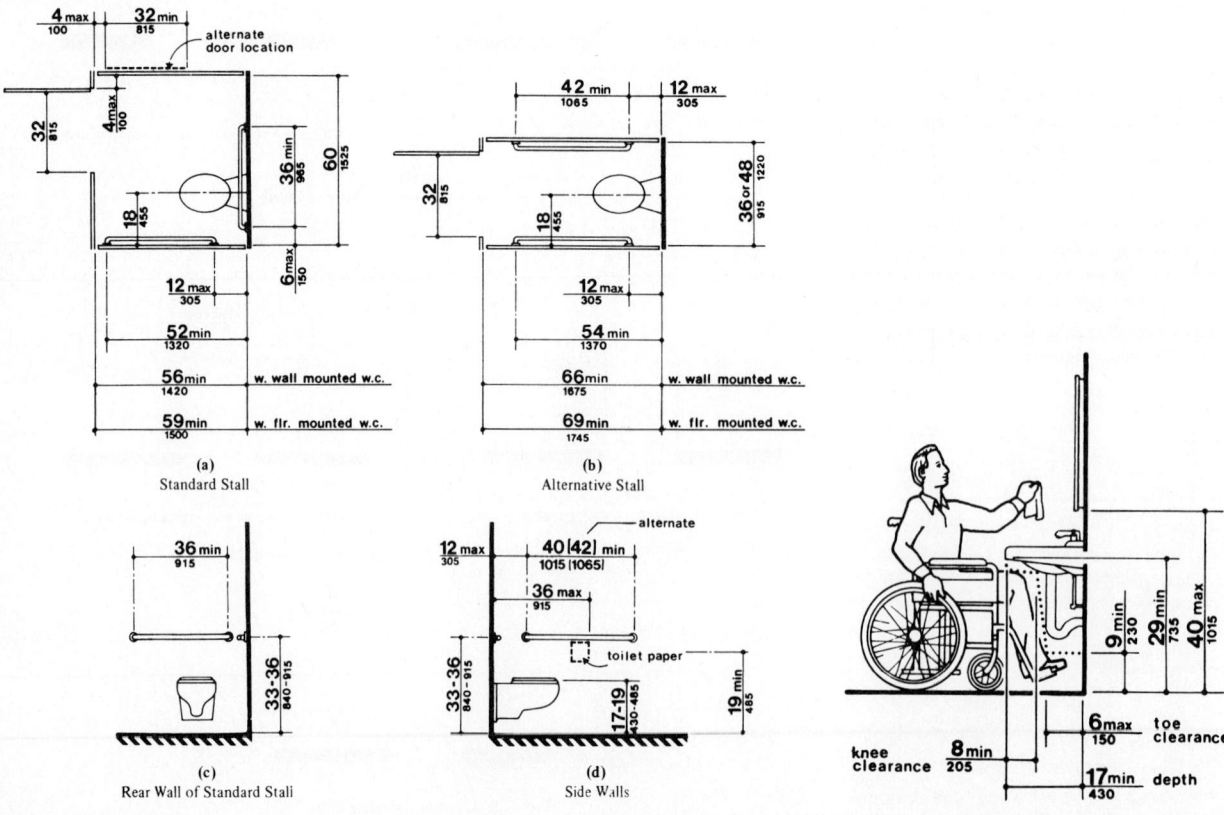

Fig. 18. Toilet stalls

Fig. 19. Lavatory clearances

for an exterior door and 5 lbf (22.2 N) for all other doors. When automatic or power-assisted doors are used they shall conform to American National Standard for Power-Operated Doors, ANSI 156.10-1979. Kick-plates 16 in (405 mm) high are recommended for heavily used doors.

Windows

The maximum force required for opening a window shall be 5 lbf (22.2 N).

Entrances

A service entrance shall not be the sole accessible entrance.

Drinking fountains

The spout shall be no higher than 36 in (915 mm) above the floor and shall be located at the front of the unit. Figure 16 shows the conditions required for a front approach. Floor-supported or recessed units can be used by a side approach.

Water closets

Clear floor space and grab bar locations for water closets not in stalls are shown in Fig. 17, and for water closets in stalls in Fig. 18. Stall front and side partitions shall provide toe clearance of at least 8 in (230 mm) above the floor.

Urinals

Wall-hung urinals shall have elongated rim not more than 17 in (430 mm) above the floor. Provide clear floor space 30 by 48 in (760 by 1220 mm) to permit forward approach. Flush control shall be not more than 44 in (1120 mm) above the floor.

Lavatories

Critical dimensions for installation of lavatory and mirror are shown in Fig. 19. Provide clear floor space 30 by 48 in (760 by 1220 mm) to permit forward approach. Hot-water pipes and drainpipes under the lavatory shall be insulated or otherwise covered.

Bathtubs

Clear floor space in front of bathtubs shall be as shown in Fig. 20. An in-tub seat or a seat at the head of the tub shall be provided. Grab bars and controls shall be located as shown in Figs. 20 and 21. A shower spray unit with a hose at least 60 in (1525 mm) long that can be used as a fixed shower head or as a hand-held shower shall be provided.

Shower stalls

Shower stall size and clear floor space shall comply with Fig. 22. A seat shall be provided in the small shower stall 17 to 18 in (430 to 485 mm) high and extending the

full depth of the stall. Grab bars and controls shall be located as shown in Fig. 23. A shower spray unit as described for bathtubs shall be provided. Curbs, if provided, for the small shower stall shall not exceed 4 in (100 mm) in height. The larger stall shall not have curbs.

Sinks

Sinks shall be a maximum of 6½ in (165 mm) deep and shall be mounted with the counter or rim no higher than 34 in (865 mm) from the floor. Knee clearance 27 in (685 mm) high, 30 in. (760 mm) wide, and 19 in (485 mm) deep shall be provided underneath sinks. Hot-water pipes and drainpipes under sinks shall be insulated or otherwise covered. Clear floor space 30 by 48 in (760 by 1220 mm) shall be provided in front of the sink to allow forward approach.

Storage

Clear floor space at least 30 by 48 in (760 by 1220 mm) shall be provided adjacent to storage facilities to allow parallel approach. Shelves and clothes rods shall be within the heights shown in Fig. 24.

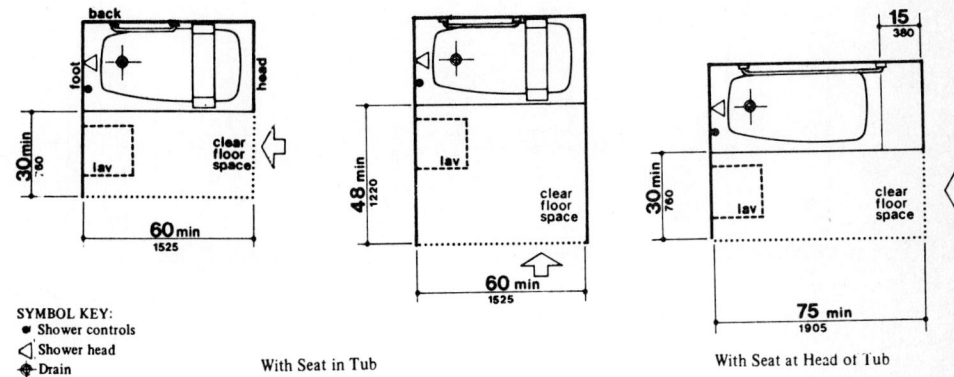

SYMBOL KEY:
- Shower controls
- Shower head
- Drain

With Seat in Tub   With Seat at Head of Tub

Fig. 20. Clear floor space at bathtubs

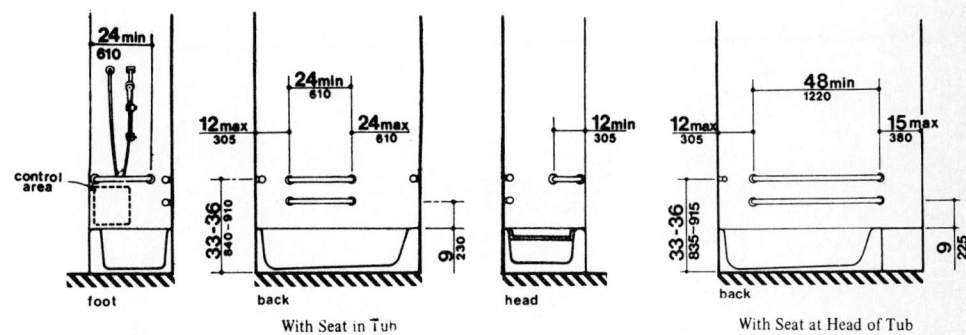

With Seat in Tub   With Seat at Head of Tub

Fig. 21. Grab bars at bathtubs

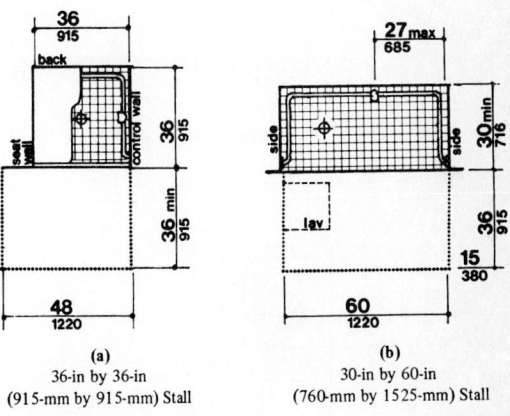

(a)
36-in by 36-in
(915-mm by 915-mm) Stall

(b)
30-in by 60-in
(760-mm by 1525-mm) Stall

Fig. 22. Shower sizes and clearances

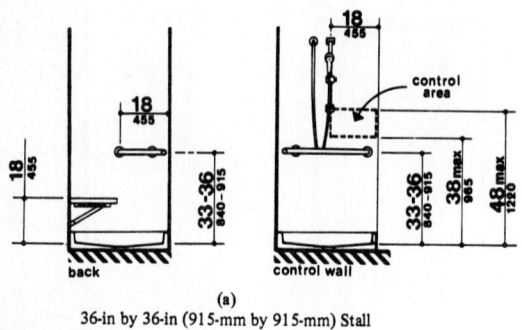

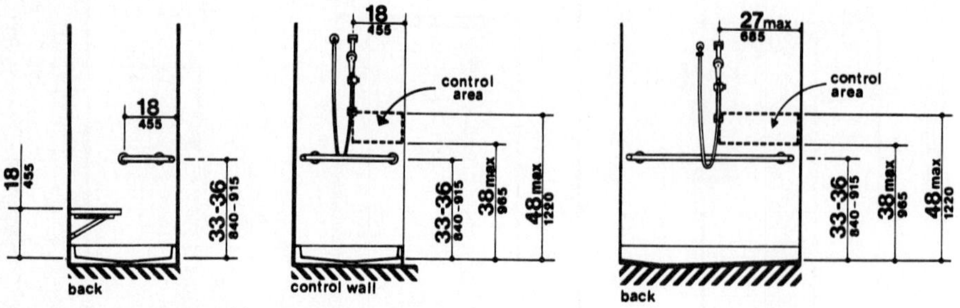

(a)
36-in by 36-in (915-mm by 915-mm) Stall

(b)
30-in by 60-in (760-mm by 1525-mm) Stall

Fig. 23. Grab bars at shower stalls

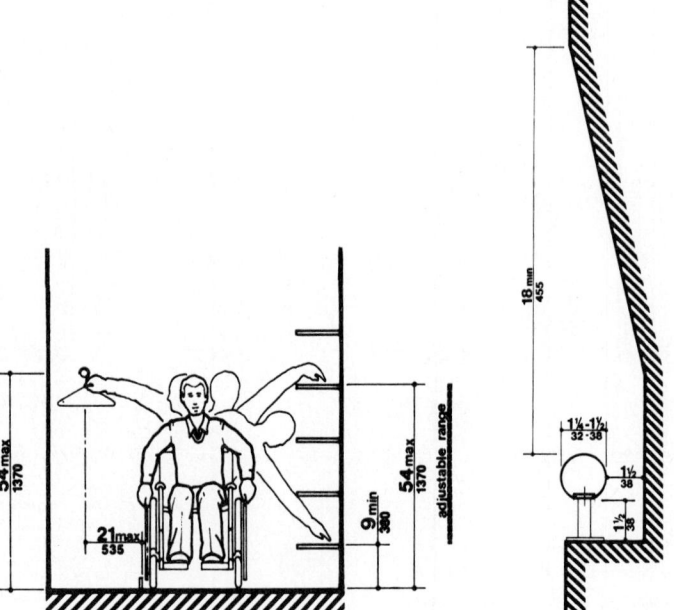

Fig. 24. Storage shelves and closets

Fig. 25. Handrail in recess

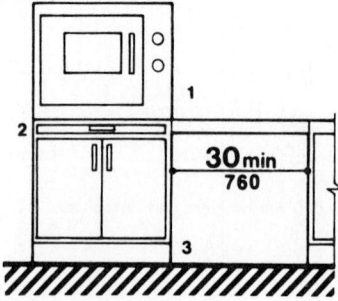

Fig. 26. Oven without self-cleaning feature
1. Countertop or wall-mounted oven.
2. Pull-out board preferred with side-opening door.
3. Clear open space.

Handrails and grab bars

The diameter or width of the gripping surface shall be 1¼ to 1½ in (32 to 38 mm) and the distance between it and the wall shall be 1½ in (38 mm). Handrail may be located in a recess if it is at least 3 in (75 mm) deep and extends at least 18 in (455 mm) above the top of the rail (Fig. 25). Grab bars, tub and shower seats, fasteners, and mounting devices shall be able to resist a load of 250 lbf (1112 N) in bending, shear, or tension (direct pull).

Telephones

Public telephones should be located so that clear floor space of 30 by 48 in (760 by 1220 mm) is provided for either front or parallel approach. The highest operable part of the telephone shall be no more than 54 in (1370 mm) above the floor. If partially enclosed, the overhang shall not exceed 19 in (485 mm) or extend below 27 in (685 mm) above the floor. If fully enclosed, the clear width of the opening shall be 30 in (760 mm) minimum. Telephones shall have pushbutton controls where such equipment is available.

Alarms

If emergency warning systems are provided, they shall include both audible and visual alarms.

Convenience receptacles

Wall-mounted units shall be mounted no less than 15 in (380 mm) above the floor.

Tables and work surfaces

If seating for people in wheelchairs is provided at tables, counters, or work surfaces, knee spaces at least 27 in (685 mm) high, 30 in (760 mm) wide, and 19 in (485 mm) deep shall be provided. Minimum space from edge of table to wall behind wheel chair shall be 36 in (915 mm). Tops of tables and work surfaces shall be from 28 to 34 in (710 to 865 mm) above the floor.

Seating in series

This type of seating, as in places of assembly, requires a minimum clear floor width of 30 in (760 mm) per wheelchair plus 6 in (150 mm) between chairs and a depth of 48 in (1220 mm) if the approach is from the front or rear or 60 in (1525 mm) if the approach is from the side.

Kitchens

Clearances between all opposing base cabinets, counter tops, appliances, or walls shall be 40 in (1015 mm) minimum, except in U-shaped kitchens where such clearance shall be 60 in (1525 mm) minimum. A clear floor space of at least 30 by 48 in (760 by 1220 mm) that allows either a forward or a parallel approach to all appliances including range, oven, refrigerator/freezer, dishwasher, and trash compactor. At least one 30-in (760-mm) wide section of counter shall be adjustable to alternative heights of 28, 32, and 36 in (710, 815, and 915 mm) measured from the floor to the top of the counter surface. Counter thickness shall be 2 in (50 mm) over the required clear area. Clear floor space of 30 by 48 in (760 by 1220 mm) shall allow a forward approach to the counter; 19 in (485 mm) of the clear space may extend under the counter. At least one shelf of all cabinets and storage shelves mounted above work counters shall be no more than 48 in (1220 mm) above the floor.

If cooktops or ovens have knee spaces

underneath, they shall be insulated or otherwise protected to prevent burns, abrasions, or electrical shock. Ovens shall be wall-hung or countertop supported. They shall be of the self-cleaning type or located adjacent to an adjustable height counter with knee space below as shown in Fig. 26. A side-hinged oven door is recommended with a pull-out board below. Controls for ovens and cooktops shall be on front panels.

Refrigerator/freezers shall have at least 50 per cent of the freezer space and 100 per cent of the refrigerator space and controls below 54 in (1370 mm) above the floor. Freezers with less than 100 per cent of the storage volume within the height limit shall be of the self-defrosting type.

Dishwashers and clothes washers and dryers shall be of front-loading type.

Tactile warnings

Tactile warning textures on walking surfaces shall consist of exposed aggregate concrete, rubber, or plastic cushioned surfaces, or raised strips or grooves having a vertical dimension of ⅛ in (3 mm). Grooves may be used indoors only. The textured area shall extend 36 in (915 mm) in the direction of travel and the full width of the walkway. Tactile warnings shall be provided at the top of all stair runs except those in dwelling units, in enclosed stair towers, or not in the line of travel. Tactile warnings shall also be installed where a walk crosses a frequently used vehicular way.

Doors to hazardous areas such as boiler rooms, loading platforms, etc., shall be made identifiable to the touch by a textured surface on the doorknob or other operating hardware. The texture may be made by knurling the metal or by applying another material.

Protruding objects

Potentially hazardous object are noticed only if they fall within the detection range of canes (Fig. 27). Visually impaired people can detect a protruding object if its lowest edge is not more than 27 in (685 mm) above the floor. Slight projections of not more than 4 in (100 mm) are not considered hazardous at any height. Projections of more than 4 in (100 mm) whose lowest edge is higher than 27 in (685 mm) are hazardous and should be protected by a wing wall as shown in Fig. 28. When an object such as a telephone is mounted on a wall or free-standing pylon perpendicular to the direction of approach it may project a maximum of 12 in (305 mm) regardless of its height (Fig. 29).

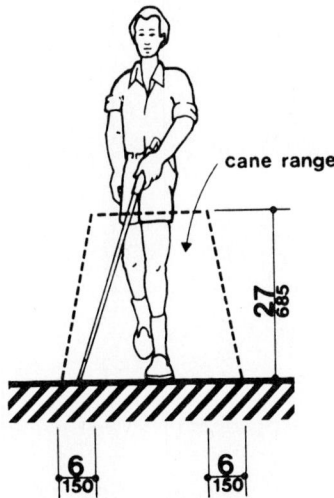

cane range

Fig. 27. Space covered by cane

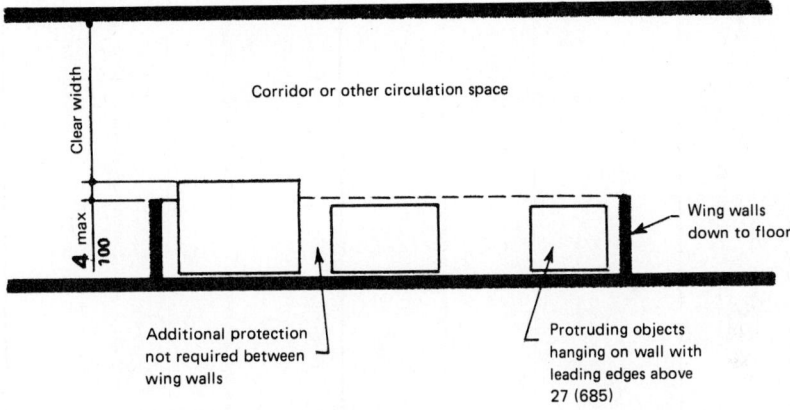

Clear width

Corridor or other circulation space

Wing walls down to floor

Additional protection not required between wing walls

Protruding objects hanging on wall with leading edges above 27 (685)

Fig. 28. Protection against protruding objects

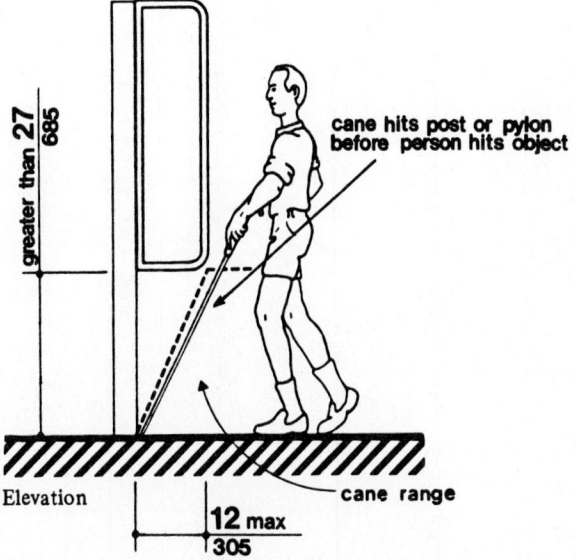

greater than 27 / 685

cane hits post or pylon before person hits object

Elevation

cane range

12 max / 305

Fig. 29. Protruding object in direction of approach

2

Structural Design

HANS J. MILTON, F.R.A.I.A., *Center for Building Technology, National Bureau of Standards*

ble 1. Densities of miscellaneous materials (Mass per unit volume)

	lb/ft³	kg/m³
tals, alloys, ores		
minum; cast-hammered	165	2640
ronze	481	7700
imony	416	6660
ss, cast-rolled	526	8430
nze, 7.9 to 14% Sn	552	8840
romium	443	7100
pper; cast-rolled	556	8910
ore, pyrites	262	4200
ld; cast-hammered	1205	19300
bars, stacked	1133	18150
coin in bags	1084	17360
n; cast, pig	450	7210
wrought	480	7690
steel	490	7850
stainless steel	500	8000
spiegel-eisen	468	7500
ferro-silicon	437	7200
ore, hematite	325	5210
ore, hematite, in bank	160–180	2560–2880
ore, hematite, loose	130–160	2080–2560
ore, limonite	237	3800
ore, magnetite	315	5050
slag	172	2760
ad	710	11370
ore, galena	465	7450
agnesium	109	1750
anganese	456	7300
ercury	848	13580
olybdenum	637	10200
ckel	545	8730
monel metal	556	8910
atinum, cast-hammered	1330	21300
ver, cast-hammered	655	10500
bars, stacked	590	9450
coin in bags	590	9450
; cast-hammered	459	7350
babbit metal	443	7100
ore, cassiterite	418	6700
ngsten	1180	18900
nadium	372	5960
c; cast-rolled	449	7190
ore, blende	253	4050
arious solids		
arbon; amorphous, graphitic	129	2070
ment, portland, loose	90	1440
nders, dry, in bulk	45	720
rk	15	240
ts	58	930
ass; common, plate	160	2560
crystal	184	2950
flint	220	3520
osphorus, white	114	1830
rcelain, china	150	2400
sins, Rosin, Amber	67	1070
bber, caoutchouc	58	930
nd, clean and dry	90	1440
river, dry	106	1700
icon	155	2480
lfur, amorphous	128	2050
ax	60	960
mber, seasoned		
(Moisture content 12%)		
sh, white	41	660
edar; white, red	22	350
estnut	30	480

	lb/ft³	kg/m³
Timber, seasoned (Cont.)		
Cypress	32	510
Ebony	76	1220
Fir; Douglas	34	540
eastern	26	420
Elm, rock	44	700
Hemlock, eastern	28	450
Hickory	51	820
Locust	48	770
Maple; hard	42	670
soft	34	540
Oak; red	44	700
white	46	740
Pine; Norway	32	510
ponderosa	28	450
white	25	400
yellow, long-leaf	41	660
yellow, short-leaf	35	560
Poplar	30	480
Redwood, California	28	450
Spruce; white, black	28	450
Walnut; black	38	610
white (butternut)	27	430
Various liquids		
Alcohol (external), 100%	49	790
Acids; muriatic 40%	75	1200
nitric 91%	94	1510
sulfuric 87%	112	1790
Oils; vegetable	58	930
mineral, lubricants	57	915
Water; 4° C. max. density	62.428	1000
100° C	59.830	958
ice	57.2	916
snow, fresh fallen	8	130
sea water	64	1030
Minerals		
Asbestos	153	2450
Barytes	281	4500
Basalt	184	2950
Bauxite	159	2550
Borax	109	1750
Chalk	137	2190
Clay, marl	137	2190
Dolomite	181	2900
Feldspar, orthoclase	159	2550
Gneiss, serpentine	159	2550
Granite, syenite	175	2800
Gravel, dry	104	1670
Greenstone, trap	187	2990
Gypsum; alabaster	159	2550
loose	70	1120
Hornblende	187	2990
Lime, hydrated; loose	32	510
compacted	45	720
Limestone, marble	165	2640
Magnesite	187	2990
Phosphate rock, apatite	200	3200
Porphyry	172	2760
Pumice, natural	40	640
Quartz, flint	165	2640
Slag; bank	70	1120
bank screenings	108	1730
machine	96	1540
sand	52	830
Sandstone, bluestone	147	2350
Shale, slate	172	2760
Soapstone, talc	169	2710

	lb/ft³	kg/m³
Plastics		
Acrylics	66–74	1050–1190
Cellulosics	71–80	1130–1280
Fluorocarbons	133–137	2130–2200
Melamine	94	1500
Phenolics	87–119	1400–1900
Polyethylene	56	900
Polystyrene	66	1060
Polyurethane	62–81	1000–1300
Reinforced Polyesters	94–131	1500–2100
Silicones	117	1880
Vinyls	74–104	1180–1670
Stone, quarried, piled		
Basalt, granite, gneiss	96	1540
Limestone, marble, quartz	95	1520
Sandstone	82	1310
Shale	92	1470
Greenstone, hornblende	107	1710
Bituminous substance		
Asphaltum	81	1300
Coal; anthracite	97	1550
bituminous	84	1350
lignite	78	1250
peat, turf, dry	47	750
charcoal, pine	23	370
charcoal, oak	33	530
coke	75	1200
Graphite	135	2160
Paraffin	56	900
Petroleum; crude	55	880
refined	50	800
benzine	46	740
gasoline	42	670
kerosene	51	820
Pitch	69	1110
Tar, bituminous	75	1200
Coal and coke, piled		
Coal; anthracite	47–58	750–930
bituminous, lignite	40–54	640–860
peat, turf	20–26	320–420
charcoal	10–14	160–220
coke	23–32	370–510
Earth, etc., excavated		
Clay; dry	63	1010
damp, plastic	110	1760
Clay and gravel, dry	100	1600
Earth; dry, loose	76	1220
dry, packed	95	1520
moist, loose	78	1250
moist, packed	96	1540
mud, flowing	108	1730
mud, packed	115	1840
Riprap; limestone	80–85	1280–1360
sandstone	90	1440
shale	105	1680
Sand, gravel, dry; loose	90–105	1440–1680
packed	100–120	1600–1920
wet	118–120	1890–1920
Excavations in water		
Sand or gravel	60	960
with clay	65	1040
Clay	80	1280
River mud	90	1440
Soil	70	1120
Stone riprap	65	1040

Values are representative of materials only, and may vary slightly.
Metric (SI) values have been converted and rounded to the nearest 10 kg/m³ (0.6 lb/ft³), except for precise values for water. Water at its maximum density (4°C) has a mass per unit volume of exactly 1000 kg/m³, or 1 kg/L; therefore, all metric values divided by 1000 provide a direct indication of the specific gravity of a material.

MINIMUM DESIGN LOADS

The following data on minimum design loads have been adapted from *American National Standard Building Code Requirements for Minimum Design Loads in Buildings and Other Structures (ANSI A58.1—1972)*, sponsored by the National Bureau of Standards.

Table 2. Dead loads—weights of building materials and constructions

Weights of masonry include mortar but not plaster. For plaster, add 5 psf for each face plastered. Average values are given. In some cases there is a considerable range of weight for the same construction; this may be as high as 25 per cent.

	Load, psf			Load, psf			Load, psf
Walls			**Partitions (Cont.)**			**Roof and wall coverings (Cont.)**	
Clay brick; 4-in., high-absorption	34		Gypsum block; 2-in.	9½		Copper or tin	1
4-in., medium-absorption	39		3-in.	10½		Corrugated asbestos-cement roofing	4
4-in., low-absorption	46		4-in.	12½		Corrugated iron	2
8-in., high-absorption	69		5-in.	14		Rigid insulation, ½-in.	¾
8-in., medium-absorption	79		6-in.	18½		Gypsum sheathing, ½-in.	2
8-in., low-absorption	89		Solid plaster; 2-in.	20		Skylight, metal frame, ⅜-in. wire glass	8
12½-in., high-absorption	100		4-in.	32		Slate; 3⁄16-in.	7
12½-in., medium-absorption	115		Hollow plaster, 4-in.	22		¼-in.	10
12½-in., low-absorption	130		Concrete block; 4-in., heavy-aggregate	30		Wood sheathing, per inch of thickness	3
17-in., high-absorption	134		4-in., light-aggregate	20		Wood shingles	3
17-in., medium-absorption	155		6-in., heavy-aggregate	42			
17-in., low-absorption	173		6-in., light-aggregate	28			
22-in., high-absorption	168		8-in., heavy-aggregate	55			Load lb per cu ft
22-in., medium-absorption	194		8-in., light-aggregate	37			
22-in., low-absorption	216		12-in., heavy-aggregate	85		**Materials**	
Sand-lime brick; 4-in.	38		12-in., light-aggregate	55		Cast-stone masonry (cement, stone, sand)	144
8-in.	74		Wood studs, 2x4-in.; unplastered	4		Cinder fill	57
12½-in.	105		plastered one side	12		Concrete, plain; cinder	108
17-in.	138		plastered two sides	20		expanded-slag aggregate	100
22-in.	173					haydite (burned-clay aggregate)	90
Concrete brick; 4-in., heavy-aggregate	46		**Glass-block masonry**			slag	132
4-in., light-aggregate	33		4-in. glass-block walls and partitions	18		stone (including gravel)	144
8-in., heavy-aggregate	89					vermiculite and perlite aggregate, nonloadbearing	25–50
8-in., light-aggregate	68		**Split furring tile**			other light aggregate, load-bearing	70–105
12½-in., heavy-aggregate	130		1½-in.	8			
12½-in., light-aggregate	98		2-in.	8½		Concrete, reinforced; cinder	111
17-in., heavy-aggregate	174					slag	138
17-in., light-aggregate	130		**Concrete slabs per inch of thickness**			stone (including gravel)	150
22-in., heavy-aggregate	216		Reinforced; stone	12½		Masonry, ashlar; granite	165
22-in., light-aggregate	160		cinder	9½		crystalline limestone	165
Brick, 4-in.; with 4-in. loadbearing structural clay-tile backing	60		lightweight	9		oolitic limestone	135
with 8-in. loadbearing structural clay-tile backing	75		Plain; stone	12		marble	173
			cinder	9		sandstone	144
Brick, 8-in., with 4-in. loadbearing structural clay-tile backing	102		lightweight	8½		Masonry, brick; hard (low-absorption)	130
Structural clay tile; 8-in. load-bearing	42		**Ceilings**			medium (medium-absorption)	115
12-in. loadbearing	58		Plaster on tile or concrete	5		soft (high-absorption)	100
Concrete block; 8-in., heavy-aggregate	55		Plaster on wood lath	8			
8-in., light-aggregate	35		Suspended metal lath and gypsum plaster	10		Masonry, rubble; granite	153
12-in., heavy-aggregate	85		Suspended metal lath and cement plaster	15		crystalline limestone	147
12-in., light-aggregate	55					oolitic limestone	138
Furring tile, 2-in., one side of masonry wall, add to above figures	12		**Roof and wall coverings**			marble	156
			Asphalt shingles	2		sandstone	137
Partitions			Cement-asbestos shingles	4		Terra cotta, architectural; voids filled	120
Clay tile; 3-in.	17		Cement tile	16		voids unfilled	72
4-in.	18		Clay tile (for mortar add 10 lb)			Timber, seasoned; commercial white ash	41
6-in.	28		2-in. book tile	12		commercial red and white oak	45
8-in.	34		3-in. book tile	20			
10-in.	40		Roman	12		Douglas fir, coast region	34
Facing tile; 2-in.	15		Spanish	19		southern cypress	32
4-in.	25		Ludowici	10		southern yellow pine	39
6-in.	38		Composition; three-ply ready roofing	1		redwood	28
			four-ply felt and gravel	5½		red, white, and Sitka spruce	28
			five-ply felt and gravel	6			

Table 2 (cont.). Dead loads—weights of building materials and constructions

Depth, in. (rib depth + slab thickness)	Width of rib, in.						Load, psf
	4	5	6	7	8	9	
	Weight, psf						

Ribbed Slabs, Stone Concrete

12-in. clay-tile fillers:

	4	5	6	7	8	9
4 plus 2	49	51	52	54		
6 plus 2	60	63	65	67		
8 plus 2½	79	82	85	87		
10 plus 3	96	100	103	106		
12 plus 3	108	112	116	120		

20-in. forms:

	4	5	6	7	8	9
6 plus 2½	45	48	50	53		
8 plus 2½	51	54	57	60		
10 plus 2½	57	60	64	68		
12 plus 2½	63	67	72	76		
14 plus 2½		74	79	84		
16 plus 2½			88	93	98	
20 plus 2½				111	118	

30-in. forms:

	4	5	6	7	8	9
6 plus 2½	41	43	45	47		
8 plus 2½	45	47	50	53		
10 plus 2½	49	52	55	58		
12 plus 2½	53	57	60	64		
14 plus 2½		62	66	70		
16 plus 2½			72	76	80	
20 plus 2½				90	95	101

(Make appropriate allowances for tapered ends)

Waffle Slabs, Stone Concrete

2-way clay-tile fillers (12 x 12):

	4	5	6
4 plus 2	61	62	64
6 plus 2	87	89	90
8 plus 2½	100	103	107
10 plus 3	121	126	131
12 plus 3	136	141	146

2-way metal forms: 19 × 19, 5 @ 24

	Load, psf
6 plus 2½	66
8 plus 2½	78
10 plus 2½	85
12 plus 2½	101

2-way metal forms: 30 × 30, 6 @ 36

	Load, psf
8 plus 3	73
10 plus 3	83
12 plus 3	95
14 plus 3	106
16 plus 3	114
20 plus 3	135

Floor Finish and Fill

	Load, psf
Double ⅞-in. wood on sleepers, light-concrete fill	19
Double ⅞-in. wood on sleepers, stone-concrete fill	28
Single ⅞-in. wood on sleepers, light-concrete fill	16
Single ⅞-in. wood on sleepers, stone-concrete fill	25
3-in. wood block on mastic, no fill	10
1-in. cement finish on stone-concrete fill	32
1-in. terrazzo on stone-concrete fill	32
Marble and mortar on stone-concrete fill	33
Linoleum on stone-concrete fill	32
Linoleum on light-concrete fill	22

Floor Finish

	Load, psf
1½-in. asphalt mastic flooring	18
3-in. wood block on ½-in. mortar base	16
Solid flat tile on 1-in. mortar base	23
2-in. asphalt block, ½-in. mortar	30
1-in. terrazzo, 2-in. stone concrete	38

Waterproofing

	Load, psf
Five-ply membrane	5

Floor Fill

	Load, psf
Cinder concrete, per inch	9
Lightweight concrete, per inch	7
Sand, per inch	8
Stone concrete, per inch	12

Wood-Joist Floors (No Plaster), Double Wood Floor

Joist size, in.	12-in. spacing, psf	16-in. spacing, psf
2x 6	6	5
2x 8	6	6
2x10	7	6
2x12	8	7
3x 6	7	6
3x 8	8	7
3x10	9	8
3x12	11	9
3x14	12	10

LIVE LOADS

Stairway and balcony railings, both exterior and interior, should be designed to resist a vertical and a horizontal thrust of 50 lb per lin ft applied at the top edge of the railing.

Floor loads: Floors should be designed to support safely the uniformly distributed live loads prescribed in Table 1 or the concentrated load in pounds given in Table 2, whichever produces the greater stresses.

Unless otherwise specified, the indicated concentration is assumed to occupy an area of 2½ ft square, so located as to produce the maximum stress conditions in the structural members.

Roof trusses: Any panel point of the lower chord of roof trusses or any point of other primary structural members supporting roofs over garage, manufacturing, and storage floors should be capable of carrying safely a suspended concentrated load of not less than 2,000 lb.

Elevators: All moving elevator loads should be increased 100 per cent for impact. The structural supports should be designed within the limits of deflection prescribed by the *American National Standard Safety Code for Elevators, Dumbwaiters, Escalators, and Moving Walks* (ANSI A17.1–1978) and *American National Standard Practice for the Inspection of Elevators (Inspectors' Manual)* (ANSI A17.2–1979).

Table 3. Minimum uniformly distributed live loads

Occupancy or use	Live load, psf	Occupancy or use	Live load, psf
Apartments (see Residential)		Office buildings:	
Armories and drill rooms	150	Offices	50
Assembly halls and other places of		Lobbies	100
assembly:		Corridors above first floor	80
Fixed seats	60	File and computer rooms require	
Movable seats	100	heavier loads based upon	
Platforms (assembly)	100	anticipated occupancy	
Balcony (exterior):	100	Penal institutions:	
On one- and two-family residences only		Cell blocks	40
and not exceeding 100 sq ft	60	Corridors	100
Bowling alleys, poolrooms, and		Residential:	
similar recreational areas	75	Multifamily houses:	
Corridors:		Private apartments	40
First floor	100	Public rooms	100
Other floors, same as occupancy		Corridors	80
served except as indicated		Dwellings:	
Dance halls and ballrooms	100	First floor	40
Dining rooms and restaurants	100	Second floor and habitable attics	30
Dwellings (see Residential)		Uninhabitable attics	20
Fire escapes	100	Hotels:	
On multi- or single-family residential		Guest rooms	40
buildings only	40	Public rooms	100
Garages (passenger cars only)	50	Corridors serving public rooms	100
For trucks and buses use AASHO*		Corridors	80
lane loads (See Table 4 for		Reviewing stands and bleachers†	100
concentrated load requirements)		Schools:	
Grandstands (see Reviewing stands)		Classrooms	40
Gymnasiums, main floors and balconies	100	Corridors	80
Hospitals:		Sidewalks, vehicular driveways, and yards	
Operating rooms, laboratories	60	subject to trucking	250
Private rooms	40	Skating rinks	100
Wards	40	Stairs and exitways	100
Corridors above first floor	80	Storage warehouse, light	125
Hotels (see Residential)		Storage warehouse, heavy	250
Libraries:		Stores:	
Reading rooms	60	Retail:	
Stack rooms (books and shelving at		First-floor, rooms	100
65 pcf) but not less than	150	Upper floors	75
Corridors above first floor	80	Wholesale	125
Manufacturing:		Theaters:	
Light	125	Aisles, corridors, and lobbies	100
Heavy	250	Orchestra floors	60
Marquees	75	Balconies	60
		Stage floors	150
		Yards and terraces, pedestrians	100

*American Association of State Highway Officials.

† For detailed recommendations, see American National Standard for Tents, Grandstands, and Air-Supported Structures Used for Places of Assembly (ANSI/NFPA 102—1967).

Table 4. Concentrated loads

Location	Load, lb
Elevator machine room grating (on area of 4 sq in.)	300
Finish light floor plate construction (on area of 1 sq in.)	200
Garages	*
Office floors	2,000
Scuttles, skylight ribs, and accessible ceilings	200
Sidewalks	8,000
Stair treads (on center of tread)	300

Floors in garages or portions of buildings used for storage of motor vehicles shall be designed for the uniformly distributed live loads of Table 3 or the following concentrated loads:

For passenger cars accommodating not more than nine passengers, 2,000 lb acting on an area of 20 sq in.

Mechanical parking structures without slab or deck, passenger cars only, 1,500 lb per wheel.

For trucks or buses, maximum axle load on an area of 20 sq in.

Machinery: For the purpose of design, the weight of machinery and moving loads shall be increased as follows to allow for impact: (1) elevator machinery, 100 per cent; (2) light machinery, shaft or motor driven, 20 per cent; (3) reciprocating machinery or power driven units, 50 per cent; (4) hangers for floors or balconies, 33 per cent; all percentages increased if so recommended by the manufacturer.

Craneways: All craneways shall have their design loads increased for impact as follows: (1) a vertical force equal to 25 per cent of the maximum wheel load; (2) a lateral force equal to 20 per cent of the weight of trolley and lifted load only, applied one-half at the top of each rail; and (3) a longitudinal force of 10 per cent of the maximum wheel loads of the crane applied at top of rail.

Reduction in live loads

Live loads 100 psf or less: For live loads of 100 psf or less, the design live load on any member supporting 150 sf or more may be reduced at the rate of 0.08 per cent per square foot of area supported by the member, but no reduction shall be made for areas to be occupied as places of public assembly, for garages, or for roofs. The reduction shall exceed neither R, as determined by the following formula, nor 60 per cent:

Table 5. Minimum roof live loads (in pounds per square foot of horizontal projection)

Roof slope	Tributary loaded area in square feet for any structural member		
	0 to 200	201 to 600	Over 600
Flat or rise less than 4 in. per ft Arch or dome with rise less than 1/8 of span	20	16	12
Rise 4 in. per ft to less than 12 in. per ft Arch or dome with rise 1/8 of span to less than 3/8 of span	16	14	12
Rise 12 in. per ft and greater Arch or dome with rise 3/8 of span or greater	12	12	12

$$R = 23 \left(1 + \frac{D}{L}\right)$$

in which R = reduction in per cent

D = dead load per square foot of area supported by the member

L = design live load per square foot of area supported by the member

Live loads exceeding 100 psf: For live loads exceeding 100 psf, no reduction shall be made except for the design live loads on columns, which may be reduced 20 per cent.

Minimum roof loads

Flat, pitched, or curved roofs: Ordinary roofs, either flat, pitched, or curved, shall be designed for the live loads as specified in Table 5 or the snow load as specified below, whichever produces the greater stresses.

Ponding: For roofs, care shall be taken to provide drainage or the load shall be increased to represent all likely accumulations of water. Deflection of roof members will permit ponding of water accompanied by increased deflection and additional ponding.

Special-purpose roofs: When used for incidental promenade purposes, roofs shall be designed for a minimum live load of 60 psf, and 100 psf when designed for roof-garden or assembly uses. Roofs to be used for other special purposes shall be designed for appropriate loads as directed or approved by the building official.

Combining loads

Except when applicable codes make other provisions, all the loads listed herein shall be considered to act in the following combinations, whichever produce the most unfavorable effects in the building, foundation, or structural member concerned.

The most unfavorable effect may occur when one or more of the contributing loads are not acting:

D	(1)
D + L	(2)
D + (W or E)	(3)
D + T	(4)
D + L + (W or E)	(5)
D + L + T	(6)
D + (W or E) + T	(7)
D + L + (W or E) + T	(8)

where D = dead load

L = live load

W = wind load

E = earthquake load

T = load due to contraction or expansion resulting from temperature changes or other causes

Probability factor

The total of the combined load effects may be multiplied by the following load combination probability factors:

a. 1.00 for combinations (1) through (4)

b. 0.75 for combinations (5) through (7)

c. 0.66 for combination (8)

SOIL AND HYDROSTATIC PRESSURE

Pressure on basement walls

In the design of basement walls and similar approximately vertical structures below grade, provision shall be made for the lateral pressure of adjacent soil. Due allowance shall be made for possible surcharge from fixed or moving loads. When a portion or the whole of the adjacent soil is below a free-water surface, computations shall be based on the weight of the soil diminished by buoyancy, plus full hydrostatic pressure.

Uplift on floors

In the design of basement floors and similar approximately horizontal construction below grade, the upward pressure of water, if any, shall be taken as the full hydrostatic pressure applied over the entire area. The hydrostatic head shall be measured from the underside of the construction.

Table 6. Live loads for storage warehouses*

Material	Pounds per Cubic Foot of Space	Height of Pile, Feet	Pounds per Square Foot of Floor
Produce, Grain, Fruit, Etc.			
Grain, in bulk			
Barley and Corn	37	8	296
Oats	26	8	208
Rye and Wheat	48	8	384
Fruit and Vegetables, in bulk			
Apples, Pears, etc	38	8	304
Potatoes, Turnips, etc	44	8	352
Miscellaneous Produce, packed			
Beans, in bags	40	8	320
Corn, in bags	31	8	248
Cornmeal, in barrels	37	6½	240
Oats, in bags	26	9	234
Rice, in bags	58	5	290
Wheat, in bags	39	8	312
Wheat Flour, in barrels	40	7	280
Hay, in bales, not compressed	14	9	126
Hay, in bales, compressed	24	9	216
Straw, in bales, compressed	19	9	171
Groceries			
Miscellaneous Articles, packed			
Butter, Lard, etc., in barrels	32	6	192
Canned Goods, Preserves, etc., in cases	58	6	348
Cheese	30	8	240
Coffee, green, in bags	39	8	312
Coffee, roasted, in bags	33	8	264
Dates and Figs, in cases, average	65	5	325
Meat, Beef, Pork, etc., in barrels	37	5	185
Molasses, in barrels	48	5	240
Salt, finely ground, in sacks	60	5	300
Soap Powder, in cases	38	8	288
Starch, in barrels	25	7	175
Sugar, in barrels	43	5	215
Tea, in chests	25	8	200
Wines, Liquors, etc., in barrels	48	5	240
Dry Goods, Cotton, Wool, Etc.			
Cotton, in bales, compressed, average	25	9	225
" unbleached goods, in bales	24	9	216
" tickings and duck, in bales	35	8	280
" printed goods, in bales	19	9	171
" printed goods, in cases	31	8	248
" quilts and flannels, in cases	16	9	144
" yarn, in cases	25	8	200
Hemp, in bales, compressed	22	8	176
" Manila, in bales, compressed	26	9	234
" Sisal, in bales, compressed	24	9	216
" Tow, in bales, compressed	29	9	261
" Burlaps, in bales, compressed	43	6	258
Jute, in bales, compressed	41	6	246
Linen, bleached goods, in cases	35	7	245
" damask goods, in cases	50	5	250
Wool, in bales, not compressed	13	9	117
" in bales, compressed	48	5	240
" dress goods, flannels, in cases	18	9	162
" worsted goods, in cases	27	9	243
Rags, in bales, compressed	19	9	171
Excelsior, in bales, compressed	19	9	171

Material	Pounds per Cubic Foot of Space	Height of Pile, Feet	Pounds per Square Foot of Floor
Drugs, Oils, Paints, Etc.			
Chemicals:			
Acids, Muriatic and Nitric, in carboys	45	1⅔	75
" Sulphuric, in carboys	60	1⅔	100
Ammonia, in carboys	30	1⅔	50
Alum, Pearl Alum, in barrels	33	7	231
Bleaching Powder, in hogsheads	31	3⅓	103
Copper Sulphate, Blue Vitriol, in bbls.	45	5	225
Soda, Caustic Soda, in iron drums	88	3⅓	294
Soda, Soda Ash, in hogsheads	62	2¾	170
Soda Crystals, Sal Soda, in barrels	30	5	150
Soda Nitrate, Niter, in barrels	45	5	225
Soda Silicate, in barrels	53	5	265
Zinc Sulphate, White Vitriol, in barrels	40	5	200
Oils, Fats, Resins, etc.:			
Glycerine, in cases	52	6	312
Oils, Animal, Lard, etc., in barrels	34	6	204
" Vegetable, Linseed, in barrels	36	6	216
" Mineral, Lubricants, in barrels	35	6	210
" Petroleum, Kerosene, in barrels	33	6	198
" Naphtha, Gasolene, in barrels	28	6	168
Rosin, in barrels	48	6	288
Shellac Gum, in boxes	38	6	228
Tallow, in barrels	37	6	222
Dye Stuffs, Paints, etc.:			
Indigo, in boxes	43	6	258
Logwood Extract, in boxes	70	4½	315
Sumac, in boxes	39	5	195
Red Lead, Litharge, dry, in barrels	132	3¾	495
White Lead, dry, in barrels	86	4¾	409
White Lead, paste, in cans	174	3½	609
Building Materials			
Cement, Natural, in barrels	59	6	354
" Portland, in barrels	73	6	438
Lime, Quick Lime, ground, in barrels	50	5	250
Plaster of Paris, ground in barrels	53	5	265
Sheet Metal and Wire			
Sheet Tin, in boxes	278	1½	417
Wire, insulated copper, in coils	63	5	315
" galvanized iron, in coils	74	4½	333
" magnet wire, on spools	75	6	450
Miscellaneous			
Chinaware, Glassware, in crates	40	8	320
" in casks	14	9	126
Glass, in boxes	60	6	360
Hardware, door and sash checks, in cases	46	6	276
" hinges, in cases	64	6	384
" locks, in cases	31	6	186
" screws, in boxes	101	4	404
Hides, raw, not compressed, in bales	13	10	130
" raw, compressed, in bales	23	10	230
Leather, in bales	16	10	160
Paper, calendered paper	50	6	300
" newspaper, manila, strawboards	35	6	210
" writing paper	64	6	384
Rope in Coils	42	6	252

This table is not from ANSI A58.1.

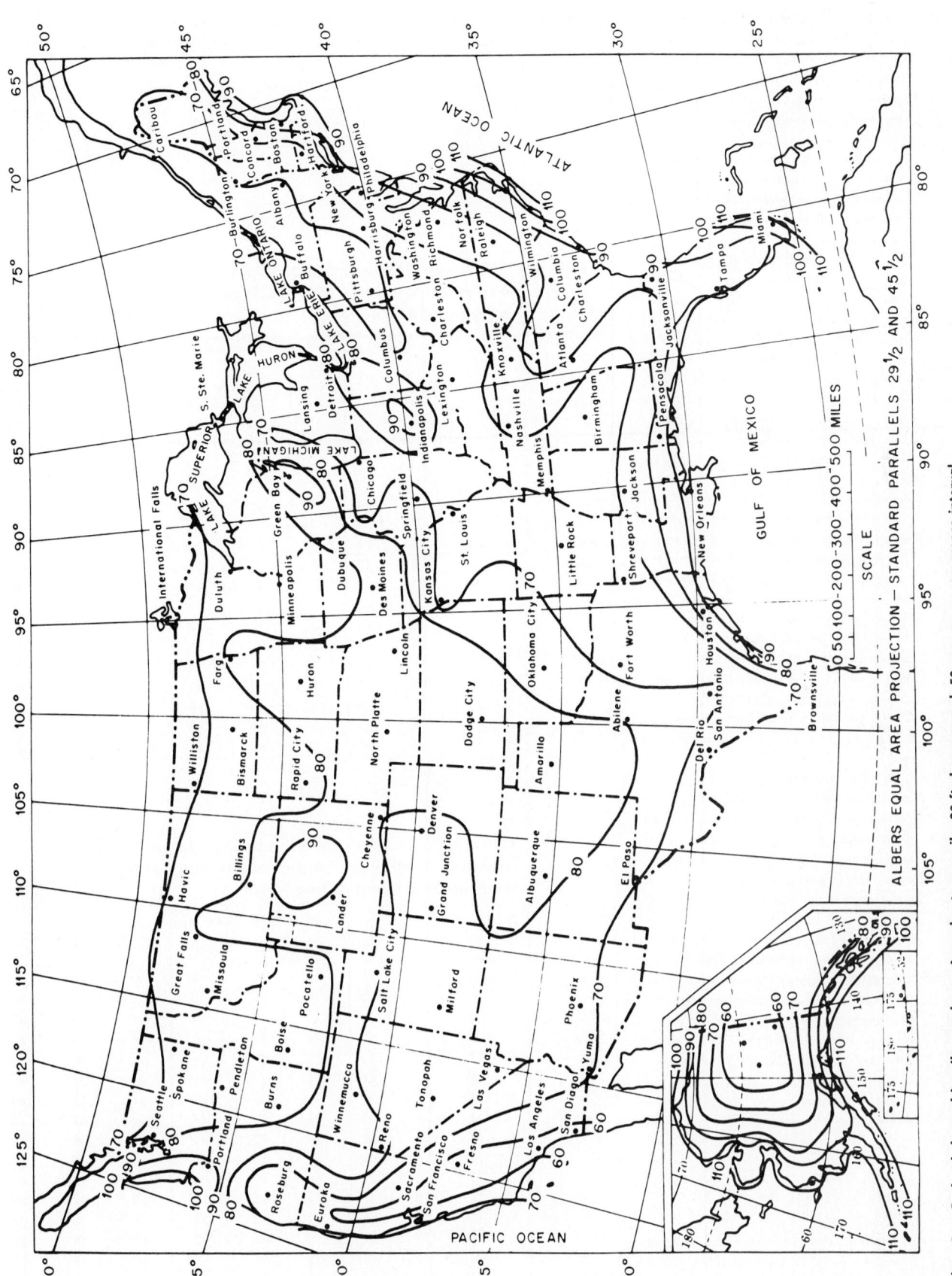

Fig. 1. Basic wind speed in miles per hour. Annual extreme-mile, 30 ft above ground, 50-year mean recurrence interval

ALBERS EQUAL AREA PROJECTION – STANDARD PARALLELS 29½ AND 45½

SCALE

0 50 100 200 300 400 500 MILES

In calculating wind loads on buildings, use is made (1) of new distributions of extreme fastest-mile winds in the United States for various mean recurrence intervals, and (2) the concept of varying load requirements based on the dynamic properties of the structure and on the nature of the surrounding terrain.

Procedure for calculating wind loads on buildings is as follows:

1. Select the appropriate mean recurrence interval depending upon the intended use and anticipated life of the building. The 50-year interval shown in Fig. 1 should be used for all buildings except those which present an unusually high degree of wind sensitivity or hazard to life in case of failure; for these a 100-year mean recurrence interval should be used. For buildings which have no human occupants, a 25-year mean recurrence interval may be used.

2. Select basic wind speed from Fig. 1 or Table 7. (Maps for 100-year and 25-year mean recurrence intervals can be found in ANSI A58.1—1972.)

3. Convert basic wind speed to effective velocity pressure by reference to Tables 8–10. (Effective velocity pressures on parts of buildings such as girts, windows, spandrels, etc., and tributary areas less than 200 sq ft are 10 to 15 per cent higher than those for whole buildings; values for a range of heights, wind speeds, and exposures are tabulated in the Standard. See section on Curtain Walls.)

4. Find design loads by multiplying effective velocity pressure by the appropriate pressure coefficients (Tables 11–17).

Pressure coefficients define the pressure acting normally at local positions on the surface of a building. Net pressure coefficients apply to the direct calculation of the wind force acting over the projected area of a structure and are dependent on its external shape and orientation with respect to the wind. In the calculation of wind loads on buildings or elements thereof, the pressure difference between opposite faces shall be taken into account. Where more than one coefficient is specified, each shall be considered in determining the maximum stresses. The net pressure shall not, in any case, be less than 10 psf for the entire building nor less than 15 psf for portions thereof. Negative values for pressure indicate pressure acting outward. Pressure coefficients given here apply to typical rectangular buildings with doors, openable windows, etc.

Walls

External pressure coefficients for walls are given in Table 11. In addition, a pressure coefficient of —2.0 shall be used at the corners of all walls and assumed to be acting on strips of width 0.1w, where w is the least width of the building. These

Table 7. - Hawaii and Puerto Rico basic wind speeds (mph)

Hawaii			
Mean recurrence interval (years)	25	50	100
Westerly exposure	60	65	75
Easterly	70	80	90
Puerto Rico			
All exposures	80	95	110

Table 8. Effective velocity pressures in pounds per square foot, exposure A—centers of large cities and very rough, hilly terrain*

Height, ft	Basic wind speed, mph								
	50	60	70	80	90	100	110	120	130
Less than 30	3	4	5	6	7	9	10	12	14
30	3	4	5	7	9	11	13	15	18
50	3	5	7	9	11	13	16	19	23
100	5	7	9	12	15	18	22	27	31
150	6	8	11	14	18	22	27	32	38
200	6	9	12	16	21	26	31	37	43
250	7	10	14	18	23	28	34	41	48
300	8	11	15	20	25	31	38	45	53
350	8	12	17	22	27	34	41	49	57
400	9	13	18	23	29	36	44	52	61
450	10	14	19	24	31	38	46	55	64
500	10	15	20	26	33	40	49	58	68
550	11	15	21	27	34	42	51	61	71
600	11	16	22	28	36	44	54	64	75
650	11	17	22	29	37	46	56	66	78
700	12	17	23	31	39	48	58	69	81
750	12	18	24	32	40	50	60	71	84
800	13	18	25	33	42	51	62	74	87

Interpolations of the values may be used for intermediate heights.

Table 9. Effective velocity pressures in pounds per square foot, exposure B—suburban areas, towns, city outskirts, wooded areas, and rolling terrain*

Height, ft	Basic wind speed, mph								
	50	60	70	80	90	100	110	120	130
Less than 30	5	6	8	10	13	16	20	23	27
30	5	7	10	13	16	20	25	29	34
50	6	9	12	15	19	24	29	34	40
100	7	11	15	19	24	30	36	43	51
150	9	12	17	22	28	34	41	49	58
200	9	14	18	24	31	38	46	54	64
250	10	15	20	26	33	41	49	59	69
300	11	16	21	28	35	43	52	62	73
350	11	16	22	29	37	45	55	65	77
400	12	17	23	31	39	48	58	69	81
450	12	18	24	32	40	50	60	72	84
500	13	18	25	33	42	51	62	74	87
550	13	19	26	34	43	53	64	76	90
600	14	20	27	35	44	55	66	79	92
650	14	20	28	36	46	57	69	82	96
700	14	21	28	37	47	58	70	83	98
750	15	21	29	38	48	59	72	86	100
800	15	22	30	39	49	61	73	87	102

Interpolations of the values may be used for intermediate heights.

local pressures shall not be included with the net external pressure when computing over-all loads.

Roofs

For buildings with a ratio of wall height to least width less than 2.5, an external pressure coefficient of −0.7 shall be used for the roof and assumed to act uniformly over the entire roof area. For buildings in which the height-width ratio is 2.5 or greater, a value of −0.8 shall be used. For arched roofs with the wind perpendicular to the axis of the arch, the coefficients shown in Table 12 shall be used. For gabled roofs with the wind perpendicular to the ridge, a pressure coefficient of −0.7 shall be used for the leeward slope together with a coefficient for the windward slope which depends on the roof slope and the height-width ratio of the building, as shown in Table 13. In addition, the local pressure coefficients given in Table 14 shall be used and assumed to be acting on a strip of width 0.1w, where w is the least width of the building normal to the ridge. These local pressures should not be included when computing overall loads. Internal pressure coefficients are given in Table 15.

Net pressure coefficients for flat or shed roofs over nonenclosed structures, such as parking garages, shelter areas, outdoor arenas, etc., are given in Table 16, where α is the angle between the wind direction and the plane of the roof and λ is the ratio of the length of the windward edge to the distance between the windward and leeward edges (aspect ratio). The resultant load may act inward or outward.

Net pressure coefficients for chimneys and tanks are given in Table 17. These coefficients apply to the projected area of the structure on a vertical plane normal to the wind direction.

Overturning and sliding

Overturning: The overturning moment due to the wind load should not exceed 66⅔ per cent of stability of the building or other structure due to the dead load only, unless the building or other structure is anchored to resist the excess overturning moment without exceeding the allowable stresses for the materials used. The axis of rotation for computing the overturning moment and the moment of stability should be taken as the intersection of the outside wall line on the leeward side and the plane representing the average elevation of the bottoms of the footings. The weight of earth superimposed over footings may be used in computing the moment of stability due to dead load.

Sliding: If the total resisting force due to friction is insufficient to prevent sliding, the building or other structure should be anchored to withstand the excess sliding

Table 10. Effective velocity pressures in pounds per square foot, exposure C—flat, open country, open flat coastal belts, and grassland*

Height, ft	Basic wind speed, mph								
	50	60	70	80	90	100	110	120	130
Less than 30	6	7	11	15	20	26	32	39	45
30	8	12	16	21	27	33	40	48	56
50	9	14	18	24	31	38	46	54	64
100	11	16	21	28	35	44	53	63	74
150	12	17	23	31	39	48	58	69	81
200	13	18	25	33	41	51	62	74	86
250	13	19	26	34	43	53	65	77	90
300	14	20	27	36	45	56	68	80	94
350	14	21	28	37	47	58	70	83	97
400	15	21	29	38	48	59	72	86	100
450	15	22	30	39	49	61	74	88	103
500	16	22	30	40	50	62	75	90	105
550	16	23	31	41	52	64	77	92	108
600	16	23	32	42	53	65	79	94	110
650	17	24	33	42	54	66	80	96	112
700	17	24	33	43	55	67	82	97	114
750	17	25	34	44	55	68	83	99	116
800	17	25	34	45	57	70	85	101	118

* Interpolations of the values may be used for intermediate heights.

Table 11. External pressure coefficients for walls

Location of wall	Pressure coefficient
Windward wall	0.8
Leeward wall— both height-width and	
height-length ratios of building ≥ 2.5	−0.6
Other buildings	−0.5
Side walls	−0.7

Table 12. External pressure coefficients for arched roofs

Type of roof	Rise-to-span ratio, r	Windward quarter	Center half	Leeward quarter
Roof on	0 < r < 0.2	−0.9		−0.5
elevated	0.2 ≤ r ≤ 0.3	(1.5r −0.3)*	(−0.7 −r)	−0.5
structure	0.3 ≤ r ≤ 0.6	(2.75r −0.68)		−0.5
Roof springing from ground level	0 < r ≤ 0.6	1.42r	(−0.7 −r)	−0.5

* When the rise-to-span ratio is (0.2 ≤ r ≤ 0.3), alternate coefficients given by (6r −2.1) shall also be used for the windward quarter.

Table 13. External pressure coefficients for windward slope of gabled roofs

h/w	θ 10–15 deg	20 deg	25 deg	30 deg	35 deg	40 deg	45 deg	50 deg	≥ 60 deg
≤ 0.3	0.01θ*	0.2	0.25	0.3	0.35	0.4	0.45	0.5	0.01θ
0.5	−1.0	−0.75	−0.5	−0.2	0.05	0.3	0.45	0.5	0.01θ
1.0	−1.0	−1.0	−0.8	−0.55	−0.3	−0.05	0.2	0.45	0.01θ
≥ 1.5	−1.0	−1.0	−1.0	−0.9	−0.6	−0.35	−0.1	0.2	0.01θ

*Except for roofs rising from ground level (h/w = 0), a coefficient of −1.0 shall be used when 10 degrees ≤ θ ≤ 15 degrees. θ = roof slope in degrees from horizontal, h = wall height at eave, w = least width of building normal to ridge.

force without exceeding the allowable stresses for the materials used. Anchors provided to resist overturning moment may also be considered as providing resistance to sliding.

Stresses during erection

Provision should be made for wind stress during erection of the building or other structure.

SNOW LOADS

Basic snow loads to be assumed in the design of buildings or other structures are given in Fig. 2, which shows the ground snow load in pounds per square foot for a 50-year mean recurrence interval. A basic snow load with a 50-year mean recurrence interval shall be used for all permanent structures except those that present an unusually high degree of hazard to life and property in case of failure, in which case a 100-year mean recurrence interval shall be used. For structures having no human occupants a 25-year mean recurrence interval may be used. Maps for 100-year and 25-year mean recurrence intervals may be found in the Standard.

Special snow regions

Special consideration shall be given to regions where no design loads are shown in Fig. 2 and where unusually high accumulations of snow may occur. The variation of ground snow loads with elevation and exposure is not yet completely understood and local differences in mountain regions are usually very significant.

Roof snow load

Minimum snow loads for the design of both ordinary and multiple series roofs, either flat, pitched, or curved, shall be determined by multiplying the ground snow load given in Fig. 2 by the appropriate coefficients. The full intensity of the roof snow load shall be applied to any one contiguous portion of the roof area with zero load on the remainder of the area if it produces a more unfavorable effect than the full intensity applied over the entire roof area.

Snow load coefficients

The basic snow load coefficient shall be taken as 0.8 and shall be increased or decreased in accordance with the following conditions:

1. Decreased load due to slide-off of snow on roofs with slopes exceeding 30 degrees
2. Decreased load due to roofs having a clear exposure in windswept areas
3. Increased load due to nonuniform accumulation on pitched or curved roofs
4. Increased load in the valleys formed by multiple series roofs
5. Increased load due to snow sliding off sloping roof areas onto adjacent roof areas
6. Increased load on the lower levels of multilevel roofs and on roof areas adjacent to projections such as penthouses, cooling towers, and parapet walls due to drifting snow

For roofs having a clear exposure to winds of sufficient intensity to remove snow and having no projections such as parapet walls, a basic snow load coefficient of 0.6 may be used. This coefficient may be applied only in those regions where the resulting reduced snow load is equal to or greater than 12 psf. Roofs shielded on any side by obstructions within a distance of 10h from the building (where h is the height of the obstruction above the level of the roof) shall not be considered to have a clear exposure.

Table 14. Local peak external pressure coefficients for roofs

Roof slope θ*	Ridges and eaves	Corners
0° to 30°	−2.4	$(0.1\theta - 5.0)$
Greater than 30°	−1.7	−2.0

*For arched roofs, θ shall be taken as the angle between the horizontal and the tangent to the roof at the springing.

Table 15. Internal pressure coefficients for buildings

n*	Openings uniformly distributed	Openings mainly in: Windward wall	Leeward wall	Side wall(s)
0 to 0.3	±0.3	$(0.3 + 1.67n)$	$(-0.3 - n)$	$(-0.3 - n)$
Greater than 0.3	±0.3	0.8	−0.6	−0.6

*n = ratio of open area to solid area of wall having majority of openings.

Table 16. Net pressure coefficients for flat plates

a	λ 1/5	1/3	1/2	1	2	3	5
10°	0.2	0.25	0.3	0.45	0.55	0.70	0.75
15°	0.35	0.45	0.5	0.68	0.83	0.88	0.83
20°	0.5	0.6	0.75	0.92	1.0	0.96	0.9
25°	0.7	0.8	0.95	1.14	1.1	1.04	0.95
30°	0.9	1.0	1.2	1.32	1.2	1.1	1.0

Table 17. Net pressure coefficients for chimneys and tanks

Shape	Type of surface	h/d 1	7	25
Square (wind normal to a face)	Smooth or rough	1.3	1.4	2.0
Square (wind along diagonal)	Smooth or rough	1.0	1.1	1.5
Hexagonal or octagonal ($d\sqrt{q} > 2.5$)	Smooth or rough	1.0	1.2	1.4
Round ($d\sqrt{q} > 2.5$)	Moderately smooth*	0.5	0.6	0.7
	Rough ($d'/d \cong 0.02$)	0.7	0.8	0.9
	Very rough ($d'/d \cong 0.08$)	0.8	1.0	1.2

h = height of structure in feet; d = diameter or least horizontal dimension in feet; d' = depth in feet of protruding elements such as ribs and spoilers; q is the effective velocity pressure, in psf, from Tables 8–10.
* = metal, timber, concrete.
For slender structures such as flagpoles, a minimum net pressure coefficient of 1.2 shall be used if $d\sqrt{q} < 2.5$

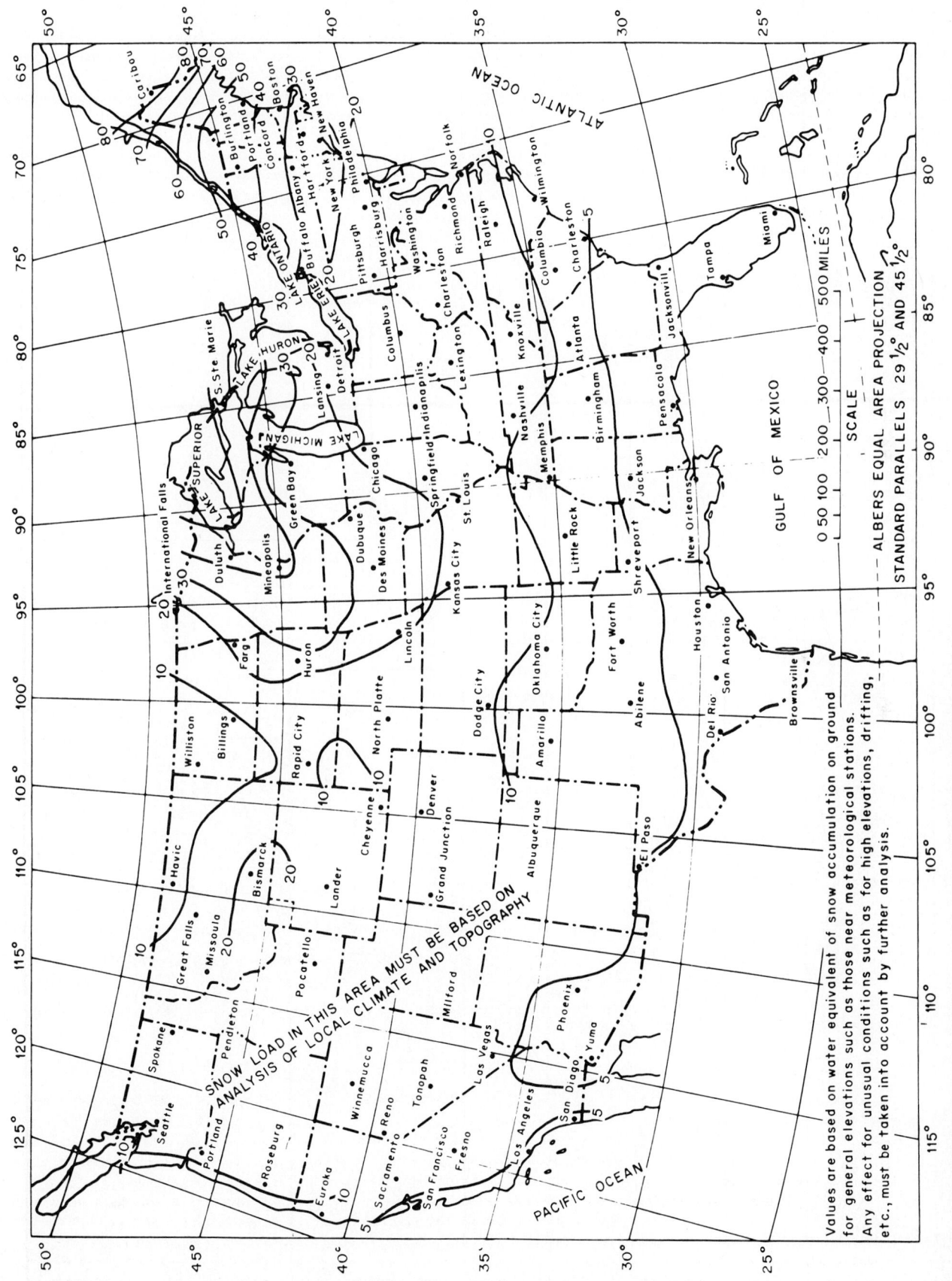

Values are based on water equivalent of snow accumulation on ground for general elevations such as those near meteorological stations. Any effect for unusual conditions such as for high elevations, drifting, etc., must be taken into account by further analysis.

Fig. 2. Snow load in pounds per square foot on the ground, 50-year mean recurrence interval

EARTHQUAKE LOADS

Lateral forces

Every building or structure and every portion thereof, and minor accessory buildings, shall be designed and constructed to resist stresses produced by lateral forces. Stresses shall be calculated as the effect of a force applied horizontally at each floor or roof level above the foundation. The force shall be assumed to come from any horizontal direction. It may be assumed that wind and earthquake loads will not occur simultaneously.

The following definitions apply only to the provisions of this section:

A space frame is a three-dimensional structural system composed of interconnected members other than shear or bearing walls and laterally supported so as to function as a complete self-contained unit with or without the aid of horizontal diaphragms or floor bracing systems.

A space frame—vertical load-carrying is a space frame designed to carry all vertical loads.

A space frame—moment-resisting is a vertical load-carrying space frame in which the members and joints are capable of resisting design lateral forces by bending moments and column shears.

A space frame—ductile moment-resisting is a moment-resisting space frame in which ductility is provided in the elastic and inelastic range in accordance with established criteria. (See *Uniform Building Code,*

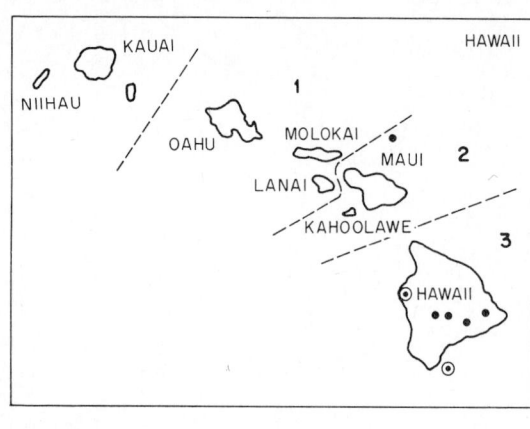

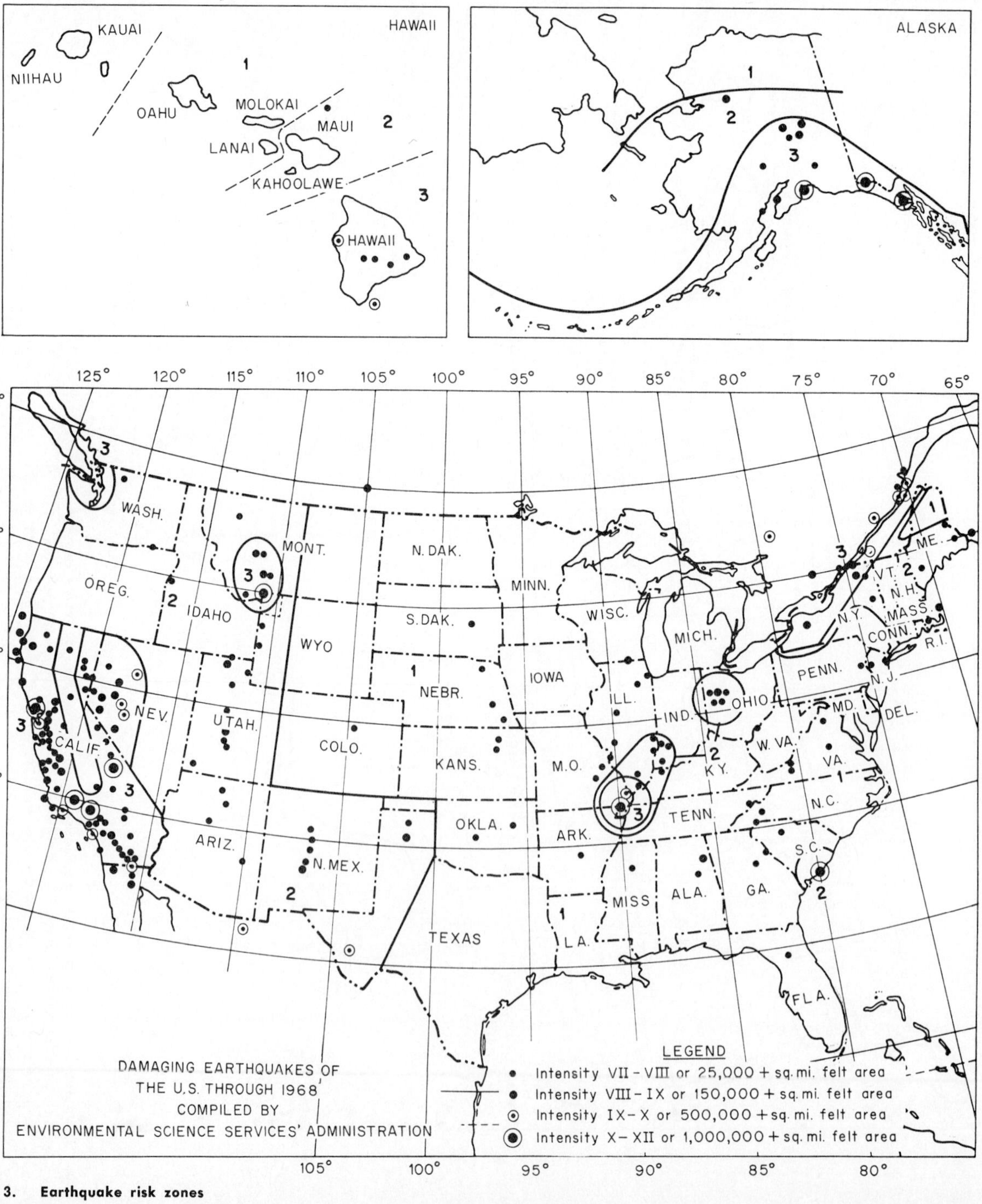

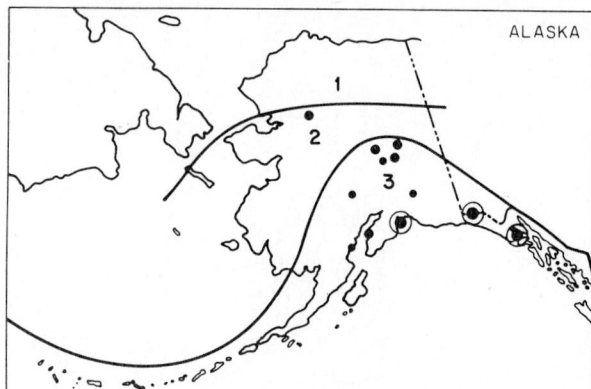

HAWAII
KAUAI
NIIHAU
OAHU
MOLOKAI
MAUI
LANAI
KAHOOLAWE
HAWAII
ALASKA
WASH.
OREG.
CALIF.
NEV.
IDAHO
MONT.
WYO
UTAH
ARIZ.
COLO.
N. MEX.
N. DAK.
S. DAK.
NEBR.
KANS.
OKLA.
TEXAS
MINN.
IOWA
M.O.
ARK.
L.A.
WISC.
ILL.
MISS
MICH.
IND.
OHIO
K.Y.
TENN.
ALA.
GA.
FLA.
S.C.
N.C.
VA.
W. VA.
PENN.
N.Y.
MD.
DEL.
N.J.
CONN.
R.I.
MASS.
VT.
N.H.
ME.
DAMAGING EARTHQUAKES OF
THE U.S. THROUGH 1968
COMPILED BY
ENVIRONMENTAL SCIENCE SERVICES' ADMINISTRATION
LEGEND
Intensity VII - VIII or 25,000 + sq. mi. felt area
Intensity VIII - IX or 150,000 + sq. mi. felt area
Intensity IX - X or 500,000 + sq. mi. felt area
Intensity X - XII or 1,000,000 + sq. mi. felt area

Fig. 3. Earthquake risk zones

1970 ed.; *Recommended Lateral Force Requirements*, 1968 rev., Seismology Committee, Structural Engineers Association of California; *Building Code Requirements for Reinforced Concrete*, ANSI A89.1–1972, ACI 318–71.)

A *box system* is a structural system without a complete vertical load-carrying space frame. In this system, the required lateral forces are resisted by shear walls.

A *shear wall* is a wall designed to resist lateral forces parallel to the wall. Braced frames subjected primarily to axial stresses shall be considered as shear walls for the purpose of this definition.

A *total lateral force* or shear at the base of the building (V), assumed to act in the direction of each of the main axes of the building, is determined in accordance with the following formula:

$$V = ZKCW$$

where Z = coefficient determined by the risk zones shown in Fig. 3. (For zone 1, $Z = 0.25$; for zone 2, $Z = 0.50$; for zone 3, $Z = 1.0$)

K = coefficient determined by structural system as shown in Table 18

C = coefficient for base shear determined with the following formula:

$$C = \frac{0.05}{\sqrt[3]{T}}$$

(Exception: $C = 0.10$ for all one- and two-story buildings.) T is the fundamental period of vibration of the building in seconds determined by the following formula:

$$T = \frac{0.05h_n}{\sqrt{D}}$$

h_n = height in feet above the base to level n (top)

D = dimension of building in feet in direction parallel to applied force

(Exception: In a building with a moment-resisting space frame which resists 100 per cent of the required lateral forces and which is not enclosed or adjoined by more rigid elements which prevent it from resisting lateral forces, $T = 0.10N$, where N = total number of stories above grade to height n.)

W = total dead load (plus 25 per cent of floor live load in warehouses)

Lateral force distribution

The total force V shall be distributed in the height of the structure in the following manner:

Table 18. Horizontal force factor K for buildings or other structures*

Type or arrangement of resisting elements	Value of K
All building framing systems except as hereinafter classified.	1.00
Buildings with a box system.	1.33
Buildings with a dual bracing system consisting of a ductile moment-resisting space frame and shear walls designed in accordance with the following criteria: 1. The frames and shear walls shall resist the total lateral force in accordance with their relative rigidities, considering the interaction of the shear walls and frames. 2. The shear walls acting independently of the ductile moment-resisting space frame shall resist the total required lateral force. 3. The ductile moment-resisting space frame shall have the capacity to resist not less than 25 per cent of the required lateral force.	0.80
Buildings with a ductile moment-resisting space frame designed to resist the total required lateral force.	0.67
Elevated tanks plus full contents on four or more cross-braced legs and not supported by a building.	3.00
Structures other than buildings.	2.00

* *Where prescribed wind loads produce higher stresses, these loads shall be used in lieu of the loads resulting from earthquake forces.*

$$F_t = 0.004V \left(\frac{h_n}{D_s}\right)^2$$

where F_t = that portion of V considered as concentrated at the top of the structure, at the level n. F_t need not exceed 0.15 and may be considered as 0 for values $\left(\dfrac{h_n}{D_s}\right)$ of 3 or less, and

$$F_x = \frac{(V - F_t)w_x h_x}{\sum\limits_{i=1}^{n} w_i h_i}$$

where x = that level of the building which is under design consideration and $i = 1$ designates the first level above the base of the building. At each level designated as x, the force F_x shall be applied over the area of the building in accordance with the mass distribution on that level. (Exception: one- and two-story buildings shall have uniform distribution.)

Pile foundations and caisson footings

Individual pile and caisson footings shall be interconnected by ties, each of which can carry a horizontal force equal to 10 per cent of the larger pile cap loading.

Distribution of horizontal shear

Total shear in any horizontal plane shall be distributed to the various elements of the lateral force-resisting system in proportion to the rigidities of the horizontal bracing system or diaphragm.

Drift

Lateral deflections or drift of a story relative to its adjacent stories shall be considered in accordance with accepted engineering practice.

Horizontal torsional moments

Provisions shall be made for the increase in shear resulting from the horizontal torsion due to an eccentricity between the center of mass and the center of rigidity. Negative torsional shears shall be neglected. Where the vertical resisting elements depend on diaphragm action for shear distribution at any level, the shear-resisting elements shall be capable of resisting a torsional moment assumed to be equivalent to the story shear acting with an eccentricity of not less than 5 per cent of the maximum building dimension at that level.

Overturning

Every building or structure shall be designed to resist the overturning effects caused by the wind forces and related requirements or the earthquake forces specified in this section, whichever governs.

At any level, the incremental changes of the design overturning moment in the story under consideration shall be distributed to the various resisting elements in the same proportion as the distribution of the shears in the resisting system. Where other vertical members are provided which are capable of partially resisting the overturning moments, a redistribution may be made to these members if framing members of sufficient strength and stiffness to transmit the required loads are provided.

Where a vertical resisting element is discontinuous, the overturning moment carried by the lowest story of that element shall be carried down as loads to the foundation.

Setbacks

Buildings having setbacks wherein the plan dimension of the tower in each direction is at least 75 per cent of the corresponding plan dimension of the lower part may be considered as a uniform building without setbacks for the purpose of determining seismic forces.

For other conditions of setbacks, the tower shall be designed as a separate building using the larger of the seismic coefficients at the base of the tower, determined by considering the tower as either a separate building for its own height or as part of the over-all structure. The resulting total shear from the tower shall be applied at the top of the lower part of the building, which shall be otherwise considered separately for its own height.

Structural systems

Buildings more than 160 ft in height shall have ductile moment-resisting space frames which (including connections) are capable of resisting not less than 25 per cent of the required seismic force for the structure as a whole. All buildings designed with a horizontal force factor K of 0.67 or 0.80 shall have ductile moment-resisting space frames.

Moment-resisting space frames and ductile moment-resisting space frames may be enclosed or adjoined by more rigid elements, which would tend to prevent the space frame from resisting lateral forces, where it can be shown that the action or failure of the more rigid elements will not impair the vertical and lateral load-resisting ability of the space frame.

Building separations: All portions of structures shall be designed and constructed to act as an integral unit in resisting horizontal forces unless separated structurally by a distance sufficient to avoid contact under deflection from seismic action or wind forces.

Exterior elements: Nonbearing nonshear wall panels or other elements which are attached to or enclose the exterior shall accommodate movements of the structure resulting from lateral forces or temperature changes. These panels or other elements shall be supported by approved means or by mechanical fasteners as follows:

1. Connections and panel joints shall allow for a relative movement between stories of not less than two times story drift caused by wind or seismic forces, or $\frac{1}{4}$ in., whichever is greater.

2. Connections shall have sufficient ductility and rotation capacity so as to preclude fracture or brittle failures at or near connections.

3. Connections to permit movement in the plane of the panel for story drift may be properly designed sliding connections using slotted or oversize holes or may be connections which permit movement by bending of ductile material.

NOMENCLATURE W= Load in lbs., L= Length in ft., R= Reaction in lbs., V= Shear in lbs., M= Bending moment in ft. lbs., D= Deflection in feet, a= Spacing, b= Spacing, x= Distance, E= Modulus of elasticity I= Moment of inertia, <= Less than, >= Greater than.

DIAGRAMS	REACTIONS = R SHEAR = V	BENDING MOMENT = M	DEFLECTION = D

CASE 1. - Beam Supported Both Ends - Continuous Load, Uniformly Distributed.

$R = R_1 = V \text{ (max.)} = \dfrac{W}{2}$

At x:

$V = \dfrac{W}{2} - \dfrac{Wx}{L}$

At center:

$M \text{ (max.)} = \dfrac{WL}{8}$

At x:

$M = \dfrac{Wx}{2L}(L-x)$

At center:

$D \text{ (max.)} = \dfrac{5}{384}\dfrac{WL^3}{EI}$

At x:

$D = \dfrac{Wx}{24\,EIL}(L^3 - 2Lx^2 + x^3)$

CASE 2. - Beam Supported Both Ends - Concentrated Load at Any Point.

$R = \dfrac{Wb}{L}$

$R_1 = \dfrac{Wa}{L}$

$V \text{ (max.)} = R$ when $a < b$ and R_1 when $a > b$

At x:

$V = \dfrac{Wb}{L}$

At point of load:

$M \text{ (max.)} = \dfrac{Wab}{L}$

At x: when $x < a$

$M = \dfrac{Wbx}{L}$

At x: when $x = \sqrt{a(a+2b) \div 3}$ and $a > b$

$D \text{ (max.)} = Wab(a+2b)\sqrt{3a(a+2b)} \div 27\,EIL$

At x: when $x < a$

$D = \dfrac{Wbx}{6\,EIL}\left[2L(L-x) - b^2 - (L-x)^2\right]$

At x: when $x > a$

$D = \dfrac{Wa(L-x)}{6\,EIL}\left[2Lb - b^2 - (L-x)^2\right]$

CASE 3. - Beam Supported Both Ends - Two Unequal Concentrated Loads, Unequally Distributed.

$R = \dfrac{1}{L}\left[W(L-a) + W_1 b\right]$

$R_1 = \dfrac{1}{L}\left[Wa + W_1(L-b)\right]$

$V \text{ (max.)} = \text{Maximum Reaction}$

At x: when $x > a$ and $< (L-b)$

$V = R - W$

At point of load W:

$M = \dfrac{a}{L}\left[W(L-a) + W_1 b\right]$

At point of load W_1:

$M_1 = \dfrac{b}{L}\left[Wa + W_1(L-b)\right]$

At x: when $x > a$ or $< (L-b)$

$M = W\dfrac{a}{L}(L-x) + W_1\dfrac{bx}{L}$

CASE 4. - Beam Supported Both Ends - Three Unequal Concentrated Loads, Unequally Distributed.

$R = \dfrac{Wb + W_1 b_1 + W_2 b_2}{L}$

$R_1 = \dfrac{Wa + W_1 a_1 + W_2 a_2}{L}$

$V \text{ (max.)} = \text{Maximum Reaction}$

At x: when $x > a$ and $< a_1$

$V = R - W$

At x: when $x > a_1$ and $< a_2$

$V = R - W - W_1$

At x: when $x = a$

$M = Ra$

At x: when $x = a_1$

$M_1 = Ra_1 - W(a_1 - a)$

At x: when $x = a_2$

$M_2 = Ra_2 - W(a_2 - a) - W_1(a_2 - a_1)$

$M \text{ (max.)} = M$ when $W = R$ or $> R$

$M \text{ (max.)} = M_1$ when $\begin{cases} W_1 + W = R \text{ or} > R \\ W_1 + W_2 = R_1 \text{ or} > R_1 \end{cases}$

$M \text{ (max.)} = M_2$ when $W_2 = R_1$ or $> R_1$

CASE 5. - Beam Fixed Both Ends - Continuous Load, Uniformly Distributed.

$R = R_1 = V \text{ (max.)} = \dfrac{W}{2}$

At x:

$V = \dfrac{W}{2} - \dfrac{Wx}{L}$

At center:

$M \text{ (max.)} = \dfrac{WL}{24}$

At supports:

$M_1 \text{ (max.)} = \dfrac{WL}{12}$

At x:

$M = \dfrac{W}{2L}\left(-\dfrac{L^2}{6} + Lx - x^2\right)$

At center:

$D \text{ (max.)} = \dfrac{1}{384}\dfrac{WL^3}{EI}$

At x:

$D = \dfrac{Wx^2}{24\,EIL}(L^2 - 2Lx + x^2)$

CASE 6. - Beam Fixed Both Ends - Concentrated Load at Any Point.

$R = W\left(\dfrac{b^2(3a+b)}{L^3}\right)$

$R_1 = W\left(\dfrac{a^2(3b+a)}{L^3}\right)$

$V \text{ (max.)} = R$ when $a < b$

$\quad = R_1$ when $a > b$

At x: when $x < a$

$V = R$

At support R:

$M_1 \left(\begin{smallmatrix}\text{max. neg. mom.} \\ \text{when } b > a\end{smallmatrix}\right) = -W\dfrac{ab^2}{L^2}$

At support R_1:

$M_2 \left(\begin{smallmatrix}\text{max. neg. mom.} \\ \text{when } a > b\end{smallmatrix}\right) = -W\dfrac{a^2 b}{L^2}$

At point of load:

$M \text{ (max.)} = Ra + M_1 = Ra - W\dfrac{ab^2}{L^2}$

At x: $M = Rx - W\dfrac{ab^2}{L^2}$

At x: when $x = \dfrac{2aL}{3a+b}$ and $a > b$

$D \text{ (max.)} = \dfrac{2W a^3 b^2}{3\,EI(3a+b)^2}$

when $x < a$

$D = \dfrac{W b^2 x^2}{6\,EIL^3}(3aL - 3ax - bx)$

Beam formulae

NOMENCLATURE W = Load in lbs., L = Length in ft., R = Reaction in lbs., V = Shear in lbs., M = Bending moment in ft. lbs., D = Deflection in feet, a = Spacing, b = Spacing, x = Distance, E = Modulus of elasticity, I = Moment of inertia, $<$ = Less than, $>$ = Greater than.

DIAGRAMS	REACTIONS = R SHEAR = V	BENDING MOMENT = M	DEFLECTION = D

CASE 7. – Beam Fixed at One End (Cantilever) – Continuous Load, Uniformly Distributed..

$R_1 = V \text{ (max.)} = W$

At x:

$V = \dfrac{Wx}{L}$

At fixed end:

$M \text{ (max.)} = \dfrac{WL}{2}$

At x:

$M = \dfrac{Wx^2}{2L}$

At free end:

$D \text{ (max.)} = \dfrac{WL^3}{8EI}$

At x:

$D = \dfrac{W}{24\,EIL}\left(x^4 - 4L^3x + 3L^4\right)$

CASE 8. – Beam Fixed at One End (Cantilever) – Concentrated Load at Any Point.

$R_1 = V \text{ (max.)} = W$

At x: when $x > a$

$V = W$

At x: when $x < a$

$V = 0$

At fixed end:

$M \text{ (max.)} = Wb$

At x: when $x > a$

$M = W(x - a)$

At free end:

$D \text{ (max.)} = \dfrac{WL^3}{6EI}\left[2 - \dfrac{3a}{L} + \left(\dfrac{a}{L}\right)^3\right]$

At point of load:

$D = \dfrac{W}{3\,EI}(L - a)^3$

At x: when $x > a$

$D = \dfrac{W}{6\,EI}\left(\begin{array}{l}-3aL^2 + 2L^3 + x^3 - \\ 3ax^2 - 3L^2x + 6aLx\end{array}\right)$

CASE 9. – Beam Fixed at One End, Supported at Other – Concentrated Load at Any Point.

$R = W\left(\dfrac{3b^2L - b^3}{2L^3}\right)$

$R_1 = W\left(\dfrac{3aL^2 - a^3}{2L^3}\right)$

At x: when $x < a$

$V = R$

At x: when $x > a$

$V = R - W$

At point of load:

$M \text{ (max.)} = Wa\left(\dfrac{3b^2L - b^3}{2L^3}\right)$

At fixed end:

$M_1 \text{ (max.)} = WL\left(\dfrac{3b^2L - b^3}{2L^3}\right) - W(L - a)$

At x: when $x < a$

$M = Wx\left(\dfrac{3b^2L - b^3}{2L^3}\right)$

At x: when $x > a$

$M = Wx\left(\dfrac{3b^2L - b^3}{2L^3}\right) - W(x - a)$

At x: when $x = a = .414L$

$D \text{ (max.)} = .0098\,\dfrac{WL^3}{EI}$

At x: when $x < a$

$D = \dfrac{1}{6\,EI}\left[\begin{array}{l}3RL^2x - Rx^3 - \\ 3\,W(L - a)^2\,x\end{array}\right]$

At x: when $x > a$

$D = \dfrac{1}{6\,EI}\left[\begin{array}{l}R_1(2L^3 - 3L^2x + x^3) - \\ 3\,Wa(L - x)^2\end{array}\right]$

CASE 10. – Beam Fixed at One End, Supported at Other – Continuous Load, Uniformly Distributed.

$R = \dfrac{3}{8}W$

$R_1 = V \text{ (max.)} = \dfrac{5}{8}W$

At x:

$V = \dfrac{3}{8}W - \dfrac{Wx}{L}$

At x: when $x = \dfrac{3}{8}L$

$M \text{ (max.)} = \dfrac{9}{128}WL$

At fixed end:

$M_1 \text{ (max.)} = \dfrac{1}{8}WL$

At x:

$M = \dfrac{Wx}{L}\left(\dfrac{3}{8}L - \dfrac{1}{2}x\right)$

At x: when $x = .4215L$

$D \text{ (max.)} = .0054\,\dfrac{WL^3}{EI}$

At x:

$D = \dfrac{Wx}{48\,EIL}\left[-3Lx^2 + 2x^3 + L^3\right]$

CASE 11. – Beam Overhanging Both Supports, Unsymmetrically Placed – Continuous Load, Uniformly Distributed.

$\dfrac{W}{a + L + b} = w = $ load per unit of length

$R = w\left[(a + L)^2 - b^2\right] \div 2L$

$R_1 = w\left[(b + L)^2 - a^2\right] \div 2L$

$V \text{ (max.)} = wa$ or $R - wa$

At x: when $x < a$ $V = w(a - x)$

At x_1: when $x_1 < L$ $V = R - w(a + x_1)$

At x_2: when $x_2 < b$ $V = w(b - x_2)$

At x_1: when $x_1 = \dfrac{R}{w} - a$

$M \text{ (max.)} = R\left(\dfrac{R}{2w} - a\right)$

At R:

$M_1 = \frac{1}{2}wa^2$

At R_1:

$M_1 = \frac{1}{2}wb^2$

At x: when $x < a$ $M = \frac{1}{2}w(a - x)^2$

At x_1: when $x_1 < L$ $M = \frac{1}{2}w(a + x_1)^2 - Rx_1$

At x_2: when $x_2 < b$ $M = \frac{1}{2}w(b - x_2)^2$

CASE 12. – Beam Overhanging Both Supports, Symmetrically Placed – Two Equal Concentrated Loads at Ends.

$R = R_1 = V \text{ (max.)} = \dfrac{W}{2}$

At x: when $x < a$

$V = \dfrac{W}{2}$

At x_1: when $x_1 < L$

$M \text{ (max.)} = \dfrac{Wa}{2}$

At x: when $x < a$

$M = \dfrac{W}{2}(a - x)$

At free ends:

$D = \dfrac{Wa^2(3L + 2a)}{12\,EI}$

At center:

$D = \dfrac{WaL^2}{16\,EI}$

By PHILIP P. PAGE, JR.; *Goldreich, Page & Thropp, Consulting Engineers*

EVALUATING THE BEARING CAPACITY OF THE SOIL

The first step in evaluating the bearing capacity of the soil is a site reconnaissance, noting existing buildings, rock outcroppings, streams, and bodies of water. A topographical survey definitely locating these items plus important trees should follow. In areas of substantial previous construction, reference to old maps may indicate features long removed from the landscape.

Subsurface investigation is most often done by borings, but test pits are also used. A typical boring rig, illustrated in Fig. 1, consists of a tripod or frame with a pulley and a small gasoline-powered winch. A hammer is raised by the winch and allowed to fall free, driving a 2½-in. pipe casing into the ground. The casing is cleaned out by a water jet. At stated intervals, normally every 5 ft, a piece of split pipe (called a spoon) is guided through the casing and driven ahead of the lead end to obtain a sample. The spoon is then withdrawn and opened so that the samples may be identified and placed in a sample jar. The number of blows necessary to drive the spoon 1 ft gives important information as to the compactness of the soil. Generally a 300-lb hammer falling 18 in. is used for advancing the casing and a 140-lb hammer falling 30 in. is used to drive the spoon. When rock is reached, a rotary power take-off on the hoist drives a core bit uncased into the rock. Rock core samples are recovered, identified, and placed in wooden sample boxes. The contractor furnishes

Table 1. Presumptive soil bearing value

Class of Material	Allowable value, tons per sq ft	
	BOCA*	NBC†
1. Massive bed rocks such as granite, diorite, gneiss	100	100
2. Foliated rock such as schist and slate	40	40
3. Sedimentary rock such as shales and sandstones	25	15
4. Soft broken bedrock	10	—
5. Compact partially cemented gravels and sand and hardpan	10	—
6. Gravel and sand-gravel mixtures	6	5
7. Loose gravel, compact coarse sand	4	4
8. Loose coarse sand and sand-gravel mixtures and compact fine sand	3	3
9. Stiff clay	2	2
Loose medium sand	2	2
10. Soft clay	1.5	1.5

* Basic Building Code, *Building Officials and Code Administrators International, Inc., 1978.*

† National Building Code, *American Insurance Association, 1976.*

the engineer with a drawing giving the location and ground elevation of the holes, a scale section of each hole showing materials encountered, and a log of the casing and spoon blows. Many codes as well as good engineering practice dictate boring locations about 50 ft on center within the building outline. Abnormal ground conditions may require closer spacing. Depth of borings should be 15 to 20 ft below foundation level with one or more borings deeper to look for weak lower levels.

Test pits give a better idea of the soil conditions but are limited to a depth of about 10 ft. Dug with a tractor-mounted backhoe, they give a good economical evaluation. Where rock is near the surface, a good picture of the rock profile is obtained.

Once the type and degree of compactness of soil has been established, the supporting power must be evaluated. Most engineers use the presumptive bearing capacity based upon visual inspection. Table 1 shows representative values for presumptive bearing capacities as listed in two national codes. Local codes may have different values.

When a soil load test is required, a 2-ft square plate is loaded to the proposed design load and held until no settlement is observed in 24 hr. The load is then increased 50 per cent and held until no settlement is observed in 24 hr. If the settlement does not exceed ¾ in. under the design load and if under the overload it does not exceed 60 per cent of that observed under the design load, the test is satisfactory.

SELECTING THE TYPE OF FOUNDATION

When good bearing material occurs directly under the building excavation, square footings are selected from prepared tables,

such as Tables 2 through 8, which were prepared using grade-60 reinforcing.

A steel billet plate distributes and reduces the concentrated load of the steel column to an acceptable load on the concrete footing, which in turn distributes the load to the soil at the allowable soil pressures; see Fig. 2. Sometimes the load is distributed, especially to lower-strength masonry such as a brick wall, by an I-beam grillage; see Fig. 3. A reinforced concrete column often bears directly on the footing and the stress in the column reinforcing is transferred to the footing by dowels; see Fig. 4.

Bearing walls have continuous footings under them; see Fig. 5. Unless the footing projections are large, the tensile stresses are so low (less than 80 psi) that reinforcement is not required. It is cheaper to thicken a footing slightly than to add reinforcing. As a rule, a footing twice as deep as its projection will require no reinforcing.

Where a lot line or interference from another footing precludes the use of square footings, a combined footing may serve two or more columns. Figure 6 shows examples of popular types of combined footings. Note that the centers of gravity of the plan area of the footing and the loads of the column must coincide.

Piers supporting grade beams extend to footings placed on bearing strata substantially below the general excavation. The grade beams, designed as flexural members, carry wall and floor loads to the piers; see Fig. 8. Above frost penetration depth, frost bevels may be placed on the beam soffits to prevent frost heave. The mass unreinforced concrete piers have a height-to-thickness ratio limit of six. Dowels develop the strength of the column reinforcing into the pier by bond. Small dowels between the pier and the footing prevent pier displacement during backfilling. In

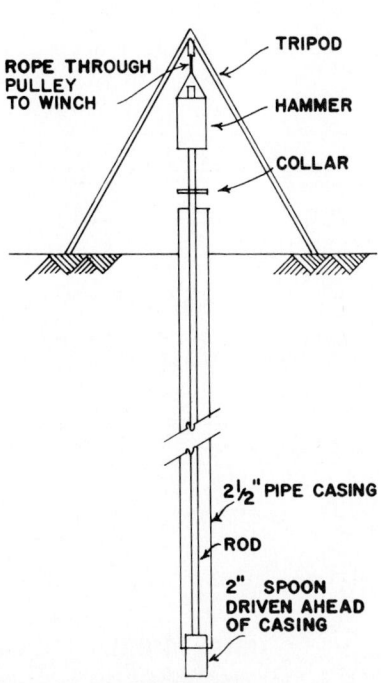

ROPE THROUGH PULLEY TO WINCH

TRIPOD

HAMMER

COLLAR

2½" PIPE CASING

ROD

2" SPOON DRIVEN AHEAD OF CASING

Fig. 1. Typical boring rig

Spread footings

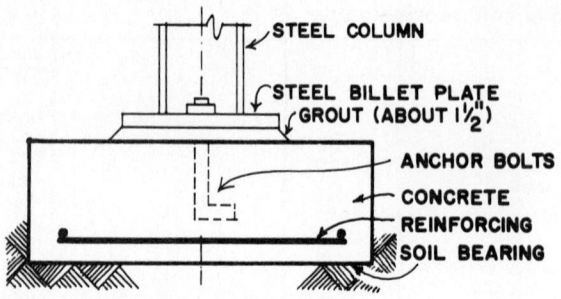

Fig. 2. Steel column on spread footing

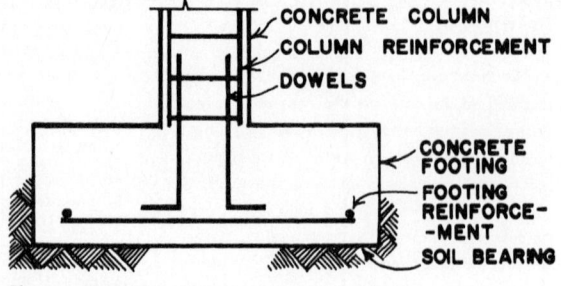

Fig. 4. Concrete column on spread footing

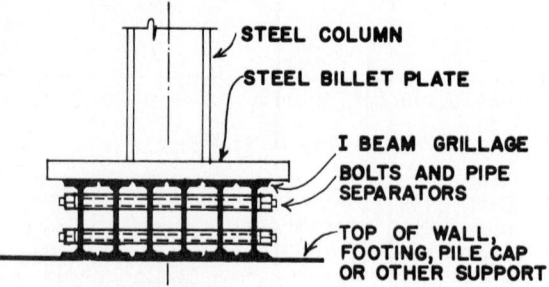

Fig. 3. Steel grillage

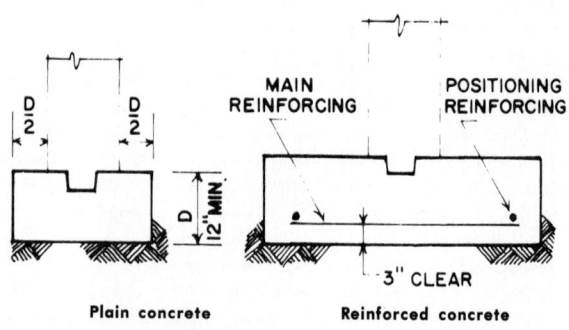

Plain concrete (most used) Reinforced concrete

Fig. 5. Typical wall footings

Table 2. Square column footings—soil bearing value, 3,000 psf*

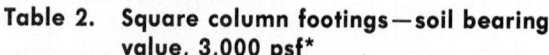

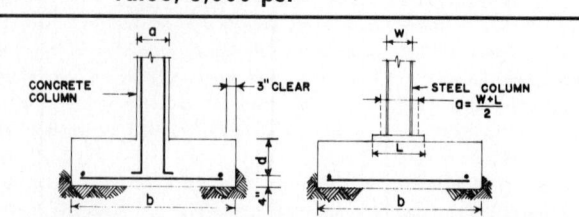

Column load, kips	b, ft	d, in.	a, in. (minimum)	Reinforcement each way
45	4'-0"	12	12	6—#4
57	4'-6"	12	12	6—#4
70	5'-0"	12	12	7—#4
85	5'-6"	12	12	5—#5
101	6'-0"	12	12	6—#5
118	6'-6"	12	12	7—#5
136	7'-0"	14	12	8—#5
156	7'-6"	14	12	7—#6
176	8'-0"	16	12	7—#6
199	8'-6"	16	12	9—#6
221	9'-0"	18	13	9—#6
246	9'-6"	18	13	8—#7
270	10'-0"	20	14	8—#7
298	10'-6"	20	14	10—#7
324	11'-0"	22	14	10—#7
354	11'-6"	22	14	9—#8
382	12'-0"	24	15	9—#8
443	13'-0"	26	15	11—#8
509	14'-0"	28	16	10—#9
580	15'-0"	30	17	11—#9
653	16'-0"	32	18	13—#9

Tables 2 through 8 have been prepared according to the 1977 ACI code ultimate design method. $f'_c = 3,000$, $f_y = 60,000$. Tabulated column loads are actual, not ultimate.

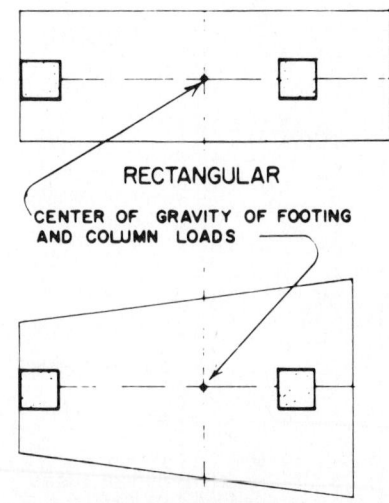

RECTANGULAR

CENTER OF GRAVITY OF FOOTING AND COLUMN LOADS

TRAPEZOIDAL

Fig. 6. Combined footings

Table 3.   Square column footings—soil bearing value, 4,000 psf

Column load, kips	b, ft	d, in.	a, in. (minimum)	Reinforcement each way
34	3'-0"	12	9	4—#4
47	3'-6"	12	9	5—#4
61	4'-0"	12	9	5—#4
77	4'-6"	12	9	4—#5
95	5'-0"	12	9	5—#5
115	5'-6"	12	10	6—#5
136	6'-0"	13	10	7—#5
158	6'-6"	14	10	6—#6
184	7'-0"	16	11	7—#6
210	7'-6"	16	12	8—#6
238	8'-0"	18	13	9—#6
268	8'-6"	19	13	7—#7
300	9'-0"	20	14	8—#7
332	9'-6"	22	14	9—#9
366	10'-0"	23	15	7—#8
403	10'-6"	24	15	8—#8
440	11'-0"	25	15	9—#8
478	11'-6"	27	16	10—#9
519	12'-0"	28	16	11—#9
604	13'-0"	30	17	10—#9
696	14'-0"	32	19	11—#9
788	15'-0"	34	20	13—#9
890	16'-0"	36	22	15—#9

Table 4.   Square column footings—soil bearing value, 5,000 psf

Column load, kips	b, ft	d, in.	a, in. (minimum)	Reinforcement each way
43	3'-0"	12	10	4—#4
59	3'-6"	12	10	5—#4
77	4'-0"	12	10	6—#4
97	4'-6"	12	10	6—#4
120	5'-0"	12	12	5—#5
144	5'-6"	14	12	6—#5
172	6'-0"	14	12	8—#5
201	6'-6"	16	12	9—#5
231	7'-0"	18	12	10—#5
264	7'-6"	20	12	8—#6
301	8'-0"	20	14	10—#6
338	8'-6"	22	14	11—#6
379	9'-0"	22	15	9—#7
420	9'-6"	24	15	10—#7
462	10'-0"	26	16	10—#7
507	10'-6"	28	16	9—#8
557	11'-0"	28	17	10—#8
605	11'-6"	30	17	10—#8
659	12'-0"	30	19	12—#8
765	13'-0"	34	20	11—#9
882	14'-0"	36	22	12—#9
1,007	15'-0"	38	23	14—#9
1,133	16'-0"	42	24	16—#9

Table 5.   Square column footings—soil bearing value, 6,000 psf

Column load, kips	b, ft	d, in.	a, in. (minimum)	Reinforcement each way
52	3'-0"	12	9	4—#4
71	3'-6"	12	9	5—#4
93	4'-0"	12	9	6—#4
117	4'-6"	12	10	5—#5
145	5'-0"	13	10	4—#6
175	5'-6"	14	11	7—#5
207	6'-0"	15	11	8—#5
242	6'-6"	17	12	7—#6
279	7'-0"	20	13	8—#6
321	7'-6"	20	14	9—#6
363	8'-0"	22	14	10—#6
408	8'-6"	24	15	8—#7
458	9'-0"	24	16	10—#7
508	9'-6"	26	16	8—#8
560	10'-0"	28	17	9—#8
615	10'-6".	30	18	10—#8
675	11'-0"	30	19	11—#8
734	11'-6"	32	19	9—#9
800	12'-0"	32	20	8—#10
933	13'-0"	34	22	10—#10
1,073	14'-0"	38	23	12—#10
1,227	15'-0"	40	25	13—#10
1,382	16'-0"	44	26	14—#10

Table 6.   Square column footings—soil bearing value, 8,000 psf

Column load, kips	b, ft	d, in.	a, in. (minimum)	Reinforcement each way
70	3'-0"	12	9	4—#4
96	3'-6"	12	9	5—#4
125	4'-0"	12	10	4—#5
157	4'-6"	14	11	5—#5
194	5'-0"	16	11	6—#5
234	5'-6"	16	12	6—#6
278	6'-0"	18	13	7—#6
325	6'-6"	20	14	8—#6
376	7'-0"	22	15	9—#6
430	7'-6"	24	16	7—#7
488	8'-0"	26	16	8—#7
549	8'-6"	28	17	9—#7
616	9'-0"	28	18	11—#7
684	9'-6"	30	19	9—#8
755	10'-0"	32	19	10—#8
832	10'-6"	32	20	12—#8
911	11'-0"	34	23	12—#8
992	11'-6"	36	23	13—#8
1,080	12'-0"	36	24	12—#9
1,259	13'-0"	40	25	14—#9
1,450	14'-0"	44	26	15—#9
1,660	15'-0"	46	28	14—#10
1,875	16'-0"	50	29	16—#10

Table 7. Square column footings—soil bearing value, 12,000 psf

Column load, kips	b, ft	d, in.	a, in. (minimum)	Reinforcement each way
106	3'-0"	12	9	4—#4
145	3'-6"	12	10	4—#5
188	4'-0"	14	11	5—#5
238	4'-6"	16	11	7—#5
294	5'-0"	17	13	6—#6
354	5'-6"	20	14	7—#6
420	6'-0"	22	15	8—#6
492	6'-6"	24	16	9—#6
570	7'-0"	25	17	8—#7
653	7'-6"	27	18	9—#7
741	8'-0"	30	19	10—#7
836	8'-6"	30	20	12—#7
936	9'-0"	32	23	13—#7
1,040	9'-6"	34	24	11—#8
1,150	10'-0"	36	24	12—#8
1,265	10'-6"	38	25	13—#8
1,387	11'-0"	39	26	15—#8
1,513	11'-6"	41	27	13—#9
1,642	12'-0"	44	28	14—#9
1,918	13'-0"	48	29	16—#9
2,220	14'-0"	50	33	15—#10
2,537	15'-0"	54	34	17—#10
2,874	16'-0"	58	36	19—#10

Table 8. Square column footings—soil bearing value, 16,000 psf

Column load, kips	b, ft	d, in.	a, in. (minimum)	Reinforcement each way
142	3'-0"	12	10	5—#4
193	3'-6"	14	11	4—#5
252	4'-0"	16	12	6—#5
318	4'-6"	18	14	7—#5
392	5'-0"	20	16	6—#6
474	5'-6"	22	16	7—#6
563	6'-0"	24	18	8—#6
660	6'-6"	26	19	10—#6
763	7'-0"	30	19	8—#7
876	7'-6"	30	20	10—#7
996	8'-0"	32	22	9—#8
1,121	8'-6"	34	24	10—#8
1,256	9'-0"	36	25	11—#8
1,396	9'-6"	38	26	10—#9
1,545	10'-0"	40	27	11—#9
1,702	10'-6"	42	28	12—#9
1,864	11'-0"	44	29	13—#9
2,035	11'-6"	46	30	14—#9
2,214	12'-0"	46	33	12—#10
2,585	13'-0"	52	34	15—#10
2,991	14'-0"	56	36	17—#10
3,420	15'-0"	60	39	19—#10
3,881	16'-0"	64	42	22—#10

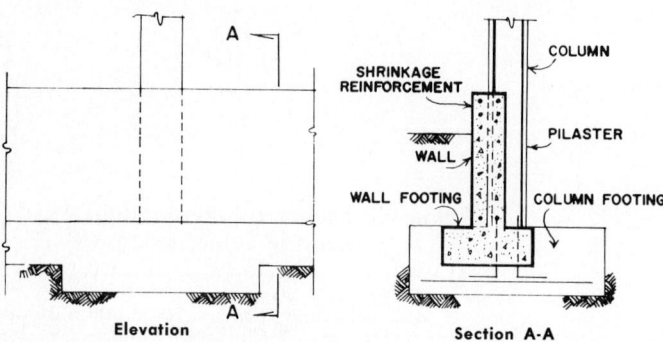

Fig. 7. Typical foundation wall and footings

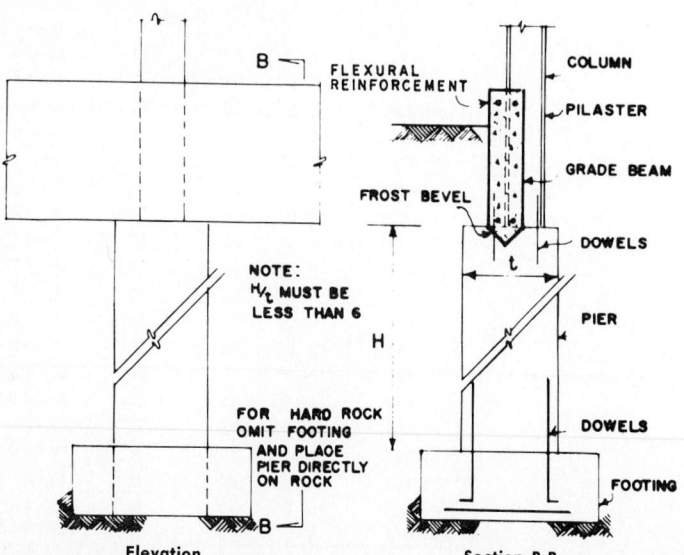

Fig. 8. Typical grade beam and pier

areas of varying and unpredictable bearing elevations, field adjustments may easily be made to the height of the pier.

For even deeper bearing strata, piles are used. Pile caps then support the columns and grade beams. The choice between walls and footings, piers and grade beams, or piles and grade beams is often determined by cost. The engineer prepares a preliminary design and cost estimate to select his foundation. The requirement of many codes, that a pile be at least 10 ft long in order to provide adequate lateral stability, often determines the changeover depth between piers and short piles.

Mats can distribute loads to large areas, permitting light soil loads on weak bearing material. Hydraulic mats resist upward water pressure. Because of the various possible arrangements and loads, each mat becomes a specialized custom design.

ECCENTRIC FOOTINGS

When it becomes impossible to place the footing directly under the column or wall, methods must be employed to prevent the resulting eccentric footing loading from causing uneven bearing pressure. Building codes generally limit the projection into the street to 1 ft beyond the property line. Thus footings under columns located on the property lines are eccentric to the columns; see Fig. 9. Straps, called pumphandles, carried back to an adjacent column for a hold-down load, remove the

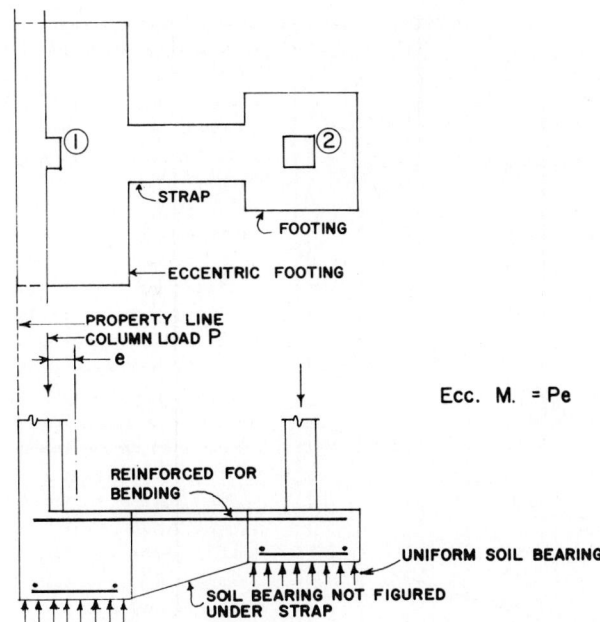

Fig. 9. Pumphandle footing

NOTE: Footing cannot be concentric with column 1 because it would cross the property line. Therefore the eccentricity is removed by the use of the strap and hold-down load of column 2.

eccentric moment. The footings are proportioned so that the pressures are uniform and similar under both footings. The strap is reinforced to resist the bending caused by the eccentricity and is not considered as furnishing bearing support. The bending caused by the eccentric loading may be resisted vertically rather than horizontally by a couple composed of tension in the first floor and compression in the basement; see Fig. 10. The wall reinforcing required may be quite substantial. At corners, walls or grade beams often act as each other's pumphandle, permitting the employment of normal footings, see Fig. 11.

FOUNDATIONS TO ROCK

Rock, having the highest bearing capacity, is often the only acceptable foundation available for heavy loads. Piers carry the loads directly to rock. On hard rock, piers require no footing, as the capacity of the rock is almost that of the concrete. Typical column and grade beam construction is employed.

Where rock occurs more than 10 to 15 ft below the grade beam soffits, piers become too costly. Clusters of piles driven to rock and encased in a pile cap can support substantial loads. For heavier loads, caissons—big holes drilled through the ground to rock and filled with concrete—are used. Piles or caissons may vary in

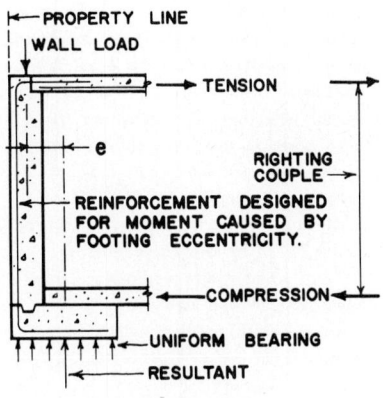

Fig. 10. Eccentric wall footing

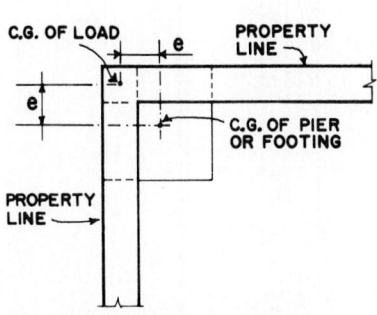

Fig. 11. Eccentric corner footing

NOTE: Eccentricities removed by walls acting as pumphandles. Each wall removes the eccentricity normal to it.

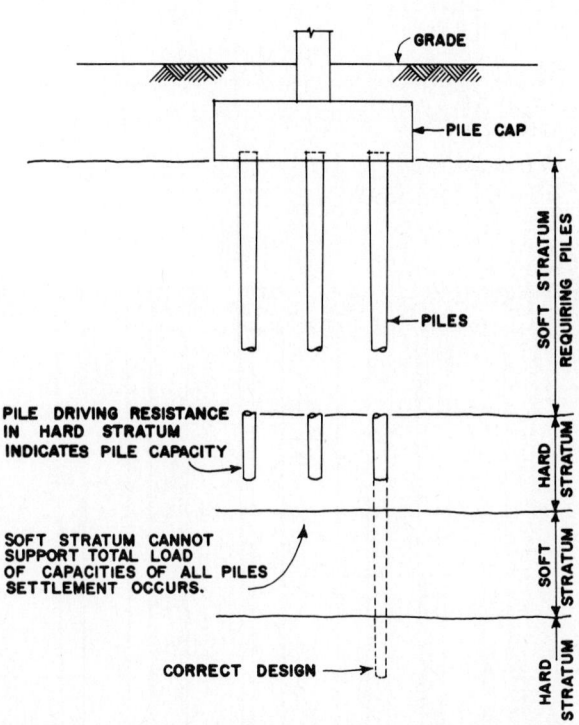

Fig. 12. Piles incorrectly seated in hard stratum above soft one

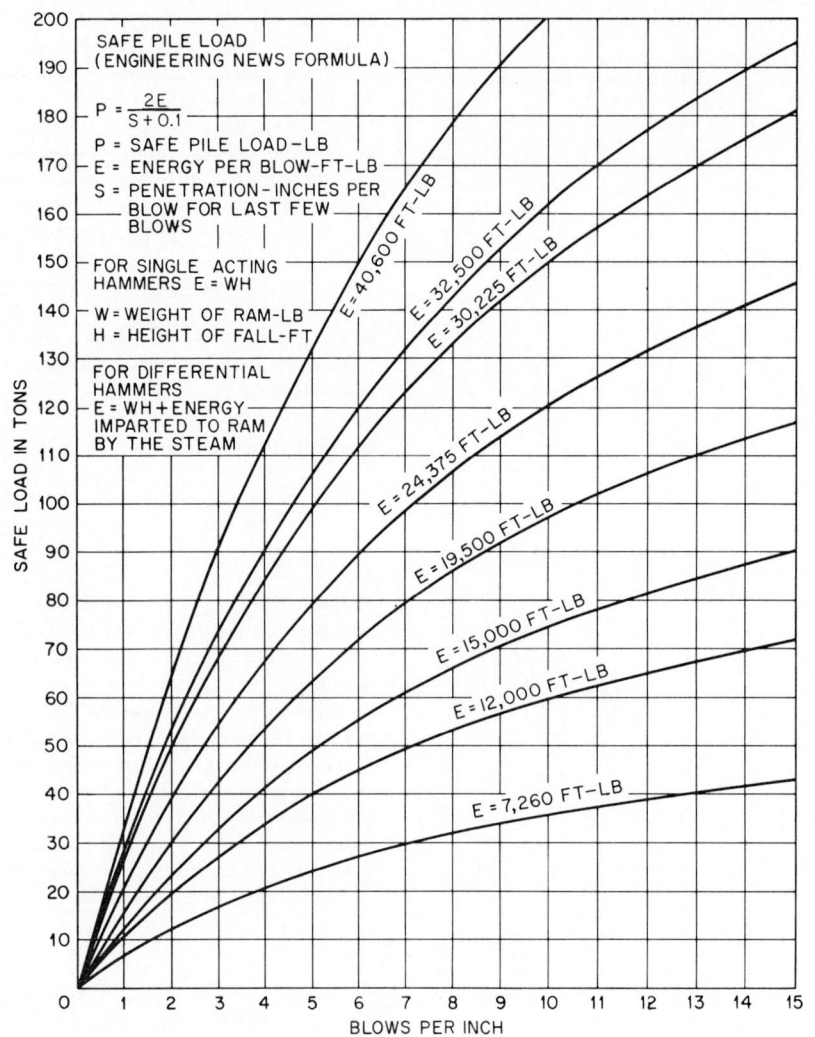

Fig. 13. Safe pile load (*Engineering News* **formula for single acting and differential hammers)**

length from 15 to over 100 ft. Pneumatic caissons in which the air pressure prevents water from entering during construction are no longer used, as the cost of the unproductive labor time during worker compression and decompression is too high.

PILES

Piles carry loads to strata below the ground surface either by end bearing (these are called bearing piles) or by skin friction along their sides (these are called friction piles). The soft material through which the pile is driven provides lateral stability, but for over-water structures the piles must be designed as columns.

Pile capacity is generally established by test load or driving resistance. Where load tests are used to establish capacity, driving resistance measurement is used to ensure that all piles are driven as hard as the test piles. The most common driving formula is the *Engineering News* formula. It translates blows per inch to safe pile capacity in tons. Figure 13 gives curves for the formula for various pile hammers. Piles are generally driven in clusters connected by pile caps.

Borings are essential to proper pile evaluation. Piles may individually test to a capacity greater than their contribution to the capacity of a cluster. A soft stratum underlying a hard one may not be able to support the total load delivered from the hard stratum, even though the resistance of the hard stratum may indicate satisfactory pile support. See Fig. 12.

Different piles shown in Fig. 14 have evolved with certain characteristics.

Types I and II are cast-in-place concrete piles. A light-gage steel shell, driven on a mandrel which is then withdrawn, is inspected and filled with concrete. Care must

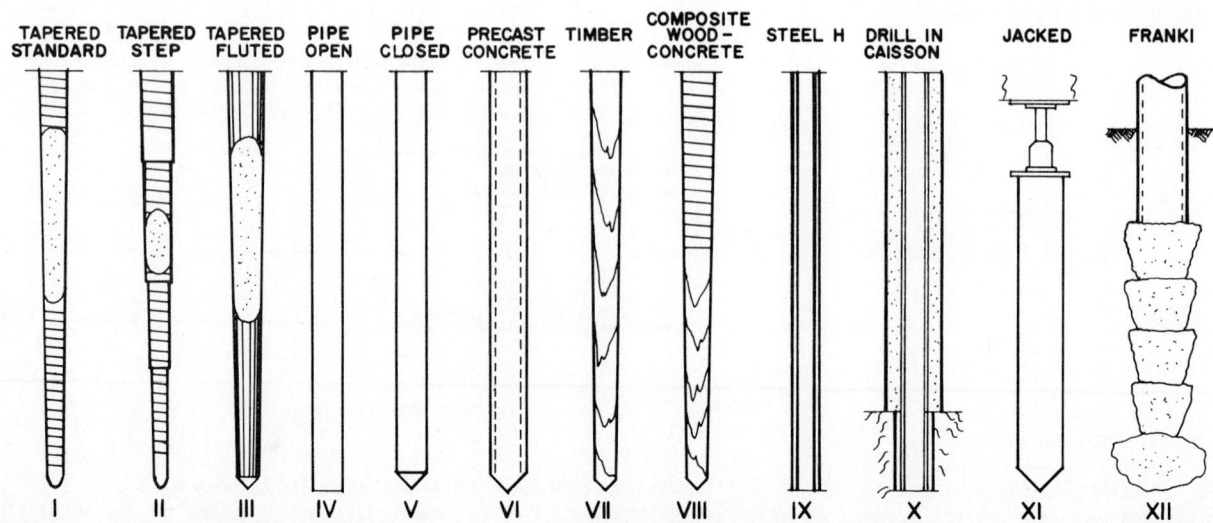

Fig. 14. Types of piles

Table 9. Standard pile caps

ACI 1977 Code—ultimate strength design. f′c = 3000 psi

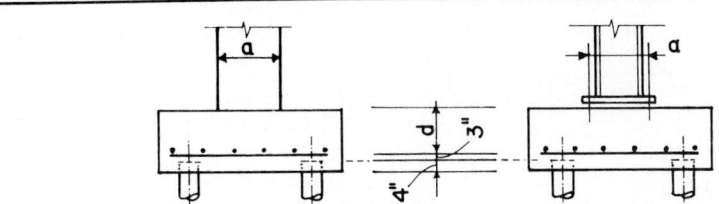

No. of piles	Plan	Pile value, kips	Column load, kips	d, in.	a, min.	Grade 40 Long way	Grade 40 Short way	Grade 60 Long way	Grade 60 Short way
1		20	18	12		3–#5	3–#5	3–#5	3–#5
		30	28	12		3–#5	3–#5	3–#5	3–#5
		40	38	12		3–#5	3–#5	3–#5	3–#5
		50	48	12		3–#5	3–#5	3–#5	3–#5
		60	58	12		3–#5	3–#5	3–#5	3–#5
		80	78	12		3–#5	3–#5	3–#5	3–#5
		100	98	12		3–#5	3–#5	3–#5	3–#5
		120	118	12		3–#5	3–#5	3–#5	3–#5
2		20	37	12	7	3–#5	4–#5	4–#4	4–#5
		30	57	15	7	5–#4	4–#5	4–#4	4–#5
		40	76	17	9	5–#4	4–#5	3–#5	4–#5
		50	96	19	9	4–#5	4–#5	5–#4	4–#5
		60	116	20	9	5–#5	4–#5	5–#4	4–#5
		80	155	22	10	4–#6	4–#5	4–#5	4–#5
		100	195	22	11	5–#6	4–#5	3–#6	4–#5
		120	235	23	12	5–#6	4–#5	5–#5	4–#5
3		20	56	15	7	3 bands of 3–#5		3 bands of 4–#4	
		30	86	15	9	3 bands of 3–#5		3 bands of 4–#4	
		40	116	17	9	3 bands of 3–#5		3 bands of 3–#5	
		50	145	18	10	3 bands of 4–#5		3 bands of 3–#5	
		60	175	19	10	3 bands of 4–#5		3 bands of 4–#5	
		80	235	20	11	3 bands of 4–#5		3 bands of 4–#5	
		100	295	21	12	3 bands of 5–#5		3 bands of 4–#5	
		120	355	21	14	3 bands of 5–#5		3 bands of 4–#5	
4		20	73	14	8	6–#5	6–#5	5–#5	5–#5
		30	113	15	9	6–#5	6–#5	6–#5	6–#5
		40	152	16	10	5–#6	5–#6	6–#5	6–#5
		50	192	17	11	6–#6	6–#6	6–#5	6–#5
		60	232	18	12	6–#6	6–#6	5–#6	5–#6
		80	312	18	14	8–#6	8–#6	5–#6	5–#6
		100	392	19	15	6–#7	6–#7	6–#6	6–#6
		120	472	20	15	7–#7	7–#7	5–#7	5–#7
5		20	90	15	9	5–#6	5–#6	5–#6	5–#6
		30	138	18	10	6–#6	6–#6	6–#6	6–#6
		40	187	21	11	7–#6	7–#6	7–#6	7–#6
		50	236	22	12	8–#6	8–#6	7–#6	7–#6
		60	285	24	14	8–#6	8–#6	8–#6	8–#6
		80	385	24	14	6–#8	6–#8	8–#6	8–#6
		100	484	25	16	7–#8	7–#8	8–#6	8–#6
		120	584	26	17	7–#8	7–#8	8–#6	8–#6

Table 9 (cont.). Standard pile caps

No. of piles	Plan	All caps			a, min	Grade 40 reinforcement		Grade 60 reinforcement	
		Pile value, kips	Column load, kips	d, in.		Long way	Short way	Long way	Short way
6		20	110	15	9	5-#7	9-#5	5-#6	8-#5
		30	168	18	10	5-#8	8-#6	6-#6	7-#6
		40	227	21	12	7-#7	9-#6	5-#7	8-#6
		50	286	22	13	8-#7	9-#6	8-#6	8-#6
		60	345	24	15	7-#8	10-#6	8-#6	9-#6
		80	465	24	15	7-#9	10-#6	6-#8	9-#6
		100	585	25	17	8-#9	8-#7	7-#8	7-#7
		120	705	26	19	7-#10	8-#7	6-#9	7-#7
7		20	127	17	10	9-#5	8-#6	6-#6	10-#5
		30	194	23	12	9-#6	10-#6	8-#6	9-#6
		40	263	25	14	7-#7	8-#7	9-#6	10-#6
		50	332	27	15	10-#6	9-#7	9-#6	8-#7
		60	401	28	16	8-#7	9-#7	7-#7	8-#7
		80	541	28	16	8-#7	9-#7	7-#7	8-#7
		100	681	28	19	9-#7	9-#7	7-#7	8-#7
		120	820	30	20	9-#7	10-#7	8-#7	9-#7
8		20	145	17	10	9-#5	8-#6	6-#6	9-#5
		30	221	23	12	9-#6	10-#6	8-#6	9-#6
		40	300	25	13	7-#7	8-#7	9-#6	10-#6
		50	378	27	15	10-#6	11-#6	9-#6	10-#6
		60	458	28	17	6-#8	9-#7	7-#7	8-#7
		80	618	28	17	8-#8	9-#8	7-#7	8-#7
		100	778	28	20	6-#10	10-#8	8-#7	9-#7
		120	936	30	22	6-#10	11-#8	7-#8	9-#7
9		20	163	17	10	10-#5	10-#5	9-#5	9-#5
		30	249	23	12	10-#6	10-#6	9-#6	9-#6
		40	338	25	14	9-#7	9-#7	10-#6	10-#6
		50	426	27	16	9-#7	9-#7	10-#6	10-#6
		60	515	28	18	10-#7	10-#7	8-#7	8-#7
		80	693	31	19	9-#8	9-#8	9-#7	9-#7
		100	872	33	20	9-#9	9-#9	7-#8	7-#8
		120	1051	34	23	9-#9	9-#9	10-#7	10-#7
10		20	176	25	12	7-#7	8-#8	8-#6	10-#7
		30	275	27	14	8-#7	9-#8	8-#6	10-#7
		40	373	29	15	7-#8	9-#8	10-#6	11-#7
		50	472	31	17	8-#8	10-#8	7-#7	9-#8
		60	570	33	19	7-#9	11-#8	8-#7	10-#8
		80	769	35	19	7-#10	11-#8	10-#7	10-#8
		100	967	37	23	9-#9	12-#8	10-#7	11-#8
		120	1166	39	24	8-#10	10-#9	7-#9	9-#9

Table 9 (cont.). Standard pile caps

No. of piles	Plan	All caps			a, min	Grade 40 reinforcement		Grade 60 reinforcement	
		Pile value, kips	Column load, kips	d, in.		Long way	Short way	Long way	Short way
11		20	194	24	11	8–#7	10–#7	8–#6	9–#7
		30	301	27	13	8–#8	11–#7	7–#7	10–#7
		40	408	30	15	7–#9	12–#7	8–#7	11–#7
		50	516	33	17	10–#8	10–#8	8–#7	9–#8
		60	623	36	19	8–#9	11–#8	9–#7	10–#8
		80	840	40	20	9–#9	10–#9	10–#7	11–#8
		100	1058	42	23	8–#10	10–#9	11–#7	9–#9
		120	1276	44	25	9–#10	11–#9	12–#7	10–#9
12		20	211	24	12	7–#8	10–#7	9–#6	9–#7
		30	328	27	14	7–#9	9–#8	8–#7	10–#7
		40	445	30	16	8–#9	9–#8	9–#7	11–#7
		50	563	33	18	9–#9	10–#8	10–#7	9–#8
		60	680	36	20	9–#9	9–#9	10–#7	10–#8
		80	917	39	21	9–#10	10–#9	9–#8	11–#8
		100	1154	42	24	9–#10	8–#10	10–#8	9–#9
		120	1391	45	26	10–#10	11–#9	8–#9	10–#9
13		20	226	22	12	8–#8	8–#8	7–#7	7–#7
		30	352	25	15	9–#8	9–#8	9–#7	9–#7
		40	489	28	17	11–#8	11–#8	10–#7	10–#7
		50	606	31	19	9–#9	9–#9	9–#8	9–#8
		60	732	34	21	10–#9	10–#9	9–#8	9–#8
		80	988	37	23	9–#10	9–#10	10–#8	10–#8
		100	1245	40	25	10–#10	10–#10	10–#8	10–#8
		120	1502	43	26	11–#10	11–#10	9–#9	9–#9
14		20	244	24	13	9–#7	10–#7	8–#7	9–#7
		30	380	27	16	11–#7	9–#8	9–#7	10–#7
		40	517	30	18	10–#8	10–#8	10–#7	9–#8
		50	653	33	20	8–#9	10–#8	10–#7	9–#8
		60	790	36	22	9–#9	11–#8	10–#8	10–#8
		80	1066	39	23	8–#10	12–#8	10–#8	9–#9
		100	1343	42	26	11–#9	10–#9	11–#8	9–#9
		120	1619	45	27	12–#9	11–#9	9–#9	10–#9
15		20	252	26	13	9–#8	10–#8	7–#8	11–#7
		30	397	29	16	9–#9	11–#8	8–#8	10–#8
		40	543	32	18	11–#9	9–#9	9–#8	11–#8
		50	688	35	20	9–#10	10–#9	10–#8	9–#9
		60	834	38	22	11–#10	11–#9	9–#9	10–#9
		80	1130	41	24	12–#10	12–#9	10–#9	11–#9
		100	1425	44	26	15–#10	10–#10	9–#10	12–#9
		120	1721	47	28	17–#10	11–#10	10–#10	10–#10

Table 10. Basement retaining walls

ACI 318–77. Ultimate strength design. $f'_c = 3,000$ psi.

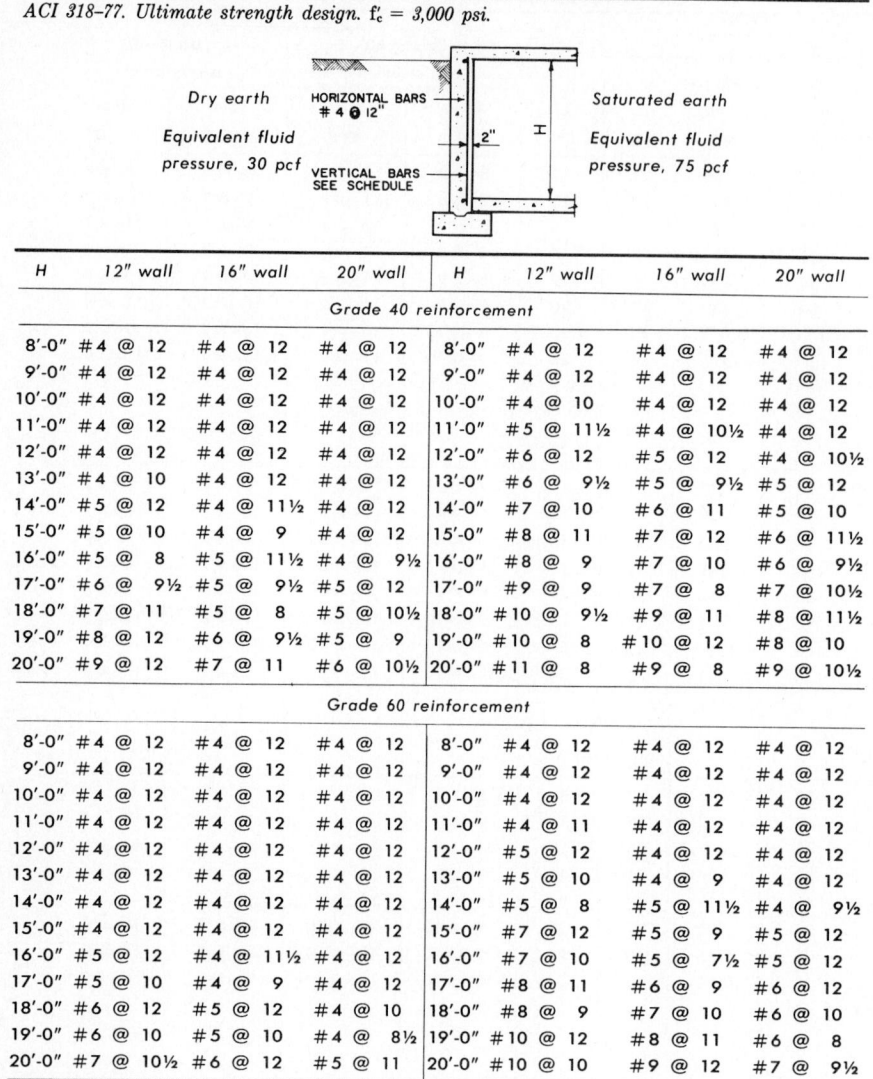

Dry earth — Equivalent fluid pressure, 30 pcf
HORIZONTAL BARS #4 @ 12"
VERTICAL BARS SEE SCHEDULE
Saturated earth — Equivalent fluid pressure, 75 pcf

H	12" wall	16" wall	20" wall	H	12" wall	16" wall	20" wall
			Grade 40 reinforcement				
8'-0"	#4 @ 12	#4 @ 12	#4 @ 12	8'-0"	#4 @ 12	#4 @ 12	#4 @ 12
9'-0"	#4 @ 12	#4 @ 12	#4 @ 12	9'-0"	#4 @ 12	#4 @ 12	#4 @ 12
10'-0"	#4 @ 12	#4 @ 12	#4 @ 12	10'-0"	#4 @ 10	#4 @ 12	#4 @ 12
11'-0"	#4 @ 12	#4 @ 12	#4 @ 12	11'-0"	#5 @ 11½	#4 @ 10½	#4 @ 12
12'-0"	#4 @ 12	#4 @ 12	#4 @ 12	12'-0"	#6 @ 12	#5 @ 12	#4 @ 10½
13'-0"	#4 @ 10	#4 @ 12	#4 @ 12	13'-0"	#6 @ 9½	#5 @ 9½	#5 @ 12
14'-0"	#5 @ 12	#4 @ 11½	#4 @ 12	14'-0"	#7 @ 10	#6 @ 11	#5 @ 10
15'-0"	#5 @ 10	#4 @ 9	#4 @ 12	15'-0"	#8 @ 11	#7 @ 12	#6 @ 11½
16'-0"	#5 @ 8	#5 @ 11½	#4 @ 9½	16'-0"	#8 @ 9	#7 @ 10	#6 @ 9½
17'-0"	#6 @ 9½	#5 @ 9½	#5 @ 12	17'-0"	#9 @ 9	#7 @ 8	#7 @ 10½
18'-0"	#7 @ 11	#5 @ 8	#5 @ 10½	18'-0"	#10 @ 9½	#9 @ 11	#8 @ 11½
19'-0"	#8 @ 12	#6 @ 9½	#5 @ 9	19'-0"	#10 @ 8	#10 @ 12	#8 @ 10
20'-0"	#9 @ 12	#7 @ 11	#6 @ 10½	20'-0"	#11 @ 8	#9 @ 8	#9 @ 10½
			Grade 60 reinforcement				
8'-0"	#4 @ 12	#4 @ 12	#4 @ 12	8'-0"	#4 @ 12	#4 @ 12	#4 @ 12
9'-0"	#4 @ 12	#4 @ 12	#4 @ 12	9'-0"	#4 @ 12	#4 @ 12	#4 @ 12
10'-0"	#4 @ 12	#4 @ 12	#4 @ 12	10'-0"	#4 @ 12	#4 @ 12	#4 @ 12
11'-0"	#4 @ 12	#4 @ 12	#4 @ 12	11'-0"	#4 @ 11	#4 @ 12	#4 @ 12
12'-0"	#4 @ 12	#4 @ 12	#4 @ 12	12'-0"	#5 @ 12	#4 @ 12	#4 @ 12
13'-0"	#4 @ 12	#4 @ 12	#4 @ 12	13'-0"	#5 @ 10	#4 @ 9	#4 @ 12
14'-0"	#4 @ 12	#4 @ 12	#4 @ 12	14'-0"	#5 @ 8	#5 @ 11½	#4 @ 9½
15'-0"	#4 @ 12	#4 @ 12	#4 @ 12	15'-0"	#7 @ 12	#5 @ 9	#5 @ 12
16'-0"	#5 @ 12	#4 @ 11½	#4 @ 12	16'-0"	#7 @ 10	#5 @ 7½	#5 @ 12
17'-0"	#5 @ 10	#4 @ 9	#4 @ 12	17'-0"	#8 @ 11	#6 @ 9	#6 @ 12
18'-0"	#6 @ 12	#5 @ 12	#4 @ 10	18'-0"	#8 @ 9	#7 @ 10	#6 @ 10
19'-0"	#6 @ 10	#5 @ 10	#4 @ 8½	19'-0"	#10 @ 12	#8 @ 11	#6 @ 8
20'-0"	#7 @ 10½	#6 @ 12	#5 @ 11	20'-0"	#10 @ 10	#9 @ 12	#7 @ 9½

$f'_c = 3,000$ psi

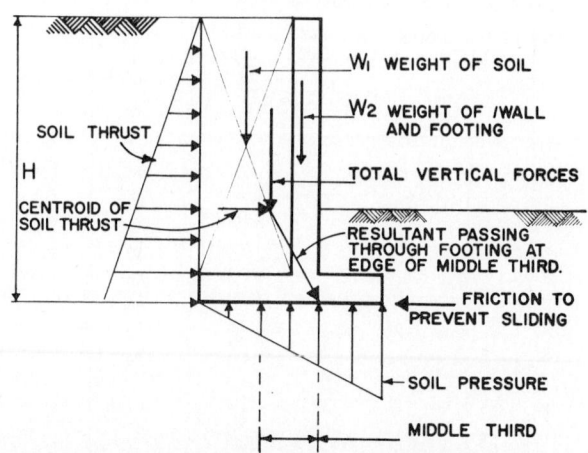

IMPERVIOUS COVER, PITCH TO DRAIN.
SELECTED FREE DRAINING BACKFILL.
WEDGE DELIVERING THRUST
1 CU. FT OF GRAVEL AT WEEP HOLE
ANGLE OF REPOSE ∅
CONCRETE WALL
STRUCTURAL REINFORCEMENT
SHRINKAGE REINFORCEMENT
WEEP HOLES 10' O.C. (ALT. TO WALL DRAIN)
POROUS PIPE WALL DRAIN
FROST PROTECTION.
BEARING STRATUM

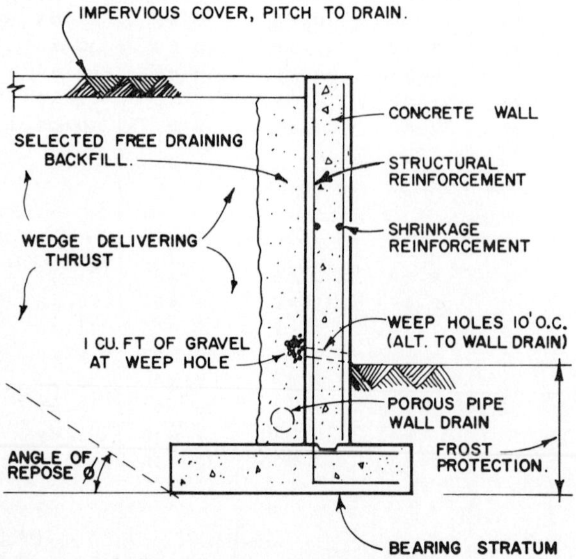

Fig. 15. Essential elements of a retaining wall

SOIL THRUST
H
CENTROID OF SOIL THRUST
W1 WEIGHT OF SOIL
W2 WEIGHT OF /WALL AND FOOTING
TOTAL VERTICAL FORCES
RESULTANT PASSING THROUGH FOOTING AT EDGE OF MIDDLE THIRD.
FRICTION TO PREVENT SLIDING
SOIL PRESSURE
MIDDLE THIRD

Fig. 16. Distribution of forces about a retaining wall
NOTE: Weight and resistance of soil over toe neglected.

be taken to avoid collapsing of the shell when an adjacent pile is driven.

Type III is similar to types I and II except that the shell gage is heavier and no mandrel is required.

Type IV is an open-end steel pipe. It is excavated, often by air jet, as it is advanced, and then filled with concrete after refusal has been reached. In lieu of reaching refusal, driving may stop while a concrete plug is placed and then redriving will seat it. The advantage is less disturbance to adjacent structures.

Type V is a closed-end pile. After driving, it is filled with concrete. Often it is used inside buildings with low head room, as short lengths are simply spliced with steel collars.

Type VI is a precast concrete pile. It is good in marine structures but requires heavy handling equipment and accurate estimation of tip elevation as it is difficult to cut off in the field.

Type VII is a wood pile—the cheapest. Where the pile will not be below the permanent water level, it must be treated with a wood preservative.

Type VIII is a composite wood and concrete pile. The timber is kept below groundwater and a greater over-all length is achieved. A closed-end pipe pile may be used in place of the timber section.

Type IX is a rolled steel H section. It is the cheapest of the higher-capacity piles. Protection must be provided when driving through cinder fill or other rust-producing material.

Type X is a drilled-in caisson. A 24-in. round pipe is driven to rock and cleaned out. A rock socket is drilled and cleaned, a steel H-section core is set, and the shell is filled with concrete. This is good for very heavy loads.

Type XI is a jacked pipe used mainly in underpinning. Jacks drive sections of steel pipe down to bearing, using the existing building as a reaction. The pipe is filled with concrete, a short steel column is

Table 11. Typical retaining walls

ACI 1977 Code ultimate strength design. $f'_c = 3,000$ psi. ASTM A-615 Grade 60 reinforcement. Soil weight 100 lb per ft³

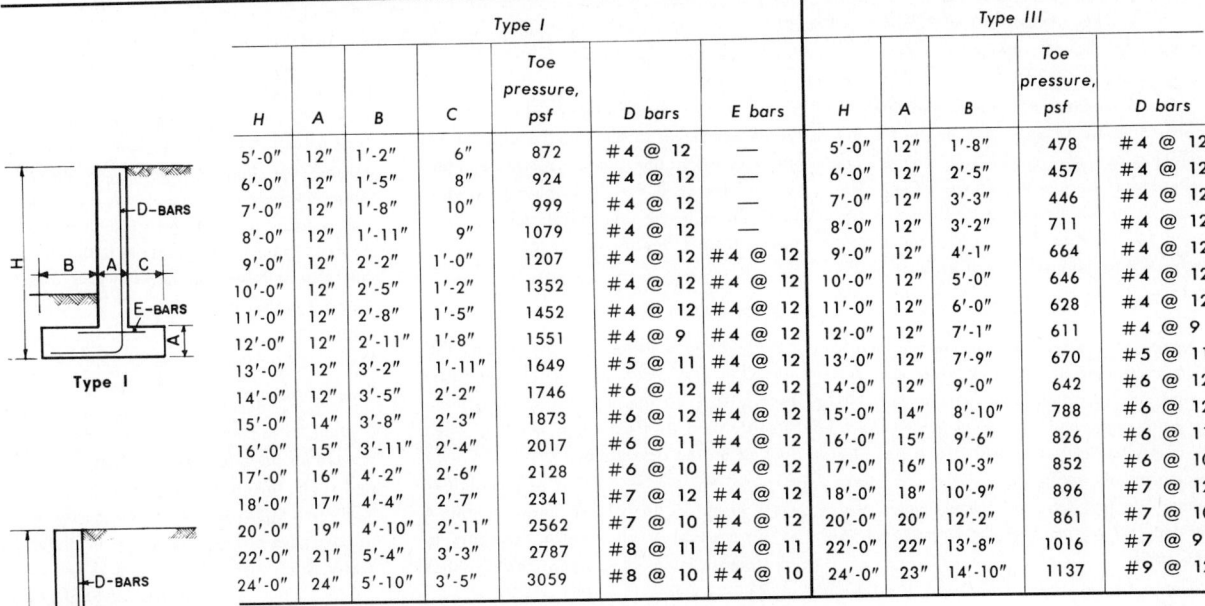

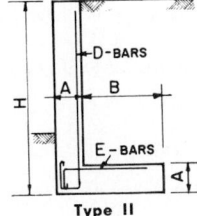

Type I

| | Type I | | | | | | | Type III | | | |
H	A	B	C	Toe pressure, psf	D bars	E bars	H	A	B	Toe pressure, psf	D bars
5'-0"	12"	1'-2"	6"	872	#4 @ 12	—	5'-0"	12"	1'-8"	478	#4 @ 12
6'-0"	12"	1'-5"	8"	924	#4 @ 12	—	6'-0"	12"	2'-5"	457	#4 @ 12
7'-0"	12"	1'-8"	10"	999	#4 @ 12	—	7'-0"	12"	3'-3"	446	#4 @ 12
8'-0"	12"	1'-11"	9"	1079	#4 @ 12		8'-0"	12"	3'-2"	711	#4 @ 12
9'-0"	12"	2'-2"	1'-0"	1207	#4 @ 12	#4 @ 12	9'-0"	12"	4'-1"	664	#4 @ 12
10'-0"	12"	2'-5"	1'-2"	1352	#4 @ 12	#4 @ 12	10'-0"	12"	5'-0"	646	#4 @ 12
11'-0"	12"	2'-8"	1'-5"	1452	#4 @ 12	#4 @ 12	11'-0"	12"	6'-0"	628	#4 @ 12
12'-0"	12"	2'-11"	1'-8"	1551	#4 @ 9	#4 @ 12	12'-0"	12"	7'-1"	611	#4 @ 9
13'-0"	12"	3'-2"	1'-11"	1649	#5 @ 11	#4 @ 12	13'-0"	12"	7'-9"	670	#5 @ 11
14'-0"	12"	3'-5"	2'-2"	1746	#6 @ 12	#4 @ 12	14'-0"	12"	9'-0"	642	#6 @ 12
15'-0"	14"	3'-8"	2'-3"	1873	#6 @ 12	#4 @ 12	15'-0"	14"	8'-10"	788	#6 @ 12
16'-0"	15"	3'-11"	2'-4"	2017	#6 @ 11	#4 @ 12	16'-0"	15"	9'-6"	826	#6 @ 11
17'-0"	16"	4'-2"	2'-6"	2128	#6 @ 10	#4 @ 12	17'-0"	16"	10'-3"	852	#6 @ 10
18'-0"	17"	4'-4"	2'-7"	2341	#7 @ 12	#4 @ 12	18'-0"	18"	10'-9"	896	#7 @ 12
20'-0"	19"	4'-10"	2'-11"	2562	#7 @ 10	#4 @ 12	20'-0"	20"	12'-2"	861	#7 @ 10
22'-0"	21"	5'-4"	3'-3"	2787	#8 @ 11	#4 @ 11	22'-0"	22"	13'-8"	1016	#7 @ 9
24'-0"	24"	5'-10"	3'-5"	3059	#8 @ 10	#4 @ 10	24'-0"	23"	14'-10"	1137	#9 @ 12

Type II

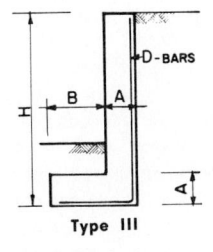

Type III

| | Type II | | | | |
H	A	B	Toe pressure, psf	D bars	E bars
5'-0"	12"	2'-1"	1141	#4 @ 12	#4 @ 12
6'-0"	12"	2'-7"	1376	#4 @ 12	#4 @ 12
7'-0"	12"	3'-2"	1576	#4 @ 12	#4 @ 12
8'-0"	12"	3'-7"	1838	#4 @ 12	#4 @ 12
9'-0"	12"	4'-0"	2097	#4 @ 12	#4 @ 12
10'-0"	12"	4'-7"	2292	#4 @ 12	#4 @ 12
11'-0"	12"	5'-2"	2483	#4 @ 12	#4 @ 10
12'-0"	12"	5'-9"	2677	#4 @ 9	#5 @ 12
13'-0"	12"	6'-4"	2870	#5 @ 11	#5 @ 9
14'-0"	12"	6'-11"	3059	#6 @ 12	#6 @ 10
15'-0"	14"	7'-3"	3330	#6 @ 12	#6 @ 10
16'-0"	15"	7'-8"	3576	#6 @ 11	#7 @ 12
17'-0"	16"	8'-3"	3761	#6 @ 10	#7 @ 10
18'-0"	18"	8'-6"	4064	#7 @ 12	#7 @ 11
20'-0"	20"	9'-6"	4493	#7 @ 10	#7 @ 9
22'-0"	22"	10'-5"	4955	#7 @ 9	#8 @ 10
24'-0"	23"	11'-3"	5460	#9 @ 12	#9 @ 10

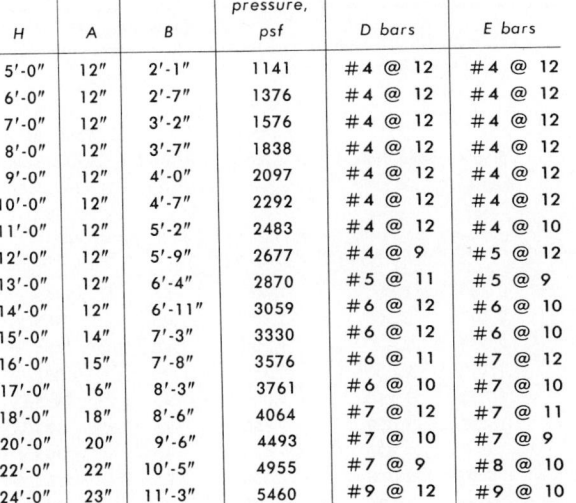

$$T = \frac{w(1 - \sin \phi)}{(1 + \sin \phi)} \frac{H^2}{2}$$

where w = unit weight of soil

ϕ = angle of repose of soil

H = height of wall

Assuming a unit weight of 100 pcf and an angle of repose of 33 degrees (a 1½ on 1 slope), the formula reduces to:

$$T = 29.5 \frac{H^2}{2}$$

The term $H^2/2$ is the expression for a fluid loading. Therefore most simple retaining walls are designed for an equivalent fluid pressure of 30 pcf. Below groundwater level the equivalent fluid pressure increases to 75 pcf. Basement retaining walls can be designed to resist this thrust, but not freestanding ones. Obviously adequate drainage is essential in economical retaining wall design.

Freestanding retaining walls are designed so that the resultant of the force of the soil pressure and the gravity loads passes through the middle third of the footing, preventing uplift. Where the soil is particularly compressible, the resultant should pass near the center of the footing to give uniform soil loading. With the resultant at the edge of the middle third, compressible soils may give differential settlement, causing the wall to rotate and the resultant to move toward the toe, thus creating a vicious circle.

For most simple cases, preengineered retaining walls may be selected, such as those shown in Table 10 for basement walls and Table 11 for freestanding walls.

placed at the top, and the jacks are removed. Pile is pretested by being jacked to an overload.

Type XII is a Franki displacement pile. A steel pipe with a wet concrete plug is driven into the ground. The plug is driven out as more concrete is rammed through the pipe, producing a large ball. The pipe is then withdrawn in steps as more concrete is rammed through the pipe to form a pedestal.

RETAINING WALLS

Retaining walls hold back or retain earth between different levels. A basement retaining wall acts as a beam between the basement and first floor. The first-floor thrust must be countered by a similar thrust on the opposite side of the building or by shear walls. Otherwise the whole building may move.

Freestanding retaining walls rely on the weight of the wall plus the weight of earth over the footing for stability. The essential elements of a retaining wall are shown in Fig. 15. The Rankine theory of earth thrust, Fig. 16, assumes that the thrust is zero at the top and a maximum at the base, giving a triangular loading. The thrust is produced by the sliding of the wedge of soil between the earth below the angle of repose and the ground surface. This thrust can be evaluated by the formula:

By Y. S. LEE, *Professor of Structural Design, School of Architecture, Pratt Institute. Associate, Severud-Perrone-Szegezdy-Sturm, Consulting Engineers*

The allowable unit stresses indicated in Table 1 apply to sawn lumber used under continuously dry conditions. Values are taken from *Design Values for Wood Construction,* a supplement to the *National Design Specification for Wood Construction,* published by National Forest Products Association (1978). For short-term loading, the allowable stresses should be increased as follows: 15 per cent for two months' duration (as for snow loads), 25 per cent for seven days' duration, 33⅓ per cent for wind or earthquake, and 100 per cent for impact. If a member is to be fully stressed to the maximum allowable stress for many years, either continuously or cumulatively, use stresses 90 per cent of those indicated in the table.

For lumber used under conditions where moisture content of the wood is at or above the fiber-saturation point, as when continuously submerged, the allowable unit stresses are subject to the adjustments given in *National Design Specification.*

Lumber classifications

Beams and stringers: Lumber of rectangular cross section, 5 in. or more in thickness and 8 in. or more in width, graded according to its strength in bending when loaded on the narrow face.

Joists and planks: Lumber of rectangular cross section, 2 to 4 in. in thickness and 4 in. or more in width, graded according to its strength in bending when loaded either on the narrow face as a joist or on the wide face as a plank.

Posts and timbers: Lumber of square or approximately square cross section, 5 by 5 in. or larger, graded primarily for use as posts or columns carrying longitudinal loads, but also suitable for miscellaneous uses in which strength in bending is not especially important.

Wood decking

Plank or laminated decks may be used in residential or industrial buildings for floors and roofs. In residential construction, where loads are light, deflection and appearance usually govern design. Since the modulus of elasticity of a species of wood remains the

(continued on page 2-38)

Table 1. Design values for visually graded structural lumber

Allowable unit stresses listed are for normal loading conditions. See National Design Specification for adjustments of tabulated values.

Species and commercial grade	Size classification	Extreme fiber in bending, F_b Single-member uses	Extreme fiber in bending, F_b Repetitive-member uses	Tension parallel to grain, F_t	Horizontal shear, F_v	Compression perpendicular to grain, $F_{c\perp}$	Compression parallel to grain, F_c	Modulus of elasticity, E
Douglas Fir—Larch (Surfaced dry or surfaced green. Used at 19% max m.c.)								
Dense Select Structural		2,450	2,800	1,400	95	455	1,850	1,900,000
Select Structural		2,100	2,400	1,200	95	385	1,600	1,800,000
Dense No. 1		2,050	2,400	1,200	95	455	1,450	1,900,000
No. 1	2" to 4"	1,750	2,050	1,050	95	385	1,250	1,800,000
Dense No. 2	thick	1,700	1,950	1,000	95	455	1,150	1,700,000
No. 2	2" to 4"	1,450	1,650	850	95	385	1,000	1,700,000
No. 3	wide	800	925	475	95	385	600	1,500,000
Appearance		1,750	2,050	1,050	95	385	1,500	1,800,000
Stud		800	925	475	95	385	600	1,500,000
Construction	2" to 4"	1,050	1,200	625	95	385	1,150	1,500,000
Standard	thick	600	675	350	95	385	925	1,500,000
Utility	4" wide	275	325	175	95	385	600	1,500,000
Dense Select Structural		2,100	2,400	1,400	95	455	1,650	1,900,000
Select Structural		1,800	2,050	1,200	95	385	1,400	1,800,000
Dense No. 1	2" to 4"	1,800	2,050	1,200	95	455	1,450	1,900,000
No. 1	thick	1,500	1,750	1,000	95	385	1,250	1,800,000
Dense No. 2	5" and	1,450	1,700	775	95	455	1,250	1,700,000
No. 2	wider	1,250	1,450	650	95	385	1,050	1,700,000
No. 3	wider	725	850	375	95	385	675	1,500,000
Appearance		1,500	1,750	1,000	95	385	1,500	1,800,000
Stud		725	850	375	95	385	675	1,500,000
Dense select structural		1,900	—	1,250	85	455	1,300	1,700,000
Select structural	Beams and	1,600	—	1,050	85	385	1,100	1,600,000
Dense No. 1	stringers	1,550	—	1,050	85	455	1,100	1,700,000
No. 1	and	1,350	—	900	85	385	925	1,600,000

Table 1 (cont.). Design values for visually graded structural lumber

Species and commercial grade	Size classification	Design values, psi						
		Extreme fiber in bending, F_b		Tension parallel to grain, F_t	Horizontal shear, F_v	Compression perpendicular to grain, $F_{c\perp}$	Compression parallel to grain, F_c	Modulus of elasticity, E
		Single-member uses	Repetitive-member uses					
Douglas Fir—Larch (Surfaced dry or surfaced green. Used at 19% max. m.c.) (cont.)								
Dense select structural		1,750	—	1,150	85	455	1,350	1,700,000
Select structural	Posts and	1,500	—	1,000	85	385	1,150	1,600,000
Dense No. 1	timbers	1,400	—	950	85	455	1,200	1,700,000
No. 1		1,200	—	825	85	385	1,000	1,600,000
Selected decking	Decking	—	2,000	—	—	—	—	1,800,000
Commercial decking		—	1,650	—	—	—	—	1,700,000
Selected decking	Decking	—	2,150	(Stresses apply at 15 per cent moisture content)				1,900,000
Commercial decking		—	1,800					1,700,000
California Redwood (Surfaced dry or surfaced green. Used at 19% max. m.c.)								
Clear Heart Structural	4" & less thick,	2,300	2,650	1,550	145	425	2,150	1,400,000
Clear Structural	and width	2,300	2,650	1,550	145	425	2,150	1,400,000
Select Structural		2,050	2,350	1,200	100	425	1,750	1,400,000
Select Structural, Open grain		1,600	1,850	950	100	270	1,300	1,100,000
No. 1	2" to 4"	1,700	1,950	975	100	425	1,400	1,400,000
No. 1, Open grain	thick	1,350	1,550	775	100	270	1,050	1,100,000
No. 2	2" to 4"	1,400	1,600	800	80	425	1,100	1,250,000
No. 2, Open grain	wide	1,100	1,250	625	80	270	825	1,000,000
No. 3		800	900	475	80	425	675	1,100,000
No. 3, Open grain		625	725	375	80	270	500	900,000
Stud		625	725	375	80	270	500	900,000
Construction	2" to 4"	825	950	475	80	270	925	900,000
Standard	thick	450	525	250	80	270	775	900,000
Utility	4" wide	225	250	125	80	270	500	900,000
Select Structural		1,750	2,000	1,150	100	425	1,550	1,400,000
Select Structural, Open grain		1,400	1,600	925	100	270	1,150	1,100,000
No. 1	2" to 4"	1,500	1,700	975	100	425	1,400	1,400,000
No. 1, Open grain	thick	1,150	1,350	775	100	270	1,050	1,100,000
No. 2	5" and	1,200	1,400	650	80	425	1,200	1,250,000
No. 2, Open grain	wider	950	1,100	500	80	270	875	1,000,000
No. 3		700	800	375	80	425	725	1,100,000
No. 3, Open grain		550	650	350	80	270	525	900,000
Stud		700	800	375	80	425	725	1,100,000
Clear Heart Structural or Clear Structural		1,850	—	1,250	135	425	1,650	1,300,000
Select Structural		1,400	—	950	95	425	1,200	1,300,000
No. 1	5" by 5"	1,200	—	800	95	425	1,050	1,300,000
No. 2	and larger	975	—	650	95	425	900	1,100,000
No. 3		550	—	375	95	425	550	1,000,000
Select Decking, Close grain	Decking	1,850	2,150	—	—	—	—	1,400,000
Select Decking	2" thick	1,450	1,700	—	—	—	—	1,100,000
Commercial Decking	6" and wider	1,200	1,350	—	—	—	—	1,000,000
Eastern Hemlock—Tamarack (Surfaced dry or surfaced green. Used at 19% max. m.c.)								
Select Structural		1,800	2,050	1,050	85	365	1,350	1,300,000
No. 1	2" to 4"	1,500	1,750	900	85	365	1,050	1,300,000
No. 2	thick	1,250	1,450	725	85	365	850	1,100,000

Table 1 (cont.). Design values for visually graded structural lumber

Species and commercial grade	Size classification	Extreme fiber in bending, F_b		Tension parallel to grain, F_t	Horizontal shear, F_v	Compression perpendicular to grain, $F_{c\perp}$	Compression parallel to grain, F_c	Modulus of elasticity, E
		Single-member uses	Repetitive-member uses					
Eastern Hemlock — Tamarack (Surfaced dry or surfaced green. Used at 19% max. m.c.) (cont.)								
No. 3	2" to 4"	700	800	400	85	365	525	1,000,000
Appearance	wide	1,300	1,500	900	85	365	1,300	1,300,000
Stud		700	800	400	85	365	525	1,000,000
Construction	2" to 4"	900	1,050	525	85	365	975	1,000,000
Standard	thick	500	575	300	85	365	800	1,000,000
Utility	4" wide	250	275	150	85	365	525	1,000,000
Select Structural	2" to 4"	1,550	1,750	1,050	85	365	1,200	1,300,000
No. 1	thick	1,300	1,500	875	85	365	1,050	1,300,000
No. 2	5" and	1,050	1,200	575	85	365	900	1,100,000
No. 3	wider	625	725	325	85	365	575	1,000,000
Appearance		1,300	1,500	875	85	365	1,300	1,300,000
Stud		625	725	325	85	365	575	1,000,000
Select Structural	Beams and	1,400	—	925	80	365	950	1,200,000
No. 1	Stringers	1,150	—	775	80	365	800	1,200,000
Select Structural	Posts and	1,300	—	875	80	365	1,000	1,200,000
No. 1	Timbers	1,050	—	700	80	365	875	1,200,000
Select	Decking	1,500	1,700	—	—	—	—	1,300,000
Commercial		1,250	1,450	—	—	—	—	1,100,000
Eastern Spruce (Surfaced dry or surfaced green. Used at 19% max. m.c.)								
Select Structural		1,500	1,750	875	65	255	1,150	1,400,000
No. 1	2" to 4"	1,300	1,500	750	65	255	900	1,400,000
No. 2	thick	1,050	1,200	625	65	255	700	1,200,000
No. 3	2" to 4"	575	675	325	65	255	425	1,100,000
Appearance	wide	1,100	1,250	750	65	255	1,050	1,400,000
Stud		575	675	325	65	255	425	1,100,000
Construction	2" to 4"	775	875	450	65	255	800	1,100,000
Standard	thick	425	500	250	65	255	675	1,100,000
Utility	4" wide	200	225	100	65	255	425	1,100,000
Select Structural		1,300	1,500	875	65	255	1,000	1,400,000
No. 1	2" to 4"	1,100	1,250	750	65	255	900	1,400,000
No. 2	thick	900	1,000	475	65	255	750	1,200,000
No. 3	5" and	525	600	275	65	255	475	1,100,000
Appearance	wider	1,100	1,250	750	65	255	1,050	1,400,000
Stud		525	600	275	65	255	475	1,100,000
Select Structural	Beams and	1,150	—	775	60	255	800	1,200,000
No. 1	Stringers	950	—	650	60	255	675	1,200,000
Select Structural	Posts and	1,100	—	725	60	255	850	1,200,000
No. 1	Timbers	875	—	600	60	255	725	1,200,000
Truss	2" to 4" thick 2" to 4" wide	1,785	2,050	1,000	65	255	1,200	1,400,000
1500 f	2" to 4" thick 5" and wider	1,500	1,700	1,000	65	255	1,100	1,400,000
Select	Decking	1,250	1,450	—	—	—	—	1,400,000
Commercial		1,050	1,200	—	—	—	—	1,200,000

Table 1 (cont.). Design values for visually graded structural lumber

Species and commercial grade	Size classification	Design values, psi						
		Extreme fiber in bending, F_b		Tension parallel to grain, F_t	Horizontal shear, F_v	Compression perpendicular to grain, $F_{c\perp}$	Compression parallel to grain, F_c	Modulus of elasticity, E
		Single-member uses	Repetitive-member uses					
Southern Pine (Surfaced dry. Used at 19% max. m.c.)								
Select Structural		2,000	2,300	1,150	100	405	1,550	1,700,000
Dense Select Structural		2,350	2,700	1,350	100	475	1,800	1,800,000
No. 1		1,700	1,950	1,000	100	405	1,250	1,700,000
No. 1 Dense	2" to 4" thick	2,000	2,300	1,150	100	475	1,450	1,800,000
No. 2	2" to 4"	1,400	1,650	825	90	405	975	1,600,000
No. 2 Dense	wide	1,650	1,900	975	90	475	1,150	1,600,000
No. 3		775	900	450	90	405	575	1,400,000
No. 3 Dense		925	1,050	525	90	475	675	1,500,000
Stud		775	900	450	90	405	575	1,400,000
Construction	2" to 4"	1,000	1,150	600	100	405	1,100	1,400,000
Standard	thick	575	675	350	90	405	900	1,400,000
Utility	4" wide	275	300	150	90	405	575	1,400,000
Select Structural		1,750	2,000	1,150	90	405	1,350	1,700,000
Dense Select Structural		2,050	2,350	1,300	90	475	1,600	1,800,000
No. 1		1,450	1,700	975	90	405	1,250	1,700,000
No. 1 Dense	2" to 4" thick	1,700	2,000	1,150	90	475	1,450	1,800,000
No. 2	5" and	1,200	1,400	625	90	405	1,000	1,600,000
No. 2 Dense	wider	1,400	1,650	725	90	475	1,200	1,600,000
No. 3		700	800	350	90	405	625	1,400,000
No. 3 Dense		825	925	425	90	475	725	1,500,000
Stud		725	850	350	90	405	625	1,400,000
Dense Standard Decking	2" to 4"	2,000	2,300	—	—	475	—	1,800,000
Select Decking	thick	1,400	1,650	—	—	405	—	1,600,000
Dense Select Decking	2" and	1,650	1,900	—	—	475	—	1,600,000
Commercial Decking	wider	1,400	1,650	—	—	405	—	1,600,000
Dense Commercial Decking	Decking	1,650	1,900	—	—	475	—	1,600,000
Dense Structural 86	2" to 4"	2,600	3,000	1,750	155	475	2,000	1,800,000
Dense Structural 72	thick	2,200	2,550	1,450	130	475	1,650	1,800,000
Dense Structural 65		2,000	2,300	1,300	115	475	1,500	1,800,000
Western Cedars (Surfaced dry or surfaced green. Used at 19% max. m.c.)								
Select Structural		1,500	1,750	875	75	265	1,200	1,100,000
No. 1	2" to 4"	1,300	1,500	750	75	265	950	1,100,000
No. 2	thick	1,050	1,200	625	75	265	750	1,000,000
No. 3	2" to 4"	600	675	350	75	265	450	900,000
Appearance	wide	1,300	1,500	750	75	265	1,100	1,100,000
Stud		600	675	350	75	265	450	900,000
Construction	2" to 4"	775	875	450	75	265	850	900,000
Standard	thick	425	500	250	75	265	700	900,000
Utility	4" wide	200	225	125	75	265	450	900,000
Select Structural		1,300	1,500	875	75	265	1,050	1,00,000
No. 1	2" to 4"	1,100	1,300	750	75	265	950	1,100,000
No. 2	thick	925	1,050	475	75	265	800	1,000,000
No. 3	5" and	525	625	275	75	265	500	900,000
Appearance	wider	1,100	1,300	750	75	265	1,100	1,100,000
Stud		525	625	275	75	265	500	900,000

Table 1 (cont.). Design values for visually graded structural lumber

Species and commercial grade	Size classification	Extreme fiber in bending, F_b Single-member uses	Extreme fiber in bending, F_b Repetitive-member uses	Tension parallel to grain, F_t	Horizontal shear, F_v	Compression perpendicular to grain, $F_{c\perp}$	Compression parallel to grain, F_c	Modulus of elasticity, E
Select Structural	Beams and	1,150	—	675	70	265	875	1,000,000
No. 1	Stringers	975	—	475	70	265	725	1,000,000
Select Structural	Posts and	1,100	—	725	70	265	925	1,000,000
No. 1	Timbers	875	—	600	70	265	800	1,000,000
Select Dex	Decking	1,250	1,450	—	—	265	—	1,100,000
Commercial Dex		1,050	1,200	—	—	265	—	1,000,000
Select Structural	Beams and	1,150	—	775	70	265	875	1,000,000
No. 1	Stringers	975	—	650	70	265	725	1,000,000
Select Structural	Posts and	1,100	—	725	70	265	925	1,000,000
No. 1	Timbers	875	—	600	70	265	800	1,000,000
Selected Decking	Decking	—	1,450	—	—	—	—	1,100,000
Commercial Decking		—	1,200	—	—	—	—	1,000,000
Selected Decking	Decking	—	1,550	(Surfaced at 15% max. m.c. and			—	1,100,000
Commercial Decking		—	1,300	used at 15% max. m.c.)			—	1,000,000

Northern Pine (surfaced dry or surfaced green. Used at 19% max. m.c.)

Species and commercial grade	Size classification	F_b Single	F_b Repetitive	F_t	F_v	$F_{c\perp}$	F_c	E
Select Structural		1,650	1,850	950	70	280	1,200	1,400,000
No. 1	2" to 4"	1,400	1,600	825	70	280	975	1,400,000
No. 2	thick	1,150	1,300	675	70	280	775	1,300,000
No. 3	2" to 4"	625	725	375	70	280	475	1,100,000
Appearance	wide	1,200	1,400	800	70	280	1,150	1,400,000
Stud		625	725	375	70	280	475	1,100,000
Construction	2" to 4"	825	950	475	70	280	875	1,100,000
Standard	thick	450	525	275	70	280	725	1,100,000
Utility	4" wide	225	250	125	70	280	475	1,100,000
Select Structural	2" to 4"	1,400	1,600	950	70	280	1,100	1,400,000
No. 1	thick	1,200	1,400	800	70	280	975	1,400,000
No. 2	5" and	950	1,100	525	70	280	825	1,300,000
No. 3	wider	575	650	300	70	280	525	1,100,000
Appearance		1,200	1,400	800	70	280	1,150	1,400,000
Stud		575	650	300	70	280	525	1,100,000
Select Structural	Beams and	1,250	—	850	65	280	850	1,300,000
No. 1	Stringers	1,050	—	700	65	280	725	1,300,000
Select Structural	Posts and	1,150	—	800	65	280	900	1,300,000
No. 1	Timbers	950	—	650	65	280	800	1,300,000
Select	Decking	1,350	1,550	—	—	—	—	1,400,000
Commercial		1,150	1,300	—	—	—	—	1,300,000

Table 2. Properties of structural lumber—sectional properties of standard dressed (S4S) sizes*

(*From* Wood Structural Design Data, *1978, National Forest Products Association*)

Nominal size b (inches) h	Standard dressed size (S4S) b (inches) h	Area of section A	Moment of inertia I	Section modulus S	Weight in lb per lin ft of piece when weight of wood per cu ft equals:					
					25 lb	30 lb	35 lb	40 lb	45 lb	50 lb
2 × 3	1½ × 2½	3.750	1.953	1.563	0.651	0.781	0.911	1.042	1.172	1.302
2 × 4	1½ × 3½	5.250	5.359	3.063	0.911	1.094	1.276	1.458	1.641	1.823
2 × 6	1½ × 5½	8.250	20.797	7.563	1.432	1.719	2.005	2.292	2.578	2.865
2 × 8	1½ × 7¼	10.875	47.635	13.141	1.888	2.266	2.643	3.021	3.398	3.776
2 × 10	1½ × 9¼	13.875	98.932	21.391	2.409	2.891	3.372	8.854	4.336	4.818
2 × 12	1½ × 11¼	16.875	177.979	31.641	2.930	3.516	4.102	4.688	5.273	5.859
2 × 14	1½ × 13¼	19.875	290.775	43.891	3.451	4.141	4.831	5.521	6.211	6.901
3 × 1	2½ × ¾	1.875	0.088	0.234	0.326	0.391	0.456	0.521	0.586	0.651
3 × 2	2½ × 1½	3.750	0.703	0.938	0.651	0.781	0.911	1.042	1.172	1.302
3 × 4	2½ × 3½	8.750	8.932	5.104	1.519	1.823	2.127	2.431	2.734	3.038
3 × 6	2½ × 5½	13.750	34.661	12.604	2.387	2.865	3.342	3.819	4.297	4.774
3 × 8	2½ × 7¼	18.125	79.391	21.901	3.147	3.776	4.405	5.035	5.664	6.293
3 × 10	2½ × 9¼	23.125	164.886	35.651	4.015	4.818	5.621	6.424	7.227	8.030
3 × 12	2½ × 11¼	28.125	296.631	52.734	4.883	5.859	6.836	7.813	8.789	9.766
3 × 14	2½ × 13¼	33.125	484.625	73.151	5.751	6.901	8.051	9.201	10.352	11.502
3 × 16	2½ × 15¼	38.125	738.870	96.901	6.619	7.943	9.266	10.590	11.914	13.238
4 × 1	3½ × ¾	2.625	0.123	0.328	0.456	0.547	0.638	0.729	0.820	0.911
4 × 2	3½ × 1½	5.250	0.984	1.313	0.911	1.094	1.276	1.458	1.641	1.823
4 × 3	3½ × 2½	8.750	4.557	3.646	1.519	1.823	2.127	2.431	2.734	3.038
4 × 4	3½ × 3½	12.250	12.505	7.146	2.127	2.552	2.977	3.403	3.828	4.253
4 × 6	3½ × 5½	19.250	48.526	17.646	3.342	4.010	4.679	5.347	6.016	6.684
4 × 8	3½ × 7¼	25.375	111.148	30.661	4.405	5.286	6.168	7.049	7.930	8.811
4 × 10	3½ × 9¼	32.375	230.840	49.911	5.621	6.745	7.869	8.933	10.117	11.241
4 × 12	3½ × 11¼	39.375	415.283	73.828	6.836	8.203	9.570	10.938	12.305	12.672
4 × 14	3½ × 13½	47.250	717.609	106.313	8.203	9.844	11.484	13.125	14.766	16.406
4 × 16	3½ × 15½	54.250	1086.130	140.146	9.418	11.302	13.186	15.069	16.953	18.837
6 × 1	5½ × ¾	4.125	0.193	0.516	0.716	0.859	1.003	1.146	1.289	1.432
6 × 2	5½ × 1½	8.250	1.547	2.063	1.432	1.719	2.005	2.292	2.578	2.865
6 × 3	5½ × 2½	13.750	7.161	5.729	2.387	2.865	3.342	3.819	4.297	4.774
6 × 4	5½ × 3½	19.250	19.651	11.229	3.342	4.010	4.679	5.347	6.016	6.684
6 × 6	5½ × 5½	30.250	76.225	27.729	5.252	6.302	7.352	8.403	9.453	10.503
6 × 8	5½ × 7½	41.250	193.359	51.563	7.161	8.594	10.026	11.458	12.891	14.323
6 × 10	5½ × 9½	52.250	392.963	82.729	9.071	10.885	12.700	14.514	16.328	18.142
6 × 12	5½ × 11½	63.250	697.068	121.229	10.981	13.177	15.373	17.569	19.766	21.962
6 × 14	5½ × 13½	74.250	1127.672	167.063	12.891	15.469	18.047	20.625	23.203	25.781
6 × 16	5½ × 15½	85.250	1706.776	220.229	14.800	17.760	20.720	23.681	26.641	29.601
6 × 18	5½ × 17½	96.250	2456.380	280.729	16.710	20.052	23.394	26.736	30.078	33.420
6 × 20	5½ × 19½	107.250	3398.484	348.563	18.620	22.344	26.068	29.792	33.516	37.240
8 × 1	7¼ × ¾	5.438	0.255	0.680	0.944	1.133	1.322	1.510	1.699	1.888
8 × 2	7¼ × 1½	10.875	2.039	2.719	1.888	2.266	2.643	3.021	3.398	3.776
8 × 3	7¼ × 2½	18.125	9.440	7.552	3.147	3.776	4.405	5.035	5.664	6.293
8 × 4	7¼ × 3½	25.375	25.904	14.802	4.405	5.286	6.168	7.049	7.930	8.811
8 × 6	7½ × 5½	41.250	103.984	37.813	7.161	8.594	10.026	11.458	12.891	14.323
8 × 8	7½ × 7½	56.250	263.672	70.313	9.766	11.719	13.672	15.625	17.578	19.531
8 × 10	7½ × 9½	71.250	535.859	112.813	12.370	14.844	17.318	19.792	22.266	24.740
8 × 12	7½ × 11½	86.250	950.547	165.313	14.974	17.969	20.964	23.958	26.953	29.948
8 × 14	7½ × 13½	101.250	1537.734	227.813	17.578	21.094	24.609	28.125	31.641	35.156
8 × 16	7½ × 15½	116.250	2327.422	300.313	20.182	24.219	28.255	32.292	36.328	40.365
8 × 18	7½ × 17½	131.250	3349.609	382.813	22.786	27.344	31.901	36.453	41.016	45.573
8 × 20	7½ × 19½	146.250	4634.297	475.313	25.391	30.469	35.547	40.625	45.703	50.781
8 × 22	7½ × 21½	161.250	6211.484	577.813	27.995	33.594	39.193	44.792	50.391	55.990
8 × 24	7½ × 23½	176.250	8111.172	690.313	30.599	36.719	42.839	48.958	55.078	61.198
10 × 2	9¼ × 1½	13.875	2.602	3.469	2.409	2.891	3.372	3.854	4.336	4.818
10 × 3	9¼ × 2½	23.125	12.044	9.635	4.015	4.818	5.621	6.424	7.227	8.030
10 × 4	9¼ × 3½	32.375	33.049	18.885	5.621	6.745	7.869	8.993	10.117	11.241
10 × 10	9½ × 9½	90.250	678.755	142.896	15.668	18.802	21.936	25.069	28.203	31.337
10 × 20	9½ × 19½	185.250	5870.109	602.063	32.161	38.594	45.026	51.458	57.891	64.323
12 × 2	11¼ × 1½	16.875	3.164	4.219	2.930	3.516	4.102	4.688	5.273	5.859
12 × 3	11¼ × 2½	28.125	14.648	11.719	4.883	5.859	6.836	7.813	8.789	9.766
12 × 4	11¼ × 3½	39.375	40.195	22.969	6.836	8.203	9.570	10.938	12.305	13.672
12 × 12	11½ × 11½	132.250	1457.505	253.479	22.960	27.552	32.144	36.736	41.328	45.920
12 × 24	11½ × 23½	270.250	12437.129	1058.479	46.918	56.302	65.686	75.069	84.453	93.837

* *For lumber surfaced 1⅝ in. thick instead of 1½ in., the area (A), moment of inertia (I), and section modulus (S) may be increased 8.33 per cent.*

Decking; ceiling joists

same for all stress grades, however, deflection does not affect grade selection. Growth characteristics are most conspicuous in the low-cost grades and may be used to provide a rustic effect. The high-priced stress grades, in which growth characteristics are negligible, are more suitable for high standards of appearance.

An important consideration in determining the stiffness and deflection of a deck is the arrangement of deck pieces that span supports. There are three basic span types. The first is the simple span, in which deck pieces of uniform length bear on two supports. This span type produces the maximum deflection. The second is the fully continuous span, in which deck pieces bear on at least three supports. This span type requires great lengths but reduces deflection to less than half that of the simple span. The third is the partially continuous span, in which at least half the deck pieces extend over one support. There are many methods of developing the latter type, but the use of random-length pieces is the method most frequently used for multiple spans—it is the most economical and reduces the deflection of the simple span by 30 per cent. Although any degree of continuity would have a similar effect on the reduction of bending moments, allowable loads are conservatively based on $M = wl^2/8$, which corresponds to the moment for a simple span.

Table 3. Total allowable loads for wood decking

The total allowable loads, including the weight of the deck, apply to seasoned lumber used under normal loading conditions.
$E = 1,760,000$ *psi and* $f = 1,200$ *psi. For other stresses or moduli of elasticity, allowable loads can be determined by direct proportion. Values for deflection are based on random-length decking using the formula*

$$\Delta = \frac{wl^4}{100EI}$$

Span length, ft	Nominal thickness of deck, in.											
	2			3			4			6		
	Deflection		Bending	Deflection		Bending	Deflection		Bending	Deflection		Bending
	$\Delta = 1/180$	$\Delta = 1/240$	$f = 1,200$	$\Delta = 1/180$	$\Delta = 1/240$	$f = 1,200$	$\Delta = 1/180$	$\Delta = 1/240$	$f = 1,200$	$\Delta = 1/180$	$\Delta = 1/240$	$f = 1,200$
	Load, lb/ft²											
6	106	80	99	489	367	278						
7	67	50	73	308	230	204						
8	45	34	56	206	154	156	567	426	305			
9	31	23	44	144	108	123	400	300	240			
10	23	17	35	105	79	100	291	217	195			
11	17	13	29	79	59	82	219	163	161	849	637	400
12	13	10	24	62	45	70	169	126	135	654	491	336
13	10	7	21	48	36	59	132	100	115	514	385	286
14				37	29	50	107	80	99	411	309	247
15				31	23	44	86	65	86	335	251	215
16				25	18	39	71	54	76	276	207	189
17				21	15	34	59	45	67	230	173	167
18							50	37	60	194	146	149
19							42	31	53	165	124	134
20							36	27	49	141	106	121

Table 4. Maximum spans for ceiling joists

$E = 1,760,000$ *psi and* $f = 1,200$ *psi. Design assumptions for deflection and bending are as follows: live load—none; dead load—weight of joist, weight of ceiling at 10 psf.*

Nominal size, in.	Spacing, center to center, in.	Deflection		Bending
		$\Delta = 1/240$	$\Delta = 1/360$	$f = 1,200$
		Span length, ft-in.		
2 × 4	12	12-13	10-7	14-7
	16	11-1	9-10	12-11
	24	9-10	8-7	10-9
2 × 6	12	18-3	15-11	21-8
	16	16-11	14-9	19-3
	24	15-0	13-1	16-2
2 × 8	12	24-3	21-0	28-0
	16	22-6	19-6	25-3
	24	19-11	17-4	21-5
2 × 10	12	28-0	26-2	28-0
	16	28-0	24-3	28-0
	24	25-0	21-11	26-10
2 × 12	12	28-0	28-0	28-0
	16	28-0	28-0	28-0
	24	28-0	26-7	28-0

Table 5. Maximum spans for attic-floor joists

$E = 1,760,000$ *psi and* $f = 1,200$ *psi. Design assumptions for deflection and bending are as follows: live load—20 psf; dead load—weight of joist, weight of floor at 2.5 psf, and weight of ceiling at 10 psf.*

Nominal size, in.	Spacing, center to center, in.	Deflection		Bending
		$\Delta = 1/240$	$\Delta = 1/360$	$f = 1,200$
		Span length, ft-in.		
2 × 4	12	8-5	7-5	8-7
	16	7-8	6-9	7-6
	24	6-9	5-11	6-2
2 × 6	12	12-11	11-3	13-0
	16	11-10	10-4	11-4
	24	10-4	9-1	9-3
2 × 8	12	17-3	15-0	17-3
	16	15-10	13-10	15-1
	24	13-10	12-2	12-6
2 × 10	12	21-7	18-11	21-7
	16	19-10	17-4	19-0
	24	17-6	15-3	15-9
2 × 12	12	26-6	23-2	26-0
	16	24-4	21-4	23-0
	24	21-6	18-10	19-0

Table 6. Maximum spans for floor joists

This table is based on the following conditions:
Deflection: Span lengths are based on a limiting deflection equal to 1/360 of the span using a modulus of elasticity of E = 1,760,000 psi. For other moduli of elasticity, multiply the span lengths given below by E/1,760,000.
Bending: Assumed dead loads are weight of joist, weight of floor at 5 psf, and weight of ceiling at 10 psf. If ceiling is not used, the live-load capacity is 10 psf greater.

Nominal size, in.	Spacing, center to center, in.	Deflection	Bending		Deflection	Bending	
		$\Delta = 1/360$	f = 1,200	f = 1,500	$\Delta = 1/360$	f = 1,200	f = 1,500
		Live load, 30 psf			Live load, 40 psf		
		Span length, ft-in.			Span length, ft-in.		
2 × 6	12	11-0	11-0	12-6	10-2	10-1	11-4
	16	10-1	9-9	10-11	9-4	8-10	9-10
	24	8-10	7-11	9-0	8-2	7-3	8-1
2 × 8	12	14-9	14-9	16-6	13-8	13-7	15-2
	16	13-6	12-9	14-6	12-6	11-10	13-2
	24	11-10	10-8	11-10	10-11	9-9	10-10
2 × 10	12	18-7	18-8	20-9	17-3	17-1	19-1
	16	17-2	16-4	18-2	15-11	15-0	16-9
	24	15-1	13-6	15-1	13-10	12-3	13-10
2 × 12	12	22-9	26-1	25-1	21-0	20-7	23-0
	16	20-11	22-10	21-11	19-4	18-0	20-2
	24	18-4	19-1	18-2	17-0	14-10	16-7
3 × 6	12	13-0	14-3	15-11	12-0	12-10	14-4
	16	11-10	12-6	13-11	11-0	11-3	12-6
	24	10-5	10-4	11-6	9-8	9-3	10-3
3 × 8	12	17-3	18-7	20-10	15-11	17-1	19-2
	16	15-10	16-4	18-3	14-9	15-0	16-9
	24	14-0	13-6	15-2	12-11	12-4	13-9
3 × 10	12	21-10	23-5	26-2	20-3	21-7	24-1
	16	20-2	20-8	23-0	18-8	18-11	21-3
	24	17-10	17-2	19-0	16-6	15-9	17-6
3 × 12	12	26-3	28-2	31-7	24-6	25-10	28-3
	16	24-3	24-10	27-9	22-6	22-10	25-6
	24	21-6	20-9	23-3	19-11	19-0	21-3
		Live load, 50 psf			Live load, 100 psf		
2 × 6	12	9-6	9-4	10-3	7-8	7-1	7-10
	16	8-8	8-1	9-1	7-0	6-2	6-10
	24	7-8	6-8	7-5	6-2	5-0	5-7
2 × 8	12	12-10	12-6	14-0	10-4	9-6	10-8
	16	11-9	10-11	12-2	9-6	8-3	9-4
	24	10-3	9-0	10-0	8-3	6-10	7-5
2 × 10	12	16-3	15-10	17-9	13-3	12-1	13-6
	16	14-10	13-9	15-6	12-1	10-6	11-9
	24	13-0	11-4	12-9	10-7	8-8	9-8
2 × 12	12	19-10	19-1	21-4	16-2	14-6	16-2
	16	18-2	16-9	18-8	14-9	12-10	14-2
	24	16-0	13-9	15-4	12-11	10-6	11-7
3 × 6	12	11-4	11-11	13-3	9-3	9-0	10-3
	16	10-4	10-4	11-6	8-5	7-11	8-9
	24	9-1	9-0	9-6	7-6	6-6	7-2
3 × 8	12	15-1	15-10	17-9	12-4	12-2	13-6
	16	13-10	13-10	15-6	11-3	10-6	11-0
	24	12-2	11-5	12-9	9-11	8-8	9-8
3 × 10	12	19-1	20-0	22-4	15-9	15-3	17-1
	16	17-7	17-6	19-6	14-4	13-5	15-0
	24	15-6	14-5	16-2	12-7	10-11	12-3
3 × 12	12	23-1	24-0	26-10	19-0	18-7	20-9
	16	21-2	21-2	23-8	17-5	16-3	18-2
	24	18-8	17-6	19-7	15-3	13-4	14-11

Rafters and roof joists

Table 7. Maximum spans for rafters and roof joists (light roofing)

This table is based on the following conditions:
Deflection: Span lengths are based on a limiting deflection equal to 1/360 of the span using a modulus of elasticity of E = 1,760,000 psi. For other moduli of elasticity,

multiply the span lengths given below by E/1,760,000.
Bending: Assumed dead loads are weight of joist, weight of sheathing at 2.5 psf, and weight of light roofing at 2.5 psf.

Nominal size, in.	Spacing, center to center, in.	Deflection $\Delta = 1/360$	Bending $f = 1,200$	Bending $f = 1,500$	Deflection $\Delta = 1/360$	Bending $f = 1,200$	Bending $f = 1,500$
		Live load, 20 psf			Live load, 30 psf		
		Span length, ft-in.			Span length, ft-in.		
2 × 6	12	12-3	14-8	16-5	11-0	12-6	14-0
	16	11-2	12-10	14-4	10-1	10-11	12-3
	24	9-10	10-7	11-10	8-10	9-0	10-1
2 × 8	12	16-4	19-5	21-7	14-9	16-9	18-7
	16	15-0	17-0	19-0	13-6	14-8	16-3
	24	13-2	14-2	15-8	11-10	12-1	13-4
2 × 10	12	20-7	24-4	26-2	18-8	21-0	23-4
	16	19-0	21-6	23-10	17-2	18-6	20-7
	24	16-9	17-10	19-10	15-1	15-4	17-0
2 × 12	12	25-0	28-0	28-0	22-8	25-2	28-0
	16	23-0	25-10	28-0	20-11	22-2	24-10
	24	20-4	21-6	24-0	18-4	18-5	20-6
3 × 6	12	14-4	18-4	20-5	12-11	15-10	17-9
	16	13-2	16-2	18-1	11-10	13-11	15-6
	24	11-7	13-5	14-11	10-5	11-6	12-10
3 × 8	12	19-0	24-1	27-0	17-3	20-11	23-4
	16	17-6	21-5	23-11	15-10	18-5	20-7
	24	15-6	17-11	19-11	14-0	15-3	17-0
3 × 10	12	23-11	30-0	32-0	21-10	26-2	29-4
	16	22-2	26-9	29-11	20-0	23-3	25-11
	24	19-8	22-6	25-1	17-10	19-4	21-7
3 × 12	12	28-8	32-0	32-0	26-3	31-4	32-0
	16	26-6	32-0	32-0	24-2	27-10	31-2
	24	23-9	27-0	30-3	21-5	23-3	26-1
		Live load, 40 psf			Live load, 50 psf		
2 × 6	12	10-2	11-2	12-5	9-6	10-1	11-4
	16	9-3	9-8	10-10	8-8	8-10	9-10
	24	8-2	7-11	8-10	7-8	7-3	8-1
2 × 8	12	13-8	14-11	16-6	12-9	13-7	15-0
	16	12-5	13-1	14-4	11-9	11-10	13-1
	24	10-11	10-9	11-10	10-3	9-9	10-9
2 × 10	12	17-4	18-10	20-10	16-3	17-1	19-0
	16	15-10	16-6	18-3	14-10	15-0	16-7
	24	13-10	13-7	15-0	13-0	12-4	13-8
2 × 12	12	21-1	22-6	25-1	19-9	20-9	23-0
	16	19-4	19-9	22-1	18-1	18-0	20-2
	24	17-0	16-4	18-3	15-11	14-10	16-7
3 × 6	12	12-0	14-1	15-9	11-4	12-10	14-4
	16	11-0	12-4	13-10	10-4	11-3	12-6
	24	9-7	10-2	11-5	9-1	9-3	10-3
3 × 8	12	16-0	18-9	20-11	15-1	17-1	19-2
	16	14-9	16-6	18-4	13-10	15-0	16-9
	24	12-11	13-7	15-2	12-2	12-4	13-9
3 × 10	12	20-4	23-6	26-3	19-2	21-6	24-2
	16	18-8	20-10	23-2	17-7	19-0	21-2
	24	16-6	17-2	19-3	15-6	15-9	17-6
3 × 12	12	24-5	28-3	31-7	23-1	25-11	28-11
	16	22-6	24-11	27-11	21-2	22-10	25-5
	24	19-11	20-9	23-2	18-8	18-11	21-2

Table 8. Maximum spans for rafters and roof joists (heavy roofing)

This table is based on the following conditions:
Deflection: Span lengths are based on a limiting deflection equal to 1/360 of the span using a modulus of elasticity of E = 1,760,000 psi. For other moduli of elasticity, multiply the span lengths given below by E/1,760,000.
Bending: Assumed dead loads are weight of joist, weight of sheathing at 2.5 psf, and weight of heavy roofing at 8 psf.

Nominal size, in.	Spacing, center to center, in.	Deflection	Bending		Deflection	Bending	
		$\triangle = 1/360$	f = 1,200	f = 1,500	$\triangle = 1/360$	f = 1,200	f = 1,500
		Live load, 20 psf			Live load, 30 psf		
		Span length, ft-in.			Span length, ft-in.		
2 × 6	12	11-6	13-3	14-10	10-6	11-7	13-0
	16	10-6	11-7	13-0	9-8	10-2	11-4
	24	9-3	9-6	10-8	8-6	8-4	9-4
2 × 8	12	15-5	17-10	19-9	14-2	15-6	17-4
	16	14-1	15-6	17-4	12-11	13-7	15-3
	24	12-6	12-9	14-4	11-4	11-2	12-6
2 × 10	12	19-5	22-2	24-10	17-10	19-6	21-10
	16	17-10	19-6	21-10	16-4	17-1	19-2
	24	15-8	16-2	18-2	14-4	14-2	15-10
2 × 12	12	23-7	26-11	28-0	21-8	23-7	26-6
	16	21-8	23-7	27-0	20-0	20-9	23-2
	24	19-2	19-7	21-11	17-7	17-2	19-3
3 × 6	12	13-5	16-9	18-9	12-4	14-9	16-6
	16	12-4	14-9	16-6	11-4	12-11	14-6
	24	10-10	12-2	13-10	10-0	10-8	11-11
3 × 8	12	17-11	22-2	24-10	16-6	19-7	21-10
	16	16-6	19-7	21-10	15-2	17-3	19-3
	24	14-8	16-3	18-2	13-4	14-3	16-0
3 × 10	12	22-8	27-8	31-3	21-0	24-7	27-6
	16	21-0	24-7	27-6	19-3	21-8	24-3
	24	18-6	20-7	22-11	17-1	18-1	20-2
3 × 12	12	27-2	32-0	32-0	25-2	29-6	32-0
	16	25-1	29-6	32-0	23-2	26-1	29-2
	24	22-4	24-10	27-10	20-6	21-9	24-4
		Live load, 40 psf			Live load, 50 psf		
2 × 6	12	9-10	10-6	11-8	9-3	9-7	10-9
	16	8-11	9-1	10-2	8-6	8-4	9-4
	24	7-10	7-6	8-4	7-5	6-10	7-8
2 × 8	12	13-3	14-0	15-8	12-6	12-10	14-5
	16	12-0	12-3	13-8	11-4	11-2	12-7
	24	10-6	10-0	11-2	10-0	9-3	10-3
2 × 10	12	16-8	17-10	19-9	15-9	16-3	18-2
	16	15-3	15-6	17-4	14-5	14-2	15-11
	24	13-5	12-9	14-3	12-8	11-10	13-1
2 × 12	12	20-3	21-4	24-0	19-3	19-9	22-0
	16	18-8	18-9	21-0	17-7	17-3	19-3
	24	16-4	15-5	17-4	15-6	14-2	15-10
3 × 6	12	11-7	13-4	14-10	10-11	12-3	13-8
	16	10-6	11-8	13-0	10-0	10-9	11-11
	24	9-3	9-7	10-9	8-9	8-10	9-10
3 × 8	12	15-5	17-9	19-10	14-8	16-4	18-3
	16	14-2	15-7	17-4	13-4	14-4	16-0
	24	12-6	12-10	14-4	11-9	11-9	13-2
3 × 10	12	19-8	22-4	25-0	18-7	20-7	23-0
	16	18-0	19-7	22-0	17-1	18-1	20-3
	24	15-10	16-4	18-2	15-0	15-0	16-8
3 × 12	12	23-7	26-11	30-0	22-4	24-10	27-9
	16	21-8	23-10	26-6	20-7	21-10	24-4
	24	19-2	19-8	22-0	18-2	18-1	20-2

Beams

Table 9 indicates the uniformly distributed loads that joists and beams may support at various span lengths. Values are based on sizes of S4S (surfaced four sides) lumber and for normal conditions of loading. Although the table is not comprehensive, it includes the most commonly used sections for each span length. Total loads, which include the weight of the beam, are given for stress condition, W, and for deflection, W_Δ, where deflection controls. The total allowable load, W, is limited by maximum allowable fiber stress in bending, f. The shear stress F_v, corresponding to the maximum load, W, is tabulated and must be checked against the allowable shear permitted for the species of wood used. Values in the table are based on 1,500 psi for f. The total allowable load limited by deflection, W_Δ, is based on a modulus of elasticity, E, of 1,760,000 psi and a maximum deflection of 1/360 of the span.

For conditions that differ from those assumed in the table, allowable loads limited by deflection, W_Δ, may be found by direct proportion. For example, if a species of wood with a modulus of elasticity of 1,540,000 psi is to be used, the total load limited by deflection can be determined by multiplying W_Δ by the factor 154/176 or 0.88. If the limiting deflection is to be 1/300 of the span, the allowable load for deflection would be W_Δ multiplied by the factor 360/300 or 1.2.

Conversion of the total allowable load, W, for different allowable stresses, f, may be accomplished by multiplying W by the ratio of the desired bending stress, f, to the tabulated bending stress. The shearing stress, F_v, must also be multiplied by the same factor.

Table 9. Total uniformly distributed loads for joists and beams

W_Δ = total uniformly distributed load in pounds for deflection of 1/360 of the span: W = total uniformly distributed load in pounds for allowable bending stress f or allowable shearing stress F_v. F_v = unit horizontal shear stress induced by load W. All values are based on the following allowable stresses: f = 1,500 psi; E = 1,760,000 psi.

| Nominal size, in. | Span length, ft | | | | | | | | | | | | | | | | | |
| | 8 | | | 9 | | | 10 | | | 11 | | | 12 | | | 13 | | |
	F_v	W	W_Δ	F_v	W	W_Δ	F_v	W	W_Δ	F_v	W	W_Δ	F_v	W	W_Δ	F_v	W	W_Δ
2 × 8	113	1,642		100	1,460		90	1,314	1,241	82	1,194	1,025	75	1,095	862	69	1,010	735
2 × 10	144	2,673		128	2,376		115	2,139		105	1,944		96	1,782		88	1,645	1,527
3 × 8	113	2,737		100	2,433		90	2,190	2,068	82	1,991	1,710	75	1,825	1,439	69	1,684	1,225
4 × 8	113	3,832		100	3,406		90	3,066	2,885	82	2,787	2,391	75	2,555	2,010	69	2,358	1,712
2 × 12	175	3,955		156	3,515		140	3,164		127	2,876		117	2,636		108	2,433	
3 × 10	144	4,456		128	3,961		115	3,565		105	3,241		96	2,970		88	2,742	2,542
2 × 14	207	5,486		184	4,876		165	4,389		150	3,990		138	3,657		127	3,376	
4 × 10	144	6,238		128	5,545		115	4,991		105	4,537		96	4,159		88	3,839	3,560
3 × 12	175	6,591		156	5,859		140	5,273		127	4,794		117	4,394		108	4,056	
3 × 14	207	9,143		184	8,127		165	7. 513		150	6,650		138	6,095		127	5,627	
4 × 12	175	9,228		156	8,203		140	7,382		127	6,711		117	6,152		108	5,679	
6 × 10	148	10,341		131	9,192		118	8,272		107	7,520		98	6,894		91	6,363	6,060
3 × 16	238	12,112		211	10,766		190	9,690		173	8,809		158	8,075		146	7,453	
4 × 14	210	13,289		187	11,812		168	10,631		153	9,664		140	8,859		129	8,177	
6 × 12	179	15,153		159	13,469		143	12,122		130	11,020		119	10,102		110	9,325	
4 × 16	242	17,518		215	15,511		193	14,014		176	12,740		161	11,678		149	10,780	
8 × 12	179	20,664		159	18,368		143	16,531		130	15,028		119	13,776		110	12,716	
6 × 14	210	20,882		187	18,562		168	16,706		153	15,187		140	13,921		129	12,850	
6 × 16	242	27,528		215	24,469		193	22,022		176	20,020		161	18,352		149	16,940	
8 × 14	210	28,476		187	25,312		168	22,781		153	20,710		140	18,984		129	17,524	

| Nominal size, in. | 14 | | | 15 | | | 16 | | | 17 | | | 18 | | | 19 | | |
	F_v	W	W_Δ	F_v	W	W_Δ	F_v	W	W_Δ	F_v	W	W_Δ	F_v	W	W_Δ	F_v	W	W_Δ
2 × 12	100	3,260		93	2,109	2,061	87	1,977	1,815	82	1,861	1,604	78	1,757	1,432	74	1,665	1,287
3 × 10	82	2,546	2,192	77	2,376	1,910	72	2,228	1,680	68	2,097	1,490	64	1,980	1,326	60	1,876	1,190
2 × 14	126	3,135		110	2,926		103	2,743		97	2,581		92	2,436	2,340	87	2,310	2,103
4 × 10	82	3,565	3,070	77	3,327	2,676	72	3,119	2,350	68	2,935	2,082	64	2,772	1,857	60	2,626	1,668
3 × 12	100	3,766		93	3,515	3,440	87	3,295	3,020	82	3,102	2,680	78	2,929	2,390	74	2,775	2,144
3 × 14	118	5,225		110	4876		103	4,571		97	4,303		92	4,063	3,900	87	3,850	3,500
4 × 12	100	5,273		93	4,921	4,813	87	4,614	4,230	82	4,342	3,750	78	4,101	3,348	74	3,885	3,000
6 × 10	84	5,709	5,225	79	5,515	4,570	74	5,170	4,010	69	4,866	3,545	65	4,596	3,160	62	4,354	2,840
3 × 16	136	6,921		127	6,460		119	6,056		112	5,700		105	5,383		100	5,100	
4 × 14	120	7,593		112	7,087		105	6,644		99	6,253		93	5,906	5,775	88	5,595	5,185
6 × 12	102	8,659		95	8,081		89	7,576	7,100	84	7,131	6,290	79	6,734	5,610	75	6,380	5,035
4 × 16	138	10,010		129	9,343		121	8,759		113	8,243		107	7,785		101	7,376	
8 × 12	102	11,808		95	11,020		89	10,332	9,690	84	9,724	8,575	79	9,184	7,650	75	8,700	6,865
6 × 14	120	11,933		112	11,137		105	10,441		99	9,827		93	9,281	9,075	88	8,792	8,140
6 × 16	138	15,730		129	14,681		121	13,764		113	12,954		107	12,234		101	11,591	
8 × 14	120	16,272		112	15,187		105	14,238		99	13,400		93	12,656	12,370	88	11,990	11,100
6 × 18	156	20,052		145	18,715		136	17,545		128	16,513		121	15,596		115	14,775	
10 × 14	120	20,611		112	19,237		105	18,035		99	16,974		93	16,031	15,680	88	15,187	14,050

Table 9 (cont.).   Total uniformly distributed loads for joists and beams

Span length, ft

Nominal size, in.	14 F_V	W	$W_\triangle$	15 F_V	W	$W_\triangle$	16 F_V	W	$W_\triangle$	17 F_V	W	$W_\triangle$	18 F_V	W	$W_\triangle$	19 F_V	W	$W_\triangle$
8 × 16	138	21,450		129	20,020		121	18,769		113	17,665		107	16,684		101	15,805	
6 × 20	174	24,897		162	23,237		152	21,785		143	20,503		135	19,364		128	18,345	
10 × 16	138	27,171		129	25,359		121	23,774		113	22,376		107	21,133		101	20,020	
8 × 18	156	27,343		145	25,520		136	23,925		128	22,518		121	21,267		115	20,148	
8 × 20	174	33,950		162	31,637		152	29,707		143	27,959		135	26,406		128	25,016	
10 × 18	156	34,635		145	32,326		136	30,305		128	28,523		121	26,938		115	25,520	
8 × 22	191	41,272		179	38,520		167	36,113		158	33,988		149	32,100		141	30,411	

Nominal size, in.	20 F_V	W	$W_\triangle$	21 F_V	W	$W_\triangle$	22 F_V	W	$W_\triangle$	23 F_V	W	$W_\triangle$	24 F_V	W	$W_\triangle$	25 F_V	W	$W_\triangle$
3 × 12	70	2,636	1,932	66	2,511	1,760	63	2,397	1,600	61	2,292	1,462	58	2,197	1,342	56	2,109	1,238
3 × 14	32	3,657	3,160	78	3,483	2,865	75	3,325	2,610	72	3,180	2,390	60	3,047	2,195	66	2,926	2,020
4 × 12	70	3,691	2,635	66	3,515	2,458	63	3,355	2,240	61	3,209	2,050	58	3,076	1,878	56	2,953	1,730
3 × 16	95	4,845	4,810	90	4,614	4,365	86	4,404	3,980	82	4,213	3,645	79	4,037	3,340	76	3,876	3,085
4 × 14	84	5,315	4,680	80	5,062	4,250	76	4,832	3,870	73	4,622	3,540	70	4,429	3,250	67	4,252	3,000
6 × 12	71	6,061	4,540	68	5,772	4,120	65	5,510	3,760	62	5,270	3,440	59	5,051	3,155	57	4,849	2,910
4 × 16	96	7,007					92	6,673	6,420	88	6,370	5,860	84	6,093	5,355	80	5,839	4,920	77	5,605	4,540
8 × 12	71	8,265	6,190	68	7,872	5,620	65	7,514	5,130	62	7,187	4,680	59	6,888	4,300	57	6,612	3,975
6 × 14	84	8,353	7,350	80	7,955	6,660	76	7,593	6,065	73	7,263	5,550	70	6,960	5,110	67	6,682	4,700
6 × 16	96	11,011		92	10,487	10,090	88	10,010	9,200	84	9,575	8,410	80	9,176	7,725	77	8,809	7,130
8 × 14	84	11,390	10,000	80	10,848	9,100	76	10,355	8,280	73	9,904	7,570	70	9,492	6,960	67	9,112	6,420
6 × 18	109	14,036		104	13,368		99	12,760		95	12,205	12,100	91	11,697	11,100	87	11,229	10,260
10 × 14	84	14,428	12,700	80	13,741	11,530	76	13,116	10,500	73	12,546	9,600	70	12,023	8,820	67	11,542	8,120
8 × 16	96	15,013		92	14,299	13,750	88	13,648	12,540	84	13,055	11,470	80	12,511	10,540	77	12,010	9,710
6 × 20	121	17,428		116	16,598		110	15,843		105	15,154		101	14,523		97	13,942	
10 × 16	96	19,019		92	18,114	17,420	88	17,290	15,870	84	16,538	14,530	80	15,849	13,350	77	15,215	12,320
8 × 18	109	19,140		104	18,229		99	17,400		95	16,644	16,500	91	15,950	15,160	87	15,312	14,000
8 × 20	121	23,765		116	22,633		110	21,605		105	20,665		101	19,804		97	19,012	
10 × 18	109	24,244		104	23,090		99	22,040		95	21,082	20,920	91	20,203	19,200	87	19,395	17,710
8 × 22	134	28,890		127	27,514		122	26,264		116	25,122		111	24,075		107	23,112	
10 × 20	121	30,103		116	28,669		110	27,366		105	26,176		101	25,085		97	24,082	
8 × 24	146	34,515		139	32,872		133	31,377		127	30,013		122	28,763		117	27,612	
12 × 20	121	36,440		116	34,705		110	33,127		105	31,678		101	30,367		97	29,152	
10 × 22	134	36594		127	34,852		122	33,267		116	31,821		111	30,495		107	29,275	
10 × 24	146	43,719		139	41,637		133	39,745		127	38,017		122	36,433		117	34,975	
12 × 22	134	44,298		127	42,189		122	40,271		116	38,520		111	36,915		107	35,439	
14 × 22	134	52,003		127	49,526		122	47,275		116	45,220		111	43,335		107	41,602	
12 × 24	146	52,923		139	50,403		133	48,112		127	46,020		121	44,103		117	42,339	
14 × 24	146	62,128		139	59,169		133	56,480		127	54,024		122	51,773		117	49,702	

Nominal size, in.	26 F_V	W	$W_\triangle$	27 F_V	W	$W_\triangle$	28 F_V	W	$W_\triangle$	29 F_V	W	$W_\triangle$	30 F_V	W	$W_\triangle$	32 F_V	W	$W_\triangle$
6 × 16	74	8,470	6,580	71	8,156	6,110	69	7,665	5,680	66	7,594	5,290	64	7,340	4,950	60	6,882	4,340
8 × 14	64	8,762	5,930	62	8,437	5,500	60	8,136	5,120	58	7,855	4,770	56	7,593	4,460	52	7,119	3,920
6 × 18	84	10,797	9,480	81	10,397	8,780	78	10,026	8,180	75	9,680	7,610	72	9,357	7,120	68	8,772	6,250
8 × 16	74	11,548	8,980	71	11,121	8,330	69	10,723	7,740	66	10,354	7,220	64	10,008	6,740	60	9,383	5,910
6 × 20	93	13,406	13,100	90	12,909	12,150	87	12,448	11,300	84	12,019	10,530	81	11,618	9,840	76	10,892	8,650
10 × 16	74	14,630	11,370	71	14,088	10,540	69	13,585	9,810	66	13,117	9,140	64	12,679	8,550	60	11,887	7,500
8 × 18	84	14,723	12,920	81	14,178	11,980	78	13,671	11,140	75	13,200	10,380	72	12,760	9,700	68	11,962	8,520
8 × 20	93	18,281	17,860	90	17,604	16,570	87	16,975	15,400	84	16,390	14,370	81	15,843	13,420	76	14,853	11,800
10 × 18	84	18,649	16,370	81	17,959	15,170	78	17,317	14,120	75	16,720	13,150	72	16,163	12,300	68	15,152	10,800
8 × 22	103	22,223		99	21,400		95	20,636		92	19,924	19,270	84	19,260	18,000	83	18,056	15,800
12 × 18	84	22,576	19,800	81	21,739	18,390	78	20,963	17,080	75	20,240	15,930	72	19,565	14,880	68	18,343	13,070
10 × 20	93	23,156	22,650	90	22,298	21,000	87	21,502	19,510	84	20,760	18,200	81	20,068	17,000	76	18,814	14,950
8 × 24	112	26,550		108	25,567		104	24,654		101	23,803		97	23,010		91	21,572	20,630
12 × 20	93	28,031	27,400	90	26,993	25,400	87	26,029	23,600	84	25,131	22,030	81	24,293	20,600	76	22,775	18,100
10 × 22	103	28,149		99	27,107		95	26,139		92	25,237	24,430	89	24,396	22,800	83	22,871	20,030
10 × 24	112	33,680		108	32,385		104	31,228		101	30,151		97	29,146		91	27,324	26,130
12 × 22	103	34,076		99	32,814		95	31,642		92	30,550	29,550	89	29,532	27,600	83	27,686	24,250
12 × 24	112	40,710		108	39,202		104	37,802		101	36,499		97	35,282		91	33,077	31,670
14 × 24	112	47,790		108	46,020		104	44,377		101	42,846		97	41,418		91	38,830	37,160

Columns

Table 10 lists safe unit axial loads (F'_c) for simple solid columns. Allowable unit stresses for l/d values from 10 to 50 in half-foot increments are computed for the range of E values from 1,000,000 to 2,400,000 psi. This tabular form provides a simple, accurate method for calculating allowable loads on columns of any size and length. The l/d ratio, however, should not exceed 50. The total allowable column load is determined by multiplying the appropriate tabular unit stress (F_c or F'_c, whichever is smaller), as adjusted for load duration, by the net cross-sectional area of the member. The tabular values for F'_c and the allowable values for F_c for the species and grade of lumber used, should be adjusted for load duration by multiplying by the following load factors:

For permanent loading (over 10 yr)	0.90
For normal loading	1.00
For snow loading (2 months)	1.15
For loading of 7 days' duration	1.25
For wind or earthquake loads	1.33
For impact loads	2.00

Table 10. Safe unit axial loads (F'_c) — simple solid columns

Obtain allowable E values from building code or the National Design Specification for Wood Construction. Calculate l/d where l = unsupported length of column, in., and d = least actual dimension of column cross section. Values of F'c from table may not exceed Fc value for species and grade of lumber used. Total allowable load on column = cross-section area, in sq in. (see Table 2) times F'c value.

l/d												
	Modulus of elasticity, E, in 1,000 psi											
	1,000	1,100	1,200	1,300	1,400	1,500	1,600	1,700	1,800	2,000	2,220	2,400
10.0	3,000	3,300	3,600	3,900	4,199	4,499	4,799	5,099	5,399	5,999	6,599	7,199
10.5	2,721	2,993	3,265	3,537	3,809	4,081	4,353	4,625	4,897	5,442	5,986	6,530
11.0	2,479	2,727	2,975	3,223	3,471	3,719	3,966	4,214	4,462	4,958	5,454	5,950
11.5	2,268	2,495	2,722	2,948	3,175	3,402	3,629	3,856	4,083	4,536	4,990	5,444
12.0	2,083	2,291	2,500	2,708	2,916	3,125	3,333	3,541	3,750	4,166	4,583	4,999
12.5	1,920	2,112	2,304	2,496	2,688	2,880	3,072	3,264	3,456	3,840	4,223	4,607
13.0	1,775	1,952	2,130	2,307	2,485	2,662	2,840	3,017	3,195	3,550	3,905	4,260
13.5	1,646	1,810	1,975	2,139	2,304	2,469	2,633	2,798	2,962	3,292	3,621	3,950
14.0	1,530	1,683	1,836	1,989	2,142	2,295	2,448	2,602	2,755	3,061	3,367	3,673
14.5	1,426	1,569	1,712	1,854	1,997	2,140	2,282	2,425	2,568	2,853	3,139	3,424
15.0	1,333	1,466	1,600	1,733	1,866	2,000	2,133	2,266	2,400	2,666	2,933	3,200
15.5	1,248	1,373	1,498	1,623	1,748	1,873	1,997	2,122	2,247	2,497	2,747	2,996
16.0	1,171	1,289	1,406	1,523	1,640	1,757	1,875	1,992	2,109	2,343	2,578	2,812
16.5	1,101	1,212	1,322	1,432	1,542	1,652	1,763	1,873	1,983	2,203	2,424	2,644
17.0	1,038	1,141	1,245	1,349	1,453	1,557	1,660	1,764	1,868	2,076	2,283	2,491
17.5	979	1,077	1,175	1,273	1,371	1,469	1,567	1,665	1,763	1,959	2,155	2,351
18.0	925	1,018	1,111	1,203	1,296	1,388	1,481	1,574	1,666	1,851	2,037	2,222
18.5	876	964	1,051	1,139	1,227	1,314	1,402	1,490	1,577	1,753	1,928	2,103
19.0	831	914	997	1,080	1,163	1,246	1,329	1,412	1,495	1,662	1,828	1,994
19.5	788	867	946	1,025	1,104	1,183	1,262	1,341	1,420	1,577	1,735	1,893
20.0	750	825	900	975	1,050	1,125	1,200	1,275	1,350	1,500	1,650	1,800
20.5	713	785	856	928	999	1,070	1,142	1,213	1,284	1,427	1,570	1,713
21.0	680	748	816	884	952	1,020	1,088	1,156	1,224	1,360	1,496	1,632
21.5	649	713	778	843	908	973	1,038	1,103	1,168	1,298	1,427	1,557
22.0	619	681	743	805	867	929	991	1,053	1,115	1,239	1,363	1,487
22.5	592	651	711	770	829	888	948	1,007	1,066	1,185	1,303	1,422
23.0	567	623	680	737	793	850	907	964	1,020	1,134	1,247	1,361
23.5	543	597	651	706	760	814	869	923	977	1,086	1,195	1,303
24.0	520	572	625	677	729	781	833	885	937	1,041	1,145	1,250
24.5	499	549	599	649	699	749	799	849	899	999	1,099	1,199
25.0	480	528	576	624	672	720	768	816	864	960	1,056	1,152
25.5	461	507	553	599	645	692	738	784	830	922	1,014	1,107
26.0	443	488	532	576	621	665	710	754	798	887	976	1,065
26.5	427	469	512	555	598	640	683	726	768	854	939	1,025
27.0	411	452	493	534	576	617	658	699	740	823	905	987
27.5	396	436	476	515	555	595	634	674	714	793	872	952
28.0	382	420	459	497	535	573	612	650	688	765	841	918
28.5	369	406	443	480	517	554	590	627	664	738	812	886
29.0	356	392	428	463	499	535	570	606	642	713	784	856
29.5	344	379	413	448	482	517	551	586	620	689	758	827

Table 10 (cont.). Safe unit axial loads (F'_c) — simple solid columns

l/d	Modulus of elasticity, E, in 1,000 psi											
	1,000	1,100	1,200	1,300	1,400	1,500	1,600	1,700	1,800	2,000	2,200	2,400
30.0	333	366	400	433	466	500	533	566	600	666	733	800
30.5	322	354	386	419	451	483	515	548	580	644	709	773
31.0	312	343	374	405	437	468	499	530	561	624	686	749
31.5	302	332	362	393	423	453	483	513	544	604	665	725
32.0	292	322	351	380	410	439	468	498	527	585	644	703
32.5	284	312	340	369	397	426	454	482	511	568	624	681
33.0	275	303	330	358	385	413	440	468	495	550	606	661
33.5	267	294	320	347	374	400	427	454	481	534	588	641
34.0	259	285	311	337	363	389	415	441	467	519	570	622
34.5	252	277	302	327	352	378	403	428	453	504	554	604
35.0	244	269	293	318	342	367	391	416	440	489	538	587
35.5	238	261	285	309	333	357	380	404	428	476	523	571
36.0	231	254	277	300	324	347	370	393	416	462	509	555
36.5	225	247	270	292	315	337	360	382	405	450	495	540
37.0	219	241	262	284	306	328	350	372	394	438	482	525
37.5	213	234	256	277	298	320	341	362	384	426	469	512
38.0	207	228	249	270	290	311	332	353	373	415	457	498
38.5	202	222	242	263	283	303	323	344	364	404	445	485
39.0	197	216	236	256	276	295	315	335	355	394	433	473
39.5	192	211	230	249	269	288	307	326	346	384	423	461
40.0	187	206	225	243	267	281	300	318	337	375	412	450
40.5	182	201	219	237	256	274	292	310	329	365	402	438
41.0	178	196	214	232	249	267	285	303	321	356	392	428
41.5	174	191	209	226	243	261	278	296	313	348	383	418
42.0	170	187	204	221	238	255	272	289	306	340	374	408
42.5	166	182	199	215	232	249	265	282	298	332	365	398
43.0	162	178	194	210	227	243	259	275	292	324	356	389
43.5	158	174	190	206	221	237	253	269	285	317	348	380
44.0	154	170	185	201	216	232	247	263	278	309	340	371
44.5	151	166	181	196	212	227	242	257	272	302	333	363
45.0	148	162	177	192	207	222	237	251	266	296	325	355
45.5	144	159	173	188	202	217	231	246	260	289	318	347
46.0	141	155	170	184	198	212	226	241	255	283	311	340
46.5	138	152	166	180	194	208	221	235	249	277	305	332
47.0	135	149	162	176	190	203	217	230	244	271	298	325
47.5	132	146	159	172	186	199	212	226	239	265	292	319
48.0	130	143	156	169	182	195	208	221	234	260	286	312
48.5	127	140	153	165	178	191	204	216	229	255	280	306
49.0	124	137	149	162	174	187	199	212	224	249	274	299
49.5	122	134	146	159	171	183	195	208	220	244	269	293
50.0	120	132	144	156	168	180	192	204	216	240	264	288

Data on this and the following two pages from Manual for House Framing, National Forest Products Association

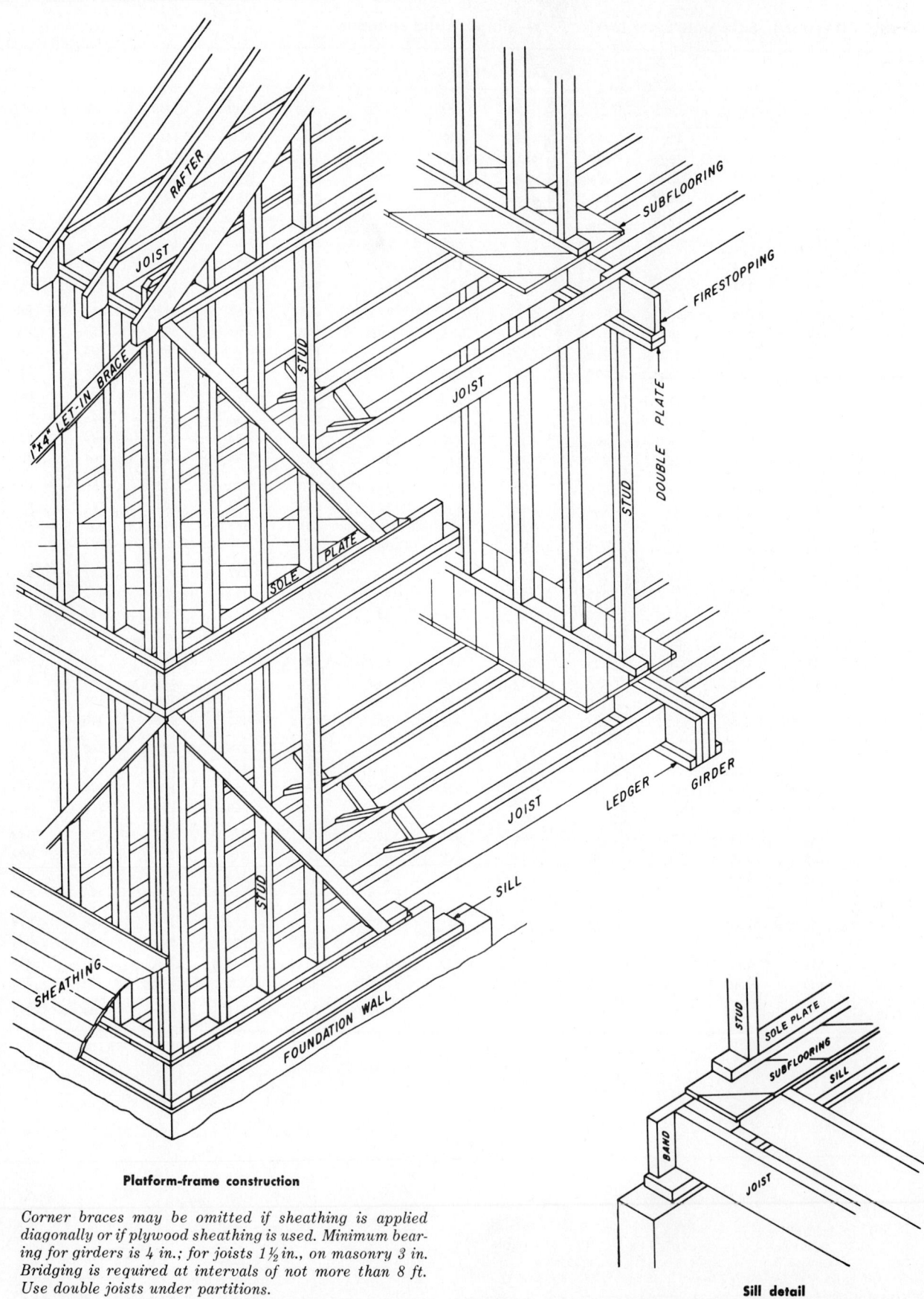

Platform-frame construction

Corner braces may be omitted if sheathing is applied diagonally or if plywood sheathing is used. Minimum bearing for girders is 4 in.; for joists 1½ in., on masonry 3 in. Bridging is required at intervals of not more than 8 ft. Use double joists under partitions.

Sill detail

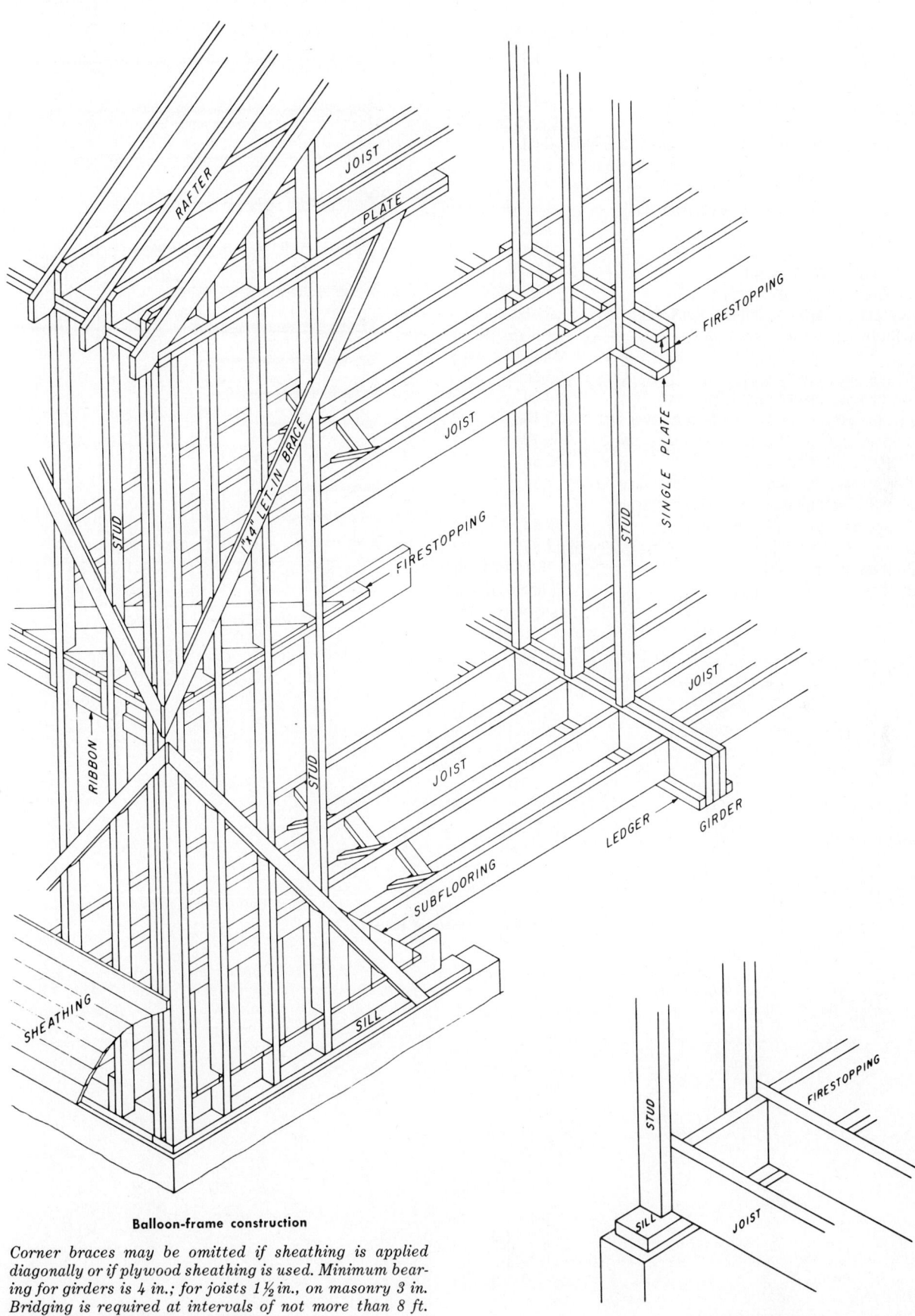

Balloon-frame construction

Corner braces may be omitted if sheathing is applied diagonally or if plywood sheathing is used. Minimum bearing for girders is 4 in.; for joists 1½ in., on masonry 3 in. Bridging is required at intervals of not more than 8 ft. Use double joists under partitions.

Sill detail

RECOMMENDED NAILING SCHEDULE USING COMMON NAILS

Joist to sill or girder, toe nail 3-8d
Bridging to joist, toe nail each end 2-8d
Ledger strip 3-16d
                               at each joist
1″ x 6″ subfloor or less to each joist, face nail . 2-8d
Over 1″ x 6″ subfloor to each joist, face nail . . . 3-8d
2″ subfloor to joist or girder, blind and face nail . 2-16d
Sole plate to joist or blocking, face nail . . . . 16d @ 16″ oc
Top plate to stud, end nail 2-16d
Stud to sole plate, toe nail 4-8d
Doubled studs, face nail . . . . 16d @ 24″ oc
Doubled top plates, face nail . . . . 16d @ 16″ oc
Top plates, laps and intersections, face nail 2-16d
Continuous header, two pieces . . . . 16d @ 16″ oc
                             along each edge
Ceiling joists to plate, toe nail 3-8d
Continuous header to stud, toe nail 4-8d
Ceiling joists, laps over partitions, face nail 3-16d
Ceiling joists to parallel rafters, face nail 3-16d
Rafter to plate, toe nail 3-8d
1-inch brace to each stud and plate, face nail . . . 2-8d
1″ x 8″ sheathing or less to each bearing,
   face nail 2-8d
Over 1″ x 8″ sheathing to each bearing, face nail 3-8d
Built-up corner studs . . . . 16d @ 24″ oc
Built-up girders and beams . . . . 20d @ 32″ oc
                             along each edge

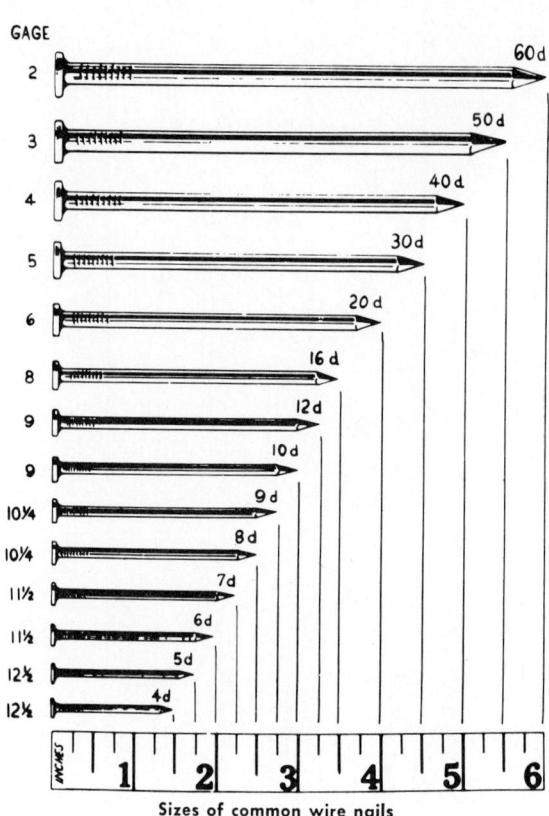

Sizes of common wire nails

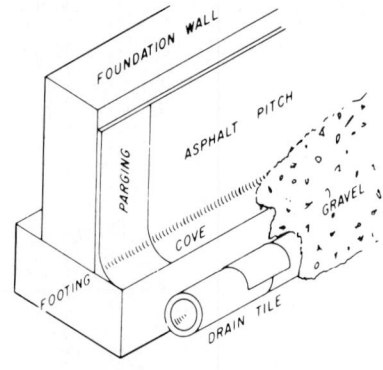

Foundation wall and footing

Footing depth is usually made equal to the foundation wall thickness, and footing width twice the wall thickness.

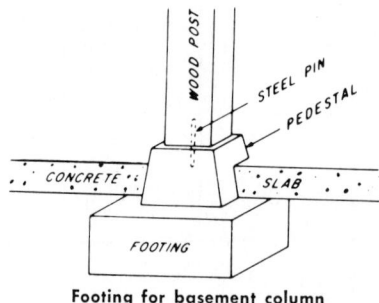

Footing for basement column

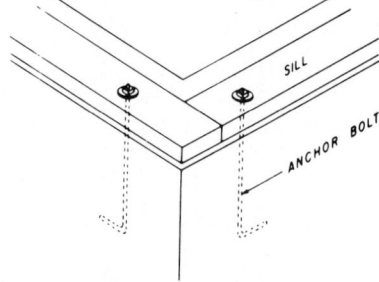

Anchorage of sill to foundation wall

Anchor bolts, ½ in. in diameter, should be spaced not more than 8 ft apart, and embedded at least 6 in. in concrete or 15 in. in masonry.

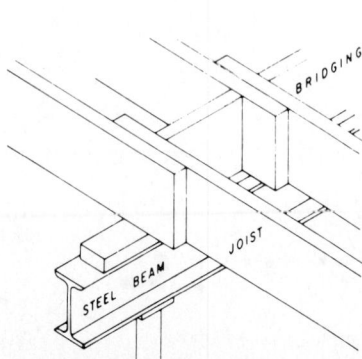

Joists on steel girder

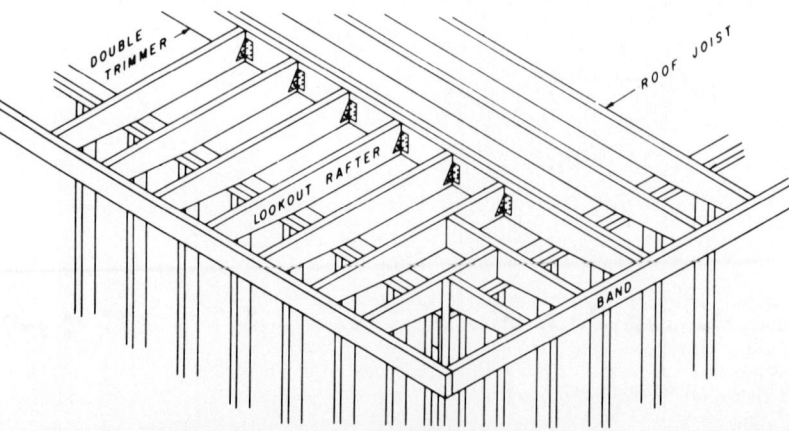

Corner detail of flat roof, with overhang of less than 3 ft

From Wood Frame House Construction, U.S. Department of Agriculture, 1970

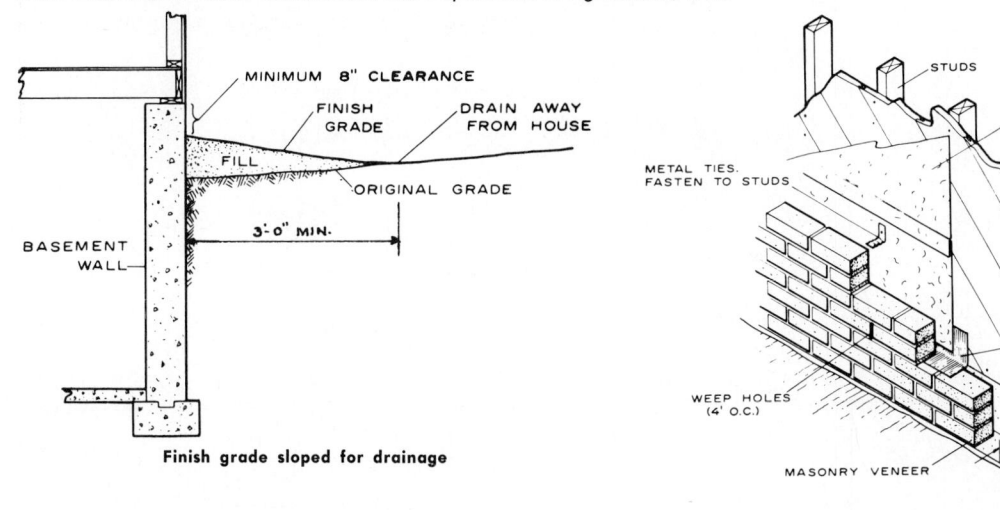

MINIMUM 8" CLEARANCE

FINISH GRADE

DRAIN AWAY FROM HOUSE

FILL

ORIGINAL GRADE

BASEMENT WALL

3'-0" MIN.

Finish grade sloped for drainage

STUDS

SHEATHING PAPER

SHEATHING

METAL TIES. FASTEN TO STUDS

BASE FLASHING EXTEND BEHIND SHEATHING PAPER

SILL

WEEP HOLES (4' O.C.)

FOUNDATION

MASONRY VENEER

Wood-frame wall with brick veneer

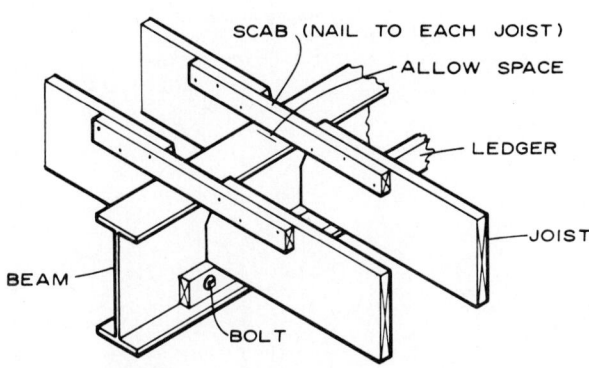

SCAB (NAIL TO EACH JOIST)

ALLOW SPACE

LEDGER

JOIST

BEAM

BOLT

Steel girder with ledger and wood scab ties

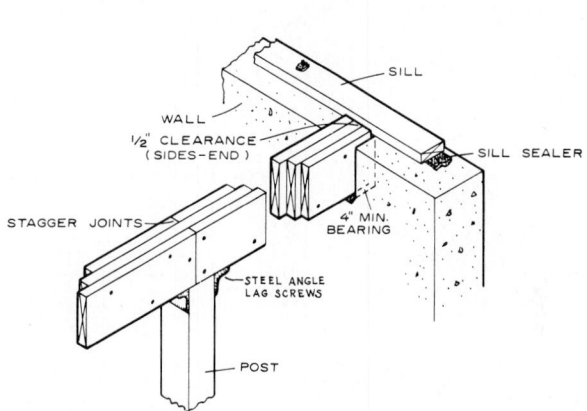

SILL

WALL

½" CLEARANCE (SIDES-END)

SILL SEALER

STAGGER JOINTS

4" MIN. BEARING

STEEL ANGLE LAG SCREWS

POST

Built-up wood girder on wood column and foundation pocket

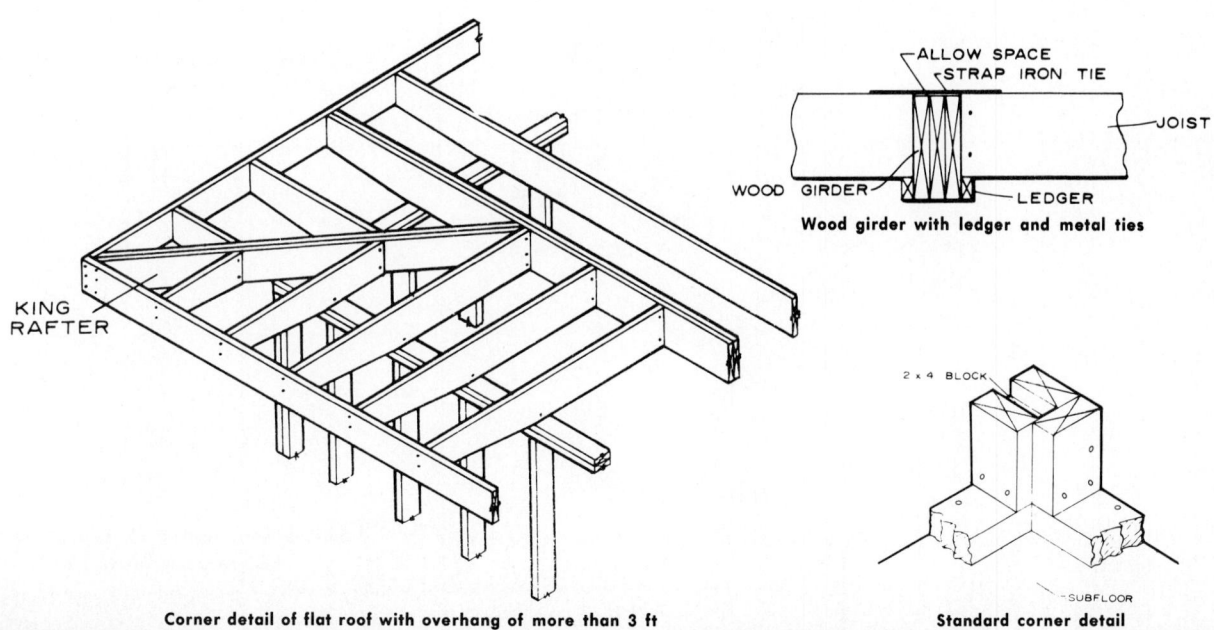

KING RAFTER

Corner detail of flat roof with overhang of more than 3 ft

ALLOW SPACE

STRAP IRON TIE

JOIST

WOOD GIRDER

LEDGER

Wood girder with ledger and metal ties

2 x 4 BLOCK

SUBFLOOR

Standard corner detail

Light wood framing

From Manual for House Framing, *National Forest Products Association*

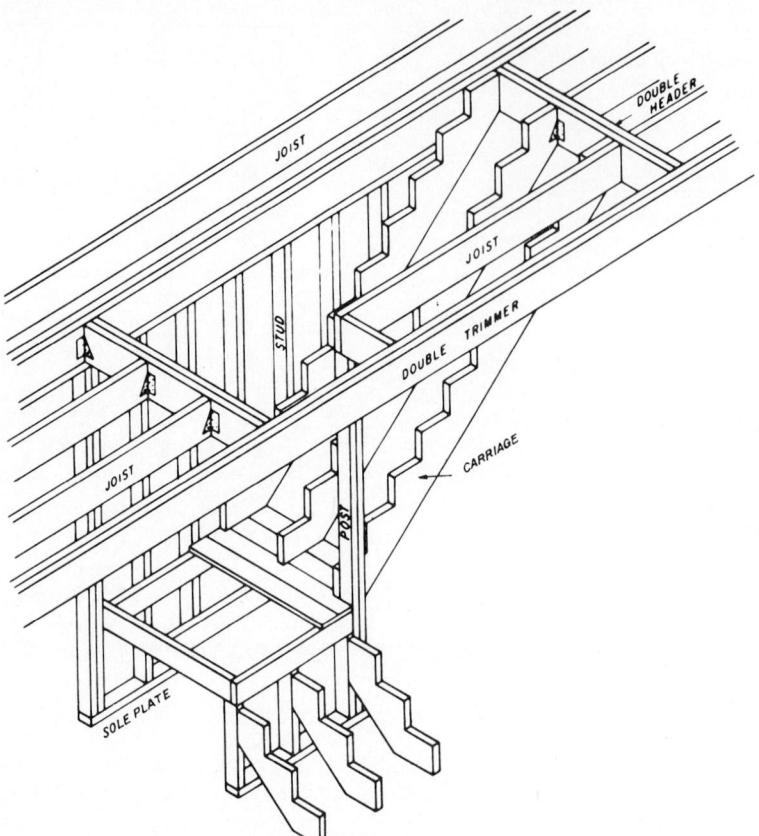

Framing for stairway with landing

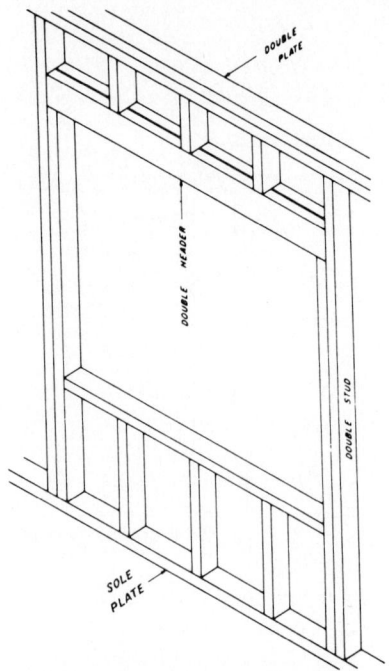

Framing around exterior wall opening

For openings over 6 ft wide, use triple studs, with the header bearing on two studs at each side.

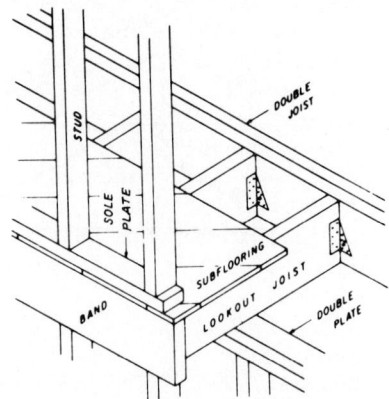

Overhanging second floor with joists parallel to wall below

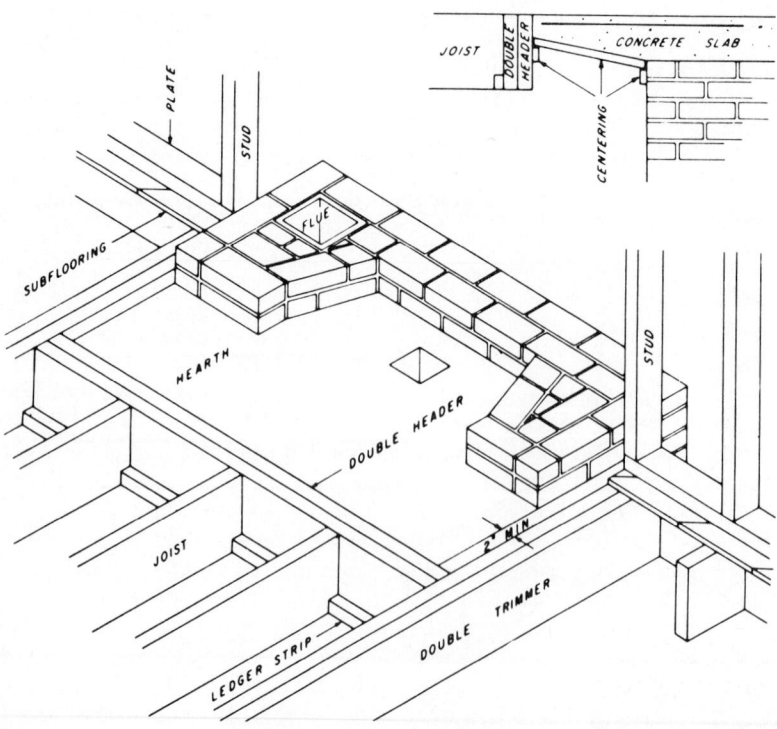

Floor framing around fireplace

Wood framing must be kept 2 in. clear of all fireplace and chimney masonry.

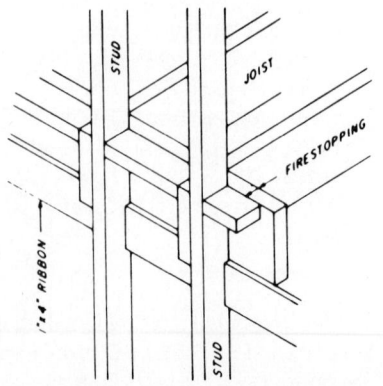

Second-floor framing at exterior wall— balloon-frame construction

By HOWARD P. VERMILYA, AIA

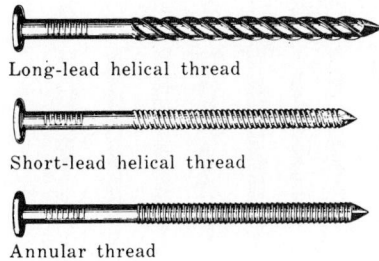

Long-lead helical thread

Short-lead helical thread

Annular thread

Nails are the oldest type of metal fastening device for wood joints. They are easily applied and inexpensive. Developments during the last 25 years made possible the mass production of properly designed threaded nails which have retained these qualities and considerably increased their effectiveness as fasteners.

Basic types
The *helically threaded nail* with medium lead angle (approximately 60° from a plane perpendicular to the nail axis) turns like a screw during hammer driving and forms a thread in the wood similar to that of the nail. The *annularly threaded nail*, with rings perpendicular to its shank, when driven forces the wood fibers over the thread crests and into the space between the thread shoulders so as to greatly resist withdrawal.

Variations
Not only may the heads and points be of the many types now available with common wire nails, but the pattern of the thread may be varied to adapt it most effectively to the specific problem. In common with plain-shank wire nails, the wire size, metal composition and finish of threaded nails may be varied. Heat treating and tempering can provide added strength and stiffness.

Uses
The threaded nail has demonstrated its merit in a number of applications. The *gypsum wallboard nail*, the heat-treated *hardwood flooring nail*, the *plywood*

sheathing nail and the *roofing nail* are only a few of those that are recognized as doing a superior job.

A further contribution is the application of threaded nails to *nailed trussed rafters*. The superiority in double shear and the stiffness of the high-carbon steel, heat-treated and hardened, helically threaded nail make it possible to build an all-nailed trussed rafter practically as stiff and equally as strong as a nail-glued one, with only two and one-half times as many nails and without the attendant problems of gluing either in the plant or in the field.

The development of threaded nails and the recognition of their advantages by users are the result to a great extent of the comprehensive research program sponsored over the last decade by the Independent Nail and Packing Company at the Virginia Polytechnic Institute's Wood Research Laboratory under the direction of Professor E. George Stern.

Advantages of threaded nails
1. When green or partially seasoned lumber is used, the threaded nail retains its holding power as the lumber is subjected to changes in moisture content or temperature. The plain-shank common wire nail, however, may lose up to four-fifths of its initial holding power, in as little as six weeks' time.
2. The threaded nail is not likely to loosen or pop as a result of creep induced by moisture or temperature changes in the wood. This same quality serves to prevent squeaky floors, caused by the loose flooring rubbing against the nail or itself.
3. V.P.I. research demonstrated that hardened-steel threaded nails may be slimmer than standard plain-shank nails when substituted for them. These thinner and stiffer nails may be driven faster with less danger of bending and less likelihood of split-

ting. This is particularly advantageous where nails must be closely spaced as in the joints of all-nailed trussed rafters.
4. When plywood diaphragms are fastened to their frames, shorter but thicker threaded nails can be used more effectively than the longer plain-shank nails, and permit easier and faster driving. (The 1½ by 0.135 in. bright threaded nail has 2.8 times the holding power of an 8d, 2½ by 0.129 in. common wire nail and 1.1 times the delayed lateral strength.)
5. The increased holding power of the threaded point end of the nail makes it possible to nail from one side only when nailing joints in single, double and multiple shear. This permits easier and faster nailing. Further, by providing clearance (a plain shank section) between the head of the nail and the threaded portion equal to the thickness of the piece to be fastened, it is possible to pull the two members together. A ⅛ in. to ¼ in. plain shank pilot can be used for the point of a threaded nail to facilitate driving into harder woods. All of these refinements in design serve to add to the usefulness of the threaded nail.

Strength factors
Both the allowable lateral strength and the withdrawal resistance of threaded nails are determined by the diameter, the configuration and slope of the thread, the composition and temper of the metal wire. Further variables are the amount of penetration and the specific gravity and moisture content of the wood into which the nails are to be driven.

Annularly threaded nails are specially resistant to *axial withdrawal* and provide maximum service as fasteners of sheet materials to plywood or softwood.

Helically threaded nails are particularly *effective in hardwoods* and in providing *resistance* to bending.

Threaded nails

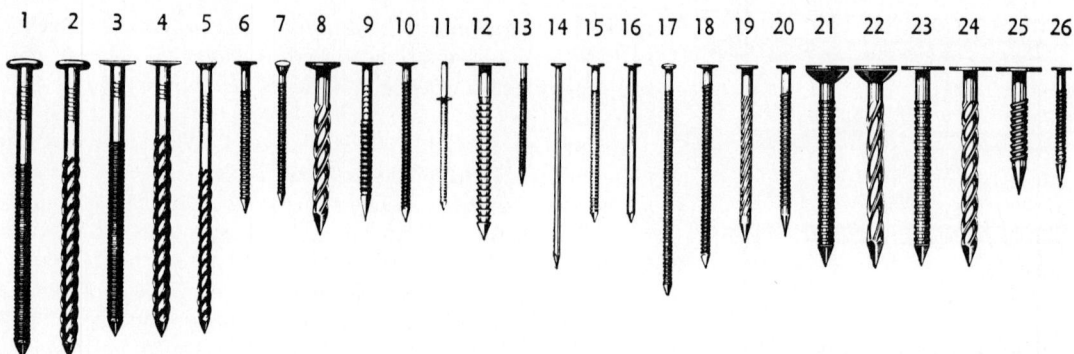

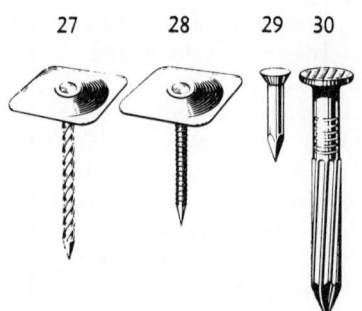

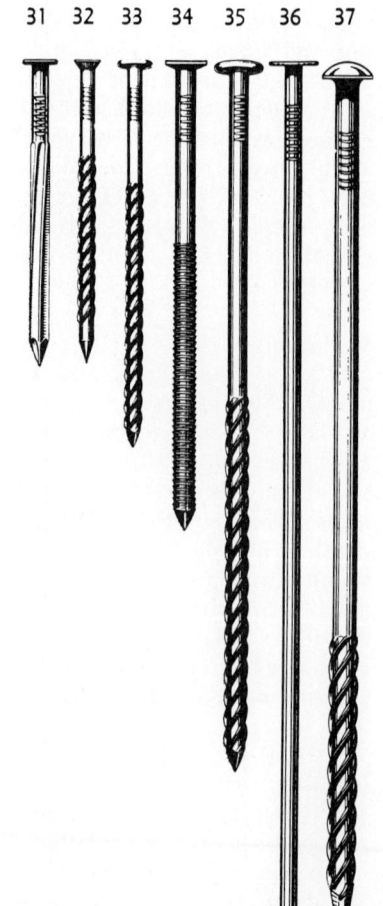

1, 2. Annular thread and spiral thread "common nails": for framing and general use.

3, 4. Annular thread and spiral thread sinkers: for sub-floors, boarding in, etc.

5. Flooring nails; hardened steel, spiral thread (prevent squeaking).

6. Underlay floor nails (prevent squeaking; eliminate bumps in linoleum, tile, carpeting).

7. Parquet floor nails.

8. Shear-resistant, spiral threaded nails: for fastening plywood diaphragms, gusset plates, etc.

9. Dry wall nails (designed to eliminate "popping and loosening").

10. Asbestos board nails; heat-treated and tempered.

11. Acoustic tile nails (can be driven without marring tile).

12. Rachet nails: for use with nailable channels.

13. Interior hardboard nails; hardened steel, small head, annular thread.

14, 15, 16. Wallboard nails.

17. Wood shingle face nails (eliminate tendency of shingles or shakes to curl).

18, 19, 20. Asbestos shingle nails; type "F" thread, annular or screw thread.

21, 22. Roofing nails with neoprene washers; annular thread and spiral thread: for application of corrugated or sheet metal material.

23, 24. Roofing nails for asphalt shingles; spiral or annular threads; or smooth.

25, 26. Roofing and siding nails: for fastening wood, asphalt or asbestos shingles and siding to plywood sheathing; roofing (25), siding (26).

27, 28. Built-up roofing nails; annular thread for wood and plywood (28); spiral thread for gypsum decking (27).

29. Concrete stub nail, hardened: for fastening plywood and metal fixtures to concrete.

30. Masonry nails: for fastening mudsills and partition plates to concrete.

31. Masonry nails: for fastening materials to brick, concrete, etc.

32. Exterior hardboard nails (eliminate predrilling).

33. Trussed rafter nails.

34. Roof decking nails: for applying insulating roof decking.

35. Pole-type construction nails.

36. Purlin nails.

37. Gutter spikes.

Drawings from Independent Mail and Packaging Co.

Lateral strength

The deformation of the nailed joint, loaded laterally, is the primary consideration in establishing an allowable lateral load. The common wire nail has about the same resistance as the low-carbon-steel helically threaded nail when driven into side-grain lumber. The high-carbon-steel, hardened, helically threaded nail, because of its greater stiffness and increased withdrawal resistance, even under lateral load conditions, can use the design value normally credited to the common wire plain-shank nail which is one gauge heavier.

Professor Stern states as a result of his work with threaded nails at Virginia Polytechnic Institute's Wood Research Laboratory that a helically threaded, hardened nail loaded in double shear can transmit twice the design load attributed to that nail in single shear, in a joint consisting of two nominal 1-in. side members and one nominal 2-in. center member. The *Douglas Fir Use Book*, however, in commenting upon plain-shank nails says that limited tests show that at design level of holding power, the nail capacity in double shear is at least twice that for single shear, but at ultimate loads, the shear efficiency is less and varies according to the ratio of the thickness of the side members to the center member. It, as well as the *National Design Specification for Stress-Grade Lumber and its Fastenings*, recommends that when a nail fully penetrates all three members, the allowable

load be increased over that for single shear by one-third when each side member is not less than about one-third the thickness of the center member, increased by two-thirds when each side member is equal in thickness to the center member. This refers to plain-shank nails whereas Professor Stern's recommendation referred specifically to high-carbon-steel, hardened, helically threaded nails.

Tests of full-size trussed rafter assemblies carried out at Wood Research Laboratory of Virginia Polytechnic Institute, with joints having multiple nails in double shear using the design values ascribed to these threaded nails by Professor Stern (namely twice that of nails in single shear), have withstood loads of from five-and-one-half to seven times the design load before failure. In all cases the failure had been in the wood members of the assembly rather than in the joints, with joint deformation held to a negligible amount.

Withdrawal strength

Nails loaded in direct withdrawal from side-grain lumber are not so efficient in strength as when loaded laterally. Withdrawal resistance of nails is materially affected by the specific gravity of the wood, varying with the density even within species. The significant loss in holding power concurrent with wood seasoning and the numerous uncertainties in joints of this type have resulted in the

practice of ascribing a factor of safety of six in determining allowable loads for plain-shank nails. Professor Stern, as a result of the higher and longer lasting holding power observed in his research with threaded nails, recommends that this factor of safety be reduced to two when applied to the ultimate test load for a properly threaded nail loaded in axial withdrawal. Consequently, withdrawal design values for such threaded nails of the same diameter or gauge can be at least three times that for plain-shank nails.

Other design factors

When more than one nail is used in the same joint the total allowable load in withdrawal or lateral resistance is the sum of the allowable loads for the individual nails. This applies provided the edge and end distances, and spacings parallel and perpendicular to the grain are sufficient to develop the full strength of the nails without splitting the member. Spacing of threaded nails should be as follows (same as for plain-shank nails): not less than five Diameters from the edge of the member, 15 D-20 D from the end, and not less than five D against and 15 D-20 D with the grain.

To further reduce the hazard of splitting, plain-shank and threaded nails may be driven into prebored holes of approximately 70 per cent of the shank or thread-root diameter in width, and 70 per cent of the depth or penetration.

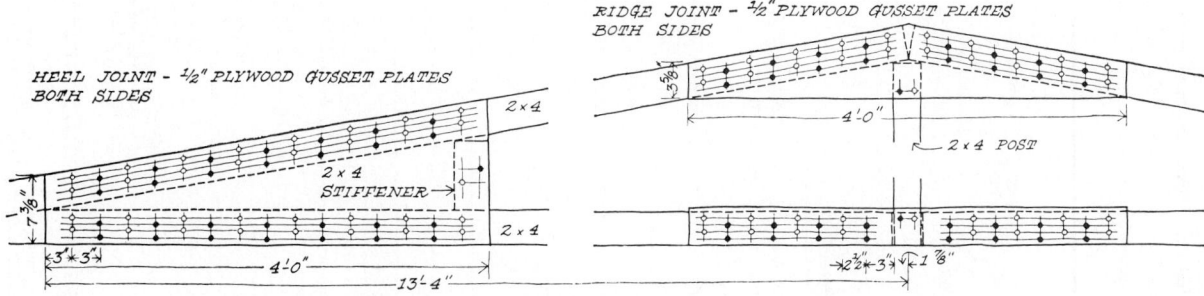

Design of an all-nailed, king-post trussed rafter, 26-ft 8-in. span

Table 11. Safe lateral load-carrying capacity (shear resistance) and withdrawal resistance

(Common Wire Nails and Threaded Nails in Douglas Fir and Southern Pine)

Penny-weight	Length, Inches	Common Wire Nail Diameter, Inches	Common Wire Nail Count per Pound	Hardened Threaded Nail Diameter, Inches	Hardened Threaded Nail Count per Pound	Safe Lateral Load per Nail in Single Shear — Common Wire Nail (Douglas Fir & Southern Pine)	Safe Lateral Load — Hardened Helically Threaded Nail* (a)	Side-Grain Common Wire — Dense Coast-Type Dougl. Fir (c')	(d')	Common Wire S.P. (e')	(c)	Side-Grain Hardened — Dense Coast-Type Douglas Fir (c')	(d)	(d')	Hardened Southern Pine (e)	(e')	(f)	End-Grain Common Wire Nail	End-Grain Hardened Southern Pine (g-e)	(g-e)	(g-f)
6d	2	0.113	181	0.105	190	63	69	29	33	42	67	81	78	93	97	116	...		81	97	...
8d	2½	0.131	106	0.120	117	78	82	34	39	48	77	92	89	106	111	133	187		92	111	156
10d	3	0.148	69	0.135	78	94	94	38	44	55	87	104	100	120	124	149	206		104	124	172
12d	3¼	0.148	63	0.135	73	94	94	38	44	55	87	104	100	120	124	149	206		104	124	172
16d	3½	0.162	49	0.148	57	107	107	42	48	60	95	114	109	131	136	164	...		114	136	...
20d	4	0.192	31	0.177	36	139	139	49	57	71	114	136	131	157	163	196	256		136	163	213
30d	4½	0.207	24	0.177	31	154	139	53	61	76	114	136	131	157	163	196	256		136	163	213
40d	5	0.225	18	0.177	27	176	139	58	67	83	114	136	131	157	163	196	256		136	163	213
50d	5½	0.244	14	0.177	23	202	139	63	72	90	114	136	131	157	163	196	256		136	163	213
60d	6	0.263	11	0.177	18	223	139	68	78	97	114	136	131	157	163	196	256		136	163	213
Shear Resistant Spiral Threaded Nail†	1½	....	....	0.135	158	...	94	...	...	...	87	104	100	120	124	149	206		104	124	172
	2½	....	....	0.135	101	...	94	...	...	...	87	104	100	120	124	149	206		104	124	172

Note: Plain-Shank Nails NOT to be Loaded in Withdrawal from End-Grain of Wood.

Based on page 65 of "National Design Specification for Stress-Grade Lumber and its Fastenings" (1960 edition), subject to adjustments (see Section 203A, etc.).

Limitations: Design values for lateral load-carrying capacity of common wire nails based on two-thirds shank penetration and those of hardened helically threaded Screw-Tite® nails based on one-half shank penetration of shortest nail of given diameter.

Selection of Design Values of Threaded Nails: Column (b) is based on derivation procedures generally accepted for common wire nails and indicates the extreme conservatism of the design values shown in Column (a). Columns (f) and (g-f) take into consideration the fact that the test values for delayed withdrawal resistance of properly threaded nails are similar to the immediate test values. This fact eliminates the need for a factor of safety of six for immediate ultimate withdrawal resistance which is customarily applied to common wire nails. A factor of safety of two is fully adequate. Again, these design values indicate the conservatism of the design values presented in Columns (c), (d), (e), and (g-e).

(a) Design values for one-gauge larger common wire nail.

(b) One-sixth of test value (page 26 of V.P.I. Wood Research Laboratory Bulletin No. 3).

(c) 1150x3x0.186 D (acc. to FPL). (d) 1150x3x0.214 D. (e) 1150x3x0.267 D.

(c') 1380x3x0.186 D (acc. to NDS). (d') 1380x3x0.214 D. (e') 1380x3x0.267 D.

Three times design value for plain-shank nail of same wire diameter.

(f) One-half of test value (page 26 of V.P.I. Wood Research Laboratory Bulletin No. 3).

(g) Five-sixths of design value for side-grain penetration (Timber News, Vol. 59, No. 2138, pp. 490-492, December, 1950).

Table prepared by Professor E. George Stern. Virginia Polytechnic Institute Wood Research Laboratory. Threaded nail values based on products of the Independent Nail & Packing Company, Bridgewater, Mass.

* tests based on use of Screw-Tite® nails made by Independent Nail & Packing Company

† tests based on use of Hi-Load® nails (For plywood diaphragms and gusset plates) made by same company

Light wood trusses, usually spaced 2'-0" on centers, are commonly called trussed rafters. They are widely used in residential and small commercial buildings. Shown here, courtesy of TECO, is a typical design for a W-truss with plate connectors for spans to 50'-0" and roof pitch 4 in 12. Data on plate sizes, number of nails, and designs for other roof pitches are available from TECO, 5530 Wisconsin Avenue, Washington, D.C. 20015. These designs are intended as suggestions only, for the use of qualified architects and engineers.

The top chord is assumed to be laterally supported by sheathing. Provide a 1 × 4

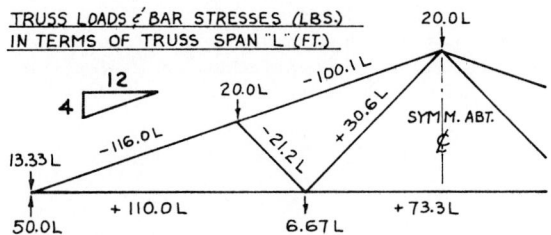

Maximum truss length for support bearing:

Lumber Species of Bearing Plate or Truss Bottom Chord	Bearing Plate Size, Placed on Wide Face		
	2 × 4	2 × 6	2 × 8
Hem-Fir	29'-7"	46'-6"	56'-0"
Douglas Fir-Larch	46'-6"	56'-0"	
Southern Pine	48'-11"	56'-0"	

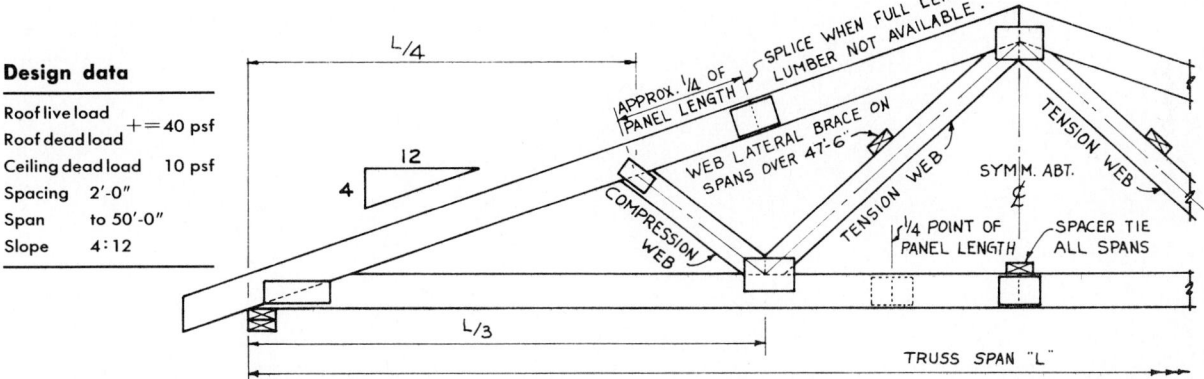

Design data

Roof live load	+= 40 psf
Roof dead load	
Ceiling dead load	10 psf
Spacing	2'-0"
Span	to 50'-0"
Slope	4:12

Lumber requirements

Species, moisture content	Commercial grade	Size classification	Allowable unit stresses				Top chord size, Max. truss span "L"				Bottom chord size, max. truss span "L"			
			F_b	F_t	F_c	$E×10^6$	2×4	2×6	2×8	2×10	2×4	2×6	2×8	2×10
Douglas fir-larch and Southern pine														
Kiln-dried 15% max.	No. 1 KD	2×4 only	1900	1100	1450	1.9	29'-10"				33'-3"			
	No. 2* KD	2×4 only	1550	925	1150	**	26'-3"				29'-4"			
	No. 1 KD	2×6 & wider	1650	1100	1450	1.9		44'-0"	50'-0"			49'-8"	50'-0"	
	No. 2* KD	2×6 & wider	1350	900	1250	**		39'-6"	50'-0"			43'-4"	50'-0"	
Dry 19% max.	No. 1	2×4 only	1750	1050	1250	1.8	28'-0"				31'-4"			
	No. 2*	2×4 only	1450	850	1000	**	24'-9"				27'-10"			
	No. 1	2×6 & wider	1500	1000	1250	1.8		41'-0"	50'-0"			46'-7"	50'-0"	
	No. 2*	2×6 & wider	1250	825	1050	**		37'-0"	48'-0"	50'-0"		41'-0"	50'-0"	
Hem-fir														
Dry 19% max.	Select Str.	2×4 only	1650	975	1300	1.5	26'-0"				30'-6"			
	No. 1	2×4 only	1400	825	1000	1.5	24'-5"				27'-2"			
	No. 2	2×4 only	1150	675	800	1.4	21'-5"				23'-8"			
	Select str.	2×6 & wider	1400	950	1150	1.5		39'-0"	50'-0"			44'-9"	50'-0"	
	No. 1	2×6 & wider	1200	800	1000	1.5		35'-7"	46'-9"	50'-0"		40'-0"	50'-0"	
	No. 2	2×6 & wider	1000	650	850	1.4		32'-0"	42'-0"	50'-0"		34'-10"	45'-9"	50'-0"

* No. 2 Southern Pine is medium grain (MG).

** Douglas fir-larch: dry 1.7; KD 1.8. Southern pine: dry 1.6; KD 1.7.

All truss members shall be of stress-grade lumber. Lumber grades, net sizes, and allowable unit stresses per American Softwood Lumber Standard PS 20-70.

Webs:

Tension and compression webs of 2 × 4 no. 3 Douglas fir-larch, or southern pine, or hem-fir, 19% max. m.c., for truss spans up to 50'-0". Web lateral bracing is indicated for spans over 47'-6".

Trussed rafters

in. continuous spacer tie across the top edge of the bottom chords at midspan of the trusses. Provide 1 × 4 to 1 × 6 in. continuous lateral web bracing where shown on the truss elevations.

Bottom chord splice for spans to 42'-0" may be located from truss centerline to ¼ points of center panel. For longer spans locate splice(s) at ¼ points only; such trusses may have two splices in the center panel.

The truss plates are to be TECO nail-on truss plates, manufactured of 20-gauge zinc-coated (hot-dip process) sheet steel (ASTM-A446) and prepunched to receive nails as specified.

Nails are to be specially manufactured of uncoated steel wire of either 0.131 in. plain round shank or 0.133 in. diameter square barbed shank (Scotch) by 1½ in. long.

Nail unit design values are 97.5 lb for Douglas fir-larch and Southern pine and 70.6 lb for hem-fir. These values are further adjusted for duration of load and joint eccentricity.

All truss members shall be accurately cut and assembled in suitable jigs so that all joints will be tight. Camber of span (ft) ÷ 60 in. is reccommended for the bottom chord and is to be introduced during fabrication. Place plates on both sides of joints. Offset plates on opposite sides of a joint ¼ in. with respect to each other.

For trussed rafters with plywood gussets see publication GT-8 by the American Plywood Association.

By WILLIAM J. LeMESSURIER, *Professional Engineer, Wm. LeMessurier Associates, Cambridge, Mass.,* and ALBERT G. H. DIETZ, *Professor of Building Engineering, Department of Architecture, Massachusetts Institute of Technology Revised 1978 by A. G. H. Dietz with assistance of American Plywood Association.*

Stressed-skin panels

In stressed-skin panels, plywood is firmly fastened to one or both edges of ribs (joists, rafters, or studs) to make the skin or skins act integrally with the ribs and provide enhanced resistance to bending or buckling. The drawings in Fig. 1 show these principles and present cross sections of stressed-skin plywood panels for floors and roofs of houses. All panels use standard 4-ft wide plywood with the face grain parallel to the joists. The lengths of the panels are variable: the maximum safe length in each case being a function of loading, joist grade, size, spacing, and plywood thickness and grade.

Structural characteristics

Structural action of a stressed-skin panel is similar to a wide-flange steel beam. The top skin carries compressive stress and the bottom carries tension. Due to the tendency of the face or faces to slip horizontally in relation to one another, important shearing stresses exist between the plywood and the ribs and also within the ribs. The only practical way to transmit this shear is by a rigidly glued joint between the plywood and joists.

The top face of the panel has additional stresses since it must carry loads between joists. When the top face serves as a floor with only an asphalt tile, linoleum, or carpet covering, it must be ⅝ in. minimum if joists are 16 in. o.c. For roof construction not intended for use as a deck, a ½-in-thick top cover is usually satisfactory.

Gluing technique

To obtain satisfactory glued joints, pressure must be applied along the glue line. The best technique, obtainable only in a shop, is to use presses to apply a pressure of at least 150 lb per square inch of contact area uniformly along the entire glue line.

In place of mechanical pressure methods, nail-gluing may be used. Nail sizes and spacings shown in the following schedule are suggested as a guide:

Nails shall be at least 4d for plywood up to ⅜ in. thick, 6d for ½ to ⅞ in. plywood, 8d for 1 to 1⅛ in. plywood. They shall be spaced not to exceed 3 in. along the framing members for plywood through ⅜ in., or 4 in. for plywood ½ in. and thicker, using one line for lumber 2 in. thick or less, and two lines for lumber more than 2 in. and up to 4 in. thick.

The glue employed is extremely important.

For panels which are not exposed to weather or high relative humidities, casein and urea resin glues will provide satisfactory bonds. For panels exposed to moisture, a highly moisture-resistant adhesive such as resorcinol formaldehyde or, with heated presses, phenol formaldehyde resins and melamine formaldehyde resins may be employed.

Framing details

Typical connections are shown in Fig. 2 on the following page. For panels longer than 8 ft, the plywood faces must be spliced, since plywood is usually not readily obtainable in longer sheets. These splices can be located anywhere within the span, but it is best to locate the splices as near the ends as possible. The splice may be made with a strip of plywood of the same thickness as the plywood joined, and glued under pressure. References: Design of Plywood Stressed-Skin Panels, U873; Fabrication of Plywood Stressed-Skin Panels, SS-8, both published by American Plywood Association.

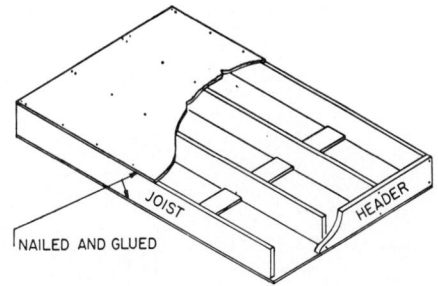

PERSPECTIVE

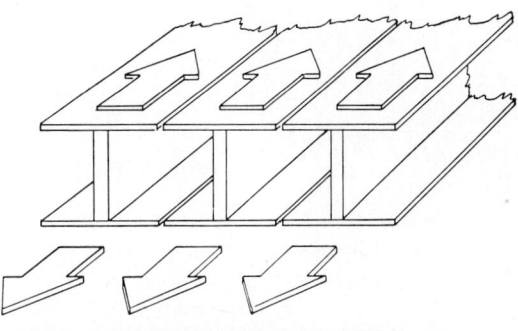

ACTION IS SIMILAR TO A SERIES OF ADJOINING BUILT-UP WOODEN I BEAMS

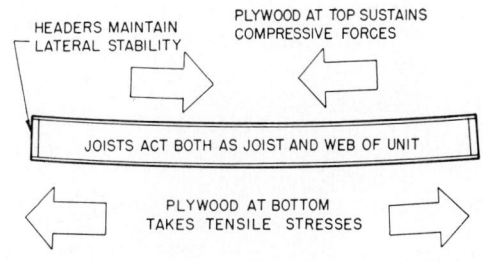

Notes for drafting
scale 1½" = 1'-0"
roof panels—5½" joists, ½" top skin, ⅜" bottom skin
      —3½" insulation in all cases
floor panel —7½" joist, ¾" top, ⅜" bottom
walls   —3½" studs, ⅜" skins
box beam —3" core, ⅜" skins

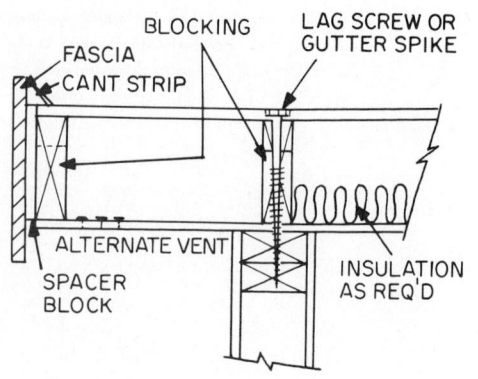

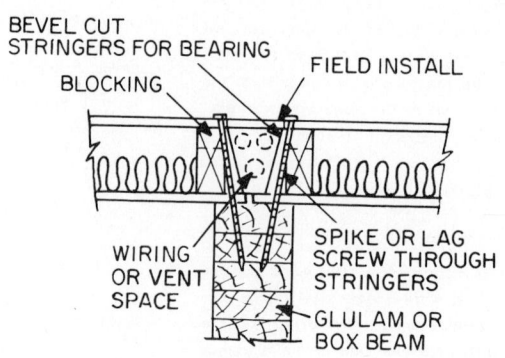

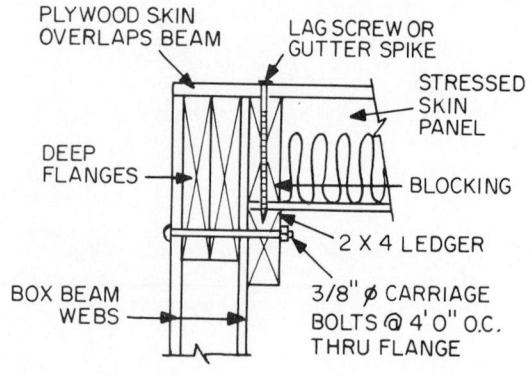

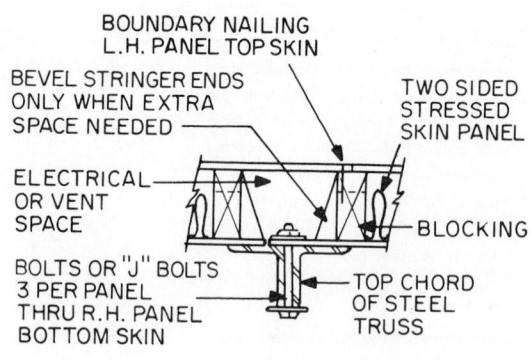

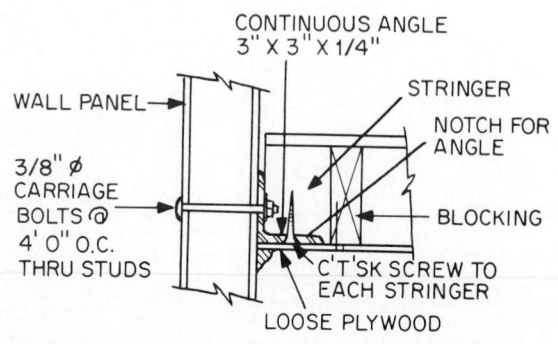

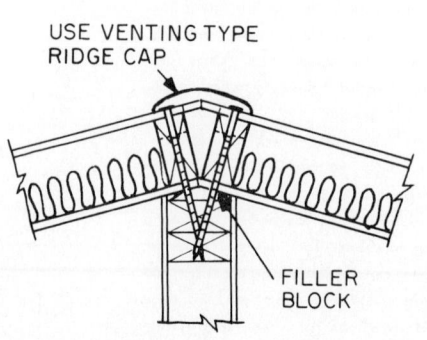

Connection details

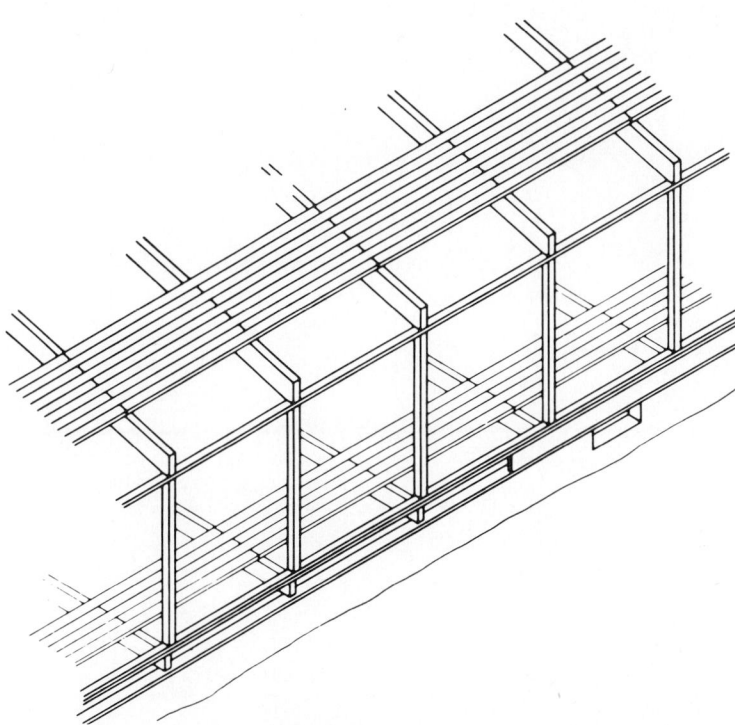

Plank-and-beam construction

From Plank and Beam Framing, *National Forest Products Association. All other data on this and the following page from* Heavy Timber Construction Details, *National Forest Products Association and* Timber Construction Manual, *American Institute of Timber Construction.*

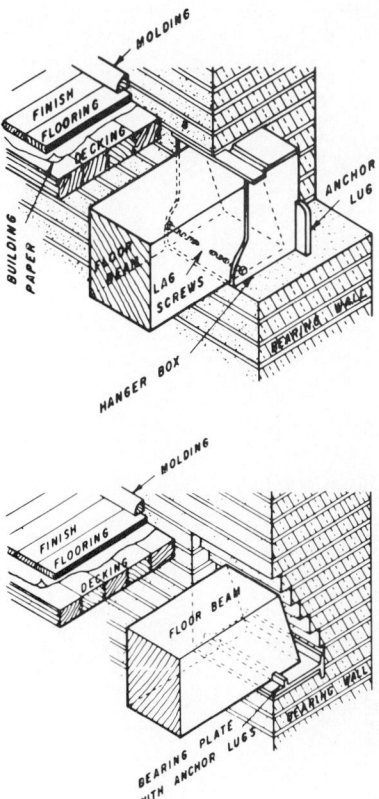

Floor framing at exterior wall

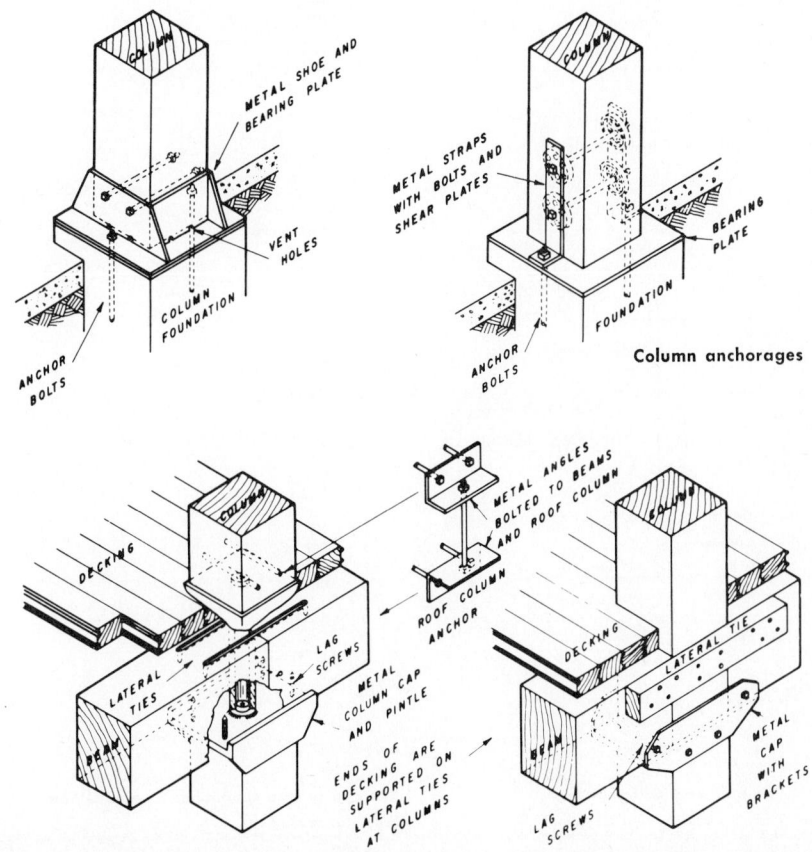

Column anchorages

Floor, beam, and column framing

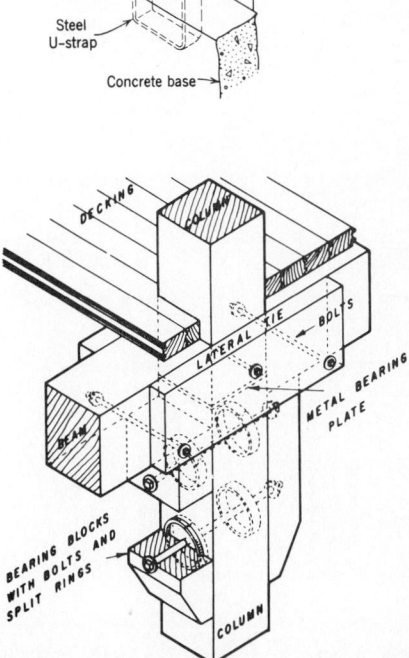

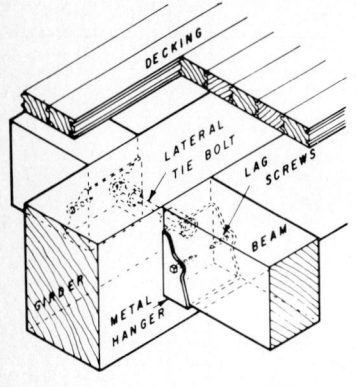

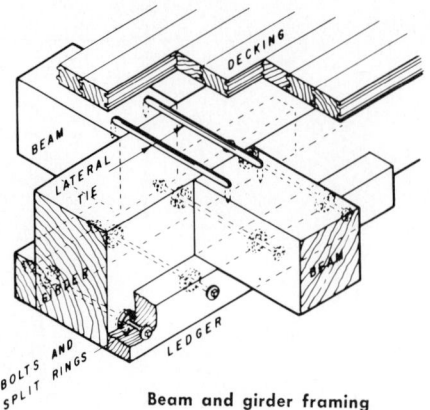

Beam and girder framing

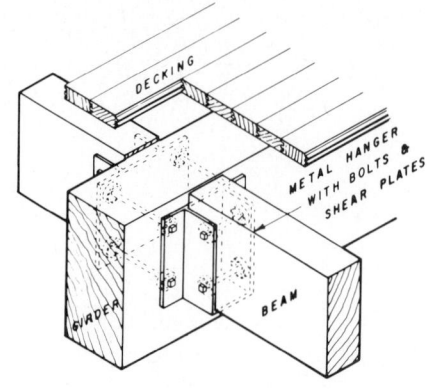

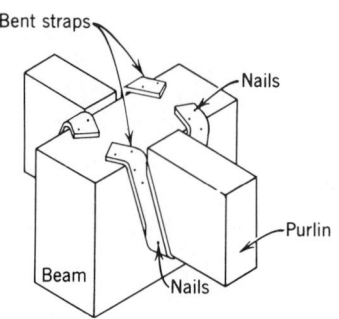

Bent strap purlin hanger

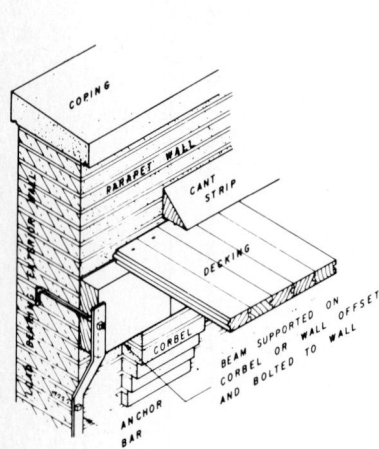

Roof framing at exterior wall

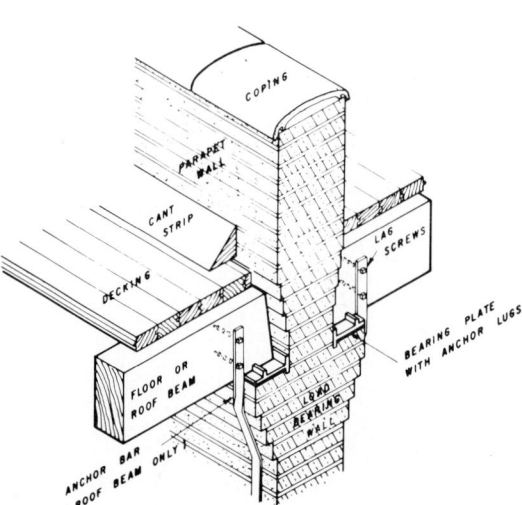

Roof framing at fire or party wall

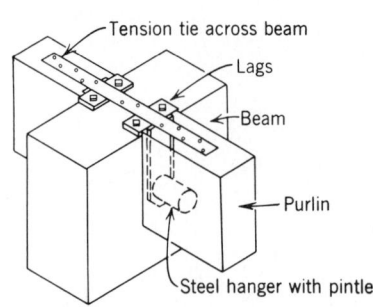

Concealed purlin hanger

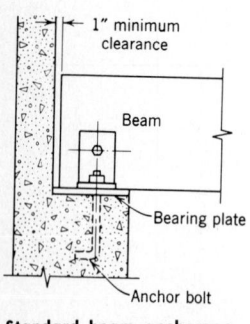

Standard beam anchorage

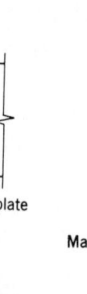

Simple beam anchorage

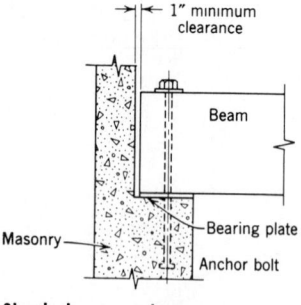

Beam to column connection—steel column

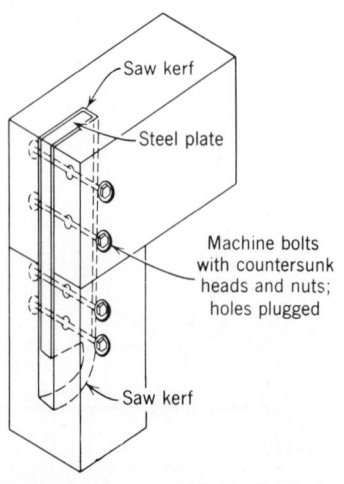

Beam to column connection—wood column— fully concealed

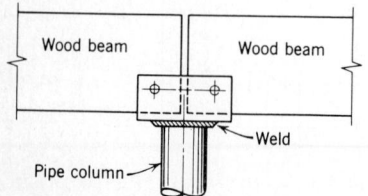

Beam to column connection—steel column

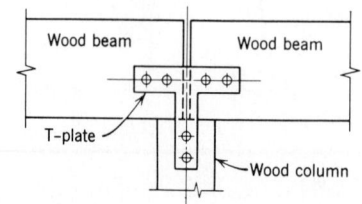

Beam to column connection—wood column

By SEYMOUR HOWARD, *Architect*
Associate Professor, School of Architecture Pratt Institute

GENERAL CONSIDERATIONS OF WOOD AS STRUCTURAL MATERIAL:

CHARACTERISTIC	CONSEQUENCE
1. Not homogeneous (orthotropic) (long cylindrical cells parallel to one axis)	1. Allowable stresses vary for pure tension & compression, tension & compression (extreme fiber) in bending, compression across grain, and also for shape of cross section ("Form factor"); depend on direction of stress with respect to direction of grain
2. Natural defects (cross-grain, spiral & diagonal; knots)	2. Allowable stresses reduced to compensate. Theory of probability used in laminated sections permits higher stresses than for solid sections
3. Decay hazard in exposed conditions	3. Preservative treatments for permanent structures. Reduced allowable stresses for temporary structures
4. Swells or shrinks with changes in humidity	4. Wood dried to expected service conditions of humidity before fabrication & assembly; for glued laminated sections, all laminations held to a 5% range of moisture content (e.g. 6% to 10% incl.)
5. Although remaining elastic, under long-term loads a permanent sag or deflection takes place	5. Use double calculated dead loads or normal $E \div 2$ for figuring allowable deflection

Note: These characteristics are listed as important differences between wood and the idealized, perfectly homogeneous and perfectly elastic material used in the mathematical analysis of strength of materials.

FIRE SAFETY

As is well known, heavy timber (6 in. nom, 5 in. min actual in least dimension) and plank construction is much better fire risk than thin sections and boarding. This fact gives glued laminated arches and frames some advantage over wood trusses and lamella arches. It also explains usual spacing of 8 ft for arches and frames, with 2 in. planking. (Next step is usually 16 to 20 ft spacing with purlins.) Small width (2 in. nom) arch rafters, spaced 24 in. o.c., with 1 in. boarding, are usually limited to farm structures and small warehouses.

RECOMMENDED SPANS (Maxima in Parenthesis)

TYPE OF STRUCTURAL UNIT	SPAN	SPACING	TYPE OF STRUCTURAL UNIT	SPAN	SPACING
Joists	Up to 24 ft	16 to 24 in.			
Sawn Beams	Up to 30 (40) ft	4 to 20 ft	TRUSSED RAFTER	20 to 60 ft	24 in.
Glued Laminated Beams	Up to 60 (100) ft	4 to 20 ft			
BOWSTRING TRUSS DEPTH/SPAN ≈ 1/1*	40 to 150 ft (200 ft)	16 to 20 ft	ARCH RAFTER OR ARCH RIB RISE/SPAN ≈ 0.45 (THREE-HINGED ARCH)	20 to 60 (80) ft	24 in.
FINK TRUSS BEST FOR SLOPES OVER 25°	40 to 60 ft (90 ft)	12 to 20 ft	TWO-HINGED ARCH RISE/SPAN - MIN 1/8 USUAL 1/6 TO 1/4	40 to 100 ft (200 ft)	8 ft or 16 to 20 ft
BELGIAN TRUSS					
PRATT TRUSS FOR SLOPES UNDER 25°			THREE-HINGED ARCH RISE/SPAN - 1/1 OR MORE	40 to 100 ft (250 ft)	8 ft or 16 to 20 ft
PRATT TRUSS (FLAT) DEPTH/SPAN ≈ 1/8† (WARREN & HOWE ALSO USED)	40 to 120 ft (150 ft)	12 to 20 ft	THREE-HINGED ARCH RISE/SPAN - MIN 1/8 USUAL 1/6 TO 1/4	40 to 100 ft (250 ft)	8 ft or 16 to 20 ft
CRESCENT TRUSS	40 to 80 ft (250 ft)	16 to 20 ft		40 to 100 ft (120 ft)	8 ft or 16 to 20 ft
LAMELLA ARCH RISE/SPAN: MIN 1/8 USUAL 1/6 TO 1/4 MAX 1/1†	40 to 120 ft (165 ft)	— —	THREE-HINGED RIGID FRAME		

Note: Glued laminated sections used in trusses for curved chords and heavily loaded straight chords and web members. Steel may be used for tension members. Glued laminated sections used for all arches and rigid frames, except that joist sections (2 by 8 to 2 by 12s) used for lamella arches.
Recommendations based on articles by Verne Ketchum (Chief Engineer, Timber Structures, Inc.) and Architectural Construction by Theodore Crane (Wiley, 1956), and other sources.
* Some authorities recommend 1/8 to 1/4 for depth/span ratio.
† Some authorities recommend 1/8 to 1/10.

FINK   BELGIAN   PRATT

TRIANGULAR ROOF TRUSSES

SCISSORS   CAMB. FINK

CAMBERED TRUSSES   BOWSTRING TRUSS

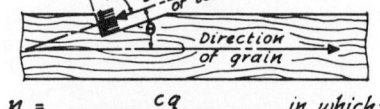
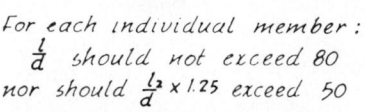

DOUBLE WARREN   FLAT TOP PRATT   SINGLE WARREN

FLAT ROOF TRUSSES

SAWTOOTH   SHED   FACTORY

FACTORY ROOF TRUSSES

Typical wood trusses

$$V = \frac{2\,b\,d^2\,F_v}{3h} \quad \text{in which.}$$

V = Maximum end reaction

F_v = Maximum permitted horizontal shear stress

b = Breadth of joist

d = Height of joist above notch

h = Total depth of joist

Beams notched at bearing points

TRUSSES

Data useful in the design of trusses are given on this and the following page. For trussed rafters, see Sheet 24.

The following data on bolted connections

$$n = \frac{c\,q}{c\,\sin^2\theta + q\,\cos^2\theta} \quad \text{in which:}$$

n = Allowable unit stress on inclined surface

c = unit stress (compression) parallel to grain

q = unit stress (compression) perpendicular to grain

θ = angle in degrees between direction of load and direction of grain

Compression on surfaces inclined to grain

(Table 12) have been derived from *National Design Specification for Wood Construction,* National Forest Products Association (1977).

For each individual member:

$\frac{l}{d}$ should not exceed 80

nor should $\frac{l_2}{d} \times 1.25$ exceed 50

Condition "a" = connector within $\frac{l}{20}$ from column end

$$P/A = \frac{0.75\,E}{(l/d)^2}$$

Condition "b" = connector from $\frac{l}{20}$ to $\frac{l}{10}$ from column end

$$P/A = \frac{0.90\,E}{(l/d)^2}$$

Spaced column

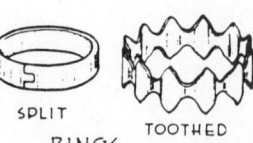

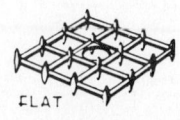

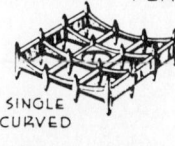
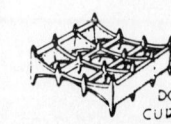
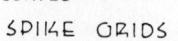

SPLIT-RING CONNECTOR   BOLT   FRAMING TIMBERS

EXAMPLE OF USE

SPLIT RINGS   TOOTHED

WITH HUB   WITHOUT HUB

CLAW PLATES

MALLEABLE FLANGED   PRESSED STEEL FLANGED

SHEAR PLATES

FLAT   SINGLE CURVED   DOUBLE CURVED

SPIKE GRIDS

CLAMPING PLATES

FLANGED

FLAT

Connectors

Table 12. Allowable loads on bolted connections

Design values, in pounds, on one bolt loaded at both ends (double shear)* for following species

Length of bolt in main member ℓ	Diameter of bolt D	ℓ/D	Projected area of bolt A=ℓxD	DOUGLAS FIR-LARCH (Dense), SOUTHERN PINE (Dense) in		ASH, Commercial White, HICKORY in		CALIFORNIA REDWOOD (Close grain), DOUGLAS FIR-LARCH, SOUTHERN PINE, SOUTHERN CYPRESS		OAK, Red & White		EASTERN HEMLOCK-TAMARACK, CALIFORNIA REDWOOD (Open grain), HEM-FIR, WESTERN HEMLOCK		MOUNTAIN HEMLOCK, WESTERN CEDARS, NORTHERN PINE	
				Parallel to grain P	Perpendicular to grain Q	Parallel to grain P	Perpendicular to grain Q	Parallel to grain P	Perpendicular to grain Q	Parallel to grain P	Perpendicular to grain Q	Parallel to grain P	Perpendicular to grain Q	Parallel to grain P	Perpendicular to grain Q
1-1/2	1/2	3.00	.750	1100	500	1080	780	940	430	830	650	800	280	750	300
	5/8	2.40	.938	1380	570	1360	880	1180	490	1050	730	1000	310	930	340
	3/4	2.00	1.125	1660	630	1630	980	1420	540	1260	820	1200	350	1120	370
	7/8	1.71	1.313	1940	700	1910	1080	1660	600	1470	900	1400	380	1310	410
	1	1.50	1.500	2220	760	2180	1170	1890	650	1690	980	1600	420	1490	450
2	1/2	4.00	1.000	1370	670	1340	1040	1170	570	1040	870	1040	370	990	400
	5/8	3.20	1.250	1820	760	1790	1170	1550	650	1380	980	1330	410	1240	450
	3/4	2.67	1.500	2210	840	2170	1300	1890	720	1680	1090	1600	460	1490	500
	7/8	2.29	1.750	2580	930	2540	1430	2200	790	1960	1200	1870	510	1740	550
	1	2.00	2.000	2960	1010	2910	1570	2520	870	2250	1310	2130	550	1990	600
2-1/2	1/2	5.00	1,250	1480	840	1450	1290	1260	720	1120	1080	1180	460	1190	500
	5/8	4.00	1,563	2140	950	2100	1460	1820	810	1620	1220	1620	520	1550	560
	3/4	3.33	1,875	2710	1060	2660	1630	2310	900	2060	1360	1990	580	1870	620
	7/8	2.86	2,188	3210	1160	3160	1790	2740	990	2440	1500	2330	630	2180	690
	1	2.50	2,500	3680	1270	3620	1960	3150	1080	2800	1640	2670	690	2490	750
3	1/2	6.00	1.500	1490	1010	1460	1460	1270	860	1130	1130	1210	550	1280	590
	5/8	4.80	1.875	2290	1140	2260	1760	1960	970	1740	1470	1810	620	1800	670
	3/4	4.00	2.250	3080	1270	3020	1950	2630	1080	2340	1630	2340	690	2230	750
	7/8	3.43	2.625	3770	1390	3710	2150	3220	1190	2870	1800	2790	760	2610	820
	1	3.00	3.000	4390	1520	4320	2350	3750	1300	3340	1960	3200	830	2990	900
3-1/2	1/2	7.00	1.750	1490	1140	1460	1460	1270	980	1130	1130	1210	640	1280	690
	5/8	5.60	2.188	2320	1330	2280	2020	1980	1130	1760	1690	1890	730	1970	780
	3/4	4.67	2.625	3280	1480	3220	2280	2800	1260	2440	1910	2580	810	2540	870
	7/8	4.00	3.063	4190	1630	4120	2510	3580	1390	3180	2100	3180	890	3030	960
	1	3.50	3.500	5000	1770	4920	2740	4270	1520	3800	2290	3710	970	3480	1050
4	1/2	8.00	2.000	1490	1180	1460	1460	1270	1010	1130	1130	1210	700	1280	790
	5/8	6.40	2.500	2330	1510	2290	2180	1990	1290	1770	1770	1900	830	2000	900
	3/4	5.33	3.000	3340	1690	3280	2590	2850	1440	2540	2170	2690	920	2770	1000
	7/8	4.57	3.500	4450	1860	4370	2870	3800	1590	3380	2400	3480	1020	3400	1100
	1	4.00	4.00	5470	2030	5380	3130	4670	1730	4160	2620	4150	1110	3960	1200
4-1/2	1/2	7.20	2.813	2330	1640	2290	2230	1990	1400	1770	1770	1890	930	2000	1010
	5/8	6.00	3.375	3350	1900	3300	2820	2860	1620	2550	2360	2730	1040	2880	1120
	3/4	5.14	3.938	4530	2090	4460	3220	3870	1790	3450	2690	3630	1140	3700	1240
	7/8	4.50	4.500	5770	2280	5680	3520	4930	1950	4390	2940	4500	1250	4380	1350
	1	3.60	5.625	7980	2670	7850	4120	6820	2280	6070	3450	5940	1460	5590	1580
5-1/2	5/8	8.80	3.438	2330	1650	2290	2150	1990	1410	1770	1770	1900	1010	1990	1190
	3/4	7.33	4.125	3350	2200	3290	2980	2860	1880	2540	2490	2730	1270	2870	1370
	7/8	6.29	4.813	4570	2550	4490	3710	3900	2180	3470	3110	3720	1400	3920	1510
	1	5.50	5.500	5930	2790	5830	4260	5070	2380	4510	3560	4820	1520	5000	1650
	1-1/4	4.40	6.875	8940	3260	8790	5040	7640	2790	6800	4210	6940	1780	6730	1930
7-1/2	5/8	12.00	4.688	2330	1480	2290	1870	1990	1260	1770	1560	1890	950	2000	1150
	3/4	10.00	5.625	3350	2130	3290	2710	2860	1820	2550	2260	2730	1320	2880	1590
	7/8	8.57	6.563	4560	2840	4480	3720	3890	2430	3460	3110	3720	1730	3910	2010
	1	7.50	7.500	5950	3550	5850	4760	5080	3030	4520	3938	4850	2060	5110	2250
	1-1/4	6.00	9.375	9310	4450	9150	6620	7950	3800	7080	5530	7580	2430	7990	2940
9-1/2	3/4	12.67	7.125	3350	1920	3290	2420	2860	1640	2550	2020	2720	1250	2870	1520
	7/8	10.86	8.313	4570	2660	4490	3360	3900	2270	3470	2810	3720	1660	3910	2010
	1	9.50	9.500	5950	3460	5850	4460	5080	2960	4520	3730	4850	2130	5110	2560
	1-1/4	7.60	11.875	9300	5210	9140	6960	7950	4450	7070	5820	7570	3040	7980	4480
	1-1/2	6.33	14.250	13410	6480	13190	9380	11460	5530	10200	7840	10910	3540	11520	3830
11-1/2	7/8	13.14	10.062	4560	1980	4490	3050	3900	2060	3470	2550	3700	1590	3930	1710
	1	11.50	11.500	5950	3240	5850	4080	5080	2770	4520	3420	4860	2040	5120	2490
	1-1/4	9.20	14.375	9300	5110	9150	6610	7950	4360	7070	5520	7570	3130	7970	3750
	1-1/2	7.67	17.250	13410	7200	13180	9570	11450	6150	10190	8000	10930	4210	11470	4640
13-1/2	1	13.50	13.500	5960	2410	5850	3730	5100	2530	4520	3120	4850	1970	5130	2410
	1-1/4	10.80	16.875	9300	4860	9140	6150	7950	4160	7070	5140	7590	3030	7990	3680
	1-1/2	9.00	20.250	13400	7070	13180	9190	11450	6040	10190	7680	10930	4340	11510	5150

* *Three (3) member joint.*
From National Design Specification for Wood Construction, 1977, National Forest Products Association.

GLUED LAMINATED TIMBER

Advantages over solid timber

Sections can have greater depth and greater length than are obtainable in solid timber.

Sections can be curved and/or of varying depth.

Outer plies can be selected for high strength and/or appearance; lower-grade wood can be used for inner plies.

Wood throughout section can be inspected before fabrication; solid timbers may contain hidden defects.

Wood throughout section can be seasoned uniformly before fabrication, reducing chances of large checks and shakes often found in solid timbers.

Inspection and seasoning before fabrication permit the use of higher design stresses than for solid timber.

(The following material has been reproduced with permission from the "Spec-Data" sheet published by the American Institute of Timber Construction, 1980.)

Definition

Structural glued laminated timber is an engineered, stress-rated product of a timber laminating plant, comprising assemblies of suitably selected and prepared wood laminations securely bonded together with adhesives. The grain of all laminations is approximately parallel longitudinally. The individual laminations shall not exceed 2 inches (51 mm) in net thickness. They may be comprised of pieces end joined to form any length, of pieces placed or glued edge to edge to make wider ones, or of pieces bent to curved form during gluing.

Materials

Lumber used for laminating is structurally graded in accordance with the standard grading provisions for the species and supplementary requirements of laminating specifications, surfaced to laminating tolerances, and dried to the required moisture content at time of gluing.

Shapes: Structural glued laminated timber members may be straight or curved to meet job specifications. Laminated beam shapes include those illustrated below:

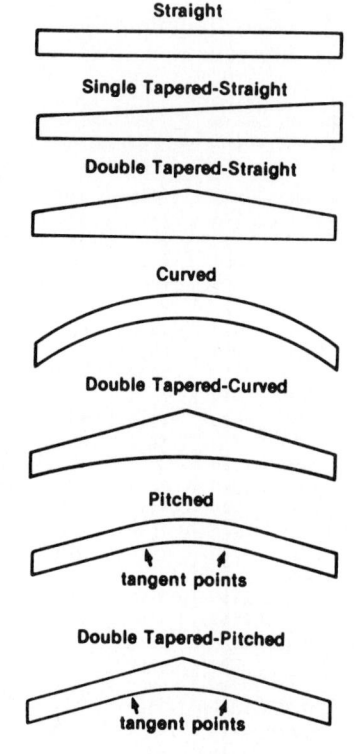

Straight

Single Tapered-Straight

Double Tapered-Straight

Curved

Double Tapered-Curved

Pitched

tangent points

Double Tapered-Pitched

tangent points

Adhesives for the production of structural glued laminated timber must comply with the specifications as contained in Voluntary Product Standard PS 56–73 for Structural Glued Laminated Timber. Laminated timber members bonded with wet-use (waterproof) adhesives must be used if the members are subject to occasional or continuous wetting; or for applications, either exterior or interior where the moisture content of the wood will exceed 16%. Examples of interior applications where wet-use adhesives should be used include: swimming pools, shower rooms, ice skating rinks, commercial laundries, car-washing operations, storage and processing operations which produce humid conditions, and when the members may be subjected to moisture exposure during transit, storage, or erection.

Preservative treatment, when required, should be in accordance with AITC 109–78, Treating Standard for Structural Timber Framing. Individual laminations may be treated before gluing, or laminated timbers may be treated after gluing if waterproof glue has been used. Species are limited to coast region Douglas fir, hem-fir, and southern pine. Preservative treatment shall be in accordance with AWPA Standards C1 and C2 and retention and penetration values in accordance with AWPA C28–78.

Sizes

Standard finished sizes of glued laminated timber are based on standard finished lumber sizes (Table 2). Other finished sizes may be produced to meet special requirements.

Depths: Dimension lumber, surfaced to 1½ inches (38 mm), is normally used to laminate straight members and those curved members having radii of curvature within the bending radius limitations for the species. Boards, surfaced to ¾ inch (19 mm), are recommended for laminating curved members when the bending radius is too short to permit the use of dimension lumber.

Widths: It is necessary to surface the glue lines of laminated members to remove adhesive squeeze-out which occurs during manufacturing and to provide a uniformly smooth surface. Therefore, the net finished widths of the glued laminated timber members are less than the net finished widths of standard industry lumber sizes. (See Table 13.)

Appearance Grades: Structural glued laminated timber is produced in three appearance grades. These are: "Industrial," which is suitable for construction in industrial plants, warehouses, garages, and for other uses where appearance is not of primary concern; "Architectural," which is suitable for construction where appearance is a factor; and "Premium," which is suitable for uses which demand the finest appearance. These appearance grades do not modify design stresses, fabrication controls, grades of lumber used, or other provisions of the applicable standards for structural glued laminated timber.

Limitations: When glued laminated timber is to be used for applications where it remains permanently exposed to the weather, measures must be taken to protect the members from decay, insect attack, checking, and weathering. Such protective measures might include special details, flashing, preservative treatments, coatings, or combinations of these methods.

Finishes: Available finishes for glued laminated timber include sealers, stains, and paints.

Surface sealers increase resistance to soiling, control grain raising, minimize checking, and serve as a moisture retardant. They fall into two classifications. Translucent penetrating sealers provide limited protection and are suitable for use when final finish requires staining or a natural finish. Primer and nonpenetrating sealer coats provide maximum protection by sealing the surface of the wood. Primer and nonpenetrating sealer coats should not be specified when the final finish requires a natural or stained finish.

Table 13. Standard finished widths of glued laminated timbers

Nominal width	Net Finished Width	
	U.S., in.	Metric, mm
3	2¼	57
4	3⅛	79
6	5⅛	130
8	6¾	171
10	8¾	222
12	10¾	273
14	12¼	311
16	14¼	362

Laminated arches may be either two-hinged or three-hinged and include the shapes illustrated. Other more complex shapes may also be fabricated.

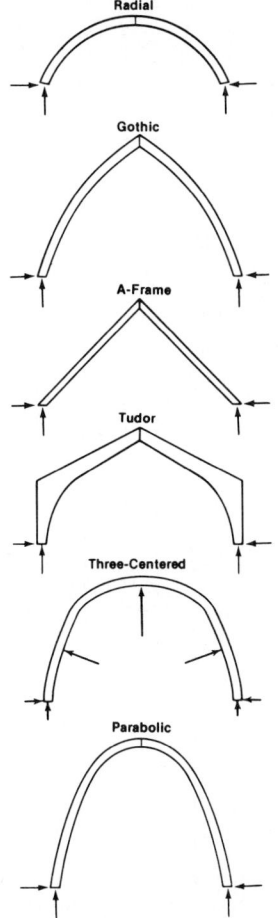

Radial

Gothic

A-Frame

Tudor

Three-Centered

Parabolic

(The following data are reproduced with permission from *Glulam Systems 1981*, published by the *American Institute of Timber Construction, Englewood, CO 80110.*)

Species

Softwoods commonly used for laminating include Western species such as Douglas fir, larch, and hem-fir; Southern pine is also used. Other species, including hardwoods, may be used. Contact AITC for additional information.

Allowable stresses are given in Tables 16 and 17 for normal conditions of loading, for dry conditions of use, and for a 12-in.-deep member with a span-to-depth ratio of 21. Modifications of stresses for other conditions are as follows:

Duration of load: See Sheet 1 of this section.

Curvature factor: For the curved portion of members, the allowable unit stress in bending is modified through multiplication by the following curvature factor $C_c = 1 - 2000(t/R)^2$ in which t = thickness of lamination in inches, R = radius of curvature in inches, and t/R should not exceed 1/

100 for hardwoods and Southern pine or 1/125 for softwoods other than Southern pine. No curvature factor is applied to stress in the straight portion of an assembly, regardless of curvature elsewhere.

The recommended minimum radii of curvature for curved structural glued laminated members are 9 ft 4 in. for a lamination thickness of ¾ in.; and 27 ft 6 in. for a lamination thickness of 1½ in. Other radii of curvature may be used with these thicknesses and other radius-thickness combinations may be used. The designer should determine availability before specifying.

Radial Tension or Compression: The radial stress induced by a bending moment in a curved member of constant cross-section is computed by the formula:

$$f_r = \frac{3M}{2Rbd}$$

in which M = bending moment in inch pounds; R = radius of curvature at centerline of member in inches; b = width of cross section in inches; d = depth of cross section in inches.

For procedures for calculating radial stresses in curved beams with varying cross-section, contact AITC.

When M is in the direction tending to decrease curvature (increase the radius), the stress is tension across the grain. For this condition, the allowable tension stress across the grain is limited to ⅓ the allowable unit stress in horizontal shear for Southern pine and California redwood for all load conditions, and for Douglas fir, hem-fir and larch for wind or earthquake loadings. The limit is 15 psi for Douglas fir, hem-fir and larch for other types of loading. These values are subject to modifications for duration of load. If these values are exceeded, mechanical reinforcing sufficient to resist all radial tension stresses is required, but in no case shall the calculated radial tension stress exceed one-third the allowable unit stress in horizontal shear.

When M is in the direction tending to increase curvature (decrease the radius), the stress is compression across the grain and is limited to the allowable unit stress in compression perpendicular to the grain for all species included herein, subject to modifications for duration of load.

Size Factor: When the depth of a rectangular beam exceeds 12 in., the tabulated unit stress in bending F_b, is reduced through multiplication by the size factor, C_F as determined from the following relationship: $C_F = (12/d)^{1/9}$ in which C_F = size factor; d = depth of member in inches (See Table 19 for values of C_F).

This size factor relationship is applicable to a bending member satisfying the following basic assumptions: (a) simply supported beam, (b) uniformly distributed load and (c) span to depth ratio (L/d) of 21. For other

ratios and leading conditions, the size factor is modified as shown in Table 14.

Lateral Stability: The tabulated allowable unit bending stress values are applicable to members which are adequately braced. When depth-to-width ratios exceed 3 to 1 the compression edge must be braced at frequent intervals. When deep, slender members are not adequately braced, a reduction to the allowable unit bending stresses must be applied based on a computation of the slenderness factor of the member, as shown in the AITC *Timber Construction Manual.*

Wet use: When the moisture content in service exceeds 16 per cent, as in outdoor locations or indoor locations of high humidity, multiply the tabular stresses by the factors shown in Table 15.

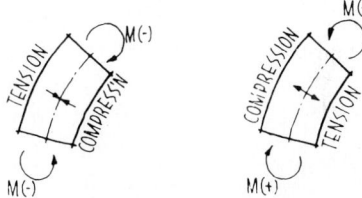

Fig. 1. Radial stress caused by bending of curved member

Table 14. Modifications of the size factor

Span to depth radio L/d	% change
7	+6.2
14	+2.3
21	0
28	−1.6
35	−2.8

Table 14A. Loading condition factors

For simply supported beams	% change
Single concentrated load	+7.8
Uniform load	0
Third point load	−3.2

Table 15. Wet-use factors

Type of stress	Wet-use factor
Bending and tension parallel to grain	0.80
Compression parallel to grain	0.73
Compression perpendicular to grain	0.67
Shear	0.88
Modulus of elasticity	0.83

Glued laminated timber

Table 16. Glulam bending and compression stresses

Combination Symbol	Outer Species Laminations/Core Laminations[3]	Bending — Loads Applied Perpendicular to Wide Faces of Laminations					Compression	
		Extreme Fiber in Bending — Tension Zone Stressed in Tension[4,5] F_{bxx}	Compression Perp. to Grain — Tension Face F_{clxx}	Compression Perp. to Grain — Compression Face F_{clxx}	Horizontal Shear F_{vxx}	Modulus of Elasticity $\times 10^{-6}$ psi E_{xx}	Compression Parallel to Grain F_c	Modulus of Elasticity $\times 10^{-8}$ psi E
VISUALLY GRADED WESTERN SPECIES								
16F-V1	DF/WW	1,600	385	385	140	1.3	1.050	1.1
16F-V2	HF/HF	1,600	385	245	155	1.4	1.300	1.3
16F-V3	DF/DF	1,600	385	385	165	1.5	1.550	1.5
20F-V1	DF/WW	2,000	450	385	140	1.4	1.200	1.2
20F-V2	HF/HF	2,000	385	245	155	1.5	1.350	1.4
20F-V3	DF/DF	2,000	450	385	165	1.6	1.600	1.5
20F-V4	DF/DF	2,000	410	385	165	1.6	1.550	1.6
The following 22F and 24F combinations may not be readily available for members 15 in. and less in depth								
22F-V1	DF/WW	2,200	450	385	140	1.6	1.250	1.3
22F-V2	HF/HF	2,200	385	385	155	1.5	1.400	1.4
22F-V3	DF/DF	2,200	450	385	165	1.7	1.650	1.6
22F-V4	DF/DF	2,200	410	385	165	1.7	1.700	1.6
24F-V1	DF/WW	2,400	450	450	140	1.7	1.400	1.4
24F-V2	HF/HF	2,400	385	385	155	1.5	1.450	1.4
24F-V3	DF/DF	2,400	450	385	165	1.7	1.700	1.6
24F-V4	DF/DF	2,400	450	450	165	1.8	1.700	1.6
24F-V5	DF/HF	2,400	450	450	155	1.7	1.600	1.5
VISUALLY GRADED SOUTHERN PINE								
16F-V1	SP/SP	1,600	385	385	200	1.4	1.450	1.3
16F-V2	SP/SP	1,600	385	385	200	1.4	1.550	1.4
16F-V3	SP/SP	1,600	450	450	200	1.4	1.500	1.3
20F-V1	SP/SP	2,000	450	385	200	1.5	1.450	1.4
20F-V2	SP/SP	2,000	450	385	200	1.6	1.500	1.4
20F-V3	SP/SP	2,000	385	385	200	1.4	1.550	1.4
The following 22F and 24F combinations may not be readily available for members 15 in. and less in depth								
22F-V1	SP/SP	2,200	450	450	200	1.6	1.650	1.5
22F-V2	SP/SP	2,200	385	385	200	1.4	1.550	1.4
22F-V3	SP/SP	2,200	450	385	200	1.6	1.500	1.4
24F-V1	SP/SP	2,400	450	385	200	1.7	1.350	1.5
24F-V2	SP/SP	2,400	450	450	200	1.7	1.600	1.5
24F-V3	SP/SP	2,400	450	450	200	1.8	1.700	1.6
Wet-Use Factors[2]		0.800	0.667	0.667	0.875	0.833	0.730	0.833

Table 17. Glulam axial stresses

Combination Symbol	Species[3]	Grade[8]	Tension Parallel to Grain F_t	Compression Parallel to Grain F_c	Modulus of Elasticity E
COMPRESSION MEMBERS					
2	DF	L2	—	1.900	1,700,000
15	HF	L2	—	1.350	1,400,000
47	SP	N2M	—	1.900	1,400,000
TENSION MEMBERS					
3	DF	L2D	1.450	—	1,800,000
16	HF	L1	1.200	—	1,600,000
48	SP	N2D	1.400	—	1,700,000
Wet-Use Factors[2]			0.800	0.730	0.833

Table 18. Section properties—use 1½″ columns in table for straight beams; use ¾″ columns in table for curved arches.

3 1/8″ WIDTH

No. of Lams 1½″	No. of Lams ¾″	Depth, d (inches)	Size Factor, C_F	Area A (inches^2)	Section Modulus, S (inches^3)	Moment of inertia, I (inches^4)
2	4	3.00	1.00	9.4	4.7	7.0
	5	3.75	1.00	11.7	7.3	13.7
3	6	4.50	1.00	14.1	10.5	23.7
	7	5.25	1.00	16.4	14.4	37.7
4	8	6.00	1.00	18.8	18.8	56.3
	9	6.75	1.00	21.1	23.7	80.1
5	10	7.50	1.00	23.4	29.3	109.9
	11	8.25	1.00	25.8	35.4	146.2
6	12	9.00	1.00	28.1	42.2	189.8
	13	9.75	1.00	30.5	49.5	241.4
7	14	10.50	1.00	32.8	57.4	301.5
	15	11.25	1.00	35.2	65.9	370.8
8	16	12.00	1.00	37.5	75.0	450.0
	17	12.75	0.99	39.8	84.7	539.8
9	18	13.50	0.99	42.2	94.9	640.7
	19	14.25	0.98	44.5	105.8	753.6
10	20	15.00	0.98	46.9	117.2	878.9
	21	15.75	0.97	49.2	129.2	1,017.4
11	22	16.50	0.97	51.6	141.8	1,169.8
	23	17.25	0.96	53.9	155.0	1,336.7
12	24	18.00	0.96	56.3	168.8	1,518.8
	25	18.75	0.95	58.6	183.1	1,716.6
13	26	19.50	0.95	60.9	198.0	1,931.0
	27	20.25	0.94	63.3	213.6	2,162.4
14	28	21.00	0.94	65.6	229.7	2,411.7
	29	21.75	0.94	68.0	246.4	2,679.5
15	30	22.50	0.93	70.3	263.7	2,966.3
	31	23.25	0.93	72.7	281.5	3,272.9
16	32	24.00	0.93	75.0	300.0	3,600.0

5 1/8″ WIDTH

No. of Lams 1½″	No. of Lams ¾″	Depth, d (inches)	Size Factor, C_F	Area A (inches^2)	Section Modulus, S (inches^3)	Moment of inertia, I (inches^4)
3	6	4.50	1.00	23.1	17.3	38.9
	7	5.25	1.00	26.9	23.5	61.8
4	8	6.00	1.00	30.8	30.8	92.3
	9	6.75	1.00	34.6	38.9	131.3
5	10	7.50	1.00	38.4	48.0	180.2
	11	8.25	1.00	42.3	58.1	239.8
6	12	9.00	1.00	46.1	69.2	311.3
	13	9.75	1.00	50.0	81.2	395.8
7	14	10.50	1.00	53.8	94.2	494.4
	15	11.25	1.00	57.7	108.1	608.1
8	16	12.00	1.00	61.5	123.0	738.0
	17	12.75	0.99	65.3	138.9	885.2
9	18	13.50	0.99	69.2	155.7	1,050.8
	19	14.25	0.98	73.0	173.4	1,235.8
10	20	15.00	0.98	76.9	192.2	1,441.4
	21	15.75	0.97	80.7	211.9	1,668.6
11	22	16.50	0.97	84.6	232.5	1,918.5
	23	17.25	0.96	88.4	254.2	2,192.2
12	24	18.00	0.96	92.3	276.8	2,490.8
	25	18.75	0.95	96.1	300.3	2,815.2
13	26	19.50	0.95	99.9	324.8	3,166.8
	27	20.25	0.94	103.8	350.3	3,546.4
14	28	21.00	0.94	107.6	376.7	3,955.2
	29	21.75	0.94	111.5	404.1	4,394.3
15	30	22.50	0.93	115.3	432.4	4,864.7
	31	23.25	0.93	119.2	461.7	5,367.6
16	32	24.00	0.93	123.0	492.0	5,904.0
	33	24.75	0.92	126.8	523.2	6,475.0
17	34	25.50	0.92	130.7	555.4	7,081.6
	35	26.25	0.92	134.5	588.6	7,725.0
18	36	27.00	0.91	138.4	622.7	8,406.3
	37	27.75	0.91	142.2	657.8	9,126.4
19	38	28.50	0.91	146.1	693.8	9.886.6
	39	29.25	0.91	149.9	730.8	10,687.8
20	40	30.00	0.90	153.8	768.8	11,531.3
	41	30.75	0.90	157.6	807.7	12,417.9
21	42	31.50	0.90	161.4	847.5	13,348.9
	43	32.25	0.90	165.3	888.4	14,325.2
22	44	33.00	0.89	169.1	930.2	15,348.1
	45	33.75	0.89	173.0	972.9	16,418.5
23	46	34.50	0.89	176.8	1,016.7	17,537.6
	47	35.25	0.89	180.7	1,061.4	18,706.4
24	48	36.00	0.88	184.5	1,107.0	19,926.0

6 3/4″ WIDTH

No. of Lams 1½″	No. of Lams ¾″	Depth, d (inches)	Size Factor, C_F	Area A (inches^2)	Section Modulus, S (inches^3)	Moment of inertia, I (inches^4)
4	8	6.00	1.00	40.5	40.5	121.5
	9	6.75	1.00	45.6	51.3	173.0
5	10	7.50	1.00	50.6	63.3	237.3
	11	8.25	1.00	55.7	76.6	315.9
6	12	9.00	1.00	60.8	91.1	410.1
	13	9.75	1.00	65.8	106.9	521.4
7	14	10.50	1.00	70.9	124.0	651.2
	15	11.25	1.00	75.9	142.4	800.9
8	16	12.00	1.00	81.0	162.0	972.0
	17	12.75	0.99	86.1	182.9	1,165.9
9	18	13.50	0.99	91.1	205.0	1,384.0
	19	14.25	0.98	96.2	228.4	1,627.7
10	20	15.00	0.98	101.3	253.1	1,898.4
	21	15.75	0.97	106.3	279.1	2,197.7
11	22	16.50	0.97	111.4	306.3	2,526.8
	23	17.25	0.96	116.4	334.8	2,887.3
12	24	18.00	0.96	121.5	364.5	3,280.5
	25	18.75	0.95	126.6	395.5	3,707.9
13	26	19.50	0.95	131.6	427.8	4,170.9
	27	20.25	0.94	136.7	461.3	4,670.9
14	28	21.00	0.94	141.8	496.1	5,209.3
	29	21.75	0.94	146.8	532.2	5,787.6
15	30	22.50	0.93	151.9	569.5	6,407.2
	31	23.25	0.93	156.9	608.1	7,069.5
16	32	24.00	0.93	162.0	648.0	7,776.0
	33	24.75	0.92	167.1	689.1	8,528.0
17	34	25.50	0.92	172.1	731.5	9,327.0
	35	26.25	0.92	177.2	775.2	10,174.4
18	36	27.00	0.91	182.3	820.1	11,071.7
	37	27.75	0.91	187.3	866.3	12,020.2
19	38	28.50	0.91	192.4	913.8	13,021.4
	39	29.25	0.91	197.4	962.5	14,076.7
20	40	30.00	0.90	202.5	1,012.5	15,187.5
	41	30.75	0.90	207.6	1,063.8	16,355.3
21	42	31.50	0.90	212.6	1,116.3	17,581.4
	43	32.25	0.90	217.7	1,170.1	18,867.4
22	44	33.00	0.89	222.8	1,225.1	20,214.6
	45	33.75	0.89	227.8	1,281.4	21,624.4
23	46	34.50	0.89	232.9	1,339.0	23,098.3
	47	35.25	0.89	237.9	1,397.9	24,637.7
24	48	36.00	0.88	243.0	1,458.0	26,244.0
	49	36.75	0.88	248.1	1,519.4	27,918.7
25	50	37.50	0.88	253.1	1,582.0	29,663.1
	51	38.25	0.88	258.2	1,645.9	31,478.7
26	52	39.00	0.88	263.3	1,711.1	33,366.9
	53	39.75	0.88	268.3	1,777.6	35,329.2
27	54	40.50	0.87	273.4	1,845.3	37,367.0
	55	41.25	0.87	278.4	1,914.3	39,481.6
28	56	42.00	0.87	283.5	1,984.5	41,674.5
	57	42.75	0.87	288.6	2,056.0	43,947.2
29	58	43.50	0.87	293.6	2,128.8	46,301.0
	59	44.25	0.87	298.7	2,202.8	48,737.4
30	60	45.00	0.86	303.8	2,278.1	51,257.8
	61	45.75	0.86	308.8	2,354.7	53,863.7
31	62	46.50	0.86	313.9	2,432.5	56,556.4
	63	47.25	0.86	318.9	2,511.6	59,337.3
32	64	48.00	0.86	324.0	2,592.0	62,208.0

8 3/4″ WIDTH

No. of Lams 1½″	No. of Lams ¾″	Depth, d (inches)	Size Factor, C_F	Area A (inches^2)	Section Modulus, S (inches^3)	Moment of inertia, I (inches^4)
6	12	9.00	1.00	78.8	118.1	531.6
	13	9.75	1.00	85.3	138.6	675.8
7	14	10.50	1.00	91.9	160.8	844.1
	15	11.25	1.00	98.4	184.6	1,038.2
8	16	12.00	1.00	105.0	210.0	1,260.0
	17	12.75	0.99	111.6	237.1	1,511.3
9	18	13.50	0.99	118.1	265.8	1,794.0
	19	14.25	0.98	124.7	296.1	2,109.9
10	20	15.00	0.98	131.3	328.1	2,460.9
	21	15.75	0.97	137.8	361.8	2,848.8
11	22	16.50	0.97	144.4	397.0	3,275.5
	23	17.25	0.96	150.9	433.9	3,742.8
12	24	18.00	0.96	157.5	472.5	4,252.5
	25	18.75	0.95	164.1	512.7	4.806.5
13	26	19.50	0.95	170.6	554.5	5,406.7
	27	20.25	0.94	177.2	598.0	6,054.8
14	28	21.00	0.94	183.8	643.1	6,752.8
	29	21.75	0.94	190.3	689.9	7,502.5
15	30	22.50	0.93	196.9	738.3	8,305.7
	31	23.25	0.93	203.4	788.3	9,164.2
16	32	24.00	0.93	210.0	840.0	10,080.0
	33	24.75	0.92	216.6	893.3	11,054.8
17	34	25.50	0.92	223.1	948.3	12,090.6
	35	26.25	0.92	229.7	1,004.9	13,189.1
18	36	27.00	0.91	236.3	1,063.1	14,352.2
	37	27.75	0.91	242.8	1,123.0	15,581.7
19	38	28.50	0.91	249.4	1,184.5	16,879.6
	39	29.25	0.91	255.9	1,247.7	18,247.5
20	40	30.00	0.90	262.5	1,312.5	19,687.5
	41	30.75	0.90	269.1	1,378.9	21,201.3
21	42	31.50	0.90	275.6	1,447.0	22,790.7
	43	32.25	0.90	282.2	1,516.8	24,457.7
22	44	33.00	0.89	288.8	1,588.1	26,204.1
	45	33.75	0.89	295.3	1,661.1	28,031.6
23	46	34.50	0.89	301.9	1,735.8	29,942.2
	47	35.25	0.89	308.4	1,812.1	31,937.7
24	48	36.00	0.88	315.0	1,890.0	34,020.0
	49	36.75	0.88	321.6	1,969.6	36,190.9
25	50	37.50	0.88	328.1	2,050.8	38,452.2
	51	38.25	0.88	334.7	2,133.6	40,805.7
26	52	39.00	0.88	341.3	2,218.1	43,253.4
	53	39.75	0.88	347.8	2,304.3	45,797.1
27	54	40.50	0.87	354.4	2,392.0	48,438.6
	55	41.25	0.87	360.9	2,481.4	51,179.8
28	56	42.00	0.87	367.5	2,572.5	54,022.5
	57	42.75	0.87	374.1	2,665.2	56,968.6
29	58	43.50	0.87	380.6	2,759.5	60,019.8
	59	44.25	0.87	387.2	2,855.5	63,178.1
30	60	45.00	0.86	393.8	2,953.1	66,445.3
	61	45.75	0.86	400.3	3,052.4	69.823.3
31	62	46.50	0.86	406.9	3,153.3	73,313.8
	63	47.25	0.86	413.4	3,255.8	76,918.8
32	64	48.00	0.86	420.0	3,360.0	80,640.0
	65	48.75	0.86	426.6	3,465.8	84,479.4
33	66	49.50	0.85	433.1	3,573.3	88,438.7
	67	50.25	0.85	439.7	3,682.4	92,519.9
34	68	51.00	0.85	446.3	3,793.1	96,724.7
	69	51.75	0.85	452.8	3,905.5	101,055.0
35	70	52.50	0.85	459.4	4,019.5	105,512.7
	71	53.25	0.85	465.9	4,135.2	110,099.6
36	72	54.00	0.85	472.5	4,252.5	114,817.5
	73	54.75	0.85	479.1	4,371.4	119.668.3
37	74	55.50	0.84	485.6	4,492.0	124,653.9
	75	56.25	0.84	492.2	4,614.3	129,776.0
38	76	57.00	0.84	498.8	4,738.1	135,036.6
	77	57.75	0.84	505.3	4,863.6	140,437.4
39	78	58.50	0.84	511.9	4,990.8	145,980.4
	79	59.25	0.84	518.4	5,119.6	151,667.3
40	80	60.00	0.84	525.0	5,250.0	157,500.0
	81	60.75	0.84	531.6	5,382.1	163,480.4
41	82	61.50	0.83	538.1	5,515.8	169,610.3
	83	62.25	0.83	544.7	5,651.1	175,891.5
42	84	63.00	0.83	551.3	5,788.1	182,326.0

10 3/4″ WIDTH

No. of Lams 1½″	No. of Lams ¾″	Depth, d (inches)	Size Factor, C_F	Area A (inches^2)	Section Modulus, S (inches^3)	Moment of inertia, I (inches^4)
7	14	10.50	1.00	112.9	197.5	1,037.0
	15	11.25	1.00	120.9	226.8	1,275.5
8	16	12.00	1.00	129.0	258.0	1,548.0
	17	12.75	0.99	137.1	291.3	1,856.8
9	18	13.50	0.99	145.1	326.5	2,204.1
	19	14.25	0.98	153.2	363.8	2,592.2
10	20	15.00	0.98	161.3	403.1	3,023.4
	21	15.75	0.97	169.3	444.4	3,500.0
11	22	16.50	0.97	177.4	487.8	4,024.2
	23	17.25	0.96	185.4	533.1	4,598.3
12	24	18.00	0.96	193.5	580.5	5,224.5
	25	18.75	0.95	201.6	629.9	5,905.2
13	26	19.50	0.95	209.6	681.3	6,642.5
	27	20.25	0.94	217.7	734.7	7,438.8
14	28	21.00	0.94	225.8	790.1	8,296.3
	29	21.75	0.94	233.8	847.6	9,217.3
15	30	22.50	0.93	241.9	907.0	10,204.1
	31	23.25	0.93	249.9	968.5	11,258.9
16	32	24.00	0.93	258.0	1,032.0	12,384.0
	33	24.75	0.92	266.1	1,097.5	13,581.7
17	34	25.50	0.92	274.1	1,165.0	14,854.1
	35	26.25	0.92	282.2	1,234.6	16,203.7
18	36	27.00	0.91	290.3	1,306.1	17,632.7
	37	27.75	0.91	298.3	1,379.7	19,143.3
19	38	28.50	0.91	306.4	1,455.3	20,737.8
	39	29.25	0.91	314.4	1,532.9	22,418.4
20	40	30.00	0.90	322.5	1,612.5	24,187.5
	41	30.75	0.90	330.6	1,694.1	26,047.3
21	42	31.50	0.90	338.6	1,777.8	28,000.1
	43	32.25	0.90	346.7	1,863.4	30,048.1
22	44	33.00	0.89	354.8	1,951.1	32,193.6
	45	33.75	0.89	362.8	2,040.8	34,438.8
23	46	34.50	0.89	370.9	2,132.5	36,786.2
	47	35.25	0.89	378.9	2,226.3	39,237.8
24	48	36.00	0.88	387.0	2,322.0	41,796.0
	49	36.75	0.88	395.1	2,419.8	44,463.1
25	50	37.50	0.88	403.1	2,519.5	47,241.2
	51	38.25	0.88	411.2	2,621.3	50,132.8
26	52	39.00	0.88	419.3	2,725.1	53,139.9
	53	39.75	0.88	427.3	2,830.9	56,265.0
27	54	40.50	0.87	435.4	2,938.8	59,510.3
	55	41.25	0.87	443.4	3,048.6	62,878.1
28	56	42.00	0.87	451.5	3,160.5	66,370.5
	57	42.75	0.87	459.6	3,274.4	69,989.9
29	58	43.50	0.87	467.6	3,390.3	73,738.6
	59	44.25	0.87	475.7	3,508.2	77,618.8
30	60	45.00	0.86	483.8	3,628.1	81,632.8
	61	45.75	0.86	491.8	3,750.1	85,782.9
31	62	46.50	0.86	499.9	3,874.0	90,071.2
	63	47.25	0.86	507.9	4,000.0	94,500.2
32	64	48.00	0.86	516.0	4,128.0	99,072.0
	65	48.75	0.86	524.1	4,258.0	103,789.0
33	66	49.50	0.85	532.1	4,390.0	108.653.3
	67	50.25	0.85	540.2	4,524.1	113,667.3
34	68	51.00	0.85	548.3	4,660.1	118,833.2
	69	51.75	0.85	556.3	4,798.2	124,153.3
35	70	52.50	0.85	564.4	4,938.3	129,629.9
	71	53.25	0.85	572.4	5,080.4	135,265.2
36	72	54.00	0.85	580.5	5,224.5	141,061.5
	73	54.75	0.85	588.6	5,370.6	147,021.1
37	74	55.50	0.84	596.6	5,518.8	153,146.2
	75	56.25	0.84	604.7	5,668.9	159,439.1
38	76	57.00	0.84	612.8	5,821.1	165,902.1
	77	57.75	0.84	620.8	5,975.3	172,537.4
39	78	58.50	0.84	628.9	6,131.5	179,347.3
	79	59.25	0.84	636.9	6,289.8	186,334.1
40	80	60.00	0.84	645.0	6,450.0	193,500.0
	81	60.75	0.84	653.1	6,612.3	200,847.4
41	82	61.50	0.83	661.1	6,776.5	208,378.4
	83	62.25	0.83	669.2	6,942.8	216,095.3
42	84	63.00	0.83	677.3	7,111.1	224,000.5
	85	63.75	0.83	685.3	7,281.4	232,096.1
43	86	64.50	0.83	693.4	7,453.8	240,384.5
	87	65.25	0.83	701.4	7,628.1	248,867.9
44	88	66.00	0.83	709.5	7,804.5	257,548.5
	89	66.75	0.83	717.6	7,982.9	266,428.8
45	90	67.50	0.83	725.6	8,163.3	275,510.8
	91	68.25	0.82	733.7	8,345.7	284,796.9
46	92	69.00	0.82	741.8	8,530.1	294,289.3
	93	69.75	0.82	749.8	8,716.6	303,990.5
47	94	70.50	0.82	757.9	8,905.0	313,902.4
	95	71.25	0.82	765.9	9,095.5	324,027.5
48	96	72.00	0.82	774.0	9,288.0	334,368.0
	97	72.75	0.82	782.1	9,482.5	344,926.3
49	98	73.50	0.82	790.1	9,679.0	355,704.5
	99	74.25	0.82	798.2	9,877.6	366,704.8
50	100	75.00	0.82	806.3	10,078.1	377,929.7

Glued laminated timber

Table 19. Simple span beam table

TABLE SPECIFICATIONS

This beam design table applies for straight, simply-supported, laminated timber beams. Other beam support systems may be employed to meet varying design conditions.

Roofs should have a minimum slope of ¼ inch per foot to eliminate water ponding.

Total load carrying capacity includes beam weight. Floor beams are designed for uniform loads of 40 psf live load and 10 psf dead load.

Allowable stresses:
Bending stress, F_b = 2400 psi (reduced by size factor C F) except those marked * in which cases F_b = 2000 psi (reduced by size factor, C_F).

Shear stress, Fv = 165 psi
Modulus of elasticity, E = 1,700,000 psi except those marked * in which cases E = 1,500,000 psi.
For roof beams, Fb and Fv were increased 15% for short duration of loading.

Deflection limits:
Roof beams — 1/180 span for total load.
Floor beams — 1/360 span for 40 psf live load only.

Values for preliminary design purposes only. For more complete design information, see the AITC "Timber Construction Manual."

SPAN FT.	SPACING FT.	ROOF BEAMS—TOTAL LOAD CARRYING CAPACITY								FLOOR BEAMS TOTAL LOAD
		20 PSF	25 PSF	30 PSF	35 PSF	40 PSF	45 PSF	50 PSF	55 PSF	50 PSF
8	4	—	—	*3⅛x4½	*3⅛x4½	*3⅛x4½	*3⅛x4½	*3⅛x4½	*3⅛x6	*3⅛x6
	6	—	—	*3⅛x4½	*3⅛x6	*3⅛x6	*3⅛x6	*3⅛x6	*3⅛x6	*3⅛x6
	8	—	—	*3⅛x6	*3⅛x6	*3⅛x6	*3⅛x6	*3⅛x6	*3⅛x6	*3⅛x7½
10	4	—	—	*3⅛x6	*3⅛x6	*3⅛x6	*3⅛x6	*3⅛x6	*3⅛x6	*3⅛x7½
	6	—	—	*3⅛x6	*3⅛x6	*3⅛x6	*3⅛x7½	*3⅛x7½	*3⅛x7½	*3⅛x7½
	8	—	—	*3⅛x6	*3⅛x7½	*3⅛x7½	*3⅛x7½	*3⅛x7½	*3⅛x7½	*3⅛x9
	10	—	—	*3⅛x7½	*3⅛x7½	*3⅛x7½	*3⅛x9	*3⅛x9	*3⅛x9	*3⅛x9
12	6	—	—	*3⅛x7½	*3⅛x7½	*3⅛x7½	*3⅛x7½	*3⅛x9	*3⅛x9	*3⅛x9
	8	—	—	*3⅛x7½	*3⅛x7½	*3⅛x9	*3⅛x9	*3⅛x9	*3⅛x9	*3⅛x10½
	10	—	—	*3⅛x9	*3⅛x9	*3⅛x9	*3⅛x10½	*3⅛x10½	*3⅛x10½	*3⅛x12
	12	—	—	*3⅛x9	*3⅛x9	*3⅛x10½	*3⅛x10½	*3⅛x10½	*3⅛x12	*3⅛x12
14	8	—	—	*3⅛x9	*3⅛x9	*3⅛x10½	*3⅛x10½	*3⅛x10½	*3⅛x10½	*3⅛x12
	10	—	—	*3⅛x9	*3⅛x10½	*3⅛x10½	*3⅛x12	*3⅛x12	*3⅛x12	*3⅛x13½
	12	—	—	*3⅛x10½	*3⅛x10½	*3⅛x12	*3⅛x12	*3⅛x13½	*3⅛x13½	*3⅛x13½
	14	—	—	*3⅛x10½	*3⅛x12	*3⅛x12	*3⅛x13½	*3⅛x13½	*3⅛x15	*3⅛x15
16	8	—		*3⅛x10½	*3⅛x10½	*3⅛x10½	*3⅛x12	*3⅛x12	*3⅛x12	*3⅛x13½
	12	—		*3⅛x12	*3⅛x12	*3⅛x13½	*3⅛x13½	*3⅛x15	*3⅛x15	*3⅛x16½
	14	—	*3⅛x12	*3⅛x12	*3⅛x13½	*3⅛x13½	*3⅛x15	*3⅛x16½	*3⅛x16½	*3⅛x16½
	16	—	*3⅛x12	*3⅛x13½	*3⅛x13½	*3⅛x15	*3⅛x16½	*3⅛x16½	3⅛x16½	*5⅛x15
18	8	—		*3⅛x12	*3⅛x12	*3⅛x12	*3⅛x13½	*3⅛x13½	*3⅛x13½	*3⅛x15
	12	—	*3⅛x12	*3⅛x13½	*3⅛x13½	*3⅛x15	*3⅛x15	*3⅛x16½	3⅛x16½	3⅛x16½
	16	—	*3⅛x13½	*3⅛x15	*3⅛x16½	*3⅛x16½	3⅛x16½	*5⅛x15	*5⅛x16½	*5⅛x16½
	20	—	*3⅛x15	*3⅛x16½	3⅛x16½	3⅛x18	3⅛x18	*5⅛x16½	5⅛x16½	5⅛x16½
20	8	—		*3⅛x12	*3⅛x13½	*3⅛x13½	*3⅛x15	*3⅛x15	*3⅛x15	3⅛x16½
	12	—	*3⅛x13½	*3⅛x15	*3⅛x15	*3⅛x16½	3⅛x16½	3⅛x16½	*5⅛x15	*5⅛x16½
	16	—	*3⅛x15	*3⅛x16½	3⅛x16½	3⅛x18	3⅛x18	*5⅛x16½	5⅛x16½	5⅛x18
	20	—	*3⅛x16½	3⅛x16½	3⅛x18	*5⅛x16½	5⅛x16½	5⅛x16½	5⅛x18	5⅛x19½
24	8	—		*3⅛x15	*3⅛x15	*3⅛x16½	3⅛x16½	3⅛x16½	3⅛x18	5⅛x16½
	12	—	*3⅛x16½	3⅛x16½	3⅛x16½	3⅛x18	*5⅛x16½	5⅛x16½	5⅛x16½	5⅛x19½
	16	—	3⅛x16½	3⅛x18	5⅛x16½	5⅛x16½	5⅛x18	5⅛x18	5⅛x19½	5⅛x21
	20	—	3⅛x18	5⅛x16½	5⅛x18	5⅛x18	5⅛x19½	5⅛x19½	5⅛x21	5⅛x22½
28	8	—	*3⅛x16½	3⅛x16½	3⅛x18	3⅛x18	5⅛x16½	5⅛x16½	5⅛x16½	5⅛x19½
	12	—	3⅛x18	5⅛x16½	5⅛x16½	5⅛x18	5⅛x18	5⅛x19½	5⅛x19½	5⅛x22½
	16	—	5⅛x16½	5⅛x18	5⅛x18	5⅛x19½	5⅛x19½	5⅛x21	5⅛x22½	5⅛x24
	20	—	5⅛x18	5⅛x19½	5⅛x19½	5⅛x21	5⅛x22½	5⅛x24	5⅛x25½	5⅛x25½
32	8	—	3⅛x18	5⅛x16½	5⅛x16½	5⅛x18	5⅛x18	5⅛x19½	5⅛x19½	5⅛x22½
	12	—	5⅛x18	5⅛x18	5⅛x19½	5⅛x19½	5⅛x21	5⅛x21	5⅛x22½	5⅛x25½
	16	—	5⅛x19½	5⅛x19½	5⅛x21	5⅛x22½	5⅛x22½	5⅛x24	5⅛x25½	5⅛x27
	20	5⅛x19½	5⅛x21	5⅛x21	5⅛x22½	5⅛x24	5⅛x25½	5⅛x27	5⅛x28½	6¾x27
36	12	—	5⅛x19½	5⅛x21	5⅛x21	5⅛x22½	5⅛x24	5⅛x24	5⅛x25½	6¾x25½
	16	—	5⅛x21	5⅛x22½	5⅛x24	5⅛x25½	5⅛x25½	5⅛x27	5⅛x28½	6¾x28½
	20	5⅛x21	5⅛x22½	5⅛x24	5⅛x25½	5⅛x27	5⅛x30	6¾x27	6¾x28½	6¾x30
	24	5⅛x22½	5⅛x24	5⅛x25½	5⅛x28½	5⅛x30	6¾x27	6¾x28½	6¾x30	6¾x33
40	12	5⅛x19½	5⅛x21	5⅛x22½	5⅛x24	5⅛x25½	5⅛x25½	5⅛x27	6¾x25½	6¾x28½
	16	5⅛x22½	5⅛x24	5⅛x25½	5⅛x27	5⅛x27	5⅛x28½	6¾x27	6¾x28½	6¾x31½
	20	5⅛x24	5⅛x25½	5⅛x27	5⅛x28½	6¾x27	6¾x28½	6¾x30	6¾x31½	6¾x34½
	24	5⅛x25½	5⅛x27	5⅛x28½	6¾x27	6¾x28½	6¾x31½	6¾x33	6¾x34½	6¾x36
44	12	5⅛x22½	5⅛x24	5⅛x25½	5⅛x27	5⅛x27	5⅛x28½	6¾x27	6¾x28½	6¾x31½
	16	5⅛x24	5⅛x25½	5⅛x27	5⅛x28½	5⅛x30	6¾x28½	6¾x30	6¾x31½	6¾x34½
	20	5⅛x25½	5⅛x28½	5⅛x30	6¾x28½	6¾x30	6¾x31½	6¾x33	6¾x34½	6¾x37½
	24	5⅛x27	5⅛x30	6¾x28½	6¾x30	6¾x31½	6¾x34½	6¾x36	6¾x37½	6¾x39
48	12	5⅛x24	5⅛x25½	5⅛x27	5⅛x28½	5⅛x30	6¾x28½	6¾x30	6¾x30	6¾x34½
	16	5⅛x25½	5⅛x28½	5⅛x30	6¾x28½	6¾x30	6¾x31½	6¾x31½	6¾x34½	6¾x37½
	20	5⅛x28½	5⅛x30	6¾x30	6¾x31½	6¾x31½	6¾x34½	6¾x36	6¾x37½	8¾x37½
	24	5⅛x30	6¾x30	6¾x31½	6¾x33	6¾x34½	6¾x37½	6¾x39	8¾x36	8¾x39

SPAN FT.	SPACING FT.	ROOF BEAMS—TOTAL LOAD CARRYING CAPACITY								FLOOR BEAMS TOTAL LOAD
		20 PSF	25 PSF	30 PSF	35 PSF	40 PSF	45 PSF	50 PSF	55 PSF	50 PSF
52	12	5⅛x25½	5⅛x27	5⅛x30	5⅛x31½	6¾x30	6¾x30	6¾x31½	6¾x33	6¾x37½
	16	5⅛x28½	5⅛x30	6¾x30	6¾x31½	6¾x33	6¾x33	6¾x34½	6¾x37½	8¾x37½
	20	5⅛x30	6¾x30	6¾x31½	6¾x33	6¾x34½	6¾x37½	6¾x39	8¾x36	8¾x40½
	24	6¾x30	6¾x31½	6¾x33	6¾x36	6¾x37½	6¾x40½	8¾x37½	8¾x39	8¾x42
56	12	5⅛x27	5⅛x30	6¾x28½	6¾x30	6¾x31½	6¾x33	6¾x34½	6¾x34½	8¾x36
	16	5⅛x30	6¾x30	6¾x31½	6¾x33	6¾x34½	6¾x36	6¾x37½	8¾x36	8¾x40½
	20	6¾x30	6¾x31½	6¾x34½	6¾x36	6¾x37½	8¾x36	8¾x37½	8¾x39	8¾x43½
	24	6¾x31½	6¾x34½	6¾x36	6¾x39	8¾x36	8¾x39	8¾x40½	8¾x42	8¾x46½
60	12	5⅛x30	6¾x28½	6¾x31½	6¾x33	6¾x34½	6¾x36	6¾x36	6¾x37½	8¾x39
	16	6¾x30	6¾x31½	6¾x34½	6¾x36	6¾x37½	6¾x39	8¾x37½	8¾x37½	8¾x43½
	20	6¾x31½	6¾x34½	6¾x36	6¾x39	8¾x37½	8¾x39	8¾x40½	8¾x42	8¾x46½
	24	6¾x34½	6¾x36	6¾x39	8¾x37½	8¾x39	8¾x42	8¾x43½	8¾x45	8¾x49½
64	12	6¾x28½	6¾x31½	6¾x33	6¾x34½	6¾x36	6¾x37½	6¾x39	6¾x40½	8¾x42
	16	6¾x31½	6¾x34½	6¾x36	6¾x37½	6¾x39	8¾x37½	8¾x39	8¾x40½	8¾x46½
	20	6¾x34½	6¾x36	6¾x39	6¾x40½	8¾x39	8¾x40½	8¾x42	8¾x45	8¾x49½
	24	6¾x36	6¾x39	8¾x37½	8¾x40½	8¾x42	8¾x43½	8¾x46½	8¾x49½	8¾x52½
68	12	6¾x30	6¾x33	6¾x34½	6¾x36	6¾x39	6¾x40½	8¾x37½	8¾x39	8¾x43½
	16	6¾x33	6¾x36	6¾x39	6¾x40½	8¾x39	8¾x40½	8¾x42	8¾x43½	8¾x48
	20	6¾x36	6¾x39	8¾x37½	8¾x40½	8¾x42	8¾x43½	8¾x45	8¾x48	8¾x52½
	24	6¾x39	8¾x37½	8¾x40½	8¾x42	8¾x45	8¾x46½	8¾x49½	8¾x52½	10¾x52½
72	12	6¾x33	6¾x34½	6¾x37½	6¾x39	6¾x40½	8¾x39	8¾x40½	8¾x42	8¾x46½
	16	6¾x36	6¾x37½	6¾x40½	8¾x39	8¾x40½	8¾x42	8¾x43½	8¾x45	8¾x51
	20	6¾x37½	8¾x37½	8¾x40½	8¾x42	8¾x43½	8¾x46½	8¾x48	8¾x51	10¾x51
	24	6¾x40½	8¾x40½	8¾x42	8¾x45	8¾x46½	8¾x49½	8¾x52½	10¾x49½	10¾x55½
76	12	6¾x34½	6¾x36	6¾x39	6¾x40½	8¾x39	8¾x40½	8¾x42	8¾x43½	8¾x49½
	16	6¾x37½	6¾x40½	8¾x39	8¾x42	8¾x43½	8¾x45	8¾x46½	8¾x48	10¾x51
	20	6¾x40½	8¾x40½	8¾x42	8¾x45	8¾x46½	8¾x48	8¾x51	10¾x48	10¾x54
	24	8¾x39	8¾x42	8¾x45	8¾x46½	8¾x49½	8¾x52½	10¾x49½	10¾x52½	10¾x58½
80	12	6¾x36	6¾x39	6¾x40½	8¾x39	8¾x42	8¾x43½	8¾x45	8¾x46½	8¾x52½
	16	6¾x39	8¾x39	8¾x42	8¾x43½	8¾x45	8¾x46½	8¾x49½	8¾x51	10¾x54
	20	8¾x39	8¾x42	8¾x45	8¾x46½	8¾x49½	8¾x51	10¾x49½	10¾x51	10¾x57
	24	8¾x42	8¾x45	8¾x46½	8¾x49½	8¾x52½	10¾x51	10¾x52½	10¾x55½	10¾x61½
84	12	6¾x37½	6¾x40½	8¾x39	8¾x42	8¾x43½	8¾x45	8¾x46½	8¾x48	10¾x51
	16	8¾x37½	8¾x40½	8¾x43½	8¾x45	8¾x48	8¾x49½	8¾x51	8¾x52½	10¾x55½
	20	8¾x40½	8¾x43½	8¾x46½	8¾x49½	8¾x51	10¾x49½	10¾x51	10¾x54	10¾x60
	24	8¾x43½	8¾x46½	8¾x49½	8¾x52½	10¾x51	10¾x52½	10¾x55½	10¾x58½	10¾x64½
88	12	6¾x39	8¾x39	8¾x42	8¾x43½	8¾x45	8¾x46½	8¾x49½	8¾x51	10¾x54
	16	8¾x40½	8¾x43½	8¾x45	8¾x48	8¾x49½	8¾x52½.	10¾x49½	10¾x52½	10¾x58½
	20	8¾x43½	8¾x46½	8¾x49½	8¾x51	10¾x49½	10¾x52½	10¾x54	10¾x55½	—
	24	8¾x45	8¾x49½	8¾x52½	10¾x51	10¾x54	10¾x55½	10¾x58½	10¾x61½	—
92	12	6¾x40½	8¾x40½	8¾x43½	8¾x45	8¾x48	8¾x49½	8¾x51	8¾x52½	10¾x55½
	16	8¾x42	8¾x45	8¾x48	8¾x49½	8¾x52½	10¾x51	10¾x52½	10¾x54	10¾x61½
	20	8¾x45	8¾x48	8¾x51	10¾x49½	10¾x52½	10¾x54	10¾x57	10¾x58½	—
	24	8¾x48	8¾x51	10¾x51	10¾x54	10¾x55½	10¾x58½	10¾x61½	10¾x64½	—
96	12	8¾x39	8¾x42	8¾x45	8¾x48	8¾x49½	8¾x51	8¾x52½	10¾x51	10¾x58½
	16	8¾x43½	8¾x46½	8¾x49½	8¾x52½	10¾x51	10¾x52½	10¾x54	10¾x57	10¾x64½
	20	8¾x46½	8¾x49½	8¾x52½	10¾x52½	10¾x54	10¾x57	10¾x58½	10¾x61½	—
	24	8¾x49½	8¾x52½	10¾x52½	10¾x55½	10¾x58½	10¾x60	10¾x64½	—	—
100	12	8¾x40½	8¾x43½	8¾x46½	8¾x49½	8¾x51	10¾x49½	10¾x52½	10¾x54	10¾x60
	16	8¾x45	8¾x48	8¾x51	10¾x51	10¾x52½	10¾x55½	10¾x57	10¾x58½	—
	20	8¾x48	8¾x52½	10¾x52½	10¾x54	10¾x57	10¾x58½	10¾x61½	10¾x64½	—
	24	8¾x51	10¾x52½	10¾x55½	10¾x58½	10¾x60	10¾x63	—	—	—

CANTILEVERED AND CONTINUOUS SPAN SYSTEMS

Cantilever beam systems may be comprised of any of the various types and combinations of beam illustrated below. Cantilever systems permit longer spans or larger loads for a given size member than do simple span systems, provided member size is not controlled by compression perpendicular to grain at the supports or by horizontal shear. Substantial design economies can be effected by decreasing the depths of the members in the suspended portions of a cantilever system.

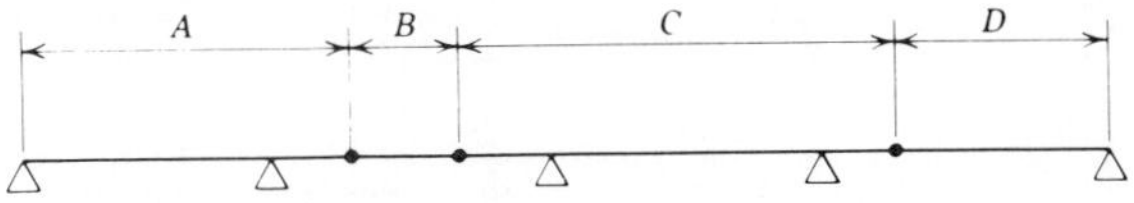

CANTILEVERED BEAM SYSTEMS. A is single cantilever, B is a suspended beam, C has a double cantilever, and D is a beam with one end suspended.

For economy, the negative bending moment at the supports of a cantilevered beam should be equal in magnitude to the positive moment.

Consideration must be given to deflection and camber in cantilevered multiple spans. When possible, roofs should be sloped the equivalent of ¼ inch per foot of horizontal distance between the level of the drain and the high point of the roof to eliminate water pockets, or provisions should be made to ensure that accumulation of water does not produce greater deflection and live loads than anticipated. Unbalanced loading conditions should be investigated for maximum bending moment, deflection, and stability.

Continuous span beams are commonly used in both building and bridge construction to reduce maximum moments, thus reducing the section size required.

Design aids for cantilever and continuous span beam systems may be found in the AITC "Timber Construction Manual."

Glued laminated timber beams are often tapered or curved to meet architectural requirements, to provide pitched roofs, or to provide a minimum depth of beam at the point of bearing.

Table 20. Cantilever beam design table

CANTILEVER BEAM TABLE ①   BEAM SPACING 20' – SEE FOOTNOTES FOR OTHER DESIGN SPECIFICATIONS.

Main Support Spacing ②, ft.	Dead Load ③, psf	Live Load, psf	TWO-SPAN SYSTEM ④ Suspended Beam	TWO-SPAN SYSTEM ④ Cantilevered Beam	THREE-SPAN SYSTEM ⑤ Suspended Beam	THREE-SPAN SYSTEM ⑤ Cantilevered Beams	THREE-SPAN SYSTEM ⑥ Suspended Beams	THREE-SPAN SYSTEM ⑥ Double Cantilevered Beam
32	10	12	*5⅛ x 16½	5⅛ x 16½	*5⅛ x 10½	5⅛ x 16½	*5⅛ x 15	*5⅛ x 15
		20	5⅛ x 16½	5⅛ x 19½	*5⅛ x 12	5⅛ x 19½	5⅛ x 18	5⅛ x 19½
		30	5⅛ x 19½	5⅛ x 25½	*5⅛ x 13½	5⅛ x 24	5⅛ x 21	5⅛ x 24
	12	12	*5⅛ x 16½	5⅛ x 16½	*5⅛ x 10½	5⅛ x 16½	*5⅛ x 16½	5⅛ x 16½
		20	5⅛ x 18	5⅛ x 21	*5⅛ x 12	5⅛ x 21	5⅛ x 18	5⅛ x 19½
		30	5⅛ x 21	5⅛ x 27	*5⅛ x 13½	5⅛ x 24	5⅛ x 21	5⅛ x 25½
	15	20	5⅛ x 19½	5⅛ x 22½	*5⅛ x 12	5⅛ x 21	5⅛ x 19½	5⅛ x 21
		30	5⅛ x 21	5⅛ x 28½	*5⅛ x 13½	5⅛ x 25½	5⅛ x 22½	5⅛ x 27
36	10	12	5⅛ x 16½	5⅛ x 18	*5⅛ x 12	5⅛ x 18	5⅛ x 16½	5⅛ x 16½
		20	5⅛ x 19½	5⅛ x 22½	*5⅛ x 13½	5⅛ x 22½	5⅛ x 19½	5⅛ x 21
		30	5⅛ x 22½	5⅛ x 28½	*5⅛ x 15	5⅛ x 27	5⅛ x 22½	5⅛ x 27
	12	12	5⅛ x 16½	5⅛ x 19½	*5⅛ x 12	5⅛ x 19½	5⅛ x 18	5⅛ x 18
		20	5⅛ x 19½	5⅛ x 24	*5⅛ x 13½	5⅛ x 24	5⅛ x 21	5⅛ x 21
		30	5⅛ x 22½	5⅛ x 30	*5⅛ x 15	5⅛ x 27	5⅛ x 24	5⅛ x 28½
	15	20	5⅛ x 21	5⅛ x 25½	*5⅛ x 13½	5⅛ x 24	5⅛ x 22½	5⅛ x 24
		30	5⅛ x 24	5⅛ x 33	*5⅛ x 16½	5⅛ x 28½	5⅛ x 25½	5⅛ x 31½
40	10	12	5⅛ x 18	5⅛ x 21	*5⅛ x 12	5⅛ x 21	5⅛ x 18	5⅛ x 18
		20	5⅛ x 21	5⅛ x 25½	*5⅛ x 15	5⅛ x 25½	5⅛ x 22½	5⅛ x 24
		30	5⅛ x 25½	5⅛ x 31½	*5⅛ x 16½	5⅛ x 30	5⅛ x 25½	5⅛ x 30
	12	12	5⅛ x 18	5⅛ x 21	*5⅛ x 12	5⅛ x 21	5⅛ x 19½	5⅛ x 19½
		20	5⅛ x 22½	5⅛ x 25½	*5⅛ x 15	5⅛ x 25½	5⅛ x 22½	5⅛ x 24
		30	5⅛ x 25½	5⅛ x 33	*5⅛ x 16½	5⅛ x 30	5⅛ x 27	5⅛ x 31½
	15	20	5⅛ x 24	5⅛ x 28½	*5⅛ x 15	5⅛ x 27	5⅛ x 24	5⅛ x 27
		30	5⅛ x 27	5⅛ x 36	5⅛ x 16½	5⅛ x 31½	5⅛ x 28½	5⅛ x 34½
44	10	12	5⅛ x 19½	5⅛ x 22½	*5⅛ x 13½	5⅛ x 22½	5⅛ x 21	5⅛ x 21
		20	5⅛ x 24	5⅛ x 28½	*5⅛ x 16½	5⅛ x 28½	5⅛ x 25½	5⅛ x 25½
		30	5⅛ x 27	5⅛ x 34½	5⅛ x 16½	5⅛ x 33	5⅛ x 28½	5⅛ x 33
	12	12	5⅛ x 21	5⅛ x 22½	*5⅛ x 13½	5⅛ x 24	5⅛ x 21	5⅛ x 21
		20	5⅛ x 24	5⅛ x 28½	*5⅛ x 16½	5⅛ x 28½	5⅛ x 25½	5⅛ x 27
		30	5⅛ x 28½	5⅛ x 36	5⅛ x 18	5⅛ x 33	5⅛ x 30	5⅛ x 34½
	15	20	5⅛ x 25½	5⅛ x 31½	5⅛ x 16½	5⅛ x 30	5⅛ x 27	5⅛ x 30
		30	5⅛ x 30	6¾ x 30	5⅛ x 18	5⅛ x 34½	5⅛ x 30	6¾ x 30
48	10	12	5⅛ x 21	5⅛ x 24	*5⅛ x 13½	5⅛ x 24	5⅛ x 22½	5⅛ x 22½
		20	5⅛ x 25½	5⅛ x 30	5⅛ x 16½	5⅛ x 30	5⅛ x 27	5⅛ x 28½
		30	5⅛ x 30	5⅛ x 37½	5⅛ x 18	5⅛ x 36	5⅛ x 31½	5⅛ x 36
	12	12	5⅛ x 22½	5⅛ x 25½	*5⅛ x 15	5⅛ x 25½	5⅛ x 24	5⅛ x 24
		20	5⅛ x 27	5⅛ x 31½	5⅛ x 16½	5⅛ x 31½	5⅛ x 28½	5⅛ x 30
		30	5⅛ x 31½	6¾ x 31½	5⅛ x 19½	5⅛ x 36	5⅛ x 31½	6¾ x 30
	15	20	5⅛ x 28½	5⅛ x 34½	5⅛ x 18	5⅛ x 33	5⅛ x 30	5⅛ x 33
		30	5⅛ x 33	6¾ x 33	5⅛ x 19½	5⅛ x 37½	5⅛ x 33	6¾ x 31½
52	10	12	5⅛ x 24	5⅛ x 27	*5⅛ x 15	5⅛ x 27	5⅛ x 24	5⅛ x 25½
		20	5⅛ x 28½	6¾ x 28½	5⅛ x 18	6¾ x 28½	5⅛ x 30	5⅛ x 31½
		30	5⅛ x 33	6¾ x 33	5⅛ x 19½	6¾ x 34½	5⅛ x 34½	6¾ x 31½
	12	12	5⅛ x 24	5⅛ x 27	*5⅛ x 16½	5⅛ x 27	5⅛ x 25½	5⅛ x 25½
		20	5⅛ x 30	6¾ x 30	5⅛ x 18	6¾ x 30	5⅛ x 30	5⅛ x 33
		30	5⅛ x 33	6¾ x 34½	5⅛ x 21	6¾ x 34½	5⅛ x 34½	6¾ x 33
	15	20	5⅛ x 31½	6¾ x 30	5⅛ x 19½	6¾ x 31½	5⅛ x 33	5⅛ x 36
		30	5⅛ x 34½	6¾ x 36	5⅛ x 21	6¾ x 36	5⅛ x 36	6¾ x 34½

CANTILEVER BEAM TABLE ①   BEAM SPACING 20′ – SEE FOOTNOTES FOR OTHER DESIGN SPECIFICATIONS.

Main Support Spacing ② ft.	Dead Load ③ psf	Live Load, psf	TWO-SPAN SYSTEM ④		THREE-SPAN SYSTEM ⑤		THREE-SPAN SYSTEM ⑥	
			Suspended Beam	Cantilevered Beam	Suspended Beam	Cantilevered Beams	Suspended Beams	Double Cantilevered Beam
56	10	12	5⅛ x 25½	5⅛ x 28½	*5⅛ x 16½	5⅛ x 28½	5⅛ x 27	5⅛ x 25½
		20	5⅛ x 31½	5⅛ x 36	5⅛ x 19½	6¾ x 31½	5⅛ x 31½	5⅛ x 33
		30	5⅛ x 36	6¾ x 36	5⅛ x 22½	6¾ x 36	5⅛ x 37½	6¾ x 34½
	12	12	5⅛ x 27	5⅛ x 30	5⅛ x 16½	5⅛ x 30	5⅛ x 27	5⅛ x 27
		20	5⅛ x 31½	6¾ x 31½	5⅛ x 19½	6¾ x 31½	5⅛ x 33	5⅛ x 34½
		30	5⅛ x 36	6¾ x 37½	5⅛ x 22½	6¾ x 37½	5⅛ x 37½	6¾ x 34½
	15	20	5⅛ x 33	6¾ x 33	5⅛ x 21	6¾ x 33	5⅛ x 34½	6¾ x 30
		30	5⅛ x 37½	6¾ x 39	5⅛ x 24	6¾ x 39	6¾ x 34½	6¾ x 37½
60	10	12	5⅛ x 27	5⅛ x 31½	5⅛ x 16½	5⅛ x 31½	5⅛ x 28½	5⅛ x 28½
		20	5⅛ x 33	6¾ x 33	5⅛ x 21	6¾ x 33	5⅛ x 34½	5⅛ x 36
		30	5⅛ x 37½	6¾ x 39	5⅛ x 24	6¾ x 39	6¾ x 34½	6¾ x 37½
	12	12	5⅛ x 28½	5⅛ x 31½	5⅛ x 18	5⅛ x 31½	5⅛ x 30	5⅛ x 30
		20	5⅛ x 34½	6¾ x 34½	5⅛ x 21	6¾ x 34½	5⅛ x 36	5⅛ x 37½
		30	6¾ x 34½	8¾ x 34½	5⅛ x 24	8¾ x 34½	6¾ x 34½	6¾ x 37½
	15	20	5⅛ x 36	6¾ x 36	5⅛ x 22½	6¾ x 36	5⅛ x 37½	6¾ x 33
		30	6¾ x 36	8¾ x 36	5⅛ x 25½	8¾ x 36	6¾ x 36	8¾ x 33
64	10	12	5⅛ x 28½	5⅛ x 33	5⅛ x 18	5⅛ x 33	5⅛ x 30	5⅛ x 30
		20	5⅛ x 33	6¾ x 36	5⅛ x 21	8¾ x 36	5⅛ x 36	6¾ x 33
		30	6¾ x 36	8¾ x 36	5⅛ x 25½	8¾ x 36	6¾ x 36	8¾ x 34½
	12	12	5⅛ x 30	5⅛ x 34½	5⅛ x 19½	5⅛ x 34½	5⅛ x 31½	5⅛ x 31½
		20	5⅛ x 36	6¾ x 36	5⅛ x 22½	6¾ x 36	6¾ x 33	6¾ x 33
		30	6¾ x 36	8¾ x 37½	5⅛ x 25½	8¾ x 37½	6¾ x 37½	8¾ x 34½
	15	20	6¾ x 33	6¾ x 37½	5⅛ x 24	6¾ x 39	6¾ x 34½	6¾ x 34½
		30	6¾ x 37½	8¾ x 39	5⅛ x 27	8¾ x 39	6¾ x 39	8¾ x 36

① This beam design table applies for straight. cantilevered. laminated timber beams. Member sizes are governed by either bending or shear. **Where building code deflection requirements apply, the member sizes must be checked.** A minimum roof slope of 1¼ in. per foot should be provided to minimize water ponding.
Specifications and allowable stresses:
  Beam spacing: 20 — 0
  Bending stress. F = 2400 psi (reduced by size factor. C_F) except those marked * in which cases F_b = 2000 psi (reduced by size factor. C_F)
  Shear stress, F_v = 165 psi
  Compression perpendicular to grain stress, $F_{c\perp}$ = 385 psi
  Duration of load factor: 1.25 for 12 psf live loads; and 1.15 for 20 and 30 psf live loads
  Member sizes are checked for full unbalanced live loading.

② Main supports are columns or bearing walls. Table is based on equal spacing of main supports.

③ Does not include weight of glulam.

④ Two-span cantilever system: Cantilevered beam extends over center support with the length of cantilever, ℓ' equal to approximately 0.20 x main support spacing, ℓ.

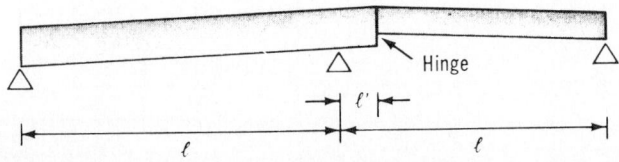

⑤ Three-span cantilever system: End members cantilevered over intermediate column supports and carrying the suspended beam. Length of cantilevers, ℓ' equal to approximately 0.25 x main support spacing, ℓ.

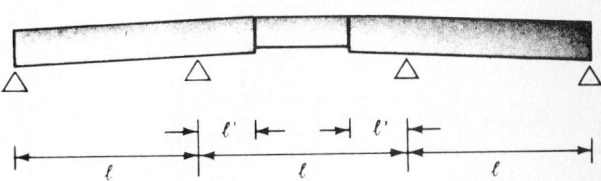

⑥ Three-span cantilever system: Center member double — cantilevered over intermediate column supports and carrying the suspended wall beams. Length of cantilevers, ℓ' equal to approximately 0.17 x main support spacing, ℓ.

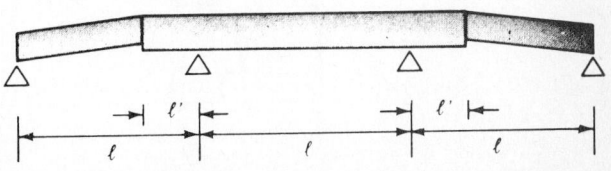

Glued laminated timber

Table 21. Arch table

Loading	Roof pitch	Wall hgt. ft.	30' span					35' span					40' span					50' span				
			Width	Base	Lower tang.	Upper tang.	Crown	Width	Base	Lower tang.	Upper tang.	Crown	Width	Base	Lower tang.	Upper tang.	Crown	Width	Base	Lower tang.	Upper tang.	Crown
VERTICAL DEAD + LIVE LOAD = 400#/FT. 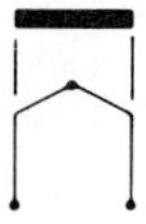	3/12	10	3⅛	8¼	12	10¾	7½	3⅛	10½	13¼	12	7½	3⅛	13¼	14½	13¼	7½	5⅛	11¾	14	13¾	7½
		12	5⅛	7½	11	10¾	7½	5⅛	7½	12	12	7½	5⅛	7½	13¼	13	7½	5⅛	10½	14¾	14½	7½
		14	5⅛	7½	12	12	7½	5⅛	7½	13½	13¼	7½	5⅛	7½	14¾	14½	7½	5⅛	9½	16¾	16¼	7½
		16	5⅛	7½	13¼	13	7½	5⅛	7½	14¾	14½	7½	5⅛	7½	16	16	7½	5⅛	8¾	18¾	17½	7½
		18	5⅛	7½	14¼	14¼	7½	5⅛	7½	16	15¾	7½	5⅛	7½	17½	17¼	7½	5⅛	8	20½	19	7½
	4/12	10	3⅛	7½	11¾	12¾	7½	3⅛	9¾	13½	12¾	7½	3⅛	12	15¼	12¾	7½	5⅛	10½	13	12¾	7½
		12	5⅛	7½	10¾	10¾	7½	5⅛	7½	11¾	11¾	7½	5⅛	7½	12¾	12½	7½	5⅛	9½	14½	13½	7½
		14	5⅛	7½	12	12	7½	5⅛	7½	13¼	13	7½	5⅛	7½	14¼	14¼	7½	5⅛	8¾	16¾	15	7½
		16	5⅛	7½	13¼	13	7½	5⅛	7½	14½	14½	7½	5⅛	7½	15¾	15½	7½	5⅛	8	18½	16½	7½
		18	5⅛	7½	14¼	14	7½	5⅛	7½	15¾	15½	7½	5⅛	7½	17	17	7½	5⅛	7½	20¼	18	7½
	6/12	12	5⅛	7½	10½	10½	7½	5⅛	7½	11½	11¼	7½	5⅛	7½	12¼	11½	7½	5⅛	8	14¾	11¾	7½
		14	5⅛	7½	11¾	11¾	7½	5⅛	7½	12¾	12¾	7½	5⅛	7½	13¾	13¼	7½	5⅛	7½	16½	12¾	7½
		16	5⅛	7½	13	12¾	7½	5⅛	7½	14	14	7½	5⅛	7½	15	15	7½	5⅛	7½	18¼	14¼	7½
		18	5⅛	7½	14	14	7½	5⅛	7½	15¼	15¼	7½	5⅛	7½	16½	16¼	7½	5⅛	7½	19¾	16	7½
	8/12	12	5⅛	7½	10¼	10	7½	5⅛	7½	11	10½	7½	5⅛	7½	12	10¼	7½	5⅛	7½	14¼	11½	7½
		14	5⅛	7½	11½	11¼	7½	5⅛	7½	12¼	12	7½	5⅛	7½	13½	11¾	7½	5⅛	7½	16	12¼	7½
		16	5⅛	7½	12¾	12½	7½	5⅛	7½	13½	13½	7½	5⅛	7½	14¾	13½	7½	5⅛	7½	17¾	13	7½
		18	5⅛	7½	13¾	13½	7½	5⅛	7½	14¾	14¾	7½	5⅛	7½	16	15	7½	5⅛	7½	19¼	14	7½
VERTICAL DEAD + LIVE LOAD = 600# FT. 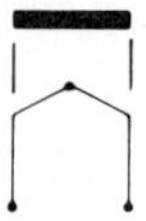	3/12	10	3⅛	12	14½	12¾	7½	5⅛	9¾	12	12¾	7½	5⅛	12¼	14	13¾	12¼	5⅛	17½	17½	15½	12¼
		12	5⅛	7½	12	12	7½	5⅛	8½	13½	13	7½	5⅛	10¾	15	13½	7½	5⅛	15½	17½	16	7½
		14	5⅛	7½	13½	13¼	7½	5⅛	7¾	15½	14¼	7½	5⅛	9¾	17½	14½	7½	5⅛	14	21	16½	7½
		16	5⅛	7½	14¾	14¾	7½	5⅛	7½	17¼	15¼	7½	5⅛	8¾	19¼	15¾	7½	5⅛	12¾	23½	17	7½
		18	5⅛	7½	16	16	7½	5⅛	7½	18¾	16¼	7½	5⅛	8	21¼	16¾	7½	6¾	9	20½	20¼	7½
	4/12	10	3⅛	11	15	15½	7½	5⅛	9	10¼	15½	7½	5⅛	11	11¼	15½	12	5⅛	15½	15½	15½	12
		12	5⅛	7½	12	12	7½	5⅛	8	13¾	12¼	7½	5⅛	9¾	15¼	12¾	7½	5⅛	14	18	15¼	7½
		14	5⅛	7½	13½	13¼	7½	5⅛	7½	15½	13¾	7½	5⅛	9	17½	13¾	7½	5⅛	12¾	21	16	7½
		16	5⅛	7½	14¾	14¾	7½	5⅛	7½	17	15	7½	5⅛	8¼	19¼	15¼	7½	5⅛	11¾	23½	16½	7½
		18	5⅛	7½	16	16	7½	5⅛	7½	18½	16¼	7½	5⅛	7½	21	16½	7½	5⅛	10¾	25½	16¾	7½
	6/12	12	5⅛	7½	12	11¼	7½	5⅛	7½	13¾	11¼	7½	5⅛	8½	15¼	11	7½	5⅛	11¾	18¼	14½	7¾
		14	5⅛	7½	13½	12¾	7½	5⅛	7½	15½	12½	7½	5⅛	7¾	17¼	12½	7½	5⅛	10¾	20¾	15¼	7½
		16	5⅛	7½	14¾	14	7½	5⅛	7½	17	14	7½	5⅛	7½	19	14	7½	5⅛	10	23	15¾	7½
		18	5⅛	7½	16	15¼	7½	5⅛	7½	18¼	15½	7½	5⅛	7½	20½	15¼	7½	5⅛	9½	25	16½	7½
	8/12	12	5⅛	7½	12	10½	7½	5⅛	7½	13½	10¼	7½	5⅛	7½	15¼	11	7½	5⅛	10	18	14	9½
		14	5⅛	7½	13¼	12¼	7½	5⅛	7½	15¼	11½	7½	5⅛	7½	17	11¾	7½	5⅛	9¼	20¼	15	8
		16	5⅛	7½	14½	13½	7½	5⅛	7½	16½	13¼	7½	5⅛	7½	18½	12¾	7½	5⅛	8¾	22¼	15¾	7½
		18	5⅛	7½	15¾	14¾	7½	5⅛	7½	18	14¼	7½	5⅛	7½	20¼	13¾	7½	5⅛	8¼	24¼	16¼	7½
VERTICAL DEAD + LIVE LOAD = 800# FT. 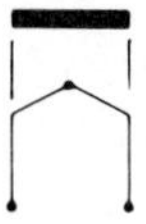	3/12	10	5⅛	10	12¼	12¼	12¼	5⅛	13	13¾	13¾	12¼	5⅛	16	16	14½	12¼	5⅛	22¾	22¾	18½	12¼
		12	5⅛	8¾	13¾	12	7½	5⅛	11¼	15¾	12½	7½	5⅛	14	17¼	13¼	7½	5⅛	20½	20½	18½	12¼
		14	5⅛	7¾	15¾	12¾	7½	5⅛	10	18¼	13¼	7½	5⅛	12¾	20½	13¾	7½	5⅛	18½	24½	19	12¼
		16	5⅛	7½	17½	13¾	7½	5⅛	9¼	20¼	14	7½	5⅛	11½	22¾	14½	7½	6¾	13	22	18¾	12¼
		18	5⅛	7½	19¼	14¼	7½	5⅛	8¼	22¼	14¾	7½	5⅛	10½	25	15¼	7½	6¾	12	24	20	12¼
	4/12	10	5⅛	9¼	9¾	18½	12	5⅛	11¾	11¾	18½	12	5⅛	14½	14½	18½	12	5⅛	20½	20½	18½	12
		12	5⅛	8	14	11½	7½	5⅛	10½	16	11¾	7½	5⅛	12¾	17¾	13	7½	5⅛	18½	20¾	17½	12
		14	5⅛	7½	16	12½	7½	5⅛	9½	18¼	12¾	7½	5⅛	11¾	20½	13½	7½	5⅛	16¾	24¾	18¼	12
		16	5⅛	7½	17½	13½	7½	5⅛	8½	20¼	13¾	7½	5⅛	10¾	22¾	13¾	7½	6¾	12	22	17¾	12
		18	5⅛	7½	19	14½	7½	5⅛	7¾	22	14¾	7½	5⅛	9¾	25	14½	7½	6¾	11	23¾	19¼	12
	6/12	12	5⅛	7½	14¼	10¾	7½	5⅛	9	16¼	10½	7½	5⅛	11	18	12½	7½	5⅛	15¼	21½	16½	11¼
		14	5⅛	7½	16	11¾	7½	5⅛	8¼	18¼	11¾	7½	5⅛	10	20¼	13¼	7½	5⅛	14¼	24½	17¼	11¼
		16	5⅛	7½	17½	13	7½	5⅛	7½	20	13	7½	5⅛	9¼	22½	13¾	7½	6¾	10¼	21½	16	11¼
		18	5⅛	7½	19	14	7½	5⅛	7½	21¾	14	7½	5⅛	8¾	24½	14¼	7½	6¾	9½	23	17½	11¼
	8/12	12	5⅛	7½	14¼	9¾	7½	5⅛	8	16	10¾	7½	5⅛	9½	17¾	12½	8	5⅛	13¼	21¼	16	11
		14	5⅛	7½	15¾	11¼	7½	5⅛	7½	18	11½	7½	5⅛	9	20	13½	7½	5⅛	12½	24	17	10½
		16	5⅛	7½	17¼	12½	7½	5⅛	7½	19¾	12	7½	5⅛	8¼	22	14	7½	6¾	9	20¾	16	10½
		18	5⅛	7½	18¾	13½	7½	5⅛	7½	21½	13	7½	5⅛	7¾	24	14½	7½	6¾	8½	22½	16½	10½
VERTICAL DEAD + LIVE LOAD = 1000# /FT. 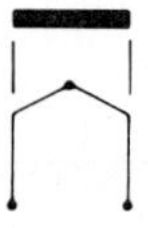	3/12	10	5⅛	12½	12½	18½	12¼	5⅛	16	16	18½	12¼	5⅛	19¾	19¾	18½	12¼	5⅛	28¼	28¼	23	17
		12	5⅛	10¾	15½	11¼	7½	5⅛	13¾	17½	13	7½	5⅛	17½	19	16	12¼	5⅛	25	25	22¼	12¼
		14	5⅛	9½	18	11¾	7½	5⅛	12½	20½	12¾	7½	5⅛	15¾	23	15¾	12¼	6¾	17½	22	18¾	12¼
		16	5⅛	8¾	20	12¼	7½	5⅛	11¼	23	12¾	7½	6¾	11	20½	17¼	12¼	6¾	16	24¾	19	12¼
		18	5⅛	8	22	12¾	7½	5⅛	10¼	25¼	13¼	7½	6¾	10	22¼	18½	12¼	6¾	14¾	27	19½	12¼
	4/12	10	5⅛	11½	11½	23	12	5⅛	14½	14½	23	12	5⅛	17¾	17¾	23	12	5⅛	25¼	25¼	23	16¾
		12	5⅛	10	15¾	11	7½	5⅛	12¾	18	13	7½	5⅛	16	19¾	15¾	12	5⅛	22½	22½	21¾	12
		14	5⅛	9	18	11¾	7½	5⅛	11½	20¾	12¾	7½	5⅛	14½	23¼	15½	12	6¾	16	22¼	18	12
		16	5⅛	8¼	20	12¼	7½	5⅛	10½	23	12½	7½	6¾	10¼	20½	16¾	12	6¾	14¾	24¾	18½	12
		18	5⅛	7½	21¾	13¼	7½	5⅛	9¾	25¼	13	7½	6¾	9½	22	18¼	12	6¾	13¾	26¾	19	12
	6/12	12	5⅛	8¾	16¼	10	7½	5⅛	11	18¼	11¾	7½	5⅛	13¾	20½	14¼	11¼	5⅛	19	24	19	11¼
		14	5⅛	8	18	11¼	7½	5⅛	10¼	20¾	12¼	7½	5⅛	12½	23¼	14½	11¼	6¾	13½	22	17¼	11¼
		16	5⅛	7½	20	12	7½	5⅛	9½	22¾	12½	7½	5⅛	11¾	25¾	15	11¼	6¾	12¾	24¼	17¾	11¼
		18	5⅛	7½	21¾	12¾	7½	5⅛	8¾	25	13	7½	6¾	8¼	21¾	17¼	11¼	6¾	11¾	26¼	18½	11¼
	8/12	12	5⅛	7¾	16	9¾	7½	5⅛	9¾	18¼	12	7½	5⅛	12	20¼	14	10½	5⅛	16¼	24	17¾	12½
		14	5⅛	7½	18	10½	7½	5⅛	9	20¼	12¾	7½	5⅛	11	22¾	14¾	10½	6¾	11¾	21½	16¾	10½
		16	5⅛	7½	19¾	11½	7½	5⅛	8½	22½	13¼	7½	5⅛	10¼	25¼	15½	10½	6¾	11	23½	17¾	10½
		18	5⅛	7½	21½	12¼	7½	5⅛	8	24½	13½	7½	6¾	7½	21	16½	10½	6¾	10½	25¼	18½	10½
VERTICAL DEAD = 240#/FT. HORIZONTAL WIND = 320#/FT. 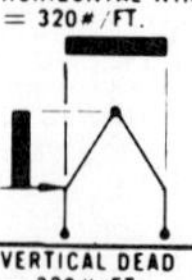	10/12	8	5⅛	7½	7½	11	7½	5⅛	7½	7½	12	10¼	5⅛	7½	8¼	13	12¾	5⅛	7½	9¼	15½	15½
		10	5⅛	7½	9¼	12½	12½	5⅛	7½	10	13¼	8	5⅛	7½	10¾	14¼	11¾	5⅛	7½	12	16¼	16¼
		12	5⅛	7½	11¼	13¾	13¾	5⅛	7½	12	14¾	7½	5⅛	7½	12¾	15¾	9¾	5⅛	7½	14¼	17½	16
	12/12	8	5⅛	7½	7½	12½	8¾	5⅛	7½	8¼	13½	12	5⅛	7½	8¾	14¾	14½	5⅛	7½	9¾	17½	17½
		10	5⅛	7½	9¾	13¾	9	5⅛	7½	10½	15	10¼	5⅛	7½	11	16¼	13¾	5⅛	7½	12½	18½	18½
		12	5⅛	7½	11¾	15¼	15¼	5⅛	7½	12½	16½	9	5⅛	7½	13¼	17½	11¾	5⅛	7½	14¾	20	18¼
	14/12	8	5⅛	7½	8¾	13¾	10½	5⅛	7½	9	15	13¾	5⅛	7½	9½	16¼	16¼	5⅛	7½	10¼	19½	19½
		10	5⅛	7½	11¼	15¼	8¼	5⅛	7½	11½	16½	12¼	5⅛	7½	12½	18	15¾	5⅛	7¾	13¼	20½	20½
		12	5⅛	7½	13¼	17	17	5⅛	7½	14	18	8¼	5⅛	7½	14½	19½	14¼	5⅛	8¼	16	22	20¾
	16/12	8	5⅛	7½	10	15	12½	5⅛	7½	10½	16¼	15¾	5⅛	7½	11	18	18	5⅛	9	11	21½	21½
		10	5⅛	7½	12¼	16½	9½	5⅛	7½	13	18	14½	5⅛	7¾	14	19½	18	5⅛	9¼	14¾	22¾	22¾
		12	5⅛	7½	14¾	18¼	7½	5⅛	7½	15½	19¾	11½	5⅛	8¼	16¼	21¼	16¾	5⅛	9¾	17½	24	23½
VERTICAL DEAD = 320# FT. HORIZONTAL WIND = 320# FT. 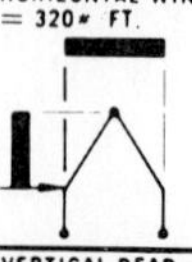	10/12	8	5⅛	7½	7½	10¾	9	5⅛	7½	8¼	11¾	11½	5⅛	7½	9	13	13	5⅛	8	10	15¾	15¾
		10	5⅛	7½	10	12	7½	5⅛	7½	10¾	13	10½	5⅛	7½	11½	14	13½	5⅛	7¾	13	16½	16½
		12	5⅛	7½	12	13¼	13¼	5⅛	7½	12¾	14¼	8½	5⅛	7½	13¾	15¼	12½	5⅛	7¾	15¾	17¼	17¼
	12/12	8	5⅛	7½	8¼	12¼	10¼	5⅛	7½	9	13¼	13¼	5⅛	7½	9½	14¾	14¾	5⅛	7¾	10½	17¾	17¾
		10	5⅛	7½	10½	13½	9	5⅛	7½	11¼	14¾	12¼	5⅛	7½	12	15¾	15¼	5⅛	7¾	13½	18¾	18¾
		12	5⅛	7½	12½	15	9	5⅛	7½	13¼	16	10¼	5⅛	7½	14¼	17¼	14¼	5⅛	7¾	16	19½	19½
	14/12	8	5⅛	7½	8¾	13½	12	5⅛	7½	9¼	14¾	14¾	5⅛	7½	10	16½	16½	5⅛	7¾	10½	19¾	19¾
		10	5⅛	7½	10¾	15	10¼	5⅛	7½	11¾	16¼	14¼	5⅛	7½	12½	17½	17¼	5⅛	7¾	13¾	20¾	20¾
		12	5⅛	7½	12¾	16½	8¼	5⅛	7½	13¾	17¾	12½	5⅛	7½	14¾	19¼	16½	5⅛	8	16½	21¾	21¾
	16/12	8	5⅛	7½	9½	15	13¾	5⅛	7½	9¾	16¼	16¼	5⅛	7½	10¼	18¼	18¼	5⅛	8¼	10¾	22	22
		10	5⅛	7½	11¾	16½	12¼	5⅛	7½	12¾	18	16¼	5⅛	7½	13	19¼	19¼	5⅛	8½	14	23	23
		12	5⅛	7½	14¼	18	7¾	5⅛	7½	14¾	19½	14½	5⅛	7½	15¾	21	18¾	5⅛	9	16¾	24¼	24¼
VERTICAL DEAD = 480#/FT. HORIZONTAL WIND = 320#/FT. 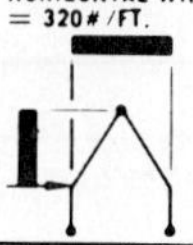	10/12	8	5⅛	7½	9	10½	10½	5⅛	7½	9¾	12	12	5⅛	8	10½	13½	13½	5⅛	10¼	11¼	16½	16½
		10	5⅛	7½	11¼	11½	10¼	5⅛	7½	12¼	12½	12½	5⅛	7¾	13¼	14	14	5⅛	10	15¼	17	17
		12	5⅛	7½	13½	12¾	8¾	5⅛	7½	14¾	13½	12½	5⅛	7¾	16	14¾	14¾	5⅛	9¾	18	17½	17½
	12/12	8	5⅛	7½	9¼	12	12	5⅛	7½	10¼	13½	13½	5⅛	7¾	11	15¼	15¼	5⅛	9¾	11¾	18½	18½
		10	5⅛	7½	11¾	13¼	11½	5⅛	7½	12¾	14¼	14¼	5⅛	7¾	13¾	15¾	15¾	5⅛	9¾	15½	19	19
		12	5⅛	7½	13¾	14½	10	5⅛	7½	15	15½	14	5⅛	7¾	16¼	16¾	16¾	5⅛	9½	18¼	19¾	19¾
	14/12	8	5⅛	7½	9¾	13¼	13¼	5⅛	7½	10½	15	15	5⅛	7¾	11¼	17	17	5⅛	9½	12	20½	20½
		10	5⅛	7½	12	14¾	13	5⅛	7½	13	16	16	5⅛	7¾	14	17¾	17¾	5⅛	9½	15½	21¼	21¼
		12	5⅛	7½	14¼	16	11½	5⅛	7½	15½	17½	15½	5⅛	7¾	16½	18¾	18¾	5⅛	9½	18½	22¼	22¼
	16/12	8	5⅛	7½	10	14¾	14¾	5⅛	7½	10¾	16¾	16¾	5⅛	7¾	11½	18¾	18¾	5⅛	9½	12	22¾	22¾
		10	5⅛	7½	12¼	16¼	14½	5⅛	7½	13¼	17¾	17¾	5⅛	7¾	14¼	19½	19½	5⅛	9½	15½	23½	23½
		12	5⅛	7½	14½	17¾	13¼	5⅛	7½	15¾	19¼	17½	5⅛	7¾	17	20¾	20¾	5⅛	9½	18¾	24½	24½

WALL HGT. FT.	60′ SPAN					70′ SPAN					80′ SPAN					90′ SPAN				
	WIDTH	BASE	LOWER TANG.	UPPER TANG.	Crown	WIDTH	BASE	LOWER TANG.	UPPER TANG.	Crown	WIDTH	BASE	LOWER TANG.	UPPER TANG.	Crown	WIDTH	BASE	LOWER TANG.	UPPER TANG.	Crown
12	5⅛	14	16¼	16¾	7½	5⅛	17¾	17¾	20	7½	5⅛	21¾	21¾	23	7½	6¾	20	20	22¾	8
14	5⅛	12¾	19½	17½	7½	5⅛	16¼	22	20¾	7½	5⅛	20	24	24	7½	6¾	18½	21½	24	7½
16	5⅛	11¾	22	17¾	7½	5⅛	15	25	21¼	7½	6¾	14¼	22½	22	7½	6¾	17¼	24¾	24¾	7½
18	5⅛	10¾	24	19¼	7½	6¾	10¾	22	21¼	7½	6¾	13¼	24½	22¾	7½	6¾	16	27	25¾	7½
20	6¾	7¾	22	22	7½	6¾	10	23½	23¼	7½	6¾	12½	26½	23	7½	6¾	15	29¼	26	7½
12	5⅛	12½	16¾	15¾	7½	5⅛	15¾	18½	18¾	7¾	5⅛	19¼	20	21½	9½	5⅛	22¾	22¾	24¼	12
14	5⅛	11½	19½	16½	7½	5⅛	14½	22	19½	7½	5⅛	17¾	24¼	22¾	8¼	6¾	16¼	21½	22¼	8½
16	5⅛	10½	21¾	17	7½	5⅛	13½	24½	20¼	7½	6¾	12¾	22	20¾	7½	6¾	15¼	24¼	23¼	7½
18	5⅛	10	23¾	17¾	7½	6¾	9¾	21½	19½	7½	6¾	12	24	21¼	7½	6¾	14¼	26½	24¼	7½
20	5⅛	9¼	25½	19¼	7½	6¾	9	23	21½	7½	6¾	11¼	25¾	22	7½	6¾	13½	28½	24¾	7½
12	5⅛	10¼	16¾	14¼	8¼	5⅛	12¾	18¾	16¾	10½	5⅛	15¼	20½	19	13¼	5⅛	18	22¼	21¼	16
14	5⅛	9½	19	15¼	7½	5⅛	12	21½	17¾	9	5⅛	14½	23¾	20¼	11½	6¾	13	21	19¾	12
16	5⅛	9	21	16	7½	5⅛	11¼	23¾	18¾	7¾	6¾	10½	21¼	18¾	8½	6¾	12¼	23¼	21	10½
18	5⅛	8½	23	16½	7½	6¾	8	20¾	17¼	7½	6¾	9¾	23	19½	7½	6¾	11¾	25¼	22	9¼
12	5⅛	8¾	16½	13½	10	5⅛	10¾	18½	15½	12¾	5⅛	12¾	20¼	17¼	16	5⅛	15	22	19¼	19¼
14	5⅛	8¼	18½	14½	8¾	5⅛	10¼	20¾	16¾	11¼	5⅛	12¼	23	18¾	14	5⅛	14¼	25¼	20¾	17
16	5⅛	7¾	20½	15½	7½	5⅛	9½	23	17¾	9¾	5⅛	11½	25½	20	12½	6¾	10¼	22¼	19½	12¾
18	5⅛	7½	22¼	16¼	7½	5⅛	9¼	25¼	18¾	8¾	6¾	8½	22	18½	9¼	6¾	10	24	20½	11½
12	5⅛	20½	20½	20¼	7½	5⅛	26¼	26¼	24	12¼	6¾	25	25	24½	12¼	6¾	29¾	29¾	27½	12¼
14	5⅛	18¾	24	21	7½	6¾	18½	22	22¼	12¼	6¾	23	23½	26	12¼	6¾	27½	27½	29¼	12¼
16	6¾	13¼	22	19	7½	6¾	17¼	25	23	12¼	6¾	21¼	27½	26¾	12¼	6¾	25½	30	30¼	12¼
18	6¾	12¼	24	20¼	7½	6¾	16	27¼	23½	12¼	6¾	19¾	30½	27¼	12¼	6¾	23¾	33½	31	12¼
20	6¾	11½	25¾	21¾	7½	6¾	14¾	29½	24	12¼	6¾	18½	33	28	12¼	8¾	17½	30	28¼	12¼
12	5⅛	18¼	20¼	19¼	7½	5⅛	23¼	23¼	22¾	12	6¾	21¾	21¾	23	12	6¾	25¾	25¾	25½	12¾
14	5⅛	17	24¼	20	7½	6¾	16½	22	21¼	12	6¾	20¼	24¼	24¼	12	6¾	24	26	27¼	12
16	6¾	12	21¾	18¼	7½	6¾	15½	24¾	21¾	12	6¾	18¾	27¼	25	12	6¾	22½	29¾	28¼	12
18	6¾	11¼	23½	18¾	7½	6¾	14½	27	22½	12	6¾	17¾	30	26	12	6¾	21¼	32¾	29¼	12
20	6¾	10½	25¼	20½	7½	6¾	13½	28¾	23	12	6¾	16¾	32¼	26½	12	8¾	15½	19¼	26¾	12
12	5⅛	15¼	21	17½	10¼	5⅛	18¾	23¼	20½	13¼	5⅛	22¾	25½	23½	16¼	6¾	20½	22¼	22¾	17
14	5⅛	14	24	18½	8¾	6¾	13½	21¾	19¼	11¼	6¾	16¼	23¾	22	12	6¾	19¼	26	24¼	14¾
16	6¾	10¼	21¼	17¼	7½	6¾	12¾	24	20	11¼	6¾	15½	26½	23	11¼	6¾	18¼	29	25½	13
18	6¾	9½	22¾	17¾	7½	6¾	12	26	21	11¼	6¾	14¾	28¾	23¾	11¼	6¾	17¼	31½	26¾	11¾
12	5⅛	13	20¾	16½	12½	5⅛	16	23¼	19	16	5⅛	19	25½	21¼	19¾	6¾	17	22¼	20½	20¼
14	5⅛	12¼	23¼	17¾	10¾	6¾	11½	21	18	12	6¾	13¾	23¼	20¼	14¾	6¾	16	25¼	22¼	18
16	6¾	8¾	20½	16½	8	6¾	11	23	19¼	10½	6¾	13	25½	21½	13¼	6¾	15½	27¾	23¾	16
18	6¾	8¼	22	17½	7½	6¾	10½	25	20	10½	6¾	12½	27½	22½	11¾	6¾	14¾	30¼	25	14½
12	5⅛	27¼	27¼	23	12¼	6¾	26¾	26¾	24¼	12¼	6¾	32½	32½	27¾	12¼	6¾	38¾	38¾	31	12½
14	6¾	19¼	22½	21¼	12¼	6¾	24½	24½	25¾	12¼	6¾	30	30	29½	12¼	8¾	28¼	28¼	29¾	12¼
16	6¾	17½	25¾	21¾	12¼	6¾	22½	28¾	26¼	12¼	6¾	27¾	31¾	30¾	12¼	8¾	26¼	29	30¾	12¼
18	6¾	16¼	28	22¼	12¼	6¾	21	31¾	26¾	12¼	8¾	20¼	29½	27¾	12¼	8¾	24½	32¼	31¾	12¼
20	6¾	15	30¼	22½	12¼	8¾	15¼	28¼	24¾	12¼	8¾	19	31¾	28½	12¼	8¾	23	34¾	32¼	12¼
12	5⅛	24¼	24¼	22	12	6¾	23½	23½	23	12	6¾	28½	28½	26	12½	6¾	33¾	33¾	29¼	15¼
14	6¾	17¼	22¾	20¼	12	6¾	21¾	25¼	24¼	12	6¾	26½	27½	28	12	6¾	31½	31½	31¼	12¾
16	6¾	16	25½	21	12	6¾	20¼	28¾	25	12	6¾	24¾	31¾	28¾	12	8¾	23	29	29	12
18	6¾	14¾	27¾	21½	12	6¾	19	31½	25¾	12	8¾	18¼	29	26½	12	8¾	21¾	31¾	29¾	12
20	6¾	13¾	29¾	22	12	6¾	17¾	33¾	26¼	12	8¾	17	31	27¼	12	8¾	20½	34	30¾	12
12	5⅛	20	24¼	20¼	12	6¾	19	22	21	13	6¾	23	23¾	23¾	16¼	6¾	27	27	26¼	19¾
14	6¾	14¼	22½	18¾	11¼	6¾	17¾	25¼	22	11¼	6¾	21½	27¾	25	14¼	6¾	25½	30	28	17½
16	6¾	13½	24¾	19¾	11¼	6¾	16¾	28	23	11¼	6¾	20¼	31	26¼	12½	6¾	24	33¾	29½	15½
18	6¾	12¾	26¾	20½	11¼	6¾	16	30½	24	11¼	6¾	19¼	33¾	27½	11¼	8¾	17¾	30¼	27¼	11¾
12	5⅛	17	24½	19	14¾	6¾	16	22	19¼	16	6¾	19¼	24	21½	19¾	6¾	22½	25¾	23¾	23¾
14	6¾	12¼	22	18	10¾	6¾	15¼	24½	20¾	14	6¾	18¼	27¼	23¼	17½	6¾	21¼	29½	25¾	21
16	6¾	11½	24	19	10½	6¾	14½	27	22	12¼	6¾	17¼	30	24¾	15½	6¾	20¼	32¾	27¼	19
18	6¾	11	26	20	10½	6¾	13¾	29¼	23	11	6¾	16½	32½	26	13¾	8¾	15¼	29	25½	14½
12	6¾	26	26	22½	12¼	6¾	32¾	32¾	26½	12¼	6¾	40½	40½	30¾	17	8¾	37¾	37¾	30¾	17
14	6¾	23½	25	23¾	12¼	6¾	30	30	28½	12¼	6¾	37¼	37¼	32¾	17	8¾	35	35	32¾	17
16	6¾	21¾	28¾	24¼	12¼	6¾	27¾	32¼	29¼	12¼	8¾	27	29¾	30½	17	8¾	32½	32½	34½	17
18	6¾	20	31½	24¾	12¼	8¾	20¼	29¾	26½	12¼	8¾	25¼	33	31	17	8¾	30¼	36	35½	17
20	8¾	14½	28	23½	12¼	8¾	18¾	31¾	27	12¼	8¾	23½	35½	31¾	17	8¾	28½	39	36	17
12	6¾	23	23	21½	12	6¾	29	29	25¼	12	6¾	35¼	35¼	29¼	16¾	8¾	32¾	32¾	28¾	16¾
14	6¾	21¼	25½	22½	12	6¾	26¾	28	27	12	6¾	33	33	31	16¾	8¾	30½	30½	31	16¾
16	6¾	19¾	28¾	23¼	12	6¾	25	32¼	27¾	12	8¾	24	29¾	28½	16¾	8¾	28¾	32	32¼	16¾
18	6¾	18¼	31¼	24	12	8¾	18¼	29¼	25½	12	8¾	22½	32½	29½	16¾	8¾	27	35½	33¼	16¾
20	6¾	17¼	33¾	24¼	12	8¾	17¼	31¼	26	12	8¾	21¼	35	30¼	16¾	8¾	25½	38¼	34¼	16¾
12	6¾	19	22	19¾	11½	6¾	23½	24¼	23¼	14¾	6¾	28½	28½	26¼	18½	6¾	33¼	33¼	29	22¾
14	6¾	17¾	25¼	21	11¼	6¾	22	28¼	24½	13	6¾	26¾	31	28	16¼	8¾	24¾	28½	27¾	16¾
16	6¾	16½	28	22	11¼	6¾	20¾	31½	25¾	11¼	8¾	19¾	29	26	15¾	8¾	23½	31½	29¼	15¾
18	6¾	15¾	30½	22¾	11¼	8¾	15¼	28¼	23¾	11¼	8¾	18¾	31¼	27	15¾	8¾	22¼	34¼	30¼	15¾
12	6¾	16¼	22	18¾	14	6¾	20	24½	21½	18	6¾	23¾	26¾	24¼	22¼	6¾	27¾	28¾	26¾	26¾
14	6¾	15¼	24¾	20¼	12¼	6¾	18¾	27¾	23¼	15¾	6¾	22½	30¾	26	19¾	6¾	26½	33¼	28¾	24
16	6¾	14¼	27¼	21¼	10¾	6¾	18	30½	24½	14	8¾	16¾	28	24¼	15	8¾	19¾	30½	27	18½
18	6¾	13¾	29½	22¼	10½	6¾	17	33¼	25¾	12½	8¾	16	30	25¾	14¾	8¾	18¾	32¾	28½	16½

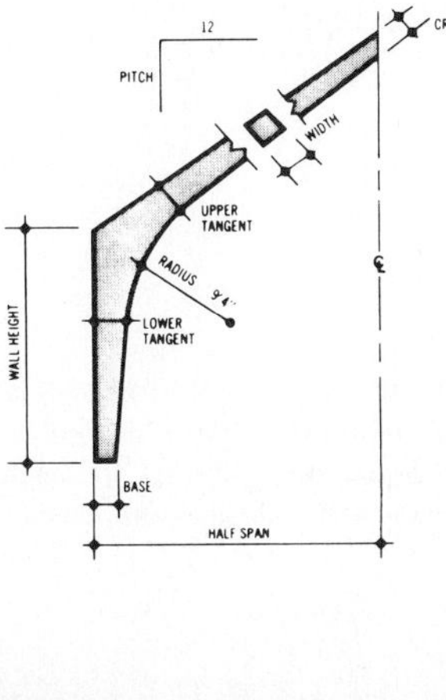
12
PITCH
CROWN
WIDTH
UPPER TANGENT
RADIUS 9'4"
LOWER TANGENT
WALL HEIGHT
BASE
HALF SPAN

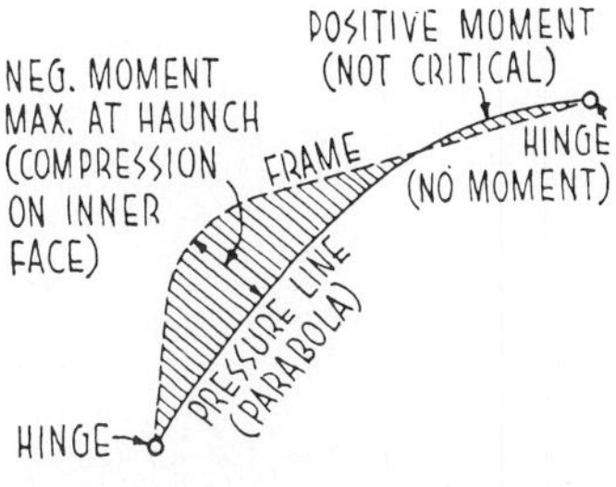
POSITIVE MOMENT (NOT CRITICAL)
NEG. MOMENT MAX. AT HAUNCH (COMPRESSION ON INNER FACE)
FRAME
HINGE (NO MOMENT)
PRESSURE LINE (PARABOLA)
HINGE

Typical moment curve of three-hinged frame arch. Uniform loading across entire span (half span only shown).

VALUES FOR PRELIMINARY DESIGN PURPOSES ONLY

For more complete design information see the AITC Timber Construction Manual. Sizes are based on Douglas fir laminated timber, developing an allowable shear stress of 165 psi and with a bending radius of 9 feet 4 inches. For Southern pine laminated timber, an allowable shear stress of 200 psi and a bending radius of 7 feet 0 inches may be used.

For roof pitches less than 10/12, the critical loading is generally the combined dead and live load on the horizontal projection of the full span. For roof pitches of 10/12 or greater, the critical loading is generally a combination of dead load and horizontal wind load. Sizes shown are determined from a uniformly distributed wind load applied on the vertical projection of the roof arm with a concentrated wind load equal to ½ the total wind load on the wall height acting at the haunch.

In the combined stress analysis, it was assumed that the bending portion of the loading exceeded the axial compression portion.

The section sizes shown in this table are in inches and are based on the following design criteria:

1. Uniform loading
2. Radius of curvature at the haunch = 9 ft 4 in.
3. Allowable stresses:

Bending stress, $F_b = 2400$ psi (reduced by curvature factor when applicable)

Shear stress, $F_v = 165$ psi

Compression parallel to grain stress, $F_c = 1500$ psi (adjusted for l/d ratio)

Modulus of elasticity, $E = 1{,}600{,}000$ psi

These stresses were increased 15% for short duration of loading and 33⅓% for wind loading when applicable.

4. Vertical arch legs are laterally supported.
5. Dead load equal to one-third of the total vertical load.

When arch deflection is a concern, arch sizes should be checked for deflection at the time of size selection.

RADIAL ARCHES

Glued laminated radial arches are well suited to achieve large, unobstructed, clear span enclosures for a variety of uses. They may be either buttressed or tied arches depending upon soil conditions and other building requirements. In the buttressed arch type, horizontal and vertical reactions are taken through concrete abutments. In the tied arch type, the horizontal reaction is taken by steel tie rods located at the ceiling height. This type of arch is usually set on masonry walls or columns.

PRELIMINARY DESIGN PROCEDURE

The following procedure may be used for determining radial arch sections for preliminary architectural planning and estimating purposes. This procedure should be used for preliminary design purposes only, since portions of it are empirical and cannot be derived rationally. In all cases, the data is subject to specific design requirements of local building codes or special conditions. A complete design check should be made in accordance with the AITC Timber Construction Manual.

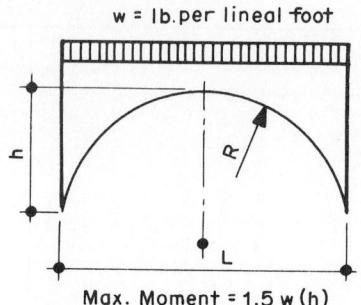

$w = lb.\ per\ lineal\ foot$

Max. Moment = 1.5 w (h)

Span (L)	= 90 ft
Rise (h)	= 30 ft
Spacing	= 16 ft
Total Load (TL)	
(live plus dead load	
on horizontal pro-	
jection)	= 50 lb/ft²
Allowable bending	
stress (F_b)	= 2400 lb/in.²

w_{TL} = (spacing) (TL) = (16)(50) = 800 plf

(1) Determine the required radius (R) either by a graphical procedure or by the formula:

$$R = \frac{4h^2 + L^2}{8h}$$

$$R = \frac{(4)(30^2) + (90^2)}{(8)(30)} = 48.75\ ft$$

(2) Maximum bending moment (M) due to total loading = 1.5 wh²

M = (1.5)(800)(30²) = 1,080,000 in.-lb

(3) Determine the limiting bending stress (F_b') using Figure 1.

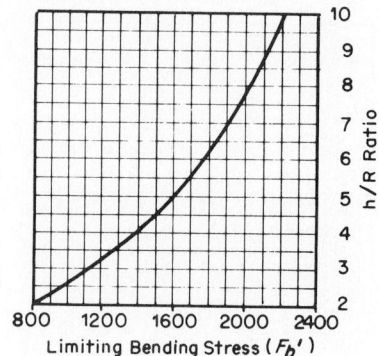

Limiting Bending Stress (F_b')

$$\frac{h}{R} = \frac{30}{48.75} = 0.62$$

Entering the graph with h/R = 0.62 determine F_b' to be 1800 psi as the limiting bending stress.

(4) Section modulus (S) required $= \dfrac{M}{F_b'C_F}$

where C_F = size factor
For preliminary purposes assume C_F = 0.90

$$S = \frac{1,080,000}{(1800)(0.90)} = 667\ in.^3$$

(5) From the Section Properties table, for a 1½" laminated thickness, select the section having the least area with a section modulus equal to, or greater than, the value calculated and having a depth to width ratio of less than 5 to 1. Select a 6¾" × 25½" section with A = 172 in.²; and S = 732 in.³

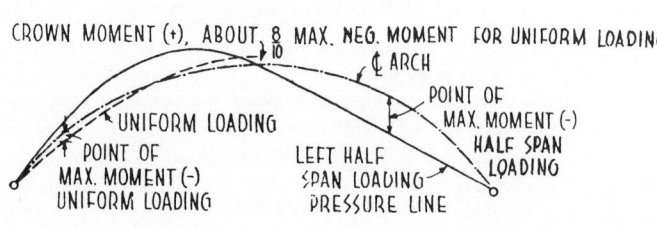

Typical bending moment curves for two-hinged and three-hinged radial arches uniformly loaded. Moment curve for half-span is also shown for the two-hinged arch (left). For a three-hinged arch the pressure line for all loadings must pass through the hinge at the crown.

As the rise-to-span ratio increases, the shape of the arch becomes more important (right). In high rise-to-span ratios, the most efficient design is one in which the centerline of the arch corresponds with the pressure curve.

TYPICAL FASTENING DETAILS

Notes: • Special details should be developed for bases of frames and arches exposed to the weather to prevent water from lying around ends of members.
• Indoors as well as outdoors, ends of members should be painted two coats or otherwise treated to reduce tendency to check.
• When more than one bolt is used (except parallel to long axis of wood) slotted holes should be used in adjoining metal plates to permit movement caused by swelling or shrinking.

BASE DETAILS

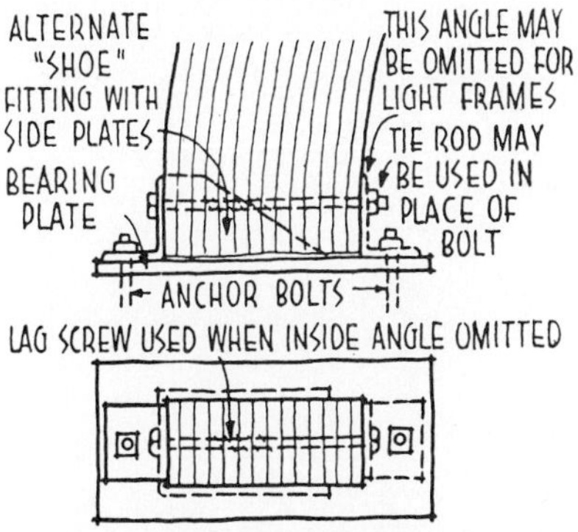

ALTERNATE "SHOE" FITTING WITH SIDE PLATES
BEARING PLATE
THIS ANGLE MAY BE OMITTED FOR LIGHT FRAMES
TIE ROD MAY BE USED IN PLACE OF BOLT
ANCHOR BOLTS
LAG SCREW USED WHEN INSIDE ANGLE OMITTED

BOLTED OR LAGSCREWED THROUGH DEPTH OF SECTION

MAY HAVE SHEAR PLATES AS WELL AS BOLTS
ANCHOR BOLTS
SLOTTED HOLE (DESIRABLE WHEN MORE THAN ONE BOLT IS USED

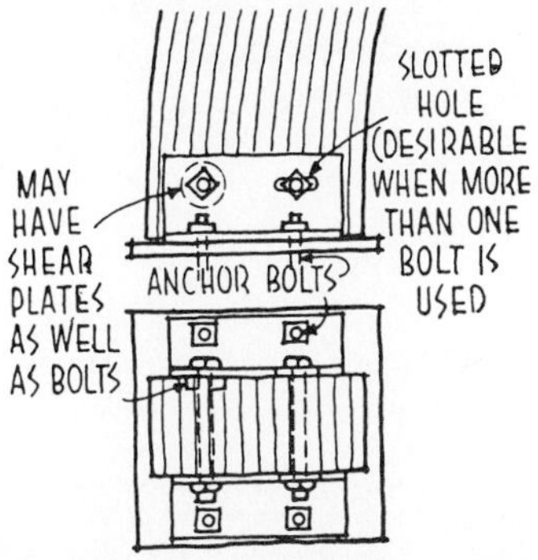

BOLTED OR LAGSCREWED ACROSS WIDTH OF SECTION

CROWN DETAILS

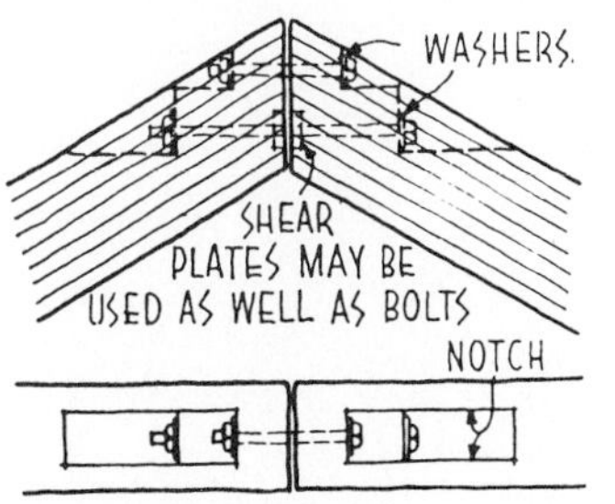

WASHERS
SHEAR PLATES MAY BE USED AS WELL AS BOLTS
NOTCH

BOLTED THROUGH DEPTH OF SECTION

PLATES MAY BE RECTANGULAR OR CUT TO FOLLOW SHAPE OF FRAME

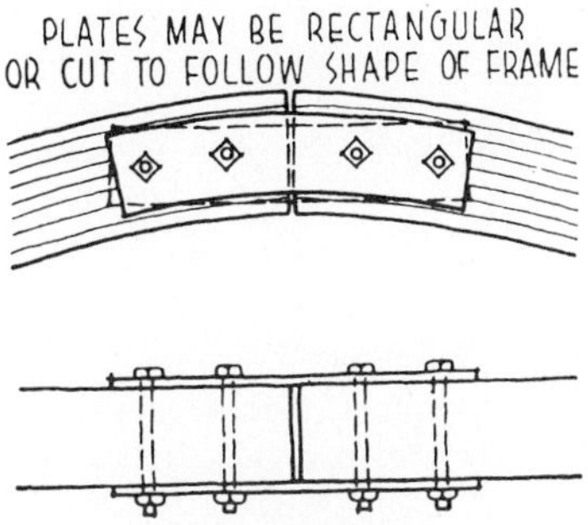

BOLTED ACROSS WIDTH OF SECTION

PURLIN DETAILS

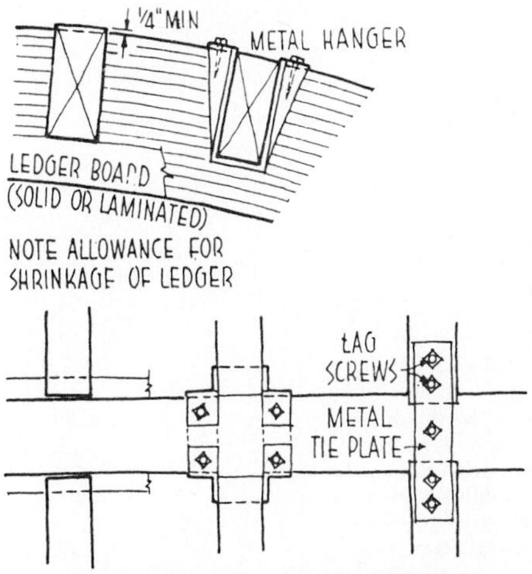

1¼" MIN
METAL HANGER
LEDGER BOARD (SOLID OR LAMINATED)
NOTE ALLOWANCE FOR SHRINKAGE OF LEDGER

LAG SCREWS
METAL TIE PLATE

THREE METHODS, TOP OF PURLIN IN SAME PLANE AS TOP OF FRAME

BOLTS
LAG SCREWS

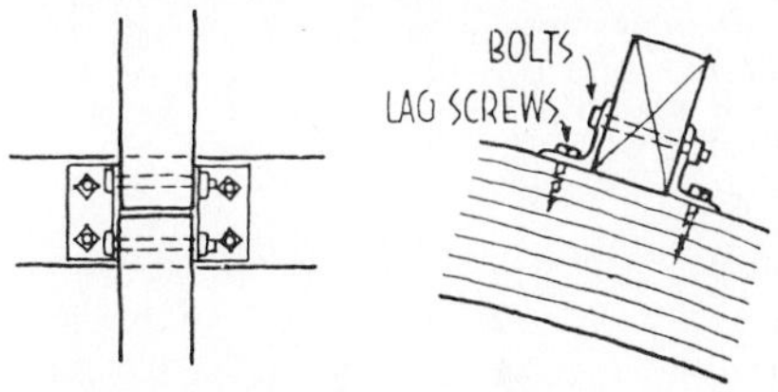

PURLIN RESTING ON TOP OF FRAME

Note: Purlins may be solid timbers or laminated.

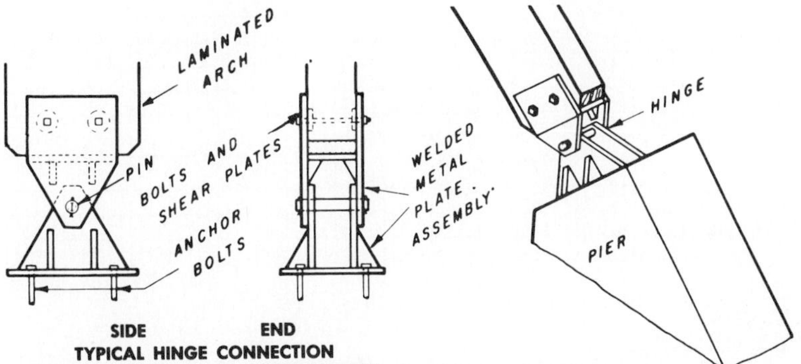

LAMINATED ARCH
PIN
BOLTS AND SHEAR PLATES
ANCHOR BOLTS
WELDED METAL PLATE ASSEMBLY

**SIDE   END
TYPICAL HINGE CONNECTION
ARCH ANCHORAGE TO EXTERIOR PIER**

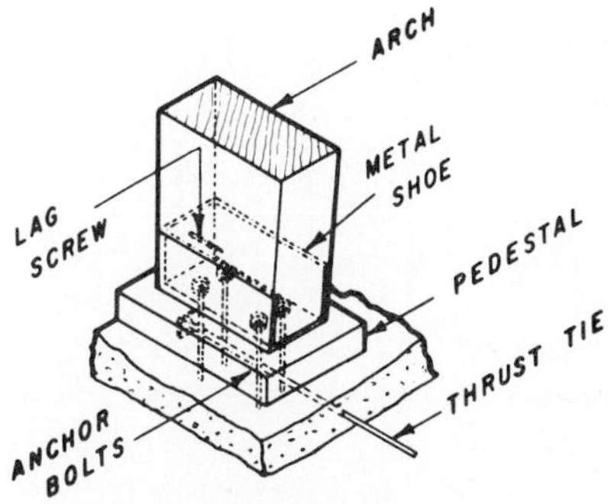

HINGE
PIER

ARCH
METAL SHOE
LAG SCREW
PEDESTAL
ANCHOR BOLTS
THRUST TIE

ARCH ANCHORAGE AT FLOOR

CANTILEVER BEAM CONNECTION WITH TENSION TIE— Vertical reaction of supported member carried by side plates and transferred to both members by bearing plates in perpendicular-to-grain bearing. Saddle rotation due to eccentric loading is resisted by tabs at top and bottom. Separate tension tie resists separation force developed between beams, as may be required in earthquake zones.

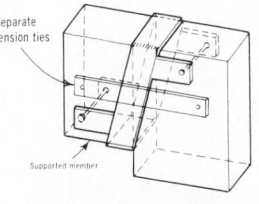

Separate tension ties
Supported member

SEPARATE TENSION TIES

By SEYMOUR HOWARD, *Architect, Associate Professor, School of Architecture, Pratt Institute*

STANDARD LAMELLA ROOF CONSTRUCTION DATA

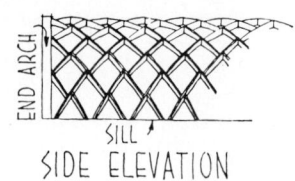

SIDE ELEVATION

END ARCH

SILL

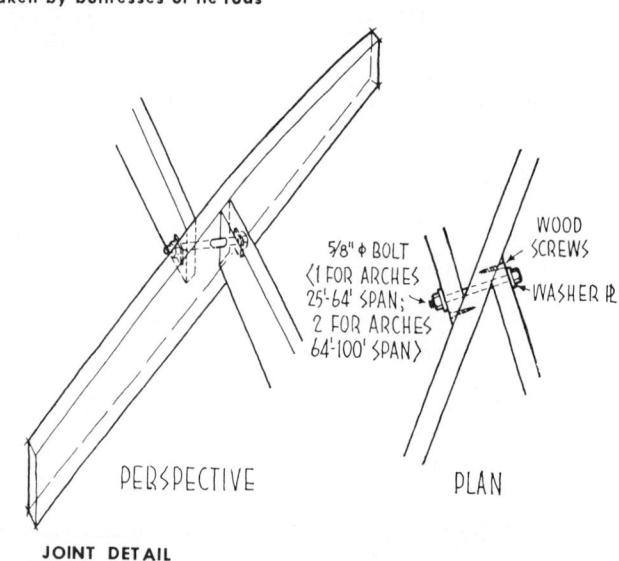

SPAN

RISE

RADIUS

SECTION

Note that this is essentially a two-hinged arch; thrust must be taken by buttresses or tie rods

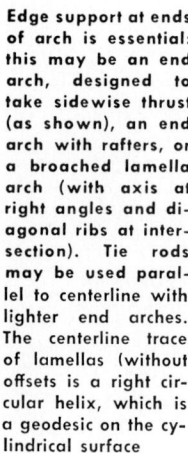

Edge support at ends of arch is essential: this may be an end arch, designed to take sidewise thrust (as shown), an end arch with rafters, or a broached lamella arch (with axis at right angles and diagonal ribs at intersection). Tie rods may be used parallel to centerline with lighter end arches. The centerline trace of lamellas (without offsets is a right circular helix, which is a geodesic on the cylindrical surface

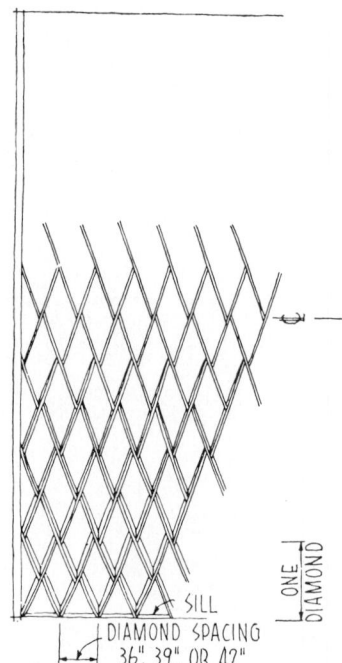

SILL

ONE DIAMOND

DIAMOND SPACING 36", 39", OR 42"

PERSPECTIVE

PLAN

5/8" φ BOLT (1 FOR ARCHES 25'-64' SPAN; 2 FOR ARCHES 64'-100' SPAN)

WOOD SCREWS

WASHER ℞

JOINT DETAIL

Note shape of lamella. Curvature is obtained by cutting upper edge only. Bolt size is minimum, and nails can replace wood screws. Special cast or welded fittings are available to eliminate the offset at the joint, such as those of Theodor Ahlborn (U.S. Patent No. 1,975,384)

TYPICAL SILL DETAILS

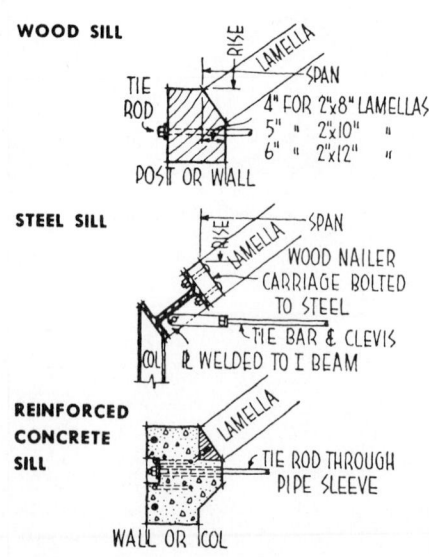

WOOD SILL

RISE

LAMELLA

SPAN

TIE ROD

4" FOR 2"x8" LAMELLAS
5"   " 2"x10"   "
6"   " 2"x12"   "

POST OR WALL

STEEL SILL

RISE

LAMELLA

SPAN

WOOD NAILER CARRIAGE BOLTED TO STEEL

TIE BAR & CLEVIS

℞ WELDED TO I BEAM

COL

REINFORCED CONCRETE SILL

LAMELLA

TIE ROD THROUGH PIPE SLEEVE

WALL OR COL

Note: Sills must be designed for both vertical & horizontal (thrust) components of reaction

"STANDARD" LAMELLA ROOF CONSTRUCTION DATA

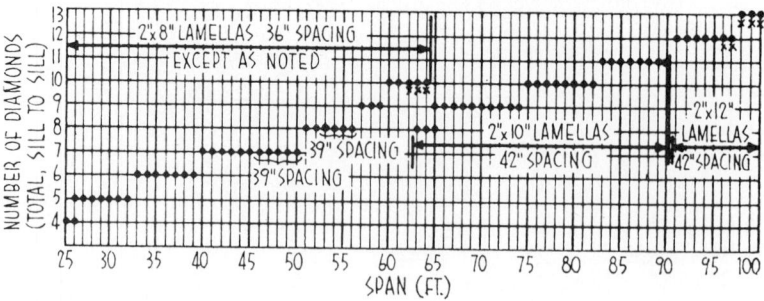

NUMBER OF DIAMONDS (TOTAL, SILL TO SILL)

2"x8" LAMELLAS 36" SPACING EXCEPT AS NOTED

39" SPACING

2"x10" LAMELLAS 42" SPACING

2"x12" LAMELLAS 42" SPACING

SPAN (FT.)

Rise   = 1/6 span
Radius = 5/6 span } Except spans marked x, for which see table

Thrust = approx (21.6 × span'−30) lbs per lin ft. Based on 20 lbs/sq ft live load

SPAN	RISE	RADIUS	SPAN	RISE	RADIUS
62 ft	10 ft– 8 in.	50 ft– 4 in.	97 ft	17 ft– 8 in.	75 ft– 5 in.
63 ft	10 ft–10 in.	51 ft– 3 in.	98 ft	17 ft–10 in.	76 ft– 3 in.
64 ft	11 ft– 8 in.	49 ft– 9 in.	99 ft	18 ft– 0 in.	77 ft– 1 in.
96 ft	16 ft–10 in.	76 ft–10 in.	100 ft	18 ft– 2 in.	77 ft–11 in.

Note: Information based on data furnished by Summerbell Roof Structures, Los Angeles 11, Calif.

By Y. S. LEE, *Associate, Severud-Perrone-Szegezdy-Sturm, Consulting Engineers Professor of Structural Design, School of Architecture, Pratt Institute*

Table 1. Types of structural steel for use in building construction

ASTM designation	Primary use in construction
Carbon steel	
A36	All-purpose carbon-grade steel used for construction of buildings and bridges.
High-strength low alloy steel	
A440	Riveted or bolted structures where weight saving is important; corrosion resistance twice that of carbon steel; not recommended for welding.
A441	Welded structures where weight saving is important; excellent impact resistance; corrosion resistance twice that of carbon steel.
A242	For exceptionally high corrosion resistance; more expensive; suitable for use in uncoated condition.
A572	Excellent formability and weldability; economical where strength and light weight are vital design objectives; the range of yield strengths offers designers a selection of steels to closely match their varied requirements.
A588	The atmospheric corrosion resistance of this steel is 4–6 times that of carbon steel; if unpainted, a tightly adhering oxide coating forms on surface to prevent progressive oxidation; for uses where weight reduction, weldability, and maintenance costs are considerations.

BEAMS

The design of steel beams must satisfy many conditions. In practice, however, the determining factor is usually the bending stress. The applicable formula in beam design is $S = M/F_b$, in which S is the section modulus in in.³, M is the bending moment in ft-kips, and F_b is the allowable bending stress in kips per square inch. Wide flange (W) sections, which are formed to develop the maximum section modulus per unit weight, are the most efficient members in resisting the bending moment.

TABULAR DATA

Data from the AISC safe-load tables[1] and the latest ASTM standard[2] have been condensed, rearranged and calculated in Table 3 to provide an immediate solution for symmetrically loaded beams for spans ranging

[1] Manual of Steel Construction *(7th ed.)*. *American Institute of Steel Construction, New York (1969).*

[2] ASTM A6–77b, *Standard Specification for General Requirements for Rolled Steel Plates, Shapes, Sheet Piling, and Bars for Structural Use. American Society for Testing and Materials (1977).*

from 9 to 60 ft. Table 3 gives W, the total allowable uniformly distributed load in kips (1,000 lb) including the weight of the beam itself, which should be deducted to find the net load that the beam will carry. It is assumed that the beams are simply supported and that their compression flanges are laterally supported. The working stress is 24,000 psi for compact sections and the stress must be reduced for non-compact sections, in accordance with the 1969 AISC specifications for A36 steel. No non-compact sections have been included in Table 3. Tabulated loads will develop live-load deflections that will not exceed $\frac{1}{360}$ of the span length when the ratio of live load to dead load is approximately 1.0. For the solution of unsymmetrically loaded beams, section moduli of the various sections are given. As an aid in detailing, the widths of flanges are also shown. Although the table does not provide a complete list of beams that may be used for each span, this will rarely be a consideration.

SPECIAL CONDITIONS

Table 3 is applicable only on the assumptions described above. Special conditions that restrict the use of the table are as follows:

1. Combined axial and bending stresses: An example of combined axial and bending stresses is a canopy beam supported by an inclined cable.

2. Unsymmetrical bending: Unsymmetrical bending indicates bending about both axes as in the case of roof purlins framing into sloping beams.

3. Web crippling: Web crippling is the presence of a high concentration of stress in the web caused by the application of a concentrated load, such as a column or an inadequate length of bearing at the support. This condition may not prohibit the use of a beam if the web is properly reinforced or stiffened.

4. Torsion stresses: Torsion stresses are developed by eccentric loading. A common example is that of a spandrel beam sup-

Table 2. Allowable stresses for structural steel

| ASTM specification | Thickness, in. | F_y Minimum yield point, ksi | Basic allowable AISC stresses, ksi | | |
| | | | 0.60 F_y | 0.66 F_y | 0.40 F_y |
			Tension	Bending*	Shear
A36	To 8″ incl.	36.0	22.0	24.0	14.5
A242	To ¾″ incl.	50.0	30.0	33.0	20.0
	Over ¾″ to 1½″ incl.	46.0	27.5	30.5	18.5
	Over 1½″ to 4″ incl.	42.0	25.2	28.0	17.0
A440	To ¾″ incl.	50.0	30.0	33.0	20.0
	Over ¾″ to 1½″ incl.	46.0	27.5	30.5	18.5
	Over 1½″ to 4″ incl.	42.0	25.2	28.0	17.0
A441	To ¾″ incl.	50.0	30.0	33.0	20.0
	Over ¾″ to 1½″ incl.	46.0	27.5	30.5	18.5
	Over 1½″ to 4″ incl.	42.0	25.2	28.0	17.0
	Over 4″ to 8″ incl.	40.0	24.0	26.4	16.0
A572					
Grade 32	To 4″ incl.	42.0	25.2	28.0	17.0
Grade 45	To 1½″ incl.	45.0	27.0	29.7	18.0
Grade 50	To 1½″ incl.	50.0	30.0	33.0	20.0
Grade 55	To 1½″ incl.	55.0	33.0	36.3	22.0
Grade 60	To 1″ incl.	60.0	36.0	39.6	24.0
Grade 65	To ½″ incl.	65.0	39.0	42.9	26.0
A588	To 4″ incl.	50.0	30.0	33.0	20.0
	Over 4″ to 5″ incl.	46.0	27.5	30.5	18.5
	Over 5″ to 8″ incl.	62.0	25.2	28.0	17.0

The beams are assumed to be compact, adequately braced members symmetrical about, and loaded in, the plane of their minor axis.

porting a wall whose center of gravity is off the centerline of the beam. This problem usually is not serious, however, because very often the indeterminate effect of this type of loading is compensated for by a reduction in the working stress.

5. *Impact and vibration:* The loads given in Table 3 are assumed to be static and gradually applied. Beams that develop dynamic loads, such as beams that support elevators or escalators, must be designed with a reduced stress as specified by the governing code to resist impact and vibration.

6. *Laterally unsupported beams:* The working stress for a beam whose compression flange (the top in a simply supported beam) is laterally unsupported is determined by its cross-sectional properties and the span length. This condition does not necessarily require a reduction in the working stress. (The procedure to be followed in this case is outlined in the AISC Manual.)

CONVERSION FACTORS

1. *Stresses:* The loads indicated in Table 3 are for ASTM Type A36 steel. If a different type of steel (A440, A441, etc.) is used, different allowable stresses are applicable. The allowable loads for these steels can be obtained by multiplying the tabulated values by the conversion factors listed in the AISC Manual.

2. *Loads:* Fig. 1 indicates the equivalent tabular loads to be used for concentrated loads. For example, a beam supporting 3 concentrated loads of 10 kips at the quarter points is equivalent to a load of 4 P or a total uniformly distributed load of 40 kips.

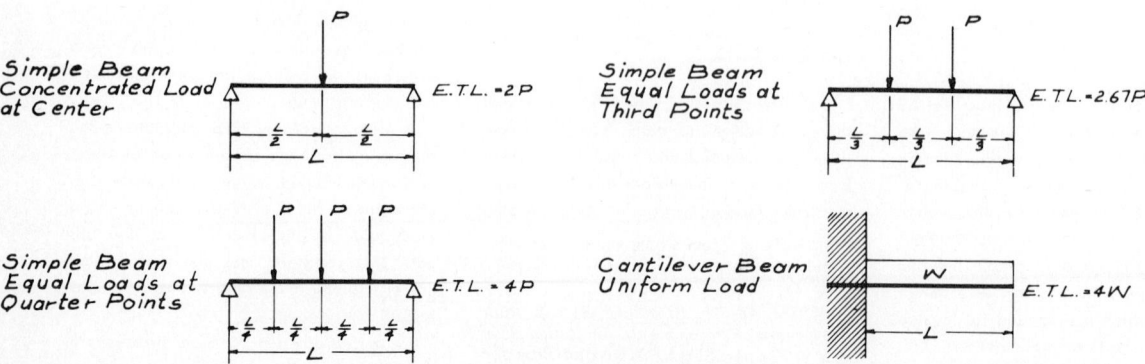

Fig. 1. Equivalent tabular load factors

Table 3. Allowable uniformly distributed loads in kips for beams laterally supported for ASTM Type A36 steel ($F_y = 36$ ksi)

Beam designation	Section modulus, in.³	Flange width, in.	\<br\>9	\<br\>10	\<br\>11	\<br\>12	Span length, ft\<br\>13	\<br\>14	\<br\>15	\<br\>16	\<br\>17	\<br\>18	\<br\>19	\<br\>20	\<br\>21	\<br\>22	\<br\>23	\<br\>24
W8 × 10	78.1	4	13.9	12.5	11.4	10.4	9.6	8.9	8.3	7.8	7.4							
W8 × 13	9.9	4	17.6	15.8	14.4	13.2	12.2	11.3	10.5	9.9	9.3							
W8 × 15	11.8	4	21.0	18.9	17.2	15.7	14.5	13.5	12.6	11.8	11.1							
W8 × 18	15.2	5¼	27.0	24.3	22.1	20.3	18.7	17.4	16.2	15.2	14.3							
W8 × 21	18.2	5¼	32.4	29.1	26.5	24.3	22.4	20.8	19.4	18.2	17.1							
S8 × 23	16.0	4⅛	28.8	25.9	23.6	21.6	19.9	18.5	17.3	16.2	15.2							
W8 × 24	20.9	6½	37.2	33.4	30.4	27.9	25.7	23.9	22.3	20.9	19.7							
W8 × 28	24.3	6½	43.2	38.9	35.3	32.4	29.9	27.9	25.9	24.3	22.9							
W10 × 12	10.9	4	19.4	17.4	15.9	14.5	13.4	12.5	11.6	10.9	10.3	9.7	9.2	8.7				
W10 × 15	13.8	4	24.5	22.1	20.1	18.4	17.0	15.8	14.7	13.8	13.0	12.3	11.6	11.0	10.5	10.0		
W10 × 17	16.2	4	28.8	25.9	23.6	21.6	19.9	18.5	17.3	16.2	15.2	14.4	13.6	13.0	12.3	11.0		
W10 × 19	18.8	4	33.4	30.1	27.3	25.1	23.1	21.5	20.1	18.8	17.7	16.7	15.8	15.0	14.3	13.7		
W10 × 22	23.2	5¾	42.2	37.1	33.8	30.9	28.6	26.5	24.8	23.2	21.8	20.6	19.5	18.6	17.7	16.9		
W10 × 26	27.9	5¾	49.6	44.6	40.6	37.2	34.3	31.9	29.8	27.9	26.3	24.8	23.5	22.3	21.3	20.3		
S10 × 25.4	24.7	4⅝	43.9	39.5	35.9	32.9	30.4	28.2	26.3	24.7	23.2	22.0	20.8	19.8	18.8			
W10 × 30	32.4	5¾	57.6	51.8	47.1	43.2	39.9	37.0	31.6	32.4	30.5	28.8	27.3	25.9	24.7			
S10 × 35	35.0	5	61	55	50	46	42	39	37	34	32	31	29	28	26	25		
W10 × 39	42.1	8	74.8	67.4	61.2	56.1	51.8	48.1	45.2	42.1	39.6	37.4	35.5	33.7	32.1	30.6		
W10 × 45	49.1	8	87.3	78.6	71.4	65.5	60.4	56.1	52.4	49.1	46.2	43.6	41.4	29.3	37.4	35.7	34.2	
W12 × 14	14.9	4	26.5	33.8	21.7	19.9	18.3	17.0	15.9	14.9	14.0	13.2	12.6	11.9	11.4	10.8	10.4	9.9
W12 × 19	21.3	4	37.9	34.1	31.0	28.4	26.2	24.3	22.7	21.3	20.0	18.9	17.9	17.0	16.2	15.5	14.8	14.2
W12 × 22	25.4	4	45.2	40.6	37.0	33.9	31.3	29.0	27.1	25.4	23.9	22.6	21.4	20.3	19.4	18.5	17.7	16.9
W12 × 30	38.6	6½	68.6	61.8	56.2	51.5	47.5	44.1	41.2	38.6	36.3	34.3	32.5	30.9	29.4	28.1	26.9	25.7
W12 × 35	45.6	6½	81.1	73.0	66.3	60.8	56.1	52.1	48.6	45.6	42.9	40.5	38.4	36.5	34.7	33.2	31.7	30.4
S12 × 31.8	36.4	5	65	58	53	49	45	42	39	36.0	34.0	32.0	31.0	29.0	28.0	26.0	25.0	24.0
W12 × 40	51.9	8	92	83	75	69	64	59	55	52	49	46	44	42	40	38	36	35
W12 × 45	58.1	8	103	93	85	78	72	67	62	58	55	52	49	47	44	42	40	39
W12 × 50	64.7	8⅛	115	104	94	86	80	74	69	65	61	58	54	52	49	47	45	43
W12 × 53	70.6	10	121	113	103	94	87	81	75	71	67	63	60	57	54	51	49	47
W14 × 22	29.0	5	51	46	42	39	36	33	31	29	27	26	24	23	22	21	20	19
W14 × 26	35.3	5	62	56	51	47	43	40	37	35	33	31	30	28	27	26	24	23
W14 × 30	41.0	6¾	74	66	60	55	51	48	44	41	39	37	35	33	32	30	29	28
W14 × 34	48.6	6¾	86	78	71	65	60	56	52	49	46	43	41	39	37	35	34	32
W14 × 38	54.6	6¾	97	88	80	73	67	63	58	55	51	49	46	44	42	40	38	36
W14 × 43	62.7	8	111	100	91	84	77	72	67	63	59	56	53	50	48	46	44	42
W14 × 48	70.3	8	125	112	102	94	86	80	75	70	66	62	59	56	53	51	49	47
W14 × 53	77.8	8	138	124	113	104	96	89	83	78	73	69	66	62	59	57	54	52
W14 × 61	92.2	10	152	148	134	123	113	105	98	92	87	82	78	74	70	67	64	61
W16 × 26	38.4	5½	68	61	56	51	47	44	41	38	36	34	32	31	29	28	27	26
W16 × 31	47.2	5½	84	76	69	63	58	54	50	47	44	42	40	38	36	34	33	31
W16 × 36	56.5	7	100	90	82	75	70	65	60	57	53	50	48	45	43	41	39	38
W16 × 40	64.7	7	115	103	94	86	80	74	69	65	61	57	54	52	49	47	45	43
W16 × 45	72.7	7	129	116	106	97	89	83	78	73	68	65	61	58	55	53	51	48
W16 × 50	81.0	7⅛	144	129	118	108	99	92	86	81	76	72	68	65	62	59	56	54
W18 × 40	68.4	6	122	109	100	91	84	78	73	68	64	61	58	55	52	50	48	46
W18 × 46	78.8	6	140	126	115	105	97	90	84	79	74	70	66	63	60	57	55	53
W18 × 50	88.9	7½	158	142	129	119	109	102	95	89	84	79	75	71	68	65	62	59
W18 × 55	98.3	7½	175	157	143	131	121	112	105	98	93	87	83	79	75	72	68	66
W21 × 50	94.5	6½	168	151	138	126	116	108	101	95	89	84	80	76	72	69	66	63
W21 × 57	111.0	6½	197	178	162	148	137	127	118	111	105	99	94	89	85	81	77	74
W21 × 62	127.0	8¼	226	203	185	169	156	145	135	127	120	113	107	102	96	92	88	85

Beams

Table 3 (cont.). Allowable uniformly distributed loads in kips for beams laterally supported for ASTM Type A36 steel (F_y = 36 ksi)

Beam designation	Section modulus, in.^{3}	Flange width, in.	Span length, ft 25	26	27	28	29	30	31	32	33	34	35	36	40	44	50	60
W14 × 22	29.0	5	19	18	17	17	16	16										
W14 × 26	35.3	5	23	22	21	20	20	19										
W14 × 30	42.0	6¾	27	26	25	24	23	22										
W14 × 38	54.6	6¾	35	34	32	31	30	29										
W14 × 53	77.8	8	50	48	46	44	43	41										
W14 × 74	112.0	10⅛	72	69	66	64	62	60										
W14 × 90	143.0	12	92	88	85	82	79	76										
W16 × 26	38.4	5½	25	24	23	22	21.0	20	20	19	19	18						
W16 × 31	47.2	5½	30	29	28	27	26	25	24	24	23	22						
W16 × 36	56.5	7	36	35	33	32	31	30	29	28	27	27						
W16 × 40	64.7	7	41	40	38	37	36	34	33	32	31	30						
W16 × 45	72.7	7	47	45	43	42	40	39	38	36	35	34						
W16 × 50	81.0	7⅛	52	50	48	46	45	43	42	41	39	38						
W16 × 57	92.2	7⅛	59	57	55	53	51	49	48	46	45	43						
W16 × 67	117.0	10¼	75	72	69	67	65	62	60	59	57	55						
W16 × 77	134.0	10¼	86	83	79	77	74	72	69	67	65	63						
W16 × 89	155.0	10⅜	99	95	92	89	86	83	80	78	75	73						
W16 × 100	175.0	10⅜	112	108	104	100	97	93	90	88	85	82						
W18 × 35	57.6	6																
W18 × 40	68.4	6	44	42	41	39	38	37	35	34	33	32	31	30				
W18 × 50	88.9	7½	57	55	53	51	49	48	46	45	43	42	41	40				
W18 × 55	98.3	7½	63	61	58	56	54	52	51	49	48	46	45	44				
W18 × 60	108	7½	69	66	64	62	60	58	56	54	52	51	49	48				
W18 × 65	117.0	7⅝	75	72	69	67	65	62	60	59	57	55	54	52				
W18 × 71	127.0	7⅝	82	78	75	73	70	68	66	64	62	60	58	56				
W18 × 76	146.0	11	93	90	87	83	81	78	75	73	71	69	67	65				
W18 × 86	166.0	11⅛	106	102	98	95	92	89	86	83	81	78	76	74				
W18 × 97	188.0	11⅛	120	116	111	107	104	100	97	94	91	89	86	84				
W21 × 57	111	6½	71	68	66	63	61	59	57	56	54	52	51	49	44	40		
W21 × 62	127	8¼	81	78	75	73	70	68	65	64	61	60	58	56	51	46		
W21 × 68	140	8¼	90	86	83	80	77	75	72	70	68	66	64	62	56	51		
W21 × 73	151	8¼	96	93	89	86	83	81	78	76	73	71	69	67	60	55		
W21 × 83	171	8⅜	109	105	101	98	94	91	88	86	83	81	78	76	68	62		
W24 × 68	153	9	98	94	91	87	84	82	79	77	74	72	70	68	61	56	49	
W24 × 76	176	9	113	108	104	101	97	94	91	88	85	83	80	78	70	64	56	
W24 × 84	197	9	126	121	117	113	109	105	102	99	96	93	90	88	79	72	63	
W24 × 94	221	9	141	136	131	126	122	118	114	111	107	104	101	98	88	80	71	
W24 × 104	258	12¾	165	159	153	147	142	138	133	129	125	121	114	115	103	94	83	
W24 × 117	291	12¾	186	179	172	166	161	155	150	146	141	137	133	129	116	106	93	
W24 × 131	329	12⅞	211	203	195	188	182	176	170	165	160	155	150	146	132	120	105	
W27 × 84	213	10	136	131	126	121	118	114	110	107	103	100	97	95	85	78	68	
W27 × 94	243	10	156	150	144	139	134	130	125	122	118	114	111	108	97	88	78	
W27 × 102	267	10	171	164	158	153	147	142	138	134	129	126	122	119	107	97	85	
W27 × 114	300	10⅛	192	185	178	171	166	160	155	150	145	141	137	133	120	109	96	
W27 × 146	411	14	263	253	244	235	227	219	212	206	199	193	188	183	164	150	132	
W30 × 99	270	10½	173	166	160	154	149	144	139	135	130	127	123	120	108	98	86	72
W30 × 108	300	10½	192	185	178	171	166	160	154	150	144	141	136	133	120	109	96	80
W30 × 116	329	10½	211	202	195	188	182	175	169	165	158	155	149	146	132	120	105	88
W30 × 124	355	10½	227	218	210	203	196	189	183	178	172	167	162	158	142	129	114	95
W33 × 118	359	11½	230	221	212	205	197	191	184	180	173	169	163	160	144	131	115	96
W33 × 130	406	11½	260	250	240	232	223	217	209	203	196	191	185	180	162	148	130	108
W33 × 141	448	11½	287	276	265	256	247	239	230	224	216	211	205	199	179	163	143	119
W36 × 135	440	12	281	271	261	251	243	235	226	220	212	207	201	196	176	160	141	117
W36 × 150	504	12	322	310	299	288	279	269	259	252	244	237	230	224	202	183	161	134

Open web steel joists are completely standardized as to lengths, depths, and carrying capacities. H-Series joists are available in depths of 8 to 30 in. in 2-in. increments, and in lengths up to 60 ft. Bearing ends are uniformly 2½ in. deep; in brick walls the bearing end will usually fit within two successive mortar joints without disturbing the brick coursing.

Open web joists permit the ready passage of pipes, ducts, and conduits within the depth of the floor structure (See Tables 14 to 16). In many cases the need for hung ceilings can be eliminated.

Open web steel joist construction can provide adequate fire resistance at low cost (See Table 13).

The light weight of open web steel joist construction permits reduction in the size of framing and footings. This is especially advantageous where poor soil conditions must be considered.

EXTENDED ENDS

H-series open web steel joists are frequently provided with extended ends. Since various manufacturers incorporate different end constructions, load tables for each manufacturer's type should be checked. As a guide to the designer, the following table of allowable loads is provided for 2½-in. depth standard ends only. The mark numbers 1 through 4 apply only to those extended ends which are separately fabricated from angle or channel sections for application to a standard joist. Where the extended end is an integral part or an extension of a standard chord member, the mark numbers used in the table do not apply.

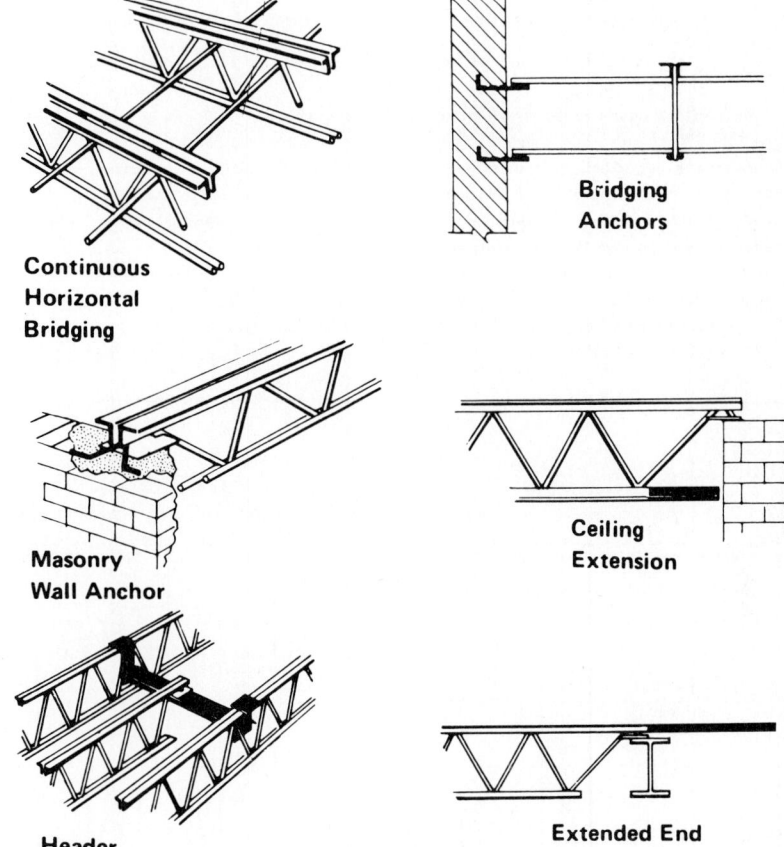

Continuous Horizontal Bridging

Bridging Anchors

Masonry Wall Anchor

Ceiling Extension

Header

Extended End

Joist accessories

Note: Because of the widespread acceptance of the high strength steel joists (H-Series, LH-Series, and DLH-Series), the J-, LJ-, and DLJ-Series were discontinued as industry standards in 1978.

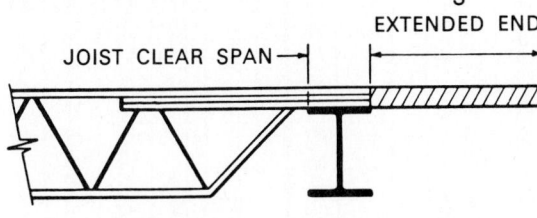

JOIST CLEAR SPAN — "S" EXTENDED END

BEARING ON STRUCTURAL STEEL

JOIST CLEAR SPAN — "S" EXTENDED END

BEARING ON MASONRY

Joists with extended ends

Table 4. Load table for standard extended ends H-Series joists

Total allowable uniform load in pounds per linear foot of extended end S

| Unsupported length of extended end | Type of standard extended ends | | | |
| | 2½" depth | | | |
	No. 1	No. 2	No. 3	No. 4
2'6"	350	350	350	350
3'0"	350	350	350	350
3'6"	285	346	350	350
4'0"	218	265	312	350
4'6"	171	208	245	306
5'0"	125	152	179	223
5'6"	94	114	134	168

Note: The total allowable uniform load in pounds per linear foot of standard extended end shall not exceed 350 lb nor shall it exceed the total allowable uniform load in pounds per linear foot of the steel joist to which the extended end applies.

Table 5. Standard load table for open web steel joists, H-series—based on a maximum allowable tensile stress of 30,000 psi††

Adopted by the Steel Joist Institute and American Institute of Steel Construction Inc., October 1, 1974

The boldface figures in the following table give the *total* safe uniformly distributed load-carrying capacities, in pounds per linear foot, of H-series steel joists. The weight of *dead* loads, including the joists, must be deducted to determine the *live* load-carrying capacities of the joists. The load table may be used for parallel chord joists installed to a maximum slope of ½ inch per foot.

The figures shown in lightface in this load table are the *live* loads per linear foot of joist which will produce an approximate deflection of 1/360 of the span. *Live* loads which will produce a deflection of 1/240 of the span may be obtained by multiplying the lightface figures by 1.5. In no case shall the total load capacity of the joists be exceeded.**

Tests on steel joists designed in accordance with the Standard Specifications have demonstrated that the Standard Load Tables are applicable for concentrated top chord loadings (such as are developed in bulb-tee roof construction) when the sum of the equal concentrated top chord loadings does not exceed the allowable uniform loading for the joist type and span and the loads are placed at spacings not exceeding 33″ along the top chord.

Loads above the heavy lines are governed by shear

Joist Designation	8H3	10H3	10H4	12H3	12H4	12H5	12H6	14H3	14H4	14H5	14H6	14H7	16H4	16H5	16H6	16H7	16H8
Nominal *Depth (in.)	8	10	10	12	12	12	12	14	14	14	14	14	16	16	16	16	16
Resist. Moment (in.-lbs.)	91,000	116,000	148,000	140,000	180,000	222,000	260,000	165,000	212,000	259,000	307,000	369,000	221,000	239,000	344,000	413,000	478,000
Max. End React. (lbs.)	2400	2500	2800	2800	3200	3600	3900	3200	3500	3800	4200	4600	3800	4300	4600	4900	5200
†Approx. Wt. (lbs./ft.)	5.0	5.0	6.1	5.2	6.2	7.1	8.2	5.5	6.5	7.4	8.6	10.0	6.6	7.8	8.6	10.3	11.4
Span in Feet																	
8	600																
9	533																
10	480 / 460	500	560														
11	436 / 345	455	509														
12	400 / 266	417	467	467	533	600	650										
13	359 / 209	385 / 337	431 / 417	431	492	554	600										
14	310 / 167	357 / 270	400 / 334	400 / 393	457	514	557	457	500	543	600	657					
15	270 / 136	333 / 219	373 / 271	373 / 320	427 / 418	480	520	427	467	507	560	613					
16	232 / 112	302 / 181	350 / 223	350 / 264	400 / 345	450 / 404	483 / 490	400 / 366	438	475	525	575	475	538	575	613	650
17		268 / 151	329 / 186	323 / 220	376 / 287	424 / 337	459 / 400	376 / 305	412 / 398	447	494	541	447	506	541	576	612
18		239 / 127	305 / 157	288 / 185	356 / 242	400 / 284	433 / 337	340 / 257	389 / 336	422 / 393	467	511	422 / 413	478	511	544	578
19		214 / 108	273 / 133	259 / 157	332 / 206	379 / 241	411 / 285	305 / 218	368 / 285	400 / 334	442 / 399	484 / 470	400 / 351	453 / 432	484	516	547
20		193 / 92	247 / 114	233 / 135	300 / 177	360 / 207	390 / 245	275 / 187	350 / 245	380 / 287	420 / 342	460 / 403	368 / 301	430 / 370	460 / 437	490	520
21				212 / 117	272 / 152	336 / 179	371 / 212	249 / 162	320 / 212	362 / 248	400 / 295	438 / 348	334 / 260	410 / 320	438 / 377	467 / 454	495
22				193 / 101	248 / 133	306 / 155	355 / 185	227 / 141	292 / 184	345 / 215	382 / 257	418 / 302	304 / 226	391 / 278	418 / 328	445 / 395	473 / 454
23				176 / 89	227 / 116	280 / 136	328 / 162	208 / 123	267 / 161	326 / 189	365 / 225	400 / 265	279 / 198	364 / 243	400 / 287	426 / 346	452 / 398
24				162 / 78	208 / 102	257 / 120	301 / 142	191 / 108	245 / 142	300 / 166	350 / 198	383 / 233	256 / 174	334 / 214	383 / 253	408 / 304	433 / 352
25								176 / 96	226 / 125	276 / 147	327 / 175	368 / 206	236 / 154	308 / 190	367 / 224	392 / 269	416 / 310
26								163 / 85	209 / 111	255 / 131	303 / 156	354 / 183	218 / 137	285 / 169	339 / 199	377 / 239	400 / 275
27								151 / 76	194 / 99	237 / 117	281 / 139	337 / 164	202 / 122	264 / 151	315 / 177	363 / 214	385 / 246
28								140 / 68	180 / 89	220 / 104	261 / 125	314 / 147	188 / 110	246 / 135	293 / 159	350 / 192	371 / 220
29													175 / 99	229 / 121	273 / 143	327 / 172	359 / 198
30													164 / 89	214 / 110	255 / 129	336 / 156	347 / 179
31													153 / 81	200 / 99	239 / 117	287 / 141	332 / 162
32													144 / 74	188 / 90	224 / 107	269 / 128	311 / 148

See page 2-84 for notes

Table 5. (cont.). For joist depths 18″ to 22″ inclusive

Joist Designation	18H5	18H6	18H7	18H8	18H9	18H10	18H11	20H5	20H6	20H7	20H8	20H9	20H10	20H11	22H6	22H7	22H8	22H9	22H10	22H11
Nominal *Depth (in.)	18	18	18	18	18	18	18	20	20	20	20	20	20	20	22	22	22	22	22	22
Resist. Moment (in.-lbs.)	325,000	383,000	466,000	540,000	627,000	705,000	814,000	365,000	406,000	499,000	602,000	701,000	789,000	912,000	422,000	526,000	653,000	776,000	873,000	1,009,000
Max. End React. (lbs.)	4500	4800	5200	5400	5900	6600	7600	4800	5100	5400	5600	6400	7000	7900	5400	5600	5800	6700	7200	8100
†Approx. Wt. (lbs./ft.)	8.0	9.2	10.4	11.6	12.6	14.0	15.8	8.4	9.6	10.7	12.2	13.2	14.6	16.4	9.7	10.7	12.0	13.8	15.2	16.9
Span in Feet																				
18	500	533	578	600																
19	474	505	547	568	621															
20	450	480	520	540	590			480	510	540	560	640								
21	429 / 409	457	495	514	562	629		457	486	514	533	610								
22	409 / 356	436 / 420	473	491	536	600		436	464	491	509	582	636		491	509	527	609		
23	391 / 312	417 / 368	452 / 441	470	513	574		417 / 380	443 / 434	470	487	557	609		470	487	504	583	626	
24	375 / 274	400 / 324	433 / 388	450 / 444	492	550	633	400 / 335	425 / 382	450	467	533	583		450 / 446	467	483	558	600	
25	347 / 243	384 / 286	416 / 343	432 / 393	472 / 428	528 / 483	608 / 548	384 / 296	408 / 338	432 / 411	448	512	560	632	432 / 395	448	464	536	576	648
26	321 / 216	369 / 255	400 / 305	415 / 349	454 / 380	508 / 429	585 / 487	360 / 263	392 / 300	415 / 365	431	492 / 476	538	608	415 / 351	431 / 426	446	515	554	623
27	297 / 193	350 / 227	385 / 272	400 / 312	437 / 340	489 / 383	563 / 435	334 / 235	371 / 268	400 / 326	415 / 392	474 / 425	519 / 480	585 / 545	386 / 313	415 / 380	430	496	533	600
28	276 / 173	326 / 204	371 / 244	386 / 280	421 / 305	471 / 344	543 / 390	310 / 211	345 / 240	386 / 292	400 / 352	457 / 381	500 / 431	564 / 488	359 / 281	400 / 341	414	479 / 468	514	579
29	258 / 155	304 / 184	359 / 220	372 / 252	407 / 274	455 / 309	524 / 351	289 / 190	322 / 216	372 / 263	386 / 317	441 / 343	483 / 388	545 / 440	335 / 253	386 / 307	400 / 379	462 / 421	497 / 473	559 / 539
30	241 / 140	284 / 166	345 / 199	360 / 227	393 / 248	440 / 280	507 / 317	270 / 171	301 / 195	360 / 238	373 / 286	427 / 310	467 / 350	527 / 397	313 / 228	373 / 277	387 / 343	447 / 381	480 / 428	540 / 487
31	225 / 127	266 / 150	323 / 180	348 / 206	381 / 224	426 / 253	490 / 287	253 / 155	282 / 177	346 / 215	361 / 259	413 / 281	452 / 317	510 / 360	293 / 207	361 / 251	374 / 311	432 / 345	465 / 387	523 / 441
32	212 / 116	249 / 137	303 / 164	338 / 187	369 / 204	413 / 230	475 / 261	238 / 141	264 / 161	325 / 196	350 / 236	400 / 255	438 / 288	494 / 327	275 / 188	342 / 228	363 / 282	419 / 314	450 / 352	506 / 401
33	199 / 106	234 / 125	285 / 149	327 / 171	358 / 186	400 / 210	461 / 238	223 / 129	249 / 147	305 / 178	339 / 215	388 / 233	424 / 263	479 / 298	258 / 172	322 / 208	352 / 257	406 / 286	436 / 321	491 / 366
34	187 / 96	221 / 114	269 / 136	311 / 156	347 / 170	388 / 192	447 / 218	210 / 118	234 / 134	288 / 163	329 / 196	376 / 213	412 / 240	465 / 273	243 / 157	303 / 190	341 / 235	394 / 261	424 / 294	476 / 335
35	177 / 88	208 / 104	254 / 125	294 / 143	337 / 156	377 / 176	434 / 200	199 / 108	221 / 123	272 / 150	320 / 180	366 / 195	400 / 220	451 / 250	230 / 144	286 / 175	331 / 216	383 / 240	411 / 269	463 / 307
36	167 / 81	197 / 96	240 / 115	278 / 132	323 / 143	363 / 162	419 / 183	188 / 99	209 / 113	257 / 137	310 / 166	356 / 179	389 / 203	439 / 230	217 / 132	271 / 160	322 / 198	372 / 220	400 / 247	450 / 282
37								178 / 91	198 / 104	243 / 127	293 / 152	341 / 165	378 / 187	427 / 212	206 / 122	256 / 148	314 / 183	362 / 203	389 / 228	438 / 260
38								169 / 84	187 / 96	230 / 117	278 / 141	324 / 153	364 / 172	416 / 195	195 / 112	243 / 136	301 / 169	353 / 187	379 / 210	426 / 240
39								160 / 78	178 / 89	219 / 108	264 / 130	307 / 141	346 / 159	400 / 181	185 / 104	231 / 126	286 / 156	340 / 173	369 / 195	415 / 222
40								152 / 72	169 / 82	208 / 100	251 / 121	292 / 131	329 / 148	380 / 168	176 / 96	219 / 117	272 / 145	323 / 161	360 / 180	405 / 205
41															167 / 89	209 / 109	259 / 134	308 / 149	346 / 167	395 / 191
42															159 / 83	199 / 101	247 / 125	293 / 139	330 / 156	391 / 177
43															152 / 78	190 / 94	235 / 116	280 / 129	315 / 145	364 / 165
44															145 / 72	181 / 88	225 / 109	267 / 121	301 / 136	347 / 154

See page 2-84 for notes.

Joists, H-series

Table 5. (cont.). For joist depths 24″ to 30″ inclusive

Joist Designation	24H6	24H7	24H8	24H9	24H10	24H11	26H8	26H9	26H10	26H11	28H8	28H9	28H10	28H11	30H8	30H9	30H10	30H11
Nominal *Depth (in.)	24	24	24	24	24	24	26	26	26	26	28	28	28	28	30	30	30	30
Resist. Moment (in.-lbs.)	462,000	576,000	716,000	851,000	957,000	1,106,000	784,000	925,000	1,040,000	1,203,000	846,000	1,000,000	1,124,000	1,300,000	909,000	1,075,000	1,207,000	1,397,000
Max. End React. (lbs.)	5600	5800	6000	7000	7500	8200	6700	7200	7600	8300	6700	7200	7700	8400	6800	7500	8100	8700
†Approx. Wt. (lbs./ft.)	10.3	11.5	12.7	14.0	15.5	17.5	12.8	14.8	16.2	17.9	13.5	15.2	16.8	18.3	14.2	15.4	17.3	18.8
Span in Feet																		
24	467	483	500	583	625													
25	448	464	480	560	600													
26	431	446	462	538	577	631	515	554	585	638								
27	415 / 375	430	444	519	556	607	496	533	563	615								
28	393 / 336	414 / 406	429	500	536	586	479	514	543	593	479	514	550	600				
29	366 / 303	400 / 365	414	483	517	566	462	497	524	572	462	497	531	579				
30	342 / 273	387 / 330	400	467 / 457	500	547	447	480	507	553	447	480	513	560	453	500	540	580
31	320 / 248	374 / 299	387 / 373	452 / 414	484 / 465	529	432 / 418	465	490	535	432	465	497	542	439	484	523	561
32	301 / 225	363 / 272	375 / 339	438 / 376	469 / 423	513 / 482	419 / 380	450 / 445	475	519	419	450	481	525	425	469	506	544
33	283 / 205	352 / 248	364 / 309	424 / 343	455 / 386	497 / 440	406 / 346	436 / 405	461 / 456	503	406 / 404	436	467	509	412	455	491	527
34	266 / 188	332 / 227	353 / 283	412 / 314	441 / 353	482 / 402	394 / 317	424 / 371	447 / 417	488 / 476	394 / 370	424	453	494	400	441	476	512
35	251 / 172	313 / 208	343 / 259	400 / 288	429 / 323	469 / 369	383 / 290	411 / 340	434 / 383	474 / 437	383 / 339	411 / 396	440	480	389	429	463	497
36	238 / 158	296 / 191	333 / 238	389 / 264	417 / 297	456 / 339	372 / 267	400 / 312	422 / 352	461 / 401	372 / 311	400 / 364	428 / 410	467	378 / 359	417	450	483
37	225 / 146	280 / 176	324 / 219	378 / 243	405 / 274	443 / 312	362 / 246	389 / 288	411 / 324	449 / 370	362 / 287	389 / 336	416 / 378	454 / 432	368 / 330	405 / 387	438 / 436	470
38	213 / 135	266 / 162	316 / 202	368 / 225	395 / 253	432 / 288	353 / 227	379 / 266	400 / 299	437 / 341	353 / 265	379 / 310	405 / 349	442 / 399	358 / 305	395 / 357	426 / 402	458
39	202 / 124	252 / 150	308 / 187	359 / 208	385 / 234	421 / 266	344 / 210	369 / 246	390 / 276	426 / 316	344 / 245	369 / 287	395 / 322	431 / 369	349 / 282	385 / 331	415 / 372	446 / 426
40	193 / 115	240 / 139	298 / 174	350 / 193	375 / 217	410 / 247	327 / 194	360 / 228	380 / 256	415 / 292	335 / 227	360 / 266	385 / 299	420 / 342	340 / 262	375 / 306	405 / 345	435 / 395
41	183 / 107	228 / 129	284 / 161	337 / 179	366 / 201	400 / 229	311 / 181	351 / 211	371 / 238	405 / 272	327 / 211	351 / 247	376 / 278	410 / 318	332 / 243	366 / 285	395 / 320	424 / 367
42	175 / 100	218 / 120	271 / 150	322 / 166	357 / 187	390 / 213	296 / 168	343 / 197	362 / 221	395 / 253	319 / 196	343 / 229	367 / 258	400 / 295	324 / 226	357 / 265	386 / 298	414 / 341
43	167 / 93	208 / 112	258 / 140	307 / 155	345 / 174	381 / 199	283 / 156	334 / 183	353 / 206	386 / 235	305 / 183	335 / 214	358 / 241	391 / 275	316 / 211	349 / 247	377 / 278	405 / 318
44	159 / 87	198 / 105	247 / 130	293 / 145	330 / 163	373 / 186	270 / 146	319 / 171	345 / 193	377 / 220	291 / 171	327 / 200	350 / 225	382 / 257	309 / 196	341 / 230	368 / 259	395 / 297
45	152 / 81	190 / 98	236 / 122	280 / 135	315 / 152	364 / 173	258 / 137	305 / 160	338 / 180	369 / 205	279 / 159	320 / 187	342 / 210	373 / 240	299 / 184	333 / 215	360 / 242	387 / 278
46	146 / 76	181 / 92	226 / 114	268 / 127	302 / 142	348 / 162	247 / 128	291 / 150	328 / 168	361 / 192	267 / 149	313 / 175	335 / 197	365 / 225	286 / 172	326 / 202	352 / 227	378 / 260
47	139 / 71	174 / 86	216 / 107	257 / 119	289 / 133	334 / 152	237 / 120	279 / 140	314 / 158	353 / 180	255 / 140	302 / 164	328 / 184	357 / 211	274 / 161	319 / 189	345 / 213	370 / 244
48	134 / 67	167 / 81	207 / 100	246 / 111	277 / 125	320 / 143	227 / 112	268 / 132	301 / 148	346 / 169	245 / 131	289 / 154	321 / 173	350 / 198	263 / 151	311 / 177	338 / 200	363 / 229
49							218 / 106	257 / 124	289 / 139	334 / 159	235 / 124	278 / 144	312 / 163	343 / 186	252 / 142	298 / 167	331 / 188	355 / 215
50							209 / 100	247 / 117	277 / 131	321 / 150	226 / 116	267 / 136	300 / 153	336 / 175	242 / 134	287 / 157	322 / 177	348 / 202
51							201 / 94	237 / 110	267 / 124	308 / 141	217 / 110	256 / 128	288 / 144	329 / 165	233 / 126	276 / 148	309 / 166	341 / 191
52							193 / 88	228 / 104	256 / 117	297 / 133	209 / 103	247 / 121	277 / 136	321 / 156	224 / 119	265 / 139	298 / 157	335 / 180
53											201 / 98	237 / 114	267 / 128	309 / 147	216 / 112	255 / 132	286 / 148	328 / 170
54											193 / 92	229 / 108	257 / 121	297 / 139	208 / 106	246 / 125	276 / 140	319 / 161
55											186 / 87	220 / 102	248 / 115	287 / 132	200 / 101	237 / 118	266 / 133	308 / 152
56											180 / 83	213 / 97	239 / 109	276 / 125	193 / 95	229 / 112	257 / 126	297 / 144
57															187 / 90	221 / 106	248 / 119	287 / 137
58															180 / 86	213 / 101	239 / 113	277 / 130
59															174 / 81	206 / 95	231 / 108	268 / 123
60															168 / 77	199 / 91	224 / 102	259 / 117

* Indicates nominal depth of steel joists only.

† Approximate weights per linear foot of steel joists only. Accessories and nailer strip not included.

*† See manufacturers' catalog for detailed information on specific joist types.

†† For an approximate total load carrying capacity at a maximum allowable tensile stress of 22,000 psi, the total load carrying capacity shown in the load table should be multiplied by the ratio 22/30.

** Section 5.9 of the Standard Specifications for Open Web Steel Joists, H-Series limits the design live load deflection as follows: Floors. 1/360 span. roofs. 1/360 of span where a plaster ceiling is attached or suspended; 1/240 of span for all other cases.

Table 6. Standard load table for longspan steel joists, LH-series—based on a maximum allowable tensile stress of 30,000 psi***

Adopted by Steel Joist Institute and American Institute of Steel Construction, Inc., October 1, 1974

The boldface figures in the following table give the total safe uniformly-distributed load-carrying capacities, in pounds per linear foot, of LH-Series joists. The weight of *dead* loads, including the joists, must in all cases be deducted to determine that *live* load-carrying capacities of the joists. The approximate *dead* load of the joists may be determined from the weights per linear foot shown in the tables.

The lightface figures in this load table are the *live* loads per linear foot of joist which will produce an approximate deflection of 1/360 of the span. *Live* loads which will produce a deflection of 1/240 of the span may be obtained by multiplying the blue figures by 1.5. (Note: The tabulated loads corresponding to these deflection limitations have been computed on the basis of 30,000 psi allowable stress provisions. For joists designed to a lower working stress these loads may be increased in the ratio of 30,000 psi to the design stress used, in order to meet the same deflection limitations.) In no case shall the total load capacity of the joists be exceeded.*

This load table applies to joists with either parallel chords or standard pitched top chords. When top chords are pitched, the carrying capacities are determined by the nominal depth of the joists at center of the span. Standard top chord pitch is 1/8 inch per foot. If pitch exceeds this standard, the load table does not apply. The load table may be used for parallel chord joists installed to a maximum slope of 1/2 inch per foot.

When holes are required in top or bottom chords, the carrying capacities must be reduced in proportion to reduction of chord areas.

The top chords are considered as being stayed laterally by floor slab or roof deck.

The approximate joist weights per linear foot shown in these tables include accessories.

Joist Designation	Approx. Wt. in Lbs. per Linear Ft.	Nominal Depth in Inches	SAFE LOAD** in Lbs. Between	CLEAR OPENING OR NET SPAN IN FEET															
			21–24	25	26	27	28	29	30	31	32	33	34	35	36				
18LH02	13	18	12000	468 313	442 284	418 259	391 234	367 212	345 193	324 175	306 160	289 147	273 135	259 124	245 114				
18LH03	14	18	13300	521 348	493 317	467 289	438 262	409 213	382 194	359 177	337 161	317 148	299 136	283 124	267				
18LH04	16	18	15500	604 403	571 367	535 329	500 296	469 266	440 242	413 219	388 200	365 182	344 167	325 153	308 141				
18LH05	17	18	17500	684 454	648 414	614 378	581 345	543 311	508 282	476 256	448 233	421 212	397 195	375 179	355 164				
18LH06	19	18	20700	809 526	749 469	696 419	648 377	605 340	566 307	531 280	499 254	470 232	443 212	418 195	396 180				
18LH07	21	18	21500	840 553	809 513	780 476	726 428	678 386	635 349	595 317	559 288	526 264	496 241	469 222	444 204				
18LH08	22	18	22400	876 577	843 534	812 496	784 462	758 427	717 387	680 351	641 320	604 292	571 267	540 246	512 226				
18LH09	24	18	24000	936 616	901 571	868 527	838 491	810 458	783 418	759 380	713 346	671 316	633 289	598 266	566 245				
			22–24	25	26	27	28	29	30	31	32	33	34	35	36	37	38	39	40
20LH02	13	20	11300	442 306	437 303	431 298	410 274	388 250	365 228	344 208	325 190	307 174	291 160	275 147	262 136	249 126	237 117	225 108	215 101
20LH03	14	20	12000	469 337	463 333	458 317	452 302	434 280	414 258	395 238	372 218	352 200	333 184	316 169	299 156	283 143	269 133	255 123	243 114
20LH04	16	20	14700	574 428	566 406	558 386	528 352	496 320	467 291	440 265	416 243	393 223	372 205	353 189	335 174	318 161	303 149	289 139	275 129
20LH05	17	20	15800	616 459	609 437	602 416	595 395	571 366	544 337	513 308	484 281	458 258	434 238	411 219	390 202	371 187	353 173	336 161	321 150
20LH06	19	20	21100	822 606	791 561	763 521	723 477	679 427	635 386	596 351	560 320	527 292	497 267	469 246	444 226	421 209	399 192	379 178	361 165
20LH07	21	20	22500	878 647	845 599	814 556	786 518	760 484	711 438	667 398	627 362	590 331	556 303	525 278	497 256	471 236	447 218	425 202	404 187
20LH08	22	20	23200	908 669	873 619	842 575	813 536	785 500	760 468	722 428	687 395	654 365	621 336	588 309	553 285	530 262	503 242	479 225	457 209
20LH09	24	20	25400	990 729	953 675	918 626	886 531	856 542	828 507	802 475	755 437	712 399	673 366	636 336	603 309	572 285	544 264	517 244	517 227
20LH10	27	20	27400	1068 786	1028 724	991 673	956 626	924 585	894 545	865 510	839 479	814 448	791 411	748 377	707 346	670 320	636 296	604 274	575 254

See page 2-87 for notes.

Longspan joists, LH-series

Table 6. (cont.). Standard load table/longspan steel joists, LH-series—based on a maximum allowable tensile stress of 30,000 psi***

CLEAR OPENING OR NET SPAN IN FEET

Joist Designation	Approx. Wt. in Lbs. per Linear Ft.	Depth in Inches	SAFE LOAD** in Lbs. Between 28–32	33	34	35	36	37	38	39	40	41	42	43	44	45	46	47	48
24LH03	14	24	11500	342	339	336	323	307	293	279	267	255	244	234	224	215	207	199	191
				235	226	218	204	188	175	162	152	141	132	124	116	109	102	96	90
24LH04	16	24	14100	419	398	379	360	343	327	312	298	285	273	262	251	241	231	222	214
				288	265	246	227	210	195	182	169	158	148	138	130	122	114	107	101
24LH05	17	24	15100	449	446	440	419	399	380	363	347	331	317	304	291	280	269	258	248
				308	297	285	264	244	226	210	196	182	171	160	150	141	132	124	117
24LH06	19	24	20300	604	579	555	530	504	480	457	437	417	399	381	364	348	334	320	307
				411	382	356	331	306	284	263	245	228	211	197	184	172	161	152	142
24LH07	21	24	22300	665	638	613	588	565	541	516	491	468	446	426	407	389	373	357	343
				452	421	393	367	343	320	297	276	257	239	223	208	195	182	171	161
24LH08	22	24	23800	707	677	649	622	597	572	545	520	497	475	455	435	417	400	384	369
				480	447	416	388	362	338	314	292	272	254	238	222	208	196	184	173
24LH09	24	24	28000	832	808	785	764	731	696	663	632	602	574	548	524	501	480	460	441
				562	530	501	460	424	393	363	337	313	292	272	254	238	223	209	196
24LH10	27	24	29600	882	856	832	809	788	768	737	702	668	637	608	582	556	533	511	490
				596	559	528	500	474	439	406	378	351	326	304	285	266	249	234	220
24LH11	29	24	31200	927	900	875	851	829	807	787	768	734	701	671	642	616	590	567	544
				624	588	555	525	498	472	449	418	388	361	337	315	294	276	259	243

Joist Designation	Approx. Wt.	Depth	SAFE LOAD 33–40	41	42	43	44	45	46	47	48	49	50	51	52	53	54	55	56
28LH05	16	28	14000	337	323	310	297	286	275	265	255	245	237	228	220	213	206	199	193
				219	205	192	180	169	159	150	142	133	126	119	113	107	102	97	92
28LH06	19	28	18600	448	429	412	395	379	364	350	337	324	313	301	291	281	271	262	253
				289	270	253	238	223	209	197	186	175	166	156	148	140	133	126	120
28LH07	21	28	21000	505	484	464	445	427	410	394	379	365	352	339	327	316	305	295	285
				326	305	285	267	251	236	222	209	197	186	176	166	158	150	142	135
28LH08	21	28	22500	540	517	496	475	456	438	420	403	387	371	357	344	331	319	308	297
				348	325	305	285	268	252	236	222	209	196	185	175	165	156	148	140
28LH09	24	28	27700	667	639	612	586	563	540	519	499	481	463	446	430	415	401	387	374
				428	400	375	351	329	309	291	274	258	243	228	216	204	193	183	173
28LH10	27	28	30300	729	704	679	651	625	600	576	554	533	513	495	477	460	444	429	415
				466	439	414	388	364	342	322	303	285	269	255	241	228	215	204	193
28LH11	29	28	32500	780	762	736	711	682	655	629	605	582	561	540	521	502	485	468	453
				498	475	448	423	397	373	351	331	312	294	278	263	249	236	223	212
28LH12	33	28	35700	857	837	818	800	782	766	737	709	682	656	632	609	587	566	546	527
				545	520	496	476	454	435	408	383	361	340	321	303	285	270	256	243
28LH13	36	28	37200	895	874	854	835	816	799	782	766	751	722	694	668	643	620	598	577
				569	543	518	495	472	452	433	415	396	373	352	332	314	297	281	266

Joist Designation	Approx. Wt.	Depth	SAFE LOAD 38–48	49	50	51	52	53	54	55	56	57	58	59	60	61	62	63	64
32LH06	18	32	16700	338	326	315	304	294	284	275	266	257	249	242	234	227	220	214	208
				211	199	189	179	169	161	153	145	138	131	125	119	114	108	104	99
32LH07	20	32	18800	379	366	353	341	329	318	308	298	288	279	271	262	254	247	240	233
				235	223	211	200	189	179	170	162	154	146	140	133	127	121	116	111
32LH08	21	32	20400	411	397	383	369	357	345	333	322	312	302	293	284	275	267	259	252
				255	242	229	216	205	194	184	175	167	159	151	144	137	131	125	120
32LH09	24	32	25600	516	498	480	463	447	432	418	404	391	379	367	356	345	335	325	315
				319	302	285	270	256	243	230	219	208	198	189	180	172	164	157	149
32LH10	26	32	28300	571	550	531	512	495	478	462	445	430	416	402	389	376	364	353	342
				352	332	315	297	282	267	254	240	228	217	206	196	186	178	169	162
32LH11	28	32	31000	625	602	580	560	541	522	505	488	473	458	443	429	416	403	390	378
				385	363	343	325	308	292	277	263	251	239	227	216	206	196	187	179
32LH12	33	32	36400	734	712	688	664	641	619	598	578	559	541	524	508	492	477	463	449
				450	428	406	384	364	345	327	311	295	281	267	255	243	232	221	211
32LH13	36	32	40600	817	801	785	771	742	715	690	666	643	621	600	581	562	544	527	511
				500	480	461	444	420	397	376	354	336	319	304	288	275	262	249	238
32LH14	37	32	41800	843	826	810	795	780	766	738	713	688	665	643	622	602	583	564	547
				515	495	476	458	440	417	395	374	355	337	321	304	290	276	264	251
32LH15	41	32	43200	870	853	837	821	805	791	776	763	750	725	701	678	656	635	616	597
				532	511	492	473	454	438	422	407	393	374	355	338	322	306	292	279

Joist Designation	Approx. Wt.	Depth	SAFE LOAD 42–56	57	58	59	60	61	62	63	64	65	66	67	68	69	70	71	72
36LH07	20	36	16800	292	283	274	266	258	251	244	237	230	224	218	212	207	201	196	191
				177	168	160	153	146	140	134	128	122	117	112	107	103	99	95	91
36LH08	20	36	18500	321	311	302	293	284	276	268	260	253	246	239	233	227	221	215	209
				194	185	176	168	160	153	146	140	134	128	123	118	113	109	104	100
36LH09	23	36	23700	411	398	386	374	363	352	342	333	323	314	306	297	289	282	275	267
				247	235	224	214	204	195	186	179	171	163	157	150	144	138	133	127
36LH10	26	36	26100	454	439	426	413	401	389	378	367	357	347	338	328	320	311	303	295
				273	260	248	236	225	215	206	197	188	180	173	165	159	152	146	140
36LH11	28	36	28500	495	480	465	451	438	425	412	401	389	378	368	358	348	339	330	322
				297	283	269	257	246	234	224	214	205	196	188	180	173	166	159	153
36LH12	32	36	34100	593	575	557	540	523	508	493	478	464	450	437	424	412	400	389	378
				354	338	322	307	292	279	267	255	243	232	222	213	204	195	187	179
36LH13	36	36	40100	697	675	654	634	615	596	579	562	546	531	516	502	488	475	463	451
				415	395	376	359	342	327	312	298	285	273	262	251	240	231	222	213
36LH14	37	36	44200	768	755	729	706	683	661	641	621	602	584	567	551	535	520	505	492
				456	434	412	392	373	356	339	323	309	295	283	270	259	247	237	228
36LH15	41	36	46600	809	795	781	769	744	721	698	677	656	637	618	600	583	567	551	536
				480	464	448	434	413	394	375	358	342	327	312	299	286	274	263	252

See page 2-87 for notes.

Table 6. (cont.). Standard load table/longspan steel joists, LH-series— based on a maximum allowable tensile stress of 30,000 psi*

CLEAR OPENING OR NET SPAN IN FEET

Joist Designation	Approx. Wt. in Lbs. per Linear Ft.	Depth in Inches	SAFE LOAD** in Lbs. Between 47–64	65	66	67	68	69	70	71	72	73	74	75	76	77	78	79	80
40LH08	20	40	16600	254	247	241	234	228	222	217	211	206	201	196	192	187	183	178	174
				150	144	138	132	127	122	117	112	108	104	100	97	93	90	86	83
40LH09	23	40	21800	332	323	315	306	298	291	283	276	269	263	256	250	244	239	233	228
				196	188	180	173	166	160	153	147	141	136	131	126	122	118	113	109
40LH10	25	40	24000	367	357	347	338	329	321	313	305	297	290	283	276	269	262	255	249
				216	207	198	190	183	176	169	162	156	150	144	139	134	129	124	119
40LH11	27	40	26200	399	388	378	368	358	349	340	332	323	315	308	300	293	286	279	273
				234	224	215	207	198	190	183	176	169	163	157	151	145	140	135	130
40LH12	32	40	31900	486	472	459	447	435	424	413	402	392	382	373	364	355	346	338	330
				285	273	261	251	241	231	222	213	205	197	189	182	176	169	163	157
40LH13	36	40	37600	573	557	542	528	514	500	487	475	463	451	440	429	419	409	399	390
				334	320	307	295	283	271	260	250	241	231	223	214	207	199	192	185
40LH14	37	40	43000	656	638	620	603	587	571	556	542	528	515	502	490	478	466	455	444
				383	367	351	336	323	309	297	285	273	263	252	243	233	225	216	209
40LH15	41	40	48100	734	712	691	671	652	633	616	599	583	567	552	538	524	511	498	486
				427	408	390	373	357	342	328	315	302	290	279	268	258	248	239	230
40LH16	47	40	53000	808	796	784	772	761	751	730	710	691	673	655	638	622	606	591	576
				469	455	441	428	416	404	387	371	356	342	329	316	304	292	282	271

Joist Designation	Approx. Wt. in Lbs. per Linear Ft.	Depth in Inches	SAFE LOAD** in Lbs. Between 52–72	73	74	75	76	77	78	79	80	81	82	83	84	85	86	87	88
44LH09	22	44	20000	272	265	259	253	247	242	236	231	226	221	216	211	207	202	198	194
				158	152	146	141	136	131	127	122	118	114	110	106	103	99	96	93
44LH10	25	44	22100	300	293	286	279	272	266	260	254	249	243	238	233	228	223	218	214
				174	168	162	155	150	144	139	134	130	125	121	117	113	110	106	103
44LH11	27	44	23900	325	317	310	302	295	289	282	276	269	264	258	252	247	242	236	232
				188	181	175	168	162	157	151	146	140	136	131	127	123	119	115	111
44LH12	31	44	29600	402	393	383	374	365	356	347	339	331	323	315	308	300	293	287	280
				232	224	215	207	200	192	185	179	172	166	160	155	149	144	139	134
44LH13	35	44	35100	477	466	454	444	433	423	413	404	395	386	377	369	361	353	346	338
				275	265	254	246	236	228	220	212	205	198	191	185	179	173	167	161
44LH14	36	44	40400	549	534	520	506	493	481	469	457	446	436	425	415	406	396	387	379
				315	302	291	279	268	259	249	240	231	223	215	207	200	193	187	181
44LH15	41	44	47000	639	623	608	593	579	565	551	537	524	512	500	488	476	466	455	445
				366	352	339	326	314	303	292	281	271	261	252	243	234	227	219	211
44LH16	47	44	54200	737	719	701	684	668	652	637	622	608	594	580	568	555	543	531	520
				421	405	390	375	362	348	336	324	313	302	291	282	272	263	255	246
44LH17	54	44	58200	790	780	769	759	750	732	715	699	683	667	652	638	624	610	597	584
				450	438	426	415	405	390	376	363	351	338	327	316	305	295	285	276

Joist Designation	Approx. Wt. in Lbs. per Linear Ft.	Depth in Inches	SAFE LOAD** in Lbs. Between 56–80	81	82	83	84	85	86	87	88	89	90	91	92	93	94	95	96
48LH10	25	48	20000	246	241	236	231	226	221	217	212	208	204	200	196	192	188	185	181
				141	136	132	127	123	119	116	112	108	105	102	99	96	93	90	87
48LH11	27	48	21700	266	260	255	249	244	239	234	229	225	220	216	212	208	204	200	196
				152	147	142	137	133	129	125	120	117	113	110	106	103	100	97	94
48LH12	31	48	27400	336	329	322	315	308	301	295	289	283	277	272	266	261	256	251	246
				191	185	179	173	167	161	156	151	147	142	138	133	129	126	122	118
48LH13	35	48	32800	402	393	384	376	368	360	353	345	338	332	325	318	312	306	300	294
				228	221	213	206	199	193	187	180	175	170	164	159	154	150	145	141
48LH14	36	48	38700	475	464	454	444	434	425	416	407	399	390	383	375	367	360	353	346
				269	260	251	243	234	227	220	212	206	199	193	187	181	176	171	165
48LH15	41	48	44500	545	533	521	510	499	488	478	468	458	448	439	430	422	413	405	397
				308	298	287	278	269	260	252	244	236	228	221	214	208	201	195	189
48LH16	47	48	51300	629	615	601	588	576	563	551	540	528	518	507	497	487	477	468	459
				355	343	331	320	310	299	289	280	271	263	255	247	239	232	225	218
48LH17	54	48	57600	706	690	675	660	646	632	619	606	593	581	569	558	547	536	525	515
				397	383	371	358	346	335	324	314	304	294	285	276	268	260	252	245

* Section 104.10 of the "Standard Specifications for Longspan Steel Joists. LH-Series and Deep Longspan Steel Joists. DLH-Series" limits the design live load deflection as follows: Floors, 1/360 of span. Roofs. 1/360 of span where a plaster ceiling is attached or suspended; 1/240 of span for all other cases.

** To solve for safe uniform load between spans shown, divide the safe load in pounds by net span in feet plus 0.67 feet. (The added 0.67 feet, 8 in., is necessary to obtain the proper span for which the load tables were developed.)
To solve for live load between spans shown, multiply the live load of the shortest net span shown in the load table by the (shortest net span plus 0.67 feet), and divide by the (actual net span plus 0.67 feet). The live load shall not exceed the safe uniform load.

*** For an approximate load carrying capacity at a maximum allowable tensile stress of 22,000 psi, the total load carrying capacity shown in the load table should be multiplied by the ratio 22/30.

Table 7. Standard load table for deep longspan steel joists, DLH-series— based on a maximum allowable tensile stress of 30,000 psi***

Adopted by Steel Joist Institute and American Institute of Steel Construction, Inc., October 1, 1974

This table was developed using 30,000 psi allowable tensile stress. Steels with allowable tensile stresses from 22,000 to 30,000 psi may be used to meet this load table. The following table gives the *total* safe uniformly distributed load-carrying capacities in pounds per linear foot of span.

All loads shown are for roof construction only. The weight of *dead* loads, including weight of joists, must in all cases be deducted to determine the *live* load-carrying capacity of the joists. Approximate weights per linear foot of joist include accessories.

The figures shown in lightface are the *live* loads per linear foot of joist which will produce an approximate deflection of 1/360 of the span. Loads which will produce an approximate deflection of 1/240 of the span may be obtained by multiplying the lightface figures by 1.5. (*Note:* The tabulated loads corresponding to these deflection limitations have been computed on the basis of 30,000 psi allowable stress provisions. For joists designed to a lower working stress, these loads may be increased in the ratio

of 30,000 psi to the design stress used, in order to meet the same deflection limitations.) For roofs, *live* load deflection is limited to 1/360 of the span where a plaster ceiling is attached or suspended; 1/240 of the span for all other cases. In no case shall the *total* capacity of the joists be exceeded.*

When holes are required in the top or bottom chords, the carrying capacities must be reduced in proportion to reduction of chord areas.

The top chords are considered as being stayed laterally by the roof deck.

The load table applies to joists with either parallel chords or standard pitched chords. When top chords are pitched, the carrying capacities are determined by the nominal depth of the joist at the center of the span. Standard top chord pitch is ⅛" per foot. If pitch exceeds this standard, the load table **does not** apply.

The load table may be used for parallel chord joists installed to a maximum slope of ½" per foot.

Joist Designation	Approx. Wt. in Lbs. per Linear Ft.	Depth in Inches	SAFE LOAD** in Lbs. Between	CLEAR OPENING OR NET SPAN IN FEET															
			61–88	89	90	91	92	93	94	95	96	97	98	99	100	101	102	103	104
52DLH10	27	52	26700	298	291	285	279	273	267	261	256	251	246	241	236	231	227	223	218
				171	165	159	154	150	145	140	136	132	128	124	120	116	114	110	107
52DLH11	29	52	29300	327	320	313	306	299	293	287	281	275	270	264	259	254	249	244	240
				187	181	174	169	164	158	153	149	144	140	135	132	128	124	120	117
52DLH12	31	52	32700	365	357	349	342	334	327	320	314	307	301	295	289	284	278	273	268
				204	197	191	185	179	173	168	163	158	153	149	144	140	135	132	128
52DLH13	36	52	39700	443	433	424	414	406	397	389	381	373	366	358	351	344	338	331	325
				247	239	231	224	216	209	203	197	191	185	180	174	170	164	159	155
52DLH14	40	52	45400	507	497	486	476	466	457	447	438	430	421	413	405	397	390	382	375
				276	266	258	249	242	234	227	220	213	207	201	194	189	184	178	173
52DLH15	45	52	51000	569	557	545	533	522	511	500	490	480	470	461	451	443	434	426	418
				311	301	291	282	272	264	256	247	240	233	226	219	213	207	201	195
52DLH16	50	52	55000	614	601	588	575	563	551	540	528	518	507	497	487	478	468	459	451
				346	335	324	314	304	294	285	276	267	260	252	245	237	230	224	217
52DLH17	55	52	63300	706	691	676	661	647	634	620	608	595	583	572	560	549	539	528	518
				395	381	369	357	346	335	324	315	304	296	286	279	270	263	255	247
			66–96	97	98	99	100	101	102	103	104	105	106	107	108	109	110	111	112
56DLH11	29	56	28100	288	283	277	272	267	262	257	253	248	244	239	235	231	227	223	219
				169	163	158	153	149	145	140	136	133	129	125	122	118	115	113	110
56DLH12	31	56	32300	331	324	318	312	306	300	295	289	284	278	273	268	263	259	254	249
				184	178	173	168	163	158	153	150	145	141	137	133	130	126	123	119
56DLH13	36	56	39100	401	394	386	379	372	365	358	351	344	338	331	325	319	314	308	303
				223	216	209	204	197	191	186	181	175	171	166	161	157	152	149	145
56DLH14	40	56	44200	453	444	435	427	419	411	403	396	388	381	375	368	361	355	349	343
				249	242	234	228	221	214	209	202	196	190	186	181	175	171	167	162
56DLH15	45	56	50500	518	508	498	488	478	469	460	451	443	434	426	419	411	403	396	389
				281	272	264	256	248	242	234	228	221	215	209	204	198	192	188	182
56DLH16	50	56	54500	559	548	537	526	516	506	496	487	478	469	460	452	444	436	428	420
				313	304	294	285	277	269	262	254	247	240	233	227	221	214	209	204
56DLH17	55	56	62800	643	630	618	605	594	582	571	560	549	539	529	520	510	501	492	483
				356	345	335	325	316	306	298	289	281	273	266	258	251	245	238	231

See page 2-89 for notes.

Table 7 (cont.). Standard load table for deep longspan steel joists, DLH-series—based on a maximum allowable tensile stress of 30,000 psi*

Joist Designation	Approx. Wt. in Lbs. per Linear Ft.	Depth in Inches	SAFE LOAD** in Lbs. Between 70–104	105	106	107	108	109	110	111	112	113	114	115	116	117	118	119	120
60DLH12	31	60	31100	295	289	284	279	274	270	265	261	256	252	248	244	240	236	232	228
				168	163	158	154	150	146	142	138	134	131	128	124	121	118	115	113
60DLH13	36	60	37800	358	351	345	339	333	327	322	316	311	306	301	296	291	286	282	277
				203	197	191	187	181	176	171	167	163	158	154	151	147	143	139	135
60DLH14	39	60	42000	398	391	383	376	370	363	356	350	344	338	332	327	321	316	310	305
				216	210	205	199	193	189	183	178	173	170	165	161	156	152	149	145
60DLH15	45	60	49300	467	458	450	442	434	427	419	412	405	398	392	385	379	373	367	361
				255	248	242	235	228	223	216	210	205	200	194	190	185	180	175	171
60DLH16	50	60	54200	513	504	494	485	476	468	460	451	444	436	428	421	414	407	400	393
				285	277	269	262	255	247	241	235	228	223	217	211	206	201	196	190
60DLH17	55	60	62300	590	579	569	558	548	538	529	519	510	501	493	484	476	468	460	453
				324	315	306	298	290	283	275	267	261	254	247	241	235	228	223	217
60DLH18	62	60	71900	681	668	656	644	632	621	610	599	589	578	568	559	549	540	531	522
				366	357	346	337	327	319	310	303	294	286	279	272	266	259	252	246

Joist Designation	Approx. Wt. in Lbs. per Linear Ft.	Depth in Inches	SAFE LOAD** in Lbs. Between 75–112	113	114	115	116	117	118	119	120	121	122	123	124	125	126	127	128
64DLH12	31	64	30000	264	259	255	251	247	243	239	235	231	228	224	221	218	214	211	208
				153	150	146	142	138	135	132	129	125	122	119	116	114	111	109	106
64DLH13	36	64	36400	321	315	310	305	300	295	291	286	281	277	273	269	264	260	257	253
				186	181	176	171	168	163	159	155	152	148	144	141	137	134	131	128
64DLH14	39	64	41700	367	360	354	349	343	337	332	326	321	316	311	306	301	296	292	287
				199	193	189	184	179	174	171	166	162	158	154	151	147	143	140	136
64DLH15	45	64	47800	421	414	407	400	394	387	381	375	369	363	358	352	347	341	336	331
				234	228	223	217	211	206	201	196	191	187	182	177	173	170	165	161
64DLH16	50	64	53800	474	466	458	450	443	435	428	421	414	407	401	394	388	382	376	370
				262	254	248	242	235	229	224	218	213	208	203	198	193	189	184	180
64DLH17	55	64	62000	546	536	527	518	509	501	492	484	476	468	461	454	446	439	432	426
				298	290	283	275	268	262	255	248	243	237	231	226	220	215	210	205
64DLH18	62	64	71600	630	619	608	598	587	578	568	559	549	540	532	523	515	507	499	491
				337	328	320	311	304	296	288	282	274	267	261	255	249	243	237	232

Joist Designation	Approx. Wt. in Lbs. per Linear Ft.	Depth in Inches	SAFE LOAD** in Lbs. Between 80–120	121	122	123	124	125	126	127	128	129	130	131	132	133	134	135	136
68DLH13	36	68	35000	288	284	279	275	271	267	263	259	255	252	248	244	241	237	234	231
				171	168	164	159	155	152	149	145	142	138	135	133	130	127	124	121
68DLH14	39	68	40300	332	327	322	317	312	308	303	299	294	290	286	281	277	273	269	266
				184	179	175	171	167	163	159	155	152	148	145	141	138	135	133	130
68DLH15	43	68	45200	372	365	360	354	348	343	337	332	327	322	317	312	308	303	299	294
				206	201	196	191	187	182	178	174	170	166	162	158	155	152	149	145
68DLH16	50	68	53600	441	433	427	420	413	407	400	394	388	382	376	371	365	360	354	349
				242	236	230	225	219	214	209	204	199	195	190	186	182	178	174	171
68DLH17	55	68	60400	497	489	481	474	467	460	453	446	439	433	427	420	414	408	403	397
				275	268	262	256	249	244	238	232	228	222	217	212	208	203	198	194
68DLH18	62	68	69900	575	566	557	549	540	532	524	516	508	501	493	486	479	472	465	459
				311	304	297	289	283	276	269	263	257	251	246	240	234	230	225	219
68DLH19	70	68	80500	662	651	641	631	621	611	601	592	583	574	565	557	548	540	532	525
				353	344	336	328	320	313	305	298	291	285	278	272	266	260	254	248

Joist Designation	Approx. Wt. in Lbs. per Linear Ft.	Depth in Inches	SAFE LOAD** in Lbs. Between 84–128	129	130	131	132	133	134	135	136	137	138	139	140	141	142	143	144
72DLH14	39	72	39200	303	298	294	290	285	281	277	274	270	266	262	259	255	252	248	245
				171	167	163	159	155	152	149	146	143	139	136	133	131	128	125	123
72DLH15	43	72	44900	347	342	336	331	326	322	317	312	308	303	299	295	291	286	282	279
				191	187	183	178	174	171	167	163	160	156	152	150	147	143	140	137
72DLH16	50	72	51900	401	395	390	384	378	373	368	363	358	353	348	343	338	334	329	325
				225	219	214	209	205	200	196	191	188	183	179	175	171	169	165	161
72DLH17	55	72	58400	451	445	438	432	426	420	414	408	402	397	391	386	381	376	371	366
				256	250	245	239	233	228	224	218	213	209	205	200	196	191	188	184
72DLH18	62	72	68400	528	520	512	505	497	490	483	479	470	463	457	450	444	438	432	426
				289	283	276	270	265	258	252	247	242	236	231	227	222	217	212	209
72DLH19	70	72	80200	619	609	600	591	582	573	565	557	549	541	533	526	518	511	504	497
				328	321	313	306	300	293	286	280	274	268	263	257	251	247	241	236

* *Section 104.10 of the "Standard Specifications for Longspan Steel Joists, LH-Series and Deep Longspan Steel Joists, DLH-Series" limits the design live load deflection as follows: 1/360 of span where a plaster ceiling is attached or suspended; 1/240 of span for all other cases.*

** *To solve for safe uniform load between spans shown, divide the safe load in pounds by net span in feet plus 0.67 feet. (The added 0.67 feet, 8 in. is necessary to obtain the proper span for which the load tables were developed.)*

To solve for live load between spans shown, multiply the live load of the shortest net span shown in the load table by the (shortest net span plus 0.67 feet)², and divide by the (actual net span plus 0.67 feet)². The live load shall not exceed the safe uniform load.

*** *For an approximate load carrying capacity at a maximum allowable tensile stress of 22,000 psi, the total load carrying capacity shown in the load table should be multiplied by the ratio 22/30.*

Joists, specifications

STANDARD PITCH 1/8 IN. PER FT

PARALLEL CHORDS, UNDERSLUNG

PARALLEL CHORDS, SQUARE ENDS

TOP CHORD PITCHED ONE WAY, UNDERSLUNG

TOP CHORD PITCHED ONE WAY, SQUARE ENDS

TOP CHORD PITCHED TWO WAYS, UNDERSLUNG

TOP CHORD PITCHED TWO WAYS, SQUARE ENDS

Fig. 2. Types of long-span joists

Warren web systems are shown, although other web systems may also be used, depending on the manufacturer.

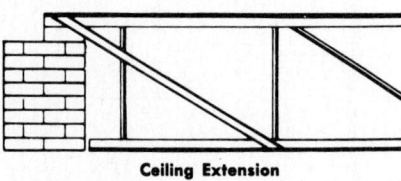

Ceiling Extension

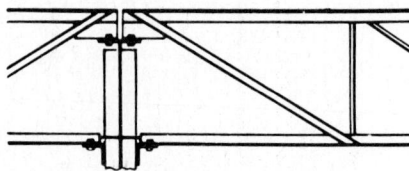

LH and DLH series joists for roof construction on structural steel columns

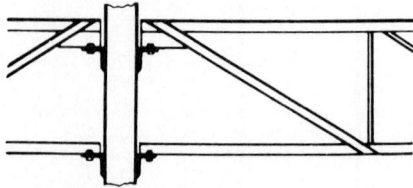

LH series joists for floor construction on structural steel columns

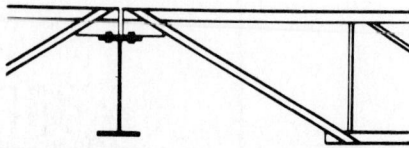

Fig. 3. Welded or bolted connections for open-web joists

Span

The clear span of a joist shall not exceed 24 times its depth.

End supports

H-series: The ends of steel joists shall extend a distance of not less than 4 in. over masonry or poured concrete supports, and not less than 2½ in. over steel supports.

LH, and DLH series: The ends of steel joists shall extend a distance of not less than 4 in. over steel supports. Due consideration of the end reactions shall be taken in the design of the supporting steel. For bearing on masonry and concrete the minimum bearing lengths, parallel to length of joists, are shown in Tables 8 and 9.

Deflection

The deflection due to the design live load shall not exceed 1/360 of the span for floors and for roofs with plaster ceilings, and 1/240 of the span for all other cases.

Bridging

The maximum spacing of lines of bridging for the different chord sizes shall not exceed the values show in Table 10-12. Spaces between rows shall be approximately uniform.

Table 8. Minimum bearing, H-series joists

Chord size*	Joist depth	Minimum bearing length, in. on masonry	on concrete
#3 thru #8	8 thru 24"	4	4
#8	26 thru 30"	5	4
#9	18 thru 30"	5	4
#10 and #11	18 thru 30"	6	4

* Last digit(s) of joist designation shown in load table.

Table 9. Minimum bearing, LH and DLH-series joists

Joist type	Minimum bearing length, in. On masonry	On concrete
LH 02 through LH 11, DLH 10, DLH 11, and DLH 12	6	6
LH 12, LH 13, LH 14, and LH 17, DLH 13, and DLH 14	8	6
LH 15, LH 16, and LH 17, DLH 15 and DLH 16	10	8
DLH 17, DLH 18 and DLH 19	12	9

Table 10. Bridging, H-series joists

Chord size*	Number of rows of bridging (Distances are clear span dimensions, ft)				
	1 row	2 rows	3 rows	4 rows	5 rows†
3	Up to 13	13 to 17	17 to 28		
4	Up to 16	16 to 21	21 to 32		
5	Up to 16	16 to 21	21 to 33	33 to 38	38 to 40
6	Up to 18	18 to 22	22 to 36	36 to 40	40 to 48
7	Up to 20	20 to 25	25 to 41	41 to 46	46 to 48
8	Up to 21	21 to 27	27 to 43	43 to 50	50 to 60
9	Up to 23	23 to 30	30 to 46	46 to 53	53 to 60
10	Up to 24	24 to 30	30 to 47	47 to 53	53 to 60
11	Up to 24	24 to 31	31 to 48	48 to 55	55 to 60

* Last digit(s) of joist designation shown in load table.
† Where five rows of bridging are required and spans are 50 ft or more, the middle row shall be diagonal bridging.

Table 11. Bridging, LH-series

Chord size*	Maximum spacing of lines of bridging
02 to 09 incl.	11'-0"
10 to 14 incl.	16'-0"
15 to 19 incl.	21'-0"

* Last two digits of joist designation shown in load table.

Table 12. Bridging DLH-series

Chord size*	Maximum spacing of lines of bridging
10	14'-0"
11 to 14 incl.	16'-0"
15 to 17 incl.	21'-0"
18 to 20 incl.	26'-0"

* Last two digits of joist designation shown in load table.

Table 13. Representative fire resistance ratings

Hours	Top slab	Ceiling
$\frac{3}{4}$	1-in. tongue and groove single wood floor on 2 × 2 in. wood strips attached to joists	$\frac{3}{4}$-in. sanded gypsum plaster on expanded metal lath
1-$1\frac{1}{2}$	2-in. reinforced concrete or 2-in. precast reinforced gypsum tile	$\frac{3}{4}$-in. portland cement or $\frac{3}{4}$-in. sanded gypsum plaster on expanded metal lath
2	$2\frac{1}{4}$-in. reinforced concrete or 2-in. reinforced gypsum tile with $\frac{1}{4}$-in. mortar finish	$\frac{3}{4}$-in. sanded gypsum plaster on expanded metal lath
2	2-in. reinforced concrete	$\frac{5}{8}$-in. UL listed acoustical tile
2	Roof deck: 1 in. noncombustible insulation board over 18- to 22-gage steel roof deck	
3	$2\frac{1}{2}$-in. reinforced concrete or 2-in. reinforced gypsum tile with $\frac{1}{2}$-in. mortar finish	1-in. neat gypsum plaster or $\frac{3}{4}$-in. gypsum-vermiculite plaster on expanded metal lath
4	$2\frac{1}{2}$-in. reinforced concrete or 2-in. reinforced gypsum plank with $\frac{1}{2}$-in. mortar finish	1-in. gypsum-vermiculite plaster on expanded metal lath

See section on Fireproofing for more examples and test data.

MAXIMUM SQUARE, CIRCULAR, AND RECTANGULAR OPENINGS IN OPEN-WEB STEEL JOISTS

Open-web construction makes it easy to install pipes, ducts, and conduits within the depth of the floor system. The following tables provide dimensions for maximum available openings in the midweb area of H-series joists to facilitate design and selection of ductwork. A minimum clearance of ¼ in. is provided from adjacent diagonal web bars for all maximum openings shown in the tables. Dimensions vary slightly with manufacturer

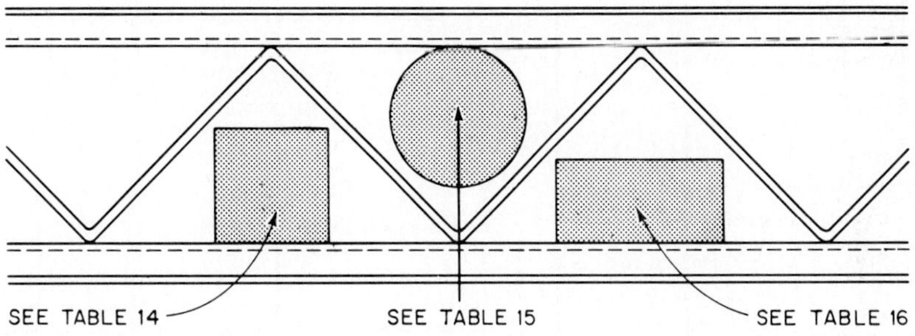

Table 14. Maximum square openings

Nominal joist depth, in.	Maximum square opening, in.
8	$4\frac{1}{8}$
10	5
12	$5\frac{5}{8}$
14	$6\frac{1}{4}$
16	$8\frac{1}{4}$
18	9
20	$9\frac{5}{8}$
22	$10\frac{1}{8}$
24	$10\frac{5}{8}$

Table 15. Maximum circular openings

Nominal joist depth, in.	Maximum circular opening, diam.— in.
8	$3\frac{1}{2}$
10	$4\frac{3}{4}$
12	$5\frac{7}{8}$
14	$7\frac{1}{8}$
16	$8\frac{1}{2}$
18	$9\frac{3}{4}$
20	11
22	$12\frac{3}{8}$
24	$13\frac{5}{8}$

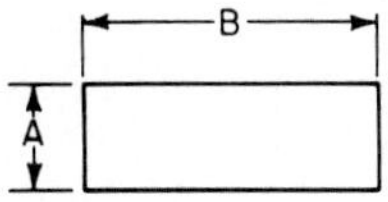

Table 16. Maximum rectangular openings, in.

Reproduced by the courtesy of Bethlehem Steel Corporation.

If A =	2	3	4	5	6	7	8	9	10	11	12
Nominal joist depth, in.						then B =					
8	10	$7\frac{1}{2}$	$4\frac{7}{8}$	$2\frac{1}{4}$							
10	$10\frac{7}{8}$	9	7	$5\frac{1}{8}$	$3\frac{1}{8}$	$1\frac{1}{4}$					
12	$11\frac{1}{4}$	$9\frac{3}{4}$	$8\frac{1}{8}$	$6\frac{5}{8}$	5	$3\frac{1}{2}$	$1\frac{7}{8}$				
14	$11\frac{3}{4}$	$10\frac{1}{2}$	$9\frac{1}{8}$	$7\frac{7}{8}$	$6\frac{5}{8}$	$5\frac{1}{4}$	4	$2\frac{3}{4}$	$1\frac{3}{8}$		
16	$19\frac{1}{4}$	$17\frac{1}{2}$	$15\frac{3}{4}$	$14\frac{1}{8}$	$12\frac{3}{8}$	$10\frac{5}{8}$	$8\frac{7}{8}$	$7\frac{1}{4}$	$5\frac{1}{2}$	$3\frac{3}{4}$	$2\frac{1}{8}$
18	$19\frac{1}{2}$	18	$16\frac{1}{2}$	15	$13\frac{1}{2}$	12	$10\frac{1}{2}$	9	$7\frac{5}{8}$	$6\frac{1}{8}$	$4\frac{5}{8}$
20	$19\frac{5}{8}$	$18\frac{3}{8}$	17	$15\frac{3}{4}$	$14\frac{3}{8}$	$13\frac{1}{8}$	$11\frac{7}{8}$	$10\frac{1}{2}$	$9\frac{1}{8}$	$7\frac{7}{8}$	$6\frac{1}{2}$
22	$19\frac{3}{4}$	$18\frac{1}{2}$	$17\frac{1}{2}$	$16\frac{1}{4}$	15	$13\frac{7}{8}$	$12\frac{3}{4}$	$11\frac{1}{2}$	$10\frac{3}{8}$	$9\frac{1}{4}$	8
24	$19\frac{7}{8}$	$18\frac{3}{4}$	$17\frac{3}{4}$	$16\frac{5}{8}$	$15\frac{5}{8}$	$14\frac{1}{2}$	$13\frac{1}{2}$	$12\frac{3}{8}$	$11\frac{3}{8}$	$10\frac{1}{4}$	$9\frac{1}{4}$

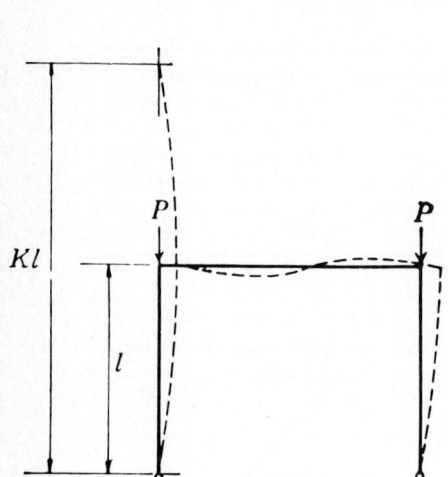

Fig. 4. Effective column length compared to actual unbraced length

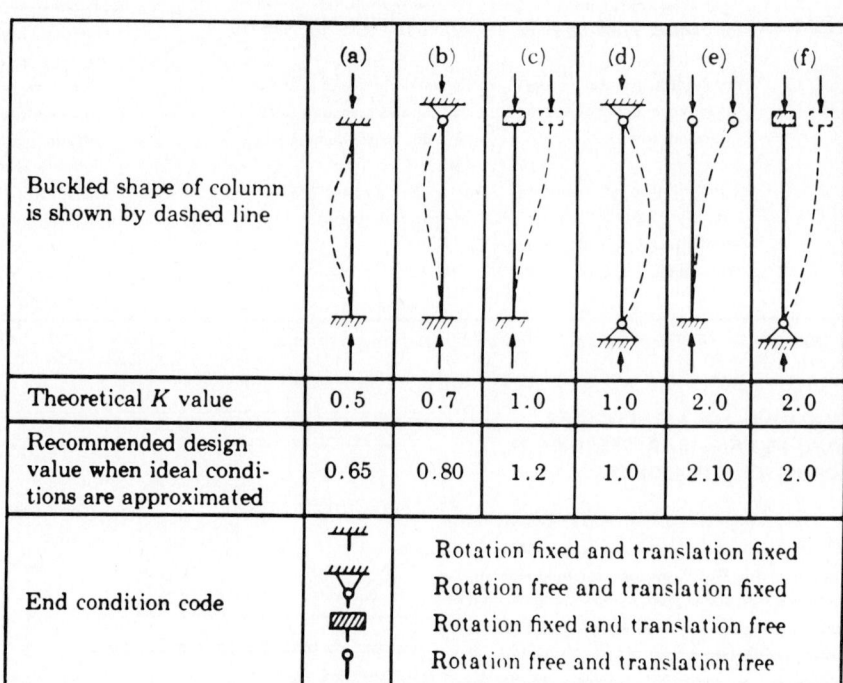

	(a)	(b)	(c)	(d)	(e)	(f)
Buckled shape of column is shown by dashed line						
Theoretical K value	0.5	0.7	1.0	1.0	2.0	2.0
Recommended design value when ideal conditions are approximated	0.65	0.80	1.2	1.0	2.10	2.0
End condition code	Rotation fixed and translation fixed Rotation free and translation fixed Rotation fixed and translation free Rotation free and translation free					

Fig. 5. K-values for various end conditions

COLUMNS

General notes

The allowable load tables which follow are for axially loaded members having the effective unsupported length indicated at the top of the table. The effective length KL is the actual unbraced length, in fact, multiplied by the effective length factor K which is dependent upon the restraint at the ends of the unbraced length and the means available to resist lateral movements. The values and notes shown here have been extracted from the *AISC Manual of Steel Construction*, 7th ed., 1969. For a complete range of values and a comprehensive discussion of the new design approach to steel columns, the Manual should be consulted.

Figure 5, which appears in the Manual, in the Commentary on the AISC Specification, affords a guide to the solution of the K factor. Interpolation between the idealized cases presented is a matter of engineering judgment.

The loads in the tables have been computed in accordance with the provisions of the AISC Specification for columns using ASTM Type A36 steel ($F_y = 36$ ksi). For columns using ASTM A242, A440, and A441, A588, A572, and A514 steel (F_y ranges from 42 to 100 ksi) see AISC Manual, 7th ed.

The loads in the tables are tabulated for main members. All values to the left of the heavy line are for Kl/r ratios equal to or less than 120. Values for Kl/r greater than 120 are shown to the right of the heavy line. Values are omitted when Kl/r exceeds 200. The radius of gyration r is taken about the Y-Y (minor) axis.

Slenderness ratio—Kl/r

One of the most important changes in column design introduced in the seventh edition of the AISC Manual concerns slenderness ratio. The following discussion is taken from the Commentary on AISC Specification.

Considerable attention has been given in the technical literature to the subject of "effective" column length (as contrasted with actual unbraced length) as a factor in estimating column strength.

Two conditions opposite in their effect upon column strength under axial loading must be considered. If enough axial load is applied to the columns in a frame dependent entirely upon its own bending stiffness for stability against sidesway, i.e., uninhibited lateral movement as shown in Fig. 4, the "effective" length of these columns will exceed their actual length. On the other hand, if the same frame were braced in such a way that lateral movement of the tops of the columns with respect to their bases (translation or sidesway) were prevented, the effective length would be less than the actual length, due to the restraint (resistance to joint rotation) provided by the horizontal member. The ratio K, effective column length to actual unbraced length, may be greater or less than 1.0.

The theoretical K-values for six idealized conditions in which joint rotation and translation are either fully realized or non-existent are tabulated in Fig. 5. Also shown are suggested design values recommended by the Column Research Council for use when these conditions are approximated in actual design. In general, these suggested values are slightly higher than their theoretical equivalents, since joint fixity is seldom fully realized.

If the column base in case (f) of Fig. 5 were truly pinned, K would actually exceed 2.0 for a frame such as that pictured in Fig. 4 because the flexibility of the horizontal member would prevent realization of full fixity at the top of the column. On the other hand, it has been shown that the restraining influence of foundations, even where these footings are designed only for vertical load, can be very substantial in the case of flat-ended column base details with ordinary anchorage. For this condition a design K value of 1.5 would generally be conservative in case (f).

While ordinarily the existence of masonry walls provides enough lateral support for tier building frames to prevent sidesway, the increasing use of light curtain wall construction and wide column spacing, for high-rise structures not provided with a positive system of diagonal bracing, can create a situation where only the bending stiffness of the frame itself provides this support.

Table 17. Columns—allowable concentric loads in kips

The loads given in this table are for main members using ASTM Type A36 steel ($F_y = 36$ ksi). Values on right of heavy line are for Kl/r ratios over 120 but not exceeding 200.

Column designation	Depth, in.	Width, in.	Effective length in feet Kl with respect to least radius of gyration: 6	8	9	10	11	12	14	16	18	20	22	24	26	28
W6 × 20	6¼	6	109	100	95	90	85	79	67	54	42	34	28	24		
W6 × 25	6⅜	6⅛	136	126	120	114	107	100	85	69	54	44	36	31		
W8 × 24	7⅞	6½	133	124	118	113	107	101	88	74	59	48	39	33	28	
W8 × 28	8	6½	155	144	138	132	125	118	103	87	69	56	46	39	33	
W8 × 31	8	8	178	170	165	160	154	149	137	124	110	95	80	67	57	49
W8 × 35	8⅛	8	201	191	186	180	174	168	155	141	125	109	91	76	65	56
W8 × 40	8¼	8⅛	229	218	212	205	199	192	177	160	143	124	104	88	75	64
W8 × 48	8½	8⅛	276	263	256	249	241	233	215	196	176	154	131	110	94	81
W8 × 58	8¾	8¼	336	320	312	303	293	283	263	240	216	190	162	136	116	100
W8 × 67	9	8¼	387	370	360	350	339	328	304	279	251	221	190	159	136	117
W10 × 33	9¾	8	189	179	173	167	161	155	142	127	112	95	78	66	56	48
W10 × 39	9⅞	8	224	213	206	200	193	186	170	154	136	116	97	81	69	60
W10 × 45	10⅛	8	260	247	240	232	224	216	199	180	160	138	115	97	82	71
W10 × 49	10	10	289	279	273	268	262	256	242	228	213	197	180	161	142	123
W10 × 54	10⅛	10	317	306	300	294	288	281	267	251	235	217	199	179	158	137
W10 × 60	10¼	10⅛	353	341	335	328	321	313	297	280	262	243	222	201	177	154
W10 × 68	10⅜	10⅛	402	388	381	372	365	357	339	320	299	278	255	230	204	177
W10 × 77	10⅝	10¼	454	439	431	422	413	404	384	362	339	315	289	261	232	202
W10 × 88	10⅞	10¼	521	504	495	485	475	464	442	417	392	364	335	304	271	237
W10 × 100	11⅛	10⅜	592	573	562	551	540	528	503	476	446	416	383	348	312	273
W10 × 112	11⅜	10⅜	663	642	631	619	606	593	565	535	503	469	433	395	355	313
W12 × 40	12	8	229	217	210	203	196	188	172	154	135	114	94	79	67	58
W12 × 45	12	8	256	243	235	228	220	211	193	173	152	129	106	89	76	66
W12 × 50	12¼	8⅛	286	271	263	254	246	236	216	195	171	146	121	102	87	75
W12 × 53	12	10	312	301	295	288	282	275	260	244	227	209	189	169	147	127
W12 × 58	12¼	10	341	329	322	315	308	301	285	268	249	230	209	187	164	142
W12 × 65	12⅛	12	389	378	373	367	361	354	341	326	311	294	277	259	240	220
W12 × 72	12¼	12	430	418	412	406	399	392	377	361	344	326	308	288	267	245
W12 × 79	12⅜	12⅛	473	460	453	446	439	431	415	398	379	360	339	317	294	270
W12 × 87	12½	12⅛	522	508	501	593	485	477	459	440	420	398	376	352	327	301
W12 × 106	12⅞	12¼	637	620	611	602	593	583	561	539	514	489	462	433	404	372
W12 × 136	13⅜	12⅜	799	779	768	757	745	732	706	679	649	618	585	550	514	475
W12 × 190	14⅜	12⅝	1142	1115	1110	1084	1068	1051	1016	978	937	894	849	802	752	700
W14 × 43	13⅝	8	244	230	223	215	207	199	181	161	140	117	96	81	69	60
W14 × 48	13⅞	8	273	258	250	242	233	224	204	182	159	133	110	93	79	68
W14 × 53	13⅞	8	302	286	277	268	258	248	226	202	177	149	123	104	88	76
W14 × 61	13⅞	10	358	345	338	330	322	314	297	278	258	237	214	190	165	142
W14 × 68	14	10	400	385	377	369	360	351	332	311	289	266	241	214	186	160
W14 × 74	14⅛	10⅛	436	421	412	403	394	384	363	341	317	292	265	236	206	177
W14 × 82	14¼	10⅛	482	365	456	446	435	425	402	377	351	323	293	261	227	196
W14 × 90	14	14½	547	536	530	524	517	511	497	482	466	449	432	413	394	374
W14 × 99	14⅛	14⅝	600	589	582	575	568	561	546	529	512	494	475	454	433	411
W14 × 109	14⅜	14⅝	661	647	640	633	626	618	601	583	564	544	523	501	478	454
W14 × 145	14¾	15½	884	869	860	851	842	832	812	790	767	743	718	691	663	634
W14 × 193	15½	15¾	1178	1157	1146	1134	1122	1110	1083	1055	1025	994	961	927	891	853
W14 × 257	16⅜	16	1569	1542	1528	1513	1497	1481	1447	1410	1372	1331	1289	1244	1198	1149
W14 × 342	17½	16⅜	2099	2064	2045	2026	2006	1985	1941	1894	1845	1793	1738	1681	1621	1559

Connection details

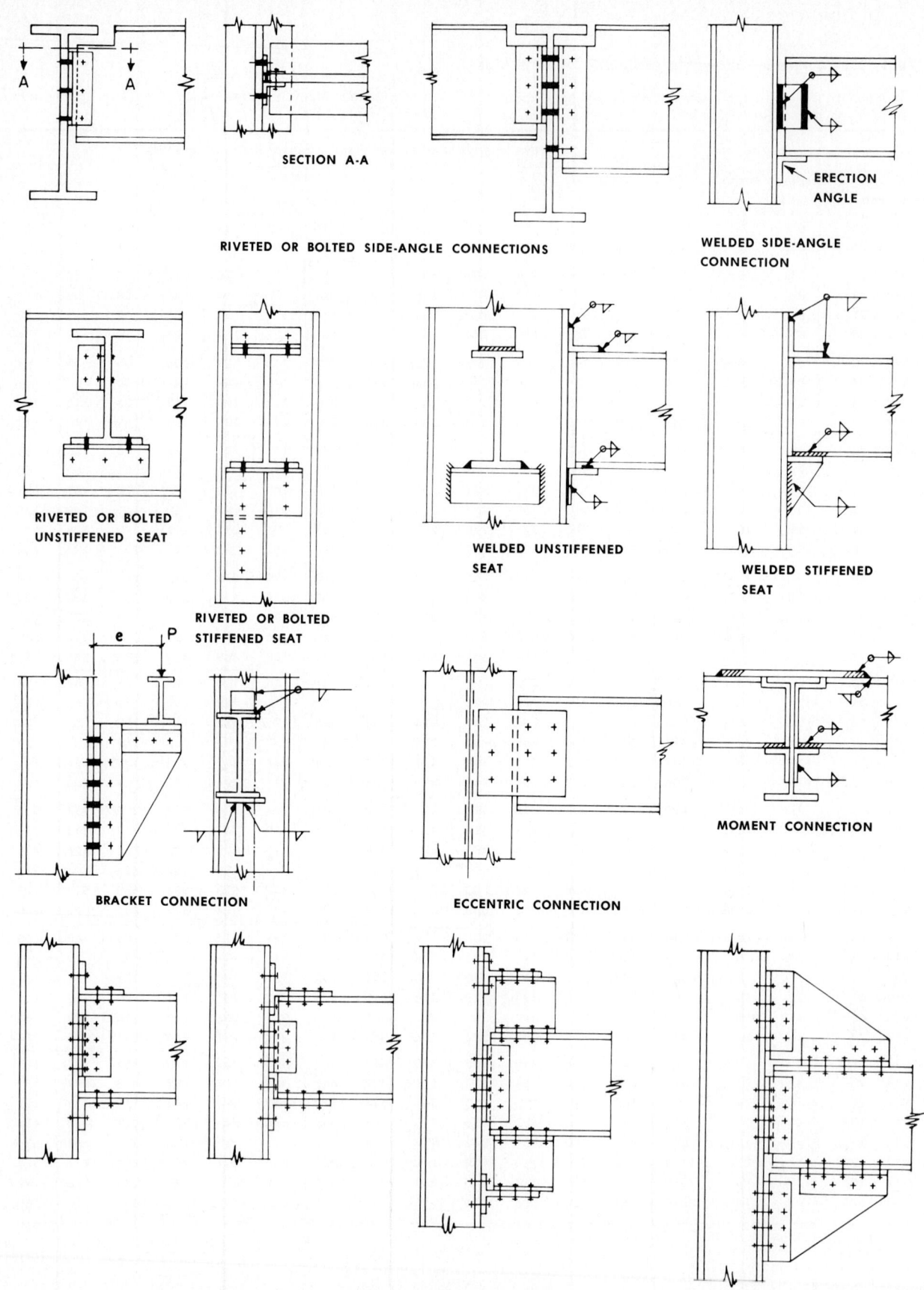

SECTION A-A

RIVETED OR BOLTED SIDE-ANGLE CONNECTIONS

WELDED SIDE-ANGLE CONNECTION

ERECTION ANGLE

RIVETED OR BOLTED UNSTIFFENED SEAT

RIVETED OR BOLTED STIFFENED SEAT

WELDED UNSTIFFENED SEAT

WELDED STIFFENED SEAT

BRACKET CONNECTION

ECCENTRIC CONNECTION

MOMENT CONNECTION

WIND MOMENT CONNECTIONS

Fig. 6.   Connection details

STANDARD AND FIREPROOF LALLY COLUMNS

Fireproofing is furnished in the specified thickness required for any fire rating by local building codes. To ensure that new steel pipe of the proper thickness is furnished, always specify the weight in pounds per foot of every column as given in the tables (for example, "SHW 8⅝ in. × 81 lb").

ECCENTRIC LOADING

The safe concentric loads in Tables 18 and 19 apply only to Lally columns and are based on all loads being applied axially. The strength of Lally columns under eccentric loading is determined as follows: For each 10,000-in.-lb bending moment due to eccentrically applied loads, add the factor f given in the tables to the sum of all vertical loads in kips.

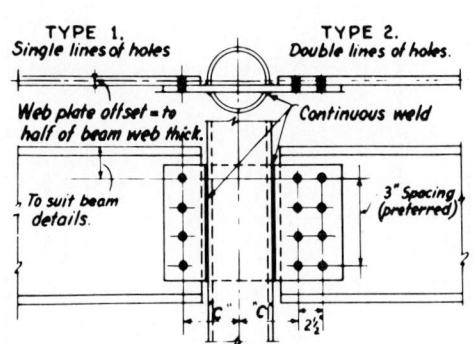

ECCENTRIC LOAD MOMENTS

The following illustrations indicate the method of determining equivalent direct loads for each 10,000-in.-lb bending moment with the use of the factor f given in the last column of the tables for safe concentric loads.

CONTINUITY IN STEEL STRUCTURES

With rare exceptions, the conventional steel building has been designed with simple, flexible connections. This practice has endured despite the fact that the notable advantages of continuity have long been established. Depth of sections and weight of members, for example, are invariably reduced in continuous structures and thus permit savings in material cost. The argument against their employment is that the required rigid connections entail an additional fabricating expense that more than nullifies savings in weight of members and is therefore not economically justifiable. This resistance has gradually lessened in recent years as a result of economical and successful use of continuous steel structures. The development of plastic design in steel and the widespread acceptance of welding are two factors that will increase the use of continuous structures.

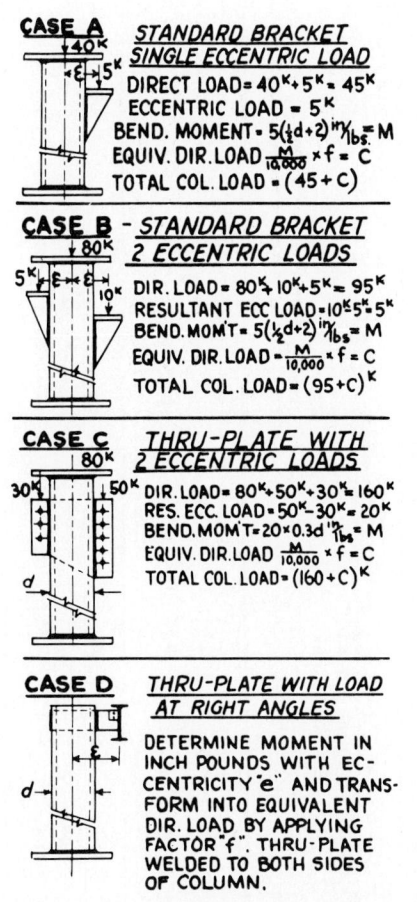

Table 18. Allowable concentric loads in kips

Outside diam., in.	Weight per foot, lb.	Area of steel, sq in.	Area of concrete, sq in.	6	7	8	9	10	11	12	13	14	15	16	17	18	19	20	22	24	26	28	30	32	34	36	38	40	Factor f
											Standard weight																		
3½	15	2.23	7.39	45	42	40	36	32	27																				15.3
4	20	2.68	9.89	58	56	53	49	45	41	36	32																		13.4
4½	24	3.17	12.73	73	70	66	63	59	55	51	46	41	36																12.0
5½	36	4.30	20.00	106	103	99	96	92	89	85	80	75	70	66	60	54													9.6
6⅝	49	5.58	28.89	144	141	139	135	131	127	123	119	114	109	104	99	93	87	81	68										8.2
8⅝	81	8.40	50.03	231	228	225	221	218	214	209	205	200	195	190	184	179	173	167	154	141	126	111							6.3
10¾	123	11.91	78.85	343	339	336	332	328	324	319	315	311	306	300	296	289	283	277	264	251	236	221	206	199	170	153			5.1
12¾	169	14.58	113.10	442	440	437	436	429	426	421	417	412	407	402	397	391	386	380	368	355	341	326	310	294	277	261	241	222	4.4
											Extra strong																		
4	22	3.68	8.90	75	71	66	61	56	51	46	39																		13.5
4½	27	4.41	11.50	93	90	86	81	76	71	65	59	52																	11.9
5½	40	6.11	18.19	139	134	130	125	120	115	110	104	98	91	84	77	69													9.6
6⅝	56	8.41	26.07	197	192	188	183	178	172	166	160	153	147	140	132	125	117	109											8.1
8⅝	91	12.76	45.66	315	309	304	300	294	289	283	277	270	263	257	250	242	234	226	209	191	171	150							6.2
10¾	133	16.10	74.66	423	419	415	410	406	401	394	389	383	377	370	363	356	349	342	326	309	291	273	254	233	211	188			5.0
12¾	178	19.24	108.44	534	530	526	521	517	512	506	501	495	490	484	477	470	464	457	442	426	409	392	374	355	334	313	291	268	4.3
											Double extra strong																		
4½	35	8.10	7.81	155	147	139	131	122	112	102	91																		12.8
5½	52	11.34	12.92	230	222	215	207	198	187	178	167	156	145	132	119														10.1
6⅝	72	15.64	18.80	327	320	312	303	293	283	272	261	250	238	225	212	198	184	169											8.5
8⅝	110	21.30	37.15	475	468	460	452	444	435	425	415	404	394	383	371	359	347	334	307	278	248								6.3

Unbraced length of column in feet up to Kh/r = 120

Note: Other sizes and wall thicknesses are available.

Table 19. Allowable concentric loads in kips—with respect to least radius of gyration

Square

Outside dimension, in.	Weight per foot, in.	Area of steel, sq in.	Area of concrete, sq in.	6	7	8	9	10	11	12	13	14	15	16	17	18	19	20	22	24	26	28	30	32	34	36	38	f, kips
3 × 3 × ¼	15	2.59	6.25	50	46	42	37	33	28																			13.4
3½ × 3½ × ¼	20	3.09	9.00	66	62	58	54	49	44	39	32																	11.4
4 × 4 × ¼	25	3.54	12.25	81	76	72	68	64	60	56	50	45	39															10.0
4 × 4 × ⅜	28	4.95	10.56	104	98	93	88	82	76	69	63	56																10.1
5 × 5 × ¼	36	4.54	20.25	113	109	105	102	98	94	90	85	81	75	71	65	59	53											8.1
5 × 5 × ⅜	40	6.45	18.06	147	141	136	132	127	122	116	110	104	97	91	84	76												8.1
5 × 5 × ½	44	8.14	16.00	176	168	164	157	151	143	136	129	120	112	103	94													8.2
6 × 6 × ¼	49	5.54	30.25	148	143	140	136	133	129	125	122	117	113	107	102	97	91	85	74									6.8
6 × 6 × ⅜	55	7.95	27.56	191	186	182	177	173	168	162	156	151	144	139	132	125	117	110	93									6.7
6 × 6 × ½	60	10.1	25.00	230	224	219	213	207	201	193	187	180	172	163	156	147	138	128										6.7
7 × 7 × ¼	66	6.48	42.25	184	179	176	173	169	166	162	159	154	150	145	140	135	130	124	113	101	87							5.9
7 × 7 × ⅜	72	9.33	39.06	237	231	227	222	218	213	209	204	198	192	186	179	173	166	159	145	129	111							5.8
7 × 7 × ½	78	11.9	36.00	284	277	272	268	262	255	248	243	235	229	221	213	206	197	188	170	150								5.7
8 × 8 × ¼	82	7.48	56.25	223	219	216	213	210	206	203	198	195	190	186	182	177	172	167	155	143	131	118	104					5.2
8 × 8 × ⅜	90	10.8	52.56	286	280	276	272	268	264	259	254	248	243	237	231	225	218	212	198	183	166	149	132					5.1
8 × 8 × ½	97	13.9	49.00	344	338	333	328	323	317	310	304	298	291	284	277	269	261	252	235	217	198	177						5.0
10 × 10 × ¼	126	9.48	90.25	309	305	302	299	296	293	290	286	282	279	274	270	265	260	256	246	235	223	211	198	184	170	154	133	4.3
10 × 10 × ⅜	135	13.8	85.56	392	387	383	380	376	371	367	363	358	352	347	341	335	330	323	311	297	282	267	249	233	215	196	176	4.2
10 × 10 × ½	145	17.9	81.00	471	465	461	456	451	446	440	434	429	422	415	408	402	394	387	370	354	336	317	298	277	255	232	208	4.1

Unbraced length of column in feet up to Kh/r = 120

Rectangular

Outside dimension, in.	Weight per foot, in.	Area of steel, sq in.	Area of concrete, sq in.	6	7	8	9	10	11	12	13	14	15	16	17	18	19	20	22	24	f, kips B-B	f, kips A-A
4 × 3 × ¼	20	3.09	8.75	61	57	52	47	41	36												10.5	12.8
5 × 3 × ¼	24	3.54	11.25	72	67	62	56	49	42												7.5	12.2
6 × 3 × ¼	28	4.04	13.75	84	78	72	65	58	51												7.2	9.5
6 × 4 × ¼	35	4.54	19.25	106	102	98	93	88	82	76	70	63	56								7.2	9.5
6 × 4 × ⅜	40	6.45	17.06	138	133	127	120	113	105	97	89	79	70	63							5.7	9.2
8 × 4 × ¼	46	5.54	26.25	134	128	123	117	110	104	96	89	79	70	63							5.6	9.2
8 × 4 × ⅜	51	7.95	23.56	174	168	160	152	143	134	124	114	103	91	81	72						5.6	9.3
8 × 4 × ½	56	10.1	21.00	210	201	191	181	171	160	146	134	120	107	91	76						5.4	
8 × 6 × ¼	64	6.48	41.25	178	175	171	168	163	159	154	149	144	138	133	126	120	113	106	92		5.3	6.6
8 × 6 × ⅜	70	9.33	38.06	231	226	221	216	210	203	198	191	185	177	170	162	153	145	136	117		5.3	6.4
8 × 6 × ½	77	11.9	35.00	277	271	265	259	251	245	236	228	220	211	201	191	181	171	160	136		4.5	6.4
10 × 6 × ¼	78	7.48	52.25	212	208	203	199	194	189	184	178	172	165	159	151	144	137	128	111	93	4.4	6.5
10 × 6 × ⅜	86	10.8	48.56	273	268	263	257	250	243	236	229	220	212	203	194	184	174	164	142	118	4.4	6.3
10 × 6 × ½	93	13.9	45.00	330	323	316	308	301	293	283	274	264	253	242	231	219	205	194	167			6.2

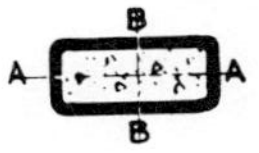

Note: Other sizes and wall thicknesses are available.

PLASTIC THEORY

The limitations of the elastic, straight-line relationship between stress and strain have long been recognized.

The plastic theory has been formulated to take into account realistically the unique characteristic of steel—ductility. The stress-strain relationship of steel (Fig. 7) is composed of an elastic (proportional) range OA and an inelastic range AD. It is in the transition AC from the elastic to inelastic deformations that the important phenomenon of plastic yielding takes place. Figure 8, in which strains are plotted to an expanded scale, illustrates this stage. The significant feature of this stage is that on reaching the yield stress, F_y (36,000 psi minimum), strains in the order of 15 times the strain at yield e_y are produced with virtually no change in stress. Within the elastic range, stresses are directly proportional to strains, which, in turn, are proportional to their distance from the neutral axis. As a result of yielding, however, virtually all fibers, independent of their dis-

tance from the neutral axis, may undergo strains that permit development of yield stress. This stage is known as plastication, from which is derived the term plastic moment (Mp), indicating the moment required for its full development. Figure 9 represents the stress and strain patterns at initial yield, at intermediate point (taken arbitrarily as $3e_u$), and at complete yielding.

Two practical effects result from plastic yielding. The first effect is the increase in the true moment capacity of a section within the limits of yield stress. For the typical rolled steel section this increase is obtained by the utilization at yield stress of the web as well as the entire flange. The ratio between plastic section modulus (Z) and elastic section modulus (S) Z/S is known as the shape factor (u). For most shapes u is equal to approximately 1.12, which indicates an increase in load capacity of 12 per cent beyond initial yield.

The second and more significant effect concerns the relative rotations that take place during yielding. The curve shown in Fig. 8 is also representative of the ideal-

ized relationship between the applied moment (stress) and the angle of rotation (strain). At yield, when the plastic moment is reached at a critical section, the moment is maintained at approximately constant value, while the section rotates in a manner simulating a hinge. This hinge action at the critical section permits a "redistribution" of larger moments to other portions of the structure.

The principles of the plastic theory can be simply illustrated in the behavior of a uniformly loaded beam with fixed ends (Fig. 10). Figure 11 shows the moments at elastic yield (phase 1) and at ultimate load (phase 2). Figures 12 and 13 indicate the rotations and moments corresponding to those loading conditions. At phase 1, the ends of the beam have reached the elastic limit, at which point they enter into the yield stage and begin hinge action. The moments at this point based on elastic analysis are $Wl/12$ at the ends and $Wl/24$ at the center of the span. As loading is increased (phase 1–2), the "hinged" ends permit the beam to act as if simply sup-

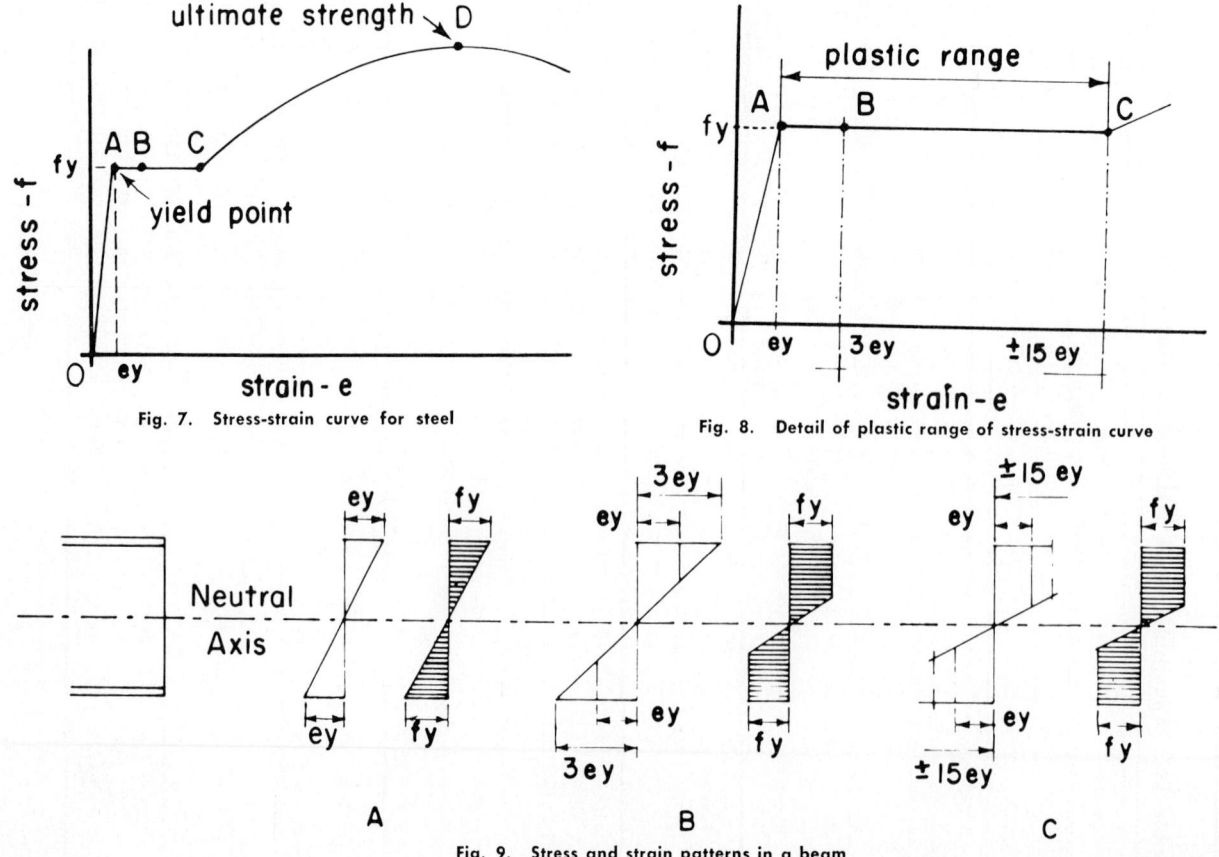

Fig. 7. Stress-strain curve for steel

Fig. 8. Detail of plastic range of stress-strain curve

Fig. 9. Stress and strain patterns in a beam

ported and to utilize the available capacity of the less stressed center portion of the beam. The shaded portion of the moment diagram in Fig. 11 represents the additional load-carrying capacity determined by the plastic theory.

Although the design is based on ultimate capacity utilizing the plastic range of yield, the structure at working loads is almost always stressed well within the elastic limit. Deflections are larger than those obtained by an elastic design but are smaller than those of simply supported members. Special consideration should be given to non-static loading, except for buildings, where loads are basically static.

The importance of the plastic theory extends beyond the practical value of producing more economical structures. Based on the ultimate capacity of a structure, it provides a clearer account of the method of collapse and a more rational design procedure. Safety (load) factors are, consequently, more consistent than in the elastic theory. Moreover, the complex analysis of indeterminate structures is simplified by avoiding approximations and assumptions that require redesign and reanalysis. Since this design method is new and relatively unfamiliar to the professional field, a standard reference is indispensable. The AISC has published two excellent design manuals—in 1956 *Plastic Design in Steel* and in 1968 *Plastic Design of Braced Multi-story Steel Frames*—which fully illustrate analysis and design procedures.

WELDING

After a long period of trial and research, welding has become fully accepted as a means of joining structural members in buildings (Fig. 14). It has the inherent advantage of fusing the metals to be joined, thereby simplifying connections and fabricating operations. In addition, it provides greater opportunities in architectural and structural design—particularly for rigid, continuous structures. Considering the extensive use of welding in other industries, such as ship building, we can hardly consider it an innovation. These industries have been largely responsible for the progress in welding equipment and the training of supervisory and working personnel. Fabricators have now acquired the necessary organization and experience to ensure reliable and economic work.

The fusion welding process most generally used in structural steel work employs an electric arc (Fig. 15). In this process, energy in the form of heat is supplied by establishing an arc between the base or parent metal (the parts to be joined) and a metal electrode. As the arc is formed, tremendous heat is concentrated at the point of welding. Instantly, the materials are at melting-point temperature. The parent metal melts in a small pool and additional metal supplied by the electrode is transferred through the arc and deposited in the pool. As the electrode continues along the joint, the molten metal left behind solidifies to form the weld. Most welding is done with coated electrodes. The function of the coating is to form a gaseous shield, which protects the arc and molten metal from contact with the air. Oxides and nitrides resulting from contact with the air tend to produce brittle welds. The coating also forms a slag-flux shield, which floats above the molten metal, protecting it from the atmosphere. The slag is easily removed after the weld has cooled.

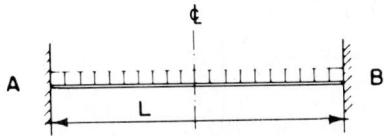

Fig. 10.   Uniformly loaded beam with fixed ends

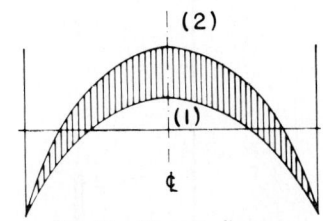

Fig. 11.   Moment diagram

1 — at elastic yield, 2 — at ultimate load; true also for Fig. 12–13.

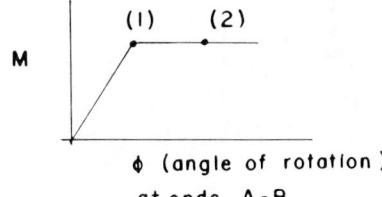

Fig. 12.   Rotation at ends of beam

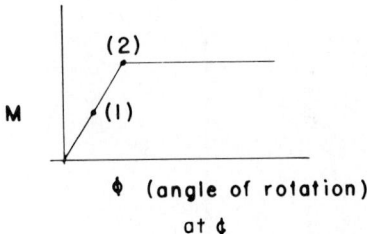

Fig. 13.   Rotation at center of beam

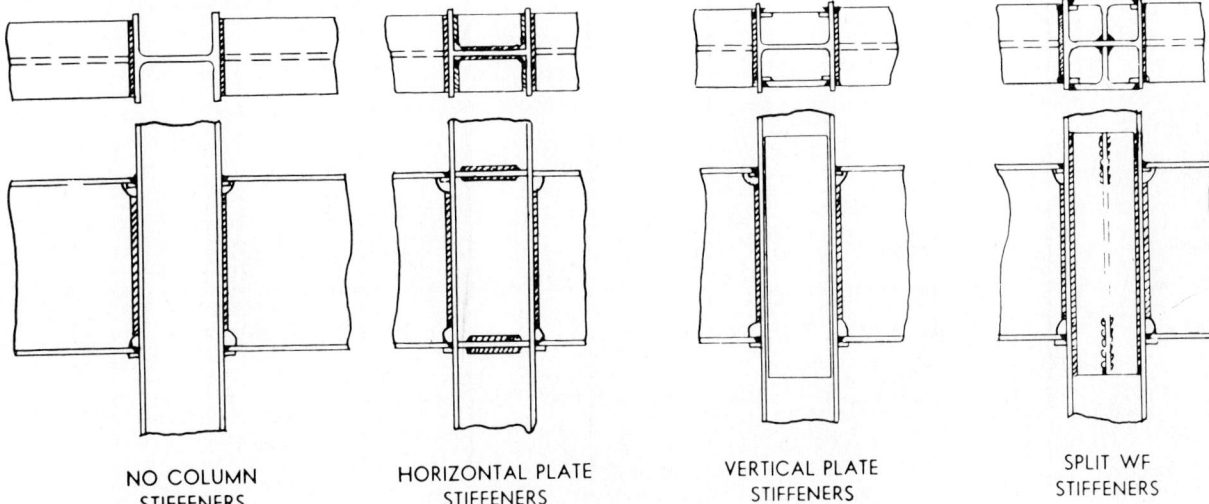

NO COLUMN STIFFENERS

HORIZONTAL PLATE STIFFENERS

VERTICAL PLATE STIFFENERS

SPLIT WF STIFFENERS

Fig. 14.   Welded column and beam connections

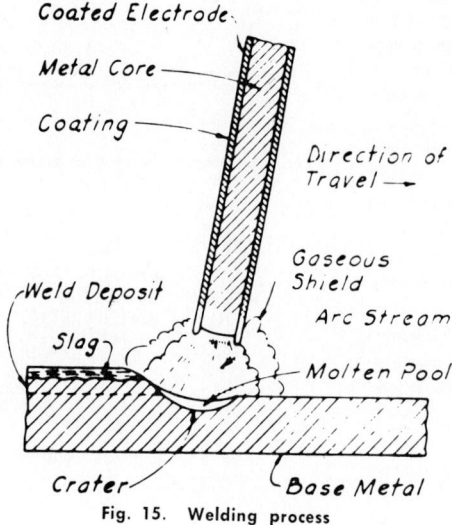

Fig. 15. Welding process

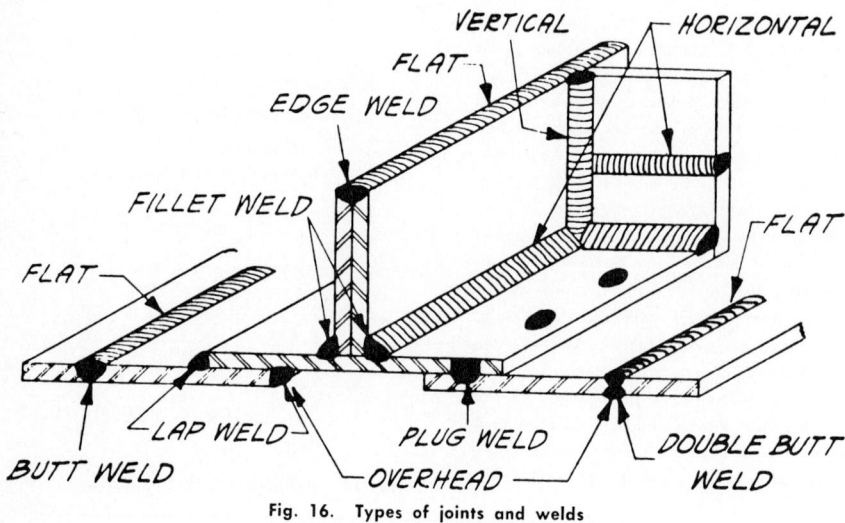

Fig. 16. Types of joints and welds

CLASSIFICATION OF WELDS

Types (Fig. 16)

1. *Fillet weld* is of approximately triangular cross section joining two surfaces approximately at right angles to each other. The size of the fillet weld is determined by the length of leg. The allowable stress may be computed on the basis of 800 pounds per linear inch per $1/16$ in. of leg size for welds made with an E60 electrode on A36 steel. For welding A36, or higher-strength steels up to $F_y = 60$ ksi, an E70 electrode should be used and the allowable stress may be computed on the basis of 930 pounds per linear inch per $1/16$ in. of leg size. The fillet weld is the most common type of weld used in structural work.

2. *Groove weld* is made by depositing filler metal in a groove between two members to be joined. The standard types of grooves are square, V, bevel-U, and J. With the exception of the square groove, all grooves may be either single or double.

3. *Plug or slot weld* is made in a circular hole (plug) or elongated hole (slot) in one member of a lap joint, joining that member to the portion of the surface of the other member that is exposed through the hole.

Positions

There are four positions in welding. In order of economy, they are the flat, horizontal, vertical, and overhead positions. Overhead welds, which are the most difficult, should be avoided whenever possible.

Joints

The three most common joints used in structural work are the butt, T, and lap joints. Other types are the edge and corner joints. Fillet welds are applicable to T, lap, and corner joints; groove welds are applicable to all joints with the exception of lap joints.

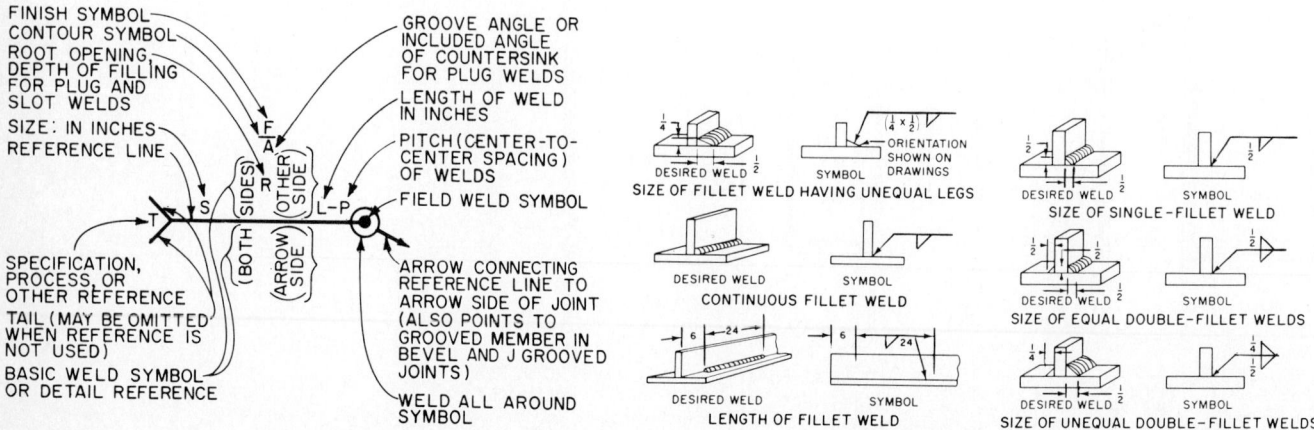

Fig. 17. Standard welding symbols

Fig. 18. Welding symbols—examples of use

By SEYMOUR HOWARD, *Architect*
Associate Professor, School of Architecture, Pratt Institute

Purpose of this section: To give the architect a description and analysis of the principal features of certain structural forms as they affect preliminary architectural design.

RIGID FRAMES IN STEEL

Shape of frame—structural considerations

For each condition of loading there exists a corresponding frame shape in which bending stresses can be eliminated. This shape is the *pressure line* and can be found from the string polygon for the given loading (Fig. 19).

A frame when built, however, is not subject to only a single condition of loading. The self-weight of the structure is constant, but the shape will be distorted by temperature changes, by axial strains, and may be deformed by foundation movement. And the imposed, live-loads will vary with weather and with the use of the structure.

These variations in loading can be properly anticipated by choosing a shape which corresponds best to the loadings expected for most of the time and which corresponds safely to the loadings expected at any time. This form will require the least material and will usually not cause tensile stresses.

Shape of frame—architectural considerations

Although they are often the most satisfying aesthetically, the curved (or polygonal) forms, and the large height-to-span ratios required by purely structural considerations, are often wasteful of cubage and expensive to construct. (See Fig. 20.)

When architectural considerations necessitate rectangular shapes, bending moments are introduced and larger sections are required. The more the shape of the frame departs from the pressure line, the greater the bending stresses introduced. In fact, the bending moment at any point on the frame can be calculated from the distance between that point and the corresponding point on the pressure line (Figs. 21, 22).

WARNING. *In no case should shapes or sizes approximated from these diagrams and tables be used without a complete structural analysis based on the specific problem, even if the conditions of loading seem to be exactly the same as those on which these diagrams and tables are based. The reference material cited in each case can be used for the more complete analysis.*

Fig. 19   *Frame shapes to eliminate bending stresses for various loadings. The bending moment or funicular curve for a simply supported beam with the same loading gives the desired curve*

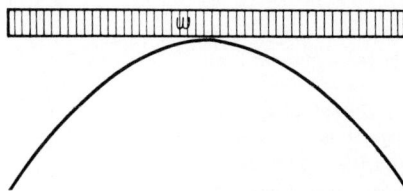

For exactly equal horizontal loading,
A Parabola

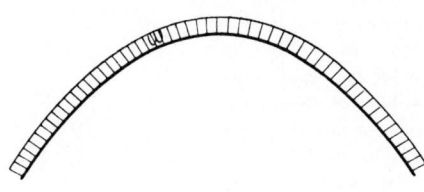

For the dead weight of a constant section,
A Catenary

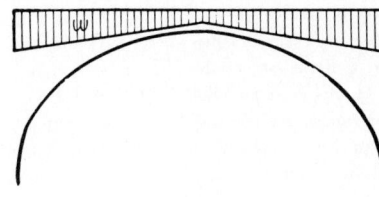

For increasing load toward the abutments,
A Third-Degree Parabola

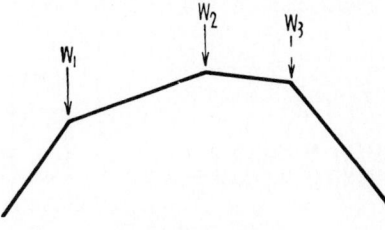

For point loads,
A Polygon

Slight changes in the shape of the pressure line with all except heavy concentrated loads have little effect on the frame design. This is true even for typical arch design where, theoretically, it is possible to make the arch axis and the pressure line coincide (for any single load condition) for the full span.

If the axis and the pressure line do not coincide, additional material is required to resist the moments induced. However, this added material is not entirely wasted because it provides an additional safety factor against unusual unbalanced load conditions. Is for this reason that unbalanced loads are so critical in the case of curved arches and are relatively of little concern in the typical rigid frame.

Where dead weight of the frame is extreme or where loads are unusual, some economies can be effected by careful study of the pressure line location.

Since rectangular frames depart the most from the usual pressure line, the diagrams have been prepared for this type. Section depths chosen on the basis of the rectangular frame can be used for preliminary purposes for other shapes as well.

Depth of section has been used as the principal function because this is usually the major consideration in preliminary design.

In making the final calculations for a frame, it may be found economical to use one depth of section for the girder and another for the column portion. These variations will affect the distribution of moments in the frame as in Fig. 23 shown below.

Whether the column and girder sections are of the same depth or not, a frame in which rolled sections are used is less expensive to fabricate than a frame of variable section, though it will require more material. Variable depth section frames are therefore more often used for long span frames, which cannot be fabricated from rolled sections (Fig. 24).

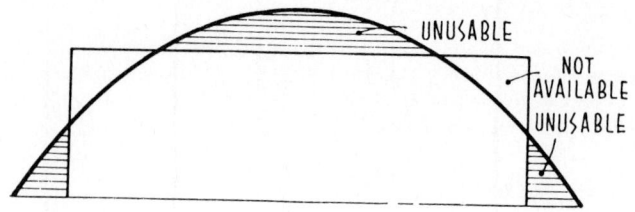

Fig. 20 *Frames following the shape of the pressure line may waste cubage*

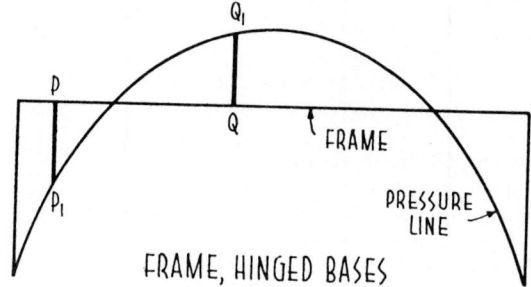

Fig. 21

Bending moment varies in proportion to the distance from the frame to the pressure line

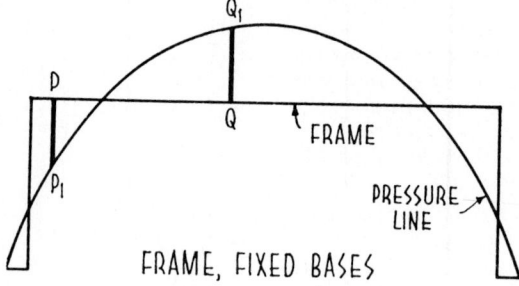

Fig. 22

Few frames are built without haunches at the knee and relatively few are built with horizontal girders. Therefore, the depths shown in Diagram 1 are somewhat larger than those normally used. Table 20 gives a comparison between a few "complete" designs (with normal knee haunches) and the recommendations of Diagram 1.

Fig. 23 *Effect of girder and column sizes on bending moments*

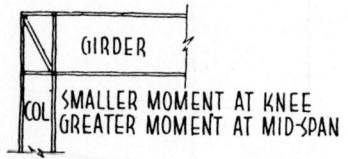

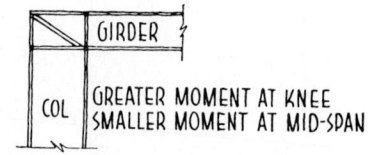

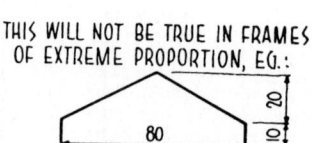

Fig. 24

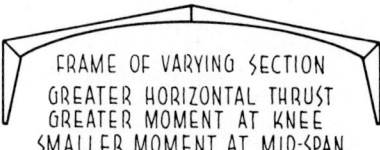

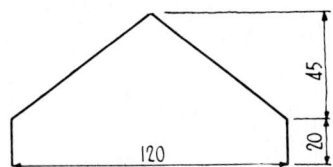

As the frame departs from a rectangular shape, moments are reduced. For a simple gable shape, the reduction will permit up to a maximum of about 20% reduction in depth of section for relatively extreme proportions as shown above right

Table 20

Span, ft	Height, ft	Column, in.	Girder, in.	Depth of Section, in.
40	12	14	12	17
60	16	18	16	22
80	16	24	24	27
100	16	30	27	32
120	16	36	30	38

Header spanning: Actual Conditions with haunched frames | Theoretical Conditions (See Diagram 1)

Note: For exact calculations for a given frame, use Single Span Rigid Frames in Steel, *by John D. Griffiths, published by American Institute of Steel Construction, Inc., New York, or standard texts on indeterminate structures.*

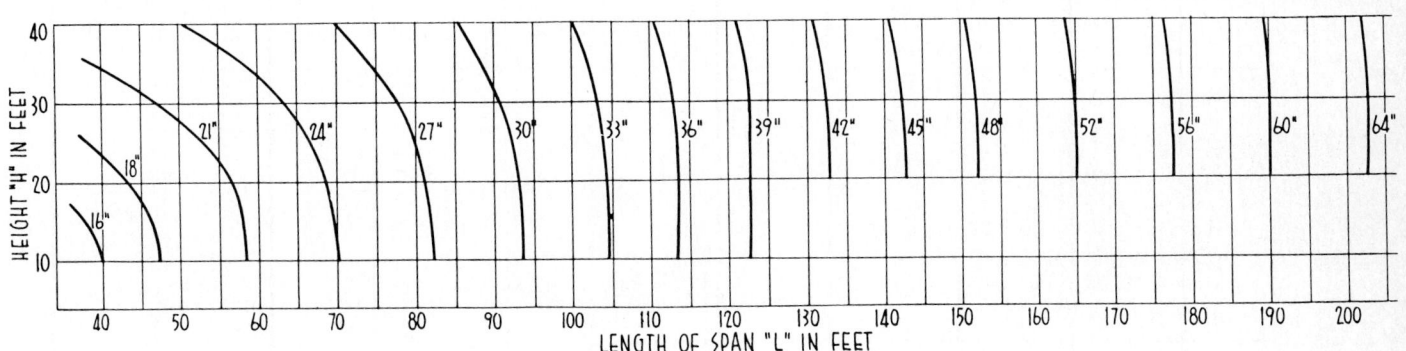

Diagram 1. Depth of section as function of length of span and height

Calculated for rectangular frames, spaced as shown in Diagram 2, and carrying total vertical load (including structure) of 50 lbs/sq ft and a horizontal load of 30 lbs/sq ft

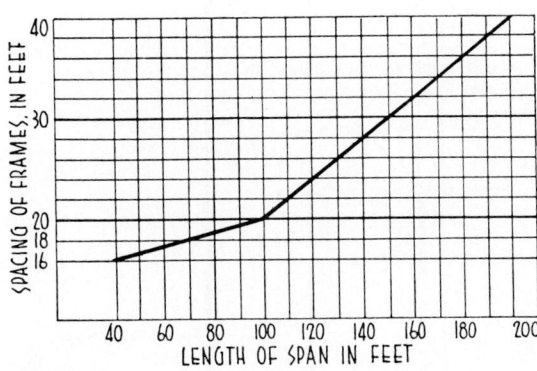

Diagram 2

Showing spacing of frames used to make calculations for Diagram 1

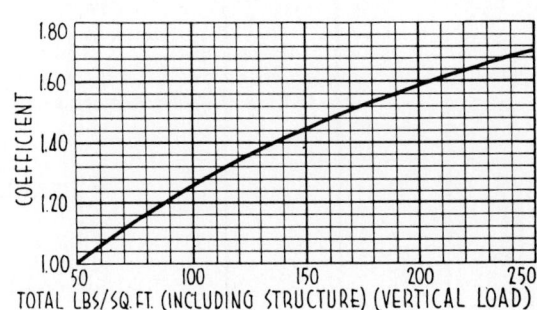

Diagram 3

Multiply depth of frame as found in Diagram 1 by coefficient corresponding to actual total load per sq ft

Fig. 25

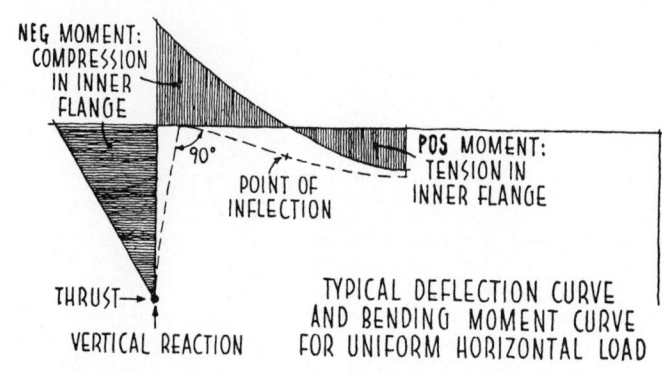

STIFFENERS IN LINE WITH INNER FLANGES AND OF SAME SECTION · DEPTH "D" · STIFFENER ON RADIAL LINE

PURLIN USED AS BRACE FOR COMPRESSION FLANGE AT KNEE

STRAIGHT KNEE

HEIGHT "H"

BASE

SPACING "S"

STRUT USED AS BRACE FOR COMPRESSION FLANGE AT KNEE

RAD.

CIRCULAR HAUNCHED KNEE

TIE BAR (IF REQUIRED)

LENGTH OF SPAN "L"

PERSPECTIVE SHOWING PRINCIPAL FEATURES OF TYPICAL SINGLE SPAN RIGID FRAME IN STEEL

Either straight knee or haunched knee (circular or polygonal) may be used. Frame can be made equally strong with either. Haunched knee increases thrust, increasing moment at knee and decreasing midspan moment

NEG MOMENT: COMPRESSION IN INNER FLANGE

90°

POINT OF INFLECTION

POS MOMENT: TENSION IN INNER FLANGE

THRUST

VERTICAL REACTION

TYPICAL DEFLECTION CURVE AND BENDING MOMENT CURVE FOR UNIFORM HORIZONTAL LOAD

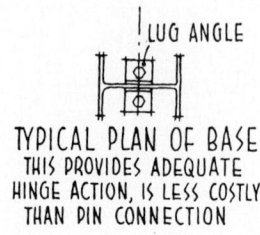

LUG ANGLE

TYPICAL PLAN OF BASE
THIS PROVIDES ADEQUATE HINGE ACTION, IS LESS COSTLY THAN PIN CONNECTION

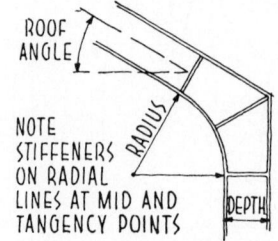

ROOF ANGLE

RADIUS

DEPTH

NOTE STIFFENERS ON RADIAL LINES AT MID AND TANGENCY POINTS

HAUNCH RADIUS	
Roof Angle	**Radius**
0°	3 x Depth
15°	2.5 x "
30°	2.0 x "
45°	1.75 x "

GENERAL CONSIDERATIONS

Advantages (compared with column & truss design)

Decrease in height (and cube) of building

Increase in clear headroom within building

Simpler maintenance

Clean appearance

Simpler erection

Disadvantages

Greater weight of steel may be required

Builder and fabricator may be unfamiliar with detailing and erection

Fig. 26 **OTHER TYPICAL ONE STORY RIGID FRAME SHAPES INCLUDE TYPES DESIGNED FOR MAXIMUM USABLE CUBAGE, FOR PARTICULAR ROOF COVERINGS AND FOR MONITOR LIGHTING**

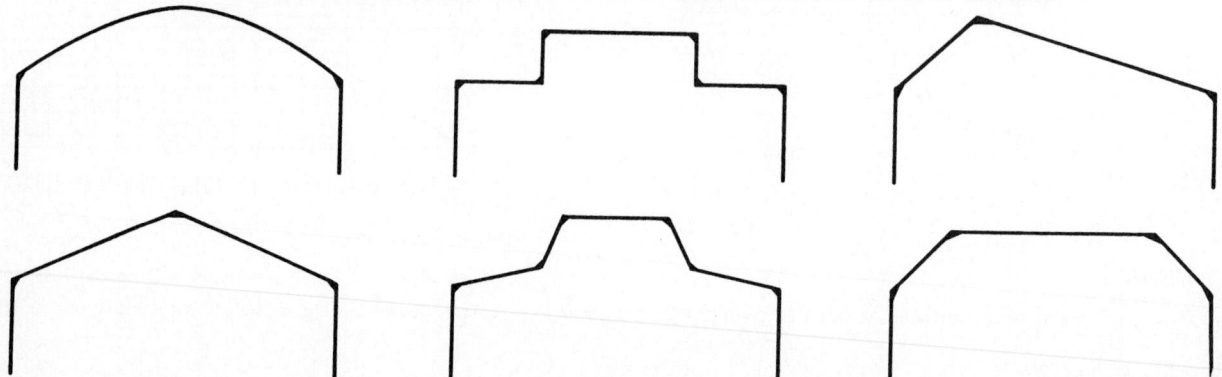

By ROBERT E. RAPP, *Regional Engineer, American Institute of Steel Construction, Inc.*

Space structures are of three general types: simple monolithic grid, double layer grid (space frame), and co-planar systems (folded or curved structures).

Grid systems are illustrated in Fig. 27. It is apparent that the analysis and fabrication costs would be less for the rectangular or diagonal arrangements than for the other types shown. The diagonal system, commonly called "diagrid," is more rigid than the rectangular type and therefore is usually preferred. The advantages of grid construction as compared to beam and girder framing are: reduction (up to 50 per cent) in required structural depth, saving (up to 25 per cent) in the amount of steel required, simplification of fabrication due to repetition of members, and better resistance to earthquake and other horizontal forces.

Double layer grids (space frames) are used for longer spans where the monolithic grid becomes too cumbersome. These three-dimensional planar systems are designed in many geometric patterns and have many names. This subject is discussed in more detail on the following pages. A typical double layer grid is shown in Fig. 28.

Domes, vaults, and folded plates are examples of co-planar space grids. Domes of several types are illustrated and discussed further on in this section. Folded plate roofs are usually simple alternations of ridges and valleys spanning rectangular areas, but they may also be used with a circular plan to produce a dome-like structure (Fig. 29). Greater spans may be achieved with the folded plate spatial grid by the use of the rhombic or lattice truss (Fig. 30). Although lattice trusses are indeterminate, they make possible the spanning of long distances with relatively light members. Spans up to 300 ft are practicl and economical with lattice structures.

Analysis. Even the simplest of the grid space systems are highly complex to analyze. The complexity may be greatly reduced by assuming that the joints are hinge-connected instead of rigid, and by ignoring the torsional forces; the results will err on the conservative side. Dr. Makowski's method (see reference below) permits the solution of rectangular or diagrid frames in a matter of minutes. If lightness of the structure is the prime factor in the design, however, more exact analysis must be employed. This analysis is highly redundant, especially with the co-planar or double layer systems. Where many complex designs are involved it would probably be advisable to use an electronic computer.

REFERENCES

Dr. Z. S. Makowski, An Analysis of Open Grid Framework, *Architectural Association Journal,* London, March, 1961.

Oliver A. Baer, Steel Frame Folded Plate Roof, *Journal of Structural Division Proceedings,* American Society of Civil Engineers, New York.

A bibliography on grid and space frames is available without charge from the American Institute of Steel Construction, Inc., Chicago, Illinois.

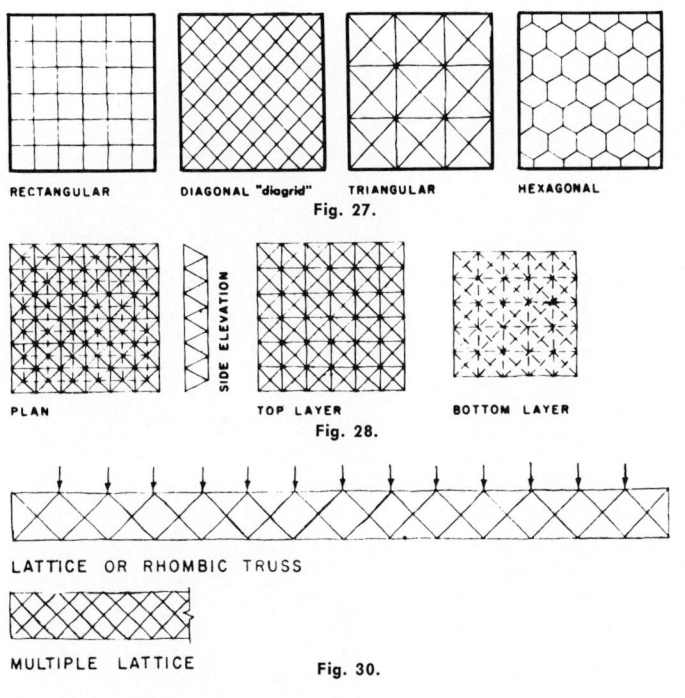

RECTANGULAR   DIAGONAL "diagrid"   TRIANGULAR   HEXAGONAL

Fig. 27.

SIDE ELEVATION

PLAN   TOP LAYER   BOTTOM LAYER

Fig. 28.

LATTICE OR RHOMBIC TRUSS

MULTIPLE LATTICE   **Fig. 30.**

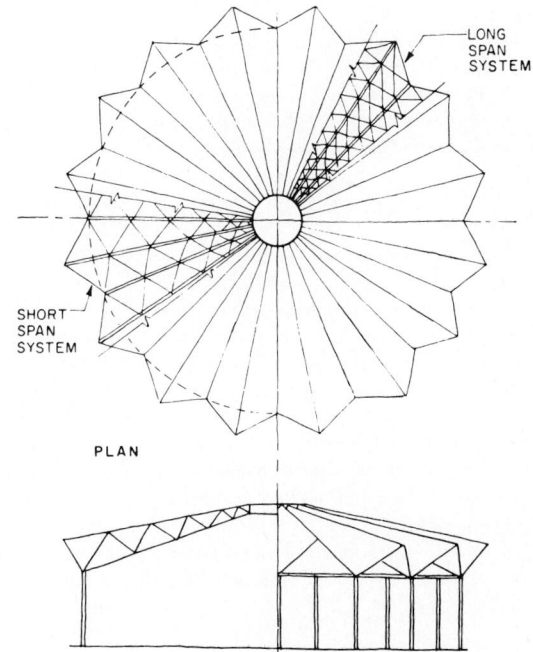

LONG SPAN SYSTEM

SHORT SPAN SYSTEM

PLAN

Fig. 29.

By SEYMOUR HOWARD, *Architect,*
Associate Professor, School of Architecture, Pratt Institute

Known also as lattice structures or three-dimensional trusses, space frames may be most simply thought of as three-dimensional equivalents of the commonly used plane trusses. Some of their characteristics are described below.

Nature of members

As for a plane truss, roof or floor decking and other elements should be so arranged that all loads are transferred to the joints of the truss. In that way all members of the truss can act as two-force members. The members should theoretically have spherical (ball-and-socket) hinges at their ends—a most difficult condition to realize in practice. The construction of the joints, even with a certain amount of restraint, is a difficult and costly problem, and is, as a result, the principal basis for patents. It is also the chief reason why space frames are not more frequently used.

Materials

Space frames can be built of reinforced concrete or, more typically, of steel or aluminum. If the joint problem is solved, space frames are feasible even of wood. In order to simplify construction, engineers tend to use members of uniform size. If all the members are made of tubes of the same outside diameter, the wall thickness can be varied (although at considerable expense) to maintain uniform stresses in the material. Otherwise the majority of the members must be oversized for the most heavily loaded not to be overstressed.

Depth

The principal purpose of the depth of any structural assembly is to provide an adequate moment arm between the upper and lower edges. The depths of space frames therefore correspond fairly closely to those of plane trusses under similar loadings. A single prismatic frame with heavy loads would require a depth of from 1/6 to 1/12 of the span. A complete floor system, however, with the top and bottom chords forming a two- or three-way grid similar to a system of closely spaced joists, would permit a minimum depth of 1/20 to 1/24 of the span.

Methods of determining forces

Most plane trusses used in building construction are statically determinate, and the forces (bar stresses) found through statics equations or Maxwell-Cremona diagrams are reasonably accurate. For three-dimensional trusses, however, even though statically determinate, the forces found through statics equations alone are often not sufficiently accurate for an economical design. Their configurations are such that one or more members at a particular joint would often be statically redundant for a given loading. The end conditions at the joints must also be taken into account. Solutions based on energy equations are more satisfactory, but are tedious. Model testing is probably the best, but is also the most costly method.

The basic geometrical unit in space frames is the tetrahedron, corresponding to the triangle in plane trusses.

The minimum number of members (m) necessary for a rigid truss, is related to the number of joints (j) by the following formula:

$$m = 3j - 6$$

Although the corresponding formula for plane trusses ($m = 2j - 3$) is seldom used, since the triangulation can usually be checked by eye, the formula for three-dimensional trusses should always be used as a check on the number of members. The hexagonal, parallel-plane space truss shown in Fig. 31, for example, would require at least three hexagons to satisfy the formula; the type S isometric space truss (Fig. 33) would require at least six squares in the upper plane.

This formula expresses a necessary condition for rigidity, but not a sufficient one. Some configurations meet this condition but still permit deformation. For such configurations additional checks such as the "zero-load test" should be made. (For an example, see *Theory of Structures* by S. Timoshenko and D. H. Young, McGraw-Hill, 1945.)

TYPES

The various types of space frames can be classified by the polyhedra from which they are built up.

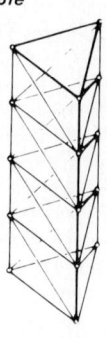
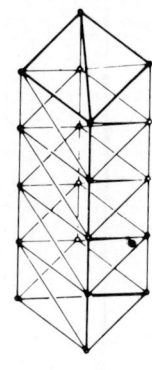
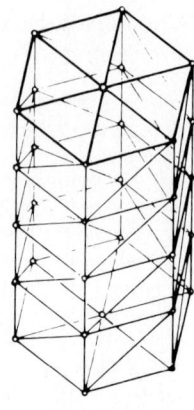

Triangular

Square

Hexagonal

Fig. 31. Space-frame towers

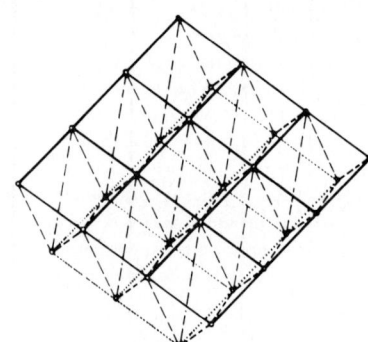

Triangular

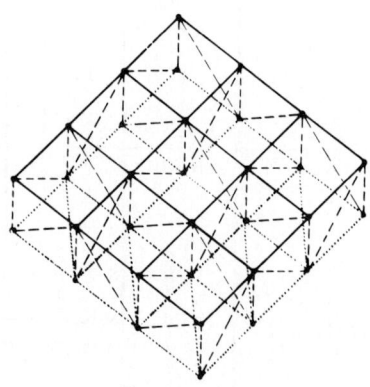

Rectangular

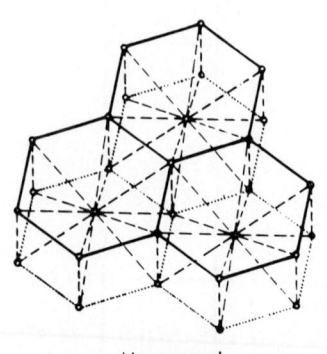

Hexagonal

Fig. 32. Space trusses for floors and roofs

For simple structures such as towers or isolated trusses, the space frame can be thought of as a single polyhedron. Any closed polyhedron whose faces are rigid (completely triangulated) must be itself rigid. Thus the triangular, square, and hexagonal towers shown in Fig. 31 can be completely hollow, provided the top and bottom planes are triangulated. Or they could be hollow if the tower were to be laid on its side as a single trussed girder.

The three towers are drawn in axonometric projection. All vertical and horizontal members can be the same length; only the diagonals on the sides and across the top and bottom of the square tower must be longer.

Other polyhedra (such as those shown on Sheets 26 and 27 of "Useful Curves and Curved Surfaces") would also be rigid space frames if all the faces were triangulated.

In searching for a space-frame pattern suitable for a complete floor or roof, we can investigate some of the lattices formed by the various space-filling polyhedra. (See the notes at the bottom of Sheet 27, "Useful Curves and Curved Surfaces.") We are interested in those lattices that give a level upper plane (floor) and a parallel lower plane (ceiling or floor). In Fig. 32, all members in the upper plane are drawn with full lines, all those in the bottom plane with dotted lines, and those in between with broken lines.

The *triangular prism*, used as the basic geometrical unit, gives two sets of plane trusses, which meet at an angle (here, 90 deg). All the trusses in one of the sets lie in parallel vertical planes; all those in the other set lie in inclined planes corresponding to the diagonal chords of the trusses in the first set.

The *cube* (or rectangular prism) also gives two sets of plane trusses. All the trusses in one of the sets lie in parallel vertical planes; all the trusses in the other set lie in parallel vertical planes at right angles to the first set. Note that diagonals are not generally provided in plan; thus, for rigidity, at least two complete edges of the floor system must be triangulated as shown. Floor or roof decking might be used to achieve this rigidity.

A system of trusses of this type was used for the Air Force Academy dining-hall roof (Skidmore, Owings, and Merrill, architects and engineers; stress analysis by J. Sbarounis and M. Gaus of that firm). In their design, the bottom chords were all in one plane, but the top chords sloped up from the roof edge to the center, giving a depth at the edge of 8 ft 6 in. and at the center of 11 ft 8 in. The clear span was 266 ft in both directions.

The *hexagonal prism* gives an upper and a lower plane of hexagons, connected vertically at each corner and diagonally from each upper corner to the diametrally opposite lower corner. Note the joint where the diagonals intersect. Three hexagonal prisms are needed for rigidity. (For an application of this system to a curved surface, see information on geodesic domes on Sheets 33 to 35 of this section.)

Octahedra plus tetrahedra give what may well be called *isometric space frames*. These lattices, which can be generated by the regular rhombohedron (itself made up of one octahedron and two tetrahedra), permit all members to be the same length. They correspond to the crystallographer's "face-centered cubic." (See diagram in Fig. 33.)

If an isometric space lattice is cut by any plane containing the faces of the octahedra (and the tetrahedra), the result is what is labeled here a type T isometric space frame (so-called because of its triangular pattern on the plan).

If, on the other hand, the lattice is cut by any plane containing the central squares of the octahedra, the result is what is labeled here a type S isometric space frame (because of the squares that appear on the plan). This truss has the advantage of conforming easily to the plan of rectangular buildings. (It has been used, for example, in two experimental structures erected for Unistrut Corp., and also as a full story-height truss in the mechanical-equipment floor of the Texas Instrument Co.) Note that the formula for the number of members is not satisfied unless there are at least six squares in the upper plane and two in the lower, and also that triangulation is required in at least one plane for rigidity.

These two isometric space frames are drawn here only in plan, section, and elevation, because their axonometric projections would be confusing. They are most easily studied in model form; models can be readily made with round toothpicks and Duco cement.

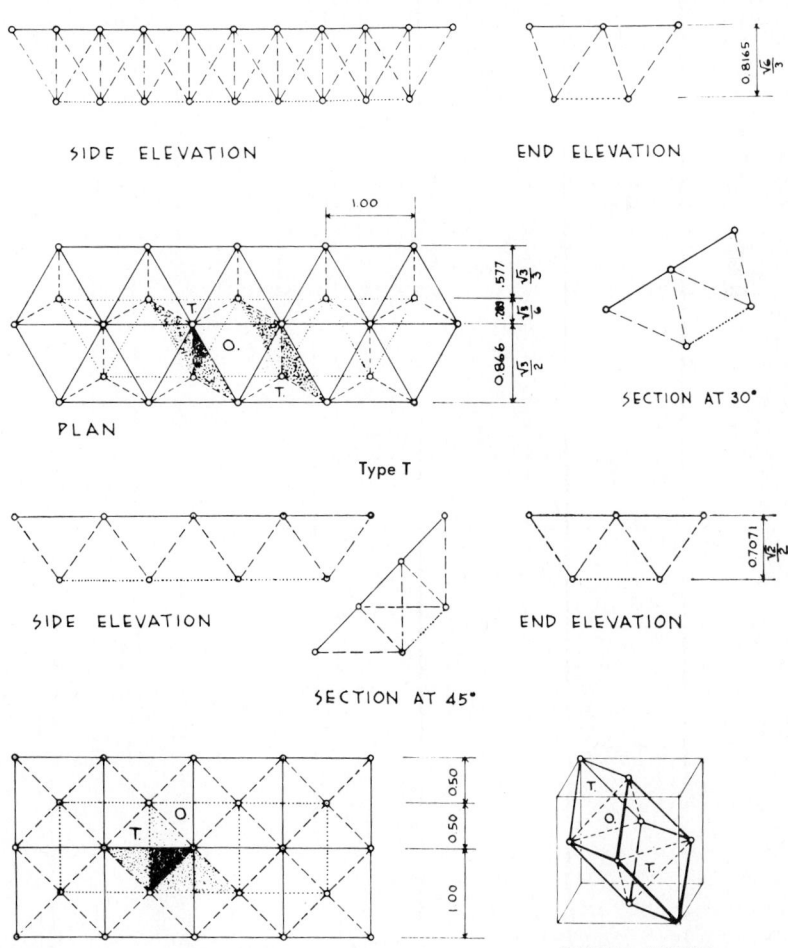

Fig. 33. Two types of isometric space truss

Metal Domes

Metal domes are generally built on some variation of the radial principle (see "Useful Curves and Curved Surfaces," Sheet 25). The principal types are illustrated in Figs. 34 and 35.

One of the initial decisions to be made is whether the dome should be a portion of a true sphere or a polyhedron. Rolled steel sections are most commonly used, since the depths of section needed can easily be found in the standard sizes. As straight members they form a polyhedron. If the members are closely spaced, however, the visual effect will be that of a sphere, particularly if the roof decking can be curved. If curved members are desired, light trusses can be fabricated to the correct radii.

Lengths of members are typically in the range of 15 to 25 ft. This will determine the spacing of radial and parallel ribs.

The most usual ratio of rise to span (diameter) is in the range $\frac{1}{5}$ to $\frac{1}{8}$. Often the span is taken as equal to the radius, which gives a ratio of 0.134.

Schwedler System

The original Schwedler dome or cupola (first published in 1866) is shown here as the "basic type with diagonals." Such a polyhedron is statically determinate and is indeformable, since the entire surface is divided into triangles. As a three-dimensional framework it satisfies the

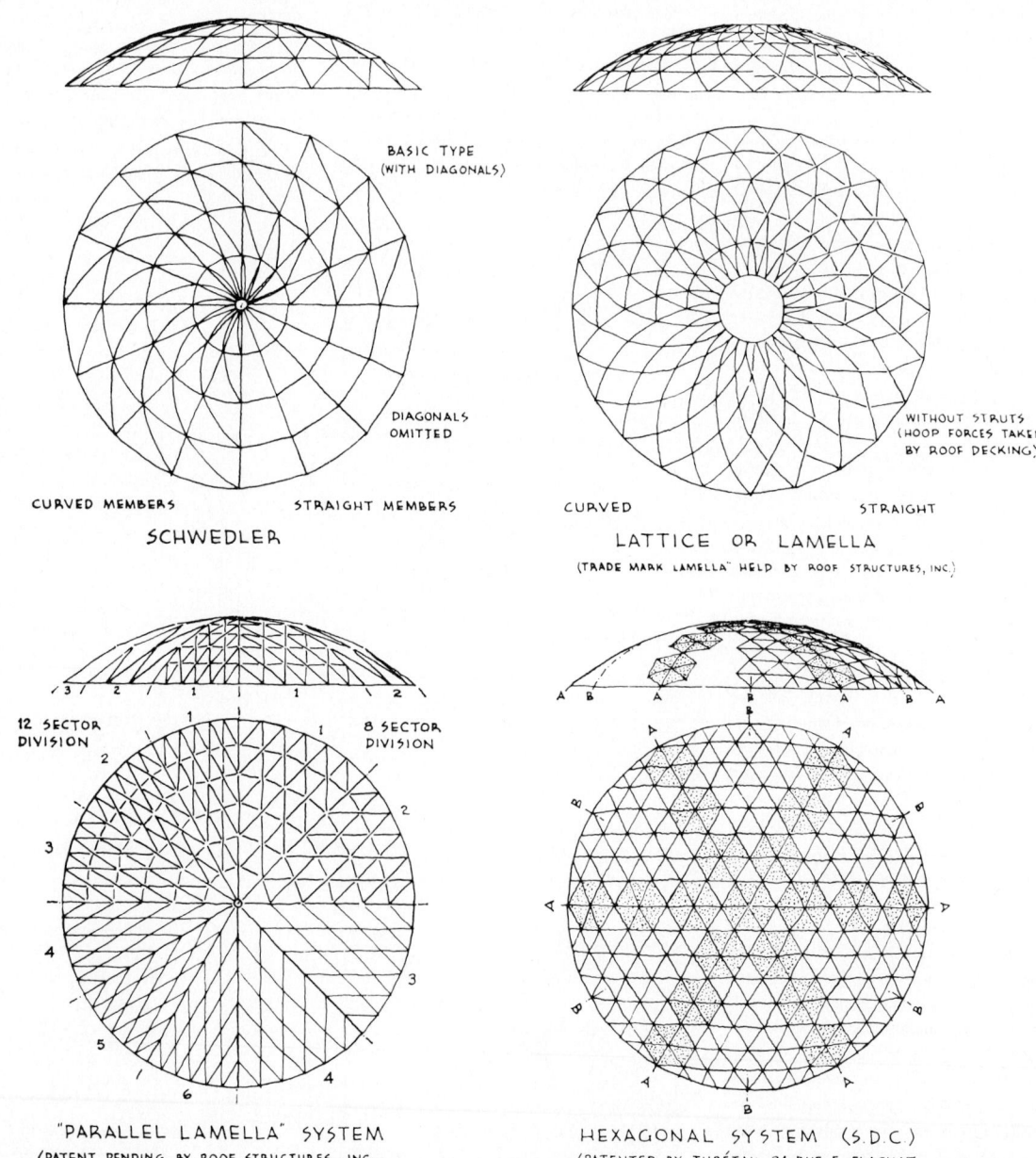

Fig. 34. Types of steel domes

statical conditions for rigidity.

Recent investigations by Professor Paul Anderson of the University of Minnesota indicate that in practice the diagonals are not necessary. The simplest type, therefore, is a Schwedler dome with diagonals omitted, consisting of straight members which are the chords of meridian (longitude) and parallel (latitude) circles.

Lamella System

In the lattice or lamella system all of the intersections of members lie on radial lines but each meridian rib is replaced by a pair of diagonal ribs. These ribs together with the struts, which are chords of latitude circles, form a triangular, three-dimensional network which is rigid. The roof decking panels can be designed to replace the struts, a technique commonly used in the case of wood lamella domes with wood planking.

The *"Parallel Lamella" System* was developed to reduce the number of ribs at the top of the dome, where the close spacing makes assembly difficult and requires a reduction in the size of members if they are not to be grossly overdesigned for the forces acting on them. Although each sector is symmetrical about its own centerline, the visual effect is to emphasize one of the radial ribs at the edge of the sector, causing an apparent dissymmetry which is somewhat disturbing esthetically.

Hexagonal System

The hexagonal system was developed for a framework of steel tubes which are fitted into special joints of cast or pressed steel and welded. The tubes in turn can support roof panels of sheet steel, steel plus concrete, terra cotta blocks covered with concrete, and so forth. Because of the characteristics of the sphere and the hexagon (see "Useful Curves and Curved Surfaces," Sheets 25–27) all of the tubes cannot be of the same length, although the variation can be kept small. The typical length of one bar is about 6 ft. In the diagram the shaded hexagons (along lines A) are all identical hexagonal pyramids; the six center bars of each must be slightly longer than the six edge bars. The lines B are axes of symmetry for the regions in between, where the lengths of bars tend to be shorter, but all the joints still lie on the surface of the sphere.

Thin Shells

Not illustrated, but occasionally used, are the ribless steel shells in which all forces are carried by the steel plating. The danger of buckling is the principal design problem. As a result the plating must be quite thick: for example, 5/8-in. plate at 25.6 lb per sq ft of surface was needed for a 200-ft diameter hemisphere built according to the specifications of the American Petroleum Institute.

Forces

An approximate idea of the magnitude of forces involved can most easily be found by assuming the spherical structure to act as a membrane. The most heavily loaded member is of course the tension ring at the lower edge. If the sphere is brought down to the ground by means of inclined piers, buttresses or A-frames, a continuous footing can be used as the tension ring; or the thrust can be taken directly by the ground if the soil is suitable.

Geodesic Domes

This type of dome might be considered as derived from an effort to construct a spherical dome solely by means of elements of uniform length. (Its inventor, R. Buckminster Fuller, describes it as "a structure impervious not only to extreme differential between internal and external loads or impact forces—yet permitting omnidirectionally effective controlled penetrability.") But the sphere is a surface which cannot be divided by any arbitrary number of arcs of the same length. Therefore, the elements must be of different lengths, although the pattern is more or less uniform. For a complete study of this problem see Sheet 25, "Useful Curves and Curved Surfaces."

One of the advantages of this type of dome is the simplicity of erection. One method is to fasten sections of the dome together like a skirt around a central mast. This portion is raised up enough so that another zone of sections can be fastened to the first portion, and so on. Or it can also be built like other domes, from the bottom up: the lowest zone erected on the piers, forming a complete circle; the next higher zone erected on the lowest, and so on. Since any complete zone is stable in itself, this procedure can be followed with a minimum of scaffolding.

Because the pattern of members or truss elements in the geodesic dome is an "overall" one, always related to the entire sphere, the perfect geodesic dome is the complete ball. As such it is ideally suited to withstand radial pressures and should prove of value in gas storage tanks and vehicles and stations for outer space. The depth of the space truss usually employed as the surface of the sphere gives it great stiffness and resistance to high winds.

When other than hemispherical or plane truncated segments are used, the edges are the main architectural problem. These lie along segments of five great circles and are sometimes supported by several piers, all at different heights. They can also be supported by arches, making only five points of support for the whole dome. These piers or edge arches must be designed to carry the thrust of the dome, and the drag and uplift due to wind loads. The connections of the dome to the piers are designed to permit a considerable amount of radial movement due to temperature changes (on the order of 3 in. for an aluminum dome with a sphere radius of 112 ft). If soil conditions are poor the piers must be held together by a tension ring of steel or prestressed concrete.

R. Buckminster Fuller, who received U.S. patents on his spherical geodesic dome in 1954, now has 100 licensees using

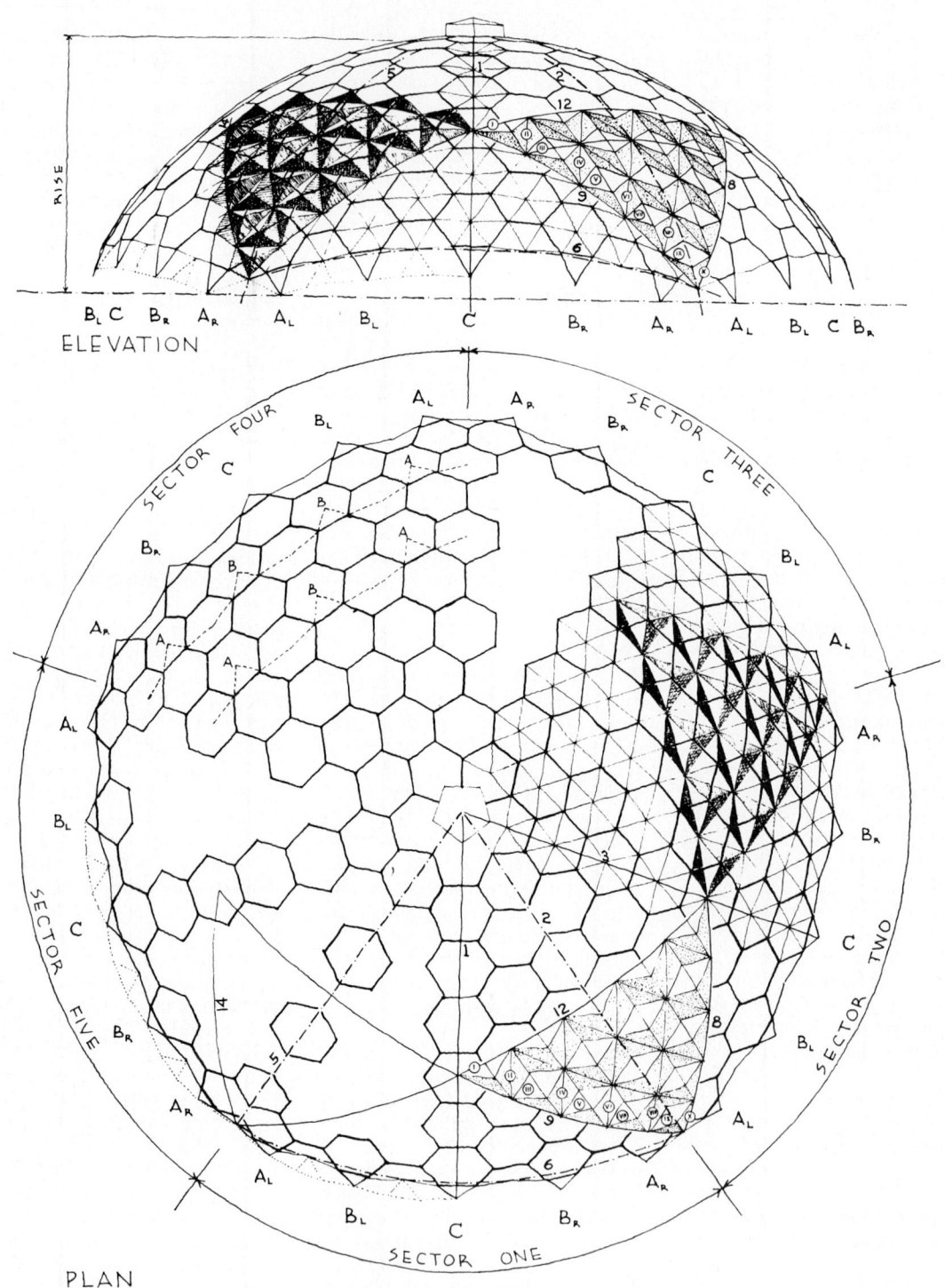

Fig. 35.   Geodesic domes

some of his principles. Synergetics, Inc., 4925 Waters Edge Dr., Raleigh, North Carolina (James W. Fitzgibbon, Executive Vice-President) has designed some of the special domes such as:

1) Steel dome for the Union Tank Car Co., in Baton Rouge, La. Plan diameter 384 ft; rise 120 ft; frequency 36; 48-in. deep space truss; 2) Aluminum dome for the American Society of Metals, near Cleveland. Plan diameter 277 ft; rise 102 ft; frequency 24; 30-in. deep space truss; 3) Projected dome for Shoppersville in Montreal. Plan diameter 525 ft; rise 96 ft above tension ring; frequency 56; 72-in. deep space truss.

All of these are designed with a space truss using an octahedron as the basic unit instead of a tetrahedron. (See Fig. 37 for octahedron unit, and Sheet 28, "Useful Curves and Curved Surfaces," for tetrahedron unit.)

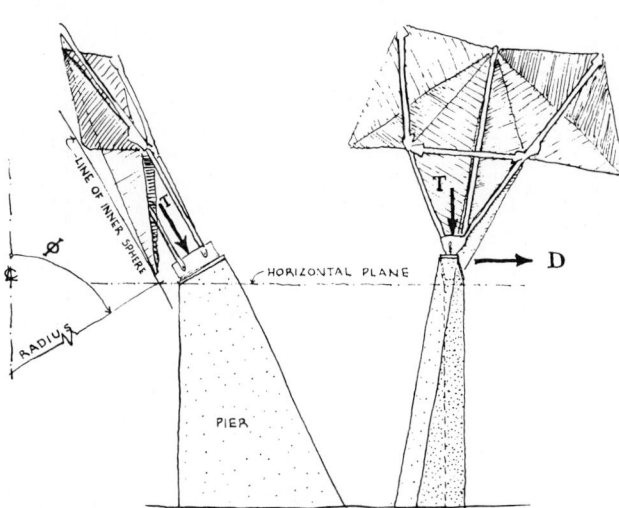

Fig. 36. Pier for geodesic dome (see Table 21)

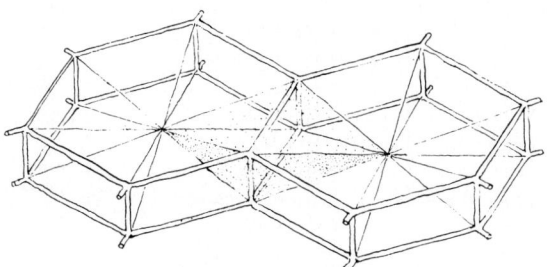

Fig. 37. Octahedron space truss

The Kaiser Aluminum and Chemical Sales Co., 919 North Michigan Ave., Chicago 11, Illinois, has designed aluminum domes based on Fuller's patents, and some of its own patents covering the system of stressed skin space truss using diamond shaped panels. Kaiser is currently marketing two basic series, each of three sizes of type A domes. (See Table 21.)

The plan and elevation shown in Fig. 35 are of Kaiser's type A-80-15.3 (approximately a quarter sphere). In plan the surface is divided into five identical sectors, corresponding to the five upper spherical triangles of the spherical icosahedron; they are joined by a pentagonal lantern at the top. Each sector is supported by five symmetrically arranged piers: C in the center (highest); B_L and A_L to the left, looking up at the dome; B_R and A_R to the right.

The geometry of the division of the dome surface is described in detail on Sheets 28–30, "Useful Curves and Curved Surfaces." A typical basic spherical triangle is shown between lines 8, 9 and 12 on both plan and elevation. The divisions are marked to correspond to those shown on Sheet 29; here the frequency (γ) is 10.

The panels and struts are drawn in detail in two other similar spherical triangles: between sectors two and three in plan and between sectors five and one in elevation.

Each unit consists of a sun-burst-crease formed, diamond shaped panel of aluminum sheet (maximum length 140 in.) with the central cambered valley approximately a chord of a great circle on the inner sphere (radius 80 ft). Six of these panels meet at a point on the inner sphere. The flanged edges of the panels go out to meet the struts, which form a hexagonal pattern with their vertices on the outer sphere (radius 81 ft). The creased valley and the four edges of the panel plus one strut comprise the six edges of the unit tetrahedron. (This has been patented by Kaiser Aluminum, Don L. Richter, inventor; other patents are pending.) Filler panels (as shown dotted in sectors five and one) can be hung from the lower edge to bring the dome down to a more uniform line.

In sector four, broken lines show the piers as they are required for the two small domes (A-80-11.5 and A-80-7.0), which can be built using the same panels but taking smaller portions of the same sphere.

Table 21. Data on Kaiser domes

Dome Code No. (Type)	Radius Inner Sphere (Add one foot for outer), Ft.	Plan Area × 10³ Sq. Ft.	Surface Area × 10³ Sq. Ft.	Volume × 10³ Cu. Ft.	Rise, Top of Lowest Pier to High Point of Inner Sphere	Frequency (ν)	Number of Piers Per Sector (5 Sectors Per Dome)	Pier Letter	Radius in Plan to Point on Inner Sphere Opposite Pier (See Fig. 36)	Ø° (See Fig. 36)	Max. Downward Thrust T with Snow Load	Max. Uplift −T with 100 m.p.h. Wind	Max Drag D (Snow or Wind)
A-80-15.3	80	15.3	21.9	603	46'-10¾"	10	5	A	72'-10"	65.6°	15.4 (30 lb. snow)	− 5.7	5.8
								B	71'-6⅛"	63.4°	21.7	− 8.3	8.6
								C	70'-11¼"	62.5°	23.2	− 9.1	7.5
A-80-11.5	80	11.5	14.5	230.7	31'-9½"	10	4	A	63'-10⅛"	53.0°	21.0 (30 lb. snow)	− 8.8	10.4
								B	61'-6⅝"	50.3°	28.2	−12.9	11.6
A-80-7.0	80	7.0	8.1	87	18'-5⅝"	10	3	A	51'-1½"	39.7°	24.6 (20 lb. snow)	−15.2	12.6
								B	48'-6¾"	37.4°	33.3	−22.7	10.3
A-112-30.0	112	30.0	42.7	1180	64'-5½"	14	7	A	101'-4½"	64.9°	22.6 (40 lb. snow)	− 7.2	10.7
								B	99'-10"	62.1°	31.4	− 9.4	13.4
								C	98'-7⅝"	61.8°	35.3	−11.1	13.5
								D	98'-2"	61.3°	36.0	−11.4	12.7
A-112-24.7	112	24.7	32.2	733	46'-5⅜"	14	6	A	92'-10½"	56.1°	32.3 (40 lb. snow)	−11.0	15.2
								B	90'-4⅜"	53.8°	42.2	−14.3	15.4
								C	88'-9⅝"	52.5°	44.5	−15.2	13.3
A-112-18.7	112	18.7	22.6	403	35'-10"	14	5	A	82'-1⅛"	47.2°	42.5 (40 lb. snow)	−15.1	18.0
								B	78'-2⅜"	44.3°	56.7	−20.2	15.4
								C	76'-10¼"	43.4°	56.9	−20.4	10.0

Note: All of these domes except A-80-7.0 can safely withstand winds of 125 m.p.h.; uplift and drag loads on piers will be increased by about 55% over those given here for 100 m.p.h. wind.

By SEMOUR HOWARD, *Architect*
Associate Professor, School of Architecture,
Pratt Institute

Of the various methods of spanning a space, suspension systems have a special appeal to the imagination because of their potential efficiency in the use of material and the long spans possible. Steel, aluminum, or fiber can be used to their maximum advantage in the form of cable or rope. All the loads can be carried in direct tension; there need be no reduction in the allowable stress to provide for the danger of buckling. The drawing of steel into wire form increases the proportional limit to stresses on the order of 160,000 psi (instead of 30,000 to 40,000 psi for structural steel) and the breaking stress to over 222,000 psi.[1] What economy of material and lightness this seems to promise!

Yet, apart from the familiar suspension bridge, very few permanent structures of this type have actually been built, because of the limitations of suspension systems.

MULTISTORY SYSTEMS: CABLES FOR VERTICAL SUPPORTS

One suspension system that crops up perennially in architectural projects is shown in Fig. 38. A series of floors are supported by tension cables that are fastened to an overhead truss.[2] The principal advantage

[1] *The modulus of elasticity, E, for a single wire (29 million psi) is not changed by wire-drawing, but the effective E when the wires are twisted into cable form goes down to 24 million psi for galvanized bridge strand and 20 million psi for the more flexible galvanized bridge rope. This reduction does not occur in the main cables of suspension bridges, which are spun in place with the wires parallel.*

[2] *Paul Chelazzi's "Suspen-Arch" system for multistory buildings is essentially the same, with the substitution of several "Suspen-Arches" at various levels instead of the single truss at the top.*

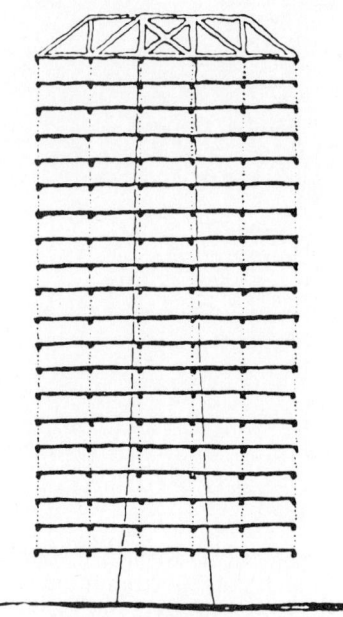

Fig. 38. Hanging floors

claimed for this type of construction is that the cross-sectional area of vertical elements is reduced to a minimum, and that, as a result, the plan provides maximum flexibility in floor layout.

Limitations

1. Although the area of the tension cables themselves is small, the addition of necessary fireproofing around them increases that area considerably.

2. The spacing of vertical supports is determined by the floor framing system. Therefore the limitations on the layout of offices are essentially the same as if the floor were supported by columns. Neither a column nor a hanger is a welcome obstruction in the middle of a room.

3. Considering the building as a whole, vertical loads must travel a path about three times as long to get to the ground as in normal columnar design.

4. Wind forces must be resisted entirely by the central compression shaft. With conventional columnar framing, on the other hand, the stiffness of all the columns can help resist horizontal forces.

5. The tendency of floors to swing horizontally can be eliminated by correct fastenings to the compression shaft. These fastenings must, however, permit relative vertical movement, because the central shaft will shorten under loading while the cables will lengthen.

SINGLE-STORY SYSTEMS: THE HANGING ROOF

If there is one general category for classifying the limitations of hanging roofs, it is *movement*. Under this broad heading can be grouped most of the problems that can be foreseen.

Nondestructive movements

1. *Changes in shape due to moving loads:* One of the advantages of tension structures is the simplicity with which one can visualize the shape of the tension elements under a load. A perfectly flexible cable or string will take a different shape for every variation in loading, according to the familiar "funicular curve" or "string polygon" (Fig. 39).

2. *Changes in shape due to unsymmetrical loading,* such as snow, over only a portion of the roof, are essentially the same as those due to moving loads. In both cases, the greater the ratio of live load to dead load, the greater the movement.

3. *Changes in shape due to wind loads:* On a roof surface, wind will act principally as an upward force (suction), unless the slope is more than about 30 deg. Some means of resisting this force must be provided: secondary tie-down cables curving upward, tie-down guy wires, or an excess of dead weight.

4. *Temperature changes* can be provided for by hinges that permit rotation as cable lengths change (Fig. 40). Particular care is

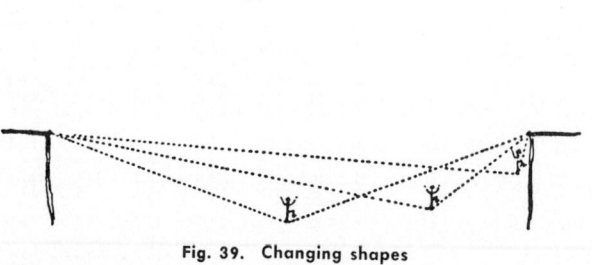

Fig. 39. Changing shapes

Fig. 40. Heat and cold

required with structures that are partly outdoors and partly indoors.

Potentially destructive movements

Vibration: Flapping, rippling, fluttering, and galloping are all forms of vibration and thus potentially destructive movements.

Every mass has its own natural period of vibration with its fundamental and higher modes. The period depends on the density of the mass, on its geometrical distribution or shape, and on the magnitude of the stresses set up by its own weight and other permanent forces acting on it. The most familiar example is a stretched wire, whose musical note depends on its material, length, and tension.

The number of half-waves formed by the vibrating wire is always a whole number; therefore one of the ways of controlling vibration is by irregular spacing of framing members, ties, and supports.

When an external pulsating force is applied to such a mass as a cable, it will be set in motion. This motion can be represented by an infinite number of superimposed modes of vibration. If one of these modes coincides with the natural frequency or fundamental mode of the mass, resonance will ensue. The amplitude or deflection will be increased, and the effect of the pulsating force may also be increased. This process could continue until the structure was destroyed.

The possible causes of vibration include wind, the most usual and the principal danger to suspended structures; and movement of vehicles and the operation of reciprocating and rotating machinery on the structure or on the ground nearby.

Wind: The flapping of simple suspended elements like a flag, a sail, or a canvas awning is very familiar, but how does the wind really act to cause a rhythmic force?

1. *Karman vortices:* If a steady wind blows against a cylinder or other obstruction, the wake takes the form of a vortex street (Fig. 41). The shedding of these vortices on the leeward side causes forces to act on the cylinder at right angles to the direction of the wind, first from one side

and then from the other. The frequency is

$$f = 0.22 \frac{V}{D}$$

in which V = velocity and D = diameter.[1]

2. *Dynamically unstable shapes:* The force of the wind on a prismatic shape is usually not in line with the direction of the wind. An analysis of its effect indicates that the force is divided into two components: drag and lift, parallel and perpendicular to the direction of the wind, as shown in Fig. 42. The magnitude of these components will vary with the angle of attack and with the section of the mass involved. Some shapes are unstable; if the wind blows at certain angles, the lift force will cause them to wobble. The dynamic stability of a given shape can be determined only by experiment. If suspension roof structures are to find more general use, experiments will have to be performed to determine the dynamic stability of various surfaces.

DAMPING

If a damping force can be provided to act in the opposite direction to that of the structure's motion when vibration starts, and if that force is proportional to the velocity of the structure (the faster it moves, the greater the damping force required), vibration can be prevented or greatly diminished. This method is often called viscous damping because a small plunger in a dashpot filled with viscous liquid will provide this type of resisting force. It is similar to the action of the cylinder of a door closer.

[1] *A Karman vortex about 39 ft long was the cause of the famous Tacoma Bridge collapse, which occurred under a steady 42-mph wind. The deck twisted about 45 deg from the horizontal in both directions until it broke. The deck was rebuilt with a box section instead of the original H section, thus increasing the resistance to torsion a hundredfold. The new section was made up of open trusses on the sides and an open-work deck, to prevent the formation of large eddies or significant pressure differences between the upper and lower surfaces.*

The curves in Fig. 43 show graphically the effect of damping. The abscissas measure the relationship:

$\dfrac{\omega}{\omega_n}$ or frequency of exciting force / natural frequency of structure

The ordinates measure the relationship:

$\dfrac{x_0}{x_{stat}}$ or amplitude of vibration due to exciting force / ampl. of deflection due to statical force of same magnitude

The curves plot the effect of various degrees of damping, from none (curve A) to perfect. In curve E, showing critical or perfect damping ($c/c_n = 1.0$), the amplitude is always less than the statical deflection, indicating that the damping has no effect if the exciting force is applied very, very slowly, but has an ever-increasing effect as the frequency of the exciting force increases.

EXAMPLES OF SUSPENSION STRUCTURES

Apart from the suspension bridge, there is to date no generally accepted body of "good practice"; relatively few suspension-structure buildings have been built. The field is new; experiments and patents are many. Among the notable buildings, however, are the following:

Transportation Building, Chicago World's Fair, 1933. Steel masts and cables, flat roof, polygonal plan. Bennett, Burnham, Holabird, Architects.

French Pavilion, Zagreb, Yugoslavia, 1935. Single layer of sheet steel, steel compression ring, 110-ft diam. Bernard Lafaille, Engineer.

North Carolina State Fair Pavilion, Raleigh, 1953. Concrete arches support single layer of cables in 300-ft roof of negative curvature (Fig. 47). William Dietrick, Architect; Mathew Nowicki, Consultant; Severud-Elstad-Krueger, Engineers.

Municipal Stadium, Montevideo, Uruguay, 1957. Single layer of cables, concrete compression ring, 308-ft diam. Mondina, Viera, Miller, Architects.

U.S. Pavilion, Brussels World's Fair, 1958. "Bicycle wheel" roof, double layer of cables,

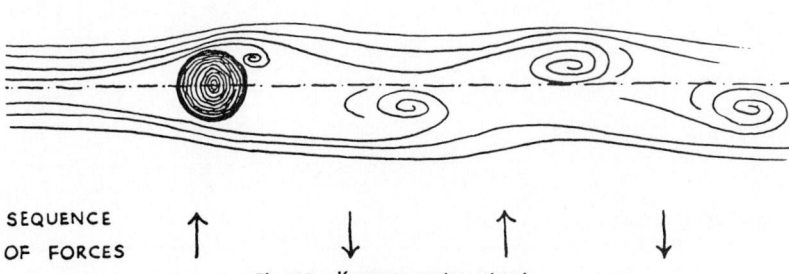

SEQUENCE OF FORCES

Fig. 41.   Karman vortex street

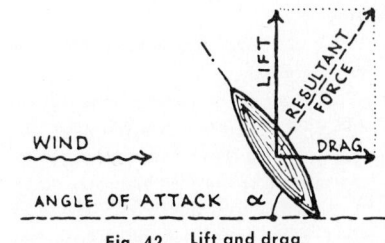

WIND

LIFT   RESULTANT FORCE   DRAG

ANGLE OF ATTACK α

Fig. 42.   Lift and drag

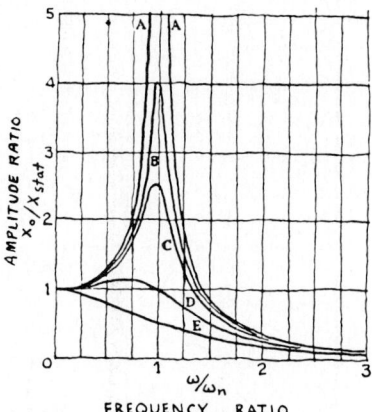

Fig. 43. Vibration with various degrees of damping

steel compression ring, 350-ft diam. Edward D. Stone, Architect.

French Pavilion, Brussels World's Fair, 1958. Steel masts and cables; roof is irregular in plan, 121 by 174 ft. Baucher, Blondel, Filippone, Architects; René Sarger, Engineer.

Hockey Rink, Yale University, 1958. Arched concrete ridge supports single layer of cables anchored to concrete side walls, lyre-shaped in plan. Eero Saarinen, Architect; Douglas Orr, Associated; Severud-Elstad-Krueger, Engineers.

Municipal Auditorium, Utica, N.Y., 1960. "Bicycle wheel" roof, double layer of cables, concrete compression ring, 240-ft diam (Fig. 44). Gehron & Seltzer, Architects; Frank Delle Cese, Associated; Lev Zetlin, Engineer.

A number of airplane hangars have been built since 1955 on the scheme shown in Fig. 40. The same principle was used with an elliptical plan for the Pan-American World Airways Passenger Terminal in New York; Tippetts-Abbot-McCarthy-Stratton, Architects; Ives, Turano, Gardner, Associated.

The first building employing the system shown in Fig. 38, scheduled for completion in 1962 in Antwerp, Belgium, for British Petroleum, Ltd., consists of twelve stories suspended from prestressed concrete roof trusses by laminated steel plate hangers. Stijnen, DeMeyer, and Reussens, Architects.

PRINCIPAL ELEMENTS OF SUSPENSION STRUCTURES

1. *Compression:* Provided by towers and masts.

2. *Tension:* Provided by main cables and hanger members.

3. *Stiffening:* For holding down against wind uplift, for preventing vibration and for maintaining shape under unsymmetrical loading. May be provided by trusses, diagonal tension stays, guy wires, secondary cables with upward curvature (these may

be prestressed), and the dead weight of the structure itself.

4. *Anchorage:* For vertical components, may be the ground (bedrock), the weight of concrete deadmen, or the dead weight of part of the structure (such as side walls). For horizontal components, may be bedrock, the resistance to sliding of concrete deadmen, or part of the structure (such as a floor, a deck, or a circumferential ring).

Principles of construction

The most promising principles for constructing roof surfaces are as follows:

1. Use two families of cables, one curved downward (concave) and the other curved upward (convex).

2. Prestress both families of cables, so that they will always be in tension and never go slack, no matter what the loading. Prestressed cables will require anchorages or edge supports able to withstand forces at least three times as great as nonprestressed cables. Force is being used instead of mass to prevent flutter, but a good deal of the avoided mass reappears in the anchorages.

If followed correctly for every part of a roof surface, these principles will ensure a "rigid" tensile membrane that can carry any load vibrations by corresponding variations in the tensile stresses in the surface. They may not by themselves *prevent* vibration, however; for this further study is required.

Some examples embodying these principles are shown in Figs. 44 to 48.

ROOFS OF NEGATIVE CURVATURE

If, as in the double dome or "bicycle wheel" roof (Fig. 44), every point is tied to two systems of cables with opposing curvature, two "surfaces" are needed. The negative or anticlastic surfaces offer another possibility. Their basic characteristics are shown in Figs. 45 to 48.

Figure 45 shows a straight-edged surface,

with the high points marked A and the low B. The framework necessary to support the surface is indicated in Fig. 46. The struts at A are necessary for the stability of the structure as a whole, the two points of support at B being insufficient unless they were built in as moment connections.

From the edges hang the principal cables, curved downward, which we can call family "a." Hanging under its own weight, each cable will describe a catenary curve. By themselves these cables would be very unstable, moving under the slightest applied load. A second set of cables is therefore laid over them to stabilize them and to resist uplift forces due to the wind. These cables are all curved upward; call them family "b." The points of intersection of the cables all lie on a surface of negative curvature.

In order to resist the considerable bending set up in the edge beams, structures have been built with the edges curved into arch form so as to resist the pull of the cables by compression alone. Figure 47 shows this design, which is familiar from the North Carolina State Fair Pavilion, and also from Frei Otto's work in Germany. Note that the edge arches need some vertical support from mullions to ensure the stability of the entire structure. In simple hanging roofs of this kind the "b" family of cables is only moderately prestressed, and flutter must be prevented by the addition of guy wires.

The next step is to provide so much prestress in the "b" cables, thus also prestressing the "a" cables (or vice versa), that the surface will be much more resistant to any changes in loading and will act like a rigid membrane. The difficulty is in prestressing the cables. One solution has been patented by René Sarger and used by him for the French Pavilion at the Brussels Fair and other structures. It consists of lowering the A-points by pulling down on the edge beam, as shown in Fig. 48.

Hyperbolic paraboloid roofs

It is important to distinguish the action

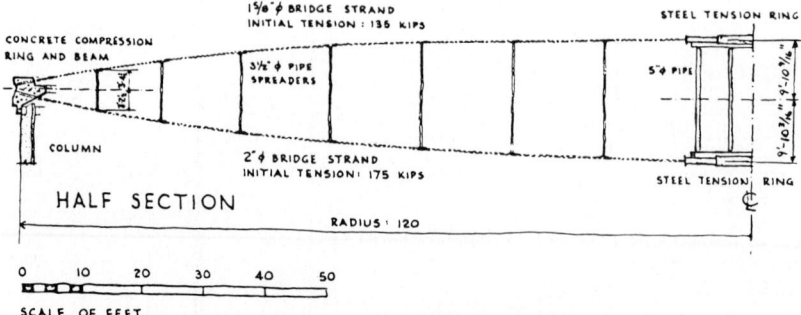

Fig. 44. Prestressed double dome ("bicycle wheel" roof)

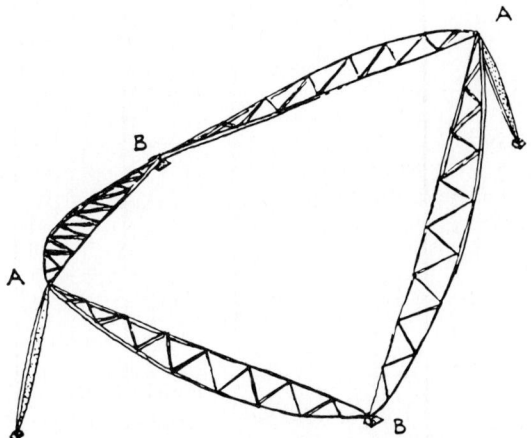

Fig. 45. Hanging roof, negative curvature

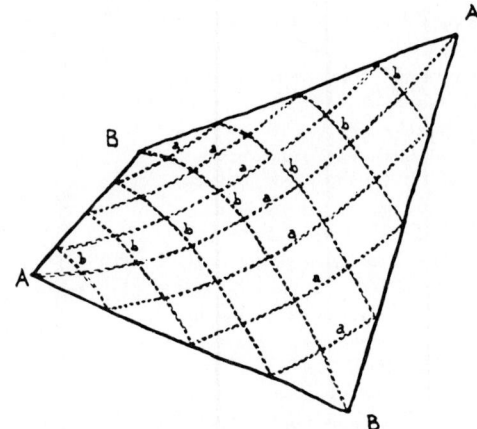

Fig. 46. Supporting framework

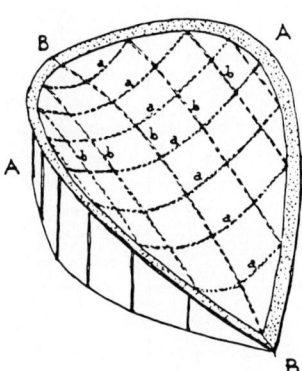

Fig. 47. Arched edges

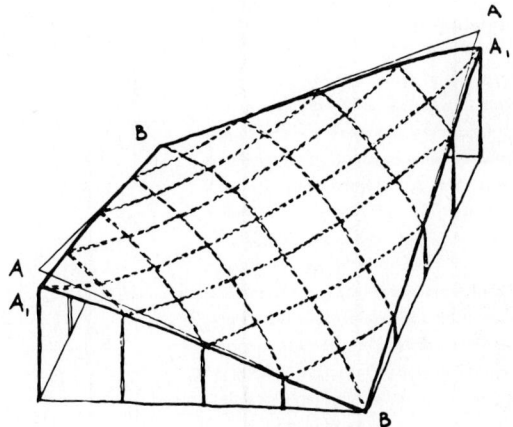

Fig. 48. Method of prestressing

of the various roof shapes that follow the hyperbolic paraboloid:

1. *The thin-shell surface*, acting as a membrane under uniform vertical loads. Tensile forces follow the lines corresponding to the "a" family and compression forces follow the "b" family. The magnitude of these membrane forces is the same at every point, and the compression and tensile forces cancel each other out at the edge. This leaves only a shearing force of the same magnitude, which the edge can support with a relatively slender column.

2. *The hanging roof, not prestressed:* Under uniform vertical loading no forces can be carried by the "b" family cables. The relatively large horizontal forces needed to support the ends of the cables of the "a" family require the edges to be designed as beams, supported at A and B. These horizontal forces will vary considerably with changes in snow and wind loads.

3. *The prestressed suspension roof:* In order to prestress both families of cables, horizontal reactive forces at least three times as large as usual must be permanently provided by the edges. However, for any variation in loading on the roof caused by snow or wind, the prestressed surface will now act similarly to the thin-shell roof, up to the point where the "compressive" force set up in the "b" family cancels out the initial tension.

Weights

Prestressed suspension roofs have been built as hyperbolic paraboloids and also as conoids (for instance, at the Brussels Fair) with remarkably light dead loads, on the order of 3 psf for cables and planking for spans of over 200 ft in both directions. These light loads were achieved, however, only by using very heavy edge beams and vertical supports, which brought the average weight up to about 40 psf.

References

Farquharson, F. B. Wind Forces on Structures: Structures Subject to Oscillation. ASCE Paper 1718.

Hartog, J. P. Den. *Mechanical Vibrations* (4th ed.). McGraw-Hill Book Co., Inc., New York (1956).

Otto, Dr. Ing. Frei. *Das Hangende Dach.* Bauwelt Verlag, Berlin (1954).

STRUCTURAL DESIGN – CONCRETE – 1
Materials

By RICHARD J. GENOVA, *Principal, Severud-Perrone-Szegezdy-Sturm, Consulting Engineers,* and
Y. S. Lee, *Professor of Structural Design, School of Architecture, Pratt Institute*

All the data contained in this section are intended exclusively for use in preliminary study and design. They provide a quick means of obtaining realistic sizes of members in a structure, and can also serve in comparing different framing schemes and column layouts. The design tables are based on the ultimate strength method in accordance with the current American Concrete Institute Building Code Requirements for Reinforced Concrete (ACI 318–77). The final design should be prepared by a structural engineer. Should the designer wish to undertake the final design, appropriate references and codes should be consulted. The final design may vary from that given by the tables because of revisions in the ACI Code and differences between the ACI Code and local building code requirements.

PLAIN CONCRETE

Concrete is a mixture composed of a paste binding together an inert filler, or aggregate. The paste is formed by the chemical reaction between cement and water. The usual proportions (by volume) range from 22 per cent paste (15 per cent water and 7 per cent cement) and 78 per cent aggregate for a lean, stiff mixture to 34 per cent paste (20 per cent water and 14 per cent cement) and 66 per cent aggregate for a rich, workable mixture. Compressive strength, in addition to being the most important quality of concrete, is indicative of its other properties. Tensile and shearing strength, modulus of elasticity, durability, and impermeability are all directly related to compressive strength.

Proportioning

The paste or cementing medium is the fundamental basis of strength development of concrete. The inherent strength of the paste is a function of the ratio of its two components expressed in gallons of water per sack of cement (known as the "water-cement" ratio). The manner in which this ratio influences the compressive strength of concrete is illustrated in Fig. 1. Type I cement is normal portland cement and Type III is high-early-strength cement. In a concrete mixture the maximum amount of aggregate should be used to produce an economical mix with low shrinkage. The amount of aggregate used depends on its effect on the workability or consistency of a mix. The limiting amount, then, is the maximum amount that can be used and still attain full compaction of the concrete. Consistency is determined by "slump" tests, which measure the number of inches a mass of concrete will settle after the slump cone has been removed from the concrete. Table

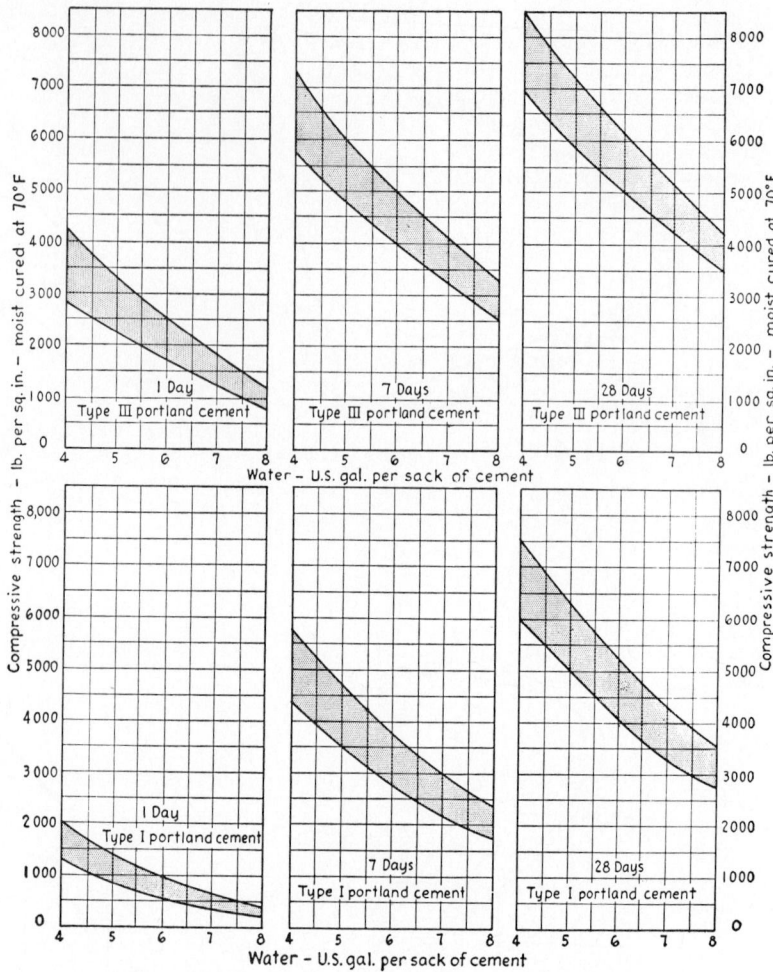

Fig. 1. Relation of compressive strength to water-cement ratio

From Design and Control of Concrete Mixes, *Portland Cement Association.*

I indicates the recommended slumps for various types of construction.

LIGHTWEIGHT AGGREGATES

Lightweight aggregates for structural concrete are now used extensively, and are a practical necessity for tall, reinforced concrete structures. These aggregates, generally produced by artificial means, are obtained by expanding, calcinating, or sintering materials such as blast-furnace slag, shale, slate, and clay. The unit weight of lightweight-aggregate concrete ranges from 90 to 115 lb per cu ft as compared with 145 to 150 lb per cu ft for normal concrete. Most of the properties of concrete using lightweight aggregate are comparable to those of concrete of the same compressive strength using normal-weight gravel or crushed stone. Flexural and bond strength are approximately equal, and the water-cement ratio is still the governing factor in strength development. Light-weight-aggregate concrete, how-

ever, generally has a lower shear or diagonal tension strength, lower modulus of elasticity, and greater shrinkage.

Table 1. Recommended slumps for various types of construction*

	Slump, in.	
Type of construction	Maxi-mum	Mini-mum
Reinforced foundation walls and footings	5	2
Plain footings, caissons, and substructure walls	4	1
Slabs, beams, and reinforced walls	6	3
Building columns	6	3
Pavements	3	2
Heavy mass construction	3	1

* If high-frequency vibrators are used, the values given should be reduced about one third.

Curing

The purpose of curing is to influence the rate of the chemical reaction between cement and water. Curing is an important consideration in structural concrete, particularly in precast and prestressed work requiring high-early-strength development. Availability of water and control of temperature are the main requirements for curing. Ponding, sprinkling, and saturating the aggregate prior to its use are three of the methods used to ensure adequate moisture for continued hydration. Minimum temperatures for the air surrounding normal concrete are 70°F for the first three days after placement or 50°F for five days. For high-early-strength concrete the requirements are 70°F for two days or 50°F for three days. If the amount of time available to develop the necessary strength is limited, the temperature should be increased. In one method, saturated steam employing temperatures in the range of 140 to 165°F is used. Insulation, which retains the heat liberated from the reaction between cement and water, will also contribute to rapid strength development.

DESIGN PROCEDURE

Since a monolithic reinforced concrete structure is inherently rigid, it produces an indeterminate system. The relative size of members, span lengths, and the effect of alternate loading all influence the magnitude of the design moments and shears and theoretically require an elastic analysis. The interaction of so many variables renders loading tables of limited value. Through the use of the ACI design coefficients (Table 2), however, design moments and shears can be determined empirically with minimum effort and time. Preliminary members can then be selected from the tables giving capacities of various sections. It is important to note that these coefficients apply only when the ratios between adjacent spans and between the uniformly distributed live and dead loads are within the required limits.

Table 3. Weight and dimensions of standard deformed bars

Bar No.	Diam, in.	Area, sq in.	Weight, lb per lin ft
2	0.250	0.05	0.167
3	0.375	0.11	0.376
4	0.500	0.20	0.668
5	0.625	0.31	1.043
6	0.750	0.44	1.502
7	0.875	0.60	2.044
8	1.000	0.79	2.670
9	1.128	1.00	3.400
10	1.270	1.27	4.303
11	1.410	1.56	5.313

Table 2. ACI design coefficients for moment and shear

This table is applicable only under the following conditions: the larger of two adjacent spans must not exceed 20 per cent of the shorter span; loads must be uniformly distributed; the unit live load must not exceed three times the unit dead load. $w =$ unit uniform load. $l' =$ span in feet.

Moment or shear	Design coefficient
Positive moment at end spans	
If discontinuous end is unrestrained	$wl'^2/11$
If discontinuous end is integral with the support	$wl'^2/14$
Positive moment at interior spans	$wl'^2/16$
Negative moment at exterior face of first interior support	
Two spans	$wl'^2/9$
More than two spans	$wl'^2/10$
Negative moment at other faces of interior supports	$wl'^2/11$
Negative moment at face of all supports for (a) slabs with spans not exceeding 10 ft, and (b) beams and girders where ratio of sum of column stiffnesses to beam stiffness exceeds eight at each end of the span	$wl'^2/12$
Negative moment at interior faces of exterior supports for members built integrally with their supports	
If the support is a spandrel beam or girder	$wl'^2/24$
If the support is a column	$wl'^2/16$
Shear in end members at first interior support	$wl'/2$
Shear at all other supports	$wl'/2$

Strength design

The present ACI code is based on the strength design method which makes use of two sets of factors. These factors, one called the *Load Factor*, the other the *Strength* or *ϕ Factor* provide respectively for conditions that result in possible understrengths. Different load factors are prescribed for the various conditions of load: dead, live, wind, and earthquake. The ϕ factors are constant for the various building components: 0.70 for tied columns, 0.75 for spiral columns and 0.90 for flexure. Since the factors vary with different combinations of the load it is only possible to tabulate the load representing ultimate usable capacity: P_u, M_u, V_u, etc.

The ACI code provides the following principal load combinations with appropriate load factors for each to compute the required strength U.

$$U = 1.4D + 1.7L$$
$$U = 0.75(1.4D + 1.7L + 1.7W)$$
$$U = 0.9D + 1.3W$$

where $L =$ live load, $D =$ dead load, and $W =$ wind load. The largest of the U values computed is to be used for design.

Other combinations of loads and factors are prescribed in the code where earthquake, lateral earth or fluid loads, impact loads, etc., are to be considered. Reference should be made to the code where these effects are to be considered.

Moment and shear

Based on two qualities of concrete, $f'_c = 3000$ psi and $f'_c = 4000$ psi, and grade 60 ($f_y = 60,000$) reinforcing steel Table 4 gives the ultimate moment capacity M_u in kip-ft and ultimate shear capacity V_u in kips for beams of rectangular section. Maximum capacities are tabulated for three percentages of reinforcement: the minimum conforming to $p_{min} = 200/f_y$ and the others are one-quarter (¼) and one-half (½) of the difference between percentage steel at 75 per cent of balance design and the minimum allowed by code. Balanced conditions are reached at a cross section where the tension reinforcement reaches its specified yield strength f_y, just as the concrete in compression reaches its assumed ultimate strain of 0.003 in. per in. The code requires that for safe practice maximum steel should be limited to 75 per cent of computed balanced design.

Since the ultimate moment M_u is proportional to the percentage of reinforcing steel, interpolation of the tables is possible for p values up to p_b, which is the steel percentage at balanced design. Flexure capacities greater than a balanced design are possible if (1) compressive reinforcement is added or (2) the design bending moment is positive (as in a single span) and the slab forms a T-section. The amount of steel required for both condition is high, however, and not recommended for good practice.

Ultimate shear capacities V_u tabulated in Table 4 are the maximum shears allowed in concrete without the addition of web reinforcement. The values are determined from

$$V_u = \frac{V_u}{\phi b_w d}$$

where

V = total shear (lb)
V_u = ultimate total design shear stress (psi)
b_w = width of the beam web (in.)
ϕ = capacity reduction factor —0.85
d = distance from extreme compression fiber to centroid of tension reinforcement (in.).

The design of reinforced concrete beams with web reinforcement consisting of vertical stirrups or inclined longitudinal bars is a normal procedure. The shear capacity of the concrete alone V_u, should not be considered, then, as a limiting value for the section. The values for V_u are included only to indicate the point at which web reinforcement would be required. Shears twice the magnitude of V_u can usually be developed with little difficulty.

Comprehensive tables that directly relate allowable loads to beam sizes for various spans are impractical for continuous reinforced concrete structures. The bending moment, which usually determines the allowable load, varies with the type of support, number of spans, and ratio of adjacent span lengths in addition to the span length. With the use of the ACI coefficients given in Table 2, however, the design moment can be readily determined. Once the design moment has been determined, either by the use of the ACI coefficients or by elastic analysis, the appropriate section can be selected from Table 4.

Allowable loads

Table 5 gives the total uniformly distributed ultimate load in kips (1000 lb) per lineal foot for f'_c = 3000 psi, f_y = 60,000 psi, and a percentage of reinforcing steel p = 50% of balanced design as defined above. One end condition of restraint is used, namely, end span free on one end and continuous on the other. In accordance with the ACI design coefficients, the design moment for the assumed end condition is equal to $wL^2/10$. By equating M_u, the resisting moment given in Table 4 to the design moment, and rearranging terms, we obtain $w = 10M_u/L^2$. Values of ultimate total loads per foot based on M_u are shown on the upper line of the table. The lower italicized figures denote the maximum allowable ultimate load per foot based on the maximum ultimate shear V_u allowed in concrete without web reinforcement. These values are obtained by setting $V_u = (wL/2)$ and solving for w. Table 6 is the same as Table 5 but for concrete of f'_c = 4000 psi. All other parameters remain the same.

Table 4. Moment and shear capacity of reinforced concrete beams

| Width (in.) | Depth (in.) | f'_c = 3000 psi | | | | f'_c = 4000 psi | | | |
| | | V_u (k) | M_u (K · Ft) | | | V_u (k) | M_u (K · Ft) | | |
			p=0.33%	p=0.65%	p=0.97%		p=0.33%	p=0.78%	p=1.24%
8	10	6.0	7.3	13.8	19.8	6.9	7.4	16.7	25.5
10		7.5	9.1	17.3	24.8	8.6	9.2	20.9	31.8
12		8.9	10.9	20.7	29.7	10.3	11.1	25.1	38.2
14		10.5	12.8	24.2	34.7	12.1	12.9	29.3	44.6
8	12	7.5	11.4	21.6	30.9	8.6	11.5	26.1	39.8
10		9.4	14.3	27.0	38.7	10.8	14.4	32.7	49.8
12		11.2	17.1	32.4	46.4	12.9	17.3	39.7	59.7
14		13.0	20.0	37.8	54.1	15.1	20.2	45.7	69.7
16		16.8	22.8	43.2	61.9	17.2	23.1	52.3	79.6
8	14	8.9	16.4	31.1	44.5	10.3	16.6	37.6	57.3
10		11.2	20.5	38.9	55.7	12.9	20.8	47.0	71.6
12		13.4	24.6	46.7	66.8	15.5	24.9	56.5	86.0
14		15.6	28.7	54.4	78.0	18.1	29.1	65.9	100
16		17.9	32.8	62.2	89.1	20.7	33.2	75.3	115
18		20.2	36.9	70.0	100	23.2	37.4	84.7	129
8	16	10.5	22.3	46.3	60.6	12.1	22.6	51.2	78.0
10		13.0	27.9	57.9	75.8	15.1	28.3	64.4	97.5
12		15.6	33.5	69.4	90.9	18.1	33.9	76.8	117
14		18.3	39.1	81.0	106	21.1	39.6	89.6	137
16		20.8	44.9	92.6	121	24.1	45.2	102	156
18		23.5	50.3	104	136	27.1	50.9	115	176
20		26.1	55.9	116	152	30.1	56.5	128	195
10	18	14.9	36.5	69.1	99.0	17.2	36.9	83.6	127
12		17.9	43.8	82.9	119	20.7	44.3	100	153
14		20.8	51.1	96.8	139	24.1	51.7	117	178
16		23.8	58.4	111	158	27.5	59.1	134	204
18		26.9	65.7	124	178	30.9	66.4	151	229
20		29.8	73.0	138	198	34.4	73.8	167	255
10	20	16.8	46.2	87.5	125	19.4	46.7	106	161
12		20.2	55.4	105	150	23.2	56.1	127	193
14		23.5	64.6	123	175	27.1	65.4	148	226
16		26.9	73.9	140	201	30.9	74.7	160	258
18		30.2	83.1	158	226	34.9	84.1	191	290
20		33.5	92.3	175	251	38.7	93.4	212	322
10	22	18.6	57.0	108	155	21.5	57.7	131	199
12		22.4	68.4	130	186	25.8	69.2	157	239
14		26.1	73.8	151	217	30.1	80.7	183	279
16		29.8	91.2	173	248	34.4	92.3	209	318
18		33.5	103	194	278	38.7	104	235	358
20		37.2	114	216	309	43.0	115	261	398
22		41.0	125	238	340	47.4	127	288	438
10	24	20.5	69.0	131	187	23.6	69.8	158	241
12		24.6	82.8	157	225	28.4	83.7	190	289
14		28.7	96.6	183	262	33.2	97.7	221	337
16		32.8	110	209	299	37.8	112	253	385
18		36.9	124	235	337	42.6	126	285	433
20		41.0	138	261	374	47.4	140	316	482
22		45.1	152	288	412	52.0	154	348	530

ASTM A615–60 grade reinforcement

Width (in.)	Depth (in.)	$f'_c = 3000$ psi				$f'_c = 4000$ psi			
		V_u (k)	M_u (K·Ft) p = 0.33%	p = 0.65%	p = 0.97%	V_u (k)	M_u (K·Ft) p = 0.33%	p = 0.78%	p = 1.24%
12		26.9	98.5	187	267	30.9	99.7	226	344
14		31.3	115	218	312	36.1	116	263	401
16	26	35.8	131	249	356	41.3	133	301	459
18		40.2	148	280	401	46.4	150	339	516
20		44.7	164	311	445	51.6	166	376	573
22		49.1	181	342	490	56.8	183	414	630
12		29.1	116	219	314	33.6	117	265	404
14		34.0	135	256	366	39.1	136	309	471
16	28	38.8	154	292	418	44.7	156	353	538
18		43.6	173	329	471	50.3	175	398	605
20		48.4	193	365	523	55.9	195	442	673
22		53.3	212	402	575	61.5	214	486	740
14		36.5	156	296	424	42.2	158	359	546
16		41.7	179	339	485	48.2	181	410	624
18	30	46.9	201	381	546	54.2	204	461	702
20		52.2	223	423	606	60.2	226	512	780
22		57.4	246	466	667	66.2	249	563	858
24		62.6	268	508	728	72.3	271	615	936
14		39.1	180	340	487	45.1	182	412	627
16		44.7	205	389	557	51.6	208	470	716
18	32	50.3	231	437	626	58.1	234	529	806
20		55.9	257	486	696	64.5	260	588	896
22		61.5	282	535	766	71.0	286	647	985
24		67.1	308	583	835	78.1	311	706	1075
16		47.7	234	442	634	55.1	236	535	815
18		53.6	263	498	713	62.0	266	602	917
20	34	59.6	292	553	792	68.9	295	669	1019
22		65.5	321	608	871	75.8	325	736	1121
24		71.5	350	664	950	82.6	354	803	1223
16		50.7	264	499	715	58.5	267	604	920
18		57.0	297	562	805	65.8	300	680	1035
20	36	63.3	330	624	894	73.1	333	755	1150
22		69.6	362	687	983	80.4	367	831	1265
24		76.0	395	749	1073	87.6	400	906	1380
26		82.3	428	812	1162	95.2	433	982	1490
18		60.4	332	630	902	69.7	336	762	1161
20		67.1	369	700	1002	77.4	374	847	1290
22		73.8	406	770	1103	85.0	411	931	1419
24	38	80.5	443	840	1203	92.7	448	1016	1547
26		87.6	480	910	1303	100	486	1100	1676
28		93.5	517	980	1403	109	523	1185	1805
30		100	554	1050	1503	117	561	1270	1934

Table 5. Total uniformly distributed loads for beam with one half of reinforcement for balanced design

$f_c' = 3000$ psi and ASTM A615–60 p $= 0.97\%$

Span length, (ft) — Ultimate loads (kips per ft)

Width (in.)	Depth (in.)	8	9	10	11	12	13	14	15	16	17	18	19	20	21	22
8	10	3.09	2.44	1.98	1.64	1.38	1.17	1.01								
		1.49	*1.33*	*1.19*	*1.09*	*1.00*	*0.92*	*0.85*								
10		3.88	3.06	2.48	2.05	1.72	1.47	1.27								
		1.86	*1.66*	*1.49*	*1.35*	*1.24*	*1.15*	*1.06*								
8	12	4.83	3.82	3.09	2.56	2.15	1.83	1.58	1.37	1.21	1.07					
		1.86	*1.66*	*1.49*	*1.35*	*1.24*	*1.15*	*1.06*	*1.00*	*0.94*	*0.88*					
10		6.05	4.78	3.87	3.20	2.69	2.29	1.98	1.72	1.51	1.34					
		2.34	*2.07*	*1.87*	*1.70*	*1.56*	*1.44*	*1.34*	*1.25*	*1.17*	*1.10*					
8	14	6.95	5.49	4.45	3.68	3.09	2.63	2.27	1.98	1.74	1.54	1.37	1.23	1.11		
		2.24	*1.98*	*1.79*	*1.62*	*1.49*	*1.38*	*1.28*	*1.19*	*1.11*	*1.05*	*1.00*	*0.94*	*0.89*		
10		8.70	6.88	5.57	4.60	3.87	3.30	2.84	2.48	2.18	1.93	1.72	1.54	1.39		
		2.81	*2.49*	*2.24*	*2.04*	*1.87*	*1.73*	*1.61*	*1.50*	*1.40*	*1.32*	*1.25*	*1.18*	*1.12*		
12		10.4	8.25	6.68	5.52	4.64	3.95	3.41	2.97	2.61	2.31	2.06	1.85	1.67		
		3.36	*2.98*	*2.69*	*2.44*	*2.24*	*2.07*	*1.92*	*1.79*	*1.68*	*1.58*	*1.50*	*1.42*	*1.34*		
8	16	9.47	7.48	6.06	5.01	4.21	3.59	3.09	2.69	2.37	2.10	1.87	1.68	1.52	1.37	1.25
		2.62	*2.32*	*2.09*	*1.90*	*1.74*	*1.61*	*1.50*	*1.39*	*1.31*	*1.23*	*1.17*	*1.11*	*1.05*	*1.00*	*0.95*
10		11.8	9.36	7.58	6.27	5.26	4.49	3.87	3.37	2.96	2.62	2.34	2.10	1.90	1.72	1.57
		3.26	*2.89*	*2.60*	*2.36*	*2.17*	*2.00*	*1.86*	*1.73*	*1.62*	*1.53*	*1.45*	*1.37*	*1.30*	*1.24*	*1.18*
12		14.2	11.2	9.09	7.51	6.31	5.38	4.64	4.04	3.55	3.15	2.81	2.52	2.27	2.06	1.88
		3.91	*3.48*	*3.13*	*2.85*	*2.61*	*2.41*	*2.24*	*2.08*	*1.96*	*1.85*	*1.73*	*1.65*	*1.56*	*1.49*	*1.42*
14		16.6	13.1	10.6	8.76	7.36	6.27	5.41	4.71	4.14	3.67	3.27	2.94	2.65	2.40	2.19
		4.57	*4.06*	*3.66*	*3.32*	*3.04*	*2.81*	*2.61*	*2.44*	*2.29*	*2.15*	*2.03*	*1.92*	*1.83*	*1.74*	*1.67*

Width (in.)	Depth (in.)	14	16	18	20	22	24	26	28	30	32	34	36	38	40	42
10	18	5.05	3.87	3.06	2.48	2.05	1.72	1.47								
		2.13	*1.86*	*1.65*	*1.49*	*1.35*	*1.24*	*1.15*								
12		6.07	4.65	3.67	2.98	2.46	2.07	1.76								
		2.55	*2.24*	*1.98*	*1.79*	*1.62*	*1.49*	*1.38*								
14		7.09	5.43	4.29	3.48	2.87	2.41	2.06								
		2.98	*2.60*	*2.31*	*2.08*	*1.90*	*1.73*	*1.61*								
16		8.06	6.17	4.88	3.95	3.27	2.74	2.34								
		3.40	*2.98*	*2.64*	*2.38*	*2.17*	*1.98*	*1.83*								
12	20	7.65	5.86	4.63	3.75	3.10	2.60	2.22	1.91	1.67						
		2.88	*2.52*	*2.24*	*2.02*	*1.84*	*1.68*	*1.55*	*1.44*	*1.34*						
14		8.93	6.84	5.40	4.38	3.62	3.04	2.59	2.23	1.94						
		3.35	*2.93*	*2.61*	*2.35*	*2.13*	*1.96*	*1.80*	*1.68*	*1.56*						
16		10.3	7.85	6.20	5.03	4.15	3.49	2.97	2.56	2.23						
		3.83	*3.36*	*2.98*	*2.69*	*2.44*	*2.24*	*2.07*	*1.92*	*1.79*						
12	22	9.49	7.27	5.74	4.65	3.84	3.23	2.75	2.37	2.07	1.82					
		3.20	*2.80*	*2.48*	*2.24*	*2.03*	*1.86*	*1.72*	*1.60*	*1.49*	*1.39*					
14		11.1	8.48	6.70	5.43	4.48	3.77	3.21	2.77	2.41	2.12					
		3.73	*3.26*	*2.90*	*2.61*	*2.37*	*2.18*	*2.01*	*1.86*	*1.74*	*1.63*					
16		12.7	9.69	7.65	6.20	5.12	4.31	3.67	2.16	2.76	2.42					
		4.26	*3.73*	*3.32*	*2.98*	*2.71*	*2.49*	*2.30*	*2.13*	*1.99*	*1.86*					
12	24	11.5	8.79	6.94	5.63	4.65	3.91	3.33	2.87	2.50	2.20	1.95				
		3.51	*3.07*	*2.73*	*2.46*	*2.24*	*2.05*	*1.89*	*1.75*	*1.64*	*1.54*	*1.45*				
14		13.4	10.2	8.09	6.55	5.41	4.55	3.88	3.34	2.91	2.56	2.27				
		4.09	*3.58*	*3.18*	*2.87*	*2.60*	*2.39*	*2.39*	*2.05*	*1.91*	*1.79*	*1.68*				
16		15.3	11.7	9.23	7.48	6.18	5.19	4.42	3.81	3.32	2.92	2.59				
		4.68	*4.11*	*3.65*	*3.28*	*2.98*	*2.74*	*2.53*	*2.35*	*2.19*	*2.05*	*1.93*				

Width, (in.)	Depth (in)	f'_c = 3000 psi and ASTM A615–60 p = 0.97% Span length, (ft) Ultimate loads (kips per ft)														
		14	16	18	20	22	24	26	28	30	32	34	36	38	40	42
14	26		12.2	9.63	7.80	6.45	5.42	4.62	3.98	3.47	3.05	2.70	2.41			
			3.91	*3.48*	*3.13*	*2.85*	*2.61*	*2.41*	*2.24*	*2.08*	*1.96*	*1.85*	*1.73*			
16			13.9	11.0	8.90	7.36	6.18	5.27	4.54	3.96	3.48	3.08	2.75			
			4.47	*3.98*	*3.58*	*3.26*	*2.98*	*2.75*	*2.56*	*2.39*	*2.24*	*2.11*	*1.99*			
18			15.7	12.4	10.0	8.29	6.96	5.93	5.11	4.46	3.92	3.47	3.09			
			5.02	*4.47*	*4.02*	*3.66*	*3.35*	*3.09*	*2.87*	*2.68*	*2.52*	*2.36*	*2.24*			
14	28			11.3	9.15	7.56	6.35	5.41	4.67	4.07	3.58	3.17	2.82	2.54		
				3.77	*3.40*	*3.09*	*2.83*	*2.62*	*2.43*	*2.27*	*2.13*	*2.00*	*1.89*	*1.79*		
16				12.9	10.5	8.64	7.26	6.18	5.33	4.64	4.08	3.62	3.23	2.90		
				4.31	*3.88*	*3.53*	*3.23*	*2.98*	*2.77*	*2.58*	*2.42*	*2.28*	*2.15*	*2.04*		
18				14.5	11.8	9.73	8.18	6.97	6.01	5.23	4.60	4.07	3.63	3.26		
				4.85	*4.36*	*3.96*	*3.64*	*3.36*	*3.11*	*2.91*	*2.72*	*2.57*	*2.42*	*2.30*		
16	30			12.1	10.0	8.42	7.18	6.19	5.39	4.74	4.20	3.74	3.36	3.03		
				4.17	*3.79*	*3.48*	*3.21*	*2.98*	*2.78*	*2.61*	*2.46*	*2.32*	*2.19*	*2.21*		
18				13.7	11.3	9.48	8.08	6.96	6.07	5.33	4.72	4.21	3.78	3.41		
				4.69	*4.27*	*3.91*	*3.61*	*3.35*	*3.13*	*2.93*	*2.76*	*2.61*	*2.47*	*2.35*		
20				15.2	12.5	10.5	8.97	7.73	6.73	5.92	5.24	4.68	4.20	3.79		
				5.22	*4.74*	*4.35*	*4.01*	*3.73*	*3.48*	*3.26*	*3.07*	*2.90*	*2.75*	*2.61*		
16	32			14.0	11.5	9.67	8.24	7.11	6.19	5.44	4.82	4.30	3.86	3.46	3.16	
				4.47	*4.06*	*3.72*	*3.44*	*3.20*	*2.98*	*2.80*	*2.63*	*2.48*	*2.36*	*2.24*	*2.13*	
18				15.7	12.9	10.9	9.26	7.99	6.96	6.11	5.42	4.83	4.34	3.91	3.55	
				5.03	*4.57*	*4.19*	*3.87*	*3.60*	*3.36*	*3.15*	*2.96*	*2.80*	*2.65*	*2.52*	*2.40*	
20				17.4	14.4	12.1	10.3	8.88	7.73	6.80	6.02	5.37	4.82	4.35	3.95	
				5.59	*5.08*	*4.66*	*4.29*	*3.99*	*3.72*	*3.49*	*3.29*	*3.10*	*2.94*	*2.80*	*2.66*	
18	34				14.7	12.4	10.6	9.09	7.92	6.96	6.17	5.50	4.94	4.46	4.04	
					4.88	*4.47*	*4.12*	*3.83*	*3.58*	*3.35*	*3.15*	*2.98*	*2.82*	*2.69*	*2.56*	
20					16.4	13.8	11.7	10.1	8.80	7.73	6.85	6.11	5.49	4.95	4.49	
					5.42	*4.96*	*4.58*	*4.26*	*3.97*	*3.72*	*3.50*	*3.31*	*3.14*	*2.98*	*2.84*	
22					18.0	15.1	12.9	11.1	9.68	8.51	7.54	6.72	6.03	5.44	4.94	
					5.96	*5.47*	*5.04*	*4.68*	*4.37*	*4.10*	*3.86*	*3.64*	*3.45*	*3.28*	*3.12*	
18	36				16.6	14.0	11.9	10.3	8.94	7.86	6.96	6.21	5.58	5.03	4.56	
					5.18	*4.74*	*4.38*	*4.07*	*3.80*	*3.56*	*3.35*	*3.16*	*3.00*	*2.85*	*2.71*	
20					18.5	15.5	13.2	11.4	9.93	8.73	7.73	6.90	6.19	5.59	5.07	
					5.76	*5.28*	*4.87*	*4.52*	*4.23*	*3.96*	*3.72*	*3.52*	*3.33*	*3.17*	*3.02*	
22					20.3	17.1	14.5	12.5	10.9	9.60	8.50	7.59	6.81	6.14	5.57	
					6.33	*5.81*	*5.36*	*4.97*	*4.64*	*4.35*	*4.10*	*3.87*	*3.66*	*3.49*	*3.32*	
20	38					17.4	14.8	12.8	11.1	9.79	8.67	7.73	6.94	6.26	5.68	
						5.59	*5.16*	*4.80*	*4.47*	*4.19*	*3.94*	*3.72*	*3.53*	*3.36*	*3.20*	
22						19.2	16.3	14.1	12.3	10.8	9.54	8.51	7.64	6.90	6.25	
						6.15	*5.68*	*5.27*	*4.92*	*4.62*	*4.34*	*4.10*	*3.89*	*3.69*	*3.51*	
24						20.9	17.8	15.3	13.4	11.8	10.4	9.28	8.33	7.52	6.82	
						6.71	*6.20*	*5.75*	*5.36*	*5.03*	*4.74*	*4.47*	*4.23*	*4.03*	*3.83*	

Table 6. Total uniformly distributed loads for beam with one half of reinforcement for balanced design

$f'_c = 4000$ psi and ASTM A615–60   p = 1.24%

Span length, (ft) — Ultimate loads (kips)

Width (in.)	Depth (in.)	8	9	10	11	12	13	14	15	16	17	18	19	20	21	22
8	10	3.98	3.15	2.55	2.11	1.77	1.51	1.30								
		1.73	*1.53*	*1.38*	*1.25*	*1.15*	*1.06*	*1.00*								
10		4.97	3.93	3.18	2.63	2.21	1.88	1.62								
		2.15	*1.90*	*1.72*	*1.56*	*1.43*	*1.32*	*1.22*								
8	12	6.22	4.91	3.98	3.29	2.76	2.36	2.03	1.77	1.56	1.38					
		2.15	*1.90*	*1.72*	*1.56*	*1.43*	*1.32*	*1.22*	*1.15*	*1.07*	*1.01*					
10		7.78	6.15	4.98	4.12	3.46	2.95	2.54	2.21	1.95	1.72					
		2.70	*2.40*	*2.16*	*1.96*	*1.80*	*1.66*	*1.54*	*1.44*	*1.35*	*1.27*					
8	14	8.95	7.07	5.73	4.74	3.98	3.39	2.92	2.55	2.24	1.98	1.77	1.59	1.43		
		2.58	*2.29*	*2.06*	*1.87*	*1.72*	*1.58*	*1.47*	*1.37*	*1.28*	*1.21*	*1.14*	*1.08*	*1.03*		
10		11.2	8.84	7.16	5.92	4.97	4.24	3.65	3.18	2.80	2.48	2.21	1.98	1.79		
		3.23	*2.87*	*2.58*	*2.35*	*2.15*	*1.99*	*1.85*	*1.73*	*1.62*	*1.52*	*1.44*	*1.36*	*1.29*		
12		13.4	10.6	8.60	7.11	5.97	5.09	4.39	3.82	3.36	2.98	2.66	2.38	2.15		
		3.87	*3.43*	*3.09*	*2.81*	*2.58*	*2.38*	*2.21*	*2.07*	*1.94*	*1.82*	*1.72*	*1.63*	*1.55*		
8	16	12.2	9.63	7.80	6.45	5.42	4.62	3.98	3.47	3.05	2.70	2.41	2.16	1.95	1.77	1.61
		3.02	*2.64*	*2.41*	*2.19*	*2.02*	*1.86*	*1.73*	*1.61*	*1.51*	*1.42*	*1.34*	*1.28*	*1.21*	*1.15*	*1.10*
10		15.2	12.0	9.75	8.06	6.77	5.77	4.98	4.33	3.81	3.37	3.01	2.70	2.44	2.21	2.02
		3.76	*3.34*	*3.01*	*2.74*	*2.51*	*2.31*	*2.15*	*2.01*	*1.88*	*1.77*	*1.68*	*1.58*	*1.51*	*1.44*	*1.37*
12		18.3	14.4	11.7	9.67	8.13	6.92	5.97	5.20	4.57	4.05	3.61	3.24	2.93	2.65	2.42
		4.53	*4.02*	*3.62*	*3.29*	*3.02*	*2.79*	*2.58*	*2.41*	*2.26*	*2.13*	*2.02*	*1.90*	*1.81*	*1.73*	*1.65*
14		21.4	16.9	13.7	11.3	9.51	8.11	6.99	6.09	5.35	4.74	4.23	3.80	3.43	3.11	2.83
		5.27	*4.68*	*4.22*	*3.83*	*3.51*	*3.25*	*3.01*	*2.81*	*2.64*	*2.48*	*2.35*	*2.22*	*2.11*	*2.01*	*1.92*

Width (in.)	Depth (in.)	14	16	18	20	22	24	26	28	30	32	34	36	38	40	42
10	18	6.48	4.96	3.92	3.18	2.62	2.21	1.88								
		2.46	*2.15*	*1.90*	*1.72*	*1.56*	*1.43*	*1.32*								
12		7.81	5.98	4.72	3.83	3.16	2.66	2.26								
		2.95	*2.58*	*2.30*	*2.07*	*1.88*	*1.73*	*1.59*								
14		9.08	6.95	5.49	4.45	3.68	3.09	2.63								
		3.43	*3.01*	*2.67*	*2.41*	*2.19*	*2.01*	*1.83*								
16		10.4	7.97	6.30	5.10	4.22	3.54	3.02								
		3.94	*3.44*	*3.06*	*2.75*	*2.51*	*2.30*	*2.12*								
12	20	9.85	7.54	5.96	4.83	3.99	3.35	2.86	2.46	2.14						
		3.32	*2.90*	*2.58*	*2.32*	*2.11*	*1.94*	*1.79*	*1.66*	*1.55*						
14		11.5	8.83	6.98	5.65	4.67	3.92	3.34	2.88	2.51						
		3.88	*3.39*	*3.01*	*2.71*	*2.47*	*2.26*	*2.08*	*1.94*	*1.81*						
16		13.2	10.1	7.96	6.45	5.33	4.48	3.82	3.29	2.87						
		4.42	*3.87*	*3.43*	*3.09*	*2.81*	*2.83*	*2.38*	*2.21*	*2.07*						
12	22	12.2	9.34	7.38	5.98	4.94	4.15	3.54	3.05	2.66	2.33					
		3.69	*3.23*	*2.88*	*2.58*	*2.35*	*2.15*	*1.99*	*1.85*	*1.73*	*1.62*					
14		14.2	10.9	8.61	6.98	5.77	4.84	4.13	3.56	3.10	2.73					
		4.30	*3.77*	*3.34*	*3.01*	*2.74*	*2.51*	*2.31*	*2.15*	*2.01*	*1.88*					
16		16.2	12.4	9.82	7.95	6.57	5.52	4.70	4.06	3.53	3.11					
		4.92	*4.30*	*3.83*	*3.44*	*3.13*	*2.87*	*2.65*	*2.46*	*2.30*	*2.15*					

Width (in.)	Depth (in.)	14	16	18	20	22	24	26	28	30	32	34	36	38	40	42
								f'c = 4000 psi and ASTM A615–60 p = 1.24% — Span length, (ft) — Ultimate loads (kips)									
12	24	14.8	11.3	8.92	7.23	5.97	5.02	4.28	3.69	3.21	2.82	2.50				
		4.06	*3.55*	*3.15*	*2.84*	*2.58*	*2.36*	*2.19*	*2.03*	*1.90*	*1.78*	*1.68*				
14		17.2	13.2	10.4	8.43	6.96	5.85	4.99	4.30	3.74	3.29	2.92				
		4.74	*4.15*	*3.68*	*3.32*	*3.02*	*2.76*	*2.55*	*2.37*	*2.21*	*2.07*	*1.95*				
16		19.6	15.0	11.9	9.63	7.96	6.68	5.70	4.91	4.28	3.76	3.33				
		5.41	*4.73*	*4.20*	*3.78*	*3.44*	*3.15*	*2.91*	*2.70*	*2.53*	*2.36*	*2.23*				
14	26		15.7	12.4	10.0	8.29	6.96	5.93	5.12	4.46	3.92	3.47	3.09			
			4.51	*4.01*	*3.61*	*3.28*	*3.01*	*2.78*	*2.58*	*2.41*	*2.26*	*2.13*	*2.01*			
16			17.9	14.2	11.5	9.48	7.97	6.79	5.86	5.10	4.48	3.97	3.54			
			5.17	*4.59*	*4.13*	*3.76*	*3.44*	*3.18*	*2.95*	*2.75*	*2.58*	*2.43*	*2.30*			
18			20.2	15.9	12.9	10.7	8.96	7.63	6.58	5.73	5.04	4.46	3.98			
			5.81	*5.16*	*4.64*	*4.22*	*3.87*	*3.57*	*3.32*	*3.09*	*2.90*	*2.73*	*2.58*			
14	28			14.5	11.8	9.73	8.18	6.97	6.01	5.23	4.60	4.07	3.63	3.26		
				4.34	*3.91*	*3.55*	*3.26*	*3.01*	*2.80*	*2.61*	*2.45*	*2.30*	*2.18*	*2.06*		
16				16.6	13.5	11.1	9.34	7.96	6.86	5.98	5.25	4.65	4.15	3.73		
				4.96	*4.47*	*4.06*	*3.72*	*3.44*	*3.20*	*2.98*	*2.80*	*2.63*	*2.48*	*2.36*		
18				18.7	15.1	12.5	10.5	8.95	7.72	6.72	5.91	5.23	4.67	4.19		
				5.59	*5.03*	*4.57*	*4.19*	*3.87*	*3.60*	*3.36*	*3.15*	*2.96*	*2.80*	*2.65*		
16	30			15.6	12.9	10.8	9.23	7.96	6.93	6.09	5.40	4.82	4.32	3.90		
				4.82	*4.39*	*4.02*	*3.71*	*3.44*	*3.21*	*3.01*	*2.84*	*2.68*	*2.53*	*2.41*		
18				17.6	14.5	12.2	10.4	8.95	7.80	6.86	6.07	5.42	4.86	4.39		
				5.42	*4.93*	*4.52*	*4.17*	*3.88*	*3.61*	*3.39*	*3.19*	*3.01*	*2.86*	*2.71*		
20				19.5	16.1	13.5	11.5	9.95	8.67	7.62	6.75	6.02	5.40	4.88		
				6.02	*5.47*	*5.02*	*4.63*	*4.30*	*4.01*	*3.77*	*3.55*	*3.34*	*3.17*	*3.01*		
16	32			17.9	14.8	12.4	10.6	9.13	7.96	7.00	6.19	5.53	4.96	4.48	4.06	
				5.16	*4.69*	*4.30*	*3.97*	*3.69*	*3.44*	*3.22*	*3.04*	*2.87*	*2.72*	*2.58*	*2.46*	
18				20.2	16.7	14.0	11.9	10.3	8.96	7.87	6.97	6.22	5.58	5.04	4.57	
				5.81	*5.28*	*4.84*	*4.46*	*4.15*	*3.87*	*3.63*	*3.42*	*3.22*	*3.06*	*2.91*	*2.76*	
20				22.4	18.5	15.6	13.3	11.4	9.96	8.75	7.75	6.91	6.21	5.60	5.08	
				6.45	*5.87*	*5.38*	*4.96*	*4.61*	*4.30*	*4.02*	*3.80*	*3.59*	*3.40*	*3.23*	*3.07*	
18	34				19.0	15.9	13.6	11.7	10.2	8.96	7.93	7.08	6.35	5.73	5.20	
					5.64	*5.17*	*4.77*	*4.43*	*4.13*	*3.88*	*3.65*	*3.44*	*3.26*	*3.10*	*2.95*	
20					21.1	17.7	15.1	13.0	11.3	9.95	8.82	7.86	7.06	6.37	5.78	
					6.26	*5.74*	*5.30*	*4.92*	*4.59*	*4.30*	*4.06*	*3.83*	*3.62*	*3.44*	*3.28*	
22					23.2	19.5	16.6	14.3	12.5	11.0	9.70	8.65	7.76	7.01	6.36	
					6.89	*6.32*	*5.82*	*5.41*	*5.05*	*4.74*	*4.45*	*4.21*	*3.99*	*3.79*	*3.60*	
18	36				21.4	18.0	15.3	13.2	11.5	10.1	8.96	7.99	7.17	6.47	5.87	
					5.98	*5.48*	*5.06*	*4.70*	*4.39*	*4.11*	*3.87*	*3.66*	*3.46*	*3.29*	*3.14*	
20					23.8	20.0	17.0	14.7	12.8	11.2	9.95	8.87	7.96	7.19	6.52	
					6.65	*6.10*	*5.63*	*5.22*	*4.87*	*4.57*	*4.30*	*4.06*	*3.85*	*3.66*	*3.49*	
22					26.1	22.0	18.7	16.1	14.1	12.4	10.9	9.76	8.76	7.91	7.17	
					7.31	*6.70*	*6.19*	*5.75*	*5.36*	*5.02*	*4.74*	*4.47*	*4.23*	*4.02*	*3.83*	
20	38					22.4	19.1	16.5	14.3	12.6	11.2	9.95	8.93	8.06	7.31	
						6.45	*5.96*	*5.53*	*5.16*	*4.84*	*4.56*	*4.30*	*4.08*	*3.88*	*3.69*	
22						24.6	21.0	18.1	15.8	13.9	12.3	11.0	9.83	8.87	8.04	
						7.08	*6.54*	*6.07*	*5.67*	*5.31*	*5.00*	*4.73*	*4.47*	*4.25*	*4.05*	
24						26.9	22.9	19.7	17.2	15.1	13.4	11.9	10.7	9.67	8.77	
						7.72	*7.13*	*6.62*	*6.18*	*5.79*	*5.45*	*5.15*	*4.88*	*4.63*	*4.41*	

Axial loads

The ACI code requires that the slenderness of a column be taken into account in designing members for axial loads and bending. For the purpose of evaluating slenderness effects the unsupported length l_u of a compression member shall be taken as the clear distance between floor slabs, girders, or other members capable of providing lateral support for the member. For rectangular compression members, the radius of gyration r may be taken as 0.30 times the overall dimension in the direction in which stability is being considered and 0.25 times the diameter for circular columns. For members braced against sidesway the effective length factor k shall be taken as 1.0. For compression members not braced against sidesway, the effective length factor k shall take into consideration cracking and reinforcement on relative stiffness, and shall be greater than 1.0. The commentary to the code states that "A compression member braced against sidesway is a member in a story in which the bracing elements such as shearwalls, shear trusses, or other type of lateral bracing, have a total stiffness, resisting lateral movement of a story, at least six times the sum of the stiffness of all the columns resisting lateral movement."

The effects of slenderness may be neglected for compression members braced

Table 7. Maximum spacing of column ties

Vertical bar size	Size and spacing of ties (in.)		
	#3	#4	#5
#5	10		
#6	12		
#7	14		
#8	16	16	
#9	18	18	
#10	18	20	
#11		22	22
#14s		24	27
#18s		24	30

Note: Maximum spacing shall not exceed least column dimension

Table 8. Axial loads for short tied columns with minimum eccentricity (0.1t)

$f'_c = 4000/psi$ bar grade 60 $\phi = 0.70$

P_u (kips)/p %

Column (in.) / Bar	10×10	10×12	10×14	10×16	12×12	12×14	12×16	12×18	14×14	14×16	14×18	14×20
4–#5	226 / 1.24	264 / 1.03										
4–#6	241 / 1.76	279 / 1.46	317 / 1.25	355 / 1.10	327 / 1.22	372 / 1.04						
4–#7	259 / 2.40	297 / 1.99	355 / 1.71	373 / 1.50	345 / 1.66	391 / 1.42	437 / 1.25	483 / 1.11	447 / 1.22	500 / 1.07		
4–#8	280 / 3.16	318 / 2.63	356 / 2.25	394 / 1.97	367 / 2.19	413 / 1.88	449 / 1.64	505 / 1.46	469 / 1.61	523 / 1.41	576 / 1.25	630 / 1.12
4–#9	303 / 4.00	341 / 3.33	379 / 2.85	417 / 2.50	391 / 2.17	437 / 2.38	483 / 2.08	528 / 1.85	494 / 2.04	548 / 1.78	601 / 1.58	655 / 1.42
6–#5	238 / 1.85			353 / 1.16	324 / 1.29	370 / 1.10						
6–#6	258 / 2.64		342 / 1.88	372 / 1.65	345 / 1.83	390 / 1.57	436 / 1.37	482 / 1.22	446 / 1.34	499 / 1.17	552 / 1.04	
6–#8	311 / 4.74	349 / 3.95	400 / 3.38	425 / 2.96	400 / 3.29	446 / 2.82	491 / 2.46	537 / 2.19	502 / 2.41	556 / 2.11	609 / 1.88	662 / 1.69
8–#6	294 / 3.52		360 / 2.51	405 / 2.20	365 / 2.44	428 / 2.09	456 / 1.83		467 / 1.79	520 / 1.57		627 / 1.25
8–#7			393 / 3.42	441 / 3.00	398 / 3.33	443 / 2.85	489 / 2.50	543 / 2.22	500 / 2.44	554 / 2.14		660 / 1.71
8–#8			432 / 4.51	470 / 3.95		493 / 3.76	539 / 3.29	584 / 2.92	540 / 3.22	593 / 2.82	647 / 2.50	700 / 2.25
8–#9							584 / 4.16	629 / 3.70	583 / 4.08	637 / 3.57	690 / 3.17	743 / 2.85
8–#10											764 / 4.03	817 / 3.62

Column (in.) / Bar	16×16	16×18	16×20	16×24	18×18	18×20	20×20	20×24	20×28	22×22	24×24	24×28	26×26	28×28	30×30
4–#8	586 / 1.23	647 / 1.09													
4–#9	612 / 1.56	673 / 1.38	734 / 1.25	856 / 1.04	744 / 1.23	813 / 1.11	891 / 1.00								
4–#10	644 / 1.98	705 / 1.76	766 / 1.58	889 / 1.32	777 / 1.56	846 / 1.41	925 / 1.27	1078 / 1.05		1088 / 1.04					

against sidesway when kl_u/r is less than $34 - (1.2\ M_1/M_2)$. For compression members not braced against sidesway, slenderness effects may be neglected when kl_u/r is less than 22.

$M_1 =$ value of the smaller factored end moment on the compression member calculated by conventional elastic frame analysis; positive if member is bent in single curvature, negative if bent in double curvature.

$M_2 =$ value of the larger factored end moment on the compression member calculated by conventional elastic frame analysis; always positive.

Design data for axial loads P_u with minimum allowed eccentricity of $0.1t$ are tabulated for various columns sizes and reinforcement that are not subject to slenderness effects. It is recommended that the column selected be tested for slenderness effects using the appropriate formulas noted

above. If the column size selected exceeds minimum values, select a larger column and test again.

The maximum spacing of column ties is shown in Table 7.

The first line in Table 8 lists the ultimate axial load, P_u, safely supported by a column of size and reinforcement noted with an eccentricity $= 0.1t$. The second line (italicized) is p, percent of steel.

$$f_c' = 4000/psi \qquad bar\ grade\ 60 \qquad \phi = 0.70$$

P_u (kips)/p %

Column (in.) Bar	16×16	16×18	16×20	16×24	18×18	18×20	20×20	20×24	20×28	22×22	24×24	24×28	26×26	28×28	30×30
4–#11	677	738	799	922	811	880	960	1112	1265	1123	1301				
	2.43	2.16	1.95	1.62	1.92	1.73	1.56	1.30	1.11	1.28	1.08				
4–#14	758	819	880	1002	893	962	1043	1196	1349	1208	1338	1571	1799	1791	2015
	3.51	3.12	2.31	2.34	2.77	2.50	2.25	1.87	1.60	1.85	1.56	1.33	2.36	1.14	1.00
6–#6	561														
	1.03														
6–#7	588	649	710		719										
	1.40	1.25	1.12		1.11										
6–#8	619	680	741	863	751		898								
	1.85	1.64	1.48	1.23	1.46		1.18								
6–#9	654	715	776	897	786	855	233	1113	1238						
	2.38	2.08	1.87	1.56	1.85	1.66	1.50	1.25	1.07						
6–#10	698	759	820	941	831	900	979	1131	1284			1502			
	2.97	2.64	2.38	1.98	2.35	2.11	1.90	1.58	1.36			1.13			
8–#6	583	644	705		714										
	1.37	1.22	1.10		1.08										
8–#7	617	675	739	870	749		896								
	1.87	1.66	1.50	1.25	1.48		1.20								
8–#8	658	719	780	913	791		938	1090		1112	1289				
	2.46	2.19	1.97	1.64	1.25		1.58	1.31		1.30	1.09				
8–#9	734	764	824	946	836		984	1136	1335	1161	1339	1507	1532	1739	
	3.12	2.77	2.50	2.08	2.46		2.00	1.66	1.42	1.65	1.38	1.19	1.18	1.02	
8–#10	760	821	882	1003	895		1043	1195	1348	1225	1403	1567	1596	1805	2028
	3.96	3.52	3.17	2.64	3.13		2.54	2.11	1.81	2.09	1.76	1.51	1.50	1.29	1.12
8–#11			939	1061	954		1105	1256	1408	1290	1470	1630	1664	1873	2097
			3.90	3.25	3.85		3.12	2.60	2.22	2.57	2.16	1.85	1.84	1.59	1.38
10–#10							1111	1263							
							3.17	2.64							
10–#11							1186	1338	1510			1714			
							3.90	3.25	2.78			2.32			
12–#10								1347		1374	1554		1748	1958	2182
								3.17		3.14	2.64		2.25	1.94	1.69
12–#11								1440	1592	1472	1653		1849	2059	2285
								3.89	3.34	3.86	3.25		2.76	2.38	2.07
12–#14													2093	2305	2532
													3.99	3.44	3.00

Construction details

Note If access to the interior of a column is necessary, a different pattern of ties may be substituted provided ties are so designed that each vertical bar is securely braced against movement in any direction
Column Steel Arranged For Bending & Direct Stress
Alternate Method Of Tie Arrangement For Elongated Columns
Typical Arrangement Of Corner Columns

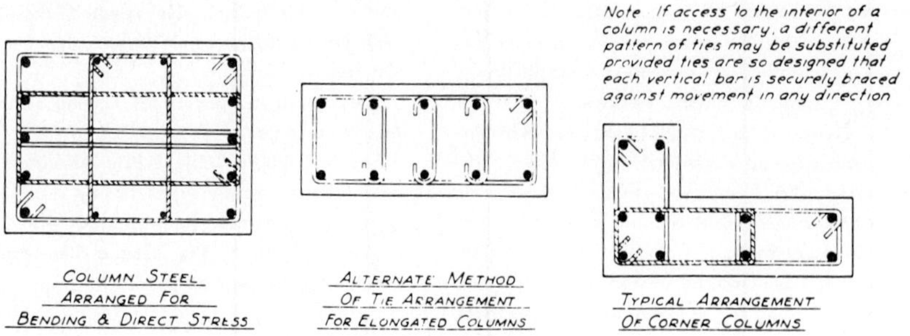

Typical special-purpose columns

Lower bar
Upper bar
Section A'-A'
A'
A'
Slope 1 to 6 maximum
4 Spaces @ 3"

Typical tied column

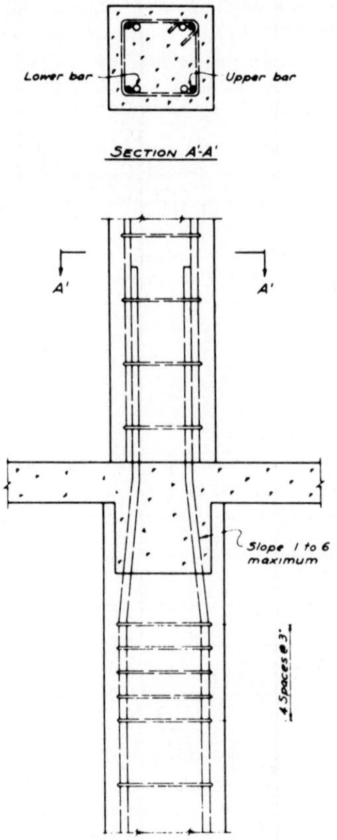

Welded Anchor Bolts.
A
A

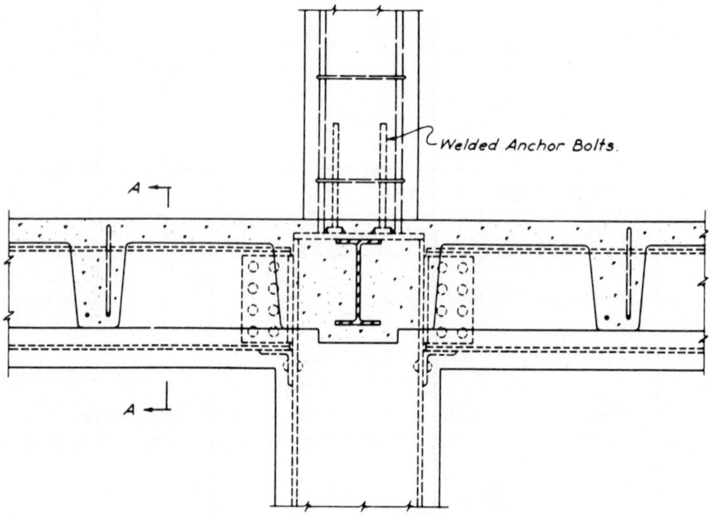

Steel construction to floor; concrete above

Fig. 2. Typical details of reinforced concrete beams, girders, and columns

From Manual of Standard Practice for Detailing Reinforced Concrete Structures, *ACI 315, American Concrete Institute.*

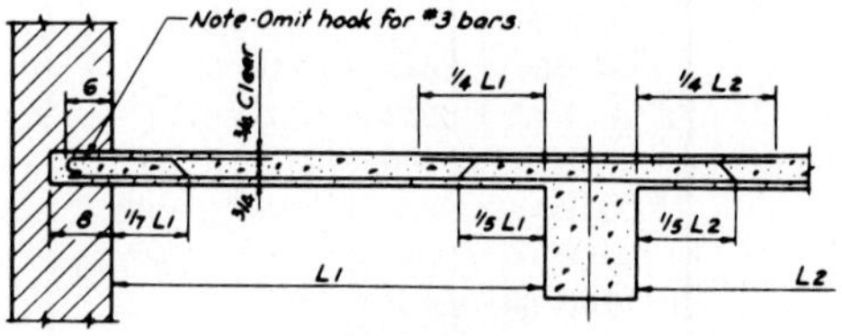

Note-Omit hook for #3 bars
6
3/4 Clear
3/4
8
1/7 L1
1/4 L1
1/4 L2
1/5 L1
1/5 L2
L1
L2

Slab detail

Section A-A

1/7 L1
Where Specified
1-0 Min.
2 For Beams
3 For Girders
1/4 Greater L
1/4 Greater L
Top Bars
#3 Stirrup Spacer
2
6
1 1/2 Clear
D
W
Section
Beams 8
Girders 12
1/7 L1
2 Clear
1 Clear
Embed 17d
1/5 L1
1/4 L2
L1
L2
This may be increased to 1/5 L1 to maintain 1-0 minimum above.

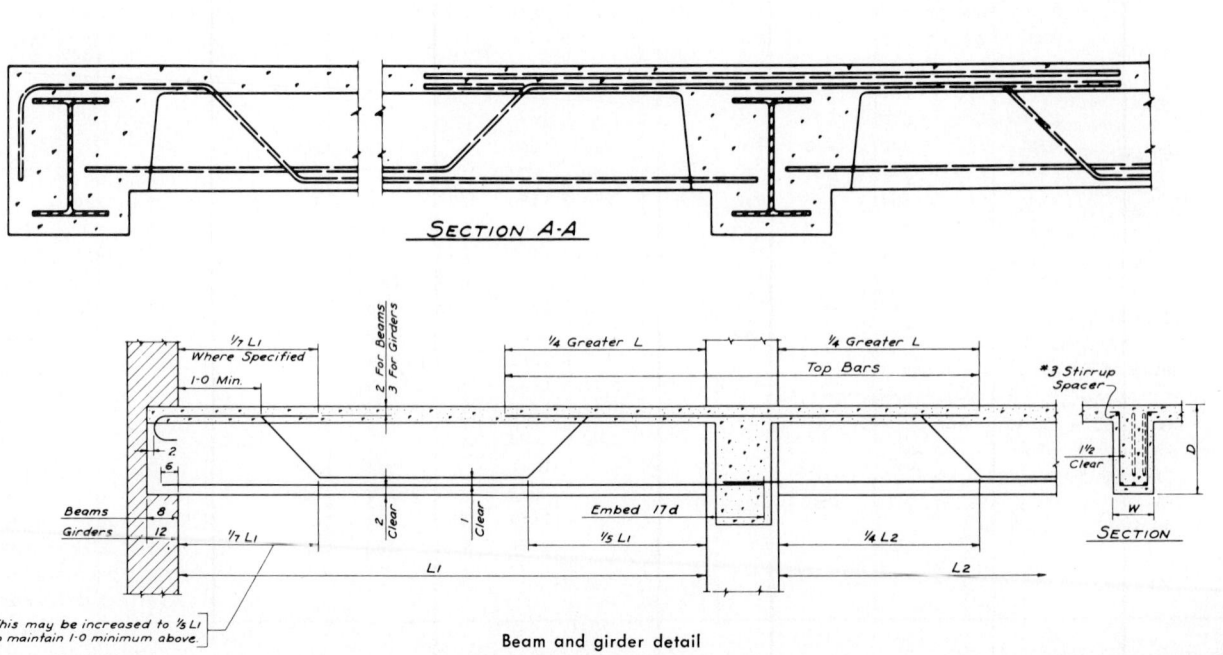

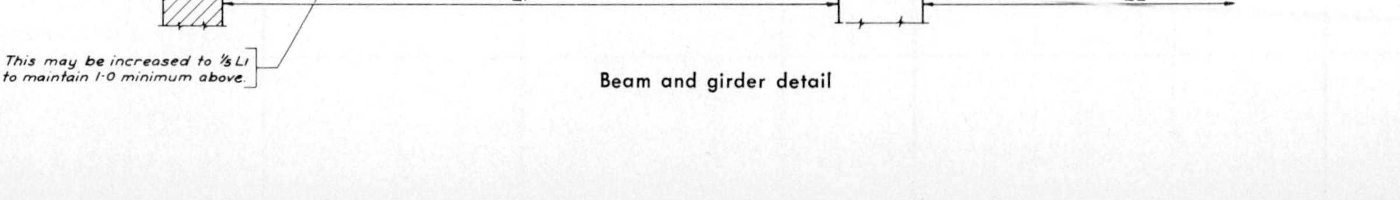

Beam and girder detail

FLAT SLABS AND TWO-WAY SLABS

Flat slabs and two-way slabs are highly indeterminate systems in which the floor slab is reinforced in two or more directions. For each system, the ACI code stipulates a minimum thickness of slab and provides an empirical method of analysis giving the flexural and shear requirements. Table 9 indicates the maximum dimensions these slabs may take in accordance with this requirement. Although the thickness of slab may be adequate to fulfill design requirements, the purpose of the table is only to establish the upper limit of the dimensions for each thickness of slab.

The minimum thickness of slabs of two-way construction having a ratio of long to short span not exceeding 2 is determined from the following relationships established by the ACI code:

$$h = \frac{l_n(800 + 0.005f_y)}{36,000 + 5000\beta[\alpha_m - 0.5(1 - \beta_s)(1 + 1\beta)]}$$

but not less than

$$h = \frac{l_n(800 + 0.005f_y)}{36,000 + 5000\beta(1 + \beta_s)}$$

where l_n = clear span in long direction, face to face of columns or beams

f_y = yield strength 60,000 psi

α = ratio of flexural stiffness of beam section to flexural stiffness of a width of slab bounded laterally by centerline of adjacent panel on each side of beam

α_m = average value of α for all beams on the edge of the panel

β = ratio of clear spans in long to short direction

β_s = ratio of length of continuous edges to total perimeter of a slab panel

An α_m value of 0.8 was used in development of Table 9.

One-way solid slabs

Table 10 gives minimum thickness of one-way solid slabs with normal weight concrete reinforced with grade 60 reinforcement. For structural lightweight concrete having unit weights of 90 to 120 lb/ft², the tabulated values shall be multiplied by $(1.65 - 0.005w_c)$ but not less than 1.09, where w_c is the unit weight in pounds per cubic foot. For steel of yield strengths other than 60,000 lb/in.² the values in the table shall be multiplied by $(0.4 + f_y/100,000)$.

The slab thickness listed for the respective spans in the table may be used without computing actual deflections.

Table 9. Minimum slab thickness for two-way slabs (in.)

Span (ft)	Number of continuous sides				
	None	1	2	3	4
10	*	*	*	*	*
12	*	*	*	*	*
14	5½	5½	*	*	*
16	6	6	6	5½	5½
18	7	7	6½	6½	6
20	7½	7½	7½	7	7
22	8½	8	8	7½	7½
24	9	9	9	8½	8
26	9½	9½	9½	9	9
28	10½	10½	10	10	9½
30	11	11	11	10½	10
32	12	12	11½	11	11
34	12½	12½	12	12	11½
36	13½	13½	13	12½	12

Thickness shall not be less than the following values:
(a) For slabs without beams or drop panels: 5"
(b) For slabs without beams but with drop panels satisfying Section 9.5.3.2 of ACI code: 4".

Table 10. Minimum thickness of one-way slabs with normal weight concrete and grade 60 reinforcement (unless deflections are computed)

Span (ft)	Simply supported (in.)	One end continuous (in.)	Both ends continuous (in.)	Cantilever (in.)
7	4½	4	4	8½
8	5	4	4	10
9	5½	4½	4	11
10	6	5	4½	12
11	7	5½	5	
12	7½	6	5½	
13	8	6½	6	
14	8½	7	6	
15	9	7½	6½	
16	10	8	7	

BEAMS

Minimum depths of beams of normal-weight concrete for spans varying from 10 to 30 ft in 2-ft increments are tabulated in Table 11 for various conditions of support. Adjustments for lightweight concrete and for steels having yield strengths other than 60,000 lb/in² shall be made in accordance with adjustments noted under one-way solid slabs above.

Reinforcement

Having established depth of beam or thickness of slab from Table 9, 10, or 11 and the ultimate moment M_u in inch-pounds, either from coefficients (Table 2) or from elastic analysis, the area of steel required can be calculated using coefficients for ultimate strength design of rectangular sections (Tables 12 and 13). Calculate M_u/bd^2, entering M_u in inch-pounds and b and d in inches. Enter chart with the M_u/bd^2 value and select p, percent of steel required, using straight-line interpolation for values of M_u/bd^2 falling between tabulated values. Since $p(\%) = 100\ A_s/bd$, by rearranging terms $A_s = p(\%)bd/100$.

The effective depth, d, used for slabs is equal to the slab thickness minus a clearance of ¾ in. plus one-half the diameter of bar.

For beams, the depth from the nearest face to the centerline of reinforcement may be taken from Table 14.

Safe Ultimate Superimposed Loads

Table 15 lists safe ultimate superimposed loads for one-way solid slabs in pounds per square foot for various spans and one condition of end restraint; end span free on

Table 12. Coefficients for ultimate strength design of rectangular beam sections

$f'_c = 3000$ psi, grade 60 steel, $A_s = pbd/100$, $\phi = 0.90$ already considered

p(%)	$\dfrac{M_u(lb\text{-}in.)}{bd^2(in.^3)}$	p(%)	$\dfrac{M_u(lb\text{-}in.)}{bd^2(in.^3)}$	p(%)	$\dfrac{M_u(lb\text{-}in.)}{bd^2(in.^3)}$
0.32	166	0.76	374	1.20	556
0.34	176	0.78	382	1.22	564
0.36	186	0.80	391	1.24	572
0.38	196	0.82	400	1.26	579
0.40	206	0.84	409	1.28	586
0.42	216	0.86	417	1.30	594
0.44	225	0.88	426	1.32	602
0.46	235	0.90	434	1.34	609
0.48	244	0.92	443	1.36	616
0.50	254	0.94	451	1.38	624
0.52	263	0.96	460	1.40	631
0.54	273	0.98	468	1.42	639
0.56	282	1.00	476	1.44	646
0.58	292	1.02	484	1.46	652
0.60	301	1.04	492	1.48	659
0.62	310	1.06	501	1.50	667
0.64	319	1.08	510	1.52	674
0.66	329	1.10	517	1.54	681
0.68	338	1.12	525	1.56	687
0.70	347	1.14	533	1.58	694
0.72	356	1.16	541	1.60	701
0.74	365	1.18	548	Use comp. reinf.	

Table 13. Coefficients for ultimate strength design of rectangular beam sections

$f'_c = 4000$ psi, grade 60 steel, $A_s = pbd/100$, $\phi = 0.90$ already considered

p(%)	$\dfrac{M_u(lb\text{-}in.)}{bd^2(in.^3)}$	p(%)	$\dfrac{M_u(lb\text{-}in.)}{bd^2(in.^3)}$	p(%)	$\dfrac{M_u(lb\text{-}in.)}{bd^2(in.^3)}$
0.32	168	0.74	373	1.40	662
0.34	178	0.76	383	1.45	683
0.36	188	0.78	392	1.50	702
0.38	198	0.80	401	1.55	722
0.40	208	0.82	410	1.60	742
0.42	218	0.84	420	1.65	761
0.44	228	0.86	429	1.70	780
0.46	238	0.88	438	1.75	799
0.48	248	0.90	447	1.80	817
0.50	258	0.92	456	1.85	836
0.52	268	0.94	465	1.90	853
0.54	278	0.96	474	1.95	869
0.56	287	0.98	483	2.00	889
0.58	297	1.00	492	2.05	907
0.60	307	1.05	514	2.10	923
0.62	316	1.10	536	2.14	938
0.64	326	1.15	558	Use comp. reinf.	
0.66	336	1.20	579		
0.68	345	1.25	601		
0.70	355	1.30	621		
0.72	364	1.35	641		

Table 11. Minimum depth of beams with normal weight concrete and grade 60 reinforcement (unless deflections are computed)

Span (ft)	Simply supported (in.)	One end continuous (in.)	Both ends continuous (in.)	Cantilever (in.)
10	8	8	8	16
12	10	8	8	18
14	10	10	8	22
16	12	12	10	24
18	14	12	12	28
20	16	14	12	30
22	18	16	14	
24	18	16	14	
26	20	18	16	
28	22	20	16	
30	24	20	18	

Table 14. Depth from nearest face of beam to centerline of bar

Bar size	#5	#6	#7	#8	#9	#10	#11
Depth, d (in.)	2.19	2.25	2.31	2.38	2.44	2.51	2.71

Table 15. Ultimate superimposed loads for one-way slabs with one end continuous $f_y = 60,000$ psi, $p = 1.0\%$

Span (ft)	Slab thickness (in.)	Ultimate superimposed loads (lb/ft²) $f'_c = 3000$ psi	$f'_c = 4000$ psi
8	4	599	622
9	4½	641	665
10	5	673	700
11	5½	700	732
12	6	721	749
13	6½	738	767
14	7	751	780
15	7½	762	792
16	8	771	801

Table 16. Ultimate superimposed loads for one-way concrete joist construction, single span

$f'_c = 4000$ psi, grade 60 steel; 5" rib 20" form, ribs @ 25" o.c.

Joist form depth + topping (in)	12	13	14	15	16	17	18	19	20	21	22	23	24
					Loads (lb/ft²)/Bottom bars								
8 + 3	620 2-#5	516 2-#5	433 2-#5										
8 + 4½				514 #5, #6	439 #5, #6								
10 + 3					578 2-#6	501 2-#6							
10 + 4½						555 2-#6	482 2-#6	420 2-#6					
12 + 3							521 2-#6	457 2-#6	402 2-#6				
12 + 4½									531 #6, #7	470 #6, #7	416 #6, #7		
14 + 3										505 #6, #7	450 #6, #7		
14 + 4½											574 2-#7	513 2-#7	460 2-#7

$f'_c = 4000$ psi, grade 60 steel, 6" rib, 20" form, ribs @ 26" o.c.

Joist form depth + topping (in)	24	25	26	27	28	29	30	31	32
16 + 3	462 2-#7	415 2-#7							
16 + 4½			392 2-#7	352 2-#7					
20 + 3					464 #7, #8	422 #7, #8	384 #7, #8		
20 + 4½							473 2-#8	431 2-#8	393 2-#8

one end and continuous on the other, for concrete strengths of $f_c' = 3000$ psi and $f_c' = 4000$ psi, and reinforcement ratio p equal to 1.0 per cent. One per cent reinforcement is considered a practical maximum amount of steel for placement in slabs. It also results in a maximum uniformly distributed load that will not exceed the allowable shear in the concrete.

In accordance with the ACI design coefficients, the design moment for the assumed end condition is equal to $wl^2/10$. Entering Table 12 or 13, select the value of M_u/bd^2 for $p = 1.05$ steel. For $f_c' = 4000$ psi and $p = 1.0\%$,

$$M_u/bd^2 = 492$$
$$M_u = 492bd^2 \quad (1)$$
$$\text{and} \quad M_u = wl^2/10 \quad (2)$$

equating (1) and (2) and solving for w

$$wl^2/10 = 492bd^2$$
$$w = 10(492)bd^2/l^2; \text{ where } b = 12 \text{ in}$$
$$= 10(492)(12)d^2/l^2$$

The ultimate superimposed load $w' = w - 1.4 \times$ weight of slab.

Using Tables 12 and 13 and the foregoing analysis, allowable loads may be calculated for any percentage of reinforcement up to 1%. Above 1% shear must be checked.

CONCRETE JOISTS

Concrete joist construction consists of narrow ribs or joists and a top slab of concrete, the whole of which is formed by creating longitudinal void spaces by means of permanent or removable forms of steel or wood. Joist widths vary from 4 in. to 7 or 8 in. Standard forms for the void spaces are usually 20 or 30 in. wide and vary in depth from 6 to 20 in. in 2-in. increments. The top slab usually varies from 2 to 4½ in. in thickness but not less than $\frac{1}{12}$ of the clear distance between ribs.

It should be noted, however, that to conform to many fire codes a minimum top slab thickness of 4½ in. is required for stone concrete and 3¼ in. for concrete of lightweight aggregates. Temperature reinforcement in the concrete top slab over forms and in a direction normal to the span of the joists may consist of either bars or welded wire fabric. For floor construction, distributing ribs with at least one No. 4 bar top and bottom are required. One rib near the center is required for spans from 20 to 30 ft and two near each third point for spans over 30 ft. The capacity of the joists can be increased by the use of tapered end forms, which are available for both 20 and 30-in.-wide forms. The recommended maximum span for joist floor construction is 16,

Table 17. Temperature and shrinkage reinforcement in one-way concrete joists

Top slab thickness (in)	Reinforcement grade 60	Welded wire fabric
2½	#3 @ 12" o.c.	4" × 12" ~ #2/#1
3	#3 @ 15" o.c.	4" × 12" ~ #2/#1
3½	#3 @ 17" o.c.	4" × 12" ~ #2.5/#1
4	#3 @ 15" o.c.	4" × 12" ~ #3/#2
4½	#3 @ 12" o.c.	4" × 12" ~ #3.5/#2

Table 18. Dome slab system: square panels 30" × 30" voids; 6" ribs @ 36" o.c.; $f_c' = 4000$ psi, Grade 60 Steel

Span and Drop panel (ft-in.)	Void depth + Top slab (in.)	Ultimate super-imposed load (lb/ft)	End panel		Exterior panel		Average cubic footage of concrete per square foot
			Min. col. size (in.)	Weight of steel (lb/ft²)	Min. col. size (in.)	Weight of steel (lb/ft²)	
18'-0" D = 6'-6" Rib on centerline	8 + 3	50	12	1.23	12	1.25	0.536
		100	12	1.23	12	1.25	
		150	12	1.32	12	1.25	
	10 + 3	50	12	1.39	12	1.40	0.611
		100	12	1.43	12	1.40	
		150	12	1.49	12	1.40	
21'-0" D = 9'-6" Rib not on centerline	8 + 3	50	12	1.33	12	1.23	0.567
		100	12	1.55	12	1.37	
		150	12	1.85	12	1.54	
	10 + 3	50	12	1.35	12	1.37	0.649
		100	12	1.51	12	1.37	
		150	12	1.66	12	1.45	
	12 + 3	50	12	1.53	12	1.54	0.748
		100	12	1.53	12	1.54	
		150	12	1.70	12	1.54	
24'-0" D = 9'-6" Rib not on centerline	8 + 3	50	12	1.47	12	1.31	0.549
		100	12	1.80	12	1.57	
		150	12	2.23	13	1.92	
	10 + 3	50	12	1.45	12	1.38	0.626
		100	12	1.65	12	1.45	
		150	12	2.07	12	1.82	
	12 + 3	50	12	1.59	12	1.55	0.721
		100	12	1.64	12	1.55	
		150	12	1.97	12	1.67	
	14 + 3	50	12	1.59	12	1.55	0.792
		100	12	1.64	12	1.55	
		150	12	1.82	12	1.64	

18.5, and 21 times the total depth of construction, respectively, depending on the conditions of end restraint.

Ultimate superimposed loads

The data in Table 16 have been derived from comprehensive tables prepared by the Concrete Reinforcing Steel Institute (CRSI). These tables give the ultimate superimposed loads for various combinations of joist width, depth of form and slab, end conditions, and reinforcement. Table 16 is mainly illustrative: it indicates the capacity of one-way joists for one set of conditions. Designs conform to the ACI code for single spans for which the design moment is equal to $wl^2/8$. Values are tabulated for joist widths of 5 and 6 in. Increasing or decreasing the joist width to 4 or 7 in. would have a corresponding effect on the loads given. Since the loads given reflect only one condition of reinforcing, the reader is referred to the CRSI *Design Handbook* which has comprehensive tables for joists of various sizes of load conditions and percent reinforcement. Temperature and shrinkage reinforcement in the concrete top slab over the forms are in a direction normal to the span of the joists and shall be bars or welded wire fabric of area equivalent to the following shown in Table 17.

TWO-WAY DOME SLABS ("WAFFLE SLABS")

The two-way dome slab has rows of joists at right angles to each other, with domes omitted around the columns to form drop panels. The columns must be of sufficient size to keep the diagonal tension within the allowable values or a flaring cap must be provided. Shallower domes are sometimes used around the drop panel to provide space for heavy top bars. Joists in each direction are divided into two bands or strips, one over the columns and extending the width of the drop panel, designed to provide reinforcement for the column strip, and the other filling in between consecutive column strips and designed to provide reinforcement for the middle strip. A second set of similar strips of joists runs at right angles to the first. If shears exceed the relatively low allowable values, flat welded stirrups are added, usually just for the length of a single dome.

The panels listed in Table 18 are in multiples of 3 ft so that the joists space out exactly. Spans of 21, 30, and 33 ft have a joist on the column center; spans of 24, 27, 36 and 39 ft have a row of domes on the column center, arranged to provide the proper size of drop panel. Narrower domes are available to fill out column spacings that are not multiples of 3 ft. Since suppliers vary considerably in standards, the designer should obtain detailed information on the types of domes most readily available at any given locality.

Although values have been given only for square panels, it is possible to estimate values for a rectangular panel by using the long side for one set of joists and the short side for the other. The ACI code limits the ratio of the long to short side to 2. Because of the considerable width of domes and the two-way nature of the slab, the designer should sketch the spacings for a typical panel and correlate them with the column spacings as a part of the early planning.

Table 18 is based on one set of stresses $f'_c = 4000$ psi and $f_y = 60,000$ psi. The allowable load represents the ultimate superimposed load including all live and dead loads except the weight of the structural concrete. The structure must have at least three consecutive panels in a row in each direction to satisfy the ACI code values for moments. If the building is narrower, a special analysis must be made. The lengths of successive spans must not differ by more

Span and Drop panel (ft-in.)	Void depth + Top slab (in.)	Ultimate super-imposed load (lb/ft)	End panel		Exterior panel		Average cubic footage of concrete per square foot
			Min. col. size (in.)	Weight of steel (lb/ft²)	Min. col. size (in.)	Weight of steel (lb/ft²)	
27'-0" D = 9'-6" Rib not on centerline	8 + 3	50	12	1.69	13	1.53	0.536
		100	12	1.98	14	1.78	
		150	12	2.33	17	2.20	
	10 + 3	50	13	1.63	13	1.43	0.611
		100	13	1.93	13	1.70	
		150	13	2.40	13	2.11	
	12 + 3	50	13	1.62	13	1.54	0.703
		100	13	1.90	13	1.67	
		150	13	2.32	13	2.00	
	14 + 3	50	13	1.62	13	1.54	0.770
		100	13	1.74	13	1.62	
		150	13	2.14	13	1.81	
	16 + 3	50	13	1.77	13	1.70	0.848
		100	13	1.84	13	1.72	
		150	13	2.08	13	1.88	
30'-0" D = 12'-6" Rib on centerline	8 + 3	50	19	1.95	15	1.86	0.557
		100	23	2.44	17	2.33	
		150	24	2.91	21	2.72	
	10 + 3	50	15	1.84	15	1.63	0.637
		100	15	2.29	15	2.02	
		150	19	2.60	18	2.38	
	12 + 3	50	15	1.86	15	1.68	0.733
		100	15	2.18	15	1.97	
		150	15	2.68	15	2.30	
	14 + 3	50	15	1.78	15	1.56	0.806
		100	15	2.07	15	1.78	
		150	15	2.55	15	2.22	
	16 + 3	50	15	1.80	15	1.74	0.888
		100	15	2.01	15	1.82	
		150	15	2.37	15	2.06	

Dome slabs

than 33 per cent of the longer span. Concrete quantities given per square foot of floor area include all structural concrete in slab and drop panel. The weight of main steel is the average weight in pounds per square foot of all longitudinal straight and truss bars. Table 19 and Figs. 3 to 6 are from CRSI *Design Handbook,* Concrete Reinforcing Steel Institute, 1972.

Table 19. Dome data

Depth (in)	Volume (cf per dome)	Weight of displaced concrete (lb per dome)	3" top slab		4½" top slab	
			Equiv. slab thickness (in)	Weight (lb/ft²)	Equiv. slab thickness (in)	Weight (lb/ft²)
30-in wide domes						
8	3.85	578	5.8	73	7.3	92
10	4.78	717	6.7	83	8.2	102
12	5.53	830	7.4	95	9.1	114
14	6.54	980	8.3	106	9.9	120
16	7.44	1116	9.1	114	10.6	133
20	9.16	1375	10.8	135	12.3	154
19-in wide domes			3" top slab		4½" top slab	
6	1.09	163	5.7	72	7.2	90
8	1.41	211	6.8	85	8.3	103
10	1.90	285	7.3	91	8.8	111
12	2.14	321	8.6	107	10.1	126

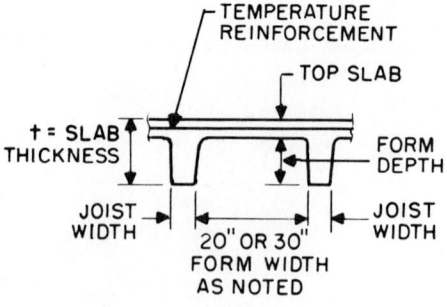

Fig. 3. Concrete joists, typical section
From CRSI Design Handbook, Concrete Reinforcing Steel Institute, 1972.

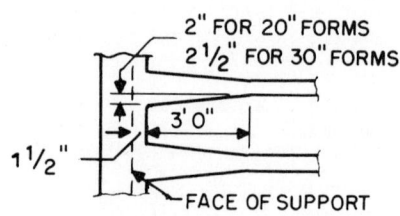

Fig. 4. Concrete joists, plan showing tapered ends

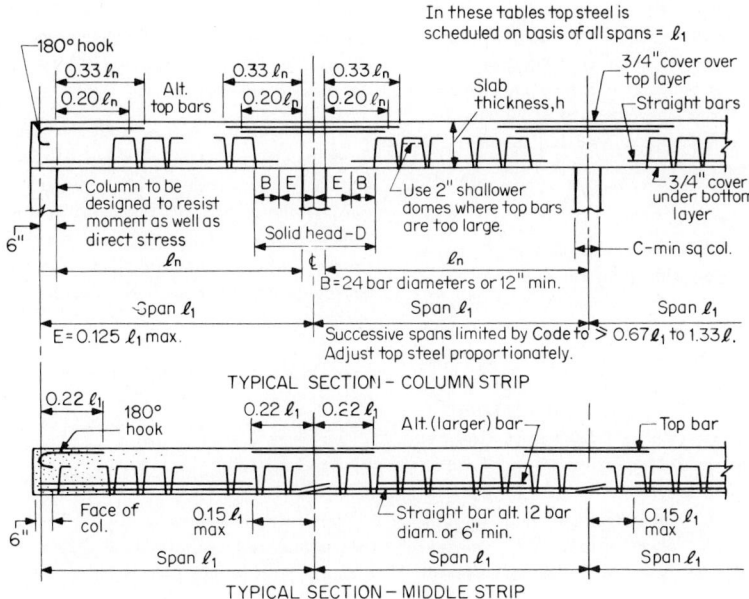

Fig. 5. Two-way dome (waffle) slab floor construction

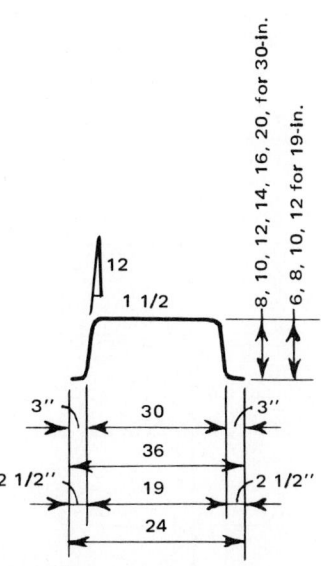

Fig. 6. Section through typical dome

Data from CRSI Design Handbook, Concrete Reinforcing Steel Institute, 1977.

LIFT-SLAB CONSTRUCTION

By JOHN G. MASCIONI, *P.E.,*
Associate Professor of Structural Design,
School of Architecture, Pratt Institute

Lift-slab construction is a method of erecting a building in accordance with the following sequence of operations:

1. Erect the columns for the building and secure their lowermost ends to the foundation.

2. Pour the first slab around these columns.

3. Apply a layer of bond-preventing material to the top of this slab.

4. Cast one, two, or more concrete slabs directly on top of the first slab, with each slab separated only by a layer of bond-preventing material.

5. Attach the lifting equipment to the columns and the slab to be lifted.

6. Lift the top slab to a predetermined elevation on the columns.

7. To prevent sidesway, maintain a sliding and guided relationship between the collars and the columns while the slab is being lifted.

8. Temporarily or permanently secure the lifted slab to the columns.

9. Connect the lifting equipment to the next lower slab or slabs to be lifted (if two or more are to be lifted together).

10. Repeat each step and extend the columns (if necessary) until all the slabs are brought to their final grades.

Lift slab is primarily a method of erection rather than design. Basically the design conforms to accepted engineering practices and codes used for formed-in-place construction. The major design difference is in the method of supporting the slabs on the columns. In lift slab, steel collars are placed around the columns for each slab connection before the concrete is placed. They become an integral part of the slab and are designed for attachment of the lifting equipment as well as to support the loads at each column. After the slabs are lifted into place, the collars are attached to the columns by welding, bolting, or pinning.

The use of lift slab will depend largely on the advantages that may occur in items affected by the operation during construction, such as forming, handling materials, speed of erection, ceiling treatment, insurance rates, and weather protection. Installation of structural materials and a large percentage of electrical and mechanical work are accomplished at ground level, where labor operations and safety are the most efficient.

No slab should be lifted until the concrete has reached a compressive strength of at least 2,700 psi as determined by standard cylinder test, and is at least 14 days old.

Vertical construction joints, where necessary, should be located at or near the midpoints of spans of slabs, beams, and walls. All continuous reinforcing should be carried through the joints.

Variable slab elevations within small areas should be avoided, although recesses for corridors and other areas create no special problems. Such recesses can be built up with cement grout, waste forms, or other forming materials for casting the next slab above. Slabs are sometimes cast directly into shallow recesses if the resulting offset in the ceiling above falls within a wall or other unobjectionable location. If each level of a split elevation covers a reasonably large area, the slabs can be divided into sections for placing and lifting.

During the preparation of a layout, efforts should be made to locate large slab openings outside of column strips and as near the center of bays as possible, or at the edge of slabs. The most desirable locations for stairwells, elevators, or other features requiring large openings are at the ends of a building or outside the slab line.

Simplicity and uniformity of building layout are the basic criteria for obtaining the maximum potential economy from lift slab.

Structural systems

Lift slab is generally used in flat-plate construction with spans ranging from 14 to 26 ft. The method is readily adaptable to almost any flat-plate project. Coffered and voided slabs are lifted for heavy loads and long spans. Inverted beams are often used for long-span roof construction. Beams or drop panels can be formed in recesses below the ground or first-floor level for one-story roof construction or for the first elevated slab in multistory buildings. Uniform and simple column arrangements are desirable and will contribute to over-all economy.

Columns can be of any type of structural steel or concrete, and can be round, square, or nearly square, in shape. Minimum sizes are desirable because the cost of slab-to-column connections increases for large columns.

Cost criteria

Lift slab generally does not change the quantities of materials required in similar types of slab systems and columns used for formed-in-place construction. The cost of the lifting operation is controlled primarily by labor and time, and may be affected by the following items:

1. *Spans:* Lifting cost generally decreases as span lengths increase because the area of slab lifted at each column increases.

2. *Height:* Lifting cost increases slightly with increases in heights of buildings. The cost can be reasonably controlled, however, by lifting two or more slabs together in multistory buildings.

3. *Welding:* Welding at column connections should be limited to that required to support the loads. Excessive welding increases time and labor unnecessarily.

Prestressing

Prestressing is frequently used in lift-slab construction and can contribute to over-all economy. Prestressing permits longer spans and reduces slab thickness, thus resulting in lower lifting costs and fewer materials. It is possible with a prestressed slab to reach virtually zero deflection for a given loading condition. This is achieved by properly placing the prestressing tendons in the slab to balance the deflections produced by the given loads.

Both normal-weight and lightweight concrete have been used in prestressed lift-slab construction. The concrete strength used is usually 4,000 psi at 28 days; the stressing

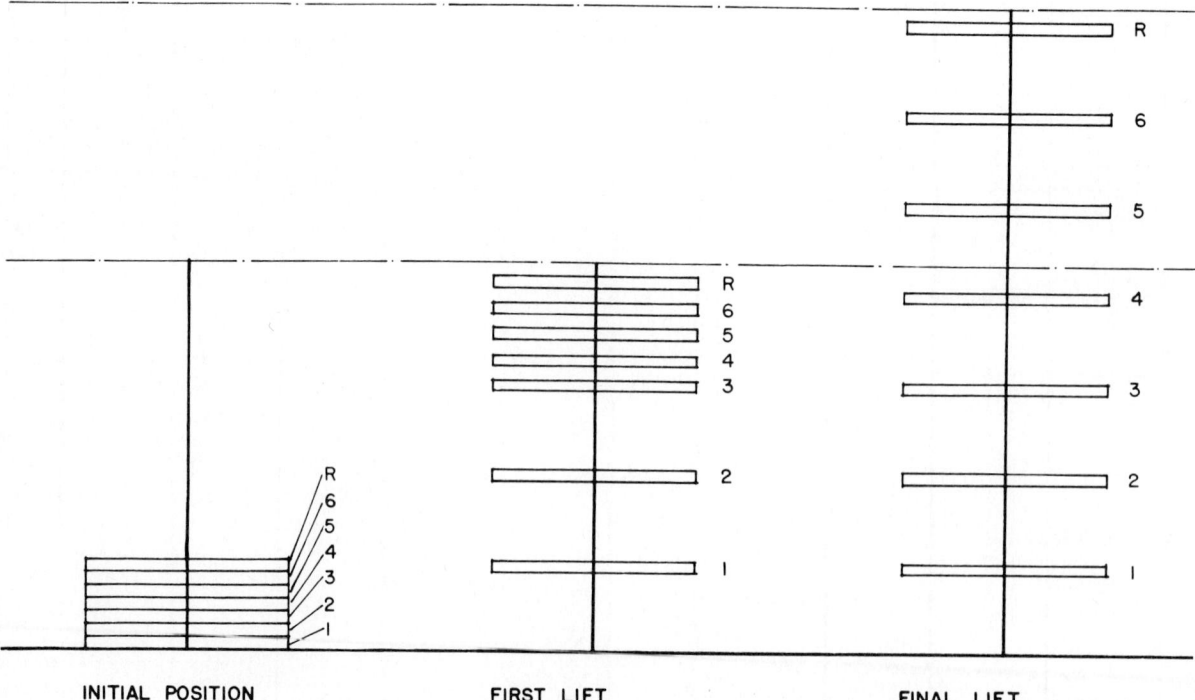

INITIAL POSITION   FIRST LIFT   FINAL LIFT

Fig. 7. Lifting procedure

takes place when the strength reaches 3,500 psi.

In general, there will be little cost advantage in prestressing slabs with spans less than 22 to 24 ft long for average loads and less than 18 to 20 ft long for heavy loads.

The prestressing usually employs some type of unbonded tendon with a button-head type of end anchorage. The size of the tendon should be small enough to permit curvature to the proper cable profile.

Limitations

1. Lift slab is limited to flat systems, except where beams or drop panels are feasible (as indicated above), or where horizontal offsets are used at the edges of successive slabs, thus permitting spandrel beams.

2. A cantilever system is desirable, but not essential. Slab edges should extend at least far enough beyond columns to permit one row of reinforcing bars to pass between the columns and the edge of the slab.

3. Close, irregular spacing of building or column lines and frequent large openings in slabs may require structural systems not appropriate for lifting.

4. Short spans averaging less than 12 ft usually are not economically feasible for lifting.

5. Lifting economy is usually limited to a minimum total slab area of 5,000 to 10,000 sq ft for a single project unless lifting can be accomplished at a time when equipment is available in the immediate area.

Other uses

Lift-slab equipment is adaptable to steel structures. It is frequently used for lifting steel roofs of existing structures to new elevations when expansion is required. The equipment is also used for lifting power-plant generators, bridges, and the super-structure of offshore oil-drilling barges.

TILT-UP CONSTRUCTION

Tilt-up construction is a special form of precast construction in which the elements, usually walls, are cast in a horizontal position on the site, tilted to the vertical position, set in place, and made an integral part of the completed structure. The principal advantages of this method are economy and reduced construction time.

The most common wall thickness is 6 in., nominal or actual, because this dimension generally meets structural requirements and permits average-size panels to be erected without extreme care. The use of the nominal dimension results in an appreciable saving because 2 by 6-in. dressed lumber can be used for the edge forms.

There are a great many different ways of designing, detailing, and erecting such structures. It will be advantageous for the designer to consult with contractors before the design and construction details are definitely established. The designer should at least consider the personnel and equipment available in the area. Even small changes in design or construction procedure may save much time and money as well as provide a better structure.

Most buildings constructed by the tilt-up method are one story in height, although some are as high as eight stories. The multistory buildings have generally been constructed by tilting the walls for one story, placing the floor above, and then repeating the process. In some instances, walls two stories in height have been cast and tilted as a unit. Various schemes using tilted platforms have been tried, but by far the most common method is to cast the wall panels on the concrete floor (using the floor as the bottom form) and then tilt them into position. In the past, improved hand equipment was used for tilting, but now most of the work is done with various types and capacities of power equipment, some of which can handle loads of up to 50 tons.

Design

Wall panels must be designed to withstand stresses both in the completed structure and during erection. The general design of the building will determine whether the walls are loadbearing or non-loadbearing with a continuous footing or supported on the column footings only. Once the walls are in position, the design requirements differ little if any from those

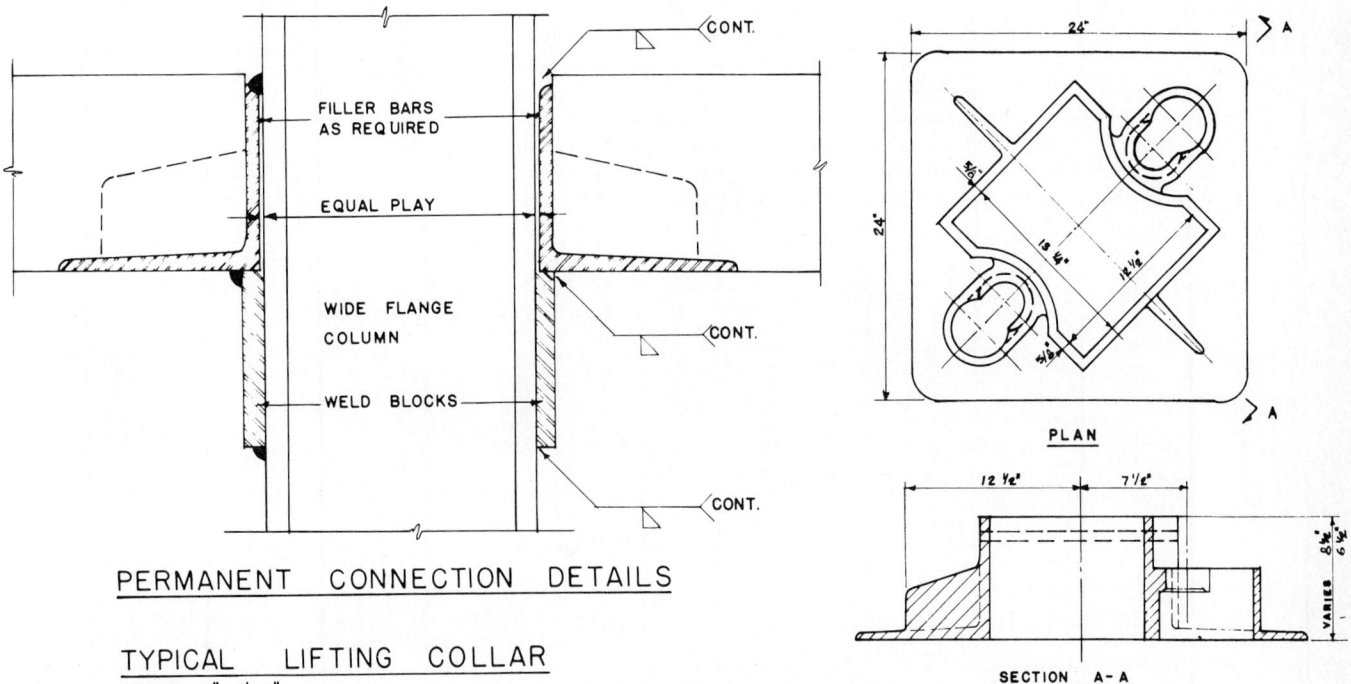

FILLER BARS AS REQUIRED

EQUAL PLAY

WIDE FLANGE COLUMN

WELD BLOCKS

CONT.

PERMANENT CONNECTION DETAILS

TYPICAL LIFTING COLLAR
SCALE 3" = 1'-0"

PLAN

SECTION A-A

Fig. 8. Connection details of lifting collars.

of conventionally built reinforced concrete walls; the only difference is in details.

Tilting a wall panel creates stresses not encountered in conventional, cast-in-place construction, and with some tilt-up arrangements an exact analysis may be complicated. The method of attaching the lifting equipment must be known in order to determine the stresses. If the attachment is to a stiff channel, or angle bolted to the top edge of the panel, then that panel will be designed as a simply supported slab. Openings present a special design problem. A general rule of thumb that is satisfactory for ordinary conditions, however, is to consider the weight of the panel as distributed over the total area including openings. The steel that would normally extend through the openings is concentrated at the sides of the openings, both horizontally and vertically. Strongbacks are advantageous where openings in the panel appreciably reduce its strength at critical sections.

Wall reinforcement is similar to that of conventional reinforced concrete walls except that special provision must be made for the stresses caused by lifting. The reinforcement may consist of bars or welded wire fabric or a combination of the two. Since lifting stresses occur only during tilting, higher unit stresses may be allowed for lifting than for other design purposes. As with reinforced concrete construction, a large number of small bars gives better crack control than the same weight of larger bars. The small bars cost slightly more per pound, however, and require a little more time to place.

Construction details

The concrete floor slab generally serves as the casting platform, although occasionally a stationary wooden platform or a tilting platform has been used. The ideal platform is a level, smoothly troweled concrete slab. Pipes or other utilities to be extended upward through the floor slab may be stopped below the floor surface and their openings temporarily closed. It should be remembered that any imperfections in the surface of the casting platform will show on the wall panel.

Many different wall finishes may be obtained economically when the wall is cast in the horizontal position. Some of these are the following: smooth float, swirled float, hand-troweled, brushed or broomed, patterned, colored, and ground. Regardless of the method employed, all panels and all parts of each panel should have a uniform finish.

Many variations of float finishes may be obtained in exactly the same manner as on floors and sidewalks. A fairly smooth float finish collects less dirt than a rough finish. Troweling provides a smooth surface but increases the possibility of surface crazing and magnifies inequalities in finishing. In harsh climates, the most severely exposed portions of the surface may gradually lose their smoothness and thus the entire surface will not retain a uniform appearance.

A pleasing finish may be produced by drawing a brush or broom over the trowel finish. This method tends to minimize any irregularities in the surface and removes laitance, which may cause surface crazing. Applying the brush marks in the vertical rather than the horizontal direction of the panel reduces the collection of dirt and increases the washing effect of rain on walls. Therefore, any horizontal brushing should be very light.

Color may be obtained by adding a colored concrete topping before the base concrete hardens. Panels may be painted, but it must be remembered that once painted they must be repainted periodically to retain a good appearance. A ground finish may be applied to wall panels while they are in the horizontal position. The same methods are used as in finishing terrazzo floors. Patterns may be made by cutting the surface with a center bead.

Wall joints

Various materials and methods have been used in forming the horizontal joint between the wall panel and its supporting member. The most common material is portland cement mortar, but premolded joint filler has also been used, either alone or in combination with mortar.

The simplest method of using mortar is to spread a layer of it on the foundation and tilt the wall onto the mortar bed. This method produces a strong, watertight joint. The main objection to the use of mortar is that it may squeeze out unevenly and permit little opportunity for adjusting the level of the wall. With some details of columns and roofs, however, a small variation is not important. A refinement of this method is to place carefully leveled pads or blocks on the foundation in order to hold the panel at the proper level until the mortar sets.

Normally rain will not penetrate very far into a vertical joint or crack even though it may be relatively wide. If, under severe conditions, rain does penetrate into the crack and runs down, no damage will be done if it drains outside the building at the bottom of the joint. Trouble may develop, however, if water accumulating at the bottom of the vertical joint drains into the building. To reduce this possibility, the top of the floor should be an inch or so above the horizontal joint. Experience has shown that with such an offset, panels can be tilted into place without difficulty (see Fig. 9).

Column joints

There are probably more variations in column details than in any other feature

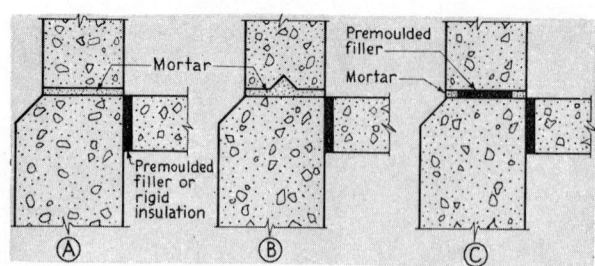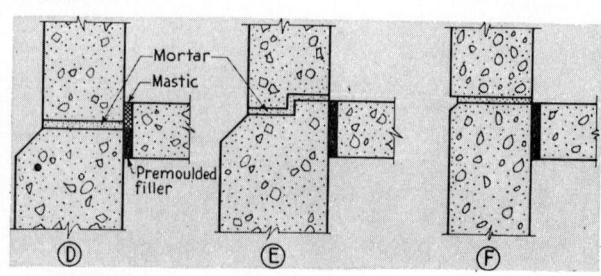

Fig. 9. Wall joints at foundation

From Tilt-up Construction, *Portland Cement Association. Shown above are typical joints subject to many variations. Sketches A and C show the simplest and most commonly used wall joints. The offset from the floor level in sketch D and the offset in the wall in sketch E reduce the possibility of leakage.*

However, if the foundation or lower wall is sloped or offset slightly (as shown in the sketches) so that there is no horizontal surface to catch the water, there is little possibility of leakage. Certainly the possibility of leakage at this point is no greater than with any unit masonry wall.

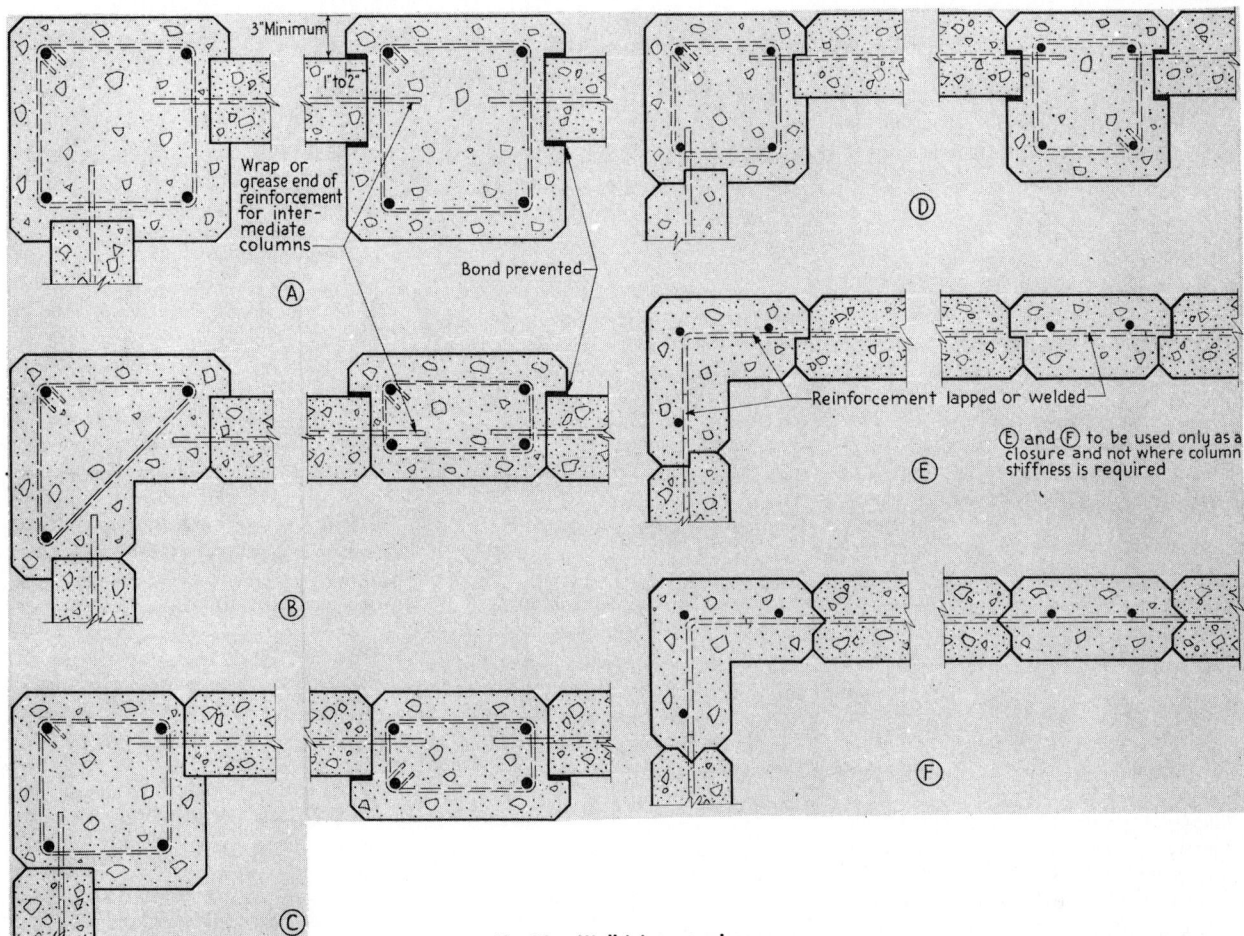

3"Minimum

1"to2"

Wrap or grease end of reinforcement for intermediate columns

Bond prevented

Ⓐ

Ⓑ

Ⓒ

Ⓓ

Reinforcement lapped or welded

Ⓔ and Ⓕ to be used only as a closure and not where column stiffness is required

Ⓔ

Ⓕ

Fig. 10. Wall joints at column

From Tilt-up Construction, *Portland Cement Association. Sketches A to D show typical joints for use where movement at the joints is desired. They can also be used for rigid joints by lapping the reinforcement and omitting the bond-prevention material.*

Even where movement is desired at intermediate columns, the corner columns are bonded to the wall panels. V-joints should be used wherever the face of the wall is flush with the column.

of tilt-up construction. Columns may be placed either after or before the panels are tilted. Both methods have advantages. On most jobs, however, the columns are cast after the panels are in place. This method permits the use of simple and economical details, particularly where the column overlaps the wall panel on both faces. Casting the column first has the advantage of greatly simplifying the temporary bracing of panels.

For large buildings in parts of the country where it is not necessary to design for earthquake forces, nearly all column connections are designed to allow relative movement between adjacent wall panels. Thus the panels can expand and contract, owing to moisture and temperature changes, without developing stresses that would tend to crack the walls. A survey of buildings constructed by the tilt-up method has shown that there is movement in the majority of

joints between panels and columns and that cracks in the panels are extremely rare.

If the columns are cast after the walls are in place, they may overlap the panels on one or both sides. This overlap hides any irregularities in the panel edges and variations in the planes of adjacent panels. Even though the space between the panels may vary because of inaccuracies in panel dimensions or setting, the overlap permits uniform column widths and repeated use of the column form without adjustments. The possibility of leakage is also reduced by overlap.

It is sometimes desirable to have the column flush with the panels on one or both sides of the wall. In such cases, a V-joint or other definite rustication should be used between the wall panel and the column. This rustication will (1) hide and protect the crack that will form at this point, (2) permit caulking if necessary, (3) provide a

straight, true joint, (4) prevent smearing of panels with leakage from concrete cast in the column, and (5) break the wall surface so that variations in the planes of adjacent panels will be inconspicuous (see Fig. 10).

Insulation

As in other types of construction, the heat-insulation value of tilt-up walls may be increased by the use of furring, blanket insulation, or rigid insulation and plaster in the usual manner after the wall has been erected. The heat-insulation value may also be increased by using lightweight concrete and, of course, by increasing the thickness. Other methods are to cast the panel on rigid insulating board that bonds to the panel, to use lightweight-aggregate concrete for the interior face of the panel, or to construct the wall as a sandwich panel.

Part of the wall thickness (on the inside

face) may be made of concrete having a high insulating value, such as that made with aggregates of very light weight. The thickness of the insulating concrete will depend on the insulation desired. From 1 to 6 in. has been used in panels with a total thickness of 6 to 8 in., although about 2 in. of insulating concrete will usually provide sufficient insulation.

Sandwich-type panels are made by placing a layer of concrete, a layer of insulation, and then a layer of concrete, the last two layers being placed before the first one has hardened. Reinforcement is placed in both layers of concrete and the two layers are fastened together by ties. The insulating material should bond to, but not be adversely affected by, the fresh concrete.

PRESTRESSED CONCRETE CONSTRUCTION
(Revised 1972 by Precast Concrete Institute)

The main purpose of prestressing is to induce desirable strains and stresses in a structure and its components. Since the tensile strength of concrete is negligible compared to its compressive strength, prestressing is necessary to counteract any significant tensile stress. Prestressing is normally accomplished by stretching high-tensile steel and then transferring the stress to the concrete by either bond or end anchorages. In a fully prestressed concrete member the entire section is in compression and therefore, is fully utilized. In contrast, a reinforced concrete member subjected to flexure utilizes less than half its concrete. This constitutes the basic difference between the two materials or systems of construction. They also differ in the use of steel. In a reinforced concrete member the steel acts with the concrete and is consequently limited by the cracking of the concrete. In a prestressed concrete member, however, the steel acts upon the concrete. A prestressed concrete member can thus be considered as a plain concrete member subjected to two types of forces: an internal prestressing force and external loads.

Design principles

If the magnitude and location of the prestressing are controlled, compressive stresses are introduced which will counteract the anticipated tensile stresses due to external loads. The effects of these two forces are considered separately in Figs. 11a and 12a and superimposed in Fig. 13a to show the final condition. Figure 11a indicates a simple rectangular beam subjected to a prestressing force, F, applied with an eccentricity, e. This condition represents the first or stressing stage. Because of the eccentric application of the prestressing force, the beam is subjected to a moment, Fe, as well as to a direct load. The stress pattern produced by the prestressing force is shown in Fig. 11d and is equal to the algebraic sum of the uniform axial stresses, F/A, and the flexural stresses due to the eccentricity, Fey/I, as shown in Fig. 11b and c. At the stressing stage, the prestressing steel and the concrete are subjected to the proof load, or worst loading condition that the member will experience. The controlling factors in the concrete (Fig. 11d) are the maximum allowable compressive stress in the bottom fiber and little or no tensile stress in the extreme top fiber. At this stage, the beam has an upward deflection or camber. In the absence of the expected superimposed loads, the camber may remain and its effects should be considered.

Shown in Fig. 12a is the beam subjected to external loads, with the corresponding stress pattern indicated in Fig. 12b. The anticipated tensile stresses that are counteracted by the prestress are shown dotted. Both the prestressing force and the external loads are shown in Fig. 13a in what is the second or working-load stage. The stress pattern at this final stage is shown in Fig. 13b and is equal to the algebraic sum of the stresses produced by the prestressing force and superimposed loads. The controlling factors in the concrete are now the allowable compressive stress in the top fiber and little or no tension in the bottom fiber. This is the opposite of the condition of the first

stage. Since tension is a controlling factor in both stages, some design procedures permit limited tension in the concrete provided that the total tensile force is small and that concrete cracking is prevented. Nonprestressed reinforcement is often added to control cracking in such cases.

The principles outlined in the above example have a wide range of applications and modifications. Slabs, shells, composite construction, and continuous beams can all benefit from prestressing. Curved or draped prestressing steel is more effective than straight steel and is usually used unless practical considerations dictate against it. Flanged shapes such as the symmetrical and unsymmetrical I- and T-sections are the most efficient and commonly used sections for prestressed concrete. Finally, it should be emphasized that the success with which prestressing counteracts stresses resulting from external loads makes it an extremely versatile structural technique.

Materials and stresses

Although many materials can be used to supply prestress, high-tensile steel is used almost universally in prestressed concrete. Prestressing steel comes in the form of wires, strands, or bars. The type of prestressing steel selected will depend on the method of prestressing, the type of anchorage, and the magnitude of the force to be applied. Specific characteristics of the steel vary with the manufacturing processes. The normal range of ultimate strength is 200,000 to 330,000 psi for wires, 240,000 to 270,000 psi for strands, and 145,000 to 160,000 psi for bars. Under service load conditions, allowable stresses in the steel at effective prestress should be the lesser value of 80 per cent of the yield strength or 60 per cent of the ultimate strength.

To fully exploit prestressing, high-strength concrete is required. If early hardening of the concrete is desirable, as in a precasting factory, high-early-strength cement is employed. Special curing procedures, such as steam curing, are extremely important in attaining high strength at an accelerated rate. The quality of concrete usually ranges from 5,000 to 8,000 psi ultimate strength at 28 days. The allowable flexural compressive stress at the service-load stage is usually 45 per cent of the ultimate compressive strength.

Prestressing methods

The two basic methods of prestressing concrete are pretensioning and posttensioning. As their names imply, the difference between them depends on whether the concrete has hardened before or after the steel is stressed. In the pretensioning method, steel is stressed in an empty form and

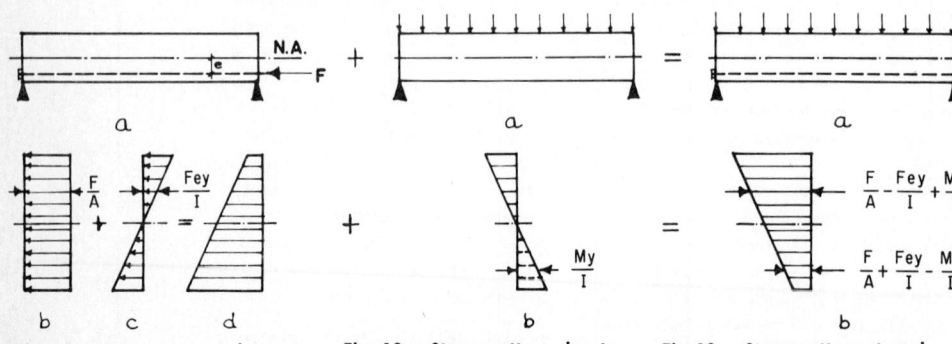

Fig. 11. Stress pattern due to prestressing

Fig. 12. Stress pattern due to superimposed loads

Fig. 13. Stress pattern at working loads

anchored to bulkheads. Concrete is then poured into the forms and the concrete becomes firmly bonded to the elongated steel. After the concrete has attained the required strength, the steel is released from the anchorages and, as the steel tends to shorten, it induces compression in the beam by transferring the prestressing force through bond to the concrete.

In the posttensioned method, the steel is stressed after the concrete has attained its design strength. To achieve this result, bond between the steel and the concrete must be prevented by lubrication of the steel or by insertion of the steel through flexible or rigid conduits which have been formed in the concrete. After the steel has been placed, it is stressed against the ends of the member. Final transfer of prestress from steel to concrete can be subsequently achieved either by bonded or unbonded tendons. In the bonded installation, prestress transfer is realized through mechanical anchorage and the bond development by grout placed in the conduits after stressing operations. Unbonded tendons transmit the prestress force through mechanical end anchorages.

An essential consideration of prestressed concrete design is the prestress loss which does occur due to concrete creep, shrinkage, and steel relaxation. Such loss is time-dependent and varies in magnitude in relation to the factors of concrete type, compressive strength, concrete stress, curing methods, temperature, and steel tensile strength. Generally, the loss will vary between 15 and 25 per cent of the initial prestress force.

The pretensioning method is particularly suitable for mass production of members. Casting beds 200 to 500 ft long permit one pouring operation and the cutting of individual members to the desired length. Additionally, this method eliminates expensive anchorage accessories and conduits. If the prestressing plant location or the size of the elements requires excessive transportation costs, the posttensioning method is recommended. Posttensioning is also recommended where cast-in-place concrete installations, continuous construction methods, or draped tendon configurations are employed.

Comparison with reinforced concrete

1. In prestressed concrete, the concrete compressive strength is often somewhat greater and the steel tensile strengths are four to five times greater than that employed for reinforced concrete.

2. By prestressing the concrete, the entire section is effective; whereas in reinforced concrete only the compressive portion on one side of the neutral axis is utilized.

3. Diagonal tension, which governs the shear capacity, is reduced in prestressed concrete due to the utilization of the increased compressive section area.

4. The higher quality and increased performance efficiency of materials used in prestressed concrete permit reduced sections, longer spans, and increased load capacities. The average member depth of a prestressed concrete section is approximately 20 per cent less than the corresponding depth of a reinforced concrete section.

5. In prestressed concrete, stresses developed in the first, or prestressing, stage are often at their design maximum; hence the member is actually pretested for working loads.

6. Both types of construction have economic advantages. The use of fewer materials, even at a higher unit cost, favors prestressed concrete; however, additional accessories and more expensive labor are frequently required. Formwork is much more complicated and expensive in prestressed concrete than in reinforced concrete. Indeed, the extent to which formwork can be reused will frequently determine the economic feasibility of prestressed concrete design and construction.

Continuity

The theoretical reasons why continuity is economical in reinforced concrete also apply to prestressed concrete. In addition, continuity in prestressed concrete has two specific advantages: first, expensive end anchorages over intermediate supports are eliminated; second, the same prestressing tendon can be used for both positive and negative moments by draping the tendon in accordance with the design requirements. Peaks of maximum negative moment, which are characteristic of continuity, are usually designed by varying the concrete section and the amount of prestressing steel (see Fig. 14).

Continuous prestressed beams can be either fully or partially continuous. For full continuity, all the tendons are prestressed in place and are generally continuous from one end to the other. Tendons may be encased in concrete during pouring, threaded through preformed conduits, or placed outside the web. Either bonded or unbonded tendons may be used. For partial continuity, each span is first precast as a simple beam and prestressed for member dead load and erection loads. After the simple elements have been erected in place, additional elements, sometimes nonprestressed, are inserted to provide continuity over the supports (see Fig. 15).

Continuity in prestressed concrete, however, has certain inherent disadvantages. Secondary stresses due to prestressing, creep and shrinkage, temperature change,

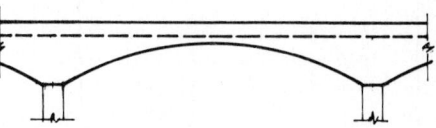

a. STRAIGHT TENDONS IN CURVED BEAMS

b. CURVED TENDONS IN HAUNCHED OR CURVED BEAMS

Fig. 14. Fully continuous beams

and settlement of supports must be controlled. The frictional loss in continuous tendons, particularly where many reversed curves exist, must be evaluated.

The possibility of a reversal of moments due to heavy live loads may prevent the economical design of a continuous prestressed concrete beam. The shortening of long continuous beams under prestress may produce excessive lateral forces and moments in the columns if they are rigidly connected to the beams.

Although prestressing has a wide variety of applications, it is most efficient when used in the manufacture of prefabricated elements. The development of standard sections similar to those used in the steel industry is most significant to the manufacturing process. The tables on the following pages provide a reasonable basis for standardization and should prove useful in preliminary study and design. They have been reprinted, with permission, from the *PCI Design Handbook*, published by the Prestressed Concrete Institute, 1971.

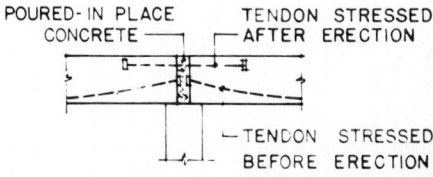

a. SHORT TENDONS STRESSED OVER SUPPORTS

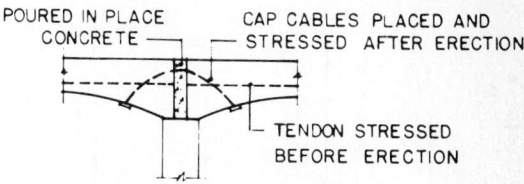

b. CAP CABLES OVER SUPPORTS

Fig. 15. Partially continuous beams

Data from PCI Design Handbook, published by Precast Concrete Institute

The load tables on the following pages give the dimensions, properties, and engineering capabilities of the shapes most commonly used throughout the industry. Designers should contact the manufacturers in the geographic area of the proposed structure to determine the availability of sections and their exact dimensions. Manufacturers often have their own load tables for sections which are not included here. The tables are based on 5,000 psi concrete; many manufacturers use higher-strength concrete, with corresponding increase in the capabilities of the sections. Topping is assumed to be 3,000 psi concrete. Prestressing strands are $7/16$- or $1/2$-in.-diameter steel having an ultimate strength of 270,000 psi. Tables show the maximum allowable loads with the usual maximum number of strands.

Typical span-to-depth ratios of flexural precast prestressed members are:

Hollow-core floor slabs	30—40
Hollow-core roof slabs	40—50
Stemmed floor slabs	25—35
Stemmed roof slabs	35—40
Beams	10—20

The required depth of a beam or slab is influenced by the ratio of live load to total load. Where this ratio is high, deeper sections may be needed.

Combinations of precast prestressed units with cast-in-place posttensioned concrete are often used. For example, single tees are sometimes spaced apart and covered by a posttensioned slab which spans between them.

On this page are shown typical connection details of precast prestressed members. These are also from the *PCI Design Handbook*.

Bearing pads are sometimes used at connections to provide uniform bearing; some types also relieve stresses caused by thermal expansion or other type of movement, either by deformation within an elastomeric pad or slippage on TFE low-friction pads.

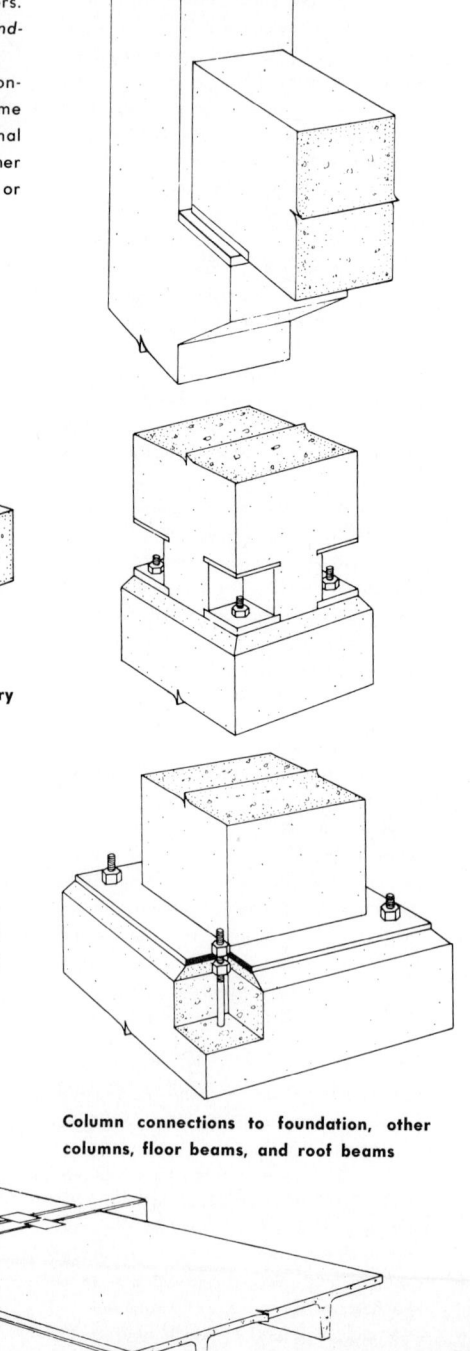

Continuous ledger beam with one-story columns

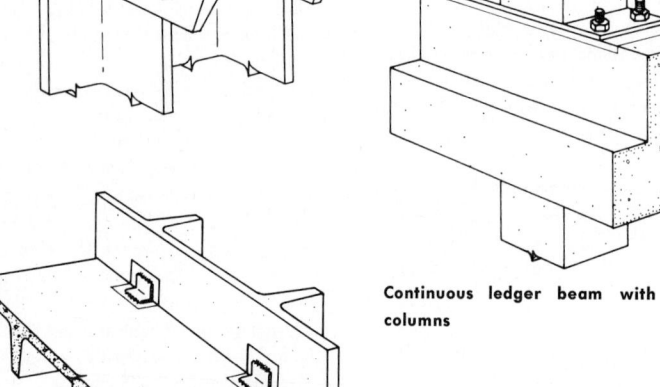

Interior bearing wall

Column connections to foundation, other columns, floor beams, and roof beams

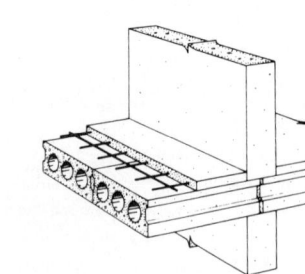

Double tees used as bearing walls

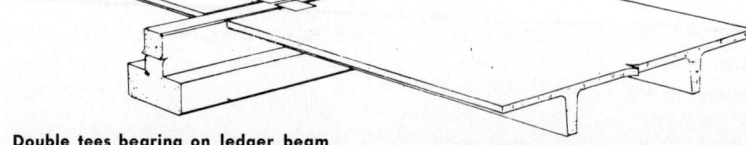

Double tees bearing on ledger beam

Fig. 16. Typical connection details

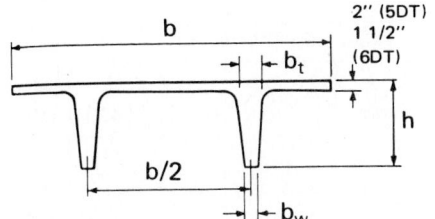

5' - 0" Wide
6' - 0" Wide
Normal Weight Concrete

Section Properties						
Designation	b (in.)	h (in.)	b_t/b_w (in.)	A (in.²)	I (in.⁴)	wt (plf)
5DT18	5'-0"	18	5.92/3.25	268	7546	278
6DT12	6'-0"	12	5.25/3.50	200	2438	208
6DT16	6'-0"	16	5.88/3.50	244	5636	254
6DT20	6'-0"	20	6.50/3.50	293	10,754	305

Table of Safe Superimposed Loads, Cambers and Deflections — No Topping

Designation	No. Strand	Span, ft.													
		50	51	52	53	54	55	56	57	58	59	60	61	62	63
5DT18	8	79*	74*	69*	65*	61	57	53	49	45	42	39	36	33	30
		1.59	1.56	1.53	1.48	1.42	1.33	1.22	1.09	0.95	0.80	0.62	0.44	0.23	0.01
		1.72	1.75	1.77	1.80	1.81	1.82	1.82	1.81	1.80	1.78	1.76	1.73	1.70	1.66

Designation	No. Strand	Span, ft.																
		38	40	42	44	46	48	50	52	54	56	58	60	62	64	66	68	70	72
6DT12	6	55*	46*	39*															
		1.44	1.40	1.30															
		1.48	1.55	1.60															
6DT16	6			67*	58*	50*	43*	37*	32*	27*									
				1.32	1.26	1.16	1.02	0.83	0.58	0.28									
				1.18	1.23	1.27	1.30	1.32	1.32	1.30									
6DT20	10										72	64	56	49	43	38	32		
											1.74	1.66	1.54	1.36	1.09	0.76	0.36		
											2.09	2.13	2.15	2.16	2.15	2.11	2.06		

Key:
72 — Safe superimposed load, psf
1.74 — Anticipated initial camber, in.
2.09 — Deflection due to superimposed load shown, in.

Section Properties					
Designation	b (in.)	h (in.)	b_t/b_w (in.)	I (in.⁴)	wt (plf)
5DT18+2	5'-0"	18	5.92/3.25	10,507	403
6DT12+2½	6'-0"	12	5.25/3.50	4244	396
6DT16+2½	6'-0"	16	5.88/3.50	9032	442
6DT20+2½	6'-0"	20	6.50/3.50	16,472	493

Table of Safe Superimposed Loads, Cambers and Deflections — 2" Normal Weight Topping

Designation	No. Strand	Span, ft.												
		46	47	48	49	50	51	52	53	54	55	56	57	58
5DT18+2	8	95*	89*	82	75	68	61	55	49	44	39	34	29	25
		1.61	1.62	1.62	1.61	1.59	1.56	1.53	1.48	1.42	1.33	1.22	1.09	0.95
		1.46	1.51	1.56	1.59	1.61	1.63	1.65	1.67	1.69	1.70	1.70	1.70	1.70

Designation	No. Strand	Span, ft.																
		22	24	26	28	30	32	34	36	38	40	42	44	46	48	50	52	54	56
6DT12+2½	4	171*	134*	106*	83*	65*	46	29											
		0.68	0.78	0.86	0.90	0.92	0.90	0.84											
		0.39	0.46	0.54	0.63	0.72	0.77	0.82											
6DT16+2½	6					175*	146*	122*	103*	86*	72*	56	42	30					
						1.00	1.09	1.17	1.25	1.31	1.35	1.32	1.26	1.16					
						0.64	0.72	0.81	0.90	0.99	1.09	1.16	1.21	1.26					
6DT20+2½	8										147*	127*	110*	95*	81*	67	54	42	32
											1.31	1.39	1.45	1.49	1.51	1.50	1.43	1.32	1.18
											0.96	1.04	1.13	1.22	1.32	1.38	1.43	1.47	1.51

*Capacity governed by ultimate strength
f'_c = 5000 psi f_{pu} = 270,000 psi

Values below heavy line require release strength higher than 3500 psi

Prestressed, double tees

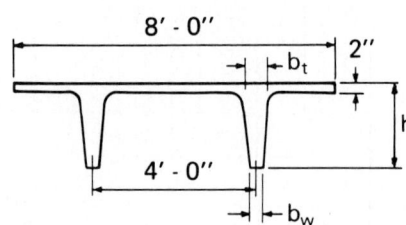

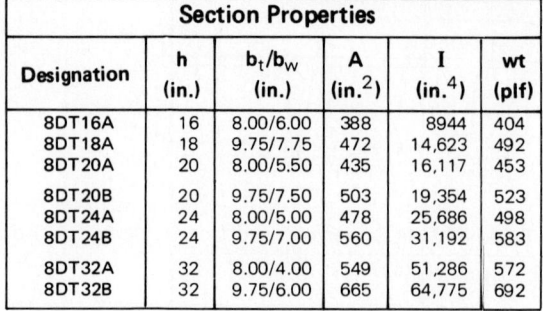

8' - 0" Wide
Wide Stem Members
Normal Weight Concrete

Section Properties					
Designation	h (in.)	b_t/b_w (in.)	A (in.²)	I (in.⁴)	wt (plf)
8DT16A	16	8.00/6.00	388	8944	404
8DT18A	18	9.75/7.75	472	14,623	492
8DT20A	20	8.00/5.50	435	16,117	453
8DT20B	20	9.75/7.50	503	19,354	523
8DT24A	24	8.00/5.00	478	25,686	498
8DT24B	24	9.75/7.00	560	31,192	583
8DT32A	32	8.00/4.00	549	51,286	572
8DT32B	32	9.75/6.00	665	64,775	692

Key

48 — Safe superimposed load, psf
0.60 — Anticipated initial camber, in.
2.05 — Deflection due to superimposed load shown, in.

Table of Safe Superimposed Loads, Cambers and Deflections

No Topping

Desig- nation	No. Strand	Span, ft.											
		48	50	52	54	56	58	60	62	64	66	68	70	72
8DT16A	12	70* 1.63 1.76	61* 1.56 1.81	53* 1.43 1.85	46* 1.20 1.87	40 0.90 1.86	34 0.53 1.82	28 0.09 1.74						
8DT18A	16			91* 1.63 1.93	81* 1.56 1.99	72* 1.43 2.04	63* 1.21 2.08	55 0.93 2.07	48 0.60 2.05	41 0.21 2.00				
8DT20A	16							64 1.82 2.49	57 1.66 2.50	50 1.45 2.49	44 1.16 2.46	38 0.77 2.41	33 0.30 2.33	
8DT20B	20							90 1.78 2.54	80 1.66 2.58	71 1.48 2.60	63 1.26 2.61	55 0.96 2.59	49 0.56 2.55	42 0.10 2.49

Desig- nation	No. Strand	Span, ft.																
		62	64	66	68	70	72	74	76	78	80	82	84	86	88	90	92	94	96
8DT24A	20	90 1.87 2.18	81 1.81 2.22	72 1.72 2.25	64 1.58 2.26	57 1.40 2.26	50 1.14 2.24	44 0.82 2.20	39 0.44 2.15	34 0.01 2.07									
8DT24B	24						82 1.72 2.98	74 1.52 2.99	66 1.26 2.98	59 0.95 2.96	52 0.56 2.91	46 0.08 2.85							
8DT32A	22												68 1.66 2.80	62 1.47 2.79	56 1.22 2.76	50 0.93 2.72	45 0.57 2.66	40 0.14 2.59	
8DT32B	28													95 1.86 3.08	87 1.69 3.09	79 1.47 3.09	72 1.21 3.07	65 0.90 3.03	58 0.53 2.98	52 0.08 2.91

*Capacity governed by ultimate strength   Values below heavy line require release strengths higher than 3500 psi
f'_c = 5000 psi f_{pu} = 270,000 psi

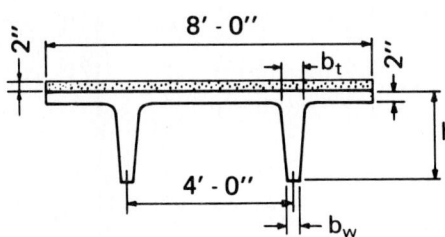

8' - 0" Wide
Wide Stem Members
Normal Weight Concrete

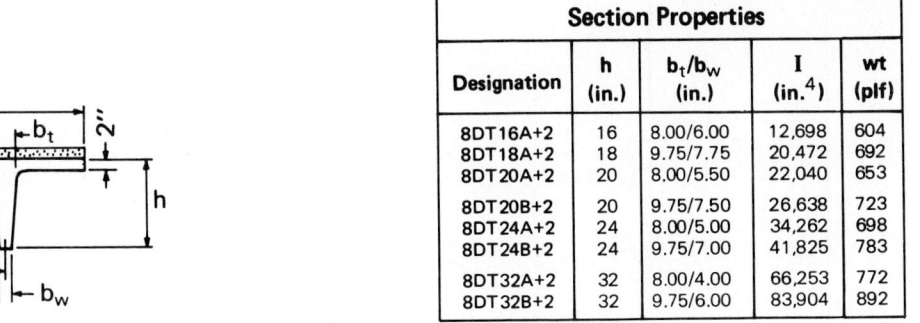

Section Properties				
Designation	h (in.)	b_t/b_w (in.)	I (in.^{4})	wt (plf)
8DT16A+2	16	8.00/6.00	12,698	604
8DT18A+2	18	9.75/7.75	20,472	692
8DT20A+2	20	8.00/5.50	22,040	653
8DT20B+2	20	9.75/7.50	26,638	723
8DT24A+2	24	8.00/5.00	34,262	698
8DT24B+2	24	9.75/7.00	41,825	783
8DT32A+2	32	8.00/4.00	66,253	772
8DT32B+2	32	9.75/6.00	83,904	892

Key

65 — Safe superimposed load, psf
1.34 — Anticipated initial camber, in.
1.78 — Deflection due to superimposed load shown, in.

Table of Safe Superimposed Loads, Cambers and Deflections   **2" Normal Weight Topping**

Designation	No. Strand	Span, ft.																	
		30	32	34	36	38	40	42	44	46	48	50	52	54	56	58	60	62	64
8DT 16A+2	8	170*	142*	119*	99*	83*	68*	56*	46*	34									
		0.92	0.99	1.03	1.05	1.05	1.02	0.96	0.87	0.73									
		0.55	0.62	0.68	0.75	0.82	0.88	0.95	1.01	1.04									
8DT 18A+2	12				190*	163*	140*	121*	104*	89*	76*	64*	53	42	31				
					1.17	1.24	1.28	1.29	1.28	1.24	1.17	1.06	0.91	0.72	0.49				
					0.78	0.85	0.92	1.00	1.07	1.14	1.21	1.28	1.33	1.34	1.35				
8DT 20A+2	12						145*	126*	110*	95*	83*	71*	60	49	39	30			
							1.44	1.51	1.56	1.59	1.60	1.59	1.51	1.38	1.21	0.99			
							1.07	1.15	1.23	1.32	1.40	1.48	1.54	1.57	1.59	1.60			
8DT 20B+2	16									150*	132*	115*	101*	88*	77*	65	53	43	33
										1.56	1.60	1.62	1.61	1.58	1.49	1.34	1.15	0.91	0.62
										1.31	1.39	1.48	1.57	1.65	1.73	1.78	1.80	1.81	1.81

Designation	No. Strand	Span, ft.																	
		50	52	54	56	58	60	62	64	66	68	70	72	74	76	78	80	82	84
8DT 24A+2	12	113*	99*	87*	75*	65*	56	46	37	28									
		1.50	1.52	1.50	1.44	1.36	1.25	1.11	0.93	0.71									
		1.13	1.19	1.26	1.32	1.38	1.43	1.45	1.45	1.45									
8DT 24B+2	16	172*	154*	138*	123*	110*	99*	88*	79*	70*	62*	55*	48*	40	33	26			
		2.67	2.79	2.90	2.99	3.07	3.12	3.14	3.07	2.97	2.82	2.62	2.38	2.08	1.73	1.32			
		1.79	1.91	2.04	2.16	2.29	2.41	2.54	2.66	2.78	2.90	3.02	3.14	3.17	3.19	3.20			
8DT 32A+2	16						137*	124*	109	96	84	73	63	53	45	37			
							1.54	1.56	1.56	1.54	1.50	1.44	1.33	1.18	1.01	0.80			
							1.40	1.47	1.51	1.55	1.58	1.61	1.62	1.64	1.64	1.63			
8DT 32B+2	20						183*	165*	150*	135*	122*	110*	99*	88	77	66	57	48	39
							1.69	1.72	1.73	1.73	1.71	1.65	1.55	1.42	1.27	1.08	0.87	0.62	0.33
							1.40	1.47	1.53	1.59	1.66	1.71	1.77	1.82	1.83	1.84	1.83	1.82	1.80

*Capacity governed by ultimate strength   Values below heavy line require release strengths higher than 3500 psi

$f'_c = 5000$ psi $f_{pu} = 270,000$ psi

Prestressed, double tees

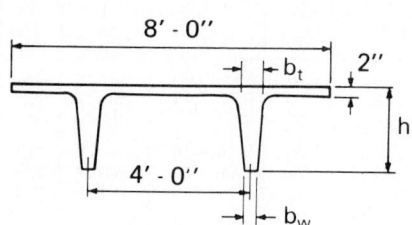

8' - 0'' Wide
Wide Stem Members
Lightweight Concrete

Section Properties

Designation	h (in.)	b_t/b_w (in.)	A (in.^{2})	I (in.^{4})	wt (plf)
8LDT16A	16	8.00/6.00	388	8944	310
8LDT18A	18	9.75/7.75	472	14,623	377
8LDT20A	20	8.00/5.50	435	16,117	347
8LDT20B	20	9.75/7.50	503	19,354	401
8LDT24A	24	8.00/5.00	478	25,686	382
8LDT24B	24	9.75/7.00	560	31,192	447
8LDT32A	32	8.00/4.00	549	51,286	439
8LDT32B	32	9.75/6.00	665	64,775	531

Key

36 — Safe superimposed load, psf
1.71 — Anticipated initial camber in.
4.06 — Deflection due to superimposed load shown, in.

Table of Safe Superimposed Loads, Cambers and Deflections

No Topping

Designation	No. Strand	52	54	56	58	60	62	64	66	68	70	72	74	76	78	80
8LDT16A	12	63 2.94 3.24	55 2.88 3.33	49 2.75 3.39	43 2.56 3.43	37 2.26 3.44	33 1.81 3.42	28 1.26 3.37								
8LDT18A	16		93 2.98 3.39	83 2.97 3.51	74 2.91 3.61	66 2.79 3.69	59 2.62 3.75	52 2.35 3.79	46 1.95 3.80	41 1.47 3.78	36 0.91 3.74	31 0.25 3.66				
8LDT20A	16										48 3.16 4.55	43 2.88 4.56	39 2.53 4.55	34 2.07 4.51	30 1.51 4.43	27 0.79 4.32
8LDT20B	16	114* 2.80 2.38	101* 2.85 2.54	89* 2.88 2.69	79* 2.86 2.85	70* 2.81 3.01	60 2.71 3.10	50 2.54 3.18	41 2.26 3.24	33 1.92 3.28	26 1.51 3.31					

Designation	No. Strand	72	74	76	78	80	82	84	86	88	90	92	94	96	98	100	102	104	106
8LDT24A	16	61 3.19 4.06	56 3.03 4.10	50 2.81 4.12	45 2.53 4.12	41 2.18 4.10	36 1.71 4.06	32 1.14 3.98	29 0.50 3.88										
8LDT24B	24						60 2.83 5.44	54 2.46 5.45	49 2.02 5.43	44 1.48 5.38	40 0.84 5.31	36 0.08 5.20							
8LDT32A	20						61 3.05 4.48	56 2.84 4.50	51 2.57 4.49	46 2.24 4.47	42 1.85 4.43	38 1.38 4.37	35 0.81 4.28	31 0.17 4.17					
8LDT32B	28											68 3.02 5.63	63 2.70 5.63	58 2.31 5.61	53 1.85 5.57	48 1.31 5.50	44 0.68 5.42		

*Capacity governed by ultimate strength   Values below heavy line required release strengths higher than 3500 psi
$f_c' = 5000$ psi $f_{pu} = 270,000$ psi

8' - 0" Wide
Wide Stem Sections
Lightweight Concrete

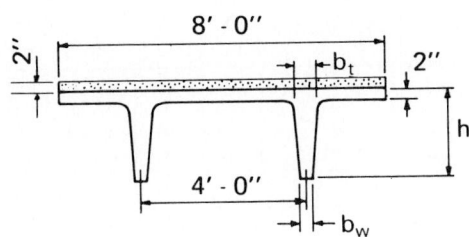

Section Properties				
Designation	h (in.)	b_t/b_w (in.)	I (in.⁴)	wt (plf)
8LDT16A+2	16	8.00/6.00	13,877	510
8LDT18A+2	18	9.75/7.75	22,426	577
8LDT20A+2	20	8.00/5.50	23,970	547
8LDT20B+2	20	9.75/7.50	29,121	601
8LDT24A+2	24	8.00/5.00	37,139	582
8LDT24B+2	24	9.75/7.00	45,562	647
8LDT32A+2	32	8.00/4.00	71,483	639
8LDT32B+2	32	9.75/6.00	90,935	731

Key

38 — Safe superimposed load, psf
1.67 — Anticipated initial camber, in.
2.05 — Deflection due to superimposed load shown, in.

Table of Safe Superimposed Loads, Cambers and Deflections **2" Normal Weight Topping**

Designation	No. Strand	Span, ft.																	
		30	32	34	36	38	40	42	44	46	48	50	52	54	56	58	60	62	64
8LDT 16A+2	8	180*	152*	128*	109*	92*	78*	66*	55*	46*	37	27							
		1.40	1.54	1.67	1.78	1.85	1.89	1.89	1.86	1.79	1.66	1.49							
		0.80	0.90	1.01	1.12	1.24	1.35	1.48	1.60	1.72	1.82	1.88							
8LDT 18A+2	12						152*	133*	115*	101*	87*	76*	66*	57*	47	38	29		
							2.05	2.18	2.27	2.32	2.32	2.28	2.20	2.08	1.90	1.67	1.38		
							1.36	1.49	1.61	1.74	1.87	2.00	2.13	2.26	2.36	2.41	2.45		
8LDT 20A+2	12										106*	93*	82*	72*	63*	53	44	36	28
											2.62	2.71	2.79	2.83	2.84	2.82	2.75	2.56	2.31
											1.99	2.14	2.29	2.43	2.58	2.68	2.76	2.83	2.88
8LDT 20B+2	16												114*	101*	89*	79*	70*	60	50
													2.80	2.85	2.88	2.86	2.81	2.71	2.54
													2.38	2.54	2.69	2.85	3.01	3.10	3.18

Designation	No. Strand	Span, ft.																	
		56	58	60	62	64	66	68	70	72	74	76	78	80	82	84	86	88	90
8LDT 24A+2	12	86*	77*	68*	59*	51	43	35	28										
		2.56	2.59	2.58	2.50	2.37	2.21	2.00	1.75										
		2.04	2.16	2.27	2.39	2.48	2.54	2.58	2.61										
8LDT 24B+2	16	123*	110*	99*	88*	79*	70*	61	52	44	36								
		2.78	2.84	2.87	2.87	2.78	2.66	2.49	2.27	2.01	1.70								
		2.16	2.29	2.41	2.54	2.66	2.78	2.88	2.94	2.98	3.00								
8LDT 32A+2	16							103*	94*	85*	76	67	58	51	44	37	31		
								2.99	3.02	3.03	3.01	2.97	2.90	2.79	2.61	2.37	2.08		
								2.59	2.71	2.82	2.92	2.98	3.04	3.09	3.13	3.15	3.17		
8LDT 32B+2	20							139*	126*	115*	105*	96*	87*	78	69	60	52	45	38
								3.03	3.07	3.08	3.07	3.03	2.97	2.84	2.65	2.42	2.15	1.84	1.48
								2.56	2.68	2.79	2.90	3.02	3.12	3.20	3.25	3.28	3.31	3.33	3.33

*Capacity governed by ultimate strength   Values below heavy line require release strengths higher than 3500 psi
f'_c = 5000 psi f_{pu} = 270,000 psi

Prestressed, single tees

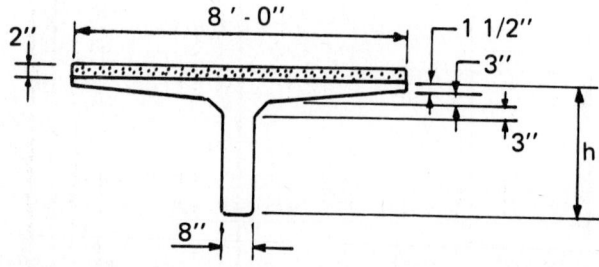

8' - 0" Wide
Normal Weight Concrete

Section Properties

Designation	h (in.)	A (in.²)	I (in.⁴)	wt (plf)
8ST 24	24	474	21,540	494
8ST 28	28	506	33,649	527
8ST 32	32	538	49,329	560
8ST 36	36	570	68,917	594

No Topping

Table of Safe Superimposed Loads, Cambers and Deflections

Designation	No. Strand	Span, ft.									
		64	66	68	70	72	74	76	78	80	82
8ST24	14	60 / 1.69 / 1.98	53 / 1.55 / 1.96	46 / 1.37 / 1.94	40 / 1.12 / 1.89	34 / 0.79 / 1.82	29 / 0.37 / 1.73				
8ST28	16					64 / 1.69 / 2.16	57 / 1.55 / 2.15	51 / 1.36 / 2.12	45 / 1.13 / 2.08	39 / 0.82 / 2.03	34 / 0.44 / 1.95

Designation	No. Strand	Span, ft.											
		80	82	84	86	88	90	92	94	96	98	100	102
8ST32	18	67 / 1.76 / 2.35	60 / 1.61 / 2.34	54 / 1.43 / 2.32	48 / 1.19 / 2.28	43 / 0.91 / 2.22	38 / 0.54 / 2.15	33 / 0.12 / 2.07					
8ST36	22								58 / 1.50 / 2.80	53 / 1.26 / 2.77	48 / 0.97 / 2.71	43 / 0.63 / 2.65	38 / 0.23 / 2.56

Key
39 — Safe superimposed load, psf
0.82 — Anticipated initial camber, in.
2.03 — Deflection due to superimposed load shown, in.

Section Properties

Designation	h (in.)	I (in.⁴)	wt (plf)
8ST 24+2	24	27,042	694
8ST 28+2	28	41,446	727
8ST 32+2	32	60,027	760
8ST 36+2	36	83,212	794

2" Normal Weight Topping

Table of Safe Superimposed Loads, Cambers and Deflections

Designation	No. Strand	Span, ft.													
		44	46	48	50	52	54	56	58	60	62	64	66	68	70
8ST 24+2	10	123* / 1.28 / 0.90	106* / 1.33 / 0.96	92* / 1.36 / 1.02	79* / 1.38 / 1.08	68* / 1.38 / 1.13	57* / 1.33 / 1.18	46 / 1.24 / 1.20	37 / 1.11 / 1.20	28 / 0.94 / 1.20					
8ST 28+2	12					118* / 1.47 / 1.11	104* / 1.51 / 1.16	91* / 1.53 / 1.22	80* / 1.54 / 1.28	70* / 1.52 / 1.33	61* / 1.49 / 1.38	51 / 1.39 / 1.40	42 / 1.26 / 1.41	34 / 1.09 / 1.40	26 / 0.89 / 1.39

Designation	No. Strand	Span, ft.														
		60	62	64	66	68	70	72	74	76	78	80	82	84	86	88
8ST 32+2	14	113* / 1.63 / 1.31	101* / 1.65 / 1.37	90* / 1.66 / 1.42	80* / 1.65 / 1.47	71* / 1.63 / 1.52	62* / 1.58 / 1.57	54 / 1.49 / 1.59	45 / 1.35 / 1.59	37 / 1.17 / 1.59	30 / 0.97 / 1.58					
8ST 36+2	16					109* / 1.78 / 1.51	99* / 1.79 / 1.57	89* / 1.78 / 1.62	80* / 1.76 / 1.67	71* / 1.71 / 1.71	63* / 1.65 / 1.76	55 / 1.55 / 1.77	47 / 1.39 / 1.77	39 / 1.21 / 1.76	33 / 0.99 / 1.75	26 / 0.75 / 1.72

*Capacity governed by ultimate strength
f'_c = 5000 psi f_{pu} = 270,000 psi

Values below heavy line require release strengths higher than 3500 psi

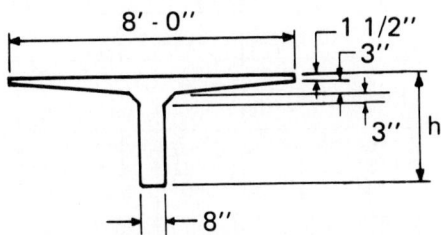

8'-0" Wide
Lightweight Concrete

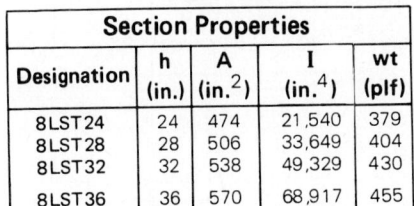

Section Properties				
Designation	h (in.)	A (in.²)	I (in.⁴)	wt (plf)
8LST24	24	474	21,540	379
8LST28	28	506	33,649	404
8LST32	32	538	49,329	430
8LST36	36	570	68,917	455

Table of Safe Superimposed Loads, Cambers and Deflections   No Topping

Desig-nation	No. Strand	Span, ft.												
		64	66	68	70	72	74	76	78	80	82	84	86	88
8LST24	12	58	52	46	41	36	32	28	24					
		2.75	2.65	2.50	2.30	2.01	1.59	1.11	0.56					
		2.87	2.90	2.91	2.90	2.86	2.80	2.72	2.61					
8LST28	14					65	58	53	48	43	38	34	30	26
						3.03	2.94	2.82	2.64	2.41	2.11	1.69	1.21	0.66
						3.26	3.29	3.31	3.31	3.29	3.25	3.19	3.11	3.00

Desig-nation	No. Strand	Span, ft.												
		82	84	86	88	90	92	94	96	98	100	102	104	106	108
8LST32	16	63	57	52	47	43	39	35	31	28					
		3.09	2.96	2.79	2.57	2.29	1.94	1.49	0.99	0.42					
		3.63	3.65	3.65	3.64	3.61	3.56	3.50	3.41	3.30					
8LST36	18					66	61	56	51	47	42	39	35	31	28
						3.22	3.08	2.90	2.68	2.41	2.08	1.67	1.18	0.65	0.06
						3.95	3.97	3.97	3.96	3.94	3.90	3.84	3.76	3.66	3.54

Key
39 — Safe superimposed load, psf
1.94 — Anticipated initial camber, in.
3.56 — Deflection due to superimposed load shown, in.

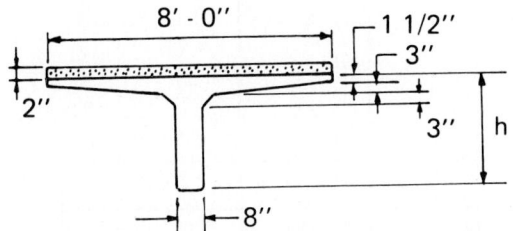

Section Properties			
Designation	h (in.)	I (in.⁴)	wt (plf)
8LST24+2	24	28,886	579
8LST28+2	28	44,109	604
8LST32+2	32	63,745	630
8LST36+2	36	88,260	655

Table of Safe Superimposed Loads, Cambers and Deflections 2"N.W.Topping

Desig-nation	No. Strand	Span, ft.												
		50	52	54	56	58	60	62	64	66	68	70	72	74
8LST 24+2	10	91*	79*	69*	60*	51	42	34	26					
		2.31	2.38	2.43	2.45	2.45	2.41	2.28	2.10					
		1.69	1.80	1.90	2.01	2.08	2.13	2.17	2.19					
8LST 28+2	12						82*	73*	65*	57	48	41	34	27
							2.67	2.71	2.72	2.72	2.68	2.61	2.47	2.25
							2.13	2.23	2.34	2.43	2.48	2.52	2.55	2.57

Desig-nation	No. Strand	Span, ft.												
		70	72	74	76	78	80	82	84	86	88	90	92	94
8LST 32+2	14	76*	68*	61	53	45	39	32	27					
		2.94	2.95	2.93	2.88	2.81	2.69	2.52	2.27					
		2.56	2.66	2.75	2.80	2.84	2.88	2.90	2.90					
8LST 36+2	16					78*	70*	63	56	49	42	36	31	26
						3.17	3.16	3.13	3.07	2.99	2.87	2.71	2.47	2.18
						2.89	2.99	3.07	3.12	3.16	3.19	3.21	3.22	3.21

*Capacity governed by ultimate strength   Values below heavy line require release strengths higher than 3500 psi
   f'_c = 5000 psi f_{pu} = 270,000 psi

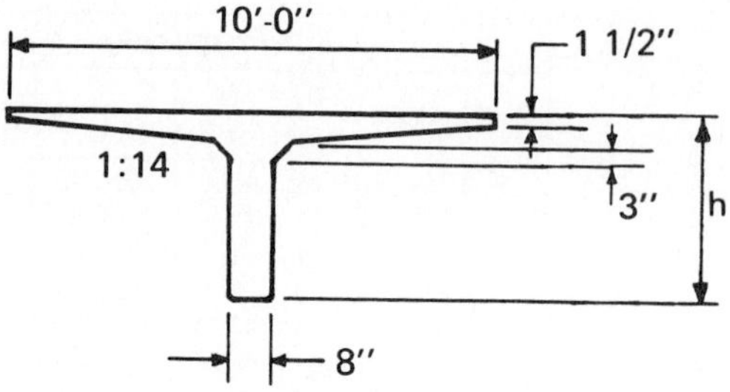

10' - 0" Wide
Normal Weight Concrete

	Section Properties			
Designation	h (in.)	A (in.²)	I (in.⁴)	wt (plf)
10ST24	24	590	22,914	615
10ST28	28	622	36,005	648
10ST32	32	654	53,095	681
10ST36	36	686	74,577	715
10ST40	40	718	100,819	748
10ST44	44	750	132,171	781
10ST48	48	782	168,968	815

Key

36 — Safe superimposed load, psf
0.86 — Anticipated initial camber, in.
1.58 — Deflection due to superimposed load shown, in.

Table of Safe Superimposed Loads, Cambers and Deflections

No Topping

Designation	No. Strand	Span, ft.																
		58	60	62	64	66	68	70	72	74	76	78	80	82	84	86	88	90	92
10ST24	14	59 1.48 1.53	51 1.37 1.52	44 1.22 1.49	37 1.00 1.44	31 0.68 1.38	26 0.31 1.29												
10ST28	16					61* 1.60 1.71	54 1.49 1.71	48 1.34 1.68	41 1.14 1.64	36 0.86 1.58	30 0.51 1.50	26 0.12 1.41							
10ST32	18									62* 1.63 1.87	56 1.51 1.86	50 1.35 1.83	44 1.15 1.79	38 0.86 1.74	33 0.53 1.67	29 0.15 1.58			
10ST36	20												69* 1.73 2.01	63 1.62 2.02	57 1.48 2.00	51 1.30 1.97	45 1.09 1.92	40 0.79 1.87	35 0.46 1.80

Designation	No. Strand	Span, ft.													
		86	88	90	92	94	96	98	100	102	104	106	108	110	112
10ST40	22	75* 1.81 2.15	69 1.71 2.16	62 1.59 2.15	56 1.43 2.12	51 1.23 2.09	46 0.99 2.04	41 0.68 1.98	36 0.34 1.91						
10ST44	24				80* 1.85 2.28	73 1.75 2.29	67 1.63 2.27	61 1.48 2.25	56 1.29 2.22	50 1.07 2.18	45 0.79 2.13	41 0.47 2.07	36 0.12 1.99		
10ST48	24				87* 1.81 2.11	80* 1.73 2.13	74* 1.62 2.14	68 1.50 2.14	63 1.34 2.12	57 1.13 2.09	52 0.89 2.05	47 0.62 2.01	42 0.32 1.95		

*Capacity governed by ultimate strength
$f'_c = 5000$ psi $f_{pu} = 270,000$ psi

Values below heavy line require release strengths higher than 3500 psi

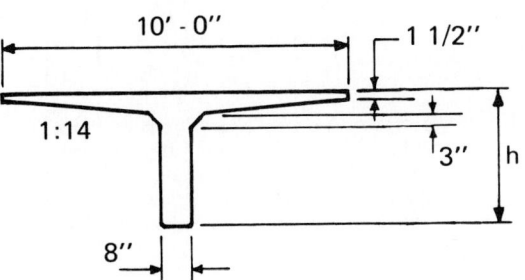

10' - 0" Wide
Lightweight Concrete

Section Properties				
Designation	h (in.)	A (in.^{2})	I (in.^{4})	wt (plf)
10LST24	24	590	22,914	471
10LST28	28	622	36,005	497
10LST32	32	654	53,095	522
10LST36	36	686	74,577	548
10LST40	40	718	100,819	573
10LST44	44	750	132,171	600
10LST48	48	782	168,968	625

Key

33 — Safe superimposed load, psf
1.93 — Anticipated initial camber, in.
3.26 — Deflection due to superimposed load shown, in.

Table of Safe Superimposed Loads, Cambers and Deflections   No Topping

Desig-nation	No. Strand	Span, ft.																	
		66	68	70	72	74	76	78	80	82	84	86	88	90	92	94	96	98	100
10LST24	14	43 2.53 2.79	37 2.33 2.76	33 2.06 2.71	28 1.70 2.63	24 1.21 2.52													
10LST28	16						43 2.64 3.12	38 2.41 3.08	33 2.11 3.02	29 1.74 2.94	26 1.24 2.83								
10LST32	18										46 2.77 3.41	41 2.55 3.38	37 2.27 3.33	33 1.93 3.26	30 1.51 3.17	26 0.97 3.06			
10LST36	20														48 2.83 3.67	44 2.61 3.65	40 2.33 3.60	36 2.00 3.54	32 1.60 3.46

Desig-nation	No. Strand	Span, ft.													
		98	100	102	104	106	108	110	112	114	116	118	120	122	124
10LST40	22	55 3.07 3.94	50 2.88 3.93	46 2.64 3.90	42 2.36 3.85	38 2.03 3.79	35 1.63 3.72	31 1.16 3.62							
10LST44	22	67 3.16 3.69	62 3.04 3.71	57 2.89 3.71	53 2.71 3.70	49 2.48 3.67	45 2.22 3.64	41 1.88 3.58							
10LST48	24			72 3.27 3.91	67 3.15 3.93	62 3.01 3.93	57 2.84 3.93	53 2.63 3.91	49 2.38 3.88	45 2.09 3.84	42 1.73 3.78	38 1.32 3.72	35 0.87 3.63	32 0.37 3.53	

*Capacity governed by ultimate strength   Values below heavy line require strengths higher than 3500 psi

f'_c = 5000 psi f_{pu} = 270,000 psi

Prestressed, rectangular beams

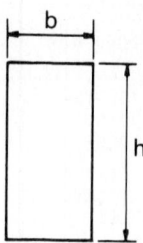

Normal Weight Concrete

Section Properties					
Designation	b (in.)	h (in.)	A (in.²)	I (in.⁴)	wt (plf)
12RB16	12	16	192	4096	200
12RB20	12	20	240	8000	250
12RB24	12	24	288	13,824	300
12RB28	12	28	336	21,952	350
12RB32	12	32	384	32,768	400
12RB36	12	36	432	46,656	450
16RB24	16	24	384	18,432	400
16RB28	16	28	448	29,269	467
16RB32	16	32	512	43,691	533
16RB36	16	36	576	62,208	600
16RB40	16	40	640	85,333	667

Key

1098 — Safe superimposed load, plf
0.43 — Anticipated initial camber, in.
0.47 — Deflection due to superimposed load shown, in.

Table of Safe Superimposed Loads, Cambers and Deflections

Desig-nation	No. Strand	16	18	20	22	24	26	28	30	32	34	36	38	40	42	44	46	48	50
12RB16	8	2721	2108	1669	1345	1098													
		0.24	0.29	0.34	0.39	0.43													
		0.23	0.28	0.34	0.40	0.47													
12RB20	8	4367	3407	2721	2213	1826	1526	1287	1094										
		0.21	0.25	0.30	0.35	0.39	0.43	0.47	0.50										
		0.19	0.23	0.29	0.34	0.40	0.46	0.52	0.58										
12RB24	8	7262	5675	4539	3700	3061	2564	2169	1851	1590									
		0.12	0.14	0.17	0.21	0.24	0.27	0.31	0.34	0.37									
		0.22	0.27	0.33	0.39	0.46	0.53	0.61	0.68	0.76									
12RB28	10			6229	5087	4219	3543	3006	2574	2220	1926	1680							
				0.15	0.17	0.20	0.23	0.26	0.29	0.32	0.35	0.38							
				0.28	0.34	0.40	0.46	0.53	0.60	0.67	0.74	0.81							
12RB32	12			6685	5553	4672	3974	3410	2949	2566	2246	1975	1743	1544					
				0.15	0.17	0.20	0.23	0.25	0.28	0.31	0.33	0.35	0.38	0.40					
				0.30	0.35	0.41	0.47	0.53	0.59	0.66	0.72	0.79	0.85	0.92					
12RB36	12				7110	5992	5104	4388	3802	3317	2910	2566	2272	2019	1799	1608			
					0.17	0.19	0.22	0.25	0.28	0.30	0.33	0.36	0.38	0.41	0.43	0.45			
					0.32	0.37	0.42	0.48	0.54	0.60	0.66	0.72	0.78	0.84	0.91	0.97			
16RB24	12		7539	6030	4914	4066	3405	2881	2458	2112	1825	1585							
			0.13	0.16	0.19	0.22	0.25	0.28	0.31	0.34	0.37	0.39							
			0.27	0.33	0.39	0.46	0.53	0.60	0.68	0.75	0.83	0.91							
16RB28	14			6768	5613	4713	4000	3424	2953	2563	2235	1958	1722	1518					
				0.17	0.19	0.22	0.25	0.28	0.31	0.34	0.36	0.38	0.40	0.42					
				0.34	0.40	0.46	0.53	0.59	0.66	0.73	0.80	0.88	0.94	1.01					
16RB32	16			7404	6230	5298	4547	3931	3422	2994	2633	2324	2058	1828	1627				
				0.17	0.20	0.23	0.25	0.28	0.31	0.33	0.35	0.38	0.40	0.41	0.43				
				0.35	0.41	0.47	0.53	0.59	0.66	0.72	0.79	0.85	0.92	0.98	1.05				
16RB36	18					6782	5830	5052	4406	3866	3408	3017	2681	2389	2135	1912	1715		
						0.20	0.23	0.25	0.28	0.30	0.33	0.35	0.37	0.39	0.41	0.42	0.43		
						0.42	0.48	0.53	0.59	0.65	0.72	0.78	0.84	0.90	0.96	1.02	1.08		
16RB40	20					7270	6309	5512	4845	4280	3798	3383	3023	2709	2434	2190			
						0.21	0.23	0.26	0.28	0.30	0.33	0.35	0.37	0.39	0.41	0.42			
						0.43	0.49	0.54	0.60	0.66	0.71	0.77	0.83	0.89	0.95	1.01			

Notes: All loads shown in this sheet are governed by ultimate.
Additional top reinforcing required.
$f'_c = 5000$ psi $f_{pu} = 270,000$ psi

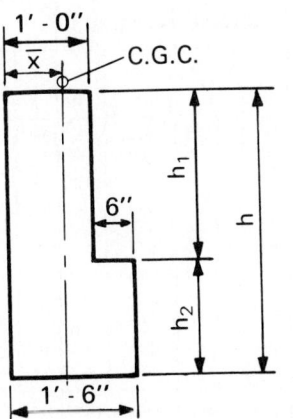

Place strand symmetrical about C.G.C.

Normal Weight Concrete

			Section Properties			
Designation	h (in.)	h_1/h_2 (in.)	A (in.^{2})	I (in.^{4})	wt (plf)	$\bar{x}$ (in.)
18LB20	20	12/8	288	9696	300	7.50
18LB22	22	14/8	312	12,894	325	7.38
18LB26	26	14/12	384	21,307	400	7.69
18LB30	30	18/12	432	32,724	450	7.50
18LB36	36	24/12	504	56,407	525	7.29
18LB40	40	24/16	576	77,568	600	7.50
18LB44	44	28/16	624	103,153	650	7.39
18LB48	48	32/16	672	133,705	700	7.29
18LB52	52	36/16	720	169,613	750	7.20
18LB56	56	40/16	768	211,264	800	7.13
18LB60	60	44/16	816	259,046	850	7.06

Key

1551 — Safe superimposed load, plf
0.39 — Anticipated initial camber, in.
0.81 — Deflection due to superimposed load shown, in.

Table of Safe Superimposed Loads, Cambers and Deflections

Designation	No. Strand	Span, ft.

Desig-nation	No. Strand	16	18	20	22	24	26	28	30	32	34	36	38	40	42	44	46	48	50
18LB20	8	6206 0.14 0.26	4841 0.17 0.33	3864 0.21 0.40	3141 0.24 0.48	2592 0.28 0.56	2164 0.32 0.64	1825 0.36 0.73	1551 0.39 0.81										
18LB22	8	7227 0.12 0.23	5642 0.15 0.29	4508 0.18 0.35	3669 0.22 0.42	3031 0.25 0.49	2535 0.28 0.56	2141 0.32 0.64	1823 0.35 0.72	1563 0.38 0.80									
18LB26	10			8089 0.13 0.25	6476 0.16 0.31	5283 0.19 0.36	4375 0.22 0.43	3669 0.25 0.49	3108 0.28 0.56	2656 0.31 0.63	2286 0.34 0.71	1979 0.37 0.78	1722 0.40 0.85	1505 0.42 0.92					
18LB30	12				8921 0.14 0.27	7295 0.17 0.33	6058 0.20 0.39	5095 0.23 0.45	4331 0.26 0.51	3715 0.29 0.58	3211 0.32 0.65	2793 0.35 0.72	2442 0.38 0.79	2146 0.41 0.86	1893 0.44 0.93	1675 0.46 1.00			
18LB36	14						8760 0.17 0.32	7386 0.20 0.38	6297 0.22 0.43	5417 0.25 0.49	4698 0.28 0.55	4101 0.31 0.61	3602 0.34 0.67	3179 0.37 0.74	2818 0.39 0.80	2507 0.42 0.87	2237 0.45 0.93	2002 0.47 1.00	1796 0.49 1.06	1614 0.51 1.12
18LB40	16							9256 0.18 0.34	7898 0.20 0.39	6803 0.23 0.45	5906 0.26 0.50	5163 0.28 0.56	4541 0.31 0.62	4014 0.33 0.68	3564 0.36 0.74	3177 0.39 0.80	2841 0.41 0.86	2549 0.43 0.92	2292 0.45 0.98	2065 0.47 1.04
18LB44	18								9765 0.19 0.37	8422 0.22 0.41	7324 0.24 0.47	6413 0.27 0.52	5650 0.29 0.58	5004 0.32 0.63	4453 0.35 0.69	3979 0.37 0.75	3567 0.40 0.81	3209 0.42 0.87	2894 0.45 0.93	2616 0.47 0.99
18LB48	20									8881 0.23 0.44	7787 0.25 0.49	6870 0.28 0.54	6094 0.31 0.60	5432 0.33 0.65	4862 0.36 0.71	4368 0.38 0.77	3936 0.41 0.83	3558 0.43 0.89	3224 0.46 0.95	
18LB52	22										9212 0.24 0.46	8136 0.26 0.51	7226 0.29 0.56	6448 0.31 0.61	5779 0.34 0.67	5199 0.36 0.72	4693 0.39 0.78	4249 0.41 0.83	3857 0.44 0.89	
18LB56	22											9240 0.24 0.46	8211 0.27 0.51	7332 0.29 0.56	6576 0.31 0.61	5921 0.34 0.66	5349 0.36 0.71	4847 0.38 0.76	4405 0.41 0.82	
18LB60	24												9575 0.26 0.48	8558 0.28 0.53	7684 0.30 0.58	6926 0.33 0.63	6264 0.35 0.68	5684 0.37 0.73	5171 0.40 0.78	

Notes: All safe loads shown on this sheet are controlled by ultimate.
Additional top reinforcing required.
f'_c = 5000 psi f_{pu} = 270,000 psi

Prestressed, inverted tee beams

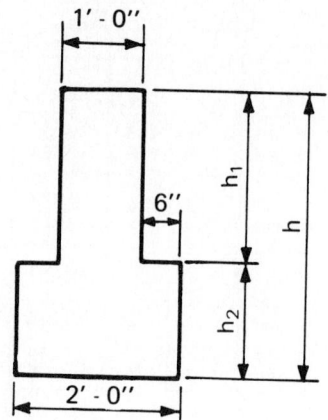

Normal Weight Concrete

Section Properties					
Designation	h (in.)	h_1/h_2 (in.)	A (in.^{2})	I (in.^{4})	wt (plf)
24IT20	20	12/8	336	10,981	350
24IT22	22	14/8	360	14,610	375
24IT26	26	14/12	456	24,132	475
24IT30	30	18/12	504	37,059	525
24IT36	36	24/12	576	63,936	600
24IT40	40	24/16	672	87,845	700
24IT44	44	28/16	720	116,877	750
24IT48	48	32/16	768	151,552	800
24IT52	52	36/16	816	192,275	850
24IT56	56	40/16	864	239,445	900
24IT60	60	44/16	912	293,460	950

Key

1576 — Safe superimposed load, plf
0.31 — Anticipated initial camber, in.
0.73 — Deflection due to superimposed load shown, in.

Table of Safe Superimposed Loads, Cambers and Deflections

Designation	No. Strand	Span, ft. 16	18	20	22	24	26	28	30	32	34	36	38	40	42	44	46	48	50
24IT20	8	6422	5001	3984	3232	2660	2214	1861	1576										
		0.12	0.14	0.17	0.20	0.23	0.26	0.29	0.31										
		0.24	0.30	0.36	0.43	0.50	0.58	0.65	0.73										
24IT22	8	7366	5742	4580	3720	3066	2557	2153	1827	1560									
		0.10	0.12	0.15	0.17	0.20	0.23	0.25	0.27	0.30									
		0.21	0.26	0.31	0.37	0.44	0.50	0.57	0.64	0.70									
24IT26	10		8397	6711	5464	4515	3777	3191	2719	2332	2012	1743	1516						
			0.11	0.13	0.16	0.18	0.21	0.23	0.26	0.28	0.30	0.32	0.33						
			0.23	0.28	0.33	0.39	0.45	0.51	0.57	0.64	0.70	0.76	0.82						
24IT30	12			9305	7599	6302	5292	4490	3844	3315	2876	2509	2198	1933	1704	1506			
				0.12	0.15	0.17	0.20	0.22	0.25	0.27	0.29	0.32	0.34	0.35	0.37	0.38			
				0.25	0.30	0.35	0.41	0.47	0.53	0.59	0.65	0.71	0.78	0.84	0.90	0.96			
24IT36	16					8556	7295	6277	5444	4754	4176	3686	3268	2909	2597	2325	2086	1876	
						0.20	0.23	0.25	0.28	0.31	0.34	0.37	0.40	0.42	0.45	0.47	0.49	0.51	
						0.38	0.44	0.50	0.56	0.62	0.69	0.75	0.82	0.89	0.96	1.02	1.09	1.15	
24IT40	16					9638	8214	7065	6125	5346	4693	4140	3668	3262	2910	2603	2333	2096	
						0.15	0.17	0.20	0.22	0.24	0.26	0.28	0.30	0.32	0.34	0.35	0.36	0.37	
						0.31	0.36	0.41	0.46	0.51	0.56	0.62	0.67	0.72	0.78	0.83	0.88	0.94	
24IT44	18							8788	7633	6676	5874	5195	4615	4116	3684	3307	2976	2684	
								0.19	0.21	0.23	0.25	0.27	0.29	0.31	0.33	0.35	0.37	0.38	
								0.38	0.43	0.48	0.53	0.58	0.63	0.69	0.74	0.79	0.85	0.90	
24IT48	20								9292	8140	7174	6357	5659	5059	4538	4084	3685	3334	
									0.20	0.22	0.24	0.26	0.28	0.30	0.33	0.34	0.36	0.38	
									0.40	0.45	0.50	0.55	0.60	0.65	0.70	0.76	0.81	0.86	
24IT52	22									9733	8590	7622	6796	6085	5469	4932	4460	4044	
										0.21	0.23	0.25	0.27	0.30	0.32	0.34	0.36	0.38	
										0.42	0.47	0.52	0.57	0.62	0.67	0.72	0.77	0.82	
24IT56	24										8995	8030	7200	6480	5852	5301	4815		
											0.24	0.26	0.29	0.31	0.33	0.35	0.37		
											0.49	0.54	0.59	0.64	0.69	0.74	0.79		
24IT60	26										9354	8396	7566	6841	6206	5645			
											0.26	0.28	0.30	0.32	0.34	0.36			
											0.51	0.56	0.61	0.65	0.70	0.75			

Notes: All safe loads shown on this sheet are controlled by ultimate.
Additional top reinforcing required.
f'_c = 5000 psi f_{pu} = 270,000 psi

HOLLOW-CORE FLOOR AND ROOF SLABS

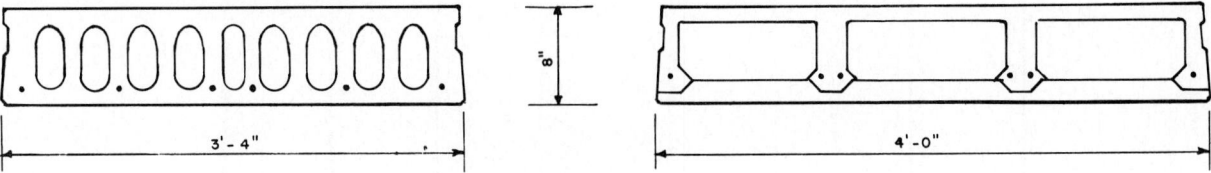

3'- 4"
8"
4'-0"

TYPICAL SECTIONS (see also sheet 35)

SPAN RANGES FOR VARIOUS DEPTHS

Maximum span to depth ratio shown is 50. Ratios above 40 (shaded areas) are not recommended for floors.

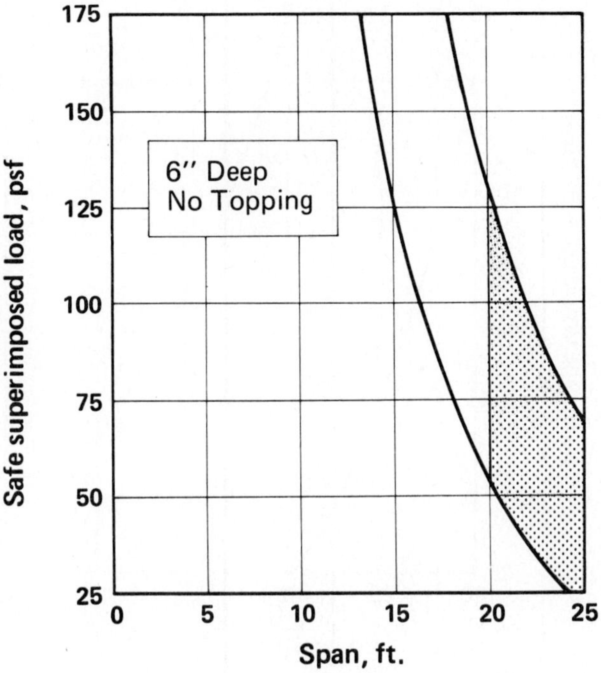

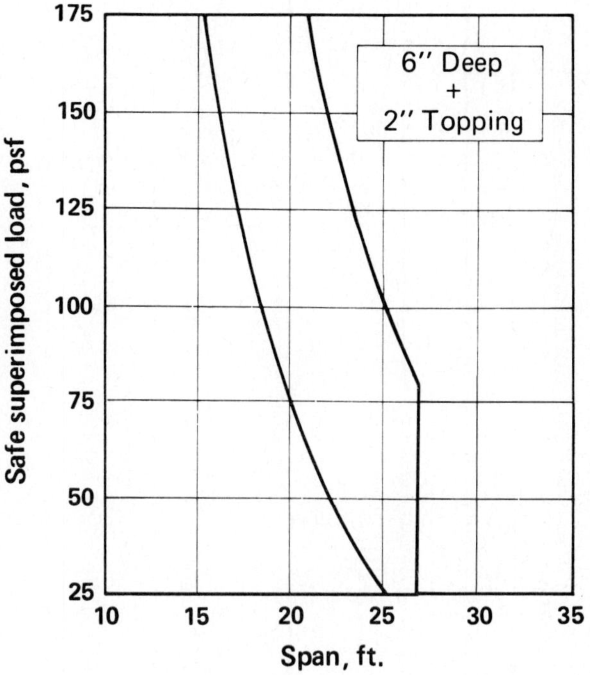

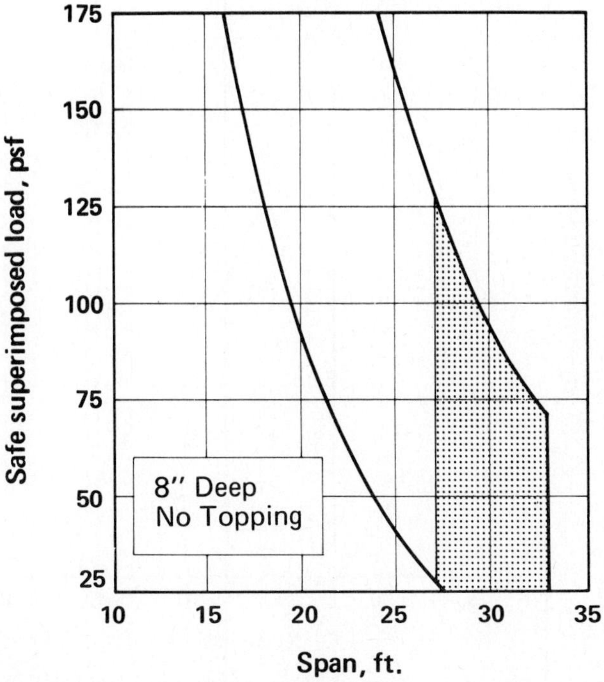

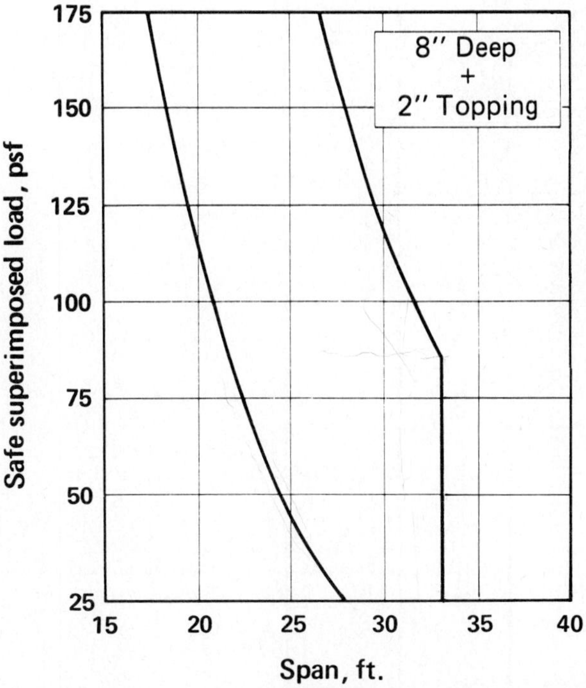

6" Deep
No Topping
Safe superimposed load, psf
175
150
125
100
75
50
25
0
5
10
15
20
25
Span, ft.

6" Deep
+
2" Topping
Safe superimposed load, psf
175
150
125
100
75
50
25
10
15
20
25
30
35
Span, ft.

8" Deep
No Topping
Safe superimposed load, psf
175
150
125
100
75
50
25
10
15
20
25
30
35
Span, ft.

8" Deep
+
2" Topping
Safe superimposed load, psf
175
150
125
100
75
50
25
15
20
25
30
35
40
Span, ft.

Note: Some types available in 8 ft widths

(From PCI Design Handbook)

Prestressed, floor and roof slabs

HOLLOW-CORE FLOOR AND ROOF SLABS

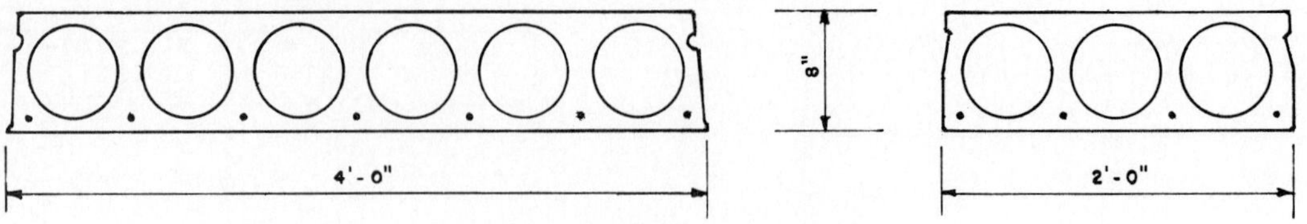
8"
4'-0"
2'-0"

TYPICAL SECTIONS (see also sheet 34)

SPAN RANGES FOR VARIOUS DEPTHS

Maximum span to depth ratio shown is 50. Ratios above 40 (shaded areas) are not recommended for floors.

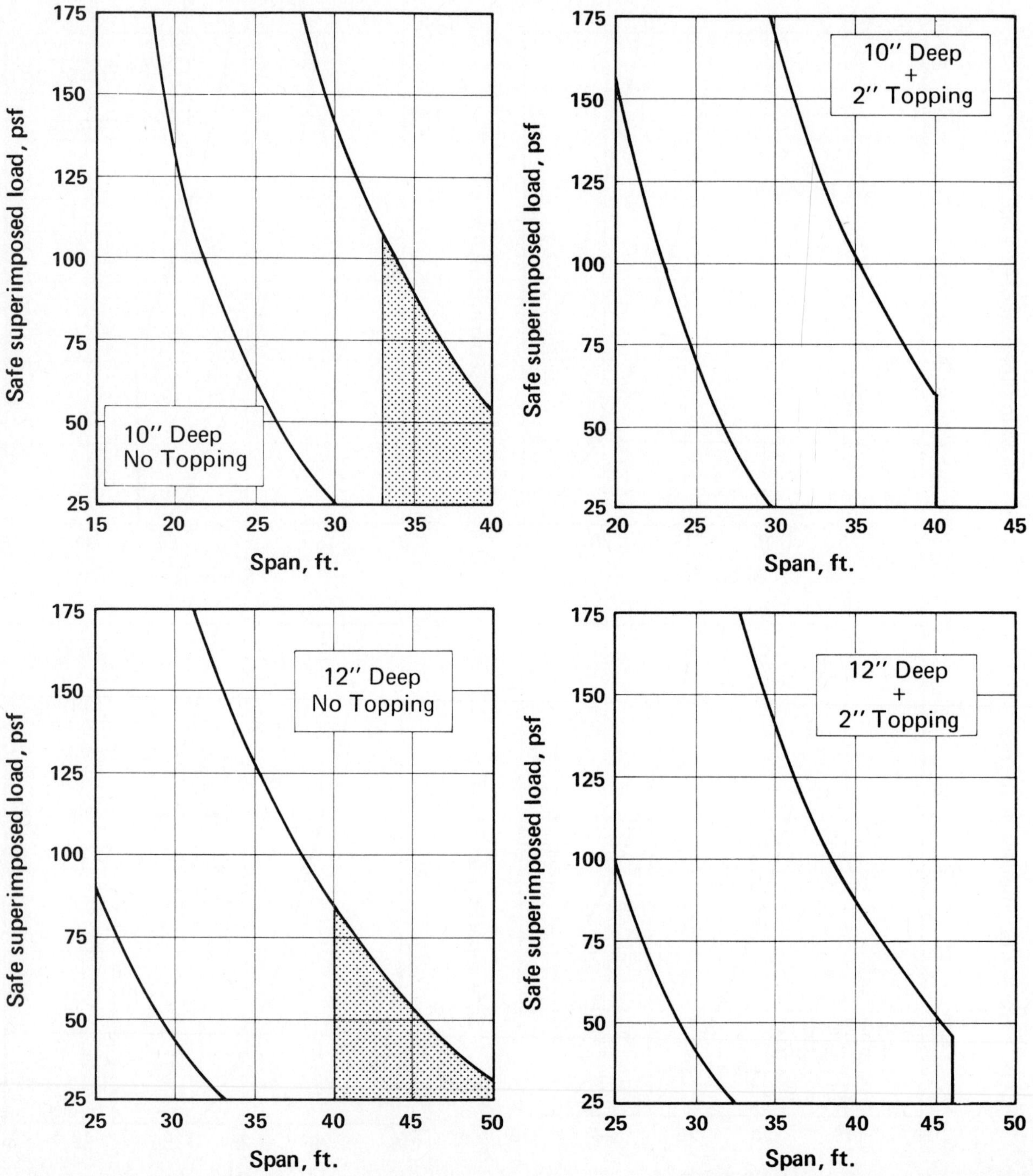
10" Deep
No Topping
10" Deep
+
2" Topping
12" Deep
No Topping
12" Deep
+
2" Topping
Safe superimposed load, psf
Span, ft.
175
150
125
100
75
50
25
15
20
25
30
35
40
45
50

Note: Some types available in 8 ft widths

(From PCI Design Handbook)

PRECAST CONCRETE CURTAIN WALLS

Precast concrete may be used as a panel material in metal-framed curtain wall construction, but it is more often used as a complete curtain wall system in which the concrete panels are attached directly to the building frame. Of the several types that have been developed, the most successful, as well as the most technologically advanced, is the concrete sandwich panel. Typical details of this type of construction are shown in Fig. 17.

Notable advantages of the precast concrete curtain wall are fire resistance, economy, large-size units, and a wide variety of finishes. Unlike metal curtain walls, which must rely upon masonry backup to meet code requirements for fire resistance,

the concrete sandwich panel is integrally fire resistant and 2-hr ratings have been obtained in several cities. In the economical "broomed" finish (a striated texture), concrete sandwich panels can compete in cost with brick and block construction and the industrial type of metal curtain walls. Panels may be obtained in sizes up to 10 by 30 ft; the large sizes and the absence of mullions or other accessory parts result in far fewer pieces to handle and fewer joints to seal than in any other curtain wall system. In addition to the broomed finish, which is also available in white cement, concrete sandwich panels are obtainable in a wide variety of colors and textures provided by exposed aggregate. The colored aggregate may be rough or smooth, or it may be ground and polished like terrazzo.

Or panels may be faced with ceramic tile that is monolithically bonded to the panel by being placed face down in the mold before the panel is poured.

Typical panels are 5 in. thick with a 1½-in.-thick core of rigid insulation which may be foamed glass, foamed plastic, or glass fiberboard. The U value is 0.14 Btu. Panels over 8 by 20 ft in size must be 6 in. thick. The 5-in. panels weigh 45 psf and the 6-in. panels 57½ psf. Reinforcing is 6 by 6 in. No. 8, or 4 by 4 in. No. 10, welded wire mesh, placed 1 in. back from each face of the panel; shear ties are 13 gage expanded metal 1½ in. diamond mesh bent into channel shape and placed around the perimeter of the panel and 2 ft on centers in the panel in the direction of the span.

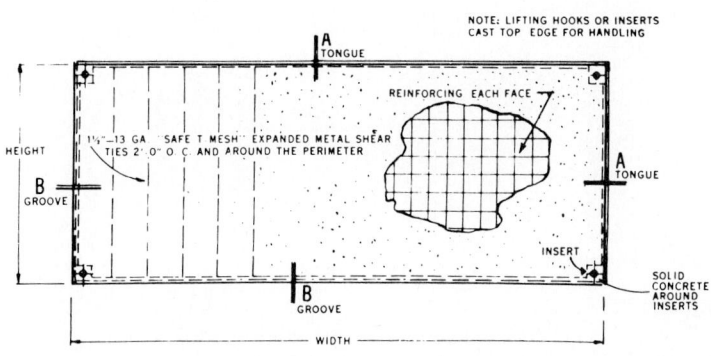

TYPICAL WALL PANEL

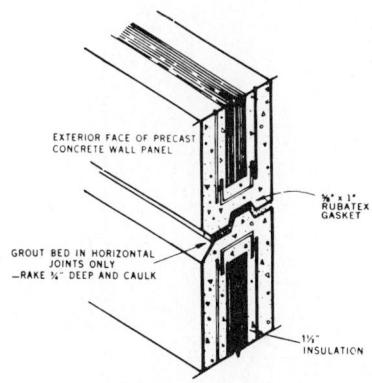

TYPICAL HORIZONTAL JOINT

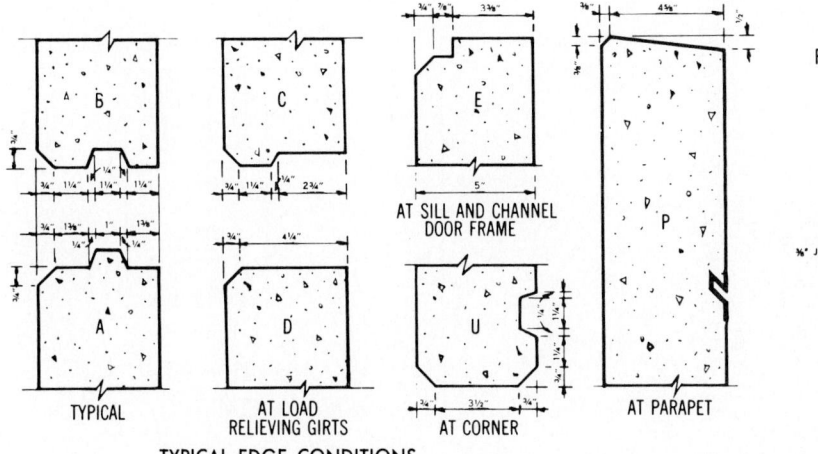

TYPICAL EDGE CONDITIONS

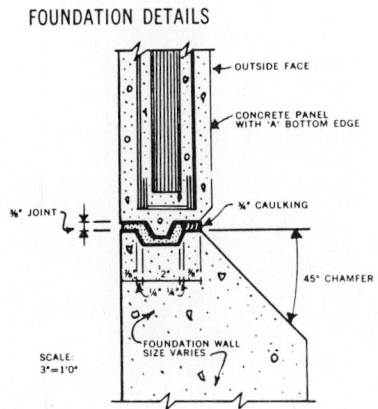

FOUNDATION DETAILS

Fig. 17. Typical construction details

Courtesy Marietta Concrete Division, American Marietta Company.

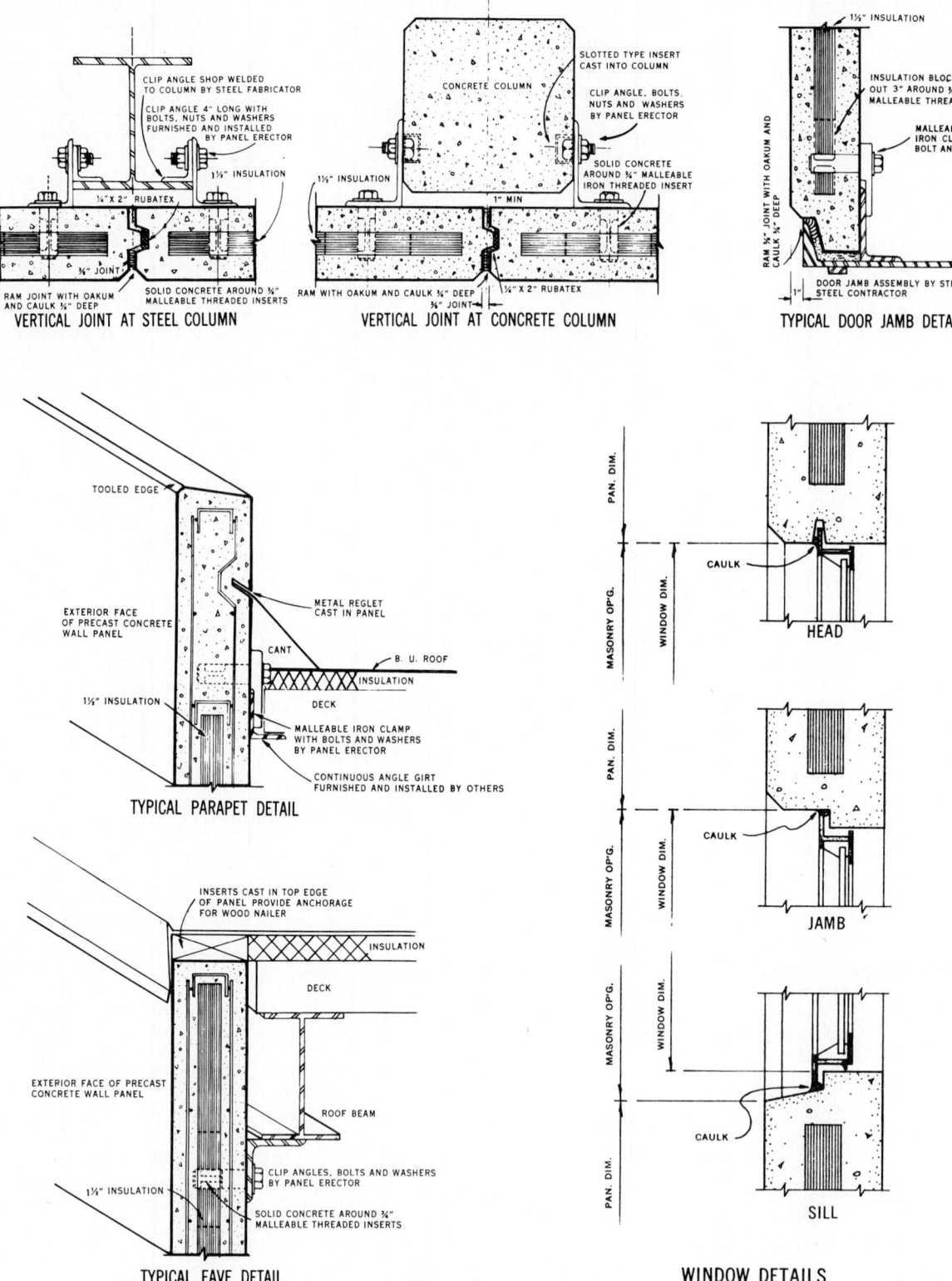

Fig. 17. (cont.) Typical construction details

By SEYMOUR HOWARD, *Architect*
Associate Professor, Pratt Institute

GENERAL CONSIDERATIONS

Advantages

1. "No other structural system makes such an economical use of materials."[1]

2. Freedom of design shapes, both in plan and in section.

3. Ease of providing natural light over large areas.

4. Great capacity to carry unbalanced loads.

5. Fireproof.

6. Great reserve strength. Local damage, even at critical point, will not cause general collapse.

Special Problems

1. Formwork must be carefully designed. Minimum of four reuses of forms required for economy.

2. Construction problems unfamiliar to most contractors.

3. Design procedure unfamiliar to many engineers; complicated shapes involve lengthy calculations. "Design of large thin shell roofs is a major engineering problem."[1]

4. Insulation must be provided, preferably above shell and ribs.

5. Surface treatment of exposed concrete must be studied for architectural effect.

[1]From *Design of Cylindrical Concrete Shell Roofs*, Manual No. 31, American Society of Civil Engineers, N. Y., 1952.

A   SHELLS CURVED IN ONE DIRECTION

Transverse stiffeners are essential. They may be:
• Integral with the supports in the form of rigid frames (as shown)
• Arches, carried on columns or directly on the ground:
• Vertical diaphragms, carried on columns or continuing to ground. (Some designs have been built with ribless stiffeners.)

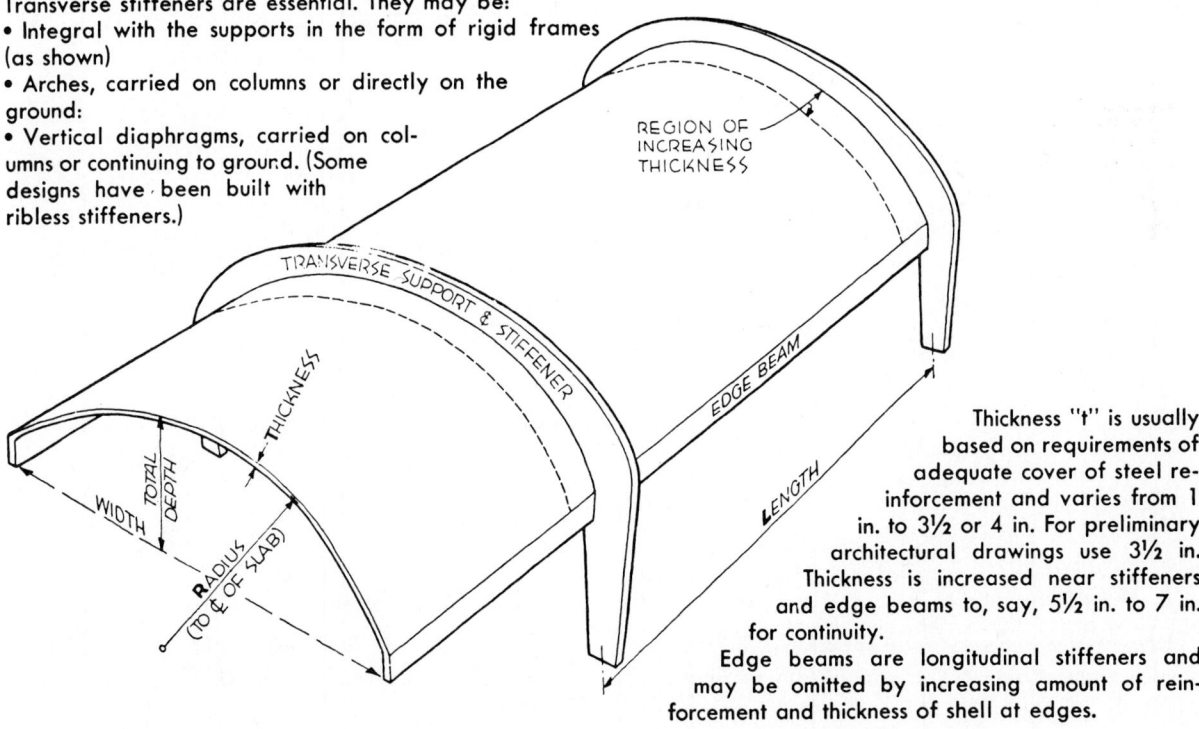

Thickness "t" is usually based on requirements of adequate cover of steel reinforcement and varies from 1 in. to 3½ or 4 in. For preliminary architectural drawings use 3½ in. Thickness is increased near stiffeners and edge beams to, say, 5½ in. to 7 in. for continuity.
Edge beams are longitudinal stiffeners and may be omitted by increasing amount of reinforcement and thickness of shell at edges.

Shells derive their strength from their ability to transfer loads by membrane stresses. These are direct stresses—compression, tension and shear—acting over the entire thickness of the shell at any point. There is no bending of an element of the shell such as exists in an element of a flat slab (except of minor magnitude caused by edge and end conditions). There is no need for continuous longitudinal support as for a masonry barrel vault incapable of supporting tensile stresses.

A(cont.)   **SHELLS CURVED IN ONE DIRECTION**

Comparison of forces acting on unit elements of shell, slab and vault. Intermediate form between long barrel shell and flat slab is tee-beam and slab.

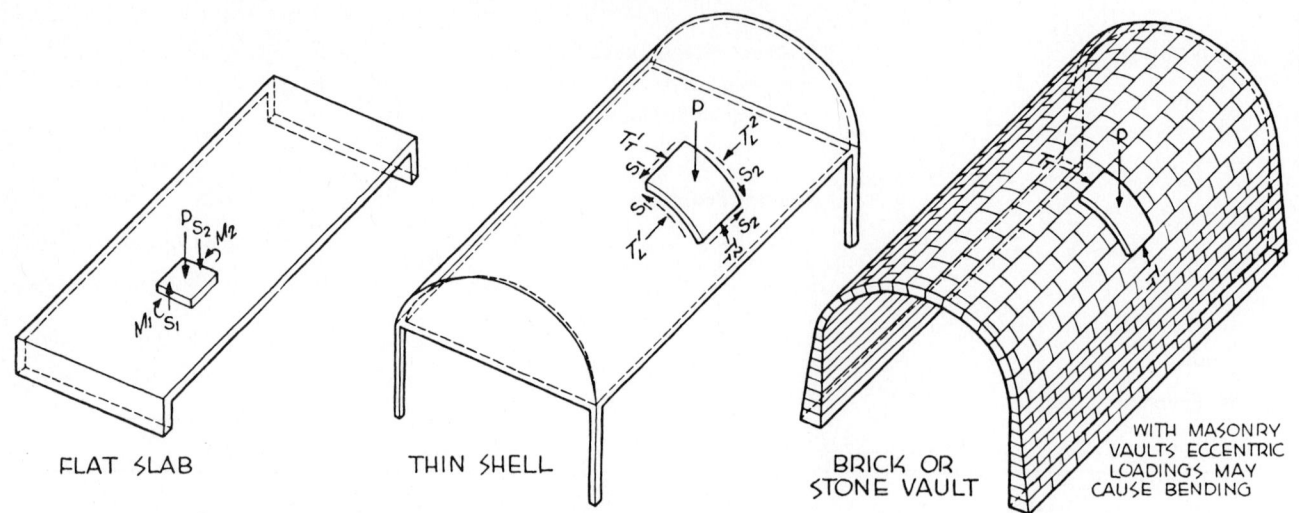

FLAT SLAB   THIN SHELL   BRICK OR STONE VAULT

WITH MASONRY VAULTS ECCENTRIC LOADINGS MAY CAUSE BENDING

A-1   **CENTER(S) OF CURVATURE BELOW SHELL**

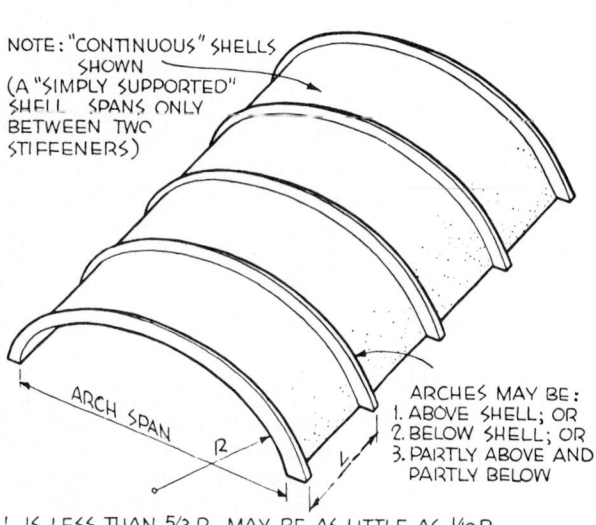

NOTE: "CONTINUOUS" SHELLS SHOWN
(A "SIMPLY SUPPORTED" SHELL SPANS ONLY BETWEEN TWO STIFFENERS)

ARCH SPAN   R   L

ARCHES MAY BE:
1. ABOVE SHELL; OR
2. BELOW SHELL; OR
3. PARTLY ABOVE AND PARTLY BELOW

L IS LESS THAN 5/3 R, MAY BE AS LITTLE AS 1/10 R

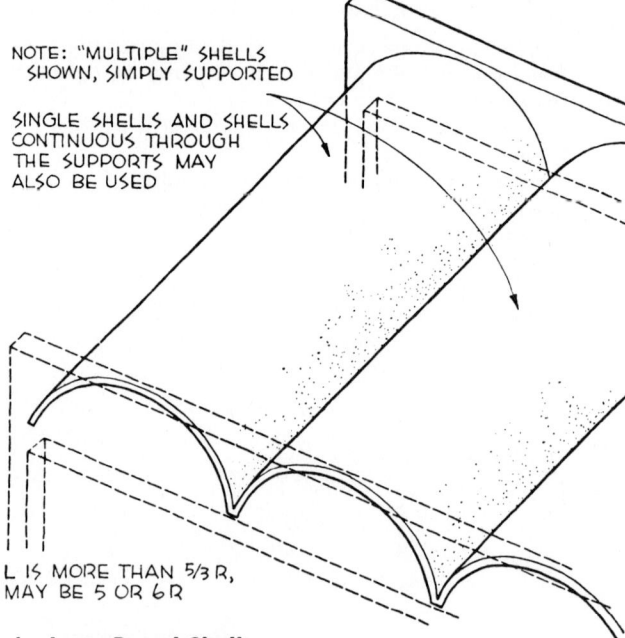

NOTE: "MULTIPLE" SHELLS SHOWN, SIMPLY SUPPORTED

SINGLE SHELLS AND SHELLS CONTINUOUS THROUGH THE SUPPORTS MAY ALSO BE USED

L IS MORE THAN 5/3 R, MAY BE 5 OR 6 R

a. Short Barrel Shells

Usually used for very wide spaces (i.e. Stiffening arch spans of over 150 ft, occasionally as short as 50 ft)

  Max. arch span built—340 ft

  Max. arch span possible—500 to 600 ft or more

  Length of shell "L" usually 20 to 40 ft

Transverse forces govern (T_T above) for shell. Arch design is primary consideration. Depth at crown varies $\frac{1}{50}$ to $\frac{1}{100}$ of arch span. Usual provisions for thrust and vertical load must be carefully designed

b. Long Barrel Shells

Max. length of shell built—236 ft (Need for expansion joints limits length). Usual lengths 50 to 135 ft

  Width of shell 30 to 50 ft

  Depth of shell including edge beam (if used) usually about $\frac{1}{10}$ length

  Longitudinal forces govern (T_L above)

Note: For calculating cylindrical short and long barrel shells, refer to "Design of Cylindrical Concrete Shell Roofs," Manual No. 31 American Society of Civil Engineers, N. Y., 1952

A-1(cont.)   CENTER(S) OF CURVATURE BELOW SHELL

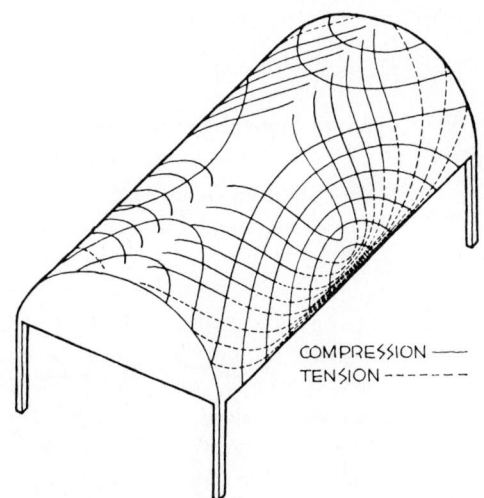

COMPRESSION ———
TENSION - - - - -

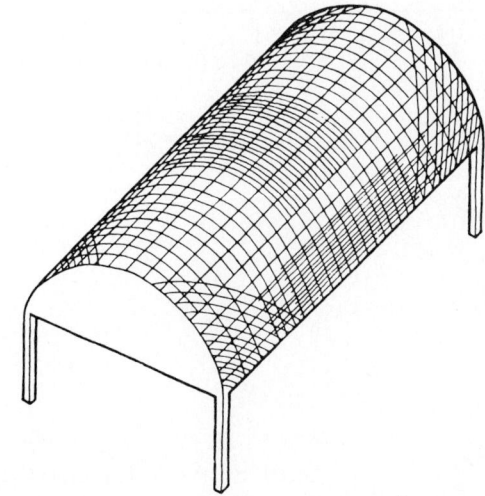

Typical stress trajectories in a simply supported, single long barrel shell

Note concentration of tensile forces at lower edge in center of shell lengths.

Horizontal component of these forces (in plan) causes lower edges of shell to move *inward* toward longitudinal Center Line. This is exactly the opposite of the movement of conventional masonry barrel vault or arch.

Typical arrangement of reinforcement in a simply supported, single long barrel shell

While it is desirable to place the reinforcement exactly along the lines of principal stress, this requires careful bending and placement. A rectilinear arrangement as shown above is easier to bend and place, although more steel will be required. Diagonal bars cannot be avoided at the lower edges of the shell near the supports.

For continuous and cantilevered shells, tensile stresses will exist at top of shell over the supports, and compressive stresses at lower edges

(See elevation diagram at bottom of page)

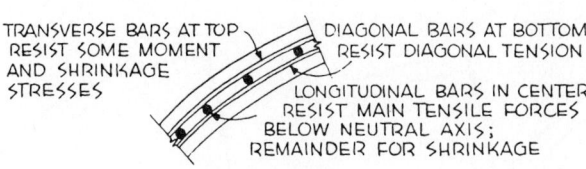

TRANSVERSE BARS AT TOP RESIST SOME MOMENT AND SHRINKAGE STRESSES

DIAGONAL BARS AT BOTTOM RESIST DIAGONAL TENSION

LONGITUDINAL BARS IN CENTER RESIST MAIN TENSILE FORCES BELOW NEUTRAL AXIS; REMAINDER FOR SHRINKAGE

Placement of bars in shell

Reinforcement may be in the form of bars or a combination of bars and mesh

Section through transverse Center Line of multiple barrel shell

The tendency of the lower edges to move inward, as shown in broken line, must be resisted by adequate transverse tensile reinforcement

Elevation of continuous long barrel shell showing stress trajectories (approximate relationships)

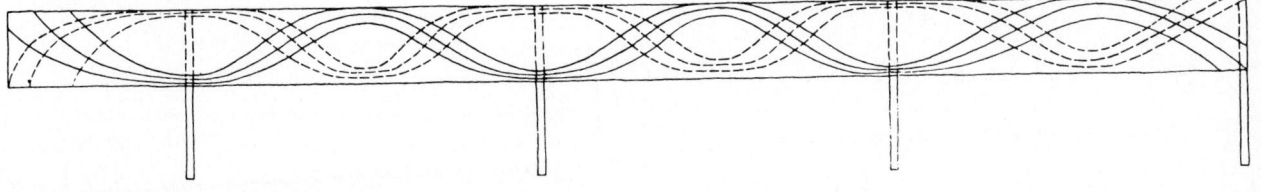

A-1(cont.)   CENTER(S) OF CURVATURE BELOW SHELL

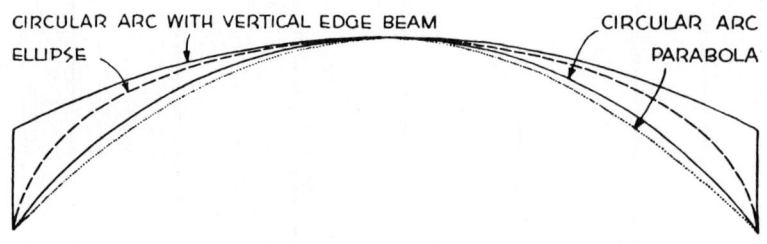

CIRCULAR ARC WITH VERTICAL EDGE BEAM

ELLIPSE

CIRCULAR ARC

PARABOLA

NOTE: *For short barrels the curve is based on the arches and follows the pressure line for them, normally close to a parabola or catenary. The catenary would lie between the parabola and the circular segment.*

Some Typical Cross Section Curves

The parabola is as flat a curve as should be used. The vertical tangents at the bottom edges of the ellipse and of a shell with edge beams will reduce or eliminate edge moments. It is not practical to place concrete at angles steeper than 45° without top forms; therefore job economy favors flatter curves. This requirement would limit depth to width ratio to 1 to 5 with circular arc. Cycloid has been used because of vertical tangent at bottom edges, but requires a depth to width ratio of 1 to π or 0.318 to 1.

Natural lighting can be provided by circular holes cut in shell, 3 ft-0 in. to 4 ft-0 in. diameter, or by glass prisms cast directly with the concrete

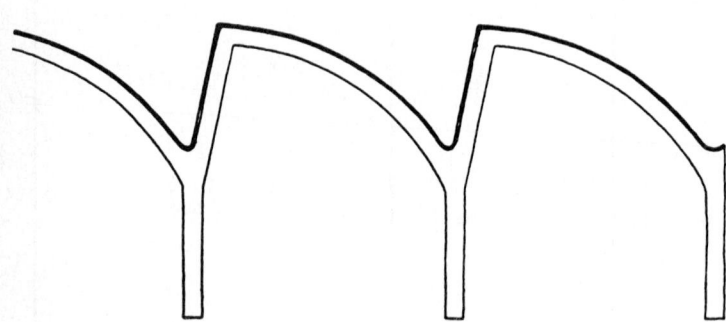

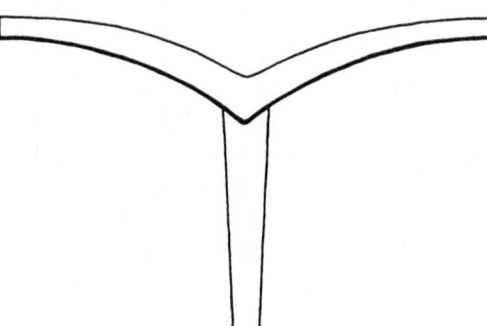

Typical "North Light" Shells

Note that, although these can be continuous, they cannot be multiple.

"Butterfly" Shell (Twin Cantilever)

Can be used as shown for train or bus platforms; also grouped in pairs with skylight between and occasional ties to eliminate need for wide, rigid footings.

A-1(cont.)   CENTER(S) OF CURVATURE BELOW SHELL

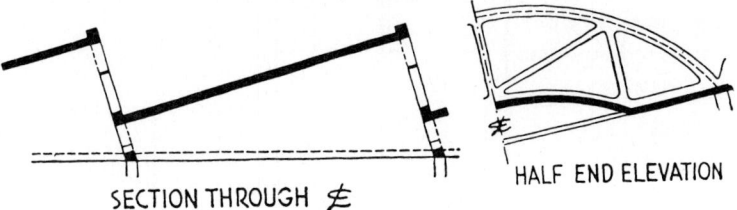

SECTION THROUGH ℄

HALF END ELEVATION

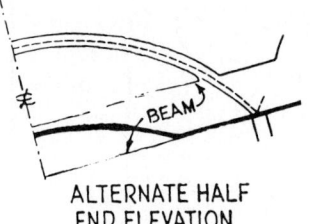

ALTERNATE HALF
END ELEVATION

Tilted Cylindrical Shell

NOTE that: Shell has same radius of curvature throughout its length; intersection of shell and flat slab traces part of an ellipse in plan.

Awkward flat areas between shells can only be eliminated by using another type of surface for the shell, such as cone (see below) or a conoid (see later sheet on B-3, shells curved in two directions); or by using another type of surface for the area between shells (such as an inverted shell).

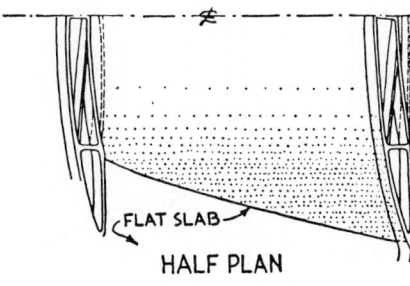

FLAT SLAB

HALF PLAN

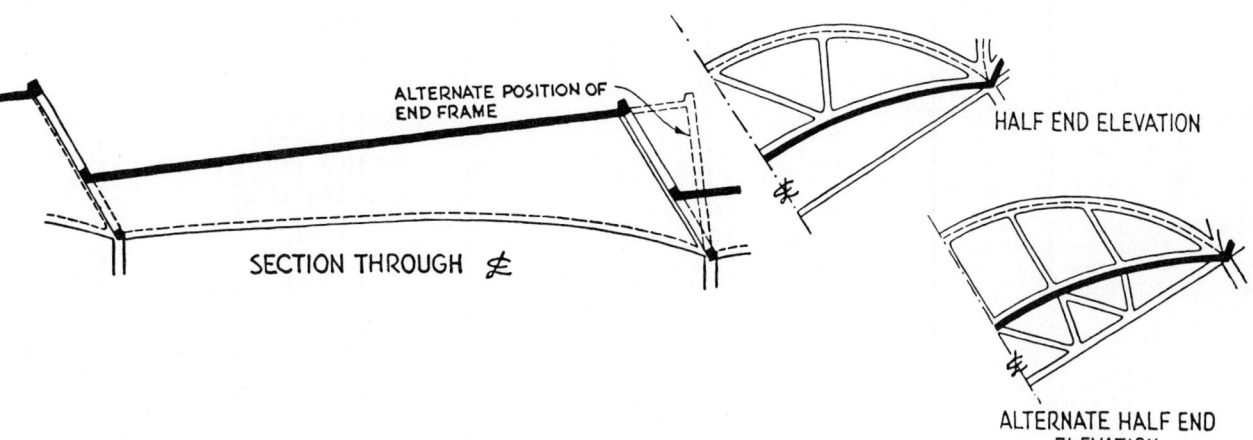

ALTERNATE POSITION OF
END FRAME

SECTION THROUGH ℄

HALF END ELEVATION

ALTERNATE HALF END
ELEVATION

Tilted Conical Shell

NOTE that: Shell has radius of curvature which varies uniformly throughout its length; intersection of adjacent shells traces part of a hyperbola in side elevation.

If cone is not tilted and if shorter radius is not used at outside curve of end elevation, large flat slab portions would have to be used between shells, similar to those formed between tilted cylinders (see above and also later sheet on A-2, center of curvature above shell).

If end frame is placed in alternate position (see section), at right angles to side of cone instead of at right angles to center line of cone, the end elevation of frame would show ellipses instead of circles.

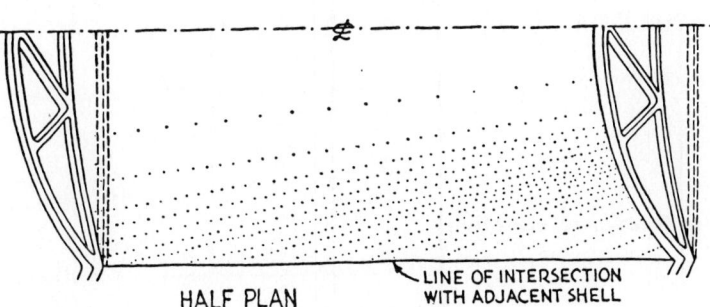

HALF PLAN

LINE OF INTERSECTION
WITH ADJACENT SHELL

A-1(cont.) CENTER(S) OF CURVATURE BELOW SHELL

For short barrel shells the arch and its abutments become the primary consideration. Some typical sections:

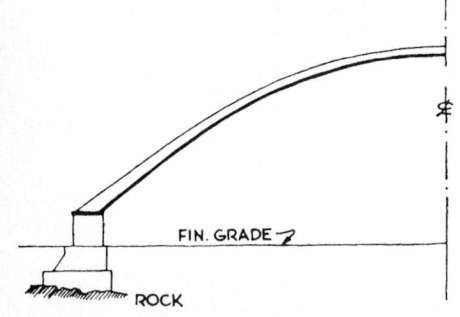

PEDESTAL AND VERTICAL BUTTRESS ON ROCK
ON POOR SOIL, USE TIE BARS

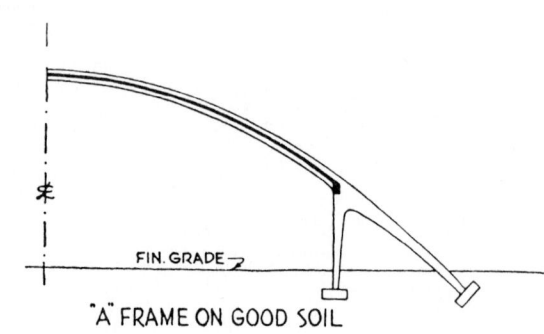

"A" FRAME ON GOOD SOIL

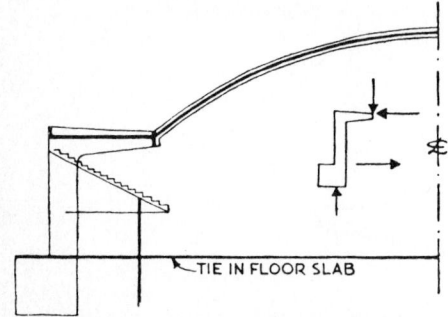

BUTTRESS WITH HORIZONTAL CANTILEVER

Horizontal component of arch thrust forms couple with tie, which is balanced by couple formed by vertical component of arch thrust and vertical reaction of foundation.

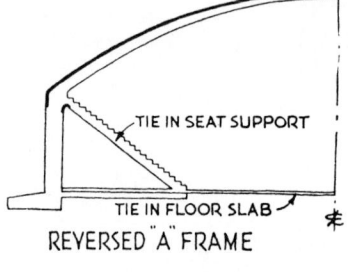

REVERSED "A" FRAME

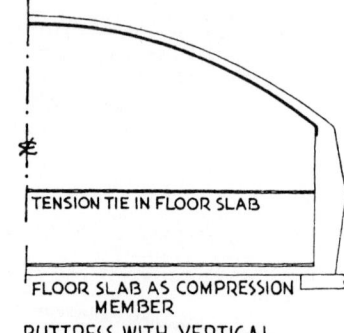

BUTTRESS WITH VERTICAL CANTILEVER

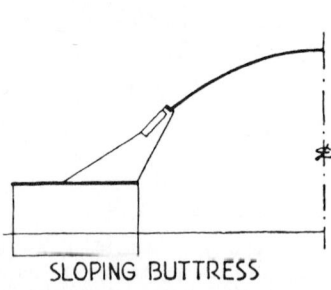

SLOPING BUTTRESS

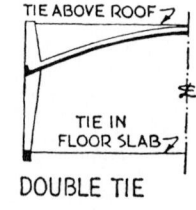

DOUBLE TIE

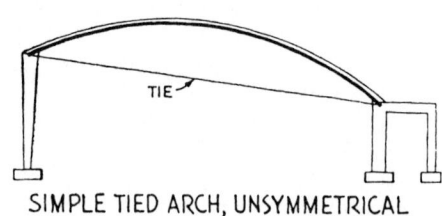

SIMPLE TIED ARCH, UNSYMMETRICAL

Transverse joints can be provided as shown in these three side elevations:

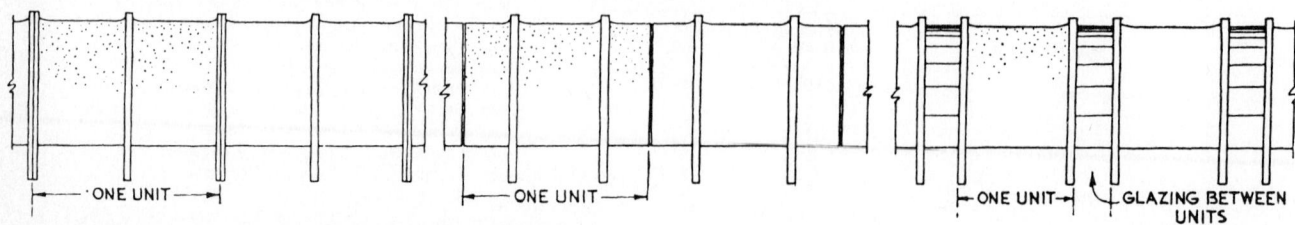

Joints are necessary for expansion, for construction convenience (limit of formwork) or to permit introduction of another element such as glazing.

A-2   CENTER(S) OF CURVATURE ABOVE SHELL

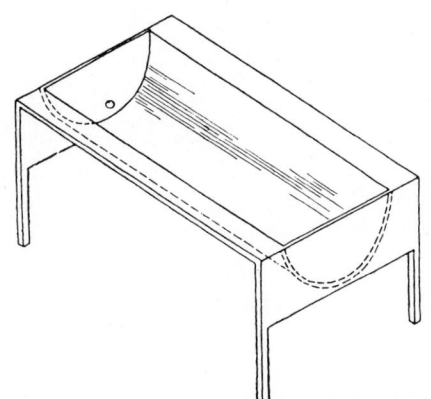

Inverted, concave shells are basically shapes best realized in tensile materials, such as wire or fiber rope, canvas, steel. The danger of buckling of the free edges of the shell requires stiffening or frequent bracing. Concave shells are therefore used chiefly as a supplement to convex shells, which have their centers of curvature below.

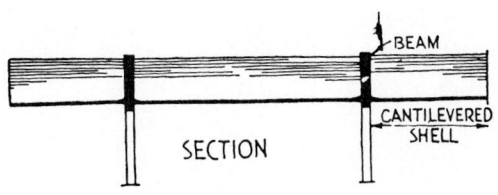

SECTION

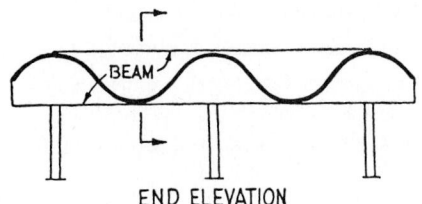

END ELEVATION

Typical Flat Corrugated Shell

Between the supports the concave part of the shell will carry the main tensile reinforcement. In the cantilevered ends the concave part will provide the main compressive strength. The shape of the corrugations has little statical importance; segments of circles are shown, but others may be used including the sine curve.

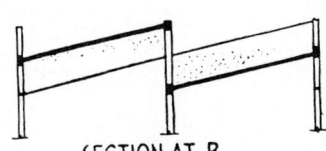

SECTION AT B

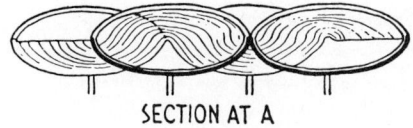

SECTION AT A

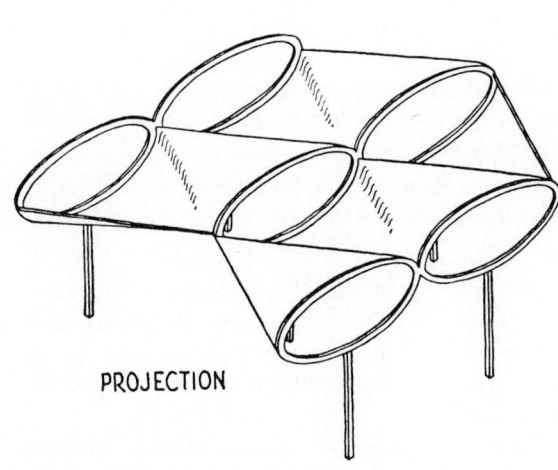

PROJECTION

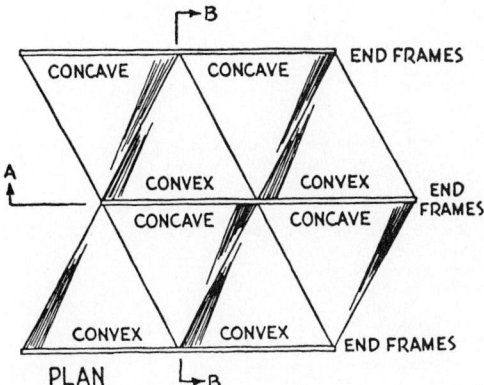

PLAN

Inverted Shells Used to Fill Spaces Between Conical Shells

(Bracing members not shown in end frames, for clarity.) (This is a scheme of Architect Horacio Carminos and Engineer Antonio B. Araciba of Argentina.)

B SHELLS CURVED IN TWO DIRECTIONS

These provide greater stiffness by their shape alone than shells curved in only one direction. Their surfaces are nondevelopable. They cannot be made by bending a flat sheet as can all surfaces curved in only one direction. The formwork, therefore, is usually more complicated and they have been used less frequently.

B-1 BOTH SETS OF CENTERS OF CURVATURE BELOW SHELL (Synclastic or Dome Surfaces)

General Case:

Surface generated by one curve ("a") sliding along another ("b") at right angles to it.

Curve "a" may vary as it slides; curve "b" may be of any shape, provided the center of curvature is always below. It is possible to vary curve "a" so that the surface will curve smoothly down to the flat plane (vertical edge frames would disappear).

Edge frames correspond to transverse stiffeners or end frames shown for shells curved in one direction. Edge frames may be: vertical diaphragm; rigid frame or truss, integral with supports or simply supported; stiffeners in edge of shell, with tension ties between points of support.

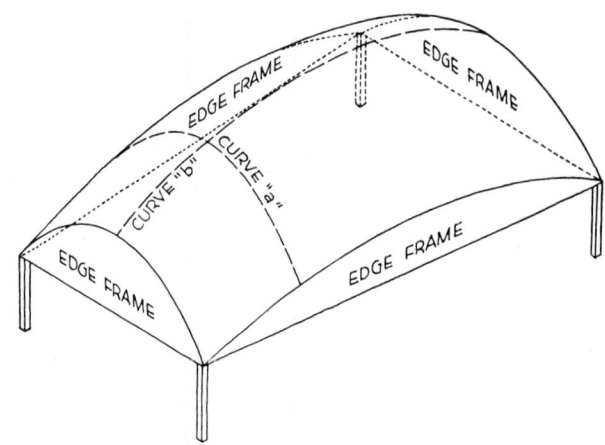

Extreme Cases:

Curve "b" of much greater radius than curve "a"

Rise may be 1/8 of length of span; width may be 1/10 of length of span; depth may be 1/10 of width of span; Max. length of span 500 ft or ▶ more. This shell approaches an arch of curved cross section. This type can be effectively combined with anticlastic shells of similar dimensions to form a corrugated surface (see B–3, Sheet 50).

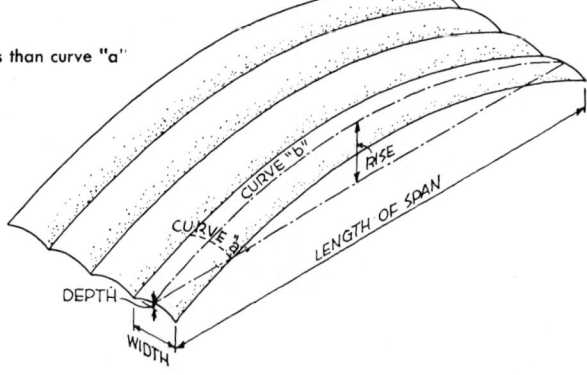

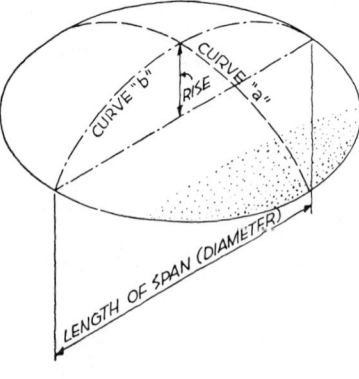

Curve "b" of same radius as curve "a"

Thickness is based on same considerations as for shells curved in one direction (see Sheet 42). Danger of buckling starts with 2 5/8 in. thickness for 100-ft radius of curvature. For nonspherical shells, thickness should be increased at points where radius of curvature decreases in comparison with radius of imaginary circumscribed sphere.

REFERENCES: As listed on Sheet 53 (see especially Eric C. Molke and J. E. Kalinka, Journal A.C.I., May–June 1938). See also International Association for Bridge and Structural Engineering, Zurich:

Vol. 1 (1932); F. Dischinger: "Contribution to theory of wall-like girders"

Vol. 4 (1936); F. Dischinger: "Shell construction in reinforced concrete"

▲

Rise may be as low as 1/8 of length of span. Max. length of span built 156 ft; much greater possible. This type is most simply considered as a surface of revolution.

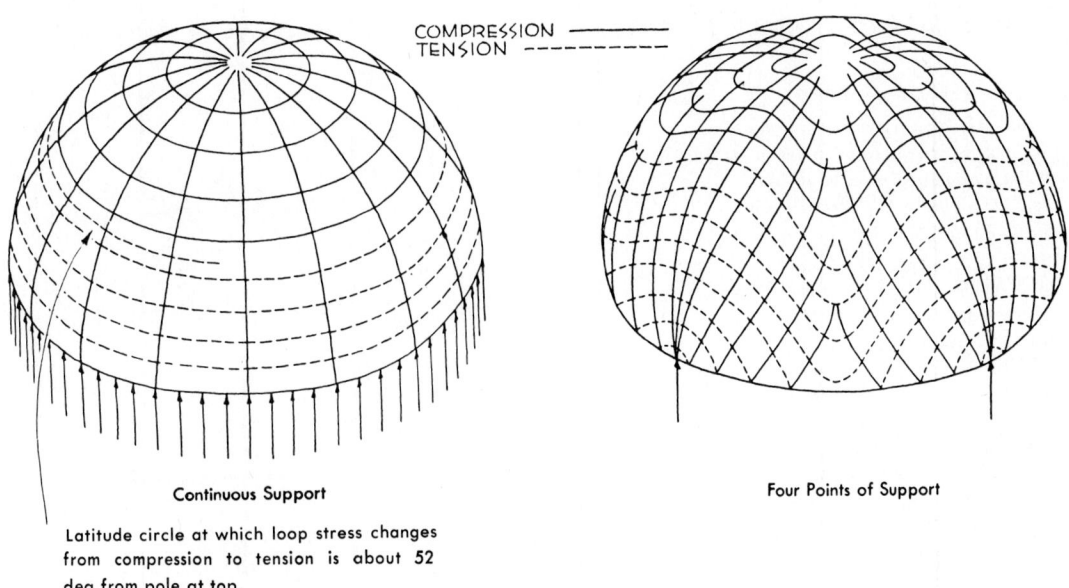

COMPRESSION ———
TENSION ---------

Continuous Support

Four Points of Support

Latitude circle at which loop stress changes from compression to tension is about 52 deg from pole at top.

Stress Trajectories for uniformly loaded spherical domes

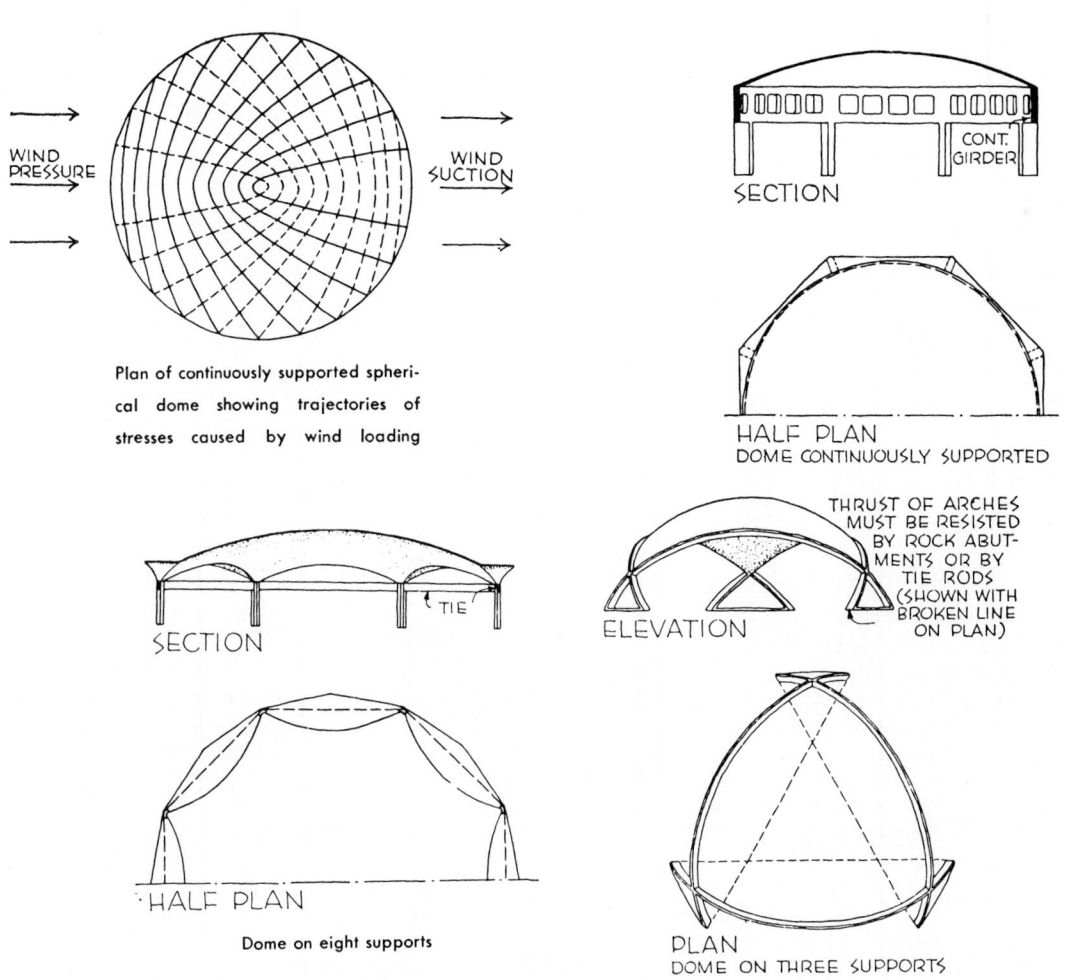

WIND PRESSURE

WIND SUCTION

Plan of continuously supported spherical dome showing trajectories of stresses caused by wind loading

SECTION
CONT. GIRDER

HALF PLAN
DOME CONTINUOUSLY SUPPORTED

SECTION
TIE

THRUST OF ARCHES MUST BE RESISTED BY ROCK ABUTMENTS OR BY TIE RODS (SHOWN WITH BROKEN LINE ON PLAN)

ELEVATION

HALF PLAN
Dome on eight supports

PLAN
DOME ON THREE SUPPORTS

Examples of various arrangements of supports

B-1 BOTH SETS OF CENTERS OF CURVATURE BELOW SHELL (synclastic or dome surfaces)

Membrane forces in spherical domes

If the thickness of a dome does not exceed 2 per cent of the radius of its sphere, the shell can be assumed to act as a membrane. In other words, only uniform tensile or compressive forces would act throughout the thickness of the dome; there could be no bending within the shell thickness. (If the shell were not continuously supported at its edges, however, some bending would probably occur in those regions.)

At any given point on the dome, specified by its colatitude or angular distance ϕ from the vertical axis, the meridian or vertical force (T_ϕ) and the hoop or horizontal force (T_θ) can be found from the diagrams and equations for a uniform dead load (weight w per unit area of dome surface), for a uniform snow load (weight w_s per unit area of plan projection), and for a uniform collar load such as an oculus (weight p per unit length of collar). These forces will have the dimensions of force per unit of length measured along the surface of the dome (that is, pounds per foot of latitude or meridian circle). To convert them to stress, divide by the thickness.

Example

Given $R = 150$ ft, thickness 4 in., and $w = 50$ psi; find the stresses at $\phi = 20$ deg. From Diagram A, we read: $T_\phi = 0.52\ Rw$, and $T_\theta = 0.43\ Rw$.

$T_\phi = 0.52 \times 150 \times 50 = 3,900$ lb per lin ft

$$\text{meridian stress} = \frac{3,900}{12\ \text{in./ft} \times 4\ \text{in.}}$$

$$= 81.2\ \text{psi (compression)}$$

$T_\theta = 0.43 \times 150 \times 50 = 3,225$ lb per lin ft

$$\text{hoop stress} = \frac{3,225}{12 \times 4}$$

$$= 67.2\ \text{psi (compression)}$$

Note from the diagrams that, for dead and snow loads, the hoop forces are compressive until quite far down (52 deg for dead load, 45 deg for snow); for collar loads, however, they are always tensile. The meridian forces are always compressive, except for an internal outward pressure or wind load (wind loads are usually not critical for a concrete dome, although they may be for a light metal frame dome).

Reactive forces in spherical domes

The lower edge of a dome must of course be supported. Unless the dome is a complete hemisphere, there will always be a horizontal component of the thrust at that

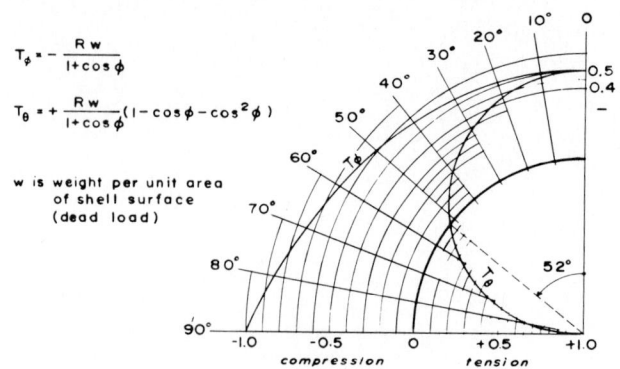

$$T_\phi = -\frac{Rw}{1+\cos\phi}$$

$$T_\theta = +\frac{Rw}{1+\cos\phi}(1-\cos\phi-\cos^2\phi)$$

w is weight per unit area of shell surface (dead load)

A. UNIFORM SHELL LOADING
multiply values by R·w

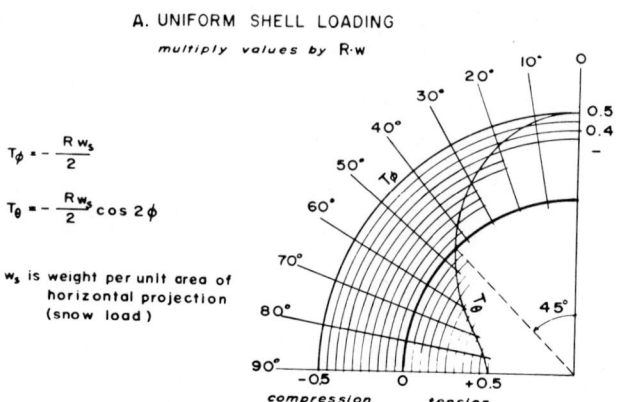

$$T_\phi = -\frac{Rw_s}{2}$$

$$T_\theta = -\frac{Rw_s}{2}\cos 2\phi$$

w_s is weight per unit area of horizontal projection (snow load)

B. UNIFORM VERTICAL LOADING
multiply values by R·w$_s$

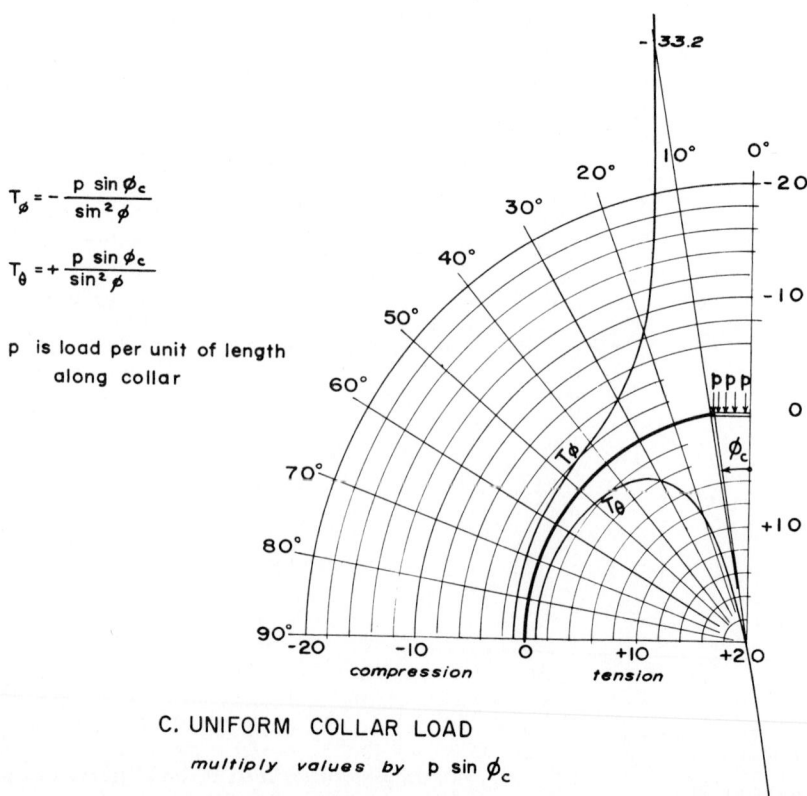

$$T_\phi = -\frac{p\ \sin\phi_c}{\sin^2\phi}$$

$$T_\theta = +\frac{p\ \sin\phi_c}{\sin^2\phi}$$

p is load per unit of length along collar

C. UNIFORM COLLAR LOAD
multiply values by p sin ϕ_c

B-1(cont.) BOTH SETS OF CENTERS OF CURVATURE BELOW SHELL

edge; this thrust is usually resisted by a tension ring. The magnitude of the total tension in the ring (usually the largest concentration of force in the structure) can be found by using the graph for coefficients, where ϕ_E is the colatitude of the lower edge. The vertical reaction at the lower edge is $T_{\phi_E} \sin \phi_E$; for convenience, the broken line in the graph gives values of $\sin \phi_E$.

Example

Given $R = 150$ ft, thickness 4 in., $w = 50$ psi, and $\phi_E = 35$ deg; find total tension in supporting ring and vertical reaction per foot of edge. From Diagram A, we read: $T_\phi = 0.55\ Rw$.

$T_\phi = 0.55 \times 150 \times 50 = 4,125$ lb per lin ft

From the graph for coefficients, we read:
$T = 0.47\ RT_{\phi_E}$.

T = total tension in ring
$= 0.47 \times 150 \times 4,125 = 291,000$ lb

From the graph for coefficients, we read:
$V = 0.57 T_{\phi_E}$.

$V = 0.57 \times 4,125$
$= 2,350$ lb per lin ft of edge

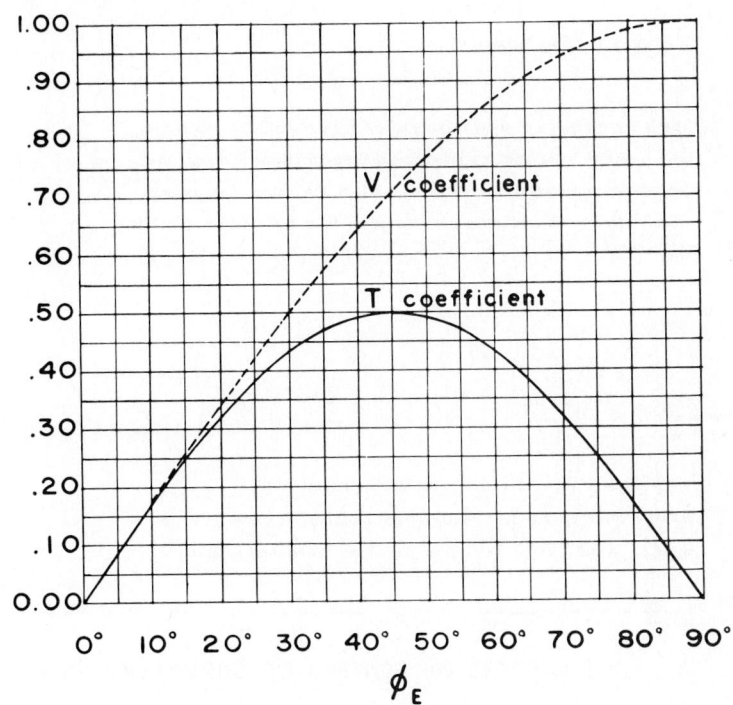

ϕ_E

COEFFICIENTS FOR T AND V

V = coefficient × T_{ϕ_E}

T = coefficient × T_{ϕ_E} × R

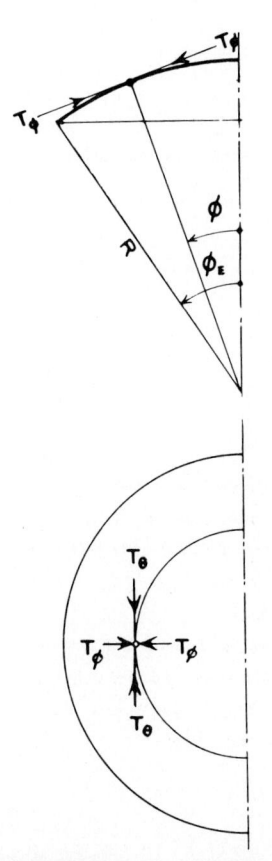

MEMBRANE FORCES

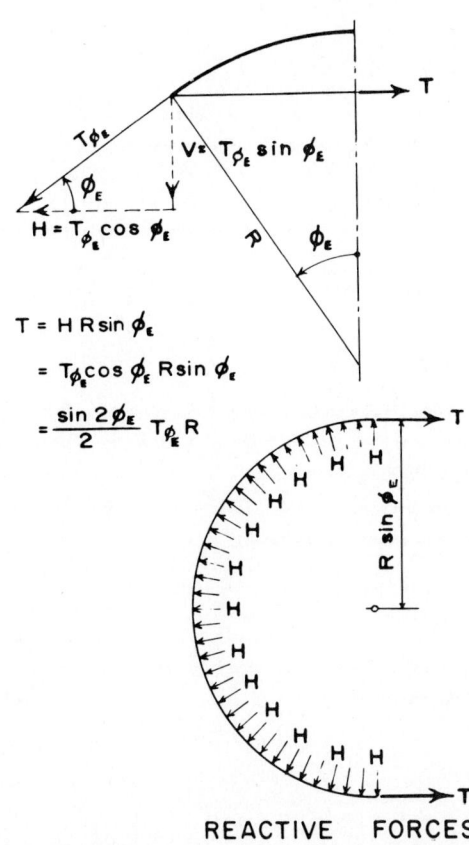

$T = H R \sin \phi_E$

$= T_{\phi_E} \cos \phi_E\ R \sin \phi_E$

$= \dfrac{\sin 2\phi_E}{2} T_{\phi_E} R$

REACTIVE FORCES

B-1(cont.)   **BOTH SETS OF CENTERS OF CURVATURE BELOW SHELL**

Polygonal Domes:

These are made up of short sections of cylindrical shells (curved in only one direction); the lines of intersection form stiffening frames. They approximate surfaces of revolution and at the same time provide simpler formwork and an easier transition to a non-circular ground plan.

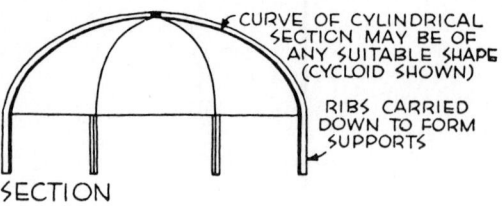

CURVE OF CYLINDRICAL SECTION MAY BE OF ANY SUITABLE SHAPE (CYCLOID SHOWN)

RIBS CARRIED DOWN TO FORM SUPPORTS

SECTION

NOTE: With symmetrical loading, no bending moments are induced in the ribs at the intersection of adjacent shell sectors

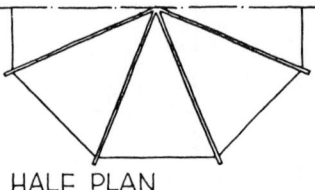

HALF PLAN

B-2   **BOTH SETS OF CENTERS OF CURVATURE ABOVE SHELL**

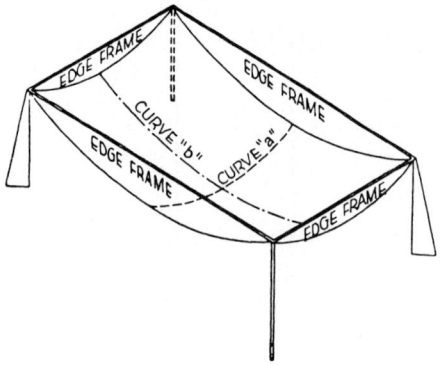

EDGE FRAME

CURVE "b"   CURVE "a"

A shell of this type is exactly the opposite of type **B-1** and the surface generated in same way, except that the center(s) of curvature of both curve "a" and curve "b" lie above the shell.

This is essentially a tensile form of relatively limited use, except for the bottoms of tanks (reservoirs, silos, etc.)

REFERENCES:

See reference noted on sheet 39; this book contains extensive bibliography.

Hajnal-Konyi: "Shell Concrete Construction" in Architect's Year Book:2. London 1947.

Felix Candela: "Simple Concrete Shell Structures." Journal American Concrete Institute December 1951.

Charles S. Whitney: "Cost of Long Span Concrete Shell Roofs." Journal American Concrete Institute June 1950.

Eric C. Molke and J. E. Kalinka: "Principles of Concrete Shell Design." Journal A.C.I. May–June 1938.

February 1953. A.C.I. Journal has three articles on shell construction:

Anton Tedesko "Construction Aspects of Thin-Shell Structures."

Charles S. Whitney "Reinforced Concrete Thin Shell Structures."

Pier Luigi Nervi "Precast concrete offers new possibilities for design of shell structures."

International Association for Bridge and Structural Engineering, Zurich; many articles in their published "Mémoires."

Interviews with:

Robert Zaborowski, of Roberts and Schaefer Co.; Boyd G. Anderson and Edward Cohen, of Ammann and Whitney; John Hogan of the Portland Cement Association.

B-3   ONE SET OF CENTERS OF CURVATURE BELOW SHELL AND ONE SET OF CENTERS OF CURVATURE ABOVE SHELL

(Anticlastic or saddle shaped surfaces)

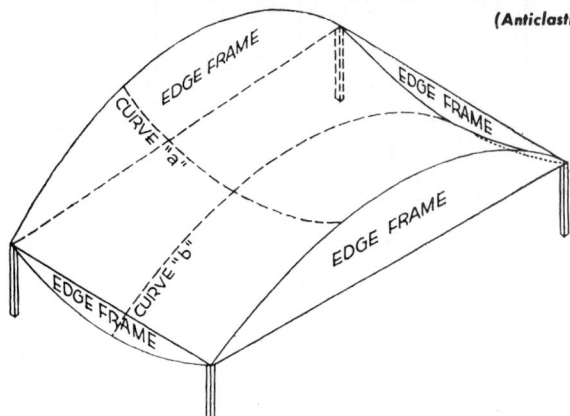

General Case

The difference between this type and B-1 & B-2 is that the centers of curvature of curve "a" are on the opposite side of the shell from the centers of curvature of curve "b."

This type of shell derives greater stiffness from its shape alone than any other type.

In practice this form is used as either a hyperbolic paraboloid or as a conoid. (Hyperboloids of one sheet also have been used.)

B-3-a   HYPERBOLIC PARABOLOIDS

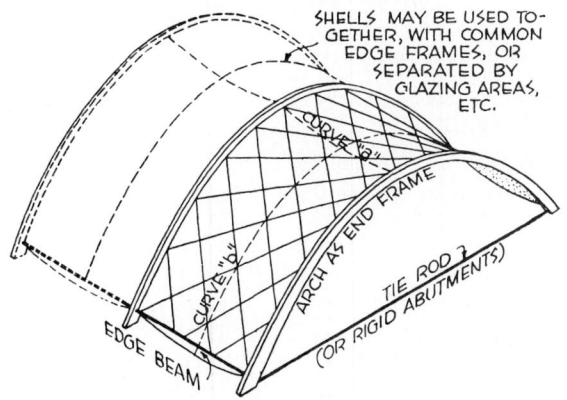

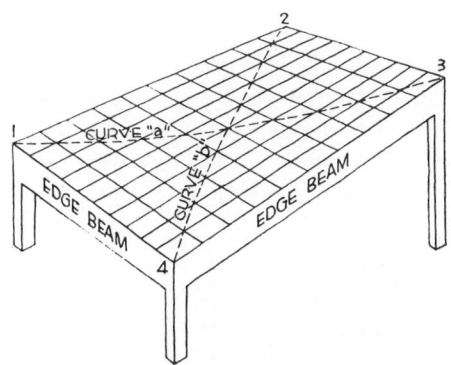

In a true hyperbolic paraboloid surface, both curves "a" and "b" are parabolas, while the traces of horizontal planes intersecting the surface are hyperbolas. The surface is generated by connecting successive points on the two arches by straight lines, which lie in parallel planes. The fact that the warped surface is created from straight lines makes formwork relatively simple. The arches can be built first and straight beams hung on them to support the form boarding. (See section of this book on "Useful Curves and Curved Surfaces")

STRAIGHT EDGED FORM

If one corner of a rectangle in plan is raised above the other three and straight lines lying in parallel planes are drawn connecting each pair of opposite sides, a hyperbolic paraboloid surface will be generated.

Corner 3 is higher than 1, 2 & 4; edges 1–2 and 3–4 are divided into equal spaces and the points are connected; similarly edges 1–4 and 2–3.

Corner 3 might also be located below instead of above the other three

Example of anticlastic and synclastic shells used together to form continuous corrugated surface

A shell of this type has been built of 330 ft span, 40 ft rise, spacing of corrugations (crest to crest) 32 ft, depth of corrugation 7 ft, shell thickness 2⅜ in., with corrugations stiffened by diaphragms. (Marignane Airport, Marseilles, 1952; Nicolas Esquillan, Engineer)

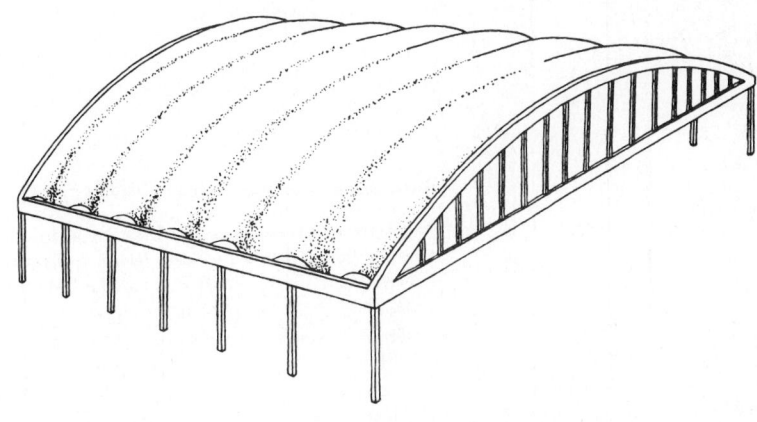

B-3-a(cont.) HYPERBOLIC PARABOLOIDS

Combinations of straight edged form

NOTE: In addition to edge stiffeners, beams or thickenings of the slab are required along lines of gables or abrupt changes (knuckles) in the surface of the shell

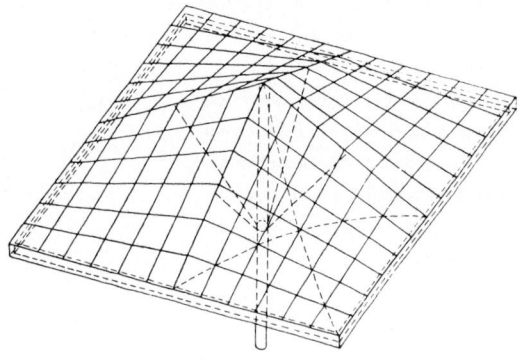

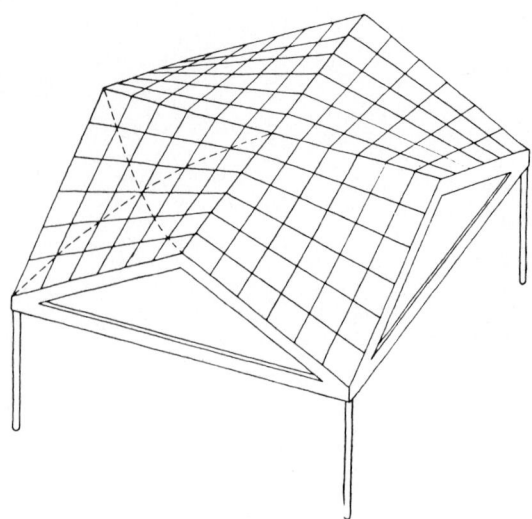

The Umbrella Form

Made by combining four hyperbolic paraboloid surfaces, each one having three low corners and one high corner. Diagonal struts may be required from column to ridges to take eccentric loading. This type would require column to be cantilevered up from wide footing if used alone. Stability can be achieved more easily by using minimum of four

The Four Gable Form

Made by combining four hyperbolic-paraboloid surfaces, each one having three high corners and one low corner.

This type can stand alone or be combined: (downspouts can be provided in the columns)

 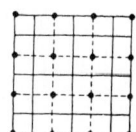

B-3-b CONOIDS

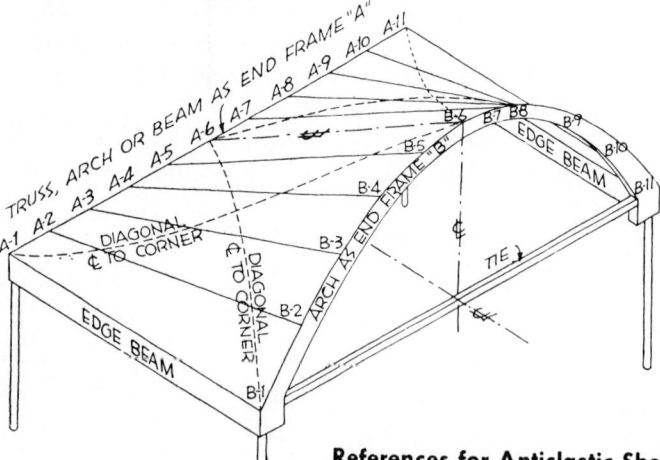

Surface generated by straight lines connecting corresponding points on opposite sides. Points are found by passing vertical planes parallel to vertical center line plane through both sides. Sides "A" and "B" may both be curved (of different curvatures), or one side may be straight and one curved (as shown).

Lines A-1 to B-1, A-2 to B-2, A-3 to B-3, etc., are all straight and all lie in planes parallel to center line plane through A-6 and B-6.

References for Anticlastic Shells

Most Important: International Association for Bridge & Structural Engineering, Zurich—Vol. 4, pp. 1–112 F. Aimond: "Étude Statique De Voiles Minces En Paraboloide Hyperbolique Travaillant Sans Flexion"
• Ditto—Vol. 2, pp. 167–179. M. Fauconnier "Essai De Rupture D'une Voute Mince Conoïde En Beton Armé"
• Ditto—Vol. 3, pp. 295–332. B. Laffaille—"Memoire Sur L'Étude Générale Des Surfaces Gauches Minces"
• American Concrete Institute Journal, March 1953—F. Candela "Skew Shells Make Unusual House Roof."

B-3-b(cont.)   CONOIDS

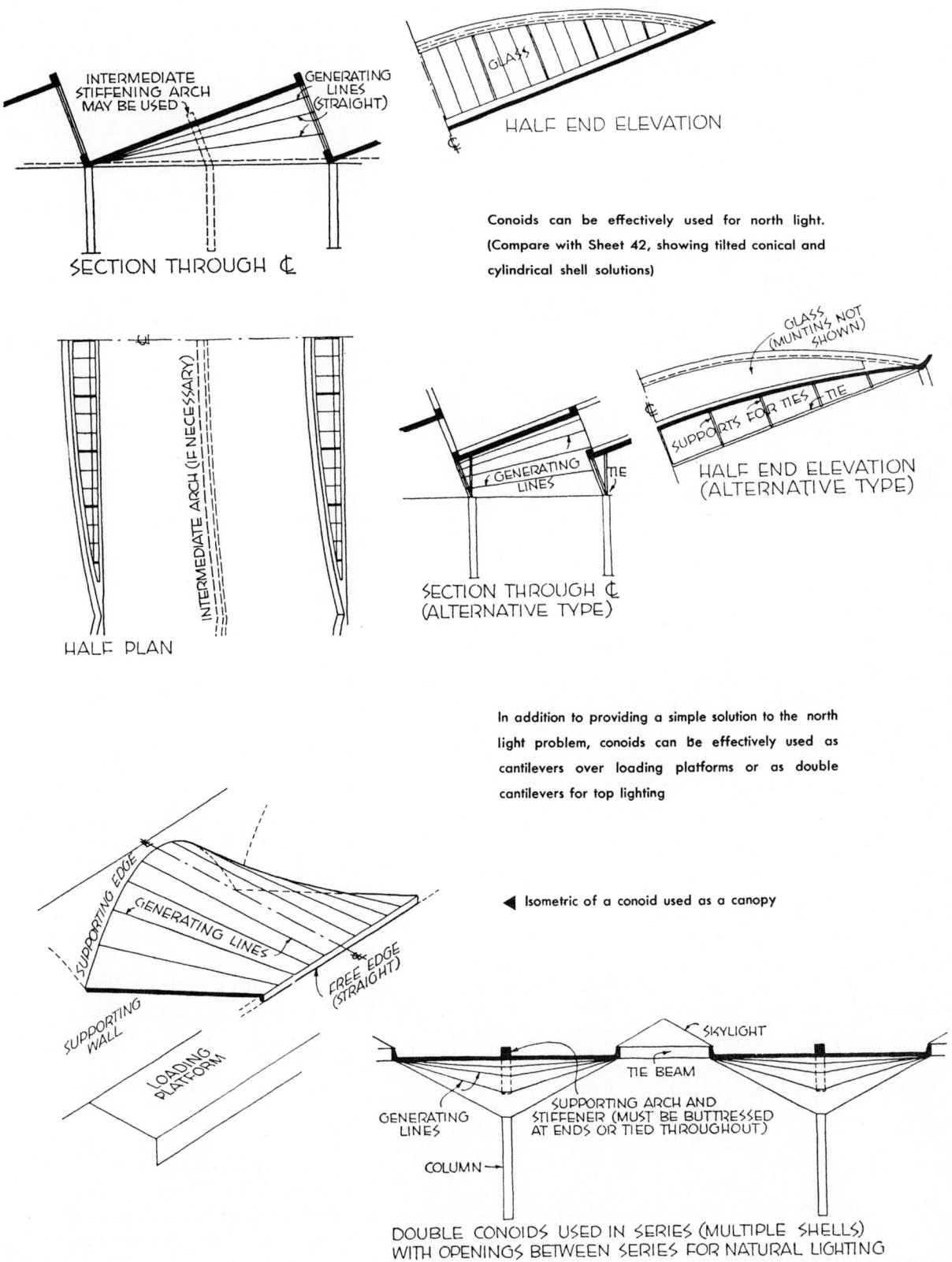

INTERMEDIATE STIFFENING ARCH MAY BE USED

GENERATING LINES (STRAIGHT)

SECTION THROUGH ℄

GLASS

HALF END ELEVATION

Conoids can be effectively used for north light. (Compare with Sheet 42, showing tilted conical and cylindrical shell solutions)

INTERMEDIATE ARCH (IF NECESSARY)

HALF PLAN

GENERATING LINES

TIE

SECTION THROUGH ℄ (ALTERNATIVE TYPE)

GLASS (MUNTINS NOT SHOWN)

SUPPORTS FOR TIES   TIE

HALF END ELEVATION (ALTERNATIVE TYPE)

In addition to providing a simple solution to the north light problem, conoids can be effectively used as cantilevers over loading platforms or as double cantilevers for top lighting

◄ Isometric of a conoid used as a canopy

SUPPORTING EDGE

GENERATING LINES

FREE EDGE (STRAIGHT)

SUPPORTING WALL

LOADING PLATFORM

SKYLIGHT

TIE BEAM

GENERATING LINES

SUPPORTING ARCH AND STIFFENER (MUST BE BUTTRESSED AT ENDS OR TIED THROUGHOUT)

COLUMN →

DOUBLE CONOIDS USED IN SERIES (MULTIPLE SHELLS) WITH OPENINGS BETWEEN SERIES FOR NATURAL LIGHTING

C   PRISMATIC SHELLS (also called folded-plate, hipped-plate, or tilted-slab construction)

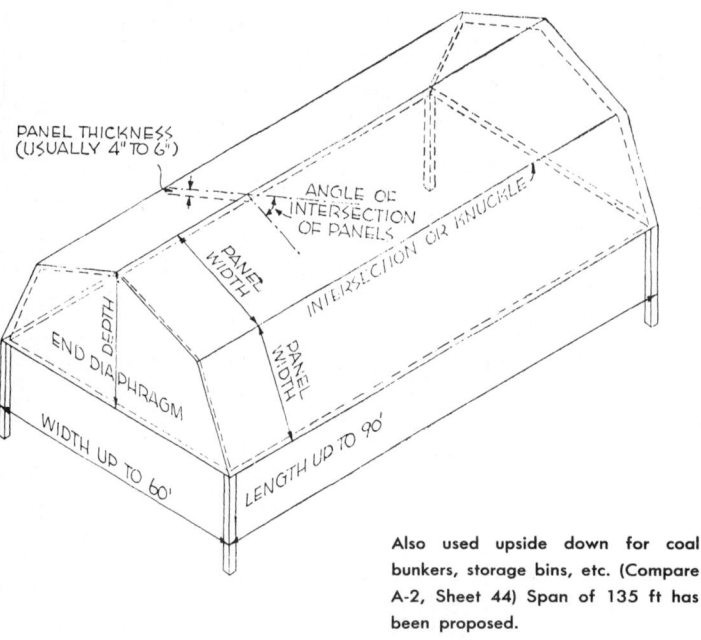

Also used upside down for coal bunkers, storage bins, etc. (Compare A-2, Sheet 44) Span of 135 ft has been proposed.

These are approximations to the curved shells made by flat panels. They bear a relationship to curved shells which is similar to that of a rigid frame to an arch. The transverse bending moments in the panel slabs are much greater than those of a curved shell, and the thickness must be greater. Each panel can be considered as supported at the intersection lines or knuckles and becomes one span in a system of continuous beams.

In the longitudinal direction there is a gradual transition from a pure shell effect for shells with panels which are wide in relation to length to a pure bending effect for shells with panels which are long compared to width. In the latter case the shell may be considered as a beam and stresses figured from the moment of inertia of the whole cross section.

Although prismatic shells are rarely used for very long spans, because the thickness of concrete and the dead load are greater than for curved shells, they may be more economical for shorter spans. The savings on formwork may offset the cost of additional concrete.

Simply Supported Single Shell (Compare A-1, Sheet 6)

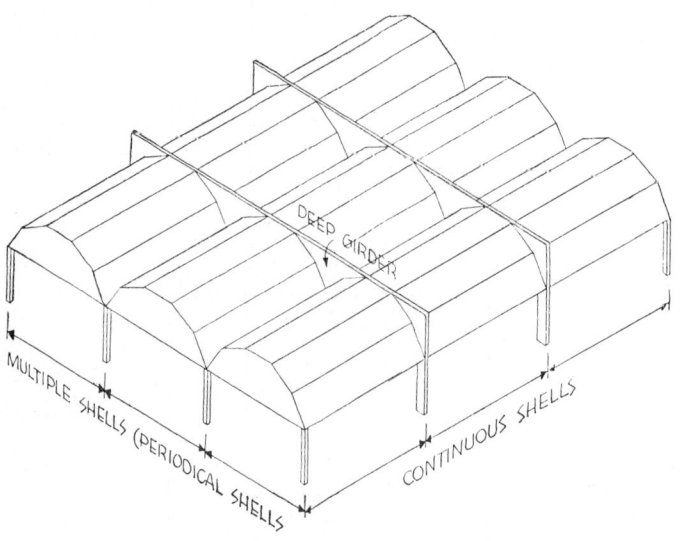

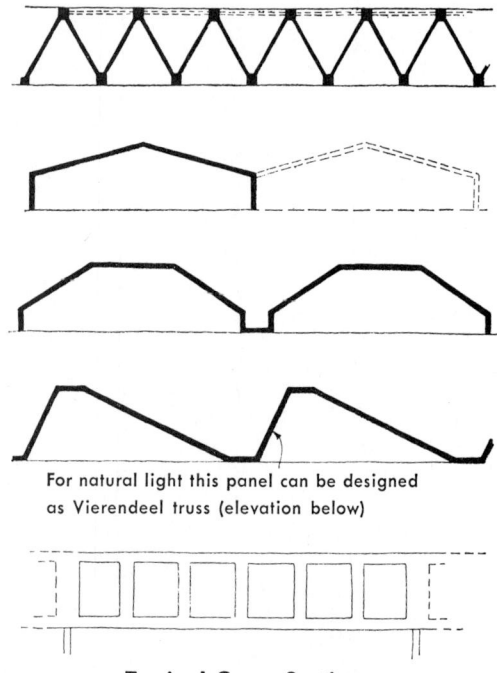

For natural light this panel can be designed as Vierendeel truss (elevation below)

Typical Cross Sections

In addition to prismatic shells which approximate the shells of single curvature, prismatic shells can also be used to approximate shells of double curvature (compare B-1, Sheet 45, and B-2, Sheet 49):

REFERENCES:

American Concrete Institute Journal, Feb., 1953. H. Craemer: "Design of Prismatic Shells."
Ditto—Jan., 1947. G. Winter and I. M. Pei "Hipped Plate Construction."
Also Articles in Publications of Int'l Ass'n For Bridge & Structural Engineering.

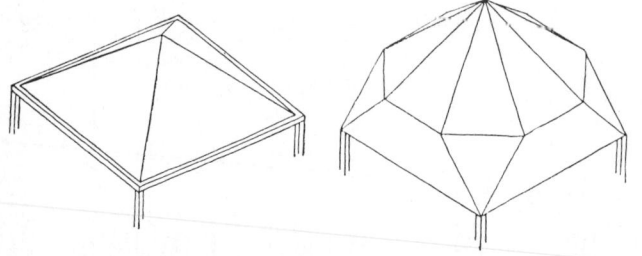

Innumerable crystalline shapes are possible. They may be used as shown or upside down.

By JOHN G. MASCIONI, *P.E., Associate Professor, School of Architecture, Pratt Institute. Revised by Y. S. LEE, Associate, Severud-Perrone-Szegezdy-Sturm, Consulting Engineers*

Basic floor framing schemes are illustrated and described on the following pages. For comparison, typical designs have been developed for each scheme. Four bay sizes, 20 by 20 ft, 20 by 24 ft, 20 by 28 ft, and 20 by 32 ft, have been investigated to note the relative effect of span length on the depth of construction. In general, the average area of the four bays, 520 sq ft, may be considered larger than the economical size bay for wood construction and solid concrete floor systems; approximately economical for the ribbed concrete floor sys-

tems; and smaller than the economical bay for steel and prestressed concrete floor systems. Design is based upon a total superimposed load of 60 lb per sq ft. All dead loads with the exception of the structural floor should be deducted to arrive at the effective live load. As the key plan shows, equal spans are assumed on the sides of the bay investigated. Beams, therefore, are designed to support loads from adjacent bays. Design of the spandrel beam, which depends on all the various construction and architectural re-

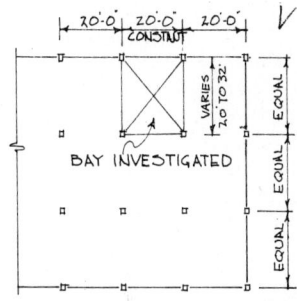

quirements, has been omitted. Reinforced concrete design is based upon 3000 psi (f_c') concrete. The allowable stress in steel for both steel framing and reinforced concrete is 20,000 psi.

Wood plank and beam

The depth of floor construction is considered the thickness of the decking which is usually a nominal thickness of 2 in., 3 in., or 4 in. Decking can be either planking laid flat or laminated lumber laid on edge and side nailed. The underside of the decking is usually left exposed. Minimum depth of construction, an important advantage, produces large deflections and limits the application of this system primarily to roofs. Random length planking in which only one end bears on a support is the most economical. Design is based upon an E = 1,760,000 psi for wood beams and 1,800,000 for glue-laminated girders. In smaller buildings a post could be placed under the beams thereby eliminating the girder.

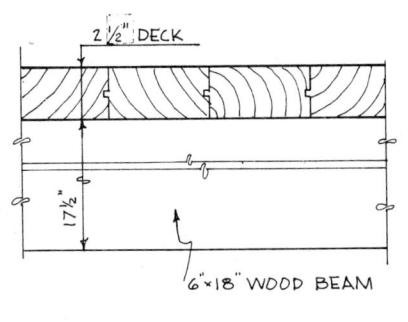

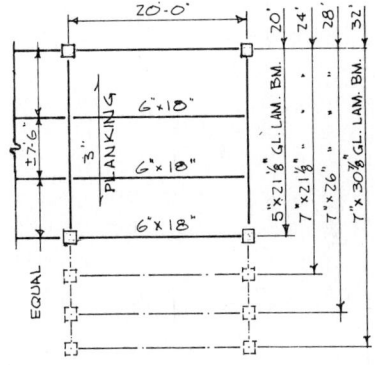

Open-web steel joists

This floor system is widely used and is very economical for light occupancy loads. In addition to the poured concrete slab shown here, it is employed with wide variety of decking and planking commercially available. Open webs facilitate the installation of pipes, ducts, and conduits. Joists tested by the Steel Joist Institute are standardized in depth up to 72 in. for spans up to 144 ft for roofs. The span of joists should not exceed 24 times the depth.

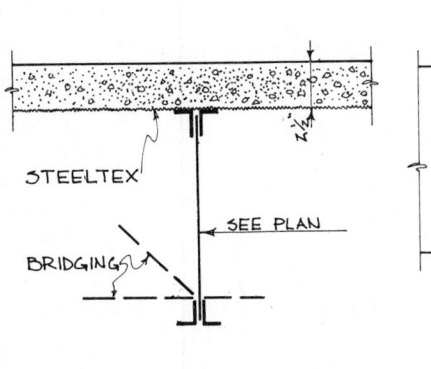

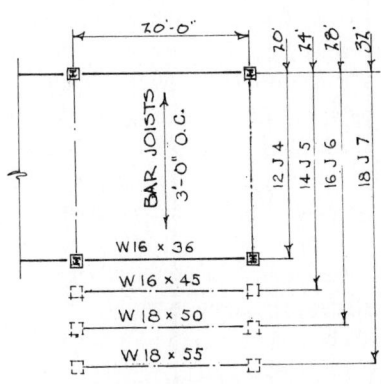

Steel beams and concrete slab

This system is one of the oldest fire-resistant floor systems. Beams should be spaced at approximately 8 ft to permit the use of welded wire fabric. Light weight concrete is used to reduce the dead load of the slab. For its principal application, office buildings, fill is required for the installation of utilities. A modification of this system consists of using lighter sections, such as Junior beams, at closer spacing so that standard plywood forms may be clipped to flanges and easily removed after the slab has hardened.

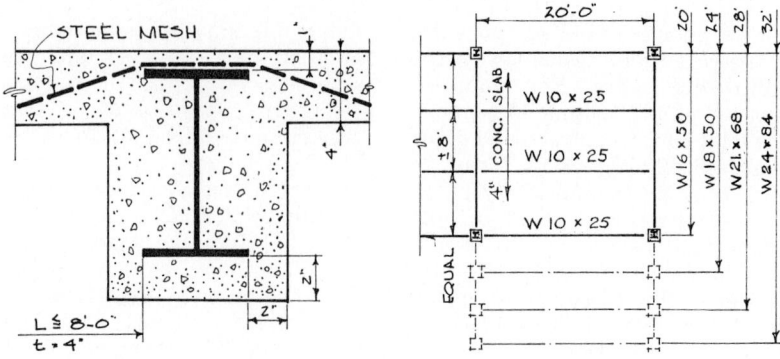

Composite construction

For many years composite construction was confined to the design of highway and bridge roadways where the relationships between deck slab and supporting steel members were ideally suited to composite design criteria. In recent years, with the introduction of metal deck doubling as forms, spray-on fireproofing displacing poured concrete haunches, etc., use of composite design in building construction has become more attractive.

By the use of steel shear connectors (usually short pieces of straight or bent steel bars or plates welded to top of steel beams), the concrete slab and supporting steel beams are made to act as a unit to resist bending moment efficiently. The steel studs transfer the horizontal shear from the steel beam to the reinforced concrete slab, making the best use of concrete in compression. The net result is a reduction in the weight and depth of steel beam required to support loads of comparable simple span steel beams. This type of design offers no economic advantage for short span construction; therefore no designs are shown for spans of less than 32 ft.

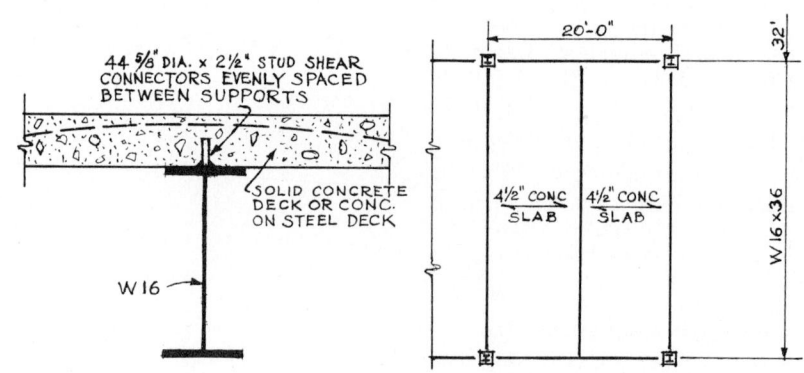

Cellular metal decking

The principal advantage of this floor system is the flexibility provided by the cells for the installation of utilities and for the location of electrical and telephone outlets. Other important advantages are light weight and fast erection. It is widely used to advantage in office buildings. Available in various depths for both short spans and long spans. Light weight concrete is not structural but serves as fill and finish and for fire protection of the top. In addition to the unit shown here, there are other similar products commercially available. For non-fireproof roofs, decking may be left exposed and the concrete fill omitted.

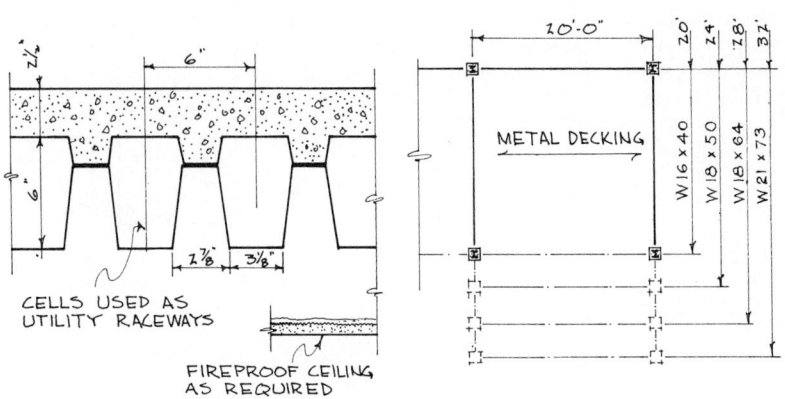

Composite metal decking

This floor system features an extremely efficient use of structural materials. The metal deck serves as positive steel reinforcement and as a form for the structural concrete slab. Like cellular metal decking, principal advantages of this system are light weight and fast erection. Decking may be either corrugated or of the rib type. On long spans temporary shoring may be required. Connections to the supporting steel are made by welding. Utilities are embedded in the concrete slab and do not affect the strength of the slab.

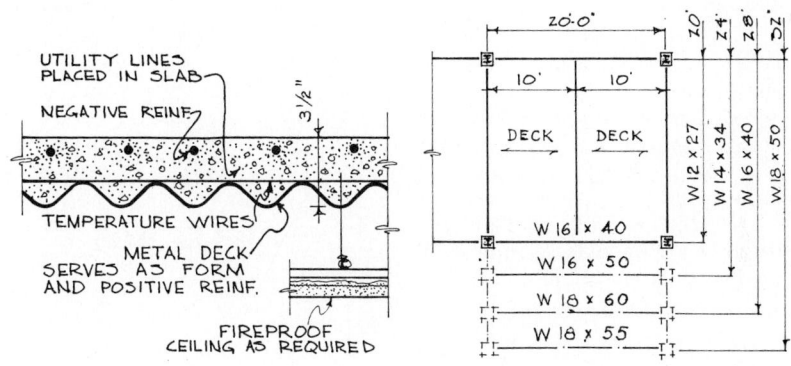

Long-span concrete plank

This floor system may be used with reinforced concrete and masonry structures as well as with steel frames. The cores may serve as the passage of utility lines and can also be utilized for warm air heating systems. The slab used in this design employs prestressing only to control deflections that would be developed by the small depths of slab. The smooth undersurface of the slab may be caulked and painted directly. Other prestressed hollow-core units are available in widths up to 8 ft -0 in. and are usually called slabs rather than plank.

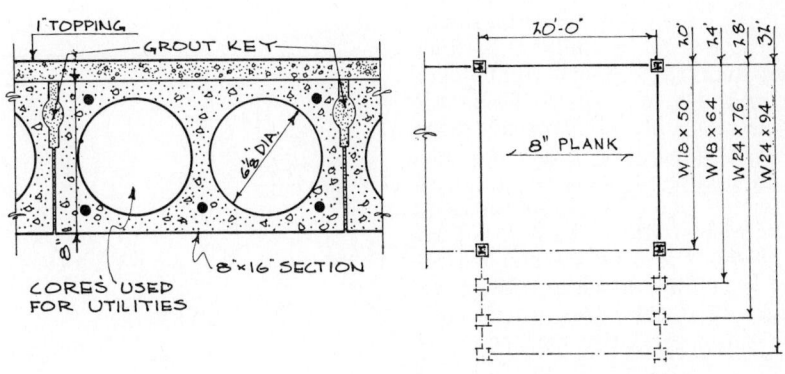

One-way solid slab

The conventional one-way solid slab with beams and girders is usually limited to smaller bays than those considered here. It is effective for supporting heavy and concentrated loads. Because of its' dead weight, this floor system is most suitable for spans less than 16 ft. The principal disadvantages of this system are the depth of construction and the formwork required for the beams and girders.

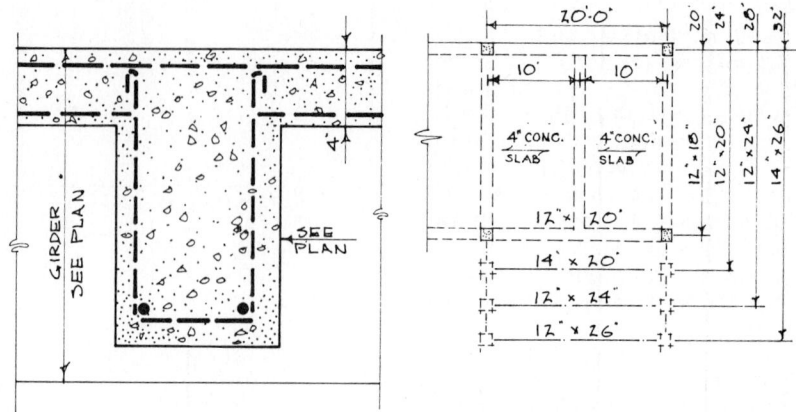

Slab band

This system is basically a one-way solid slab system with wide and shallow beams, called slab bands. It has been used for apartment buildings by Fred N. Severud, Consulting Engineer. The desirable reduction in beam depth increases the amount of reinforcement; however, this is compensated by a saving in slab reinforcement due to the slab haunches. Slab bands do not have to be centered on columns and exterior and interior columns may be placed independently of each other.

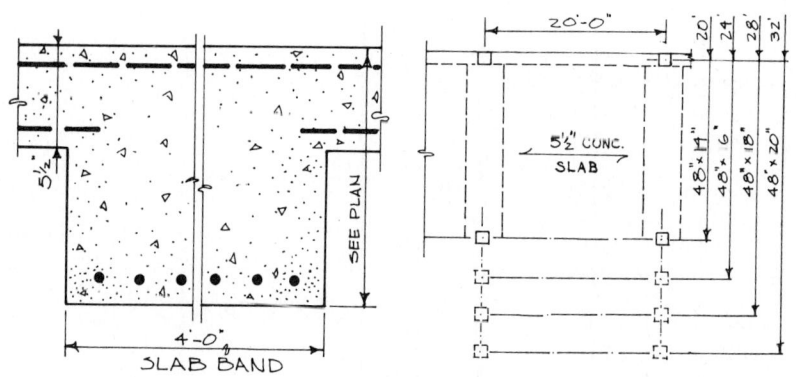

One-way concrete joist

The elimination of concrete that provides little or no moment resistance reduces the dead weight and permits this floor system to support light loads for fairly long spans. Re-usable metal or plastic pans are used for this purpose. Shear and moment capacity may be increased by the use of tapered forms at supports. Other methods of reducing the dead weight are the use of filler block and the placing of paper tubes in the slab. Both of the latter methods have the advantage of providing a flat under-surface that may be easily finished as a ceiling.

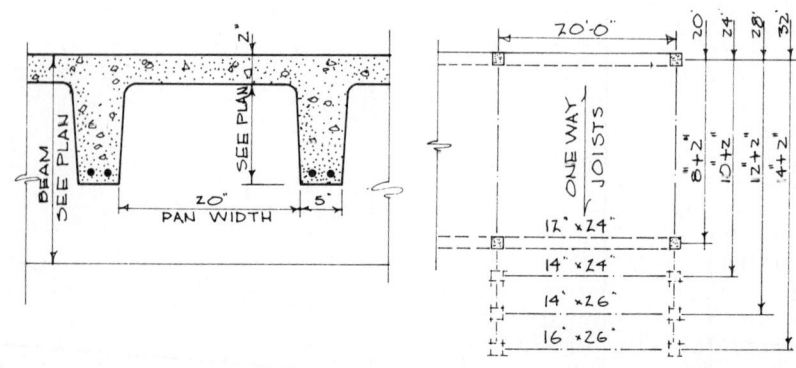

Two-way solid slab

The reinforcement and support of a slab in two directions makes this system very efficient structurally, particularly for heavy and concentrated loads, up to 30-ft spans. A practical limit for two way action is a ratio of long span to short span of approximately 1.7. All two-way systems should be used with fairly square bays for maximum efficiency. A modification of this system is a two-way joist or rib system in which unnecessary concrete is replaced by dome pans or filler blocks.

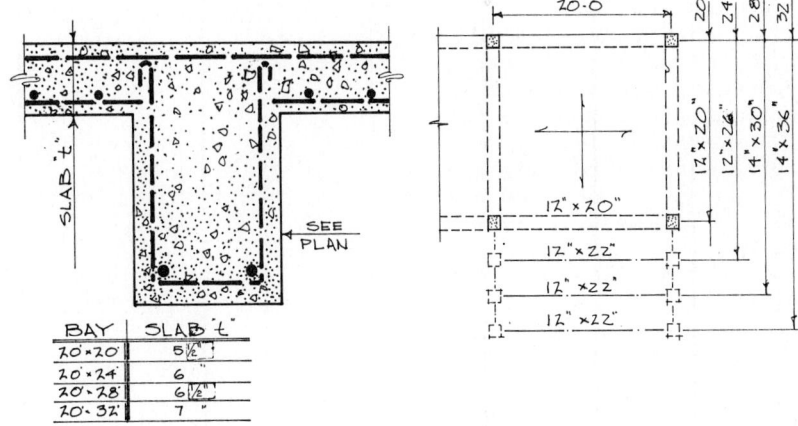

BAY	SLAB t
20 × 20	5½"
20 × 24	6
20 × 28	6½"
20 × 32	7"

Flat plate

Flat plate is a special type of flat slab construction in which column capitals and drop panels, as well as beams, are eliminated. It is used primarily for relatively light loads and modest spans. Shear at the columns is often the governing factor but may be controlled by special shearhead reinforcement. The increased amount of reinforcement due to shallow depth is usually offset by advantages of the flat plate system. These include minimum depth of construction, and simple and economical formwork which increases the speed of construction. Flat plate also permits flexibility in the location of columns.

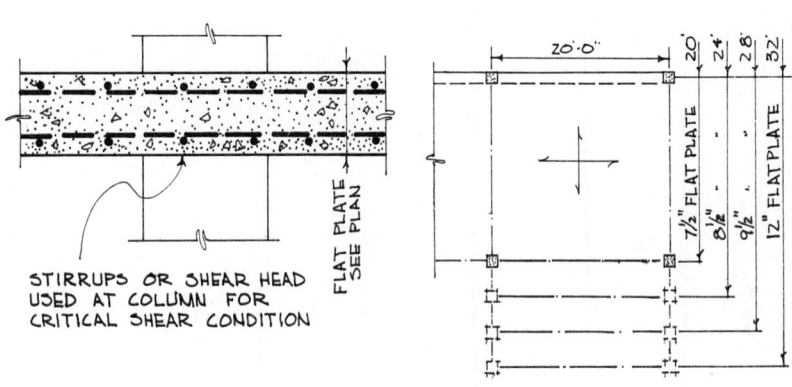

STIRRUPS OR SHEAR HEAD USED AT COLUMN FOR CRITICAL SHEAR CONDITION

Waffle slab

A waffle slab is a solid flat plate with dome forms placed in the slab to produce ribs or joists in two directions. The elimination of the dead weight of concrete not needed to resist moment increases the spans for which this system may be used. For the critical moments and shears that occur at the columns a solid area of concrete is required approximately equal to one third the span in each direction. Filler blocks, instead of dome forms, may also be used to replace concrete.

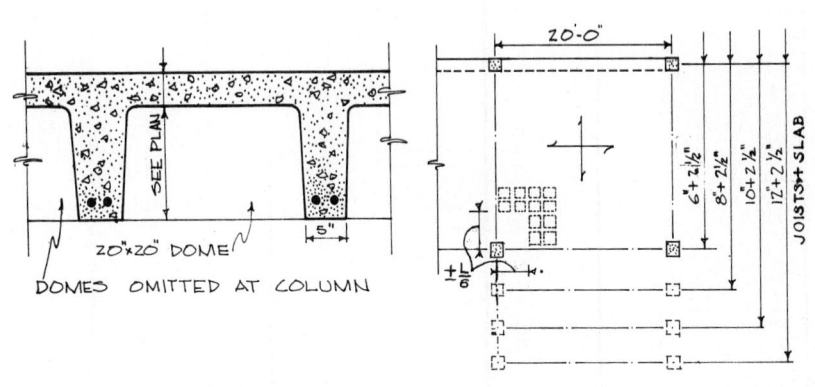

20"×20" DOME

DOMES OMITTED AT COLUMN

Prestressed concrete

The use of manufactured precast and prestressed concrete elements permits a wide variety of framing solutions. In addition to the double tee shown here, prestressed channels, joists, tee's and planks could be used. The feasibility of using prestressed elements will often depend upon the accessibility of a manufacturing plant. Prestressed concrete elements are of little advantage for short spans but can be used to advantage for long spans with all types of construction. Prestressing, in the form of posttensioning, may also be used effectively to increase the spans and capacity of cast-in-place concrete systems.

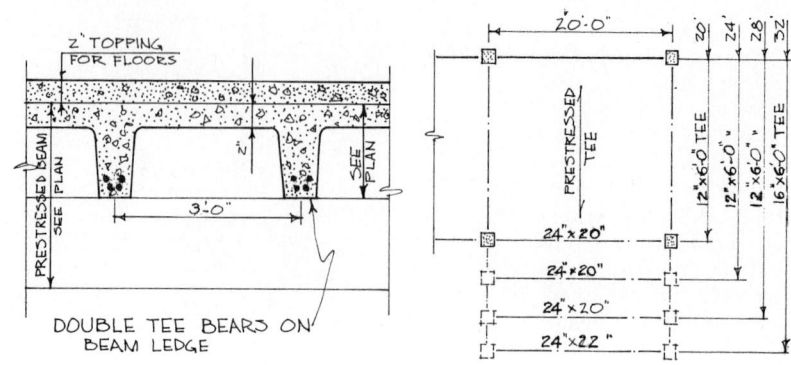

DOUBLE TEE BEARS ON BEAM LEDGE

Prepared with the assistance of the Brick Institute of America

REFERENCES

Masonry may be designed in accordance with any of four different standards. The standards used for the design will be dictated by the type of masonry material being used and by the type of design, whether standard empirical design or engineered masonry design. Each of these standards is complete in its approach to the design of masonry. However, the theory and assumptions within the standards differ, and thus the designer should not—under most circumstances—attempt to combine them. The four standards are:

1. *American National Standard Building Code Requirements for Masonry*, ANSI A41.1 —1953, R1970. This standard covers the design of nonreinforced masonry constructed of brick, structural clay tile, concrete masonry units, glass block, stone, and plain concrete. It covers the design of these materials used independently or in combination. The standard provides minimum wall thickness, maximum heights, and maximum lateral support requirements. Because it is for all masonry units, it is based on conservative compressive stresses.

2. *American National Standard Building Code Requirements for Reinforced Masonry*, ANSI A41.2—1960, R1970. This standard covers the design of reinforced masonry constructed of brick, structural clay tile, concrete masonry units, or a combination of these materials.

3. *Building Code Requirements for Engineered Brick Masonry, Brick Institute of America*, 1969. This standard provides for minimum requirements for the design and construction of brick masonry of solid masonry units both plain (nonreinforced) and reinforced. It does not include requirements for construction using hollow units or requirements for fire protection.

4. *Specifications for the Design and Construction of Loadbearing Concrete Masonry*, NCMA, 1970. This specification provides minimum requirements for the design and construction of loadbearing concrete masonry, both plain and reinforced.

MASONRY MATERIALS

Masonry materials should conform to the following standards of quality of the American Society for Testing and Materials (ASTM), American National Standards Institute (ANSI), and American Concrete Institute (ACI):

Brick, clay or shale, solid, building (common): ANSI/ASTM C62-75a, Grade SW for use in contact with earth subject to freezing and for all floors regardless of exposure,

Table 1. Mortar types (ASTM C270–73)

Mortar type	Minimum average compressive strength of three 2-in. cubes at 28 days, psi	Parts by volume			
		Portland cement	Masonry cement	Hydrated lime or lime putty	Aggregate measured in damp, loose condition
M	2,500	1	1 (Type II)		Not less than 2¼ and not more than 3 times the sum of the volumes of the cements and lime used.
		1		¼	
S	1,800	½	1 (Type II)		
		1		Over ¼ to ½	
N	750		1 (Type II)		
		1		Over ½ to 1¼	
O	350		1 (Type I or II)		
		1		Over 1¼ to 2½	
K	75	1		Over 2½ to 4	

Table 2. Types of mortar required for various kinds of masonry

Kind of masonry	Types of mortar required
Foundations:	
Footings	M or S
Walls of solid units	M, S, or N
Walls of hollow units	M or S
Hollow walls	M or S
Masonry other than foundation masonry:	
Piers of solid masonry	M, S, or N
Piers of hollow units	M or S
Walls of solid masonry	M, S, N, or O
Walls of solid masonry, other than parapet walls or rubble stone walls, not less than 12 in. thick nor more than 35 ft. in height, supported laterally at intervals not exceeding 12 times the wall thickness	M, S, N, O, or K
Walls of hollow units; loadbearing or exterior, and hollow walls 12 in. or more in thickness	M, S, or N
Hollow walls, less than 12 in. in thickness where assumed design wind pressure:*	
(a) exceeds 20 psf	M or S
(b) does not exceed 20 psf	M, S, or N
Glass-block masonry	M, S, or N
Nonbearing partitions or fireproofing composed of structural clay tile or concrete masonry units	M, S, N, O, or gypsum
Gypsum partition tile or block	Gypsum
Fire brick	Refractory air-setting mortar
Linings of existing masonry, either above or below grade	M or S
Masonry other than above	M, S, or N

* For design wind pressures, see section on Design Loads.

Grade MW for all other exterior uses, Grade NW for all interior uses except floors.

Brick, clay or shale, solid, facing: ANSI/

ASTM C216-75a, Grade SW for use in contact with earth subject to freezing and for all floors, Grade MW elsewhere; Type FBS having a normal range of variation in color and dimension, Type FBX having a minimum of such variations, and Type FBA having a maximum nonuniformity in color, texture, and dimension for architectural effect.

Brick, clay or shale, hollow, building and facing: ANSI/ASTM C652-75, having a solid area not less than 60 nor more than 75 percent of gross area; Grades SW and MW as above; Types HBS, HBX, HBA as above, plus Type HBB for use where appearance is not a consideration.

Brick, sewer and manhole: ANSI/ASTM C32-73.

Brick, paving: ANSI/ASTM C7-42 (1972).

Brick, industrial floor: ASTM C410.

Brick, calcium silicate (sand-lime): ANSI/ASTM C73-67 (1972), Grade MW or SW as above.

Brick, concrete, building: ANSI/ASTM C55-71, Grade A where exposed to weather or soil.

Tile, structural clay, loadbearing, wall: ANSI/ASTM C34-62 (1975), Grade LBX where exposed to weather or soil, Grade LB elsewhere.

Tile, structural clay, nonloadbearing: ANSI/ASTM C56-71.

Tile, structural clay, facing: ANSI/ASTM C212-75, Grade FTX having minimum variation in color and dimension, Grade FTS having a normal range of variation and some minor defects.

Tile, structural clay, facing, ceramic glazed (also covers ceramic glazed brick and solid masonry units): ANSI/ASTM C126-71, Grade S for use with narrow joints, Grade SS having minimum variation in dimension; Type I, single-faced units; Type II, two-faced units.

Block, concrete, hollow, loadbearing: ANSI/ASTM C90-70, Grade A where exposed to weather or soil.

Block, concrete, hollow, nonloadbearing: ANSI/ASTM C129-73.

Block, concrete, solid, loadbearing: ANSI/ASTM C145-71.

Cast stone: ACI 704.

Chemical resistant masonry units: ANSI/ASTM C279-54 (1972).

Gypsum tile and block: ANSI/ASTM C52-54 (1972).

Mortar materials:

Hydrated lime: ANSI/ASTM C207-76, Type S.

Hydraulic hydrated lime: ANSI/ASTM C141-67.

Quicklime: ANSI/ASTM C5-59 (1974).

Masonry cement: ANSI/ASTM C91-71.

Natural cement: ANSI/ASTM C10-70a.

Portland cement: ANSI/ASTM C150-76, Type I, II, or III.

Air-entraining portland cement: ASTM C175, Type IA, IIA, or IIIA.

Blast-furnace-slag portland cement: ASTM C595, Type IS or ISA.

Gypsum: ANSI/ASTM C22-50 (1972).

Aggregate: ANSI/ASTM C144-76.

Mortar for unit masonry: ASTM C270-73. For types and proportions see Table 1. Mortar should be mixed with the maximum amount of water that it is possible to use and still produce a workable mix.

Mortar, portland cement-lime, for brick masonry: BIA MI-72.

Grout for unreinforced masonry: Type M, S, or N mortar to which sufficient water should be added to produce a pouring consistency.

Grout for reinforced masonry: ASTM C476-63 (1969); aggregate: ASTM C404-70.

Gypsum mortar: proportions by weight are one part gypsum to not more than three parts aggregate.

Table 3. Allowable compressive stresses in masonry

Construction; grade of unit	Allowable compressive stresses on gross cross-sectional area (except as noted), psi				
	Type M mortar	Type S mortar	Type N mortar	Type O mortar	Type K mortar
Solid masonry of brick and other solid units of clay or shale; sand-lime or concrete brick:					
8,000 psi or more	400	350	300	200	100
4,500 to 8,000 psi	250	225	200	150	100
2,500 to 4,500 psi	175	160	140	110	75
1,500 to 2,500 psi	125	115	100	75	50
Grouted solid masonry of brick and other solid units of clay or shale; sand-lime or concrete brick:					
4,500 psi or more	350	275	200		
2,500 to 4,500 psi	275	215	155		
1,500 to 2,500 psi	225	175	125		
Solid masonry of solid concrete masonry units:					
Grade A	175	160	140	100	
Grade B	125	115	100	75	
Masonry of hollow units	85	75	70		
Piers of hollow units, cellular spaces filled	105	95	90		
Hollow walls (cavity or masonry bonded)*					
Solid units:					
Grade A or 2,500 psi or more	140	130	110		
Grade B or 1,500 to 2,500 psi	100	90	80		
Hollow units	70	60	55		
Stone ashlar masonry:					
Granite	800	720	640	500	
Limestone or marble	500	450	400	325	
Sandstone or cast stone	400	360	320	250	
Rubble stone, coursed, rough, or random	140	120	100	80	

* On gross cross-sectional area of wall minus area of cavity between wythes (leaves). The allowable compressive stresses for cavity walls are based upon the assumption that the floor loads bear upon only one of the two wythes. When hollow walls are loaded concentrically, the allowable stresses may be increased by 25 per cent.

USES OF MORTAR TYPES

Table 2, from ANSI A41.1, gives the types of mortar required for various kinds of masonry. Brick Institute of America (BIA) recommends mortar uses for clay masonry as follows:

Selection of a particular mortar type is usually a function of the needs of the finished structural element. Where high winds are expected, high lateral strength is required, and hence mortar with high tensile bond strength is chosen. For loadbearing walls, high compressive strength may be the governing factor. Or considerations of durability, color, flexibility, etc. may be of utmost concern. Factors which improve one property of mortar often do so at the expense of others. For this reason, when selecting a mortar, evaluate properties of each type and choose that mortar which will best meet particular end-use requirements. Recommended general uses for mortars are discussed in the following paragraphs.

Type N mortar: Type N mortar is a medium-strength mortar suitable for general use in exposed masonry above grade. It is specifically recommended for parapet walls, chimneys, and exterior walls wherever these are subject to severe exposure.

Type S mortar: Tests indicate that the tensile bond strength between brick and Type S mortar approaches the maximum obtainable with cement-lime mortars. Type S mortar also has reasonably high compressive strength. It is recommended for use in reinforced masonry, for unreinforced masonry where maximum flexural strength is required, and for use where mortar adhesion is the sole bonding agent between facing and backing as it is, for example, with some ceramic veneers.

Type M mortar: Type M mortar has high compressive strength and somewhat greater durability than other mortar types. It is specifically recommended for unreinforced masonry below grade and in contact with earth, as in foundations, retaining walls, walks, sewers, and manholes.

Type O mortar: Type O mortar is a low-strength mortar suitable for general interior use in nonloadbearing masonry. It may be used for loadbearing walls of solid masonry where compressive stresses do not exceed 100 psi provided that exposures are not severe. In general, do not use Type O mortar where it will be subject to freezing action.

Allowable stresses on various types of masonry with the several types of mortar are given in Table 3, from ANSI A41.1.

EMPIRICALLY DESIGNED MASONRY (Summarized from ANSI A41.1)

Lateral support: The ratio of the unsupported height or length of a wall to its thickness should not exceed 20 for bearing walls of solid masonry laid in Type M, S, N, or O mortar, nor 12 if laid in Type K mortar, and should not exceed 18 for hollow walls or wall of hollow units regardless of the type of mortar used. To compute the ratio for cavity walls, the thickness should be taken as the sum of the thicknesses of the inner and outer wythes. The distance between lateral supports of nonbearing partitions should not exceed 36 times the actual thickness of the partition including plaster.

Lateral support, measured horizontally,

may be obtained from cross walls, piers, or buttresses; and measured vertically, from floors and roofs. Where floor or roof joists are parallel to the wall, metal anchors spaced not less than 6 ft apart horizontally, should engage at least three joists, which should be solidly bridged at these points.

For isolated piers, the ratio of unsupported height to the smallest dimension should not exceed 10; if built of hollow units, the ratio should not exceed 4, unless the cellular spaces are filled solidly with concrete or with Type M or S mortar.

Maximum heights and minimum thicknesses of bearing walls and foundation walls are given in Figs. 1 and 2, respectively.

ENGINEERED BRICK MASONRY

The 1969 BIA standard provides minimum requirements for the design and construction of engineered brick masonry. These requirements are predicated on a general analysis of the structure and are based on generally accepted analysis procedures.

In order to realize the full benefits of the stresses provided for in the standard, there is a requirement for architectural or engineering inspection of the workmanship. The inspection should be of such nature as to ascertain, in general, if the construction and workmanship are in accordance with the contract drawings and specifications.

The frequency of inspections should be such that the inspector can observe the various stages of the construction and that the work is being properly performed.

When there is no architectural or engi-

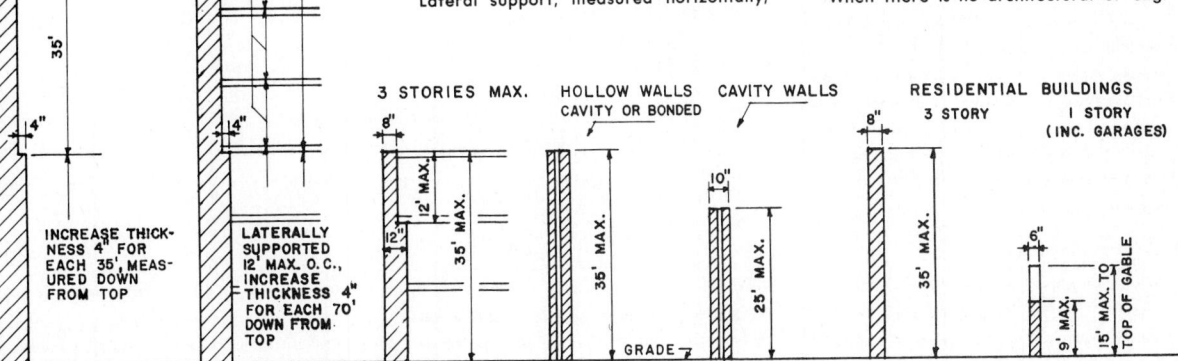

Fig. 1. Minimum thicknesses of masonry bearing walls

Rubble stone should be 4 in. thicker than shown above, but not less than 10 in. in any case. Poured concrete may be 2 in. thinner than shown above, but not less than 8 in. except where 6-in. walls are permitted. Non-bearing walls may be 4 in. thinner than shown above, but not less than 8 in., except where 6-in. walls are permitted.

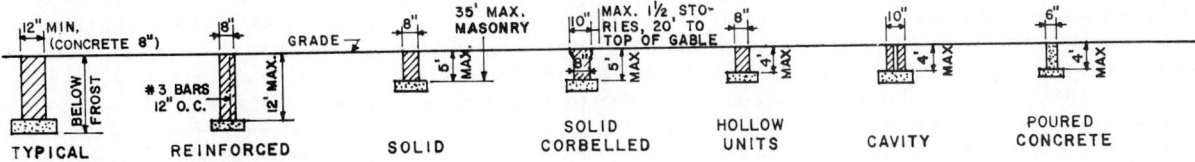

Fig. 2. Minimum thicknesses of masonry foundation walls

neering inspection as described above, the reduced allowable stresses and values provided in the standard must be used.

Materials

The strength (compressive, shearing, and transverse) of brick masonry is affected both by the properties of the brick units and the mortar in which they are laid. The compressive strength of the brick units has the greater effect on the compressive strength of the brick masonry. Although mortar is also a factor in compressive strength, its greater effect is on the transverse and shearing strengths of brick masonry.

For these reasons, there are specific requirements and limitations on materials for use with this standard.

Brick: Brick must conform to the requirements for grade MW or SW as specified in ASTM C62 or C216. In addition, brick used in loadbearing or shear walls must comply with the dimension and distortion tolerances specified for types FBS of ASTM C216. If the brick do not comply with these tolerance requirements, they may be used providing the ultimate compressive strength of the masonry (f'_m) is determined by prism tests. Used or salvaged brick are not permitted in engineered brick masonry construction.

Mortar: Most of the test data, on which the allowable stresses for brick masonry in the BIA standard are based, were obtained on specimens built with portland cement-lime mortar. The standard provides for three mortar types: M, S, and N as described in ASTM C270, except that the mortar must consist of mixtures of portland cement (Type I, II or III), hydrated lime (Type S, non-airentrained), and aggregate when the allowable stresses included in the standard are used. The standard provides, however, that "Other mortars . . . may be used when approved by the building official, provided strengths for such masonry construction are established by tests. . . ."

Structural requirements

Determination of f'_m: The allowable stresses in the standard are based, for the most part, on the compressive strength of brick masonry, f'_m. This factor may be determined in accordance with prism testing or may be assumed, based on the compressive strength of the brick units and the type of mortar used.

Determination of allowable stresses: The allowable stresses—compressive (f_m), tensile (f_t), and shearing (f_v)—in nonreinforced brick masonry should not exceed the values shown in Table 5.

Selection of stress reduction factors: Two stress reduction factors are used in calculating allowable loads on walls and columns. They are the slenderness coefficient, C_s, and the eccentricity coefficient, C_e.

Table 4. Assumed compressive strength of brick masonry

| Compressive strength of units, psi (MPa) | Assumed compressive strength of brick masonry f'_m, psi (MPa) | | | | | |
| | Without inspection | | | With inspection | | |
	Type N mortar	Type S mortar	Type M mortar	Type N mortar	Type S mortar	Type M mortar
14,000 plus	2140	2600	3070	3200	3900	4600
(96.527 plus)	(14.755)	(17.926)	(21.167)	(22.063)	(26.890)	(31.716)
12,000	1870	2270	2670	2800	3400	4000
(82.737)	(12.893)	(15.651)	(18.409)	(19.305)	(23.442)	(27.579)
10,000	1600	1930	2270	2400	2900	3400
(68.948)	(11.032)	(13.307)	(15.651)	(16.547)	(19.995)	(23.442)
8,000	1340	1600	1870	2000	2400	2800
(55.158)	(9.240)	(11.032)	(12.893)	(13.790)	(16.547)	(19.305)
6,000	1070	1270	1470	1600	1900	2200
(41.369)	(7.377)	(8.756)	(10.135)	(11.032)	(13.100)	(15.168)
4,000	800	930	1070	1200	1400	1600
(27.579)	(5.516)	(6.412)	(7.377)	(8.274)	(9.653)	(11.032)
2,000	530	600	670	800	900	1000
(13.790)	(3.654)	(4.137)	(4.620)	(5.516)	(6.205)	(6.895)

Table 5. Allowable stresses in nonreinforced brick masonry

| Description | Allowable stresses, psi | |
	Without inspection*	With inspection*
Compressive, axial		
Walls, f_m	$0.20f'_m$	$0.20f'_m$
Columns, f_m	$0.16f'_m$	$0.16f'_m$
Compressive, flexural		
Walls, f_m	$0.32f'_m$	$0.32f'_m$
Columns, f_m	$0.26f'_m$	$0.26f'_m$
Tensile, flexural		
Normal to bed joints		
M or S mortar, f_t	24	36
N mortar, f_t	19	28
Parallel to bed joints		
M or S mortar, f_t	48	72
N mortar, f_t	37	56
Shear		
M or S mortar, V_m	$0.5\sqrt{f'_m}$, but not to exceed 40	$0.5\sqrt{f'_m}$, but not to exceed 80
N mortar, V_m	$0.5\sqrt{f'_m}$, but not to exceed 28	$0.5\sqrt{f'_m}$, but not to exceed 56
Bearing		
On full area, f_m	$0.25f'_m$	$0.25f'_m$
On one-third area or less, f_m	$0.375f'_m$	$0.375f'_m$
Modulus of elasticity, E_m	$1,000f'_m$, but not to exceed 2,000,000 psi	$1,000f'_m$, but not to exceed 3,000,000 psi
Modulus of rigidity, E_v	$400f'_m$, but not to exceed 800,000 psi	$400f'_m$, but not to exceed 1,200,000 psi

* *Where f'_m is determined in accordance with "brick tests," values of f'_m shall be based on Table 1. Where f'_m is determined in accordance with "prism tests," values of f'_m shall be reduced by one-third when there is no engineering or architectural inspection.*

Determination of e_1/e_2: At the top and bottom of any wall or column a virtual eccentricity of some magnitude (including zero) occurs. The ratio of the smaller virtual eccentricity to the larger virtual eccentricity is e_1/e_2. Since e_1 is always the smaller, the absolute value of the ratio is always less than or equal to 1.0. Where e_1 or e_2 or both are equal to zero, e_1/e_2 is assumed to be zero. Where the member is bent in single curvature (top and bottom virtual eccentricity occurring on the opposite sides of a wall or column centroidal axis), the ratio e_1/e_2 is positive. Where the member is bent in double curvature (top and bottom virtual eccentricity occurring on the same side of a wall or column centroidal axis), the ratio e_1/e_2 shall be negative (see Fig. 3 for illustration).

Determination of e/t: The ratio of the

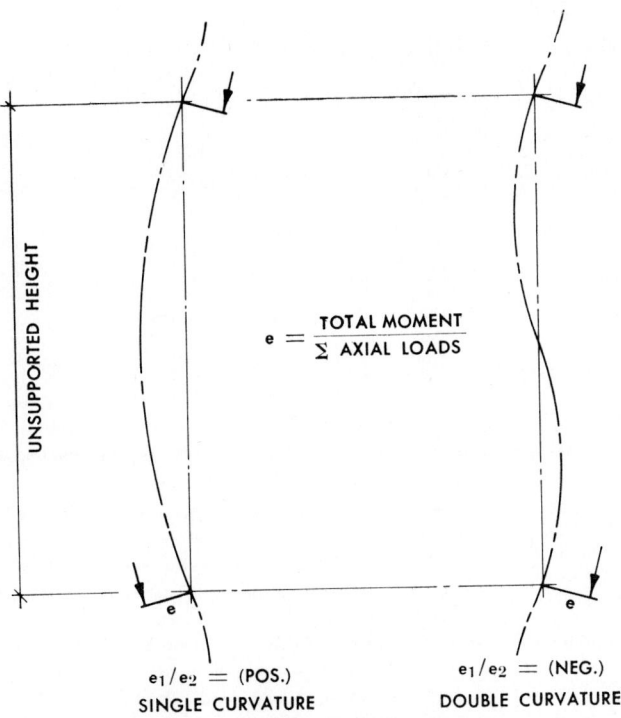

$$e = \frac{\text{TOTAL MOMENT}}{\Sigma \text{ AXIAL LOADS}}$$

$e_1/e_2 =$ (POS.)
SINGLE CURVATURE

$e_1/e_2 =$ (NEG.)
DOUBLE CURVATURE

Fig. 3.   Eccentricity in a column or bearing wall

maximum virtual eccentricity to the wall thickness, e/t, is used in selecting the eccentricity coefficient, C_e. The design of a non-reinforced member requires that e/t be less than or equal to $1/3$.

Selection of C_e: The eccentricity coefficient, C_e, may be selected from Table 6 or calculated from the formulae shown below Table 6 by using the proper e_1/e_2 and e/t ratios. Linear interpolation is permitted within the table.

Selection of C_s: The slenderness coefficient, C_s, may be selected from Table 7 or calculated from the formula below Table 7 by using the proper e_1/e_2 and h/t ratios. Linear interpolation is also permitted within the table.

Allowable axial loads: Allowable axial

Table 6.   Eccentricity coefficients C_e

$\frac{e}{t}$	-1	$-\frac{3}{4}$	$-\frac{1}{2}$	$-\frac{1}{4}$	0	$+\frac{1}{4}$	$+\frac{1}{2}$	$+\frac{3}{4}$	$+1$
0 to $\frac{1}{20}$ (0.05)	1.00	1.00	1.00	1.00	1.00	1.00	1.00	1.00	1.00
$\frac{1}{12}$ (0.083)	0.90	0.90	0.89	0.89	0.88	0.88	0.87	0.87	0.87
$\frac{1}{8}$ (0.125)	0.82	0.81	0.80	0.79	0.78	0.77	0.76	0.75	0.74
$\frac{1}{6}$ (0.167)	0.77	0.75	0.74	0.72	0.71	0.69	0.68	0.66	0.65
$\frac{5}{24}$ (0.208)	0.73	0.71	0.69	0.67	0.65	0.63	0.61	0.59	0.57
$\frac{1}{4}$ (0.250)	0.69	0.66	0.64	0.61	0.59	0.56	0.54	0.51	0.49
$\frac{7}{24}$ (0.292)	0.65	0.62	0.59	0.56	0.53	0.50	0.47	0.44	0.41
$\frac{1}{3}$ (0.333)	0.61	0.57	0.54	0.50	0.47	0.43	0.40	0.36	0.32

If $0 < e/t \leq 0.05$, then $C_e = 1.0$

If $0.05 < e/t \leq 0.167$, then $C_e = \dfrac{1.3}{1 + 6\frac{e}{t}} + \dfrac{1}{2}\left(\dfrac{e}{t} - \dfrac{1}{20}\right)\left(1 - \dfrac{e_1}{e_2}\right)$

If $0.167 < e/t \leq 0.333$, then $C_e = 1.95\left(\dfrac{1}{2} - \dfrac{e}{t}\right)$
$+ \dfrac{1}{2}\left(\dfrac{e}{t} - \dfrac{1}{20}\right)\left(1 - \dfrac{e_1}{e_2}\right)$

Table 7.   Slenderness coefficients C_s

$\frac{h}{t}$	-1	$-\frac{3}{4}$	$-\frac{1}{2}$	$-\frac{1}{4}$	0	$+\frac{1}{4}$	$+\frac{1}{2}$	$+\frac{3}{4}$	$+1$
5.0	1.00	1.00	1.00	1.00	1.00	1.00	1.00	1.00	1.00
7.5	1.00	1.00	1.00	1.00	1.00	0.98	0.96	0.93	0.90
10.0	1.00	0.99	0.98	0.96	0.93	0.91	0.88	0.84	0.80
12.5	0.95	0.94	0.92	0.90	0.87	0.83	0.79	0.75	0.70
15.0	0.90	0.88	0.86	0.83	0.80	0.76	0.71	0.66	0.60
17.5	0.85	0.83	0.81	0.77	0.73	0.69	0.63	0.57	0.50
20.0	0.80	0.78	0.75	0.71	0.67	0.61	0.55	0.48	0.40
22.5	0.75	0.73	0.69	0.65	0.60	0.54	0.47	0.39	
25.0	0.70	0.67	0.64	0.59	0.53	0.47	0.39		
27.5	0.65	0.62	0.58	0.53	0.47	0.39			
30.0	0.60	0.57	0.52	0.47	0.40				
32.5	0.55	0.52	0.47	0.41					
35.0	0.50	0.46	0.41						
37.5	0.45	0.41							
40.0	0.40								

$$C_s = 1.20 - \frac{h/t}{300}\left[5.75 + \left(1.5 + \frac{e_1}{e_2}\right)^2\right] \leq 1.0$$

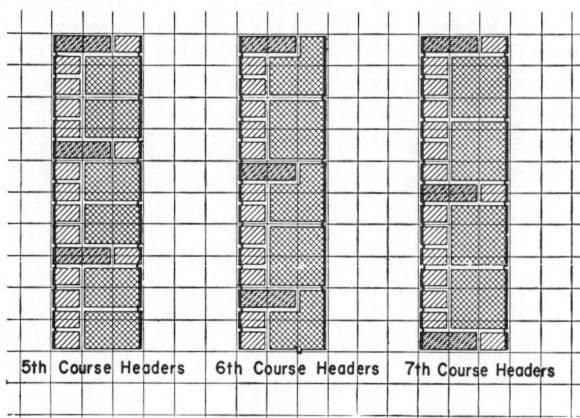

Fig. 4. Bonding of solid masonry walls

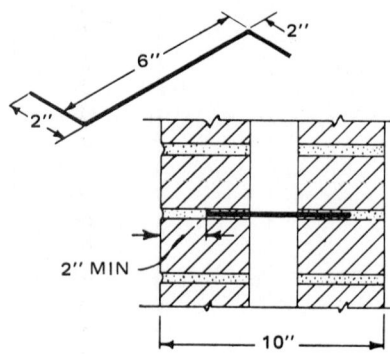

Fig. 5. Bonding walls of hollow units

loads *(P)* on nonreinforced brick masonry walls and columns can be computed by using the following formula:

$$P = C_e \, C_s \, f_m \, A_g$$

where A_g = gross cross-sectional area.

Structural bond

Structural bonding of masonry walls may be accomplished in three ways: (1) by the overlapping (interlocking) of the masonry units, (2) by the use of metal ties embedded in connecting joints, and (3) by the adhesion of grout to adjacent wythes of masonry.

Masonry bonders

In walls of solid masonry, bonders (also known as headers) should make up not less than 4 per cent of the wall area. Bonders should extend not less than 4 in. into the backing and should be spaced not more than 24 in. apart horizontally or vertically (Fig. 4).

In ashlar masonry, bondstones should be uniformly distributed and should constitute not less than 10 per cent of the area of the wall. In rubble masonry, bondstones should be spaced not more than 3 ft vertically or horizontally; if the wall is more than 24 in. thick, bondstones should be provided for each 6 sq ft of wall surface on each side.

In walls of hollow masonry more than one unit in thickness, bonders lapping at least 4 in. over the unit below should occur at vertical intervals of not more than 34 in., or bonders that are at least 50 per cent greater in thickness than the units below shall be used at vertical intervals not exceeding 17 in. (Fig. 5).

Metal ties

Metal ties must be used for the bonding of cavity walls and may be used for the bonding of solid walls (Fig. 6). Ties should be 3/16-in. (4.8 mm)-diam steel rods or other material of equivalent stiffness, with ends bent at a 90-deg angle to form hooks

not less than 2 in. (51 mm) long. For walls built of hollow masonry units, ties of rectangular shape should be used. Metal ties should be made of, or coated with, corrosion-resistant metal, and should be embedded in the horizontal joints of the masonry. There must be not less than one metal tie for each 4½ sq ft of wall area. Ties in alternate courses should be staggered and the vertical distance between courses should not exceed 24 in.; the horizontal distance between ties should not exceed 36 in. (Fig. 7).

Cavity walls

Cavity walls must be bonded with metal ties, as described above. Additional bonding ties should be provided at all openings, spaced not more than 3 ft (914 mm) apart around the perimeter and withint 12 in. (305 mm) of the opening. The cavity must be kept clear of mortar droppings and be properly flashed and drained at the bottom. (See sheets 24–26)

Grouted masonry

Masonry units in outer wythes should be laid with full head and bed joints of Type M or S mortar. Interior joints should be filled with grout, and longitudinal joints should be not less than ¾ in. wide. Each grout pour should be stopped 1½ in. below the top of the masonry units and properly stirred. Headers should not be used (metal ties are required).

Chases and recesses

Chases and recesses should be not deeper than one-third the wall thickness, nor longer

than 4 ft. horizontally, and should have at least 8 in. of masonry at the back and sides. The total area of chases and recesses should not exceed one-fourth the wall area. In residential buildings not over two stories high, vertical chases 4 in. deep and not over 4 sq ft in area are permitted in 8-in. walls;

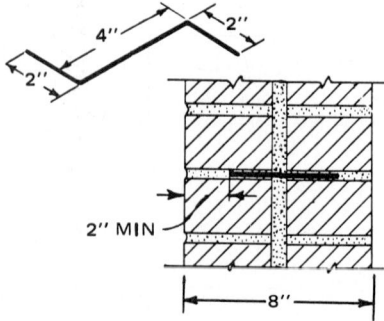

Fig. 6. Size and location of metal ties.

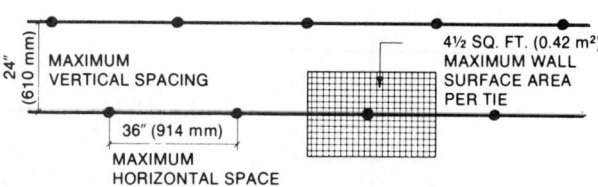

Fig. 7. Spacing of metal ties.

lintels should be used above chases or recesses more than 12 in. wide.

Corbeling

Projection of a masonry unit should not exceed one-half its vertical dimensions; projection of brick should not exceed 1 in. per course. Total projection should not exceed one-half the wall thickness.

WORKMANSHIP

High-absorption brick (having absorption rates exceeding 20 g (0.7 oz) per min for 30 sq in. of brick surface immersed in ⅛ in. of water) must be thoroughly wetted before laying; sprinkling is not sufficient. However, brick should be surface dry when laid. All bed and head joints should be completely filled. The mortar bed should be thick and uniform, and furrowed only lightly, if at all; it should be spread over only a few brick at a time. Mortar should be applied to the ends of brick and to the entire side of header brick before they are laid: "slushing" the head joints will not completely fill all the voids. Holes caused by the removal of nails or line pins should be plugged immediately. Proper tooling of exterior joints reduces water penetration of the wall; concave joints are best for this purpose. Additional insurance against leakage may be obtained by parging or back-plastering with mortar the face of the backup before the facing is laid. Solid metal-tied walls are recommended by BIA for superior resistance to water penetration, especially for 8-in. walls.

ARCHES

Data and illustrations on this and the following page have been derived from *Technical Notes on Brick Construction*, published by the Brick Institute of America.

An arch is a form of construction in which a number of units span an opening by transferring vertical loads laterally to adjacent units and thus to the supports. It is essentially a beam curved in the plane of the loads. Any section in an arch, therefore, may be subjected to moment and shear, as in an ordinary beam. In addition it is subjected to thrust from components of vertical loads in the direction of the arch axis.

In a fixed arch, as all masonry arches are, three conditions must be maintained to ensure pure arch action:

1. The length of the span must remain constant.
2. The elevation of the ends must remain unchanged.
3. The inclination of the skewback must be fixed.

If any of these conditions is violated by sliding, settlement, or rotation of the abut-

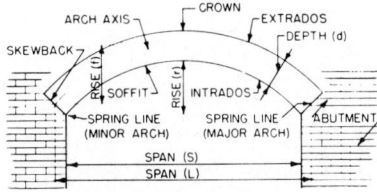

Fig. 8. Arch terminology

ments, critical stresses, for which the arch was not designed, may develop. Such stresses may result in failure of the arch.

STRUCTURAL DESIGN

All theories for the design of masonry arches are in fact methods of verification. Dimensions of the arch are first assumed, based on common practice or an empirical formula, and the assumed arch is then tested by one or more of the theories.

There are two classes of theories of the stability of a masonry arch: line of thrust and the elastic deformation. The line-of-thrust theories consider the stability of the arch ring as depending upon the friction and the reactions between the several arch sections or voussoirs. The elastic theories consider the arch as a curved beam whose stability depends upon internal stresses.

In general, the line-of-thrust theories are most applicable to symmetrical masonry arches loaded uniformly over the entire span or subjected to symmetrically placed concentrated loads. For such arches, the line of resistance, which is the line connecting the points of application of the resultant forces transmitted to each voussoir, is required to fall within the middle third of the arch section so that neither the intrados nor extrados of the arch will be in tension.

For arches subjected to nonsymmetrical

loading, which may develop tensile stresses in the arch, the elastic theories provide a more accurate method of analysis than the line-of-thrust theories.

Line-of-thrust analysis

One of the oldest line-of-thrust theories is based upon the hypothesis of least crown thrust. This hypothesis can be applied to the analysis of an arch by static methods, provided the external forces acting upon the arch are known and the point of application and direction of the crown thrust are assumed.

It is customary to assume the direction of the crown thrust as horizontal and its point of application at the upper extremity of the middle third of the section; that is, two-thirds the arch depth from the intrados.

With the above assumptions, the forces acting on each section of the arch may be determined by analytical and graphic methods. The first step in such an analysis is to determine the joint of rupture. This is that joint for which the tendency of the arch to open at the extrados is the greatest and which, therefore, requires the greatest crown thrust applied at the upper extremity of the middle third to prevent the joint from opening. At this joint the line of resistance of the arch will fall on the lower extremity of the middle third of the section.

For segmental arches of short spans (not exceeding 6 ft) and of low rise-to-span ratios (not exceeding 0.15), the joint of rupture may be assumed to be the skewback of the arch. Based on this assumption and the hypothesis of least crown thrust, the magnitude of the crown thrust and the magnitude and direction of the reaction at the skewback may be determined graphically (Fig. 9).

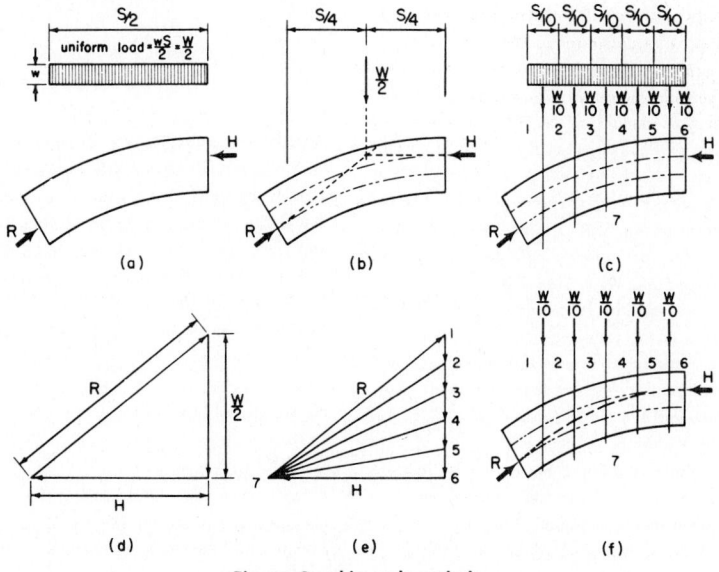

Fig. 9. Graphic arch analysis

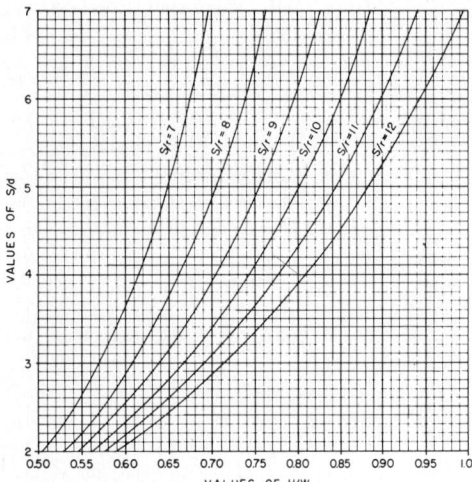

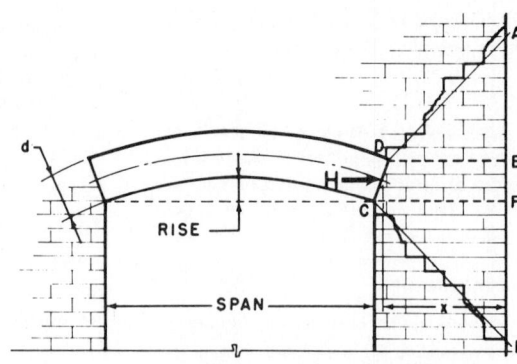

Fig. 11. Calculating resistance to horizontal thrust

In this analysis, since the arch is symmetrical and uniformly loaded over the entire span, one-half the arch is considered. Figure 9a shows the external forces acting upon the arch section. For equilibrium, the lines of action of these three forces $W/2$, H, and R must intersect at one point, as shown in Fig. 9b. Since H is assumed to act horizontally, this determines the direction of force R. Its magnitude may be obtained by constructing a force diagram (Fig. 9d).

The next step in the graphic analysis is to divide the arch into voussoirs and to transform the uniform load into the equivalent concentrated loads, acting on each voussoir or section (Fig. 9c). Starting at any convenient point (in this example, the point between the reaction and the first load segment past the skewback), we place numbers between each pair of forces (Fig. 9c). Now each force is identified by a number; for example, the reaction is 7-1 and the first vertical load is 1-2.

The side of the force diagram representing $W/2$ is divided into the same number of equivalent loads as was done in Fig. 9c. The numbers previously used for identification are placed in the manner shown to identify the forces in the force diagram. Thus, 7-1 is the skewback reaction, 6-7 the horizontal thrust, and so on. From the intersection of H and R (7-1 and 6-7), a line is drawn to each intermediate point on the leg representing $W/2$. (See Fig. 9e.)

The equilibrium polygon may now be drawn in the following manner: Extend the line of the reaction until it intersects the line of action of 1-2. Through this point draw a line parallel to the line 7-2, of Fig. 9e, until it intersects the line of action of 2-3. Through this point draw a line parallel to 7-3 of Fig. 9e. Complete the equilibrium polygon in this manner. (See Fig. 9f.)

If the polygon lies completely within the middle third, the arch is stable.

Elastic deformation analysis

Many methods of elastic analysis suitable for arches have been developed; in most instances, however, the application is complicated and time-consuming. *Frames and Arches* by Valerian Leontovich (McGraw Hill Book Co., 1959) provides equations for the design of parabolic arches of both constant and variable cross section which substantially simplify this type of analysis.

MINOR ARCH DESIGN

There are three methods of failure of unreinforced masonry arches: by rotation of one section of the arch about the edge of a joint, by the sliding of one section of the arch on another or on the skewback, and by crushing of the masonry.

Rotation: The assumption that the equilibrium polygon lies entirely within the middle third of the arch section, precludes the rotation of one section of the arch about the edge of a joint or the development of tensile stresses in either the intrados or extrados.

Sliding: The coefficient of friction between the units composing a brick or tile masonry arch is at least 0.50, without considering the additional resistance to sliding resulting from bond between mortar and the masonry units. This coefficient corresponds to an angle of friction of approximately 27 deg. If the angle that the line of resistance of the arch makes with the normal to the joint between arch sections is less than the angle of friction, the arch is stable against sliding. This first angle can be determined graphically.

For minor segmental arches, the angle between the line of resistance and the normal to the joint is greatest at the skewback.

For segmental arches with radial joints, the angle γ between the skewback and the vertical is

$$\gamma = \tan^{-1} \frac{4rS}{S^2 - 4r^2}$$

or in terms of the radius of curvature

$$\gamma = \sin^{-1} \frac{S}{2R}$$

in which

S = span
r = rise
R = radius of curvature

Figure 10 is a graphic representation of thrust coefficients, H/W, for segmental arches subjected to uniform load over the entire span. Once the thrust coefficient is determined for a particular arch, the horizontal thrust H may be determined as the product of the thrust coefficient and the total load W. To determine the proper thrust coefficient, one must first determine the characteristics of the arch, S/r and S/d, in which d = the depth of the arch and S, r, and d are all expressed in the same units.

Once the horizontal thrust has been determined, the maximum compressive stress in the masonry is determined by the following formula:

$$f_m = \frac{2H}{bd}$$

in which

f_m = maximum compressive stress in the arch, psi
H = horizontal thrust, lb
b = breadth of the arch, in.
d = depth of the arch, in.

Thrust resistance

Resistance to horizontal thrust, developed by the arch, is provided by the adjacent mass of masonry. In areas where limited masonry is available, such as corners and openings, it may be necessary to check the resistance of the wall to the horizontal thrusts. Figure 11 illustrates how such resistance may be calculated.

It is assumed that the thrust of the arch attempts to move a volume of masonry enclosed by the boundary lines ABCD. For calculating purposes the area CDEF is equivalent in resistance. It can be seen that the thrust is acting against two planes of resistance, CF and DE. The resistance to arch thrust is determined by the following formula:

$$H_r = v_m n x t$$

$H_r =$ resisting thrust, lb

$v_m =$ allowable shearing stress in masonry wall, psi

$n =$ number of resisting shear planes

$x =$ distance from the center of skewback to end of wall, in.

$t =$ wall thickness, in.

The minimum distance from a corner or opening at which an arch may be located is easily determined by writing the formula to solve for x, substituting actual arch thrust for resisting thrust:

$$x = \frac{H}{v_m n t}$$

For brick with mortar Type M or S, $v_m = 50$; with mortar Type N, $v_m = 35$.

REINFORCED MASONRY

Reinforced masonry utilizes steel in combination with masonry to produce greatly increased resistance to tensile, shear, and compressive forces. The basic principle is the same as that of reinforced concrete, and the method of design and the terminology employed are very similar to those used in reinforced concrete design.

Design and construction of reinforced masonry are governed by local codes and by the *American National Standard Building Code Requirements for Reinforced Masonry* (ANSI A41.2-1960, R1970). The principal provisions of the latter code, excluding those which are the same as in the ANSI Code for Masonry (A41.1), are summarized below.

Reinforcement should conform to the following standards of quality: Deformed reinforcing bars—ANSI/ASTM A706-75; billet-steel bars—ANSI/ASTM A615-72a; rail-steel bars—ANSI/ASTM A616-72; welded steel fabric—ANSI/ASTM A185-70; steel for bridges and buildings—ANSI/ASTM A36-74.

Aggregate for masonry grout: ASTM C404-70, coarse aggregate No. 8.

Mortar proportions by volume: 1 part portland cement, ¼ to ½ part hydrated lime or lime putty, and fine aggregate consisting of 2¼ to 3 times the sum of the separate volumes of the cement and lime. (These proportions correspond to mortar Type S, ASTM C270.)

Grout proportions by volume (ASTM C476-71): Type MG (mortar grout)—1 part portland cement, ¼ part hydrated lime or lime putty, and fine aggregate consisting of 2¼ to 3 times the sum of the separate volumes of the cement and lime (mortar Type M, ASTM, C270), to which sufficient water should be added to cause the mixture to flow readily. Stir at frequent intervals to prevent separation of materials. Type PG

(pea gravel grout)—1 part portland cement, ¼ part hydrated lime or lime putty, 2¼ to 3 parts fine aggregate, and 1 to 2 parts coarse aggregate; the sum of the volumes of the fine and coarse aggregates should not exceed 4 times the sum of the volumes of the cement and lime.

Allowable stresses

Compressive strength of masonry (f'_m) should be determined preferably by test of a masonry prism, following the procedure described in ANSI A41.2. In the absence of a test, compressive strength of masonry should be as shown in Table 8. Allowable stresses in reinforcement (longitudinal f_s and web f_v) should not exceed those shown in Table 9. Allowable stresses in reinforced masonry (f_m) should not exceed those shown in Table 10.

Reinforced grouted masonry

Masonry units should be laid in full head and bed joints, with no mortar fins projecting into spaces to be filled with grout. Metal ties should be used to bond the two outer wythes of the wall to each other. Longitudinal joints to receive grout should be not less than ¾ in. wide. If the longitudinal joint (core) is less than 2 in. wide, the maximum height of grout pour should be 12 in. If the longitudinal joint is 2 in. or more in width, the maximum height of grout pour should not exceed 48 times the joint width for MG grout or 64 times the joint width for PG grout, but not to exceed a height of 12 ft. in lifts of 4 ft. (Fig. 12). Grout pour should be stopped 1½ in. below the top of masonry units. In walls built of hollow masonry units, minimum dimensions of continuous vertical cores should be 2 by 3 in. and the maximum height of grout pour should be 4 ft. (Fig. 13).

Table 8.   Compressive strength of masonry

Values shown are for gross area of solid masonry units, net area of hollow masonry units.

Compressive strength of the units, psi	Assumed compressive strength of masonry (f'_m) psi
1,000 to 1,500	900 to 1,150
1,501 to 2,500	1,151 to 1,550
2,501 to 4,000	1,551 to 2,000
4,001 to 6,000	2,001 to 2,400
6,001 to 8,000	2,401 to 2,700
8,001 to 10,000	2,701 to 2,900
10,001 to 12,000	2,901 to 3,000
Over 12,000	3,000

Table 9.   Allowable stress in reinforcement (f_s or f_v)

Condition	Grade of steel	Stress, psi
Tensile	Structural (bars and shapes)	18,000
	Intermediate and hard*	20,000
Compressive (column verticals)	Intermediate	16,000
	Hard*	20,000

* Billet, rail, or axle steel.

Table 10.   Allowable stresses in reinforced masonry

Description	Symbol	Allowable stress
Compressive:*		
Axial: Walls ($h/t = 10$ or less)	f_m	$0.20f'_m$
($h/t = 25$)	f_m	$0.15f'_m$
Flexural	f_m	$0.33f'_m$
Shear: Beams with no web reinforcement	v_m	50 psi†
Beams with web reinforcement	v	150 psi
Bond: Plain bars	u	80 psi
Deformed bars (ASTM A706)	u	160 psi
Bearing	f_m	$0.25f'_m$
Modulus of elasticity	E_m	$1,000f'_m$
Modulus of rigidity	E_v	$400f'_m$

* For allowable stress on columns, see Section 9.4 of ANSI A41.2.
† See Section 8.7.1 (c) of ANSI A41.2.

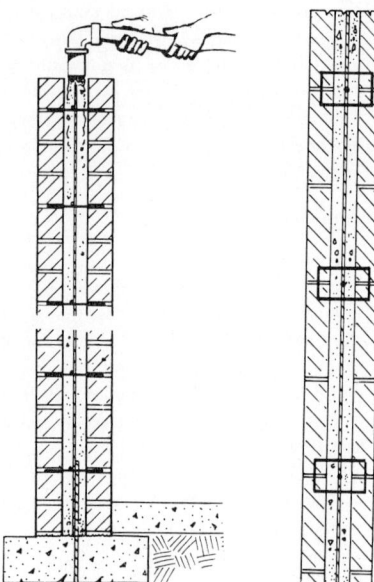

Fig. 12. "High-lift" grouted reinforced masonry; section and plan

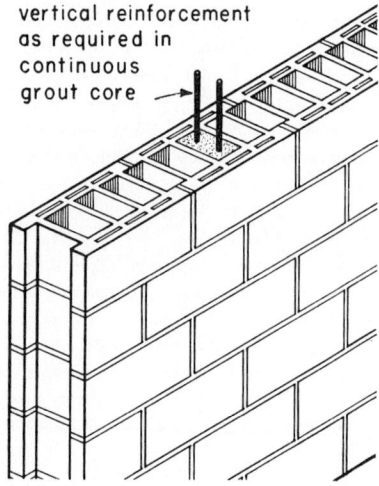

vertical reinforcement as required in continuous grout core

Fig. 13. Reinforced structural facing tile

Reinforcement should be completely embedded in grout. The minimum distance between parallel bars is one diameter. The minimum coverage of bars is 3 in. at the bottom of footings, 2 in. in vertical members exposed to weather or soil, 1½ in. in columns and on bottoms and sides of girders and beams, ¾ in. in walls not exposed to weather or soil, and one diameter but not less than ¾ in. above all horizontal bars not exposed to weather or soil.

Minimum joint thickness: The thickness of grout or mortar between masonry units and reinforcement bars should be not less than ¼ in., except that ¼-in.-diam bars may be placed in ½-in. horizontal joints.

Columns

Columns should be not less than 12 in. in either dimension, and the unsupported height should not exceed 20 times the smallest dimension. The ratio of area of the vertical reinforcement to gross area of column section should be not less than 0.005 nor more than 0.04. Reinforcement should consist of at least 4 bars of not less than ½-in. diam. Ties should be not less than ¼-in. diam, spaced not more than 16 bar diameters, 48 tie diameters, smallest dimension of column, or 16 in.

Walls

Bearing walls should be not less than 6 in. thick, and the unsupported height should not exceed 25 times the thickness. Nonbearing walls may have an unsupported height of 30 times the thickness. The area of steel reinforcement should be not less than 0.002 times the cross-sectional area of the wall; maximum spacing of reinforcement should not exceed 6 times the wall thickness, or 48 in. Horizontal reinforcement should be provided in the top of footings, at the bottom and top of wall openings, at the floor and roof levels, and at the top of parapet walls. In addi-

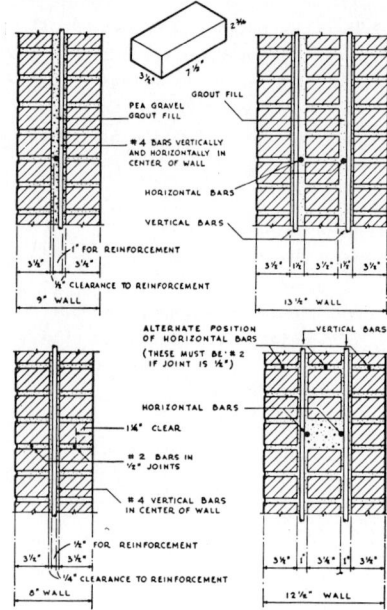

Fig. 15. Typical wall sections using modular brick

tion there should be not less than one ½-in. diam bar around all window and door openings and extending at least 24 in. beyond the corners of the openings (Fig. 14).

Reinforced masonry walls of modular brick are shown in Fig. 15.

Nonbearing curtain or panel walls of reinforced brick masonry 4 in. thick may be designed to span 20 ft or more horizontally between columns or piers. Figure 18 shows such a wall with typical one-way reinforcement, furring, insulation, and interior finish. A detail section through the wall is given in Fig. 16. Flexible anchorages, as shown in Fig. 17, rather than the rigid type shown in Fig. 21, should be used to secure the 4-in. curtain wall to the columns.

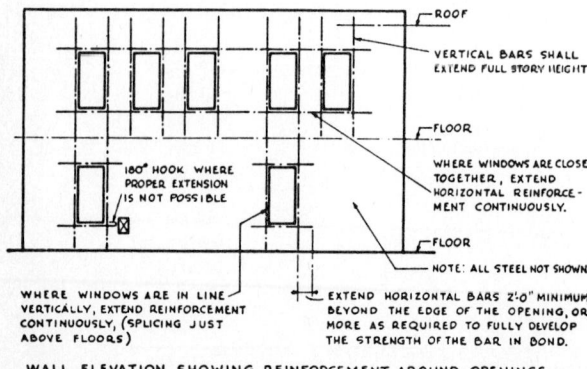

WALL ELEVATION SHOWING REINFORCEMENT AROUND OPENINGS

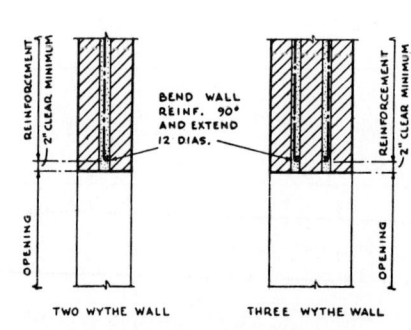

SECTIONS AT EDGE OF OPENINGS

Fig. 14. Typical reinforcement around wall openings

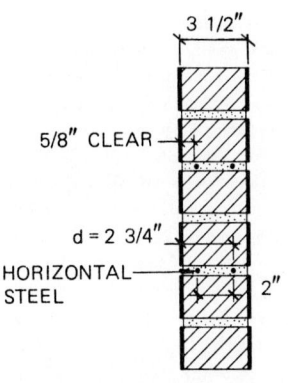

Fig. 16. Section through 4-in. reinforced brick curtain wall

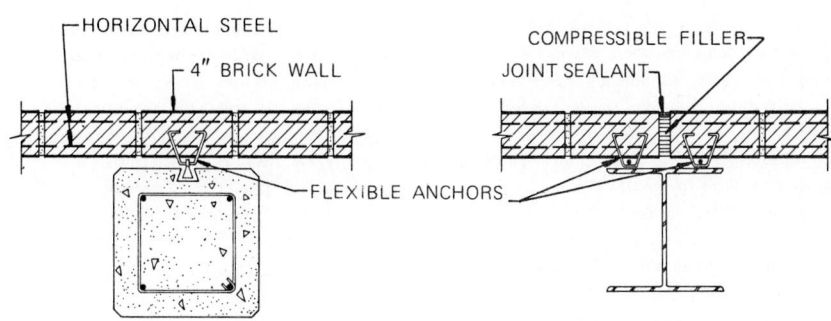

Fig. 17. Flexible anchorages for 4-in. reinforced brick curtain walls

Reinforced masonry is well suited to the resistance of lateral forces and is widely used in the seismic areas of the Pacific coast. It is also well adapted to the construction of blast-resistant structures (Fig. 20). Reinforced masonry may be used as curtain walls in framed structures. If such walls are tied rigidly to the frame they can be designed to resist all or most of the lateral forces acting on the building (Fig. 21).

Reinforced masonry is most often used for vertical elements such as walls and columns. Since no formwork is required, the cost is competitive with that of rein-

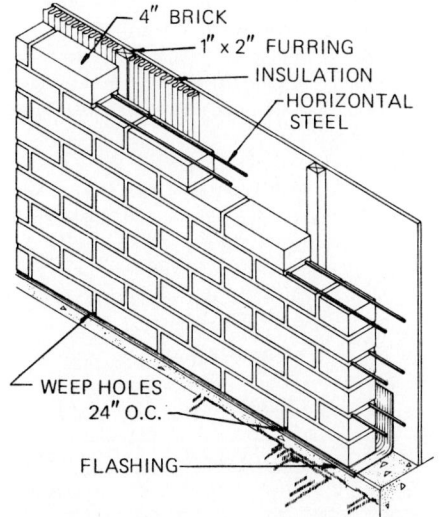

Fig. 18. Isometric of 4-in. reinforced brick curtain wall with furring, insulation, and interior finish

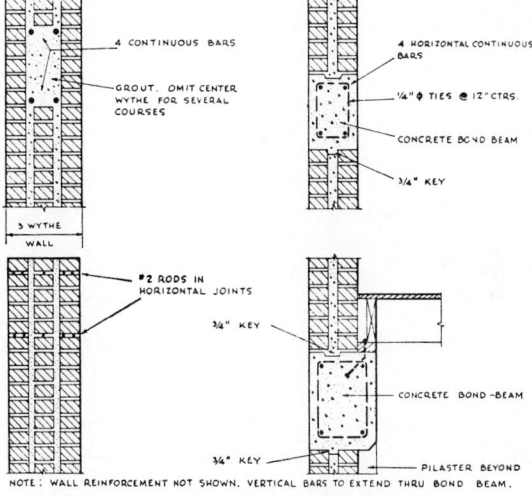

Fig. 19. Sections through typical bond beams

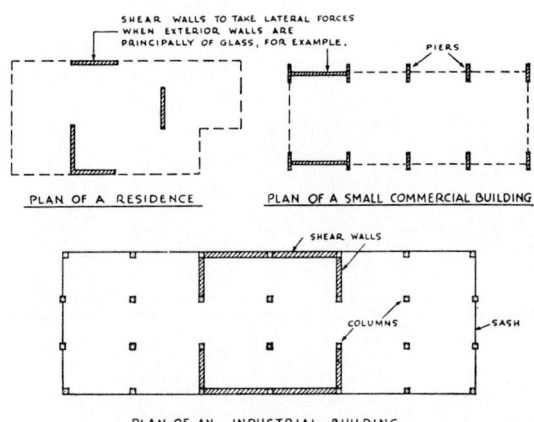

Fig. 20. Reinforced masonry shear walls

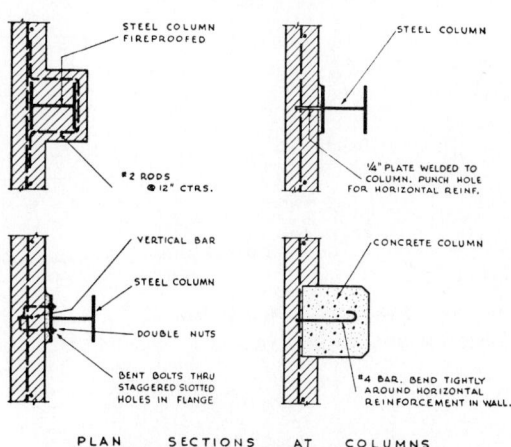

Fig. 21. Attachment of reinforced masonry curtain walls to structural columns

Reinforced masonry retaining walls

forced concrete. Reinforced masonry is also frequently used for bond beams (Fig. 19) and for lintels. Continuous bond beams at each floor level are recommended for all buildings with loadbearing walls.

"High-lift" grouting (Fig. 12) has been approved by local and ANSI Codes. The wall may be built as shown, with a minimum cavity width of 2 in., to a maximum height of 12 ft before grouting. Cleanout spaces must be provided at the base of the wall so that the cavity can be cleaned daily during construction. The wall must be allowed to cure for at least three days (five days in wet weather) before grouting. The first grout should be a cement-sand slurry (1 part cement to 2 parts sand) poured to a depth of 2 in., followed by regular PG grout poured at a constant rate: maximum of 1 ft in 10 minutes, minimum of 1 ft in 20 minutes; after each 3 ft of pour, wait 30 to 60 minutes. Intermittent vibration is necessary during all stages of grouting.

Data and illustrations on this and the following pages have been derived from *Technical Notes on Brick Construction,* published by the Brick Institute of America.

Retaining walls

Reinforced masonry is frequently used for minor retaining walls, especially in locations where appearance is important. The masonry may be hollow block with grouted cells or grouted cavity wall as shown in Fig. 22. Table 11 may be used for the structural design of the type of wall shown in Fig. 22 for various heights up to 6 ft. (Walls higher than 6 ft should be designed by an engineer.) Table 11 is based on the following assumptions:

Soil weight 100 lb/ft³
No surcharge
Brick minimum compressive strength 6000 psi
Type M mortar
Steel design tensile strength 20,000 psi
Concrete minimum compressive strength 2500 psi
Wall thickness (actual) 9½ in. with reinforcing steel in center ($d = 4.75$)
Horizontal reinforcing, one #3 bar 20 in. o.c. vertically, or #9 guage galvanized truss or ladder-type reinforcement 16 in. o.c.

Materials and workmanship should be in accordance with the ANSI Code as described on previous pages. Brick should be Type SW, facing or building, with an absorption rate between 5 and 20 grams per minute on a 30-sq-in. surface, and a minimum compressive strength of 5,000 psi.

Every effort should be made to keep water out of the wall. A suitable cap should be provided and the back surface should be parged and/or coated with asphalt or other waterproofing material.

Provision for adequate drainage is important in the design of any retaining wall. Weep holes, larger than those normally used in building construction, should be placed at intervals above the finished grade in the front of the wall. Instead of, or in addition to, weep holes, a continuous drain may be installed behind the wall at the base of the stem (Fig. 22). The drain pipe should be perforated or laid with open joints and covered with a pervious material, such as gravel or broken stone.

LINTELS, STEEL

A lintel is a horizontal member or beam placed over a wall opening to carry the superimposed weight above. Lintels may be of structural steel, reinforced masonry, or reinforced concrete. Masonry arches, widely used in the past, are rarely employed today.

Structural steel shapes are the most commonly used type of lintel. Steel angles are the simplest shapes and are suitable

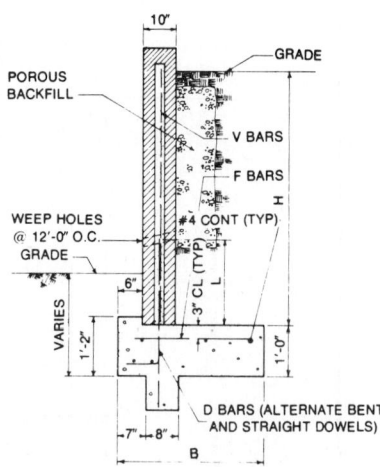

Fig. 22. Section through typical low, reinforced masonry retaining wall

Table 11. Steel required for low reinforced masonry retaining walls

H	B	L	D BARS	V BARS	F BARS
2'-0''	1'-9''	1'-10''	#3 @ 40''		#3 @ 40''
2'-6''	1'-9''	2'-4''	#3 @ 40''		#3 @ 40''
3'-0''	2'-0''	2'-10''	#3 @ 40''		#3 @ 40''
3'-6''	2'-0''	3'-4''	#3 @ 40''		#3 @ 40''
4'-0''	2'-4''	1'-4''	#3 @ 27'' #4 @ 40''	#3 @ 27'' #3 @ 40''	#3 @ 27'' #3 @ 40''
4'-6''	2'-8''	1'-6''	#3 @ 19'' #4 @ 35''	#3 @ 38'' #3 @ 35''	#3 @ 19'' #3 @ 35''
5'-0''	3'-0''	1'-8''	#3 @ 14'' #4 @ 25'' #5 @ 40''	#3 @ 28'' #3 @ 25'' #4 @ 40''	#3 @ 14'' #3 @ 25'' #4 @ 40''
5'-6''	3'-3''	1'-10''	#3 @ 11'' #4 @ 20'' #5 @ 31''	#3 @ 22'' #4 @ 40'' #4 @ 31''	#3 @ 11'' #3 @ 20'' #4 @ 31''
6'-0''	3'-6''	2'-0''	#3 @ 8'' #4 @ 14'' #5 @ 20''	#3 @ 16'' #4 @ 28'' #5 @ 40''	#3 @ 8'' #3 @ 14'' #4 @ 20''

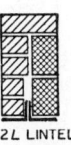  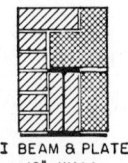

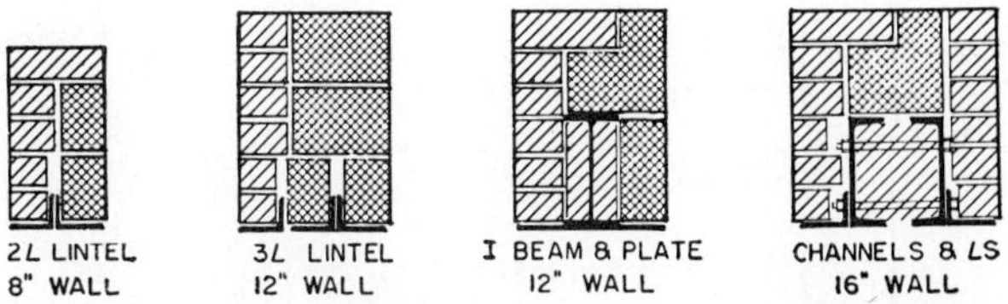

2L LINTEL 3L LINTEL I BEAM & PLATE CHANNELS & LS
8" WALL   12" WALL   12" WALL   16" WALL

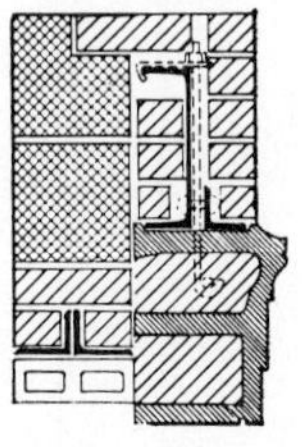

TERRA COTTA LINTEL

Fig. 23. Typical steel lintels

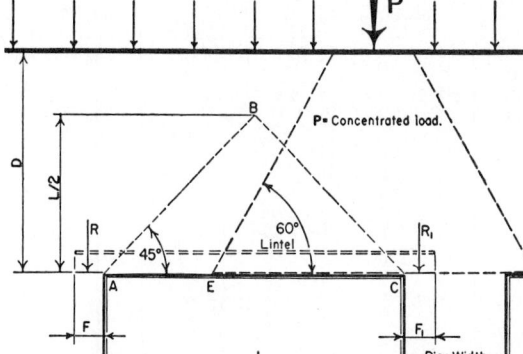

Fig. 24. Computing loads on a lintel

for spanning openings of moderate width and where the superimposed loads are not excessive. Wide openings or heavy loads may require steel channels, I-beams, or combinations of these with angles or plates (Fig. 23). The outstanding leg of the angle or plate should be at least 3½ in. to support a nominal 4-in. wythe of masonry. The specifications of the American Institute of Steel Construction require that the minimum thickness of such exterior members, if partially exposed to the weather, be $\frac{5}{16}$ in. for one- and two-story structures, and $\frac{7}{16}$ in. for stuctures over two stories in height. Table 12 gives allowable uniform loads on steel angles used as lintels. (For wide-flange sections, see load tables in "Structural Design—Steel: Beams.")

Load calculations: Determination of the load to be supported by the lintel is illustrated in Fig. 24. The weight of the masonry above the opening can be safely assumed as the weight of a triangular section whose height is one-half of the clear span of the opening. In other words, the lintel supports a triangle of masonry (ABC) in which the sides form a 45-deg angle with the base. Corbelling action of the masonry above the top of the opening may be counted upon to support the weight of the masonry outside the triangle.

To the dead load of the wall must be added the uniform dead and live loads of floors and roofs that frame into the wall above the opening and below the apex of the 45-deg triangle. Any such load above the apex may be neglected. In Fig. 24, D is greater than $L/2$, so the floor load may be ignored. If, however, D were less than $L/2$, the uniform dead and live loads of the floor would be added to the uniform dead load of the triangular section of the wall (ABC).

Concentrated loads from beams, girders, or trusses framing into the wall above the opening must also be considered. Such loads may be distributed over a wall length equal to the base of a triangle whose apex is at the point of load application and whose sides form an angle of 60 deg with the horizontal. In Fig. 24, the portion of the concentrated load P carried by the lintel would be distributed over the length EC.

Bearing area: In order to determine the over-all length of a steel lintel, the required bearing area must be determined. The stress in the masonry supporting each end of the lintel must not exceed the allowable unit stress for the type of masonry used. (See Table 3, Allowable compressive stresses in masonry.)

Deflection: Structural cracks in the masonry above the lintel are usually caused

Table 12. Allowable uniform superimposed load in pounds per foot for A-36 steel angle lintels ($F_b = 22{,}000$ psi)

Angle size, in.*	Weight per foot, lb	Span in feet (center to center of required bearing)									
		3	4	5	6	7	8	9	10	11	12
3 × 3½ × ¼	5.4	956	517	262	149	91	59				
× $\frac{5}{16}$	6.6	1166	637	323	184	113	73				
× ⅜	7.9	1377	756	384	218	134	87	59			
3½ × 3½ × ¼	5.8	1281	718	406	232	144	94	65			
× $\frac{5}{16}$	7.2	1589	891	507	290	179	118	80			
× ⅜	8.5	1947	1091	589	336	208	137	93	66		
4 × 3½ × ¼	6.2	1622	910	580	338	210	139	95	68		
× $\frac{5}{16}$	7.7	2110	1184	734	421	262	173	119	85	62	
× ⅜	9.1	2434	1365	855	490	305	201	138	98	71	
× $\frac{7}{16}$	10.6	2760	1548	978	561	349	230	158	113	82	60
4 × 4 × $\frac{7}{16}$	11.3	2920	1638	1018	584	363	239	164	116	85	62
× ½	12.8	3246	1820	1141	654	407	268	185	131	95	70
5 × 3½ × ¼	7.0	2600	1460	932	636	398	264	184	132	97	73
× $\frac{5}{16}$	8.7	3087	1733	1106	765	486	323	224	161	119	89
× $\frac{7}{16}$	12.0	4224	2371	1513	1047	655	435	302	217	160	120
× ½	13.6	4875	2736	1746	1177	736	488	339	244	179	134
6 × 3½ × ¼	7.9	3577	2009	1283	888	650	439	306	221	164	124
× $\frac{5}{16}$	9.8	4390	2465	1574	1090	798	538	375	271	201	151
× ⅜	11.7	5200	2922	1865	1291	945	636	443	320	237	179
× ½	15.3	6828	3834	2448	1695	1228	818	570	412	305	230
6 × 4 × ¼	8.3	3739	2099	1340	928	679	458	319	231	171	129
× $\frac{5}{16}$	10.3	4552	2556	1632	1129	827	562	391	283	209	158
× ⅜	12.3	5365	3012	1923	1331	974	665	463	335	248	187
× $\frac{7}{16}$	14.3	6178	3469	2214	1533	1122	764	532	384	284	215
× ½	16.2	6990	3925	2506	1734	1270	857	597	431	319	241

* Dimensions given are vertical leg by horizontal leg by thickness.
Note: Allowable loads to the left of the heavy line are governed by moment, and to the right by deflection of 1/600 of span.

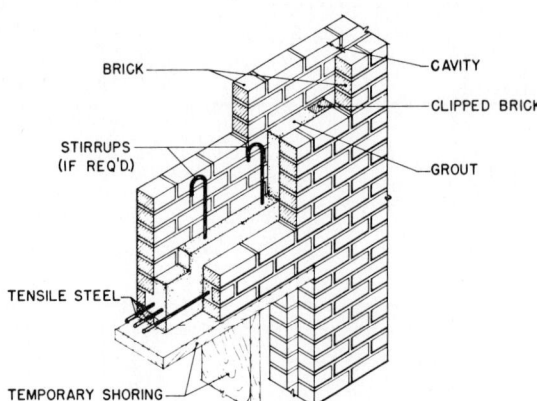

Fig. 25. Reinforced brick lintel in cavity wall

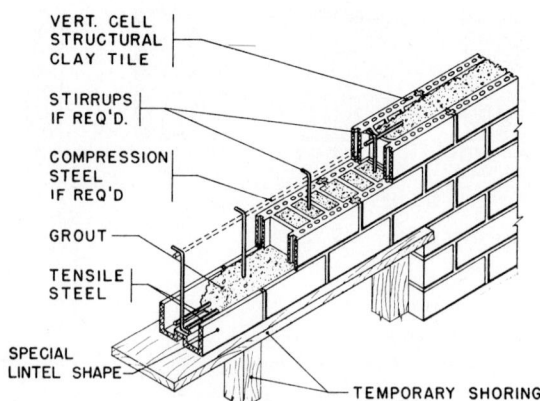

Fig. 26. Reinforced tile lintel in tile wall

by excessive deflection of the lintel. To avoid such cracks, deflection of the lintel should be limited to 1/600 of the span.

Fireproofing: Code requirements for the fireproofing of lintels should be carefully checked and provided for in the design.

Flashing: The design of a steel lintel is not complete until provision has been made for adequate flashing. It is always good insurance to provide weep holes in the facing at the lowest point of the flashing so that any accumulated moisture can easily escape.

REINFORCED MASONRY LINTELS

Reinforced masonry lintels offer certain advantages over structural steel lintels: savings obtained by a reduction in the amount of steel used and by the elimination of painting, and additional safety through built-in fireproofing.

Reinforced brick and tile lintels are simply special applications of reinforced masonry, described on previous pages, and should be designed in accordance with the ANSI Code for Reinforced Masonry (A41.2).

Materials

All standard clay masonry units—solid and hollow, brick and tile, glazed and unglazed—are adaptable to reinforced masonry design. In addition, special soffit shapes are often available for lintel design. Mortar must be of portland cement, lime, and sand, conforming to ASTM Specification C 270, Type M or S. The use of masonry cements in mortar for reinforced masonry is not allowed. Grout may be Type MG, which is generally used on jobs requiring a small amount of reinforced masonry, or Type PG, which is more economical for large jobs.

Load

Determination of the load to be supported by the lintel is the same as that described on the previous page for steel lintels.

Design

Reinforced masonry lintels are usually designed as simple beams. In short or deep lintels, there is little likelihood of cracking due to deflection or end rotation. In relatively long, shallow, or heavily loaded lintels, there is a possibility of cracking, and in such cases it may be advisable to use top, or negative, steel. For such steel to be effective it must be continuous with column steel or must extend into the wall beyond the jamb. Often the easiest solution is to provide a continuous bond beam around the building.

Shear: The maximum allowable shear in lintels with no web reinforcement is 50 psi. If the shearing stress is above 50 psi, but less than 150 psi, stirrups are required. Shearing stress in a lintel must never exceed 150 psi.

Bond: The perimeter of tension steel must be sufficient to ensure that bond stress does not exceed the allowable. Tension steel should extend a minimum of 4 in. beyond the face of the supports. Special anchorage may be accomplished by hooking the bars.

Positioning of steel: There must be at least a 1/4-in. clearance between steel reinforcement and adjacent masonry, except that 1/4-in. bars may be placed in 1/2-in. mortar joints and No. 6 gage wire or smaller may be placed in 3/8-in. mortar joints.

Parallel bars for main reinforcing should have a clearance of one diameter between bars.

Tabular data

Tables 13 to 21 give resisting moments and shears for various brick and tile lintel sections. The tables have been compiled for modular units with 1/2-in. mortar joints, as indicated in the figures accompanying

the tables. The tables, therefore, are conservative for lintels of slightly larger dimensions. Other assumptions, under which the tabulated values have been compiled, are given in Fig. 27. For masonry having an ultimate compressive strength, f'_m less than 2,000 psi, these tables are not valid. For masonry of greater compressive strength, the tables are conservative.

Resisting moments tabulated in the tables are those determined by masonry or by reinforcing steel, whichever governs design. Where resisting moments are governed by the steel, values are in bold face type.

Tabulated are two values of resisting shears, one as diagonal tension in the masonry, V_m, and another as bond on the tensile steel, V_o. For lintels in which no stirrups are provided, the smaller resisting shear governs. V_m is based upon an allowable working stress in diagonal tension of 50 psi. The allowable working stress for shear as diagonal tension, when web reinforcement is provided, is 150 psi. Accordingly, resisting shears could have values 3 times as great as those indicated in column V_m, if stirrups are provided. A glance at the table will indicate that, before such high shearing stresses are reached, bond may govern design. In Tables 13 and 14, bond governs all shear values and, therefore, values of V_m are not given.

For brick laid 3 courses to 8 in. vertically, the effective depth may be expressed in courses (for example, 2c = 2 courses) for purposes of selecting values from the tables. Through the use of this method, it becomes unnecessary to calculate the effective depth in inches in order to use the tables. The effective depths listed in the tables have been rounded off to the nearest 0.1 in.

The effective depth d, in Tables 13 and 14, is based upon a 1/4-in. reinforcement centered within mortar joints. In Tables 15

DESIGN ASSUMPTIONS

f'_m = 2000 psi.

f_s = 20,000 psi.

v = 50 psi. (no stirrups)

v = 150 psi. (stirrups)

u = 80 psi. (plain bars)

u = 160 psi. (deformed bars)

n = 15

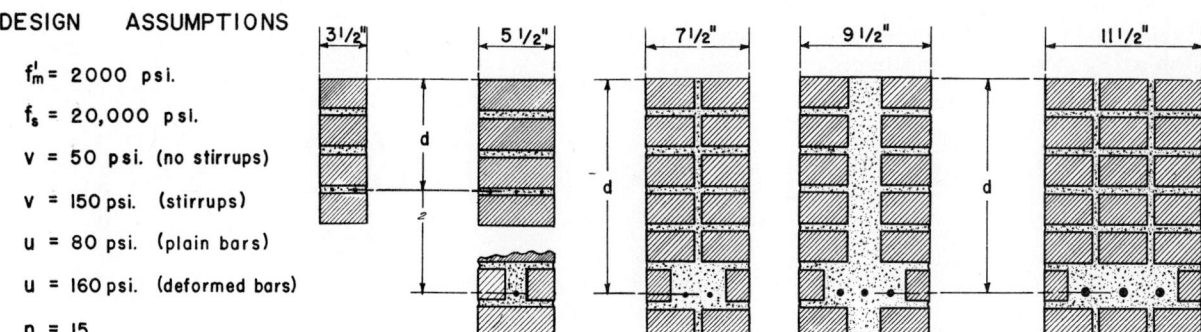

Fig. 27. Typical sections, reinforced brick lintels

Tables 13–18. resisting moments and shears for reinforced brick lintels

Table 13. Nominal 4-in. lintels
Reinforcing in bed joint.

Depth	d = 5.1″	(2c)	d = 7.8″	(3c)	d = 10.5″	(4c)
Reinf.	M	V_o	M	V_o	M	V_o
1—#2	390	220	605	455	820	620
2—#2	750	430	1180	890	1600	1210

Table 14. Nominal 6-in. lintels
Reinforcing in bed joint.

Depth	d = 5.1″	(2c)	d = 7.8″	(3c)	d = 10.5″	(4c)	d = 13.1″	(5c)	d = 15.8″	(6c)
Reinf.	M	V_o	M	V_o	M	V_o	M	V_o	M	V_o
2—#2	780	440	1200	905	1630	1230	2060	1550	2490	1400
3—#2	1140	645	1770	1340	2410	1820	3040	2290	3670	2080

Table 15. Nominal 6-in. lintels
Reinforcing in grout space.

Depth	d = 4.6″		(2c)	d = 7.3″		(3c)	d = 10.0″		(4c)	d = 12.6″		(5c)	d = 15.3″		(6c)	d = 18.0		(7c)
Reinf.	M	V_m	V_o	M	V_m	V_o	M	V_m	V_o	M	V_m	V_o	M	V_m	V_o	M	V_m	V_o
1—#3	770	*	790	1230	*	1260	1700	*	1730	2170	*	2230	2640	*	2720	3120	*	3200
1—#4	1060	*	1010	2160	*	1630	3000	*	2260	3840	*	2890	4700	*	3550	5530	*	4180
1—#5	1190	1060	1210	2600	1730	1970	4400	2410	2750	5810	3090	3540	7120	3800	4330	8410	4480	5120

Table 16. Nominal 8-in. lintels

Depth	d = 4.6″		(2c)	d = 7.3″		(3c)	d = 10.0″		(4c)	d = 12.6″		(5c)	d = 15.3″		(6c)	d = 18.0″		(7c)
Reinf.	M	V_m	V_o	M	V_m	V_o	M	V_m	V_o	M	V_m	V_o	M	V_m	V_o	M	V_m	V_o
2—#3	1380	1540	1550	2420	2480	2500	3350	3420	3440	4280	4380	4400	5220	5340	5360	6160	6300	6340
3—#3	1570	1500	2260	3360	2430	3660	6310	3360	5070	6310	4310	6490	7690	5250	7920	9100	6210	9360
2—#4	1630	1470	1970	3530	2380	3200	5890	3310	4450	7560	4250	5700	9230	5190	6960	10900	6140	8240
2—#5	1800	1410	2350	4000	2300	3860	6820	3210	5380	10170	4140	6930	13970	5070	8500	16600	6010	10100
2—#6	1910	1350	2720	4350	2230	4480	7510	3120	6290	11300	4040	8110	15600	4950	9950	20500	5880	11800

Table 17. Nominal 10-in. lintels

Depth	d = 7.3″		(3c)	d = 10.0″		(4c)	d = 12.5″		(5c)	d = 15.3″		(6c)	d = 18.0″		(7c)	d = 20.6″		(8c)
Reinf.	M	V_m	V_o	M	V_m	V_o	M	V_m	V_o	M	V_m	V_o	M	V_m	V_o	M	V_m	V_o
2—#3	2450	*	2510	3380	*	3470	4310	*	4430	5260	*	5400	6200	*	6370	7150	*	7350
3—#3	3600	3110	3710	4980	4300	5120	6380	5510	6560	7780	6720	8020	9190	7930	9440	10600	9150	10900
2—#4	4130	3060	3230	5950	4240	4480	7630	5440	5760	9320	6640	7020	11000	7850	8300	12700	9060	9580
3—#4	4630	2990	4750	7960	4160	6610	11200	5340	8480	13700	6530	10400	16300	7730	12300	18800	8930	14200
2—#5	4720	2950	3900	7980	4120	5460	11500	5300	7010	14100	6490	8590	16700	7680	10200	19300	8890	11800
2—#6	5170	2870	4540	8850	4020	6380	13300	5180	8220	18300	6350	10100	23300	7540	12000	26900	8730	13900
3—#5	5320	2880	5710	9110	4030	8000	13700	5190	10300	18800	6360	12600	24600	7540	15000	28500	8720	17300
2—#7	5530	2780	5150	9600	3910	7250	14500	5060	9380	20200	6220	11500	26500	7400	13700	33400	8560	15900
3—#6	5750	2790	6660	9980	3910	9310	15100	5060	12000	21000	6210	14800	27500	7380	17600	34800	8550	20400

Table 18. Nominal 12-in. lintels

Depth	d = 10.0″		(4c)	d = 12.6″		(5c)	d = 15.3″		(6c)	d = 18.0″		(7c)	d = 20.6″		(8c)	d = 23.3″		(9c)
Reinf.	M	V_m	V_o	M	V_m	V_o	M	V_m	V_o	M	V_m	V_o	M	V_m	V_o	M	V_m	V_o
2—#4	5990	*	4530	7680	*	5810	9380	*	7070	11100	*	8370	12800	*	9650	14500	*	10900
3—#4	8840	5080	6670	11300	6520	8540	13800	7970	10400	16400	9420	12400	18900	10900	14300	21500	12400	16200
2—#5	9060	5040	5500	11600	6480	7070	14200	7920	8660	16800	9370	10200	19500	10800	11800	22100	12300	13400
4—#4	9800	5010	8750	14800	6430	11200	18200	7870	13800	21600	9310	16300	25000	10800	18800	28300	12200	21400
2—#6	10100	4920	6450	15000	6330	8300	19800	7770	10200	23500	9210	12100	27100	10600	14000	30800	12100	15900
3—#5	10400	4940	8080	15500	6350	10400	21000	7780	12800	24900	9220	15100	28700	10700	17500	32600	12100	19800
2—#7	11000	4800	7340	16500	6190	9470	23000	7610	11600	30100	9030	13800	36400	10500	16000	41400	11900	18200
4—#5	11300	4850	10600	17000	6250	13600	23500	7670	16800	30700	9090	19900	37800	10500	23000	43000	12000	26100
3—#6	11400	4800	9440	17200	6200	12200	23800	7600	14900	31200	9020	17700	39400	10400	20500	45500	11900	23400
4—#6	12400	4710	12300	18800	6090	16000	26100	7480	19600	34300	8880	23300	43400	10300	27000	53200	11700	30700
3—#7	12400	4670	10700	18800	6040	13900	26200	7430	17100	34500	8840	20300	43500	10300	23500	53300	11700	26800
4—#7	13300	4590	14000	20300	5940	18200	28400	7310	22400	37500	8690	26600	47600	10100	30900	58600	11500	35100

Tables 19–21. Resisting moments and shears for reinforced tile lintels

Table 19. Nominal 4-in. lintels

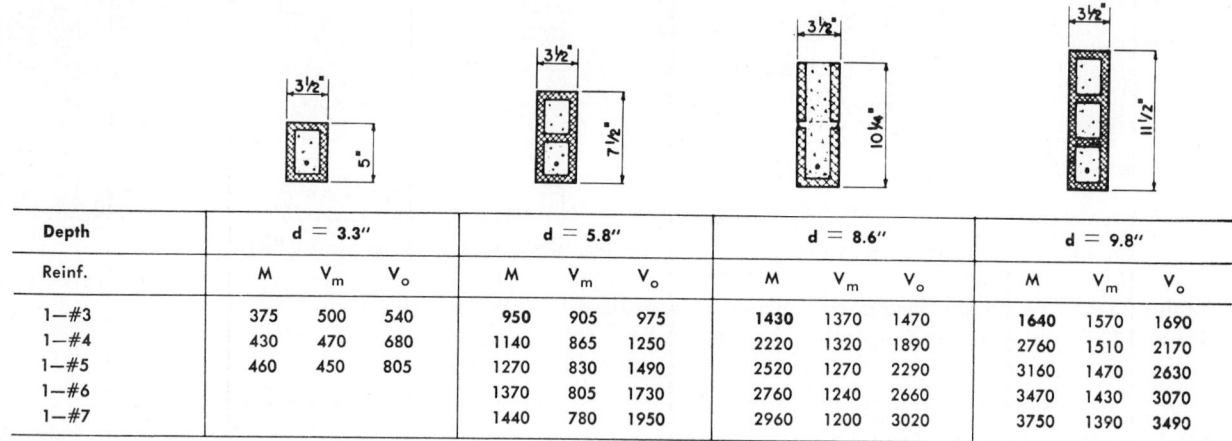

Depth	d = 3.3″			d = 5.8″			d = 8.6″			d = 9.8″		
Reinf.	M	V_m	V_o	M	V_m	V_o	M	V_m	V_o	M	V_m	V_o
1—#3	375	500	540	**950**	905	975	**1430**	1370	1470	**1640**	1570	1690
1—#4	430	470	680	1140	865	1250	2220	1320	1890	2760	1510	2170
1—#5	460	450	805	1270	830	1490	2520	1270	2290	3160	1470	2630
1—#6				1370	805	1730	2760	1240	2660	3470	1430	3070
1—#7				1440	780	1950	2960	1200	3020	3750	1390	3490

Table 20. Nominal 6-in. lintels

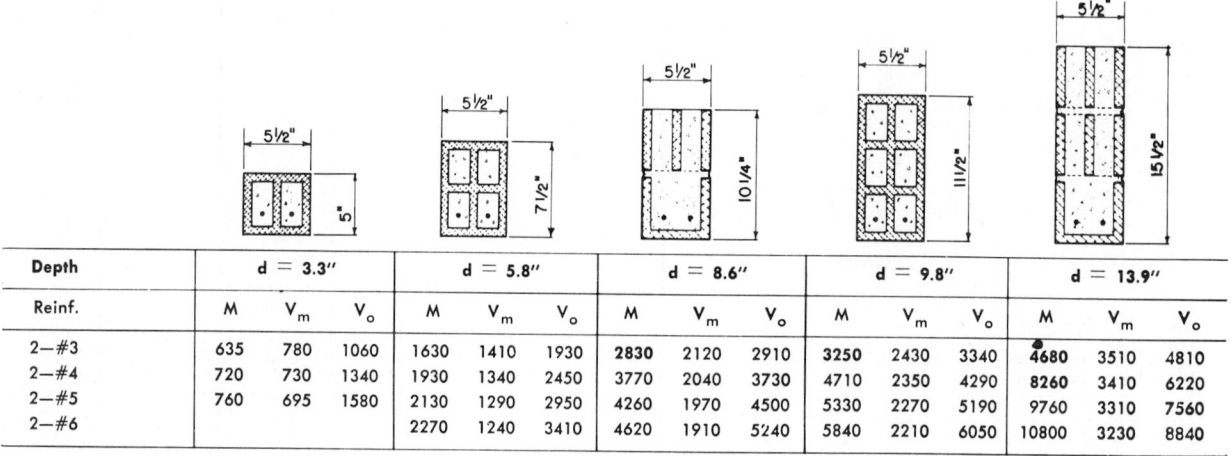

Depth	d = 3.3″			d = 5.8″			d = 8.6″			d = 9.8″			d = 13.9″		
Reinf.	M	V_m	V_o	M	V_m	V_o	M	V_m	V_o	M	V_m	V_o	M	V_m	V_o
2—#3	635	780	1060	1630	1410	1930	**2830**	2120	2910	**3250**	2430	3340	**4680**	3510	4810
2—#4	720	730	1340	1930	1340	2450	3770	2040	3730	4710	2350	4290	8260	3410	6220
2—#5	760	695	1580	2130	1290	2950	4260	1970	4500	5330	2270	5190	9760	3310	7560
2—#6				2270	1240	3410	4620	1910	5240	5840	2210	6050	10800	3230	8840

Table 21. Nominal 8-in. lintels

Depth	d = 3.3″			d = 5.8″			d = 8.6″			d = 9.8″			d = 13.9″		
Reinf.	M	V_m	V_o	M	V_m	V_o	M	V_m	V_o	M	V_m	V_o	M	V_m	V_o
2—#3	790	1080	1080	**1900**	1950	1960	**2870**	2930	2950	**3290**	3360	3380	**4730**	4840	4870
2—#4	905	1020	1360	2400	1860	2500	4630	2830	3800	5790	3260	4360	8380	4710	6310
2—#5	975	968	1620	2670	1790	3000	5300	2740	4590	6630	3160	5290	12000	4590	7690
2—#6				2890	1730	3480	5800	2660	5350	7290	3070	6170	13400	4480	9010
2—#7				3030	1670	3920	6220	2590	6070	7870	2990	7010	14600	4370	10300
2—#8				3150	1620	4350	6570	2520	6760	8350	2910	7810	15600	4280	11500

The tables apply to all solid grouted tile lintels of the over-all dimensions shown.

Resisting moments are given in foot-pounds.

Resisting moments in bold face type are controlled by the steel; others are controlled by the masonry.

Resisting shears are given in pounds.

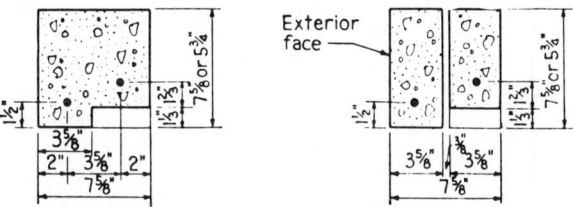

Fig. 28. One-piece lintel (see Table 22) and split lintel (see Table 23)

Table 22. Lintels with wall load only

Size of lintel		Clear span of lintel ft.	Bottom reinforcement	
Height in.	Width in.		No. bars	Size of bars
5¾	7⅝	Up to 7	2	⅜-in. round deformed
5¾	7⅝	7 to 8	2	⅝-in. round deformed
7⅝	7⅝	Up to 8	2	⅜-in. round deformed
7⅝	7⅝	8 to 9	2	½-in. round deformed
7⅝	7⅝	9 to 10	2	⅝-in. round deformed

Table 23. Split lintels with wall load only

Size of lintel		Clear span of lintel ft.	Bottom reinforcement	
Height in.	Width in.		No. bars	Size of bars
5¾	3⅝	Up to 7	1	⅜-in. round deformed
5¾	3⅝	7 to 8	1	⅝-in. round deformed
7⅝	3⅝	Up to 8	1	⅜-in. round deformed
7⅝	3⅝	8 to 9	1	½-in. round deformed
7⅝	3⅝	9 to 10	1	⅝-in. round deformed

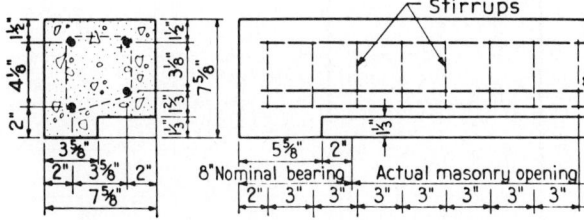

Fig. 29. One-piece lintel with stirrups (see Table 24)

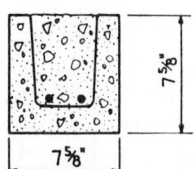

Fig. 30. Lintel block

through 18, the effective depths are based upon reinforcement placed in grout with a ½-in. clearance between the steel and the top of the adjacent unit immediately below. True effective depth, therefore, varies with the bar diameter. This variation, however, is small in the range of bar sizes chosen for these tables. The effective depths shown are listed primarily to aid the designer when using units that are not laid 3 courses to 8 in. vertically (such as roman brick or oversize brick).

REINFORCED CONCRETE LINTELS

The tables and illustrations shown on this page are from *Concrete Masonry Handbook*, published by the Portland Cement Association.

Design data

Design data for one-piece and split (two-piece) lintels, supporting wall loads only, are shown in Fig. 28 and Tables 22 and 23. Data for lintels that support both wall and floor loads are shown in Fig. 29 and Table 24. All designs are based on concrete having an ultimate strength of 2,000 psi.

Split lintels should never be used to support combined wall and floor loads, because it is difficult to design the inner section for the same deflection as the outer section, which carries wall loads only. Differences in deflection of the two sections would probably result in cracking of the masonry wall. Split lintels are light in weight and easy to handle. The air space between the sections provides some insulation.

Reinforced concrete lintels should have a minimum bearing area of at least 8 in. at each end. Larger bearing areas are required for lintels that have long spans or carry heavy loads. All but short simple lintels act as reinforced concrete beams and should be designed by an engineer.

In locations where it is desirable that lintels have a surface texture matching that of the concrete masonry wall, special cast-in-place or precast lintels can be made by using channel-shaped lintel block (Fig. 30).

Table 24. Lintels with wall and floor loads

Floor load is assumed to be 85 psf with 20-ft span.

Size of lintel		Clear span of lintel ft.	Reinforcement		Web reinforcement No. 6 gage wire stirrups. Spacings from end of lintel—both ends the same
Height in.	Width in.		Top	Bottom	
7⅝	7⅝	3	None	2—½-in. round	No stirrups required
7⅝	7⅝	4	None	2—¾-in. round	3 stirrups, Sp.: 2, 3, 3 in.
7⅝	7⅝	5	2—⅜-in. round	2—⅞-in. round	5 stirrups, Sp.: 2, 3, 3, 3, 3 in.
7⅝	7⅝	6	2—½-in. round	2—⅞-in. round	6 stirrups, Sp.: 2, 3, 3, 3, 3, 3 in.
7⅝	7⅝	7	2— 1-in. round	2— 1-in. round	9 stirrups, Sp.: 2, 2, 3, 3, 3, 3, 3, 3 in.

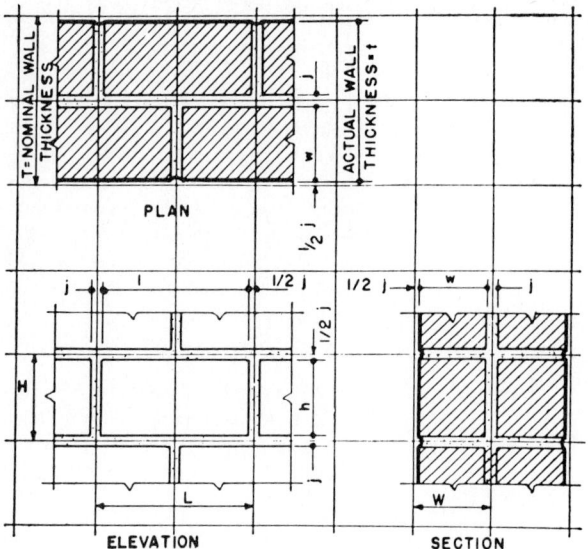

Fig. 31. Modular masonry dimensions

Capital letters signify nominal dimensions. Lower-case letters signify standard or specified dimensions. Thickness of standard mortar joint is indicated by "j." Actual unit dimensions may vary from standard or specified dimensions by not more than the permissible tolerances for variations of dimensions.

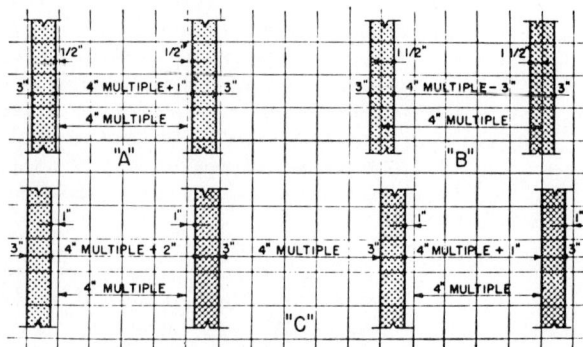

Fig. 32. Grid locations of masonry walls

Table 25. Nominal modular sizes of brick (in inches)

Thickness	Face dimension in wall		Modular coursing, in.
	Height	Length	
4	2	12	2C-4
4	2⅔	8 or 12	3C-8
4	3⅕	8 or 12	5C-16
4	4	8 or 12	1C-4
4	5⅓	8 or 12	3C-16

Table 26. Nominal modular sizes of structural clay load-bearing backup tile (in inches)

Thickness	Face Dimension in Wall	
	Height	Length
4	5⅓	12
4	8	8 or 12
4	10⅔	12
6	5⅓	12
6	8	12 [1]
6	10⅔	12
8	5⅓	12 [1]
8	8	8 or 12 [1]
8	10⅔	12

[1] Includes stretcher and header units.

Data and illustrations on this and the following three pages have been derived from *Technical Notes on Brick Construction*, published by the Brick Institute of America.

UNIT DIMENSIONS

Modular clay masonry units are designated by nominal dimensions, equal to the standard or actual dimension plus the thickness of the mortar joint with which the unit is designed to be laid, as illustrated in Fig. 31. For example, a modular unit whose nominal length is 12 in. would actually be 11½ in. if the unit were designed to be laid with a ½-in. mortar joint, or 11⅝ in. if designed for a ⅜-in. joint.

The standard mortar joint thicknesses for modular clay masonry units are ¼ in. for glazed brick and tile, ⅜ in. or ½ in. for facing brick and unglazed facing tile, and ½ in. for building brick and structural tile.

Sizes of brick: Table 25 lists the sizes of modular brick currently available. However, since few manufacturers produce all the sizes listed, the purchaser should ascertain the sizes available in any locality before proceeding with the design.

Sizes of structural clay tile: Modular nominal sizes of structural clay tile are given in Tables 26, 27, and 28. Only the dimensions of the full-size stretcher units are shown. Half lengths and half heights, as well as corner and jamb units, are available in most series for bonding. Here also, few if any manufacturers will produce all of the sizes listed.

Sizes of partition tile: No modular standards have as yet been established for sizes of partition tile by the American National Standards Institute.

MODULAR DETAILS (see section on *Modular coordination*)

Modular details show the relation of the building parts to the 4-in. grid, and thus their relation to one another. This rela-

Table 27. Nominal modular sizes of structural clay load-bearing wall tile (in inches)

Thickness	Face Dimension in Wall	
	Height	Length
4	5⅓	12
4	8	8 or 12
4	12	12 [1]
6	5⅓	12
6	12	12 [1]
8	5⅓	12
8	8	8, 12 or 16
8	12	12 [1]
10	5⅓	12
10	8	12
10	12	12 [1]
12	12	12 [1]

[1] Partition tile.

Table 28. Nominal modular sizes of structural clay facing tile (in inches)

Thickness	Face Dimension in Wall	
	Height	Length
2, 4, 6 and 8	4	8 and 12
2, 4, 6 and 8	5⅓	8 and 12
2, 4, 6 and 8	8	12 and 16 [1]

[1] 16-in. lengths in 2 and 4 in. thicknesses only.

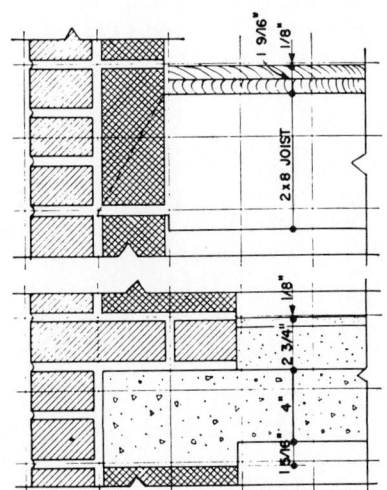

Fig. 33. Modular masonry walls with two types of floor construction

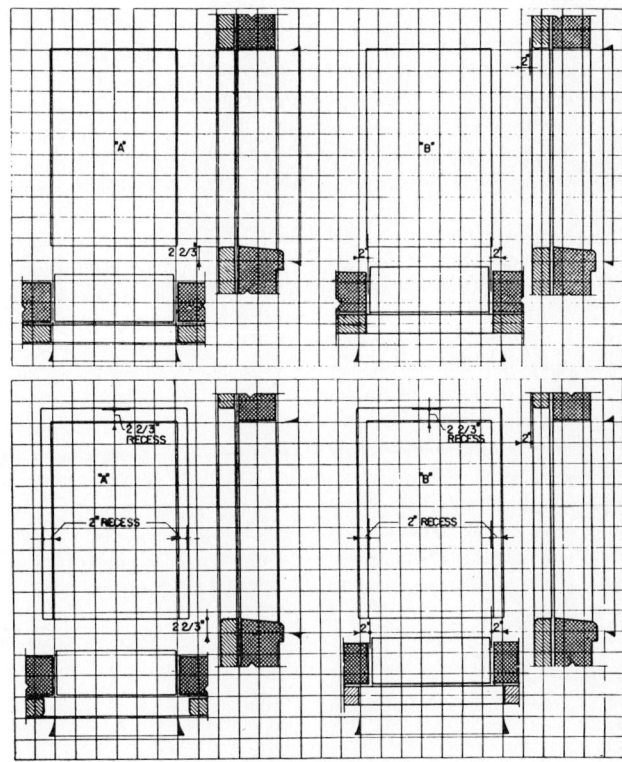

Fig. 34. Grid positions of openings

tionship is shown by reference dimensions to grid lines on the large-scale details. In order to correlate building layouts with details, layout dimensions must maintain the grid positions of the modular details. For this reason, the selection of grid locations of critical parts of the structure, such as walls and floors, is one of the first steps to be taken in the development of a modular design.

Grid locations of masonry walls: Alternate grid locations for walls are shown in Fig. 32. Symmetrical grid positions for walls (either centered between or on grid lines) have certain fundamental advantages. In details "A" and "B," the difference between grid dimensions and actual dimensions is a single constant. In detail "C," however, there are three alternate values for this difference and they must be identified on the plans.

Grid location of floors: The surface of finished floors bearing on masonry walls should be placed ⅛ in. below the grid line in order to maintain a constant relation between the floor masonry openings for exterior doors. Figure 33 illustrates modular details of two types of floor construction and their relationship to the grid and the exterior masonry wall.

Grid position of openings: Opening details involve the coordination of many products, such as modular masonry (both facing and backup), windows, doors, glass block, and trim. Because of the interchangeability provided by coordination, the jamb, head, and sill details are each referenced to the standard grid, permitting them to be drawn as separate modular

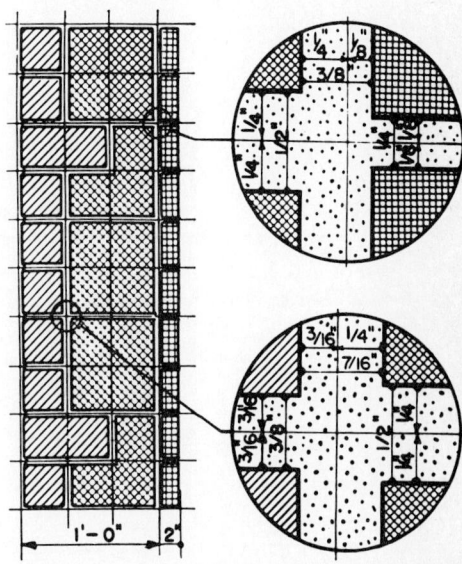

Fig. 35. Coordination of modular masonry products

Exterior facing brick are shown with ⅜-in. joints, backed up with structural clay tile with ½-in. joints. Inside facing of glazed-tile soaps is laid with ¼-in. joints.

details. The combination for any one job may then be selected and shown by the architect. Since it is essential for their correct combination that these separate details be referenced to the same grid lines, the grid opening is used and identified by the half-arrow symbol as shown in Fig. 34.

The conformation of openings at jamb and head may be flush or may include a recess. The depth of recesses at jambs is always 2 in., and, at the head, 1⅓ in. or 2⅔ in. The conformation at sills is determined by the window or door installation detail and the type of sill used. Windows and doors should be placed horizontally in a symmetrical grid position so that the same modular detail will apply to each jamb. This placement does not apply to the vertical position since head and sill details are essentially different.

It is usually essential that the head of an opening coincide with a horizontal mortar joint.

ESTIMATING QUANTITIES

Except for the nonmodular "standard brick" (3¾ by 2¼ by 8 in.) and some oversize brick (3¾ by 2¾ by 8 in.), virtually all the brick produced and used in the United States are sized to fit the modular system. Since there is still a considerable production of nonmodular brick, this section includes estimating information for nonmodular as well as modular units.

Because of its simplicity and accuracy, the most widely used estimating procedure is the "wall-area" method. It consists simply of multiplying known quantities of material required per square foot by the net wall area (gross areas less areas of all openings).

Estimating material quantities is greatly simplified under the modular system. For a given nominal size, the number of modular masonry units per square foot of wall will be the same regardless of mortar joint thickness—assuming, of course, that the units are to be laid with the thickness of joint for which they are designed. There are only

three standard modular joint thicknesses: ¼ in., ⅜ in., and ½ in.

In contrast, the number of nonmodular standard brick required per square foot of wall will vary with the thickness of the mortar joint.

In the estimating procedure, determine the net quantities of all material before adding any allowances for waste. Allowances for waste and breakage vary, but, as a general rule, at least 5 per cent should be added to the net brick quantities and 10 to 25 per cent to the net mortar quantities. Particular job conditions or experience may dictate different factors.

ESTIMATING TABLES

Table 29 gives net quantities of brick and mortar required to construct walls 1 wythe in thickness with nonmodular brick in the two most used sizes and the two most common joint thicknesses (⅜ in. and ½ in.). Mortar quantities are for full bed and head joints.

Table 29. Nonmodular brick and mortar required for single-wythe walls in running bond (no allowances for breakage or waste)

Size of brick, in.			With ⅜-in. joints			With ½-in. joints		
t	h	l	Number of brick per 100 sq ft	Cubic feet of mortar per 100 sq ft	Cubic feet of mortar per 1,000 brick	Number of brick per 100 sq ft	Cubic feet of mortar per 100 sq ft	Cubic feet of mortar per 1,000 brick
3¾ × 2¼ × 8			655	5.8	8.8	616	7.2	11.7
3¾ × 2¾ × 8			551	5.0	9.1	522	6.4	12.2

Table 30. Modular brick and mortar required for single-wythe walls in running bond (no allowances for breakage or waste)

Nominal size of brick, in.			Number of brick per 100 sq ft	Cubic feet of mortar			
				Per 100 sq ft		Per 1,000 brick	
t	h	l		⅜-in. joints	½-in. joints	⅜-in. joints	½-in. joints
4 × 2⅔ × 8			675	5.5	7.0	8.1	10.3
4 × 3⅕ × 8			563	4.8	6.1	8.6	10.9
4 × 4 × 8			450	4.2	5.3	9.2	11.7
4 × 5⅓ × 8			338	3.5	4.4	10.2	12.9
4 × 2 × 12			600	6.5	8.2	10.8	13.7
4 × 2⅔ × 12			450	5.1	6.5	11.3	14.4
4 × 3⅕ × 12			375	4.4	5.6	11.7	14.9
4 × 4 × 12			300	3.7	4.8	12.3	15.7
4 × 5⅓ × 12			225	3.0	3.9	13.4	17.1
6 × 2⅔ × 12			450	7.9	10.2	17.5	22.6
6 × 3⅕ × 12			375	6.8	8.8	18.1	23.4
6 × 4 × 12			300	5.6	7.4	19.1	24.7

Table 31. Bond correction factors for walls of Tables 29 and 30* (add to facing and deduct from backing)

Bond	Correction factor
Full headers every fifth course only	⅕
Full headers every sixth course only	⅙
Full headers every seventh course only	⅐
English bond (full headers every second course)	½
Flemish bond (alternate full headers and stretchers every course)	⅓
Flemish headers every sixth course	1/18
Flemish cross bond (Flemish headers every second course)	⅙
Double-stretcher, garden wall bond	⅕
Triple stretcher, garden wall bond	⅐

Correction factors are applicable only to those brick which have lengths of twice their bed depths.

Table 32. Cubic feet of mortar for collar joints*

Cubic feet of mortar per 100 sq ft of wall		
¼-in. joint	⅜-in. joint	½-in. joint
2.08	3.13	4.17

$$* \; Cu\ ft\ per\ 1{,}000\ units = \frac{10 \times cu\ ft\ per\ 100\ sq\ ft\ of\ wall}{number\ of\ units\ per\ sq\ ft\ of\ wall}$$

Table 34. Average specific gravities and unit weights*

Material	Specific gravity	Unit weight, lb per cu ft
Portland cement	3.15	94
Lime	2.25	40
Water	1.00	62.4

Values for sand are not listed because they vary considerably. Obtain precise values from laboratory tests (or from supplier).

Table 33. Material quantities per cubic foot of mortar

	Quantities by volume				Quantities by weight			
	Mortar type and proportions by volume				Mortar type and proportions by volume			
	M	S	N	O	M	S	N	O
Material	1:¼:3	1:½:4½	1:1:6	1:2:9	1:¼:3	1:½:4½	1:1:6	1:2:9
Cement	0.333	0.222	0.167	0.111	31.33	20.89	15.67	10.44
Lime	0.083	0.111	0.167	0.222	3.33	4.44	6.67	8.89
Sand	1.000	1.000	1.000	1.000	80.00	80.00	80.00	80.00

Table 30 provides similar information for walls constructed with modular brick of various sizes.

The brick and mortar quantities in Tables 29 and 30 are for running (or stack) bond which contains no headers. For bonds requiring full headers, the correction factors given in Table 31 must be applied. Also, when estimating quantities for multi-wythe walls, the mortar quantities for interior vertical longitudinal collar joints given in Table 32 must be added.

Table 33 contains the quantities of portland cement, hydrated lime, and sand required for 1 cu ft of four types of mortar. Although ASTM C270 permits a range of proportions for each mortar type (see Table 1), the quantities in Table 32 have been based on a single set of proportions for each of these types. For convenience in estimating, quantities based upon both weight and volume are included in the table. Mortar is generally proportioned by volume on the job, although proportioning by weight is the more accurate method.

Mortar yield

By rule of thumb: For jobs where mortar yield calculations are not critical, use the following rule of thumb to determine approximate mortar yield:

For each 1 cu ft of damp loose sand, the mortar yield will be 1 cu ft.

By calculation: For given volumes of materials, mortar yield depends upon proportions, water content, and air content. Water content will vary with sand gradation, lime and cement content, and, quite often, the judgment of the brick mason.

Mortar yield calculations are based upon absolute volume. To determine yield, first obtain:

1. Unit weights and specific quantities of all materials (see Table 34).

2. Total volume of water used in mortar mix, including mixing water and the water present in the sand.

Sand: When a relatively small amount of water (4 to 10 per cent) is added to dry sand, it *bulks*; that is, it increases in volume far in excess of the volume of water added. This increase can be as much as 50 per cent, depending largely upon the gradation of the sand. Because of bulking, volumetric measurement of sand is not very accurate.

Although weighing sand is a more accurate method of measurement, it is, perhaps, not nearly so convenient as measuring volume. For proportion specifications, ASTM C270 assumes that 1 cu ft of damp loose sand (bulked sand) is equal to 80 lb of dry sand (and that it has bulked approximately 38 per cent).

Specific gravity of sand: Obtain the specific gravity of sand from the supplier. Procedure for determining specific gravities of sands is given in ASTM C128, *Standard Method of Test for Specific Gravity and Absorption of Fine Aggregate.* An average value for silica sands is 2.65.

Moisture content of sand: In any given sand, the moisture content may vary from day to day or even from hour to hour. While this variation exists, it is not as critical in mortars as it is in portland cement concrete. Most damp loose sands contain approximately ½ to 1 gal of water per cu ft of sand. For many yield calculations, an assumption of this amount of water may be sufficient. Where greater accuracy is desired, determine moisture content according to the procedure given in ASTM C70, *Standard Method of Test for Surface Moisture in Fine Aggregate.*

Weight of sand: To accurately determine mortar yield requires knowledge of the sand's moisture content, specific gravity, and unit weight (bulked and dry). To deter-

mine bulked unit weight, weigh 1 cu ft of bulked sand. The standard method for determining unit weight of aggregate is given in ASTM C29, *Standard Method of Test for Unit Weight of Aggregate.* When moisture content and bulked weight are known, the weights of water and dry sand are easily computed.

Water: Use the total weight of water in yield calculations; i.e., sum of the weights of mixing water and water present in the sand. If the moisture content of the sand is known, it is a simple matter to calculate the weight of water in the sand. Add the weight of water present in the sand to the weight of mixing water added to the batch at the mixer. To convert gallons of mixing water to pounds, multiply by 8.33.

Absolute volume: The absolute solid volume of a material is the volume of its solid portion only; voids are not included. Thus

$$V_m = \frac{W_m}{62.4 G_m} \qquad (1)$$

where V_m = absolute solid volume of any given material, cu ft

W_m = batch weight of the material, lb

G_m = specific gravity of the material

The absolute volume of mortar is the sum of the absolute volumes of all ingredients (cement, lime, sand, and water)

$$V_M = V_C + V_L + V_S + V_W \qquad (2)$$

Mortar yield: Mortar yield is equal to its absolute volume (V_M) plus the volume of entrapped air. When the air content of mortar is known, the yield may be found from the relationship

$$Y = \frac{100 V_M}{100 - a} \qquad (3)$$

where Y = volume of mortar yield, cu ft

V_M = absolute solid volume of mortar, cu ft, from Eq. (2)

a = air content of freshly mixed mortar, per cent

Air contents of freshly mixed portland cement-lime mortars are in the order of 10 per cent.

Brick, coursing tables

Table 35. Vertical coursing table for nonmodular brick*

No. of	2 1/4" high units		2 5/8" high units		2 3/4" high units	
courses	3/8" joint	1/2" joint	3/8" joint	1/2" joint	3/8" joint	1/2" joint
1	0'-2 5/8"	0'-2 3/4"	0'-3"	0'-3 1/8"	0'-3 1/8"	0'-3 1/4"
2	0'-5 1/4"	0'-5 1/2"	0'-6"	0'-6 1/4"	0'-6 1/4"	0'-6 1/2"
3	0'-7 7/8"	0'-8 1/4"	0'-9"	0'-9 3/8"	0'-9 3/8"	0'-9 3/4"
4	0'-10 1/2"	0'-11"	1'-0"	1'-0 1/2"	1'-0 1/2"	1'-1"
5	1'-1 1/8"	1'-1 3/4"	1'-3"	1'-3 5/8"	1'-3 5/8"	1'-4 1/4"
6	1'-3 3/4"	1'-4 1/2"	1'-6"	1'-6 3/4"	1'-6 3/4"	1'-7 1/2"
7	1'-6 3/8"	1'-7 1/4"	1'-9"	1'-9 7/8"	1'-9 7/8"	1'-10 3/4"
8	1'-9"	1'-10"	2'-0"	2'-1"	2'-1"	2'-2"
9	1'-11 5/8"	2'-0 3/4"	2'-3"	2'-4 1/8"	2'-4 1/8"	2'-5 1/4"
10	2'-2 1/4"	2'-3 1/2"	2'-6"	2'-7 1/4"	2'-7 1/4"	2'-8 1/2"
11	2'-4 7/8"	2'-6 1/4"	2'-9"	2'-10 3/8"	2'-10 3/8"	2'-11 3/4"
12	2'-7 1/2"	2'-9"	3'-0"	3'-1 1/2"	3'-1 1/2"	3'-3"
13	2'-10 1/8"	2'-11 3/4"	3'-3"	3'-4 5/8"	3'-4 5/8"	3'-6 1/4"
14	3'-0 3/4"	3'-2 1/2"	3'-6"	3'-7 3/4"	3'-7 3/4"	3'-9 1/2"
15	3'-3 3/8"	3'-5 1/4"	3'-9"	3'-10 7/8"	3'-10 7/8"	4'-0 3/4"
16	3'-6"	3'-8"	4'-0"	4'-2"	4'-2"	4'-4"
17	3'-8 5/8"	3'-10 3/4"	4'-3"	4'-5 1/8"	4'-5 1/8"	4'-7 1/4"
18	3'-11 1/4"	4'-1 1/2"	4'-6"	4'-8 1/4"	4'-8 1/4"	4'-10 1/2"
19	4'-1 7/8"	4'-4 1/4"	4'-9"	4'-11 3/8"	4'-11 3/8"	5'-1 3/4"
20	4'-4 1/2"	4'-7"	5'-0"	5'-2 1/2"	5'-2 1/2"	5'-5"
21	4'-7 1/8"	4'-9 3/4"	5'-3"	5'-5 5/8"	5'-5 5/8"	5'-8 1/4"
22	4'-9 3/4"	5'-0 1/2"	5'-6"	5'-8 3/4"	5'-8 3/4"	5'-11 1/2"
23	5'-0 3/8"	5'-3 1/4"	5'-9"	5'-11 7/8"	5'-11 7/8"	6'-2 3/4"
24	5'-3"	5'-6"	6'-0"	6"-3"	6'-3"	6'-6"
25	5'-5 5/8"	5'-8 3/4'	6'-3"	6'-6 1/8"	6'-6 1/8"	6'-9 1/4"
26	5'-8 1/4"	5'-11 1/2"	6'-6"	6'-9 1/4"	6'-9 1/4"	7'-0 1/2"
27	5'-10 7/8"	6'-2 1/4"	6'-9"	7'-0 3/8"	7'-0 3/8"	7'-3 3/4"
28	6'-1 1/2"	6'-5"	7'-0"	7'-3 1/2"	7'-3 1/2"	7'-7"
29	6'-4 1/8"	6'-7 3/4"	7'-3"	7'-6 5/8"	7'-6 5/8"	7'-10 1/4"
30	6'-6 3/4"	6'-10 1/2"	7'-6"	7'-9 3/4"	7'-9 3/4"	8'-1 1/2"
31	6'-9 3/8"	7'-1 1/4"	7'-9"	8'-0 7/8"	8'-0 7/8"	8'-4 3/4"
32	7'-0"	7'-4"	8'-0"	8'-4"	8'-4"	8'-8"
33	7'-2 5/8"	7'-6 3/4"	8'-3"	8'-7 1/8"	8'-7 1/8"	8'-11 1/4"
34	7'-5 1/4"	7'-9 1/2"	8'-6"	8'-10 1/4"	8'-10 1/4"	9'-2 1/2"
35	7'-7 7/8"	8'-0 1/4"	8'-9"	9'-1 3/8"	9'-1 3/8"	9'-5 3/4"
36	7'-10 1/2"	8'-3"	9'-0"	9'-4 1/2"	9'-4 1/2"	9'-9"
37	8'-1 1/8"	8'-5 3/4"	9'-3"	9'-7 5/8"	9'-7 5/8"	10'-0 1/4"
38	8'-3 3/4"	8'-8 1/2"	9'-6"	9'-10 3/4"	9'-10 3/4"	10'-3 1/2"
39	8'-6 3/8"	8'-11 1/4"	9'-9"	10'-1 7/8"	10'-1 7/8"	10'-6 3/4"
40	8'-9"	9'-2"	10'-0"	10'-5"	10'-5"	10'-10"
41	8'-11 5/8"	9'-4 3/4"	10'-3"	10'-8 1/8"	10'-8 1/8"	11'-1 1/4"
42	9'-2 1/4"	9'-7 1/2"	10'-6"	10'-11 1/4"	10'-11 1/4"	11'-4 1/2"
43	9'-4 7/8"	9'-10 1/4"	10'-9"	11'-2 3/8"	11'-2 3/8"	11'-7 3/4"
44	9'-7 1/2"	10'-1"	11'-0"	11'-5 1/2"	11' 5 1/2"	11'-11"
45	9'-10 1/8"	10'-3 3/4"	11'-3"	11'-8 5/8"	11'-8 5/8"	12'-2 1/4"
46	10'-0 3/4	10'-6 1/2"	11'-6"	11'-11 3/4"	11'-11 3/4"	12'-5 1/2"
47	10'-3 3/8"	10'-9 1/4"	11'-9"	12'-2 7/8"	12'-2 7/8"	12'-8 3/4"
48	10'-6"	11'-0"	12'-0"	12'-6"	12'-6"	13'-0"
49	10'-8 5/8"	11'-2 3/4"	12'-3"	12'-9 1/8"	12'-9 1/8"	13'-3 1/4"
50	10'-11 1/4"	11'-5 1/2"	12'-6"	13'-0 1/4"	13'-0 1/4"	13'-6 1/2"
100	21'-10 1/2"	22'-11"	25'-0"	26'-0 1/2"	26'-0 1/2"	27'-1"

* *Brick positioned in wall as stretchers. Vertical dimensions are from bottom of mortar joint to bottom of mortar joint.*

Table 36. Vertical coursing table for modular brick*

No. of	Nominal height (h) of unit†				
courses		2 2/3"	3 1/5"	4"	5 1/3"
1	0'-2"	0'-2 11/16"	0'-3 3/16"	0'-4"	0'-5 5/16"
2	0'-4"	0'-5 5/16"	0'-6 3/8"	0'-8"	0'-10 11/16"
3	0'-6"	0'-8"	0'-9 5/8"	1'-0"	1'-4"
4	0'-8"	0'-10 11/16"	1'-0 13/16"	1'-4"	1'-9 5/16"
5	0'-10"	1'-1 5/16"	1'-4"	1'-8"	2'-2 11/16"
6	1'-0"	1'-4"	1'-7 3/16"	2'-0"	2'-8"
7	1'-2"	1'-6 11/16"	1'-10 3/8"	2'-4"	3'-1 5/16"
8	1'-4"	1'-9 5/16"	2'-1 5/8"	2'-8"	3'-6 11/16"
9	1'-6"	2'-0"	2'-4 13/16"	3'-0"	4'-0"
10	1'-8"	2'-2 11/16"	2'-8"	3'-4"	4'-5 5/16"
11	1'-10"	2'-5 5/16"	2'-11 3/16"	3'-8"	4'-10 11/16"
12	2'-0"	2'-8"	3'-2 3/8"	4'-0"	5'-4"
13	2'-2"	2'-10 11/16"	3'-5 5/8"	4'-4"	5'-9 5/16"
14	2'-4"	3'-1 5/16"	3'-8 13/16"	4'-8"	6'-2 11/16"
15	2'-6"	3'-4"	4'-0"	5'-0"	6'-8"
16	2'-8"	3'-6 11/16"	4'-3 3/16"	5'-4"	7'-1 5/16"
17	2'-10"	3'-9 5/16"	4'-6 3/8"	5'-8"	7'-6 11/16"
18	3'-0"	4'-0"	4'-9 5/8"	6'-0"	8'-0"
19	3'-2"	4'-2 11/16"	5'-0 13/16"	6'-4"	8'-5 5/16"
20	3'-4"	4'-5 5/16"	5'-4"	6'-8"	8'-10 11/16"
21	3'-6"	4'-8"	5'-7 3/16"	7'-0"	9'-4"
22	3'-8"	4'-10 11/16"	5'-10 3/8"	7'-4"	9'-9 5/16"
23	3'-10"	5'-1 5/16"	6'-1 5/8"	7'-8"	10'-2 11/16"
24	4'-0"	5'-4"	6'-4 13/16"	8'-0"	10'-8"
25	4'-2"	5'-6 11/16"	6'-8"	8'-4"	11'-1 5/16"
26	4'-4"	5'-9 5/16"	6'-11 3/16"	8'-8"	11'-6 11/16"
27	4'-6"	6'-0"	7'-2 3/8"	9'-0"	12'-0"
28	4'-8"	6'-2 11/16"	7'-5 5/8"	9'-4"	12'-5 5/16"
29	4'-10"	6'-5 5/16"	7'-8 13/16"	9'-8"	12'-10 11/16"
30	5'-0"	6'-8"	8'-0"	10'-0"	13'-4"
31	5'-2"	6'-10 11/16"	8'-3 3/16"	10'-4"	13'-9 5/16"
32	5'-4"	7'-1 5/16"	8'-6 3/8"	10'-8"	14'-2 11/16"
33	5'-6"	7'-4"	8'-9 5/8"	11'-0"	14'-8"
34	5'-8"	7'-6 11/16"	9'-0 13/16"	11'-4"	15'-1 5/16"
35	5'-10"	7'-9 5/16"	9'-4"	11'-8"	15'-6 11/16"
36	6'-0"	8'-0"	9'-7 3/16"	12'-0"	16'-0"
37	6'-2"	8'-2 11/16"	9'-10 3/8"	12'-4"	16'-5 5/16"
38	6'-4"	8'-5 5/16"	10'-1 5/8"	12'-8"	16'-10 11/16"
39	6'-6"	8'-8"	10'-4 13/16"	13'-0"	17'-4"
40	6'-8"	8'-10 11/16"	10'-8"	13'-4"	17'-9 5/16"
41	6'-10"	9'-1 5/16"	10'-11 3/16"	13'-8"	18'-2 11/16"
42	7'-0"	9'-4"	11'-2 3/8"	14'-0"	18'-8"
43	7'-2"	9'-6 11/16"	11'-5 5/8"	14'-4"	19'-1 5/16"
44	7'-4"	9'-9 5/16"	11'-8 13/16"	14'-8"	19'-6 11/16"
45	7'-6"	10'-0"	12'-0"	15'-0"	20'-0"
46	7'-8"	10'-2 11/16"	12'-3 3/16"	15'-4"	20'-5 5/16"
47	7'-10"	10'-5 5/16"	12'-6 3/8"	15'-8"	20'-10 11/16"
48	8'-0"	10'-8"	12'-9 5/8"	16'-0"	12'-4"
49	8'-2"	10'-10 11/16"	13'-0 13/16"	16'-4"	12'-9 5/16"
50	8'-4"	11'-1 5/16"	13'-4"	16'-8"	22'-2 11/16"
100	16'-8"	22'-2 11/16"	26'-8"	33'-4"	44'-5 5/16"

* *Brick positioned in wall as stretchers.*

† *For convenience in using table, nominal 1/3", 2/3", and 1/5" heights of units have been changed to nearest 1/16". Vertical dimensions are from bottom of mortar joint to bottom of mortar joint.*

Fig. 36. Running bond

Fig. 37. Common bond with headers every sixth course

Fig. 38. Common bond with Flemish headers every sixth course

TYPES OF BONDS

The five pattern bonds in most common use today are running bond, common or American bond, Flemish bond, English bond, and English cross or Dutch bond. Variations of these basic bonds include double-stretcher Flemish, garden wall, stack or block, and others too numerous to mention here. (For a more detailed discussion, see *Bonds and Mortars in the Wall of Brick*, Structural Clay Products Institute.)

Running bond is the simplest of the basic pattern bonds and consists entirely of stretchers. Since there are no headers, metal ties must be used for structural bond. Running bond is used largely in cavity-wall construction and in brick-veneered walls. Figure 36 shows conventional running bond with vertical joints centered on the stretchers above and below. With Roman brick, nominally 12 in. long, the vertical joints often occur at the third points of the units above and below. This arrangement is commonly known as "one-third bond."

Common or American bond is a variation of running bond with a complete course of full-length headers at regular intervals—the interval depending upon the size of the units and the bonding requirements. These headers provide structural bonding as well as a definite pattern on the wall surface. Header courses usually occur at every fifth, sixth, or seventh course. Figure 37 shows common bond with headers at every sixth course. A "three-quarter" brick must start each header course at the corner and a three-quarter brick closer must be used in the face of

the wall in which the end of the starter brick appears. Common bond may be varied by using a Flemish header course (Fig. 38) instead of continuous headers.

Flemish bond (Fig. 39) consists of alternate stretchers and headers, with the headers centered on the stretchers above and below. Headers used outside the structural bonding courses may be "blind headers" or half brick. Two methods are used for starting the corners of Flemish bond work. Shown on the left is the "Dutch corner," in which a three-quarter brick is used to start each course. On the right is the "English corner," in which a 2-in. or quarter-brick closer is used.

English bond (Fig. 40) has alternate courses of headers and stretchers. The headers are centered on the stretchers and the joints between stretchers. The vertical joints between stretchers in all courses line up vertically. Blind headers of half brick may be used in courses that are not required to be structural bonding courses.

English cross or Dutch bond is a variation of English bond and differs only in the lack of alignment of the vertical joints between the stretchers in alternate courses. These joints center on the stretchers themselves in the courses above and below. Either an English or a Dutch corner may be used to start English or Dutch bond.

Block or stack bond is a pure pattern bond; all vertical joints are aligned and there is no overlapping of the units in the face of the wall. Metal ties are usually employed to provide structural bond between the facing and the backup. Stack bond is also used extensively in facing-tile work, with structural bond provided by the use of extra-wide stretcher units

or metal ties. Curved walls, where radial stretcher brick are not available, are usually built entirely of headers, which may be laid in running bond but are more frequently laid in stack bond.

TYPE OF JOINT

Joints are of great importance in the appearance of the wall. Four types of exposed joints are shown in Fig. 41: (1) Weathered, (2) Flush, (3) V, and (4) Concave. All are superior in weather resistance to struck joints (not illustrated), which may, however, be used for interior work. Tooled joints (3 and 4), which compress and spread the mortar after it has partially set, result in the best weathering properties. The color of the joints is also extremely important for the over-all appearance of the wall; if other than natural color is desired, mortar color should be specified.

CAVITY WALLS

Cavity walls consist of two wythes of masonry separated by an air space, and tied together with corrosion-resistant metal ties. (See Fig. 42.) The exterior masonry wythe is brick or hollow brick, and the interior masonry wythe can be brick, hollow brick, structural clay tile, or hollow or solid concrete masonry units, depending on the required wall properties and features. The cavity of 2 to 4½ in. (51 to 114 mm) between the two wythes may be either insulated or left as air space. In either case, parging of the cavity face of either wythe is neither necessary, nor recommended. The interior surface of the cavity wall may be left exposed or finished in a normal way.

DUTCH CORNER   ENGLISH CORNER

Fig. 39. Flemish bond

ENGLISH CORNER   "DUTCH" CORNER

Fig. 40. English bond

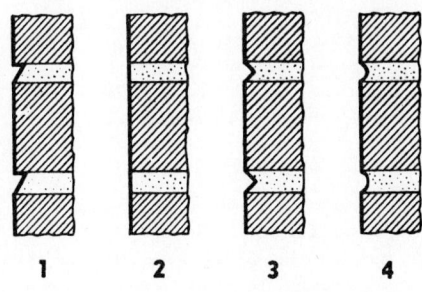

1   2   3   4

Fig. 41. Joint treatments

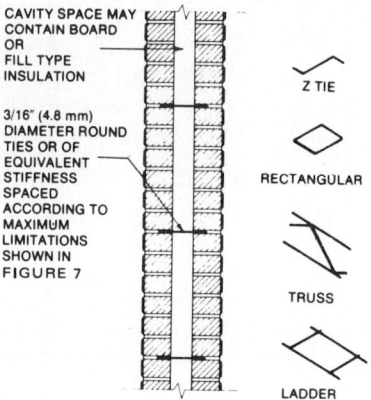

CAVITY SPACE MAY CONTAIN BOARD OR FILL TYPE INSULATION

3/16" (4.8 mm) DIAMETER ROUND TIES OR OF EQUIVALENT STIFFNESS SPACED ACCORDING TO MAXIMUM LIMITATIONS SHOWN IN FIGURE 7

Z TIE

RECTANGULAR

TRUSS

LADDER

Fig. 42. Cavity wall ties

Table 37. Allowable compressive stresses in cavity walls
ANSI A41.1-1953 (R 1970)

Compressive strength of units	Allowable compressive stresses, net cross-sectional area, lb/ft² ᵃ (MPa)		
	Mortar type		
	M	S	N
Solid units			
2500 psi (17.237 MPa) plus	140 (0.965)	130 (0.896)	110 (0.758)
1500 (10.342 MPa) to 2500 psi (17.237 MPa)	100 (0.689)	90 (0.621)	80 (0.552)
Hollow units	70 (0.483)	60 (0.414)	55 (0.379)

ᵃ Net cross-sectional area of cavity walls is the nominal gross cross-sectional area of the wall minus area of cavity between wythes. The allowable compressive stresses are based upon the assumption that floor and roof loads bear upon but one of the two wythes. Where hollow walls are concentrically loaded, the allowable stresses may be increased 25%.

Cavity walls are used extensively in all types of low- and high-rise buildings. The primary reasons for their popularity are superior rain penetration resistance, excellent thermal capabilities, good sound transmission resistance, and high fire resistance.

PROPERTIES OF CAVITY WALLS

Resistance to moisture penetration

One of the major functions of an exterior wall is to resist rain penetration. A masonry cavity wall, properly designed and built, is totally resistant to rain penetration through the wall assembly. Any moisture which may pass through the exterior wythe will run down the cavity face of that wythe to the bottom of the cavity where it is diverted to the outside by continuous flashing and weep holes.

Thermal properties

Heat losses and heat gains through masonry walls are minimized by the use of cavity wall construction. Resistance to heat transmission may be further increased by the use of insulation in the cavity. Steady-state U values can range from 0.40 (2.27 W · m⁻² · K⁻¹) for an 8 in. (203 mm) uninsulated cavity wall to 0.06 (0.34 W · m⁻² · K⁻¹) for a cavity wall with 2-in. (51 mm) polyurethane board insulation. This is further enhanced when considering dynamic conditions. See sheets 26 and 27 for further information about insulated cavity walls.

Sound transmission

Resistance to transmission of sound is accomplished in two ways: the use of heavy massive walls, or the use of discontinuous construction. The cavity wall employs both of these, i.e., the weight of the two masonry wythes plus the partial discontinuity of the cavity. A 10-in. (254 mm) cavity wall has an STC (Sound Transmission Class) rating of 50, which is usually sufficient for substantially reducing typical outside noises entering the building through the wall.

Fire resistance

The results of ASTM E119 fire resistance tests clearly show that masonry cavity walls have excellent fire resistance. Fire resistance ratings of cavity walls range from 2 to 4 h, depending upon the wall thickness and other factors.

Structural properties

Properly designed, detailed and constructed cavity walls may be used in any building requiring loadbearing or nonloadbearing walls in the same manner as other masonry walls.

The increased flexibility afforded by the separation of the wythes and the use of metal ties permits more freedom of differential movement between the wythes. This is extremely important in today's construction which makes use of increasingly more combinations of dissimilar materials.

DESIGN OF CAVITY WALLS

Structural design

The structural design of cavity walls can be by either of two methods. The rational design method is based on the properties of the wall materials and engineering analysis. (See sheets 4 and 5) This method may be used for high-rise bearing wall buildings, auditoriums, churches, gymnasiums, warehouses, and other structures where high walls are a necessity. The empirical method is generally satisfactory for one- and two-story buildings consisting of light construction, and limited floor spans and wall heights; and for multi-story buildings where unsupported wall heights are not excessive. (See sheet 3)

Allowable stresses: The allowable compressive stresses included in Table 37, based on ANSI A41.1, are adequate for the design of most structures in which loadbearing cavity walls are used. However, for buildings in which higher compressive stresses are developed, it may be desirable to design the interior wythe of the cavity wall as the loadbearing element and to consider the exterior wythe as a veneer or curtain wall.

Thickness: ANSI A41.1 states that for loadbearing walls, ". . . 10-inch [254 mm] cavity walls shall not exceed 25 feet [7.620 m] in height above the support of such walls. The facing and backing of cavity walls shall each have a thickness of at least 4 inches [102 mm] and the cavity shall be not less than 2 inches [51 mm] (actual) nor more than 3 inches [76 mm] in width."

Lateral support: ANSI A41.1 requires that the ratio of unsupported height to nominal thickness or the ratio of unsupported length to nominal thickness (one or the other, but not necessarily both) should not exceed 18 for cavity walls. In computing this ratio, the value for the thickness of the cavity wall is taken as the sum of the *nominal* thicknesses of the inner and outer wythes.

Lateral support in the vertical direction may be provided by floors, roofs, or spandrel beams. Lateral support in the horizontal direction, where the length of the wall is the controlling factor, may be provided by cross walls, columns, buttresses, or pilasters.

Bonding: The facing and backing (adjacent wythes) of cavity walls should be tied together with corrosion resistant 3/16-in. (4.8 mm) diameter steel ties, or metal tie wire of equivalent stiffness, embedded in the horizontal mortar joints. (See Fig. 42) There should be at least one metal tie for each 4½ sq ft (0.418m²) of wall area. Individual ties in alternate courses should be staggered; the maximum vertical distance between ties should not exceed 24 in. (610 mm) and the maximum horizontal distance should not exceed 36 in. (914 mm). (See Fig. 7) The ends of the ties should be bent to 90 deg angles to provide hooks not less than 2 in. (51 mm) long, or ties bent to a rectangular shape should be used. Additional ties should be provided at all openings spaced not more than 3 ft (914 mm) apart around the perimeter and within 12 in. (305 mm) of the opening. Where the cavity width exceeds 3½ in. (89 mm) but is less than 4½ in. (114 mm), there should be at least one metal tie for each 3 sq ft (0.279 m²) of wall area. It should be noted that crimping of the metal ties in the middle to form a drip is not necessary, and could decrease the strength of the tie.

When continuous wall ties (joint reinforcement) are used, they may be either truss or ladder type with at least one side wire in each wythe (Fig. 42). Where the cavity wall is composed of a brick exterior wythe and a 6-in. (152 mm) or greater hollow concrete block inner wythe, the reinforcement should consist of three wires (Fig. 43), or two wires with rectangular ties.

Continuous horizontal wall reinforcement should be properly lapped where necessary [a minimum of 8 in. (203 mm)] in accordance with the recommendations of the Concrete Reinforcing Steel Institute. To provide additional continuity, the reinforcement should be carried around corners, especially in the exterior wythe (see Fig. 43). Horizontal reinforcement *must* be discontinuous at all movement joints (see Fig. 44).

Flashing and weep holes: Good flashing details are an absolute necessity in cavity wall construction. In order to divert moisture out of the cavity through the weep holes, continuous flashing should be installed at the bottom of the cavity, and wherever the cavity is interrupted by elements such as shelf angles or lintels.

Since the purpose of the flashing is to collect moisture so it may be diverted to the outside, weep holes must be provided wherever flashing is used. Weep holes are located in the joints of the outer wythe immediately above the flashing. Spacing of weep holes should be approximately 2 ft (610 mm) o.c. maximum, except for those using a wick material which should be 16 in. (406 mm) o.c. maximum (see Fig. 45).

Shelf angles: When the wall height or the number and location of openings necessitate supporting the outer wythe of a cavity wall on shelf angles attached to the structural

frame, it is recommended that horizontal pressure relieving joints be placed immediately beneath each angle. This is particularly important in reinforced concrete frame buildings.

Pressure-relieving joints may be constructed by either leaving an air space or placing a *fully* compressible material under the shelf angle and sealing the joint with a permanent elastic sealant (see Fig. 46).

When the exterior wythe of a masonry wall is supported on shelf angles, proper anchorage and shimming of the angles must be insured so that they cannot rotate and induce concentrated stresses in the masonry. A small space should be left between lengths of angles to allow for horizontal thermal movements and the holes for anchor bolts should be horizontally slotted to allow for greater ease of construction and any horizontal movement.

Expansion joints: The movement of the outer brick wythe due to thermal and moisture expansion may be greater than the movement in solid or composite walls exposed to the same environment. This is due to the greater differences between the mean maximum and mean minimum temperatures of the outer wythe of the cavity wall, and the absence of restraint usually provided by dead and live loads, masonry bonders, or filled collar joints in solid walls. This is particularly true for nonloadbearing cavity walls used in skeleton-frame construction, especially if they are insulated. For this reason, it is recommended that expansion joints be provided through the outer wythe of the cavity wall on each side of an external corner where the walls are 50 ft (15.240 m) or more in length. Where possible this joint may be placed in line with the jambs of the windows nearest the corner.

In certain situations it may prove advantageous to use continuous horizontal joint reinforcement as temperature steel in the exterior brick wythe. This reinforcement may consist of No. 9 gauge wire spaced 16 in. (406 mm) o.c. vertically.

When brick is used in the exterior wythe with solid or hollow concrete masonry in the inner wythe, special care must be exercised in the detailing. Control joints must be placed in the concrete wythe, along with suitable joint reinforcement, to control cracking from shrinkage due to initial drying. Control joints may be placed 20 ft (6.096 m) o.c., or as recommended by the National Concrete Masonry Association. The locations of these control joints may or may not coincide with those of the expansion joints in the brick wythe (Fig. 44).

Anchorage: The flexible anchorage of masonry walls to skeleton frames, to permit differential movement of the walls and frame, is discussed on sheets 59 and 60.

A modification of these recommendations is used for cavity walls enclosing skeleton-frame structures. The exterior wythe may be supported on the foundation, with lateral support provided by anchoring the outer

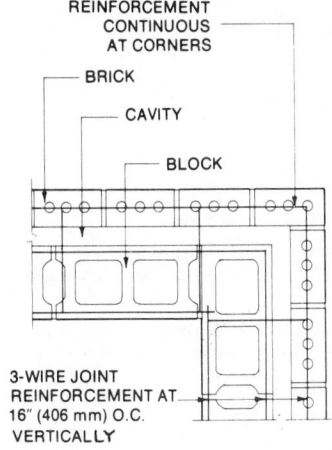

Fig. 43. **Continuous horizontal wall reinforcement**

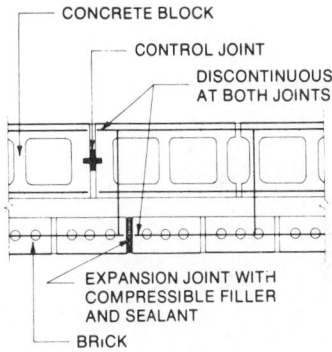

Fig. 44. **Expansion and control joint detail**

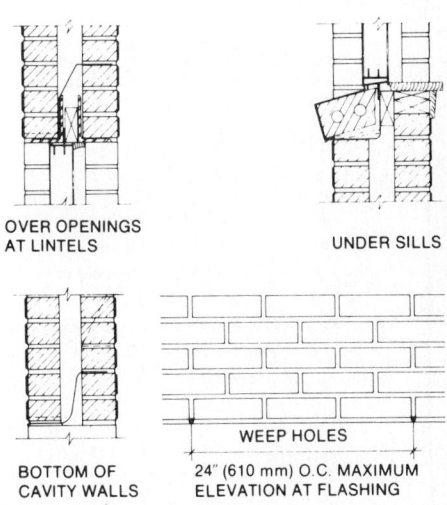

Fig. 45. **Flashing and weep holes**

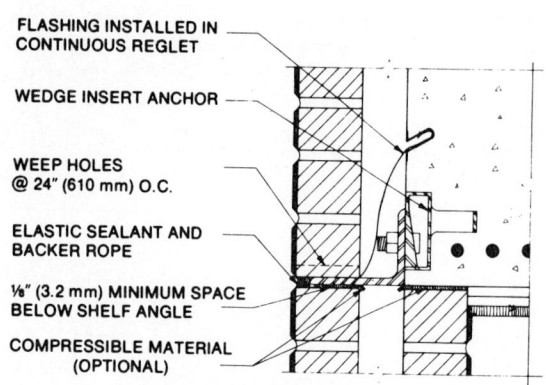

Fig. 46. Steel shelf angles

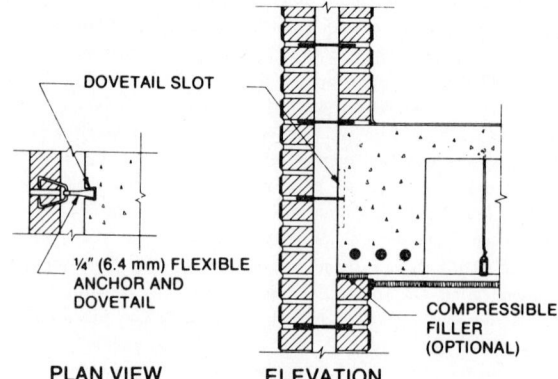

Fig. 47. Flexible anchorage to concrete frame

Table 38. Insulation material properties[a]

Material	Density lb/ft³ (kg/m³)	Thermal conductivity k Btu/(h · ft² · °F) (W · m⁻² · K⁻¹)	Thermal resistance R (per in.) °F/(Btu · h · f²) (K · W⁻¹ · m⁻²)	Permeance, perm-in.	Vapor resistance ft² · h (in. Hg)
Granular Fills:					
Vermiculite (water repellent)	5–9 (80–144)	0.44 (2.50)	2.27 (0.40)	62[e]	0.0163[e]
Perlite (silicone-treated)	5–8 (80–130)	0.37 (2.10)	2.70 (0.48)	N.A.[d]	N.A.[d]
Rigid Boards:					
Expanded Polystyrene, Extruded	3.5 (56)	0.19 (1.08)	5.26 (0.92)	1.2	0.8333
Expanded Polystyrene, Molded Beads	0.9–1.1 (14–18)	0.28 (1.59)	3.57 (0.63)	2.0–5.8	0.5–0.1724
Expanded Polyurethane, Extruded	1.5 (24)	0.16 (0.91)	6.25 (1.10)	0.4–1.6	2.5–0.625
Perlite Aggregate	11 (176)	0.38 (2.16)	2.63 (0.46)	25	0.04
Rigid Urethane	2 (32)	0.16[c] (0.91)[c]	6.25[c] (1.10)[c]	2	0.50
Cellular Glass	9 (144)	0.35–0.44[b] (1.99–2.33)[b]	2.86–2.44[b] (0.50–0.41)[b]	0	Very High
Preformed Fiberglass	4–9 (64–144)	0.21–0.26 (1.19–1.48)	4.76–3.86 (0.84–0.68)	Very High	Very Low

[a] *Tabulated values are from varied sources. Designers should check with manufacturers and other sources for more precise values.*
[b] *From 0 to 90°F (−18 to 32°C).*
[c] *Based on aged k-factor.*
[d] *N.A. = Not available.*
[e] *Material thickness is 2.5 in.*

wythe to the inner wythe and the frame on which the inner wythe is supported. The anchors or ties, providing lateral support for the outer wythe, should be capable of resisting both tension and compression, but should be designed to permit movement parallel to the plane of the wall in both a vertical and horizontal direction (Fig. 47).

MATERIALS

Brick: Brick must conform to the requirements for Grade MW or SW. For insulated cavity walls in freezing climates, only Grade SW should be used in the exterior wythe.

Mortar: The mortar has an important effect on the strength of a cavity wall. Tests have shown that the bond between mortar and brick is the most important single factor affecting wall strength when the load is applied horizontally. Type S mortar is recommended for use in cavity walls in locations where wind velocities are expected to exceed 80 mph (128.7 km/h). For other locations Type N may be used.

Weep holes: Weep holes may be formed by oiled metal rods, removed after the mortar is set, or by plastic tubing or rope wicks left in place. Cotton sash cord or nylon rope act as wicks, drawing moisture out of the cavity.

Expansion joints: Expansion joint material can be of 20-oz copper, premolded compressible elastic filler, or specially formed rubber or plastic sections.

INSULATED CAVITY WALLS

Insulating materials

To be suitable for use in cavity walls insulating materials must meet the following criteria:

1. They must permit the free drainage of

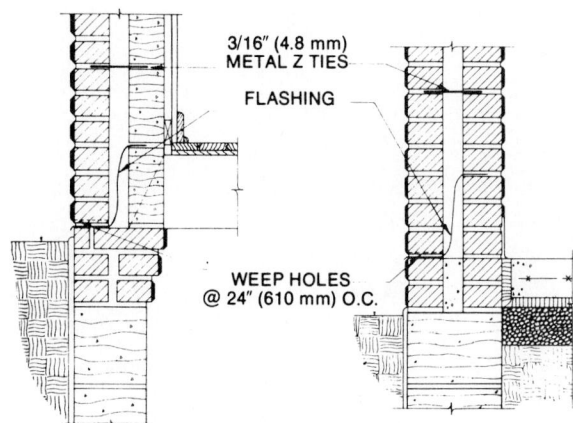

Fig. 48. Foundation details

LUBRICATED BEARING SURFACES
AND SLOTTED HOLES IN BEARING
SEATS OF STEEL JOISTS

CONCRETE SLAB OVER
STEEL DECKING AND
STEEL JOISTS

3/16" ((4.8 mm) DIAMETER
METAL TIES

2" (51 mm) MINIMUM CAVITY

Fig. 49. Anchorage of steel floor joists

moisture through the cavity without transmission to the interior wythe.

2. Insulating efficiency must not be impaired by retained moisture.*

3. Granular fill materials must support their own weight without settlement.

4. The materials must be resistant to rot, fire, and vermin.

Granular fills

Two types of granular fill insulation have been found to meet the above criteria. These are water repellent vermiculite masonry fill and silicone-treated perlite loose fill insulation. Granular fill insulation is usually poured directly into the cavity from the bag or from a hopper placed on top of the wall. Pours can be made at any convenient interval. Rodding or tamping is not necessary and might reduce the thermal resistance of the material. The insulation in the wall should be protected from the weather during construction.

Rigid boards

Expanded or molded polystyrene, expanded polyurethane, rigid urethane, cellular glass, preformed fiberglass, and perlite board have all been used as insulation in cavity walls. Rigid board insulation is installed horizontally in the air space against the cavity face of the interior wythe. A minimum of 1 in. (25 mm) should be left between the cavity face of the external wythe and the insulation board, in order to permit the cavity to drain freely. Care should be taken to ensure that all boards abutt at their ends and between ties and fit flush against the inner wythe. Adhesive

Water entrapped in insulation can destroy the thermal-insulating value. Water vapor can flow wherever air can flow—between fibers, through interconnected open cells, or where a closed cell structure breaks down. Wherever water replaces air, the insulating value drops drastically since water's thermal conductivity exceeds that of air by 20 times.

should be used to hold the insulation in place.

Thermal properties

Properties of typical insulating materials suitable for use in cavity walls are shown in Table 38. Overall heat transmission (*U*-values) through four types of cavity wall with various insulating materials are given in Table 39.

Vapor barrier

Tests have shown that no vapor barrier is required in insulated cavity walls if the following three conditions are met: (1) each wythe must have a vapor permeance not exceeding three perms (a 4-in. wythe of brick has a permeance of about 2.2 perms), (2) average interior relative humidity conditions for heated and air-conditioned buildings should not exceed 50 per cent, and (3) the vapor pressure gradient should be not more than 1 in. (25 mm) of mercury for a period of not more than 30 days.

These conditions are satisfied by most residential, commercial, institutional, and industrial buildings in the continental United States. Laundries, cold-storage facilities, indoor swimming pools, hockey rinks, and buildings with high relative humidities are examples of buildings where the use of a vapor barrier may be required.

If required, the vapor barrier must have a vapor permeance not exceeding 1 perm, and it must be placed on the warm side of the insulation. Commonly used vapor barriers are asphalt-coated paper, aluminum foil, and polyethylene film.

Table 39. *U*-values of typical masonry cavity walls

8-in. Cavity wall (3-in. brick both wythes)	U^a	10-in. Cavity wall (4-in. brick both wythes)	U^a
No fill	0.40 (2.27)	No fill	0.37 (2.10)
2-in. Vermiculite fill	0.18 (1.02)	2-in. Vermiculite fill	0.17 (0.97)
2-in. Perlite fill	0.15 (0.85)	2-in. Perlite fill	0.14 (0.79)
2-in. Polystyrene board	0.08 (0.45)	2-in. Polystyrene board	0.08 (0.45)
2-in. Polyurethane board	0.06 (0.34)	2-in. Polyurethane board	0.06 (0.34)
9-in. Cavity wall (3-in. brick, 4-in. lightweight concrete block)	U^a	10-in. Cavity wall (4-in. brick, 4-in. lightweight concrete block)	U^a
No fill	0.28 (1.59)	No fill	0.27 (1.53)
2-in. Vermiculite fill	0.15 (0.85)	2-in. Vermiculite fill	0.15 (0.85)
2-in. Perlite fill	0.13 (0.74)	2-in. Perlite fill	0.13 (0.74)
2-in. Polystyrene board	0.07 (0.40)	2-in. Polystyrene board	0.07 (0.40)
2-in. Polyurethane board	0.06 (0.34)	2-in. Polyurethane board	0.06 (0.34)

^{a} Units are Btu/(h · ft² · °F)

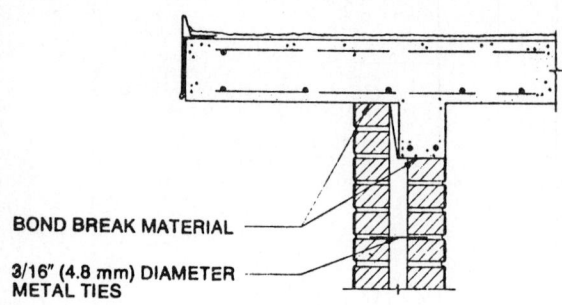

BOND BREAK MATERIAL

3/16" (4.8 mm) DIAMETER METAL TIES

Fig. 50.   Concrete roof slab

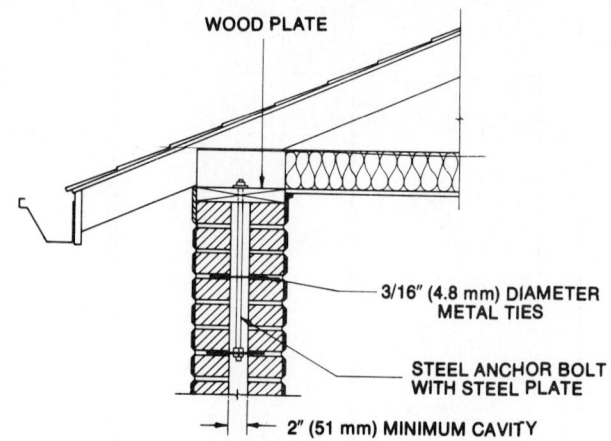

WOOD PLATE

3/16" (4.8 mm) DIAMETER METAL TIES

STEEL ANCHOR BOLT WITH STEEL PLATE

2" (51 mm) MINIMUM CAVITY

Fig. 51.   Anchorage of wood roof framing

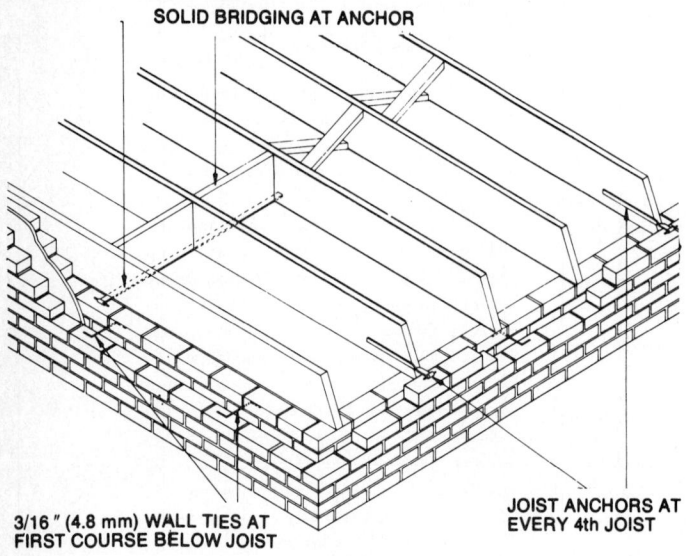

LATERAL SUPPORT METAL ANCHORS @ 8' (2.44 m) O.C. MAXIMUM

SOLID BRIDGING AT ANCHOR

3/16" (4.8 mm) WALL TIES AT FIRST COURSE BELOW JOIST

JOIST ANCHORS AT EVERY 4th JOIST

Fig. 52.   Anchorage of wood floor framing

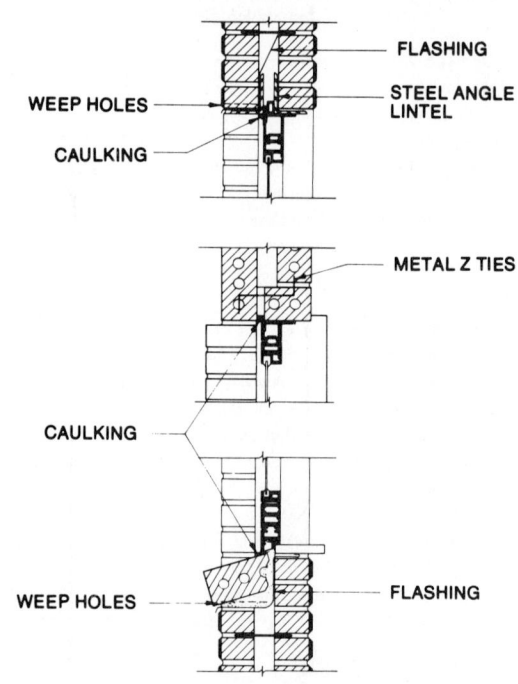

FLASHING

WEEP HOLES

STEEL ANGLE LINTEL

CAULKING

METAL Z TIES

CAULKING

WEEP HOLES

FLASHING

Fig. 53.   Commercial metal window

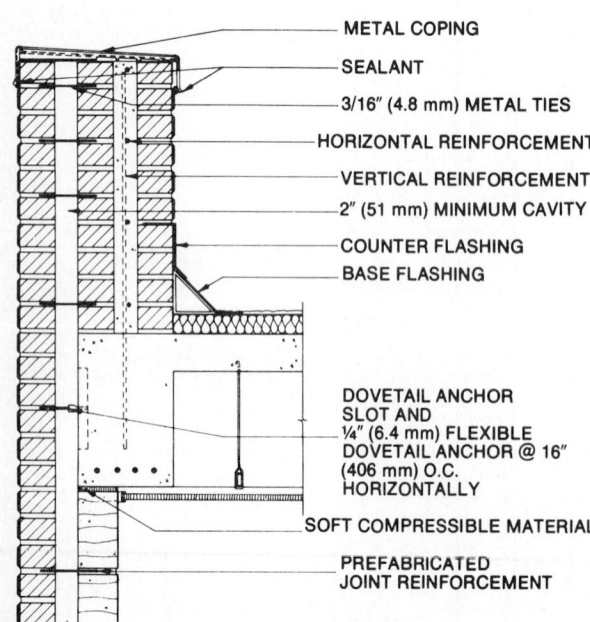

METAL COPING

SEALANT

3/16" (4.8 mm) METAL TIES

HORIZONTAL REINFORCEMENT

VERTICAL REINFORCEMENT

2" (51 mm) MINIMUM CAVITY

COUNTER FLASHING

BASE FLASHING

DOVETAIL ANCHOR SLOT AND ¼" (6.4 mm) FLEXIBLE DOVETAIL ANCHOR @ 16" (406 mm) O.C. HORIZONTALLY

SOFT COMPRESSIBLE MATERIAL

PREFABRICATED JOINT REINFORCEMENT

Fig. 54.   Reinforced parapet wall

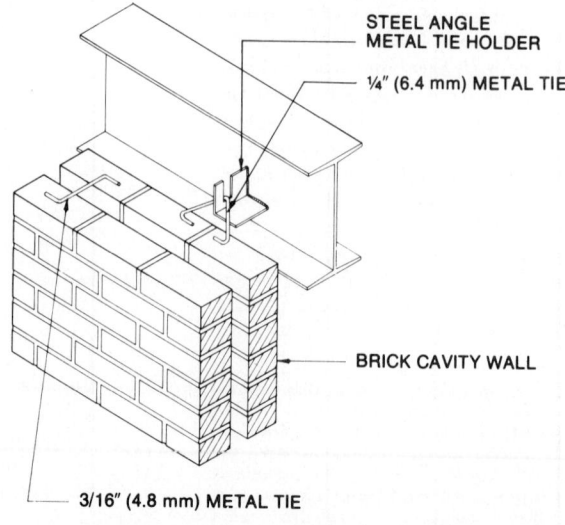

STEEL ANGLE METAL TIE HOLDER

¼" (6.4 mm) METAL TIE

BRICK CAVITY WALL

3/16" (4.8 mm) METAL TIE

Fig. 55.   Flexible anchorage to steel beam

Most building codes now permit the use of 6-in. single-wythe masonry loadbearing walls for all types of one-story buildings. Six-in. masonry units of brick, tile, and block are generally available. Units are usually 12 in. long, in order to permit the use of half bonds, and are available in several heights, the most popular being the modular 2⅔ in. (3 courses in 8 in.). Most 6-in. masonry units are cored.

Six-inch masonry walls should be furred on the inside in order to prevent the infiltration of moisture and to provide space for the installation of insulation and electric wiring. Two- by two-inch furring is recommended, fastened by clips which hold the strips at least ¼ in. clear of the masonry (Fig. 62). This permits air circulation back of the clips and the free drainage of any moisture that may be present on the back surface of the masonry wall. The bottom of the furred space should be flashed and drained with weep holes as in a cavity wall.

Typical construction details are shown in Figs. 56 to 59. Lintels for 6-in. masonry walls may be steel, wood, or reinforced masonry (Fig. 60). Safe spans for 6-in. reinforced brick lintels are given in Fig. 61.

The fire resistance rating of a 6-in. brick wall without furring and interior finish is 2½ hours. U-values for 6-in. brick walls with various finishes and insulations are given in Table 40.

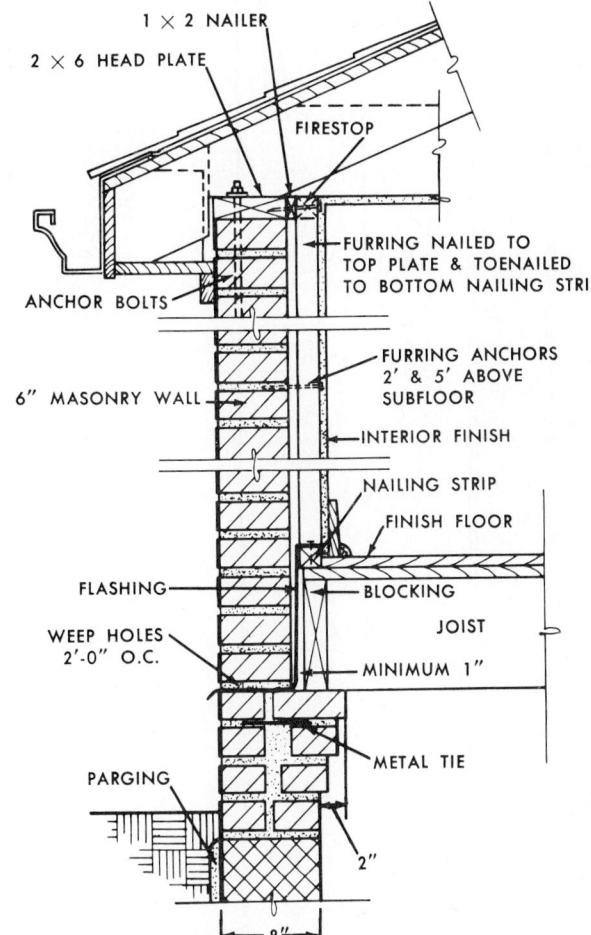

Fig. 56. Typical wall section; 8-in. foundation

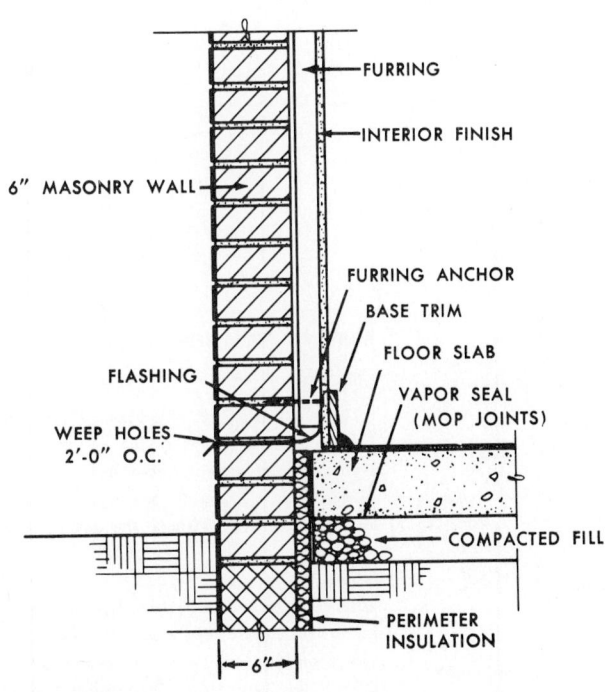

Fig. 57. Section at sill; slab on grade, 6-in. foundation

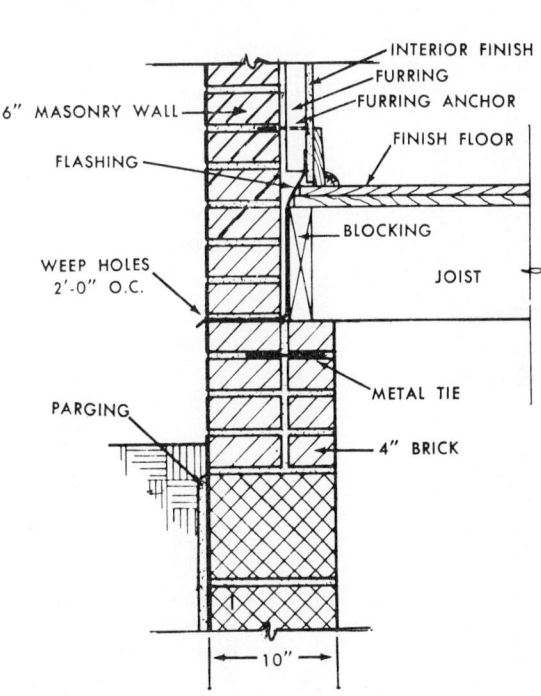

Fig. 58. Section at sill; 10-in. foundation

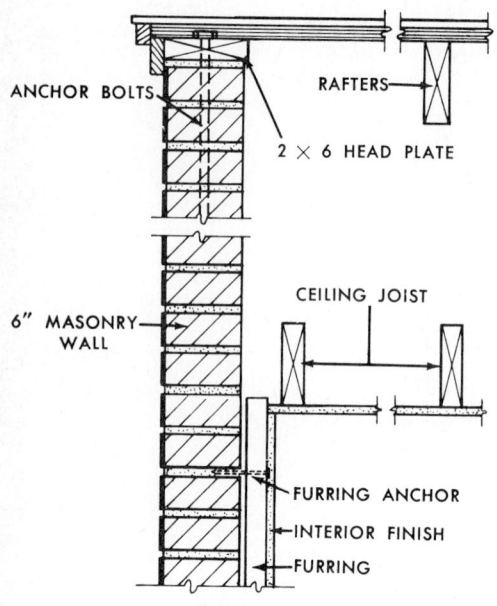

Fig. 59. Section at gable

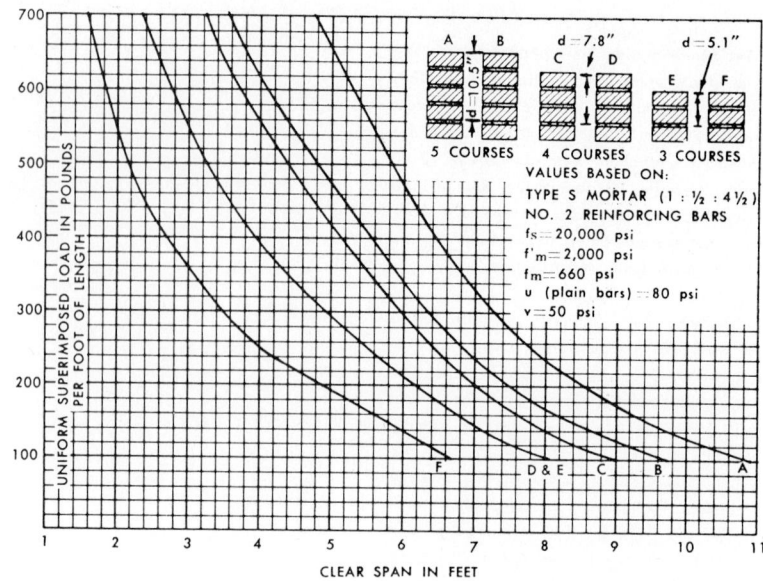

Fig. 61. Safe spans for uniformly loaded 6-in. reinforced brick lintels

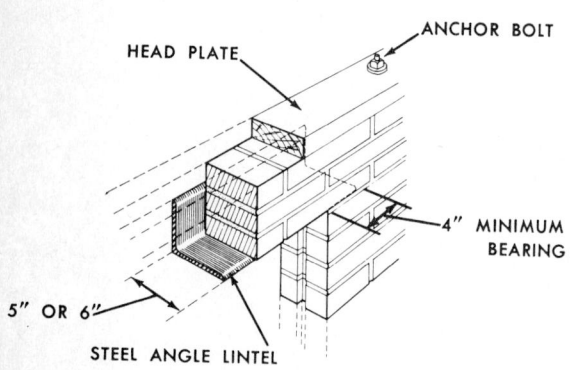

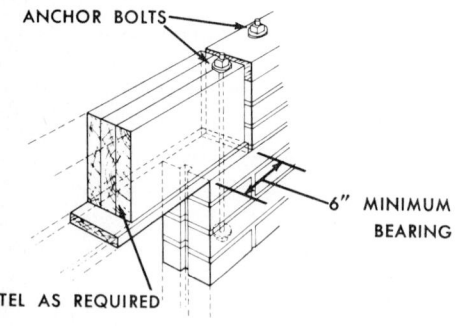

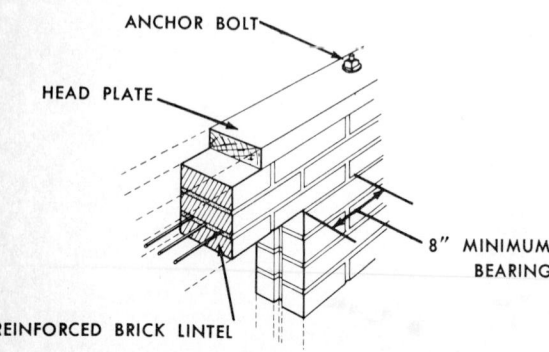

Fig. 60. Lintel construction

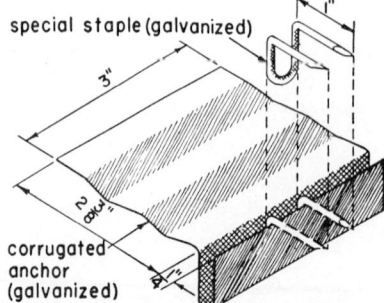

Fig. 62. Recommended type of furring clip

Table 40. Heat-transmission coefficients for 6-in. brick walls

Heat-transmission coefficients for SCR brick walls with various interior finishes and insulations are corrected for 15-mph wind velocity.

Type of interior finish and insulation (2x2-in. furring)	U factor
1-in. roll insulation, ½-in. insulating board lath, ½-in. vermiculite plaster	0.12
1-in. roll insulation, ⅜-in. gypsum board (dry wall)	0.16
1-in. roll insulation, metal lath, ¾-in. gypsum plaster	0.16
⅜-in. gypsum lath with aluminum foil, ½-in. vermiculite plaster	0.23
½-in. insulating board lath, ½-in. vermiculite plaster	0.23
½-in. gypsum board (dry wall) with aluminum foil	0.26
⅜-in. gypsum lath, ½-in. vermiculite plaster	0.33
Metal lath, ¾-in. gypsum plaster	0.40

SURFACE TREATMENTS

Efflorescence

The formation of efflorescence requires (1) water-soluble salts in the masonry, (2) water in contact with these salts for sufficient time to dissolve them, and (3) a construction that permits the solution to migrate to the surface of the masonry where the salts are deposited upon evaporation of the water. Obviously, if masonry could be constructed which contained no water-soluble salts or if no water penetrated the masonry, efflorescence would not occur. In masonry exposed to the weather, however, neither of these conditions can be met completely. Consequently, the practical way to eliminate efflorescence is to reduce all contributing factors to a minimum. The following procedures are recommended as a means to that end.

1. Reduce the amount of soluble salts in the masonry materials by:
   a. Specifying that all wall facing and trim materials pass a "wick test" for efflorescence (ASTM C67).
   b. Testing mortar for efflorescence; if necessary add calcium stearate (0.2 per cent by weight of combined cement and lime).
2. Prevent contact between facing and backup by use of cavity-wall construction or flashing.
3. Keep moisture out of wall by use of:
   a. Hard-burned brick or tile facing.
   b. Cavity-wall or solid metal-tied wall construction.
   c. Good workmanship (all joints thoroughly filled).
   d. Protection of the tops of walls during construction.
   e. Projecting sills and copings, with drip slots underneath (Fig. 63).
   f. Flashing, especially at all intersections of wall and roof, under all horizontal elements such as copings and sills, and just above finished grade, to prevent rise of moisture by capillarity from the foundation.
   g. Caulking, carefully applied, around all door and window frames.
   h. Vapor barrier and ventilation to prevent condensation within walls.

Cleaning

New buildings: Many buildings have been irreparably damaged by improper cleaning. Commonest causes of such damage are (1) failure to saturate masonry before application of cleaning agent, (2) use of too strong acid solution, and (3) failure to protect windows and trim. It is recommended that any cleaning agent be tried first on a sample wall (minimum area of 20 sq ft) and left for at least a week.

To clean *unglazed masonry surfaces*, remove large particles with a wood paddle and saturate the surface with water. Apply a 10 per cent solution of muriatic acid (not more than 1 part acid to 9 parts water) to an area of not more than 15 to 20 sq ft. Then wash the surface with clear water.

To cut labor costs, high-pressure water is sometimes used; nozzle pressures range between 400 and 700 lb/in² (2750 to 4850 kPa) at a flow rate of 3 to 8 gal/min (0.2 to 0.5 L/s). Two hoses may be used, one with cleaning solution, the other with plain water. Dry sandblasting is also sometimes used.

To clean *glazed surfaces*, scrub with soap and water only. Use no acid and no metal scrapers on glazed surfaces.

Efflorescence can usually be removed with soap and water and a stiff scrubbing brush. If necessary, use dilute muriatic acid, as described above. A type of efflorescence known as "green stain" may be caused by the action of muriatic acid on some types of masonry. Since this type cannot be foreseen it is important to make a preliminary test on a sample wall. Green stain is difficult to remove: try oxalic acid (2 lb per 5 gal of water) brushed or sprayed on and washed off after several hours; if necessary follow with sodium hydroxide ("Drano"—one 12-oz can per qt of water) applied liberally with paint brush and hosed off after three days.

Old buildings: Cleaning methods listed in order of frequency of use are as follows:

1. *High-pressure steam*—best for relatively impervious facing materials.
2. *Sand blasting*—used mostly on porous materials such as limestone, sandstone, and unglazed brick; cannot be used on glazed or polished surfaces.
3. *Hand washing*—expensive; used only on small buildings.
4. *High-pressure cold water*—good if there is ample water supply and suitable method of disposing of waste.
5. *Chemical and steam*—used for removing coatings such as paint.

Before deciding upon the cleaning of an old building, consider carefully whether it is advisable. The "dirt" may be simply weathered masonry, not accumulated deposits, and the cleaning process may remove the actual surface of the masonry.

Stains

The removal of stains, such as those caused by rust, smoke, copper, oil, and the like, requires special treatment appropriate to the type of stain and the type of masonry. See *Technical Notes on Brick Construction No. 20 Revised,* published by the Brick Institute of America.

Painting

Paints are applied to masonry walls for decorative effect and as a barrier to rain penetration. They must not, however, prevent the wall from "breathing," that is, prevent moisture within the wall from escaping by evaporation from the surface. Cement-based paints and water-thinned emulsion paints are highly permeable to water vapor and are recommended for exterior use. New masonry walls intended to be painted should not be cleaned with acid.

Cement-based paint should be applied to a wall only after it has cured for at least a month and has been dampened thoroughly by spraying. Apply heavy coats with a stiff brush, allowing at least 24 h between coats. During this time and for several days after the final coat keep the wall damp by periodic spraying. Water-thinned emulsion paints, commonly called latex paints, can be applied to damp uncured walls; since they are quick-drying, additional coats can be applied without waiting. Polyvinyl acetate and acrylic emulsions are generally the most satisfactory of the water-thinned paints.

Solvent-thinned paints should be applied only to completely dry, clean surfaces. Oil-based and alkyd paints are nonpermeable and are not recommended for exterior masonry. Oil-based paints are highly susceptible to alkalies and new masonry must be thoroughly neutralized before being painted; zinc chloride or zinc sulfate solution, 2 to 3½ lb per gallon of water is often used for this purpose. Several days of drying is usually required between coats. Synthetic rubber and chlorinated rubber paints can be applied to damp, alkaline surfaces, and can be used on exterior masonry.

Waterproofing

Silicones are widely used for waterproofing, or more correctly dampproofing, masonry walls. Without actually sealing openings, silicones retard water absorption by creating a negative capillarity which repels water. Silicones may be water-based or solvent-based and may be applied by brush or spray. Normally, silicones cause no perceptable color change, but they sometimes bleach artifically colored mortar. They penetrate the masonry to a depth of ⅛ to ¼ in. and their effective life is from 5 to 10 years.

Foundation walls below grade should be waterproofed with one or preferably two ⅜-in. coats of portland cement mortar (1 : 1½); after curing apply hot bituminous coating or a cold asphalt emulsion coating.

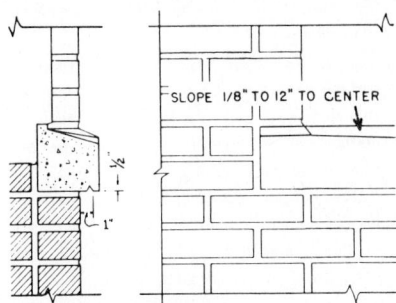

Fig. 63. Sill detail to prevent wash

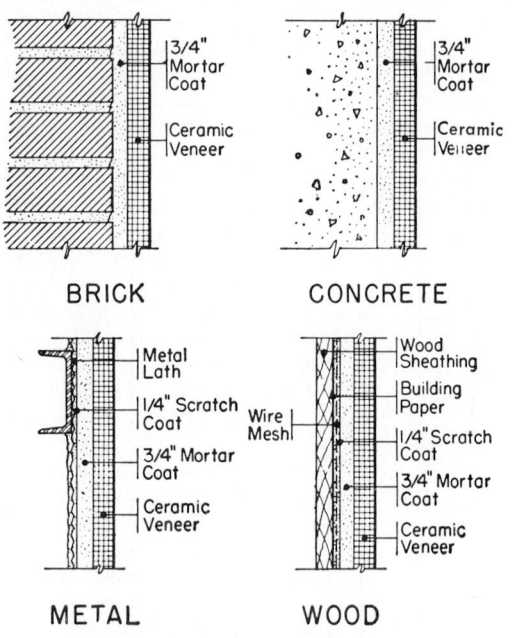

Fig. 64. Adhesion-type ceramic veneer

This veneer is adaptable to both new and remodeling work and, as illustrated here, for attachment to various types of backings.

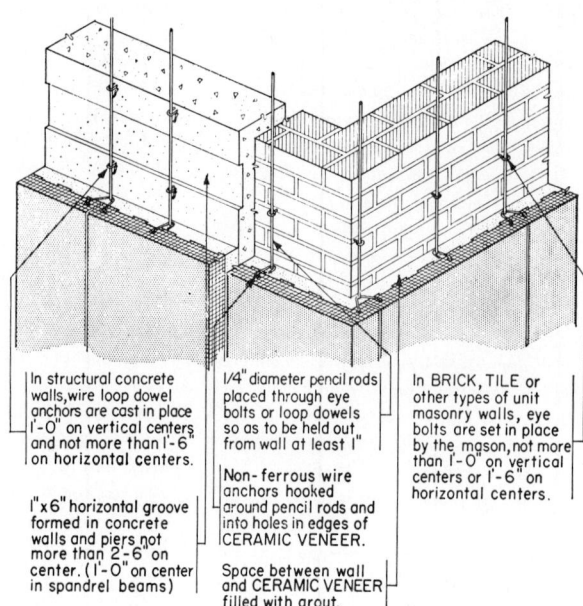

In structural concrete walls, wire loop dowel anchors are cast in place 1'-0" on vertical centers and not more than 1'-6" on horizontal centers.

1"x6" horizontal groove formed in concrete walls and piers not more than 2'-6" on center. (1'-0" on center in spandrel beams)

1/4" diameter pencil rods placed through eye bolts or loop dowels so as to be held out from wall at least 1"

Non-ferrous wire anchors hooked around pencil rods and into holes in edges of CERAMIC VENEER.

Space between wall and CERAMIC VENEER filled with grout.

In BRICK, TILE or other types of unit masonry walls, eye bolts are set in place by the mason, not more than 1'-0" on vertical centers or 1'-6" on horizontal centers.

Fig. 65. Anchored-type ceramic veneer

The ceramic-veneer slabs may be set with the ribs or scoring in a horizontal position or, as shown here, in a vertical position.

CERAMIC VENEER

Ceramic veneer is used extensively on large plain areas of modern buildings. The present discussion will be confined to the installation of adhesion- and anchored-type ceramic veneer.

Adhesion type

Adhesion-type ceramic veneer (Fig. 64) is commonly called "thin ceramic veneer," since the maximum over-all thickness of the slab is 1⅛ in. The maximum face area of individual slabs does not exceed 540 sq in. The maximum over-all face dimensions, therefore, are about 18 by 30 in. or 20 by 27 in. This type of ceramic veneer requires no metal anchorage, but is held in place by the adhesion of the mortar to the ceramic-veneer body and the backing wall. The over-all thickness from the face of the ceramic veneer to the face of the backing wall will be only 1¾ to 2 in.

Extensive shear tests on adhesion-type ceramic-veneer wall panels indicate that the shearing strengths developed by such a method of anchorage are much greater than those required by building codes.

The mortar recommended for adhesion-type ceramic veneer consists of 1 part portland cement, ½ part high calcium lime putty, and 4 parts sand, by volume. To this mixture may be added ammonium stearate, or the equivalent, in the proportions recommended by the manufacturer.

The units should be so dimensioned that they may be set with uniform joints approximately ¼ in. in width. The face lengths and widths should not vary by more than ¹⁄₁₆ in. from the dimensions called for on the setting drawings, and the faces of the units should not vary from a true plane by more than an average of ¹⁄₁₆ in. per sq ft.

Erection

1. Dampen wall; if recommended by manufacturer, soak units in water for 1 hr.
2. Apply brush coat of cement and water to back of unit and to wall.
3. Apply mortar to back of unit and to wall.
4. Set unit, plumb and level, tap to remove air pockets; use wood wedges in joints.
5. Tool or rake face joints ½ in. deep and point.
6. Wash with clean water and soap, if necessary; use no acid.

Anchored type

Anchored-type ceramic veneer (Fig. 65) is recommended if the architect desires a large-scale slab. Ribs or scoring are provided on the backs of such units, and the over-all slab thicknesses range from 2 to approximately 2½ in. Depending on the slab thickness, a total of 3 to 4½ in. is required from rough wall to finished veneer surface to provide adequate grout space between the veneer and the backing. Anchor holes are provided in the

bed edges of the slabs for the installation of the anchors, which, in turn, are fastened to pencil rods anchored to the backing or inserted in dovetail slots in the backing. Once the anchors are in place, the units are bonded to the wall by a reinforced grout core, keyed into the horizontal groove in the rough masonry backing. The ribs on the back of the panel are keyed into the grout.

The cement grout used with anchored-type ceramic veneer consists of 1 part portland cement, 1 part sand, and 5 parts graded pea gravel passed through a ¼-in. sieve. Sufficient water is added to cause the mixture to flow readily.

Erection

1. When pencil rods are used, insert ¼-in. diam rods vertically through loops of dowel anchors in rough wall.
2. Set ceramic-veneer unit with wood wedges in joints. Insert wire anchors in top edge, and tie to vertical rods.
3. When one horizontal course is complete, pour grout in space between backs of units and rough wall.
4. Point joints and wash surface, as described above.

Acid cleaning or the use of abrasives is not recommended for ceramic-glazed surfaces, nor should metal cleaning tools be used. If hard lumps of mortar must be removed, sharpened wood paddles are recommended.

STRUCTURAL CLAY TILE PARTITIONS

Unit dimensions

Structural clay partition tile have 12 by 12-in. faces and thicknesses of 2, 3, 4, 6, 8, 10, and 12 in. In nonmodular tile, these are the actual dimensions. In modular tile, the actual dimensions are smaller by the thickness of one joint, usually ½ in. All units have three cells in width. Units up to and including 6 in. in thickness have one cell; units thicker than 6 in. are two cells deep.

Physical properties

The following physical properties of structural clay tile partitions are covered in the tables: weight, Table 41; stability (maximum heights), Table 42; and sound resistance, Table 43 (National Bureau of Standards tests, reported in BMS 17 and supplements).

Plaster adhesion

For many years, scored surfaces were considered necessary to obtain a strong bond between plaster and tile. Extensive tests at the National Bureau of Standards and other laboratories have indicated that ample bond strength is developed between plaster and tile surfaces that are smooth, combed, or roughened (wire cut).

Construction

Nonbearing partitions, where suspended ceilings do not occur, should extend from the top of the structural floor to the bottom surface of the floor construction above and should be wedged with small pieces of tile. The top joint should then be filled with mortar.

Partitions should be bonded at intersections and properly anchored to door bucks and adjoining masonry walls. Partitions that abut intersecting walls should be anchored with metal ties or clips at least ⅞ in. wide and of not less than No. 16 gage galvanized iron, at vertical intervals of not more than 4 ft.

Multiple-unit nonbearing tile partitions should be bonded at vertical intervals not exceeding 34 in. by lapping one unit at least 3¾ in. over the unit below; by lapping with units at least 50 per cent greater in thickness than the units below at vertical intervals not exceeding 17 in.; or by galvanized corrugated metal ties at least ⅞ in. wide and not lighter than No. 22 gage, or other approved ties. At least one tie should be used for each 2 sq ft of wall area with ties spaced not farther apart than 24 in. either vertically or horizontally.

In plastered construction, wood or steel channel door bucks should be approximately 1½ in. wider than the thickness of the tile to act as grounds for the plaster.

Table 41. Average weights of clay tile partitions*

| | \multicolumn{6}{c}{Nominal thickness, in.} | | | | | |
	2	3	4	6	8	12
Weight, psf	15	16	17	24	32	46

No plaster finishes are included.

Table 42. Maximum heights of clay tile partitions
Cells may be vertical or horizontal.

| | \multicolumn{7}{c}{Nominal thickness, in.} | | | | | | |
	2	3	4	6	8	10	12
Maximum unsupported height, ft	9*	12	15	20	25	30	36

Maximum unsupported horizontal length is 6 ft.

Table 43. Sound-transmission loss in decibels

Material in Test Panel	Weight psf.	Average Reduction Factors*
12″ Hollow Tile—two different types of units, plaster both sides, brown and white finish.	65	48.6
12″ Hollow Tile—two different types of units, plaster both sides, brown and white finish.	66	50.0
8″ Hollow Tile—plaster both sides, brown and smooth white finish.	48	49.8
6″ Hollow Tile—plaster both sides, brown coat and smooth white finish.	39	47.1
6″ Hollow Tile—plaster both sides, brown coat and smooth white finish.	37	45.7
4″ Hollow Tile—plaster both sides, brown coat and smooth white finish.	29	44.0
4″ Hollow Tile—plaster both sides, brown coat and smooth white finish.	29	43.5
3″ Hollow Tile—plaster both sides, brown coat and smooth white finish.	28	44.4
8″ Hollow Tile (Heath cubes)—plaster both sides, brown coat and smooth white finish.	55	51.0
4″ Hollow Tile—wood furring, paper, metal lath and plaster both sides.	34	57.5
4″ Hollow Tile (on pads)—wood furring, paper, metal lath and plaster both sides.	34	58.3
8″ Hollow Tile—2 units, 1¾″ apart, filled with Flax-li-num and ½″ Flax-li-num pads at top, bottom and sides of one wythe.	50	59.2

"Average transmission loss" ratings are less accurate than "sound transmission class" (STC) ratings now generally used.

STRUCTURAL CLAY FACING TILE PARTITIONS

Properties of fifteen walls using structural clay facing tile, alone or in combination with other materials, are given in Table 44; wall sections are shown in Fig. 66. Both are from the Facing Tile Institute.

Allowable load has been computed from the unit working stresses prescribed in the *American National Standard Building Code Requirements for Masonry.* Allowable loads are computed on the net area and the following working stresses: Type M mortar, 85 psi; Type S mortar, 75 psi; Type N mortar, 70 psi.

Material quantity: Mortar quantities shown are for tile laid with ¼-in. joints. If ⅜-in. joints are used, mortar quantities should be increased by 40 per cent.

Lateral-support requirements conform to the ANSI Code, which generally permits a 100 per cent increase in required spacing of supports for nonloadbearing partitions as compared to loadbearing partitions. Lateral support may be obtained horizontally from across walls or piers and vertically from floors or roofs.

Wall weights are taken from *American National Standard Building Code Requirements for Minimum Design Loads for Buildings and Other Structures* (ANSI A58.1). For plastered walls, add 5 psf for ⅝-in. gypsum plaster.

Sound resistance: Sound-transmission losses are based on test results, where available. In other cases, they have been computed in accordance with National Bureau of Standards Research Paper No. 48.

Modular design: All structural clay facing tile manufactured by members of the Facing Tile Institute are designed for modular coordination. All wall sections on the following three pages are drawn on the standard 4 by 4-in. modular grid.

Stack bond

In addition to the conventional half, third, and quarter bonds, structural clay facing tile is often laid in stack bond (block or plumb bond), in which all joints, vertical as well as horizontal, are aligned. The units may be placed with their long axes in either a horizontal or a vertical direction, and are referred to on this page as "stretcher stack bond" and "soldier stack bond," respectively.

Unit

If structural clay facing tile is laid in stack bond, it is particularly important that the size of units be within extremely close tolerances, since the continuous joints accentuate any variation in size between adjacent units. In order to ensure minimum variation of face dimensions, it is recommended that the units be specified as "Select Quality, Gaged" or "Select Quality, Ground Edge." Permissible tolerances for this grade are plus or minus ¹⁄₁₆ in.; the maximum difference between the largest and smallest unit in one lot is ³⁄₃₂ in. Standard face dimensions are 5, 7¾, 11¹¹⁄₁₆, and 15¾ in. All three of the most common series of structural facing tile (4D—nominal face size 5⅓ by 8 in.; 6T—5⅓ by 12 in.; 8W—8 by 16 in.) are readily adaptable for use in stack bond. No special shapes are needed, although standard shapes may sometimes be used in unconventional positions.

Bonding

Figure 67 shows seven typical wall sections in which structural clay facing tile is used in stack bond, both soldier and

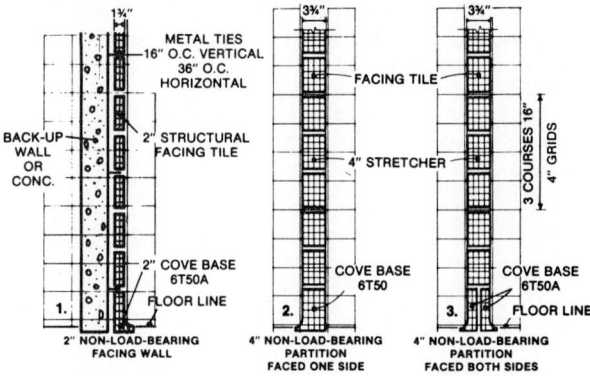

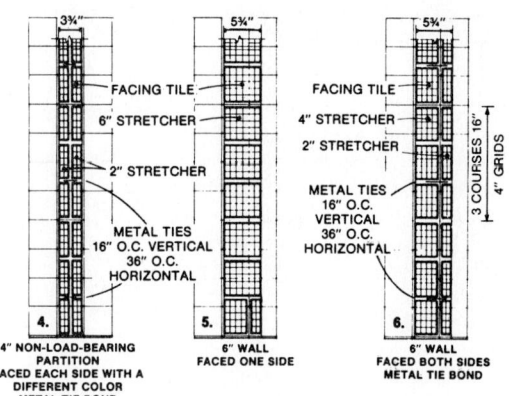

Fig. 66. Typical wall sections

Table 44. Properties of wall sections

WALL NUMBER		1	2	3	4	5	6
Allowable Load (lb. per lin. ft.)	Type M Mortar (85 psi)					5,870	5,870
	S (75 psi)	—	—	—	—	5,180	5,180
	N (70 psi)					4,830	4,830
Material Quantity (per 100 sq. ft.)	Mortar (cu. ft.) 25% waste added	1.30	2.19	2.19	2.19	3.36	3.36
	Units (F.T.)[5] 2% waste added	230	230	230	460	230	230
	(F.T.)[5] 2% waste added	—	—	—	—	—	230
	Metal Ties 2% waste added	25.5	—	—	25.5	—	25.5
U Valve (BTU per sq.ft. per hr. per °F)	Unplastered Partition	—	0.40	0.40	0.39	0.35	0.34
Lateral Support Spacing Required (ft.)	Non-Load-Bearing	—	12	12	12	18	18
	Load-Bearing	—	—	—	—	9	9
Wall Weight (lb. per sq. ft.)	Unplastered	20	30	30	33	41	47
Sound Resistance (db)	Unplastered	—	45	45	46	47	48
Fire Resistance	Regular Coring	—	*	—	1	1	2
	Fire Rated Coring	—	1	1	1	2	3

*Note: ¾" plaster on back of these units will produce 1 hr. rating.

stretcher. As may be seen, structural bonding of stretcher stack bond walls is similar to conventional methods. Although most of the sections shown indicate masonry bond between the various wythes of the wall, bonding by means of noncorrosive metal ties is equally suitable.

Acoustical facing tile

Acoustical facing tile has random perfora- tions in the face and Fiberglas pads in the cores. Its sound absorption coefficients are given in Table 45 and may be compared with those of brick, plaster, and other materials given in Table 2 of the section on Acoustics. Acoustical facing tile makes it possible to have a sound-absorbing wall which is rugged, fireproof, and loadbearing, and can be scrubbed or even steam cleaned.

Table 45. Average sound absorption coefficients

Sound Frequency, Hertz	125	250	500	1000	2000	4000	NRC
Sound Absorption Coefficients, Sabins Per Square Foot	0.31	0.50	0.67	0.91	0.43	0.43	0.60

Courtesy of Facing Tile Institute.

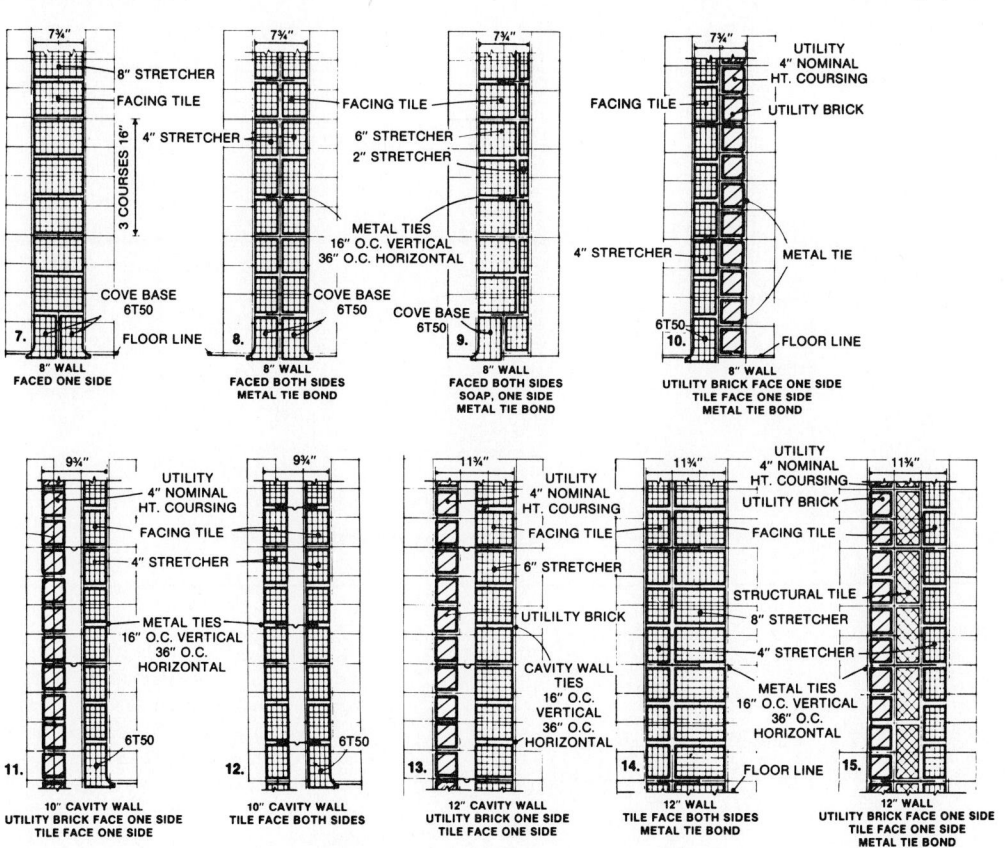

Fig. 66 (cont.). Typical wall sections

Table 44 (cont.). Properties of wall sections

WALL NUMBER		7	8	9	10	11	12	13	14	15
Allowable Load (lb. per lin. ft.)	Type M Mortar (85 psi)	7,900	7,900	7,900	7,900	6,300[3]	6,300[3]	7,970[3]	12,000	12,000
	S (75 psi)	6,980	6,980	6,980	6,980	5,400[3]	5,400[3]	6,840[3]	10,580	10,580
	N (70 psi)	6,510	6,510	6,510	6,510	4,950[3]	4,950[3]	6,270[3]	9,860	9,860
Material Quantity (per 100 sq. ft.)	Mortar (cu. ft.) 25% waste added	4.53	4.53[1]	4.53[1]	9.57	6.97	4.38	8.14	9.32	16.59
	Units (F.T.)[5] 2% waste added	230	460	230[4]	230	230	460	230	230[2]	230
	(S.T.) 2% waste added	—	—	—	471	471	—	471	—	153
	(Brick) 5% waste added	—	—	—	471	471	—	471	—	471
	Metal Ties 2% waste added	—	25.5	25.5	25.5	25.5	25.5	25.5	25.5	25.5
U Valve (BTU per sq. ft per hr. per °F)	Unplastered Partition	0.31	0.30	0.30	—	—	—	—	—	—
	Exterior Wall	—	—	—	0.41	0.30	0.25	0.23	0.30	0.31
	2-in. Insulation	—	—	—	—	0.08	0.08	0.08	—	—
Lateral Support Spacing Required (ft.)	Non-Load-Bearing	24	24	24	24	24	24	30	36	36
	Load-Bearing	12	12	12	12	12	12	15	18	18
Wall Weight (lb. per sq. ft.)	Unplastered	50	60	58	67	67	60	79	80	89
Sound Resistance (db)	Unplastered	49	50	50	52	54	52	58	57	57
Fire Resistance	Regular Coring	2	2	2	3	3	3	4	4	4
	Fire Rated Coring	—	4	4	3	4	4	4	—	4

[1] If collar joint is filled, add 2.6 cu. ft. per 100 sq. ft. of wall.
[2] 230 each of 4" and 8" stretchers.
[3] Eccentrically loaded. For concentric loading increase allowable load 25%.
[4] 230 each of 2-in. and 6-in. stretchers.
[5] Tile quantity based on nominal 5"x 12" facing tile.

Structural clay facing tile partitions; chemical-resistant brick and tile

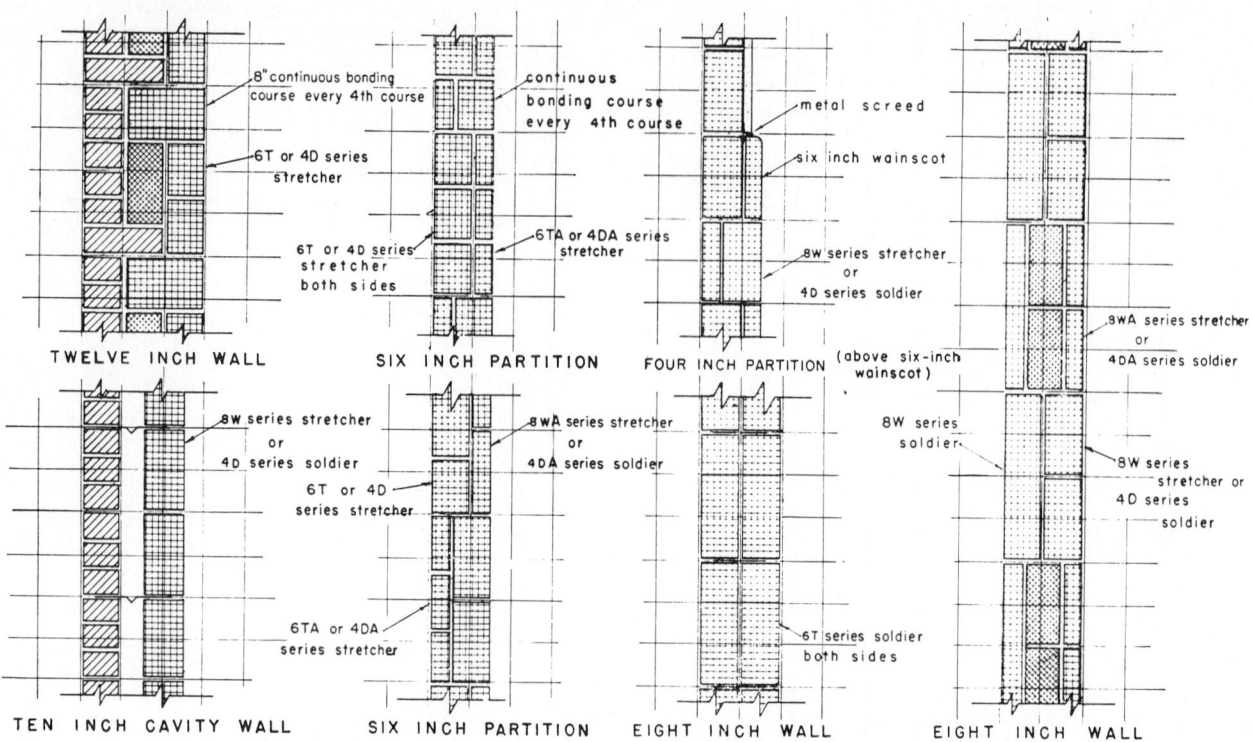

Fig. 67. Typical wall sections using structural clay facing tile in soldier and stretcher stack bond

CHEMICAL-RESISTANT BRICK AND TILE

Determining the required protection

Foremost in the design of a chemical-resistant element is the proper determination of the type and severity of the expected and/or possible corrosive environment.

Primary considerations are the following:

1. The chemical agent or agents and their nature (liquid, dry solid, wet solid, dry gas, or moist gas).

2. The expected temperature or temperature range.

3. The expected concentration or range of concentration.

4. The expected state of the agent (stationary or flowing).

5. The expected exposure (continuous or intermittent).

Masonry units: Nearly all well-burned clay masonry units have a high degree of chemical resistance, including facing brick (ASTM C216), building brick (ASTM C62), sewer brick (ASTM C32), paving brick (ASTM C7), industrial floor brick (ASTM C410), structural clay facing tile (ASTM C212), and ceramic glazed brick and tile (ASTM C126). However, for extreme exposures chemical-resistant clay masonry units (ASTM C279) are recommended, especially for use with special chemical-resistant mortars. With the exception of hydrofluoric acid, clay masonry units are relatively immune to direct chemical attack. Where hydrofluoric acid is a consideration, special

"carbon" brick are available from some manufacturers.

Standard specifications

Chemical-Resistant Masonry Units, ASTM C279.

Chemically Setting Silicate and Silica Chemical-Resistant Mortars, ASTM C466.

Chemical-Resistant Resin Mortars, ASTM C395.

Chemical-Resistant Sulfur Mortar, ASTM C287.

Chemical-resistant mortars

The duration of satisfactory performance and life of a chemical-resistant installation depends to a large degree on the selection of the proper mortar jointing material. In addition to chemical properties, the physical and mechanical properties of the mortar are also important to the performance of the selected system (see Table 46). Expected reactions and recommended uses are indicated in Table 47, which has been condensed from a much longer list published by American Concrete Institute.

Types of mortars: There are many types of formulations of chemical-resistant mortars, several of which are described here. It should be pointed out that the descriptions, capabilities, and properties listed here and in Tables 46 and 47 are general, and these properties may in many cases be varied by altering the formulations.

1. *Portland cement mortars.* Conventional portland cement mortars can be used in many so-called chemical-resistant installations. There are many chemicals which do not attack conventional mortar. Among these are neutral salts, most carbonates, nitrates, some chlorides and fluorides, silicates, and weak alkaline solutions. In addition, petroleum products and coal-tar distillates, when free of fatty oils and other potentially acidic materials, are normally harmless although they may cause undesirable discoloration and staining. The chemical-resistant properties of conventional mortars can, however, be altered and improved by various means, including the addition of waterproofing agents and other special admixtures to modify portland cement mortar.

2. *Sulfur mortars.* Sulfur mortars are applied as hot-melt materials containing an inert silica or carbon filler. Plasticized sulfur mortars are available as proprietary materials. The plasticizers reduce brittleness and improve the other mechanical properties. Sulfur mortars are particularly useful for protection against oxidizing acids and, when carbon filled, for protection against combinations of oxidizing acids and hydrofluoric acid. The heat resistance of sulfur mortars is relatively low, usually limited to approximately 190° F. Chemical resistance to alkaline solutions and some organic solvents is poor.

3. *Silicate mortars.* Silicate mortars have been successfully used in chemical-resistant brickwork for over fifty years. Originally they were solutions of silicate of soda mixed with a siliceous filler which air-hardened on drying out. More recently the air-hardening silicate mortars have been replaced by "chemically hardening" silicate mortars which include a mild acid solid or other reactive agent in the filler. Silicate mortars have excellent chemical resistance to all strong acids with the exception of hydrofluoric and related acids. The heat resistance is good up to a temperature of 750°F. They have, however, been formulated and used at temperatures of 1500°F and higher. Silicate mortars have good resistance to oils, fats, and solvents and excellent resistance to hot, strong solutions of such acids as sulfuric, nitric, and chromic. Some disadvantages are the high porosity, permeability, lack of alkali resistance, and poor resistance to neutral and weak acid solutions.

4. *Phenolic resin mortars.* Phenolic resin mortars are phenolformaldehyde resin binders with inert powder fillers containing an acid catalyst. The filler may be silica flour, carbon, coke flour, barytes, or asbestos. Ordinary phenolformaldehyde resin mortars have good resistance to most mineral acids and solutions of inorganic salts and mildly oxidizing solutions. They are rapidly attacked by strong oxidizing agents such as nitric acid, chromic acid, and concentrated sulfuric acid. They perform satisfactorily in mild alkaline solutions and in many solvents but have poor resistance to strong alkalies.

Recently there have been developed so-called modified phenolic resin mortars, which show improved resistance to alkalies and solvents. The recommended upper temperature limit for phenolic resin mortars is 350°F, or less where warpage and porosity are considerations.

5. *Furan resin mortars.* Furan resin mortars have been used with chemical-resistant brick and tile vessel linings for nearly thirty years. They are generally supplied as two-part systems comprised of liquid furan resin and powder filler containing an acid catalyst. The powder filler is usually carbon, coke flour, or silica. Furan mortars have a wide range of chemical resistance and are suitable for service with nonoxidizing acids, alkalies, salts, gases, oils, greases, detergents, and most solvents at temperatures up to 375°F. Chemical resistance and heat performance may be varied depending upon the formulation and the type of filler.

6. *Polyester resin mortars.* Polyester resin mortars have been used with brick and tile units for chemical-resistant applications for over fifteen years. They may be single or two-component systems. The filler is usually silica, but carbon has also been used. Polyester resin mortars are used in bleach vessels and for mild oxidizing agents but lack resistance to strong alkalies and many solvents. Heat resistance is relatively low, generally limited to 250°F. It should be noted, however, that by varying formulations their physical properties can be changed materially.

7. *Epoxy resin mortars.* The epoxy resin mortars are approximately twelve years old.

They are furnished in two- and three-component systems containing inert fillers. In general, epoxy resin mortars have excellent physical and mechanical properties as well as excellent resistance to nonoxidizing acids and to alkalies. Their resistance to solvents and heat are not outstanding but can be greatly enhanced by special formulations. For usual formulations, temperatures of 200 to 250°F are generally maximum.

8. *Other chemical-resistant mortars.* Many synthetic resins in liquid form or which can be dissolved in a solvent are used for chemical-resistant mortar applications. Many specialty mortars can be produced to conform to specific requirements in addition to chemical resistance. These requirements may involve such diverse considerations as color, appearance, food laws, mechanical and physical properties, etc. A wide variety of these are used with brick and tile as mortars, including vinyls, coumaroneindenes, urea-formaldehyde, melamines, acrylates, polyamides, rubbers, and others.

Asphaltic and bituminous materials have also been used for low-temperature service, both with and without fillers. They have been used as joint mortar but are more often used as a membrane behind the chemical-resistant layer or barrier.

Conclusion

The field of chemical-resistant masonry is a highly specialized one. Therefore, it is strongly recommended that the engineering advice, services, and recommendations of the manufacturing specialists in this field be used in the design and construction of installations of this nature.

Table 46. Typical physical and mechanical properties of chemical-resistant mortars*

Property	Sulfur	Silicate	Phenolic resin	Furan resin	Polyester resin	Epoxy resin
Density, lb per cu ft	138	125	112†	95	125	95–125
Apparent porosity, per cent	< 1	> 12	1	< 1	< 1	< 1
Tensile strength, psi	600	350	1,200	1,400	1,400	1,600
Compressive strength, psi	6,000	3,500	10,000	12,000	12,000	16,000
Modulus of rupture, psi	1,400	750	1,400	1,600	1,750	1,800
Modulus of elasticity, 10^6 psi	1.2	1.0	0.6	1.0	1.5	1.3
Coefficient of linear expansion, 10^{-6} in. per in. per °F	18.2	6.0	8.0	11.5	18.0	14.0
Maximum service temperature, °F	190	750–1,600	350	375	250	250
Working time of mixed mortar at 70°F, min	. . .	40	30–120	30	60	45
Final setting time, days	. . .	3	3–4	2	2	2
Linear shrinkage on setting, per cent	. . .	1.0	0.8	0.4	1.2	0

* Adapted from the Journal of the American Concrete Institute, *December 1966.*
† *Silica-filled.*

Table 47. Effect of chemical agent and commonly used protective treatments*

Material	Effect on portland cement mortar	Mortars†
Acetic acid, < 10 per cent‡	Disintegrates slowly	Fu, Ph, S, Ep, Si
Acetone	Liquid loss by penetration. May contain acetic acid as impurity (which see)	Fu, Si, Ep
Acid waters (pH of 6.5 or less)	Disintegrates slowly	Fu, Ph, Ep, PE, Si, S
Aluminum chloride	Disintegrates rapidly	Fu, Ph, S, Ep, PE
Aluminum sulfate‡	Disintegrates	Fu, Ph, S, Ep, PE
Ammonium carbonate‡	Not harmful	Fu, Ep, Ph, Asph
Ammonium chloride‡	Disintegrates slowly	Fu, Ph, S, Ep, PE
Ammonium nitrate	Disintegrates	Fu, Ph, S, Ep, PE
Ammonium sulfate‡	Disintegrates	Fu, Ph, Ep, S, PE
Ammonium superphosphate	Disintegrates	Fu, Ep, Ph
Automobile and diesel exhaust gases	May disintegrate by action of carbonic, nitric, or sulfurous acid	Fu, Ep, Ph
Beef fat‡	Solid fat disintegrates slowly, melted fat more rapidly	Fu, EP
Beer‡	May contain, as fermentation products, acetic, carbonic, lactic, or tannic acids (which see)	Ep, Fu
Buttermilk‡	Disintegrates slowly	Ep, PE, Fu
Calcium chloride‡	In porous or cracked mortar, attacks steel	Fu, Ph, S, Ep, PE
Carbon dioxide‡	Gas may cause permanent shrinkage (see also carbonic acid)	Fu, Ph, S, Ep, PE
Carbon tetrachloride‡	Liquid loss by penetration	Fu, Ph
Carbonic acid‡	Disintegrates slowly	Fu, Ph, S, Ep, PE
Castor oil	Disintegrates, especially in presence of air	Fu, Ph, PE
China wood oil	Liquid disintegrates slowly. Dried or drying films harmless	Fu
Chlorine gas	Slowly disintegrates	Si, PE
Cider‡	Disintegrates slowly (see acetic acid)	Ep, Fu, PE
Coal	Sulfides leaching from damp coal may oxidize to sulfurous or sulfuric acid (which see)	Fu, Ph, Ep, S
Coconut oil‡	Disintegrates, especially in presence of air	Fu, Ph, Ep, PE
Cod liver oil‡	Disintegrates slowly	Fu, Ph, Ep, PE
Copper sulfate	Disintegrates mortar of inadequate sulfate resistance	Fu
Corn syrup‡	Disintegrates slowly	Fu, Ph, Ep
Cottonseed oil‡	Disintegrates, especially in presence of air	Fu, Ph, PE
Creosote	Phenol present disintegrates slowly	Fu, Ph, Si
Ethylene glycol‡	Disintegrates slowly	Fu, Ph, Ep, S
Fermenting fruits, grains, vegetables, or extracts‡	Industrial fermentation processes produce lactic acid. Disintegrates slowly (see lactic acid)	
Ferric sulfate	Disintegrates mortar of inadequate quality	Fu, Ph, S, Ep, PE
Fish oil‡	Disintegrates slowly	Fu, Ph, PE
Flue gases	Hot gasses (400–1100 °F) cause thermal stresses. Cooled, condensed sulfurous, hydrochloric acids disintegrate slowly	Si, FC
Formaldehyde, 37 per cent‡	Formic acid, formed in solution, disintegrates slowly	Fu, Ph, S, Ep
Fruit juices‡	Hydrofluoric, other acids, and sugar all cause disintegration (see also fermenting fruits, grains, vegetables, extracts)	Fu, Ph, Ep
Glucose‡	Disintegrates slowly	Fu, Ph, Ep
Glycerine‡	Disintegrates slowly	Fu, Ph, S, Ep
Hydrochloric acid‡	Disintegrates rapidly, including steel	Fu, Ph, S, Si, Ep
Hydrofluoric acid§	Disintegrates rapidly, including steel	Ph, Fu, S
Hydrogen sulfide	Not harmful, but in moist, oxidizing environments converts to sulfurous acid (see text), disintegrates slowly	Fu, Ph, S, Ep, PE
Lactic acid‡	Disintegrates slowly	Fu, Ph, Ep, PE
Lard and lard oil‡	Lard disintegrates slowly, lard oil more rapidly	Fu, Ph, PE, Ep
Lead nitrate	Disintegrates slowly	Fu, Ph, S, Ep, PE

* *Adapted from the* Journal of the American Concrete Institute, *December 1966.*
† *Key to symbols used:*

Symbol	Material		Symbol	Material
Asph	*Asphalt*		*PE*	*Polyester*
Btmn	*Bituminous*		*Ph*	*Phenolic*
Ep	*Epoxy*		*S*	*Sulfur*
FC	*Fire clay*		*Si*	*Silicate*
Fu	*Furan*			

‡ *Sometimes used in food processing or as food or beverage ingredient. Ask for advisory opinion of Food and Drug Administration.*
§ *Requires special "carbon brick"; see text.*

Table 47 (cont.). Effect of chemical agent and commonly used protective treatments*

Material	Effect on portland cement mortar	Mortars†	Material	Effect on portland cement mortar	Mortars†
Linseed oil‡	Liquid disintegrates slowly. Dried or drying films are harmless	Fu, Ph, Ep, PE	Sewage	Usually not harmful (see hydrogen sulfide)	Fu, Ph, Ep, S, PE
Lubricating oil	Fatty oils, if present, disintegrate slowly	Fu, Ph, Ep, PE	Silage	Acetic, butyric, lactic acids (and sometimes fermenting agents of hydrochloric or sulfuric acids) disintegrate slowly	Fu, Ph, Ep
Magnesium chloride‡	Disintegrates slowly	Fu, Ph, S, Ep			
Magnesium sulfate‡	Disintegrates mortar of inadequate sulfate resistance	Fu, Ph, S, Ep, PE	Sodium hydroxide‡	Disintegrates mortar	Ep, Fu
Manure	Disintegrates slowly	Fu, Ph, Ep	Sodium nitrate‡	Disintegrates slowly	Fu, Ph, S, Ep, PE
Margarine‡	Solid margarine disintegrates slowly, melted margarine more rapidly	Fu, Ph, Ep, PE	Sodium sulfate	Disintegrates mortar of inadequate sulfate resistance	Fu, Ph, S, Ep, PE
Mash, fermenting	Acetic and lactic acids, and sugar disintegrate slowly	Fu, Ep	Sour milk‡	Lactic acid disintegrates slowly	Fu, Ep, PE
Methyl ethyl ketone	Liquid loss by penetration	Fu, Ph	Soybean oil‡	Liquid disintegrates slowly. Dried or drying films harmless	Fu, Ph, Ep
Mineral spirits	Liquid loss by penetration	Fu, Ph, Ep, PE	Sugar‡	Disintegrates slowly	Fu, Ph, Ep, PE
Molasses‡	At temperatures $\leq 120°$ F, disintegrates slowly	Fu, Ph, Ep	Sulfuric acid, 30 per cent‡	Disintegrates rapidly	Fu, Ph, S, Ep, Si
Nitric acid, ≥ 30 per cent	Disintegrates rapidly	S, Si	Sulfurous acid	Disintegrates rapidly	Fu, Ph, S, PE
Olive oil‡	Disintegrates slowly	Fu, Ph, Ep			
Oxalic acid	Not harmful	Fu, Ph, S, Ep	Tallow and tallow oil	Disintegrates slowly	Fu, Ph, Ep, PE
Peanut oil‡	Disintegrates slowly	Fu, Ph, Ep, PE	Tannic acid	Disintegrates slowly	Fu, Ph, Ep, Si
Petroleum oils	Liquid loss by penetration. Fatty oils, if present, disintegrate slowly	Fu, Ph, PE	Tung oil	Liquid disintegrates slowly. Dried or drying films are harmless	Fu, Ph, Ep
Phenol	Disintegrates slowly	Fu, Ph, Si	Turpentine	Mild attack. Liquid loss by penetration	Fu, Ph
Phosphoric acid‡	Disintegrates slowly	Fu, Ph, S, Ep			
Potassium nitrate‡	Disintegrates slowly	Fu, Ph, Ep, S	Vinegar	Disintegrates slowly (see acetic acid)	
Potassium sulfate‡	Disintegrates mortar of inadequate sulfate resistance	Fu, Ph, S, Ep, PE	Wood pulp	Not harmful	Fu, Ep, S, Ph, PE
Sea water‡	Disintegrates mortar of inadequate sulfate resistance. Attacks steel in porous or cracked masonry	Fu, Ph, Ep, PE	Zinc chloride‡	Disintegrates slowly	Fu, Ph, S, Ep, PE
			Zinc sulfate	Disintegrates slowly	Fu, Ph, S, Ep, PE

Clay tile solar screens

By HOWARD P. VERMILYA, *AIA*

Much has been written about masonry solar screens as shading devices and about how they may be most effective in reducing the sun's heat,* especially for air-conditioned buildings, but little information has been given on their structural aspects.

From their very nature, screen walls are rarely, if ever, load-bearing and while they may be of a variety of materials, those using hollow clay or concrete masonry units are more generally used.

Structural stability is attained by providing the screen wall with lateral support at proper intervals and by avoiding excessive compressive loads. Lateral support may be obtained by cross walls, piers, buttresses or columns when the limiting distance between lateral supports is measured horizontally, or by floors and roofs when the limiting distance is measured vertically (ANSI Building Code Requirements for Masonry). The distance between these supports may be computed by the use of the following formulas:

(1) for restrained ends

$$L = 6.33 \times t \sqrt{\frac{A_b}{w \times k}}$$

(2) for simply supported ends

*See section on "Heating, Ventilating, and Air Conditioning: Sun Angles, and Solar Loads." See also the book *Solar Control and Shading Devices* by Olgyay and Olgyay, Princeton University Press, 1976.

$$L = 5.17 \times t \sqrt{\frac{A_b}{w \times k}}$$

Where:

L = allowable distance between lateral supports in feet

t = actual wall thickness in inches

A_b = ratio of actual bed joint length in a horizontal longitudinal plane to the total wall length.

(A_b = 1 for stack, running or common bond, and 0.5 for split bond patterns where each unit is lapped ⅓ over the lower unit.)

w = design wind pressure in pounds per square foot as taken from wind pressure map and wind pressure tables for height zones above ground.

k = ratio of solid wall area to total wall area.

DESIGN CONSIDERATIONS

1. If the solar screen is supported by building it into a reinforced concrete structure, the end condition is fixed to a degree justifying the 1/12th moment coefficient used in Formula 1, while if the screen is supported on a steel shelf angle with ⅛th moment coefficient is indicated as in Formula 2.

2. Provisions should be made to anchor clay masonry solar screens to the building frame to prevent them from being sucked off their supports. The coefficient of static friction of

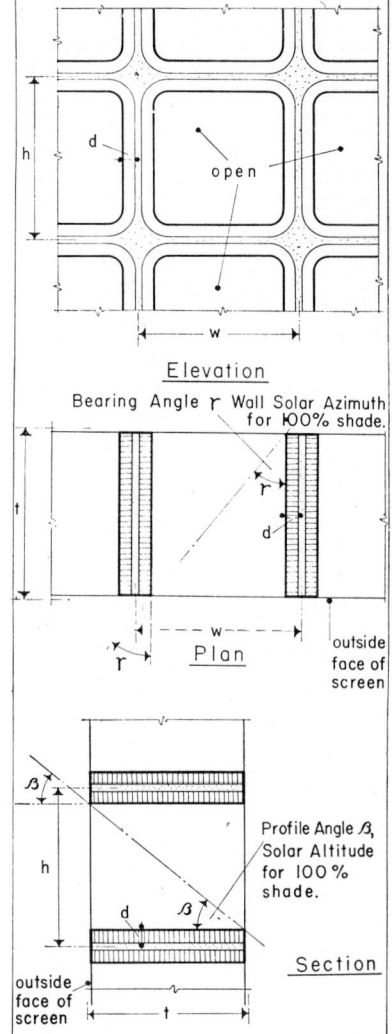

Elevation

Bearing Angle r Wall Solar Azimuth for 100% shade.

Plan

outside face of screen

Profile Angle β, Solar Altitude for 100% shade.

Section

outside face of screen

Table 48. Design data—clay masonry solar screens

Rectangular Sizes				Structural Data		Shading Data		Units	Estimating Data			
Nominal Modular Dimensions in inches*			Specified Dimension in inches			100% Shading			Mortar			
									Cu. ft. per sq. ft. of Wall Area		Cu. ft. per 1000 Units	
h Face Height	w Face Width	t Length in Wall Thickness	d Shell Thickness	k Ratio of Solid Wall Area to Total Wall Area	Approximate Weight per sq. ft. of Wall Area in lb.	Profile Angle B	Bearing Angle r	No. per sq. ft. of Wall	½" joints	⅜" joints	½" joints	⅜" joints
4	8	6	⅝	.56	40	23°	49°	4.5	.092	.069	20.3	15.2
4	8	8	⅝	.56	54	17°	40°	4.5	.125	.094	27.8	20.8
4	8	12	⅝	.56	80	12°	29°	4.5	.193	.145	42.5	31.9
8	8	6	⅝	.39	30	49°	49°	2.25	.061	.046	27.1	20.3
8	8	8	⅝	.39	40	40°	40°	2.25	.828	.622	36.8	27.6
8	8	12	⅝	.39	60	29°	29°	2.25	.127	.095	56.5	42.4
8	12	6	¾	.375	30	48°	62°	1.5	.051	.382	34.5	26.9
8	12	8	¾	.375	40	39°	54°	1.5	.700	.525	46.6	35.0
8	12	12	¾	.375	60	28°	42°	1.5	.108	.081	72.0	54.0
12	12	6	⅞	.34	25	61°	61°	1.0	.042	.032	42.0	31.5
12	12	8	⅞	.34	33	53°	53°	1.0	.057	.043	57.2	43.0
12	12	12	⅞	.34	50	41°	41°	1.0	.880	.66	88.2	66.1

*Manufactured dimensions are ⅜ in. to ½ in. smaller than the nominal modular dimensions shown, depending on the manufacturer.

masonry on concrete, 0.70, and masonry on steel, 0.30, is not always sufficient to prevent horizontal movement of light-weight walls. Strap anchors can be employed to resist this movement.

Clay masonry screens which butt against or pass vertical members of concrete should be anchored in slots built into the concrete. Anchors, made of not less than 16-gage galvanized iron, should be at least ⅞-in. wide and spaced not more than 18 in. on center vertically.

3. Mortars for clay masonry units should conform to ASTM standard specifications, "Mortars for Unit Masonry" C 270. Types M or S shall be used when the distance between lateral supports exceeds 0.7 of the maximum permitted by Formula 1 or 2; when the distance is 0.7 or less, Type N mortar may be used. Mortar bed joints should be completely filled.

4. For structural considerations, units in split bond should not lap over the units below less than one third of their horizontal projection area.

5. L, the distance between lateral supports, may be measured either horizontally between walls or columns or vertically between floor slabs or beams when stack, running or common bond is used, but only vertically when split bond is used.

Table 49. Physical properties of clay masonry solar screen units

Raw Materials:
  Units shall be made of surface clay, shale, fire clay or mixtures thereof.

Finish:
  Exposed ends shall be uncored and reasonably free from cracks, chips, surface roughness and other defects detracting from the appearance of the wall when viewed from a distance of 20 ft.

Water Absorption:
  Maximum per cent by 1 hr. boiling;
    Where the weathering index is more than 100

Average of 5 units	9%
Individual units	11%

    Where the weathering index is less than 100

Average of 5 tests	16%
Individual units	19%

Dimensional Variation:
  Maximum variation plus or minus from specified dimension in width, w; height, h; or length, t 3%
  The shell thickness, d, shall be not less than $1/16$ in. under nor more than $1/4$ in. over the specified dimension given in Table 52.

EXAMPLE:

Location: Dallas, Texas, 5th floor.
Material: 8-by-8-by-8-in. hollow clay units in stack bond.
Frame or supports: reinforced concrete.
Mortar: Type S.
Wind Pressure Map (Fig. 1 in Design Loads section) shows that the wind speed for Dallas is 70 mph. Table 1 in the section on Curtain Walls shows wind pressure 50 ft above ground is 21 lb/ft².
k: Table 48 shows 0.39 for 8-by-8-by-8-in. unit having shell thickness of ⅝ in. with ⅜-in. mortar joints.
A_b: 1 for stack bond
t: 7.5-in. actual thickness

$$L = 6.33 \times 7.5 \sqrt{\frac{1}{21 \times .39}}$$

$$L = 16.7 \text{ ft}$$

If solar screen had been laid in type N mortar, allowable distance between supports could not exceed 0.7 of 16.7 ft or 11.7 ft.

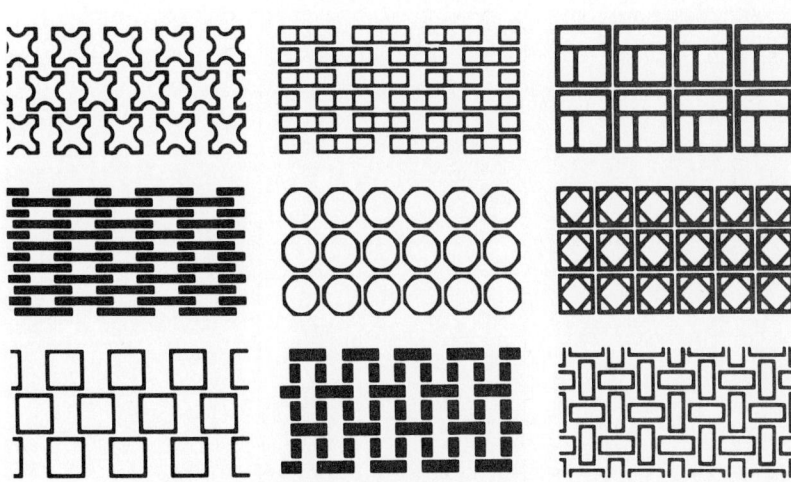

Fig. 68. Pattern variations in brick, tile, and terra cotta screens

Concrete masonry, dimensions and properties

From data supplied by the National Concrete Masonry Association

Standards for concrete masonry and mortar are given on Sheets 1 and 2 of this section. Mortar types and uses and allowable compressive stresses on concrete masonry are given in Tables 1, 2, and 3 of this section. Reference should also be made to *Specification for Concrete Masonry Construction* (ACI 531.1-76) published by the American Concrete Institute.

Sizes: All concrete masonry units are modular in size. The larger units, called blocks, have nominal face dimensions of 8 in. in height by 16 in. in length and nominal thicknesses of 4, 6, 8, 10, or 12 in. Actual dimensions are in all cases 3/8 in. less to allow for the thickness of the joint. Permissible dimensional tolerance is 1/8 in., but in practice deviation rarely exceeds 1/32 in. Hollow units, defined as those having core-void areas greater than 25 per cent of the gross area, may be of two-core or three-core design at the option of the manufacturer. Minimum allowable thicknesses of face shells and interior webs are given in Table 50.

Weight of concrete units can be calculated from the equivalent solid thicknesses given in Table 52 provided that the density of the concrete is known. In the absence of specific information, the following values may be assumed.

	lb/cu ft
Pumice concrete	75
Expanded shale concrete	85
Expanded slag and cinder concrete	95
Air-cooled slag concrete	120
Crushed stone and gravel concrete	135

Fire resistance: Concrete masonry is highly fire-resistant, the lightweight units being more efficient in this respect than the heavyweight units. The fire resistance of concrete masonry can be considered as a function of the type of aggregate used in

Table 50. Minimum thickness of face shell and webs (ASTM C90-70T)

Nominal width of units, in.	Face shell thickness, min. in.*	Web thickness — Webs, min. in.*	Web thickness — Equivalent web thickness, min. in. per lineal ft†
4	3/4	3/4	1 5/8
6	1	1	2 1/4
8	1 1/4	1	2 1/4
10	1 3/8 (1 1/4)‡	1 1/8	2 1/2
12	1 1/2 (1 1/4)‡	1 1/8	2 1/2

* *Average of measurements on 5 units taken at the thinnest point.*
† *Sum of measured thickness of all webs in unit, times 12, divided by length of unit.*
‡ *Face shell thickness shown in parentheses is applicable where allowable design load is reduced in proportion to the reduction in thickness from basic shell thicknesses shown.*

Table 51. Estimated fire-resistance ratings of concrete masonry

Aggregate type	Minimum equivalent thickness, in., for rating of — 1 hr	2 hr	3 hr	4 hr
Pumice	1.8	3.0	4.0	4.7
Expanded slag	2.2	3.3	4.2	5.0
Expanded shale or clay	2.5	3.7	4.7	5.5
Limestone, scoria, cinders, or un-expanded slag	2.7	4.0	5.0	5.9
Calcareous gravel	2.8	4.2	5.3	6.2
Siliceous gravel	3.0	4.5	5.7	6.7

Table 52. Gross and solid volumes and equivalent solid thickness of hollow stretcher units (data based on units 7 5/8 in. high by 15 5/8 in. long)

Width, in.	Gross. volume, cu in. (cu ft)	Minimum thicknesses — Shell, in.	Web, in.	3-core units — Per cent solid volume	Equivalent solid thickness, in.	2-core units — Per cent solid volume	Equivalent solid thickness, in.
3 5/8	432 (0.25)	0.75	0.75	63	2.28	64	2.32
		1.00	1.00	73	2.66	73	2.66
5 5/8	670 (0.388)	1.00	1.00	59	3.32	57	3.21
		1.12	1.00	63	3.54	61	3.43
		1.25	1.00	66	3.71	64	3.60
		1.37	1.12	70	3.94	68	3.82
7 5/8	908 (0.526)	1.25	1.00	56	4.27	53	4.04
		1.37	1.12	60	4.57	57	4.35
		1.50	1.12	62	4.73	59	4.50
9 5/8	1145 (0.664)	1.25	1.12	53	5.10	48	4.62
		1.37	1.12	55	5.29	51	4.91
		1.50	1.25	58	5.58	54	5.20
11 5/8	1385 (0.803)	1.25	1.12	49	5.70	44	5.12
		1.37	1.12	51	5.93	46	5.35
		1.50	1.25	54	6.28	49	5.70
		1.75	1.25	57	6.63	52	6.05

the concrete. The fire resistance of any concrete masonry wall can be estimated from Tables 51 and 52; or, conversely, the thickness of masonry required to meet a specific fire-resistance requirement may be determined. Fire-resistance ratings of concrete masonary walls of various thicknesses are given in the section on "Fireproofing."

Special shapes are made for many purposes. Some of the most widely used are shown in Fig. 69. Shape names may derive from the function they perform or from the shape itself, as illustrated in the following list:

Functional:

Stretcher	Column	Bond beam
Corner	Grade	Manhole
Header	Sill	Chimney
Corner return	Sash	Screen
	Jamb	Soffit
L-corner	Control joint	Floor filler
Partition	Coping	Back up
Pier	Lintel	Pilaster insert
Pilaster	Flue liner	Joist unit

Shape name:

Solid	Brick	Plain end
Hollow	Split	Open end
Solid top	Batter	(single and
Single bull nose	Fluted	double)
	Frog	Recessed
Double bull nose		Jumbo brick
		Slump
Half		

Insulation value: U values for walls of concrete masonry of various types are given in the section on Insulation. The insulating value of lightweight units is generally 35 to 40 per cent greater than that of heavyweight units. The cells of hollow units may be filled with insulation, which should be the special water-repellent type previously mentioned in the section on Cavity Walls. The use of this type of insulation cuts the U value of the wall approximately in half. Table 53 gives resistance (R) values for hollow concrete block walls with cells empty and with cells filled with poured insulation.

Acoustical properties: Noise Reduction Coefficient (NRC): Exposed concrete masonry walls will absorb from 26 to 50 per cent of the sound waves striking them. The variation depends more on the surface texture than on the type of aggregate used. Paint applied to any acoustically absorbent material tends to close the pores and reduce its value for sound control. Spray painting reduces the value less than brush painting, and water-base paints less than oil-base paints.

Sound transmission class (STC): Concrete masonry, like any other masonry, is an effective sound isolation material. Where sound isolation is desirable, a transmission loss of 40 db or more is usually required. Table 54 lists the many types of lightweight concrete masonry walls meeting this requirement.

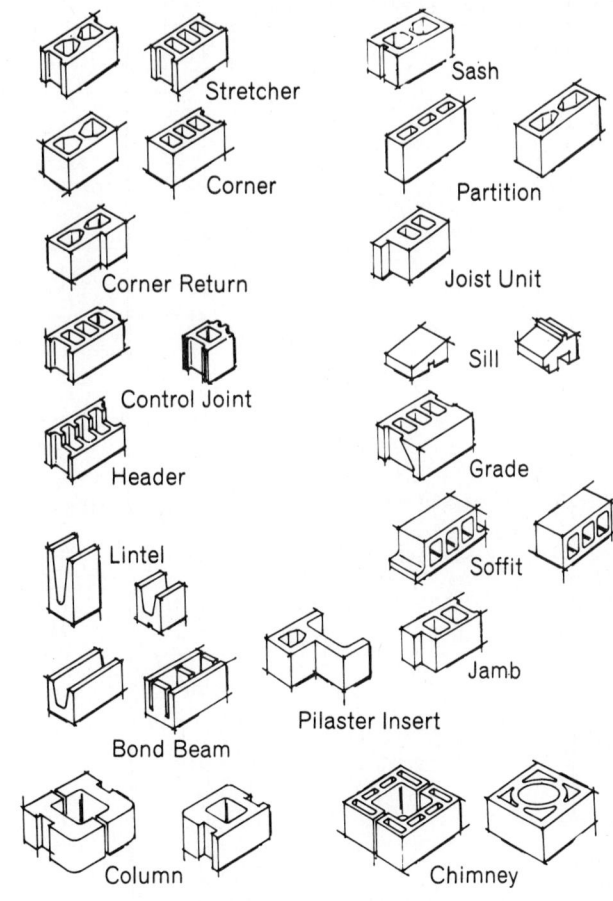

Fig. 69. Typical shapes of concrete masonry units

DESIGN OF CONCRETE MASONRY WALLS

Modular design is recommended (see section on "Modular Coordination"). For economy in construction, walls should be laid out to make maximum use of full- and half-length units (see Tables 55–56). This minimizes cutting and fitting units on the job—operations that slow up construction. All dimensions such as over-all length and height of wall, width and height of door and window openings, and wall areas between doors, windows, and corners should be planned to use full- and half-sized units that are commonly carried in stock (see Fig. 70). Full advantage of modular design for concrete masonry requires that window and door frames be of modular dimensions that fit modular full- and half-size units. All horizontal dimensions will then be in multiples of nominal half-length units, and all vertical dimensions will be multiples of nominal full-height units. Thus, with the nominal 8 by 8 by 16-in. block, both horizontal and vertical dimensions should be designed to be in multiples of 8 in.

Table 53. Resistance values ($R = 1/C$) of single-wythe concrete masonry walls with hollow cells empty and filled with bulk insulation

Thickness, in.	Insulation in cells	Unit weight of concrete, lb/cu ft				
		60	80	100	120	140
4	Filled	3.36	2.79	2.33	1.92	1.14
	Empty	2.07	1.68	1.40	1.17	0.77
6	Filled	5.59	4.59	3.72	2.95	1.59
	Empty	2.25	1.83	1.53	1.29	0.86
8	Filled	7.46	6.06	4.85	3.79	1.98
	Empty	2.30	2.12	1.75	1.46	0.98
10	Filled	9.35	7.46	5.92	4.59	2.35
	Empty	3.0	2.40	1.97	1.63	1.08
12	Filled	10.98	8.70	6.80	5.18	2.59
	Empty	3.29	2.62	2.14	1.81	1.16

Table 54. Sound transmission classes (STC) of concrete masonry walls

Thickness, in.	Description	Weight, lb/sq ft of wall area	STC
	Hollow block:		
4	Unpainted and unplastered	18	40
4	Unpainted and unplastered	26.5	41
4	Painted both sides	34.1	43
6	Unpainted and unplastered	21	44
4	Painted both sides	32.3	44
4	Plastered both sides	34.8	44
8	Unpainted and unplastered	30	45
4	½-in. gypsum board on furring, both sides	24.5	45
8	Painted both sides	30	46
6	Plastered both sides	31	46
8	Painted both sides	33.5	48
4	Plastered both sides	30	48
6	⅝-in. gypsum board on furring, both sides	35.1	49
4	Plastered both sides	32	49
8	Painted one side, gypsum board on furring, one side	43.3	50
4	Plastered both sides	42	50
	Solid block:		
6	Plastered both sides	54	52
	Hollow block:		
8	Plastered one side	38	52
6	Painted one side, ½-in. gypsum board on furring, one side	27	53
10	Plastered both sides	49	55
	Solid block:		
12	Unpainted and unplastered	121	55
8	Plastered both sides	67	56
10	Plastered both sides	81	58
12	⅝-in. gypsum board on furring, one side	124	58

Table 56. Nominal length of concrete masonry walls by stretchers

Actual length of wall is measured from outside edge to outside edge of units and is equal to the nominal length minus ⅜″ (one mortar joint.)

No. of stretchers	Nominal length of concrete masonry walls	
	Units 15⅝″ long and half units 7⅝″ long with ⅜″ thick head joints.	Units 11⅝″ long and half units 5⅝″ long with ⅜″ thick head joints.
1	1′ 4″	1′ 0″
1½	2′ 0″	1′ 6″
2	2′ 8″	2′ 0″
2½	3′ 4″	2′ 6″
3	4′ 0″	3′ 0″
3½	4′ 8″	3′ 6″
4	5′ 4″	4′ 0″
4½	6′ 0″	4′ 6″
5	6′ 8″	5′ 0″
5½	7′ 4″	5′ 6″
6	8′ 0″	6′ 0″
6½	8′ 8″	6′ 6″
7	9′ 4″	7′ 0″
7½	10′ 0″	7′ 6″
8	10′ 8″	8′ 0″
8½	11′ 4″	8′ 6″
9	12′ 0″	9′ 0″
9½	12′ 8″	9′ 6″
10	13′ 4″	10′ 0″
10½	14′ 0″	10′ 6″
11	14′ 8″	11′ 0″
11½	15′ 4″	11′ 6″
12	16′ 0″	12′ 0″
12½	16′ 8″	12′ 6″
13	17′ 4″	13′ 0″
13½	18′ 0″	13′ 6″
14	18′ 8″	14′ 0″
14½	19′ 4″	14′ 6″
15	20′ 0″	15′ 0″
20	26′ 8″	20′ 0″

Table 55. Nominal height of concrete masonry walls by courses

For concrete masonry units 7⅝″ and 3⅝″ in height laid with ⅜″ mortar joints. Height is measured from center to center of mortar joints.

No. of courses	Nominal height of concrete masonry walls	
	Units 7⅝″ high and ⅜″ thick bed joint	Units 3⅝″ high and ⅜″ thick bed joint
1	8″	4″
2	1′ 4″	8″
3	2′ 0″	1′ 0″
4	2′ 8″	1′ 4″
5	3′ 4″	1′ 8″
6	4′ 0″	2′ 0″
7	4′ 8″	2′ 4″
8	5′ 4″	2′ 8″
9	6′ 0″	3′ 0″
10	6′ 8″	3′ 4″
15	10′ 0″	5′ 0″
20	13′ 4″	6′ 8″
25	16′ 8″	8′ 4″
30	20′ 0″	10′ 0″
35	23′ 4″	11′ 8″
40	26′ 8″	13′ 4″
45	30′ 0″	15′ 0″
50	33′ 4″	16′ 8″

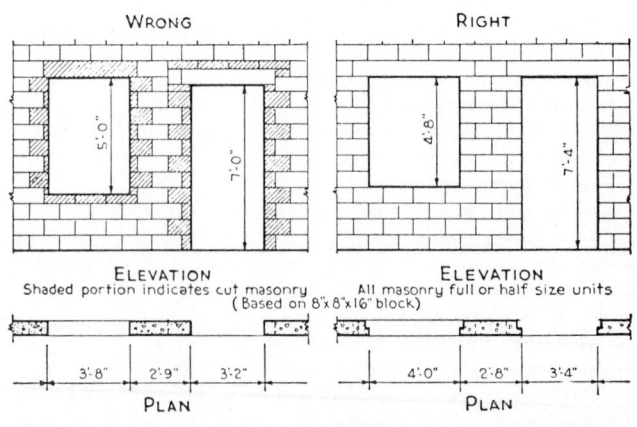

Fig. 70. Examples of wrong and right planning of concrete masonry wall openings

Concrete masonry, estimating tables; engineered concrete masonry

Table 57. Mortar and concrete masonry requirements for 100 sq ft of wall area

(Wall is assumed to be one masonry unit in thickness.)

Nominal height and length of units, in.	Number of units per 100 sq ft	Cu ft of mortar per 100 sq ft
8 x 16	112.5	6.0
8 x 12	150.0	7.0
5 x 12	221.0	8.5
4 x 16	225.0	9.5
2¼ x 8*	675.0	14.0
4 x 8†	450.0	12.0
5 x 8‡	340.0	11.0
2 x 12§	600.0	15.0
2 x 16§	450.0	15.0

* ¼ Modular concrete brick (2¼ × 3⅝ × 7⅝).
† Jumbo concrete brick (3⅝ × 3⅝ × 7⅝).
‡ Double concrete brick (4⅞ × 3⅝ × 7⅝).
§ Roman concrete brick: (1⅝ × 3⅝ × 11⅝), (1⅝ × 3⅝ × 15⅝).

Table 58. Typical values for number* of concrete masonry units laid per 8-hr day by a single mason

Size of masonry unit, in. W x H x L	Number of units per 8-hr day
4 x 8 x 16	200
6 x 8 x 16	180
8 x 8 x 16	160
10 x 8 x 16	140
12 x 8 x 16	120
Concrete brick:	
Modular	800–900
Jumbo	600–700
Double	400–500
Roman	250–350

* Decrease by 10 per cent for normal-weight and heavyweight units.
Increase by 3–5 per cent for 12-in.-long units.
Increase 15 per cent for 4-in.-high units.

Table 59. Quantities of materials for a cubic yard of concrete masonry mortar

Mortar type, ASTM C270	Sand, damp, loose volume	Cementitious materials (bags of material or cubic feet)*		
		Portland cement	Masonry cement	Lime
Type M	1.0 cy	4.5	4.5	
Type M	1.0 cy	7.5	...	2.0
Type S	1.0 cy	3.0	6.0	
Type S	1.0 cy	6.0	...	3.0
Type N	1.0 cy	...	9.0	
Type N	1.0 cy	4.5	...	4.5
Type O	1.0 cy	...	9.0	
Type O	1.0 cy	3.0	...	6.0

* Cementitious materials are usually one cubic foot volume per bag.

Table 60. Insulation required for 100 sq ft of concrete masonry wall

Wall	Insulation, CF, for 100 sq ft wall
Cavity wall:	
2-in. cavity	16.7
2½-in. cavity	20.0
4-in. cavity	33.4
Single-wythe wall:	
6-in. hollow CMU	19.0
8-in. hollow CMU	27.6
10-in. hollow CMU	35.0
12-in. hollow CMU	50.0

ENGINEERED CONCRETE MASONRY

Principles of engineered masonry design and construction, discussed on Sheets 3, 4 and 5 for brick masonry, are equally applicable to concrete masonry. Application of these principles is set forth in detail in *Specifications for the Design and Construction of Load-Bearing Concrete Masonry,* published by the National Concrete Masonry Association in 1970.

Engineering inspection is required for this type of construction; if not provided, allowable stresses must be reduced by half. Materials must conform to ASTM standards. The ultimate compressive strength of the masonry (f'_m) may be determined by prism test or by the compressive strength of the units and the type of mortar used, as shown in Table 61.

Allowable stresses in nonreinforced concrete masonry shall not exceed the following values:

Axial $0.20f'_m$
Flexural $0.30f'_m$

Shear and tension in flexure shall not exceed the values given in Table 62.

Allowable shear on steel bolts and anchors shall not exceed the values given in Table 63.

The slenderness ratio is the ratio of the effective height to the effective thickness, and for both walls and columns it shall not exceed 20. When a wall or column has full lateral support at the top and bottom, its effective height is its actual height. In the absence of top support, the effective height shall be twice the actual height. The effective thickness of a column and of a wall without pilasters is its actual thickness. The effective thickness of a wall with pilasters is its actual thickness times the coefficient shown in Table 64, where T_p = pilaster thickness and T_w = wall thickness. The effective thickness of cavity walls loaded on both wythes is two-thirds of the actual thickness excluding the cavity. The effective thickness of cavity walls loaded on one wythe is the actual thickness of the loaded wythe.

Axial loads on walls shall be computed by:

$$P = 0.20f'_m \left[1 - \left(\frac{h}{40t} \right)^3 \right] A_n$$

where h = effective height
t = effective thickness
A_n = net cross-sectional area

Axial loads on columns shall be computed by the following formula:

$$P = 0.18f'_m \left[1 - \left(\frac{h}{30t} \right)^3 \right] A_n$$

Where the virtual eccentricity on a wall or column exceeds one-third of the thickness or the value which will produce tension in the masonry, the member shall be redesigned as reinforced masonry.

Allowable stresses and design procedures for the design of reinforced masonry are also given in the NCMA specifications.

Engineered concrete masonry; construction details

Table 61. Compressive strength of masonry

(Gross area for masonry of solid units; net area for masonry of hollow units)

Compressive strength of the units, psi	Assumed compressive strength of masonry, f'_m, psi	
	Type M and S mortar	Type N mortar
Over 1,500 to 2,500	1,151 to 1,550	875 to 1,100
Over 2,500 to 4,000	1,551 to 2,000	1,101 to 1,250
Over 4,000 to 6,000	2,001 to 2,400	1,251 to 1,350
Over 6,000	2,400	1,350

Table 63. Allowable shear on bolts and anchors*†

Bolt or anchor diameter, in.	Embedment, in. ‡	Allowable shear, lb
¼	4	270
⅜	4	410
½	4	550
⅝	4	750
¾	5	1,100
⅞	6	1,500
1	7	1,850
1⅛	8	2,250

* *Without engineering inspection, reduce stresses by half.*
† *In determining the stresses in concrete masonry, the eccentricity due to loaded bolts and anchors shall be considered.*
‡ *Bolts and anchors shall be solidly embedded in mortar or grout.*

Table 62. Allowable stress in shear and tension in flexure for nonreinforced concrete masonry*

Allowable stresses	Masonry construction of			
	Hollow units		Grouted or solid units	
	Type M or S mortar	Type N mortar	Types M or S mortar	Type N mortar
Shear, psi	34§	23§	34	23
Tension in flexure: ¶				
Normal to bed joints†	23§	16§	39	27
Parallel to bed joints‡	46§	32§	78	54

* *If no engineering inspection, reduce stresses by one-half.*
† *Direction of stress is normal to bed joints, vertically in normal masonry construction.*
‡ *Direction of stress is parallel to bed joints, horizontally in normal masonry construction. If masonry is laid in stack bond, tensile stresses in the horizontal direction shall not be permitted in the masonry.*
§ *Net mortar bedded area.*
¶ *For computing flexural resistance due to horizontal load, the section modulus of a cavity wall shall be assumed to be equal to the sum of the section moduli of each wythe.*

Table 64. Coefficients for stiffened walls

Ratio: pilaster spacing (O.C.) / pilaster width	$\dfrac{T_p}{T_w} = 1$	$\dfrac{T_p}{T_w} = 2$	$\dfrac{T_p}{T_w} = 3$
6	1.0	1.4	2.0
8	1.0	1.3	1.7
10	1.0	1.2	1.4
15	1.0	1.1	1.2
20 or more	1.0	1.0	1.0

CONSTRUCTION DETAILS

Footings must be placed on undisturbed earth, below the frost line. Footing drains must be kept above the level of the bottoms of the footings.

Concrete masonry units must be dry when laid. The first course should be laid on a full mortar bed; all subsequent courses should be laid with face-shell bedding only, except that mortar should be applied to all sides of a core which is to be filled with grout. All joints should be ⅜ in. thick; exterior joints should be tooled unless the wall is to be plastered or parged. The top course, supporting the floor and/or wall, should be made solid by (1) filling the cores of the top course with mortar or concrete, (2) using solid or solid-topped units, or (3) providing a reinforced bond beam in place of the top course.

Joists running parallel to the foundation wall should be anchored to it, as shown in Fig. 77, at intervals of not more than 8 ft.

Walls above grade should be built to the following dimensional tolerances: deviation from plumb, ¼ in. in 10 ft, ⅜ in. in 20 ft, ½ in. in 40 ft; deviation from level, ¼ in. in 20 ft, ½ in. in 40 ft; deviation from cross-sectional dimensions of columns, −¼ in., +½ in.

Cracking of masonry walls is often caused by movement resulting from temperature or moisture changes. Three measures which can be taken to control this type of cracking are as follows:

1. Specify products which limit movement due to moisture (Type I moisture-controlled concrete masonry units).

2. Use steel reinforcement to increase resistance to cracking (bond beams spaced 4 ft apart vertically or horizontal joint reinforcing spaced 8, 16, or 24 in. apart vertically).

3. Provide control joints and other devices which accommodate movement.

Control joints are vertical separations built into the wall at locations where cracking is likely to occur. Common methods of constructing control joints are illustrated in Fig. 78. The joints permit free longitudinal movement but have sufficient shear and flexural strength to resist lateral loads. Maximum spacing of control joints is shown in Table 66. Other locations for control joints include:

1. Changes in wall height or thickness

2. At construction joints in foundation, in roof, and in floors

3. At chases and recesses for piping, columns, fixtures, etc.

4. At abutment of wall and columns.

5. At return angles in L-, T-, and U-shaped structures

6. At one or both sides of wall openings

Table 65. Maximum depth below grade (height of fill) for unreinforced concrete masonry basement walls

Material of foundation wall	Nominal thickness	Maximum depth below grade* when walls support:		
		Wood frame	Wood frame with masonry veneer	Masonry
Hollow masonry units	8″	4′(6′)	4′-6″(6′)	5′(7′)
	10″	5′(7′)	5′-6″(7′)	6′(7′)
	12″	7′	7′	7′
Solid masonry units	8″	5′(7′)	5′-6″(7′)	6′(7′)
	10″	6′(7′)	6′(7′)	6′-6″(7′)
	12″	7′	7′	7′

* Where soil is well-drained and equivalent liquid weight is not more than 25 pcf, figures in parentheses may be used. Based on National Building Code, 1976.

10″ and 12″ walls require special consideration at corners L-corner units or fill in with brick

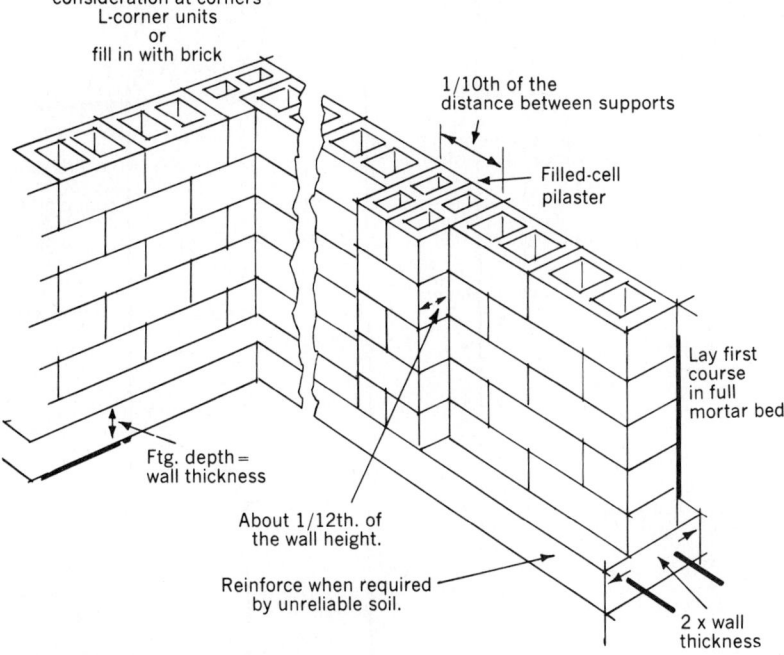

1/10th of the distance between supports

Filled-cell pilaster

Lay first course in full mortar bed

Ftg. depth = wall thickness

About 1/12th. of the wall height.

Reinforce when required by unreliable soil.

2 x wall thickness

Fig. 71. Foundation wall with pilasters

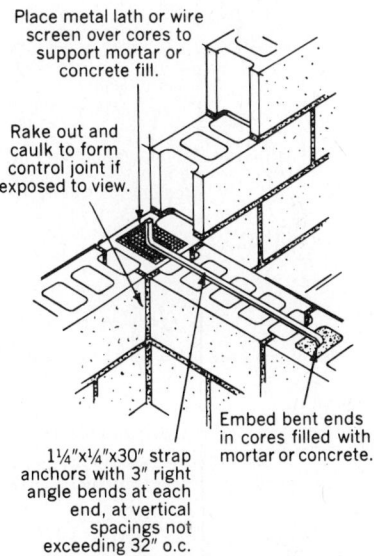

Place metal lath or wire screen over cores to support mortar or concrete fill.

Rake out and caulk to form control joint if exposed to view.

Embed bent ends in cores filled with mortar or concrete.

1¼″x¼″x30″ strap anchors with 3″ right angle bends at each end, at vertical spacings not exceeding 32″ o.c.

Fig. 72. Anchorage of intersecting bearing walls

RECOMMENDED PROTECTIVE COATINGS FOR WATERPROOFING EXTERIOR FACE OF WALLS:
1) Two ¼ inch coats of portland cement plaster, or,
2) One ¼ inch coat of portland cement plaster plus two brush coats of bituminous waterproofing, or,
3) One heavy troweled-on coat of cold, fiber-reinforced asphaltic mastic.

Gravel or stone fill.

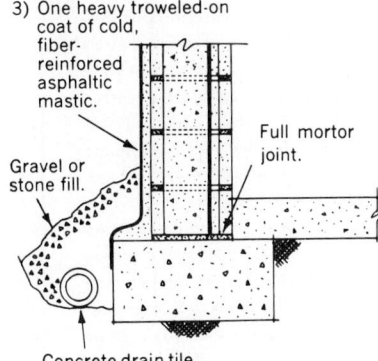

Full mortor joint.

Concrete drain tile.

WELL DRAINED SOILS

Fig. 73. Typical footing detail

RECOMMENDED PROTECTIVE COATINGS FOR WATERPROOFING EXTERIOR FACE OF WALLS:
1) Two ¼ inch thick coats of portland cement plaster plus two brush coats of bituminous waterproofing, or,
2) One ¼ inch thick coat of portland cement plaster plus one heavy troweled-on coat of cold, fiber-reinforced asphaltic mastic.

Bituminous joint.

Gravel or stone fill.

Waterproof membrane

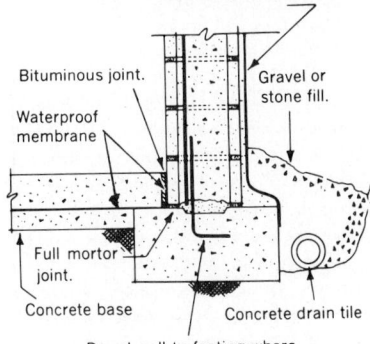

Full mortor joint.

Concrete base

Concrete drain tile

Dowel wall to footing where floor cannot be assumed to support wall laterally; as where bituminous joint is used between floor and wall.

WET AND IMPERMEABLE SOILS

Fig. 74. Footing detail for very wet soil

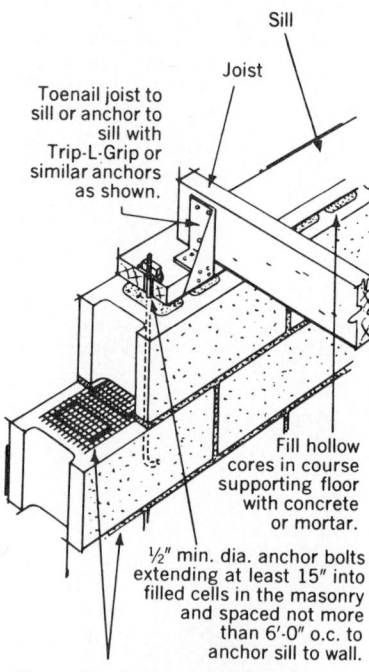

Construction details; reinforced concrete masonry

Sill
Joist
Toenail joist to sill or anchor to sill with Trip-L-Grip or similar anchors as shown.
Fill hollow cores in course supporting floor with concrete or mortar.
½" min. dia. anchor bolts extending at least 15" into filled cells in the masonry and spaced not more than 6'-0" o.c. to anchor sill to wall.
Place wire screen or metal lath in joint under cores to be filled to prevent filling of cores below.

Fig. 75. Anchoring wood sill to foundation

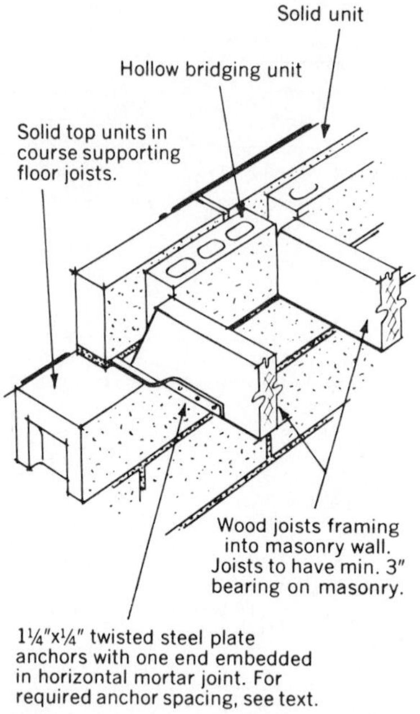

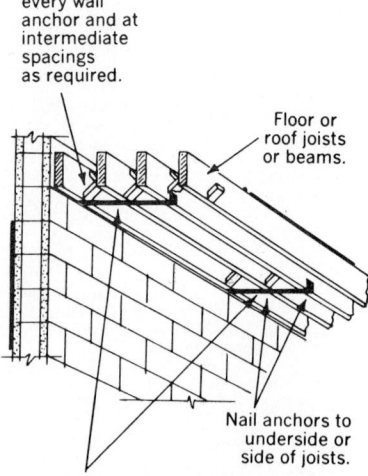

Solid unit
Hollow bridging unit
Solid top units in course supporting floor joists.
Wood joists framing into masonry wall. Joists to have min. 3" bearing on masonry.
1¼"x¼" twisted steel plate anchors with one end embedded in horizontal mortar joint. For required anchor spacing, see text.

Fig. 76. Anchoring wood joists to masonry wall

Cross bracing at every wall anchor and at intermediate spacings as required.
Floor or roof joists or beams.
Nail anchors to underside or side of joists.
Wall anchors at required intervals (see text). Anchors should have split end embedded in mortar joint or end bent down into block core and core filled with mortar. Length of anchor should be sufficient to engage at least three joists.

Fig. 77. Anchoring parallel joists to masonry wall

Table 66. Control-joint spacing for moisture-controlled type I concrete masonry units*

Recommended spacing of control joints	Vertical spacing of joint reinforcement			
	None	24"	16"	8"
Expressed as ratio of panel length to height, L/H	2	2½	3	4
With panel length (L) not to exceed: [regardless of height (H)]	40'	45'	50'	60'

* *When bond beams spaced 4' vertically are employed in lieu of joint reinforcement, control joints may be spaced 60' maximum.*

BUILDING PAPER
CONCRETE FILL
RAKE JOINT AND CAULK
SPECIAL CONTROL JOINT UNITS
PREFORMED GASKET
SASH UNITS
RAKE AND CAULK
RAKE AND CAULK

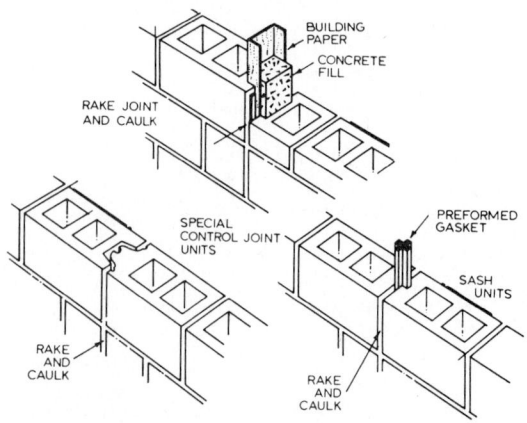

Fig. 78. Typical control joint details

REINFORCED CONCRETE MASONRY

Reinforced concrete masonry walls can be designed in accordance with *American National Standard Building Code Requirements for Reinforced Masonry* (ANSI A41.2-1960, R1970) or in accordance with the principles of engineered masonry as described in *Specifications for the Design and Construction of Load-Bearing Concrete Masonry,* published in 1970 by the National Concrete Masonry Association. Allowable stresses under the ANSI code are given in Table 10 of this section.

Typical construction details for reinforced concrete masonry are illustrated in Fig. 79. Grouting may be "low-lift" or "high-lift" as described earlier in this section. If high-lift grouting is used, it should be poured in 4-ft lifts, with an interval of ½ hour or more before the next pour. High-lift grouting also requires the provision of cleanout openings at the base of the wall.

Equivalent solid wall thicknesses for reinforced hollow block walls are given in Table 67. From these figures axial compressive loads can be readily calculated (Fig. 80*a*). In the case of concentrated loads, the wall length considered effective is (1) the distance between loads or (2) the width of the bearing plus four times the wall thickness.

Shear calculations in reinforced concrete masonry walls follow reinforced concrete design procedures also except that the factor (j) is still employed, and web reinforcement is provided to carry the entire shear when the computed shear stress exceeds that allowed on the plain masonry.

$$v = \frac{V}{bjd}$$

where v = shear stress
V = total shear
b = width of compression face of flexural member
d = distance from extreme compression fiber to centroid of tension reinforcement
j = ratio of distance between centroid of tension and centroid of compression to the depth, d

In flexural compression, the effective design section of a retained hollow-unit concrete masonry wall is similar to a T-beam, Fig. 80*b*. Width of the compression flange, b, is assumed equal to six times the nominal wall thickness, t, when the wall is laid in running bond, and three times wall thickness when laid stack bond. The width of the T-beam stem, b', is equal to the width of the filled core plus the adjacent cross webs

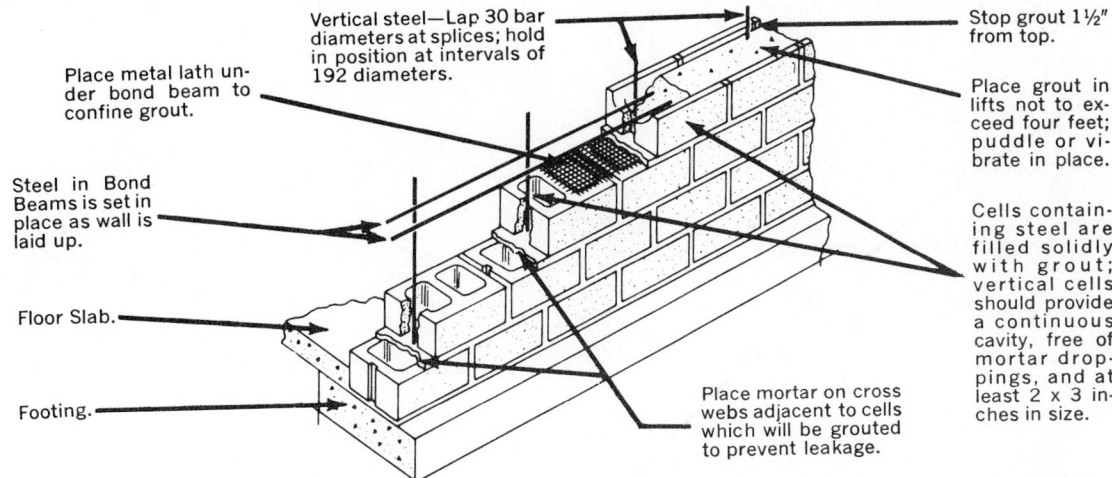

Vertical steel—Lap 30 bar diameters at splices; hold in position at intervals of 192 diameters.

Place metal lath under bond beam to confine grout.

Steel in Bond Beams is set in place as wall is laid up.

Floor Slab.

Footing.

Stop grout 1½" from top.

Place grout in lifts not to exceed four feet; puddle or vibrate in place.

Cells containing steel are filled solidly with grout; vertical cells should provide a continuous cavity, free of mortar droppings, and at least 2 x 3 inches in size.

Place mortar on cross webs adjacent to cells which will be grouted to prevent leakage.

Fig. 79. Typical reinforced concrete masonry construction

(a)

a. Area assumed effective in axial compression

Table 67. Equivalent solid wall thicknesses

Wall construction	Wall thickness		
	6"	8"	12"
	Equiv. net solid thickness		
Solid grouted wall	5.6	7.6	11.6
Vertical cores grouted at			
16" o.c.	4.5	5.8	8.5
24" o.c.	4.1	5.2	7.5
32" o.c.	3.9	4.9	7.0
40" o.c.	3.8	4.7	6.7
48" o.c.	3.7	4.6	6.5
No grout in wall	3.4	4.0	5.5

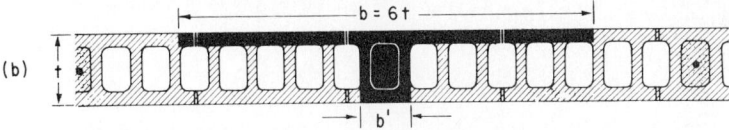

(b)

$b = 6t$

t

b'

b. T-beam section assumed in flexural compression

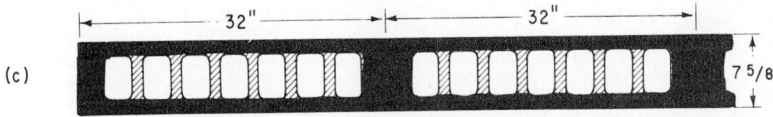

(c)

32"   32"   7 5/8"

c. Area assumed effective in longitudinal shear

Fig. 80.   Structurally effective areas of reinforced concrete masonry wall. Walls 8 in. thick; vertical cores grouted 32 in. on center; equivalent solid thickness (Table 67) = 4.9 in.

(normally 6 in. for a three-core block). Location of T-beam neutral axis and computations then follow procedures standard for reinforced concrete.

Walls subject to both axial and flexural compressive stresses are proportioned so that the summation of the ratios of calculated to allowable stresses does not exceed unity.

Combined stresses:

$$\frac{f_m}{F_m} + \frac{f_a}{F_a} \text{ not to exceed } 1.0$$

where f_a = computed axial unit stress
f_m = computed flexural unit stress
F_a = allowable axial stress
F_m = allowable flexural stress

Of special interest in the design of multistory loadbearing structures, Fig. 80c shows the wall section assumed effective in longitudinal shear walls.

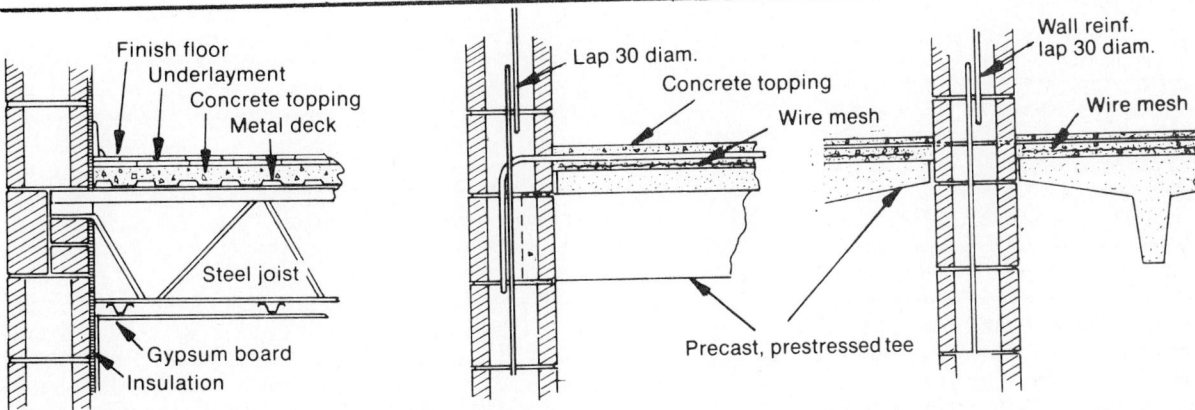

Finish floor
Underlayment
Concrete topping
Metal deck

Steel joist

Gypsum board
Insulation

Lap 30 diam.

Concrete topping

Wire mesh

Precast, prestressed tee

Wall reinf. lap 30 diam.

Wire mesh

Fig. 81.   Construction details, reinforced concrete masonry

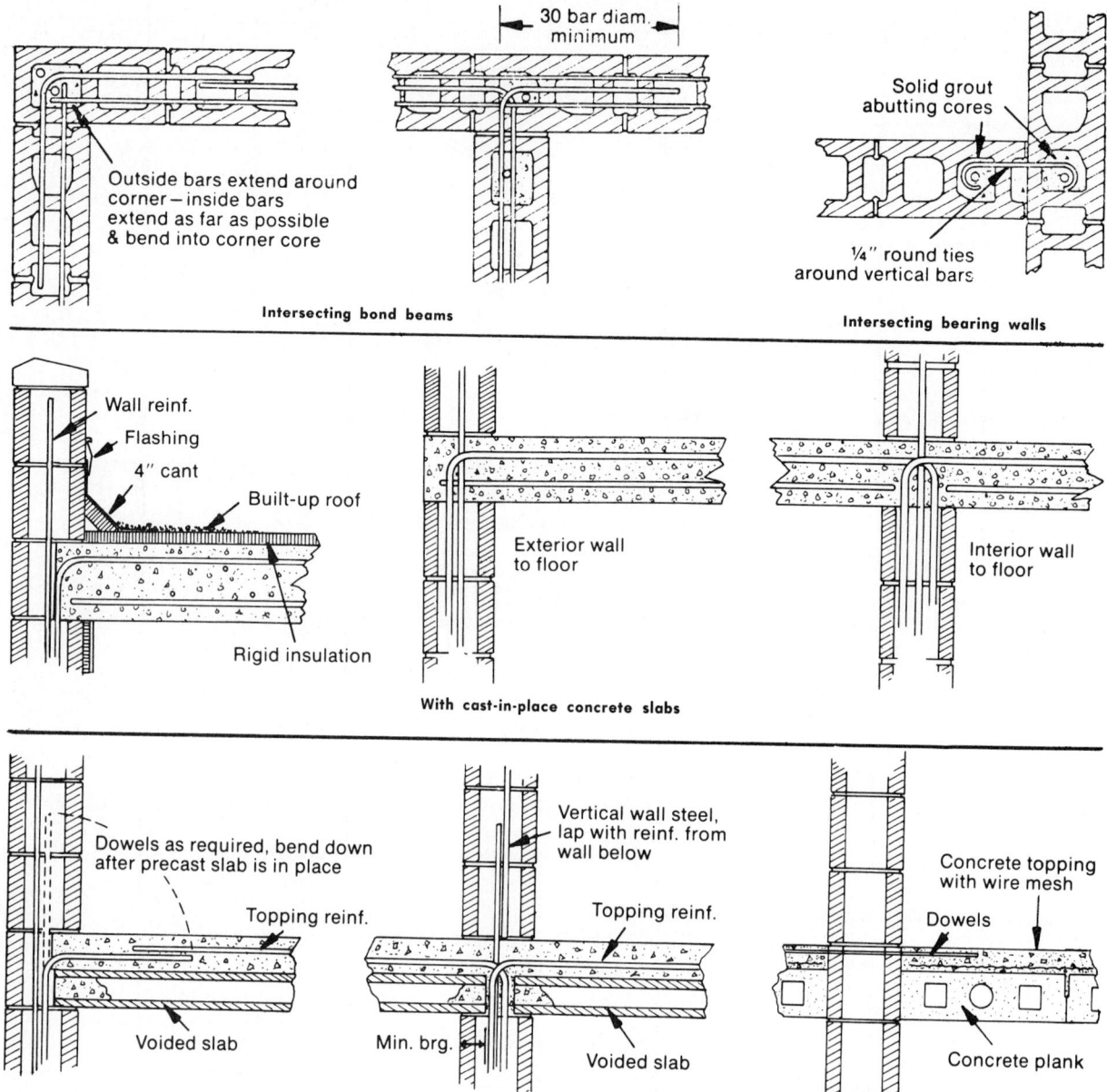

Intersecting bond beams

Outside bars extend around corner – inside bars extend as far as possible & bend into corner core

30 bar diam. minimum

Solid grout abutting cores

¼" round ties around vertical bars

Intersecting bearing walls

Wall reinf.

Flashing

4" cant

Built-up roof

Rigid insulation

Exterior wall to floor

Interior wall to floor

With cast-in-place concrete slabs

Dowels as required, bend down after precast slab is in place

Topping reinf.

Voided slab

Vertical wall steel, lap with reinf. from wall below

Topping reinf.

Min. brg.

Voided slab

Concrete topping with wire mesh

Dowels

Concrete plank

With precast hollow-core floor slabs

Fig. 81 (cont.). Construction details, reinforced concrete masonry

RETAINING WALLS

Design

The main forces acting on a retaining wall are the pressures exerted by the earth it retains. These pressures are both horizontal and vertical in direction. Vertical pressure is the weight of the soil.

Designs herein are based upon an assumed soil weight of 100 pcf. Horizontal pressure is based upon an equivalent fluid weight for the soil. Equivalent fluid weight used in these designs is 45 pcf. This equivalent fluid weight is considered satisfactory for most purposes.

The horizontal pressure exerted by the retained earth can cause (1) the retaining wall to break at the junction of the wall and its footing, (2) overturning of the wall and footing intact, or (3) horizontal sliding of the wall and footing.

Walls shown herein were designed with a safety factor against overturning of not less than 2 and a safety factor against horizontal sliding of not less than 1.5. In computing the allowable wall heights, h, shown in Table 73, it was assumed that the backfill has a level, horizontal surface.

Construction

Dowels must be provided to connect the wall to the footing. Locate them at verti- cal wall rods and as near to the back (ten- sion face) of the wall as possible in order to assure maximum reinforcement effi- ciency.

Allow masonry walls to set at least 24 hr after completion before grouting. Pour grout in layers of 4 ft, allowing 1 hr between suc- cessive layers. Compact grout thoroughly by puddling or vibration.

Provision should be made to prevent ac- cumulation of water behind a retaining wall. Four-inch-diameter weep holes located at 5- to 10-ft spacing along the base of the wall should be sufficient. Place about 1 cu ft of gravel or crushed stone around the intake of each weep hole. A continuous longitudinal drain along the back of the wall may be used in lieu of weep holes.

Waterproofing the back face of the retaining walls is recommended (1) in areas subject to severe frost action, (2) in areas of heavy rainfall, (3) when backfill material is relatively impermeable, and (4) when wall is constructed of porous masonry units. Of course, the tops of masonry retaining walls should be capped or otherwise protected to prevent the entry of water into unfilled hol- low cells and spaces.

Long retaining walls should be broken in- to panels 20 to 30 ft in length by means of vertical control joints.

Backfilling should not be permitted until at least seven days after grouting. Where heavy equipment is used in backfilling walls designed to resist earth pressure only, such equipment should not approach closer to the top of the wall than a distance equal to the height of the wall.

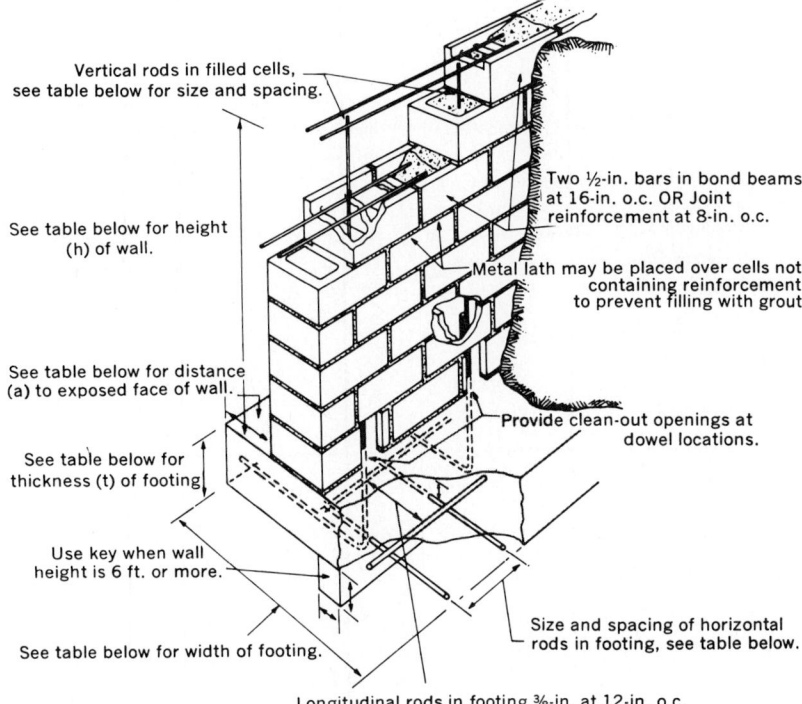

Vertical rods in filled cells, see table below for size and spacing.

See table below for height (h) of wall.

See table below for distance (a) to exposed face of wall.

See table below for thickness (t) of footing

Use key when wall height is 6 ft. or more.

See table below for width of footing.

Two ½-in. bars in bond beams at 16-in. o.c. OR Joint reinforcement at 8-in. o.c.

Metal lath may be placed over cells not containing reinforcement to prevent filling with grout

Provide clean-out openings at dowel locations.

Size and spacing of horizontal rods in footing, see table below.

Longitudinal rods in footing ⅜-in. at 12-in. o.c.

Fig. 82. Reinforced concrete masonry retaining wall

Table 68. Reinforced concrete masonry retaining walls

Height of wall, h	Width of footing	Thickness of footing, t	Distance, a, to face of wall	Size and spacing of vertical rods in wall	Size and spacing of horizontal rods in footing
			8″ walls		
3′-4″	2′-4″	9″	8″	⅜″ @ 32″	⅜″ @ 27″
4′-0″	2′-9″	9″	10″	½″ @ 32″	⅜″ @ 27″
4′-8″	3′-3″	10″	12″	⅝″ @ 32″	⅜″ @ 27″
5′-4″	3′-8″	10″	14″	½″ @ 16″	½″ @ 30″
6′-0″	4′-2″	12″	15″	¾″ @ 24″	½″ @ 25″
			12″ walls		
6′-8″	4′-6″	12″	16″	¾″ @ 24″	½″ @ 22″
7′-4″	4′-10″	12″	18″	⅞″ @ 32″	⅝″ @ 26″
8′-0″	5′-4″	12″	20″	⅞″ @ 24″	⅝″ @ 21″
8′-8″	5′-10″	14″	22″	⅞″ @ 16″	¾″ @ 26″
9′-4″	6′-4″	14″	24″	1″ @ 8″	¾″ @ 21″

COATINGS

Fill coats

Fill coats or primer-sealers are used to fill the voids in porous concrete masonry and on open or coarse-textured masonry before the application of finish coats. Fill coats contain regular portland cement as a binder and some form of finely graded siliceous sand filler. Acrylic latex or polyvinyl acetate latex is sometimes combined with the portland cement binder. Fill coats are applied by brushing the material into the voids of the surface, which requires good workmanship for successful results. Those fill coats which do not contain latex require application to a moist surface and moist curing for hydration of the portland cement constituent. The fill- ers containing latex do not require moist curing because the latex retards evapora- tion of moisture, thereby making it available for hydration of the cement binder.

Portland cement paints: These paints are sold in powdered form in a variety of colors and are mixed with water just before use. They are produced in standard and heavy- duty types. The standard type contains a minimum of 65 per cent portland cement by weight and is suitable for general use. The heavy-duty type contains 80 per cent port- land cement and is used where there is ex- cessive and continuous contact with mois- ture, such as in swimming pools. Each type is available with a siliceous sand additive for use as a filler on porous surfaces. Portland cement paints set by hydration of the ce- ment which bonds to the masonry surface. They are applied to moist surfaces by stiff brush and dampened by fine water spray for 48 to 72 hours until the cement cures. Port- land cement paints contain little organic material and are not subject to attack from alkali found in new concrete. They have a long history of success in waterproofing ma- sonry when properly applied and cured.

Latex paints: Latex paints, inherently re- sistant to alkali, are made of water emul- sions of resinous materials. They dry throughout as soon as the water of emulsion has evaporated, usually within 1½ hours. Styrene-butadiene is one of the original syn- thetic chemical coatings and is still in use. Other latex coatings such as polyvinyl ace- tate and acrylic resin are presently in greater demand and are also available as clear coatings for colorless applications. All latex paints are available as opaque coat- ings. Latex paints may be applied to damp or dry surfaces and require no curing. Al- though acrylic latex is somewhat higher in cost than the other latex waterproofing materials, it has demonstrated superior re- sistance to penetration by rain and shown greater overall durability.

Oil-base paints: Oil-base paints are man- ufactured from natural oil resins or synthetic alkyd resins. Similar to conventional house paints, the oil-base paints designed for use on masonry are usually reinforced by certain resins to improve their resistance to alkali. They may be applied by brush, roller, or spray. A dry masonry surface is required at the time of application and the effective alkalinity of the surface must be reduced through aging the masonry or application of surface pretreatments. Oil-base paints which are subjected to dampness from within the masonry may fail from blistering and peeling.

Chlorinated rubber-base paints: These paints are composed of chlorinated natural rubber which is blended with pigments and resins. Often termed rubber-base paints, they may be applied to dry or slightly damp surfaces. The heavy consistency of these paints contributes toward filling the voids of porous surfaces and is conducive to application by roller. They possess good resistance to alkali. They are highly impermeable to vapor, but show a tendency to lose adhesion, especially near a break in the film.

Epoxy coatings: These coatings are based on epoxy or urethane resins to which a catalyst is added just before application. The epoxies are highly resistant to alkali and form an impervious film. Outdoor exposure of epoxy paints results in chalking, which must be removed by washing with soap and water to restore the original appearance. The high cost of the material and difficulty experienced in application have limited the use of epoxies to specialized requirements. They are not recommended for general use on concrete masonry.

Silicone-based coatings: Silicone is a colorless resinous material produced by a synthetic process from silicon dioxide. When applied to masonry surfaces, silicone-based coatings do not cause a change in color or texture. Without actually sealing openings, silicones retard water absorption by changing the contact angle between water and the walls of capillary pores in the masonry. Silicones do not bridge large openings;

therefore, fill coats are desirable on coarse-textured masonry. Application of silicone-based coatings is commonly accomplished by flooding the surface with a low-pressure spray head.

Bituminous coatings: These coatings are produced from coal tar or asphalt and are furnished in solid form to be melted for hot application. They are also available in liquid form, either diluted in solvent or emulsified with water, for application at normal temperature. Hot application of bituminous coatings may be made alone or in combination with felt or other reinforcing fabric to form a built-up membrane. Where considerable hydrostatic pressure is exerted upon the coating, the built-up membrane has the distinct advantage of maintaining continuity of waterproofing over possible imperfections in the wall. The low cost and excellent resistance to penetration of water favor the use of bituminous coatings where appearance is not important, such as below-grade portions of basement walls.

Table 69. Concrete masonry coatings

| Type of coating | Suitability for concrete masonry walls | | | | Comparative factors of coatings | | | | | | | | | |
| | Above grade | | Below grade | | | | | | | | | | | |
	Interior surface	Exterior surface	Interior surface	Exterior surface	Permeable film (breathing)	Alkali-resistant	Surface condition required	Usual application	Moist curing required	Type thinner used	Type finish	Coats generally required	Resultant coating	Expected service life (years)
Fill coats	✕	✕	✕		Yes	Yes	Moist	Brush	Yes	Water	Flat	1	Opaque	5–8
Portland cement paints	✕	✕	✕		Yes	Yes	Moist	Brush	Yes	Water	Flat	2	Opaque	5–8
Latex paints	✕	✕	✕		Yes	Yes	Dry or moist	Brush Roller Spray	No	Water	Flat	2–3	Opaque or clear	4
Oil base paints	✕				No	No	Dry	Brush Roller Spray	No	Solvent	Flat Gloss	2	Opaque	4
Chlorinated rubber-base paints	✕				No	Yes	Dry or moist	Roller Brush	No	Solvent	Semi-gloss	2	Opaque	5
Silicone-based coatings		✕			Yes	Yes	Dry	Spray Flood	No	Water Solven	Flat	2	Clear	5–8
Bituminous coatings				✕	No	Yes	Dry or moist Emulsion	Spray Brush	No	Water Solvent Emulsion	Flat	2	Opaque	Indefinite

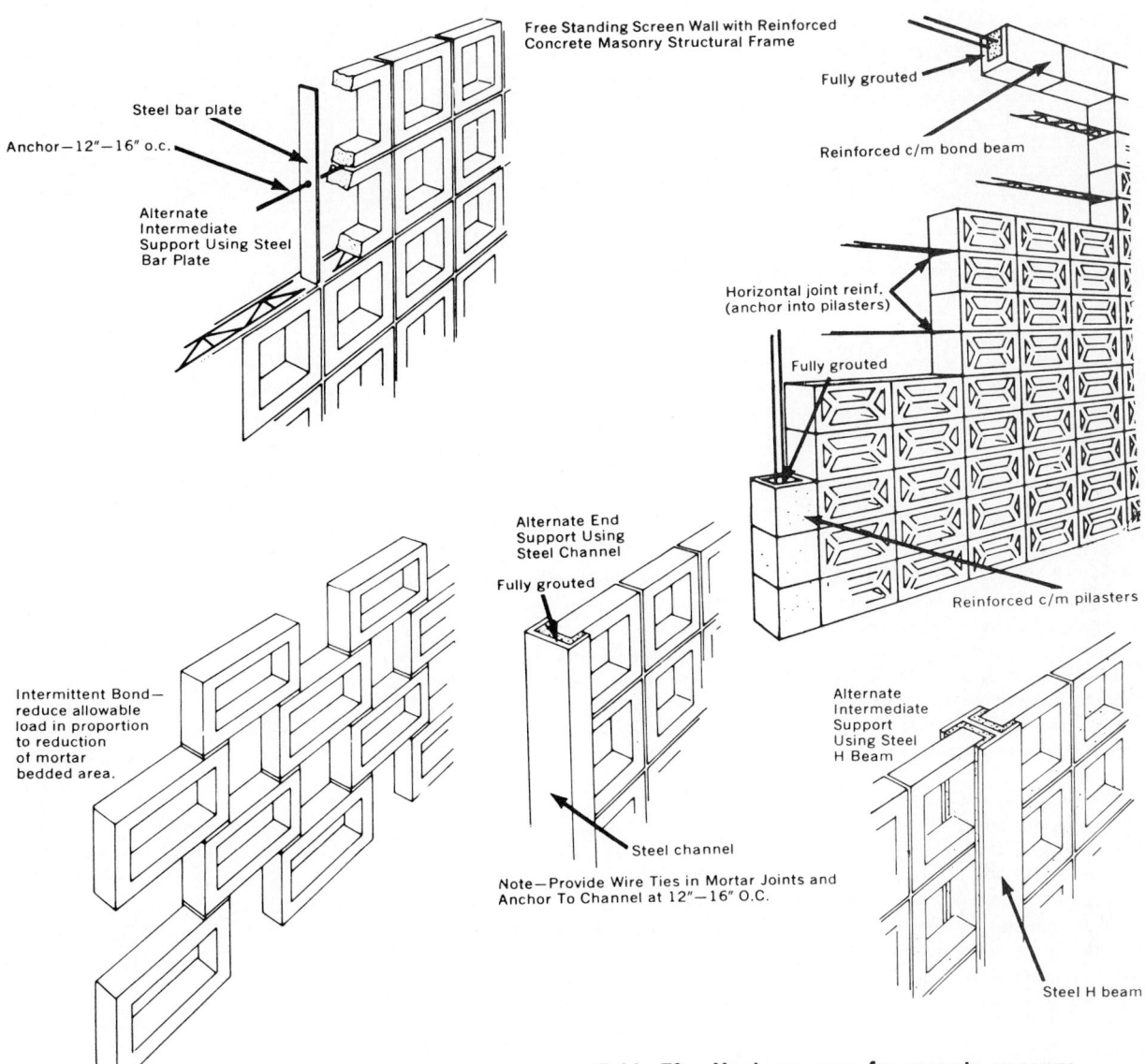

Free Standing Screen Wall with Reinforced Concrete Masonry Structural Frame

Steel bar plate

Anchor—12"–16" o.c.

Alternate Intermediate Support Using Steel Bar Plate

Fully grouted

Reinforced c/m bond beam

Horizontal joint reinf. (anchor into pilasters)

Fully grouted

Reinforced c/m pilasters

Intermittent Bond— reduce allowable load in proportion to reduction of mortar bedded area.

Alternate End Support Using Steel Channel

Fully grouted

Steel channel

Note—Provide Wire Ties in Mortar Joints and Anchor To Channel at 12"–16" O.C.

Alternate Intermediate Support Using Steel H Beam

Steel H beam

Steel T beam

Alternate Intermediate Support Using Steel T Beam

Anchor 12"–16" o.c.

Fig. 83. Construction details, screen walls

Table 70. Maximum span for concrete masonry screen walls

Construction	Maximum distance between lateral supports		
	Nominal thickness of wall, in.*		
	4	6	8
Nonloadbearing			
Reinforced†			
Exterior	10'-0"	15'-0"	20'-0"
Interior	16'-0"	24'-0"	32'-0"
Nonreinforced			
Exterior	6'-8"	10'-0"	13'-4"
Interior	12'-0"	18'-0"	24'-0"
Loadbearing			
Reinforced†	Not recom-	12'-6"	16'-8"
Nonreinforced	mended	9'-0"	12'-0"

Minimum thickness for nonloadbearing walls, 4 in.; for loadbearing walls, 6 in.

†*Total steel area, including joint reinforcement, not less than 0.002 times the gross cross-sectional area of the wall, not more than ⅔ of which may be either horizontal or vertical.*

Cold weather construction

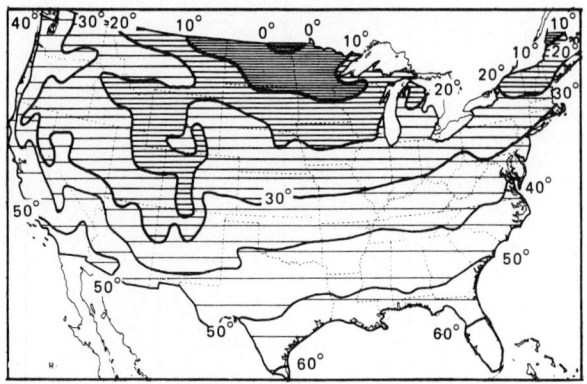

Fig. 84. Average daily mean temperatures in January

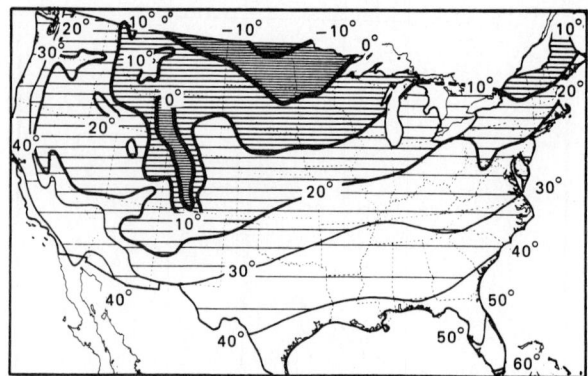

Fig. 85. Average daily minimum temperatures in January

Cold weather construction, long familiar in northern Europe and Russia, is now being increasingly practiced in this country. The advantages of earlier occupancy and the reduction of construction time, with its heavy carrying charges, more than compensate for the additional cost which, according to a recent Canadian study, averages between ¾ and 1½ per cent of the total construction cost.

The maps (Figs. 84 and 85) show the part of the United States where cold weather construction is a problem. In general, it is that area lying north of the 30-degree line in Fig. 84 or the 20-degree line in Fig. 85. It should be noted that the recommendations given below call for supplementary heat only when the daily mean temperature is 20 degrees or lower, a condition which is normal in only a small portion of this country.

A clear distinction should be made between cold weather concreting and masonry construction. Generally concrete is placed in forms which absorb little water from the concrete and prevent evaporation into the atmosphere. On the other hand, in masonry construction thin layers of mortar are placed between thicker absorbent units which absorb water from the mortar and stiffen it. The degree of saturation of the mortar is therefore lowered and the water-cement ratio is reduced. Hence little water is actually left to freeze in the mortar and cause damage by expansion. Unfortunately, most building codes do not recognize this distinction and require more protection than is necessary.

After extensive research, the International Masonry Industry All-Weather Council issued in 1970 *Guide Specifications for Cold Weather Masonry Construction,* the principal provisions of which are summarized here: All materials must be delivered dry and kept fully covered at all times. Brick should be more absorbent than those used in nor-

SPECIAL CANTED PURLIN

TARPAULIN OR POLYETHYLENE

Fig. 86. Scaffold-type enclosure

Table 71. Wind chill effect

When thermometer reads (°F)	When the wind blows at the mph below, it reduces effective temperature to					
	5	10	15	20	25	30
+40	37	28	22	18	16	13
+30	27	16	9	4	0	−2
+20	16	4	−5	−10	−15	−18
+10	6	−9	−18	−25	−29	−33
0	−5	−21	−36	−39	−44	−48
−10	−15	−33	−45	−53	−59	−63
−20	−26	−46	−58	−67	−74	−79
−30	−36	−58	−72	−82	−88	−94
−40	−47	−70	−88	−96	−104	−109

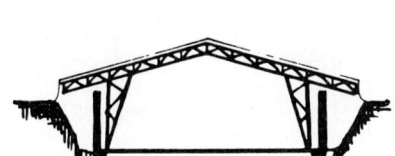 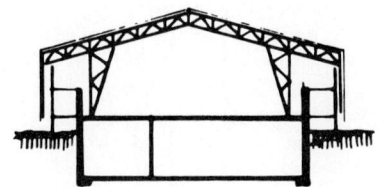 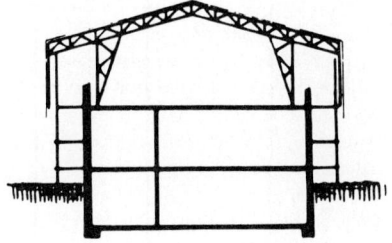

Fig. 87. Roof-type enclosure for multistory buildings

mal construction, suctions of 20 to as much as 40 gm per min per 30 sq in. being permissible. Absorbent brick should be sprinkled before laying with heated water, above 70°F if the units are above 32°, and above 130° when the units are below 32°F.

Type S or Type M mortar is recommended, or the use of mortar made with Type III portland cement (ASTM C150—high early strength). Sand, if frozen, must be heated before mixing. Ideal mortar temperature is 70 ± 10°F; the mixing temperature selected should be maintained within

10°. Admixtures in general, and antifreezes in particular, are not recommended. Accelerators, such as calcium chloride, may be used up to a maximum of 2 per cent of the portland cement by weight provided that the masonry does not contain metal, which is severely corroded by the salt. Coloring pigments should be limited to 10 per cent (carbon black to 2 per cent) of the cement content by weight; they may retard the setting of the mortar, which is an undesirable effect in cold weather construction. Masonry units below 20°F in temperature

should be heated to at least 20° and preferably 30°.

Masonry must not be laid on a frozen or snow- or ice-covered bed. Such a bed must be heated until it is dry to the touch. Masonry damaged by freezing must be removed before continuing construction.

Enclosures may be of many types. Small buildings are often completely enclosed in a tent or inflated structure. A simple type of scaffold enclosure is shown in Fig. 86. A roof enclosure suitable for multistory buildings is shown in Fig. 87.

Table 72. Summary of recommendations for cold weather construction

Temperature,* °F	Construction	Protection
40–32	Heat sand or mixing water to produce mortar temperatures between 40 and 120°F.	Protect top of masonry from rain or snow by waterproof membrane extending down sides a minimum of 2 ft for 24 hr.
32–25	Heat sand and water to produce mortar temperatures between 40 and 120°F. Maintain temperatures of mortar on boards above freezing.	Cover masonry completely with waterproof membrane for 24 hr.
25–20	Heat sand and water to produce mortar temperatures between 40 and 120°F. Maintain mortar temperatures on boards above freezing. Provide supplementary heat on both sides of walls. Provide windbreaks when wind is over 15 mph (Table 76).	Cover masonry completely with insulating blankets for 24 hr.
20 and below	Heat sand and water to provide mortar temperatures between 40 and 120°F. Provide enclosure and supplementary heat to maintain air temperature above 32°F. Temperature of units when laid shall be not less than 20°F.	Maintain masonry temperature above 32°F for 24 hr by enclosure and supplementary heat supplied by electric blankets, infrared lamps, or other methods.

Air temperature at time of construction, and mean daily air temperature during period of protection.

The elements which make up a building are in a constant state of motion relative to each other. The movement itself is not visible but its results frequently are. Movement may be caused by many things, such as curing, changes in moisture content, structural loading, plastic flow, or foundation settlement; but by far the most prevalent cause of movement is thermal expansion.

Two types of temperature variation induce movement in a structure (Fig. 88). The first of these is the slow, seasonal change from winter to summer; the second, relatively rapid fluctuations which take effect within a few hours. Design of almost any large building involves consideration of both. In small buildings, the rapid fluctuations are more likely to cause damage.

Fortunately, concrete and medium steel have similar coefficients of expansion (Table 73). Where buffers must be provided between stressed materials, expansion joints, properly protected against wear and weather, usually suffice.

EXPANSION JOINTS

Where a large building—or one of its parts—is restrained from moving by the pressure of an adjoining building, or other mass, provision must be made to take up the thrust. Expansion joints (Fig. 89), therefore, normally occur between new and old buildings and also between a wing of a building over 150 ft long and the main body of the structure.

Movement also takes place between parts of the same structure exposed to different temperatures. Ordinarily, roofs become much hotter, and expand more than walls, especially shaded walls. To prevent damage, roofs are frequently ringed with expansion joints. In addition, the roof structure, particularly if it is rigid, may be large enough to require a transecting expansion joint—one which passes through the roof, walls, and sometimes lower floors. Such transecting expansion joints vary in size and design with the size and construction of the building and the location of the joint.

In monolithic reinforced concrete buildings, expansion joints should completely divide the structure, cutting roof, walls, and floors. Joints are sometimes provided 100 ft on centers. The usual practice is to space them every 200 ft. With the use of longitudinal reinforcing, buildings up to 300 ft in length have been successfully constructed without expansion joints.

Steel-framed buildings: Practice varies in the steel-framed building with curtain walls. Although expansion joints that completely divide the buildings are also used in this type, 200 to 250 ft on centers, many successful slab-roofed buildings have been constructed with expansion joints in roofs and top-floor walls only, stopping at the top floor line. The expanding roof slab moves faster and farther than do the walls. Flexibility of the top-floor steel columns is relied upon to yield to the thrust set up by the roof slab, completely absorbing it and preventing its transmission to lower stories. Movement of masonry in lower floors is taken up in individual joints, and is further restrained by the steel framing.

Solid masonry buildings: Freestanding solid masonry buildings usually require joints about 100 ft on centers. With an average winter-summer temperature differential of about 100°F, a masonry wall will expand about 0.4 in. in every 100 ft of length. Expansion joints at 100-ft intervals must be approximately ½ in. wide, and are easily concealed in the average mortar joint.

PROVISIONS AT GRADE

Provision must be made for the building equipped with transecting expansion joints to slip on its foundation. In solid masonry buildings, the mortar joint between the concrete foundation and the masonry wall provides a satisfactory slipping surface. Monolithic buildings, however, require slip joints between the walls and foundation to permit movement of the superstructure. Since the foundation is buried in the ground, and thus has little temperature differential to influence it, it is not affected by temperature fluctuations of the air.

SPECIAL BUILDING TYPES

Structures in which unusually low summer temperatures are maintained, as in breweries and cold-storage warehouses, must allow for much greater expansion than other building types.

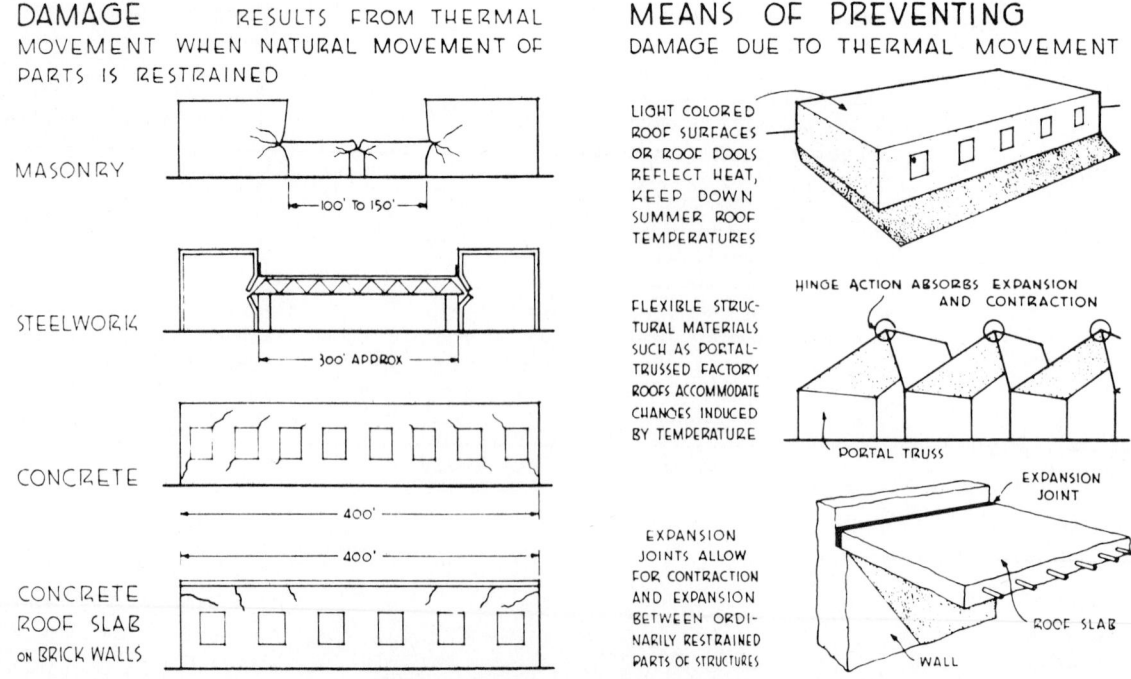

DAMAGE RESULTS FROM THERMAL MOVEMENT WHEN NATURAL MOVEMENT OF PARTS IS RESTRAINED

MASONRY — 100' TO 150'

STEELWORK — 300' APPROX

CONCRETE — 400'

CONCRETE ROOF SLAB ON BRICK WALLS — 400'

MEANS OF PREVENTING DAMAGE DUE TO THERMAL MOVEMENT

LIGHT COLORED ROOF SURFACES OR ROOF POOLS REFLECT HEAT, KEEP DOWN SUMMER ROOF TEMPERATURES

FLEXIBLE STRUCTURAL MATERIALS SUCH AS PORTAL-TRUSSED FACTORY ROOFS ACCOMMODATE CHANGES INDUCED BY TEMPERATURE

HINGE ACTION ABSORBS EXPANSION AND CONTRACTION

PORTAL TRUSS

EXPANSION JOINTS ALLOW FOR CONTRACTION AND EXPANSION BETWEEN ORDINARILY RESTRAINED PARTS OF STRUCTURES

EXPANSION JOINT

ROOF SLAB

WALL

Fig. 88. Damage due to thermal movement

Table 73. Coefficients of linear expansion (in./in./°F)

METALS, ALLOYS	
aluminum	0.0000128
brass	0.0000104
bronze	0.0000101
copper	0.0000093
cast iron	0.0000059
steel, hard	0.0000073
steel, structural	0.0000067
steel, stainless	0.0000096
MASONRY	
ashlar masonry	0.0000035
brick masonry	0.0000031
cement, Portland	0.0000059
concrete	0.0000079
concrete masonry	0.0000067
granite	0.0000047
limestone	0.0000044
marble	0.0000056
plaster	0.0000092
rubble masonry	0.0000035
sandstone	0.0000061
slate	0.0000058
TIMBER, parellel to fiber	
fir	0.0000021
maple	0.0000036
oak	0.0000027
pine	0.0000030
TIMBER, transverse	
fir	0.000032
maple	0.000027
oak	0.000030
pine	0.000019

EXPANSION JOINTS ARE NEEDED:

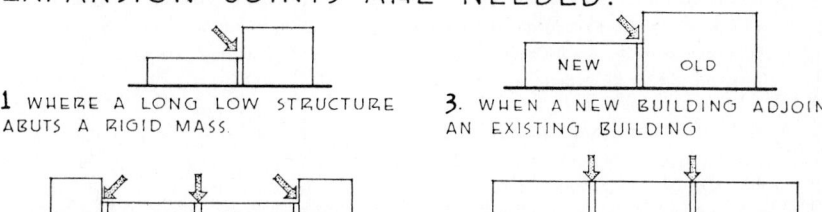

1. WHERE A LONG LOW STRUCTURE ABUTS A RIGID MASS.

2. AT ENDS OF A LOW STRUCTURE BETWEEN TWO HEAVY MASSES AND AT APPROPRIATE INTERVALS — USUALLY EVERY 150 FEET.

3. WHEN A NEW BUILDING ADJOINS AN EXISTING BUILDING

4. IN FREE STANDING BUILDINGS, THROUGH EXPANSION JOINTS ARE REQUIRED AT INTERVALS OF APPROXIMATELY 200 FT.

5. WHEN INTERIOR AND EXTERIOR TEMPERATURE DIFFERENTIALS ARE EXCESSIVE, AS IN A COLD STORAGE BUILDING

FUNCTIONS:

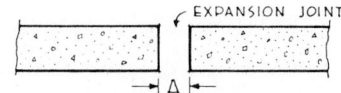

MUST PROVIDE FOR MAXIMUM THERMAL-INDUCED MOVEMENT LIKELY TO BE ENCOUNTERED. [WIDTH OF JOINT "A" = SPAN (INCHES) X 100 (AVERAGE WINTER-SUMMER TEMP. DIFF.) X n (COEFFICIENT OF EXPANSION OF THE MATERIAL)]

MUST BE CONCEALED IF IT IMPAIRS APPEARANCE

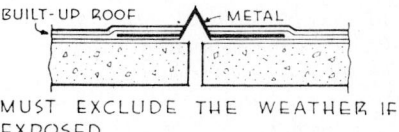

MUST EXCLUDE THE WEATHER IF EXPOSED

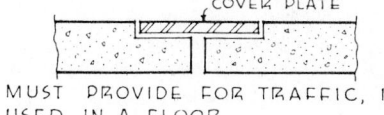

MUST PROVIDE FOR TRAFFIC, IF USED IN A FLOOR.

TYPICAL EXPANSION JOINTS:

NOTE: DRAWINGS NOT TO SCALE

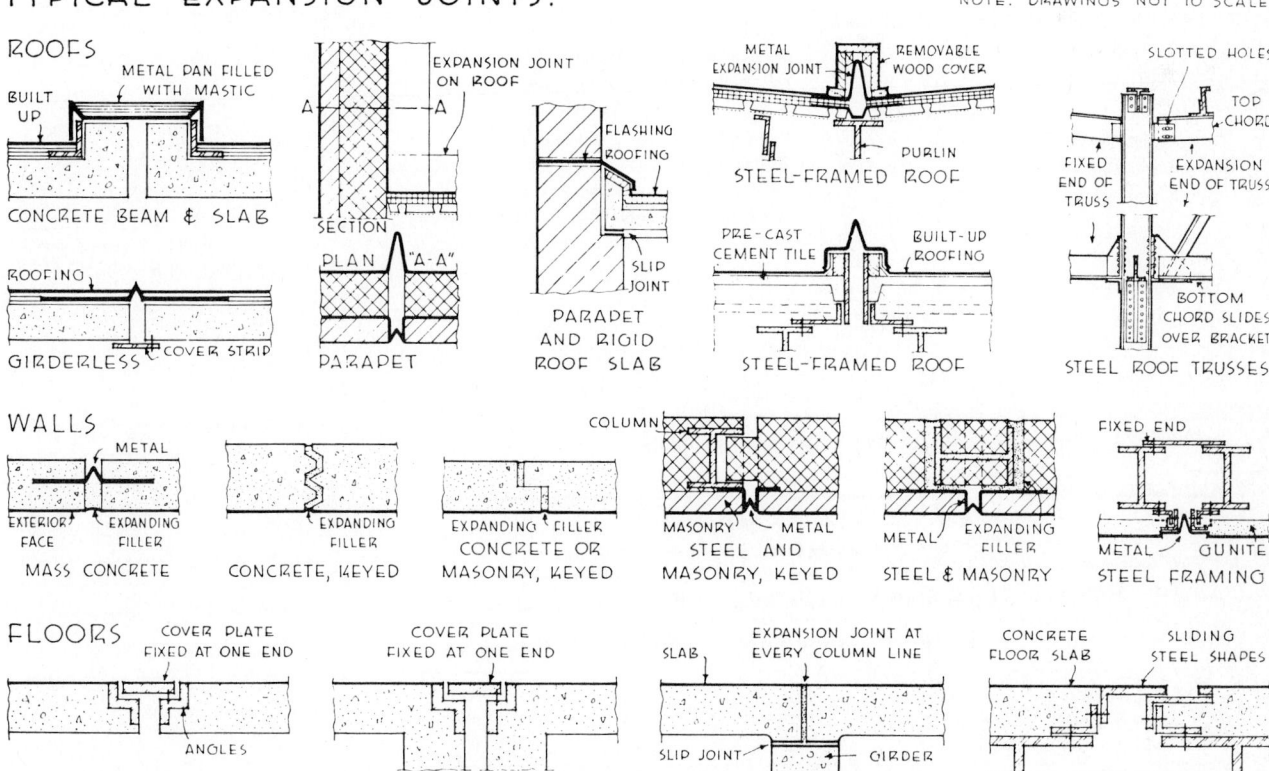

Fig. 89. Typical expansion joints and their functions

Thermal expansion

Data and illustrations on this and the following two pages have been derived from *Technical Notes on Brick Construction,* published by the Brick Institute of America.

Recent investigations have shown that thermal expansion and contraction contribute to the cracking of masonry walls and that former recommendations for the location and spacing of expansion joints should be revised.

There are several reasons why greater provision must be made for thermal movement now than was required several decades ago:

1. *Thin walls:* Codes now permit the use of thinner masonry walls, especially for nonloadbearing curtain walls. Temperature variations are greater in thin walls because of reduced heat storage capacity.

2. *Insulation:* Increased use of insulation on the inside of masonry walls results in greater temperature variations in the masonry.

3. *Composite walls:* Increased use of walls faced with brick and backed up with hollow units (tile or concrete) that have different coefficients of expansion results in differential thermal movement.

4. *Sills and lintels:* Sills and lintels also produce differential movement, which, in the case of metal window and door frames and lintels, can be relatively large.

5. *Parapets and foundations:* There is often a substantial temperature difference between parapets and building walls and between building walls and foundation, particularly in heated buildings, which results in differential movements of these elements.

Masonry failures resulting from thermal movement may be classified under two headings: cumulative expansion and differential expansion.

1. *Cumulative expansion:* In the absence of restraint, a brick wall 100 ft long may be expected to expand ⅜ in. owing to a temperature increase of 100°F. When the wall contracts, however, its tensile strength is not sufficient to overcome frictional resistance, and thus one or more cracks will appear. The same cumulative expansion causes failure of walls at offsets where the masonry at right angles to the long wall is placed in bending and shear by the thermal expansion of the long wall.

2. *Differential expansion:* The effect of differential movements of different materials in a composite masonry wall may be sufficient to cause cracking of one of the wall elements, generally the one having the lowest coefficient of expansion. Differential movement between masonry and metal that may be built into it is much greater than the movement between masonry materials, and numerous examples may be found of masonry cracking caused by expansion of metal members.

COEFFICIENTS OF EXPANSION

Table 73 gives average coefficients of expansion of masonry materials and of steel and aluminum, the metals most commonly used in conjunction with masonry.

RECOMMENDATIONS

Offsets and junctions: In general, expansion joints should be located at offsets, provided the wall expanding into the offset is 50 ft or more in length, and at junctions of walls in L-, T-, or U-shaped buildings. Figure 90 shows such locations and Fig. 91 shows details of typical expansion joints.

Long walls: Recommended spacing of expansion joints in long walls is given in Table 74. Such joints should be approximately ¾ in. thick and, where two or more expansion joints are required, it is suggested that the distance from the corner to the nearest expansion joint not exceed one-half the distances given in Table 74. Figure 92 shows details of typical expansion joints in long walls.

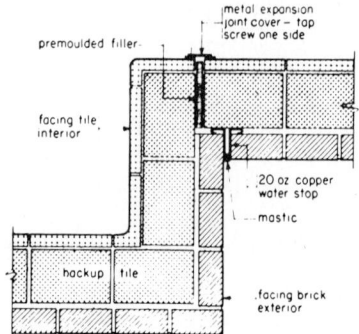

Fig. 90.   Location of expansion joints

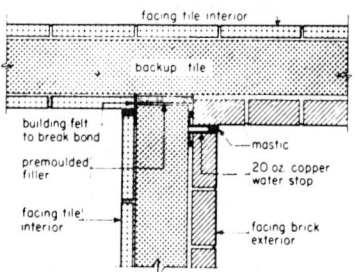

EXPANSION JOINT AT
WALL OFFSET

EXPANSION JOINT AT JUNCTURE
OF INTERSECTING WALLS
Fig. 91.   Expansion joints in walls

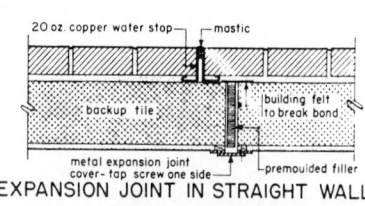

EXPANSION JOINT IN STRAIGHT WALL

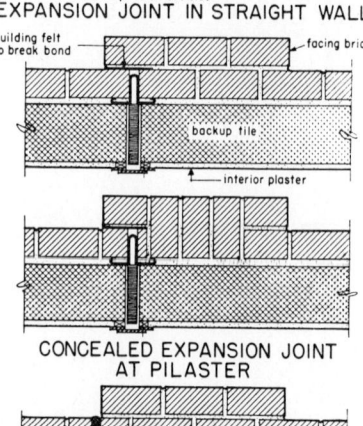

CONCEALED EXPANSION JOINT
AT PILASTER

EXPANSION JOINT AT PILASTER

Fig. 92.   Expansion joints in straight walls

Table 74.   Recommended spacing of expansion joints

Outside Temperature Ranges F*	Maximum Length of Wall, ft.			
	Unheated or Insulated		Heated not Insulated	
	Solid	Openings†	Solid	Openings†
100 and over	200	100	250	125
Less than 100	250	125	300	150

*The range from the lowest average temperature to the highest.
†Openings 20 per cent more of wall area.

Masonry walls in skeleton-frame construction are especially susceptible to cracking caused by thermal and other kinds of movement. In addition to thermal movement within the wall itself (discussed on the previous page), there may be differential movement between the wall and the building frame. Perhaps even more important is the fact that skeleton frames are more flexible than masonry walls and undergo greater deflection due to floor loads and to wind and other lateral forces.

A solution to this problem is the use of flexible ties between the masonry walls and the columns and spandrel beams of the building frame. Recommended details of such flexible anchorages are shown on this and the following page.

If the building is not too high, the exterior walls can be erected completely independent of the columns and beams for vertical support. The walls then carry their own dead weight to the foundation, and thus reduce the size and cost of the frame. The skeleton frame provides the wall with lateral support and carries all other vertical loads. The wall is tied to the frame by flexible anchors that take tension and compression, but no shear, and thus permit differential longitudinal and vertical movements between the frame and the wall (Figs. 94–97). A schematic diagram for such a structural system is shown in Fig. 93.

Metal ties should be No. 6 gage galvanized steel or other noncorrosive metal of equal strength. To avoid buckling of the ties, the distance between the inside face of the wall and the anchor seat should not exceed 3 in., and preferably not more than ¾ in. The size and spacing of ties is based on tensile and compressive loads induced by wind suction and pressure on the wall. Table 75 shows the maximum spacing of No. 6 gage ties on spandrel beams for three wind pressures, based on the maximum distance between lateral supports for several wall types. If lateral support is provided only by columns, the spacing of ties should be the same as shown in Table 75.

Steel or concrete columns, beams, and spandrels should not be surrounded with masonry unless absolutely necessary. It is especially important that masonry not be placed in contact with columns. Physical

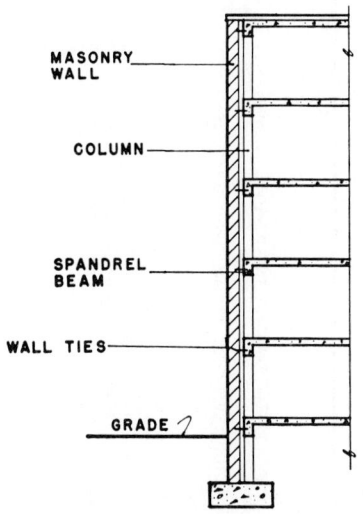

Fig. 93. Masonry wall braced but not supported by building frame

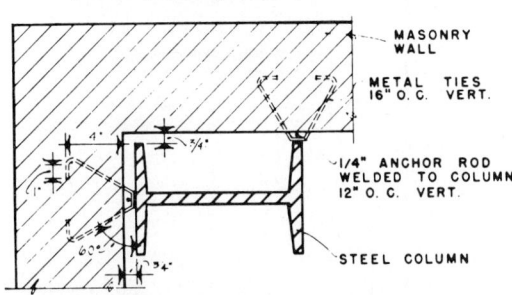

PLAN OF WALL ANCHORAGE TO STEEL COLUMN

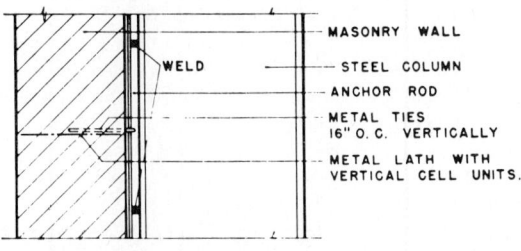

ELEVATION OF WALL ANCHORAGE TO STEEL COLUMN

Fig. 94. Wall anchorage to steel column

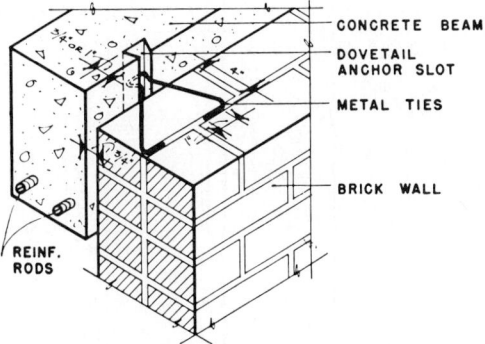

WALL ANCHORAGE TO CONCRETE BEAM

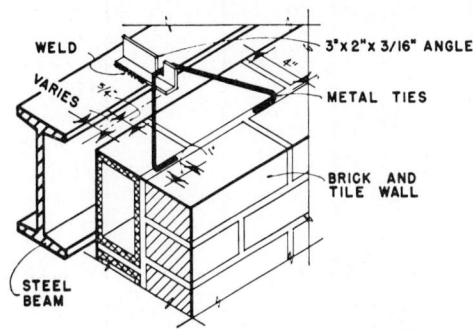

WALL ANCHORAGE TO STEEL BEAM

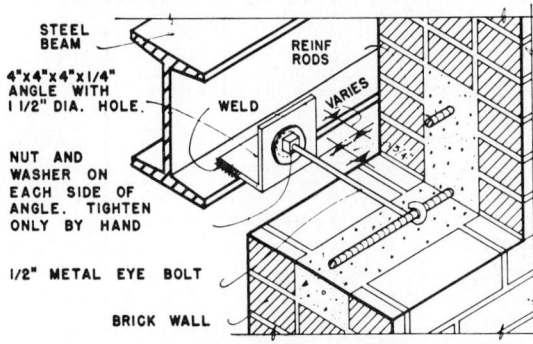

ALTERNATE WALL ANCHORAGE TO STEEL BEAM

Fig. 95. Typical beam-wall anchorage

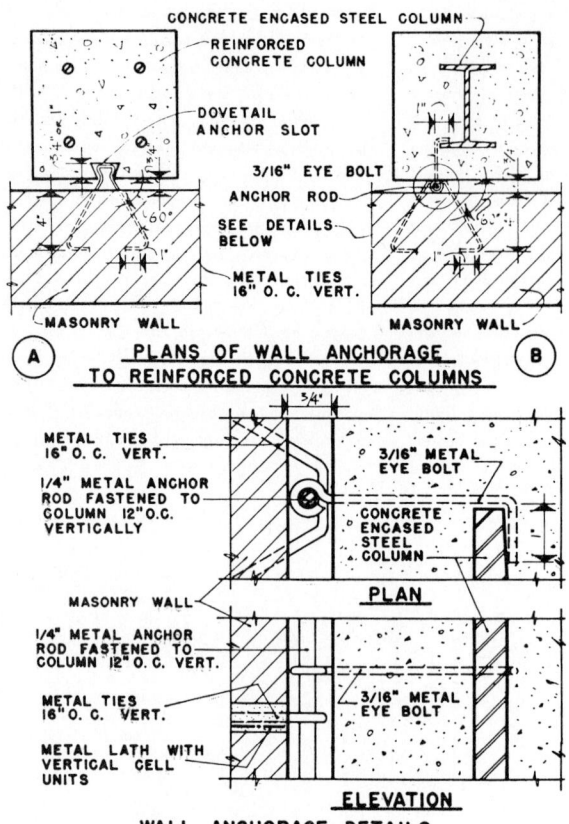

Fig. 96. Wall anchorage details

Fig. 97. Column partially encased in masonry wall

Table 75. Spacing of wall ties

Wall type	Maximum distance between lateral supports for walls	Maximum spacing of no. 6 gage tie anchors at lateral supports		
		40 psf	30 psf	20 psf
6" brick	10' 0"	1' 6"	2' 0"	2' 0"
8" tile	12' 0"	1' 3"	1' 8"	2' 0"
8" brick	13' 4"	1' 3"	1' 6"	2' 0"
12" tile	18' 0"	1' 0"	1' 6"	1' 8"
12" brick	20' 0"	0' 8"	1' 0"	1' 6"

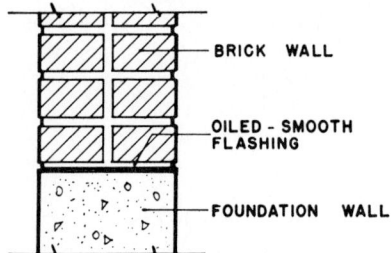

Fig. 98. Prevention of bond at foundation

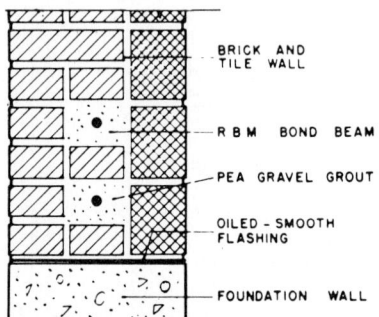

Fig. 99. Reinforcement of wall at foundation

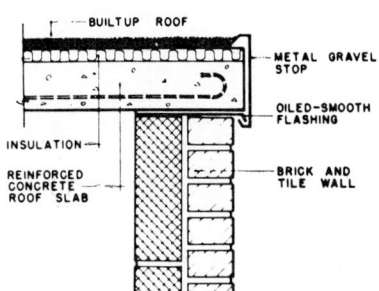

Fig. 100. Prevention of bond between masonry wall and roof slab

contact between the edges of decks or floor slabs and the inside face of masonry walls should be prevented. If steel columns are fire-protected by masonry or other material, the fireproofing should not be in contact with the masonry wall.

If it is considered necessary to encase columns, the encasement should not exceed 4 in. in a 12-in. wall (Fig. 97). Columns should not be encased in an 8-in. wall.

To prevent cracks resulting from differential movement between the foundation and the wall, the detail shown in Fig. 98 will break the bond between the two and permit each to move independently. This detail may be used in structures for which it is not necessary to anchor the walls to the foundation. In general, such anchorage is unnecessary for skeleton-frame structures in which the enclosing walls may be anchored to the frame.

Additional resistance to cracking resulting from any forces that may be transmitted to the wall by friction may be obtained by incorporating a reinforced "bond beam" in the base of the wall (Fig. 99).

A somewhat similar condition occurs where masonry bearing walls support a concrete floor or roof slab. Investigations have shown that such slabs as a rule not only shrink horizontally but also curl upward at the corners. If the walls are tied rigidly to the slab, cracking of the masonry is almost certain to result. This condition is most severe in roof slabs, and in such cases it is recommended that parapets be eliminated and that positive means be provided to break the bond between wall and slab. A suggested detail for this condition is shown in Fig. 100. The natural struggle between the inside and outside portions of a wall becomes most intense at the juncture of roof and parapet wall. This struggle may continue until there is, literally, an explosion. Indeed, cracked or broken parapet walls, particularly at roof corners, are quite common.

Every wall of any thickness is strained by the differences in exposure and temperature between inside and outside. The outer surface, or outer layer, gets wet and then is heated by the sun, or, more to the point, it is subject to freezing temperature while the inner layer is heated. Thus the outside layer wants to contract, the inner one to expand. Sooner or later each goes its own way and an explosion follows, leaving a break in the wall.

This problem is especially important in the design of parapets. For here differences in exposure and temperature reach the extreme, above the point where the outside wall gets any heat at all from inside. Heat in the top story rises to the underside of the roof slab, causing it to expand. Insulation on top will free the slab from the influence of the cold outside, and the slab will stretch comfortably. But the parapet wall, exposed to the cold, will shrink from each free end, toward the center. (The free end refers only to the top of the wall; the bottom is fixed at the roof line.) At the corner, the pull is along each wall. The roof slab is pushing the bottom corner of the parapet wall outward; the top of each wall is being pulled inward. Thus the corner cracks often take the pattern shown in Fig. 101.

Masonry wall cracks at or near the junction of parapet and roof line are perhaps the most difficult of all types of masonry cracking to eliminate. This difficulty is due to the severe exposures to which the parapet is subjected, to its relatively light weight, to movements between parapet and building walls, and perhaps to other factors often hard to identify.

There is no single solution of the problem of cracking of parapet walls. Many methods have been tried by different designers with varying success. Figure 102 shows a reinforced parapet wall construction recommended by the Brick Institute of America to minimize vertical cracking. Figure 103 shows standard details used in the office of Fred N. Severud, Consulting Engineer. These details, despite the similarity of the

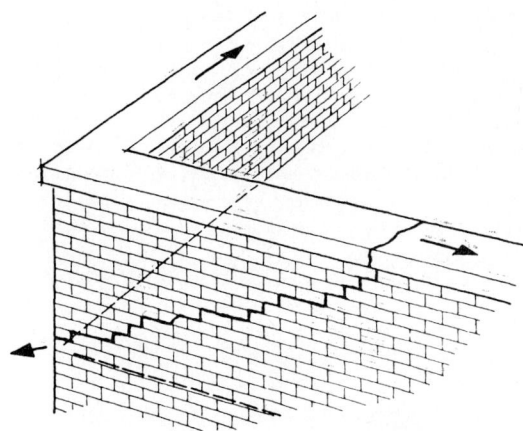

Fig. 101. Typical corner crack on parapet walls

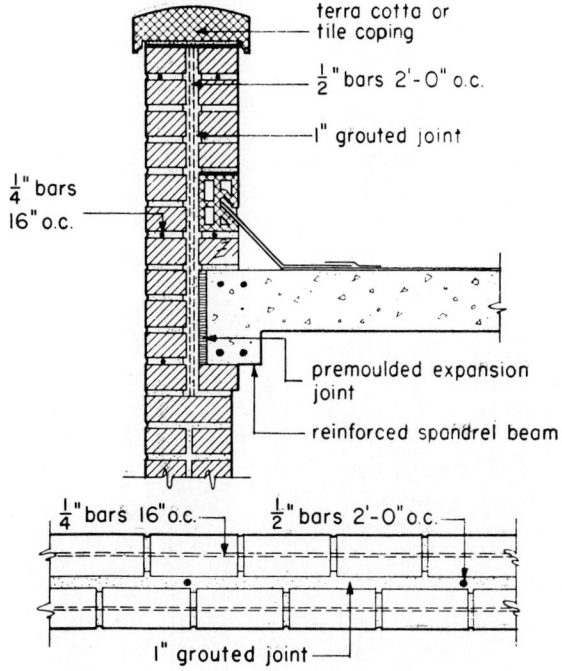

terra cotta or tile coping

$\frac{1}{2}$" bars 2'-0" o.c.

1" grouted joint

$\frac{1}{4}$" bars 16" o.c.

premoulded expansion joint

reinforced spandrel beam

$\frac{1}{4}$" bars 16" o.c. $\frac{1}{2}$" bars 2'-0" o.c.

1" grouted joint

Fig. 102. Reinforced parapet wall (see also Fig. 54)

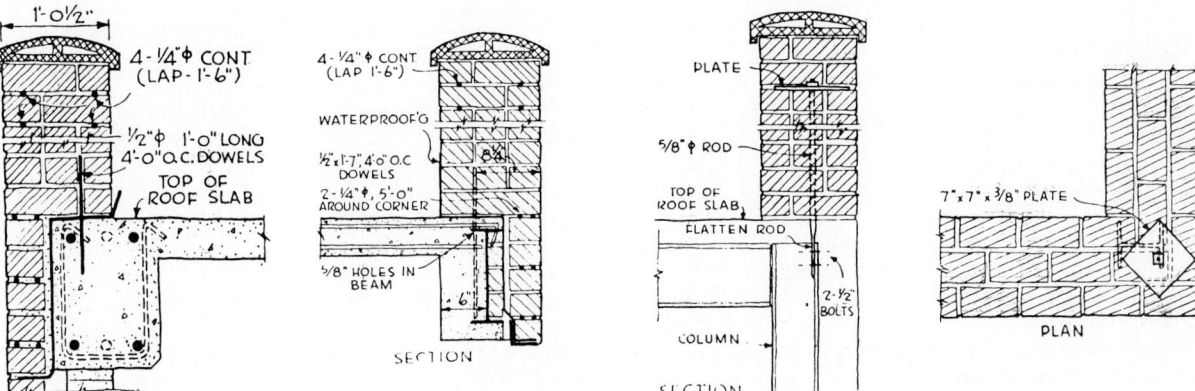

Fig. 103. Standard details for parapet wall

horizontal reinforcing, differ significantly, the BIA design provides flexibility between the wall and the spandrel beam, whereas the Severud designs anchor the two firmly together. The more recent design by BIA shown in Fig. 54 combines both principles: the reinforced parapet wall is anchored firmly to the spandrel beam, but the outer wythe of the cavity wall is tied to the beam by a flexible anchor.

An entirely different approach is shown in Fig. 104, in which a concrete fence is substituted for the parapet wall. Concrete struts, poured with the spandrel beams, act as fence posts; precast concrete planks are set in slots in the posts.

The only sure way to prevent the cracking of parapet walls is to eliminate the parapet entirely. BIA and many other authorities in this field recommend the elimination of parapets wherever possible. Figure 105 shows a standard detail of the New York City Housing Authority for a pipe railing instead of a parapet. See also the eave detail shown in Fig. 100.

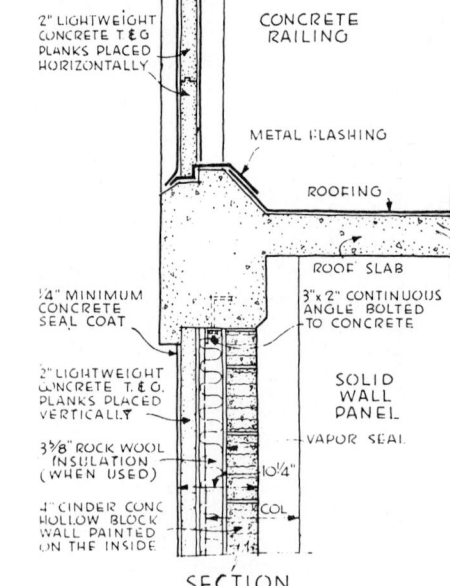

Fig. 104. Concrete fence for parapet wall

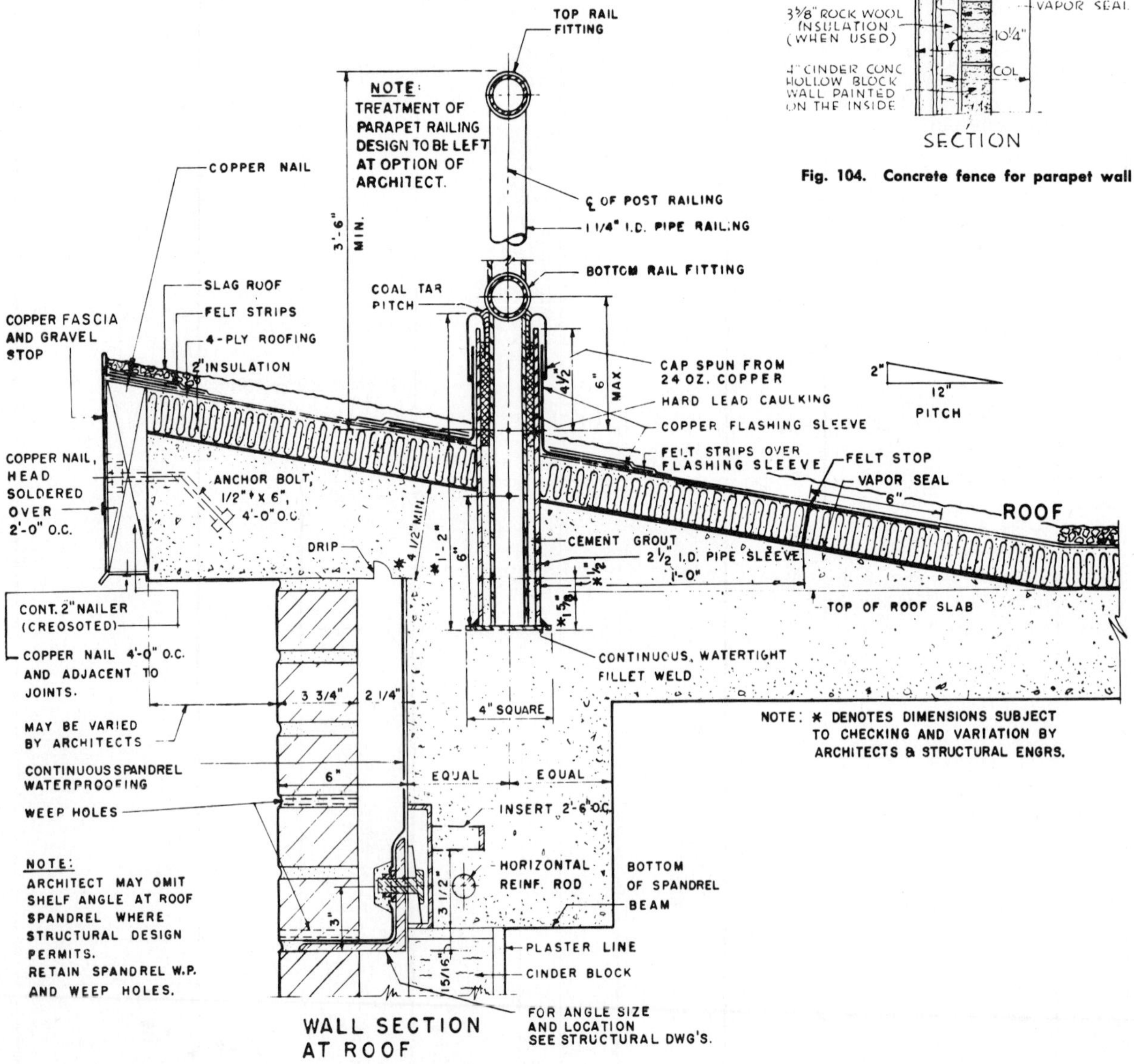

Fig. 105. Pipe railing for parapet wall

Data and illustrations on this and the following page have been derived from *Technical Notes on Brick Construction*, published by the Brick Institute of America.

ATTACHING WOOD TRIM

The most common method of anchoring such items as baseboards, chair rails, and picture moldings to masonry walls is by the use of wood nailing blocks placed in vertical mortar joints by the mason as he builds the wall. These blocks should be of seasoned soft wood and creosoted to prevent shrinkage or rot. They should never be placed in horizontal mortar joints.

Metal nailing or "wall" plugs (Fig. 106) provide better construction. They are made of galvanized metal, either with or without a wood or fiberboard insert. Like the wood nailing blocks, the metal wall plugs are built into the joints as the masonry is erected. Their exact location is not a serious problem when used to fasten baseboards or chair rails, but it may be difficult to predetermine their location for fixtures, cabinets, shelving, and the like.

Attaching fixtures and cabinets: Several methods of attaching fixtures, cabinets, shelving, and trim are shown in Fig. 107. The methods illustrated in Fig. 107*a, b,* and *d* can be used only with structural clay tile

walls and are installed after the walls are built and the exact loaction of the fixture is determined.

Figure 107*c* illustrates a method of fastening that can be used with either brick or tile construction, by building the wood plug in as the wall is built, or by driving it into a hole drilled into the masonry after it has been erected.

Fig. 107*e* and *f* show two methods that may be used with either brick or tile construction. Usually, the expansion shields or fiber plugs are placed in holes drilled in the mortal joints. As required, such holes may be drilled through the face shells of tile, or into the mortar joints with hard steel or carbide tipped drills. In some cases where softer tile are used, as in plastered partitions, small holes may be made by the use of an ordinary 1/8-in. punch and hammer.

A relatively new method of attaching to solid masonry walls employs a power-actuated tool that, in effect, "rams" or drives an anchor or pin into the masonry instantaneously. There are suitable pins for almost any type of anchorage desired. Three typical pins are illustrated in Fig. 108.

Furring applications: Although there are many examples of brick, structural clay tile, and composite brick and tile walls with plaster finish applied directly to the interior masonry surface, furring on 8-in. walls is recommended, particularly in northern areas and for residential construction.

Furring may be of wood, metal, or hollow tile, depending upon the type of construction and the local building requirements.

Several typical methods of attaching wood furring are shown in Fig. 109. The wood furring strips are either 1x2 in. or 2x2 in. and are applied vertically to the wall at intervals usually 16 in. on center. The wood strips may be attached by nailing into wood nailing blocks or metal wall plugs as shown in Fig. 109*c,* or directly into the mortar joints by the use of case-hardened "cut" nails or special spiral-threaded masonry nails as shown in Fig. 109*d.* Special anchor nails fastened to the masonry wall with an adhesive cement is a recent development for installing furring and is illustrated in Fig. 109*a.* Such fastenings are easily and quickly installed without drilling, plugging, or nailing. Brick-size porous clay nailing blocks are available in some areas. Since such blocks are completely inert, there is no danger of nail disintegration from chemical reaction. The use of such blocks is illustrated in Fig. 109*b.*

Metal furring strips consist of standard light steel channels fastened by either tie wires built into the mortar joint or by special clips designed for this purpose.

Tile furring may be either attached or free-standing. Hollow or cored structural clay units for use as attached furring may be 2, 3, or 4 in. in nominal thickness. The

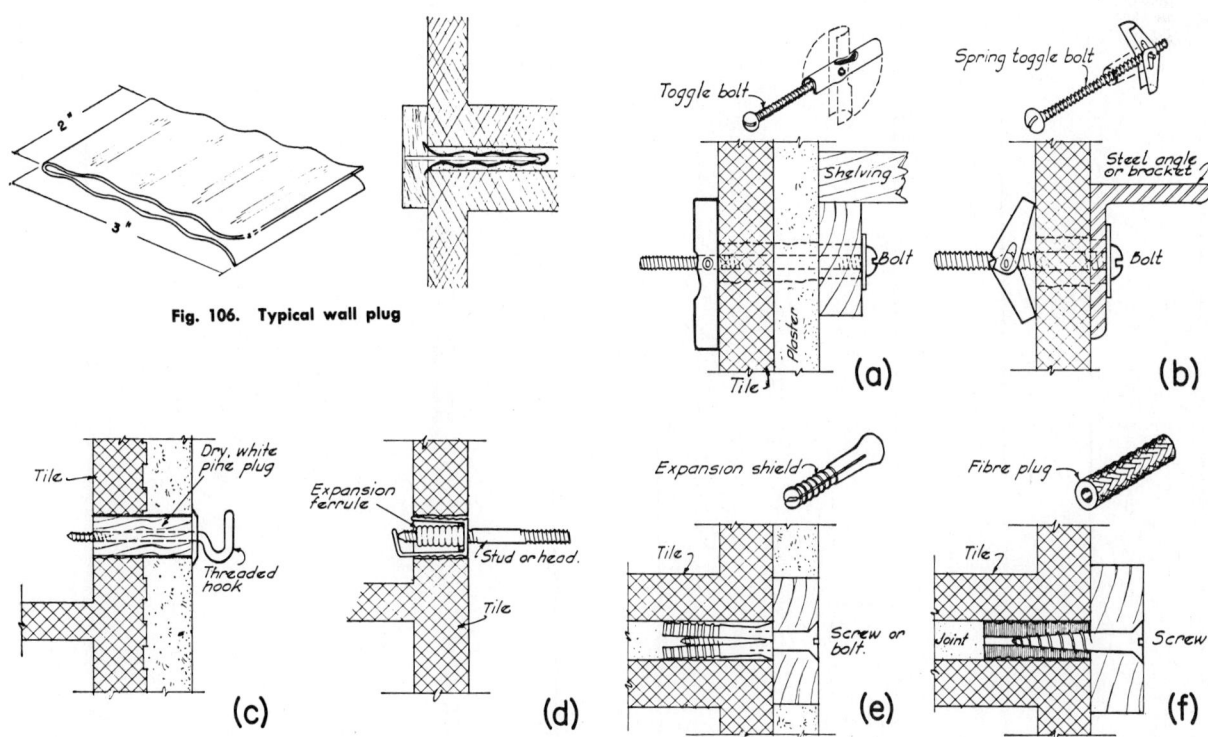

Fig. 106. Typical wall plug

(a)   (b)

(c)   (d)   (e)   (f)

Fig. 107. Wall plugs

2-in. thickness is available either as a solid-back unit or as "split" furring. The split units should always be applied directly to the wall without mortar on the back of the ribs, thus providing an uninterrupted air space. Since the solid-back furring tile have one or more air cells through their thicknesses, the space between the units and the wall may be filled with mortar, if desired for greater rigidity or where exterior wall parging is specified. Figure 110 illustrates a typical method of applying split furring tile.

Several different methods of attaching tile furring to masonry walls may be used. Table 76 gives the proper spacing of anchors or ties for attached furring, together with height and length limitations of the furring itself.

Nailing: Drive 10d nails into the mortar joints of the main wall and clinch the heads of the nails down into the cells of the tile or over the ends of the split tile as shown in Fig. 110.

Wire ties: Heavy wire ties, not less than No. 11 gage, may be built into the mortar joints of the wall as the masonry is erected, and bent down into the cells of the furring tile as they are erected.

Corrugated or crimped metal ties should be at least $\frac{7}{8}$ in. wide and not lighter than No. 22 gage.

Wire mesh should be at least 4 in. wide strips of $\frac{1}{2}$-in. mesh, No. 20 gage galvanized wire fabric. These ties should extend at least 3 in. into the masonry wall and to within $\frac{1}{2}$ in. of the face of the furring.

Anchors: Tile furring is attached to concrete by the use of dovetail anchors inserted into metal slots embedded in the concrete. These anchors should be at least $\frac{7}{8}$ in. wide and not lighter than No. 16 gage.

Grout or adhesives: When solid-back hollow units are used they may often be applied directly to the structural wall without metal anchors or ties by utilizing the high adhesive bond obtained by filling the back space with cement grout. Or a waterproof adhesive may be used.

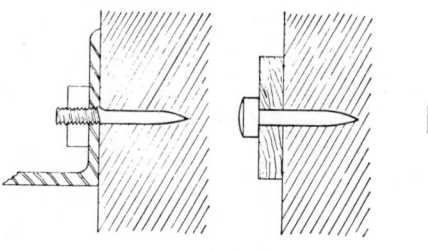
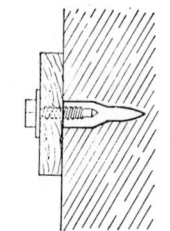

Fig. 108. Pins

Table 76. Height and length limitations for attached furring tile and spacing of metal ties and anchors

Type and Thickness of Furring	Maximum Allowable Spacing of Ties		
	No Ties Required	24" Vertical 24" Horizontal	16" Vertical 24" Horizontal
2-in. Split	—	Up to 14 ft.	14 to 35 ft.
2-in. Hollow	9 ft.[1]	9 to 14 ft.	14 to 35 ft.
3-in. Hollow	12 ft.	12 to 18 ft.	18 to 35 ft.
4-in. Hollow	15 ft.	15 to 22 ft.	22 to 35 ft.

[1] Not over 6 ft. in length.

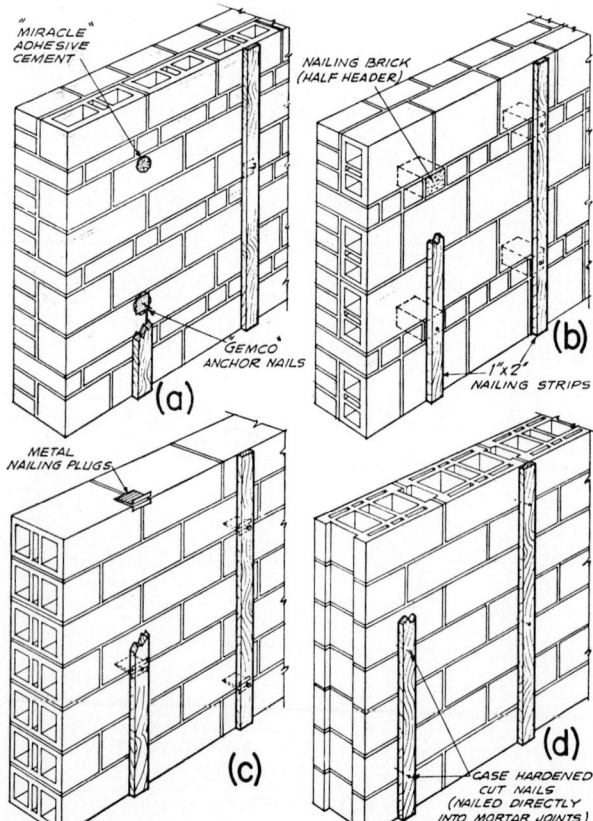

Fig. 109. Methods of attaching wood furring

"MIRACLE" ADHESIVE CEMENT

NAILING BRICK (HALF HEADER)

GEMCO ANCHOR NAILS

(a)

(b)

1"x2" NAILING STRIPS

METAL NAILING PLUGS

(c)

(d)

CASE HARDENED CUT NAILS (NAILED DIRECTLY INTO MORTAR JOINTS)

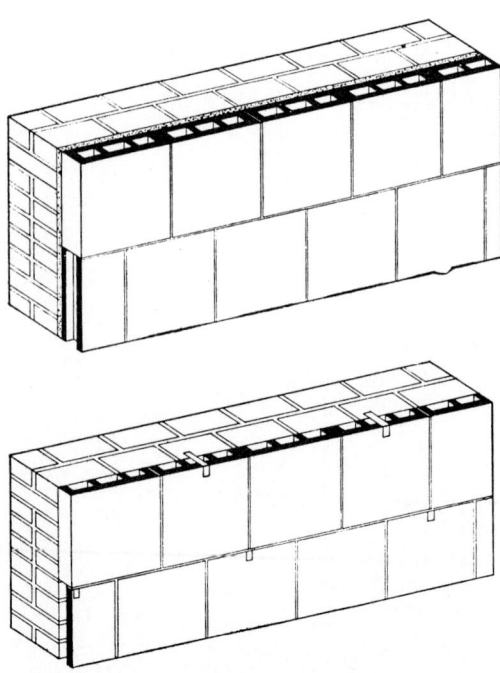

Fig. 110. Solid-back and split furring tile

3

Building Materials, Components, and Techniques

By PHILIP P. PAGE, JR., Goldreich, Page, and Thropp, Consulting Engineers

An understanding of the problems involved in foundation drain design can best be had by studying the nature of groundwater. Groundwater is water in the pores of the soil, and as such it follows the laws of hydraulics. Its origin is rainwater, which seeps through the soil until it is stopped by some impervious layer. This layer may be at a very great depth. The top of this water in the soil is called the groundwater level. The water flows through the soil until it emerges aboveground in a body of water. The friction between the soil and the water flowing through it is overcome by building up a higher groundwater level away from the point of emergence. Therefore, the following points can be made about groundwater:

1. The groundwater level varies seasonally with the amount of rainfall.
2. The groundwater level follows the general contour of the land, but is closer to the surface in low ground and farther from the surface in high ground.
3. The direction of groundwater flow is always in the direction of the lower groundwater level.

Hydrostatic Head

Groundwater, following the laws of hydraulics, always produces a hydrostatic head or water pressure which at any point is equal to the depth of that point below groundwater level times the unit weight of water, 62.4 psf. The effect of this pressure upon a building is illustrated at right. The earth pressure is reduced (from 240 to 100 psf) because of the buoyant effect of the water on the soil particles, but the total pressure is greatly increased.

Purpose of Foundation Drains

Foundation drains lower the groundwater, thus preventing building up of a hydrostatic head against the walls or floor of a building with resultant leakage or structural damage. A drainage system should consist of footing drains of sufficient size and an adequate outfall or method of water disposal. The enlarged detail at right shows the basic elements of a foundation drain.

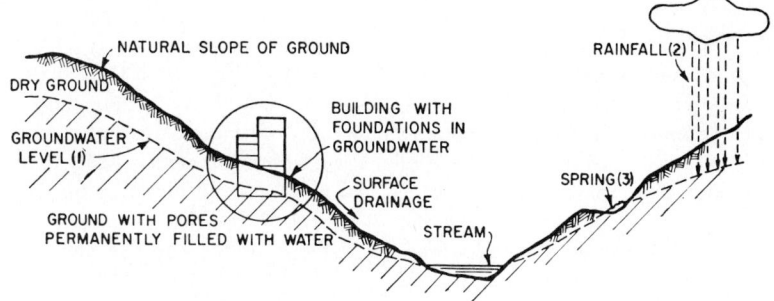

BASIC FACTORS AFFECTING GROUNDWATER LEVEL

(1) Groundwater level tends to follow ground contour—deeper on hills, shallower in valleys.
(2) Rainfall percolates through ground to recharge groundwater. Groundwater level varies with amount of rainfall. (3) Springs occur where local ground depressions place ground level below groundwater level.

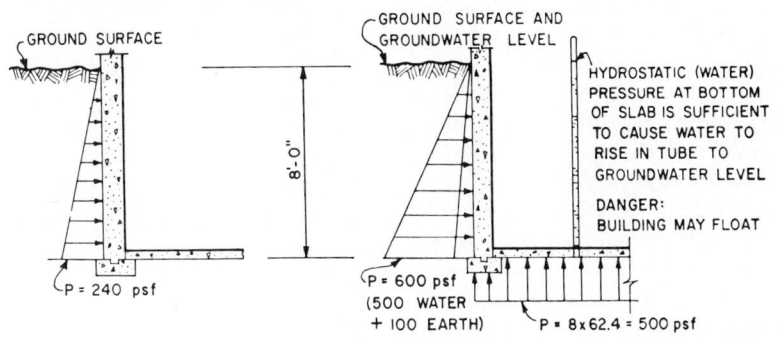

EFFECT OF HYDROSTATIC PRESSURE ON A BUILDING

Note: Waterproofing is not sufficient in itself to protect walls against groundwater unless they can take heavy earth and water loads

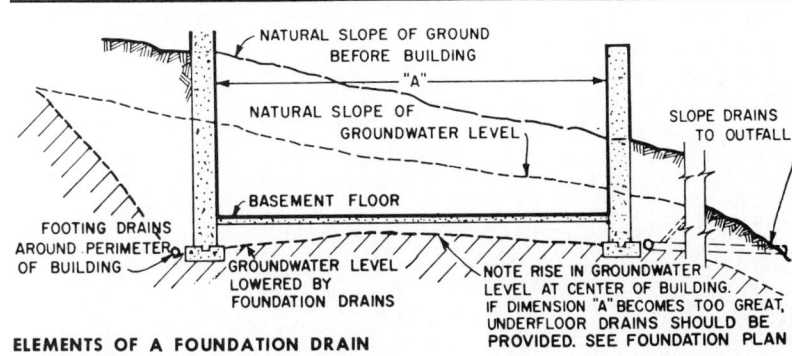

ELEMENTS OF A FOUNDATION DRAIN

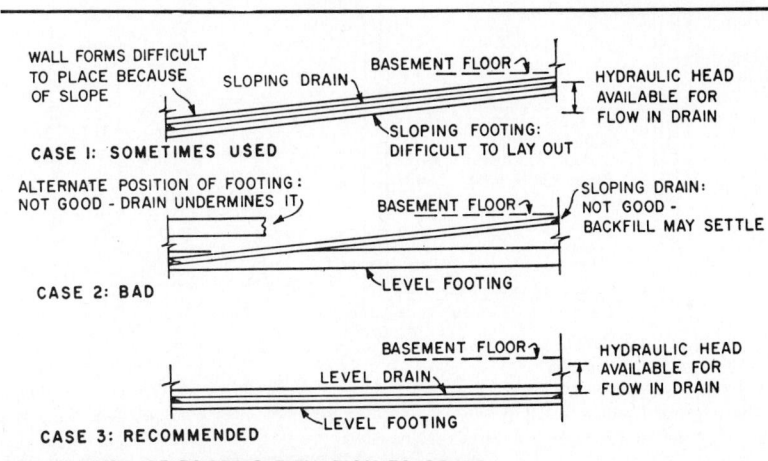

RELATIONSHIP OF FOOTING ELEVATION TO DRAIN

Estimation of Infiltration

The amount of infiltration varies according to the type of soil and height of groundwater above footings. Clays have such a small flow of groundwater that nominal 4-in. drains are satisfactory for all but the largest installations. Silts have more flow. Sands and gravels can have such a heavy flow that pumping tests are required to determine the flow quantity.

Location of Drains

Drains are placed around the periphery of a building far enough below floor level to develop sufficient hydraulic head for drainage. The footing is always placed at least 4 in. below the invert of the drain (bottom of the inside diameter) to prevent groundwater flowing under the footing from washing out soil fines, with resultant settlement of the structure. For buildings covering a large area it may be necessary to place underfloor drains to prevent the building up of head in the center.

Selection of Size of Drain

Once the infiltration has been established and the plan of the drains laid out, the size of pipe and elevation of invert must be established. The nomograph at right can be used. The selection of the proper drain then requires an economic study.

Example

Given: Inflow of 100 gpm, established by a pumping test during excavation

Length of drain—350 ft

Friction factor for pipes—$n = 0.015$

Find: Underdrainage design required to keep cellar dry

Solution: Assume a 6-in. pipe. From nomograph, required slope for a 6-in. pipe and 100 gpm discharge is 0.0024. Hydraulic drop is $350 \times 0.0024 = 0.84$ ft. Bottom of drain should be, therefore, $0.84 + 0.5$ (thickness of floor slab) $= 1.34$ ft below surface of floor.

To adjust for $n = 0.019$, multiply inflow by $0.019/0.015$ and then use nomograph.

To adjust for $n = 0.013$, multiply inflow by $0.013/0.015$ and then use nomograph.

Example

Inflow of 100 gpm

Friction factor—$n = 0.019$

Solution

$100 \times 0.019/0.015 = 126$

Taking line from 126 on Discharge bar through 6-in. Drain Diam. gives Slope of 0.0040

The required hydraulic head is increased as pipe diameter is decreased, as can be seen in the nomograph. When drain is lowered to increase head, footing must be lowered to stay below level of drain and thus prevent silt from being washed away from under footing. Selection of drain size usually depends on cost differential between small pipe—and therefore more excavation for lowering of footings—and more costly large pipe but less digging. See detail below.

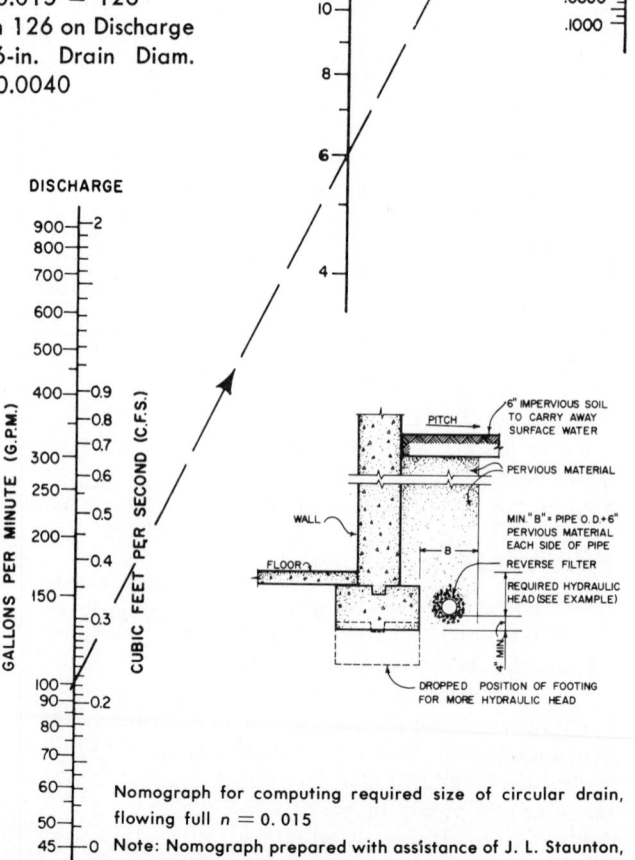

Nomograph for computing required size of circular drain, flowing full $n = 0.015$

Note: Nomograph prepared with assistance of J. L. Staunton, Staunton and Freeman.

PLAN

ON SOME BUILDINGS UNDERFLOOR DRAINS MAY BE REQUIRED TO PREVENT WATER FROM RISING UNDER FLOOR

Note: If gravity outflow is not practical or possible, a sump has to be used with a pump to draw out groundwater

Type of Drain

To permit the entry of water but prevent the entry of soil a reverse filter surrounds the foundation drain. This reverse filter consists of coarse gravel next to the pipe followed by layers of coarse and then fine sand. Porous or perforated pipe is preferable to open joint pipe. The table below shows the basic characteristics of the main types of pipe used. The pipe generally is laid level, without slope, to avoid the problem of sloping footing bottoms, as shown on Sheet 1. A footing seal of impervious material should be provided to prevent the flow of water under the footing.

Outfall

Disposal of the water collected in the drains must be given careful thought. Too often drawings simply indicate an arrow to an outfall or a dry well. The outfall must be capable of taking the discharge without becoming surcharged. Generally the connection to sanitary sewers is prohibited by law and certainly is not to be encouraged.

Dry wells should not be specified, for obvious reasons, when they would be below the water table. Dry wells are satisfactory, though, when they will stay above the water table and when this soil is permeable enough to dissipate the inflow.

Good outfalls consist of storm sewers or other drainage devices located at a lower elevation than that of the footings. Sometimes such an outfall is impossible to reach and it becomes necessary or more economical to collect the water in a sump and to pump out to surface drainage.

Basic characteristics of drain pipes

POROUS CONCRETE TO PERMIT INFILTRATION OF WATER

CONCRETE LOCKING JOINT

HOLES TO PERMIT INFILTRATION OF WATER

JOINT

HOLES ON BOTTOM 1/3 OF PIPES

COUPLING

HOLES IN BOTTOM FOR WATER

TAR PAPER ON TOP TO PREVENT ENTRY OF SILT

OPEN JOINT TO ALLOW ENTRY OF WATER

TAR PAPER ON TOP TO PREVENT ENTRY OF SILT

OPEN JOINT TO ALLOW ENTRY OF WATER

BELL & SPIGOT JOINT

SOMETIMES HOLES ARE PROVIDED ON BOTTOM FOR INFLOW

SLIP-ON COUPLING

HOLES IN BOTTOM FOR WATER

SPLIT COUPLING

SAW CUTS EVERY THIRD CORRUGATION

Type	n	Advantages	Disadvantages
Porous concrete	0.015	Freedom from silting, erosion and corrosion; easily laid; resists surcharge load	Most expensive
Perforated concrete	0.015	Same as porous	Expensive
Perforated metal	0.019	Freedom from silting; resists surcharge load	Possible corrosion; high n value
Open joint concrete	0.015	Strong; resists surcharge load	Joints may permit entry of silt, which clogs line; harder to lay; backfill must be laid with more care
Open joint clay	0.019	Least expensive; resists corrosion	Joints may silt up; high n value; more easily broken by careless backfill or surcharge
Vitrified clay	0.013	Low n value; best for runs to outfall; resists corrosion and erosion	Least effective entry of water
Perforated bituminous fiber	0.015	Inexpensive; freedom from corrosion; easily laid	Easily broken by careless backfill or surcharge load
Corrugated polyethylene	0.019	Freedom from corrosion; resists surcharge load; flexible; easily laid in long lengths	Expensive; high n value; sawcuts may permit silting

Foundation drains

From data supplied by R. W. SEXTON

PROTECTION OF UNDERGROUND CONSTRUCTION

The problem should be considered from three angles, 1. The causes and conditions, 2. Preventive measures, and 3. Cures.

In times past little effort was made to waterproof buildings. Most of the important public or private buildings were built on high ground for natural drainage, if possible. The cellars of houses were expected to leak after exceptionally heavy rainstorms. Waterproofing first became vitally important when the tall building, with deep basement containing mechanical equipment, entered the field of construction. Today, the economy of the times makes it imperative to plan buildings in which all available space is put to practical use. Basements of houses, which in times past would have been used only for storage, are now planned to contain livable rooms. It is not feasible to put permanent interior finishes into such rooms unless the surrounding walls and the floors are built to exclude water, moisture, and dampness.

FOOTING DRAIN

DETAIL OF JOINT AT JUNCTION OF FLOOR AND WALL
SCALE – 1½" = 1'-0"

UNDERFLOOR DRAIN
SCALE – 3/8" = 1'-0" EXCEPT WHERE NOTED

STONE CATCH BASIN
TO COLLECT WATER AND CARRY IT AWAY FROM A BUILDING

CAUSES AND CONDITIONS: LOCATION, SOIL, WATER TABLE

The foundations of the simplest building go below frost line, and water conditions of some kind are almost sure to be encountered. A large portion of the earth's surface consists of bedrock and soil underlaid with water. The water flows through the materials themselves, if they are porous, and through the open spaces between the different geological substances. The water table is the name given to the surface of this ground water. The height of the water table varies somewhat with the amount of rainfall, and with the type of substance of which the ground is made, but it generally follows the contour of the ground, coming nearer the surface in the valleys than on the ridges. Irregularities of distribution of soft and hard materials often cause the level of the water to rise and drop perceptibly within a comparatively small area.

Above the level of the water table the soil contains surface water. This is sometimes called capillary water because it lies in minute pores so close to one another that capillary action takes place. The rate at which this water is transmitted through the ground depends upon the size of the pores of the various substances of which the ground is made. The pores of clay are usually filled with water even though the underground water level is many feet below. As oil will rise in a lampwick, surface water will come to the surface by capillary action from a considerable depth. Capillary water cannot be drained out of the soil by any system of drainage.

Occasionally a building site will prove to have definite upward water pressure, similar to a true artesian well. On sites which are near rivers subject to floods, or on low marshy land, steady or intermittent heads of water will often be encountered. Because of marked variation in the properties of soil and rock within short distances and at different depths, it is always well to investigate underground conditions by means of test pits or borings. The porosity of the soil, besides being related to the possibility of infiltration of water, also has a bearing on the amount of weight foundations will support. It is not unusual to find soil with high bearing power underlaid with material with less resistance to weight.

PREVENTIVE MEASURES

Since prevention may be cheaper than cure, every effort should be made to keep water away from foundations where it can be harmful. In large buildings with deep foundations this may not be possible. In rare cases, where a plentiful source of power is near at hand, it may be more economical to pump water out of basements than to build walls strong enough to resist its entry. In a majority of cases, however, it is possible to drain water away from basements, especially when buildings are placed on land higher than their immediate surroundings. When it is known that the site of a building is going to be wet, every effort should be made, at the very outset of the job, to correct the condition. Catch basins, with or without drainage lines, may be installed around the perimeter of the proposed location to collect the water and carry it away to lower ground. Basements in which water 2 or 3 ft. deep has collected during the excavation period, are sometimes made entirely dry by installation of such drains. When drains cannot be installed, sump pumps placed in pits below the basement floor, operated electrically or hydraulically, may serve the same purpose. They are useful on rocky ground where blasting out trenches would be difficult and expensive.

Footing drains are the best means of attracting and collecting water that is present in the immediate vicinity of foundations. They consist of lines of drain tile placed around the outside or the inside of foundation walls, connected to some suitable outlet.

PERMEABILITY OF CONCRETE

Poured concrete, if well made, can be practically watertight. The impermeability will depend largely upon the care with which it is mixed and placed. All the aggregates should be of low absorption value, and the cement should adhere to each particle. The materials should be carefully selected, the proportions accurately calculated, and the workmanship rigorously supervised. To produce the dense, yet plastic and workable mix that is desirable, there should not be over 6 gals. of water per bag of cement. The mixture should be tamped with rods or agitated by electric vibrators to secure proper density. The hydration of the cement—that is, combining the cement and the water —takes time. Strength is gained and porosity is reduced during the period of hardening or curing. These changes take place rapidly during the first few days, more slowly thereafter. Most concrete should be kept wet for at least 7 days. Fabric coverings, straw, or other coatings are used to retain the water. The tendency of concrete to dry rapidly is usually noticeable in the hot, dry days of summer. The accompanying chart shows, for three different mixes of concrete, the relation of curing time to permeability.

Though concrete may not permit the passage of water through it, moisture may creep in. Even if the pores are very minute and compacted they may connect with one another. They may act as capillary tubes, drawing in and filling themselves with water. This action may cause the wall to be damp.

RECOMMENDED CONCRETE MIXTURES FOR FOUNDATION WALLS AND BASEMENTS

KIND OF WORK	STRENGTH IN LBS/ SQ. IN. AT 28 DAYS	GALLONS OF WATER FOR EACH ONE-SACK BATCH IF SAND IS:			TRIAL MIXTURE FOR FIRST BATCH			MAX. SIZE OF AGGREGATE, INCHES
		DAMP	WET	VERY WET	CEMENT	SAND	PEBBLES	
ORDINARY RESIDENTIAL FOUNDATIONS	2000	6¼	5½	4¾	1	2¾	4	1½
WATERTIGHT FOUNDATIONS FOR POORLY DRAINED SOIL	3000	5½	5	4¼	1	2¼	3	1½

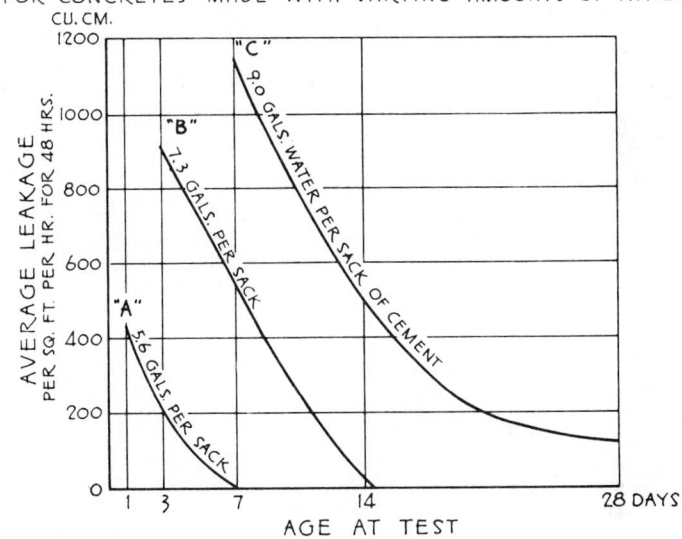

EFFECT OF CURING TIME ON PERMEABILITY
FOR CONCRETES MADE WITH VARYING AMOUNTS OF WATER

MIX "A" BECAME WATERTIGHT IN 7 DAYS.
MIX "B" BECAME WATERTIGHT IN 14 DAYS (BUT WAS FAR FROM IT IN 7 DAYS).
MIX "C" WAS NOT WATERTIGHT AFTER 4 WEEK CURE.

THESE DATA FROM PORTLAND CEMENT ASSOCIATION.

CRACKS AND JOINTS IN MASONRY

All types of masonry walls are subject to cracking due to settlement or to shrinkage caused by temperature changes. Even the well-proportioned concrete wall will crack unless there are a sufficient number of expansion joints. Brick, stone, and concrete block walls, besides being made of porous materials, have a large number of joints. Particularly when such walls are built in water-logged soil, great care should be exercised to keep the joints, which are the weakest link in the barrier against the entry of water, as tight as possible. All forms of construction seams are critical spots from the standpoint of waterproofing. The junction between the floor slab and the walls, generally known as the "floor line," is particularly vulnerable. A concrete slab may shrink as it sets, pull away from the surrounding walls and leave an opening for water. It is sometimes advisable to purposely make an open joint and later fill it

with impervious material. Pieces of bevelled siding, greased so that they will come out easily, may be set in place before the slab is poured. When the slab has set, the boards are removed, and a rich mixture of concrete, or bituminous waterproofing placed in the crack.

HYDROSTATIC PRESSURE

When measurable water pressure is encountered, precautions to keep it out of basements become engineering problems. A permanent 1 ft. head of water above the bottom of a slab will exert an upward pressure of 62½ lb. per sq. ft. on the slab. When the head is 10 ft. the pressure will become 625 lb. per sq. ft. The slab must be designed and reinforced to resist the pressure to which it is subjected. Sometimes thickening and reinforcing the floor slab will hold the water out.

Water pressure around the foundations of many large buildings is severe, and there is frequently no way to relieve it either by drainage or by pumping. When a concrete wall or slab is made thicker, the impermeability of the material is not proportionally increased, but the additional weight offers greater resistance to the pressure of the water.

Sometimes the pressure of the water will be greater than the normal dead load on the floor. In such cases buildings may be designed to carry the upward force of the water to the points of load concentration above. There are cases where it may be more economical to thicken the upper floors to obtain weight rather than thickening the lowest slab which is subjected to the direct force of the water. This is because every foot of depth added to the lowest slab (if the floor heights are kept constant) will increase the hydrostatic head, and the only gain would be the difference between the weight of the concrete and the weight of the water. The construction of some basements under high pressure is similar to the construction of tanks, except that they are built to resist pressure from without rather than from within. Study of the soil conditions and distribution of horizontal and vertical reactions must be studied.

INTEGRAL WATERPROOFING

The method consists of putting a compound, designed to increase impermeability, into the concrete mix. Experience has shown that few, if any, compounds are able to give the concrete a degree of perfection greater than would be obtainable if it were possible perfectly to grade, proportion and place the ingredients of the concrete itself. One kind of compound, which comes in powdered form, is designed to improve the workability of the concrete, thus reducing the number of interstices which might be formed if the mixture was not rich enough or of the proper consistency. Another type contains water-repellent admixtures which reduce absorption and retard penetration of water by capillary attraction. Tests have shown that some compounds have an injurious effect on the strength of the concrete. More desirable results have been obtained by the use of compounds made of inert materials such as clay, sand, and lime, which help to fill the voids, than by use of compounds in which chemical changes create water-repellent action.

MEMBRANE WATERPROOFING

The membrane method is the oldest form of waterproofing and until recently was the one in most common use. The older type membrane consists of the application of alternate layers of bituminous material such as asphalt, coal tar, or pitch — and fabric, like felt, burlap, canvas, or fiber glass. The bituminous substance is heated and mopped onto the surface to be protected and onto the alternating layers of fabric. Recently membranes consisting of sheets of butyl or other synthetic rubber with lapped and cemented joints have been used. These sheets are bonded to vertical surfaces but generally not to horizontal ones. The materials used should be elastic and cohesive as well as waterproof, because they are subjected to strains which will tend to make them crack and to dryness which will decrease their flexibility. A well-applied membrane seals the pores of a wall against penetration of moisture and obstructs the flow of any water.

Membranes should never be put on the inside of a foundation wall if it is possible to put them on the outside. Effective installations provide for con-

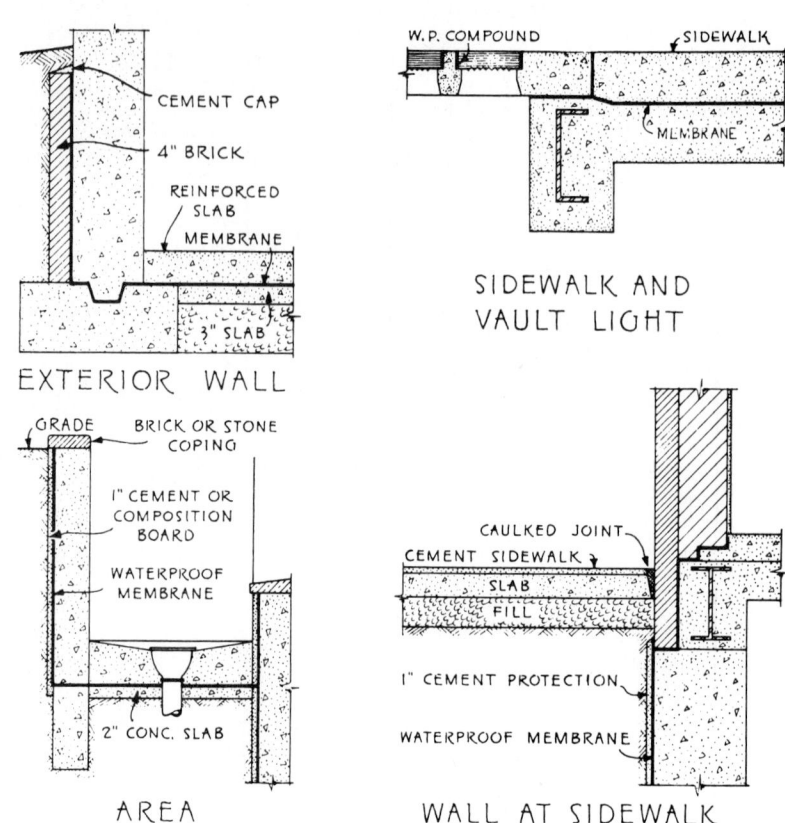

EXTERIOR WALL

SIDEWALK AND VAULT LIGHT

AREA

WALL AT SIDEWALK

SCALE OF THESE DRAWINGS ⅜" = 1'-0"

Number of plies of waterproofing material required for varying heads of water

Head of water, ft	Coal tar and felt	Commercial asphalt and felt
0	2	2
1–3	3	3
4–10	4	4
11–25	5	5

tinuous barrier of protection. Where a wall meets a floor, the membrane is usually run through a keyed footing. A similar key is used at the intersection of an interior partition with an exterior wall.

The protection of the membrane is very important. On the outside, if it is in direct contact with earth, it is subject to upheaval by frost, puncture by roots of trees, deterioration by acids in the soil. Several methods of protection are employed, all of which consist of placing another material between the membrane and the earth. A thin wall of brick or concrete is often

built. Composition board may also be used. Some boards available are manufactured to resist termites, dry rot, fungus, and other cellulose destroying agencies. They are also insoluble, and have insulating value. Their low conductivity will protect the bitumen in the membrane from the heat of the sun during the period of application. Such boards are embedded in the outer layer of fabric when it is given its final mopping. Blows with a wooden mallet insure overall contact of the board and the underlying surface. Bitumen is then mopped on the outside, to protect the board and the joints.

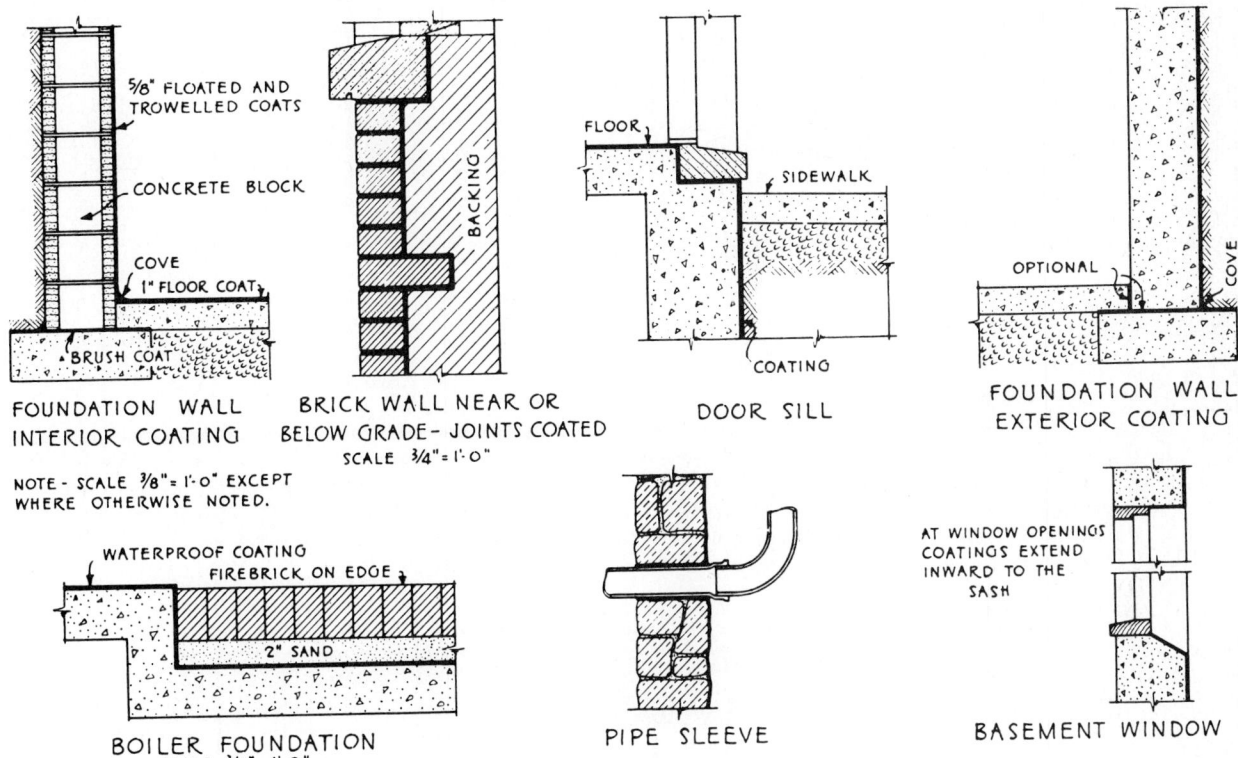

FOUNDATION WALL INTERIOR COATING

5⁄8" FLOATED AND TROWELLED COATS
CONCRETE BLOCK
COVE
1" FLOOR COAT
BRUSH COAT

BRICK WALL NEAR OR BELOW GRADE – JOINTS COATED
SCALE 3⁄4" = 1'·0"
BACKING

DOOR SILL
FLOOR
SIDEWALK
COATING

FOUNDATION WALL EXTERIOR COATING
OPTIONAL
COVE

NOTE – SCALE 3⁄8" = 1'·0" EXCEPT WHERE OTHERWISE NOTED.

BOILER FOUNDATION
SCALE 3⁄4" = 1'·0"
WATERPROOF COATING
FIREBRICK ON EDGE
2" SAND

PIPE SLEEVE

BASEMENT WINDOW
AT WINDOW OPENINGS COATINGS EXTEND INWARD TO THE SASH

CEMENT-BASE WATERPROOF COATINGS

There are several compounds available today, which, when applied to either the interior or the exterior surface of any type of basement wall, or to the upper surface of a floor slab, will render the wall or floor waterproof by sealing the pores. Most of these materials achieve and retain their hold on the surface by the bonding of Portland Cement. The basic ingredient of most of the compounds is cement, but some are sold in paste, powder, or liquid form to be mixed with cement by the consumer. These materials should not be confused with cement-base paints. The coatings have a hard wearing surface, and have been known to resist a hydrostatic head of 190 ft.

One type of coating contains ingredients of an organic nature, another type has a mineral base, being composed principally of iron.

A mineral type of compound which is commonly known as iron coating, takes advantage of the fact that iron, when it oxidizes, will expand to several times its original volume. Properly prepared iron will retain its ability to expand even when mixed with sand, cement, and water. In so doing, it fills the voids left by the water when it evaporates, leaving the surface to which it has been applied sheathed with dense iron-cement that will withstand considerable pressure.

Before application of either type of coating is made, any hydrostatic pressure which exists should be relieved, either by pumping or by drainage. Holes made for this purpose may later be filled and finished. Sometimes a steel drum is placed below the level of the floor and the water is pumped out of it. When the waterproofing of the space has been completed, the drum itself is left in place and given a coating, and the floor is built over it.

Smooth surfaces which are to receive plaster coatings must first be roughened with cold chisels, bush hammers, or sandblasting so that a satisfactory bond will be secured. They should then be cleaned with scrubbing brushes, and rinsed until all traces of alien matter have disappeared. While the surface is wet, plaster coatings should then be floated on with a trowel. If two coats are to be applied, the second coat should go on while the initial set of the first coat is taking place. Coatings on inside walls are usually ½ or ⅝ in. thick, on floors 1 in. thick. Walls and floors should be done, insofar as possible, in one operation. The coatings will not absorb water, after the water with which they are made has evaporated.

Iron undercoats are put on with a brush. Enough time should elapse between two coats to allow for complete oxidation of the iron. The first coats are made of iron compound mixed with water, the final coat is iron mixed with water, cement, and sand, and it may be put on either with a brush or with a trowel. Since iron coatings are not suitable wearing surfaces, when they are used on floors they must be covered with 1 in. topping of cement.

It is generally preferable to use cement-base coating on the inside of buildings. If walls are subject to freezing temperatures, they may be furred and the coating put on the furring. Being rigid, plaster coats are subject to cracking. They should never cover expansion joints. Coatings on the inside are accessible for easy and economical repair, and they may be applied to various parts of the building as it goes up without interfering with the normal progress of the work.

NECESSITY FOR SUPERVISION

Too much emphasis cannot be placed on the necessity of consulting men who have made a special study of waterproofing. The success of any job will depend on the skill and experience of the men who supervise and do the work.

Mat foundations, roofs, walls

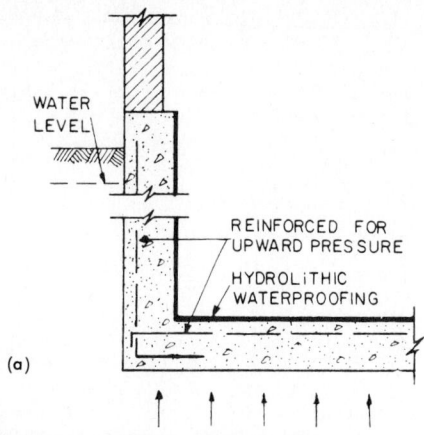

(a)

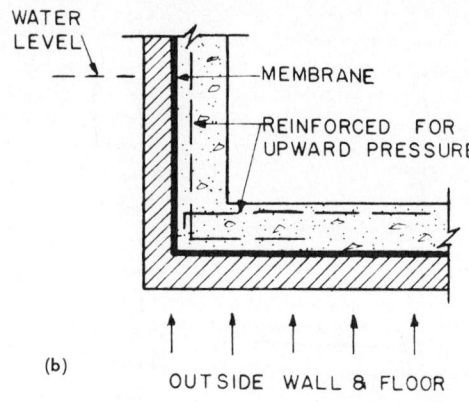

(b)

REINFORCED CONCRETE MAT OR RAFT

Reinforced concrete mats or rafts are floor slabs and walls designed to resist the head of water expected. They are usually waterproofed.

(a) Hydrolithic waterproofing consists of the application of coats of cement plaster containing iron filings or a similar type of waterproof plaster to the inside surfaces of the floors and walls.

(b) Membrane waterproofing consists of the application of two or more plies of asphalt and felt to the outside surfaces of the floors and walls. It thus has the disadvantage that secondary walls or floors must be provided for its application or protection and that a leak may be difficult to locate and repair.

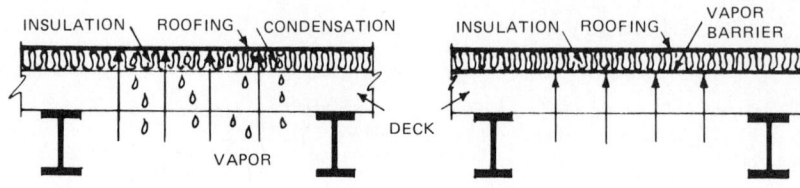

VAPOR BARRIERS

If the vapor barrier for a roof is applied underneath the insulation, the moist air coming up against it will meet a relatively warm surface and the moisture will not condense. If the vapor barrier is placed on top of the insulation, the moist air coming up against the cold surface of the roofing membrane will tend to condense and come back into the insulation as free water, with deleterious results.

WALL WATERPROOFING

Important considerations for obtaining waterproof walls:

(a) Thorough workmanship in laying the brick, full mortar beds, no voids, etc.

(b) Lime cement mortar, that is, ASTM C270-73. Type N or S.

(c) Reasonably porous face brick for bond.

(d) Parging back of face brick with mortar.

(e) Continuous spandrel flashing at floors.

(f) An independent free-standing furring.

(g) Coating back of wall with hot asphalt emulsion applied with a spray or trowel.

(h) Drips on all overhanging edges.

(i) Sills projecting beyond the jambs, not ending flush at jambs.

(j) Pointing of face with "weathered" or "concave" joints.

(k) Lintel flashings turned up at ends.

(l) Preformed bituminous waterproofing units may be built into the wall.

(m) Test-hosing water between furring and wall may be required as a test.

PARAPET WALL WATERPROOFING

Suggestions to obtain waterproof parapet walls:

(a) A through wall cap flashing to seal off and lead down the water in the upper part of the parapet.

(b) Shear anchorage of dowels or masonry offsets to prevent creeping, particularly under corners, of the parapet wall relative to the main wall—a common defect.

(c) Avoidance of sealing in the water in the parapet wall with a bituminous coating. It will cause the wall to freeze and scale off brick.

(d) Use of face brick or a hard burned brick in the rear of parapet walls.

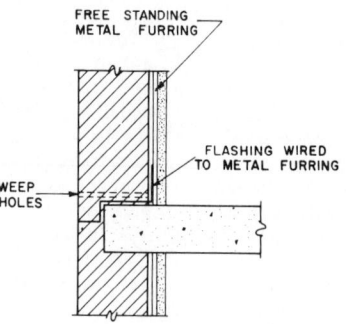

CORRECTION OF LEAKY WALLS

Driving rains may come through walls, even if flashings are correctly inserted. The use of silicones and acrylic solutions has proved disappointing because of their failure to bridge hairline cracks. Defective mortar joints are a more common cause than masonry porosity. Raking defective joints to a depth of ¾ in. and repointing them should suffice. Waterproofing solutions may help after joint repair.

The most difficult type of leak to control seems to be one where the water comes down in or on the inside face of the wall and reaches the floor, where it spreads out, staining the ceiling or wall below. Attempts to meet this with a spandrel flashing have not been entirely successful because of:

(a) Failure to provide weep holes in the wall to assist in draining the water out. (b) Failure to provide an adequate continuous water-tight gutter clear of mortar droppings to catch water coming down the inside face of the wall.

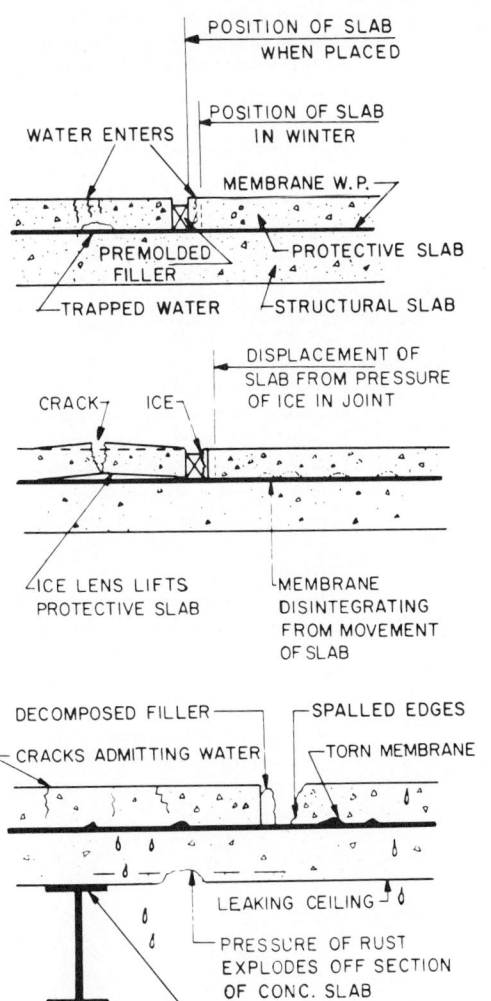

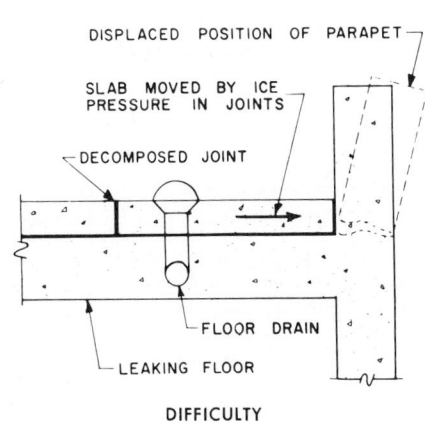

DIFFICULTY

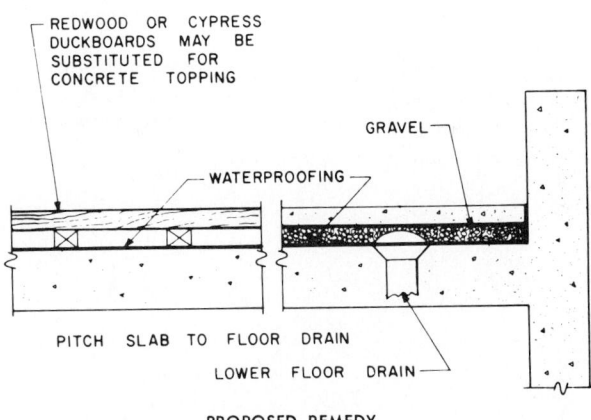

PROPOSED REMEDY

WATERPROOFING PAVED AREAS OVER OCCUPIED SPACES

The membrane is to be preferred for structures where the seepage is downward, such as sidewalk vault ceilings. The danger here is that the membrane which lies between the finished surface and the main supporting slab will trap water and cause the protective slab to freeze and heave, perhaps breaking the membrane.

To avoid this, drains must be installed at the membrane level and gravel or porous fill should be placed on top of the finished membrane before the finish surface is placed.

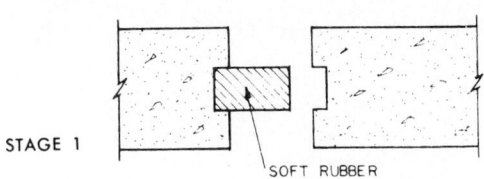

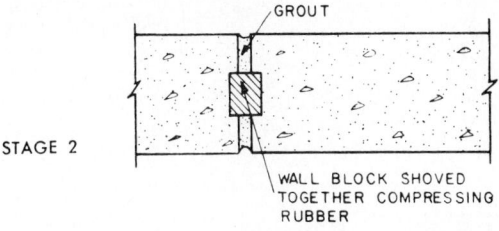

PRECAST MASONRY UNITS

Problems in connection with precast masonry units include:

The exposed concrete should be waterproofed with integral waterproofing to avoid wet diaper appearance after a rainstorm.

Horizontal joints should be tongue-and-grooved in such a way as to throw out the water coming down the surface.

Vertical joints must depend upon mastic or cement and, as there are considerable volumetric changes due to temperature and shrink-

age, an elastic mastic must be relied upon to caulk the joints. In recent years new sealants have been introduced that are far superior to the conventional oil-based compounds, which have a short life when exposed to sunlight and weather. Polysulfides, silicones, and urethanes are excellent for caulking glass, curtain walls, and masonry (see section on Curtain Walls). Vertical joints may be set with compressed live or foam rubber between them, as shown.

From HUD Minimum Property Standards, 1973 Edition, Revised 1975. *U.S. Department of Housing and Urban Development*

TERMITE PROTECTION

Provide protection against termites in those areas where they are determined to be a hazard. Methods of protection are divided into two types, chemical and physical barriers. With the exception of treated lumber, all barriers shown are effective only for subterranean termites. Where damp-wood, drywood, and Formosan termites present a hazard, additional precautions, must be taken.

Physical barriers

Acceptable physical barriers are as follows:

1. Concrete foundations, free of cracks and porous areas, for basement and crawl space types of construction except where masonry or masonry veneer walls extend below top of foundation wall and are less than 8 in. above finish grade.
2. Monolithic framed concrete slab, reinforced with at least 6 × 6 10/10 wwf in areas where winter design temperature exceeds +15°F, extending from wall to wall without openings or joints. Piping, ductwork, and other penetration of slab shall be thoroughly sealed with coal tar pitch. Interior and exterior sill plates in contact with the concrete slab shall be treated wood or foundation grade Redwood.
3. Foundations caps of cast-in-place con-

crete, not less than 4-in. thick, reinforced with two No. 3 bars. Cap shall be placed continuously on top of all unit masonry foundations and piers and shall be the full width of wall, extending through voids in masonry veneer or faced masonry walls.

Chemical barriers

Chemical barriers consist of soil poisoning and pressure treated lumber.

Soil poisoning: When soil poisoning is used, the rate of application of the approved chemicals should be not less than that recommended by the U.S. Department of Agriculture publication "Subterranean Termites," Home and Garden Bulletin No. 64. Soil should not be treated when excessively wet or immediately after heavy rains, in order to avoid movement of the toxicant from the site. Unless the treated areas are to be immediately covered, precautions shall be taken to prevent disturbance of the treatment. Chemical soil treatment should not be used where there is a possibility of contamination of a water source or supply.

Pressure treated lumber: Lumber or plywood treated for protection against termite infestation should be labeled with a permanent mark, indicating conformance with the applicable standard, and the information required by the standard shall appear on the label. The label shall be an approved quality-mark of an independent inspection agency.

When treated lumber is used, the members to be treated are:

1. Frame construction. Basement or crawl space: sill plate, joists, header joists, girders, columns, sole plate, subfloor and wood sheathing below the level of the first floor. Sheathing shall be treated wood, treated plywood or noncellulosic material.
2. Frame construction. Slab-on-ground other than monolithic: partitions, sole plate, studs, top plate, blocking and wood sheathing, but not siding. Sheathing shall be treated wood, treated plywood or noncellulosic material. In two-story structures, treat as above up to bottom of second floor joists.
3. Masonry veneer construction. Treat as 1 and 2 as applicable.
4. Masonry wall construction. Basement or crawl space: joists, girders, columns, and subfloor below first floor line. Above first floor: all wood, except millwork, in contact with or framing into exterior wall, but not including ceiling and roof construction.
5. Masonry wall construction. Slab-on-ground, all wood, except millwork in contact with or framing into exterior wall, but not including ceiling and roof construction; all wood partitions including studs, plates and blocking, up to ceiling construction in one-story structures and to second floor construction in two-story structures.

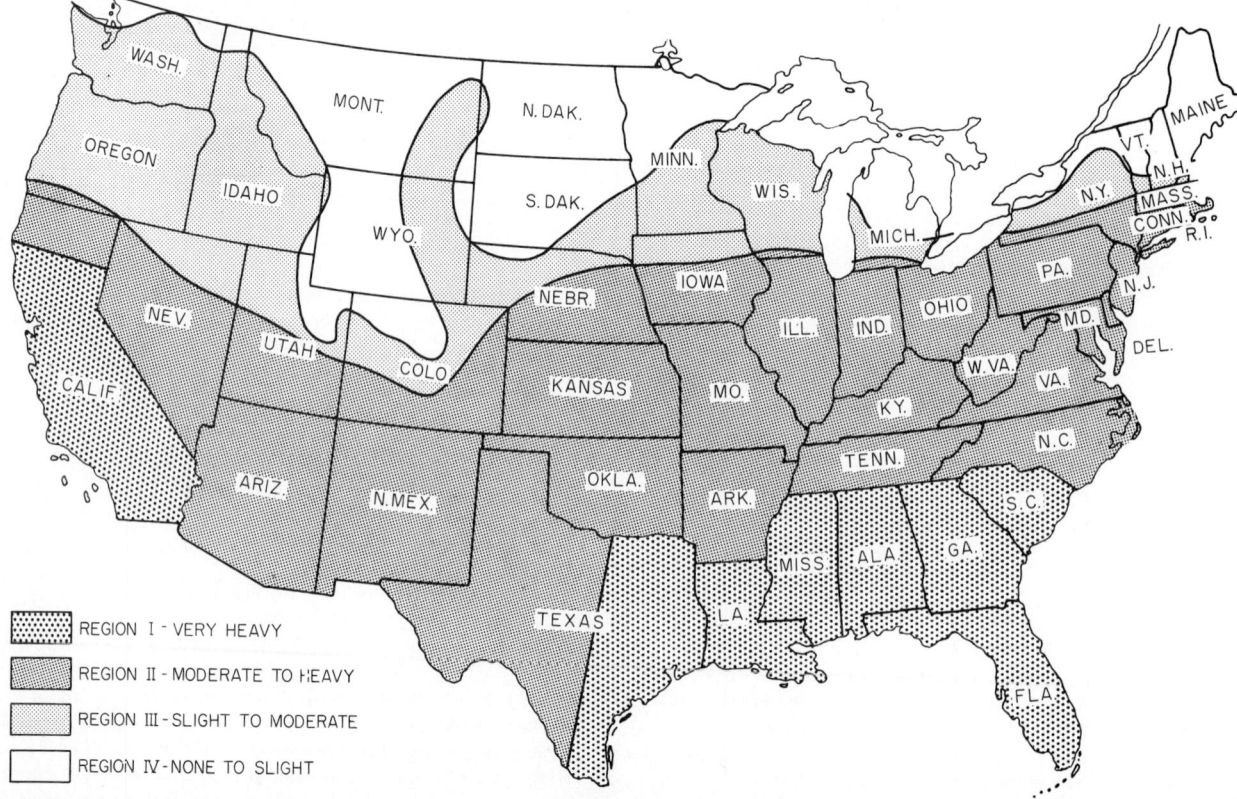

REGION I - VERY HEAVY

REGION II - MODERATE TO HEAVY

REGION III - SLIGHT TO MODERATE

REGION IV - NONE TO SLIGHT

Geographic distribution of termite infestation

From a study by the Building Research Advisory Board

In addition to protective measures, periodic inspection is necessary.

The protective measures assume complicance with the following general standards of good construction, all of which have as their purpose the reduction of moisture in the soil and in the building, thereby reducing the likelihood that wood will rot and thus furnish food for termites.

1. Adequate drainage for the site and building
2. Minimum clearance (8 in.) between ground and wood
3. Adequate ventilation of structural spaces
4. Proper flashing
5. Installation of vapor barriers and sheathing papers where required
6. Removal of all stumps, roots, wood scraps, etc., from the building site

The map shown on the previous page gives the approximate degree of hazard to be expected from termites in different parts of the country. Local distribution may be spotty and a given site may be more or less hazardous than indicated by the map. Protection is required in all cases in Region I and in most cases in Region II. Protection is usually not required in Region III and never in Region IV.

Although HUD requirements no longer mention metal shields among physical barriers, it is believed that this form of protection will continue to be used by many architects, especially in areas of heavy termite infestation. The following data on metal shields has been furnished by the Copper Development Association. Metals other than copper can be used, of course, but the application details would be the same.

Termites require damp, rotting wood, and will carry in moisture and fungi to rot sound wood so they can feed on it. This requires a constant source of moisture, usually obtained from the soil. Entrance to unprotected structures is gained through cracks in concrete or masonry foundations or walls, through the wood portion of the house frame, or by building tunnel-like structures called shelter tubes over foundation posts and walls.

Properly installed shields will not only prevent termites from invading the wooden portion of the structure but will also act as an effective moisture barrier.

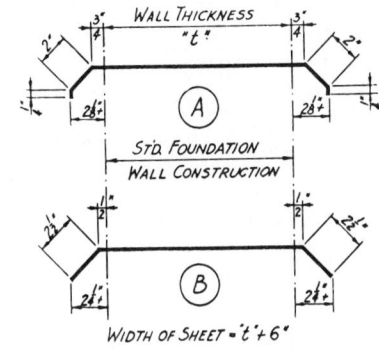

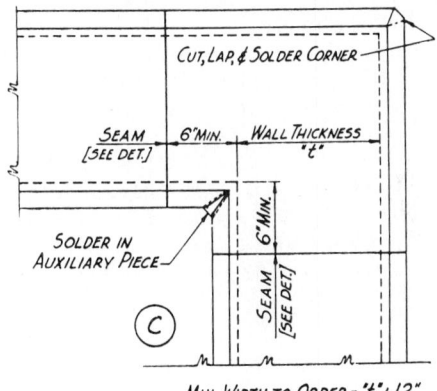

Drawings above and below show details for using cold rolled copper sheet

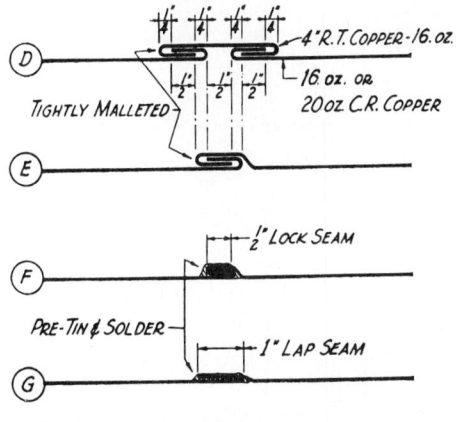

FIGURE 1

BARRIER SHIELD In installations where inspection of the shield is impossible, a barrier type is required. It is designed so that termites building up over the stone or concrete foundations are blocked from entry into the woodwork of the house above by the projection of the shield. Two basic barrier type shields are shown in A and B of *Figure 1*.

The A type with a vertical turn-down edge is preferable, but the B type is also satisfactory and under some conditions easier to apply. The sharp edge of the metal, either vertical or at 45°, provides a 180° angle around which the termites are unable to construct a shelter tube. (A shelter tube is a tunnel-like structure

built by termites over foundation walls and posts through which they can bring fungi and moisture to dry wood.) Some shield designs have a rolled edge, but they are not recommended because shelter tubes might be built around the roll.

At corners, as in standard types of through-wall flashing, it is better to use a specially formed piece as in C than to have a diagonal seam across the corner. Four types of cross seams are shown at D, E, F, and G. Types D and E should be tightly malleted. When the soldered types (F or G) are used, the edge of the sheets should be pre-tinned to ensure a solid joint. Any loose joint provides access for termites to enter the structure.

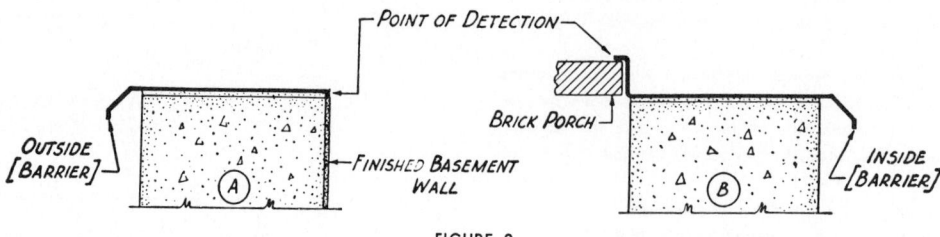

FIGURE 2

DEFLECTOR SHIELD This shield, illustrated in *Figure 3b,* does not in itself provide an impossible barrier to the termites. It is employed only in areas accessible for periodic inspections, such as the interior wall of a basement recreation room, or on the outside of a brick porch.

Termites building a shelter tube from the ground moisture to house woodwork are forced to move out around the shield as indicated at the "point of detection" *(Figure 2).* The shelter tube, exposed at this point, can be easily broken off and the termites that have gained access to the building are cut off from their essential moisture. This simple procedure, repeated several times, apparently discourages the tube-building termites.

VENTILATION Termites in a building isolated by shields generally make a strong effort to restore contact with ground moisture. If a shallow, unexcavated area is available they have been known to connect a joist to the ground by means of a shelter tube. Proper ventilation however, should defeat such attempts. Under moist conditions, lengthy shelter tubes can be formed, but under dry conditions the tubes have the consistency of sand and tend to crumble and collapse.

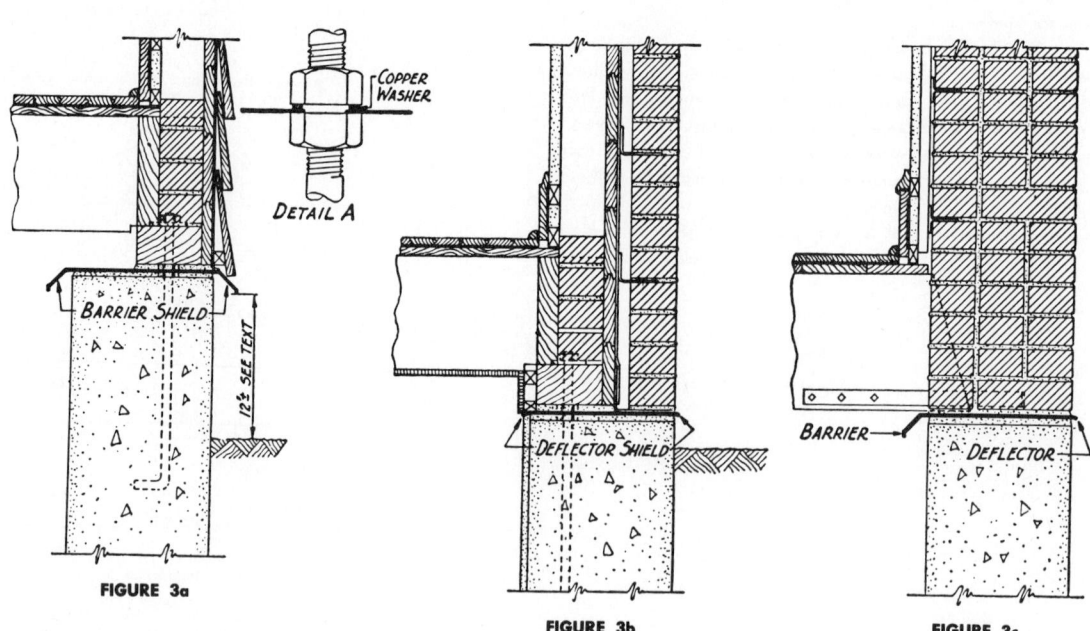

FIGURE 3a

FIGURE 3b

FIGURE 3c

TYPICAL FOUNDATION WALLS *Figure 3a* shows the foundation wall installation of a shield for a frame house. Here a barrier type is necessary. With veneer construction, as shown in *Figure 3b,* a deflector shield is generally satisfactory. Similarly, a deflector shield generally is used in solid masonry construction, *Figure 3c,* although in this illustration the interior has been assumed to be inaccessible for periodic inspection; therefore, a barrier shield is shown installed on the inside.

In the southern part of the United States the shield should be from 12 to 18 in. above ground level; in the northern part, from 9 to 15 in. is usually sufficient. The degree of local infestation also must be considered in determining proper clearance.

When there is objection to the line of shielding shown on the outside of the house it often can be camouflaged with shrubbery, or a modification of a true barrier type can be employed. This design, of course, will demand periodic inspections to discover if any termite shelter tubes have been built and care should be taken that shrubbery does not provide a by-pass of the shield.

Detail A *(Fig. 3a)* shows how an anchor-bolt penetrating the shield is made termite-proof. Instead of the washer as shown, special nuts with grooves may be used. In either case, the two should be drawn so tightly that termites can't squeeze through.

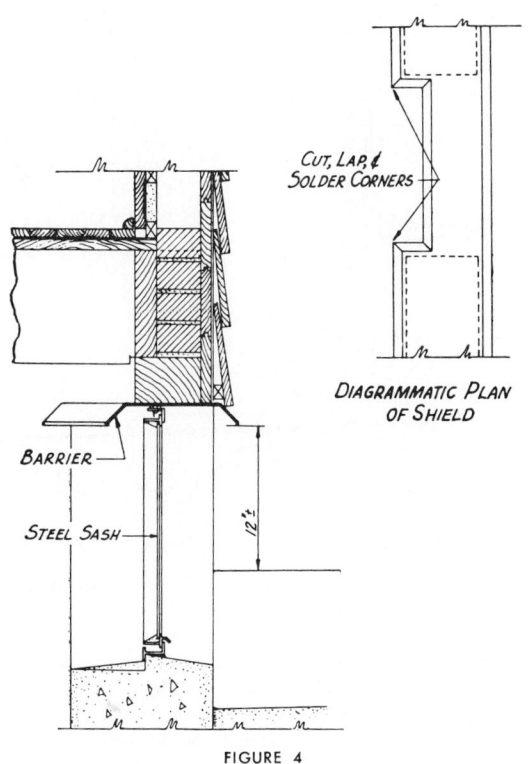

FIGURE 4

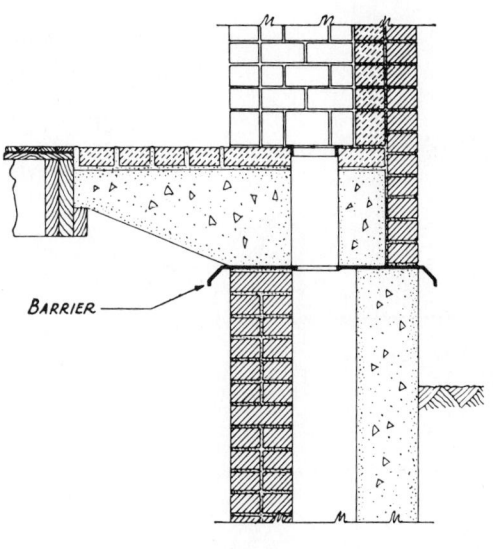

FIGURE 5

TYPICAL CELLAR WINDOW *Figure 4* shows a detail of shielding construction at a typical cellar window. As the window itself is below the level of the shield, to secure complete protection the window should be a metal one. When the window is above the ground level, a shield beneath the window will give ample protection.

FIREPLACE *Figure 5* shows a fireplace protected by a barrier shield over the foundation wall. The ash-dump is above the shield and the ash-flue below. Utmost caution should be exercised in the installation of the termite shield under the fireplace. The seal should be tight and permanent. Termites can squeeze through the narrowest of crevices.

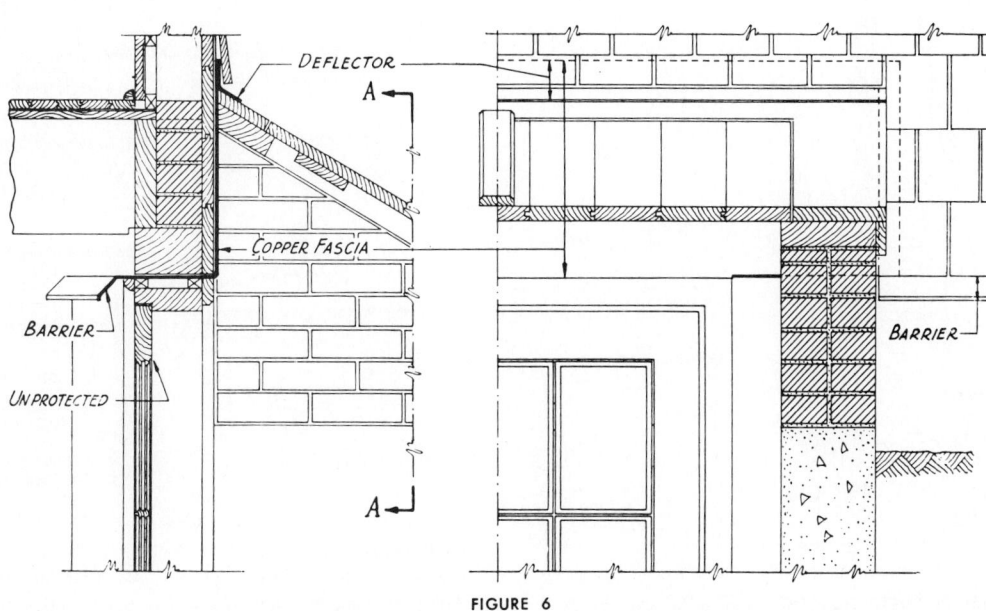

FIGURE 6

CELLAR HATCHWAY *Figure 6* shows a typical cellar hatchway installation. Note that this application combines barrier with partial deflector type shields, because where the shield extends vertically it is conceivable that shelter tubes might be built around it. The combination of shields, plus inspection, will ensure protection of the building. In this example the door shown is of wood construction and it is located beneath the protection of the shield. To be termite-proof the door and frame (unless treated) should be metal.

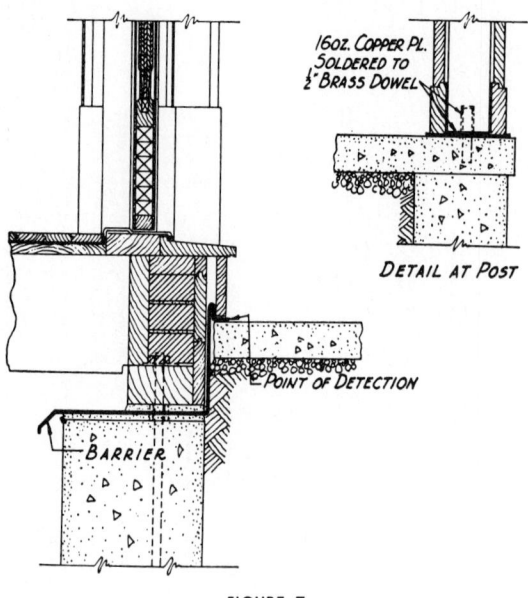

FIGURE 7

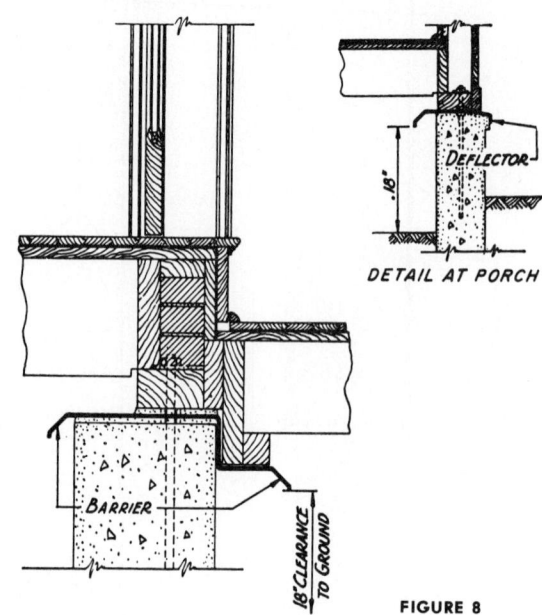

FIGURE 8

DOOR SILL *Figure 7* shows another combination shield applied under a door sill adjoining a concrete (or brick) porch. A deflector type is used on the outside because of ease of inspection, while the inner one is a true barrier type. Note that the shield is bent up behind the kickboard to form a water stop. The detail at the upper right illustrates a deflector shield inserted under a wood post resting on a concrete (or brick) porch.

PORCHES *Figure 8* shows shielding applied at a house wall adjoining a porch of wood construction. A barrier shield is necessary throughout, particularly as the area under the porch is rarely easy to inspect. This area should also be well ventilated. The detail at the upper right shows a shield at the outside of the porch. When exposed, a deflector shield can be employed as illustrated, otherwise a barrier type should be used.

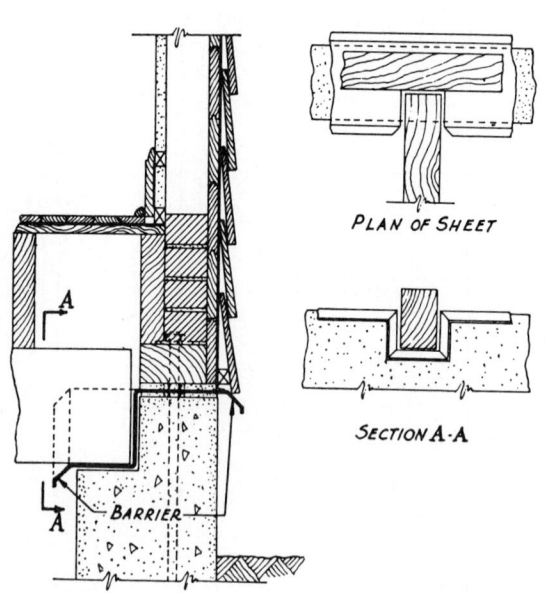

FIGURE 9

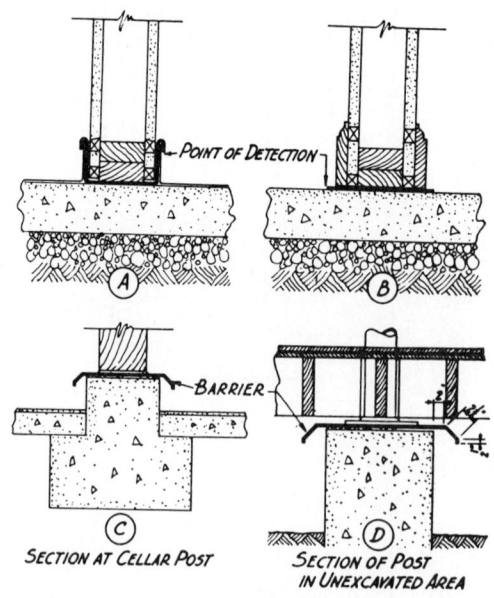

FIGURE 10

CELLAR BEAM POCKETS *Figure 9* shows a barrier shield installed at a cellar beam pocket. In this application the shield must be cut, fitted and soldered to meet the dimensional specifications of the beam, thickness of wall, etc. If a bolt is inserted through the termite shield, extreme care must be taken to assure an absolutely tight joint.

PARTITIONS *Figure 10* shows shield details for cellar partitions and other miscellaneous areas. A and B illustrate methods of deflector shield installations between a cellar floor and a cellar partition. Similar applications can be made between a partition and a cellar side wall. Inspection for shelter tubes should be made regularly.

The barrier shield shown in detail C protects the cellar post. Detail D is self-explanatory.

Information on this and the following page was collected and prepared by Ronald Allwork from publications of the British Building Research Station, the Copper Development Association, and the National Association of Sheet Metal Contractors.

MOISTURE PENETRATION

Moisture penetrates masonry walls because of (1) the porous nature of the wall material or (2) the opening up of joints as a result of expansion and contraction. The depth to which moisture penetrates cannot be precisely determined; it averages about 4½ in. but under severe conditions may be as much as 9 in. (These figures do not apply to walls subject to continuous or prolonged wetting.) The diagrams on the following page show possible courses of penetration for typical walls. Note that the points of final penetration (designated by the circles) often occur immediately after the water has encountered a change of material in its downward course.

Parapet walls are exposed to weather on both sides and on top. Because few forms of construction will withstand such exposure, particularly penetration from the top, the coping is of first importance.

Copings provide greater protection for walls if they are (1) made of a material of low permeability and good frost resistance, (2) given an overhang and provided with a drip, (3) designed to shed water in the direction of the roof, and (4) provided with saddle-back (or similar) joints.

DESIGN OF WALL FLASHINGS

1. Consider the effective life of a flashing material in relation to the life of the wall.
2. Bear in mind the corrosion factor of the flashing material due to (a) local atmospheric conditions and (b) contact with wall materials.
3. Investigate the suitability of the flashing material from the standpoint of (a) tensile strength to withstand perforation, (b) flexibility to conform to the mortar bed, and (c) resistance to squeezing out because of the weight of the wall.
4. Study the location of flashings to provide for the diversion of water to the exterior surface of the wall at its vulnerable points.
5. Provide for the stability of the masonry above through-wall flashings by the use of dowels, keying, steps, or other means.

TYPES OF FLASHINGS

Sheet metal, metal-and-paper, and fabric (or membrane) flashings are available either as basic sheet materials, from which flashings are job-fabricated, or as preformed flashings. Most preformed flashings are patented types offered under various trade names. Fabric flashings are also available with integral reinforcing, and both metal and fabric types can be obtained in special shapes (or with other special provisions) for maintaining an effective masonry bond.

COPPER FLASHING

Temper: Cold-rolled (cornice-temper) copper should be used for all flashings, whether exposed or concealed. Because of its greater strength, cold-rolled copper is better able to resist the thermal and other stresses to which flashings may be subjected than is soft (roofing-temper) copper.

Weight: Where flashings are fully exposed and subject to severe stresses, as in copings and gravel stops, use 20-oz copper. Through-wall flashings partly exposed should be 16-oz; under stone belt-courses and sills, 20-oz. Fully concealed through-wall flashings may be 10 oz. Spandrel flashing may be a 6-oz sheet, or a membrane consisting of 3-oz copper on reinforced kraft paper. This membrane is also suitable for flashing around door and window openings. With slate or tile roofs, open valley flashings should be 20 oz and closed valley flashings 24 oz. For all other flashings, use 16 oz. (For the thicknesses of copper sheets of various weights, see "Architectural Metals," Sheet 8.)

Expansion: Continuous runs of any type of metal flashing must be provided with expansion joints spaced not more than 30 ft apart. A loose-locked joint filled with elastic cement or white lead is generally used for this purpose.

Fastenings: All nails and screws used with copper flashing must be copper or copper alloy. Flashings more than 12 in. wide should be secured by 2-in. cleats of 16-oz copper spaced 12 in. on centers.

Lead-coated copper may be used for flashings adjacent to light-colored stone or white-painted wood which might be stained by the weathering of bare copper.

Other metals, such as galvanized or aluminum-clad steel, aluminum, stainless steel, lead, and monel, may also be used for flashing. Installation details are generally similar to those shown here for copper flashing.

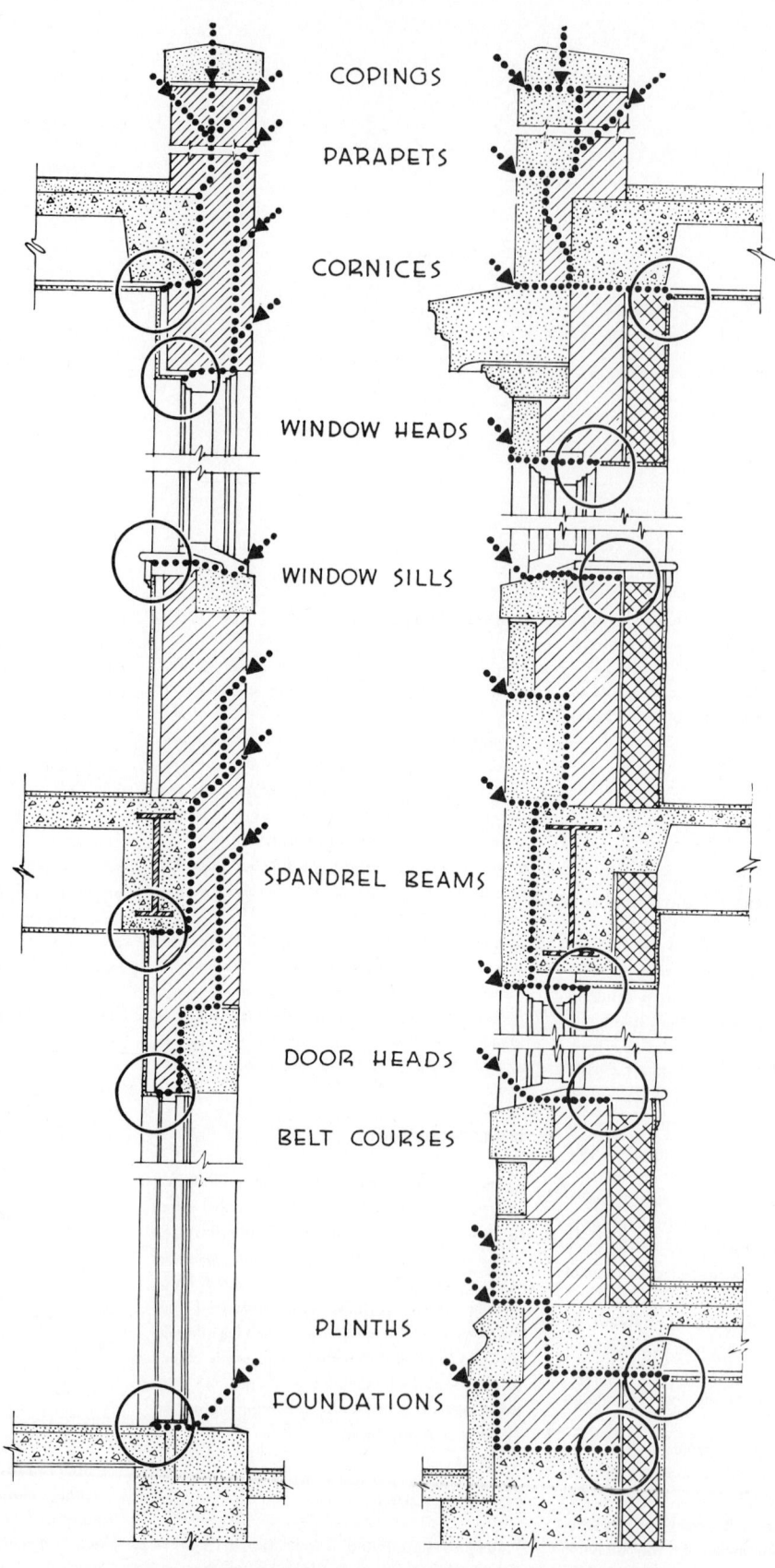

COPINGS

PARAPETS

CORNICES

WINDOW HEADS

WINDOW SILLS

SPANDREL BEAMS

DOOR HEADS

BELT COURSES

PLINTHS

FOUNDATIONS

Moisture penetration of multistory masonry walls

Data from Modern Applications of Sheet Copper in Building Construction, Copper Development Association, Inc.

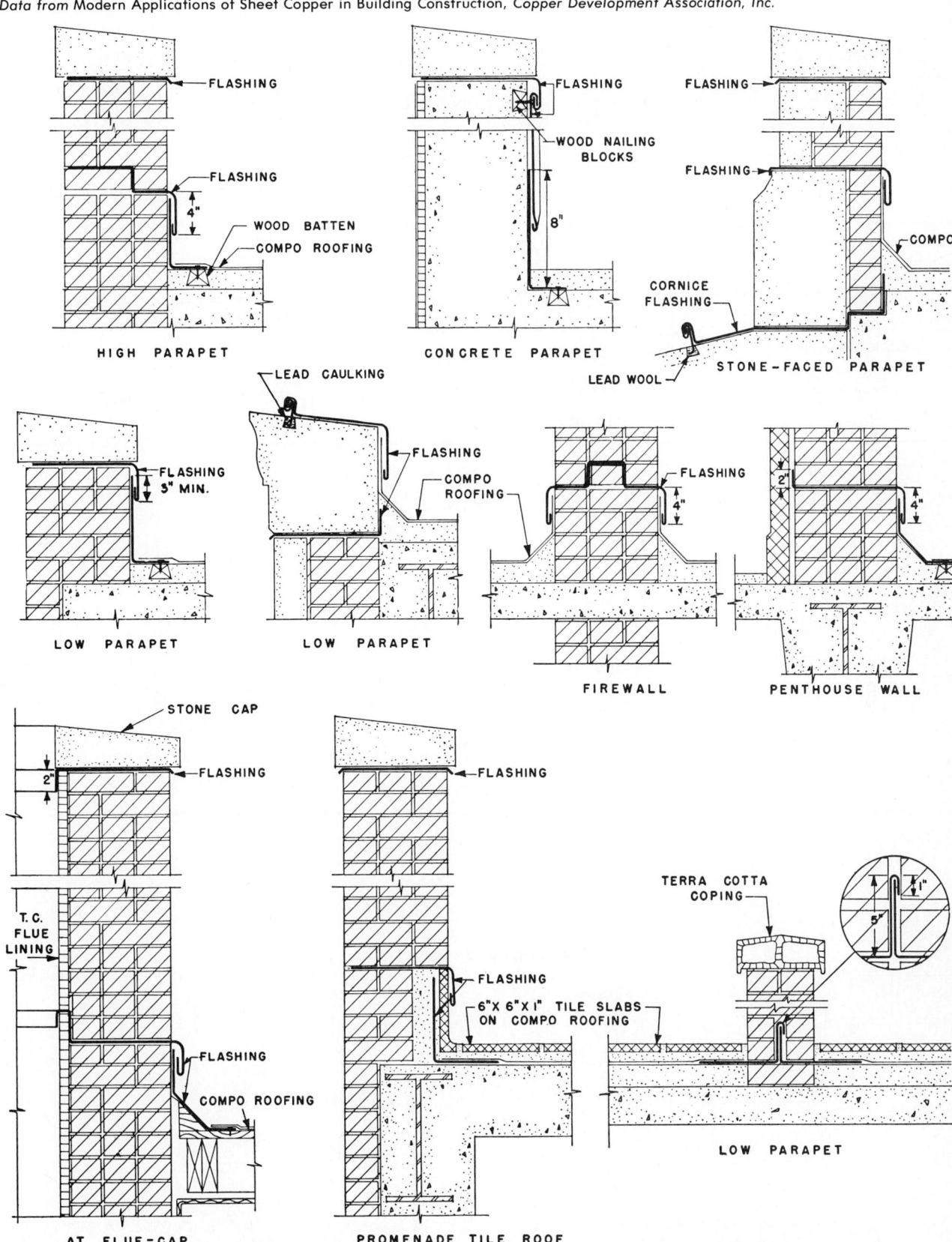

Flashing for walls and parapets

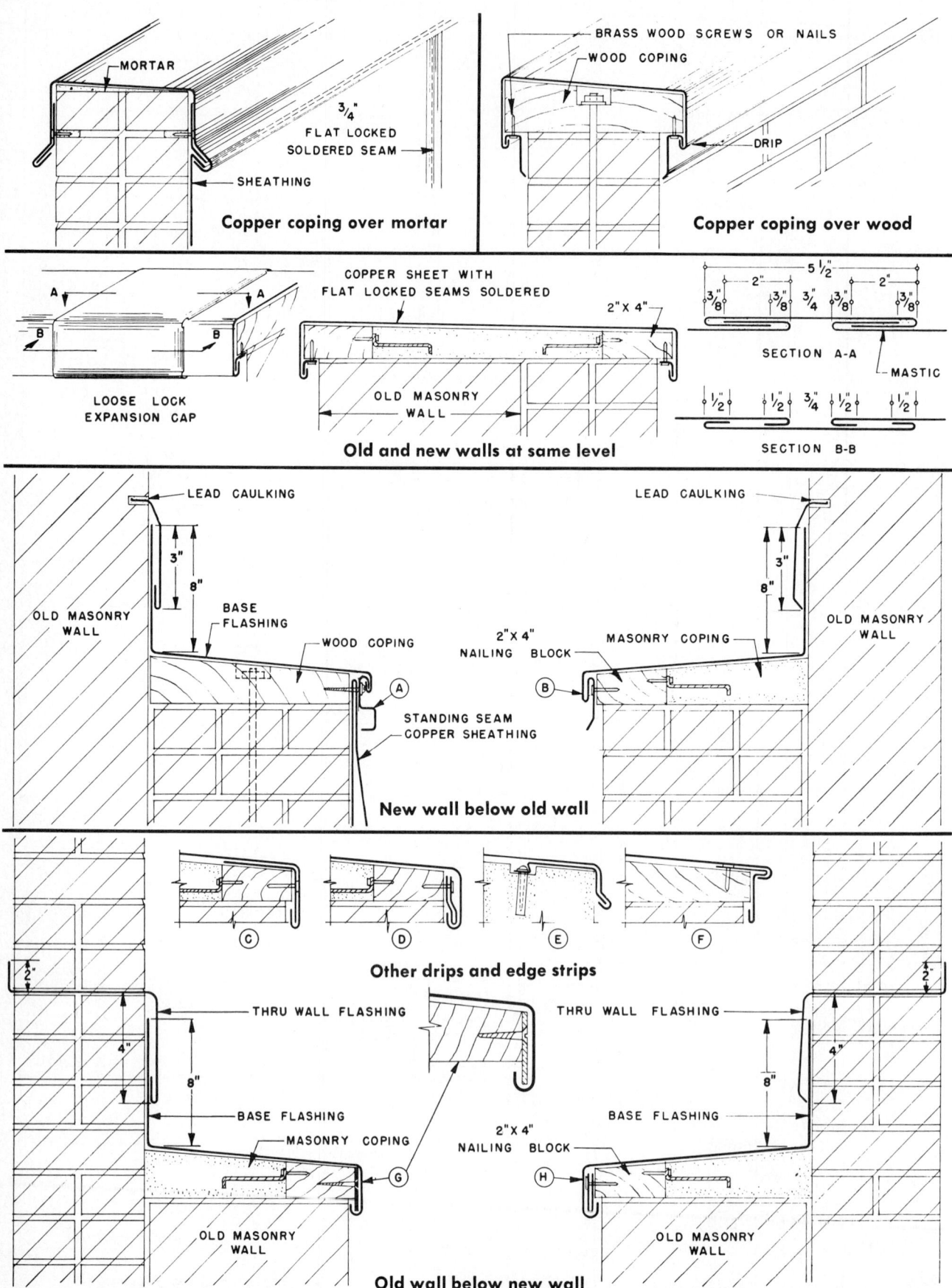

Copper coping over mortar

Copper coping over wood

Old and new walls at same level

New wall below old wall

Other drips and edge strips

Old wall below new wall

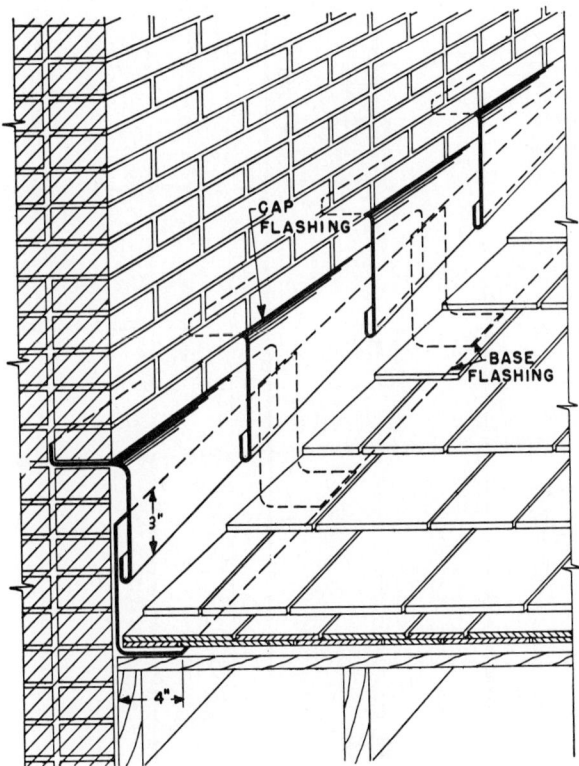

Side wall flashing, shingle roof against brick

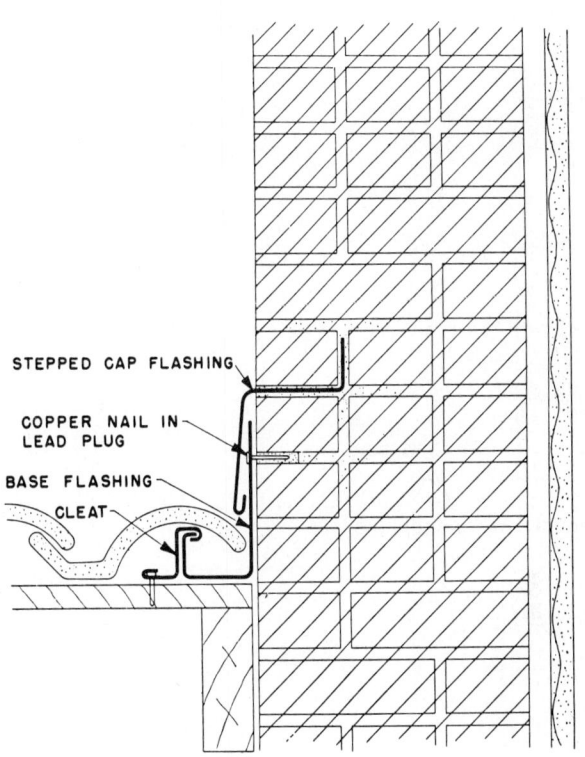

Side wall flashing, tile roof against brick

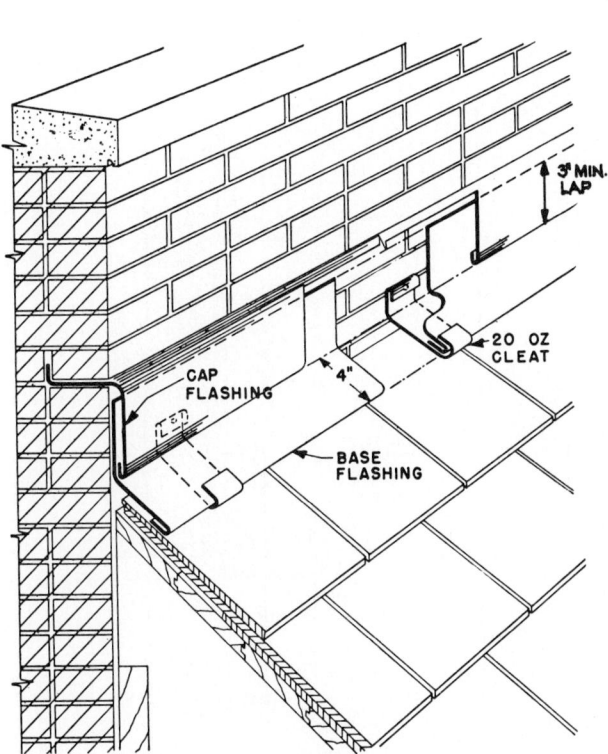

Head wall flashing, shingle roof against brick

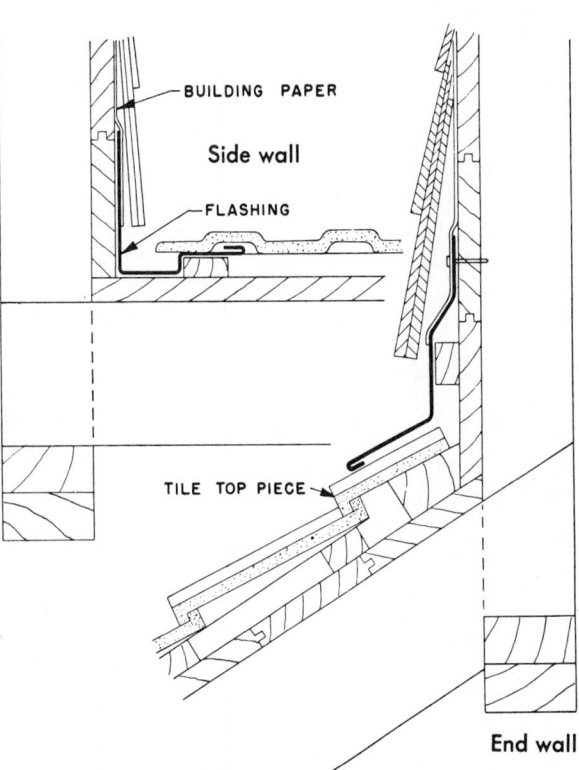

Head wall flashing, tile roof against frame

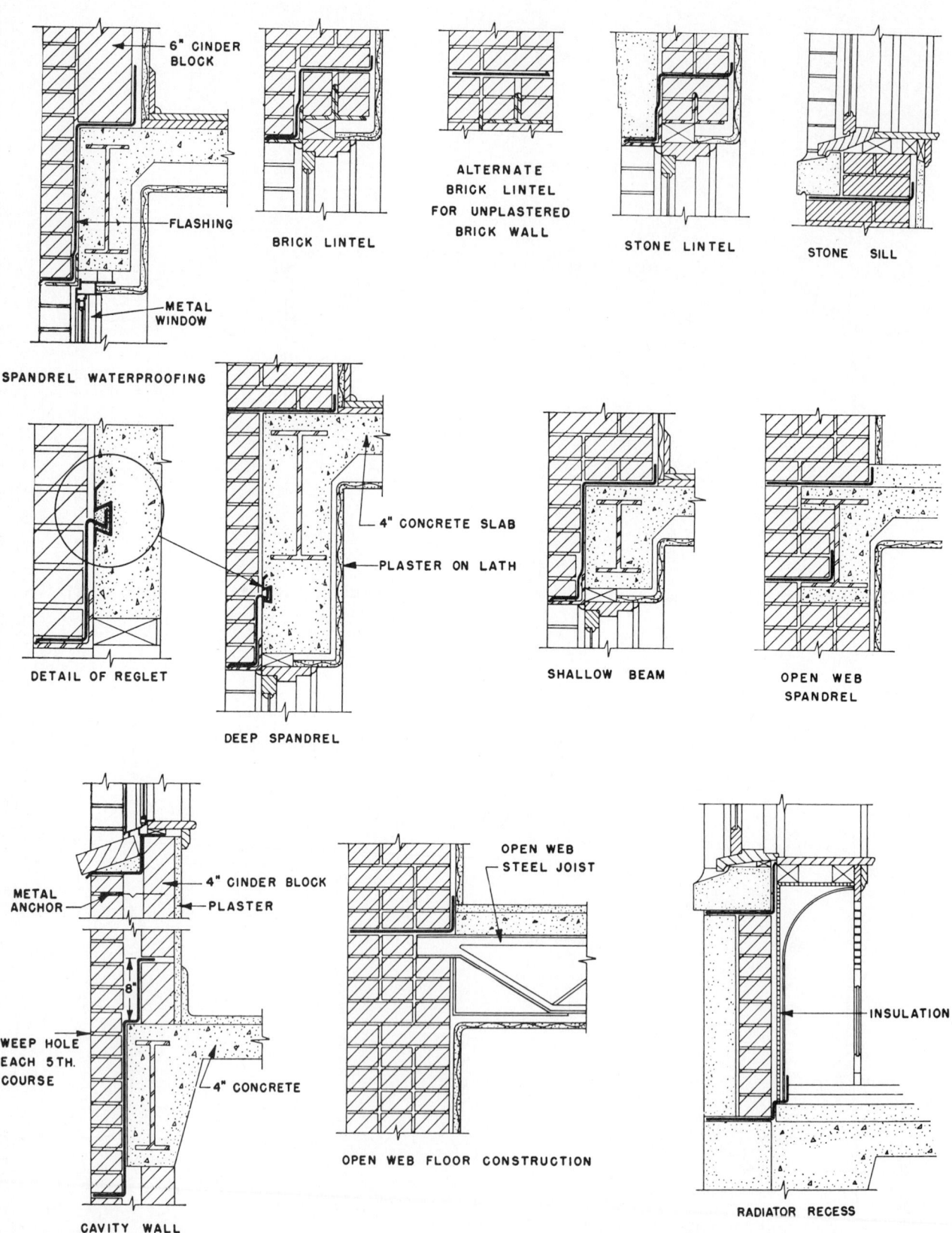

6" CINDER BLOCK

FLASHING

METAL WINDOW

SPANDREL WATERPROOFING

BRICK LINTEL

ALTERNATE BRICK LINTEL FOR UNPLASTERED BRICK WALL

STONE LINTEL

STONE SILL

DETAIL OF REGLET

DEEP SPANDREL

4" CONCRETE SLAB

PLASTER ON LATH

SHALLOW BEAM

OPEN WEB SPANDREL

METAL ANCHOR

4" CINDER BLOCK

PLASTER

8"

WEEP HOLE EACH 5TH. COURSE

4" CONCRETE

CAVITY WALL CONSTRUCTION

OPEN WEB STEEL JOIST

OPEN WEB FLOOR CONSTRUCTION

INSULATION

RADIATOR RECESS

Flashing for spandrels and windows

Wood-frame construction

Brick veneer on wood frame

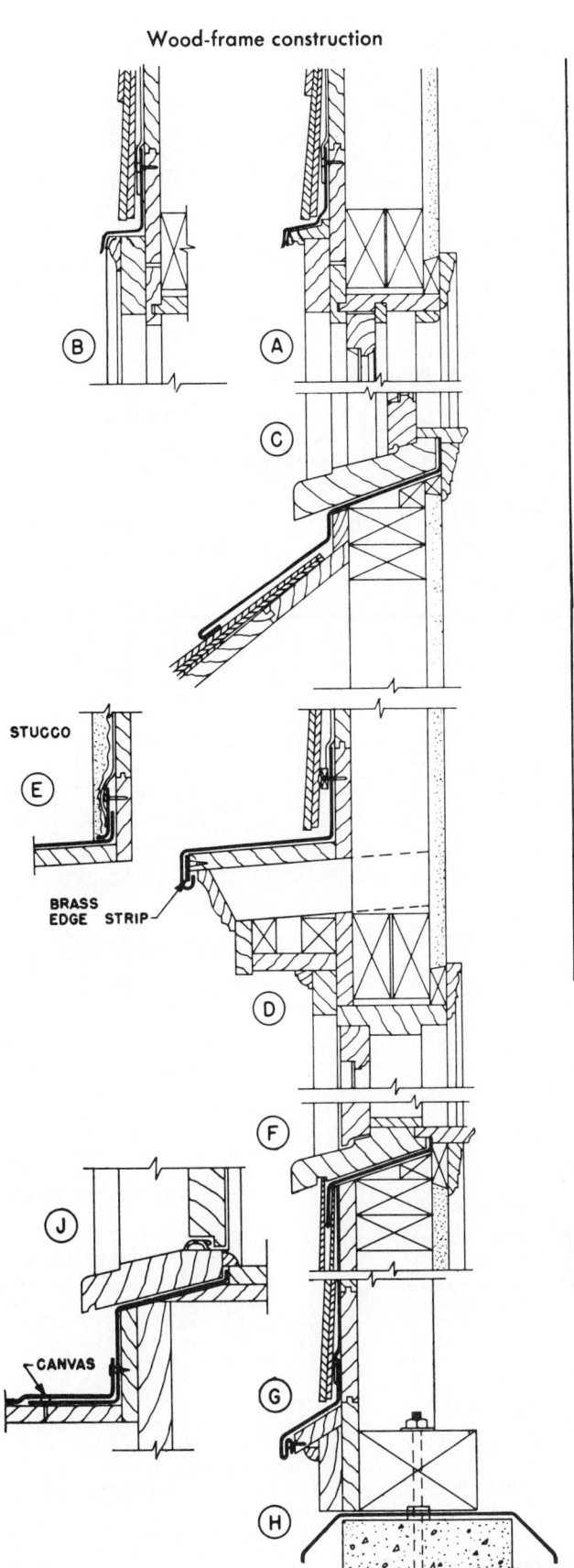

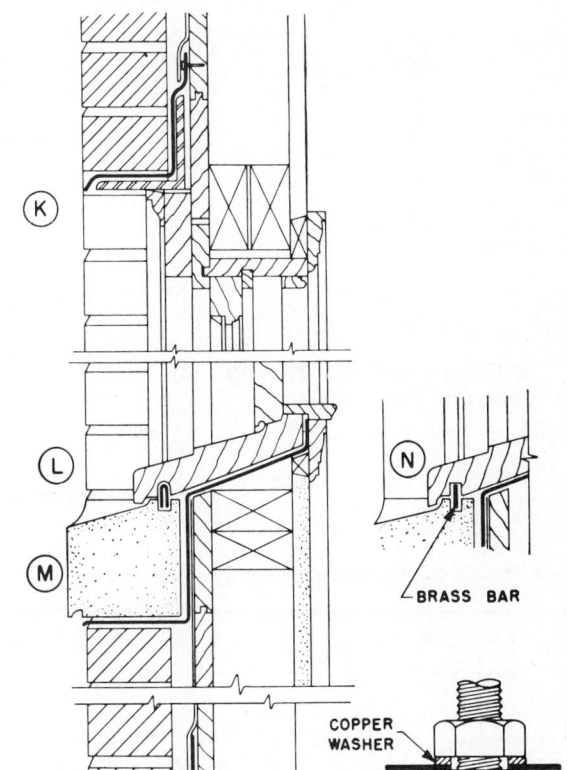

BRASS BAR

COPPER WASHER

STUCCO

BRASS EDGE STRIP

CANVAS

A — CASING FLASHING - DRIP CAP
B — CASING FLASHING - MOLDING
C — DORMER SILL FLASHING
D — WINDOW HEAD CORNICE - SHINGLES
E — WINDOW HEAD CORNICE - STUCCO
F — CASEMENT WINDOW SILL FLASHING - HIDDEN
G — WATER TABLE FLASHING
H — TERMITE SHIELD ON FOUNDATION WALL
J — DOOR SILL ABOVE CANVAS DECK
K — WINDOW HEAD FLASHING
L — WATER BAR - COPPER
M — WINDOW SILL FLASHING
N — ALTERNATE WATER BAR - BRASS
O — WATER TABLE FLASHING
P — TERMITE SHIELD
Q — ANCHOR BOLT FLASHING

Flashing for window and sill

Gravel stops; doorheads

Gravel stops

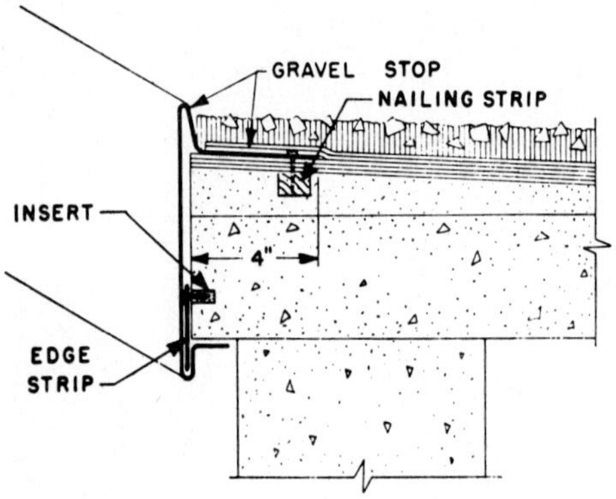

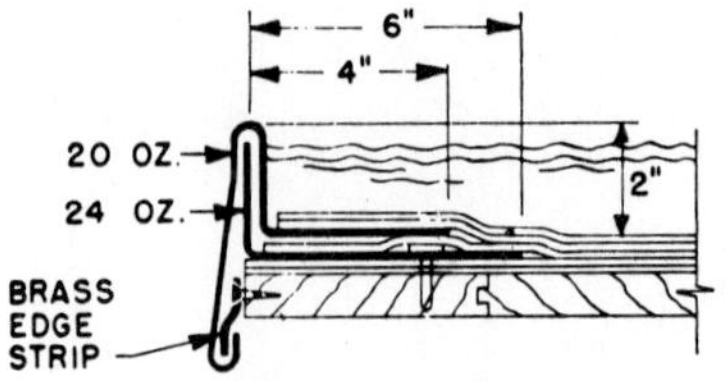

GRAVEL STOP
NAILING STRIP
INSERT
4"
EDGE STRIP

Built-up roofing (sloping) on concrete slab

6"
4"
20 OZ.
24 OZ.
2"
BRASS EDGE STRIP

Dam for roof pond

4"
BRASS EDGE STRIP

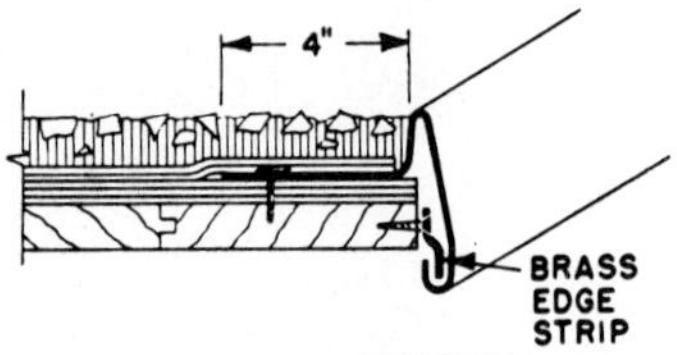

Built-up roofing (level) on wood

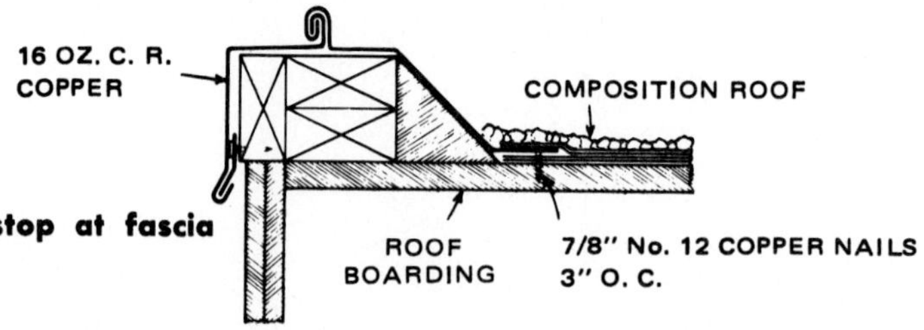

16 OZ. C. R. COPPER
COMPOSITION ROOF
ROOF BOARDING
7/8" No. 12 COPPER NAILS 3" O. C.

Set back gravel stop at fascia board

(For extruded aluminum gravel stops, see Sheet 12.)

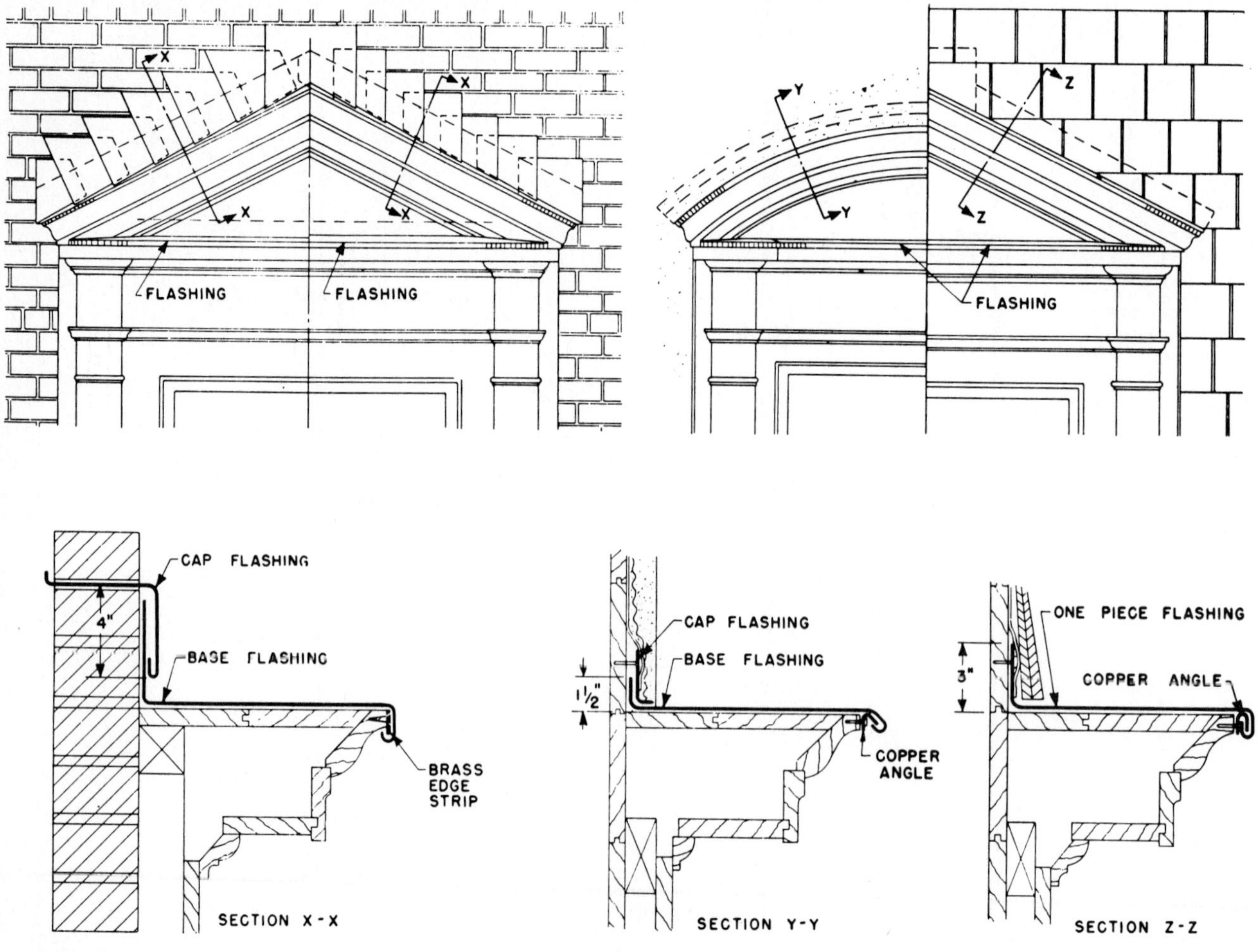

X
X
X
X
FLASHING
FLASHING
Y
Y
Z
Z
FLASHING
CAP FLASHING
4"
BASE FLASHING
BRASS EDGE STRIP
SECTION X-X
CAP FLASHING
BASE FLASHING
1½"
COPPER ANGLE
SECTION Y-Y
ONE PIECE FLASHING
3"
COPPER ANGLE
SECTION Z-Z

Flashing for doorheads

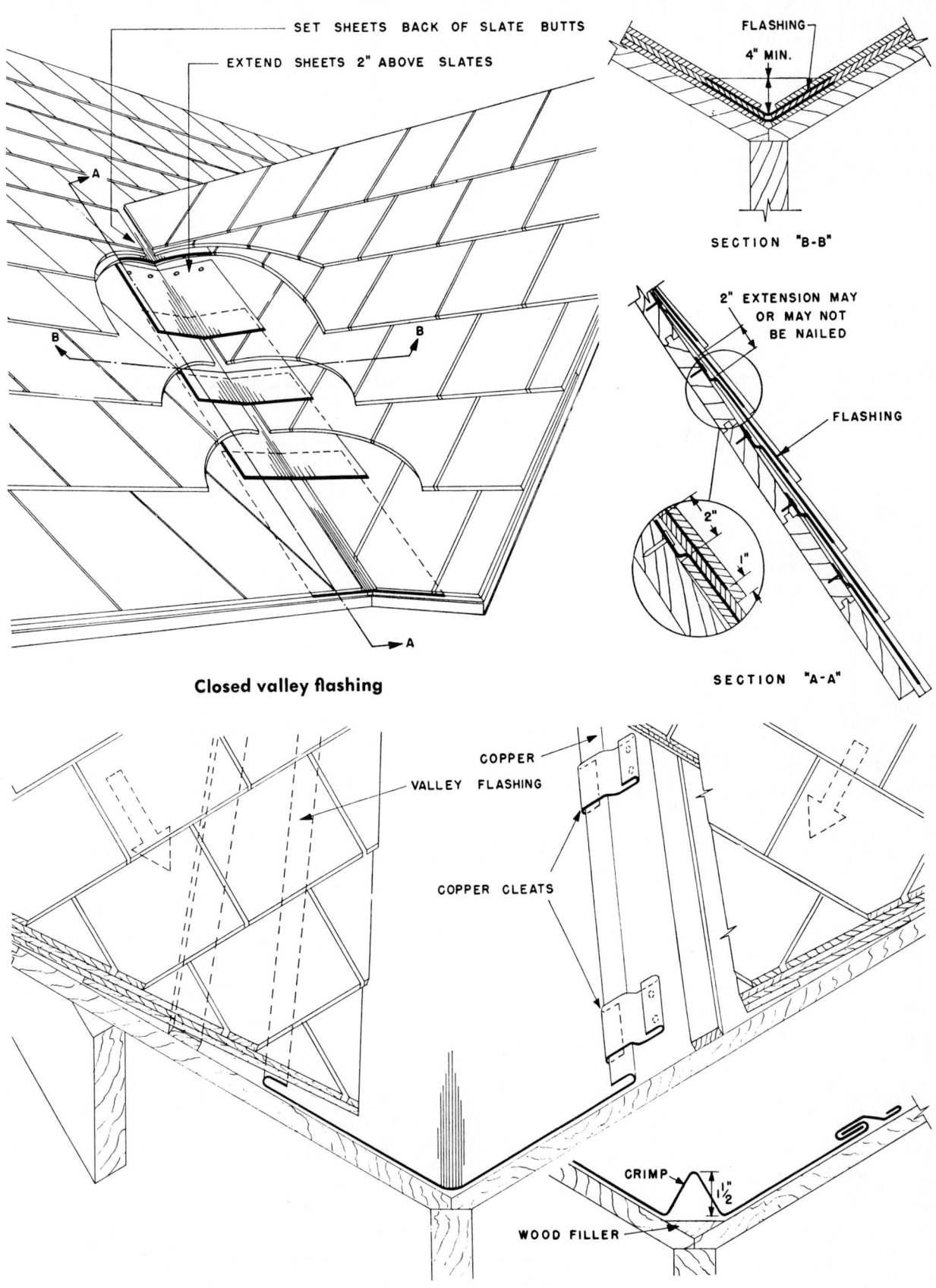

SET SHEETS BACK OF SLATE BUTTS

EXTEND SHEETS 2" ABOVE SLATES

FLASHING

4" MIN.

SECTION "B-B"

2" EXTENSION MAY OR MAY NOT BE NAILED

FLASHING

2"

1"

SECTION "A-A"

Closed valley flashing

COPPER

VALLEY FLASHING

COPPER CLEATS

CRIMP

1½"

WOOD FILLER

Open valley flashing

When two roof slopes deliver unequal amounts of water to a valley, the larger amount may force the smaller amount to back up and overflow the top of the flashing. To prevent this backup, a 1½-in. crimp is formed in the copper at the bottom of the valley, as shown in the detail.

VENT FLASHING

In tile roofs, flashing of a vent pipe is essentially the same as for a shingle roof. For built-up roofing, horizontal flashing should extend on the roof 6 in. in all directions. It must be placed on several layers of felt and covered with at least two layers.

On shingle or slate roofs, the lower edge of the base flashing has to overlap the shingles at least 4 in., whereas the sides and top normally extend 6 in. and are placed under the shingles. The edges of the flashing to the side are folded over ½ in. to prevent water from driving under the shingles. If the flashing is 12 in. or more in width, the lower edge should be turned back on itself ½ in. to stiffen the metal.

CHIMNEY FLASHING

On shingle, slate, or flat tile roofs, the base flashing extends out on the shingles 4 to 6 in. at the bottom, with the edge turned back on itself ½ in. for stiffness. Flashing is also carried up the chimney so that the cap flashing will lap at least 4 in. over it.

The lowest shingle flashing on each side folds around the corner of the chimney and is soldered to the base flashing. Separate shingle flashings, which serve as base flashings up the sides, are inserted with each course of shingles, and are hooked over the top edge of the shingles. Each shingle flashing should lap the one below at least 3 in., and the roofing should lap over the metal 4 in. at the sides.

Base and shingle flashings are cap-flashed as shown. Along the lower side, where cap flashing is horizontal, it is continuous, but up the sides it is made of separate pieces, stepped as required by the slope of the roof. The separate sheets should have side laps of at least 3 in. and should lap the base flashings everywhere at least 4 in. Cap flashings should be inserted as the chimney is constructed, carried all the way through to the inside, and turned up 1 in. against the flue linings. If this is not possible, the mason can leave sand courses at joints where the flashings will come. The sand courses are easily removed, after which the flashings are inserted to a depth of at least 2 in. into the brickwork and secured by lead plugs 1 in. wide and 8 in. apart. Joints are finished with roofing cement.

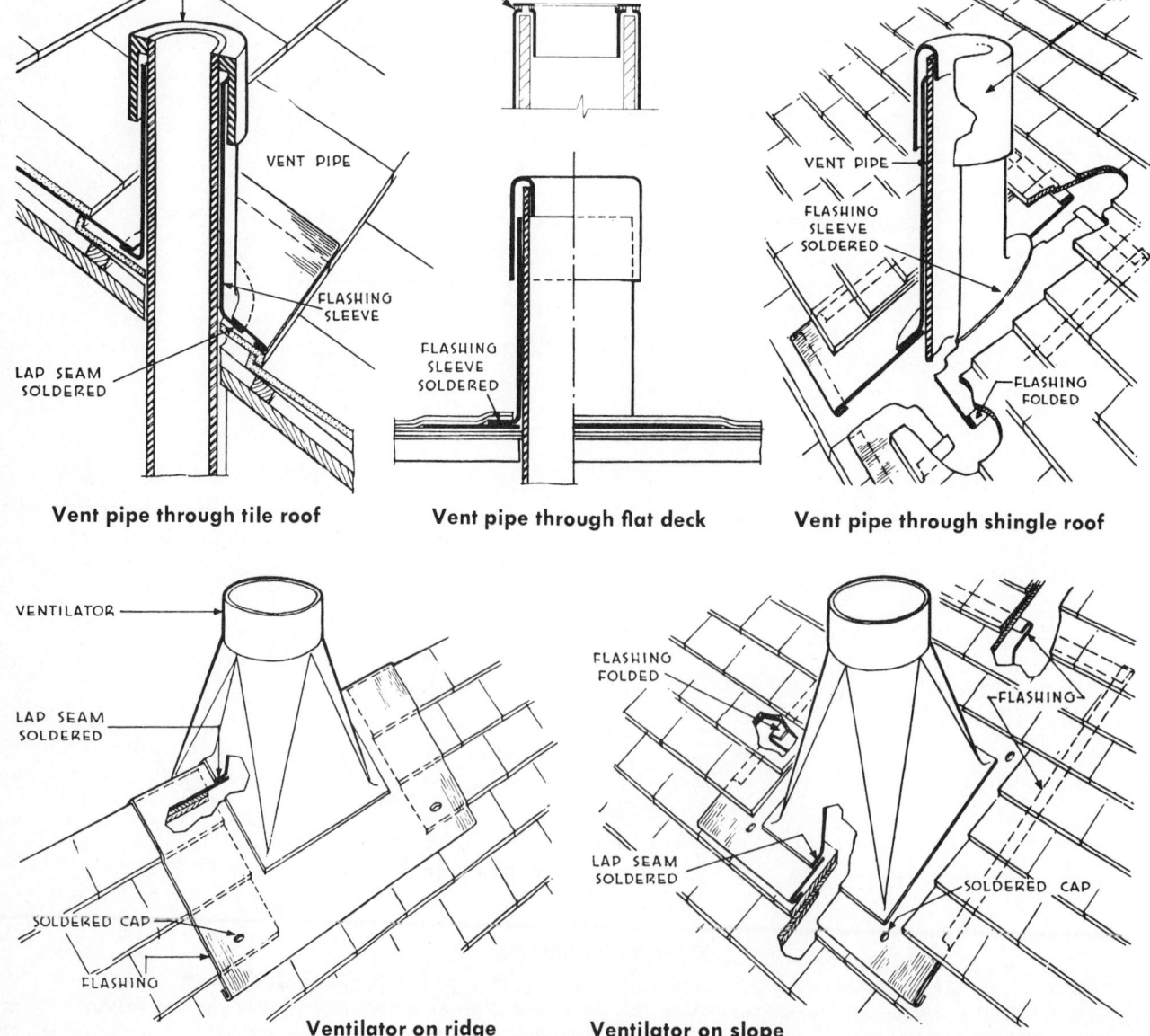

Vent pipe through tile roof

Vent pipe through flat deck

Vent pipe through shingle roof

Ventilator on ridge

Ventilator on slope

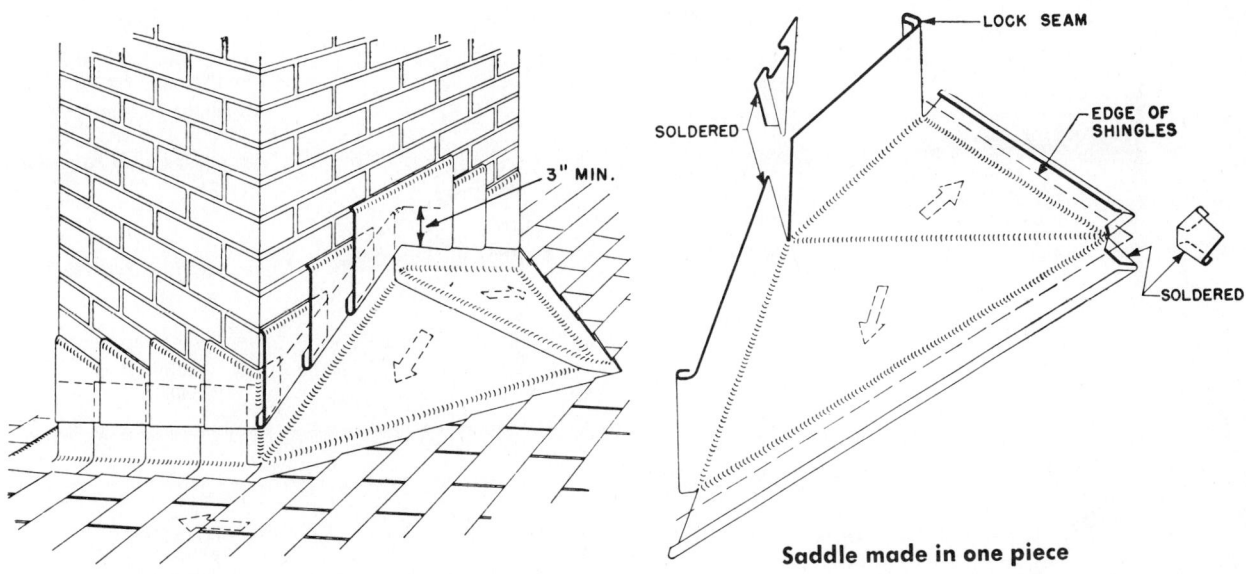

Detail of saddle or cricket (stepped cap flashing)

Saddle made in one piece

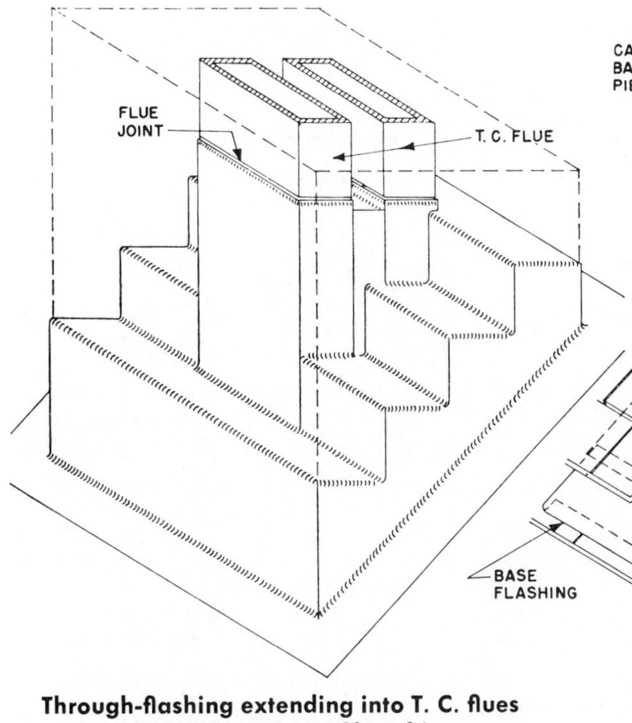

Through-flashing extending into T. C. flues
(See also section on Sheet 3.)

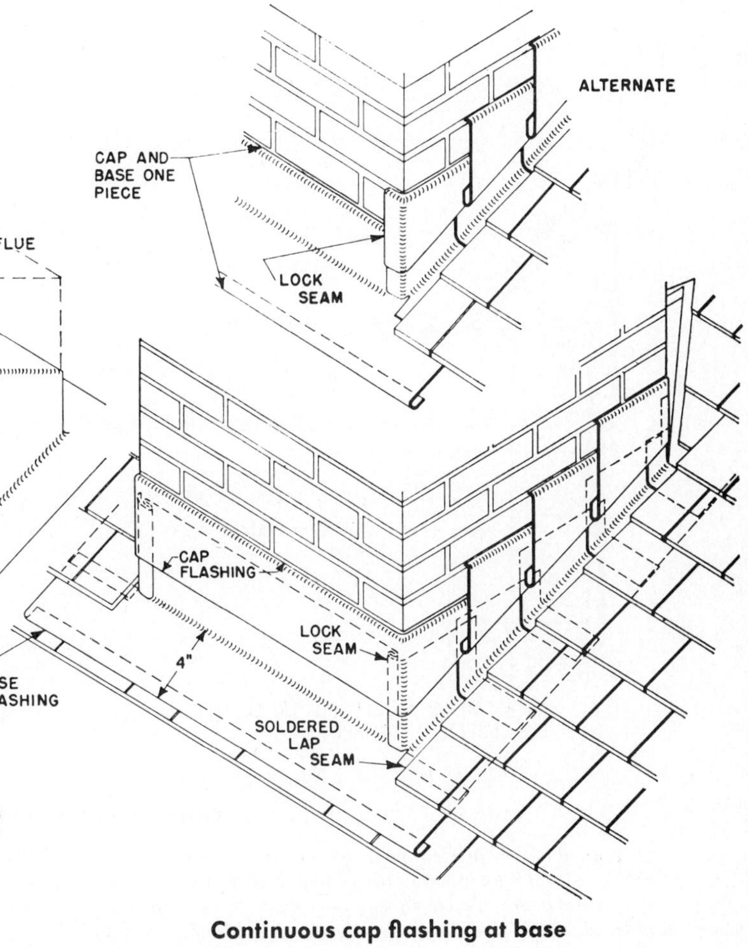

Continuous cap flashing at base

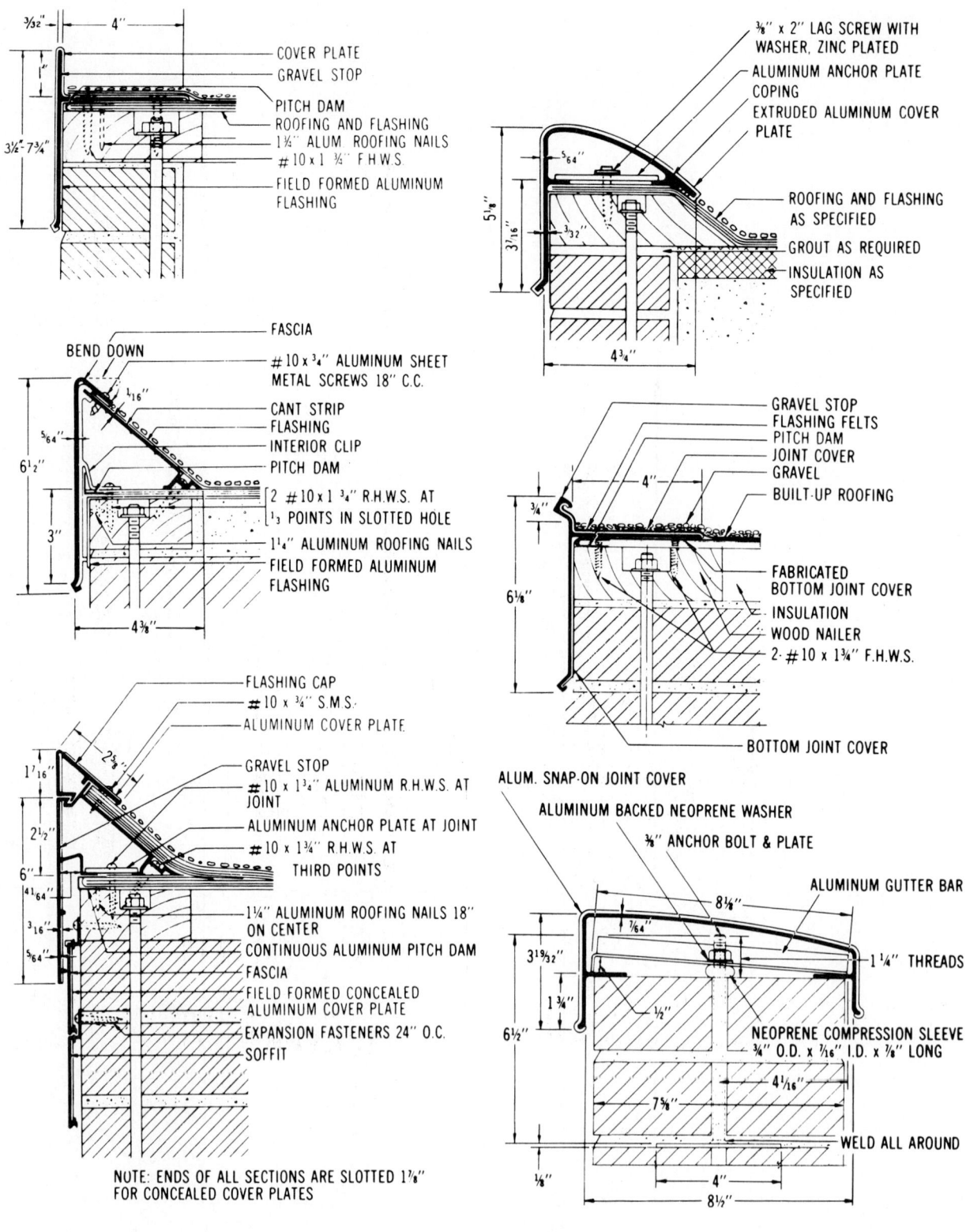

Gravel stops and copings

Extruded aluminum copings, gravel stops, and fascias are available as proprietary products from several manufacturers. Those shown here (courtesy of Reynolds Metals Company) are typical, but many other *designs are available. All types include provision for expansion, waterproof joint covers (usually concealed), and all necessary clips and accessories.*

By HOWARD P. VERMILYA, *AIA*

RESISTANCE TO WIND AND WIND-DRIVEN RAIN

New materials and methods of application offer solutions to former difficulties with asphalt shingle roofs caused by high winds and low-sloped roofs. High winds could lift tabs and permit wind-driven water to penetrate the roof. If winds were strong enough, they could rip off the tabs. Previously the industry-recommended minimum roof slope for asphalt shingles was 4 in 12, because lower roof slopes were susceptible to wind-driven rain penetration. Now, however, the industry recommends the use of asphalt shingles for slopes as low as 2 in 12.

This was made possible through the technique of cementing the shingle tabs with a quick-setting adhesive as they are laid. More recently new products have been introduced to achieve the same result and these include:

1. A factory-applied self-sealing adhesive which is activated after application by pressure and/or solar heat.
2. Interlocking tabs (square butt strip shingle).
3. Increased size and weight, resulting in increased stiffness and triple coverage.

Material standards

Asphalt shingles—ANSI/ASTM D225
—FS SS-S-1534
Underlayment —ANSI/ASTM D226
—FS HH-R-595

APPLICATION

1. The standard 210-lb, 12-by-36-in. square butt strip shingle providing double coverage at exposure of 5 in. is applied as follows:

Roof pitch	Underlayment
a. 7 or more in 12	none
b. 4 thru 6 in 12	single layer
c. 2 thru 3 in 12	double layer*

2. The heavy 300 lb, 15-by-36-in. square butt strip shingle providing triple coverage at exposure of 5 in. is applied as follows:

Roof pitch	Underlayment
a. 4 or more in 12	none
b. 3 in 12	single layer
c. 2 in 12	double layer

• Single layer of No. 15 asphalt saturated felt underlayment is applied with a 2-in. headlap and a 6-in. endlap.

* *Cement tabs of strip shingles, use self-sealing strip shingle, or use lock tab type shingle.*

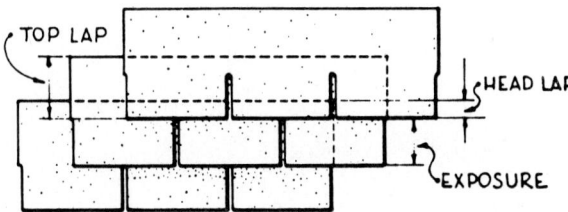

Fig. 1. TERMS relating to lapping of shingles

• Double layer of underlayment is applied with a 19-in. headlap and a 6-in. end-lap.
• Starter course of shingles shall be doubled and project about ⅜ to ½ in.
• Eaves flashing (Where design temperature is 25 F or colder):

1. Provide double layer of underlayment extending back from eaves to a line 24 in. inside the inner face of exterior wall, and
2. Where roof slope is less than 4 in 12, seal lap of double underlay with continous layer of asphalt cement.

• Roofing nails should be corrosion resistant with deformed shanks made from 11 or 12 gauge wire with at least a ⅜-in. head. The nail should penetrate the roof deck at least 1 in. At least four and preferably six nails should be used in each strip. Special fasteners may be used if recommended.

TERMINOLOGY

Weight Approximate shipping weight per square.

Square of roofing Amount of roofing which, when applied at the usual exposure, will cover 100 sq ft of roof surface.

End or Side Lap Shortest distance in inches by which horizontally adjacent roofing elements overlap each other.

Headlap Distance from the lower edge of an overlapping shingle to the upper edge of the one in the second course below.

Exposure Distance between exposed edges of overlapping shingles.

Coverage Number of layers of shingle covering a given area, usually double or triple for strip shingles. Cutouts less than ¾ in. are ignored.

Underlayment Asphalt felt weighing 15 lb per square is recommended.

Plastic Asphalt Cement Usually used as part of a flashing assembly where roof meets a wall, chimney or other vertical surface.

Lap Cement Usually used where one sheet overlaps another.

Quick-Setting Adhesive Cement Adhesive of either brush, trowel or gun consistency, is usually used for sealing tabs of strip shingles or for sealing laps of roll roofing.

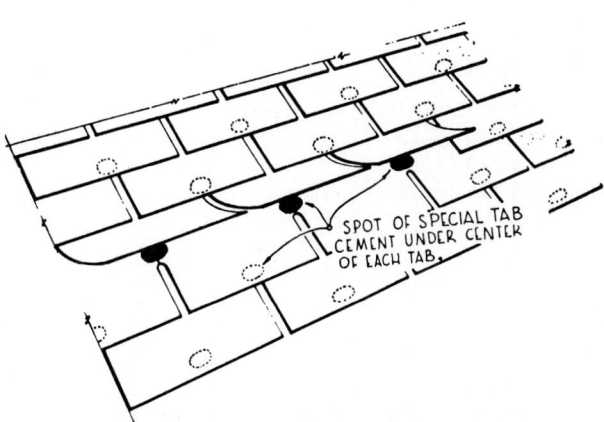

Fig. 2. CEMENTING of shingle tabs is used for low-slope roofs and for roofs in windy areas

GENERAL APPLICATION PROCEDURES

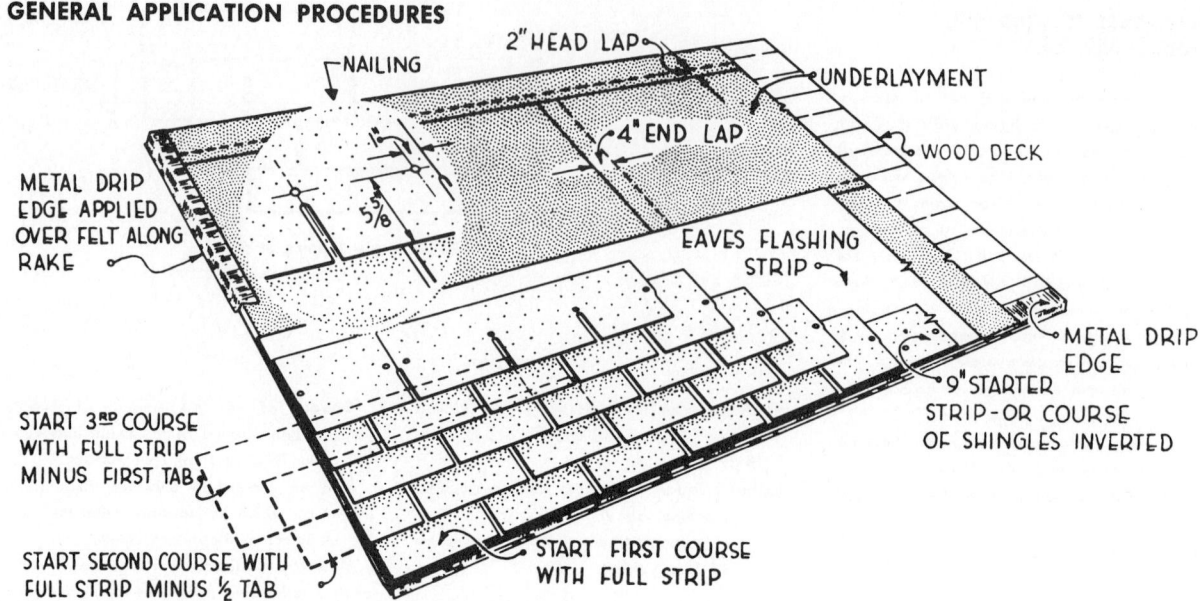

NAILING

2" HEAD LAP

UNDERLAYMENT

4" END LAP

WOOD DECK

METAL DRIP EDGE APPLIED OVER FELT ALONG RAKE

5⅝

EAVES FLASHING STRIP

METAL DRIP EDGE

9" STARTER STRIP-OR COURSE OF SHINGLES INVERTED

START 3ᴿᴰ COURSE WITH FULL STRIP MINUS FIRST TAB

START SECOND COURSE WITH FULL STRIP MINUS ½ TAB

START FIRST COURSE WITH FULL STRIP

Fig. 3 PROCEDURE FOR APPLYING square-butt asphalt shingles

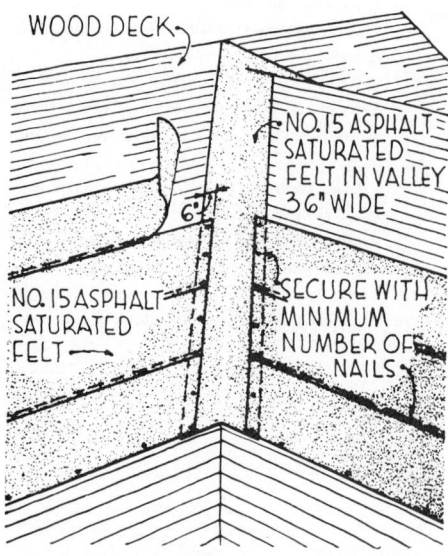

WOOD DECK

NO. 15 ASPHALT SATURATED FELT IN VALLEY 36" WIDE

SECURE WITH MINIMUM NUMBER OF NAILS

NO. 15 ASPHALT SATURATED FELT

6"

Fig. 4 DECK PREPARATION for a valley. Saturated felt underlayment is centered in the valley and secured with only enough nails to hold it in place until the shingles are applied. The courses of felt underlay are cut to overlap the valley strip by not less than 6 in. The eave flashing strip is then applied.

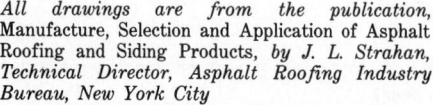

All drawings are from the publication, Manufacture, Selection and Application of Asphalt Roofing and Siding Products, *by J. L. Strahan, Technical Director, Asphalt Roofing Industry Bureau, New York City*

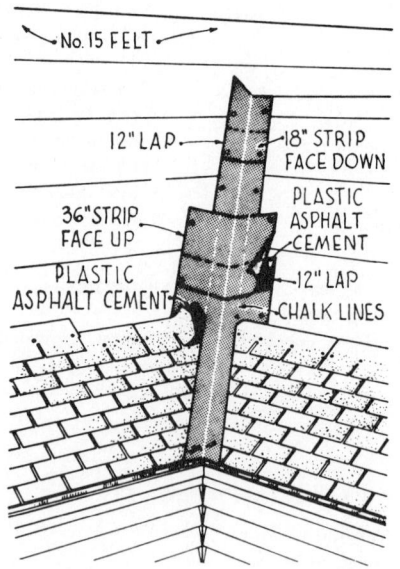

No. 15 FELT

12" LAP

18" STRIP FACE DOWN

36" STRIP FACE UP

PLASTIC ASPHALT CEMENT

PLASTIC ASPHALT CEMENT

12" LAP

CHALK LINES

Fig. 5 VALLEY FLASHINGS are made from mineral surfaced asphalt roll roofing. An 18-in.-wide layer of mineral surfaced roll roofing is centered in the valley, surfaced side down, and the lower edge is cut to conform to and be flush with the eave flashing strip. When necessary to splice the material, the ends of the upper segments overlap the lower segments and are secured with plastic asphalt cement as shown. Only enough nails are used in rows 1 in. in from each edge to hold the strip smoothly in place. The upper corner of each end shingle is clipped as shown to prevent water from penetrating between the courses. The roofing material is cemented to the valley lining.

LOW SLOPE APPLICATION

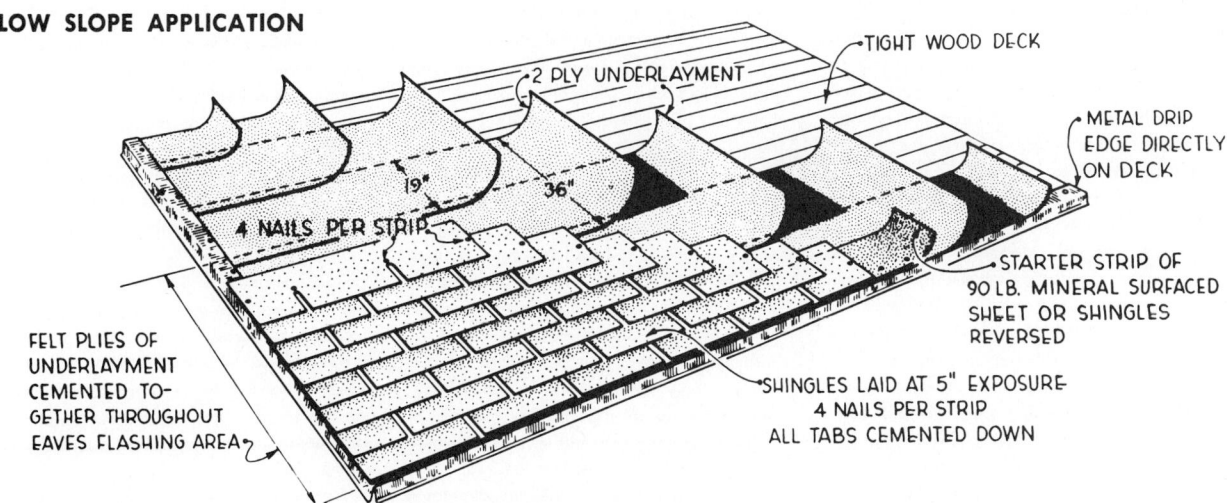

2 PLY UNDERLAYMENT

TIGHT WOOD DECK

METAL DRIP EDGE DIRECTLY ON DECK

19"

36"

4 NAILS PER STRIP

STARTER STRIP OF 90 LB. MINERAL SURFACED SHEET OR SHINGLES REVERSED

FELT PLIES OF UNDERLAYMENT CEMENTED TO-GETHER THROUGHOUT EAVES FLASHING AREA

SHINGLES LAID AT 5" EXPOSURE 4 NAILS PER STRIP ALL TABS CEMENTED DOWN

Fig. 6 SQUARE-TAB STRIP SHINGLES are recommended for use on decks having a slope lower than 4 in 12 but not less than 2 in 12 when special application methods are used to compensate for the slower water run-off resulting from the lower roof slope. These application methods involve: (a) double underlayment; (b) a special cemented eaves flashing strip; (c) use of quick-setting cement to fasten shingle tabs.

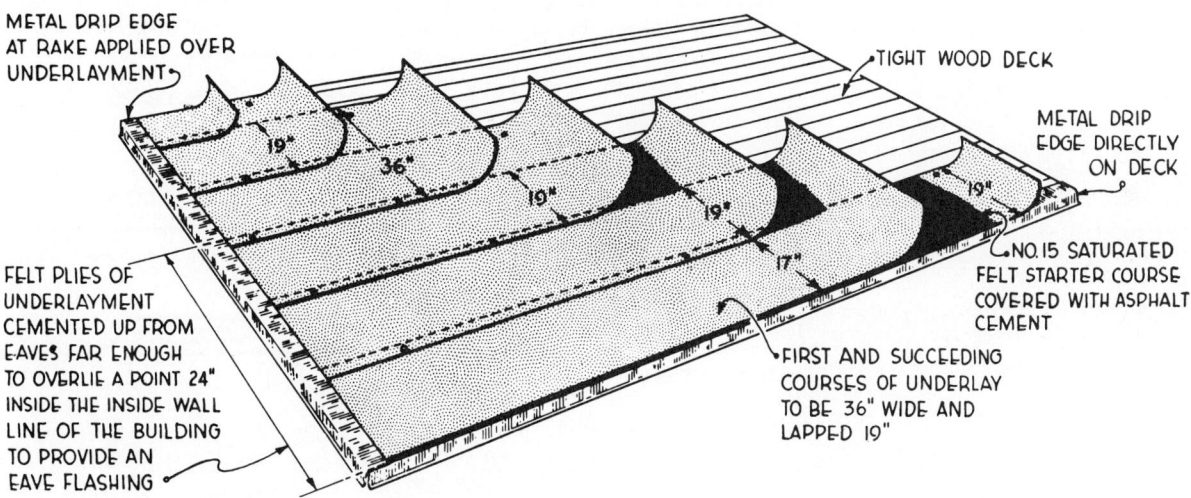

METAL DRIP EDGE AT RAKE APPLIED OVER UNDERLAYMENT

TIGHT WOOD DECK

METAL DRIP EDGE DIRECTLY ON DECK

19"

36"

19"

19"

17"

19"

FELT PLIES OF UNDERLAYMENT CEMENTED UP FROM EAVES FAR ENOUGH TO OVERLIE A POINT 24" INSIDE THE INSIDE WALL LINE OF THE BUILDING TO PROVIDE AN EAVE FLASHING

NO.15 SATURATED FELT STARTER COURSE COVERED WITH ASPHALT CEMENT

FIRST AND SUCCEEDING COURSES OF UNDERLAY TO BE 36" WIDE AND LAPPED 19"

Fig. 7 FELT UNDERLAY application on a low slope deck.

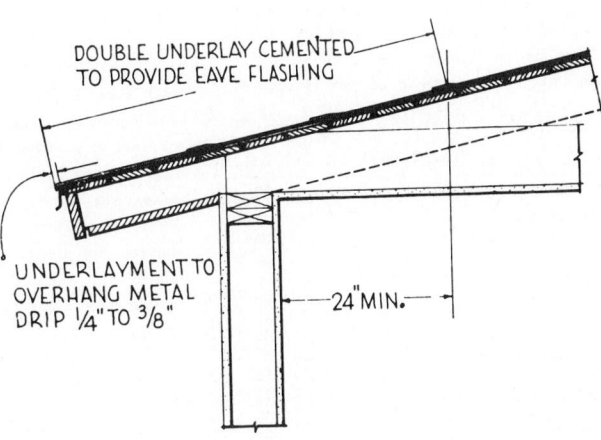

DOUBLE UNDERLAY CEMENTED TO PROVIDE EAVE FLASHING

UNDERLAYMENT TO OVERHANG METAL DRIP ¼" TO ⅜"

24" MIN.

Fig. 8 EAVE FLASHING. The felt underlay that extends from the eave up the roof far enough to overlie a point 24 in. from the inside wall line of the building is treated as follows: A continuous layer of plastic asphalt cement is applied to the surface of the underlay starter course before the first full course is applied, and also to the 19-in. underlying portion of each succeeding course which lies within the eaves flashing area, before placing the next course. Fig. 6 shows how the shingles are applied over the underlayment. The exposure is 5 in. and four nails are required.

Data and illustrations from Modern Applications of Sheet Copper in Building Construction, Copper Development Association, Inc.

Copper is one of the oldest of roofing materials. Although more expensive initially than some other roofing materials, copper is extremely durable and, if properly installed, is practically maintenance-free. Weathering of copper produces a blue-green patina which protects the surface from further corrosion. Copper is highly ductile and readily conforms to the contours of domes and other curved and irregular shapes. Copper roofs, like those of other metals (except lead), are light in weight (see Table 1), and thus require less structural framing than is necessary with heavier roofing materials. The three standard types of metal roofing—batten seam, standing seam, and flat seam—are described on the following pages.

Copper is produced in two standard grades of hardness or temper: "soft" (roofing temper) and "cold-rolled" (cornice temper). In general, cold-rolled copper is recommended for all sheet metal work in building construction, except standing- and batten-seam roofing, and for caps and through-wall flashings. The thickness of copper sheet is denoted by the weight in ounces per square foot of sheet; for equivalent thicknesses in inches, see Table 10 in section on "Architectural Metals."

Common types of seams in sheet metal work are shown in Figs. 9–13. Of these, probably the commonest is the lock seam. All fastenings for sheet copper must be of copper or copper alloy. All copper sheets more than 12 in. wide should be secured in such a manner as to permit free movement. The standard technique for this purpose is the cleat, shown in Fig. 14.

Surfaces on which copper roofing is to be laid must be smooth and free of all small projections, such as nailheads, and must be absolutely dry. Wood sheathing, after being laid, should be allowed to weather for several days, protected from rain. Well-seasoned shiplap sheathing is recommended. For maximum durability, use kiln-dried, pressure-treated sheathing. Concrete decks should be smoothed by a wash of neat cement or by heavy coats of asphalt paint; in the latter case the asphalt must be covered by rosin-sized or similar building paper before copper is applied.

Table 1. Weights of roofing materials

Material	Approx. Weight of 100 Sq. Ft. Laid
Clay Shingle Tile	1000 – 2000 lbs.
Clay Spanish Tile	800 – 1500 "
Slate	600 – 1600 "
Hard Lead Sheet (about ⅛")	600 – 800 "
Felt and Gravel (Slag 100 lbs. less)	550 – 650 "
Asbestos Shingles	265 – 650 "
Asphalt Shingles	130 – 325 "
Wood Shingles	200 – 300 "
22 g. Galv. Iron (Corrugated)	175 "
16-oz. Copper	116 – 145 "
26 g. Galv. Iron (Standing Seam)	100 – 125 "
Tinned Steel	65 – 100 "
Aluminum	35 – 60 "

Some provision, such as wood battens or nailing inserts, must be made for receiving the nails that fasten the cleats. Various nailing concretes are available. Cinder concrete is injurious to copper and should be covered with a heavy coating of asphalt paint.

A layer of roofing felt covered by a layer of smooth (such as rosin-sized) building paper should be placed under all copper roofing, valleys, and gutter linings. The National Board of Fire Underwriters recommends an asphalt-saturated asbestos felt weighing about 14 lb per 100 sq ft.

Copper need not be painted for protection. It may be painted, if desired, for decoration or to prevent the staining of adjacent materials. In either case, or where the appearance of lead is desired, lead-coated copper may be used to advantage.

BATTEN SEAM

Batten (or ribbed) seam roofing (Fig. 15) may be used on slopes of 3 in. or more to the foot, although in localities where ice and snow collect on the roof it should not be used on a slope as low as 3 in 12. Battens should be of wood, well seasoned and straight, and impregnated against rot. Nail-, screw-, or boltheads must be countersunk. Battens are usually spaced 20 to 30 in. apart, the exact spacing being adjusted to fit the stock widths of copper sheets, which are available in multiples of 2 in. From the mechanical standpoint, narrow spacing (24 in. or less) is recommended. With the type of batten shown in Fig. 16, the width of the sheets will be 3 in. greater than the center-to-center spacing of the battens. Standard sheet length is 96 in.

STANDING SEAM

Standing seam roofing (Figs. 17–21) is the simplest and most economical form of metal roofing. It is applicable to the same building types and the same roof pitches as batten seam roofing. Standing seams are usually made 1 in. high, which results in a spacing between seams of 3¼ in. less than the sheet width. Spacing of seams is a matter of architectural scale, but for economy, stock sheet widths should be used. Recommended maximum sheet size is 20 by 96 in., resulting in a seam spacing of 16¾ in. For most conditions, 12-oz cold rolled or 16-oz sheets should be used; for seam spacings greater than 20 in., 20-oz sheets are recommended. For economy, small houses may be roofed with 10-oz copper in 16-in. widths, formed into seams ¾ in. high, spaced 13¾ in. apart.

FLAT SEAM

Flat seam roofing is used mostly on flat roofs and decks but also on the curved and warped surfaces of spires, domes, and cupolas, where the small size of the sheets is an advantage in fitting them to the curved surface. Sheets of 20-oz copper, either 16 by 18 or 18 by 24 in., with ¾-in. seams flat-locked and soldered, are recommended. Pretinning the seams assures a stronger, more durable joint. On domes and steeples where there is no possibility of water collecting on the roof, seams may be left unsoldered and filled with white lead. Sheets are held down by 2-in. copper cleats, two on each of two adjacent sides; the other two sides are held by the edges of the adjacent sheets already cleated. Since soldered flat seams, unlike batten or standing seams, do not provide for expansion, expansion joints must be installed at approximately 37-ft intervals in each direction, as illustrated in Fig. 22.

Flat seam roofing may also be used to line the bottom of planting areas in roof gardens or elsewhere. A detail is shown in Fig. 23.

OTHER METALS

The installation details shown here for copper roofing also apply, with minor variations, to other metals used for roofing, such as galvanized steel, terneplate, aluminum, stainless steel, and monel.

Fig. 9. Lap seam, soldered

Fig. 10. Common lock, or hook, seam

Fig. 11. Flat-lock seam

Fig. 12. Flat-lock seam with cleat

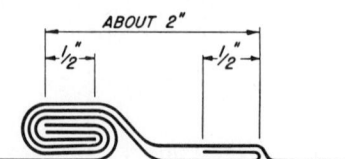

Fig. 13. Double-lock seam with cleat

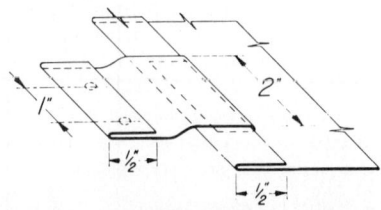

Fig. 14. Cleat

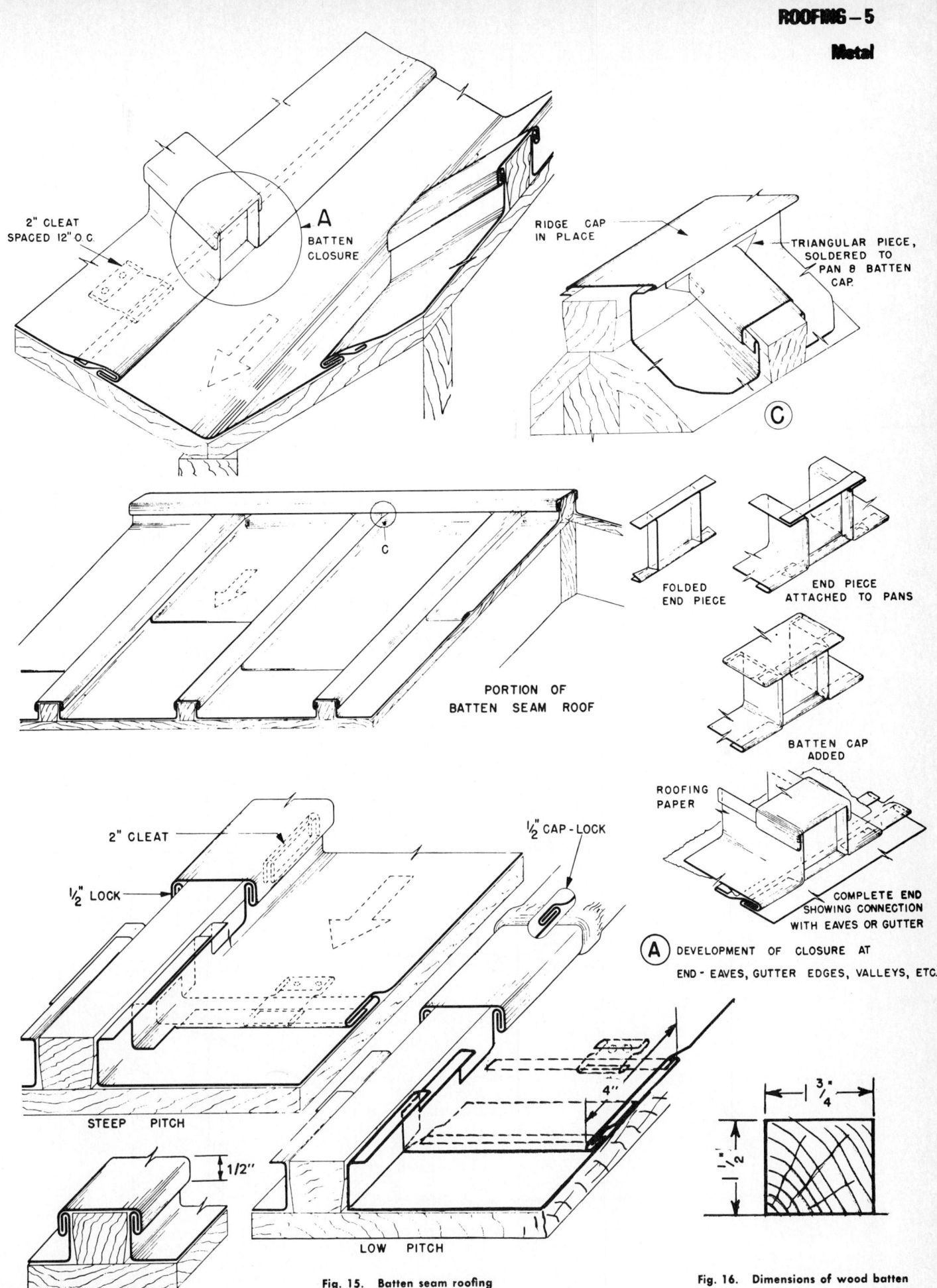

2" CLEAT SPACED 12" O.C.

A BATTEN CLOSURE

RIDGE CAP IN PLACE

TRIANGULAR PIECE, SOLDERED TO PAN & BATTEN CAP.

C

PORTION OF BATTEN SEAM ROOF

FOLDED END PIECE

END PIECE ATTACHED TO PANS

BATTEN CAP ADDED

ROOFING PAPER

COMPLETE END SHOWING CONNECTION WITH EAVES OR GUTTER

A DEVELOPMENT OF CLOSURE AT END - EAVES, GUTTER EDGES, VALLEYS, ETC.

2" CLEAT

½" LOCK

½" CAP-LOCK

STEEP PITCH

1/2"

LOW PITCH

4"

3/4"

1/2"

Fig. 15. Batten seam roofing

Fig. 16. Dimensions of wood batten

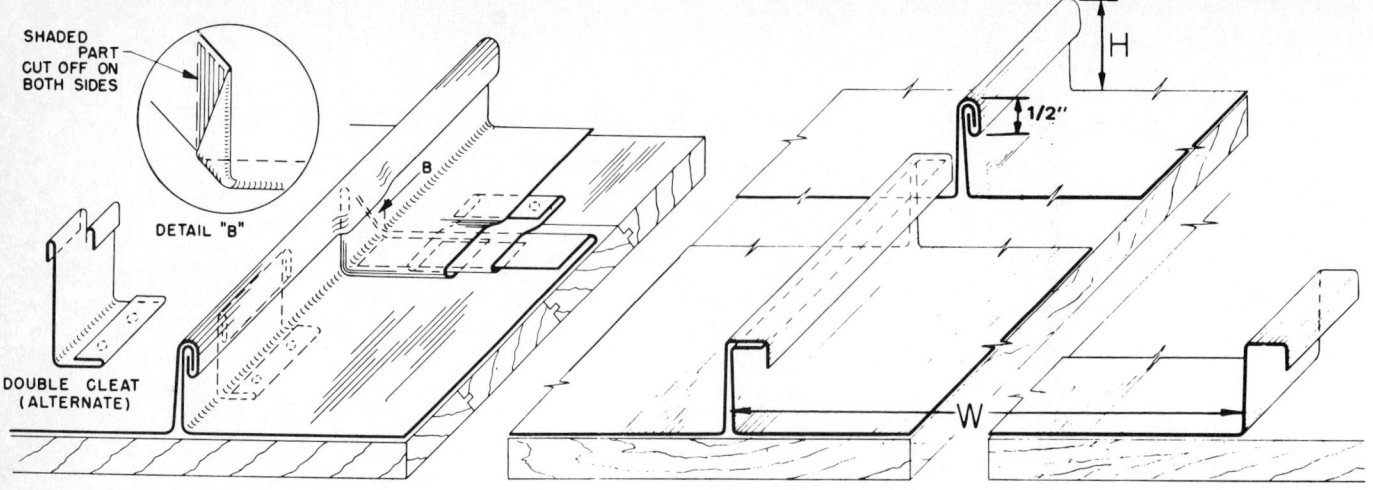

SHADED PART CUT OFF ON BOTH SIDES

DETAIL "B"

B

DOUBLE CLEAT (ALTERNATE)

H

1/2"

W

Fig. 17. Standing seam roofing—formed in place

Fig. 18. Standing seam roofing—preformed pans

PAN WIDTH "W"			
WIDTH OF SHEET	SEAM HEIGHT—H		
	$\frac{7}{8}$	1	$1\frac{1}{4}$
20	$17\frac{1}{4}$	$16\frac{3}{4}$	$16\frac{1}{4}$
22	$19\frac{1}{4}$	$18\frac{3}{4}$	$18\frac{1}{4}$
24	$21\frac{1}{4}$	$20\frac{3}{4}$	$20\frac{1}{4}$
26	$23\frac{1}{4}$	$22\frac{3}{4}$	$22\frac{1}{4}$
28	$25\frac{1}{4}$	$24\frac{3}{4}$	$24\frac{1}{4}$

ALL DIMENSIONS IN INCHES

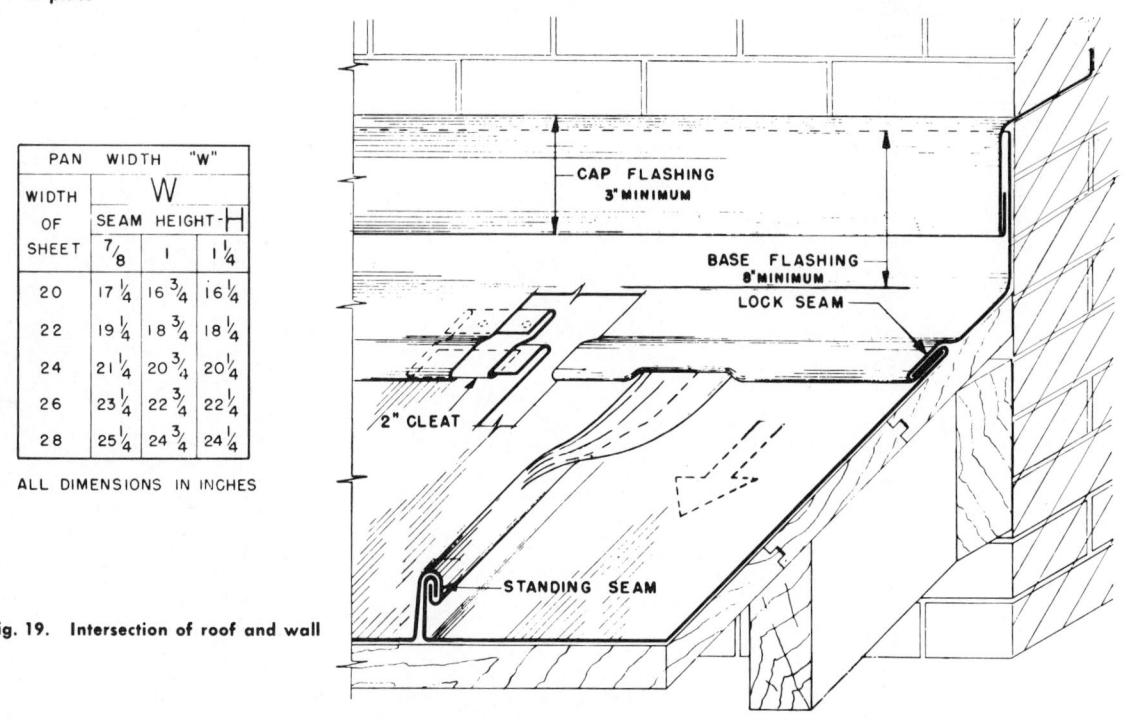

CAP FLASHING 3" MINIMUM

BASE FLASHING 8" MINIMUM

LOCK SEAM

2" CLEAT

STANDING SEAM

Fig. 19. Intersection of roof and wall

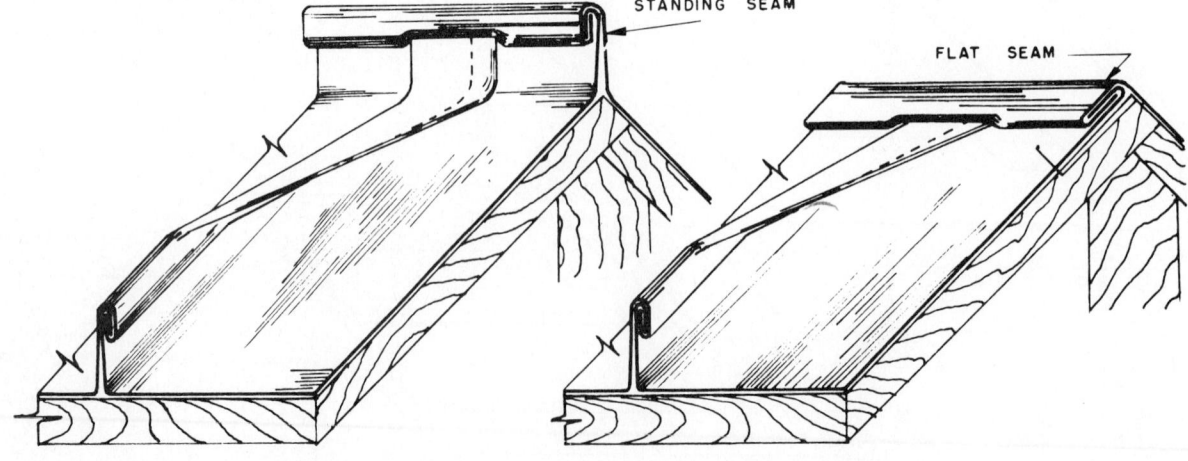

STANDING SEAM

FLAT SEAM

Fig. 20. Gable and ridge details

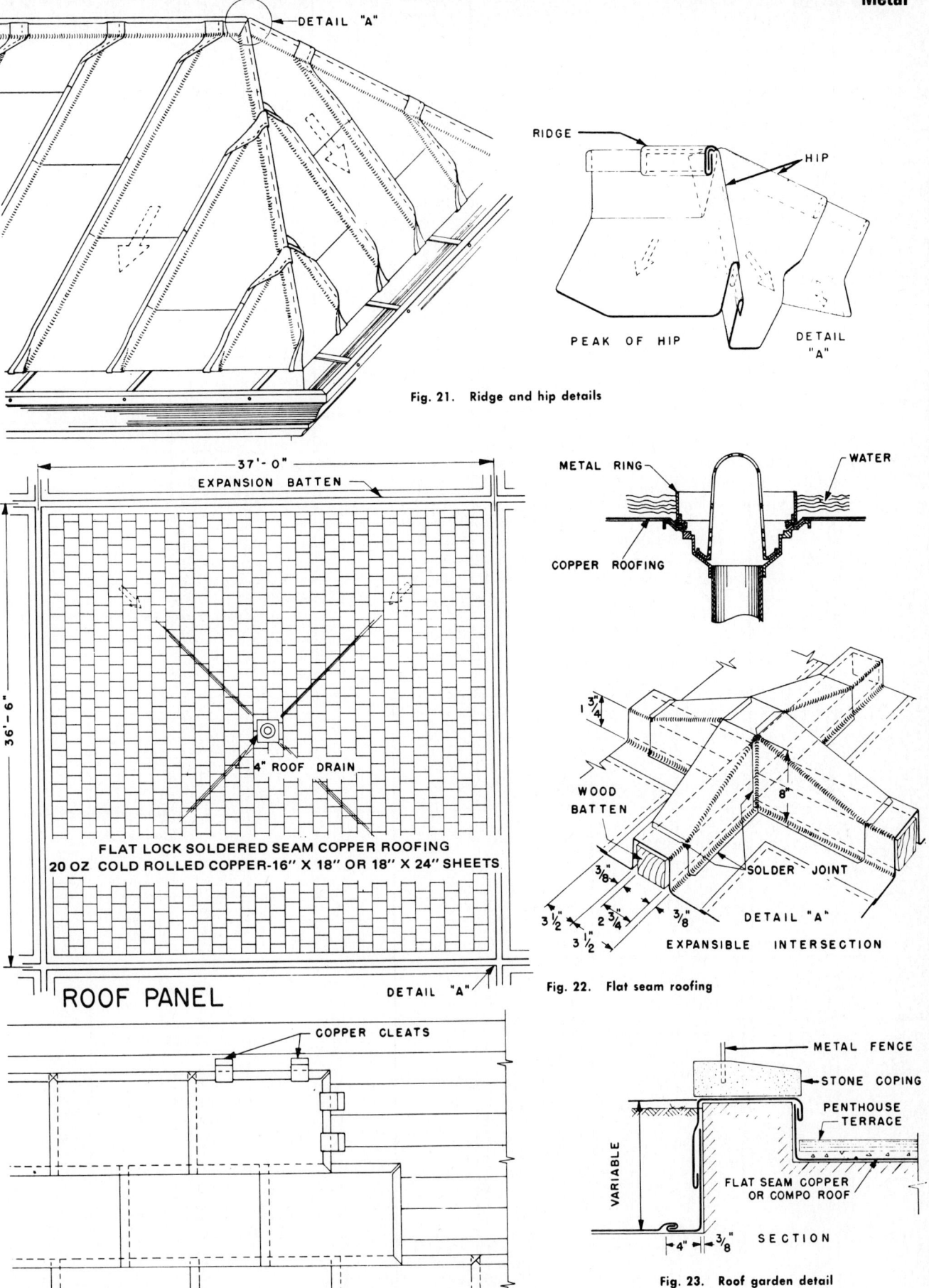

DETAIL "A"

RIDGE

HIP

PEAK OF HIP

DETAIL "A"

Fig. 21. Ridge and hip details

37'-0"

EXPANSION BATTEN

36'-6"

4" ROOF DRAIN

FLAT LOCK SOLDERED SEAM COPPER ROOFING
20 OZ COLD ROLLED COPPER-16" X 18" OR 18" X 24" SHEETS

ROOF PANEL

DETAIL "A"

COPPER CLEATS

METAL RING

WATER

COPPER ROOFING

1 3/4"

8"

WOOD BATTEN

SOLDER JOINT

3/8"

3 1/2"

2 3/4"

3/8"

3 1/2"

DETAIL "A"

EXPANSIBLE INTERSECTION

Fig. 22. Flat seam roofing

METAL FENCE

STONE COPING

PENTHOUSE TERRACE

VARIABLE

FLAT SEAM COPPER OR COMPO ROOF

4"

3/8"

SECTION

Fig. 23. Roof garden detail

By SIDNEY M. SHELOV, AIA

The roof is one of the most essential parts of a building as it protects occupants, contents, and interior of the structure from the elements. Once an architect has determined the kind of roof he intends to use, he must give equal attention to the design of the roof drainage system.

Factors to be considered in the design of roof drainage systems are the area to be drained, size of gutters, downspouts, outlets, slope of roof, type of building, and appearance.

ROOF AREA TO BE CONSIDERED

The design capacity for a roof drainage system depends on the quantity of water to be handled. The quantity of water in turn depends on the roof area, slope, and rainfall intensity.

In considering the roof area, it must be remembered that rain does not necessarily fall vertically and that maximum conditions exist only when rain falls perpendicular to a surface. Since the roof area would increase as its pitch increases, it would not be advisable to use the plan area of a pitched roof in the calculation of a drainage system.

Experience has taught that use of the true area of a pitched roof often leads to oversizing of gutters, downspouts, and drains. To determine the design area for a pitched roof, Table 1 is used.

Table 1. Design areas for pitched roofs

Pitch	B*
Level to 3 in./ft	1.00
4 to 5 in./ft	1.05
6 to 8 in./ft	1.10
9 to 11 in./ft	1.20
12 in./ft	1.30

To determine the design area, multiply the plan area by the factor in column B.

Table 2. Rainfall intensity and drainage factors

	A Storms which should be exceeded only once in 5 years		B Storms which should be exceeded only once in 10 years		C Maximum record Storms	
	Intensity in Ins./Hr. lasting 5 minutes	Sq. Ft. of actual roof drained per Sq. In. of Leader area	Intensity in Ins./Hr. lasting 5 minutes	Sq. Ft. of actual roof drained per Sq. In. of Leader area	Intensity in Ins./Hr. lasting 5 minutes	Sq. Ft. of actual roof drained per Sq. In. of Leader area
Albany, N. Y.	6	200	7	175	7	175
Atlanta, Ga.	7	175	7	175	11	110
Boston, Mass.	5	210	6	200	7	175
Buffalo, N. Y.	5	210	5	210	10	120
Chicago, Ill.	6	200	7	175	8	150
Detroit, Mich.	6	200	6	200	10	120
Duluth, Minn.	5	210	6	200	7	175
Kansas City, Mo.	7	175	8	150	10	120
Knoxville, Tenn.	5	210	6	200	7	175
Louisville, Ky.	6	200	7	175	9	130
Memphis, Tenn.	5	210	6	200	9	130
Montgomery, Ala.	7	175	7	175	8	150
New Orleans, La.	7	175	7	175	9	130
New York City, N. Y.	6	200	8	150	9	130
Norfolk, Va.	6	200	7	175	8	150
Philadelphia, Pa.	6	200	7	175	8	150
Pittsburgh, Pa.	6	200	6	200	9	130
St. Louis, Mo.	6	200	8	150	8	150
St. Paul, Minn.	6	200	6	200	8	150
San Francisco, Cal.	2	600	2	600	1	300
Savannah, Ga.	6	200	7	175	9	130
Seattle, Wash.	3*	100	3*	100	3.5*	370
Washington, D. C.	6	200	7	175	10	120

*From local records

Table 3. Dimensions of standard leaders

Type	Area in Sq. In.	Leader Sizes
Plain Round	7.07	3"
	12.57	4"
	19.63	5"
	28.27	6"
Corrugated Round	5.94	3"
	11.04	4"
	17.72	5"
	25.97	6"
Polygon Octagonal	6.36	3"
	11.30	4"
	17.65	5"
	25.10	6"
Square Corrugated	3.80	1¾" x 2¼" (2")
	7.73	2⅜" x 3¼" (3")
	11.70	2¾" x 4¼" (4")
	18.75	3¾" x 5" (5")
Plain Rectangular	3.94	1¾" x 2¼"
	6.00	2" x 3"
	8.00	2" x 4"
	12.00	3" x 4"
	20.00	3¾" x 4¾"
	21.00	1" x 6"
S.P.S. Pipe	7.38	3"
	12.72	4"
	20.00	5"
	28.88	6"
Cast Iron Pipe	7.07	3"
	12.57	4"
	19.64	5"
	28.27	6"

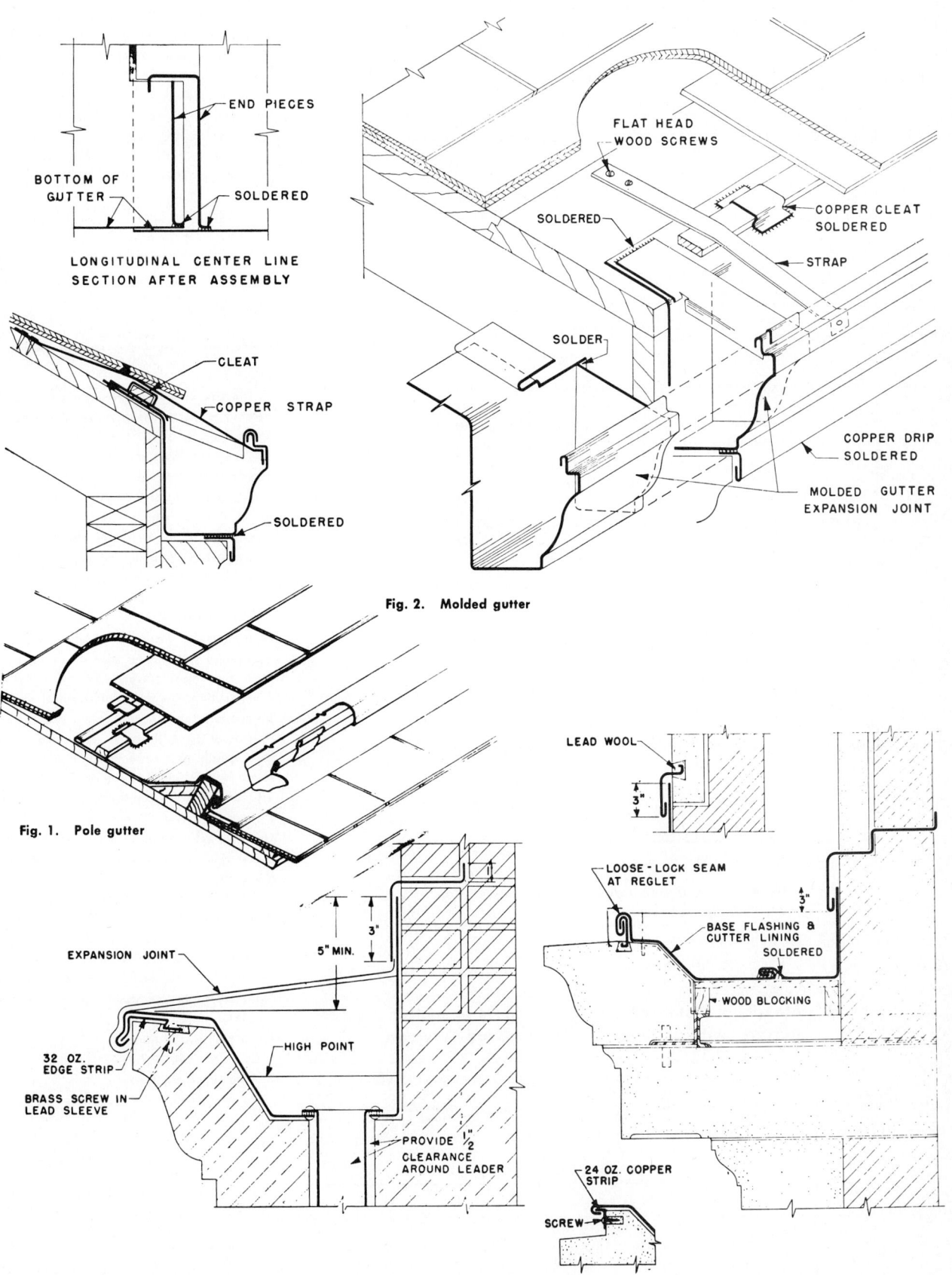

END PIECES

BOTTOM OF GUTTER

SOLDERED

LONGITUDINAL CENTER LINE
SECTION AFTER ASSEMBLY

CLEAT

COPPER STRAP

SOLDERED

FLAT HEAD
WOOD SCREWS

SOLDERED

SOLDER

COPPER CLEAT
SOLDERED

STRAP

COPPER DRIP
SOLDERED

MOLDED GUTTER
EXPANSION JOINT

Fig. 2. Molded gutter

Fig. 1. Pole gutter

EXPANSION JOINT

32 OZ.
EDGE STRIP

BRASS SCREW IN
LEAD SLEEVE

5" MIN.

3"

HIGH POINT

PROVIDE 1/2"
CLEARANCE
AROUND LEADER

LEAD WOOL

3"

LOOSE-LOCK SEAM
AT REGLET

3"

BASE FLASHING &
GUTTER LINING
SOLDERED

WOOD BLOCKING

24 OZ. COPPER
STRIP

SCREW

Fig. 3. Stone cornice and built-in gutter

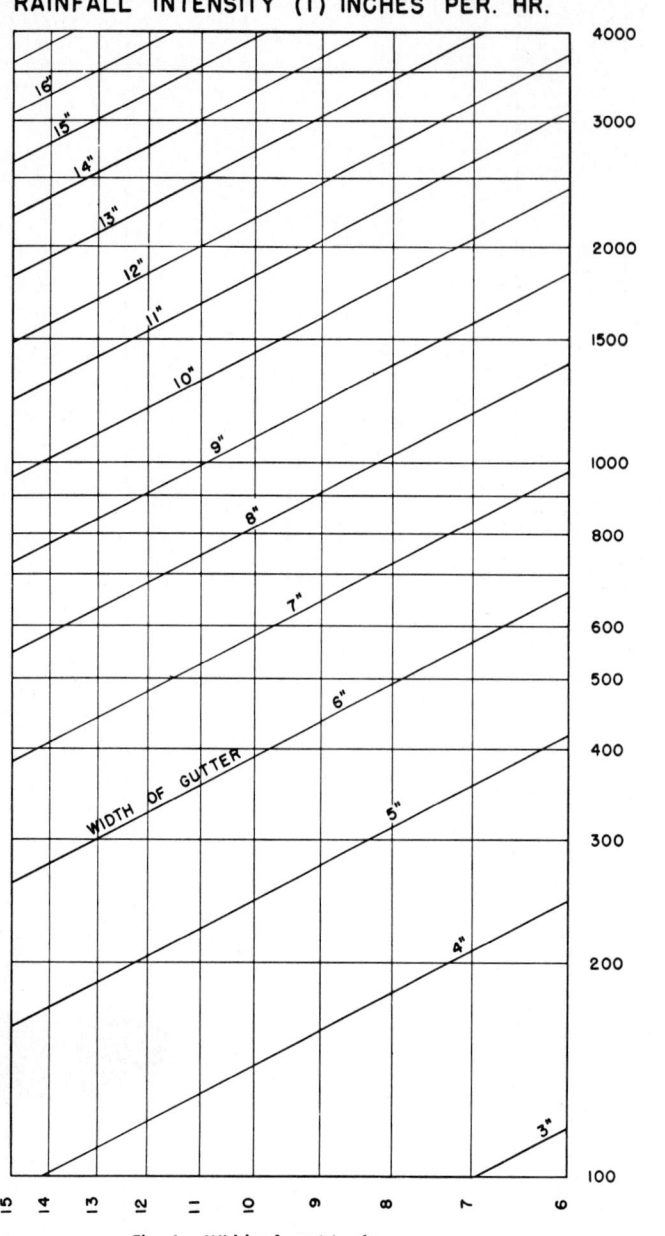

RAINFALL INTENSITY (I) INCHES PER. HR.

WIDTH OF GUTTER

AREA (A) SQ. FT.

Fig. 4. Width of semicircular gutters

GUTTERS

In sizing gutters, the following considerations apply:

1. Spacing and size of outlet openings. (The gutter can never be any more effective than the downspout selected to drain it.)

2. Slope of the roof. (The gutter must be of such a design that water from a steep roof will not by its own velocity tend to spill over the front edge.)

3. Style of gutters to be used. (All gutters are not effective for their full depth and width.)

4. Expansion joint location. (Water cannot flow past an expansion joint.)

The size of rectangular gutters depends upon these factors:

1. Area to be drained. (A, Fig. 6.)
2. Rainfall intensity per hour. (I, Fig. 6.)
3. Length of gutter in ft. (L, Fig. 6.)
4. Ratio of depth to width of gutter. (M, Fig. 6.)

The size of half-round gutters is directly related to the downspout size. If the downspout spacing is 20 ft or less, the gutter size can be the same as the downspout size (but not less than 4 in.). If the downspout spacing is between 20 and 50 ft, add 1 in. to the downspout size for the gutter. Although it is not recommended, wherever it is necessary to drain more than 50 ft of gutter into one downspout, the gutter should be 2 in. larger than the downspout.

The required sizes of gutters other than rectangular or round can be determined by finding the semicircular or rectangular area that most closely fits the irregular cross section. The depth of a gutter should be not less than half nor more than three-fourths of its width; gutter sizes are therefore usually expressed in width only. Half-round gutters are economical and highly efficient; they are commonly used as eaves, troughs, and less often as built-in gutters. Other common types of gutter are the pole gutter (Fig. 1), molded gutter (Fig. 2), and the built-in gutter (Fig. 3).

For built-in gutters in large buildings the following formulas, and Figs. 4 and 6 which were derived from them, are recommended. These formulas were developed empirically from tests conducted by the National Bureau of Standards in Washington, D.C.

For semicircular gutters:

$$W = 1.3 \, Q^{2/5}$$

For rectangular gutters:

$$W = 0.481 \, m^{-4/7} \, I^{3/28} \, Q^{5/14}$$

Table 4. Maximum distances between leaders of built-in copper gutters (with expansion joints midway between)

Width of Gutter Bottom in Inches	Side Angles of 45° and 60°				Side Angles of 60° and 90°			
	Weight of Sheet				Weight of Sheet			
	16 oz.	20 oz.	24 oz.	32 oz.	16 oz.	20 oz.	24 oz.	32 oz.
	Distance Between Downspouts in Feet							
8	30	35	45	—	35	45	55	—
12	20	30	40	65	25	35	45	80
16	—	25	30	55	—	30	40	70
20	—	20	25	50	—	25	35	60
24	—	—	25	45	—	—	30	55

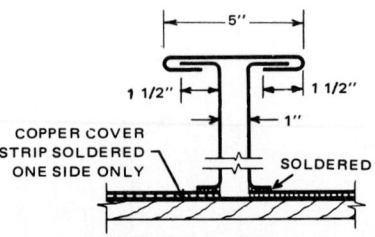

COPPER COVER STRIP SOLDERED ONE SIDE ONLY

SOLDERED

Fig. 5. Typical expansion joint

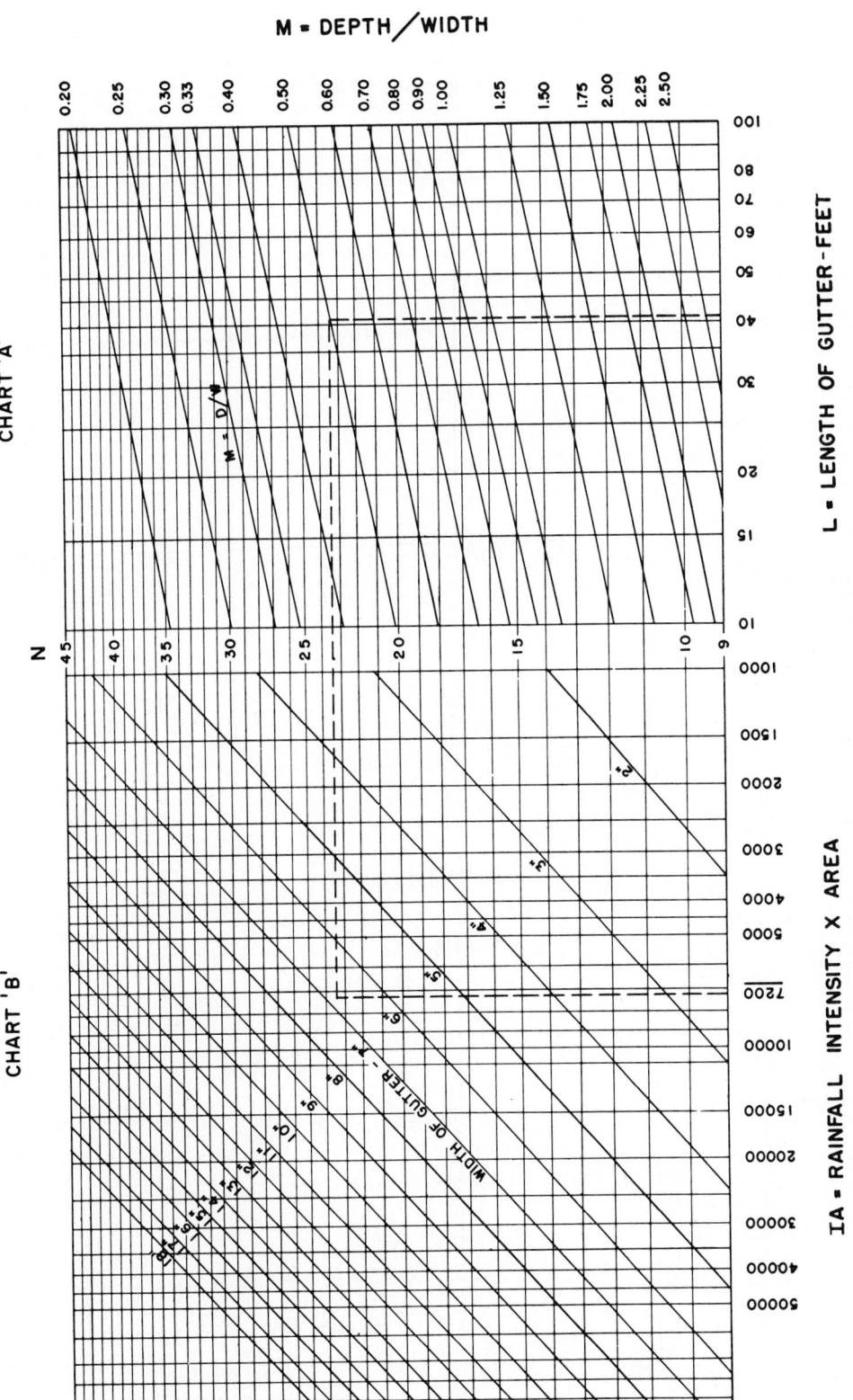

Fig. 6. Width of rectangular gutter for given roof areas and rainfall intensities.

Enter at the bottom of Chart A at given value for L. Follow vertical line to intersection with oblique line for given value of M. Proceed horizontally into chart B to intersection with vertical line for given value of IA. The nearest oblique line above the intersection gives width of the gutter. Dashed line illustrates an example where L = 40 ft, M = 0.59, and IA = 7,200; width of gutter is 7 in.

in which,

W = width of gutter, ft
m = depth/width
l = length of gutter, ft
Q = total gutter inflow, cu ft per sec

These formulas are for level gutters. Where the slope exceeds 2 per cent, the gutter should be narrowed and deepened.

Gutter cross sections must be such as to prevent an expansive thrust of ice from splitting the seams. The top should be wider than the bottom, and the depth less than the bottom width. A slope of 60 deg from the horizontal is recommended for at least one side of the gutter. Gutters and the linings of built-in gutters must be unre-strained except at the outlet. Maximum distances between outlets are shown in Table 3.

EXPANSION

Gutters of all types must be designed with provision for longitudinal expansion. The standard expansion joint is illustrated in principle in Fig. 5. In practice it necessarily varies with the shape of the gutter and may be fairly complex. The expansion joint is usually placed at the high point of the slope of the gutter, midway between outlets. It is often treated as the meeting of the closed ends of two separate gutters, as shown in Fig. 2.

OUTLETS

Outlets (Fig. 7) should be elliptical or rectangular in plan, with the longer dimension in the direction of gutter flow. The longer dimension should be the same as the gutter width and the shorter dimension about two-thirds of the gutter width. For larger gutters the width of the outlet may be the same as the width of the gutter and the length of the outlet about half again as long. The outlet should be tapered to the size of the leader within a length of 1½ to 2 times the diameter of the leader, but not less than the maximum dimension of the outlet.

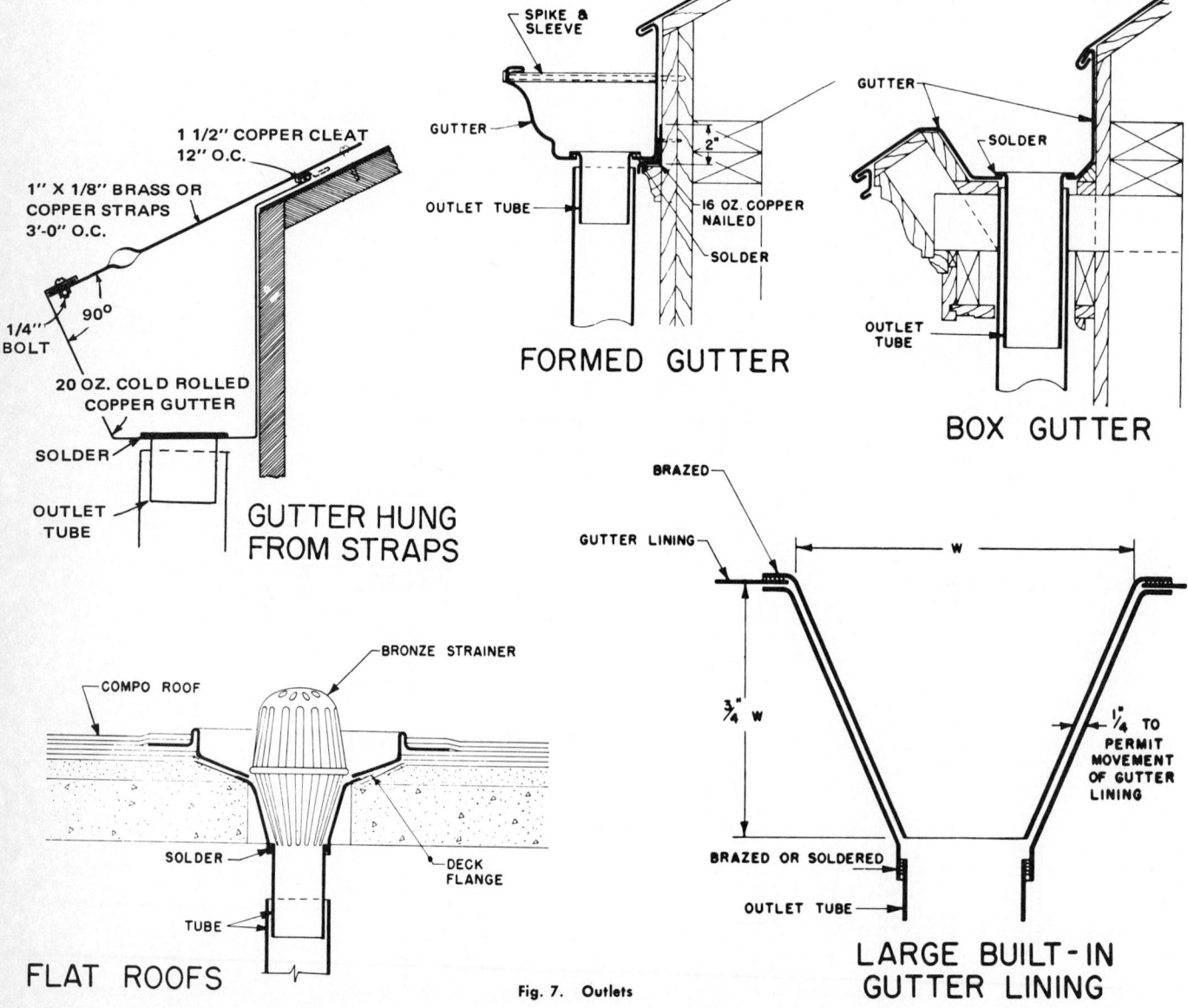

FORMED GUTTER

BOX GUTTER

GUTTER HUNG FROM STRAPS

FLAT ROOFS

LARGE BUILT-IN GUTTER LINING

Fig. 7. Outlets

The outlet should be soldered to the gutter but not to the leader; it should extend about 6 in. into the leader. There should be enough space between the outlet and the leader to prevent the formation of a vacuum.

FACTORY-MADE ROOFING PRODUCTS

In Fig. 8 are shown the various parts of gutters, leaders, and accessories made and stocked by manufacturers and distributors throughout the country. Molded gutters, including the half-round type, are made in several designs, two of which are shown in Fig. 9. The most commonly used is the 16-oz single-bead half-round eaves trough. Standard length is 10 ft, available with either lap-joint or slip-joint ends. Slip joints provide for expansion and contraction in long runs of gutter; they are used for every third length, or 30 ft apart; the intervening lap joints are soldered. Several types of stock gutter hangers are shown in Fig. 10.

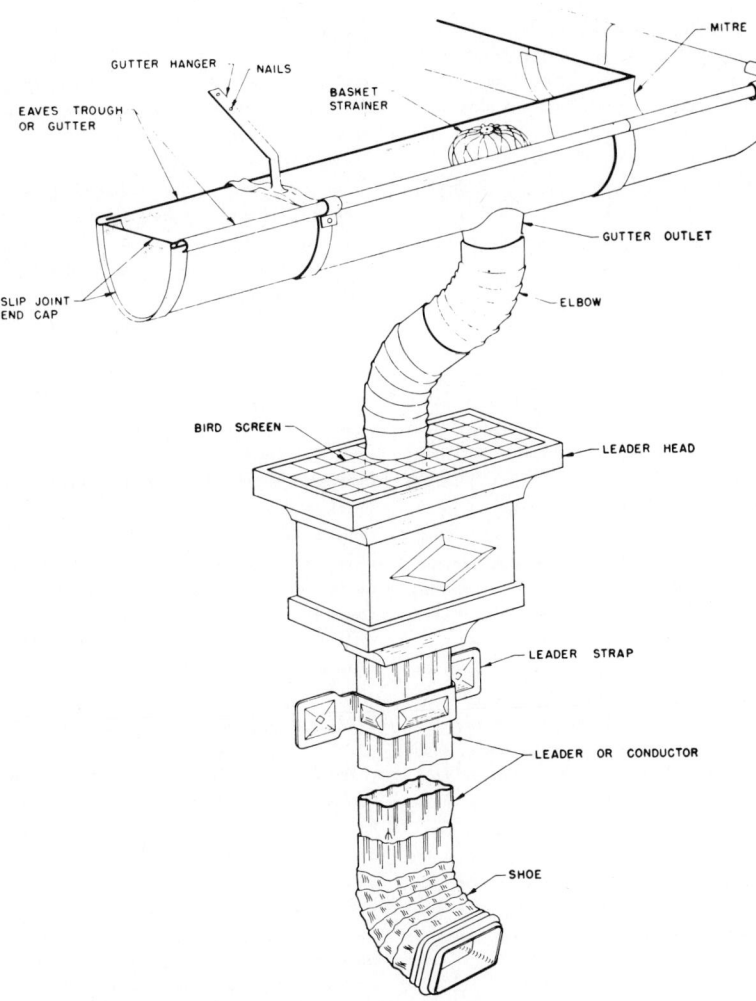

Fig. 8.   Factory-made roof drainage products

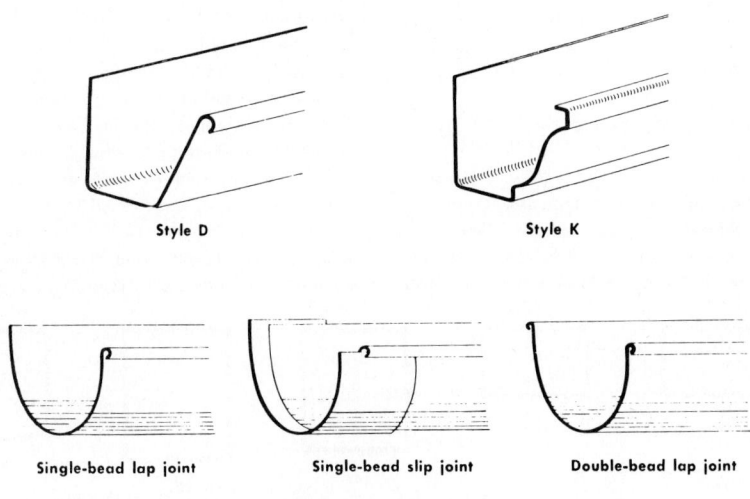

Style D

Style K

Single-bead lap joint

Single-bead slip joint

Double-bead lap joint

Half-round type

Fig. 9.   Molded gutters

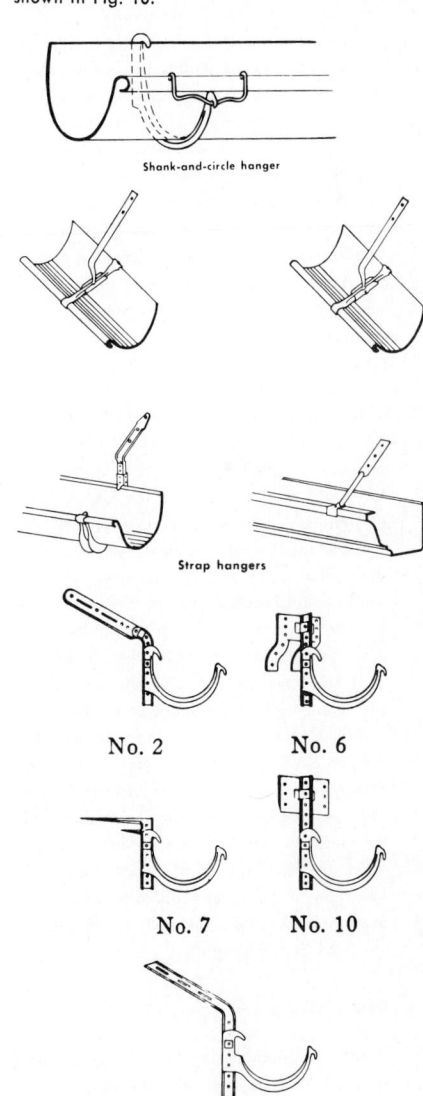

Shank-and-circle hanger

Strap hangers

No. 2

No. 6

No. 7

No. 10

No. 12

Fig. 10.   Gutter hangers

Number 12 has bronze circle for double-bead gutters; other circles are for single-bead gutters.

By JOHN HANCOCK CALLENDER, *Professor of Architecture, Pratt Institute*

Traditionally, the window was considered an "opening" in the wall, and many building codes and building professionals still use that term. With the increasing use of glass, however, windows now often form the entire wall, and thus the traditional distinction between wall and window is no longer valid. Most metal window manufacturers now offer complete curtain wall systems (see "Curtain Walls").

Windows, or window walls, perform several distinct functions. The most important of these is normally the admission of *light*, both from a practical standpoint and for its psychological and aesthetic effect on the interior space. A second function of windows is *ventilation*. Although the rapid increase in the use of air conditioning has reduced the need for natural ventilation in many types of buildings, nevertheless this is still one of the major purposes of windows. A third function of windows is to permit *vision*, in or out. This, too, is both practical and psychological. Fourth, windows sometimes serve as an *emergency escape*. Finally, windows are *elements of architectural composition* and, especially today, are extremely important in the total aesthetic effect created by a building.

LIGHT

The amount of light admitted depends on the number, size, location, and transparency of the windows. The higher the window head, the deeper the penetration of light into the room. The lower the sill, the less shadow on the floor near the window. The more nearly the area of the window approaches that of the wall, the greater the amount of light admitted and the more even its distribution. Reflected light from the ground or from roof decks will enter adjacent windows; if the horizontal surfaces have a high reflectivity, the amount of reflected light admitted through the windows, at an upward angle, will be considerable. The orientation of the windows will have an important effect upon the quality of the light admitted. The type of glass used will also affect the quality of the light, as well as the quantity (see "Daylighting").

VENTILATION

Where windows are used for ventilation, the requirements vary with the season and the climate. In cold weather the principal requirement is freedom from drafts. This is usually achieved by the use of a window (such as the hopper type) that will deflect the entering air upward. In hot dry summer weather, on the other hand, it is often desirable to admit as much breeze as possible. Here windows with 100 per cent opening are preferable. If the direction of the wind can be predicted, the use of larger windows on the leeward side than on the windward side will increase the velocity of the air passing through the room. In hot rainy climates, it is highly desirable to have windows (such as the awning type) that can be left open in the rain.

VISION

The vision function of glass in windows works both ways, permitting one to look out as well as to look in. For many uses "looking out" has disadvantages in that it may be distracting or unpleasant. In such cases the sill height may be raised or translucent glass used. If the object is to prevent someone from looking in, the same devices may be employed or curtains or shades may be used to ensure privacy. Where looking out is a pleasure that can be indulged, large clear glass areas should be used with as few divisions as possible located where they will not interfere with the lines of sight. The use of large glass areas not only permits the view to be enjoyed but also makes the room itself seem more spacious. In the design of large fixed glass areas, consideration should be given to the problems of solar heat gain, accessibility of the outside for cleaning, and the danger of injury from failure to see the glass.

ESCAPE

Windows used for emergency escape must be easy to open, have reasonably low sills, and openings large enough to go through without difficulty. Screens and storm sash must be easily and quickly removable.

WEATHER RESISTANCE

Windows must be sufficiently weatherproof for their intended use. There is a considerable range in the degree of weathertightness that may be acceptable; some industrial buildings, for example, may tolerate a degree of air (or even water) infiltration that would not be acceptable in a residence. Weatherstripping is usually necessary if a high degree of weathertightness is required. Some types of windows are inherently more weatherproof than others; the double-hung window is probably the best in this respect and the jalousie the worst; out-opening windows are generally more weathertight than in-opening windows.

MATERIALS

Windows are commonly made of wood, steel, and aluminum; less often of stainless steel or bronze. Wood windows are inexpensive and provide good insulation, but shrink and swell with changes in moisture content. Steel windows have strength and dimensional stability. Aluminum windows do not require painting. All metal windows, however, provide poor insulation and are subject to condensation on their inner surfaces.

TYPES OF OPERATION

Window vents may slide horizontally or vertically (double-hung); they may be hinged at the side (casement), top (awning), or bottom (hopper); or they may be pivoted horizontally (industrial) or vertically. Combinations of two or even three of these vent types in a single window are not uncommon. Shown on this page are standard symbols used on elevation drawings to indicate the type of vent operation.

Out-opening windows must be screened on the inside—an arrangement that puts the screen where it can easily be kept clean, but necessitates the use of through- or under-screen operators. Pivoted windows are almost impossible to screen. In-opening windows interfere with shades and draperies and may be hazardous to people in the room. Windows opening out on a terrace or walkway are also a hazard. Some types of windows, such as double-hung and jalousie, are difficult to clean.

The principal types of windows, with notes on their characteristics and appropriate uses, are shown on the following pages.

  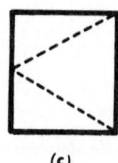  

(a)   *(b)*   *(c)*   *(d)*   *(e)*

Fig. 1. Standard symbols for ventilator operation (windows viewed from the outside)

(a) Hinged at top open out; (b) Hinged at bottom open in; (c) Hinged at left; (d) Hinged at right; (e) Pivoted—vertically or horizontally.

SPECIAL WINDOW TYPES

For use in prisons and mental institutions, special windows have been developed which offer differing degrees of detention and appearance of detention. Many types are available in steel and a few in reinforced aluminum. A similar type of window, called a "security window," is used in warehouses and many other types of buildings to prevent forcible entry.

For use in air-conditioned buildings, a special type of vertically pivoted window has been developed which can be opened only by key for cleaning.

"Classroom windows" consist of a large fixed glass area with two or more small awning or hopper vents at the bottom. They are intended for use in one-story schools where ventilation is supplied mechanically. Special "escape windows" have also been developed for use in this type of school.

"Fire windows" required by building codes and insurance inspection agencies are usually designed to meet the requirements of the National Fire Protection Association Standards (NFPA No. 80) and must bear the seal of the Underwriter's Laboratory Inc. They are permitted in walls of Class E (moderate) and Class F (light) exposure and may be of hollow metal or solid sections. Glass areas are limited to 720 sq in. and must not exceed 54 in. in height and 48 in. in width for Class E; and are limited to 2,916 sq in. and must not exceed 54 in. in height or width for Class F. Sash must be glazed with ¼-in. fire-resistant wire glass. Reference should be made to the standard for more detailed requirements regarding the design and installation of window units.

Because of their large scale, "church windows" have traditionally required special treatment, and several firms specialize in this and other types of custom work. These specialists make to order windows of any material.

ACCESSORIES

The following accessories are generally available from window manufacturers: anchors, clips, fins, subframes, metal sills, mullions, mullion covers, casings and other trim, window cleaning anchors, glazing beads, special hardware for pole or chain operation, mechanical operators (manual or power), screens, and storm sash.

Wood windows are usually sold glazed and are installed by carpenters. Metal windows are usually unglazed and are installed by the manufacturer or a special subcontractor.

SHADES AND SHADING DEVICES

Window frames should provide, when necessary, means for attaching roller-type shades. In designing interior window surrounds, attachments and clearances for other shading devices such as venetian blinds, vertical blinds, or curtains and draperies should be considered. The orientation of the window may necessitate exterior shading, particularly if air conditioning is contemplated. The more nearly the window faces the west the more significant and the more difficult shading becomes. Shading-type insect screening, roof overhangs, horizontal or vertical louvers, and open lattice-like screens of wood, metal, or masonry have been used effectively when properly designed for the particular application. Heat-absorbing or tinted glass may also be used to reduce the solar heat load (see "Glass").

WINDOW TYPES

Double-hung

Available in wood, steel, aluminum, and kalamein, in a wide variety of weights and sizes. Single-hung, triple-hung, and combination with hopper vent also available. Counterweights or spring balances used for larger sizes, spiral balances for smaller. Maximum opening 50 per cent. Hard to clean. Some residential types have sash removable for cleaning. Double-hung windows are used for all types of buildings except industrial.

Wood, steel, aluminum, bronze. Made in a variety of weights for uses varying from residential to monumental. Maximum opening 100 per cent. Screens and storm sash must be on inside and under-screen operators provided. Maximum width of ventilator about 2 ft. Extension hinges permit cleaning of outside surface. Used mostly in residential buildings.

Casement

Reversible

Available in wood and steel. Similar to double-hung in appearance, but may be tilted for better control of ventilation, or reversed for cleaning. Maximum opening 50 per cent. Used for residential and industrial buildings.

Wood, steel, aluminum. Construction similar to residential casements or industrial windows. Used wherever inexpensive utilitarian windows are required.

Basement and utility

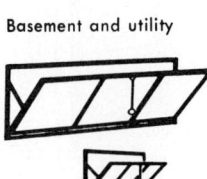

Austral

Wood and steel. When closed, similar to double-hung in appearance. Upper and lower sash counterbalanced on arms pivoted to frame; upper and lower sash operate simultaneously. Maximum opening 50 per cent. Good ventilation. Difficult to screen, shade or curtain. Used in schools, hospitals and other institutional buildings.

Wood, aluminum. Maximum opening 50 per cent. Sash usually removable for cleaning. Large sash sizes are practical. Used mostly in residential buildings.

Horizontally sliding

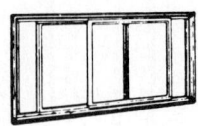

Projected

Available in steel and aluminum. Ventilators operate by either projecting out at bottom as top slides down or in at top as bottom slides up ("hopper vent"). Can be left open in rain. Inside screens required with through-screen operators. Used for commercial, institutional, and public buildings.

Available in steel and aluminum. Inexpensive windows for use in industrial and utilitarian buildings. Often used continuously horizontally and vertically to form entire walls. Mechanical operators available. Screens impractical.

Horizontally pivoted

Combination

Steel, aluminum. Combination of casement and projected ventilators. Used for commercial, institutional, and public buildings.

Steel, aluminum. Similar to above in construction and use, but the projected ventilators give better control of ventilation, permit screening, and may be left open in the rain. Mechanical operators are available.

Commercial projected

Awning

Wood, steel, aluminum. Ventilators operate in unison by manual control or by concealed mechanical operators. Maximum opening 100 per cent. Can be left open in rain. Heavy type in steel or aluminum used for industrial and institutional buildings. Lighter type in wood or aluminum used for residential buildings. Awning windows with shallow ventilators are sometimes called "louver windows." Types with ventilators 6 in. or less in height may be used for light security or detention purposes.

Steel, aluminum. Made of the same "industrial" sections used for the previous two types, but are better made and more weathertight. Often used in office portions of industrial buildings and in many types of commercial and institutional buildings.

Architectural projected

Steel only. Heavy construction top-hung windows for mechanical operation only. Available in heights of 3, 4, 5, and 6 ft and lengths in multiples of 2 ft. Typically used in monitors of industrial buildings, hence, often called "monitor windows."

Continuous

Jalousie

Aluminum only. A louver window in which the ventilators are strips of glass 3 or 4 in. high which are held in metal frames only at the sides. Louvers are operated simultaneously by crank and mechanical operator concealed in frame. Maximum opening 100 per cent. Screens and storm sash are installed on inside. Louvers when open do not project beyond building line. Used mostly on residential buildings.

Steel. For use in commercial and other types of buildings to prevent forcible entry. Muntins form continuous grille in window frame; ventilator and frame superimposed on inner surface of grille. Ventilators usually project in. For greater protection, a type is available having maximum grille openings of 88 sq in.

Security

Vertically pivoted

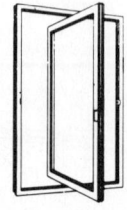

Aluminum, stainless steel. Opens by key for cleaning only, not for ventilation. Large sizes are practical. For use in high-class air-conditioned commercial or public buildings.

Steel. Similar to security windows except that the purpose is to prevent forcible exit from the building; often called "guard windows." Made of heavy steel sections. For use in prisons and psychiatric hospitals.

Detention

Table 1. Characteristics of various types of windows

From "Selection of Windows," Technical Reprint No. 5, Building Research Institute.

X indicates characteristics	double hung	double hung (reversible)	casement (out)	casement (in)	awning, canopy	pivoted (vertical)	pivoted (horizontal)	top hinged (out)	bottom hinged (in)	fixed sash	jalousie	monitor, continuous	projected	horizontal sliding
ADVANTAGES														
not apt to sag	x	x			x	x	x	x	x	x		x		x
screen & storm sash easy to install	x	x		x	x			x						x
provides 100% vent opening			x	x	x	x	x	x	x		x	x		
easy to wash with proper hardware		x		x		x	x		x					
will deflect drafts			x	x	x	x	x		x		x	x		
offers rain protection while partly open						x		x	x		x	x	x	
diverts inflowing air upward						x	x		x		x	x	x	
odd sizes economically available											x			x
large sizes practical										x				x
DISADVANTAGES														
only 50% of area openable	x	x												x
does not protect from rain when open	x	x	x			x								x
inconvenient operation when over an obstruction	x	x					x	x						x
presents a hazard if vent low and close to walkways			x		x	x	x	x				x	x	
requires weather stripping	x	x	x	x		x	x	x	x					x
horizontal members obstruct view	x	x			x		x				x	x	x	
vertical members obstruct view			x	x										x
will sag if not structurally strong			x	x										
glass soils quickly when vent open					x		x	x	x		x	x	x	
inflowing air cannot be diverted downward	x	x	x		x	x		x	x		x		x	x
excessive air leakage											x			
hard to wash											x			
interferes with furniture drapes, blinds, etc.				x		x	x		x					
screens—storm windows difficult to provide						x	x							x
sash has to be removed for washing	x								x	x	x			x

By HOWARD P. VERMILYA, AIA

Although wood windows are still made to custom designs—as double-hung units for institutional buildings and as fixed and operating sash in custom residential work (Figs. 8-10)—the vast majority of wood windows produced today are of stock design and manufactured as separate sash and frames or more often as complete window units.

Under the auspices of the National Woodwork Manufacturers Association (NWMA) and the U.S. Department of Commerce, the following Commercial Standards have been established for the production of wood windows:

CS163-59—*Ponderosa Pine Windows, Sash, and Screens:* This standard covers 1⅜-in.-thick check-rail windows and casement and cellar sash; 1⅛-in.-thick plain-rail windows and storm and cellar sash and screens; and ¾-in.-thick screens. Standard sizes are listed for each (Table 2, 4, 5, and 6, Figs. 2, 3 and 4).

CS190-59—*Standard Stock Double-Hung Wood Window Units:* This standard provides minimum requirements for double-hung wood window units including assembly of the component parts, window frames, 1⅜-in. double-hung check-rail windows (sash), balancing, weatherstripping, 1⅛-in. storm sash, and ¾-in. and 1⅛-in. window screens. Weatherstripping should limit air infiltration to not more than 0.75 cfm per lin ft of sash-crack perimeter when submitted to wind pressure equivalent to 25 mph.

CS193-53—*Standard Stock Ponderosa Pine Insulating-Glass Windows and Sash:* This standard provides minimum requirements for 1⅜-in.-thick windows and sash to accommodate ½-in.-thick insulating glass, and for 2¼-in.-thick stationary sash to accommodate 1-in.-thick insulating glass (Tables 7 and 8, Figs. 5 and 6, respectively). Sizes of glass are also specified.

CS204-59—*Standard Stock Wood Awning Window Units and Projected Awning and Stationary Sash Units:* This standard provides minimum requirements for material, construction, grading, and tolerances for frames, sash, operating mechanism, weatherstripping, storm sash, screens, and assembly of component parts into a wood awning unit of projected awning and stationary sash unit. Operative sash should be weatherstripped to prevent air infiltration in excess of 0.5 cfm per lin ft of sash-crack perimeter when subjected to wind pressure equivalent to 25 mph.

CS205-59—*Standard Stock Wood Casement Window Units:* This standard provides minimum requirements for material, construction, assembly, grading, and tolerances of units. Essential construction require-

ments cover casement frames, sash, operating mechanism, weatherstripping, storm sash, screens, and assembly ot component parts into a wood casement unit. Sizes are not specified. Weatherstripping should limit air infiltration to not more than 0.5 cfm ft of sash perimeter when subjected to wind pressure equivalent to 25 mph.

CS208-57—*Standard Stock Exterior Wood Windows and Door Frames:* This standard provides minimum specifications for standard stock exterior window and casement and cellar sash frames and exterior door frames. Data include construction, grading, and tolerances.

STANDARD OPENING SIZES

The opening sizes for windows, sash, and screens given in the tables are normally employed in structures of modular design, and were designed to meet the basic requirements of *American National Standard Basis for the Coordination of Dimensions of Building Materials and Equipment,* ANSI A62.1 (see Fig. 7 and section on "Modular Coordination").

PRESERVATIVE TREATMENT

Water-repellent wood preservative treatment of all wood parts after machining is required by all these standards. The preservative as well as the method of treatment must conform to NWMA Industry Standard I.S.-4 "Water-Repellent Preservative Non-Pressure Treatment for Millwork."

WOOD SPECIES AND GRADE

Ponderosa pine in shop grades is almost universally used for stock window units; other softwoods are occasionally used. The wood should be dried to a moisture content of 6 to 12 percent. Sash and frame exposed to view should be free from blue stains, knots, pitch pockets, or surface checks larger than ⅛ in. deep by 2 in. long. Finger jointing is allowed in the frame only. When an opaque finish is factory applied, the above noted visual defects are permitted and finger joints are allowed in sash.

ADHESIVES

Adhesives used in the manufacture of sash and frames should meet or exceed wet-use adhesive requirements of ASTM D 3110.

CLASSES AND PERFORMANCE REQUIREMENTS

NWMA Industry Standard for Wood Window Units, I.S. 2-73 (ANSI A200.1-1974) establishes two classes, A and B, and sets

performance requirements for each. The following tests are required:

Concentrated load on sash members in plane of window and perpendicular to plane of window

Air infiltration (ASTM E 283)

Water infiltration (ASTM E 331)

Uniform load deflection (ASTM E 330)

Physical load test (ASTM E 330)

WEATHERSTRIPPING, STORM SASH, SCREENS

Weatherstripping may be factory applied or installed at the site. It reduces air infiltration anywhere from 50 to 85 per cent, depending upon how well the window and frame are fitted and upon the quality of the weatherstripping. *Storm sash* also serve to reduce air leakage, in addition to reducing heat loss through the glass. Storm sash are available for all standard-size window openings. *Screens* also may be obtained in stock sizes (in either half- or full-size) to fit standard double-hung window openings (Table 3). Aluminum frame screens should conform to C.S. 240 and Screen Manufacturers Association SMR 1003.

HARDWARE

Stock window units usually come with all hardware applied and ready to set in place. If sash and frames are assembled at the job, hardware is usually field applied, using the type recommended by the manufacturer.

WOOD WINDOW TYPES

In addition to the double-hung, casement, and awning windows, for which standards have been established, other types of window units are generally available. These include the *sliding window* with one sliding and one fixed sash, two sliding sash, or two sliding and one fixed (center) sash, and with two sliding sash under a picture or fixed sash. Sizes have not been standardized but range from approximately 2 ft to 4 ft 6 in. in height and sometimes higher, and from 3 ft to 5 or 6 ft in width for the two sash openings. Sash are usually removable for cleaning. Some are available with double glazing; others are available with combination self-storing storm sash and sash screens. The *picture window* has received much recent development. It is incorporated in a single frame, usually as the center element, with double-hung, awning, or casement windows. It has been developed as a bow window unit with or without operating

Table 2. Check-rail windows, 1⅜ in. thick

The windows on this page are made ⅛ in. narrower and ¹⁄₁₆ in. shorter than window opening sizes listed. Dimensions for wood parts such as stiles, muntins, etc. are face measurements.

Window opening sizes in feet and inches (width x height)	Glass sizes in inches (width x height)					
	2 Lt	4 Lt high	Top 2, 3, 4 Lt w	Top 4, 6, 8 Lt	12 Lt	8, 16 Lt
			(Top 2 Lt w)	(Top 4 Lt)		(8 Lt)
1–8 x 3–2	16 x 16	16 x 7¾	7⅞ x 16	7⅞ x 8	———	8 x 8
3–6	18	8¾	18	9	———	9
3–10	20	9¾	20	10	———	10
4–2	22	10¾	22	11	———	11
4–6	24	11¾	24	12	———	12
4–10	26	12¾	26	13	———	13
5–2	28	13¾	28	14	———	14
5–6	30	14¾	30	15	———	———
5–10	32	15¾	32	16	———	———
			(Top 3 Lt w)	(Top 6 Lt)		
2–0 x 2–6	20 x 12	20 x 5¾	6½ x 12	6½ x 6	———	———
2–10	14	6¾	14	7	———	———
3–2	16	7¾	16	8	6²¹⁄₃₂ x 8	10 x 8
3–6	18	8¾	18	9	9	9
3–10	20	9¾	20	10	10	10
4–2	22	10¾	22	11	11	11
4–6	24	11¾	24	12	12	12
4–10	26	12¾	26	13	13	13
5–2	28	13¾	28	14	14	14
5–6	30	14¾	30	15	15	15
5–10	32	15¾	32	16	———	16
2–4 x 2–6	24 x 12	24 x 5¾	7²⁷⁄₃₂ x 12	7²⁷⁄₃₂ x 6	———	———
2–10	14	6¾	14	7	8 x 7	———
3–2	16	7¾	16	8	8	———
3–6	18	8¾	18	9	9	———
3–10	20	9¾	20	10	10	———
4–2	22	10¾	22	11	11	———
4–6	24	11¾	24	12	12	12 x 12
4–10	26	12¾	26	13	13	———
5–2	28	13¾	28	14	14	14
5–6	30	14¾	30	15	15	———
5–10	32	15¾	32	16	———	16
2–8 x 2–10	28 x 14	28 x 6¾	9⁵⁄₃₂ x 14	9⁵⁄₃₂ x 7	9¹¹⁄₃₂ x 7	———
3–2	16	7¾	16	8	8	———
3–6	18	8¾	18	9	9	———
3–10	20	9¾	20	10	10	———
4–2	22	10¾	22	11	11	———
4–6	24	11¾	24	12	12	———
4–10	26	12¾	26	13	13	———
5–2	28	13¾	28	14	14	———
5–6	30	14¾	30	15	15	———
5–10	32	15¾	32	16	16	14 x 16
			(Top 4 Lt w)	(Top 8 Lt)		(16 Lt)
3–0 x 2–10	32 x 14	32 x 6¾	7¹³⁄₁₆ x 14	7¹³⁄₁₆ x 7	10²¹⁄₃₂ x 7	———
3–2	16	7¾	16	8	8	7¹³⁄₁₆ x 8
3–6	18	8¾	18	9	9	9
3–10	20	9¾	20	10	10	10
4–2	22	10¾	22	11	11	11
4–6	24	11¾	24	12	12	12
4–10	26	12¾	26	13	13	13
5–2	28	13¾	28	14	14	14
5–6	30	14¾	30	15	15	———
5–10	32	15¾	32	16	16	———
3–4 x 2–10	36 x 14	36 x 6¾	8¹³⁄₁₆ x 14	8¹³⁄₁₆ x 7	———	———
3–2	16	7¾	16	8	———	8¹³⁄₁₆ x 8
3–6	18	8¾	18	9	———	9
3–10	20	9¾	20	10	———	10
4–2	22	10¾	22	11	———	11
4–6	24	11¾	24	12	12 x 12	12
4–10	26	12¾	26	13	———	13
5–2	28	13¾	28	14	14	14
5–6	30	14¾	30	15	———	15
5–10	32	15¾	32	16	16	16
3–8 x 3–6	40 x 18	40 x 8¾	9¹³⁄₁₆ x 18	9¹³⁄₁₆ x 9	———	———
3–10	20	9¾	20	10	———	———
4–2	22	10¾	22	11	———	———
4–6	24	11¾	24	12	———	———
4–10	26	12¾	26	13	———	9¹³⁄₁₆ x 14
5–2	28	13¾	28	14	———	15
5–6	30	14¾	30	15	———	16
5–10	32	15¾	32	16	———	

				Top 4, 6, 8 Lt	12 Lt	8, 16 Lt
Stiles			1²⁹⁄₃₂"	St. ... 1²⁹⁄₃₂"	St. ... 1²¹⁄₃₂"	St. ... 1²⁹⁄₃₂"
Top Rail			1²⁹⁄₃₂"	T.R. ... 1²⁹⁄₃₂"	T.R. ... 1²¹⁄₃₂"	T.R. ... 1²¹⁄₃₂"
Bottom Rail			3"	B.R. ... 3"	B.R. ... 2¾"	B.R. ... 2¾"
Vertical Bar			³⁄₁₆"	V.B. ... ³⁄₁₆"	V.B. ... ³⁄₁₆"	V.B. ... ³⁄₁₆"
Horizontal Bar			⁷⁄₁₆"	Mun. ... ³⁄₁₆"	Mun. ... ³⁄₁₆"	Mun. ... ³⁄₁₆"
Check Rail			1³⁄₃₂"	C.R. ... 1³⁄₃₂"	C.R. ... 1³⁄₃₂"	C.R. ... 1³⁄₃₂"

Other standard types are 4, 6, 15, 18, 20, and 24 light and cottage windows.

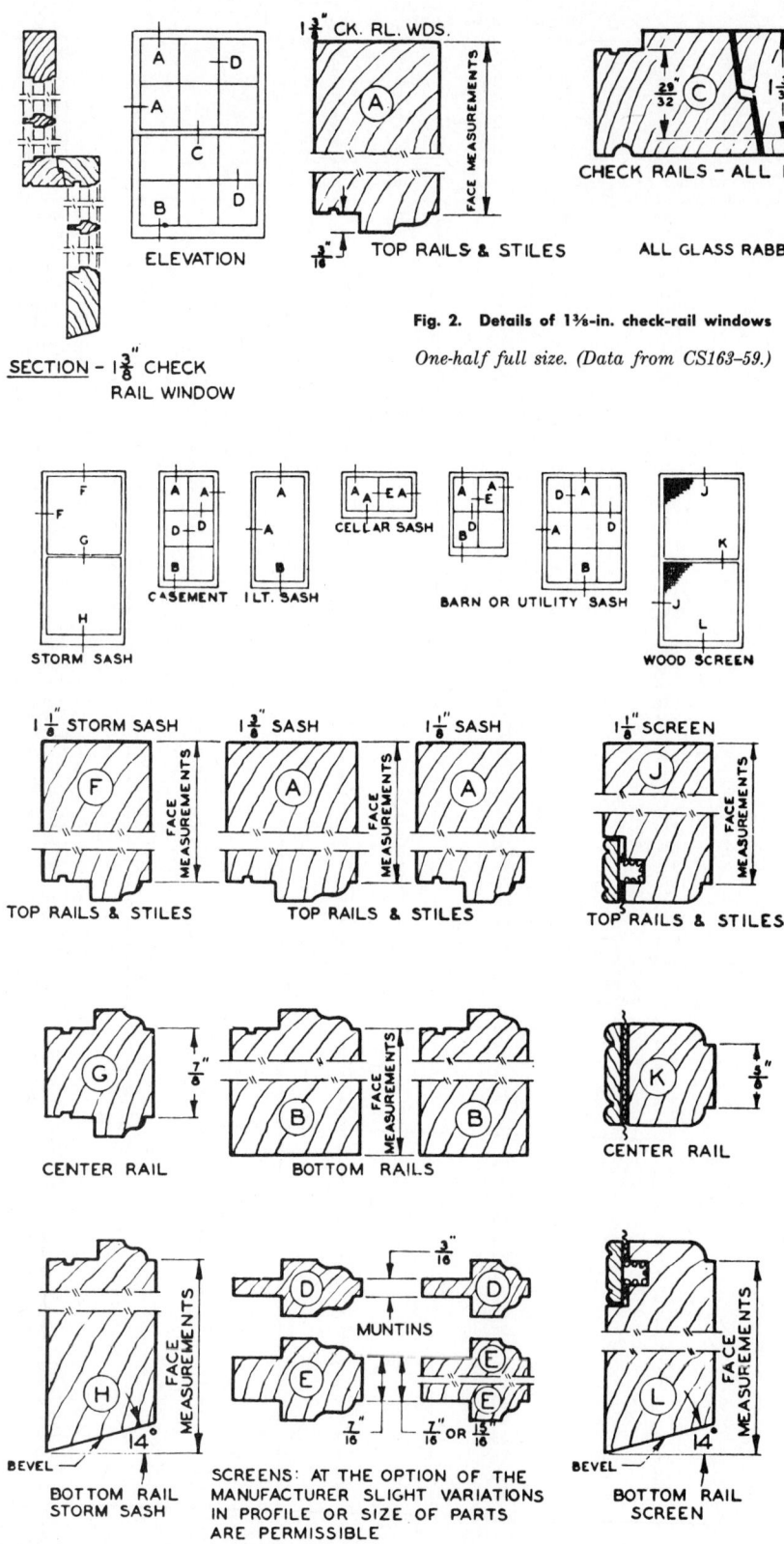

SECTION – 1⅜" CHECK RAIL WINDOW

ELEVATION

1⅜" CK. RL. WDS.

TOP RAILS & STILES

CHECK RAILS – ALL 1⅜" CK. RL. WDS.

ALL GLASS RABBETS – 3/16" DEEP

Fig. 2. Details of 1⅜-in. check-rail windows

One-half full size. (Data from CS163–59.)

BOTTOM RAILS

14° BEVEL

STORM SASH

CASEMENT 1 LT. SASH

CELLAR SASH

BARN OR UTILITY SASH

WOOD SCREEN

1⅛" STORM SASH

1⅜" SASH

1⅛" SASH

1⅛" SCREEN

TOP RAILS & STILES

TOP RAILS & STILES

TOP RAILS & STILES

CENTER RAIL

BOTTOM RAILS

CENTER RAIL

BOTTOM RAIL STORM SASH

BEVEL 14°

3/16"

MUNTINS

1/16" 1/16" OR 1 5/16"

SCREENS: AT THE OPTION OF THE MANUFACTURER SLIGHT VARIATIONS IN PROFILE OR SIZE OF PARTS ARE PERMISSIBLE

BOTTOM RAIL SCREEN

BEVEL 14°

Fig. 3. Details of storm sash, single sash, and screens

One-half full size. (Data from CS163–59.)

sash of the awning, casement, or projected type. Heights range from about 3 ft 6 in. to 6 ft 8 in., and widths from about 6 to 12 ft. Other popular combinations with the picture window are one or more operating sash (awning or sliding) above or below the fixed sash. Another recent development is the *window wall* constructed of stacked, projected, and fixed window units. Some of these units may be reversed as hopper units to open in, or even used as casements when placed on their sides. They are available with either double glass or storm sash, and with screens.

INSTALLATION

The NWMA recommends that sash be installed after the plaster is thoroughly dry, at the same time that trim is applied to the inside of the building. Openings can be closed during construction with plastic film.

Table 3. Dimensions of storm sash and screens

(Data from CS163-59)

Storm Sash		Screens	
St.	1 29/32″	St.	1 27/32″
T.R.	1 29/32″	T.R.	1 27/32″
B.R.	4 1/16″	B.R.	3″
C.R.	7/8″	C.R.	5/8″

Storm Sash and Screens are made ⅛″ narrower and 1″ longer than window opening sizes.

Available for all modular-sized window or sash openings.

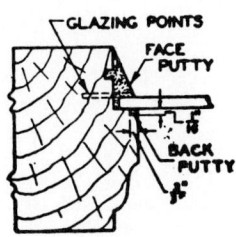

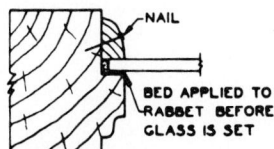

Fig. 4.   Glazing details in 1⅜-in. sash

One-half full size. (Data from CS163–59.)

Table 4. Standard sizes of casement sash, 1⅜ in. thick

Sash are made ⅛ in. narrower and 1/32 in. shorter than the opening sizes listed. (Data from CS163–59.)

Prefit face measurements (in.)

Stiles	1 21/32	Vertical bar	3/16
Top rail	1 29/32	Muntin	3/16
Bottom rail	3		

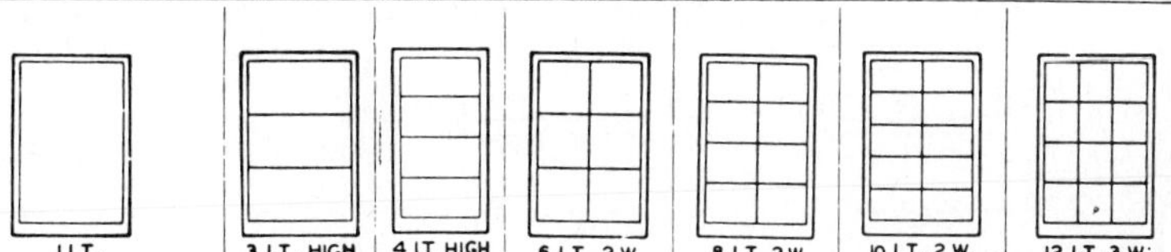

	1 LT.	3 LT. HIGH	4 LT. HIGH	6 LT. 2 W.	8 LT. 2 W.	10 LT. 2 W.	12 LT. 3 W.

Opening sizes	Glass sizes						
ft and in.	*in.*	*in.*	*in.*	*in.*	*in.*	*in.*	*in.*
0-11½×2-6	8×25	8×8 5/32	8×6 1/16	....	....	....	....
2-10	29	9½	7 1/16	....	....	....	....
3-2	33	10 13/16	8 1/16	....	....	....	....
3-6	37	12 9/32	9 1/16	....	....	....	....
3-10	41	13½	10 1/16	....	....	....	....
4-2	45	14 13/16	11 1/16	....	....	....	....
4-6	49	16 5/32	12 1/16	....	....	....	....
4-10	53	17½	13 1/16	....	....	....	....
5-2	57	18 13/16	14 1/16	....	....	....	....
1-3½×2-6	12×25	12×8 5/32	12×6 1/16	5⅞×8 5/32	5⅞×6 1/16	....	....
2-10	29	9½	7 1/16	9½	7 1/16	....	....
3-2	33	10 13/16	8 1/16	10 13/16	8 1/16	....	....
3-6	37	12 9/32	9 1/16	12 9/32	9 1/16	5⅞×7 3/16	....
3-10	41	13½	10 1/16	13½	10 1/16	8	....
4-2	45	14 13/16	11 1/16	14 13/16	11 1/16	8 25/32	....
4-6	49	16 5/32	12 1/16	16 5/32	12 1/16	9 19/32	....
4-10	53	17½	13 1/16	17½	13 1/16	10 13/32	....
5-2	57	18 13/16	14 1/16	18 13/16	14 1/16	11 3/16	....
1-7½×2-6	16×25	16×8 5/32	16×6 1/16	7⅞×8 5/32	7⅞×6 1/16	....	....
2-10	29	9½	7 1/16	9½	7 1/16	....	....
3-2	33	10 13/16	8 1/16	10 13/16	8 1/16	....	....
3-6	37	12 9/32	9 1/16	12 9/32	9 1/16	7⅞×7 3/16	5 5/32×9 1/16
3-10	41	13½	10 1/16	13½	10 1/16	8	10 1/16
4-2	45	14 13/16	11 1/16	14 13/16	11 1/16	8 25/32	11 1/16
4-6	49	16 5/32	12 1/16	16 5/32	12 1/16	9 19/32	12 1/16
4-10	53	17½	13 1/16	17½	13 1/16	10 13/32	13 1/16
5-2	57	18 13/16	14 1/16	18 13/16	14 1/16	11 3/16	14 1/16
1-11½×2-6	20×25	20×8 5/32	20×6 1/16	9⅞×8 5/32	9⅞×6 1/16	....	....
2-10	29	9½	7 1/16	9½	7 1/16	....	....
3-2	33	10 13/16	8 1/16	10 13/16	8 1/16	....	....
3-6	37	12 9/32	9 1/16	12 9/32	9 1/16	9⅞×7 3/16	6½×9 1/16
3-10	41	13½	10 1/16	13½	10 1/16	8	10 1/16
4-2	45	14 13/16	11 1/16	14 13/16	11 1/16	8 25/32	11 1/16
4-6	49	16 5/32	12 1/16	16 5/32	12 1/16	9 19/32	12 1/16
4-10	53	17½	13 1/16	17½	13 1/16	10 13/32	13 1/16
5-2	57	18 13/16	14 1/16	18 13/16	14 1/16	11 3/16	14 1/16
2-3½×2-6	24×25	24×8 5/32	24×6 1/16	11⅞×8 5/32	11⅞×6 1/16	....	....
2-10	29	9½	7 1/16	9½	7 1/16	....	....
3-2	33	10 13/16	8 1/16	10 13/16	8 1/16	....	....
3-6	37	12 9/32	9 1/16	12 9/32	9 1/16	11⅞×7 3/16	7 27/32×9 1/16
3-10	41	13½	10 1/16	13½	10 1/16	8	10 1/16
4-2	45	14 13/16	11 1/16	14 13/16	11 1/16	8 25/32	11 1/16
4-6	49	16 5/32	12 1/16	16 5/32	12 1/16	9 19/32	12 1/16
4-10	53	17½	13 1/16	17½	13 1/16	10 13/32	13 1/16
5-2	57	18 13/16	14 1/16	18 13/16	14 1/16	11 3/16	14 1/16

[1] Certain modifications in size may be necessary for modular coordination, depending upon the type and design of frame used.

Table 5.   Standard sizes of picture sash, 1⅜ in. thick

Sash are made ⅛ in. narrower and 1/32 in. shorter than the opening sizes listed. (Data from CS163–59.)

Prefit face measurements (in.)			
Stiles 12 9/32 Bottom rail 2¾			
Top rail 12 1/32 Bars and muntins 7/16			
4 HORIZ. LTS.	12 LT. 3 W.	16 LT. 4 W.	20 LT. 5 W.

Opening sizes	Glass sizes			
ft and in.	*in.*	*in.*	*in.*	*in.*
4–4×4–6 5–2	48×12 14	15 21/32×12 14	11 5/8×12 14	---------- ----------
5–0×4–6 5–2	56×12 14	---------- ----------	13 5/8×12 14	10 13/16×12 14
5–8×4–6 5–2	------ ------	---------- ----------	15 5/8×12 14	12 13/32×12 14

Table 6.   Standard sizes of cellar sash, 1⅜ and 1⅛ in. thick

Sash are made ⅛ in. narrower and ⅛ in. shorter than the opening sizes listed. (Data from CS163–59.)

Prefit face measurements (in.)		
Stiles 12 1/32	12 1/32	
Top rail 12 9/32	12 9/32	
Bottom rail 12 9/32	12 9/32	
Vertical bar 7/16	7/16	
2 LT.		3 LT.

Opening sizes	Glass sizes	Opening sizes	Glass sizes
ft and in.	*in.*	*ft and in.*	*in.*
1–8×1–4	8×12	2–0×1–0	6 21/32×8
2–0×1–4 1–8 2–0	10×12 16 20	2–4×1–4 1–8	8×12 16
		2–8×1–0 1–4 1–8 2–0	9 11/32×8 12 16 20
2–4×1–4 1–8 2–0	12×12 16 20	3–0×1–4 1–8 2–0	10 21/32×12 16 20
2–8×1–4 1–8 2–0	14×12 16 20	3–4×1–4 1–8 2–0 2–4	12×12 16 20 24

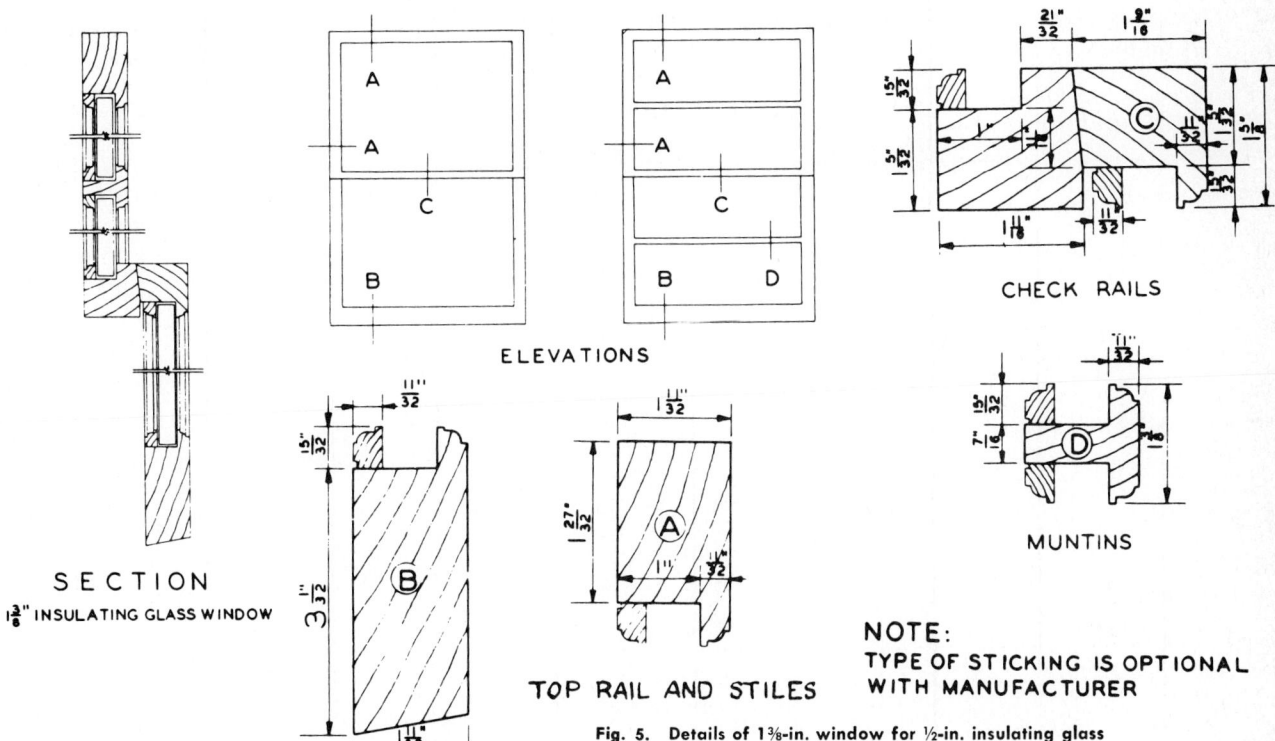

SECTION

1⅜" INSULATING GLASS WINDOW

ELEVATIONS

CHECK RAILS

MUNTINS

BOTTOM RAIL

TOP RAIL AND STILES

NOTE:
TYPE OF STICKING IS OPTIONAL
WITH MANUFACTURER

Fig. 5. Details of 1⅜-in. window for ½-in. insulating glass

One-half full size. (Data from CS193–53.)

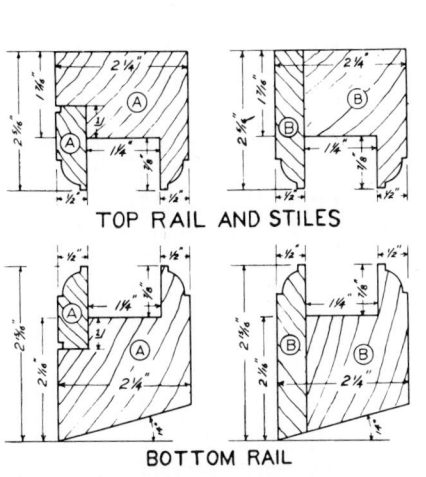

TOP RAIL AND STILES

BOTTOM RAIL

Fig. 6. Details of 2¼-in. stationary sash for 1-in. insulating glass

One-half full size. Stationary sash may be made in accordance with either of the above details at the option of the manufacturer. Depth of the rabbet is optional, but must not be less than ½ in. (Data from CS193–53.)

Fig. 7. Relation of window to grid opening in brick wall

Data from CS163–59.

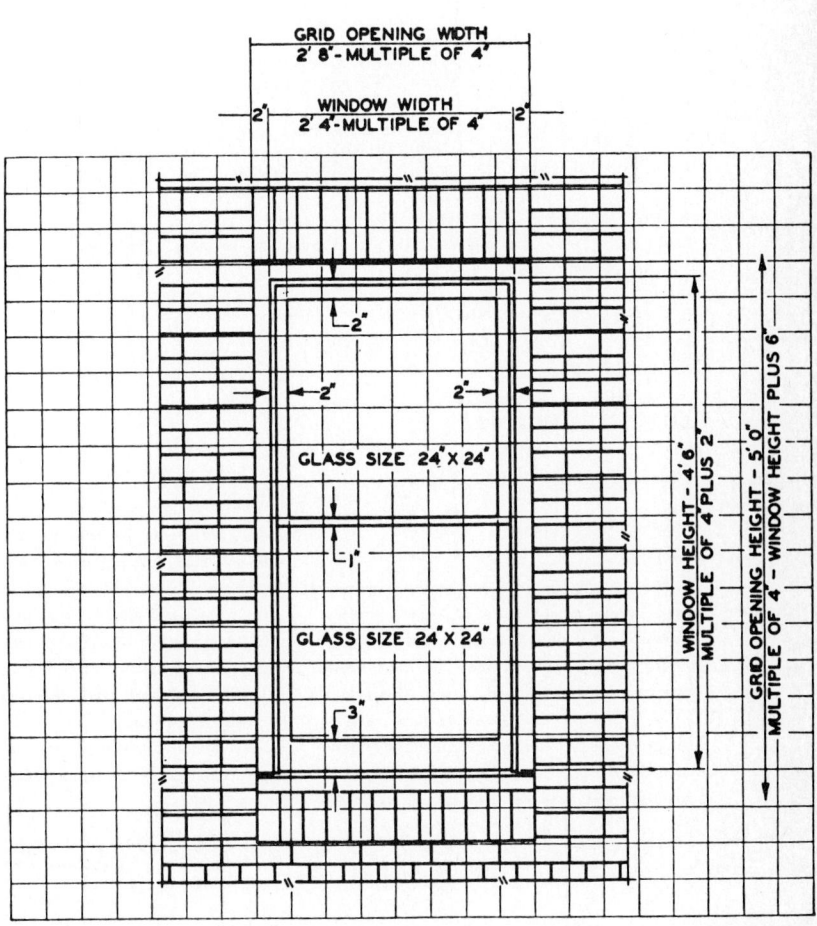

GRID OPENING WIDTH
2' 8"- MULTIPLE OF 4"

WINDOW WIDTH
2' 4"- MULTIPLE OF 4"

GLASS SIZE 24" X 24"

GLASS SIZE 24" X 24"

WINDOW HEIGHT - 4'- 6"
MULTIPLE OF 4 PLUS 2

GRID OPENING HEIGHT - 5'- 0"
MULTIPLE OF 4 - WINDOW HEIGHT PLUS 6

Table 7. Standard sizes of insulating-glass check-rail windows, 1⅜ in. thick

Windows are made ⅛ in. narrower and 1/16 in. shorter than the sash opening sizes listed. (Data from CS193–53.)

Prefit face measurements (in.)

Stiles	1 27/32	Check rails	1 5/32
Top rail	1 27/32	Muntins	7/16
Bottom rail	3 1/32		

Sash opening sizes	TWO-LIGHT WINDOWS		FOUR-LIGHT WINDOWS	
	Glass sizes	Glass opening sizes	Glass sizes	Glass opening sizes
ft. and in.	in.	in.	in.	in.
2-0 × 4-6	20 × 24	20 3/16 × 24 3/16	20 × 11 11/16	20 3/16 × 11 7/8
5-2	28	28 3/16	13 11/16	13 7/8
2-4 × 3-2	24 × 16	24 3/16 × 16 3/16	--------------	--------------
4-6	24	24 3/16	24 × 11 11/16	24 3/16 × 11 7/8
5-2	28	28 3/16	13 11/16	13 7/8
2-8 × 3-2	28 × 16	28 3/16 × 16 3/16	--------------	--------------
4-6	24	24 3/16	28 × 11 11/16	28 3/16 × 11 7/8
5-2	28	28 3/16	13 11/16	13 7/8
3-0 × 3-2	32 × 16	32 3/16 × 16 3/16	--------------	--------------
4-6	24	24 3/16	32 × 11 11/16	32 3/16 × 11 7/8
5-2	28	28 3/16	13 11/16	13 7/8
3-4 × 4-6	36 × 24	36 3/16 × 24 3/16	36 × 11 11/16	36 3/16 × 11 7/8
5-2	28	28 3/16	13 11/16	13 7/8

Table 8. Standard sizes of insulating-glass stationary sash, 2¼ in. thick

Prefit sash are made ⅛ in. less in width than the sash opening sizes listed. (Data from CS193–53.)

Prefit face measurements (in.)

Stiles	1 7/16
Top rail	1 7/16
Bottom rail	2 1/16

Sash opening sizes	Glass sizes	Glass opening sizes
ft. and in.	in.	in.
4-4 × 4-6	48 1/2 × 50	49 × 50 1/2
5-2	58	58 1/2
5-0 × 4-6	56 1/2 × 50	57 × 50 1/2
5-2	58 1/8	58 1/2
5-8 × 4-6	64 1/2 × 50	65 × 50 1/2
5-2	58	58 1/2
6-4 × 4-6	72 1/2 × 50	73 × 50 1/2
5-2	58	58 1/2
7-0 × 4-6	80 1/2 × 50	81 × 50 1/2
5-2	58	58 1/2
8-4 × 4-6	96 1/2 × 50	97 × 50 1/2
5-2	58	58 1/2

CUSTOM WINDOWS

Courtesy of Architectural Woodwork Institute

SPECIES SELECTION

The pine species are the most commonly used in the manufacture of wood window frames and sash (excepting window walls, where other materials may be preferable due to costs of thicker members). This popularity is due to their even texture, dimensional stability, excellent paintability, low cost, and ready availability. The mahoganies and redwood, however, are gaining in popularity and should be considered. To help in this selection, all pertinent information on the characteristics of woods for exterior use is contained in Table 9. This table has been adapted from the Wood Characteristic Table in the manual, *Guide to Wood Species Selection*, published by the Architectural Woodwork Institute.

See section on "Wood" for AWI grades, specifications, and moisture content requirements.

PRESERVATIVE TREATMENT

Treatment of all exterior window frames and sash with pentachlorophenol preservative and a water repellent additive is recommended. (For more information read "Effects of Humidity on Wood" and "Preservative Treatment of Wood" in AWI's *Guide to Wood Species Selection*.) The water repellent and preservative treatment prevents water absorption, eliminates rotting and greatly reduces staining, checking and dimension change. Dry wood that has minimum shrinkage or swelling holds paint better and therefore lasts longer.

PROTECTIVE COATINGS

Painting In almost all cases, architectural woodwork receives further protective and decorative coating. If the final finish is to be paint, it may be desirable to have the priming coat applied at the mill. This is particularly true in areas of high humidity. Second and third coats should be applied as soon after installation as possible.

Staining Long-lasting, economical finishes are now obtainable by the use of pigmented stains. All stain coatings should contain the water repellent and preservative ingredients as well as the pigmented penetrating stain foundation, since the penetrating stains are only decorative and do not keep water out of the wood. Only one coat is usually used on the first application when the wood surfaces are new and smooth, and penetration is only moderate. Two coats should be used on rough-sawed textured surfaces. After weathering for 1 or 2 years, the exposed surfaces develop a slight roughness and some fine checking. This roughness makes the wood very receptive to penetrating stains and thus greatly increases the finish durability. A second application should be made after roughness has developed for optimum results.

GLAZING

Regular putty or oil-based glazing compounds must be covered with paint in order to be fully effective. The paint should cover about 1/16-in. of the glass to insure a seal. Insulating glass or large lights of plate glass are usually glazed with wood or aluminum stops, and polybutylene or rubber-based extruded glazing tapes and special bedding compounds. These materials may be used on both sides of the glass or on just one side, with wood or metal channel stops. Where they are used on only one side for bedding, and a metal channel is used on the other, gunning type liquid acrylic polymer is recommended to fill and seal any small voids next to the glass. All the new methods and materials that have been developed over the last few years for use on large high-rise buildings, mainly for metal sash, are in many cases just as applicable for use on wood. See sections on "Glass" and "Curtain Walls."

Table 9. Wood species recommended for window frames and sash

Species	Relative cost	Practical size limitations: Maximum thickness[2]	Maximum width	Maximum length	Hardness	Dimensional stability[3]	Finishing: Paint	Penetrating pigmented stain	Remarks
[1]**Cypress**	100	2¾"	9½"	16′	Medium	8/64"	Good	Good	Has become scarce. Check local availability. Mostly of inland variety. All heart not available.
[1]**Fir** Douglas—Flat Grain	75	2¾"	11"	16′	Medium	10/64"	Fair	Fair	Tendency to splinter and grain raise.
Fir Douglas—Vertical Grain	80	1⅝"	11"	16′	Medium	6/64"	Good	Good	Good stability. Some splintering.
[1]**Mahogany** African—Plain Sawn	120	2¾"	11½"	16′	Hard	7/64"	Good	Excellent	Moderate price, excellent stability, good overall properties.
[1]**Mahogany** Tropical American—"Honduras"	170	2¾"	11½"	16′	Hard	6/64"	Good	Excellent	Similar to African mahogany, slightly finer texture, more expensive.
Tanguile "Dark Philippine Mahogany"—Plain Sawn	120	1¾"	11"	16′	Medium	12/64"	Fair	Good	Philippine hardwood closest to true mahogany; best of "Philippine mahoganies."
[1]**Oak** White—Plain Sawn	120	1⅝"	7½"	12′	Very Hard	11/64"	Fair	Good	Hard and wear-resistant. Use generally limited to door frames.
Pine Idaho	80	1¾"	11"	16′	Soft	8/64"	Excellent	Good	Excellent workability and good properties for general use. These pines can be specified interchangeably when preservative-treated, as required by AWI Quality Standards.
Pine Northern	80	2¾"	9½"	14′	Soft	8/64"	Excellent	Good	
[1]**Pine** Ponderosa	75	2¾"	11"	16′	Soft	8/64"	Excellent	Good	
Pine Sugar	80	2¾"	11"	16′	Soft	7/64"	Excellent	Good	
Pine Yellow Shortleaf	65	2¾"	11"	16′	Medium	10/64"	Fair	Fair	An economical hard pine, somewhat prone to checking.
Red Cedar Western (Heartwood)	90	1⅝"	11"	16′	Soft	6/64"	Good	Excellent	High natural decay resistance, very stable. Soft. Limited supply.
Redwood Flat Grain (Heartwood)	85	2¾"	11"	20′	Soft	6/64"	Good	Good	Superior exterior wood. High natural decay resistance, low flammability. Plentiful.
[1]**Redwood** Vertical Grain (Heartwood)	90	2¾"	11"	20′	Soft	3/64"	Excellent	Excellent	Superior exterior wood. High natural decay resistance, low flammability. Good supply in most sizes.
Spruce Sitka	75	1¾"	11"	16′	Medium	10/64"	Good	Good	Strong, straight-grained; used mostly on square edge material. Not generally molded.
[1]**Teak** East Indian	430	2⅝"	9½"	14′	Very Hard	6/64"	Good	Excellent	Most outstanding wood for all uses. Very expensive.

[1] *Indicates species represented by a color plate, showing its appearance in the natural state and with two types of stain, in the AWI publication,* Guide to Wood Species Selection.
[2] *Without laminating.*
[3] *These figures represent possible width change in a 12" board when moisture content is reduced from 10% to 5%.*
[4] *To be used in determining allowable connector loads, with "1" representing the weakest group.*
[5] *Estimate based on density.*

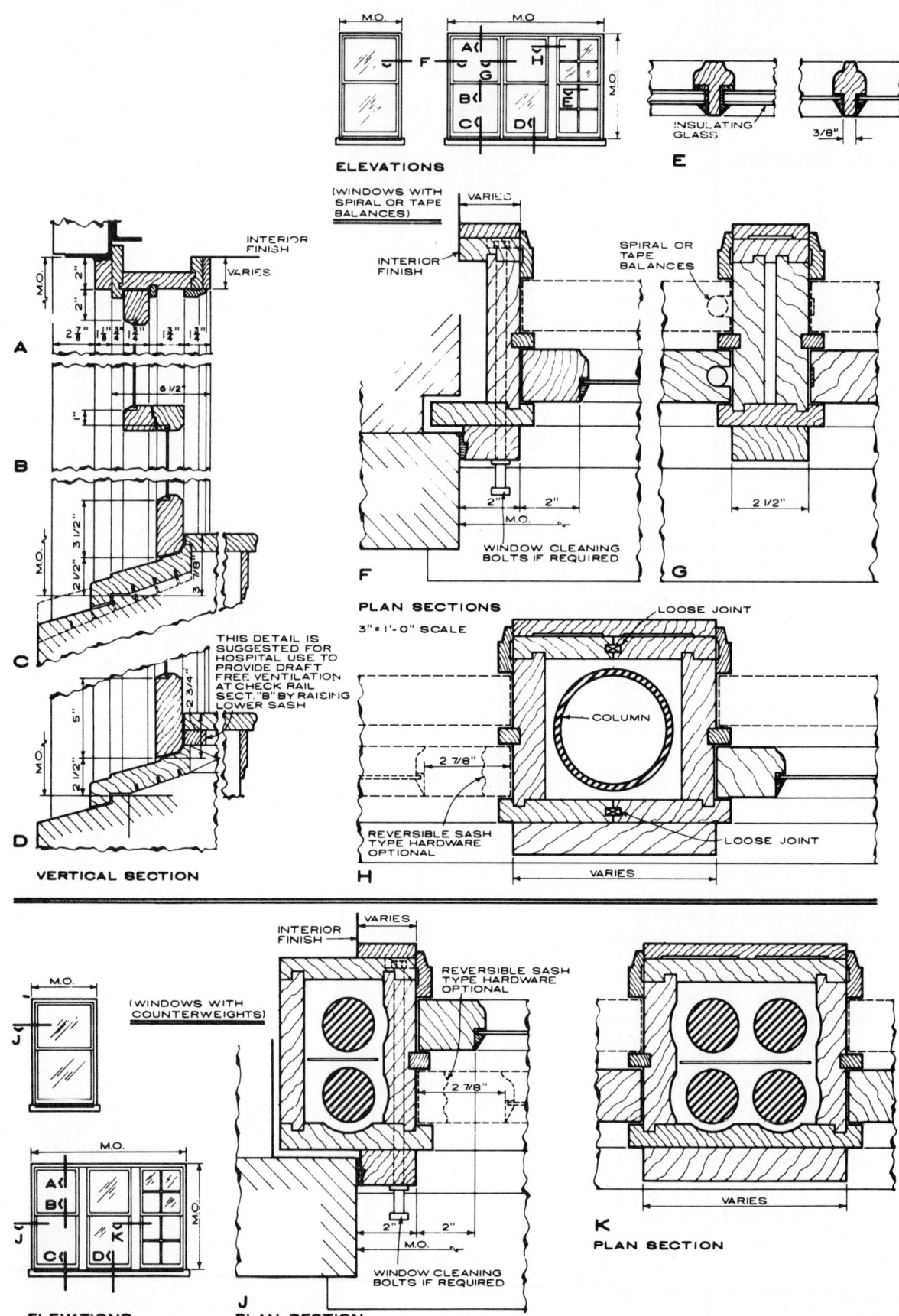

Fig. 8. Typical details, double-hung windows

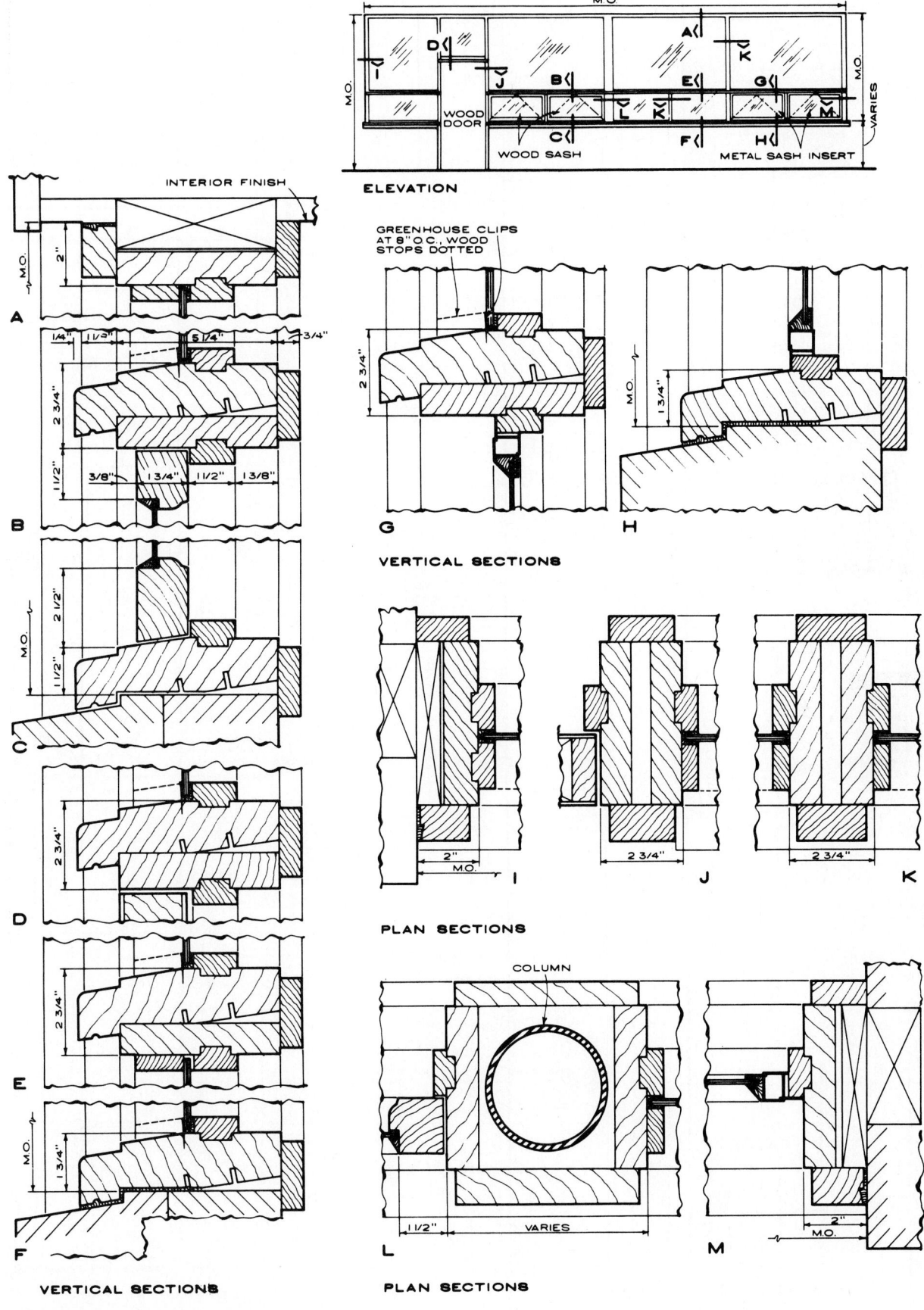

ELEVATION

VERTICAL SECTIONS

PLAN SECTIONS

PLAN SECTIONS

VERTICAL SECTIONS

Fig. 9. Typical details, window walls

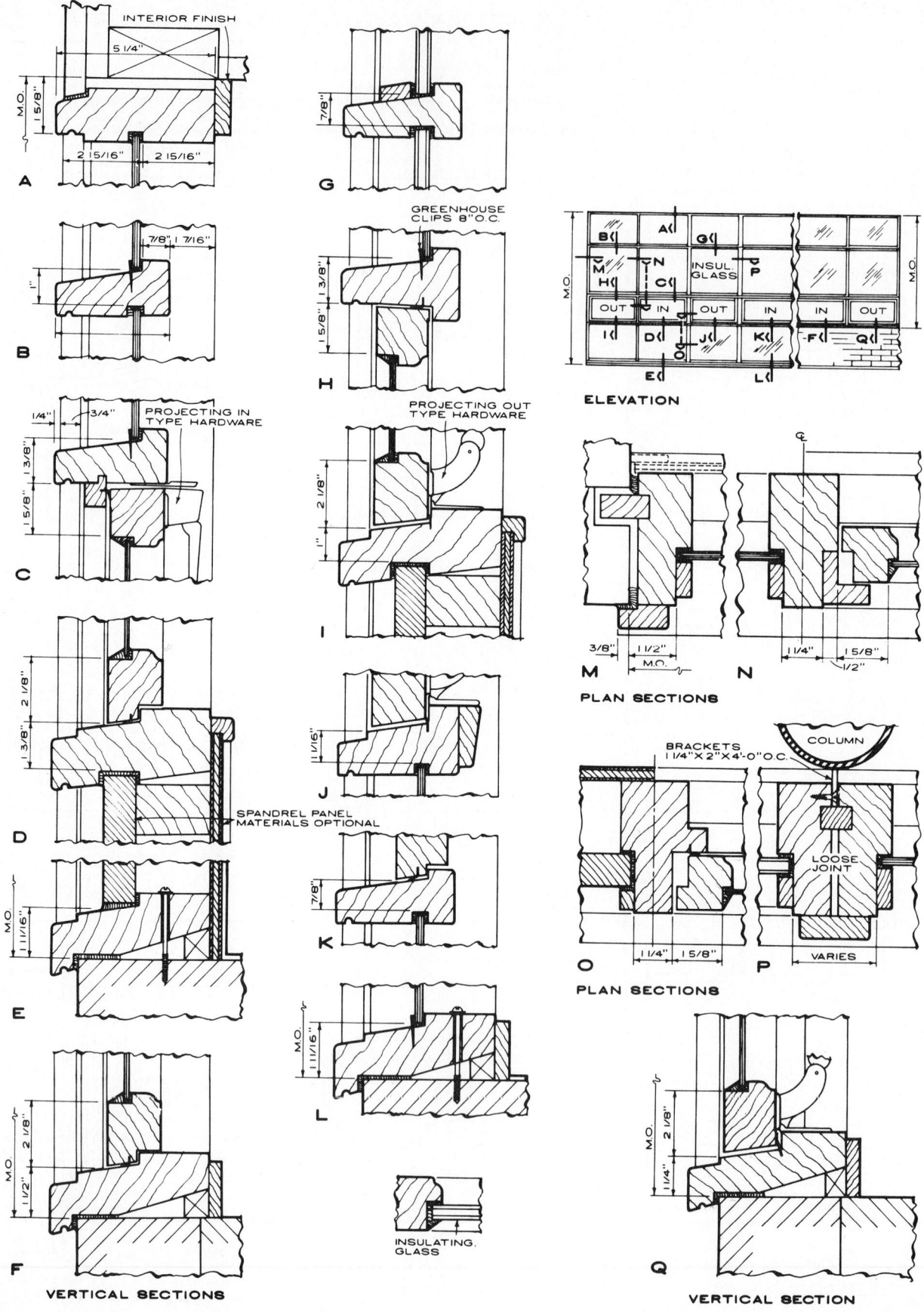

Fig. 10. Typical details, curtain walls

By HOWARD P. VERMILYA, AIA

Steel windows are made in a wide variety of type and grade combinations of ventilator openings. The sizes and types have been largely standardized through the efforts of the Steel Window Institute. Except for residential casements, all standard types are sized in accordance with the principles of modular coordination described in American National Standards Institute ANSI A62.1. Within the range of standard sizes established, those designated as warehouse types are available for immediate delivery; other sizes are available on order from the factory.

WINDOW TYPES

The classification of window types is based generally on the grade for a common or probable use, often with several weights and design types for each grade. The types listed in the Steel Window Institute's *Recommended Specifications for Steel Windows* are as follows:

Residential
   Casement
   Basement
   Utility
   Ranch
   Picture
Commercial, industrial, institutional
   Projected
   Casement
   Combination
   Classroom
   Guard
   Psychiatric
   Awning
   Architectural projected
   Commercial projected
   Security
   Continuous
   Steel subframe

Types other than those listed above are manufactured but have not been standardized as to size or specification. Among these are: *double-hung* (heavy) for commercial and institutional buildings, *vertically pivoted* (stainless steel) for high-class air-conditioned buildings, and *escape* windows (intermediate) for educational buildings.

Grades of steel windows are determined by the weight of the combined outside frame and ventilator members in pounds per linear foot or by the depth and thickness of the individual sections. Standards establish maximum vent sizes and infiltration requirements and other items pertinent to the particular type of window. Screens are supplied for most types, with provision for window operation where nec-

essary. Storm sash are available from some manufacturers. Insulating glass up to ½ in. thick can be installed in most types. All glazing is done at the site by the glazing contractor.

Shop finish comprises cleaning in a hot alkali solution, rinsing, bonderizing, rinsing, and dipping or spraying on a coat of paint, then preferably baking for at least 30 min at a temperature not less than 300°F. Double-hung windows must be electrogalvanized or tight-coat hot-galvanized before forming. The weight of the galvanized coating should conform to Class B2, ASTM A386-55.

One manufacturer has developed an alternate finish consisting of a bonderizing treatment, followed by an epoxy-resin-type primer baked on, over which an alkydamine-type enamel is baked on as a finish coat. This coating complies with Federal Specifications TT-E-489b and TT-R-266a.

Residential windows

Casement, *picture*, and *ranch* windows should have frames and ventilators made of hot-rolled structural steel sections having a minimum depth of 1 in. and a minimum weight of 2 lb per lin ft. At a wind velocity of 25 mph, the maximum infiltration permitted is 1 cu ft per lin ft of ventilator perimeter. *Basement* and *utility* windows should have frames and ventilators of hot-rolled steel sections having a minimum depth of 1 in. and a minimum weight of 1.7 lb per lin ft.

Maximum casement ventilator size is 1 ft 11¼ in. in width by 4 ft 1⅜ in. in height. Two types of casement operation are standard: *roto* (crank-operated, under screen) and *simplex* (manually operated, with friction hinges). In the latter case screens are provided with a sliding wicket to give access to the window. Muntins may be omitted if desired (some manufacturers only). Typical installation details of residential casement windows are shown in **Fig. 11.**

Casement, basement, and utility windows have been standardized in size, as shown in Fig. 12. Picture windows have not been standardized, but they are usually available in the standard casement heights of 3 ft 2⅜ in., 4 ft 2⅝ in., and 5 ft 3 in. Ranch windows also have not been standardized as to size, but most manufacturers base their designs on a fixed glass size of 24 in. by 36 in. This results in window widths of approximately 3 ft 1 in., 6 ft 2 in., and 9 ft 3 in., and heights of 2 ft 1 in., 4 ft 2 in., and 6 ft 3 in. For more precise information on ·ranch and picture windows, consult manufacturers' catalogs.

Double-hung windows (light) are made

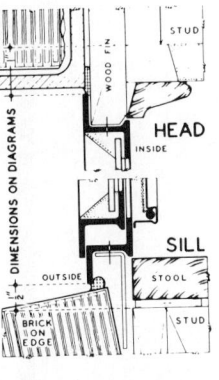

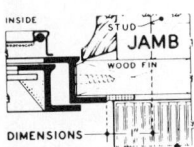

Fig. 11. Residential casement window in brick-veneer construction—scale 3 in. = 1 ft.

Courtesy Hope's

from cold-formed strip steel that has been galvanized before forming. The minimum depth of the frame is 3¾ in.; the minimum thickness of the sill is 0.060 in., of all other members of the frame and ventilators, 0.048 in. Parting strips may be extruded aluminum, and muntins may be hot-rolled steel tees, ungalvanized. Maximum width is 4 ft; maximum height is 7 ft 1½ in. or, with sill ventilator, 8 ft 1½ in. At a wind velocity of 25 mph, maximum infiltration is 1 cu ft per lin ft of ventilator perimeter and maximum glass thickness is ¼ in. Screens are installed on the outside and may be top-hinged or sliding. Standard sizes are shown in Fig. 13 and typical details in Fig. 14.

Intermediate windows

Intermediate windows are made of heavier and better constructed sections than those used for residential windows. They are made in a number of window types and are intended for a wide range of uses. *Projected*, *casement*, and *combination* windows are long-established types and are widely used in the better class of commercial and institutional buildings. *Classroom* windows are intended primarily for use in school buildings but are well suited to many other applications. They consist of a large, fixed glass area for light and view, with one or more small projected ventilators at the bottom for controlled ventilation. The four window types mentioned above have been standardized as to size (Figs. 15-18). Other intermediate types that have not been standardized will be noted later.

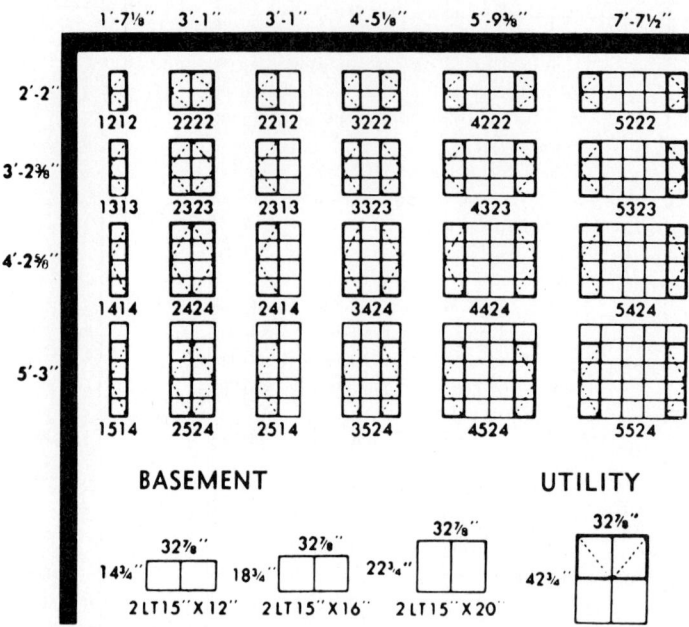

Fig. 12 Residential casement windows: types and sizes

Eastern sizes shown apply to all states except California, Oregon, Washington, Idaho, Nevada, Utah, and Arizona. For western sizes consult manufacturers' catalogs. All sizes shown are warehouse types. Dimensions are over-all out-to-out measurements. Single ventilators may swing from right or left. Fixed types furnished for all sizes shown. (From "Recommended Specifications for Steel Windows," Steel Window Institute.)

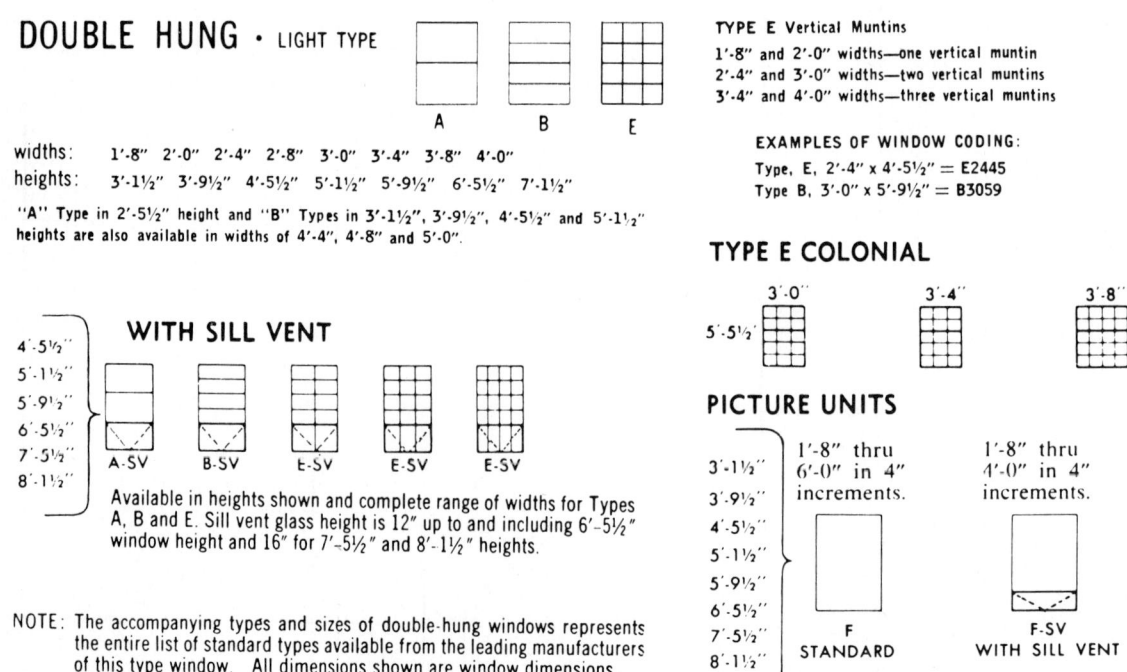

DOUBLE HUNG · LIGHT TYPE

widths: 1'-8" 2'-0" 2'-4" 2'-8" 3'-0" 3'-4" 3'-8" 4'-0"

heights: 3'-1½" 3'-9½" 4'-5½" 5'-1½" 5'-9½" 6'-5½" 7'-1½"

"A" Type in 2'-5½" height and "B" Types in 3'-1½", 3'-9½", 4'-5½" and 5'-1½" heights are also available in widths of 4'-4", 4'-8" and 5'-0".

WITH SILL VENT

Available in heights shown and complete range of widths for Types A, B and E. Sill vent glass height is 12" up to and including 6'-5½" window height and 16" for 7'-5½" and 8'-1½" heights.

NOTE: The accompanying types and sizes of double-hung windows represents the entire list of standard types available from the leading manufacturers of this type window. All dimensions shown are window dimensions.

TYPE E Vertical Muntins

1'-8" and 2'-0" widths—one vertical muntin
2'-4" and 3'-0" widths—two vertical muntins
3'-4" and 4'-0" widths—three vertical muntins

EXAMPLES OF WINDOW CODING:
Type, E, 2'-4" x 4'-5½" = E2445
Type B, 3'-0" x 5'-9½" = B3059

TYPE E COLONIAL

PICTURE UNITS

F
STANDARD

F-SV
WITH SILL VENT

Fig. 13. Residential double-hung windows: types and sizes

From "Recommended Specifications for Steel Windows," Steel Window Institute.

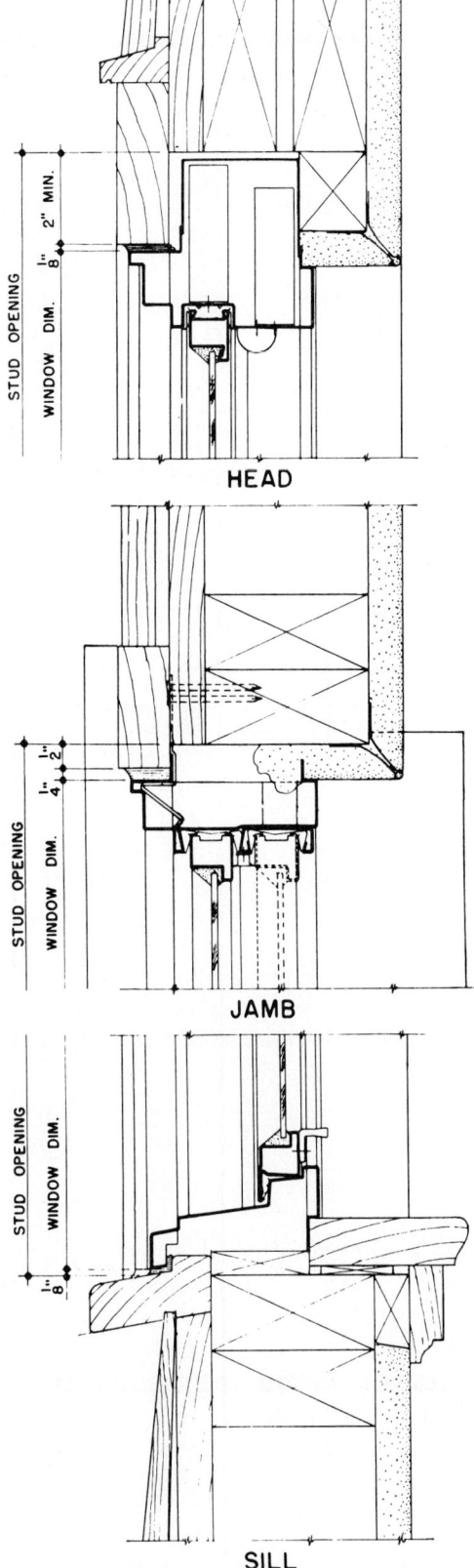

Fig. 14. Residential double-hung window in wood-frame construction—scale: 3 in. = 1 ft

Courtesy Truscon

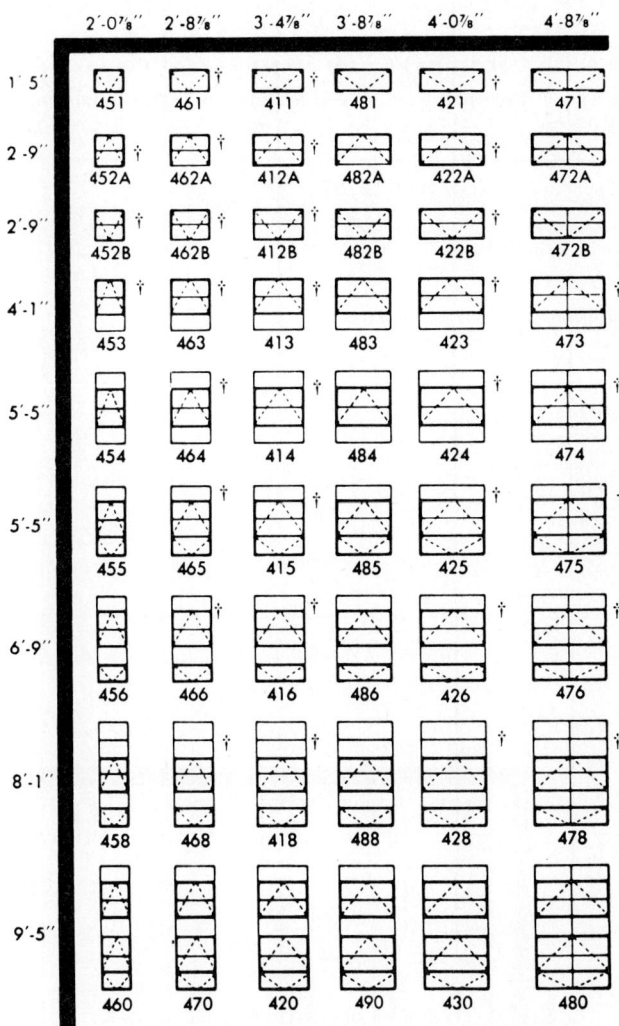

(Swing of vents only as indicated)

Fig. 15. Intermediate* projected windows: types and sizes

*Architectural projected windows are available in the same types and sizes including warehouse types, shown above. To specify architectural projected windows, change the first digit of the code number from 4 to 2 (251, 261, etc.). Fixed or stationary units may be supplied for all types shown. *For heavy intermediate, add the suffix "H"; for heavy custom, add the suffix "HC." (From "Recommended Specifications for Steel Windows," Steel Window Institute.) The symbol † indicates warehouse types and sizes.*

Intermediate windows are manufactured from hot-rolled structural steel, in three weights or grades, standard, heavy, and heavy custom. Minimum weights and dimensions of the members and maximum sizes of the vents for each grade are shown in Table 10. At a wind velocity of 25 mph, maximum infiltration permitted is 1 cu ft per lin ft of ventilator perimeter.

Casement ventilators that exceed 5 ft 6 in. in height should have three hinges and a two-point-connected locking device. Projected ventilators whose top edges are more than 6 ft 6 in. above the floor should be provided with hardware designed for pole or chain operation.

A typical installation detail of an intermediate projected window is shown in Fig. 19, and various glazing details for intermediate windows are given in Fig. 20.

Guard windows are designed for use in jails and correctional institutions. They are available in standard sizes and in three types of construction that provide "minimum," "moderate," or "maximum" detention. The basic design employs fixed main

Table 10. Specification for intermediate windows

Data from Recommended Specifications for Steel Windows, *Steel Window Institute.*

	Standard intermediate	Heavy intermediate	Heavy custom
Minimum combined weight of frame and vent members, lb per lin ft	3.0	3.5	4.2
Minimum depth (front to back) of frame and vent members, in.	1¼	1⁵⁄₁₆	1½
Maximum vent size			
Casement:			
Width, ft–in.	2–3	2–6	3–0
Height, ft–in.	5–6	6–0	8–0
Area, sq ft			24
Projected			
Width, ft–in.	4–8	5–0	6–0
Height, ft–in.	2–8	3–0	4–0
Area, sq ft			20

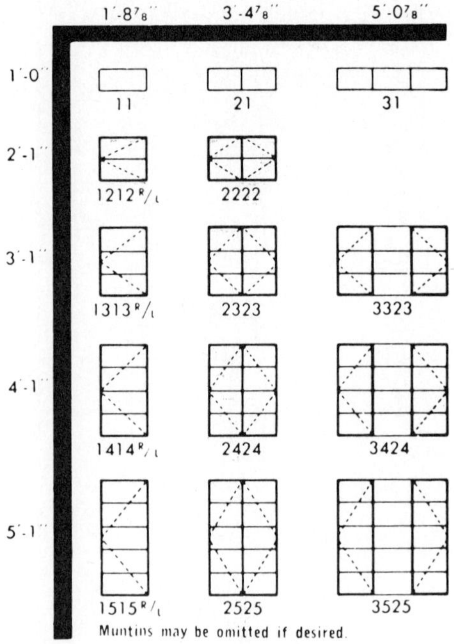

Fig. 16. Intermediate casement windows: types and sizes

Figures 16, 17, and 18 from "Recommended Specifications for Steel Windows," Steel Window Institute.

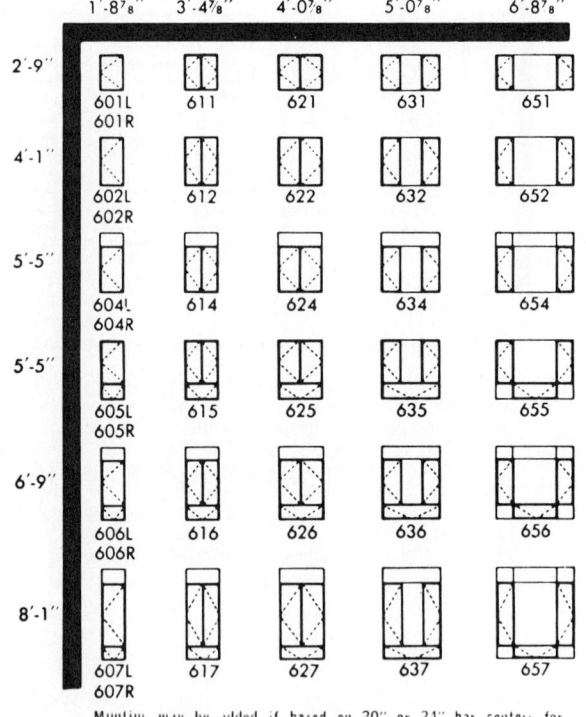

Muntins may be added if based on 20" or 24" bar centers for width and 16" bar centers for height. Sill vents may be omitted in favor of fixed light at sill.

FIXED or STATIONARY UNITS may be supplied for all types shown.
(*) For HEAVY INTERMEDIATE, add the suffix "H"
    For HEAVY CUSTOM, add the suffix "HC"

Fig. 17. Intermediate combination windows: types and sizes

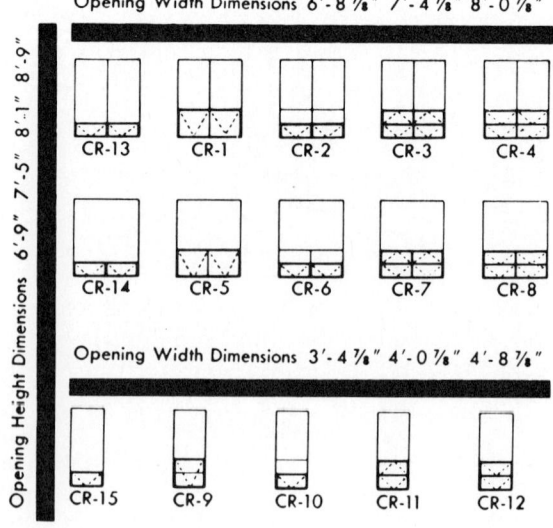

Fig. 18. Intermediate classroom windows: types and sizes

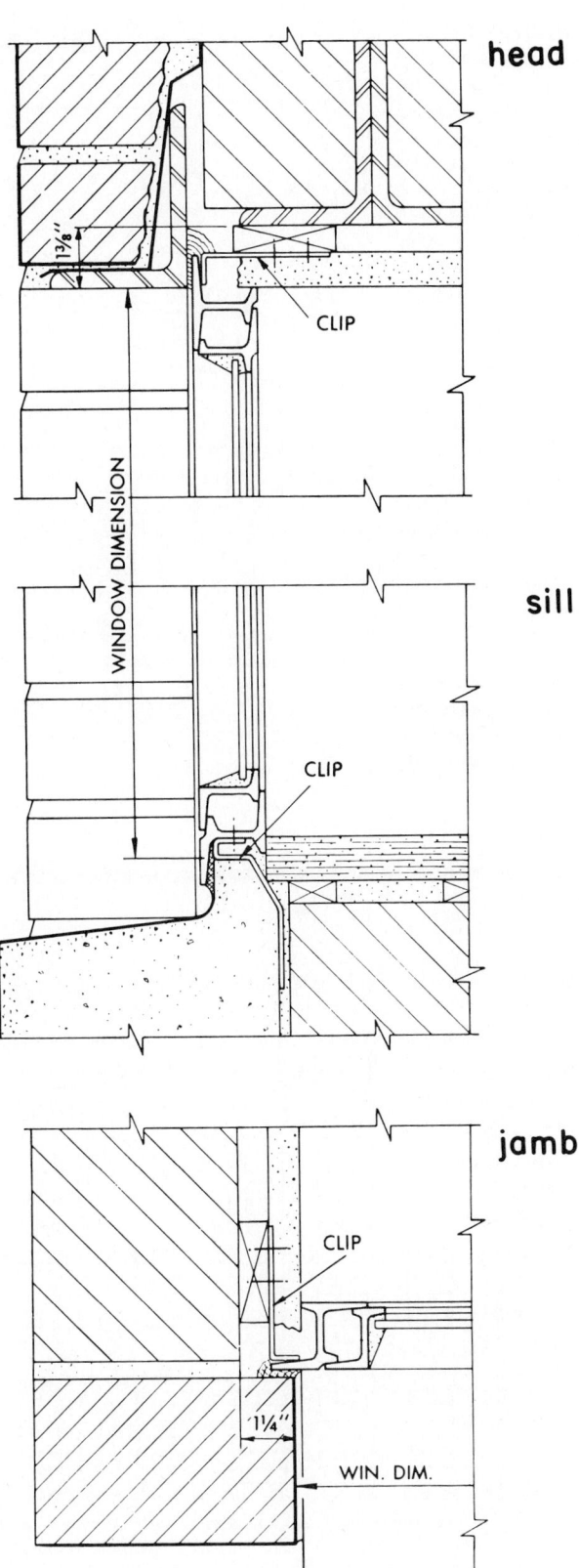

head

sill

jamb

CLIP

CLIP

CLIP

WINDOW DIMENSION

1³⁄₈"

1¼"

WIN. DIM.

Fig. 19. Intermediate projected window in masonry construction—scale: 3 in. = 1 ft

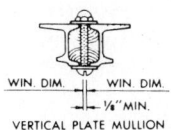

Equal-leg frames, available from most manufacturers, may be used to form narrow mullions, as shown in the two small details.

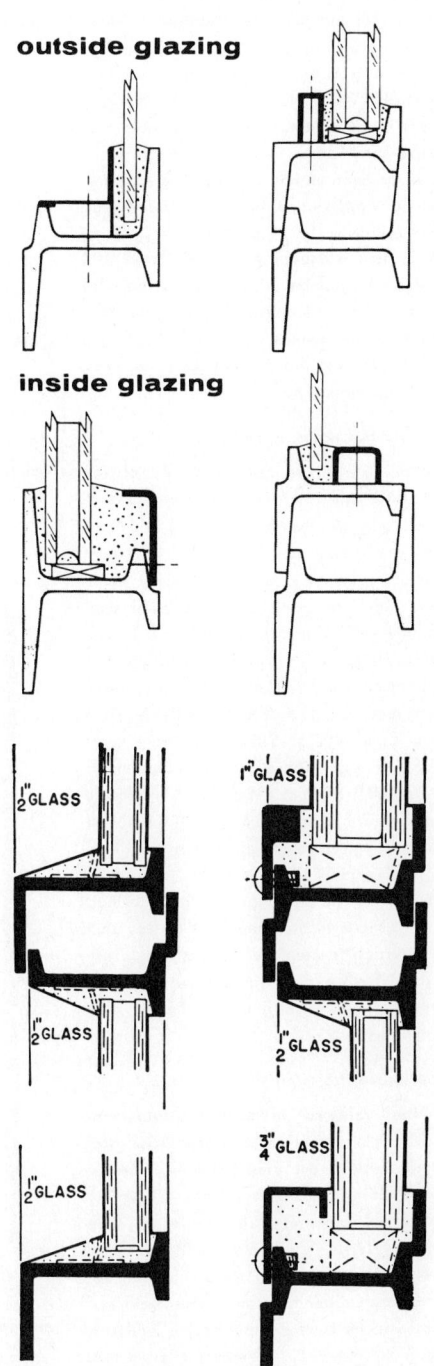

outside glazing

inside glazing

Fig. 20. Glazing details for intermediate windows: glazing clips and various thicknesses of insulating glass—one-half full size

frames or grilles with restricted glass openings and superimposed ventilators attached to the inside or outside of the grille (see manufacturers' catalogs).

Psychiatric windows are designed for use in mental institutions. Heavy intermediate sections and construction are used in conjunction with restricted glass openings and ventilator heights and with special hardware and screens. Ventilators may open in or out (see manufacturers' catalogs).

Awning windows provide a series of ventilators projecting outward and operating in unison. They are made of intermediate, heavy intermediate, and heavy custom materials and construction. Although sizes have not been standardized in the industry, awning windows are made in a wide range of sizes up to 16 ft in height or 20 ft in width. Size is usually limited to about 100 sq ft by the number of ventilators that can be opened by one operator. Some manufacturers provide awning windows with narrow, louver-type ventilators that can be used for detention purposes.

Architectural projected windows

Architectural projected windows occupy a middle place between intermediate projected and commercial projected windows. They are widely used in the less expensive types of commercial and institutional buildings. They are made from hot-rolled steel sections with a minimum depth of 1⅜ in. (1¼ in. if corners are welded and ground) and a minimum thickness of ⅛ in. Maximum vent size is 5 ft 0 in. wide by 2 ft 8 in. high, with a vertical muntin in vents over 4 ft wide. There are no requirements as to infiltration. Architectural projected windows are made in the same types and sizes as intermediate projected windows, shown in Fig. 16. Vents shown to project out may be made to project in, provided that all vents in the same unit do so. Outside glazing is standard, but inside glazing is available on order from some manufacturers. Typical installation details are shown in Fig. 21.

Commercial projected windows

Often referred to as "industrial windows" or "factory sash," commercial projected windows are used not only in industrial buildings but also in many types of commercial buildings. The projected type has now largely replaced the *horizontally pivoted* type, which, however, is still obtainable on order from most manufacturers. Sizes are the same for both types and are shown in Fig. 22. Commercial projected, like architectural projected, windows are made from hot-rolled steel sections with a minimum depth of 1⅜ in. (1¼ in. if corners are welded) and a minimum thickness

of ⅛ in. Maximum vent size is 5 ft 0 in. wide by 2 ft 8 in. high, with vertical muntins as shown. Again, there are no requirements as to infiltration. All sash are designed for inside glazing. Screens are available except for the pivoted type. Windows bearing underwriters' labels (Class E, moderate fire exposure) are available from some manufacturers, subject to the established limitations of size, installation, and glazing. Typical details of commercial projected windows are given in Figs. 23 and 24.

Security

Security windows are similar to commercial projected except that the frame and muntins form a continuous fixed grille on which the ventilator is superimposed. Ventilators open in. Security windows are used in warehouses, stores, factories, and other buildings, to prevent forcible entry. Standard sizes are shown in Fig. 25.

Continuous

Continuous windows are used in monitor or sawtooth roofs in factories and similar buildings. The SWI "Standards" classifies continuous windows as a specialty and

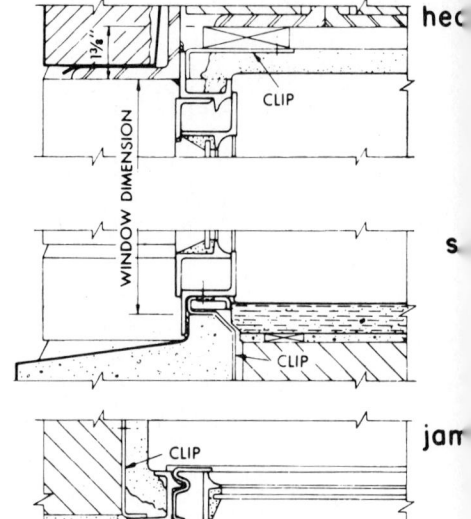

Fig. 21. Architectural projected windows in masonry construction—scale: 3 in. = 1 ft

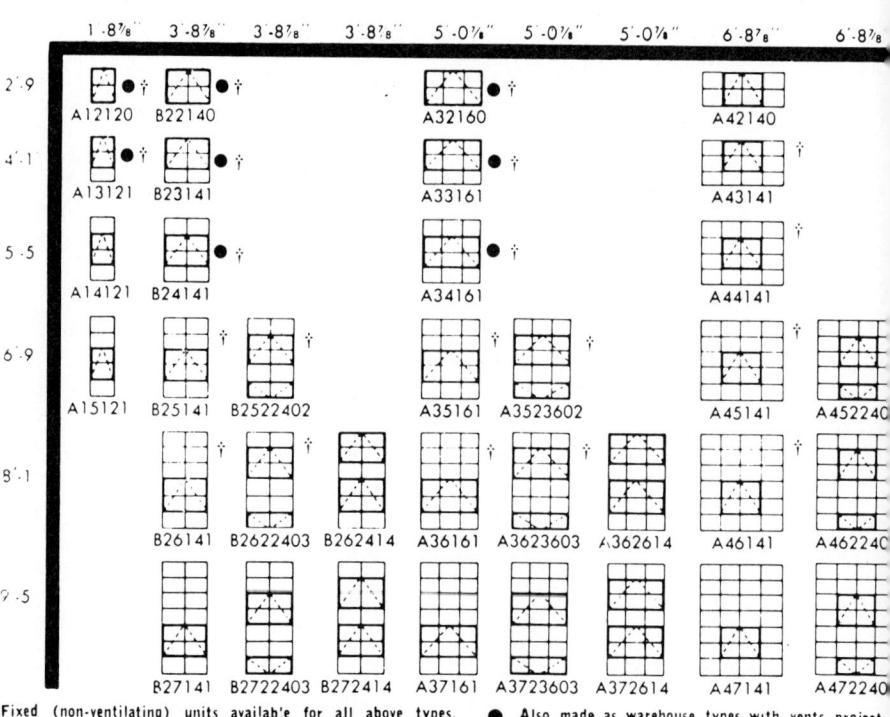

Fixed (non-ventilating) units available for all above types.   ● Also made as warehouse types with vents project

Fig. 22. Commercial projected windows: types and sizes

Horizontally pivoted windows are available on special order in the various sizes and ventilating sash arrangements indicated for commercial projected windows. Consult individual manufacturer's catalog for availability. (From "Recommended Specifications for Steel Windows," Steel Window Institute.)

The symbol † indicates warehouse types and sizes.

Grid
Window Dimen.
HEAD
Grid
Window Dimen.
JAMB
Grid
Window Dimen.
Clip
SILL

NOT LESS
CLIP
WINDOW DIMENSION
TIE RODS FOR LONG SPANS
CLIP
NOT LESS
7/16" HOLES NOT OVER 20" ℄ TO ℄ BY STEEL CONTR.
TYPICAL HORIZONTAL MULLION
CLIP

Fig. 23. Commercial projected windows in masonry (left) and concrete construction—scale: 3 in. = 1 ft

Courtesy Lupton

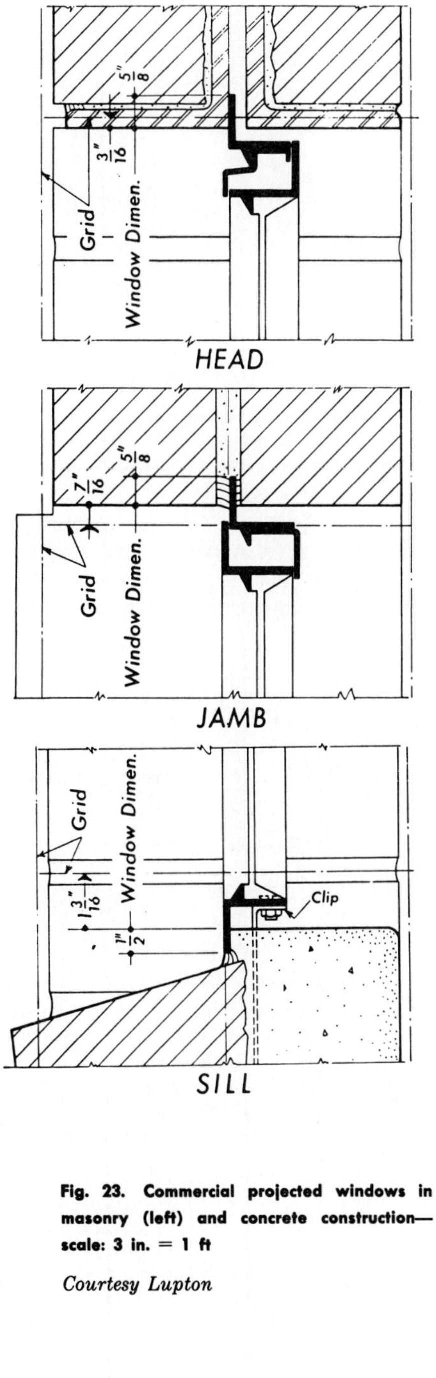

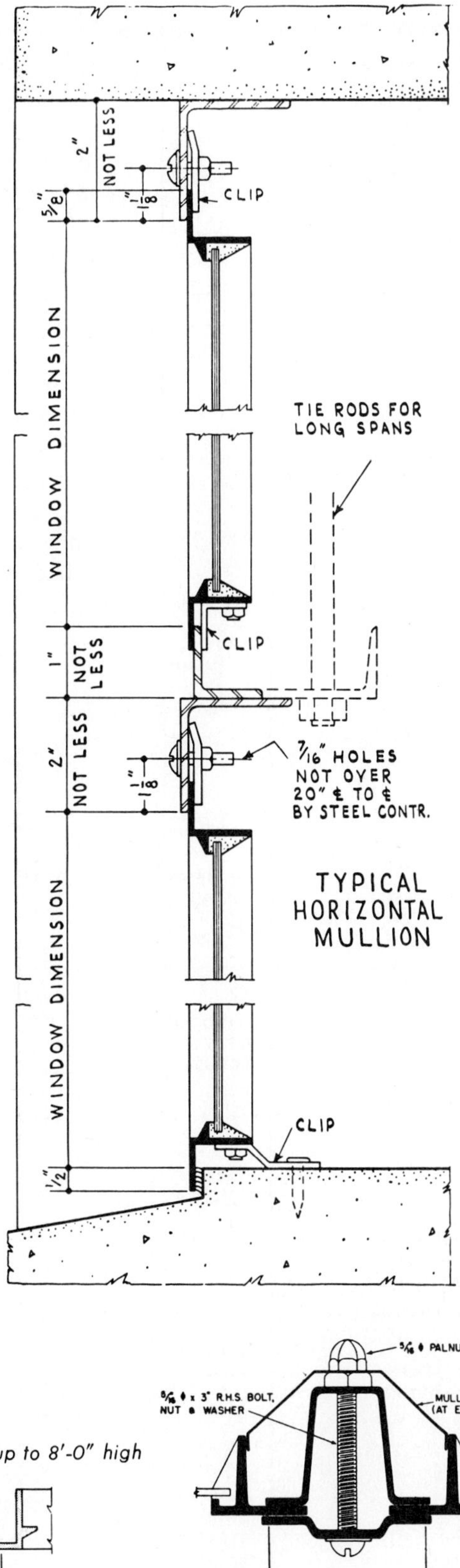

gives neither specifications nor sizes. The following information from the 1960 SWI "Standards" will serve to give a general idea of the sizes and construction of these windows. The principal members should be made of hot-rolled steel sections having the following minimum weights in pound per linear foot: top rail, 1.6; bottom rail, 3.0; end rails, 1.2. Window units are manufactured in heights of 3, 4, 5, and 6 ft and in even-foot lengths, with vertical muntins on 2-ft centers. The outswinging ventilator units must overlap, by about 2 ft, stationary storm panels at each end. The 3-ft high windows open to a maximum horizontal distance of 22 in.; the larger sizes open to 30 in.

Multiple units

Multiple units for large openings are formed by the use of standard mullions of various shapes, depending upon the height of the windows (Fig. 24). Mullions are 3⅛ in. wide, but in most cases the space between window units can be reduced to 2⅛ in. by compressing the detail. The sizes of openings formed by the use of multiple units of intermediate and commercial projected windows are shown in Tables 11 and 12, respectively. Since commercial projected windows are often used continuously past columns, Table 12 also gives suggested selections of multiple units for various column spacings.

MECHANICAL OPERATORS

Manual or motor-driven mechanical operators are used for opening and closing groups of windows. Standard types are as follows: The *lever-arm* operator (manual only) provides rapid opening for short runs of pivoted or projected ventilators. The *rack-and-pinion* operator (manual or motor) acts more slowly but can control longer runs. It is also suitable for short runs of continuous top-hung windows. *Tension* operators (motor only) are designed for opening and closing continuous top-hung windows.

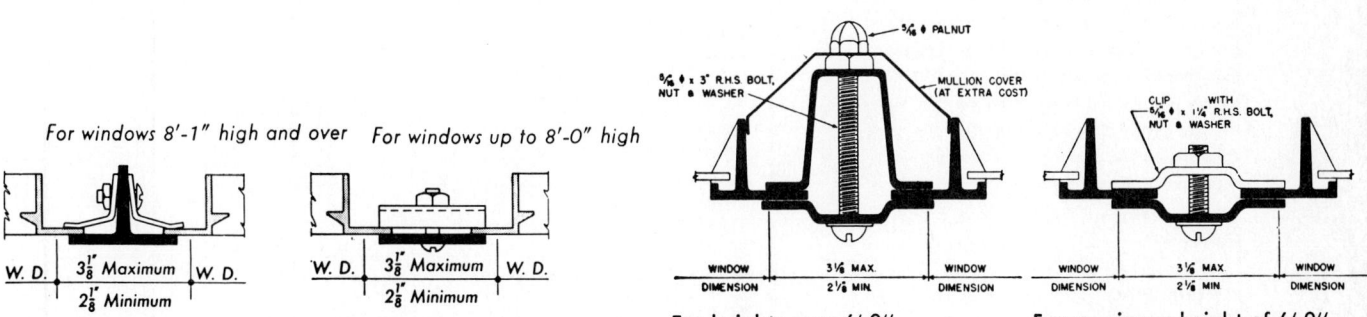

For windows 8'-1" high and over
W. D.
3⅛" Maximum
W. D.
2⅛" Minimum
For windows up to 8'-0" high
W. D.
3⅛" Maximum
W. D.
2⅛" Minimum
5/16 ⌀ PALNUT
5/16 ⌀ x 3" R.H.S. BOLT, NUT & WASHER
MULLION COVER (AT EXTRA COST)
WINDOW DIMENSION
3⅛ MAX.
2⅛ MIN.
WINDOW DIMENSION
For heights over 6'-9"
CLIP WITH 5/16 ⌀ x 1¼ R.H.S. BOLT, NUT & WASHER
WINDOW DIMENSION
3⅛ MAX
2⅛ MIN
WINDOW DIMENSION
For maximum height of 6'-9"

Fig. 24. Typical mullions for commercial projected windows—scale: 3 in. = 1 ft

Courtesy Lupton, above; Bogert and Carlough, below.

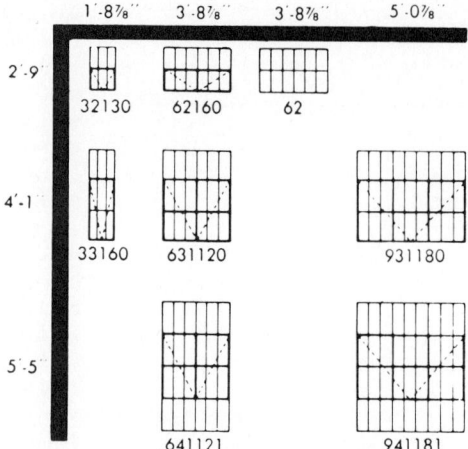

Fig. 25. Security windows: types and sizes

All items shown are warehouse types.

> *From "Recommended Specifications for Steel Windows," Steel Window Institute.*

Ventilators or guard bars are super-imposed. Ventilators open in behind fixed unit muntins as shown.

Screw-type operators (manual only) are designed for group control of pivoted or projected ventilators in vertical arrangement, as in power houses, auditoriums, and similar structures. Recommended lengths of runs of windows controlled from a single power station are indicated in Table 13. The power unit for the tension-type operator should be located at the end of the run. For all other operators, the power unit should be located approximately at the center of the run. If power must be located at the end of the run, reduce lengths shown in the table by one-third. Manual power may be applied by chain and sprocket or by solid shaft with gear and crank. Lever-arm and rack-and-pinion operators and chain control are shown in Fig. 26.

FINS, SUBFRAMES, SURROUNDS

Metal fins or clips for anchoring windows to adjacent construction are available for most window types. Metal subframes or surrounds and metal trim are available for some types of windows. Subframes are made of No. 12 or 14 gage cold-formed steel sheet; they are installed as the wall is built; the windows can then be installed in the subframes after the wall construction is complete. Wood fins and surrounds are available for some residential windows, to aid installation in wood-frame construction.

CURTAIN WALLS

Complete curtain wall systems are offered by most steel window manufacturers (see "Curtain Walls").

Table 11. Multiple unit windows: intermediate and architectural projected

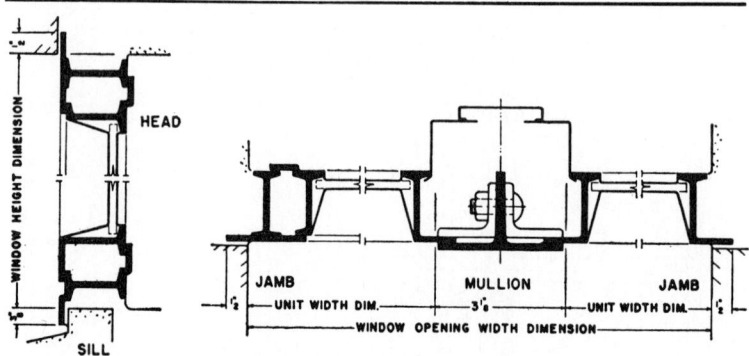

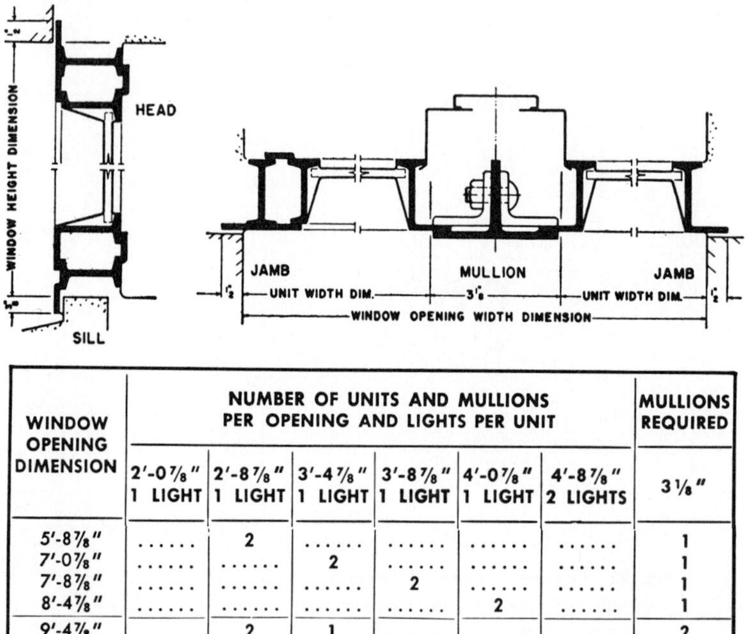

WINDOW OPENING DIMENSION	NUMBER OF UNITS AND MULLIONS PER OPENING AND LIGHTS PER UNIT						MULLIONS REQUIRED
	2'-0⅞" 1 LIGHT	2'-8⅞" 1 LIGHT	3'-4⅞" 1 LIGHT	3'-8⅞" 1 LIGHT	4'-0⅞" 1 LIGHT	4'-8⅞" 2 LIGHTS	3⅛"
5'-8⅞"	......	2	......	......	......	......	1
7'-0⅞"	......	......	2	......	......	......	1
7'-8⅞"	......	......	......	2	......	......	1
8'-4⅞"	......	......	......	......	2	......	1
9'-4⅞"	......	2	1	......	......	......	2
9'-8⅞"	......	......	......	......	......	2	1
10'-8⅞"	......	......	3	......	......	......	2
11'-4⅞"	......	......	2	......	1	......	2
11'-8⅞"	......	......	......	3	......	......	2
12'-8⅞"	......	......	......	......	3	......	2
13'-4⅞"	......	......	......	......	2	1	2
14'-0⅞"	......	......	......	......	1	2	2
14'-8⅞"	......	......	......	......	......	3	2
15'-8⅞"	......	......	......	4	......	......	3
16'-4⅞"	......	......	......	2	2	......	3
17'-0⅞"	......	......	......	......	4	......	3
18'-0⅞"	......	......	5	......	......	......	4
19'-8⅞"	......	......	......	......	......	4	3
21'-4⅞"	......	......	......	......	5	......	4
23'-4⅞"	......	......	......	......	2	3	4
24'-8⅞"	......	......	......	......	......	5	4
25'-8⅞"	......	......	......	......	6	......	5
27'-0⅞"	......	......	......	......	4	2	5
28'-4⅞"	......	......	......	......	2	4	5
29'-8⅞"	......	......	......	......	......	6	5
30'-8⅞"	......	......	......	......	6	1	6
32'-0⅞"	......	......	......	......	4	3	6

Table 12.   Multiple unit windows: commercial projected and pivoted windows

Courtesy Michael Flynn Manufacturing Company.

For Steel or Masonry Openings

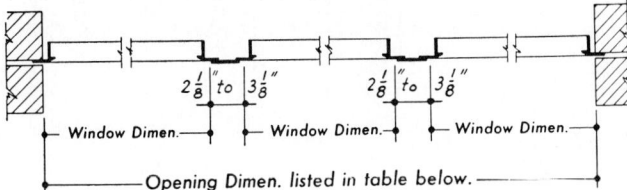

Combinations of units that can be arranged symmetrically

WIDTH OF OPENING		DESIGN			
2⅛″ MULLIONS	3⅛″ MULLIONS	QUANTITY AND SIZE OF UNITS	UNITS WIDE	LIGHTS WIDE	QUANT. MULLS.
7′– 7⅞″	7′–8⅞″	2@ 3′–8⅞″	2	4	1
8′–10⅞″	9′–0⅞″	2@ 1′–8⅞″ 1@ 5′–0⅞″	3	5	2
9′– 6⅞″	9′–8⅞″	1@ 1′–8⅞″ 2@ 3′–8⅞″	3	5	2
10′– 3⅞″	10′–4⅞″	2@ 5′–0⅞″	2	6	1
11′– 6⅞″	11′–8⅞″	3@ 3′–8⅞″	3	6	2
12′– 2⅞″	12′–4⅞″	1@ 1′–8⅞″ 2@ 5′–0⅞″	3	7	2
12′–10⅞″	13′–0⅞″	2@ 3′–8⅞″ 1@ 5′–0⅞″	3	7	2
13′– 7⅞″	13′–8⅞″	2@ 6′–8⅞″	2	8	1
14′– 2⅞″	14′–4⅞″	1@ 3′–8⅞″ 2@ 5′–0⅞″	3	8	2
14′– 6⅞″	14′–8⅞″	2@ 3′–8⅞″ 1@ 6′–8⅞″	3	8	2
15′– 5⅞″	15′–8⅞″	4@ 3′–8⅞″	4	8	3
15′– 6⅞″	"	3@ 5′–0⅞″	3	9	2
17′– 2⅞″	17′–4⅞″	2@ 5′–0⅞″ 1@ 6′–8⅞″	3	10	2
17′– 6⅞″	17′–8⅞″	1@ 3′–8⅞″ 2@ 6′–8⅞″	3	10	2
18′– 1⅞″	18′–4⅞″	2@ 3′–8⅞″ 2@ 5′–0⅞″	4	10	3
18′–10⅞″	19′–0⅞″	1@ 5′–0⅞″ 2@ 6′–8⅞″	3	11	2
19′– 4⅞″	19′–8⅞″	5@ 3′–8⅞″	5	10	4
20′– 6⅞″	20′–8⅞″	3@ 6′–8⅞″	3	12	2
20′– 8⅞″	21′–0⅞″	4@ 3′–8⅞″ 1@ 5′–0⅞″	5	11	4
20′– 9⅞″	"	4@ 5′–0⅞″	4	12	3
21′– 5⅞″	21′–8⅞″	2@ 3′–8⅞″ 2@ 6′–8⅞″	4	12	3
22′– 0⅞″	22′–4⅞″	3@ 3′–8⅞″ 2@ 5′–0⅞″	5	12	4
23′– 3⅞″	23′–8⅞″	6@ 3′–8⅞″	6	12	5
24′– 1⅞″	24′–4⅞″	2@ 5′–0⅞″ 2@ 6′–8⅞″	4	14	3
24′– 8⅞″	25′–0⅞″	1@ 3′–8⅞″ 4@ 5′–0⅞″	5	14	4
25′– 4⅞″	25′–8⅞″	3@ 3′–8⅞″ 2@ 6′–8⅞″	5	14	4
25′– 2⅞″	"	1@ 1′–8⅞″ 6@ 3′–8⅞″	7	13	6
26′– 0⅞″	26′–4⅞″	5@ 5′–0⅞″	5	15	4
27′– 2⅞″	27′–8⅞″	7@ 3′–8⅞″	7	14	6
27′– 5⅞″	"	4@ 6′–8⅞″	4	16	3
27′– 8⅞″	28′–0⅞″	1@ 6′–8⅞″ 4@ 5′–0⅞″	5	16	4
28′– 6⅞″	29′–0⅞″	6@ 3′–8⅞″ 1@ 5′–0⅞″	7	15	6
29′– 4⅞″	29′–8⅞″	1@ 1′–8⅞″ 4@ 6′–8⅞″	5	17	4
31′– 1⅞″	31′–8⅞″	8@ 3′–8⅞″	8	16	7
31′– 4⅞″	"	1@ 3′–8⅞″ 4@ 6′–8⅞″	5	18	4
31′– 3⅞″	"	6@ 5′–0⅞″	6	18	5
32′– 8⅞″	33′–0⅞″	1@ 5′–0⅞″ 4@ 6′–8⅞″	5	19	4
33′– 0⅞″	33′–8⅞″	1@ 1′–8⅞″ 8@ 3′–8⅞″	9	17	8
33′– 2⅞″	"	1@ 1′–8⅞″ 6@ 5′–0⅞″	7	19	6

Variations—Variations from widths shown above may be made by varying the mullion dimension between 2⅛″ and 3⅛″.

For Continuous Bands Set in Front of Columns

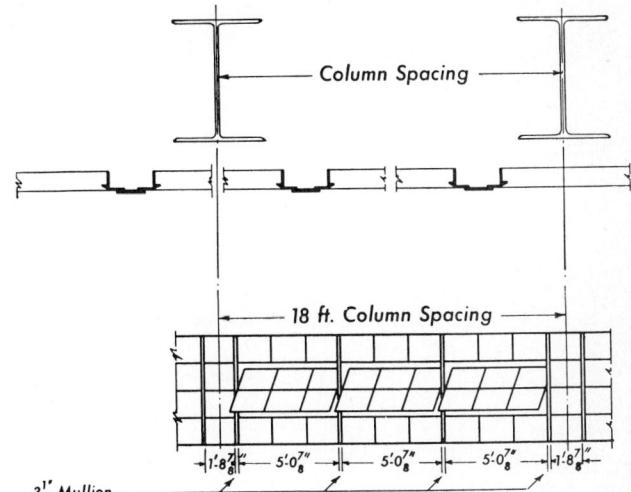

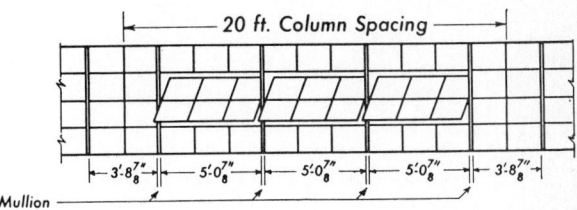

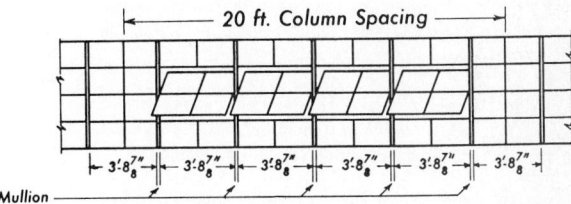

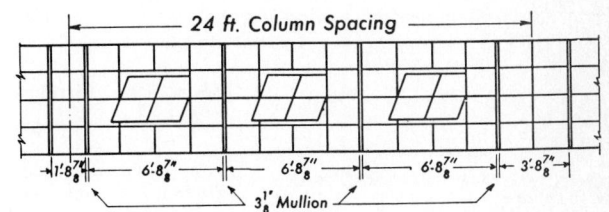

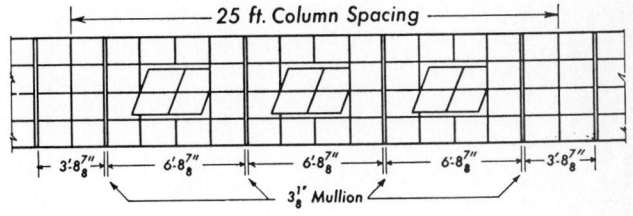

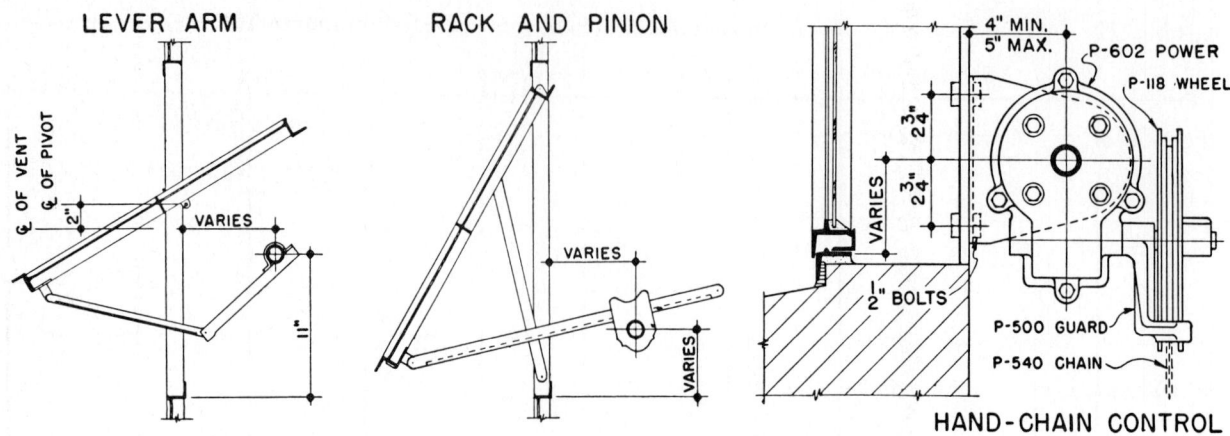

Fig. 26. Mechanical operators—scale: left and center, ¾ in. = 1 ft; right, 1½ in. = 1 ft

Courtesy Truscon.

CHECK LIST FOR SPECIFYING STEEL WINDOWS

(Courtesy of Federal Windows Manufacturing Company, Inc.)

SAFETY: Are there windows in passageways that should swing out to clear pedestrian traffic? Are there any on lot lines which should swing in? Does Code require underwriters' labels or similar construction?

HAZARD: Is some special arrangement of ventilators or operating hardware necessary for self-closing in fire or automatic opening in explosion?

CLEANING: Will ventilator arrangement permit washing from inside building? Should there be provision for outside cleaning?

MATERIAL: Have you adequately identified the quality of window required by weight, depth and industry classification?

FINISH: Is standard bonderizing and prime coat of paint required; or galvanizing before shop painting? Is first field coat specified to be applied promptly after windows are received on the job and before glazing?

GLAZING: Is glazing to be outside with glazing compound, inside with glazing beads or outside with glazing beads?

HARDWARE: Is hardware to be polished bronze, solid bronze unpolished, white bronze, die cast lacquered or iron? Is hardware within reach from floor or should windows be operated by pole or other special arrangement? How many poles are required?

SUBFRAMES: What gage of metal is wanted? Are joints to be welded and ground smooth?

TRIM: Is trim such as closures, column covers, stools or other miscellaneous material to be furnished by window manufacturer?

SCREENS: Are insect screens required, and if so, for which windows? Are screens to have wickets for access to locking handles or be flat with hardware operating through or under the screen?

SHADES: Is preparation for mounting shades required? If dark shades are used, is special head and jamb framing required? Who furnishes shade brackets?

ERECTION: Have you specified that windows are to be installed by the manufacturer or an approved responsible company specializing in this kind of work?

CAULKING: Is bedding in mastic specified under "Windows" and caulking under "Masonry"? Is a particular kind of compound required?

Table 13. Maximum lengths of run for mechanical operators

From "Recommended Specifications for Steel Windows," Steel Window Institute, 1969.

LIMITS IN LENGTHS of RUNS (lineal feet)	LEVER ARM				RACK and PINION				
	dust shield		oil enclosed		dust shield		oil enclosed		
	chain	rod	chain	rod	chain	rod	chain	rod	elect.
PROJECTED	—	—	—	—	100	90	140	120	200
PIVOTED	100	80	150	120	160	140	200	180	240

CONTINUOUS TOP HUNG	TENSION TYPE					RACK and PINION				
	vert.	sloped 30° from vert.				vert.	sloped 30° from vert.			
	6'0"	3'0"	4'0"	5'0"	6'0"	6'0"	3'0"	4'0"	5'0"	6'0"
Manual	200	160	140	120	100	150	120	100	80	60
Electric	300	240	210	180	150					

By HOWARD P. VERMILYA, *AIA*

In recent years aluminum has become one of the foremost materials for window construction. Many manufacturers of aluminum windows were originally, and still are, producers of steel windows. With some types (double-hung, combination, classroom, pivoted, and projected), it is possible to procure windows for the same-sized openings in either steel or aluminum, although the largest sizes of aluminum may not be available from all sources. On the other hand, aluminum casements are available in the same sizes but offer a wider range than do the intermediate steel-casement sizes.

Practically all shapes or sections are made from aluminum alloys designed for extruding. The most widely used alloy is 6063-T5, which has an ultimate tensile strength of 27,000 psi. Some use is also made of alloy 6063-T6, with a tensile strength of 35,000 psi, particularly where a thinner section or a harder surface is desired. The *Aluminum Window Specifications* of the Architectural Aluminum Manufacturers Association (ANSI/AAMA 3029-1977) requires a minimum tensile strength of 22,000 psi and a minimum yield strength of 16,000 psi. Alloy 3003 or 5050 sheet may be used for cold-formed work, mullion covers, trim, and screens.

WINDOW TYPES

Aluminum window types, as established by the Architectural Aluminum Manufacturers Association, and for which specifications with performance standards and use grades have been formulated, are as follows:

DH-B1—Double-hung (and single-hung) windows for residential-type buildings

DH-A2—Double-hung (and single- and triple-hung) windows for commercial-type buildings

DH-A3—Double-hung (and single- and triple-hung) windows for monumental-type buildings

DH-A4—Double-hung (and single- and triple-hung) windows for monumental-type buildings

C-B1—Casement windows for residential-type buildings

C-A2—Casement windows for commercial-type buildings

C-A3—Casement windows for monumental-type buildings

P-B1—Projected windows for residential-type buildings

P-A2—Projected windows for commercial-type buildings

P-A2.50—Projected windows for commercial-type buildings

P-A3—Projected windows for monumental-type buildings

A-B1—Awning windows for residential-type buildings

A-A2—Awning windows for commercial-type buildings

HS-B1—Horizontal sliding (double and single) windows for residential-type buildings

HS-B2—Horizontal sliding (double and single) windows for light commercial-type buildings

HS-A2—Horizontal sliding (double and single) windows for commercial-type buildings

HS-A3—Horizontal sliding (double and single) windows for monumental-type buildings

J-B1—Jalousie windows for residential-type buildings

JA-B1—Jal-awning windows for residential-type buildings

VS-B1—Vertical sliding windows for residential-type buildings

TH-A2—Top-hinged (inswinging) windows for commercial-type buildings

TH-A3—Top-hinged (inswinging) windows for monumental-type buildings

VP-A2—Vertically-pivoted windows for commercial-type buildings

VP-A3—Vertically-pivoted windows for monumental-type buildings

HP series—Any of the above designations followed by "HP" indicates that the aluminum window complies with the requirements pertaining to high performance.

Additional types of windows manufactured in aluminum are as follows:

Industrial (horizontally pivoted)

Folding

Classroom

Emergency-exit

Detention (security)

Corridor

Ribbon (glass-block installations).

The *Specifications* of the Architectural Aluminum Manufacturers Association sets certain minimum requirements for all aluminum windows. These refer to:

1. Alloys, their composition and strength.
2. Minimum section thickness of 0.062 for frames, sash, and muntins.
3. Fasteners, hardware, and anchors—aluminum, nonmagnetic stainless steel or other noncorrosive material compatible with aluminum. Concealed fasteners may be coated steel if hidden when window is open. Plated or coated hardware must be insulated from aluminum. Steel anchors may be used if insulated from aluminum.
4. Joints are either mechanical or welded. Both provide satisfactory joints if well designed and well fabricated. Casement and projected windows are usually welded.

5. Weatherstrip material (plastic, woven, or metallic) must be compatible with aluminum.
6. Aluminum-to-aluminum contact between hardware parts or window members that move against one another is not permitted.
7. All windows except sliding and jalousie windows are to be assembled at the factory.
8. Standard glazing practice is to design for ⅛-in. glass except for jalousies. Other glass thicknesses may be used when specified. Compound or glazing beads compatible with aluminum may be used, depending on the manufacturer's design and practice. Glazing compound should meet Federal Specification TT-G-00410 for aluminum windows and not require paint protection.
9. Finishes may be any of the following when offered by manufacturers.
   a. Mill finish—natural finish after cleaning.
   b. Satin finish produced by etching in caustic, belt polishing, or rubbing with emery cloth or steel wool.
   c. Bright finish produced by buffing.
   d. Anodized finish—an electrolytic finish—provides a thicker oxide coating than is naturally produced on aluminum. It may be specified for any of the first three finishes.
10. Protective coatings are used to protect the window from:
    a. Construction abuses—preferred coating is clear water-white methacrylate-type lacquer resistant to mortar and plaster.
    b. Steel or wood subframes—protect with alkali-resistant bituminous paint or zinc-chromatic primer in the case of steel and with wood preservative in the case of wood.

The *Specifications* of the Architectural Aluminum Manufacturers Association also gives the particular requirements of each window design and use type. It includes references to materials, construction, and hardware and gives performance requirements relating to horizontal, vertical, and uniform load tests and to air infiltration tests. Ventilator torsion tests are required for monumental casements and commercial and monumental projected windows. Hardware load tests are required for commercial and monumental casements, residential projected, awning, and jalousie windows. Water-resistance tests are required for

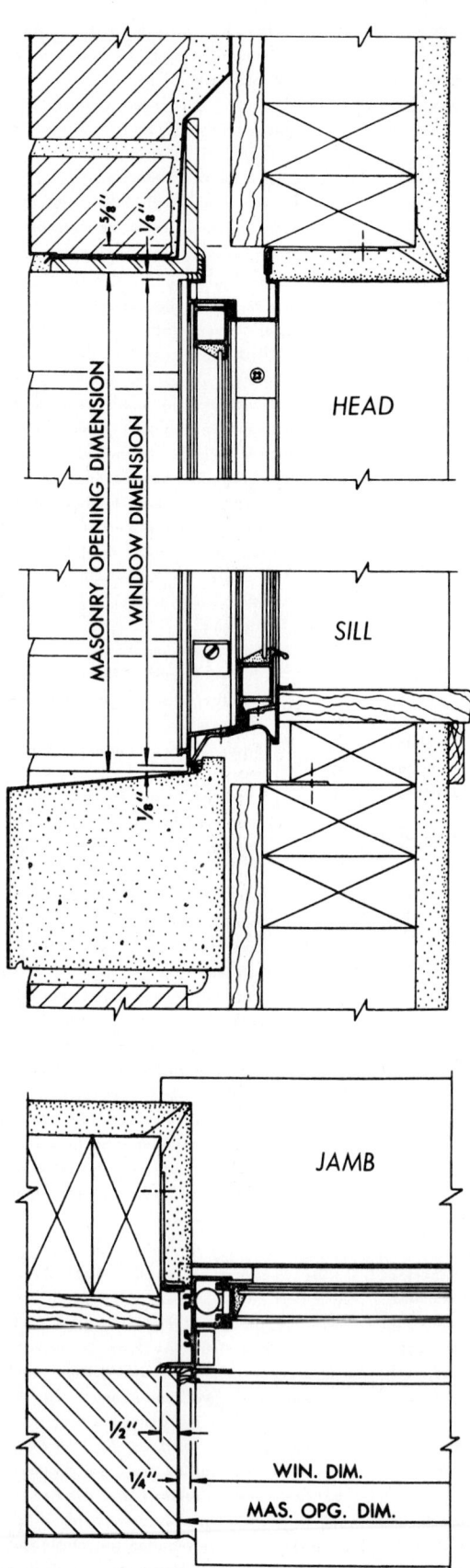

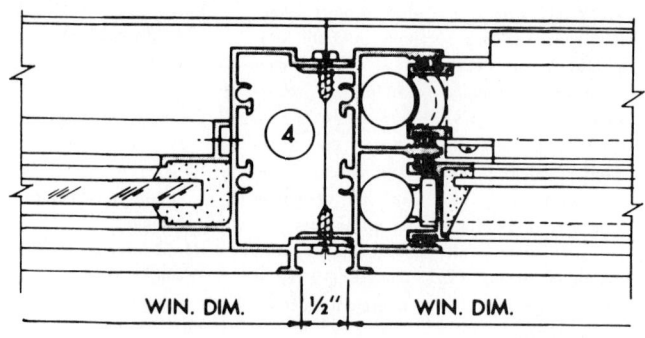

Residential picture window combined with double hung

Details *Scale 3" = 1'-0"*

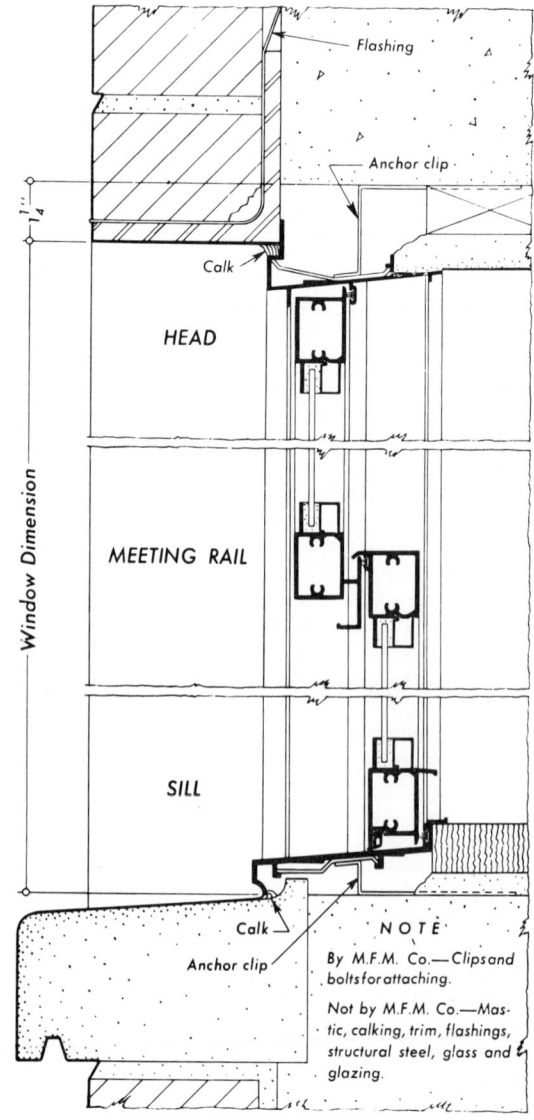

Double-hung, residential windows—brick veneer

Double-hung monumental window

Courtesy Lupton

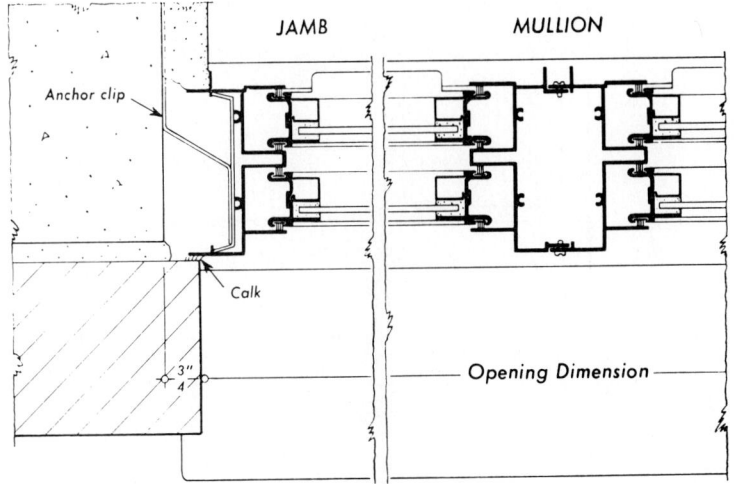

JAMB   MULLION

Anchor clip

Calk

3/4"

Opening Dimension

Double-hung monumental window

Courtesy Lupton

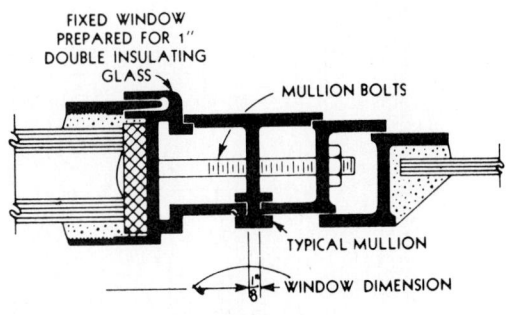

FIXED WINDOW PREPARED FOR 1" DOUBLE INSULATING GLASS

MULLION BOLTS

TYPICAL MULLION

WINDOW DIMENSION

Residential casement

Courtesy Lemco

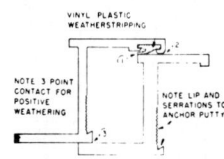

VINYL PLASTIC WEATHERSTRIPPING

NOTE 3 POINT CONTACT FOR POSITIVE WEATHERING

NOTE LIP AND SERRATIONS TO ANCHOR PUTTY

Residential casement

Courtesy Truscon

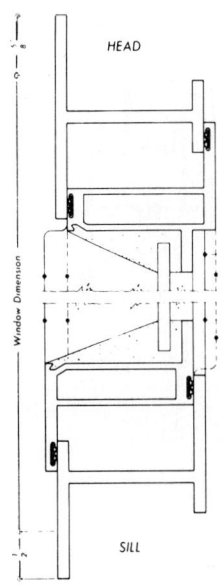

HEAD

Window Dimension

SILL

Projected windows—weatherstripped

Courtesy Lupton

JAMB

Window Dimension

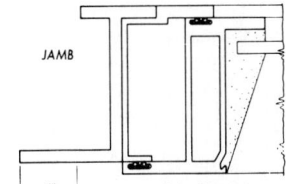

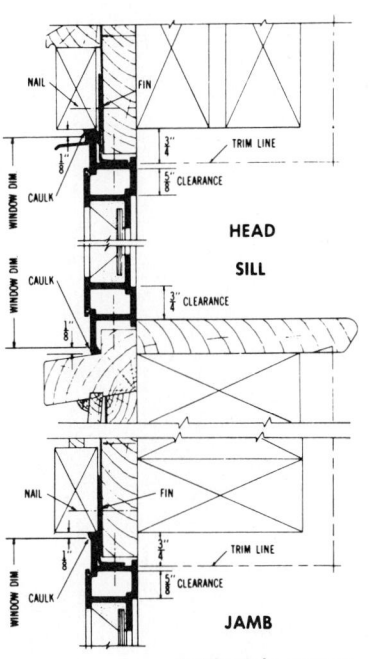

NAIL   FIN

TRIM LINE

CLEARANCE

WINDOW DIM

CAULK

HEAD

SILL

CLEARANCE

WINDOW DIM

CAULK

NAIL   FIN

TRIM LINE

CLEARANCE

WINDOW DIM

CAULK

JAMB

Residential casement

Courtesy Reynolds

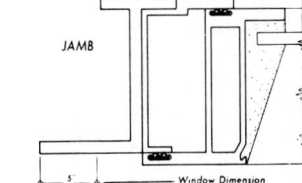

Inside snap-on bead glazing
(alternate)

Outside snap-on bead glazing
(alternate)

Weatherstripped projected windows

Courtesy Lupton

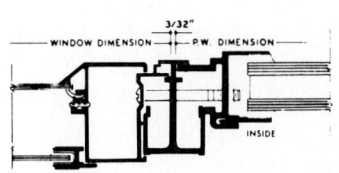

WINDOW DIMENSION   3/32"   P.W. DIMENSION

INSIDE

Residential awning window

Combination ventilating window—1-in. insulating glass. (Courtesy Lemco)

head

jamb

sill

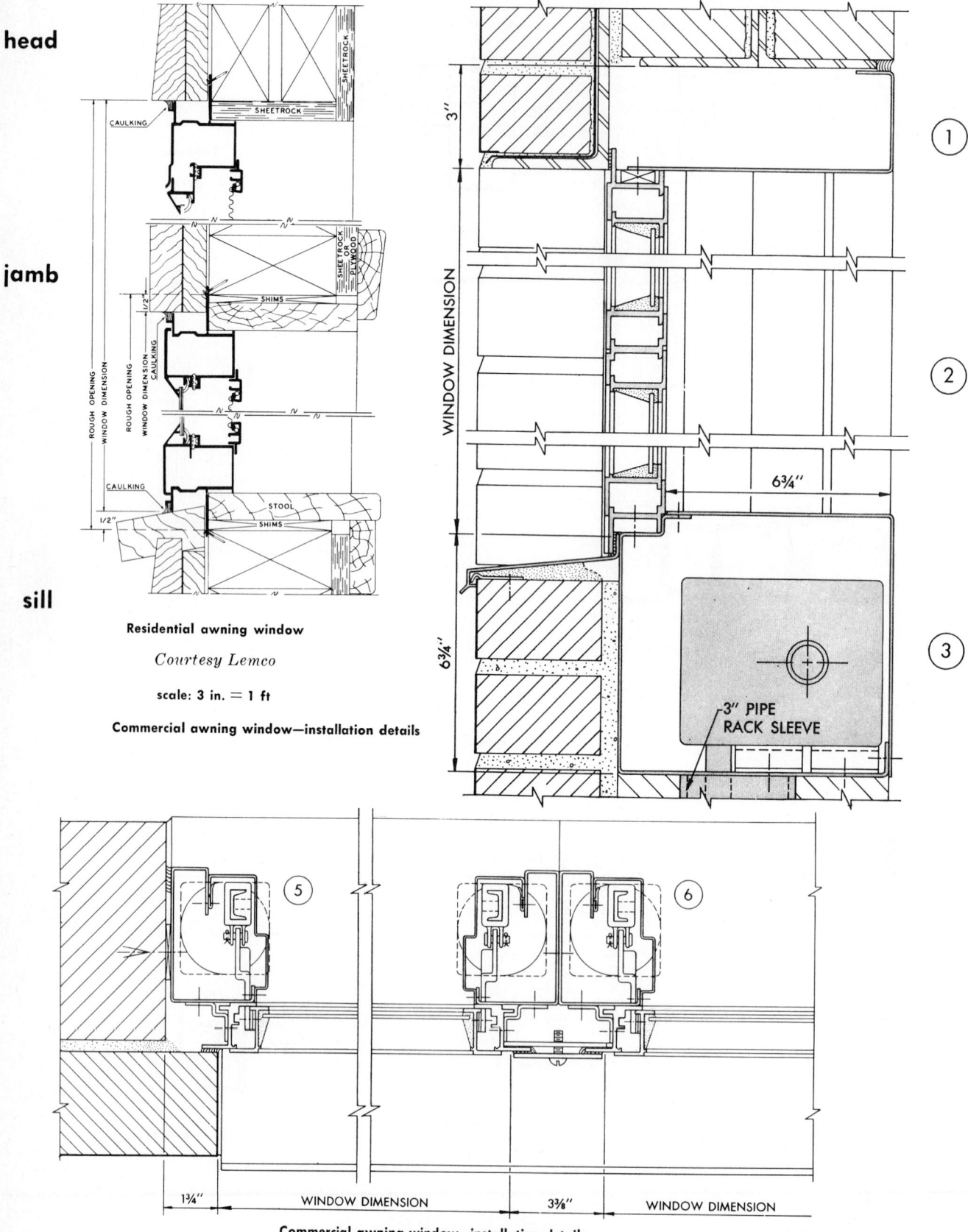

Residential awning window

Courtesy Lemco

scale: 3 in. = 1 ft

Commercial awning window—installation details

Commercial awning window—installation details

(See next page for key elevation.)

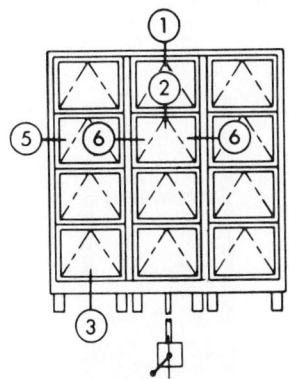

Key elevation for commercial awning window details shown on previous page

awning type, Class II sliding windows, and jalousie windows. These tests are similar in method as applied to the various grades of windows but have differing applied loads and limits for determining performance. Residential-type windows are subject to less severe conditions of use and therefore are not required to comply with the more rigorous tests given to the commercial or monumental types.

The results of these tests are of value to architects in judging the relative merits of windows of various grades and of various manufacturers within grades. The air infiltration and water resistance test results are useful in evaluating different types of windows.

Hurricane specifications require certain tests in addition to those required of all window types. Air infiltration tests are the same. Water-resistance tests are the same as those required of awning, horizontal sliding, and jalousie windows. Physical load tests require a uniform load of 40 psf on the entire outside area (equal to a 127-mph wind) to be followed by a load of 20 psf on the interior surface, each applied for a period of 10 seconds, without glass breakage or permanent damage causing the window to be inoperable.

Table 14. Minumum requirements for air infiltration

Window types	Air infiltration,* cu ft per linear ft
DH-B1	0.50
-A2, A3, A4	0.50
C-B1, A2, A3	0.50
P-B1, A2, A3	0.50
-A2.50	0.375
A-B1	0.50
-A2	0.50
HS-B1, B2, A2	0.50
-A3	0.50
J-B1	1.50†
JA-B1	0.50
VS-B1	0.50
TH-A2	0.375
-A3	0.50
VP-A2	0.375
-A3	0.50

Tested in accordance with ASTM E283-73; pressure difference, 6.24 psf.
†*Cu ft per sq ft of ventilated area (not linear ft of ventilator perimeter).*

CURTAIN WALLS

Many manufacturers of aluminum windows offer their products assembled or for assembly as curtain walls in one- or two-story sections or assemblies, and in various widths. These assemblies include a variety of mullion types, both vertical and horizontal, and insulated or uninsulated panels with optional finishes and cores (see "Curtain Walls").

SPECIAL TYPES

Custom-made windows represent a large portion of the production facilities of the industry with some companies specializing in this type of work. Church windows rep-

resent the great variety that is possible with some manufacturers. Others limit their custom products to variations in openings, muntins, glazing methods, and sizes. Some manufacturers have facilities for making windows and assemblies including curtain walls of bronze or stainless steel, in addition to aluminum.

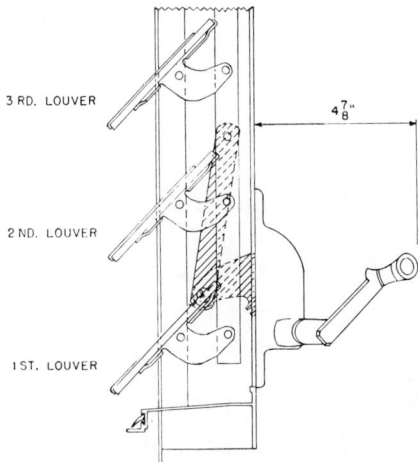

Jalousie operator location up to and including 17 louvers

Jalousies over 63 in. high are dual operated. Obscure glass may be used in the lower louvers for privacy. (Courtesy Truscon.)

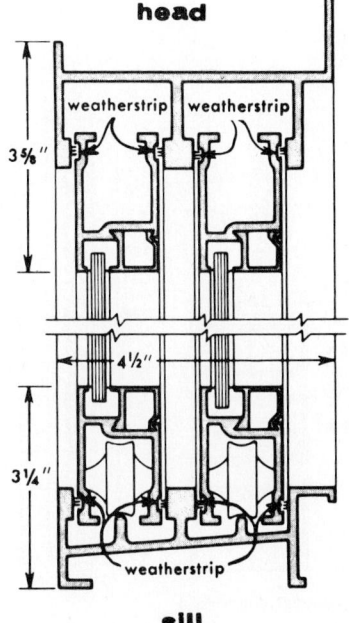

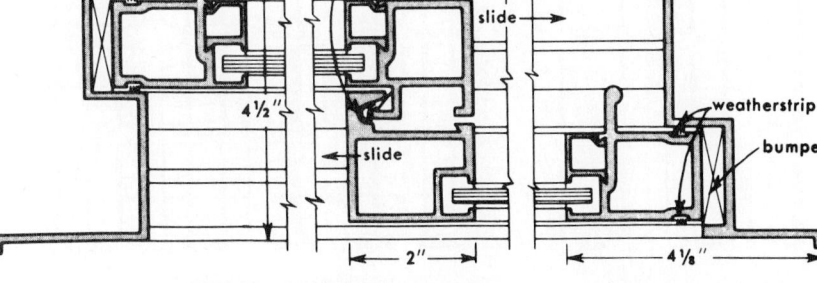

jamb	meeting rail	jamb

Horizontal sliding window—horizontal section

Courtesy Albro

Horizontal sliding window—vertical section

Courtesy Albro

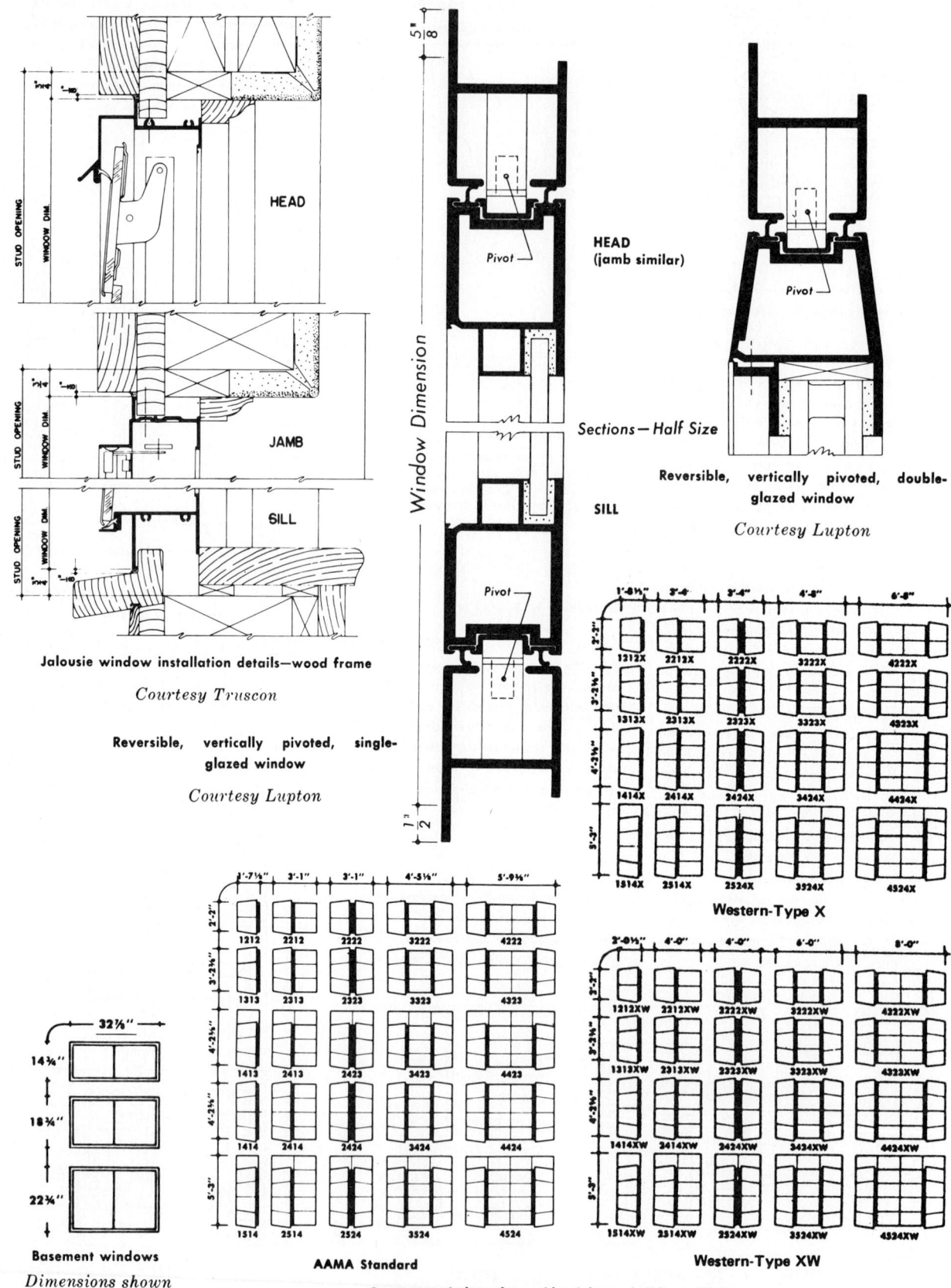

Jalousie window installation details—wood frame

Courtesy Truscon

Reversible, vertically pivoted, single-glazed window

Courtesy Lupton

Sections—Half Size

Reversible, vertically pivoted, double-glazed window

Courtesy Lupton

Western-Type X

Western-Type XW

Basement windows

Dimensions shown are window dimensions.

AAMA Standard

Casement windows for residential-type buildings (C-B1)

Units with single ventilator may be hinged either right or left. Fixed types are furnished for all sizes shown. Dimensions shown are window dimensions.

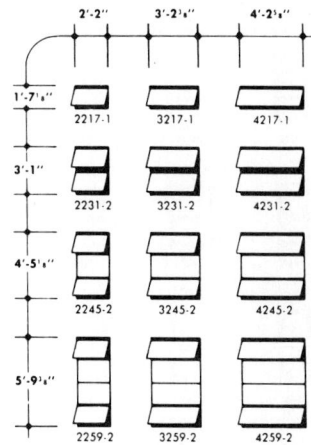

Projected windows for residential-type buildings (P-B1)

Dimensions shown are window dimensions.

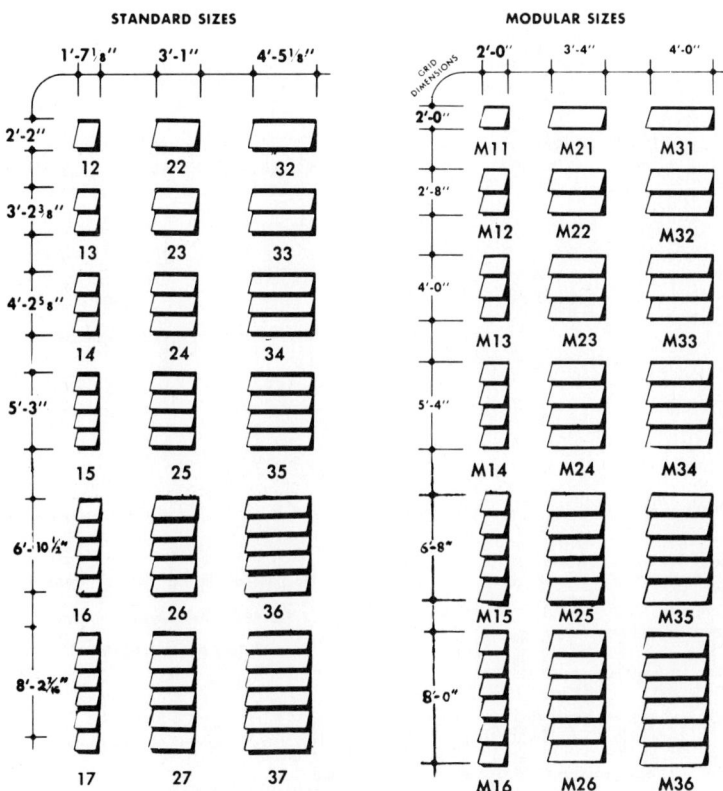

STANDARD SIZES   **MODULAR SIZES**

Awning windows for residential- and commercial-type buildings (A-B1 and A-A2)

All dimensions are out-to-out of sash frame, 1 in. greater than window dimension.

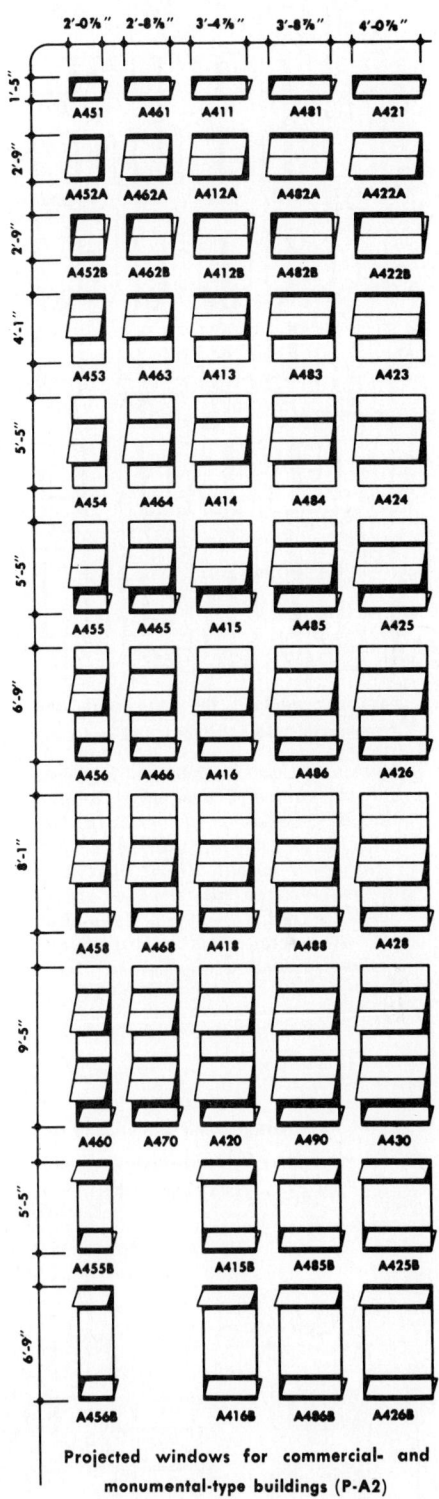

Projected windows for commercial- and monumental-type buildings (P-A2)

Dimensions shown are window opening dimensions.

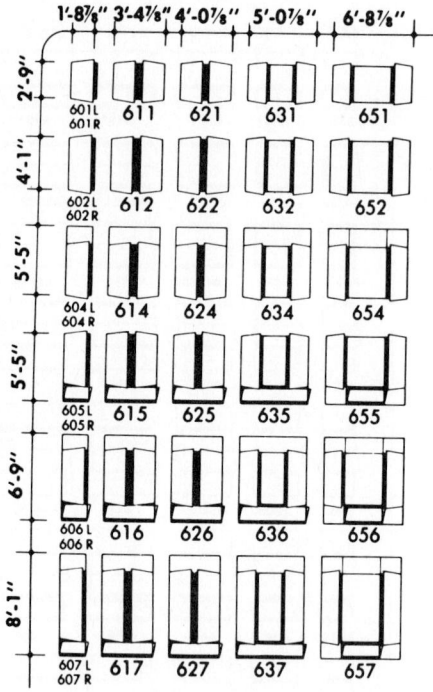

Casement windows for commercial- and monumental-type buildings (C-A2 and C-A3)

Horizontal and/or vertical muntins may be added if desired, provided they are based on 20 or 24-in. bar centers for width, and 16-in. bar centers for height. Fixed light may be provided at sill in place of sill vents. Fixed types are furnished for all sizes shown. Dimensions shown are window dimensions.

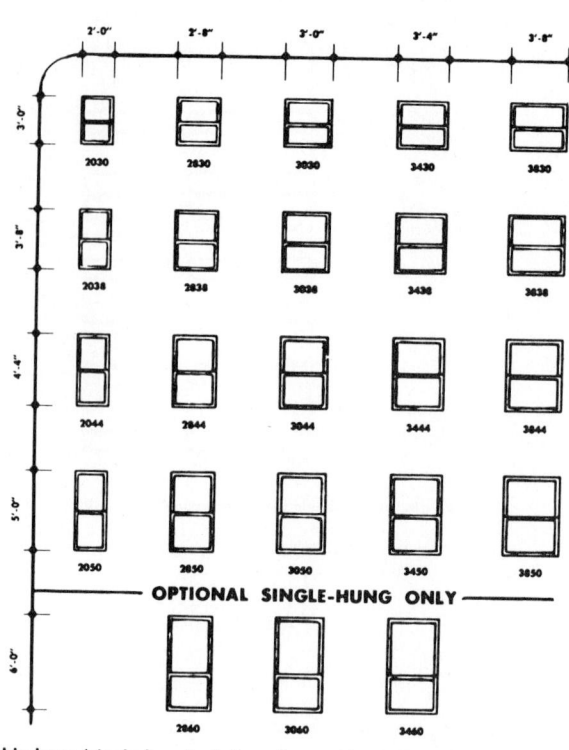

Double-hung (single-hung) windows for residential-type buildings (DH-B1)

Dimensions shown are maximum dimensions for that portion of the frame that fits into the rough opening.

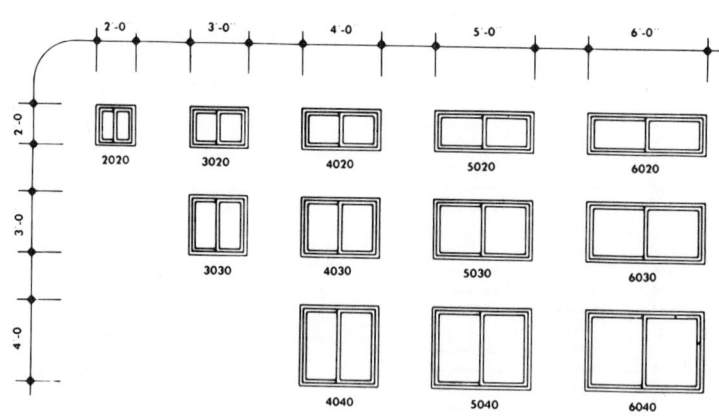

Horizontal sliding (double and single) windows for residential-type buildings (HS-B1 and HS-B2)

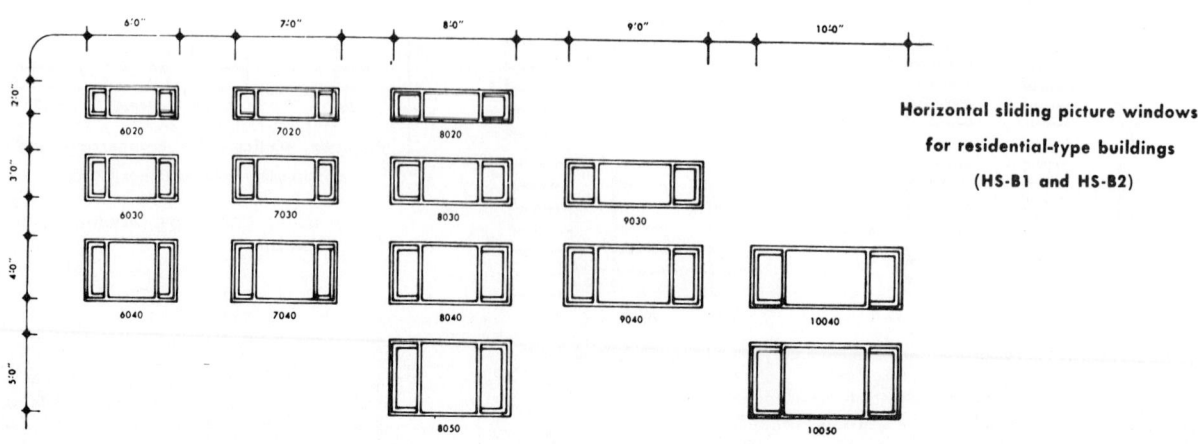

Horizontal sliding picture windows for residential-type buildings (HS-B1 and HS-B2)

By HOWARD P. VERMILYA, *AIA*

Sliding glass doors are usually framed with aluminum extrusions, although a few companies produce them in steel and wood.* The industry originally developed in California but has spread throughout the country in recent years. Consequently, a greater emphasis has been placed on the weathering qualities of the doors to meet the more severe requirements of colder climates. Originally used only in houses, they are now found in apartments, hotels, institutions, and commercial buildings.

Standardization has become increasingly important as the industry has sought to improve its product through research and the establishment of performance standards. The Architectural Aluminum Manufacturers Association has established specifications for aluminum sliding glass doors: ANSI/AAMA 402.9-1977. The specifications set standards for materials, finish, and hardware and establish performance requirements and test procedures pertaining to strength, weather resistance, and operation. The specifications differentiate between four grades of doors: SGD-B1 for residential-type buildings, SGD-B2 for residential-type buildings where increased size and/or better performance are required, SGD-A2 for commercial-type buildings, and SGD-A3 for monumental-type buildings. In addition any of the foregoing designations followed by "HP" indicates conformance to the section of the specifications pertaining to high wind loading.

DOOR SIZE AND TYPE

Sizes of doors are based on panel unit sizes and combinations of panels. The

* *See* Wood Siding Patio Doors. *ANSI/NWMA I.S. 5-73.*

stock types of doors include two, three, and four panels, some stationary and others movable (Fig. 1). For the most part, only one track is used, but some custom multiple sliding door installations use three or four tracks. Sizes are limited in height by the frame section used and in width by the standard sizes of double insulating glass. For single glazing, the size is limited by the thickness of the glass and the design wind load for the locality (see section on "Glass").

POCKET DOORS

Pocket doors are available from several companies. These doors are generally used on interior installations but also may be designed for exterior wall locations. Obscure translucent glass may be used where visual privacy is desired. The wall pocket into which the doors slide may be built wide enough to take one, two, or three door panels using the same number of tracks. Pockets may be built on both sides, each to take one half of the panels used in the opening. Although these openings are usually special designs, panels are of the same sizes as are used for standard openings.

DESIGN

Most manufacturers supply bottom-rolling doors with adjustable sealed-bearing sheaves on either aluminum or stainless-steel sill tracks. Stainless-steel tracks are usually inserted in the aluminum sill; alternatively, they may cap the aluminum sill track. Some types roll on overhead tracks. The movable panel is usually designed to slide inside the stationary panel. It is good practice to avoid aluminum-to-aluminum contact of moving parts. Such

contact is usually prevented by using a silicone-treated woven wool pile weatherstripping, which provides protection against air and water infiltration. Neoprene and vinyl are also used as weatherstripping. Sliding panels are designed for removal in the unlocked position. Sills for interior installations are usually horizontal and recessed flush with the finished floor. Sills for exterior wall locations usually slope or step down and contain provisions for drainage of possible condensation. Screens, using either glass fiber or aluminum mesh in aluminum frames, slide on rollers on a track in the sill, usually outside the stationary panel. Although screens are a standard item they must be ordered specially if desired.† Latches that can be locked from the inside are usually supplied as standard equipment, but cylinder locks may be obtained on special order. Latches should be so designed that they will not be damaged if the panel is closed while the latch is in the locked position.

SECTIONS

Sections of frame and sliding or stationary panels are extrusions, usually of 6063-T5 aluminum alloy having an ultimate strength of 27,000 psi and a yield strength of 21,000 psi. The AAMA specifications require a minimum ultimate strength of 22,000 psi, a yield strength of 16,000 psi, and a section thickness of 0.062 in. The sections may be tubular- or H-shaped or other open types. Tubular-shaped sections are generally considered stronger but any section that passes the performance tests should be satisfactory. Strength and deflection data for sections used by the manu-

† See Specifications for Aluminum Sliding Screen Doors, *ANSI/SMA 2005-1975.*

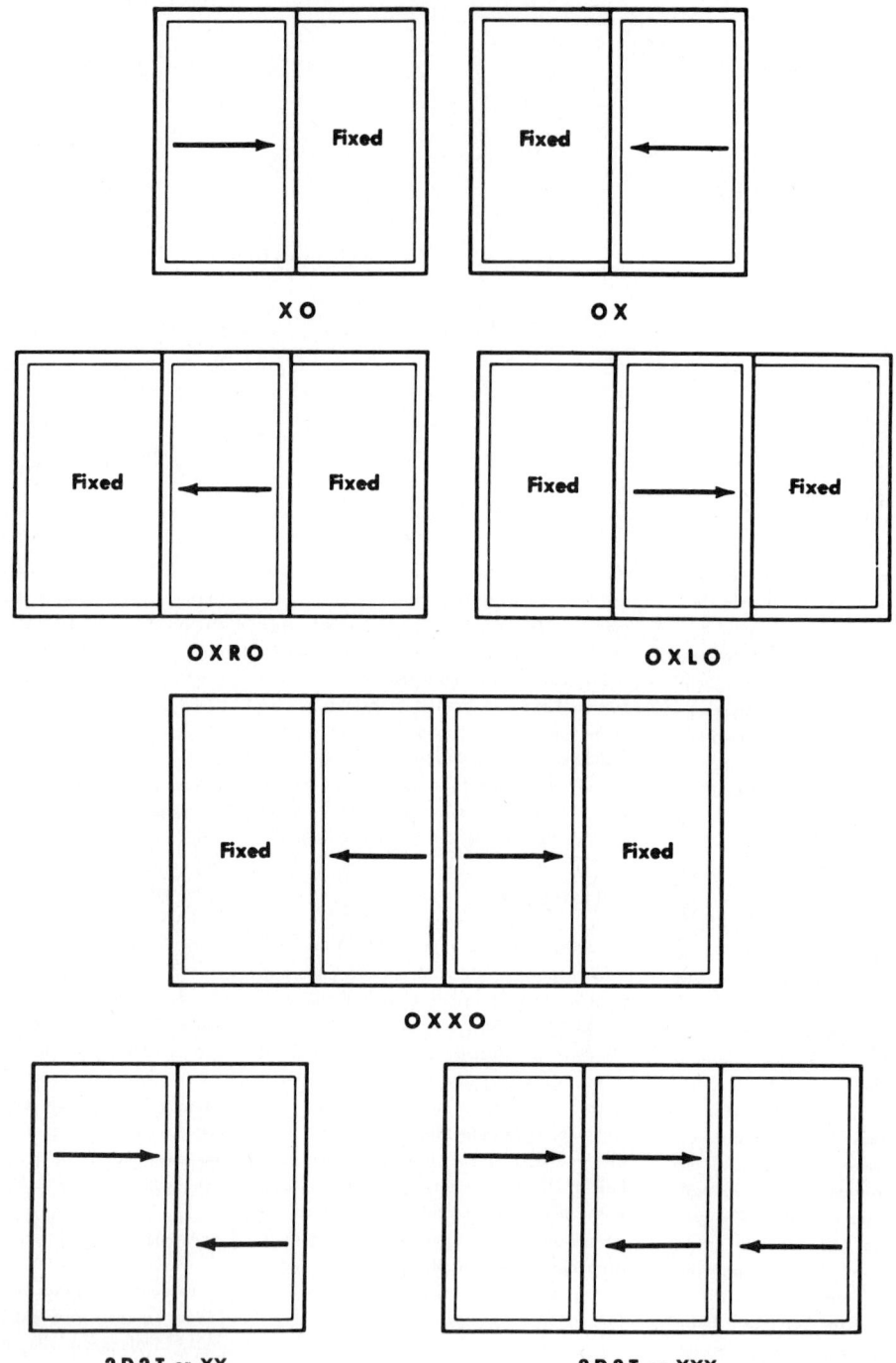

XO   OX

OXRO   OXLO

OXXO

2D2T or XX   3D3T or XXX

Fig. 1.   Standard sizes and nomenclature for sliding glass doors
(Courtesy Architectural Aluminum Manufacturers Association.)

The standard nominal sizes of sliding glass doors are derived from width modules of 3', 4' and 5' with heights being nominally 6' 9" and 8' 0". Manufacturer's literature should be consulted for exact sizes and availability of panel arrangements. Exact dimensions of sliding doors are governed by standard insulating glass sizes which are:

34" × 76"	*34" × 92"*
46" × 76"	*46" × 92"*
58" × 76"	*58" × 92"*

Sliding door arrangements, locks, handles, and accessories are determined as viewed from the outside looking in.

O—Fixed Panel
X—Moving Panel
D—Moving Panel
T—Track
R—Right
L—Left
DIGIT—Number of moving panels or number of tracks

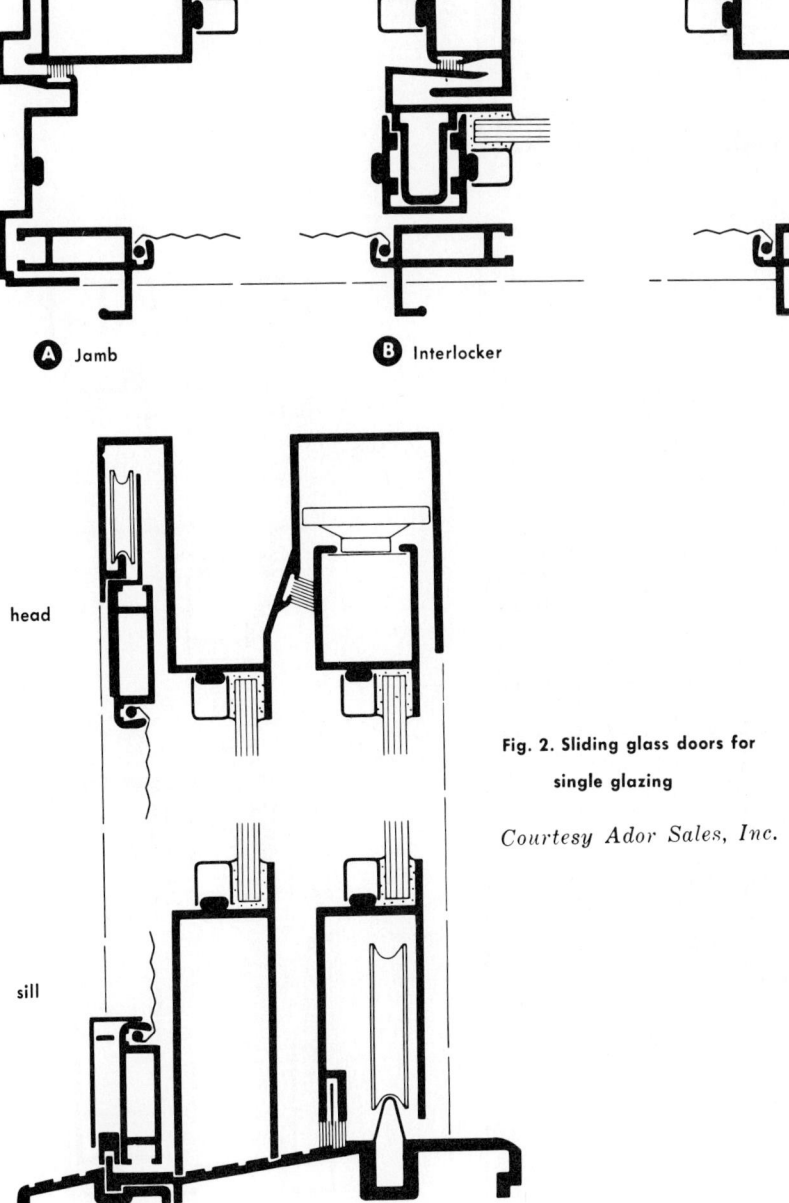

A Jamb **B** Interlocker **H** Meeting stile

head

sill

Fig. 2. Sliding glass doors for
single glazing

Courtesy Ador Sales, Inc.

tection during construction. The better
classes of doors usually have an anodized
finish of either 0.4 mil (0.0004-in.) thickness
or heavier, protected by a coating of methacrylate lacquer.

One manufacturer offers an epoxy coating in a range of colors. This coating has
been subjected to weatherometer and salt-
spray tests and is reported to be durable
and impact- and chip-resistant.

GLAZING

Sliding doors are usually glazed by the
installer, although some companies offer
preglazed sash. Glass must be of the safety
type meeting the requirements of ANSI
297.1-1975; see section on Glass. The
panels may be obtained for either single or
double glazing; some manufacturers provide interchangeable glazing beads to permit the use of either type of glass. Formed
vinyl glazing strips or channels are generally
used, rather than glazing compounds. The
aluminum glazing bead, if used, may be of
the snap-on type or may be screwed in
place. Construction details of doors for
single glazing are shown in Figs. 2 and 3
and for double glazing in Fig. 4.

WEATHER RESISTANCE

Manufacturers can generally furnish data
on the rate of air and water infiltration
under various wind conditions and rates
of rainfall. These figures should be obtained when comparing various classes of
doors made by several manufacturers. Air
infiltration for class B1 should not exceed
1 cfm per sq ft of frame area with a wind of
25 mph. For classes B2 and A2, infiltration
should not exceed ½ cfm. For class A3,
infiltration should not exceed ½ cfm with
a wind of 50 mph. For class HP, no water
should penetrate beyond the threshold under
conditions simulating a 2-in. rainfall and a
50-mph wind for a period of 15 min.

facturer should be available upon application. The strength and weather resistance
of the section determine the major differences between the various grades of doors.
Connections of panels and frames at
corners should be rigid and designed to
permit complete weatherstripping. Connections are usually mechanical to permit KD
shipment and local assembly, but some
manufacturers use welded connections.
Connectors should be noncorrosive and are
usually aluminum or stainless steel. Muntins are available from some manufacturers.

Condensation on the aluminum frames
is a serious problem in cold climates. To
combat this, some manufacturers have eliminated the through-conductivity of the metal
by inserting less conductive material between the inner and outer parts of sections for both panels and frames.

FINISH

The AAMA specifications require that all
sliding doors and frames have a protective coating. The minimum coating is a
clear lacquer, intended principally for pro-

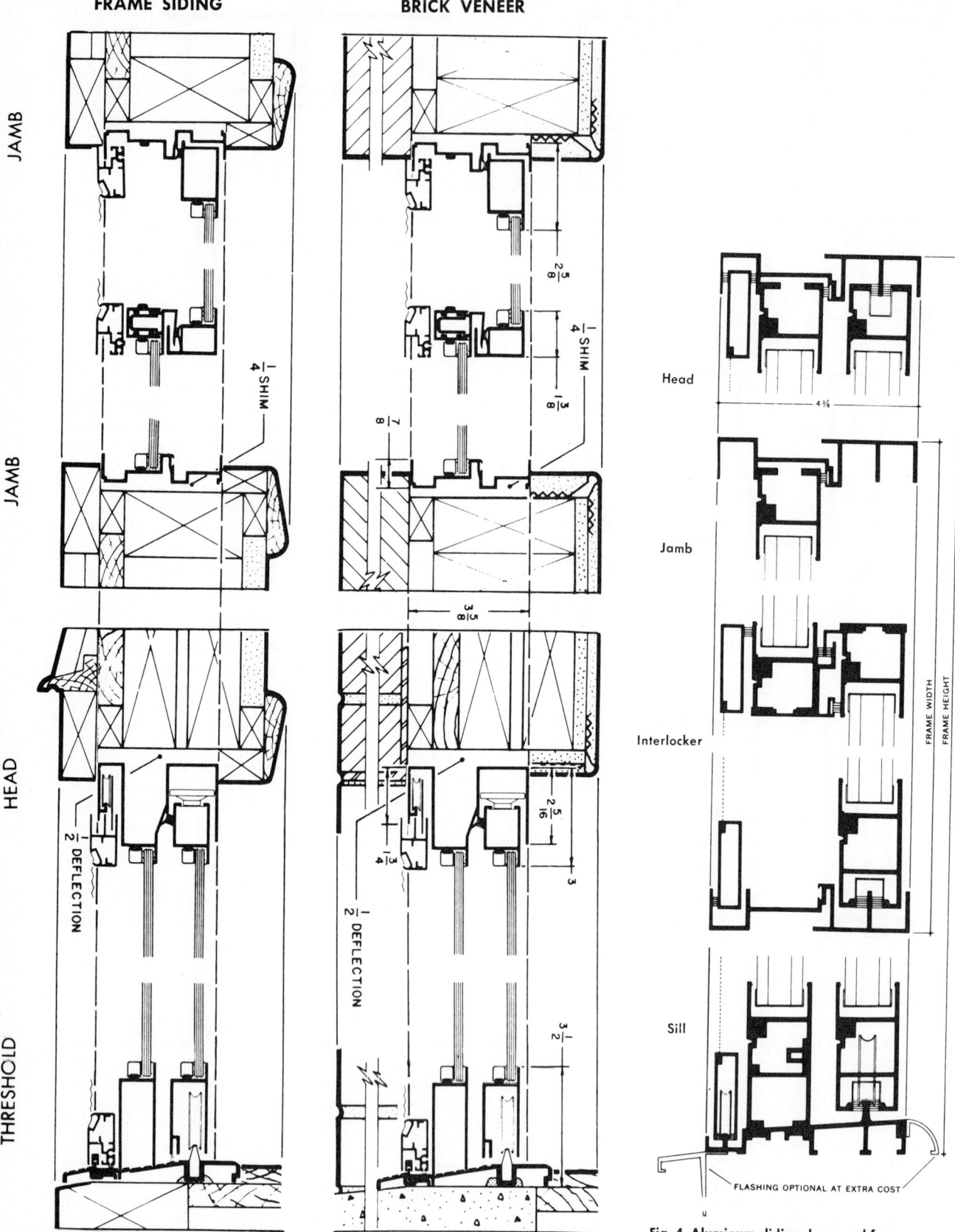

FRAME SIDING

BRICK VENEER

JAMB

JAMB

HEAD

THRESHOLD

Head

Jamb

Interlocker

Sill

FLASHING OPTIONAL AT EXTRA COST

Fig. 3. Sliding glass doors for single glazing

Courtesy Ador Sales, Inc.

**Fig. 4. Aluminum sliding doors and frames
for insulating glass**

*Courtesy Miller Sliding Glass
Door Co., Inc.*

By HOWARD P. VERMILYA, AIA, and JOHN HANCOCK CALLENDER, *Professor of Architecture, Pratt Institute*

Skylights serve primarily to admit light through the roofs of buildings. They may also supply ventilation or access to the roof, and they may serve as fire or explosion vents. Skylights make possible an even distribution of natural light in enclosed spaces of any size, without the structural complexities of clerestories or monitors. Since skylights are part of the roof, they must of course be absolutely weatherproof, which is not always easy to achieve. Other problems of skylight design, all resulting from their overhead location, are sunlight and sun heat, shading, condensation, and the hazard from glass breakage.

PLASTIC SKYLIGHTS

Plastic skylights are now the most widely used type. They are sold as a complete unit ready to install and, being light in weight, they are very simple to install. Plastic skylights eliminate the hazard from broken glass and, since they have few or no joints, they greatly reduce the likelihood of leaks. A wide variety of sizes and types is available.

Most plastic skylights have frames made of aluminum extrusions (usually 6063-T5) that fit over a curb and are fastened to it. The frame, which is usually in two pieces, forms a condensation gutter on the inside and a drip on the outside (Fig. 1). Some types provide integral frame, curb, and flashing (Fig. 2). Insulated curbs and aluminum well liners are available on some models. A "self-flashing" type which has no frame and requires no curb is installed directly on the roof deck, and the roofing felts are mopped over the flanges (Fig. 3).

Skylights may provide for ventilation in any of several ways: fixed or operable louvers or ventilating fans in the sidewalls (Fig. 4), or devices for opening the skylight itself. Opening mechanisms are usually manually controlled, but they may be equipped with fusible links so that the skylight will open automatically in the event of fire.

Other common skylight accessories include plastic diffusing panels, plastic eggcrate grilles, operable aluminum louvers, and roller shades; these items are all placed at or near the plane of the ceiling (Fig. 5). If ceiling diffusers are used, artificial lighting is often installed in the well below the skylight. The skylight thus becomes a lighting fixture and ensures that all light, natural and artificial, will come from the same source.

Plastic skylights may consist of a single thickness ot plastic, or two sheets with sealed edges and an air space between,

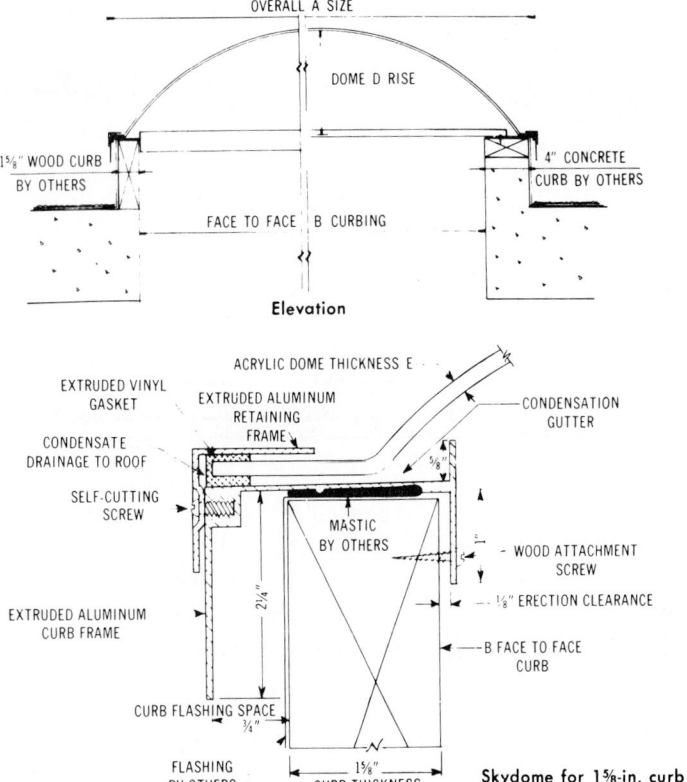

Fig. 1. Typical plastic dome skylight

Courtesy Wasco.

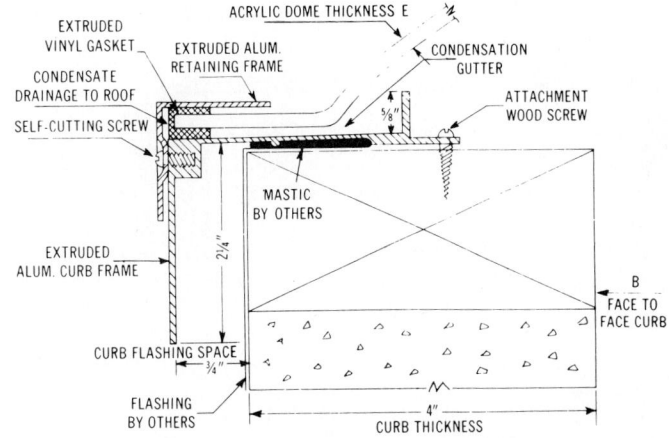

Fig. 2. Extruded frame, double dome skydome

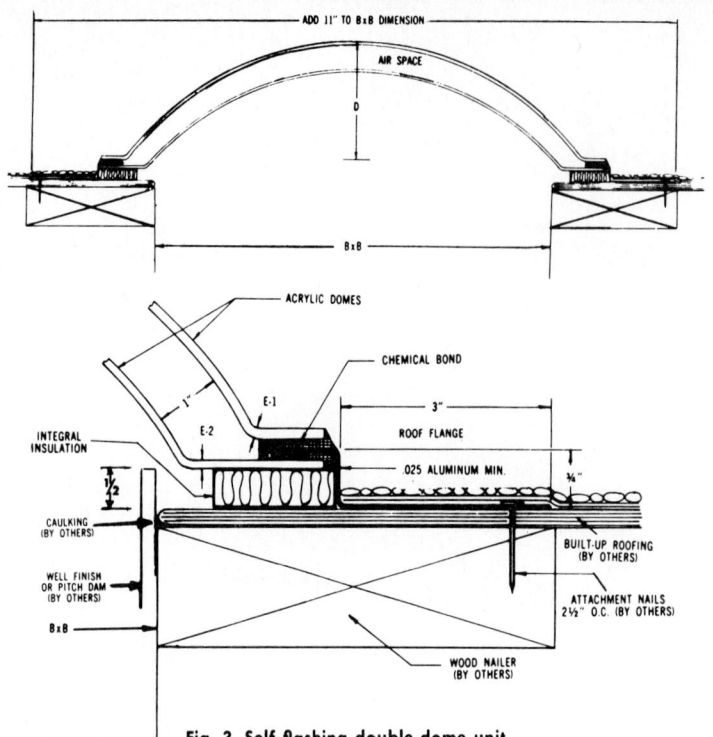

Fig. 3. Self-flashing double dome unit

or even three sheets with two air spaces. Double and triple "glazing" greatly improves the thermal characteristics of skylights and reduces or eliminates condensation; it also improves light diffusion (Figs. 2, 3, and 7).

The translucent plastic is usually an acrylic or a glass fiber reinforced polyester. Acrylic plastics may be transparent or translucent and are characteristically used in the domed form. They are available in various degrees of light transmission, diffusion, and heat gain; one manufacturer offers as many as eight types. Polyester sheets are translucent only, and may be white or colored. They are characteristically used in either flat or corrugated sheets.

Skylights that are circular, square, or nearly square in plan are generally domed acrylic plastic. Long, rectangular skylights are usually corrugated polyester, slightly arched (Fig. 6). Completely flat panels are available in the form of polyester-faced sandwich panels with aluminum eggcrate cores and frames. Both the corrugated and the sandwich-type polyester skylights are available in the curbless or "low silhouette" model as well as in the models for installation over a curb (Fig. 7).

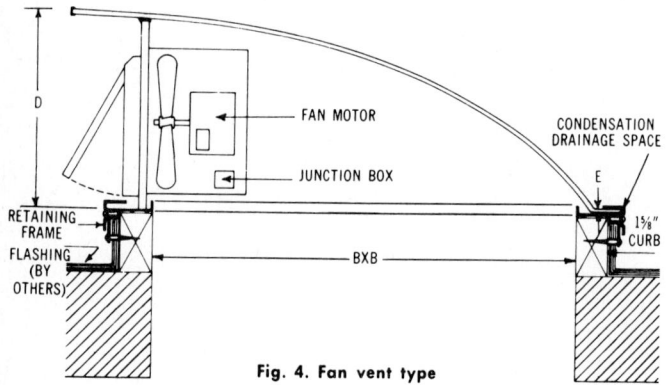

Fig. 4. Fan vent type

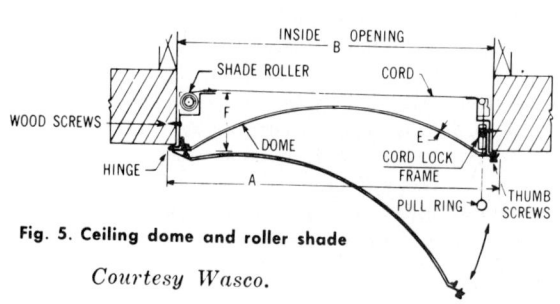

Fig. 5. Ceiling dome and roller shade

Courtesy Wasco.

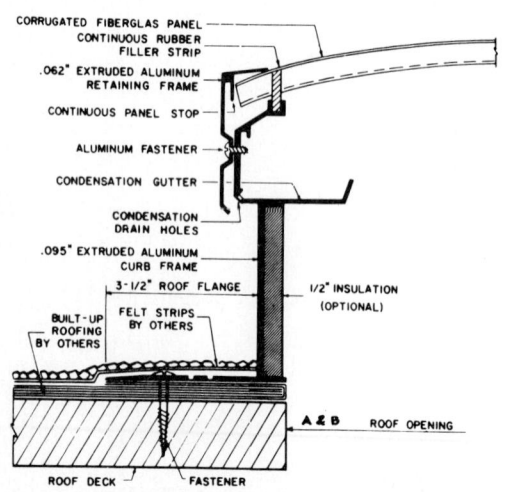

Fig. 6. Corrugated-plastic, integral-curb skylight

Courtesy Vanco.

Fig. 7. Sandwich panel, aluminum-grid-core skylight

Courtesy Kalwall.

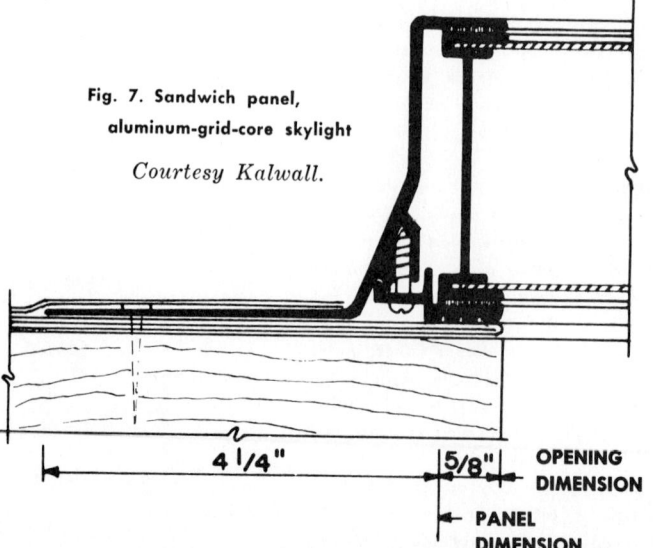

Table 1. Types and sizes of skylights

The thickness of the plastic and the height of the dome vary with the size of the skylights. The thickness varies from ⅛ to ¼ in., the dome height from 1½ to 25 in.

Type	Inside curb measurement, in.		
	Small	Medium	Large
Square dome on 1⅝-in. curb	14¼x14¼	37 x 37	99½x 92½
Rectangular dome on 1⅝-in. curb	14¼x22¼	37 x 75	93¼x113¼
Round dome inside curb—diameter	24	43	91
Corrugated rectangular, inside frame*	23½x39½	35½x109½	71½x144½
Plastic-faced aluminum grid 1⁹⁄₁₆ in. thick	22¼x22¼	37 x 37	44½x 92½
Plastic-faced aluminum grid 2¾ in. thick	44½x92½	44½x140½	44½x236½

* Supports are required under panel laps if the width dimension between frames exceeds 47½ in.

Sizes of skylights are not uniform, although there is some similarity within the industry. Table 1 indicates the range of types and sizes available.

Corrugated polyester sheets may be used without frames to form economical skylights in roofs built of corrugated metal or asbestos cement. The corrugated plastic matches the corrugations of the roofing and is installed at the same time and by the same techniques as the roofing sheets (Fig. 8). Corrugated polyester sheets may also be nailed directly to wood purlins to form entire roofs over porches, patios, and the like (Fig. 9).

METAL SKYLIGHTS

Metal skylights are usually custom made of aluminum extrusions or galvanized steel. Other metals such as copper, lead-coated copper, monel, stainless steel, and aluminum-clad steel are sometimes used. Metal skylights are made in certain standard shapes or styles (Fig. 10). Although most often used in single units, skylights can be designed to cover an entire roof, as in a baseball cage or a museum. Besides light they can provide various types of ventilation as well as access to the roof.

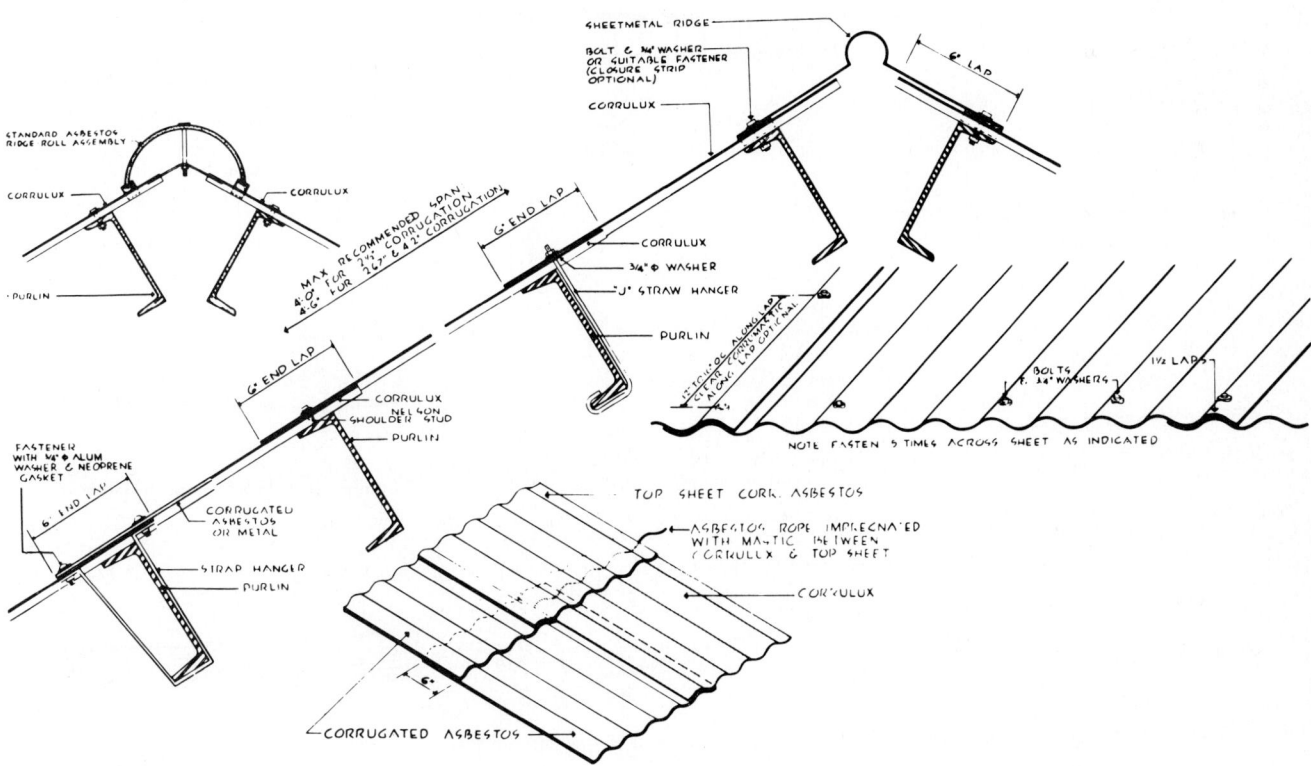

Fig. 8. Corrugated plastic with corrugated metal roofing for skylights

Courtesy Corrulux.

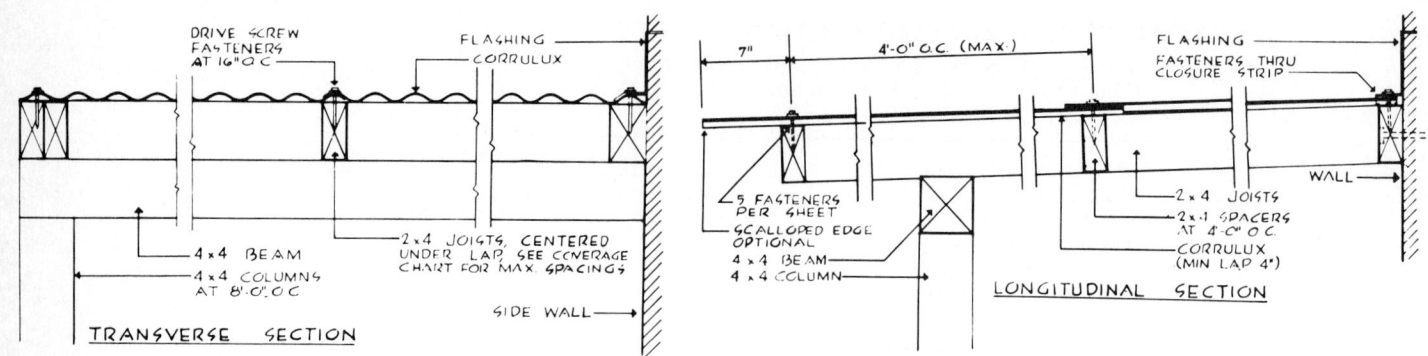

Fig. 9. Corrugated plastic on wood purlins for skylights

Courtesy Corrulux.

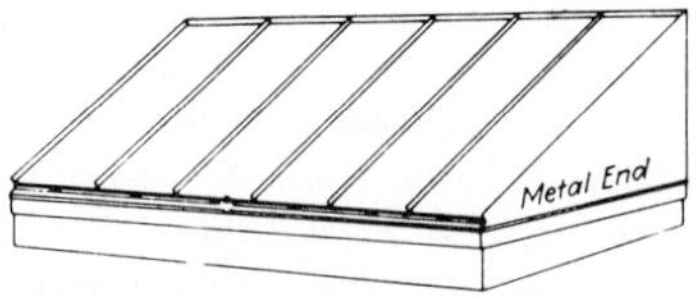

Single-pitch skylight

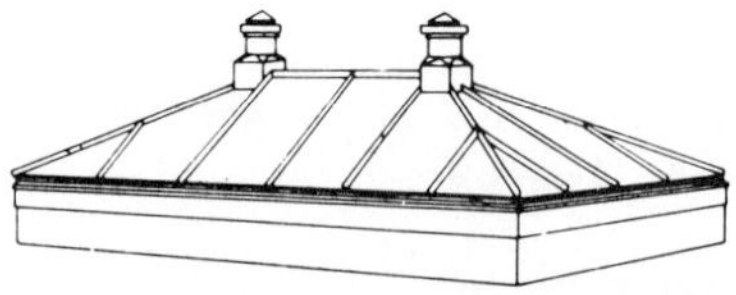

Hipped skylight with tubular ventilators

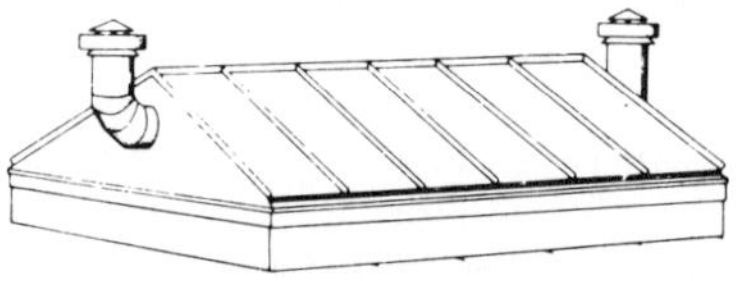

Double-pitch skylight with tubular ventilators at ends

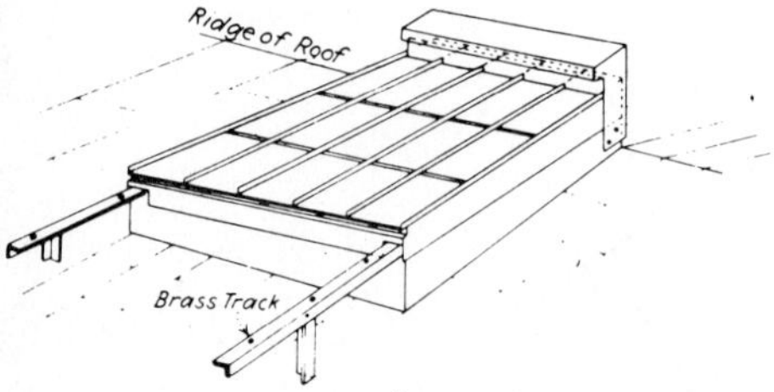

Theater stage skylight of the rolling type; may also be double pitch or hipped

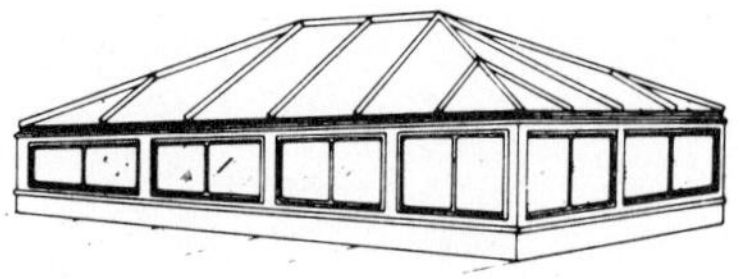

Stationary or movable sash under hipped skylight

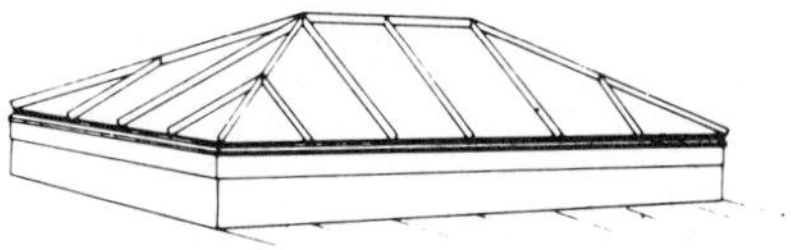

Plain hipped skylight

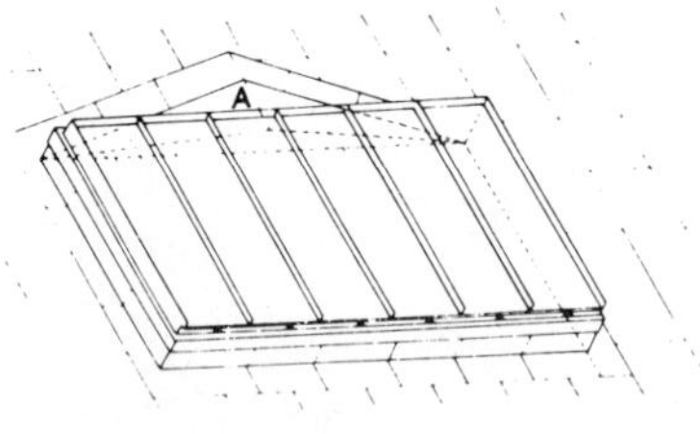

Double-pitch skylight

Flat skylight on pitched roof; may be hinged to serve as scuttle

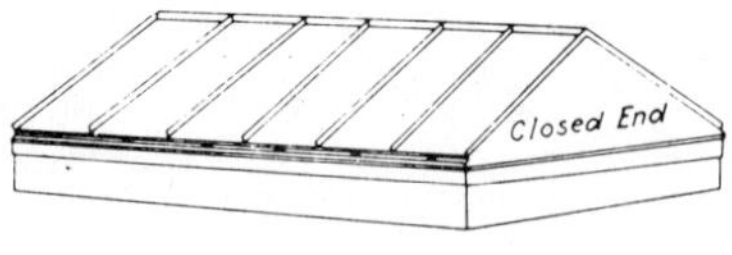

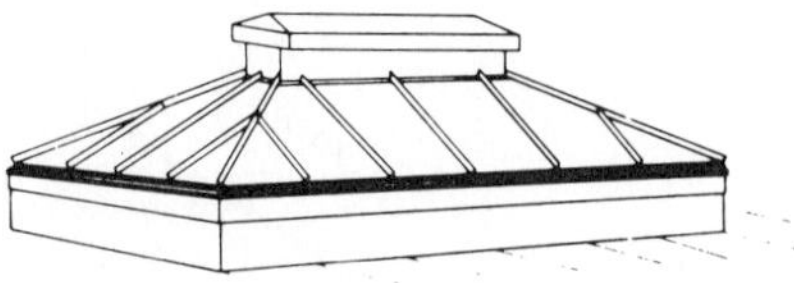

Hipped skylight with ridge ventilator

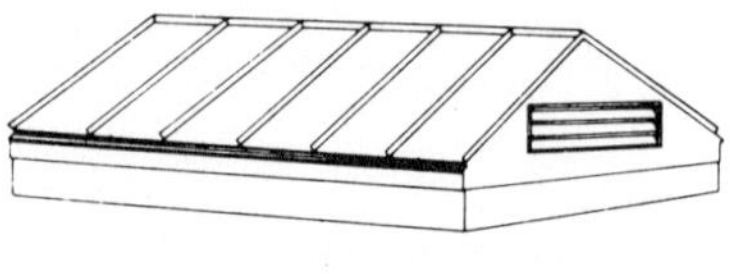

Double-pitch skylight with stationary or movable louvers at ends

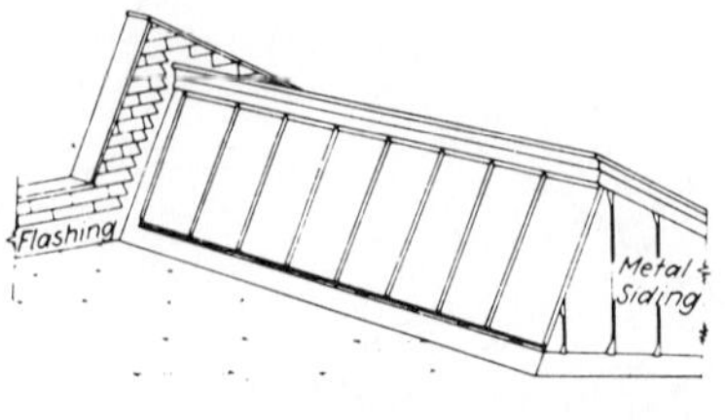

Partial view of sawtooth or north-light skylight

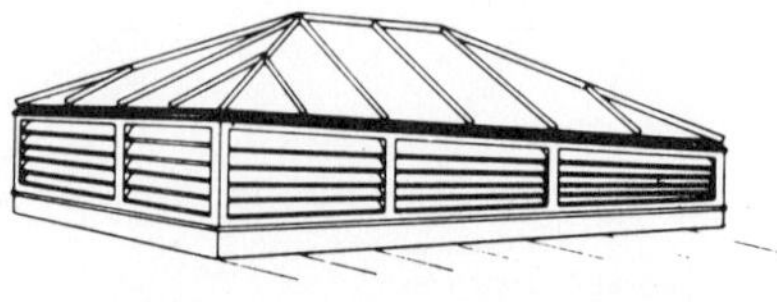

Stationary or movable louvers under hipped skylight

Fig. 10. Sheet metal skylights

From Standard Practice in Sheet Metal Work, Sheet Metal Contractors National Association, Inc.

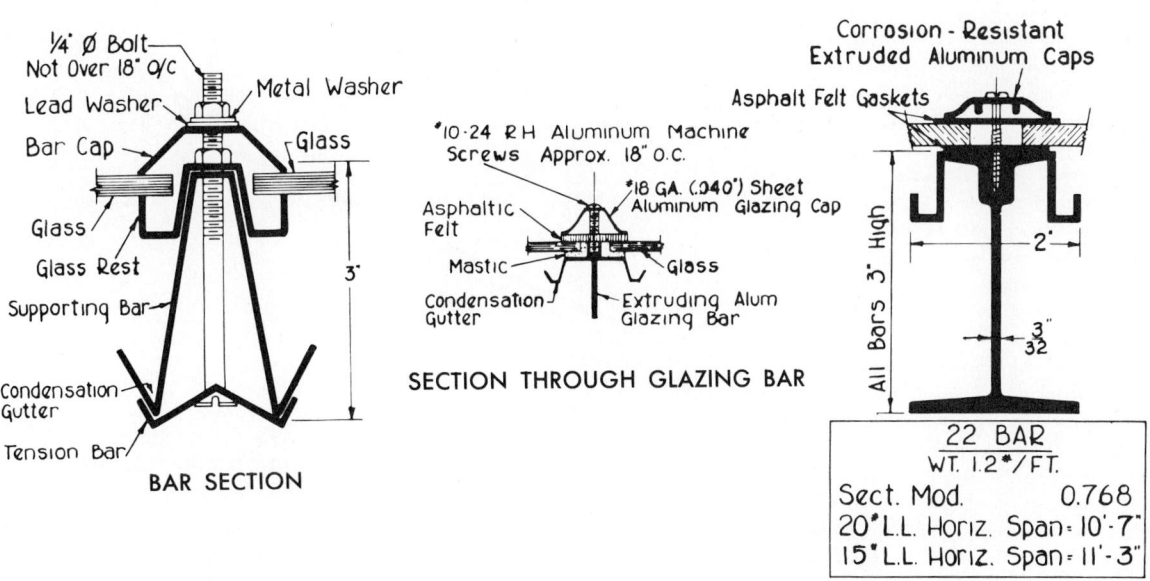

¼" Ø Bolt Not Over 18" O/C
Metal Washer
Lead Washer
Bar Cap
Glass
Glass
Glass Rest
Supporting Bar
Condensation Gutter
Tension Bar

BAR SECTION

#10-24 RH Aluminum Machine Screws Approx. 18" O.C.
#18 GA. (.040") Sheet Aluminum Glazing Cap
Asphaltic Felt
Mastic
Glass
Condensation Gutter
Extruding Alum Glazing Bar

SECTION THROUGH GLAZING BAR

Corrosion - Resistant Extruded Aluminum Caps
Asphalt Felt Gaskets
All Bars 3" High
2"
3/32"

22 BAR	
WT. 1.2#/FT.	
Sect. Mod.	0.768
20# L.L. Horiz. Span =	10'-7"
15# L.L. Horiz. Span =	11'-3"

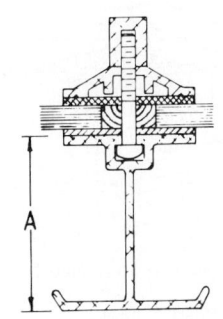

A

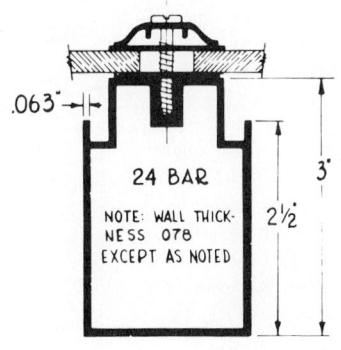

.063"
24 BAR
NOTE: WALL THICKNESS .078 EXCEPT AS NOTED
3"
2½"

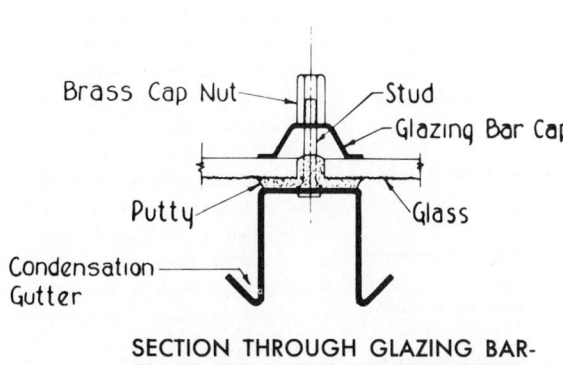

Brass Cap Nut
Stud
Glazing Bar Cap
Putty
Glass
Condensation Gutter

SECTION THROUGH GLAZING BAR- STANDARD PUTTY CONSTRUCTION

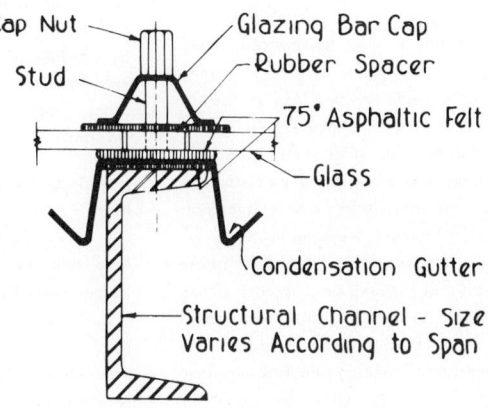

Cap Nut
Stud
Glazing Bar Cap
Rubber Spacer
75° Asphaltic Felt
Glass
Condensation Gutter
Structural Channel - Size Varies According to Span

SECTION THROUGH GLAZING BAR

Fig. 11. Glazing bar sections

From Standard Practice in Sheet Metal Work, *Sheet Metal Contractors National Association, Inc.*

The essential element in the metal skylight is the "sash bar" or "glazing bar" (Fig. 11), many of which are patented. Most designs include condensation gutters with weep holes for drainage. Details have been developed which eliminate putty and the maintenance problem it presents; some designs use direct metal-to-glass contact, others use felt, cork, or other composition as gaskets or cushions. Standard designs are usually based on a glass width of 24 in.

The glass used in skylights is generally ¼-in. wired glass in ribbed, hammered, or rough patterns with the smooth face out, and is limited in size to 24 in. in width and 48 in. in length. Other types of glass such as sheet, plate, tempered, safety, heat-absorbent, or glare-reducing may be used, as may various types of plastic sheets. Double glazing with two separate sheets of glass with an air space between may be incorporated in the design, or sealed double glass may be used.

In addition to the standard types shown in Fig. 10, two others should be noted. One is the curbless, depressed-head skylight used on pitched roofs (Fig. 12). The other is the automatic stage ventilator, which is required by law in many cities (Fig. 13).

Metal skylights need not be limited to the standard types. Possibilities in custom-designed skylights are limited only by the imagination of the architect. An example of imaginative design is shown in Fig. 14.

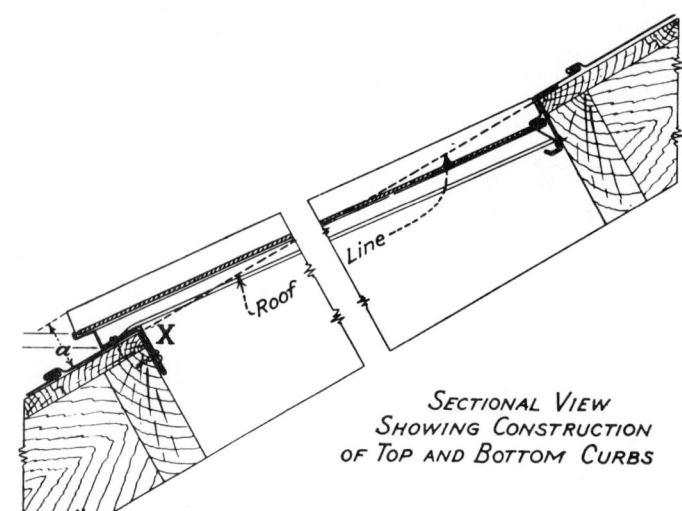

SECTIONAL VIEW SHOWING CONSTRUCTION OF TOP AND BOTTOM CURBS

Fig. 12. Curbless flat skylight on pitched roof

From Standard Practice in Sheet Metal Work, *Sheet Metal Contractors National Association, Inc.*

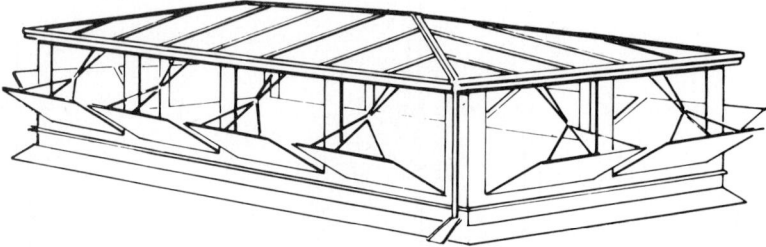

Fig. 13. Automatic stage ventilators

Courtesy Vanco.

FIRE PROTECTION

To provide against emergencies resulting from fires, the glass in the skylight should be plain glass not thicker than ⅛ in. so that it may be pierced easily. This type of skylight is used over theater stages to provide venting for a fire on the stage in order to prevent its spread to the auditorium (Fig. 13). It is also used at the top of required exit stair enclosures and vent shafts. Where thin glass is required, screens (removable to permit cleaning) are commonly provided above the glass as protection against flying brands and below as protection against falling glass. Plastic skylights with fusible links operating opening mechanisms have been developed to serve as automatic vents, but are not as easily pierced from the outside as is thin glass.

When skylights are used primarily for light or light and ventilation the *National Building Code* (1976) of the American Insurance Association requires that they have sashes and frames of noncombustible material and be glazed with ¼-in. wire glass, approved glass block, or an approved plastic that does not present a fragmentation hazard. (Wood frames may be used by special permission in foundries and where acid fumes are present.) Where plastic is used the Code establishes the following requirements for skylights:

1. They shall have curbs at least 4 in. high.
2. They shall not exceed 100 sq ft in area and the total area shall not exceed 20 per cent of the floor area.
3. They shall be separated by at least 5 ft.
4. They shall be not closer than 30 ft to a wall in which the openings are required to be protected, or 10 ft to the edges of roofs of fire-resistant construction.
5. Skylights having a slope of less than 20° above the horizontal shall be screened from flying brands.

GLASS-BLOCK SKYLIGHTS

Glass block may also be used in skylights. They offer the advantages of excellent light diffusion and good thermal insulation. The blocks may be preassembled in aluminum or concrete grids, or they may be installed individually in job-built grids of reinforced concrete (Figs. 15 and 16). In the latter case the concrete may be poured directly around the blocks to seal them as well as support them, or they may be installed in waterproof mastic so that a unit can be easily replaced if damaged. One type of block is specially designed to exclude summer sunlight striking at a high angle, but to admit winter sun that strikes at a low angle, and to admit north light at all times. These units must be installed with correct orientation. All glass-block skylights must be installed with a minimum pitch of ¼ in. per ft for drainage.

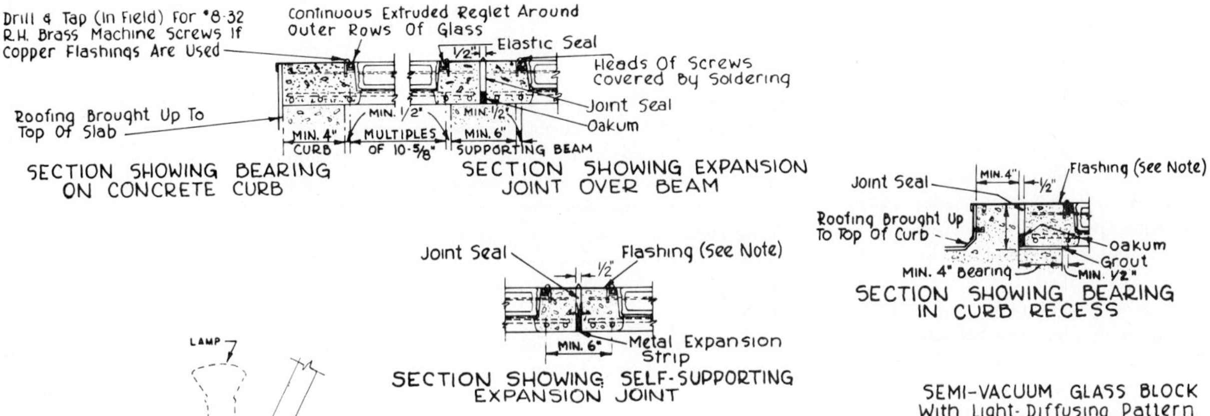

Drill & Tap (In Field) For #8-32 R.H. Brass Machine Screws If Copper Flashings Are Used

Continuous Extruded Reglet Around Outer Rows Of Glass

Elastic Seal

Heads Of Screws Covered By Soldering

Roofing Brought Up To Top Of Slab

Joint Seal

Oakum

MIN. 4" CURB

MIN. 1/2"

MULTIPLES OF 10-5/8"

MIN. 1/2"

MIN. 6"

SUPPORTING BEAM

SECTION SHOWING BEARING ON CONCRETE CURB

SECTION SHOWING EXPANSION JOINT OVER BEAM

Joint Seal

Flashing (See Note)

MIN. 4"

1/2"

Roofing Brought Up To Top Of Curb

Oakum

Grout

MIN. 4" Bearing

MIN. 1/2"

SECTION SHOWING BEARING IN CURB RECESS

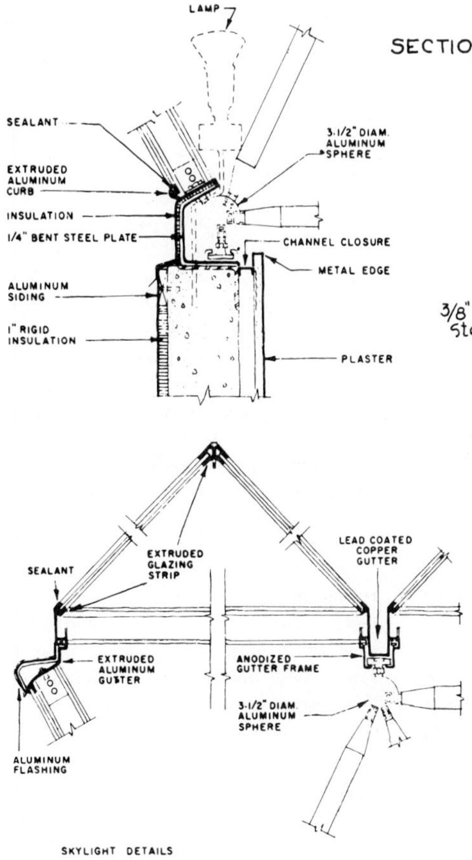

Joint Seal

Flashing (See Note)

1/2"

MIN. 6"

Metal Expansion Strip

SECTION SHOWING SELF-SUPPORTING EXPANSION JOINT

SEMI-VACUUM GLASS BLOCK With Light-Diffusing Pattern On Inner Surfaces

Extruded Coverplate-Continuous In One Direction With Intermediate Lengths In Lateral Direction

Waterproof Seal

No. 10 Compression Rods

3/8" Diam. Deformed Steel Rods

Bedding

3 7/8"

10 5/8" On Centers Both Ways

SECTION SHOWING DETAIL OF CONSTRUCTION

LAMP

SEALANT

EXTRUDED ALUMINUM CURB

INSULATION

1/4" BENT STEEL PLATE

ALUMINUM SIDING

1" RIGID INSULATION

3-1/2" DIAM. ALUMINUM SPHERE

CHANNEL CLOSURE

METAL EDGE

PLASTER

SEALANT

EXTRUDED GLAZING STRIP

LEAD COATED COPPER GUTTER

EXTRUDED ALUMINUM GUTTER

ANODIZED GUTTER FRAME

3-1/2" DIAM. ALUMINUM SPHERE

ALUMINUM FLASHING

SKYLIGHT DETAILS

Fig. 14. Space-frame skylight

A space frame of bright aluminum rods and spheres supports a gutter system of extruded aluminum sections which in turn holds the 1/4-in. wire glass in such a fashion that movement is possible without leakage. Reynolds Building, Detroit; Yamasaki, Architect.

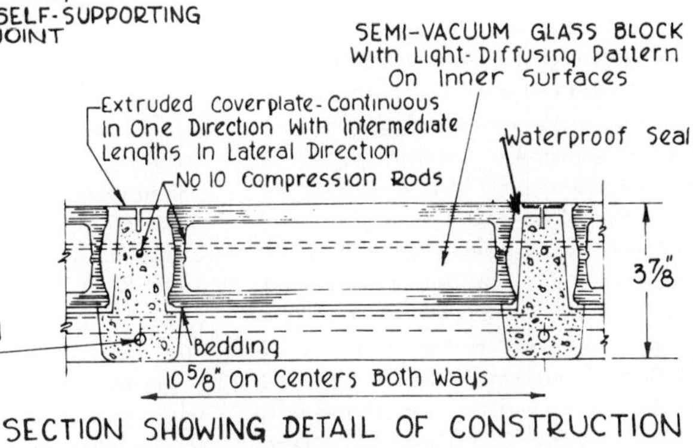

STRUCTURAL DATA

MAXIMUM PANEL SIZES:-
Factory Glazed Panels:
4 Units By 7 Units Or Approx. 28 Sq. Ft Area.
Factory Finished Grids (Glass Set At Job Site)
5 Units By 7 Units Or Approx. 35 Sq. Ft. Area.
MONOLITHIC PANELS (CONSTRUCTED AT JOB SITE)
8 Units By 12 Units Or Approx. 85 Sq. Ft. Site)
MAXIMUM SPAN BETWEEN SUPPORTS:-
Width-Not Over 7'-2"
Length-Unlimited (Using Self-Supporting Joints)
MINIMUM PITCH:-
Provide For Minimum 1/4" TO 12" Pitch.
WEIGHT PER. SQ. FT:-
Approx. 35-40 Lbs. (Glazed)
LIVE LOAD:-
40 lbs. Plus Per. Sq. Ft.

NOTE :-FLASHINGS-
Flashings Consisting Of 2 Plies Membrane Fabric Cemented To Concrete Surfaces With Hot Asphalt Mopping Between Plies And On Outer Surfaces To Be Furnished And Installed By Roofing Or Sheet Metal Contractor. If Desired, Membrane Flashings May Be Covered With 18 Oz. Lead-Coated Copper As Shown In Details Above.

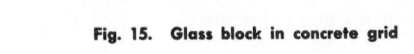

SCHEDULE OF UNIT MULTIPLES AT 10-5/8" CENTERS					
1 = 0'-10-5/8"	4 = 3'-6 1/2"	7 = 6'-2 3/8"	10 = 8'-10 1/4"		
2 = 1'-9 1/4"	5 = 4'-5 1/8"	8 = 7'-1"	11 = 9'-8 7/8"		
3 = 2'-7 7/8"	6 = 5'-3 3/4"	9 = 7'-11 5/8"	12 = 10'-7 1/2"		

Fig. 15. Glass block in concrete grid

From Standard Practice in Sheet Metal Work, *Sheet Metal Contractors National Association, Inc.*

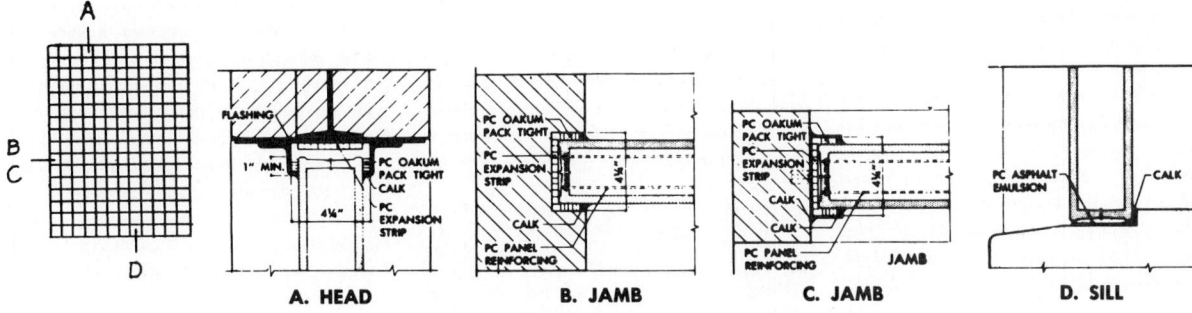

FLASHING

1" MIN.

PC OAKUM PACK TIGHT

CALK

4 1/4"

PC EXPANSION STRIP

A. HEAD

PC OAKUM PACK TIGHT

PC EXPANSION STRIP

4 1/4"

CALK

PC PANEL REINFORCING

B. JAMB

PC OAKUM PACK TIGHT

PC EXPANSION STRIP

4 1/4"

CALK

CALK

PC PANEL REINFORCING

JAMB

C. JAMB

PC ASPHALT EMULSION

CALK

D. SILL

A

B

C

D

Fig. 16. Glass block in aluminum grid *Courtesy of Pittsburgh Corning.*

CURTAIN WALLS – 1
Types

By JACK M. ROEHM, PE, *Director of Technical Services,*
Architectural Aluminum Manufacturers Association

INTRODUCTION

The modern metal curtain wall gained wide architectural acceptance in the early 1950s as a means of enclosing building structures. This type of wall construction made possible the extensive use of glass facades with clean, trim metal supporting frameworks. The components of these metal and glass facades were capable of being manufactured to relatively precise tolerances in the factory, easily shipped to the job site because of their light weight, and rapidly installed on the building structure. These favorable features combined to produce not only an attractive and economical wall system but also a system which permitted faster enclosure and earlier occupancy of the building than was obtainable by wall systems which required a great deal of on-site work. For these reasons the metal curtain wall has been widely used throughout the world. Over the years new methods of finishing metals have become available; glasses which provide insulation and reflect solar radiation have been produced; sealants which are capable of performing excellently under the extremes of weather to which walls are subjected have been developed, so that today the architect has available materials and techniques which offer great design versatility plus a capability of achieving whatever performance level is required of the wall system.

Satisfactory performance depends on proper design. Metal and glass, like all other construction materials, impose their own disciplines upon the designer. Their performance is governed by fundamental laws of physics, and a properly designed metal curtain wall necessarily reflects a proper regard for these laws. Since these materials react in their own ways to the ever-present forces of nature—heat, wind, water, gravity, light, and sound—a clear understanding of these forces is essential to the design of satisfactorily performing metal curtain walls.

The covering of a field-constructed frame with a factory-fabricated wall requires a degree of dimensional control in construction and a coordination of construction with the wall fabricator beyond what was called for in the older, on-site methods of wall construction.

Thus a review of the design principles dictated both by the nature of the materials and by the technique associated with their fabrication and assembly becomes a necessary prerequisite to good metal curtain wall design. Reference: *Aluminum Curtain Wall Design Guide Manual,* Architectural Aluminum Manufacturers Association, 1979.

DEFINITION

A metal curtain wall is generally defined as an exterior nonloadbearing wall which may consist entirely or principally of metal or may be a combination of metal, glass, and other surfacing materials supported by or within a metal framework.

It is important to note that the determining distinction in this widely accepted definition is the material used in the supporting framework, rather than that used for surfacing the wall. Many materials, such as glass, masonry, or plastic, may be used for the "infilling" panels, which may cover a large part of the wall surface, but if these materials are carried in a metal framework to provide a nonbearing wall system, the term "metal curtain wall construction" properly applies. It is obviously not necessary, therefore, that the design include metallic panels in order to qualify under this definition.

CLASSIFICATION OF CURTAIN WALLS

Variations in metal curtain wall construction are almost infinite, and it is impossible to pigeonhole the many types in certain clearly defined categories. Early research, both in the Princeton studies[1] and by the Building Research Institute,[2] proposed three bases of classification: (1) Visual characteristics, (2) Method of support, and (3) Method of assembly. Although this system of classification may have been valid and useful in the earlier days of metal curtain wall, it no longer has very much significance. It has now become common practice to classify metal curtain walls by type and system, the type designating whether or not the design is unique and the system designation referring to the method of installation. The following explanation of this classification method, along with the accompanying illustrations, is quoted, with permission of the publishers, from the publication *Aluminum Curtain Walls.*[3]

Wall types

Because of the wide and increasing variety of aluminum curtain wall designs, it is difficult, if not impossible, to precisely identify every design as representing one or another of a few basic types. Certain broad distinctions can usually be made, but in some cases accurate classification under one of a limited number of subcategories becomes subjective and therefore debatable. Nevertheless, because there are so many variations, some generally accepted

[1] *J. H. Callender et al.* Curtain Walls of Stainless Steel. *School of Architecture, Princeton University, Princeton (1955).*
[2] *Charles R. Koehler, ed.* Architectural Metal Curtain Wall Workshop—Conference. *Report of Five Workshops, Building Research Institute, Washington (1956).*
[3] Aluminum Curtain Walls, *vol. 1 (October, 1970), Architectural Aluminum Manufacturers Association.*

system of identifying the most common design forms becomes essential.

One method of identification which is useful and all-inclusive is based on the extent to which the wall design is unique. Any aluminum wall is either (1) a custom type, (2) a standard type, or in some cases (3) a combination of the two. The two basic types are described as follows:

Custom type walls are those which are designed specifically for one project (either a single building or a group of related buildings). Such walls usually, though not necessarily, have substantial areas of glass and may be used on buildings of any type or size. Typically they are chosen for the more glamorous high-rise structures and for commercial, institutional, and monumental buildings of high quality.

Standard type walls are those which employ components and details which are designed and standardized by their manufacturer. They may be assembled in stock units, but more often their arrangement is dictated by the architect's design. Standard walls may be either of two types:

Architectural: Walls having formed framing members (usually extrusions) and sizable areas of glass, often with opaque panel areas also.

Industrial: Walls composed either of preformed metal sheets made in stock patterns and sizes, used in combination with standard windows, or of large metal-faced insulated panels, used either with or without fenestration. Typical usage of such walls is on industrial type structures.

The term "standard" should not be interpreted as in any way implying rigidly fixed or static design concepts. Standard designs vary from one manufacturer to another and are adaptable to a broad range of esthetic expression. It has been suggested, in fact, that three subcategories of standard architectural walls should be recognized—"stock standard," "modified standard," and "custom standard"—to indicate the degree of design flexibility offered in the so-called standard types and the fact that distinction between standard and custom walls may be nebulous.

As a rule, the standard architectural type of wall, because of the economies inherent in quantity production, tends to be less expensive than custom walls, but this is not always the case. Some of the more complex standard designs may cost as much or more than the simplest custom designs, and on large projects, where quantities are sufficient to warrant large-scale production methods, custom work may impose little if any cost premium.

Wall systems

Both custom and standard walls may be further classified according to their "sys-

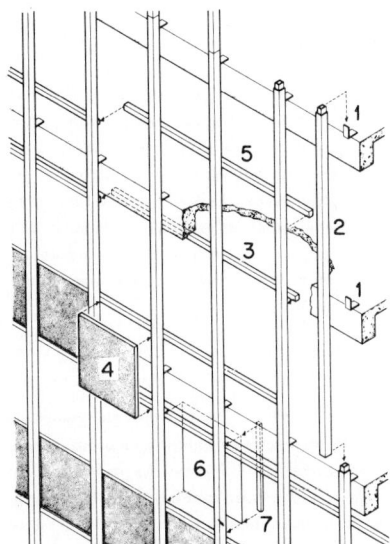

Fig. 1. Stick system—schematic of typical version. (1) Anchors, (2) mullion, (3) horizontal rail (gutter section at window head), (4) spandrel panel (may be installed from inside building), (5) horizontal rail (window sill section), (6) vision glass (installed from inside building), (7) interior mullion trim.

Other variations: Mullion and rail sections may be longer or shorter than shown. Vision glass may be set directly in recesses in framing members, may be set with applied stops, may be set in subframe, or may include operable sash.

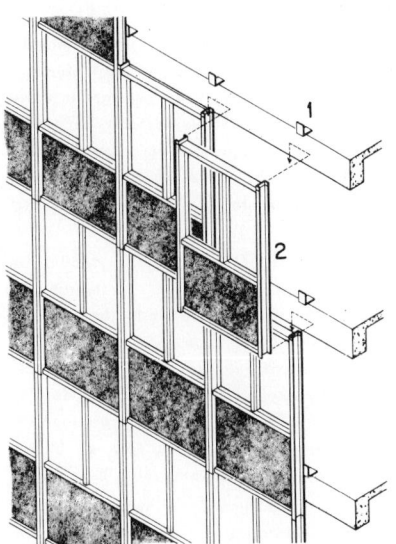

Fig. 2. Unit system—schematic of typical version. (1) Anchor, (2) preassembled framed unit.

Other variations: Mullion sections may be interlocking "split" type or may be channel shapes with applied inside and outside joint covers. Units may be unglazed when installed or may be preglazed. Spandrel panel may be either at top or bottom of unit.

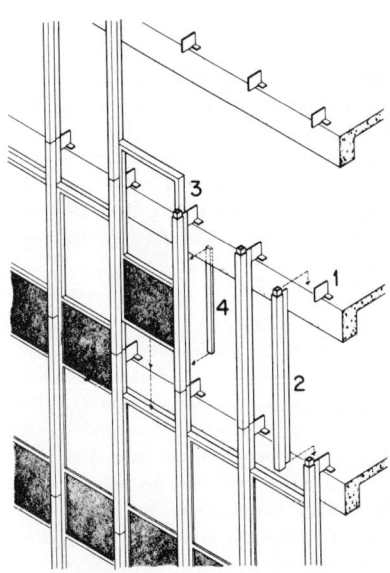

Fig. 3. Unit-and-mullion system—schematic of typical version. (1) Anchors, (2) mullion (either one- or two-story lengths), (3) preassembled unit—lowered into place behind mullion from floor above, (4) interior mullion trim.

Other variations: Framed units may be full-story height (as shown) either unglazed or preglazed, or may be separate spandrel cover units and vision glass units. Horizontal rail sections are sometimes used between units.

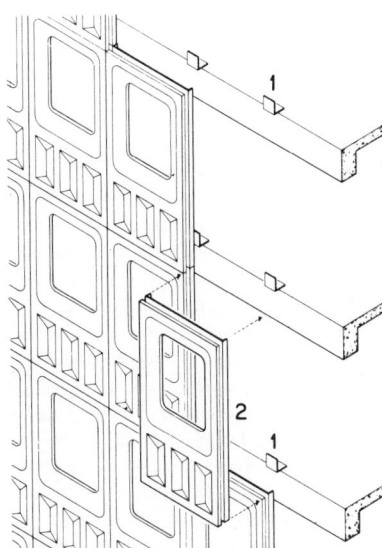

Fig. 4. Panel system—schematic of typical version. (1) Anchor, (2) panel.

Other variations: Panels may be formed sheet or castings, may be full-story height (as shown) or smaller units, and may be either preglazed or glazed after installation.

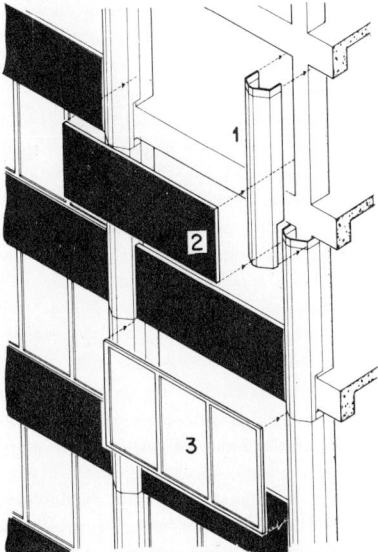

Fig. 5. Column-cover-and-spandrel system —schematic of typical version. (1) Column cover section, (2) spandrel panel, (3) glazing infill.

Other variations: Column covers may be one piece or an assembly, may be of any cross-sectional profile, and either one or two stories in height. Spandrel panel may be plain, textured, or patterned. Glazing infill may be a preassembly, either glazed or unglazed, or be assembled in place.

tem" or method of installation. The majority of curtain walls built to date may be identified as representing one of five different systems, but some of the newer designs do not fall neatly into any of these categories.

The five generally recognized systems referred to are these: (1) the stick system, (2) the unit system, (3) the unit-and-mullion system, (4) the panel system, and (5) the column-cover-and-spandrel system. Each of these systems is illustrated schematically and is briefly described in the following.

In the stick system (Fig. 1) the wall is installed piece by piece. Usually the mullion members are installed first, followed in turn by the horizontal rail members, the panels (if any), and finally the glazing or window units. However, in designs accenting the horizontal lines, the process may be altered to first install the larger horizontal members. In either case, both the horizontal and vertical framing members are often long sections designed to overlap or extend through at their intersections.

The stick system was used extensively in the early years of metal curtain wall development and is still in wide use in greatly improved versions. Some manufacturers consider it to be superior to other systems. The advantages of this system are its relatively low shipping and handling costs, because of minimal bulk, and the fact that it offers some degree of dimensional adjustment to site conditions. Among its disadvantages are the necessity of assembly in the field, rather than under controlled factory conditions, and the fact that preglazing is obviously impossible.

In the unit system (Fig. 2), the wall is composed entirely of large framed units preassembled at the factory, complete with spandrel panels (if any) and sometimes also preglazed. The vertical edges of the units join to form mullion members, top and bottom members join to form horizontal rails, and the units may be one, two, or sometimes three stories in height. This system provides assembly under controlled shop conditions, where the work can be carefully inspected, and facilitates rapid enclosure of the building with a minimum of field labor and relatively few field joints. On the other hand, the units are bulky and require more space for shop assembly, shipping, and on-site storage. They also necessitate more elaborate protective measures, both in transit and in storage at the site prior to installation. Another problem sometimes encountered is the detailing and installation of "leave-out" units. Typical wall units are designed for sequential interlocking installation, and when openings have to be left in the wall to facilitate the handling of construction materials, the units installed later to close these openings usually require special joint details and installation procedures.

The unit-and-mullion system (Fig. 3), as the term implies, is a compromise between the two previously described systems. In this system the mullion members are separately installed first, then preassembled framed units are placed between them. These units may be full story height, or they may be divided into a spandrel unit and a vision glass unit. The system is often employed when the mullion sections are unusually deep or large in cross section, making it impractical to incorporate them as part of a preassembled unit.

The advantages and disadvantages of this system are generally comparable to those of the unit system. The shipping bulk of the units themselves is somewhat less, because of the omission of the mullion section, but the amount of field labor, field jointing, and erection time is likely to be somewhat greater.

The panel system (Fig. 4) is similar in concept to the unit system, the chief difference being that the panels are not preassembled framed units but homogeneous units formed from sheet metal or as castings, with few if any internal joints except at the glass periphery. The panels may be full story height, with or without openings for glazing, or they may be smaller units. Unlike the other three systems, the panel system usually provides an overall pattern for the wall, rather than a grid pattern or a design having strong vertical or horizontal accents.

Two kinds of panel system should be recognized; those of an "architectural" character and those used in industrial walls. The architectural type (shown in Fig. 4) is always custom-made and consequently relatively expensive, whereas the industrial type panels are produced in large quantity, as standard products, by roll- or brake-forming, and are relatively inexpensive.

The architectural panel system offers all of the advantages of the unit system, with probably a wider range of design flexibility, and has the added advantage of a minimal amount of shop labor. However, with present techniques, the cost of dies (if panels are formed by stamping) or of molds (if formed by casting) makes this system economically attractive only when a large number of identical panels are to be used.

The column-cover-and-spandrel system (Fig. 5) is a relatively recent development compared with the other four systems. As its name implies, the elements of this system consist of column cover sections, long spandrel units which span between the column covers, and infill glazing units which may be either preassemblies or separate framing members and glass.

This type of system, unlike the other four described, provides a facade design which clearly expresses the structural frame of the building, rather than a superimposed grid or overall pattern. It permits a wide latitude of esthetic expression in all three of its basic components, and because column spacings and spandrel depths vary with almost every building, its use is necessarily limited to custom type walls.

Using this method of classification, a wall might be identified as a custom wall of the unit-and-mullion system, a standard wall of the stick system, a custom column-cover-and-spandrel system, a standard industrial wall, and so forth. As previously mentioned, however, variations in metal curtain wall design are limitless, and new concepts are constantly appearing. The distinction between custom and standard types is usually not difficult, but sometimes systems other than the five most common, listed above, are used. For the present these may be referred to simply as "other systems," but some of these may well become popular enough to warrant adding other categories to the list of commonly used systems.

MATERIALS

By definition, metal is the principal structural material in these walls, although it is frequently not the most conspicuous material. Sometimes a large portion of the wall area is sheathed with metal, but more often the apparent quantity of metal is only the minimum required to provide necessary support and stiffness for the nonmetallic infilling materials.

The metals used include carbon steel, aluminum, stainless steel, and bronze.

Most carbon steels, though relatively low in cost, require painting to protect them from corrosion. But with the availability of superior long-lived coatings, this is no longer a serious handicap, and painted steel curtain walls are being used even on high-rise buildings.

Aluminum has been used much more extensively, in all types of curtain walls, than any other metal. By far its most common use, in custom and standard walls, is in the form of extruded shapes for mullion members and rail and sash sections, but it is also often used in the form of sheet or plate for column covers, fascias, soffits, and panels. Stainless steel, being a more costly metal, has been used to a lesser extent and generally only in custom walls. This metal is typically used either in sheet form or in sections that are brake-formed or roll-formed from sheet or strip material. Bronze has been the least commonly used of all the architectural metals in metal curtain wall work, because of its relatively high cost. Like aluminum, it may be easily extruded or cast, or it may be used in the form of sheet or plate.

Many types of glass are used in metal curtain wall construction. Clear, tinted, and reflective glass are used for transparent glazing, and the opaque colored "structural" types of glass are widely used as panel materials. Many outstanding buildings have walls almost entirely of glass, with a minimum of exposed metal framing.

Numerous other materials are also used as infilling panels. Porcelain-enameled metal, either carbon steel or aluminum, has long been a popular material, used as the exterior facing of hollow insulated panel and sandwich-panel constructions. Several types of masonry materials—marble, slate, tile, and stone—are also used in panel areas. Ceramic tile facings, applied either to precast concrete slabs or to rigid, nonmetallic sheet materials, are popular in many areas. Additionally, plastic materials have been used as panel facings, although their use has, to date, been comparatively limited.

DESIGN WIND LOADS

Introduction

Wind loads are the primary concern in the structural design of aluminum curtain walls. It is these loads that dictate the necessary stiffness and strength of framing members, the thickness of glass, and the strength of the anchorage details. Compared with those wind loads used by the structural engineer in designing the building frame, the loads acting upon the walls and governing their design are somewhat different, and the designer of the wall should have a clear understanding of their nature and magnitude.

Fundamentals of wind load design

In determining the wind loads to be used in designing aluminum curtain walls for a rectangular building, the following factors must be considered:

The geographic location of the building.

The wind velocity to be expected in that location.

The degree of shielding or exposure provided by surroundings.

The height of the building.

The location on the building facade of the wall area in question.

If the building were not rectangular in plan, its shape would be another important factor to be considered.

Location and basic wind velocity

Thanks to readily available data accumulated over a long period of time by the U.S. Environmental Science Services Administration (formerly the U.S. Weather Bureau), maximum wind velocities to be expected in any location in continental U.S. can be found simply by reference to wind velocity maps such as shown in Figure 1 in the section on Design Loads (p. 2-11). The data on which these maps are based have been obtained by anemometer readings taken at some 128 airport locations throughout the country.

The wind velocities shown on the map are referred to as the *basic wind speed*, which is the fastest-mile speed, at 30 ft above the ground, recorded within a certain period of time or "recurrence interval." Maps are available for 2, 10, 25, 50 and 100-year intervals. Only the latter three intervals are significant in building design and the 50-year interval is most often used in the United States. Maximum velocities increase somewhat, but not a great deal, with the increase of the interval from 50 to 100 years.

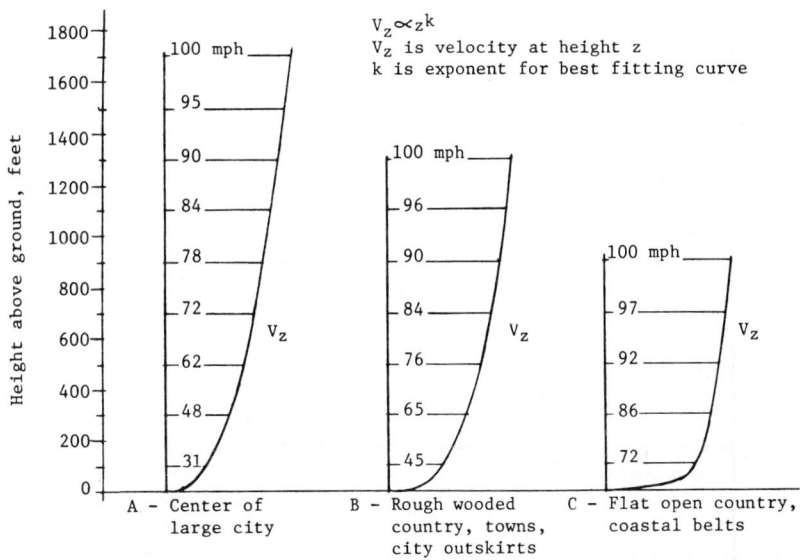

Fig. 6. Mean velocity profiles over terrain with three different roughness characteristics for gradient wind of 100 mph

Conversion of velocity to pressure

Wind is considered to act essentially as a fluid and according to the laws of physics the theoretical static pressure exerted by a flowing fluid on a stationary plate is expressed by the following equation:

$$q = 0.00256V^2$$

where q = static or *velocity pressure* in pounds per square foot

V = velocity in miles per hour

Note that *velocity pressure is not to be confused with design pressure* which is usually quite different as will be explained later.

Effects of height and surroundings

It has long been common knowledge that wind velocities increase with height above ground. At ground level the wind velocity is low because of the friction or drag. Above the ground, wind velocity increases in an exponential relationship with height, $V_z \propto z^k$, reaching its maximum design effect at 1000 to 2000 ft, depending on the drag effect of the terrain over which the wind is blowing. For example, wind blowing at 40 mph at a height of 30 ft may have a velocity of from 50 to 65 mph at an elevation of 200 ft.

Accumulated data, based on many anemometer readings, showed that wind velocities are 40 to 50 per cent greater in open country, such as at airports, than in nearby built-up areas. This has led to the requirement, in the newer codes, that design wind loads take into account the terrain effect and be determined in accordance with one of three types of exposure:

Exposure A Heavily built-up urban locations protected by surrounding tall buildings, and locations in very rough, hilly terrain.

Exposure B Suburban areas, towns, city outskirts, wooded areas and rolling terrain.

Exposure C Flat, open country, open flat coastal belts and grasslands, fully exposed to a long fetch of wind.

The theoretical wind velocities at various heights, characteristic of each of these three exposures, are seen in Figure 6, which shows the "velocity profiles." The "gradient wind" is the wind velocity at the gradient level, where the frictional effect of the terrain becomes negligible. In ANSI Standard A58.1-1972 "Building Code Requirements for Minimum Design Loads in Buildings and Other Structures," the average power-law exponents, k, for determining the exponential relationship of wind velocity to height for different terrain conditions are 1/3, 1/4.5 and 1/7 for exposures A, B and C respectively.

Gust effects

The "fastest mile" velocity shown on the wind velocity maps is the wind speed, in mph, based on the shortest recorded time interval in which one mile of wind passed the recording instrument. It is *not* the greatest wind velocity to be anticipated at that location, however, because gusts of much shorter duration often occur, and these may have significantly greater speed. A "gust factor" must therefore be applied to provide for this, in computing the design wind load.

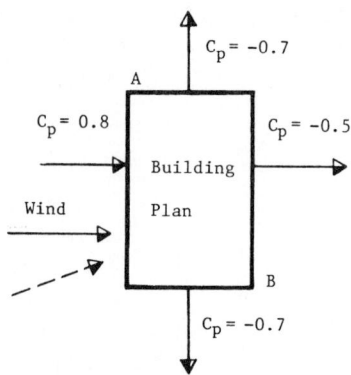

C_p = External Pressure Coefficient

Fig. 7. Loading effects of wind forces acting on a rectangular building

This factor varies with height, being highest near the ground, as well as with exposure, being highest in Exposure A. In all cases the gust factor increases the wind velocity—and the design load, the amount of increase varying from as little as 5% to over 100%.

External pressure coefficients

Wind forces acting on a building of rectangular plan shape produce quite different loading effects on the four facades. As illustrated in Fig. 7, only the windward side of the building is subjected to positive (inward acting) loads; the other three sides are subjected to negative (outward acting), or suction, loads. The diagram of Fig. 7 is, of course, oversimplified, because the wind direction is seldom normal to one face of the building. More frequently it is angular to the building, as indicated by the dashed arrow, and in such cases high negative pressures are created on the leeward side of exposed corners, in areas A and B. In these areas the pressure coefficient may be a negative value of −2.0 or more.

Internal pressure coefficients

Another important consideration, in the design of the building *enclosure,* is the pressure existing within the building. This pressure is the cumulative effect of wind action, mechanical ventilation and air conditioning, and stack effect. The latter depends on the exterior–interior temperature difference, and so is particularly significant in tall buildings in the colder climates. The net internal pressure is variable in character, and seldom can be predicted with accuracy, but it is more often positive than negative in the upper stories of high-rise buildings during the heating season. On the basis of information gathered to date, the coefficient usually used *for wind action only* is ±0.3 for buildings with uniformly distributed openings in the walls.

Design wind load

The design wind load is computed by taking all of the above factors into account. Basically, the procedure involves first determining, by reference to the appropriate map, the basic wind velocity and computing the velocity pressure, then modifying this pressure by applying the appropriate height, exposure, and gust factors and the external and internal pressure coefficients.

In practice the procedure is usually simplified by the use of tables. Tables 1, 2, 3, and 4 are taken from ANSI Standard A58.1-1972. Table 1 shows the effective velocity pressures for parts and portions of buildings and structures, which includes exterior walls, for exposure C. Table 2 shows the external pressure coefficients for walls. The effective velocity pressure is multiplied by the appropriate pressure coefficients to determine the external pressure exerted on the wall. Table 4 shows the effective velocity pressures for calculating internal pressures for exposure C. Table 3 shows the internal pressure coefficients for buildings. Again, the effective velocity pressure is multiplied by the appropriate pressure coefficient to determine the internal pressure exerted on the wall. The sum of the external and internal pressures gives the total pressure on the wall due to wind. This is the design wind pressure. However, this is not the total pressure to which the wall may be subjected. Stack action in high-rise buildings can be quite significant, particularly in cold climates. The pressures created by heating and air-conditioning equipment will also affect the wall loading, although in high-rise buildings the effect will not be as great as the effect of stack action. External factors such as the proximity of another building may result in a channeling effect which will increase negative pressures.

ANSI Standard A58.1-1972 is available from the American National Standards Institute, 1430 Broadway, New York, NY 10018. It covers in a very comprehensive manner wind loads on rectangular buildings. It provides a very clear distinction between wind loads as they affect the building structure and wind loads as they affect parts and portions of the building, the latter being the loads for which a curtain wall and its various components must be designed.

For most situations the ANSI standard will provide the data needed to calculate design wind loads. For other situations where, for example, building shape is other than rectangular in plan, the site location may have unusual wind conditions, the building may be critically located with respect to other nearby buildings, a cold climate may cause high internal pressure from stack action, and thus wind tunnel testing and special engineering studies may be essential to determine the required design wind loads.

ANSI A58.1 gives wind pressure values up to a height of 800 ft. This height represents a building of considerable height. There could be many unknowns in the way wind acts on such a building. Wind tunnel testing and special engineering studies may also be essential on buildings of much less height than this—even 300 ft or less—in order to determine safe design wind loads. Reference may be made to AAMA Technical Information Report TIR-A2-1975 "Design Wind Loads for Aluminum Curtain Walls" for more information on this subject.

Local wind loads and overall loads on building structure

There are two aspects of wind loading that must be considered in the design of most buildings. First, there is the overall wind load—the composite effect of positive and negative pressures—that governs the design of the building structure. It is this overall loading that the structural engineer is concerned with in determining the required strength and stiffness of the building frame. Second, there are the "local" wind loads which act on the various areas of the building enclosure, dictating the strength and stiffness of wall and roof elements and the adequacy of their fastenings. It is these loads, of course, that govern curtain wall design. The two types of loading differ significantly, and it is imperative that these differences be understood.

For one thing, these two kinds of wind load normally represent differing areas of concern and responsibility. While it is usually the structural engineer who is responsible for determining the overall load and designing the "bones" of the structure, it is generally the architect's responsibility to design the building "skin" to withstand the local wind loads. The inherent differences between the two types of wind loading are these:

1. The overall load is the net result of all loads occurring simultaneously at any time on all building surfaces, whereas the local load is the maximum load that may occur at any time at any location on any wall surface.

2. Under any given condition of wind direction and velocity, the overall load is considered to have a specific intensity, but both the intensity and character of local loading differ considerably on various parts of the building surface.

3. Generally, only gusts of about 2 sec or longer duration are significant in determining the critical overall loading, but the critical local loading is momentary in nature.

4. Local loads are greatly influenced by the configuration of the building surface on which they act, whereas the facade configuration of rectangular buildings has lit-

Table 1. Effective velocity pressures (lb/ft^2) for parts and portions of buildings and structures, q_P (Exposure C*)

Height (ft)	Basic wind speed (mph)								
	50	60	70	80	90	100	110	120	130
30 or less	10	14	19	24	31	38	46	55	64
50	11	15	21	27	34	42	51	61	72
100	12	18	24	31	39	49	59	70	82
150	13	19	26	34	43	53	65	77	90
200	14	20	28	36	46	57	69	82	96
250	15	21	29	38	48	59	72	86	101
300	15	22	30	39	50	61	74	88	104
350	16	23	31	41	52	64	77	92	108
400	16	24	32	42	53	66	80	95	111
450	17	24	33	43	54	67	81	96	113
500	17	25	34	44	56	69	84	99	117
550	18	25	34	45	57	70	85	101	119
600	18	26	35	46	58	72	87	104	122
650	18	26	36	46	59	72	88	104	123
700	19	27	36	48	60	74	90	107	126
750	19	27	37	48	61	76	91	109	128
800	19	28	37	49	62	76	92	110	129

* C: Flat, open country, open flat coastal belts, and grassland. Interpolations of the values of q$_P$ may be used for intermediate heights.

Table 2. External pressure coefficients for walls, C_p

Location of wall	Pressure coefficient
Windward wall	+0.8
Leeward wall, both height-width and height-length ratios of building ≥ 2.5	—0.6
Leeward wall, other buildings	—0.5
Side walls	—0.7
Building corners, within vertical strip whose width is 1/10 the least width of the building	—2.0*

* Not to be included in net external pressure when computing overall wind load on building.

Table 3 Internal pressure coefficients for buildings, C_{pi}

n*	Openings uniformly distributed	Openings mainly in		
		Windward wall	Leeward wall	Side wall(s)
0 to 0.3	±0.3	(0.3 + 1.67n)	(—0.3 — n)	(—0.3 — n)
Greater than 0.3	±0.3	0.8	—0.6	—0.6

* n = ratio of open area to solid area of wall having majority of openings.

Table 4. Effective velocity pressures (lb/ft^2) for calculating internal pressures, q_M (Exposure C*)

Height (ft)	Basic wind speed (mph)								
	50	60	70	80	90	100	110	120	130
30 or less	6	9	13	16	21	26	31	37	43
50	7	11	15	19	24	30	36	43	50
100	9	13	18	23	29	36	44	52	61
150	10	15	20	26	33	40	49	58	68
200	11	16	22	28	36	44	53	63	74
250	12	17	23	30	38	47	57	67	79
300	12	18	24	32	40	49	60	71	83
350	13	19	25	33	42	51	62	74	87
400	13	19	26	34	43	54	65	77	90
450	14	20	27	35	45	55	67	80	93
500	14	21	28	37	46	57	69	82	96
550	15	21	29	38	47	59	71	84	99
600	15	22	29	38	49	60	73	87	102
650	15	22	30	39	50	61	74	88	104
700	16	23	31	40	51	63	76	91	106
750	16	23	31	41	52	64	77	92	108
800	16	24	32	42	53	65	79	94	110

* C: Flat, open country, open flat coastal belts, and grassland. Interpolations of the values of q$_M$ may be used for intermediate heights.

tle or no effect on the overall loading.

5. Maximum local loads are of greater intensity than the overall load, and the most critical local loads are usually negative in character.

6. Overall loads are seldom of critical concern on low buildings of large floor area, whereas local loads are significant on buildings of all sizes and shapes.

7. Internal pressures have no effect on the overall load but usually have a very significant effect on local loads.

The relative significance of inadequate provision for these two types of wind loading is quite obvious. Certainly the results of underestimating the overall wind load on a building of consequence would likely be tragic, as compared with the loss of some of its windows, wall panels, or roofing in a windstorm. Fortunately, very few, if any, important buildings have been toppled by winds; there are no classic examples of building failures comparable to the Tacoma bridge disaster. On the other hand, local failures of roofs, windows, and wall cladding are not uncommon and, in aggregate, such failures have cost millions of dollars. It should be remembered, too, that when extensive damage to the building enclosure does occur, it usually begins with some small local failure. It seems evident, therefore, that while adequate provision seems to have been made for the overall wind loads in building design, the intensity of local wind loading has sometimes been underestimated.

The theoretical determination of the actual wind pressure or suction existing at a given point on the surface of a building, under a given wind direction and velocity, is a very complex, if not impossible, problem. Contributing to this fact are the vagaries of wind action as influenced both by adjacent surroundings and the configuration of the wall surface itself. Much more research is needed on the microeffects of such architectural features as projecting mullions and column covers, and deep window reveals. In the meantime we have been relying

increasingly on two methods of obtaining more information about wind loads on building surfaces: model testing in boundary layer wind tunnels and field measurements on the walls of actual buildings. The latter will be briefly discussed later in this article.

Probably the most important fact established by these tests and measurements is that the negative or outward-acting wind loads on wall surfaces are greater and more critical than had formerly been assumed. As noted earlier, when the wind direction is normal or nearly normal to one face of a rectangular building, the other three faces are subjected to negative loading, that on the sides parallel to the wind being nearly as great, in psf, as the positive loading on the windward side. Under the action of diagonal, or "cornering" winds, the negative load on the leeward side of the outer corners becomes much higher. It may be as much as twice the amount of the positive loading or higher.

Some architects may still think of wind loads in terms of inward-acting pressure only. In doing so they overlook the importance of negative loading in curtain wall design, despite the teachings of experience. In most instances of local wall failure, glass or panels have been blown *off* of the building, not into it, and the majority of such failures have occurred in areas near the building corners. Obviously this underlines the vital importance of giving careful attention to the design of both anchorage and glazing details to resist outward-acting forces, especially near the corners of highrise buildings. In some cases architects, cognizant of the problem, have specified greater glass thickness in openings near the corners of tall buildings.

Another finding that has resulted from model testing and field investigations is the fact that wind loads, both positive and negative, on the taller buildings at least, do *not* vary in proportion to height above ground. Typically the positive pressure contours, instead of being horizontal, as illustrated in Fig. 8a, are usually found to follow a more concentric pattern such as illustrated

diagramatically in Fig. 8b, with the highest pressure being near the upper center of the facade, and pressures at the very top being somewhat less than those a few stories below the roof. Negative pressures, as illustrated in Fig. 8c, are greatest in the regions of the building corners and roof edge.

STRUCTURAL DESIGN

In detailing the design of the wall, it is essential to have up-to-date information as to the unit stresses to be used for the metal itself. Except for the copper alloys, the recommended design stresses have been pretty well established by the associations representing the prime producers of the various metals, and this information is readily available in standard references. The publications to be consulted for this data are the following: For aluminum: (1) *Aluminum Standards and Data.* (2) *Specifications for Structures of Aluminum Alloys, Aluminum Construction Manual, Section A.* Both of these publications are available from The Aluminum Association, 818 Connecticut Avenue NW, Washington, DC 20006. For copper alloys: contact the Copper Development Association, Inc., 405 Lexington Avenue, New York City 10017. For light-gage carbon and low alloy steels: *Light Gage Cold-formed Steel Design Manual,* available from American Iron and Steel Institute, 1000 6th Street, Washington, DC 20036. For structural steels: *Manual of Steel Construction, Part 5, Specification for the Design, Fabrication and Erection of Structural Steel for Buildings,* available from American Institute of Steel Construction, Inc., 400 N. Michigan Avenue, Chicago, IL 60611. For stainless steel: *Design of Light Gage Cold-formed Stainless Steel Structural Members,* available from American Iron and Steel Institute, 1000 6th Street, Washington, DC 20036.

In walls where panels of glass, metal, or other materials are set within surrounding metal frames, these panels usually transmit the wind loads to the frame through a relatively soft sealing material. The wall framing, in turn, carries the loads to the structural building frame through the wall connections at the points of anchorage. Consequently, the sealing material must have sufficient compressive strength, extensibility, and recovery ability to serve its function under countless cycles of positive and negative loading, and anchor connections must be adequate to resist similar but far greater and highly concentrated loading effects. The problem is compounded, of course, by the concurrent movements in expansion and contraction due to temperature changes and by the necessity of maintaining an effective over-all seal against penetration by water or air under these combined effects.

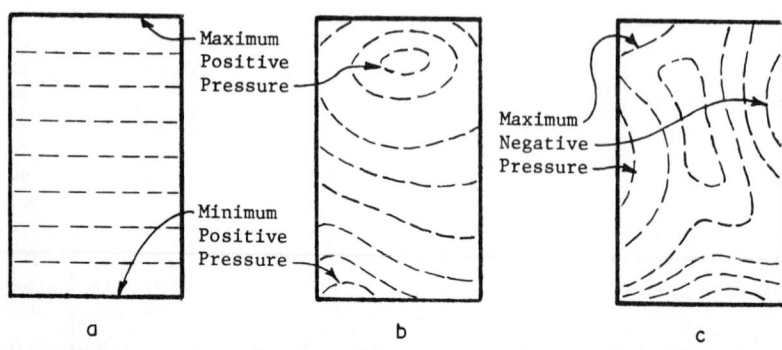

Fig. 8. Distribution of wind loads over facade

Structural capacity implies both strength and stiffness. The elements of the wall may have ample strength to carry without damage the loads imposed on them yet may lack the stiffness needed to prevent excessive bending when the loads are applied. Thus, under heavy wind loads the wall, although adequately strong, may bow or bulge conspicuously, frightening the building's occupants. Improperly designed framing members could, without exceeding their safe strength, deflect enough to permit glass to break or even blow out. In some cases, then, the flexibility of the glass itself may be the limiting factor in determining required stiffness.

Permissible deflection-span ratios have generally been established on rather arbitrary bases. A deflection of $1/360$ of the span, or 1 in. in 30 ft, has long been the accepted reasonable maximum where plaster surfaces are involved. Approximately twice this amount, or $1/175$ of the span, is recommended as the "psychological" limit beyond which the average observer may feel insecure.

In this connection, the AAMA *Metal Curtain Wall, Window, Store Front and Entrance Guide Specifications Manual* (1976)* stipulates that "The deflection of any framing member in a direction normal to the plane of the wall when subjected to a uniform load deflection test at design pressures specified, in accordance with ASTM E 330–70, shall not exceed $1/175$ of its clear span except that when a plastered surface subjected to bending is affected, the deflection shall not exceed $1/360$ of the span. For thin metal panel walls commonly used in industrial buildings the deflection shall not exceed $1/60$ of the span."

Formulas for calculating the deflection of uniformly loaded simple and fixed beams are given in Fig. 12 and illustrated as applied to vertical members loaded horizontally.

The permissible deflection of framing members due to vertical dead loads (such as panels and glass) is of course limited also, but here the actual *distance* the member deflects is usually more critical than the deflection-span ratio.

The AAMA guide specification states that "the deflection of any member in a direction parallel to the plane of the wall, when carrying its full dead load, shall not exceed an amount which will reduce the glass bite below 75% of the design dimension and the member shall have $1/8$" minimum clearance between itself and the top of the fixed panel, glass, or other fixed part immediately

* *Architectural Aluminum Manufacturers Association, 35 East Wacker Drive, Chicago, IL 60601.*

below. The clearance between the member and an operable window or door shall be at least $1/16$".

From the standpoint of structural efficiency, considerably greater lateral deflections might be permissible within safe stress limits, particularly under intermittent loading such as that produced by wind forces. So long as the stresses are well below the yield point, some designers may feel justified in accepting greater deflections because of the economic advantages to be gained. Other designers may feel that even smaller limits than these specifications permit should be designated, but it must be recognized that such restrictions might make heavier and more expensive sections necessary.

Some of the more monumental curtain wall buildings, especially those with all fixed glass and complete air conditioning, include permanently installed window-washing equipment operated from mobile cranes on the rooftop. In such installations mullion members must usually be designed to serve as guide rails for the mechanically operated cleaning platforms. This loading may be a critical design factor, requiring careful analysis based on loading data obtained from the manufacturer of the cleaning equipment.

Another important aspect of structural design is the selection of the proper metal to be used for fasteners. Obviously they must be corrosion resistant; but the corroding effects of weather alone are not the only ones to be considered. The corrosion of dissimilar metals by electrolysis is even more critical and, in fact, generally determines the selection. (See Sheet 2 of section on "Architectural Metals.")

PROVISION FOR MOVEMENT

Adequate provision for movement is one of the most important considerations in metal curtain wall design. Movements are continually taking place within the various components themselves, these parts are moving in relation to one another, and the whole wall is moving in relation to the building frame. The entire structure, in fact, is actually, though often unnoticeably alive and active. To consider it otherwise, as a static assembly, is to ignore the facts.

The chief causes of movement are:
Thermal expansion and contraction
Wind loads
Gravity forces
Loads and vibrations affecting the building frame.

If some components of the wall are of absorptive materials, dimensional changes due to the effects of moisture must also be considered.

The effects of expansion and contraction induced by temperature changes are especially significant in metal curtain wall construction. In comparison with older types of construction, these walls involve the use of materials that have (1) much higher expansion coefficients, (2) relatively larger units, and (3) smaller heat capacities. These factors acting in concert obviously magnify the problems of movement.

Temperatures inside modern buildings are controlled within a narrow range the year around; the fluctuation in outdoor temperature and the resulting through-wall temperature differentials dictate the requirements of the wall design. The actual metal (surface) temperature may vary daily, in winter, as much as 100° F in most parts in the country and 150° F in some northern areas. If the metal surface is dark-colored and nonreflective, these variations may be even higher.

Whatever may be the cause of movement in the wall, the problem of providing for it reduces essentially to the problem of joint design, because it is in the joints that movement is typically accommodated. Experienced designers all agree that the proper detailing of joints is usually the most difficult and important part of metal curtain wall design. If the wall units are large factory-made assemblies, shipped and erected as complete wall sections, their expansion and contraction under temperature changes are usually accommodated at the joints *between* these units, rather than at joints *within* the unit. Since the "working" joints are thus reduced to only those between units, it is often argued that the units should be made as large as possible in order to minimize the number and total length of these joints. It should be remembered, however, that the amount of thermal movement in any component is proportional to its size, and as the number of joints is decreased, the amount of movement to be accommodated in each increases. Beyond a certain point, then, the maintenance of weathertightness obviously becomes much more difficult.

Naturally, the effects of thermal movement are more conspicuous in the larger panels and longer sections. Metal-faced panels, however constructed, deform to some degree with changes in ambient temperature. Laminated panels, being essentially bimetallic plates, tend to bulge inward on cold, cloudy days and outward when heated by the sun. Hollow panels and unstiffened sheets, when restricted at their edges, tend to bow or "oil-can" in an unpredictable fashion. Therefore, all panels must be framed with ample edge clearance in order to permit movement in the plane of the wall.

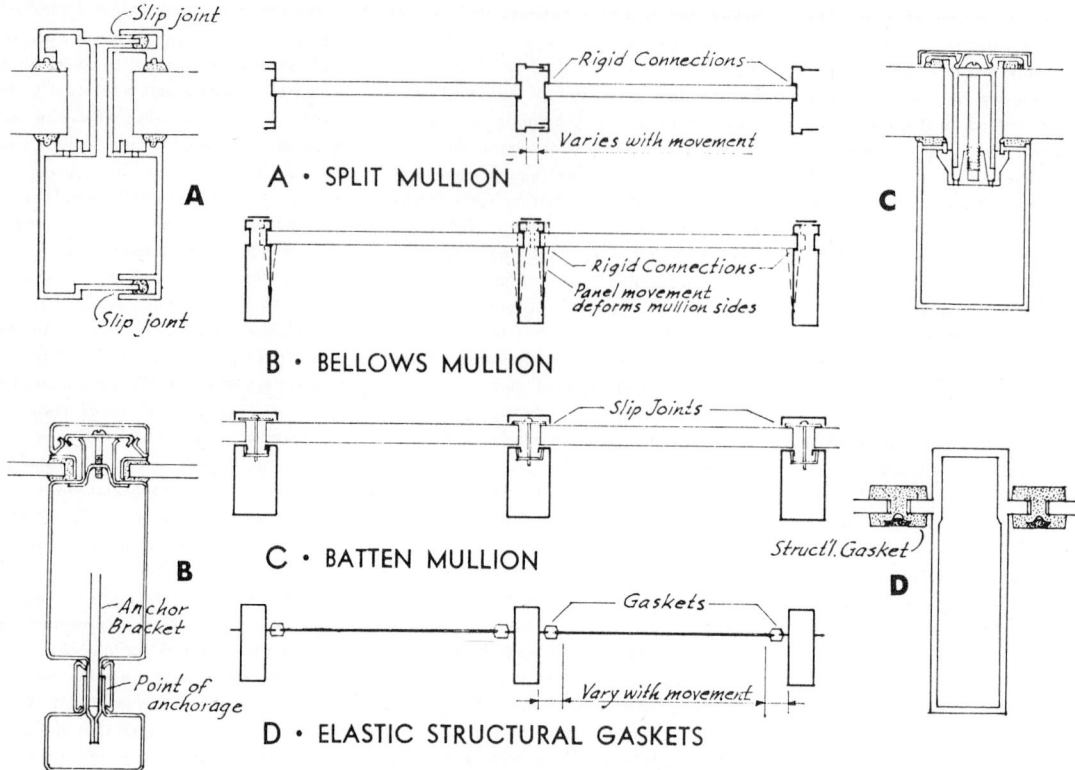

Fig. 9. Methods of providing for movement

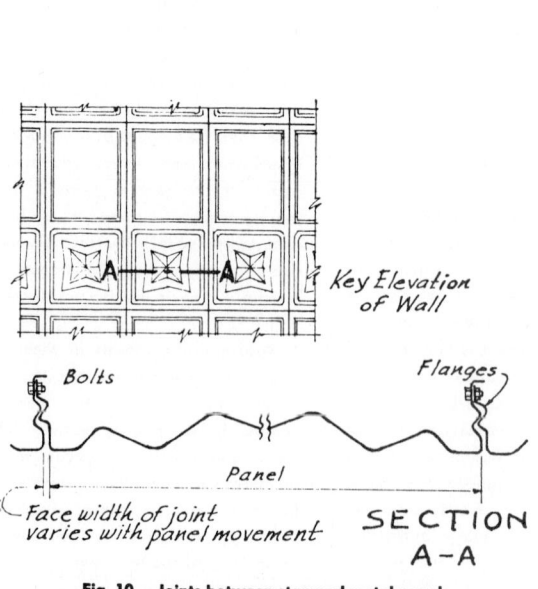

Fig. 10. Joints between stamped metal panels

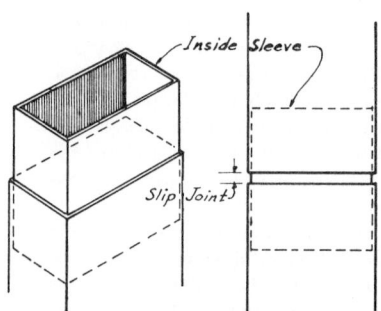

Fig. 11. Typical joint in vertical mullion.

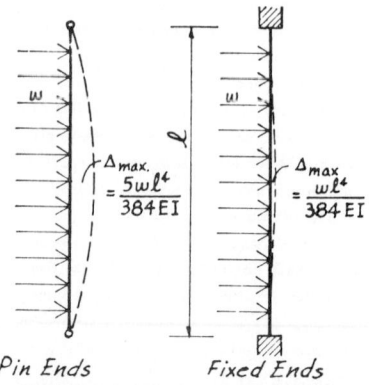

Fig. 12. Deflection of vertical beams

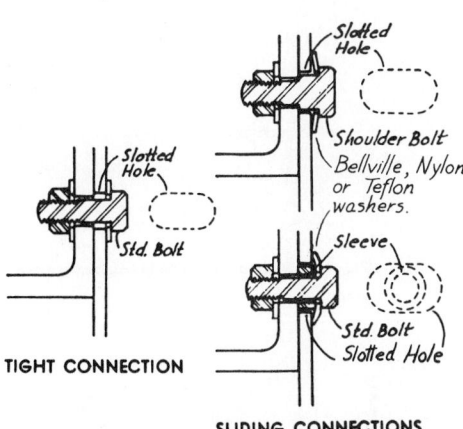

Fig. 13. Bolted anchorage connections

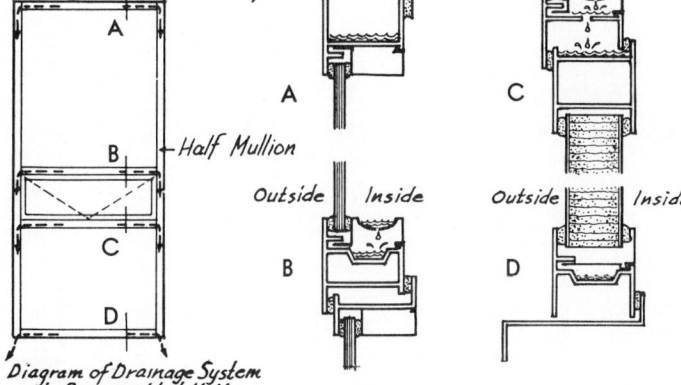

Fig. 14. Diagram of interior drainage system in a preassembled unit

Lengthwise expansion in long metal members such as mullions must also of course be accommodated at the end joints between sections, with provision being made for both vertical and horizontal movement in the plane of the wall. These movements may be absorbed by (1) relative displacement (slipping) of the joining parts, (2) deformation (bending) of the member, (3) increase in internal stresses, or (4) a combination of these effects. To avoid permanent deformation, stresses must of course be kept below the yield point of the metal, and in framing members it should not be sufficient to cause noticeable bending.

If movement is entirely restrained, thermal forces may build up sufficient stresses within the member to cause buckling or even failure. In some cases a certain amount of deformation is a calculated design feature, but when deformation must be avoided, either the necessary displacement must be accommodated or the member must be designed with enough strength and stiffness to resist the imposed stresses. Loads on mullion members resulting from temperature changes, for example, can be severe if the members are rigidly anchored top and bottom. This condition is most often found in single-story construction. The most critical situation occurs on hot summer days when long aluminum mullions tend to expand far more than the building frame to which they are anchored.

In wall designs employing mullion framing members (grid designs), it is common practice to provide for horizontal movement at each mullion. Four common ways of accomplishing this are illustrated in Fig. 9. In the split mullion system (A), the two channel-shaped halves of the mullion are not rigidly joined but are permitted to move relative to each other; in the bellows mullion (B), the projecting mullion jambs are sufficiently flexible to permit the mullion width to vary as the panels expand and contract; in the batten mullion (C), inner and outer cap sections clamp the edges of adjacent panels but are not directly connected to them; and in the structural gasket system (D), the elastic gasket provides a flexible link between the panel and mullion.

Whether the design of the wall is one of the common grid types or some other design, the details must still allow for movement. One variation of the panel system, for example, may employ heavy-gage stamped metal panels directly joined at their edges and concealing or eliminating the supporting framework (Fig. 10). When formed metal units of this kind are used, they are typically designed with deep corrugated flanges rigidly connected along their inner edges, as shown in the detail. Thermal forces can thus be accommodated by a combination of stress and deformation in these flexible flanges.

In multistory buildings, movement in a vertical direction is typically accommodated in the wall design at one or two story intervals. When the wall components are two stories in height, correspondingly greater movement must of course be provided for. Mullion sections are often spliced with some form of telescoping slip joint (Fig. 11). Instead of using an inside sleeve as shown, the designer may offset the upper end of the lower member by swaging to accomplish the same purpose.

Anchorage details, too, may be very significant in determining the effect of stresses in the vertical framing members. The deflection of a member under wind loading may be limited by providing some degree of fixity, rather than a simple pin joint, at its ends. A mullion acts as a vertical beam, and when simply supported its maximum deflection under uniform loading is five times that caused by the same loading if the ends are rigidly fixed. Complete rigidity in end connections is seldom practical, and most end conditions are likely to be nearer a pin-joint condition than a fixed condition, but in some instances added rigidity can be supplied to advantage (Fig. 12).

Movement at anchorage points is often permitted, theoretically at least, by the use of slotted holes. The true functional value of this device as typically used, however, is often questionable. The bolts may be drawn up so tightly that the value of the slot is eliminated by friction, if not by subsequent corrosion. Frequently this type of connection resists movement until high stresses accumulate, and then it may suddenly release with a cracking sound. If slotted holes are to ensure the displacement intended, either shoulder bolts or sleeves should be used, as shown in Fig. 13, with Bellville or molded nylon or Teflon washers to provide light but positive pressure and to prevent rattling.

WATER PENETRATION AND AIR INFILTRATION

Ideally, a wall would permit no water to penetrate its exterior surface from outside but at the same time would permit any moisture within the wall to escape through this same surface to the atmosphere. Needless to say, this ideal function is rarely if ever realized, since we do not yet have a surfacing material with the requisite characteristic of one-way permeability.

In the AAMA metal curtain wall guide specifications, water penetration is defined as "the appearance of uncontrolled water other than condensation on the indoor face of any part of the wall," with the explanation that "uncontrolled" water is any that is not contained and drained back to the outside (or "controlled"), with no damage to the wall or adjacent construction or finishes. This guide specification then further stipulates that "no uncontrolled water penetration shall occur when the curtain wall is

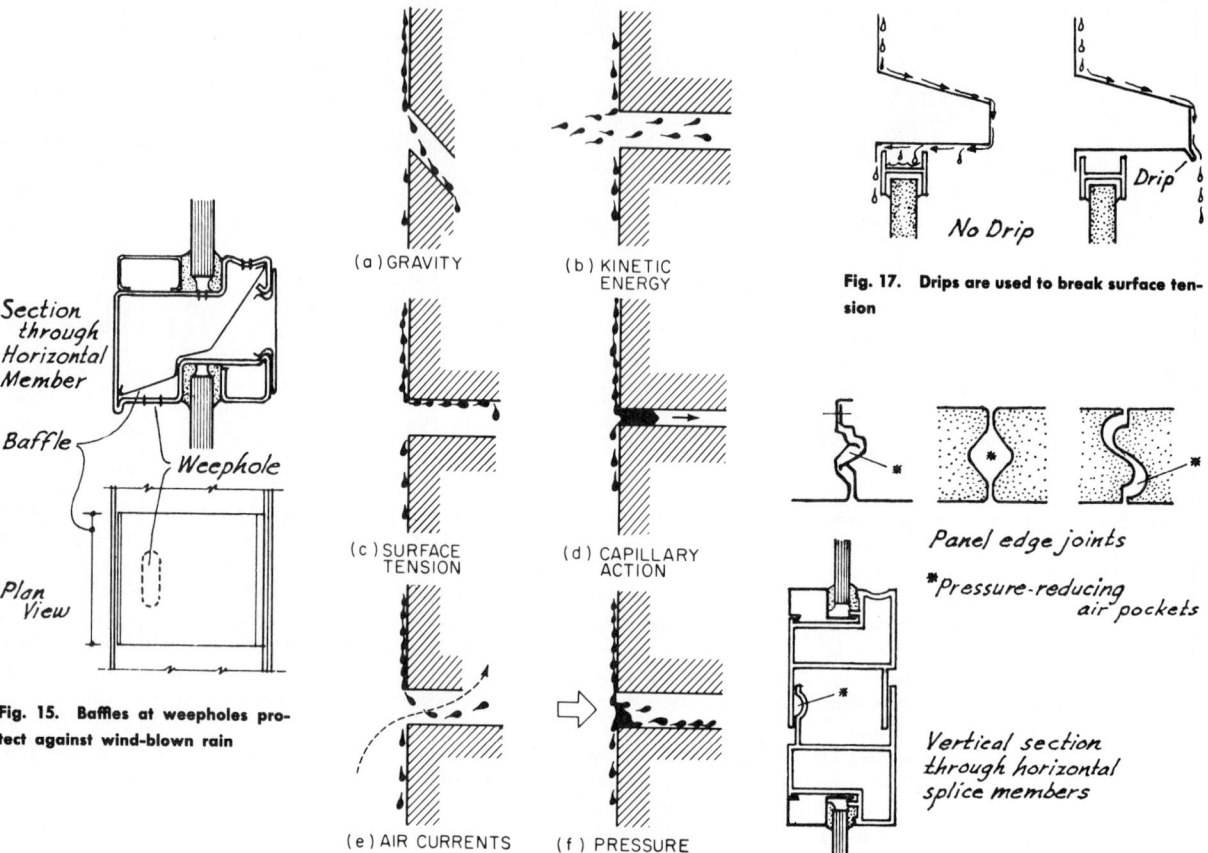

(a) GRAVITY

(b) KINETIC ENERGY

(c) SURFACE TENSION

(d) CAPILLARY ACTION

(e) AIR CURRENTS

(f) PRESSURE DIFFERENCE

Section through Horizontal Member

Baffle

Weephole

Plan View

Fig. 15. Baffles at weepholes protect against wind-blown rain

Fig. 16. Forces acting to move water through an opening

No Drip

Drip

Fig. 17. Drips are used to break surface tension

Panel edge joints

*Pressure-reducing air pockets

Vertical section through horizontal splice members

Fig. 18. Typical capillary breaks in joints

tested in accordance with ASTM E 331 at a differential static pressure of 20% of the inward acting design pressure." The AAMA specification provides for an optional test which stipulates that "no uncontrolled water penetration shall occur when the wall is tested in accordance with AAMA Standard TM-1-76 using dynamic pressure." The severity of the tests employed in verifying water tightness vary somewhat with the type of wall and its intended location. In all cases, however, the outdoor face of the test wall is completely and continuously covered with water, applied at the rate of 5 gallons per square foot of wall per hour, while being subjected to either static pressure (a static test) or the pressure from an artificially produced, high velocity air stream (a dynamic test). On some walls both tests are used. The dynamic test may reveal weaknesses in a pressure-equalized wall design which would not show up in a static test.*

* For information on all types of curtain wall testing, see Aluminum Curtain Walls, *vol. 1 (October, 1970), published by Arch'l. Aluminum Manufacturers Assoc. (AAMA).*

High winds cause rainwater to flow in all directions over the windward surface of a wall, and on surfaces of impervious materials much of it tends to collect at the joints —the major points of vulnerability. Experience has proved that to provide all wall joints at their outer surface with a permanently waterproof seal is virtually impossible because of their continual movement. Instead, two other methods have been developed for preventing leakage in metal curtain walls, and either of these, when intelligently applied, is highly dependable. One is referred to as the "internal drainage" or "secondary defense" system and has long been used by competent designers. The other is the "pressure equalization method." Both these methods are applicable to the design of windows as well as complete wall systems.

The internal drainage method is based on the philosophy that it is impractical if not impossible to totally eliminate, for an indefinite period, all leakage at all points in the outer skin of the wall, but that such minor leakage as does occur can be prevented from penetrating to the indoor face

of the wall or even remaining within the wall. This is accomplished by providing within the wall itself a system of flashing and collection devices, with ample drainage outlets to the outdoor face of the wall.

One way of doing this is to so detail the wall that water penetrating the seals around glazed or panel areas will be collected, either directly or indirectly, inside hollow mullion sections that serve as downspouts. The sketches in Fig. 14 indicate diagrammatically how this is accomplished. on highrise buildings, though, the advisability of using this type of drainage system is questionable, because the quantity of water accumulated in long runs of mullions may be excessive, and it is difficult to provide drainage from the mullions at intermediate levels. The preferred practice in tall buildings, therefore, is to drain the horizontal members themselves directly to the outdoors by means of baffled weepholes (Fig. 15).

Any interior drainage system within the wall should be intended to function only under extreme conditions and should not be considered as the primary defense against leakage. The proper detailing of joints and their sealing should always be the chief deterrent to water penetration under normal conditions.

The method of pressure equalization, employing the "rain screen principle," is generally a more sophisticated and complex solution, but it is claimed by its proponents to be practically infallible when properly applied.

The rain screen principle is based on the fact that for leakage to occur in a wall there must be three essentials: (1) water, (2) an opening, and (3) some force to move the water through the opening. If any one of these essentials is lacking, there can be no leakage. Instead of attempting to eliminate the opening by complete sealing, it may be preferable to eliminate the force. Several types of force must be considered, some of which are not related to wind action. These forces, as illustrated in Fig. 16, are gravity, kinetic energy, surface tension, capillary action, air currents, and pressure difference. With the exception of the latter, all these can be controlled by well-known techniques such as baffling (Fig. 15) and the provision of drips (Fig. 17) and capillary breaks (Fig. 18). But the force created by a pressure difference, the most critical of all, can be eliminated only by equalizing the pressures existing on both sides of the opening. This can be accomplished by providing an air space within the wall, behind the exterior facing, in which the air pressure is at least as great at all points and at all times as the outdoor pressure. The equalization of pressures on the two sides of the outer skin, or rain screen, is produced by *not* tightly sealing its joints but purposely leaving many or all of them open and providing openings in protected locations to connect the air space behind it with the outdoors. To maintain this air pressure, it is essential that the indoor face of the wall, on the other hand, be sealed as tightly as practicable. Thus the primary seal, being on the inner wall face, is in a relatively dry location and is not subjected to *both* water and pressure.

It should be recognized that, due to the vagaries of wind-driven rain, the successful use of the pressure equalization method is seldom a simple matter. It requires not only an understanding of the principle involved but also careful attention to details. For a comprehensive discussion of its design implications, the reader is referred to *Aluminum Curtain Walls,* vol. 2, February, 1971, published by the Architectural Aluminum Manufacturers Association. A typical method of providing pressure equalization in a metal curtain wall system is shown in Fig. 19 taken from this publication.

Ample weepholes, judiciously located, are important features of most curtain wall designs. With internal drainage systems, they serve as outlets, and when pressure equalization is employed, they act as "connectors" between the inner air space and the outdoors. In both cases they function as drains for condensate which may occur on cold surfaces within the wall. But if they are not carefully designed, they may also be points of weakness in the defense against water penetration. In heavy storms the pressure of high winds on the wall face often forces rainwater to flow *upward* on the wall, thus entering openings in soffit areas which would not be subject to penetration under normal rainfall conditions. It is imperative, therefore, that they be either so located that penetration by wind-driven rain is impossible or so backed up by baffles that no damage will result from such penetration.

The phenomenon of surface tension—that property of water which causes it to adhere to a surface—is of special significance in metal-wall constructions. The provision of positive-drip profiles at the outer edges of soffit areas is therefore of even greater importance than in masonry construction, where more absorptive materials are used (Fig. 17).

Capillary action is another characteristic of water to be recognized in the detailing of a metal wall. Because of it, water may travel surprising distances between adjacent surfaces, even in defiance of gravity and without abnormal pressure. This may be a source of leakage, particularly in "dry" or uncaulked joints, and the capillary effect is

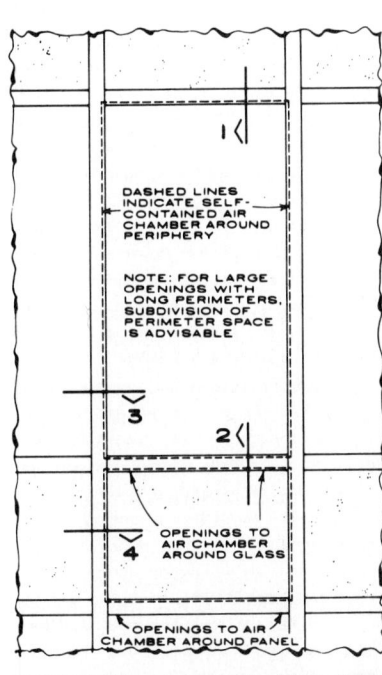

ELEVATION OF TYPICAL WALL AREA

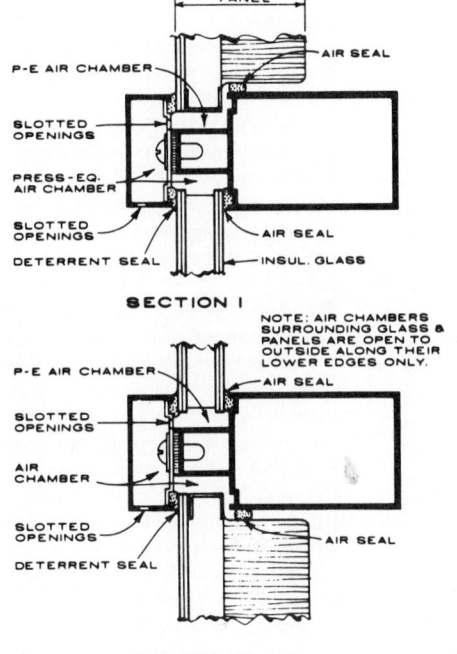

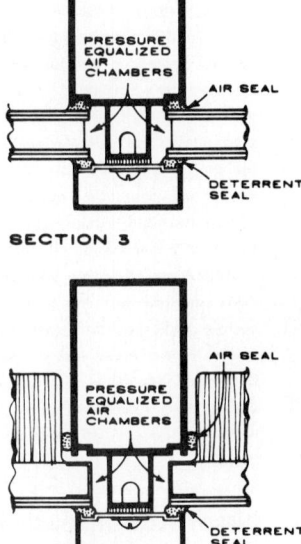

Fig. 19. Pressure-equalized standard wall system

greatly aggravated, of course, by wind pressure. To discourage water infiltration by capillarity, it is often advisable to provide "capillary breaks" in detailing vulnerable joints. This is done by deforming or grooving the contacting surfaces in such a way as to form interrupting gaps in the narrow space between them, instead of permitting the parts to be in close contact for the full depth of the joint (Fig. 18).

The infiltration of air is much less likely than water infiltration to have a damaging effect on the building interior. To some degree air infiltration may be desirable, but the amount must be controlled within permissible limits to avoid drafts and maintain comfort. Up to a point, such infiltration as may occur through the wall tends to vary with wind velocity, but with higher wind velocities this relationship no longer holds.

Control of air infiltration through the typical metal wall depends chiefly on two factors: the tightness of joint seals and the presence of operable sash. With proper design of the former and tight weather-stripping of the latter it will seldom be significant.

When preformed elastomeric or plastic gaskets are used as periphery seals around panels or glass, it is important, unless the perimeter void is pressure-equalized, that no gaps be permitted at their corner joints. Unless continuity is provided, the abutting strips must be carefully and tightly fitted at corners, and positive contact must be permanently maintained under constant compression.

Some types of operable sash are available in pressure-equalized designs, and in these, tight weatherstripping at the indoor face is essential to provide an effective air seal. On the more common types of sash, not so designed, double weatherstripping, with ample weathering overlaps, is usually advisable. In either case, all weatherstripping should be readily accessible for replacement when worn or deteriorated. Window hardware, too, must be adequately strong and rigid to lock windows tightly shut, assuring a good seal all around.

AAMA metal curtain wall guide specifications stipulate that "air leakage through the curtain wall shall not exceed 0.06 cfm per square foot of fixed wall projected area plus the permissible allowance specified for operable windows or doors within the test area, when tested in accordance with ASTM E283."

ENERGY FLOW THROUGH WALLS

A basic understanding of energy flow through the wall is essential to the design of metal curtain wall systems which will provide an energy efficient building.

Table 5. Specific heat, density, and thermal conductivity of building materials

Construction materials	Specific heat Btu/lb/°F	Density lb/ft³	Thermal conductivity (k) Btu/h/ft²/°F/in.
Aluminum (1100)	0.214	171	1536
Brick, building	0.2	120	5
Brick, facing	—	130	9
Brass, red	0.09	548	1044
Brass, yellow	0.09	519	828
Bronze	0.104	530	204
Cement plaster or stucco	0.16	116	5
Concrete (stone)	0.156	140	12
Copper (electrolytic)	0.092	556	2724
Gypsum plaster	—	105	5.6
Marble	0.21	162	18
Steel (mild)	0.12	489	314
Steel, stainless (302)	—	501	113
Wood, hard	0.45-0.65	23-70	0.78-1.78
Wood, soft	0.65	27	0.82

Insulating Materials

Cellular glass	0.24	9	0.40
Glass fiber board	0.19	4-9	0.25
Expanded polystyrene (extruded, plain)	0.29	1.8	0.25
Expanded polystyrene (molded beads)	0.29	1.0	0.28
Expanded polyurethane	0.38	1.5	0.16
Mineral fiber board	0.17	15	0.29

Glazing Materials

Acrylic	0.35	73	1.20
Glass	0.21	158	6.48
Polycarbonate (unfilled)	0.30	74	1.36

Heat transfer is one form of energy flow. Heat transfer through walls occurs by: (1) conduction from the high temperature side to the low temperature side, (2) convection of the air on the wall surfaces, (3) absorption and emission of radiation, and (4) infiltration and exfiltration of air. When considering conductive heat transfer through a wall it must be remembered that the heat transfer occurs between the inside air and the outside air.

The conductive heat flow through the wall, both outward and inward, is determined by the resistance to thermal transmission provided by the materials composing the wall assembly. Heat is very readily conducted through metals, much less readily through glass, and very slowly through light, porous, insulating materials and across confined air spaces. Methods of calculating thermal transmission through walls are given in the section on Insulation, which also lists the coefficients of conductivity of most building materials. For convenience, coefficients of the materials most often used in curtain walls are given in Table 5.

Typically, the thermal values advertised for walls are those of certain components of the wall rather than of the complete assembly, though it is the latter that is of chief significance. The true over-all U value of the wall assembly (Btu per hour per square foot per degree of temperature difference between air on the outside and inside surfaces) is the result of the complex interrelationship of the transmission values of the individual component materials. It is difficult to calculate theoretically and can be determined accurately only by actual testing of the whole assembly.

The growing scarcity and ever-increasing costs of fossil fuels has stimulated manufacturers to produce windows and wall systems which have excellent thermal performance. As a means of evaluating thermal performance AAMA developed a method of testing windows, sliding glass doors and walls which permits determination of the condensation resistance of the assembly and the resistance to heat flow. The method of testing is described in AAMA 1502.7 *Voluntary Standards and Tests of Thermal Performance of Insulating Windows, Doors and Exterior Wall Sections*. In a good metal curtain wall design the performance of the metal framing elements should match the performance of the glass. This will mean that insulating metal framing sections will be used with insulating glass. Insulating metal framing will incorporate thermal breaks to eliminate through metal conduction from the inside air to the outside air. Typical methods of achieving thermal breaks are shown in Fig. 23.

The fact that over-all thermal values are generally inferior to those of some of the principal components is due chiefly to the presence of metal parts extending through the wall and serving as heat conductors. Even in moderate climates, therefore, it is important that the amount of such through-metal be minimized, and in cold climates it is mandatory.

The thermal insulating value of the wall is usually an important consideration in all parts of the country, whether the prime concern be to prevent heat loss in cold weather or to minimize heat gain during the warm season. Summer air conditioning has become an established requirement even in the northern states, and because the cost of cooling, per Btu, is much higher than the cost of heating, the thermal performance of the wall has become increasingly important.

The location of the wall insulation in respect to the structural frame of the building is an important consideration. In the interests of economy, it is better to locate the insulation *outside* the building frame, as shown in Fig. 20, for two reasons: (1) The uninsulated floor edges and spandrel beams act as heat-exchange fins, contributing to heat loss and resulting in cold floors near the perimeter of the building, and (2) the exterior structural framing, when insulated, remains at relatively constant temperature, and its thermal movements are minimized. Since any such movements are necessarily cumulative (no expansion joints being provided in the frame), they can be the cause of major sealing problems and high maintenance costs. When design requirements dictate that structural framing elements be exposed outside the curtain wall, an insulative covering of these members becomes highly advisable, particularly on tall buildings.

In many metal curtain walls the proportion of transparent glazed area is large, varying between 50 and 80 per cent of the total wall area. Since glass has a relatively poor over-all insulating value as compared with most wall panels, both the proportion and the type of glass used largely determine the over-all thermal value of the wall. Therefore a reduction of heat flow through the glazed areas may be highly significant in improving this value. Regular ¼-in. plate

or float glass has a thermal conductivity (*U* value) of about 1.13, whereas factory-sealed insulating glass has a *U*-value of 0.55 if clear glass is used and an average *U*-value of about 0.40 when made with reflective glass. Thus the use of insulating glass has a major effect on the thermal value of the wall, especially if the glass area is large (Fig. 21). Admittedly the initial cost of insulating glass is higher, but usually the cost difference is reclaimed in lower installation and operating expenses for heating and cooling within a few years, and substantial savings result thereafter.

Invariably, as insulation of the wall is increased, by whatever means, the costs of heating and air conditioning are lowered. There are usually limits, however, beyond which the addition of more insulation is not economically justified, when the interest on the capital investment exceeds the return in savings. This limit varies with local conditions and costs. It cannot be determined by any rule of thumb but always deserves careful attention in wall designs that involve long-term costs.

The proportional value of insulation in the solid or opaque areas of the wall varies with the extent of the transparent glazed area, as well as with the type of glass used. This value increases as the glazed area is reduced, and as Fig. 21 illustrates, it has greater significance when insulating glass is used than when the glazing is of a single thickness. Regardless of the proportion of glazed to solid-wall area, however, each unit of heat transfer eliminated represents the same amount of saving, and the time required to amortize the cost of insulation by such saving remains the same.

Increasing the insulated opaque area of a wall and reducing the glass area does not necessarily reduce the heat loss through a wall during the heating season. In fact, depending on the window orientation, just

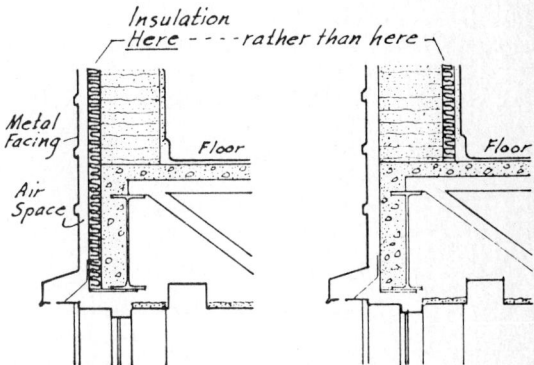

Fig. 20. Location of wall insulation

the opposite may occur. The heat loss may be increased. With orientations from east through south to west there can be a desirable solar heat gain through the glass area which will more than offset conductive heat loss, providing a net heat gain for the season and thereby reducing fuel consumption by the central heating system. However, while solar heat gain could be desirable in the winter it could be highly undesirable in the summer because of the increase in the air conditioning load. Therefore a wall design which will effectively use solar heat gain in the winter must incorporate shading devices which will offer the necessary protection from the sun in the summer.

Daylighting is another possible energy conserving advantage offered by glass. Daylighting makes it possible to cut down on the use of electric lighting and the energy saved in this way can more than offset the reduction in conductive heat loss which would occur if an insulated opaque wall were used in place of glass and electric lighting was therefore required.

From a purely functional standpoint, the logical location for wall insulation would be

Calculated approximate thermal values

Allowance has been made for conduction of aluminum frame.

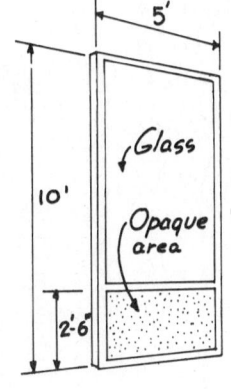

Opaque area (aluminum facing)	U value of opaque area	Over-all U value of 5 × 10 ft unit		
		Single glass (U: 1.13)	Insulating glass	
			Clear glass (U: 0.55)	Reflective glass (U: 0.40)
2-in. paper honey-comb	0.27	1.09	0.70	0.59
2-in. glass fiber	0.12	1.06	0.65	0.55
2-in. glass fiber plus 8-in. lightweight concrete block	0.09	1.05	0.65	0.55

Fig. 21. Effect of insulation in the opaque area of a panel on its over-all heat loss

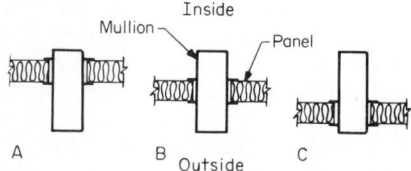

Fig. 22. Location of mullion in relation to plane of wall

outside the metal wall framework itself, but this is inconsistent with present design concepts. In grid designs, the pattern of the framing elements is the dominant design feature, and insulated panels are not placed outside these elements but between them. It follows that if the metal elements themselves do not have thermal breaks they will serve as highly conductive paths by which heat readily penetrates the wall. Not only does this result in undesirable heat loss or gain but it may also result in the formation of condensation on the inside surfaces of the metal in cold weather.

The extent of this effect depends a great deal on the details of the mullion design. As illustrated in Fig. 22 the proportion of the member exposed to inside air is highly significant, because of the warming effect on the member. When a large proportion of it is exposed to the outside temperature, as in Sketch A, the inside warming effect will be small. This is the worst condition for interior condensation but unfortunately a popular practice. Sketch B illustrates a compromise arrangement that will perform satisfactorily in mild climates. Sketch C is the best arrangement as far as the effect

of "fin heat loss" is concerned. Most of the metal surface is inside the building, and the relatively small area exposed to the cold is not large enough to lower the temperature of the inner face to the point where condensation will occur except in severe climates.

Present practice is to use framing systems incorporating thermal breaks where condensation could be a problem and where good thermal performance is desired (Fig. 23).

Although the effects of solar radiation have been mentioned, the foregoing paragraphs have dealt primarily with heat transmission through conduction. As pointed out previously heat is also transmitted by convection, radiation and air leakage.

When radiant energy strikes the surface of a body, the energy is in part reflected, transmitted, or absorbed, depending on the nature of the material and the wavelength of the incident radiation. For opaque materials, such as aluminum, negligible amounts of the energy are transmitted in the ultraviolet, visible and infrared regions of the spectrum so that the sum of the energy reflected and the energy absorbed is essentially equal to the incident energy striking the surface. For transparent materials, such as clear glass, most of the radiant energy is transmitted. The capacity of a body to absorb radiant energy is called *absorptivity*. Once a body has absorbed energy, it in turn reradiates, or emits, a portion of that energy to its surroundings, the term *emissivity* describes the capacity of a body to emit energy by radiation. Surfaces with low emissivity, such as polished aluminum, have high resistance to radiant heat transfer whereas surfaces with high emissivity, such as black

anodized aluminum, have low resistance to radiant heat transfer.

The resistance to heat transfer by convection depends on the nature of the air flow over the surface, that is, on the wind speed, if there is a wind, or on the air movement caused by temperature differences in the air when there is no wind.

The surface resistance on the exterior of a wall in the winter time, under 15 mph wind velocity, is 0.17. On the interior surface the value of the resistance is 0.68. The reciprocals of these numbers, 5.88 and 1.47 respectively, are referred to as surface heat transfer coefficients. In the summer time, under the effects of solar radiation, the outside surface resistance may increase to 0.40.

For single glass and for metal framing without a thermal break, it is the air film at the surface and the surface properties which provide practically all of the resistance to heat transmission.

Air leakage through the joints of curtain walls and the cracks around operating windows can significantly affect the performance of a building, particularly on a building that relies primarily on mechanical heating and cooling systems. This air leakage is caused by air pressure differences across the wall resulting from wind action, chimney or stack action, and mechanical ventilating equipment. For good thermal performance air leakage should be held to a minimum.

A reference on the subject of thermal performance is AAMA *Aluminum Curtain Walls,* Volume 9, "Design for Energy Conservation in Aluminum Curtain Walls."

Fig. 23. Methods of preventing heat flow through mullions and framing
(a) Integral cast-in place polyurethane plastic thermal break
(b) Mechanically locked-in-place extruded PVC thermal break
(c) Structural elastomeric gasket locked in mullion and supporting glass or panels
(d) Structural elastomeric batten supporting glass or panels on split mullion
(e) Extruded PVC spacer between mullion and batten

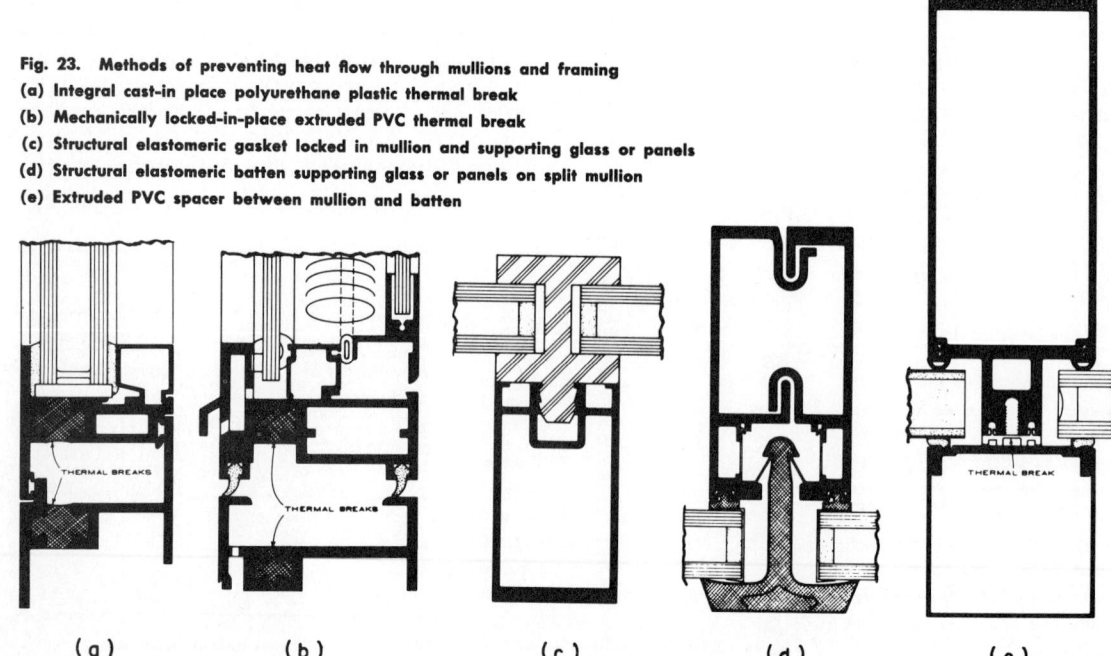

(a) (b) (c) (d) (e)

By WAYNE F. KOPPES, FAIA, *Architectural Consultant*

WATER VAPOR AND CONDENSATION

The presence of condensed moisture on the inner face of a wall is always annoying, and if it collects within the wall itself it may cause serious damage. With present-day knowledge of water-vapor movement and behavior, condensation within buildings and in the shell construction itself can be avoided if proper attention is given to the matter in the planning stage, but it may be both difficult and expensive to correct poor design if trouble develops in an occupied building. When moisture appears on the inner surface of a wall it is usually an indication of improper design, ill-advised use of materials, or unforeseen moisture-producing operations within the building.

A brief review of some of the elementary principles of physics will suggest how condensation in and on building walls can be prevented. Water evaporates into the atmosphere, changing from a liquid to a gas and becoming invisible water vapor. The amount of vapor the air can contain depends on the air temperature; the warmer the air, the more water it can hold. Thus, if warm moisture-laden air is cooled, it releases its excess vapor, which again takes the form of water. Such reduction in temperature may be caused by the air coming in contact with a cooler surface, in which case the water is deposited on this surface as condensation. Everyone has observed this phenomenon on the outside of a glass containing a cold drink or on dew-laden grass in the cool of a summer evening. Appropriately enough, the temperature of the air at which its contained moisture begins to condense is known as its "dew point."

In designing for moisture control, it is essential to recall certain important facts concerning the nature of water vapor:

1. Vapor in the air results in pressure, just as with any other gas. As the amount increases, in absolute terms of grains of water per pound of dry air, the greater becomes the vapor pressure. Cold air has a lower vapor pressure than equally saturated warm air, and as the relative humidity increases, these differences in vapor pressure between cold and warm air also increase.

2. The movement of water vapor is largely determined by differences in vapor pressure, much as air movement (wind) is caused by differences in atmospheric pressure. Like the air in a toy balloon, it is always seeking to escape from high-pressure areas, such as a heated building, to areas of lower pressure, such as the colder out-of-doors.

3. Water vapor movement may be independent of that of the air containing it, and it is even independent of gravity. Just as with heat, however, the transfer of vapor may be affected by a moving air stream, especially if the air is moving toward an area of lower vapor pressure. Thus ventilation, even by natural forces, is an important deterrent to condensation.

4. Water vapor can penetrate microscopic openings through which even air cannot pass.

5. Water vapor condenses on surfaces that impede its normal flow and are colder than the dew point of the air containing it.

It becomes apparent, then, that the effect of water vapor on a wall construction depends chiefly upon two factors: (1) The vapor pressures existing on the two sides of the wall, and (2) The permeability characteristics of the wall's component materials. The first factor is generally predetermined by the conditions of use and location of the building, but the second imposes on the designer not only the necessity of selecting the proper materials but also the importance of using them in their proper relationships.

Building materials vary widely in vapor **permeance, as indicated in Table 6.** In general terms, those having a permeance of less than unity are considered to be *relatively* good vapor barriers. Metals, even in foil thickness, are for all practical purposes perfect barriers, and it is principally this fact that makes proper moisture control so important in the design of metal curtain wall construction.

Moisture within nonresidential buildings may come from a variety of sources (Table **7). In new buildings most of it may have** been introduced in large amounts with wet materials of construction. In older buildings, moisture is constantly being released in many ways—by industrial processes, by washing of floors, by plant life, by human respiration and perspiration, and often, during the heating season at least, by artificial means of humidification. Within the wall itself, moisture may also result from external leakage through weepholes or through exterior joints in the wall construction.

The condensation of moisture from such sources will usually occur on the room-side face of the wall only in cold weather, and even then it will be negligible if the heating system is designed to sweep these surfaces with sufficient warm air to keep their temperatures above the dew point of the impinging air. If the heating system is not so designed, the condensation on single glazed and cold metal surfaces on cold

days may be troublesome, but since it can be seen and removed, it is seldom dangerous. Far more critical is the occurrence of condensation hidden within the wall itself. Here the undetected collection of moisture may deteriorate organic materials, impair the value of insulation, and cause corrosion of metallic parts by galvanic action, if not by rusting.

The significance of these facts leads to four important rules governing the design of the wall:

1. Provide a vapor barrier on or near the warm side of the wall.

2. Provide sufficient insulation to keep critical surfaces warmer than the dew-point temperature of the indoor air. (A critical surface is one that tends to impede the flow of water vapor).

3. Provide for vapor release on the cold side of the wall.

4. Avoid using a tight vapor barrier on both sides of the wall. This creates a vapor trap in which condensation can accumulate.

The logic of these principles is illustrated in Fig. 24. As indicated, some vapor will pass through even the best barrier materials, at their joints or seams, and moisture is likely to enter the wall also by leakage from the outside. Therefore, in an ideal wall the outer skin will have a permeance rating at least five times that of the inner skin. With metal walls this ideal situation is often impossible—in fact the reverse may be true. Either both skins are of metal (a perfect vapor barrier), or the outer skin is of metal and the inner skin is of some relatively permeable material. In both cases, ventilation within the wall is a necessity, regardless of whether or not insulation is provided for in the space. Condensation is almost certain to occur on the inner side of the outer

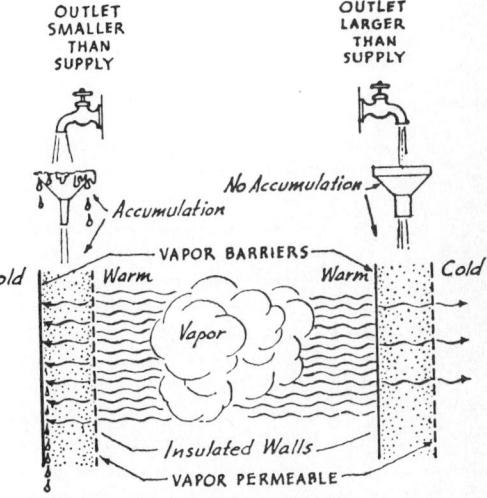

Fig. 24. Vapor barriers and vapor releases

Table 6. Approximate permeability characteristics of building materials

Material	Permeance (perms)	Permeability (perm-in.)
Aluminum foil, 0.0006-in., on paper	0.02	
Aluminum foil, 0.004-in.	0.00	
Polyethylene film, 0.001-in.	0.67	
0.004-in.	0.17	
0.008-in.	0.08	
Cellular glass		0.00
Foamed polystyrene		1.0–2.0
Asphalt-coated paper, glossy, 10 lb/sq	0.35	
Laminated kraft building paper, 7.5 lb/sq	0.42	
Oilcloth	0.96	
Paint:		
2 coats asphalt paint on plywood	0.43	
2 coats aluminum paint on plywood	1.29	
3 coats exterior paint on wood	0.3–1.0	
¼-in. DF plywood, exterior type	0.72	
interior type	1.86	
Vegetable fiber insulating board, uncoated	20.0–50.0	
Glass fiber insulating board	50.0–90.0	
Plaster, ¾-in. on metal lath	15.0	
½-in. on gypsum lath	20.0	
Gypsum wall board, ⅜-in.	50.0	
Concrete, 1-2-4 mix		3.2
4-in. brick wall	0.8–1.1	
Still air		120.0

Table 7. Sources of indoor moisture (in approximate amounts of water)

Occupants	Average of 2¼ lb per person per 8-hr day in sedentary occupations
Plant life	About 1¾ lb per plant in 24 hr
Washing floors	3 lb per 100 sq ft per washing
Construction	Stone concrete— 2 lb per sq ft of 4-in. slab ⎫
	Gypsum concrete— 5.4 lb per sq ft of 2-in. roof slab ⎬ must eventually be evaporated
	Gypsum plaster— 1.6 lb per sq ft of 1-in. plaster ⎭
	Heating salamander—1.3 gal of water per gal of oil burned

metal skin if the construction is reasonably tight, and this must be prevented, or at least the moisture must be evaporated, by permitting air to circulate behind it. In addition, a means should be provided for draining any excess moisture that may accumulate at the bottom of this vent space.

In metal-clad walls of the industrial type **Fig. 25**, these principles may govern the design of a large portion of the total wall area and are of special importance, of course, when it is a question of housing industrial processes requiring high humidities. In standard architectural and custom walls proper moisture control can usually be provided in the panel areas. It is important there, whether the panels be simply facings over masonry backup or a composite, insulated assembly comprising the complete wall. In the former case, as illustrated in **Fig. 26**, the insulation should preferably be placed outside the masonry, and a well-ventilated and drained space should always be provided behind the facing.

It has sometimes been recommended that the edges of composite panels be completely sealed with a film impermeable to vapor. This is logical only if (1) the air within the panel is dehumidified before the edge seal is applied, and (2) it can be guaranteed that the hermetic seal will remain perfect during the life of the building. Some means of fulfilling these requirements may eventually be developed, as it has been for insulating glass. Otherwise, the sealing of panel edges against the passage of vapor is ill advised and results in a vapor trap. With the bellows action that occurs in a sealed hollow panel

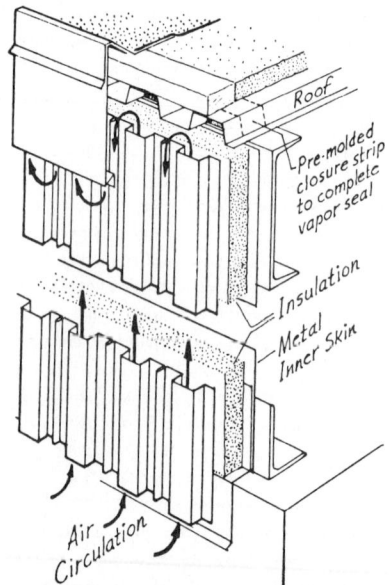

Fig. 25. Ventilation of industrial-type curtain wall

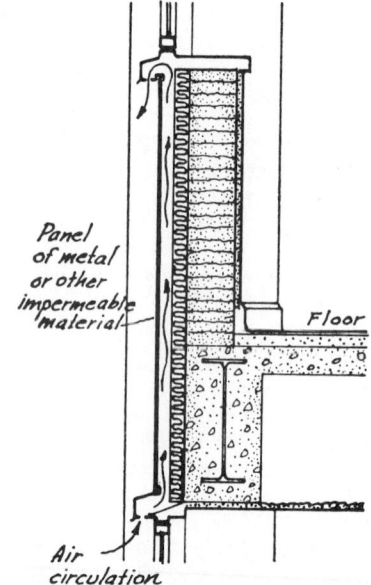

Fig. 26. Ventilation of metal wall panel with masonry backup

because of fluctuating air temperatures and volume, vapor is sucked in through any microscopic opening in the seal as the panel cools and is likely to condense at the low point of the temperature cycle. Over a period of time the panel becomes a reservoir of water, and trouble follows.

In composite panel assemblies, whether they be the laminated- or hollow-pan type, ventilation is usually essential. The only exception is laminated construction employing a core material of closed-cell structure, which in itself is a good vapor barrier.

Instead of being sealed, the edges of most panel constructions should be highly permeable to vapor and deliberately ventilated. The ventilation must of course be provided in such a way as to prevent the entrance of rain or snow, but this is a common feature of good panel designs. With some types of laminated panels it may be advisable to apply protective tape around the edges to prevent damage in transit and handling, but such tape should either be removed or be deliberately punctured, in areas to be protected from the weather, before the panels are installed.

JOINTS

The successful functioning of any metal curtain wall depends largely upon the design of the joints between the component parts. Proper detailing of the joints is the most critical, and often the most difficult, part of the whole wall design. As discussed previously, relative movement of the wall components is a prime factor affecting the entire design concept, and it is chiefly in the detailing of the joints that this movement must be accommodated. Consequently an analysis of the functions and characteristics of joints is essential to an intelligent approach to the joint problem.

Wall assemblies in general include two broad categories of joints:

1. *Closed joints,* which are intended to effect a tight seal against the entrance of weather at all times

2. *Operable joints,* such as those surrounding a ventilator sash, which may on occasion be deliberately opened but when closed are intended to provide a weathertight contact of the joined parts.

Since it is the closed joints which present most of the problems in metal curtain wall design, the discussion will be concerned primarily with that category.

The typical closed-joint assembly is composed of three basic elements:

1. The *joint shape,* or the conformation of the joining parts

2. The *joint seal,* or the material or technique used to make the assembly weathertight

3. The *fasteners,* upon which the structural integrity of the assembly depends.

It should be recognized, however, that some joints, notably some bellows-flange mating joints, are designed to function without the necessity of adding a sealing material.

Criteria of good design require that any closed joint perform certain functions and have certain characteristics. It should:

1. Give durable protection from the infiltration of air and moisture

2. Provide structural and thermal insulation values comparable to those of the adjacent wall areas

3. Have few parts and ample dimensional tolerances

4. Facilitate installation and replacement of the wall components.

Durable protection

The most important function of the joint assembly is to exclude water, dust, and air from the building interior, but it must also protect the wall construction itself and insure its durability. If the joining components themselves are invulnerable to moisture, the penetration of water into the joint between them may not be harmful, provided electrolytic action is prevented and prompt drainage to the exterior is effected. If water contained in a joint should freeze, however, either movement or stress, or both, result, and these must be accommodated without damage to the wall.

The sealing material is typically the most critical element of the joint assembly affecting durability. Good, long-lived seals are more expensive than short-lived sealing material, and there is often a temptation to "economize" on this detail, with concern only for initial cost and little thought for later maintenance expense. Particularly on large buildings sealing material that will require maintenance should be avoided at all costs. The charges for such work are likely to be far greater than the original cost of using even the best and most durable (but commensurately expensive) material; thus, to select a sealing material on the basis of initial cost alone is a false economy.

Structural value

Joints between wall components must have sufficient strength to transmit forces from either joined part to the other. These forces, imposed principally by the wind or by temperature changes, may subject the joint assembly to any of the usual structural forces of shear, tension, compression, or flexure. The nature and intensity of the forces will of course vary with the position and function of the joint.

When members are rigidly and continuously joined, as by welding, the functions of sealing and fastening are performed simultaneously by the joining technique and the strength of the assembly is determined by the "seal" itself. Typically, however, the joint seal is provided by a nonrigid material which contributes only partially, if at all, to the strength of the assembly. In most cases, therefore, it is the joint shape and the fasteners which must provide the essential structural value.

Thermal insulation

In general, joint details have relatively little effect on the over-all thermal insulation value of the wall, but poor joint design may result in objectionable cold spots on the building interior. As previously noted, the use of through-metal in the joint assembly should always be avoided but is particularly objectionable in cold climates. Fasteners are the most frequent offenders in this respect, but a poor choice of joint shape may be even more critical in reducing thermal insulation value.

Number of parts

The simplest design that will meet all the critical requirements is usually the best. The number of loose parts, such as battens, gaskets, and splines, should be as small as possible, and no more fasteners should be used than are necessary to provide adequate strength and stiffness. It is always desirable to keep to a minimum the number of types of joints used and to employ the same joint shape, sealing method, and fastening device as widely as possible throughout the installation. Uniformity in these respects not only permits lower manufacturing and erection costs but also provides for greater interchangeability of similar parts.

Dimensional tolerances

Costs of manufacture and installation are greatly affected also by the degree of precision required. If these costs are to be kept within reasonable limits, the necessity of close dimensional tolerances should be avoided. Metal curtain wall construction usually involves the marriage of factory-made units to a field-constructed frame, thus relating two widely differing concepts of precision. This should be recognized in the design of joints. Factory tolerances may readily be held to a few thousandths of an inch, but field construction tolerances are measured in major fractions of an inch. Since field conditions necessarily govern installation, designs based on "machine-fit" assemblies and tolerances are unrealistic. Unless ample allowance is made for dimensional variations, particularly in the joint shape, expensive field adjustments are likely to result.

Facility of installation and replacement

Alignment of parts should be largely automatic, and the necessity of tedious positioning or force-fitting should always be avoided. Wherever possible, the joining and anchoring methods should be such that the wall can be installed with few

and simple tools and without exterior scaffolding. A joint shape may require that components be installed in some definite order or that the last panel installed be of a special type; preferably, however, the design should permit wide latitude in the order of assembly.

It is advantageous, too, if the joint assembly can be designed to allow for removal of any panel or unit for replacement without the necessity of disturbing a number of adjacent units. Such facility is a feature which metal curtain walls can offer as an advantage over masonry construction, where replacement of wall units, if required, is usually a major operation.

BASIC JOINT TYPES

By JACK M. ROEHM, PE,
Consulting Engineer

The material presented in this section is taken from AAMA *Aluminum Curtain Walls,* Volume 6, "Joints in Aluminum Curtain Walls." Sealant technology is advancing rapidly. Every effort has been made to present current data in this article but manufacturers should be checked for latest technical data when sealants are being specified.

Joint sealant performance is dependent on the design of the joints, the proper selection of sealing materials and their proper installation. Whether they be "working joints," designed to accommodate movement, or "non-working joints," secured by fasteners, some kind of seal is usually employed.

The joint seal may be one of several types: (1) A compound which is a flowable adhesive material applied either in bulk form by means of a gun or knife, or in some preformed extruded shape, (2) A preformed, cellular compression seal with adhesive on one or two sides which is usually supplied in tape form or (3) a gasket, which is a dry, precured shape available in a wide variety of extruded forms. In some instances these types may be used in combination.

There are many shapes or configurations used as edge profiles of joining members, and some of the more common of these are illustrated in Fig. 27. Basically, however, these reduce to three types: 1) the butt joint, 2) the lap joint, and 3) some combination of these two forms, such as the "surround," or glazing type joint. In metal curtain wall construction the combination form is by far the most common.

Butt joints: Butt joints usually subject the

sealant to tensile and compressive stresses. The most important consideration in designing a butt joint to receive a wet sealant is the width of the joint and the sealant depth to width ratio. Joints should be designed to permit the necessary cleaning and drying of the substrates, application of a primer if required, and proper installation of the sealant itself.

In most butt joints, an important consideration is a proper backing for the sealant. This is essential, both to control the depth of sealant contact with the joining parts and to provide proper sealant configuration. The back up material must, of course, be compressible, compatible with the sealant, non-staining and non-contaminating to both the sealant and substrate materials. Recommended materials are closed cell polyethylene foam, polyurethane foam and neoprene or butyl rod or tubing. Back up materials are not and should not be used as a secondary seal. Oakum or bituminous impregnated materials should never be used. The width or diameter of the back up should be approximately 25% greater than the joint width, and compressed when inserted so that it fits tightly in the joint. It should never be stretched longitudinally to facilitate its installation nor should it be punctured. The sealant should not adhere to the back up material. A release film of some type should be used, when necessary, to prevent this. (Sealant manufacturer's recommendations should be followed.)

Lap joints: Lap joints subject the sealant primarily to shear stresses which are less critical than tensile or compressive stresses. Lap joints generally have the advantage that the sealant is partially protected from direct exposure to the weather. However, unless the sealant can be applied before, the joining parts are put together, lap joints are more difficult to seal. Preparation of substrate surfaces and application of a primer may be difficult or virtually impossible after the joining members are in position. Due to component and installation tolerances, the joint thickness may be too small for proper sealant performance.

Surround joints: The "surround" type of joint, used at the periphery of glass or panels, is probably the most common, and certainly one of the most critical of all joints in the curtain wall. In most cases there are far more lineal feet of such joints exposed to the weather than of any other joint type.

Details of peripheral seals used in surround joints for metal and glass are reviewed in the article on Glass and Glazing. Panel materials and constructions vary widely, however, and some of them are particularly susceptible to relatively large movement under temperature fluctuations and

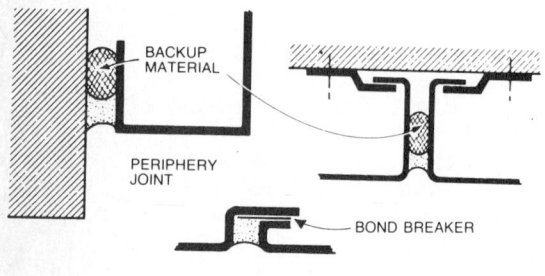

BACKUP MATERIAL

PERIPHERY JOINT

BOND BREAKER

BUTT JOINTS

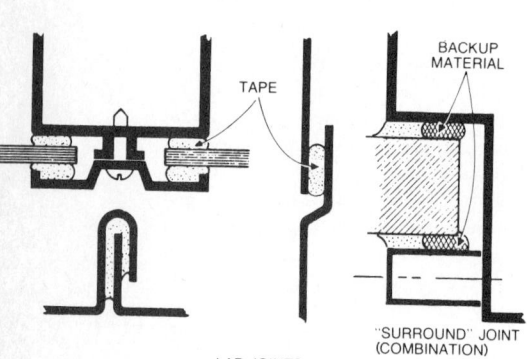

TAPE

BACKUP MATERIAL

LAP JOINTS

"SURROUND" JOINT (COMBINATION)

Working Joints

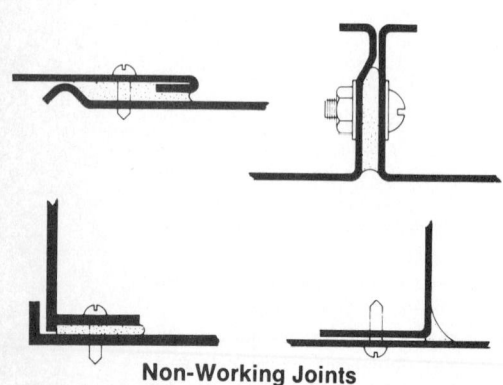

Non-Working Joints

Fig. 27. Representative joint types

due consideration must be given to this problem.

SEALANTS

Critical sealant properties

Sealants, like other building materials, have specific physical characteristics which determine how they will react under conditions of use. The design of joint systems must take into account such factors.

The most critical properties of a sealant are its adhesive strength, cohesive strength, recovery ability after deformation, modulus, and durability under the effects of weathering. The importance of adhesive and cohesive strength is self-evident. Unless the sealant bonds securely and continuously to the substrates when subjected to tensile stress, the sealant will fail. In many cases, depending on the substrate material, a primer may be required to promote the bonding action. Clearly, cohesive strength is equally important. A material which lacks the strength to "hold itself together" under repeated stress cannot provide a suitable seal.

Sealants may accommodate movement by either of two mechanisms. One of these is internal flow under stress, a characteristic variously referred to as stress relaxation, creep, cold flow, or plastic flow. Subjected to stress, the sealant deforms by flowing in the manner of a viscous fluid. An entirely different mechanism is the accommodation of movement by means of a rubber-like property — the ability to deform under stress but, when the stress is removed, to recover.

The properties of many sealant materials vary with temperature. The temperature range occurring on the surface of a building is sufficient to cause changes in the properties of some types of sealant — changes sufficient to cause failure in some cases. It is essential, too, that the basic properties of the sealant do not change significantly with age. Should such changes occur, the assumptions regarding their behavior which originally governed the joint design are no longer valid.

It is most important that the critical properties — adhesive strength, cohesive strength, and modulus — be kept in proper balance in conjunction with the proper joint design and sealant configuration. If the modulus is high and the adhesive strength is low, then adhesive failure may occur. If the modulus is high and the adhesive strength is high, substrate failure may occur. If the modulus is low and the adhesive strength is high, then cohesive failure may occur. Some low modulus sealants will fail in working joints.

Classification of sealants*

Many factors must be considered in choosing the right sealant for a given application. In the final analysis, however, performance is the prime consideration. Various inherent characteristics determine the quality of performance in use, and most of these are subject to evaluation by standard methods of test, as will be discussed later.

Sealant compounds vary considerably in the amount of extension and compression movement they can withstand before failure. It is this fact that has led, in recent years, to general acceptance of the following performance classification, which is reflected in current Federal Specifications and ASTM standards.

Low-range sealants: Those having a maximum predicted cyclic movement capability of ±5%, through their useful life in relatively stable joints. (No table is provided for such sealants, however they are frequently used in aluminum windows and masonry.) Federal Specification TT-C-00598 and modifications covers the essential requirements for sealants in this class. ASTM C 834 describes test methods for evaluating specific characteristics such as staining, degree of bond, extrudability, shrinkage, tack-free time, and set.

Medium-range sealants: Those having a predicted cyclic movement capability of ±5 to ±10% through their useful life. Federal Specification TT-S-001657 covers butyl rubber-based, solvent release type, single component, sealing compounds. (See Table 8.)

High-range sealants: Those which have a predicted cyclic movement capability of ±12½ to ±25% through their useful service life. Those with the lower movement capability are designated as Class B in Federal Specifications TT-S-00227, TT-S-00230 and TT-S-001543 (with current modifications) and in class 12½ in ASTM C719, "Standard Method of Test For Adhesion and Cohesion of Elastomeric Joint Sealants Under Cyclic Movement." Those with the higher capability are designated as Class A in these Federal Specifications and as Class 25 in ASTM C 719, (See Table 9).

Some preformed tapes and gaskets can accommodate the cyclic movement in the low, medium, and high range categories through their useful lives. Information relative to specific performance characteristics

* The classification and performance characteristics of the three ranges are based on the assumption that the compounds referred to are manufactured to meet the established performance criteria.

and properties may be found in AAMA 810.1, ASTM C 509 and D 1056, or directly from the manufacturer of the particular product under consideration.

In all cases, the movement capability is the maximum percentage of width change in a butt joint, in extension and/or compression, *from the originally installed joint width.* For example, a joint that is 1-in. wide at the time of sealant installation must not be extended beyond 1¼ in. or compressed to less than ¾ in., for a sealant that has a movement capability of ±25%.

It should be noted that while the term "sealant" by definition, technically applies to the three classifications of products, it is common practice in many segments of the industry to think of only the medium and high range products—those having elastomeric properties—as being "sealants." While this may lead to some confusion in semantics, it is a practice which is likely to continue. As referred to hereinafter, in this section "sealants" are bulk products and not preformed tapes or gaskets.

Low-range sealants or "caulks:" Generic materials used for these compounds include: oil- and resin-based compounds, bituminous-based caulks, and mastics sometimes modified with rubber, polybutene, latex compounds, etc. The major advantages of these products are their ease of installation, a fair range of colors (except for bituminous materials), and relatively low cost. Their major disadvantages are that they can absorb relatively little movement and they may shrink. Some of the low-range sealants do not cure and allow dirt particles to adhere. Additionally, some of the components in the compound may migrate and will contaminate the surrounding surfaces (porous as well as nonporous). Sealants of this class are appropriate for use in joints where little or no movement is expected. Life expectancy is directly related to the mass, type of substrate, joint movement, and exposure.

Medium-range sealants: Included in this group are the acrylics, butyls (both skinning and nonskinning varieties), neoprene, and other synthetic resins not identified as to composition by their manufacturers, vinyl-latex compounds, etc. Comparative characteristics are summarized in Table 8.

While the sealants in the medium-range group have better extensibility and recovery properties than those in the low-range category, their use is normally confined to non-working joints and those working joints where relatively small movement is expected. The nonskinning butyls and polyisobutylenes are frequently used for "buttering" thin metal-to-metal joints even where a cap bead of high-range sealant is to be applied later. However, if a cap bead of a high-range

Table 8. Medium-Range Sealants (Maximum cyclic movement capability ±5 to ±10%)*

Types	Butyls, skinning type	Butyls, nonskinning type, polybutene, polyisobutylene	Acrylic (nonaqueous) Acrylic (aqueous) neoprene and others
Chief ingredients	Polymers, solvents, inert reinforcing pigments, nonvolatizing plasticizers, polymerizing drying vehicles	Polymers, solvents, inert reinforcing pigments, nonvolatizing and nondrying plasticizers	Polymers, solvents, inert reinforcing pigments, non-volatile plasticizers, curing agents
Curing process	Solvent release, usually oxidation of drying oil. Forms skin on exposed surface	Noncuring	Solvent release
Staining of masonry	None, if product meets FS TT-S-001657	Not generally recommended for use against masonry.†	None
Primer	As recommended.	As recommended.	As recommended.
Ultraviolet resistance	Fair to good	Fair, but not recommended for exposed application	Good
Hardness (Shore A @ 75°F)	15–50	5–20	10–40
Resistance to extension	Low to moderate	Low	Moderate
Resistance to compression	Moderate	Low	Moderate

Advantages	All Types:	Low to moderate cost. Good adhesion to most substrates. Good workability and flexibility. May be self-healing.
Limitations	All Types:	High shrinkage; may be 30% or more.† High dirt pickup. Slow set or cure; may require 3 mos. or more. Remains soft. May stain porous surfaces.†
Precautions:	All Types:	Failures of seals may result when sealants are: (1) applied to moisture-containing materials such as concrete. (2) subject to long periods of immersion in water, and (3) in contact with other sealants with which they are incompatible. Manufacturers should be consulted on these matters. See the section on Installation of Sealants.
Typical applications	Skinning Types:	Sealing of lap joints subject to limited movement. Narrow nonworking butt joints in window frame assemblies. Supplementary seals in glazing.‡
	Nonskinning Types:	Concealed lap or interlocking metal-to-metal joints where there is no danger of the non-drying sealant contaminating an adjoining surface on which a curing-type sealant may be installed.

Refer to paragraph on Movement Capability.
† If product meets Federal Specification TT-S-001657, it will not stain masonry, and shrinkage does not exceed 25%.
‡ Refer to manufacturers' information for compatibility with insulating and laminated glass.

Table 9. High-Range Sealants (Maximum cyclic movement capability ±12½ to ±25%)*

	Multicomponent	Single-component
Types	Polymercaptans, polysulfides, polyurethanes, silicones	Polymercaptans, polysulfides, polyurethanes, silicones, solvent-release acrylics
Chief ingredients	Base component: polymers, prepolymers, activators, pigments, non-volatizing plasticizers, inert fillers Curing agent: activators, accelerators and extenders	Polymers, prepolymers, activators, pigments, nonvolatizing plasticizers, inert fillers, and integral curing agents
Curing process	Chemical cure by mixing of curing agent with base compound	Temperature and/or humidity moisture cure or dormant curing triggered by humidity or oxidation
Staining of masonry	May occur with some types; check by testing in accord with ASTM C510	
Primer requirements	Required on some materials with some types of sealant Consult manufacturer for requirements	
Ultraviolet resistance	See specific manufacturer for information.	
Hardness (Shore A @ 75°F)	See specific manufacturer for information.	
Resistance to extension at low temp.	See specific manufacturer for information.	
Resistance to compression at high temp.	See specific manufacturer for information.	
Advantages	Good adhesion to properly prepared surfaces, good weathering, negligible shrinkage, good flexibility and elasticity. Moderate to high recovery. Good to excellent low-temperature flexibility. Available in a wide range of colors.	
	Early firm cure. Some available in pourable, self-leveling form.	Premixing unnecessary.
Limitations	Proper mixing is critical. Limited pot life after mixing.	Cure rate depends on moisture and humidity (slower than multicomponent sealants). Daily temperature changes and wind loading may adversely change sealant configuration if not cured.
Precautions:	All Types:	Failures of seals may result when sealants are: (1) applied to moisture-containing materials such as concrete, (2) subject to long periods of immersion in water, and (3) in contact with other sealants with which they are incompatible. Manufacturers should be consulted on these matters. See the section on Installation of Sealants.
Typical applications		Where high cyclic movement is anticipated.

* *Refer to paragraph on Movement Capability.*

Sealants, preformed

is to be applied, care should be taken to ensure the compatibility of sealant to sealant and that there are no migratory compounds to prevent or destroy the bond and integrity of the cap bead. Some installation contractors consider this a mandatory precautionary practice, for example, in the sealing of lap joints between mullion sections, because it provides a secondary defense in the event that excessive movement causes failure of the cap bead.

High-range sealants: The types included in this category are polymercaptans, polysulfides, polyurethanes, silicones, solvent-release acrylics, and combinations of polymers.

The most critical concern, in evaluating sealants of this range, is their ability to perform satisfactorily under dynamic joint movement. As previously mentioned, it is no single characteristic, but a proper balance of several essential properties, that determines performance. The sealant will perform properly only as long as this balance is maintained. Comparative characteristics are summarized in Table 9.

This class of sealants is used far more extensively than any others in aluminum curtain walls because of the prime necessity of accommodating significant amounts of movement in wall joints. Each generic type in this class may have its own characteristics, and may also have certain relative merits or limitations. The particular manufacturer should be consulted for specifics.

Forms of sealant

Within each of the categories of sealant, products made from the same base polymer may take more than one form. The various forms and consistencies are the following:

Knife grade: A suitable viscosity for handling with a putty knife.

Gunnable nonsag grade: A viscosity suitable for application in a hand operated or power gun without sagging, under the manufacturer's conditions, when applied in a vertical or overhead joint.

Tapes: These are preformed, continuous shapes, usually square, rectangular, round, or wedgelike, extruded from butyl-based compounds or as cured cellular materials with adhesive. These types are normally used under compression in lap joints and are commonly employed in peripheral joints. The manufacturer should be consulted to determine necessary percentages of compression and application techniques. These general characteristics, advantages, limita-

tions and typical applications are summarized in Tables 10 and 11.

Preformed resilient shapes

Currently, most *resilient shapes* are being produced either in vinyl (polyvinyl chloride) or neoprene, although butyl rubbers also have entered the field.

The resilient gaskets typically depend on flexibility and elasticity, rather than adhesion, for their sealing action. Their effectiveness for specific purposes is largely determined by the appropriateness of the compound and shape used, and their proper functioning depends to a great extent also on meticulous design. As contrasted with the bulk materials, which are suitable for an infinite variety of applications, the resilient shapes are generally designed for specific applications, with performance characteristics "built in" to suit requirements.

It is important to recognize the difference between the plastic material, vinyl, and the elastic materials, neoprene and butyl, in respect to the effects of heat and cold. Vinyl, being a thermoplastic material, is more affected by temperature changes, tending to become stiffer at low temperatures and more susceptible to plastic flow at elevated temperatures. On the other hand, being heat-

Table 10. Preformed Tapes (100% solids sealing material)*

Types	Nonresilient	Semiresilient	Resilient
Chief ingredients	Polybutenes and selected inert fillers	Polybutenes, polyisobutylenes, and selected fillers.	Polybutene or polyisobutylene and fillers.
Curing process	None	None	None
Staining of masonry	Yes	May occur	May occur
Primer	Consult manufacturer for requirements		
Ultraviolet resistance	Fair	Fair to good	Fair to good
Hardness (Shore A @ 75°F)	Putty-like.	5–25	5–30
Resistance to extension	Very low	Low to moderate	Moderate to high
Resistance to compression	Very low	Low to moderate	Moderate to high
Resiliency	None	Low to moderate	Moderate to high
Advantages, All types:	No special equipment normally required for installation. Forms functional seal immediately. Initial adhesion even at low temperature. No shrinkage. Good to excellent weatherability.		
Precautions:	All Types:	Failures of seals may result when sealants are: (1) applied to moisture containing materials such as concrete, (2) subject to long periods of immersion in water and (3) in contact with other sealants with which they are incompatible. Manufacturers should be consulted on these matters. See the section on Installation of Sealants.	

* *Consult manufacturer for compatibility with sealed insulating glass.*

Table 11. Cellular Preformed Tapes

Types	Closed or noninterconnecting cellular, compression seals. Not to include impregnated open-cell products.
Chief ingredients	Polyvinyl chloride, vinyl nitrile, neoprene, polyurethane.
Adhesive systems	Pressure-sensitive or contact.
Curing process	Solvent-dry only with contact adhesives.
Percent compression required	Consult manufacturer.
Resiliency	Moderate to high.
Ultraviolet resistance	Consult manufacturer.
Resistance to extension	Consult manufacturer.
Advantages:	Forms functional seal immediately; no waiting for cure except for contact adhesives. Permanent, quick, accurate installation. No shrinkage. Good to excellent weatherability. No special equipment normally needed for installation.
Limitations:	Must be held under compression. Tolerances must be close to insure continuous compression. Joint movement should be limited depending upon tape formulation (consult manufacturer).
Precautions: All Types:	Failures of seals may result when sealants are: (1) applied to moisture-containing materials such as concrete. (2) subject to long periods of immersion in water and (3) in contact with other sealants with which they are incompatible. Manufacturers should be consulted on these matters. See the section on Installation of Sealants.
Typical applications:	Peripheral joints, singularly and in combination with other sealants.

sealable, vinyl shapes are customarily supplied in continuous coils and can be cut to length and readily "welded" at abutting corners with a hot blade. The sealing of joints in elastomeric materials must be done by vulcanizing, using special equipment—a process which is not feasible at the job site. When resilient gaskets alone are used to seal joints around panels or glass, the joining of the gasket strips at corners is critical in preventing leakage. Careful fitting to provide positive compression of the abutting pieces may accomplish this, but to achieve complete continuity, heat-sealing or vulcanizing is always preferable. Neoprenes, EPDM, and vinyl are compared in Table 12.

Movement dictates joint design

It is generally recognized that the movement expected in a sealant joint determines the design dimensions of the joint. A cause of trouble in butt joints is the failure to provide a sufficient joint width. This may be due to any of several reasons: neglecting to calculate the probable amount of movement, inability to provide sufficient width because of job conditions, or a misunderstanding of the movement capability of the sealant.

The principles governing joint size apply to all types of joints, but are most easily illustrated by reference to the width of butt joints.

The movement capability limits are a percentage of the joint width when the sealant is installed. If the anticipated joint movement is ±⅛″ and all other factors are equal or similar; the following joint dimensions will apply:

	Joint Width
High-range sealants ± 25%	⅛″ × 4 = ½″
Medium-range sealants ± 12½%	⅛″ × 8 = 1″
Low-range sealants ± 5%	⅛″ × 20 = 2½″

When using high-range sealant in a butt joint, the designed joint width should be four times the maximum anticipated change. The importance of selecting the right sealant to maintain a reasonable joint width is apparent.

Temperature is one of the chief factors causing movement. Because surface temperature at the time of installation is seldom predictable, it is recommended that, to ensure against overstressing the sealant, a temperature gradient of at least 180°F should always be used in determining the amount of movement to be accommodated. Joints are widest in cold weather when the joining parts contract and narrowest in hot weather when they expand. This is illustrated diagrammatically in Figure 28. Assuming that surface temperatures of materials may vary from −20°F to 160°F, it is this 180°F temperature change that should be assumed to predict the total overall amount of joint movement.

In lap joints, it is the width of the sealant that is critical. Relative over-sliding movement of the joining parts subjects the sealant to shear stress which, as previously noted, is usually less critical than direct tension or compression. But under shear stress, too, there is a practical limit to the amount of movement permissible for a long period of time. Consequently the width of sealant required is proportional to the amount of movement anticipated, but for practical reasons it should not in any case be less than ⅛″ in a working joint. Most sealants in the medium- and high-range classes are capable of repeatedly resisting without damage a shear displacement m, equal to one-half the width of the joint, as shown in Fig. 29. As recommended, a maximum temperature gradient of 180°F should be assumed in determining the amount of movement likely to occur.

Table 12. General characteristics of gasket materials

	Cellular neoprene (closed cell)	Noncellular neoprene (dense)	EPDM	Vinyl
Basic ingredients	Neoprene polymer compounded with small amounts of reinforcing filler (usually carbon black) and nonvolatizing plasticizers. Cured with appropriate zinc compounds.		Ethylene propylene polymers and terpolymers, reinforcing fillers, nonvolatizing plasticizers. Curing system varies with manufacturer.	Polyvinyl chloride polymers, with limited amounts of fillers and nonvolatizing plasticizers.
	Expanded with blowing agents			
Typical characteristics: Weather resistance	Excellent	Excellent	Not yet fully established	Good
Life expectancy	30 years	30 years		20 years
Resiliency	High	High	Moderate	Fair to moderate
Compressibility	High	Displacement pressures vary with durometer and configuration		
Compression set	Low	Low	Moderate to low	Moderate to high
Moisture pickup	Low	Low	Low	Low
Flammability rating	Self-extinguishing	Self-extinguishing	Supports combustion	Varies with compound
Colors	Black unless coated	Black (color not dependable)	Can be colored	Wide range of colors
Appropriate uses: Compression gaskets	Suitable for any glass or sheet materials; also for expansion and control joints	Limited uses in glazing with plate glass and spandrel glass	New material; appropriate uses being evaluated	Glazing of storefronts, entrances, doors and some types of windows
Structural gaskets	Not appropriate	H-type gaskets for glazing fixed glass or panels in metal frames; raglet-type gaskets for fixed glazing in precast concrete	Being used to some extent experimentally	Not appropriate
Other uses	Backup material for joint sealants	Setting blocks, shims, spacers, etc. for glass and panels	Being evaluated	Continuous wedges for interior applications
Applicable specifications	ASTM: C-509	Compression gaskets: AAMASG-1-76 *Specifications for Dense Rubber-Like Compression Gasket Materials.* Structural gaskets: ASTM: C-542 with NAAMM modifications	None yet available	

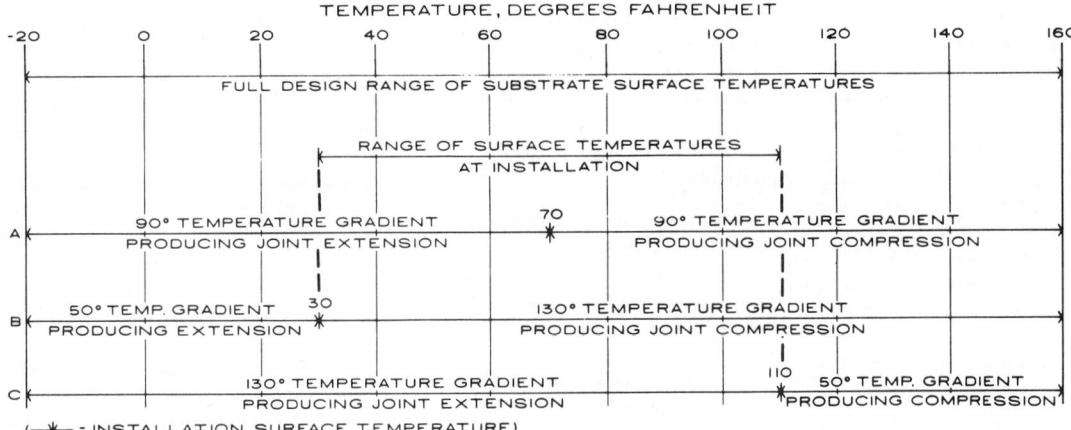

Fig. 28. Effect of installation surface temperature on installed joint width

Joint movements in aluminum curtain walls are often caused by forces other than temperature. They are produced by wind loading, deformation or displacement of the building frame, vibrations and other causes. The probability of such movements must be taken into account in design.

The movements within and between building components, whether due to temperature or other causes, are seldom uniform and continuous. Because of frictional and other restraints, internal stresses build up within building parts as they are subjected to various forces. When these stresses become high enough to overcome restraints and inertia, then movement occurs. Consequently, more often than not, the joints between parts open and close in a series of short "stick-and-slip" displacements, rather than at a uniform rate of movement.

Sealant characteristics and their evaluation

There are various standard laboratory methods for measuring and evaluating the most essential properties and characteristics of sealants, and these are incorporated in many of the sealant specifications listed in Table 13. It must be recognized, however,

that laboratory testing, while quite dependable as a means of comparing products, cannot be expected to accurately predict the in-use performance of a given sealant. The reasons for this are quite obvious. Laboratory tests are necessarily conducted on small specimens and under ideal conditions of cleanliness, with careful attention to procedure and workmanship. It is seldom possible to provide such conditions at the job site.

Adhesion and cohesion: These critical properties of medium- and high-range sealants are generally measured in two ways: (1) by the "durability," or adhesion-cohesion tests required in the Federal Specifications for elastomeric compounds and in ANSI 116.1, and (2) by the adhesion-in-peel type of test.

In essence, the durability test involves the casting of ½" x ½" x 2" joint sections between plates of aluminum, glass and concrete, and then, after curing, subjecting these joint specimens to lateral stress at various temperatures. Both the Federal Specifications and the ASTM Test Method C 719 require first a 7-day immersion of the specimen in water, then 7 days of heat aging under compression, followed by cycled com-

pression and extension, both at room temperature and at alternating high and low temperatures.

The adhesion-in-peel test, also required in most specifications, involves embedding a strip of strong fabric in a bed of sealant, allowing the sealant to cure and then measuring the force required to peel the fabric from the sealant by pulling at an angle of 180°F. *For sealants to be used in a glazing channel, this test should be preceded by subjecting the specimen to ultraviolet light passing through glass.* See Test Methods no. 4 and no. 12 in AAMA 820.1 for testing information.

Hardness: Hardness is the ability to resist surface penetration by a blunt probe. It is determined by using a durometer, which measures the extent of the probe's penetration into the sealant. The term "Shore A" denotes a specific type of durometer made by the Shore Instrument Company and equipped with an "A" scale of hardness measurement ranging from 0 (no penetration resistance) to 100 (complete resistance). On this scale the resistance of a stationer's rubber band is approximately 40, while that of a rubber heel would be about 70.

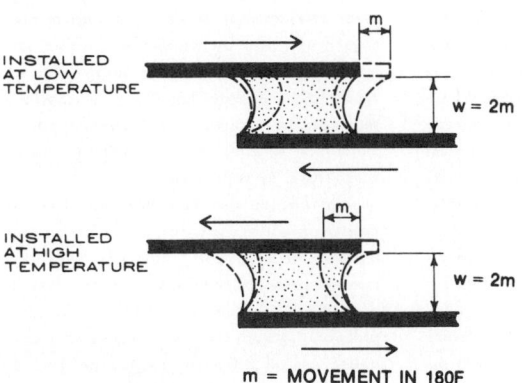

m = MOVEMENT IN 180F

Fig. 29. Movement in lap joints

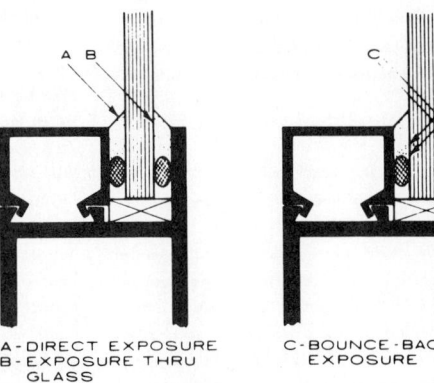

A - DIRECT EXPOSURE
B - EXPOSURE THRU GLASS

C - BOUNCE-BACK EXPOSURE

Fig. 30. Ultraviolet exposure

Sealant hardness may be important at two stages: (1) initially, after curing, and (2) after aging. The effect of long-term exposure on hardness is of utmost importance, as a significant change can radically affect the sealant's ability to function. Hardness may be changed by solar effects on the plasticizers or the base polymer itself, by heat from other sources, by a faulty curing mechanism, or by a combination of factors.

Elastic recovery is the ability of the cross-linked sealant to recover from a constant external deformation. The elastic recovery is a measure of the crosslinking density of the system. A higher degree of recovery indicates a higher degree of crosslinking or chemical cure that will result in a better fatigue modulus and superior performance of the sealant. The elastic recovery is lost completely at the brittle point of the sealant. This elastomeric property is expressed as percent recovery or the ratio between the recovered length to original length.

Permanent set occurs when a sealant is stretched, released, and does not return to its original length but remains longer. The increase in length, expressed as percent of the original length, is called permanent set. It depends principally on the amount and time of deformation, the state of cure, and the degree and type of loading.

Compression set (cold flow): Compression set occurs when a sealant is subjected to a compression load for some time and does not return to its original dimension when the load is removed. A high compression set is undesirable in a sealant, as it reduces the extension capabilities and may cause further degradation of performance as the sealant ages.

Effects of ultraviolet exposure: It is essential that sealants have high resistance to the effects of ultraviolet (UV) exposure. The degrading effects of three types of exposure must be considered.

(1) Direct exposure, as in any joint exposed to sunlight.
(2) Exposure through glass, as at the indoor interface of a glazing sealant. Adhesive bond to the glass may be affected.
(3) "Bounce-back" exposure, as at the outdoor interface of a glazing sealant.

These three types of exposures are illustrated in Fig. 30.

Compatibility with contacting materials: Compatibility is the ability of two or more materials to exist and perform properly when in direct contact. This is an essential characteristic which is often overlooked. Incompatibility may result in staining, inadequate adhesion or a complete breakdown of one or more of the sealing components. The specifier should make certain, by testing if necessary, that the products to be used are completely compatible.

Sealants, tapes, and gaskets, used in conjunction with insulating glass and laminated glass, which contact the edge of the glass, must be evaluated for compatiblity before use.

PRECAUTIONS

Because of the multiplicity of building materials, substrates, coatings, treatments, sealants, etc., tests should be conducted to determine the compatibility of the particular materials under consideration for use where data on the combinations is not available. Manufacturers of sealants will often conduct tests and provide data on compatiblity of substrate and sealant candidates. The use of the testing services offered by manufacturers of sealants if recommended.

Installation of sealants

A preinstallation inspection and conference is advisable. One reason for this is that, since weatherproofing is usually one of the last operations on the building exterior, sealants often have to correct, or compensate for, prior errors and miscalculations. As already mentioned there is a "performance gap" between laboratory test results on sealants and their actual performance in the field. Actual job-site conditions are not known until sealant installation begins.

Precautions

Where sealants are to be applied to a material which may contain moisture, such as concrete, wood, or other porous products, special application procedures may be necessary in order to avoid failures of the seal due to the moisture.

If a sealant is to be used in a joint which may be subject to long periods of immersion in water resulting from rain, condensation, or other causes, special treatments may be required to reduce the possibility of failure. Wherever possible, joints should be designed so that water does not collect but is drained to the outside of the wall. This is particularly critical in the case of organically sealed insulating glass.

Successful performance of sealants, when in contact with each other, depends on their being compatible. One type of sealant may not be compatible with another type. Where such incompatible sealants come in contact, a sealant failure can be expected. Care must be taken in the selection of joint sealants to be used with organically sealed insulating glass. Where an improper selection is made, an insulating glass seal failure can be anticipated. Curtain-wall seal failures can also be anticipated because of incompatible sealants, and because some joints are internal it becomes virtually impossible to effect an economic repair to stop the water leakage.

Sealant manufacturers should be consulted about their products and what should

be done if any of the three aforementioned conditions, namely, a moist substrate, long periods of water immersion, and contact between different sealants, are to be encountered.

Sealant application: The sealing contractor should inspect the job along with a qualified representative of the sealant manufacturer before work begins. Trial application on a wall mockup, with subsequent tests of performance, is also recommended.

Surface preparation: A prime essential of satisfactory performance of any sealant is the quality of surface preparation. Inadequate surface preparation may result in bond failure, regardless of the quality of the sealant or how carefully it is put in place.

Surface contamination is the major hazard. In general, dust, dirt, incompatible sealants, moisture protectives and release coatings are the chief contaminants. In addition to these, the following may be present on specific substrates and should be removed:

On metal. Oil or grease films, wax, stryrenated coatings, lacquer coatings, release coatings, etc. These can usually be readily removed by an appropriate solvent followed by wiping with a dry cloth (avoid refilming). Solvents such as mineral spirits or kerosene that leave an oil deposit, must not be used. The question of lacquer on metal surfaces has long been argued. Most sealant literature and labels call for removal of any lacquer coating. The bond of the sealant will be no better than that of the lacquer. It is usually difficult to remove lacquer at the job site. Therefore, to ensure proper sealant performance, no lacquer should be applied to surfaces where a sealant is to be applied.

On glass. Fruit juices, coffee, soft drinks, and other contaminants, and the transferred slip-sheet chemical or slip coating applied by the manufacturer, the latter of which is water-soluble.

On concrete or masonry. Friable surfaces, laitance, form release coatings, polishes, lubricants, residue from reaction with muriatic acid, and transparent waterproofing or preservatives. Masonry with loose, friable surfaces should first have the loose material removed, and may have to be specially treated. The sealant manufacturer's advice should be solicited as to a suitable primer to be used in such cases.

Joint backup and bondbreakers: The necessity of, and reasons for, providing backup material in deep butt joints has been discussed earlier. In some joints of this general type there is insufficient depth for a compressible backup, the joint depth being controlled by an offset or tongue on one of the joining parts. In such cases, for optimal performance, the sealant should not bond to the bottom of the joint recess. Instead,

Table 13. Specifications for building joint sealants

Type of Sealant	Specification Number	Date	Responsible Agency (addresses given below)
Two-part polymers	TT-S-00227e	1970	General Services Administration (NBS)*
	ANS A116.1†	1967	American Society for Testing and Materials
Two-part polysulfide	19GP-3M	1976	Canadian Specifications Board
	TBTPS II	1971	Thiokol Chemical Corporation
Two-part polyurethane	19GP-15M	1976	Canadian Specifications Board
Two-part silicone	19GP-19	1970	Canadian Specifications Board
One-part polymers	TT-S-00230c	1970	General Services Administration (NBS)*
One-part acrylic	19GP-5M	1976	Canadian Specifications Board
One-part butyl	TT-S-001657	1970	General Services Administration (NBS)*
	19GP-14M	1976	Canadian Specifications Board
One-part polysulfide	19GP-13M	1976	Canadian Specifications Board
	TBTPS IV	1971	Thiokol Chemical Corporation
One-part silicone	TT-S-001543A	1971	General Services Administration (NBS)*
	19GP-9M	1976	Canadian Specifications Board
	19GP-18	1970	Canadian Specifications Board
One-part polyurethane	19GP-16a	1971	Canadian Specifications Board
Ductile back-bedding compounds	AAMA 802.3	1976	Architectural Aluminum Manufacturers Association
Narrow joint sealants	AAMA 803.3	1976	Architectural Aluminum Manufacturers Association
Ductile back-bedding glazing tape	AAMA 804.1	1970	Architectural Aluminum Manufacturers Association
Bonding-type back-bedding compound	AAMA 805.2	1971	Architectural Aluminum Manufacturers Association
Bonding-type back-bedding glazing tape	AAMA 806.1	1969	Architectural Aluminum Manufacturers Association
Cured-rubber-type back-bedding tape	AAMA 807.1	1969	Architectural Aluminum Manufacturers Association
Exterior perimeter sealing compound	AAMA 808.3	1976	Architectural Aluminum Manufacturers Association
Nondrying sealants	AAMA 809.2	1972	Architectural Aluminum Manufacturers Association
Expanded cellular glazing tape	AAMA 810.1	1977	Architectural Aluminum Manufacturers Association
Test methods for sealants	AAMA 820.1	1976	Architectural Aluminum Manufacturers Association

* *National Bureau of Standards (NBS) is responsible for technical preparation.*
† *This specification, available from ANSI, has been under the jurisdiction of ASTM Committee C24 since first issued in 1960. As some of its provisions are now outdated, however, it will likely soon be replaced by a new ASTM specification.*

SOURCES OF ABOVE SPECIFICATIONS:
American National Standards Institute (ANSI), 1430 Broadway, New York City 10018
American Society for Testing and Materials, 1916 Race Street, Philadelphia, PA 19103
Architectural Aluminum Manufacturers Association, 35 East Wacker Drive, Chicago, IL 60601
Canadian Specifications Board, National Reserach Council, Ottawa, Ontario, Canada KIA OS5
Federal Specifications Business Service Center, General Services Administration, 7th and D Streets S.W., Washington, DC 20407
Thiokol Chemical Corporation, Chemical Division, P.O. Box 1296, Trenton, NJ 08607

a bond breaker should be installed on the bedding surface, as shown in Fig. 31, to permit the sealant to absorb movement without creating any excessive concentrated stresses. A suitable release material such as polyethylene tape should be laid on the bedding surface to prevent this.

Primer or surface conditioner: Some sealants require a primer or surface conditioner to obtain satisfactory adhesion to substrates. The printed instructions provided by the sealant manufacturer should state whether the product being used requires such a primer, what primer to use on various materials, and how to apply it. These instructions should be followed implicitly. Primers or surface conditioners supplied by one manufacturer should not be used with sealants made by another. Specific primers should be used for the intended substrate surfaces. Coatings may require priming to obtain adhesion.

Before proceeding with the primer application it is always advisable to check for possible staining or deterioration of the substrate materials. Only clean brushes or daub-ers should be used for the application. Some primers must be dry before installing the sealant, while with others a tacky surface is essential. Refer to manufacturers' recommendation for quantity of primer required. In all cases the exposed joint surface must be completely coated.

Application of the sealant: Multicomponent sealants consist of separately packaged base compound and curing agent which must be properly and thoroughly mixed prior to use. Their "pot life," or time available for use before curing advances too far, is limited, and varies with temperature and humidity. The single-component sealants are ready for use as supplied.

Either type of sealant must be applied with sufficient pressure and in sufficient volume to completely fill the joint. Butt joints, in particular, should be tooled after the sealant is applied, to ensure full contact with the substrate interfaces, as shown in Fig. 32. Only in this way can proper adhesion to the forming parts be obtained.

Finally, it is important that any sealant smeared or dropped on adjacent surfaces be immediately cleaned off, as removal is likely to be difficult once the sealant has cured.

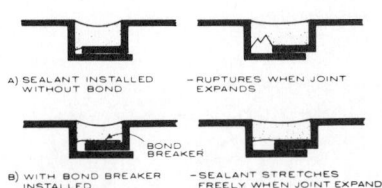

Fig. 31. Function of bond breaker

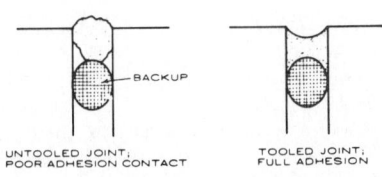

Fig. 32. Importance of tooling joint

By DR. PETER V. PAULUS, *Director Research and Development, Standard Products Co.*[9]

Functional principle

Lockstrip gaskets are preformed and cured elastomeric mechanical seals used to install glass or solid infill panels in a supporting framework. To facilitate installation and provide the pressure required to secure and seal the installed material, the gaskets are made in two parts: (1) the main body of the gasket, having a grooved recess in one face, and (2) a separate wedgelike continuous locking strip which is inserted into this recess. The gasket body is first placed on or into the frame

[9] *Abridged from an article in* Aluminum Curtain Walls *with the permission of the publisher, Architectural Aluminum Manufacters Association.*

without the locking strip; the glass or panel is then positioned in the gasket, and finally the lockstrip is inserted. Insertion of the lockstrip forces the gasket lips against both the installed material and the surrounding frame and places the entire gasket under sufficient compression to produce the sealing pressure. The elastomer used for the lockstrip is harder than that used for the main body of the gasket. This facilitates the insertion of the strip and also increases the pressure exerted by it. The effectiveness of the seal depends upon the properties of the elastomer used, the control of critical dimensions, and the design characteristics of the total system.

In typical openings, where the glass is of medium thickness and not too large in area, gaskets and glass are routinely in-

stalled and lockstrip is locked or "zipped" into place as described. However, the growing number of curtain wall designs having high performance requirements, as well as those using very large lights of glass, insulating glass, tinted glass, or subdivided lights within a single frame has led to the need for improved and more sophisticated installation techniques which heretofore have not been well defined.

ASTM Standard C542-76, Standard Specification for Elastomeric Lockstrip Glazing and Panel Gaskets, stipulates the physical requirements of the finished gasket. These are shown in Table 14. Currently the elastomers being used for this purpose are neoprene, butyl, and EPDM, an ethylene-propylene polymer formerly identified as EPT.

Table 14. Physical requirements for lockstrip gaskets—ASTM C542-76

Property	Requirements	Test method
Tensile strength, min*	2,000 psi (14 MPa)	D 412
Elongation at rupture, min, per cent	175	D 412
Tear resistance, min	120 lb per linear in. (214 N per linear cm)	D 624 (die C)
Hardness, durometer A*	75 ± 5	D 2240
Compression set, max, per cent, 22 h at 212°F (100°C)	35	D 395 (method B)
Brittleness temperature, min	−40°F (−40°C)	D 746
Ozone resistance, 1 ppm		
100 h at 100°F (37.7°C), 20 per cent elongation	no cracks	D 1149
Heat aging, 70 h at 212°F (100°C)		D 573
Change in hardness, max	+10 −0 durometer points	
Loss in tensile strength, max, per cent	15	
Loss in elongation, max, per cent	40	
Flame propagation†	Gaskets must not propagate flame	As specified
Lip seal pressure‡		
Extruded section, min	4 lb per linear in. (7 N per linear cm)	As specified
Corners, min	4 lb per linear in. (7 N per linear cm)	As specified

* If a separate stock is used for the locking strip, it may have a hardness of 80 ± 5 durometer points and a minimum tensile strength of 1,800 psi (12.5 MPa). In all other respects, it must meet these specifications.
† This requirement may be waived (see *).
‡ In the case of molded corners with integral sealing devices, the requirement for corner lip seal pressure may be lowered by the architect or professional engineer.

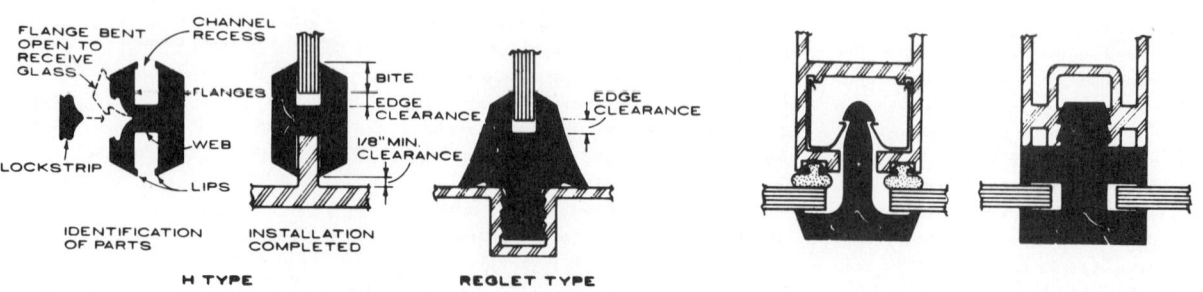

MOST COMMONLY USED TYPES   **REPRESENTATIVE PROPRIETARY TYPES**

Fig. 33. Types of lockstrip gaskets

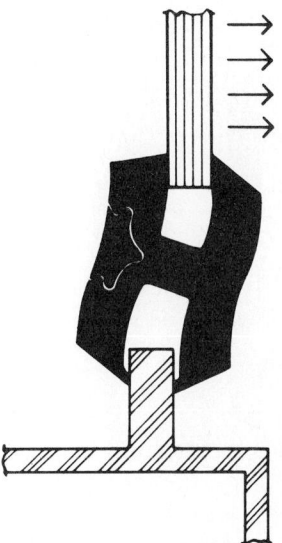

Fig. 34. Gasket "roll-off" due to excessive edge clearance and high wind load

Types

There are many variations in the design of lockstrip gaskets, several of which are shown in Fig. 33. The two most commonly used types are the H-type and the reglet type, the former being the most commonly used in aluminum curtain wall work. This H gasket fits over a flange or lip on the surrounding frame, whereas the reglet gasket fits into a recess in the frame. In most cases either one or the other of these types is used exclusively within an opening, but in some instances they may be used in combination. Generally the reglet type has the greater strength and versatility. It is the type usually preferred when the framing material is concrete, and it is frequently used also in aluminum frames.

Characteristics

The many forces that cause movement in aluminum curtain walls also affect the ability of any glazing material to maintain a tight seal. The high resiliency of lockstrip gaskets permits wall movement to be accommodated rather than resisted, and the gaskets readily adjust to normal amounts of movement, an inherent advantage of this type of gasket.

Most lockstrip gaskets, preformed as continuous closed frames, are made by extruding the straight sections and then connecting them at the corners by a process known as transfer molding or extrusion molding. The gasket is purposely made to be slightly (about 1 per cent) larger than the opening of the frame into which it is to be installed. As a consequence it is normally seated tightly against the frame and is under a slight linear compression. As lip pressure is likely to be lowest at the gasket corners, this linear compression assures that the lockstrip will exert pressure around the corner. Thus the gasket should be installed by beginning at the middle of a straight side and working toward the corners, stretching the gasket as little as possible, and ending at the corner with a little excess length which is forced into the groove.

The frame: This must have sufficient strength and stiffness to support the load imposed on it. The part of the frame in contact with the gasket must be smooth and flat; heavy extrusion die lines, roughness, irregularities, or offsets at joints may cause leaks. The thickness of the flanges engaged by the gasket must be held within a tolerance of $\pm\frac{1}{32}$ in., and the intersection of flanges at the corners must be within $\frac{1}{64}$ in. of true alignment. The projection of the flanges must be such as to provide clearance of not less than $\frac{1}{8}$ in. (see Fig. 33). Opening dimensions of rectangular frames must be held within the following tolerances: sides, $\pm\frac{1}{16}$ in. for lengths of 6 ft or less, $\pm\frac{1}{8}$ in. for greater lengths; the two diagonal dimensions of any opening, $\pm\frac{1}{8}$ in.

The contained glass or panel: Elastomeric gaskets have unique advantages when tinted glass is being used because they permit the edges of the glass to remain at nearly the same temperature as that of the rest of the glass, thus minimizing the internal stresses due to temperature differences. With other types of glazing this difference may be as much as 60° F and even more on opaque spandrel glass.

The dimensional relation of the gasket to the contained glass or panel becomes critical as the area of the opening becomes larger. The larger the infill, the greater the total pressure exerted upon it by wind forces and the more important it becomes that the gasket engage or "bite" as much of the infill edge as possible. The wind load factor plus the weight factor in these cases may cause failure by "roll-off," as shown in Fig. 34. The greater the bite, the greater the resistance to roll-off. Therefore the gasket manufacturers recommend an edge

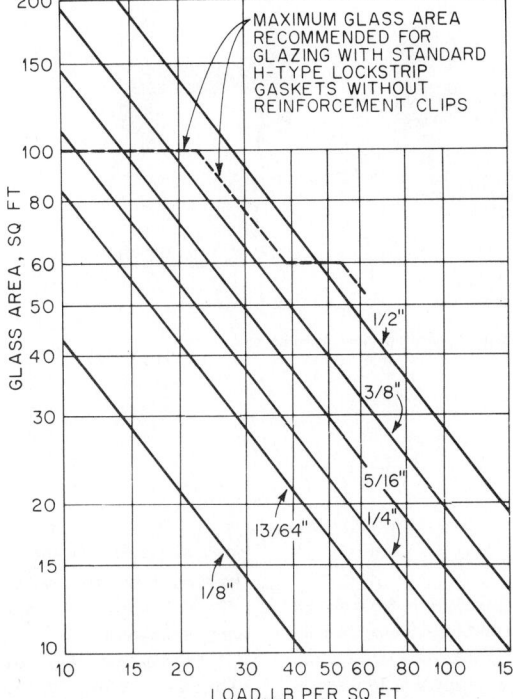

Fig. 35. Maximum glass area for "standard practice" installations of H-type lockstrip gaskets (for vertical windows supported on four sides)

NOTES: *Loads are based on minimum glass thicknesses allowed in Federal Specification DD-G-00451D. Design factor = 2.5.*
Loads apply to glass lights having a length-to-width ratio of 3 or less; for higher l/w ratios, consult glass manufacturers' literature.
Maximum loads are for 1-minute uniform loading, representative of "fastest mile wind."
For insulating glass, maximum load is 1.5 times load shown for the thinner light used in the unit. Maximum area currently available is 72 square feet.

clearance of $3/32$ in. But the glass manufacturers, in view of the cutting tolerances of $\pm 1/16$ in. for $1/4$-in. glass to $1/8$ in. for $1/2$-in. glass, favor an edge clearance of $3/16$ in. Since the more tightly the glass fits into the gasket, the longer it takes to install it, the glaziers also favor an edge clearance of $3/16$ in. A reasonable compromise would be $1/8$ in.

Standard practice versus high performance: Standard practice, as already described, is appropriate up to certain limits of opening size and wind loading, as shown in Fig. 35. Beyond these limits, "high-performance" practice is required. In such cases the designer has two alternatives: he may use heavier and more expensive gaskets or he may provide reinforcement for the standard H-gasket at small additional cost. The use of metal reinforcing clips, as shown in Fig. 36, results in a dramatic increase in the resistance of the gasket to roll-off. By this means it is possible to accommodate edge clearances of as much as $3/16$ in., facilitate installation, and still meet the structural requirements of high wind loading. Experience has proved that negative (outward-acting) wind loads are much more critical than positive wind loads. Therefore the clips are usually placed on the exterior side to prevent the glass from blowing out, but if necessary they may be used on the interior side also.

As mentioned earlier, certain sections such as the reglet type and the supported-T type (Fig. 33) can provide as much as 50 per cent greater roll-off resistance than the standard H-section. But with these sections too, the addition of supplementary clips will provide additional safety factors.

Setting strips: These are required at the bottom of all lockstrip gaskets, the length of the strips depending upon the weight of the glass to be supported. The purpose of the strips is threefold: to prevent the glass from cutting into the gasket as it vibrates under wind loading, to facilitate installation of the glass by equalizing the bite at head and sill, and to keep the bottom edge of insulating glass and laminated glass free from moisture which may accumulate in the gasket channel. The pressure on the strips should not exceed 15 psi; this limit will not be exceeded if 1 lineal inch of strip is used for each square foot of glass (thus a sheet of glass with an area of 48 sq ft would require two 24-in. strips). The strips should be symmetrically placed, with the outer ends no nearer the corners of the glass than 6 in. The width of the strips should be no greater than the glass thickness. The hardness of the strips should be between 80 and 90, Shore A durometer.

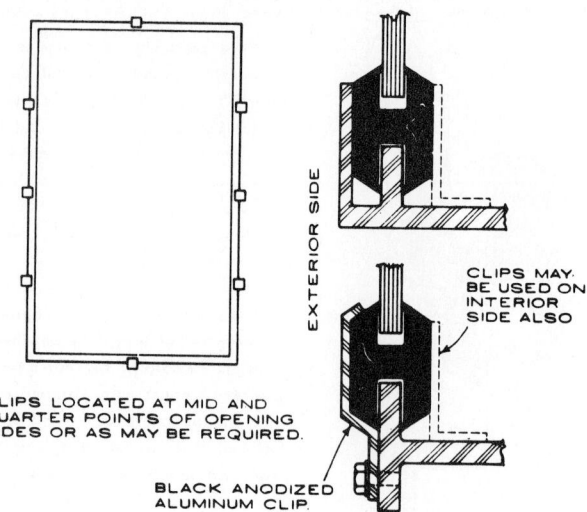

CLIPS LOCATED AT MID AND QUARTER POINTS OF OPENING SIDES OR AS MAY BE REQUIRED.

EXTERIOR SIDE

CLIPS MAY BE USED ON INTERIOR SIDE ALSO

BLACK ANODIZED ALUMINUM CLIP.

Fig. 36. Reinforcement clips for "high performance" gasket glazing

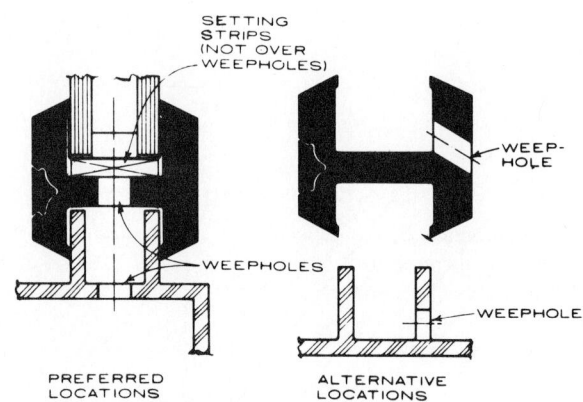

SETTING STRIPS (NOT OVER WEEPHOLES)

WEEP-HOLE

WEEPHOLES

WEEPHOLE

PREFERRED LOCATIONS

ALTERNATIVE LOCATIONS

Fig. 37. Weepholes for insulating glass installations

Weepholes and drainage

A properly designed weep or drainage system is often desirable in many glazing installations and is imperative when using insulating or laminated glass in a lockstrip gasket system. Properly designed, a weephole system is more than simply a means of draining accumulated water; it utilizes the pressure equalization concept to prevent potential water penetration to the building interior, either at the frame side or the glass side of the gasket. Sectional views of typical weephole locations, with insulating glass, are shown in Fig. 37.

It is recommended that the following rules be observed:

1. Not less than three weepholes should be provided at the sill, one located near each end and one at the center, at the lowest part of the gasket channel.

2. Weepholes should be at least $1/4$ in., and preferably $3/8$ in., in diameter, to prevent plugging by construction debris or insects.

3. Weepholes should not be placed on the lockstrip side of the gasket.

By WAYNE F. KOPPES, FAIA, *Architectural Consultant*

PANELS

A great variety of materials is used in the opaque panel areas of metal curtain wall construction. Where fire-resistant construction in these areas is required by local building codes, masonry backup is usually employed, and in such cases the panels are essentially decorative in nature and may or may not include thermal insulation. When such requirements do not govern, the panels may constitute the complete wall construction, providing within one thin, preassembled unit the exterior facing, the interior finish, and the intermediate insulation.

The numerous common panel types may be considered under four principal categories:

1. *Solid sheets:* Uninsulated panels made from such materials as heavy-gage metal, structural glass, plastic, or thin slabs of marble, slate, or other stone are typically employed as facings over masonry backup. With such panels, insulation is often provided separately.

2. *Hollow metal pans:* Panels formed by flanging metal sheets into shallow pans, attached back-to-back to form hollow panels which usually contain insulation. They may be used either as facing panels over masonry or more often to provide the complete wall construction.

3. *Laminated ("sandwich") assemblies:* Composite constructions having thin dense surfaces adhesively bonded onto both sides of a low-density core material. In most cases good thermal insulating qualities are provided by using a lightweight porous material as the core, and such "sandwiches" may either comprise the complete wall or be used simply as facing panels. Thin, noninsulating sandwich panels with denser cores are often used as flat surfacing materials.

4. *Precast concrete units:* Panels made of reinforced concrete, either in solid form or with a core of insulating material, and with various integral or applied surface finishes.

Most panel constructions may be readily classified as one of these four principal types, although some constructions combine the characteristics of two or more types and others belong to none of these classifications. A closer look at these four varieties (particularly the second and third), however, will provide basic information about the common panel constructions and the important considerations relative to their design and use.

Solid sheet panels

Most facing panels of this type are of either glass or metal. Two types of "structural" glass are appropriate for this use:

1. *Colored structural glass,* which is made by the continuous batch method, with metal oxides incorporated in the mix to produce a variety of opaque colors. It is available in polished, rough, and "suede" or "twill" finishes and in thicknesses ranging from ¼ to 1¼ in.

2. *Ceramic colored glass,* which is made by fusing color onto the back of ¼-in. plate or float glass. A large variety of colors is available, and both polished and textured finishes are standard, with a number of special finishes and custom colors obtainable on special order.

The colored structural glass should be "heat-strengthened" (tempered) for exterior use, especially in the darker colors; the ceramic colored glass is heat-strengthened in its process of manufacture and is intended specifically for exterior uses. Because heat-strengthened glass cannot be cut in the field, it is essential that sizes be accurately predetermined and that any required notching or drilling be completely detailed for factory fabrication.

Metal sheet panels may be constructed in several ways. They may be:

1. Thin plate material, with smooth or polished finish
2. Sheet metal press-formed into sculptural designs
3. Corrugated or ribbed metal sheets, produced by roll- or brake-forming
4. Assemblies of interlocking extruded shapes
5. Single castings or assemblies of castings.

The chief problem with the first type of panel is to achieve a sufficiently flat surface to avoid the appearance of waviness or "oil-canning." Since the visual effect of waviness is a function of light reflection, it is proportional to the degree of polish used on the surface. Waviness is seldom objectionable on relatively flat, nonreflective dark matte surfaces. It is impractical, in any case, to require "optical flatness" on panel surfaces because this is virtually impossible to accomplish, and a requirement of "visual flatness" is not definitive. Flatness criteria based on the *slope* of the surface, as suggested in the Princeton studies of stainless-steel curtain walls, seem the most logical and are recommended in the NAAMM *Metal Curtain Wall Specifications.*

Hollow metal pans (mechanically assembled)

This is a common type of panel construction in both custom and standard walls. Typically these panels consist of an outer pan of porcelain-enameled steel, usually 16 gage, and an inner pan of galvanized iron, often prime-painted. Occasionally the outer pan does not have a flat surface but may be fluted or otherwise deformed. The two pans are flanged in a variety of conformations and are connected by mechanical means at their edges to form a hollow box containing lightweight inorganic insulation. Many manufacturers also offer a variation of this construction in which the outer pan, especially in panels of large area, is partially filled with a cementitious material to improve its rigidity and flatness.

Most frequently the insulation used is of the flexible blanket type, and it must of course be permanently positioned within the panel, either by adhesive attachment to the inner pan or by the use of noncorrosive spacers. If its thickness is less than the full panel depth, the resulting air space should be between the insulation and the *outer* panel face, and a natural circulation of air should occur in this space to minimize the collection of moisture due to condensation.

For best results, manufacturers generally recommend that, when the outer pan is not reinforced by a backup material, the face area of these panels should be limited to 16 sq ft, or 24 sq ft when cementitious fill is used. These limitations are imposed both by considerations of flatness and by the fact that typical production equipment cannot accommodate widths greater than 52 in. The over-all thickness of the panels usually ranges from 1¼ to 2½ in.

A number of typical variations of edge shapes and details are illustrated in Fig. 38.

Laminated (sandwich) assemblies

This type includes by far the greatest variety of constructions, since a large num-

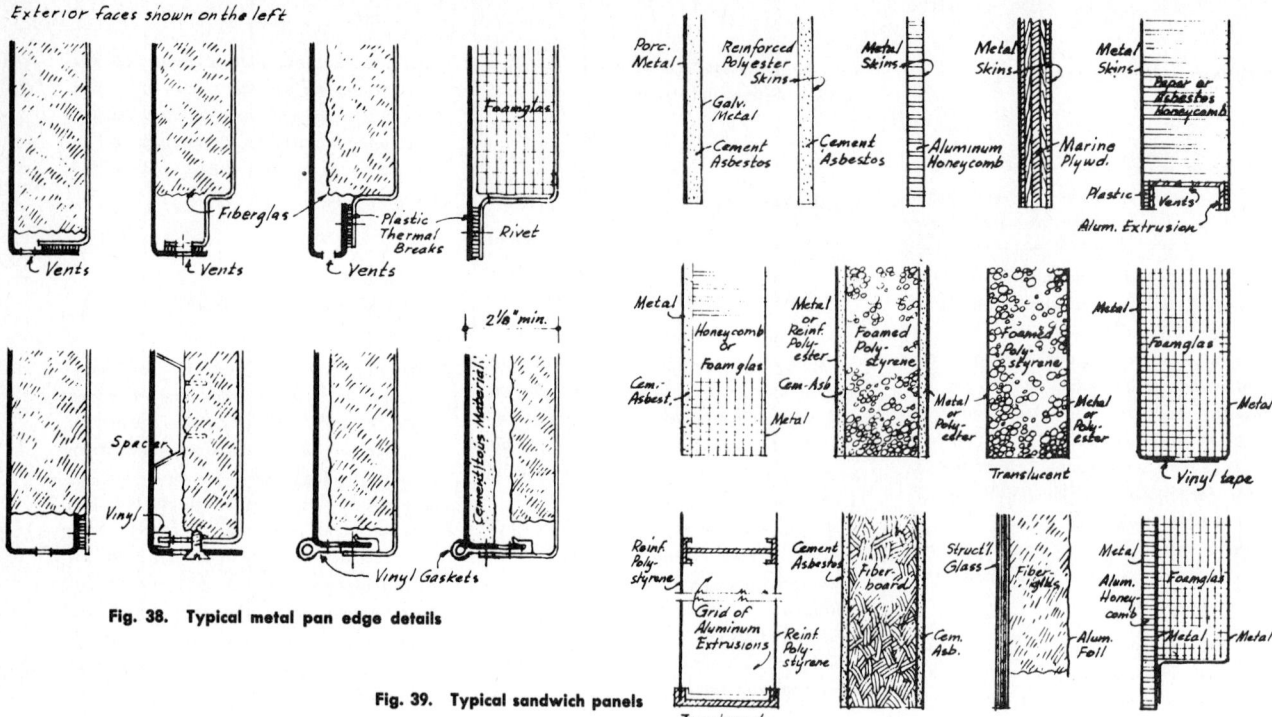

Exterior faces shown on the left

Fig. 38. Typical metal pan edge details

Fig. 39. Typical sandwich panels

ber of both skin and core materials can be assembled in innumerable combinations. Among the materials most commonly used are the following:

Core materials
Insulating (low density):
Kraft paper honeycomb (impregnated)
Foamed glass
Plastic foams
Asbestos paper honeycomb
Aluminum honeycomb
Aluminum "eggcrate"
Fiberboard
Low-density cementitious materials
Noninsulating (high density):
Cement-asbestos board
Plywood
Hardboard

Skin materials
Porcelain-enameled steel
Aluminum: anodized, polished, or porcelain-enameled; smooth or textured
Stainless steel: polished or colored, smooth or textured
Ceramic tile (on sheet backing)
Polyester, reinforced with glass fiber
Cement-asbestos
Glass
Marble
Precast concrete

It is common practice with the light-gage metals, and sometimes with the polyester facings, to use a composite skin, consisting of the thin facing material laminated to a thicker, rigid backup sheet of non-metallic material such as cement-asbestos board or hardboard, to provide the required stiffness, flatness, and resistance to indentation. By this means, metals of almost foil thinness have been successfully used, both in smooth and textured finishes, as the outer skin material.

All these sandwich constructions depend entirely on adhesive bonding, usually under heat and high pressure, for their structural integrity, and they are generally characterized by more-than-adequate strength and stiffness. In the absence of mechanical fastenings, thorough testing is essential to insure against eventual failure of the assembly by delamination, and testing procedures for this purpose have become pretty well standardized over a period of years (ASTM D-1037). With the help of present-day adhesives and improved manufacturing techniques, these laminated constructions have found wide acceptance, not only in exterior building panels but in many other building applications as well, and when made by reputable manufacturers have proved wholly satisfactory.

Some of the denser noninsulating laminates, such as metal-faced plywood, cement-asbestos board and hardboard, and also cement-asbestos-faced fiberboard, are available in large-size standard sheets which can be cut to desired dimensions. With these exceptions, low-density-core assemblies are apt to be produced only on order, to meet specific requirements of size, finish, thermal insulating value, and the like.

Representative details of some of the more common types of laminated assemblies are shown in Fig. 39. For discussion of the structural theory of sandwich panels, see section on Structural Sandwiches.

Edge sealing and venting of panels

With most types of metal-faced composite panels, ventilation of the panel interior is an important consideration, and it becomes particularly important when the insulation used is capable of absorbing moisture. As discussed in connection with "Water Vapor and Condensation," the attempt to hermetically seal the panel edges can rarely be justified and is even more rarely accomplished with success. Instead of being sealed, the edges of most composite-panel constructions, whether of the hollow-pan or laminated type, should be highly permeable to water vapor and deliberately ventilated.

If proper venting is to result, the manner in which the periphery sealing of the panels is accomplished within the supporting framework also deserves careful attention. It does little good to provide vents in the edge of the panel itself if their function is impeded by the use of impermeable sealing materials around the panel. Instead of using a solid setting bed of compound or full-depth gaskets at these locations, seals should ideally be placed only at the outer and inner panel faces (Fig. 40), leaving the space adjacent to the weepholes clear for venting and drainage.

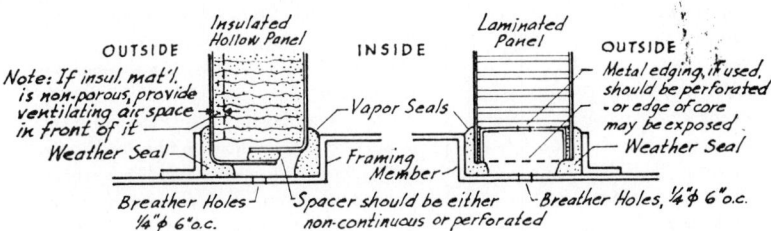

DETAILS OF VENTING BOTTOM EDGES OF COMPOSITE PANELS

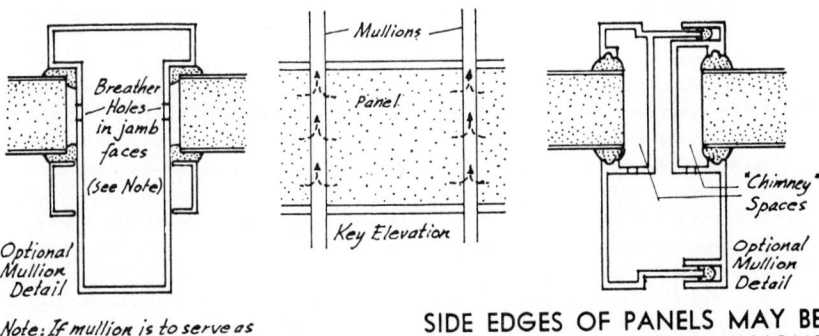

SIDE EDGES OF PANELS MAY BE VENTED INTO HOLLOW MULLIONS

Fig. 40. Methods of venting interiors of panels

By JACK M. ROEHM, PE, *Consulting Engineer*

CURTAIN WALL SPECIFICATIONS

To a large extent, the achievement of satisfactory results with a metal curtain wall design depends on the quality of the architect's specifications. In fact, in many respects the specifications may be more important than the drawings. Manufacturers usually prefer to develop their own details, even for custom walls, but complete and explicit specifications are always essential if the architect's requirements are to be correctly interpreted.

The *Metal Curtain Wall, Window, Store Front and Entrance Guide Specifications Manual* published by the Architectural Aluminum Manufacturers Association is the most complete guide to the preparation of specifications published to date. It contains references to accepted standards for most of the components and materials used in metal curtain wall construction. This publication is the result of impartial and objective collaboration by technical experts in many fields. The guide specifications are accompanied by a commentary text which explains the reasons for, and significance of, the specification clauses. The information presented here will treat only the more important general principles to be observed in specifying

metal curtain wall construction; for detailed information the AAMA manual should be consulted.

To begin with, it is advisable to list "Metal Curtain Walls" as a separate section of the architectural specifications, even for small jobs. This is preferable to specifying the metal work under one section, the glass under another, and other parts and materials under still different headings.

Grouping everything relating to the wall in a separate section ensures that the wall contractor knows what is involved in the entire job, can bid accurately and can schedule the installation efficiently. A single contractor generally assumes the total responsibility for the wall work. The store front work may or may not be included in the wall section of the specification. Often store front work is done by a different contractor.

Specifications which follow the recommendations of the Construction Specifications Institute will have a three-part format. These will be Part 1—General, Part 2—Products and Part 3—Execution. The AAMA manual follows the CSI recommendations in order to facilitate its use by specifiers.

Following is a complete outline of items which may appear in the architect's specification. This outline is taken directly from the AAMA manual.

PART I—GENERAL

1.01 **Description of Product**
1.02 **Related Work Specified Elsewhere**
1.03 **Items Furnished But Not Installed**
1.04 **Items Installed But Not Furnished**
1.05 **References**
1.06 **Wall Contractor**
1.07 **Quality Assurance**
    A. Qualifications
    B. Mock-ups
    C. Performance and Testing Requirements
        1. Provision for Thermal Movements
        2. Structural Properties
        3. Water Penetration
        4. Air Leakage
        5. Thermal, Light and Sound Transmission Performance
        6. Fire Resistance Requirements
        7. Field Check for Water Leakage
        8. Other Performance Requirements and Tests
1.08 **Submittals**
    A. Shop Drawings
    B. Samples
    C. Structural Calculations
    D. Test Reports
    E. Certification and Labeling
1.09 **Identification, Delivery and Storage of Materials**
1.10 **Warranty**
1.11 **Reimbursement for Special Provisions**

PART 2—PRODUCT

2.01 **Metals**
    A. Metals Schedule
    B. Aluminum Alloys
    C. Copper Alloys
    D. Carbon Steel
    E. High Strength, Low Alloy Steel
    F. Stainless Steel
    G. Patterned Metal Sheets
2.02 **Fastener Metals for Joining Various Metal Combinations**
    A. Aluminum to Aluminum
    B. Aluminum to Stainless Steel or Carbon Steel
    C. Copper Alloys to Copper Alloys
    D. Copper Alloys to Aluminum
    E. Copper Alloys to Stainless Steel
    F. Copper Alloys to Carbon Steel
    G. Carbon Steel to Carbon Steel
    H. Stainless Steel to Stainless Steel
    I. Fastener Alloy Types, Designations and Standards
2.03 **Protective Materials for Metals**
    A. Standards
2.04 **Finishes**
    A. Aluminum
    B. Copper Alloys
    C. Carbon Steel
    D. Weathering Steel
    E. Stainless Steel
    F. Organic Coatings

G. Porcelain Enamel

2.05 Curtain Wall System

A. Curtain Wall Units and Components Schedule

B. Metal Framing Performance

C. Metal Framing Alloy and Finish

D. Framing Clearance

E. Framing Glazing

F. Framing Component Accommodation

G. Panel Removal

H. Anchors

I. Column Covers

J. Other Components

K. Flashings

L. Performance Requirements

2.06 Store Front and Entrance Framing System

A. Store Front and Entrance Framing System Schedule

B. Metal Framing Performance

C. Metal Framing Alloy and Finish

D. Framing Clearance

E. Framing Glazing

F. Framing Component Accommodation

G. Panel Removal

H. Framing Reinforcing Members

I. Framing Anchors

J. Weatherstripping

K. Flashings

L. Performance Requirements

2.07 Entrance Doors

A. Entrance Door Schedules
1. Swing Door Entrances
2. Revolving Door Entrances
3. Sliding Door Entrances
4. Hardware
5. Automatic Power Operators

B. Performance Requirements

C. Metal

D. Glass and Glazing

E. Weatherstripping

2.08 Panels

A. Panel Schedule

B. Panel Performance

C. Materials and Construction
1. Metal Facing Panels, Single Thickness
2. Adhesively Bonded Panels—Metal Faced
3. Adhesively Bonded Panels—Glass Faced
4. Mechanically Assembled Panels
5. Non-metallic Panels

D. Fabrication and Workmanship

2.09 Glass and Plastic Glazing Materials

A. Glass and Glazing Schedule

B. Performance Requirements

C. Flat Glass Quality

D. Insulating Glass

E. Tempered, Heat Strengthened and Spandrel Glass

F. Plastic Sheet Products

G. Safety Glazing

2.10 Setting Blocks, Edge Blocks and Spacers

A. Setting Blocks

B. Edge Blocks

C. Spacers

D. Requirements

2.11 Windows and Doors

A. Operable Window and Door Schedule

B. Operable Window and Door Performance

C. Operable Aluminum Windows and Sliding Door Standards

D. Operable Steel Windows

E. Other Operable Metal Windows

F. Glazing

G. Finishes

H. Glass or Plastic Sheet

I. Screens

J. Screening

K. Operating Hardware

2.12 Other Proprietary Wall Components

2.13 Field Installed Insulating Materials

A. Insulation Installation Schedule

B. Materials Specifications

C. Fire Resistance Requirements

D. Installation Materials and Accessories

2.14 Sealing and Glazing Materials

A. Sealing and Glazing Schedule

B. Materials Specifications

2.15 Fabrication

A. General

B. Joints in Metal Work

C. Shop Assembly

D. Exposed Fasteners

E. Protection of Metals

F. Welding

G. Soldering and Brazing

H. Fabrication of Stainless Steel, Copper and Copper Alloys

I. Fabrication of Weathering Steel

J. Shop Painting of Steel

K. Use of Sealing Materials

L. Shop Glazing

PART 3—EXECUTION

3.01 Lines and Grades

A. Curtain Walls and Store Fronts

B. Correction of Errors

3.02 Prior Inspection of the Structure

3.03 Installation

A. Curtain Wall and Store Front Framing

B. Panels

C. Column Covers

D. Windows and Doors

3.04 Erection Tolerances

3.05 Installation Within Masonry Openings

3.06 Anchorage

3.07 Welding

3.08 Use of Sealing Materials

3.09 Postponement of Complete Enclosure

3.10 Field Glazing

A. Glass and Glazing

B. Setting Blocks and Spacers

C. Specifications

D. Plastic Sheets

E. Application of Tapes

3.11 Field-Applied Insulation

3.12 Removal of Debris

3.13 Protection and Cleaning

In defining performance requirements, methods of testing, materials, finishes, sealants, insulation and other items, reference to existing standards of AAMA, ANSI, ASTM, AWS, CGSB, GSA, PEI, and other recognized organizations will be found very helpful, and this is a practice which is recommended. However, it is essential that the specification writer be certain that the standard to which he or she refers will in fact provide the performance or the material which is required for the job. As a guide to the specification writer, the AAMA guide specifications manual references appropriate standards throughout.

Although writing a good specification is of prime importance, the architect's responsibility does not end here. Like any law, this contract document is only as effective as its enforcement, and just as with laws, honest and rigid enforcement is usually rewarded with respect. Respect for a good architectural specification is evidenced in better workmanship, both in the factory and in the field. Well-written specifications, designating specific materials and definite performance requirements instead of dealing in vague generalities, will result in more accurate and reliable bidding and are an invaluable aid to competent and effective field supervision.

by WAYNE F. KOPPES, FAIA, *Architectural Consultant*

ELECTROLYTIC CORROSION

Data courtesy of Copper Development Association, Inc.

When dissimilar metals are in contact in the presence of an electrolyte, such as water containing very small amounts of acid, they set up a galvanic action that results in the deterioration of one of them. The following is a list of the more common commercial metals according to what is known as the electrochemical series:

1. Aluminum	6. Tin
2. Zinc	7. Lead
3. Steel	8. Copper
4. Iron	9. Stainless steel
5. Nickel	

When any two metals in this list are in contact, with an electrolyte present, the one with the lower number is corroded. The galvanic action increases as the metals are farther apart in the electrochemical series.

Insulation between dissimilar metals will prevent galvanic action. Recommended insulators, in order of preference, are asbestos, lead, heavy tinning of ferrous metal, good-quality moisture-proof building paper or felt, or a heavy coat of asphalt paint.

FINISHES

All data on finishes condensed from NAAMM Metal Finishes Manual.

The important subject of finishes for architectural metals is both broad and complex, and to be well informed on the matter requires extensive study and experience. The intent here is simply to present certain basic information regarding the more common types of finish, how they are produced and how they may be identified. For more comprehensive information on the subject, the architect is referred to NAAMM's *Metal Finishes Manual,* 1976 edition.

It should be kept in mind, in considering the selection of finishes, that the cost is usually proportional to the service value. The over-all cost significance of even the most expensive finish is relatively small, and selection on the basis of low initial cost may result in excessive long-term expense. And another point: when appearance is a critical factor, as it often is, range samples of the intended finish should be required for approval, with the understanding that the finish provided must fall within the approved range.

MECHANICAL FINISHES

The mechanical finishes are generally produced by polishing, buffing, and rubbing.

They vary somewhat from one metal to another, and each industry has its own terminology. In addition to the numerous standard mechanical finishes, the producers of all the architectural metals offer many special proprietary finishes, which should be specified by name or number and name of the producer. The costs of various mechanical finishes differ significantly, and an inappropriate choice may involve needless expense. In the interests of economy, therefore, the architect should investigate comparative costs before making his selection.

Descriptions of and designations for mechanical finishes on aluminum, as established by the Aluminum Association, are shown in Table 6, and similar information regarding these finishes for the copper alloys, as provided by the Copper Development Association, is given in Table 13. The American Iron and Steel Institute's descriptions and designations applying to mechanical finishes on stainless steel will be found in Table 18.

Table 1. Thickness equivalents of sheet metal gages

These data are provided primarily for reference purposes, rather than to facilitate the use of gage numbers in specifying metal thicknesses. Because the lack of consistency between the various gage systems frequently leads to confusion and errors, the thickness of metal should be specified in decimal inches instead.

	Thickness in inches			
	Manufacturers' Standard gage	Galvanized Sheet gage	U.S. Standard gage	Browne & Sharpe gage
Gage number	Uncoated steel sheets and electrolytically zinc-coated sheets	Hot-dip galvanized sheet	Stainless steel sheet and strip	Nonferrous sheets and wire
0			0.3125	0.3249
1			0.28125	0.2893
2			0.26563	0.2576
3	0.2391		0.250	0.2294
4	0.2242		0.23438	0.2043
5	0.2092		0.21875	0.1819
6	0.1943		0.20313	0.1620
7	0.1793		0.1875	0.1443
8	0.1644	0.1681	0.17188	0.1285
9	0.1495	0.1532	0.15625	0.1144
10	0.1345	0.1382	0.14063	0.1019
11	0.1196	0.1233	0.125	0.0907
12	0.1046	0.1084	0.10938	0.0808
13	0.0897	0.0934	0.09375	0.0720
14	0.0747	0.0785	0.07813	0.0641
15	0.0673	0.0710	0.07031	0.0571
16	0.0598	0.0635	0.0625	0.0508
17	0.0538	0.0575	0.05625	0.0453
18	0.0478	0.0516	0.050	0.0403
19	0.0418	0.0456	0.04375	0.0359
20	0.0359	0.0396	0.0375	0.0320
21	0.0329	0.0366	0.03438	0.0285
22	0.0299	0.0336	0.03125	0.0253
23	0.0269	0.0306	0.02813	0.0226
24	0.0239	0.0276	0.025	0.0201
25	0.0209	0.0247	0.02188	0.0179
26	0.0179	0.0217	0.01875	0.0159
27	0.0164	0.0202	0.01719	0.0142
28	0.0149	0.0187	0.01563	0.0126
29	0.0135	0.0172	0.01406	0.0113
30	0.0120	0.0157	0.0125	0.0100

CHEMICAL FINISHES

Chemical finishes of one kind or another are used on both ferrous and nonferrous metals, but their chief uses are on the latter. On the copper alloys their most important use in architectural work is in the form of conversion coatings, which are employed to both alter the color of the metal and provide a final finished surface. On aluminum, though, they are often used as pretreatments for other subsequent finishes and change only the surface texture of the metal.

The so-called caustic etch finish used on aluminum is relatively inexpensive, being obtained by treating the work in a solution that is basically caustic soda or equivalent. This process removes the natural oxide surface film from the metal, but this film reforms upon exposure to the atmosphere. When caustic etch is to be the final finish, the etched surfaces should be coated with a clear organic coating for protection during handling and erection. The organic coating should have a minimum thickness of 0.5 mil. An etch is often used before anodizing, particularly when dealing with large flat areas, where the control of color matching is important.

The descriptions and designations of chemical finishes for aluminum are shown in Table 7 while those for the copper alloys are given in Table 14.

ELECTROCHEMICAL FINISHES

In the architectural field, electrochemical finishes are currently used almost exclusively on aluminum in the process known as anodizing.

The anodized finishes are oxide coatings obtained by immersing the work in an electrolytic bath, using an electrolyte such as sulphuric or other acid. The metal is made the anode in this process, and the surface is converted into essentially aluminum oxide which is an integral part of the metal.

The architect is cautioned that there is a wide range of quality in anodizing work, and some of the competitive commercial work in this field is of doubtful value. In specifying anodized finishes the critical characteristics to be insisted upon are the proper thickness, density, and seal of the coating.

Color is produced in anodic coatings either by impregnating the oxide coating with suitable dyes or pigments, by electro-deposition of the color or by the nature of the alloy itself. The silicon alloys (4000 series), for example, produce various shades of gray when anodized. Whether the colors are inherent or are added by absorption, the pores of the anodic coating are subsequently sealed to produce a stain-resistant and durable surface.

By far the most important development in architectural aluminum finishes during recent years has been the development of the "hard-coat" color anodics, which have become very popular. These finishes, which are produced by proprietary integral color processes, range from light gold to dark bronze and from gray to black, the color depending upon both the alloy and the process used. The voltages and current densities required are higher than with conventional anodizing processes, and accurate control of the bath temperature is a critical factor. These hard-coat finishes are heavier, denser, and more abrasion-resistant than coatings provided by other anodizing methods.

Because of the nature of the finishing process, minor shade variations can be expected from one colored element to another, particularly between sheet and extrusions. This inherent characteristic of the finish need be no problem if properly anticipated in the design.

Color anodizing is largely custom work, with each prime producer using his own proprietary process. In specifying this type of work, the architect should follow the recommendations of the manufacturer or supplier whose process is to be used. Table 8 lists two classes of anodizing, both approved for exterior architectural use. A Class II finish provides the thinner coating and is intended for work that will be regularly maintained, such as store fronts, doors, and entrance trim. No thinner coating than this should be used. Class I finishes provide a thicker coating and should be specified for all items subject to maximum abrasion (such as push bars) and for areas not likely to receive regular maintenance care.

APPLIED FINISHES

The term "applied finishes" refers to those finishes involving the use of some added material as a surface coating, as opposed to converting the surface of the metal itself into an integral coating. These applied finishes are often protective as well as decorative in nature and may be either organic or inorganic.

Table 2. Weights of architectural metals in sheet thicknesses

Density, lb/in.³	Aluminum 0.100	Bronze† 0.303	Carbon steel 0.284	Stainless steel* 0.287
Thickness (inches)		*Pounds per square foot*		
0.006	0.086	0.262	0.244	0.248
0.008	0.115	0.349	0.326	0.331
0.010	0.144	0.436	0.409	0.413
0.012	0.173	0.524	0.492	0.496
0.016	0.230	0.698	0.654	0.661
0.020	0.288	0.873	0.818	0.827
0.025	0.360	1.09	1.02	1.04
0.032	0.461	1.40	1.31	1.32
0.040	0.576	1.74	1.64	1.65
0.050	0.720	2.18	2.04	2.07
0.063	0.907	2.75	2.58	2.60
0.080	1.15	3.49	3.26	3.30
0.090	1.30	3.93	3.69	3.72
0.100	1.44	4.36	4.09	4.13
0.125	1.80	5.45	5.12	5.17
0.160	2.30	6.98	6.54	6.61
0.190	2.74	8.29	7.78	7.85
0.250	3.60	10.91	10.22	10.33
0.313	4.51	13.66	12.81	12.94
0.375	5.40	16.36	15.34	15.50
0.500	7.20	21.82	20.45	20.67
0.750	10.80	32.72	30.67	31.00
1.000	14.40	43.63	40.90	41.33

* *Weights given are for 300 series; weights of 200 series slightly less*
† *Muntz Metal 280*

Organic coatings include a wide variety of materials ranging from paints and air-drying enamels to the sophisticated newer types of thermally cured synthetic coatings. Paints and air-drying enamels are used chiefly on ferrous products, baked enamels, and high performance synthetic coatings on either ferrous or aluminum products. In all cases the service life of the coating depends a great deal upon the surface preparation and pretreatment of the metal and the proper choice and application of the primer coat.

Factory-applied organic coatings may be either clear or pigmented. Clear lacquers are often used as short-term protective coatings over mechanical or chemical finishes on aluminum and the copper alloys, but their use on stainless steel is not recommended. Many of the factory-applied pigmented coatings are enamels, which have a high proportion of resin content and provide hard, resistant finishes. Some of these cure by air-drying, some contain binders that are thermosetting and require heat to harden them, and others are heated to hasten their chemical cure.

The factory-applied high performance (organic) exterior metal finishes have been rapidly growing in importance during the past decade. Such coatings are very durable, some having a life expectancy of 20 years or more, and they are available in a wide range of colors. They include the air-drying epoxies and urethanes and the thermally cured fluorocarbons (such as "Kynar 500") and siliconized polyesters (such as "Duracron"). These finishes are proprietary products not covered by industry standards, and each type has its own characteristics and limitations which should be clearly understood before specifying.

The inorganic coatings are chiefly either metallic, in which the added material is one or more other metals, or vitreous porcelain enamel, in which an opaque glass-like pigmented coating is bonded to the metal by fusion.

Among the metallic coatings, galvanizing, or the application of a zinc coating on steel, is by far the most common. There are several methods of application, but the hot dip method and electro-deposition are those generally used. The hot dip method, used on sheet, strip, and fabricated parts, usually produces coatings 0.90 oz/ft² or heavier, though lighter coatings may also be provided. Electrolytic coatings, used on sheet, strip and small hardware items, are much lighter, ranging from a "flash" coat (no minimum weight specified) to a weight of 0.165 oz/ft².

Porcelain enamel, the most durable of all applied finishes, is not as widely used now as it was before the introduction of the colored anodics and the high performance organic coatings. It can be applied to any of the architectural metals, but is usually

Table 3. Thermal expansion of building materials (in temperature range of from 68 to 212°F unless otherwise noted)

Material	In. per in. per °F ($\times 10^{-6}$)	In. in 10 ft for a temperature rise of 100°F	In. in 10 ft for a temperature rise of 150°F
Wood:			
Perpendicular to grain	19 to 32	—	—
Parallel to grain	2.1 to 3.6	0.025 to 0.043	0.038 to 0.065
Brick masonry	3.1	0.037	0.056
Limestone masonry	3.5	0.042	0.063
Cellular glass	4.0	0.048	0.072
Plate glass	5.1	0.061	0.092
Stainless steel, Type 430	5.8	0.070	0.104
Concrete	6.5	0.078	0.117
Structural steel	6.7	0.080	0.121
Plaster	9.2	0.110	0.166
Copper, 110	9.4	0.113	0.169
Stainless steel, Type 302	9.6	0.115	0.173
Red brass, 230	10.0	0.120	0.180
Architectural bronze, 385	11.0	0.132	0.198
Muntz metal, 280	11.0	0.132	0.198
Aluminum	12.9	0.155	0.232
Lead	15.9	0.190	0.286
Zinc, rolled	17.3	0.208	0.311
Plastics:			
Phenolics	8.5 to 25	0.102 to 0.300	0.153 to 0.450
Glass-reinforced polyesters	10 to 14	0.120 to 0.168	0.180 to 0.252
Acrylics*	40 to 50	0.480 to 0.600	0.720 to 0.900

Temperature range, 60 to 120°F.

Table 4. Schedule of fastener metals*

Metallic fasteners joining metal parts shall be made of the metals listed in the following table, at the intersection of the column and line headed by the respective metals to be joined.
Courtesy of National Association of Architectural Metal Manufacturers.

Metals joined	Stainless steel	Copper alloys	Carbon steel	Aluminum
Aluminum	Stainless steel	Stainless steel (nonmagnetic)†	Stainless steel	Aluminum or stainless steel (nonmagnetic)
Carbon steel	Stainless steel	Brass or bronze	Metallic-coated carbon steel	
Copper alloys	Stainless steel, brass, or bronze	Brass or bronze		
Stainless steel	Stainless steel			

Alloys used for fasteners shall be as follows:

Fastener metal	Types or alloys
Stainless steel:	
Where exposed to weather	300 series
Protected or interior locations	300 or 400 series
Copper alloys:	
Brass	C2800, Muntz metal; C46400, naval brass; or C46500, leaded naval brass
Bronze	C65100, low-silicon bronze B or C 65500, high-silicon bronze A
Aluminum:	
Screws and bolts	2024, 6061
Nuts	6262
Rivets	1100, 6053, or 6061

In addition to the fastener metals shown, metallic-coated carbon steel may be used in all cases in locations not exposed to dampness or moisture.

†*Joining of these metals not normally recommended; consult metal producers.*

Aluminum Alloys

Table 5. Guide for the selection of aluminum alloys
Courtesy Architectural Aluminum Manufacturers Association

Typical applications	Alloy	Comments
SHEET AND PLATE		
Panels, fascias, column covers, sunshades, ductwork, gutters, flashings, etc.		General-purpose non-heat-treatable alloys:
	3003	Most widely used general-purpose sheet alloy. Economical for sheets having fair mechanical properties and excellent formability. Takes on a slight brownish yellow cast when anodized and is susceptible to structural streaking that is particularly noticeable in large flat areas.
	5052	Slightly better mechanical properties and higher cost than Alloy 3003. Good workability and excellent corrosion resistance, even in salt air exposures. Excellent weldability. Assumes yellowish cast when anodized and is susceptible to structural streaking, particularly in large flat areas.
		Non-heat-treatable alloys suitable for anodizing:
	1100	Low-strength alloy, appropriate for applications requiring high degree of formability. Finishes well but susceptible to structural streaking when anodized, particularly noticeable in large flat areas.
	1135	Somewhat higher purity than Alloy 1100 and gives a brighter finish. Mechanical properties are similar to those of Alloy 1100.
	5005	Commonly used for low-cost all-purpose sheets having good formability and finishing characteristics. Slightly better mechanical properties than Alloy 1100. Good anodized appearance match with 6063 extrusions but susceptible to structural streaking, particularly noticeable in large flat areas.
		For proprietary alloys designed for quality applications where excellent anodized appearance is critical, consult the aluminum producers.
		For proprietary alloys developed specifically for this use, consult the aluminum producers.
		Heat-treatable alloys:
	6061	Most economical and versatile of the heat-treatable alloys. Used chiefly for roll-formed structural shapes and other applications requiring high strength. Good anodized appearance match with 6061 extrusions but not with 6063 extrusions. May take on yellowish cast when anodized.
		General note regarding clad alloys:
		Improved finishing characteristics may be obtained by cladding aluminum alloys with a thin layer of aluminum that is metallurgically bonded to a core alloy. The cladding may be of the same or different alloy than the core.
		Caution: When buffing clad products, care must be exercised not to wear through the cladding. Clad products to be anodized should not be ground.
		For proprietary alloys developed specifically for this use, consult the aluminum producers.
EXTRUSIONS Mullions, sash, fascias, copings, thresholds, handrails, trim, etc.	6063	Most commonly used extrusion alloy. Good anodized appearance match with Alloys 1100, 5005, and proprietary natural anodizing sheets.
	6061	Used for extrusions requiring high strength. See above under "Sheet and Plate" for general characteristics.
		For proprietary alloys designed for quality applications where excellent anodized appearance is critical, consult the aluminum producers.
Roofing and siding	Alclad 3004	Used for standard corrugated, ribbed, and V-beam industrial roofing and curtain wall sheets. Not generally anodized.
Porcelain enameling	6061	See above under "Sheet and Plate" for general alloy characteristics.
		Proprietary alloys developed specifically for this use:
	Alcoa:	Nos. 1 and 4 Porcelain Enameling Extruded Shapes.
	Olin:	Porcelain Enamel Quality Extrusions.
	Reynolds:	6061, Porcelain Enameling Quality.
CASTINGS Decorative panels, hardware items, etc.	43	Used for ornamental castings in which strength is not a critical requirement. Castings turn gray after anodizing.
	F214	Stronger than Alloy 43; produces best anodized appearance match with 6063 extrusions.
	356	High-strength casting alloy; turns gray after anodizing.
FASTENERS		
	1100	Used for low-strength rivets and for washers.
	2024	Used for bolts and screws.
	5056	Used for nails.
	6053	Used for medium-strength rivets.
	6061	Used for nails and high-strength rivets, bolts, screws, and washers.
	6062	Used for nuts.
		Note: All fasteners except nails may be either plain or anodized.

used on either enameling iron (or steel) or on aluminum. Only certain alloys of aluminum, however, are suitable for receiving this type of finish.

The Porcelain Enamel Institute, Inc. (PEI) has long been active in promoting high quality standards in architectural porcelain enamel work of all kinds, and has formulated standards and specifications for such work which are observed throughout the industry. Copies of these are available to the architect upon request from PEI.

Table 6. Standard designations for mechanical finishes for aluminum

All designations are to be preceded by the letters AA to identify them as Aluminum Association designations. From Designation System for Aluminum Finishes, *Aluminum Association, 1976.*

Type of finish	Designation	Description	Examples of method of finishing
As fabricated	M10	Unspecified	
	M11	Specular as fabricated	
	M12	Nonspecular as fabricated	
	M1x	Other	To be specified
Buffed	M20	Unspecified	
	M21	Smooth specular	Polishing with grits coarser than 320 and finishing with 320 grit, using peripheral wheel speed of 6,000 fpm. Then buffing with aluminum oxide buffing compound, using peripheral wheel speed of 7,000 fpm
	M22	Specular	Buffing with aluminum oxide compound, using peripheral wheel speed of 7,000 fpm
	M2x	Other	To be specified
Directional, textured	M30	Unspecified	
	M31	Fine satin	Wheel or belt polishing with aluminum oxide grit of 320 to 400 size, using peripheral wheel speed of 6,000 fpm
	M32	Medium satin	Wheel or belt polishing with aluminum oxide grit of 180 to 220 size using peripheral wheel speed of 6,000 fpm
	M33	Coarse satin	Wheel or belt polishing with aluminum oxide grit of 80 to 100 size; peripheral wheel speed of 6,000 fpm
	M34	Hand rubbed	Hand rubbing with stainless steel wool lubricated with neutral soap solution. Final rubbing with No. 00 wool
	M35	Brushed	Brushing with rotary stainless steel wire brush (wire diameter 0.0095 in., peripheral wheel speed 6,000 fpm); or various proprietary satin finishing wheels or satin finishing compounds with buffs
	M3x	Other	To be specified
Nondirectional, textured	M40	Unspecified	
	M41	Extra fine matte	Air blasting with finer than 200-mesh washed silica sand or aluminum oxide, using 45-lb pressure with gun held 8–12 in. from work at 90-degree angle
	M42	Fine matte	Air blasting with 100- to 200-mesh silica sand or aluminum oxide. Air pressure 30 to 90 lb depending on metal gage; gun held 12 in. from work at angle of 60 to 90 degrees
	M43	Medium matte	Air blasting with 40- to 50-mesh silica sand or aluminum oxide. Air pressure 30 to 90 lb depending on metal gage; gun held 12 in. from work at angle of 60 to 90 degrees
	M44	Coarse matte	Air blasting with 16- to 20-mesh silica sand or aluminum oxide. Air pressure 30 to 90 lb depending on metal gage; gun held 12 in. from work at angle of 60 to 90 degrees
	M45	Fine shot blast	Shot blasting with cast steel shot of ASTM size 70-170 applied by air blast or centrifugal force
	M46	Medium shot blast	Shot blasting with cast steel shot of ASTM size 230-550 applied by air blast or centrifugal force
	M47	Coarse shot blast	Shot blasting with cast steel shot of ASTM size 660-1320 applied by air blast or centrifugal force
	M4x	Other	To be specified

Table 7. Standard designations for chemical finishes for aluminum

All designations are to be preceded by the letters AA to identify them as Aluminum Association designations. From Designation System for Aluminum Finishes, *Aluminum Association, 1976.*

Type of finish	Designation	Description	Examples of method of finishing
Nonetched, cleaned . . .	C10	Unspecified	
	C11	Degreased	Treatment with organic solvent
	C12	Chemically cleaned	Use of inhibited chemical cleaner
	C1x	Other	To be specified
Etched	C20	Unspecified	
	C21	Fine matte	Use of tri-sodium phosphate, 3–6 oz per gal, at 140–160°F for 3–5 min
	C22	Medium matte	Use of sodium hydroxide (caustic soda), 4–6 oz per gal, at 140–150°F for 5 to 10 min
	C23	Coarse matte	Use of sodium fluoride, 1½ oz plus sodium hydroxide, 4-6 oz per gal, at 140-150°F for 5 to 10 min
	C2x	Other	To be specified
Brightened	C30	Unspecified	
	C31	Highly specular	Use of bright dip solution of a proprietary phosphoric-nitric acid type or proprietary electro-brightening or electropolishing treatment
	C32	Diffuse bright	Use of etched finish C22 followed by brightening finish C31
	C3x	Other	To be specified
Chemical conversion coatings	C40	Unspecified	
	C41	Acid chromate-fluoride	Use of proprietary chemicals producing clear to typically yellowish color
	C42	Acid chromate-fluoride-phosphate	Use of proprietary chemicals producing clear to typically greenish color
	C43	Alkaline chromate	Use of proprietary chemicals producing clear to typically gray color
	C4x	Other	To be specified

Table 8. Standard designations for anodic coatings on aluminum

All designations are to be preceded by the letters AA to identify them as Aluminum Association designations. From Designation System for Aluminum Finishes, *Aluminum Association, 1976.*

Type of finish	Designation	Description	Examples of method of finishing
General	A10	Unspecified anodic coatings	
	A11	Preparation for other applied coatings	0.1 mil coating produced in 15% sulfuric acid used at 70 ± 2°F, 12 amp/sq ft for 10 min
	A12	Chromic acid coating	To be specified
	A13	Hard, abrasion-resistant coating	To be specified
	A1x	Other	To be specified
Protective and decorative (coating less than 0.4 mil thickness)	A21	Clear coating	Coating thickness to be specified. 15% sulfuric acid used at 70 ± 2°F, at 12 amp/sq ft
	A211	Clear coating anodizing	Coating thickness—0.1 mil min; weight—4 mg/in.^{2} min
	A212	Clear coating anodizing	Coating thickness—0.2 mil min; weight—8 mg/in.^{2} min
	A213	Clear coating anodizing	Coating thickness—0.3 mil min; weight—12 mg/in.^{2} min
	A22	Coating with integral color	Coating thickness to be specified. Color dependent on alloy and process used
	A221	Coating with integral color	Coating thickness—0.1 mil min; weight—4 mg/in^2 min
	A222	Coating with integral color	Coating thickness—0.2 mil min; weight—8 mg/in^2 min
	A223	Coating with integral color	Coating thickness—0.2 mil min; weight depends on process—12 mg/in^2 min
	A23	Coating with impregnated color	Coating thickness to be specified. 15% sulfuric acid used at 70 ± 2°F, 12 amp/sq ft, followed by dyeing with organic or inorganic colors
	A231	Coating with impregnated color	Coating thickness—0.1 mil min; weight—4 mg/in.^{2} min
	A232	Coating with impregnated color	Coating thickness—0.2 mil min; weight—8 mg/in.^{2} min
	A233	Coating with impregnated color	Coating thickness—0.3 mil min; weight—12 mg/in.^{2} min
	A24	Coating with electrolytically deposited color	Coating thickness to be specified. 15% sulfuric acid used at 70 ± 2°F, 12 amp/sq ft, followed by electrolytic deposition of inorganic pigment, in coating
	A2x	Other	To be specified

Table 8 (cont.). Standard designations for anodic coatings on aluminum

Type of finish	Designation	Description	Examples of method of finishing
Architectural Class II (coatings with 0.4 to 0.7 mil thickness)	A31	Clear coating	Treatment with 15% sulfuric acid at 70 ± 2°F, 12 amp/sq ft for 30 min, or equivalent
	A32	Coating with integral color	Color dependent on alloy and process specified
	A33	Coating with impregnated color	Treatment with 15% sulfuric acid at 70 ± 2°F, 12 amp/sq ft for 30 min, followed by dyeing with organic or inorganic colors
	A34	Coating with electrolytically deposited color	15% sulfuric acid at 70 ± 2°F, 12 amp/sq ft for 30 min, followed by electrolytic deposition of inorganic pigment in coating
	A3x	Other	To be specified
Architectural Class I (coatings of 0.7 mil or greater)	A41	Clear (natural)	Treatment with 15% sulfuric acid at 70 ± 2°F, 12 amp/sq ft for 60 min or equivalent
	A42	Coating with integral color	Color dependent on alloy and process specified
	A43	Coating with impregnated color	Treatment with 15% sulfuric acid at 70 ± 2°F, 12 amp/sq ft for 60 min, followed by dyeing with organic or inorganic color or equivalent
	A44	Coating with electrolytically deposited color	15% sulfuric acid at 70 ± 2°F, 12 amp/sq ft for 60 min, followed by electrolytic deposition of inorganic pigment in the coating
	A4x	Other	To be specified

Table 9. Appearance matching of natural anodized aluminum alloys (alloys having same preparatory and Class I anodizing treatment)*

Courtesy Architectural Aluminum Manufacturers Association

Match with alloy	Sheet and plate			Extrusions		Castings
	Alloy 1100	Alloy 3003	Alloy 5005	Alloy 6061	Alloy 6063	Alloy F214
1100	Good	Poor	Good	Poor	Good	Good
3003	Poor	Good	Poor	Fair	Poor	Poor
5005	Good	Poor	Good	Poor	Good	Good
6061	Poor	Fair	Poor	Good	Poor	Poor
6063	Good	Poor	Good	Poor	Good	Good

For color matching of anodized proprietary alloys, consult the metal producer.

NOTE: It is important to recognize that color uniformity is not always obtainable, even with items of the same alloy. Matches indicated as "Good" in the above table, even though the best obtainable, should not necessarily be assumed to be consistently excellent.

Table 10. Thickness of copper sheet and strip*

Weight, ounces per sq ft	Theoretical thickness, in.	Minimum thickness, in. at any point
32	0.0431	0.0405
24	0.0323	0.0295
20	0.0270	0.0245
16	0.0216	0.0190
12	0.0163	0.0141
10	0.0135	0.0120
8	0.0108	0.0090

Applicable to sheet and strip furnished flat up to 36″ wide, inclusive, and up to 120″ long, inclusive. Thickness calculated for a unit weight of 0.322 pounds per cubic inch.

Data supplied by the Copper Development Association, Inc.

Copper and its alloys were the first metals used by man. Many bronze artifacts exist today which were made more than 5000 years ago, proving the remarkable durability of this metal.

The Copper Development Association lists a total of 178 standard coppers and copper alloys, classified in nine groups: coppers, brasses, leaded brasses, tin brasses, phosphor bronzes, silicon bronzes, nickel silvers, cupro-nickels, and beryllium copper.

Fortunately for the architect only a few of these alloys are generally used in building construction. They are:

Alloy 110—copper
122—copper
220—commercial bronze
230—red brass
260—cartridge brass
280—Muntz metal
385—architectural bronze
655—silicon bronze
745—nickel silver
796—leaded nickel silver

Data on the composition, color, and physical properties of these ten alloys are given in Table 12.

Alloy 110 (copper) is used principally in the form of sheet and strip for roofing, flashing, and gutters. It is generally specified by weight in ounces per square foot. Equivalent thicknesses in decimals of an inch are shown in Table 10.

Historically, bronze has been defined as

Table 11. Color matching of copper alloys

COLOR MATCHING: alloys to be used in various forms, for best color match with certain sheet and plate alloys. Color of surfaces compared after identical grinding or polishing.

Sheet and plate alloys	Forms to be matched in color					
	Extrusions	Castings	Fasteners	Tube & pipe	Rod & wire	Filler metals
Alloy 110 Alloy 122 copper	Alloy 110 copper (simple shapes)	Copper (99.9 min.)	Alloy 651 low-silicon bronze (fair)	Alloy 122 copper	Alloy 110 copper	Alloy 189 copper
Alloy 220 commercial bronze, 90%	Alloy 314 leaded commercial bronze	Alloy 834	Alloy 651 low-silicon bronze	Alloy 220 commercial bronze, 90%	Alloy 220 commercial bronze, 90%	Alloy 655 high-silicon bronze
Alloy 230 red brass, 85%	Alloy 385 architectural bronze	Alloy 836*	Alloy 651 low-silicon bronze (fair) Alloy 280 Muntz metal	Alloy 230 red brass, 85%	Alloy 230 red brass, 85%	Alloy 655 high-silicon bronze (fair)
Alloy 260 cartridge brass, 70%	Alloy 260 cartridge brass, 70% (simple shapes)	Alloys 852, 853	Alloy 260 cartridge brass, 70% Alloy 360 Alloy 464 Alloy 465	Alloy 260 cartridge brass, 70%	Alloy 260 cartridge brass, 70%	Alloy 681 low-fuming bronze (poor)
Alloy 280 Muntz metal	Alloy 385 architectural bronze	Alloys 855* 857	Alloy 651 low-silicon bronze (fair) Alloy 280 Muntz metal	Alloy 230 red brass, 85%	Alloy 280 Muntz metal	Alloy 681 low-fuming bronze
Alloy 655 high-silicon bronze	Alloy 655 (simple shapes)	Alloy 875	Alloy 651 low-silicon bronze Alloy 655 high-silicon bronze	Alloy 651 low-silicon bronze Alloy 655 high-silicon bronze	Alloy 651 low-silicon bronze Alloy 655 high-silicon bronze	Alloy 655 high-silicon bronze
Alloy 745 nickel-silver	Alloy 796 leaded nickel-silver	Alloy 973	Alloy 745 nickel-silver	Alloy 745 nickel-silver	Alloy 745 nickel-silver	Alloy 773 nickel-silver

There is a color-matching casting alloy occasionally used by architectural metals fabricators in lieu of Alloys 836 and 855. It has a nominal composition of 82.0% copper, 2.5% tin, 2.5% lead, and 13.0% zinc.

Table 12. Composition, color, and physical properties of copper alloys

ALLOY NUMBER—COMPOSITION—COLOR	PHYSICAL PROPERTIES	ENGLISH	METRIC	FORMS AVAILABLE (commonly used forms are in boldface type)	SPECIFICATION STANDARDS
110 copper nominal composition: 99.9% copper color: natural—salmon red weathered—from reddish-brown to gray-green patina in six years	coefficient of thermal expansion	.0000094 per F	.0000170 per C	lead coated sheet	ASTM B101
				bar rod	ASTM B133
	modulus of elasticity	17.000.000 psi	117.200 Mpa	**strip** **sheet** plate	ASTM B152
	tensile strength:			building construction—sheet strip	ASTM B370
	cold rolled temper sheet	36.000 psi	248 Mpa	pipe	
	cold rolled high yield sheet	40.000 psi	276 Mpa	tube	
				wire	
122 copper nominal composition: 99.9% copper .02% phosphorous color: natural—salmon red weathered—from reddish-brown to gray-green patina in six years	coefficient of thermal expansion	.0000094 per F	.0000170 per C	pipe	ASTM B42
				rod	ASTM B133
	modulus of elasticity	17.000.000 psi	117.200 Mpa	plate sheet strip rolled bar	ASTM B152
				threadless pipe	ASTM B302
				welded tube	ASTM B447
	tensile strength:			**tube**	ASTM B75
	cold rolled high yield sheet	40.000 psi	276 Mpa		ASTM B88
220 commercial bronze nominal composition: 90% copper 10% zinc color: natural—red gold weathered—from brown to gray-green patina in six years	coefficient of thermal expansion	.0000102 per F	.0000184 per C	plate sheet **strip** rolled bar	ASTM B36
	modulus of elasticity	17.000.000 psi	117.200 Mpa	**wire**	ASTM B134
				tube	ASTM B135
	tensile strength:			**rod**	
	half hard sheet	52.000 psi	360 Mpa	**bar**	
230 red brass nominal composition: 85% copper 15% zinc color: natural—reddish yellow weathered—from chocolate brown to gray-green patina in six years	coefficient of thermal expansion	.0000104 per F	.0000187 per C	bar plate sheet **strip**	ASTM B36
	modulus of elasticity	17.000.000 psi	117.200 Mpa	**pipe**	ASTM B43
				wire	ASTM B134
	tensile strength:			**tube**	ASTM B135
	half hard sheet	57.000 psi	393 Mpa	rod	
260 cartridge brass nominal composition: 70% copper 30% zinc color: natural—yellow	coefficient of thermal expansion	.0000111 per F	.0000199 per C	plate sheet **strip** rolled bar	ASTM B26
	modulus of elasticity	16.000.000 psi	110.300 Mpa	wire	ASTM B134
				tube	ASTM B135
	tensile strength:			pipe	
	half hard sheet	62.000 psi	427 Mpa	rod	

Table 12 (cont.).   Composition, color, and physical properties of copper alloys

ALLOY NUMBER COMPOSITION—COLOR	PHYSICAL PROPERTIES	ENGLISH	METRIC	FORMS AVAILABLE (commonly used forms are in boldface type)	SPECIFICATION STANDARDS
280 Muntz metal **nominal composition:** 60% copper 40% zinc **color:** natural—reddish yellow weathered—from red brown to gray-brown in six years	coefficient of thermal expansion modulus of elasticity tensile strength: half hard sheet	.0000110 per F 15,000,000 psi 70,000 psi	.0000208 per C 103,400 Mpa 483 Mpa	tube bar **plate** **sheet** **strip** bar rod **strip** wire	ASTM B135 QQ-B-613 (federal specification) QQ-B-626
385 architectural bronze **nominal composition:** 57% copper 3% lead 40% zinc **color:** natural—reddish yellow weathered—from russet-brown to dark brown in six years	coefficient of thermal expansion modulus of elasticity tensile strength	.0000116 per F 14,000,000 psi 60,000 psi	.0000209 per C 96,500 Mpa 414 Mpa	**extrusions** **bar** **rod** wire	ASTM B455
655 silicon bronze **nominal composition:** 97% copper 3% silicon **color:** natural—reddish old gold weathered—from russet brown to finely mottled dark grey-brown in four years	coefficient of thermal expansion modulus of elasticity tensile strength	.0000100 per F 15,000,000 psi 78,000 psi	.0000180 per C 103,400 Mpa 538 Mpa	**plate** **sheet** **strip** rolled bar bar rod shapes wire **pipe** **tube**	ASTM B97 ASTM B98 ASTM B99 ASTM B315
745 nickel silver **nominal composition:** 65% copper 25% zinc 10% nickel **color:** natural—warm silver weathered—from gray-brown to finely mottled gray-green in six years	coefficient of thermal expansion modulus of elasticity tensile strength	.0000091 per F 17,500,000 psi 73,000 psi	.0000164 per C 120,700 Mpa 503 Mpa	plate **sheet** **strip** bar rod wire **tube**	ASTM B122 ASTM B151 ASTM B206
796 leaded nickel silver **nominal composition:** 45% copper 42% zinc 10% nickel 2% manganese 1% lead **color:** natural—warm silver weathered—from gray-brown to finely mottled gray-green in six years	coefficient of thermal expansion modulus of elasticity tensile strength: extrusions	.000011 per F 16,000,000 psi 60,000 psi	.0000198 per C 110,300 Mpa 414 Mpa	**bar** **extrusions** **rod**	none applicable

Table 13. Standard designations for mechanical finishes for copper alloys

Courtesy National Association of Architectural Metal Manufacturers.

Type of finish	Designation	Description	Example of methods of finishing
As fabricated	M10	Unspecified mill finish	Optional with finisher
	M11	Specular as fabricated	Cold rolling with polished steel rolls
	M12	Matte finish as fabricated	Cold rolling followed by annealing; hot rolling, extruding, casting
	M1x	Other	To be specified
Buffed	M20	Unspecified	Optional with finisher
	M21	Smooth specular	Cutting with aluminum oxide or silicon carbide compounds, starting with relatively coarse grits and finishing with 320 grit, using a peripheral wheel speed of 6,000 fpm, followed by buffing with aluminum oxide buffing compounds using a peripheral wheel speed of 7,000 fpm
	M22	Specular	Cutting with compounds as for the M21 finish, followed by a final light buffing
	M2x	Other	To be specified
Directional textured	M30	Unspecified	Optional with finisher
	M31	Fine satin	Wheel or belt polishing with aluminum oxide or silicon carbide abrasives of 180–240 grit, using a peripheral speed of 6,000 fpm
	M32	Medium satin	Wheel or belt polishing with aluminum oxide or silicon carbide abrasives of 120–180 grit, using a peripheral wheel speed of 6,000 fpm
	M33	Coarse satin	Wheel or belt polishing with aluminum oxide or silicon carbide abrasives of 80–120 grit, using a peripheral wheel speed of 6,000 fpm
	M34	Hand rubbed	Hand rubbing with No. 0 stainless steel wool and solvent, No. 0 pumice and solvent, nonwoven abrasive mesh pad or Turkish oil and emery
	M35	Brushed	Brushing with rotary stainless steel, brass, or nickel silver wire wheel. Coarseness of finish controlled by diameter and speed of wheel and pressure exerted
			Wheel polishing with aluminum oxide or silicon carbide abrasive compounds of 50–150 grit on packed or loose muslin buffs at peripheral speeds of from 3,500–5,500 fpm
	M36	Uniform	Wheel or belt polishing in a single pass with aluminum oxide or silicon carbide abrasives of 60–80 grit, using a peripheral speed of 6,000 fpm
	M3x	Other	To be specified
Nondirectional textured	M40	Unspecified	Optional with finisher
	M41	(Number unassigned)	
	M42	Fine matte	Air blast with No. 100–200 mesh silica sand or aluminum oxide. Air pressure 30–90 lb. Gun 12 in. from work at an angle of 60–90 deg
	M43	Medium matte	Air blast with No. 40–80 mesh silica sand or aluminum oxide. Air pressure 30–90 lb. Gun 12 in. from work at an angle of 60–90 deg
	M44	Coarse matte	Air blast with No. 20 mesh silica sand or aluminum oxide. Air pressure 30–90 lb. Gun 12 in. from work at an angle of 60–90 deg
	M45	Fine shot blast	Air blast with S-70 metal shot
	M46	Medium shot blast	Air blast with S-230 metal shot
	M47	Coarse shot blast	Air blast with S-550 metal shot
	M4x	Other	To be specified

Table 14. Standard designations for chemical finishes for copper alloys

Courtesy National Association of Architectural Metal Manufacturers

Type of finish	Designation	Description	Example of methods of finishing
Nonetched cleaned	C10	Unspecified	Optional with finisher
	C11	Degreased	Treatment with organic solvent
	C12	Chemically cleaned	Use of inhibited chemical cleaner
	C1x	Other	To be specified
Conversion coatings	C50	Ammonium chloride *(patina)*	Saturated solution of commercial sal ammoniac, spray or bush applied. Repeated applications may be required.
	C51	Cuprous chloride Hydrochloric acid *(patina)*	In 500 ml of warm water, dissolve 164 g cuprous chloride crystals, 117 ml hydrochloric acid, 69 ml glacial acetic acid, 80 g ammonium chloride, 11 g arsenic trioxide. Dilute to 1 liter. Apply by spray, brush, or stippling. Repeated applications may be required. Avoid use of aluminum containers.
	C52	Ammonium sulfate *(patina)*	Dissolve in 1 liter of warm water, 111 g ammonium sulfate, 3.5 g copper sulfate, 1.6 ml concentrated ammonia. Spray apply. 6–8 applications may be required under high humidity conditions.
	C53	Carbonate *(patina)*	Various formulations utilizing copper carbonate as the major constituent.
	C54	Oxide *(statuary)*	Principal formulations utilize aqueous solutions of copper sulfates and copper nitrates at temperatures of from 85°C to boiling or permanganate solutions at temperatures of from 80°C to boiling, using immersion periods of from 30 sec to 5 min.
	C55	Sulfide *(statuary)*	2–10% aqueous solutions of ammonium sulfide, potassium sulfide, or sodium sulfide. Solutions swabbed or brushed on. Repeated application increases depth of color.
	C5x	Other	To be specified.

an alloy in which the chief constituents are copper and tin, and brass as an alloy in which the chief constituents are copper and zinc. Based on this definition, only the present architectural casting alloy could be classified as a bronze; the other copper alloys in common architectural use would be brasses since they contain no tin. The justification for designating these alloys as "bronzes" is that they resemble tin bronze in color, both in the natural finish and in the weathered state. It is unlikely that the use of the word "bronze" for the principal copper alloys used in architectural work will ever be superseded.

Not all alloys are available in all forms. It is therefore necessary for the architect to know which alloys are good color matches. The most widely used combination of color-matching alloys is architectural bronze for extrusions, Muntz metal for sheets and fastenings, and red brass for drawn shapes such as tubes and bars. Full data on the color matching of copper alloys is provided in Table 11.

Cartridge brass is the familiar yellow brass used mostly indoors for hardware, lighting fixtures, railings, fireplace equipment, candlesticks, and the like.

Nickel silver contains no silver; its white color results from the presence of nickel and zinc.

Standard designations for mechanical and chemical finishes for copper alloys are given in Tables 13 and 14, respectively.

By E. S. KOPECKI, *Committee of Stainless Steel Producers, American Iron and Steel Institute*

The most striking characteristics of the stainless steels for architectural applications are outstanding resistance to corrosion, great strength, excellent formability, and enduring beauty. They are contemporary materials that have been proven by extensive use both in and on buildings for more than a half a century. Although stainless steels were once regarded as luxury items, their economic benefits are now widely recognized.

TYPES OF STAINLESS STEEL

There are 57 stainless steels recognized by American Iron and Steel Institute (AISI) as standard compositions. Also available are numerous proprietary or special-purpose stainless steels.

Technically speaking, stainless steels are iron-base alloys containing 10 per cent or more chromium, which imparts corrosion resistance. Other alloying elements may be added to enhance certain characteristics, such as formability, weldability, machinability, strength, hardness, corrosion resistance, or a combination thereof. Nickel, for example, improves fabrication characteristics and corrosion resistance to acid environments. High chromium content improves corrosion and oxidation resistance, especially at elevated temperatures whereas molybdenum in small quantities increases resistance to corrosion in chloride environments, such as at sea coast locations.

Stainless steels used in architecture are grouped into three metallurgical categories, with alloys in each category tending to have similar characteristics. These categories are *austenitic, ferritic,* and *martensitic.*

Austenitic stainless steels contain iron, chromium, and nickel as the principal alloying elements, and they are identified by AISI 200 or 300 Series numbers. Characterized as having excellent corrosion resistance, unusually good fabricability, and good strength, which is increased by cold working, the austenitic stainless steels are the most frequently used types. The general-purpose austenitic grade is *Type 304,* which contains about 18 per cent chromium and 8 per cent nickel. It is sometimes referred to as 18-8 stainless, and is widely used for architectural purposes.

Ferritic stainless steels, which are identified by AISI 400 Series numbers, contain about 17 per cent chromium, but no nickel. Consequently they have good corrosion resistance but are only slightly hardenable by cold working. The general-purpose grade of this group is *Type 430,* which is frequently used for interior architectural applications.

Martensitic stainless steels, which are also identified by AISI 400 Series numbers, are likewise straight-chromium types. The chromium levels in this group, however, are around 12 per cent, such as in the general-purpose *Type 410,* so they have considerably less corrosion resistance as compared to the ferritic and austenitic types. They do not contain nickel, and they are not hardenable by cold working. But the carbon content is adjusted so as to allow hardening by thermal treatment, much in the same manner as martensitic steels.

The 200 and 300 Series stainless steels are generally not attracted to a magnet, whereas the 400 Series types are strongly magnetic. This serves as a quick method of identification.

For architectural applications, the appropriate types have been well established through years of practical experience, namely types 201, 301, 302, 304, 316, 410, and 430.

Type 302 is an often-specified alternate to Type 304, but for architectural applications there is virtually no difference between the two.

Type 316 contains 2 to 3 per cent molybdenum and is sometimes used for architectural applications where chlorides may be present in the environment, such as along sea coasts or in heavily industrialized areas.

Type 301 has a slightly different chromium-nickel ratio than Type 304 thereby giving it higher strength properties resulting from cold working, as would occur with roll-formed structural components. For example, tensile strengths exceeding 200,000 lb/in.^{2} can be achieved with Type 301, yet it maintains good ductility.

Type 201 is approximately equivalent to Type 301, but it has somewhat higher strength. in Type 201, manganese substitutes for some of the nickel.

STRENGTH PROPERTIES

Table 15 lists the chemical composition ranges and typical mechanical property val-

ues for the seven "architectural" stainless steels. Designers should note that the table shows *nominal* values and should refer to appropriate ASTM standard specifications for specific design data, as suggested in Table 16.

Because of the unusual strength characteristics of stainless steels, such as the significant effect of cold working on the austenitic grades, the design formulae developed for carbon steel as found in AISC specifications should not be applied (see Fig. 1). Available from AISI is a publication entitled "Stainless Steel Cold-Formed Structural Design Manual—1974 Edition" that will help architects and specifiers better understand and more effectively use the higher strength characteristics of stainless steels for structural applications.

ASTM A666-72 provides minimum strength values for types 201, 301, 302, 304 and 316 in four grades or conditions. ¼-hard, and half-hard tempers. In brief:

Grade A   30,000 lb/in.^{2} minimum yield
Grade B   40,000 lb/in.^{2} minimum yield
Grade C   75,000 lb/in.^{2} minimum yield
Grade D   100,000 lb/in.^{2} minimum yield

BASIC USE

Typical exterior applications of stainless steels include curtain walls, spandrel panels, mullions, windows, entrances, storefronts, doors, flashings, roofs, railings, column covers, facias, louvers, and grilles. Interior applications include wall panels, railings, elevator doors and interiors, stairways, escalators, and kitchen equipment. Hidden applications for stainless steel include anchors, snap ties, and through-wall flashing.

In selecting stainless steels for these applications, a number of characteristics should be considered. These include:

Appearance and durability
Compatibility with other materials
Strength
Minimum maintenance
Fabricability

Appearance and durability are directly related to corrosion resistance. The resistance of stainless steels to atmospheric corrosion is excellent except where high levels of chlo-

Stainless steels

Table 15. Composition and mechanical and physical properties of the principal stainless steels

	AISI TYPE						
	201	301	302	304	316	410	430
Nominal Composition %							
Chromium	16-18	16-18	17-19	18-20	16-18	11.5-13.5	16-18
Nickel	3.50-5.50	6-8	8-10	8-10.5	10-14	—	—
Manganese	5.50-7.50	2.0Max	2.00Max	2.0Max	2.0Max	1.0Max	1.0Max
Molybdenum	—	—	—	—	2-3	—	—
Carbon	0.15Max	0.15Max	0.15Max	0.08Max	0.08Max	0.15Max	0.12Max
Representative Mechanical Properties (sheet & strip annealed)							
Tensile 1000psi (MPa)	95(6551)	110(758)	90(621)	84(579)	84(579)	70(483)	75(517)
Yield 1000psi (MPa) (0.2% Offset)	45(310)	40(276)	40(276)	42(290)	42(290)	45(310)	50(345)
Elongation in 2" %	40	60	50	55	50	25	25
Modulus of Elasticity, psi x 10⁶ (GPa)	28.6(197)	28.0(193)	28.0(193)	28.0(193)	28.0(193)	29.0(200)	29.0(200)
Hardness, Rockwell B	90	85	85	80	79	80	85
Physical Properties							
Weight, lb/cu.in. (kg/m³)	0.28(7780)	0.29(8060)	0.29(8060)	0.29(8060)	0.29(8060)	0.28(7780)	0.28(7780)
Thermal Conductivity at 212°F (100°C) btu/sq.ft./hr/deg F/ft (W/m·K)	9.4(0.113)	9.4(0.113)	9.4(0.113)	9.4(0.113)	9.4(0.113)	14.4(0.174)	15.1(0.182)
Coefficient of Thermal Expansion in/in/deg F x 10⁻⁶ 32 to 212°F (cm/cm/deg C x 10⁻⁶ 0 to 100°C)	8.7(15.7)	9.4(17.0)	9.6(17.3)	9.6(17.3)	8.9(15.9)	5.5(9.9)	5.8(10.4)

ride (or salt) content are encountered. Therefore, proximity to the ocean or other sources of chloride contamination could be a major concern. Sulfur contamination, which can cause atmospheric corrosion of other metals, is not particularly significant with stainless steels. The amount of rainfall is important only insofar as it reduces through natural washing the concentration of chlorides on the steel surface.

In rural or urban atmospheres types 301, 302, and 304 are generally used and give long service without significant changes in appearance. In industrial atmospheres free of chloride contamination, the same steels will provide long-time service and will remain free of rust staining. A film of dirt can be expected to form on the surface but when this film is removed the stainless steel will be found to be unattacked and to have retained its original bright appearance.

In marine atmospheres, types 301, 302, or 304 may develop some rust staining when exposed to salt sprays. The staining is usually superficial and can be easily removed. Type 316, which contains molybdenum, is essentially resistant to rust staining in marine environments.

Compatibility: Stainless steels are compatible both chemically and aesthetically with almost all common building materials. They can be used safely in contact with, or imbedded in stone, concrete, masonry, plaster or any other building materials. They do not stain marble or other light-colored materials with which they may be in contact, nor does the wash from stainless steels stain adjacent materials.

The relatively low coefficient of expansion in comparison to aluminum—⅛ in. in 10 ft per 100°F of temperature change (9.4 x 10⁻⁶ in./in./°F)—permits stainless steels to be used in long members or large panels and minimizes the need for expansion joints.

The flexibility and elasticity of stainless steel permit the use of higher temper stainless steel with "spring-back" for bellows construction to provide for the differential movement between wall panels and supporting structure caused by thermal expansion and contraction. Flexibility and elasticity also permit the use of snap-in components such as glazing stops and mullion covers. At the other extreme, fully annealed or "dead soft" stainless steel has no spring-back and is suitable for conditions where on-site fabrication—as in flashing—is common.

Strength: Stainless steels are by far the strongest of the architectural metals. For instance, in some hardened and tempered grades, tensile strengths of up to 300,000 lb/in.² (2068 MPa) (0.2 per cent offset) can be achieved.

Maintenance: Stainless steels are basically self cleaning in that when they are boldly exposed to the washing effects of rain, they remain clean and bright, thus minimizing the need for maintenance. In dry climates or where surfaces are protected from the elements, periodic cleaning will keep stainless steels looking their best.

Fabricability: Because the manufacture of some architectural products may involve machining or cold-heading operations, other stainless steel types are sometimes used for improved productivity. For instance, if machining is involved in the manufacture of a product, a free-machining stainless steel will provide better machining rates at lower cost. If either type 302 or 304 were selected for a particular application, type 303 stainless steel is the free-machining grade that has similar qualities. The free-machining counterparts for types 410 and 430 are types 416 and 430F, respectively.

Some products may be formed in cold-heading machines, in which case it would be more desirable for the manufacturer to use a stainless steel with better cold-working characteristics. One widely used grade is type 305, which has better cold-forming characteristics than type 304.

SIZES AND SHAPES

Stainless steels are available from steel producers and steel service centers as sheet, strip, plate, bar, wire, tubing, and pipe. Table 17 shows how the various mill forms are classified by size. Familiarity with each of these mill product forms can help the specifier achieve simple and economical solutions to design problems. It is suggested that specifiers check with stainless steel producers prior to specifying mill products, to verify suitability of application and availability.

Gages

Economy in the use of stainless steel generally is needed to be competitive with other architectural metals. The architect can compensate for the higher initial unit cost of stainless steel by utilizing its greater strength and corrosion resistance to reduce the thickness of sections or to eliminate the need for secondary framing. For maximum economy, the architect can consider the following possibilities:

Use the least expensive type of stainless steel and product form suitable for the application.

Use rolled finishes.

Use the thinnest gage possible. Consider textured patterns or continuously backed sheets.

Use standard roll-formed sections, and keep them simple.

Use long lengths to minimize joints.

Suggestions on specific thicknesses to use with various applications are shown in Fig. 2.

When working with thin-gage material, there is potential for optical distortion, espe-

Table 16. ASTM standards

| Product Form | Stainless Steel Type | | | | | | |
	201	301	302	304	316	410	430
Plate	A412	A167	A167	A167	A167	A176	A176
	——	A177	A177	——	——	——	——
	A480	A480	A480	A480	A480	A480	A480
	——	A666	A666	A666	A666	——	——
Sheet and	A412	A167	A167	A167	A167	A176	A176
Strip	——	A177	A177	——	——	——	——
	A480	A480	A480	A480	A480	A480	A480
	——	A666	A666	A666	A666	——	——
Bar	A429	——	A276	A276	A276	A276	A276
	A484	——	A484	A484	A484	A484	A484
Wire	——	A368	A368				
	——	——	A492	A492	A492	——	——
	——	——	A580	A580	A580	A580	A580
Pipe and Tubing	——	A554	A554	A544	A554	——	A554

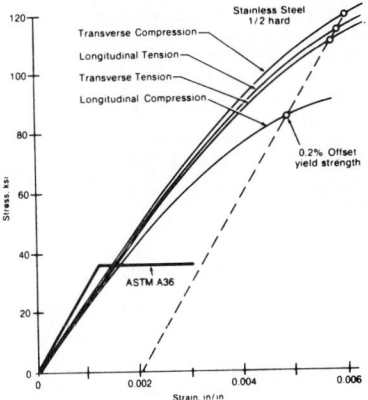

Fig. 1. Representative stress–strain curve for half-hard stainless steel and mild steel

cially in large flat panels. The principal contributing factors are failure to provide adequate stiffness in the component and failure to accommodate movement, such as might be caused by wind loading or thermal expansion.

An excellent method for enhancing stiffness is to curve the panel concavely. Or long, flat panels can be stiffened by formed grooves, flutes, or ribs, or large panel areas can be given a sculptured effect by brake forming. Textured or embossed sheets also increase panel stiffness, or stiffeners can be attached to the back. One technique is to laminate a thin-gage sheet to a continuous rigid backing, such as exterior grade plywood or hardboard. Channels, tees, or angles (roll-formed of light-gage stainless) can be attached to the back for stiffness. In adding attachments to the back, allowances should be made to accommodate movement. Stainless steel panels with honeycomb cores provide strong, light-weight, flat modular units.

Teflon washers and sufficiently large slots for mounting fasteners will allow the various components in a panel section to move. Also, good design will allow for movement between panels, and between panels and the building.

Other factors can also help. These include stretcher-leveled sheets, appropriate finish, proper fabrication, and correct installation.

FINISHES

The unique combination of attractive surface and inherent resistance to corrosion is often the reason stainless steels are selected for ornamental architectural metalwork. Because of these exceptional properties, mechanical finishes, (rolled-and-polished finishes) are predominantly specified. However, coatings or chemical and electro-chemical finishes, which include painting and porcelain enameling, acid etching, electropolishing and oxide conversion surface coloring, are also used to a limited extent in architecture.

Mechanical finishes are produced by three basic methods. These are (1) rolling between polished or textured rolls; (2) polishing and/or buffing with abrasive wheels, belts or pads; (3) blasting with abrasive grit or glass beads. The resulting surface textures vary from the dull appearance produced by hot or cold rolling to mirror-bright surfaces. The most widely used are the mechanically polished finishes, which are characterized by fine parallel grit lines.

The finishes resulting from rolling are unpolished surface textures resulting from the initial forming of the metal. They are the simplest and lowest cost finishes obtainable, yet they are available in a wide range of appearances. Rolls can be highly polished to produce a bright, reflective finish or etched to produce a dull matte finish.

Patterned finishes are also imparted to sheet by rolling, and they are available in a wide variety of sculptural designs and textures. These are produced either by passing mill finish sheet between two machined-matched design rolls, impressing patterns on both sides of the sheet, or by a variation of this process, and they generally contribute added stiffness as well as a decorative texture, while reducing optical distortions. These

finishes are supplied by some mills and by secondary processors.

Polished finishes are produced by successive processes of grinding and polishing, and sometimes buffing, which vary in cost depending on the number of operations involved. The standard AISI finish designations (Table 18) adequately describe these finishes.

Blast finish methods employ special equipment which bombards the stainless steel surface with abrasive grit or glass beads to produce a nondirectional matte finish. With the development of portable blast equipment, blast finishes offer the advantage of blendability and permit shop or field refinishing after welding and grinding.

Electropolishing produces a finish with a bright luster on either polished or unpolished surfaces by means of an electrolytic bath.

Coatings and surface conversion finishes are used for architectural applications of stainless steel to a limited extent. Coatings such as porcelain enamel, are occasionally used to produce colored finishes on stainless steel. Since applied coatings are not required for protection against corrosion, their use is largely restricted to color accent and trim.

Oxide conversion coatings are produced by carefully controlled chemical and heat treatment of the metal surface. This process provides colors ranging from pale gray to black. A matte finish can be produced by acid etching.

Finishing can be performed at any of several stages in the production/fabrication/installation sequence. Sheet and strip are available as stock items in a choice of standard mechanical finishes. In addition, producers offer a variety of rolled and polished proprietary finishes.

The fabricator usually finishes or refinishes assemblies or components to meet specified appearance requirements or to remove tool or weld marks. Since fabricator finishes vary

Table 17. Classification of stainless steel product forms

Item	Description	Dimensions		
		Thickness	Width	Dia. or Size
Sheet	Coils and cut lengths; Mill finishes Nos.			
	1, 2D & 2B	under 3/16"	24" & over	——
	Pol. finishes Nos.			
	3, 4, 6, 7 & 8	" "	all widths	——
Strip	Cold-finished, coils or cut lengths	under 3/16"	under 24"	——
Plates	Flat rolled or forged	3/16" & over	over 10"	——
Bars	Hot-finished rounds, squares, octagons and hexagons	——	——	1/4" & over
	Hot finished flats	1/8" & over	1/4" to 10" incl.	——
	Cold-finished rounds, squares, octagons and hexagons	——	——	over 1/2"
	Cold-finished flats	1/8" & over	3/8" & over	——
Wire	Cold-finished only: round, square, octagon, hexagon, flat wire	0.010" to under 3/16"	1/16" to under 3/8"	1/2" & under
Pipe and Tubing	Several different classifications, with differing specifications, are available. For information on standard sizes consult Committee of Stainless Steel Producers.			
Extrusions	Not considered "standard" shapes, but of potential architectural interest. Currently limited in size to approximately 6½" diameter circle, or structurals to 5" diameter.			

1" = 25.4 mm

Fig. 2. General thickness guidelines for architectural applications

1" = 25.4mm

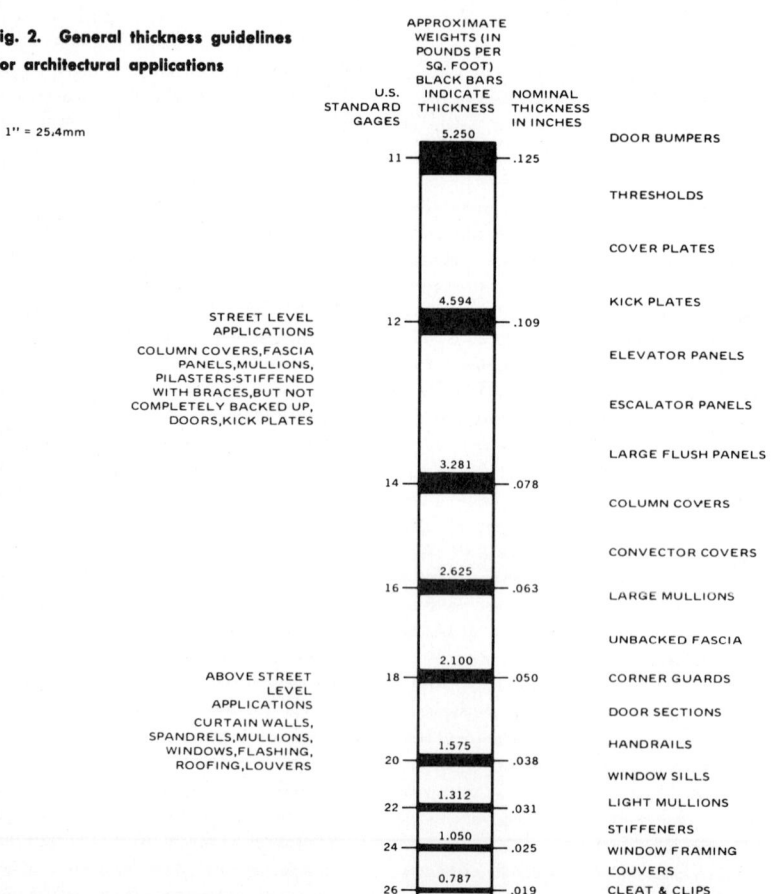

This chart is intended as a general guide only. For recommendations on specific applications, the designer should contact a stainless steel producer or fabricator.

in appearance from industry standards due to differences in equipment and finishing techniques, specifications and verbal descriptions should be supplemented by actual finish samples to assure desired appearance.

Selection of finish is normally determined by both functional and aesthetic requirements. For example, installations that require the removal of evidence of exposed welds preclude the use of rolled, nondirectional finishes that cannot be blended or refinished.

Sheet finishes are described broadly by the operations used to obtain them, as shown in Table 18. Stainless steel strip has three standard finishes, described by the finishing operations employed in their production. No. 1 strip finish is approximately the same as No. 2D sheet finish. It varies in appearance from dull gray matte to a fairly reflective surface, depending largely upon the composition of the alloy. No. 2 strip finish is approximately the same as No. 2B sheet finish. It is a smoother, more reflective finish than No. 1 strip finish, and likewise varies with the composition of the alloy. A bright annealed finish is also available. It is a prior highly reflective finish retained by final annealing in a controlled-atmosphere furnace. For architectural uses a final buffing is often employed.

Samples: Since standard finishes vary on different products and because many nonstandard finishes are available, the architect should consult producers or fabricators and examine samples before making finish selection.

Finish availability: Sheet and strip products are available in all of the AISI standard mechanical finishes. However, No. 2B cold-rolled finish, which is usually subsequently refinished by the fabricator, and No. 4 polished finish are the most commonly used in architecture and are generally available in stocked sheet.

It is important to remember that most architectural finishes have a directional quality, which, if ignored, can result in a crazy-quilt like pattern when erected. Unless the architect plans to create special visual effects by mixing finishes, the specifier should call for one type of finish and to specify that all panels be fabricated and installed with the grain parallel and running in the same direction.

LIMITATIONS

Stainless steels have few limitations. Care in handling is always important with stainless as it is with any architectural metal, to preserve the surface finish from damage. Materials used to clean masonry, such as muriatic, hydrochloric, and other chloride-base acids can damage stainless steels, so they should be used with care and promptly

Table 18. Standard mechanical sheet finishes

Unpolished or Rolled Finishes:

No. 1   A rough, dull surface which results from hot rolling to the specified thickness followed by annealing and descaling.

No. 2D   A dull finish which results from cold rolling followed by annealing and descaling, and may perhaps get a final light roll pass through unpolished rolls. A 2D finish is used where appearance is of no concern.

No. 2B   A bright, cold-rolled finish resulting in the same manner as No. 2D finish, except that the annealed and descaled sheet receives a final light roll pass through polished rolls. This is the general-purpose cold-rolled finish that can be used as is, or as a preliminary step to polishing.

Polished Finishes;

No. 3   An intermediate polish surface obtained by finishing with a 100-grit abrasive. Generally used where a semifinished polished surface is required. A No. 3 finish usually receives additional polishing during fabrication.

No. 4   A polished surface obtained by finishing with a 120–150 mesh abrasive, following initial grinding with coarser abrasives. This is a general-purpose bright finish with a visible "grain" which prevents mirror reflection.

No. 6   A dull satin finish having lower reflectivity than No. 4 finish. It is produced by Tampico brushing the No. 4 finish in a medium of abrasive and oil. It is used for architectural applications and ornamentation where a high luster is undesirable, and to contrast with brighter finishes.

No. 7   A highly reflective finish that is obtained by buffing finely ground surfaces but not to the extent of completely removing the "grit" lines. It is used chiefly for architectural and ornamental purposes.

No. 8   The most reflective surface, which is obtained by polishing with successively finer abrasives and buffing extensively until all grit lines from preliminary grinding operations are removed. It is used for applications such as mirrors and reflectors.

---

and thoroughly washed away. Salt-laden marine environments can stain surfaces and even cause pitting of the metal if they are not rinsed off regularly with fresh water. In highly polluted industrial areas, such as around chlorine plants or where a history of corrosion problems exist, attention should be given to the selection of the proper alloy.

GALVANIC RELATIONSHIPS

In addition to having excellent resistance to corrosion, stainless steels are among the least aggressive metals in causing galvanic corrosion with other architectural metals. The possibility of galvanic corrosion is of concern where dissimilar metals are in contact with one another, especially if galvanized or mild steel fasteners or aluminum are used to join stainless steel components. (See Sheet 1 and Table 4).

FABRICATION

In general, stainless steels are formed and assembled very much like mild steel. The stainless steels can be formed, cut, sheared, sawed, drilled, hammered, pressed, spun, rolled, forged, stretched, riveted, soldered, brazed, welded, and bolted by most of the conventional methods used in industry today.

There are differences, however, and understanding the differences is a requisite to successful and economical fabrication of stainless steels into architectural components.

For instance, the stainless steels in the 200 and 300 Series work-harden, which means that forming and bending equipment should be of the heavy-duty type, and it is sometimes necessary to anneal a workpiece between fabrication steps, or to select a grade that has better cold-forming characteristics — such as using type 305 instead of type 304.

If machining is an important manufacturing step, such as for fasteners or anchors, it would be useful to consider a free-machining stainless steel — such as type 303 instead of type 304.

Joining: In welding, it is well to know that stainless steels are poor conductors of heat; therefore, lower heat settings should be used on the welding machines. Welding rods should be selected according to the material being welded. In soldering, acid fluxes containing chlorides should be avoided. Instead, phosphoric acid type fluxes are preferred.

Mechanical Fastening: The methods and devices used for mechanical fastening of stainless steel parts are essentially the same as those used for other metals. A full selection of screws, bolts, studs, clips, and other fastening hardware is available in stainless steel. When joining stainless steel components, it is always good practice to use stainless steel fasteners.

Adhesive Fastening: Structural adhesives offer some interesting advantages and are gaining acceptance. Adhesives may be used to provide strong invisible attachments or continuous watertight seams, with no damage to the metal finish.

The technology of structural adhesives is developing at such a rapid pace that generalizations are inadvisable. Various adhesives are being used successfully to join or to laminate stainless steel to itself, to other metals, and to other materials. Because the adhesives cure with little or no applied heat, problems of heat-developed stresses or impairment of mechanical properties are avoided.

In some cases, acceptable joints can be made faster with adhesives than with other available methods.

Finishing: Stainless steels used in architectural applications are usually finished by the manufacturer or contractor prior to arrival at the job site. Little post installation work is necessary other than the removal of any protective films or paper that may have been applied to the stainless steel surface for protection during fabrication and shipment. Following the removal of the protective papers, the metal surfaces should be cleaned to remove adhesive residue.

MAINTENANCE

It should be emphasized that stainless steel performs best when clean and exposed to the atmosphere. Temporary protective coatings (film or paper) should be removed promptly after the need has ceased. Before washing and as work progresses, metal debris such as nails, filings, cuttings, drillings, etc., should be removed to avoid surface discoloration and possible localized surface pitting. Stainless steel may be cleaned after installation with ordinary detergent and clean water.

Muriatic (builder's) acid for cleaning masonry or similar hydrochloric acid-type cleaners must immediately be neutralized and scrubbed off with clean water if splashed, sprayed, spilled or otherwise brought into contact with a stainless steel component.

Porcelain enamel

By Porcelain Enamel Institute

Porcelain enamel is a highly durable alumina-borosilicate glass fused to metal under extreme heat. It has a wide variety of uses in the construction of commercial, industrial, and residential buildings.

Among the more important uses are curtain wall, veneer and fascia panels; roofing; siding; architectural graphics, including both electrical and non-illuminated signs; toilet partitions; escalator cladding; solar collector plates; sun shields; chalkboards; and industrial and medical clean rooms.

Porcelain enamel's design versatility plus the character of its impervious, inorganic, vitreous surface makes the material suitable for use wherever color stability, cleanability, ease of maintenance, freedom from reaction to chemicals, durability, and resistance to heat, abrasion, and corrosion are necessary or desirable.

APPLICATIONS

As an exterior wall material, the most popular current uses of porcelain-enameled panels are as curtain walls and fascias. Here the possibilities of color (almost unlimited), design, embossing, textures, and patterns can be fully exploited. Veneer panels are often used over masonry in new construction. They also provide architects with considerable design flexibility in modernizing the facades of existing buildings. Among the many advantages of porcelain-enamel veneer panels are light weight, ease of attachment, fast erection, minimum preparation of the existing facade, and little interference with the daily use of a building during modernization.

Porcelain enamel is commonly used for shower, toilet, and lavatory partitions. As an interior wall material, it is specially functional in bathrooms, kitchens, and industrial laboratory and hospital "clean" rooms. Matching enameled moldings are available.

METAL SUBSTRATES

The metal base (in architecture, generally steel, aluminum, or aluminized steel) to which the porcelain enamel is fused is usually fully fabricated prior to finishing to ensure the effectiveness of the coating. This requires complete forming, with joints and lugs welded and holes drilled.

Three principal types of steel are used for architectural porcelain enameling: (1) enameling steel of low metaloid and copper content, (2) "zero-carbon" steels designed for special porcelain-enamel application, and (3) conventional cold-rolled sheet steel.

Aluminum companies produce specially developed alloys for porcelain enameling. They are formulated for various end uses and yield various properties after being enameled. In most cases, the companies that developed them have labeled them with their own designations, but there are also several readily available alloys carrying industrywide designations that are recommended. Alloys 1100, 3003, and 6061 are usually used for sheet applications and 6061 and 7014 for extrusions. For castings, alloys 43 and 356 are generally used.

BASIC MATERIAL

With conventional processing systems, frit, water, clay, opacifiers, color oxides, and electrolytes are ground in a ball mill, producing a thick, creamy liquid substance called "slip." In the case of steel substrates, after the fabricated part has been thoroughly cleaned, acid-etched, and given a thin coating of nickel, the component is either sprayed or dip- or flow-coated with slip. Following a drying process to remove the water, the part is passed through an enameling furnace at high temperature (generally between 1400 and 1550° F) where the coating is fused to the metal. Steel architectural components are almost always given two coats of enamel—first a ground coat to promote adherence and then a cover coat for desired color. When multicolor designs are specified, as in signs and murals, the number of firings can go much higher. Steel panels are coated both front and back to ensure equal firing and panel flatness

and to give complete corrosion protection.

Frits formulated for application on aluminum and aluminized steel are modified, usually by the addition of lead, to give them a lower melting point and a higher coefficient of expansion. Before being coated, aluminum is also thoroughly cleaned and given a mild etch. Furnace temperatures for fusing enamel to aluminum are above 980° F but seldom higher than 1000° F. Because of its noncorrosive nature, some field fabrication can be carried out on porcelain-enameled aluminum—for example, holes can be drilled and certain types of panels can be cut.

Though most porcelain enamel architectural components are still produced by these conventional methods, recent technological breakthroughs now make it possible for porcelain enamel to be electrostatically applied in dry powder form, resulting in substantial savings in energy, materials, and labor. Vastly streamlined metal preparation procedures which eliminate the traditional acid-etch are also among the promising new developments in porcelain enamel processing.

PROPERTIES

The relative importance of various properties in a given situation may determine the composition of the porcelain enamel as well as the type of base metal used. There are acid- or alkali-resistant types of enamel. A standard Porcelain Enamel Institute test classifies enamels as AA, A, B, C, and D in descending order of their acid resistance.

Table 19. Properties and characteristics of porcelain enamel

Courtesy of Porcelain Enamel Institute

Hardness (Mohs')	3½–6
Abrasion resistance (PEI), %*	30–65 plus residual specular reflectance
Abrasion resistance (Taber), gm†	0.0078 for best types
Torsion resistance (PEI), in.‡	0.016, 50–60; 0.009, 80–120
Acid resistance	Excellent when specified
Alkali resistance	Excellent when specified
Solvents, organic	Resistant to all
Heat resistance, ° F	700–1500§
Ultraviolet light	Not affected
Diffuse reflectance	As desired up to +88%¶
Total reflectance	As desired up to +90% #
Weathering	Acid-resistant grades not affected
Dielectric strength	100–450 volts/mil
Thermal conductivity	6–9 Btu/(hr) (sq ft) (° F) (in.)

*By same test, good plate glass retains 50 per cent specular gloss.
† 16,000 cycles with 1,000-gm load and CS17F wheel.
‡ Right-angle-shaped specimens 12 in. long and having 3/16-in. radius at right-angle bend, twisted until failure at radius of bend.
§ Higher temperatures are resisted by special types of enamels—up to 2000° F.
¶ For normal application weights. Higher values have been obtained in special circumstances. Normal commercial diffuse reflectances on appliances average about 78 percent.
# As total reflectance is related to diffuse reflectance, note ¶ applies here also.

There is a strong correlation between acid resistance and weatherability. The PEI-recommended specifications for exterior architectural components call for either AA or A enamels to be used on steel substrates and grade B or higher on aluminum. A recent report issued by the National Bureau of Standards on a 30-year exposure test of enamel panels said that the majority of enamels with good acid resistance showed only barely perceptible changes in color and gloss.

GLOSS AND COLOR

Porcelain-enamel coatings can be supplied in a broad range of specular reflectance. Glossy finishes will generally have specular gloss readings of from 45 to 60, semiglosses from 25 to 45, and mattes 25 and below. The architect should bear in mind that a two- or three-number difference on the scale is barely perceptible to the eye and final determination of degree of glossiness should be made from actual samples supplied by the manufacturer.

There are literally thousands of colors available in porcelain enamel. To provide the designer with a solid base from which to begin specifying color, PEI has established a series of 19 glossy colors and 16 "NatureTone" colors—soft, low-chroma colors selected to blend with other construction materials. These colors are available throughout the industry and may be specified by number from the color guide furnished by PEI. As in the case of degree of glossiness, final determination of color should be made from actual porcelain-enamel samples rather than from ink or other organic color chips.

PANEL FABRICATION

Insulated porcelain-enamel panels can be totally custom-designed or standard units. Custom panels permit the architect to design the panel's shape and specify its color or colors, finish, texture, insulation, backup finish, and the method of installation. If formed or embossed panels are desired but the size and design of a structure does not require enough panels to justify the cost of new dies, porcelain enamelers have standard dies that can be utilized. They also have standard colors, textures, insulations, and backup panels.

An interesting development is the continuous-process porcelain enameling of light-gage steel coils. Finished material is laminated to rigid insulation and backup sheets and then normally used as inserts in curtain wall systems. These panels are available in a complete range of colors,

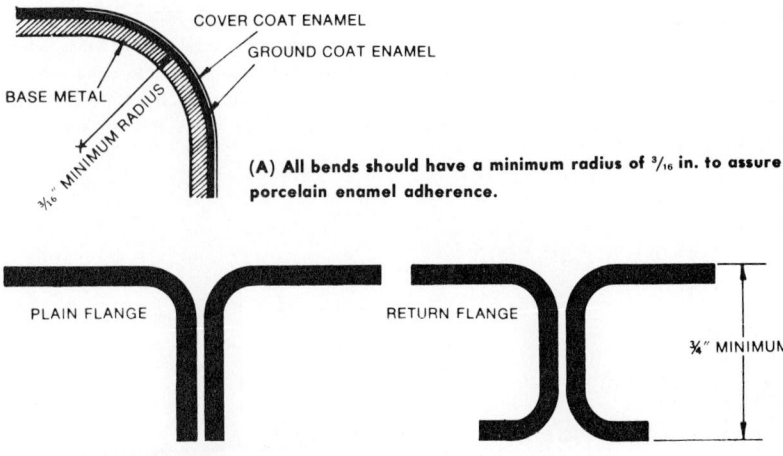

(A) All bends should have a minimum radius of ³⁄₁₆ in. to assure porcelain enamel adherence.

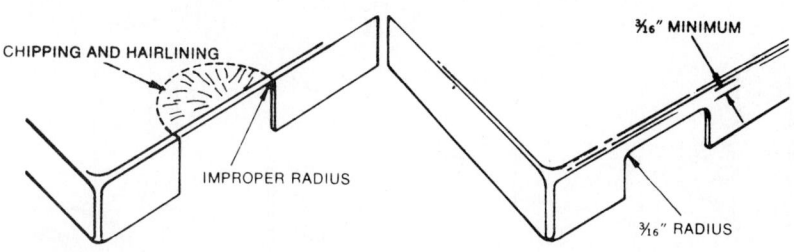

(B) Panel flanges should be a minimum of ³⁄₄ in. deep.

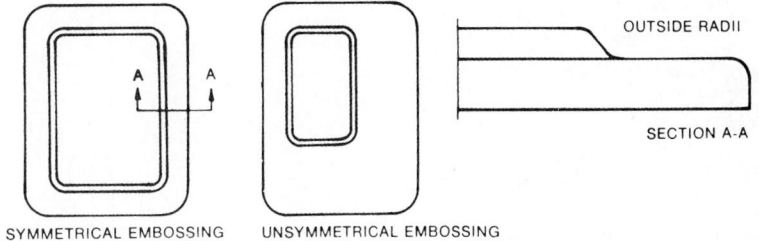

(C) When cutouts and notches cannot be avoided, radius should be maintained as shown in (A) above.

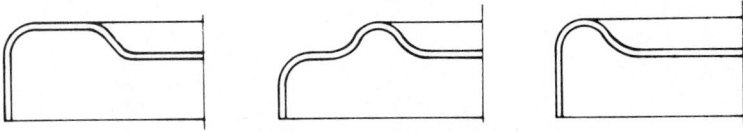

(D) Embossings should be symmetrical or carefully balanced to avoid uneven stresses.

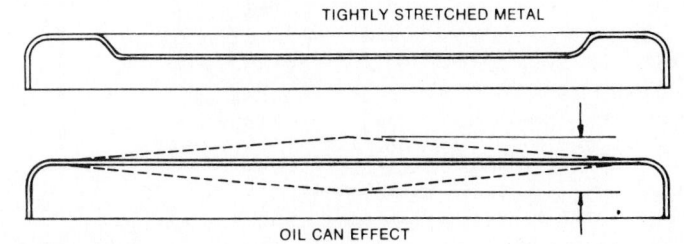

(E) Here are a few of the conventional methods of embossing.

(F) Embossing takes up excess metal in a panel to remove the "oil can" effect, assuring greater rigidity and flatness.

Fig. 3. Fabrication details

finishes, and textures in a generous variety of widths and lengths.

There are four basic types of insulation—solid, honeycomb, foams, and batts—in a variety of materials providing a range of U values, sound absorption, and fire resistance. Behind the insulation or what would be the interior wall surface, some type of rigid backup sheet as an integral part of the panel is usually used. This backup sheet may be porcelain enamel, the same as the facing sheet. Or any number of prefinished materials may be laminated to the insulating core or mechanically fastened to the facing sheet.

From coil stock, panels up to 35 ft long have been fabricated while heavy-gage laminated panels have been produced up to 6 by 12 ft. Size limits of uninsulated pan panels depend upon the design of the panel and its application.

Formed steel panels are normally fabricated from 20- to 16-gage metal, and formed aluminum substrates are from 0.030 to 0.125 in. thick. Laminated steel panels are made from coil stock in the range of 28- to 18-gage and unflanged aluminum panels use metal thicknesses from 0.020 to 0.040 in.

From *Guide to Designing with Architectural Porcelain Enamel on Steel,* Porcelain Enamel Institute, 1970

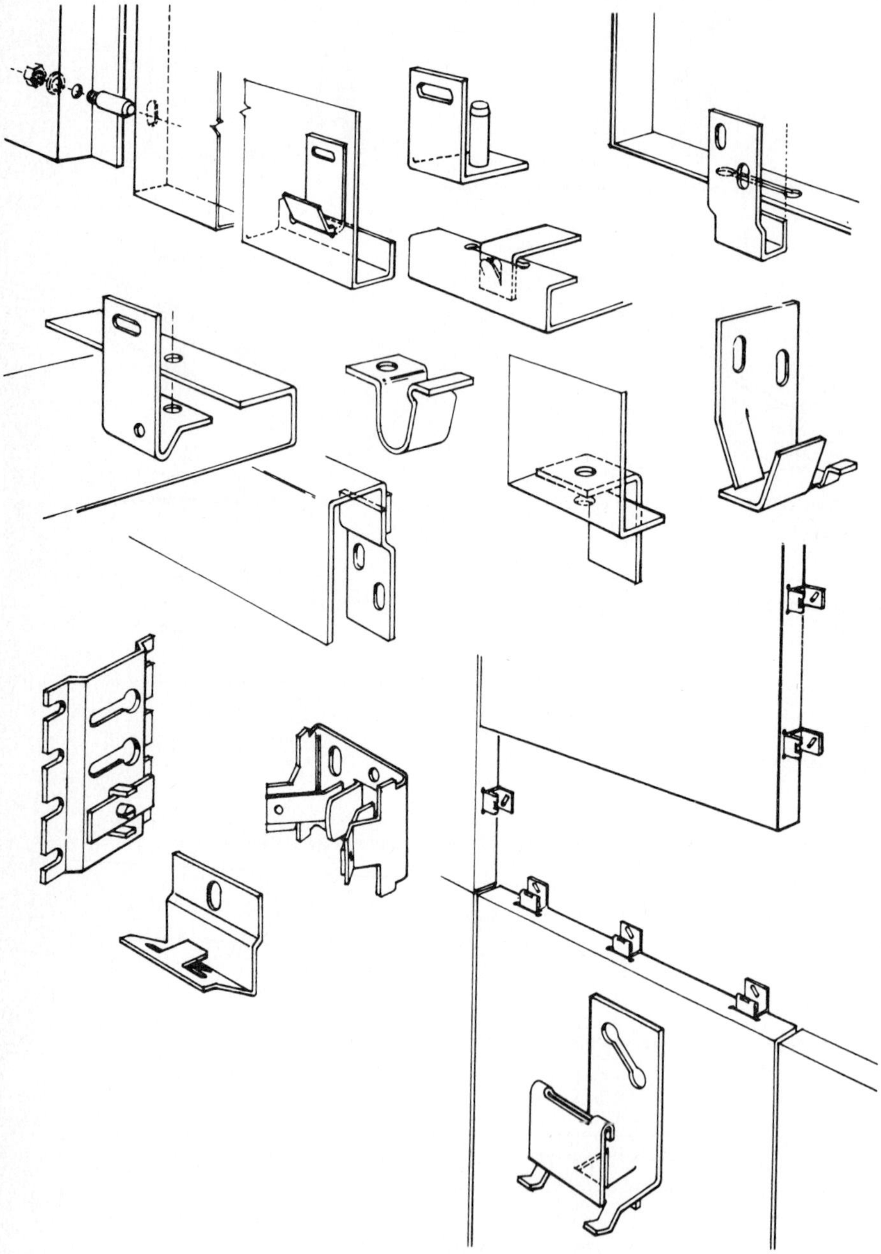

FABRICATION CONSIDERATIONS

Architectural porcelain enamel offers outstanding design flexibility. Even so, there are some fabrication considerations that will help the designer reach his intended goals.

For example, proper flanging for edge strength and light embossing to add strength across the panel help assure that large flat surfaces will stay flat. Lamination to a rigid insulation material, standard practice with light-gage facing sheets, permits the use of panels with especially large flat surfaces.

Flanges should be at least ¾ in. in depth for panels up to 10 or 12 sq ft. Larger panels should have at least 1-in. flanges. A return flange is considered preferable to a plain flange. Embossings should be symmetrical or balanced to avoid setting up uneven stresses that can cause warping (see Fig. 3).

Whether designing flanges or embossings, all bends should have a minimum radius of ³⁄₁₆ in. inside or outside. Taking this into consideration during design avoids production changes that might alter the designer's intent.

To these general recommendations for designing with porcelain enamel may be added one more. When in doubt, consult an experienced porcelain enameler. No matter what your problem, chances are that he has solved it many times before.

Fig. 4. Typical fasteners

FASTENERS

A wide variety of fastening systems for veneer and insulated porcelain-enamel

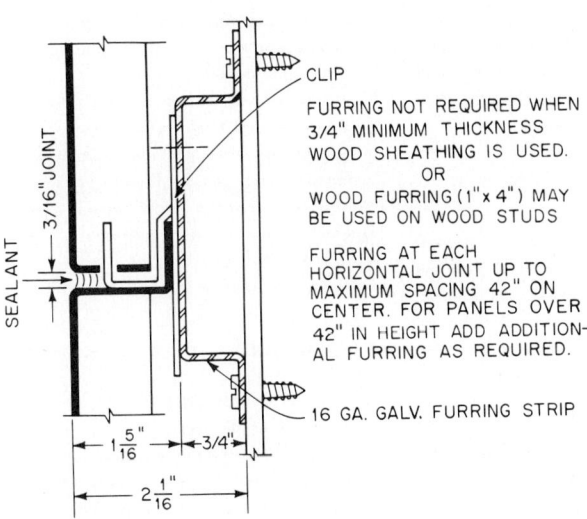

CLIP

FURRING NOT REQUIRED WHEN 3/4" MINIMUM THICKNESS WOOD SHEATHING IS USED. OR WOOD FURRING (1" x 4") MAY BE USED ON WOOD STUDS

FURRING AT EACH HORIZONTAL JOINT UP TO MAXIMUM SPACING 42" ON CENTER. FOR PANELS OVER 42" IN HEIGHT ADD ADDITIONAL FURRING AS REQUIRED.

16 GA. GALV. FURRING STRIP

3/16" JOINT

SEALANT

$1\frac{5}{16}$"   3/4"

$2\frac{1}{16}$"

Fig. 5. Horizontal joint

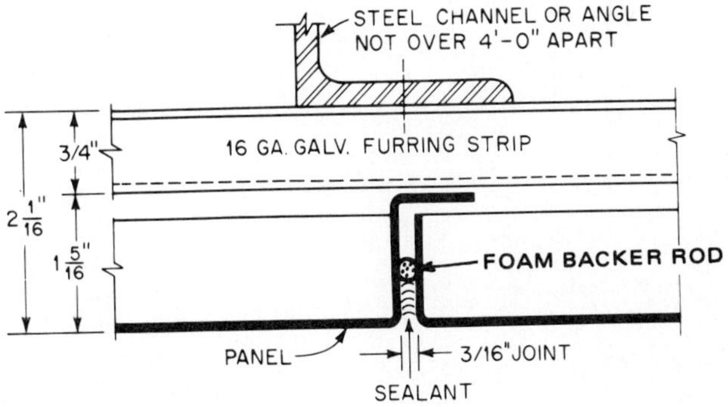

STEEL CHANNEL OR ANGLE NOT OVER 4'-0" APART

16 GA. GALV. FURRING STRIP

3/4"

$2\frac{1}{16}$" $1\frac{5}{16}$"

FOAM BACKER ROD

PANEL

3/16" JOINT

SEALANT

Fig. 6. Vertical joint

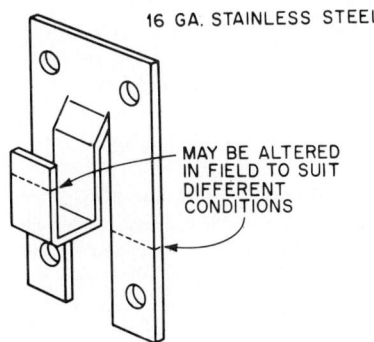

16 GA. STAINLESS STEEL

MAY BE ALTERED IN FIELD TO SUIT DIFFERENT CONDITIONS

Fig. 7. Fastening clip

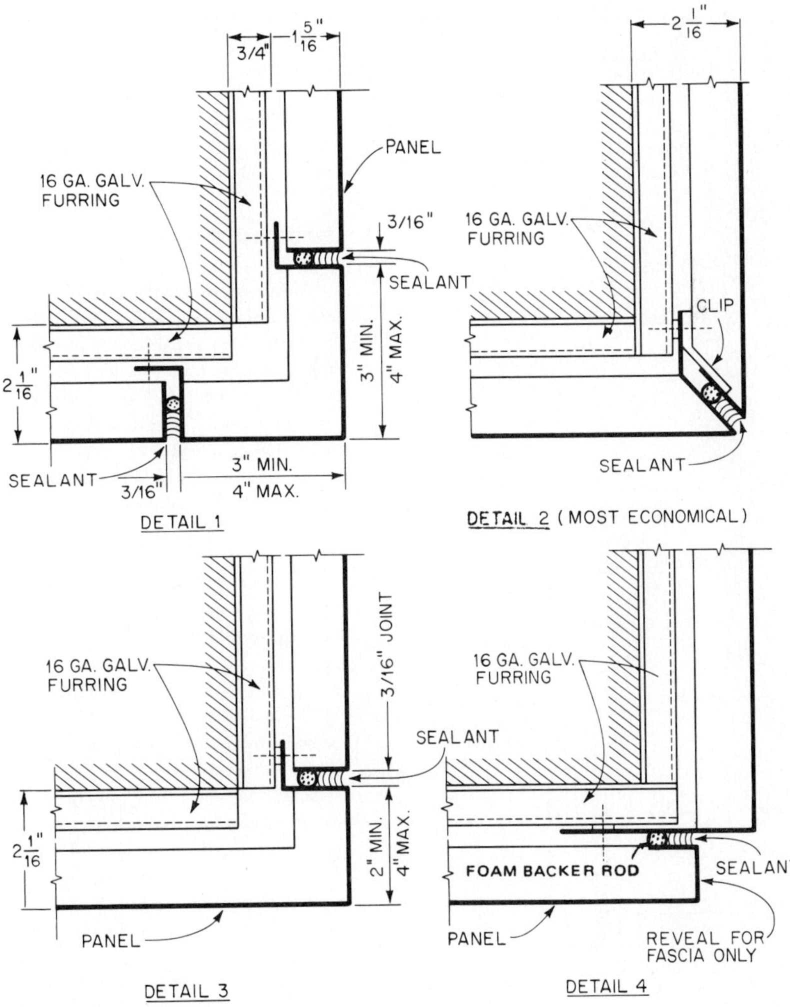

panels has been developed and refined through the years. They are readily available from the engineering departments of architectural porcelain enamelers.

The system illustrated in Fig. 4 are representative of the most popular types, covering all but the most unusual porcelain enamel applications. This group of fasteners is not exhaustive, but it does provide a point of departure for the architectural designer.

As an aid to achitectural specifiers, the Porcelain Enamel Institute has available a published specification, PEI: S-100, *Specification for Architectural Porcelain*

DETAIL 1

3/4" $1\frac{5}{16}$"

16 GA. GALV. FURRING

PANEL

3/16"

SEALANT

3" MIN. 4" MAX.

$2\frac{1}{16}$"

SEALANT   3/16"

3" MIN. 4" MAX.

DETAIL 2 (MOST ECONOMICAL)

$2\frac{1}{16}$"

16 GA. GALV. FURRING

CLIP

SEALANT

DETAIL 3

16 GA. GALV. FURRING

3/16" JOINT

SEALANT

2" MIN. 4" MAX.

$2\frac{1}{16}$"

PANEL

DETAIL 4

16 GA. GALV. FURRING

SEALANT

FOAM BACKER ROD

PANEL

SEALANT

REVEAL FOR FASCIA ONLY

Fig. 8. Corner details

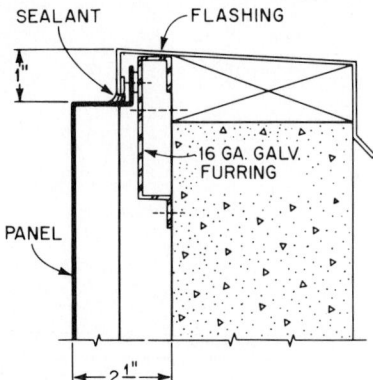

Fig. 9. Coping detail

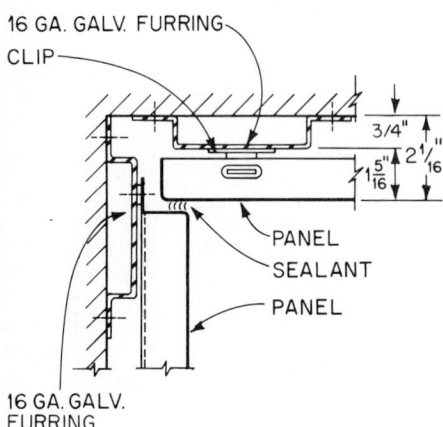

Fig. 10. Soffit detail

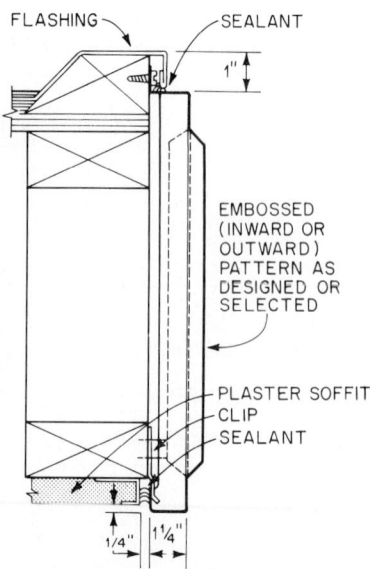

Fig. 11. Fascia detail

Enamel on Steel for Exterior Use, which covers all technical aspects. When specifying architectural porcelain-enameled components, architects should also consider the following variables:

BASE METALS

Type: The substrate should be (1) special-purpose "enameling iron or steel" of low metaloid and carbon content, (2) special-type steels designed for porcelain enamel application, or (3) conventional cold-rolled sheets which have been shown suitable for enameling.

Thickness: Thickness of the metal should be agreed upon during consultation with the enameler. Full consideration should be given to size, shape, and duty which the component will perform in the building.

Shop drawings: Complete shop drawings should show forming details; location of clips, lugs, bracing, and other attachments; and location of completed component in the structure. Dimensional tolerances should be included on all drawings.

Flatness: There should be complete agreement between the designer and the enameler as to the allowable variations from flatness. Measurement of flatness should be made with the panel in the position in which it will be installed.

PORCELAIN-ENAMEL FINISH

Gloss: Architectural porcelain enamels can be supplied in a wide range of degree of glossiness. The architect should select the degree desired from actual samples supplied by the manufacturer. It is recommended that the finish be of a type that will not reflect distinct images. Reproducible, quantitative measurements of image-gloss can be made using the equipment and procedure described in PEI Bulletin T-20; *Image Gloss Test.*

Color: Color of a porcelain-enamel finish should be specified by manufacturer's catalog or PEI number or by a suitable color chip, but final determination should be made only from actual samples supplied by the manufacturer. In production, some colors are more easily controlled than others. When difficult-to-control colors are selected, an agreement should be reached as to allowable tolerances. Compliance with color specification may be determined by visual matching under viewing conditions mutually agreed upon by contracting parties, or they may be determined instrumentally.

Texture: Normally porcelain-enamel finishes are smooth and nontextured. Special textures are available and may be specified, but final determination should be made only from actual samples supplied by the manufacturer.

Thickness of finish: Thin porcelain-enamel coatings are preferable to thicker ones because they provide maximum resistance to damage from flexure and impact. When heavy coatings are necessary to meet specific appearance requirements, they should only be specified after consultation with the manufacturer.

TEST METHODS

There are three generally accepted test methods for determining the weather resistance of porcelain enamel.

Acid spot test: This test is fully described in PEI Bulletin T-21, *Test for Acid Resistance of Porcelain Enamel (Citric Acid Spot Test).* This is the test normally used.

Cupric sulfate test: This test described in PEI Bulletin T-22, *Cupric Sulfate Test for Color Retention,* is used for red, yellow, and orange porcelain enamels.

Boiling acid test: This test is described in ASTM C283-54. It is an alternative to the acid spot test and is used on enamels of especially low specular gloss.

PACKAGING AND SHIPPING

Consideration should be given to the methods of packing, shipping, and handling of completed porcelain-enameled architectural components which will protect them in transit and at the same time be practical for the supplier, shipper, and erector.

REFERENCES

Specification for Architectural Porcelain Enamel on Steel for Exterior Use (PEI: S-100), Porcelain Enamel Institute, 1965.

Architectural Metals Finishes Manual, National Association of Architectural Metal Manufacturers, 1976.

Color Guide for Architectural Porcelain Enamel, Porcelain Enamel Institute.

Design and Fabrication of Sheet Steel Parts for Porcelain Enameling, Porcelain Enamel Institute, 1966.

Light Gage Cold Formed Steel Design Manual, American Iron and Steel Institute, 1968.

The Making, Shaping and Treating of Steel, United States Steel Corporation, 1964.

Metal Curtain Wall, Window, Store Front and Entrance Guide Specification Manual, Architectural Aluminum Manufacturers Association, 1976.

Guide to Designing with Architectural Porcelain Enamel on Steel, Porcelain Enamel Institute, 1970.

By DONALD J. VILD, P.E.

TYPES OF GLASS USED IN BUILDINGS

There are four primary types of glass produced for buildings: float glass, sheet glass, patterned glass, and wired glass. All other types are some variation of these four. Plate glass is no longer produced.

Float glass

Produced by flowing molten glass over a bath of molten tin and slowly cooling. This produces glass with very uniform thickness and flatness.

Float glass is available in thicknesses from $\frac{1}{8}$" to $\frac{7}{8}$". This glass has excellent optical quality and is suitable for mirrors as well as for windows, curtain walls, and doors. For use in vision areas of buildings "glazing select" quality is generally specified.

Sheet glass

All sheet glass is drawn either flat or vertically, is not mechanically polished, and contains slight wave distortions more detectable in large sheets than in small ones. These distortions, or "draws" run in one direction, and for best appearance, should be placed horizontally when glazing. To ensure this, the width dimension should always be stated first when listing sizes.

Sheet glass for buildings is generally single strength (0.085"–0.101" thick) or double strength (0.115"–0.134" thick). For vision areas "glazing A" or "glazing B" quality is used. Applications are limited to small sizes in windows and doors.

Patterned glass

Patterned glass (sometimes referred to as "figured" or "rolled" glass) is a flat glass having a pattern or texture impressed on one or both sides in the process of rolling. It is commonly available in thicknesses of $\frac{1}{8}$", $\frac{3}{16}$", and $\frac{7}{32}$". Numerous designs are offered—including flutes, ribs, grids, and a variety of other regular and random patterns—all of which provide translucency and some degrees of obscurity. Patterns are classified as decorative or glazing; i.e., used primarily for their functional properties. If the pattern is directional, the width dimension should be stated first in listing sizes.

Wire glass

Wire glass may be patterned, smooth rolled, or ground and polished. Most wire glass is nominally $\frac{1}{4}$" thick although some $\frac{7}{32}$" glass is available. Three types of wire configurations are produced: square-welded mesh, diamond-welded mesh, and linear parallel wires. Wired glass is used primarily in fire rated windows and doors, skylights, and applications requiring a safety glazing material.

Heat-absorbing glass

Because of the need to control solar heat and glare in large glass areas, glass manufacturers offer a variety of tinted glasses designed to have improved performance characteristics over clear glass. Three colors of heat-absorbing glass are presently available: bronze, gray, and green-tinted.

Both heat absorption and glare reduction are accomplished by incorporating small quantities of colorants in the glass. This reduces the transmittance of both visual light and the sun's radiant energy as well as changing the appearance. Any tinted glass may properly be termed "heat-absorbing" as long as it meets the following limits established in Federal Specification DD-G-451D.

Glass thickness	Maximum solar transmission, per cent
$\frac{1}{8}$"	67
$\frac{3}{16}$"	56
$\frac{1}{4}$"	52
$\frac{5}{16}$"	45
$\frac{3}{8}$"	39
$\frac{1}{2}$"	36

The glass is termed "higher light transmission" if its daylight transmission is greater than those listed below; if it is lower, the glass is termed "lower light transmission."

Glass thickness in.	Daylight transmission, per cent
$\frac{1}{8}$	80
$\frac{3}{16}$	75
$\frac{1}{4}$	70
$\frac{5}{16}$	65
$\frac{3}{8}$	60
$\frac{1}{2}$	50

A listing of some nonproprietary types of glass, with their thermal and optical properties, is given in Table 1.

Heat-absorbing glass may be obtained in thicknesses of $\frac{3}{16}$" and $\frac{1}{4}$" for green-tinted type and $\frac{1}{8}$" through $\frac{1}{2}$" for grey and bronze colors. Heat-absorbing glasses are all float glass.

Tinted glasses, i.e., glasses with tint but which do not meet the requirements for heat-absorbing glasses, are available in sheet glass.

Reflective-coated glass

This is glass with a coating of metal or a metal compound factory applied on one surface. The coating reflects light and solar heat. Coatings are applied by pyrolytic, chemical-deposition, sputtering, or vacuum-deposition processes. The latter two produce the more uniform quality. Some coatings, such as chromium and tin oxide, are durable and can be furnished on single glass. These may be used for vision areas or, when heat-strengthened or fully tempered, for spandrels. Other coatings such as copper, gold, and aluminum are less durable and are available only on products where they are protected, as in insulating and laminated glasses. Coatings may be applied on any type of glass and thicknesses up to $\frac{1}{2}$". In some cases coatings applied to heat-absorbing glasses may require the glass to be heat-strengthened or fully tempered because of added solar absorption.

Maximum sizes available vary with each manufacturer and type of coating. The largest for any type is 120 x 144 in. There are numerous colors and levels of heat and light transmittance available. Consult the various manufacturers.

Insulating glass

The term "insulating glass" refers to a factory assembled unit consisting of two or more panes of glass separated by air spaces. The periphery of the air spaces is hermetically sealed. There are two types of these sealed units:

Organic seal type: Two or more panes of glass separated by air spaces sealed at their edges with an organic seal. Polysulfide, butyl, and silicone are common sealants

Table 1. Thermal and optical properties of heat-absorbing glasses

Thickness (in.)	Daylight transmission (per cent)			Total solar transmission (per cent)	Shading coefficient*
	bronze	gray	green-tinted		
$\frac{1}{8}$	68	62	——	64	0.83
$\frac{3}{16}$	58	51	78	55	0.75
$\frac{1}{4}$	50	42	74	46	0.68
$\frac{5}{16}$	43	34	——	38	0.62
$\frac{3}{8}$	37	28	——	32	0.57
$\frac{1}{2}$	28	19	——	23	0.50

*The shading coefficient is the total solar heat gain for the glass listed divided by the total solar heat gain for DS sheet glass.

Table 2. Bow (warpage) tolerances* in inches for fully tempered and heat-strengthened glasses

Length of span, in.	Glass thickness, in.					
	1/8, 3/16	7/32	1/4	5/16	3/8	1/2 and over
Up to 36	0.188	0.150	0.125	0.109	0.093	0.063
36 to 48	0.282	0.235	0.188	0.171	0.141	0.093
48 to 60	0.374	0.312	0.250	0.219	0.187	0.141
60 to 72	0.470	0.392	0.375	0.281	0.235	0.187
72 to 84	0.561	0.498	0.500	0.328	0.282	0.235
84 to 96	0.940	0.750	0.625	0.437	0.375	0.282
96 to 108	–	–	0.750	0.562	0.500	0.375
108 to 120	–	–	0.875	0.687	0.625	0.500
120 to 132	–	–	–	–	0.750	0.625

Values apply for glass held vertically and supported on two setting blocks.

used. Glass thicknesses furnished are generally in the range of 1/8 to 1/4 in. For very large sizes, thicker glasses may be used. Air-space widths range from 1/4 to 3/4 in. with 1/4, 3/8, and 1/2 in. being the more common. Insulating glass is available in various combinations of glass. Reflective-coated, heat-absorbing, clear, tempered, laminated, wired, and patterned glass are used. Consult manufacturers for availability, sizes, requirements for tempering, etc.

Glass edge type: Two sheets of clear single-strength or double-strength glass fused together at their edges, enclosing a nominal 3/16 in. air space. This type of glass is not produced with multiple air spaces. Sizes and availability are limited and the product is generally available only as a component of factory assembled windows.

Fully tempered glass

Tempered glass is produced by heating the glass to just below its softening temperature and then cooling it suddenly under carefully controlled conditions. It becomes three to five times more resistant to most types of impact and thermal stress. When tempered glass is broken, it disintegrates into small pieces which do not usually present a serious hazard. Tempered glass cannot be cut or drilled after fabrication. The exact size required and any holes, notches, edge work, etc., must be specified when ordering.

All float and sheet glass 1/8-in thick or thicker and of all types can be tempered. Most reflective-coated glasses must be tempered before coating. Wired glass and certain patterned glasses with deep patterns cannot be tempered. Tempered glass can be used in insulating glass and laminated glass assemblies. Fully tempered glass is classified as a safety glazing material by standards and codes.

Allowable bow (warpage) for fully tempered, heat-strengthened, and ceramic colored (spandrel) glasses are listed in Table

2. These are from Federal Specification DD-G-1403B. This bow is inherent in the fabrication of these products.

Laminated glass

Laminated glass consists of two or more plies of glass bonded together with sheets of transparent polyvinyl butyral plastic. Heat and pressure bond the layers into one unit. The elasticity and adhesion of the plastic tend to hold the glass particles in place when fractured. For architectural applications, the thickness of the plastic interlayer is usually 0.015 in. In cases where this glass must meet requirements for safety glazing materials used in buildings, the plastic is 0.030 or 0.045 in. depending upon the thickness of the glass plies. "Burglar-resisting glasses" with superior penetration resistance incorporate a 0.060-in. or thicker plastic interlayer. Multiple laminations consisting of four or more glass plies to a total thickness of 3/4 to 3 in. produce "bullet-resisting glass."

Heat-strengthened glass

This glass and fully tempered glass are produced in similar ways. The resistance to impact and thermal stresses of heat-strengthened glass is increased two to three times as compared with regular glass. When it breaks, unlike fully tempered glass, the fragments are large. This glass cannot be altered after fabrication.

Heat-strengthened glass is not considered a safety glazing material.

Spandrel (ceramic colored) glass

Colored ceramic glass is a heat-strengthened or fully tempered product designed for exterior spandrel use. It is made by fusing opaque color onto the back of 1/4-in. float glass. A large variety of colors is available. Smooth surfaces are standard, but a number of patterned surfaces and custom colors may be obtained on order. Glass other than 1/4-in. thickness is occasionally used. As with any tempered or heat-strengthened glass, it cannot be drilled or cut after firing. Conse-

quently the exact size and all fabrication details must be accurately specified when ordering. Thickness and cut-size tolerances are within the limits specified in Federal Specification DD-G-1403B. This specification also establishes limits on the properties of the base glass and ceramic backing. Spandrel glass should always be used with an opaque backup.

REQUIREMENTS FOR SAFETY GLAZING

On July 6, 1977 Federal Safety Standard 16 CFR 1201 for Architectural Glazing became effective. The standard mandates the use of safety glazing material in sliding doors, storm doors, interior and exterior doors, tub and shower enclosures, and certain fixed panels exposed to possible human impact. Willful violations may be considered criminal offenses under the Consumer Product Safety Act. Fully-tempered glass, laminated glass with a 0.030 or 0.045-in. plastic interlayer, wired glass, and certain rigid plastics comply with the standard.

INDUSTRY STANDARDS

Federal Specification DD-G-451D, Glass, Float or Plate, Sheet, Figured (Flat, for Glazing, Mirrors and Other Uses), establishes dimensional and quality limits for all types of base glass including wired glass and heat-absorbing glasses.

Federal Specification DD-G-1403B, Glass, Plate (Float), Sheet, Figured, and Spandrel (Heat-Strengthened and Fully Tempered), presents specifications for heat-strengthened and fully tempered glass used in windows, doors, and spandrel applications. Quality limits for the base glass from which the above are fabricated are the same as in Federal Specification DD-G-451D. DD-G-1403B covers dimensional tolerances, allowable bow (warpage), durability of ceramic colored (spandrel) glasses, and strength requirements.

American National Standard Z97.1-1975, Performance Specifications and Methods of Test for Safety Glazing Material Used in Buildings, covers the safety requirements for fully tempered, laminated, and wired glass and rigid plastics. It is directed primarily toward assuring that safety glazings have fail-safe characteristics.

Federal Safety Standard 16 CFR 1201 for Architectural Glazing Materials includes test criteria for safety glazing materials (similar to Standard Z97.1-1975) and specifies areas where safety glazing materials must be used.

ASTM Proposed Specification P3 for Sealed Insulating Glass Units establishes test procedures and end-point criteria for insulating glass units.

WIND-LOAD STRENGTH

The ability of glass to withstand wind loads is based on a complex relationship of the glass type, thickness and dimensions, support conditions, and the dynamic characteristics of the wind. The wind forces must be interpreted by the design professional into equivalent uniform static loads before available data may be used.

The procedure for determining design wind loads is described in detail in American National Standard Building Code Requirements for Minimum Design Loads in Buildings and Other Structures (ANSI A58.1-1972). Wind velocities for any U.S. location can be determined by referring to the wind map, Fig. 1 in the section on Design Loads. Wind velocities can be converted to wind pressures by reference to Tables 1 to 4 in the section on Curtain Walls. Wind pressures are assumed to be equivalent to uniform static loads.

Information presented here applies only to glass exposed to uniform static loads of 30–60 sec duration. Figures 1 and 2 show the relationship between size, thickness, and strength of annealed glass using a design factor of 2.5 (average breaking pressure divided by 2.5). Figure 1 is for glass firmly supported on all four edges and Fig. 2 is for glass supported on two opposite edges. It is general professional practice to use a design factor of 2.5 for glass in building exteriors. This is the basis for most building codes and ordinances. In practical terms, a design factor of 2.5 means that if all glass in a building is subjected to exactly the maximum allowable uniform static load, 8 out of 1000 lights would fail. The failure rate in a building is further dependent upon the design wind load used and the statistical probability of these loads being experienced on the different areas of the building facade.

For various design factors, the statistical probabilities of failure are as follows:

Design factor	Predicted breakage
2.0*	23 out of 1000
2.5	8 out of 1000
3.0	4 out of 1000
5.0	0.7 out of 1000
10.0	0.2 out of 1000

A design factor of less than 2.0 should not be used in choosing glass for buildings.

Should a design factor of 2.5 not be appropriate, adjustments may be made based on personal engineering judgment and experience. The necessary adjustment in design load can be computed using the following formula:

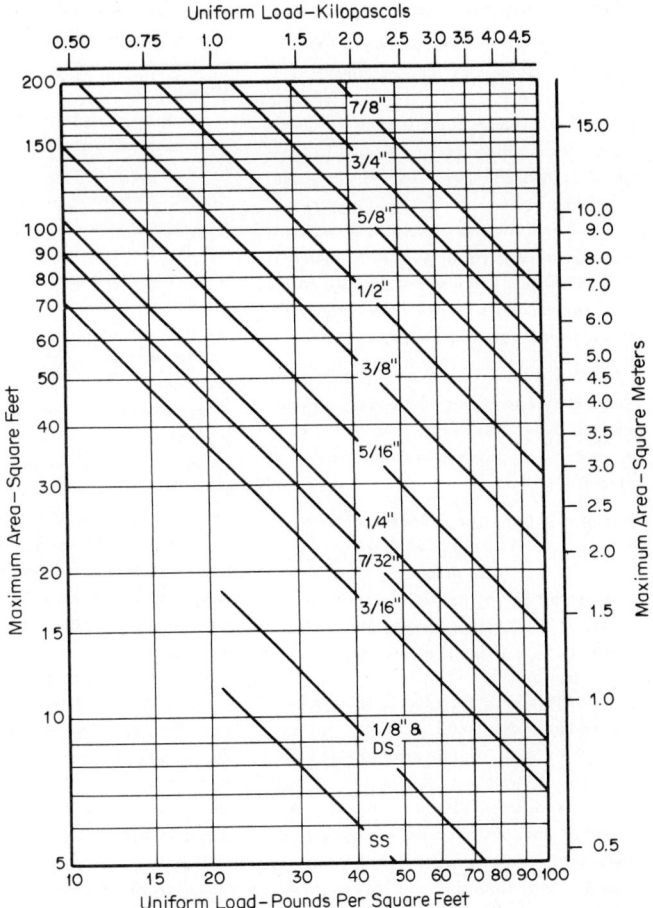

Fig. 1. Maximum area of glass versus uniform load. Design factor = 2.5. Glass firmly supported on all four edges.

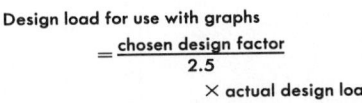

Design load for use with graphs
$$= \frac{\text{chosen design factor}}{2.5}$$
$$\times \text{ actual design load}$$

Figure 1 applies to rectangular lights of glass with length-to-width ratios no more than 5 : 1 firmly supported on all four edges.

To determine the strength of other than annealed glass held four sides, use the appropriate multiplying factor listed below.

Regular float and sheet	1.0
Fully tempered glass	4.0
Heat-strengthened glass	2.0
Insulating glass (both lights same thickness)	1.5
Laminated glass, wired glass	0.6

These multiplying factors cannot be used with Fig. 2. Only single tempered glass or single annealed glass of appropriate thickness should be used in two-side support systems. The allowable span for tempered glass is 2 times that for annealed glass of the same thickness for a given uniform load.

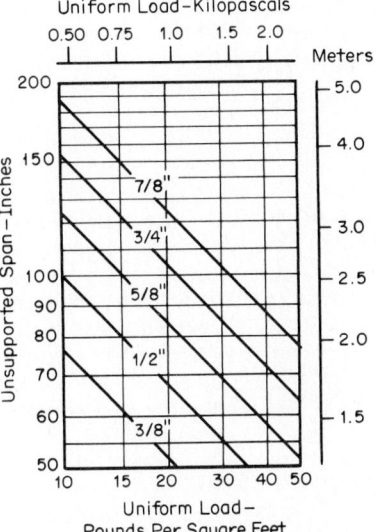

Fig. 2. Maximum span of glass versus uniform load. Design factor = 2.5. Glass firmly supported on two opposite edges.

GENERAL GLAZING GUIDELINES

The design of a good glazing system incorporates experience and judgment and considers glass type, framing system, method of erection, and associated tolerances. The glazing system should be designed to minimize loads on the glass due to building movement. To adequately retain glass in the framing system and prevent breakage caused by glass-to-metal contact or by mechanical and thermal stresses, architect's specifications should include the following general glazing guidelines.

Framing system: The framing system must structurally support the glass and provide openings which are within specified limits for squareness, corner offset, and bow. These limits are:

Square	⅛-in. difference in the lengths of the diagonals
Corner offset	1/32-in. at each corner
Bow	1/16-in. in any 4-ft length of framing

The deflection of the glass framing members under design loads must not exceed either the length of the span divided by 175 or ¾ in., whichever is less. The deflection of horizontal members due to the weight of the glass should be limited to minimize bite and thermal stress at the glass edge. For heat-absorbing and coated, high-performance glasses, a limit of ⅛ in. or 25 per cent of the design edge clearance of the glass or panel below, whichever is less,

is recommended. Twisting of the sill member due to the dead load of the glass should be limited to 1 degree between ends and center.

Anchors, expansion joints: Anchors and expansion joints should be designed so that loads are not applied on the glass framing due to movement of the structure. For a stick system, there should be a vertical expansion joint at every floor and preferably at a horizontal support member. Vertical expansion joints should never be placed along an edge of insulating glass. Horizontal expansion joints should be placed either at each column line or within 30 ft of each other, whichever is less.

Thermal movement: In wall design and erection, thermal movement must be properly considered. Movement due to thermal expansion and contraction cannot be limited in a specific wall design, since it is a function of temperature and thermal expansion properties of the wall. For example, a curtain wall with most of the metal within the building will have less movement than a wall with large projecting exterior fins. Expansion joint widths should be based on the conditions that exist during erection. The design should be such that it is practical for the erector to install the wall with the joints nearly full open in cold weather and nearly closed in hot weather.

Clearance and bite: The glazing system should provide for minimum face clearances, edge clearances, and nominal bite as shown in Table 3. Excessive bite can increase thermal stresses at the glass edge, especially

for high-performance coated and heat-absorbing products.

Edge damage: Glass should be handled and glazed carefully to prevent edge damage. Edge damage may occur when glass is rotated or "pitched" on its corner on hard surfaces prior to glazing. It is recommended that a "rolling block" be used by glaziers to rotate the unit.

Setting blocks: Lights larger than 6 ft² or thicker than ⅛ in. should be set on two identical neoprene or EPDM setting blocks with a Shore A durometer hardness of 85 ± 5. Preferably, these blocks should be centered at the bottom quarter points. When this is impractical, the end of the setting block can be moved to within either 6 in. or one-eighth the width of the glass from the vertical glass edge, whichever distance is greater. Setting blocks should always be equidistant from the centerline of the glass.

The length of each setting block should be 0.1 in. for each square foot of glass area but no less than 4 in. in length. The setting blocks should be 1/16 in. less than full channel width and high enough to provide the recommended nominal and minimum edge clearance for the glass. In the case of lock-strip gasket systems, the setting blocks should be sized so that the length of each setting block is 0.4 in. for each square foot of glass area and have the height recommended by the gasket manufacturer. For ½-in. and thicker lights of monolithic glass where the length of neoprene blocks may become prohibitive, lead blocks may be used. Lead blocks should not be used with insulating, laminated, or wire glass or in lock-strip gasket applications. The length of each lead setting block should be 0.05 in. for each square foot of glass area but no less than 4 in. total in any case.

Glass positioning: Glass should be centered in the opening vertically and horizontally. For large lights in dry glazing systems, an edge cushion should be used in each vertical jamb to prevent lateral "walking" of the light. Shore A 65 ± 5 durometer hardness neoprene is preferred. The bumper should be at least 3 in. in length. A nominal ⅛-in. clearance should be allowed between the edge of the glass and the bumper.

Shims: Intermittent face shims should be discouraged. Face clearances should be provided by a continuous neoprene gasket or spacer. The durometer range may vary depending on the intended purpose. For example, a low-durometer neoprene material may be used as a backup material for a gunned-in-place sealant while high-durometer neoprene may be used to apply adequate pressure to preshimmed glazing tape.

Sealant: To provide a watershed, the sealant should be limited to an approximate height of 1/16 in. beyond the sightline of the glass framing members.

Table 3. Recommended cover and clearances, in.*

Glass type and thickness	Nominal cover	Minimum clearance	
		Edge	Face
Single glass:			
SS	¼	⅛	1/16
DS-⅛	¼	⅛	⅛
3/16	5/16	3/16	⅛
7/32	⅜	¼	⅛
¼†	⅜	¼	⅛
5/16	7/16	5/16	3/16
⅜†	7/16	5/16	3/16
½	½	⅜	¼
⅝	⅝	⅜	¼
¾	¾	½	¼
⅞	⅞	½	¼
Spandrel glass:			
¼	½	¼	3/16
⅜	½	¼	3/16
Insulating glass using:			
SS	⅜	3/16	1/16
DS-⅛	⅜	3/16	⅛
3/16	½	¼	3/16
¼	½	¼	3/16

* Do not apply for lockstrip gaskets. Consult gasket manufacturer.
† Except for spandrel glasses.

Weep systems: The glazing system must be designed so that moisture does not accumulate in the glazing channel for prolonged periods. For lock-strip gasket glazing, either an auxiliary sealant around the entire periphery or an adequate weep system, or both, must be used. A weep system should incorporate enough weep holes to ensure adequate drainage. When the weep system consists of weep holes at the sill, the holes should be at least ⅜ in. in diameter when they are in a location that may be subjected to driving rain. The holes can be smaller in protected areas.

In systems with glazing channels, the channel should not be completely filled with glazing sealant. Instead, a void should be left between the edge of the glass and the glazing channel. Systems requiring a heel or toe bead should use a material that is permanently pliable in the temperature range to which it will be subjected. Care should be exercised in application not to fill the edge void or interfere with the weep system.

ADDITIONAL GLAZING GUIDELINES FOR LAMINATED GLASS

1. The edges of laminated glass must not be exposed to cleaners or solvents. The glazing system must be designed so that moisture does not accumulate in the glazing channel for prolonged periods.
2. For coated laminated glass, the high-performance ply must be placed to the exterior.
3. Polysulfide, silicone, butyl rubber, or polybutene base sealants may be used if they are 100 per cent solids, containing no solvents.
4. Laminated glass must not be butt-jointed in exterior applications. Even with the sophisticated sealants available today, moisture vapor transmission can occur through the sealant and may result in eventual delamination.

ADDITIONAL GLAZING GUIDELINES FOR INSULATING GLASS

1. The glazing system must be designed so that moisture does not accumulate in the glazing channel for prolonged periods.
2. In dry glazing systems, the compressive pressure on the glass edge should be a minimum of 4 lb/lin in. of edge to provide some assurance of an adequate seal. The pressure on the glass edge should not exceed 10 lb/lin in. Excessive pressure on the glass can increase mechanical stresses and contribute to glass breakage.
3. The etched label should be glazed in a horizontal position at the bottom of the opening.
4. When heat-absorbing or coated glass is used, the high-performance light must be glazed to the exterior.
5. Glazing materials must be resilient, nonhardening compounds, tapes, or elastomeric gaskets. Polysulfide or silicone compounds, butyl, or polybutene tapes may be used if they are made essentially of solids, containing no solvents.
6. Glazing compounds must not be thinned with chlorinated solvents (dry cleaning fluids) or benzene-related compounds such as toluene.
7. When a heel or toe bead is necessary, compatibility between this material and the insulating glass sealants is required.

DETAILING

Annealed glass, particularly heat-absorbing and reflective types, should be isolated from the surround and not glazed into high heat capacity materials, such as directly into a concrete reglet.

Breakage of annealed glass can occur when the temperature differential within the glass is large. The design and location of hot air outlets should be carefully considered to direct heat away from the glass and prevent high temperature differences between the center and edge of the glass. When heating systems are initially activated during low-temperature periods, special care should be exercised to shield the glass.

Draperies, venetian blinds, or other interior shading devices must be hung away from the glass so that space is provided at the bottom and top, or bottom and one side, to provide natural air movement over the roomside face of the glass. For blinds or drapes in open or closed position, a 2-in. minimum clearance between the frame and the shading device must be observed. If these clearances cannot be provided in the case of venetian blinds, a positive stop or lock-out that limits the movements of the blinds should be used. For horizontal blinds, for instance, the lock-out should limit the rotation of the blinds so that they are in a position 60° off the horizontal in the most closed position. For vertical blinds, the lock-out should limit the movement of the blinds so that a ½-in. spacing exists between the blinds in the most closed position.

Suspended ceiling soffits must be well to the room side, or should include vent slots to allow roomside air convection.

DAMAGE TO GLASS SURFACES

The surface of glass may be damaged by certain causes. Among these are sparks from welding. Glass near welding operations should be protected. Other sources of glass surface damage are alkaline materials and oxidizing steel. Run-off from these materials may be deposited on the glass and stain the surface. Frequent cleaning of the glass during building construction, and possibly for a period after completion, may be necessary.

Glass must be stored so that it is not subjected to cyclic wetting and drying. This wetting and drying action can cause staining or etching of the glass surface. Glass in cases should be stored in a dry, well ventilated area. On a job site, the cases should be stored in the building interior and protected from all moisture. Glass stored out of the case should always be stored with interleaving or spacing between the individual lights of glass.

GLAZING MATERIALS

Wood-sash putty

Wood-sash putty is generally a mixture of pigment and linseed oil. Application of a suitable primer, such as priming paints or boiled linseed oil, to wood sash before applying putty is a necessary practice. Putty should not be painted until it is thoroughly set. All putty should be painted for proper protection. Do not use for insulating glass or laminated glass. Do not use except for small windows located at low elevations.

Metal-sash putty

Metal-sash putty differs from wood-sash putty in that it is formulated to adhere to a nonporous surface. It is used for the glazing of aluminum or steel sash, either inside or outside. Metal-sash putty should be painted within two weeks after application, but should be thoroughly set and hard before painting commences. Do not use for insulating glass or laminated glass.

Elastic glazing compound

These compounds differ from wood- and metal-sash putties both in composition and performance. They are used for either inside or outside glazing, and should surface dry but remain slightly soft and plastic underneath for considerable periods of time. This soft or plastic condition is desirable where windows or doors are subject to twisting or vibration. The glazing compound does not have to be painted but may be, if desired. Certain compounds are available in a range of colors.

Polybutene tape

This material is a nondrying mastic which is available in extruded ribbon shapes of varying widths and thicknesses. The tape remains plastic or resilient over extremely long periods of time. It possesses great adhesion

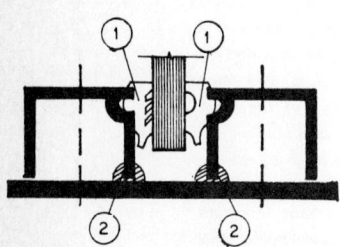

(a) (1) Vinyl or neoprene bead; (2) Butyl or polysulfide (do not use for laminated, wired, or insulating glass unless the system is weeped).

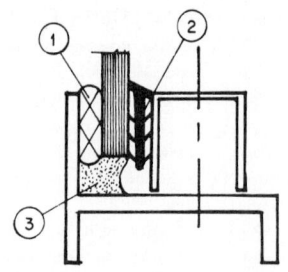

(b) (1) Butyl tape (use type with integral core if glass size is over 100 united inches); (2) Vinyl spline; (3) Noncuring acrylic.

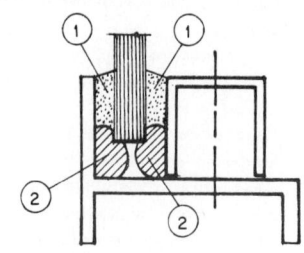

(c) (1) Butyl tape, silicone, or polysulfide; (2) Neoprene rod, 30 Durometer A.

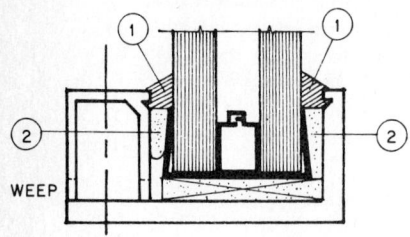

(d) (1) Neoprene bead; (2) Silicone, polysulfide, or acrylic.

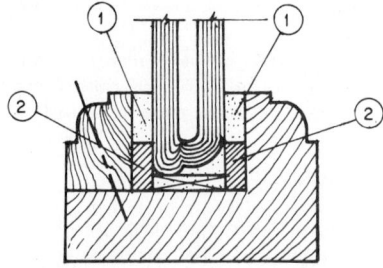

(e) (1) Polysulfide or butyl tape; (2) Neoprene spacers, 60 Durometer A, 24 in. on center.

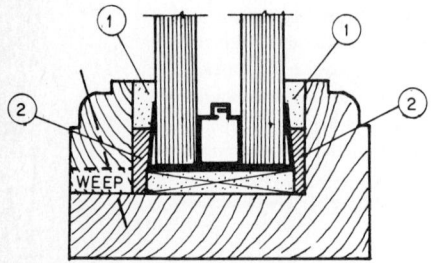

(f) (1) Silicone or polysulfide; (2) Butyl tape.

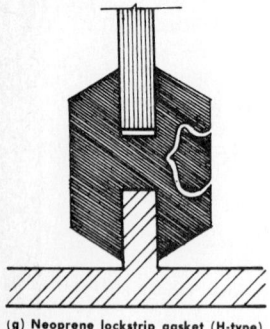

(g) Neoprene lockstrip gasket (H-type).

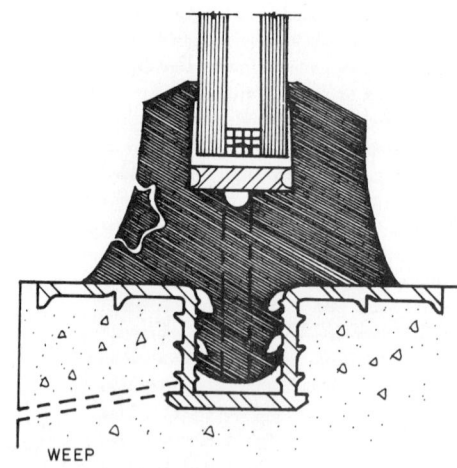

(h) Neoprene lockstrip gasket (spline type).

Fig. 3. Representative glazing systems

qualities. It should not be used as a substitute or replacement for spacers. This tape must be pressure applied for proper adhesion.

Polysulfide elastomer sealing compound

This material is a two-part synthetic rubber based on a polysulfide polymer. Its consistency after mixing is similar to a caulking compound. The mixed compound is applied by either caulking gun or spatula. It is well suited to many applications in modern curtain wall construction. Good performance requires that the sealing surfaces be extremely clean. Excess and spilled material must be removed and surfaces cleaned during the working time of the material as it is almost impossible to remove with solvents when set.

Silicone sealing compound

This is a one-part material with superior adhesion to glass and excellent resistance to moisture and ultraviolet exposure. It is furnished as a gun-grade material only. Surfaces must be cleaned. Metal surfaces must be primed. Silicones can be applied at extremes of temperature.

Compression materials: neoprene, vinyl, EPDM

These materials are extruded or molded in various shapes; channel, angle, etc. They may be used as a continuous gasket or intermittently as spacer shims. The varying thicknesses and cross sections are dependent upon the particular type of glazing or glazing material combinations. To establish and maintain a weathertight joint, the gasket must be compressed not less than 15 per cent, assuming no flow or adhesion (see also sealing materials in "Curtain Walls").

Sash preparation

Remove all rivet, screw, bolt, or nail heads, welding fillets, and other projections from specified clearances in glazing rabbet.

Seal all sash corners and fabrication intersections to make sash weathertight. Weep rabbet outdoors at sill.

Prime paint all sealing surfaces of wood sash and of carbon steel sash. Use appropriate solvents to remove greases, lacquers, and other organic protective finishes from sealing surfaces of aluminum sash. All sealing surfaces must be clean, dry, and dust free before glazing begins.

Typical glazing systems

Figure 3 shows representative typical glazing systems which have proved satisfactory when proper glazing techniques are used. With the rapid advancement in glazing technology and the development of new sealants, there are many other adequate systems.

By ALBERT G. H. DIETZ,
Professor of Building Engineering,
Department of Architecture,
Massachusetts Institute of Technology

CHARACTERISTICS

Chemists describe plastics as organic "polymers" and can explain why similarities in the structure of plastics' molecules give rise to many similarities in engineering properties. Fairly safe generalizations can be made about the physical characteristics of these materials, just as with metals and other materials. Further, it is useful to recognize the basic division among plastics, which is reflected in their engineering properties. Not unlike the distinctions between "non-ferrous" and "ferrous," or "hardwoods" and "softwoods," the two major divisions into one of which all the plastics must fall are:

The Thermoplastics, which become soft when exposed to sufficient heat and harden when cooled, no matter how often the process is repeated. Although some need more heat than others, softening with heat is their distinguishing characteristic, very much like the behavior of candle wax.

The Thermosets, which are set into permanent shape with or without heat during forming. Subsequent heating will not soften them, and the only change that can be brought about by increasing heat is actual chemical decomposition—analogous to the charring and burning of wood.

Ten characteristics of plastics in general have an important bearing on building applications. They are exhibited in varying degree, often being especially marked in one or the other of the two basic subclasses—thermoplastic and thermosetting plastics.

1. *Excellent electrical-insulating properties,* in terms both of resistivity and dielectric strength. There are also other good electrical properties which are important in specific applications that are of more significance in electrical engineering than in building.

2. *Good corrosion resistance.* At least one plastic material can be found to resist practically any corrosive condition found in building. Many instances can be cited—in industrial piping, for example—where plastics have far out-performed costlier metals, such as copper or stainless steel, under corrosive conditions.

3. *Creep.* Some plastics, especially the thermosets, are essentially elastic within certain limits of stress: deformation in proportion to the load applied which disappears quickly when the load is released. Others, especially the thermoplastics, exhibit plastic behavior: they flow, or "creep," when stressed, depending not only on the load, but also on the rate at which it is applied and its duration, and increasing with increases in temperature. This characteristic is comparable to that of steel or other metals when stressed, perhaps at high temperatures, beyond the elastic limit. When the load is removed, the material may eventually recover part of the deformation, or all of it. Creep may be so small as to be unnoticeable, or too large to be acceptable in a given application.

4. *Low to moderate tensile strength* is generally characteristic of unreinforced plastics, although in laminated or reinforced form, plastics can compare quite favorably with metals.

5. *Low modulus of elasticity* is also characteristic, but glass-fiber-reinforced thermosetting plastics offer roughly the same range of stiffness as wood or concrete. Carbon, graphite, and aramids, while expensive, provide much higher elastic moduli in composites.

6. *Low maximum service temperatures.* In contrast with a number of structural building materials in common use, plastics in general are best used at temperatures below the wood-char point of 380-400 deg F. This is only an approximate statement, due to the varied conditions of actual use and to differing combinations of temperature-affected properties that may be relevant: tensile strength, creep, chemical stability, and the like.

7. *High thermal coefficient of expansion.* Plastics typically **expand,** per unit of temperature increase, several times as much as metals. Thermoplastics, as a group, have a higher coefficient than thermosets.

8. *Flammability.* In the sense that they can be destroyed by fire, plastics can be grouped with all other organic materials. However, a number of them—including certain thermoplastics—will extinguish themselves once the igniting flame has been removed, as in standard tests. (See Fire Behavior, below.)

9. *Low thermal conductivity.* Typical "k-value" for the plastics in common use is about 1.5, or slightly higher than wood. As low-density foams, plastics provide some of the most efficient thermal insulators available for building; a 2 lb per cu ft polystyrene foam, for example, might offer a "k" of 0.25, and polyurethane still lower.

10. *Light weight,* per unit volume. Unmodified with fillers, reinforcements, or other additives, the more common of these materials range from a specific gravity of just under 0.9 (polypropylene) to roughly 1.5 (polyvinyl chloride, PVC). Strength-to-weight ratios thus compare favorably with those of other materials.

Tensile strength of plastics is comparable to wood and concrete, but increases to the range of metal alloys when reinforced or laminated with other materials or when drawn into fine filaments. Although plastics are inherently low in stiffness, when reinforced they range higher even than wood and concrete. Forming into structural shapes also increases stiffness. Thermal conductivity is about as low as wood, making plastics excellent insulators. Although most plastics are damaged above about 200°F, many do not support their own combustion, or burn with difficulty in standard tests.

TERMINOLOGY

A certain amount of chemical-industry terminology cannot be avoided in discussing plastics. A few of the

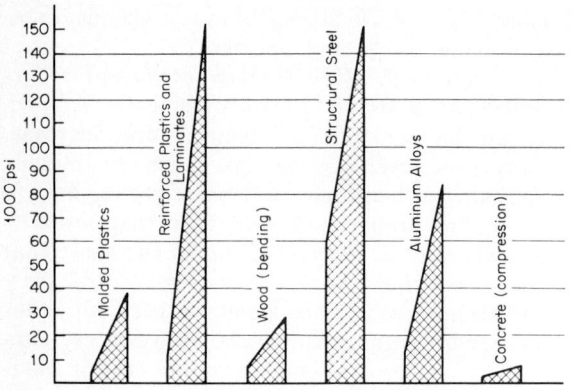

Fig. 1. Tensile strength of plastics and other materials

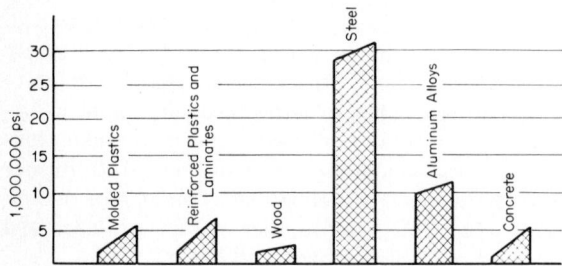

Fig. 2. Modulus of elasticity of plastics and other materials

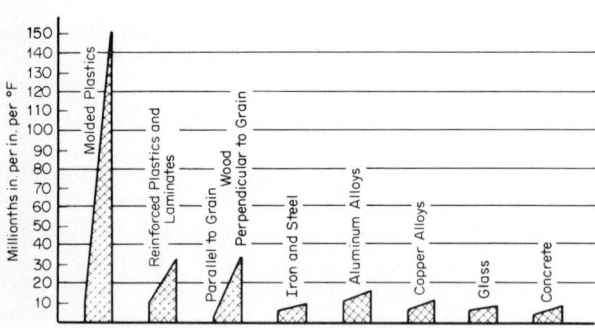

Fig. 3. Thermal expansion of plastics and other materials

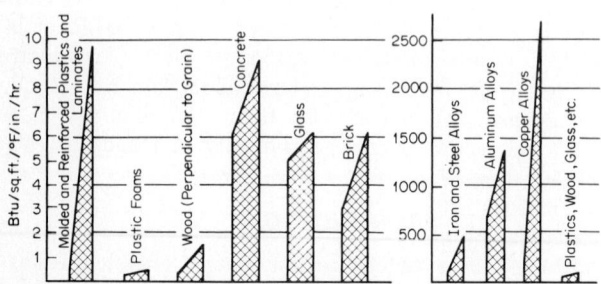

Fig. 4. Thermal conductivity of plastics and other materials

following terms are included because their meanings in this context are somewhat more precise than in common parlance.

COLD FLOW:
Creep occurring at room temperature.

COPOLYMER:
A substance consisting of long-chain molecules formed from two or more different monomers.

CREEP:
The change in dimension of a plastic under load over a period of time. Does not include the initial instantaneous elastic deformation.

CROSS-LINKING:
The chemical union of polymer molecules to form a three-dimensional network. Cross-linked polymers are usually infusible thermosets.

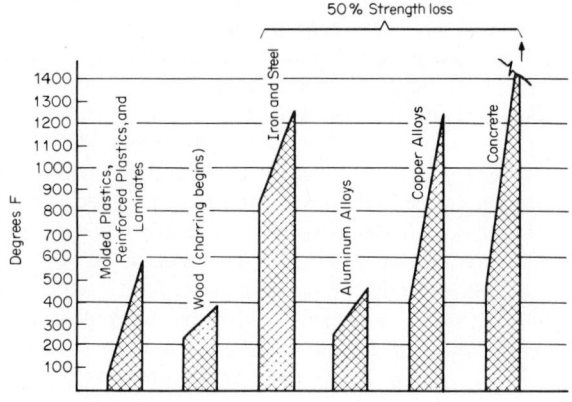

Fig. 5. Maximum continuous service temperature of plastics and other materials

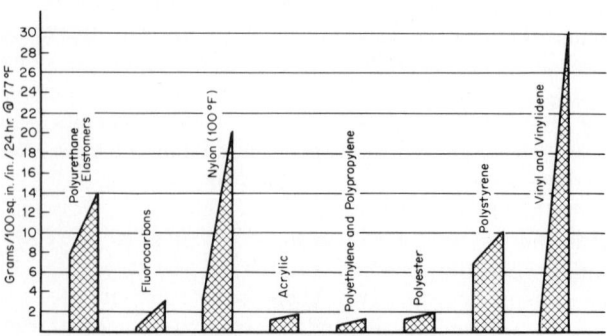

Fig. 6. Water vapor permeability of plastics films 0.001-in. thick

Note: Figures 1 through 6 adapted from *Plastics for Architects and Builders* by Albert G. H. Dietz, MIT Press, 1970.

CURE:
Changing physical properties of a material by chemical reaction—usually to a harder or more permanent form.

DEFLECTION TEMPERATURE:
Degrees Fahrenheit at which a plastic material under fixed stress distorts as temperature increases, according to standard ASTM test procedure. (D 648-56).

DEGRADATION:
Molecular change to the polymer, usually from exposure to light, fire, or heat, becoming apparent as charring, discoloration, clouding of transparent plastics, embrittlement, or other loss of original properties.

DISPERSION:
A liquid with finely-divided insoluble particles scattered uniformly throughout. Called a "colloid" if particles are fine enough. "Dispersion" and "suspension" contrast with a "solution."

ELASTOMER:
A material which at room temperature can be stretched repeatedly to at least twice its original length and, upon release of the stress, will return instantly and with force to its approximate original length.

EXOTHERMIC:
Adjective indicating a chemical reaction that gives off heat.

FILM:
Sheeting of nominal thickness not greater than 10 mils.

FLASH:
Extra plastic attached to a molding along the parting line. It must be removed before the piece can be considered finished.

HIGH-PRESSURE LAMINATES:
Laminates molded and cured at pressures not lower than 1000 psi, (commonly 1200-2000 psi).

INHIBITOR:
A substance that slows down chemical reaction—often used to prolong "shelf" or storage life.

LATEX:
A suspension in water of fine particles of rubber, (which today includes synthetic rubber).

LINEAR:
Adjective to describe a long-chain molecule with a minimum of side-chains or branches.

MONOFILAMENT:
A continuous thread made up of only one filament.

MONOMER:
A substance constituted of a simple molecule, of relatively low molecular weight, that is capable of reacting with like molecules to form long-molecular-chain "polymers" (or, with both like and unlike molecules, to form "copolymers").

ORGANIC:
Adjective to distinguish those compounds, like plant and animal matter, which contain the very prevalent carbon atom. "Inorganic" compounds are those that do not contain carbon.

PLASTICIZER:
Materials added to a plastic to improve flexibility or to facilitate compounding.

POLYMER:
A substance consisting of long-chain molecules formed by the union of many small molecules that are alike. (See "monomer.")

POLYMERIZATION:
The process by which polymers and copolymers are formed.

POSTFORMING:
Bending phenolic laminates or certain other thermosetting sheet materials into simple (substantially permanent) shapes by heat and pressure after initial cure.

REINFORCED PLASTICS (formerly called low-pressure laminates):
In general, laminates molded and cured in the range of pressures from 400 psi down to and including pressures obtained by the mere contact of the plies, or incorporation of fibrous reinforcement by other means such as spray-deposition or filament winding.

RESIN (SYNTHETIC):
Polymeric synthetic products having some of the characteristics of natural resins. Some serve as base ingredients of plastics; others are important ingredients of finishes, adhesives, etc.

RESORCINOL:
Generic noun for a group of synthetic polymers, much like the phenolics, that are chiefly used as heat and water resistant adhesive.

ROVING:
A form of fibrous glass in which spun strands are woven into a tubular rope.

SUSPENSION:
A liquid with small, solid particles dispersed more or less uniformly throughout.

THERMOPLASTIC:
Term identifying that category of plastics which soften whenever heated sufficiently.

THERMOSET AND THERMOSETTING:
Terms identifying the other category of plastics, which undergo a chemical change and harden permanently when heated (in contradistinction to the thermoplastics).

THIXOTROPIC:
Said of materials that are gel-like at rest, but fluid when agitated (desirable in paints).

VACUUM FORMING:
Method of sheet forming in which the plastic sheet is clamped in a stationary frame, heated and drawn down by a vacuum into a mold.

VINYL:
Alone, this word has a precise meaning to chemists. But as used in building, it is a vague term for certain polymers or copolymers. It is safe to assume that "vinyl" means, in connection with latex paints, "polyvinyl acetate" or—anywhere else in building—"polyvinyl chloride" (PVC), or a preponderantly-PVC copolymer .

PRINCIPAL TYPES OF PLASTICS
Thermoplastics
ABS PLASTICS:
Compounds of acrylonitrile, butadiene, and styrene. Important characteristics are toughness, chemical resistance, and non-brittleness at low temperatures.

ACETATE:
See "Cellulosics."

ACRYLICS:
Popularly known trade names are "Lucite" or "Plexiglas"; chemical

name, "polymethyl methacrylate." These materials combine the transparency of glass with plastics' shatter-resistant quality. Their weathering performance has been better than other common plastics, and is being constantly improved.

BUTYRATE:

See "Cellulosics."

CELLULOSICS:

(Primarily cellulose acetate or butyrate.) Also transparent, "acetate" is well known as photographic safety-film. These plastics are tough—one common use is tool handles.

FLUOROCARBONS:

A group of extremely inert plastics. As resins, dispersions, oils, greases, and waxes, they have high thermal stability and excellent resistance to chemical attack.

METHYL MECHACRYLATE:

See "Acrylics."

NYLON:

Molded-nylon products are tough, have a low frictional coefficient, and they resist mechanical wear better than many metals. Nylon's high softening temperature is exemplified by its replacement of brass for mixing-valves in automatic washers.

POLYCARBONATE:

A polymer offering outstanding impact strength, dimensional stability under varying humidity or temperature, heat resistance, weather resistance, and clarity.

POLYETHYLENE:

Waxy and chemically inert, flexible even at low termperatures, this material is one of the best known plastics. It is a water barrier and retards the passage of water vapor. The plain, colorless substance is short lived in sunlight, but carbon-black-pigmented polyethylene has a good weathering record. (A "linear" high-density polyethylene has greater stiffness and temperature resistance than standard low-density polyethylene.)

POLYPROPYLENE:

A thermoplastic material composed of polymers of propylene. The lightest of all commercial plastics, its properties are roughly comparable with those of linear polyethylene.

POLYSTYRENE:

Non-water-absorbent, brittle, it has a wide range of colors. Copolymers of styrene with rubber, such as ABS, can be very tough. Polystyrene is one of several plastics used in electric-lighting diffusers. In foamed form, it has become an important thermal insulation.

PVC (POLYVINYL CHLORIDE):

The resin itself is rigid; plasticizers and copolymerization add flexibility to excellent resistance to wear and abuse.

POLYVINYLIDENE CHLORIDE:

A cousin of PVC, chemically as well as in its properties. Unlike PVC, which must be "stabilized" against degradation under ultraviolet light, it performs well outdoors without special formulation. Well-known trade names are Saran and Geon.

Thermosets

ALKYDS:

These appear chiefly as molded electrical parts. They are also important constituents of certain paints.

EPOXY:

Epoxy is used in building because of its excellent adhesive qualities and chemical resistance.

MELAMINE AND UREA:

Hard, durable, and dimensionally stable, these quite similar plastics are resistant to chemicals, electrical potential, and heat. With a wider color range, melamine is well known to the public in the form of molded dishes and laminates, such as counter tops.

PHENOLIC:

Familiar for years in the old, black telephone handsets, it is strong, durable, and both electrical- and heat-resistant. This low-cost "workhorse" plastic is limited to dark colors.

POLYESTER:

Appears in film form but has been known longer as the plastic most commonly used in large glass-fiber-reinforced translucent panels and molded shapes that are strong, rigid, and impact-resistant. Polyester's resistance to abrasion can be poor, as can its ultraviolet-light resistance, but properties vary widely with differences in formulation.

Polyesters replace portland cement as the matrix in polyester concrete. Compressive, tensile, shear, and impact strengths are higher than in portland-cement concrete, and porosity is lower because nothing evaporates. One use is as thin finished-concrete facings on sandwich panels with foamed plastic cores.

Polymers, including acrylics, polyester, and others, are employed to impregnate standard concrete, increasing compressive and impact strengths, durability, and resistance to moisture penetration.

POLYURETHANE:

Thermosetting polymer, appearing as flexible and rigid foams and coatings, also as adhesives and, in elastomeric form, as sealants.

SILICONES:

Being semi-inorganic substances, silicones might not be classified strictly as "plastics." In building, they are applied to masonry to improve its water-repellance and weatherability and are also used as sealants.

APPLICATIONS

Solid finish surfacing*

FLOOR COVERING

Plastics typically employed—PVC; vinyl-asbestos.

Preferred because—Permanent color; chemical and wear resistance.

Remarks—Share some problems of all resilient floorings, such as shrinkage, selection of proper adhesives and indentation.

COUNTERTOPS

Plastics typically employed—Melamine on phenolic laminate; PVC or polyester laminated to hardboard or other substrate.

Preferred because—Ease of cleaning, no maintenance, withstand abuse and variety of colorful designs.

Remarks—Best heat resistance offered by decorative melamine-surfaced laminates. But the others are more adaptable to complex shapes.

INTERIOR WALL SURFACING

Plastics typically employed—PVC, either in sheets (often fabric-backed) or impregnated in fabric; polyester, often factory- or field-applied to masonry.

Preferred because—Variety of colorful designs; easy maintenance; withstand abuse.

Remarks—PVC provides top-quality wall coverings for such hard-use installations as hotels and insti-

* as contrasted with liquid-applied paints and coatings.

tutions. Field-applied polyesters' uses include sanitary locations such as dairies and bakeries.

EXTERIOR WALL SURFACING

Plastics typically employed—Polyester (reinforced with glass fibers); acrylic, (often similarly reinforced); PVC, polycarbonate, fluorocarbons. (See also polyester concrete under POLYESTER.)

Preferred because—Integral color; large-area units possible, with fewer joints than brick, shingles, etc.; lightweight; relatively easy to clean.

Remarks—These building materials have been in use long enough to begin to establish weatherability comparisons. Architectural possibilities offered by added feature of translucency only beginning to be explored. Flammability and fire resistance are discussed below.

GLAZING

Plastics typically employed—(see also translucent exterior wall surfacing, above). Acrylic; polyester; PVC; polyethylene; polycarbonate.

Preferred because—Shatter-resistant; conducts heat only ¼ as fast as glass; because readily formed, offers self-flashing shapes such as single-unit skylights.

Remarks—Optically, acrylics are as good as the best glass; others may not be, but decorative possibilities are unlimited. Polyethylene uses temporary only, as during construction.

Water and vapor barriers

MEMBRANES, FLASHING, TAPES

Plastics typically employed—Polyethylene; PVC; polyvinylidene chloride; polyurethane.

Preferred because—Flexible; sealable, thus offering waterproof sheeting of any size. Sufficient elasticity can be formulated to accommodate building's movements, also to seal around penetrating nails, pipes, etc.

Remarks—Plastic foams employed as thermal insulation often double as vapor barriers; so can plastic films applied to sheets such as plywood. With flashing and tapes, it must be kept in mind that some plastics are formulated only for placement within the construction, not for exposure to ultra-violet and weather.

WEATHERSTRIPPING, WATERSTOPS

Plastics typically employed—PVC; polyurethane.

Preferred because—Can be formulated for elasticity approaching that of synthetic rubbers, which are also common in these applications. No corrosion; no staining. Thermoplastics, such as PVC, readily joined at mitered corners by "welding," or thermal-pressure-joinery.

Remarks—Such flexible materials, in extruded form, offer water-stop-expansion-joint between adjacent pours of concrete slab or wall. Another class of synthetics somewhat related to plastics is also important in building as water-barriers: "elastomers" (i.e. rubbery materials) such as neoprene gaskets and sheeting, polysulfide, acrylic, polyurethane, and butadiene sealants, silicone polymers, synthetic-rubber roof coatings, and the like.

Thermal insulation

Plastics typically employed—Polystyrene, polyurethane (foams).

Preferred because—Insulating properties not reduced by wetting; density readily controlled; special properties possible: adhesiveness, vapor barrier, some structural strength, decorative translucence.

Remarks—Where desirable to fill voids, may be foamed-in-place. Although these foams burn when held in a flame, they can be self-extinguishing.

Structural elements

Plastics typically employed—Polyester or epoxy, reinforced with glass fibers; rigid PVC.

Preferred because—Corrosion resistance; high strength-to-weight ratios.

Remarks—Plastics have been used in sandwich panels for faces, adhesives and cores. Phenolic impregnated kraft honeycomb and polystyrene and polyurethane foams are most commonly used as cores. Reinforced plastics are used as shells and folded plates, as well as corrugated and flat sheets, the latter frequently as sandwich facings.

Finish hardware

Plastics typically employed—Almost all the thermoplastics listed here and most of the thermosets.

Preferred because—Good decorative characteristics; minimal mainte-nance; inexpensive even when intricately shaped. Certain properties often determine specific applications; for instance, nylon's wear-resistance has introduced it into hardware.

Remarks—Plastic or plastic-coated insect screening popular because noncorroding. Plastic drawers and chairs are common. Plastics safer than glass or ceramic for knobs and handles, towel bars.

Electrical components

Plastics typically employed—All.

Preferred because—Superior electrical properties, especially under adverse conditions such as prolonged dampness, vibration, etc. Translucency the basis for widespread use as electric-light diffusers, including "luminous ceilings."

Remarks—First major commercial area for plastics (in the 1920's) was electrical applications; this continues to broaden with the increase of electrical and electronic complexity in buildings.

Plumbing

Plastics typically employed—For fixtures and fittings, reinforced polyester, rigid PVC, ABS; for piping, polyethylene, PVC, and various butadiene blends akin to ABS.

Preferred because—No corrosion. Easy to handle, to assemble. Fewer joints; easy maintenance.

Remarks—Widely used for drain, waste, and vent piping, water supply to building, irrigation. Newer formulations available to resist hot fluids, including water, under pressure.

Miscellaneous construction aids

Translucent polyethylene film provides temporary enclosure for wintertime construction. The same material is widely used as an inexpensive tarpaulin to protect equipment or materials stored on site. A top-quality, very durable tarpaulin is PVC-coated nylon fabric. Plastic chairs to support reinforcing rods in concrete make good use of the non-corrosive properties of plastics. Various plastic coatings for concrete forms produce smoother concrete, prolong the life of the forms, and make their removal easier. Strippable plastic coatings are used to protect plumbing fixtures and finished metal surfaces during construction.

The synthetic resins upon which most paints are based today are closely identified with the plastics discussed here; so, too, are a number of adhesives and binders that are important in building: phenolic adhesives for exterior-grade plywood, phenolic binders for glassfiber insulating batts and boards, urea particleboard binders, resorcinol or epoxy adhesives, and similar materials.

DESIGNING FOR PLASTICS
Thermal coefficient

Thermal expansion and contraction of plastics is typically high; the coefficient is five or more times that of metals. This calls for special care in detailing, keeping in mind movement in the major axis or plane of the component. Thus means should be devised for avoiding or disguising distortion of large sheets. In the same general connection, an important advantage of plastics for use in building is their capability of being formed fairly readily to resist stress concentrations, whether arising from thermal movement or other causes.

Durability

Weathering of plastics outdoors and the general durability of plastics when not exposed to the weather, are questions uppermost in the minds of designers and specifiers. Unfortunately, the plastics industry has not yet succeeded in developing accelerated laboratory tests that reliably predict the weathering performance of materials over periods of 20 years and more.

The record of actual exposures, of course, grows longer and more complete all the while. There are acrylics that have stood up well under outdoor exposures exceeding 25 years. A few other plastics can point to exterior installations 15 years or more old, with negligible deterioration. With new formulations constantly appearing, the designer can only cautiously weigh the variables. The more easily replaceable components —glazing, for example—might not have to prove themselves by decades of actual exposure-history if replacement costs were counterbalanced by other factors: low initial installed cost, good appearance, resistance to damage, ease of maintenance.

Aside from weather-erosion and deterioration under ultra-violet light, the general durability of plastics in typical building applications has been good. PVC for example provides perhaps the best resilient flooring from the viewpoint of standing up under neglect. According to accelerated tests, nylon outwears bronze mechanically. Many plastics offer impact resistance that makes them more durable than alternative materials for the same application. (The success of plastic and plastic-coated luggage illustrates this.) Sometimes the properties which provide durability in plastics also enhance their attributes for safety. For example, the use of plastics in shower doors and room dividers is appropriate since it is almost impossible to fall through them.

Corrosion and stain resistance

Another aspect of plastics' durability which can be all-important to the designer is that they are not subject to chemical corrosion or to electrolytic action. This generalization must be modified, however, by pointing out that some plastic materials are selectively attacked by certain classes of solvents—mostly chemicals that are not likely to be found outside laboratory or industrial buildings. (Where a plastic is to be put to a new use, the designer would be wise to check the possibilities against a listing of the degree to which a number of chemicals will attack it. Such tabulations are available from the producer of the basic material.) This absence of ordinary corrosion may mean absence of staining as well as increased durability.

Fire behavior

Being organic materials, all plastics can be destroyed by fire. Although some plastics burn of themselves, many are self-extinguishing when the flame igniting them in standard tests has been removed. Among these flammable plastics, there is a great range of the degree of ease of ignition.

Flammability, as with other materials, is highly dependent upon conditions. A material that rates "self-extinguishing" or even "nonflammable" in a standard test may burn readily in a large fire. Smoke evolution may be low, moderate, or severe depending upon the type of fire and the composition of the material. As with other organic materials, carbon monoxide is the most prevalent toxic gas given off (again depending upon fire conditions), but other noxious and toxic gases may be generated, depending upon the composition of the material and the nature of the fire. Where actual fire hazards may be present, specific properties of the material must be considered. Thermoplastics, for instance, will soften—perhaps melt—before a fire even reaches them. Partly depending on the softening temperature, this may be bad or good: approval for ceiling light diffusion is commonly given for those plastics that can be relied upon in case of fire to fall out of position soon enough so as not to interfere with the effectiveness of sprinklers placed above the suspended ceiling.

If building codes do not take ease of ignition into account, the designer should do so wherever this could bear on fire safety. Codes do emphasize two characteristics of materials, both of which presuppose an out-of-control blaze already going: One is fire retardation, and this is something only for heavy constructions of brick, concrete, etc.—not for organic materials, except, perhaps, when used as insulating cores in construction in which the facings provide suitable protection against fire penetration. The other is the rate at which flame may spread across the surface of a flammable material. Especially in spaces used by the public, this can become a fire- and panic-hazard. According to the various standard tests used for measuring this characteristic, the flammable plastics present a wide range of surface-flame-travel. Some will hardly spread flame at all; others will do so faster than wood.

Deformation under load

"Creep" is a property of most materials, but, with traditional materials of construction, it is reasonable to assume elastic behavior within certain limits of stress. However, many plastics, especially the thermoplastics, exhibit time-dependent plastic behavior: flow, or creep, of the material under load, so deformation depends not only on the load, but also on the rate at which it is applied and on its duration. Further, this phenomenon is greater at elevated temperatures. In the case of many plastics, these relationships are of major significance and must be taken into account; otherwise, failures may occur. Appropriate stress levels and factors of safety must be employed. For materials exhibiting no sharply defined yield points or elastic limits, the working stresses are likely to depend upon the degree of creep that can be tolerated.

Interior finish and trim

Plastic materials must conform to the requirements of the code.

Glazing of openings

Plastics may be employed for glazing doors, sash, and framed openings not required to be fire-resistive, in unprotected frame construction, and in factory and industrial buildings. In other buildings in which such openings need not be fire-resistance rated, additional limitations are:

1. In any story, area not greater than 25 per cent of wall area.
2. Above first story, area of pane not greater than 16 ft², not more than 4 ft high. At least a 3-ft spandrel between stories.
3. Plastics not more than 75 ft above grade.
4. If continuous architectural projection (canopy) at least 3 ft wide at each floor, area of approved thermoplastics may be increased to 50 per cent of wall area in structures less than 150-ft high. Sizes and dimensions not limited except by structural requirements. No spandrel limitations.

If a complete approved automatic fire-suppressant system is provided, the foregoing permissible glazings may be doubled.

Exterior wall panels

Plastics may be used as panels in exterior walls not required to have a fire-resistance rating except in buildings such as homes for the ill and infirm, hospitals, jails, prisons, mental institutions and similar buildings, and buildings used for the storage of hazardous materials. The limitations are summarized in Table 1.

Roof panels

Except for homes for the infirm and ill, hospitals, jails, prisons, mental institutions and similar buildings, and storage of hazardous materials, approved plastic roof panels may be installed:

1. In roofs of buildings protected by complete fire-suppressant systems.
2. Where the roof need not have a fire-resistance rating.

FIRE RESISTANCE REQUIREMENTS

The three model building codes contain sections respecting light-transmitting plastics and plastics foams. The following summary is based largely upon the BOCA and ICBO codes, but all three are quite similar in their provisions respecting plastics. They relate mostly to light-transmitting and foamed plastics.

General

An approved thermoplastic, thermosetting, or reinforced plastic must have a self-ignition temperature of at least 650°F (ASTM D1929), and a smoke density rating of no more than 450 (ASTM E84) or 75 (ASTM D2843).

Classification

Class C-1 plastics have a burning extent less than 1 in., and Class C-2 plastics have a burning rate less than 2.5 in. per minute, respectively (ASTM D635), in nominal 0.60-in. thickness or the thickness intended for use.

Structural requirements

Plastic materials, assemblies, connections, and fastening must be of adequate strength and durability to withstand loads and forces specified in the code. Provision must be made for expansion and contraction.

Table 1. Area limitation and separation requirements for plastic wall panels*

Fire separation	Class of plastic	Max. % area of ext. wall in plastic panels	Max. ft² single area	Minimum separation of panels (ft) Vertical	Horizontal
6 ft or less	——	NP†	NP	——	——
6 ft or more but less than 11 ft	C1	10	50	8	4
	C2	NP	NP	——	——
11 ft or more but less than 30 ft	C1	25	90	6	4
	C2	15	70	8	4
Over 30 ft	C1	50	Not limited	3‡	0
	C2	50	100	6‡	3

* *Combinations of plastic wall panels and glazing subject to same limitations as wall panels.*
From *BOCA Code, 1978. Building Officials and Code Administrators International, Inc.*
† *Not permitted.*
‡ *No vertical separation if a projection at least 3-ft wide provides an effective fire canopy.*

Table 2. Area limitations for roof panels

Class of plastic	Max. area individual panel (ft²)	Max. aggregate area (% of floor area)	Separation horizontally (ft)
C1	300	30	4*
C2	100	25	4*

* *When exterior wall openings must be fire-resistance rated, roof panels must be at least 6 ft from such walls.*

Table 3. Area limitations for skylight assemblies*

Class of plastic	Max. area per unit (ft²)	Aggregate area (% floor area)	Horizontal separation (ft)	Curb height above roof (in.)	Height domed skylight
C1	100	33†	4‡	4	10 % of span,
C2	100	25†	4‡	4	or at least 5 in.

* Need not be applied if building is one-story high, at least 30 ft from other buildings, and space below roof not classified as high hazard or institutional use or means of egress, or plastic material meets fire-resistive requirements of roof.
† May be doubled if used as fire-venting system or building has complete fire-suppressant system, except for mental hospitals, prisons, and similar buildings, and buildings for storage hazardous materials.
‡ When exterior wall openings must be fire-resistance rated, skylight assemblies must be at least 6 ft from such walls.

3. If panels meet the requirements for roof covering of the occupancy group.

Area limitations are given in Table 2. Exceptions are:

1. One-story building up to 16-ft high, not exceeding 1200 ft², not closer than 11 ft from another building or lot line.
2. Low-hazard buildings, e.g., swimming pool shelters and greenhouses not more than 5000 ft² and not closer than 11 ft from property line or other buildings.
3. Roofs of terraces, patios of one- and two-family dwellings.

Skylight assemblies

Except for buildings for storage of hazardous materials, plastics skylight assemblies may be employed under limitations shown in Table 3.

Light-diffusing systems

Plastic light-diffusing systems are not permitted in institutional buildings, high-hazard-materials storage buildings, or exitways unless protected with a fire-suppressant system. They must comply with interior-finish requirements unless they will fall before igniting at ambient temperature at least 200°F below ignition temperature but stay in place at ambient 175°F at least 15 minutes. Individual panels must not exceed 10 ft in length nor 30 ft² in area. In exitways and corridors they must not exceed 30 per cent of the ceiling area. If a fire-suppressant system is installed, areas are not limited, but sprinklers must be above and below the panels unless specifically approved for installations only above.

Partitions, bathroom accessories, awnings, and greenhouses

Plastics must comply with requirements for partitions. They are permitted for glazing in showerstalls, bathtub enclosures, and similar uses. Plastic awnings must comply with general provisions. Plastics may replace plain glass in greenhouses.

FOAM PLASTICS

General

Except as specified below, foam plastics must have a flame-spread rating of 75 or less and smoke-developed rating of 450 or less (ASTM E84).

Specific requirements

Trim: Plastic foam trim may cover not more than 10 per cent of a wall or ceiling area, density must be 20 lb/ft³ or more, thickness not greater than ½ in. and width not greater than 4 in.

Locations: Within cavity of masonry or concrete wall.

On room side of conforming surfaces provided that the foam is protected by thermal barrier equal to ½-in. gypsum board having a finish rating of not less than 15 minutes. Barrier must stay in place at least 15 minutes.

Within wall cavity or as an element of combustible nonfire-resistant wall with same protection as above.

Within wall cavity of combustible fire-resistant walls provided the same protection is provided as above, or fire tests are made.

In cold storage and similar applications, foam plastics 10 in. thick may be employed if flame-spread rating of material 4 in. thick is 75 or less, if the space is protected by automatic fire-extinguishing systems, and the foam is protected by ½-in. portland cement plaster or other thermal barrier having a 15-minute finish rating.

If foam plastic has a flame-spread rating of 25 or less, it may be used not more than 4 in. thick if covered with 0.032 in. aluminum or 26-gauge galvanized steel sheet, provided that automatic sprinklers are used and fire-resistant construction is not required.

Foam plastic may be part of Class A, B, or C roofing assembly if the foam nearest the interior of the building has an approved barrier. Ordinary roof coverings, other than A, B, or C, may be applied over plastic foam separated from the interior of the building by ½-in. exterior-grade plywood with supporting blocking, or by equivalent protection.

Where doors without fire-resistant ratings are permitted, foam plastic with flame-spread rating of 25 or less may be used as cores of doors with 0.032-in. aluminum or 26-gauge steel sheet facing.

Foam plastic having fire-spread ratings of 75 or less may be used as backer board ⅜-in. thick or less, if heat content is 2000 Btu/ft² or less and backer board is separated from the building interior by 2 in. or more of mineral insulation or equivalent.

By ALBERT G. H. DIETZ, *Professor of Building Engineering, Department of Architecture, Massachusetts Institute of Technology*

STRUCTURAL PRINCIPLES

As employed in building, a structural sandwich consists essentially of two relatively thin, hard, dense, strong, stiff facings bonded to a relatively thick, light, less strong, and less stiff core. The structural principle is similar to that of an I-beam, box beam, or stressed-skin panel; the facings are similar to the flanges and the core is similar to the web, the difference being that the core of a sandwich is spread over the entire width of the facing whereas the web of an I-beam is concentrated. The geometry in both cases puts the flanges or facings as far from the neutral axis as possible, resulting in a high moment of inertia and stiffness modules with consequent maximum resistance to imposed bending moments and to deflection under load (Fig. 1). The facings of the sandwich provide the resistance to tension and compression in the internal resisting moment couple; the core provides resistance to shear. In a sandwich, the core has the additional function of supporting the thin compression facing against buckling or wrinkling so that it can develop its full compressive strength. The adhesive that bonds facings and core together must be able to withstand the shear and tensile stresses induced between them.

Because of their relatively low stiffnesses, core materials often have low shearing moduli. This means that the shear stresses set up in the core may cause more marked shear distortion than is usually the case in stiff structural materials such as steel, concrete, or wood. The further result is that a structural sandwich may deflect more under load than would ordinarily be predicted by the visual simplified deflection formulas, which ignore shear deflection. Shear deflection is marked only in relatively short, heavily loaded sandwiches; as the span to depth ratio becomes large, the factor diminishes.

MATERIALS

Many materials can be and are employed for the facings and cores of structural sandwiches. Among the facing materials are metal (steel and aluminum, mainly), plywood, hardboard, cement-asbestos board, gypsum board, thin slabs of reinforced concrete, concrete slabs utilizing polyester resin in place of portland cement, high-pressure laminates, glass-fiber reinforced plastics, transparent plastics such as acrylics, other plastics such as rigid polyvinyl chloride, and any other suitable material for the particular installation. Cores include plastics foams such as polystyrene and polyurethane, foamed glass, foamed silicate, foamed concrete, fiberboard, particle board, and a variety of grids such as the honeycomb based on a phenolic-resin-impregnated kraft paper. Facings and cores may be composites of several constituents.

Just as many materials may be employed for facings and cores, so the adhesives that bond them together may be based on many materials. Typically, they are polymeric substances that bond well to a variety of surfaces. Among them are epoxies, phenol formaldehyde, resorcinol formaldehyde, urea formaldehyde, melamine formaldehyde, rubber-based adhesives, and many others. The strong and waterproof but brittle adhesives such as phenol formaldehyde may be modified with elastomers such as synthetic rubber to provide flexibility and toughness needed to resist differential temperature stresses set up between facings and cores. No additional adhesive is required in the case of foamed-in-place polyurethane cores which adhere tenaciously to all the usual facing materials.

In addition to their structural functions, building sandwiches must provide thermal

DEFLECTION

The expression for deflection of a sandwich beam, including shear deflection is

$$d = k_b \, P \, L^3/D + k_s \, PL/N$$

where $D = E_f \, b \, (h^3 - C^3)/12$
$N = (h + c) \, b \, G_c/2$
P = load
L = length of beam or span
E_f = elastic modulus of facing
G_c = core shear modulus
b = width of sandwich
h = overall thickness of sandwich
c = thickness of core

k_b and k_s are coefficients depending upon the loading condition. A few values are given in Table 1.

Table 1. Values of K_b and k_s

Load	Beam ends	Deflection at	k_b	k_s
Uniform	Simply supported	Midspan	5/384	1/8
Uniform	Both clamped	Midspan	1/384	1/8
Concentrated, midspan	Simply supported	Midspan	1/48	1/4
Concentrated, midspan	Both clamped	Midspan	1/192	1/4
Uniform	Cantilever	Free end	1/8	1/2
Concentrated, free end	Cantilever	Free end	1/3	1

and acoustical barriers as in walls and partitions. If the thermal transmission coefficients, k, of the various constituents of a sandwich are known, the overall thermal coefficient, U, can easily be calculated by standard formulas (see section on "Insulation"). Because light weight is often a desired attribute of a structural sandwich, its acoustical isolation characteristics may or may not be satisfactory, depending upon the level desired, the acoustical "limpness" of its constituents, and the efficiency of the seals around the sandwich panel (see section on "Acoustics— Sound isolation").

If a sandwich panel is to remain flat with changes in temperature or moisture content that may cause expansion and contraction of the various layers, it must have "balanced" construction; that is, the corresponding layers on each side of the central plane must have corresponding expansion and contraction characteristics.

A few examples of sandwich panels are:
Cement-asbestos board facings, fiberboard core
Plywood facings, honeycomb core
Glass-fiber reinforced plastics facings, aluminum grid core
Polyester concrete facings reinforced with glass fiber, polyurethane foam core
Hardboard facings, particle board core
Metal facings, foam and honeycomb core
For additional examples and further discussion of this subject, see section on "Curtain Walls."

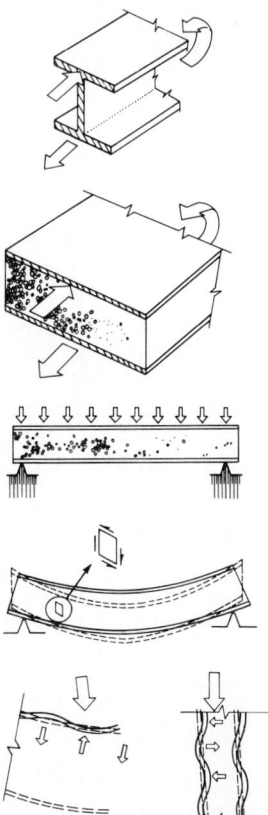

Fig. 1. Behavior of sandwich beams. Facings, analogous to flanges of I-beam, provide tension-compression internal resisting couple; core resists shear similarly to web of I-beam. Shear distortion of core leads to increased deflection. Core supports compression facings against wrinkling or buckling.

(From A. G. H. Dietz, Plastics for Architects and Builders, copyright by MIT Press, 1970.)

Data from International Cut Stone Contractors and Quartymen's Association.

Characteristics of Various Building Stones

Limestone

Oolitic — a calcite-cemented calcareous stone formed of shells and shell fragments, practically non-crystalline in character. It is found in massive deposits, located almost entirely in Lawrence, Monroe and Owen Counties, Indiana, and in Alabama, Kansas and Texas. This limestone is characteristically a freestone, without cleavage planes, possessing a uniformity of composition, texture and structure. It possesses a high internal elasticity, adapting itself without damage to extreme temperature changes.

Dolomitic — a limestone rich in magnesium carbonate, frequently somewhat crystalline in character. It is found in ledge formations in a wide variety of color tones and textures. Generally speaking, its crushing and tensile strengths are greater than the oolitic limestones, and its appearance shows greater variety in texture.

Crystalline — a limestone which is predominantly composed of calcium carbonate crystals, though not of the re-crystallized nature characteristic of marble. It is high in crushing and tensile strength, very low in absorption, and usually shows only slight variations from a uniform light gray color and smooth texture.

Sandstone

A sedimentary rock consisting usually of quartz cemented with silica, iron oxide or calcium carbonate. Sandstone is durable, has a very high crushing and tensile strength, and a wide range of colors and textures.

Quartzite

A compact granular rock composed of quartz crystals, usually so firmly cemented as to make the mass homogeneous and as hard as many granites. The stone is generally quarried in stratified layers, the surfaces of which are unusually smooth. Its crushing and tensile strengths are extremely high. The color range is wide.

Rubble (ledge stone), Flagging

A natural cleft stone, which may be limestone, sandstone or quartzite, particularly adaptable as a veneer. Since a large number of stones can be classified as rubble, there is also a wide variety of colors and textures. This stone is broken to standard widths and in random lengths from 6 in. to whatever the various quarries supply.

Chesapeake-Hue (Maryland quartzite) split face, random ashlar

Indiana Limestone (oolitic) shot sawed finish

Indiana Limestone (oolitic) split face

Penn-Kress Stone (Pennsylvania quartzite) split face veneer

Colorado Red Sandstone (quartzite sandstone) split face

Sunset Stone (Wisconsin limestone) split face, random ashlar

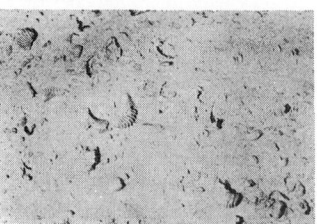

Cordova Shell Limestone (Texas oolitic) smooth machine finish veneer

Tennquartz (Tennessee Stone quartzite) strip rubble veneer, random lengths

Carthage Stone (Missouri crystalline limestone) split face, random lengths, coursed

Winona Travertine Stone (Minnesota dolomitic limestone) split face, random ashlar

Classifications of Building Stone

Cut Stone

This includes all stone cut or machined to a given size, dimension or shape, and produced in accordance with working or shop drawings which have been developed from the architect's structural drawings.

Ashlar Facing

Strictly speaking, any exposed stone facing made from broken or cut stone, set at random or in uniform courses, is an ashlar facing. In this sense, cut stone may be set as an ashlar facing, or the word ashlar may apply to various forms of facing with stone which is not measured and cut, according to shop drawing specifications, but is set at the discretion of the stone mason on the job. Ashlar facing may be of several surface finishes, viz:

Split Face. (Sawed Bed) This is customarily furnished in unit heights, generally speaking 4 in. on the beds, and is delivered to the job in strips or lengths from 18 in. to 4 ft. Usually split face is sawed on the beds and is split either by hand or with machine so that the surface face of the stone exhibits the natural quarry texture.

Strip Rubble. Strip rubble, generally speaking, comes from a ledge quarry. The beds of the stone, while uniformly straight, are of the natural cleft as the stone is removed from the ledge, and then split by machine to approximately 4 in. widths.

Sawed Face. This is a plain stone, the surface of which is the natural sawed finish. Like split face, it is furnished in unit heights, 4 in. on the bed and in lengths of 2 ft to 5 ft.

Rock (Pitch) Face. This is similar to split face, except that the face of the stone is pitched to a given line and plane, producing a bold appearance rather than the comparatively flush face obtained in split face. It occasions additional labor and necessarily an increased cost over split face.

Flagstone

Sawed — So furnished it is sawed from dimension blocks of limestone or sandstone, usually in 2 in. thicknesses. Monotones of buff or gray or variegated are obtainable in this type.

Ledgestone — The majority of flagstones come from ledge quarries and are furnished in thicknesses from 1_2 in. to 2 in. Such flagging comes in various colors: tan, brown, gray, red, blue, white, green, pink, buff, purple, yellow, orange and combinations of these. Most quarries furnish it either in random, irregular sizes, or broken to definite or pre-determined dimensions.

Color and Pattern in Building Stone

Color

Building stone is available today in very wide variety of colors. It is true, of course, that some of the startling "decorator" hues which have become common for interior decoration will not be found in natural stone. The basic colors themselves are there, but always reduced in intensity. There are reds and greens, blues, yellows, grays, and various mixtures, either as solid colors, or as variegated combinations.

Some stones, like the limestones, gain effectiveness through the quality of the material, even though the color be monotone. Others, such as the strip rubble stones, frequently offer a wide range of hues which are normal to the stone as it comes from the quarry.

PATTERN can be established by variations in size, setting methods, color, finish

Surface Finishes of Cut Stone

Surface finishing of cut stone is frequently an important factor in its final quality as set in a job. Variations in texture which result from different finishes, increase greatly the working palette of the architect, since the original wide range of stones is made broader still by a consideration of the choice of finishes.

Not all stones, of course, take every finish. And where a finish is applicable, it should be analyzed for cost, particularly if hand labor is required.

More detailed information than can be provided here may be obtained from any of the Stone Association members.

Smooth Planer Finish

This is the finish left on the stone as it comes from the planer, with such tool marks as may exist being carefully removed from the finished surface of the stone. It is the finish most generally specified.

Carbo-Finish

This is a very smooth finish produced by the use of a carborundum machine instead of a planer.

Rubbed Finish

This requires the rubbing of the stone with an abrasive, after the stone has been planed. Today, with carboloy tipped planer tools, this operation is generally unnecessary, since the planer tool takes the stone down to a finish comparable to a rubbed finish. Rubbing stone adds to the cost.

Sawed Finish, Sand-Sawed

This is the finish which is left as the stone comes from the gang-saw. As such, it provides a moderately smooth, granular surface, varying in texture with the type of stone.

Sawed Finish, Chat-Sawed

Finish is produced by sawing with coarse chat under the sawing blade, resulting in an interesting, rough surface texture.

Sawed Finish, Shot-Sawed

Finish is similar to chat-sawed, except that chilled steel shot is used under the blades. The finished surface is heavily ribbed with irregular, roughly parallel grooves.

Tooled Finishes

Since tooled finishes are usually costly, they seldom are used in modern construction. It is recommended that an Association member be consulted before specifying these finishes.

Hand Finishes

There is also a wide variety of hand finishes applicable to cut stone. These are usually expensive and should be considered only when cost is not an important factor. Information about such finishes as bush hammer, crandal, pick point, stripping, etc., is available from any of the Association members.

Planer Finish

Rubbed Finish

Sand Sawed Finish

Chat Sawed Finish

Shot Finish

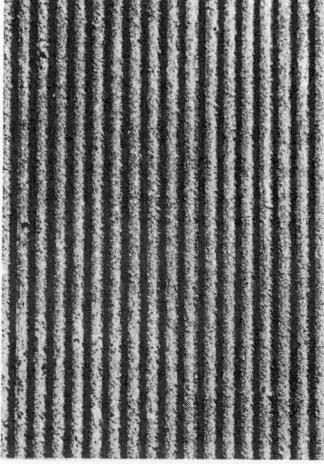
Tooled Finish

Checklist of principal building stones

State	Name	Crushing strength, psi	Wt., pcf	Texture	Color
			Sandstone		
Ark.	Cherry Blend	—	—	Medium	Brown, gray, cream, buff, pink
	Multi-ledge	—	—	—	Brown, pink, gray, variegated
	Rainbow Ledge	13,400	159	Medium	Brown, tan, yellow, pink, white, gray
	Harmony Ledge	13,667	159	Fine	Pink, brown, gray
Ariz.	Canyon	13,600	—	Coarse	Pink, buff, tan
	Dunbar	—	—	—	"Grand Canyon colors"
	Kaibab Arizona	13,600	—	Medium	Buff, pink, tan, red, yellow, variegated
Ind.	Sienna	4,000	150	Fine	Red, pink, brown, tan, yellow, cream, buff
Kans.	Bandera	8,446	—	—	Gray, buff
Mass.	Brownstone	4,500	155	Fine	Brown
Mo.	Clear Creek	—	—	Fine	Buff, gold, brown
Nev.	Kaibab Neva	18,069	—	Medium	Red, white, brown, yellow, purple
	Yasu	17,000	158	Medium	White, yellow, pink, purple, red, brown
N.Y.	Bluestone	12,500	160	Fine	Blue, gray, buff, lilac, green, tan
	Lenroc	27,500	165	Fine	Blue, gray, brown, rust, tan
	Mountain Hue	—	—	—	Blue green, gray, lilac, buff
Ohio	Berea, Amherst, Cleveland	8,500	140	—	Gray, buff, variegated
	Briar Hill Golden Tone	5,000	150	Fine	Gray, buff, brown, pink, tan
	Pearl	—	—	Fine	Gray, buff, brown, pink
Pa.	Delaware	3,800	180	Medium	Brown, gray, russet, tan, rose
	Penn-Kress	—	—	—	Gray, green, purple
Utah	Bear Valley Green	—	—	Medium	Green
			Nugget sandstone		
Utah	Sandy	—	—	Fine	Buff, gray, red, purple
			Quartzitic sandstone		
Ala.	Oneonta	5,228	160	Fine	Pink, buff, gray, brown
Colo.	Berthoud Pink, B. Variegated	6,000	159	Fine	Pink, orchid, variegated
	Colorado Pink, C. Rose, C. Red	—	162	—	Pink, rose, red, buff, cream, gray, variegated
	Loveland Buff	—	150	Medium	Buff, white, gray, brown stripes
	Lyons Redstone	—	155	Medium	Red, pink, rose, white stripes, brown, blue
N.Y.	Adirondack Hue	37,400	157	Fine	Pink, buff, gray
Utah	New Park Mining	14,400	154	Fine	Buff to red
			Quartzite		
Ga.	Pine Log	7,000	160	Coarse	Ivory, tan, red, gray, brown, buff
Md.	Chesapeake-hue	20,400	170	—	Gray, blue, brown, beige, cream, green, rust
Pa.	Allegheny	—	—	Fine	Blue, green, red, lilac, gray
Tenn.	Crab Orchard	19,060	162	Fine	Pink, buff, tan, blue, gray
	Tennessee Variegated	20,850	162	—	Pink, tan, buff, gray, variegated
	Tennquartz	26,833	162	—	Pink, tan, buff, gray, variegated
Utah	Turquoise	7,000	150	Coarse	Turquoise, green
			Oolitic limestone		
Ala.	Rockrange, Rockwood	4,553	145	Fine	Buff, gray, white
	Veined Gray	4,553	145	Fine	Gray with darker stripes
Ind.	Indiana Limestone	{ 2,500 10,000	135 180 }	Fine	Buff, gray, variegated

(Continued on following page)

Checklist of principal building stones (cont.)

State	Name	Crushing strength, psi	Wt., pcf	Texture	Color
	Victor Huro	17,500	185	Fine	Buff
	Victor Rouge, V. Travertine	5,500	175	Coarse	Rouge, buff
Kans.	Junction City, Silverdale	4,706	130	Fine	Buff
Tex.	Cordova Cream, Liberty Hill Cream	{ 2,070 2,300	124	Fine	Cream
	Cordova Shell, Liberty Hill Shell	{ 1,070 2,005	119	Shelly	Light golden
	Dolomitic limestone				
Calif.	Santa Maria	21,700	—	—	White, cream, rust
Ind.	Laurelstone	20,000+	—	—	Buff, brown, gray
Minn.	Kasota Cream, K. Pink	15,000	157	Fine	Cream, pink
	Mankato Buff, M. Cream, M. Gray	{ 13,500 15,000	157	—	Buff, cream, gray
	Plum Valley	—	—	—	Pink, tan
	Winona Travertine	17,000	158	Travertine	Yellow, white, buff, pink, gray
Mo.	Ste. Genevieve	—	155	—	Cream
Wis.	Conco Lannon	22,200	—	Fine	Ivory, gray, buff
	Fond du Lac	—	180	Fine	White, gray, blue, rose, tan
	Halquist Lannon	31,936	—	—	White, cream, buff, rust, blue
	Lannon	35,000	170	Fine	Blue, gray, rust
	Quality Lannon	—	—	Fine	Blue, green, gray, lilac, buff
	Sunset	16,078	159	Fine	Variegated
	Silicified limestone and chert				
Calif.	Flagstone, Mossback, Oatmeal, Ornamental, Plaster Rock, Specimen, Waterwash	—	—	{ Medium Coarse	White, gray, buff, variegated
	Crystalline limestone				
Mo.	Carthage	20,000	167	—	Light gray
	Marble (see section on Marble)				
Ga.	Crystal White, Etowah Pink, Creole, Cherokee, Pale Pink, Golden Vein, Variegated	{ 10,356 13,590	155	—	White with gray, black, or gold veins; pink; pink with gray or black veins
Tenn.	Tennessee Marble	{ 14,000 18,000	170	Fine	Pink, gray, brown
Vermont	Emerald White, Emerald Green, Sunset Blue	—	169	Fine	White with green veins, green with white clouds, blue-gray with white clouds
	Agate				
Utah	Desert Onyx	16,710	150	Fine	White, pale peach
	Mica schist				
Pa.	Pennsylvania Mica	{ 2,000 4,000	160	—	Gray, gold, brown
	Granite				
Conn.	Mt. Coral Pink	—	—	—	Wide variations in color and texture
Ga.	Blue Diamond, Keershaw Pink, Congaree	25,180	165	{ Fine to coarse	Gray or pink with dark specks
	Salisbury	—	—	—	Orange pink

(Continued on following page)

Checklist of principal building stones (cont.)

State	Name	Crushing strength, psi	Wt., pcf	Texture	Color
Maine	Deer Island, Sherwood Pink	—	—	Medium	Gray, pink
	Moose-a-Bec Pink	—	—	—	Pink-brown
	North Jay	—	—	Fine	White, light gray
	Swenson Pink	—	—	Medium	Pink with black waves
Mass.	Chelmsford Bullfinch, C. Gray, C. White	—	—	Fine	Buff, gray, white
	Extra Dark Quincy	—	—	—	Occasional small black spots
	Milford Buff, M. Pink	—	—	Medium	Brown or pink with dark spots
	Plymouth, Weymouth	—	—	—	Soft grays and greens, buff, tan, yellow, brown, purple
	Rockport Gray	—	—	—	Medium gray
Minn.	Cold Spring Agate	—	—	Medium	Brownish red
	Cold Spring Diamond Pink	—	—	Medium	Gray buff with black spots
	Cold Spring Rainbow	—	—	Fine	Pink and black
	Crystal Gray	—	—	Coarse	Dark gray to purple
	Diamond Gray	—	—	Medium	Light gray
	Opalescent	—	—	Coarse	Dark green-gray with brown and black spots
	Oxford Gray	—	--	Fine	Dark gray
	Rockville	—	—	Coarse	Light to medium gray
	Ruby Red	—	—	Fine	Brownish red
Mo.	Mission Red	—	—	—	Occasional thin dark veins
N.H.	Bears Den Quarry	—	—	Medium	Green-gray and brown variegated
	Conway Green	—	—	Coarse	Dark green-gray with black spots
	Conway Pink	—	—	Coarse	Pink with gray and black spots
	Mason	—	—	Medium	Dark to greenish gray
	Souhegan White	—	--	—	Uniform texture
	Swenson Buff Antique, S. Gray	—	—	Fine	Light to medium brown, gray
N.Y.	Westchester	34,500	166	Fine	Dark to medium gray with pink specks
N.C.	Balfour Pink	34,700	165	Medium	Pink, pale to reddish
	Carolina White	51,900	165	Medium	Light gray with small flecks
	Mount Airy	29,233	165	Medium	White, light gray
	Rowan Pink	34,700	165	Medium	Gray white to pale pink
Pa.	French Creek Black	40,000	190	Fine	Black
S.Dak.	Cold Spring Carnelian	—	—	Fine	Brownish red
	Imperial Mahogany	—	—	—	Some waves and veining
Tex.	Texas Pink	—	—	Coarse	Pink
Wis.	Cold Spring Bright Red	—	—	Fine	Bright red
	Cold Spring Veined Ebony	—	—	Medium	Black (bronze)
Argillite					
N.J.	Princeton	11,600	150	Fine	Dark brown, blue, purple, gray, buff
Slate					
N.Y.	Yorkmont	—	—	—	Green, gray, black, purple, red
Pa.	Pennsylvania Black	—	—	—	Blue-black
Vt.	Vermont Slate	—	—	—	Red, green, purple, gray, mottled
Va.	Buckingham	—	—	—	Blue-black
Soapstone					
Va.	Albarene	—	—	—	Dark green

Data from International Cut Stone Contractors and Quarrymen's Association, Granite Association, and various manufacturers.

By ARTHUR HOCKMAN, *National Bureau of Standards, U.S. Department of Commerce*

PHYSICAL PROPERTIES OF 113 DOMESTIC MARBLES

Marble has always been regarded as an attractive and durable building material. In recent years the use of thin marble in the form of panels, slabs, and through-the-wall units in curtain wall structures has become more prevalent. For this reason, the National Bureau of Standards has compiled pertinent data regarding some of its physical properties.

The following sheets give the results of tests for abrasive hardness, absorption and specific gravity for 113 samples of domestic marbles originally obtained from 25 quarries located in nine states.

Geologically, marble is defined as a metamorphic, recrystallized limestone composed predominantly of crystalline grains of calcite or dolomite or both, having interlocking or mosaic structure. Commercially, marble is any crystalline rock capable of taking a high polish and composed predominantly of one or more of the following minerals: calcite, dolomite or serpentine. About 85 per cent of the samples were in the class of marble as defined from the geological standpoint, while the remaining 15 per cent were classed as commercial marbles.

MARBLE CLASSIFICATION

The marble samples have been classed by the producers into four groups—A, B, C or D. The groups are defined by the Marble Institute of America in their Marble Engineering Handbook as follows:

GROUP A—"Sound marbles and stones with uniform and favorable working qualities."

GROUP B—"Marbles and stones similar in character to those in Group A, but with somewhat less favorable working qualities. They may have occasional natural faults. A limited

amount of waxing[1] and sticking may be necessary."

GROUP C—"Marbles and stones of uncertain variation in working qualities. Geological flaws, voids, veins and lines of separation are common. Standard shop practice is to repair these variations of nature by sticking, waxing and filling. These techniques have recently been greatly improved by the use of new adhesives. Rodding,[2] liners,[3] and other forms of reinforcement may be freely employed when necessary."

GROUP D—"Marbles and stones similar to Group C, subject to the same methods of finishing and manufacture, but with a larger proportion of natural faults. These have also a maximum variation in working qualities. This group comprises many of the highly colored marbles prized for their decorative qualities."

Marbles that are used for monumental, structural or veneer purposes and are to be exposed to the weather are generally selected from Group A. Marbles in Groups B, C, and D are usually selected for their color and decorative effects. Occasionally carefully selected marbles from these groups are used on surfaces exposed to the weather.

[1] Waxing, sticking and filling are methods used in the marble trade to repair and improve the appearance of marbles containing natural flaws, voids, veins, etc. Materials such as wax, shellac, coloring and marble dust are used for this purpose.

[2] Rodding is a method of reinforcing a slab of marble by cementing stainless steel or aluminum rods to the back of the slab.

[3] Liner is a thin slab of marble that is cemented to the back of the original slab in order to reinforce it.

DESCRIPTION OF SAMPLES

Most of the domestic samples were in the form of hand specimens 3- by 5-in., ranging in thickness from $\frac{1}{4}$ in. to $\frac{7}{8}$ in. With the small size and number of samples available for the tests, the test results should not be interpreted to represent the entire marble deposit available from each respective source.

The physical properties of marble as determined by laboratory test are given in Table 1. Tests also show that the flexural strength of marble is reduced by aging. To compensate for the aging effect, the ultimate flexural strength of marble is considered to be half of its actual tested strength. To calculate allowable stress in the design of transversely loaded marble walls, multiply one half the ultimate failure stress by 40 per cent. This produces a total safety factor of 5, which the Marble Institute recommends for contemporary curtain wall and veneer design. Where marble is used for stair treads, lintels, or otherwise as a loadbearing material, a safety factor of 10 is recommended. The actual strength of the marble being used should be determined, and this value should be used for the final design.

TEST PROCEDURES

ASTM Standard Test C241–51, *Abrasion Resistance of Stone Subjected to Foot Traffic.*

ASTM Standard Test C97–47, *Absorption and Bulk Specific Gravity of Natural Building Stone.*

ASTM Standard Test C97–47, *Bulk Specific Gravity.*

Table 1. Physical properties of marble *

PROPERTY	DIRECTION OF LOAD TO BEDDING PLANE	HIGHEST VALUE OBTAINED	LOWEST VALUE OBTAINED	AVERAGE VALUE OBTAINED
Compressive Strength (psi)	Parallel	15,331	6,012	10,223
	Perpendicular	16,750	7,537	10,974
Transverse Strength (psi) (Mod. of Rupture or Flexural Strength)	Parallel	2,580	1,095	1,930
	Perpendicular	2,709	1,092	1,927
Shear Strength (psi)	Parallel	4,812	1,683	3,358
	Perpendicular	4,331	2,351	3,204
Modulus of Elasticity (Millions psi)	Parallel	13.00	1.97	8.35
	Perpendicular	14.85	4.33	9.56
Density (lbs. cu. ft.) (Weight)		172.4	163.0	168.0
Absorption (%) (48 hour soak)		.61	.07	.17
Thermal Conductivity (k) (BTU in/hr/sq.ft./°F)		15.65	10.45	13.58
Moisture Transmission (Perm inches)		4.46	.32	1.72
Coefficient of Thermal Expansion (in/in/°F)		.000012	.000004	.000007
Creep Deflection (inches) (after 24 hours)		.00033	.00000	.00008

* *Test procedures available from Marble Institute of America, Inc. on request.*

SOURCE, DESCRIPTION AND PROPERTIES OF DOMESTIC MARBLES

NO.	SOURCE	DESCRIPTION [1]	ABRASIVE HARDNESS (H_a value) [3]	ABSORPT'N (48 hr) %	BULK [4] SPECIFIC GRAVITY	GROUP [5]
1	ALABAMA	[2]IVORY CREAM, TRANSLUCENT, very few green markings	14	.11	2.71	B
2		WHITE AND CREAM, TRANSLUCENT, bold prominent markings	14	.14	2.70	A
3		WHITE, TRANSLUCENT, well-distributed prominent markings	13	.13	2.70	A
4		CREAM, TRANSLUCENT, uniform clouded markings	9	.14	2.70	A
5		CREAM, TRANSLUCENT, some veining or clouding	11	.14	2.70	A
6		IVORY-CREAM, TRANSLUCENT, occasional traces of color	10	.14	2.70	A
7		WHITE, green veining predominating	20	.11	2.71	B
8		WHITE AND CREAM, very bold and prominent markings	18	.10	2.71	B
9		WHITE, prominent light clouds	16	.08	2.71	A
10		WHITE, light clouds	11	.09	2.71	A
11	ARKANSAS	DARK GRAY, light gray spottings	38	.14	2.69	B
12		GRAY WITH BROWN TONE, and white spots	18	.34	2.68	B
13		RED, WHITE AND GOLD spots, red veining	17	.19	2.65	C
14		ROSE, white and yellow spots	13	.23	2.67	C
15		GRAY WITH BROWN TONE, golden spots and veins	26	.27	2.68	B
16		DARK BROWN, abundance of small white spots	13	.43	2.66	C
17		DARK BROWN, abundance of small white spots	24	.22	2.68	C
18	COLORADO	LIGHT BROWN TO CREAM, some light rose (travertine)	13	1.10	2.47	C
19		LIGHT BROWN TO RED (travertine)	20	.75	2.52	C
20		CREAM, light brown to red veining (travertine)	18	1.58	2.46	C
21	GEORGIA	WHITE, profusion of blue-black veining	17	.09	2.71	A
22		GRAY, dark gray, wavy veins	16	.11	2.71	A
23		WHITE, gray veins and clouding	16	.12	2.71	A
24		WHITE, few gray veins and clouds	16	.10	2.71	A
25		ROSE TO LIGHT PINK, dark green and gray veining	13	.08	2.71	A
26	MARYLAND	DARK GREEN, mottled veins and markings (serpentine)	55	1.03	2.66	C
27		LIGHT GREEN, mottled veins and markings (serpentine)	43	1.56	2.63	C
28	MISSOURI	LIGHT GRAY, distinct darker gray veining	16	.59	2.64	A
29		LIGHT GRAY, gray veins resembling clouds	19	.83	2.64	A
30		GRAY, without any distinct veining	17	.86	2.63	A
31		ROSE, gray fossil markings	16	.14	2.69	C
32		LIGHT ROSE, numerous light and dark fossils	15	.16	2.68	C
33		GRAY, dark gray veinings, light brown markings	15	.63	2.64	C
34		LIGHT TO DARK GRAY, light brown veining	17	.36	2.68	C
35		GRAY, yellow or golden veins, fossil markings	20	.18	2.68	C
36		LIGHT GRAY AND GOLD, yellow veins	18	.40	2.67	C
37		LIGHT TO MEDIUM GRAY, many light and dark fossils	17	.30	2.67	C
38		MEDIUM BROWN, light and dark veining	19	.43	2.68	C
39		LIGHT TO MEDIUM GRAY, fine pencil-like markings	17	.46	2.64	A
40	N. CAROLINA	GRAY, blue-black wavy veining	19	.07	2.72	A
41	TENNESSEE	DARK PINK, dark veins	24	.07	2.70	A
42		GRAY, SLIGHT TINT OF RED, blue veinings	22	.07	2.70	A
43		DARK BROWN, white spots	25	.07	2.70	A
44		BROWNISH RED, with white veinings and markings	31	.06	2.71	A
45		VARIEGATED RED AND GRAY, white veinings	28	.07	2.71	C
46		GRAYISH PINK, blue veining and white spots	25	.07	2.71	A
47		GRAYISH RED, small blue veinings	23	.08	2.70	A
48		BLACK, occasional white markings	38	.15	2.72	B
49		DARK BROWN, white and red spots	27	.07	2.71	A
50		DARK BROWN, pinkish-gray spots	26	.05	2.70	A
51		REDDISH BROWN, white spots	22	.07	2.70	A
52		BROWNISH RED, variegated with white markings	44	.06	2.71	C
53		DEEP BROWNISH RED, mixed with gray markings, white spots	37	.02	2.71	C
54		BROWNISH RED, variegated with white markings	39	.01	2.71	C
55		BROWNISH RED, mixed with gray and white markings	27	.05	2.71	C

[1] The various descriptions of the samples were supplied by the respective producers.
[2] Capitalized portion of the description signifies the background color of the marble.
[3] The H_a value is an expression of wear resistance and is the reciprocal, multiplied by 10, of the volume of material abraded in a 5 min tests, using the National Bureau of Standards Abrasion Machine. The higher the H_a value, the more resistant to abrasion is the material.
[4] The weight per cubic foot can be determined by multiplying the bulk specific gravity by 62.4.
[5] As defined in the text.

SOURCE, DESCRIPTION AND PROPERTIES OF DOMESTIC MARBLES (cont.)

NO.	SOURCE	DESCRIPTION[1]	ABRASIVE HARDNESS (H_a value)[3]	ABSORPT'N (48 hr) %	BULK SPECIFIC GRAVITY	GROUP[5]
56	TENNESSEE	[2]GRAYISH PINK, mottled with white, pink, red and black	27	.05	2.71	A
57		BROWN, dark brown veinings, white spots	21	.09	2.70	A
58		DEEP BROWNISH PINK, fine dark veining	26	.04	2.71	A
59		DEEP RICH RED, small blue veining	22	.05	2.70	A
60		DARK TO MEDIUM GRAYISH RED, white spots	25	.07	2.70	A
61		VARIEGATED GRAYISH PINK TO RED, blue veinings	23	.08	2.70	A
62		LIGHT TO DARK PINK, small blue veinings	25	.06	2.70	A
63		MEDIUM TO LIGHT PINK, blue veinings	23	.05	2.70	A
64		GRAYISH PINK TO RED, dark veins, some fossils	22	.07	2.70	A
65		LIGHT PINK, dark colored veining	24	.09	2.70	A
66		GRAYISH RED, white spots	23	.01	2.70	A
67		GRAYISH LIGHT RED, white spots	27	.05	2.71	A
68		GRAYISH RED, white spots, red veining	28	.06	2.70	A
69		LIGHT PINK, blue veining	25	.06	2.70	A
70		GRAY, SLIGHT TINGE OF PINK, small blue veining	22	.07	2.70	A
71		GRAYISH PINK, darker veins	23	.08	2.70	A
72		GRAYISH PINK, small blue veining	24	.07	2.70	A
73		CREAM, yellowish brown veins, some fossils	21	.09	2.70	A
74		GRAYISH PINK, blue veining	21	.10	2.70	A
75		PINK AND GRAY, white clouds, veins, fossils	26	.05	2.70	C
76		PINK AND GRAY, reddish veining, some fossils	28	.11	2.69	C
77		DEEP RED TO PINK AND GRAY, dark veins	22	.06	2.70	A
78		GRAY WITH SLIGHT PINK, blue veinings	22	.10	2.70	A
79		GRAY, very close dark veinings	23	.09	2.70	A
80		LIGHT GRAY, few dark veinings	20	.11	2.69	A
81		PEARL, some blue-black veinings, clouds	23	.10	2.69	A
82		LIGHT AND GRAYISH PINK, dark veins, shell markings	21	.06	2.70	A
83		GRAY, scattering of white spots	28	.06	2.70	A
84		LIGHT CREAM, irregular gold veining	25	.58	2.65	C
85		DEEP ROSE, dark brown spots, white and gray markings	29	.02	2.71	C
86		LIGHT TO DARK ROSE, irregular blue veining	27	.07	2.71	C
87		LIGHT BROWN, white and gray fossils	28	.05	2.70	A
88	VERMONT	WHITE, gray clouds	13	.12	2.70	A
89		GRAY, darker gray veining	10	.14	2.70	A
90		WHITE, gray clouds	10	.12	2.70	A
91		WHITE, gray green clouds	11	.15	2.70	A
92		LIGHT GRAY, dark gray clouds	13	.11	2.70	A
93		NEARLY BLACK, gray flecks	24	.14	2.70	A
94		DARK GREEN, white veins (serpentine)	77	.18	2.72	C
95		MAHOGANY RED, white spots	34	.16	2.81	C
96		WHITE, faint flecks	8	.20	2.70	A
97		WHITE, faint green clouds	7	.20	2.70	A
98		WHITE, light green markings	8	.19	2.70	A
99		WHITE, light green clouds	9	.19	2.70	A
100		WHITE, CREAM, light green veining	10	.20	2.70	A
101		WHITE, light green veining	8	.17	2.70	A
102		CREAM, faint green veining	12	.17	2.71	A
103		WHITE, narrow green stripes	11	.21	2.70	A
104		WHITE, wide green bands	11	.17	2.70	A
105		WHITE, light green mottle	9	.16	2.71	A
106		LIGHT GREEN, occasional tan markings	9	.16	2.72	A
107		LIGHT GRAY, dark green veining	9	.19	2.72	A
108		GREEN, white clouds	10	.21	2.71	A
109		WHITE, heavy green clouds	9	.18	2.71	A
110		WHITE, abundant green clouds	8	.17	2.71	A
111		GRAY, darker gray clouds	9	.15	2.70	A
112		WHITE, gray veining	11	.15	2.70	A
113	VIRGINIA	BLACK, SLIGHT GREENISH CAST, occasional white or gray veins	53	.07	2.86	A

[1] The various descriptions of the samples were supplied by the respective producers.
[2] Capitalized portion of the description signifies the background color of the marble.
[3] The H_a value is an expression of wear resistance and is the reciprocal, multiplied by 10, of the volume of material abraded in a 5 min tests, using the National Bureau of Standards Abrasion Machine. The higher the H_a value, the more resistant to abrasion is the material.
[4] The weight per cubic foot can be determined by multiplying the bulk specific gravity by 62.4.
[5] As defined in the text.

Stone veneer is attached to the building structure by means of metal anchors and supports, such as those illustrated in Fig. 1. Marble veneers are usually 2 in. or less in thickness; other stone veneers are generally 3 or 4 in. thick. Typical details for the attachment of marble veneer are shown in Fig. 2, and for limestone veneer in Figs. 3 and 4. Stone veneer used in curtain wall construction is shown in Figs. 5 and 6. Details of more conventional applications are given in Figs. 7 and 8.

RESIDENTIAL

Stones commonly used in residential work are available in several patterns, as illustrated in Fig. 9. Veneer thickness averages 3½ to 4 in. Joint widths vary from ½ in. for sawed-bed ashlar to a maximum of 3 in. for rubble and mosaic. Joints may be flush or raked ⅜ in. deep. In many types of stones sawed-bed ashlar is available with modular vertical dimensions, the height of the larger stones being multiples of the height of the smallest stone plus the

width of one joint. The term "2, 3, or 4 rise" refers to this type of masonry, the numbers indicating the number of heights. In laying this type of masonry, the following rules should be observed for the most pleasing appearance: no vertical joint should extend above the top of the highest stones; stones of the same height should not be laid end to end; no horizontal joint should exceed the length of two stones. The method of attaching stone veneer to wood-frame or masonry walls is shown in Fig. 10.

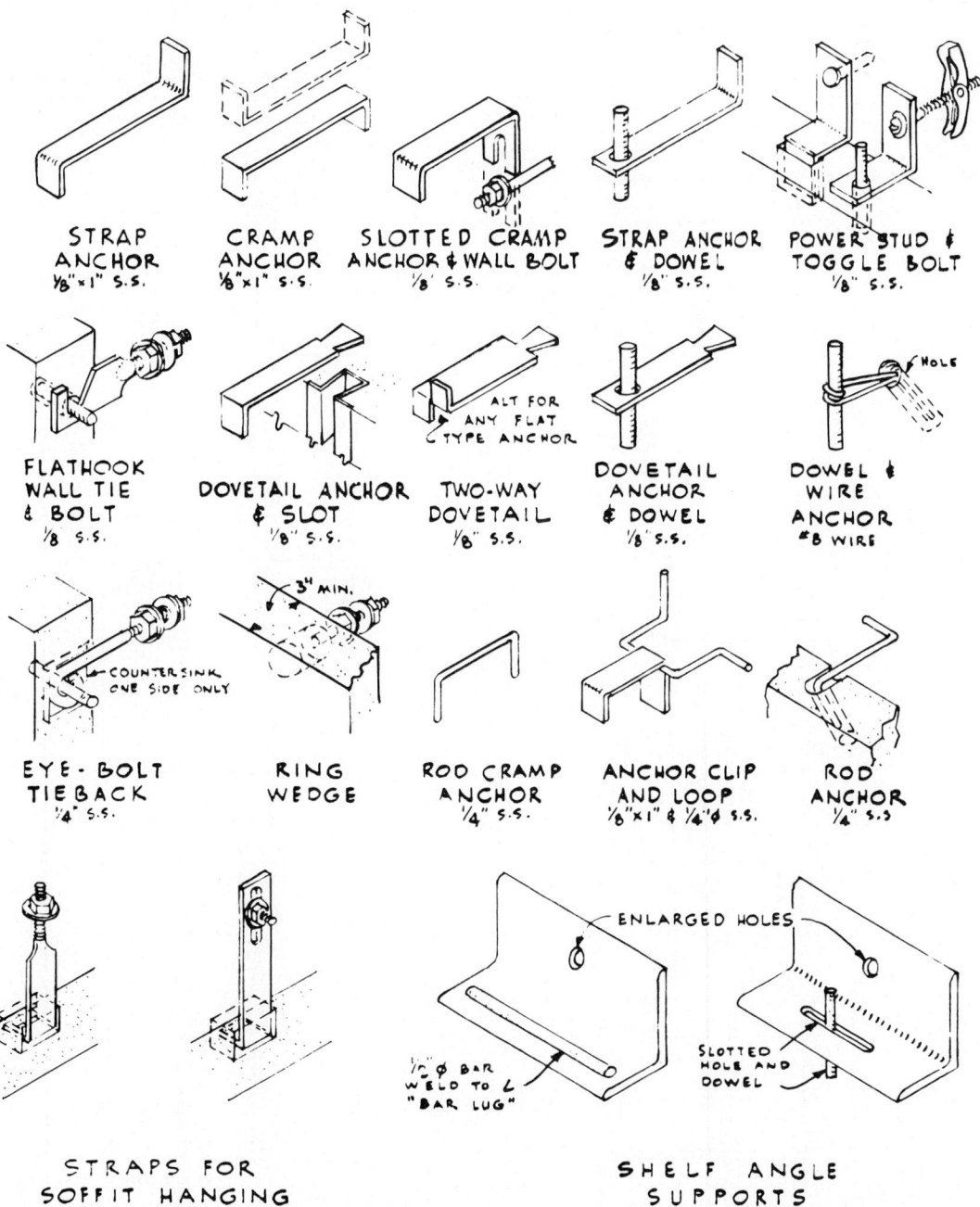

Fig. 1.   Anchors and supports for stone veneer

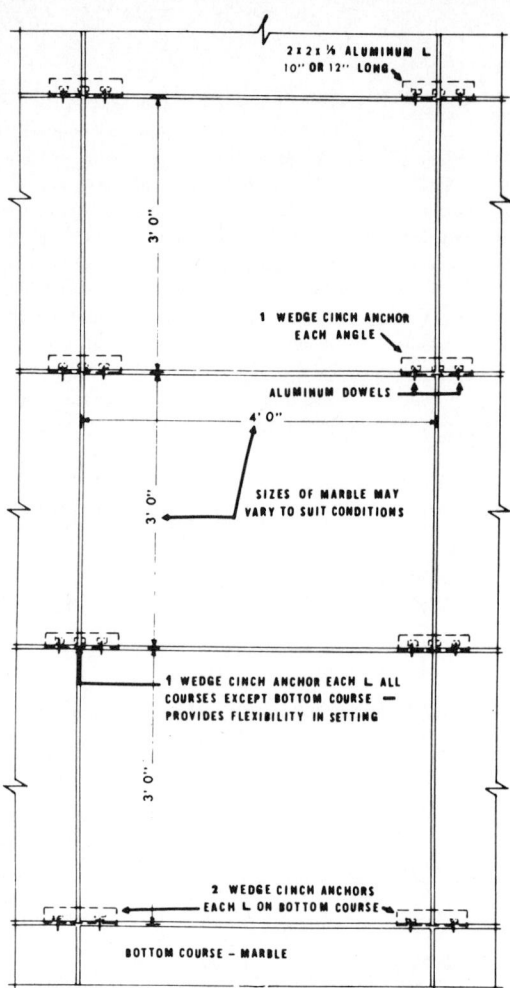

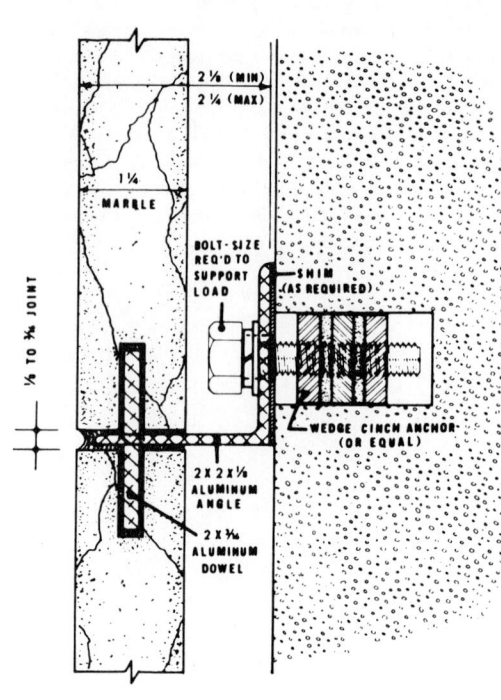

Fig. 2.   Anchorage and support for thin marble veneer

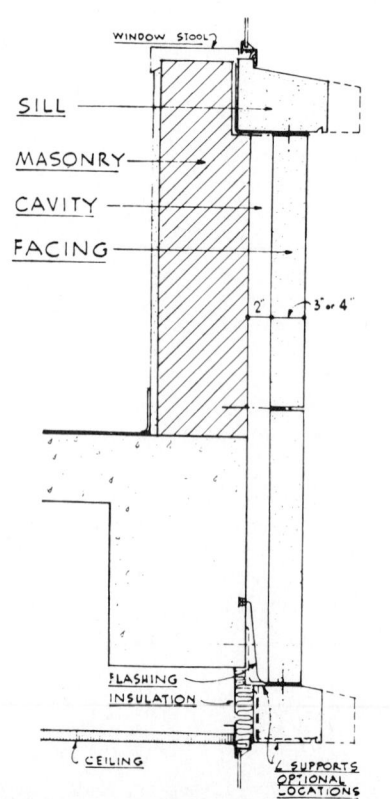

Fig. 3.   Limestone spandrel with masonry backup

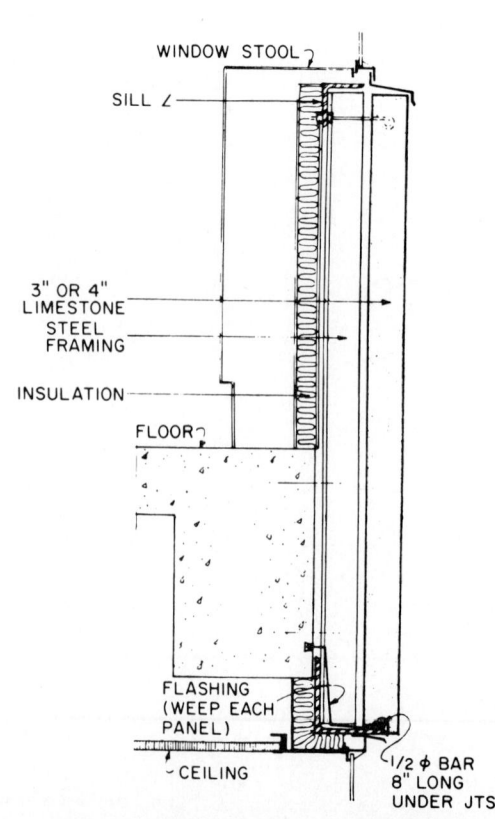

Fig. 4.   Limestone spandrel on insulated metal frame

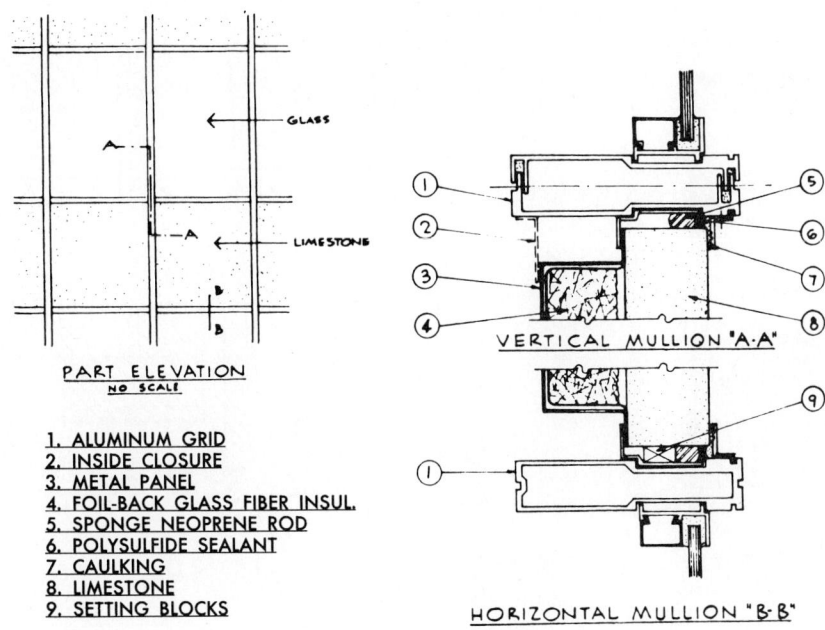

PART ELEVATION
NO SCALE

1. ALUMINUM GRID
2. INSIDE CLOSURE
3. METAL PANEL
4. FOIL-BACK GLASS FIBER INSUL.
5. SPONGE NEOPRENE ROD
6. POLYSULFIDE SEALANT
7. CAULKING
8. LIMESTONE
9. SETTING BLOCKS

VERTICAL MULLION "A-A"

HORIZONTAL MULLION "B-B"

Fig. 5. Limestone insulated curtain wall panel
Thickness 3⅞ in., weight 26 psf, *U* value 0.14

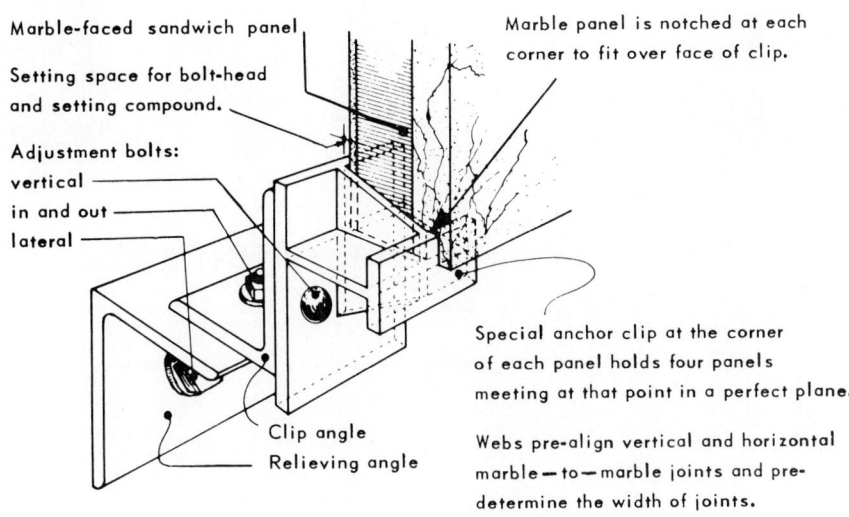

Marble-faced sandwich panel

Setting space for bolt-head
and setting compound.

Adjustment bolts:
vertical
in and out
lateral

Clip angle
Relieving angle

Marble panel is notched at each
corner to fit over face of clip.

Special anchor clip at the corner
of each panel holds four panels
meeting at that point in a perfect plane.

Webs pre-align vertical and horizontal
marble — to — marble joints and predetermine the width of joints.

Fig. 6. Marble insulated curtain wall panel

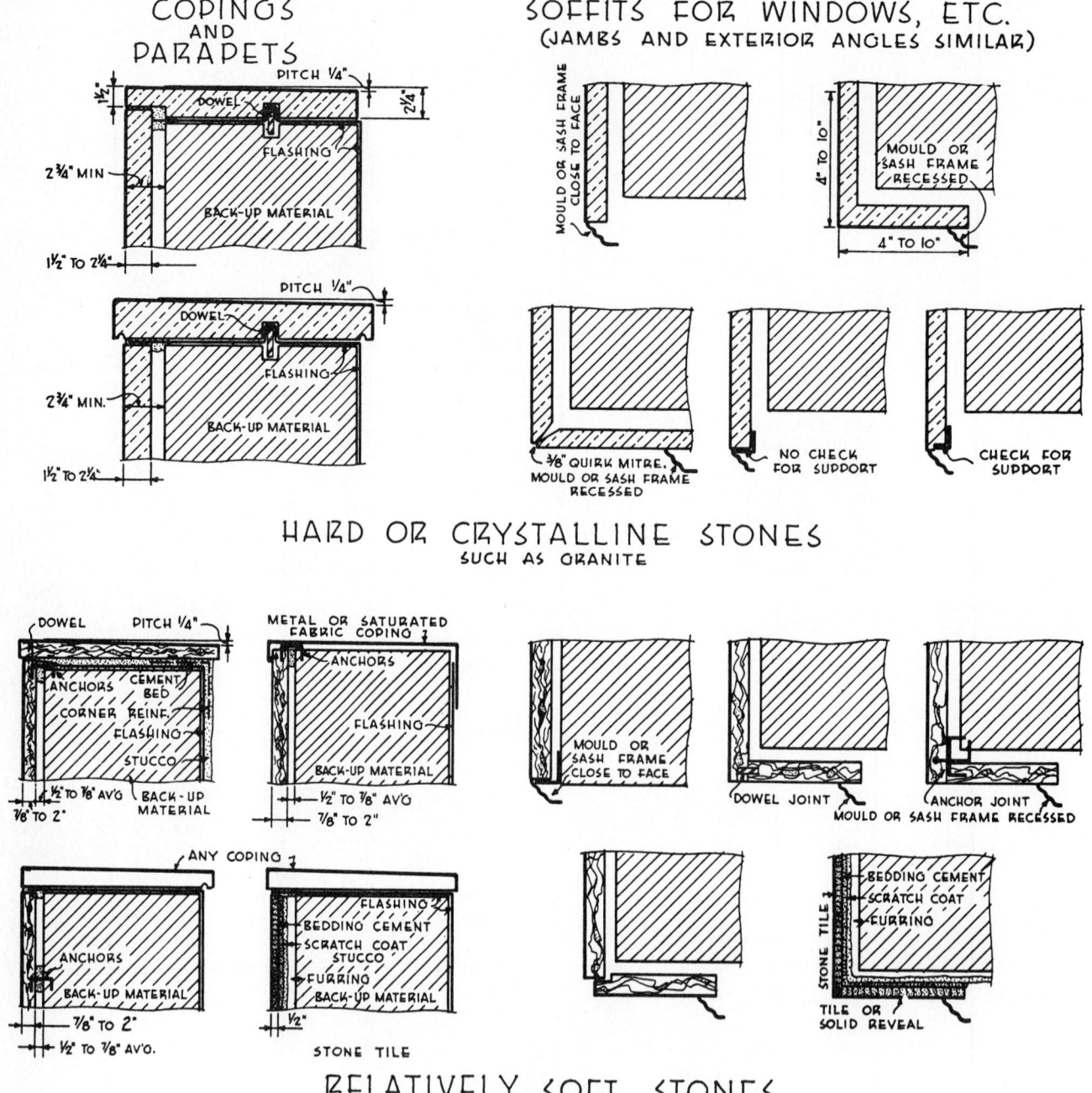

Fig. 7. Details of stone veneer construction—copings and window reveals

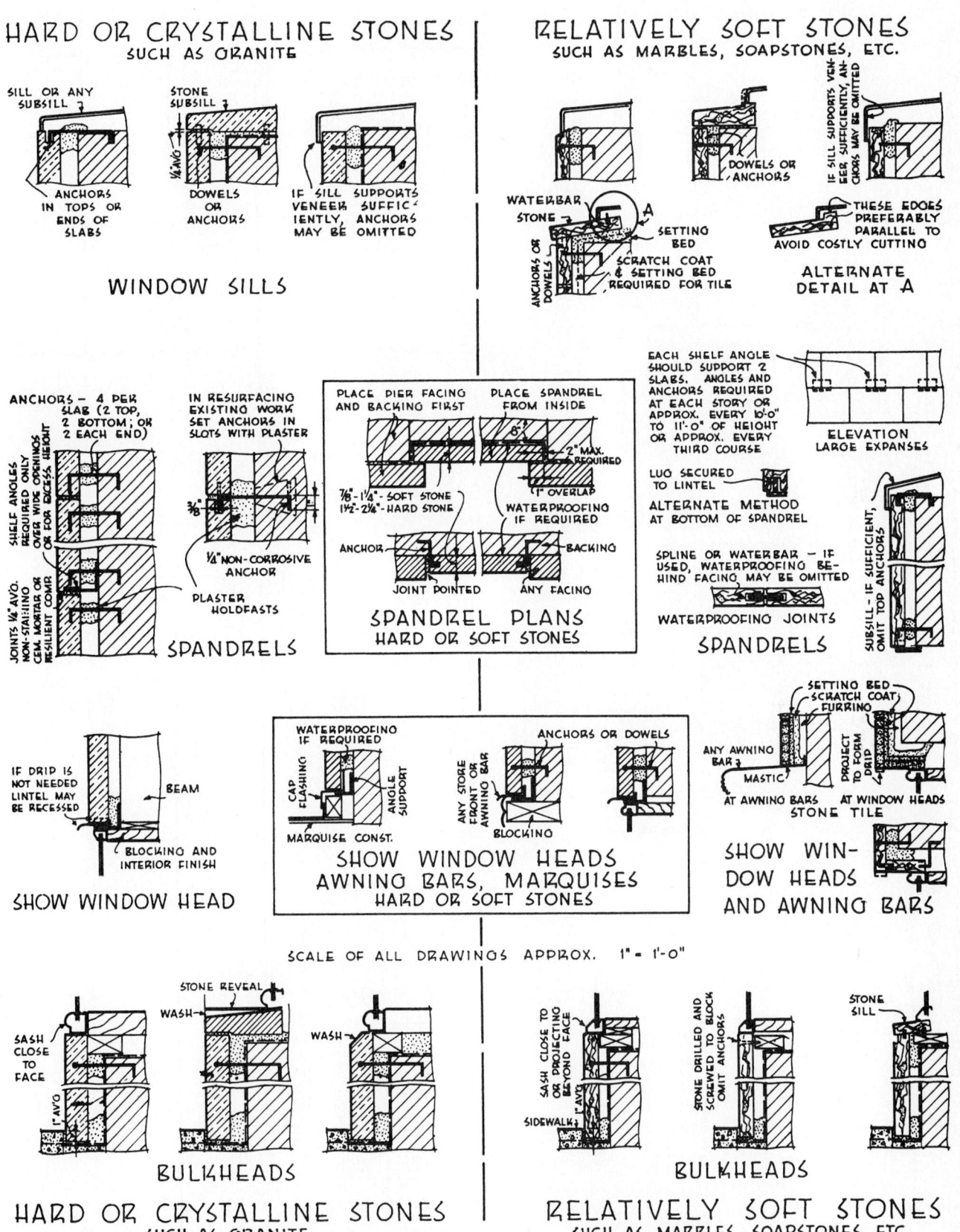

Fig. 8.   Details of stone veneer construction—window sills, spandrels, and bulkheads

a. Coursed ashlar

b. Coursed ashlar

c. Random ashlar, sawed bed

d. Random ashlar, sawed bed, 3-rise

e. Random ashlar, hand cut

f. Random ashlar, hand cut

g. Random rubble

h. Mosaic

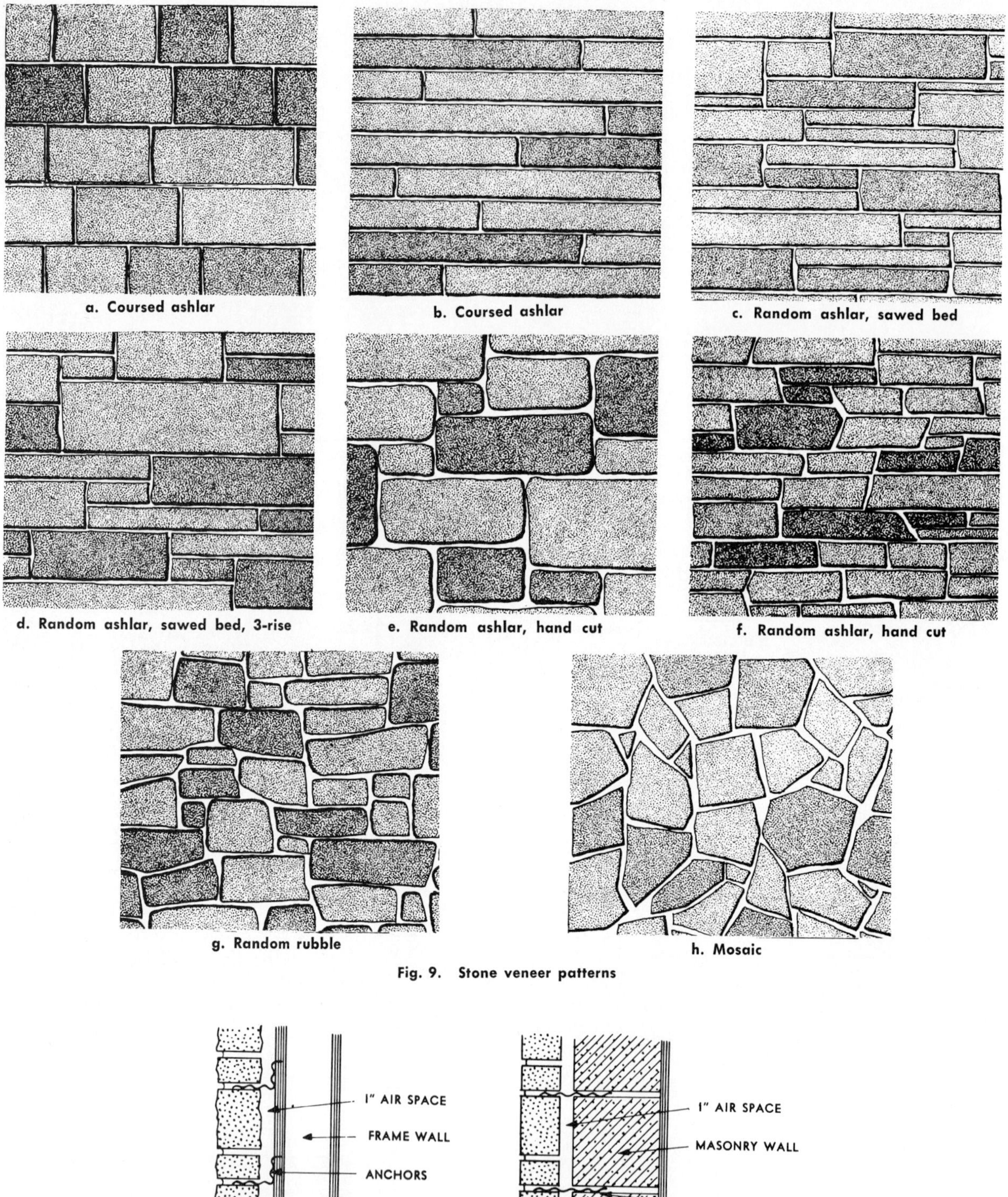

Fig. 9.   Stone veneer patterns

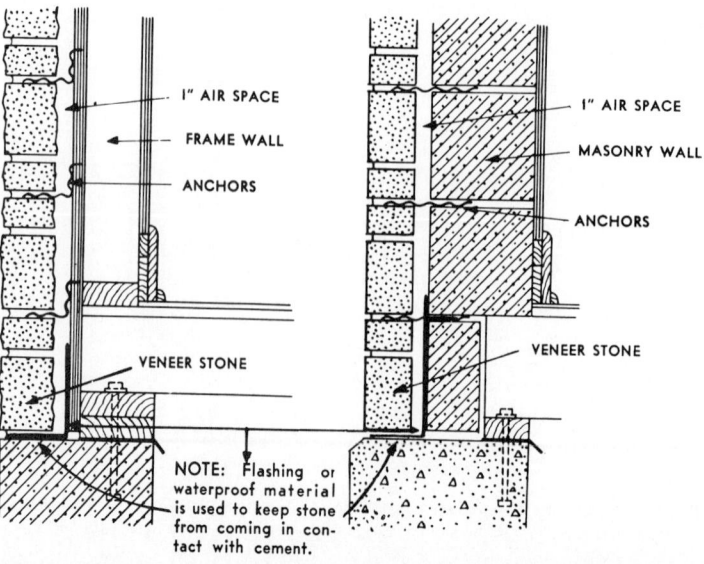

1" AIR SPACE

FRAME WALL

ANCHORS

1" AIR SPACE

MASONRY WALL

ANCHORS

VENEER STONE

VENEER STONE

NOTE: Flashing or waterproof material is used to keep stone from coming in contact with cement.

Fig. 10.   Anchorage of stone veneer to wood-frame wall and to masonry wall

By HOWARD P. VERMILYA, AIA

The primary interior stones are the various marbles and slate. Exterior stones are also often used for dramatic effects as interior wall materials in residential and commercial structures and in churches. The smooth-surfaced marbles are more likely to be found as wall or flooring material in monumental or institutional buildings and in commercial buildings such as banks and quality office buildings. Slate and other flagging have their major interior use as a flooring material in residential, ecclesiastical, and institutional buildings.

MARBLE

Interior marble

Interior marble is usually ⅞ in. thick when used in large slabs as standing marble or as tile on floors. Wall tile ½ in. thick is now furnished in modular sizes 8 by 8 in., 8 by 12 in., or 12 by 12 in. Standard (⅞-in.) floor tile sizes are 8 by 16 in., 12 by 12 in., and 10 by 20 in. Wall tile may be used on floors where traffic is not heavy, as in residences. Toilet stall partitions of marble are usually ⅞ in. thick, but the stiles should be 1¼ in. thick. Standard window stools and lavatory tops are ⅞ in. thick. Stair risers are ⅞ in. thick and treads 1¼ in. thick unless heavy traffic is anticipated. Some manufacturers provide for antislip inserts in stair treads. Thicker slabs (1½ in. and 2 in.) are used for counters. Standard thicknesses of marble are ⅞, 1¼, 1½, and 2 in.

Standing interior marble

Standing interior marble (Fig. 11) is set by spotting with plaster of Paris and using concealed corrosion-resistant wire anchors secured to the wall backing. Joints, usually 1/16 in. wide, should be fully buttered with plaster of Paris as each slab is set. When standing marble is set in wet locations or in unheated places subject to moisture or condensation, however, spotting should consist of portland cement plus a shrinkage-reducing accelerator.

The optimum setting space, that is, the distance from rough wall backing to the finish face of the marble, is 1½ in.; where liners are required the setting space should be 2½ in. External angles are usually butt joints. The use of quirk mitre joints (not recommended on base courses) should be specially noted in the specifications as they are not standard practice.

If the optimum setting space is not available, plasticized synthetic resin-based, nonstaining, moisture-resistant bonding cements or dry-set mortars may be used. Thin marble tile is usually set with bonding cements or dry-set mortars similar to those used on ceramic tile. Elastic, nonstaining, pointing and caulking mastics are also used instead of plaster of Paris or portland cement, particularly with thin marble tile. Joints should be ⅛ to 3/16 in. thick.

Floor marble

For floor marble, the concrete base or cinder fill above the slab floor should be within 2½ in. of the finish floor line (Fig. 12a). The cement bed should be mixed quite dry and the marble tamped until fully bedded to the proper level of the floor. The marble tile is then removed and the back parged with wet cement or the bed sprinkled with water and cement and back of tile wet. Fully buttering edges of tile as it is laid is also an approved method. Joints are 1/16 in. They should be grouted with neat cement later if not buttered when laid.

The standard specifications of the Marble Institute of America approve several methods for the installation of marble flooring. Method No. 1 calls for a sand or tar paper cleavage bed between the rough floor slab and the setting bed. Method No. 2 employs a minimum ⅛-in. dry-set portland cement mortar setting bed (Fig. 12b). Method No. 3 for thin (½-in.) marble tile, specifies a setting bed of portland cement permitting a minimum 1¼-in. distance from the rough concrete slab to the finish floor (Fig. 12c). Method No. 4, for thin marble tile, calls for a ⅛-in.-thick dry-set portland cement mortar setting bed as in Method No. 2 above (Fig. 12d).

Finishes

Finishes for interior marble are as follows:

1. Natural finish, produced by sawing with sand.
2. Sand-rubbed or wet sand finish, a smooth surface produced on a cast-iron rubbing bed with sand and water. Used for treads and floors, sometimes after floors have been set.
3. Grit finish, a smooth, dull finish between sand and hone, produced by grits. On floors the finish is produced by surfacing after setting.
4. Hone or egg shell finish, a dull gloss surface giving relatively little reflection, produced by hand or machine. Used on floors and standing marble.
5. Polish finish, a gloss surface that will reflect light and emphasize color and markings, produced by a buffer with putty powder applied to a honed surface. It is generally used for standing marble.

As noted on a previous page, marbles are classified in four groups (A, B, C, and D) according to the characteristics and working qualities in finishing.

Manufactured granite or marble

Manufactured granite or marble is a masonry material used for either exterior or interior facing. Granite or marble aggregates in a wide variety of colors are formed by special bonding agents to produce slabs of great density and strength and low absorption. The slabs are usually formed in 1½ or 2¼-in. thicknesses for use in a manner similar to standing marble, but they may be formed in deeper sections to include reinforcing as lintels or for other structural purposes. They are often finished with a high polish. Erection is similar to other building stone surfacing units.

SLATE

Slate is used for roofing, exterior and interior wall panels, flooring, and other uses such as window sills, stair treads and risers, toilet stall partitions, and blackboards. The slate may be split to provide a natural cleft surface, or it may be sawed, planed, semirubbed, sand rubbed, or honed and polished. Edges may be sheared, smooth sawed, sand rubbed, or honed. The honed finish is rarely used on floors or treads. Exposed edges are usually sand rubbed. Colors, which vary with the quarry, are slate gray, blue-black, green, mottled green and purple, purple and red.

Interior slate flooring nominally ½ in. thick varies from ½ to ⅝ in. in actual thickness; 1-in. flooring varies from ⅞ to 1⅛ in. The ½-in. thickness is generally used unless exceptionally heavy traffic is anticipated. The slate is manufactured in a wide variety of standard sizes—from a nominal 6 by 6 in. up to 18 by 24 in.—many of which permit the development of patterns using one, two, or three sizes. Slate is also widely used in precut random rectangular patterns, as well as in quarry run irregular flagging. Some manufacturers provide slate sawn to a uniform thickness of ⅜ in. and cut to standard size for use as tile. Slate is laid similarly to floor marble over a concrete base in a portland cement mortar setting bed with joints ½ in. or more in width.

FLAGSTONE

Flagstone is the generic name for any stone used for paving an area to be walked on. Any hard stone that splits easily into large, relatively thin slabs may be used for this purpose. In addition to slate, many varieties of sandstones, quartzite, and limestone are commonly used as flagging, depending upon local availability and preferences. In the Middle Atlantic States the word flagstone has long meant only bluestone, a hard sandstone quarried in New York and Pennsylvania. Any stone used for flagging must be smooth enough for comfortable walking, but not so smooth as to be slippery when wet. For indoor use, smoother finishes and narrower joints are usually specified. Common flagstone patterns are shown in Fig. 13 and installation details are shown in Fig. 14.

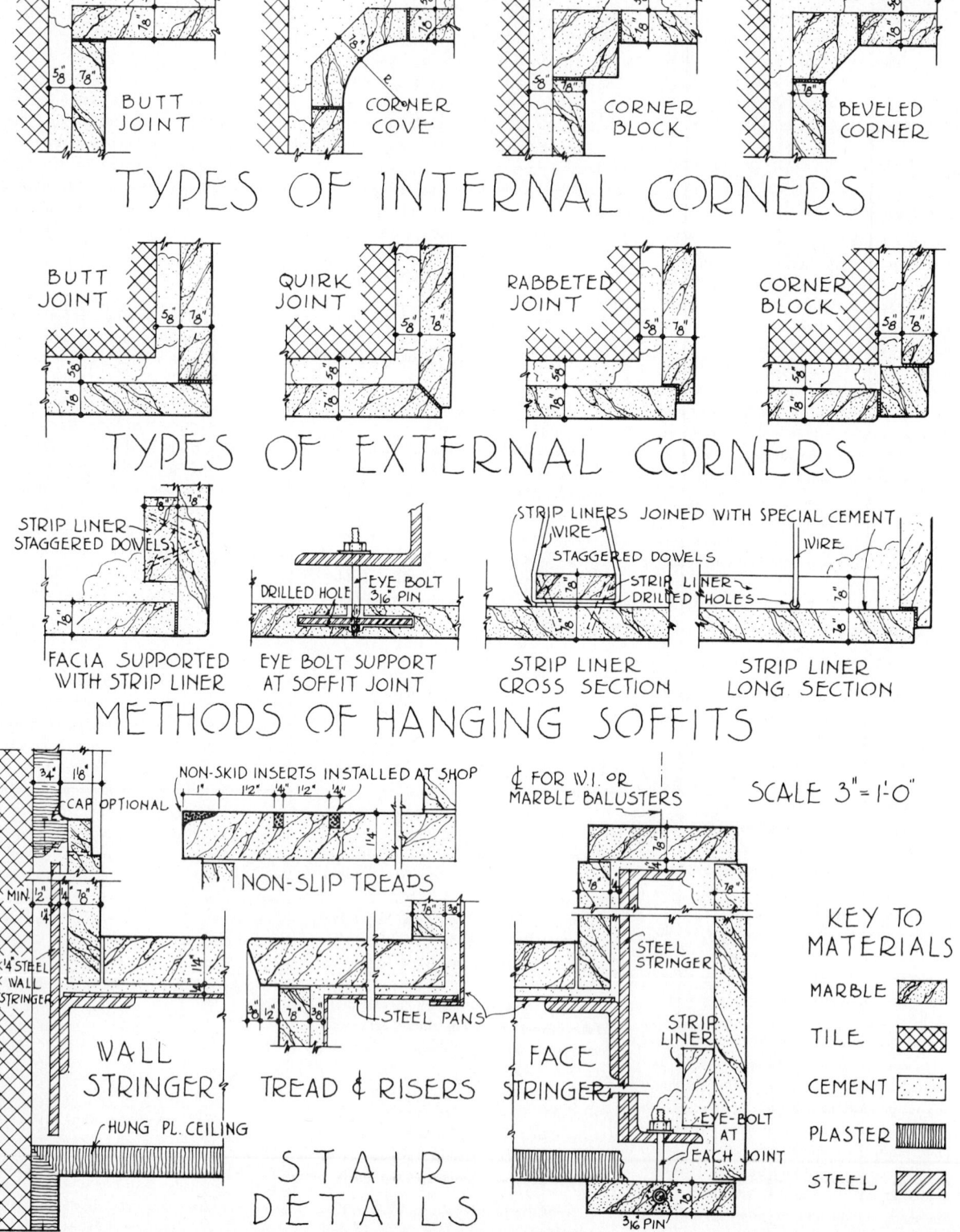

Fig. 11.   Interior marble details

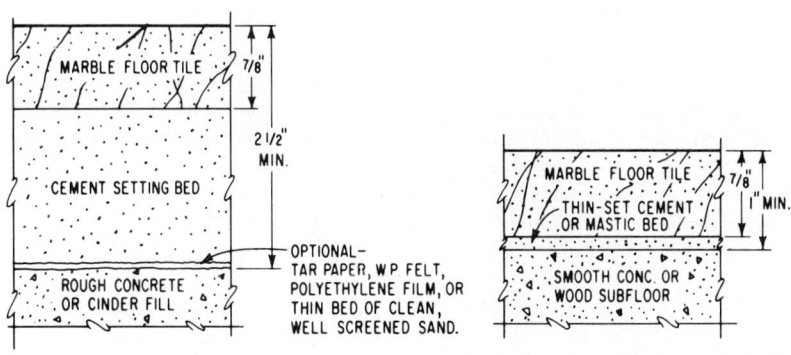

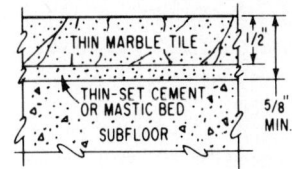

c. Thin marble tile, preferred method

a. Standard floor tile, preferred method   b. Standard floor tile, thin-set method

d. Thin marble tile, thin-set method

Fig. 12. Marble floor setting methods

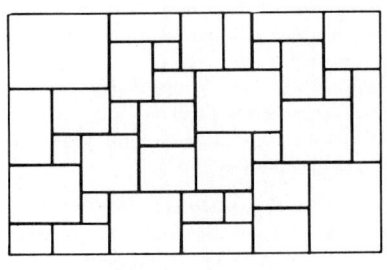

a. Random rectangular

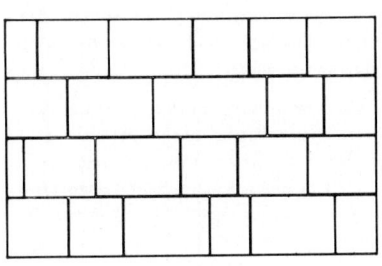

b. Coursed

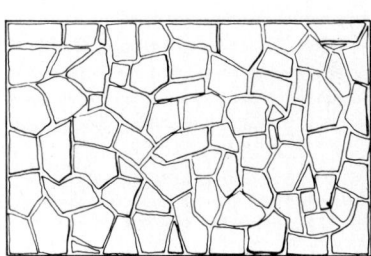

c. Irregular or mosaic

Fig. 13. Flagging patterns

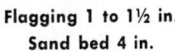

a. On sand bed

Flagging 1 to 1½ in.
Sand bed 4 in.

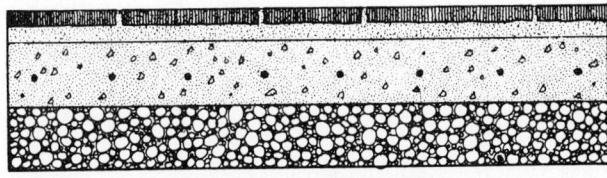

b. On concrete slab on grade

Flagging ¾ to 1 in.
Setting bed 1 to 1½ in.
Reinforced concrete slab 4 in.
Gravel or cinders 4 in.

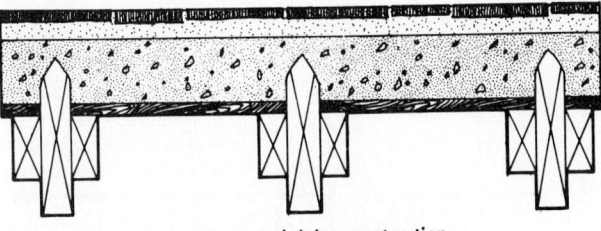

c. On wood joist construction

Flagging ¾ to 1 in.
Setting bed 1 to 1½ in.
Reinforced concrete slab 4 in.
Wood subfloor ¾ in.

Fig. 14. Flagstone setting methods

The following material is based largely on "Fire-Resistant Steel-Frame Construction," American Iron and Steel Institute, 1974.

BUILDING CODE REQUIREMENTS

Modern building codes specify minimum fire-resistance requirements based on studies by fire protection engineers. The degree of fire hazard in each type and size of construction and for each class of occupancy is evaluated, and the degree of fire resistance required for each building component is determined. The degree of fire resistance required for any structural component is expressed in terms of its ability to withstand fire exposure in accordance with the requirements of the standard time-temperature fire test of the American Society for Testing and Materials.

The ASTM Method of Fire Tests of Building Construction and Materials" (E119) is the universally accepted standard for classifying the duration and intensity of fires and for measuring the degree of fire resistance provided by building materials and constructions. The fire-resistance rating is expressed as the time, in hours, that the assembly is able to withstand exposure to the standard fire (Fig. 1) before the first critical point

[1] *This term, although technically inaccurate, is so well established in the building industry, that it seems best to continue using it.*

in its behavior is reached. These tests indicate the length of time that structural members, such as columns and beams, maintain their strength and rigidity, and that floors, roofs, walls, and partitions remain intact and prevent the spread of fire and the passage of flame, hot gases, and excessive heat when subjected to the standard fire. Actual tests of building assemblies form the basis of the fire-resistance rating and are now generally accepted by all nationally recognized model building codes that use this performance requirement in determining the degree of fire resistance for each construction and occupancy.

CONSTRUCTION MATERIALS

To qualify as both safe and dependable, fire-protection materials for modern steel-framed buildings should display the following characteristics:

- Noncombustibility and the added attribute of not producing smoke or toxic gases when subjected to elevated temperatures Thermal protective capability when tested in accordance with the Standard Fire Test—ASTM E119

- Product reliability giving positive assurance of consistent and uniform protection characteristics
- Availability in a form that permits efficient and uniform application
- Sufficient bond strength and durability to prevent either dislodgement or surface damage during normal construction operations
- Resistance to weathering or erosion resulting from atmospheric conditions

The characteristics outlined above are primary requisites; the additional qualities, listed below, are given because they are desirable for certain applications:

- Attractive surface finish to eliminate the need for additional finishing
- Good acoustical properties for optimum sound absorption and minimum sound transmission
- Minimum health hazards to applicators
- Paintability or attractive integral coloring, washability
- Dry rather than wet application
- Direct contact application
- Minimum clean-up requirements during and after construction.

Briefly discussed below are a number of acceptable fire-protection materials that meet all of the principal characteristics listed above and, in varying degrees, some special qualitites.

Gypsum

Gypsum, a mineral with unusual fire-resistant qualities, slowly releases water of crystallization in quantities up to one-half its volume when subjected to high temperatures. Until this water has been completely released and the gypsum has been dehydrated, the side away from the fire remains at approximately 212°F. Gypsum plaster, machine or manually applied to metal or gypsum lath, is very satisfactory fireproofing material. It may be combined with lightweight aggregates, wood fiber, or sand. Poured or precast gypsum slabs may be used with cellular steel floors, steel deck, or other floor or roof systems. Gypsum wallboard, in the form of lath or finish material, and gypsum tile are used as components of fire-resistant constructions.

Vermiculite and perlite

Vermiculite and perlite are lightweight aggregates possessing high thermal insulation qualities. They are used both in gypsum and cement plaster and in concrete. The weight of these aggregates is one-tenth that of sand. They are also used as ingredients in acoustical plaster with excellent fire-resistant as well as acoustical

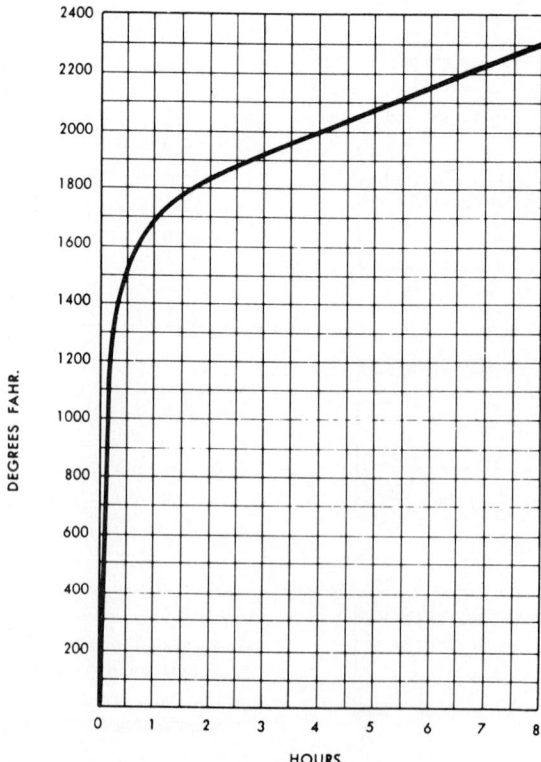

Fig. 1. ASTM time-temperature curve

In the standard fire test, air temperature rises to 1000°F in only 5 minutes, reaches 1,700°F at 1 hour, and 2,000°F at 4 hours.

and insulating properties. Acoustical plaster usually consists of a colloidal clay or gypsum binder, vermiculite or perlite aggregate, mineral fibers, and a foaming agent added to create porosity. The plaster may be machine-applied directly to the underside of light-gage steel floors or roof decks, columns or beams, or to gypsum or metal lath.

Mineral fiber

Mineral fiber,[2] combined with a mineral binder, air, and water, forms a very efficient and extremely lightweight fireproofing material. Applied with a special spray gun, the material will bond directly to steel, metal lath, and to most other clean rigid surfaces such as gypsum lath and concrete. In some constructions an adhesive is applied to the surface, and then the mineral fiber is sprayed on while the adhesive is still tacky, to increase the bond to the backing material. Mineral fiber has excellent fire-resistant qualities as well as acoustical qualities when applied to the underside of floors and roofs and also to steel structural members, such as columns, beams, girders, and trusses. Mineral fiber acoustical tile has also demonstrated excellent fire-resistant qualities when densely packed, tongued and grooved, and faced with a finish coating.

Portland cement

Portland cement concrete continues to be useful as a fireproofing material. When subjected to high temperatures, it releases water in a manner similar to gypsum, although to a lesser degree. The selection of aggregate is critical to the fire resistance of concrete. Aggregate containing 60 per cent or more of quartz, chert, or granite is not as fire-resistant as limestone or trap rock and therefore the concrete must be increased in thickness to obtain a comparable fire rating. The use of light aggregates instead of stone greatly improves the fire resistance of concrete. Concrete is now used largely for fire protection in reinforced concrete, over steel floor and roof decks, and for steel columns (where it also provides protection from abrasion due to traffic). Portland cement plaster is also used for fire protection. Mixing it with lightweight aggregates and mineral fiber greatly improves its fire resistance. It is preferred to gypsum plaster if there is exposure to the weather or high humidity.

Masonry

Masonry (brick, clay tile, concrete or cinder blocks, gypsum tile) is mainly used for walls and partitions, for protection to spandrels, and as backup for curtain walls. Its weight and thickness have caused it to be less used than formerly in steel-framed buildings.

Intumescent coatings are mixtures of resins, binders, pigments, ceramics, and refractory fillers. They are spray-applied directly to the steel surfaces that are to be protected. After application, these materials adhere and harden in a manner similar to paint. Resultant coatings are textured and, unlike soft plaster and mineral fiber protections, can often resist abrasion without additional covering or finishing.

At an elevated temperature, a chemical reaction occurs that causes the coating to swell to many times its applied thickness, thus forming an insulating blanket that protects the steel against heat penetration. Intumescent mastic fire-protection systems have achieved ratings of up to 2 hr for both beams and columns.

LIGHTWEIGHT CONSTRUCTION

Lightweight fire-resistant construction is a development of recent years. Concrete, steel-cellular, or composite-form floors and roofs, steel and precast concrete joists, junior beams, and corresponding wall elements have to a great extent replaced earlier heavier construction. Combinations of these elements with lightweight plaster and concrete, insulation, and sprayed-on or membrane fireproofing have made possible this lighter fire-resistant construction. The new performance codes using the ASTM fire ratings, instead of the old specification codes requiring a thickness of a specified number of inches, have aided this development.

The reduction in weight of the fireproofing alone has been significant. Lighter beams, girders, columns, and footings, or wider spacings with more free space, have been obtained. The American Institute of Steel Construction reports that if lightweight plaster or sprayed acoustical ceiling were suspended under a 24 by 24-ft floor bay designed for a 50-psf live load, the elimination of individual concrete fireproofing encasement of the supporting floor beams could reduce the dead load of that bay by more than 35 psf or 10½ tons. The Institute reports also that the use of a cellular or composite-form floor with thin topping could eliminate another 8 tons, a total saving of 18½ tons for a single bay.

MEMBRANE FIREPROOFING

Membrane fireproofing of floors and roofs consists of a thin, lightweight, fire-resistant ceiling interposed between the fire source and the incombustible floor or roof to be protected. The membrane may be directly attached to the lower surfaces of the framing members, or furred or suspended below them, and extends from wall to wall. Ducts, piping, wiring, and other mechanical equipment may be housed in the space between the floor or roof and the finished, fireproofing membrane ceiling below. Ceilings of vermiculite-, perlite-, or sand-gypsum plaster on metal or gypsum lath have served as membranes. All three aggregates are satisfactory for ratings up to and including 2 hr; the lightweight aggregates must be used for greater exposures. Most building code and fire insurance authorities recognize the equivalence of perlite and vermiculite aggregates for fire-resistance ratings. Thus their use is generally interchangeable. Gypsum lath used is ⅜ in. thick perforated. It is attached to furring channels with special clips; for greater fire resistance, 14 gage wire is inserted between lath and clip. For 4-hr resistance, 20 gage galvanized 1-in. hexagonal wire mesh is wire-tied beneath the gypsum lath. Tested fire-resistance ratings have been established for suspended ceilings pierced for ducts and electric outlets. These tested ratings show that the openings have little effect on the fire resistance if their total area is not greater proportionately than 100 sq in. per 100 sq ft of ceiling, or if the openings are protected. Acoustical plaster and sprayed mineral fiber on metal or gypsum lath, and mineral fiber acoustical tiles on suspension systems as membranes, have also received excellent fire ratings. Membrane fireproofing has made unnecessary the individual fireproofing of beams and girders supporting the incombustible floor or roof above and at the same time gives valuable protection to the hidden equipment, thus reducing fire losses significantly.

CONTACT FIREPROOFING

Contact fireproofing is applied directly to the surface of the structural component to be protected. In floor and roof systems, acoustical plaster or sprayed mineral fiber (usually proprietary products) is machine-applied directly to the underside of cellular or composite-form steel floors. With contact fireproofing, all supporting beams and girders must also be protected. This may be done by encasing them with lath or by spraying the plaster or fiber directly on the beam, maintaining a uniform thickness over exposed surfaces of flanges and web. In addition to their fireproofing char-

---

[2] *Asbestos, formerly the major ingredient in this type of insulation, has recently been banned in most cities as being injurious to the health of the workers. Rockwool and other mineral fibers continue to be used.*

acteristics these materials provide excellent sound absorption and thermal insulation.

A perforated-metal hung ceiling may be installed for appearance without impairing the sound absorption, and it may also be used as a conditioned-air diffuser.

ACOUSTICAL TILE CEILINGS

The use of acoustical tile ceilings as fire protection to incombustible and combustible

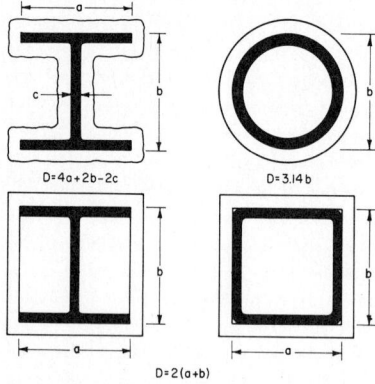

Fig. 2. Method of calculating D factor

floor and roof decks is now common. Fire-resistant tile (Federal Specification SS-A-118b, Class A), 12 by 12 in. or larger, ⅜ or ¾ in. thick, in fissured or perforated patterns, are used in a special steel suspension system. Fire-resistance ratings of up to 4 hr can be attained by the use of this system below unprotected steel beams or joists supporting an incombustible floor deck. Ratings of up to 1½ hr (combustible) can be achieved for wood floors supported on wood joists.

STEEL AT ELEVATED TEMPERATURES

The behavior and properties of steel at high temperatures has been intensively investigated, especially in connection with heating equipment, incinerators, and the like. But this condition of continuous exposure to high temperature is quite different from the condition encountered in a building fire — a relatively short exposure to rapidly rising temperature. At 1000°F the yield strength of the steel is slightly below the allowable design stress. Thus in the standard fire test, failure occurs when the average

temperature of a structural steel section reaches 1000°F.

In a building fire, or in a fire test, a structural steel section is rarely heated uniformly. Temperature differences of 600°F between the upper and lower flanges of a beam have been measured in standard fire tests. In heavy steel sections there may be considerable differences between surface and interior temperatures.

Steel expands 1 per cent of its length when heated to 1300°F. Thus a 25-ft beam would expand 3 in. in length. If restrained, even if only by its cooler ends, it will buckle. The distortion of steel members in a fire is caused by thermal expansion as well as by reduced strength under load.

No permanent loss of strength results from fire exposure. If a steel member can be straightened *in situ*, it need not be replaced.

Tests have clearly shown significant improvement in fire endurance when the ends of the test specimen are restrained against expansion. Recent major revisions of ASTM E119 have introduced dual ratings for floor and roof assemblies and for individual beams, based on the condition of their end supports—restrained or unrestrained. The standard defines restraint as follows:

> Floor and roof assemblies and individual beams in buildings shall be considered restrained when the surrounding or supporting structure is capable of resisting substantial thermal expansion throughout the range of anticipated elevated temperatures. Constructions not complying with this definition are assumed to be free to rotate and expand and shall therefore be considered as unrestrained.

Under this definition most members in steel-framed buildings are considered to be restrained; structural continuity is not required. An example of unrestrained construction is where roof beams and assemblies are supported on a bearing wall.

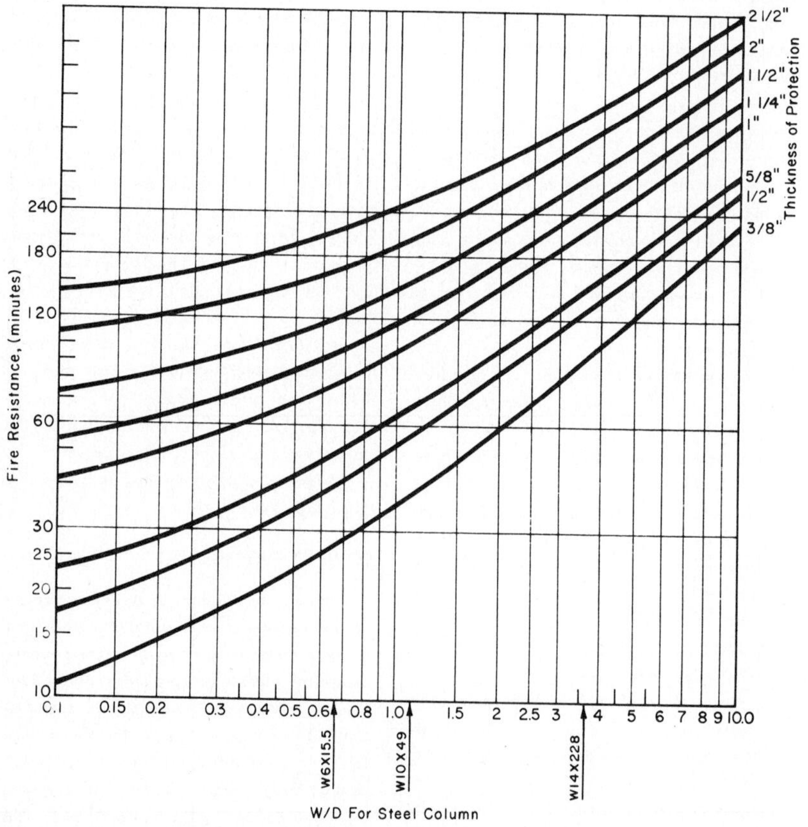

FIRE RATINGS

An index of fire-resistant constructions is given in Table 1. There are so many possible combinations of materials, thicknesses, and methods of installation that it is not feasible to list them all here. The designer should choose the type of fire protection he or she wishes to use and then obtain the pertinent test reports from the laboratories listed.

Beams: Most tests have employed various sizes of light-weight beams from 6 to 12 in. in depth. Ratings are not applicable to sizes smaller than those tested.

Columns: Most tests have employed W10x49 or W14x228 as representative of light and heavy columns. Ratings are not applicable to sizes smaller than those tested.

Fig. 3. Thickness of gypsum wallboard required for fire resistance for various sizes of steel columns.

From *"Designing Fire Protection for Steel Columns," American Iron and Steel Institute, 1978.*

In general, the heavier the section, the less the thickness of insulation required to achieve a specific rating. Extensive research and testing have resulted in the development of a formula for calculating the fire-resistance rating of steel sections:

$$R = \left(\frac{20W}{DP} + C\right) L$$

R = Fire resistance in hours
W = Weight of steel in lb/ft
D = Perimeter of protection, at the interface between protection and steel (inner face of protection), in inches
P = Density of insulation in lb/ft³
L = Thickness of insulation in inches
C = Constant as follows:
  C = 0.5 for protection materials such as sprayed fibers, and dense ($P \geq$ 20 lb/ft³) mineral wool
  C = 1.2 for protections containing portland cement or gypsum, such as plasters and cementitious mixtures

The two most significant factors are the shape of the fire-protection material (D) and the mass of the steel section (W). Methods of calculating D are shown in Fig. 2. It is worthy of note that the box type of membrane insulation shown at the lower left of Fig. 2, requires less thickness of insulation for a given rating than the direct applied contact insulation shown at the upper left. This is not because of the enclosed air space but because of the reduced perimeter of protection. Fig. 3 shows the thickness of gypsum wallboard required to achieve various fire ratings for different column sections.

Floor-roof assemblies: The great majority of fire tests have been in this field. Openings in fire-resistive ceilings for electrical fixtures, air-conditioning diffusers, etc. are limited in area as indicated in Item 34 in Table 1. Duct openings are usually protected by dampers equipped with fusible links, but mineral fiber board or gypsum board may be used.

REFERENCES

Fire-resistance Ratings. American Insurance Association (1967).

Fire-resistant Steel-frame Construction. American Iron and Steel Institute (1974).

Lathing and Plastering Assemblies. National Bureau for Lathing and Plastering, Inc.

Fire Resistance Design Manual, 1978, Gypsum Association.

Metal Lath Membrane Fireproofing for Steel Buildings. Technical Bulletin No. 3, Metal Lath Manufacturers Association.

National Building Code. American Insurance Association (1976).

Table 1. Fire-rated constructions

(From *Fire-Resistant Steel-Frame Construction,* American Iron and Steel Institute, 1974)

Note: *In the summaries that follow, the authority listed is either the agency that conducted the fire test and assigned the rating, or the agency whose published list of ratings is generally acknowledged as authoritative by the building industry and public officials. The following agencies are referred to by the indicated abbreviations:*
AIA: *American Insurance Association*
NBS: *National Bureau of Standards*
UL: *Underwriters Laboratories, Inc.*

1. BEAMS: Membrane Ceiling Protection	BASIC CONSTRUCTION	RATING (hours)	AUTHORITY REF.
	1. Floor or roof that develops required fire resistance		
	2. Steel beam. (Tests use beams 6 to 12 in. deep)		
	3. Ceilings:	1,1½,2,3,4	UL-A000,-D000,-G000, and -P000 series
	Acoustical tiles, concealed grid		
	Acoustical tiles, exposed grid	.3	UL-G200 series
	Lay-in panels, exposed grid	1,1½,2,3,4	UL-A200,-D200,-G200, and -P200 series
	Steel pans with mineral wool	1,1½,2,4	UL-A000,-D000,-G000, and -P000 series
	Wallboards, gypsum	1,1½	AIA
		2,3	UL-G500 series
	Mineral and fiber boards	2	AIA
	Mineral fibers on metal lath	1½,2,2½	NBS
		4	UL-A400
	Mineral fibers on gypsum lath	3	AIA
	Plaster on metal lath:		
	Cementitious mixture	3,4	UL-A400,-D400,-G400 series
	Perlite-gypsum	2,3,4	AIA
			UL-A400 and -P400 series
	Sand-gypsum	1,1½,2, 3,3½	NBS-BMS92
	Sand-portland cement	1½,2	NBS-BMS92
	Vermiculite-gypsum	2½,3,4	NBS-BMS92
		3,4	UL-A400 and -D400 series AIA
	Wood-fibered gypsum	2½,3,4	NBS-BMS92
	Plaster on gypsum lath:		
	Cementitious mixture	1	AIA
	Perlite-gypsum	1,1½,2, 2½,3,4	AIA

Table 1 (cont.). Fire-rated constructions

2. BEAMS: Encased Protection	BASIC CONSTRUCTION	RATING (hours)	AUTHORITY REF.
	1. Floor or roof that develops required fire resistance		
	2. Steel beam		
	3. Solid insulation:		
	Concrete (poured)	*1,2,3,4	AIA
	Gypsum (poured)	*1,2,3,4	AIA
	Masonry units:		
	Concrete block and fill	*1,2,3	AIA
	Clay tile and fill	*1,2,3	AIA

3. BEAMS: Enclosed Protection	BASIC CONSTRUCTION	RATING (hours)	AUTHORITY REF.
	1. Floor or roof that develops required fire resistance		
	2. Steel beam. Tests use beams 6 to 12 inches deep		
	3. Enclosure:		
	Masonry units—brick, clay tile, gypsum tile, concrete	*1,2,3,4	AIA
	Mastic and wallboard	2	UL-N600 series
	Mineral fibers on metal lath	1½,2,3	UL-A800,-D800,-N800, and -P800 series
	Plaster on gypsum lath:		
	Perlite-gypsum	3	AIA
	Vermiculite-gypsum	3	AIA
	Plaster on metal lath:		
	Cementitious mixture	2,3,4	UL-A700,-D700,-N400, and -P800 series
	Perlite-gypsum	1,4	UL-A400,-D400,-D900, and -P900 series
	Sand-gypsum	*1,2½	AIA
	Sand-portland cement	*1,2	AIA
	Vermiculite-gypsum	1,2,3,4	UL-A800,-D700,-P900,-P600, and -N400 series
	Wallboard-gypsum	2,3	UL-N500 series
	Mineral and fiber boards	1½,2	UL-N300 series

4. BEAMS: Direct Applied	BASIC CONSTRUCTION	RATING (hours)	AUTHORITY REF.
	1. Floor or roof that develops required fire resistance		
	2. Steel beam. Tests use 6- to 12-inch beams.		
	3. Sprayed insulation:		
	Cementitious mixture	1,1½,2,3,4	UL-A700,-D700,-N700,-P600, -P700,-P900 series
	Mineral fibers	¾,1,1½, 2,3,4	UL-A800,-D800,-D900,-J800, -N800,-P800 and -P900 series
	Mastic	¾,1,2	UL-N600 series

Estimated.

5. COLUMNS:
Pipe and Tubular
(Metal Enclosed)

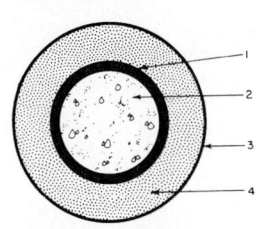
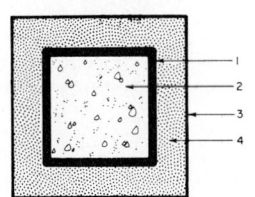

BASIC CONSTRUCTION	RATING (hours)	AUTHORITY REF.
1. Steel column: pipe and tubular sections		
2. Fill: concrete, structural grades		
3. Metal enclosure, non-bearing		
4. Insulating fill	2,3,4	UL-X100 series

6. COLUMNS:
Pipe and Tubular (Plaster)

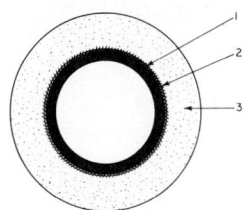

BASIC CONSTRUCTION	RATING (hours)	AUTHORITY REF.
1. Steel column: pipe and tubular sections		
2. Metal lath		
3. Insulation:		
Vermiculite-gypsum plaster	2	UL-X400 series

7. COLUMNS
W Shapes: *
Solid Encased Protection
(Metal Enclosed)

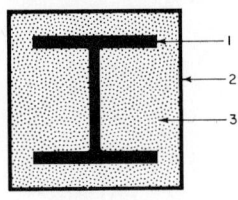

BASIC CONSTRUCTION	RATING (hours)	AUTHORITY REF.
1. Steel column:		
W type sections		
2. Metal enclosure, non-bearing		
3. Insulating fill	2,3,4	UL-X100 series

8. COLUMNS
W Shapes: *
Solid Encased Protection
(Concrete)

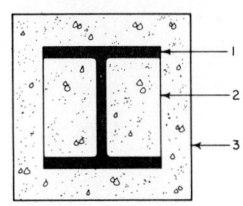

BASIC CONSTRUCTION	RATING (hours)	AUTHORITY REF.
1. Steel column:		
W type sections		
2. Reinforcement (where required in fire test):		
Steel wire or mesh		
3. Insulation:		
Concrete, structural grades**	1,2,3,4	NBS-BMS124
Gypsum-concrete	4	NBS-No. RP563

W refers to the designation of steel shapes as given in the Manual of Steel Construction, American Institute of Steel Construction.
**Depending on grade of concrete and total area of steel and concrete.*

Table 1 (cont.). Fire-rated constructions

9. COLUMNS
W Shapes:*
Enclosed Protection
(Masonry Units)

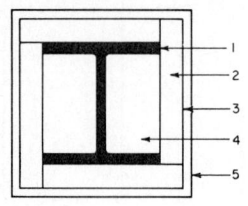

BASIC CONSTRUCTION	RATING (hours)	AUTHORITY REF.
1. Steel column: W type sections		
2. Masonry units:		
Brick	1,4	NBS-BMS92
Gypsum block, hollow or solid	2,4	UL-X500 series
		NBS-BMS92
Cinder concrete block, hollow	4	NBS-BMS92
Clay or shale tile, hollow	1,2,3,4	NBS-BMS92
3. Ties, only where noted in test: Steel straps or wire mesh		
4. Fill, only where noted in test: Concrete or broken masonry and mortar		

5. Additional insulation, only where noted in test:
    Sand-gypsum plaster
    Gypsum wallboard		

10. COLUMNS
W Shapes:*
Enclosed Protection
(Mineral Wool)

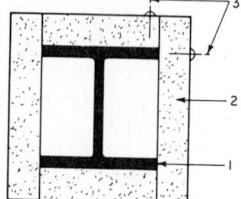

BASIC CONSTRUCTION	RATING (hours)	AUTHORITY REF.
1. Steel column: W type sections		
2. Mineral wool: Batts or blankets	4	UL-X200 series

3. Fasteners:
    Welded steel studs
    Alt.—light gage steel barbed corner angles with straps		

11. COLUMNS
W Shapes:*
Enclosed Protection
(Mineral and Fiber Boards)

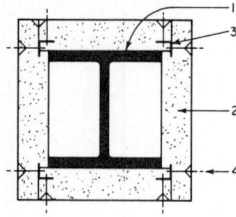

BASIC CONSTRUCTION	RATING (hours)	AUTHORITY REF.
1. Steel column: W type sections		
2. Mineral and fiber boards	1,1½,2,3,4	UL-X200 series
3. Corner angles: Light gage steel		
4. Screws		

W refers to the designation of steel shapes as given in the Manual of Steel Construction, American Institute of Steel Construction.

12. COLUMNS W Shapes:* Enclosed Protection (Gypsum Wallboard)	BASIC CONSTRUCTION	RATING (hours)	AUTHORITY REF.

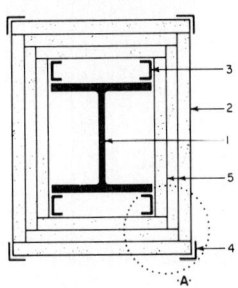

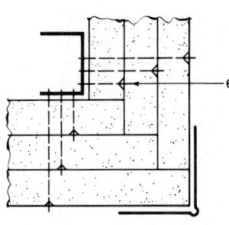

DETAIL AT ·A·

1. Steel column:
   W type sections
2. Gypsum wallboard, one to four layers — RATING: 2,3,4 — AUTHORITY: NBS, UL-X500 series

3. Spacer, continuous light gage galvanized steel stud, typical of most tests. In some tests, spacer is located between first layer (in contact with column flange) and second layer. In others, without spacers, wallboard is in contact with column flanges
4. corner beads, light gage galvanized steel angles
5. Tie wires where used
6. Screws

13. COLUMNS W Shapes:* Enclosed Protection (Gypsum Block)	BASIC CONSTRUCTION	RATING (hours)	AUTHORITY REF.

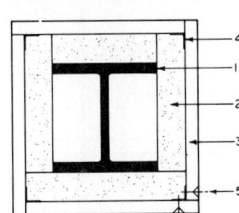

1. Steel column:
   W type sections
2. Insulation:
   Gypsum block, solid or hollow
   Gypsum plank — RATING: 4 — AUTHORITY: UL-X500 series
3. Ties, steel straps at ¼ points
4. Corner angle, light gage steel
5. Screws

Table 1 (cont.). **Fire-rated constructions**

14. COLUMNS
W Shapes:
Enclosed Protection
(Plasters)

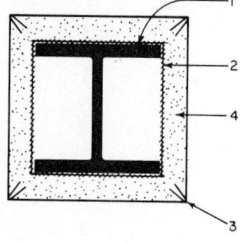

BASIC CONSTRUCTION	RATING (hours)	AUTHORITY REF.
1. Steel column: W type sections		
2. Backing: Gypsum lath or wallboard Metal lath or wire fabric		
3. Corner bead, light gage steel (typical of most tests)		
4. Plaster* on metal lath:		
Vermiculite-gypsum	4	AIA
	3,4	UL-X400 series
Perlite-gypsum	2,3,4	UL-X400 series
Cementitious mixtures	4	UL-X400 series
Sand-gypsum	1	NBS-BMS92
Sand-portland cement	1	NBS-BMS92
Wood fibered gypsum	4	NBS-BMS92
Plaster* on wire fabric:		
Vermiculite-portland cement	4	UL-X400 series
Perlite-portland cement	4	UL-X400 series
Plaster* on gypsum lath:		
Vermiculite gypsum	3	UL-X400 series
	4	NBS-BMS135
Perlite-gypsum	2,2½,3,4	NBS-BMS135
	3	AIA
	4	UL-X400 series
Cementitious mixture	4	UL-X400 series
Sand-gypsum	1,1½,2	NBS-BMS135
	2,3	AIA

15. COLUMNS
W Shapes:
Enclosed Protection
(Mastic)

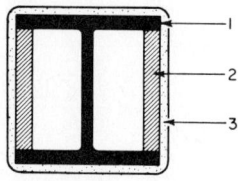

BASIC CONSTRUCTION	RATING (hours)	AUTHORITY REF.
1. Steel column: W type sections		
2. Backing: Gypsum wallboard, secured to column with spring steel clips		
3. Intumescent mastic	1½,2	UL-X600 series

16. COLUMNS
W Shapes:
Direct Sprayed Protection
(Cementitious, Mineral
Fibers, Mastic)

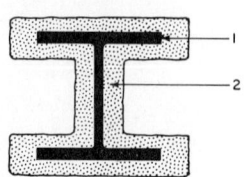

BASIC CONSTRUCTION	RATING (hours)	AUTHORITY REF.
1. Steel column: W type sections		
2. Sprayed insulation:*		
Cementitious mixtures	1½,2,3,4	UL-X700 series
Mineral fibers	2,3,4	UL-X800 series
Mastic	1	NBSTR10215-3; FR3601
	1½,2,3	UL-X600 series

* Materials applied in one or two coats, of thickness prescribed in test reports.

17. FLOOR AND ROOF ASSEMBLIES
Cellular Steel:
Membrane Ceiling Protection

BASIC CONSTRUCTION	RATING (hours)	AUTHORITY REF.
1. Topping:		
Sand-gravel concrete		
Sand-limestone concrete		
Perlite-portland cement concrete		
2. Cellular steel units: all configurations		
3. Ceiling:*		
Acoustical tiles, concealed grid	2,3,4	UL-A000 series
Lay-in panels, exposed grid	1½,2,3	UL-A200 series
	2	UL-D200 series
Metal pans with mineral wool	1,2	UL-A000 series
Mineral fibers on metal lath	4	UL-A400 series
Plaster on gypsum lath:		
Perlite gypsum	3	AIA
Plasters on metal lath:		
Cementitious mixture	3,4	UL-A400 series
Perlite-gypsum	3,4	UL-A400 series
Vermiculite-gypsum	3,4	UL-A400 series
		NBS-BMS92
Neat gypsum	3,4	NBS-BMS92

18. FLOOR AND ROOF ASSEMBLIES
Cellular Steel:
Direct Applied Protection

BASIC CONSTRUCTION	RATING (hours)	AUTHORITY REF.
1. Topping:		
Sand-gravel concrete		
Sand-limestone concrete		
Lightweight aggregate concrete		
2. Cellular steel units; all configurations		
3. Insulation:		
Mineral fibers	1½,2,3,4	UL-A800 series
Plaster: Cementitious mixture	1½,2,3	UL-A700 series
	2,3,4	AIA

19. FLOOR AND ROOF ASSEMBLIES
Blended Cellular and
Formed Steel Units:
Membrane Ceiling Protection

BASIC CONSTRUCTION	RATING (hours)	AUTHORITY REF.
1. Topping:		
Sand-gravel concrete		
Sand-limestone concrete		
Lightweight aggregate concrete		
2. Steel Units:		
Blended cellular or formed; all configurations		
3. Ceiling:		
Acoustical tiles, concealed grid	1½,2,3	UL-D000 series
	3	AIA
Lay-in panels, exposed grid	1½,2,3,4	UL-D200 series
	2,3	AIA
Metal pans with mineral wool	3	UL-D000 series
Plaster on metal lath:		
Cementitious mixture	3,4	UL-D400 series
Perlite-gypsum	3,4	UL-D400 series
Vermiculite-gypsum	4	UL-D400 series

For general information on permissible openings see Item 34 on page 3-194.

Table 1 (cont.).   Fire-rated constructions

20. FLOOR AND ROOF ASSEMBLIES
Blended Cellular and Formed Steel Units: Direct Applied Protection

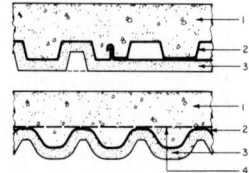

BASIC CONSTRUCTION	RATING (hours)	AUTHORITY REF.
1. Topping:		
Sand-gravel concrete		
Sand-limestone concrete		
Lightweight aggregate concrete		
2. Steel Units:		
Blended cellular or formed; all configurations		
3. Insulation:		
Mineral fibers	¾,1,1½, 2,3,4	UL-D800 series
Plaster: cementitious mixture	1,1½,2,3,4	UL-D700 series
	2,3	AIA
4. Reinforcement:		
Steel rods or wire fabric (where required)		

21. FLOOR AND ROOF ASSEMBLIES
Blended Cellular and Formed Steel Units: Unprotected

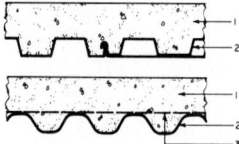

BASIC CONSTRUCTION	RATING (hours)	AUTHORITY REF.
1. Topping:		
Sand-gravel concrete		
Sand-limestone concrete		
Lightweight aggregate concrete		
2. Steel Units:	¾,1,1½,2,3	UL-D900 series
Blended cellular or formed; all configurations	1½	AIA
No membrane or insulation		
3. Reinforcement:		
Steel rods or wire fabric (where required)		

22. FLOOR AND ROOF ASSEMBLIES
Reinforced Concrete Slabs: Poured in Place; Membrane Ceiling Protection

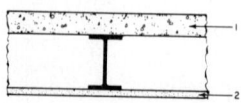

BASIC CONSTRUCTION	RATING (hours)	AUTHORITY REF.
1. Reinforced concrete slab:		
Sand-limestone concrete		
2. Plaster on metal lath:		
Vermiculite-gypsum	3,4	AIA

23. FLOOR AND ROOF ASSEMBLIES
Steel Joists:
Membrane Ceiling
Protection

BASIC CONSTRUCTION	RATING (hours)	AUTHORITY REF.
1. Topping:		
Sand-gravel concrete		
Sand-limestone concrete		
Cinder concrete with topping		
Perlite-portland cement concrete		
Gypsum tiles		
Gypsum tiles with topping		
Gypsum concrete		
2. Forming: (where required)		
Metal lath*		
Formed steel		
Gypsum boards		
Paper-backed wire fabric		
3. Steel Joists:		
Open web types. See test reports for minimum size		
4. Ceiling:**		
Acoustical tiles, concealed grid	1,1½,2,3	UL-G000 series
Lay-in panels, exposed grid	1,1½,2,3	UL-G200 series
Metal pans with mineral wool	2	UL-G000 series
Gypsum wallboard	¾,1,1½,2,3	UL-G500 series
Mineral fibers:		
on gypsum lath	3	AIA
on metal lath	1½,2,2½	NBS-TRBM44
Mineral and fiber boards	2	AIA
Plaster on metal lath:		
Cementitious mixture	2	UL-G400 series
Neat gypsum	2½,3	NBS-BMS92
Perlite-gypsum	3	AIA
Vermiculite-gypsum	4	UL-G400 series
	2½,3,4	NBS-BMS92
Sand-gypsum	1½,2	NBS-BMS92
	3	AIA
Sand-portland cement	1½	NBS-BMS92
Plaster on gypsum lath:		
Cementitious mixtures	¾,1	UL-G500 series
Perlite-gypsum	1	UL-G500 series
	1,1½,2,2½,3,4	NBS-BMS141

24. FLOOR AND ROOF ASSEMBLIES
Reinforced Concrete Slabs:
Poured in Place: Unprotected

BASIC CONSTRUCTION	RATING (hours)	AUTHORITY REF.
1. Reinforced concrete slabs:		
Type aggregate:		
Slag	2½,4	AIA
Shale	4	AIA
Trap rock	2,3	AIA
Limestone	1,3	AIA
Siliceous gravel	¾,1,1½,2	NBS-TRBM44
Calcareous gravel	2	AIA

25. FLOOR AND ROOF ASSEMBLIES
Reinforced Concrete Solid Units:
Direct Applied Protection

BASIC CONSTRUCTION	RATING (hours)	AUTHORITY REF.
1. Concrete planks with tongue and groove joints		
2. Insulation:		
Sprayed mineral fibers	1,1½	UL-J800 series

* S11 Technical Digest No. 4, "Design of Fire-Resistive Assemblies with Steel Joists" published by Steel Joist Institute.
** For general information on permissible openings see Item 34 on Sheet 13.

Table 1 (cont.). Fire-rated constructions

26. FLOOR AND ROOF ASSEMBLIES Reinforced Concrete Cellular Units: Direct Applied Protection	BASIC CONSTRUCTION	RATING (hours)	AUTHORITY REF.

	1. Topping:
	  Lightweight aggregate concrete
	2. Reinforced concrete cellular units
	3. Insulation:
	  Sprayed mineral fibers
		
		1½,2
			
			UL-J800 series

27. FLOOR AND ROOF ASSEMBLIES Reinforced Concrete Cellular Units: Unprotected	BASIC CONSTRUCTION	RATING (hours)	AUTHORITY REF.

	1. Reinforced concrete hollow core units:
	  Normal weight aggregates
	  Lightweight aggregate
	2. Topping:
	  Expanded shale concrete
	  Normal weight aggregate concrete
	  No topping, grouted joints
		
		3
		1,1½,2,3,4
		¾,1,2
			
			AIA
			UL-J900 series
			UL-J900 series

28. ROOF ASSEMBLIES Steel Decks: Direct Applied Protection	BASIC CONSTRUCTION	RATING (hours)	AUHORITY REF.

	1. Roof covering:
	  Class A, B or C per UL listing
	2. Insulation:
	  Mineral and fiber boards
	  Vermiculite-portland cement concrete
	3. Decking:
	  Corrugated or fluted steel
	4. Insulation:
	  Cementitious mixture
	
	  Mineral fibers
		
		1,1½
		2
		1,1½,2
			
			UL-P700 series
			AIA
			UL-P800 series

29. ROOF ASSEMBLIES Steel Decks on Steel Joists: Membrane Ceiling Protection	BASIC CONSTRUCTION	RATING (hours)	AUTHORITY REF.

	1. Roof covering:
	  Class A, B, or C, per UL listing
	2. Insulation:
	  Mineral and fiber boards
	  Perlite-portland cement concrete
	  Vermiculite-portland cement concrete
	3. Decking:
	  Corrugated, ribbed, or fluted; painted or galvanized steel
	4. Steel joists:
	  Minimum size and maximum center to center spacing as given in test reports
	5. Ceiling:
	  Lay-in panels, exposed grid
	  Plaster on metal lath:
	    Perlite gypsum
	    Vermiculite-gypsum		

		¾,1,2 2,3 2	UL-P200 series UL-P400 series UL-P400 series

30. ROOF ASSEMBLIES Concrete Decks: Precast Units Unprotected	BASIC CONSTRUCTION	RATING (hours)	AUTHORITY REF.

	1. Roof covering:
	  Class A, B, or C, per UL listing
	2. Decking:
	  Perlite-portland cement concrete—joints grouted
		
		¾,2
			
			UL-P900 series

31. ROOF ASSEMBLIES
Concrete Decks: Precast Units on Steel Joists: Membrane Ceiling Protection

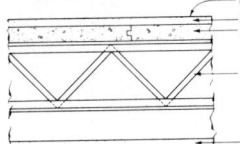

BASIC CONSTRUCTION	RATING (hours)	AUTHORITY REF.
1. Roof covering:		
Class A, B, or C, per UL listing		
2. Insulation (where indicated in test):		
Mineral and fiber boards		
3. Decking:		
Concrete units		
Gypsum concrete units		
Cement-fiber units		
4. Steel joists:		
Minimum size and maximum center to center		
spacing of joists as given in test reports		
5. Ceiling:		
Acoustical tiles, concealed grid	2	UL-P000 series
Lay-in panels, exposed grid	2	UL-P200 series
Plaster:		
Perlite-gypsum	2	UL-P400 series

32. ROOF ASSEMBLIES
Concrete Decks: Poured in Place Unprotected

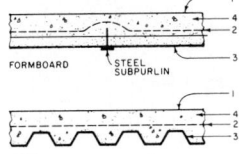

FORMBOARD   STEEL SUBPURLIN

STEEL

BASIC CONSTRUCTION	RATING (hours)	AUTHORITY REF.
1. Roof covering:		
Class A, B or C, per UL listing		
2. Reinforcing steel:		
Wire fabric		
3. Forming:		
Steel:		
Corrugated or fluted		
Formboard:		
Mineral and fiber boards		
Gypsum wallboard		
Cement-fiber units		
4. Decking:		
Gypsum concrete	1,2	UL-P600 series
Cellular concrete	2	UL-P900 series
Perlite-portland cement concrete	1,2	UL-P900 series
Vermiculite-portland cement	1	UL-P600 series
Concrete	2	UL-P900 series

33. ROOF ASSEMBLIES
Concrete Decks: Poured in Place on Steel Joists: Membrane Ceiling Protection

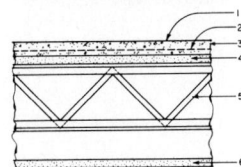

BASIC CONSTRUCTION	RATING (hours)	AUTHORITY REF.
1. Roof covering:		
Class A, B or C, per UL listing		
2. Reinforcing steel:		
Welded wire fabric (where indicated in test)		
3. Decking:		
Gypsum-wood fibered concrete		
Perlite-gypsum		
Perlite-portland cement concrete		
4. Form board:		
Gypsum wallboard		
Mineral and fiber boards		
Paper backed wire fabric		
5. Steel joists:		
Minimum size and maximum center to center		
spacing as given in test reports		
6. Ceiling:		
Acoustical tiles, concealed grid	1½,2	UL-P000 series
Lay-in panels, exposed grid	1½,2	UL-P200 series
Plaster on metal lath: Perlite-gypsum	2,3	UL-P400 series

Table 1 (cont.). Fire-rated constructions

34. MEMBRANE CEILING OPENINGS FOR FLOOR AND ROOF ASSEMBLIES

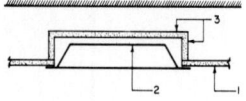

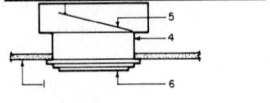

1. Fire-rated membrane ceiling. Tests with openings have been made on all type membranes.
2. Steel housing for fluorescent lamps. Generally 2 ft by 4 ft, spaced so that their area does not exceed 25 ft² per each 100 ft² of ceiling area. This is maximum; see test report for applicable limitation.
3. Light fixture protection:
   Batts and blankets
   Mineral and fiber boards
   Gypsum wallboard
4. Galvanized steel air duct.
5. Outlet protection:
   Damper with fusible link or UL approved alternate protection system.
6. Outlet opening of 576 in.² (total or individual) per each 100 ft² of ceiling area with maximum dimension of opening of 30 in. This is the maximum opening tested; see test report for applicable limitation.

35. WALLS AND PARTITIONS: Hollow

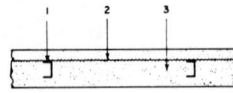

BASIC CONSTRUCTION	RATING (hours)	AUTHORITY REF.
1. Cold-formed steel studs: single channels or wire truss		
2. Insulation fill: (Where indicated in test reports) Mineral wool batts Mineral fibers Cementitious mixture		
3. Insulation wall:		
Gypsum wallboard	1,2	UL-U400 series
	1	AIA
Mineral and fiber boards	1	UL-U400 series
	1	AIA
Plater on metal lath:		
Cementitious mixture	4	UL-U400 series
Perlite-gypsum	1	UL-U400 series
	2	AIA
Sand-gypsum	1,1½,2	AIA & NBS-BMS92
Sand-portland cement	4	UL-U400 series
	1,1½	AIA
Vermiculite-gypsum	4	UL-U400 series
Wood-fibered gypsum	½,2	NBS-BMS92
Plaster on gypsum lath:		
Perlite-gypsum	1,2,2½	AIA
Sand-gypsum	1,1½	AIA
	1	UL-U400 series

36. WALLS AND PARTITIONS: Solid

BASIC CONSTRUCTION	RATING (hours)	AUTHORITY REF.
1. Cold-formed steel studs: channels and lath		
2. Lath: type indicated below		
3. Insulation wall:		
Plaster on metal lath		
Perlite-gypsum	1	AIA
	2	UL-U400 series
Sand-gypsum	1,1½,2	NBS-BMS92
	1	AIA
Vermiculite-gypsum	2	AIA
Wood fibered-gypsum	2	AIA
Plaster on gypsum lath (no studs):		
Perlite-gypsum	1,2	NBS
Sand-gypsum	1	AIA
Vermiculite-gypsum	1,2	NBS
Concrete:		
Perlite-portland cement on wire mesh	4	AIA
Sand-portland cement on steel reinforcing bars	1,3	AIA
Vermiculite-portland cement on paper backed wire fabric	4	UL-U200

37. WALLS AND PARTITIONS: Hollow Exterior Load Bearing Wall	BASIC CONSTRUCTION	RATING (hours)*	AUTHORITY REF.
	1. Exterior wall: brick veneer		
	2. Insulation:		
	Mortar on paper-backed wire fabric		
	Mortar plus fiberboard sheathing		
	Gypsum wallboard		
	Fiber board sheathing		
	3. Cold-formed steel studs: single channels		
	4. Insulation:		
	Plaster:		
	Sand-gypsum on gypsum lath	2	AIA
	Sand-gypsum on metal lath or paper-backed wire fabric, over mineral wool blanket	4	
	Neat gypsum on metal lath	1½	NBS-BMS92
	Vermiculite-gypsum on metal lath	2	
	Sand-gypsum on metal lath	1¾	

Ratings are for interior fire exposure; ratings for fire on brick side are greater.

EXAMPLES OF FIRE-RATED CONSTRUCTIONS

The only fire-rated constructions (or "assemblies" as they are called by fire-resistance professionals) are those which have been tested by a reputable laboratory in accordance with ASTM E119. Exact duplicates of fire-rated constructions will be accepted by all code authorities, but the slightest departure from the tested construction may result in rejection. Full scale fire tests are expensive and time-consuming; there are only a few laboratories in the country equipped to perform the standard ASTM test.

A compendium of fire-rated constructions, "Fire-resistance Ratings," is published by the American Insurance Association, 85 John Street, New York, New York 10038. The 1968 edition is now being updated.

"Fire Resistance Design Manual, 1978 Edition," published by the Gypsum Association, 1603 Orrington Avenue, Evanston, Illinois 60201, describes more than 200 fire-rated constructions, limited of course to those employing gypsum products. The manual also lists sound isolation ratings (STC) for all wall and floor/ceiling constructions. A representative selection from the manual is given in Table 2. Code initials used in Table 2 for testing laboratories are as follows:

Fire

BMS	Building Materials & Structures, National Bureau of Standards
FM	Factory Mutual Research Corporation
SFT	Standard Fire Test, Fire Prevention Research Institute
NBS	National Bureau of Standards
PCA	Portland Cement Association
UL	Underwriters Laboratories, Inc.
OSU	The Ohio State University
UC	University of California
GET	George E. Troxell, P.E., Consulting Engineer
WHI	Warnock Hersey International

Sound

ACI	Acoustical Consultants, Inc.
BMS	Building Materials & Structures, National Bureau of Standards
BBN	Bolt, Beranek and Newman, Inc.
CK	Cedar Knolls Acoustical Laboratories
G&H	Geiger and Hamme
KAL	Kodaras Acoustical Laboratories
KG	Kaiser Acoustical Laboratories
NBS	National Bureau of Standards
NGC	Gold Bond Building Products, Division of National Gypsum Company, Acoustical Laboratories
OCF	Owens-Corning Fiberglas Product Testing Laboratories
OR	Ohio Research Corporation
RAL	Riverbank Acoustical Laboratories
USG	United States Gypsum Company Acoustical Research Center
WHI	Warnock Hersey International

Table 2. Fire and sound ratings of various constructions

(From "Fire Resistance Design Manual, 1978 Edition," published by Gypsum Association)

Fire rating hr	Sound rating STC	Description	Section, data, references — Fire	Section, data, references — Sound
		INTERIOR WALLS AND PARTITIONS		
1	45–49	**Construction Type: Gypsum Wallboard, Mineral Fiber, Metal Studs** One layer ½" type X gypsum wallboard or veneer base applied parallel to each side of 2½" metal studs 24" o.c. with 1" type S drywall screws 8" o.c. to edges and 12" o.c. to intermediate studs. 2" mineral fiber 2.5 pcf friction fit in stud space. Also fire tested with 1½" mineral fiber 3.0 pcf stapled to board in stud spaces. Stagger joints 24" o.c. each side. (NLB)	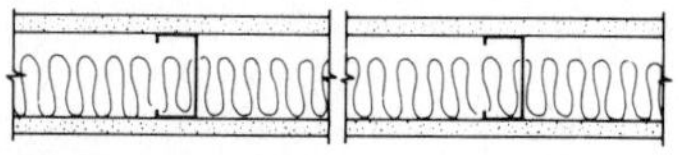 Thickness: 3½" Limiting Height: 13' 5" Approx. Weight: 5 psf Fire Test: FM WP 51-1, 9-22-66	Sound Test: RAL TL 69-42, 10-17-68
1	55–59	**Construction Type: Gypsum Wallboard, Metal Studs** Base layer ¼" gypsum wallboard applied parallel to each side of 2½" metal studs 24" o.c. with ⅞" typs S drywall screws 12" o.c. Face layer ⅝" X gypsum wallboard or veneer base applied on each side parallel to studs with 1⁵⁄₁₆" type S drywall screws 12" o.c. Stagger joints 24" o.c. each layer and side. Sound tested using 1½" mineral fiber in stud space. (NLB)	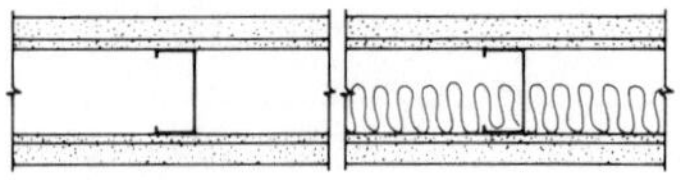 Thickness: 4¼" Limiting Height: 13' 10" Approx. Weight: 8 psf Fire Test: See WP 1051	Sound Test: CK 684-14, 8-13-68
1	40–44	**Construction Type: Gypsum Veneer Base, Veneer Plaster, Metal Studs** One layer ½" type X gypsum veneer base applied parallel or at right angles to each side of 2½" metal studs 24" o.c. with 1" type S drywall screws 8" o.c. to edges or ends and 12" o.c. to intermediate studs. Omit screws in top and bottom runners. Stagger joints 24" o.c. each side. ¹⁄₁₆" gypsum veneer plaster applied over both sides. Sound tested with 3" glass fiber in stud space and with studs 16" o.c. (NLB)	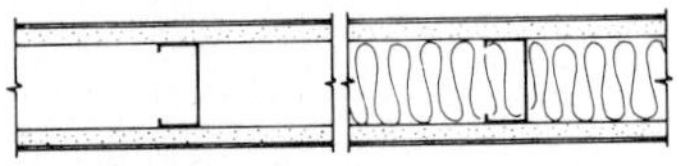 Thickness: 3⅝" Limiting Height: 14' 8" Approx. Weight: 5 psf Fire Test: UC, 8-5-63; UC, 11-1-63; UC, 5-31-66	Sound Test: G & H NG-269FT, 12-20-65
1	40–44	**Construction Type: Gypsum Lath, Gypsum Plaster, Metal Studs** ½" 1:2 gypsum-sand plaster applied over face of ⅜" plain gypsum lath fastened at right angles to each side of 2½" open web metal studs 16" o.c. with 12 gage galvanized wire clips. 16 gage furring channel stiffener installed horizontally at mid-height through web of studs and wire tied. Stagger end joints each lath on each side with end joint clips at lath corners. (NLB)	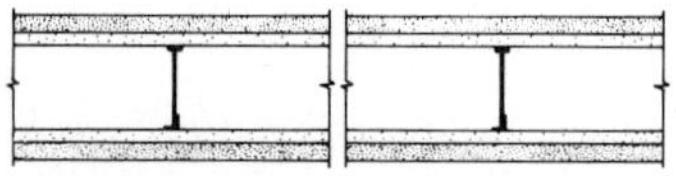 Thickness: 4¼" Limiting Height: 11' 2" Approx. Weight: 14 psf Fire Test: FM WP-65-1, 1-10-67	Sound Test: NGC 3042, 2-20-69
1	35–39	**Construction Type: Gypsum Wallboard, Semi-Solid Gypsum Studs** One layer ⅝" type X gypsum wallboard or veneer base applied parallel to each side of 6" wide gypsum studs 24" o.c. made of 2 or 3 layers of laminated gypsum panels. Attach wallboard to gypsum studs with 1" type G drywall screws 20" o.c. and with laminating compound. Fire tested with 1" thick gypsum studs. Sound tested using ⅝" thick gypsum studs. (NLB)	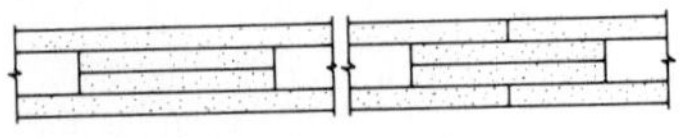 Thickness: 2½" Limiting Height: 12' 0" Approx. Weight: 8 psf Fire Test: UL R 2717-19, 21 Design U510, 6-3-57	Sound Test: G & H BW-8 FT,
1	35–39	**Construction Type: Gypsum Plaster, Metal Lath, Solid Metal Channel** 2" solid 1:1-1:2 gypsum-sand plaster applied over 2.5 lb. metal lath wire tied 6" o.c. to ¾" cold rolled channel studs 16" o.c. embedded in plaster. (NLB)	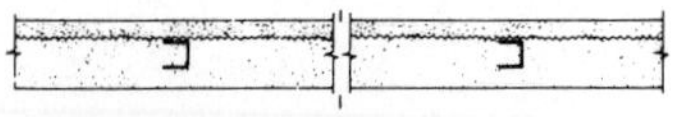 Thickness: 2" Limiting Height: 12' 6" Approx. Weight: 18 psf Fire Test: OSU T-129, 3-16-48	Sound Test: BMS 144/523, 2-25-55 & NBS Monograph 77, 11-30-64

Fire rating hr	Sound rating STC	Description	Section, data, references	
			Fire	Sound
2	55–59	**Construction Type: Gypsum Wallborad, Mineral Fiber, Metal Studs** Base layer ⅝" type X gypsum wallboard or veneer base applied parallel to each side of 3⅝" metal studs 24" o.c. with 1" type S drywall screws 32" o.c. Staple 2" glass fiber 0.9 pcf to one side in stud space. Face layer ⅝" type X gypsum wallboard or veneer base applied parallel to one side of studs with 1⅝" type S drywall screws 12" o.c. to edges and 24" o.c. to intermediate studs. On opposite side second layer ½" type X gypsum wallboard or veneer base applied parallel to studs with 1⅝" type S drywall screws 12" o.c. Third face layer ¼" or ⅜" gypsum wallboard or veneer base laminated parallel to studs with ¾" daubs of adhesive spaced 12" o.c. each way. Stagger joints 24" o.c. each layer and side. (NLB)	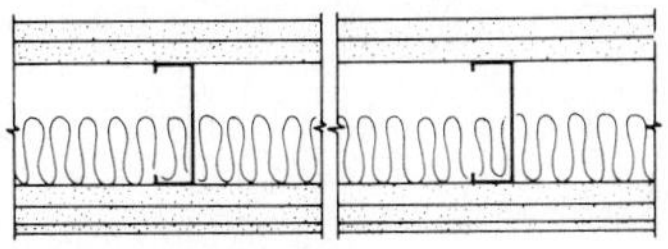 Thickness: 6¼" Limiting Height: 19' 5" Approx. Weight: 11 psf Fire Test: UL R3560-1 Design U403, 8-21-68 Sound Test: RAL TL 69-118, 12-16-68	
2	50–54	**Construction Type: Gypsum Wallboard, Metal Studs** Base layer ½" type X gypsum wallboard or veneer base applied parallel to each side of 1⅝" metal studs 24" o.c. with 1" type S drywall screws 12" o.c. Face layer ½" type X gypsum wallboard or veneer base applied on each side parallel to studs with 1⅝" type S drywall screws 12" o.c. Stagger joints 24" o.c. each layer and side. Sound tested using 1½" mineral fiber in stud space. (NLB)	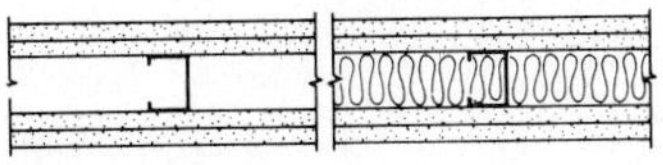 Thickness: 3⅝" Limiting Height: 12' 4" Approx. Weight: 9 psf Fire Test: UC, 12-7-64 Sound Test: ACI 1131 a, 7-14-64	
2	50–54	**Construction Type: Gypsum Veneer Base, Veneer Plaster, Metal Studs** Base layer ½" type X gypsum veneer base applied parallel to each side of 2½" metal studs 24" o.c. with 1" type S drywall screws 24" o.c. Face layer ½" type X gypsum veneer base applied on each side parallel to studs with 1⅝" type S drywall screws 12" o.c. No screws in runners. Apply 3/32" gypsum-veneer plaster over each face. Stagger joints 24" o.c. each layer and side. Sound tested using 1" mineral fiber in stud space. (NLB)	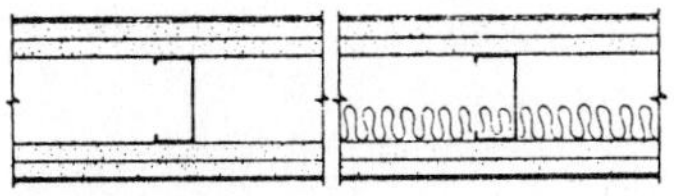 Thickness: 4¾" Limiting Height: 15' 10" Approx. Weight: 10 psf Fire Test: UL R5085-7 Design U303, 12-1-66 Sound Test: CK 654-66, 12-29-65	
2	40–44	**Construction Type: Gypsum Plaster, Gypsum Lath, Metal Studs** ¾" 1:2 gypsum-perlite plaster applied over ⅜" perforated gypsum lath attached at right angles to each side of 2½" open web metal studs spaced 16" o.c. with 12 gage wire clips. End joint clips at lath corners. (NLB)	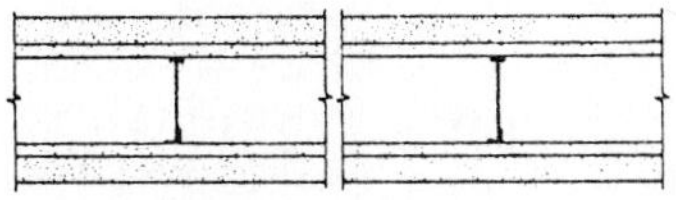 Thickness: 4¾" Limiting Height: 11' 2" Approx. Weight: 13 psf Fire Test: OSU T-1813, 5-29-61	
2	40–44	**Construction Type: Gypsum Plaster, Metal Lath, Metal Studs** ¾" 1:1, 1:1 fibered gypsum sand plaster applied over 3.4 lb. metal lath wire tied at right angles to each side of 2½" open web metal studs 16" o.c. (NLB)	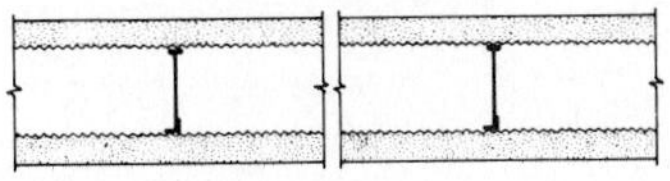 Thickness: 4¼" Limiting Height: 11' 2" Approx. Weight: 16 psf Fire Test: UL R4024-9, 10, 1-5-67	
2	35–39	**Construction Type: Solid Gypsum Wallboard** One layer ½" type X gypsum wallboard or veneer base applied parallel to each side of 1" tongue and groove gypsum coreboard with laminating compound combed over entire surface. Stagger joints 24" o.c. each layer and side. (NLB)	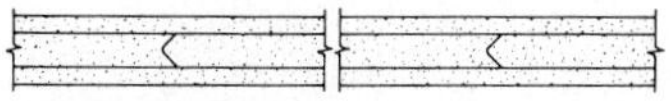 Thickness: 2" Limiting Height: 11' 0" Approx. Weight: 9 psf Fire Test: OSU T-1339, 4-8-60 Sound Test: See WP 1310	

Table 2 (Cont.)   Fire and sound ratings of various constructions

(From "Fire Resistance Design Manual, 1978 Edition," published by Gypsum Association)

Fire rating hr	Sound rating STC	Description	Section, data, references	
			Fire	Sound
2	35–39	**Construction Type: Semi-Solid Gypsum Wallboard** Base layer ½" type X gypsum wallboard or veneer base applied parallel to each side of 1⅝" x 6" type X gypsum board studs 24" o.c. with laminating compound combed over entire surface of gypsum studs and 2" type G drywall screws at 24" o.c. to studs. Face layer ½" type X gypsum wallboard or veneer base applied parallel to studs on each side with laminating compound combed over entire contact surface and 2" type G drywall screws spaced 24" o.c. into gypsum studs. Edges secured to top and bottom channels with 1½" type S drywall screws 24" o.c. Stagger joints 24" o.c. for each layer and side. (NLB)	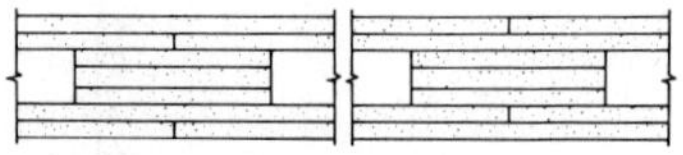 Thickness: 3⅝" Limiting Height: 14' 0" Approx. Weight: 10 psf Fire Test: UC, 2-8-62	
2	34 30–39	**Construction Type: Gypsum Plaster, Solid Metal Channel, Metal Lath** 2½" solid 1:2:2 gypsum-perlite plaster applied over each side of 3.4 lb. metal lath wire tied to one side of ¾" cold rolled channels 16" o.c. embedded in plaster. (NLB)	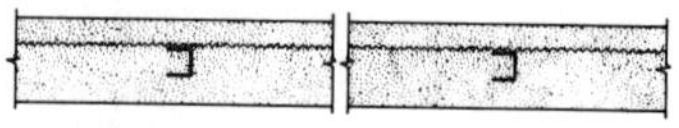 Thickness: 2½" Limiting Height: 12' 0" Approx. Weight: 12 psf Fire Test: UL R3453, 2-13-52	
2	35–39	**Construction Type: Gypsum Block, Gypsum Plaster** ½" 1:3 gypsum-sand plaster applied over both sides of 3" thick hollow gypsum block. (NLB)	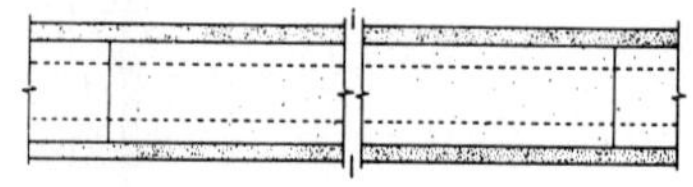 Thickness: 4" Approx. Weight: 21 psf Fire Test: OSU T-118-27, 28, 7-18-50	
*	50–54	**Construction Type: Gypsum Wallboard, Mineral Fiber, Wood Studs** One layer ⅝" proprietary type X gypsum wallboard or veneer base applied parallel to resilient channels 24" o.c. with 1" type S drywall screws in edges and center row 12" o.c. End joints back-blocked with resilient channels. Resilient channels attached at right angles to 2" x 4" wood studs 16" or 24" o.c. with 1¼" type S drywall screws. 3" mineral fiber 2.0 or 2.3 pcf in stud space. On opposite side one layer ⅝" type X gypsum wallboard or veneer base applied at right angles to studs with 1¼" type W drywall screws 12" o.c. Stagger vertical joints 48" o.c. each side. Sound test based on studs 16" o.c. and open face of 2.0 pcf mineral fiber blankets toward resilient side of stud space. (LB)	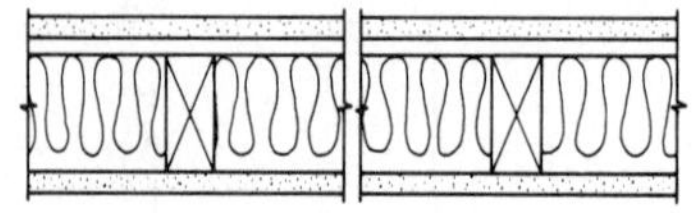 Thickness: 5⅜" Approx. Weight: 7 psf Fire Test: UL R1319-93, 94, 129 Design U311, 8-10-66 Sound Test: BBN 760903, 9-17-76	
*	50–54	**Construction Type: Gypsum Wallboard, Wood Studs** Base layer ⅝" type X gypsum wallboard or veneer base applied at right angles to each side of 2" x 4" wood studs 16" o.c. staggered 8" o.c. on 2" x 6" wood plates with 6d coated nails 1⅞" long, 0.085" shank, ¼" heads, 24" o.c. Face layer ⅝" type X gypsum wallboard or veneer base applied on each side at right angles to studs with 8d coated nails 2⅜" long, 0.113" shank, 9/32" heads, 8" o.c. Stagger vertical joints 16" o.c. each layer and side. (LB)	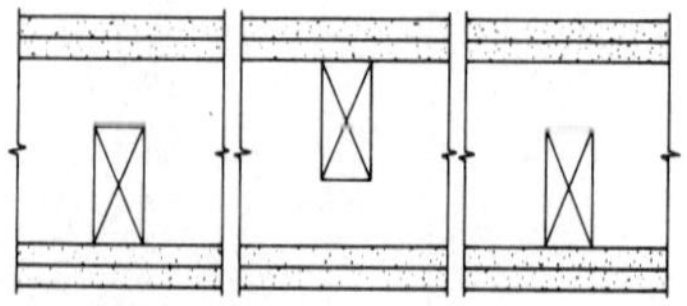 Thickness: 8" Approx. Weight: 13 psf Fire Test: See WP 4135 Sound Test: NGC 2377, 5-19-70	

* *Combustible.*

Fire rating hr	Sound rating STC	Description	Section, data, references	
			Fire	Sound

Construction Type: Gypsum Wallboard, Metal Studs

| 2 | 55–59 | Base layer ⅝" type X gypsum wallboard or veneer base applied parallel to a double row of 1⅝" metal studs 24" o.c. and 6¼" apart with 1" type S drywall screws 8" o.c. at edges, 12" o.c. in field. 25 gage by 9½" long runner pieces located at ⅓ points used as cross braces and attached with two No. 8 x ½" self-drilling steel screws at each end. Optionally ⅝" gypsum board pieces 12" wide x 9½" long may be used as cross braces fastened to stud pairs with three 1" type S drywall screws at each end of brace. Face layers ⅝" type X gypsum wallboard or veneer base applied parallel to studs with 1⅝" type S drywall screws 8" o.c. at joints and top and bottom runners, 12" o.c. in field. Stagger joints each layer and side. Sound tested using 3½" glass fiber stapled to one side in cavity. (NLB) | 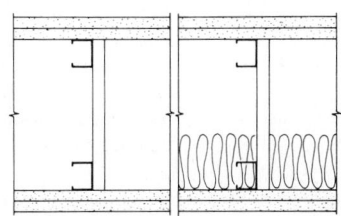
Thickness: 12"
Limiting Height: 16' 0"
Approx. Weight: 10 psf
Fire Test: UL R4024-14
    Design U420, 11-17-76
Sound Test: RAL TL 76-156, 6-7-76 | |

Construction Type: Double Solid Gypsum Wallboard

| 2 | 55–59 | One layer ½" regular gypsum wallboard or veneer base applied with ⅜" beads of laminating compound 2" o.c. to exterior side only of 1" gypsum coreboards placed on each side of 1" air space. Coreboard fastened with No. 6 x 1⅝" type S screws, three per board, into floor and ceiling runners (track). Sound tested with 3" air space and 1½" mineral fiber stapled on one side in cavity. (NLB) | 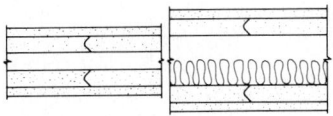
Thickness: 4"
Limiting Height: 8' 6"
Approx. Weight: 12 psf
Fire Test: UC, 4-25-61
Sound Test: ACI 109006c, 6-29-64 | |

FLOOR–CEILING ASSEMBLIES

Construction Type: Steel Joists, Concrete Slab, Gypsum Wallboard

| 2 | 45–49 | ⅝" proprietary type X gypsum wallboard or veneer base applied perpendicular to rigid furring channels with 1" type S drywall screws 12" o.c. Rigid furring channels 24" o.c. attached with 18 gage wire ties to open web steel joists 24" o.c. and supporting ⅜" rib metal lath and 2" concrete slab. Double channel at wallboard end joints. (Two hour restrained and unrestrained.) | 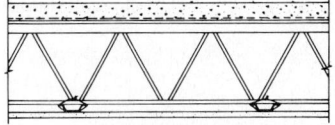
Approx. Ceiling Weight: 2½ psf
Fire Test: UL R2717-43
    Design G505, 7-29-66 | |

Construction Type: Steel Joists, Concrete Slab, Metal Lath, Gypsum Plaster

| 2 | 45–49 | ⅝" gypsum-vermiculite plaster or ⅞" gypsum-wood fiber plaster applied to ⅜" rib metal lath wire tied with 18 gage wire 5" o.c. to open web steel joists 24" o.c. supporting ⅜" rib metal lath and 2" concrete slab. | 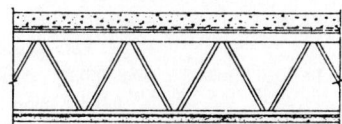
Approx. Ceiling Weight: 3 psf
Fire Test: BMS 92/43, 10-7-42 | |

Construction Type: Concrete Slab, Pan Joists, Gypsum Wallboard

| 2 | 45–49 | ⅝" type X gypsum wallboard or veneer base screw attached perpendicular to rigid furring channels with 1" type S drywall screws 8" o.c. Furring channels 24" o.c. suspended from 2½" precast reinforced concrete joists 35" o.c. with 21 gage galvanized steel hanger straps fastened to sides of joists. Joist leg depth, 10". Double channel at wallboard end joints. | Approx. Ceiling Weight: 3 psf
Fire Test: PCA 1281-1, 10-67 | |

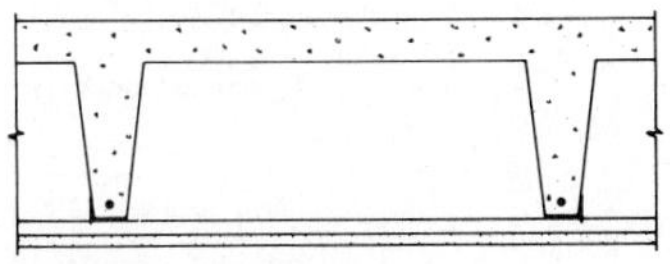

Table 2 (Cont.) Fire and sound ratings of various constructions

(From "Fire Resistance Design Manual, 1978 Edition," published by Gypsum Association)

Fire rating hr	Sound rating STC	Description	Section, data, references Fire	Sound
3	45–49	**Construction Type: Steel Joists, Concrete Slab, Gypsum Lath, Gypsum Plaster** ½" 1:2 gypsum-perlite plaster applied over ⅜" perforated gypsum lath clip attached providing continuous support across the lath and additionally supported with 1" hexagonal mesh 20 gage galvanized wire fabric to ¾" cold rolled channels 16" o.c. wire tied with 18 gage wire to open web steel joists 24" o.c. supporting ⅜" rib metal lath and 2" concrete slab.	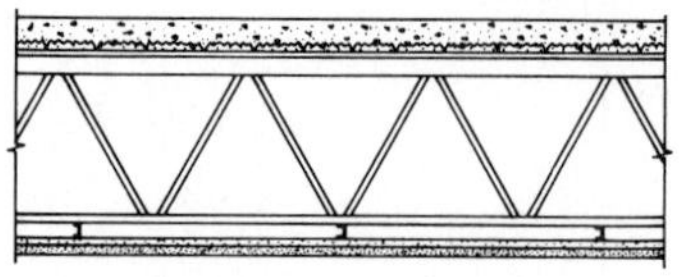 Approx. Ceiling Weight: 4 psf Fire Test: NBS 312, 3-4-52	
3	45–49	**Construction Type: Steel Joists, Metal Lath, Gypsum Plaster** ⅝" 1:2-1:3 gypsum-vermiculite plaster or ⅞" neat-wood fiber gypsum plaster applied over 3.4 lb. metal lath wire tied with 18 gage wire 5" o.c. to open web steel joists 24" o.c. supporting ⅜" rib metal lath and 2½" concrete slab.	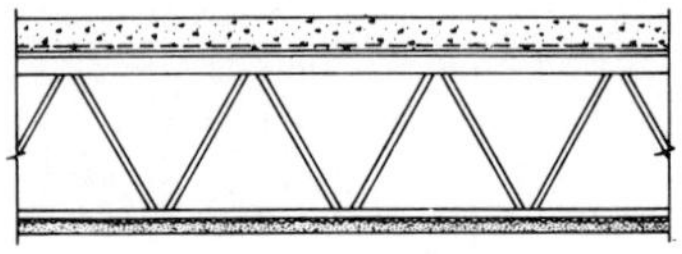 Approx. Ceiling Weight: 4 psf Fire Test: BMS 92/43, 10-7-42	
3	45–49	**Construction Type: Concrete Slab, Cellular Steel Deck, Metal Lath, Gypsum Plaster** ⅝" thick mill-mixed gypsum-perlite plaster applied over 3.4 lb. metal lath wire tied to ¾" cold rolled channels 12" o.c. wire tied to 1½" cold rolled channels 48" o.c. suspended 16" with 8 gage steel wire 36" o.c. from 2" concrete slab over 3" cellular steel deck supported by steel beam. (Three hour restrained and unrestrained.)	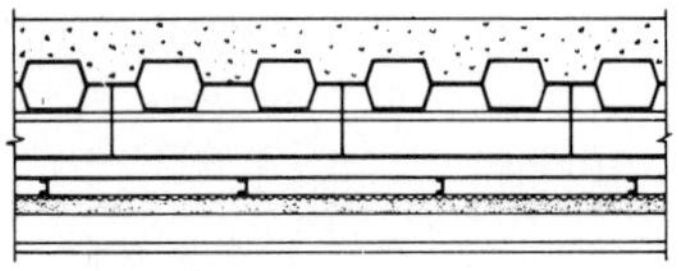 Approx. Ceiling Weight: 2½" psf Fire Test: UL R3574-6 Design A403, 7-25-57	
4	45–49	**Construction Type: Steel Joists, Concrete Slab, Gypsum Lath, Gypsum Plaster** 1" 1:2-1:3 gypsum-perlite plaster applied over ⅜" perforated gypsum lath clip attached providing continuous support across the lath and additionally supported with 1" hexagonal mesh 20 gage galvanized wire fabric to ¾" cold rolled channels 12" o.c. wire tied to open web steel joists 24" o.c. supporting ⅜" rib metal lath and 2" concrete slab.	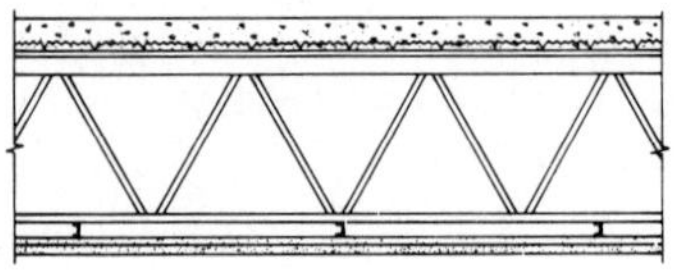 Approx. Ceiling Weight: 5½" psf Fire Test: NBS 311, 1-8-52	
1*	50–54	**Construction Type: Wood Joists, Gypsum Wallboard, Mineral Fiber** ½" type X gypsum wallboard or veneer base applied at right angles to resilient furring channels with 1" type S drywall screws 8" o.c. on ends and 12" o.c. in field. Gypsum board end joints fastened to additional pieces of furring channels. Resilient channels applied 24" o.c. at right angles to wood joists 16" o.c. with 6d coated nails 1⅞" long, 0.085" shank, ¼" heads, two per joist. Wood joists supporting ⅝" interior plywood with exterior glue subfloor and ⅜" particle board 1.5 psf. 3½" thick glass fiber insulation batts 0.7 pcf friction fit in joist cavities supported alternately every 12" by wire rods and resilient furring channels. Sound tested with carpet and pad and with insulation stapled to joists.	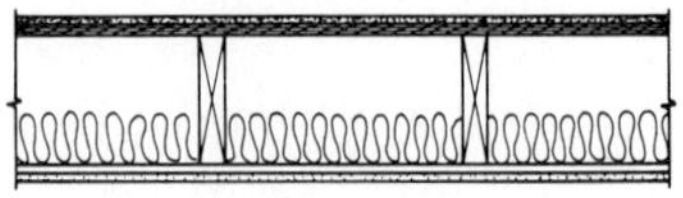 Approx. Ceiling Weight: 2 psf Fire Test: FM FC-181, 8-31-72 Sound Test: G & H OC-3 MT, 10-13-71 IIC & Test: (73 C & P) G & H OC-3 MT, 10-13-71	
1*	50–54	**Construction Type: Wood Joists, Gypsum Wallboard, Electric Heating Panel, Mineral Fiber** One layer ⅝" proprietary type X gypsum board electrical radiant heating panels attached with 1" type S screws 5¾" o.c. at right angles to resilient furring channels spaced 24" o.c. installed at right angles to 2" x 10" wood joists 16" o.c. with 3½" glass fiber, 0.75 pcf friction fit in joist space. Wood floor of nominal 1" T & G or ½" plywood subfloor and nominal 1" T & G or ⅝" plywood finish floor.	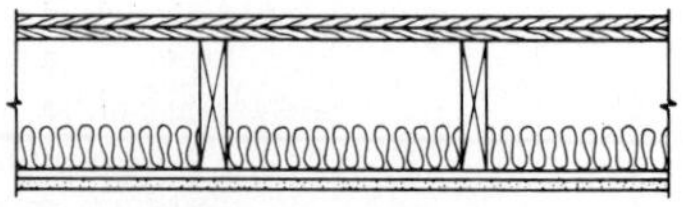 Approx. Ceiling Weight: 3 psf Fire Test: FM FC-137, 1-30-70 IIC & Test: 43 (62 C & P) NGC 5026, 6-23-66	

* *Combustible.*

Fire rating hr	Sound rating STC	Description	Section, data, references	
			Fire	Sound

ROOF DECKS

2		**Construction Type: Metal Edged Gypsum Plank, Steel Joists, Suspended Acoustical Ceiling** 2″ precast metal-edged gypsum plank clipped to open web steel joists 7′ 0″ o.c. Suspended ceiling of acoustical ceiling board. (Two hour restrained and unrestrained assembly.)	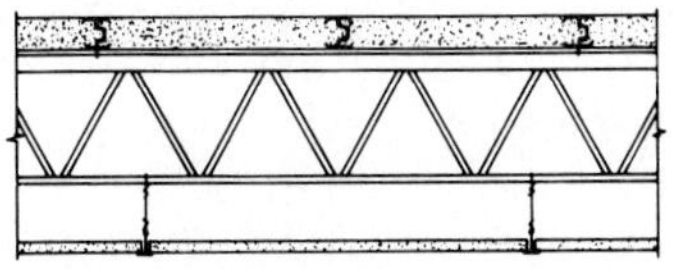 Fire Test: UL R5403-3 Design P213, 9-22-67	
2		**Construction Type: Gypsum Concrete, Mineral Fiber Acoustical Formboard, Subpurlins** 2″ gypsum concrete roof reinforced with 2″ hexagonal 19 gage and 16 gage reinforcing mesh covered with Class A, B or C, built-up roof covering. Deck laid on 1″-1½″ mineral fiber formboard supported by trussed tee subpurlins spaced 32¾″ o.c. over steel beams not more than 7′ 0″ apart. (Two hour restrained and unrestrained assembly.)	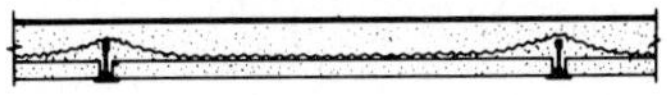 Fire Test: UL R5169-1 Design P677, 1-14-66	

COLUMNS — NOTE: All columns are 10WF49 unless otherwise specified. Heavy columns are 14WF228. Protection for heavy steel columns does not apply to lighter columns.

2		**Construction Type: Metal Studs, Gypsum Wallboard** Two layers of ⅝″ type X gypsum wallboard or veneer base, screw attached to 1⅝″ metal studs located at each corner of columns with 1″ type S screws 24″ o.c. for base layer and 1⅝″ type S drywall screws 12″ o.c. for face layer. 1¼″ metal beads at corners attached with 6d coated nails 1¾″ long, 0.0915″ shank, ¼″ heads, 12″ o.c.	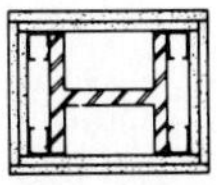 Fire Test: UL R2717-34 Design X517, 5-15-64	
2		**Construction Type: Metal Lath, Gypsum Plaster** 1″ 1:2-1:3 gypsum-perlite plaster over 3.4 lb. self-furring expanded diamond mesh metal lath and 2½″ wide flanged expanded metal corner beads wire tied with 18 gage galvanized wire 6″ o.c.	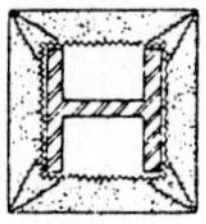 Fire Test: UL R3187-4, 5, 7 Design X402, 7-30-52	
3		**Construction Type: Metal Studs, Gypsum Wallboard** Three layers of ⅝″ type X gypsum wallboard or veneer base screw attached to 1⅝″ metal studs located at each corner of column. Base layer attached with 1″ type S drywall screws 24″ o.c., second layer with 1⅝″ type S drywall screws 12″ o.c. and 18 gage wire tied 24″ o.c. Face layer attached with 2¼″ type S drywall screws 12″ o.c. and 1¼″ corner bead at each corner nailed with 6d coated nails, 1⅞″ long, 0.0915″ shank, ¼″ heads, 12″ o.c.	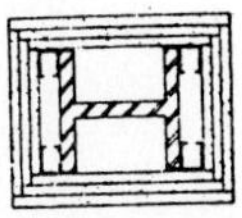 Fire Test: UL R2717-31 Design X509, 2-20-64; R3501-36 Design X510, 7-31-64	
3		**Construction Type: Metal Studs, Gypsum Wallboard** Two layers ½″ type X gypsum wallboard or veneer base. Base layer screw attached to 1⅝″ steel studs located at corners of heavy steel column with 1″ type S drywall screws 24″ o.c. Face layer attached with 1⅝″ type S drywall screws 12″ o.c. into studs. 1″ corner bead applied each corner with 4d coated nails 1⅜″ long, 0.067″ shank, ¹³⁄₆₄″ heads, 12″ o.c.	 Fire Test: UL R3501-61 Design X513, 7-16-69	

Table 2 (Cont.)   Fire and sound ratings of various constructions

(From "Fire Resistance Design Manual, 1978 Edition," published by Gypsum Association)

Fire rating hr	Sound rating STC	Description	Section, data, references	
			Fire	Sound
4		**Construction Type: Gypsum Plaster, Metal Lath** 1½" 1:2-1:3 gypsum-perlite plaster over 3.4 lb. metal lath wire tied with 18 gage wire 24" o.c. set 7/16" away from the column with ¾" cold rolled channels.	 Fire Test: UL R3187-6 Design X406, 8-7-52	
4		**Construction Type: Gypsum Block, Gypsum Plaster** ⅝" 1:3 gypsum-sand plaster over 2" solid gypsum blocks enclosing column providing ¼" clearance from flange with ⅜" gypsum mortar bed in vertical and horizontal joints. Reentrant space not filled.	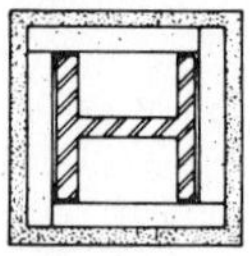 Fire Test: BMS 92/40, 10-7-42	

BEAMS AND GIRDERS

Fire rating hr	Sound rating STC	Description	Section, data, references	
2		**Construction Type: Steel Frame, Gypsum Wallboard** Two layers of ⅝" type X gypsum wallboard or veneer base around beam. Base layer attached with 1¼" type S drywall screws 16" o.c., face layer attached with 1¾" type S drywall screws 8" o.c. to frame of 25 gage runner and corner angles suspended from 25 gage channel brackets 24" o.c. Runners attached to steel deck units with fasteners 12" o.c. ½" space provided between beam and angle edges all around. Outside corners protected by 20 gage corner bead crimped or nailed. (Two hour restrained and unrestrained beam.)	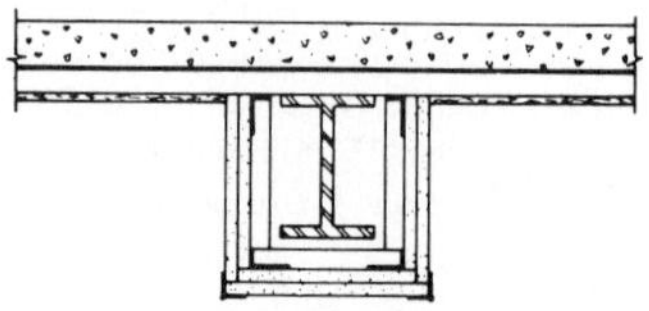 Fire Test: UL R4024-5 Design N501, 9-14-66	
3		**Construction Type: Metal Lath, Gypsum Plaster** 1¼" mill-mixed gypsum-perlite plaster over 3.4 lb. diamond mesh metal lath attached to beam with 11 gage steel clips 9" o.c. (Three hour restrained beam.)	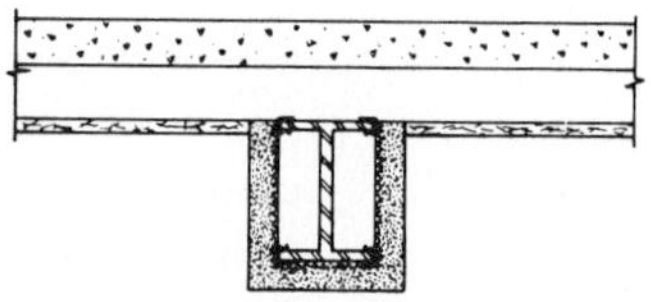 Fire Test: UL R4197-1 Design 19-3, 1-29-59	
3		**Construction Type: Ceiling Membrane Fireproofing, Metal Channels, Gypsum Wallboard** Suspended ceiling of ½" type X gypsum wallboard or veneer base screw attached with 1" type S drywall screws 12" o.c. to furring channels spaced 24" o.c. attached with 18 gage tie wire or 11 gage clips to bottom chord of steel joists spaced 24" o.c. supporting 2½" of concrete. (Three hour unrestrained beam.)	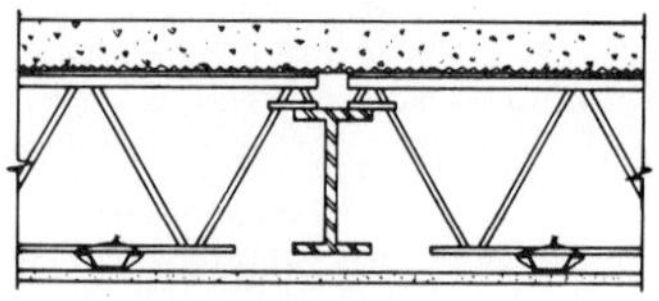 Fire Test: UL R3501 Design G514, 7-22-66	
4		**Construction Type: Gypsum Plaster, Metal Lath** ¾" 1:2 mill-mixed gypsum-perlite plaster over suspended 3.4 lb. diamond mesh metal lath wire tied with 18 gage wire to ¾" cold rolled channels 12" o.c. wire tied to 1½" cold rolled channels 48" o.c. and suspended from steel deck and 2" concrete slab. 3½" min. clearance from lower beam flange to top of ceiling. (Four hour unrestrained beam.)	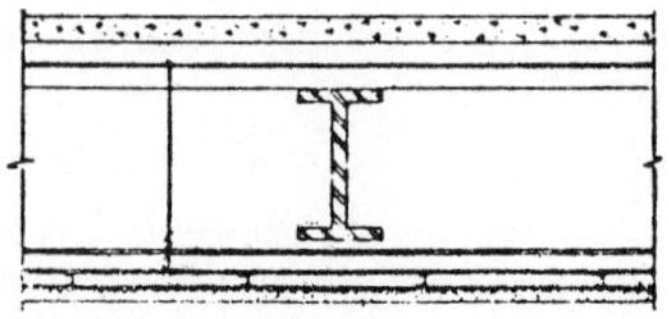 Fire Test: UL R3574-6 Design A403, 7-25-57	

By HOWARD P. VERMILYA, *AIA*

Plaster as a finish material for exterior and interior walls and ceilings dates back to the ancient Egyptians. Its greatest practical advantage is that it can provide a continuous surface without joints. It is also useful for concealing rough construction and the spaces for piping and wiring. Because it is completely inorganic, plaster is fireproof, rot proof, and vermin proof. As its name implies, it has no characteristic form—it can be flat or curved, smooth or rough, textured or molded, hard or soft. It can be integrally colored and serve as the finish surface, or it may form a base for the application of other finish materials such as paint, paper, textiles, tile, marble, plastic, and plywood. Plaster can be mixed and applied by hand or by machine.

PLASTERING MATERIALS

Plaster is composed of a mixture of cementitious materials, aggregates, and water. Admixtures are sometimes added, preferably at the mill, to retard or accelerate the setting. Of the three cementitious materials used in plaster, *lime*, the oldest, is now used primarily for the finish coats, and as a plasticizer in the base and finish coats with other cementitious materials; *portland cement* is used primarily for service applications where strength and resistance to moisture are paramount considerations; *calcined gypsum* is now the most widely used material for basecoat and finish plaster.

Standard specifications for various plastering materials are listed in Table 1.

Gypsum

Gypsum is commercially available in four forms for basecoat work.

1. Neat plaster contains no aggregate but may or may not contain fibers.

2. Ready-mix plaster contains aggregate mixed in by the manufacturer and requires only the addition of water to be ready for use.

3. Wood-fiber plaster contains no less than 0.75 per cent by weight of non-staining wood fibers. Sand, if used, may be added at the site.

4. Bond plaster is designed to be used for direct application to properly prepared monolithic concrete surfaces.

Gypsum is commercially available in the following five forms for finish coat work.

1. Ready-mix finish plasters are proprietary products designed for use over gypsum basecoats. They may or may not include fine aggregates and are available for various finishes. They may be painted as soon as they have set.

2. Acoustical plasters are proprietary products designed for sound absorption.

3. Gaging plasters are combined with lime putty. They are designed for slow, normal, or quick set or for strength.

4. Molding plaster is used for molding or casting.

5. Keene's cement, which is calcined at higher temperatures, is used to produce high-density plaster. It is usually mixed with lime to increase the plasticity.

Gypsum plasters are designed for application over metal lath, fiberboard lath, gypsum lath, and gypsum tile. The set is controlled by the use of admixtures by the manufacturer. Gypsum plasters, other than Keene's cement, should not be retempered.

Lime

Lime, used in building, is classified as either finishing lime or mason's lime; the former is usually used in plaster base and finish coats. These are further classified as quicklime or hydrated lime. Finishing hydrated limes are available as normal (Type N) or special (Type S) hydrated limes. Quicklime requires slaking for use as lime putty, a slow and time-consuming process, whereas Type N hydrated lime requires soaking 12 to 16 hours (overnight) and Type S hydrated lime may be mixed with water to develop its plasticity almost instantly. In addition Type S is apt to provide greater plasticity since the unhydrated oxides are limited to 8 per cent whereas there is no limit to them for Type N. Mill-fibered hydrated lime is available.

Lime basecoats are mixed using lime putty (a stiff paste resulting from slaking quicklime or soaking hydrated lime in water), sand, and water. Gaging plaster, which may be gypsum gaging plaster, Keene's cement, or portland cement, is often added to produce early strength and counteract possible shrinkage in setting.

Lime finish coats are made from the same ingredients as basecoats except that finer sand is used as aggregate.

Portland cement

Portland cement plaster is usually made from Type I or II portland cement or from types IA or IIA air-entrained portland cement; Type II is more resistant to sulphate attack and freezing damage. For interior plastering, portland cement is usually mixed with an aggregate, either sand or lightweight, and lime putty or dry hydrated lime (Type S). Portland cement with or without aggregate is used for base and

Table 1. Standard specifications for plastering materials and applications

Materials	Specifications	
	ANSI/ASTM	Federal
Gypsum plaster, including ready-mixed, neat, wood-fibered, and gaging	C28	SS-P-00402B Types I, II, III
Gypsum casting and molding plaster	C59	—
Gypsum Keene's cement	C61	SS-C-00161
Gypsum veneer plaster	C587	SS-P-00402B, Type VI
Portland cement, Types I-V	C150	SS-C-192b
Portland cement, air-entraining, Types IA, IIA, IIIA	C175	SS-C-192b
Quicklime	C5	SS-Q-351
Finishing hydrated lime, normal	C6	—
Finishing hydrated lime, special	C206	SS-L-351
Inorganic aggregates	C35	—
Bonding compounds	C631	—
Galvanized steel wire	A641	—
Metal lath	—	QQ-B-101C
Gypsum lath	C37	SS-L-0030D, Type I
Gypsum base for veneer plaster	C588	SS-L-0030D, Type VI
Gypsum partition tile or block	C52	—
Furring and lathing	C841	—
Gypsum plastering	C842	—
Application of gypsum base for veneer plaster	C844	—
Gypsum veneer plastering	C843	—
Gypsum plastering	ANSI A42.1	—
Portland cement plastering	ANSI A42.2	—
Furring and lathing for portland cement plaster	ANSI A42.3	—
Interior lathing and furring	ANSI A42.4	—

Table 2. Sieve analysis of aggregates for gypsum plaster (ASTM C35)

| | Percentage retained on each sieve | | | | | |
| | Perlite by volume | | Vermiculite by volume | | Sand by weight | |
Sieve size	Max	Min	Max	Min	Max	Min
No. 4	0	—	0	—	0	—
No. 8	5	0	10	0	5	0
No. 16	60	10	75	40	30	5
No. 30	95	45	95	65	65	30
No. 50	98	75	98	75	95	65
No. 100	100	88	100	90	100	90

Table 3. Types and weights of metal lath and maximum permissible spacing of supports*

(From ANSI/ASTM C841-76)

| | | Maximum permissible spacing of supports center to center, in. (mm) | | | | |
| | | Walls (partitions) | | | Ceilings | |
Type of metal plastering base	Minimum weight of metal base, lb/yd² (kg/m²)	Wood studs	Solid partitions	Steel studs wall furring, etc.	Wood or concrete	Metal
Expanded metal lath:						
Diamond mesh	2.5 (0.08)	16 (406)	16 (406)	13.5 (343)	12 (305)	12 (305)
	3.0 (0.1)	16 (406)	12 (305)	12 (305)	12 (305)	12 (305)
	3.4 (0.12)	16 (406)	16 (406)	16 (406)	10 (254)	16 (406)
Flat rib	2.5 (0.08)	16 (406)	12 (305)	12 (305)	12 (305)	12 (305)
	2.75 (0.09)	16 (406)	16 (406)	16 (406)	16 (406)	16 (406)
	3.0 (0.1)	16 (406)	16 (406)	16 (406)	16 (406)	13 (330)
	3.4 (0.12)	19 (482)	24 (610)	19 (482)	19 (482)	19 (482)
⅜-in. (9.5-mm) rib	3.0 (0.1)	19 (482)	N/A§	16 (406)	16 (406)	16 (406)
	3.4 (0.12)	24 (610)	N/A	19 (482)	19 (482)	19 (482)
	3.5 (0.12)	24 (610)	N/A	19 (482)	19 (482)	19 (482)
	4.0 (0.14)	24 (610)	N/A	24 (610)	24 (610)	24 (610)
¾-in. (19-mm) rib	5.4 (0.18)	24 (610)	N/A	24 (610)	36 (914)	36 (914)
Sheet lath	4.5 (0.15)	24 (610)	N/A	24 (610)	24 (610)	24 (610)
Wire lath welded	1.4 (0.05)†	16 (406)	16 (406)	16 (406)	16 (406)	16 (406)
	1.95 (0.07)‡	24 (610)	24 (610)	24 (610)	24 (610)	24 (610)

* *If paper-backed lath is used, limit to lath having an absorbent and a perforated slotted paper separator only.*
† *Welded wire paper-backed lath, 16-gage.*
‡ *Welded wire, paper-backed lath, 16-gage face wire.*
§ *Not applicable.*

finish coats on masonry, roughened monolithic concrete, and metal lath. It is not recommended for use over wood, fiberboard, or gypsum laths or over gypsum tile or basecoats. It is used where resistance to humidity, wetting and drying, and freezing and thawing are desired, in addition to strength. It is available in ready-mix form, with color added if desired.

Aggregates

Aggregates are used in plaster to provide dimensional stability and bulk. Since they are less expensive than the cementitious material, there is a possibility that lime and gypsum plasters may be mixed with more aggregate than they can properly bond. Strength of plaster basecoats is related to proportion of aggregate, and cracking is related to strength. The lightweight aggregates serve to reduce the over-all weight of the plaster, from 104 to 120 lb per cu ft for sanded plaster to 50 to 55 lb per cu ft for vermiculite or perlite plaster. They increase the sound absorption and fire resistance and lower the heat transmission values. Aggregates also serve to provide color and texture. They should be inert, clean, graded in size from coarse to fine and sharp and rough rather than round and smooth in shape.

Sand should be clean and washed if necessary. The variation in chemical composition of sand from local sources has caused manufacturers of gypsum plasters to vary the admixtures in some localities in order to offset the influence of the sand on setting times. American Society for Testing and Materials standards are used for sieve analysis (Table 2) and for determining the amount of inorganic impurities and water-soluble chemicals in sand (ASTM C-40).

Vermiculite, a micaceous material, when expanded by heat treatment becomes a lightweight aggregate weighing from 7.5 to 10 lb per cu ft. It is manufactured in five types according to size. Type III is used in plastering and when combined with gypsum or special binder produces acoustical, insulating, or fire-resistant plaster. It is used in basecoats; when used in finish coats as fines or as acoustical plaster it should be applied only over vermiculite basecoats. It has a tannish color.

Perlite, an inert siliceous volcanic rock, when expanded by heat treatment becomes a lightweight aggregate weighing from 7.5 to 15 lb per cu ft. It is similar to vermiculite in function but has a grayish white color. It is used quite generally in gypsum ready-mix plaster as an aggregate.

Pumice is similar in structure to perlite but its weight, 28 to 32 lb per cu ft, limits its use to areas where it is produced.

Wood fiber, added to neat gypsum plaster preferably at time of manufacture, improves the working qualities and produces the strongest of commonly used basecoats. ASTM C 28 specifies not less than 0.75 per cent wood fiber by weight.

Hair, sisal, manila, or glass fiber may be added to gypsum plaster scratch coats and should be added to lime and lime—portland cement scratch and brown coats for all bases, and to portland cement scratch coats over metal lath. Fiber is sometimes added to hydrated lime at the mill.

Water should be potable. Water containing salt or lime will accelerate and water containing organic or vegetable material will retard the set of plaster. Too much water decreases the strength of plaster and also its density.

Admixtures are added to the cementitious material to control the time of setting. Retarders usually serve to lower the strength. They are better added by the manufacturer.

Acoustical plasters are usually proprietary products, some being applied over basecoats and others being sprayed directly onto the structure, including steel decks, beams and girders, and columns. Since they are softer than other plasters their use is generally confined to ceilings and to walls above door head height.

PLASTER BASES

Plaster bases for the most part consist of lath or masonry. Lath is used where it is necessary to span open spaces between vertical or horizontal structural members. It is also used over masonry walls to provide a key, or where the wall has been dampproofed with a bituminous coating. Spacing of supports for various types of lath is given in Table 3.

Metal lath is made from cold-rolled sheets of mild low-carbon steel with 0.25 per cent copper added. All metal lath, unless galvanized, is coated with a rust-inhibitive paint. It is the most versatile plaster base, being used for interiors and exteriors, and where curved forms are used. Diamond mesh lath is produced by expanding sheet steel, and sheet lath is produced by punching it.

Diamond mesh metal lath is suitable for all types of plastering. It is available in 2.5 and 3.4 lb per sq yd weights painted, and in 3.4 lb galvanized. The standard sheet sizes are 24 or 27 in. wide by 96 in. long, although they are available in longer lengths for use in solid partitions. Self-furring diamond lath in the same sizes is available for use over masonry walls and ceilings and old surfaces, and for wrapping around steel columns. Paper-backed diamond mesh lath is used for machine application.

Rib lath has V-shaped ribs to provide the stiffness necessary for widely spaced supports. For plastering it comes in two forms: (1) flat ribbed lath with ⅛-in. ribs, weighing 2.75 and 3.4 lb per sq yd, and (2) ⅜-in. ribbed lath weighing 3.4 or 4.0 lb per sq yd. Ribbed lath sheet sizes are the same as for diamond mesh.

Sheet lath comes in 4.5 lb per sq yd and heavier sheets.

Table 4. Properties of gypsum job-mixed basecoat plasters

Property	Sand		Perlite		Vermiculite		Wood Fibered to Sand	
	1 : 2	1 : 3	1 : 2	1 : 3	1 : 2	1 : 3	1 : 0	1 : 1
Compressive Strength Pounds per sq. in.	775-1050	525-700	600-800	450-600	400-525	250-325	1750-2350	
Tensile Strength Pounds per sq. in.	150-200	100-150	165-170	90-150	130-160	70-100	280-400	240-250
Modulus of Elasticity Pounds per sq. in. x 10⁶	1.0	1.15-1.20	0.21-0.33			0.028	0.65-0.75	
Density In-Place Pounds per cu. ft.	104-120	104-120	50-56	41-45	50-55	42-45	79-82	
Coefficient of Linear Expansion inches/inch/degree F x 10⁻⁶	6.50	6.75	7.35	7.30	8.35	8.60	9.30	
Thermal Conductivity BTU/sq. ft./hour/°F/ inch thickness	5.51	5.60	1.64	1.31	1.74	1.42	3.15	

Source: Gypsum Association.

Table 5. Properties of gypsum finish coat plasters

Materials	Ready-mix finish plaster	Gypsum gaging-lime putty plasters		Keene's cement		Acoustical plaster	Ready-mix colored plaster
		Regular	High strength	Medium	Hard		
Mix (dry weight)	Neat	1:2	1:1	2:1	4:1	Neat	Neat
Compressive strength, psi	—	2,000–3,000 avg 1,200 min	5,000 min	4,000–5,000 avg 2,500 min		Low	—
Hardness, kg*	55	56	108	50	70	Soft	Hard
Setting time, minutes	—	20–40	20–40	20–360		—	—
Workability	Fair	Very good	Good	Fair	Poor	Poor	Poor
Remarks	May be painted as soon as set, no alkali reaction with paint		Requires less water than standard gaging plaster	Can be retempered, less susceptible to moisture than regular calcined gypsum		Good sound absorption	Float finish

* Kilograms required to force a 10-mm ball 0.01 in. into plaster face.

Bases; mixes and coats

Wire lath is made of No. 19 U.S. gage wire with 2½ meshes per inch coated with zinc or rust-inhibitive paint. V-stiffened wire lath is made from No. 20 U.S. gage wire with No. 24 U.S. gage V-rib stiffeners spaced not more than 8 in. apart.

Paper-backed wire fabric consists of No. 16 U.S. gage zinc-coated wire spaced not to exceed 2x2 in. with stiffening ribs spaced not to exceed 5 in. o.c. with absorptive paper backing attached with No. 17 U.S. gage stitch wire 2 in. o.c.

Metal lath accessories are composed of such items as metal grounds, corner beads, screeds, expansion joints, picture molds, casing beads, studs, tracks, clips, runners, channels, base and chair rails, and access panel frames. There are several varieties of each to choose from and most are proprietary, being related to a particular assembly.

Gypsum lath has a core of gypsum plaster between two layers of absorbent paper. It may be plain, perforated with ¾-in. holes on 4-in. centers, or insulating lath, backed with aluminum foil to provide a vapor barrier and reflective insulation. It is available in ⅜ and ½ in. thicknesses and in sheets 16 or 24 in. wide and 48 in. long. Longer lengths may be specified for use in special systems such as solid partitions.

Fiberboard insulation lath (Federal Specification LLL-F-321b) may be single or multiple ply board in ½ in., ¾ in., and multiples of ½ in. thicknesses, in widths of 16, 18, or 24 in. and 48-in. lengths.

Foamed plastic is also used as a plaster base, as noted below.

MIXING AND APPLICATION

Plaster formulas

The selection of the plaster ingredients is concerned with the choosing of the cementitious material and aggregate whose properties when combined provide the kind of finish desired and are compatible with the plaster backing and mixing method used. (See ANSI/ASTM C842 and ANSI A42.1 for recommended specifications for gypsum plastering.) The properties of gypsum basecoat and finish plasters are given in Tables 4 and 5.

Water when mixed with the cementitious material forms a paste which coats the aggregate particles and when it dries bonds them together. Only enough water should be added to provide plasticity or workability, since greater amounts reduce the strength and density of the plaster. The amount, shape, and size of aggregates, especially where there is an excess of fines, affect the plasticity and strength since more cement is required to coat the particles.

Tables 6 and 7 give the recommended mixes and maximum amounts of aggregate for basecoats over various backings and finish coats, without reference to the amount of water to be used. Measurement equivalents are shown in Table 8.

Plaster thickness cannot be overemphasized as a factor in the strength of plaster. Recommended thicknesses are shown in Table 9. Rigidity, stiffness, deflection, and cracking are all related to the thickness of plaster.

The number of coats in which plaster is applied may vary from one to two to three—more for solid partitions. The usual practice is to use two or three coats, depending on the plaster or base used. When two-coat work is used, the scratch and brown coats are applied without an interval to permit the scratch coat to set. The Contracting Plasterers' and Lathers' International Association in its recommended Specification for Lathing Furring and Plastering states as follows: "Plastering with gypsum, Keene's cement, lime, portland cement, or portland cement—lime plaster shall consist of not less than three coats, scratch, brown, and finish, when applied over metal

Table 6. Base coat proportions*

(From ANSI/ASTM C841-76)

| | Aggregates† | | |
| | Sand | | |
Plaster base	By volume, ft³ (m³), damp and loose	By weight, lb (kg) damp and loose	Perlite or vermiculite‡ By volume, ft³ (m³)
Over Gypsum Lath			
Two-coat work:			
Base coat	2½ (0.071)	250 (91.5)	2 (0.05)
Three-coat work:			
Scratch coat	2 (0.056)	200 (90.7)	2 (0.05)
Brown coat	3 (0.085)	300 (136)	2 (0.05)
or			
Scratch and brown coats	2½ (0.071)	250 (91.5)	——
Over Metal Lath			
Three-coat work:			
Scratch coat	2 (0.056)	200 (90.7)	2 (0.05)
Brown coat	3 (0.085)	300 (136)	2 (0.05)
or			
Scratch and brown coats	2½ (0.071)	250 (91.5)	——
Over Unit Masonry			
Two-coat work:			
Base coat	3 (0.085)	300 (136)	3 (0.085)
Three-coat work:			
Scratch coat	3 (0.085)	300 (136)	3 (0.085)
Brown coat	3 (0.085)	300 (136)	3 (0.085)
Over Monolithic Concrete§			

* The proportions are applicable for both hand and machine application of plaster. See plaster manufacturer's instructions for application of machine-applied plaster.

† Use of an accurate device to measure quantities, such as a measuring box or container of known capacity, is highly encouraged. Where such a device is not available, six No. 2, square-edge (not scoop) shovels, with a blade approximately 8½ in. (216 mm) wide and 11 in. (279 mm) long, with the maximum depth of sides not more than 1½ in. (38 mm) higher than the face of the blade, and filled to an average depth of 4 in. (102 mm) of damp, loose sand, may be considered as the approximate equivalent to 1 ft³ (0.028 m³).

‡ Where the plaster is 1 in. (25 mm) or more in total thickness, or where the finish coat is sand float or acoustical, the proportions for the brown coat may be increased to 3 ft³ (0.085 m³).

§ For use of bonding compounds for plastering on monolithic concrete, see footnotes in Table 9.

Table 7. Finish coat proportions

(From ANSI/ASTM C842-76)

| | Dry | | | | | | Lime putty wet equivalent | | |
| | Weight, lb (kg) | | | Volume, ft³ (m³) | | | ft³ (m³) | U.S. gal (litres) | lb (kg) |
	Gypsum	Lime	Aggregate	Gypsum	Lime	Aggregate			
Troweled Finishes:									
Lime putty with:*									
Gypsum gauging	100 (45.36)	225 (102.06)	0	1 (0.0283)	4½ (0.1273)	0	6.75 (0.1910)	52.5 (198.71)	450 (204.12)
Gypsum Keene's cement:									
Medium	100 (45.36)	50 (22.68)	0	1 (0.0283)	1 (0.0283)	0	1⅛ (0.0283)	8¾ (33.19)	100 (45.36)
Hard	100 (45.36)	25 (11.34)	0	1 (0.0283)	½ (0.0142)	0	⅝ (0.0177)	4½ (17.03)	50 (22.68)
Ready-mixed gypsum	100 (45.36)	0	0	1 (0.0283)	0	0	0	0	0
Gypsum vermiculite	100 (45.36)	0	7 to 15 (3.18) to (6.8)	1 (0.0283)	0	1 (0.0283)	0	0	0
Floated Finishes:									
Lime putty with:									
Gypsum gauging	100 (45.36)	225 (102.06)	200 (90.72)	1 (0.0283)	4½ (0.1273)	2 (0.0566)	6.75 (0.1910)	52.5 (198.71)	450 (204.12)
Gypsum Keene's cement:									
Medium	150 (68.04)	100 (45.36)	450 (204.12)	1½ (0.0424)	2 (0.0566)	4½ (0.1273)	2¼ (0.0637)	17½ (66.24)	200 (102.06)
Ready-mixed gypsum†	100 (45.36)	0	0	1 (0.0283)	0	0	0	0	0
Gypsum-vermiculite	100 (45.36)	0	7 to 15 (3.18) to (6.8)	1 (0.0283)	0	1 (0.0283)	0	0	0
Gypsum-sand (job-mixed)‡	100 (45.36)	0	200 (90.72)	1 (0.0283)	0	2 (0.0566)	0	0	0

* *If additional hardness of finish coat is desired, increased amounts of gypsum may be used; however, hard finishes should not be used over lightweight aggregate base coats.*
† *Mixed with water only, in accordance with manufacturers' printed directions.*
‡ *Gypsum shall be neat, unfibered plaster.*

Table 8. Measurement equivalents

Gypsum	1 bag = 100 lb
	1 cu ft = 60 lb
Portland cement	1 bag = 94 lb = 1 cu ft
Hydrated lime	1 bag = 50 lb
Lime putty	1 cu ft = 40 lb of dry material plus water
Sand	1 cu ft = 100 lb = 7 No. 2 shovelsful
Perlite	1 cu ft = 7.5–15 lb
Vermiculite	1 cu ft = 6–10 lb
Water	1 cu ft = 62.5 lb = 7.48 gal

Table 9 Thickness of plaster

(Measured from face plane of plaster base)

Plaster base	Thickness of plaster including finish coat, in. (mm)
Metal plaster base	⅝ (15.87) min
All other types of plaster base	½ (12.70) min
Unit masonry	⅝ (15.87) min
Monolithic concrete surfaces:*	
Vertical†	⅝ (15.87) min
Horizontal‡	⅜ (3.17 to ⅜ (9.52)

* *Base coat plastering of the same proportions as specified herein for unit masonry may be applied over plain or reinforced monolithic concrete, provided the surface is first covered with a metal plaster base or first coated with a bonding compound.*

† *Finish coat plaster applied direct to a bonding compound over vertical monolithic concrete shall not exceed 3/16 in. (4.76 mm) in thickness. Where more than 3/16 in. of finish coat is required to bring such vertical surface to a true plane, a base coat of plaster shall first be applied to the bonding compound.*

‡ *Where horizontal or vertical monolithic concrete surfaces require more than 3/8 in. (9.52 mm) or 5/8 in. (15.87 mm) of plaster, respectively, to produce required lines or surfaces, metal plaster base shall be attached to the concrete before application of plaster. Where concrete surface requires the application of more than 1 in. (25.4 mm) of plaster to produce required lines or surfaces, lath shall be applied over furring secured to the concrete.*

lath, wire lath, or wire fabric, and shall consist of not less than two coats when applied over wood lath, gypsum lath, or fiber insulation lath, or unit masonry and shall consist of a bond coat and finish coat when applied direct to concrete."

Basecoats, in addition to the cementitious material and aggregate, should contain hair or fiber either as "mill fibered" (added by the manufacturer) or added as mixed. Basecoats of lime or portland cement plaster, individually or in combination, should not be applied directly to fiber insulation lath or gypsum lath or gypsum tile, nor should portland cement plaster be applied directly to wood lath. Both scratch and brown coats should be scratched to provide a mechanical key. Cracking is related to strength of basecoats. This in turn is related to thickness and proportion and type of aggregate used in basecoats.

Finish coats generally use one of three finishing methods: troweling, floating, or spraying. Trowel finishes are used to create a flat smooth surface usually for further decoration by painting or papering. The use of not less than ½ cu ft fine silica sand or perlite to each 100 lb of gaging plaster or Keene's cement increases the factor of safety in preventing cracking in trowel finishes. Varying degrees of

hardness can be obtained by care in the troweling. Float finishes are used where a surface texture is wanted. The texture will vary with the type of aggregate used and the type of float (wood, carpet, sponge, etc.). Float finishes tend to show less cracking than trowel finishes. These plasters are used with float finishes: gypsum-sand, lime-Keene's cement-sand, gypsum–lightweight aggregate fines, colored plaster, and portland cement–sand. Spray finishes, being machine applied, provide great latitude in texture, depending on the techniques and machines. It is usually desirable to work from a previously agreed upon sample developed with the application contractor. Acoustical plaster finishes may be sprayed on or hand troweled, usually in two coats, to a thickness of ½ in.

PLASTERING SYSTEMS AND ASSEMBLIES

Walls and partitions are based upon three basic systems. The factors affecting the selection of the system are cost, fire resistance, weight, thickness or space occupied, sound transmission or absorption, and concealment of equipment (see Table 10).

Hollow walls may be bearing or nonbearing and are framed with wood or

Table 10. Comparative analysis of partition systems for initial selection of partition type

Partition type*	Weight, lb per lin ft for 8' ht			Floor area occupied, sq ft per lin ft			Fire-resistance rating, hr			Sound transmission loss, db			Cost index		
	High	Low	Avg	High	Low	Avg	High	Low	Avg	High	Low	Avg	High	Low	Avg
Unit masonry	337	169	232	0.97	0.25	0.53	7.0*	0.5	2.92	58	37	44	1 sample L.W. conc. 142		
Solid plaster	203	70	135	0.25	0.13	0.19	2.5	0.42	1.19	47	33	38.7	126	100	113
Metal studs	214	65	130	0.83	0.21	0.42	2.5	0.5	1.33	55	30	44.9	137	114	125
Wood studs	160	77	122	0.61	0.22	0.45	2.0	0.42	0.89	55	33	43.1	135	110	120

All partitions plastered both sides.

metal studs, the latter often involving a proprietary system. The thickness is determined by the load, the stiffness, the sound resistance, and the need for concealment of equipment. Wood studs are 2 by 4s or 2 by 6s and may be doubled or staggered for increased concealment or sound resistance. Metal studs may be prefabricated in 1⅝ to 6-in. widths (Fig. 1) or site fabricated from ¾ to 2-in. channels (Fig. 2). With channels, spacers or stiffeners are usually employed but may be omitted to improve the sound quality of the wall. Most metal-stud hollow systems use floor and ceiling runners, although some use clips. The lath is applied with nails, clips, wire, or staples. When resilient clips are used they serve to reduce the sound transmission.

Solid plaster partitions are economical, highly fire resistant, and occupy a minimum of space. However, they have limitations in height and length and offer very little space for concealment of electrical and mechanical equipment. They may be constructed (1) with metal or gypsum lath stretched vertically between floor and ceiling runners as studless partitions (Figs. 3 and 4) or (2) with vertical channel studs extending from floor to ceiling runners, to which lath is applied, as solid stud partitions (Fig. 5): These assemblies are embedded in plaster. Solid partitions are limited to a minimum thickness of 2 in. by the American National Standard Specifications for Gypsum Plastering (ANSI A42.1). The Contracting Plasterers' and Lathers' International Association in its specifications limits the height of studless gypsum lath solid partitions to 12 ft and metal lath solid partitions to 9 ft 6 in. Solid stud partitions may be built to a height of 24 ft at a thickness of 3¼ in.; lengths, however, are limited when the height is over 10 ft.

Solid plaster partitions are braced temporarily on one side until after the scratch coat of plaster has been applied to the other side and has set, then the bracing is removed to permit the application of the scratch or back up and brown coats to the previously braced side. After the latter sets, the brown coat is applied over the first scratch coat. Finish coats can then be applied to either side.

Masonry walls are customarily furred on the inside because of the likelihood of moisture penetration through the masonry. (The inside surface of cavity walls may be plastered directly.) The furred space provides some insulation and a place for the concealment of electrical and mechanical equipment. Furring may be of wood (1 by 2 in. or 2 by 2 in.) or metal (¾-in. channels) and is normally applied vertically. Insulation may be placed between the furring strips.

Foamed plastic (expanded polystyrene) slabs applied to the inside of exposed walls with ¼ in. of masonry cement mortar provide furring, insulation, vapor barrier, and lath, all in one operation. Manufacturer's application directions should be followed carefully. Material is available in thicknesses of 1 to 4 in. in multiples of ½ in. and in widths of 12, 16, or 24 in. and lengths of 8 and 9 ft.

Masonry partitions of concrete block, common brick (medium hard), medium hard structural clay tile, and many types of stone provide the best masonry bases for direct plastering. High suction units such as soft common brick, soft or porous structural tile, gypsum tile, and lightweight concrete block require more care, as they have a tendency to withdraw the mixing water from the plaster at excessive rates. The denser masonry units such as hard burned brick, glazed tile, and some stone, having low suction rates, present problems of bonding. All can be used as bases for either gypsum or portland cement plasters with the exception of gypsum tile, which requires gypsum plaster. Bonding can be improved with high suction units by dampening the base surface before plastering, and spray curing after applying basecoats, and with low suction units by using those materials which provide an adequate key for a mechanical bond. The joints should be struck flush and the surfaces clean. Self-furring metal lath may be applied directly to these surfaces, if necessary.

Monolithic concrete, to be an adequate base for plaster, must also be clean and provide a mechanical key for an effective bond. Three approaches have been taken towards the providing of a positive key: (1) prior treatment of the forms, by using rough boards or by treating boards with ammonia to raise the grain, or by lining forms with materials or devices that deform the surface so as to provide a mechanical bond, (2) treatment of the concrete surfaces by stripping forms early to permit wire brushing or scratching, or by applying a retarder to the forms so that the slower setting surface of concrete can be brushed more easily, or by repeated etching of the surface with muriatic acid, and (3) coating the concrete surface with bond plaster consisting of a rich low-consistency cement and sand mixture as a dash coat (not considered as a base coat), or by application of bonding agents, which are usually proprietary water-based emulsions sprayed on to provide a built-up base equivalent to scratch and brown coats, to which the finish coat of plaster may be applied.

Ceilings

Contact ceilings have the lath or plaster applied directly to the under side of the floor or floor framing. For direct application of plaster to monolithic concrete ceilings see above. Special fireproofing and acoustical plasters (proprietary mixes) are also sprayed directly to the underside of steel decks and their supports. Where the floor framing consists of wood, light-gage steel or reinforced concrete joists, it is customary where spacing permits (24 in. or under) to apply lath directly to the underside of the floor framing (Fig. 6). The type of fastener and its spacing must be adequate to support the lath and plaster. Cellular steel decks with punched flaps permit contact fastening of lath with wire ties.

Furred ceilings are used where the spacing of framing members is too great to permit direct application of lath, or where it is necessary to level or straighten the

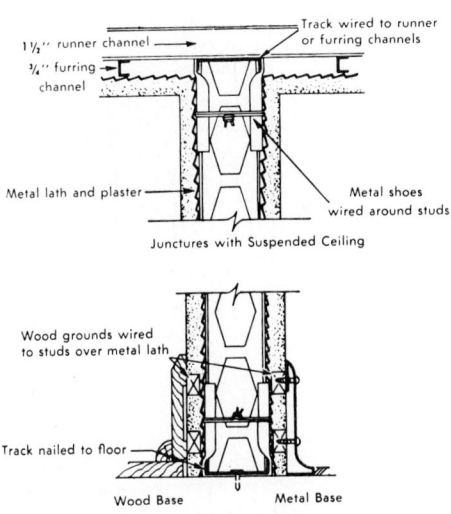

1½" runner channel
¾" furring channel
Track wired to runner or furring channels
Metal lath and plaster
Metal shoes wired around studs

Junctures with Suspended Ceiling

Wood grounds wired to studs over metal lath
Track nailed to floor

Wood Base Metal Base

Junctures with floor

Fig. 1. Hollow partition—prefabricated metal stud

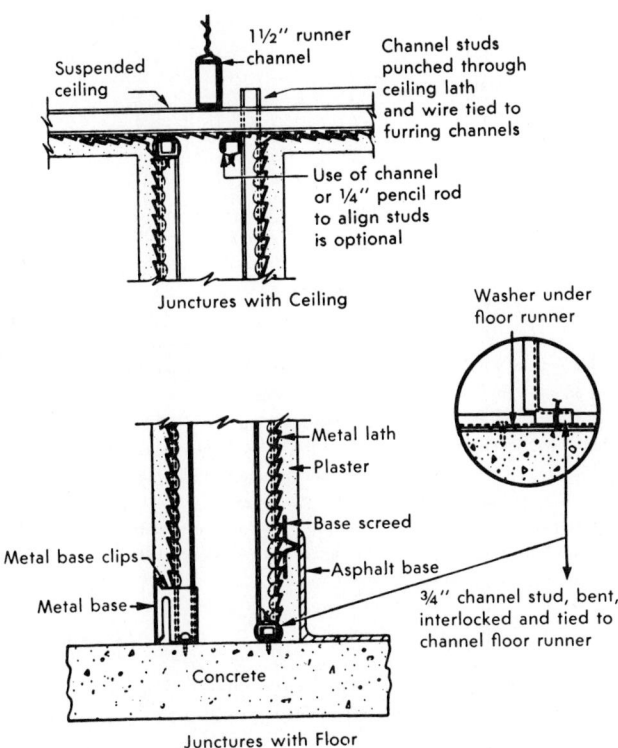

Suspended ceiling
1½" runner channel
Channel studs punched through ceiling lath and wire tied to furring channels
Use of channel or ¼" pencil rod to align studs is optional

Junctures with Ceiling

Washer under floor runner

Metal lath
Plaster
Base screed
Metal base clips
Asphalt base
Metal base
Concrete
¾" channel stud, bent, interlocked and tied to channel floor runner

Junctures with Floor

Fig. 2. Hollow partition—channel studs

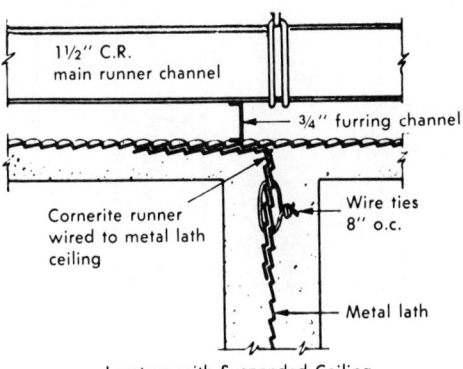

1½" C.R. main runner channel
¾" furring channel
Cornerite runner wired to metal lath ceiling
Wire ties 8" o.c.
Metal lath

Juncture with Suspended Ceiling

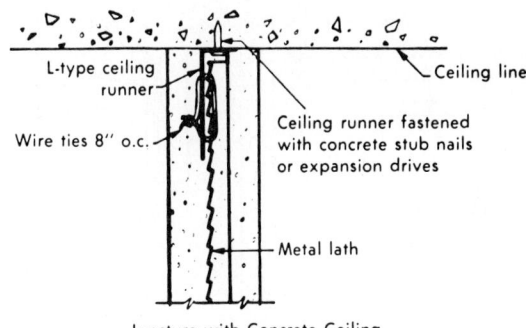

L-type ceiling runner
Wire ties 8" o.c.
Ceiling line
Ceiling runner fastened with concrete stub nails or expansion drives
Metal lath

Juncture with Concrete Ceiling

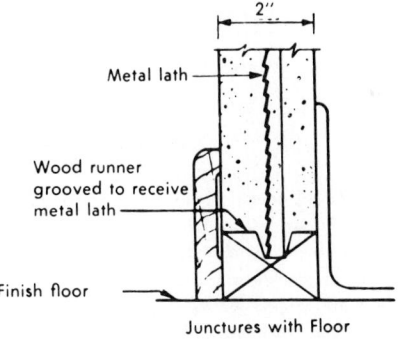

2"
Metal lath
Wood runner grooved to receive metal lath
Finish floor

Junctures with Floor

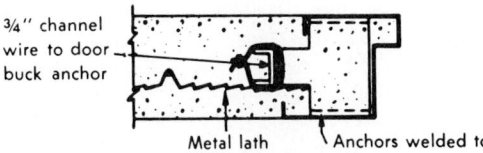

¾" channel wire to door buck anchor
Metal lath
Anchors welded to door buck

Metal Door Buck

Fig. 3. Solid partition—studless—metal lath

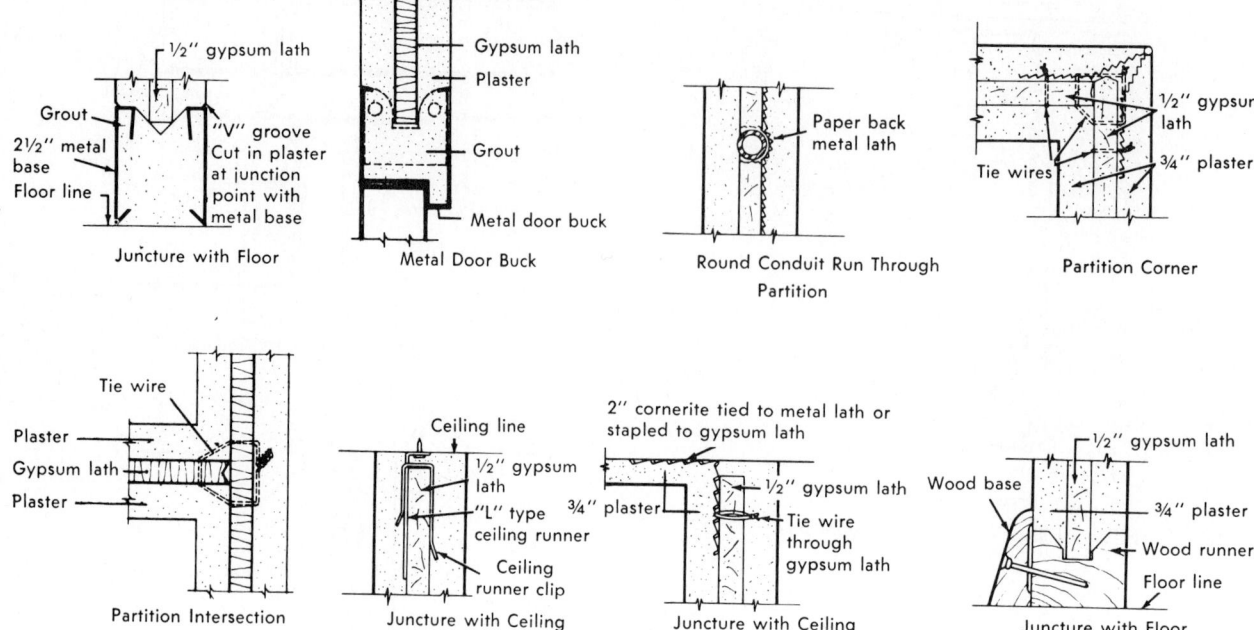

Fig. 4. Solid partition—studless—gypsum lath

ceiling, or where improved sound conditions are desired. The furring may consist of wood strips, steel channels, round rods, clips, or other devices to provide a frame to which the lath may be applied. Because of the greater concentration of loads, fasteners need more consideration. Direct pull on fasteners in wood and nailable steel joists should be avoided (Fig. 7).

Suspended plaster ceilings, in which the ceiling framing is hung below the floor or roof system, usually are used to conceal lighting or mechanical equipment and often to permit formed ceilings of varying shapes. These frames consist of main runners and cross runners hung from the structure above with wire, rods, or flat hangers. The lath is fastened with wire

or clips to the runners (see Fig. 8 and Tables 11–13).

Less cracking will usually be experienced when the joint between ceilings and walls uses unrestrained rather than restrained perimeter construction (Fig. 9 and Table 14). Control joints are recommended for large ceiling areas (60 ft or more in length).

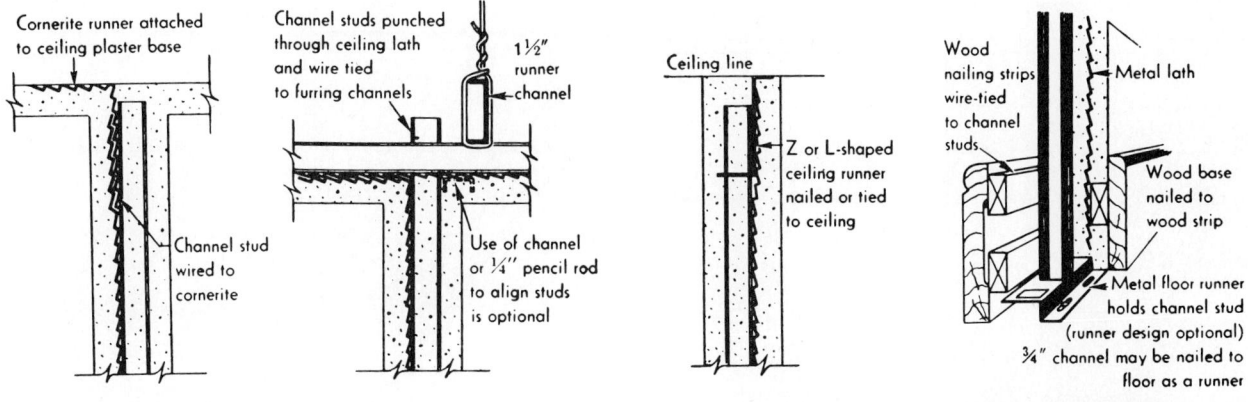

Cornerite runner attached to ceiling plaster base

Channel stud wired to cornerite

Channel studs punched through ceiling lath and wire tied to furring channels

1½" runner channel

Use of channel or ¼" pencil rod to align studs is optional

Ceiling line

Z or L-shaped ceiling runner nailed or tied to ceiling

Wood nailing strips wire-tied to channel studs

Metal lath

Wood base nailed to wood strip

Metal floor runner holds channel stud (runner design optional) ¾" channel may be nailed to floor as a runner

METAL FLOOR RUNNER AND WOOD BASE

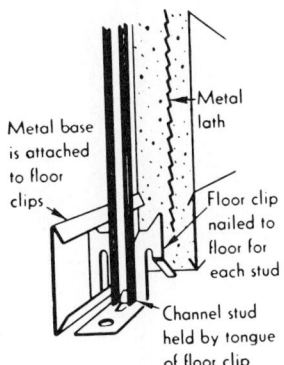

Design of metal base and floor clips varies among manufacturers

Metal base is attached to floor clips

Metal lath

Floor clip nailed to floor for each stud

Channel stud held by tongue of floor clip

Fig. 5.   Solid partition—channel studs

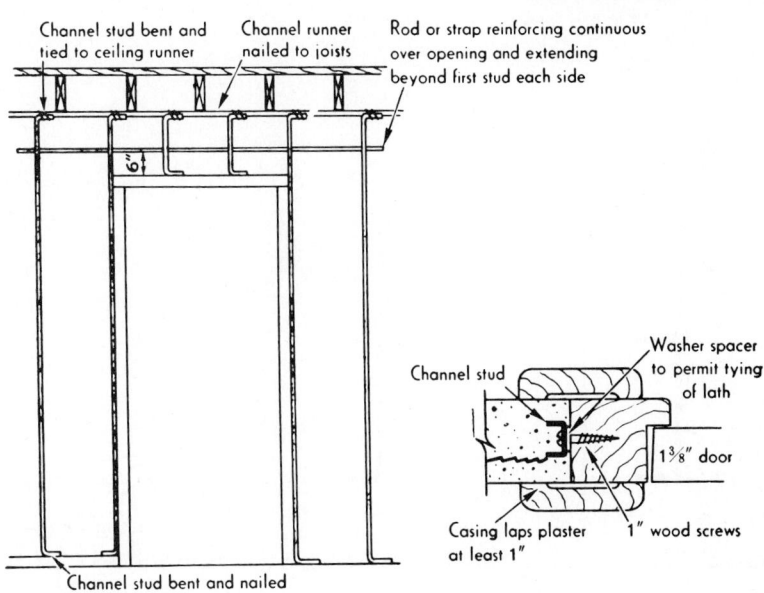

Channel stud bent and tied to ceiling runner

Channel runner nailed to joists

Rod or strap reinforcing continuous over opening and extending beyond first stud each side

6"

Channel stud bent and nailed to floor or wood runner

Channel stud

Washer spacer to permit tying of lath

1⅜" door

Casing laps plaster at least 1"

1" wood screws

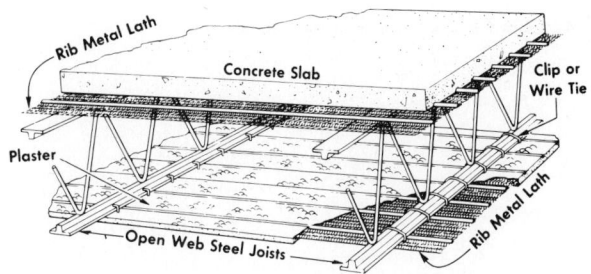

Rib Metal Lath

Concrete Slab

Clip or Wire Tie

Plaster

Open Web Steel Joists

Rib Metal Lath

Fig. 6.   Contact ceiling—steel joist

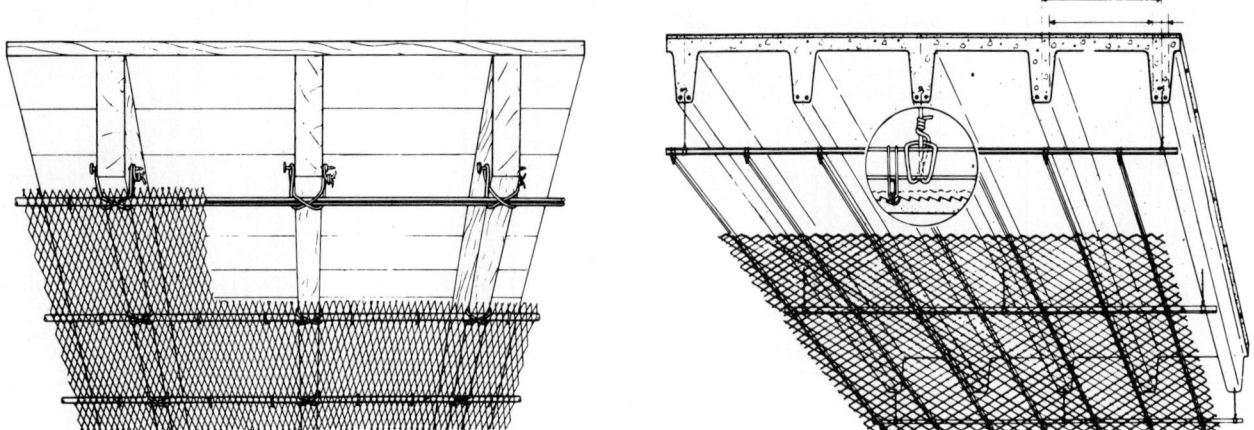

Fig. 7. Furred ceiling—wood joists   **Fig. 8. Suspended ceiling—concrete joists**

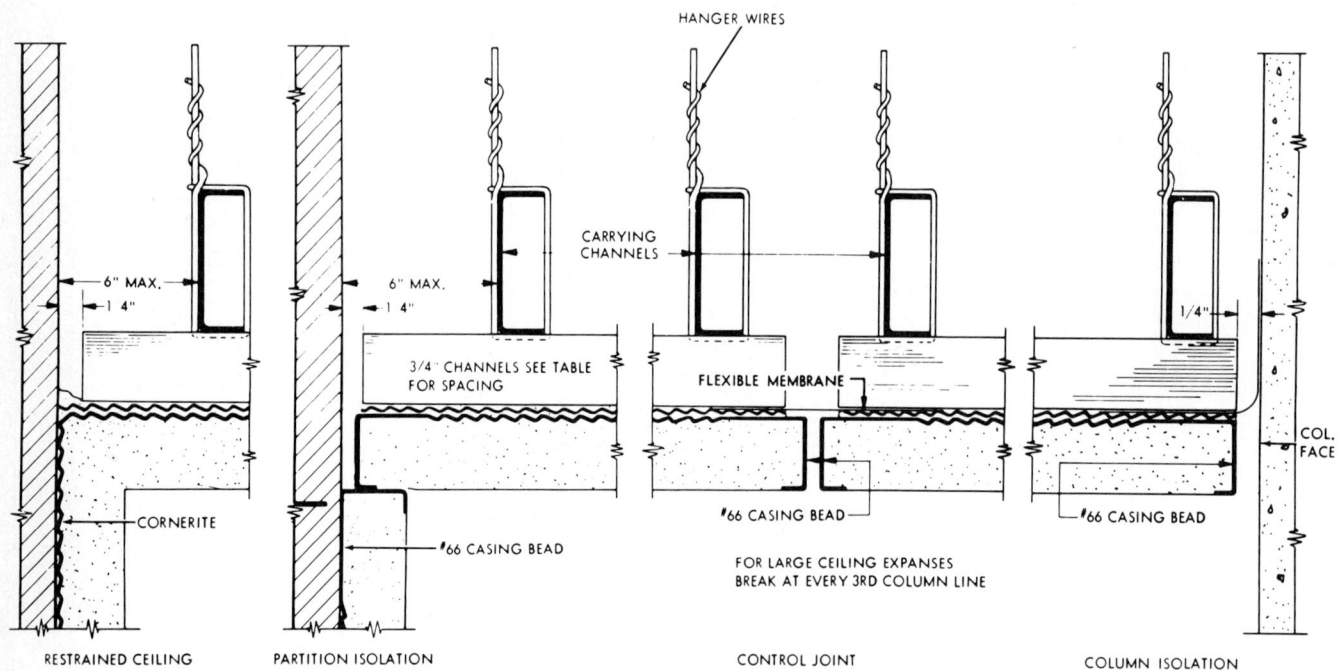

HANGER WIRES

CARRYING CHANNELS

6" MAX.
4"

6" MAX.
4"

3/4" CHANNELS SEE TABLE FOR SPACING

FLEXIBLE MEMBRANE

1/4"

CORNERITE

#66 CASING BEAD

#66 CASING BEAD

#66 CASING BEAD

COL. FACE

FOR LARGE CEILING EXPANSES BREAK AT EVERY 3RD COLUMN LINE

RESTRAINED CEILING   PARTITION ISOLATION   CONTROL JOINT   COLUMN ISOLATION

Fig. 9. Restrained and unrestrained ceilings and control joints

Table 11. Hangers for suspended ceilings

Maximum ceiling area supported, sq ft	Minimum size of hangers
12.5	9 gage wire
16	8 gage wire
18	3/16-in. diameter, mild steel rod*
20	7/32-in. diameter, mild steel rod*
22.5	1/4-in. diameter, mild steel rod*
25.0	1x3/16 in. mild steel flat†

It is highly recommended that all rod hangers be protected with a zinc or cadmium coating.

†*It is highly recommended that all flat hangers be protected with a zinc or cadmium coating or with a rust-inhibitive paint.*

Table 12. Spans and spacings of main runners*

(From "American National Standard Specifications for Installation of Interior Lathing and Furring," ANSI/ASTM C841-76)

Minimum size and type	Maximum span between hangers or supports, in.	Maximum center-to-center spacing of runners, in.
3/4 in.–0.3 lb per ft, cold or hot rolled channel	24	36
1 1/2 in.–0.475 lb per ft, cold rolled channel	36	48
1 1/2 in.–0.475 lb per ft, cold rolled channel	42	42
1 1/2 in.–0.475 lb per ft, cold rolled channel	48	36
1 1/2 in.–1.12 lb per ft, hot rolled channel	48	54
2 in.–0.59 lb per ft, hot rolled channel	60	48
2 in.–1.26 lb per ft, hot rolled channel	60	60
1 1/2 x 1 1/2 x 3/16 angle	60	42

These spans are based on webs of channels being erected vertically. Other sections of hot or cold rolled members of equivalent beam strength may be substituted for those specified.

Table 13. Spans and spacings of cross furring*

(From "Specifications for Installation of Interior Lathing and Furring," ANSI/ASTM C841-76)

Minimum size and type	Maximum span between runners or supports, in.	Maximum center-to-center spacing of cross furring members, in.
1/4 in. diameter pencil rods	24	12
3/8 in. diameter pencil rods	24	19
3/8 in. diameter pencil rods	30	12
3/4 in.–0.3 lb per ft, cold or hot rolled channel	36	24
	42	19
	48	16
1 in.–0.410 lb per ft, hot rolled channel	48	24
	54	19
	60	12

These spans are based on webs of channels being erected vertically. Other sections of hot or cold rolled members of equivalent beam strength may be substituted for those specified.

Table 14. Relative performance of lath and plaster systems with respect to crack resistance

(Source: Gypsum Association)

G = gypsum lath—3-coat plastering
G2 = gypsum lath—2-coat plastering
M = metal lath—3-coat plastering
*WF = neat wood fiber scratch and gypsum sanded brown**
S = sanded plaster: 1:2†; 1:3‡

P = perlited plaster: 1:2¶
V = vermiculited plaster: 1:2¶
*F = sand float finish**
*T = smooth trowel finish**

	RESTRAINED CONSTRUCTION			UNRESTRAINED CEILING CONSTRUCTION		
PERFORMANCE	LATH BASE	PLASTER BASECOAT	FINISH COAT	LATH BASE	PLASTER BASECOAT	FINISH COAT
EXCELLENT	G or M	WF	F	G or M	WF	F
	G or M	S	F	G	S or P	F
				G or M	WF	T
				G	S	T
				M	S	F
GOOD	G or M	WF	T	G2	S or P	F
	G	P	F	G	V	F
	G	S	T	M	P	F
	G2	S	F	G2 or M	S	T
	G	V	F	G	P or V	T
	G2 or M	P	F	M	V	F
	G2 or M	S	T			
	G	P	T			
ACCEPTABLE	G2 or M	V	F	G2	V	F
	G	V	T	G2 or M	P	T
	G2 or M	P	T			
NOT RECOMMENDED	G2 or M	V	T	G2 or M	V	T

* All proportioning of basecoat and finish coat plaster as recommended in ANSI 42.1.
† Scratch.

‡ Brown, 1:2½ for 2-coat work over gypsum lath.
¶ Scratch and brown.

STUCCO

Stucco (exterior plaster) is applied directly to masonry and can be applied to frame structures by either of two methods. One, known as the "open-frame method," consists of stucco applied to metal reinforcement that is attached directly to the structural frame. The second, known as "sheathed construction," differs from the first only in that sheathing and waterproof paper are interposed between the structural members and the metal reinforcement. If the frame is sufficiently rigid, open-frame construction is generally considered to have greater crack resistance than sheathed construction. This is especially true if back plastering is used. Metal reinforcement should in all cases be furred out sufficiently from the studs or sheathing to provide for complete embedment in the stucco. In open-frame construction that is not back plastered, paper-backed wire mesh is often used. As an alternate, 18 gage horizontal wires are stretched across the face of the studs at 6-in. intervals to support waterproof building paper, which is attached to the studs before the metal reinforcement is applied. American National Standard Specifications for portland cement stucco (ANSI A42.2 and A42.3) recommend 12-in. stud spacing for either of these alternate constructions, but 16-in. spacing is more generally used. For light steel framing, The standards recommend maximum stud spacings as follows: for open-frame: back-plastered construction, 32 in., provided rigid cross furring is applied at 16-in. intervals; sheathed frame, 24 in.; open-frame not back-plastered, 16 in.

Data courtesy of Gypsum Association

DEFINITION

Gypsum board, as defined in ASTM C11, is "the generic name for a family of non-combustible sheet products consisting of a core primarily of gypsum and a paper surfacing."

Gypsum board panels are mainly used as the surface layer of interior walls and ceilings; as a base for ceramic, plastic and metal tile; for exterior soffits; for elevator and other shaft enclosures; and to provide fire protection to structural elements.

TYPES OF GYPSUM BOARD

Regular gypsum board is used as a surface layer on walls and ceilings.

Type X gypsum board is available in ½-in. and ⅝-in. thickness and has an improved fire resistance made possible through the use of special core additives. It is also available with a predecorated finish. Type X gypsum board is used in most fire rated assemblies.

Predecorated gypsum board has a decorative surface which does not require further treatment. The surfaces may be coated, printed, or have a vinyl film. Other predecorated finishes include factory painted and various textured patterns.

Water-resistant gypsum board has a water-resistant gypsum core and water-repellent paper. It serves as a base for application of ceramic or plastic wall tile or plastic finish panels in bath, shower, kitchen and laundry areas. It is available with a regular or type X core and in ½- and ⅝-in. thicknesses.

Gypsum backing board is designed to be used as a base layer or backing material in multi-layer systems. It is available with aluminum foil backing and with regular and type X cores.

Gypsum coreboard is available as a 1-in.-thick solid coreboard or as a factory laminated board composed of two ½-in. boards. It is used in shaft walls and laminated gypsum partitions with additional layers of gypsum board applied to the coreboard to complete the wall assembly. It is available in 24-in. widths with a variety of edges.

Gypsum sheathing is used as a protective, fire-resistive membrane under exterior wall-surfacing materials such as wood siding, masonry veneer, stucco and shingles. It also provides protection against the passage of water and wind and adds structural rigidity to the framing system. The noncombustible core is surfaced with firmly bonded water-repellent paper. In addition, a water-repellent material may be incorporated in the core. It is available in 2- and 4-ft. widths, ½- and ⅝-in. thick. The latter is also available with type X core.

Gypsum board substrate for floor or roof assemblies has a type X core ½-in. thick and is available in 24- or 48-in. widths. It is used under combustible roof coverings to protect the structure from fires originating on the roof. It can also serve as an underlayment when applied to the top surfaces of floor joists and under subflooring. It may also be used as a base for builtup roofing applied over steel decks.

Gypsum form board has a fungus-resistant paper and is used as a support and permanent form for poured-in-place reinforced gypsum concrete roof decks.

Gypsum lath and *gypsum base for veneer plaster* are described in the section on Plaster.

Standard specifications for gypsum wallboard materials and application are shown in Table 1.

Gypsum board products are available with insulating aluminum foil backing which provides an effective vapor barrier for exterior walls when applied with the foil surface against the framing. With a minimum of ¾ in. enclosed air space adjacent to the foil, additional insulating efficiency is achieved. This combination effectively reduces outward heat flow in the cold season and inward heat flow in the warm season. (Foil-backed gypsum board should not be used as a backing material for tile, a second-face ply on a two-ply system, in conjunction with heating cables, or when laminating directly to masonry, ceiling and roof assemblies).

SIZES

Standard gypsum boards are 4 ft wide and 8, 10, 12 or 14 ft long. Other lengths and widths are available from the manufacturer on special order.

The various thicknesses of gypsum wallboard available in regular, type X, and predecorated board are as follows:

¼-in. —a lightweight, low cost board used as a base in a multilayer application for improving sound control, or to cover existing walls and ceilings in remodeling.

⁵⁄₁₆-in. —a lightweight gypsum board developed for use in manufactured construction, primarily mobile homes.

⅜-in. —a lightweight board principally applied in a double-layer system over wood framing and as a face layer in repair or remodeling.

½-in. —generally used as a single-layer wall and ceiling construction in residential work and in double-layer systems for greater sound and fire ratings.

⅝-in. —used in quality single-layer and double-layer wall systems. The greater thickness provides additional fire resistance, higher rigidity, and better impact resistance.

1-in. —either a single one-inch board or two ½ inch factory laminated boards used as a liner or as a coreboard in shaft walls, semi-solid or solid gypsum board partitions.

Table 1. Standard specifications for gypsum wallboard materials and application

Materials	Specifications	
	ANSI/ASTM	Federal
Gypsum wallboard	C36	SS-L-30D, Type III
Gypsum sheathing	C79	SS-L-30D, Type II
Gypsum backing board or core board	C442	SS-L-30D, Type IV
Gypsum water-resistant backing board	C630	SS-L-30D, Type VII
Joint treatment materials	C475	SS-J-750
Nails for application of gypsum board	C514	FF-N-105B
Adhesives for fastening gypsum board to wood framing	C557	
Adhesives for laminating gypsum board	C475	
Steel studs and furring channels for screw application of gypsum board	C645	
Screws for application of gypsum board to light gage steel studs	C646	
Installation of steel framing members to receive screw-attached gypsum board	ANSI A97.2	
Gypsum wallboard finishes	ANSI A97.1	

EDGES

The standard edges are tapered, square edge, beveled, rounded, tongue and grooved, and featured joint edge. (Fig. 1)

APPLICATION

Gypsum board panels can be applied over wood or metal framing or furring. They can be applied to masonry and concrete surfaces, either directly or to furring strips.

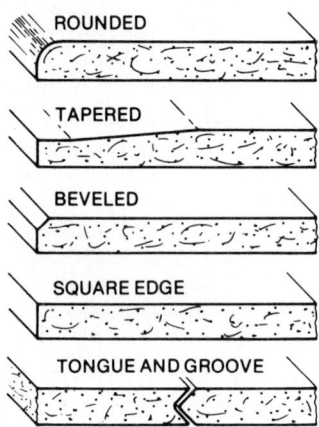

ROUNDED

TAPERED

BEVELED

SQUARE EDGE

TONGUE AND GROOVE

Fig. 1. Standard edge shapes

Most common in residential construction is the standard gypsum wallboard system with the joints between the panels and internal corners reinforced with tape and covered with joint treatment compound to prepare them for decoration. External corners are normally reinforced with metal corner beads which in turn are covered with joint compound. Exposed edges are covered with metal or plastic trim. The result is a smooth, unbroken surface ready for final decoration of paint, textures, wallpaper, tile, paneling or other materials. When predecorated board is used, no further finishing is necessary, but moldings or battens can be applied to cover the joints if desired.

Single- and multi-ply application

In light commercial and residential construction, single-ply gypsum board systems are commonly used. Generally, they are adequate to meet normal usage, fire resistance, and sound control requirements.

Multi-ply systems have two or more layers of gypsum board and therefore can increase sound isolation and fire-resistive performance. They also provide better surface quality because face layers are usually laminated over base layers thereby reducing the number of fasteners. As a result, surface joints of the face layer are reinforced by the continuous base layers of gypsum board.

Application of single-ply gypsum board

Maximum spacing of framing members for single-ply gypsum board construction is shown in Table 4.

Gypsum board panels may be applied parallel to or perpendicular to framing members, as shown in Fig. 2. Perpendicular application is stronger and usually results in less total length of joints requiring treatment.

Nailing schedule is shown in Table 5. Nail spacing for single nailing is shown in Fig. 2. Nail spacing for double nailing, a recommended alternate, is shown in Fig. 3.

When screws are used in lieu of nails, they should be spaced a maximum of 12 in. (305 mm) o.c. for ceilings and 16 in. (406 mm) o.c. for walls where the framing members are 16 in. o.c. Screws should be spaced a maximum of 12 in. o.c. for ceilings and walls where framing members are 24 in. (610 mm) o.c. Screws are Type W for wood, Type S for sheetmetal, and Type G for solid gypsum construction. Type S screws are self drilling and self tapping. Screws are generally power driven.

Staples are recommended only for attaching base ply to wood members in multi-ply construction. They should be 16 gauge, flattened, galvanized wire with a minimum $\frac{7}{16}$-in.-wide crown and spreading points. Staples should provide a minimum of $\frac{5}{8}$ in. penetration into supports.

Table 2. Fire-resistance ratings

Material	Floor-ceiling construction	Loadbearing wood-stud partitions*
⅝-in. Type X gypsum wallboard	1 hr	1 hr
½-in. Type X gypsum wallboard	45 min	45 min
2 layers ⅜-in. regular gypsum wallboard		1 hr
½-in. regular gypsum wallboard	40 min	
⅜-in. regular gypsum wallboard	25 min	

Fire-resistance ratings per Underwriters Laboratory, Chicago, Illinois, and the National Bureau of Standards.

Table 3. Thermal conductivity values*

Thickness		Conductance "C"	Resistance "R"
Inch	mm	Btu/(hr · ft² · °F)	(hr · ft² · °F)/Btu
⅜	9.5	3.00	0.333
½	12.7	2.36	0.424
⅝	15.9	1.88	0.532
1	25.4	1.20	0.850

For values for enclosed air spaces, including those enclosed by foil back gypsum board, see section on Insulation.

Table 4. Maximum framing spacing for single-ply gypsum board

Single ply gypsum board (thickness)		Application to framing	Maximum o.c. spacing of framing	
Inches	mm.		Inches	mm.
Ceilings:				
†⅜	9.5	*Perpend	16	406
½	12.7	Perpend	16	406
½	12.7	*Parallel	16	406
⅝	15.9	Parallel	16	406
½	12.7	*Perpend	24	610
⅝	15.9	Perpend	24	610
Sidewalls:				
⅜	9.5	Perpend or Parallel	16	406
½	12.7	Perpend or Parallel	24	610
⅝	15.9	Perpend or Parallel	24	610

On ceiling to receive a waterbase spray texture finish, gypsum board should be applied perpendicular to framing and board thickness increased from ⅜ in. (9.5 mm) to ½ in. (12.7 mm) for 16 in. (406 mm) o.c. framing and from ½ in. (12.7 mm) to ⅝ in. (15.9 mm) for 24 in. (610 mm) o.c.
†*Should not support thermal insulation.*

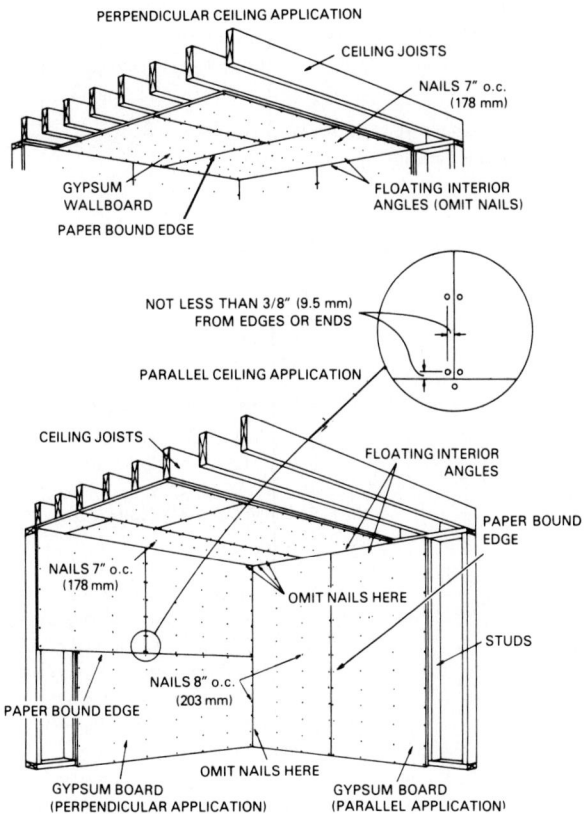

Fig. 2. Single-ply application of gypsum board

Floating interior angles

To minimize possibility of fasteners popping in areas adjacent to wall and ceiling intersections, the floating-angle method of application may be used for either single- or double-layer application of gypsum board to wood framing. This method is applicable where single nailing, double nailing or screw attachment is used. Gypsum board should be applied to ceiling first. (See Fig. 4). Floating interior angles should not be used where fire ratings are required.

Adhesive-and-fastener application

Adhesive may be used in the application of gypsum board to wood or metal framing with resulting reduction in the number of fasteners required and improvement in the overall stiffness of the structure. Adhesive should be applied in a straight bead ¼

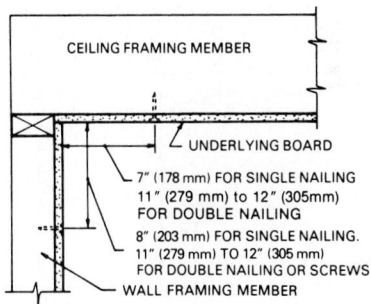

Fig. 4. Floating angle at ceiling-wall intersection

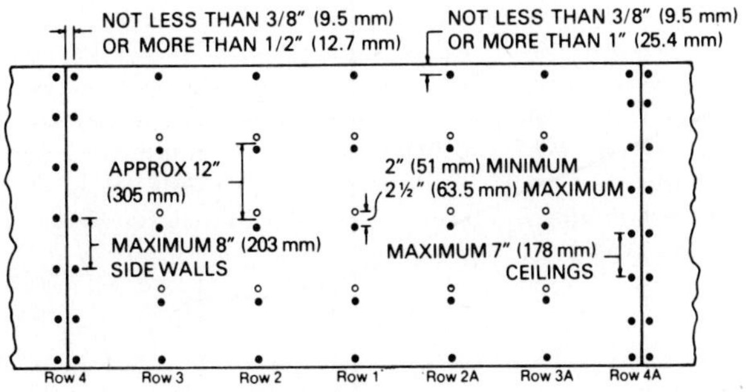

Fig. 3. Double nailing:

(1) Starting at center of board, nails shown by dot · are applied in row 1, then rows 2 and 2A, 3 and 3A, 4 and 4A, etc., always nailing from center to edges of sheet

(2) Apply second nails shown by circle ° in same manner as first nails, also starting at row 1

Table 5. Nailing schedule for single-ply gypsum board*

Gypsum board thickness		Minimum nail length†	
Inches	mm.	Inches	mm.
¼	6.4		
⅜	9.5	1-¼	32
½	12.7	1-⅜	35
⅝	15.9	1-½	38

* *Where a specific degree of fire resistance is required for gypsum board assemblies and constructions, nails of same or larger length, shank diameter, and head bearing area, as those described in the test report may be used.*

† *For application over existing solid surfaces, nail should have a flat or concave head, a diamond point, and such length as to provide not less than ⅞ in. (22 mm), or ¾ in. for annular ringed nails, penetration into the nailing members. For fire-rated assemblies 1⅛ to 1¼ in. penetration is generally required.*

Table 6. Fastener spacing* with adhesive application

Framing member spacing	Ceilings		Partitions load-bearing		Partitions non-load-bearing	
	Nail	Screw	Nail	Screw	Nail	Screw
16 in. o.c.	16 in.	16 in.	16 in.	24 in.	24 in.	24 in.
24 in. o.c.	12 in.	16 in.	12 in.	16 in.	16 in.	24 in.

12 in. = 305 mm, 16 in. = 406 mm, 24 in. = 610 mm

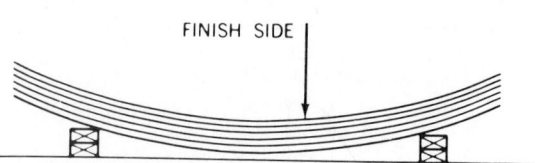

Fig. 5. Prebowing keeps gypsum board in tight contact with adhesive after it is applied

Table 7. Base-ply fastener spacing

Location	Nail spacing		Screw spacing		Staple spacing	
	Laminated face ply	Nailed face ply*	Laminated face ply†	Screwed face ply†	Laminated face ply	Nailed or screwed face ply*
Walls	8 in. o.c. (203 mm)	16 in. o.c. (406 mm)	16 in. o.c. (406 mm)	24 in. o.c. (610 mm)	7 in. o.c. (178 mm)	16 in. o.c. (406 mm)
Ceilings	7 in. o.c. (178 mm)	16 in. o.c. (406 mm)	16 in. o.c. (406 mm)	24 in. o.c. (610 mm)	7 in. o.c. (178 mm)	16 in. o.c. (406 mm)

Fastener spacing for face ply shall be the same as for single layer application.
† 12 in. o.c. for both ceilings and walls when supports are spaced 24 in. o.c.

in. in diameter to the face of all framing members except plates. Where two gypsum board panels abut on a framing member two beads of adhesive should be applied, one near each edge of the framing member. Perimeter fastener spacing for adhesive application is shown in Table 6. Fasteners 24 in. on center are required in the field of ceiling panels only. Where fasteners at vertical joints are undesirable, as in the case of predecorated panels, they may be eliminated by using prebowed panels, nailed or screwed at top and bottom plates only. Prebowing of the panels may be accomplished by stacking them face up with the ends supported by 2-in. blocking and the center resting on the floor, and leaving them overnight or until permanently bowed (Fig. 5).

Two-ply application

Base ply may be backing board, with or without aluminum foil backing; it may be nailed, screwed, or stapled, with or without adhesive; joint treatment is not required. Face ply may be laminated (attached by adhesive) or nailed or screwed. If face ply is to be laminated, base ply should be applied with fasteners spaced as for single-ply construction. If face ply is to be nailed or screwed without adhesive, base ply should be nailed 16 in o.c. or screwed 24 in. o.c., and the face ply fastener spacing should be the same as for single ply-construction (Table 7). Face-ply joints should be offset at least 10 in. from joints in base ply. Face-ply application may be by sheet, strip, or spot lamination — terms which describe methods of applying the adhesive. The adhesive most commonly used is the same joint compound used for embedding tape, but some manufacturers make a special laminating adhesive. The face ply must be held firmly against the base ply with temporary or permanent fasteners or temporary bracing. Permanent fasteners are generally used in the field of ceiling panels.

SELF-SUPPORTING GYPSUM PARTITIONS

Noncombustible, non-loadbearing partitions can be constructed of multi-ply gypsum board without supporting framework. Only floor and ceiling runners (tracks) are required to stabilize the partitions. These partitions can be prefabricated, site fabricated, or built in place.

Self-supporting gypsum partitions are classified as:

semisolid, utilizing gypsum studs between face plies, and
solid with a coreboard inner ply

All gypsum board components such as studs, coreboard, backing board, wallboard, and predecorated board are installed vertically.

Semisolid partitions

Semisolid partitions provide vertical interior passages for mechanical and electrical services. They consist of single- or two-ply faces of gypsum board separated by vertical gypsum strips, 6-in. wide, at least 1-in. thick, placed 2 ft on center (Fig. 6). These strips are commonly called studs, but they are 6 in. shorter than the panels and do not bear on anything. If they are made 1⅝ in. thick, then standard electrical outlet boxes can be used.

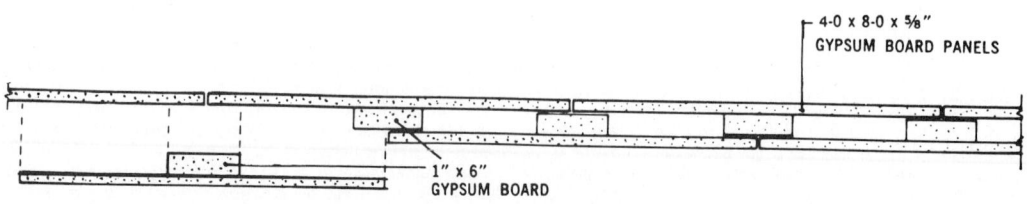

Fig. 6. Semisolid gypsum board partition

Separated stud construction to improve sound isolation qualities can be provided in either single or two-ply partitions. Installation is essentially the same as for regular gypsum stud partitions, but twice as many studs are required. These are spaced 12 in. o.c. and staggered on opposite sides of the partition.

Solid partitions

Solid gypsum partitions have gypsum board faces laminated to each side of a coreboard. Vertical joints in the face ply should be offset at least 3 in. from joints in the coreboard. The face ply typically is attached by sheet lamination with supplemental drywall screws. Double solid partitions separated by an air space provide improved sound isolation and space for mechanical and electrical services.

Solid partitions can easily be designed to be demountable, as shown in Fig. 7.

GYPSUM SUBSTRATE UNDER COMBUSTIBLE PANELING

The use of gypsum board substrate under combustible paneling provides improved fire resistance, sound control, and impact resistance, as shown in Table 8. Backing board, ⅜- or ½-in. thick, is recommended, applied as for single-ply construction. Joints need not be taped. Combustible panel should be applied using a bead of adhesive over each stud and midway between studs (Fig. 8). Joints in the face ply should be staggered

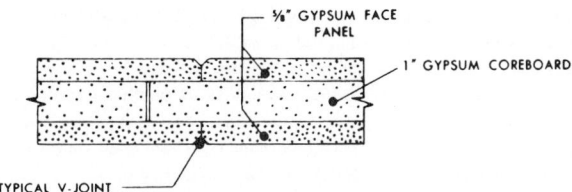

1/8" GYPSUM FACE PANEL

1" GYPSUM COREBOARD

TYPICAL V-JOINT

Fig. 7. Demountable solid gypsum board partition

Table 8. Properties of combustible paneling over gypsum board

	¼" Paneling (no gypsum board)	¼" Paneling with ⅜ in. gypsum board	¼" Paneling with ½ in. gypsum board
Burn-through time	8 min.	42 min.	73 min. (plus)
Sound rating	28 STC	40 STC	40 STC
Impact resistance	130 ft-lb	410 ft-lb	410 ft-lb

from those of the base ply of gypsum board. Secure the paneling at top and bottom with 4d finishing nails, 12 in. o.c. and with one nail at mid-height per stud.

JOINT TREATMENT

Joint adhesives are of three general types:

1. a taping or bedding compound used to adhere the tape to board
2. a finishing or topping compound used especially for finishing
3. an all-purpose compound to be used for both embedding and finishing the joint.

The groove formed by the tapered edges when gypsum boards join should be prefilled with joint embedding compound. Center reinforcing tape and press it down into the joint compound. Apply additional joint treatment compound using a 5- or 6-in. finishing knife.

The initial tape embedding can also be done with a semi-automatic tool that applies the joint compound and tape simultaneously.

After the embedding coat is completely dry 24 hours or more, apply a second coat feathered about 2 in. beyond edges of the first coat. Spot fastener heads and allow to dry (Fig. 9).

After the second coat is dry, sand lightly

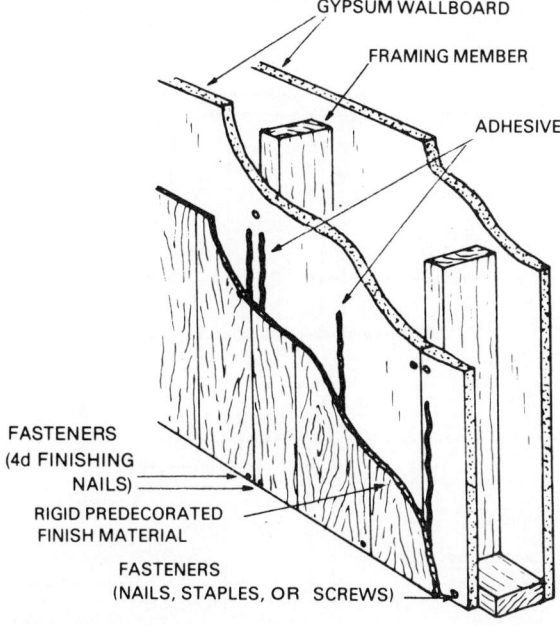

GYPSUM WALLBOARD

FRAMING MEMBER

ADHESIVE

FASTENERS (4d FINISHING NAILS)

RIGID PREDECORATED FINISH MATERIAL

FASTENERS (NAILS, STAPLES, OR SCREWS)

Fig. 8. Combustible paneling over gypsum board substrate

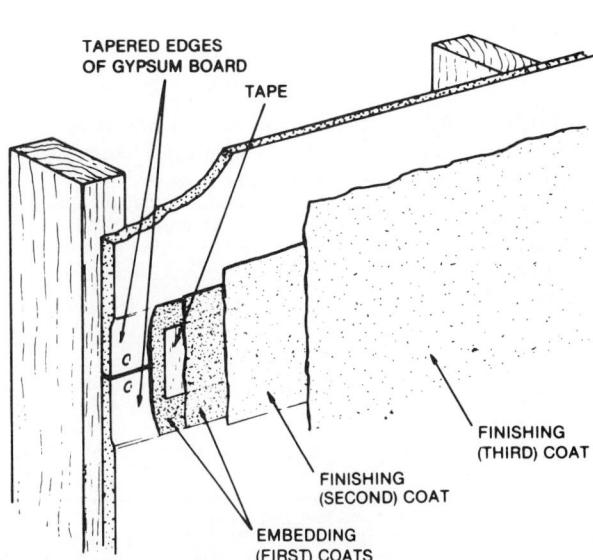

TAPERED EDGES OF GYPSUM BOARD

TAPE

FINISHING (THIRD) COAT

FINISHING (SECOND) COAT

EMBEDDING (FIRST) COATS

Fig. 9. Joint treatment

and apply a thin finishing coat to joints and fastener heads. Feather edges to about 6 in. from the center of the joint. When dry, sand lightly, taking care not to raise nap of paper surface of board.

Precreased tape is available for use in interior corners and at the intersection of wall and ceiling. Exterior corners should be reinforced with metal cornerite, installed with nails or screws, coated with joint compound and finished like a taped joint. Exposed edges of gypsum board should be covered with metal trim.

DECORATION

Gypsum board surfaces can be decorated with paint, paper, textures, fabric or vinyl wall coverings. Seal or prime the surface with a good quality emulsion paint. The sealer allows the wall coverings to be removed more easily without marring the surface. Glue-size, shellac, and varnish are not suitable as sealers or primers.

Latex paints do not raise the fibers in the face paper as oil base paints do, and therefore are preferred for sealing and priming and may also be used for the finish coat when two more applications are made. Paints may be spray, brush, or roller applied. The final coat can be textured if desired.

METAL STUD PARTITIONS

Gypsum board and metal stud partitions are widely used in commercial and industrial buildings, in high rise office buildings, apartment houses, and wherever noncombustible lightweight partitions are required. There are a variety of framing systems, many of them proprietary, for both loadbearing and nonloadbearing partitions. More than 20 gyp-

sum board and metal stud partitions, having fire ratings of 1 to 2 hours and STC ratings of 40 to 59, are detailed in *Fire Resistance Design Manual 1978*, published by the Gypsum Association. Some systems are demountable and can be re-erected without loss of fire or sound rating.

Typical metal studs for non-loadbearing partitions are C-shaped of 25-gage galvanized steel. They are available in 1⅝-, 2½-, 3¼-, 3⅝-, 4-, and 6-in. depths and in lengths of 6 to 16 ft.

Maximum height limitations for typical gypsum board and metal stud partitions are given in Table 9, based on a load of 5 lb/ft² and a deflection limit of $\frac{1}{120}$ of the height. A higher degree of performance may be desirable for office and institutional buildings, as compared to industrial buildings.

Partitions in high-rise buildings may suffer damage from building movement. This has led to the development of special perimeter relief details (Fig. 10) which are now in general use in high-rise construction. These details do not impair fire resistance or sound isolation ratings.

MOISTURE-RESISTANT CONSTRUCTION

Water-resistant gypsum board is suitable for exterior use as ceiling canopies, covered walkways, porches, breezeways, carports, and eave soffits. Framing should be no more than 16 in. o.c. for ½-in. board, and not more than 24 in. o.c. for ⅜-in. board. Edges should be protected by wood or metal trim. Gypsum board should be primed and finished with two coats of exterior paint.

Water-resistant gypsum backing board is recommended for use in bathrooms, laundries, kitchens, utility rooms and other areas

subject to moisture. It is used as a base for the adhesive application of ceramic and plastic tile and plastic finished wall panels in shower and tub enclosures. (See section on "Tile.") Water-resistant gypsum board subjected to moisture should not be foil backed or applied directly over a vapor barrier, and is not recommended for use in areas subject to extreme exposure to moisture, such as saunas, steam rooms, and gang shower rooms.

Water-resistant gypsum backing board should be applied horizontally with the factory bound edge spaced a minimum of ¼ in. above the lip of the shower pan or tub (see Figs. 11 and 12). Shower pans, or tubs should be installed prior to the installation of the gypsum board. Shower pans should have an upstanding lip or flange a minimum of 1 in. higher than the threshold. Suitable blocking should be provided approximately 1 in. above the top of tub or pan, and

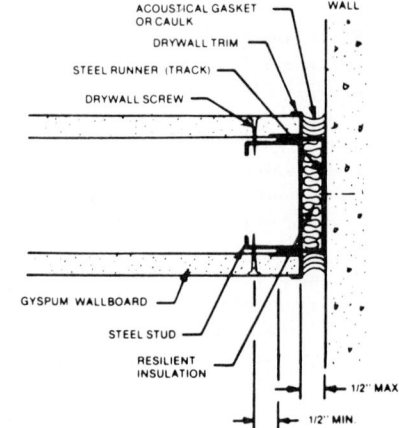

Steel stud partition—plan at wall

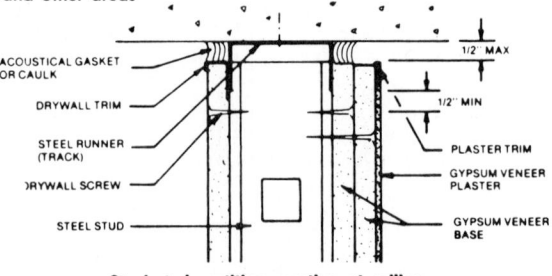

Steel stud partition—section at ceiling

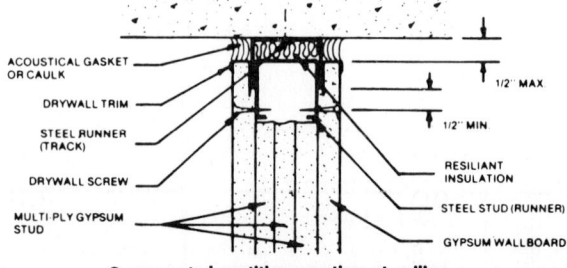

Gypsum stud partition—section at ceiling

Fig. 10.   Perimeter relief details for nonbearing partitions

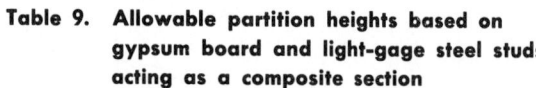

Table 9.   Allowable partition heights based on gypsum board and light-gage steel studs acting as a composite section

Stud spacing (in.)	Facing on each side	Stud depth (in.)			
		1⅝	2½	3⅝	4
		Height in feet and inches			
16	½"-one-ply	11'0"	14' 8"	19'5"	20'8"
24	½"-one-ply	10'0"	13' 5"	17'3"	18'5"
24	½"-two-ply	12'4"	15'10"	19'5"	20'8"

(1) *Steel studs and runners (track) comply with ASTM C 645; steel screws comply with ASTM C 646 and are spaced in accordance with Gypsum Association Recommended Specifications for the Application and Finishing of Gypsum Board.*

(2) *Where solid core or double doors are used in partitions built to maximum height, it is recommended that door closers be used or the door frame be reinforced.*

behind the horizontal joint of the gypsum board above the tub or pan. Studs must be at least 3½ in. deep and not more than 16 in. o.c. for ceramic tile application.

Water-resistant gypsum backing board should be attached with nails or screws spaced not more than 8 in. o.c. When ceramic tile more than ⅜ in. thick is to be applied, the nail or screw spacing should not exceed 4 in. o.c.

Cut edges and openings around pipes and fixtures should be caulked flush with waterproof, nonhardening caulking compound or with the adhesive used for setting the tile. Joints do not generally need to be treated. If joint treatment is considered necessary, do not use joint compound, but instead use caulking compound or tile adhesive. The caulking compound, if used, must be compatible with the tile-setting adhesive.

ELECTRIC RADIANT HEATING SYSTEMS

Packaged electric panel heating systems utilizing gypsum board as the base material are commercially available and can be installed as a complete system in new or existing structures. Also on-site systems can be fabricated in-place utilizing gypsum backing board, electric heating cable, a filler material and a face ply of gypsum board. Radiant heating systems should not be operated with wire temperature exceeding 125°F.

It is recommended that a base layer of gypsum backing board at least ½ in. thick be attached perpendicularly to ceiling supports with nails 7 in. o.c. or with screws spaced 12 in. o.c. Taping of joints is not required. Electric heating cables should be securely attached to the backing board in accordance with the recommendations of the cable manufacturer and the requirements of the National Electrical Code. Cables should be parallel to and between framing members with at least 1¼-in. clearance from center of framing member on each side so that at least a 2½ in. wide unobstructed strip is provided under each framing member. Cables should cross framing members only at ends of ceiling 4 to 6 in. from the wall. There should be at least a 4-in. space clear of cables completely around the perimeter of each ceiling (Fig. 14). Cables should be kept at least 8 in. clear of all openings such as light fixtures.

All inspections and testing of the heating system should be completed before the application of the filler material.

The heating cable must be completely embedded with a nonshrinking, noninsulating filler applied ¼ in. thick, leveled and finished to a smooth surface. The filler material should be allowed to dry before the face board is installed.

To prevent striking heating cables where they cross framing members, attach the face layer of gypsum board (no thicker than ½ in.) with nails or screws 8 to 10 in. away from the wall around the perimeter of the ceiling. The spacing of fasteners should be the same as the base layer application, allowing ⅞ in. penetration into the framing members for nails and ⅝ in. for screws. A minimum of one week (two weeks in cold conditions) drying time is necessary before operating the heating system.

Decoration should not proceed until the heating system has been tested a minimum of 24 hr. The heating system should then be turned off and allowed to cool before decorating.

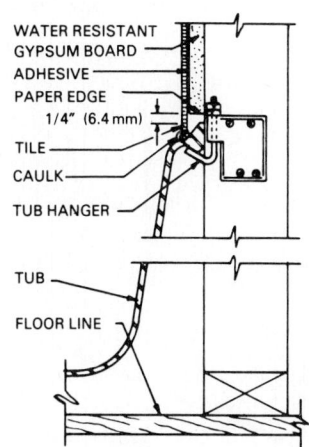

Fig. 11. Wall tile on gypsum board at bathtub rim

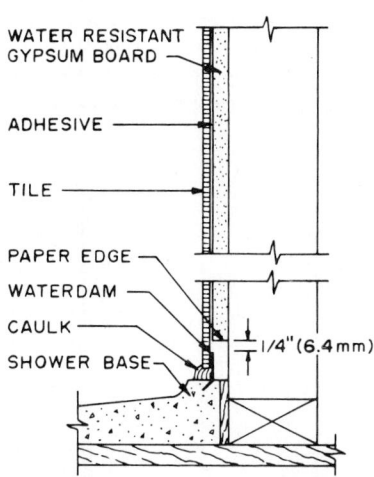

Fig. 12. Wall tile on gypsum board at shower base

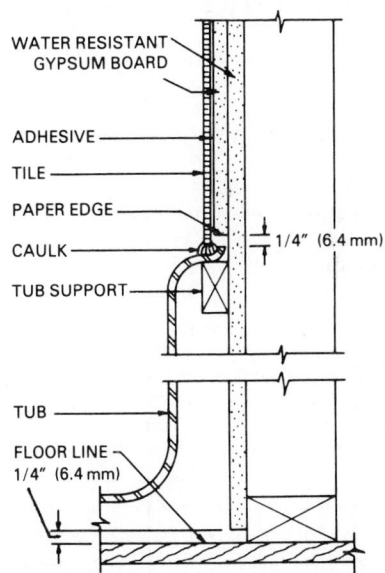

Fig. 13. For fire- or sound-rated construction gypsum board must be continuous from ceiling to floor

Table 10. Bending radii of gypsum board

Gypsum board thickness		Bent lengthwise		Bent widthwise	
In.	mm	Ft	Meter	Ft	Meter
¼	6.4	5	1.5	15	4.6
⅜	9.5	7.5	2.3	25	7.7
½	12.7	*10	3.0	—	—

Bending two ¼ in. (6.4 mm) pieces successively permits radii shown for ¼ in. (6.4 mm).

Note: By moistening face and back paper thoroughly and allowing water to soak well into core, board may be bent to still shorter radii. When board dries thoroughly, it will regain its original hardness.

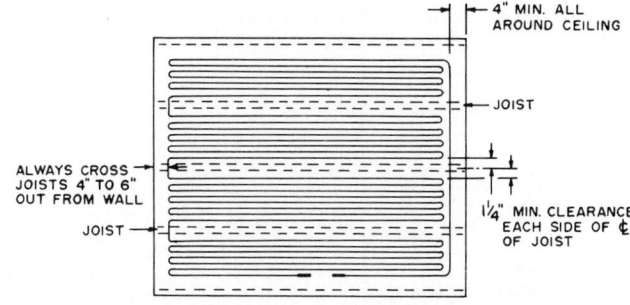

Fig. 14. Reflected plan of ceiling showing typical heating cable layout

Insulation board

By HOWARD P. VERMILYA, AIA

Insulation board, sometimes called "fiberboard" or "rigid insulation," is a generic term used to describe wood or vegetable fibers that have been compressed or felted to form rigid boards. The term is not generally used for boards made of inorganic fibers such as glass, asbestos, or mineral wool. The first wood-fiber insulating board was developed by the Insulite Company in 1914 and the first vegetable-fiber board, using bagasse or sugarcane fibers, was produced by the Celotex Corporation in 1920.

USES

Originally designed as an insulator, insulation board now has many uses:

1. Exterior sheathing
2. Interior wall and ceiling finish (building board)
3. Acoustical tile
4. Roof insulation
5. Roof deck
6. Form board (for gypsum or concrete decks)
7. Shingle backer strips
8. Exterior siding
9. Plaster lath
10. Floor underlayment
11. Panels (sandwich)

In order to meet the requirements of all the above, various modifications have been made in the basic product. Insulation board may be obtained which has been specially treated, integrally or by impregnation, to improve its resistance to moisture, rot, termites, and fire. For certain uses, densities have been increased to improve structural properties, particularly for sheathing and form board. Layers of board have been laminated to increase insulation and structural properties. These laminated boards are also used as cores for sandwich panels faced with other materials. A wide variety of decorative surfaces have been developed. Acoustical properties have been improved by drilling holes in the exposed face.

STANDARDS

Insulation board is manufactured to uniform industry standards established by the Insulation Board Institute and to comply with the following national standards:

1. Federal Specification LLL-F-321
2. Federal Specification SS-S-118 (acoustical tile)
3. ANSI Voluntary Product Standard PS 57-73
4. American Society for Testing and Materials: ASTM-C-208, Class E (sheathing), Class C (roof insulation)
5. Federal Specification LLL-1-535 (sheathing and roof insulation)

The physical properties covered by these standards include density, thermal conductivity, transverse load without rupture, deflection at breaking load, tensile strength, water absorption, linear expansion, and decay and rot resistance. The standards are also concerned with the surface finishes for interior boards, plank, and tile, and provide test procedures for determining their compliance with flame-resistance standards.

Standard types and sizes of insulation board are given in Table 11. Types of fasteners used for the installation of insulation board are listed in Table 12.

EXTERIOR SHEATHING

Exterior sheathing is used to replace wood boards on walls and roofs and thereby reduce air infiltration and provide additional insulation. Sheathing boards are generally 4 by 8 or 4 by 9 ft, $\frac{25}{32}$ in. thick, and are impregnated, integrally treated, or coated with asphalt. These boards, when properly nailed to the frame, 3 in. on center at edges and 6 in. on center on intermediate studs, stiffen it so as to eliminate the need for corner bracing (Fig. 15). For horizontal application, sheathing boards 2 by 8 ft with V-joints along the long edges, are also available in this thickness, although they do not provide

equivalent bracing (Fig. 16). A more recent development is a high-density, asphalt-treated board, 4 by 8 ft or 4 by 9 ft by ½ in. thick. This board has increased nail-holding power, which not only provides the required stiffness to permit omission of corner bracing but also permits the board to be used as a nailing base, with screw-type or annular-ring nails (Fig. 17), for the

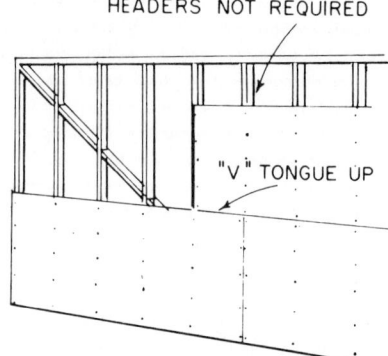

Fig. 16. Insulation board sheathing, 2 by 8 ft, applied horizontally

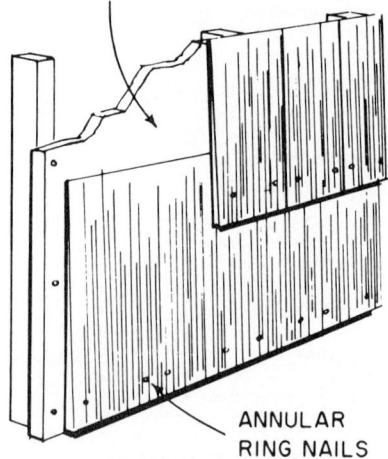

Fig. 17. Application of shingles to high-density insulation board sheathing

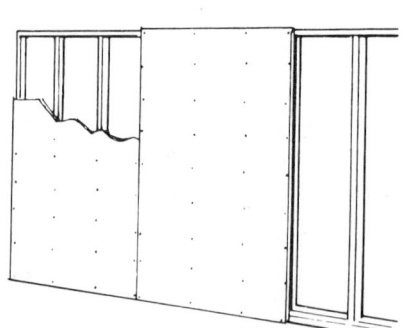

Fig. 15. Insulation board sheathing, 4 by 8 or 4 by 9 ft, applied vertically

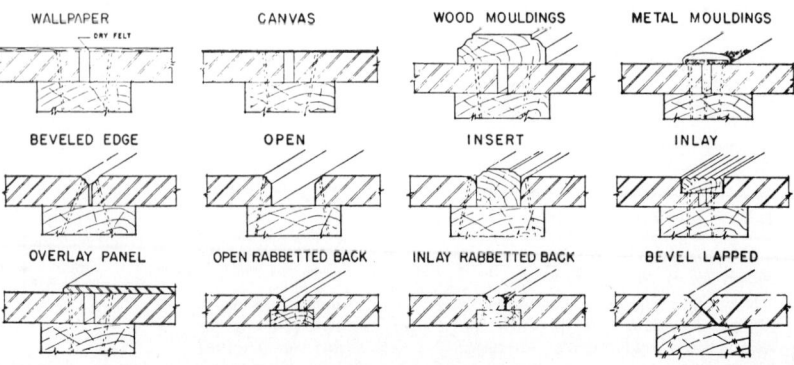

Fig. 18. Joint treatments for building board

Table 11. Standard sizes and thicknesses of structural insulation board products*

Courtesy Insulation Board Institute

Product	Thickness *	Sizes *	Edges	Major uses
Building board	½"	4'x6' 4'x7' 4'x8' 4'x9' 4'x10' 4'x12'	Square	General purpose structural insulating board; decorative interior finish; base for plastic paints, wall coverings and other interior decorative finishes
Insulating roof deck	C value 1½" 0.24 2" 0.18 3" 0.12	2'x8'	Fabricated long edges; short edges interlocking or square	Three-in-one product, roof deck, insulation, and interior finish for flat, pitched or shed-type open-beamed-ceiling roof construction
Roof insulation	C value ½" 0.72 1" 0.36 1½" 0.24 2" 0.19 2½" 0.15 3" 0.12	23"x47" 24"x48"	Varies	For roof insulation under built-up roofing on flat roofs and under certain types of roofing on pitched roofs. Floor insulation for masonry floors. Protection course for membrane waterproofing
Tile, plain or perforated	½"	12"x12" 12"x24" 16"x16" 16"x32"	Fabricated edges	Decorative, insulating wall and ceiling finish. Frequently used in conjunction with building board and/or plank
Plank	½"	8"x8' 8"x10' 12"x8' 12"x10' 16"x8' 16"x10'	Fabricated long edges	Decorative, insulating wall and ceiling finish. Frequently used in conjunction with building board and/or tileboard
Sheathing, regular density	½" or $\frac{25}{32}$"	4'x8' 4'x9' 4'x10' 4'x12'	Square	Wall sheathing under brick veneer, siding, shingles, or stucco
	½" or $\frac{25}{32}$"	2'x8'	Long edges fabricated; short edges square	
Sheathing, high-density	½"	4'x8' 4'x9'	Square	High-density product designed for use without supplementary corner bracing
Sheathing, nail-base	½"	4'x8' 4'x9'	Square	High-density product designed for use in frame construction to permit the direct attachment of exterior siding materials such as wood and asbestos shingles. The super strength of this material also eliminates the need for supplementary corner bracing
Shingle backer	⁵⁄₁₆" or ⅜"	11¾"x48" 13½"x48" 15"x48" 15½"x48"	Square	Undercoursing for wood or asbestos-cement shingles applied over insulation board sheathing
Insulating form board	1" or 1½"	24", 32" and 48" widths; 4' to 12' in length	Square	Designed for use as a permanent form for reinforced gypsum or lightweight aggregate concrete poured-in-place roof construction

* For additional thicknesses and sizes, consult manufacturer.

direct application of asbestos or wood shingles. Sheathing paper may be omitted over asphalt-treated boards.

BUILDING BOARD

Building board is used as an interior finish material for walls and ceilings. It is usually manufactured ½ in. thick, although some manufacturers supply it in ⅜, ⅝, 1, 1⅜, and 1⅞-in. thicknesses. Others laminate ½-in. boards to achieve greater thicknesses. In the ⅜-in. thickness it is usually called

utility board. All manufacturers make it in 4 by 8-ft sheets and some supply it also in sheets up to 14 ft in length and 8 ft in width. The ½-in. board is intended for use over studs 16 in. on center and it should be supported on all edges. It is available with various predecorated finishes, plain or wood-grain, or primed for later painting. Various joint treatments are shown in **Fig. 18**. Plank in 8, 12, 16, and 24-in. widths, 8 and 10 ft long, is supplied predecorated for finishing walls. Ceiling tile, 12 by 12, 12 by 24, 16 by 16, and 16 by

32 in., is also made with various surface finishes for application to solid backing or to furring strips. Both the plank and tile have tongue and groove (T and G) or other edges which permit concealed fastening at the joints (Fig. 19). They may also be applied with adhesives.

ACOUSTICAL TILE

Acoustical tile made from insulation board may be obtained prefinished with a standard, coated finish or with a flame-re-

Table 12. Fasteners most commonly used for structural insulation board products

Courtesy Insulation Board Institute

Product	Application	Thickness, in.	Size and type of fastener
Building board	Framing 16 in. o.c.; fasteners 3 in. o.c. on edges and 6 in. o.c. on intermediate framing and ⅜ in. from edges	½	1½-in. 4d common nail 1½-in. galv. roofing nail 1½ in. 4d finishing nail
Insulating roof deck	Framing not less than 3 in. nom. width; spacing of framing members not more than 16 times thickness of deck; applied across roof beams with nails spaced approx. 4½ in. o.c. on each roof beam; 8 in. o.c. at all edges, ridges, eaves, and openings	1½ 2 3	3-in. 10d galv. or bright nail 3½-in. 16d galv. or bright nail 4½-in. 30d galv. or bright nail
Roof insulation	Wood decks—nail 12 in. o.c. (no vapor barrier)	½, 1, 1½, 2 2½, 3	Large headed galv. roofing nail with minimum ⁷⁄₁₆-in. head with sufficient length to penetrate the roof deck at least ¾ in.
Tile, plain or perforated	Nail or staple at three corners and 8 in. o.c. along framing members; 16 in. tile on 8 in. o.c. framing; 12 in. tile on 12 in. o.c. framing	½	3d brad 3d finishing 3d box ½ or ⁹⁄₁₆-in.-long staples
Plank	Planks applied at right angles to framing; nailed through nailing flange at each support; planks applied parallel to framing; space nails 6 in. apart	½	3d brad 3d finishing 3d box
Sheathing	4x8-ft and 4x9-ft board applied vertically; framing 16 in. o.c.; nailed or stapled 3 in. o.c. on edges and 6 in. o.c. on intermediate framing; 2x8-ft board applied horizontally with nails or staples spaced 4 in. o.c. at vertical edges and 8-in. o.c. at intermediate supports	½ ²⁵⁄₃₂	1½-in. galv. roofing nail 1¾-in. galv. roofing nail 1⅛-in. galv. staple, 16 gage with ⁷⁄₁₆-in. crown 1¾-in. galv. roofing nail 2-in. galv. roofing nail 8d common nail 1½-in. galv. staple, 16 gage with ⁷⁄₁₆-in. crown
Shingle backer	Applied over insulation board sheathing. Backer nailed with a 7d galv. box nail at each stud with ½-in. sheathing and 8d galv. box nails at each stud with ²⁵⁄₃₂-in. sheathing	⁵⁄₁₆ and ⅜	7d galv. box 8d galv. box
	Use 2-in. galv. annular-grooved nail for wood shingles		2-in. galv. annular-grooved

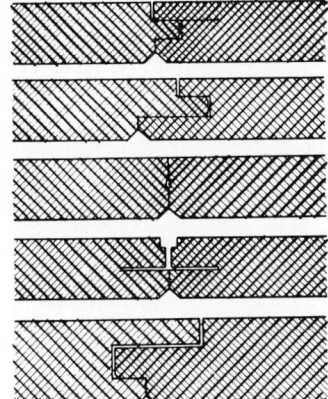

Fig. 19. Joint treatments for ceiling tile

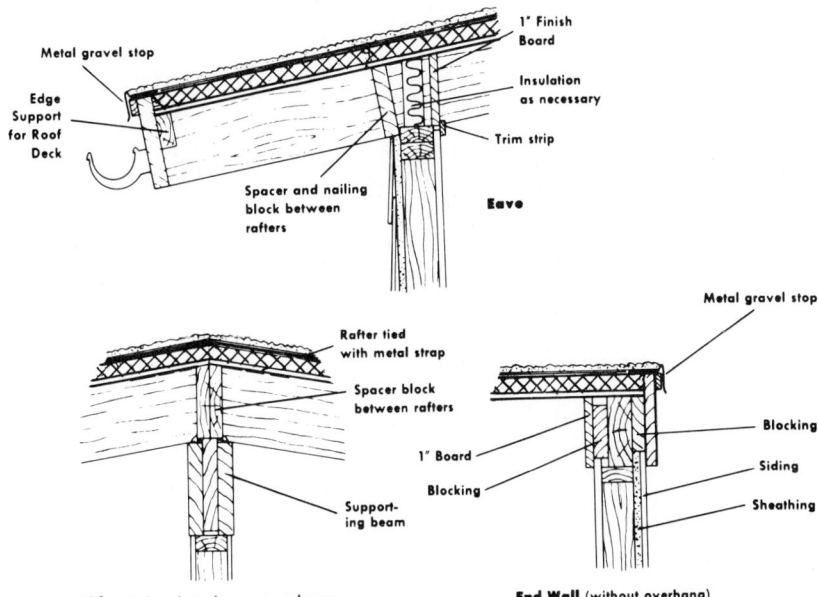

Fig. 20. Details of insulating roof deck

sistant surface treatment. Under Federal Specification SS-S-118, these finishes are Class D and Class C, respectively. In addition, the surface may be textured, fissured, striated, or have drilled holes in regular or random patterns. The drilled types are commonly called "perforated," although the holes do not penetrate the entire thickness of the board. Acoustical tile is produced in ½, ¾, and 1-in. thicknesses, and sizes range in multiples of 12 in., from 12 by 12 up to 24 by 48 in. The edges are generally designed for concealed fastening by nails or staples, some are designed for use with suspension systems, and all types are suitable for adhesive application. The finishes are designed to clean easily and to permit repainting with nonbridging paints.

ROOF INSULATION

Roof insulation, usually of the same density as the building board, is applied over any type of roof decking as a base for built-up roofing. It is supplied plain, or coated or impregnated with asphalt, in thicknesses ranging from ½ up to 3 in. in increments of ½ in. Sheet size is 24 by 48 in. Edges may be square, T and G, or shiplap. The insulation is usually laid on a mopped-on vapor barrier. Edge and cant strips are provided by several manufacturers. The weight ranges from 0.72 psf for ½-in. board to 4.79 psf for 3-in. board, and the thermal conductance (C factor) ranges from 0.72 to 0.12.

ROOF DECK

Insulating roof deck is a laminated board in thicknesses of 1½, 2, and 3 in., 2 ft wide by 8 ft long. It is designed for use in exposed-beam construction, in which the underside of the roof deck forms the finished ceiling. Roof deck can be applied to flat or sloping roofs and provides (1) a structural roof deck, (2) insulation, and (3) a prefinished ceiling. Details of the construction are shown in Fig. 20. The bottom layer of board is usually plain insulation building board; the upper layers may be plain or asphalt-impregnated. Some manufacturers also provide an acoustical treatment to the ceiling with surface treatments complying with Federal Specification SS-S-118 Class C (slow-burning) and Class D. For use in climates where the average daily January temperature may fall below 40°F, a board is available which has a vapor barrier applied between the bottom two

Table 13. Insulating roof deck

Information shown is for board size of 2 by 8 ft

Thickness, in.	Maximum framing c. to c., in.	Weight, psf	U value (inc. roofing)
1½	24	2.3	0.19
2	32	3.1	0.15
3	48	4.5	0.11

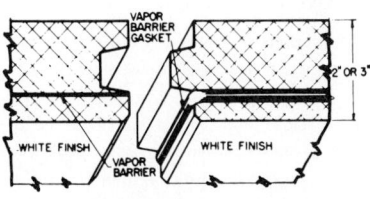

Fig. 21. Insulating roof deck with vapor barrier

layers in the 2 and 3-in. thicknesses (Fig. 21). The long edges have T and G joints, and special gasket-type inserts are available for boards incorporating vapor barriers. The short edges which must occur over framing members may be interlocking or square. The end joints, which should be staggered, are caulked to prevent passage of water vapor. All open edges and surfaces must be protected from exposure. Minimum rafter thickness should be 3 in. to provide proper bearing. Rafter spacing is shown in Table 13. Built-up or selvedge-edge roll roofing may be applied in the normal way. Rigid shingles should be applied to furring strips. Asphalt shingles may be applied directly to the 2 and 3-in.-thick roof decks with galvanized or aluminum 1½-in. annular-ring nails, as recommended by the roofing manufacturer. Some manufacturers may recommend that self-sealing tab shingles be used or that tabs be cemented down. This would seem a wise precaution in windy areas.

FORM BOARD

Insulating form board in standard thicknesses of 1 in., widths of 24, 32, or 48 in., and lengths up to 12 ft, is used as a permanent form below poured roof decks such as gypsum or lightweight concrete. Thicknesses of ¾ and 1½ in. are also available. Form board is usually precut to fit between roof subpurlins (Fig. 22). Spacing of subpurlins is generally 32⅝ in. for gypsum decks and 24⅝ in. for lightweight concrete. End joints may be T and G to avoid the need for additional supports. Long

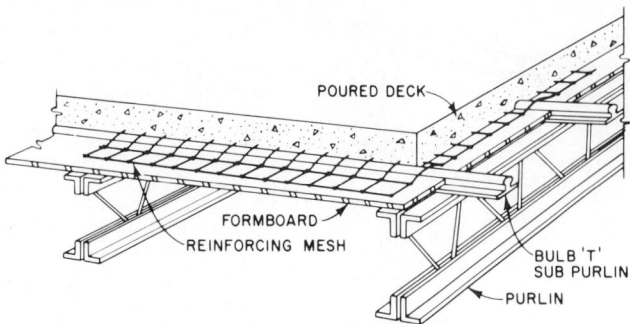

Fig. 22. Insulating form board between subpurlins

edges are square. The board is treated to resist mildew and termites, and the bottom surface is either unfinished or primed for later painting, since it may be water-stained during the pouring of the roof deck. *U* values of form board roofs are given in Table 14.

Acoustical form board, with the lower surface drilled for acoustical absorption, is made in the same sizes as regular form board and also in tiles 12 by 24 and 24 by 24 in. High-density board, sometimes asphalt impregnated in the upper laminations, provides strength, whereas low-density material in lower laminations provides the sound absorption.

Table 14. *U* value of roofs with 1-in. form board and built-up roofing

Deck thickness, in.	Gypsum	Vermiculite concrete 1:4	Perlite concrete 1:4
2	0.20	0.18	0.16
3	0.18	0.15	0.13

SHINGLE BACKER BOARD

Shingle backer board (Table 15 and Fig. 23) is manufactured in $\frac{5}{16}$ and $\frac{3}{8}$-in. thicknesses and 48-in. lengths. The width varies from $11\frac{3}{4}$ to $15\frac{1}{2}$ in., depending upon the size of shingle with which it is to be used. The uses and functions of backer board are

Table 15. Shingle backer boards

Shingle backer width, in.	Shingle	Shingle exposure, in.
$11\frac{3}{4}$	12-in. asbestos cement	$10\frac{1}{2}$
$13\frac{1}{2}$	16-in. wood	12
15	16-in. wood	$13\frac{1}{2}$
$15\frac{1}{2}$	18-in. wood	12–14

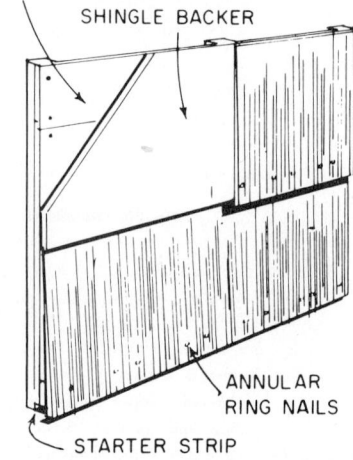

Fig. 23. Application of shingle backer board

similar to those of the under course of wood shingles in double coursing, using similar exposures. It provides insulation and a heavier shadow line with less nailing.

EXTERIOR SIDING

Some manufacturers make a high-density, water-resistant board suitable for use as exterior siding. It is available in nominal $\frac{1}{2}$ or $\frac{5}{8}$-in. thicknesses in plain or V-grooved sheets 4 by 8 up to 8 by 14 ft. As lap siding, it comes in 12-in. widths for a $10\frac{3}{4}$-in. exposure, and in 8 to 16-ft lengths.

INSULATING LATH

Insulating lath is used as the base for plaster (see section on "Plaster").

FLOORS

Insulating fiberboard is used in 4 by 4 or 4 by 8-ft sheets under wood subflooring as insulation and to reduce the transmission of airborne and impact sound. It is also used as underlayment on concrete or wood floors for wall-to-wall carpeting, resilient tile at least $\frac{3}{16}$ in. thick, or wood tile. When laid over concrete, an asphalt-impregnated or integrally treated board should be used,

cemented to the slab with hot-asphalt or cold-asphalt mastic. When recommended by the manufacturer of the underlayment, an adhesive may also be used.

PANELS

Sandwich panels with cores of laminated fiberboard and faces of asbestos-cement board or hardboard are available and have been used as exterior walls and as partitions and roof decks. Asbestos-cement-faced panels are available in $\frac{11}{16}$, $1\frac{1}{8}$, $1\frac{9}{16}$, and 2-in. thicknesses, 4-ft widths, and up to 12-ft lengths. The thicker panels are recommended for roof decks. The 4 by 8-ft panels, supported at all four edges, will carry 50 and 62.5 lbs per sq ft, respectively, for the $1\frac{9}{16}$ and 2-in. thicknesses. Curtain wall and partition systems have been developed by the manufacturers (Fig. 24). Hardboard-faced panels are available in thicknesses of $\frac{5}{8}$, $1\frac{9}{16}$, and $1\frac{5}{8}$ in., widths of 2 or 4 ft, and lengths of 8, 9, or 10 ft. The hardboard may be surfaced with a vinyl finish simulating wood grain. Long edges are grooved for splines.

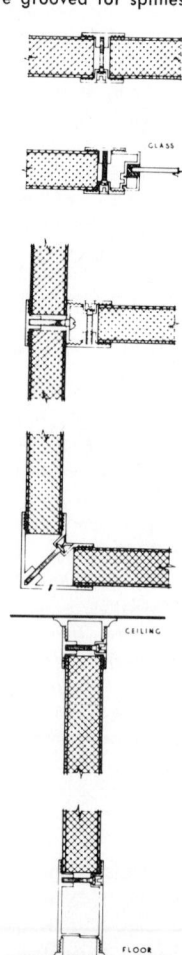

Fig. 24. Movable partition system utilizing sandwich panels and aluminum framing

By SIDNEY M. SHELOV, AIA

"Hardboard" is the generic name for a panel manufactured primarily of felted lignocellulosic fibers, consolidated under heat and pressure to a density of 31 pcf ($0.5 g/cm^3$) or more. Other materials or procedures may be used during manufacture to improve certain properties. The most important of these is the process known as *tempering*, which substantially improves the properties of stiffness, strength, hardness and resistance to water and abrasion.

Hardboard ranges in color from yellow to dark brown, depending on the manufacturing process used. It is dense and uniform in appearance and can easily be sawed, planed, sanded, drilled, or punched. It can be nailed, screwed, stapled, or glued in place and bent to smaller radii than can

most other boards. It takes paint and other finishes well.

Hardboard is produced to industry standards established by the American Hardboard Association (AHA-IS-1-71). This standard divides the field into three broad categories: basic hardboard, hardboard siding, and prefinished hardboard paneling. These three categories are covered by the following ANSI Voluntary Product Standards: PS 58-73, PS-59-73, and PS 60-73, respectively.

Basic hardboard is classified into five quality grades (called types): Tempered, Standard, Service-tempered, Service, and Industrialite. Each type is further divided into two classes of surface finish (S1S and S2S) resulting from the method of manu-

facture. Physical and mechanical properties of all ten types of basic hardboard are given in Table 16. These properties are established by tests conducted in accordance with ASTM D1037-64, *Standard Methods of Evaluating the Properties of Wood-base Fiber and Particle Panel Materials.*

Basic hardboard is manufactured in widths of 4 or 5 ft and in lengths to order. In practice, lengths vary from 3 to 10 ft in increments of 1 ft and from 10 to 16 ft in increments of 2 ft. Thicknesses vary from $\frac{1}{12}$ to 1 in. as shown in Table 16, which also shows the tolerances for thickness. Tolerances for length and width are $\pm \frac{1}{16}$ in. Tolerances for squareness and straightness are $\frac{1}{64}$ in. per foot of length or width. *Pre-finished hardboard wall paneling* can be

Table 16. Physical and mechanical properties of basic hardboard

Type designation	Surface	Nominal thickness designations, in.	Thickness limits (min–max avg per panel), in.*	Modulus of rupture (min avg per panel), psi*	Tensile strength (min avg per panel)		Water resistance	
					Parallel to surface, psi	Perpendicular to surface, psi	Water absorption (max per panel), per cent	Thickness swelling (max per panel), per cent
Tempered	S1S	$\frac{1}{12}$	0.070–0.090	7,000	3,500	150	30	25
		$\frac{1}{10}$	0.090–0.110				20	16
		$\frac{1}{8}$	0.115–0.155				15	11
		$\frac{3}{16}$	0.165–0.205				12	10
		$\frac{7}{32}$	0.205–0.250				12	10
		$\frac{1}{4}$	0.220–0.265				10	8
		$\frac{5}{16}$	0.290–0.335				8	8
		$\frac{3}{8}$	0.350–0.400				8	8
Tempered	S2S	$\frac{1}{10}$	0.090–0.110	7,000	3,500	150	25	20
		$\frac{1}{8}$	0.115–0.155				20	16
		$\frac{3}{16}$	0.165–0.205				18	15
		$\frac{7}{32}$	0.205–0.250				18	14
		$\frac{1}{4}$	0.220–0.265				12	11
		$\frac{5}{16}$	0.290–0.335				11	10
		$\frac{3}{8}$	0.350–0.400				10	9
Standard	S1S	$\frac{1}{12}$	0.070–0.090	5,000	2,500	100	35	30
		$\frac{1}{10}$	0.090–0.110				25	22
		$\frac{1}{8}$	0.115–0.155				20	16
		$\frac{3}{16}$	0.165–0.205				18	14
		$\frac{7}{32}$	0.205–0.250				18	14
		$\frac{1}{4}$	0.220–0.265				16	12
		$\frac{5}{16}$	0.290–0.335				14	10
		$\frac{3}{8}$	0.350–0.400				12	10
Standard	S2S	$\frac{1}{12}$	0.070–0.090	5,000	2,500	100	35	30
		$\frac{1}{10}$	0.090–0.110				30	25
		$\frac{1}{8}$	0.115–0.155				25	18
		$\frac{3}{16}$	0.165–0.205				25	18
		$\frac{7}{32}$	0.205–0.250				20	16
		$\frac{1}{4}$	0.220–0.265				18	14
		$\frac{5}{16}$	0.290–0.335				15	12
		$\frac{3}{8}$	0.350–0.400				12	10
Service-tempered	S1S	$\frac{1}{8}$	0.115–0.155	4,500	2,000	100	20	15
		$\frac{3}{16}$	0.165–0.205				18	13
		$\frac{7}{32}$	0.205–0.250				18	13
		$\frac{1}{4}$	0.220–0.265				15	13
		$\frac{3}{8}$	0.350–0.400				14	11

any basic hardboard type, with or without specially textured surfaces, on which one of a variety of finishes has been applied for decorative or utilitarian uses.

Finishes are classified on the basis of performance as follows:

Class I— A finish which has the highest degree of wear, stain, abrasion, and moisture resistance. Where additional hardness and scratch resistance are required, the finish is applied to tempered hardboard.

Class II— A finish which is resistant to most household stains, has a moderate degree of wear and abrasion resistance, and can be cleaned with soap and water. It is usually applied to standard and service type hardboard. This finish is not recommended for long exposures to high heat, steam, or high humidity conditions.

Finishes are required to be "commercially free" from the following appearance defects: orange peel, waviness, sagging, uneven coating distribution, scratches, pin and pit holes, dirt specks. Finishes must be tested for the following properties, in accordance with the appropriate ASTM tests: adhesion, washability, scrape adhesion, fade resistance, flame spread, steam resistance, heat resistance, high humidity resistance, abrasion resistance, and stain resistance against the following staining agents: trisodium phosphate, mineral oil, nail polish remover, household bleach (5.5 per cent sodium hypochlorite), alcohol (190 proof), homogenized milk, household ammonia (10 percent), carbonated cola drink, reconstituted lemon juice (10 percent citric acid), nonsmearing lipstick, china-marking pencil, and freshbrewed strong coffee. Class I finishes should show no effect from any of the staining agents or from steam and no more than a slight color change from heat or high humidity.

Pre-finished hardboard wall paneling is available in widths of 4 and 5 ft, lengths of 5, 6, 7, 8, 9, and 10 ft, and thicknesses $\frac{1}{8}$, $\frac{3}{16}$, $\frac{7}{32}$, and $\frac{1}{4}$ in. Tolerance on length and width is $\frac{1}{16}$ in.; tolerance on thickness is as shown in Table 16.

Hardboard siding is basic hardboard adapted for use as siding on buildings; it is available unfinished or with the exposed surface and edges factory primed. It may have one side embossed or machined with a pattern or texture.

Unfinished hardboard siding must have the physical and mechanical properties shown in Table 17. Factory-primed siding must have these same properties and in addition those properties listed in Table 18.

Lap siding is available in lengths of 8 to 16 ft in increments of 2 ft, in widths up to 12 in., and in thicknesses of $\frac{3}{8}$ and $\frac{7}{16}$ in. Panel siding is available in lengths

Table 16 (cont.). Physical and mechanical properties of basic hardboard

Type designation	Surface	Nominal thickness designations, in.	Thickness limits (min–max avg per panel), in.*	Modulus of rupture (min avg per panel), psi*	Tensile strength (min avg per panel)		Water resistance	
					Parallel to surface, psi	Perpendicular to surface, psi	Water absorption (max per panel), per cent	Thickness swelling (max per panel), per cent
Service-tempered	S2S	$\frac{1}{8}$	0.115–0.155	4,500	2,000	100	25	22
		$\frac{3}{16}$	0.165–0.205				20	18
		$\frac{7}{32}$	0.205–0.250				20	16
		$\frac{1}{4}$	0.220–0.265				18	14
		$\frac{3}{8}$	0.350–0.400				18	14
Service	S1S	$\frac{1}{8}$	0.115–0.155	3,000	1,500	75	30	25
		$\frac{3}{16}$	0.165–0.205				25	15
		$\frac{7}{32}$	0.205–0.250				25	15
		$\frac{1}{4}$	0.220–0.265				25	15
		$\frac{3}{8}$	0.350–0.400				25	15
		$\frac{7}{16}$	0.410–0.460				25	15
Service	S2S	$\frac{1}{8}$	0.115–0.155	3,000	1,500	75	30	25
		$\frac{3}{16}$	0.165–0.205				27	22
		$\frac{7}{32}$	0.205–0.250				27	22
		$\frac{1}{4}$	0.220–0.265				27	22
		$\frac{3}{8}$	0.350–0.400				27	22
		$\frac{7}{16}$	0.410–0.460				27	22
		$\frac{1}{2}$	0.475–0.525				18	14
		$\frac{5}{8}$	0.600–0.650				15	12
		$\frac{11}{16}$	0.660–0.710				15	12
		$\frac{3}{4}$	0.725–0.775				12	9
		$\frac{13}{16}$	0.785–0.835				12	9
		$\frac{7}{8}$	0.850–0.900				12	9
		1	0.975–1.025				12	9
Industrialite	S1S or S2S	$\frac{3}{8}$	0.350–0.400	2,000	1,000	35	25	20
		$\frac{7}{16}$	0.410–0.460				25	20
		$\frac{1}{2}$	0.475–0.525				25	20
		$\frac{5}{8}$	0.600–0.650				22	18
		$\frac{11}{16}$	0.660–0.710				22	18
		$\frac{3}{4}$	0.725–0.775				20	16
		$\frac{13}{16}$	0.785–0.835				20	16
		$\frac{7}{8}$	0.850–0.900				20	16
		1	0.975–1.025				20	16

Minimum or maximum average per panel is the lowest or the highest allowable value an individual panel can have when all test values for the given property of an individual panel have been averaged.

Table 17. Physical and mechanical properties of unfinished hardboard siding*†

						Water resistance	
Impact, min value, in.	Hardness, min value, lb	Modulus of rupture, min avg per panel, psi	Nailhead pull thru, min value, lb	Lateral nail resistance, min value, lb	Weather-ability, max value, in.	Water absorption, max per panel, per cent	Thickness swelling, max per panel, per cent
9	450	1800	150	150	0.010 Swelling and no visible fiber raising	20	15

These requirements apply only to hardboard siding used as a siding material and do not apply to hardboard combined with other materials as a siding.

† Each manufacturer, after establishing his siding manufacturing specifications and prior to marketing siding, shall test representative samples in accordance with the ASTM D 1037-64, Accelerated Aging test method and determine that his siding, after cycling, retains 50 per cent of the original modulus of rupture when calculated on the basis of the original board thickness.

Table 18. Physical properties of factory-primed hardboard siding

Water resistance			
Water absorption, max. per panel, per cent	Thickness Swelling, max. per panel, per cent	Minimum Sealing	Weatherability of prime coat
15	10	No visible flatting	No visible fiber raising, checking, erosion, or flaking

of 4, 6, 7, 8, 9, 10, 12, and 16 ft, width of 4 ft, and thicknesses of ¼, ⅜, and ⁷⁄₁₆ in. Thickness tolerances are as follows:

  ¼ in.—0.220–0.265 in.
  ⅜ in.—0.325–0.375 in.
  ⁷⁄₁₆ in.—0.376–0.450 in.

In addition to the standard products described above, manufacturers produce a wide variety of special products. Some of these are among the most widely used types of hardboard.

Underlayment is a basic hardboard meeting the strength requirements of ⁷⁄₃₂ and ¼ in. Service type, planed or sanded on one side to a thickness of 0.215 ± 0.005 in. It is used primarily as an underlay for linoleum, asphalt tile, plastic tile, and similar resilient flooring materials. It is usually

available in 3 × 4 and 4 × 4 ft sizes.

Concrete forms are made of tempered hardboard, ¼ in. thick, which has been given additional processing to provide maximum performance when used as panels and liners in concrete form work.

Door panels: Hardboard ⅛ in. thick is extensively used for the faces of hollow-core flush doors and, in thicknesses of ³⁄₁₆ or ¼ in., for inserts for panel doors.

Cores for high-pressure plastic laminates are characterized by high perpendicular tensile strength and a very smooth surface. Cores for low-pressure plastic sheets and wood veneer have to have good perpendicular tensile strength, machinability, and a smooth surface.

Laminated hardboard consists of two or

more panels of hardboard laminated together. It is manufactured to obtain greater thickness or two smooth surfaces.

Perforated hardboard is a basic hardboard, plain or decorated, which has punched or drilled holes spaced 1 in. on center or, on special order, ½ in. on center. The diameter of the holes is ³⁄₁₆ in. on ⅛-in. board and ⁹⁄₃₂ in. on ¼-in. board. These boards are used as decoration and also, with specially designed hangers, to provide flexible and decorative wall mounting and storage facilities. When backed with a 1- or 2-in.-thick glass-fiber blanket of ¾ lb per cu ft density, the perforated board has a noise-reduction coefficient ranging from 0.60 to 0.75, depending upon the thickness of the blanket and the spacing of the holes (Fig. 25).

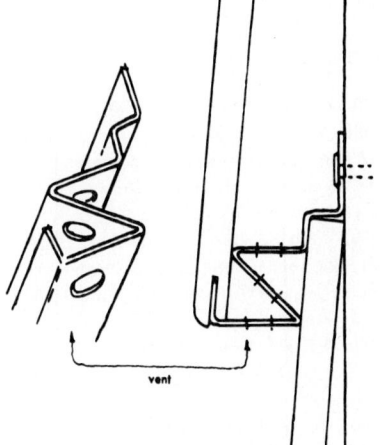

Fig. 26. Hardboard siding attached by means of aluminum strip

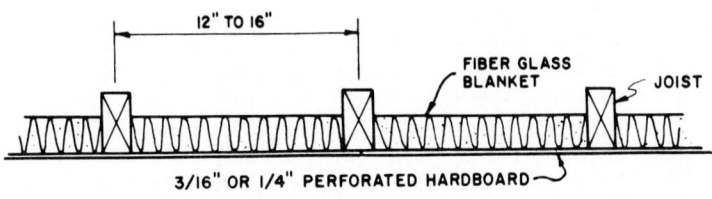

Fig. 25. Perforated hardboard used as an acoustical ceiling

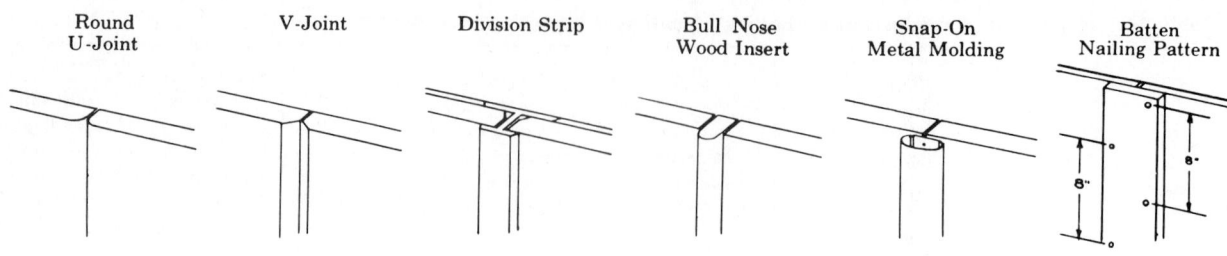

Round U-Joint V-Joint Division Strip Bull Nose Wood Insert Snap-On Metal Molding Batten Nailing Pattern

Fig. 27. Hardboard joint treatments

Embossed or machined patterns include simulated leather, wood graining, basketweave, fluting, striation, and probably the most widely used of all— scoring in 4-in. squares simulating wall tile. This latter pattern then receives a Class I decorative finish, as described above, and is then generally called tile board.

Decorative overlaid board. This is hardboard on which a film or sheet has been laminated; it may be of a solid color or of simulated wood grain or other design.

Prefinishing. Various manufacturers offer partially or fully prefinished products. Factory-sealed, filled, primed, or coated hardboard panels are available as well as fully prefinished hardboard siding.

Super high-density hardboard is usually in the density range from 80 to 90 pcf and is available from the manufacturer in heavier thicknesses and in single or multiple plies laminated with a reinforced thermosetting bond. It is usually smooth on two sides (S2S) and given various treatments during manufacture for special electrical and machining properties. It is also usually characterized by hard surfaces, low water absorption, and high modulus of rupture.

APPLICATION

Workability: Hardboard may be cut, drilled, routed, shaped, or fastened with the usual carpenter's tools but power tools can do an even better job. Carbide-tipped saw blades are recommended. Twist high-speed drills perform better than auger bits; for routing and shaping, high-speed equipment with high-speed steel bits should be used.

Nailing (see Table 19): Drive nails perpendicular to panel surface, nailing center of panel first and edges last. Nails should penetrate 1 in. into backing material on interior applications and 1½ in. on exterior applications. Space 8 in. on center on intermediate supports and 4 in. at edges.

Edge clearance should be ¼ to ⅜ in. minimum. Do not toenail or nail into the edge.

Screws: Predrill holes and countersink for flathead screws that are long enough to penetrate 1 in. into supports. Sheet metal screws and bolts also hold well.

Staples: Divergent chisel-point staples (⅞ in.) driven with a power stapler or air gun may be used.

Clips designed for the particular application are often shipped by the manufacturer with decorated board to permit concealment of the fasteners and alignment of the joints.

Adhesives, for interior applications only, may be waterproof tile or linoleum adhesive, or contact cement. When attaching to a solid surface, apply adhesive with a notched trowel over the entire surface. Contact cement should be applied to both surfaces and may be used to apply board directly to wood framing.

Bending: The minimum radii of bends depend upon the thickness of the board, the density, the side exposed, and the method of bending. A ¾-in. radius is possible when using some 1/10-in. boards, but a radius of 7 to 12 in. is more common (see manufacturers' literature for recommendations for their board). Cold dry bends are made only over permanently supported framework. Cold moist bends can be made around a pattern and allowed to dry, using the soaking or wetting method to make the board more pliable.

Conditioning: The moisture content of hardboard varies with humidity conditions, as do other cellulose products. Conditioning, by allowing the board to adapt to prevailing humidities or, in the case of exterior applications, by wetting the back side of the board and letting it stand for 24 hours before application, is recommended.

Backing: Over open framing 16 in. on center, use a 3/16, ¼, or 5/16-in. thickness;

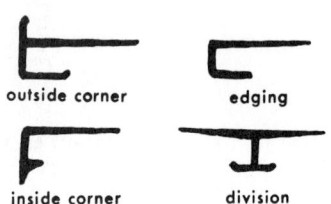

outside corner edging

inside corner division

Fig. 28. Metal moldings for the attachment of hardboard

thinner boards should be applied over solid backing of wood, plywood, gypsum board, or plaster. Masonry exterior walls should be dampproofed and furred before applying hardboard; a vapor barrier is also desirable.

Joint treatments: Many joint treatments are possible using the square-edge boards (Fig. 27). Do not butt joints tightly; allow some space between panels—at least 1/16 in. for exterior panels. Manufacturers provide machined tongue-and-groove and shiplap joints for panel and plank edges, or metal moldings may be used, either plain or decorated to match the hardboard (Fig. 28).

Perforated board: To receive the hangers designed for use with perforated board, space them away from solid backing at least ¼ in. for ⅛-in. board and ½ in. for ¼-in. board.

Finishing: Every type of finish suitable for wood can be used with hardboard. These include oil and rubber-base paints, lacquer, enamels, penetrating sealers (for floors and work surfaces), stains, water-emulsion paints, varnish, shellac, and wax, when applied in accordance with manufacturers' recommendations. Finishes may be applied with brush, roller, or spray. Primers are recommended for most finishes, especially oil and enamel paints. Most latex paints are good sealers. Enamel undercoaters and alkyd-base primers and sealers are usually satisfactory. Clear filler-sealers, not varnish, resin, or penetrating-type, may be used as primers. Varnish should be applied over a sealer only.

Table 19. Application of hardboard

Courtesy Georgia-Pacific Plywood Company

Application	Type of hardboard	Maximum open framing, in.	Thickness, in.	Nail spacing		Fastening methods: any of the following for these hardboard applications
				Intermediate supports, in.	Around edges, in.	
Interior walls and ceilings	Standard, tempered	Solid backing, 16	⅛ ³⁄₁₆ ¼	8 8 8	4 4 4	Nails: 1¼" casing 1½" casing 1¼" finishing 1½" finishing 1¼" countersunk 1¼" box 1¼" 18 gage brads
	Factory-finished hardboard					
	Perforated hardboard (leave ⅜" or more open space between hardboard and wall)	16 16 16	⅛ ³⁄₁₆ ¼	8 8 8	4 4 4	Adhesives: The following waterproof adhesives may be used when applied according to manufacturers' recommendations: linoleum cement tileboard cement contact cement
Underlayment (floor)	Underlayment hardboard		0.215	6	4	Nails: 1¼" drive screws (flat head) 1¼" ring-grooved
Finish flooring	Tempered hardboard		¼	12	6	Nails: 1¼" coated casing
Protected exteriors	Standard or tempered hardboard	16	¼	6	4	Nails: 1¾" box, siding, or sinker
Panel siding	(With or without sheathing)					Nails: 2¼" galvanized siding 2¼" galvanized box
	Tempered hardboard, grooved or ungrooved	16	⅜	8	4	
Lap siding	(With or without sheathing)					Nails: galvanized siding galvanized box 2" where wood, plywood, or no sheathing is used 2½" over all other types of sheathing
	Tempered hardboard, 12" or 16" wide	16	⅜	16 along bottom edge into studs		

Particle board

By SIDNEY M. SHELOV, *AIA*

Particle board consists of particles of wood bonded together with synthetic resin or other binder. Particles are classified for size, dried to a uniform moisture content, mat-formed, compressed to a uniform density, and cured under heat and pressure. Some manufacturers make a three-ply board with outer layers made of finely cut flakes to provide smooth hard surfaces and a core of more coarsely cut material. Additives to impart greater dimensional stability, fire resistance, resistance to fungi and insects, or other desired properties may be incorporated in the board at the time of manufacture.

Particle board has the following characteristics: uniformity of thickness and density, freedom from knots and other defects, no grain, no warp, dimensional stability (compared to wood), excellent glue-bond surface, high nail- and screw-holding ability, resistance to indentation, and ease of workability with standard woodworking tools.

The principal use of particle board is as core stock for high-pressure plastic laminates and hardwood veneers. As core stock it is used by manufacturers of furniture, cabinets, countertops, wall paneling, partitions, and doors of all types.

Edge banding may be done with high-pressure laminates, metal or wood strips or moldings, or wood veneers, or the edges may be filled for staining, lacquering, or painting (Fig. 29). Raw edges should not be exposed to moisture, wear, or abrasion.

Particle board is also used with clear or stained finishes or, when the surface is filled with wood paste or other filler (factory-applied in some cases), it may be painted for paneling, shelving, and doors. In this form it is often used for sliding closet doors (Fig. 31) and demountable office partitions with wood or metal framing members (Fig. 32).

Particle board is usually made in panels measuring 4 ft in width by 8 ft or more in length and in thicknesses ranging from $\frac{1}{8}$ in. to 2 in. in increments of $\frac{1}{16}$ or $\frac{1}{8}$ in. Tolerances for length and width are $\pm \frac{1}{16}$ in., for thickness, $\pm \frac{1}{64}$ in.

The National Particleboard Association has established industry standards (CS236–66) for various types of particleboard and the physical properties for each type (Table 20). There are two use types (interior and exterior), three density grades, and two strength classes. Conformance to the standards is determined by tests carried out in accordance with ASTM D 1037–64.

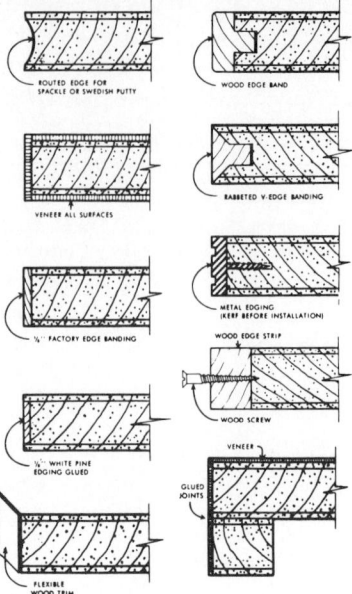

Fig. 29. Edge treatments

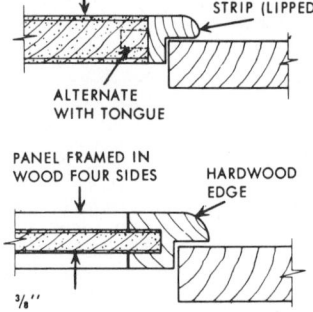

Fig. 30. Cabinet door edges

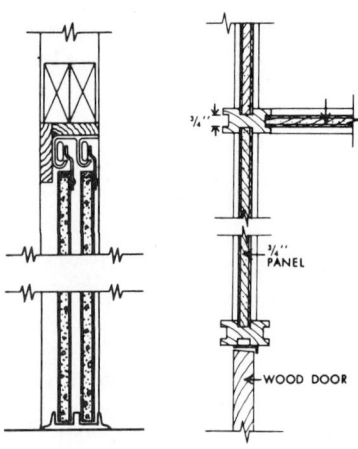

Fig. 31. Sliding closet doors   **Fig. 32. Movable partitions**

Table 20. Physical properties* of particle board

Type (use)	Density (grade) min avg	Class§	Modulus of rupture, min avg, psi	Modulus of elasticity, min avg, psi	Internal bond, min avg, psi	Linear expansion, max avg, per cent	Screw holdings Face, min avg, lb	Edge, min avg, lb
1†	A: (high density, 50 pcf and over)	1	2,400	350,000	200	0.55	450	
		2	3,400	350,000	140	0.55		
	B: medium density, between 37 and 50 pcf	1	1,600	250,000	70	0.35	225	160
		2	2,400	400,000	60	0.30	225	200
	C: low density, 37 pcf and under	1	800	150,000	20	0.30	125	
		2	1,400	250,000	30	0.30	175	
2‡	A: (high density, 50 pcf and over)	1	2,400	350,000	125	0.55	450	
		2	3,400	500,000	400	0.55	500	350
	B: (medium density, between 37 and 50 pcf)	1	1,800	250,000	65	0.35	225	160
		2	2,500	450,000	60	0.25	250	200

* *Tested in accordance with ASTM D-1037-64.*
† *Type 1: Mat-formed particle board (generally made with urea-formaldehyde resin binders) suitable for interior applications.*
‡ *Type 2: Mat-formed particle board made with durable and highly moisture- and heat-resistant binders (generally phenolic resins) suitable for interior and certain exterior applications when so labeled.*
§ *Class: Strength classifications based on properties of panels currently produced.*

Plastic laminate is a hard, durable surfacing material which is resistant to moisture, heat, and most chemicals. It is extensively used for the tops of tables, desks, bars, and counters, and for kitchen and bathroom cabinets, shower and tub enclosures, wall paneling and doors.

High-pressure laminates consist of 8 to 10 layers of resin-impregnated papers converted by heat and pressure into a plastic-like material. The face is a transparent sheet of melamine-treated paper; the second layer is the pattern or color sheet, also melamine-impregnated; the balance of the plies are phenolic resin-impregnated kraft papers. Press heat of approximately 265 to 305°F and pressures of 800 to 1200 lb/in.² for periods of 60 to 90 minutes effect the conversion.

Under the standard of the National Electric Manufacturers Association, NEMA LD 3-1975 (Revised 1978), high-pressure decorative laminates are produced in seven types:

1. *General-purpose type* laminate is designed for both horizontal and vertical applications where good appearance, durability, resistance to stains and resistance to heat up to 275°F are required.
2. *Postforming-type* laminate is similar to the general-purpose type but can be thermoformed under controlled temperature and pressure in accordance with the manufacturer's recommendations.
3. *Cabinet-liner-type* laminate is a backing material which has a color or pattern sheet to enhance its appearance and which is intended for use in cabinet interiors.
4. *Backer-type* laminate is a high-pressure laminate without a decorative face intended for use as a balancing back in panel construction.
5. *Specific-purpose-type* laminate is similar to the general-purpose type but provides improved physical properties.
6. *High-wear-type* laminate is similar to the general-purpose type but provides exceptionally high surface wear resistance.
7. *Fire-rated-type* laminate is similar to the general-purpose type in surface properties, but provides lower fire-hazard characteristics as determined by the test methods required by the authority having jurisdiction.

The seven types and their thicknesses and some of their properties are given in Table 21. The standard describes tests for a total of fifteen properties and specifies minimum performance requirements for each.

High-pressure laminates are made in three surface finishes varying only in the degree of gloss: satin finish, furniture finish, and gloss finish.

High-pressure laminate has one wood-like characteristic: grain. The grain (called "machine direction" or MD) is determined by the direction in which the paper was made. Like wood, plastic laminates shrink and swell with changes in humidity and this movement is greatest across the grain ("cross-machine direction" or CD).

High-pressure laminates are surfacing materials only and are normally applied by adhesive to a substrate. Adhesives used are of the following types:

Urea formaldehyde—satisfactory for most uses; may be hot-pressed or room-temperature bonded.

Resorcinol and phenol-resorcinol—recommended for use where high water and heat resistance are required; hot or room-temperature bonding.

Casein—generally satisfactory for use under dry conditions; room-temperature bonding only.

Epoxy—no volatile components, therefore recommended for bonding to impervious substrates such as metal; hot or room-temperature bonding.

Polyvinyl acetate (PVA)—satisfactory for use where resistance to water and high heat are not required, such as furniture, cabinets, office partitions; not recommended for sink tops; room-temperature bonding only.

Contact—suitable for room-temperature bonding to all substrates including metal; does not restrict the movement of the laminate caused by changes of humidity to the same extent as the "rigid" adhesives.

Substrates or cores most commonly used are particle board and plywood; hardboard and metal are sometimes used. Particle board, in 40-lb density, is recommended for most uses. Hardwood-faced plywood may be used where additional strength is required; for use under conditions of high moisture, exterior-type plywood should be used. Rotary-cut Douglas fir plywood is not recommended because the pronounced grain pattern sometimes "telegraphs" through the face of the laminate. Neither gypsum board nor plaster is recommended as a substrate.

Laminate-faced panels should be balanced by a backing-type laminate adhered to the back of the substrate. The backing laminate should be the same thickness as

Table 21. Types and properties of high-pressure laminates

(from NEMA LD3-1975 (revised 1978)

Types	Nominal thickness, in.	Wear resistance, cycles (min)	Impact resistance, in. (min)	Dimensional change*	
				% MD (max)	% CD (max)
General-purpose	0.050	400	50	0.5	0.9
General-purpose	0.038	400	35	0.6	1.0
General-purpose†	0.028	200	20	0.7	1.2
General-purpose†	0.022	200	15	0.8	1.3
Postforming‡	0.042	400	30	1.1	1.4
Postforming†‡	0.030	300	20	1.1	1.4
Postforming†‡	0.022	200	15	1.1	1.4
Cabinet liner	0.020	50	10	1.2	2.0
Backer	0.020	—	—	—	—
Backer	0.050	—	—	—	—
Specific-purpose	0.125	400	75	0.3	0.7
Specific-purpose	0.062	400	55	0.5	0.9
High-wear	0.120	3000	75	0.3	0.7
High-wear	0.080	3000	40	0.4	0.8
High-wear	0.062	3000	35	0.5	0.9
Fire-rated§	0.062	400	55	0.5	0.9
Fire-rated§	0.050	400	45	0.5	0.9
Fire-rated§	0.032	300	20	0.7	1.2

* *See discussion in text.*
† *Not recommended for all applications; consult the manufacturer for recommended uses.*
‡ *Minimum bending radius: 0.042–⅝ in.; 0.030–½ in.; 0.022–⅜ in.*
§ *Consult the manufacturer for specific flame resistance properties such as flame spread rating, fuel contribution values, and smoke generation characteristics since these NEMA Standards do not specify these properties.*

the face and the machine direction of the two laminates should be parallel.

Panel edges are most commonly finished with strips of laminate, applied by hand or by special edge-banding machine. The use of thinner material (0.038 or 0.028 in.) is recommended in order to minimize the exposure of the inner plies of the laminate. Mitering of the face and edge laminates is not recommended. It is very difficult to do and if successfully achieved it results in both an edge so sharp as to be dangerous and one that is easily damaged.

Natural wood edges are often used, either for design contrast, or where the edge will be subjected to severe service, since wood can be easily repaired or refinished. Typical wood edge details are shown in Fig.

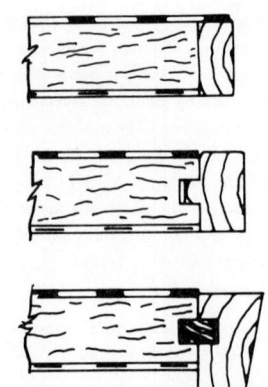

Fig. 33. Typical wood edge details

Inside band   Outside band

Fig. 34. One-piece postformed countertop

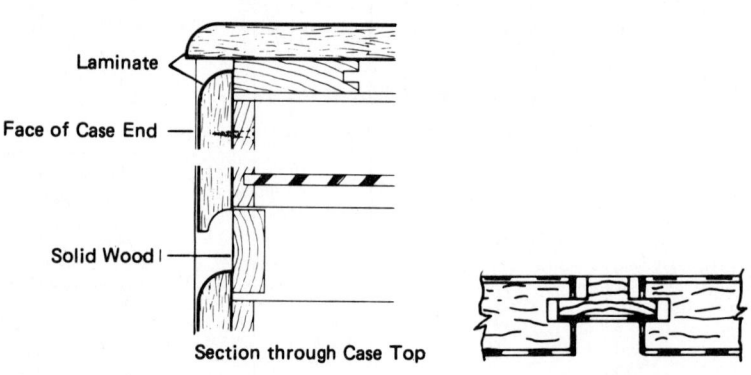

Laminate

Face of Case End

Solid Wood

Section through Case Top

Fig. 35. Postformed desk top and drawer fronts

Fig. 36. Expansion joint for long vertical panels

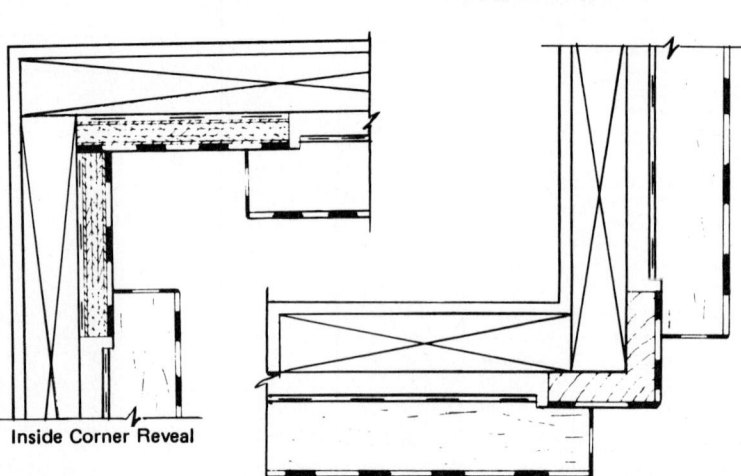

Inside Corner Reveal

Outside Corner Reveal

Fig. 38. Corner details, wall panels

(All figures courtesy Architectural Woodwork Institute)

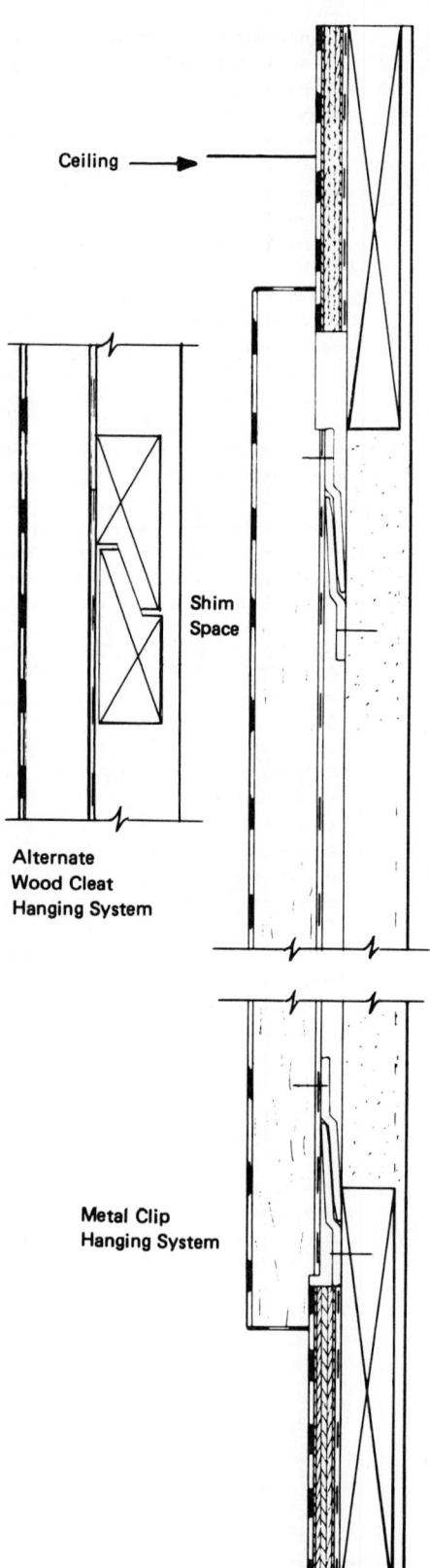

Ceiling

Shim Space

Alternate Wood Cleat Hanging System

Metal Clip Hanging System

Fig. 37. Method of installing wall panels

33. Note that in each case a completely flush surface with the laminate is avoided. This permits the wood to be sanded without scratching the laminate and also visually delineates the wood finish from the laminate surface.

High-pressure laminates are being increasingly used in cabinet work of all types. The most practical cabinet design is that in which the doors and drawer fronts overlay the frame (see "Types of Casework" in the section on Wood). Avoid if possible the "exposed face frame" type. Laminate thickness for vertical surfaces can be 0.038 or 0.028 in.; for counter tops it must be 0.050 in. general-purpose type (Fig. 34) or 0.042 in. postforming type (Fig. 34). Postformed edges can be used for doors and drawer fronts where a curved edge is acceptable (Fig. 35). If extensive areas are to be laminate covered, such as counter fronts exceeding 96 in. in length, an expansion joint should be provided (Fig. 36).

High-pressure laminates used for wall paneling require maximum flatness and dimensional stability. For this purpose the following measures are recommended:

1. Minimum core thickness should be ¾ in.
2. For panel widths of 24 in or less laminate thickness of 0.038 cr 0.028 in. may be used. For wider panels 0.050 in. thickness must be used. Balancing backing sheet of same thickness as face must be used.
3. To permit free panel movement and avoid visible fastenings, panels should be hung from metal clips or interlocking wood cleats, as shown in Fig. 37. Joints between panels and at corners should be similarly treated with reveals (Fig. 38).

PLYWOOD

The following information has been derived from PS1-74 and from the following publications of the American Plywood Association: *Plywood Construction Guide*, Y300, 1978; *Plywood Design Specifications*, Y510, Revised 1978.

Plywood is made of an odd number of layers of thin wood (veneer) bonded together in such a way that the direction of the grain of adjacent layers is at right angles. The outside plies are called faces (or face and back), and the center ply (or plies) is called the core. In the case of five or more ply construction, the inner plies that are bonded directly and at right angles to the faces are called crossbands. Faces and crossbands are usually veneer, while the core

may be of veneer, lumber, or other material (see Fig. 39).

The principal advantages of plywood as compared with solid wood are (1) equalization of the strength along the length and across the width of the panel; (2) equalization and reduction of dimensional changes due to moisture; (3) greater resistance to checking, splitting, and warping; (4) reduction in construction labor, weight, and thickness resulting from the availability of wood in wallboard form. The greater the number of plies for a given total thickness, the more nearly equal are the strength and shrinkage properties along and across the panel and the greater is the resistance to splitting. Resistance to warping or twisting is the result of *balanced construction*, which means that the plies are arranged in matching pairs on either side of the core; this is why plywood normally consists of an odd number of plies.

Plywood, like other forms of wood, is divided into softwood and hardwood, which are defined as the wood from coniferous and broad-leafed trees, respectively. This division has resulted in two separate plywood industries, each with its own standards and trade associations. In general, the softwood plywood industry is located on the West Coast; its principal product is rotary-cut Douglas fir, and its end use is predominantly structural. The hardwood plywood industry is located generally in the South and Middle West; its products include a wide variety of species and cuts, and their end use is principally for furniture, wall paneling, and doors.

SOFTWOOD

Practically all softwood plywood is manufactured from softwood species growing in the northwestern section of the United States and Western Canada. Softwood plywood is covered by ANSI/Voluntary Product Standard PS1-74, "Construction and Industrial Plywood," sponsored by American Plywood Association and developed in cooperation with National Bureau of Standards.

The major uses for softwood plywood, particularly Douglas fir, are structural. Its use as a finishing material is increasing, especially where structural and finish functions are combined. Manufacturing emphasis is being placed upon factory finishing techniques to make it more attractive as a finish material.

Structurally, plywood is employed where its large sheet size may function advantageously to brace the structure and to reduce the labor of installation. Among such uses are as sheathing on walls and roofs, as subfloors, as panel faces, and as

concrete forms. It is also used as an underlayment for resilient flooring and wall-to-wall carpeting, and as a backing for ceramic and other tiles on floors and walls. It is employed extensively in cabinetwork and as shelving.

Softwood plywood is manufactured in two *types* and six *grades*. Type is determined by the glue bond and grade by the quality of the veneers used.

TYPE

Plywood is manufactured in two basic types: exterior type with 100 per cent waterproof glueline and interior type with either water-resistant (interior) or waterproof (exterior) glue. Most interior-type panels are

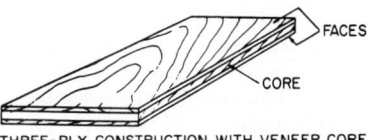

THREE-PLY CONSTRUCTION WITH VENEER CORE.

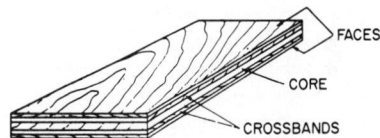

FIVE-PLY CONSTRUCTION WITH VENEER CORE.

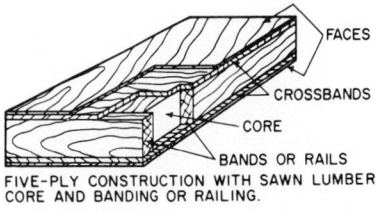

FIVE-PLY CONSTRUCTION WITH SAWN LUMBER CORE AND BANDING OR RAILING.

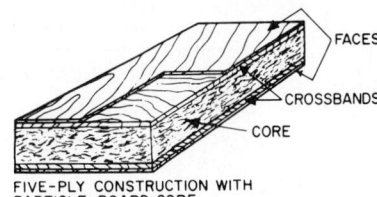

FIVE-PLY CONSTRUCTION WITH PARTICLE-BOARD CORE.

Fig. 39. Typical plywood constructions

Courtesy of Hardwood Plywood Institute

manufactured with exterior glue. These may be used for applications subject to temporary exposure to moisture or high humidity. However, because the grade of veneer used for backs and inner plies of interior-type panels may affect glueline performance, only exterior-type plywood should be used for permanent exposure to moisture or the weather.

GRADE

Within each type of plywood is a variety of plywood grades. These are generally identified in terms of the veneer grade used on the face and back of the panel, e.g., C-D, A-B, etc. Veneer grades define appearance of the panel in terms of allowable numbers and sizes of repairs that may be made in veneers during manufacture, and natural unrepaired growth characteristics. (See Table 22.) The best looking veneer grades are N and A. The minimum grade of veneer permitted in exterior type plywood is C grade. D-grade veneer is used only for backs and inner plies of interior type plywood.

Although all softwood plywood grades have structural properties, panel grades fall into two general categories: "appearance" grades and "engineered" grades. (See Tables 23 and 24.) Plywood siding and sanded plywood comprise the appearance grades. These are designed for use where, as the name suggests, appearance is an important consideration. The engineered grades, on the other hand, are the workhorse grades, those used for concrete forming, sheathing, subflooring and other applications where bending strength and stiffness are of greater importance than appearance.

GROUP NUMBER

Plywood may be manufactured from over 70 species of wood. These species are divided on the basis of strength and stiffness into five Groups under U.S. Product Standard PS 1. Strongest woods are in Group 1; the next strongest in Group 2, and so on. The Group number that appears in some APA grade-trademarks is based on the species used for face and back veneers. Where face and back veneers are not from the same species Group, the higher Group number is used, except for sanded and decorative panels ⅜ in. thich or less. These are identified by face species because they are chosen primarily for appearance and used in applications where structural integrity is not critical. Some species are used widely in plywood manufacture, others rarely. Check local availability if a particular species is desired.

SPAN RATINGS

Identification Index

The *Identification Index* is the set of two numbers separated by a slash that appears in the grade-trademark on C-D Interior, C-D Interior with exterior glue (CDX), C-C Exterior and Structural I and II C-D and C-C sheathing grades. The left-hand number indicates the maximum recommended center-to-center spacing of supports in inches when the panel is used for roof decking with *face grain across supports*. The right-hand number indicates the maximum recommended spacing of supports in inches when the panel is used for subflooring in double-layer construction with *face grain across supports*.

A panel marked 32/16, for example, may be used for roof decking over supports 32 in. o.c. or for subflooring over supports 16 in. o.c. In all cases, plywood is assumed continuous over two or more spans.

The Identification Index numbers are based on both panel thickness and the species group used for face and back. Since properties vary with each group, the same index number may appear on panels of different thickness. For example, 24/0 appears on both ⅜-in. and ½-in. C-D INT sheathing because, in the latter, species of lower strength and stiffness have been used on the face and back. Conversely, panels of the same thickness may be marked with as many as three different index numbers. For example, ⅜-in. C-D INT may be marked 16/0, 20/0, or 24/0, depending on the species used on the face and back. The higher the index number, the greater the strength and stiffness.

Span Index

The *Span Index* — or maximum recommended spacing of supports—is the number that appears in the grade-trademark on APA Sturd-I-Floor® and 303® Siding panels. Sturd-I-Floor panels are designed specifically for single-floor (combined subfloor-underlayment) applications and are manufactured with Span Indexes of 16, 20, 24 and 48 in. Sturd-I-Floor panels in a given thickness may be manufactured in more than one Span Index. (See Table 25.) Panels with a Span Index greater than the actual joist spacing may be substituted for panels of the same thickness with a Span Index matching the actual joist spacing. For example, 19/32-in.-thick Sturd-I-Floor 20 o.c. may be substituted for 19/32-in.-thick Sturd-I-Floor 16 o.c. over joists 16 in. o.c.

APA 303 Sidings are produced with Span Indexes of 16 and 24 in. and may be used direct to studs or over nonstructural sheathing (Sturd-I-Wall construction), or over nailable plywood or lumber sheathing (conventional construction). Panels with a Span Index of 16 in. may be applied vertically to studs spaced 16 in. o.c. Panels bearing a Span Index of 24 in. may be used vertically over studs 24 in. o.c. All 303 Siding panels may be applied horizontally direct to studs 16 or 24 in. o.c., provided horizontal joints are blocked. When 303 Siding is used over nailable plywood or lumber sheathing, the Span Index refers to the maximum recommended spacing of vertical rows of nails rather than to stud spacing.

Note: Spacings referred to in the Identification and Span Indexes are accepted by most major building codes. Local interpretations may vary, however, so make sure your construction complies with your local code.

Table 22. Veneer grades

N	Smooth surface "natural finish" veneer. Select, all heartwood or all sapwood. Free of open defects. Allows not more than 6 repairs, wood only, per 4 x 8 panel, made parallel to grain and well matched for grain and color.
A	Smooth, paintable. Not more than 18 neatly made repairs, boat, sled, or router type, and parallel to grain, permitted. May be used for natural finish in less demanding applications.
B	Solid surface. Shims, circular repair plugs and tight knots to 1 in. across grain permitted. Some minor splits permitted.
C Plugged	Improved C veneer with splits limited to ⅛-in. width and knotholes and borer holes limited to ¼ x ½ in. Admits some broken grain. Synthetic repairs permitted.
C	Tight knots to 1½ in. Knotholes to 1 in. across grain and some to 1½ in. if total width of knots and knotholes is within specified limits. Synthetic or wood repairs. Discoloration and sanding defects that do not impair strength permitted. Limited splits allowed. Stitching permitted.
D	Knots and knotholes to 2½-in. width across grain and ½ in. larger within specified limits. Limited splits are permitted. Stitching permitted. Limited to interior grades of plywood.

Table 23 Guide to appearance grades of plywood*

(Specific grades and thicknesses may be in locally limited supply. See your dealer before specifying.)

Type	Grade designation†	Description and most common uses	Face	Inner plies	Back	Most common thicknesses (inch)					
Interior Type	N-N, N-A, N-B INT-APA	Cabinet quality. For natural finish furniture, cabinet doors, built-ins, etc. Special order items.	N	C	N,A, or B						¾
	N-D-INT-APA	For natural finish paneling. Special order item.	N	D	D	¼					
	A-A INT-APA	For applications with both sides on view, built-ins, cabinets, furniture, partitions. Smooth face; suitable for painting.	A	D	A	¼		⅜	½	⅝	¾
	A-B INT-APA	Use where appearance of one side is less important but where two solid surfaces are necessary.	A	D	B	¼		⅜	½	⅝	¾
	A-D INT-APA	Use where appearance of only one side is important. Paneling, built-ins, shelving, partitions, flow racks.	A	D	D	¼		⅜	½	⅝	¾
	B-B INT-APA	Utility panel with two solid sides. Permits circular plugs.	B	D	B	¼		⅜	½	⅝	¾
	B-D INT-APA	Utility panel with one solid side. Good for backing, sides of built-ins, industry shelving, slip sheets, separator boards, bins.	B	D	D	¼		⅜	½	⅝	¾
	DECORATIVE PANELS–APA	Rough-sawn, brushed, grooved, or striated faces. For paneling, interior accent walls, built-ins, counter facing, displays, exhibits.	C or btr.	D	D		5⁄16	⅜	½	⅝	
	PLYRON INT-APA	Hardboard face on both sides. For counter tops, shelving, cabinet doors, flooring. Faces tempered, untempered, smooth, or screened.		C & D					½	⅝	¾
Exterior Type	A-A EXT-APA	Use where appearance of both sides is important. Fences, built-ins, signs, boats, cabinets, commercial refrigerators, shipping containers, tote boxes, tanks, ducts.‡	A	C	A	¼		⅜	½	⅝	¾
	A-B EXT-APA	Use where the appearance of one side is less important.‡	A	C	B	¼		⅜	½	⅝	¾
	A-C EXT-APA	Use where the appearance of only one side is important. Soffits, fences, structural uses, box-car and truck lining, farm buildings. Tanks, trays, commercial refrigerators.‡	A	C	C	¼		⅜	½	⅝	¾
	B-B EXT-APA	Utility panel with solid faces.‡	B	C	B	¼		⅜	½	⅝	¾
	B-C EXT-APA	Utility panel for farm service and work buildings, boxcar and truck lining, containers, tanks, agricultural equipment. Also as base for exterior coatings for walls, roofs.‡	B	C	C	¼		⅜	½	⅝	¾
	HDO EXT-APA	High Density Overlay plywood. Has a hard, semi-opaque resin-fiber overlay both faces. Abrasion resistant. For concrete forms, cabinets, counter tops, signs, tanks.‡	A or B	C or C plgd	A or B			⅜	½	⅝	¾
	MDO EXT-APA	Medium Density Overlay with smooth, opaque, resin-fiber overlay one or both panel faces. Highly recommended for siding and other outdoor applications, built-ins, signs, displays. Ideal base for paint.‡§	B	C	B or C			⅜	½	⅝	¾
	303 SIDING EXT-APA	Proprietary plywood products for exterior siding, fencing, etc. Special surface treatment such as V-groove, channel groove, striated, brushed, rough-sawn. Stud spacing indicated on grade stamp.	(¶)	C	C			⅜	½	⅝	
	T 1-11 EXT-APA	Special 303 panel having grooves ¼" deep, ⅜" wide, spaced 4" or 8" o.c. Other spacing optional. Edges shiplapped. Available unsanded, textured and MDO.	C or btr.	C	C				19⁄32	⅝	
	PLYRON EXT-APA	Hardboard faces both sides, tempered, smooth or screened.		C					½	⅝	¾
	MARINE EXT-APA	Ideal for boat hulls. Made only with Douglas fir or western larch. Special solid jointed core construction. Subject to special limitations on core gaps and number of face repairs. Also available with HDO or MDO faces.	A or B	B	A or B	¼		⅜	½	⅝	¾

* Sanded both sides except where decorative or other surfaces specified.
† Available in Group 1, 2, 3, 4, or 5 unless otherwise noted.
‡ Also available in STRUCTURAL I (all plies limited to Group 1 species) and STRUCTURAL II (all plies limited to Group 1, 2, or 3 species).
¶ C or better for 5 plies; C plugged or better for 3 plies.
§ Also available as a 303 siding.

Table 24. Guide to engineered grades of plywood

(Specific grades and thicknesses may be in locally limited supply. See your dealer before specifying.)

	Grade designation	Description and most common uses	Veneer grade			Most common thicknesses (inch)				
			Face	Inner plies	Back					
Interior Type	C-D INT-APA	For wall and roof sheathing, subflooring, industrial uses such as pallets. Most commonly available with exterior glue. Specify exterior glue where construction delays are anticipated and for treated-wood foundations.[a]	C	D	D	5/16	3/8	1/2	5/8	3/4
	STRUCTURAL I C-D INT-APA and STRUCTURAL II C-D INT-APA	Unsanded structural grades where plywood strength properties are of maximum importance: structural diaphragms, box beams, gusset plates, stressed-skin panels, containers, pallet bins. Made only with exterior glue. See (5) for species group requirements. Structural I most commonly available.	C[b]	D[b]	D[b]	5/16	3/8	1/2	5/8	3/4
	UNDERLAYMENT INT-APA	For underlayment or combination subfloor-underlayment under resilient floor coverings, carpeting in homes, apartments, mobile homes. Specify exterior glue where moisture may be present, such as bathrooms, utility rooms, or where construction is delayed, as in site-built floors. Touch sanded. Also available in tongue-and-groove.[d,e]	C Plugged	C[c] & D	D		3/8	1/2	5/8	3/4
	C-D PLUGGED INT-APA	For built-ins, wall and ceiling tile backing, cable reels, walkways, separator boards. Not a substitute for UNDERLAYMENT as it lacks UNDERLAYMENT's indentation resistance. Touch sanded. Also made with exterior glue.[d,e]	C Plugged	D	D	5/16	3/8	1/2	5/8	3/4
	2·4·1 INT-APA	Combination subfloor-underlayment. Quality base for resilient floor coverings, carpeting, wood strip flooring. Use 2·4·1 with exterior glue in areas subject to moisture or where construction is delayed, as in site-built floors. Unsanded or touch-sanded as specified. Can be special ordered in Exterior type for porches, patio decks, roof overhangs, exterior balconies. Available in tongue-and-groove.[f]	C Plugged	C[c] & D	D			1 1/8		
Exterior Type	C-C EXT-APA	Unsanded grade with waterproof bond for subflooring and roof decking, siding on service and farm buildings, crating, pallets, pallet binds, cable reels, treated-wood foundations.[a]	C	C	C	5/16	3/8	1/2	5/8	3/4
	STRUCTURAL I C-C EXT-APA and STRUCTURAL II CC-EXT-APA	For engineered applications in construction and industry where full Exterior type panels are required. Unsanded. See (5) for species group requirements.	C	C	C	5/16	3/8	1/2	5/8	3/4
	UNDERLAYMENT C-C Plugged EXT-APA C-C PLUGGED EXT-APA	For underlayment or combination subfloor-underlayment under resilient floor coverings where severe moisture conditions may be present, as in balcony decks. Use for tile backing, refrigerated or controlled atmosphere rooms, pallets, fruit pallet bins, reusable cargo containers, tanks and boxcar and truck floors and linings. Touch-sanded. Also available in tongue-and-groove.[d,e]	C Plugged	C[c]	C		3/8	1/2	5/8	3/4
	B-B PLYFORM CLASS I & CLASS II EXT-APA	Concrete form grades with high reuse factor. Sanded both sides. Mill-oiled unless otherwise specified. Special restrictions on species. Available in HDO and STRUCTURAL I. Class I most commonly available.	B	C	B				5/8	3/4

[a] *Made in many different species combinations. Specify by Identification Index.*
[b] *Special improved grade for structural panels.*
[c] *Special construction to resist indentation from concentrated loads.*
[d] *Available in Group 1, 2, 3, 4, or 5.*
[e] *Also available in STRUCTURAL I (all plies limited to Group 1 species) and STRUCTURAL II (all plies limited to Group 1, 2, or 3 species).*
[f] *Made only from certain wood species to conform to APA specifications.*

GRADE-TRADEMARKS

Typical APA grade-trademarks and their explanations are shown in Fig. 40. Appearance grades with both sides of appearance quality (bottom example) are edge stamped. All other grades are back stamped. The Group, Span, and Identification Index numbers shown are examples only; the proper specification will depend on the panel application. See "Group Number," "Span Index," and "Identification Index" for explanations and availability, and the following floor, wall, and roof sections for plywood grade and thickness recommendations.

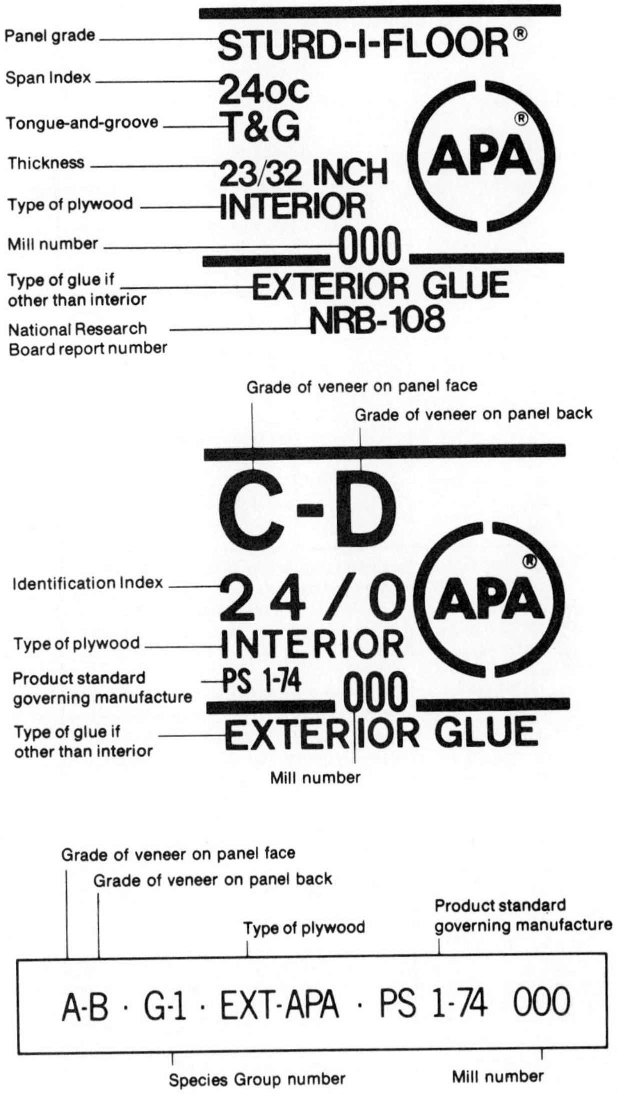

Panel grade — **STURD-I-FLOOR®**
Span Index — **24oc**
Tongue-and-groove — **T&G**
Thickness — **23/32 INCH**
Type of plywood — **INTERIOR**
Mill number — **000**
Type of glue if other than interior — **EXTERIOR GLUE**
National Research Board report number — **NRB-108**

Grade of veneer on panel face
Grade of veneer on panel back

C-D
Identification Index — **24/0** APA
Type of plywood — **INTERIOR**
Product standard governing manufacture — **PS 1-74** **000**
Type of glue if other than interior — **EXTERIOR GLUE**
Mill number

Grade of veneer on panel face
Grade of veneer on panel back
Type of plywood
Product standard governing manufacture

A-B · G-1 · EXT-APA · PS 1-74 000

Species Group number   Mill number

Fig. 40. Typical APA grade-trademarks

FLOOR CONSTRUCTION

APA Sturd-I-Floor®

Sturd-I-Floor is a new span-rated APA proprietary product designed specifically for use in single-layer floor construction beneath nonstructural finish flooring. The product provides all of the proven cost-saving and performance benefits of combined subfloor-underlayment construction. It is recognized by the National Research Board (under Report No. NRB-108), which is sponsored jointly by the three model code organizations—promulgators of the Basic Building Code, Uniform Building Code, and Standard Building Code. Maximum recommended spacing of floor joists—or Span Index—is stamped on each panel back. Panels are manufactured with Span Indexes of 16, 20, 24, and 48 in.

Sturd-I-Floor 48 o.c. incorporates all the features of panels formerly designated 2·4·1. Application recommendations remain the same—install panels over 2x joists spaced 32 in. o.c. or over 4x girders 48 o.c. For the 48 o.c. method, supports may be 2x joists spiked together, 4x lumber, lightweight steel beams, or open web joists.

Plywood subflooring

The limiting factor in the design of plywood floors is deflection under concentrated loads at panel edges. The Identification Indexes in Table 26 apply to C-D INT-APA, C-C EXT-APA, Structural I and II C-D INT-APA, and Structural I and II C-C EXT-APA grades only, and are the minimum recommended for the spans indicated. The spans assume plywood continuous over two or more spans with *face grain across supports*. Nailing recommendations are given in Table 26.

Plywood underlayment

For maximum stiffness, place face grain across supports and end joints over framing. When floor members are dry, make sure fasteners are flush with or below floor surface just prior to installation of thin floor coverings such as tile, linoleum or vinyl. Fasteners should be set if green framing will present nail-popping problems upon drying. *Do not* fill nail holes. Fill and thoroughly sand edge joints of panels to receive resilient floor covering (except carpet). Fill any other damaged or open areas such as splits and sand all surface roughness.

Where floors may be subject to unusual moisture, use panels with exterior glue or Underlayment C-C Plugged EXT-APA. Nailing recommendations are given in Table 27.

Table 25. APA Sturd-I-Floor®a

Span index (Maximum joist spacing) (in.)	Panel thicknessᵇ (in.)	Fastening: Glue-nailedᶜ			Fastening: Nailed-only		
		Nail size and type	Spacing (in.)		Nail size and type	Spacing (in.)	
			Panel edges	Intermediate		Panel edges	Intermediate
16	$^{19}/_{32}$, $^{5}/_{8}$	6d deformed-shankᵈ	12	12	6d deformed-shank	6	10
20	$^{19}/_{32}$, $^{5}/_{8}$ $^{23}/_{32}$, $^{3}/_{4}$	6d deformed-shankᵈ	12	12	6d deformed-shank	6	10
24	$^{23}/_{32}$, $^{3}/_{4}$	6d deformed-shankᵈ	12	12	6d deformed-shank	6	10
	$^{7}/_{8}$	8d deformed-shankᵈ	12	12	8d deformed-shank	6	10
48 (2-4-1)	$1^{1}/_{8}$	8d deformed-shankᵉ	6	ᶠ	8d deformed-shankᵉ	6	ᶠ

ᵃ Special conditions may impose heavy traffic and concentrated loads that require construction in excess of the minimums shown. Heavy duty floor recommendations are available from APA.

ᵇ As indicated above, panels in a given thickness may be manufactured in more than one Span Index. Panels with a Span Index greater than the actual joist spacing may be substituted for panels of the same thickness with a Span Index matching the actual joist spacing. For example, $^{19}/_{32}$-in.-thick Sturd-I-Floor 20 o.c. may be substituted for $^{19}/_{32}$-in.-thick Sturd-I-Floor 16 o.c. over joists 16 in. o.c.

ᶜ Use only adhesives conforming to APA Specification AFG-01 applied in accordance with the manufacturer's recommendations.

ᵈ 8d common nails may be substituted if deformed-shank nails are not available.

ᵉ 10d common nails may be substituted with 1-$^{1}/_{8}$-in. panels if supports are well seasoned.

ᶠ Space nails 6 in. for 48-in. spans and 10 in. for 32-in. spans.

Table 26. Plywood subflooring

(C-D INT-APA, C-C EXT-APA, Structural I and II C-D INT-APA, Structural I and II C-C EXT-APA)

Panel identification index (or group number)	Plywood thickness (in.)	Maximum span (in.)	Nail size & type	Nail spacing (in.)	
				Panel edges	Intermediate
$^{30}/_{12}$ᵃ	$^{5}/_{8}$	12ᵇ	8d common	6	10
$^{32}/_{16}$	$^{1}/_{2}$, $^{5}/_{8}$	16ᶜ	8d commonᵈ	6	10
$^{36}/_{16}$ᵃ	$^{3}/_{4}$	16ᶜ	8d common	6	10
$^{42}/_{20}$	$^{5}/_{8}$, $^{3}/_{4}$, $^{7}/_{8}$	20ᵉ	8d common	6	10
$^{48}/_{24}$	$^{3}/_{4}$, $^{7}/_{8}$	24	8d common	6	10
$1^{1}/_{8}$" Groups 1 & 2ᵃ	$1^{1}/_{8}$	48	10d common	6	6
$1^{1}/_{4}$" Groups 3 & 4ᵃ	$1^{1}/_{4}$	48	10d common	6	6

ᵃ Check dealer for availability.

ᵇ May be 16 in. if $^{25}/_{32}$-in. wood strip flooring is installed at right angles to joists.

ᶜ May be 24 in. if $^{25}/_{32}$-in. wood strip flooring is installed at right angles to joists.

ᵈ 6d common nail permitted if plywood is $^{1}/_{2}$ in.

ᵉ May be 24 in. if $^{25}/_{32}$-in. wood strip flooring is installed at right angles to joists, or if a minimum $1^{1}/_{2}$ in. of lightweight concrete is applied over plywood.

Table 27. Plywood underlayment

Plywood grades[a] and species group	Application	Minimum plywood thickness (in.)	Fastener size and type	Fastener spacing (in.)[b]	
				Panel edges	Intermediate
Groups 1, 2, 3, 4, 5 UNDERLAYMENT INT-APA (with interior, or exterior glue) UNDERLAYMENT Ext-APA C-C Plugged EXT-APA	Over plywood subfloor	¼	18 ga. staples or 3d ring-shank nails[c,d]	3	6 each way
	Over lumber subfloor or over uneven surfaces.	⅜	16 ga. staples[d]	3	6 each way
			3d ring-shank nails[d]	6	8 each way
Same grades as above, but Group 1 only.	Over lumber floor up to 4" wide. Face grain must be perpendicular to boards.	¼	18 ga. staples or 3d ring-shank nails	3	6 each way

[a] When ¹⁹⁄₃₂ in. or thicker, Sturd-I-Floor—APA may be specified.
[b] If green framing is used, space fasteners so they do not penetrate framing.
[c] Crown width ⅜ in. for 16 ga., ³⁄₁₆ in. for 18 ga. staples, length sufficient to penetrate completely through, or at least ⅝ in. into, subflooring.
[d] Use 3d ring-shank nail also for ½-in. plywood and 4d ring-shank nail for ⅝-in. or ¾-in plywood.

Table 28. APA Sturd-I-Wall®

(Direct to studs or over monstructural sheathing)

Plywood panel siding description (All species groups)	Nominal thickness (in.)	Max. stud spacing (in.)		Nail size (Use nonstaining box, siding or casing nails)*	Nail spacing (in.)	
		Face grain vertical	Face grain horizontal		Panel edges	Intermediate
MDO EXT-APA	¹¹⁄₃₂ & ⅜	16	24	6d for panels ½" thick or less;	6	12
	½₂ & thicker	24	24			
303-16 o.c. Siding EXT-APA	¹¹⁄₃₂ & thicker	16	24	8d for thicker panels.		
303-24 o.c. Siding EXT-APA	¹⁵⁄₃₂ & thicker	24	24			

* If siding is applied over sheathing thicker than ½ in., use next regular nail size.

Table 29. Exterior plywood siding over nailable plywood or lumber sheathing

Plywood siding			Maximum spacing (in.) of vertical rows of nails		Nail size (Use nonstaining box, siding or casing nails)	Nail spacing (in.)	
	Description (All species groups)	Nominal thickness (in.)	Face grain vertical	Face grain horizontal		Panel edges	Intermediate
Panel Siding	MDO EXT-APA	¹¹⁄₃₂, ⅜	16	24	6d for panels ½" thick or less; 8d for thicker panels.	6	12
		½ & thicker	24	24			
	303-16 o.c Siding EXT-APA	¹¹⁄₃₂ & thicker	16	24			
	303-24 o.c. Siding EXT-APA	¹⁵⁄₃₂ & thicker	24	24			
Lap Siding	MDO EXT-APA	¹¹⁄₃₂ & thicker	—	24	6d for siding ⅜" thick or less; 8d for thicker siding.	4 @ vertical butt joints; 6 along bottom edge.	8 (if siding wider than 12".)
	303 Siding EXT-APA	¹¹⁄₃₂ & thicker	—	24			

Table 30. Plywood wall sheathing[a,b]

(Plywood continuous over 2 or more spans)

Panel identification index	Panel thickness (in.) & construction	Maximum stud spacing (in.) exterior covering nailed to:		Nail size[c]	Nail spacing (in.)[c]	
		Stud	Sheathing		Panel edges (when over framing)	Intermediate (each stud)
¹²/₀, ¹⁶/₀, ²⁰/₀	⁵/₁₆	16	16[d]	6d	6	12
¹⁶/₀, ²⁰/₀, ²⁴/₀, ³²/₁₆	³/₈ & ½ (3 ply)	24	16 24	6d	6	12
²⁴/₀, ³²/₁₆	½ (4 & 5 ply)	24	24	6d	6	12

[a] When plywood sheathing is used, building paper and diagonal wall bracing can be omitted.
[b] In dry conditions, space panel edges ⅛-in., panel ends ¹/₁₆-in. In wet or humid conditions double spacing.
[c] Common, smooth, annular, spiral-thread, or galvanized box, or T-nails of the same diameter as common nails (0.113-in. dia. for 6d) may be used. Staples also permitted at reduced spacing.
[d] Apply plywood with face grain across studs.

Table 31. Interior plywood paneling

Plywood thickness	Maximum support spacing (in.)	Nail size (Use casing or finishing nails)	Nail spacing (in.)	
			Panel edges	Intermediate
¼	16*	4d	6	12
⁵/₁₆	16†	6d	6	12
³/₈	24	6d	6	12
½	24	6d	6	12
⅝	24	8d	6	12
¾	24	8d	6	12
Texture 1-11	24	8d	6	12

* Can be 20 in. if face grain of paneling is across supports.
† Can be 24 in. if face grain of paneling is across supports.

WALL CONSTRUCTION

APA Sturd-I-Wall®

The APA Sturd-I-Wall system consists of APA 303 plywood panel siding applied directly to studs or over nonstructural fiberboard, gypsum, or rigid foam insulation sheathing. (Nonstructural sheathing is defined as sheathing not recognized by building codes as meeting bending and racking strength requirements.)

The system is accepted by HUD and the model codes. And since the single layer of plywood panel siding is strong and rack resistant, it eliminates the cost of installing separate structural sheathing or diagonal wall bracing. Panel sidings are normally installed vertically, but may also be placed horizontally (face grain across supports) if horizontal joints are blocked. Maximum stud spacings for both applications are given in Table 28.

Plywood panel and lap siding over nailable plywood or lumber sheathing

See recommendations in Table 29.

Plywood wall sheathing

Plywood wall sheathing easily meets building code requirements for bending and racking strength without let-in corner bracing. Recommendations in Table 30 for plywood wall sheathing apply to all species groups.

Interior plywood paneling

Plywood lends itself to a number of decorative surface treatments for attractive interior paneling and accent walls. Such treatments include saw-textured relief grain, embossed, striated, and grooved. Support and nail spacing recommendations are given in Table 31. Recommendations apply to all species groups.

ROOF CONSTRUCTION

Plywood roof sheathing

The recommendations for plywood roof sheathing in Table 32 apply to C-D INT-APA, C-C EXT-APA, Structural I and II C-D INT-APA, and Structural I and II C-C EXT-APA. Values include the effects of a 5 lb/ft² dead load; uniform load deflection limits are 1/180 of span under live load plus dead load, and 1/240 under live load only. Plywood is assumed continuous over two or more spans with *face grain across supports.* Allowable live loads may have to be decreased for slate or tile roofs with dead loads greater than 5 lb/ft².

Roof trusses spaced 24 in. o.c. are widely recognized as the most economical construction for residential roofs, particularly when ³/₈-in. 24/0 sheathing with panel clips is used. However, using fewer supports with thicker plywood—e.g., ¾-in. 48/24 plywood over framing 48 in. o.c.—is also cost-effective for long-span flat or sloped roofs. Fastening recommendations are given in Table 33.

When support spacing exceeds the maximum length of an unsupported edge (see Table 31), provide adequate blocking, tongue-and-groove edges, or other edge support such as panel clips.

Table 32. Allowable uniform live loads for roof decking

(C-D INT-APA, C-C EXT-APA, Structural I and II C-D INT-APA and structural I and II C-C EXT-APA)

Identification index	Plywood thickness (in.)	Maximum span (in.)	Unsupported edge-max. length (in.)	Allowable live loads (psf) Spacing of supports center-to-center (in.)									
				12	16	20	24	30	32	36	42	48	60
12/0	5/16	12	12	150									
16/0	5/16, 3/8	16	16	160	75								
20/0	5/16, 3/8	20	20	190	105	65							
24/0	3/8, 1/2	24	20, 24*	250	140	95	50						
32/16	1/2, 5/8	32	28	385	215	150	95	50	40				
42/20	5/8, 3/4, 7/8	42	32		330	230	145	90	75	50	35		
48/24	3/4, 7/8	48	36			300	190	120	105	65	45	35	
48/24†	3/4, 7/8	48	36				225	125	105	75	55	40	
2-4-1‡	1⅛	72	48				390	245	215	135	100	75	45
1⅛" Grp. 1 & 2	1⅛	72	48				305	195	170	105	75	55	35
1¼" Grp. 3 & 4	1¼	72	48				355	225	195	125	90	65	40

* *Maximum unsupported length 20 in. for ⅜-in. plywood, 24 in. for ½-in. plywood.*
† *Loads apply only to C-C EXT-APA, Structural I C-D INT-APA, and Structural I C-C EXT-APA. Check availability of these grades before specifying.*
‡ *2·4·1 is synonymous with Sturd-I-Floor 48 o.c.*

Table 33. Plywood roof deck fastening recommendations

Plywood thickness (in.)	Nailing[a]			Stapling[b,c]			
		Spacing (in.)				Spacing (in.)	
	Size	Panel edges	Intermediate	Leg length		Panel edges	Intermediate
5/16	6d	6	12	1¼		4	8
3/8	6d	6	12	1⅜		4	8
1/2	6d	6	12	1½		4	8
5/8, 3/4, 7/8	8d	6	12[d]	—		—	—
1⅛, 1¼	8d or 10d	6	12[d]	—		—	—

[a] *Use common smooth or deformed-shank nails with plywood to 1 in. thick. For 1-⅛-in. and 1-¼-in. panels, use 8d deformed-shank or 10d common smooth-shank nails.*
[b] *All values are for 16 ga. galvanized wire staples with a minimum crown width of ⅜ in.*
[c] *For stapling asphalt shingles to 5/16-in. and thicker plywood, use staples with a ¾-in. minimum crown width and a ¾-in. leg length. Space according to shingle manufacturer's recommendations.*
[d] *For spans 48 in. or greater, space nails 6 in. at all supports.*

CONCRETE FORMS

(Abstracted from *Plywood for Concrete Forming*, copyright 1973 by American Plywood Association, revised 1979.)

A major use of plywood is for concrete forms. Recommended grades (all exterior-type) are given in Table 34. Usual thicknesses are ⅝ or ¾ in. but other thicknesses are sometimes used; thinner sections may be necessary for curved forms. For curved forms the bending radii shown in Table 35 can be considered practical minimums for average panels bent dry. Shorter radii can be obtained by selecting panels free of knots or other defects and/or by wetting or steaming.

Concrete pressures on column and wall forms vary with the temperature and the rate of pour, as shown in Table 36, which is based on a concrete density of 150

Table 34. Grade-use guide for concrete forms*

Use these terms when you specify plywood	Description	Veneer grade	
		Faces	Inner plies
B-B PLYFORM Class I & II† APA	Specifically manufactured for concrete forms. Many reuses. Smooth, solid surfaces. Mill-oiled unless otherwise specified.	B	C
High Density Overlaid PLYFORM Class I & II† APA	Hard, semiopaque resin-fiber overlay, heat-fused to panel faces. Smooth surface resists abrasion. Up to 200 reuses. Light oiling recommended between pours.	B	C Plugged
STRUCTURAL I PLYFORM† APA	Especially designed for engineered applications. All Group 1 species. Stronger and stiffer than PLYFORM Class I and II. Recommended for high pressures where face grain is parallel to supports. Also available with High Density Overlay faces.	B	C or C Plugged

Commonly available in ⅝" and ¾" panel thicknesses (4' x 8' size).
† Check dealer for availability in your area.

Table 35. Minimum bending radii

Plywood thickness (in.)	Across the grain (ft.)	Parallel to grain (ft.)
¼	2	5
5/16	2	6
⅜	3	8
½	6	12
⅝	8	16
¾	12	20

Table 36. Concrete pressures for column and wall forms

Pour rate (ft/hr)	Pressures of vibrated concrete (lb/ft²)*†			
	50° F		70° F	
	Columns	Walls	Columns	Walls
1	330	330	280	280
2	510	510	410	410
3	690	690	540	540
4	870	870	660	660
5	1050	1050	790	790
6	1230	1230	920	920
7	1410	1410	1050	1050
8	1590	1470	1180	1090
9	1770	1520	1310	1130
10	1950	1580	1440	1170

Maximum pressure need not exceed 150h, where h is maximum height of pour.
† Based on concrete with density of 150 pcf and 4 in. slump.

Table 37. Allowable pressures (lb/ft²) on plyform Class I (deflection limited to 1/360th of the span)

Support spacing (in.)	Face grain across supports*					
	Plywood thickness (in.)					
	½	⅝	¾	⅞	1	1⅛
4	3265	4095	5005	5225	5650	6290
8	970	1300	1650	2005	2175	2420
12	410	575	735	890	1190	1370
16	175	270	370	475	645	750
20	100	160	225	295	410	490
24		120	160	230	280
32				105	130
36					115
	Face grain parallel to supports*					
4	1860	2350	2910	3450	4615	5455
8	605	905	1120	1325	1775	2100
12	215	360	670	820	1100	1300
16		150	300	480	725	895
20		105	210	290	400	495
24			110	180	255	320

Plywood continuous across two or more spans.

lb/ft². Allowable pressures on Plyform Class 1 are shown in Table 37, from which panel thickness and support spacing may be determined. If deflection of 1/270 instead of 1/360 is acceptable, then allowable pressures at spacings over 12 in. may be increased.

STRUCTURAL COMPONENTS

Prefabricated nailed-glued assemblies of lumber and plywood are being increasingly used in many types of buildings. Such components include long span box beams, trussed rafters, stressed skin panels, sandwich panels, folded plate construction, diaphragm floor and roof construction, shear walls, and curved panels for vaulted roofs. Components may be shop or site fabricated, but should be designed by a structural engineer. Technical publications on each type of component are available from American Plywood Association, P.O. Box 11700, Tacoma, Washington, 98411.

REFERENCES

Formwork for Concrete, M. K. Hurd, American Concrete Institute, 1974

Formwork for Concrete Structures, R. L. Peurifoy, McGraw-Hill, 1964

Concrete Forming and Wood Foundation Systems, American Plywood Association, C60

Plywood Concrete Form Surfaces, Coatings, and Treatments, American Plywood Association, Z394

HARDWOOD

Hardwoods of more than 200 species from all parts of the world are used in making hardwood plywood. Those most commonly used and generally available in stock are listed in Table 38.

Most hardwood plywood manufactured in the United States conforms to NBS Voluntary Product Standard PS-51 *Hardwood and Decorative Plywood*. It is made in four types, six grades, and three core constructions (see Fig. 39).

Types

Technical (Ext.): Fully waterproof bond. The construction is designed to provide approximately equal strength in both directions. Maximum veneer thickness: A species, $\frac{1}{12}$ in.; B species, $\frac{1}{10}$ in.; C species, $\frac{1}{8}$ in. Core must be all veneer. Bond must withstand boiling and shear test and be unaffected by microorganisms.

Type I (Ext.): Fully waterproof bond. Maximum veneer thickness: A species, $\frac{1}{8}$ in.; B species, $\frac{3}{16}$ in.; C species, $\frac{1}{4}$ in. Bond must withstand boiling and shear test and be unaffected by microorganisms.

Type II (Int.): Water-resistant bond. Bond must withstand three cycles of cold-soaking test.

Type III (Int.): Moisture-resistant bond. Bond must withstand two cycles of cold-soaking test.

Grades

Premium (1): Veneers must be full length and edge-matched.

Good (1): For natural finish—sharp contrasts in color or pattern not permitted.

Sound (2): For smooth paint finish—minor defects filled.

Utility (3): Defects permitted, but less than in Grade 4.

Backing (4): Defects permitted.

Specialty (SP): Custom-made panels, such as architectural plywood, with special veneer selection and/or grain matching; also curved, molded, impregnated, or overlaid panels.

Core constructions

All-veneer plywood usually has three or five plies, but may have more. Inner plies may be either hardwood (Grades 2 or 3) or softwood (Grades B or C); if face veneer is less than $\frac{1}{16}$ in. thick, a softwood veneer immediately below it must be Grade B.

Lumber-core plywood is usually five-ply construction, with the grain of the core parallel to that of the face. It is used principally for furniture and cabinetwork because it can be doweled, splined, dovetailed, and butt-hinged. Low-density, even-grained hardwoods or softwoods with moderate shrinkage characteristics are suitable for lumber cores; poplar and basswood are most often used. The maximum width of the core strips varies with the density of the veneer species: A species, $2\frac{1}{2}$ in.; B species, 3 in.; C species, 4 in. Mixing of species is not permitted. Grades of lumber core are as follows:

1. Clear—with full-length or finger-jointed strips; no patches or plugs
2. Sound—with full-length or finger-jointed strips
3. Regular—strips of random length, tight end joints
4. Clear edge—regular core with clear full-length edge strips $1\frac{1}{2}$ in. or more wide
5. Banded—regular core banded with clear strips on one or more edges, as specified
6. Mitered bands—or other special banding, as specified

Composite panels are those having cores of other than veneer or lumber. Cores may be solid (particle board, foamed plastic, mineral composition) or hollow (wood or fiberboard eggcrate, plastic-impregnated paper honeycomb, sections of paper cylinders). Solid-core panels are usually five-ply; hollow-core panels are often seven-ply. Both types are usually banded with wood on all edges. These core constructions are used principally in the manufacture of doors.

Sizes

Sizes generally available in stock (in inches) are as follows:

Widths—24, 30, 36, 42, 48.
Lengths—48, 60, 72, 84, 96, 120.
Thicknesses—three ply, $\frac{1}{8}$, $\frac{3}{16}$, $\frac{1}{4}$; five ply, $\frac{5}{16}$, $\frac{3}{8}$, $\frac{1}{2}$, $\frac{5}{8}$; seven ply, $\frac{5}{8}$, $\frac{3}{4}$; nine ply, $\frac{3}{4}$; lumber core five ply, $\frac{3}{4}$.

Table 38. Categories of commonly used species based on specific gravity ranges[1]

Category A species (0.56 or more specific gravity)	Category B species (0.43 through 0.55 specific gravity)	Category C species (0.42 or less specific gravity)
Ash, Commercial White	Ash, Black	Alder, Red
Beech, American	Avodire	Aspen
Birch, Yellow, Sweet	Bay	Basswood, American
Bubinga	Cedar, Eastern Red[2]	Box Elder
Elm, Rock	Cherry, Black	Cativo
Madrone, Pacific	Chestnut, American	Cedar, Western Red[2]
Maple, Black (hard)	Cypress[2]	Ceiba
Maple, Sugar (hard)	Elm, American (white, red, or gray)	Cottonwood, Black
Oak, Commercial Red	Fir, Douglas[2]	Cottonwood, Eastern
Oak, Commercial White	Gum, Black	Pine, White and Ponderosa[2]
Oak, Oregon	Gum, Sweet	Poplar, Yellow
Paldao	Hackberry	Redwood[2]
Pecan, Commercial	Lauan, (Philippine Mahogany)	Willow, Black
Rosewood	Limba	
Sapele	Magnolia	
Teak	Mahogany, African	
	Mahogany, Honduras	
	Maple, Red (soft)	
	Maple, Silver (soft)	
	Prima Vera	
	Sycamore	
	Tupelo, Water	
	Walnut, American	

[1] Based on ovendry weight and volume at 12 percent moisture content.
[2] Softwood.

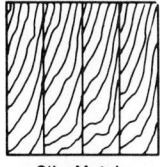  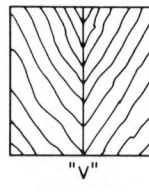  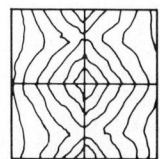

Slip Match   Herringbone   "V"   Book Match   Four-way Center and Butt

   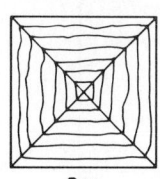 

Diamond   Reverse Diamond   Checkerboard   Box   Reverse Box

Fig. 41. Veneer matching patterns

Lengths of 144 in. are available from many sources, and still longer and wider panels are available on special order. The smaller sizes are more economical. Some mills cut panels to size on large orders.

Tolerances in length and width are plus or minus $\frac{1}{32}$ in.; in square, plus or minus $\frac{3}{32}$ in.; in thickness (sanded), plus 0, minus $\frac{3}{64}$ in.

Sanding

Type of sanding and number of surfaces to be sanded must be specified.

1. No sanding—tape not removed.
2. Rough sanding.
3. Regular sanding—surface clean and free of tape; may show sander streaks.
4. Polish sanding—clean and smooth.

Note: In no case is mill-sanded plywood to be considered as ready for painter's finish.

Special plywoods

Fire-retarded. Plywood, veneers, and lumber cores may be treated with chemicals which make them resistant to decay, ter-

mites, and fire. Where appearance is important, the face veneer may be left untreated.

Metal-faced. Plywood may be faced on one or both sides with sheet metal for increased strength, abrasion resistance, or fire resistance. Its principal use is for truck bodies.

Plastic-faced. Plywood may be faced with plastic sheets of various types, for improved resistance to wear or checking, or as a type of prefinished panel.

Counterfronts. Plywood panels having the

Panel joints

Tongue and groove

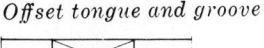

Offset tongue and groove

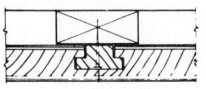

Concealed batten spline

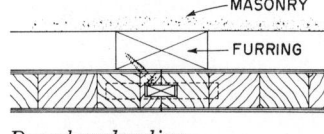

Dowel and spline

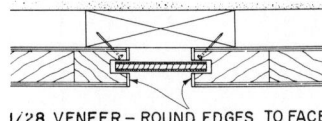

1/28 VENEER – ROUND EDGES TO FACE

Exposed spline

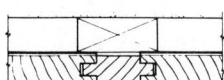

Decorative batten

Fig. 42. Lumber core plywood wall paneling

Panel joints

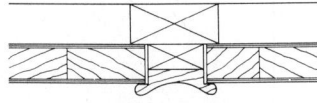

Exposed batten spline

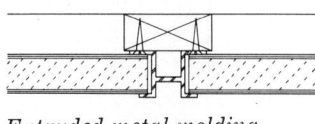

Extruded metal molding

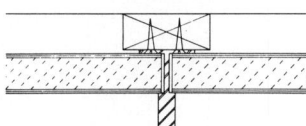

Extruded metal molding

Corners

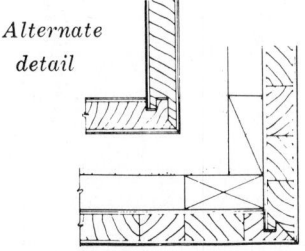

Alternate detail

Outside corner

Corners

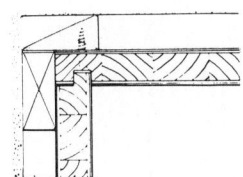

Inside corner

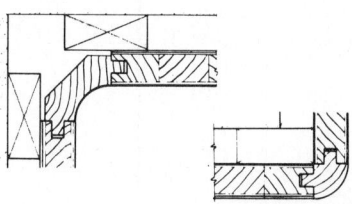

Hardwood corners

Cabinetwork

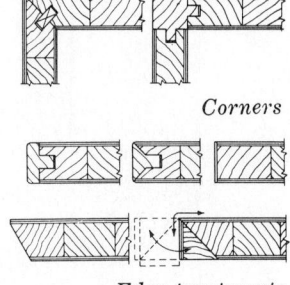

Corners

Edge treatments

Courtesy of Architectural Woodwork Institute

grain of the face veneer running the short way of the panel are available; their principal use is for store fixtures.

Prefinished. Prefinished wall paneling is available in a wide variety of species and finishes; it is usually ¼ in. thick, 16 to 48 in. wide, and 7 to 12 ft long. Fastenings may be concealed. Finishes include wax stains, lacquers, synthetic resins, and plastics. Prefinished flooring squares are also generally available.

Architectural plywood is custom made from veneer selected by the architect in the flitch. Veneers are sequence-matched in the pattern specified (Fig. 41); shop drawings are furnished and the panels are numbered. Architectural plywood is usually ¾-in. lumber core; face veneers are 1/20 to 1/28 in. and crossbands 1/10 to $\frac{1}{16}$ in. thick. Typical installation details are shown in **Fig. 42.** Architectural plywood is also furnished in ¼ or ⅜-in. thickness; in this case it should be applied over a backing of $\frac{5}{16}$-in. plywood installed horizontally. Panels should be sealed or back-primed before installation.

Ordering plywood

Specify the following: number of pieces, width, length, thickness, number of plies, core construction, grade of face, grade of back, type, sanding, special requirements. All dimensions should be given in inches. "Width" means across the grain and "length" means parallel to the grain of the face veneer, regardless of the shape of the panel.

REFERENCES

Structural Design Guide for Hardwood Plywood, HPMA 5G-71

Truax, Dr. T. R.: *Hardwood Plywood Manual,* Hardwood Plywood Institute (1962).

Architectural Woodwork Quality Standards, Architectural Woodwork Institute (1978).

By FREDERICK F. WANGAARD, *Associate Professor of Forest Products, Yale University*

INTERIOR FINISHES *

Plywood is adapted to a wide variety of finishing treatments including natural, stained, blonde, enameled, or painted finishes, or it may be covered with wallpaper. The most distinctive effects are, of course, obtainable only with finishes that permit the natural beauty of wood to be revealed.

Modern finishing treatments for plywood emphasize (1) the natural effect of the grain, color, and figure of the wood obtained through clear finishes or (2) the light effects which may be achieved without losing the distinctive characteristics of texture, grain, and figure by subduing the normal grain contrast of the wood with pigmented sealers. Prior to finishing, all nails should be countersunk and the holes filled with wood putty of matching color. The panel is then lightly sanded with 2/0 sandpaper and wiped clean.

Recommended finishing schedules vary with the species, but are illustrated by the following examples:

1. **Walnut:** Light natural finish. A coat of clear brushing lacquer is first applied. This coat should be steel wooled after drying (3–4 hours) and a second lacquer coat applied. This second coat is also rubbed with steel wool when dry and then rubbed with a good paste wax. A full finish, involving a third coat of lacquer, may be desired on trim or doors where heavy wear is anticipated.

2. **Rift white oak:** Blonde finish. Following preliminary sanding, a white pigmented resin sealer, which has been thinned 10–20 per cent with turpentine or mineral spirits, is brushed on the plywood. After setting for 3–5 minutes, it is rubbed into the pores of the wood, wiped clean, and allowed to dry for 24 hours. The surface is then lightly sanded with 2/0 sandpaper and finished with two coats of lacquer and wax as de-

* See also section on Finishes and "Stains and Paints on Plywood," published by American Plywood Association.

scribed for walnut.

Finishing recommendations for other hardwood species vary in certain details from the relatively simple treatments described here and are available through plywood dealers. It is advisable, in any case, to sample any prescribed finishing treatment on scrap pieces of plywood before starting the job.

Light stain-glaze finishes which subdue the normal grain contrast of the species are very popular and effective finishing treatments for Douglas fir plywood. Steps in the treatment include (1) Application of interior white undercoat paint thinned with turpentine in the ratio 1 part undercoat to 1 part thinner. Within 10–20 minutes excess undercoat is wiped off with a cloth following the grain to attain the desired show-through of grain. When the surface is dry, it is lightly sanded with fine sandpaper. (2) A coat of thinned white shellac or clear resin sealer, the surface is again lightly sanded when dry. (3) Application of a color coat which may be a tinted interior undercoat, thinned enamel, color in oil, or a light stain. Only a thin color coat is applied and wiped or dry-brushed to the desired appearance. The surface is again sanded lightly when dry. (4) A final coat of flat varnish is then applied, and after drying, it is buffed with 3/0 steel wool.

Variations of the foregoing method include substitution of a white pigmented sealer (applied as described for blonde white oak) for steps 1 and 2. Another possibility is the elimination of step 1 (the white undercoat), otherwise following the procedure outlined.

A simple one-step finishing treatment for Douglas fir consists of a coat of stain wax, which is applied with a cloth or brush. This is wiped down after a few minutes to the desired shade.

The basic procedure for obtaining a **"bleached" or blonde finish** with Douglas fir consists of the application of thinned white undercoat which is wiped down following the grain to

the desired tone before it becomes tacky. After drying, the surface is lightly sanded and finished with a coat of clear shellac, flat varnish, or clear lacquer.

The only maintenance normally required for finishes of the types previously described is an occasional application of wax.

Highest quality enameled walls without visible joints are obtained by the following treatment of Douglas fir or gum plywood. For this type of finish, panels should be butted together closely and all nail holes, hammer marks, and joints filled with Swedish putty. The wood is next primed with thinned flat white oil paint followed by the application of inexpensive unbleached muslin (tobacco cloth grade). The muslin is applied similarly to wallpaper using ordinary wallpaper paste, which has been strained to remove lumps. After drying, a coat of glue size is brushed on. Any conventional enamel finishing system may be employed satisfactorily over this base. This type of treatment is especially desirable in kitchens and bathrooms.

Conventional wall and woodwork paint finishes are, of course, used successfully on plywood walls and built-ins. When water thinned paints are used, the plywood should first be sealed with a clear resin sealer, shellac, or a flat white paint to prevent raised grain.

Wallpapered walls require the close butting of plywood panels, which are commonly of Douglas fir, but may include some of the more economical hardwoods such as gum. Joints should be filled with Swedish putty and the surface primed with a thin flat white paint. The surface is next coated with wheat flour paste to which gelatin glue size has been added. Next is applied a layer of 3/4-pound deadening or lining felt, which is treated with the same paste and size. After butting the felt neatly at the joints, and rolling it smooth, wallpaper may be hung in the usual manner, using ordinary wheat flour paste.

By JOHN HANCOCK CALLENDER, *Professor of Architecture, Pratt Institute,* and HOWARD P. VERMILYA, *AIA*

Wood is extensively used as an interior and exterior finishing material. Both hardwoods and softwoods are used in solid form as well as in plywood.

Dimensional stability

All wood shrinks and swells with changes in moisture content. The art of designing in wood is to know the extent and direction of the movement and the measures that can be taken to minimize it. Some species of wood are more dimensionally stable than others. Table 1 classifies the principal species according to this characteristic. While the difference between the woods in the first and last groups is significant, the difference between adjacent groups may be hardly discernible in actual use.

It is important that wood have the appropriate moisture content when purchased, and that it be protected from moisture before and after installation. Moisture content is appropriate when it corresponds to the average atmospheric conditions to which the wood will be exposed, indoors or out (Table 2). Kiln drying is essential for interior wood finish. Kiln-dried wood should not be brought to the job until the building is fully enclosed and the plaster thoroughly dry.

All lumber species used for exterior work, except the heartwood of Redwood and Western Red Cedar, must be treated by not less than a 3-min dip in a 5 per cent solution of pentachlorophenol with water repellent added in accordance with Commercial Standards C.S. 262-63, and the solution must be in accordance with Federal Specification TT-W-572B, May 28, 1969.

While the above two woods do not need this treatment to prevent decay, treatment

Table 1. Dimensional stability of various woods

Data supplied by Architectural Woodwork Institute

Hardwoods				
Group I (most stable)	Group II		Group III	Group IV (least stable)
White ash	Red alder	Rock elm	Beech	Cottonwood
Butternut	Black ash	Soft elm	Red gum	Sap gum
Cherry	Blue ash	Hard maple	Magnolia	Sycamore
Chestnut	Basswood	Soft maple		Tupelo
Poplar	Birch	Red oak		
Walnut	Hackberry	White oak		
Willow				

Softwoods		
Group I	Group II	Group III
Cedar, Alaska	Cedar, Port Orford	Douglas fir (coast and inland types)
Cedar, eastern red	Cypress, southern	Hemlock, western
Cedar, western red	Douglas fir (Rocky Mountain type)	Larch, western
Cedar, northern white	Fir, balsam	Pine, longleaf
Pine, northern white	Fir, white	Pine, Norway
Pine, sugar	Hemlock, eastern	Pine, shortleaf
Redwood	Pine, ponderosa	Pine, Idaho
	Spruce, Engelmann	Spruce, Sitka

should be considered where transparent or penetrating pigmented finishes are to be applied for the benefits obtained from the water repellent action of the treatment. The tendency of these woods to stain from water soluble extractives is reduced and fungus and mildew discolorations are also minimized.

The region of maximum decay and termite damage includes coastal and southern California, Arizona, western New Mexico, the Texas border, the entire Gulf coast, and the Atlantic coast north to Virginia. For important buildings in this region, architects may wish to specify pressure treatment for exterior woodwork. Pressure treatment utilizing waterborne salts should not be used for finish woodwork; AWI recommends the use of the same 5 per cent solution of pentachlorophenol with added water repellent, as used in the dip method. With either method, freshly made end cuts must be promptly brush-coated.

Coatings on the surface of the wood

Table 2. Recommended moisture content for woodwork at time of installation—in percentage of oven-dry weight

Data supplied by Architectural Woodwork Institute

Service condition	Quantity	Southwestern states (Nevada, Utah, Arizona)	Southern coastal states, including Southern California coast	Remainder of the United States	Alberta, Saskatchewan, and Manitoba	Ontario and Quebec	East and west coast provinces, including Newfoundland
Interior wood finish	Average	6	11	8	6	7	10
	Range permitted in individual pieces	4–9	8–13	5–10	4–9	5–9	8–12
Exterior trim	Average	9	12	12	12	12	13
	Range permitted in individual pieces	7–12	9–14	9–14	10–15	10–15	11–15

Table 3. Lumber grades for architectural woodwork

(Data supplied by Architectural Woodwork Institute

Species groups [1]	Premium grade		Custom grade		Economy grade		Longest length available [3]
	Min. clear area required, in.², sample piece size in ( )	No. of defects [2] permitted in sizes larger than min.	Min. clear area required, in.², sample piece size in ( )	No. of defects [2] permitted in sizes larger than min.	Min. clear area required, in.², sample piece size in ( )	No. of defects [2] permitted in sizes larger than min.	
Clear natural Ash, Birch, Basswood, Hard & Soft Maple, [4] Poplar (contain heartwood & sapwood	630 (4½" x 140")	1	486 (4½" x 108")	2	336 (4½" x 75")	4	13'-6"
Select Red Birch Select Brown Ash (no sapwood allowed in clear pieces)	567 (4½" x 126")	1 and 5% sapwood	432 (4½" x 96")	2 and 10% sapwood	294 (4½" x 65")	4 and 20% sapwood	11'-6"
Select White Birch, Select White Hard Maple, [4] Select White Ash (no heartwood allowed in clear pieces)	567 (4½" x 126")	1 and 5% heartwood	432 (4½" x 96")	2 and 10% heartwood	294 (4½" x 65")	4 and 20% heartwood	11'-6"
Red Oak, White Oak, Mahogany, Teak	630 (4½" x 140")	2	486 (4½" x 108")	3	336 (4½" x 75")	5 and 10% sapwood	13'-6"
Rift or quarter sawn Red or White Oak	384 (4½" x 85")	1	189 (4½" x 42")	2 and 20% plain & quarter sawn	No economy grade		11'-6"
Walnut (sapwood allowed), [5] Cherry, Butternut (no sapwood allowed in clear pieces)	384 (4½" x 85")	2 and 20% sapwood in Walnut	189 (4½" x 42")	4 and 30% sapwood in Walnut	No economy grade		11'-6" Cherry 9'-6" Walnut & Butternut
Clear heart Redwood (no sapwood), clear natural Redwood (contains sapwood & heartwood)	1044 (7¼" x 144")	2	693 (7¼" x 96")	2	540 (7¼" x 74")	3	15'-8" (to 19'-8" on special order)
Southern Yellow Pine, Ponderosa Pine, Sugar Pine, Northern White Pine, Douglas Fir, Spruce, Cypress, Western Red Cedar, Inland Cedar	960 (7¼" x 132")	2	640 (7¼" x 88")	3	500 (7¼" x 69")	4	15'-8"

[1] *All plain sawn except as noted. Grouping species required since cutting potential varies in hardwoods*
[2] *Defects in hardwoods consists of tight pin knots not larger than ¼" and/or checks not larger than 0.03" x 3". Sapwood or heartwood may be a defect where so listed in the table. Defects in softwoods consist of tight knots and/or checks or pitch pockets of the sizes shown:*

	Premium grade	Custom grade	Economy grade
Knots	½"	¾"	1"
Checks	0.03" x 5"	0.05" x 7"	0.08" x 10"
Pitch pockets	0.06" x 4"	0.09" x 8"	unlimited

[3] *Longest length available is limited to 10% of the total footage required for the job in any given thickness.*
[4] *Mineral stain in Hard and Soft Maple is limited as follows: Premium grade, none allowed; Custom grade, none allowed in 75% of all members; Economy grade, no limit.*
[5] *Sapwood in Walnut is permitted in varying proportions in all grades. If objectionable, it can be eliminated by sap-staining or toning, as part of the finishing work.*

also reduce dimensional changes. While no coating is entirely moistureproof, a standard three-coat application of paint, varnish, or enamel will greatly lower the amount of moisture reaching the wood and penetrating into it.

The way a board is sawed from the log has an important effect on its stability. Quarter-sawed or edge-grain (vertical-grain) lumber shrinks and swells less and cups and twists less than plain-sawed and flat-grain lumber.

Architectural woodwork

Architectural woodwork includes *millwork,* consisting of trim and paneling, and *cabinetwork,* consisting of cabinets and other built-in furniture. Since the distinction between these two classifications is no longer precise, architects preparing specifications are advised to include all such work, regardless of the degree of mill or site fabrication, in a single section called "architectural woodwork."

The *Quality Standards of the Architectural Woodwork Industry* cover the following categories of work:

Standing and running trim—casings, stops, stools, cornices, fascias, soffits, and board or plywood wall covering
Casework—cabinets, counters, enclosures
Panelwork—stiles and rails with flush or raised panels
Closet shelving
Miscellaneous ornamental items—mantels, columns, pediments, grilles, church items, etc.
Stairwork
Exterior frames, sash, screens, blinds, and shutters
Doors

Grades. It has long been traditional for architects to specify for millwork and cabinetwork lumber grades A or B Select for natural finish and C Select for paint finish (or Clear, Select, and Sound, respectively, for certain hardwoods). However, the Architectural Woodwork Institute recommends that lumber grades *not* be used for architectural woodwork, since even the highest grades permit defects, which makes them unacceptable for this type of work. The AWI has therefore established its own grades of Premium, Custom, and Economy, which are used not only for lumber (Table

3) and plywood, but also for details of construction and workmanship.

Not included in the standard lumber grades or in the AWI grades are the special forms of several species which are selected for certain abnormal features. Examples are knotty pine, wormy chestnut, pecky cypress, and wattled walnut.

In some species there is little difference in appearance between heartwood and sapwood, while in others the difference in color is marked. Where this contrast is not considered aesthetically desirable, the sapwood can be stained to match the heartwood as part of the finishing operation. Only redwood and western red cedar are available in all-heartwood grades. For other species, if all-heartwood is required, it must be cut from the regular grade, which may seriously limit the maximum sizes that can be provided.

Dimensions of milled lumber vary slightly in different areas of the country. Lengths are in 2-ft increments beginning with 6 or 8 ft. The usual maximum length is 16 ft, but some softwoods are available in 18- and 20-ft lengths. Actual length should be assumed to be 2 in. less than nominal length, to allow for end checking and shrinkage resulting from seasoning or kiln drying. For custom molding, it should be noted that the maximum capacity of most molding machines is 4 by 11½ in.

The Quality Standards of AWI permit the gluing of large members. In hardwood species, pieces may be glued for thickness and width as follows: thickness exceeding 1 1/16 in.; width exceeding 4¼ in. for rift sawn oak, red and white birch, walnut, and butternut; width exceeding 7¼ in. for other species. Softwoods may be glued if width exceeds 11¼ in.

Exterior trim, as well as siding, is usually of softwood. Important considerations are resistance to decay and paint-holding characteristics. Redwood, cypress, and western red cedar are notably resistant to decay and are therefore sometimes called the "durable woods." Other species should be treated with a preservative. In paint-holding ability, the three durable woods, along with all the other cedars, constitute Group 1 (best) in the Forest Product Laboratory's classification. Ponderosa pine, of which much stock millwork is made, is in Group 3. Douglas fir and southern yellow pine are in Group 4 (poorest). Fastenings for exterior trim should be of noncorroding metal, such as galvanized steel, aluminum, or stainless steel; note that cement-coated nails are not rustproof.

American softwoods

The principal softwoods used in finishing work are listed below, along with a brief summary of their characteristics pertinent to this use.

Cedar, Alaska (Chamaecyparis nootkatensis). Pacific Coast. Heartwood and sapwood clear yellow. Texture fine and uniform; works and finishes well. Decay resistant. Very low shrinkage.

Cedar, incense (Libocedrus decurrens). Pacific Coast. Reddish-brown with some contrasting cream-colored sapwood. Distinctive knots range from medium to large in size. Flourishes of grain.

Cedar, inland red. Northwest. Color varies from dark reddish-brown to light yellow; generally, this is the darkest of the cedars. Interesting grain flourishes; medium and larger knots.

Cedar, Port-Orford (Chamaecyparis lawsoniana). Pacific Coast. Heartwood light yellow to pale brown. Fine and uniform texture with straight grain. Moderately light, strong, and shock resistant. Shrinks moderately with little warping. Heartwood very decay resistant.

Cedar, western red (Thuja plicata). Northwest. Heartwood reddish-brown and highly resistant to decay. Light, soft, easily worked; very low shrinkage. Holds paint well. Available in all-heartwood grade.

Cedar, white (Chamaecyparis occidentalis and *C. thyoides).* North and East Coast. Heartwood light reddish-brown; sapwood lighter, sometimes nearly white. Texture fine and uniform. Light, soft, brittle, splits easily. Low shrinkage. Heartwood resistant to decay.

Cypress, southern (Taxodium distichum). Southeast. Heartwood varies from light yellowish-brown to dark brownish-red, brown, or chocolate. Sometimes contains decay pockets known as pecks. Shrinkage moderate. Highly resistant to decay. Holds paint well.

Douglas fir (Pseudotsuga taxifolia). Northwest. Orange-red in color with narrow, light-colored sap ring. Grain is distinct. Strong, hard, heavy. Knots are of medium size and blend with the color of the wood. Does not hold paint well.

Fir, balsam (Abies balsamea). Northeast and north. Nearly white, with little figure. Light in weight, soft, low in strength.

Fir, white (Abies concolor and *A. grandis).* West. White with reddish tinge. Interesting grain pattern. Light, soft, straight-grained, uniform texture, easily worked. The whitest commercial softwood.

Hemlock, eastern (Tsuga canadensis). North and northeast. Heartwood is pale brown with reddish hue, coarse and uneven in texture. Knots characteristically small. Moderately light in weight and low in strength.

Hemlock, western (Tsuga heterophylla). Northwest. Heartwood and sapwood are almost white with a purplish tinge. Fine and uniform texture; straight grain. Many small tight black knots. Moderately light and strong with high shrinkage.

Larch, western (Larix occidentalis). Northwest. Heartwood mostly reddish with small amount of straw-colored sapwood. Interesting grain pattern. Little contrast between knot and wood color; knots usually small. Does not hold paint well.

Pine, Idaho, or western white (Pinus monticola). Northwest. Color varies from light to pale reddish-brown. Unusually straight and even grain. Characteristic red knots are neat, small to medium in size. High shrinkage.

Pine, lodgepole (Pinus contorta). West. Deep straw to creamy white in color with satiny sheen. Knots range in size from small to medium and are neat in appearance. Light in weight, low in strength.

Pine, northern white (Pinus strobus). North and northeast. Heartwood ranges from cream to light brown, often with a reddish tinge. Very uniform texture and straight grain. Easily worked; takes glue and paint well. Very low shrinkage.

Pine, ponderosa (Pinus ponderosa). West. Creamy white to deep straw color. Gentle grain configuration. Knots are generally smooth, small to large in size. Uniform texture; easy to work.

Pine, red, or Norway (Pinus resinosa). North. Heartwood pale red to reddish-brown; sapwood nearly white with yellowish tinge. Generally straight grain, coarse and uneven in texture, and somewhat resinous. High shrinkage.

Pine, southern yellow, including *longleaf (Pinus palustris),* shortleaf *(P. echinata),* loblolly or North Carolina *(P. taeda).* Southeast. Heartwood reddish-brown, sapwood yellowish-white. Longleaf pine is heavy, strong, and hard, but the less dense types are used for finishing lumber because they work more easily and hold finishes better. North Carolina pine is lighter and softer.

Pine, sugar (Pinus lambertiana). West. Soft-toned creamy white, darkens to pale brown, sometimes tinged with pink. Grain often shows light brown flecks. Knots medium to large, red in color. Low shrinkage. Unusually wide boards available.

Redwood (Sequoia sempervirens). Pacific Coast. Heartwood light cherry to dark mahogany color; narrow sapwood almost white. Straight-grained, easily worked, holds paint well, shrinks very little. Highly resistant to decay. Unusually wide boards obtainable. Available in all-heartwood grade.

Spruce, eastern (Picea rubra, P. glauca, P. mariana). North and northeast. Heartwood ranges from cream to light brown, often with a reddish tinge. Uniform texture, straight grain, easily worked, moderate shrinkage.

Spruce, Engelmann (Picea engelmannii). West. One of the whitest of western woods, its grain is nearly invisible from a short distance away. Characterized by neat array of small knots.

Spruce, Sitka (Picea sitchensis). Pacific Coast. Heartwood light pinkish-brown, sapwood creamy white. Fine uniform texture with straight grain. High shrinkage. Light but strong for its weight.

REFERENCES

Wood Handbook, Forest Products Laboratory, U.S. Department of Agriculture.

Architectural Woodwork Quality Standards, Architectural Woodwork Institute, Chicago (1978). Also other publications of the Institute.

Publications of the following trade associations:

California Redwood Association, San Francisco, Calif.

National Hardwood Lumber Association, Chicago, Ill.

Southern Forest Products Association, New Orleans, La.

West Coast Lumbermen's Association, Portland, Ore.

Western Wood Products Association, Portland, Ore.

By BURDETT GREEN, *Executive Vice President, Fine Hardwoods Association,*
and JAMES ARKIN, *AIA, Consultant, Architectural Woodwork Institute*

BIRCH, DOMESTIC AND CANADIAN

There are two species of commercial importance that are often marketed together, as listed below. They are so similar that it is not necessary to specify them. However, one should specify either "Natural Birch," "Selected White Birch" or "Selected Red Birch." Natural Birch combines both sapwood and heartwood. Selected White Birch includes only sapwood, and Selected Red Birch only heartwood.

BIRCH, SWEET (*Betula lenta*) — Black Birch, Cherry Birch
Source: Mainly from Adirondack and eastern Appalachian areas, although also as far south as northern part of Gulf States
Color: Brown tinged with red; thin, light brown or yellow sapwood
Pattern: Grain distinct but not prominent
Characteristics: Heavy; very strong and hard; close-grained
Uses: All cabinetwork where strength and hardness is desired
Availability: Abundant as both veneer (rotary, sliced) and lumber
Price Range: Medium

BIRCH, YELLOW (*Betula alleghaniensis,* formerly *Betula lutea*) — Gray Birch, Silver Birch, Swamp Birch
Source: Canada, Lakes states, New England south to North Carolina
Color: Cream, light brown tinged with red; thin, nearly white sapwood
Pattern: Plain and often curly or wavy
Characteristics: Heavy; strong; hard; close-grained; even texture
Uses: Interiors; furniture; doors; store fixtures; accessories; etc.
Availability: Veneer (both rotary and sliced) and lumber abundant. As veneers, sapwood of rotary birch is sold as "selected white" and heartwood as "selected red." Greater volume produced is "natural birch," and contains a normal combination of color tones
Price Range: Medium

MAPLE

The three species of maple described below are grown in widely separated areas and vary greatly in physical properties.

MAPLE, HARD (*Acer saccharum*) — Birds Eye Maple, Northern Maple, Rock Maple, Sugar Maple
Source: Lakes states, Appalachians, Northwest U. S., Canada
Color: Cream to light reddish-brown heartwood; thin white sapwood tinged slightly with reddish-brown
Pattern: Usually straight-grained; sometimes found highly figured with *curly, blistered, quilted, birds eye* or *burl grain,* scattered over entire tree or in irregular stripes and patches
Characteristics: Heavy; hard; strong; close-grained; tough; stiff; uniform texture. Excellent resistance to abrasion and indentation
Uses: Interiors; furniture; fixtures; flooring; decorative inlays
Availability: *Plain maple* veneer (quartered, sliced, half-round, rotary) plentiful. *Figured maple* (including birds eye, butts, etc.) veneer (quartered, sliced, half-round, rotary) rare
Price Range: *Plain maple* — medium. *Figured maple* — costly

MAPLE, SOFT (*Acer saccharinum*) — Silver Maple
Same general characteristics as hard maple, but not nearly so hard or strong. Usually shows considerable dark (mineral) streaks.
Availability: Plentiful as both veneer and lumber
Price Range: Medium to inexpensive

MAPLE, OREGON (*Acer macrophyllum*) — Big Leaf Maple
A true maple, but not so hard or strong as silver maple.
Source: Pacific Coast and Southern Canada
Availability: As both lumber and veneer, locally. As figured veneers (blistered, burl, etc.), rare
Price Range: Inexpensive for plain types. Moderate to costly for quilted and burls

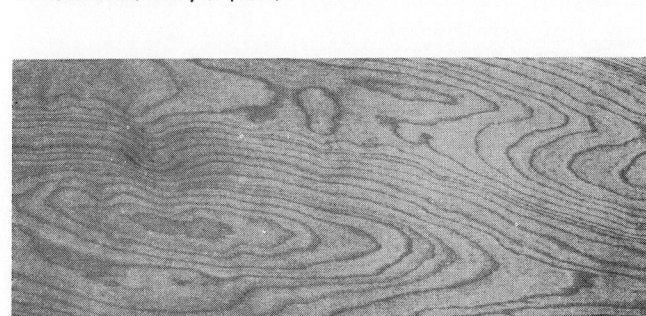
Birch, Natural, rotary (1 piece)

Birch, Selected White, rotary (1 piece)

Maple, plain rotary (2 pieces, book-matched)

Maple, birds eye (1 piece)

MAHOGANY

An often misused name, applied to many woods not of the mahogany family. The three authentic commercial species of mahogany are *Swietenia mahogani*, *Swietenia macrophylla* and *Khaya ivorensis*. (All true mahoganies are the *Meliaceae* family, *genera Swietenia* or *Khaya*.) Their descriptions follow:

Mahogany, African, swirl (1 piece)

MAHOGANY, AFRICAN (*Khaya ivorensis*)
Source: Africa (Ivory Coast, Gold Coast, French Cameroon, Cape Lopez, Nigeria)
Color: Light pink to reddish-brown and tannish brown
Pattern: Although pores are distributed, this wood produces a very distinct, pleasing grain. The most lavishly figured mahogany offered in plain stripe, broken stripe, mottle, fiddleback, fine crotches and faux swirl
Characteristics: Available in great lengths and widths; milder textured with slightly larger pores than other mahogany species; relatively hard; works well; highly lustrous; polishes well; durable
Uses: Interiors, furniture; accessories and art objects; etc.
Availability: Veneer (quartered, sliced, half-round, rotary) abundant. Lumber abundant
Price Range: Medium; costly for highly figured veneers

Mahogany, African, quartered ribbon-striped (1 piece)

MAHOGANY, CUBAN (*Swietenia mahogani*)
One of the finest of the several mahogany species. However, the exportation of this species from Cuba is no longer permitted

Source: Cuba, also throughout the West Indies
Color: Light red; yellowish-tan when cut; darkens rapidly to deep rich golden brown or brown-red; exceptionally fine color
Pattern: Highly figured, mottled, fiddle-back crotches, also plain stripes
Characteristics: Heavier and harder than the other mahoganies; wears exceptionally well; extremely durable; close-grained; takes excellent finish; has good strength and bending properties; ideal wood for turning and carving
Uses: Fine cabinetry
Availability: Haiti, Puerto Rico, and the Dominican Republic

Mahogany, Tropical American, plain flat cut (1 piece)

MAHOGANY, TROPICAL AMERICAN, including PERUVIAN and BRAZILIAN MAHOGANY (*Swietenia macrophylla*). (Brazilian Mahogany marketed as Amazon Mahogany)
Source: Mexico, Brazil, Peru and Central America (especially Honduras)
Color: Varies from a light reddish or yellowish-brown to a rich, dark red, depending upon country of origin and situation. Most supplies tend to be yellowish-tan, changing on brief exposure to rich, golden brown
Pattern: A considerable variety of figures, similar to African mahogany except crotches are not readily available. Straighter grain generally. Location influences appearance also
Characteristics: Lighter and softer than Cuban; mostly straight-grained but even when interlocked is exceptionally stable; more mellow texture than Cuban (West Indian); extremely good strength properties; works well; stains and finishes well; durable and decay-resistant. Central America produces more figured logs for fancy veneers
Uses: Paneling; furniture; fine joinery; exterior uses
Availability: Central American veneer (quartered, sliced, half-round) abundant. Lumber plentiful. Brazilian and Peruvian plentiful
Price Range: Inexpensive to medium

Mahogany, Tropical American, figured flat cut (1 piece)

OAK, AMERICAN

Includes several species from the Red Oak and White Oak groups. Except for source and color, Red Oak and White Oak, the two leading American species, are very similar. Characteristics they have in common are:

Pattern: Quartered oak has a striking "flake" pattern caused by extremely large and wide rays that reflect light. Plain flat-sliced or sawn oak has an attractive figure of stripes and leafy grain caused by the distinct layers of springwood and summerwood and the large pores, especially concentrated in the springwood. Rift-cut (half-round) oak has a fine pin stripe. Rotary-cut oak has a distinct watery figure with great contrast

Characteristics: A heavy, ring-porous hardwood with larger, more prominent pores in the springwood than summerwood; very strong and very hard; stiff and heavy; durable under exposure; great wear-resistance; holds nails and screws well. Red and white oak look very similar when finished, and because of its large pores, oak takes a great variety of fine filled or textured finishes

Uses: Flooring (both solid and plywood tiles); furniture; paneling; general construction; display and store fixtures; handles

Availability: Veneer (quartered, sliced, half-round, rotary) plentiful. Lumber available

Price Range: Medium

OAK, RED (*Quercus borealis*)

Source: Throughout the eastern United States; especially in the Appalachians, Ohio, Kentucky

Color: Slightly redder tinge than white oak (though hard for an untrained eye to tell), and more uniform in color

Pattern: Flake figure less prominent than white oak

Characteristics: Slightly coarser grain, with large, rounded, open pores. Easier to finish than white oak, though both are excellent

Uses: All the same purposes as White Oak

OAK, WHITE (*Quercus alba*)

Source: Entire eastern United States, especially produced in the Central States and down through the Appalachian region

Color: From light brown with a grayish tinge in the heartwood to shades of ochre in the sapwood

Pattern: More pronounced and longer rays than red oak, and more frequently rift-sawn for the comb-grain, pin-striped figure than red oak. Occasionally crotches, swirls and burls

Characteristics: Pores are angular and very numerous and filled with a glistening substance called tyloses, which makes this wood especially suitable where water-resistance is required. Tannic acid in the wood protects it from fungi and insects. Closer grained than red oak

Uses: Nearly all common uses of hardwoods, and especially popular where strength and durability are required. Also for watertight or water-resistant purposes

OAK, ENGLISH BROWN will be treated in a later issue.

CHERRY, BLACK (*Prunus serotina*) — Rum Cherry, Wild Black Cherry

Source: Maine to Dakotas and Appalachians; production largely Pennsylvania to West Virginia

Color: Light reddish-brown

Pattern: Straight-grained; satiny; some figured. Small gum pockets are normal markings

Characteristics: Light; strong; rather hard; fine-grained

Uses: Woodwork; fine furniture

Availability: Veneer (quartered, sliced, half-round) plentiful. Very fine figured cherry available for architectural use. Lumber plentiful

Price range: Medium

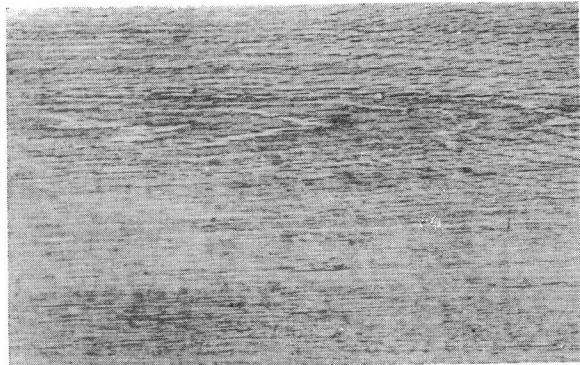

Oak, White, plain flat cut (1 piece)

Oak, White, rift cut (2 pieces, book-matched)

Oak, White, quartered (2 pieces, book-matched)

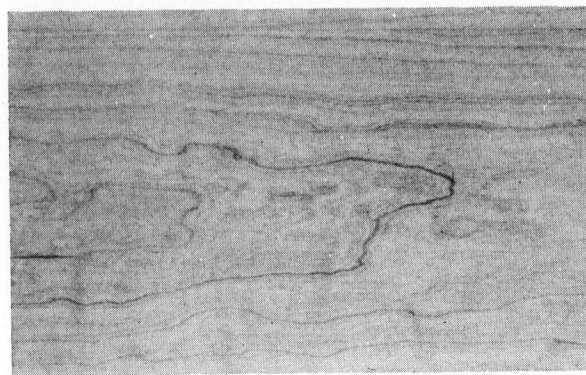

Cherry, plain sliced (1 piece)

WALNUT, AMERICAN (*Juglans nigra*)

Better than 95 per cent of all walnut used in the United States comes from one genus, *Juglans nigra*, formerly referred to as American Black Walnut. The wood itself is not black but a light to chocolate brown, sometimes slightly purplish brown. In specifying plywood or veneers, it is not enough simply to indicate "Walnut," or even "American Walnut," because this one species is available in more different figure or grain types than any other wood.

Source: Grows throughout the United States and Southern Canada, but its commercial range is confined largely to some fifteen Central States

Color: Light gray-brown to dark purplish brown

Pattern: Plain to highly figured. Produces a greater variety of figure types than any other hardwood (approached only by mahogany): longwood (flat-cut; half-round; quarters, both plain and figured), crotches, swirls, stumpwood and occasionally burls. Four of the most readily available types are described below:

Plain Flat Cut—Comes in reasonably good widths, from 8 to 18 in., and occasionally in "half-round" to even wider stocks. Flitches (or individual stock) usually contain from 1200 to 1800 sq ft. In lengths, 9 to 10 ft predominate; however, fine architectural logs may be had up to 12 or 14 ft and occasionally to 16 ft long

Figured Flat Cut—Leafy grain character caused by annual growth rings is the same as in "plain flat cut," but, in addition, one or more types of "cross figures," "roll figure" or "mottle" appear, usually distributed more or less evenly over the face. Uniformity over large areas should not be expected, because the figure varies even within one log

Quartered Plain—The growth rings on the sides of flat cut walnut produce a quartered effect. By cutting out the leafy heart (flat) grain, pure quarters result. Certain large logs are often quarter-cut to give the entire sheet a stripe. Quarters, which come from only one-quarter of the log, are therefore much narrower in width, ranging from 5 to 10 in., mostly 5 to 8 in. However, panels of any width may be obtained by matching in either of two ways: book matching or slip matching

Quartered Figured—As explained above, a small percentage of the logs that may be quartered have "cross figure." When book-matched, they produce a "fiddle-back" effect. Other types of cross figure may be had by specifying "slightly figured quarters" or "highly figured quarters"

Characteristics: Moderately heavy; very strong for its weight, exceptionally stable. Even "plain" types are often characterized by dapples (pin knots, which are really not knots) and slight variations in color. When chosen for this informal character, the wood is described as "Enchanted Walnut"

Uses: Architectural woodwork; furniture

Availability: Veneer abundant. Lumber plentiful

Price Range: Medium to costly for highly figured types

WALNUT, CLARO (*Juglans hindsii*)—California Walnut

There is considerable confusion as to the exact species of *Juglans* that produces fast-growing Claro Walnut. Some authorities claim it comes from *Juglans regia*. (Photograph on Sheet 5.)

Source: California and southern Oregon, east of Coast Range

Color: Tannish brown with dark brown

Pattern: Wavy grain; prominent light stripes

Characteristics: Moderately heavy; hard; rather open-grained

Uses: Highly decorative areas of fine furniture and paneled interiors

Availability: Quartered veneers rare. Lumber not available

Price Range: Medium to costly

Walnut, American, plain flat cut (1 piece)

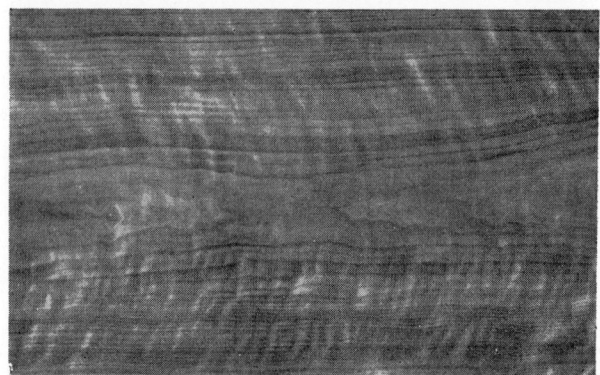

Walnut, American, figured flat cut (1 piece)

Walnut, American, quartered sliced (2 pieces book-matched)

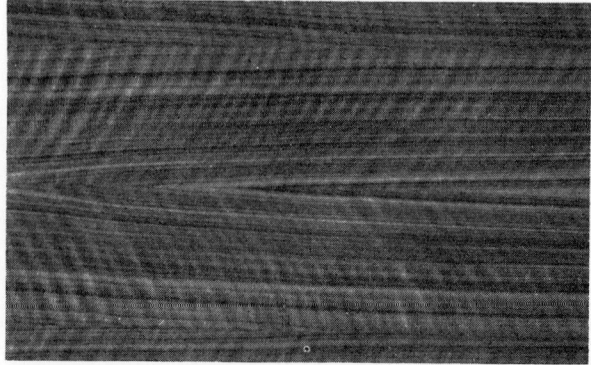

Walnut, American, quartered figured (2 pieces, book-matched)

WALNUT, EUROPEAN *(Juglans regia)*

Although walnut grows rather widely (though sparsely) over most of the world, only a small amount is imported, and it is mainly from Europe. The European walnuts are all from the same genus, *Juglans regia*, or Royal Walnut. Each type normally takes the name of the country of origin. The most important are:

WALNUT, CIRCASSIAN

Source: Europe
Color: Tawny
Pattern: Variegated streaks of black or dark brown (these pigment streaks passing across the growth rings are typical of Circassian Walnut). Occasionally crotches and swirls
Characteristics: Not so strong or hard as American Walnut, but otherwise about the same properties
Uses: Woodwork; highly decorative furniture
Availability: Veneer rare. Lumber scarce
Price Range: Expensive

WALNUT, ENGLISH OR FRENCH

Source: England and France
Color: Soft and quite gray-brown; lighter in color than American Walnut
Pattern: Fine, smooth grain; less prominent growth lines than Circassian Walnut
Characteristics: Very much like Circassian
Uses: Same as Circassian
Availability: Scarce
Price Range: Expensive

WALNUT, PERSIAN

Persian Walnut is the wood of European-Asiatic trees. It is grown in many countries and marketed as English, Italian, Turkish, Bulgarian, Spanish, Austrian and Russian Walnut, according to locale or source

BUTTERNUT *(Juglans cinerea)* — White Walnut

A true walnut.

Source: North Central States and Southern Canada
Color: Pale brown
Pattern: Satiny wood with leafy grain
Characteristics: Soft to medium textured, with occasional dark spots or streaks
Uses: Interior finish of houses; furniture
Availability: Veneer (sliced) and lumber somewhat more than "rare"
Price Range: Medium

ORIENTALWOOD *(Endiandra Palmerstoni)* — Australian Laurel, Australian Walnut, Oriental Walnut; formerly "Queensland Walnut"

Although this wood was introduced into America in the late 1920's as "Oriental Walnut," it is not related to the walnut family (see botanical names).

Source: Australia
Color: Pinkish-gray to brown
Pattern: Somewhat like plain quartered Claro Walnut but with dark stripes and even broader ones
Characteristics: Medium weight; turns and polishes well; firm to hard
Uses: Furniture; cabinetry
Availability: Veneer (quartered) scarce
Price Range: Costly

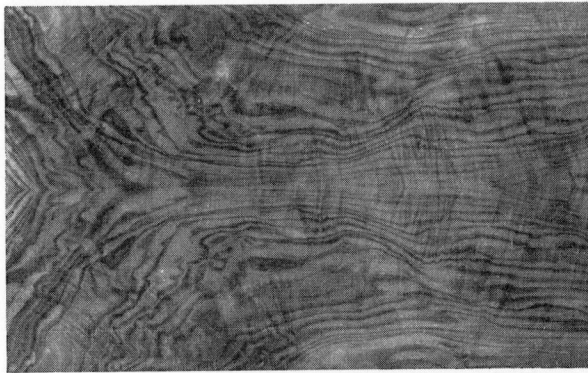

Walnut, Claro, flat cut (2 pieces, book-matched)

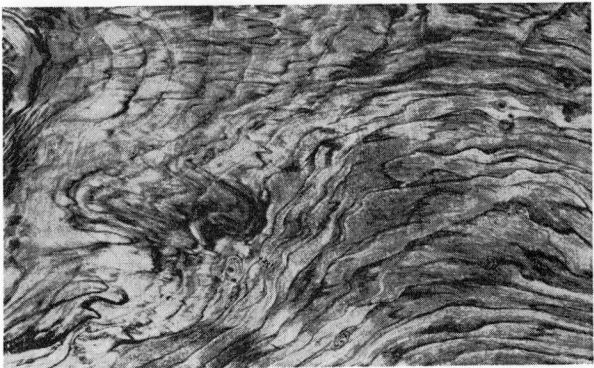

Walnut, Circassian (one piece)

Butternut, plain flat cut (1 piece)

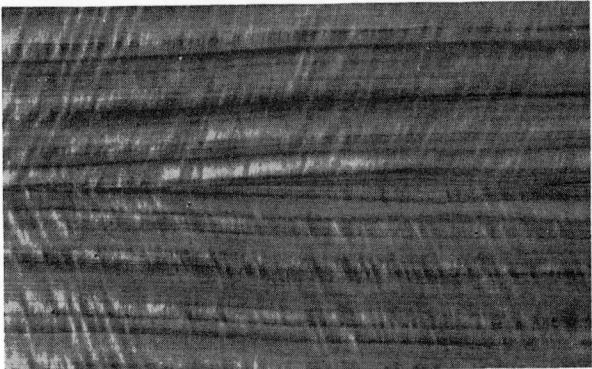

Orientalwood (2 pieces, book-matched)

ASH, AMERICAN

There are many American species of ash, but the three major commercial ones are, in order of importance:

ASH, BLACK *(Fraxinus nigra)*—Brown Ash, Hoop Ash, Swamp Ash
Source: Principally the Lakes States
Color: Warm brown heartwood with a thin white or light brown sapwood
Pattern: Clusters of eyes occasionally scattered over plain wood
Characteristics: Extremely stable; heavy; rather soft; tough
Uses: Veneer for faces of decorative plywood; lumber for solid plank wall panels and for chairs, especially bent frames
Availability: Veneers (largely rotary, rarely burls) rare to plentiful
Price Range: Medium

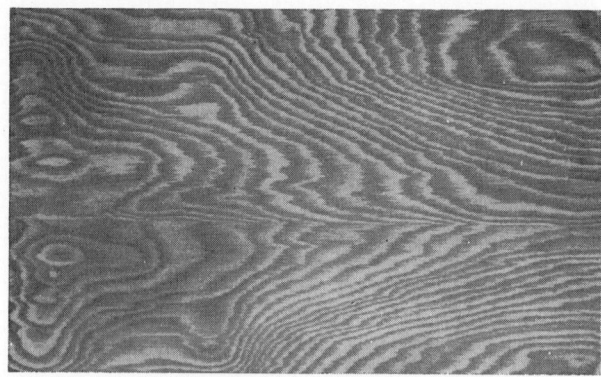

Ash, Brown (2 pieces, book-matched)

ASH, GREEN *(Fraxinus pennsylvanica lanceolsta)*—Swamp Ash, Water Ash; lumber sold as White Ash
Source: Principally South Atlantic States and Mississippi Valley
Color: Cream to very light brown heartwood with thick, lighter colored sapwood
Pattern: Both flat-cut and quartered; moderately open grain
Characteristics: Heavy; hard; strong; medium-grained; tough
Uses: Interiors; furniture
Availability: Largely for commercial veneers
Price Range: Medium

Ash, White (2 pieces, book-matched)

ASH, WHITE *(Fraxinus americana)*
Source: Principally Lakes States, also New England and Central States
Color: Cream to very light brown heartwood with thick, lighter colored sapwood
Pattern: Both flat-cut and quartered; moderately open grain
Characteristics: Heavy; hard; strong; medium-grained; tough
Uses: Interiors; furniture
Availability: Veneer (quartered, sliced, half-round, rotary) plentiful, (butts and figured sliced), rare. Lumber plentiful
Price Range: Medium

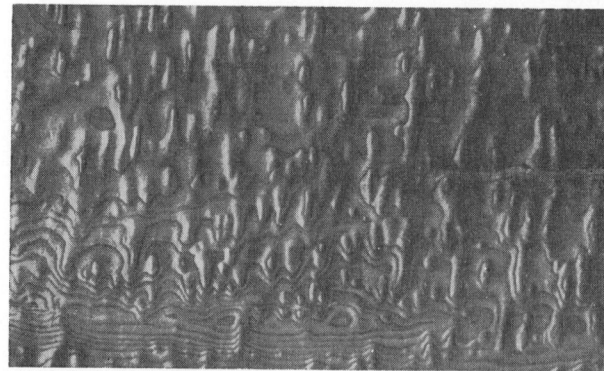

Ash, Japanese (1 piece)

ASH, JAPANESE *(Fraxinus sieboldiana)*—Damo, Tamo
Source: Japan
Color: Brownish-tan through gray to almost white
Pattern: Plain to highly varied with swirls, fiddle-back mottle and a "peanut shell" figure. Extreme grain character
Characteristics: Bends easily; lighter weight than American and European Ash; glues well; finishes well; strong for its weight
Uses: Decorative interiors and furniture; inlays and overlays
Availability: Veneer (half-round) scarce
Price Range: Costly

AVODIRE *(Turraeanthus africana)*—Apaya
Source: African Gold Coast, Ivory Coast (Liberia, Cameroons)
Color: White to creamy gold
Pattern: Largely figured with a mottle; crotches and swirls
Characteristics: Medium texture; firm, clean grain; usually wavy or irregularly interlocked; lustrous; moderately hard; weighs about the same as African Mahogany
Uses: Architectural panels; furniture; fixtures
Availability: Veneer (quartered, sliced, half-round) plentiful, also crotches and swirls. Lumber available
Price Range: Moderate

Avodire, rope figure (2 pieces, book-matched)

BUBINGA (*Guibourtia demeusii*)—African Rosewood, Akume, Kewazinga

Source: West Africa

Color: Red with streaks or lines of ornamental dark purple

Pattern: From a rather plain stripe to a heavy mottle which occurs in the quarter-cut wood. Occasionally cut sliced and half-round

Characteristics: Very hard. While described as having a close grain, it has conspicuous and fairly large pores. Capable of being worked into fine cabinetry

Uses: General cabinetry

Availability: Plentiful in the form of veneers. Largely produced as longwood, but occasionally as crotches and swirls

Price Range: Medium to costly

Bubinga, quartered (2 pieces, bock-matched)

CEDAR, AROMATIC RED (*Juniperus virginiana*)—Eastern Red Cedar, Juniper, Pencil Cedar, Red Cedar, Southern Red Cedar, Tennessee Red Cedar

Although Cedar is not one of the hardwoods, since it is a coniferous or needle-bearing tree rather than a "broad-leaf," which generally depicts hardwoods, this species is commonly produced by the hardwood industry. It is a very fine-textured wood which is used extensively along with hardwoods by the cedar chest industry and also for lining interiors of closets and cabinetry to be used for storage.

Source: Occurs over most of the eastern two-thirds of United States. Largest production in Southeastern and South Central States

Color: Light red with streaks of light sapwood

Pattern: Knotty, with other natural characteristics always present

Characteristics: Although brittle, it is regarded as a fine wood to work

Uses: Cedar storage chests; linings of closets and chests; small articles of woodenware

Availability: Veneer (sawn or sliced) plentiful; lumber plentiful, both in rather small sizes

Price Range: Medium

Cedar, Aromatic Red (3 pieces, unmatched)

ELM, AMERICAN (*Ulmus americana*)—Soft Elm, Water Elm, White Elm

Although there are several varieties of Elm that vary but slightly in character, the two commonly available types are Northern Brown Elm and Southern Elm.

Source: United States, east of the Rockies

Color: Light brownish

Pattern: Conspicuous growth pattern, like Ash

Characteristics: Heavy; hard; strong; tough; difficult to split; coarse-grained; bends exceedingly well

Uses: Widely used as veneers for containers; some for furniture. Although for years the most widely used wood for berry baskets and cther containers, less of it is used for that purpose today and more of it is cut into veneers and lumber for both architectural plywood and fine furniture

Availability: Veneer (quartered, sliced, rotary) plentiful. Lumber available

Price Range: Medium

Elm, Northern Brown, flat cut (2 pieces, book-matched)

ELM, CARPATHIAN BURL (*Ulmus campestris*)—English Elm

Although not pictured here, it is a type of true Elm described as Carpathian Elm Burl and was rather widely used in the furniture and fixture trade during the 1920's. Although an especially highly figured burl, it is usually quite defective and is rarely used today.

Elm, American, quartered (3 pieces, book-matched)

GUMWOOD (*Liquidambar styraciflua*)

For years Gumwood has been one of the most widely used hardwoods in the furniture and woodworking industries. For many years it was extensively used for interior trim and woodwork, especially in areas to be painted. In certain sections of the country it was commonly finished natural. Today Sap Gum is most frequently used in a lumber form for the structural parts of furniture carrying plywood surfaces of other woods. Sap Gum, too, is widely used for the inner plies of "bonded" or plywood construction. Heartwood and sapwood are sold separately as Red Gum and Sap Gum.

GUM, RED (*Heartwood*) —Hazelwood, Southern Gum, Sweet Gum

Source: Wide range in the United States, but commercial production largely from lower Mississippi Valley
Color: Reddish-brown
Pattern: Dark streaks
Characteristics: Moderately heavy; hard; straight; close-grained; not exceedingly strong. Often selected for its attractive figure
Uses: Outside and inside finish of houses; cabinetry
Availability: Veneer (sliced, rotary) plentiful. Lumber available
Price Range: Medium

GUM, SAP (*Sapwood*)

Source: Same as Red Gum
Color: Pinkish-white, often blued by sap stains
Pattern: Plain but not strong; usually watery
Characteristics: Same as Red Gum except not as durable
Uses: Plywood (interiors) and lumber for furniture; architectural woodwork for paint; most widely used species for veneers in the United States
Availability: Veneer (rotary) abundant. Lumber abundant
Price Range: Inexpensive

HAREWOOD, ENGLISH GRAY (*Acer pseudoplatanus*)—Sycamore

The name "Sycamore" is normally applied to this species in its country of origin, England. As noted by its botanical name, *Acer*, it is a true maple, and it is a great deal like our Northern Hard Maple. *Pseudoplatanus* further indicates that it is a false *platanus*, which is the botanical name of plane-tree or sycamore.

Source: England
Color: Natural white. Called English white before dyeing. Usually dyed silver gray
Pattern: Both plain and figured
Characteristics: Same as Maple
Uses: Marquetry; inlay; paneling
Availability: Veneer (quartered, sliced) scarce. Lumber available
Price Range: Costly

IREME (*Terminalia ivorensis*)—African Teak, Black Afara, Emeri, Framerie, Idigbo, Iroko

In the European trade this is a very valuable timber of a light grayish-brown color. The grain is firm and hard and the wood machines well. It has been used for many years in England and France, and limited quantities have been brought into the United States.

Source: Africa, Gold Coast
Color: Pale yellow to light brown
Pattern: Faint ribbon stripe with intermediate grain and noticeable rays
Uses: Panels and cabinetwork
Availability: Plentiful as veneers
Price Range: Moderate

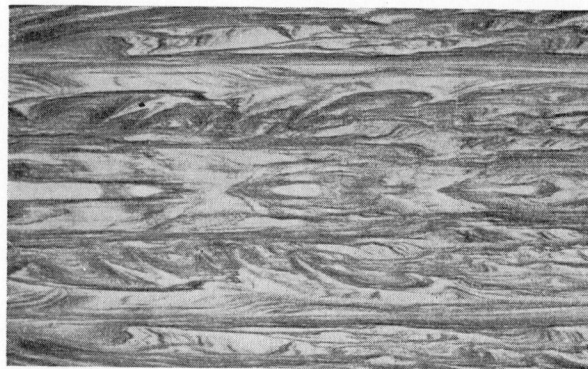

Gum, Red, figured (2 pieces, book-matched)

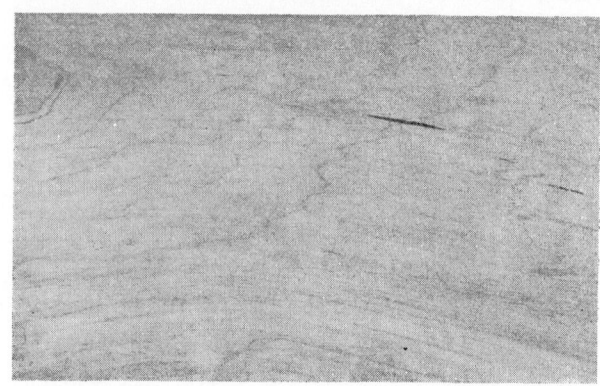

Gum, Sapwood (1 piece)

Harewood, English Gray, figured (1 piece)

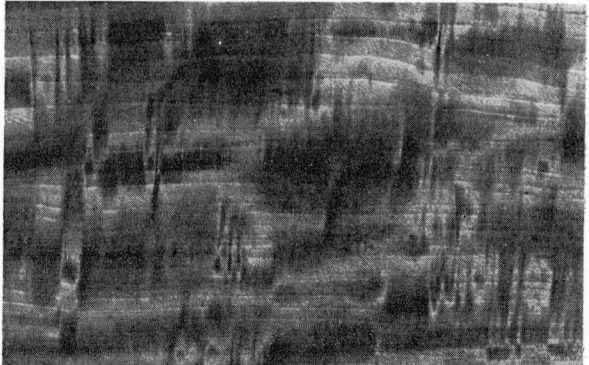

Ireme, mottled (1 piece)

LAUAN or PHILIPPINE HARDWOODS

The Philippine Islands are the source of a great variety of hardwoods only a few of which are imported into the United States. The greatest volume comes from a group sold commercially as "Philippine Mahogany," although it is not related to the true mahoganies. Several fine hardwoods from the Philippine Islands and that part of the world are known and marketed under their own names, such as Narra, Almon, Bella-Rosa, Sonora and Paldao. Those classified and sold as Philippine Mahogany are quite varied in color and texture. They include the softer species of *Shorea*, which are light-colored to reddish-brown in color, and the species of *Parashorea* and *Pentacme*. This group is divided into two classes, as follows: (1) Red Lauan (*Shorea negrosensis*), Tanquile (*Shorea polysperma*) and Tiaong (*Shorea spp.*); (2) Almon (*Shorea almon*), White Lauan (*Pentacme contorta*), Bagtikan (*Parashorea picata*) and Mayapis (*Shorea squamata*). In general, these woods, as compared with the Tropical American and African Mahoganies, are more coarse-grained and stringy. They require a greater amount of sanding to produce a finishing surface and are much less stable under atmospheric (moisture) changes. Pictured here are the less common type of Red Lauan showing butterfly pattern and the run-of-mine type of Lauan that is reaching this country today, which has a mild ribbon stripe and is nearly all quartered.

LAUAN, RED (*Shorea negrosensis*)

Also called "Philippine Mahogany." Sold as Philippine Hardwoods.

Source: Philippine Islands
Color: Red to brown
Pattern: Ribbon stripe; interlocking grain
Characteristics: Coarse texture; large pores
Uses: Furniture; doors; cabinetry
Availability: Veneer (quartered, sliced, rotary) abundant. Lumber available
Price Range: Medium to inexpensive

LAUAN, WHITE (*Pentacome contorta*)

Same as above but for color.

NARRA (*Pterocarpus indicus, Pterocarpus echinatus*)—Angsena, Sena

Although this wood is another one of the Philippine Hardwoods, it has properties distinctly superior to those described above.

Source: Dutch East Indies, Philippines
Color: Rose to deep red. Some are golden yellow
Pattern: Distinct grain character; some ripple
Characteristics: Heavy and hard; not strong; durable
Uses: High-grade furniture; interior finish of ships and vehicles
Availability: Veneer (quartered) rare
Price Range: Costly

MAKORI (*Mimusops heckelii*)—African "Cherry," Baku, Cherry "Mahogany," Makore

Source: African Gold Coast, Nigeria
Color: Pinkish-brown to blood red or red-brown
Pattern: Somewhat similar to a close-grained Mahogany, but with dark red growth lines and smaller pores, as found in Cherry. Some logs are straight-grained and show figure like African Mahogany stripes; others have a striking, checkered figure sometimes streaked with darker color
Characteristics: Finer textured than true mahoganies, and denser, harder and heavier; tough; stiff; large sizes; strong; gummy and lustrous; glues well; works fairly easily
Uses: Furniture and cabinetry
Availability: Veneer (quartered, sliced) plentiful
Price Range: Medium

Lauan, Red, flat cut (2 pieces, book-matched)

Lauan, White (2 pieces, slip-matched)

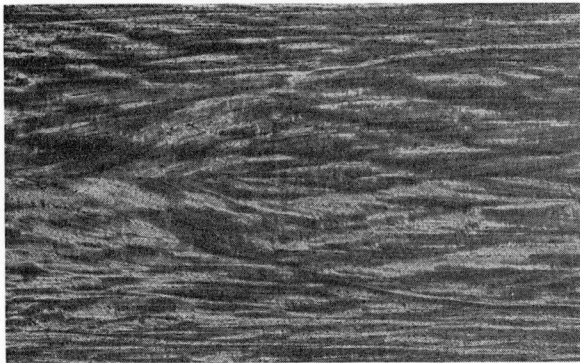

Narra, semi-figured (2 pieces, book-matched)

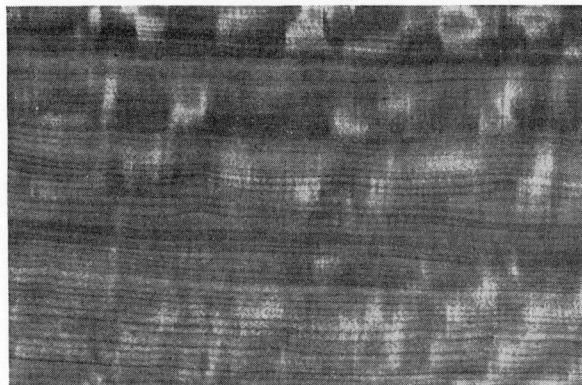

Makori, quartered, mottled (1 piece)

LACEWOOD (*Cardwellia sublimis*)—Australian Silky Oak, Queensland Silky Oak, Selano, Silky Oak.

Source: Queensland, Australia

Color: Light pink with silvery sheen

Pattern: Small flaky grain due to large rays

Characteristics: Very attractive over-all pattern when used on small areas

Uses: Often as borders and limited, highly figured areas of fine furniture

Availability: Veneer (quartered) scarce

Price Range: Costly

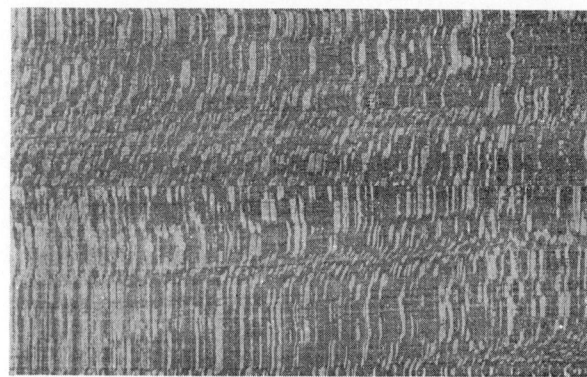
Lacewood, quartered (one piece)

LAUREL, EAST INDIAN (*Terminalia tomentosa*)—East Indian Walnut

This species is closely related to Ireme (note botanical name). However, the Laurel principally imported into this country is a very important wood growing throughout India and Burma. It varies widely in color from a yellowish-brown through all stages to a rich, warm brown with dark streaks, handsomely marked, and many types of figure. Another type of Laurel produced in the United States, which is an entirely different species known as California Laurel or Oregon Myrtle, is usually produced in burl or clustered figure. This should not be confused with the Laurel from the Far East (*Terminalia*).

Source: India and Burma

Color: Gray or brown with black lines

Pattern: Striped; occasional block-mottle or fiddleback figure; indistinct rays

Characteristics: Coarse-grained; hard and brittle; pores not numerous

Uses: Fine cabinetry

Availability: Veneer (quartered) scarce. Lumber scarce

Price Range: Costly

Laurel, East Indian, quartered (2 pieces, book-matched)

LIMBA (*Terminalia superba*) — "Korina," Afara, Frake, Offram

Another *Terminalia* which has been widely publicized under the trade-name of "Korina." In recent years this species has become one of the most popular naturally blond woods brought into this country. It has an especial appeal for architectural use in view of the fact that it is available in large sizes, as is Mahogany, and as both veneers (plywood) and lumber.

Source: West Africa

Color: Pale yellow to light brown

Pattern: Rays fine and irregular; pores scarce, but large enough to give an interesting grain character

Characteristics: Medium texture and hardness; a naturally blond wood of good working properties

Uses: Architectural paneling and woodwork; contemporary furniture

Availability: Veneer (quartered, sliced) plentiful. Lumber available

Price Range: Medium

Limba ("Korina"), quartered (one piece)

MYRTLE (*Umbellularia californica*)—Acacia Burl, Baytree, California Laurel, Oregon Myrtle, Pepperwood (at times called Acacia but no relation)

Source: West Coast of United States, especially Southern Oregon and Northern California

Color: Golden-brown and yellowish-green. Wide range from light to dark

Pattern: Mixture of plain wood, mottle, cluster, blistered, stump and burl figure with a scattering of dark purple blotches

Characteristics: Hard, strong pores the size and distribution of Walnut; a magnificent, highly figured veneer

Uses: Decorative panels for architectural interiors, store fixtures and furniture; novelties; many fine turnings, trays and carvings

Availability: Veneers (half-round), lengths usually under 5 ft although up to 8 ft, rare to scarce. Lumber scarce

Price Range: Costly

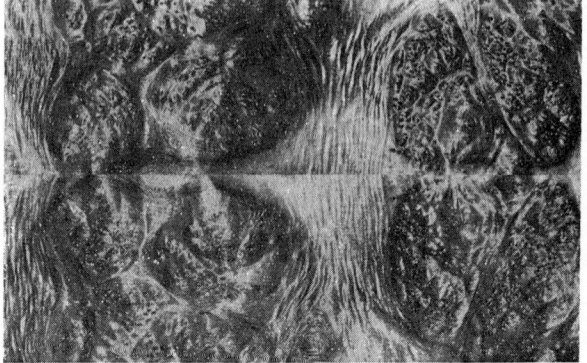
Myrtle Cluster, rotary (2 pieces, book-matched)

OAK, ENGLISH BROWN (*Quercus robur, L. Q.; Quercus sessiliflora, Salisb.*)—European Oak, Pollard Oak

Source: England

Color: Light tan to deep brown

Pattern: Black spots, sometimes creating an effect much like tortoise shell

Characteristics: Noticeable figure and grain character; especially pronounced flakes due to the medullary rays showing on the quartered surface

Uses: Architectural woodwork; some fine furniture

Availability: Veneer (quartered, sliced) scarce. Lumber scarce

Price Range: Costly

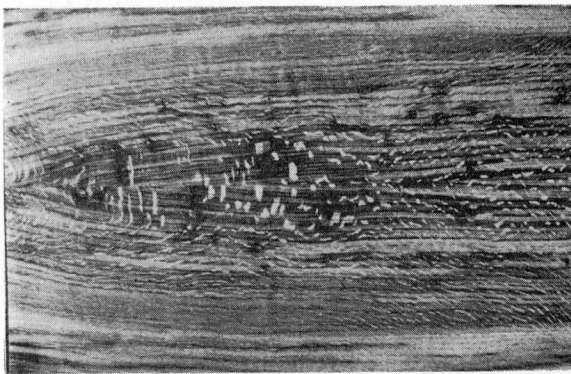

Oak, English Brown, sliced (2 pieces, book-matched)

PALDAO (*Dracontomelum dao*)—Dao

Source: Philippines, Indo-China and East Indies

Color: Gray to reddish brown

Pattern: Varied grain effects usually with irregular stripes, some occasionally very dark; occasional crotch or swirl

Characteristics: Pores are large, partially plugged; fairly hard; an exotic appearing wood

Uses: Architectural woodwork and furniture

Availability: Veneer (quartered, half-round) plentiful. Lumber available

Price Range: Medium

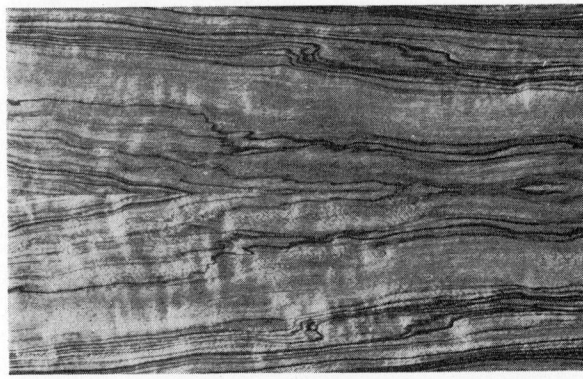

Paldao, quartered (2 pieces, book-matched)

PRIMA VERA (*Cybistax Donnell-smithii*)—Durango, Palo Blanco, San Juan (sometimes misnamed "White Mahogany")

Source: From Central Mexico, south through Guatemala and Honduras into Salvador (other species of *Tabebuia* found in northern South America)

Color: Yellow-white to yellow-brown

Pattern: Straight grain. Although often plain, it usually shows large mottle or diagonal block figure

Characteristics: Odorless and tasteless; medium to coarse textured; straight to somewhat striped grained; moderately light in weight

Uses: A fine, general-use cabinetwood

Availability: Veneer (quartered, sliced) scarce. Lumber available

Price Range: Costly

Prima Vera, quartered (2 pieces, book-matched)

SATINWOOD

There are several somewhat similar woods imported under this name. The two most important are:

SATINWOOD, CEYLON (*Chloroxylon swietenia, D.C.*)—East Indian Satinwood

Source: Ceylon and southern India

Color: Pale gold

Pattern: Ripples, straight stripes; bee's wing mottled

Characteristics: Hard; dense; interlocking grain; inclined to check

Uses: Furniture

Availability: Veneer (quartered, sliced, half-round) rare. Lumber rare

Price Range: Costly

SATINWOOD, WEST INDIAN (*Zanthoxylum flavum, Vahl.*)—San Domingan Satinwood

Source: Puerto Rico, British Honduras

Color: Creamy golden yellow

Pattern: Wavy grain

Characteristics: Fine grained; hard and quite heavy; works well with most tools

Uses: Furniture; marquetry; inlaying; turnery

Availability: Veneer (sliced) scarce. Lumber available

Price Range: Costly

Satinwood, Ceylon, figured quartered (2 pieces, book-matched)

SAPELE (*Entandrophragma cylindricum*)—Aboudikrou, Sipo, Tiama

Source: African Ivory Coast, Nigeria

Color: Dark red-brown

Pattern: Stripe and bee's wing

Characteristics: Considerable variation in grain; light portions of stripes lustrous; works fairly well with hand and machine tools; tough; harder and heavier than African Mahogany

Uses: Veneers for furniture; cabinetwork; interior decoration

Availability: Veneer (quartered) plentiful. Lumber available

Price Range: Medium

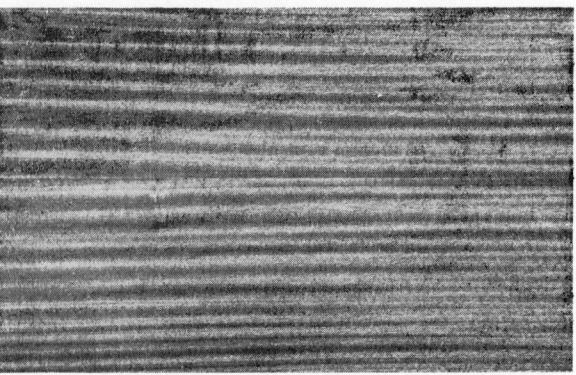

Sapele, quartered (2 pieces, book-matched)

TEAK (*Tectona grandis*)—Burma Teak, Rangoon Teak

Source: Burma, Java, East India, Indo-China

Color: Tawny yellow to dark brown, often with lighter streaks, not black as many think

Pattern: A great deal like Walnut, sometimes mottled and fiddle-back

Characteristics: Strong; tough; oily. Like Walnut, except for oiliness, and is one of the finest cabinetwoods

Uses: Paneling; furniture; floors; ship decking

Availability: Veneer (quartered, sliced) plentiful. Lumber available

Price Range: Costly

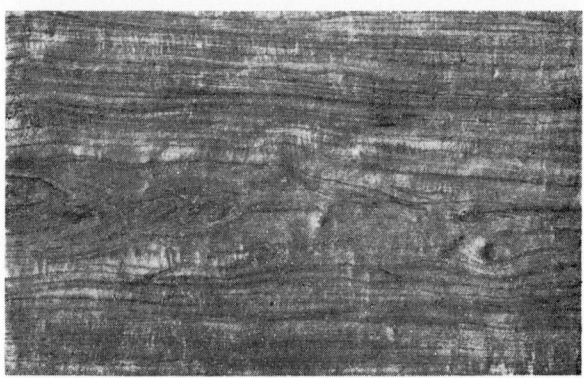

Teak, flat cut, semi-figured (one piece)

TIGERWOOD (*Lovoa klaineana*)—Congowood (often misnamed African "Walnut," Benin Walnut and Nigerian Golden "Walnut")

Source: West Africa

Color: Gray-brown to gold with black streaks

Pattern: Pronounced ribbon stripe

Characteristics: Easily worked; transverse grain shows irregularly sized, scattered pores

Uses: Furniture; paneling

Availability: Veneer (quartered) plentiful. Lumber available

Price Range: Medium

Tigerwood, quartered (4 pieces, book-matched)

YEW

Two species of genuine Yew are available:

YEW, AMERICAN (*Taxus spp.*)—Florida, Pacific or Western Yew

Source: Pacific Coast and Southwestern Canada

Color: Reddish-brown

Pattern: Close-grained; often highly grain figured

Characteristics: Heavy; hard; available in very small sizes

Uses: Veneers—decorative areas of fine furniture

Availability: Rare as both veneers and lumber

Price Range: Costly

YEW, ENGLISH (*Taxus, baccata*)

Source: England

Color: Pale red, somewhat like Cherrywood or Pencil Cedar

Pattern: Smooth, lustrous grain. Wild grain gives much character

Characteristics: Strong; elastic

Availability: In small sizes, individual pieces often being only 4 to 6 in. wide and 2 to 6 ft long

Price Range: Costly

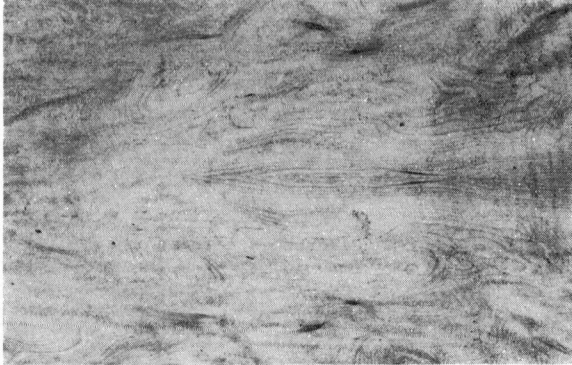

Yew, sliced (2 pieces, book-matched)

To conclude this series of better than fifty of the most interesting fine hardwoods that are both suitable and available for architectural interiors and fine furnishings, we present twelve fine hardwoods from Almon to Zebrawood, with a wide range of color and character. Actually, there are 99,000 different hardwoods in the world, of which some 200 are made available by the hardwood industry to American and Canadian specifiers and users. Of that 200, many are available for but limited use, due to quantity, size, cost, etc. In this Time-Saver Standards series we have presented "those most likely to succeed" along with the old reliables which are again being presented as "something new" when finished imaginatively.

ALMON (*Shorea almon*)

This wood is not to be confused with almond (*Prunus communis*), which is one of the rare nut woods.

Source: Philippine Islands
Color: Light cream or straw
Pattern: Quartered or rotary figure
Characteristics: Light; works well although stringy; finishes well; coarse-textured; cross-grained; moderately hard
Availability: Veneer (quartered, rotary) plentiful. Lumber available
Uses: Occasionally for cabinetry
Price Range: Inexpensive

CAPOMO (*Brosium Alicastrum*) — Breadnut, Capone, Laredo Ogechi, Ojoche, Ramon
Source: Central America
Color: Yellowish sapwood; reddish heartwood
Pattern: Cross ripple, lustrous. May be had in plain as well as figured types (such as is pictured here)
Characteristics: Hard
Uses: Furniture
Availability: Veneer (quartered) plentiful
Price Range: Medium

CHEN CHEN (*Antiaris africana*) — Ako, Quen Quen
Source: African Gold Coast to Cameroons
Color: White to yellow gray
Pattern: Stripe
Characteristics: Soft; works well; light in weight
Uses: Furniture; wall paneling
Availability: Not much Chen Chen lumber is used in America, nor is it widely used as veneers. However, it is available in good sizes and in clear grades of the prominent lustrous stripes
Price Range: Low to medium

CHERRY, BLACK (*Prunus serotina*) — Rum Cherry, Wild Black Cherry

Although this species has been reviewed previously (Sheet 6), only plain sliced cherry of the type used in considerable volume by the furniture industry was pictured. The photograph of figured sliced Cherry shown here illustrates the architectural type or those types which, as a result of the current popularity of Cherry for transitional and modern furniture, make available at below value prices unusually attractive forms of a well-known cabinetwood.

Source: Maine to Dakotas and Appalachians; production largely Pennsylvania to West Virginia
Color: Light reddish-brown
Pattern: Straight-grained; satiny; some figured. Small gum pockets are normal markings
Characteristics: Light; strong; rather hard; fine-grained
Uses: Fine furniture, woodwork and engraver's blocks
Availability: Veneer (quartered, sliced, half-round) plentiful. Lumber plentiful
Price Range: Medium

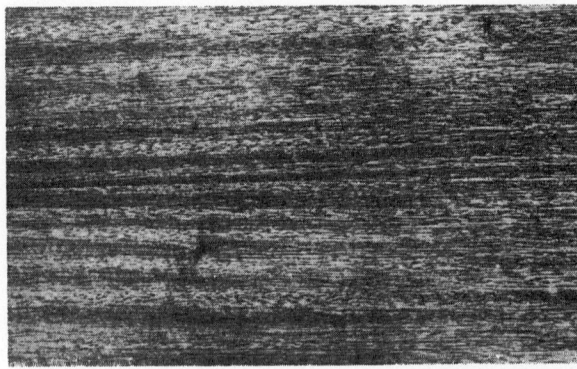

Almon, quartered (2 pieces, book-matched)

Capomo, figured (3 pieces, book-matched)

Chen Chen, sliced (2 pieces, book-matched)

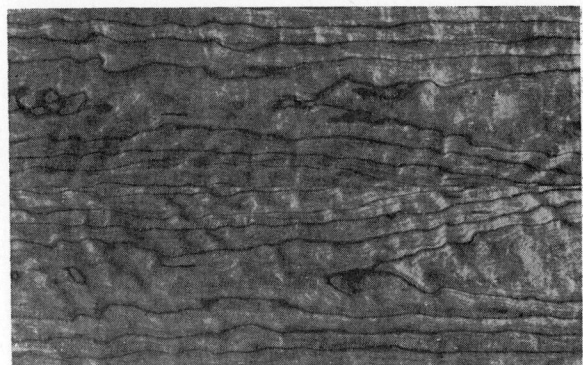

Cherry, figured (2 pieces, book-matched)

EBONY

Three types have come into the American market:

EBONY, BLACK (*Diospyros tomentosa*; also *Diospyros ebenum* and *Diospyros assimilis*)
Source: Northern India, Himalaya
Color: Black
Pattern: Rays very fine, joined at right angles by similar fine light-colored bars, forming a minute pattern
Characteristics: Exceedingly minute pores somewhat scarce; hard; dense and of great weight
Uses: Inlays and marquetry; handles
Availability: Scarce as veneer or lumber
Price Range: High

EBONY, GABOON (*Diospyros dendo*) — Black Ebony, Calabar, Gabun, Lagos
Source: Africa
Color: Very deep black
Pattern: Very indistinct grain
Characteristics: Hard
Uses: Turnery; inlaid work; fancy goods
Availability: Rare
Price Range: Costly

EBONY, MACASSAR (*Diospyros melanoxylon*) — Marblewood
Source: East Indies
Color: Dark brown to black; large proportion of logs streaked with yellow or yellowish-brown
Pattern: Rays fine and very indistinct; grain markings largely from brown streaks on black background
Characteristics: Dense, close grain
Uses: Ornamental work, such as brush backs and handles
Availability: Veneer (quartered, sliced) scarce. Lumber rare
Price Range: Costly

HACKBERRY (*Celtis occidentalis*) — Sugarberry
Source: New England to Virginia and west through Iowa, Missouri and Kansas
Color: Yellowish
Pattern: Rather distinct; fine sparkle from small rays when quartered
Characteristics: Heavy; moderately hard; not strong; coarse-grained
Uses: Furniture
Availability: Veneer (quartered, slices, half-round, rotary) plentiful. Lumber available
Price Range: Inexpensive to medium

KOA (*Acacia Koa*)
Source: Hawaii
Color: Golden brown with dark streaks
Pattern: Brown streaks, lustrous sheen. Occasionally develops a perfect fiddleback figure or other cross figure
Characteristics: Walnut-like texture, but not as hard
Uses: Fine furniture
Availability: Veneer (quartered, sliced) scarce. Lumber available
Price Range: Costly

REDWOOD, BURL (*Sequoia sempervirens*) — Big Tree
Source: California — northern coastal region
Color: Pink to deep red heartwood
Pattern: Clusters of eyes (burls)
Characteristics: Soft; light; close-grained; heartwood exceptionally durable; easily worked; except somewhat splintery
Uses: Decorative areas of cabinetry
Availability: Veneer (half-round) scarce. Lumber abundant
Price Range: Costly as burl veneers

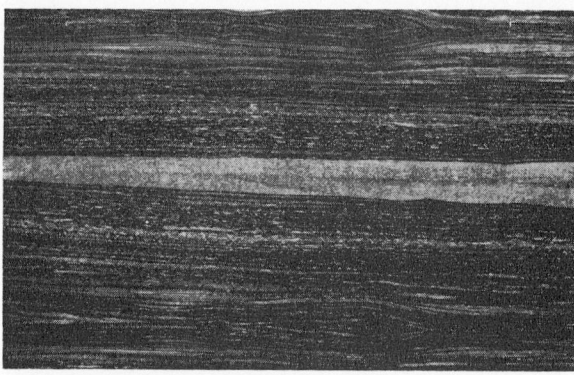

Ebony, Macassar (4 pieces, book-matched)

Hackberry, rotary (one piece)

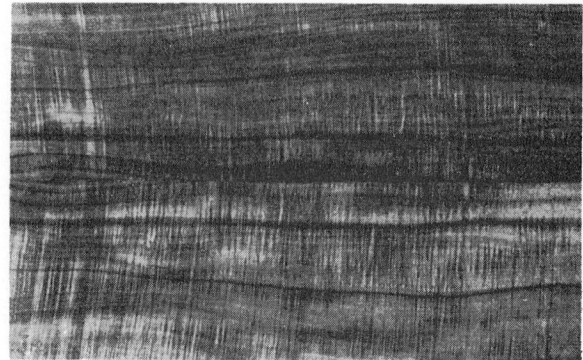

Koa, figured (2 pieces, book-matched)

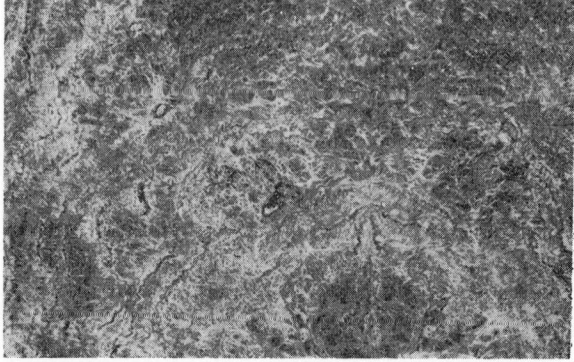

Redwood, burl (2 pieces, book-matched)

ROSEWOOD

Many woods are produced under the name of "Rosewood" in various parts of the world. The more important are these:

ROSEWOOD, BRAZILIAN (*Dalbergia nigra*) — Jacaranda, Rio Rosewood, Bahia Rosewood
Source: Brazil
Color: Various shades of dark brown — chocolate to violet; conspicuous black streaks
Pattern: Streaks of dark brown or black pigment lines
Characteristics: Rather large pores exceedingly irregular both in size and position
Uses: Limited use for walls and furniture
Availability: Veneer (quartered, sliced, half-round, rotary) scarce. Lumber available
Price Range: Costly

Rosewood, Brazilian (one piece)

ROSEWOOD, EAST INDIAN (*Dalbergia latifolia*) — Bombay Rosewood, Blackwood locally, Malobar
Source: Southern India and Ceylon
Color: Dark purple to ebony; streaks of red or yellow
Pattern: Small to medium pores in wavy lines; exceedingly fine rays; occasionally crotches and swirls
Characteristics: Stands up exceptionally well under all conditions; texture is close, firm and hard; requires rather a sharp tool to secure a smooth surface; very moderate shrinkage
Uses: Patternmaking (locally); fine furniture
Availability: Veneer (quartered, sliced, half-round) scarce
Price Range: Costly

Rosewood, East Indian, quartered (2 pieces, book-matched)

ROSEWOOD, MADAGASCAR (*Dalbergia Greveana*) — Madagascar Pilisander, French Rosewood
Source: Madagascar
Color: Dark to light rose-pink
Pattern: Pronounced lines of darker red shades
Characteristics: Very hard
Uses: Limited use for walls and furniture
Availability: Veneer scarce
Price Range: Costly

ROSEWOOD, MEXICAN (probably *Dalbergia Stevensonii*. However, there are about fifteen different species of Rosewood [*Dalbergia*] that produce good quality timber out of 250 species of trees and shrubs in this group)

Yellowpoplar, sliced (2 pieces, book-matched)

YELLOWPOPLAR (*Liriodendron tulipifera*) — Tuliptree, Whitewood
Source: New England to Michigan, Appalachians to Gulf
Color: Canary color, sometimes with slightly greenish cast and occasionally with rather dark streaks
Pattern: Even texture; straight grain
Characteristics: Light to medium weight; strong; soft; easily worked
Uses: As veneers, widely used for cross-banding and backs of plywood. As lumber, interior finish or fixtures (usually to be painted)
Availability: Veneer (quartered, sliced, half-round, rotary, occasionally burls) abundant. Lumber available
Price Range: Inexpensive

ZEBRAWOOD (*Microberlinia brazzavillanensia* or *Brachy-stegia*) — Zebrano, Zingana
Source: African Cameroon, Gaboon, West Africa
Color: Straw, dark brown; exceptionally pronounced fine stripes
Pattern: Striped; dark brown stripes; lustrous surface
Characteristics: Heavy; hard; with somewhat coarse texture
Uses: As veneer, inlays
Availability: Veneer (quartered) rare to available
Price Range: Costly

Zebrawood, quartered (one piece)

PURPOSE

Information in this section can be used as a general guide in the selection of wood, character of workmanship and types of joints for the detailing and specification of cabinet work. Drawings show only typical conditions and therefore cover a wide range of applications. They are intended to indicate principles of good joining rather than solutions to specific problems.

SELECTION OF WOOD

For painted surfaces wood must be fine grained, free from knots, sap or pitch and easy to work, with a surface that will not raise. Eastern white pine is ideal. Due to its scarcity, other woods are usually employed. Whitewood, redwood, and California, Idaho and Ponderosa pine are satisfactory materials. Basswood, poplar, sugar pine and gum are less satisfactory. The pines are often knotty but are used for paneling. Birch is harder and is adaptable to more expensive work containing carvings and mouldings.

For natural finishes woods with a decorative grain, as oak, walnut, mahogany and numerous imported woods, are most adaptable. These can be stained, oiled, varnished or waxed. So can gum, redwood, and white, Idaho or Ponderosa pine.

Seasoning is a requisite for cabinet work. All woods should be thoroughly kiln-dried and cabinet work should never be installed until all moisture within the building has been dissipated and plaster is bone-dry.

WORKMANSHIP

Differences between various classes of woodwork lie entirely in the workmanship; that is, in the character of the joining and finish. Types may be divided as follows:

Carpentry is least expensive, being done entirely on the job by more or less skilled mechanics.

Millwork is to some extent prefabricated. Mouldings, certain types of joints, and all exposed surfaces are run through machines and may or may not be assembled and machine-sanded before delivery, depending on the grade of work. Work must usually be scraped and sanded on the job. Joints are almost always assembled with finishing nails or screws and are of simplest type, avoiding undercuts, etc., requiring multiple machining or expensive workmanship.

Cabinet Work ("Joinery"), the most expensive class of architectural woodwork, is almost always shop-assembled, scraped and sanded. Joints must be absolutely accurate, depend principally on glue for strength, and consequently require expert craftsmen and expensive machinery. Work should be hand sanded after installation.

Furniture. A distinct class of work not usually related to architectural construction. Some methods, types of joints, etc., are adaptable to cabinet work.

All four classes overlap to some extent. Millwork and cabinet work are particularly considered here. In these classes, joints should be inconspicuous, of a type to control or eliminate shrinkage, and should conceal end wood unless part of the design. Surfaces and profiles should be clean cut and free from defects. Means of installation should be concealed.

CHARACTERISTICS OF JOINTS

Joints may be divided into four general types: *Butted, Shiplapped, Tongued-and-grooved,* and *Mitered.* Used in their simple basic form, none is satisfactory for cabinet work except the tongued-and-grooved type in certain instances. However, when variously combined or when reinforced with gluing and dowels or splines, satisfactory joints can be developed.

Butt joint. A simple but weak joint that opens easily and may show end wood when used at angles. Strength and range of use is greatly increased by use of the *mortise and tenon* and *dowels* and even more when a *straight spline* is included. Use of a glued *butterfly spline* with a butt joint produces an extremely strong joint. These variations are widely used to produce large flush surfaces of solid wood or backing for veneers.

Shiplap joint. Stronger than a butt joint but subject to opening from shrinkage. Rarely used in a simple form in cabinet work except for door rebates. It is often moulded to conceal shrinkage in quirks or combined as a *miter and shoulder* for corners. Another variation is the *shoulder joint.*

Tongue-and-groove joint. A strong joint, widely used for re-entrant angles. Effect of wood shrinkage is concealed when

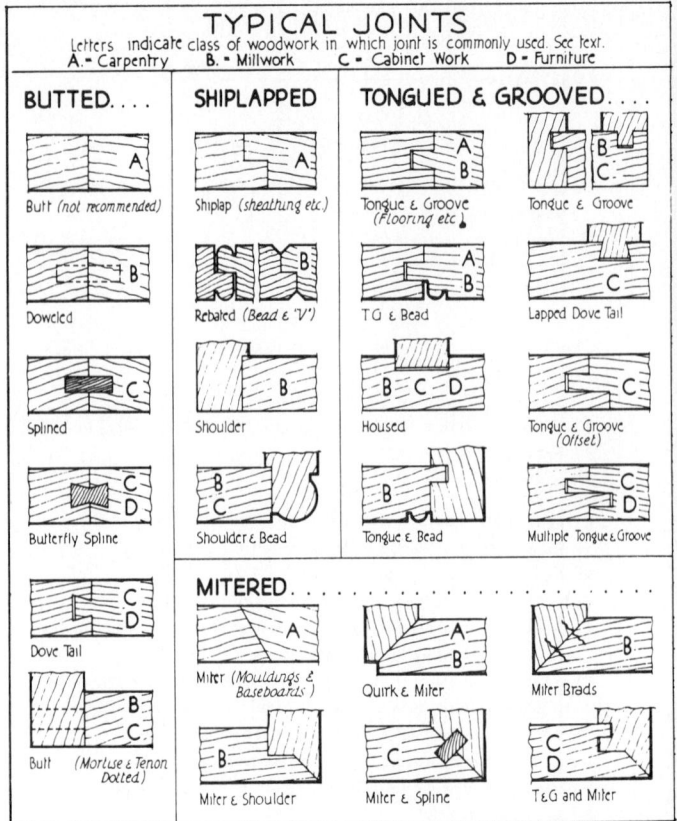

the joint is beaded or otherwise moulded. In expensive cabinet work glued *dovetail* and *multiple tongue-and-groove* are used.

Miter joints are weak and difficult to fit if used alone. Joints with *miter brads* are sufficiently strong for short lengths. Joints made in combination with other forms, as a *tongue-and-groove miter,* are tight and sturdy.

USE OF JOINTS

Use of certain types of joints depends to a large degree upon the type of work and workmanship involved. The following notes indicate use of joints in various categories, but cannot be regarded as an inclusive check list.

For panels, shelving, etc. or wherever the end of one piece butts against the face of another; *housed joint,* with or without cover mould, or some type of *tongue-and-groove* joint. Omit glue to avoid splitting due to swelling or shrinkage.

For joining stiles and rails: *mortise and tenon,* glued in better work. Dowels may be used or hardwood wedges may be driven and glued into ends of tenons in high grade work.

For re-entrant corners: *shoulder joints* for inexpensive work. *Tongue-and-groove* is sturdier. Both should be glued, are often screwed together and may be glued to a rough frame.

For external corners: simple *miter* and *quirk and miter* both lack strength. *Miter brads* are practical only for short lengths. *Miter and shoulder* glued and face-screwed or nailed is satisfactory (generally "millwork"). *Miter and spline* is preferable. In high grade work exterior corners are reinforced by gluing to a corner post or short lengths of blocking.

Glued joints: when screws, nails, etc., can not be used, or when fine work is to be veneered, strength of the joint depends on accuracy of milling and total glue surface. Glue surface may be tremendously increased by using multiple or offset tongues and grooves, by forming miter cuts into waves, multiple shoulders, tongues and grooves, etc. Such work is cabinet work. If done by a reliable cabinet maker, a guarantee should be obtained and joint detail and composition of glue left to him.

Mouldings should be applied in continuous lengths if possible. Use simple miter for necessary joints, cope re-entrant angles unless excessively undercut, miter external corners.

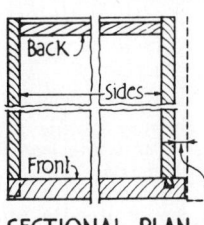

SECTIONAL PLAN

When any type of patented drawer slide is used, consult man'f's catalogue for this dimension. The lapped front conceals slide

Dust-Panels & top face of drawer Runners should be flush

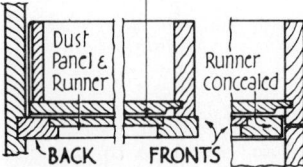

Bottom rabeted to front and sides; secured to front only.
Runners & Guides preferably hardwood; Panels either veneer or solid

DRAWERS

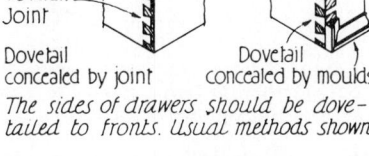

The sides of drawers should be dovetailed to fronts. Usual methods shown

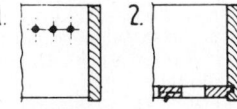

1 Bottomless – For towels, etc.
2 Flush Lattice Bottom – Permits air circulation for linens, etc.

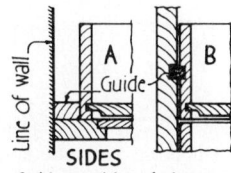

SIDES

.A Guide at side of drawer, fastened to Drawer Runner
B Guide (Hardwood) rabeted into side of Drawer.

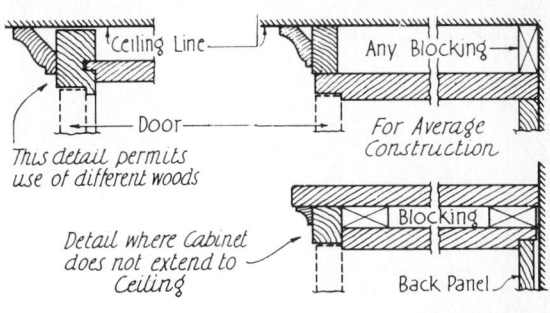

This detail permits use of different woods

For Average Construction

Detail where Cabinet does not extend to Ceiling

CORNICE

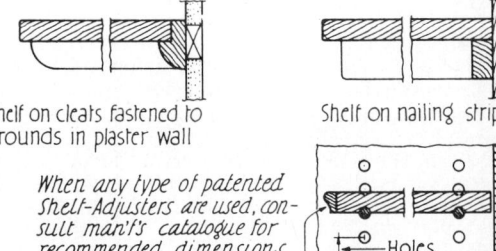

Shelf on cleats fastened to grounds in plaster wall

Shelf on nailing strips

When any type of patented Shelf-Adjusters are used, consult man's catalogue for recommended dimensions Shelf edge may be Hardwood

Adjustable Shelf on Wood Pegs

SHELVES

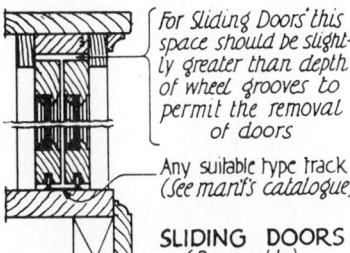

For Sliding Doors this space should be slightly greater than depth of wheel grooves to permit the removal of doors

Any suitable type track (See man'f's catalogue)

SLIDING DOORS
(Removable)

Flush Front Panel Doors

Felt Backing
Plate Glass Mirror
Removable Mouldings

DOOR WITH MIRROR

Miter & Shoulder Joint
Removable Mouldings
Tongue & Groove Joint
Glass

DETAILS FOR GLAZED DOORS

Miter Joint & Hardwood Spline
Invisible Hinges Optional
Miter Joint with Miter Brads
Integral & Applied Stops

DETAILS FOR PANELED DOORS
(Panels may be either plain or ply-wood)

DOORS

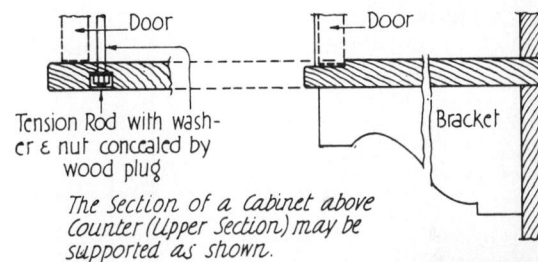

Tension Rod with washer & nut concealed by wood plug

Bracket

The Section of a Cabinet above Counter (Upper Section) may be supported as shown.

SUPPORTS

1 With drawer below   3 With Backboard
2 With moulding   4 Backboard with Cove Corner

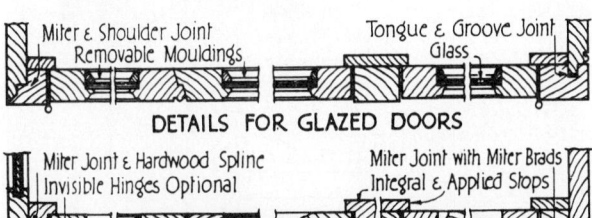

Door
Drawer

Ground

COUNTERS

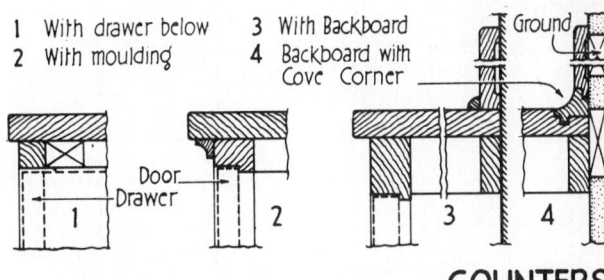

Door

This detail permits the use of different woods

Any Blocking

Base-board
Finish Floor
Rough Floor

This detail may be used if Cabinet extends to Finish Floor

BASES

Toe Space with Sanitary Cove

Floor Covering may finish against bottom of Cabinet

3½" (min)

Any Blocking
Rough Floor

Door

Floor Covering butts against base

4" (min.)

Blocking

TOE SPACE

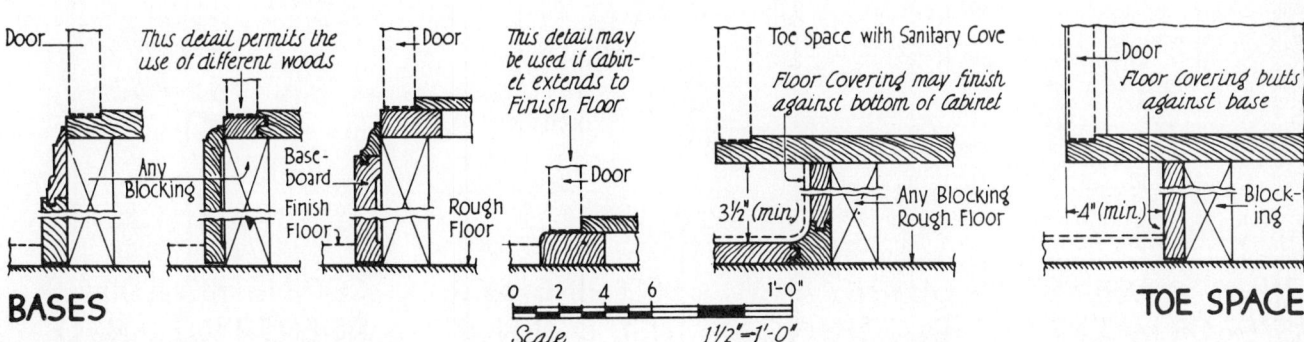

0 2 4 6   1'-0"
Scale   1½"=1'-0"

PURPOSE

Information on this sheet outlines methods of assembly and installation of common cabinet work. Solutions of typical problems are presented without attempting to detail specific cabinets.

ASSEMBLY

High grade cabinet and veneered work is assembled as far as possible at the shop. Joints are glued and blocked, and sometimes secured with finishing nails or screws. Carpentry and millwork are generally put together with finishing nails if of soft wood, or with screws if of hardwood. Hardwood should be drilled to prevent splitting before using nails or screws, and heads should be countersunk and concealed by cover moulds, moulding quirks, or putty, plastic wood or other filler, colored to match the finish. No nails, screws or joints should be visible unless they are intentionally incorporated in design.

Shrinkage and warping effects can be largely eliminated by proper detailing and construction. *Wide flat surfaces* (solid or veneered) should be made up of several narrow strips glued and doweled, splined, or dovetailed together. Cleats may also be screwed or keyed to backs of wide surfaces. *Joints in corners, sheathing, etc.* should be concealed within quirks of moulds (as in moulded tongue-and-groove) or return faces (shoulder joints). *Panels* should be rigidly secured on one side only, and are often left entirely loose. Housed joints, not glued, permit panels to expand and contract without splitting.

Large moulded surfaces (such as cornices or mantels) should always be shop-assembled and delivered with scribe-moulds (see "Scribing" below) loosely tacked to assembled units.

INSTALLATION

All grades of woodwork should be preservative treated or back painted before erection, preferably before delivery to the job. Satisfactory priming coats are aluminum paint or white lead in linseed oil, thinned with turpentine or mineral spirits.

Preparation. On frame walls plaster may be limited to one or two coats, may be recessed between studs or may be omitted. In the latter case, building paper should be used between woodwork and studs. On masonry, plaster may consist of one or two coats or may be omitted. Masonry surfaces, particularly exterior walls, should be waterproofed or woodwork should be protected by a layer of waterproof paper and should always be furred out. When finish of the interior of cabinets is plaster, either plain or canvas covered, the final coat of plaster is applied after erection of cabinet.

Grounds of soft wood for attaching cabinet work must be accurately located, are secured directly to framing members or furring, and must be concealed.

Blocking of rough lumber should be erected for supporting raised floors and large or heavy cabinet work, if it can be concealed. Blocking must be accurately placed and secured with nails.

Shimming. Minor irregularities in blocking, furring, or placement of studs may be corrected by using shims (wedge shaped pieces of wood, often shingles) to bring completed work to plumb and level lines. Shimming should be concealed.

Scribing is the practice of fitting edges of cabinet work accurately to all irregularities of finish plaster, masonry or other abutting surfaces. Wood mouldings, panel frames or cabinet returns to be scribed should be provided with a beveled edge.

Prefabricated woodwork is generally delivered knocked down for assembly on the job and is erected similarly to custom-made work. Consult manufacturers' data.

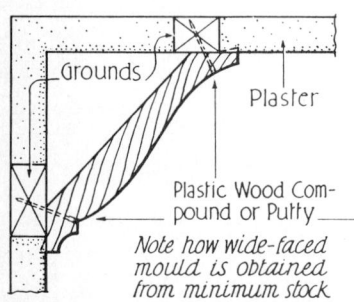

Note how wide-faced mould is obtained from minimum stock

NAILING TO GROUNDS

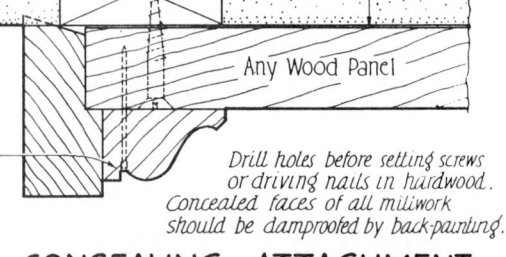

Drill holes before setting screws or driving nails in hardwood. Concealed faces of all millwork should be dampproofed by back-painting.

CONCEALING ATTACHMENT OF HARDWOODS

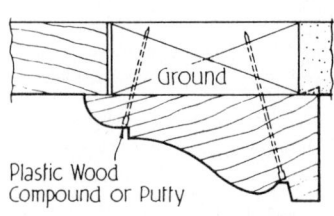

NAILING IN QUIRKS

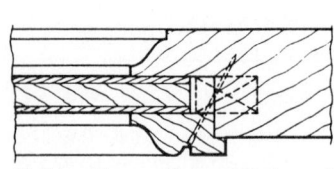

Nail to stiles or rails; avoiding panel

NAILING PANEL MOULD

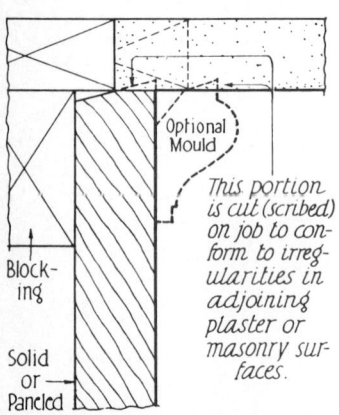

This portion is cut (scribed) on job to conform to irregularities in adjoining plaster or masonry surfaces.

SCRIBING AGAINST PLASTER OR MASONRY

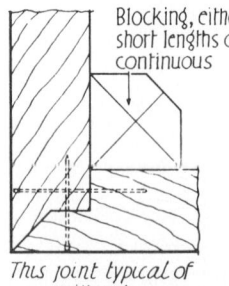

This joint typical of millwork

Nailing & gluing a mortise and shoulder provides a strong, reasonably permanent joint

GLUING AND BLOCKING

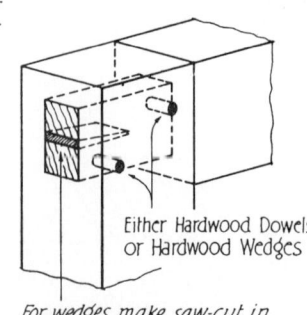

Either Hardwood Dowels or Hardwood Wedges

For wedges, make saw-cut in tenon before assembling. Holes for dowels may be offset to draw joint tight.

SECURING MORTISE & TENON

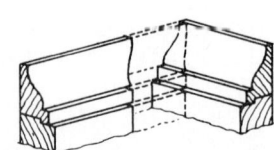

Cope by hand on job unless excessively undercut; if so, use miter. Flat members may be butted or Tongued-and-Grooved.

COPING MOULDINGS RE-ENTRANT ANGLE

TYPES OF CASEWORK

Exposed face frame—flush (also often known as *conventional flush* construction) is the basic design in architectural woodwork. The drawer and door faces are flush with the face frame. This design is highly functional and allows the use of different thicknesses of wood for doors and drawer fronts. Heavy-duty as well as concealed hinges are readily available for a variety of door thicknesses. The exposed face frame has the advantage of providing a solid surround for the operating doors and drawers which keeps them aligned. This type of construction is recommended for hard-service applications because of its superior strength and rigidity. It is, however, a more expensive design, due to the necessity of careful fitting and aligning of the doors and drawers, and the close tolerances required by the exposed joinery in the face frame. For these reasons this design does not lend itself to the economical use of plastic laminate covering.

Exposed face frame—lipped design has most of the advantages and is similar in construction to the flush design. Provided that edge banding is not required on the doors, the lipped design is a more economical style, since the fitting tolerances of the doors and drawers are less critical.

Flush overlay provides an attractive appearance, since only the door and drawer fronts are visible on the face of the cabinet. A matched-grain effect can be achieved, if specified, by having all doors and drawer fronts cut from the same panel. It also lends itself ideally to the use of laminated plastic for the exposed surfaces. A requirement of the flush overlay design is heavy-duty hardware. The absence of a face frame requires careful site preparation and installation to maintain the proper alignment of the doors and/or drawers to one another.

Reveal overlay is a variation of the flush overlay design that presents a "raised panel" effect. Although it requires a face frame, it is for the most part concealed and, as with lipped design, requires less demanding fitting tolerances. The reveal between the doors and drawer fronts reduces the problem of alignment. It incorporates most of the advantages of the flush overlay and exposed face frame designs. The architect has the option of utilizing the reveals vertically and/or horizontally, and the width of the reveal is variable.

Note: For kitchen cabinets see ANSI A161.1, Minimum Construction and Performance Standards for Kitchen and Vanity Cabinets

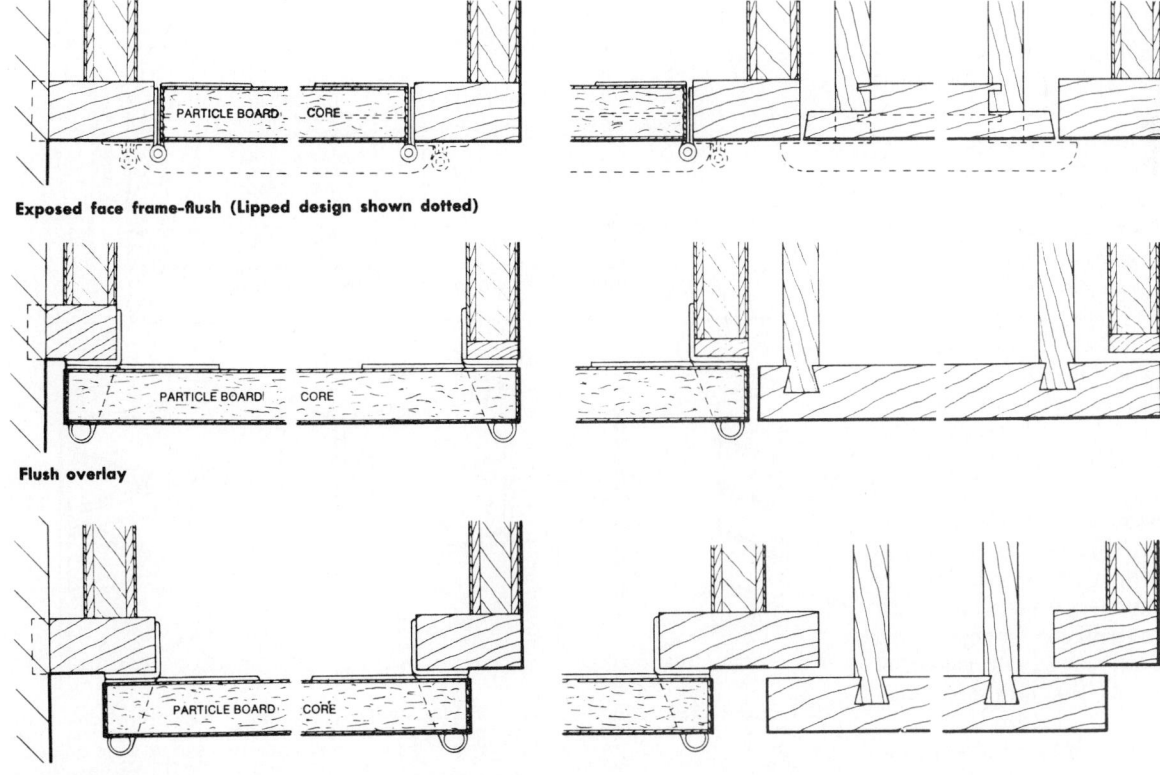

Exposed face frame-flush (Lipped design shown dotted)

Flush overlay

Reveal overlay

Three types of cabinet design—typical jamb and mullion details

Courtesy of Architectural Woodwork Institute

Based on information from Nuroco Woodwork, New Rochelle, N.Y.

Tʜᴇ amount of woodwork and cabinet-work used in contemporary building, particularly residences, has increased by such leaps and bounds that it often constitutes one of the largest dollar outlays in a new house. A knowledge of standard modern woodworking practices, therefore, should not only stimulate design, but should be a means of exploiting valuable technical economies and eliciting fair and comparable estimates from woodworking contractors.

WOODWORK TRENDS

Four principal factors account for the great increase in residential woodwork. They are: (1) greater use of glass (accompanied by a more widespread use of jalousies, blinds and louvers); (2) the open-closed plan (when achieved by means of light, flexible walls of rolling, sliding or folding doors or wood panels); (3) built-in furniture and storage; and (4) a swing towards more natural interior finishes and greater texturing of interior surfaces.

Some traditional woodwork forms are undergoing change — trim is being simplified and emboldened in scale. The fussy classic mantel is being replaced by simpler wood frames that are more in scale with clean-lined contemporary furniture. Stair rails, balusters and newels are being given more unconventional expression. Some old forms have almost disappeared — false ceiling beams, the awesome front doorway and porchwork with its columnar dignity.

Woodwork trim, in other words, is going to work. The hackneyed melange of moldings which used to surround doors and windows indiscriminately is being replaced by moldings with more architectural effectiveness. Doorways "on ax" may be given bold-scale trim for emphasis; secondary doors, simply functional hairline moldings for impact- and wear-resistance. As in all phases of design, there is less orthodoxy than ever before.

The technique of woodwork manufacture has been changed only by the more common use of plywoods and

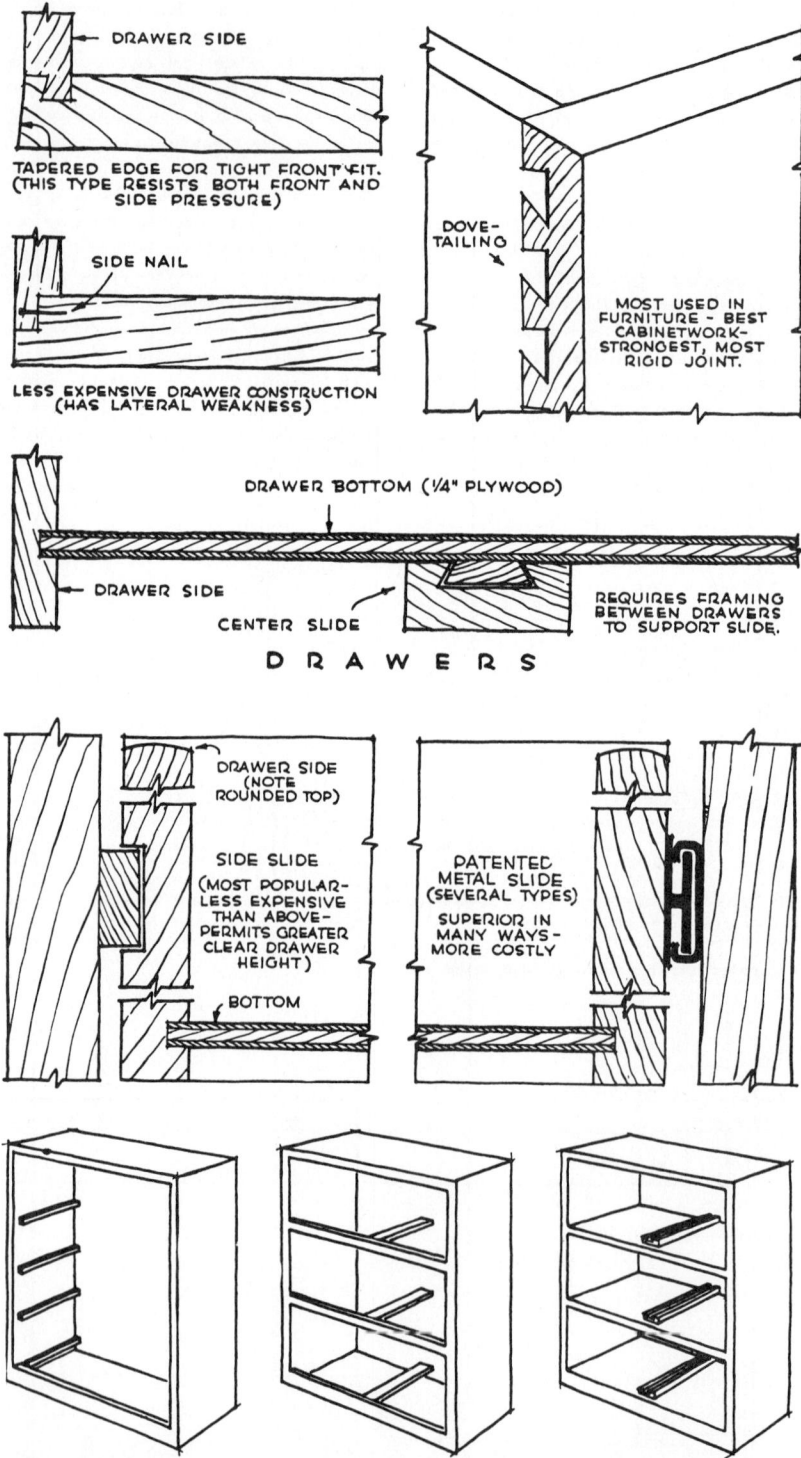

TAPERED EDGE FOR TIGHT FRONT FIT. (THIS TYPE RESISTS BOTH FRONT AND SIDE PRESSURE)

LESS EXPENSIVE DRAWER CONSTRUCTION (HAS LATERAL WEAKNESS)

DOVE-TAILING

MOST USED IN FURNITURE - BEST CABINETWORK-STRONGEST, MOST RIGID JOINT.

DRAWER BOTTOM (¼" PLYWOOD)

REQUIRES FRAMING BETWEEN DRAWERS TO SUPPORT SLIDE.

D R A W E R S

DRAWER SIDE (NOTE ROUNDED TOP)

SIDE SLIDE (MOST POPULAR-LESS EXPENSIVE THAN ABOVE-PERMITS GREATER CLEAR DRAWER HEIGHT)

BOTTOM

PATENTED METAL SLIDE (SEVERAL TYPES) SUPERIOR IN MANY WAYS-MORE COSTLY

LEAST EXPENSIVE. PERMITS SIDE SLIDES ONLY. ALLOWS MAXIMUM DRAWER DEPTH.

OPEN FRAME PERMITS USE OF CENTER SLIDES OR SIDE SLIDES. FRONT FRAMING STIFFENS CONSTRUCTION BUT REDUCES DRAWER HEIGHT, CREATES AN EDGE WHICH MAY SNAG DRAWER CONTENTS.

DUST TIGHT. PERMITS USE OF CENTER OR SIDE SLIDES USED IN BEST DRAWER CONSTRUCTION. SOLID SHELF PREVENTS SNAGGING OF DRAWER CONTENTS.

C H E S T S

FIXED SHELVES

veneers. Although new methods of gluing and joining seem to offer promise of producing cheaper, stronger assemblies, there are many difficulties still to be overcome before they achieve fullest use. It is practically impossible, for example, to glue end-butt joints sufficiently strong to meet the requirements of ordinary service. End-to-side-grain joints are also difficult to glue properly. For these and other reasons, the traditional glued wood joinings (dowel, mortise and tenon, dado, tongue and rabbet, slip or lock corner, dovetail, blocked and tongue and groove) remain standard practice.

Some chemical applications are extending the usefulness of woodwork. Treatments to improve the rot and termite-resistance of wood and to control warping, shrinking, and swelling will not discolor the wood and will permit the use of natural finishes. Densifying processes that greatly increase the hardness of wood offer the possibility of endowing soft woods with the hardness of oak. The same process permits through-coloring of the treated lumber.

Plywoods with machine or chemically made textures are being increasingly used in cabinetwork. Striations, embossings, exaggerated grainings are examples. The use of such improvisations will undoubtedly increase to offset the shortage of hardwoods, and to meet the growing demand for more arresting surfaces.

HOW TO TELL GOOD WOODWORK
Surface

The surface should be free of all disfiguring defects such as raised grain, stains, evidences of poor and uneven

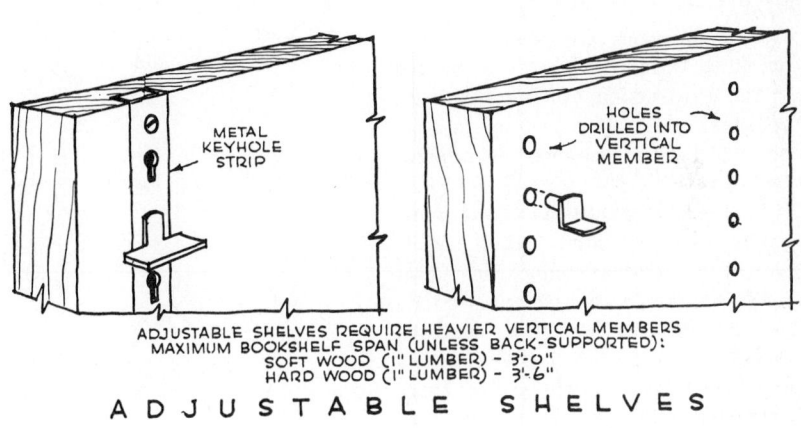

ADJUSTABLE SHELVES REQUIRE HEAVIER VERTICAL MEMBERS
MAXIMUM BOOKSHELF SPAN (UNLESS BACK-SUPPORTED):
SOFT WOOD (1" LUMBER) – 3'-0"
HARD WOOD (1" LUMBER) – 3'-6"

ADJUSTABLE SHELVES

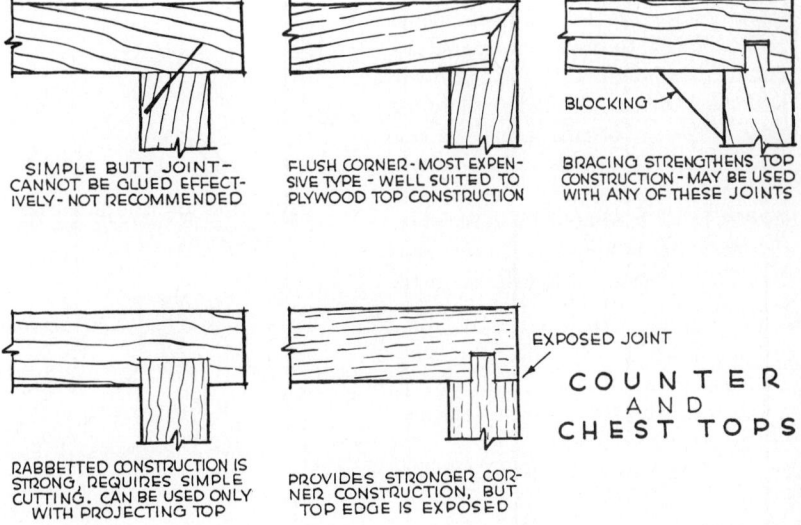

COUNTER
AND
CHEST TOPS

planing, sanding, tool marks, gouges, scratches, dirt. Moldings should have clean edges, arrises and profiles. They should be crisp. There should be no chatter marks, caused by too rapid cutting, or any splintered edges. At the miters, profiles should match perfectly — evidence of perfect cutting.

If the material is to receive a natural finish, the color and graining should be uniform (or correctable with staining).

Joints

All joints should be cleanly matched, tight. Verticals should be plumb.

Look for signs of warping, splitting, checking, shrinking. If plywood is used in the construction, examine treatment of panel edges. If edges are face-veneered, check appearance and application of veneer.

Poor woodwork betrays itself in its joints. Low-cost joints often replace correct (and costlier) connections. Good woodwork has dado cuts in vertical pieces to support horizontal members, rabbetted construction to stiffen vertical members joined at right angles. Large mitered moldings should be doweled or secured by means of metal or wood splines. Blocking should be used to stiffen larger pieces and to secure tops to dressers, wardrobes and similar pieces.

Working Parts

Cheap construction of working parts, such as drawers and doors, makes for quick obsolescence. Drawer fronts should be dovetailed to sides, or secured by some other interlocking joint. Drawer backs and bottoms should be let into the sides. Drawer bottoms should be sufficiently strong to support the drawer contents without sagging. Drawer sides should be of hardwood to resist wear, unless drawer is supported on side runners. Drawer should fit snugly, not bind, snag, or rattle.

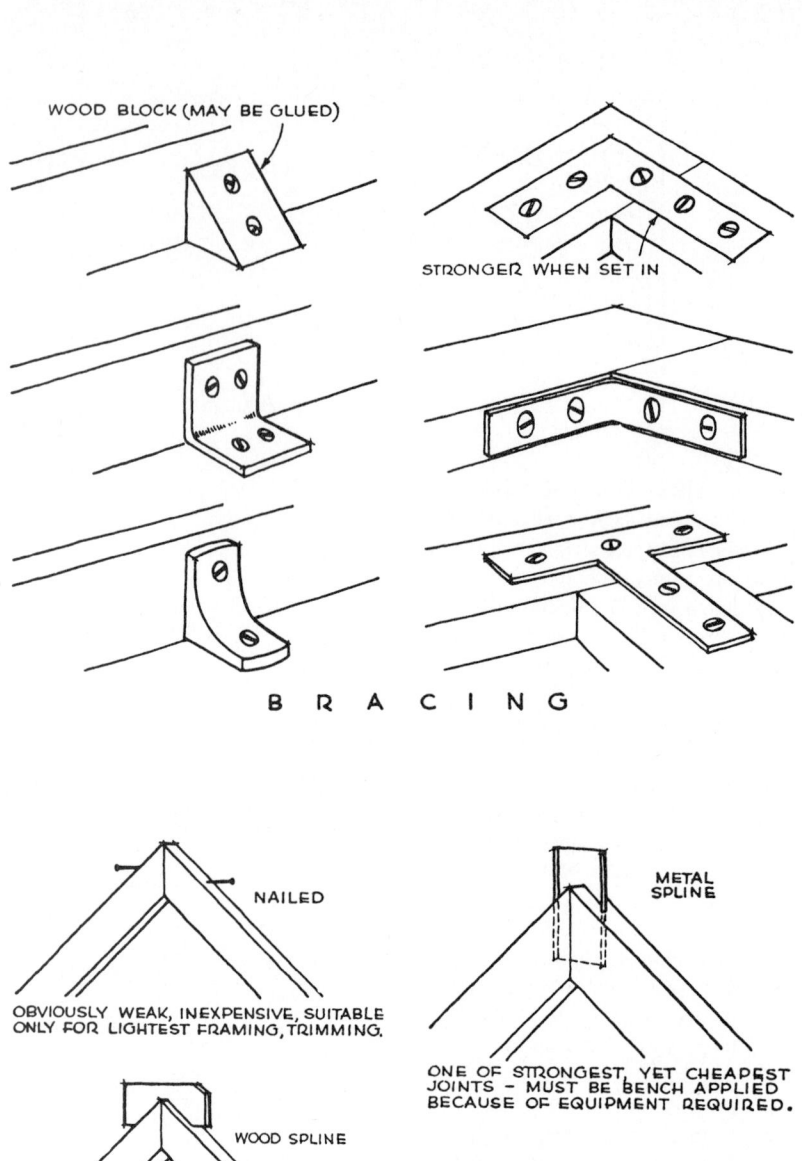

WOOD BLOCK (MAY BE GLUED)

STRONGER WHEN SET IN

B R A C I N G

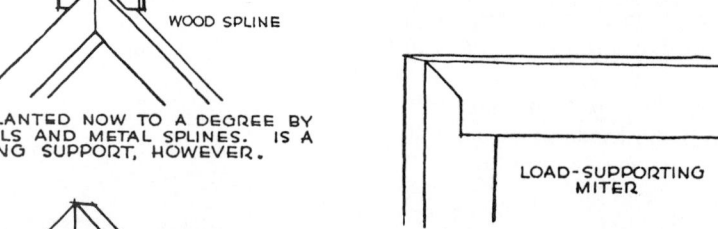

NAILED

OBVIOUSLY WEAK, INEXPENSIVE, SUITABLE ONLY FOR LIGHTEST FRAMING, TRIMMING.

METAL SPLINE

ONE OF STRONGEST, YET CHEAPEST JOINTS – MUST BE BENCH APPLIED BECAUSE OF EQUIPMENT REQUIRED.

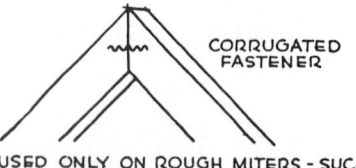

WOOD SPLINE

SUPPLANTED NOW TO A DEGREE BY DOWELS AND METAL SPLINES. IS A STRONG SUPPORT, HOWEVER.

CORRUGATED FASTENER

USED ONLY ON ROUGH MITERS – SUCH AS SCREENS, WHERE ACCURACY IS UNESSENTIAL.

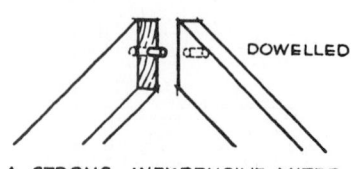

DOWELLED

A STRONG, INEXPENSIVE MITER.

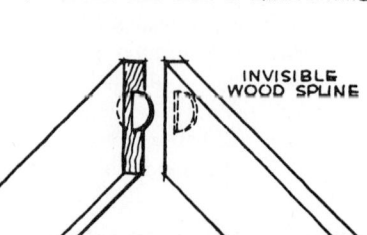

LOAD-SUPPORTING MITER

THIS IS ONE OF FEW MITERS THAT WILL CARRY A SUPERIMPOSED STRESS. MORE COSTLY BECAUSE OF EXTRA CUTTING

INVISIBLE WOOD SPLINE

WOOD SPLINE PRODUCES STRONG MITER. HAS ADVANTAGE OF BEING COMPLETELY INVISIBLE.

M I T E R S

PANELING

THE FRAME

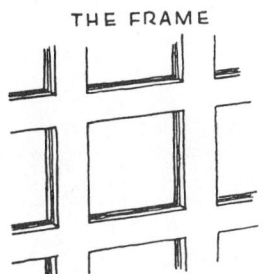

THE FRAME MUST BE RIGID. PANELS FLOAT FREE, THEIR EDGES HELD IN GROOVES IN THE FRAME.

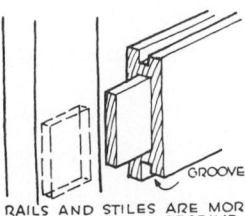

RAILS AND STILES ARE MORTISED. GROOVES RECEIVE SPLINES OR PANEL EDGES.

PANEL TYPES

SOLID STICKING PANEL - MAY BE USED IN EITHER SOLID OR PLYWOOD PANELS. USUAL PANEL CONSTRUCTION.

PANELS MAY ALSO BE SECURED BY MEANS OF APPLIED MOLDINGS, NAILED INTO WOOD SPLINES SLIPPED INTO GROOVES OF STILES AND RAILS. (IT COSTS LESS TO CUT GROOVES AND INSERT SPLINES THAN TO MAKE COMPLEX PROFILE WITH SPLINES INTEGRAL IN THE STILES).

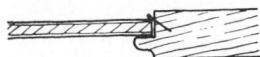

LEAST EXPENSIVE METHOD- USED WHERE BACK OF PANEL IS NOT EXPOSED.

TRUE PANELING
(IN WHICH PANEL IS SET FREE IN A FRAME)

THE PANEL

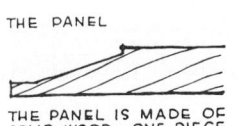

THE PANEL IS MADE OF SOLID WOOD - ONE PIECE,

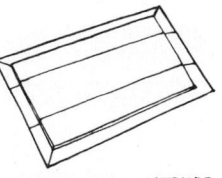

OR OF SEVERAL MATCHED PIECES GLUED TOGETHER,

OR OF PLYWOOD,

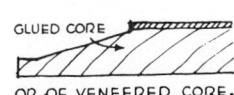

GLUED CORE

OR OF VENEERED CORE.

THE ADVANTAGE OF PLYWOOD PANELS IS THAT THEY PERMIT PERFECT MATCHING OF COLOR AND GRAIN IN ALL PANELS. PLYWOOD, TOO, EXPANDS AND CONTRACTS LESS THAN SOLID WOODS. DISADVANTAGE IS THAT PLYWOOD PANELS ARE DIFFICULT TO BEVEL. WHERE BEVELING IS REQUIRED, HERE ARE SOLUTIONS:

PLYWOOD / SOLID

USES SOLID WOOD FOR BEVEL; CALLS FOR CAREFUL MATCHING OF PLYWOOD IF PANEL IS TO BE NATURALLY FINISHED.

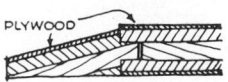

PLYWOOD

USES STRIPS FROM SAME PLYWOOD PANEL TO ACHIEVE PERFECT MATCH. SUPERIOR TO ABOVE; MAY BE COSTLIER.

WARDROBE AND CABINET DOORS

I. PLYWOOD FLUSH DOORS

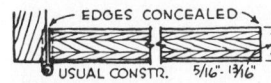

EDGES CONCEALED

USUAL CONSTR.   5/16"- 13/16"

LEAST EXPENSIVE FLUSH DOOR. SELECT FOR UNIFORMITY OF GRAIN, PATTERN (IF NATURALLY FINISHED), GOOD CRUMBLE-FREE CORE. FOR METHODS OF TREATING EXPOSED PLYWOOD EDGES SEE "PLYWOOD EDGE TRIMMING."

EDGE EXPOSED

CAN BE USED ONLY AT CORNERS. - PRODUCES SIMPLE MODERN EFFECT.

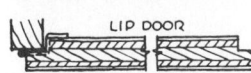

LIP DOOR

PRODUCES RAISED PANEL EFFECT. ESPECIALLY STRIKING WHEN MANY LIKE-SIZED PANELS ARE USED.

II. PANEL DOORS

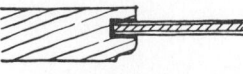

USUAL CONSTRUCTION - USED WITH SOLID OR PLYWOOD PANELS.

BACK NAILING STRIP

BACK STRIP IS USED MAINLY TO SECURE GLASS PANELS. MAY ALSO BE USED TO SECURE WOOD PANELS IN SAME DOOR.

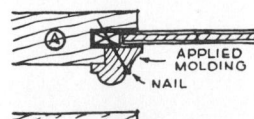

Ⓐ APPLIED MOLDING   NAIL

Ⓑ NAIL

APPLIED MOLDINGS ARE USED WHERE SHAPE OF MOLDING MAKES CUTTING IT FROM STILE WASTEFUL Ⓐ, OR WHERE PROFILE OF MOLDING PRECLUDES USE OF COPING AT CORNERS Ⓑ, OR WHERE MORE THAN ONE MOLDING DESIGN MAY BE USED IN A DOOR.

WARDROBES AND CABINETS

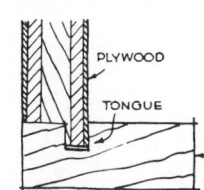

PLYWOOD   TONGUE   SOLID MEMBER

TYPICAL GOOD OUTSIDE CORNER CONSTRUCTION WHERE SOLID MEMBER FORMS WARDROBE DOOR FRAME.

GOOD OUTSIDE CORNER CONSTRUCTION WHERE NATURAL FINISH CONTINUES AROUND CORNER. RECOMMENDED WHERE BOTH MEMBERS ARE PLYWOOD. COSTLIER.

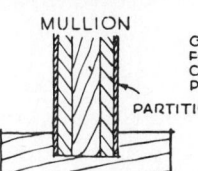

MULLION   PARTITION

GOOD MULLION CONSTRUCTION FOR WARDROBES AND OTHER CABINETS. PARTITION OF ¾" PLYWOOD IS LET INTO MULLION.

PLYWOOD EDGE TRIMMING

MOST COMMON SOLUTION – REQUIRES EXPENSIVE CUTTING, GLUING. CORNERS ARE WEAK. GOOD WHEN ALL SIDES ARE EXPOSED.

WEAK HERE

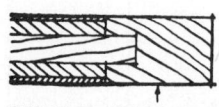

PROVIDES STRONG EDGE FOR HINGES, ABRASIVE WEAR, OR MOLDED WORK. INTRODUCES DIFFERENT WOOD GRAIN AND TEXTURE.

THIS PIECE MAY BE MOLDED

PROVIDES STRONG, WEAR-RESISTANT EDGE FOR WORK TOPS AND TABLES. TYPE SHOWN IS FLEXIBLE – CAN BE BENT TO FOLLOW MOST CURVES. FOR GOOD SEAL STRIP, SHOULD BE CEMENTED AND SCREWED TO THE TOP. USED MOSTLY FOR SERVICE TOPS.

METAL EDGE

TOP LIP HOLDS DOWN TOP VENEER-MAKES STRONGER, MORE DURABLE EDGE. WILL NOT BEND READILY.

METAL

UNTRIMMED EDGES

THIS CORNER TENDS TO BE WEAK. RECEDING EDGE HELPS CONCEAL EXPOSED EDGES OF PLIES.

STRONGER AT TOP. CURVED EDGE HELPS CONCEAL EDGES OF PLIES.

IF SURFACE IS TO BE PAINTED NO EDGE FINISH IS NECESSARY.

TABLE LEGS, APRONS
METHODS OF ATTACHING TOPS TO LEGS

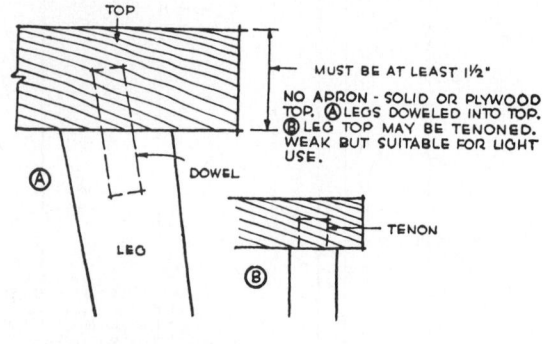

TOP

MUST BE AT LEAST 1½"

NO APRON – SOLID OR PLYWOOD TOP. Ⓐ LEGS DOWELED INTO TOP. Ⓑ LEG TOP MAY BE TENONED. WEAK BUT SUITABLE FOR LIGHT USE.

Ⓐ DOWEL LEG

Ⓑ TENON

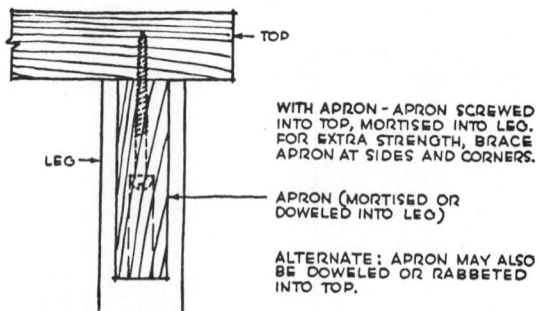

TOP

LEG

WITH APRON – APRON SCREWED INTO TOP, MORTISED INTO LEG. FOR EXTRA STRENGTH, BRACE APRON AT SIDES AND CORNERS.

APRON (MORTISED OR DOWELED INTO LEG)

ALTERNATE: APRON MAY ALSO BE DOWELED OR RABBETED INTO TOP.

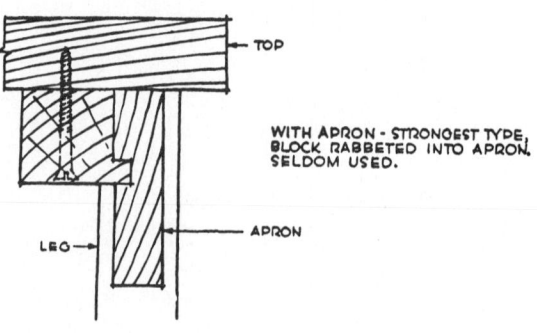

TOP

WITH APRON – STRONGEST TYPE, BLOCK RABBETED INTO APRON. SELDOM USED.

LEG APRON

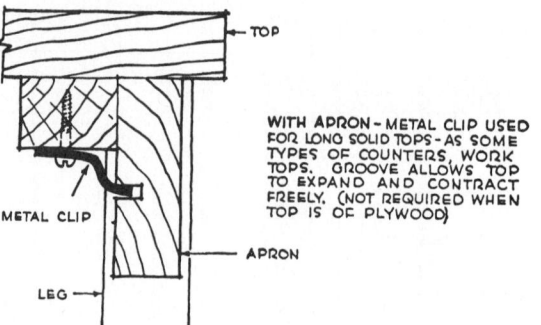

TOP

METAL CLIP

WITH APRON – METAL CLIP USED FOR LONG SOLID TOPS – AS SOME TYPES OF COUNTERS, WORK TOPS. GROOVE ALLOWS TOP TO EXPAND AND CONTRACT FREELY. (NOT REQUIRED WHEN TOP IS OF PLYWOOD)

APRON

LEG

For information on finishes for cabinet work, see section on Finishes.

By HOWARD P. VERMILYA, AIA

A tile is a relatively small, nonstructural, surfacing unit which is thin in relation to its width and length. Tiles may be made of various materials (such as stone, cement, plastic, metal, fiberboard, glass, rubber, asphalt, and cork), but clay is by far the most common, so much so that the Federal Trade Commission has ruled that the word "tile" when unmodified refers to a baked clay or ceramic product.

Ceramic tile

Ceramic tile, one of man's oldest building materials, has unique functional and decorative properties. Its imperviousness and its smooth surface have caused it to be widely used in hospitals, kitchens, bathrooms, swimming pools, dairies, bakeries, and the like—wherever the utmost in sanitation and easy maintenance is required. Other physical properties of tile, such as its hardness, durability, and fire resistance, may also be important functionally. As a decorative material, ceramic tile offers an almost unlimited choice of colors and patterns which do not fade, and it is practically indestructible. The decorative use of tile was carried to a very high point in medieval Islamic architecture ranging from Persia to Spain. It is also widely used in contemporary architecture.

Ceramic tile is made from clay, or a mixture of clay and other materials which is called the body of the tile. The tile may or may not have a glazed face and it is fired at a temperature above red heat, sufficiently high to result in specific physical properties and characteristics.

Standards are in general use throughout the industry. The principal standards pertaining to the manufacture and installation of ceramic tile are as follows:

ASTM C242 *Standard Definitions of Terms Relating to Ceramic Whitewares and Related Products*

SPR R61, *Clay Tiles for Floors and Walls.* Department of Commerce, Simplified Practice Recommendation

Federal Specification SS-T-308b, *Tile, Floor, Wall, and Trim Units, Ceramic*

ANSI/TCA A137.1—1967, *Specification for Ceramic Tile*

ANSI A118.1—1976, *Specifications for Dry-Set Portland Cement Mortar*

ANSI A118.2—1967 (R 1976), *Conductive Dry-Set Portland Cement Mortar*

ANSI 118.3—1976, *Chemical Resistant, Water Cleanable, Tile-Setting Epoxy*

ANSI A118.4—1973 (R 1976), *Specifications for Latex-Portland Cement Mortar*

ANSI A136.1—1967 (R 1976), *Organic Adhesives for Installation of Ceramic Tile, Type I and Type II*

ANSI A108.1—1976, *Specifications for Glazed Ceramic Wall Tile Installed with Portland Cement Mortar*

ANSI A108.2—1967, *Specifications for Ceramic Mosaic Tile Installed with Portland Cement Mortar*

ANSI A108.3—1967, *Specifications for Quarry Tile and Paver Tile Installed with Portland Cement Mortar*

ANSI A108.4—1976, *Specifications for Ceramic Tile Installed with Water-Resistant Organic Adhesives*

ANSI A108.5—1976, *Specifications for Ceramic Tile Installed with Dry-Set Portland Cement Mortar*

ANSI A108.6—1976, *Specifications for Ceramic Tile Installed with Chemical Resistant, Water Cleanable, Tile-Setting Epoxy*

ANSI A108.7—1967 (R 1976), *Specifications for Electrically Conductive Ceramic Tile Installed in Conductive Dry-Set Portland Cement Mortar*

NFPA Bulletin no. 56 *Code for Use of Flammable Anesthetics,* National Fire Protection Association

Manufacturing processes: Two processes are in general use:

Dust-pressed process, in which the clays are ground to dust and mixed with a minimum of water, shaped in steel dies, and then fired

Plastic process, in which the clays are made plastic by mixing with water, shaped by extrusion or in molds, and then fired

Both processes are used to produce glazed or unglazed tile of various sizes, densities, and degrees of water absorption.

Grades are established by SPR R61 for ceramic mosaic, quarry tile, and glazed tile (except faience), as follows:

Standard grade (blue label): within specified limits as to dimension, warpage, blemishes, and other defects; 5 per cent seconds permitted

Seconds (yellow label): permits many but not all the defects prohibited in the standard grade.

Master-grade certificates covering an entire shipment will be issued if requested before shipment is made.

Sizes are shown in Table 1.

Classes: Ceramic tile is broadly classified as unglazed or glazed.

Unglazed tile is a hard, dense tile of homogeneous composition. Its colors and characteristics are determined by the materials used in the body, the method of manufacture, and the thermal treat-

Table 1. Sizes of ceramic tile, in.

Ceramic mosaic		Wall tile		Quarry tile	
Square					
3/8 x 3/8 #	A	1 3/8 x 1 3/8 #	D	2 3/4 x 2 3/4 x 1/2	G
1/2 x 1/2 #	C	2 1/16 x 2 1/16 #	E	4 x 4 x 1/2	H
3/4 x 3/4	A	3 x 3 #	D	6 x 6 x 1/2	G
15/16 x 15/16	B	4 1/4 x 4 1/4	E	6 x 6 x 3/4	I
1 1/16 x 1 1/16	C	6 x 6	D	9 x 9 x 3/4	J
1 3/16 x 1 3/16	A				
1 15/16 x 1 15/16	B				
2 3/16 x 2 3/16	C				
Oblong (rectangular)					
1 3/16 x 3/4	A	6 x 3 #	D	6 x 2 3/4 x 1/2	G
1 15/16 x 15/16	B	6 x 4 1/4 #	DE	8 x 4 x 1/2	H
2 3/16 x 1 1/16	C	8 1/2 x 4 1/4 #	E	8 x 4 x 3/4	
		6 x 9 #	D	8 x 3 7/8 x 3/4 #	
				8 x 3 3/4 x 3/4 #	
Hexagonal				8 x 2 3/8 x 3/4 #	
1 in.				8 x 2 1/4 x 3/4	
				9 x 6 x 3/4	IJ

NOTES: Paver tiles are usually 6 x 6, but may be smaller.

Sizes shown include all of the standard sizes of SPR R61 and some nonstandard sizes (indicated by #) which are generally available. Not all companies produce all the sizes shown, and some produce other sizes than those shown.

The capital letter following a size indicates that it is coordinated in dimension with the other sizes followed by the same letter.

Tile thicknesses are as follows: ceramic mosaic, 1/4; wall tile, 5/16, 3/8 #; paver tile, 1/2 #; quarry tile, 1/2, 3/4.

Tile joint widths are as follows: 2 3/16 square or smaller, 1/32 to 7/64, usually 1/16; over 2 3/16 to 4 1/4 square, 1/16 to 1/4, usually 1/8; 6 x 6 and larger, 1/4 to 3/4; quarry, 3/8 to 3/4; faience, all sizes, 1/8 to 1/2.

Shapes available other than square and oblong include diagonal half-tiles, pentagons, hexagons, octagons, equilateral triangles, diamonds, dots, and half-hexagons.

ment. It is used primarily for floors and walks.

Glazed tile has an impervious face of ceramic materials fused onto the body of the tile, which may be of any type. The glazed surface may be clear, white, or colored. Standard glazes may be *bright* (glossy), *semimatte* (less glossy), *matte* (dull), or *crystalline* (mottled and textured; good resistance to abrasion). Glazed tile is used principally for walls; crystalline glazed tile may be used for light-duty floors.

Bodies: Tile bodies are classified by ASTM C242 as to their degree of water absorption as follows:
Impervious: 0.5 per cent or less
Vitreous: 0.5 to 3 per cent
Semivitreous: 3 to 7 per cent
Nonvitreous: over 7 per cent

Types of tile

Porcelain: a ceramic mosaic or paver generally made by the dust-pressed process, with a composition that is dense, fine-grained, and smooth, and has a sharply formed face. Colors are usually clear and luminous; they may have a granular blend

Natural clay tile: a tile, made by either the dust-pressed method or the plastic method from clays that produce a dense body, with a distinctive, slightly textured appearance

Ceramic mosaic: tile made by either the dust-pressed or plastic process, usually ¼ to ⅜ in. thick, and having a facial area of less than 6 sq in. It is usually mounted on sheets of paper, approximately 1 by 2 ft in size, to facilitate setting. Ceramic mosaic may be of either porcelain or natural clay composition

and comes plain or with an abrasive mixture throughout. It may be unglazed or glazed

Pavers: unglazed porcelain or natural clay tile formed by the dust-pressed process, with a composition similar to that of ceramic mosaics but relatively thicker and having a facial area of 6 or more sq in

Quarry tile: unglazed tile, usually having 6 or more sq in. of surface area, made by the plastic extrusion process from natural clay or shales

Faience tile: glazed or unglazed tile, generally made by the plastic process, showing characteristic variations in the face, edges, and glaze that give a hand-crafted, nonmechanical effect

Faience mosaic: faience tile less than 6 sq in. in facial area. It is ⁵⁄₁₆ to ⅜ in. thick and is usually mounted

Glazed interior-wall tile: a glazed tile

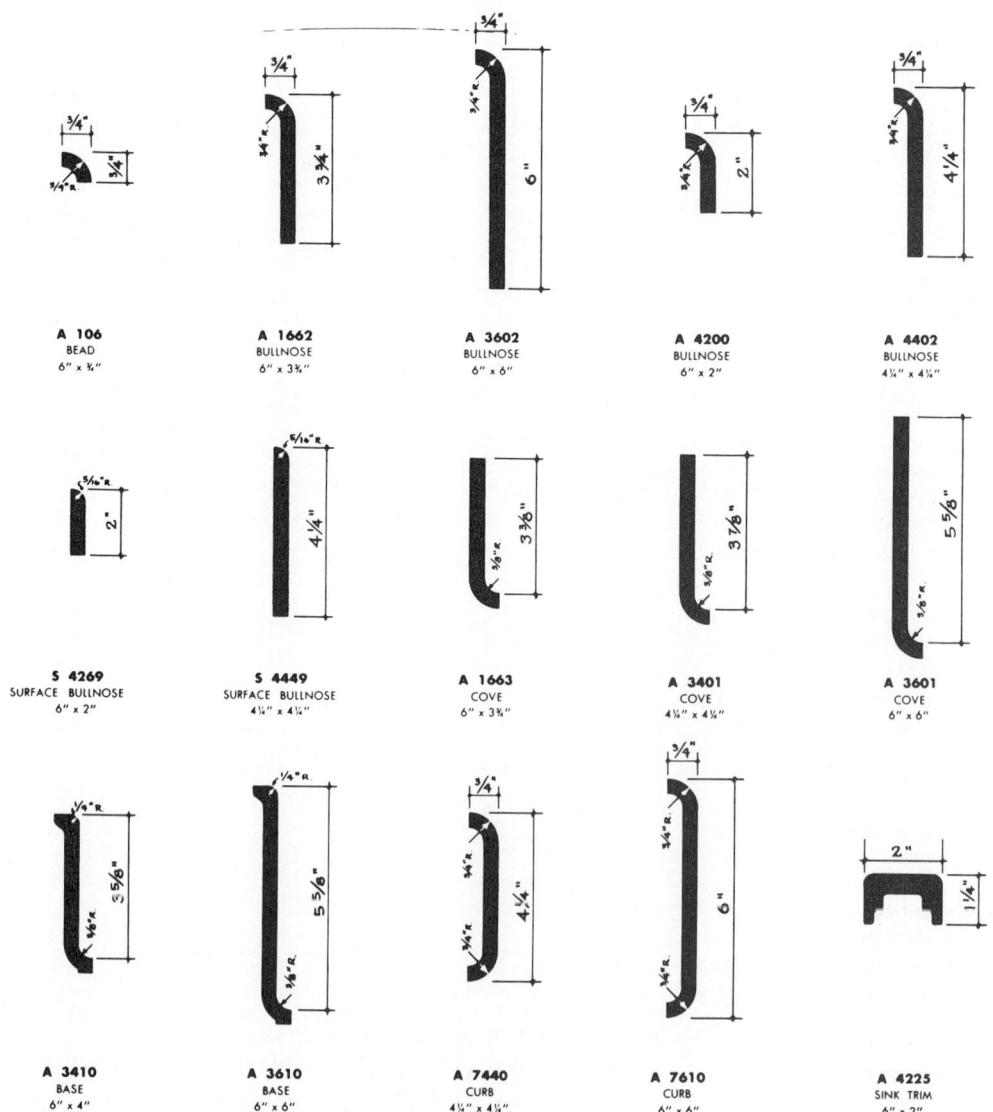

Fig. 1. Standard trim shapes and sizes

"A" numbers designate units for setting in conventional mortar bed. "C" numbers designate ceramic mosaic trim, conventional type. "S" numbers designate "surface type" units, including ceramic mosaic, for use with dry-set mortar or adhesive. (From Simplified Practice Recommendation R-61.)

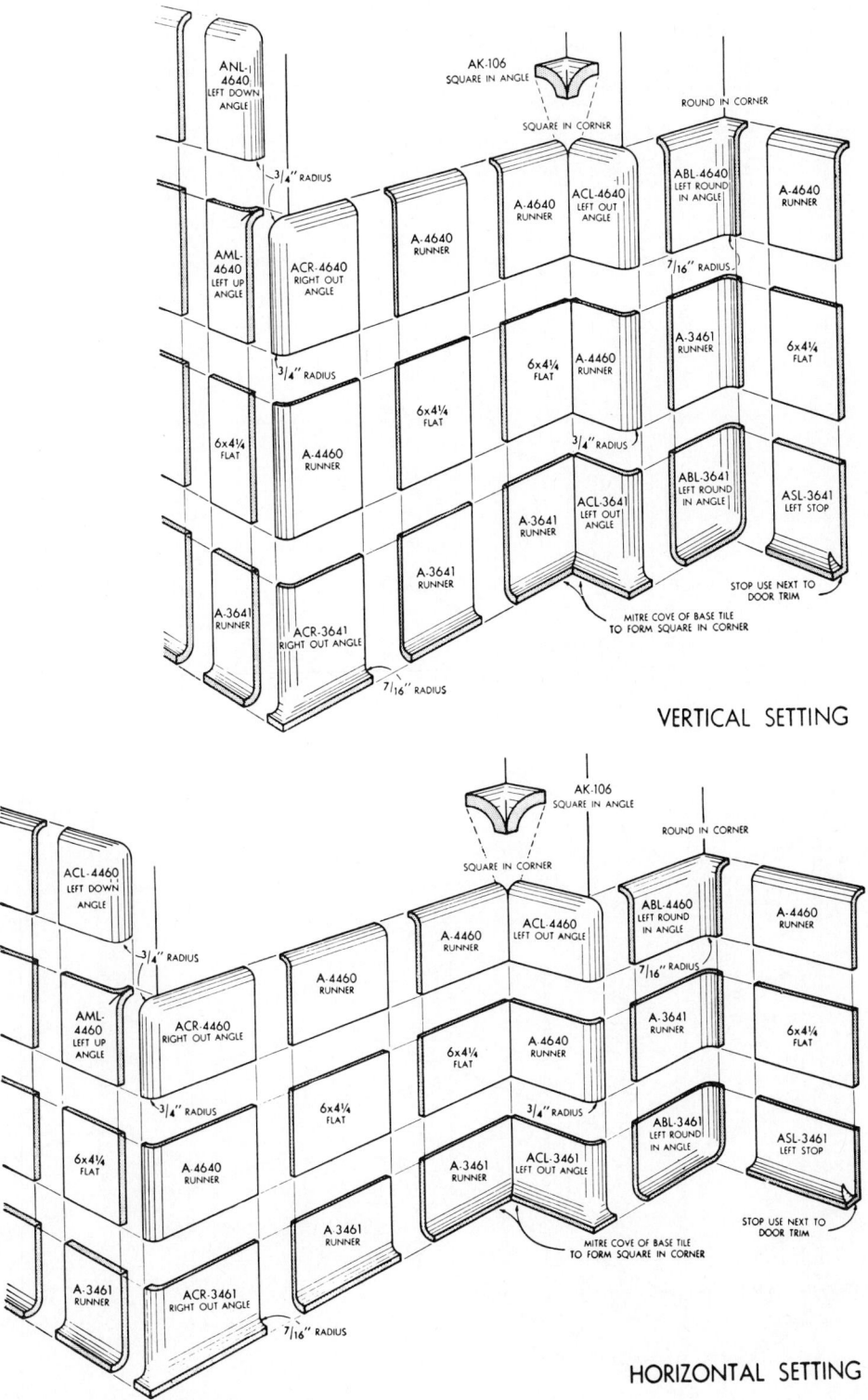

VERTICAL SETTING

HORIZONTAL SETTING

Fig. 2.   Standard trim shapes and designations

6 by 4¼ in. wall tile set in conventional mortar bed. (Courtesy American-Olean Tile Company.)

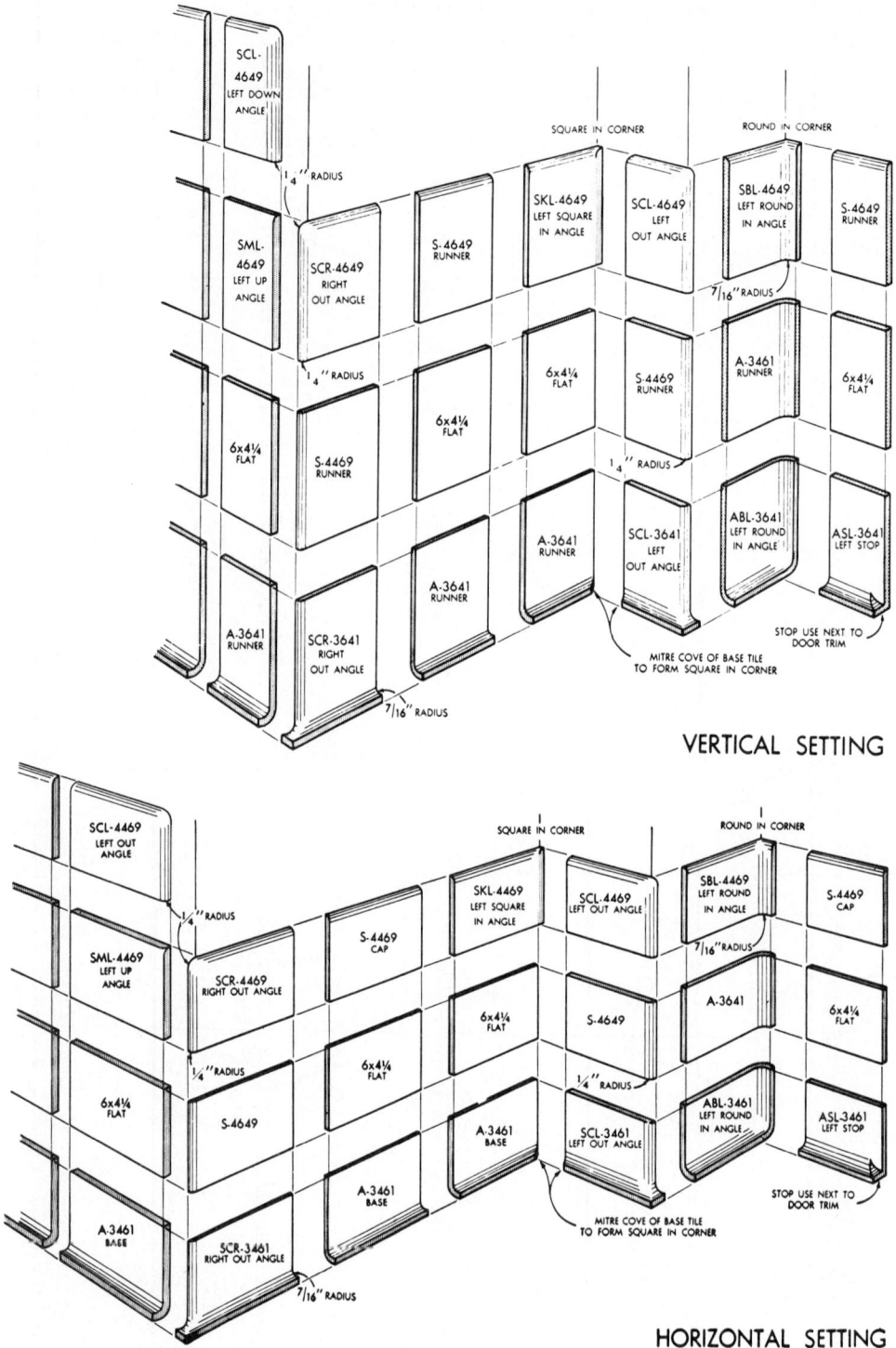

Fig. 3. Standard trim shapes and designations

6 by 4¼ in. wall tile set in dry-set mortar or adhesive. (Courtesy American-Olean Tile Company.)

with a body, usually nonvitreous, suitable for general interior use but not designed to withstand excessive impact or freezing and thawing conditions

Special-purpose tile: a tile, either glazed or unglazed, made to meet the requirements of particular uses. Some examples of special-purpose tile are:

Nonslip tile: produced by the addition of abrasive substances such as silicon carbide or other gritty particles to the body of unglazed or to the glaze of glazed tiles to be used for flooring

Frostproof tile: glazed or unglazed tile made on an impervious or vitreous body for use on exterior areas subject to freezing and also for interior surfaces of refrigerators and freezers

Acid-, alkali-, and stain-resistant tile: used principally for floors and counter tops in food processing and chemical plants, laboratories, and the like. Special grout must be used. Stain-resistant tile has been developed for use in chemically treated swimming pools

Ship or galley tile: a special quarry tile having an indented face pattern for nonslip effect

Packing-house tile: similar to quarry tile but thicker

Conductive tile: used to prevent static electrical discharge where such discharge might cause an explosion, as in a hospital operating room, munitions plant, laboratory, etc. Conductive tile, usually ceramic mosaic, has an impervious, unglazed body into which have been introduced certain iron oxides or acetylene black to provide moderate electrical conductivity for personnel and equipment in contact with the floor. The NFPA Standard requires an electrical resistance not greater than 500,000 ohms nor less than 25,000 ohms, with no single tile having a greater resistance than 2½ million ohms. Warranty to that effect will be furnished by the manufacturer if requested before shipment. Conduc-

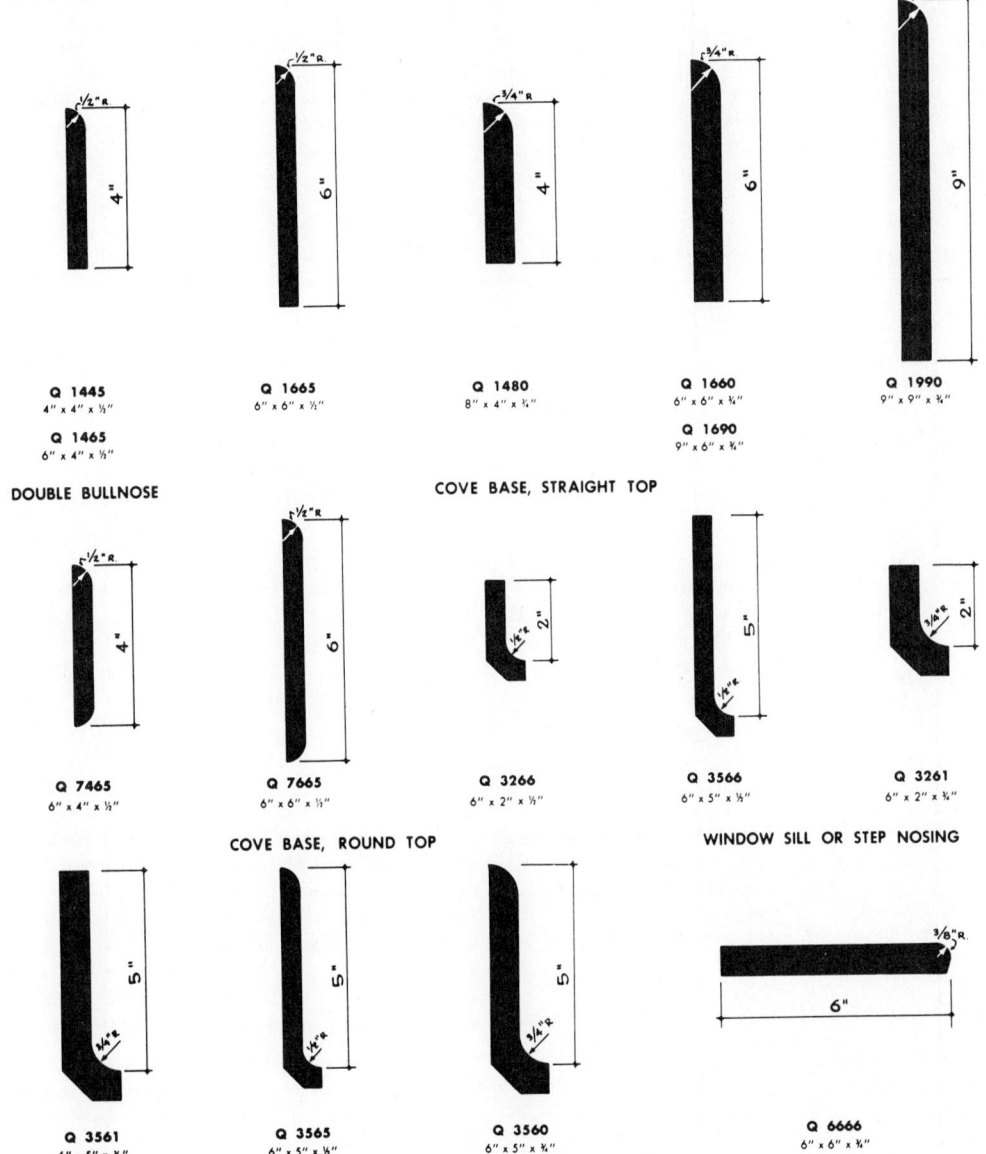

Fig. 4. Quarry tile trim shapes and sizes

"Q" numbers designate quarry tile trim. (From SPR R61)

tive tile must be set in a special conductive cement bed or adhesive

Trim units: These are variously shaped ceramic units such as caps, bases, coves, bullnoses, corners, etc., which are necessary for edging a tile field or making a transition betwen intersecting planes. Trim is made to match flat tile in color and texture and to coordinate with it in dimension. It is made for both thick-bed and thinset applications.

Accessories: Bathroom accessories such as the soap dish, paper holder, tumbler holder, towel bars, grab bars, hooks, and shelf brackets are made to match face-tile colors and textures. The units are glazed over ceramic or china bases and may be either flush or flange type; the latter fits over and conceals the cut edges of the wall tile.

Edges: Two types are in common use: the *square* edge, used with flush grouted joints, and the *cushion* edge, which permits the joints to be recessed slightly from the face of the tile. Some tiles are provided with *self-spacing* lugs on two adjacent edges to facilitate spacing the tile for uniform joint widths.

Mounted tile: Ceramic mosaic is usually furnished mounted on sheets of paper approximately 1½ to 2 sq ft in area. Until recently the paper mounting was always on the face of the tile and was soaked off after the tile had been permanently installed. Rear-mounted tile, using a perforated paper which permits adequate bonding of the tile to the setting bed, is now available. This enables the tile setter to see what he is doing and to exercise closer control over joint widths, levels, and patterns.

Installation: There are three accepted methods for installing ceramic tile (Table 2):

1. The conventional method using a portland cement mortar bed.
2. The dry-set portland cement mortar method.
3. The organic adhesive method.

The *conventional mortar-bed method,* also known as the "thick-bed method," should be used wherever the utmost protection is needed against moisture, for floors subject to heavy traffic, and for most exterior applications. The procedure is as follows:

1. Waterproof membrane should be applied over unstable surfaces such as wood subfloors or wood or steel wall framing; also over gypsum plaster, gypsum block, or gypsum wallboard.

2. Self-furring or self-supported metal reinforcing in middle of setting bed—mandatory when waterproof membrane is used.

3. Expansion joints not over 16 ft on center in both directions. Should cut entirely through setting bed. Mandatory in exterior tile work, desirable with large wood surfaces.

4. For floors and decks, mortar setting bed should be ¾ to 1¼ in. thick, consisting of 1 part (vol) portland cement, 5 to 6 parts sand, and 1/10 part hydrated lime type S. Waterproof cement or admixtures may be used. For walls and ceilings the mortar setting bed should be ¼ to ¾ in. thick, consisting of 1 part (vol) portland cement, 4 to 5 parts sand, and ½ part hydrated type S lime. On walls mortar setting bed may be applied to scratch, or scratch and leveling, coats of cement plaster after they have dried for 24 hours or if the one-*float-coat method* is used, the setting bed is applied directly to the reinforcing mesh.

Table 2.   Mortars for installation of ceramic tile

Mortar type	Areas of use	Remarks	American National Standard specifications
1. Conventional portland cement and sand mortar	For general use over masonry, wood frame, metal studs, etc. Requires wire lath over all unstable substructures.	Requires soaking of all non-vitreous, wall tile. — Grouting is usually done with standard portland cement grout; however, all presently available grouts can be used.	A108.1—1976, A108.2—1967, A108.3—1967 *Glazed Ceramic Wall Tile, Ceramic Mosaic Tile, Quarry Tile and Paver Tile Installed with Portland Cement Mortar*
2. Dry-set portland cement mortar—with or without sand	For use over cinder block, concrete, gypsum wallboard, scratch coat and all other sound masonry surfaces.	Permits use of dry non-vitreous, wall tile, and thin (1/16 in. minimum) mortar layers. — Requires special dry-wall grouts.	A118.1—1976 *Dry-Set Portland Cement Mortar* A108.5—1976 *Ceramic Tile Installed with Dry-Set Portland Cement Mortar*
3. Organic adhesive, wall type and floor type	For use over all flat and reasonably smooth nondusting surfaces; usually cement plaster, asbestos-cement board, fir plywood, or gypsum wallboard.	Only dry tile can be installed with organic adhesives. They do not have indefinite life of portland cement mortars, but they can take more movement of substructure without installation damage. — Requires special dry-wall grouts.	A136.1—1967 (R 1976) *Organic Adhesives for the Installation of Ceramic Tile, Type I and Type II* A108.4—1976 *Ceramic Tile Installed with Water-Resistant Organic Adhesives*
4. Acid-alkali resistant mortars. Various types are available. They are generally thin setting (mortar layer ¼ in. or less).	For use in corrosive areas, generally with quarry tile in industrial installation.	Special techniques required for mortars of this type. — Grouting is usually done with same material used for mortar.	A118.3—1976 *Chemical-Resistant, Water Cleanable Tile-Setting Epoxy* A108.6—1976 *Ceramic Tile Installed with Chemical Resistant, Water Cleanable Tile-Setting Epoxy*

Table 3. Grouts for ceramic tile joints

Grout type	Use	Remarks	Colors
1. Portland cement conventional types	For grouting vitreous and wet non-vitreous tiles, usually in conventional portland cement and sand installations.	Used neat for most narrow ($\frac{1}{16}$ in.) wide grout joints, and with sand for quarry tile grout joints. Many proprietary formulations improve texture and shrinkage characteristcis.	White or gray; can be colored with inert pigment.
2. Dry-wall portland cement types	For grouting ceramic tile installations with dry-set portland cement or organic adhesives.	This type will not lose water to absorptive surfaces it contacts, as will conventional portland cement types.	White or gray; can be colored with inert pigments.
3. Organic types	For grouting all kinds of tile where impermeable, nonstaining surface is desired.	Relatively new category of tile grout, being pioneered by Tile Council of America. Resistant to acid and alkali attack.	White. Can be colored.
4. Flexible grouts	For grouting floors where some flexibility is desired.	Two-part grouts to be mixed on job.	Dark gray and black.
5. Acid-alkali resistant grout	For use in corrosive areas, generally with quarry tile in industrial installations.	Special technique required for most grouts of this type.	White, red, gray and black.
6. Tub caulks	For caulking between tub lip and tile walls.	Available in tubes from any hardware or building supplier.	White
7. Expansion joint fillers	For filling expansion and contraction joints.	Mostly two parts—to be mixed at job site.	Black, gray and aluminum.

5. While the setting bed is still plastic, trowel or dust on a $\frac{1}{32}$- to $\frac{1}{16}$-in. thickness of neat cement paste (float method) or apply to back of tile (buttering method), and set tile firmly on bed. Soak glazed wall tile before setting. Joint width is determined by strings, pegs, spacers, or other methods.

6. Beat tile into mortar bed. Cut through setting bed horizontally or vertically every 17 to 24 in.

7. Grout, clean, and prevent too rapid drying—damp-curing for three days is recommended. All recognized types of grout (portland cement, commercial-waterproof, flexible, and nonstaining) may be used (Table 3).

The *dry-set portland cement mortar method* uses a relatively new type of mortar developed by the Tile Council of America and produced under license by manufacturers. In the dry-set mortar, inorganic admixtures have been incorporated with the portland cement to increase water retentivity and the bonding action of the cement. This process makes it unnecessary to soak absorptive tile or damp-cure the setting bed; damp-curing of dry-set grout is recommended, however, particularly on floors, exteriors, and in wet locations.

The dry-set mortar method may be used in wet locations, showers, tub-shower recesses, etc., directly over portland cement plaster, concrete, concrete masonry, structural clay tile or brick, and in dry locations over ½-in. or ⅝-in. gypsum wallboard, when properly installed with taped and treated joints. Dry-set mortar over a compatible primer sealer has been used over gypsum wallboard in recessed tub-showers and in shower compartments. A water-proof cleavage membrane and a reinforced portland cement mortar setting bed ¾ to 1¼ in. thick should be used over wood floors to receive tile. Dry-set mortar may be used neat or mixed with fine sand according to the thickness of the bed and the type of tile used. The ratio of sand to cement used should follow the manufacturer's directions.

The procedure is as follows:

1. Float mortar over backing, using flat side of trowel, to a minimum thickness of $\frac{1}{16}$ in. for walls and ceilings, ⅛ in. for floors.

2. Comb mortar with notched trowel within 10 min of applying tile.

3. Soaking porous tile is unnecessary but may be done if desired or if conventional portland cement grout is to be used.

4. Press tile into bed, tap and beat into place. Ribbed-back tile may require application of mortar to back of tile to obtain full contact. If mounted tile is used, soak off paper, using as little water as possible, before initial set.

5. Grout and clean. Damp-cure for at least three days if conventional portland cement or dry-set mortar is used for grouting.

In the *Organic Adhesive Method*, the adhesive used should comply with ANSI A136.1, which requires container labels to provide instructions regarding storage, handling on job, tools to be used, effective solvents, and warnings of improper applications, conditions, and locations, including toxicity and flammability. Use only the type of adhesive recommended by the manufacturer for the particular function and conditions. The adhesive method can be used in dry areas directly over such backing materials as waterproof plywood, asbestos-cement board, hardboard, metal, gypsum board, and other materials. When the backing is properly waterproofed it may be used in wet locations. In either location the adhesive manufacturer's directions with reference to appropriate backing materials should be carefully followed.

The procedure is as follows:

1. Apply underlayment recommended by manufacturer, if surface needs leveling. This applies particularly to remodeling work over existing tile, terrazzo, or concrete floors, or other irregular surfaces.

2. Apply primer sealing coat to backing material or underlayment when recommended by manufacturer.

3. Set tile using either the float or the buttering method. The float method is usually recommended for ceramic mosaics, glazed tile, and faience mosaics; the buttering method, or combination float and buttering method, for pavers, quarry tile, and faience tile. The *float method* consists of spreading adhesive over the backing surface with a special trowel, notched as recommended by manufacturer, and pressing tile into it. The *buttering method* reverses the former procedure by applying the adhesive directly to the back of the tile in a thin layer and then pressing the tile onto the backing material.

4. Carefully remove all adhesive from face of tile, using only solvents recommended by adhesive manufacturer.

5. Grout may be portland cement mortar, in which case porous tile should be soaked, dry-set grout, commercial waterproof grout, flexible grout, or nonstaining grout.

A *conductive-tile mortar bed* may be the conventional portland cement mortar bed (1¼ in. thick), or a dry-set portland cement mortar or organic-adhesive setting bed, with additives to make it electrically conductive. These are usually proprietary products and the manufacturer's instructions should be carefully observed. The grout need not be conductive.

Acid- and alkali-resistant mortar beds and grouts are also generally proprietary products. They are usually of the thin-set type, mortar or adhesive. They are used principally in industrial and laboratory applications, usually with quarry tile. Manufacturer's directions should be followed strictly.

A two-component epoxy-resin setting bed and grout has been developed by the Tile Council of America and designated AAR-II. After mixing, it is troweled over the subsurface to a minimum thickness of ⅛ in., and the tile is installed in the usual manner. Grouting is normally done the following day, and the floor may be put into service the day after, although the resin does not attain its full strength for 28 days. Excess resin may be cleaned off the face of the tile and off tools with water.

Metal tile

Tile made of metal is available for wall and ceiling finish. It is made of several dif-

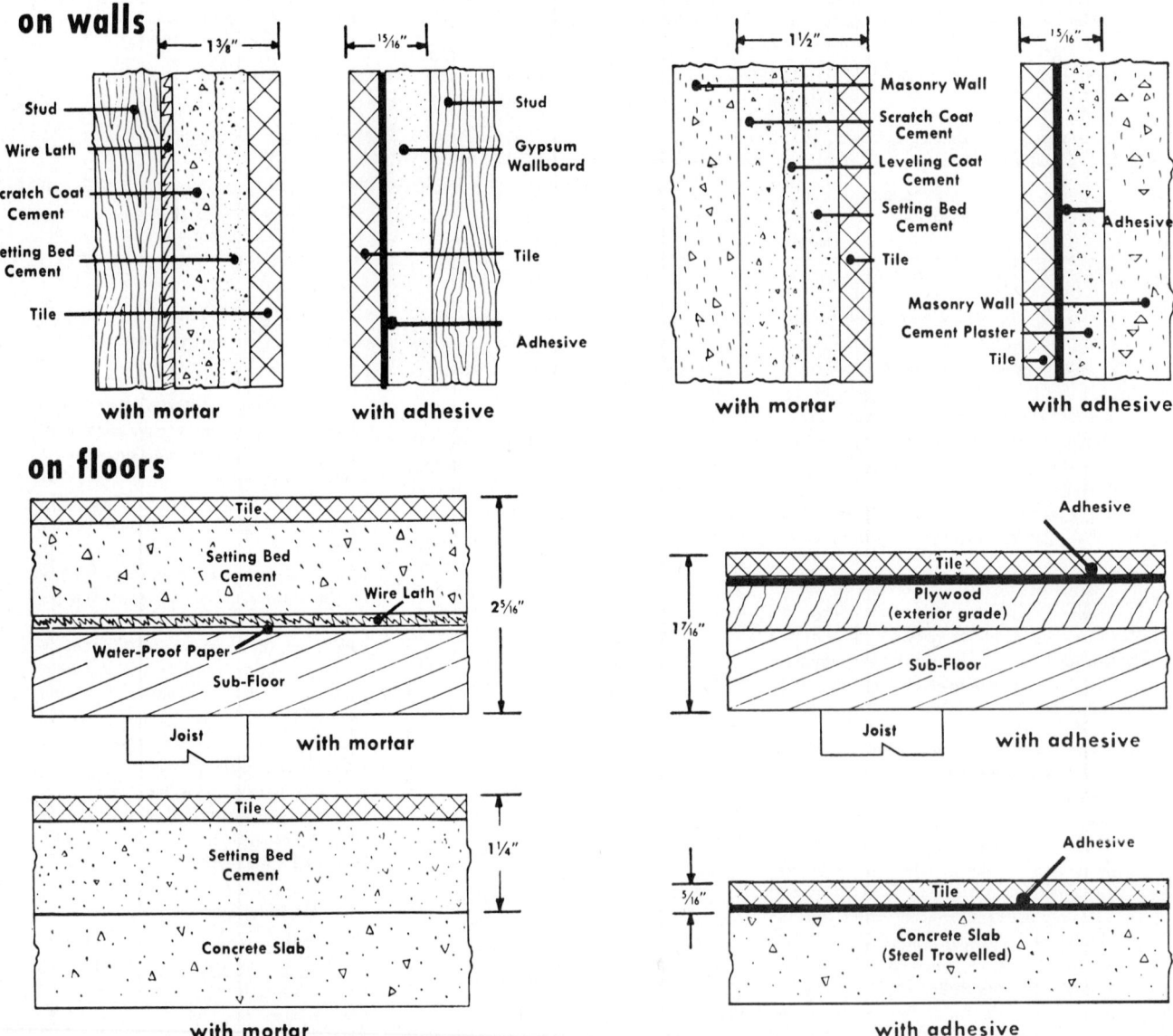

Fig. 5. Typical details of tile installations on walls and floors—One-half full size

Courtesy Minnesota Mining and Manufacturing Company.

ferent metals, which may have various finishes. The principal advantages of metal as compared with ceramic tile are its light weight (1 lb per sq ft in place) and its thinness (⅛ to 3/32 in., including the adhesive). In other respects it has many of the desirable characteristics of ceramic tile, being smooth and impervious, which makes it sanitary and easy to clean, hard and durable, heat-resistant, and decorative.

Base metal: Tile may be formed from strip steel, aluminum, copper, brass, or stainless steel. Steel, 0.015 in. thick, is zinc-plated, bonderized, and spray-coated with zinc chromate before finishing. Aluminum is usually alloy 3003 half-hard; it is 0.020 in. thick for resin-enamel finish and 0.025 in. thick for porcelain enamel. Copper, brass, and stainless steel are 0.015 in. thick.

Finishes: The finish may be a clear or colored resin enamel, baked on at a temperature in excess of 300°F, or a porcelain enamel of either the low-temperature (on aluminum) or high-temperature type. The latter is very similar to the glaze on ceramic tile and has approximately the same characteristics. Exposed metals are usually given a brushed or satin finish. Brass, copper, and aluminum are protected from oxidation by a clear resin-enamel baked-on coating. Stainless steel needs no protection. Exposed metals may be had with a "hammered" pattern, if desired.

Sizes: Flat tile is available in three sizes: 4¼ by 4¼, 4¼ by 8½, and 8½ by 8½ in.

Trim: Three types of trim are available (Fig. 7): (1) Flat-cap, using the standard tile depth; (2) Bullnose-cap, showing a slightly bulbous projection to give an illusion of greater thickness to the tile; (3) Extended-depth, providing a rounded return at the top to give an even greater appearance of depth than the bullnose-cap. Each system employs related coves or bases, corners, and angles to provide a complete wall installation. The resin-enamel tile may be bent around corners, but the porcelain-enamel tile requires special corner shapes.

Installation: Metal tile is affixed to the backing material by the float method, using mastic. Brown-coat plaster or the various wallboards make excellent bases. Porous materials need sealing with primers. Two types of mastic are used:

1. *Oil-type mastic* with white lead or with titanium pigment, which must be applied with a notched trowel over two coats of orange shellac. The tile may be applied immediately to the mastic, which may also serve as grout between the tiles.

2. *Resinous-type mastic,* which may be applied without the use of a sealer but does require waiting before application of tile and does require the use of a grouting

compound. Also, a special cleaner is required to remove excess mastic from the face of the tile.

Plastic tile

Plastic tile is made by the injection molding process from a polystyrene molding compound to which fillers and pigments have been added. Its manufacture and installation are controlled by an industry standard, U.S. Department of Commerce Commercial Standard CS168-50 *Polystyrene Plastic Wall Tiles and Adhesives for Their Application.* This standard establishes requirements for thickness, size, heat resistance, color fastness, opacity, and defects not permitted. Minimum thickness is 0.062 in., and the lip must extend at least 0.033 in. beyond the back of the tile.

Plastic tile is as thin as metal tile and even lighter in weight (¾ lb per sq ft in place). It has an unlimited range of colors, plain or mottled, and the pattern extends through the thickness of the tile. It is available in various surface finishes: glossy, matte, striated, scored, or other textured finish. It is moisture-resistant and nonabsorptive, hence sanitary and easily cleaned but it is not as hard as metal or ceramic tile and it can be scratched. Plastic tile should not be used outdoors nor should it be subjected to continued direct radiation from sun lamps or germicidal lights. It is combustible but not hazardous, since it does not ignite easily and it burns slowly. It is adversely affected by certain chemicals, such as paste waxes and spray insecticides.

Sizes range from 1 in. sq to 12 in. sq, with the 4¼-in. size being the most generally used. The edges of the tile are rounded or cushioned to give an appearance of depth. Projections have been molded to the back of the tile by some manufacturers to minimize the concaving of the tile in the larger sizes. Spacer-type edges are provided by some manufacturers to facilitate spacing and alignment. Secondary ribs parallel to the edges have been molded in by some manufacturers to improve water resistance; mastic trapped in these grooves prevents moisture from entering the cavity behind the tile.

Installation: Plastic tile may be applied to walls or ceilings that are smooth, straight, dry, and structurally sound or rigid. The surface may be plaster, gypsum board, plywood, hardboard, fiberboard, asbestos-cement board, or concrete. Walls subject to moisture penetration or condensation should be furred-out and resurfaced. In wet locations, such as shower recesses, it may be desirable to prime the wall first. The adhesive manufacturer's directions should be followed carefully. Towel bars and other bath accessories should be fastened to the structural wall and not to the tile.

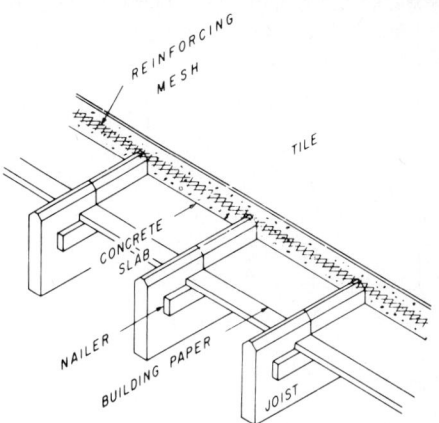

Fig. 6. Detail of thick-bed tile floor over wood joists

This detail is used to keep tile floor at same level as other finish floors. (Courtesy National Forest Products Association.)

The mastic is applied with a notched trowel. Removal of a tile should show at least 75 per cent coverage of the tile with adhesive. Follow the manufacturer's directions as to rate of spread and thickness, as adhesives vary with reference to speed of drying, thickness required, and open times. Tile is usually set about ⅛ in. away from adjacent tile and then slid into place, allowing a small space at least 0.005 in. between tile. The mastic squeezed between the tile is then pointed or smoothed out to provide a grouted joint. Grout may be added if necessary. The tile may be set in place close to the adjacent tile if an ungrouted (clean joint) is desired. Tile never should be butted together tightly; room for expansion should be allowed, particularly when it is installed at a temperature below 70°F.

Special shapes of tile are available for caps, cove bases, and corners. Tile should either be cut with a guillotine-type cutter or sawed; snips or scissors should not be used. No attempt should be made to clean the tile until the mastic has set; then a special cleaner should be used with a soft cloth.

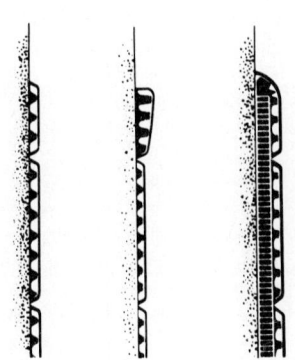

Fig. 7. Metal tile—sections through three types of caps: Flat, Bullnose, Extended depth

Courtesy Vikon Tile Corporation.

By HOWARD P. VERMILYA, AIA,

Terrazzo is a type of marble mosaic that utilizes a portland cement matrix. It is an extremely durable surface of great beauty and variety, made possible by the wide choice of colors and sizes of the marble chips, the design of the divider strips, and the possibility of using metal or mosaic inserts. Although its principal use is for interior and exterior floors, terrazzo, cast in place or precast, is also used for bases, wainscots, partitions, shower receptors, stairs, and many other items. As precast tile, usually made with large chips or broken marble, it is used on both floors and walls.

Marble is vulnerable to attack by acids and strong alkalies. Therefore terrazzo, being essentially a marble product, should *not* be used where it may come in contact with acids or strong alkali concentrations.

Terrazzo topping

The following types of terrazzo topping are included in "Specifications and Technical Data," issued by the National Terrazzo and Mosaic Association, Inc.:

1. *Standard.* Composed of equal parts of No. 1 and No. 2 (and sometimes No. 3) marble chips (see Table 1); minimum thickness, ⅝ in.; uses 1¼-in.-deep divider strips.

2. *Venetian.* Composed of No. 1 through No. 8 marble chips; minimum thickness, 1 in.; uses 1½-in.-deep divider strips.

3. *Berliner* (Palladiana). Composed of broken marble ranging in size from 4 to 140 sq. in., with joints of standard terrazzo ranging in width from ½ to 5 in.; minimum thickness, 1 in.

4. *Rustic* (Washed). A standard or venetian topping which is washed or broomed before it has set and is later treated with acid; may or may not be ground; used principally outdoors.

5. *Conductive.* Same as standard type but includes acetylene carbon black in matrix and underbed to make it electrically conductive; used principally in hospital operating rooms.

6. *Abrasive.* Same as standard or venetian but includes abrasive aggregates or aluminum oxide in the matrix; used to prevent slipping in shower receptors, around swimming pools, and outdoors.

The last three types are discussed in more detail below.

Colors of terrazzo floors are those of the marbles used, and they may be mixed as desired. The National Terrazzo and Mosaic Association maintains a catalog of color plates which may be referred to by architects in specifying colors. The marble chips constitute at least 70 per cent of the terrazzo surface. The cement matrix may be white or gray cement, or it may be colored, using pigments which are nonfading and not affected by alkali.

The mix should be in the proportion of 200 lb of aggregate (marble chips) to 94 lb (1 bag) of portland cement (Type 1, ASTM C150), with not more than 5½ gal of water.

Installation. Once it is in place, the topping is rolled and then hand-troweled to an even surface exposing the top of the divider strips. After curing (minimum six days), the surface is machine-rubbed, while covered with water, using No. 24 grit or finer abrasive stones and followed with No. 80 grit or finer stones. Then a neat-cement grout is applied to the cleaned surface to fill the surface voids. Not less than 72 hours later, all surplus grout should be removed by regrinding in water, using No. 80 grit or finer abrasive stones. After cleaning, a terrazzo sealer should be applied and the floor buffed.

Abrasive terrazzo floors fall into three different types:

1. *Normal:* Abrasive aggregate sprinkled over topping before rolling (¼–½ lb abrasive aggregate per sq ft).

2. *Quarter-inch:* Standard terrazzo topping placed to within ¼ in. of finished floor level; abrasive mix containing 10–40 per cent abrasive to total aggregate (standard ratio of aggregate to cement being maintained) is placed immediately to bring to finished level.

Table 1. Marble chip sizes (adopted by National Terrazzo and Mosaic Association)

Chip size number	Passes through screen Inches	Retained on screen Inches
0	⅛	1⁄16
1	¼	⅛
2	⅜	¼
3	½	⅜
4	⅝	½
5	¾	⅝
6	⅞	¾
7	1	⅞
8	1⅛	1

3. *Abrasive mixed throughout:* Abrasive mix to consist of 10–40 per cent abrasive to total aggregate. This type, which is placed in the same manner as standard terrazzo topping, is used only for very heavy-duty floors.

The surface in all types should show at least 70 per cent aggregate, marble and abrasive.

Conductive terrazzo floors require careful workmanship to meet the requirements of the National Fire Protection Association (Bulletin 56), which call for an electrical resistance of less than 1 million ohms and greater than 25,000 ohms. To prevent the development of static electricity, acetylene carbon black is mixed into the terrazzo topping and the underbed, a total minimum thickness of 1¾ in. Three pounds (dry weight) of acetylene black is added to the underbed mix and 2 lb is added to the topping for each 94 lb (1 bag) of cement; only 5 gal of water is used per bag of cement. The acetylene black is introduced as a thin paste mixed with a 1½ per cent solution of isopropyl alcohol, using ¾ gal for each pound. Machine mixing of this paste into the entire batch for a minimum of 1 min and a maximum of 3 min is required to obtain uniform dispersion. Excess mixing destroys the function of the acetylene black. Galvanized-iron reinforcing mesh (not grounded) is used in the underbed to provide uniform conductivity. Heavy-top nonconductive plastic divider strips on galvanized steel bottoms with suitable anchorage are used to divide the floor into 2- by 2-ft squares. Floors are cured for a minimum of fourteen days, then ground and grouted, and 2 lb of acetylene black per 94 lb of cement are added to the grout. Finishing should be done not earlier than seven days later. The floor is then cleaned, re-ground, and sealed. Sealers and cleaners should not leave a film which may destroy conductivity of the floor. Acids must not be used to clean terrazzo floors.

Rustic finish, usually used only on outdoor terrazzo, is achieved by washing the surface before it has set with water under pressure or with a stiff broom, to a depth of approximately 1⁄16 in., taking care not to disturb the marble chips. After curing, the surface is saturated with water and then washed with a 10 per cent solution of muriatic acid, after which it is thoroughly cleaned with water. Surface is usually not ground, although it may be lightly ground when laid as a patio floor or swimming pool deck.

Underbeds

Underbed thicknesses vary with the type of construction. It is conventional to express this thickness in terms of the over-all thickness of the underbed and the terrazzo topping, ½ in. for standard or 1 in. for venetian.

1. *Bonded terrazzo,* where the underbed is bonded with a neat-cement coating to the structural slab; minimum thickness, 1¾ in. (outdoors, 2 in.) (Fig. 1).

2. *Sand-cushion terrazzo,* where the underbed is laid with reinforcing mesh over a waterproof-membrane-covered sand bed ¼ in. thick; minimum total thickness, 2½ in. (Fig. 2).

3. *Terrazzo over wood,* where the underbed is laid with reinforcing mesh over a waterproof membrane laid on a tight wood deck; minimum thickness, 2½ in. (Fig. 3).

Underbed used in the above types of construction is a mixture of one part portland cement (Type I) to four parts of sand. Reinforcing mesh is 2 by 2-in., galvanized, welded wire mesh. Waterproof membrane is 5-lb, asphalt-saturated roofing felt.

4. *Monolithic terrazzo,* where the topping is placed directly on a fresh, structural concrete slab, which must be at least 4 in. thick and reinforced. If the slab is on grade, as is usually the case, it should be poured over a waterproof and vaporproof membrane laid on a thoroughly compacted drainage bed of broken stone or gravel. Topping should be installed preferably not later than 24 hours, and in no case more than 6 days, after the structural slab is poured.

The sand-cushion method offers the best assurance of a sound floor without cracks due to vibration or movement of the structure. The same principle of isolating the terrazzo from a substrate in which movement can be expected is used over wood construction. Monolithic terrazzo was developed to provide an attractive and durable floor finish at low initial cost, primarily for residences.

Divider strips

Divider strips are used to control and localize any shrinkage or flexure cracks. (If terrazzo is properly installed, shrinkage cracks will not occur.) The strips fulfill an important decorative purpose by creating scale and pattern and permitting changes of color to be made with ease and accuracy. They also serve, during installation of the topping, as grounds for establishing the level of the finished surface. Finally, they facilitate repair or replacement of damaged sections of topping.

The strips should be carried through the border to the wall or to the edge of the terrazzo. They should be placed over beams, girders, columns, and bearing walls, around stair openings, and wherever there is likely to be a change of stress in the floor. Expansion-type strips with neoprene cores should be placed not more than 30 ft apart in corridors and other places where considerable movement can be anticipated. In monolithic terrazzo, which is usually installed before the partitions, strips should be located under the partitions wherever there are significant changes of area, and they should be used to divide large areas into panels. Panel sizes vary from 16 to 50 in., depending upon the size of the floor area. Small panels are preferable but more expensive. Outdoor panels should not exceed 3 ft; conductive panels should not exceed 2 ft.

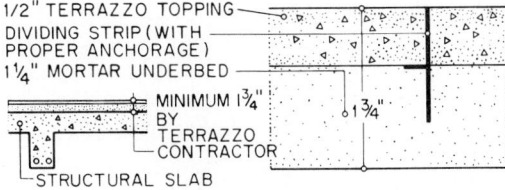

1/2" TERRAZZO TOPPING
DIVIDING STRIP (WITH PROPER ANCHORAGE)
1¼" MORTAR UNDERBED
MINIMUM 1¾" BY TERRAZZO CONTRACTOR
STRUCTURAL SLAB
1¾"

Fig. 1. Bonded terrazzo

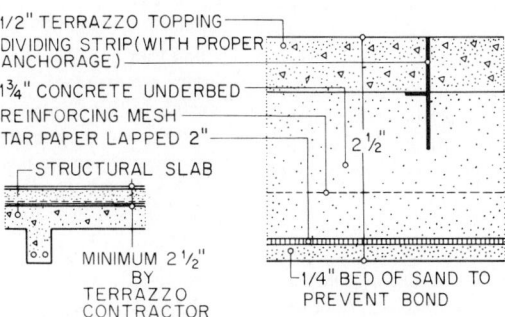

1/2" TERRAZZO TOPPING
DIVIDING STRIP (WITH PROPER ANCHORAGE)
1¾" CONCRETE UNDERBED
REINFORCING MESH
TAR PAPER LAPPED 2"
STRUCTURAL SLAB
2½"
MINIMUM 2½" BY TERRAZZO CONTRACTOR
1/4" BED OF SAND TO PREVENT BOND

Fig. 2. Sand-cushion terrazzo

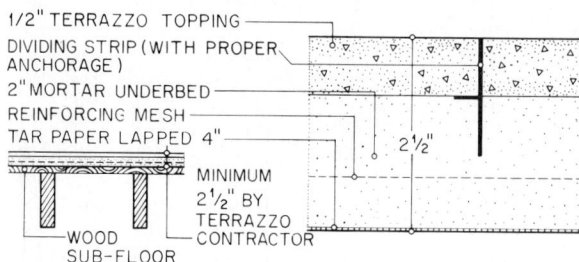

Fig. 3. Terrazzo on wood construction

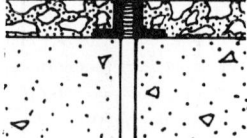

Fig. 4. Monolithic terrazzo with expansion-type divider strip

(Note) All figures courtesy of National Terrazzo and Mosaic Association.

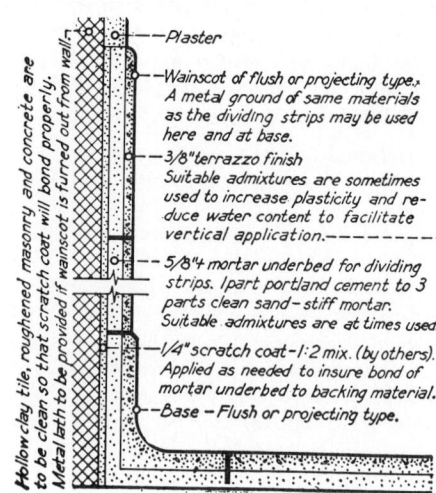

Fig. 6. Terrazzo wainscot

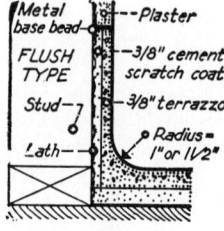
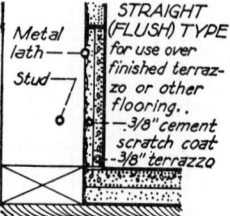
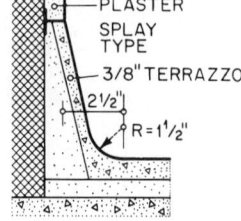

Fig. 5. Terrazzo bases

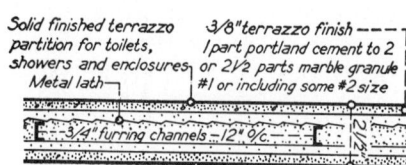

Fig. 7. Solid partition

Divider strips are made from half-hard brass, white alloy zinc (99 per cent zinc), or plastic (acetate butyrate) in a number of colors. Zinc strips should not be used outdoors. Thickness ranges from 18 gage (minimum) to ¼ in. or more. Strips ⅛ in. and thicker are of the heavy-top type, with a thin bottom member. These are usually fabricated to the architect's design in shops specializing in this work. Strips for standard terrazzo are 1¼ in. deep; for Venetian terrazzo they are 1½ in. deep. They are installed in the underbed while it is semiplastic, before the topping is placed. Strips for monolithic terrazzo are T- or L-shaped and ⅝ in. deep. They are fastened to the green underbed by cement nails or are set in grout. Expansion-type strips (Fig. 4) should be used over control or expansion joints in the structural slab.

Bases

Terrazzo bases are usually installed integrally with the floor. They may be flush, projected, or splayed, and the intersection with the floor may be a right angle or cove (Fig. 5). The bases are capped with a metal bead. Divider strips should align with those of the floor; the usual practice is to continue every other floor divider through the base. A precast terrazzo base is sometimes used, especially with other flooring materials.

Wainscots and partitions

Terrazzo wainscots and partitions consist of ⅜ in. topping and ⅝ in. underbed, applied to masonry or to a cement-plaster scratch coat on metal lath (Fig. 6). Solid partitions should be formed with ¾-in. furring channels 12 in. on center; a cement-plaster scratch coat is applied to both sides of the metal lath, to receive terrazzo underbed and topping (Fig. 7). Underbed for wainscots and partitions consists of a 1 to 3 mix of portland cement and sand. Divider strips should be spaced not more than 30 in. apart.

Stairs

Terrazzo is often used as a finish for stairs. Treads and risers may be poured in place or precast, and they may be installed over a concrete or steel base (Fig. 8). Topping for poured-in-place treads and risers should be ½ in. and the over-all thickness not less than 1½ in. for treads and 1 in. for risers. Strings may have ⅜ in. topping and ⅝ in. underbed. On steel stairs the underbed must be reinforced and anchored to the steel; NTMA recommends an over-all thickness of 2 in. for treads and 1½ in. for risers. However, risers are usually omitted here.

Shower receptors

The detail of a cast-in-place shower receptor is shown in Fig. 9. Precast types are also available.

Precast terrazzo

Precast terrazzo, also known as artificial marble, is used for floor and wall tile, bases, stair treads and risers, window stools, door saddles, shower receptors, counter tops and various specialty items. The mix is usually 2½ parts aggregate (marble chips) to 1 part cement, by weight.

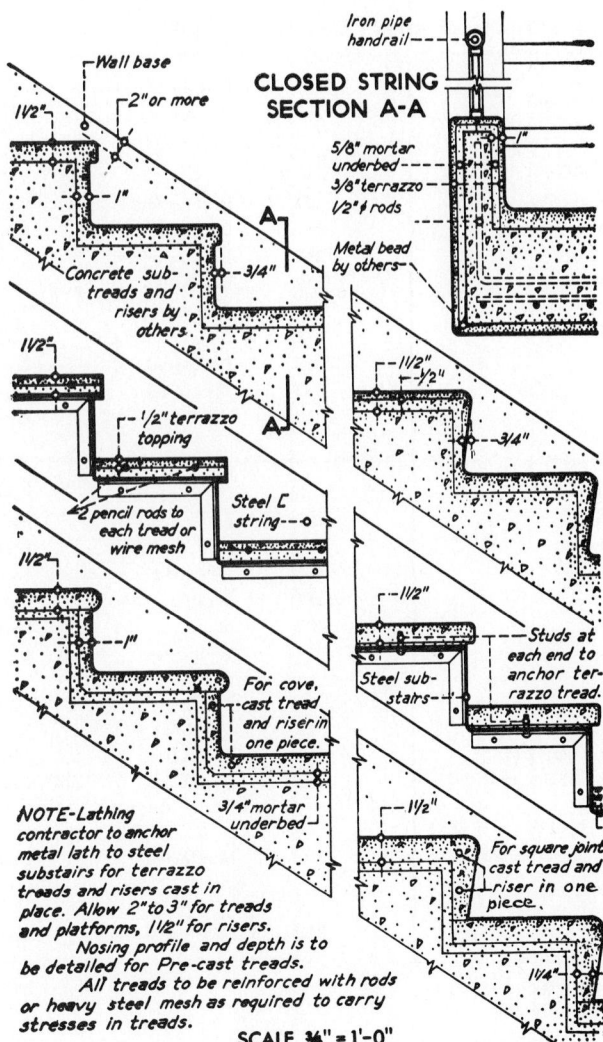

Fig. 8. Terrazzo stair details. Top: poured in place on concrete, two nosing designs. Center: on steel; left, poured in place; right, precast. Bottom: precast on concrete; two nosing designs.

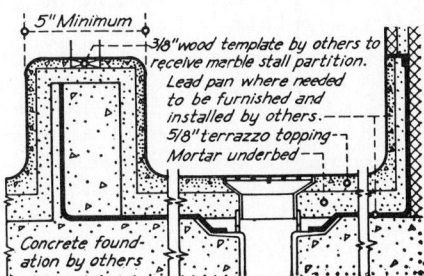

Fig. 9. Terrazzo shower receptor (poured in place)

It is cast by a compression and vibration process in watertight metal molds.

Thin-set terrazzo

Several types of thin-set terrazzo have been developed in recent years. Their principal advantage is the elimination of the underbed (1 to 2 in. thick). This not only reduces the dead load on the structure but also, in many cases, eliminates the need for depressing the structural slab where terrazzo meets another flooring material. Another important advantage is reduction in installation time from the ten days or more required for conventional terrazzo to as little as two days for some thin-set types. Most thin-set systems are proprietary; strict compliance with the manufacturer's instructions is necessary. Skilled workmanship is as important in thin-set as in conventional terrazzo installation.

The principal types of thin-set terrazzo are:

1. *Bonding agent.* An organic adhesive (polysulfide, neoprene, vinyl, or epoxy) is applied to the structural slab before the topping is poured. The topping is standard portland cement type, $\frac{1}{2}$ in. thick, installed and finished in the conventional way. Divider strips are required; they are L-shaped and are set in adhesive.

2. *Admixtures.* The addition of acrylic or vinyl emulsions to the standard topping mix results in a notable increase in the tensile and flexural strength of the terrazzo. Thickness of the topping may be reduced in some cases to as little as $\frac{1}{4}$ in. The use of a bonding agent is advisable. Divider strips are not required but are recommended for locations where stresses can be anticipated; they are set in adhesive. Over substrates subject to movement, glass-fabric reinforcement may be bedded in the adhesive.

3. *Plastic matrix.* In this type of terrazzo a plastic (epoxy or neoprene) replaces portland cement as the matrix. The cured topping has an extremely high tensile strength and can be as thin as the size of the marble chips will permit. In practice, epoxy terrazzo is usually $\frac{1}{8}$ to $\frac{3}{8}$ in. thick, and neoprene terrazzo is $\frac{3}{8}$ to $\frac{5}{8}$ in. thick. Divider strips are not required but are recommended for locations subject to stress. Since the epoxy has a limited "pot life," the strips may be used to mark off areas that can be completed within the time limit. Divider strips must be metal and are set in epoxy adhesive. A liquid primer is usually required; it is applied 2 to 3 hours before the installation of the terrazzo mix.

Epoxy

By GERALD R. WEISSMAN, *Director, Coatings Department, Foster D. Snell, Inc., Consulting Chemists*

Epoxy toppings for industrial floors

The outstanding advantage of epoxy toppings for concrete floors in industrial and laboratory buildings is their high degree of resistance to chemical attack from acids, alkalies, and solvents. The general range of this resistance is indicated in the accompanying table. The destructive effect of any chemical is determined by three things: concentration, temperature, and duration of exposure. The conditions occurring in a given plant are virtually impossible to duplicate in laboratory tests; therefore, whenever possible, it is prudent to subject samples to conditions similar to those which will be encountered in the building being designed. Usually, this can be done by putting various samples in one of the owner's present buildings.

Epoxy floor toppings develop ultimate compressive strengths of 10,000 to 15,000 psi. In abrasion resistance they are superior to average concrete floors, but not as resistant as the highest-quality concrete topping. In comparison with other industrial floor toppings epoxies are thin (⅛ to ¹⁄₁₆ in.), light in weight, jointless, and quick-curing. They can usually be put into service within 1 to 3 days, and they attain their maximum strength within 1 week. Where appearance is a factor, the glossy finish and wide choice of colors in epoxy is an advantage in its favor.

The principal ingredients in an epoxy floor are (1) silica sand, or some material with a high silicate content, or materials like glass cloth or crushed stone, which are inert to most chemical attack; (2) epoxy resin, which in its fully concentrated form also is inert to many chemicals. These ingredients are analogous in function to aggregate and cement in a concrete floor. Epoxy resin is the binder which holds the mass together and bonds it to the base slab. Aggregate adds impact strength and brings the coefficient of thermal expansion of the epoxy closer to that of the concrete to which it is bonded.

In addition, a curing agent and a flexibilizer also are used. The curing agent converts the liquid epoxy resin to a solid. Numerous agents are available, but to withstand industrial floor usage, only one type is normally suitable—an aliphatic amine curing agent that produces the best combination of temperature, chemical, and mechanical properties.

The flexibilizer improves crack and impact resistance. Thus, when stresses are set up by differences in thermal expansion between the epoxy and the concrete base, for example, during steam cleaning, the epoxy will not crack. The amount of flexibilizer used is critical: too little leaves

Chemical resistance of epoxy flooring composition*

Material	Time, hr	Appearance of test sample	Evaluation of chemical resistance
MINERAL ACIDS			
Sulfuric-conc. (96%)	24	Disintegrated	Poor
Sulfuric—50%	312	Discolored	Fair-Good
Sulfuric—20%	312	Unaffected	Good
Sulfuric—10%	312	Unaffected	Good
Nitric-conc. (78%)	24	Disintegrated	Poor
Nitric—40%	312	Discolored slightly	Good
Nitric—20%	312	Discolored	Good
Hydrochloric-conc. (38%)	312	Discolored	Good
Phosphoric-conc. (86%)	312	Unaffected	Good
ORGANIC ACIDS			
Acetic, glacial (99.5%)	48	Disintegrated	Poor
Acetic—50%	100	Badly etched	Poor
Acetic—20%	150	Badly etched	Poor
Acetic—10%	312	Whitened	Fair-Good
Acetic—5%	312	Slightly whitened	Good
Lactic (100%)	200	Slightly etched	Poor-Fair
Oleic (100%)	312	Unaffected	Good
BASES			
Sodium hydroxide—50%	312	Discolored	Fair-Poor
Sodium hydroxide—25%	312	Unaffected	Excellent
Ammonium hydroxide conc. (57%)	312	Discolored	Good
SALTS			
Sodium bisulfite (saturated)	312	Unaffected	Good
SOLVENTS			
Mineral spirits, Xylol, Benzene, Ethyl acetate, Methyl ethyl ketone, Methyl cellosolve acetate, Butyl cellosolve, carbitol	312	Unaffected	Excellent (except for benzene which is rated as good)

* Note: Samples listed were tested at room temperature. Compressive strength before exposure was 14,500 psi.

the floor brittle; too much reduces the floor's strength.

The maximum amount of aggregate that can be used without seriously impairing the properties of the topping is four times the combined weight of the epoxy resin and the curing agent. Much of the effectiveness of an epoxy floor depends on the way it is installed. A 100 per cent epoxy, correctly formulated, is not in itself a guarantee that the floor will live up to expectations. As in many phases of construction, workmanship is important.

An important factor in connection with adhesion of the epoxy topping to the base slab is adequate preparation of the base slab. Despite epoxy's fame for great adhesion, good bond will not occur unless the base slab surface is clean, dry, and roughened. Slab preparation is done either

by sand blasting or chemical etching. Workmen must do every inch of the floor carefully since only one defective spot is sufficient to cause trouble.

A properly prepared slab will permit the epoxy to achieve a bond strength greater than the internal strength of concrete, which is assurance that the bond will not fail under stress.

One other installation procedure is critical: the temperature. To achieve proper cure, the floor should be applied when the temperature is 70 to 80°F. Epoxies should never be installed if the temperature is below 60°F or above 105°F. At the lower temperature curing will not occur for an excessively long time, and at the higher temperature curing will occur so fast that it might be impossible to install the topping properly.

By HOWARD P. VERMILYA, AIA

Hardwoods commonly used as flooring are oak (white and red), hard (sugar) maple, birch, beech, and pecan. Walnut, teak, and other fine hardwoods are occasionally used. Softwoods used are generally the denser species such as Douglas fir and southern yellow pine. Redwood and western red cedar, although quite soft, are used for porch floors and outdoor decks because of their resistance to decay. All species are available in both quarter-sawed (vertical or edge-grain) and plain-sawed (flat-grain). Vertical-grain flooring wears better, especially in the softwoods, and has less tendency to cup and warp. End-grain wood blocks of southern yellow pine, upland oak, or hard maple are used for heavy-duty industrial flooring. The physical properties of the principal woods used for flooring are given in Table 2. Standard sizes of strip flooring are shown in Tables 3–5.

Oak, both red and white, is used principally as strip flooring, but also as plank, parquet, and block flooring. It is the most widely used of all species, especially for residential purposes. It is available in two grades of quarter-sawed and five grades of plain-sawed strip, either square-edged or tongued-and-grooved and end-matched. Red and white oak are graded separately in grades above No. 2 common, but color within the species is not considered. Both are light in color, white oak having a brownish tinge and red oak a pinkish cast. Oak strip flooring is covered by Commercial Standard CS56-60 of the U.S. Department of Commerce and Product Standard PS-56. Standard grades are as follows:

Quarter-sawed or plain-sawed:

Clear: The face shall be practically clear, admitting an average of ⅜ in. of bright sap. Bundles are to be 2 ft and up; average length, 4¼ ft.

Select: The face may contain sap, small streaks, pin worm holes, burls, slight imperfections in working, and small tight knots which do not average more than one to every 3 ft. Bundles are to be 2 ft and up; average length, 3¾ ft.

Plain-sawed only:

No. 1 common: This shall be of such nature as will lay a good residential floor and may contain varying wood characteristics such as flags, heavy streaks and checks, worm holes, knots, and minor imperfections in working. Bundles are to be 2 ft and up; average length, 3 ft.

No. 2 common: This may contain sound natural variations of the forest product and manufacturing imperfections. The purpose of this grade is to furnish an economical

floor suitable for homes or general utility use, or where character marks and contrasting appearance are desired. Bundles are to be 1¼ ft and up; average length, 2½ ft.

1¼ ft shorts: Pieces may range from 9 to 18 in. long, but they must average 15 in. There are two grade classifications: No. 1 (common and better), and No. 2 (common).

Prefinished oak flooring is available in the following grades (red and white oak are separated in each grade):

Prime: The face shall be selected for appearance after finishing, but sapwood and the natural variations of color are permitted. The minimum average length is 4 ft; bundles are to be 2 ft and longer.

Standard and better: A combination of prime and standard to contain the full product of the board except that no pieces are to be lower than standard grade. The minimum average length is 3½ ft; bundles are to be 1¼ ft and longer.

Standard: This will contain sound wood characteristics which are even and smooth after filling and finishing and will lay a sound floor without cutting. The minimum average length is 3 ft; bundles are to be 1¼ ft and longer.

Tavern: This shall be of such nature as will make and lay a serviceable floor without cutting, but shall purposely contain typical wood characteristics which are to be properly filled and finished. The minimum average length is 2½ ft; bundles are to be 1¼ ft and longer.

Hard maple, beech, and birch are available in four standard grades which do not consider color variation and in three special grades selected for color. Maple is the species most used for gymnasium floors

and is also widely used for industrial flooring. It is available in several heavy-duty thicknesses (Table 4). Grades (as listed in the Maple Flooring Manufacturers' *Specifications Manual*) are as follows:

First grade: 25/32 in. and thicker, its face shall be practically free of all defects, but the varying natural color of the wood shall not be considered a defect. Standard lengths in all widths in this grade shall be in 2-ft bundles and longer as the stock will produce. Not over 30 per cent of the total footage shall be in bundles under 4 ft.

Second grade: 25/32 in. and thicker, it admits of tight, sound knots and slight imperfections in dressing, but must lay without waste. Standard lengths in all widths in this grade shall be in 2-ft bundles and longer as the stock will produce. Not over 45 per cent of the total footage shall be in bundles under 4 ft.

Third grade: 25/32 in. and thicker, it must be of such character as will lay and give a good serviceable floor. Standard lengths in all widths of this grade shall be in 1¼-ft bundles and longer as the stock will produce. Not over 65 per cent of the total footage shall be in bundles under 4 ft.

Fourth grade: 25/32 in. and thicker, it may contain defects of all character, but must lay a serviceable floor, with some cutting. Standard lengths in all widths shall be in 1¼-ft bundles and longer as the stock will produce.

Special grades:

Selected first-grade light northern hard maple: This grade is carefully selected for uniformity of light color. The color tones in individual strips will vary somewhat,

Table 2. Physical properties of woods used for flooring

Species	Specific gravity*	Hardness†	
		End	Side
Beech, American	0.64	1590	1300
Birch, yellow	0.62	1480	1260
Pecan	0.66	1930	1820
Hickory, shagbark	0.72	—	—
Maple, sugar	0.63	1840	1450
Oak:			
Northern red	0.63	1580	1290
Southern red	0.59	1020	1060
White	0.68	1520	1360
Douglas fir, coast type	0.48	900	710
Pine, southern yellow shortleaf	0.51	750	690

* Moisture content, 12%.
† Load required to embed 0.044-in. steel ball to one-half its diameter.

SOURCE: Wood Handbook, Forest Products Laboratory, U.S. Department of Agriculture.

but after laying, this grade provides a luxurious "light"-appearing floor.

Selected first-grade amber northern hard maple: This grade is carefully selected for uniformity of amber color. The color tones in individual strips will vary somewhat, but after laying, this grade provides a luxurious "amber"-appearing floor.

Selected first-grade red: This grade is produced from all-red faced northern beech or birch and is selected especially for color. The color is a rich, warm tint peculiar to these woods.

Lengths are the same as for standard first grade.

Pecan is available in three standard grades and three special grades selected for color. Pecan, a species of hickory, is denser than the other hardwoods used for flooring. It is sometimes mixed with true hickory, an even denser wood, as strip flooring for industrial use. Grades are as follows:

First grade: It shall be practically free of defects, but the varying natural color of the wood shall not be considered a defect. Bundles shall be 2 ft and longer; not over 25 per cent of the footage shall be 2 and 3 ft.

First-grade red: This is the same as first grade except that the face shall be all heartwood.

First-grade white: This is the same as first grade except that the face shall be all bright sapwood.

Second grade: This will admit of tight, sound knots or their equivalent, pin worm holes, streaks, light stains, and slight imperfections in working. It shall be of such nature as to lay a sound floor without cutting. Bundles shall be 1¼ ft and longer; the proportion of 1¼- to 3-ft bundles shall not exceed 40 per cent of the footage.

Second-grade red: This is the same as second grade except that the face shall be all heartwood.

Third grade: This must be of such character as will give and lay a good, serviceable floor. Bundles shall be 1¼ ft and longer; the proportion of 1¼- to 3-ft bundles shall not exceed 60 per cent of the footage.

Prefinished beech and pecan is furnished in one grade only:

Tavern and better: A combination of prime, standard and tavern containing the full product of the board except that no pieces are to be lower than tavern grade. The minimum average length is 3 ft, bundles are 1¼ ft and longer.

Douglas fir is graded B or better, C, and D in vertical grain and C or better, D, and E in flat grain or mixed grain.

The vertical-grain grades are widely used

Table 3. Hardwood strip flooring sizes, counts, and weights

SOURCE: *Specification Manual of the National Oak Flooring Manufacturers' Association*

"Nominal" is the size designation used by the *trade*, but it is not always the actual size. Sometimes the actual thickness of hardwood flooring is 1/32-inch less than the so-called nominal size. "Actual" is the *mill* size for thickness and face width, excluding tongue width. "Counted" size determines the board feet in a shipment. Pieces less than 1 inch in thickness are considered to be 1 inch.

Oak			
NOMINAL	ACTUAL	Counted	Weights M Ft.
Tongued and Grooved-End Matched			
²⁵⁄₃₂ x 3¼ in.	²⁵⁄₃₂ x 3¼ in.	1 x 4 in.	2300 lbs.
²⁵⁄₃₂ x 2¼ in.	²⁵⁄₃₂ x 2¼ in.	1 x 3 in.	2100 lbs.
²⁵⁄₃₂ x 2 in.	²⁵⁄₃₂ x 2 in.	1 x 2¾ in.	2000 lbs.
²⁵⁄₃₂ x 1½ in.	²⁵⁄₃₂ x 1½ in.	1 x 2¼ in.	1900 lbs.
³⁄₈ x 2 in.	¹¹⁄₃₂ x 2 in.	1 x 2½ in.	1000 lbs.
³⁄₈ x 1½ in.	¹¹⁄₃₂ x 1½ in.	1 x 2 in.	1000 lbs.
½ x 2 in.	¹⁵⁄₃₂ x 2 in.	1 x 2½ in.	1350 lbs.
½ x 1½ in.	¹⁵⁄₃₂ x 1½ in.	1 x 2 in.	1300 lbs.
Square Edge			
⁵⁄₁₆ x 2 in.	⁵⁄₁₆ x 2 in.	face count	1200 lbs.
⁵⁄₁₆ x 1½ in.	⁵⁄₁₆ x 1½ in.	face count	1200 lbs.
Beech, Birch, Hard Maple and Pecan			
NOMINAL	ACTUAL	Counted	Weights M Ft.
Tongued and Grooved-End Matched			
²⁵⁄₃₂ x 3¼ in.	²⁵⁄₃₂ x 3¼ in.	1 x 4 in.	2300 lbs.
²⁵⁄₃₂ x 2¼ in.	²⁵⁄₃₂ x 2¼ in.	1 x 3 in.	2100 lbs.
²⁵⁄₃₂ x 2 in.	²⁵⁄₃₂ x 2 in.	1 x 2¾ in.	2000 lbs.
²⁵⁄₃₂ x 1½ in.	²⁵⁄₃₂ x 1½ in.	1 x 2¼ in.	1900 lbs.
³⁄₈ x 2 in.	¹¹⁄₃₂ x 2 in.	1 x 2½ in.	1000 lbs.
³⁄₈ x 1½ in.	¹¹⁄₃₂ x 1½ in.	1 x 2 in.	1000 lbs.
½ x 2 in.	¹⁵⁄₃₂ x 2 in.	1 x 2½ in.	1350 lbs.
½ x 1½ in.	¹⁵⁄₃₂ x 1½ in.	1 x 2 in.	1300 lbs.
Special Thicknesses (T and G, End Matched)			
¹⁷⁄₁₆ x 3¼ in.	³³⁄₃₂ x 3¼ in.	5/4 x 4 in.	2400 lbs.
¹⁷⁄₁₆ x 2¼ in.	³³⁄₃₂ x 2¼ in.	5/4 x 3 in.	2250 lbs.
¹⁷⁄₁₆ x 2 in.	³³⁄₃₂ x 2 in.	5/4 x 2¾ in.	2250 lbs.
Jointed Flooring— i.e., Square Edge			
²⁵⁄₃₂ x 2½ in.	²⁵⁄₃₂ x 2½ in.	1 x 3¼ in.	2250 lbs.
²⁵⁄₃₂ x 3¼ in.	²⁵⁄₃₂ x 3¼ in.	1 x 4 in.	2400 lbs.
²⁵⁄₃₂ x 3½ in.	²⁵⁄₃₂ x 3½ in.	1 x 4¼ in.	2500 lbs.
¹⁷⁄₁₆ x 2½ in.	³³⁄₃₂ x 2½ in.	5/4 x 3¼ in.	2500 lbs.
¹⁷⁄₁₆ x 3½ in.	³³⁄₃₂ x 3½ in.	5/4 x 4¼ in.	2600 lbs.

NOTE: Oak, Beech, Birch, Hard Maple and Pecan Flooring are bundled by averaging the lengths. A bundle may include pieces from 6 in. under to 6 in. over the nominal length of the bundle. No piece shorter than 9 in. admitted.

The percentages under 4 ft. referred to in the grading rules on this page apply on total footage in any one shipment of the item.

¾-in. allowance shall be added to the face length when measuring the length of each piece.

Flooring shall not be considered of standard grade unless the lumber from which the flooring is manufactured has been properly kiln-dried.

Table 4. Maple strip flooring sizes in inches

From the Specification Manual of the Maple Flooring Manufacturers' Association

Tongued-and-grooved flooring				
Thickness	Widths			
³⁄₈	1½	2	2¼	
½	1½	2	2¼	
⁵⁄₈	1½	2	2¼	
²⁵⁄₃₂	1½	2	2¼	3¼
³³⁄₃₂	1½	2	2¼	3¼
⁴¹⁄₃₂			2¼	3¼
⁵³⁄₃₂			2¼	3¼

* *Jointed flooring (square-edge): all thicknesses in 2½ and 3¼ in. widths; also special widths 2¼, 3⅜, and 3½ in.*

Table 5. Softwood strip flooring sizes

Thickness, in.		Widths, in.	
Nominal	Dressed minimum	Nominal	Dressed minimum
⅜	⁵⁄₁₆	2	1½
½	⁷⁄₁₆	3	2⅜
⅝	⁹⁄₁₆	4	3¼
1	²⁵⁄₃₂	5	4¼
1¼	1¹⁄₁₆	6	5³⁄₁₆
1½	1⁵⁄₁₆		

Table 6. Nailing schedule for hardwood flooring

SOURCE: *Specification Manual of NOFMA*

Tongued and Grooved Flooring Must Always Be Blind-Nailed, Square-Edge Flooring Face-Nailed.

Size Flooring	Type and Size of Nails	Spacing
(Tongued & Grooved) 25/32 x 3¼	7d or 8d screw type or cut steel nail*	10-12 in. apart
(Tongued & Grooved) 25/32 x 2¼	Same as above	Same as above
(Tongued & Grooved) 25/32 x 1½	Same as above	Same as above
(Tongued & Grooved) ½ x 2, ½ x 1½	5d screw type or cut steel or wire nail	10 in. apart
Following flooring must be laid on wood sub-floor:		
(Tongued & Grooved) ⅜ x 2, ⅜ x 1½	4d bright casing nail — wire, cut or screw nail	8 in. apart
(Square-Edge) 5/16 x 2, 5/16 x 1½	1-in. 15 gauge fully barbed flooring brad, preferably cement coated	2 nails every 7 in.

*If steel wire flooring nail is used, it should be 8d, preferably cement coated. Newly developed machine-driven barbed fasteners of the size recommended by the manufacturer are acceptable.

in institutional and industrial buildings where a serviceable floor, under conditions of moderate wear, is desired. The flat-grain grades are used where little wear is expected and are also used as underlayment for other floor coverings.

Southern yellow pine is graded similarly to Douglas fir, and as strip flooring has similar uses. It is available in thicknesses of 2, 2½, 3, 4, and 5 in. for use as factory flooring. It is also used as *end-grain-block* flooring in industrial and other heavy traffic areas, often creosoted or otherwise treated with preservatives.

Grading rules are administered by the following agencies:

Oak, pecan, maple, beech, and birch—National Oak Flooring Manufacturers Association, Memphis, Tennessee.

Maple, beech, and birch—Maple Flooring Manufacturers Association, Chicago, Ilinois.

Douglas fir—West Coast Bureau of Lumber Grades and Inspection, Portland, Oregon.

Southern yellow pine—Southern Pine Inspection Bureau, New Orleans, Louisiana.

INSTALLATION

Strip flooring is usually applied over a subfloor, although in thicknesses of 1 in. nominal or greater, it may be applied directly at right angles to the floor framing or to screeds (sleepers) over concrete floors. When so applied, the spacing of the supports should not exceed 16 in. on center for 1-in. flooring.

Subfloors are usually 1-in. wood boards, preferably square edge and not over 6 in. wide, spaced ¼ in. apart (1½ in. over screeds). At least two 8d or 10d nails should be used at each bearing. Good practice recommends that subflooring be laid diagonally over joists or screeds to provide bracing and to permit the finish flooring to be laid in either direction, parallel or perpendicular to the framing. Subfloors may also be plywood, which should be installed with the grain of the face plies perpendicular to the framing.

The maximum spacing of framing members is 16 in. for ½-in.-thick five-ply C-D structural interior grade Douglas fir plywood; 20 in. for ⅝ in., and 24 in. for ¾ in. If strip flooring is laid at right angles to the framing members, the spacing for ½- and ⅝-in. plywood may be 24 in. Western softwood plywood should be ⅛ in. thicker than Douglas fir for similar spans.

Over concrete slabs on grade, wood floors must be protected against moisture and dampness. Good practice calls for the installation of a moisture barrier above or below the slab. For installation on top of the slab, which is preferred, an asphalt primer should first be applied to the concrete, followed by a 2-mil or heavier polyethylene film laid in cold asphalt mastic, or a two-ply asphalt-felt membrane laid in hot asphalt. For installation under the slab a 4- or 6-mil polyethylene should be used with the seams taped. In any case the moisture barrier should be carried up the sides of the foundation to the finished floor level.

Screeds or sleepers should be pressure-treated with a preservative other than creosote, which may bleed through the nail holes and stain the finish floor. For standard double-floor construction, screeds should be spaced 16 in. on center; if the subfloor is to be omitted, screeds must be spaced not more than 12 in. on center. For the mastic-bedded method of installation, which is now generally used, sleepers should be 2 by 4 in. in random lengths

from 24 to 36 in. They are laid flat in asphalt mastic, spaced 16 in. on center, with joints staggered and space between the butts for air circulation. Mastic, if used over the entire surface of the floor, should be ³⁄₃₂ in. thick; if used in "rivers" under the screeds only, it should be ¼ in. thick. For FHA single-floor installations, the 2 by 4-in. screeds should be from 18 to 30 in. long, laid 12 in. on center, with joints staggered and ends lapped 4 in. or more.

The older and more expensive method of installing screeds by anchoring them mechanically to the slab is still used, especially in large installations (Figs. 11, 12). For this method, screeds are usually 2 by 2 or 2 by 3 in. in long lengths, securely attached to the slab by means of power-driven anchors, and wedged or shimmed level. Chair anchor inserts are less often used today because they interfere with concrete-finishing machines. Beveled screeds set in the slab or held in place by fill are not recommended because they can not be shimmed and they do not stay in place well.

Good nailing (Table 6) is essential if loose or squeaky floors are to be avoided. Nailing is done through the tongue at an angle of approximately 45 deg (Fig. 10); a nail set should be used to drive the nail home. The screw-type nail, because of its greater holding power, is largely replacing the traditional cut nail. Finish strip flooring is usualy laid parallel to the longest dimension of the room. Short lengths are used in closets and other inconspicuous places. Since strip flooring is kiln-dried, care must be taken to protect it from moisture at time of delivery and before laying, if cupping or buckling is to be avoided. Plastering should have been completed and allowed to dry before flooring is delivered to the job. Space for expansion should be allowed at all edges of the room. This space, usually 1 in. wide, is easily covered by base and shoe moldings, which are nailed to the wall and not to the flooring (Fig. 13).

Plank flooring is laid the same as strip flooring with blind-edge nailing spaced similarly. In addition, it is fastened to the subfloor with at least two screws at each end and others along the length of the piece arranged to provide adequate holding and an attractive pattern. All screws are countersunk and covered with a glued-in-place walnut plug. Planks should not be driven tightly together.

Block and parquet flooring may be nailed or laid in mastic on a wood subfloor; over a concrete base, the mastic method must be used. Nailing is done through the tongues, as in strip flooring application. The mastic, either cold or hot, in which the flooring is embedded is usually applied over asphalt felt (30 lb) on wood subfloors and over a dampproofing membrane on concrete floors (Figs. 13, 14). In either case the manufacturer's recommendations, since they vary somewhat

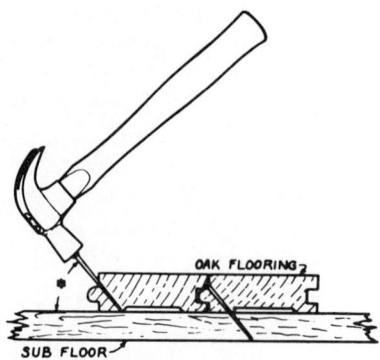

*40 to 50° dependent upon the type of nail used.

Fig. 10. Blind nailing tongued-and-grooved strip flooring

From Commercial Standard CS56-60

based upon experience with the flooring, should be followed.

Block flooring (sometimes called wood "squares" or "tiles" to distinguish it from end-grain blocks used for industrial flooring) is produced in walnut, teak, and cherry, as well as the usual domestic hardwoods. Squares are usually 9 by 9 or 12 by 12 in., tongued and grooved, ⅜ to ¾ in. thick, unfinished or prefinished. There are two major types, unit-blocks and laminated blocks. In unit-blocks, each composed of several small strips of flooring, the two tongue edges are at right angles to each

other. This product is covered by Voluntary Product Standard PS-27. In laminated blocks, made of three or five plies bonded with moisture-resistant glue, the tongues are on opposed sides. This product is covered by *Laminated Hardwood Block Flooring Standard,* ANSI 010.2—1975, and *Laminated Hardwood Floor Tile Standard,* ANSI/HPMA-LFT—1978. Allowance for expansion must be made with unit-blocks (see Fig. 13) but is unnecessary with laminated ones. Both kinds may be laid in squares or diagonal patterns. Shapes other than square (rectangular, herringbone, end-to-end) are available in unit-blocks.

Institutional and industrial floors often present special problems, which have resulted in the development of many proprietary systems. Gymnasium and armory floors cover large unbroken areas, and must be resilient, smooth but not slippery, and easy to maintain. Industrial floors may also be very large in area, and they are often subjected to heavy, wheeled traffic and severe impact. Floors of this type are usually installed over concrete slabs on grade. They may be floated in mastic directly on the slab or installed on screeds anchored to the slab. Metal-channel screeds with interlocking metal clips for attaching the flooring are often used instead of wood screeds and nailing. Mastic-floated construction is used not only for blocks (squares), as previously mentioned, but also for end-grain blocks, herringbone par-

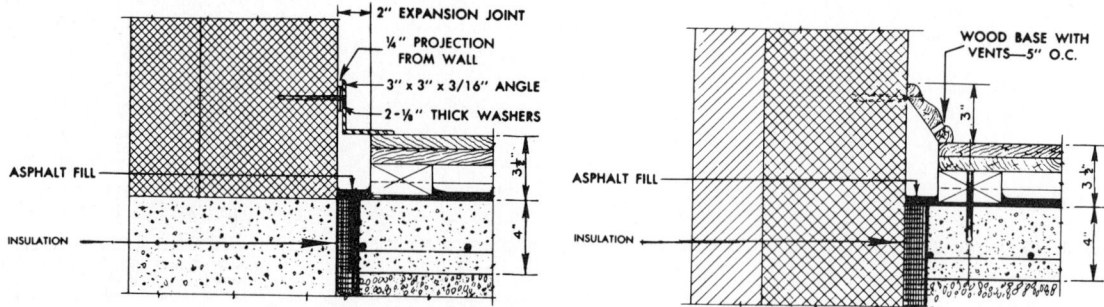

Fig. 11. Strip flooring on screeds on concrete slab with ventilating base in wood or metal

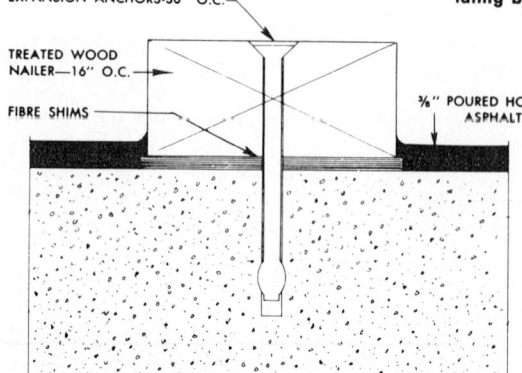

Fig. 12. Detail of wood screed anchored to concrete slab

Courtesy Wood and Synthetic Flooring Institute

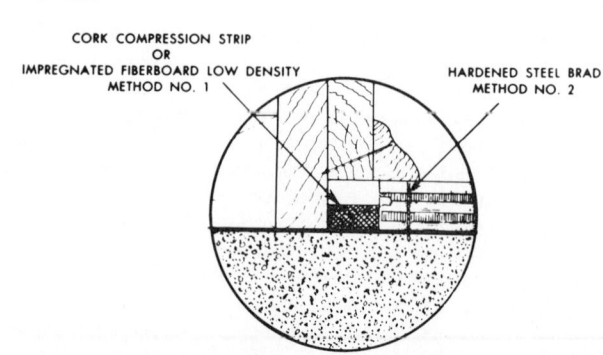

Fig. 13. Block flooring in mastic on concrete slab. Two methods of securing blocks at perimeter

Courtesy Wood and Synthetic Flooring Institute

quet (Fig. 14), and steel-splined flooring (Fig. 15). The latter is 5/4-in. strip flooring in 12-in. lengths, with interlocking steel splines across the ends. The mastic-floated method is also used for bedding the subfloor in "mastic-nailed" construction. In this method, the pieces of subflooring, 5/4 by 4 in. and 18 in. long, are laid in mastic ½ in. apart, with end joints staggered. The spaces between the pieces are later filled with mastic and the surface is covered with mastic before the finish floor is nailed in place (Fig. 16).

The *resilience* of mastic-floated floors can be improved by the use of an underlayer of ½-in. corkboard, installed in mastic, over which the flooring is installed, also in mastic (Fig. 16). Extra resilience for floors on screeds can be provided by the use of cork or rubber pads under the screeds at each anchor.

Ventilation of the spaces between the screeds is important and, for large floor areas, mechanical ventilation is often used, especially if the floor is below grade or subject to adverse moisture conditions. The Wood Flooring Institute recommends that for floors up to 80 ft wide a ventilation trench 6½ by 15 in. be provided underneath and at right angles to the screeds; for floors more than 80 ft wide, two such trenches should be provided.

Adequate space for *expansion* must be provided on all sides of all wood flooring. The minimum space for all types except laminated block is 1 in. per 100 linear ft of flooring. In large floor areas on screeds the minimum edge space should be 1½ in. and preferably 2 in., in order to help ventilate the underfloor space; the base should be drilled or otherwise adapted to permit the circulation of air past it (Fig. 11). The edge pieces of mastic-floated floors must be held in place by resilient filler, steel springs, or similar devices (Figs. 13, 14).

FINISHING

Unfinished wood floors require sanding before *finishing*. This is usually done with electric sanding machines. The first traverse, using No. 2 sandpaper, may be made across the grain or at a 45 deg angle (except for maple flooring, which should only be sanded with the grain); succeeding traverses should be made with the grain, using No. ½, then No. 0, and successively finer paper, depending upon the number of sandings desired. The first two sandings usually employ a drum sander and the final a rotary-disk sander. Hand sanding is done or edgers or scrapers used near walls, in corners and closets, and around pipes. The final sanding or hand buffing should not be done until immediately before finishing is to start, to prevent

the grain of the unprotected wood from rising.

Open-grain flooring such as oak requires a filler; paste types have proved very satisfactory. Stain, if used, should be applied before the filler. An oil stain is advisable. Often it is combined with the filler as a pigmented filler. Three types of finish are employed most extensively: floor seal, varnish, or shellac, and occasionally lacquer. Floor seal penetrates the wood and wears with it. Worn spots can be retouched without the complete refinishing required by other types of finish.

Floors are usually finally finished with paste wax, which provides a sheen and protection to the finish. Water-base waxes or the self-finishing liquid waxes are not recommended, as they have a tendency after frequent use to raise the grain and roughen the floor.

The Maple Flooring Manufacturers' Association offers a list of finish materials which are recommended for use with general-purpose maple flooring and for use with special flooring such as that in gymnasiums.

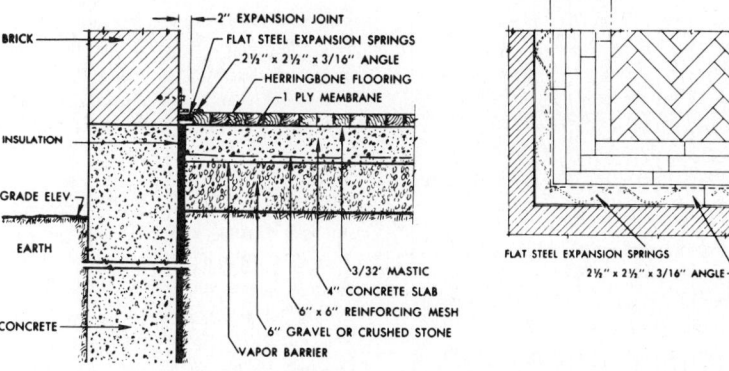

Fig. 14. Herringbone flooring in mastic on concrete slab; steel springs secure the edge pieces

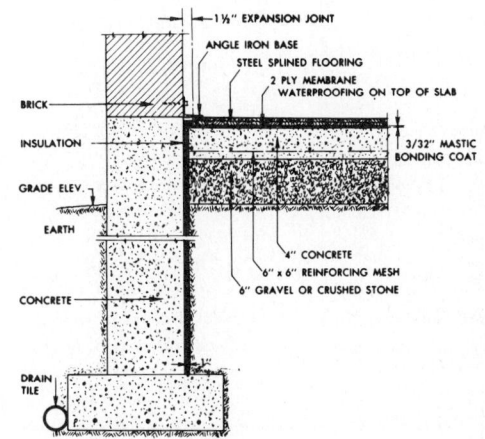

Fig. 15. Steel-splined flooring in mastic on concrete slab

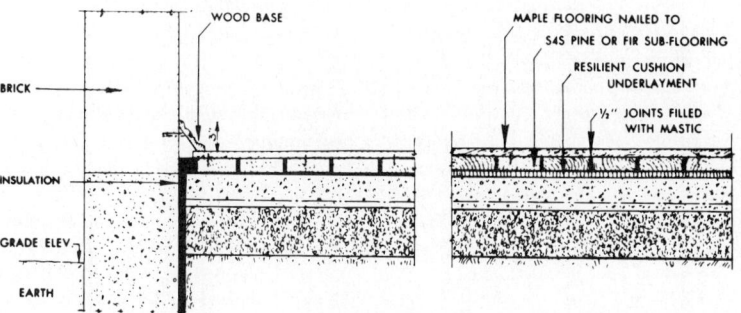

Fig. 16. Mastic-nailed flooring on concrete slab with and without resilient cushion underlayment

Courtesy Wood and Synthetic Flooring Institute

By HOWARD P. VERMILYA, *AIA*

Resilient flooring materials are produced in sheet or tile form in thicknesses ranging from $\frac{1}{16}$ to $\frac{3}{16}$ in. They are made of various compositions of resins, plasticizers, fibers, pigments, and fillers, formed under heat and pressure. Smooth-surface resilient flooring materials include asphalt tile, vinyl-asbestos tile, vinyl tile or sheet (backed or homogeneous), rubber tile or sheet, and cork tile (plain or vinyl-covered). Essential data on all types of resilient flooring are summarized in Table 7; additional data on each type will be found in the following text. Federal specifications and industry standards are listed in Table 8.

Asphalt tile. Composed through full thickness of asphaltic or resinous binder with asbestos or other fibers, fillers, and pigments, pressure-formed while hot. Sizes 12 by 12 and 18 by 24 in. available from some manufacturers. Classified by color as follows:

Group A—solid, dark colors
Group B—dark background colors
Group C—medium to light background colors
Group D—light background colors, including white

Group A is the lowest and Group D the highest in cost. Asphalt tile is the lowest in first cost and the least resilient of all types. Recommended for commercial, light industrial, and residential use. Not recommended for shower, toilet, or laundry rooms, for display windows, or for exterior use. Softens under heat. Not grease-resistant. *Grease-resistant* asphalt tile is available in two types:

Class 1—edible oil-resistant
Class 2—mineral oil-resistant

Slip-resistant type is also available; it is similar in all other respects to regular aphalt tile.

Vinyl-asbestos tile

Composed through full thickness of vinyl resins, plasticizers, pigments, fillers, and asbestos fibers, formed under pressure while hot. Sizes 12 by 12 and 18 by 24 in. available from some manufacturers. Excellent grease, alkali, and abrasion resistance; easy maintenance, poor resilience, moderate cost. In ⅛-in. gage, recommended for severe commercial use; in thinner gages for residential use. Not recommended for toilets, showers, laundries, show windows, or sun rooms. Slip-resistant, heat-resistant, and conductive types are available.

Vinyl (-backed) sheet and tile

Wearing layer composed of vinyl resin, plasticizers, pigments, and fillers, overlaid on a backing of asphalt-saturated felt or an alkali-resistant material. Excellent grease, alkali, and abrasion resistance; fair resilience. Alkali-resistant sheet is also available in thicknesses of 0.070 and 0.090 in.

Vinyl (homogeneous) sheet and tile

Composed through full thickness of vinyl resin, plasticizers, pigments, and fillers, formed under pressure while hot. Sheet is available in widths of 27, 36, 45, and 54 in. in the three gages shown in Table 7. Tile is also available in ³⁄₁₆-in. thickness and in special sizes up to 36 by 36 in. and special shapes such as diamonds, hexagons, and octagons. Excellent resilience and resistance to indentation; excellent grease, alkali, and abrasion resistance; high cost. Conductive type is available.

Rubber sheet and tile

Composed through full thickness of natural, synthetic, or reclaimed rubber, or a combination of these, with reinforcing fibers, pigments, and fillers, vulcanized and molded under pressure. Also available in ¼-in. thickness. Tile also available in 12 by 12- and 18 by 36-in. sizes. Excellent resilience and resistance to indentation; good resistance to grease, alkali, and abrasion. Also available with cellular backing for extra comfort and quietness under foot.

Linoleum sheet and tile

Wearing layer composed of oxidized linseed oil or other oleo-resinous binder, ground cork, wood flour, mineral fillers, and pigments, pressed on a backing of burlap or asphalt-saturated felt; tile may be unbacked. Linoleum tile is also available in 12 by 12-in. size. Tile may be considerably denser than sheet, with better resistance to indentation but less resilience; can be used on suspended floors only. Excellent grease resistance, good resistance to abrasion, easy maintenance, poor alkali resistance. Heavy gage with burlap backing recommended for severe commercial uses; lighter gages for residential use. Conductive type available in heavy gage.

Cork tile

Composed through full thickness of compressed granulated cork bonded with a heat-processed resinous binder. Surface may be unfinished or finished with wax, lacquer, or resin. Thicknesses of ¼ and ½ in. are available on special order. In addition to the standard 9 by 9 in., the following sizes are available: 6 by 6, 6 by 12, 12 by 12, 12 by 24, and 36 by 36 in. Edges may be beveled or square. Excellent resilience—most comfortable and quiet of all resilient floors. Not recommended for heavy traffic locations.

Vinyl-faced cork tile

Wearing layer of clear vinyl sheet fused by heat and pressure to regular cork tile. It is available in the same sizes as regular cork tile and in thicknesses of ⅛ and ³⁄₁₆ in., with square or beveled edges. Approximate installed cost is $1.75 to $1.85 per sq ft. It may be used on suspended or on-grade floors, but not below grade. Its thermal conductivity (*k*) is 0.7 btu. Maximum static load without permanent indentation varies with the manufacturer from 75 to 150 psi. On the scale used in Table 7, it is judged to be very good in comfort, warmth, quietness, alkali resistance, and ease of maintenance, and to be excellent in grease resistance. Recommended for commercial use, moderate to heavy traffic.

Accessories

Borders, feature strips, inserts (standard and custom designs), bases, and edging strips are available from most manufacturers. Stair treads with integral nosings are available, made of heavy-gage rubber or homogeneous vinyl sheet, in colors and patterns to match flooring.

Selection of resilient flooring

Selection should be based upon consideration of the following factors, in the order given:

1. Moisture conditions, subfloor and surface
2. Functional qualities desired
3. Cost factors, initial and long-range
4. Visual or aesthetic considerations

Subfloor moisture causes some types of resilient flooring and some types of adhesives to deteriorate. It has therefore become customary to classify flooring materials as to their suitability for use above grade, on grade, or below grade (Fig. 17). These classifications are the same whether the flooring is applied directly to a concrete slab or to a wood subfloor on screeds. An inadequately ventilated crawl space has the same effect as a floor on grade.

Excessive surface moisture, such as that to be expected around the equipment in laundries and lavatories, may affect adversely the adhesive, the backing, or the underlayment. Materials recommended for on-grade installation will generally give satisfactory service under surface moisture conditions if they are installed with a waterproof adhesive. Sheet material, having fewer seams than tile, is recommended for such conditions.

The performance requirements of the flooring should be the designer's next consideration. These include such factors as resilience, ease of maintenance, and dura-

Table 7. Summary of data on resilient flooring materials

Source: *Installation and Maintenance of Resilient Smooth-surface Flooring, Building Research Institute*

Type of flooring	Asphalt		Vinyl — Backed types					Vinyl — Flexible homogeneous	Rubber		Linoleum		Cork§
	Regular	Grease-proof	Semi-flexible asbestos	Regular		Alkali resistant							
Form available	Tile	Tile	Tile	Sheet	Tile	Sheet	Tile‡	Tile	Sheet	Tile	Sheet	Tile	Tile
Dimensions*													
Size or width, in.	9 x 9	9 x 9	9 x 9	72	9 x 9	45, 72	9 x 9	9 x 9	36	9 x 9	72	9 x 9	9 x 9
Thickness, in.	0.125 0.1875	0.125 0.1875	0.0625 0.080 0.09375 0.125	0.0625 0.070	0.0625	0.0625 0.080	0.0625 0.080	0.080 0.09375 0.125	0.080 0.125 0.1875	0.080 0.125 0.1875	0.070 0.090 0.125	0.065 0.090 0.125	0.09375 0.125 0.1875 0.3125
Cost: Approximate relative installed cost for thickness indicated	0.125" Low 0.1875" Low	0.125" Low 0.1875" Moderate	0.0625" Low 0.125" Moderate	0.0625" Low 0.070" Moderate	0.0625" Low	0.0625" Moderate 0.080" Medium	0.0625" Moderate 0.080" Medium	0.080" Medium 0.09375" High 0.125" Very high	0.080" Moderate 0.125" Medium 0.1875" High	0.080" Moderate 0.125" Medium 0.1875" High	0.070" Low 0.090" Low 0.125" Moderate	0.065" Low 0.090" Low 0.125" Medium	0.09375" Low 0.125" Moderate 0.1875" Medium 0.3125" High
Use level†													
Suspended	Yes	Yes	Yes	Yes	Yes	Yes	Yes	Yes	Yes	Yes	Yes	Yes	Yes
On grade	Yes	Yes	Yes	No	Yes	Yes	Yes	Yes	Yes	Yes	No	No	Yes
Below grade	Yes	Yes	Yes	No	No	Yes	Yes	Yes	Yes	Yes	No	No	No
Physical characteristics:													
Thermal conductivity Btu/hr./sq. ft/°F/in.	3.1	3.1	3.1	1.4	1.4	1.2-3.3	1.2-3.3	5.3	5.3	5.3	1.5	1.5	0.5
Relative maximum static load without permanent indentation expressed in psi	25 (Fair)	25 (Fair)	25 (Fair)	75 (Good)	75 (Good)	75 (Good)	75 (Good)	200 (Excellent)	200 (Excellent)	200 (Excellent)	75 (Good)	75 (Good)	75 (Good)
Under foot comfort	Fair	Fair	Good	Good	Good	Good	Good	Excellent	Excellent	Excellent	Good	Good	Excellent
Apparent warmth to touch	Fair	Fair	Good	Good	Good	Good	Good	Good	Good	Good	Good	Good	Excellent
Quietness (noise level)	Fair	Fair	Good	Good	Good	Good	Good	Very good	Very good	Very good	Good	Good	Excellent
Surface alkali resistance	Excellent	Excellent	Excellent	Excellent	Excellent	Excellent	Excellent	Excellent	Good	Good	Fair	Fair	Fair
Grease resistance	Poor	Very good	Excellent	Excellent	Excellent	Excellent	Excellent	Excellent	Good	Good	Excellent	Excellent	Fair
Ease of maintenance	Fair	Good	Good	Very good	Very good	Very good	Very good	Very good	Good	Good	Very good	Very good	Fair

Slipperiness — Varies with finish and waxing, normally all are slip-resistant when dry.
Impact resistance — All are resistant to shattering, splitting, cracking, or other damage under normal conditions.
Light reflectivity — Varies from almost zero to 65% depending on color, surface texture and finish—consult manufacturer.
Durability — All show excellent durability under use conditions for which they are individually suitable when installed and maintained as recommended by manufacturer.

* Nominal commercial dimensions only are shown—other sizes, shapes, thicknesses and widths vary with manufacturer.
† When installed in accordance with the specific precautions and recommendations of the manufacturer.
‡ Also available in sheet; see text.
§ For data on vinyl-faced cork tile; see text.

bility. Resilience has two aspects: comfort under foot and quietness, the absorption of impact noises. Durability includes not only resistance to abrasion (traffic) but also to grease, alkalies, and chemicals, and to indentation. Other factors, such as warmth to the touch, slipperiness, light reflectivity, fire resistance, or electrical conductivity, must sometimes be considered. Where sanitation is of primary importance, sheet material should be used in preference to tile. Besides having fewer joints generally, it can be coved up at the walls to eliminate the joint at the base. The seams of vinyl flooring can be heat-fused to form a jointless floor.

Installed costs range from $0.20 per sq ft to over $2.00. Cost varies not only with the type of material but also with the complexity of the design and the use of such accessories as feature strips and inserts. The shape of the floor area to be covered also affects the cost. Where long-range costs are an important consideration, special attention should be given to maintenance characteristics, resistance to wear, and ease of repair or replacement.

The appearance of the finished floor is affected by its resistance to indentation and by its dimensional stability, color fastness, and light reflectivity, in addition to the color and pattern selected by the designer. Permanent indentation not only impairs the use and maintenance of the floor but also has a disastrous effect on appearance. Indentation caused by static loads such as furniture can generally be prevented by attention to the limits of the material (Table 7) and the use of protective devices. Impact loads are less predictable, but they may also cause permanent indentation. The stiletto heels worn today can produce impact loads well in excess of 2,000 psi and can leave permanent indentations in all types of resilient flooring except rubber and homogeneous vinyl.

Lack of dimensional stability may result in buckling or in the opening of seams or joints. Exposure to direct sunlight sometimes causes shrinking or fading of flooring materials. Neutral colors have the best resistance to fading; pastel colors, especially yellows and pinks, are the poorest. Cork may become lighter after prolonged exposure to sunlight. Sheet materials resist shrinkage better than tiles.

Light reflectivity of the flooring is sometimes an important functional factor, and it also has an important effect upon the appearance of the floor. Glossy finishes have less total reflectivity than matte finishes and therefore appear somewhat darker, but they produce specular reflections which may be very bright when

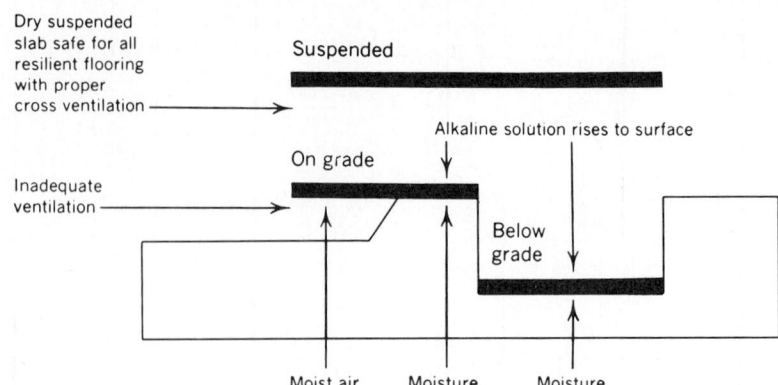

Fig. 17. Location of floors with respect to grade

Courtesy Armstrong Cork Company

viewed directly. High-gloss finishes tend to show up minor irregularities in the subfloor; extra care is therefore necessary in the preparation of the subfloor; extra maintenance is also required. Light reflectivity values are generally available from the manufacturers for each color and pattern of each type of flooring.

The selection of color and pattern may be safely left to last because there is now such a wide choice of these in every type of flooring. Having determined the type of flooring from considerations of use, function, and cost, the designer can usually achieve, with the colors and patterns available in that type, the aesthetic effect he wants.

Installation

Resilient floors over concrete require careful selection of resilient materials and the adhesives used and, since resilient floors reflect the condition of the surface on which they are laid, care in finishing the subfloor. Many of the problems can be eliminated or minimized by protective measures taken as the slab is being laid and by proper curing of the concrete. For slabs on or below grade, membranes of vapor-resisting materials such as polyethylene film 0.004 or 0.006 in. thick, butyl rubber sheet, or 55-lb asphalt roofing felt under the slabs serve to prevent transmission of moisture from the ground. Adequate curing time, sometimes several months, is necessary to permit slabs to dry sufficiently to assure bonding of adhesives even on suspended slabs. Tests should be made to determine the moisture conditions within the slab and the adhesive to be used. Excess moisture may cause mold growth in flooring containing oleo-resinous binders or cellulosic fibers. Alkaline salts from concrete in solution can destroy the bond and leave salt deposits in cracks in the tile. Curing, hardening, and parting

compounds as well as oil, grease, and paint on old floors, all prevent bonding of adhesives to concrete. Lightweight concrete in densities of from 20 to 90 lb per cu ft should receive a 1-in. topping of standard concrete. If the density of light aggregate concrete exceeds 90 lb per cu ft and the surface is well-troweled so as to be smooth and even, it may be used as the subfloor. Only floorings which are alkali-resistant should be used over light aggregate floors, since the latter have much slower drying times, particularly when they are on grade, than floors of regular concrete. Cracks, minor holes, and crevices should be filled with a crack filler.

Underlayments of the latex, asphalt, or polyvinyl acetate type are used over rough, uneven, or worn concrete subfloors. These mastic underlayments contain resin binders in the mix and may be safely applied in thin layers or feathered out at the edges. Latex underlayments are troweled on to a maximum thickness of ⅛ in.; greater thicknesses require additional costs. They should not be used with solvent-type asphalt adhesives. Asphalt-type underlayments may be applied in greater thicknesses, approximately ½ in., with a minimum of ⅜ in., except for small areas which may be feathered. The asphalt type also should not be used with solvent-type adhesives or with certain types of chemical-set waterproof cements. Emulsion-type adhesive may be used with either underlayment. (NOTE: Since some manufacturers are prone to conceal their formulations, the reactions of underlayments and adhesives and their use should be checked with suppliers. Whenever possible it is advisable to specify flooring, adhesive, and underlayment from the same manufacturer.) Polyvinyl acetate resins mixed with portland cement as an additive provide the plastic qualities which permit its use as a thin underlayment, ranging from $\frac{1}{16}$ in. thick to featheredge, when applied over a prime coat of polyvinyl acetate concrete bonding compound.

Resilient materials over wood floors do not require board types of underlayment when applied over well-laid double floors using tongued-and-grooved face boards not over 3 in. wide, or over single layers of plywood ⅞ in. thick, where all edges are supported, or over 1⅛ in. 2-4-1 T and G Douglas fir plywood combination subfloor and underlayment. Square-edged board floors should be covered with 25/32-in. T and G wood flooring 3 in. or less in width, or with ½-in.-thick plywood (C-D plugged interior- or C-C plugged exterior-grade Douglas fir or western softwood plywood) underlayment. Underlayment-grade plywood, ¼ or preferably ⅜ in. thick, may be used over single tongued-and-grooved floors of narrow boards 3 in. or less in width, over double floors of tongued-and-grooved boards 4 in. or wider, or over ½- or ⅝-in. plywood subfloors supported on all edges and with the face-ply grain perpendicular to the floor framing, which should not be spaced more than 16 in. on center. Exterior-grade plywood should be used where surface moisture may be anticipated, as in bathrooms. Hardboard (not tempered) may also be used in lieu of ¼-in. plywood. Particle board is not recognized now as an acceptable underlayment in the specifications of resilient flooring associations. However, the National Particleboard Association recently established an underlayment performance standard for wood particle board which has been accepted by the Federal Housing Administration for use under resilient flooring materials.

Wood floors should be sanded, particularly if strip flooring is used. Nails should be set and all cracks should be filled. Latex underlayment is recommended where wood floors are uneven or cupped. The installation specifications of the Asphalt and Vinyl Asbestos Tile Institute provide that a 15-lb fully saturated asphalt-felt membrane be pasted down over wood-strip subfloors, subject to the tile manufacturers' recommendations. Lining felt should be omitted where latex underlayment is used and may be omitted where plywood is used. Wood subfloors not covered by felt or underlayment should be sealed with a prime coat of shellac or other sealer to prevent moisture absorption.

Adhesives are a most important factor in the life of a resilient floor. They also affect the ease of application and later removal, should that be desired. They vary widely in cost. Disregarding cost, the

Table 8. Federal specifications and industry standards

Federal specifications

Tile, floor, asphalt	SS—T—312A Type I
Tile, floor, asphalt, grease-resistant	SS—T—307
Tile, floor, vinyl-asbestos	SS—T—312A Type IV
Tile, floor, flame-retardant	MIL—T—18830 Navy Bureau of Ships
Flooring, vinyl plastic (homogeneous); sheet or tile	SS—T—312A Type III
Flooring, vinyl sheet (backed)	L—F—475
Floor covering, rubber, sheet or tile	SS—T—312A Type II
Linoleum, battleship	LLL—L—351b
Linoleum, plain, jaspe, and marbleized, sheet or tile	LLL—F—1238A
Floor covering (linoleum), felt-backed	LLL—F—471
Tile, floor, cork:	LLL—T—431b
Class 1. Wax, lacquer, or resin finish	
Class 2. Clear-plastic-film finish	
Paste, linoleum	OP—106
Asphalt, emulsion-type	Interim SS—A—00138
Asphalt, cut-back type	Interim SS—A—128
Adhesive, linoleum and plastic tile	MIL—C—21016C
Underlayment: Basic hardboard	PS-58, ANSI A135.4
Particle board (Type I-B1)	CS-236
Plywood	PS-1

Standard specifications, for materials only, are available from: Rubber and Vinyl Flooring Council of the Rubber Manufacturers Association, and Asphalt and Vinyl-Asbestos Tile Institute; both are in New York. Installation specifications are not standard but are issued by the various manufacturers for their own products. Manufacturers' specifications should be scrupulously observed, particularly as to type and condition of the subfloor and type of adhesive to be used.

selection of an adhesive is based upon: the type of resilient flooring to be used, the type of subfloor, the location of the subfloor with reference to moisture, the type of underlayment used, and the probability of surface moisture. In general, it is advisable to use the adhesives recommended by the manufacturer of the resilient flooring. The following is a list of the major types of adhesives:

Paste (linoleum)—water-soluble: an all-purpose adhesive for above-grade installations for lining felt, backed sheet materials, and tile other than asphalt and vinyl-asbestos.

Cement—waterproof-latex type: for concrete surfaces on or below grade for backed sheet materials and all tile permitted in these locations except asphalt and vinyl-asbestos. Alkali- and moisture-resistant.

Primer—solvent type: sealer for concrete surfaces before application of adhesives for asphalt and vinyl-asbestos tile. Should not be used over latex or asphalt-type underlayments.

Cut-back asphalt: on concrete surfaces at all grades and on lining felt over wood surfaces for asphalt and vinyl-asbestos tile—resists alkaline moisture—should not be used over latex or asphalt-type underlayment.

Emulsion-type—clay and asphalt base: all-purpose adhesive for asphalt and vinyl-asbestos tile at all grades. May be used over latex and asphalt-type underlayments. Resists alkali and moisture.

Brushing cement—asphalt and rubber-base: all types of subfloors—eliminates need for lining felt—used for vinyl-asbestos tile and asphalt tile—may be used over latex and asphalt-type underlayments.

Chemical-set waterproof—latex and powder: used for on- or below-grade concrete for rubber or vinyl tile—resists surface moisture.

Cement—resin-base: used on or above grade for cork or vinyl-cork and above grade for linoleum or vinyl sheet or tile where surface moisture is anticipated.

By HOWARD P. VERMILYA, AIA

VINYL

Vinyl wall coverings are tough, flexible materials, supplied in rolls, which can be applied by standard paper-hanging techniques to a variety of wall surfaces. They provide a durable, cleanable, stain-resistant wall finish especially suitable for institutional and commercial use where hard wear is anticipated. The material is supplied in widths of 24, 48, 50, and 54 in., and in lengths ranging from 6 to 35 yd. The wider rolls have the advantage of requiring fewer seams. A very wide range of colors and textures is available, many of them simulating other materials such as leather, fabric, straw, wood, and the like.

Vinyl-coated wall coverings (Federal Specification CCC-W-408) are made of pigmented vinyl resins and plasticizers which are applied to a backing material and covered by a clear vinyl surfacing sheet which is fused to the base sheet by heat and pressure. The backing is usually a tightly woven preshrunk cotton fabric, but other materials including nonwoven types may be used. Vinyl coverings designed for use on upholstery often have a knit or other type of stretchable backing which generally makes them unsuitable for use on walls.

Cotton preshrunk woven fabric backing

Types and weights most often used

Osnaburg	(2.35)*	38x28 threads/in.	3.6 oz/sq yd
Sheeting	(2.40)*	56x56 threads/in.	3.7 oz/sq yd
Drill	(1.85)*	68x40 threads/in.	4.9 oz/sq yd
Broken twill	(1.06)*	76x52 threads/in.	8.6 oz/sq yd

* lineal yards per pound in greige, 58–60 in. wide.

The weight of the wall covering has an appreciable bearing upon the wear resistance. The following tabulation classifies vinyl coverings as light, medium, or heavy by weight.

Vinyl wall coverings

Weight, oz/sq yd

Classification	Backing	Vinyl coating	Total	Range
Light weight	3.7	9.3	13.0	12–16
Medium weight	4.8	13.8	18.6	14–20
Heavy weight	8.6	15.4	24.0	20–26

Another classification gives as standard a wall covering weighing 9.5 oz per sq yd, and as heavy duty, one weighing 17.5 oz per sq yd. The lightweight material is recommended for use in areas where it replaces paint to eliminate maintainance; the medium-weight material, for areas where there is average traffic, such as offices, reception rooms, hospital wards, and dining rooms; and the heavyweight material, for such areas as corridors, schoolrooms, gymnasiums, and service areas where there is heavy traffic and hard wear, even that involving movable equipment.

Tests of vinyl wall coverings are usually in accordance with methods specified in Federal Specification CCC-T-191(b) involving weight of backing, coating, and thickness, and other factors such as tensile and tear strength, shrinkage, resistance to ultraviolet light, cold, heat, wear, and staining; also accelerated aging, adhesion, and cracking. Flame spread rate is determined by NFPA 255 or ASTM E84-61 based on the Underwriters' Laboratories, Inc., tunnel test; rating is affected by the adhesive used as well as by the wall surface to which it is applied. Most vinyl wall coverings can achieve a flame spread rate of 10 (the usual required rating) when applied with special adhesives to a noncombustible wall surface such as plaster.

Application. A vinyl wall covering may be applied to any smooth, rigid surface such as plaster, asbestos–cement board, gypsum wallboard, or plywood, and to smooth-faced concrete or terra cotta blocks. Where the surface is porous, a primer is usually recommended. Previously painted surfaces require special care, particularly if water-sensitive paints have been used. Glass and metal surfaces require special adhesives. Most manufacturers advise using their own adhesives and caution against the use of wheat or starch pastes. Joints should be butted and not lapped, as vinyl wall covering will not adhere to itself, and should not be made in or at corners formed by intersecting walls. The heavy materials are more difficult and costly to apply than the lighter ones.

Another type of vinyl wall covering is supplied in *sheets,* usually 23 by 95 in. and approximately 15 sq ft in area. The manufacturer of this product uses textured fabrics, ferns, leaves, and butterflies as elements in design. These are inserted between a layer of clear vinyl, which provides the durable surface, and a base layer of colored vinyl, behind which is a layer of aluminum foil which acts as a vapor barrier. This assembly is laminated to a paper backing. The sheets are designed for both edge and end butting, so they may be used with any ceiling height. They are applied by standard paper-hanging techniques.

FLEXIBLE WOOD VENEER

Very thin (0.012 in. or less) veneer is bonded to a backing material to make a wall covering similar to wallpaper. The veneer is treated to make it flexible so that it can be bent around corners parallel to the grain. It is provided as strips in widths up to 24 in. and in lengths up to 12 ft, depending on the woods selected and the matching pattern desired. It is installed like wallpaper.

One manufacturer supplies flexible wood veneer in rolls 27½ in. wide, in three lengths—40, 27, and 13 ft—and also in 25 by 25-in. squares. The veneer has a moisture-resistant finish, and the backing is paper. Other manufacturers supply the material bonded to a woven cotton fabric, with the veneer unfinished for finishing on the job in the same manner as wall paneling. "Architectural" grades of matched veneers are available, as well as random grades, in many species of wood.

The finished appearance is no better than the surface to which it is applied. Since the veneer is comparatively thin, a smooth surface is essential. Its flexibility makes it especially adaptable to curved walls or surfaces. When applied to an incombustible wall, it is permitted by building codes in many locations where untreated solid wood or plywood is not allowed.

COLD–GLAZED

Field-applied cold-glazed wall coatings are characterized by a hard, glossy surface which resembles a ceramic glaze, which has led to their sometimes being referred to as "vitreous surfacings." They are well suited for use in industrial, commercial, and institutional buildings where a tough, sanitary, and easily cleaned surface is desired, at a cost less than that of ceramic tile. These glazed finishes have the advantage of being jointless; they are resistant to abrasion and impact and are not affected by most chemicals. They are available in a wide range of colors, including mottled and flecked patterns of two or more colors.

Cold-glazed coatings are usually spray-applied, but some types may be applied by brush or roller. Thicknesses vary from 5 to 70 mils, or from the thickness of a standard three-coat paint film to about $\frac{1}{16}$ in. Glazed coatings may be applied to almost any clean, dry, stable surface such as masonry, concrete, plaster, gypsum board, or asbestos–cement board. Porous surfaces, such as cinder blocks, usually require the prior application of a primer-filler. Masonry joints should be tooled, since the coating will not conceal them. These finishes are used mostly on interior walls and ceilings, but some types are suitable for use on exterior surfaces. All are proprietary products, and the manufacturer's directions should be carefully followed; experienced and skilled applicators are essential.

Cold-glazed coatings vary widely in composition, application techniques, and physical properties; there are no industry standards. The coatings may be classified on the basis of their composition into two general groups—cement-plastic and all-plastic. The former consists of products composed of portland cement and plastic in varying proportions, ranging from a basically cement product with organic additives to a basically plastic product with cement filler. Portland cement is, of course, inorganic and incombustible; it produces a hard surface of known durability which is waterproof but not vaporproof; it must be moist-cured. Plastics are organic and therefore combustible, to a greater or lesser degree;

being relatively new, their durability is not positively known; they are quick-drying, waterproof, and in most cases vaporproof. A vaporproof finish is highly desirable for an interior wall or ceiling, but is generally undesirable for an exterior surfacing. If a vapor barrier is used on the exterior surface of a wall, provision should be made for ventilating the interior of the wall.

Cement type. This is the oldest of the glazed finishes, having been used, mostly in Europe, for some 40 years. It is composed of white portland cement, finely ground silica sand, mineral oxide pigments, and organic hardeners and sealers. The glaze is said to be produced by crystallization of the cement molecules and therefore to be integral with the base coat. This type requires multiple-stage application and moist curing; including the latter, the complete process consists of six or seven applications. It is incombustible and vaporporous. Scraffito designs are feasible in this type.

PLASTIC

Plastic-cement type. This more recently developed type consists of a plastic emulsion base with portland cement added as a filler. It is somewhat less expensive than the cement type since it is only a two- or three-stage operation and moist curing is not required. Hardness and glaze are supplied by the all-plastic sealer coat. Depending upon the relative proportions of plastic and portland cement, this type may be combustible or incombustible and permeable or impermeable to vapor.

All-plastic type. Plastic coatings are also fairly new. They are usually applied in two coats and are therefore likely to be thinner than other types of glazed finish, although still considerably thicker than the usual three-coat paint film. The principal plastics used as field-applied coatings are epoxy, polyester, urethane, vinyl, and hypalon. Of these the first three are most nearly comparable with the cold-glazed finishes. They produce surfaces which are glossy and easily cleaned; they are very hard and tough, with good resistance to

abrasion and impact and to most chemicals. Epoxy, polyester, and urethane are thermosetting; they are cured by means of a heat-generating catalyst which is added just prior to application. These two-part materials have a very limited pot life and require experience and skill in their application. They are impervious to vapor. The materials are combustible; but when applied to an incombustible surface in the small thicknesses usually employed, they present no serious hazard. They will withstand heat up to 300 or even 400°F.

Vinyl and hypalon are in a somewhat different category. They do not produce a hard, glossy surface, but rather a resilient, tough, flexible surface with a satin finish. *Vinyl* is the "cocoon" material used to protect the Navy's "mothball fleet" after World War II. It is completely waterproof and weatherproof and may be used on interior or exterior surfaces including roofs and swimming pools. It can be applied in thicknesses ranging from 5 to 40 mils or more; for ordinary interior applications a thickness of 10 mils is recommended; for heavy-duty interiors and all exteriors, 20 to 25 mils; for roofs, 30 to 35 mils. Vinyl is a thermoplastic and will soften at temperatures above 170°F. Permeability to vapor varies with the thickness, but is sufficiently low to classify the material as a vapor barrier. It is combustible (slow-burning) and in the heavier thicknesses can be considered a hazard because of the heavy black smoke given off.

Hypalon is Du Pont's trade name for their recently developed synthetic rubber coating intended primarily for exterior use. Being a true rubber, it is waterproof and highly elastic (300 per cent elongation), but it differs from other rubbers in that it is very durable when exposed to the weather. Unlike its cousin neoprene, it can be obtained in white or light colors as well as dark. In addition to a primer, two coats are required and three are recommended. Neoprene, being less expensive, is sometimes used for the undercoats. Hypalon is used mostly for roofs but is occasionally used on exterior walls.

Paints

By RAY E. CUMRINE, *AIA, Ketchum & Sharp, Architects*

Specifications of paints for various surfaces and conditions

Specification of paints has become much more complicated as new materials have been developed through modern paint technology for practically every surface and service condition. Below is a check list of the principal paint types and their applications.

CHECK LIST

EXTERIOR SURFACE	PRIMER	FINISH
Concrete and Concrete Block	1. Polyvinyl Acetate 2. Acrylic 3. Styrene-butadiene 4. Cement	1. Polyvinyl Acetate or Styrene-butadiene 2. Acrylic 3. Styrene-butadiene 4. Cement
Brick, Cement Asbestos	1. Polyvinyl Acetate 2. Acrylic 3. Styrene-butadiene	1. Polyvinyl Acetate or Styrene-butadiene 2. Acrylic 3. Styrene-butadiene
Aluminum	1. Zinc Chromate	1. Linseed Oil
Galvanized Metal	1. Zinc Dust and Zinc Oxide, Zinc Chromate or Aluminum 2. Vinyl-alkyd wash	1. Linseed Oil or Alkyd 2. Vinyl-alkyd
Iron and Steel	1. Red Lead, Blue Lead or Zinc Chromate	1. Linseed Oil or Alkyd
Chemical-Resistant		
	1. Neoprene 2. Wash Primer and Zinc Chromate Vinyl Resin 3. Phenolic Resin 4. Epoxy 5. Vinyl-alkyd wash	1. Neoprene 2. Vinyl Resin 3. Phenolic Resin 4. Epoxy 5. Vinyl-alkyd
Hot Metal (To 500°)	1. Zinc Dust or Aluminum	1. Aluminum
Metal Under Water	1. Phenolic Type Zinc Chromate 2. Neoprene	1. Phenolic Type Zinc Chromate 2. Neoprene
Wood	1. Linseed Oil 2. Alkyd 3. Acrylic	1. Linseed Oil 2. Alkyd 3. Acrylic
Plaster (Stucco)	1. Polyvinyl Acetate 2. Acrylic 3. Styrene-butadiene	1. Polyvinyl Acetate or Styrene-butadiene 2. Acrylic 3. Styrene-butadiene
INTERIOR SURFACE	**PRIMER**	**FINISH**
Concrete and Concrete Block	1. Linseed Oil 2. Cement 3. Chlorinated Rubber 4. Styrene-butadiene 5. Acrylic 6. Epoxy or Acrylic 7. Polyester 8. Polyvinyl Acetate 9. Alkyd	1. Linseed Oil 2. Cement 3. Chlorinated Rubber 4. Styrene-butadiene 5. Acrylic 6. Epoxy 7. Polyester 8. Polyvinyl Acetate, Styrene-butadiene or Alkyd 9. Alkyd
Brick, Cement Asbestos	1. Polyvinyl Acetate 2. Alkyd 3. Styrene-butadiene	1. Polyvinyl Acetate or Alkyd 2. Alkyd 3. Styrene-butadiene
Aluminum	1. Zinc Chromate	1. Alkyd
Galvanized Metal	1. Zinc Dust and Zinc Oxide, Zinc Chromate or Aluminum	1. Linseed Oil or Alkyd
Iron and Steel	1. Red Lead, Blue Lead or Zinc Chromate	1. Linseed Oil or Alkyd
Wood	1. Linseed Oil 2. Alkyd	1. Linseed Oil 2. Alkyd
Plaster	1. Alkyd or Polyvinyl Acetate 2. Polyvinyl Acetate or Styrene-butadiene 3. Acrylic	1. Alkyd 2. Styrene-butadiene 3. Acrylic

INTERIOR AND EXTERIOR

Paint is a medium which imparts to a surface, in addition to decor, both durability and protection against deteriorating elements to a degree that depends upon the ingredients in the solution and the type of surface. In this summary the qualities of the general categories of paints and finishes are presented with an eye toward their most practical applications to particular types of surfaces: interior masonry, interior wood trim, exterior masonry, exterior wood, floors and metal surfaces. No attempt has been made to include special waterproofing coatings, as these are a study in themselves.

With the exception of the most recently developed acrylic finishes, practically all conventional paints and accessory materials required for architectural uses are adequately covered by Federal Specifications, which are available from the U. S. Government Printing Office. These specifications provide criteria for the selection of paints and can be employed as a basis of quality and performance.

Definitions

Vehicles are the liquid portions of pigmented paints. They serve as "carriers" for the pigments. The vehicle usually contains *both* volatile and non-volatile components. The volatile, or solvent, component, such as mineral spirits or water, serves two major purposes: (1) it facilitates application of the paint, and (2) by its evaporation it contributes to the drying of the paint film. The non-volatile component, referred to as the "binder," remains as an integral part of the paint film to bind the pigment particles together. Durability of the paint and adhesion of the film to the surface are largely functions of the binder. Typical binders or non-volatile vehicles include drying oils (linseed, tung), alkyd and phenolic resins and acrylic and vinyl resin emulsions (latexes).

Pigments include natural and synthetic, organic and inorganic types. For example, titanium dioxide is a synthetic inorganic pigment, while toluidine red and yellow are synthetic organic pigments. Pigments are employed to impart color and hiding power, as well as to protect the organic vehicle binder from the damaging rays of the sun. Hiding power, or the ability of the paint to obscure underlying color, varies with the different types of pigments. Dark pigments are more effective than light pigments. Of the commonly used white pigments, titanium dioxide is the most effective, while white lead is the least effective. Fading and color change result partly from instability of the pigmentation. Blue and green pigments generally are most susceptible to fading outdoors, with even some variation among these.

Clear coatings include varnishes, unpigmented lacquers, shellacs, clear sealers, wax polishes and water-repellent coatings. In general, they do not have the same protection against sunlight as pigmented coatings.

Varnish is a homogeneous solution of resin, drying oil, drier and solvent. Varnish dries by evaporation of the solvent followed by oxidation and polymerization of the drying oils and resins. It is commonly used as the vehicle in pigmented paints and enamels of the quick-drying, smooth-leveling types.

Lacquer is any type of organic coating that dries rapidly and solely by evaporation of the solvent. Typical solvents are acetates, alcohols and ketones. Although lacquers were generally based on nitrocellulose, manufacturers currently use vinyl resins, plasticizers and reacted drying oils to improve adhesion and elasticity.

Shellac is a solution of refined lac resin in denatured alcohol. It dries by evaporation of the alcohol. The resin is generally furnished in orange and bleached grades. Shellac comes in various "cuts," which indicate the amount of resin in pounds added to 1 gal of solvent: 4-, 4.5- and 5-lb cuts cover the range of light, medium and heavy grades used. Shellac can be used to seal knots in wood prior to painting.

Emulsion paints generally employ synthetic emulsion resins today and are water-thinned.

Interior: Masonry, Plaster, Wallboard

New interior surfaces of plaster, wallboard and masonry should be coated first with a primer-sealer and then with finish coats. Alkyd-type primer-sealers are used more extensively today than conventional oil types, especially under alkyd paints, although they can be used under finishes of any base. The new acrylic primer-sealers, which can be used under any type finish, are finding wider use because of their ease of application, resistance to alkalinity and rapid drying time. Common finishes are listed below:

Acrylic resin emulsion paint	Excellent durability
	Excellent washability immediately upon drying
	Excellent resistance to moisture
	Excellent hiding power in colors, fair in white
Latex paint	Good durability, except on hot surfaces
	Excellent washability, contingent upon chemical curing, which varies from 30 to 90 days
	Excellent hiding power in white, fair in colors
Alkyd flat enamel	Good durability
	Good resistance to moisture and washing
	Excellent hiding power and appearance
Oil flat paint	Good durability
	Fair resistance to moisture and washing
	Good hiding power and appearance
Casein and alkyd resin emulsion paints	Still used, but to a much lesser extent because of poor resistance to moisture and washing

Prepared with the assistance of Benjamin J. Harris, Maintenance Coatings Co., Inc. and John C. Moore, National Paint, Varnish and Lacquer Association, Inc.

Exterior: Wood

Pigmented paints for exterior wood surfaces are generally of the ready-mixed, linseed-oil-vehicle type. The pigments, apart from extenders, usually consist of white lead, titanium dioxide and zinc oxide. When combined in the proper proportions, they provide the optimum in hiding power, durability and repainting characteristics. Especially recommended for areas where industrial fumes are present are the high-quality titanium dioxide paints without lead pigments. They are white initially and stay white even in heavy fume areas where other white paints containing lead turn to gray, yellow and brown. Although three-coat painting of exterior wood has been conventional, it is now possible to apply two coats if properly executed. Regardless of the number of coats, the total thickness should be about the same. For two coats the primer should be applied at about 450 sq ft per gal and the finish coat at 550. For three coats the primer should be applied at 550 sq ft per gal and the succeeding finish coats at about 650.

Exterior oil paint	Zinc oxide hardens film and prevents mildew growth Chalking-type titanium imparts self-cleaning and good repainting characteristics Very slow drying
Oil trim enamel	Retains gloss well Good resistance to fading Very slow drying
Spar varnish	Excellent for doors, handrails, thresholds, etc., where maximum outdoor durability is desired
Stain	Good shingle stains, in various shades of red, brown and green, permit "breathing"

Floors: Wood

Wood floor finishes are usually formulated with a varnish vehicle for weatherability and effective penetration into the wood. Two coats are usually applied.

Oil-base enamel	Good wear resistance Good moisture resistance Recommended for softwood porches, steps and floors, both inside and outside
Varnish	Penetrating varnish is an effective sealer and leaves a thin but durable coating
Shellac	Seals wood and leaves a hard-gloss finish
Polishing-type wax	Protects a clear-finished surface and improves its appearance
Wax emulsion	Practical for an inexpensive, no-buffing floor treatment

Exterior: Masonry

For concrete, plaster, stucco, asbestos-cement siding, concrete masonry, brick and cinder block the exterior finishes listed below are used. Washability is not important in exterior paints. Many are formulated to "chalk" gradually, thus becoming self-cleaning.

Acrylic resin emulsion paint	Excellent durability Excellent alkali resistance Excellent color retention Fast drying
Latex (styrene/butadiene) paint	Excellent alkali resistance Good durability Color retention not so good as the acrylics Overnight drying
Polyvinyl acetate (p.v.a.) emulsion paint	Excellent alkali resistance Good durability Color retention not so good as the acrylics Overnight drying
Cement base paint	Suitable for coarse, rough surfaces. Smooth or glazed surfaces must be specially treated for roughening Excellent alkali resistance Good durability against moisture Overnight drying
Exterior oil paint	Good durability when applied to old masonry Vulnerable to attack by alkali

Floors: Concrete

Coatings on concrete floors do not vary much in appearance, at least not to an important degree. Their most important effects are the qualities they impart to the floor. Vehicles are usually selected on the basis of hardness and toughness, but they should not be so hard that they will be brittle and chip off when bumped. In addition to pigmentation to produce color and hiding power, inert pigments are sometimes added to contribute to the over-all wear and foot traffic resistance of the finish.

Epon resin base enamel	Excellent abrasion resistance Excellent alkali resistance Excellent adhesion Excellent resistance to grease and oil
Chlorinated rubber paint	Excellent wear resistance Excellent alkali resistance Excellent for damp floors
Varnish-base paint	Good wear resistance Good moisture resistance Excellent for dry, aged floors

Interior: Wood Trim

Interior wood trim can be painted with enamel or with a flat finish to be consistent with flat finishes on interior walls. Of course, semi-gloss and full-gloss finishes are still applied too. Pigmented paints for interior wood surfaces are generally formulated with quick-drying vehicles, such as varnish, alkyd resin or a mixture of varnish with linseed oil. New wood must have a prime coat before application of the finish coat. Three coats of pigmented paint are usually applied. However, two coats are often satisfactory. For estimating purposes, a coverage of approximately 400 to 500 sq ft per gal may be assumed. If treated with reasonable care, a good paint job on interior woodwork will last many years before repainting is required.

Alkyd flat enamel	Excellent leveling properties
	Excellent washability
	Excellent mar resistance
	Good durability
	Overnight drying
Acrylic resin emulsion paint	Excellent washability within 1 hr after application
	Very good durability
	Very good mar resistance
	Good leveling properties
	Fast drying
Oil flat paint	Good leveling properties
	Fair washability
	Fair durability
	Fair mar resistance
	Slow drying

Latex paint	Excellent washability, contingent upon chemical curing, which takes from 30 to 90 days
	Good durability after curing
	Good leveling properties
	Good mar resistance
Alkyd semi-gloss paint	Very good washability
Alkyd or oil-base full-gloss paint	Good hiding power
Varnish	Good, clear finish for trim
Stain	Frequently used in clear finish systems to intensify or modify the original color of the wood

Metal Surfaces

Before being finished with the desired type of protective and/or decorative coating, a metal surface must be properly cleaned and primed with a rust-inhibiting primer. The surface should be free of rust, scale, grease, oil, wax or other contaminant that will impair the adhesion of the primer. The function of the primer is to seal the surface to which it is applied, to inhibit corrosion of the metal surface, and to ensure good adhesion of the finish coat. Most of the finish paints described before for masonry and wood surfaces provide satisfactory finishes. Of the emulsion paints, the acrylics are best for primed hot radiator surfaces. In addition, a whole series of new paints has been developed, incorporating the resins of vinyl, epon, neoprene, phenolic, furane, etc., which resist acids and alkalies. This quality makes them particularly valuable for chemical plants, breweries, dairies, etc. Primers useful for metal surfaces are listed below, classified by pigment and vehicle, both of which are important. Regardless of which primer is used, the primed surface should be finish-coated in a reasonable length of time after application, because the primers are not intended to be weather-resistant.

Red lead pigment	Excellent for ferrous metalwork which cannot be cleaned of all rust
	Best for exterior use
	Most commonly used with oil vehicle
Zinc chromate pigment	Excellent for ferrous metalwork which is clean, bright, rust-free
	Most commonly used with alkyd resin vehicle
Zinc dust pigment	Good for all metal surfaces
	Excellent rust-inhibitive action
	Good for galvanized surfaces
Iron oxide pigment	Most commonly used to provide thick coating over thin zinc chromate coating
	Sometimes combined with zinc chromate to provide color
	Little rust-inhibitive action

Alkyd vehicle	Most commonly used with zinc pigments, but can be used with others
	Quick drying
Oil-base vehicle	Oil (about 25%) often added to other primers to get under old rust and so hold paint film better
	Slow drying
Phenolic vehicle	Good for metals which will be exposed to dampness or water immersion
	Quick drying
Vinyl vehicle (wash coat)	Excellent for non-ferrous metals, such as aluminum, copper, brass, etc. A thin, tightly adherent film is obtained over which any type paint can be applied
	Most commonly used with zinc chromate pigment
	Quick drying

Specifications recommended by the National Association of Store Fixture Manufacturers

TERMINOLOGY FOR FINISHING

Woods

1. *Fine textured woods*—Woods such as maple, beech, birch, gum, basswood, yellow poplar and sycamore, having small pores.

2. *Coarse textured woods*—Woods such as oak, walnut, Honduras mahogany, African mahogany, Philippine mahogany, ash, and elm having large, visible, open pores.

Stains

1. *Oil stain*—A transparent solution of a dye powder soluble in aromatic hydrocarbons. Normally dry to recoat in 2-4 hours. Need sealers over them which do not dissolve the stain and create bleeding. Shellac is normally used.

2. *Water stain*—A transparent solution of water soluble dye powders. Causes raised grain in most woods and requires long air drying before recoating.

3. *N.G.R.* (*non-grain-raising stain*) —A transparent solution of water stain powders, in solvents other than water, which does not swell the wood fibers and create raised grain.

4. *Pigmented wiping stain*—A thin oleo-resinous varnish with added specially ground color pigments, either earth or chemical. Must be kept agitated or settling occurs. Dries in 4 hours or more at moderate room temperature.

5. *Washcoat*—A thin solution of a sealer. A lacquer washcoat is normally a 4-6 per cent solids solution of a lacquer sealer. A shellac washcoat is normally the equivalent of a ½ lb cut of shellac. (See definition.) Primary purposes of the washcoats are: (1) to stiffen raised grain fibers and allow clean sanding, (2) to form a sealing layer between stain and succeeding color coats of finish, and (3) to allow cleaner, easier filler wiping.

This material was prepared by GLENN P. BRUNEAU of the Department of Wood Technology, University of Michigan, and appeared in "Specifications for the Manufacture of Store Fixtures," a publication prepared under the supervision of Dr. STEPHEN B. PRESTON and under the direction of the Specifications Committee of the National Association of Store Fixture Manufacturers.

6. *Lacquer sealer*—A quick drying lacquer, so formulated as to provide quick dry, good holdout of succeeding coats, and containing sanding agents such as zinc stearate to allow dry sanding of sealer. Requires constant stirring to avoid separation of ingredients. Usually contains 15-20 per cent solids at spray consistency. One full wet coat (see the definition) deposits approximately 1 mil of dry film thickness.

Lacquers

1. *Water-white lacquer*—A transparent lacquer having no apparent color, normally used over light colored surfaces. Usually contains approximately 1 mil of dry film thickness.

2. *Clear lacquer*—A transparent lacquer, unpigmented, but having some natural color, usually a light amber. Normally used over surfaces where slight darkening by topcoats is allowable. Usually contains approximately 20 per cent solids at spray consistency. One full wet coat deposits approximately 1 mil of dry film thickness.

3. *Flat lacquer*—A clear or water-white lacquer to which clear pigments have been added to diffuse light reflection from the surface of the dried film and simulate a rubbed surface. Usually contains approximately 20 per cent solids at spray consistency. One full wet coat deposits approximately 1 mil of dry film thickness.

4. *Hot lacquer*—A lacquer formulate for spraying at elevated temperatures, usually 160 F. Normally contains 30 per cent or greater solids content. Produces in two sprayed coats the equivalent of three coats of normal cold sprayed lacquer. Normally produces 1½ mils or greater dry film thickness in one sprayed coat.

5. *Lacquer enamel*—A clear lacquer to which has been added coloring pigments, bulking pigments and others. Forms an opaque film. Requires constant agitation to prevent color changes due to settling out of pigments. Usually contains 35 per cent or greater solids content at spray consistency. One full wet coat deposits approximately 2 mils or greater dry film thickness.

Other Finishing Materials

1. *Full wet coat*—A coat of finishing material applied in such manner as to exhibit an all over wet appearance (as contrasted to a dry or sandy spray). Usually considered to be near the maximum amount that can be applied on a vertical surface without sags or runs.

2. *Cut (of shellac)*—Number of pounds of resin added to each gallon of solvent. Liquid shellac is often supplied as a "4-lb cut." Equal parts of a "4-lb cut" of shellac and alcohol produce the accepted equivalent of a "2-lb cut." One part of a "4-lb cut" of shellac to seven parts of alcohol produces the accepted equivalent of a "½-lb cut".

3. *Uniforming*—Application of colored finishing materials to wood surfaces, finished or unfinished, to minimize variations in color or intensity of color. Usually performed where different woods are used in the same construction or to even up the color of all units in a group. Major use is on transparent and toned finishes.

4. *Lacquer undercoater*—A heavily pigmented lacquer enamel. Formulated to provide filling sealing and coloring. Can normally be sanded without lubricant. Air dries in 1 hour or more.

5. *Toner*—A thin lacquer enamel containing specially ground chemical and earth pigments. Thin applications have high hiding power. Dries rapidly, in 15 minutes or longer.

6. *Paste wood filler*—A mixture of oleo-resinous varnish, coloring pigments, bulking pigments (silex, others) and other ingredients. Usually reduced for application with VM&P naphtha at following rates: For walnut, Honduras mahogany and similar woods, 8-10 lb filler/gallon reducer. For oak, Philippine mahogany, ash and similar woods, 10-12 lb filler/gallon VM&P naphtha. Primary purpose is to fill and color vessels or pores of the wood and provide a level surface for succeeding coats. Formulated to air dry in 4 hours or more.

7. *Orange peel*—Roughness of a sprayed surface, resembling the surface of an orange peel, caused by lack of flow of sprayed finish droplets.

FINISH PROCEDURES
FOR EXPOSED
HARDWOOD SURFACES

1. Natural finish for exposed hardwood surfaces:

A. *Natural finish for coarse textured woods*

(1) Apply washcoat of lacquer sealer. Dry and sand lightly with 6/0 opencoat abrasive paper.

(2) Apply paste wood filler over all open grained wood. Filler should be allowed to "flash off" until a flat or dull appearance is noted. At this point, surfaces are padded by machine or by hand, with downward pressure across the grain, pushing excess filler into the pores. This initial padding is followed with a clean wipe across the grain to remove excess filler. After this operation, lightly wipe parallel to the grain with a clean cloth to remove all cross wipe marks. Excess filler in corners, carving or similar depressions should be brushed out or picked out cleanly. Dry filler thoroughly before sealing.

(3) Apply full wet coat of lacquer sealer. Dry.

(4) Sand out all roughness with 6/0 opencoat abrasive paper. Dust off thoroughly with air jet.

(5) Apply full wet coat water white lacquer. Dry.

(6) Scuff with 6/0 opencoat abrasive paper to remove any roughness present. Dust off with air jet.

*(7) Apply second full wet coat water white lacquer. Dry.

B. *Natural finish for fine textured woods*

(1) Follow exact procedure for "Natural finish for coarse textured woods," 1.A., except for elimination of steps (1) and (3). (Eliminate initial washcoating and filling operations.)

2. Stained finish for exposed hardwood surfaces:

A. *Stained finish for coarse textured woods*

(1) Apply one coat of stain (water, N.G.R., oil or pigmented wiping stain).

(a) If water stain is used: Dry thoroughly after staining and apply even washcoat of lacquer sealer (4-6 per cent solids). Scuffs sand when dry with 6/0 abrasive paper to remove raised fibers.

(b) If N.G.R. stain is used: Dry thoroughly, apply even washcoat of lacquer sealer (4-6 per cent solids). Scuff lightly when dry with 6/0 opencoat abrasive paper.

(c) If oil stain is used: Dry thoroughly according to manufacturer's directions. Apply even washcoat of white shellac (½-lb cut). Dry completely and scuff sand lightly with 6/0 opencoat abrasive paper.

(d) If pigmented wiping stain is used: Wipe evenly and cleanly, removing accumulations in crevices, inside corners, etc. by dry brush or wiping. Dry according to manufacturer's directions and follow with a washcoat of lacquer sealer (4-6 per cent solids). Sand washcoat lightly with 6/0 opencoat. Avoid cutting through stain.

(2) Apply paste wood filler (following procedure shown under 1.A. step (2). Dry thoroughly.

(3) Apply one full wet coat lacquer sealer (15-20 per cent solids). Dry thoroughly.

(4) Sand sealer to remove all roughness and dust off with air jet.

(5) Apply one full wet coat clear lacquer (water white may be specified but is not essential for dark stained finishes). Dry completely.

(6) Apply second full wet coat clear lacquer (or water white if specified). Dry completely

B. *Stained finish for fine textured woods*

(1) Follow exact procedure under 2.A. except eliminate the filling operation, step (2).

3. Bleached finish for exposed hardwood surfaces:

A. *Bleach all exposed surfaces.* For bleaches requiring a neutralizing wash, neutralize according to manufacturer's directions. Since any free

alkali left on the bleached surface may have a serious effect on subsequence coats, each bleached surface should be tested for alkalinity, after neutralizing, as follows:

(1) A test solution containing the following ingredients should be formulated:

1 part phenolpthalein
50 parts ethyl alcohol
50 parts water

(2) Several drops of this test solution should be placed at different points on the neutralized surface. If the spots turn red or pink, even momentarily, the surface is still alkaline.

(3) If the above test indicates alkalinity, the surface should be reneutralized with a 5-15 per cent solution of acetic acid and then sponged with clear water to remove bleaching residues.

Certain bleaches do not require a neutralizer. If not, eliminate neutralizing wash. All bleached surfaces should be dried thoroughly before recoating.

B. *Sand bleach surfaces* to remove all roughness with 6/0 abrasive paper. Any sandthrough of bleached surface to unbleached wood should be spot bleached to uniform surface color.

C. At this point, staining is to be done according to specification.

4. Toner finish for exposed hardwood surfaces:

A. *Toner finish for coarse textured woods*

(1) Spray uniform coat of toner over all surfaces. Avoid excessive buildup of coating at overlaps of spray pattern to avoid streaks. Natural pattern of the wood should not be obscured by toner application. Dry completely.

(2) Apply water white lacquer washcoat evenly over all exposed surfaces. Dry completely. Scuff sand lightly to remove roughness with 6/0 opencoat abrasive paper. Dust off thoroughly with air jet.

(3) Apply paste wood filler of correct color and consistency and complete schedule outlined under 1.A. starting with step (2), the filling operation.

---

*In any finish schedule, if hot lacquers (at 30-35 per cent solids) are used as the topcoats, two hot sprayed coats shall be considered sufficient to replace three coats of normal cold spray lacquer (20 per cent solids)

4. Toner finish for exposed hard-wood surfaces (continued):

B. *Finish for fine-textured woods*

(1) Toner finish—plain*

(a) Apply toner. Spray one light coat parallel to the grain of the wood, followed immediately by a second coat to even up coloration. The amount of toner sprayed should create a uniform color without closing the pores of the wood.

(b) Spray water-white lacquer wash-coat and dry.

(c) Sand lightly with 6/0 opencoat abrasive paper. Dust off with air jet. Avoid cutting through to bare wood. Sandthrough to wood should require touch-up with toner and washcoat re-application.

(d) Apply lacquer sealer and dry.

(e) Sand with 6/0 opencoat abrasive. Dust with air jet.

(f) Spray water-white lacquer top-coat and dry.

(g) Spray second topcoat water-white lacquer and dry.

(2) Toner-glaze finish.*

(a) Spray toner parallel to grain to uniform coloration. Dry thoroughly.

(b) Spray lacquer washcoat.

(c) Sand lightly with 8/0 opencoat abrasive paper, parallel to grain, and dust off with air jet.

(d) Apply glaze in thin coat over all toned surface. Wipe in circular pattern to deposit glaze evenly in small pores. Follow by wiping with a clean soft cloth parallel to the grain. A uniform color should be maintained overall. Deposits of glaze in corners and similar places should be removed.

(e) Spray lacquer sealer and dry.

(f) Sand sealer with 6/0 opencoat abrasive and dust with air jet.

(g) Spray topcoat of water-white lacquer and dry.

(h) Spray second topcoat of water-white lacquer and dry.

5. Opaque or pigmented finish for exposed hardwood surfaces:

A. *Opaque finish for coarse textured woods*

(1) Apply paste wood filler according to directions for filling under 1.A.(2).

(2) Dry thoroughly.

(3) Apply full wet coat of approved undercoating lacquer enamel. This undercoat shall be an appreciably different color from the finish coat to assure against skips in the spray pattern, and of a proper ground color with relation to the aforesaid finish coat. Dry.

(4) Sand all undercoated surfaces with 5/0 opencoat abrasive paper or finer, to complete removal of all roughness.

(5) Apply full wet coat of lacquer enamel. Dry thoroughly and scuff sand with 6/0 opencoat abrasive paper to remove accumulated roughness. Dust off completely with air jet.

(6) Apply second coat of lacquer enamel. Dry completely.

B. *Opaque finish for fine textured woods*

(1) Follow exact procedure outlined for coarse textured woods (5.A.) but eliminate step (1), the filling operation.

6. Finishing exposed particle board:

A. *Natural finish*

(1) Follow procedure under 1.B.

B. *Stained finish*

(1) Follow procedure under 2.B.

C. *Opaque or pigmented finish*

(1) Follow procedure under 5.B.

7. Opaque or pigmented finish for exposed paper-overlaid particle board:

Follow exact procedure outlined under 5.B., except eliminate second lacquer enamel topcoat.

8. Finishes for exposed fiberboard:

A. Natural—Follow procedure outlined under 1.B. (water-white lacquer shall not be mandatory).

B. Opaque or pigmented finish—Follow procedure under 5.B. eliminating second lacquer enamel topcoat.

RUBBING AND POLISHING

For each wood material used, and each finishing schedule used, the rubbing and polishing method should be selected by the architect from the fol-

lowing systems. He should specify which areas (tops, sides, etc.) will be rubbed and/or polished.

1. No rubbing or polishing:

Unexposed interior areas, drawer sides and interiors, shelving, and similar parts should not require any rubbing or polishing, other than removal by fine abrasive paper of any roughness created by the finishing process used.

2. Steel wool—Dull satin:

A. 3/0 steel wool should be used parallel to the grain of the wood, to remove roughness and create an all-over dull satin sheen in those areas specified by the designer.

(or) B. 4/0 steel wool should be used, parallel to the grain of the wood, to remove roughness and create an all-over dull satin sheen in those areas specified by the architect. 4/0 steel wool will create a slightly higher luster than 3/0 steel wool.

3. Dull satin:

A. Machine or hand sand, with 320 grit silicon carbide abrasive paper, using a non-blooming lubricant. All rubbing should be done parallel to the grain of the wood. Follow with an even rub in long continuous strokes with 4/0 steel wool. All lubricant and rubbing slush must be removed. Surface shall be clean and dry before waxing.

(or) B. Repeat procedure in (A) above, except use 360 grit silicon carbide abrasive paper in place of 4/0 steel wool.

4. Period satin:

A. Machine or hand sand with 320 or 360 grit silicon carbide abrasive paper, using a non-blooming lubricant, until all orange peel and other irregularities in surface film are removed. Follow this by hand rubbing with 3-F pumice using a soft felt pad, in long continuous strokes. All residual pumice and rubbing slush shall be removed. Dry completely before waxing.

(or) B. Repeat procedure outlined in (A) above, but substitute 500 grit silicon carbide abrasive paper for the

---

*In either schedule for fine textured woods, if the toner is one having a high lacquer binder content, washcoating may be eliminated. Light sanding with 8/0 opencoat abrasive paper should be used to smooth toned surfaces before proceeding. Any sandthrough of toned surface should require re-application of toner to match surrounding area and resanding with 8/0 abrasive paper

3-F pumice. Rub in long continuous strokes parallel to the grain of the wood. Clean up thoroughly, dry and wax.

5. High sheen satin:

A. Sand, by machine or hand, with 360 grit silicon carbide abrasive paper, using a non-blooming lubricant, to remove all surface film irregularities. Follow with 4-F pumice by machine or hand, with soft felt rubbing pads. If a higher sheen is desired, small amounts of rotten-stone shall be added to the 4-F pumice.

6. High luster:

A. Sand surface, parallel to the grain, by machine or hand, with 320 or 360 grit silicon carbide abrasive paper, using a non-blooming lubricant. Follow with a final sanding with 400 grit silicon carbide abrasive paper to create an all-over fine scratch pattern. Irregularities in flat surfaces missed by these two operations should be rubbed by hand with soft felt pad, using 4-F pumice. Clean the surface so that no abrasive particles or pumice remain. Apply rubbing compound and buff with rotary buffer to all-over even sheen. Clean up excess compound and then polish lightly with rotary buffer and clean lambs wool pad. Care should be exercised in both the compounding and polishing operations to prevent burning or softening of finish by frictional heat.

FINISH FOR UNEXPOSED AREAS

1. Unexposed drawer surfaces:

A. Apply one coat of lacquer sealer on all inside surfaces of drawers and outside surfaces of drawer sides and back. Skips, in corners or elsewhere, shall not be allowed. When dry, hand sand with 6/0 opencoat abrasive paper to remove roughness. Dust thoroughly with air jet.

2. Accessible interior parts (shelves, partitions, etc.):

A. Apply one coat lacquer sealer. Dry.

B. Remove any roughness by scuff sanding with 6/0 open coat abrasive paper.

UNIFORMING OF COLOR

1. Used where noticeable color differences exist on a unit, or between units in the same group.
2. Uniforming color should be applied without obvious lap marks or streaks, and shall not obscure the grain of the wood.
3. Wherever possible uniforming should be done on the last sealer coat, followed by a protective topcoat.
4. Uniforming colors should be formulated to give excellent adhesion to the surface on which they are applied.
5. Uniforming colors should have fade resistance equal to that of the entire finish system used.
6. Application of uniforming color on the final topcoat, instead of the sealer, should not create a surface roughness or sheen different from that of the topcoat.

FIELD PAINTING

1. Large panels and other items which cannot be satisfactorily finish painted in the shop may be painted in the field when specified by the architect.

A. All such items should be factory primed in a manner appropriate to the selected finish coat.

B. Finish painting in the field should conform to the appropriate preceding paragraphs presented in this article and the previous one (August).

WORKMANSHIP; PREPARATION
Workmanship Specifications

1. All workmanship shall be the very best with all materials evenly and smoothly applied. Runs, sags, bubbles, brush marks, heavy orangepeel, and other detrimental surface effects shall not be allowed. All finishing shall be performed under expert supervision.
2. Unless otherwise specified herein, all materials shall be applied in strict accordance with printed directions of the finishing-material manufacturer.
3. No finish shall be applied over a preceding coat unless the preceding coat is completely dry.
4. Doors and other components that are free to warp shall be given a sufficient number of coats of finishing material on opposite side and edges

to equalize moisture gain or loss and thus minimize warpage.
5. Holes for locks and catch strike plates shall be touched up to match adjoining surfaces.

Preparation for Finishing

1. Before any finish is applied, all wood surfaces shall be thoroughly sanded, by machine or hand sanding.

A. All sanding shall be done parallel to the grain of the wood.

B. A succession of grit sizes shall be used, each removing in turn all the coarser grooves created by the preceding grit.

2. For all exterior or exposed surfaces, a final grit size of 4/0 or finer shall be used.
3. Sandthrough at edges, corners or other areas of veneered surfaces shall not be allowed, except for opaque finishes.
4. Veneered panels having excessive bleedthrough of adhesive due to hot- or cold-press gluing shall be admitted for opaque finishes.
5. No cross-grain sanding marks shall be admissible for any finish system on veneered or solid wood members.
6. For surfaces to be water stained, the 4/0 sanding shall be followed by an application of glue sizing (one part, by volume, hot animal glue to 10 parts water at approximately 140 F) applied lightly and evenly over all sanded surfaces. The sized surfaces shall be thoroughly dried and then lightly sanded with 5/0 opencoat abrasive paper, by machine or hand, to remove all raised grain created by sizing. Water staining can then proceed with a minimum of raised grain.
7. All knife-edge corners shall be carefully eased with 4/0 abrasive paper.
8. All wood surfaces shall be kept free of dust, dirt, oil, adhesives, or other substances which would interfere with normal finishing procedure.
9. On surfaces to receive opaque finishes, dents, cuts, nail holes and similar damage shall be filled, dried completely and then sanded flush with 4/0 abrasive paper. The filling material selected shall be one giving excellent adhesion to uncoated wood surfaces.

PURPOSE

Data in this section make possible the quick solution of any stair problem ordinarily encountered in architectural practice. These data include a chart of proportional treads and risers and tabular material giving handrail heights, headroom, and stair gradients for stairs with risers from 5 to 9 inches.

Material in this section has been adapted from data originally developed by Ernest Irving Freese.

PROPORTIONAL TREAD AND RISER DIAGRAM

It has been found that dimensions of stair treads and risers are proportional to one another and can be plotted on a hyperbola, reproduced here in the form of a working chart. Rules for its use are given in the caption. No formulae are required to produce results desired, for dimensions are accurate to the nearest ⅛ in., a tolerance that is not ordinarily excessive in building practice.

In all cases the width of tread is exclusive of a nosing.

Use of this diagram makes unnecessary any adherence to former "rules" for proportioning of tread and riser. Both usual rules for stair layout are violated in the diagram. These are, "the sum of tread and riser shall not exceed 17½ in." and, "the product of tread and riser shall not exceed 75."

However, the average of the risers shown, 7 in., is proportional to a tread of 11 in., a combination that produces a stair which is comfortable to use and generally economical of floor space. At the lower extreme, a riser of 5 in. produces a tread of 16 in. which approximates the proportions of a brick step with a tread equal to two stretchers and a rise equal to two courses.

For the design of garden stairs see the section on Landscaping in *Time-Saver Standards for Building Types*, 1st ed., p. 1048.

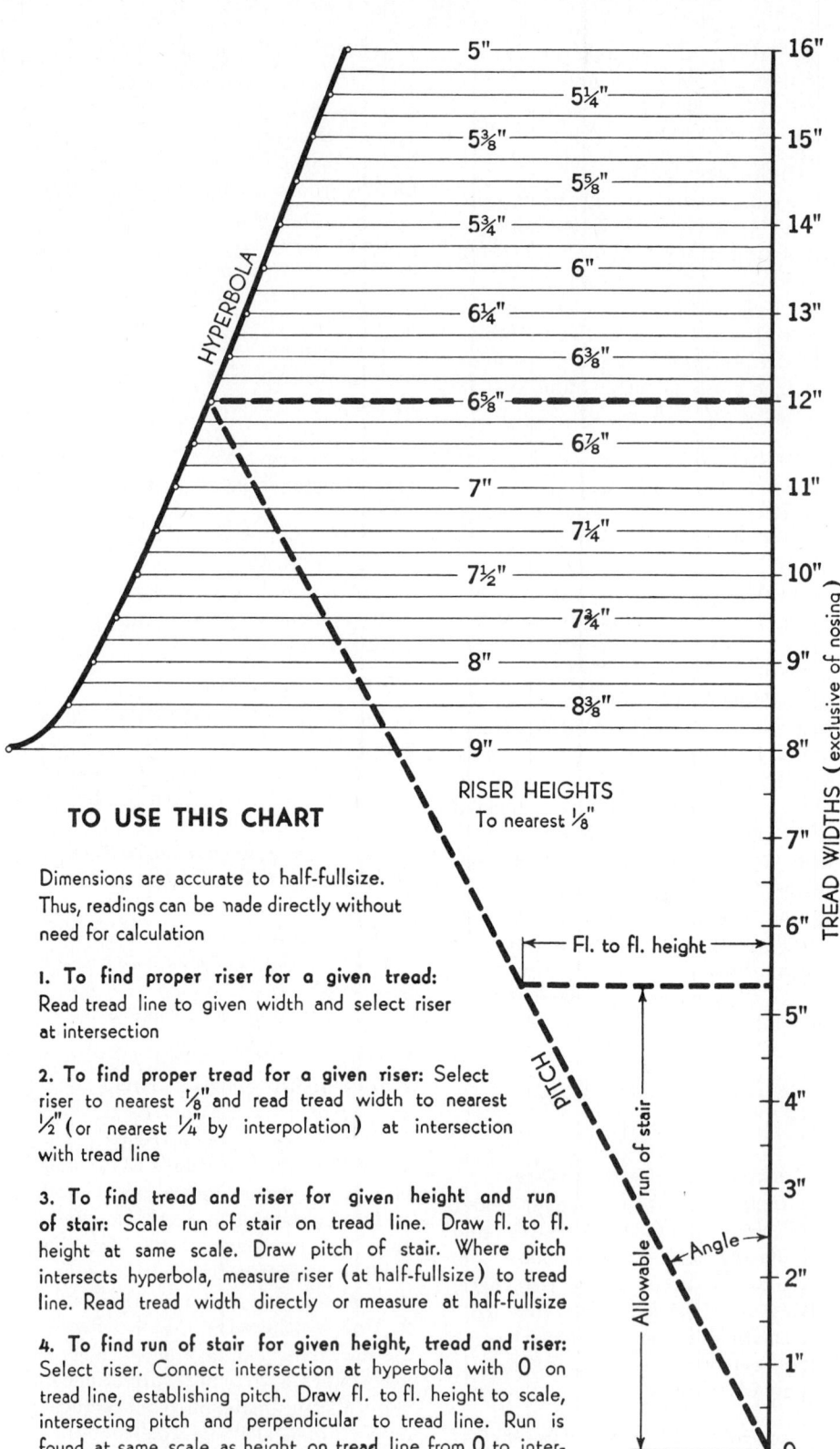

TO USE THIS CHART

Dimensions are accurate to half-fullsize. Thus, readings can be made directly without need for calculation

1. To find proper riser for a given tread: Read tread line to given width and select riser at intersection

2. To find proper tread for a given riser: Select riser to nearest ⅛" and read tread width to nearest ½" (or nearest ¼" by interpolation) at intersection with tread line

3. To find tread and riser for given height and run of stair: Scale run of stair on tread line. Draw fl. to fl. height at same scale. Draw pitch of stair. Where pitch intersects hyperbola, measure riser (at half-fullsize) to tread line. Read tread width directly or measure at half-fullsize

4. To find run of stair for given height, tread and riser: Select riser. Connect intersection at hyperbola with 0 on tread line, establishing pitch. Draw fl. to fl. height to scale, intersecting pitch and perpendicular to tread line. Run is found at same scale as height on tread line from 0 to intersection of fl. to fl. height

PROPORTIONAL TREAD AND RISER DIAGRAM

All Dimensions are at ½ Full Size

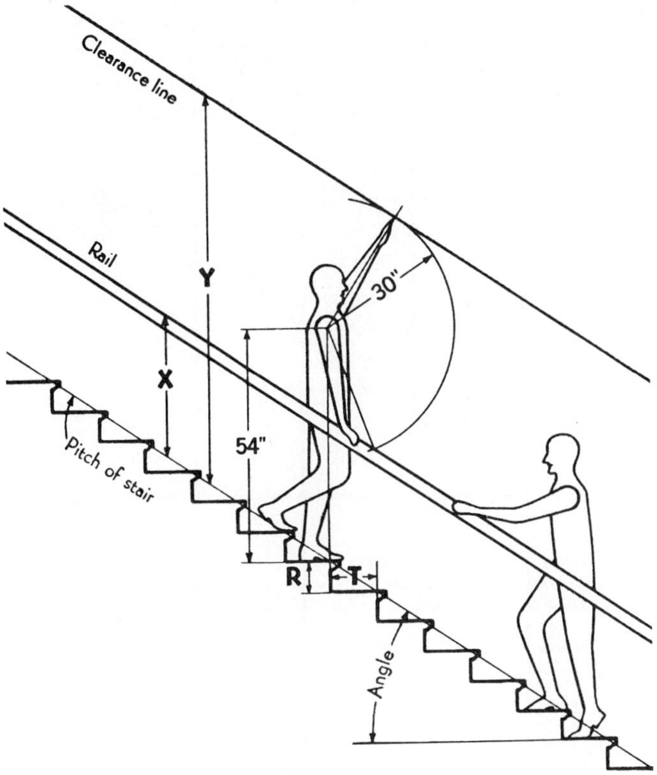

STAIRWAY LAYOUTS

Comfortable stairways cannot be designed except in relation to dimensions of the average human figure. As applied to stairways these dimensions and the equivalent of the average comfortable walking stride of about 24 in. fix the gradient of stairways, the proportional relation of treads and risers, the height of the handrail and the minimum necessary headroom.

The accompanying diagram indicates the influence of human figure dimensions and suggests the desirability of varying ceiling clearances and handrail heights according to variations in stair gradients. These variations are included in the table as related to dimensions of treads and risers developed from the Proportional Tread and Riser Diagram.

Treads and risers in curved stairs should be proportioned on an assumed "line of travel" 18 in. from the inner (smaller radius) handrail.

For the sake of practical classification a stairway can be defined as follows:

"A stepped footway having a gradient not less than 5:16 *pitch, or* 31¼ *per cent, or an angle of* 17 *degrees and* 21 *minutes; and not greater than* 9:8 *pitch or* 112½ *per cent, or an angle of* 48 *degrees and* 22 *minutes." (See gradient diagram on Sheet* 9.)

Below these limits, footways become ramps; above them stepladders. Both types of footways are subject to rules similar to those applicable to stairway design.

All building codes have strict specifications for stairs which are required exits. The National Building Code of the American Insurance Association and the New York City code both require that treads and risers be proportioned by the formula $T \times R = 70$ to 75, with risers not over 7¾ in. high and treads not less than 9 in. wide, exclusive of nosings. Minimum stair width for most uses is 44 in., based on two 22-in. lanes of traffic. Handrails are required on both sides and may project a maximum of 3½ in. into the required width. Winders and open risers are prohibited. The maximum vertical rise permitted between landings is 12 ft; in places of assembly it is 8 ft. Stairs must be designed for a live load of 100 psf.

In single-family houses HUD will permit stairs as steep as 8¼-in. rise and 9-in. tread, but for main stairs HUD recommends a gradient between 30 and 35 deg. For exterior stairs risers should not exceed 6 in. and treads should not be less than 12 in.; the maximum rise permitted between landings is 5 ft, and handrails are required.

NOSINGS

Nosings extending ¾ to 1½ in. (usually 1¼ in.) beyond the face of the riser are functionally necessary and are required by most building codes. Nosings may be provided by extending the treads or by sloping the risers. The latter method is customary in concrete stairs because of easier forming (see Sheet 8), and in any type of stair where carpet is to be installed. This type of nosing is also recommended for stairs to be used by the handicapped.

DIMENSIONS FOR STAIRWAYS

Step dimensions		Gradient designations		Headroom*	Handrail height
Riser **R** in inches	Tread **T** in inches	Per cent grade	Angle in degrees, minutes	**Y** in inches	**X** in inches
5	16	31.25	17-21	85	33½
5¼	15½	33.87	18-43	86	
5½	14¾	37.28	20-27		
5¾	14	41.07	22-20		
6	13½	44.44	23-58	87	33
6¼	13	48.07	25-40		
6½	12¼	53.06	27-57	88	
6¾	11¾	57.44	29-52		
7	11	63.63	32-28	89	
7¼	10½	69.04	34-37	90	
7½	10	75	36-52	91	
7¾	9½	81.57	39-12	93	33½
8	9	88.88	41-38	94	
8¼	8½	97.05	44-9	96	
8½	8¼	103.02	45-51	97	
8¾	8⅛	107.07	46-57	98	34
9	8	112.5	48-22	99	

NOTES

1. 7" by 11" is the proportion by which all steps are laid out
2. Risers from 5" to 6½" are suitable for exterior and "grand" interior stairs
3. Risers from 6⅝" to 7⅝" are most comfortable and most suitable for interior stairs
4. Risers for cellar and attic stairs may be up to 9" high
5. Width - minimum for single-file travel, 30"
6. Width - minimum for comfort, 36"
7. Width - desirable (for furniture passage etc.), 42"
8. Consult local building codes on all stair problems

Minimum for head clearance only can be safely taken as 84 in. for all gradients; HUD permits 80 in.

Critical dimensions and clearances

STAIR TABLE

Dimensions indicated on the accompanying diagram and listed in the table determine the vertical and horizontal areas and headroom clearances for stair systems with tread and riser proportions shown. They can be used directly in developing sketches or working drawings and eliminate the need for experimental stair plans or sections. All dimensions refer to face of treads without nosing.

Tabular data refer only to minimum conditions for straight run stairs. All figures may be adjusted according to requirements of design or stair use. For similar dimensional information controlling other types of stairways, see the following pages.

Widths of stairways may vary with these requirements. For passage of furniture minimum clear widths should be selected from the table on Sheet 4.

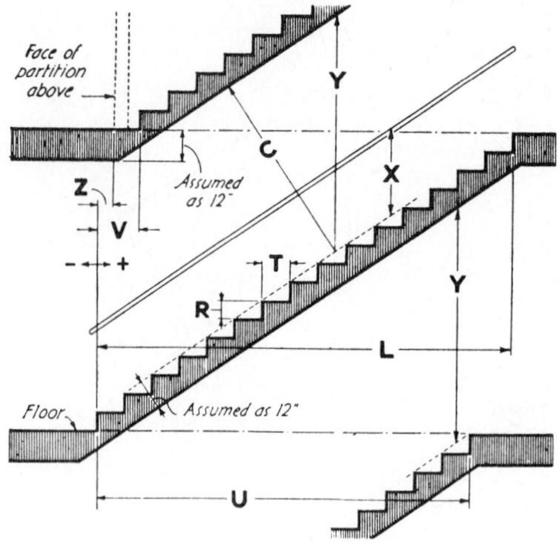

STAIR TABLE.... Dimensions in feet and inches

Floor to Floor Height		No. of Risers	Riser R	Tread T	Total Run L	Min. Headroom Y	Handrail X	Clearance C	Partition Above Z*	First Riser Below - U	First Riser Above - V*
8'-0"	†	11	8.73"	8¼"	6'-10½"	8'- 2"	2'-10"	5'- 8"	– 1'-10"	8'- 6"	– 1'- 7"
	†	12	8.00	9	8- 3	7-10	2- 9½	5-10½	– 1- 8½	9- 7½	– 1- 4
		13	**7.38**	**10¼**	**10- 3**	**7- 7**	**2- 9**	**6- 2**	**–1- 8½**	**11- 6**	**– 1- 1½**
		14	**6.86**	**11½**	**12- 5½**	**7- 4**	**2- 9**	**6- 4**	**–1- 7**	**13- 5½**	**– 9½**
	Δ	15	6.40	12½	14- 7	7- 3	2- 9	6- 7½	– 1- 6½	15- 5½	– 7½
	Δ	16	6.00	13½	16-10½	7- 3	2- 9	6- 7½	– 1- 9	17- 6	– 8
8'-6"	†	12	8.50	8½	7- 9½	8- 1	2- 9½	5- 8½	– 1- 3½	8-10	–11
	†	13	7.85	9¼	9- 3	7- 9	2- 9½	5-10½	– 1- 1	9-10	– 7½
		14	**7.29**	**10½**	**11- 4½**	**7- 6**	**2- 9**	**6- 2**	**–10½**	**12- 9**	**– 4**
		15	**6.80**	**11½**	**13- 8½**	**7- 4**	**2- 9**	**6- 4**	**–10½**	**13-10**	**– 1½**
	Δ	16	6.38	12½	15- 7½	7- 3	2- 9	6- 5½	– 7	15- 5½	+ 3½
	Δ	17	6.00	13½	18- 0	7- 3	2- 9	6- 7	– 7	17- 8	+ 5
9'-0"	†	12	9.00	8	7- 4	8- 3	2-10	5- 6	– 11	8- 1	– 8
	†	13	8.31	8½	8- 6	8- 0	2- 9½	5- 9	– 9	8-11½	– 5
		14	**7.71**	**9½**	**10- 3½**	**7- 9**	**2- 9½**	**6- 0**	**– 6**	**10- 5**	**– ½**
		15	**7.20**	**10½**	**12- 3**	**7- 6**	**2- 9**	**6- 2½**	**– 3**	**11-10**	**+ 4½**
		16	**6.75**	**11¾**	**14- 8¼**	**7- 4**	**2- 9**	**6- 4**	**+ 2**	**13-11**	**+ 1- 0**
	Δ	17	6.35	12½	16- 8	7- 3	2- 9	6- 5½	+ 5	15- 5½	+ 1- 4
	Δ	18	6.00	13½	19- 1½	7- 3	2- 9	6- 7½	+ 6	17- 8	+ 1- 6
9'-6"	†	13	8.77	8	8- 0	8- 2	2-10	5- 5½	– 3½	8- 2	– ½
	†	14	8.14	9	9- 9	7-10	2- 9½	5- 9½	± 0	9- 5½	+ 5
		15	**7.60**	**9¾**	**11- 4½**	**7- 7**	**2- 9**	**5-11½**	**+ 4½**	**10- 7**	**+10½**
		16	**7.13**	**10¾**	**13- 5¼**	**7- 5**	**2- 9**	**6- 2**	**+ 9½**	**12- 2**	**+ 1- 5½**
		17	**6.71**	**11¾**	**15- 8**	**7- 4**	**2- 9**	**6- 4**	**+1- 1½**	**13-11½**	**+ 1-11**
	Δ	18	6.33	12½	17- 8½	7- 3	2- 9	6- 5½	+ 1- 5½	15- 7	+ 2- 4
	Δ	19	6.00	13½	20- 3	7- 3	2- 9	6- 8	+ 1- 8	17- 9	+ 2- 7½
10'-0"	†	14	8.57	8½	9- 2½	8- 1	2- 9½	5- 8½	+ 2	8- 8	+ 6
	†	15	8.00	9	10- 6	7-10	2- 9½	5-10½	+ 6½	9- 7	+11
		16	**7.50**	**10**	**12- 6**	**7- 7**	**2- 9**	**6- 1**	**+ 1- 1**	**10-11½**	**+ 1- 6½**
		17	**7.06**	**11**	**14- 8**	**7- 5**	**2- 9**	**6- 2½**	**+ 1- 7½**	**12- 5½**	**+ 2- 2½**
		18	**6.67**	**12**	**17- 0**	**7- 4**	**2- 9**	**6- 5**	**+2- 0**	**14- 3½**	**+ 2- 9**
	Δ	19	6.32	12½	18- 9	7- 3	2- 9	6- 6	+ 2- 5	15- 8	+ 3- 2½
	Δ	20	6.00	13½	21- 4½	7- 3	2- 9	6- 7½	+ 2-10	17- 9	+ 3- 8½
10'-6"	†	14	9.00	8	8- 8	8- 3	2-10	5- 5½	+ 6	8- 0	+ 9
	†	15	8.40	8½	9-11	8- 1	2- 9½	5- 8½	+ 9½	8-10	+ 1- 1
		16	7.88	9¼	11- 6¾	7- 9	2- 9½	5-10½	+ 1- 3½	9-10	+ 1- 8½
		17	**7.41**	**10**	**13- 4**	**7- 7**	**2- 9**	**6- 1**	**+ 1- 9½**	**11- 0**	**+ 2- 3½**
		18	**7.00**	**11**	**15- 7**	**7- 5**	**2- 9**	**6- 2¼**	**+ 2- 5**	**12- 7½**	**+ 0- 0½**
		19	**6.63**	**12**	**18- 0**	**7- 4**	**2- 9**	**6- 4½**	**+2-11**	**14- 4**	**+ 3- 8½**
	Δ	20	6.30	12½	19- 9½	7- 3	2- 9	6- 6	+ 3- 5½	15- 7	+ 4- 3½
	Δ	21	6.00	13½	22- 6	7- 3	2- 9	6- 7½	+ 4- 0	17- 9	+ 5- 0
11'-0"	†	15	8.80	8	9- 4	8- 2	2-10	5- 6	+ 1- 0½	8- 1	+ 1- 2½
	†	16	8.25	8¾	10-11¼	8- 0	2- 9½	5-10	+ 1- 5	9- 2½	+ 1- 9
		17	**7.76**	**9½**	**12- 8**	**7- 9**	**2- 9½**	**6- 0**	**+2- 0**	**10- 3½**	**+ 2- 4½**
		18	**7.33**	**10¼**	**14- 6¼**	**7- 6**	**2- 9**	**6- 1½**	**+2- 7½**	**11- 4½**	**+ 3- 1½**
		19	**6.95**	**11**	**16- 6**	**7- 5**	**2- 9**	**6- 3**	**+3- 3**	**12- 8**	**+ 3- 9**
		20	**6.60**	**12**	**19- 0**	**7- 4**	**2- 9**	**6- 5**	**+3-10½**	**14- 5½**	**+ 4- 7½**
	Δ	21	6.29	12½	20-10	7- 3	2- 9	6- 6	+ 4- 5	15- 8	+ 5- 3
	Δ	22	6.00	13½	23- 7½	7- 3	2- 9	6- 7½	+ 5- 1	17- 8	+ 6- 0

Notes: Figures in bold face indicate stairs recommended for most interiors.

† Indicates stairs allowable only for attics and cellars but not recommended.

Δ Indicates stairs for exterior or monumental use.

* Dimensions given plus or minus; i.e. behind or in front of first riser (see diagram above).

CLEARANCES FOR FURNITURE PASSAGE

The information on this page supplements that contained in the Stair Table on the previous page. Width is not always a critical factor of stairway design but is important when the layout involves one or more turns with straight runs. Typical layouts for such stairways include the Long L, Double L, Wide U, Wide L, and Narrow U. (See the following pages for layouts and tabular data on these types.)

Stairways used solely as circulation from floor to floor can be 2'-0" wide for comfortable passage of one individual or 3'-6" for two, side-by-side. When furniture must be taken up and down, minimum clear widths of straight runs and landings must be carefully selected or corners will constitute obstructions in many instances.

Recommended minimum clear widths as shown in the table are not necessarily the width of stairs, either rough or wall-to-wall. Projections of newels, handrails or baseboards can obstruct passage of furniture and must be taken into account when determining actual stair widths.

Headroom is also a controlling factor of design. With minimum headroom conditions shown in the Stair Table, clear widths for furniture passage must be greater in most cases than may be necessary if headroom is unlimited or equal at least to the ceiling height. This is particularly important at the first riser and at turns, where the under rake of the first stair limits the vertical clearance of the stairway below. Therefore, if stairs must be comparatively narrow and if furniture must be transported over them, headroom, or vertical clearance, must be increased accordingly.

Landing widths may be increased to provide greater turning space for maneuvering furniture. If this is done, minimum clear widths can be proportionately decreased. However, this expedient is not effective unless hallways at either end of the stairway are at least equal to the landing widths. Narrow hallways often offer as great an obstruction to furniture maneuvering as low headroom, narrow runs or cramped turns.

Open-well stairways give more opportunity to maneuver furniture, since even very bulky but light pieces may often be lifted over rails or newels. In general, a closed-string stair should be wider than an open-string type for the same degree of convenience.

Tabular data on this page reflect safe *average* clearances for transportation of items listed. Dimensions of furniture are subject to wide variations. Consequently, the minimum clear widths recommended here are susceptible to adjustment in certain instances.

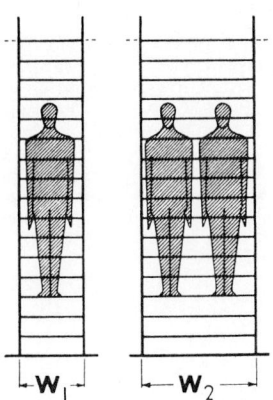

MINIMUM HUMAN PASSAGE

MINIMUM STAIR WIDTHS

Above: Stairs designed for comfortable human passage only may be relatively narrow. W_1 may be 2'-0" but 2'-6" is better. W_2 should be at least 3'-6".
Right: Furniture passage demands greater width. If stair landing is increased or headroom unlimited, W_F may be decreased. See table below.

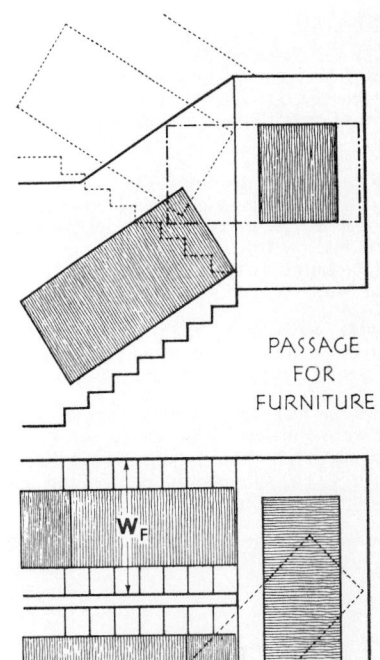

PASSAGE FOR FURNITURE

RECOMMENDED MINIMUM CLEAR WIDTHS OF STAIRS (W_F)*
for furniture movement

| Furniture | | Min. Headroom ▲ | | Unlimited Headroom | | |
| Article | Size | Wide U Type | Narrow U Type | Wide and Narrow U | Narrow U only● | |
					Stair	Landing
Double Bed Box Spring	4'-6"x 6'-6"x 8"	3'- 2"	3'- 2"	2'- 3"		
Dressing Table	1'-10"x 4'-0"x 2'-6"	2'- 5"	2'- 5"	2'- 5"		
Bureau	2'-0"x 4'-0"x 3'-0"	2'- 8"	2'- 8"	2'- 8"		
Chiffonier	1'-8"x 3'-4"x 4'-8"	2'- 6"	2'- 6"	2'- 6"		
Chest of Drawers	1'-9"x 3'-4"x 4'-8"	2'- 7"	2'- 7"	2'- 7"		
Divan - Club	3'-6"x 7'-2"x 2'-9"	4'- 8"	4'- 8"	3'- 4"	3'-0"	3'-8"
Divan - Average	3'-0"x 6'-8"x 2'-6"	4'- 4"	4'- 4"	2'-11"		
Piano - Concert Grand	9'-0"x 5'-4"x 1'-8"	4'- 8"	4'- 8"	3'- 2"■	3'-0"■	3'-4"■
Piano - Music Room Grand	7'-3"x 5'-2"x 1'-6"	3'-10"	3'-10"	3'- 0"		
Piano - Drawing Room Grand	6'-9"x 5'-0"x 1'-4"	3'- 6"	3'- 6"	2'-10"		
Piano - Baby Grand	5'-8"x 4'-10"x 1'-2"	3'- 0"	3'- 0"	2'- 8"		
Piano - Standard Upright	2'-2"x 5'-10"x 4'-6"	4'- 0"	3'- 9"	3'- 3"	3'-0"	3'-6"
Highboy - Large	2'-0"x 3'-6"x 7'-6"	4'- 4"	4'- 4"	2'-10"		
Highboy - Average	1'-8"x 3'-4"x 6'-0'	3'- 6"	3'- 6"	2'- 6"		
Secretary - Large	1'-10"x 3'-8"x 7'-2"	4'- 0"	4'- 0"	2'-10"		
Secretary - Average	1'-10"x 3'-0"x 6'-10"	3'-10"	3'-10"	2'- 6"		
Sideboard	1'-9"x 5'-0"x 3'-2"	2'- 6"	2'- 6"	2'-10"		
Buffet	2'-1"x 3'-3"x 6'-6"	4'- 0"	4'- 0"	2'-10"		
Dresser	1'-9"x 6'-0"x 5'-6"	4'- 4"	3'- 6"	3'- 4"	3'-0"	3'-8"
Table (6 People)	3'-6"x 5'-0"x 2'-6"	3'- 2"	3'- 2"	3'- 2"	3'-0"	3'-4"
Table (8 People)	3'-6"x 7'-0"x 2'-6"	4'- 8"	4'- 4"	3'- 2"	3'-0"	3'-4
Table (10 People) Rd.	6'-4" Diam.	4'- 8"	4'- 8"	3'- 0"		
Desk - Slope Top	2'-6"x 3'-8"x 3'-4"	3'- 3"	3'- 2"	3'- 2"	3'-0"	3'-4"
Desk - Flat Top	3'-0"x 5'-6"x 2'-6"	3'- 2"	3'- 0"	3'- 0"		
Desk - Executive's	3'-2"x 6'-0"x 2'-6"	4'- 2"	4'- 2"	3'- 1"	3'-0"	3'-2"
Trunk - Wardrobe	1'-11"x 2'-6"x 3'-7"	2'- 5"	2'- 5"	2'- 5"		

Notes : **✱** Clear width between faces of rails, newels etc. or between rail or newel and finish wall.
▲ Headroom limited to minimum for comfortable human passage (see "Stair Table" and text).
● Narrow stairs and wide landings.
■ Absolute minimum not recommended (see text).

PURPOSE

The six diagrams on this and the following sheet represent unit plans for types of non-winder stairways which are most frequently encountered in the average residential planning problem. Tabular information with each was developed from data contained in the Stair Table.

Unit plans are drawn to ⅛" scale and therefore can be supplied directly as a check of stair layouts to sketch plans and elevations. Each represents an average condition with a stair pitch well within the comfort zone. The basis is a 9'-6" floor-to-floor height with 16 risers each 7.13" in height. Width is 3'-0" from wall to wall.

Tabular data with each unit plan indicates dimensional variations which occur when stairways of substantially similar pitches are planned for floor-to-floor heights from 8 to 11 feet.

Width is the only critical dimension missing from this unit plan information. This varies with requirements of design and stair use and should be selected from data on previous page. Width is a dimension controlling critical clearances on all stairs that contain a turn.

Winders have not been included in these unit plans because they represent a stair condition generally regarded as unde-

sirable. However, use of winders is sometimes necessary due to cramped space. In such instances, winders should be adjusted to replace landings so that the narrow portions of treads at the inside of the turn are at least equal to ¾" T. When this is done, dimensions of L_1 and L_2 are decreased by approximately ½T, the exact figure depending upon the width selected. The practice of adding a winder-riser to bisect the landing diagonally from the corner of a newel is to be avoided in all cases for it produces a dangerously narrow step in a particularly undesirable place.

APPLICATION OF UNIT PLANS

Diagrammatic data can be used on sketches as a graphic check as noted. Tabular data can be applied to either sketches or working drawings to eliminate the necessity of developing experimental stairway sections to determine run, proportional rise, horizontal and vertical areas and location of under-rake minimum headroom.

Dimensional data have been confined to a single pitch for all floor-to-floor heights. The pitch indicated is that most generally desirable for human comfort. Data for other pitches listed as tread and riser proportions in the Stair Table can be substituted for values of L_1, L_2, and M.

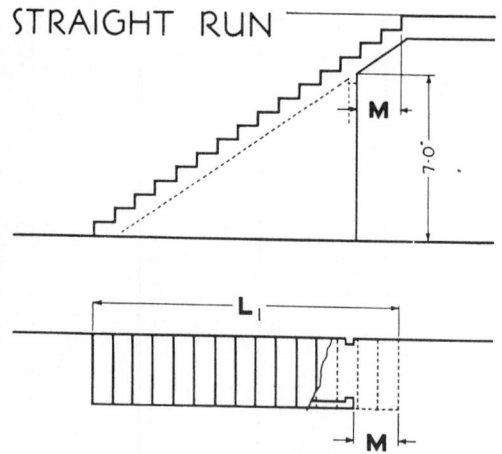

STRAIGHT RUN

HEIGHT FLOOR TO FLOOR	NO OF RISERS	RISER	TREAD	L_1	M
8'-0"	13	7.38	10¼"	10'-3"	—
8'-6"	14	7.29	10½"	11'-4½"	4½"
9'-0"	15	7.20	10½"	12'-3"	1'-1½"
9'-6"	16	7.13	10¾"	13'-5¼"	1'-11¼"
10'-0"	17	7.06	11"	14'-8"	2'-9½"
10'-6"	18	7.00	11"	15'-7"	3'-7"
11'-0"	19	6.95	11"	16'-6"	4'-5"

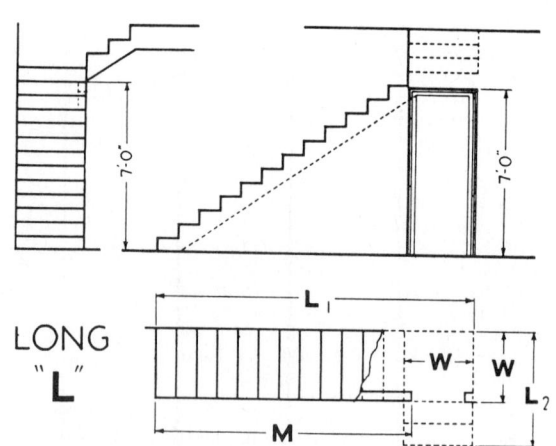

LONG "L"

HEIGHT FLOOR TO FLOOR	Nº RISERS	RISER	TREAD	Nº RISERS	L_1	Nº RISERS	L_2	M
8'-0"	13	7.38	10¼"	13	10'-3" + W	0	W	10'-3"
8'-6"	14	7.29	10½"	13	10'-6" + W	1	W	10'-6"
9'-0"	15	7.20	10½"	13	10'-6" + W	2	10½" + W	10'-6"
9'-6"	16	7.13	10¾"	13	10'-9" + W	3	1'-9½" + W	11'-0"
10'-0"	17	7.06	11"	13	11'-0" + W	4	2'-9" + W	11'-4"
10'-6"	18	7.00	11"	13	11'-0" + W	5	3'-8" + W	11'-5"
11'-0"	19	6.95	11"	13	11'-0" + W	6	4'-7" + W	11'-6"

WIDE "L"

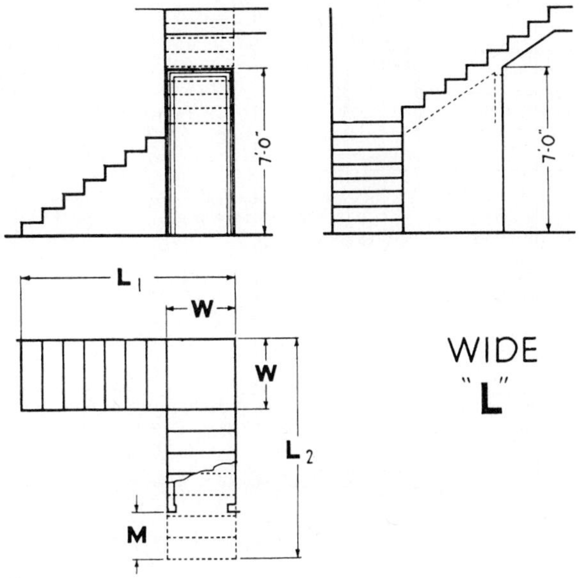

HEIGHT FLOOR TO FLOOR	Nº RISERS	RISER	TREAD	Nº RISERS	L_1	Nº RISERS	L_2	M
8'-0"	13	7.38	10¼"	7	5'-1½"+W	6	4'-3¼"+W	–
8'-6"	14	7.29	10½"	7	5'-3"+W	7	5'-3"+W	4½"
9'-0"	15	7.20	10½"	8	6'-1½"+W	7	5'-3"+W	1'-1½"
9'-6"	16	7.13	10¾"	8	6'-3¼"+W	8	6'-3¼"+W	1'-11¼"
10'-0"	17	7.06	11"	9	7'-4"+W	8	6'-5"+W	2'-9½"
10'-6"	18	7.00	11"	9	7'-4"+W	9	7'-4"+W	3'-7"
11'-0"	19	6.95	11"	10	8'-3"+W	9	7'-4"+W	4'-5"

NARROW "U"

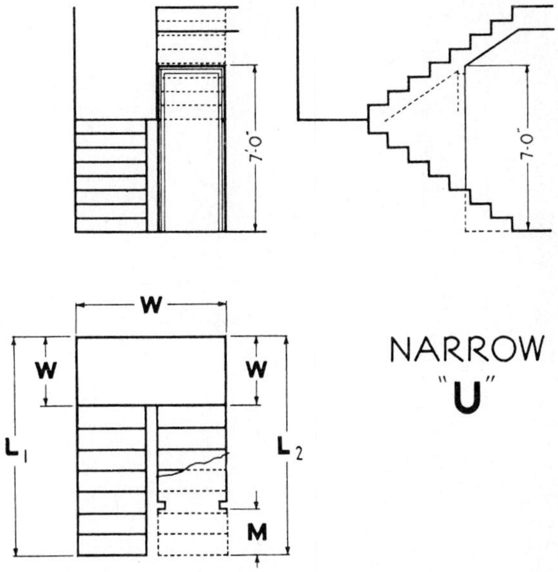

HEIGHT FLOOR TO FLOOR	Nº RISERS	RISER	TREAD	Nº RISERS	L_1	Nº RISERS	L_2	M
8'-0"	13	7.38	10¼"	7	5'-1½"+W	6	4'-3¼"+W	–
8'-6"	14	7.29	10½"	7	5'-3"+W	7	5'-3"+W	4½"
9'-0"	15	7.20	10½"	8	6'-1½"+W	7	5'-3"+W	1'-1½"
9'-6"	16	7.13	10¾"	8	6'-3¼"+W	8	6'-3¼"+W	1'-11¼"
10'-0"	17	7.06	11"	9	7'-4"+W	8	6'-5"+W	2'-9½"
10'-6"	18	7.00	11"	9	7'-4"+W	9	7'-4"+W	3'-7"
11'-0"	19	6.95	11"	10	8'-3"+W	9	7'-4"+W	4'-5"

DOUBLE "L"

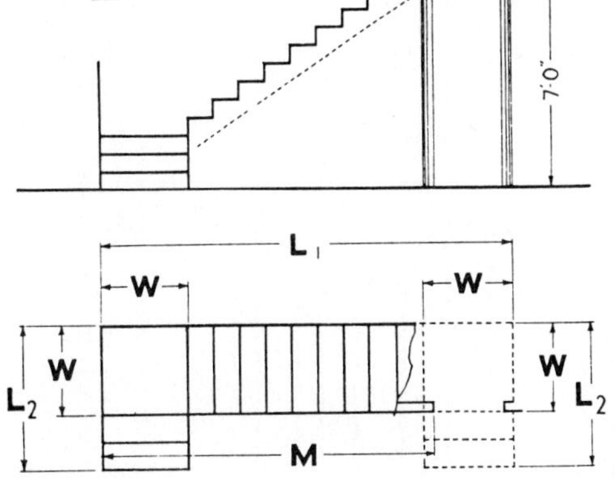

HEIGHT FLOOR TO FLOOR	Nº RISERS	RISER	TREAD	Nº RISERS	L_1	Nº RISERS	L_2	M
8'-0"	13	7.38	10¼"	13	10'-3"+2W	0	W	10'-3"+W
8'-6"	14	7.29	10½"	12	9'-7½"+2W	1	W	9'-7½"+W
9'-0"	15	7.20	10½"	11	8'-9"+2W	2	10½"+W	8'-9"+W
9'-6"	16	7.13	10¾"	10	8'-0¾"+2W	3	1'-9½"+W	8'-3¾"+W
10'-0"	17	7.06	11"	9	7'-4"+2W	4	2'-9"+W	7'-8"+W
10'-6"	18	7.00	11"	8	6'-5"+2W	5	3'-8"+W	6'-10"+W
11'-0"	19	6.95	11"	7	5'-6"+2W	6	4'-7"+W	6'-0"+W

WIDE "U"

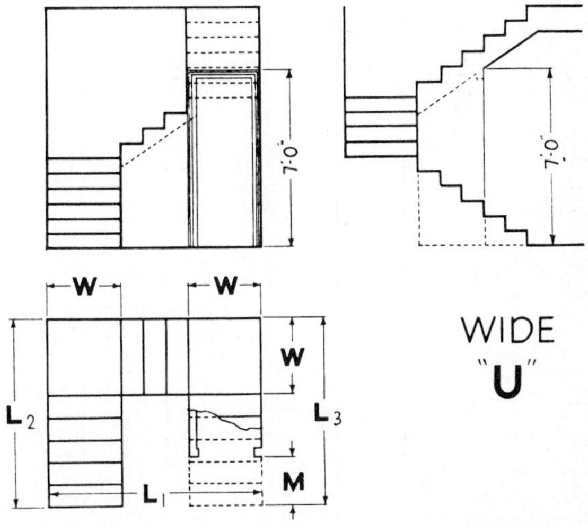

HEIGHT FLOOR TO FLOOR	Nº RISERS	RISER	TREAD	Nº RISERS	L_1	Nº RISERS	L_2	Nº RISERS	L_3	M
8'-0"	13	7.38	10¼"	4	2'-6¾"+2W	4	2'-6¾"+W	5	3'-5"+W	–
8'-6"	14	7.29	10½"	4	2'-7½"+2W	5	3'-6"+W	5	3'-6"+W	4½"
9'-0"	15	7.20	10½"	4	2'-7½"+2W	5	3'-6"+W	6	4'-4½"+W	1'-1½"
9'-6"	16	7.13	10¾"	4	2'-8¼"+2W	6	4'-5¾"+W	6	4'-5¾"+W	1'-11¼"
10'-0"	17	7.06	11"	4	2'-9"+2W	6	4'-7"+W	7	5'-6"+W	2'-9½"
10'-6"	18	7.00	11"	4	2'-9"+2W	7	5'-6"+W	7	5'-6"+W	3'-7"
11'-0"	19	6.95	11"	4	2'-9"+2W	7	5'-6"+W	8	6'-5"+W	4'-5"

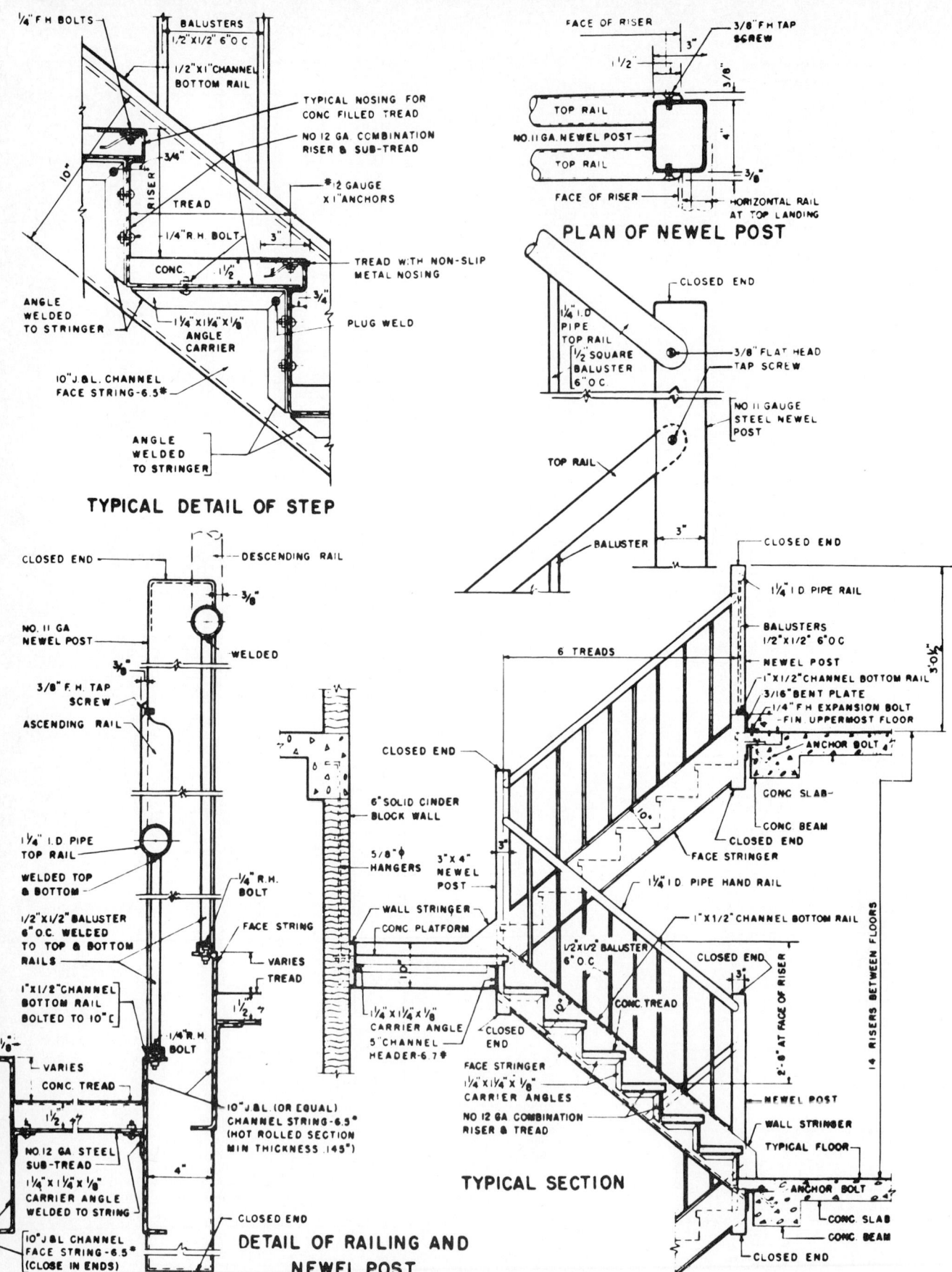

TYPICAL DETAIL OF STEP

PLAN OF NEWEL POST

DETAIL OF RAILING AND NEWEL POST

TYPICAL SECTION

Typical steel stair construction (standard detail of the New York City Housing Authority)

Scale: section ⅜ in. = 1 ft; details 1½ in. = 1 ft. (Note: See also Metal Stairs Manual *published by National Association of Architectural Metal Manufacturers, 1971.)*

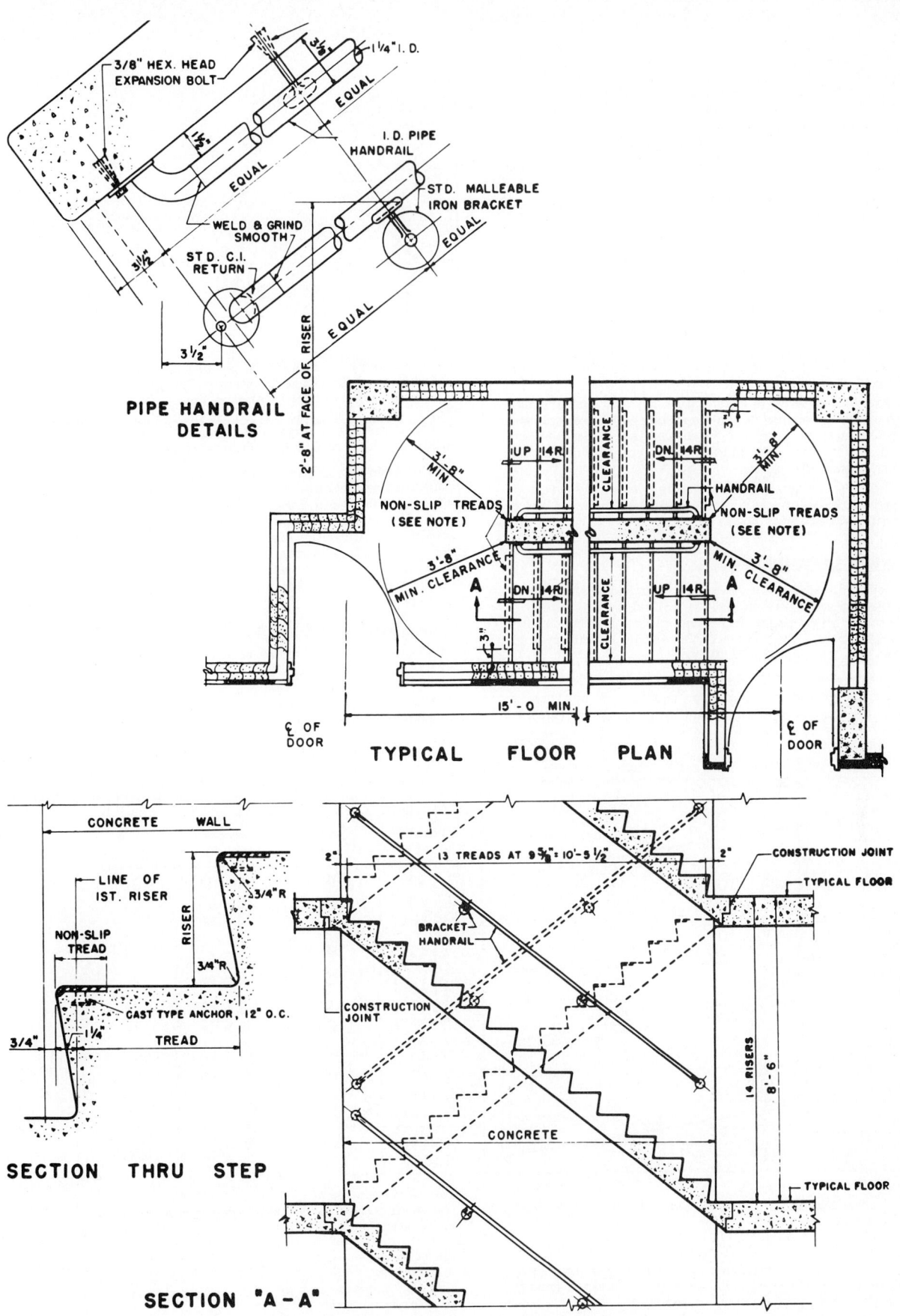

PIPE HANDRAIL DETAILS

TYPICAL FLOOR PLAN

SECTION THRU STEP

SECTION "A-A"

Typical reinforced concrete scissors stair
(standard detail of New York City Housing Authority)

Scale: plan and section ¼ in. = 1 ft; details 1½ in. = 1 ft.

PURPOSE

Design of ladders and pedestrian ramps is more directly influenced by conditions of location and use than by theory. Exact formulae have not been developed. However, data on this sheet give such information as has been found to be practical. Tabular material has been adapted from data formulated by Ernest Irving Freese, from the New York City Building Code and from recommendations of the Workmen's Compensation Service Bureau.

DEFINITIONS

Ramps as considered here are inclined pedestrian passages without vertical risers and of a lower pitch than stairs. In general, they are easier to ascend or descend than stairs.

Ladders have a greater pitch than stairs. No ladder is comfortable, though some may be easier to climb than others. They can be divided into two classifications:

(1) Stepladders are lower in pitch than 75° and require flat treads. Risers may be either "open" or "closed" (see below). Handrails may or may not be provided. In this classification belong most fire escapes and ladders for boiler rooms, fly galleries, attics, decks, etc.

(2) Rung ladders are pitched more steeply than 75°, require extremely narrow treads or round rungs to provide knee-room and do not require additional handrails.

LAYOUTS AND REQUIREMENTS

Ramps steeper than 10% require non-slip surfaces and handrails. If possible, these safety measures should be included in all ramps. Most building codes limit the pitch, the maximum being about 2:12 or 16 2/3%. See Table I for recommended pitches, widths, handrail heights and clearances.

Stepladders require handrails on both sides when not confined between walls or when risers are "closed." When risers are "open," treads or the ladder frame may serve as hand-

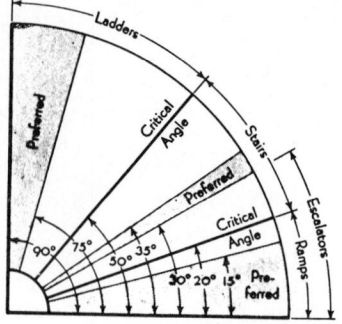

Diagram shows recommendations of the Workmen's Compensation Service Bureau for pitch of ramps, stairs and ladders. Pitches close to "critical angles" should be avoided wherever possible as these are uncomfortable and unsafe

holds. However, handrails should be provided wherever possible. Stepladders are normally "single-file" footways. Being used only where limitations of space will not permit installation of stairs they should be as narrow as possible. See Table II for dimensions and clearances. In all cases consult local building codes and fire regulations.

Rung ladders should have round rungs if possible to provide a maximum of knee-room. Rungs need not be evenly spaced between floors, but irregular spaces should occur at the lower landing for safety. Rung spacing and clearances may be determined graphically as shown in Table III or taken directly from Table III, Columns 4 and 5. Ladders necessary for proper maintenance or fire safety of buildings are specified in most building codes and fire regulations.

PREFABRICATED STAIRS AND LADDERS

Various types of counterbalanced disappearing stairs are available, as well as iron pit-ladders, fire-escape equipment, etc. Manufacturers' reference data should be consulted for necessary tolerances, structural requirements and recommended installation practices.

TABLE I - RAMPS - 0° to 20° Pitch

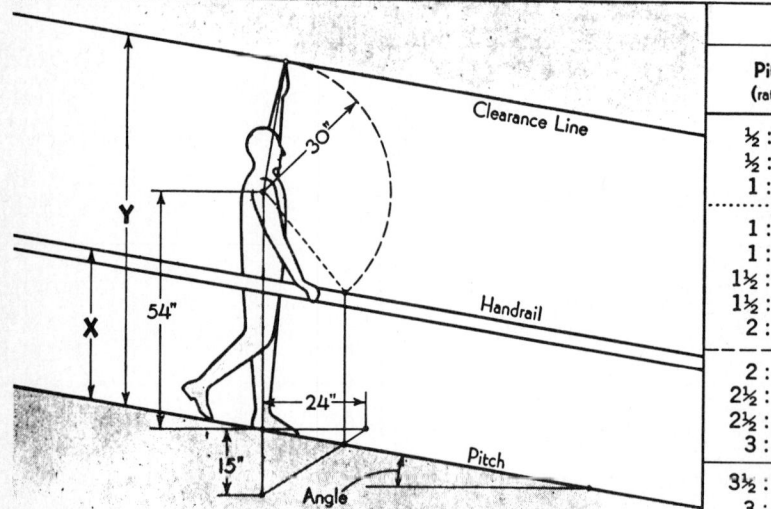

GRADIENT			HANDRAIL HEIGHT	CLEARANCE
Pitch (ratio)	Grade (%)	Angle (deg. - min.)	X (inches)	Y (inches)
½ : 12	4⅙	2 – 23	35	
½ : 10	5	2 – 52	35	
1 : 12	8⅓	4 – 46	34½	
1 : 10	10	5 – 43	34½	
1 : 8 }	12½	7 – 7	34	84
1½ : 12 }				
1½ : 10	15	8 – 23	34	
2 : 12	16⅔	9 – 28	34	
2 : 10	20	11 – 19	34	
2½ : 12	20⅚	11 – 46	33½	
2½ : 10 }	25	14 – 2	33½	85
3 : 12 }				
3½ : 12	29⅙	16 – 16	33½	
3 : 10	30	16 – 42	33½	

NOTES:

Overhead clearances and handrail heights may be determined graphically from the diagram

Maximum pitch:
(1) Values below the dotted line......are prohibited by the New York City Building Code for theatre aisles, except for runs not exceeding 10' - 0" which may be pitched a maximum of 1:8
(2) Values below the dash line-- are prohibited by most other building codes
(3) All values above the solid line—— are approved by the Workmen's Compensation Service Bureau

(4) HUD requires pitch of 1:10 or lower
(5) ANSI A117.1 recommends maximum slope 1:12. See section on Design for Handicapped.

Minimum width:
(1) For single file traffic = 30" }
(2) For furniture passage = 36" } *determined by*
(3) Preferred single file min. = 42" } *Ernest Irving Freese*
(4) For theatre aisles = 36", increasing 1½" every 5'-0" of run (N.Y.C. Bldg. Code)

TABLE II - STEPLADDERS - 50° to 75°

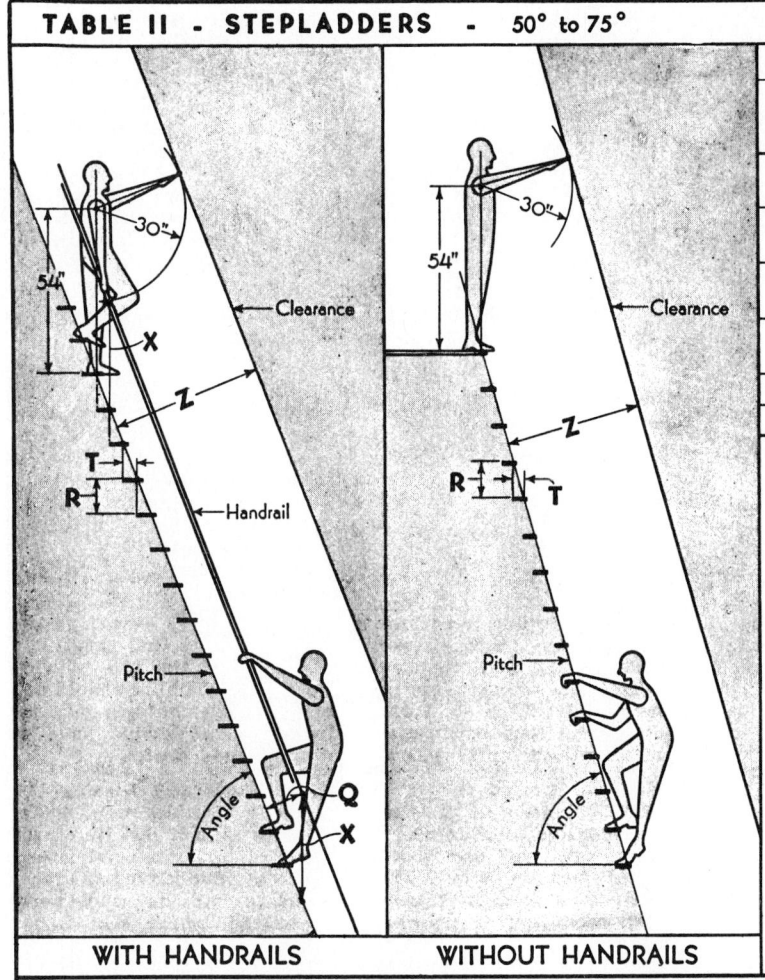

WITH HANDRAILS	WITHOUT HANDRAILS

STEP DIMENSIONS		GRADIENT		CLEAR-ANCE Z (inches)	HANDRAIL HEIGHT X (inches)
Riser R (inches)	Tread T (inches)	Grade (%)	Angle (deg. - min.)		
9⅜	7½	125	51 – 21	64	
9¾	7	139.28	54 – 19	62	34½
10⅛	6½	155.75	57 – 18	59	
10½	6	175	60 – 16	57	35
10⅞	5½	197.72	63 – 10	54	
11¼	5	225	66 – 2	52	35½
11⅝	4½	258.66	68 – 50	50	
12	4	300	71 – 34	47	36
12⅜	3½	353.21	74 – 12	45	36½
12¾	3	425	76 – 46	42	37

NOTES:

Clearance and handrail height may be determined graphically if desired

Handrails are required on both sides of stepladders if risers are not left "open" or if not confined between side walls

Maximum and minimum widths:

    With handrails: 21" to 24"
    Without handrails: variable
    Between sidewalls: 24" minimum

HUD requires slope between 50 and 60°; trends 6 in. min; risers 12 in. max; width, 20 in. min, 30 in. max; handrails both sides extending 30 in. above upper floor.

FORMULAE:

$$Tread = T = 20 - \frac{4}{3}R$$

$$Riser = R = 15 - \frac{3}{4}T$$

Perpendicular distance, pitch line to handrail =

$$Q = X \div \sqrt{\left(\frac{R}{T}\right)^2 + 1}$$

TABLE III - RUNG LADDERS - 75° to 90°

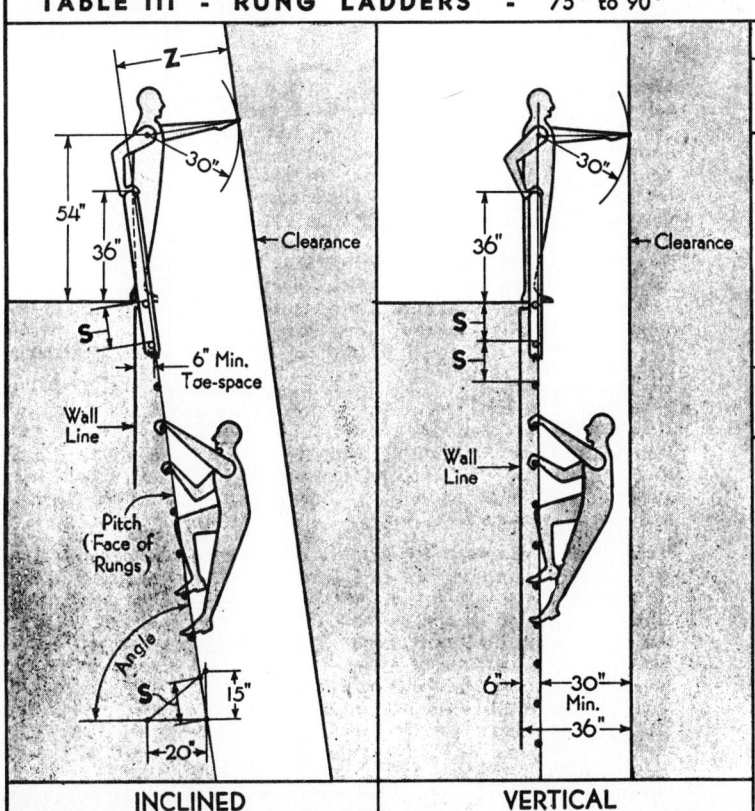

INCLINED	VERTICAL

	GRADIENT		RUNG SPACING S (inches)	CLEAR-ANCE Z (inches)
Pitch (ratio)	Grade (%)	Angle (deg. - min.)		
12 : 2½	480	78 – 14	13¼	41
12 : 2	600	80 – 33	13½	39
12 : 1½	800	82 – 53	13¾	37
12 : 1	1200	85 – 14	14¼	35
12 : ½	2400	87 – 37	14½	32
Vertical		90 – 0	15 maximum 12 minimum	30

NOTES:

Clearances and handrail heights may be determined graphically if desired. Ladder frame should extend 3'-0" above platform

Widths:

    Minimum = 15"
    Desirable = 18"
    Minimum between sidewalls = 24"

PURPOSE

Correct proportions and mandatory requirements for the design of interior fireplaces, smoke chambers and fireplace flues are indicated on Sheet 2.

GENERAL

Dimensions of correctly designed fireplaces are proportional within certain limits, the basis for proper proportions being the width of the fireplace opening. The accompanying table includes simple formulae for various widths. When followed within the limits indicated, adequate draft is assured, thus eliminating the smoke nuisance always present in poorly designed fireplaces.

CONSTRUCTION DETAILS

Fireplace. Design practice common to some localities has produced fireplaces with proportions other than those recommended on this sheet. Much variation, however, from the proportions indicated here will tend to interfere with proper draft. These dimensions are also recommended for the construction of fireplaces designed to throw a maximum of heat into the room. For fireplaces larger than 84 inches similar proportions should obtain. However, such fireplaces usually require metal hoods to lower the effective height (H). The same result may be obtained by raising the back hearth. Lowering the back hearth from 2″ to 4″ will aid in keeping ashes within the back-hearth area. Effective height of the fireplace (H) is always height of clear opening.

The reflecting wall at the back should always be built as a plane surface sloping up into the lower edge of the throat and terminating slightly above the level of the lintel. When the back is built in a vertical curve, air currents are deflected under the lintel, thus causing smoke to roll past the throat and into the room.

Throat. This should extend the full width of the fireplace opening. Limiting dimensions for throats are given in the table on the next page. Unless a metal throat (see below) or masonry arch is used, iron or steel is usually required to support masonry lintels. Maximum thickness of masonry at the lintel in front of the opening ranges from 4 to 6 inches depending on the material used.

Smoke Shelf (also called "wind shelf"). This element is required in all fireplaces to prevent downdraft in the chimney from destroying the updraft and thus blowing smoke into the room. In all cases, parging on the smoke shelf is recommended as indicated in the detail. When this is done the normal downdraft tends to circle up, to mingle with hot gases and aid updraft through the chimney flue. Otherwise, a pocket may be formed within the smoke chamber which may produce uneven, turbulent downdraft currents and consequently, a smoky fireplace.

A smoke chamber is an essential part of fireplace construction. It provides space for the smoke to mix with cold chimney air before the flue is sufficiently heated to carry heated gases up the chimney through normal convection. Actual construction will vary with the type of throat and the size of the fireplace. In all cases, however, the smoke chamber should be constructed with a 60° slope from throat to chimney flue as indicated in the accompanying drawings, and should have a smooth interior surface so as not to impede drafts.

Flues. The proper size of flue has an important bearing on efficient operation of the fireplace. When possible, round flues are preferable to square or oblong flues; and a flue lining is recommended for use with fireplaces of all types and sizes. Unlined flues are usually rough. Deposits of inflammable creosote distilled from fireplace fuels tend to form on rough surfaces, producing a constant fire hazard which should be avoided. Effective areas of flues, particularly the rectangular type, are always less than the actual cross-sectional inside area. Sizes of square and round flue linings and of unlined flues are shown in the accompanying table of recommended flue dimensions.

Clay flue lining should conform to ASTM Specification C315–56. Square and rectangular flue linings are normally designated by their outside dimensions, round flue linings by their inside diameters. Flue linings are also available in modular sizes for use with modular masonry, in conformance with ANSI A62.4 *Sizes of Clay Flue Lining*. Dimensions and effective areas of modular flue linings are shown in Table 1. Nonmodular sizes are shown in Tables 2 and 3. All tables are courtesy of the Clay Flue Lining Institute.

Ash dumps and pits. The ash dump should be fitted with a hinged cast-iron cover. It is common practice to locate the ash dump in the center of the back hearth. However, in certain cases where sub-construction makes it possible, the ash dump may be conveniently located on either side of the back hearth. The passage from ash dump to pit should be lined with at least an 8½″ x 8½″ flue tile if the pit is to serve more than one fireplace, or if it is not possible to construct a straight passage. Any bend in the ash passage should not be less than 60° to avoid the possibility of clogging. Floors of ash pits should be parged with mortar or otherwise sloped to a cast-iron cleanout door for convenience in removing ashes. The bottom of a cleanout door should be at least 8″ above the cellar floor to permit use of an ash receptacle when the pit is being cleaned.

Wood framing members must be kept at least 2″ away from all fireplace or chimney masonry. In addition, it is recommended that wood mantels and trim be kept 8″ back from the fireplace opening at the sides and 12″ clear above the opening, although custom or local ordinances often permit much less clearance.

Prefabricated fireplace equipment. All dimensions and details of construction shown on this sheet may be subject to some adjustment to conform to installation requirements of prefabricated metal dampers, throats, smoke chamber linings, ash dumps and cleanout doors. Each of these units is manufactured in a number of types. No common standard of dimensions has been established and manufacturers' data should be consulted in all cases prior to a selection for specific use.

Circulating fireplaces are also manufactured in a variety of types and sizes. Installation requirements of these units are also subject to variations noted and proportional dimensions given here should be carefully adjusted to their use in accordance with manufacturers' data.

Table 1. Square and rectangular clay flue linings—modular sizes

Minimum net inside area, sq in.	Nominal dimensions, in.*	Outside dimensions, in.	Minimum wall thickness, in.	Approx. maximum outside corner radius, in.
15	4x 8	3.5x 7.5	0.5	1
20	4x12	3.5x11.5	0.625	1
35	8x 8	7.5x 7.5	0.625	2
57	8x12	7.5x11.5	0.75	2
87	12x12	11.5x11.5	0.875	3
120	12x16	11.5x15.5	1.	3
162	16x16	15.5x15.5	1.125	4
208	16x20	15.5x19.5	1.25	4
262	20x20	19.5x19.5	1.375	5
320	20x24	19.5x23.5	1.5	5
385	24x24	23.5x23.5	1.625	6

* *Cross section of flue lining shall fit within rectangle of dimension corresponding to nominal size.*

Table 2. Square and rectangular clay flue linings—nonmodular sizes

Minimum net inside area, in.	Outside width of short side, in.	Outside width of long side, in.	Wall thickness, in.
22	4½	8½	⅝
36	4½	13	¾
51	8½	8½	¾
79	8½	13	⅞
108	8½	17¾	1
125	13	13	⅞
168	13	17¾	1
232	17¾	17¾	1¼
279	20	20	1⅜
338	20	24	1½
420	24	24	1⅝

Table 3. Round clay flue linings

Minimum net inside area, sq in.	Inside diameter, in.	Thickness, in.
26	6	⅝
47	8	¾
75	10	⅞
108	12	1
171	15	1⅛
240	18	1¼
330	21	1⅝
433	24	1¾
551	27	2
683	30	2⅛
990	36	2½

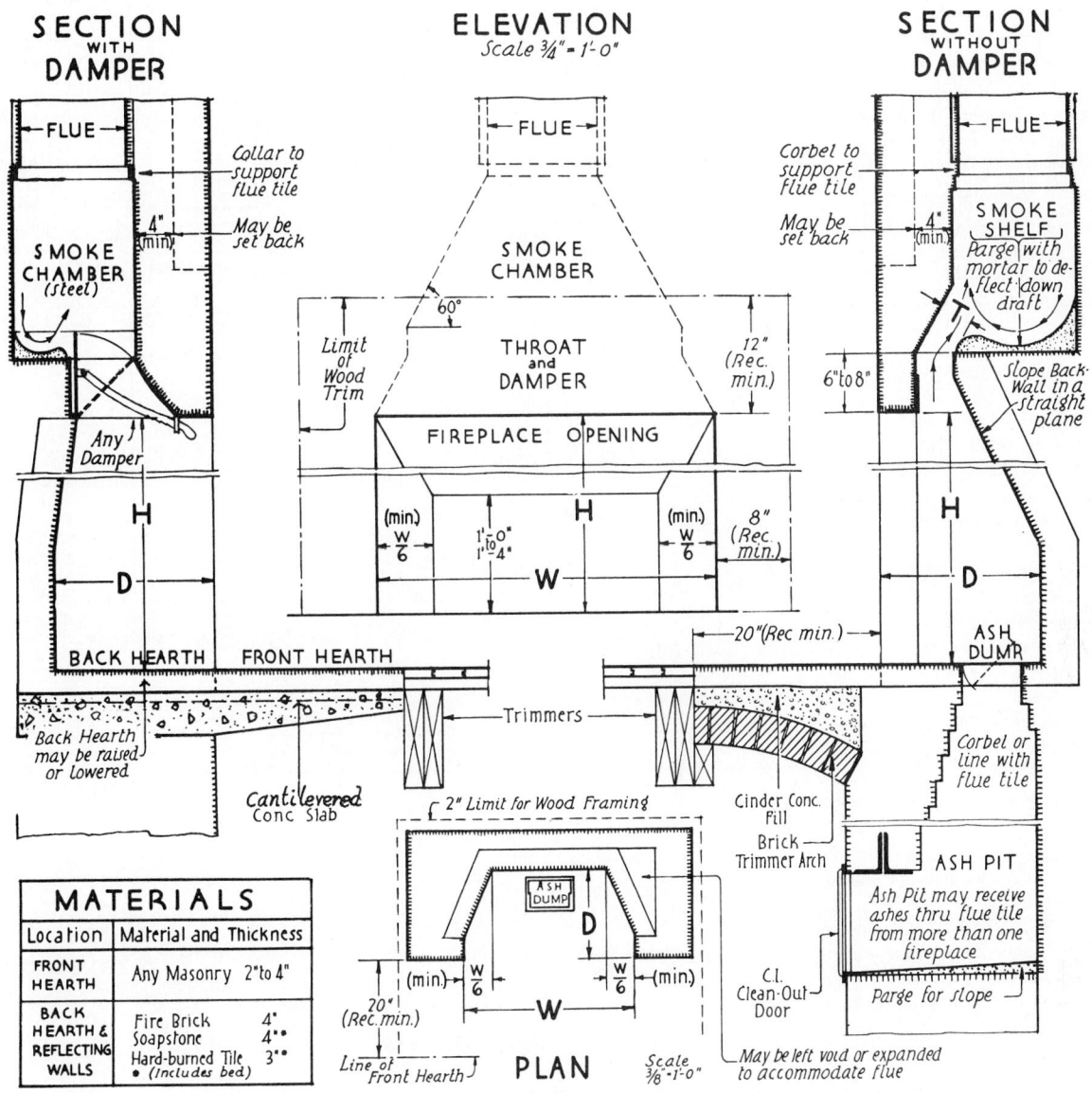

SECTION WITH DAMPER

FLUE

Collar to support flue tile

May be set back

4" (min.)

SMOKE CHAMBER (steel)

Any Damper

H

D

BACK HEARTH   FRONT HEARTH

Back Hearth may be raised or lowered

Cantilevered Conc. Slab

Trimmers

ELEVATION
Scale ¾" = 1'-0"

FLUE

SMOKE CHAMBER

60°

THROAT and DAMPER

FIREPLACE OPENING

Limit of Wood Trim

12" (Rec. min.)

(min.) W/6   1'-0" to 1'-4"   (min.) W/6   8" (Rec. min.)

H

W

20" (Rec. min.)

SECTION WITHOUT DAMPER

FLUE

Corbel to support flue tile

May be set back

4" (min.)

SMOKE SHELF

Parge with mortar to deflect down draft

6" to 8"

T

Slope Back Wall in a straight plane

H

D

ASH DUMP

Cinder Conc. Fill

Brick Trimmer Arch

C.I. Clean-Out Door

Corbel or line with flue tile

ASH PIT

Ash Pit may receive ashes thru flue tile from more than one fireplace

Parge for slope

May be left void or expanded to accommodate flue

PLAN
Scale ⅜" = 1'-0"

2" Limit for Wood Framing

ASH DUMP

D

(min.) W/6   W/6 (min.)

W

20" (Rec. min.)

Line of Front Hearth

MATERIALS	
Location	Material and Thickness
FRONT HEARTH	Any Masonry 2" to 4"
BACK HEARTH & REFLECTING WALLS	Fire Brick 4• Soapstone 4•• Hard-burned Tile 3•• • (Includes bed)

FIREPLACE DIMENSIONS (In Inches)		RECOMMENDED FLUE SIZES (In Inches)					
		FIREPLACE WIDTH **W**	RECTANGULAR FLUES			EQUIVALENT ROUND	
			Nominal or Outside Dimension	Inside Dimension	Effective Area	Inside Diameter	Effective Area
W	24 to 84						
H	⅔ to ¾ W	24	8½ x 8½	7¼ x 7¼	41••	8	50.3••
D	½ to ⅔ H {16 to 24 (Rec) for Coal / 18 to 24 (Rec) for Wood}	30 to 34	8½ x 13	7 x 11½	70••	10	78.54••
FLUE (Effective Area)	⅛ WH for unlined flue 1/10 WH for rectangular lining 1/12 WH for circular lining	36 to 44	13 x 13	11¼ x 11¼	99••	12	113.0••
		46 to 56	13 x 18	11¼ x 6¼	156••	15	176.7••
T (Area)	5/4 to 3/2 FLUE AREA	58 to 68	18 x 18	15¾ x 5¾	195••	18	254.4••
T (Width)	3" minimum to 4½" maximum	70 to 84	20 x 24	17 x 21	278••	22	380.13••

Data supplied by Steel Door Institute

Standard nomenclature for steel doors and frames, as proposed by the Steel Door Institute, is shown in Figs. 1 and 2, respectively.

Steel doors and frames should conform to one of the following commercial standards, published by the U.S. Department of Commerce:

CS242-62: Standard Stock Commercial 1¾-inch Thick Steel Doors and Frames*

PS4-66: Flush-type Interior Steel Doors and Frames

The principal provisions of CS242 are as follows:

Standard opening sizes are shown in Table 1. Doors are sized to fit these openings with ⅛ in. clearance at head and jambs and a maximum of ¾ in. at the sill.

Minimum steel thicknesses are shown in Table 2.

Flush doors may be of hollow steel construction or of composite metal face construction. In the latter type, the face sheets must be bonded to the core with waterproof adhesive and welded to perimeter channels on all four edges.

Frames may be of the knocked-down type or welded. In either case they must be rigid and present a neat appearance when erected. Frames must be provided with not less than three wall anchors per jamb and an anchor to the floor at each jamb. Anchors should be at least 18 gage (0.0449 in.) steel.

Doors and frames should be prepared to receive locks, strikes, and hinges. Mounting and location of locks should be in accordance with ANSI Specification for Door and Frame Preparation for Hardware, A115.1—A115.14. Lock and latch sets should conform to Federal Specification FF-H-00106b (Hardware, Builders'; Locks and Door Trim), Series 86 (Mortise locks), Series 90 (Mortise unit type locks), Series 140 (Mortise integral type locks), or Series 161 (Bored or cylindrical locks). Center line of strike should be located $40\frac{5}{16}$ in. above the finished floor. Provision should be made for three regular weight hinges, 4½ by 4½ in.

Performance tests for standard steel doors, frames, anchors, hinge reinforcings, and exit device reinforcings are given in ANSI A151.1—1969.

Interior steel doors (PS4-66) are of lighter construction and are not more than 3 ft wide. Standard opening sizes are shown in Table 3 and minimum steel thicknesses in Table 4.

Specifications for custom hollow metal doors and frames are published by National Association of Architectural Metal Manufacturers. Standards for architectural door trim are given in ANSI/BHMA 1001.

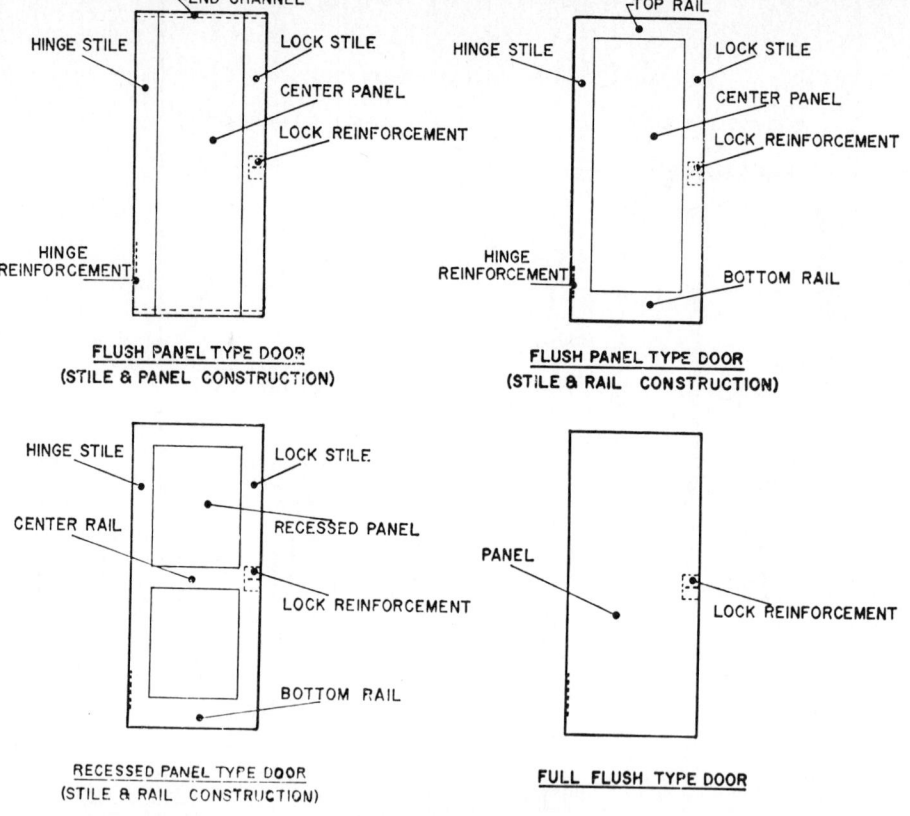

Fig. 1. Nomenclature for steel doors

From ANSI A123.1—1974

Table 1. Standard opening sizes (CS242-62)

WIDTH & HEIGHT	WIDTH & HEIGHT	WIDTH & HEIGHT
2'0" x 6'8"	2'0" x 7'0"	2'0" x 7'2"
2'4" x 6'8"	2'4" x 7'0"	2'4" x 7'2"
2'6" x 6'8"	2'6" x 7'0"	
2'8" x 6'8"	2'8" x 7'0"	2'8" x 7'2"
3'0" x 6'8"	3'0" x 7'0"	3'0" x 7'2"
3'4" x 6'8"	3'4" x 7'0"	3'4" x 7'2"
3'6" x 6'8"	3'6" x 7'0"	
3'8" x 6'8"	3'8" x 7'0"	3'8" x 7'2"
4'0" x 6'8"	4'0" x 7'0"	4'0" x 7'2"

[1] Sizes shown are for single doors only, for pairs of doors use twice the width indicated.

Table 2. Thickness of steel for component parts (CS242-62)

	Minimum gage of sheet metal	
	Gage No.	Equivalent Gage thickness
Door Frames	16	0.0598
Reinforcements for surface applied hardware	16	.0598
Doors—hollow steel construction Panels and stiles	18	.0478
Reinforcements for surface applied hardware	16	.0598
Doors—composite construction		
Perimeter channel	18	.0478
Surface sheets	22	.0299
Lock and strike reinforcements	16	.0598
Hinge reinforcements	[3]10	.1345
Flush bolt reinforcements	16	.0598
Glass moldings	20	.0359
Glass muntins	22	.0299

Table 3. Standard opening sizes (PS4-66)

1⅜-in.-thick doors	1¾-in.-thick doors
2'0'' x 6'8''	2'6'' x 6'8''
2'4'' x 6'8''	2'8'' x 6'8''
2'6'' x 6'8''	3'0'' x 6'8''
2'8'' x 6'8''	
3'0'' x 6'8''	2'6'' x 7'0''
	2'8'' x 7'0''
	3'0'' x 7'0''

Table 4. Thickness of steel for component parts (PS4-66)

Item	Gage	Equivalent thickness
	No.	*Inch*
Frames, 1⅜ in. thick	18	0. 0478
Frames, 1¾ in. thick	16	. 0598
Stiles for doors	20	. 0359
Panels for doors	20	. 0359
Lock and strike reinforcements	16	. 0598
Hinge reinforcements	11	. 1196
Closer reinforcements	14	. 0747

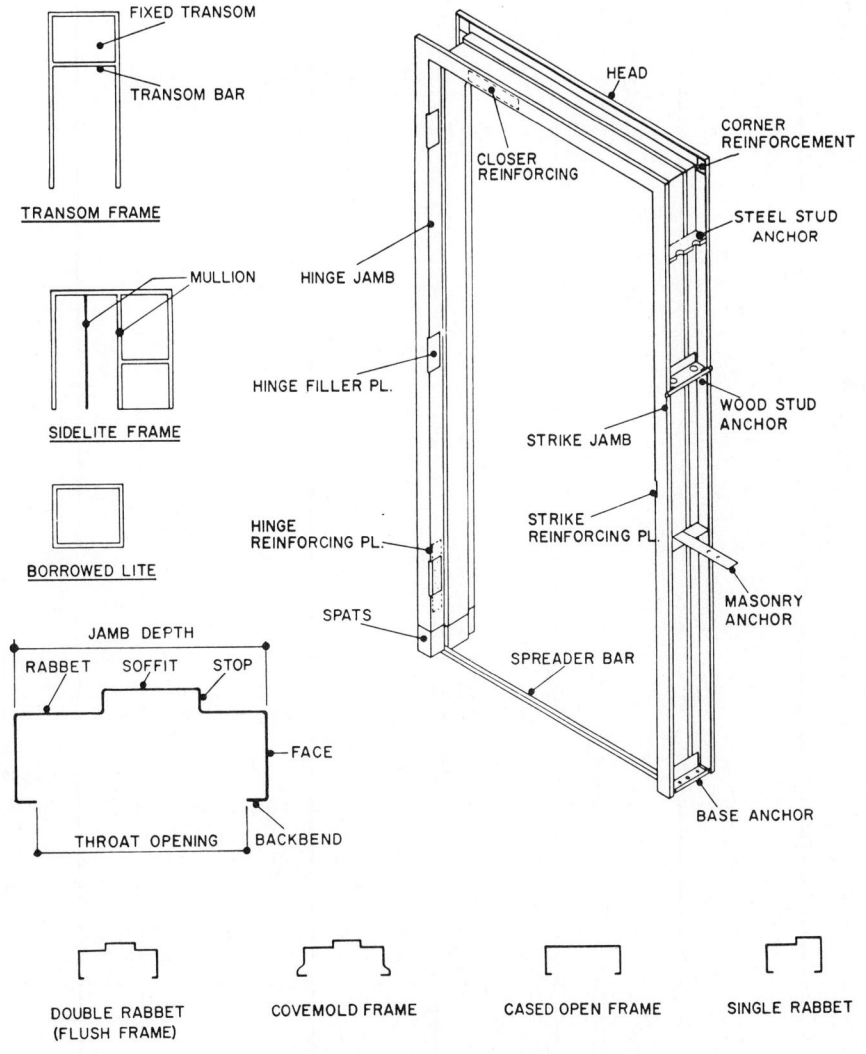

Fig. 2. Nomenclature for steel door frames

From ANSI A123.—1974

PLASTER CRACKING

The control of chip cracking of plaster at steel door frames requires simple attention to a few details in design and specifications. If the door frame is free to twist upon impact or the trim returns are free to vibrate, the movement of the frame will loosen small pieces of finish coat and base coat plaster, and unsightly spalling will result.

The following comments and sketches illustrate the improper elements as well as the suggested recommendations, which are the result of field inspection of good and bad installations together with laboratory and field experiments.

The basic considerations are relatively simple:

1. The frame must be securely anchored in place.
2. The partition must enter the frame so that the two work as a unit. This includes both the structural elements of the partition, the plaster base and the plaster.
3. Vibration of the frame, especially the trim returns, must be dampened.
4. The steel door frame must be sufficiently wide to allow full plaster grounds.

Ear cracking off the corners of a door frame is not controlled as easily as chip cracking. The cause of ear cracking is difficult to isolate. It occurs in reinforced concrete walls, masonry walls and lath and plaster constructions. Apparently impact alone is not the cause since cracking will occur over the openings prior to installation of the doors.

The continuity of the wall or partition is broken by the opening and the weakest plane of the construction is at the opening. Ear cracking can be minimized by attention to the construction at the head of framed opening; the following details are important:

Masonry

1. Workmanship — Masonry units should be laid up with proper bond, full mortar bed and end joints.
2. Lintels should be used over all openings and not supported by the head of the steel door frame. The lintels should extend out from the door jamb sufficiently to eliminate a weak vertical joint adjacent to the face of the door jamb.
3. Reinforce the base coat plaster at the corner of door frame by using self-furring metal lath, 12 in. by 18 in., diagonally at the corner. The dimple of the self-furring metal lath holds the mesh out into the face of the base coat plaster, where the reinforcement is needed.

Studs (Steel or Wood)

1. Gypsum Lath in 16 in. by 96 in. sheets should be used over door frames to eliminate butt joints over or closely adjacent to the door frame.
2. Reinforce the base coat plaster by stapling a 12 by 18-in. piece of self-furring metal lath diagonally over the corners of the door frame. The self-furring metal lath will hold the mesh out at the face of the base coat plaster where the reinforcing is effective. Conventional diamond mesh lath flat against the lath is ineffective.

PLASTER GROUNDS

Masonry Partitions — Plaster grounds on all masonry partitions are ⅝ in.

Metal Lath — Plaster grounds are ⅝ in. from the face of the metal lath. Diamond mesh metal lath and plaster totals ¾ in.

Gypsum Lath — Plaster grounds are ½ in. from face of lath; plaster and lath = ⅞ in.

Note: Because gypsum is rigid and can be held away from structural members by attachment shoes, wire ties, etc., the overall thickness of the gypsum and plaster over *steel studs* must be detailed as 1 *in.*

PARTITION THICKNESS

Masonry	Partition
3 in.	4¼ in.
4 in.	5¼ in.
6 in.	7¼ in.
8 in.	9¼ in.

Steel Studs	Dia. Mesh Lath and Plaster	Gypsum Lath or ⅜ in. Rib-lath and Plaster
2½ in.	4 in.	4½ in.
3¼ in.	4¾ in.	5¼ in.
4 in.	5½ in.	6 in.
6 in.	7½ in.	8 in.

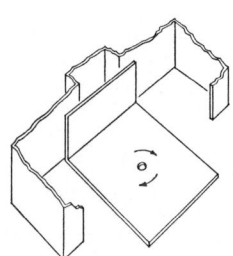

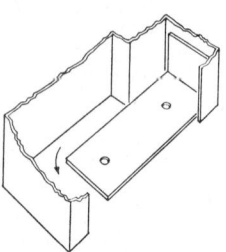

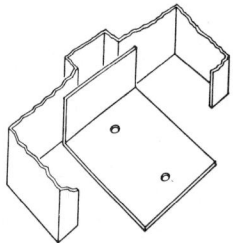

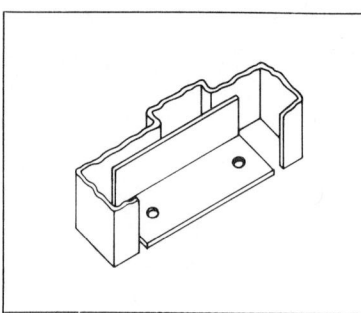

BASE PLATES

Very Poor (Top left) Single pin allows door frame to pivot on impact. Trim returns acting as plaster stops are free to vibrate on impact. All contribute to chip cracking and plaster spalling

Poor (Above) The double pin resists twisting of frame; since it is only attached to the jamb face it leaves trim returns free to vibrate on impact

Very Poor (left) Double pin holds the base plate from pivoting but the frame is anchored at one edge and twists. The end trim return is free to vibrate on impact

Good Base plate anchored with double pins resists twisting of frame

ANCHORAGES

Very Poor Concrete nails have short penetration and cause spalling making a very insecure attachment

Very Good Ackerman, rawl or plastic screw anchors provide secure attachment

Very Good Powder actuated drives provide secure anchorage

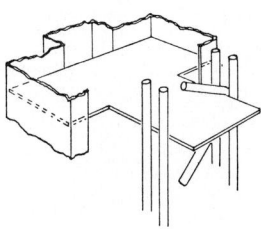

Very Poor Wire tying a stud strut to a loose masonry anchor makes an insecure attachment. The stud is outside the frame and will not resist twisting. The anchor doesn't prevent vibration of the trim returns

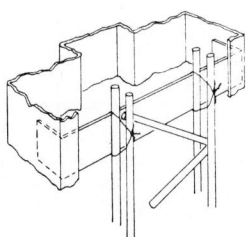

Poor Strap insert ties the trim returns together and dampens the vibration, but saddle tying the strut to the flat strap does not prevent the frame from sliding on impact

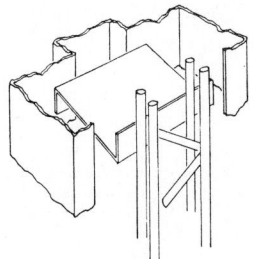

Very Poor The Z-shaped clip provides poor anchorage for the strut and fails to tie the trim returns together

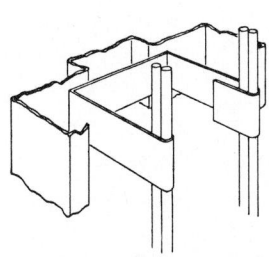

Very Poor Wrap around strap allows frame to shift on impact, and the trim returns are free to vibrate

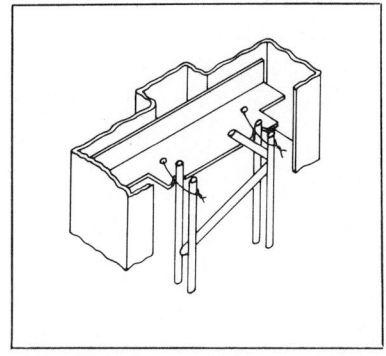

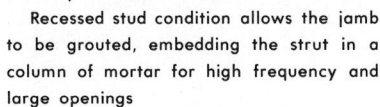

Very Good Anchor welded to rabbet of frame notched to provide full plaster penetration. Wire stud is nested in notches and securely wire-tied to the anchor.

Recessed stud condition allows the jamb to be grouted, embedding the strut in a column of mortar for high frequency and large openings

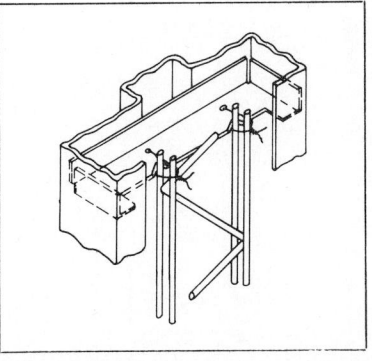

Very Good Lock-in anchor has same advantages as welded-in anchors, with greater flexibility. Additional anchors can be added or relocated to suit the door opening requirements

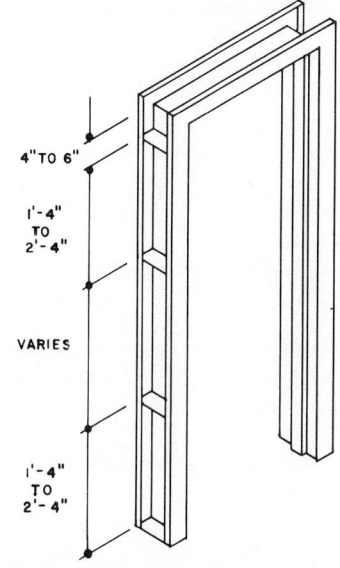

4" TO 6"

1'-4"
TO
2'-4"

VARIES

1'-4"
TO
2'-4"

* May vary with door height

Good Minimum of three jamb anchors spaced as shown and one base anchor. For frames over 7 ft 6 in. in height, use four jamb anchors per jamb

RECOMMENDED INSTALLATION

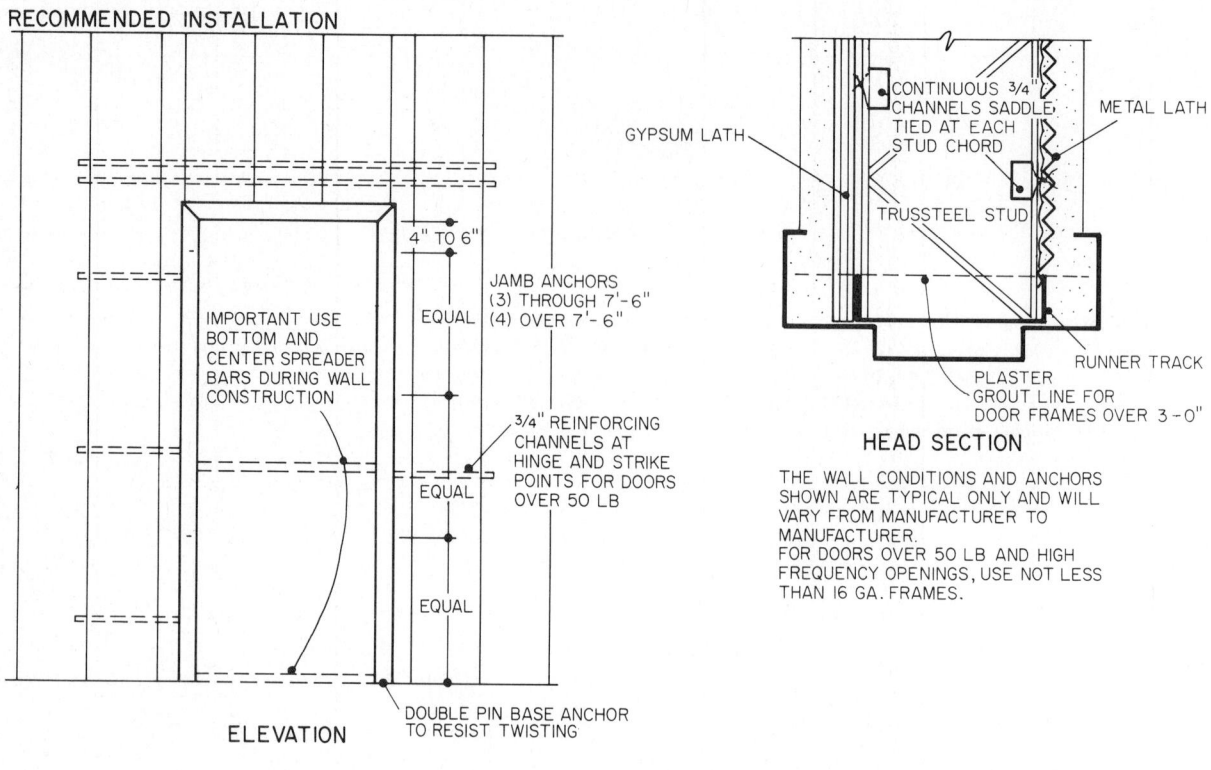

ELEVATION

IMPORTANT USE BOTTOM AND CENTER SPREADER BARS DURING WALL CONSTRUCTION

4" TO 6"

JAMB ANCHORS (3) THROUGH 7'-6" (4) OVER 7'-6"

EQUAL

EQUAL

EQUAL

3/4" REINFORCING CHANNELS AT HINGE AND STRIKE POINTS FOR DOORS OVER 50 LB

DOUBLE PIN BASE ANCHOR TO RESIST TWISTING

HEAD SECTION

GYPSUM LATH

CONTINUOUS 3/4" CHANNELS SADDLE TIED AT EACH STUD CHORD

METAL LATH

TRUSSTEEL STUD

RUNNER TRACK

PLASTER GROUT LINE FOR DOOR FRAMES OVER 3-0"

THE WALL CONDITIONS AND ANCHORS SHOWN ARE TYPICAL ONLY AND WILL VARY FROM MANUFACTURER TO MANUFACTURER.
FOR DOORS OVER 50 LB AND HIGH FREQUENCY OPENINGS, USE NOT LESS THAN 16 GA. FRAMES.

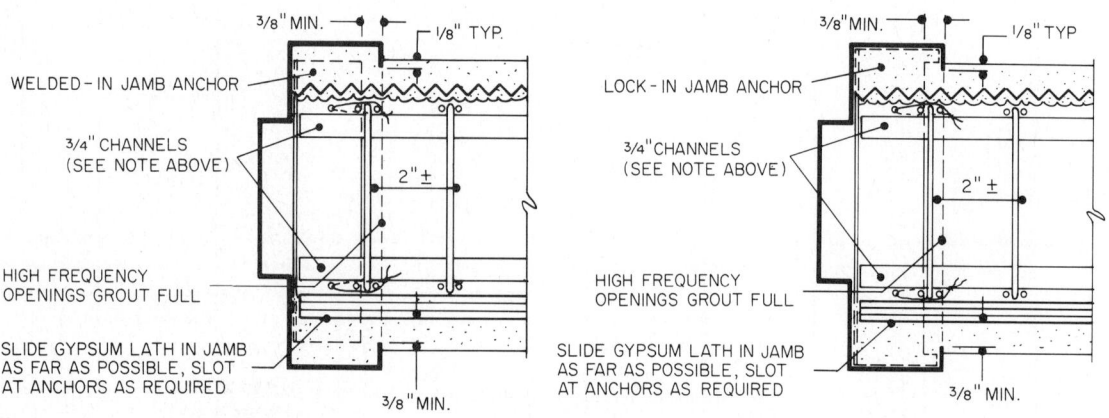

3/8" MIN.　1/8" TYP.

WELDED-IN JAMB ANCHOR

3/4" CHANNELS (SEE NOTE ABOVE)

2"±

HIGH FREQUENCY OPENINGS GROUT FULL

SLIDE GYPSUM LATH IN JAMB AS FAR AS POSSIBLE, SLOT AT ANCHORS AS REQUIRED

3/8" MIN.

3/8" MIN.　1/8" TYP

LOCK-IN JAMB ANCHOR

3/4" CHANNELS (SEE NOTE ABOVE)

2"±

HIGH FREQUENCY OPENINGS GROUT FULL

SLIDE GYPSUM LATH IN JAMB AS FAR AS POSSIBLE, SLOT AT ANCHORS AS REQUIRED

3/8" MIN.

JAMB SECTIONS

NOT RECOMMENDED INSTALLATION

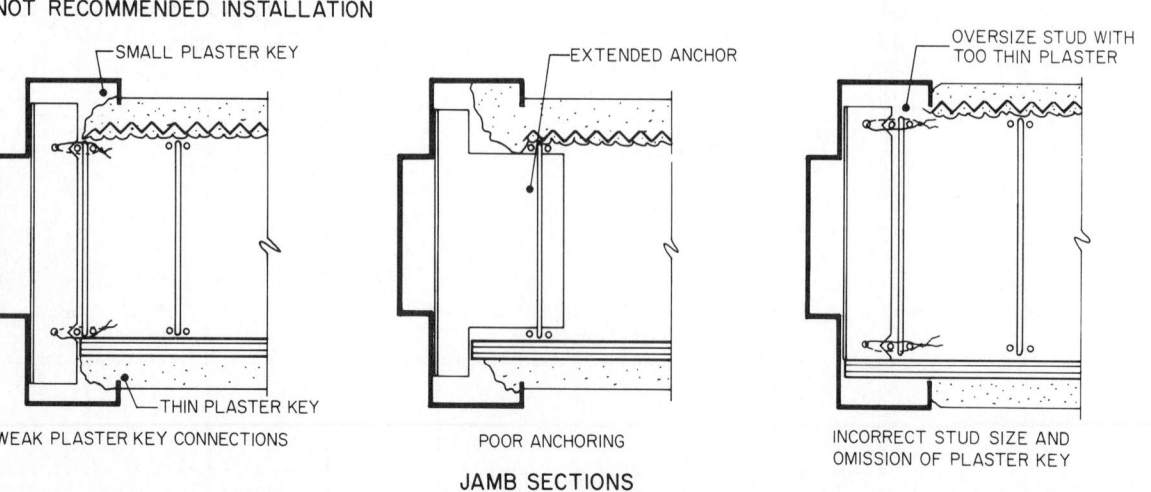

SMALL PLASTER KEY

THIN PLASTER KEY

WEAK PLASTER KEY CONNECTIONS

EXTENDED ANCHOR

POOR ANCHORING

OVERSIZE STUD WITH TOO THIN PLASTER

INCORRECT STUD SIZE AND OMISSION OF PLASTER KEY

JAMB SECTIONS

By SEYMOUR HOWARD, *Architect, Associate Professor, Pratt Institute*

The following data on hardware have been prepared in cooperation with the American Society of Architectural Hardware Consultants and the Builders Hardware Manufacturers Association.

FINISHES

The finish of the metal must be carefully distinguished from the base metal. Some finishes can be obtained by electroplating on a different metal; indeed, for some finishes (such as chromium) this is the only method. A magnet can be used to detect iron or steel base metal beneath the plating.

DURABILITY

The durability of the finish is greater on unplated metals, when the finishing process is applied directly to the base metal. Non-ferrous base metals and stainless steels finished in natural color are the most durable. Improvements in chromium plating make this a long-lasting finish.

BASE METAL

The base metal may be either wrought (fabricated) from thin sheet material or extruded, forged, or cast. Cast designs are usually heavier and more expensive.

STANDARD FINISHES

The Builders Hardware Manufacturers Association standard lists 88 finishes; the federal specification about one quarter of that number. The table above gives a selection of the finishes most often used, listed by BHMA number followed by the nearest equivalent US number. The BHMA code, unlike the federal specification, assigns separate numbers to finishes applied to each separate base material except when brass or bronze can be used without affecting the final finish.

Samples of finishes in categories A and B together with selected samples from category C are available for purchase at the BHMA office, 60 East 42 Street, New York, N.Y. 10017.

Comparative finishes should match when viewed approximately 2 ft apart and 3 ft away on the same plane and under the same environment.

BHMA categories are defined as follows:
A. Those that will match BHMA match plates when viewed according to the formula described above.
B. Those that are unstable and vary when

Table 1. Standard finishes for builders' hardware

From BHMA Materials and Finishes Standard 1301; 1969

BHMA code	Nearest U.S. equivalent*	Finish description	Base material	BHMA category
600	USP	Primed for painting	Steel	D
601	US1B	Bright japanned	Steel	D
602	US2C	Cadmium plated	Steel	D
603	US2G	Zinc plated	Steel	D
605	US3	Bright brass, clear-coated	Brass	A
606	US4	Satin brass, clear-coated	Brass	A
609	US5	Satin brass, blackened, satin-relieved, clear-coated	Brass	C
611	US9	Bright bronze, clear-coated	Bronze	A
612	US10	Satin bronze, clear-coated	Bronze	A
613	US10B	Oxidized satin bronze, oil-rubbed	Bronze	B
616	US11	Satin bronze, blackened, satin-relieved, clear-coated	Bronze	C
618	US14	Bright nickel-plated, clear-coated	Brass, bronze	A
619	US15	Satin nickel-plated, clear-coated	Brass, bronze	A
622	US19	Flat black-coated	Brass, bronze	A
624	US20A	Dark oxidized, statuary bronze, clear-coated	Bronze	C
625	US26	Bright chromium-plated	Brass, bronze	A
626	US26D	Satin chromium-plated	Brass, bronze	A
627	US27	Satin aluminum, clear-coated	Aluminum	A
628	US28	Satin aluminum, clear-anodized	Aluminum	A
629	US32	Bright stainless steel	Stainless steel 300 series	A
630	US32D	Satin stainless steel	Stainless steel 300 series	A

* *Federal Specification (interim) FF-H-00106b, 1967.*

applied to different alloys and forms of base metal. These finishes are compatible with the BHMA match plates, but it is to be understood that these finishes cannot and do not match from one alloy or form of metal to the next and from one manufacturer to the next.
C. Includes ornamental finishes found on all forms of metal. The metal is blackened or oxidized or relieved or highlighted, usually by hand. Aesthetically, it is not desirable that they match but they should be compatible.
D. A functional protective finish in which appearance is not a factor.

Practically all metals used are alloys of two or more elements, and each manufacturer may vary the chemical analyses of his alloys. Brass is essentially an alloy of copper and zinc. Technically, bronze is a copper-tin alloy; commercially, however, the term includes not only copper-tin alloys but also certain copper-zinc alloys having

a typical bronze color. White bronze refers to a large number of copper-nickel-zinc alloys in which the copper predominates. Monel-metal, a nickel-copper alloy in which the nickel is 67 per cent, is well known for its great durability and corrosion resistance.

Aluminum is widely used as a hardware metal, with various alloys being employed to produce cast, wrought, extruded, or forged members. Exposed surfaces are usually given an anodic treatment which produces a surface film that preserves the original color.

Stainless steel is increasingly employed despite its relatively high cost. No surface treatment other than polishing or scouring is needed, nor is maintenance required to preserve this finish. Hardware in this metal is usually produced from sheets or extrusions, although some casting has been achieved. Its strength, durability, and resistance to corrosion make it highly desirable for heavy-duty use.

Conventions for the hand of hardware must be determined accurately so that there is no misunderstanding between specification writer, dealer, and manufacturer.

Hardware in general is of three main types: universal, reversible, and handed.

1. *Universal* can be used in any position (example, door stop).

2. *Reversible* can have the "hand" changed by revolving from left to right or by turning upside down or by reversing some part of the mechanism (example, many types of locks and latches).

3. *Handed* (not reversible) can be used only on doors of the hand for which the hardware is designed (example, most bevel or rabbeted front locks and latches, loose-joint butt hinges).

Although the hardware item specified may be reversible, or even universal, it is safe practice to state the hand completely, in accordance with the conventions shown here.

For all doors (except casements and doors with cremone bolts) the hand is determined from the outside. The outside is the side from which security is necessary. In a series of connecting rooms (as for a hotel suite) the outside will be the side of each successive door as you come to it proceeding from the entrance in. For two rooms of equal importance with a passage between, the outside is the passage side.

Strictly speaking, the door itself is only right or left hand; the locks and latches may be reverse bevel. It is best, however, to include the term reverse bevel and to specify in accordance with the conventions shown here. The specification writer can thus prevent any confusion over which side is the outside, particularly important when "split finishes" are desired. This method also places the responsibility for the correct choice on the hardware dealer or manufacturer.

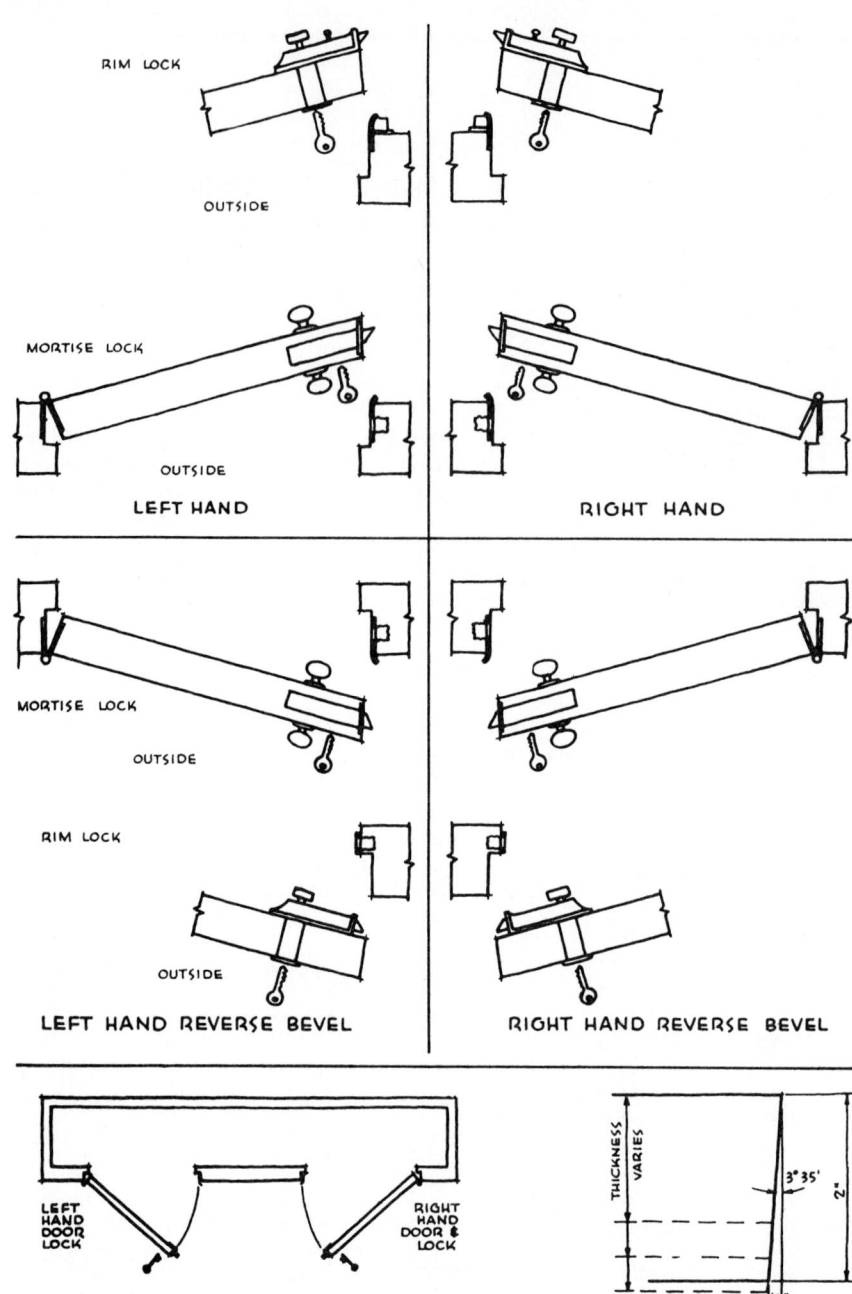

LEFT HAND

RIGHT HAND

LEFT HAND REVERSE BEVEL

RIGHT HAND REVERSE BEVEL

CUPBOARDS, CABINETS, BOOKCASES
Note: Refrigerator doors follow these conventions

STANDARD BEVEL

THUMB LATCH

Oldest type; simple to install; difficult to adjust; may be padlocked. Made generally. Often used instead of outside knob for period front doors.

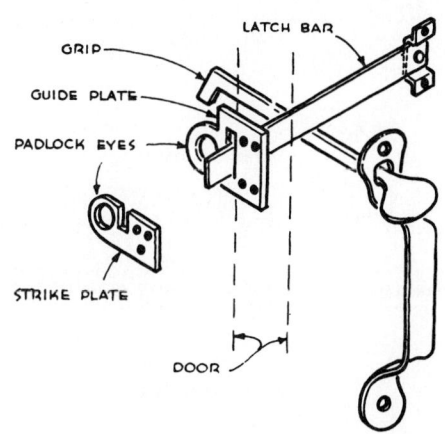

RIM LOCKS & LATCHES

Case and strike both mounted on face of door and trim without mortising; colonial design.

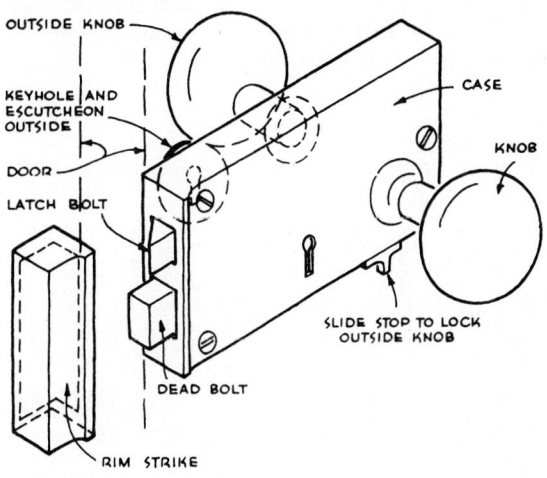

OTHER TYPES, SUCH AS RIM NIGHT LATCHES, OFTEN USED IN REMODELING WORK.

MORTISE LOCKS & LATCHES

Developed historically from rim types; wood doors must be mortised to receive it; hollow metal doors are easily fabricated to template to receive case, cylinder and spindle. Size of case and accessibility of mechanism make economically possible the maximum number and variety of key and latch functions. Made generally.

INTEGRAL LOCKS AND LATCHES
A mortise-type lock with integral front and lock in knob; factory assembled.

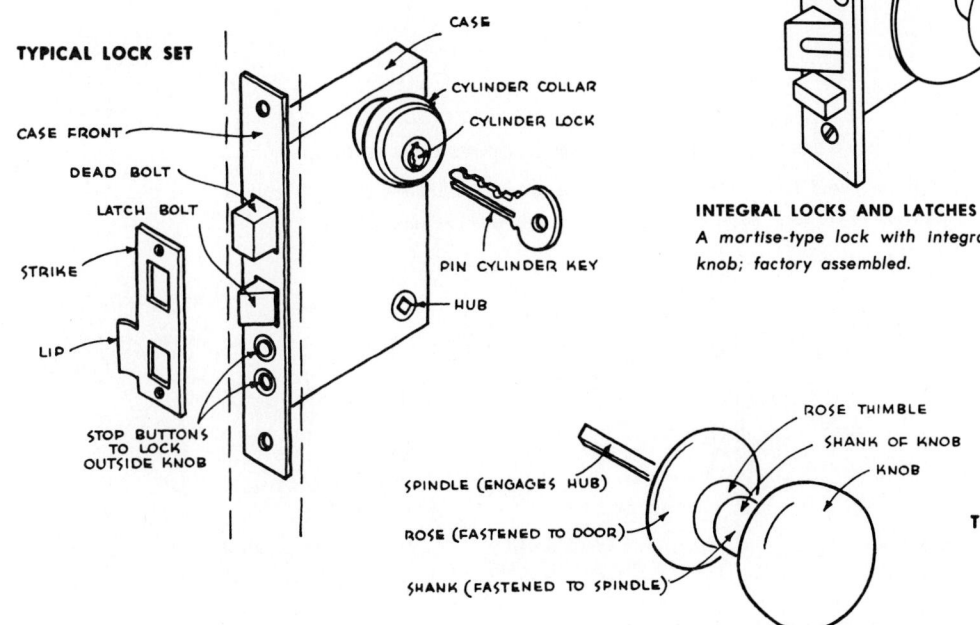

Note: *For mounting height, see sheet 19.*

PREASSEMBLED (UNIT) LOCKS & LATCHES

Complete factory assembly eliminates much adjustment on job. Unit slid into notch cut on job (wood) or prepared at shop (metal doors). Dead bolt may be omitted to make simple latch set to match. Lock-set also made without dead bolt but with button in inside knob to prevent outside knob from turning (for bathroom, bedroom, etc.); made by relatively few manufacturers; available in heavy duty only.

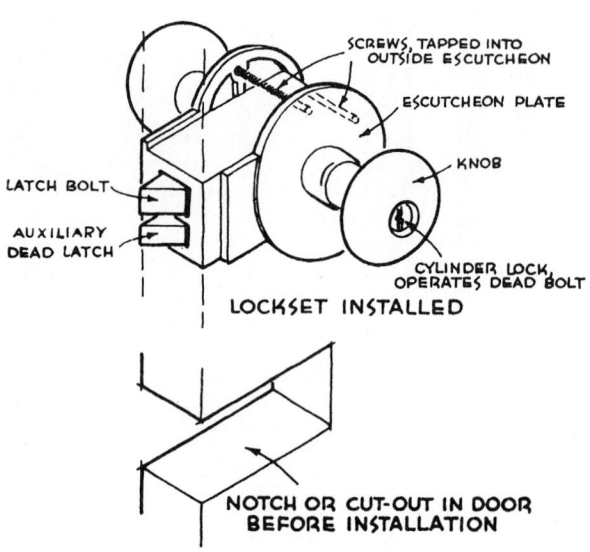

LATCH BOLT
AUXILIARY DEAD LATCH
SCREWS, TAPPED INTO OUTSIDE ESCUTCHEON
ESCUTCHEON PLATE
KNOB
CYLINDER LOCK, OPERATES DEAD BOLT

LOCKSET INSTALLED

NOTCH OR CUT-OUT IN DOOR BEFORE INSTALLATION

BACKSETS & PROJECTIONS

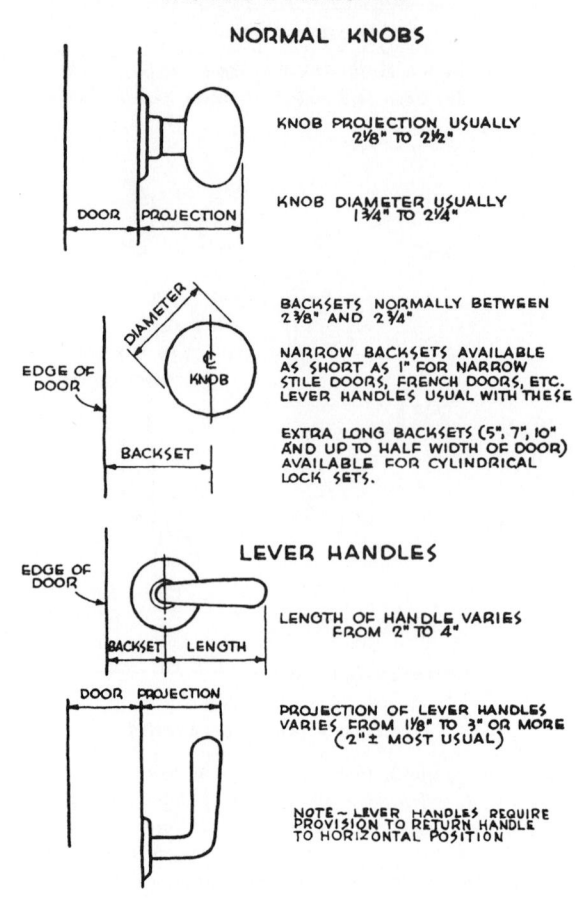

NORMAL KNOBS

DOOR | PROJECTION

KNOB PROJECTION USUALLY 2⅛" TO 2½"

KNOB DIAMETER USUALLY 1¾" TO 2¼"

DIAMETER — € KNOB

EDGE OF DOOR

BACKSET

BACKSETS NORMALLY BETWEEN 2⅜" AND 2¾"

NARROW BACKSETS AVAILABLE AS SHORT AS 1" FOR NARROW STILE DOORS, FRENCH DOORS, ETC. LEVER HANDLES USUAL WITH THESE

EXTRA LONG BACKSETS (5", 7", 10" AND UP TO HALF WIDTH OF DOOR) AVAILABLE FOR CYLINDRICAL LOCK SETS.

LEVER HANDLES

EDGE OF DOOR
BACKSET | LENGTH

LENGTH OF HANDLE VARIES FROM 2" TO 4"

DOOR | PROJECTION

PROJECTION OF LEVER HANDLES VARIES FROM 1⅛" TO 3" OR MORE (2"± MOST USUAL)

NOTE – LEVER HANDLES REQUIRE PROVISION TO RETURN HANDLE TO HORIZONTAL POSITION

BORE-IN LOCKS & LATCHES (TUBULAR & CYLINDRICAL TYPES)

Simple to install in wood doors; only two holes to bore and shallow mortise for case front; metal doors also can be easily fabricated to receive these types.

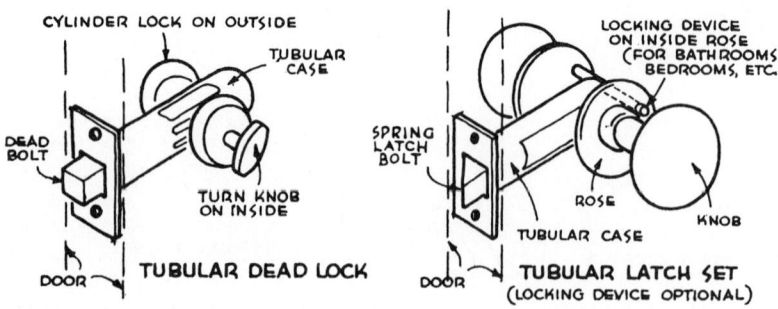

CYLINDER LOCK ON OUTSIDE
TUBULAR CASE
DEAD BOLT
TURN KNOB ON INSIDE
DOOR

TUBULAR DEAD LOCK

LOCKING DEVICE ON INSIDE ROSE (FOR BATHROOMS, BEDROOMS, ETC.)
SPRING LATCH BOLT
ROSE
TUBULAR CASE
KNOB
DOOR

TUBULAR LATCH SET (LOCKING DEVICE OPTIONAL)

CYLINDRICAL CASE
LOCKING BUTTON IN KNOB; CYLINDER (PIN OR WAFER) LOCK CAN ALSO BE USED HERE
DEADLOCKING LATCH BOLT

CYLINDRICAL LOCK SET
ALSO AVAILABLE AS SIMPLE LATCH SET
AVAILABLE WITH LONG (5", 7", 10" ETC.) BACKSET

SEPARATE TUBULAR LOCK SETS AND LATCH SETS MADE BY MANY MANUFACTURERS.

THIS TYPE MADE TO DATE ONLY BY A FEW MANUFACTURERS.

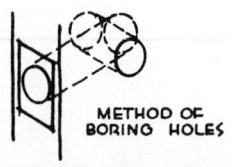

METHOD OF BORING HOLES

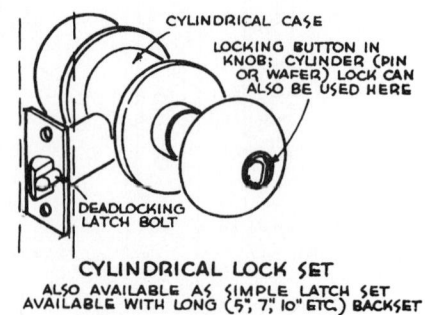

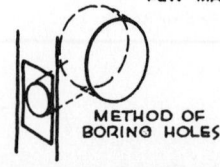

METHOD OF BORING HOLES

Table 2. Lock functions

From *ANSI/BHMA 601—1975, LOCKS AND LOCK TRIM; MORTISE LOCKS AND LATCHES, Federal specification number: series 85, 86, and 87 (fire doors)*

BHMA number	Mortise locks and latches—description of functions	BHMA number	Mortise locks and latches—description of functions
F01	Passage or Closet Latch: Latch bolt operated by knob from either side at all times.	F14	Store Door Lock: Latch bolt operated by knob from either side. Dead bolt operated by key from either side.
F02	Privacy, Bedroom or Bath Lock: Latch bolt operated by knob from either side. Dead bolt operated by turn from inside and by emergency key from outside.	F15	Hotel Guest Room Lock: Latch bolt operated by key from outside or by rotating inside knob. Outside knob is always inoperative. Dead bolt operated by turn from inside which shuts out all keys except emergency and display key. Auxiliary dead latch. Indicator button. When so specified, inside knob will retract both bolts.
F03	Communicating Lock: Latch bolt operated by knob from either side. Two dead bolts or split dead bolt operated independently by turns from both sides. Should not be used on doors in rooms that have no other entrance.	F16	Dead Lock: Dead bolt operated by key from either side.
F04	Entry Lock: Latch bolt operated by knob from either side except when outside knob is made inoperative by a stop or mechanical means other than key. When outside knob is locked, latch bolt may be retracted by key from outside or by rotating inside knob. Auxiliary dead latch.	F17	Dead Lock: Dead bolt operated by key from outside and by turn from inside.
		F18	Dead Lock: Dead bolt operated by key from outside only.
F05	Classroom Lock: Latch bolt operated by knob from either side except when outside knob is locked from outside by key. When outside knob is locked, latch bolt may be retracted by key from outside or by rotating inside knob. Auxiliary dead latch.	F24	Apartment or Store Doorhandle Lock: Latch bolt operated by thumb piece on both sides except when outside thumb piece is locked by key from inside. When outside thumb piece is locked, latch bolt may be retracted by key outside or by thumb piece inside. Auxiliary dead latch.
F06	Classroom or Hospital Lock: Latch bolt operated by knob from either side except when outside knob is locked from outside by key. Latch bolt may be locked in a retracted position by key. When outside knob is locked, latch bolt may be retracted by key from outside or by rotating inside knob unless latch bolt has been locked in a retracted position. Auxiliary dead latch.	F25	Store Doorhandle Lock: Latch bolt operated by thumb piece from either side. Dead bolt operated by key from either side.
F07	Storeroom or Closet Lock: Latch bolt operated by key from outside or by rotating inside knob. Outside knob is always inoperative. Auxiliary dead latch.		

Note: The preassembled lock is available only in Grade #1 (Heavy duty). Federal specification number: series 90 and 98 (fire doors)

BHMA number	Mortise locks and latches—description of functions	BHMA number	Preassembled (unit) locks and latches—description of functions
F08	Front Door Lock: Latch bolt operated by knob from either side except when outside knob is made inoperative by a stop or mechanical means other than key. Dead bolt operated by turn inside. Key outside operates both bolts. Rotating inside knob always operates latch bolt.	F36	Passage or Closet Latch Set: Latch bolt operated by knob from either side at all times.
F09	Apartment, Exit, or Public Toilet Lock: Latch bolt operated by knob from either side except when outside knob is locked by key from inside. When outside knob is locked, latch bolt may be retracted by key from outside or by rotating inside knob. Auxiliary dead latch.	F37	Privacy, Bedroom or Bath Lock: Latch bolt operated by knob from either side. Outside knob is locked by pushbutton inside and unlocked by emergency key outside, rotating inside knob, or closing door.
F10	Apartment Corridor Door Lock: Latch bolt operated by knob from either side except when outside knob is made inoperative by a stop or mechanical means other than key. Dead bolt operated by turn inside. Key outside operates both bolts. Dead bolt has 1 in. throw. Hardened steel rollers in bolt when so specified. Rotating inside knob always operates latch bolt.	F38	Patio or Privacy Lock: Latch bolt operated by knob from either side. Outside knob is locked by pushbutton inside and unlocked by rotating inside knob or closing door. Auxiliary dead latch. Should not be used on doors in rooms that have no other entrance.
F11	Dormitory or Exit Lock: Latch bolt operated by knob from either side except when outside knob is made inoperative by a stop or mechanical means other than key. Dead bolt projected by key from either side. Dead bolt retracted by key from outside. Both bolts retracted by inside knob.	F39	Communicating Lock: Latch bolt operated by knob from either side. Turn button in either knob locks or unlocks opposite knob. Auxiliary dead latch. Should not be used on doors in rooms that have no other entrance.
F12	Dormitory or Exit Lock: Latch bolt operated by knob from either side except when outside knob is made inoperative by a stop or mechanical means other than key. Dead bolt projected by key from outside and by turn from inside. Dead bolt retracted by key from outside. Both bolts retracted by inside knob.	F40	Entrance or Storeroom Lock: Latch bolt operated by knob from either side except when outside knob is locked by turn button in inside knob. When outside knob is locked, latch bolt may be retracted by key from outside or by rotating inside knob. Turn button must be manually rotated to unlock outside knob. Auxiliary dead latch.
F13	Dormitory or Exit Lock: Latch bolt operated by knob from either side. Dead bolt projected by key from outside and turn from inside. Rotating inside knob retracts both bolts.	F41	Entry Lock: Latch bolt operated by knob from either side except when outside knob is locked by pushbutton in inside knob. When outside knob is locked, operating key from outside or rotating inside knob retracts latch bolt and releases pushbutton. Closing door does not release pushbutton. Auxiliary dead latch.
		F42	Classroom Lock: Latch bolt operated by knob from either side except when outside knob is locked from outside by key. When outside knob is locked, latch bolt may be retracted by key from outside or by rotating inside knob. Auxiliary dead latch.

Table 2 (cont.). Lock functions

BHMA number	Preassembled (unit) locks and latches— description of functions
F43	Classroom or Hospital Lock: Latch bolt operated by knob from either side except when outside knob is locked from outside by key. Latch bolt may be locked in a retracted position by key. When outside knob is locked, latch bolt may be retracted by key from outside or by rotating inside knob unless latch bolt has been locked in a retracted position. Auxiliary dead latch.
F44	Storeroom or Closet Lock: Latch bolt operated by key from outside or by rotating inside knob. Outside knob is always fixed. Auxiliary dead latch.
F45	Apartment, Exit or Public Toilet Lock: Latch bolt operated by knob from either side, except when outside knob is locked by key from inside. When outside knob is locked, latch bolt may be retracted by key from outside or by rotating inside knob. Auxiliary dead latch.
F46	Store Door Lock: Latch bolt operated by knob from either side except when bolt knobs are locked by key from either side. Auxiliary dead latch.
F47	Store Door Lock: Latch bolt operated by knob from either side. Dead bolt operated by key from either side.
F48	Hotel Guest Room, Clubhouse, Dormitory, or Apartment Entrance Lock: Latch bolt operated by knob from inside at all times. Outside knob always fixed. Latch bolt by key from outside except when pushbutton inside is depressed, thus shutting out all keys except emergency key. Depressing pushbutton operates visual indicator in face of cylinder, showing room is occupied. Turning inside knob or closing door releases indicator and shut-out feature except when pushbutton is turned to shut-out position with special key, shutting out all keys except emergency key. Auxiliary dead latch.

Note: The integral type lock is available only in Grade #1 (Heavy duty) Functions 54, 55, and 56 available for 1⅜" thick doors; all functions available for 1¾" doors Federal specification number: series 140

BHMA number	Integral type locks and latches— description of functions
F54	Passage or Closet Latch: Latch bolt operated by knob from either side at all times.
F55	Privacy, Bedroom or Bath Lock: Latch bolt operated by knob from either side. Dead bolt operated by turn from inside and by emergency key from outside.
F56	Communicating Lock: Latch bolt operated by knob from either side. Two dead bolts operated independently by turns from both sides. Should not be used on doors in rooms that have no other entrance.
F57	Patio or Privacy Lock: Latch bolt operated by knob from either side except when outside knob is locked by stop in front. Rotating inside knob always operates latch bolt. Auxiliary dead latch.
F58	Patio or Play Court Lock: Latch bolt operated by knob from either side except when outside knob is locked from inside by key. Rotating inside knob always operates latch bolt. Auxiliary dead latch.
F59	Entry Lock: Latch bolt operated by knob from either side except when outside knob is locked by stop in front. When outside knob is locked, latch bolt may be retracted

BHMA number	Integral type locks and latches— description of functions
	by key from outside or by rotating inside knob. Auxiliary dead latch.
F60	Entrance or Storeroom Lock: Latch bolt operated by knob from either side. Dead bolt operated by key from outside or turn from inside.
F61	Classroom Lock: Latch bolt operated by knob from either side except when outside knob is locked from outside by key. When outside knob is locked, latch bolt may be retracted by key from outside or by rotating inside knob. Auxiliary dead latch.
F62	Classroom or Hospital Lock: Latch bolt operated by knob from either side except when outside knob is locked from outside by key. When outside knob is locked, latch bolt may be retracted by key from outside or by rotating inside knob. Auxiliary dead latch. Latch bolt and auxiliary dead latch may be locked in a retracted position by key.
F63	Storeroom or Closet Lock: Latch bolt operated by key from outside or by rotating inside knob. Outside knob is always fixed. Auxiliary dead latch.
F64	Utility, Asylum or Institutional Lock: Latch bolt operated by key from either side. Both knobs always fixed. Auxiliary dead latch.
F65	Front-door Lock: Latch bolt operated by knob from either side except when outside knob is locked by stop in front. Dead bolt operated by turn inside. Key outside operates both bolts. Rotating inside knob always operates latch bolt.
F66	Apartment, Exit, or Public Toilet Lock: Latch bolt operated by knob from either side except when outside knob is locked by key from inside. When outside knob is locked, latch bolt may be retracted by key from outside or by rotating inside knob. Auxiliary dead latch.
F67	Service Station or Exit Lock: Latch bolt operated by knob from inside. Outside knob is always fixed. Latch bolt operated from outside by key and from inside by knob. Dead bolt operated from outside by key and from inside by turn.
F68	Store Door Lock: Latch bolt operated by knob from either side. Dead bolt operated by key from either side.
F69	Hotel Guest Room Lock: Latch bolt operated by knob inside. Dead bolt operated from outside by all keys unless projected from inside by turn, then all keys are shut out except display and emergency keys. Emergency keys acts as shut-out key. Outside knob always fixed. Equipped with indicator button.

Federal specification number: series 150, 150Y, 159, 160, 161.

BHMA number	Bored locks and latches— description of functions
F75	Passage or Closet Latch: Latch bolt operated by knob from either side at all times.
F76	Privacy, Bedroom or Bath Lock: Latch bolt operated by knob from either side. Outside knob is locked by pushbutton inside and unlocked by emergency key outside, rotating inside knob, or closing door.

Table 2 (cont.).   Lock functions

BHMA number	Bored locks and latches—Description of functions	BHMA number	Bored locks and latches—description of functions
F76A	Privacy, Bedroom or Bath Lock: Latch bolt operated by knob from either side except when both knobs are in locked position by locking device on inner side. Locking device must be in unlocked position before inside knob can be operated. Emergency release on outside must permit outside knob to operate latch bolt.		button on inside knob. When knobs are locked, latch bolt is operated by key in outside knob. Turn button must be manually rotated to unlock knobs.
F76B	Privacy, Bedroom or Bath Lock: Latch bolt operated by knob from either side. Outside knob is locked by pushbutton inside and unlocked by emergency key outside, rotating inside knob and/or closing door.	F83	Exit Lock: Dead-locking latch bolt operated by knob from either side, except when outside knob is locked by turn button in inside knob. Turn button must be manually rotated to unlock outside knob. Rotating inside knob always operates latch bolt.
F77	Patio or Privacy Lock: Dead-locking latch bolt operated by knob from either side. Outside knob is locked by pushbutton inside and unlocked by rotating inside knob or closing door. Should not be used on doors in rooms that have no other entrance.	F84	Classroom Lock: Dead-locking latch bolt operated by knob from either side except when outside knob is locked from outside by key. When outside knob is locked, latch bolt is operated by key in outside knob or by rotating inside knob.
F77A	Patio or Privacy Lock: Dead-locking latch bolt operated by knob from either side, except when both knobs are in locked position by locking device on inner side. Locking device must be in the unlocked position before inside knob can be operated. Should not be used on doors in rooms that have no other entrance.	F85	Classroom or Hospital Lock: Dead-locking latch bolt operated by knob from either side except when outside knob is locked from outside by key. Latch bolt may be locked in a retracted position by key. When outside knob is locked, latch bolt is operated by key in outside knob or by rotating inside knob unless latch bolt has been locked in a retracted position.
F77B	Patio or Privacy Lock: Dead-locking latch bolt operated by knob from either side. Outside knob is locked by pushbutton inside and unlocked by rotating inside knob and/or closing door. Should not be used on doors in rooms that have no other entrance.	F86	Storeroom or Closet Lock: Dead-locking latch bolt operated by key in outside knob or by rotating inside knob. Outside knob is always fixed.
F78	Communicating Lock: Dead-locking latch bolt operated by knob from either side. Turn button in either knob locks or unlocks opposite knob. Should not be used on doors in rooms that have no other entrance.	F87	Utility, Asylum, or Institutional Lock: Dead-locking latch bolt operated by key in knob from either side. Both knobs always fixed.
F79	Communicating Lock: Dead-locking latch bolt operated from outside by knob and from inside by thumb turn. Turning button in knob locks both knob and thumb turn. Button does not release unless manually restored to unlocked position. Lock may be opened by manually restoring button to unlocked position.	F88	Apartment, Exit, or Public Toilet Lock: Dead-locking latch bolt operated by knob from either side, except when outside knob is locked by key from inside. When outside knob is locked, latch bolt may be retracted by key in outside knob or by rotating inside knob.
F80	Communicating Lock: Dead-locking latch bolt operated by knob from either side. Turning key in either knob locks or unlocks its own knob independently. Should not be used on doors in rooms that have no other entrance.	F89	Exit Latch: Dead-locking latch bolt retracted by knob from inside at all times. Outside knob is always fixed.
F81	Entrance or Storeroom Lock: Dead-locking latch bolt operated by knob from either side except when outside knob is locked by turn button in inside knob. When outside knob is locked, latch bolt is operated by key in outside knob or by rotating inside knob. Turn button must be manually rotated to unlock outside knob.	F90	Corridor Lock: Dead-locking latch bolt operated by knob from either side except when outside knob is locked by pushbutton in inside knob. Key in outside knob or rotating inside knob releases pushbutton except when slotted pushbutton is turned to a locked position. Closing door does not release pushbutton. Inside knob always operates.
F82	Entry lock: Dead-locking latch bolt operated by knob from either side except when outside knob is locked by pushbutton in inside knob. When outside knob is locked, operating key in outside knob or rotating inside knob retracts latch bolt and releases pushbutton. Closing door does not release pushbutton.	F91	Store Door Lock: Dead-locking bolt operated by knob from either side except when both knobs are locked by key in knob from either side.
F82A	Entry Lock: Dead-locking latch bolt operated by knob from either side except when both knobs are in locked position by locking device on inner side. Key from outside unlocks locking device. Locking device must be in unlocked position in order that inside knob can be operated.	F92	Service Station Lock: Dead-locking latch bolt operated by knob from either side except when outside knob is locked by pushbutton inside. Key outside, rotating inside knob or closing door, releases button unlocking outside knob except when slotted pushbutton is rotated to a locked position. Inside knob always operates.
F82B	Entry Lock: Dead-locking latch bolt operated by knob from either side except when both knobs are locked by turn	F93	Hotel Guest Room, Clubhouse, Dormitory, or Apartment Entrance Lock: Dead-locking latch bolt operated by knob from inside at all times. Outside knob always fixed. Latch bolt by key from outside except when pushbutton inside is depressed, thus shutting out all keys except emergency key. Depressing pushbutton operates visual indicator in face of cylinder, showing room is occupied. Turning inside knob or closing door releases indicator and shut-out feature except when pushbutton is turned to shut-out position with special key, shutting out all keys except emergency key.

Lock dimensions

Table 3.   Government specification locks (FF-H-00106b)

All dimensions are minimum, in inches

Series no. and type	Case	Backset	Front	Bolt	Bolt throw	Door thickness
3 Mortise, Bit-Key	3½ high x 3¼ deep x ⁹⁄₁₆ thick	2½ to 2¾ ± ¹⁄₃₂	5½ x ⅞	latch ⁹⁄₁₆ x ⁷⁄₁₆ dead ¹³⁄₁₆ x ⅜	⅜ ⁷⁄₁₆	1⅜
8 French door, cyl. lock	5½ x backset + 1 x ¾	1½ ± ¹⁄₃₂ (2 may be specif.)	7⅞ x 1¹⁄₁₆	latch ²⁷⁄₃₂ x ⅝ dead 1⅛ x ⁷⁄₁₆	½ ½	1¾
85 Mortise, cyl. lock	5½ x 3½ x ⅝	2½ to 2¾ ± ¹⁄₃₂	7¾ x ⅞	latch ²⁷⁄₃₂ x ⅝ dead 1⅛ x ⁷⁄₁₆	½ ½	1⅜
86 Mortise, cyl. lock	5½ x 3¾ x ¾	2¾ ± ¹⁄₃₂	8 x 1¼ beveled	latch 1 x ⅝ dead 1⅛ x ½	½ ½	1¾
87 Mortise, cyl. lock (fire doors)	same as 86	same as 86	same as 86	latch (plain or antifriction) 1 x ⅝	¾	1¾
90 Unit lock (preassembled)	1¾ high	2¾ ± ¹⁄₃₂ (3¾ may be specif.)	part of case, beveled	latch (hinged) ⅝ x 1 dead ¾ x ⅞	½ ½	1¾ (can be specif. 1⅜ min, 3 max ¾
98 Same as 90 (fire doors)	same as 90	same as 90 ⅝ x 1	same as 90 ⁵⁄₁₆	latch (hinged) ⅝ x 1 auxil. latch	¾ ⁵⁄₁₆	same as 90
121 Entrance door, cyl. lock, mortise, handle one side	5¼ x 3½ x ⅝	2½ to 2¾ ± ¹⁄₃₂	7⅝ x ⅞	latch ²⁷⁄₃₂ x ¹⁹⁄₃₂ dead 1⅛ x ⁷⁄₁₆	½ ½	1¾
123 Same as 121, Handle both sides	5¼ x 3¾ x ¾	2¾ ± ¹⁄₃₂	7¾ x 1¼	latch 1 x ⅝ dead 1⅛ x ½	½ ½	1¾
140 Mortise, Integral-type (factory assembled)	3 x 2⅜	2¾ ± ¹⁄₃₂	4¼ x 1¼	latch ⅝ x ²⁷⁄₃₂ auxil. ¼ x ²⁷⁄₃₂ dead ¼ x ²⁷⁄₃₂	½ ⅜ ½	1¾ (can be specif. up to 2¼)
150, 150Y Bored, tubular, cyl. lock (light duty)	edge bore ¾ to 1 diam x 3¾ deep max	2⅜ to 2½	2 x ⅞	⁹⁄₁₆ x ½	⅜	1⅜ to 1¾
159 Bored, cyl, cyl lock (light duty)	Cross bore 2⅛ diam Edge bore ⅞ to 1 diam	2⅜ or 2½	2¼ x 1 x .060	⅝ x ½	⅜	1⅜ to 1¾
160 Bored cyl, cyl. lock (medium duty)	Cross bore 2⅛ diam Edge bore ⅞ to 1 diam	2⅜ or 2½ (can be specif. 2¾	2¼ x 1 x .085	latch ¹¹⁄₁₆ x ½	⅜	1⅜ to 2-max
161 Bored, cyl, cyl. lock, (heavy duty)	Cross bore 2⅛ diam Edge bore 1 diam	2¾ (can be specif. 5)	2¼ x 1⅛ x .085 beveled	latch ⅞ x ⅝	½ (¾ can be specified)	1⅜ to 2
181, 182 Bored tubular, cyl, dead locks & night latches	Edge bore ⅞ to 1 diam x 3¾ max.	2⅜ to 2¾ ± ¹⁄₃₂	2 x 1	⅝ x ½	½	1⅜ to 2
183 Mortise, cyl. lock, night latch	3¼ x 3¼ x ¾	2⅜ to 2¾ ± ¹⁄₃₂	5 x 1⅛	¾ x ⁹⁄₁₆	½	
184 Mortise, knob, latch	1⅝ x 3⅛ x ⁹⁄₁₆	2⅜ to 2¾ + ¹⁄₃₂	3⅜ x ¹³⁄₁₆	⁹⁄₁₆ x ⁷⁄₁₆	⅜	1⅜
185 Mortise, knob, latch	2¼ x 3½ x ⅝	2¾ ± ¹⁄₃₂	4 x 1	¹¹⁄₁₆ x ⁹⁄₁₆	½	1¾
189 Mortise, bit-key, dead-lock	2⅛ x 3⅜ x ⅝	2⅜ to 2¾ ± ¹⁄₃₂	4 x 1	⅞ x ⁷⁄₁₆	⁷⁄₁₆	
190, 191 Mortise, cyl. dead-lock	2⅜ x 3⅝ x ¾	2⅜ to 2¾ ± ¹⁄₃₂ (can be specif. 1½ or 2)	4⅛ x 1¹⁄₁₆	¹⁵⁄₁₆ x ½	½	
192 Asylum, (mortise) bit-key, dead-lock	3 x 4 x ¹³⁄₁₆	3 ± ¹⁄₃₂	5½ x 1¼	1¾ x ⅝	⁹⁄₁₆	

See *Exit Devices, ANSI/BHMA 701.*

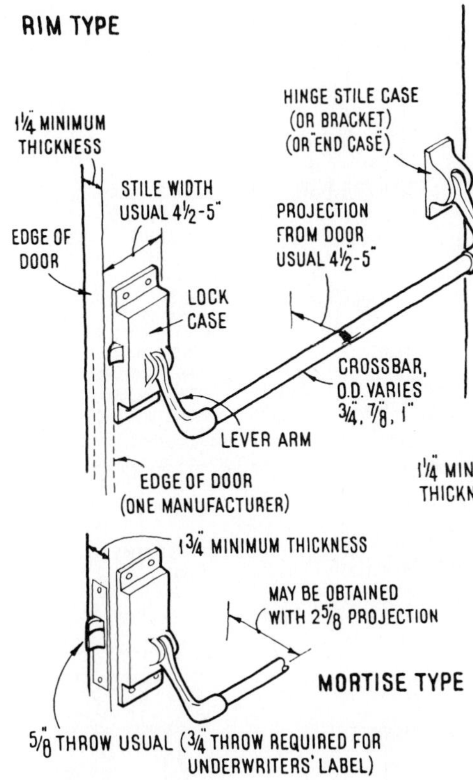

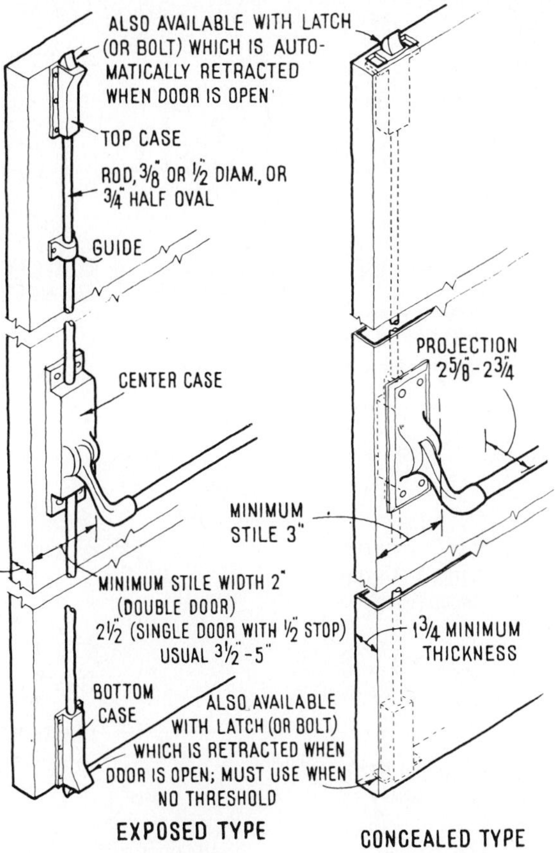

RIM TYPE

1¼ MINIMUM THICKNESS

EDGE OF DOOR

STILE WIDTH USUAL 4½-5"

LOCK CASE

HINGE STILE CASE (OR BRACKET) (OR END CASE)

PROJECTION FROM DOOR USUAL 4½-5"

CROSSBAR, O.D. VARIES 3/4", 7/8", 1"

LEVER ARM

EDGE OF DOOR (ONE MANUFACTURER)

1¼ MINIMUM THICKNESS

ALSO AVAILABLE WITH LATCH (OR BOLT) WHICH IS AUTO-MATICALLY RETRACTED WHEN DOOR IS OPEN

TOP CASE

ROD, 3/8 OR ½ DIAM., OR 3/4 HALF OVAL

GUIDE

CENTER CASE

MINIMUM STILE 3"

PROJECTION 2 5/8 - 2 3/4

MINIMUM STILE WIDTH 2" (DOUBLE DOOR) 2½ (SINGLE DOOR WITH ½ STOP) USUAL 3½ - 5"

BOTTOM CASE

ALSO AVAILABLE WITH LATCH (OR BOLT) WHICH IS RETRACTED WHEN DOOR IS OPEN; MUST USE WHEN NO THRESHOLD

1¾ MINIMUM THICKNESS

1¾ MINIMUM THICKNESS

MAY BE OBTAINED WITH 2 5/8 PROJECTION

MORTISE TYPE

5/8 THROW USUAL (3/4 THROW REQUIRED FOR UNDERWRITERS' LABEL)

EXPOSED TYPE   **CONCEALED TYPE**

CENTER LATCH BOLT TYPES

Used for: (1) single door
(2) active door of a pair (standard for underwriters' labeled fire door)
(3) both doors of a pair with mullion (removable or fixed)

VERTICAL ROD TYPES

Used for: (1) inactive door of a pair (standard for underwriters' labeled fire door)
(2) both doors of a pair
(3) single door (reduces chances of warping or springing)

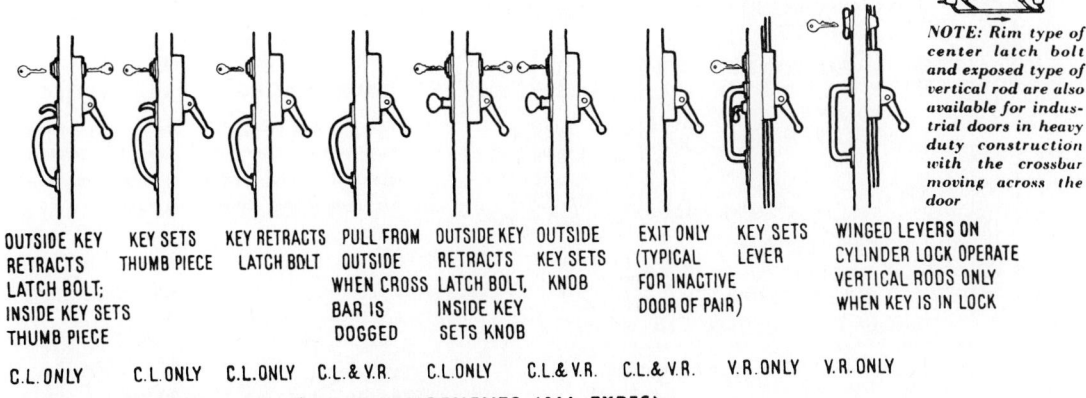

OUTSIDE KEY RETRACTS LATCH BOLT; INSIDE KEY SETS THUMB PIECE

KEY SETS THUMB PIECE

KEY RETRACTS LATCH BDLT

PULL FROM OUTSIDE WHEN CROSS BAR IS DOGGED

OUTSIDE KEY RETRACTS LATCH BOLT, INSIDE KEY SETS KNOB

OUTSIDE KEY SETS KNOB

EXIT ONLY (TYPICAL FOR INACTIVE DOOR OF PAIR)

KEY SETS LEVER

WINGED LEVERS ON CYLINDER LOCK OPERATE VERTICAL RODS ONLY WHEN KEY IS IN LOCK

C.L. ONLY   C.L. ONLY   C.L. ONLY   C.L. & V.R.   C.L. ONLY   C.L. & V.R.   C.L. & V.R.   V.R. ONLY   V.R. ONLY

NOTE: Rim type of center latch bolt and exposed type of vertical rod are also available for industrial doors in heavy duty construction with the crossbar moving across the door

TYPICAL FUNCTION AND TRIM ARRANGEMENTS (ALL TYPES)

Note: Devices should be U.L. labeled for panic. When used with fire doors, they carry an additional label and are referred to as Fire Exit Hardware. Crossbar can be dogged down with latch in retracted position, permitting door to be used push and pull. (Dogging not allowed on Fire Exit Hardware.)

MECHANISMS vary with manufacturer and cost. Latches are pivoted type, usually retracted by cam and spring action, though some are made with lever arm acting directly on latch. With vertical rod operation, either pivoted type latch or sliding bolt may be used, actuated by springs, cams and gravity.

METALS: drop forged, extruded and cast brass (or bronze) or malleable iron for formed members; stainless steel or monel for pivots and pins; bars and rods extruded or rolled brass (or bronze) or steel. Tensile, strength, resilience and hardness should be checked against type of use expected.

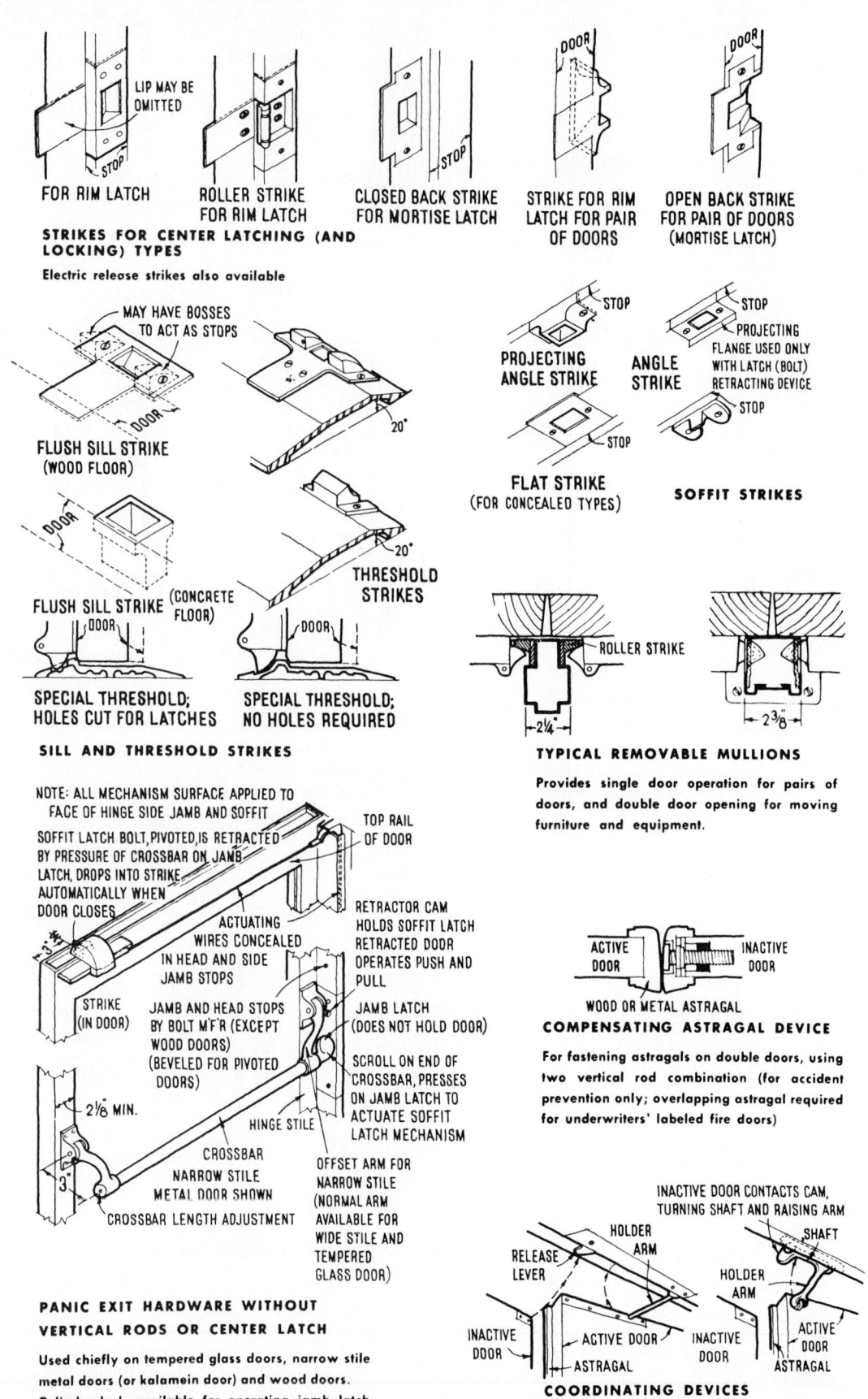

STRIKES FOR CENTER LATCHING (AND LOCKING) TYPES

FOR RIM LATCH • ROLLER STRIKE FOR RIM LATCH • CLOSED BACK STRIKE FOR MORTISE LATCH • STRIKE FOR RIM LATCH FOR PAIR OF DOORS • OPEN BACK STRIKE FOR PAIR OF DOORS (MORTISE LATCH)

Electric release strikes also available

SILL AND THRESHOLD STRIKES

FLUSH SILL STRIKE (WOOD FLOOR) — MAY HAVE BOSSES TO ACT AS STOPS

FLUSH SILL STRIKE (CONCRETE FLOOR)

THRESHOLD STRIKES

SPECIAL THRESHOLD; HOLES CUT FOR LATCHES • SPECIAL THRESHOLD; NO HOLES REQUIRED

SOFFIT STRIKES

PROJECTING ANGLE STRIKE • ANGLE STRIKE — PROJECTING FLANGE USED ONLY WITH LATCH (BOLT) RETRACTING DEVICE

FLAT STRIKE (FOR CONCEALED TYPES)

TYPICAL REMOVABLE MULLIONS

ROLLER STRIKE — 2¼" — 2⅜"

Provides single door operation for pairs of doors, and double door opening for moving furniture and equipment.

PANIC EXIT HARDWARE WITHOUT VERTICAL RODS OR CENTER LATCH

NOTE: ALL MECHANISM SURFACE APPLIED TO FACE OF HINGE SIDE JAMB AND SOFFIT

SOFFIT LATCH BOLT, PIVOTED, IS RETRACTED BY PRESSURE OF CROSSBAR ON JAMB LATCH, DROPS INTO STRIKE AUTOMATICALLY WHEN DOOR CLOSES

TOP RAIL OF DOOR

ACTUATING WIRES CONCEALED IN HEAD AND SIDE JAMB STOPS

RETRACTOR CAM HOLDS SOFFIT LATCH RETRACTED DOOR OPERATES PUSH AND PULL

STRIKE (IN DOOR)

JAMB AND HEAD STOPS BY BOLT M'F'R (EXCEPT WOOD DOORS) (BEVELED FOR PIVOTED DOORS)

JAMB LATCH (DOES NOT HOLD DOOR)

SCROLL ON END OF CROSSBAR, PRESSES ON JAMB LATCH TO ACTUATE SOFFIT LATCH MECHANISM

2⅛" MIN.

HINGE STILE

CROSSBAR NARROW STILE METAL DOOR SHOWN

OFFSET ARM FOR NARROW STILE (NORMAL ARM AVAILABLE FOR WIDE STILE AND TEMPERED GLASS DOOR)

CROSSBAR LENGTH ADJUSTMENT

Used chiefly on tempered glass doors, narrow stile metal doors (or kalamein door) and wood doors. Cylinder lock available for operating jamb latch from exterior. Minimum jamb thickness to accommodate lock 1¾ in.

COMPENSATING ASTRAGAL DEVICE

ACTIVE DOOR • INACTIVE DOOR

WOOD OR METAL ASTRAGAL

For fastening astragals on double doors, using two vertical rod combination (for accident prevention only; overlapping astragal required for underwriters' labeled fire doors)

COORDINATING DEVICES

INACTIVE DOOR CONTACTS CAM, TURNING SHAFT AND RAISING ARM

HOLDER ARM • RELEASE LEVER • SHAFT

INACTIVE DOOR • ACTIVE DOOR • ASTRAGAL

Assure closing of inactive door before active door when overlapping astragal is used

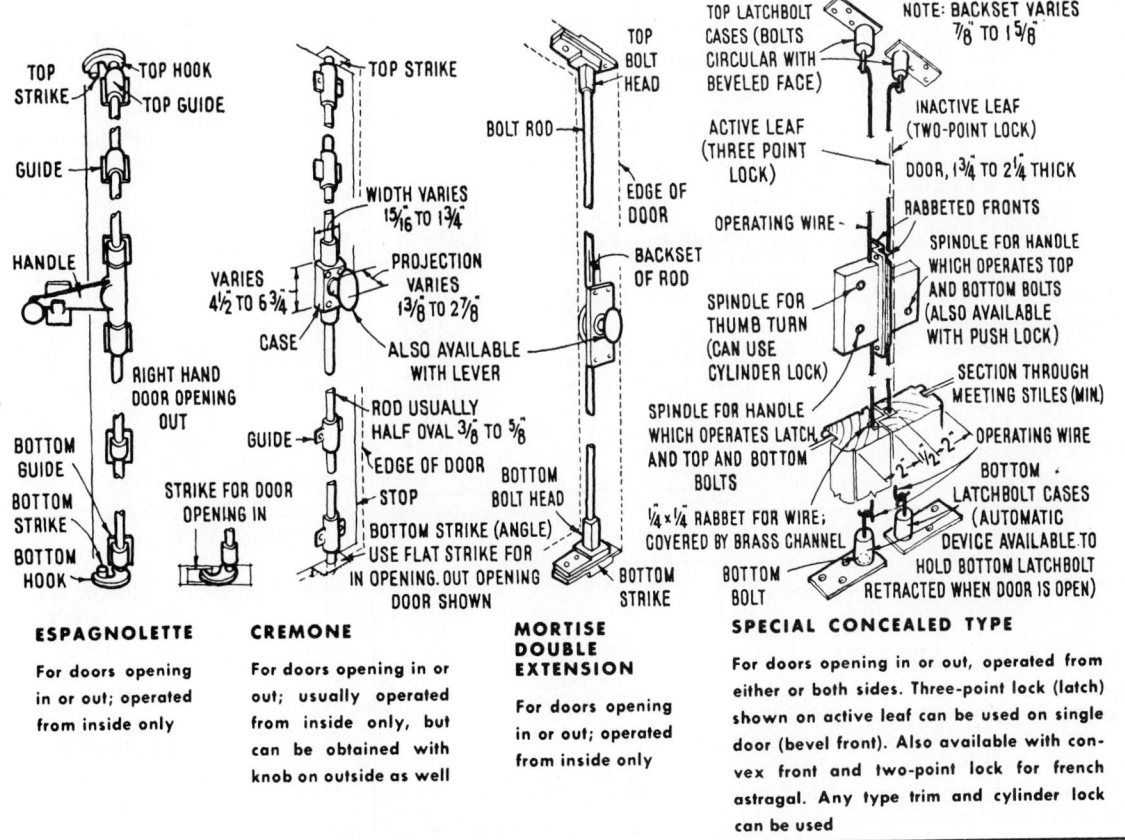

ESPAGNOLETTE

For doors opening in or out; operated from inside only

CREMONE

For doors opening in or out; usually operated from inside only, but can be obtained with knob on outside as well

MORTISE DOUBLE EXTENSION

For doors opening in or out; operated from inside only

SPECIAL CONCEALED TYPE

For doors opening in or out, operated from either or both sides. Three-point lock (latch) shown on active leaf can be used on single door (bevel front). Also available with convex front and two-point lock for french astragal. Any type trim and cylinder lock can be used

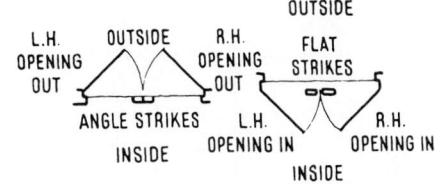

"HAND" CONVENTIONS, ESPAGNOLETTE AND CREMONE BOLTS

Note: for double doors, inactive (standing) leaf may be held by rabbet or by french astragal on active leaf, or have its own bolts

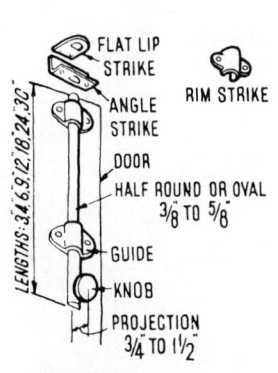

SURFACE

Also available with guide concealed in width of ½ in. half round rod

Note: Check availability of sizes and exact details with manufacturers

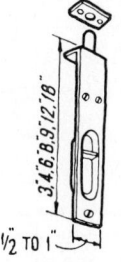

FLUSH

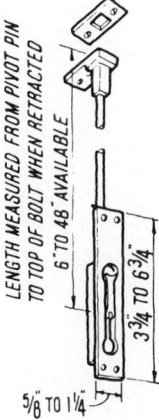

EXTENSION FLUSH

Can be set in edge of inactive door of a pair. Also available for application on face of stile, with knob (see double extension bolt)

Hinges are commonly classified as *full mortise, half mortise, full surface,* and *half surface,* also *olive knuckle, pivot, concealed,* and various special-purpose types. A *butt* hinge is one designed to be mortised into the butt edge of the door and into the rabbet of the door frame, as shown in the drawing at the right. Hinges are available in wrought steel, brass, bronze, and stainless steel; nonferrous hinges should be equipped with stainless steel pins. Unless specified otherwise, pins should be loose (removable with a moderate degree of force) but non-rising. Pins should fit with close tolerances to prevent undue wear. Button tips are standard for pins; sloping "hospital tips" are available on order, as are ball, steeple, and other "decorator tips." Bearings may be plain, ball, oil-impregnated, or antifriction; plain bearings should not be used for heavy doors or those equipped with door-closing devices. Ball bearings may be specified to be concealed within the hinge barrel.

HOW TO SPECIFY HINGES

Number (in pairs), type of bearings, type of tips, type of screws, type of hinge, metal, height, width (required only for full mortise hinges), weight, finish. Number of hinges per door varies with the height of the door: two for doors up to 5 ft high, three for doors between 5 ft and 7 ft 6 in. high, and one additional hinge for each additional 30 in. of height. Size of hinges depends upon the weight of the door, width of the door, and the frequency of use. The following may be used as a guide:

Table 4. Hinge guide

Door Thickness (Inches)	Door Width	Minimum hinge Height (Inches)
⁷⁄₈ or 1	Any	2 ½
1 ⅛	To 36"	3
1 ⅜	To 36"	3 ½
1 ⅜	Over 36"	4
1 ¾	To 41"	4 ½
1 ¾	Over 41"	4 ½ Heavy
1 ¾ to 2 ¼	Any	5 Heavy*

* To be used for heavy doors of high frequency or unusual stress.

Hinge width should be sufficient to provide clearance for trim. For mounting heights, see Sheet 19.

TEMPLATE HINGES

Template hinges are made to standard templates (in accordance with U.S. Department of Commerce Commercial Standard CS9-65 and ANSI/BHMA 111) to ensure exact matching of hinge and its screw holes with doors and jambs, either metal or wood, made by others.

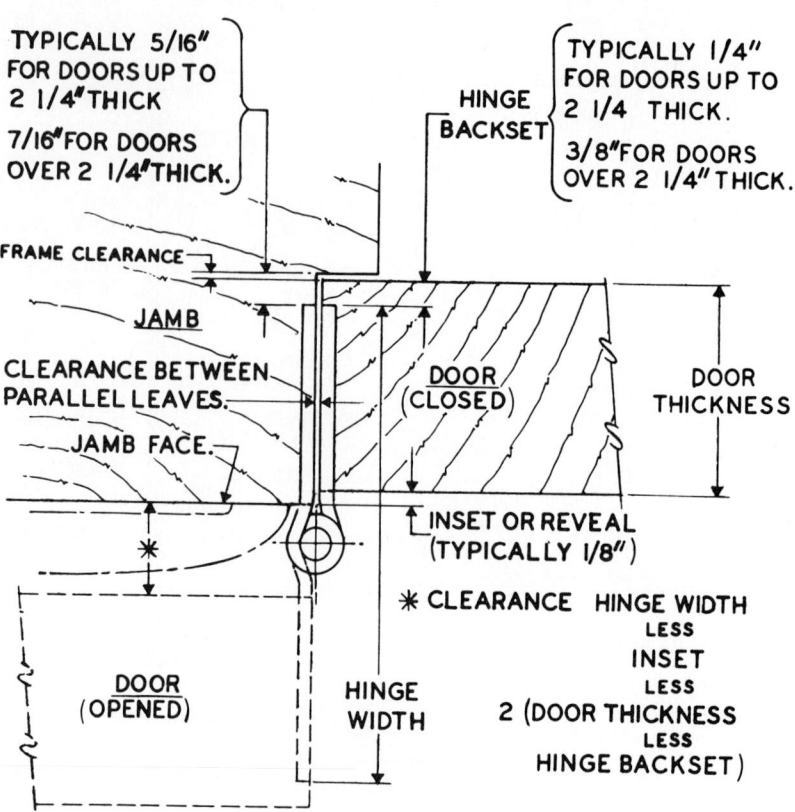

TYPICALLY 5/16" FOR DOORS UP TO 2 1/4" THICK

7/16" FOR DOORS OVER 2 1/4" THICK.

TYPICALLY 1/4" FOR DOORS UP TO 2 1/4" THICK.

3/8" FOR DOORS OVER 2 1/4" THICK.

HINGE BACKSET

FRAME CLEARANCE

JAMB

CLEARANCE BETWEEN PARALLEL LEAVES.

JAMB FACE.

DOOR (CLOSED)

DOOR THICKNESS

DOOR (OPENED)

HINGE WIDTH

INSET OR REVEAL (TYPICALLY 1/8")

* CLEARANCE HINGE WIDTH
LESS
INSET
LESS
2 (DOOR THICKNESS
LESS
HINGE BACKSET)

TYPICAL MORTISE HINGE INSTALLATION

(From American National Standard Butts and Hinges, ANSI/BHMA 101)
Notes: A typical location for olive knuckle and paumelle hinges is ¼ in. from knuckle side of door to edge of hinge leaf.

Some products of hollow metal doors and frames employ ¼-in-backset for the jamb and a ³⁄₁₆-in. hinge backset for the door.

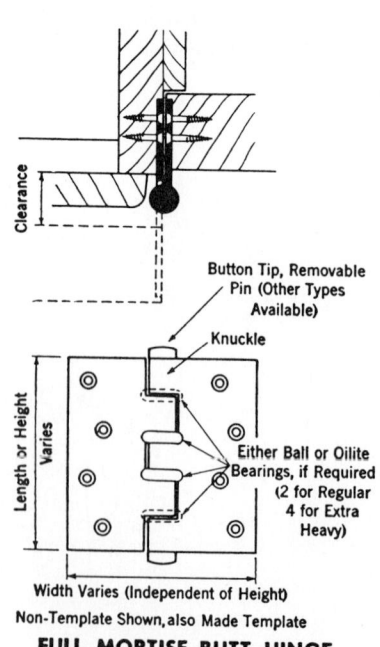

Clearance

Button Tip, Removable Pin (Other Types Available)

Knuckle

Length or Height Varies

Either Ball or Oilite Bearings, if Required (2 for Regular 4 for Extra Heavy)

Width Varies (Independent of Height)

Non-Template Shown, also Made Template

FULL MORTISE BUTT HINGE

Non-Template: for Wood Doors and Wood Jambs (All Wood Screws)

Template: for Wood Doors and Pressed Metal Jambs (Order ½ Machine Screws); or for Hollow Metal Doors and Pressed Metal Jambs (Order All Machine Screws)

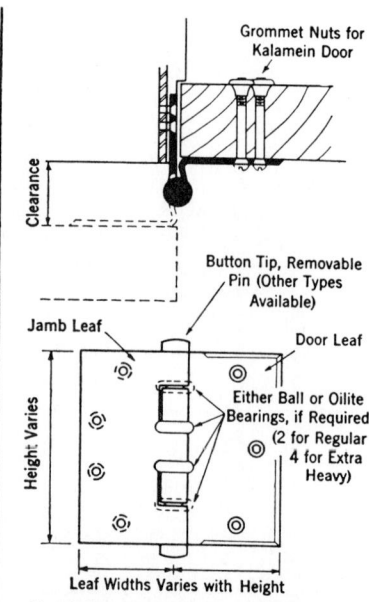

Grommet Nuts for Kalamein Door

Clearance

Button Tip, Removable Pin (Other Types Available)

Jamb Leaf

Door Leaf

Height Varies

Either Ball or Oilite Bearings, if Required (2 for Regular 4 for Extra Heavy)

Leaf Widths Varies with Height

Template Shown, also Made Non-Template

HALF SURFACE BUTT HINGE

Non-Template: for Wood Doors and Jambs (All Wood Screws); or for Kalamein Doors and Kalamein Jambs (Order ½ Machine Screws with Grommet Nuts)

Template: for Kalamein Doors and Pressed Metal Jambs (Order All Machine Screws, ½ with Grommet Nuts)

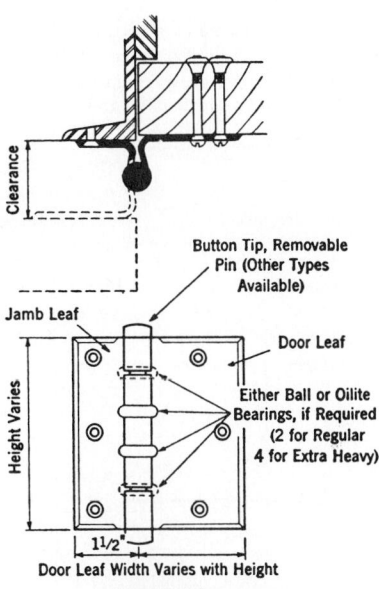

FULL SURFACE HINGE FOR KALAMEIN DOOR
(CHANNEL IRON FRAME)

Labels in figure: Clearance; Button Tip, Removable Pin (Other Types Available); Jamb Leaf; Door Leaf; Either Ball or Oilite Bearings, if Required (2 for Regular, 4 for Extra Heavy); Height Varies; 1½"; Door Leaf Width Varies with Height; Template Only

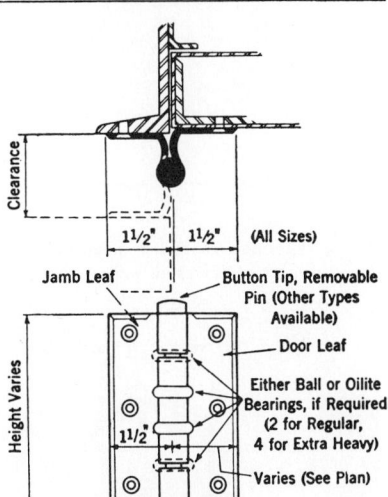

FULL SURFACE HINGE FOR ANGLE IRON DOOR
(CHANNEL IRON FRAME)

Labels in figure: Clearance; 1½"; 1½" (All Sizes); Jamb Leaf; Button Tip, Removable Pin (Other Types Available); Door Leaf; Either Ball or Oilite Bearings, if Required (2 for Regular, 4 for Extra Heavy); 1½"; Varies (See Plan); Height Varies; Template Only

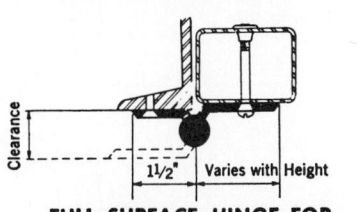

FULL SURFACE HINGE FOR TUBULAR STEEL DOOR

(Elevation as Shown for Hinge for Angle Iron Door)

Labels in figure: Clearance; 1½"; Varies with Height

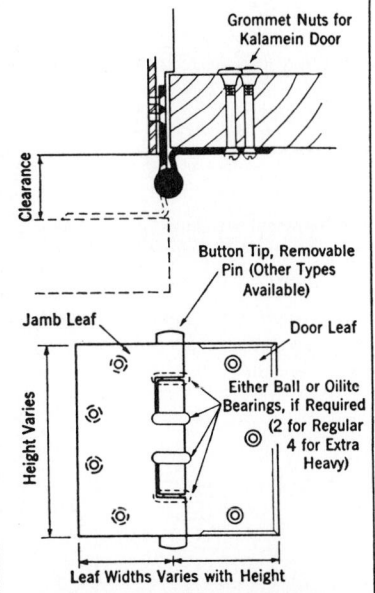

HALF SURFACE BUTT HINGE

Labels in figure: Grommet Nuts for Kalamein Door; Clearance; Button Tip, Removable Pin (Other Types Available); Jamb Leaf; Door Leaf; Either Ball or Oilite Bearings, if Required (2 for Regular 4 for Extra Heavy); Height Varies; Leaf Widths Varies with Height; Template Shown, also Made Non-Template

Non-Template: for Wood Doors and Jambs (All Wood Screws); or for Kalamein Doors and Kalamein Jambs (Order ½ Machine Screws with Grommet Nuts)

Template: for Kalamein Doors and Pressed Metal Jambs (Order All Machine Screws, ½ with Grommet Nuts)

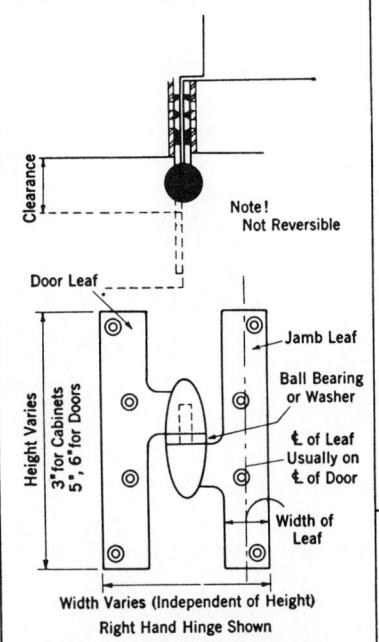

OLIVE KNUCKLE (PAUMELLE) HINGE

Labels in figure: Clearance; Door Leaf; Note! Not Reversible; Jamb Leaf; Ball Bearing or Washer; ℄ of Leaf Usually on ℄ of Door; Width of Leaf; Height Varies; 3" for Cabinets 5", 6" for Doors; Width Varies (Independent of Height); Right Hand Hinge Shown

Type of Loose Joint Hinge, Therefore Handed. Knuckle Alone Visible when Door Closed. Made Template and Non-Template (See Notes Under Full Mortise Butt Hinge)
Note: for Clearances, See Manufacturers Catalogs

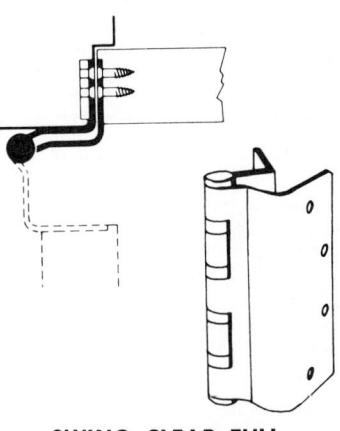

SWING CLEAR FULL MORTISE HINGE

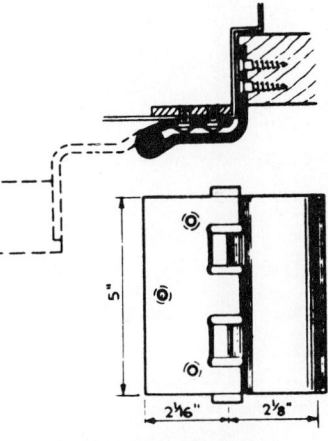

SWING CLEAR HALF MORTISE HINGE

Labels in figure: 5"; 2¹⁄₁₆"; 2⅛"

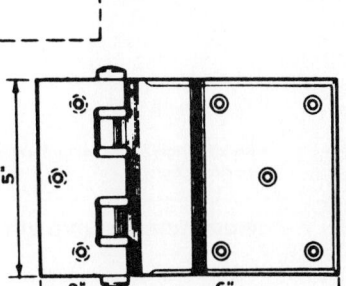

SWING CLEAR FULL SURFACE HINGE

Labels in figure: 5"; 2"; 6"

Table 5. Hinge sizes available

Sizes are based on height (same as length) of hinge. Full mortise butt hinges are usually made of same width as their height (e.g.: 4½ x 4½ in., 6 x 6 in.) but are available in other widths. When clearance for trim (see Hinges, Sheet 12) make these widths unsuitable (e.g., trim very narrow or omitted or very wide plinth or trim), specify width desired, to nearest larger ½-in. dimension, and manufacturer will be able to furnish. Half surface, full surface, and half mortise hinge widths are not variable.

Size of hinge, length or height, in.	Thickness of metal — Non-template and template wrought metal (gov. stnds, CS9-65) in.	Diam of knuckle, usual, in.	Full mortise, non-template	Full mortise, template	Half surface, template	Full surface, template (kal. doors)	Full surface, template (angle iron doors)	Full surface, template (tubular steel doors)	Half mortise, template	Half surface, non-template	Olive knuckle template and non-template
			Sizes listed in government standards or generally available from manufacturers							Other sizes and types available from manufacturers	
2	0.083		X	X						X	
2½	0.089		X	X						X	
3	0.092	0.515	X	X	X					X	X
3½	0.123	0.632	X	X	X					X	
4	0.130	0.632	X	X	X					X	
4, heavy	0.170			X							
4½	0.134	0.695	X	X	X	X	X		X	X	
4½, heavy	0.180	0.831	X	X	X	X	X	X	X		
5	0.146	0.731	X	X	X	X	X		X	X	X
5, heavy	0.190	0.831	X	X	X	X	X	X	X		
6	0.160	0.784	X	X							X
6, heavy	0.203	0.906	X	X	X	X	X	X	X		X
8, heavy	0.203	0.971	X	X							

Note: For cabinet hardware see ANSI/BHMA 101.

SPRING HINGES

Simplest closing device. Energy stored in spring closes door. No closing speed control unless additional device is used, such as surface type door check without spring.

DOUBLE ACTING SPRING BUTT HINGES

Note: Button tip now standard instead of ball tip shown.

Double Acting

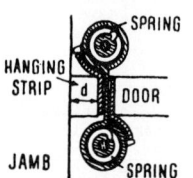

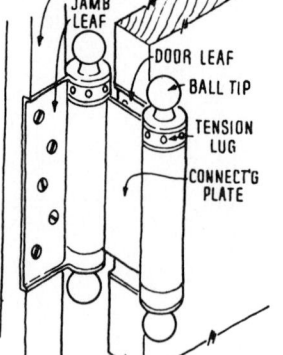

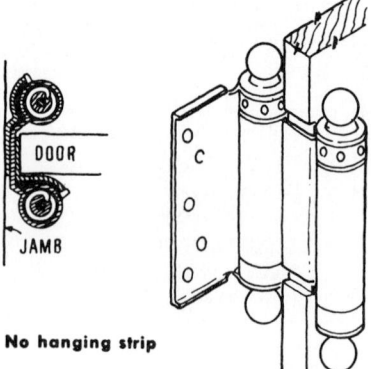

With hanging strip

Also available with clamp flanges and bolts for kalamein doors.

No hanging strip

SINGLE ACTING SPRING BUTT HINGES

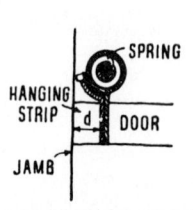

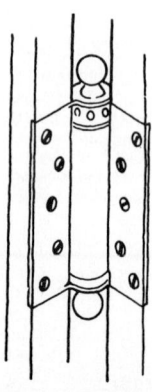

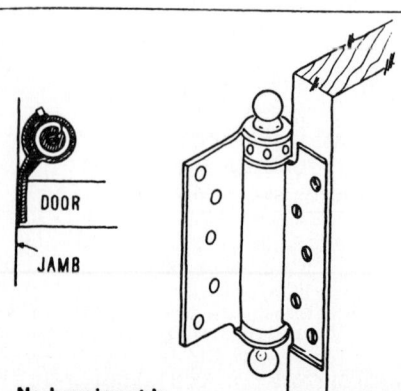

With hanging strip

(If jamb face is in line with door face, this type can be used without additional hanging strip).

Also available as half surface hinge for kalamein doors with pressed steel jambs (4, 6, and 7 in. sizes)

No hanging strip

Table 6. Hinge dimensions

SIZES OF SPRING BUTT HINGES	Size	Min Door Thickness	Max Door Thickness Wood	Max Door Thickness Metal	Max Door Width	Max Door Weight	Depth (d) Hanging Strip (if required)	General Rules
Note: Check all information and details for exact cases carefully with mfr.'s catalogs.	3″	¾″	1″	⅞″	2′-2″	30 lb.	½″	1. Use largest size hinge that thickness of hardwood and kalamein doors will permit
	4	⅞ (1)	1¼	1⅛	2-4	42	⅝	2. Use min door thickness only for light wood doors
Variations in door thickness for hinges of different mfrs. shown in parentheses.	5	1⅛ (1)	1½	1⅜	2-6	56	⅝	3. Use three hinges for doors that are extra heavy or frequently used. Place third hinge down ⅓ distance between upper and lower hinges.
	6	1¼ (1⅛)	1¾	1½	2-8	72	¾	
* For hanging strip only.	7	1⅜ (1¼)	2	1¾	2-9	90	⅞	
	8	1½	2¼	2	2-10	110	1	
	10	1¾	2½	2⅛	3-0	150	1⅛	
	12*	2¼	3	2⅝	3-2	190	1¼	

SPRING PIVOT HINGES

Double Acting

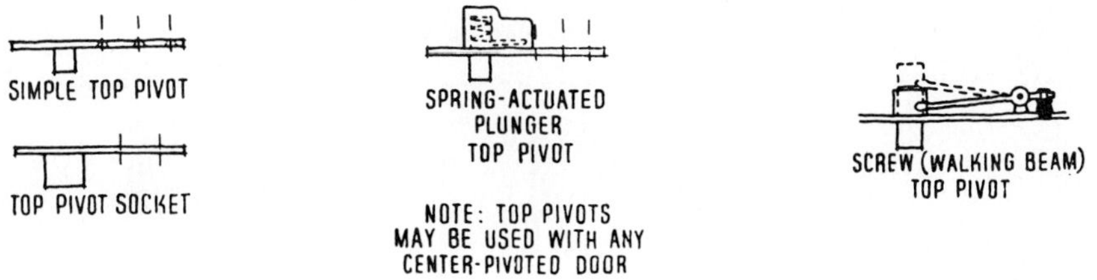
SIMPLE TOP PIVOT
TOP PIVOT SOCKET
SPRING-ACTUATED PLUNGER TOP PIVOT
NOTE: TOP PIVOTS MAY BE USED WITH ANY CENTER-PIVOTED DOOR
SCREW (WALKING BEAM) TOP PIVOT

Horizontal Type

For doors 1⅛ to 2¾ in. thick

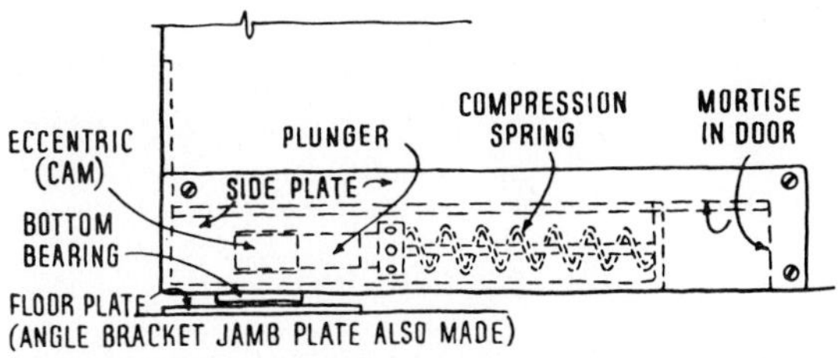
ECCENTRIC (CAM)
PLUNGER
COMPRESSION SPRING
MORTISE IN DOOR
SIDE PLATE
BOTTOM BEARING
FLOOR PLATE
(ANGLE BRACKET JAMB PLATE ALSO MADE)

Vertical Type

For doors 1⅛ to 2¾ in. thick

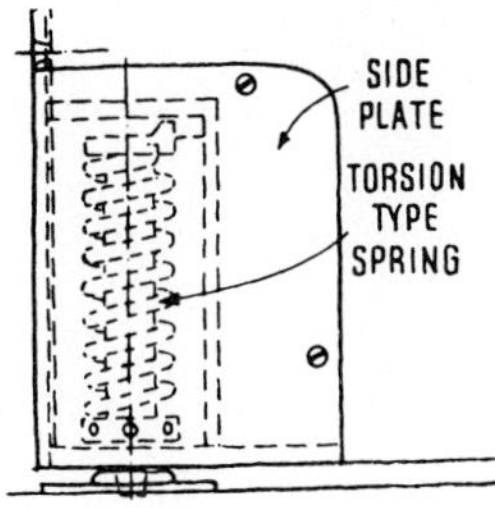
SIDE PLATE
TORSION TYPE SPRING

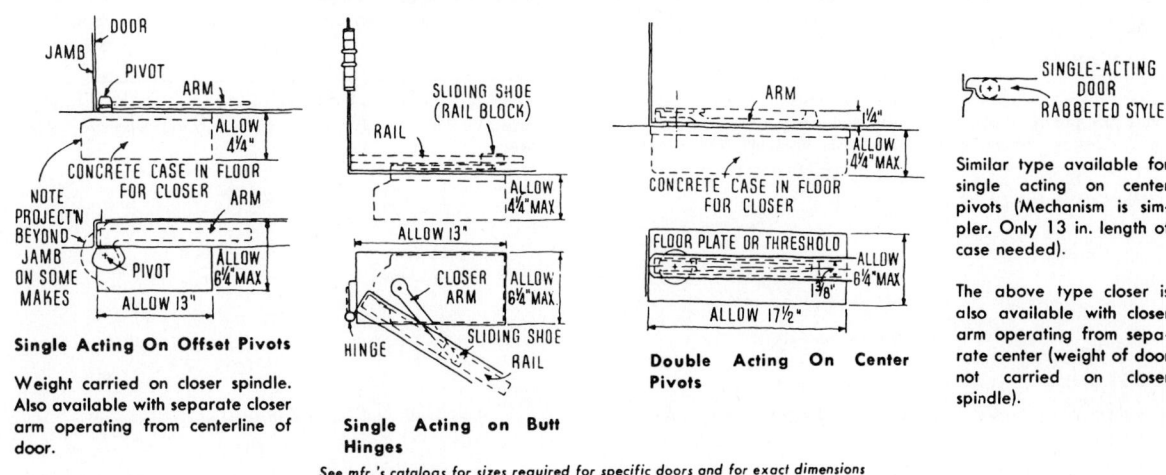

FLOOR CLOSERS (CHECKING FLOOR HINGES, FLOOR CHECKS)

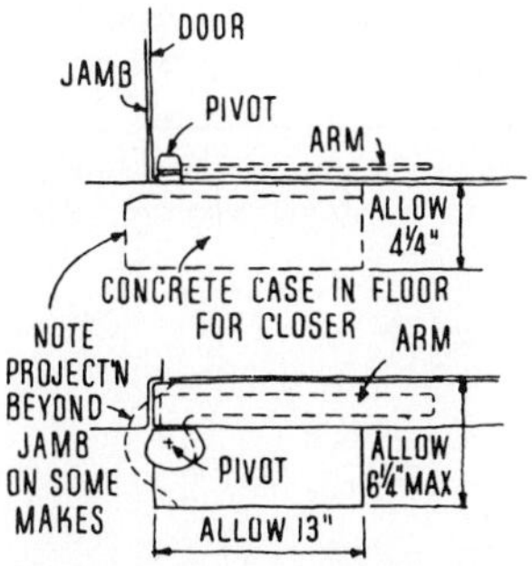
DOOR
JAMB
PIVOT
ARM
ALLOW 4¼"
CONCRETE CASE IN FLOOR FOR CLOSER
NOTE PROJECT'N BEYOND JAMB ON SOME MAKES
ARM
PIVOT
ALLOW 6¼" MAX
ALLOW 13"

Single Acting On Offset Pivots

Weight carried on closer spindle. Also available with separate closer arm operating from centerline of door.

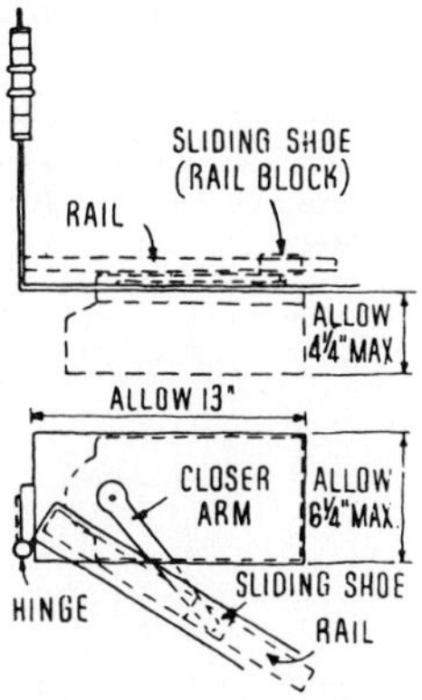
SLIDING SHOE (RAIL BLOCK)
RAIL
ALLOW 4¼" MAX
ALLOW 13"
CLOSER ARM
ALLOW 6¼" MAX
SLIDING SHOE
HINGE
RAIL

Single Acting on Butt Hinges

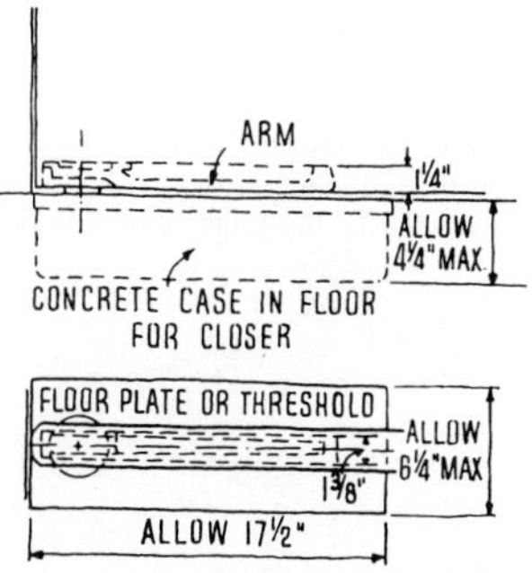
ARM
¼"
ALLOW 4¼" MAX
CONCRETE CASE IN FLOOR FOR CLOSER
FLOOR PLATE OR THRESHOLD
ALLOW 6¼" MAX
1⅞"
ALLOW 17½"

Double Acting On Center Pivots

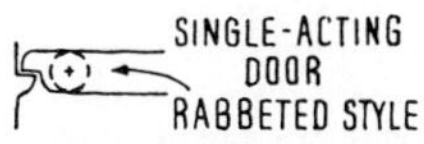
SINGLE-ACTING DOOR RABBETED STYLE

Similar type available for single acting on center pivots (Mechanism is simpler. Only 13 in. length of case needed).

The above type closer is also available with closer arm operating from separate center (weight of door not carried on closer spindle).

See mfr.'s catalogs for sizes required for specific doors and for exact dimensions

Door Closers—see ANSI/BHMA 1001, Door Control (Closers).

Sizes of Overhead Door Closers *(From Dept. of Commerce CS22-40)*

Where strong drafts are encountered and as noted above under bracket and parallel arm installations, use next larger size.

Size	Description, Max Door Size (Approx.)
I	Ordinary screen, light interior doors 1⅛ in. by 2 ft-6 in. by 6 ft-6 in.
II	Heavy screen doors, 1⅜ in. by 3 ft by 7 ft Light interior doors, 1⅜ in. by 2 ft-8 in. by 7 ft Closet doors, 1¾ in. by 2 ft-8 in. by 7 ft
III	Light exterior doors, 1¾ in. by 2 ft-6 in. by 7 ft Corridor or office doors, 1¾ in. by 3 ft by 7 ft
IV	Ordinary exterior doors, 1¾ in. by 3 ft by 7 ft-6 in. Heavy interior doors, 2¼ in. by 4 ft by 7 ft-6 in.
V	Heavy exterior doors, 2¼ in. by 3 ft-6 in. by 7 ft-6 in. Heavy interior doors subject to strong drafts
VI	Extra heavy entrance doors 3 in. thick or over, or doors of unusual height or width, refrig. doors, etc.

DOOR CLOSERS

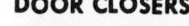
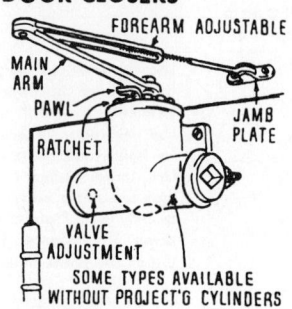

Surface Type

Dimensions approx. Check with mfr. for exact sizes

Angle to which door may be opened is set by: closer to jamb distance; length of main arm (may be available in different sizes) and fore arm (adjustable); jamb and butt conditions; projection of closer. When specifying, state max opening angle desired.

OVERHEAD CLOSERS

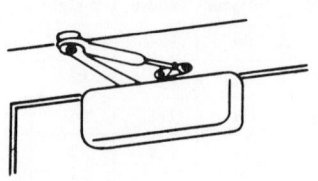

The traditional design shown at the left has now been generally superseded by the more modern design shown above.

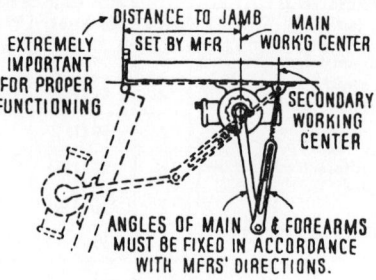

Mounted on door, hinge side, with regular (exposed) arm.

Door weight carried on hinges or pivots

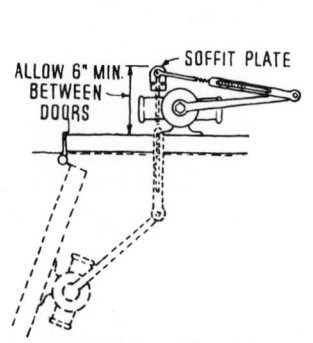

Parallel Arm

Mounted on stop side of door. Used where min clearance is required; e.g. between two doors. Effective power reduced; use next larger size.

Soffit Bracket

Soffit bracket usual type. Distance from jamb to main working center maintained for full effectiveness.

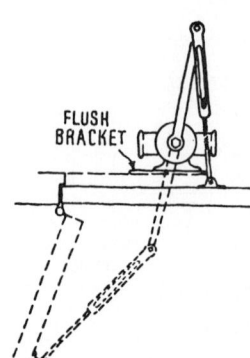

Mounted on brackets on stop side to keep closer out of weather, to hide, or when trim interferes.

Flush Bracket

Flush type mounted on face of opposite side when soffit is narrow. Working center distance maintained.

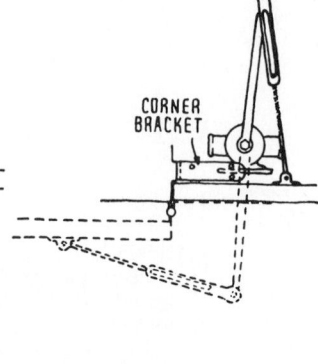

Corner Bracket

Corner bracket used to obtain 180° opening or for less obstruction. Effective power reduced; use next larger size.

Special Arms Available: Two or three point hold open arms for hospitals (private—about 10° for ventilation; semi-private—about 45°; passage—about 95°); and hold open arms with fusible links for automatic closing in case of fire. Hold open arms cannot always be depended on for exterior doors opening out; use separate holder if necessary.

Fully Concealed Types

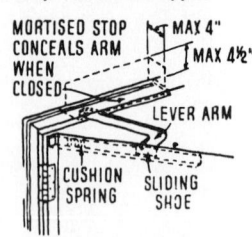

Housed in head above door. For doors on hinges, offset or center pivots.

Housed in head above door. Projecting arm gives greater power than concealed arm. Door on hinges or pivots. Arm projects on stop side. Also used on outswinging wood doors when door top is not weather protected.

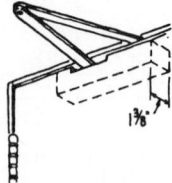

Housed in door. For interior doors only. Also available with concealed arm. Door hung on hinges or pivots.

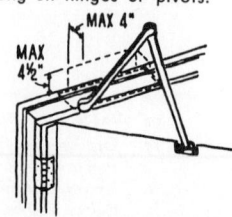

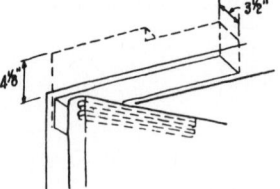

For double acting interior doors, hung on center pivots. Housed in head above door.

For heavy and exterior double acting doors, hung on center pivots. Housed in head above door.

Note: For specific details and sizes, consult manufacturers' catalogs.

OVERHEAD HOLDERS AND STAYS

See ANSI/BHMA 311, Door Controls (Overhead Holders)

General Notes for All types

1. In determining hold-open angle, be sure clearance is available for slight swing past angle to allow shock absorber to function.
2. Slide and track types available (concealed or exposed) with friction shoes which hold door open against light drafts at any position (no predetermined hold-open angle).
3. Similar types also available as simple stays (stops), to prevent door opening beyond a fixed angle, but without hold-open mechanism.

Concealed Type

Available for: 1. Single hung on butts;
2. Single hung on offset pivots;
3. Single hung on center pivots;
4. Double hung on center pivots.

Automatically holds door open at predetermined angle (up to about 110 deg); released by simple pull on door.
1. Release hold open mechanism (acts as stay only);
2. Lock hold open mechanism (door can be shut only by turning knob).

Exposed Types

Available for: 1. Single hung on butts;
2. Single hung on offset pivots;
3. Single hung on center pivots.

Operation similar to concealed type.

SLIDE CONTAINING HOLDING MECHANISM

JAMB BRACKET, APPLIED TO STOP

CONTROL LEVER (TURN TO RELEASE MECHANISM, ACTS AS STAY ONLY)

TRACK

JAMB BRACKET, APPLIED TO STOP

SHOCK ABSORBER

CONTROL HANDLE (TURN TO RELEASE MECHANISM, ACTS AS STAY ONLY)

SHOCK ABSORBER

MAX. DEPTH ABOUT 2"

JAMB BRACKET, APPLIED TO RABBET

SLIDING SHOE

CONTROL KNOB
HOLD-OPEN MECHANISM

JAMB BRACKET, APPLIED TO STOP

THE HOLD-OPEN ENGAGES AND RELEASES THE DOOR AUTOMATICALLY. HOLD-OPEN TENSION CAN BE ADJUSTED OR DISENGAGED.

ROLLER STOPS (BUMPERS)

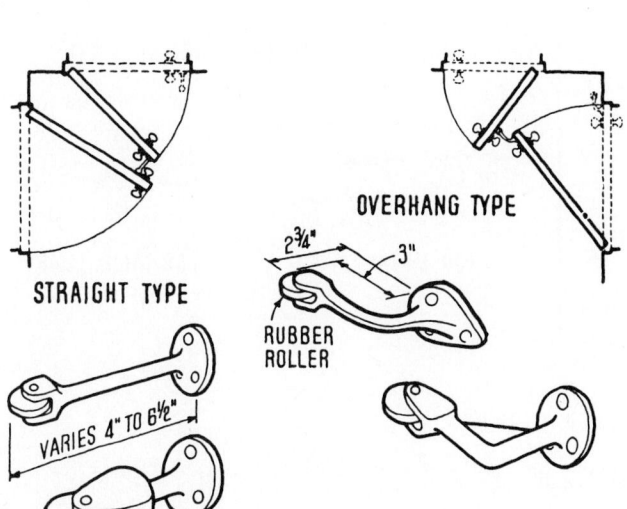

STRAIGHT TYPE

VARIES 4" TO 6½"

OVERHANG TYPE

2¾" 3"

RUBBER ROLLER

CABIN DOOR HOOKS

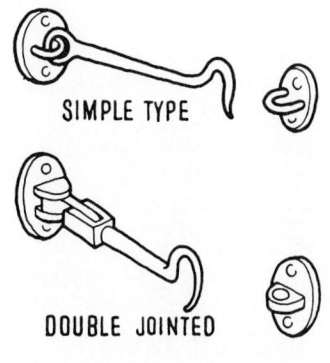

SIMPLE TYPE

DOUBLE JOINTED

LENGTHS USUALLY AVAILABLE
2½", 3", 3½", 4", 6", 8"

Note: For specific details and sizes, consult manufacturers' catalogs.

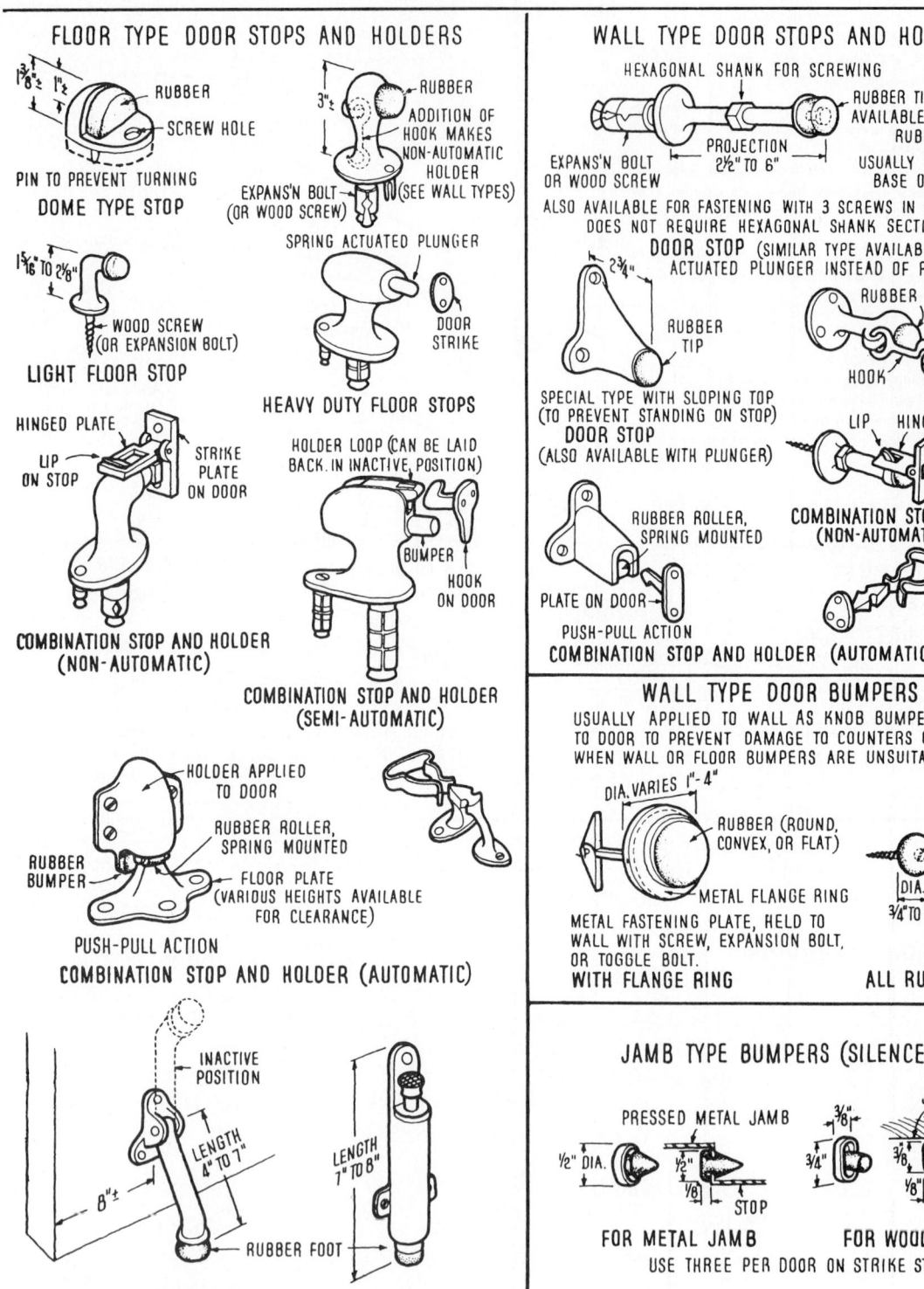

FLOOR TYPE DOOR STOPS AND HOLDERS

RUBBER
SCREW HOLE
PIN TO PREVENT TURNING
DOME TYPE STOP

RUBBER
ADDITION OF HOOK MAKES NON-AUTOMATIC HOLDER (SEE WALL TYPES)
EXPANS'N BOLT (OR WOOD SCREW)

WOOD SCREW (OR EXPANSION BOLT)
LIGHT FLOOR STOP

SPRING ACTUATED PLUNGER
DOOR STRIKE
HEAVY DUTY FLOOR STOPS

HINGED PLATE
LIP ON STOP
STRIKE PLATE ON DOOR
COMBINATION STOP AND HOLDER (NON-AUTOMATIC)

HOLDER LOOP (CAN BE LAID BACK IN INACTIVE POSITION)
BUMPER
HOOK ON DOOR
COMBINATION STOP AND HOLDER (SEMI-AUTOMATIC)

HOLDER APPLIED TO DOOR
RUBBER ROLLER, SPRING MOUNTED
RUBBER BUMPER
FLOOR PLATE (VARIOUS HEIGHTS AVAILABLE FOR CLEARANCE)
PUSH-PULL ACTION
COMBINATION STOP AND HOLDER (AUTOMATIC)

INACTIVE POSITION
LENGTH 4" TO 7"
8"±
RUBBER FOOT
LEVER TYPE HOLDER

LENGTH 7" TO 8"
PLUNGER TYPE HOLDER

WALL TYPE DOOR STOPS AND HOLDERS

HEXAGONAL SHANK FOR SCREWING
EXPANS'N BOLT OR WOOD SCREW
PROJECTION 2½" TO 6"
RUBBER TIP (SNAP-ON). ALSO AVAILABLE WITH THREADED RUBBER TIPS.
USUALLY APPLIED TO BASE OF WALL
ALSO AVAILABLE FOR FASTENING WITH 3 SCREWS IN BASE; THIS TYPE DOES NOT REQUIRE HEXAGONAL SHANK SECTION.
DOOR STOP (SIMILAR TYPE AVAILABLE WITH SPRING ACTUATED PLUNGER INSTEAD OF RUBBER TIP)

RUBBER TIP
SPECIAL TYPE WITH SLOPING TOP (TO PREVENT STANDING ON STOP)
DOOR STOP (ALSO AVAILABLE WITH PLUNGER)

RUBBER
HOOK
PLATE ON DOOR
RIGHT HAND TYPE SHOWN. LEFT HAND ALSO AVAILABLE

LIP HINGED PLATE
STRIKE PLATE ON DOOR
NOT HANDED
COMBINATION STOP AND HOLDER (NON-AUTOMATIC TYPES)

RUBBER ROLLER, SPRING MOUNTED
PLATE ON DOOR
PUSH-PULL ACTION
COMBINATION STOP AND HOLDER (AUTOMATIC TYPES)

WALL TYPE DOOR BUMPERS

USUALLY APPLIED TO WALL AS KNOB BUMPERS. ALSO TO DOOR TO PREVENT DAMAGE TO COUNTERS OR FURNITURE WHEN WALL OR FLOOR BUMPERS ARE UNSUITABLE.

DIA. VARIES 1"- 4"
RUBBER (ROUND, CONVEX, OR FLAT)
METAL FLANGE RING
METAL FASTENING PLATE, HELD TO WALL WITH SCREW, EXPANSION BOLT, OR TOGGLE BOLT.
WITH FLANGE RING

SCREW HEAD COVERED BY RUBBER
DIA. ¾" TO 1⅛"
ALL RUBBER

JAMB TYPE BUMPERS (SILENCERS)

PRESSED METAL JAMB
½" DIA.
½"
⅛"
STOP
FOR METAL JAMB

JAMB
⅜"
¾"
⅜"
⅛"
STOP
FOR WOOD JAMB

USE THREE PER DOOR ON STRIKE STOP

Note: For specific details and sizes, consult manufacturers' catalogs.

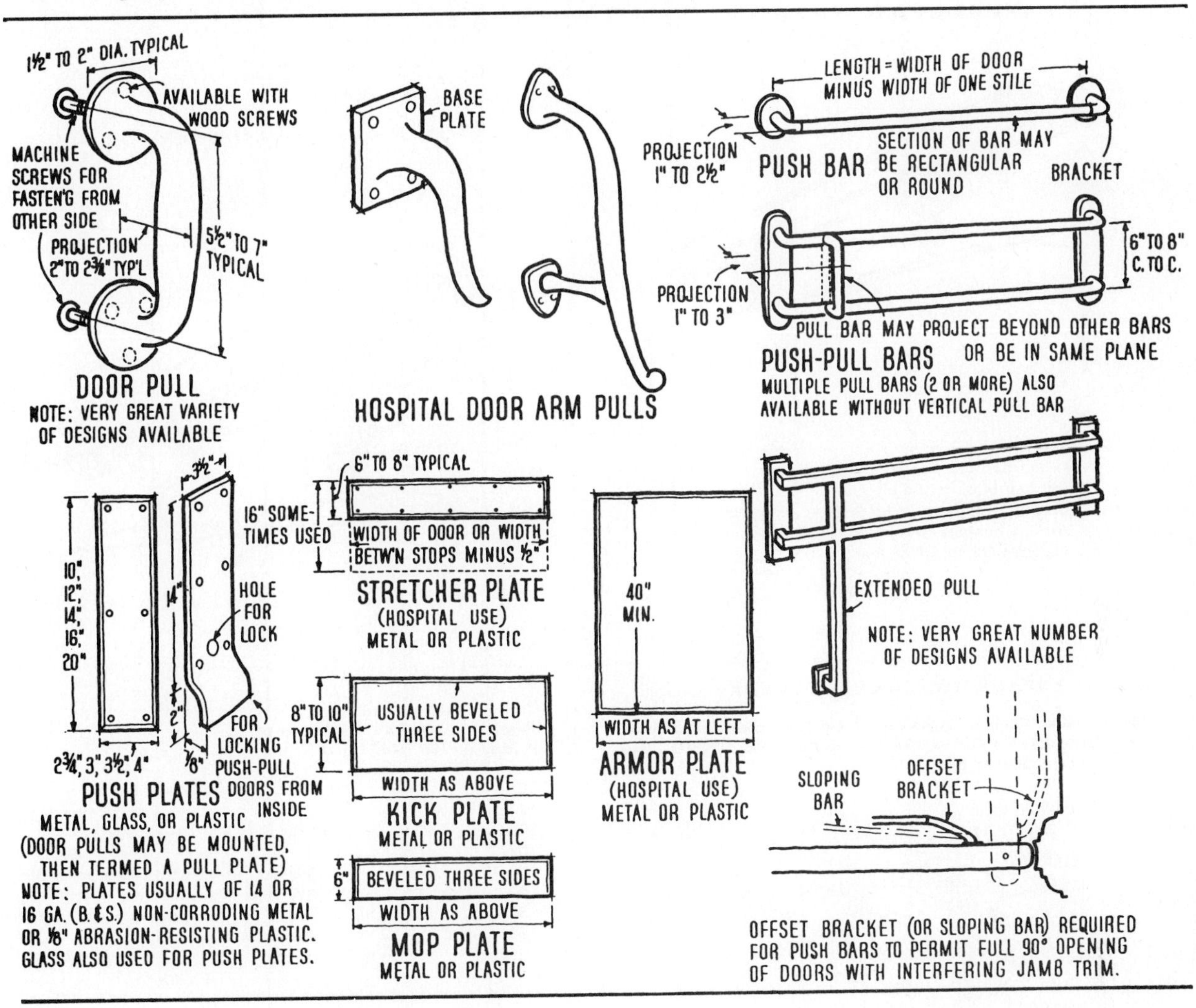

1½" TO 2" DIA. TYPICAL

AVAILABLE WITH WOOD SCREWS

MACHINE SCREWS FOR FASTEN'G FROM OTHER SIDE

PROJECTION 2" TO 2¾" TYP'L

5½" TO 7" TYPICAL

DOOR PULL
NOTE: VERY GREAT VARIETY OF DESIGNS AVAILABLE

BASE PLATE

HOSPITAL DOOR ARM PULLS

LENGTH = WIDTH OF DOOR MINUS WIDTH OF ONE STILE

PROJECTION 1" TO 2½"

PUSH BAR

SECTION OF BAR MAY BE RECTANGULAR OR ROUND

BRACKET

PROJECTION 1" TO 3"

6" TO 8" C. TO C.

PULL BAR MAY PROJECT BEYOND OTHER BARS OR BE IN SAME PLANE

PUSH-PULL BARS
MULTIPLE PULL BARS (2 OR MORE) ALSO AVAILABLE WITHOUT VERTICAL PULL BAR

10", 12", 14", 16", 20"

3½"

HOLE FOR LOCK

14"

2"

⅛"

FOR LOCKING PUSH-PULL DOORS FROM INSIDE

2¾", 3", 3½", 4"

PUSH PLATES
METAL, GLASS, OR PLASTIC
(DOOR PULLS MAY BE MOUNTED, THEN TERMED A PULL PLATE)
NOTE: PLATES USUALLY OF 14 OR 16 GA. (B. & S.) NON-CORRODING METAL OR ⅛" ABRASION-RESISTING PLASTIC. GLASS ALSO USED FOR PUSH PLATES.

6" TO 8" TYPICAL

16" SOMETIMES USED

WIDTH OF DOOR OR WIDTH BETW'N STOPS MINUS ½"

STRETCHER PLATE
(HOSPITAL USE)
METAL OR PLASTIC

8" TO 10" TYPICAL

USUALLY BEVELED THREE SIDES

WIDTH AS ABOVE

KICK PLATE
METAL OR PLASTIC

6"

BEVELED THREE SIDES

WIDTH AS ABOVE

MOP PLATE
METAL OR PLASTIC

40" MIN.

WIDTH AS AT LEFT

ARMOR PLATE
(HOSPITAL USE)
METAL OR PLASTIC

EXTENDED PULL

NOTE: VERY GREAT NUMBER OF DESIGNS AVAILABLE

SLOPING BAR

OFFSET BRACKET

OFFSET BRACKET (OR SLOPING BAR) REQUIRED FOR PUSH BARS TO PERMIT FULL 90° OPENING OF DOORS WITH INTERFERING JAMB TRIM.

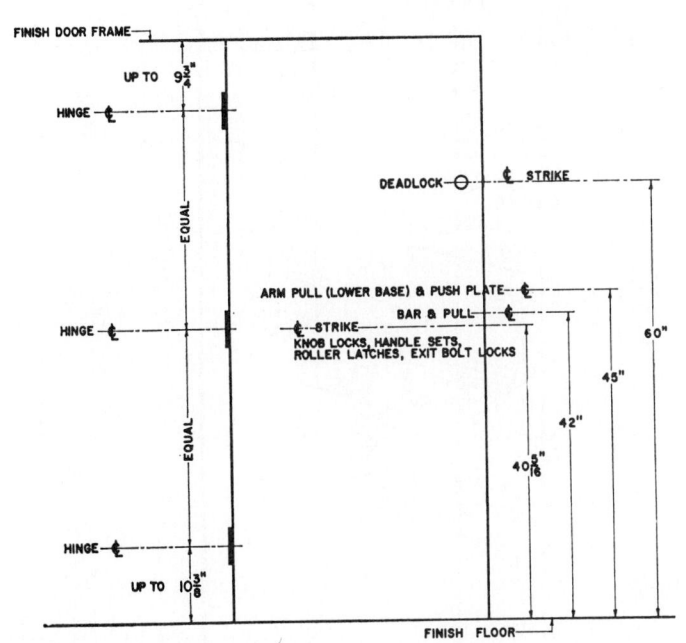

FINISH DOOR FRAME

UP TO 9¾"

HINGE ℄

DEADLOCK ℄ STRIKE

EQUAL

ARM PULL (LOWER BASE) & PUSH PLATE ℄

BAR & PULL ℄

HINGE ℄

℄ STRIKE

KNOB LOCKS, HANDLE SETS, ROLLER LATCHES, EXIT BOLT LOCKS

60"

45"

42"

40⅝"

EQUAL

HINGE ℄

UP TO 10⅜"

FINISH FLOOR

STANDARD STRIKE

Dimensions meet the following standards of the American National Standards Institute: A115.1 through A115.14. Holes in strike may vary to suit many lock functions, including those with both latch and dead bolts.

LOCATION DIAGRAM

Note: These dimensions are only a general guide in the absence of other specifications. They would be unsuitable for some types of buildings such as schools. Some dimensions are determined by door manufacturers, whose templates should be consulted.

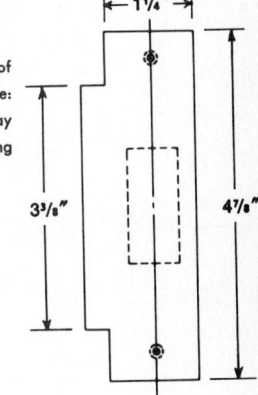

1¼"

3⅜"

4⅞"

OVERHEAD SUPPORT

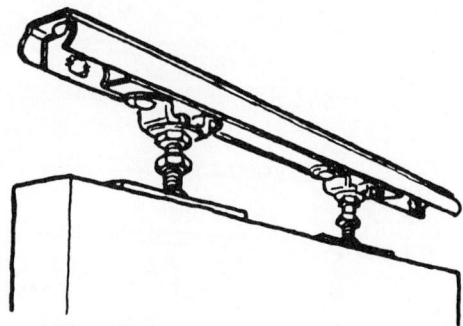

BALL SUPPORTED

(2 rows of ball bearings, in line horizontally)

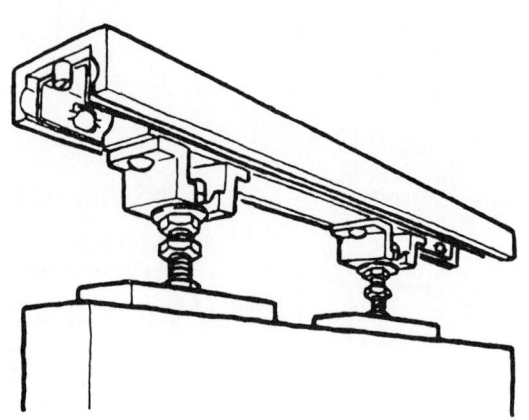

A ball bearing hanger featuring twin rows of ball bearings, accurately hand fitted. Three adjustments compensate for header irregularities. Various hangers are available for loads ranging from 35 to 1,000 lb.

WHEEL SUPPORTED, CHANNEL TRACK

TRACK: rolled steel, formed steel, or extruded aluminum. BEARING: plain, bushed, Oilite bushed, steel balls or steel rollers. WHEELS: steel, brass, fibre, rubber or plastic.

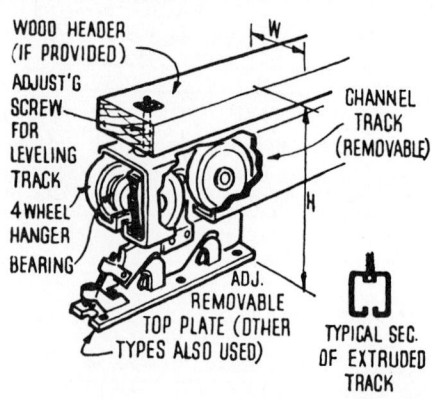

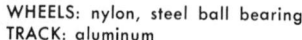

Weight limit (lbs.)	Width "W" (in.)	Clearance "H" (in.)	Notes
125	2¼	6¼	2 wheels only ⎱
175	2¼	6¼	4 wheels only ⎰ as shown
300	3¼	8½	4 wheels only ⎰
100	1⅝	3	With header omitted,
200	1¾	3⅛	non-removable top plate,
300	2⅛	3½	bracket support for track,
50	1	2⅜	and adjustable pendant bolt
50	1	1⅛	Non-adjustable

Also available with special hangers for folding and accordion doors:

Weight (lbs.)	W (in.)	H (in.)
80	3⅝	4⅜ — 4⅞ (higher "H" for folding doors)
110	3⅝	5⅜ — 5⅞
225	5⅝	6⅞ — 7¼

WHEEL SUPPORTED, I-BEAM TRACK, TOP MOUNTED, ADJUSTABLE

WHEELS: nylon, steel ball bearing
TRACK: aluminum

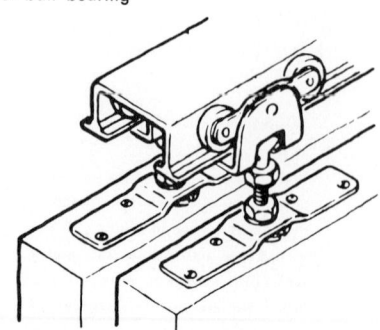

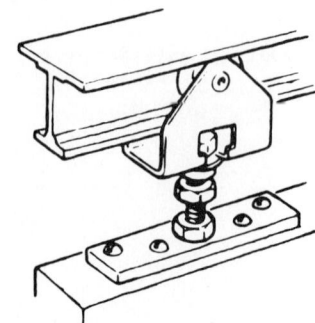

OVERHEAD SUPPORT

WHEEL SUPPORTED

Many variations of track section are available. TRACK: steel or aluminum; double sections are available for by-passing doors. WHEELS: steel, fibre, plastic, rubber or brass. BEARINGS: Oilite, ball bearing or plain. TRACK: may be fastened directly with screws (non-adjustable) or hung from brackets. CARRIER: may be fastened directly or by an intermediary of bracket.

Note: Dimensions, track profiles, hanger styles, vary with manufacturers. Check with catalogs

---

TYPICAL EXTRUDED SECTION FOR BY-PASSING DOORS

TYPICAL DOOR FASTENING DEVICES

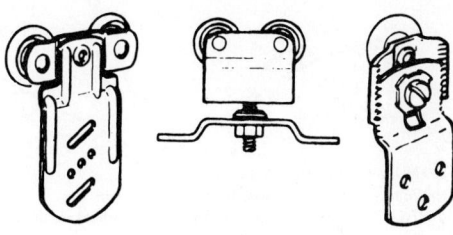

TYPICAL FLOOR GUIDES & TRACK

CONVERGING DOOR GUIDE

THRESHOLD TYPE

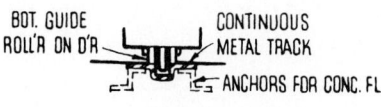

BOT. GUIDE ROLL'R ON D'R — CONTINUOUS METAL TRACK — ANCHORS FOR CONC. FL.

FLUSH TYPE

TRACK FOR FOLDING & ACCORDION DOORS

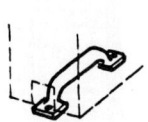

SLOT IN DOOR

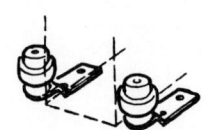

FOR POCKET DOORS ONLY

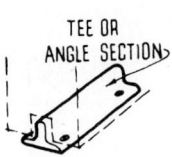

TEE OR ANGLE SECTION

SLOT IN DOOR

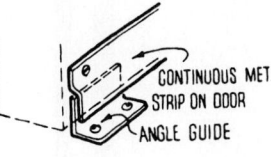

CONTINUOUS MET. STRIP ON DOOR — ANGLE GUIDE

FLOOR SUPPORT

TYPICAL HEAD GUIDES

Note: space "S" must be allowed to permit lifting door up off track.

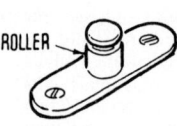

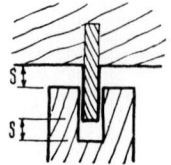

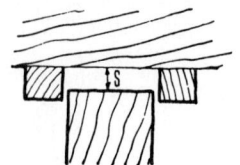

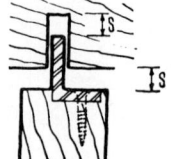

ROLLER GUIDE (1 pair per door). Can run in groove in head, in channel or between hardwood strips

HARDWOOD STRIP IN HEAD, GROOVE IN DOOR.

TWO HARDWOOD STRIPS ON HEAD.

METAL ANGLE ON DOOR, GROOVE IN HEAD.

TYPICAL SHEAVES

Wheels have square edge for channel track, concave edge for T or W shaped track.

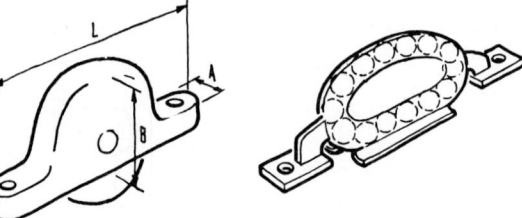

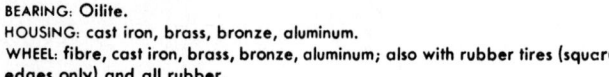

BALL BEARING TYPE
Use with T shaped track.

BEARING: Oilite.
HOUSING: cast iron, brass, bronze, aluminum.
WHEEL: fibre, cast iron, brass, bronze, aluminum; also with rubber tires (square edges only) and all rubber.

TYPICAL TRACK SECTIONS

Special extruded sections are also available with weather-stripping.

Max. Door Weight (1 pr sheaves)	Wheel Dia. (in.)	Housing (in.)		
		A	B	L
50	1 1/16	15/32	7/8	2 15/16
125	1 7/8	11/16	1 15/16	4 3/8
200	3	1 3/16	2 7/8	6

TRACK: brass, bronze, aluminum, stainless steel.

SLIDING DOOR POCKET

All steel pocket frame for vanishing sliding doors. Warp-proof, split jamb and studs consisting of channel sections with wood inserts to which wall panels can be nailed. Designed to take any type of wall material. For 1 3/8 or 1 3/4-in. doors.

TYPICAL PLANS OF SLIDING DOORS Overhead support shown, but plans are similar for floor support.

For center-folding and edge-folding accordion doors, see section on "Folding Partitions."

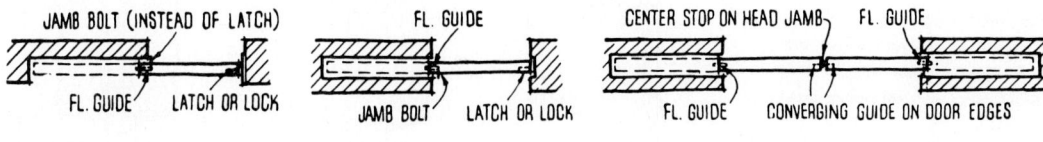

OPEN SIDE POCKET   WALL POCKET

SINGLE SLIDING DOORS

May be used with open side pockets.

BI-PARTING DOORS—May have jamb bolts on both doors or latch (lock) at center.

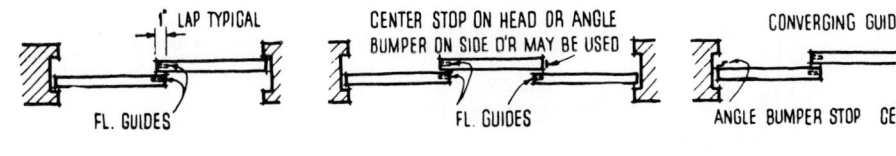

TWO DOORS

Two floor guides required for center door if stop is not used.
THREE DOORS

FOUR DOORS

BY-PASSING DOORS (Parallel Doors)

TYPICAL PULLS, JAMB BOLTS, LATCHES & LOCKS (applicable to all types)

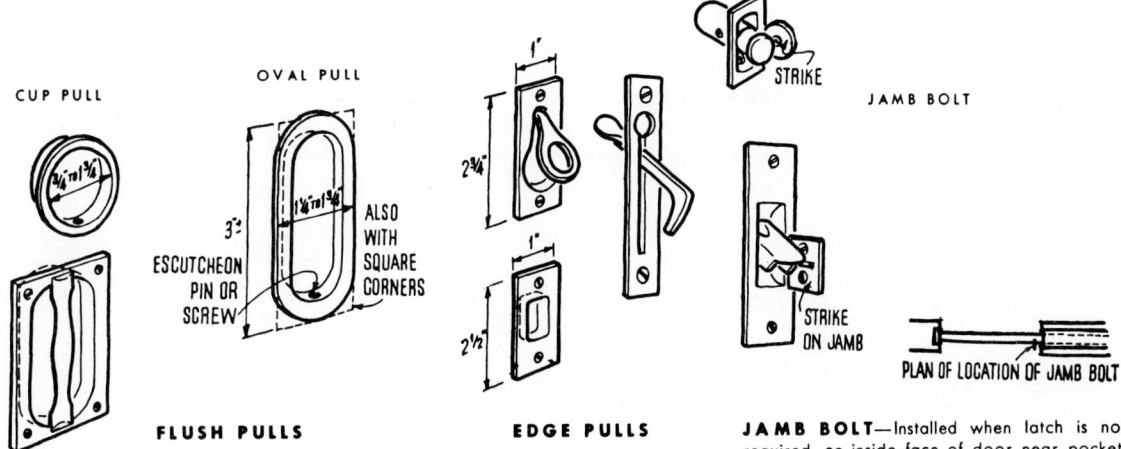

CUP PULL   OVAL PULL   STRIKE   JAMB BOLT

FLUSH PULLS   **EDGE PULLS**   **JAMB BOLT**—Installed when latch is not required, on inside face of door near pocket.

STRIKE ON JAMB

PLAN OF LOCATION OF JAMB BOLT

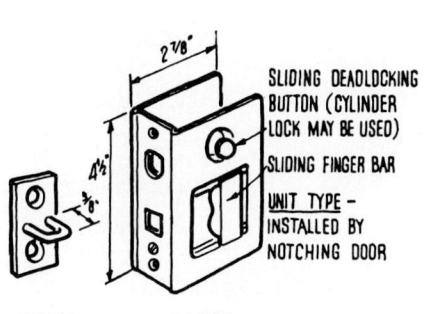

SLIDING DEADLOCKING BUTTON (CYLINDER LOCK MAY BE USED)

SLIDING FINGER BAR

UNIT TYPE—INSTALLED BY NOTCHING DOOR

STRIKE   LATCH

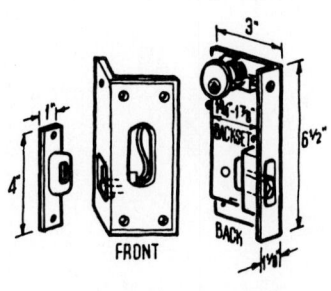

FRONT   BACK

LOCK, Half Mortise, Latch Type
Fed. Spec. No. 197.

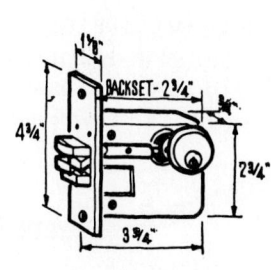

LOCK, Mortise, Deadlock Type
Fed. Spec. No. 198.

HINGES

BUTT HINGES: See Hardware Sheets 12–15. Use removable pin (except for combination doors). Butts should be galvanized or cadmium plated steel with brass pin, or solid brass, bronze or other non-corroding metal

SPRING HINGES (See also Hardware Sheets 14–15)

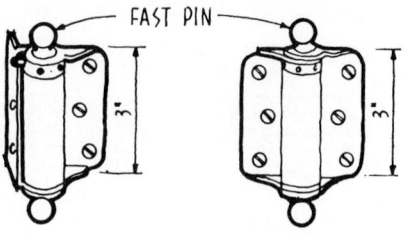

HALF SURFACE ADJUSTABLE TENSION   **FULL SURFACE ADJUSTABLE TENSION**   **FULL SURFACE NON ADJUSTABLE**

ALSO AVAILABLE WITH SPRING ENCLOSED IN BARREL

LATCHES AND CATCHES

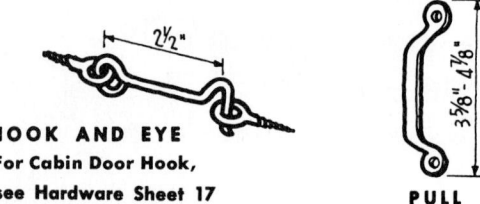

HOOK AND EYE
For Cabin Door Hook, see Hardware Sheet 17

PULL

SPRING CATCH

Thumb Latch can be used for these doors; see Hardware Sheet 3

RIM LATCH
Typical Backset 1½ in.

TUBULAR LATCH
Also available with rose instead of escutcheon; typical backsets: 1¼, 1⅜ in.

MORTISE LATCH
Also available with slide stop instead of dead bolt; typical backsets: 1¼, 1⅜ in.

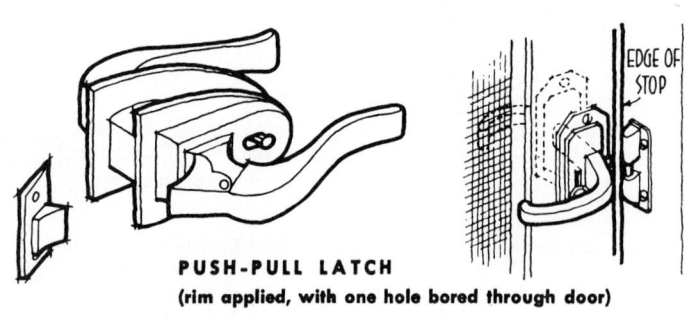

PUSH-PULL LATCH
(rim applied, with one hole bored through door)

CLOSING DEVICES

1. **SPRING HINGES** (see top of page)
2. **COIL SPRING** attached to eyes screwed to jamb and to door

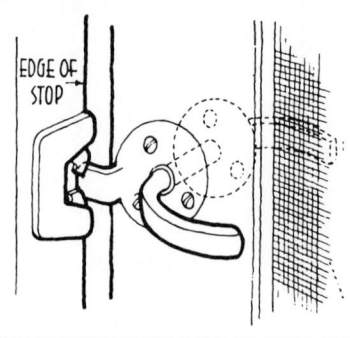

3. **LIQUID CLOSER** (Hardware Sheet 16) best applied to outside of door; parallel arm installation possible between doors if 6 in. clearance provided. This type is used for storm doors and extra heavy screens. Glass in storm doors presents large surface to wind. Strong closing action required and also stay or stop to prevent wind from opening door too far

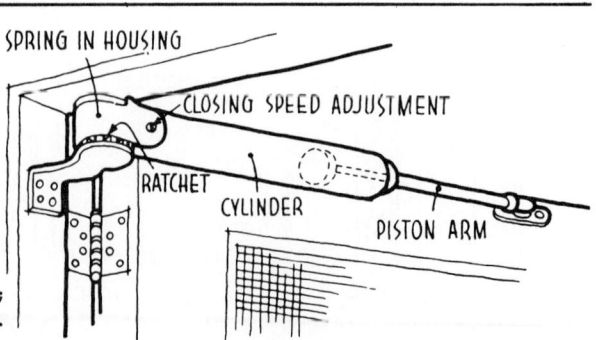

4. **PNEUMATIC CLOSER** operation similar to liquid closers, but checking element uses air instead of liquid

4

Environmental Control

By ROBERT B. NEWMAN and the staff of Bolt Beranek and Newman Inc., Consultants in Acoustics

INTRODUCTION

This section should help the building designer understand the basic principles of architectural acoustics and help him to design buildings in which later "correction" will be unnecessary. The proper acoustic environment for any kind of activity in a building can be determined in advance, and the necessary provisions can be made during the design.

Often acoustics problems are not recognized explicitly by the designer or owner of a building. Everyone knows, for example, that special attention to acoustics is required for an auditorium or a school of music, but too few people realize that every motel and apartment house, every office building and hospital also has acoustical problems that must be solved. Many of these problems can be handled with little added expense.

Each element of the design and construction of a building has some influence on its acoustical characteristics, and unless all of the factors involved are clearly understood and properly incorporated during the design of the building, satisfactory results will seldom be achieved. The important thing is to understand how much and what kind of influence these various elements have.

As will be shown in this section, acoustics should influence not only the choice of finish materials in rooms, but also the basic disposition of the elements of the building—locating noisy rooms far away from quiet rooms, for example. Much expense for special noise-isolating construction can be avoided simply by using good common sense.

SOURCE, PATH, RECEIVER

Almost every acoustical situation can be described in terms of a source of sound, a path for transmission of sound, and a receiver of the sound. Sometimes the source strength can be increased or reduced, the path can be made less or more effective, and the receiver can be made more attentive by removing distraction, or he can be made more tolerant to disturbance.

If, for example, a noisy air-conditioning unit (source) bothers the occupant of an office (receiver), the problem must be analyzed in terms of what can be done about reducing the noise at the source (selection of the quietest available equipment, proper mountings, etc.), what can be done about reducing the transmission (path) by way of structure and ducts (resilient separation, absorbent lining, etc.), and what can be done to get the receiver to tolerate a bit of noise. Attack on any single aspect of the problem may result in overdesign or an unsatisfactory solution.

BASIC PROBLEMS AND CRITERIA

Acoustics is one of the many aspects of the environment in which we live. Sounds can distract us; they can make us happy or sad. The quantity of sound we hear and its context determine the over-all effect. The loud noise of an airplane flying overhead may interfere with a telephone conversation or it may bring on a feeling of fear. Laughter in an adjoining classroom may prove quite distracting to students attending a lecture: the knowledge that something funny is going on in the next room will distract the students, although the level of sound transmitted may not interfere with the audibility of speech.

The basic purpose of architectural acoustics is to provide a *satisfactory acoustic environment* for whatever use the space is intended. In the office building the designer may wish to provide freedom from distraction or privacy for conversation. In the concert hall he may wish to provide maximum communication between the performers and the listeners, allowing the room itself to enhance the quality of the musical sounds. In almost any situation one can determine just what the environmental requirements are, and then proceed to design the building to satisfy them.

FACTORS INFLUENCING THE ACOUSTIC ENVIRONMENT

Qualities that characterize the desired acoustic environment vary widely depending on how the space is to be used, how fussy the users may be, and how the space relates to other parts of the building. A library reading room, for example, should certainly be free from distraction. This freedom can be achieved either by having the reading room quiet (forbidding all sorts of disturbing sound) or by allowing the reading room to have a moderate, continuous background sound level of an unobtrusive, unrecognizable character which hides or masks the many minor intrusions that inevitably come along (people entering and leaving, books being delivered from the stacks, typewriters in operation, etc.). The latter is clearly the more realistic approach. In a large business office one might be able to accept even more noise, but here again there are limits beyond which workers would find it difficult to perform their tasks. People usually tolerate a noise conveying no information better than they do one which tells them something about activities in an adjoining space. An expected noise is often more tolerable than an unexpected one of the same magnitude.

In addition to describing the magnitude and dynamic characteristics of the background sound, we should also describe the character of the occupied space. If a room is finished in materials that are highly sound-reflective, then sounds will persist for a long time and will seem to come from all directions; the space will probably be less pleasant than one which has a moderate amount of sound-absorptive finish. Everyone knows the experience of going into an empty house before the furniture has been put in place—how much more pleasant it is after rugs, curtains and upholstered chairs have been moved in. A room can be too "dead," however, and therefore quite oppressive. There are optimum ranges for reverberation time in occupied spaces. All these matters must be thought through carefully when planning a building.

An important aspect of the acoustic environment, often overlooked, is the opportunity to introduce a sequence of sound qualities as one goes from space to space in a building. A uniform acoustic environment throughout a building can be just as monotonous as a uniform lighting environment. It is pleasant to go from a reverberant space where this quality adds a sense of monumentality, to a "dead" space where, perhaps, communication is important, or where one may merely wish to sit down and read, or experience a feeling of enclosure and quiet. Both kinds of space gain by contrast. It is certainly to be hoped that the old specification of "acoustical tile on all ceilings" is now out-of-date!

FACTORS INFLUENCING HEARING CONDITIONS

If the environment is to be favorable to good hearing conditions

1. It must be completely quiet.

2. The desired sounds must be sufficiently loud.

3. The sounds must be well distributed through the room to give a desirable degree of acoustic uniformity, and to avoid disturbing echoes, focusing, or "islands" of low intensity.

4. The reverberation time must be long enough to give proper blending of sounds and yet be short enough so that there is no excessive overlapping and confusion.

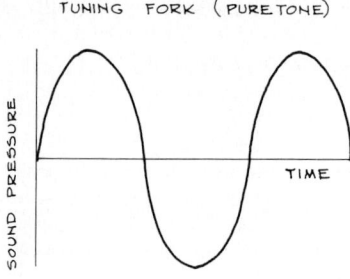

TUNING FORK (PURE TONE)

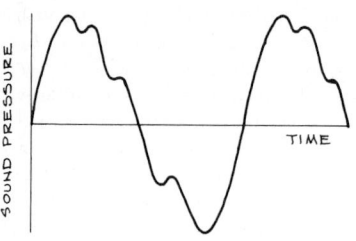

MUSICAL NOTE
(COMBINATION OF SEVERAL PURE TONES)

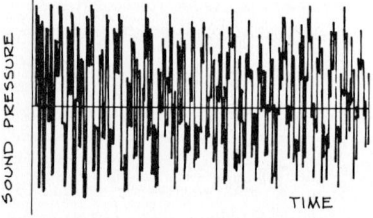

SPEECH, MUSIC, NOISE

Fig. 1. Schematic representations of a pure tone, a musical note, and more complex sounds (speech, music, and noise), showing the variation of sound pressure with time

These simple criteria, if satisfied, will result in good hearing conditions in any space. Sometimes we can use the natural sounds in the space and, by proper design of the enclosing surfaces, achieve all of the requirements for even the most weak-voiced speakers. In large or noisy spaces it may be necessary to use a carefully designed electronic sound reinforcement system. But whatever the requirements or whatever the space, good hearing conditions can be achieved for any type of use. The important thing, as in all aspects of acoustics, is to recognize the problems in advance and solve them in the design stage of the project, not after it is finished.

BASIC TERMINOLOGY AND DEFINITIONS

To deal effectively with acoustics problems in building design, the architect must be familiar with some of the basic acoustical concepts and terminology. The intelligent evaluation of a product often hinges on simple matters of acoustical terminology. Obviously it is not possible to include here all of the terms and concepts that will be encountered, but it is hoped that those outlined below will cover many practical situations. (For more detailed information, refer to references cited with succeeding sections.)

TERMS DEALING WITH THE CHARACTER OF SOUND

Frequency (f): Frequency is the rate of repetition of a periodic phenomenon. That rate, and therefore that frequency, determines the pitch of a sound. Sound waves are basically periodic phenomena. For example, in air they consist of a series of compressions and rarefactions of air particles moving outward from some vibrating source.

Frequency is basic to the description of sounds and materials to control sound. The frequency is the reciprocal of the time period, or the time necessary for the phenomenon to repeat. The unit is the cycle per second (cps) or the numerically equal Hertz (Hz).

The frequency range for the human ear extends from about 20 to about 20,000 Hz for young persons with acute hearing. Some musical instruments encompass almost this entire range, notably the pipe organ. The range of human speech which is most important for understanding extends from about 600 to about 4,000 Hz. On the other hand, if we are concerned with the annoyance of speech sounds, not only with their intelligibility, the lower frequency parts of the speech range may also be important, and these may extend down to below 200 Hz.

Pure tone: A pure tone is the simplest kind of sound because it is composed entirely of sound waves of a single frequency. A pure tone can be generated by striking a tuning fork, but very few of the sounds around us are this "pure."

Musical tone: A musical tone is actually a combination of many pure tones. For example, striking a piano key at middle C (256 Hz) would give rise to a tone composed of this fundamental frequency plus integral multiples of this frequency, called harmonics. These harmonics are what determine the quality or "timbre" of the musical tone.

Common sounds (speech, music, noise): In real life the sounds that surround us are much more complex than the simple pure tone or musical tone discussed above. These more complex sounds include speech, music, and a much wider range of sounds which we call noise if they are sounds we do not want to hear. Figure 1 shows graphically these various kinds of sounds as well as a pure tone and a musical tone.

Frequency band: For the measurement and specification of matters pertaining to sound it is often convenient to divide the audible frequency range into sections. One common division of the frequency range is into octave bands which divide the frequency range into sections centered at the following frequencies:

Octave Band Center Frequencies, Hz

31.5	250	2,000
63	500	4,000
125	1,000	8,000

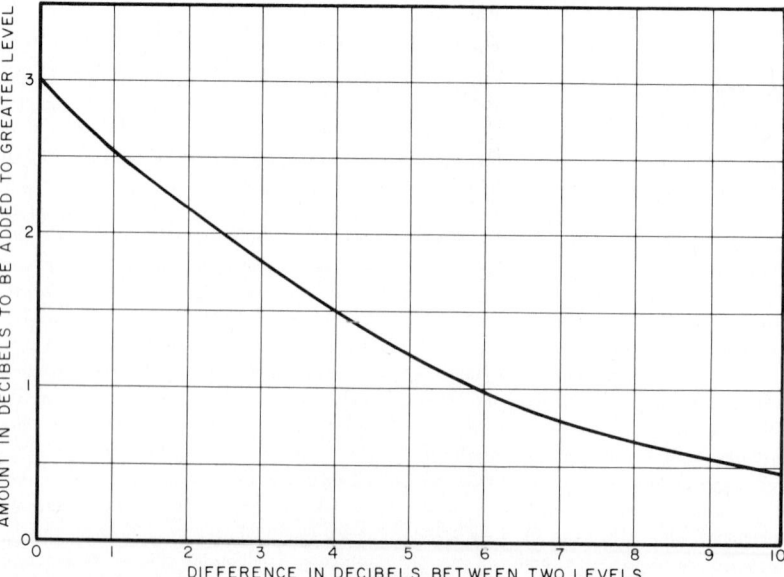

Fig. 2. Chart for adding two sound-pressure levels (SPL) or intensity levels (IL)

Further breakdowns of the frequency range are used for more detailed analyses of sound problems. These include ½ octave bands, ⅓ octave bands, and even smaller divisions of the frequency range.

Velocity of sound (c): A sound wave travels at a velocity that depends primarily on the elasticity and the density of the medium. In air at normal temperature and pressure the sound velocity is approximately 1130 ft/s (344 m/s). This is extremely slow when compared with the velocity of light, which is 186,000 miles per second (300,000 km per sec).

Wavelength (λ): Knowing the velocity of sound, one can calculate at any frequency the wavelength of the sound (i.e., the distance that the sound wave travels in one cycle) by the following expression:

$$\lambda = \frac{c}{f}$$

where λ = wavelength, ft or m
c = velocity of sound, fps or mps
f = frequency of sound, Hz

A few simple calculations will reveal that high-frequency sounds are characterized by short wavelengths and low-frequency sounds by long wavelengths. For example, at 100 Hz the wavelength of sound in air is about 11 ft (3.5 m), while at 1,000 Hz the wavelength is only 1 ft (35 cm).

TERMS DEALING WITH THE MAGNITUDE OF SOUND

Sound power (W): Sound power in watts describes the energy of the sound source. This power may be: (1) the total power radiated by the source over its entire frequency range; (2) the power radiated in a limited frequency range; or (3) the power radiated in each of a series of frequency bands. Obviously the frequency range of sound power (or any of the other quantities dealing with the magnitude of sound discussed below) should be clearly specified.

Sound intensity (I): The sound intensity is the power radiated in a specified direction through unit area normal to this direction; e.g., watts per square foot or watts per square centimeter. This term is analogous to light intensity.

Sound pressure (p): The sound pressure is the variation from normal atmospheric pressure caused by the flow of sound energy as a to-and-fro motion of the molecules in the air. Most equipment for measuring sound is pressure-sensitive, and it is usually easier to measure pressure fluctuations than intensities.

The commonly used unit for pressure (cgs system) is the microbar (1 dyne/cm²). In the SI system, the unit is the pascal (1 newton per square meter (N/m²). 1 pascal = 10 microbars.

Decibels (dB): The decibel is a dimensionless unit for expressing the ratio of two numerical values on a logarithmic scale. It is convenient to use decibels in dealing with sound power, sound intensity, or sound pressure because of the tremendous range of values of these quantities that can be perceived by the ear. For example, the range of sound intensities than can be perceived by the normal ear extends all the way from the faint rustle of leaves up to the roar of a jet engine, which encompasses a ratio of sound intensities from one million-million to one. The number of decibels is ten times the logarithm to the base 10 of the numerical ratio of the two quantities. For example, let W_1 and W_2 designate two powers, or I_1 and I_2 designate two sound intensities, and p_1 and p_2 designate two pressures, then the corresponding number of decibels (M in each case) is

$$M \text{ (sound power)} = 10 \log \frac{W_1}{W_2} \text{ (decibels)}$$

$$M \text{ (sound intensity)} = 10 \log \frac{I_1}{I_2} \text{ (decibels)}$$

$$M \text{ (sound pressure)} = 10 \log \left(\frac{p_1}{p_2}\right)^2 \text{ (decibels)}$$

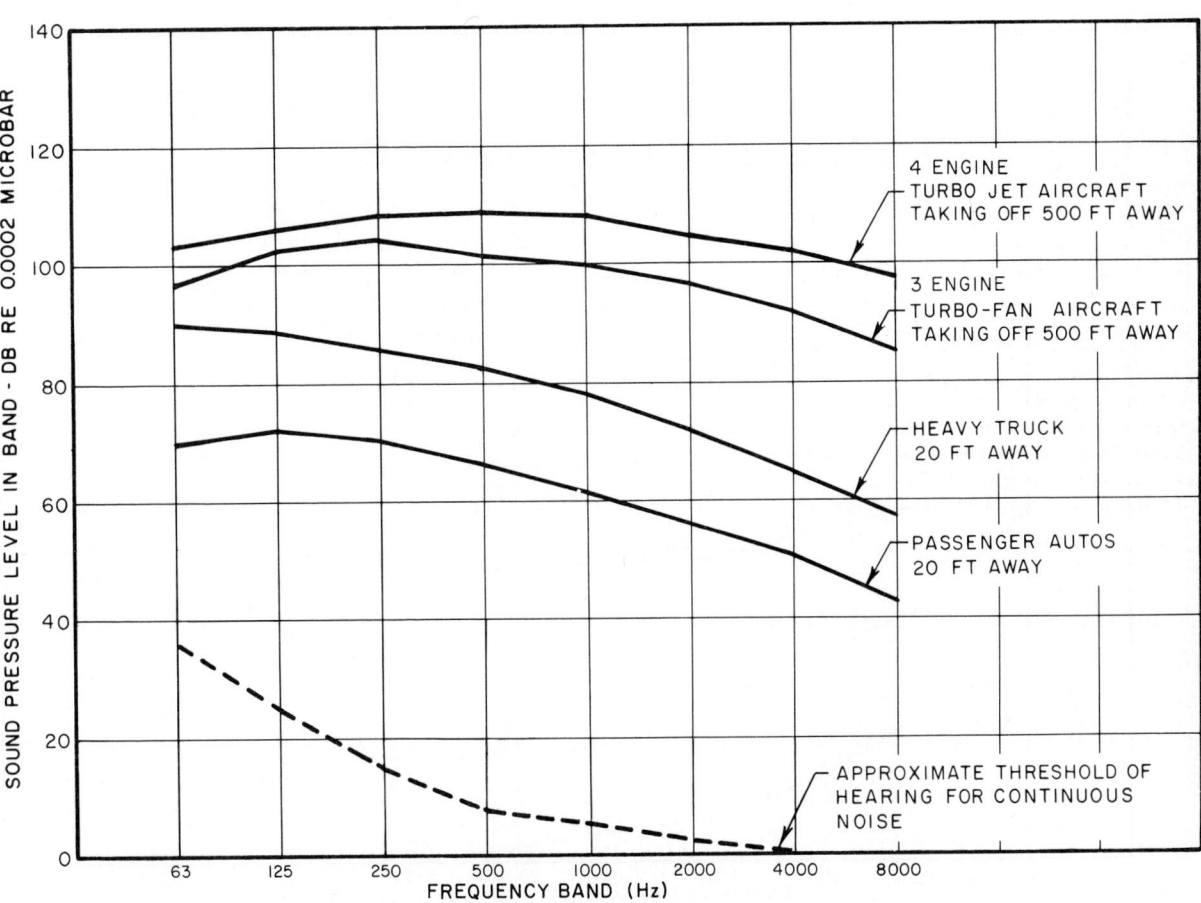

Fig. 3. Sound-pressure levels for some noise sources; measured outdoors

Addition of decibels: Decibels, since they are logarithmic units and not like ordinary units such as feet and meters, cannot be added directly. One must convert back to power, intensity, or pressure, add these quantities, and finally convert the total back to decibels. In other words, 50 dB plus 50 dB is not 100 dB but rather 53 dB. A simplified chart for adding quantities in decibels is given in Fig. 2.

Sound-power level (PWL): Sound-power level is the designation in decibels of the ratio of two sound powers. The reference power is usually taken to be 10^{-12} watt Therefore,

$$PWL = 10 \log\left(\frac{W}{10^{-12}}\right) \text{ decibels}$$

Sound-intensity level (IL): Sound-intensity level is the designation in decibels of the ratio of two intensities. The reference intensity is usually taken to be 10^{-16} watt/sq cm. Therefore,

$$IL = 10 \log\left(\frac{I}{10^{-16}}\right) \text{ decibels}$$

Sound-pressure level (SPL): Sound-pressure level is the designation in decibels of the ratio of two pressures squared. The reference pressure is usually taken to be 0.0002 microbar (0.0002 dyne/cm²). In SI units, the reference pressure is 20 μPa (2×10^{-5} N/m²). The sound-pressure level in decibels is the same with either reference pressure. Therefore,

$$SPL = 10 \log\left(\frac{P \text{ (microbars)}}{0.0002 \text{ microbar}}\right)^2 \text{ or}$$

$$= 10 \log\left(\frac{p \text{ (Pa)}}{2 \times 10^{-5} \text{ Pa}}\right)^2$$

Instruments that measure sound level give sound pressure level in decibels. But in most circumstances the sound pressure level and the sound intensity level of a given sound are numerically equal and can be used interchangeably. Some typical measured sound-pressure levels are shown in Figs. 3 and 4.

Sound level: Simple sound-measuring devices are available to record the physical magnitude of sound in terms of single numbers. Single-number sound levels are defined as the quantity read on a standard sound-level meter with an appropriate frequency-weighting network. A commonly used system of single numbers are A-scale readings which, for relatively low over-all sound levels, correspond to the way our ears respond to the sound (i.e., they weight or "ignore" the low-frequency end of the sound spectrum). The frequency-weighting network must always be known in order to evaluate single-number readings. Fig. 5 shows the range of some common sounds measured in terms of average levels obtained from sound-level meter readings, using the standard A-scale frequency-weighting.

Noise reduction (NR): Noise reduction is the difference in decibels of the sound-pressure levels or the sound-intensity levels at two points along a sound path. Alternatively, it is the difference in decibels of the sound-pressure levels or sound-intensity levels existing at a single point before and after a change of acoustical treatment to a space. Therefore, the following expressions are often used:

$$NR = IL_1 - IL_2 \text{ (decibels)}$$
$$NR = SPL_1 - SPL_2 \text{ (decibels)}$$

Attenuation: Attenuation, or the reduction in sound level, is often used in the same sense as noise reduction described above.

SOUND UNDER FREE-FIELD CONDITIONS

Inverse square law: Under free-field conditions of sound radiation (i.e., no reflecting surfaces around the sound source) the sound intensity is reduced by ¼ each time the distance from the sound source is doubled. This is expressed as follows:

$$\frac{I_1}{I_2} = \frac{d_2^2}{d_1^2}$$

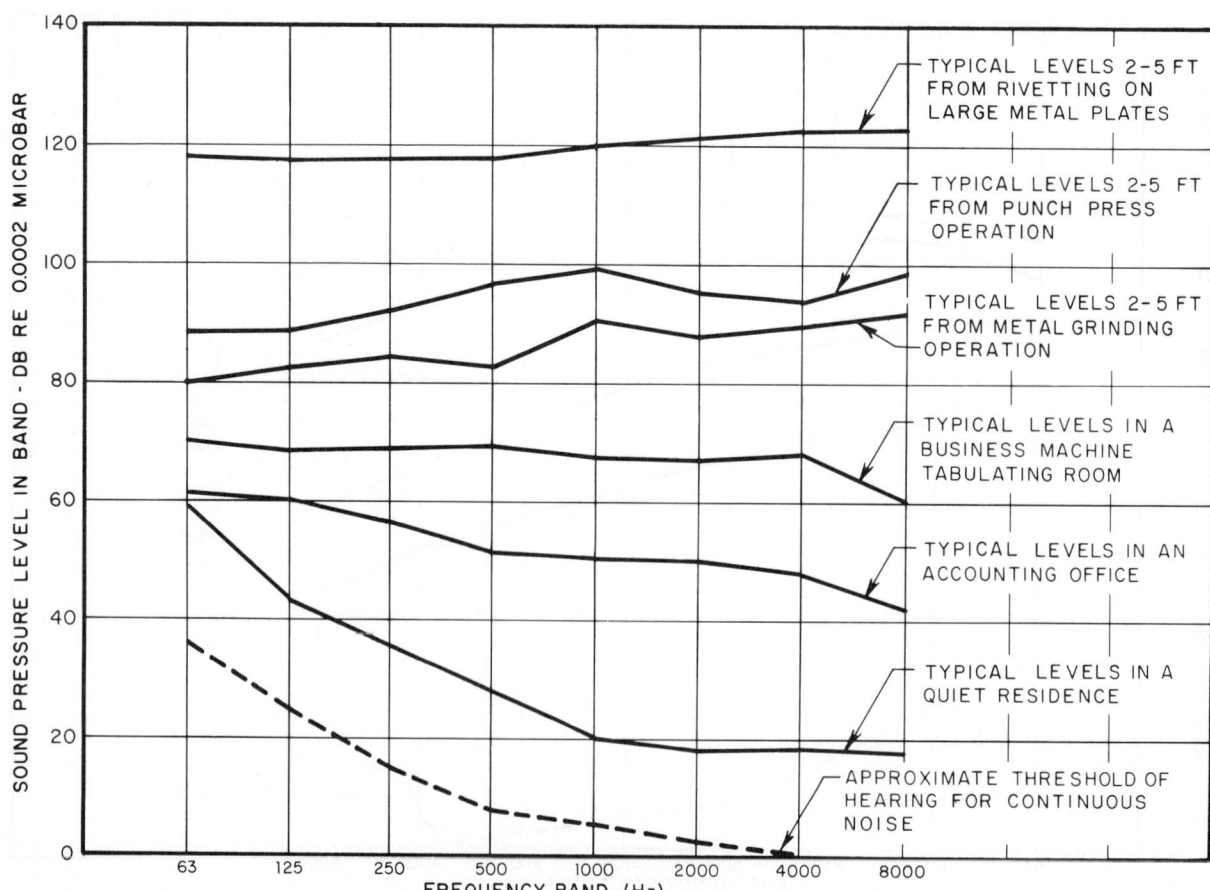

Fig. 4. Sound-pressure levels for some noise sources; measured indoors

where I_1 and I_2 are the sound intensities at distances d_1, and d_2 from the sound source. This phenomenon is analogous to the reduction of light intensity as one moves away from a source of light under free-field conditions. In terms of sound levels (*IL* or *SPL*) the inverse square law means that the level is decreased by 6 dB each time the distance from the source is doubled.

SOUND IN ROOMS

Reflection and absorption: When a sound source is placed within an enclosure, reflection of the sound wave traveling outward from the sound source occurs at the boundaries, and the sound waves continue to reflect between the boundaries themselves. If the sound source is continuous, this reflection of sound will establish relatively constant levels within a normal-sized room (except very near the source). These "built-up" or reverberant levels are dependent on the amount of absorption of the sound energy that takes place at each encounter of the sound wave with the enclosing surface. Most hard surfaces (concrete, plaster, glass, etc.) absorb very little sound and are generally classed as sound-reflecting surfaces. Other materials (usually porous, or thin panel materials) absorb appreciable amounts of sound and are termed sound-absorbing material (see section on "Criteria for the Acoustic Environment").

Sound-absorption coefficient (α): The absorption coefficient is the fraction of incident sound energy that is absorbed by a surface. Random incidence of the impinging sound is assumed unless otherwise specified.

Absorption units (A): Absorption units are usually expressed in sabins and equal the area of a surface S times its absorption coefficient α. Usually several kinds of surfaces or materials are included in a room, and the total absorption is the sum of the areas times their absorption coefficients.

Noise-reduction coefficient (NRC): The noise-reduction coefficient for a sound-absorbing material is the arithmetic average of the absorption coefficients at 250, 500, 1,000, and 2,000 Hz, rounded off to the nearest multiple of 0.05.

Dead room: A dead room is one characterized by large amounts of absorption.

Live room: A live room is one characterized by very small amounts of absorption.

Room noise reduction (NR): The intensity levels or sound-pressure levels in a room built up by repeated reflections of sound from the enclosing surfaces are affected by the amount of absorption present. The difference in levels given by two conditions of total room absorption is as follows:

$$NR = 10 \log\left(\frac{A_2}{A_1}\right) \text{ (decibels)};$$

where A_1 and A_2 are the total absorbing

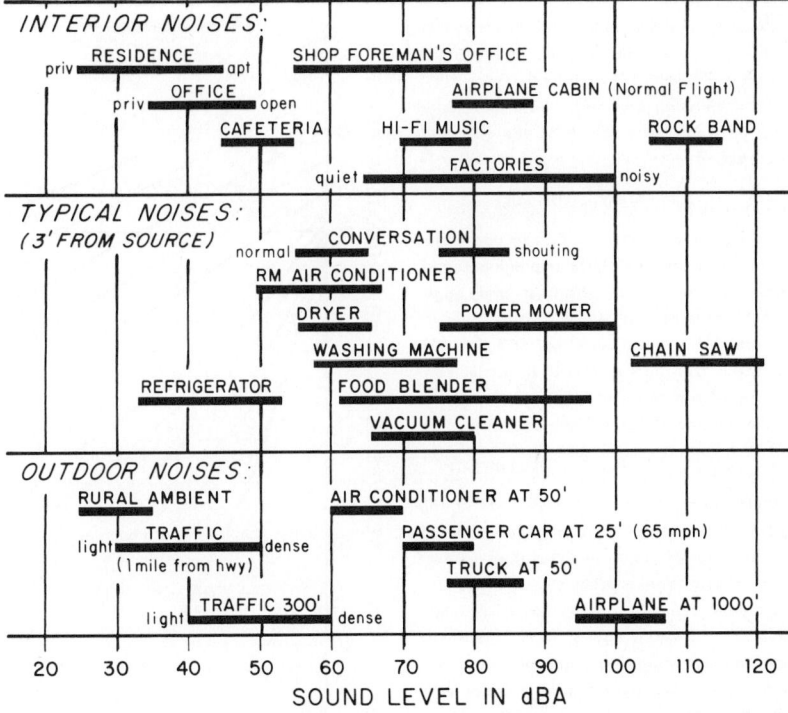

Fig. 5. Range of sound levels in dBA found in typical environments from a variety of sources. Single-number sound level readings must be used with caution when analyzing noise problems

units in sabins in the room before and after treatment.

Reverberation: Reverberation is the persistence of sound after the source of sound has stopped. It is due to the repeated reflections of the sound remaining between the enclosing surfaces.

Reverberation time (T): The reverberation time of a room is by definition the time required for the sound level to decrease 60 dB after the source is stopped. The reverberation time is given approximately by the following expression:

$$T = .05 \frac{V}{A} \text{ (sec)}$$

where V = volume of the space, cu ft
A = total room absorption, sabins

In metric units:

$$T = 0.16 \frac{V}{A} \text{ (s)}$$

where V = volume of space, m³
A = total room absorption, metric sabins

Diffusion: Ideally a diffuse sound field is one in which the sound level is everywhere the same. Diffusion is a desirable characteristic for many listening spaces (see section on "Design For Good Hearing").

Echo: An echo is a sound wave reflected or otherwise returned with sufficient magnitude and delay so as to be perceived as a sound distinct from the directly transmitted sound.

Flutter echo: A flutter echo is a rapid

succession of reflected sound waves resulting from a single initial sound pulse. This effect often occurs with a sound source between two hard parallel walls and is sometimes confused with reverberation.

Creep: Creep is the reflection of sound along a curved surface. It occurs when a sound source is located close to surfaces such as domes, vaults, etc., so that the reflected sound energy is conserved and can be heard distinctly at some point further along the surface; for example, a "whispering gallery" (see Fig. 35).

Focusing: Focusing occurs when sound waves are reflected from concave surfaces and build up the reflected sound levels at some point or area away from the reflecting surface.

Standing waves: In small rooms, in particular, sound waves can build up nodes and antinodes which are characterized by regions of maximum sound-pressure level and minimum sound-pressure level. Standing-wave effects are usually restricted to the low-frequency range.

SOUND TRANSMISSION BETWEEN ROOMS

Transmission coefficient (τ): The transmission coefficient is the fraction of incident energy that is transmitted through a barrier. Thus

$$\tau = \frac{W_2}{W_1}$$

where W_1 is the sound energy in watts incident on the barrier and W_2 is the sound energy in watts transmitted.

Transmission loss (TL): The transmission loss of a barrier is given by the following expression:

$$TL = 10 \log \frac{1}{\tau} \text{ (decibels)}$$

It is a basic property of a barrier and varies with the frequency of the impinging sound, the surface weight, stiffness, and edge-mounting condition of the barrier.

Effective transmission loss (Eff TL): The effective transmission loss of a barrier consisting of two or more different materials is given by the following expressions:

$$Eff\ TL = 10 \log \frac{\Sigma S}{\Sigma \tau S} \text{ (decibels)},$$

where ΣS is the sum of the areas of the parts of the barrier in square feet, and $\Sigma \tau S$ is the areas of materials times their respective transmission coefficients.

Sound transmission class (STC): A single number rating assigned to a measured transmission-loss curve obtained by comparison to a standard curve in accordance with recommended rules given in ASTM E413-73 (see also discussion in section on "Sound Isolation").

Room-to-room noise reduction (NR): The difference in sound-intensity levels *(IL)* or sound-pressure levels *(SPL)* between a "source" room and a "receiving" room is given approximately by the following expression:

$$NR = TL - 10 \log \frac{S}{A_2} \text{ (decibels)},$$

where *TL* is the effective transmission loss of the barrier in decibels, *S* is the total area of the barrier in square feet, and A_2 is the total absorption in the receiving room in sabins.

Attenuation factor: Attenuation factor is sometimes used to describe the room-to-room noise reduction of a particular construction. For example, the noise reduction values through suspended ceiling configurations over two adjacent test rooms are reported in terms of attenuations in decibels (see section on "Sound Isolation").

Impact transmission: This is what happens when a structure is in direct contact with a vibrating source or is struck by an impulsive force such as footfall. The resulting vibration of the structure causes radiation of airborne sound into adjoining spaces.

Structure-borne transmission: Structure-borne transmission refers to sound waves transmitted within a structure. These structure-borne waves may be induced by airborne sound impinging on a barrier or by direct impact sound sources. If the structure-borne waves are of sufficient magnitude, they may be reradiated into a space as air-borne sound.

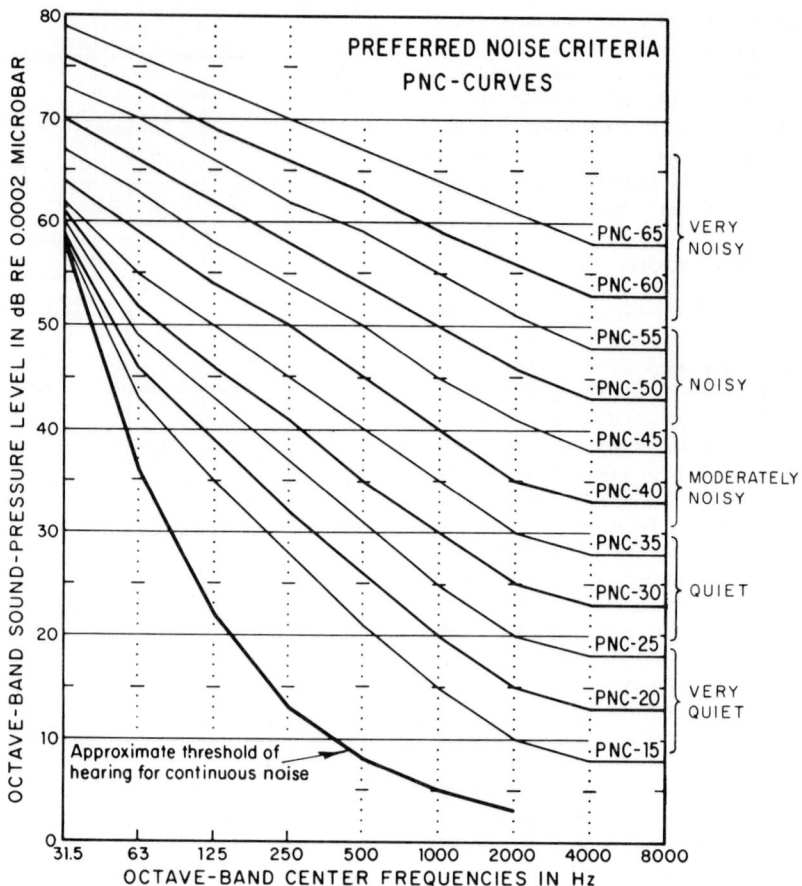

Fig. 6.   **Preferred noise criteria (PNC) curves**

Background noise: Background noise refers to the ambient or all-encompassing noise associated with a given environment and is usually due to a composite of sounds from many sources near and far.

Masking noise: This usually refers to a background noise that has the ability to cover up some specific intruding sound. It is sometimes called "acoustical perfume."

Speech privacy: Speech privacy is a condition of sound isolation of a room in which the occupant feels he has sufficient freedom from intruding speech sounds, so that he can conduct his work in an undisturbed manner. This is usually achieved when the speech levels transmitted to the space are unintelligible or very nearly so.

Table 1.   Recommended noise criteria for various uses

Type of space	Recommended noise criteria (range or maximum)	Approximate sound level in dBA
Broadcast and recording studios, concert halls	PNC 15	25
Legitimate theaters (no amplification), churches	PNC 20	30
Large conference rooms (for 50 or so), small auditoriums, music rehearsal rooms, motion picture theaters	PNC 25	33
Classrooms, conference rooms (for 20 or so)	PNC 30	37
Bedrooms (hotels, apartment houses, hospitals, residences)	PNC 25–40	34–47
Private or semiprivate offices, living rooms, libraries	PNC 30–40	38–47
Sports coliseums (amplification)	PNC 35–45	42–52
Restaurants, stores	PNC 35–45	42–52
General offices (typing, etc.)	PNC 40–50	47–56
Factories	PNC 50–75	56–80

CRITERIA FOR THE ACOUSTIC ENVIRONMENT

Before the designer can begin actual engineering work on a building, he must establish his criteria. Basically, a satisfactory acoustic environment is one in which the character and magnitude of all sounds are compatible with the satisfactory use of the space for its intended purpose. While this is a reasonable objective, it is not always easy to express it in quantitative terms. In talking about the thermal environment, for example, one cannot simply say that 70° F is comfortable but must also talk about humidity, air movement, etc. In lighting, one cannot simply say that 100 foot-candles is an ideal light intensity but must also consider other factors in the luminous environment, such as specular glare, color, continuity, etc. Similarly in acoustics, we cannot just say how much noise we want but rather we must specify what kind of noise, what pitch, whether it is continuous, expected, or contains information, etc.

Human beings are highly adaptable to the various physical phenomena of heat, light, and sound, and their sensitivity varies widely. The human ear can detect the sound-intensity levels of less than 10 dB (the gentle rustle of leaves) and yet can survive without permanent hearing damage the powerful roar of a jet engine—as much as 120 dB, almost a million-million times the intensity of the leaf rustle sound.

Psychologists and research workers in acoustics have laid a good deal of the ground work that enables us to understand how much and what kind of noise will affect speech communication, annoyance, and fatigue. Work has also been done on the problem of hearing damage due to high-intensity noise levels, but this is seldom an important problem in ordinary buildings. Although the research results are far from complete, they do lead us to certain generally accepted specifications on the noise environment in many of the kinds of spaces we design.

Buildings are often built on sites near airports or other loud noise sources. Recent work on acoustical criteria has included consideration of allowable levels of intruding sound from these sources into occupied spaces and also methods of predicting "acoustic suitability" of sites. In critical spaces, infrequent intrusion of noise can be permitted to be as much as 5 dB above the normal background without degradation of the environment. If the space is not one that requires a very low background, occasional intrusions of up to 10 dB above the normal background may be acceptable. More than 10 dB of intrusion will normally be unacceptable and cause major complaints or even legal action.

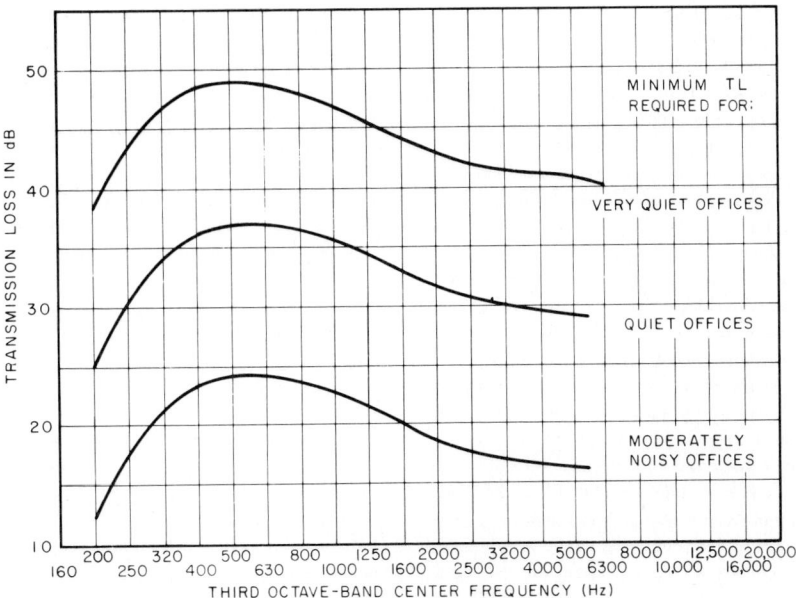

Fig. 7. Approximate transmission-loss criteria for speech privacy between offices

Some recommended noise criteria for various types of occupancy are indicated in Table 1.

As one might expect, spaces where listening is important require low background levels, and business offices and factories where speech communication is restricted to short distances can have higher background levels.

BACKGROUND NOISE CRITERIA

Although single-number sound level readings (dBA) give us some idea of how much noise we have, a much better method of specifying continuous background noise level is the use of noise criteria (PNC) curves (see Fig. 6). The PNC curves are a further refinement of the formerly used NC curves, taking more nearly into account the noise spectrums actually observed in a great many building situations. The PNC curves provide a system of rank-ordering various noise spectrums in terms of specified sound pressure levels in each of nine octave frequency bands. Octave bands are convenient for dividing the audible frequency range into segments for purposes of measurement. The PNC numbers are the arithmetic average of the sound pressure levels in the 500, 1,000, and 2,000 Hz bands. These frequency bands are very closely related to the important frequencies for speech intelligibility. Thus, the presence of noise in these bands can interfere with speech, and most people rate the noisiness of the environment with speech interference.

Also shown in Fig. 6 is the subjective evaluation that a listener might give to a particular acoustic environment that has octave band sound levels approximating these curves. Below PNC 25, for example, most people would judge a space "very quiet"; above PNC 55, "very noisy"; and between these extremes, "quiet," "moderately noisy," and "noisy." In terms of speech communication, a background sound spectrum of PNC 30 would permit understanding of speech at normal voice levels at distances up to about 20 ft. A PNC-40 spectrum would permit a raised voice to be understood at 20 ft but would only permit normal voice communication at distances up to about 6 ft. With a background spectrum of PNC 50, a raised voice would be required to be heard clearly at more than 3 ft between speaker and listener. Even higher levels than PNC 50 would be permissible in a factory, where speech communication and annoyance is not too important. However, if the continuous background noise levels exceed PNC 70, it is impossible to use the telephone; and with spectrum levels as high as PNC 80, there may be a possibility of permanent hearing damage after long exposure.

The Walsh-Healey Public Contracts Act relating to industrial hygiene was amended in 1969 to include the specification of maximum safe levels of noise for various exposure periods for people working in industries doing work for the government. The Occupational Safety and Health Act of 1970 incorporates the Walsh-Healey requirements and applies to all industries in the United States. These noise specifications are given in terms of dBA rather than in terms of detailed octave band spectrums. For example, the maximum level of ambient noise may not exceed 90 dBA if a worker is exposed to it for eight hours a day. Higher levels are permitted for shorter exposures.

It should be emphasized that we are often just as interested in the minimum as in the maximum permissible levels as described in Table 1. In an office or even in a residence it may be desirable to have a certain amount of masking noise to assure adequate acoustical privacy between spaces, and it may well be that our *PNC* curve would be used to specify the bottom limit of background noise levels as well as the maximum. For example, in a small private office the occupant may not object to the noise of a continuous background sound spectrum as high as *PNC* 35 or *PNC* 40. Often, such a background spectrum is provided by the ventilating system in the building. If the ventilating system will not make enough noise, a noisier grille may be selected so that adequate privacy is achieved with the lightweight, movable wall construction separating one office from another. In other words, while we do not want the background noise to exceed a specified criterion spectrum, at the same time we do not want it to fall much below this spectrum.

In an auditorium, however, where we do not need any masking noise we should achieve as near inaudibility of background as possible, *PNC* 20 or less.

The ASHRAE Guide in its chapter on Sound Control describes in detail methods for calculating noise levels due to air-handling equipment and also considers in greater detail the criteria for background level design. With the information provided in the Guide and in the manufacturers' literature the architect today is in an excellent position to specify the acoustic environment and then to select the proper materials and equipment to meet the design goals.

CRITERIA FOR SPEECH PRIVACY BETWEEN OFFICES

As will be pointed out in a later section, speech privacy between rooms is determined not only by the transmission loss of the separating partitions, but also by the background noise in the spaces. In the special situation of office privacy, we can give some approximate recommendations for the transmission loss that must be provided by the partitions for particular background noise conditions. These criteria, giving the required transmission loss as a function of frequency in ⅓ octave bands, are shown in Fig. 7. The subjective ratings of background noise correspond with those shown in Fig. 6. It must be carefully noted, however, that Fig. 7 gives approximate criteria values for transmission loss and assumes average levels of speech effort in the adjacent office, and that the office occupant expects average privacy (not complete secrecy).

CRITERIA FOR REVERBERATION IN ROOMS

Every occupied space has some sort of reverberation characteristic. It may be live or it may be dead but there is always a certain amount of return of energy reflected from distant surfaces to the listener that gives him a "feel" of the space. There are no criteria for exactly what reverberation time one should have in a house or in an office but experience shows that, unless such occupied spaces are furnished or finished with reasonable amounts of sound-absorbing material, they will not be comfortable. The next section contains a discussion of the procedure for calculating reverberation time in a space as well as the effect of the amounts of sound-absorbing treatment in a room on the general sound level in the room. However, the quality of the sound in the space is usually a more important factor than the absolute level, at least within the ordinary range of interest. Sound-absorbing treatment in a space reduces the spreading of sound and localizes the direction of sources: sounds do not seem to come from everywhere, and the annoyance level from all sorts of noise sources is less. In a restaurant sound-absorbing materials to reduce reverberation time are very important in making an acceptable acoustic environment. With hard surfaces in such spaces the din often becomes unbearable, and corrective measures must be taken

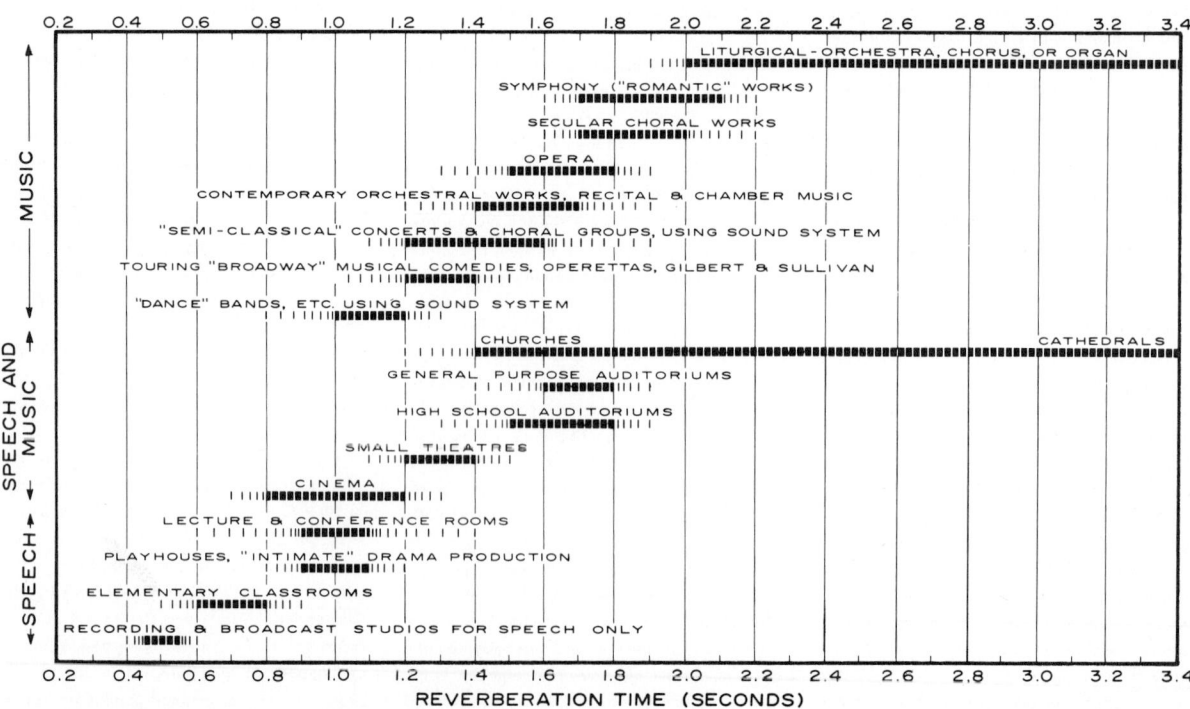

Fig. 8. **Optimum reverberation (500-1000 Hz) for auditoriums and similar facilities**

later. In the house with an open plan and sparse furnishings some sound-absorbing material on floor or ceiling surfaces can do a great deal to improve the acoustic environment.

In larger rooms where hearing is important, we can put definite numbers on the range of reverberation times which seem to most listeners to be satisfactory. A small conference room or lecture room used primarily for speech needs a relatively low reverberation time in order to achieve high articulation and separation of successive sounds for maximum audibility. At the other end of the scale is the large cathedral church where liturgical music is of major importance and where the audibility of a sermon can be handled with a carefully designed sound reinforcement system and where maximum blending of the musical sounds must be the criterion for design. Between these extremes lie the whole range of types of performance. In general, the reverberation time of an auditorium of any size should lie somewhere between 1 and 2 sec for best results. In general, the larger the hall, the longer the reverberation time must be for satisfactory listening conditions. But for every situation there is considerable latitude in the choice of a design reverberation time that will give satisfaction. In Fig. 8 we show the range of reverberation times generally considered acceptable for various types of use. The preferred range for most uses is shown as a black bar for the given function, and is extended with the dotted sections showing what might be called the extremes of acceptability. An auditorium which must serve many functions may be designed with a compromise reverberation time. A better solution is to provide large but variable areas of sound absorbing treatment to accommodate functions demanding less reverberation than the basic design provides. A chart such as this should be considered only a guide for design, and the selection of the criterion for each particular situation should be considered very carefully in the light of the actual proposed uses of the space.

SOUND ABSORPTION

The architect is concerned with the amount of sound absorption in a space for any or all of the following purposes:

1. To reduce noise levels (noise control)

2. To shorten or prolong reverberation (reverberation control)

3. To eliminate echo (echo control), or other undesirable sound reflections (focusing or flutter control)

For example, in a typical school classroom, noise control (i.e., the reduction of

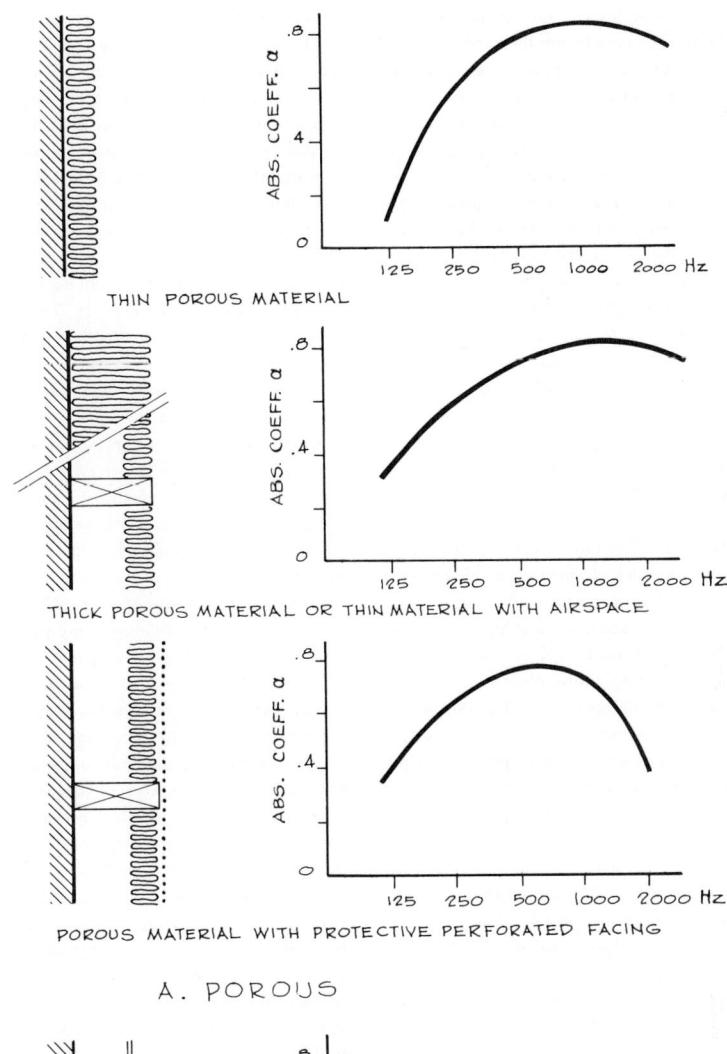

THIN POROUS MATERIAL

THICK POROUS MATERIAL OR THIN MATERIAL WITH AIRSPACE

POROUS MATERIAL WITH PROTECTIVE PERFORATED FACING

A. POROUS

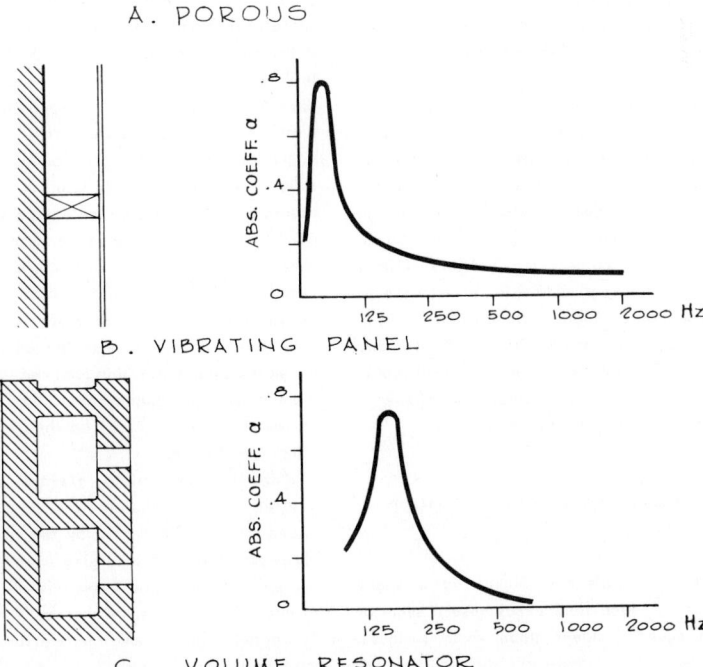

B. VIBRATING PANEL

C. VOLUME RESONATOR

Fig. 9. Basic types and relative efficiencies of sound-absorbing materials

activity noise levels built up by repeated reflections of sound from the room surfaces) may be just as important as reverberation control (the avoidance of excessive persistence of reflected sound after the source has stopped). In the latter case, excessive reverberation would result in overlapping of successive syllables and make speech difficult to understand. In a concert hall design, on the other hand, the architect may avoid introducing any sound absorption besides that provided by the audience itself, in order to achieve the longest possible reverberation time. Even the inclusion of sound-absorbing material for echo control may prove undesirable in a concert hall. A preferable solution may be to redesign any offending surfaces so that the reflected sound is redirected and no longer heard as a discrete echo.

Thus, the first job of the designer is to determine which of these requirements must be met in the space and to what extent; that is, as in every acoustics problem, the design objective must be clearly defined. The success in meeting these objectives depends largely upon the designer's knowledge and skill in the selection and use of materials.

It should be emphasized that the principal uses of sound-absorbing materials are for the control of sound *within* a space and not for the control of sound transmission between spaces. There is much confusion on this point and much disappointment has resulted from the misapplication of sound "insulating" materials to room surfaces or in the stud space of some partition constructions. Such use of sound-absorbing material often makes no significant difference in the sound transmission between spaces. For the most part, sound-absorbing materials, especially porous lightweight ones, offer little resistance to sound transmission. There are, however, some new specially designed materials (suspended acoustical tile ceilings in particular) which act as both sound absorbers and sound-reducing barriers. (These combination materials will be discussed in the section on Sound Isolation.) However, in general, one should view cautiously any "cure-alls" which promise to solve all acoustics problems with a single homogeneous material of practically no thickness.

THE BASIC MECHANISM OF SOUND ABSORPTION

All materials and objects in a space where a sound field exists absorb some of the sound incident upon their surfaces. Porous, fibrous materials such as carpets, draperies, upholstered furniture, and clothing, and specially designed sound-absorbing materials are capable of appreciable sound

absorption (that is, they do not reflect very much of the sound energy which strikes them). Impervious, thin, flexible panels (plywood, etc.) absorb sound also, but their effectiveness is usually limited to the low-frequency range of the audible spectrum. By contrast with these absorbers, most common building materials (brick, concrete, glass, plaster, etc.) are very poor sound absorbers and most often absorb less than 5 per cent of the incident sound energy in the frequency range of interest. In fact, these latter materials may be classified as sound-reflecting materials and can be used effectively in auditorium design to distribute the desired sounds properly.

Sound absorption results when the impinging sound energy is converted to heat energy in the body of the absorber (although the amount of heat is quite small). In the porous type of sound absorber this occurs as the pressure of the air increases and decreases with the arrival of successive sound waves causing the air molecules near the porous surface to migrate into the labyrinth of capillary-like tunnels in rapid to-and-fro motion. Part of the acoustical energy is thus converted to heat by frictional drag. The amount of friction, and hence absorption, provided by the material is, of course, determined by the actual physical properties of the porous layer: thickness, density, porosity, the orientation of the fibers or passageways, and, of prime importance, the resistance the material offers to the passage of air. The careful design and control of these parameters is the domain of the acoustical researcher and manufacturer. However, it is important for the architect to have some basic understanding of what is involved in absorption by the porous materials that are most commonly used. Only then can he understand why a very thin layer of a so-called "acoustical paint" cannot possibly absorb sound efficiently where, on the other hand, a carefully designed perforated thin sheet material such as that used for sound-absorbing luminous ceiling applications can be an effective sound absorber. But even with these latter materials the absorption depends on the material in combination with the enclosed air volume behind, and in this context they may actually be thought of as "thick" materials.

With thin, impervious, flexible panels, absorption results when the surface is set in to-and-fro flexural motion by the alternating pressure of the impinging sound wave, and part of the sound energy is converted to heat through internal viscous damping. Few panel absorbers are manufactured and marketed as such, and the architect must rely on the information published in acoustical texts for the effect such materials may have on his room design. Broadly speak-

ing, however, the absorption of thin panels is confined primarily to the low-frequency range.

Another type of absorber called the volume resonator (or Helmholtz resonator, in honor of its discoverer) uses a restrained volume of air with a small opening or tunnel exposed to the impinging sound wave. This type of absorber has somewhat specialized and limited uses in architectural acoustics but may be carefully designed into a particular room to give effective absorption at particular frequencies. Of course, volume resonators of varying sizes may be distributed throughout the room to give absorption over a wider frequency range. The basic absorption mechanism is, however, the conversion of sound energy to heat by frictional drag of the air molecules in and around the neck leading to the restrained volume of the air behind.

Figure 9 shows the three basic types of sound absorption and their relative characteristics in terms of absorption coefficients.

SOUND-ABSORPTION COEFFICIENT

The effectiveness of any material as a sound absorber is given by its absorption coefficients over the frequency range of interest. The sound-absorption coefficient a describes the fraction of the incident sound energy that the material absorbs. For most architectural materials the coefficients given are those for random incidence of the impinging sound. Theoretically, the coefficient can vary from 0 (no sound absorption) to 1.0 (all the incident sound is absorbed), but practically speaking, all materials lie between these extremes. The most commonly used frequencies for reporting the sound-absorption coefficient are the following: 125, 250, 500, 1,000, 2,000, and 4,000 Hz. Table 2 lists the absorption coefficients for many common building materials and furnishings as well as for audience and seats. Most of these coefficients have either been derived from laboratory measurements or calculated from measurements in finished rooms. These coefficients are not absolute and may vary in actual practice by as much as 5 or 10 per cent for a given material depending upon different methods of applying the material, amounts of material used or variation sample characteristics and other factors.

Most manufacturers of acoustical materials publish bulletins showing test data on their products. The sound absorption coefficients at standard test frequencies are measured in accordance with a standard test procedure (ASTM Test Method C423-77). These data can be used to compare the relative performance of various products,

Table 2. Absorption coefficients of common building materials and furnishings

Coefficients for proprietary materials are available from manufacturers. This short list is useful in making reverberation calculations and in comparing the performance of various materials.

Materials	Absorption Coefficients (Hz)					
	125	250	500	1000	2000	4000
Brick, unglazed	0.03	0.03	0.03	0.04	0.05	0.07
Brick, unglazed, painted	0.01	0.01	0.02	0.02	0.02	0.03
Carpet, heavy, on concrete	0.02	0.06	0.15	0.35	0.60	0.65
Same on 40 oz hairfelt or foam rubber	0.10	0.25	0.55	0.70	0.70	0.70
Same, with impermeable latex backing on 40 oz hairfelt or foam rubber	0.10	0.25	0.40	0.40	0.50	0.60
Concrete block, painted	0.10	0.08	0.06	0.07	0.09	0.08
Fabrics						
Light velour, 10 oz per yd² hung straight, in contact with wall	0.03	0.04	0.11	0.17	0.25	0.35
Medium velour, 14 oz per yd² draped to half area	0.07	0.30	0.50	0.65	0.70	0.70
Heavy velour, 18 oz per yd² draped to half area	0.14	0.35	0.55	0.70	0.75	0.80
Heavy cotton flannel, 14 oz per yd² hung flat 6″ away from wall	0.25	0.55	0.65	0.60	0.75	0.90
Floors						
Concrete, terrazzo, marble or ceramic tile	0.01	0.01	0.02	0.02	0.02	0.02
Linoleum, asphalt, rubber, vinyl, or cork tile on concrete	0.02	0.03	0.03	0.03	0.03	0.02
Wood on joists	0.15	0.11	0.10	0.07	0.06	0.07
Wood parquet in asphalt on concrete	0.04	0.04	0.07	0.06	0.06	0.07
Glass						
Large panes of heavy plate glass	0.15	0.06	0.04	0.03	0.02	0.02
Ordinary window glass	0.25	0.15	0.10	0.07	0.05	0.03
Gypsum board, ½ in. nailed to 2 × 4's 16 in. o.c.	0.30	0.10	0.05	0.04	0.07	0.09
Openings						
Proscenium, average, curtain open	0.30	0.35	0.40	0.45	0.50	0.55
Under-balcony, upholstered seats	0.35	0.45	0.60	0.70	0.70	0.65
Plaster, gypsum or lime						
on tile or brick	0.02	0.02	0.02	0.03	0.04	0.04
on lath	0.14	0.10	0.06	0.05	0.04	0.04
suspended	0.20	0.12	0.08	0.05	0.04	0.04
Plywood panelling, ⅜ in.	0.28	0.22	0.17	0.09	0.10	0.11
Air at 50% R.H.						
sabins per 1000 ft³				0.9	2.9	7.4
metric sabins per 100 m³				0.29	0.96	2.44

	Absorption Coefficients for Audience and Seating* (Hz)					
	125	250	500	1000	2000	4000
Audience, seated in upholstered seats	0.39	0.57	0.80	0.94	0.92	0.87
Unoccupied cloth-covered upholstered seats	0.19	0.37	0.56	0.67	0.61	0.59
Unoccupied plastic-covered upholstered seats	0.35	0.45	0.50	0.55	0.50	0.40
Unoccupied wooden pews with cushions	0.20	0.25	0.30	0.45	0.45	0.45
Unoccupied metal or wood seats, or pews	0.04	0.04	0.05	0.07	0.07	0.07

* Audience area must be calculated to include an edge effect equal in area to a strip 0.5 m wide for each aisle bordering the seating. No edge effect is added where seating abuts a wall or balcony front.

Table 3. Classification of common manufactured acoustical materials

Regularly perforated cellulose fiber tile

Random perforated cellulose fiber tile

Textured, finely perforated, fissured, or simulated fissured cellulose tile

Cellulose fiber lay-in panels

Perforated mineral fiber tile

Fissured mineral fiber tile

Textured, finely perforated, or smooth mineral fiber tile

Mineral fiber lay-in panels

Perforated metal pans with mineral fiber pads

Perforated metal lay-in panels with mineral fiber pads rated as part of fire resistive assemblies

Mineral fiber tile rated as part of fire resistive assemblies

Perforated asbestos cement board panels with mineral fiber pads

Special acoustical panels and systems

Sound-absorbent duct lining

and to help in selecting an appropriate material for a given task.

NOISE-REDUCTION COEFFICIENT

A single-number rating that is often used for specifying sound-absorbing products is the noise-reduction coefficient (NRC). This is the arithmetic average of the sound-absorption coefficients at 250, 500, 1,000 and 2,000 Hz. Note that this average does not include the coefficients at 125 Hz where absorption is often needed but difficult to obtain. Thus, caution should be exercised in the selection of acoustical materials on the basis of NRC. The preferred method for specifying products for use in room acoustics design is to specify minimum sound-absorption coefficients at each of the six test frequencies from 125 to 4,000 Hz. The NRC may be adequate, however, where low-frequency absorption is not particularly critical or where the acoustics problem is not serious (for example, lobbies, corridors, general activity spaces, etc.).

SELECTING ACOUSTICAL MATERIALS

The ever-increasing number of building materials specifically designed to meet the demands for effective sound absorption often makes the actual selection difficult. Basically, however, there are four broad categories of acoustical materials. Some of these may be delivered to the job ready for installation; others may require on-site assembly or application:

1. Prefabricated, factory-finished materials
2. Plastic (or "wet") applied materials
3. Special site-assembled materials
4. Suspended baffles or "space" absorbers

Prefabricated materials

This category includes most of the products listed in the manufacturers' bulletins referred to above. Basically, these are factory-finished products or systems. Table 3 gives some idea of the scope of this category of materials.

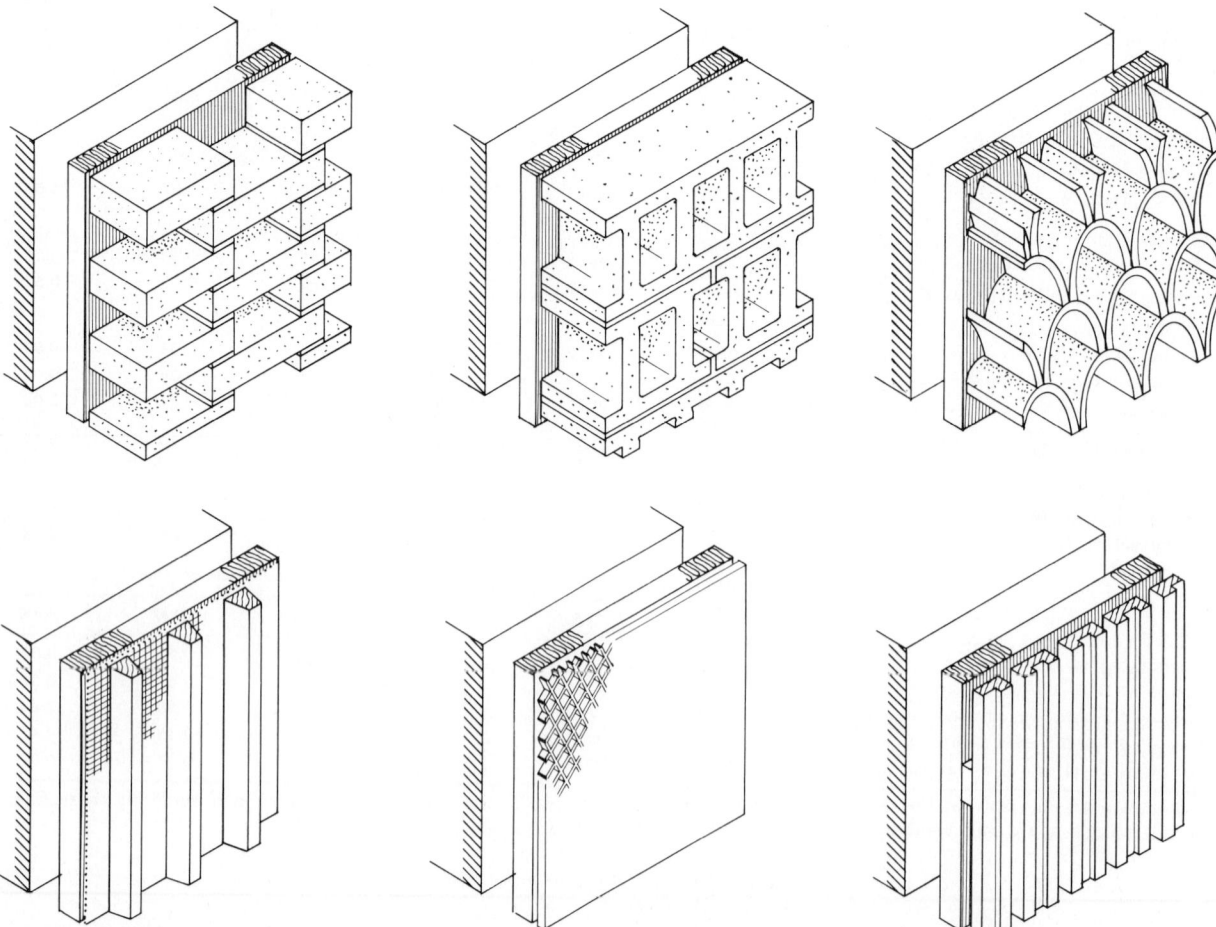

Fig. 10.   Examples of some "open" architectural materials that can be used as facings for sound-absorbing treatments

As discussed previously, the thickness and method of mounting are important in the determination of the absorption coefficient at various frequencies. The thicker the material or the more air space behind it, the greater will be the low frequency absorption. When evaluating a product, therefore, on the basis of sound-absorption coefficients, it is important to know what mounting was used in testing.

Plastic-applied materials

This category includes plaster and mineral or cellulose fiber products to which a binding agent and water are added at the time of application. They are applied in a wet, semiplastic state either by hand troweling or spraying on by machine. Thus, these materials have visual continuity without modular lines or joints. However, the absorption achieved in the field by these products is strongly dependent on careful installation. Coefficients determined from field measurements have been significantly lower than those reported on carefully prepared laboratory samples.

Acoustical plaster uses an aggregate of vermiculite or perlite with a "setting" type of binder, such as gypsum or lime, or a "nonsetting" binder, such as bentonite. These materials must be applied to a hard, back-up surface of scratch or brown-coat plaster or concrete or masonry surfaces, and can rarely be installed in greater than 1 in. total thickness; the more usual application is ½ in. or less. Thus, the low-frequency absorption which can be achieved is quite small and seldom adequate to control sound reflections, especially from curved surfaces that may be causing echo or focusing difficulties in a room. Surface porosity is sometimes improved by wire brush or nail roller stippling, but generally speaking, most acoustical plasters are easily sealed and rendered ineffective by painting. Refinishing and cleaning must follow the manufacturer's instructions very closely to avoid any further reduction of the sound-absorbing properties of the material. Acoustical plaster should *never* be used when an effective sound absorbing treatment is required.

Mineral or cellulose fiber base products are combined with a binding agent and water in a special spray gun and applied either directly on a hard back-up surface or on an open lath. Greater thickness (up to 3 in.) of this somewhat soft, porous, lightweight material are possible than with acoustical plasters, and the possibility of application on an open lath takes advantage of the airspace behind the surface, thus increasing the low-frequency absorption. Some sprayed products, because they are relatively soft, may be easily damaged, and

matching the color and finish of the remaining area is often difficult in a patching or clean-up process. Despite this disadvantage sprayed fiber products have a certain advantage for the acoustical treatment of domes and other curved shapes, where focusing echoes would seriously interfere with satisfactory hearing conditions.

Special job assembled—composite

In spite of the tremendous variety of "off the shelf" materials, there are occasions when acoustical or visual requirements require a "custom" design. Very often the desired acoustical result can be achieved with a porous sound-absorbing material (1 or 2-in. thick mineral fiber blanket) with or without an airspace behind to increase the low-frequency absorption. The architectural problem then is in the selection and detailing of an acoustically transparent facing or screening that would have the least effect on the efficiency of the sound-absorbing material. Generally speaking, the effect of a facing is to reduce the high-frequency absorption of the composite construction, or in other words, the facing cuts off the high-frequency absorption above some given frequency. This is because sound energy is reflected from the solid material between the holes or openings in the facing at a frequency where the wavelength of the impinging sound is equal to or less than the dimension of the solid area. For example, spaced wood strips about 3 in. wide would reflect considerable sound at and above the frequency of about 2,000 Hz and would, therefore, not be a suitable treatment for an auditorium rear wall where one might want effective echo control. On the other hand, a flattened expanded metal, having 30 to 40 per cent open area with solid dimensions less than 3/16 in., would be satisfactory over the entire frequency range. For reverberation or noise control high-frequency absorption may not be critical, especially if other high-frequency absorbing materials are present in the space. Therefore, relatively large-dimensioned grille elements (perforated brickwork, etc.) may be perfectly acceptable. Figure 10 illustrates a few of the possibilities for imaginative architectural facing treatment of porous sound-absorbing materials. Many of these have been used effectively in contemporary and traditional spaces where no other available treatment adequately solves both acoustical and visual problems.

The procedures for calculating the precise effects of various facings on the sound-absorbing efficiency of a material are quite difficult and beyond the scope of the present discussion. However, the point to be made here is that the opportunity for satisfying the requirements for sound absorption, even

in the most monumental of spaces, is often limited only by the designer's imagination.

Suspended baffles or space absorbers

Prefabricated special sound-absorbing units (for example, flat baffles, cones, prisms, parallelepipeds, tetrahedrons, etc.) constructed of porous materials with integral or applied facing materials form a class of products which are particularly useful where a continuous application of conventional materials is not feasible. Such baffles or space absorbers have application in industrial plants where the ceiling surfaces are often remote from the source of noise or must be kept free for access to ducts, pipes, etc.

The conventional method of reporting sound-absorption coefficient data on a per unit area basis is not applicable in these instances since the efficiency of the unit depends largely upon the spacing between units. As the spacing between units is increased, the efficiency per unit increases to a maximum at a given spacing which may be determined experimentally for the particular product. The measurements are reported in sabins per unit (1 sabin is equivalent to 1 sq ft of a material having unity sound-absorption coefficient) for given spacings and geometric arrays. The characteristics of one such unit with various on-center spacings are shown in Fig. 11.

Although the efficiency per unit rises with increasing spacing, it may not always be possible to achieve sufficient total absorption in a given room due to the limited num-

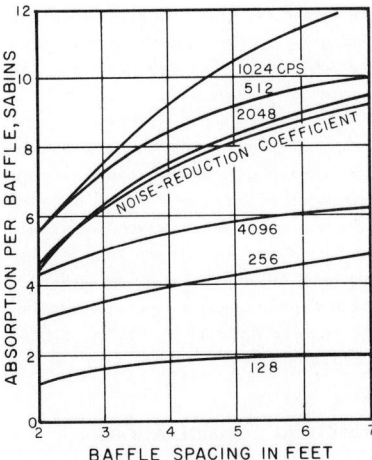

Fig. 11. Absorption per baffle (2 by 4 ft noise stop baffle)

Measured in sabins at several frequencies for spacings of the baffles ranging between 2 and 7 ft. (Courtesy of Owens-Corning Fiberglas Corporation.)

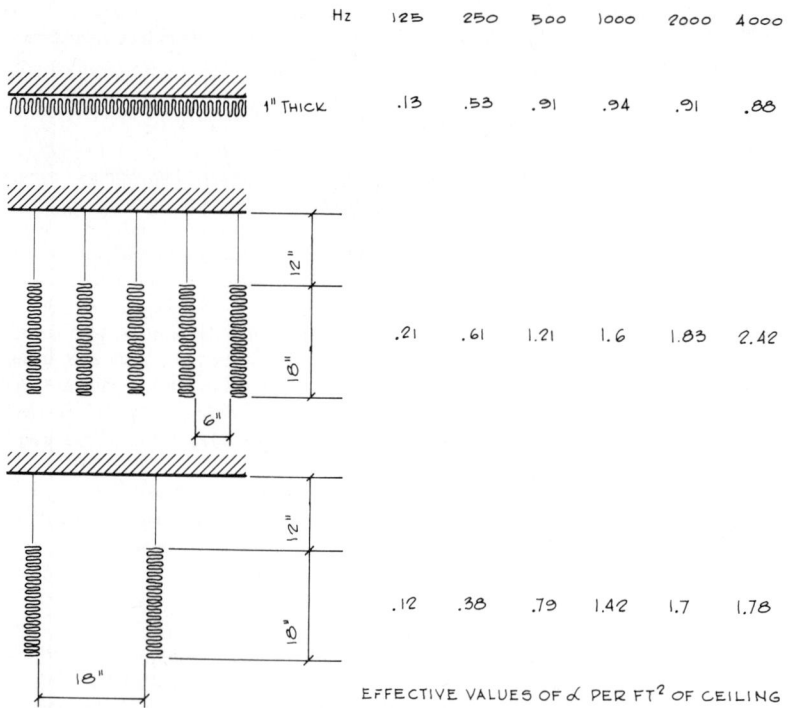

Hz	125	250	500	1000	2000	4000
1" THICK	.13	.53	.91	.94	.91	.88
	.21	.61	1.21	1.6	1.83	2.42
	.12	.38	.79	1.42	1.7	1.78

EFFECTIVE VALUES OF α PER FT² OF CEILING

Fig. 12. Comparative values of the effective sound-absorption coefficient (α per square foot of reflected ceiling area) for a porous material used in a flat ceiling application versus baffle configurations

ber of units that can practically be installed. The optimum design for noise control would be the one which produces the most absorption (in sabins) with the least number of units. A comparison may be made of the effectiveness of the suspended array by dividing absorption (sabins per unit times the number of units) by the area of the ceiling (sq ft). The result is comparable to the sound-absorption coefficient per unit area of a typical continuous ceiling treatment. Such a comparison is drawn in Fig. 12 for a ceiling finish of 1-in. fibrous material and two configurations of continuous horizontal baffles made of the same material. Note that it is possible to have effective ceiling coefficients greater than unity in these instances. This does not mean, however, that the absorption coefficient per square foot of the material of which the baffle is made exceeds unity.

PRACTICAL CONSIDERATIONS

Since absorption in porous materials requires access by the impinging sound to the interstices of the material, the sound-absorbing efficiency may be seriously affected if the openings are blocked. Common sense dictates that materials having very tiny pores can be easily sealed by repeated painting while large perforations, slots, and fissures are not so easily bridged. Manufacturers usually have specific instructions on their particular products; these should be strictly adhered to if the original acoustical design of the room is not to be altered in the future.

Light reflection and flame resistance, although of no acoustical concern, are often important considerations in the selection of acoustical materials. The manufacturers' bulletins referred to earlier also give information of this type for the various products listed.

SOME FUNDAMENTAL ROOM ACOUSTICS CALCULATIONS

Reverberation

The reverberation time of a room is given approximately by the following expression:

$$T = \frac{0.05V}{A}$$

where V = room volume, cu ft

A = total room absorption, sabins

This expression is sufficiently accurate for design purposes in most rooms where the total absorption is not very large (as it may be in broadcast studios, special laboratory test rooms, etc.). The proportions of the room should also not be extreme—dimensional ratios of about 3:1 are the limit for validity. A typical calculation for the small lecture auditorium shown in Fig. 13 is given below the illustration.

Example: Calculate the reverberation time at 500 Hz for the auditorium shown in Fig. 13 (1) with no audience and (2) with an audience of 200 people.

Since the absorption coefficients for most materials vary with frequency, it is usually necessary to perform this calculation for other representative frequencies (e.g., at 125 Hz and at 2,000 Hz). The optimum values for reverberation time are discussed in the section on "Criteria for the Acoustic Environment."

Room noise reduction

With a steady sound source in a room the sound levels are highest very near the source and fall off as one moves away from the sound source until at some distance (usually within a few feet) the levels become relatively constant throughout the remainder of the room. These constant levels (sometimes called average or reverberant levels) are primarily due to the buildup of reflected sound from the enclosing room surfaces. The reduction of reverberant sound levels is often of interest and is achieved by introduction of absorption on enclosing surfaces. The amount of noise reduction that can be achieved is given by the following expression:

$$NR \text{ (in decibels)} = 10 \log \frac{A_2}{A_1}$$

where A_1 and A_2 are the total amounts of sound absorption present in the space before and after the introduction of the additional absorption. The total absorption in both cases is equal to the sum of the areas of the materials in square feet times their respective absorption coefficients (that is, $A = \Sigma S a$).

A few calculations will show that it is relatively easy to get between 5 and 10 dB of noise reduction by adding absorption to an untreated room.

However, it is considerably more difficult to get greater than 10 dB of reduction in most practical situations.

Example: What reduction in reverberant sound levels would be realized by finishing the ceiling of a bare concrete room 15 by 20 by 10 ft high with an acoustical tile having a sound-absorption coefficient of 0.80 at 500 Hz?

Condition 1:

concrete floor,	300 sq ft × 0.02 =	6.0
concrete ceiling,	300 sq ft × 0.02 =	6.0
concrete walls,	700 sq ft × 0.02 =	14.0
	A_1 =	26.0
		sabins

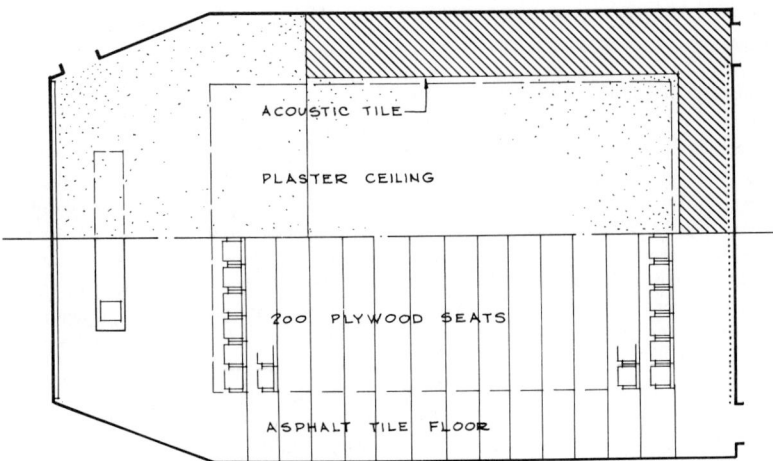

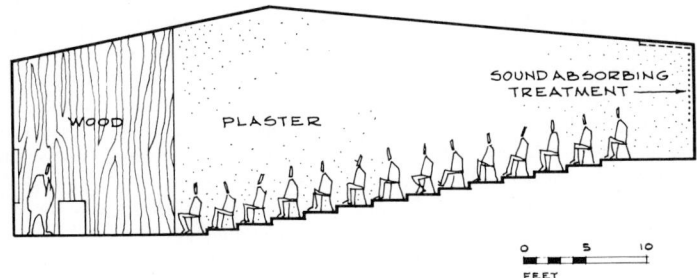

Figure. 13 Lecture room design in sample reverberation time calculation shown below for 500 Hz.

Material	Area S, sq ft	α 500	S α
1. Empty room condition:			
Ceiling:			
Plaster	1,550	0.06	93
¾-in. acoustical tile	350	0.8	280
Walls			
Wood	800	0.17	136
Plaster on masonry	1,220	0.02	24
Sound-absorbing treatment	210	0.7	147
Floor:			
Asphalt tile	950	0.03	30
Plywood seats	950	0.05	48
Total absorption, A			758 sabins

Reverberation time, empty,

$$T = \frac{0.05(25,200)}{758} = 1.66 \text{ s}$$

Material	Area S, sq ft	α 500	S α
2. Occupied room condition:			
Total absorption in empty room (less absorptive value of seats)			710
Occupied seating area	950		
edge effect, 1.5 ft			
all around	200		
	1,150	0.80	920
Total absorption, A			1,630 sabins

Reverberation time, full audience

$$T = \frac{0.05 (25,200)}{1,630} = 0.77 \text{ s}$$

Condition 2:

concrete floor,   300 sq ft × 0.02 =   6
acoustical ceiling, 300 sq ft × 0.80 = 240
concrete walls   700 sq ft × 0.02 = 14

$$A_2 = 260 \text{ sabins}$$

therefore,

$$NR = 10 \log \frac{A_2}{A_1} = 10 \log \frac{260}{26} = 10 \text{ dB}$$

This means that, if we were to measure a sound level of 50 dB in the bare concrete room, the level would be reduced to 40 dB by the introduction of this amount of sound-absorbing treatment on the ceiling. Note that the absorption coefficients for most materials vary with frequency and that this calculation should actually be performed at the several representative frequencies for which the coefficients are given. Also, note that the noise reduction discussed above has no effect at all on the noise levels heard very near the source of sound in the room.

REFERENCES

Beranek, L. L. *Noise Reduction.* McGraw-Hill Book Company, Inc., New York (1960).

Beranek, L. L. *Noise and Vibration Control.* McGraw-Hill Book Co. Inc., New York (1971).

Harris, Cyril M. *Handbook of Noise Control.* McGraw-Hill Book Company, Inc., New York, 2d Ed. (1979).

Parkin, P. H., and H. R. Humphreys, *Acoustics, Noise and Buildings.* Faber and Faber, Ltd., London (1958).

Kundsen, V. O., and C. M. Harris, *Acoustical Designing in Architecture.* John Wiley and Sons, Inc., New York (1950).

Design for Hearing, *Progressive Architecture* (May, 1959), pp. 143-206.

SOUND ISOLATION

Control of the transmission of unwanted sound into any space within a building is often the major concern of the designer interested in assuring a satisfactory acoustic environment. The undesired sound may be automotive or aircraft noise from the outside, or it may be sound generated in surrounding spaces such as speech in an adjacent classroom, or music or recorded sounds in an adjacent apartment. Or it may be direct impact-induced sound such as footfalls of persons walking on the floor above, rain impact on a lightweight roof construction, or vibrating mechanical equipment.

As far as the designer is concerned, all of these problems can be grouped under the general category of sound isolation but, obviously, the design criterion for the particular intruding sound will vary considerably, depending not only on the use of the space involved but also on the characteristics of the intruding noise source itself. For example, in an auditorium, or any other listening space for that matter, little or no intruding sound of any kind can be tolerated. On the other hand, in a private office, the major concern may be the elimination of intelligible sounds (such as speech from the occupant next door, footfalls from the corridor, etc.), while relatively high levels of continuous bland sounds like the rush of air from an overhead air-conditioning diffuser may be quite acceptable.

Sound-isolation problems in any building can be quite complex from the point of view not only of analyzing the many potential sources of intruding sound, but also of evaluating what levels of intruding sound can be tolerated by the occupants of the space. The designer must not only have some fundamental knowledge of the general aspects of the analysis of a sound-isolation problem, but also some understanding of the important physical characteristics of barriers and how these can best be used to isolate a given space from both air-borne and structure-borne sounds.

The problems of sound isolation are usually considerably more complicated than problems of sound absorption and involve reductions of sound level which are of greater orders of magnitude than can be achieved by either absorption or separation of the noise sources from the listener. These large reductions of sound level from one space to another can be achieved only by continuous and massive impervious barriers and, if the problem involves structure-borne sound as well, it may be necessary to introduce discontinuities or resilient layers into the barrier also.

The significant point is that sound-absorbing materials and sound-isolating materials are used for entirely different purposes. Just as one does not expect much sound absorption from an 8-in. concrete wall, there is not much reason to expect high sound isolation from a porous, lightweight material that may be applied to the surfaces of the room. The basic mechanisms of sound absorption and sound isolation are quite different. This point cannot be emphasized too strongly. Architects and building designers continue to rely on sound absorbing materials for sound isolation. Sound absorbing materials are almost worthless for sound isolation.

THE SIMPLE CASE OF ROOM-TO-ROOM SOUND TRANSMISSION

In order to illustrate a number of the important variables in any sound-isolation problem, we will try to visualize a simple case of air-borne sound transmission between two rooms separated by a common barrier (Fig. 14). One of the rooms (called the source room) contains a continuously operating noise source, and the other (called the receiving room) has a listener. To keep the situation simple, we will assume that the only way for sound to get to the receiving room is through the common wall which is completely airtight so that all the sound has to go through the material itself. The source room sound which is relatively uniform throughout the room, except very near the source, impinges on the barrier at many angles of incidence. In essence, when the sound impinges, it tries to move the barrier and to the extent that it does move it, sound is reradiated by the barrier to the receiving room. The level of transmitted sound in the receiving room (not very near the wall) is dependent primarily on three factors: (1) the transmission loss (TL) of the wall, (2) the area of the wall, and (3) the amount of absorption in the receiving space.

This can be expressed approximately by the following equation:

$$NR = TL - 10 \log \frac{S}{A_2}$$

where NR is noise reduction, dB (the difference in reverberant sound levels between the two spaces in question, in this case $SPL_1 - SPL_2$); TL is transmission loss of the wall, dB; S is area of the wall, sq ft; A_2 is total sound absorption of the receiving room in sabins (A is the sum of the areas of various materials in the room, sq ft, times their respective sound-absorption coefficients).

The transmission loss accounts for the largest part of the room-to-room noise reduction but, as can be seen, the area of the wall and the amount of sound-absorbing material in the receiving space also have some effect. The larger the wall area is, the more sound energy will be transmitted. The more sound-absorbing material there is in the receiving space, the lower the reverberant sound level will be. In most practical situations, the correction term which accounts for the area of the wall and the receiving room absorption, usually affects the room-to-room noise reduction by not more than about ±5 dB. However, this amount may be quite significant in many sound-isolation designs.

NOISE REDUCTION, NR = $SPL_1 - SPL_2$
= $TL - 10 \log \frac{S}{A_2}$

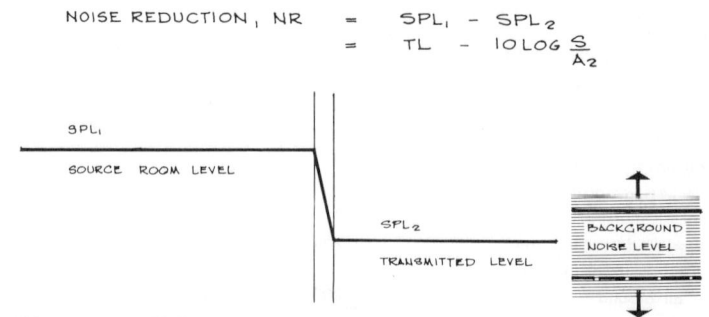

Fig. 14. Illustration of the simple case of air-borne sound transmission between adjacent rooms through a common barrier

With a sound source in one room the transmitted sound level is dependent not only on the transmission loss of the barrier, but also on the area of the barrier and the receiving room absorption. The actual background "masking" noise levels determine whether or not the transmitted sound will be heard.

THE ROLE OF MASKING NOISE IN SOUND ISOLATION

Whether or not the transmitted sound will be heard in the receiving room depends on another factor which we have thus far neglected: the level of the background sound in the receiving room. Whether we are aware of it or not, there is always a certain amount of continuous background noise present in any space due to the air-conditioning system, the noise of distant traffic, the noise of activities in other parts of the building, or even crickets or wind noise if we happen to be out in the country. The effect of this masking sound on any sound-isolation problem is perhaps as important as the sound-isolating properties of the barrier itself. This effect is shown schematically in Fig. 14. With a given construction between two spaces, the level of intruding sound is determined by the level of sound in the source room, the transmission loss and area of the barrier, and the absorption in the receiving space. The background sound, on the other hand, may vary considerably in any building, depending on whether or not the air-conditioning system is on or off; the presence of other activities within the building; or the nature of the exterior noise situation. For example, the background sound in a typical office building may vary by as much as 15 to 20 dB, and this variation in background sound level can mean that it will fall either above or below the transmitted sound level. Masking occurs when the

Table 4. Air-borne sound transmission-loss values for some common building constructions derived from field measurements

Building construction	Transmission loss (dB) at listed frequencies (Hz)						
Walls	125	250	500	1,000	1,000	4,000	STC
2¼-in. laminated plasterboard and coreboard demountable partition (9 psf)	29	29	30	32	37	38	34
2-in. solid gypsum sand-aggregate plaster (18 psf)	31	32	33	38	45	53	38
4-in. hollow-core gypsum block, ⅝-in. sand-aggregate plaster both sides (25 psf)	30	31	33	39	42	46	38
4-in. pumice block, unpainted (16 psf)	18	19	26	32	35	40	38
6-in. hollow concrete block, painted (28 psf)	30	33	36	41	46	51	41
4½-in solid brick, plastered both sides (45 psf)	34	35	40	51	57	60	46
7-in. stone-aggregate concrete (90 psf)	44	42	52	58	66	70	55
2 x 4 wood studs, ½-in. gypsum board both sides (6 psf)	20	30	36	41	43	42	39
2 x 4 wood studs, ½-in. sand-aggregate plaster on ⅜-in. gypsum lath both sides (16 psf)	27	25	31	44	34	50	34
2½-in. wire studs, ⅝-in. sand-aggregate plaster on metal lath both sides (19 psf)	26	24	37	31	37	50	34
3⅝-in. sheet metal stud, ½ in. gypsum board both sides, 2½-in. insulation in airspace (16 psf)	27	36	48	56	50	46	46
Two separate rows of ¾-in. furring channels 2¾-in. on center, ⅝-in. sand plaster on metal both sides (4¾ in. total thickness) (17 psf)	29	35	44	43	46	55	44
2½-in. wire studs, ½-in. sand-aggregate plaster on ⅜-in. gypsum lath on ½-in. resilient metal, clips both sides (12 psf)	30	37	43	48	43	60	45
Double row 2 x 4 studs on separate 2 x 4 plates, total of 7-in. insulation in 8-in.-wide cavity. One layer of ½-in. gypsum board each side (8 psf)	33	47	58	64	65	62	54
4-in. hollow concrete block wall (24 psf) painted, with ½-in. gypsum board on resilient furring channels on 1 x 2 strapping one side only, with 1-in. insulation in airspace	27	44	57	64	61	55	51
2 x 4 studs, 16 in. on center, ⅝-in. gypsum board both sides, with 24 in. on center, resilient metal furring channels one side only, 2½-in. insulation in airspace, resilient caulked peripheral joint (6 psf)	30	41	55	58	50	56	51
Two wythes of plastered 4½-in. solid brick, 2-in. airspace between (sound-absorbing material in airspace—bridging at edge only) (90 psf)	43	50	52	61	73	78	59
Two wythes of plastered 4½-in. solid brick, 12-in. airspace between (wythes completely isolated) (90 psf)	57	70	83	93	—	—	81
Floors—Ceilings							
Typical residential floor-ceiling; wood finish and subfloor on wood joists, gypsum lath and plaster below (about 15 psf)	24*	32*	40*	48*	51*	54*	43
3½ in. concrete floor slab, ½-in. plaster finish coat below (about 45 psf)	43*	40*	44*	53*	56*	58*	50
Oak flooring on ½-in. plywood subfloor on 2 x 10 joists, 16 in. on center ⅝-in. gypsum board ceiling on resilient metal furring channels, 3½-in. insulation in airspace (10 psf)	35	39	45	52	58	63	50
Doors							
1¾-in. hollow or solid-core door, normally hung, ungasketed, ½-in. undercut	7	9	13	14	13	12	13
1¾-in. solid wood door, fully gasketed	22	25	25	26	30	34	28
1¾-in. special double-panel construction acoustically-rated door (STC 40)	31	33	37	40	44	44	40

Number is not a transmission-loss value but a room-to-room noise reduction value adjusted for a receiving room, with a 0.5-sec reverberation time at the listed frequency. The actual transmission loss value should be within ± 2 dB of the listed noise reduction value.

Sources: Beranek, L. L. (ed.), Noise Reduction, chap. 13. McGraw-Hill Book Company, Inc., New York (1960); and Bolt Beranek and Newman Inc., unpublished data.

Note: STC ratings for a number of wall and floor-ceiling constructions are given in Table 2 of Fireproofing section.

background sound either completely covers up the transmitted sound or, at least, the part of it that conveys information. A dripping faucet can be extremely annoying in the deathly silence of the night. However, during the daytime, the same level of noise from this faucet may be completely obscured by the general activity sounds that are present.

In any space whose activities require extreme quiet, the background sound itself must be very low, and thus the barriers are called upon to provide large amounts of reduction of any intruding sound. This explains why a concert hall, a broadcast studio, or a special laboratory may need very elaborate, double wall construction. On the other hand, in office buildings, considerably higher background sound levels can be tolerated as long as they are continuous and bland in character. This of course places less of a demand on the sound isolation that must be provided by the structure.

Open plan offices

The importance of masking noise is providing speech privacy in open-plan offices or "office landscapes" cannot be overemphasized. In such spaces, some sound isolation for speech privacy can be provided by extensive and efficient sound absorbing treatment on all surfaces that might reflect sound from one person to another. In addition, partial height screens can be used to cut off line of sight between people. This reduces sound transmission. Such screens should be made of plywood or similar lightweight solid material, should have sound absorbing surface treatment, and should extend well above head height to be effective.

A continuous and unobtrusive background noise for masking, however, is essential for speech privacy. This can sometimes be provided by the air-conditioning system, but the requirement for combining the function of thermal comfort control with noise generation is often too much to ask. This is especially true with variable volume systems. The spectrum of this masking noise should correspond approximately to the PNC 40 noise criterion curve but with decreasing levels above 2000 Hz. Activity noise, although relatively high in such spaces, is intermittent and variable and cannot be relied on for masking purposes. In order to provide speech privacy in open-plan offices, a carefully designed electronic background noise system is almost always required. Such a system normally consists of solid-state noise generators and amplifiers plus filters and controls for adjusting the character and level of the noise. Loudspeakers are distributed in or above the ceiling and provide a uniform, bland, innocuous sound throughout the

space, ensuring maximum speech masking and minimum annoyance.

Much research is under way to try to arrive at a better understanding of the masking effects of background sound on various kinds of intruding noise. For speech-isolation problems, these effects are well understood. It is possible to achieve a good balance among partition selection, sound absorbing treatment, and the background noise to solve speech privacy problems with assurance.

There has been some criticism of the use of masking noise as "unnatural" and harmful—gives people headaches, etc. If the masking noise in an open-plan office is so loud that it is noticeable or interferes in any way with desirable communication, the system is badly designed. There is not a shred of evidence that a well-designed

masking noise system has any adverse effects on people. It has been demonstrated clearly that freedom from distraction and the sense of privacy afforded by such background noise is a definite benefit in the office environment.

The precise effect of masking on other intermittent, intruding sounds, such as mechanical equipment noise, music, and so on are less well understood and, for the time being, the designer must provide a safety factor in the sound-isolation design so that the transmitted sound will be reduced somewhat below the lowest background noise levels that will actually exist in the space.

TRANSMISSION LOSS

With the understanding that there is more to any sound-isolation problem than the

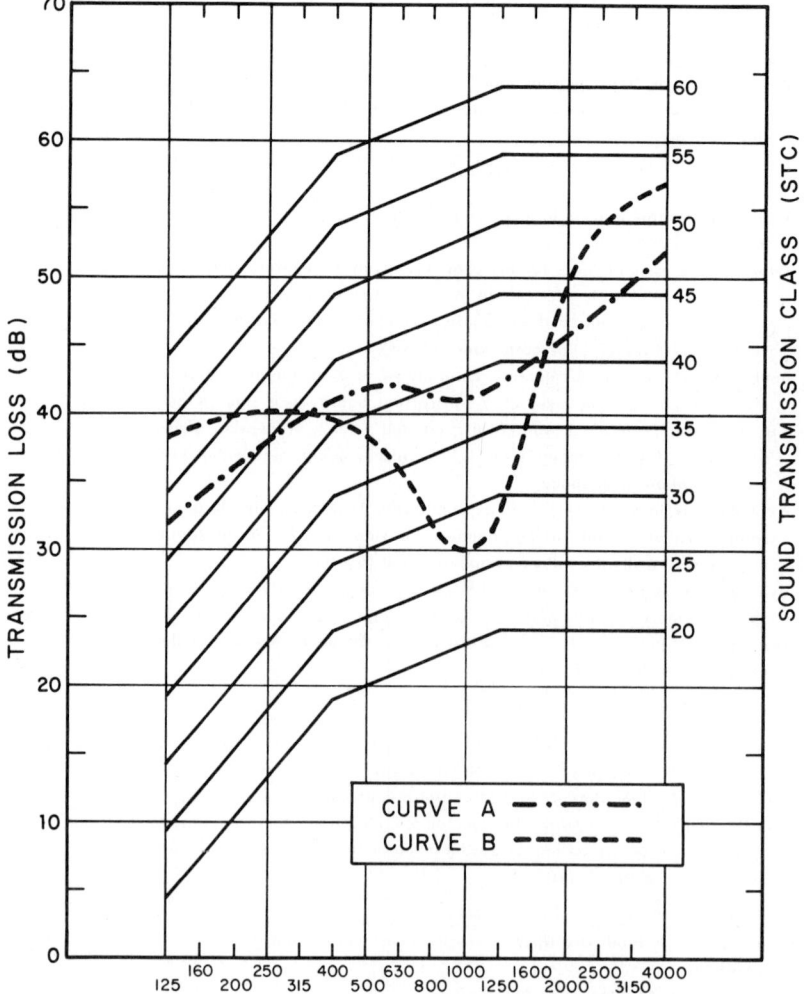

Fig. 15. Example of the determination of the STC rating from a partition transmission-loss curve

The STC for Curve A is 44 and for Curve B 35. See text and ASTM E413-70T for further discussion of the rating procedure.

transmission loss of a barrier, we can proceed to discuss intelligently the important variables that affect transmission loss. The transmission loss of a barrier is the ratio expressed in decibels of the acoustical energy transmitted from the barrier to the acoustical energy incident upon it. It can range from 0 dB for no barrier to practical limits of 70 dB or so at certain frequencies for elaborate-heavy constructions. This represents a range in the ratio of transmitted to incident sound energy of from 1, for a *TL* of 0 dB, to 1/10,000,000 for a *TL* of 70 dB. The measure of this property of a barrier is derived from carefully controlled laboratory or field measurements. Its value is dependent on the size of the panel tested, edge-mounting conditions, the weight and stiffness of the panel, and other factors. The transmission loss of a barrier varies with frequency and, as with sound-absorbing materials, test results are usually reported at a number of frequencies in the range between 125 and 4,000 Hz. Typical transmission-loss data for some common constructions are given in Table 4. See also Tables 37 and 59 of *Structural Design—Masonry* for sound transmission losses for various masonry wall constructions. Transmission-loss data are published in bulletin form by laboratories such as the National Bureau of Standards, or they may be found in texts on architectural acoustics and in manufacturers' literature. Some precautions, however, must be observed in evaluating any transmission-loss data because different methods of testing can lead to widely differing results. (For further information, see section on FHA multifamily standards.)

Sound transmission class

To supersede the average transmission-loss rating and to overcome many of the objections to this simple arithmetic average of test results, a single-number rating procedure has been developed and is described in ASTM E413-73, *Determination of Sound Transmission Class.* This rating procedure yields a single number called the *sound transmission class (STC)* by comparing the measured sound transmission-loss curves for a construction with a set of hypothetical transmission-loss contours of a given shape. Figure 15 shows the *STC* contours at 5-dB intervals, but there can be intermediate classifications since all the *STC* contours have exactly the same shape. The *STC* for a construction to be rated corresponds to the contour that fits the measured transmission-loss curve according to the following rules:

1. The sum of the deficiencies for the 16 one-third octave bands (that is, the deviations below the contour) shall not be greater than 32 dB.

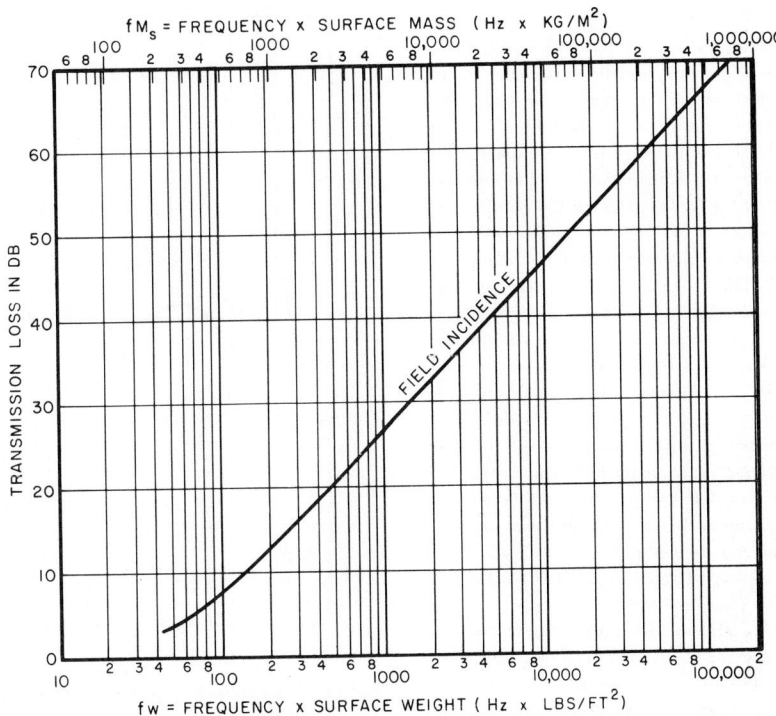

Fig. 16. Theoretical "mass law" curves for estimating transmission loss of single homogeneous panels on the basis of their surface weight alone

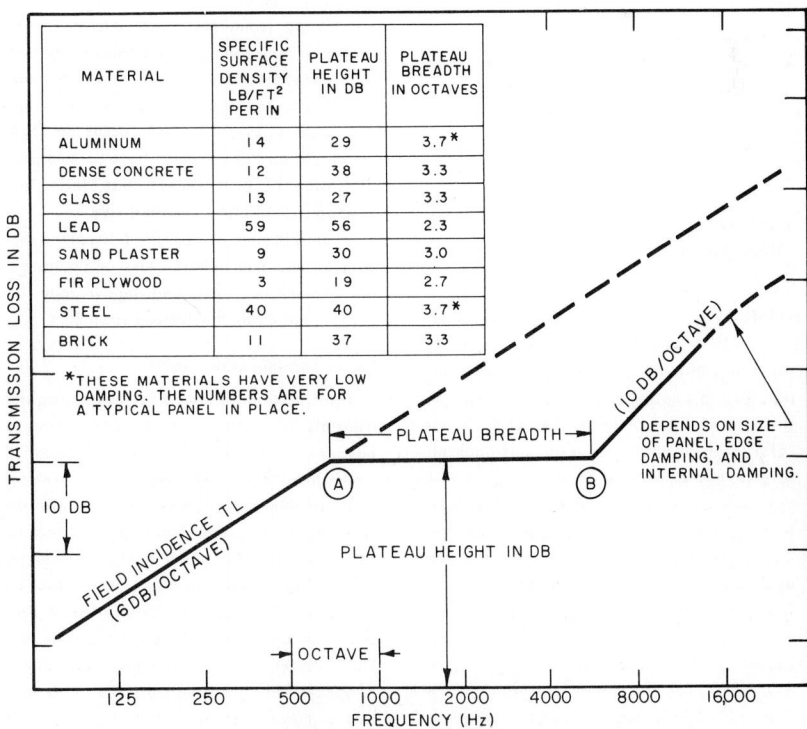

Fig. 17. Design chart for estimating transmission loss of single homogeneous panels considering both surface weight and stiffness

2. The maximum deficiency in any one-third octave band shall not exceed 8 dB.

3. When the contour is adjusted to the highest value (in integral decibels) that meets the above requirements (1 and 2), the sound transmission class for the specimen is the *TL* value corresponding to the intersection of the contour and the 500 Hz ordinate.

Figure 15 also shows two measured transmission-loss curves, A and B, and how their *STC* values compare with their average transmission-loss values. The 11-frequency average *TL* value for curve A is 41.8 dB and for curve B is 41.6 dB. In other words, their average transmission-loss values are very close in spite of the significant dip in the transmission-loss characteristic of the construction represented by curve B. The *STC* values, on the other hand, do reflect the significance of deficiencies, such as that exhibited by curve B. The *STC* value for curve A is 44 and for curve B is 35. The *STC* value for curve A is set by the sum of the deficiencies which is 30 for *STC* 44. (Moving up one contour would result in a sum of 40 deficiencies, which exceeds the allowable 32.) The *STC* rating for curve B, on the other hand, is set by the maximum allowable deficiency of 8 dB which occurs in the 1,000 Hz band, even though the sum of the deficiencies is only 19. The *STC* procedure gives no credit to a construction whose transmission loss is better than it needs to be at certain frequencies.

It should be noted that STC is not affected by transmission loss at frequencies below 125 HZ. Therefore, where low-frequency isolation is important—for example, when isolating live music—octave band or even more detailed data should be used, not STC numbers.

LABORATORY VERSUS FIELD TRANSMISSION LOSS

Obviously, if laboratory results of sound transmission-loss tests are to be typical of real installations, the laboratory-test samples should duplicate, in so far as possible, the actual field conditions of erection. Laboratory tests on small panel samples generally give higher values of transmission loss than will be achieved in the field. Similarly, tests on unrealistic panel samples (for example, testing only the intermediate panel of a demountable partition system when the field conditions will always consist of an assembly of the panel along with its connecting posts, molding strips, etc.) can give misleading results. Some laboratories are equipped for testing relatively large-size panel samples which duplicate in almost

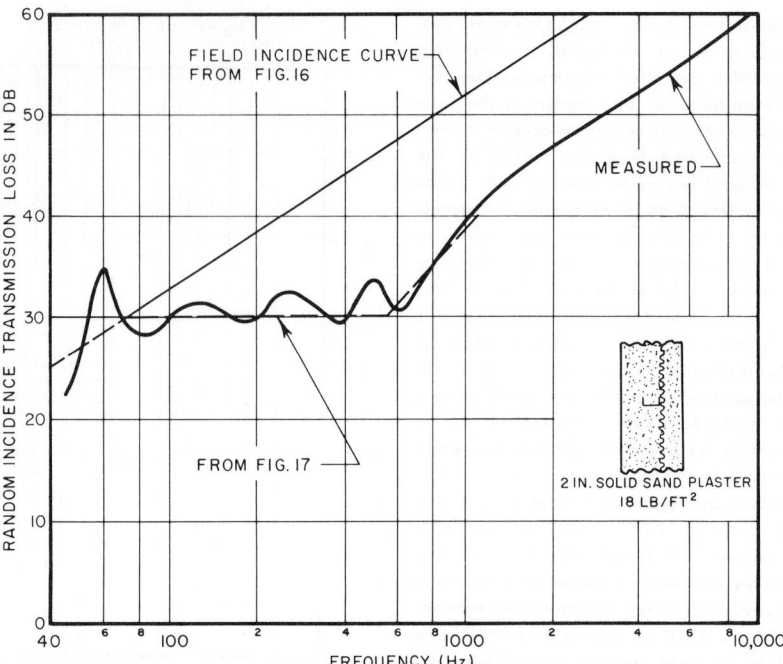

Fig. 18. Comparison of measured versus estimated transmission loss of a panel, from Figs. 16 and 17

every detail the actual field conditions of erection. Transmission-loss data from different laboratories are not generally comparable, often because of different-sized panel test openings, but also because of the different testing techniques used. ASTM E90-75 provides standardization of laboratory testing procedures and requires that the construction being tested include all the essential details as they will occur in field installations. Panels must have a minimum dimension of 8 ft except that doors and windows should be of normal size.

In the absence of realistic laboratory test data on the transmission loss of a barrier, the procedures described below may be used to estimate the transmission loss.

Single homogeneous walls

The traditional method for estimating the transmission loss of single homogeneous barriers has been on the basis of so-called "mass law." Figure 16 shows the theoretical field incidence transmission-loss curve for what might be called "ideal" panels; that is, the weight of the panel is the controlling factor. This curve describes the situation that is encountered most often in field conditions of room-to-room sound transmission. The performance of a partition will be slightly better if all the sound arrives at its surface at normal incidence and slightly poorer for completely random incidence. Note that

the abscissa is given in frequency times surface weight ($f \times w$) so that once the weight of the material is established, we can readily construct a graph or a table of the transmission loss versus frequency for field incidence of the impinging sound.

You might conclude, on comparing a manufacturer's test data with the values given in Fig. 16, that his data are in error, possibly because of an inadequate measuring technique or due to some other reason. The transmission loss for a single homogeneous partition cannot exceed the theoretical mass law limits. The only way to beat the mass law, as will be discussed below, is to go to a special double or multilayer construction in which case the partition could no longer be considered homogeneous.

Actually very few homogeneous common building materials follow the mass law curve accurately due to the internal stiffness of the materials themselves. Lead and steel sheets, due to their very low stiffness, are among the few materials that follow mass law over a large portion of the frequency range. Most materials—plaster, glass, concrete, etc.—exhibit significant dips in their transmission-loss characteristics at some frequency range depending on the stiffness of the material involved. A procedure for estimating the transmission loss of common homogeneous materials is given in Fig. 17. The process is outlined as follows:

1. Select a piece of graph paper such as that used to draw Fig. 17. The abscissa should be labeled "frequency in Hz" and should be on a logarithmic scale so that each octave (doubling) of frequency has the same extent along the scale. Label the ordinate "TL in dB."

2. From data in the table of Fig. 17 and the thickness of the panel, determine the surface weight of the panel. For example, 2-in. sand plaster will weigh 18 lb/sq ft.

3. From the field incidence curve of Fig. 16 select the transmission-loss of the panel from some frequency times surface weight combination (for example, $f \times w = 125 \times 18 = 2250$. The transmission-loss from Fig. 17 at this $f \times w$ combination $= 33$ dB. Therefore, the transmission loss at 125 Hz for the 18 lb/sq ft sand plaster barrier $= 33$ dB). Plot this value on the graph and draw a 6 dB per octave slope through it, sloping upwards with rising frequency. This is what the partition transmission-loss would look like if the plaster construction had no internal stiffness.

4. Determine the plateau height from the table in Fig. 17 and draw a horizontal line through it, intersecting the field incidence line at point A (for plaster, this is at 30 dB).

5. Determine the plateau breadth from the table and, starting at point A, mark off the number of octaves on the horizontal line. (For plaster, the plateau breadth is 3 octaves; label the end point of the plateau point B.)

6. Above point B, the transmission loss will rise at the rate of about 10 dB per octave.

Fig. 18 shows the estimated transmission-loss for a 2-in. plaster barrier calculated using the above procedure and also compares the estimate with an actual field measurement of the transmission loss of a 2-in. standard plaster partition.

Nonhomogeneous single walls

The procedure for estimating the transmission loss of nonhomogeneous single walls is a great deal more complicated. Such walls might include plaster on stud constructions, hollow masonry block walls, metal sandwich panels, etc. For complex nonhomogeneous single wall constructions the designer is referred to texts on acoustics, or he might attempt to make an estimate, using the procedures discussed above, and assuming plateau heights and breadths for constructions which, on the basis of stiffness, most closely resemble the structure in question.

Double walls

The procedure for estimating the transmission loss of double walls is even more

complex. Figure 19 shows schematically the effect on transmission loss of splitting a single wall of a given weight into two separate layers. As can be seen, significant improvement can be achieved except at certain resonant frequencies. With very thin-layered constructions and with very small air spaces such as occur in some thermal glass products (air spaces in the order of ¼ in.), the resonant dips may occur in an important frequency range, and thus, the effective improvement in transmission loss may not be significant. In such cases, it may actually be better to use a single-layer construction of the same total weight. Also, the improvement implies true separation of the layers which can only be approximated in actual practice by careful detailing. Figure 20 provides a simplified approximate method for estimating the transmission loss for double constructions.

Example: Assume that it is required to estimate the improvement in transmission loss at 500 Hz of a wall consisting of two 4-in. thick concrete layers, separated by a 3-in. air space over a single 8-in. thick concrete wall. Assume the density of concrete as 150 pcf.

Surface weight of 8-in. wall (w) = 100 psf
Frequency (f) = 500 Hz
$f \times w$ = 50,000

TL (8-in. concrete) = 60 dB (from field incidence curve of Fig. 16)

Improvement in TL = 6 dB (from Fig. 20)

TL (for double concrete) = 66 dB

In the above example, to get an improvement of 6 dB in transmission loss by weight alone rather than by a double construction, it would be necessary to double the weight of the single 8-in. wall (to 16 in.). (See Fig.

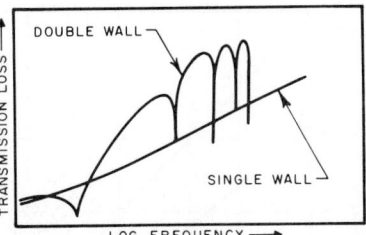

Fig. 19. Curves showing the theoretical transmission-loss improvement of a double wall over a single wall of the same total weight

16.) Improvement of transmission loss by weight alone very rapidly reaches a point of diminishing return in which the thickness and other practical considerations of the wall become excessive. However, it is extremely important to remember that if the improvement suggested above is really to be achieved in practice, very careful detailing is required to assure that the two layers of the construction are not rigidly bridged by wall ties, conduit or piping, etc.

Composite walls

Most walls contain a number of different constructions. For example, a door or glass transom or a mullion filler panel may occur in the common barrier between two rooms. Figure 21 gives a procedure for calculating the effective transmission loss from the transmission-loss data for the individual elements.

Example: It is required to estimate the effective transmission loss at a particular

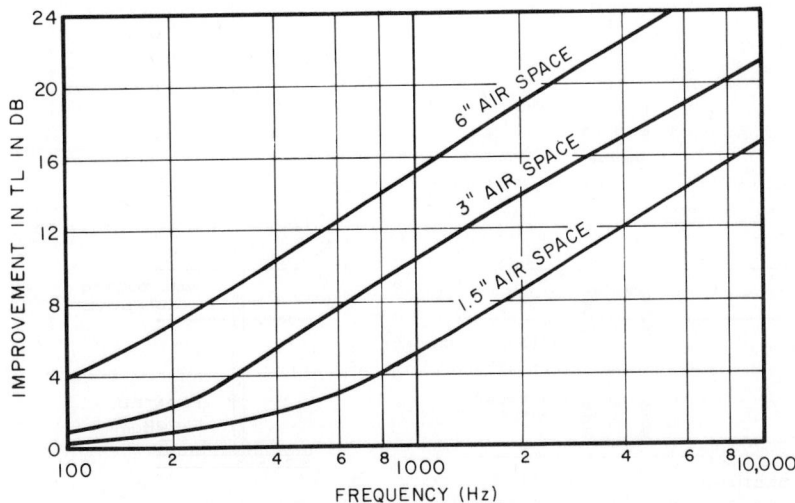

Fig. 20. Curves for estimating the improvement in transmission loss of splitting a wall of a given weight into two separate walls with various spacings

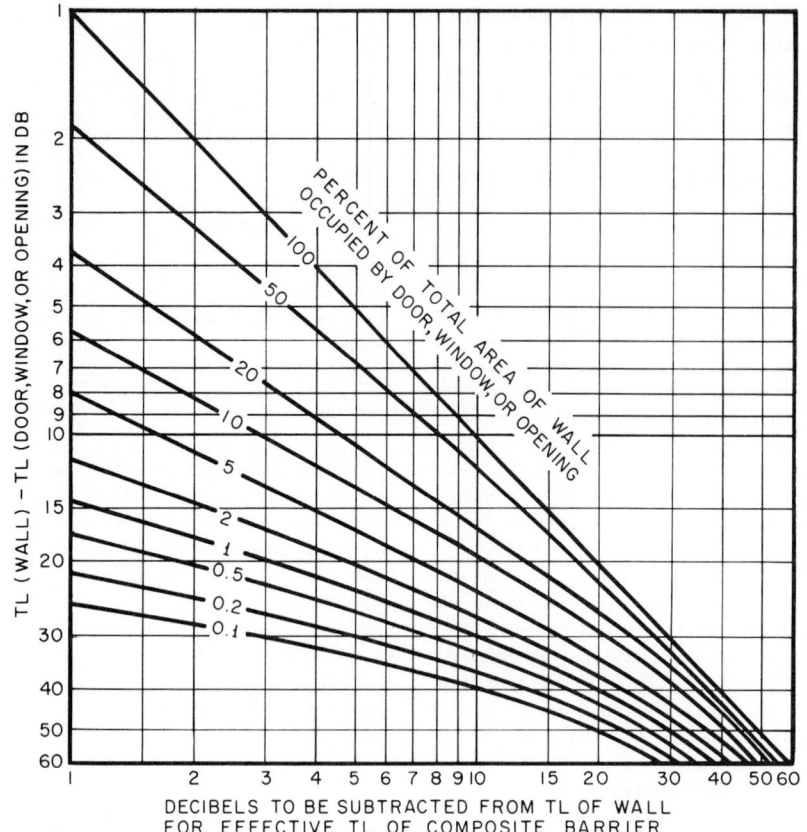

Fig. 21.   Chart for calculating the effective transmission loss of a composite barrier

frequency range for a composite wall containing a door. Assume the following:

$$\text{Wall} + \text{Door} = 100 \text{ sq ft}$$
$$TL \text{ (Wall)} = 40 \text{ dB}$$
$$\text{Door} = 20 \text{ sq ft}$$
$$TL \text{ (Door)} = 15 \text{ dB}$$

Door occupies 20 per cent of wall suface

Then, TL (Wall) — TL (Door) = 40 dB — 15 dB = 25 dB

Entering the vertical scale of Fig. 21 at 25 dB, and reading horizontally to the 20 per cent curve, then vertically to the top horizontal scale, it can be seen that the transmission loss of the composite barrier is 18 dB less than the barrier without a door, or an effective transmission loss of 22 dB (40 dB — 18 dB).

Obviously, to achieve a higher degree of transmission loss for the composite structure in the example, it would be necessary to select a door with a higher transmission loss for a greater composite efficiency. On the other hand, if it is assumed that a transmission loss of 22 dB is acceptable (presumably, a very marginal requirement for noise or speech isolation), then a wall having a transmission loss of only 25 to 30 dB would provide an acoustically balanced design at considerably less cost.

Effect of holes, openings, etc.

A hole has a transmission loss of 0 dB, and if one does a few sample calculations with Fig. 21 he will soon discover that it takes very little hole area to reduce the effective transmission loss of a barrier. Cracks around doors, back-to-back light switches, electrical service outlets, pipe penetrations, openings above partitions, etc. are, therefore, extremely important considerations in partition design. Figure 23 illustrates a number of common leaks that are found in building constructions. Obviously, these leaks must be carefully sealed if the full effectiveness of a particular construction is to be achieved. Such leaks can be controlled by inserting solid, impervious barriers in the openings or, at the smaller cracks and holes, by packing with resilient materials and calking with mastic. Care and skill on the part of the designer in the drawing stage of a project can do much to eliminate the need for detective work when trying to find the sound leaks once the building has been completed.

FLANKING OF SOUND

Thus far, we have concerned ourselves with the transmission of sound between rooms only through a common barrier. It is usually important to consider other paths for sound transmission between spaces. These may be referred to as "flanking" paths

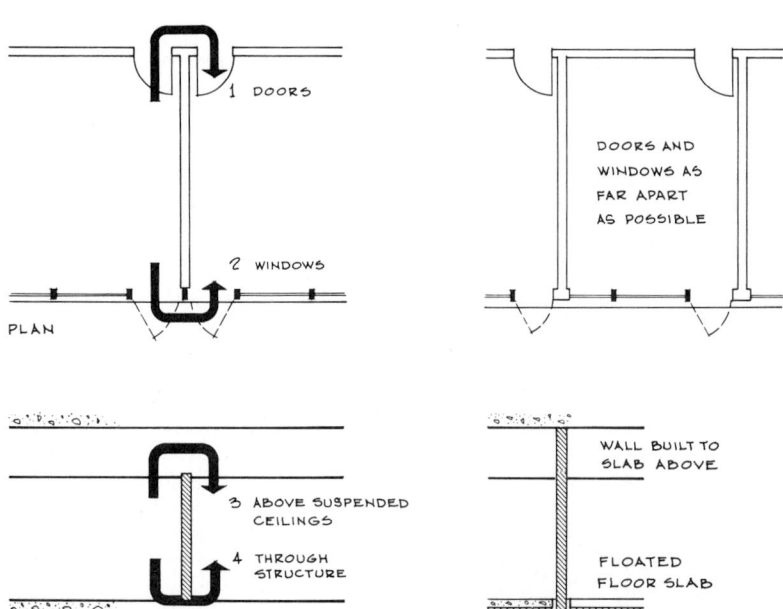

Fig. 22.   Some "flanking" paths for sound between rooms around a common barrier and their remedies

In general, the higher the transmission-loss requirements of the common barrier are, the more serious the flanking problem is.

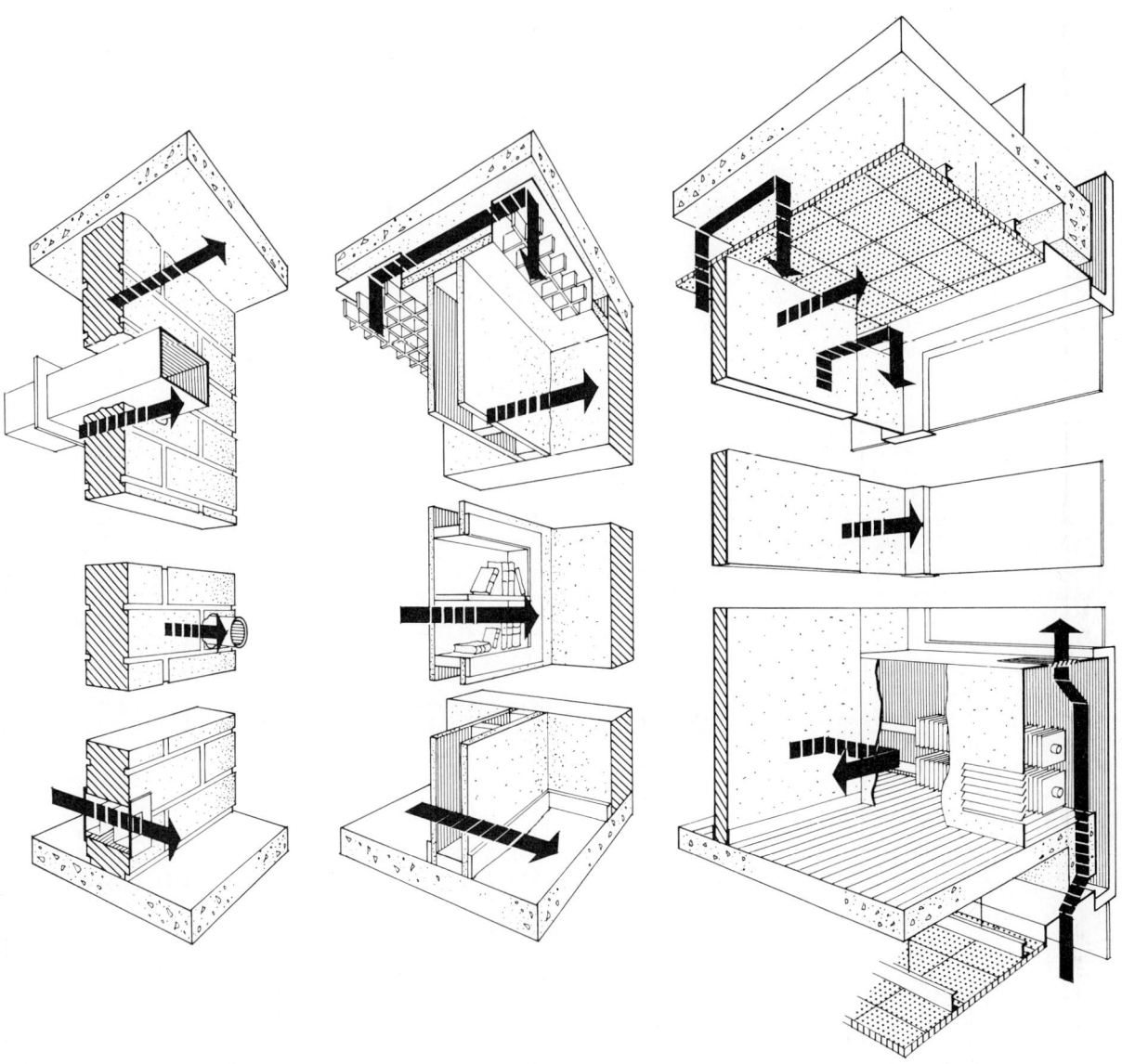

Fig. 23.   Some sound-leakage paths commonly found in field constructions

These must be sealed by proper detailing if the full effectiveness of any construction is to be realized.

since they bypass the common barrier between the spaces. A number of common flanking problems are shown schematically in Fig. 22.

Doors should be widely separated and gasketed if a high-transmission-loss construction is required between separate rooms. To improve the door problem, illustrated as path 1 in Fig. 22, the revised location for the door in one of the rooms would be advisable. Similarly, with operable sash (flanking path 2), the preferred window opening arrangement is shown.

Flanking of sound through the structure (path 4) is important if high transmission loss is required between rooms. For example, special "floated" floors or ceilings may be required if high levels of air-borne sound

are anticipated in a room which would excite the common lightweight floor or ceiling slab construction and reradiate into the adjacent space. This degree of concern for air-borne—to—structure flanking of sound is important only if the common barrier between the spaces in question requires high-transmission-loss construction. Such requirements do exist for many broadcast studio spaces, music classroom spaces, etc.

Flanking of sound through suspended ceiling constructions (path 3) is perhaps the most common problem in office buildings today, where large open spaces must be designed for flexible partition arrangement. The obvious solution is, of course, to continue the partition construction beyond the level of the suspended ceiling to the under-

side of the structure above. However, such a solution is not practical in many situations and really defeats the very flexibility that may be desired. In these instances, it makes more sense to think in terms of a horizontal barrier at the level of the suspended ceiling. The sound-isolation requirement of the horizontal barrier may not be as great as that which would be required for a vertical barrier, especially if one considers that sound must travel through the barrier in one room, along the plenum space, and thence down through the horizontal barrier into the second space. Reduction of sound energy occurs each time the sound passes through the ceiling, provided the material is reasonably impervious or has an impervious backing. Additional loss of sound energy occurs as the sound proceeds through the plenum space, especially if some sound absorption is provided in the plenum, either on top of the suspended ceiling or on the underside of the floor structure above in the form of sprayed-on porous fireproofing material.

The Acoustical and Insulating Materials Association (AIMA) has sponsored some research on this particular problem, leading toward the development of a test procedure which evaluates the sound-isolation effectiveness of various ceiling products. The procedure is to measure the sound reduction between two test rooms over which the ceiling material is placed in its normal suspension system. To assure that only the sound reduction of the ceiling-plenum-ceiling path is measured, a high-transmission-loss wall is used as the common barrier between the test rooms; this extends up to the level of the suspended ceilings. The result of such tests are reported in terms of "attenuation" in decibels at several frequencies between 125 and 4,000 Hz. Note that the term "attenuation" is used here rather than "transmission loss" because the reported sound reduction is not a physical property of the ceiling material but rather a room-to-room reduction of sound energy for a particular suspended ceiling-plenum arrangement. In general, however, in selecting a ceiling system in sound-isolation design, the attenuation of the ceiling configuration should be equal to or slightly greater than the transmission loss of the common barrier between any two spaces in order to assure a balanced acoustical design.

STRUCTURE-BORNE SOUND

Structure-borne sound waves travel quite efficiently (i.e., with little loss of energy) from one part of a rigid structure to another. If the level of sound or vibrational energy which excites these waves is strong enough, they may be reradiated as air-borne sound from the structure. Common structure-borne sound problems in buildings are due to sources which act directly on the structure such as the impact of footfalls or vibrations from pianos and from rigidly mounted mechanical equipment. Also, as mentioned previously, high levels of air-borne sound in a space excite structure-borne sound waves which reradiate in adjacent spaces, especially if the common floor or ceiling constructions are relatively lightweight. Some methods for controlling these problems are shown in Figs. 24 and 25. Careful detailing to isolate direct vibration-inducing sources and to avoid bridging of resilient constructions is extremely important where structure-borne sound-transmission problems exist.

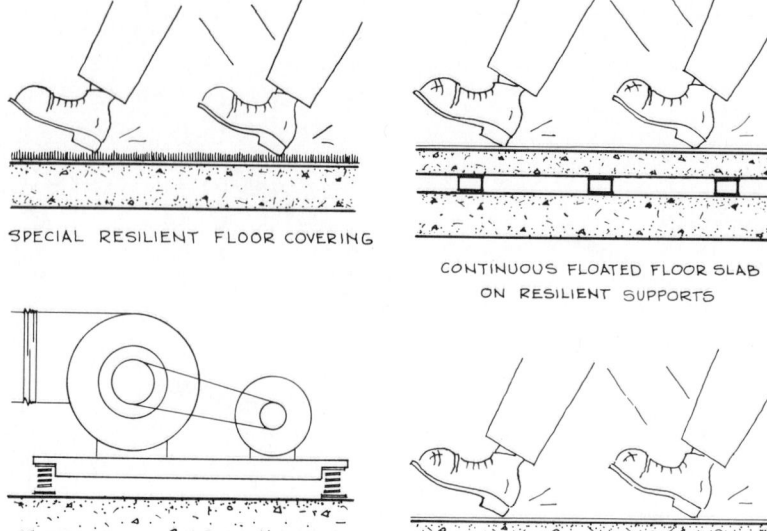

SPECIAL RESILIENT FLOOR COVERING

CONTINUOUS FLOATED FLOOR SLAB ON RESILIENT SUPPORTS

SPECIAL RESILIENTLY HUNG CEILING

SPECIAL RESILIENTLY HUNG CEILING

Fig. 24. Typical corrective measures for structure-borne sound problems involving vibration-inducing noise sources and direct impact sources

IMPACT NOISE ISOLATION

"Impact noise" refers to a special kind of structure-borne sound, namely, the noise radiated into the room beneath a floor on which impacts are occurring, such as footsteps (particularly with leather or steel-tipped heels), dropping of toys, or scraping of furniture being moved.

The method for measuring impact noise and assessing impact isolation is quite different from the methods used to evaluate air-borne sound isolation, which were discussed above. When we measure the transmission loss of a party wall, we produce in the room on one side a steady sound that contains energy at all frequencies of interest. The sound levels are measured, at all frequencies, on both sides of the wall and the difference between the sound levels on the two sides is a measure of the *isolation* provided by the wall: the greater the difference, the better the isolation.

But this method does not work with impact noise. In fact, the air-borne noise in the source room due to impacts on the floor has practically no relation to the noise radiated into the room below. One can see this intuitively by considering a concrete slab on which is floated a simple plywood floor resting on a thick, soft blanket of some kind: this floating plywood floor drastically reduces communication of the sound of footsteps to the room below because of the

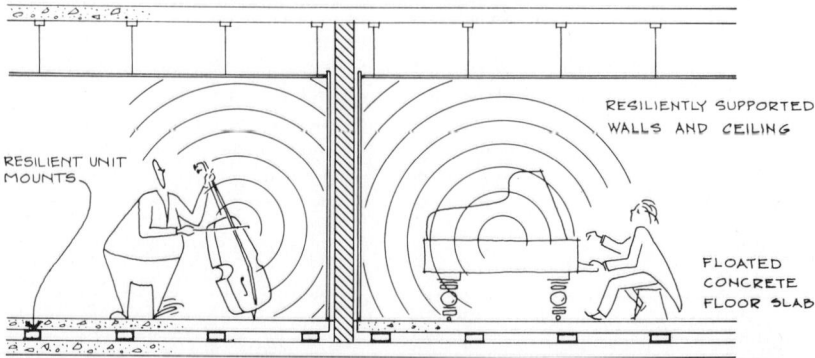

RESILIENT UNIT MOUNTS

RESILIENTLY SUPPORTED WALLS AND CEILING

FLOATED CONCRETE FLOOR SLAB

Fig. 25. Schematic representation of constructions required to control the transmission of high levels of air-borne and structure-borne sound

soft blanket, but the free-floating plywood may actually amplify the sound of the impacts on it as heard in the upper room. On the other hand, the addition of carpeting to the slab, instead of the floated plywood, would reduce the impact sound in both upper and lower rooms. Obviously, the difference in *air-borne* sound levels on the two sides of a floor is not a valid measure of impact isolation.

We use instead a standard method of generating constant and known impacts: a standard "tapping machine," which produces a series of uniform impacts at a uniform rate on the floor under test (see ASTM E492-77, *Laboratory Measurement of Impact Sound Transmission Through Floor-Ceiling Assemblies Using the Tapping Machine*). The impact sound pressure level (ISPL, measured in decibels) thus produced by this standard tapping as received in the room below, is measured and analyzed into different bands of frequency, so that a curve can be plotted showing how the sound energy in the receiving room is distributed over the audible frequency range: the lower the sound levels in the room below, the better the floor/ceiling construction.

It is assumed that a construction which will transmit little noise with the standard tapping machine will also give low noise with other types of impacts. This assumption has been called into question frequently and, in fact, it is known in some cases to be quite wrong: for semiresilient floor coverings, particularly, the rank ordering of various floor coverings is not the same under excitation with the tapping machine as with ladies' high-heeled shoes. Generally, the tapping machine tends to exaggerate, in comparison with real footfalls, the improvement to be gained by adding a semiresilient floor covering to the bare floor. Nevertheless, the tapping machine and the test method based on it are currently the best means we have for evaluating impact noise isolation.

Table 5. Impact noise ratings (INR and IIC) for various floor/ceiling constructions

Type of construction	*INR*	*IIC*
Reinforced concrete slab 6½-9½ in. thick; floor ⅝-in. composition, or none; ceiling ½-in. plaster, or none	−17	34
Reinforced concrete slab 4½ in. thick; floor ¾-in. cement; ceiling suspended gypsum lath and plaster 1 in. thick	−4	47
Reinforced concrete slab 5 in. thick; floor ⅛-in. linoleum on 2-in. concrete on 1-in. glass fiber blanket; ceiling ½-in. plaster	+1	52
Reinforced concrete slab 6 in. thick; floor ¾-in. t-and-g boards on 1½ by 2 in. battens on ½-in. pads of fiberboard, asbestos, or cork; ceiling ½-in. plaster	+3	54
Same except 1-in. glass fiber blanket instead of pads	+7	58
Reinforced concrete slab 6½ in. thick; floor ¼-in. cork tile; ceiling ½-in. gypsum board on metal clips on furring strips	+4	55
Wood joists 2 by 8 in., 16 in. on center; floor ¾-in. t-and-g boards; ceiling ⅜ in. gypsum board nailed to joists	−18	33
Wood joists 2 by 8 in., 16 in. on center; floor ⅞-in. boards on 2 by 2 in. battens on 1-in. glass fiber blanket; ceiling ⅜-in. gypsum board with skim coat of plaster	−8	43
Same except standard lath and plaster ceiling instead of gypsum board	−4	47
Wood joists 2 by 8 in., 16 in. on center; floor ¾-in. t-and-g boards; ceiling ⅝-in. gypsum board screwed to resilient metal runners 12 in. on center nailed to joists	−5	46
Wood joists 2 by 10 in., 16 in. on center; floor ⅜-in. nylon carpet on ¼-in. foam rubber pad, on ½-in. plywood underlay, on ⅝-in. plywood subfloor; ceiling ½-in. gypsum board nailed to joists	+5	56
Steel bar joists 8 in. deep, 27 in. on center; floor ⅛-in. vinyl-asbestos tile on 2-in. concrete slab on ⅜-in. ribbed lath; ceiling ½-in. plaster on ⅜-in. gypsum lath clipped to furring channels 16 in. on center tied to bottom of joists	−10	41
Same except floor finish ⅜-in. vinyl carpet on ¼-in. foam rubber pad, instead of ⅛-in. vinyl-asbestos tile	+26	77

Single-number ratings for impact noise isolation

It is often convenient for comparison purposes to have a single number with which to characterize the impact isolation of a floor rather than refer to the entire test curve of impact noise at the various frequencies. Like the assignment of the sound transmission class, in the similar case of rating transmission loss, we can assign a single-number rating for impact isolation by comparing the measured curve of impact sound pressure level (*ISPL*) against a standard criterion curve, which is translated vertically along the curve of measured data until they nearly match (according to carefully specified rules). The rating is given in terms of the amount by which the standard curve must be displaced to match best the measured curve.

Two such ratings have been proposed, and both are in current use: they are identical in principle in the way they are assigned, and for practical purposes they are readily converted one into the other.

The impact noise rating (*INR*), introduced by the FHA in the early sixties (*Impact Noise Control in Multifamily Dwellings*, FHA no. 750, January, 1963) covers a range of values for various floor constructions centered around zero, and carries with it an implied criterion of suitability. A floor with an impact noise rating of zero is just adequate to achieve freedom from intrusion of impacts when the background noise is *NC* 20 to 25. Floors with negative ratings (such as −17) will provide less than adequate isolation; floors with positive ratings are better than just adequate and are to be used in dwellings of higher quality or where the background noise is lower. A difference of about 5 units is just noticeable in practice.

Some people were confused by the use of what appeared to be "negative attenuation" values in the impact noise ratings; therefore, in subsequent supplementary recommendations made by HUD (*A Guide to Airborne, Impact, and Structure-borne Noise Control in Multifamily Dwellings*, HUD, FT/TS-24, January, 1968) the rating system was modified slightly, so that the range of rating values for different floors runs through about the same range (all positive numbers) as the sound transmission class for walls and floors. The name was changed to impact insulation class (*IIC*) in parallelism with *STC*, and the numerical values run about 51 units higher than the *INR* values for the same floors. Thus, if the *INR* of a floor is zero, the *IIC* is about 51; if the *INR* is −10, the *IIC* is about 41, etc.

Table 5 shows the impact noise ratings for various floor/ceiling constructions.

Figure 26 shows the relative improvement to be gained in impact sound isolation over a bare concrete floor slab, using various floor finish materials. Note that the carpet and special resilient tiles are effective but their effectiveness is limited to the mid- and upper-frequency range. In other words, by using such materials we may be able to eliminate the annoying "click" of footfall noise, but the low-frequency "thud" may still be heard in the floors below. If it

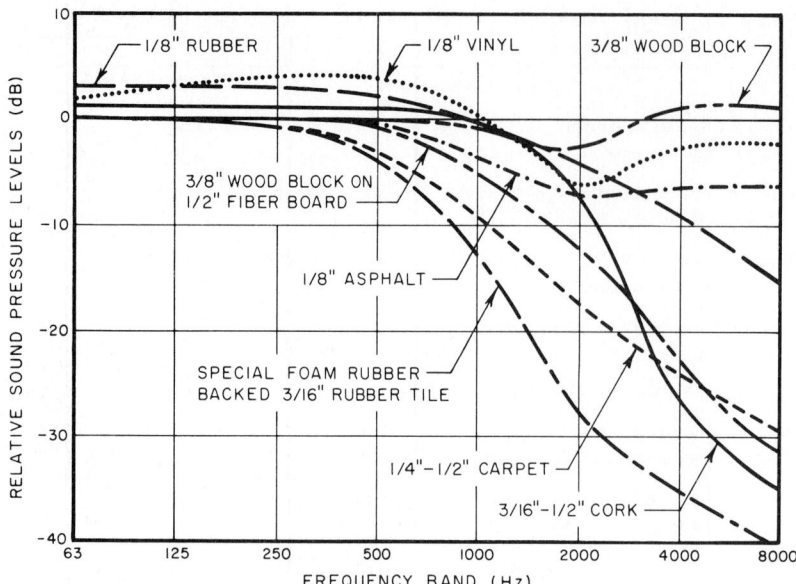

Fig. 26. Curves showing the relative improvement in reducing impact sound transmission of various flooring materials on concrete over a bare concrete slab itself

is necessary to achieve high values of impact sound reduction over the entire frequency range (as it may be between apartments or for critical listening spaces above one another), more elaborate constructions such as floated floors or special resiliently hung ceilings may be required.

SOUND ISOLATION FOR AIR-CONDITIONING SYSTEMS AND EQUIPMENT

One of the principal sources of noise in buildings is the air-conditioning and other mechanical systems. There is airborne and

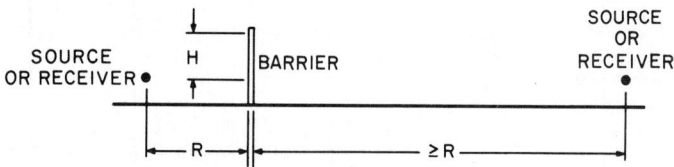

APPROXIMATE ATTENUATION DUE TO BARRIER

$$NR = 10 \, LOG_{10} \, \frac{H^2}{R} + 10 \, LOG \, f - 17 \, dB$$

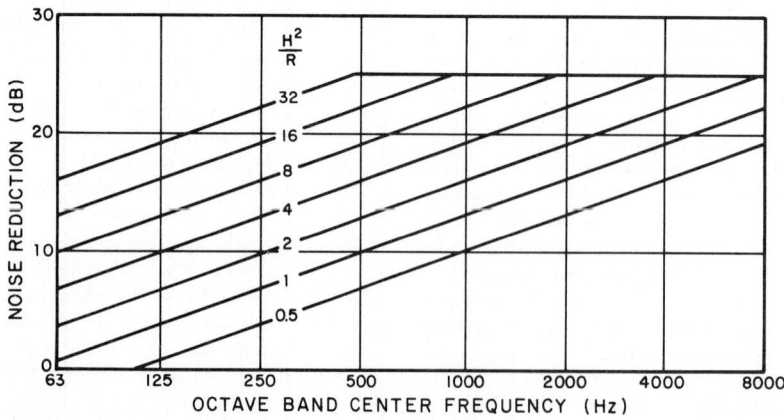

Fig. 27. Chart for estimating the noise reduction between a sound source and observer due to wall of height H (all dimensions in feet)

This procedure applies only to outdoor situations and indoor situations having extensive sound absorbing treatments.

structure-borne noise from the mechanical equipment itself and from the associated piping and ductwork. Ducts (both supply and return) can carry fan noise to occupied spaces unless proper mufflers and sound-absorbing linings are used. Grilles, diffusers, fan coil units and other terminal devices can also generate noise at the point of air delivery. This noise, if it is not too loud, can be useful as masking noise to improve speech privacy, but it would be intolerable in an auditorium.

The noise control procedures for air-conditioning systems are covered thoroughly in the *ASHRAE Handbook* (see "References"). It may be useful here, however, to take note of some typical noise control problems often found in buildings.

Mechanical equipment rooms should be as remote as possible from acoustically sensitive spaces. The walls, floors, and ceilings of such equipment rooms should be of heavy concrete and masonry construction with careful attention to air-tight seals at all openings and penetrations. Wherever ducts, pipes, or conduits penetrate a wall, floor, or ceiling of a mechanical equipment room, there should be a ½-in. clearance all around that is filled with a soft fibrous material and sealed with a non-hardening caulking—never cement grout! Doors to these rooms should be of heavy, solid construction without grilles and with complete air-tight gaskets.

Sound-absorbing treatment (2-in. glass fiber) should cover conveniently available wall and ceiling areas of mechanical equipment rooms to reduce the noise level in the rooms and, thus, that available for transmission to other spaces. Heavy compressors and other large pieces of floor mounted equipment should be located on slab-on-grade if possible. Where this is not possible or practical, equipment should be located near major columns or bearing walls or over major beams. Suspended equipment should be hung from beams or heavy joists, not from lightweight slabs.

Floor-mounted equipment is often placed on "housekeeping pads" about 4-in. high. This added concrete keeps the vibration isolation devices off the floor protecting them from rust and corrosion and also gives greater stiffness and inertia to the supporting structure.

Perhaps the biggest problem of all in noise control for mechanical equipment is the resilient isolation of all vibrating components. All electrical service must be through very flexible (floppy) conduit. There can be no rigid connection of any sort between the isolated machine or piping and the building structure. Refrigerant, and chilled-water pipes, as well as drainpipes, both large and small, must be resiliently supported at each floor and wall penetration and the space between pipe and sleeve must be packed and sealed with soft materials—never filled with grout. Even domestic water pipes should be wrapped with glass fiber or neoprene at every penetration of joist or stud and at every support point. These vibrating sources radiate noise to surrounding spaces only when rigidly coupled to walls and floors which then become sounding boards.

The selection of proper vibration isolators for machines and pipes (steel springs, neoprene isolation, etc.) is, or should be, the job of the mechanical engineer. But when the architect sees a spring isolator mashed flat or hanging in the air, or a pipe isolator plastered into a partition, he or she should know that something is wrong. Excessive noise will inevitably result unless *every* detail of resilient isolation is carefully carried out. Only the most scrupulous supervision of installation will give good and quiet results.

PARTIAL HEIGHT BARRIERS

Very little room-to-room sound isolation can be expected with partial height barriers as can be seen from the previous discussion on composite walls. All one has to do is assume a transmission loss of 0 dB for the open space above a partial height wall between two rooms, and a calculation of the effective transmission loss based on the relative areas involved will soon reveal the ineffectiveness of such barriers. In outdoor noise situations, on the other hand, where there are no enclosing surfaces to contain the sound source and build up reverberant levels, walls may have some limited effectiveness under certain conditions. This may also be true indoors if the room surfaces are treated with sound-absorbing material, thereby approximating outdoor acoustical conditions. A barrier will give no reduction at all if the receiver can see the source—there must be no line of sight. The following example, using the data from Fig. 27 will serve to illustrate the effectiveness and the limitations of this method of sound isolation.

Example: Assume that it is necessary to know the noise reduction due to a vertical wall 15 ft high constructed on a residential property line. The wall is parallel to and 25 ft from the center line of a moving lane of automobile traffic on one side and 100 ft from a terrace adjoining a residence on the other side. Since the "line-of-sight" between the listener's ear and the sound source is elevated approximately 5 ft above the ground, we estimate that the effective height of the wall is 10 ft. Therefore,

$$N = \frac{2}{\lambda} \left\{ R(\sqrt{1 + H^2/R^2 - 1}) \right.$$
$$\left. + D(\sqrt{1 + H^2/D^2 - 1}) \right.$$

$$N \approx \frac{H^2}{\lambda R} \text{ if } D \gg R \geq H$$

where $R = 25$ ft
$H = 10$ ft

$$\frac{H^2}{R} = 4$$

From Fig. 27:

Frequency Hz	NR, dB
63	7
125	10
250	13
500	16
1,000	19
2,000	22
4,000	25
8,000	25

From this it can be seen that the acoustical shielding provided by the wall with the assumed conditions produces a significant sound reduction in the middle and higher frequency range (500 Hz and higher) where the intruding noises could interfere with speech intelligibility. At the lower frequencies we can expect only a very slight improvement. All this is based on the assumption that the wall is reasonably solid—a row of trees would do nothing.

When the example is viewed in plan, it can be seen that while H remains constant, R can vary considerably, depending on the location of the sound source along the road with respect to the terrace. Thus, spot-checking several arbitrary positions along the source path is advisable. Obviously, if the wall is not continuous around the property, any flanking will reduce the expected attenuation, depending on the configuration of the wall.

The transmission of sound in out-of-doors situations is actually affected by temperature, humidity, atmospheric turbulence, wind direction, and the nature of the ground cover. However, where distances less than a few hundred feet or a hundred meters are involved, these effects may be neglected. In any event, the procedure for calculating noise reduction of outdoor barriers given in Fig. 27 and in the above example should give the designer some general idea of how high a wall must be in order to get any significant relief from an outdoor noise problem. Perhaps the solution may be to find another site for the building. Since there is more emphasis on outdoor living in contemporary architecture, and at the same time, an increase in outdoor noise problems, particularly automotive and truck traffic, the shielding effects provided by walls and terrain features may prove important in sound-isolation design.

REFERENCES

Beranek, L. L. *Noise Reduction*, chaps. 13 and 23. McGraw-Hill Book Company, Inc., New York (1960).

Laboratory Measurement of Air-Borne Sound Transmission Loss of Building Partitions, ASTM E90-75 American Society for Testing and Materials, Philadelphia.

Beranek, L. L. *Acoustic Measurements.* John Wiley and Sons, Inc., New York (1949).

Beranek, L. L. *Acoustics.* McGraw-Hill Book Company, Inc. New York, 1954.

The Use of Architectural Acoustic Material: Theory and Practice, AIA No. 39-A. American Institute of Architects. Washington, D.C.

Doelle, Leslie L. *Acoustics in Architectural Design.* Division of Building Research, National Research Council (Canada), Ottawa (1965).

Noise in Hospitals, U.S. Dept. of Health, Education & Welfare, Public Health Service, PHS Pub. No. 930-D-11, U.S. Government Printing Office, Washington, D.C. (1963).

A Guide to Impact Noise Control in Multi Family Dwellings. FHA Report No. 750, Federal Housing Administration, Washington, D.C.

Sound Insulation of Wall, Floor and Door Construction. National Bureau of Standards, Building Materials and Structures, Report No. 144 with supplements, U.S. Government Printing Office, Washington, D.C. (1955).

ASHRAE Handbook, Chapter on Sound Control, published periodically by the American Society of Heating, Refrigerating and Air Conditioning Engineers, Inc., New York.

DESIGN FOR GOOD HEARING

Good hearing conditions in almost any kind of indoor or outdoor auditorium can be assured in advance if the four basic requirements discussed in the Introduction are satisfied: (1) quiet background; (2) sufficient loudness; (3) proper distribution; and (4) adequate blending and separation of sounds.

QUIET

Really excellent hearing conditions, either indoors or outdoors, can only be achieved when the listening area is quiet. If we have too much noise, there is no point in worrying about the other factors which make for good hearing conditions. Outdoors, the noise may come from aircraft, from automotive traffic, or even from wind in the trees. Inside buildings, we not only have some of these outdoor noises transmitted through the shell of the building, but we have many noise generators such as air-conditioning systems and adjoining

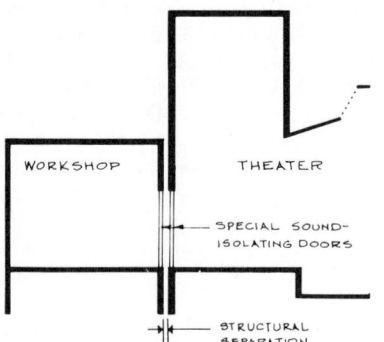

Fig. 28. Stage-scenery workshop isolation

spaces (lobbies, stage workshops, other auditoriums) that must be kept under control. The techniques of noise control are discussed in the section on "Sound isolation" but unless these are all observed with great care, it is unlikely that an excellent auditorium will result, no matter how carefully the other aspects of room acoustics are considered.

Outdoors, the best noise control technique is to place the audience far away from noise sources. High quality concert music simply cannot be presented outdoors on a noisy site in modern city traffic. High solid walls or earth berms can help reduce traffic noise, but trees and shrubs are useless as noise barriers—they are only a visual help.

The indoor auditorium can be made quiet even in a noisy city location. The audience chamber must be treated as an isolated area separated from all other areas by heavy wall and roof construction, closed doors, lined ducts, and other positive noise control measures. Noises in surrounding areas should be reduced as much as possible at the source. Lobbies, for example, should have heavy sound-absorbing treatment and should always be shut off from the auditorium with closed doors, preferably weather-stripped. If there is a scenery workshop

adjoining the stage, it should be separated with a complete structural break (Fig. 28) with double sound-isolating doors to eliminate the noise from hammering and sawing. If one auditorium is located above or next to another, the two must be separated with double construction to permit simultaneous use (see Fig. 25).

The ventilating system for an auditorium should be inaudible. This means that the associated ductwork must be lined with sound-absorbing materials or that special sound traps must be installed. The fans and compressors must either be remotely located or carefully isolated with resilient mountings and heavy housings.

Dampers for balancing must be located far upstream of the grills or diffusers to avoid generation of noise at the point of distribution. Special grilles or diffusers may be needed to assure silent air delivery and extraction. Normal "commercial practice" is *never* good enough for an auditorium.

LOUDNESS AND DISTRIBUTION

It is obvious that the sounds we want to hear should be loud enough, and that all sounds should be uniformly distributed. People in the front of the seating area should not receive great quantities of sound while those in the back barely hear at all.

A "dead spot," an area where reflected sound arrives too late to be integrated with the original signal, can be just as unsatisfactory as a seat in which a person hears everything twice due to long-delayed echoes. Adequate loudness and good distribution of sound are determined almost entirely by the size, shape, and surface finishes of the room and, in some cases, by the use of carefully designed sound-reinforcing equipment. In most moderate-sized auditoriums, however, it is not necessary to resort to electronic aid. If the space is designed carefully with well-chosen materials, the enclosure itself provides the needed sound reinforcement and good distribution.

In the small conference room or office there is seldom a problem of adequate loudness, but there can be problems of distribution caused either by concave walls or ceilings, or by flutter echoes between parallel, uninterrupted surfaces. At the other end of the scale, the large sports arena must depend almost entirely on amplified sound for hearing speech or music, and the enclosure is treated so that it will be as absorptive as possible to reduce troublesome echoes and unwanted confusion.

Figure 29 shows the typical distribution of sound to an audience seated on level ground outdoors (or in a large sound-absorbing room). The spherical sound waves radiate outward from the speaker, and the intensity of sound in these waves decreases inversely as the square of the distance. However, as it grazes over the clothing and hair of the sound-absorptive audience, additional losses occur which can amount to as much as 2 dB per row. This means that people seated near the back of an audience not only receive less sound energy because they are far away from the sound source, but they are also deprived of sound energy by the people in front of them. Thus, in outdoor, flat audience areas the loudness and distribution requirements are poorly met. In any listening situation the better the sight line for vision, the better will be the hearing.

In the ancient Greek and Roman theaters this problem was solved by placing the audience on steep hillsides (in quiet locations: no airplanes, trucks, trains or cars). When the audience is placed on a very steep angle (Fig. 30), there is very little energy loss in the freely advancing sound wave, and until the audience is quite far away from the source, there is no great difficulty in hearing, at least when actors speak with raised voice. In the writings of Vitruvius, good hearing in the ancient theaters is attributed to buried resonant urns. This is sheer poetic bunk!

However, placing the audience on a steep hillside is not the only solution; we can get the same result by raising the sound source position with respect to the audience, or even more simply by using "mirrors." If the sound from the original source is reflected from a hard ceiling surface over the audience, it appears to come to the audience from the virtual image position overhead, and thus, does not experience the grazing incidence losses of the original sound from the source (see Fig. 31). The action of the ceiling as a reflector, bringing sounds down on top of the audience, is extremely important in all auditorium situations. This sound mirror (the ceiling) is probably the most important surface in the room for determining good distribution and adequate loud-

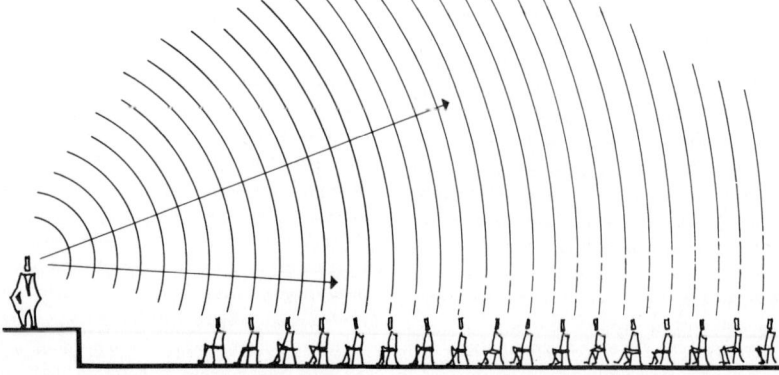

Fig. 29. Sound distribution outdoors over audience

ness. The walls are important too, especially where long reverberation time is wanted.

To be useful in giving added loudness, clarity, or definition to the sound, the reflection must arrive at the listener's ear not more than about 30 milliseconds after the original sound arrives. This means that the difference in path between the direct sound and the useful reflected sound should not be more than about 30 ft. This determines the maximum height for sound-reflecting surfaces above the audience.

The shape of an auditorium can be varied and refined in many ways but, basically, the ceiling of any room where hearing is important should be hard and sound reflective and should *never* be treated with sound-absorbing materials except in very special situations (e.g., large sports arena).

Figure 32 illustrates some possible refinements in ceiling design which provide more uniform distribution to an audience. The problems that come from using deep balconies are shown in Fig. 33. For good distribution and adequate loudness a listener must be seated properly in the auditorium so that he receives not only direct sound from the source but also reflected sound from the ceiling and walls. He must be able to "see" the ceiling and if he is seated deep under a balcony (or side aisle in a church) and cannot receive this reflected sound from the ceiling, he will hear poorly. If the balcony is handled as shown in the right-hand side of Fig. 33, people under the balcony will hear well. If the ceiling is made with concave sections, either barrel- or dome-shaped (see Figs. 34 and 35), there will inevitably be concentrations of sound in certain areas of the seating. The only solution for shapes of this sort is to make them highly diffusing (discussed further on in this section) or to make them highly absorptive (in which case, we no longer have an auditorium but a noise control environment or an anti-auditorium).

Plan influence on loudness and distribution

The plan of an auditorium should be determined by many factors including the gross seating capacity; the possible need for short viewing distances; whether the hall is primarily to be a concert hall or primarily an assembly or lecture hall; conditions of the site; and dozens of other factors (see Fig. 36 for an inept approach).

The provision of good sightlines is most important, and this should be worked out even before much acoustic design is done. To hear well, we must also see well. These senses are not completely separate. Viewing distances should be made as short as possible, especially for live performances, and everyone in the audience should be able to see all of the performing area.

Although traditionally the seating is laid out on radial lines, there is no reason why

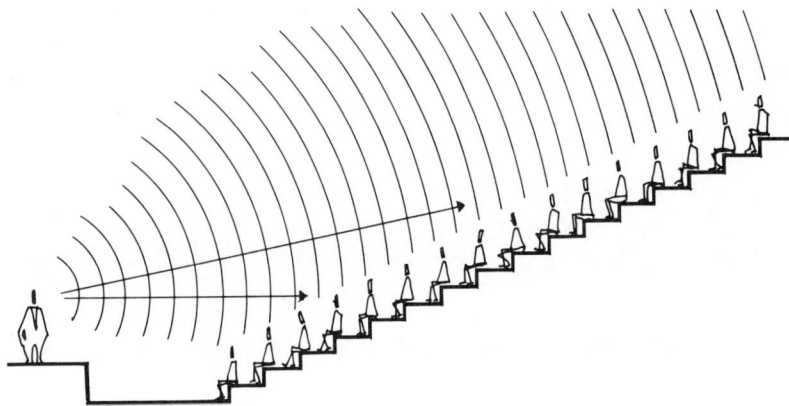

Fig. 30. Steep seating minimizes audience attenuation

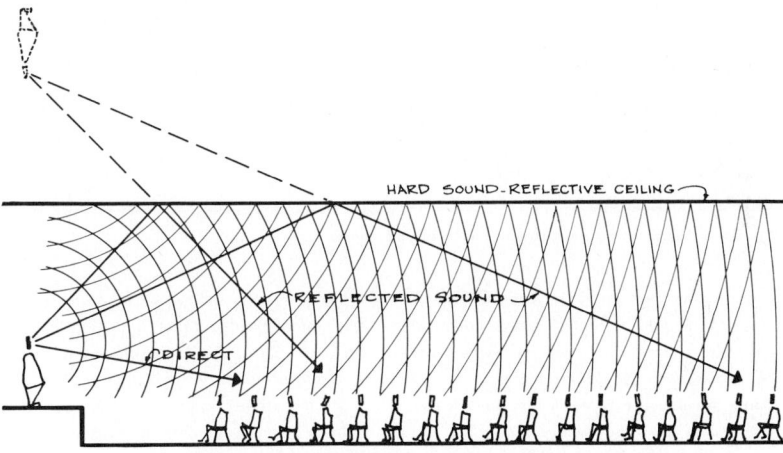

Fig. 31. A sound-reflecting ceiling reinforces the direct sound to the audience

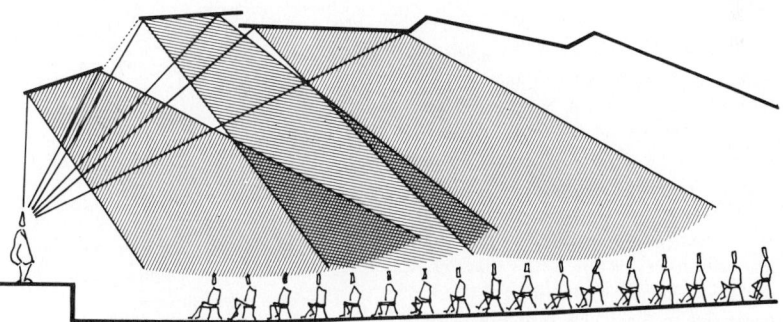

Fig. 32. Uniform distribution of reflected sound can be assured by proper ceiling design

very handsome and adequate arrangements cannot be made with straight sections of seating. Curved plan elements should be avoided whenever possible because they always give rise to troublesome echo problems. The rear wall of an auditorium should never be curved unless it is absolutely necessary and if it is a smooth, concave curve in plan, it must be treated very heavily with sound-absorbing material to reduce the possibility of echo. this often adds more permanent sound-absorbing material to the room than may be desirable. A straight or seg-

mented rear wall is always a less troublesome surface. If sound-absorbing treatment must be used to control echo, the facings must be very open (see section on "Sound absorption"). Balcony fronts generally should be either open railings or tilted so that they do not reflect sound to the front of the room.

There is no "best" plan or section for an auditorium. Every scheme must be considered on its own merits. Certain types of plans are more troublesome than others, especially when the hall becomes quite

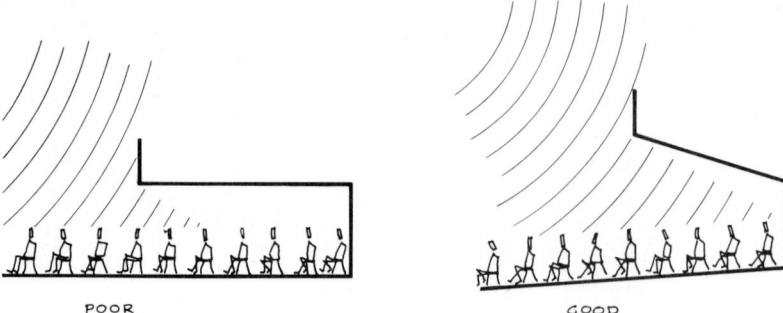

Fig. 33. Deep underbalconies deprive some seats of useful reflected sound

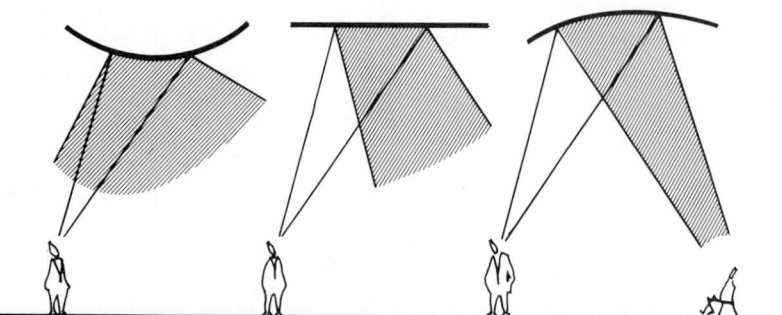

Fig. 34. Effect of surface shape on reflected sound

wide and the time delay between arrival of initial sound and reflected sound becomes great. In general, side wall surfaces near the proscenium should be tilted to direct sounds toward the rear of the hall rather than across the room where long time delays would result (see Fig. 37).

REFLECTION AND DIFFUSION OF SOUND

We have discussed at some length the reflection of sound from the enclosing surfaces of a room, but it is important to keep in mind that, unless the surfaces or the elements of the surface are large compared with the wavelengths of sound involved, they will not reflect sound in a geometric fashion. The reflecting surfaces should have minimum dimensions of 3 to 6 ft. if they are to act as true sound mirrors over a useful frequency range. Small objects of a few inches or less will merely allow sound to pass by and will have little effect on the sound field (see Fig. 38). Thus, a pulpit canopy or suspended sound-reflecting panels over an orchestra or in the ceiling of an auditorium, or the elements of a faceted ceiling or side wall, must be sizable to handle sound reflection in a predictable fashion.

On the other hand, it is usually desirable to have a certain amount of random scattering or diffusion in the sound-reflecting property of the enclosure, and we try to introduce a great deal of irregularity in the enclosing surfaces of rooms. Coffers, splayed panels, or offset surfaces of scale ranging from 3 to 10 ft or more with depth of perhaps 1 or 2 ft give good diffusion of sound while at the same time they give good reflection of sound from source to listener. This means that for any of the possible source positions in the room, sound is quite likely to be reflected to all of the listening positions. The analogy can be drawn with a glossy paint surface as compared with a matte surface. There is a general reflection of light from the latter but without the "hot spots" which are seen in a glossy surface. It is especially important for good balance in a concert hall to have a high degree of diffusion of sound surrounding the performers so that they can all hear each other very clearly. This achievement of good mixing and blending of the sound at the start almost always gives better results than very smooth enclosing surfaces.

REVERBERATION

The reverberation time of an auditorium is probably its most talked-about characteristic. Reverberation time can be measured, and in many cases it can be calculated and predicted in advance. However, the common practice of shouting or clapping the hands and looking at a stopwatch will only give a crude approximation to the true value. The details for calculating reverberation time are discussed in the section on "Sound absorption."

Reverberation is something quite different from echo, and there is often confusion on this point. Echo is the distinct repetition of a sound reflected from a distant surface (see Fig. 39); it is almost always undesirable. Reverberation, on the other hand, is the smooth decay of sound as it reflects from surface to surface around the room, gradually losing energy on each contact with the absorbing elements in the space. Some reverberation is always desirable in a room to give it life and character. The absence of reverberation indicates an overabundance of sound-absorbing material and energy waste. The designer's problem is to adjust reverberation to an optimum value and to conserve all the sound energy he possibly can for the benefit of listeners.

At least as important as reverberation time in determining the listening "quality" of a space is the balance between the "early" and the "late" sound energy—the direct sound including reflections (up to about 50 m/s) and the later reflections that constitute reverberation. This balance will be different for various types of performances—more "early" sound for speech and less for music.

Another factor of considerable importance is the direction from which the reflected sound arrives. In general, clarity as required for speech is associated with strong frontal sound, but the spatial qualities of music are enhanced if the listener receives strong lateral and other nonfrontal reflections.

The reverberation time of an auditorium is largely controlled by the area occupied by the sound-absorbing audience and by the actual cubic volume of the space. These two factors set a limit on how much reverberation one can have, while the sound-absorbing materials added for the control of echo and unwanted reflections have only a minor effect. The shape of the auditorium is very important in determining the reverberation time and smoothness of decay of sound. The sound must have an opportunity to travel around the room and should not all be quickly grounded in the sound-absorbing audience. The more rectangular shapes seem to give the finest reverberation characteristics, expecially for musical performances and provide the best potential for good balance between early and reverberant energy.

In many older concert halls the audiences were more tightly packed than in modern halls with their more luxurious seating. Consequently, for the same volume a larger number of people could be accommodated, and therefore, the reverberation time could be higher than in a modern hall

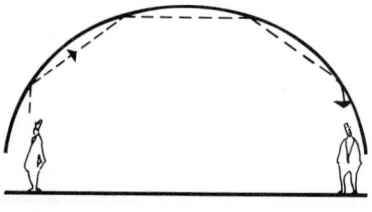

CREEP, OR THE WHISPERING GALLERY

Fig. 35. Sound reflection along curved surfaces often results in strange effects

with the same seating capacity unless the volume is also increased. But, increasing the volume also reduces the total energy density and if the hall gets too big, the sound tends to lose its "punch."

As we saw in an earlier section, the criteria for reverberation time in auditoriums for various uses show a wide range of acceptable values. These go from less than a second for certain types of speech activity to two or more seconds for liturgical music.

If an auditorium must accommodate a very wide variety of functions, it may be necessary to introduce mechanisms for varying the reverberation characteristics. However, if sound-absorbing panels or curtains or other elements are to be introduced to reduce the reverberation time from a high value for music performances to low values for speech, it is necessary to change large areas of the wall surfaces from hard to soft. A significant change cannot be accomplished merely by turning a few panels around or making other minor modifications. Remember that the seating area is a large "flywheel" of absorption, and that, unless one introduces an area of sound-absorbing material equal to a good fraction of the seating area, the reverberation time will not be reduced very much. Figure 40 shows a possible scheme for storing such retractable draperies. It should also be evident that the seating area should have a fairly constant sound-absorbing characteristic regardless of audience size. Thus, fabric-upholstered seats are an acoustical necessity in *any* well-designed auditorium.

BUILDINGS WHERE HEARING CONDITIONS ARE IMPORTANT

Schools

Often overlooked in today's quest for flexibility and new structural forms in school design is the basic need for good hearing conditions in all of the spaces, either with or without folding partitions.

In the lower elementary classroom the problem is usually one of noise suppression; thus, an over-all treatment of the ceiling area with a sound-absorbing material is advised. However, in the secondary school classroom where lecture teaching is normal, it is generally better to use the central part of the classroom ceiling as a sound reflector to make the communication between teacher and pupil easier: it is really a small auditorium. A very rough rule-of-thumb says that only about half the ceiling area should be covered with sound-absorbing material in an ordinary thirty-pupil classroom.

Open-plan schools, like open-plan offices, should have as much sound-absorbing surface as possible to minimize the spreading of sound from one group to another. Instruction in such spaces is usually limited to small groups.

Music rehearsal rooms should have sub-

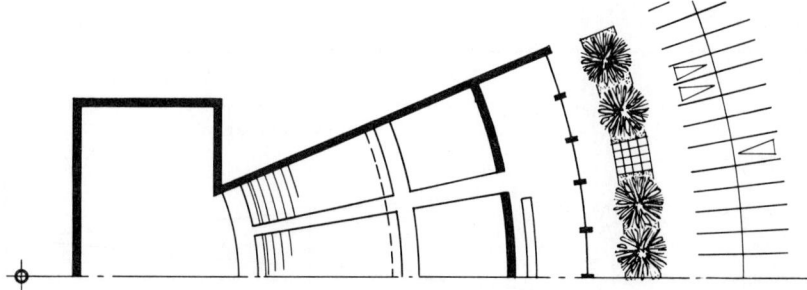

Fig. 36. The beam compass approach to auditorium design results in poor sound distribution

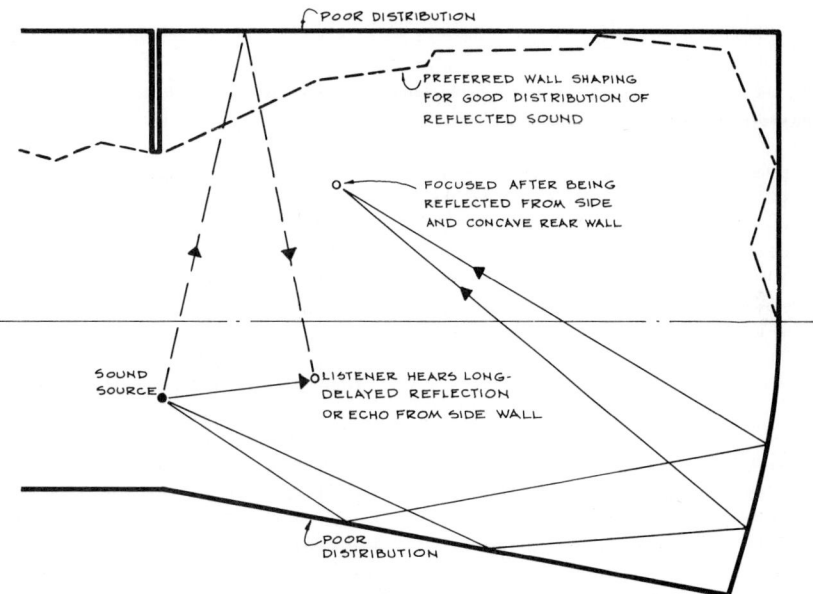

Fig. 37. Effect of wall shaping on sound distribution

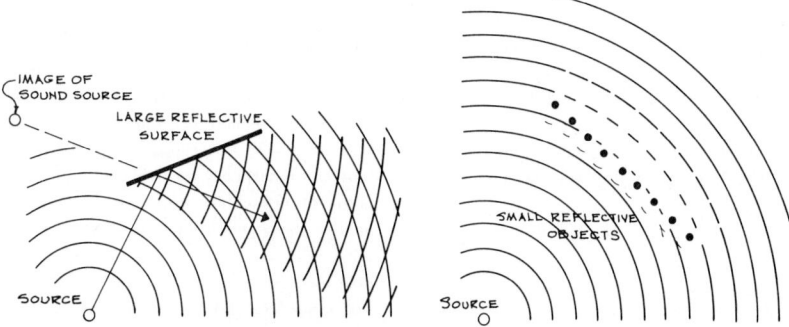

Fig. 38. Effect of size of surface on sound reflection

stantially higher ceilings than ordinary classrooms, usually at least 15 ft and preferably 20 ft, and some effort should be made to introduce sound-diffusing elements in the enclosing surfaces. It is almost hopeless to ask a large school band to rehearse comfortably in a room with a 9 ft ceiling covered with acoustical tile! These rooms should be isolated as much as possible from the rest of the building, but if they must be placed close to other classrooms, special double constructions must be used to separate them.

The music department often contains, in addition to the large rehearsal rooms, small practice rooms which must have special attention to isolation details (discussed in section on "Sound isolation"). It is usually a good idea not to open the practice rooms directly into the rehearsal room but rather to have an intervening corridor or sound lock so that the rooms can be used simultaneously.

If the school has an auditorium, its design should follow the basic principles outlined

Design for good hearing

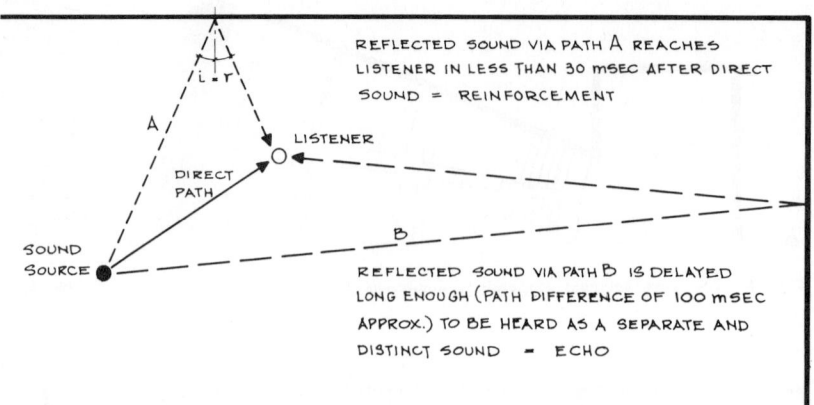

Fig. 39. **Early reflections are useful reinforcement, but long-delayed reflections of sufficient intensity may be heard as distinct echoes.**

earlier. There should always be a sound-reflecting ceiling in the stage area for the use of musicians when they perform. This can be permanent or removable depending on the program. Also, hopefully, the auditorium will have fabric-upholstered seats so that it will be as satisfactory for rehearsals when empty or for small groups as it will be for full occupancy. When an auditorium can be used for a variety of functions and audience size it is an achievement of true flexibility.

Often the gymnasium must serve the function of an auditorium, and if it does, a good compromise can be achieved by treating only part of the ceiling with sound-absorbing material for noise and reverberation control leaving the central portion hard for sound-reinforcing reflection. If the stage is at one end of the room, the opposite end can be treated with a sound-absorbing material to reduce echo (see Fig. 41), and sometimes a sound-reflecting panel can be arranged at the platform end of the room to give additional sound-reinforcing reflections. The gymnasium is probably the only space in a school besides the auditorium

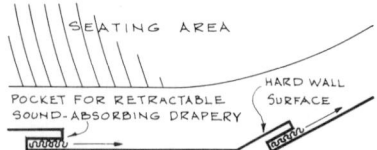

Fig. 40. **Example of a method for introducing "variable" sound absorption in room design**

where a speech reinforcing system may be required and only the highest quality components should be used. These systems should not be merely an extension of the basic paging and announcement system for the school.

Multipurpose auditoriums

Large auditoriums intended for conventions, concerts, plays, ballet, and every other conceivable type of performance are being built in many cities throughout the world. To be really successful, these buildings should not be designed to seat more than 2,500 to 3,000 people.

If concert music is an important part of the program of use, the maximum desirable reverberation time of the hall would be something like 2 s at midfrequencies. The required volume of the hall will then be uniquely determined by the absorption provided by the audience and performers. On the other hand, there will be many musical as well as speech events where a less reverberant environment is required, maybe as little as 1.4 s. This range of reverberation time can realistically be achieved with large areas of retractible draperies as discussed earlier. The point is, however, that reverberation time can only be decreased by adjustable devices. It cannot be increased beyond the upper limit set by the volume and the sound absorbing audience.

In an earlier section we have seen that for good distribution of sound in an auditorium, people seated under a balcony must have good upward-looking sight lines to the

main ceiling (Fig. 33). This is equally important for receiving sound from the reverberant field in the upper part of the room. A person seated in a deep underbalcony space is "out of it." There is no hard and fast rule for depth of underbalcony seating, but the more open this area is to the main volume of the room, the better.

If there is a stage house to accommodate flown scenery, an orchestra enclosure must be provided for concert uses. This helps to make the performing area acoustically part of the auditorium. It provides some sound reflection to the audience, but is most important to other musicians on stage so that they can hear each other and achieve good balance. One cannot expect an orchestra or a chorus to perform in the usual stage house full of sound-absorbing scenery and draperies. An enclosure for the stage must be made of heavy, sound-reflecting material (plywood, steel, etc.)—it cannot be light painted canvas—and it must be so arranged that it can be put in place and taken down with a minimum of effort (see Fig. 42).

The placement of an organ, if it is to be provided, presents a most difficult problem in the multipurpose auditorium with stage house. If it is only to be used for recitals, the pipes and console can be placed at one side of the hall near the proscenium opening. But in that position it cannot be used for accompanying a choir on stage or as part of an orchestral performance. Balance and ensemble problems are simply too difficult with this physical separation. The only really satisfactory location for the organ is at the back of the stage immediately behind the orchestra and/or choir within the orchestra enclosure. In a number of multipurpose auditoriums this problem has been solved by mounting the whole instrument on casters, making it portable. It can then be stored offstage, sometimes in an adjoining room—to be used there for practice. The organ is a musical instrument like a piano. It must be placed so the organist is with the other musicians if it is used in performance with them.

Because the volume of the hall is determined by the need for a long reverberation time for concerts, the ceiling will likely be quite high. Thus, reflections from the ceiling will be too late for "early" (within 50 ms) reinforcement of sound to listeners in the front half of the main-floor seating. It is usually necessary to provide a layer of sound-reflecting panels at an intermediate height extending for some distance from the proscenium out over the audience to give these "early" reflections (see Fig. 43). The exact height, shape, and size of these reflecting panels and their extent will be determined by the particular geometry of the hall.

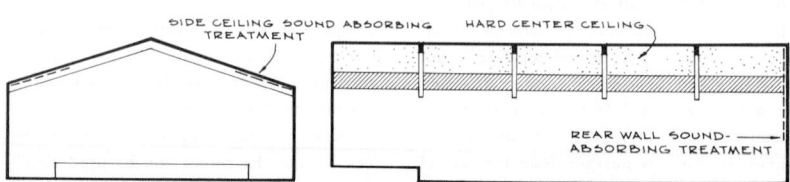

Fig. 41. **Example of a simple acoustical treatment for a multipurpose room**

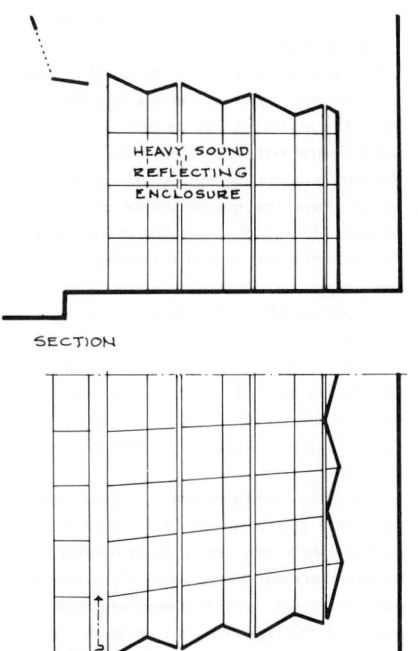

HEAVY SOUND REFLECTING ENCLOSURE

SECTION

HALF REFLECTED PLAN

Fig. 42. Example of an orchestral enclosure for a large multipurpose stage

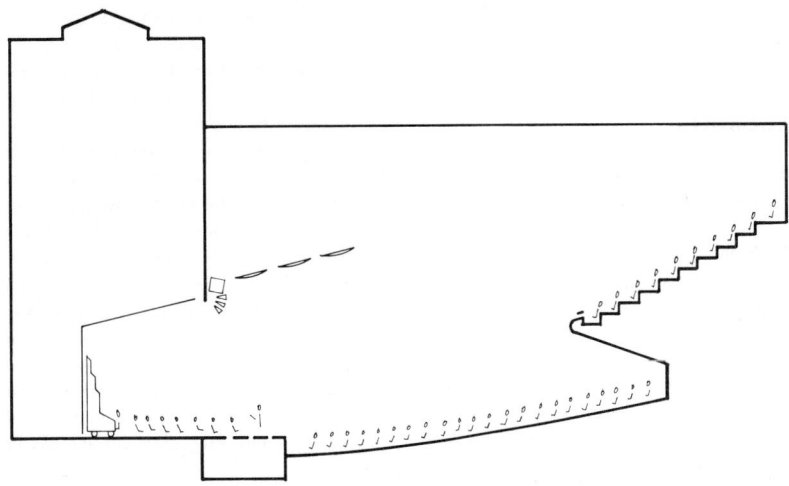

Fig. 43. Section through a typical multipurpose auditorium showing orchestra enclosure, portable organ, sound system, and sound-reflecting panels

Churches

All of the basic requirements for good hearing must be met in the church, but there are a number of specific matters peculiar to this building type that the designer must take into account. Usually, the form of the church itself will not be governed quite so much by acoustical considerations as would a school auditorium, but basically difficult shapes, such as domes, barrel vaults, etc., should be avoided at all cost. The reverberation time in the church should be designed to be fairly high (upwards of 1.6 sec), and this means special attention must be directed to problems of speech intelligibility. In the larger church (300 seats or more), it will often be necessary to provide either a speech-reinforcing system or a carefully designed pulpit canopy. The latter is often an excellent device to bring direct speech sound to the listeners without the use of electronic reinforcement. The pulpit canopy, of course, does nothing for speech at the altar and in the lectern, but many churches up to 1,000 seats have been designed with good pulpit canopies and no sound amplification with excellent results (see Fig. 44).

An important function of the enclosing surfaces in a church is to give strong, mutually reinforcing reflections to the congregation. This gives every member of the congregation the sense of being part of a group of people singing and praying, and encourages participation in common worship. A church with a sound-absorptive ceiling that does not reflect sound from one part of the room to another leaves each member of the congregation feeling alone and conspicuous, and thus nonparticipating.

Another important acoustics problem in the church is the placement of the choir and the organ and their relation to the congregation. The choir should be out in the open, it should be grouped in as nearly a square array as possible, and it should be immediately in front of the organ (the pipes, not the console) where the singers can hear the organ as the congregation will hear it (see Fig. 45). The choir should *not* be tucked in a low-ceilinged alcove, nor divided across a wide chancel, nor strung out in a long line, nor should the organ pipes be widely distributed. If the organ and choir are well placed in the church, at either front or rear, if the ceiling and wall surfaces are so arranged that the congregation is in the same space as the musicians, and if all the people

Fig. 44. A pulpit canopy may provide effective natural reinforcement of speech in churches

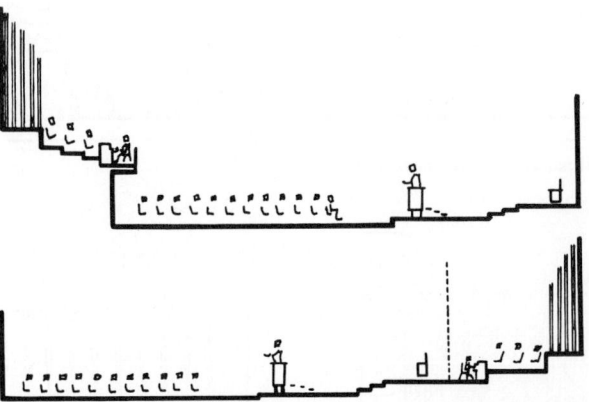

Fig. 45. The organ, choir, and console must be considered a unit of inseparable parts with unobstructed acoustical "line-of-sight" to the congregation. Front or rear gallery locations can be equally effective

Sound reinforcement systems

in the church receive reinforcing reflections from the enclosing surfaces, almost inevitably good results will be obtained.

REFERENCES

Beranek, L. L. *Music Acoustics and Architecture.* John Wiley and Sons, Inc., New York (1963).

Knudsen, V. O. and C. M. Harris. *Acoustical Designing in Architecture.* John Wiley and Sons, Inc., New York (1950).

Better Architecture for the Performing Arts, *Architectural Record* (December, 1964).

Newman, R. B. (ed.) Design for Hearing, *Progressive Architecture* (May 1959).

Schultz, T. J. Acoustics of the Concert Hall, *IEEE Spectrum* (June, 1965).

Kutruff, H. *Room Acoustics,* John Wiley and Sons, N.Y. (1973).

SOUND REINFORCEMENT SYSTEMS*

In many situations, to obtain adequate loudness and good distribution of sound, it is necessary to augment the natural transmission of sound from source to listener by means of a sound system. In large sports arenas, in airport terminal buildings, and in other noisy locations, it is almost always necessary to provide sound reinforcement. Even in rooms where most strong-voiced speakers can be heard clearly, the weaker voices must be amplified, and there is often the need to reproduce recorded material or movie sound. In all cases, however, the design of the sound reinforcement system must be carefully integrated with the design

See also section on "Sound Systems."

of the room and with its acoustical characteristics.

There are two principal types of sound reinforcement systems: central and distributed. The preferred type in most situations is the central system in which a loudspeaker (or cluster of loudspeakers) is located directly above the actual source of sound. Only one loudspeaker position is used in a system of this sort, and it is capable of giving maximum realism. The listener with his two ears is readily able to localize the direction of the source of sound, and if the amplified signal comes from the same direction as the original sound, he gets an impression merely of increased loudness or clarity but not of artificial "amplified" sound (Fig. 46).

The other principal type of sound reinforcement system is the distributed type. In this system, one uses a large number of loudspeakers distributed uniformly over the audience areas. With loudspeakers located overhead, this type of system operates much like downlighting. We cover the room with small "pools" of sound, each listener receiving sound from only the closest loudspeakers. This type of system is used in any situation where the ceiling height is inadequate to use a central system or where all listeners cannot have "line of sight" on a central loudspeaker. It is also used in such spaces as large convention rooms, where there must be a very flexible arrangement of the space for amplifying sources of sound in any position in the hall. It is the logical system for most airport terminal buildings, where the amplified signal usually must be somewhat higher in level in order to override the high background noise levels due to aircraft operations. The distributed system is a flexible system, and while it does not give maximum realism in reinforcing live activities, it can be made to provide high intelligibility in many difficult situations (Fig. 47).

In spaces with very high ceilings or when other considerations will not permit mounting the loudspeakers in the ceiling, loudspeakers in a distributed system can be installed within the audience areas. They can be attached to the backs of the seats in conference rooms, mounted in the desks in assembly rooms or legislative chambers, or installed in the backs of church pews.

Although it is very common practice, one should never locate loudspeakers at the two sides of the proscenium opening for sound reinforcement (see Fig. 48). This always gives poor quality and unrealistic amplification, disassociating the speaker's voice from his or her visible location. Even worse is the cross-fire from loudspeakers distributed along both sides of a room, or in the four

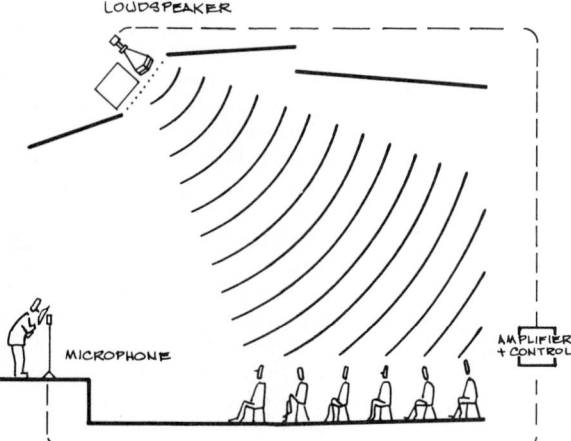

Fig. 46.   Central loudspeaker system

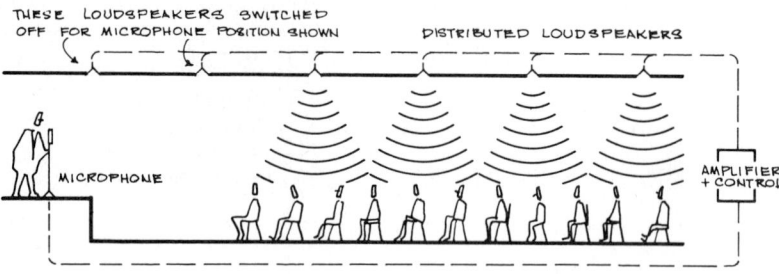

Fig. 47.   Distributed loudspeaker system

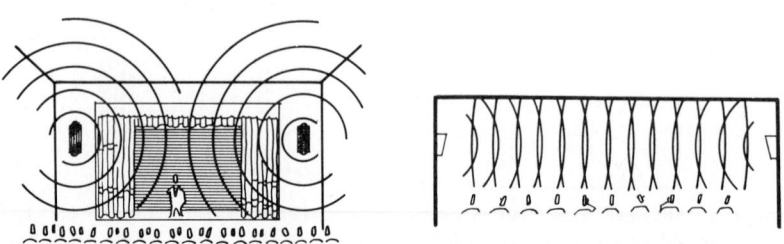

Fig. 48.   Poor loudspeaker placement can mean ineffective sound reinforcement

corners. Hearing conditions can almost always be improved by shutting off such systems.

CENTRAL SYSTEMS

The loudspeaker for a central system usually consists of a cluster of directional horns, some of which handle the high-frequency end of the audible spectrum, and larger loudspeakers which handle the low-frequency end of the spectrum. The high-frequency horns are usually exponential, multicell, or radial horns and are arranged in clusters to give coverage of specific areas of the seating. It is important that the horn arrays be designed to have proper directional characteristics and that the level of sound from the several units be individually adjustable. One cannot achieve high-quality sound amplification without loudspeakers with carefully controlled directional characteristics. If a loudspeaker system is to be used only for speech purposes, the system need not have any low-frequency loudspeakers and can be housed in a smaller space than a full-frequency-range system (used for music). Usually, a speech system is cut off at approximately 300 Hz (i.e., these loudspeakers do not amplify sounds below that frequency). This results in no loss in realism and actually improves intelligibility in rooms with "boomy" characteristics.

The designer of an auditorium incorporating a loudspeaker system must realize that the system will take a great deal of space and that it cannot be tucked conveniently into a 1-ft slot. The grille in front of the loudspeaker must be completely transparent to sound and must contain no large-scale elements (see Fig. 49). Every listener in the room must have line-of-sight on the loudspeaker; one cannot count on reflection of sound from room surfaces to fill in any areas not covered by direct line of sight.

When listeners are far away from the central loudspeaker cluster, or if they do not have line-of-sight to the cluster, auxiliary loudspeakers can be placed in nearby overhead locations (with appropriate time delay) to give coverage.

The operator of the sound system should be located toward the rear of the seating area where he can hear the system as it is heard by the audience. He should not be behind a glass window in a booth receiving sound only from a monitor loudspeaker. The power amplifiers can be in any convenient location, but the actual controls must be "in the room."

Microphones must be placed near the sources of sound. If there are to be many sources, as in a play, there must be a sufficient number of microphones provided with-

ALTERNATIVE GRILLE LOCATIONS SHOWING HOW COVERAGE PATTERNS OF LOUDSPEAKERS DETERMINE MINIMUM SIZE OF GRILLE OPENING

LOW FREQUENCY ENCLOSURE

HIGH FREQUENCY HORNS

COVERAGE PATTERN MUST NOT BE OCCLUDED BY FRAMING MEMBERS

0 1 2 3 4 5 FT.

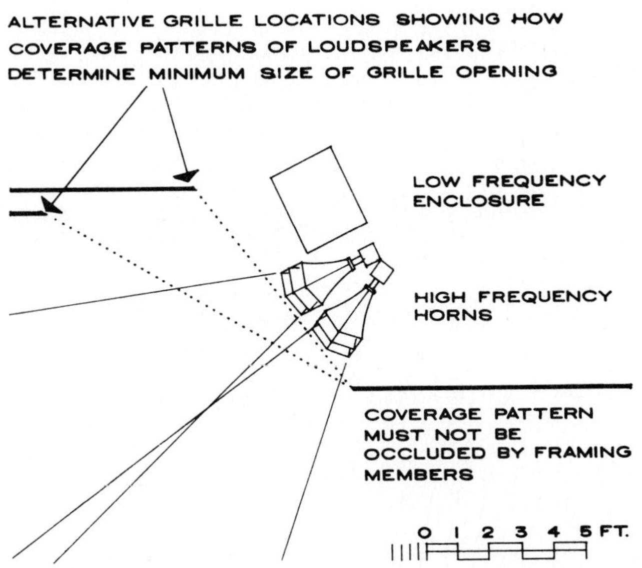

Fig. 49. Loudspeaker grille sizes are determined by the coverage patterns of the loudspeakers behind them

in the acting area, concealed in the scenery, etc., that the actors are always relatively close to these pickup devices.

There is also the important problem of feedback of sound energy from loudspeaker to microphone, and the relative locations of microphones to the loudspeakers must be carefully considered to avoid the familiar squealing or howling of a poorly designed and operated system. This is a matter for detailed consideration by the designer of the system and is not primarily an architectural question except insofar as relative location of loudspeaker to microphone is concerned. In the large arena or sports building, the central cluster of loudspeakers is usually suspended without any attempt at concealment, and some central position can usually be found giving everyone clear line of sight on the unit.

In some situations, line-source or column loudspeakers are preferable to radial or multicellular horns (see Fig. 50). These units give a restricted coverage in the vertical plane that is advantageous in confining the distribution to audience head level. The horizontal distribution is fairly nondirectional. These loudspeakers must always be mounted vertically or tilted slightly down, never placed horizontally.

DISTRIBUTED SYSTEMS

In this type of sound-amplifying system it is extremely important to have an adequate number of loudspeaker units. They are generally placed in the ceiling, facing down and sounding through appropriate grillage. Each loudspeaker unit is considered to cover be-

tween 60 and 90 degrees, depending on the type selected. Even the highest-quality units with the most suitable grilles do not cover more than 90 degrees adequately; when concealed behind fake diffusers, they are far less satisfactory (Fig. 51). Unfortunately, many loudspeakers employed in such systems beam high-frequency energy rather sharply. Uniform, high speech intelligibility is not possible with such systems; also, they must be operated at an uncomfortably high level to permit listeners between loudspeakers to hear properly.

In order to prevent feedback, a switching system is usually provided, so that certain loudspeakers can be shut off when a source of sound is to be placed immediately under one of the units in a space for flexible use.

As mentioned earlier, loudspeakers should never be placed along the side walls of a room, producing "cross firing." This cross firing always causes the listener to hear from many loudspeakers at the same time, with multiple time delays reducing speech intelligibility. In a church, the loudspeakers might be located in the bottoms of chandeliers (over the heads of the worshippers) or column loudspeakers can be located slightly above head height, either on structural columns or along the side walls. These systems are really successful only when provisions for time delay are included. The amplified sound arrives at the listener's ears just after the direct sound from the speaker has been received. There is then no awareness of the nearby loudspeakers as the source. Results can be incredibly good. This type of system is especially effective in highly reverberant spaces where a central

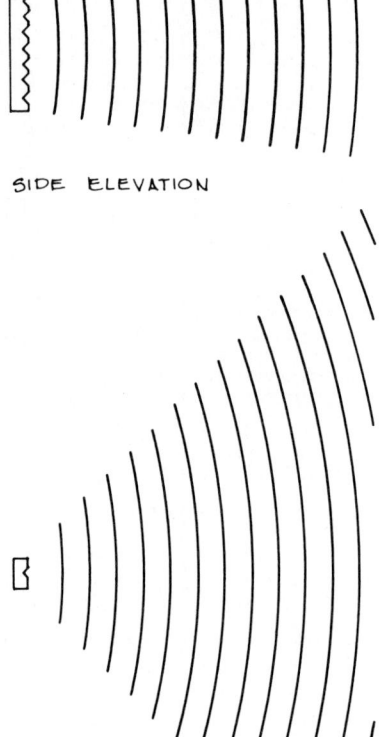

SIDE ELEVATION

PLAN

Fig. 50. A line-source or column loudspeaker and its coverage characteristics

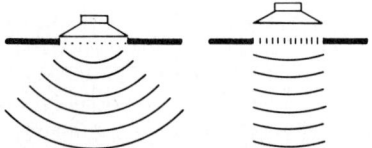

Fig. 51. Poorly chosen loudspeaker grille materials can markedly affect the sound distribution from any loudspeaker

cluster would only add loudness and confusion.

The availability of relatively inexpensive digital time-delay units has made possible the uniform coverage of seating area in many "difficult" spaces. As suggested earlier, when it is not possible for all listeners to have direct line-of-sight on the central loudspeaker cluster, nearby overhead loudspeakers can fill in. The sound from these auxiliary units is usually delayed about 10

ms after the sound from the live source or central cluster of loudspeakers has arrived at the listener's position. Even when listeners in a large auditorium can see the central cluster, it is sometimes better to cover a balcony area from auxiliary overhead units rather than try to do the whole job from the central loudspeaker. This reduces the size of the central unit and gives better control of distribution.

The most important characteristic of a good sound amplification system is that it sounds natural and that the sound appears to come from the live source. This can be done only with a system carefully designed for the given space that has been properly installed and, most important of all, intelligently and sensitively operated.

NOISE CONTROL REQUIREMENTS IN UNITED STATES BUILDING CODES

For many years the United States was one of the few highly developed countries in the world that had no requirements in its building codes for the control of noise. This resulted in the progressive deterioration of acoustical privacy and comfort and in an increasing number of complaints from the occupants of multifamily buildings. By contrast, more and more countries abroad, having become concerned over the intrusion of noise and its effect on the health and happiness of their people, have instituted control measures based on careful and thorough investigations.

FHA/HUD regulations

In 1963, for the first time, an important American code established standards in this field. The Federal Housing Administration (FHA) in its *Minimum Property Standards for Multifamily Housing* (FHA no. 2600, November, 1963) set minimum requirements for the control of both air-borne sound and impact sound transmission that represent a substantial improvement over previous general practice, even for high-rental apartment buildings.

These Minimum Property Standards have been revised from time to time. The 1976 version as issued by the U.S. Department of Housing and Urban Development (of which the FHA is a part) is shown in Table 6 for multifamily and for one- and two-family housing. The requirements are the same for both categories although some footnotes such as those relating to elevators, and so on, do not apply to one- and two-family housing.

In 1968, HUD adopted a set of recommendations (A *Guide to Airborne, Im-*

pact, and Structure-Borne Noise-Control in Multifamily Dwellings, HUD, FT/TS-24, January, 1968) for the control of airborne noise and impact noise that are somewhat more detailed and somewhat more stringent than those of the *Minimum Property Standards*. Presumably, since these later limitations are presented only as "recommendations" and not requirements, they may be regarded as supplementing the earlier document to provide guidance on what performance would be appropriate in situations where better than minimum performance is desired.

In HUD's supplementary recommendations of 1968, descriptive definitions of three different grades of acoustic environment are given in order to deal effectively with the wide range of urban development, geographic locations, economic conditions, and other factors encountered in United States housing. Construction that meets the criteria, respectively, for these different grades will provide good sound isolation and satisfy most occupants.

Grade I is applicable primarily in suburban residential areas, i.e., "quiet" locations where the nighttime exterior noise levels might be about 35–40 dBA or lower. Here the recommended interior noise environment should be NC 20-25. In addition, the insulation criteria of this grade are applicable in certain special cases, such as dwelling units above the eighth floor in high-rise buildings and the better class or "luxury" buildings, regardless of location.

Grade II is the most important category and is applicable primarily in residential urban and suburban areas with "average" noise environment. Here the nighttime exterior noise levels might be about 40–45 dBA, and the interior noise environment should not exceed NC 25–30.

Grade III criteria should be considered as minimal recommendations and are applicable in "noisy" urban areas. Here the nighttime exterior noise levels might be about 55 dBA or higher; the interior noise environment should not exceed NC 35.

Tables 7 and 8 give the recommended values of sound transmission class (STC) and impact insulation class (IIC) for all three grades of acoustical environment for wall structures and floor/ceiling structures separating different apartments. Table 9 gives recommended values of transmission loss for partitions within a single dwelling unit.

Figures 52 and 53 show the relations between HUD's basic (bedroom-to-bedroom) criteria and the requirements or recommendations in other countries.

NEW YORK CITY BUILDING CODE

Only one United States city, New York, has adopted extensive noise control measures in its building code (local law no. 76 for the year 1968, subarticle 1208.0, *Noise Control in Multiple Dwellings*). A few other cities have articles in their building codes intended to deal with one or another aspect of noise control, but these are typically fragmentary or poorly worded and are difficult to enforce.

New York's code requires that walls, partitions, and floor/ceiling constructions built before January, 1972, shall have a minimum *STC* of 45 and after this date of 50. This requirement does not apply to dwelling unit entrance doors; however, for

buildings completed before January, 1972, such doors must fit closely and not be undercut; after that date, entrance doors must have an *STC* of at least 35.

Floor/ceiling constructions separating dwelling units from each other or from public halls or corridors must have a minimum impact noise rating *(INR)* of zero.

Detailed criteria are also given in the New York code for the maximum sound power level in mechanical spaces adjoining dwelling units, for the maximum sound power levels permitted for exterior mechanical equipment, for the sound pressure levels

inside a dwelling unit due to exterior mechanical equipment, and the maximum permissible sound power level from terminal units of the ventilating system. In all cases, the maximum permitted levels are 3–8 dB lower for buildings built after January, 1972.

Constructions that meet the criteria

For constructions that meet the various requirements for transmission loss in terms of the sound transmission class *(STC)*, see Table 4 in the section on Sound Isolation. For floor/ceiling constructions that meet the impact isolation requirements in terms of

Table 6. Sound-transmission limitations

Location of partition	STC (6)	
Living unit to living unit, corridor (1), or public space (average noise) (2)	45	
Living unit to public space and service areas (high noise) (3),(5)	50	
Location of floor-ceiling	*STC*	*IIC (7)*
Floor-ceiling separating living units from other living units, public space (4), or service areas (2)	45	45
Floor-ceiling separating living units from public space and service areas (high noise) (3) including corridor floors over living units	50	50

Notes
(1) *These values assume floors in corridors are carpeted; otherwise increase STC by 5.*
(2) *Public space of average noise includes lobbies, storage rooms, stairways, etc.*
(3) *Areas of high noise include boiler rooms, mechanical equipment rooms, elevator shafts, laundries, incinerator shafts, garages, and most commercial uses.*
(4) *Does not apply to floor above storage rooms where noise from living units would not be objectionable.*
(5) *Increase STC by 5 when over or under mechanical equipment which operates at high noise levels.*
(6) *STC determined in accordance with ASTM E 413.*
(7) *IIC determined in accordance with ASTM E 492-73T.*

Table 7. Criteria for airborne sound insulation of wall partitions between dwelling units*

Partition function between dwellings, Apt. A to Apt. B	Grade I, STC	Grade II, STC	Grade III, STC
Bedroom to bedroom	55	52	48
Living room to bedroom	57	54	50
Kitchen to bedroom	58	55	52
Bathroom to bedroom	59	56	52
Corridor to bedroom	55	52	48
Living room to living room	55	52	48
Kitchen to living room	55	52	48
Bathroom to living room	57	54	50
Corridor to living room	55	52	48
Kitchen to kitchen	52	50	46
Bathroom to kitchen	55	52	48
Corridor to kitchen	55	52	48
Bathroom to bathroom	52	50	46
Corridor to bathroom	50	48	46

* *Where the partition between dwelling units is common to several functional spaces, the partition must meet the highest criterion value.*

Table 8. Criteria for airborne and impact sound insulation of floor-ceiling assemblies between dwelling units*

Partition function between dwellings, Apt. A to Apt. B	Grade I		Grade II		Grade III	
	STC	IIC	STC	IIC	STC	IIC
Bedroom above bedroom	55	55	52	52	48	48
Living room above bedroom	57	60	54	57	50	53
Kitchen above bedroom	58	65	55	62	52	58
Family room above bedroom	60	65	56	62	52	58
Corridor above bedroom	55	65	52	62	48	58
Bedroom above living room	57	55	54	52	50	48
Living room above living room	55	55	52	52	48	48
Kitchen above living room	55	60	52	57	48	53
Family room above living room	58	62	54	60	52	56
Corridor above living room	55	60	52	57	48	53
Bedroom above kitchen	58	52	55	50	52	46
Living room above kitchen	55	55	52	52	48	48
Kitchen above kitchen	52	55	50	52	46	48
Bathroom above kitchen	55	55	52	52	48	48
Family room above kitchen	55	60	52	58	48	54
Corridor above kitchen	50	55	48	52	46	48
Bedroom above family room	60	50	56	48	52	46
Living room above family room	58	52	54	50	52	48
Kitchen above family room	55	55	52	52	48	50
Bathroom above bathroom	52	52	50	50	48	48
Corridor above corridor	50	50	48	48	46	46

* See discussion in section on "Impact Noise Isolation," under "Sound Isolation."

either the impact noise rating (INR) (introduced in the earlier FHA requirements and also used in the New York code) or the later impact insulation class (IIC) a modification adopted by HUD to be more in line with international standards, see Table 5 in the section on Sound Isolation.

How do we get good noise control in buildings?

It has been reported that of all complaints property managers hear about apartments, lack of soundproofing heads the list. Why is this, when we have the technology and materials to get good sound isolation? It is usually because the building components are ineptly put together. Selection of a good floor, ceiling, or partition construction is not enough to ensure privacy. The excellent isolation that a floating raft floor can provide may, for example, be nullified by careless detailing that permits conduits, ducts, or plumbing to "short circuit" the isolation or by poor supervision that permits the raft floor to be attached solidly to the walls at the edges. Any leaks or cracks can largely nullify the sound-isolating properties of an otherwise adequate construction.

What is really important is the actual noise reduction achieved between spaces, not what components are used. A soufflé can fall even when made with the finest ingredients!

In recognition of this fact, the Environmental Protection Agency (EPA) in 1978 proposed a new model building code. This includes a performance specification for ad-

Table 9. Criteria for airborne sound insulation within a dwelling unit

Partition function between rooms	Grade I, STC	Grade II, STC	Grade III, STC
Bedroom to bedroom* †	48	44	40
Living room to bedroom* †	50	46	42
Bathroom to bedroom* †	52	48	45
Kitchen to bedroom* †	52	48	45
Bathroom to living room†	52	48	45

* Closets may be used as "buffer" zones providing unlouvered doors are used.
† Doors leading to bedrooms and bathrooms should be of solid-core construction and gasketed to assure a comfortable degree of privacy.

equate sound isolation, to be demonstrated by acoustical tests in the finished building.

A code will be successful only if it is both feasible and effective. Noise control provisions are feasible if they can be easily understood and accomplished without exotic constructions and are enforcible and readily adaptable to existing codes. They are effective if, when enforced, they actually lead to good acoustical quality in buildings.

The EPA proposals are aimed at high effectiveness. The mandatory final acoustical test might discourage adoption, but EPA has suggested pilot programs to demonstrate the general improvement in acoustical performance that results when ordinary good-quality constructions are used. This could help convince local builders that significant improvement in quality can be achieved without unusual construction or heroic effort. It is a matter of avoiding construction goofs and getting one's money's worth out of materials already bought and paid for.

Codes should specify some reliable types of construction that have been used many times with predictable sound-isolation performance. The only way that we can know that the building has been properly assembled, however, is with an acoustical test in the finished building, since acoustical faults are seldom visible.

The function of compliance tests in the finished building is to force responsible people to apply already existing technology instead of ignoring it, utilize good design, and follow it through with careful attention to detail in construction. That is the formula for good acoustical quality in buildings.

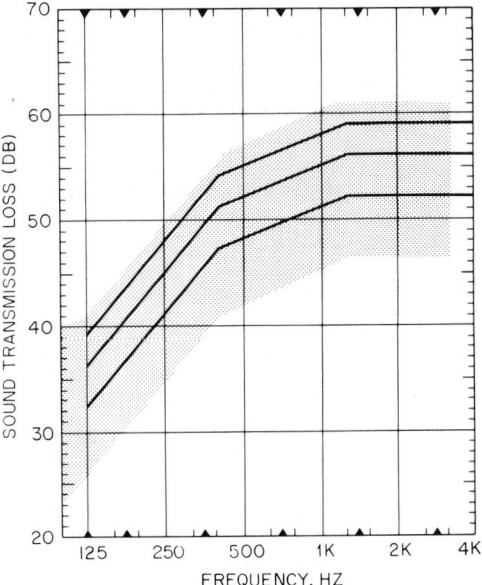

Grade I   STC = 55
Grade II STC = 52
Grade III STC = 48

Approximate range of airborne sound insulation requirements or recommendations of other countries

Fig. 52.   Air-borne sound isolation criteria

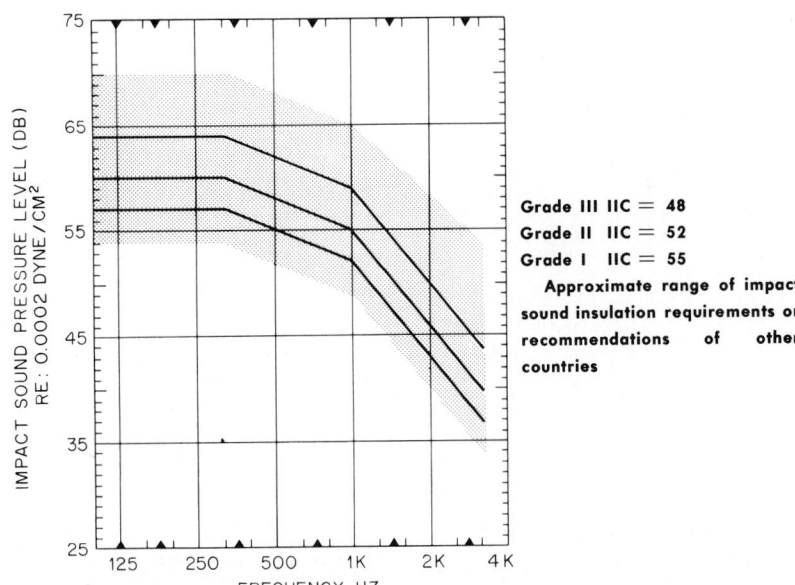

Grade III IIC = 48
Grade II IIC = 52
Grade I   IIC = 55

Approximate range of impact sound insulation requirements or recommendations of other countries

Fig. 53.   Impact sound isolation criteria

INSULATION – 1

Types; theory

By LAURENCE SHUMAN, *Consulting Engineer*
With additional material from ASHRAE Handbook of Fundamentals, *1977*

This section on thermal insulation, based on recent research results, covers: theory of heat transmission (briefly), a method for calculating insulation economies, and tables of heat transmission factors. Advances in this field have been primarily in insulating materials themselves—types and efficiency, new heat transmission data on building sections insulated with reflective materials, methods for calculating insulation requirements for concrete slabs on grade, and a greater recognition of the problems of condensation. A feature of this section is the comprehensive, easy-to-use set of tables on *U*-factors.

THERMAL INSULATION

Thermal insulating efficiency is a factor in: (1) temperatures of inside surfaces which affect comfort of occupants and aid or deter condensation, and (2) heat transmission through building sections which determines energy requirements for both heating and cooling. Economies in fuel consumption can be calculated with reasonable accuracy (see Sheet 2) and balanced against initial cost of insulation and cost of heating-cooling system.

In addition to their primary function, insulating materials are often used in buildings to perform other functions. Among these are structural uses (sheathing, lath), finish materials (wallboard, ceiling tile, spray-applied ceiling finish), fire resistance (ceiling tile, spray-applied insulation), noise control (ceiling tile, spray-applied ceiling, floor underlay, blankets), and vibration control (pads under machines).

Thermal insulation is made of the following basic materials:

1. *Mineral fibrous* material, such as asbestos, rock, slag, or glass wool
2. *Mineral cellular* material, such as foamed glass, calcium silicate, perlite, vermiculite, foamed concrete, or ceramic
3. *Organic fibrous* material, such as wood, cane, cotton, hair, cellulose, or synthetic fiber
4. *Organic cellular* material, such as cork, foamed rubber, polystyrene, or polyurethane

Thermal insulation is available in the following physical forms:

1. Loose fill—dry granules or nodules, poured or blown in place
2. Flexible or semirigid—blankets and batts of wool-like material
3. Rigid—boards and blocks
4. Membrane—reflective insulation
5. Spray applied—mineral fiber or insulating concrete
6. Poured in place—insulating concrete
7. Foamed in place—polyurethane

COEFFICIENT OF HEAT TRANSMISSION, *U*; DEFINITION

Calculations of heating or cooling loads are usually based on rate of heat flow through building sections, along with ventilation and moisture requirements. The symbol *U* designates the over-all coefficient of heat transmission for any section of building shell. The units for *U* are Btu per sq ft of section per hr per deg F temperature difference between inside air and outside air. It is practically always less than one.

MECHANISM OF HEAT TRANSFER

The heat flow through any structural section is retarded by several elements associated with or incorporated in the section:

1. The outside surface traps a thin film of air which resists heat flow. This film varies with wind velocity and with physical character of the surface.
2. Each layer of material contributes resistance to heat flow. Usually heavy compact materials have less resistance than light ones.
3. Each measurable air space adds to the over-all resistance. Resistances vary with dimensions of the space and character of surfaces facing the space.
4. Inside surface of the section also traps an air film. This film is usually thicker than the outside film due to much lower air velocity.

The sum of these resistances gives the over-all resistance (*R*), whose reciprocal is *U*.

Heat absorbed by, or lost from, a building section is a combination of heat transfer by radiation, convection, and conduction. Radiation is controlled by character of the surfaces (emissivity) and temperature difference between surface and opposed objects, buildings, etc. Convection and conduction are functions of the roughness of the surface, air movement, and temperature difference between air and surface.

Thermal resistance of materials: When a material is homogeneous, such as insulating board, its ability to transfer heat, thermal conductivity *k*, is measured as Btu per hr, per sq ft, per degree F, per in. of thickness. The reciprocal $1/k$ is the resistivity. The resistance of any thickness of material is its resistivity per inch times the total thickness. In calculating *U* values, only the resistances are used.

Non-homogeneous materials, such as hollow building blocks or composite plaster and lath, are laboratory-tested for their actual thicknesses instead of per inch of thickness. The resistance is calculated for the entire thickness. The reciprocal of resistance is conductance. Both are included in Table 5.

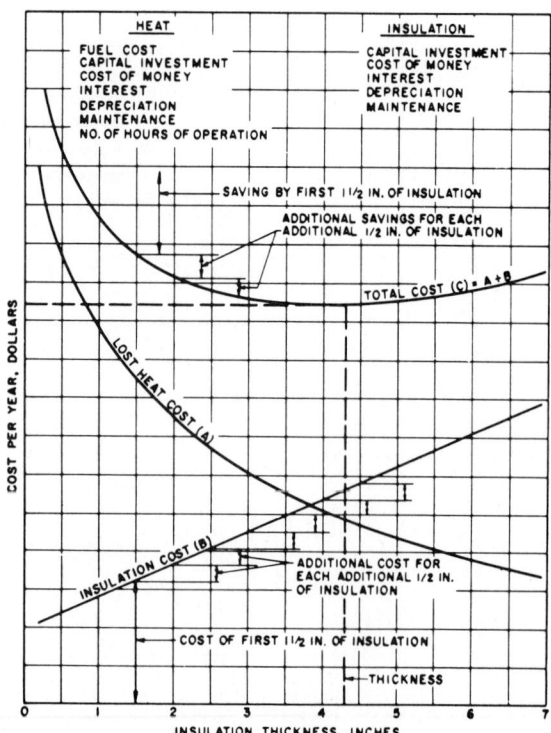

Fig. 1. Determination of economic thickness of insulation.
(*Reproduced by permission from* ASHRAE Handbook of Fundamentals, *1972*.)

Thermal resistance of air spaces: Heat flow across an air space involves the resistance of the air in the space and the materials bounding the space.

Heat passes across the space by conduction from one face to air, then by convection through the space, and finally by conduction to the opposite face. This portion of heat flow is controlled by the dimensions and shape of the air space, the texture of the materials facing the space, the mean temperature of the space, and direction of heat flow.

Heat also crosses the space by radiation from the warm face to the colder face. It is practically unaffected by the depth of the space. It is controlled by the difference in temperature of the two faces and by their relative ability to emit or absorb radiant heat (emissivity). Factors of convection and radiation vary independently in ordinary construction. Emissivities of ordinary building materials are usually high, 0.80 or more, whereas those of metals are low, around 0.05.

When heat flow is upward, the proportion of convective heat to radiant heat is high, and the relative importance of emissivity is low. The reverse is true for heat flow downward. Low emissivity factors are most useful for the latter case, for resistance to solar heat in roofs and ceilings and for reduction of heat losses in floors over unheated areas.

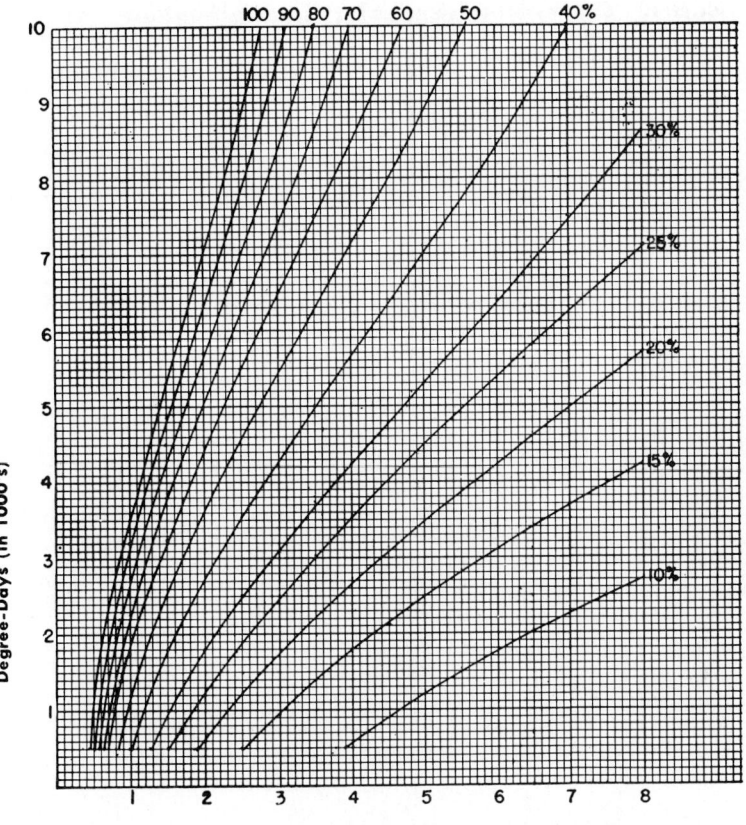

Fig. 2. Fuel requirements chart for $U = 1.00$

CALCULATION OF U-VALUES

To calculate the U-value for any wall, floor, ceiling, or roof section, proceed as follows:

1. Select the resistance R or the resistivity $1/k$ of each material, air space or exposed surface of the given section from Tables 3–5.

2. Where resistivity (per in.) is used, multiply by the actual thickness of the material.

3. Total the sum of the various resistances and divide it into 1.00 to get the reciprocal.

4. The result is the coefficient of heat transmission U in Btu per sq ft per hr per degree F.

Intelligent selection can be made from the wide variety of methods for adding thermal protection when the cost factors are known. Economy of operation may be sufficient to offset additional charges for better insulation. Use of insulation beyond that required for structural and comfort conditions should be based on economic analysis, and such insulation methods should be capable of repaying their costs. (See Fig. 1.)

A method for evaluating operating economies of insulation treatments is given here. Fuel costs and savings are expressed in terms of fuel units per unit area of building section involved. Where several possible construction assemblies are being considered, it is possible to compare the annual expense of each in terms of fuel requirements through use of their U values.

FUEL REQUIREMENTS CHART

Cost of any building section in terms of fuel units per year can be obtained from curves on the Fuel Requirements Chart (Fig. 2) and Tables 1 and 2. The curves show the approximate number of therms (1 therm = 100,000 Btu) required by each square foot of section for various heating plant efficiencies and for the appropriate number of degree-days when the U-factor = 1.00. Multiplying this number of fuel units by the actual U-values of the sections being studied gives the approximate annual fuel requirement.

The chart curves are derived from formulas published in the *ASHRAE Guide*, with some modifications to indicate the additional fuel requirements in those areas where the heating load is light. Calculations based on the chart are approximately correct to 5 per cent, and take into consideration night cutback to 55 F. Where no cutback is expected, the values should be increased by about 7 per cent, and where longer cutbacks, weekend shutdowns, etc., are contemplated, individual judgment will have to be exercised for adjustments.

USE OF CHART

The chart is used as follows:

1. Determine the number of degree-days for the locality of construction from Table 8 in the section on Heating, Ventilating, and Air Conditioning, or from the National Weather Service or from local sources such as fuel dealers.

2. Select the appropriate heating efficiency curve. The efficiency will vary with construction quality and design, heating plant design and quality, accuracy of installation, operating control methods and apparatus, and tenant habits. Suggested efficiencies are given in Table 1 and in Table 32 in the HVAC section.

3. Locate degree-days on the vertical scale and proceed horizontally to the appropriate efficiency curve. From this point drop vertically to the horizontal fuel scale, which is an annual number of therms where U = 1.00.

4. Multiply this number by the number of

Table 1.   Suggested efficiencies for use with the chart

TYPE OF FUEL	FIRING	TYPE OF HEATING APPARATUS			
		Boilers (steam or hot water)	Warm-air furnaces		Overflow heaters (space heaters)
			Forced	Gravity	
Gas	Designed for gas	80	70–80	70	70
	Conversion burners	70	60–70	60	—
Oil	Designed for oil	75	65–75	65	60
	Conversion burners	70	60–70	60	—
Anthracite or coke	Hand-fired:				
	No controls	60	50–60	50	40
	With controls	70	60–70	60	—
	Stoker-fired	75	65–75	65	—
Bituminous coal	Hand-fired:				
	No controls	50	40–50	40	40
	With controls	60	50–60	50	—
	Stoker-fired	65	55–65	55	—

Tables 1 and 2 can be used in conjunction with the Fuel Requirements Chart.
See also Table 32 in section on Heating, Ventilating, and Air Conditioning.

Table 2.   Fuel requirements

Multiply number of therms by factor in left-hand column to find fuel requirements in units at right

Factor	Cu Ft of Gas at
91	1100 Btu/cu ft
100	1000 Btu/cu ft
111	900 Btu/cu ft
125	800 Btu/cu ft
143	700 Btu/cu ft
167	600 Btu/cu ft
200	500 Btu/cu ft

Factor	Lb of Coal at
7.1	14,000 Btu/lb
7.7	13,000 Btu/lb
8.3	12,000 Btu/lb
9.1	11,000 Btu/lb
10.1	10,000 Btu/lb

Factor	Gal of Fuel Oil
0.75	No. 1
0.71	No. 2
0.67	No. 4
0.66	No. 5
0.65	No. 6

square feet of building section and by the *U* factor.

5. Convert the number of therms to the particular type of fuel to be used by Table 2.

Note: for another method of calculating fuel consumption, see sheet 56 of the HVAC section.

COST ANALYSIS

The annual fuel consumption for each building section allows comparisons of economy to be done as follows:

1. Set up the initial cost of each of the building sections being considered as a yearly charge covering interest and amortization.

2. Add the excess fuel cost for the sections having greater fuel consumption than the one having the least.

3. Totals will show the approximate differences in cost for each type.

For a more refined analysis, such costs as maintenance, repair, etc., should be considered. Also the heating plant may be reduced in size if heating load is cut sufficiently by insulation.

From ASHRAE Handbook of Fundamentals, *1977.*
American Society of Heating, Refrigerating and Air Conditioning Engineers.

OVER-ALL COEFFICIENTS AND THEIR PRACTICAL USE

The values in Tables 3, 4, and 5, for component elements and materials were selected by the ASHRAE Technical Committee as representative. They are based on available published data obtained by the guarded hot plate method (ASTM C177) or by the guarded hot box method (ASTM C236). Because there are variations in commercially available materials of the same type, not all of these selected representative values will be in exact agreement with data for individual products. The exact value for a certain manufacturer's material can be secured from unbiased tests or from guaranteed data of the manufacturer.

The most exact method of determining the heat transmission coefficient for a given combination of building materials assembled, as a building section is to test a representative section in a guarded hot box. However, it is not practicable to test all the combinations which may be of interest in building construction. Experience has indicated that *U*-values for many constructions—when calculated by the methods given in this chapter, using accurate values for the component materials, and when corrections are made for framing member heat loss—are in good

agreement with values determined by guarded hot box measurements.

SIMPLIFIED PROCEDURE FOR DETERMINING *U*-VALUES

Tables 6A through 6K and Tables 7A and 7B illustrate the procedure which enables the engineer to determine and compare values for many types of construction. The procedure is to determine the *U*-value for the uninsulated construction in Tables 6A through 6K; the benefit derived from the addition of insulating materials is shown in Tables 7A and 7B. The final *U*-value can be adjusted for framing by use of the equation given below. Additional summer values for ventilated and nonventilated attics are given in Table 8.

Special attention must be given to vapor barriers, as outlined in section on Condensation Control. Moisture from condensation or other sources materially reduces the heat-flow resistance of insulation.

VALUES USED IN CALCULATION OF *U*-VALUE TABLES

Tables 6A through 6K are based on values given in Tables 3 through 5 and the following conditions:

Equilibrium or steady-state heat transfer, eliminating effects of heat capacity

Surrounding surfaces at ambient air temperatures

Exterior wind velocity of 15 mph for winter (surface $R = 0.17$) and 7.5 mph for summer (surface $R = 0.25$)

Surface emissivity of ordinary building materials, $\epsilon = 0.90$

Air space resistance values used were interpolated from Table 4.

Adjustments for framing were made on basis of parallel heat flow through 2×4 in. (nominal) studs, 16 in. on centers, the framing covering about 20 per cent of wall area.

Actual thicknesses of lumber assumed to be as follows:

Nominal	Actual
1 in. (S-2-S)	$\frac{3}{4}$ in.
$1\frac{1}{2}$ in. (S-2-S)	$1\frac{1}{4}$ in.
2 in. (S-2-S)	$1\frac{1}{2}$ in.
$2\frac{1}{2}$ in. (S-2-S)	2 in.
3 in. (S-2-S)	$2\frac{1}{2}$ in.
4 in. (S-2-S)	$3\frac{1}{2}$ in.
Finish flooring (maple or oak)	$\frac{3}{4}$ in.

It should be noted that the effects of poor workmanship in construction and installation have an increasingly greater percentage effect on heat transmission as the coefficient becomes numerically smaller. Failure to meet design estimates may be caused by lack of proper attention to exact compliance with specifications. A factor of safety may be employed as a precaution when it is desirable.

INSULATED CONSTRUCTIONS

Table 7A provides a means of determining, without calculation, the U-value of the between-framing area of various types of construction with added insulation installed in the air space.

Table 7B is constructed and used in a manner similar to Table 7A. However, after having selected the desired U-value for a roof deck insulation, the values are shown in conductance C of roof deck insulation. This is done to facilitate the specification of materials, since roof deck insulations are marketed by conductance values (C).

ADJUSTMENT FOR FRAMING

Adjustment for parallel heat flow through framing and insulated areas may be made by using the following equation:

$$U_{av} = \frac{S}{100}(U_s) + \left(1 - \frac{S}{100}\right)(U_i)$$

where U_{av} = average U-value for building section.

U_i = U-value for area between framing members.

U_s = U-value for area backed by framing members.

S = percentage of area backed by framing members.

Example: Parallel heat flow through framing (studs, joists, plates, furring, etc.) and insulated areas is calculated by the equation. Consider a frame wall with R-11 insulation, a U_i-value across the insulated space of 0.069 ($R = 14.43$), and a U_s-value across the framing of 0.128 ($R = 7.81$). Assuming a 20 per cent framing (typical for 16-in. in o.c. framing including multiple studs, plates, headers, sills, band joists, etc.), the average U-value of this wall can be calculated.

$$U_i = 0.069; \ U_s = 0.128; \ S = 20$$

$$U_{av} = (0.2)(0.128) + (0.8)(0.069)$$
$$= 0.026 + 0.055 = 0.081$$

For a frame wall with 24-in. o.c. stud space, the framing factor is estimated at 15 per cent. In this case, the average U-value becomes 0.078. Depending on the care and installation of the insulation, U-values obtained in practice may be higher than those calculated here.

For those systems with complicated geometry, U_{av} should be measured by laboratory tests on a large, representative area of the building section including the framing system.

Table 3. Surface conductances and resistances for air

(Reproduced by permission from *ASHRAE Handbook of Fundamentals*, 1977.)
All conductance values expressed in Btu/(hr·ft²·°F).
A surface cannot take credit for both an air space resistance value and a surface resistance value. No credit for an air space value can be taken for any surface facing an air space of less than 0.5 in.

SECTION A. Surface conductances and resistances*							SECTION B. Reflectivity and emittance values of various surfaces and effective emittances of air spaces				
		Surface Emittance								Effective Emittance E of Air Space	
Position of Surface	Direction of Heat Flow	Non-reflective $\epsilon = 0.90$		Reflective $\epsilon = 0.20$		Reflective $\epsilon = 0.05$	Surface	Reflectivity in Percent	Average Emittance ϵ	One surface emittance ϵ; the other 0.90	Both surfaces emittances ϵ
		h_i	R	h_i	R	h_i R					
STILL AIR											
Horizontal	Upward	1.63	0.61	0.91	1.10	0.76 1.32	Aluminum foil, bright	92 to 97	0.05	0.05	0.03
Sloping—45 deg	Upward	1.60	0.62	0.88	1.14	0.73 1.37	Aluminum sheet	80 to 95	0.12	0.12	0.06
Vertical	Horizontal	1.46	0.68	0.74	1.35	0.59 1.70	Aluminum coated paper, polished	75 to 84	0.20	0.20	0.11
Sloping—45 deg	Downward	1.32	0.76	0.60	1.67	0.45 2.22	Steel, galvanized, bright	70 to 80	0.25	0.24	0.15
Horizontal	Downward	1.08	0.92	0.37	2.70	0.22 4.55	Aluminum paint	30 to 70	0.50	0.47	0.35
MOVING AIR (Any Position)		h_0 R		h_0 R		h_0 R	Building materials: wood, paper, masonry, nonmetallic paints	5 to 15	0.90	0.82	0.82
15-mph wind (for winter)	Any	6.00 0.17					Regular glass	5 to 15	0.84	0.77	0.72
7.5-mph wind (for summer)	Any	4.00 0.25									

* Conductances are for surfaces of the stated emittance facing virtual blackbody surroundings at the same temperature as the ambient air. Values are based on a surface-air temperature difference of 10°F and for surface temperature of 70°F.

Coefficients of air spaces

Table 4. Thermal resistances of plane air spaces[a,e]

(Reproduced by permission from *ASHRAE Handbook of Fundamentals*, 1977.)

All resistance values expressed in (hour)(square foot)(degree Fahrenheit temperature difference) per Btu

Values apply only to air spaces of uniform thickness bounded by plane, smooth, parallel surfaces with no leakage of air to or from the space.

Thermal resistance values for multiple air spaces must be based on careful estimates of mean temperature differences for each air space.

Position of Air Space	Direction of Heat Flow	Mean Temp,[b] (F)	Temp Diff,[b,d] (deg F)	0.5-in. Air Space[a] Value of E[b,c]					0.75-in. Air Space[a] Value of E[b,c]				
				0.03	0.05	0.2	0.5	0.82	0.03	0.05	0.2	0.5	0.82
Horiz.	Up	90	10	2.13	2.03	1.51	0.99	0.73	2.34	2.22	1.61	1.04	0.75
		50	30	1.62	1.57	1.29	0.96	0.75	1.71	1.66	1.35	0.99	0.77
		50	10	2.13	2.05	1.60	1.11	0.84	2.30	2.21	1.70	1.16	0.87
		0	20	1.73	1.70	1.45	1.12	0.91	1.83	1.79	1.52	1.16	0.93
		0	10	2.10	2.04	1.70	1.27	1.00	2.23	2.16	1.78	1.31	1.02
		−50	20	1.69	1.66	1.49	1.23	1.04	1.77	1.74	1.55	1.27	1.07
		−50	10	2.04	2.00	1.75	1.40	1.16	2.16	2.11	1.84	1.46	1.20
45° Slope	Up	90	10	2.44	2.31	1.65	1.06	0.76	2.96	2.78	1.88	1.15	0.81
		50	30	2.06	1.98	1.56	1.10	0.83	1.99	1.92	1.52	1.08	0.82
		50	10	2.55	2.44	1.83	1.22	0.90	2.90	2.75	2.00	1.29	0.94
		0	20	2.20	2.14	1.76	1.30	1.02	2.13	2.07	1.72	1.28	1.00
		0	10	2.63	2.54	2.03	1.44	1.10	2.72	2.62	2.08	1.47	1.12
		−50	20	2.08	2.04	1.78	1.42	1.17	2.05	2.01	1.76	1.41	1.16
		−50	10	2.62	2.56	2.17	1.66	1.33	2.53	2.47	2.10	1.62	1.30
Vertical	Horiz.	90	10	2.47	2.34	1.67	1.06	0.77	3.50	3.24	2.08	1.22	0.84
		50	30	2.57	2.46	1.84	1.23	0.90	2.91	2.77	2.01	1.30	0.94
		50	10	2.66	2.54	1.88	1.24	0.91	3.70	3.46	2.35	1.43	1.01
		0	20	2.82	2.72	2.14	1.50	1.13	3.14	3.02	2.32	1.58	1.18
		0	10	2.93	2.82	2.20	1.53	1.15	3.77	3.59	2.64	1.73	1.26
		−50	20	2.90	2.82	2.35	1.76	1.39	2.90	2.83	2.36	1.77	1.39
		−50	10	3.20	3.10	2.54	1.87	1.46	3.72	3.60	2.87	2.04	1.56
45° Slope	Down[d]	90	10	2.48	2.34	1.67	1.06	0.77	3.53	3.27	2.10	1.22	0.84
		50	30	2.64	2.52	1.87	1.24	0.91	3.43	3.23	2.24	1.39	0.99
		50	10	2.67	2.55	1.89	1.25	0.92	3.81	3.57	2.40	1.45	1.02
		0	20	2.91	2.80	2.19	1.52	1.15	3.75	3.57	2.63	1.72	1.26
		0	10	2.94	2.83	2.21	1.53	1.15	4.12	3.91	2.81	1.80	1.30
		−50	20	3.16	3.07	2.52	1.86	1.45	3.78	3.65	2.90	2.05	1.57
		−50	10	3.26	3.16	2.58	1.89	1.47	4.35	4.18	3.22	2.21	1.66
Horiz.	Down[d]	90	10	2.48	2.34	1.67	1.06	0.77	3.55	3.29	2.10	1.22	0.85
		50	30	2.66	2.54	1.88	1.24	0.91	3.77	3.52	2.38	1.44	1.02
		50	10	2.67	2.55	1.89	1.25	0.92	3.84	3.59	2.41	1.45	1.02
		0	20	2.94	2.83	2.20	1.53	1.15	4.18	3.96	2.83	1.81	1.30
		0	10	2.96	2.85	2.22	1.53	1.16	4.25	4.02	2.87	1.82	1.31
		−50	20	3.25	3.15	2.58	1.89	1.47	4.60	4.41	3.36	2.28	1.69
		−50	10	3.28	3.18	2.60	1.90	1.47	4.71	4.51	3.42	2.30	1.71

Position of Air Space	Direction of Heat Flow	Mean Temp,[b] (F)	Temp Diff,[b,d] (deg F)	1.5-in. Air Space[a] Value of E[b,c]					3.5-in. Air Space[a] Value of E[b,c]				
				0.03	0.05	0.2	0.5	0.82	0.03	0.05	0.2	0.5	0.82
Horiz	Up	90	10	2.55	2.41	1.71	1.08	0.77	2.84	2.66	1.83	1.13	0.80
		50	30	1.87	1.81	1.45	1.04	0.80	2.09	2.01	1.58	1.10	0.84
		50	10	2.50	2.40	1.81	1.21	0.89	2.80	2.66	1.95	1.28	0.93
		0	20	2.01	1.95	1.63	1.23	0.97	2.25	2.18	1.79	1.32	1.03
		0	10	2.43	2.35	1.90	1.38	1.06	2.71	2.62	2.07	1.47	1.12
		−50	20	1.94	1.91	1.68	1.36	1.13	2.19	2.14	1.86	1.47	1.20
		−50	10	2.37	2.31	1.99	1.55	1.26	2.65	2.58	2.18	1.67	1.33
45° Slope	Up	90	10	2.92	2.73	1.86	1.14	0.80	3.18	2.96	1.97	1.18	0.82
		50	30	2.14	2.06	1.61	1.12	0.84	2.26	2.17	1.67	1.15	0.86
		50	10	2.88	2.74	1.99	1.29	0.94	3.12	2.95	2.10	1.34	0.96
		0	20	2.30	2.23	1.82	1.34	1.04	2.42	2.35	1.90	1.38	1.06
		0	10	2.79	2.69	2.12	1.49	1.13	2.98	2.87	2.23	1.54	1.16
		−50	20	2.22	2.17	1.88	1.49	1.21	2.34	2.29	1.97	1.54	1.25
		−50	10	2.71	2.64	2.23	1.69	1.35	2.87	2.79	2.33	1.75	1.39
Vertical	Horiz.	90	10	3.99	3.66	2.25	1.27	0.87	3.69	3.40	2.15	1.24	0.85
		50	30	2.58	2.46	1.84	1.23	0.90	2.67	2.55	1.89	1.25	0.91
		50	10	3.79	3.55	2.39	1.45	1.02	3.63	3.40	2.32	1.42	1.01
		0	20	2.76	2.66	2.10	1.48	1.12	2.88	2.78	2.17	1.51	1.14
		0	10	3.51	3.35	2.51	1.67	1.23	3.49	3.33	2.50	1.67	1.23
		−50	20	2.64	2.58	2.18	1.66	1.33	2.82	2.75	2.30	1.73	1.37
		−50	10	3.31	3.21	2.62	1.91	1.48	3.40	3.30	2.67	1.94	1.50
45° Slope	Down[d]	90	10	5.07	4.55	2.56	1.36	0.91	4.81	4.33	2.49	1.34	0.90
		50	30	3.58	3.36	2.31	1.42	1.00	3.51	3.30	2.28	1.40	1.00
		50	10	5.10	4.66	2.85	1.60	1.09	4.74	4.36	2.73	1.57	1.08
		0	20	3.85	3.66	2.68	1.74	1.27	3.81	3.63	2.66	1.74	1.27
		0	10	4.92	4.62	3.16	1.94	1.37	4.59	4.32	3.02	1.88	1.34
		−50	20	3.62	3.50	2.80	2.01	1.54	3.77	3.64	2.90	2.05	1.57
		−50	10	4.67	4.47	3.40	2.29	1.70	4.50	4.32	3.31	2.25	1.68
Horiz.	Down[d]	90	10	6.09	5.35	2.79	1.43	0.94	10.07	8.19	3.41	1.57	1.00
		50	30	6.27	5.63	3.18	1.70	1.14	9.60	8.17	3.86	1.88	1.22
		50	10	6.61	5.90	3.27	1.73	1.15	11.15	9.27	4.09	1.93	1.24
		0	20	7.03	6.43	3.91	2.19	1.49	10.90	9.52	4.87	2.47	1.62
		0	10	7.31	6.66	4.00	2.22	1.51	11.97	10.32	5.08	2.52	1.64
		−50	20	7.73	7.20	4.77	2.85	1.99	11.64	10.49	6.02	3.25	2.18
		−50	10	8.09	7.52	4.91	2.89	2.01	12.98	11.56	6.36	3.34	2.22

[a] Credit for an air space resistance value cannot be taken more than once and only for the boundary conditions established.

[b] Interpolation is permissible for other values of mean temperature, temperature differences, and effective emittance E. Interpolation and moderate extrapolation for air spaces greater than 3.5 in. are also permissible.

[c] Effective emittance of the space E is given by $1/E = 1/e_1 + 1/e_2 - 1$, where e_1 and e_2 are the emittances of the surfaces of the air space (See section B of Table 3.)

[d] Resistances of horizontal spaces with heat flow downward are substantially independent of temperature difference.

[e] Thermal resistance values were determined from the relation $R = 1/C$, where $C = h_c + Eh_r$, h_c is the conduction-convection coefficient, Eh_r is the radiation coefficient $\cong 0.00686E\,[(460 + t_m)/100]^3$, and t_m is the mean temperature of the air space. For interpretation from Table 4 to air space thicknesses less than 0.5 in. (as in insulating window glass), assume $h_c = 0.795\,(1 + 0.0016)$ and compute R-values from the above relations for an air space thickness of 0.2 in.

Table 5. Thermal properties of typical building and insulating materials—(design values)[a]

These coefficients are expressed in Btuh-ft² (deg F difference in temperature between the air on the two sides),
and are based on an outside wind velocity of 15 mph

These constants are expressed in Btu per (hour) (square foot) (degree Fahrenheit temperature difference). Conductivities (k) are per inch thickness, and conductances (C) are for thickness or construction stated, not per inch thickness. All values are for a mean temperature of 75°F, except as noted by an asterisk (*) which have been reported at 45°F.

Description	Density (lb/ft³)	Conductivity (k)	Conductance (C)	Resistance[b] (R) Per inch thickness (1/k)	Resistance[b] (R) For thickness listed (1/C)	Specific Heat, Btu/(lb) (deg F)	SI Unit Resistance[b] (R) (m·K)/W	SI Unit Resistance[b] (R) (m²·K)/W
BUILDING BOARD								
Boards, Panels, Subflooring, Sheathing								
Woodboard Panel Products								
Asbestos-cement board	120	4.0	—	0.25	—	0.24	1.73	
Asbestos-cement board 0.125 in.	120	—	33.00	—	0.03			0.005
Asbestos-cement board 0.25 in.	120	—	16.50	—	0.06			0.01
Gypsum or plaster board 0.375 in.	50	—	3.10	—	0.32	0.26		0.06
Gypsum or plaster board 0.5 in.	50	—	2.22	—	0.45			0.08
Gypsum or plaster board 0.625 in.	50	—	1.78	—	0.56			0.10
Plywood (Douglas Fir)	34	0.80	—	1.25	—	0.29	8.66	
Plywood (Douglas Fir) 0.25 in.	34	—	3.20	—	0.31			0.05
Plywood (Douglas Fir) 0.375 in.	34	—	2.13	—	0.47			0.08
Plywood (Douglas Fir) 0.5 in.	34	—	1.60	—	0.62			0.11
Plywood (Douglas Fir) 0.625 in.	34	—	1.29	—	0.77			0.19
Plywood or wood panels 0.75 in.	34	—	1.07	—	0.93	0.29		0.16
Vegetable Fiber Board								
Sheathing, regular density 0.5 in.	18	—	0.76	—	1.32	0.31		0.23
0.78125 in.	18	—	0.49	—	2.06			0.36
Sheathing intermediate density 0.5 in.	22	—	0.82	—	1.22	0.31		0.21
Nail-base sheathing 0.5 in.	25	—	0.88	—	1.14	0.31		0.20
Shingle backer 0.375 in.	18	—	1.06	—	0.94	0.31		0.17
Shingle backer 0.3125 in.	18	—	1.28	—	0.78			0.14
Sound deadening board 0.5 in.	15	—	0.74	—	1.35	0.30		0.24
Tile and lay-in panels, plain or acoustic	18	0.40	—	2.50	—	0.14	17.33	
0.5 in.	18	—	0.80	—	1.25			0.22
0.75 in.	18	—	0.53	—	1.89			0.33
Laminated paperboard	30	0.50	—	2.00	—	0.33	13.86	
Homogeneous board from repulped paper	30	0.50	—	2.00	—	0.28	13.86	
Hardboard								
Medium density	50	0.73	—	1.37	—	0.31	9.49	
High density, service temp. service underlay	55	0.82	—	1.22	—	0.32	8.46	
High density, std. tempered	63	1.00	—	1.00	—	0.32	6.93	
Particleboard								
Low density	37	0.54	—	1.85	—	0.31	12.82	
Medium density	50	0.94	—	1.06	—	0.31	7.35	
High density	62.5	1.18	—	0.85	—	0.31	5.89	
Underlayment 0.625 in.	40	—	1.22	—	0.82	0.29		0.14
Wood subfloor 0.75 in.	—	—	1.06	—	0.94	0.33		0.17
BUILDING MEMBRANE								
Vapor-permeable felt	—	—	16.70	—	0.06			0.01
Vapor-seal, 2 layers of mopped 15-lb felt	—	—	8.35	—	0.12			0.02
Vapor-seal, plastic film	—	—	—	—	Negl.			
FINISH FLOORING MATERIALS								
Carpet and fibrous pad	—	—	0.48	—	2.08	0.34		0.37
Carpet and rubber pad	—	—	0.81	—	1.23	0.33		0.22
Cork tile 0.125 in.	—	—	3.60	—	0.28	0.48		0.05
Terrazzo 1 in.	—	—	12.50	—	0.08	0.19		0.01
Tile—asphalt, linoleum, vinyl, rubber	—	—	20.00	—	0.05	0.30		0.01
vinyl asbestos						0.24		
ceramic						0.19		
Wood, hardwood finish 0.75 in.			1.47		0.68			0.12
INSULATING MATERIALS								
BLANKET AND BATT								
Mineral Fiber, fibrous form processed from rock, slag, or glass								
approx.[e] 2–2.75 in.	0.3–2.0	—	0.143	—	7[d]	0.17–0.23		1.23
approx.[e] 3–3.5 in.	0.3–2.0	—	0.091	—	11[d]			1.94
approx.[e] 5.50–6.5 in.	0.3–2.0	—	0.053	—	19[d]			3.35
approx.[e] 6–7 in.	0.3–2.0	—	0.045	—	22[d]			3.87
approx.[d] 8.5 in.	0.3–2.0	—	0.033	—	30[d]			5.28

Notes are located at the end of the table.

Coefficients of materials

Table 5 *(cont.).* **Thermal properties of typical building and insulating materials—(design values)[a]**

Description	Density (lb/ft³)	Conductivity (k)	Conductance (C)	Resistance[b] (R) Per inch thickness (1/k)	Resistance[b] (R) For thickness listed (1/C)	Specific Heat, Btu/(lb) (deg F)	Resistance[b] (R) (m·K)/W	Resistance[b] (R) (m²·K)/W
BOARD AND SLABS								
Cellular glass	8.5	0.38	—	2.63	—	0.24	18.23	
Glass fiber, organic bonded	4–9	0.25	—	4.00	—	0.23	27.72	
Expanded rubber (rigid)	4.5	0.22	—	4.55	—	0.40	31.53	
Expanded polystyrene extruded Cut cell surface	1.8	0.25	—	4.00	—	0.29	27.72	
Expanded polystyrene extruded Smooth skin surface	2.2	0.20	—	5.00	—	0.29	34.65	
Expanded polystyrene extruded Smooth skin surface	3.5	0.19	—	5.26	—		36.45	
Expanded polystyrene, molded beads	1.0	0.28	—	3.57	—	0.29	24.74	
Expanded polyurethane[f] (R-11 exp.)	1.5	0.16	—	6.25	—	0.38	43.82	
(Thickness 1 in. or greater)	2.5							
Mineral fiber with resin binder	15	0.29	—	3.45	—	0.17	23.91	
Mineral fiberboard, wet felted Core or roof insulation	16–17	0.34	—	2.94	—		20.38	
Acoustical tile	18	0.35	—	2.86	—	0.19	19.82	
Acoustical tile	21	0.37	—	2.70	—		18.71	
Mineral fiberboard, wet molded Acoustical tile[g]	23	0.42	—	2.38	—	0.14	16.49	
Wood or cane fiberboard Acoustical tile[g] ... 0.5 in.	—	—	0.80	—	1.25	0.31		0.22
Acoustical tile[g] ... 0.75 in.	—	—	0.53	—	1.89			0.33
Interior finish (plank, tile)	15	0.35	—	2.86	—	0.32	19.82	
Wood shredded (cemented in preformed slabs)	22	0.60	—	1.67	—	0.31	11.57	
LOOSE FILL								
Cellulosic insulation (milled paper or wood pulp)	2.3–3.2	0.27–0.32	—	3.13–3.70	—	0.33	21.69–25.64	
Sawdust or shavings	8.0–15.0	0.45	—	2.22	—	0.33	15.39	
Wood fiber, softwoods	2.0–3.5	0.30	—	3.33	—	0.33	23.08	
Perlite, expanded	5.0–8.0	0.37	—	2.70	—	0.26	18.71	
Mineral fiber (rock, slag or glass) approx.[e] 3.75–5 in.	0.6–2.0	—	—		11	0.17		1.94
approx.[e] 6.5–8.75 in.	0.6–2.0	—	—		19			3.35
approx.[e] 7.5–10 in.	0.6–2.0	—	—		22			3.87
approx.[e] 10.25–13.75 in.	0.6–2.0	—	—		30			5.28
Vermiculite, exfoliated	7.0–8.2	0.47	—	2.13	—	3.20	14.76	
	4.0–6.0	0.44	—	2.27	—		15.73	
ROOF INSULATION[h]								
Preformed, for use above deck Different roof insulations are available in different thicknesses to provide the design C values listed.[h] Consult individual manufacturers for actual *thickness of their material.*			0.72 to 0.12		1.39 to 8.33		— —	0.24 to 1.47
MASONRY MATERIALS								
CONCRETES								
Cement mortar	116	5.0	—	0.20	—		1.39	
Gypsum-fiber concrete 87.5% gypsum, 12.5% wood chips	51	1.66	—	0.60	—	0.21	4.16	
Lightweight aggregates including expanded shale, clay or slate; expanded slags; cinders; pumice; vermiculite; also cellular concretes	120	5.2	—	0.19	—		1.32	
	100	3.6	—	0.28	—		1.94	
	80	2.5	—	0.40	—		2.77	
	60	1.7	—	0.59	—		4.09	
	40	1.15	—	0.86	—		5.96	
	30	0.90	—	1.11			7.69	
	20	0.70		1.43			9.91	
Perlite, expanded	40	0.93		1.08			7.48	
	30	0.71		1.41			9.77	
	20	0.50		2.00		0.32	13.86	
Sand and gravel or stone aggregate (oven dried)	140	9.0	—	0.11		0.22	0.76	
Sand and gravel or stone aggregate (not dried)	140	12.0	—	0.08			0.55	
Stucco	116	5.0	—	0.20			1.39	
MASONRY UNITS								
Brick, common[i]	120	5.0	—	0.20	—	0.19	1.39	
Brick, face[i]	130	9.0	—	0.11	—		0.76	

Table 5 *(cont.)*. **Thermal properties of typical building and insulating materials—(design values)[a]**

Description	Density (lb/ft³)	Conductivity (k)	Conductance (C)	Resistance[b] (R) Per inch thickness (1/k)	Resistance[b] (R) For thickness listed (1/C)	Specific Heat, Btu/(lb)(deg F)	SI Unit Resistance[b] (R) (m·K) W	SI Unit Resistance[b] (R) (m²·K) W
Clay tile, hollow:								
1 cell deep ....3 in.	—	—	1.25	—	0.80	0.21		0.14
1 cell deep ....4 in.	—	—	0.90	—	1.11			0.20
2 cells deep..........................6 in.	—	—	0.66	—	1.52			0.27
2 cells deep..........................8 in.	—	—	0.54	—	1.85			0.33
2 cells deep.........................10 in.	—	—	0.45	—	2.22			0.39
3 cells deep.........................12 in.	—	—	0.40	—	2.50			0.44
Concrete blocks, three oval core:								
Sand and gravel aggregate ....4 in.	—	—	1.40	—	0.71	0.22		0.13
....8 in.	—	—	0.90	—	1.11			0.20
....12 in.	—	—	0.78	—	1.28			0.23
Cinder aggregate ....3 in.	—	—	1.16	—	0.86	0.21		0.15
....4 in.	—	—	0.90	—	1.11			0.20
....8 in.	—	—	0.58	—	1.72			0.30
....12 in.	—	—	0.53	—	1.89			0.33
Lightweight aggregate....................3 in.	—	—	0.79	—	1.27	0.21		0.22
(expanded shale, clay, slate ....4 in.	—	—	0.67	—	1.50			0.26
or slag; pumice) ....8 in.	—	—	0.50	—	2.00			0.35
....12 in.	—	—	0.44	—	2.27			0.40
Concrete blocks, rectangular core.*[j]								
Sand and gravel aggregate								
2 core, 8 in. 36 lb.[k]* .:	—	—	0.96	—	1.04	0.22		0.18
Same with filled cores[j]*	—	—	0.52	—	1.93	0.22		0.34
Lightweight aggregate (expanded shale,								
clay, slate or slag, pumice):								
3 core, 6 in. 19 lb.[k]*	—	—	0.61	—	1.65	0.21		0.29
Same with filled cores[l]*	—	—	0.33	—	2.99			0.53
2 core, 8 in. 24 lb.[k]*	—	—	0.46	—	2.18			0.38
Same with filled cores[l]*	—	—	0.20	—	5.03			0.89
3 core, 12 in. 38 lb.[k]*	—	—	0.40	—	2.48			0.44
Same with filled cores[l]*	—	—	0.17	—	5.82			1.02
Stone, lime or sand........................	—	12.50	—	0.08	—	0.19	0.55	
Gypsum partition tile:								
3 × 12 × 30 in. solid	—	—	0.79	—	1.26	0.19		0.22
3 × 12 × 30 in. 4-cell	—	—	0.74	—	1.35			0.24
4 × 12 × 30 in. 3-cell	—	—	0.60	—	1.67			0.29
PLASTERING MATERIALS								
Cement plaster, sand aggregate	116	5.0	—	0.20	—	0.20	1.39	
Sand aggregate ....0.375 in.	—	—	13.3	—	0.08	0.20		0.01
Sand aggregate ....0.75 in.	—	—	6.66	—	0.15	0.20		0.03
Gypsum plaster:								
Lightweight aggregate.................0.5 in.	45	—	3.12	—	0.32			0.06
Lightweight aggregate...............0.625 in.	45	—	2.67	—	0.39			0.07
Lightweight agg. on metal lath ....0.75 in.	—	—	2.13	—	0.47			0.08
Perlite aggregate.........................	45	1.5	—	0.67	—	0.32	4.64	
Sand aggregate...........................	105	5.6	—	0.18	—	0.20	1.25	
Sand aggregate......................0.5 in.	105	—	11.10	—	0.09			0.02
Sand aggregate....................0.625 in.	105	—	9.10	—	0.11			0.02
Sand aggregate on metal lath..........0.75 in.	—	—	7.70	—	0.13			0.02
Vermiculite aggregate.....................	45	1.7	—	0.59	—		4.09	
ROOFING								
Asbestos-cement shingles.....................	120	—	4.76	—	0.21	0.24		0.04
Asphalt roll roofing	70	—	6.50	—	0.15	0.36		0.03
Asphalt shingles	70	—	2.27	—	0.44	0.30		0.08
Built-up roofing ....0.375 in.	70	—	3.00	—	0.33	0.35		0.06
Slate.............................0.5 in.	—	—	20.00	—	0.05	0.30		0.01
Wood shingles, plain and plastic film faced	—	—	1.06	—	0.94	0.31		0.17
SIDING MATERIALS (On Flat Surface)								
Shingles								
Asbestos-cement..........................	120	—	4.75	—	0.21			0.04
Wood, 16 in., 7.5 exposure...............	—	—	1.15	—	0.87	0.31		0.15
Wood, double, 16-in., 12-in. exposure	—	—	0.84	—	1.19	0.28		0.21
Wood, plus insul. backer board, 0.3125 in........	—	—	0.71	—	1.40	0.31		0.25
Siding								
Asbestos-cement, 0.25 in., lapped.............	—	—	4.76	—	0.21	0.24		0.04
Asphalt roll siding	—	—	6.50	—	0.15	0.35		0.03
Asphalt insulating siding (0.5 in. bed.)	—	—	0.69	—	1.46	0.35		0.26
Hardboard siding, 0.4375 in.	40	1.49	—	0.67	—	0.28	4.65	
Wood, drop, 1 × 8 in...................	—	—	1.27	—	0.79	0.28		0.14

Coefficients of materials; coefficients of walls

Table 5 *(cont.).* Thermal properties of typical building and insulating materials—(design values)[a]

Description	Density (lb/ft³)	Conductivity (k)	Conductance (C)	Resistance[b] (R) Per inch thickness (1/k)	Resistance[b] (R) For thickness listed (1/C)	Specific Heat, Btu/(lb) (deg F)	SI Unit Resistance[b] (R) (m·K)/W	SI Unit Resistance[b] (R) (m²·K)/W
Wood, bevel, 0.5 × 8 in., lapped..............	—	—	1.23	—	0.81	0.28		0.14
Wood, bevel, 0.75 × 10 in., lapped.............	—	—	0.95	—	1.05	0.28		0.18
Wood, plywood, 0.375 in., lapped	—	—	1.59	—	0.59	0.29		0.10
Aluminum or Steel[m], over sheathing								
Hollow-backed..........................	—	—	1.61	—	0.61	0.29		0.11
Insulating-board backed nominal								
0.375 in..............................	—	—	0.55	—	1.82	0.32		0.32
Insulating-board backed nominal								
0.375 in., foil backed....................			0.34		2.96			0.52
Architectural glass........................	—	—	10.00	—	0.10	0.20		0.02
WOODS								
Maple, oak, and similar hardwoods..............	45	1.10	—	0.91	—	0.30	6.31	
Fir, pine, and similar softwoods.................	32	0.80	—	1.25	—	0.33	8.66	
Fir, pine, and similar softwoods.........0.75 in.	32	—	1.06	—	0.94	0.33		0.17
...................................1.5 in.		—	0.53	—	1.89			0.33
...................................2.5 in.		—	0.32	—	3.12			0.60
...................................3.5 in.		—	0.23	—	4.35			0.75

Notes for Table 5

[a] Representative values for dry materials were selected by ASHRAE Technical Committee on Insulation and Moisture Barriers. They are intended as design (not specification) values for materials in normal use. For properties of a particular product, use the value supplied by the manufacturer or by unbiased tests.

[b] Resistance values are the reciprocals of C before rounding off C to two decimal places.

[c] Also see Insulating Materials, Board.

[d] Does not include paper backing and facing, if any. Where insulation forms a boundary (reflective or otherwise) of an air space, see Tables 3 and 4 for the insulating value of air space for the appropriate effective emittance and temperature conditions of the space.

[e] Conductivity varies with fiber diameter. Insulation is produced in different densities; therefore, there is a wide variation in thickness for the same R-value among manufacturers. No effort should be made to relate any specific R-value to any specific thickness. Commercial thicknesses generally available range from 2 to 8.5.

[f] Values are for aged board stock. Conductivity increases slowly with time as air permeates the cells.

[g] Insulating values of acoustical tile vary, depending on density of the board and on type, size, and depth of perforations.

[h] The U. S. Department of Commerce, *Simplified Practice Recommendation for Thermal Conductance Factors for Preformed Above-Deck Roof Insulation,* No. R 257-55, recognizes the specification of roof insulation on the basis of the C-values shown. Roof insulation is made in thicknesses to meet these values.

[i] Face brick and common brick do not always have these specific densities. When density is different from that shown, there will be a change in thermal conductivity.

[j] Data on rectangular core concrete blocks differ from the above data on oval core blocks, due to core configuration, different mean temperatures, and possibly differences in unit weights. Weight data on the oval core blocks tested are not available.

[k] Weights of units approximately 7.625 in. high and 15.75 in. long. These weights are given as a means of describing the blocks tested, but conductance values are all for 1 ft² of area.

[l] Vermiculite, perlite, or mineral wool insulation. Where insulation is used, vapor barriers or other precautions must be considered to keep insulation dry.

[m] Values for metal siding applied over flat surfaces vary widely, depending on amount of ventilation of air space beneath the siding; whether air space is reflective or nonreflective; and on thickness, type, and application of insulating backing-board used. Values given are averages for use as design guides, and were obtained from several guarded hotbox tests (ASTM C236) or calibrated hotbox (BSS 77) on hollow-backed types and types made using backing-boards of wood fiber, foamed plastic, and glass fiber. Departures of ±50% or more from the values given may occur.

Table 6A. Coefficients of transmission *(U)* of frame walls*
(Reproduced by permission from *ASHRAE Handbook of Fundamentals,* 1977)
These coefficients are expressed in Btuh·ft² (deg F difference in temperature between the air on the two sides),
and are based on an outside wind velocity of 15 mph

Replace Air Space with 3.5-in. R-11 Blanket Insulation (New Item 4)

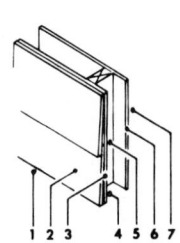

Construction	1 Resistance (R) Between Framing	1 Resistance (R) At Framing	2 Resistance (R) Between Framing	2 Resistance (R) At Framing
1. Outside surface (15 mph wind)	0.17	0.17	0.17	0.17
2. Siding, wood, 0.5 in.× 8 in. lapped (average)	0.81	0.81	0.81	0.81
3. Sheathing, 0.5-in. asphalt impregnated	1.32	1.32	1.32	1.32
4. Nonreflective air space, 3.5 in. (50 F mean; 10 deg F temperature difference)	1.01	—	11.00	—
5. Nominal 2-in. × 4-in. wood stud	—	4.38	—	4.38
6. Gypsum wallboard, 0.5 in.	0.45	0.45	0.45	0.45
7. Inside surface (still air)	0.68	0.68	0.68	0.68
Total Thermal Resistance (R)	R_i=4.44	R_s=7.81	R_i=14.43	R_s=7.81

Construction No. 1: $U_i = 1/4.44 = 0.225$; $U_s = 1/7.81 = 0.128$. With 20% framing (typical of 2-in. × 4-in. studs @ 16-in. o.c.), $U_{av} = 0.8 (0.225) + 0.2 (0.128) = 0.206$ (See Eq 9)

Construction No. 2: $U_i = 1/14.43 = 0.069$; $U_s = 0.128$. With framing unchanged, $U_{av} = 0.8(0.069) + 0.2(0.128) = 0.081$

* See text section on overall coefficients for basis of calculations.

Table 6B. Coefficients of transmission (U) of solid masonry walls*
(Reproduced by permission from *ASHRAE Handbook of Fundamentals*, 1977)

Coefficients are expressed in Btuh·ft² (deg F difference in temperature between the air on the two sides), and are based on an outside wind velocity of 15 mph

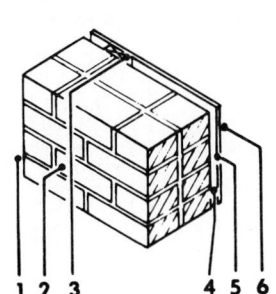

Replace Furring Strips and Air Space with 1-in. Extruded Polystyrene (New Item 4)

	1		2
	Resistance *(R)*		
Construction	Between Furring	At Furring	
1. Outside surface (15 mph wind)	0.17	0.17	0.17
2. Common brick, 8 in.	1.60	1.60	1.60
3. Nominal 1-in. ×3-in. vertical furring	—	0.94	—
4. Nonreflective air space, 0.75 in. (50 F mean; 10 deg F temperature difference)	1.01	—	5.00
5. Gypsum wallboard, 0.5 in.	0.45	0.45	0.45
6. Inside surface (still air)	0.68	0.68	0.68
Total Thermal Resistance (R)	$R_i = 3.91$	$R_s = 3.84$	$R_i = 7.90 = R_s$

Construction No. 1: $U_i = 1/3.91 = 0.256$; $U_s = 1/3.84 = 0.260$. With 20% framing (typical of 1-in. × 3-in. vertical furring on masonry @ 16-in. o.c.)
$U_{av} = 0.8 (0.256) + 0.2 (0.260) = 0.257$
Construction No. 2: $U_i = U_s = U_{av} = 1/7.90 = 0.127$

* See text section on overall coefficients for basis of calculations.

Table 6C. Coefficients of transmission (U) of frame partitions or interior walls*
(Reproduced by permission from *ASHRAE Handbook of Fundamentals*, 1977)

Coefficients are expressed in Btuh·ft² (deg F difference in temperature between the air on the two sides), and are based on still air (no wind) conditions on both sides

Replace Air Space with 3.5-in. R-11 Blanket Insulation (New Item 3)

	1		2	
	Resistance (R)			
Construction	Between Framing	At Framing	Between Framing	At Framing
1. Inside surface (still air)	0.68	0.68	0.68	0.68
2. Gypsum wallboard, 0.5 in.	0.45	0.45	0.45	0.45
3. Nonreflective air space, 3.5 in. (50 F mean; 10 deg F temperature difference)	1.01	—	11.00	—
4. Nominal 2-in. × 4-in. wood stud	—	4.38	—	4.38
5. Gypsum wallboard, 0.5 in.	0.45	0.45	0.45	0.45
6. Inside surface (still air)	0.68	0.68	0.68	0.68
Total Thermal Resistance (R)	$R_i = 3.27$	$R_s = 6.64$	$R_i = 13.26$	$R_s = 6.64$

Construction No. 1: $U_i = 1/3.27 = 0.306$; $U_s = 1/6.64 = 0.151$. With 10% framing (typical of 2-in. × 4-in. studs @ 24-in. o.c.), $U_{av} = 0.9 (0.306) + 0.1 (0.151) = 0.290$
Construction No. 2: $U_i = 1/13.26 = 0.075$, $U_s = 1/6.64 = 0.151$. With framing unchanged, $U_{av} = 0.9(0.075) + 0.1(0.151) = 0.083$

* See text section on overall coefficients for basis of calculations.

Table 6D. Coefficients of transmission (U) of masonry walls*
(Reproduced by permission from *ASHRAE Handbook of Fundamentals*, 1977)

Coefficients are expressed in Btuh·ft² (deg F difference in temperature between the air on the two sides), and are based on an outside wind velocity of 15 mph

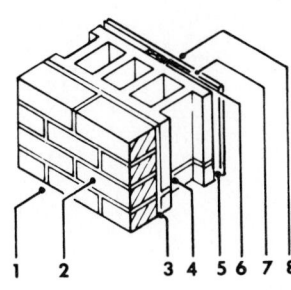

Replace Cinder Aggregate Block with 6-in. Light-weight Aggregate Block with Cores Filled (New Item 4)

	1		2	
	Resistance (R)			
Construction	Between Furring	At Furring	Between Furring	At Furring
1. Outside surface (15 mph wind)	0.17	0.17	0.17	0.17
2. Face brick, 4 in.	0.44	0.44	0.44	0.44
3. Cement mortar, 0.5 in.	0.10	0.10	0.10	0.10
4. Concrete block, cinder aggregate, 8 in.	1.72	1.72	2.99	2.99
5. Reflective air space, 0.75 in. (50 F mean; 30 deg F temperature difference)	2.77	—	2.77	—
6. Nominal 1-in. × 3-in. vertical furring	—	0.94	—	0.94
7. Gypsum wallboard, 0.5 in., foil backed	0.45	0.45	0.45	0.45
8. Inside surface (still air)	0.68	0.68	0.68	0.68
Total Thermal Resistance (R)	$R_i = 6.33$	$R_s = 4.50$	$R_i = 7.60$	$R_s = 5.77$

Construction No. 1: $U_i = 1/6.33 = 0.158$; $U_s = 1/4.50 = 0.222$. With 20% framing (typical of 1-in. × 3-in. vertical furring on masonry @ 16-in. o.c.), $U_{av} = 0.8 (0.158) + 0.2 (0.222) = 0.171$
Construction No. 2: $U_i = 1/7.60 = 0.132$, $U_s = 1/5.77 = 0.173$. With framing unchanged, $U_{av} = 0.8(0.132) + 0.2(0.173) = 1.40$

* See text section on overall coefficients for basis of calculations.

Table 6E.   Coefficients of transmission *(U)* of masonry cavity walls*
(Reproduced by permission from *ASHRAE Handbook of Fundamentals*, 1977)
Coefficients are expressed in Btuh·ft² (deg F difference in temperature between the air on the two sides), and are based on an outside wind velocity of 15 mph

Replace Furring Strips and Gypsum Wallboard with 0.625-in. Plaster (Sand Aggregate) Applied Directly to Concrete Block-Fill 2.5-in. Air Space with Vermiculite Insulation (New Items 3 and 7.

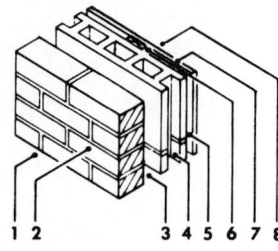

Construction	1 Resistance (R)		2
	Between Furring	At Furring	
1. Outside surface (15 mph wind)	0.17	0.17	0.17
2. Common brick, 8 in.	0.80	0.80	0.80
3. Nonreflective air space, 2.5 in. (30 F mean; 10 deg F temperature difference)	1.10*	1.10†	5.32‡
4. Concrete block, stone aggregate, 4 in.	0.71	0.71	0.71
5. Nonreflective air space 0.75 in. (50 F mean; 10 deg F temperature difference)	1.01	—	
6. Nominal 1-in. × 3-in. vertical furring	—	0.94	—
7. Gypsum wallboard, 0.5 in.	0.45	0.45	0.11
8. Inside surface (still air)	0.68	0.68	0.68
Total Thermal Resistance (R)	R_i = 4.92	R_s = 4.85	$R_i = R_s$ = 7.79

Construction No. 1: U_i = 1/4.92 = 0.203; U_s = 1/4.85 = 0.206. With 20% framing (typical of 1-in. × 3-in. vertical furring on masonry @16-in. o.c.), U_{av} = 0.8(0.203) + 0.2(0.206) = 0.204

Construction No. 2: U_i = U_s = U_{av} = 1.79 = 0.128

* See text section on overall coefficients for basis of calculations.
† Interpolated value from Table 4.
‡ Calculated value from Table 5.

Table 6F.   Coefficients of transmission *(U)* of masonry partitions*
(Reproduced by permission from *ASHRAE Handbook of Fundamentals*, 1977)
Coefficients are expressed in Btuh·ft² (deg F difference in temperature between the air on the two sides), and are based on still air (no wind) conditions on both sides

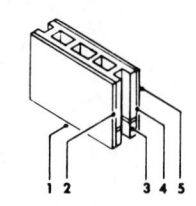

Replace Concrete Block with 4-in. Gypsum Tile (New Item 3) Construction	1	2
1. Inside surface (still air)	0.68	0.68
2. Plaster, lightweight aggregate, 0.625 in.	0.39	0.39
3. Concrete block, cinder aggregate, 4 in.	1.11	1.67
4. Plaster, lightweight aggregate, 0.625 in.	0.39	0.39
5. Inside surface (still air)	0.68	0.68
Total Thermal Resistance(R)	3.25	3.81

Construction No. 1: U = 1/3.25 = 0.308

Construction No. 2: U = 1/3.81 = 0.262

* See text section on overall coefficients for basis of calculations.

Table 6G.   Coefficients of Transmission *(U)* of frame construction ceilings and floors*
(Reproduced by permission from *ASHRAE Handbook of Fundamentals*, 1977)
Coefficients are expressed in Btuh·ft² (deg F difference between the air on the two sides), and are based on still air (no wind) on both sides

Assume Unheated Attic Space above Heated Room with Heat Flow Up—Remove Tile, Felt, Plywood, Subfloor and Air Space—Replace with R-19 Blanket Insulation (New Item 4)

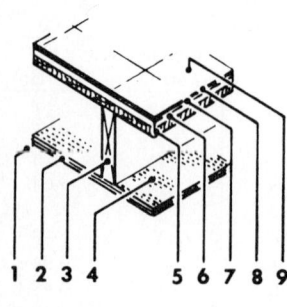

Construction (Heat Flow Up)	Heated Room Below Unheated Space 1 Resistance (R)		2	
	Between Floor Joists	At Floor Joist	Between Floor Joists	At Floor Joists
1. Bottom surface (still air)	0.61	0.61	0.61	0.61
2. Metal lath and lightweight aggregate, plaster, 0.75 in.	0.47	0.47	0.47	0.47
3. Nominal 2-in. × 8-in. floor joist	—	9.06	—	9.06
4. Nonreflective airspace, 7.25-in.	0.93†	—	19.00	—
5. Wood subfloor, 0.75 in.	0.94	0.94	—	—
6. Plywood, 0.625 in.	0.78	0.78	—	—
7. Felt building membrane	0.06	0.06	—	—
8. Resilient tile	0.05	0.05	—	—
9. Top surface (still air)	0.61	0.61	0.61	0.61
Total Thermal Resistance (R)	R_i = 4.45	R_s = 12.58	R_i = 20.69	R_s = 10.75

Construction No. 1 U_i = 1/4.45 = 0.225; U_s = 1/12.58 = 0.079. With 10% framing (typical of 2-in. joists @ 16-in. o.c.), U_{av} = 0.9 (0.225) + 0.1 (0.079) = 0.210

Construction No. 2 U_i = 1/20.69 = 0.048; U_s = 1/10.75 = 0.093. With framing unchanged, U_{av} = 0.9 (0.048) + 0.1 (0.093) = 0.053

* See text section on overall coefficients for basis of calculations.
† Use largest air space (3.5 in.) value shown in Table 4.

Table 6H. Coefficients of transmission *(U)* of flat masonry roofs with built-up roofing, with and without suspended ceilings*† (winter conditions, upward flow)

(Reproduced by permission from *ASHRAE Handbook of Fundamentals*, 1977)

These coefficients are expressed in Btuh·ft² (deg F difference in temperature between the air on the two sides),
and are based upon an outside wind velocity of 15 mph

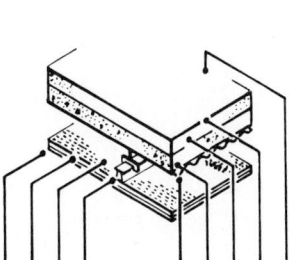

Add Rigid Roof Deck Insulation, $C = 0.24$ $(R = 1/C)$ (New Item 7) Construction (Heat Flow Up)	1	2
1. Inside surface (still air)	0.61	0.61
1. Metal lath and lightweight aggregate plaster, 0.75 in.	0.47	0.47
3. Nonreflective air space, greater than 3.5 in. (50 F mean; 10 deg F temperature difference)	0.93‡	0.93‡
4. Metal ceiling suspension system with metal hanger rods	0§	0§
5. Corrugated metal deck	0	0
6. Concrete slab, lightweight aggregate, 2 in.	2.22	2.22
7. Rigid roof deck insulation (none)	—	4.17
8. Built-up roofing, 0.375 in.	0.33	0.33
9. Outside surface (15 mph wind)	0.17	0.17
Total Thermal Resistance (R)..........................	4.73	8.90

Construction No. 1: $U_{av} = 1/4.73 = 0.211$
Construction No. 2: $U_{av} = 1/8.90 = 0.112$

* See text section on overall coefficients for basis of calculations.
† To adjust *U*-values for the effect of added insulation between framing members, see Table 7 or 8.
‡ Use largest air space (3.5 in.) value shown in Table 4.
§ Area of hanger rods is negligible in relation to ceiling area.

Table 6I. Coefficients of transmission *(U)* of wood construction flat roofs and ceilings* (winter conditions, upward flow)

(Reproduced by permission from *ASHRAE Handbook of Fundamentals*, 1977)

Coefficients are expressed in Btuh·ft² (deg F difference in temperature between the air on the two sides),
and are based upon an outside wind velocity of 15 mph

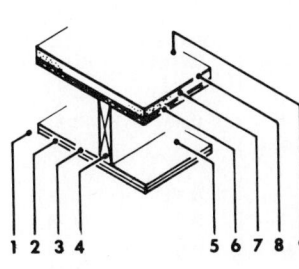

Replace Roof Deck Insulation and 7.25-in. Air Space with 6-in. R-19 Blanket Insulation and 1.25-in. Air Space (New Items 5 and 7)	1		2	
	Resistance (R)			
Construction (Heat Flow Up)	Between Joists	At Joists	Between Joists	At Joists
1. Inside surface (still air)	0.61	0.61	0.61	0.61
2. Acoustical tile, fiberboard, glued, 0.5 in.	1.25	1.25	1.25	1.25
3. Gypsum wallboard, 0.5 in.	0.45	0.45	0.45	0.45
4. Nominal 2-in. × 8-in. ceiling joists	—	9.06	—	9.06
5. Nonreflective air space, 7.25 in. (50 F mean; 10 deg F temperature difference)	0.93†	—	1.05‡	—
6. Plywood deck, 0.625 in.	0.78	0.78	0.78	0.78
7. Rigid roof deck insulation, c = 0.72, $(R = 1/C)$	1.39	1.39	19.00	—
8. Built-up roof	0.33	0.33	0.33	0.33
9. Outside surface (15 mph wind)	0.17	0.17	0.17	0.17
Total Thermal Resistance (R)	R_i=5.91	R_s=14.04	R_i=23.64	R_s=12.65

Construction No. 1 $U_i = 1/5.91 = 0.169$; $U_s = 1/14.04 = 0.071$. With 10% framing (typical of 2-in. joists @ 16-in. o.c.), $U_{av} = 0.9$ $(0.169) + 0.1 (0.071) = 0.159$
Construction No. 2 $U_i = 1/23.64 = 0.042$; $U_s = 1/12.65 = 0.079$. With framing unchanged, $U_{av} = 0.9 (0.042) + 0.1 (0.079) = 0.046$

* See text section on overall coefficients for basis of calculations.
† Use largest air space (3.5 in.) value shown in Table 4.
‡ Interpolated value (0°F mean; 10°F temperature difference).

Table 6J. Coefficients of transmission *(U)* of metal construction flat roofs and ceilings*
(winter conditions, upward flow)
(Reproduced by permission from *ASHRAE Handbook of Fundamentals,* 1977)
Coefficients are expressed in Btuh·ft² (deg F difference in temperature between the air on the two sides),
and are based on upon outside wind velocity of 15 mph

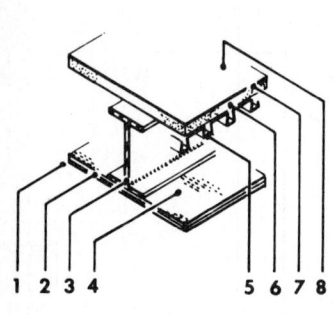

1 2 3 4   5 6 7 8

Replace Rigid Roof Deck Insulation (C = 0.24) and Sand Aggregate Plaster with Rigid Roof Deck Insulation, C = 0.36 and Lightweight Aggregate Plaster (New Items 2 and 6)

Construction (Heat Flow Up)	1	2
1. Inside surface (still air)	0.61	0.61
2. Metal lath and sand aggregate plaster, 0.75 in	0.13	0.47
3. Structural beam	0.00†	0.00†
4. Nonreflective air space (50 F mean; 10 deg F temperature difference	0.93‡	0.93‡
5. Metal deck	0.00†	0.00†
6. Rigid roof deck insulation, C = 0.24(R = 1/c)	4.17	2.78
7. Built-up roofing, 0.375 in.	0.33	0.33
8. Outside surface (15 mph wind)	0.17	0.17
Total Thermal Resistance (R)	6.34	5.29

Construction No. 1: *U* = 1/6.34 = 0.158
Construction No. 2: *U* = 1/5.29 = 0.189

* See text section on overall coefficients for basis of calculations.
† If structural beams and metal deck are to be considered, the technique shown in ASHRAE Handbook may be used to estimate total *R*. Full-scale testing of a suitable portion of the construction is, however, preferable.
‡ Use largest air space (3.5 in.) value shown in Table 4.

Table 6K. Coefficients of transmission *(U)* of pitched roofs*†
(Reproduced by permission from *ASHRAE Handbook of Fundamentals,* 1977)
Coefficients are expressed in Btuh·ft² (deg F difference in temperature between the air on the two sides), and are based on an outside wind velocity of 15 mph for heat flow upward and 7.5 mph for heat flow downward

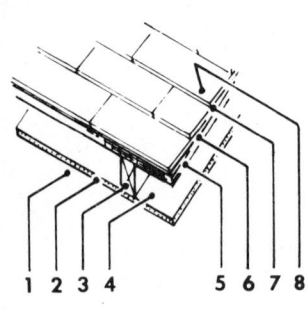

1 2 3 4   5 6 7 8

Find U_{av} for same Construction 2 with Heat Flow Down (Summer Conditions)

Construction 1 (Heat Flow Up) (Reflective Air Space)	1		2	
	Between Rafters	At Rafters	Between Rafters	At Rafters
1. Inside surface (still air)	0.62	0.62	0.76	0.76
2. Gypsum wallboard 0.5 in., foil backed	0.45	0.45	0.45	0.45
3. Nominal 2-in. × 4-in. ceiling rafter	—	4.38	—	4.38
4. 45 deg slope reflective air space, 3.5 in. (50 F mean, 30 deg F temperature difference)	2.17	—	4.33	—
5. Plywood sheathing, 0.625 in.	0.78	0.78	0.78	0.78
6. Felt building membrane	0.06	0.06	0.06	0.06
7. Asphalt shingle roofing	0.44	0.44	0.44	0.44
8. Outside surface (15 mph wind)	0.17	0.17	0.25§	0.25§
Total Thermal Resistance (R)	R_i=4.69	R_s=6.90	R_i=7.07	R_s=7.12

Construction No. 1: U_i=1/4.69= 0.213; U_s = 1/6.90 = 0.145. With 10% framing (typical of 2-in. rafters @16-in. o.c.), U_{av}= 0.9 (0.213) + 0.1 (0.145) = 0.206
Construction No. 2: U_i=1/7.07 = 0.141; U_s = 1/7.12 = 0.140. With framing unchanged, U_{av}= 0.9 (0.141) + 0.1 (0.140) = 0.141

Find U_{av} for same Construction 2 with Heat Flow Down (Summer Conditions)

Construction 1 (Heat Flow Up) (Non-Reflective Air Space)	3		4	
	Between Rafters	At Rafters	Between Rafters	At Rafters
1. Inside surface (still air)	0.62	0.62	0.76	0.76
2. Gypsum wallboard, 0.5 in.	0.45	0.45	0.45	0.45
3. Nominal 2-in. × 4-in. ceiling rafter	—	4.38	—	4.38
4. 45 deg slope, nonreflective air space, 3.5 in. (50 F mean; 10 deg F temperature difference)	0.96	—	0.90‡	—
5. Plywood sheathing, 0.625 in.	0.78	0.78	0.78	0.78
6. Felt building membrane.	0.06	0.06	0.06	0.06
7. Asphalt shingle roofing	0.44	0.44	0.44	0.44
8. Outside surface (15-mph wind)	0.17	0.17	0.25§	0.25§
Total Thermal Resistance (R)	R_i=3.48	R_s=6.90	R_i=3.64	R_s=7.12

Construction No. 3: U_i = 1/3.48 = 0.287; U_s = 1/6.90 = 0.145. With 10% framing typical of 2-in. rafters @ 16-in. o.c.), U_{av}= 0.9 (0.287)+ 0.1 (0.145) = 0.273
Construction No. 4: U_i = 1/3.64 = 0.275; U_s = 1/7.12 = 0.140. With framing unchanged, U_{av}= 0.9 (0.275) + 0.1 (0.140) = 0.262

* See text section on overall coefficients for basis of calculations.   ‡ Air space value at 90°F mean, 10°F temperature difference.
† Pitch of roof—45 deg.   § 7.5-mph wind.

Table 7A. Determination of *U*-value resulting from addition of insulation to the total area[e] of any given building section

(*Reproduced by permission from* ASHRAE Handbook of Fundamentals, *1977.*)

Given Building Section Property[a,b]		Added R[c,d,e]						
		R=4	R=6	R=8	R=12	R=16	R=20	R=24
U	R	U	U	U	U	U	U	U
1.00	1.00	0.20	0.14	0.11	0.08	0.06	0.05	0.04
0.90	1.11	0.20	0.14	0.11	0.08	0.06	0.05	0.04
0.80	1.25	0.19	0.14	0.11	0.08	0.06	0.05	0.04
0.70	1.43	0.19	0.13	0.11	0.07	0.06	0.05	0.04
0.60	1.67	0.19	0.13	0.10	0.07	0.06	0.05	0.04
0.50	2.00	0.18	0.13	0.10	0.07	0.06	0.05	0.04
0.40	2.50	0.16	0.12	0.10	0.07	0.05	0.05	0.04
0.30	3.33	0.14	0.11	0.09	0.07	0.05	0.04	0.04
0.20	5.00	0.11	0.09	0.08	0.06	0.05	0.04	0.03
0.10	10.00	0.06	0.06	0.06	0.05	0.04	0.04	0.03
0.08	12.50	0.06	0.06	0.05	0.04	0.04	0.03	0.03

[a] *For U- or R-values not shown in the table, interpolate as necessary.*
[b] *Enter column 1 with U or R of the design building section.*
[c] *Under appropriate column heading for Added R, find U-value of resulting design section.*
[d] *If the insulation occupies a previously considered air space, an adjustment must be made in the given building section R-value.*
[e] *If insulation is applied between framing members use equation given on sheet 4 to determine average U-value.*

Table 7B. Determination of *U*-value resulting from addition of insulation to uninsulated building sections

(*Reproduced by permission from* ASHRAE Handbook of Fundamentals, *1977.*)

U Value of Roof without Roof-Deck Insulation[a]	Conductance C of Roof-Deck Insulation					
	0.12	0.15	0.19	0.24	0.36	0.72
	U	U	U	U	U	U
0.10	0.05	0.06	0.07	0.07	0.08	0.09
0.15	0.07	0.08	0.08	0.09	0.11	0.12
0.20	0.08	0.09	0.10	0.11	0.13	0.16
0.25	0.08	0.09	0.11	0.12	0.15	0.19
0.30	0.09	0.10	0.12	0.13	0.16	0.21
0.35	0.09	0.10	0.12	0.14	0.18	0.24
0.40	0.09	0.11	0.13	0.15	0.19	0.26
0.50	0.10	0.12	0.14	0.16	0.21	0.29
0.60	0.10	0.12	0.14	0.17	0.22	0.33
0.70	0.10	0.12	0.15	0.18	0.24	0.35

[a] Interpolation or mild extrapolation may be used.

Note: for U-values for solid wood doors and for glass windows, doors; also see Tables 3 and 4 in section on Heating, Ventilating, and Air Conditioning.

Table 8. Effective resistance of ventilated attics[a] (summer condition)

(*Reproduced by permission from* ASHRAE Handbook of Fundamentals, *1977.*)

PART A. NONREFLECTIVE SURFACES

Ventilation Air temp., F	Sol-air[d] temp., F	No Ventilation		Natural Ventilation		Power Ventilation[e]					
		Ventilation rate, cfm/sq ft									
		0		0.1[b]		0.5		1.0		1.5	
		1/U Ceiling resistance, R[c]									
		10	20	10	20	10	20	10	20	10	20
80	120	1.9	1.9	2.8	3.4	6.3	9.3	9.6	16	11	20
	140	1.9	1.9	2.8	3.5	6.5	10	9.8	17	12	21
	160	1.9	1.9	2.8	3.6	6.7	11	10	18	13	22
90	120	1.9	1.9	2.5	2.8	4.6	6.7	6.1	10	6.9	13
	140	1.9	1.9	2.6	3.1	5.2	7.9	7.6	12	8.6	15
	160	1.9	1.9	2.7	3.4	5.8	9.0	8.5	14	10	17
100	120	1.9	1.9	2.2	2.3	3.3	4.4	4.0	6.0	4.1	6.9
	140	1.9	1.9	2.4	2.7	4.2	6.1	5.8	8.7	6.5	10
	160	1.9	1.9	2.6	3.2	5.0	7.6	7.2	11	8.3	13

PART B. REFLECTIVE SURFACES[f]

Ventilation Air temp., F	Sol-air temp., F	0		0.1		0.5		1.0		1.5	
		10	20	10	20	10	20	10	20	10	20
80	120	6.5	6.5	8.1	8.8	13	17	17	25	19	30
	140	6.5	6.5	8.2	9.0	14	18	18	26	20	31
	160	6.5	6.5	8.3	9.2	15	18	19	27	21	32
90	120	6.5	6.5	7.5	8.0	10	13	12	17	13	19
	140	6.5	6.5	7.7	8.3	12	15	14	20	16	22
	160	6.5	6.5	7.9	8.6	13	16	16	22	18	25
100	120	6.5	6.5	7.0	7.4	8.0	10	8.5	12	8.8	12
	140	6.5	6.5	7.3	7.8	10	12	11	15	12	16
	160	6.5	6.5	7.6	8.2	11	14	13	18	15	20

[a] *The term effective resistance is used when there is attic ventilation. A value for no ventilation is also included. The effective resistance of the attic may be added to the resistance (1/U) of the ceiling (Table 6G) to obtain the effective resistance of the combination based on sol-air (see section on HVAC) and room temperature. These values apply to wood frame construction with a roof deck and roofing having a conductance of 1.0 Btu/(hr·ft²·°F).*
[b] *When attic ventilation meets the requirements of Table 2 in section on Condensation Control, 0.1 cfm/ft² may be assumed as the natural summer ventilation rate for design purposes.*
[c] *Resistance is one (hr·ft²·°F)/Btu. Determine ceiling resistance from Tables 6G and 7A and adjust for framing. Do not add the effect of a reflective surface facing the attic to the ceiling resistance from Table 6G, as it is accounted for in Table 8, Part B.*
[d] *Roof surface temperature rather than sol-air temperature may be used if 0.25 is subtracted from the attic resistance shown.*
[e] *Based on air discharging outward from attic.*
[f] *Surfaces with effective emissivity E of 0.05 between ceiling joists facing the attic space.*

If the basement is *heated* to a specified temperature, heat loss is calculated in the usual manner, based on proper wall and floor U-values and outdoor air and ground temperatures. Heat loss through windows and walls above-grade is based on outdoor air temperatures and proper air-to-air U-values. In addition, heat loss due to air leakage is calculated for this portion of the wall. Heat loss through basement walls below-grade is based on floor and wall U-values for surfaces in contact with the soil, and on proper ground temperature.

Rules of thumb have been established, by experiment and analysis, over the past 30 years, for heat loss through basements of residential buildings. It was felt adequate to adopt a uniform or average heat loss per square foot of wall of 0.2 and of floor of 0.10 Btuh/(ft²) for each °F of temperature difference between basement and ground water temperature. (See Table 9.)

Using the rule of thumb, accurate estimates of heat loss cannot be made, and it is impossible to estimate the depth below-grade to which it is economical to carry insulation. It has been shown that heat loss through the soil surrounding a house basement can be calculated on the basis of steady state heat flow around concentric circular paths centered on the intersection of the ground surface and the basement wall. For the floor, these paths are continued around circular arcs centered on the intersection of the basement floor and wall (Fig. 3).

WALLS BELOW GRADE

The heat loss/ft²/°F between basement and external temperatures is given in Table 11 for uninsulated concrete walls as well as walls to which 1, 2, or 3 in. of insulation have been added.

BASEMENT FLOORS

It is possible to calculate heat loss through the basement floor for each ft² in the same way as for the wall, using longer heat flow paths around the arcs of two circles (see Fig. 3). Table 11 indicates, however, that the heat loss from the 7 ft of the uninsulated basement wall is only a small fraction of the total loss through the wall; thus, it can readily be appreciated that (with the much longer heat flow path) the loss through each ft² of basement floor rapidly becomes a negligible part of the total basement heat loss. It is reasonable, therefore, to take an average value for the loss through the basement floor. Typical values are given in Table 10.

Heat loss from the below-grade portion of the basement per deg F temperature difference can be estimated using figures in Tables 10 and 11. For the wall, the values for heat loss through each ft² are selected

(*All data reproduced by permission from ASHRAE Handbook of Fundamentals, 1977.*)

Table 9. Below-grade heat losses for basement walls and floors

Ground Water Temperature	Basement Floor Loss,[a] Btu/Sq Ft	Below Grade Wall Loss,[b] Btu/Sq Ft
40	3.0	6.0
50	2.0	4.0
60	1.0	2.0

[a] Based on basement temperature of 70 F and U of 0.10.
[b] Assumed twice basement floor loss.

Table 10. Heat loss through basement floors [Btu(h)(ft²)(°F)]

Depth of foundation wall below grade (ft)	Width of house			
	20 (ft)	24 (ft)	28 (ft)	32 (ft)
5	0.032	0.029	0.026	0.023
6	0.030	0.027	0.025	0.022
7	0.029	0.026	0.023	0.021

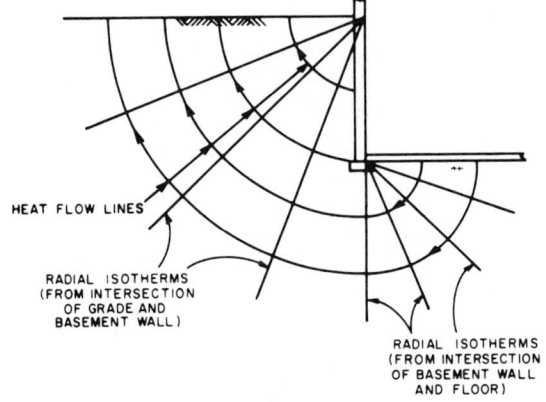

HEAT FLOW LINES

RADIAL ISOTHERMS (FROM INTERSECTION OF GRADE AND BASEMENT WALL)

RADIAL ISOTHERMS (FROM INTERSECTION OF BASEMENT WALL AND FLOOR)

Fig. 3. Heat flow from basement

Table 11. Heat loss below grade in basement walls[a] [Btuh/(ft²)(°F)]

Depth (ft)	Path length through soil (ft)	Heat loss			
			Insulation		
		Uninsulated	1-in.	2-in.	3-in.
0–1 (1st)	0.68	0.410	0.152	0.093	0.067
1–2 (2nd)	2.27	0.222	0.116	0.079	0.059
2–3 (3rd)	3.88	0.155	0.094	0.068	0.053
3–4 (4th)	5.52	0.119	0.079	0.060	0.048
4–5 (5th)	7.05	0.096	0.069	0.053	0.044
5–6 (6th)	8.65	0.079	0.060	0.048	0.040
6–7 (7th)	10.28	0.069	0.054	0.044	0.037

[a] $k_{soil} = 9.6(Btuh)(in.)/(ft²)(°F)$; $k_{insulation} = 0.24(Btuh)(in.)/(ft²)(°F)$.

from Table 11, added together, and the total multiplied by the perimeter of the house. For the floor, the average heat loss per ft² is estimated from Table 10 and multiplied by the floor area. The resulting two values may then be added together and multiplied by the appropriate design temperature difference to give the maximum rate of heat loss from that portion of the basement below grade.

DESIGN TEMPERATURES

Selecting the appropriate design temperature difference can be a problem. Although internal design temperature is given, none of the usual external design air temperatures are applicable. However, ground surface temperature is known to fluctuate about a mean value by an amplitude A, which will vary with geographic location and surface cover. Thus, suitable external design temperatures can be obtained by subtracting A for the location from the mean annual air temperature, $\bar{t}_a$. Values for $\bar{t}_a$ can

be obtained from meteorological records; and A can be estimated from the map in Fig. 4.

Example: Consider a basement 28 ft wide by 30 ft long sunk 6 ft below grade, with 2 in. of insulation applied to the top 2 ft of wall below grade. Assume an internal air temperature of 70°F and an external design temperature ($\bar{t}_a - A$) of 20°F.

Solution:

Wall (Using Table 11):

1st ft below grade	0.093 Btuh/(ft)(°F)
2nd ft below grade	0.079 Btuh/(ft)(°F)
3rd ft below grade	0.155 Btuh/(ft)(°F)
4th ft below grade	0.119 Btuh/(ft)(°F)
5th ft below grade	0.096 Btuh/(ft)(°F)
6th ft below grade	0.079 Btuh/(ft)(°F)
Total per ft length of wall	0.621 Btuh/(ft)(°F)

Basement perimeter
$$= 2(28 + 30) = 116 \text{ ft}$$

Total wall heat loss
$$= 0.62 \times 116 = 71.92 \text{ Btuh/°F}$$
$$\sim 72 \text{ Btuh °F}$$

Floor (Using Table 10):

Average heat loss per ft²
$$= 0.025 \text{ Btuh/(ft)(°F)}$$

Floor area

28×30
$$= 840 \text{ ft}^2$$

Total floor heat loss

$0.025 \times 840 = 21 \quad$ Btuh/°F

Total

Total basement heat loss below grade
$$= 72 + 21 = 93 \text{ Btuh/°F}$$

Design temperature difference
$$= 70 - 20 = 50°F$$

Hence, the maximum rate of heat loss from the below-grade basement
$$= 93 \times 50 = 4650 \text{ Btuh}$$

UNHEATED BASEMENTS

If a basement is unheated, its temperature normally will range between that in the rooms above and that of the ground. Of course, basement windows will lower basement temperature when it is cold outdoors,

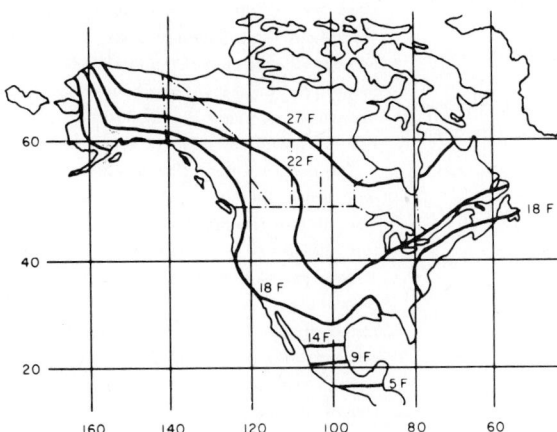

Fig. 4. Lines of constant amplitude

Table 13. Floor heat loss to be used when warm air perimeter heating ducts are embedded in slabs[a]

Btuh per (linear foot of heated edge)

Outdoor Design Temperature, F	Edge Insulation		
	1-in. Vertical Extending Down 18 in. Below Floor Surface	1-in. L-Type Extending at Least 12 in. Deep and 12 in. Under	2-in. L-Type Extending at Least 12 in. Down and 12 in. Under
−20	105	100	85
−10	95	90	75
0	85	80	65
10	75	70	55
20	62	57	45

[a] Factors include loss downward through inner area of slab.

Table 12. Heat loss of concrete floors at or near grade level per foot of exposed slab edge, Btuh

Outdoor Design Temperature, F	Total Width of Insulation, In.	Value of F for Unheated Slab[a]			Value of F for Heated Slab[b]		
		R = 5.0	R = 3.75	R = 2.50	R = 5.0	R = 3.33	R = 2.50
−30 and colder	24	34	51	67	46	69	92
−25 to −29	24	32	48	64	44	66	88
−20 to −24	24	30	45	60	41	61	82
−15 to −19	24	28	43	57	39	59	78
−10 to −14	24	27	40	54	37	55	74
− 5 to − 9	24	25	38	51	35	52	70
0 to − 4	24	24	36	48	32	48	64
+ 5 to + 1	24	22	33	44	30	45	60
+10 to + 6	18	21	31	42	25	38	50
+15 to +11	12	21	31	42	25	38	50
+20 to +16	Edge only	21	31	42	25	38	50

R = Thermal resistance of insulation, $1/C$.
[a] Where perimeter insulation is not required, use $F = 50$ for unheated slabs or $F = 75$ for heated slabs.
[b] Slab floors having heating pipes or ducts under the slab shall be considered as *heated slabs*.

Reproduced by permission from ASHRAE Handbook of Fundamentals, 1977, except equation and Table 12 which are from the 1972 edition.

and heat given off by the heating plant will increase the basement temperature. The exact basement temperature is indeterminate. In general, heat from the heating plant sufficiently warms the air near the basement ceiling to make an allowance unnecessary for floor heat loss from rooms located over the basement.

FLOOR SLABS ON GRADE

Two types of concrete floors used in basementless houses are (1) the unheated floor, relying for warmth on heat delivered above floor level by the heating system, and (2) the heated floor containing heated pipes or ducts that constitute a radiant slab or portion thereof for complete or partial heating of the house.

For type 1, the floor heat loss, economically considered, is of minor importance since it generally comprises about 10 per cent of the total heat loss of the house. From the comfort standpoint, however, it may be most important, since houses with cold floors are not successfully heated. In this connection, it should be remembered that a well-insulated floor does not assure comfort if downdrafts from windows or exposed walls create pools of chilly air over considerable areas of the floor. For this reason, a floor of type 1 should not be used in a severe climate except with a heating system that delivers enough heat near the floor to counteract the downdrafts of the exterior walls and the heat transmission through the floor.

The heat loss from a concrete slab floor on grade is more nearly proportional to the perimeter than to the area of the floor, and the heat loss can be estimated by means of the equation

$$H = FP$$

where H = heat loss of floor, Btuh
F = heat loss coefficient, Btuh (per linear foot of exposed edge)
P = perimeter or exposed edge of floor, linear feet

The F values in Table 12 are considered to be sufficiently accurate for design calculations. The insulation should extend under the floor horizontally for 2 ft. The insulation can also be located along the vertical foundation wall with equal effectiveness if the insulation extends 2 ft below the floor level.

Example: Calculate the heat loss from a floor 12 by 15 ft with two exposures. The floor is an unheated concrete slab which is insulated at the edge with 2 in. of insulation extending horizontally for a distance of 2 ft from the edge. The outdoor design temperature is − 5° F and thermal resistance of the insulation is 3.75.

Solution: From Table 12, the heat loss per foot of exposed edge is 38 Btuh. The length of exposed edge is 12 ft + 15 ft = 27 ft. The total edge loss is then 27 × 38 = 1026 Btuh.

Floors of type 2, containing heating pipes or ducts, are now in common use. The heat loss downward into the ground and outward through the edges of the floor slab is called the reverse loss. The same equation noted above can be used to calculate the reverse loss when warm-air perimeter heating ducts are used. To make the results of this application more usable, values corresponding to those shown in Table 12 for unheated floors are given in Table 13 for concrete floors with a warm-air perimeter duct.

The desirability of edge insulation is apparent. One inch of water-resistant material is the minimum thickness of edge insulation that should be used, but a 2-in. thickness is recommended. The values of edge loss in Table 13 indicate that the reverse heat loss of heated slabs is likely to be about 20 per cent of the total heat loss of many types of present-day houses and may exceed 20 per cent if only 1 in. of insulation is used at the edge of the floor.

The concrete floor slab is usually placed on a gravel fill 4 in. thick or more, both to insulate the floor from the earth and to retard the rise of groundwater by capillarity. A vaporproof membrane should be installed over the gravel fill. Obviously, it is important that such floors be laid several inches above grade and that effective subsoil drainage be provided to avoid slabs soaked by rain or melting snow and consequent excessive heat loss.

Insulating material standards: (From HUD Minimum Property Standards, 1973, Revised 1978)

Cork board	FS HH-I-525
Cellular glass	FS HH-I-551
Cellulose, vegetable or wood fiber	FS HH-I-515
Expanded polystyrene insulation board	FS HH-I-524

HUD INSULATION REQUIREMENTS
(From HUD Minimum Property Standards, 1973, Revised 1978)

Table 14. Maximum *U*-values of ceilings, walls, and openings

Winter degree days	Flat roof deck[1]	Masonry wall Construction		Frame wall construction		Doors and windows
		ceilings	walls	ceilings	walls	
4500 or less	0.14	0.05	0.10	0.08	0.08	1.13
4501 to 8000	0.09	0.05	0.10	0.05	0.08	0.65
8001 or more	0.09	0.04	0.10	0.04	0.08	0.65

[1] *Indicates construction with rigid roof insulation and exposed structural system. When roof cavity is available use column for ceilings.*

Table 15. Maximum *U*-value of floor sections over unheated basements, garages, or crawl spaces

Winter degree days	Structural slab	Wood and metal framing
2500 or less	No requirement	No requirement
2501 to 4500	0.15	0.10
4501 or more	0.12	0.08

Table 16. Maximum *U*-values of foundation walls enclosing heated basements or crawl spaces

Winter degree days	Maximum U-value
2500 or less	No Requirement
2501 to 4500	0.24
4501 or More	0.17

Fiberboard	FS LLL-I-535 Class C or E or ASTM C-208
Insulation board (urethane)	FS HH-I-530
Mineral fiber, board (roof)	FS HH-I-526
Mineral fiber, insulation blanket	FS HH-I-521
Mineral fiber, pneumatic or poured	FS HH-I-1030
Perimeter insulation	FS-HH-I-524 Type II FS HH-I-558, Form A, Class 1 or 2
Reflective, thermal	FS HH-I-1252
Structural fiberboard insulating roof deck	AIMA IB Spec. No. 1
Vermiculite	ASTM C-516
Perlite	FS-HH-I-574

Maximum U-Values

All buildings shall be constructed to comply with the maximum U-values shown in Tables 14, 15 and 16. U-values shown do not include adjustments for framing in walls, ceilings or floors, nor for the sash frame in windows or glass doors.

In areas of 4500 or less winter degree days and 400 or more summer cooling hours, buildings to be mechanically cooled shall be insulated as for areas of 4501 to 8000 winter degree days, except for glazing.

Basement or Crawl Space Foundation Walls

Insulation may be omitted from floors over heated basement areas or heated crawl spaces if foundation walls are insulated. Foundation walls of heated basements need not be insulated except where habitable rooms are provided or where 50 percent of the wall is exposed to outside air. The U-value of foundation wall sections shall not exceed the value shown in Table 16.

Crawl space plenum walls

When a crawl space is used as a supply or return plenum, the crawl space perimeter wall shall be insulated to provide a maximum heat loss of 35 Btuh per lineal foot of perimeter wall assuming a crawl space air temperature of 70°F for return plenums and 110°F for supply plenums.

Slab-on-Ground Floors

Edge heat loss of concrete slabs around the perimeter of heated spaces shall not exceed a maximum value per linear foot of exposed edge of 42 Btuh for unheated slabs and 50 Btuh for heated slabs. Calculations of heat loss through concrete slabs shall be made using the formula $H = F \times P$ and Table 12.

Adapted from A Study of Slab-on-Ground Construction of Residences, conducted by the Building Research Advisory Board for FHA

BASIC DESIGN CONSIDERATIONS

The physical characteristics of the site and the nature of the soil are the controlling factors. The type of soil, its load-bearing and capillary characteristics must be known in order to have an efficient and effective slab-on-ground design. Surface drainage in every direction is essential, and, if necessary, a positive underground drainage system must be provided. Proper elevation of the slab above the finished grade is critical. Many moisture problems will not occur if elevation of the slab and drainage are properly handled. A moisture condition may cause a failure of the flooring surface material, and increase thermal problems.

Moisture control involves controlling the water transfer by capillarity and by vapor phase migration. The capillary rise of water can be broken by using a layer of granular base material under the slab. A vapor barrier separating the slab from the ground will limit vapor transmission and may also serve as a water stop. Under most conditions, it is wise to use both of these protective measures.

The major thermal consideration is to provide comfort. A less important consideration is to achieve some economy from heat loss through the slab. Essential is a suitable insulation material, correctly placed around the perimeter of the slab.

Site Grading and Drainage

(1) Finish grades should slope downward away from structures having slab-on-ground construction, a minimum of 12 in. for a distance of 25 ft in all directions (4 per cent slope).

(2) Wherever less than a 4 per cent slope is used adjacent to the structure, such as for a terrace, a positive means of drainage should be provided.

(3) In side-hill locations, the site should be so graded that surface water will be diverted around the structure. In addition, a positive system of underground drainage may be required for certain conditions.

Height of Floor above Finish Grade

(1) For an unheated slab or where heating coils are embedded in the slab, the finish grade at the outside wall should be not less than 8 in. below the top of the concrete slab.

(2) Where warm air ducts are used in or under the slab, the finish grade at the outside wall should be not less than 2 in. below the bottom of ductwork adjacent to the foundation wall.

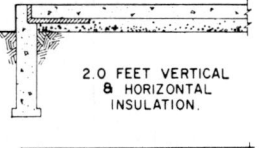

2.0 FEET VERTICAL & HORIZONTAL INSULATION.

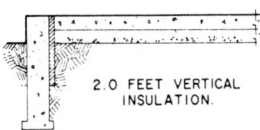

2.0 FEET VERTICAL INSULATION.

Soil Capillarity

The underside of a concrete slab should not be in contact with liquid water. Capillary water rises through soil from the water-level or water-table to various heights depending on the type of soil. (See Fig. 5.) A base material of limited capillarity of sufficient thickness will break the capillary rise of water. Effective drainage will prevent the base from being a reservoir of water.

Material of limited capillarity

In order for a material to be considered of limited capillarity the capillary rise of liquid water in the material should not exceed 2 in. Coarse gravel is such a material.

Capillary Material

Clay, silt, sands, bank-run gravel, or other soils are capillary materials (see Table 17). This classification applies to both undisturbed soil and foundation fill.

Base

A base for a concrete slab-on-ground must be at least 4 in. in thickness and consist of clean coarse gravel or other material of limited capillarity. The base should be

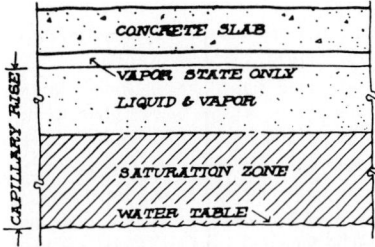

Fig. 5. Moisture and vapor in covered soil

Table 17. Capillarity of soils

Capillary rise above the water table in various soils

Gravel	0.0 ft
Coarse sand	2.6 ft
Fine sand	7.5 ft
Silt	11.5 ft
Clay	11.5 ft

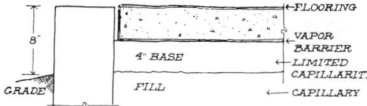

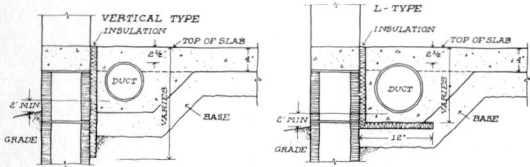

Fig. 6. Slab on grade with perimeter warm-air heating system.

thoroughly compacted by rolling or tamping to assure uniform support for the slab.

Vapor Barrier

(1) The permeance of vapor barriers should not exceed 0.20 perms when tested by the ASTM methods.

(2) Vapor barrier joints should be lapped a minimum of 6 in. Sealing is not required.

(3) Vapor barriers should be capable of withstanding handling and construction traffic without puncture or displacement.

INSULATION

Properties

(1) Insulation should be required to be non-capillary, not permanently harmed by wetting, or harmed by contact with wet concrete mix, and not subject to damage by termites or fungi.

(2) Insulation for horizontal use must have compressive strength sufficient to support a dead load of 50 lb/ft² and a live load of 40 lb/ft².

Location

(1) The slab perimeter must be insulated in its entirely.

(2) If the highest known water-table of a site is 2 ft. or more below outside grade, perimeter insulation may be placed in either a vertical or horizontal position.

(3) If the highest known water-table is less than 2 ft below the outside grade, perimeter insulation must be placed in a horizontal or L-shaped position. An exception should be made if a special drainage system is provided to prevent moisture from reaching the insulation.

Thermal Resistances

It is recommended that the method of establishing thermal resistances for the selection of insulation be determined by using the outdoor design temperatures for the region (see Table 12).

CRAWL SPACES

By RUDARD A. JONES, AIA; Architectural Consultants: F. M. LESCHER and W. H. KAPPLE
Data used by permission of the University of Illinois Small Homes Council from its copyrighted publication Crawl-Space Houses

Crawl-space houses should, and can, be constructed so that: (1) they are free from problems of moisture, (2) they resist termite attack, and (3) the floor and rooms above crawl space can be kept at comfortable temperatures.

MOISTURE

Excessive moisture within a house can result from dampness in a crawl space due to improper grading of the lot for drainage or due to the omission of moisture control devices, such as ground cover, vapor barrier and ventilation openings. An uncorrected moisture problem can cause decay of wood and eventually structural failure of the house.

The only satisfactory way of avoiding moisture problems is to prevent moisture (vapor and liquid) from entering the crawl space.

Moisture in the crawl space can be due to:

1. High ground-water level in the area.
2. Surface water.
3. Capillary rise of ground moisture.
4. Moisture from the house.

SOURCE OF MOISTURE

1. GROUND WATER

Sometimes the level of the water in the ground (water table) is raised above the bottom surface of the crawl space due to:

a. Heavy or prolonged rains.

b. A spring which appears only in wet seasons and is not discovered when the house is built.

RECOMMENDATIONS: Crawl-space construction is not recommended if ground-water level in an area is so high that it can flood the crawl space periodically.

Where a spring is discovered during or after construction, or where unexpected flooding occurs, install drainage collector lines within the crawl space. Grade the bottom of the crawl space so that any water will drain to the tile. Cover the crawl-space area with coarse, washed gravel (fine gravel or sand tends to block the tile).

2. SURFACE WATER

Rain water on ground or from roof passes through, or under, the foundation walls.

In some areas, heavy soils may retain surface drainage and cause water pressure against the walls of the crawl space.

RECOMMENDATIONS: Surface drainage problems usually occur because the floor of the crawl space is 2 to 3 ft below finished grade. To avoid such problems:

a. Grade the lot so that drainage is away from the house and no water is allowed to stand on the site. Slope of the grade should be at least 6 in. in 25 ft.

b. Use wide overhangs and/or gutters and downspouts. (Do not connect downspouts to footing drains.)

c. Install a footing drain of field tile with open joints.

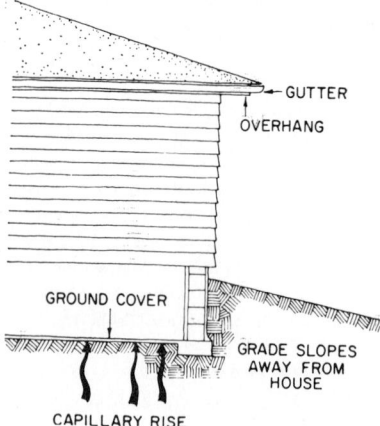

Fig. 8. Typical corner of a crawl space house.

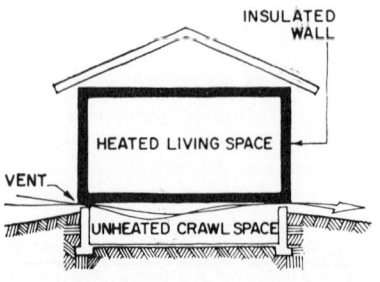

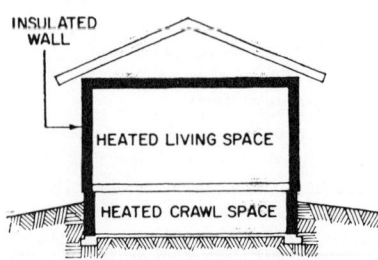

Fig. 7. Open and closed crawl space designs.

d. Waterproof the outside of the walls with a bituminous coating. Masonry walls should have a half inch coat of mortar applied first.

3. CAPILLARY RISE OF GROUND MOISTURE

Moisture travels upward from lower layers of certain soils by capillary action (as much as 18 gal. per day have been noted under a 1000 sq ft house) and evaporates within the crawl space.

Capillary rise occurs in nearly all crawl spaces built in areas where the soil is clay or silt. Such moisture is present even though the ground in the crawl space may seem dry and dusty.

RECOMMENDATION: Moisture from capillary rise can be kept out of the crawl space by using a vapor-barrier type of ground cover which is not susceptible to damage by fungi. Grade and smooth the ground before installing the ground cover. Turn up ground cover 4 to 6 in. on the walls of the crawl space.

4. MOISTURE FROM THE HOUSE

Theoretically in a cold open crawl space, excessive moisture from the house may travel downward through the floor into the crawl space. The moisture may condense on walls or floor of the crawl space if they are cold.

RECOMMENDATION: To prevent downward flow of moisture into an open crawl space, install a vapor barrier above the floor insulation—either directly above it, or between the subfloor and the finish flooring.

VENTILATION

Before the effectiveness of ground cover was proven, large ventilation openings were required in the foundation wall to allow moisture to escape from the crawl space. With the use of ground cover which prevents moisture rise from the ground into the crawl space, a minimum amount of ventilation[1] is needed. Provide at least four corrosion-resistant foundation vents which can be closed during the heating season. Four 8-in. by 16-in. units will satisfactorily vent a house up to 1400 sq ft—install an additional vent for each additional 350 sq ft. (Screen the vents with 1/8-in. corrosion-resis-

[1] HUD regulation: A minimum of two vents, giving a total free area of ventilation equivalent to 1/1500 of the crawl-space area, is required when ground cover is used. Without ground cover, ten times as much ventilation area is required. See Sheet 5 of section on Condensation Control.

tant mesh—64 openings per sq in.—to keep out insects.)

OPEN CRAWL SPACES

To achieve warm floors in a crawl-space house, either (1) insulate the floor above an open crawl space, or (2) insulate the exterior walls of a closed crawl space.

Open crawl spaces are those which are ventilated to such an extent that the temperature within the crawl space approaches that of the outside air. In cold areas, it is necessary to insulate water pipes in such crawl spaces to protect against freezing, heating pipes or ducts to prevent excessive heat loss, and floors to make them comfortable.

RECOMMENDATIONS FOR RESISTANCE OF FLOOR INSULATION

Table 18 shows the minimum amount of insulation required to maintain the surface temperature of a hardwood floor over a plywood subfloor at 65 F (the minimum temperature recommended for comfort) or higher. These insulation requirements will also limit heat loss through the floor to 5.5 Btu/hr/sq ft. (See HUD requirements, Table 15.)

CLOSED CRAWL SPACES

The moisture control provided by ground cover is so effective that crawl-space ventilators can usually be kept closed during the heating season. This "closed" crawl-space construction is recommended except under severe moisture conditions since it provides maximum floor comfort with a minimum expenditure for insulation. Insulation around water pipes and heat ducts and pipes is not needed; furthermore, a closed crawl space can also serve as the plenum for a warm-air heating system.

If the temperature of the crawl space can be maintained at 70 F., the surface temperatures of the floors in the rooms above will also be a comfortable 70 F. Heat from uninsulated warm-air ducts or hot-water heating pipes can often keep a well-insulated, closed crawl space near the 70 F. level.

The walls enclosing the crawl space must be insulated to reduce heat loss and to help maintain the temperature of the crawl space at 70 F. (Heat loss to the ground through the earth floor of a crawl space is small.) To accomplish this:

a. The box-sill headers and the end joists of the floor must be insulated, preferably

with a flexible-type insulation (batt or blanket) which has a vapor barrier on one side. The vapor barrier should face the interior of the crawl space.

b. For the exterior walls, insulation in sheet or block form is most easily applied. Tempered nails or an adhesive mastic are suggested. Insulation should be of a type not affected by termites or dampness. If it is not vaporproof, a vapor barrier should be installed on the inside face of the insulation since moisture condensation is otherwise likely to occur between the insulation and the wall, or within the wall cavity.

HEATING SYSTEMS

Heating systems which supply heat near the floor along the exterior walls of the house reduce uncomfortable drafts along the floor. For this reason, perimeter heating or baseboard heating is recommended.

In a warm-air perimeter system, the heat can be distributed (1) through ducts in the crawl space, or (2) by using the crawl space, if it is closed, as a plenum.

When a closed crawl space is used as a plenum the temperature in the space will approach 100 F. See Table 19 for recommendations for wall insulation. Insulation and ground cover selected for a plenum-type crawl space should be fire-resistant.

Table 18.   Resistance of floor insulation

Outside design temperature	Resistance of insulation
−30°	13.26
−20°	11.42
−10°	9.58
0°	7.74
10°	5.90
20°	4.06
30°	2.22

Table 19.   Resistance of heated crawl space insulation

Outside design temperature	For closed crawl space	For crawl space as plenum
−30	5.03	7.61
−20	4.25	6.74
−10	3.45	5.85
0	2.71	5.03
10	1.98	4.25
20	1.27	3.45
30	.59	2.71

FOUNDATION-WALL INSULATION FOR HEATED CRAWL SPACES

The recommended minimum insulation shown in the table will limit the heat loss to 50* Btu/hr per lineal foot of wall around the crawl space. These insulation standards are based on economy since, with a warm crawl space, floor comfort is no problem. The more thoroughly a wall is insulated, the lower is the heat loss and the greater is the fuel saving.

CONSTRUCTION DETAILS

The minimum depth of the crawl space should be 2 ft under the floor joists or 18 in. under the girder.

Two types of crawl-space construction for houses are presented on this page: (1) foundation-wall construction for a closed crawl space (illustrated), and (2) pier construction.

* *HUD requires maximum of 35 Btu.*

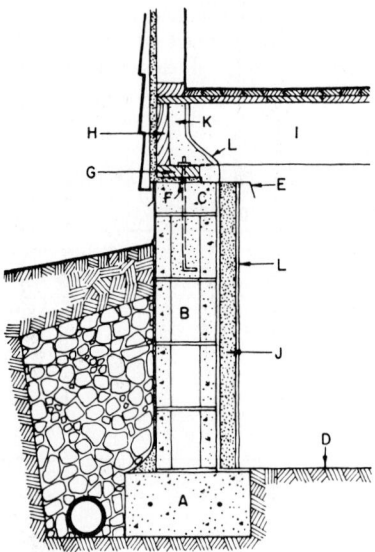

Fig. 9. Foundation detail of a crawl space house.

FOUNDATION-WALL CONSTRUCTION (Key to illustration)

A. *POURED CONCRETE CONTINUOUS WALL FOOTING*

B. *FOUNDATION WALLS FOR FRAME HOUSES,* 8-in masonry or 6-in. poured concrete. (Check local building code.)

Where the exterior walls to be supported by the foundation are thicker (as in an 8-in. solid brick house), the foundation wall must be correspondingly thicker.

Foundation wall should extend at least 8 in. above grade and remain exposed at least 6 in.

C. *HOLLOW-MASONRY FOUNDATION WALL* must be capped with (1) a course of solid masonry, or (2) a 4-in. poured concrete cap reinforced by No. 14 wire mesh 2 by 2 in.

D. *GROUND COVER.*

E. *METAL TERMITE SHIELD.* Where anchor bolts penetrate the shield, the area should be well sealed with coal-tar pitch or tight lead washers.

F. *SEALER FOR THE SILL PLATE.* Use material similar to expansion joint.

G. *SILL PLATE* 2 by 6 in., anchored with ½-in. bolts, 8 ft on center—minimum of two bolts to each piece of sill. Pressure treated lumber is recommended.

H. *HEADER OF BOX SILL.*

I. *JOISTS.*

J. *FOUNDATION-WALL INSULATION.*

K. *CORNER-PACK INSULATION.*

L. *VAPOR BARRIER.*

PIER CONSTRUCTION

Where the outside walls and the outer edge of the floor of a house rest upon a beam supported by piers, the crawl space is usually enclosed by non-loadbearing (curtain) walls placed between the piers. (In some instances, the curtain wall may support the masonry veneer walls above it.)

Piers are usually 8-in. diameter concrete or 8 by 12 in. solid masonry. Curtain walls are usually 4-in. solid or hollow masonry. Maximum height for 4-in. hollow masonry is 40 in. Unbalanced fill against a 4-in. curtain wall should not be higher than 2 ft.

From ASHRAE Handbook of Fundamentals, 1977. *American Society of Heating, Refrigerating, and Air Conditioning Engineers*

Water vapor

Moisture is present as vapor in all air. Water vapor originates from such necessary living requirements as cooking, laundering, bathing, and the breathing and perspiration of people. In a typical family of four, the average daily production of water vapor from these sources may be as much as 25 lb, and it may be much greater where such appliances as humidifiers, automatic washers, and dryers are used. Another large source of water vapor is sometimes the bare earth in a crawl space or basement. Also, in new construction, moisture is added by poured concrete slabs, masonry construction, and new plaster. All this water vapor must escape from the dwelling.

Water vapor in air is a gas which occupies all the space along with the air present. In many ways, the water vapor can act independently of the air, since in general its properties do not depend on the presence of the air. It exerts its own vapor pressure and can move about through air in a space, or move through materials under differences in its own vapor pressure, independently of the air. However, when the air is moved suddenly or is heated or cooled, the water vapor present is similarly affected, so that it is usually necessary to consider it as a part of an air-vapor mixture.

Water vapor may also be transferred as a part of a moving air stream caused by convection currents or air infiltration. This means of water vapor transfer is similar to that of transfer of heat by air leakage, and in many instances it constitutes the major means.

Condensation

Change of moisture from the gaseous state to the liquid or solid state is called condensation. This may occur as a result of reduction of temperature over a period of time, or as a result of migration of vapor to regions of lower temperature. Condensation may be no more than a nuisance, as when it occurs on windows. But it may and often does occur within the building structure, hidden from sight, where it may cause serious damage.

The behavior of vapor in the air at different air temperatures is shown in full in the psychrometric chart. For illustrative purposes, a simplified version of the chart is shown in Fig. 1.

A common condition inside buildings, 70° F and 40 per cent relative humidity, is represented by point A. The vapor pressure of the water present in the air, although not shown on the chart, can be calculated readily from the vapor pressure at saturation and the relative humidity, since relative humidity is equal to the ratio of the actual vapor pressure to the saturation pressure at the existing temperature.

The increasing relative humidity accompanying cooling from the condition represented by A on the chart to point B can readily be followed. At B, however, at 44.6° F, the relative humidity becomes 100 per cent, and the air-vapor mixture is said to be saturated. The temperature at which this particular air-vapor mixture, upon cooling, becomes saturated is its dew-point temperature. Upon further cooling, to 35° F, the original amount of water vapor can no longer be retained and is reduced by condensation to the condition represented by C, from 0.0633 lb per lb dry air to 0.0427 lb per lb dry air. The process ABC is typical of that which an air-vapor mixture experiences when it comes in contact with a cool window surface. Cooling from B to C results in visible condensation on the glass surface. If the point C were below 32° F, the condensation would be in the form of frost.

Effect of surface temperature at or below dew point

Once the temperature drops below the dew point, or frost point if below 32° F, the vapor pressure at the condensing surface is also reduced, thereby establishing a gradient of vapor pressure from the room air to the window surface. This gradient will operate, in conjunction with the convective action within the room, to move water vapor continuously to the window surface to be condensed so long as the concentration of water vapor in the room is maintained.

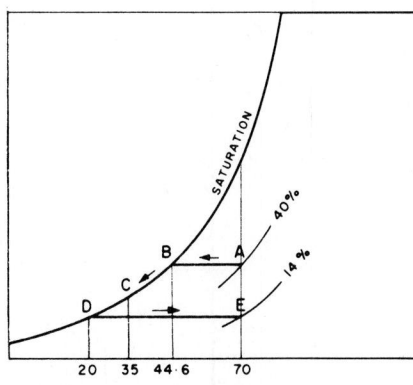

Fig. 1. Two typical heating and cooling processes in air within buildings shown on psychrometric chart

A common winter process is that shown by DE, showing air at 20° F, saturated, being heated to 70° F with a resulting large decrease in relative humidity. This explains, in part, the greatly reduced relative humidities experienced in houses in extreme cold weather, when cold outdoor air enters the house and is heated.

Moisture in building materials

The effect of moisture on building materials is deleterious in several ways. One is the increase in dimension caused by moisture in most organic materials, most strikingly in wood and wood fiber products such as paper. Less generally recognized but a real factor is the dimensional change which moisture produces in masonry. More serious than dimensional change is the deterioration of many building materials in the presence of moisture, resulting in the rotting of wood, the rusting of steel, and the spalling of masonry from frost action. Condensation of water vapor, although not the only means by which wetting may be brought about, is nevertheless a most insidious one, particularly in respect to freeze-thaw breakdown, since from its nature it is most likely to occur at points of low temperature at where there may later be risk of freezing while the material remains in a saturated condition. Finally, the presence of moisture increases the thermal transmission of all building materials except such impervious ones as glass or metal, resulting in increased fuel consumption and lower interior surface temperatures, hence reduced comfort.

Vapor transmission

Vapor transmission through a material or assembly of materials of any thickness is called *permeance* and is measured in *perms*, a unit equal to 1 grain/(ft²)(hr)(in.) of mercury pressure difference. Water-vapor transmission through a material 1 in. thick is called *permeability* and is measured in *perm-inches*. Permeance or permeability figures on a number of materials are given in Table 1.

Resistance *(R)* to vapor flow provided by a sheet or board is the reciprocal of the permeance and correspondingly, the overall resistance *(R$_t$)* of an assembly (like a wall) of materials in series is the sum of the resistances of its component parts:

$$R_t = R_1 + R_2 + R_3 + \cdots R_n$$

The overall permeance *(M$_t$)* of the assembly is the reciprocal of the overall resistance:

$$M_t = 1/R_t$$

Effect of location on condensation probability

The average winter temperature and its duration are factors in the condensation problem. In Fig. 2 the map of the United States is divided into condensation zones based on winter weather conditions. The solid lines separating the zones follow state lines and are those recommended by the Department of Housing and Urban Development for the guidance of owners, builders, and architects. The dashed lines are the − 20° F, 0° F, and + 20° F isotherms of winter design temperature. It will be noted that there is reasonably good correlation between the zones determined by the two sets of lines.

Condensation inside walls

When water vapor is allowed to enter a wall and condensation occurs on its outer cold elements, it appears as frost or liquid.

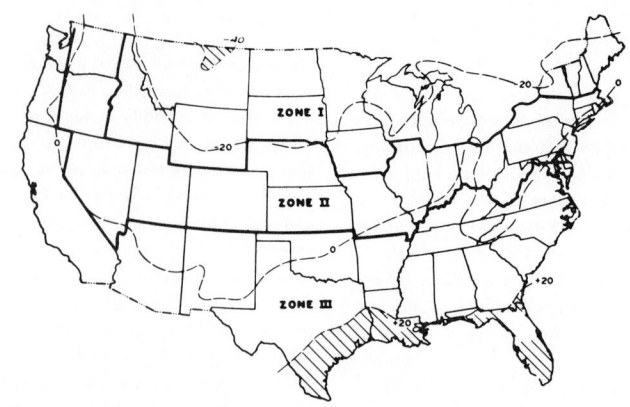

Fig. 2. Condensation zones in the United States
Zones include areas with design temperatures about as follows: Zone I, − 20°F and lower; Zone II, 0 to − 20°F; Zone III, above 0°F. Note that crosshatched areas are outside Zones I and III.

Table 1. Permeance and permeability of materials to water vapor[a]

Reprinted by permission from ASHRAE Handbook of Fundamentals, 1977.

Material	Permeance (Perm)	Resistance[1] (Rep)	Permeability (Perm-in.)	Resistance/in.[1] (Rep/in.)
Materials used in construction				
Concrete (1:2:4 mix)			3.2	0.31
Brick masonry (4-in. thick)	0.8[f]	1.3		
Concrete block (8-in., cored, limestone aggregate)	2.4[f]	0.4		
Tile masonry, glazed (4-in. thick)	0.12[f]	8.3		
Asbestos cement board (0.2-in. thick)	0.54[d]	1.8		
Plaster on metal lath (0.75 in.)	15[f]	0.067		
Plaster on wood lath	11[e]	0.091		
Plaster on plain gypsum lath (with studs)	20[f]	0.050		
Gypsum wall board (0.375 in., plain)	50[f]	0.020		
Gypsum sheathing (0.5 in., asphalt impreg.)			20[d]	0.050
Structural insulating board (sheathing qual.)			20–50[f]	0.050–0.020
Structural insulating board (interior, uncoated. 0.5 in.)	50–90[f]	0.020–0.011		
Hardboard (0.125 in., standard)	11[f]	0.091		
Hardboard (0.125 in., tempered)	5[f]	0.2		
Built-up roofing (hot mopped)	0.0			
Wood, sugar pine			0.4–5.4[f,b]	2.5–0.19
Plywood (douglas fir, exterior glue, 0.25 in. thick)	0.7[f]	1.4		
Plywood (douglas fir, interior glue, 0.25 in. thick)	1.9[f]	0.53		
Acrylic, glass fiber reinforced sheet, 56 mil	0.12[d]	8.3		
Polyester, glass fiber reinforced sheet, 48 mil	0.05[d]	20		
Thermal insulations				
Air (still)			120[f]	0.0083
Cellular glass			0.0[d]	∝
Corkboard			2.1–2.6[d], 9.5[e]	0.48–0.38
Mineral wool (unprotected)			116[e]	0.0086
Expanded polyurethane (R-11 blown) board stock			0.4–1.6[d]	2.5–0.62
Expanded polystyrene—extruded			1.2[d]	0.83
Expanded polystyrene—bead			2.0–5.8[d]	0.50–0.17
Unicellular synthetic flexible rubber foam			0.02–0.15[d]	50–6.7
Plastic and metal foils and films[c]				
Aluminum foil (1 mil)	0.0[d]			
Aluminum foil (0.35 mil)	0.05[d]	20		
Polyethylene (2 mil)	0.16[d]	6.3		3100
Polyethylene (4 mil)	0.08[d]	12.5		3100
Polyethylene (6 mil)	0.06[d]	17		3100
Polyethylene (8 mil)	0.04[d]	25		3100
Polyethylene (10 mil)	0.03[d]	33		3100
Polyester (1 mil)	0.7[d]	1.4		
Cellulose acetate (125 mil)	0.4[d]	2.5		
Polyvinylchloride, unplasticized (2 mil)	0.68[d]	1.5		
Polyvinylchloride plasticized (4 mil)	0.8–1.4[d]	1.3–0.72		

Table 1 (cont.). Permeance and permeability of materials to water vapor[a]

Material	Permeance (Perms)			Resistance[1] (Rep)		
	Dry-cup	Wet-cup	Other	Dry-cup	Wet-cup	Other
Building paper, felts, roofing papers[g]						
Duplex sheet, asphalt laminated, aluminum foil one side (43)[h]	0.002	0.176		500	5.8	
Saturated and coated roll roofing (326)[h]	0.05	0.24		20	4.2	
Kraft paper and asphalt laminated, reinforced 30-120-30 (34)[h]	0.03	1.8		3.3	0.55	
Blanket thermal insulation back up paper, asphalt coated (31)[h]	0.04	0.6–4.2		2.5	1.7–0.24	
Asphalt-saturated and coated vapor barrier paper (43)[h]	0.2–0.3	0.6		5.0–3.3	1.7	
Asphalt-saturated but not coated sheathing paper (22)[h]	3.3	20.2		0.3	0.05	
15-lb asphalt felt (70)[h]	1.0	5.6		1.0	0.18	
15-lb tar felt (70)[h]	4.0	18.2		0.25	0.055	
Single-kraft, double (16)[h]	31	42		0.032	0.024	
Liquid-applied coating materials						
Paint—2 coats						
Asphalt paint on plywood		0.4			2.5	
Aluminum varnish on wood	0.3–0.5			3.3–2.0		
Enamels on smooth plaster			0.5–1.5			2.0–0.66
Primers and sealers on interior insulation board			0.9–2.1			1.1–0.48
Various primers plus 1 coat flat oil paint on plaster			1.6–3.0			0.63–0.33
Flat paint on interior insulation board			4			0.25
Water emulsion on interior insulation board			30–85			0.03–0.012
Paint-3 coats						
Exterior paint, white lead and oil on wood siding	0.3–1.0			3.3–1.0		
Exterior paint, white lead-zinc oxide and oil on wood	0.9			1.1		
Styrene-butadiene latex coating, 2 oz/sq ft	5.5			0.18		
Polyvinyl acetate latex coating, 4 oz/sq ft	5.5			0.18		
Chloro-sulfonated polyethylene mastic, 3.5 oz/sq ft	1.7			0.59		
7.0 oz/sq ft	0.06			16		
Asphalt cut-back mastic, 1/16 in., dry	0.14			7.2		
3/16 in., dry	0.0			—		
Hot melt asphalt, 2 oz/sq ft	0.5			2		
3.5 oz/sq ft	0.1			10		

[a] *Table 1 gives the water transmission rates of some representative materials. The data are provided to permit comparisons of materials; but in the selection of vapor barrier materials, exact values for permeance or permeability should be obtained from the manufacturer of the materials under consideration or secured as a result of laboratory tests. A range of values shown in the table indicated variations among mean values for materials that are similar but of different density, orientation, lot or source. The values are intended for design guidance and should not be used as design or specification data. The compilation is from a number of sources; values from dry-cup and wet-cup methods were usually obtained from investigations using ASTM E96 and C355; values shown under others were obtained from investigations using such techniques as two-temperature, special cell, and air-velocity.*

[b] *Depending on construction and direction of vapor flow.*

[c] *Usually installed as vapor barriers, although sometimes used as exterior finish and elsewhere near cold side where special considerations are then required for warm side barrier effectiveness.*

[d] *Dry-cup method.*

[e] *Wet-cup method.*

[f] *Other than dry- or wet-cup method.*

[g] *Low permeance sheets used as vapor barriers. High permeance used elsewhere in construction.*

[h] *Basic weight in lb per 500 ft².*

[i] *Resistance and resistance/in. values have been calculated as the reciprocal of the permeance and permeability values, respectively.*

If the weather temperature rises frequently, frost melts and, becoming liquid, is likely to penetrate capillary materials like wood or run down when the surface is nonabsorbing or is already saturated with water. In weather that is continuously cold for a long period, the frost may build back into a cavity or fibrous insulation and, when it reaches a warmer plane, will run to lower, cooler levels where it forms a mass of ice. Water seepage to the weather side may occur harmlessly in masonry walls when the weather is above freezing, but water seepage into the building must obviously be avoided. In typical frame construction with wood sheathing, which has large water absorbing capacity, seepage is rare and occurs only after a long period of steady cold weather. More generally, moisture accumulates in wood sheathing and siding through the colder months and reaches a peak in late winter, after which the drying of spring and summer complete the annual cycle.

Under-roof condensation

In roofs, the condensation problem is much the same as in walls. The covering of a flat roof is even more resistant to the escape of vapor than wall coverings such as paint; and while paint is likely to be ruptured by excessive moisture, no such relief can occur in roofs. Thus roofs furnish conspicuous examples of rapid decay in lumber.

Crawl space condensation

In crawl spaces over uncovered, damp ground, a large water evaporation sometimes occurs and causes condensation on the outer ends of floor joists and other members that are below the floor line and near the outdoors. Water vapor from the crawl space may also enter walls, be transported by rising air in a stack effect, and even reach the attic by this route when the wall structure permits. Ventilation, as discussed later in this chapter, is an important correction factor in these cases.

Effect of insulation

Insulation in a wall or roof reduces heat loss and lowers the temperature of the outer elements of the structure, thus increasing the possibility of condensation if the vapor path to the cold surface is not blocked. Since low vapor resistance is a characteristic of fibrous insulation, the needed vapor resistance must be provided by other means. It is to be noted that in typical residential conditions, condensation does not occur in fibrous insulation itself except when frost has formed on sheathing and gradually built backward among the fibers. Wet insulation may result from this condition or from liquid condensation seeping down from a higher level.

CONTROL OF CONCEALED CONDENSATION

An excessive accumulation of moisture in walls (or roofs) can be prevented by one or more of the following measures: (1) providing a vapor and air barrier to limit vapor entrance into the wall, (2) ventilating the building to reduce vapor pressure therein, or (3) ventilating the wall cavity to remove vapor that has entered.

1. *Vapor barrier.* A vapor barrier is the principal and most obvious correction, but each measure is more effective if aided by the effect of another. In habitations, some ventilation of the living space, either incidental or planned, is necessary. Also, a small amount of cavity ventilation is essential in cases where the vapor inflow is not completely stopped and the moisture storing capacity of the outer wall elements is slight. This applies to some prefabricated designs using metal siding.

Vapor-barrier sheets are often built into the wall near the warm surface. In wood frames they may be applied to the inside surface of the studs. They are sometimes attached to the warm side of the insulating materials, or they may be applied on the cold side of plaster base materials.

The necessary barrier resistance depends on a number of factors. When the vapor

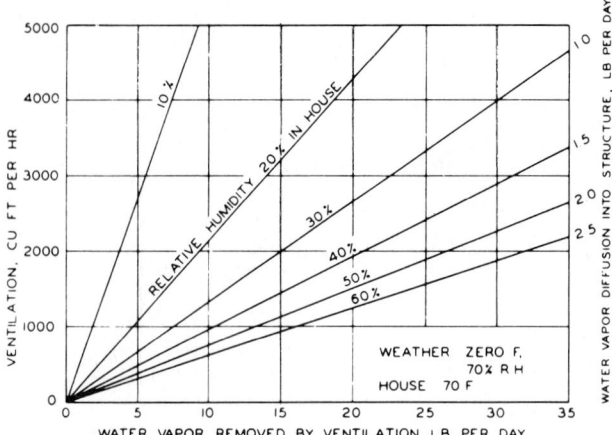

Fig. 3.   Water vapor balance in a dwelling
(Vapor barrier, 1 perm; wall and ceiling area, 2,000 sq ft, insulated.)

flow occurs in annual cycles, as in heated buildings, the requirement is not as exacting as it is for a cold storage room, where there is no chance for drying out an accumulation of moisture. In a heated structure, covered on the outside with materials highly resistant to water vapor such as paint or roll roofing, the winter season is a time of moisture accumulation in the cold outer elements, and their safe moisture holding capacity is an important factor in determining the barrier requirement. A house without sheathing requires a better barrier. A prefabricated design with only

a sheet of metal outside of the insulation, requires a very high resistance barrier on the warm side. Materials such as plastic faced sidings, aluminum siding and decorative metal panels may present problems of condensation directly behind the cold side finish. The interior vapor pressure and the length and severity of the winter are also important.

For typical frame dwellings with wood sheathing and siding in the northern United States, a barrier permeance of 1 perm or less has been found satisfactory. There are cases, however, in residential construction

Table 2.   Recommended good practice—loft and attic ventilation[1]

Type of roof and occupancy	Condensation zone[2]		
	I	II	III
(a) Flat roof—Slope 3 in. in 12 in. or less. No occupancy contemplated.	Total net area of ventilation should be 1/300th[3] distributed uniformly at the eaves *plus* a vapor barrier in the top story ceiling. Free circulation must be provided through all spaces.	Same as for zone I.	Same as for zone I.
(b) Gable roof—Slope over 3 in. in 12 in. No occupancy contemplated.	Total net area of at least two louvers on opposite sides located near the ridge to be 1/300th[3] *plus* a vapor barrier in the top story ceiling.	Same as for zone I.	Same ventilation as for zone II. A vapor barrier is not considered necessary.
(c) Hip roof—No occupancy contemplated.	Total net area of ventilation should be 1/300th[3] with 1/600th[2] distributed uniformly at the eaves *and* 1/600th[3] located at the ridge with all spaces interconnected. A vapor barrier should also be used in the top story ceiling.	Same as for zone I.	Same ventilation as for zone II. A vapor barrier is not considered necessary.
(d) Gable or hip roof— With occupancy contemplated.	Total net area of ventilation should be 1/300th[3] with 1/600th[2] distributed uniformly at the eaves *and* 1/600th[3] located at the ridge with all spaces interconnected. A vapor barrier should also be used on the warm side of the top full story ceiling, the dwarf walls, the sloping part of the roof, and the attic story ceiling.	Same as for zone I.	Same as for zone I except that a vapor barrier is not considered necessary if insulation is omitted.

[1] *It is recognized that in many areas increased ventilation may be desirable for summer comfort.*
[2] *The zone numbers refer to Fig. 2.*
[3] *Refers to area enclosed within the building lines at the eave level.*

where a 1-perm barrier would not be adequate, and there are also many industrial applications in which a very much higher vapor resistance is required.

In applying vapor resistance to a wall, there are certain fundamental principles that should be followed. First, the vapor barrier should be placed as near to the warm surface of the wall as practicable. Second, it should be continuous, with no direct openings through the barrier. Good workmanship and application are very important.

2. *Ventilation of living space.* The second measure listed for the control of concealed condensation is ventilation of the house. This measure is obviously necessary as an accompaniment to a vapor barrier since, if the barrier blocks entrance into the walls, the water vapor must be removed by other means. No great volume of air change is necessary, however, and normal infiltration alone is frequently all that is required in winter weather.

The effectiveness of ventilation with outdoor air is shown in Fig. 3, which also shows the small amount of water vapor escaping into the barrier-equipped, well-insulated walls and ceilings (2,000 sq ft) of a typical small dwelling, the floor being neglected. Evidently, ventilation of 2,000 cfh will remove 21 lb of vapor per day with the relative humidity at 40 per cent, while at the same time 1.5 lb escapes into the structure. The total vapor production (22.5 lb) is a typical amount. By reference to the section on "Heating, Ventilating and Air Conditioning," 2,000 cfh appears to be near the minimum for odor control, and ventilation would have to be higher when cooking is done. By reference to the same section, it appears that usual infiltration will normally supply the necessary air change but that supplementary ventilation may be necessary in kitchen and laundry for proper vapor control and for the reduction of peaks in relative humidity that would otherwise occur in those areas.

Table 3.   Net and gross ventilator areas

Gross ventilator area = net area × factor A	
Ventilator covering	A
¼ in. mesh hardware cloth	1
Screening, 8 mesh to the in.	1¼
Insect screen, 16 mesh to the in.	2
Louvers and ¼ in. mesh hardware cloth	2
Louvers and screening, 8 mesh to the in.	2¼
Louvers and insect screen, 16 mesh to the in.	3

3. *Ventilation of structure.* The third measure listed for the control of concealed condensation is ventilation of the structure itself. It is effective in certain cases, especially as a supplement to warm-side vapor resistance which is considerable but not of itself fully adequate. Air from outdoors is used. The vents must be shielded from the entrance of rain and insects.

Attics and crawl spaces may be considered as parts of the structure, and for these portions ventilation is practically a necessity. Attic ventilation has long been an established practice, but its effectiveness is likely to be diminished by the newer practice of adding insulation to ceilings. Insulation requires added ventilation, which in turn necessitates adequate insulation. The recommended ventilation shown in Table 2 for dwellings is based on such insulation. The *net area* refers to the total of all openings free from obstructions (see Table 3). The use of louvers and 8-mesh screen (usually recommended) requires a gross area 2.25 times that listed. In Zone I of Fig. 2, a ceiling vapor barrier is recommended for all constructions. It is also necessary that stray openings from walls into the attic or around a loose-fitting attic door be avoided. The *stack effect* allows a large inflow of warm air from the dwelling, transporting much vapor to a danger area. Methods of ventilating attic spaces are shown in Fig. 4.

Crawl spaces under dwellings where the earth is damp and uncovered require a high rate of ventilation. At least four openings, one at each corner, as high as possible, should be provided. Their total net area may be calculated by the formula

$$a = \frac{2L}{100} + \frac{A}{300}$$

where L = the perimeter of the crawl space, linear feet

A = the area of the crawl space, square feet

a = the total net area of all vents (or the gross area if a ¼-in.-mesh screen is used), square feet

This ventilation is usually sufficient but cools the first floor so much that insulation is needed. A better control measure is a cover on the damp ground. This cover may be a concrete slab, or heavy roll roofing (55 lb), or 0.004-0.006-in.-thick polyethylene plastic film laid on a graded surface with its edges lapped 2 in. (but not necessarily cemented). With this barrier, the vent area may be reduced to 10 per cent of that calculated by the equation.

In building walls, cavity ventilation can be applied in a moderate climate as the sole vapor control system. However, wall air passages designed to remove an unre-

stricted vapor supply are unduly large and may waste considerable heat. On the other hand, a barrier as the only control measure would, in some cases, require so high a resistance as to be impractical. Ventilation of the structure in conjunction with a vapor barrier is a procedure with important applications, but its general utility has not been fully investigated. Ventilation is most effective when each structural space has a clearly defined air passage with an inlet and outlet. In walls, a small convective effect may be utilized by locating one vent at the bottom and one at the top of each space.

The best time to vapor-proof a building is during its construction. After a building is completed, ventilation of the occupied space is the most easily applied of the three basic control measures. Paint that is chosen for its low vapor permeance can be applied as a barrier on the interior with good results, care being taken that all areas, including parts of partitions and ceilings which offer an indirect vapor path to the cold wall, are covered. Ventilation of the wall cavity is effective in certain cases, especially to supplement the foregoing measures. When such venting is required, each cavity space isolated by framing should be separately vented, with an inlet and outlet judiciously placed, to accomplish proper air change.

VISIBLE CONDENSATION

Visible condensation usually occurs on glass but may occur on any surface whose temperature is below the dew point of the interior air. Conditions under which condensation will occur are shown in Fig. 5. To prevent surface condensation, increase the temperature of the surface or reduce the relative humidity of the air, or both. The inside surface temperature of glass may be increased by the use of double glass or by passing a current of warm air across it. The inside surface temperature of other material may be increased by the use of insulation. The relative humidity of the inside air may be lowered by ventilation (exhaust fans in kitchens, baths, laundries, etc.) or by reducing the output of humidifiers, or both.

Visible condensation may also occur in summer. It is often seen on basement concrete walls and floors that are cooled by the earth and on exposed cold-water pipes. Being massive, they tend to hold a constant temperature from day to day while the weather dew-point temperature rises. As an operating problem, the solution may be to reduce ventilation at times of high weather dew point, to warm the surfaces, or to dehumidify the space. A practical and fully

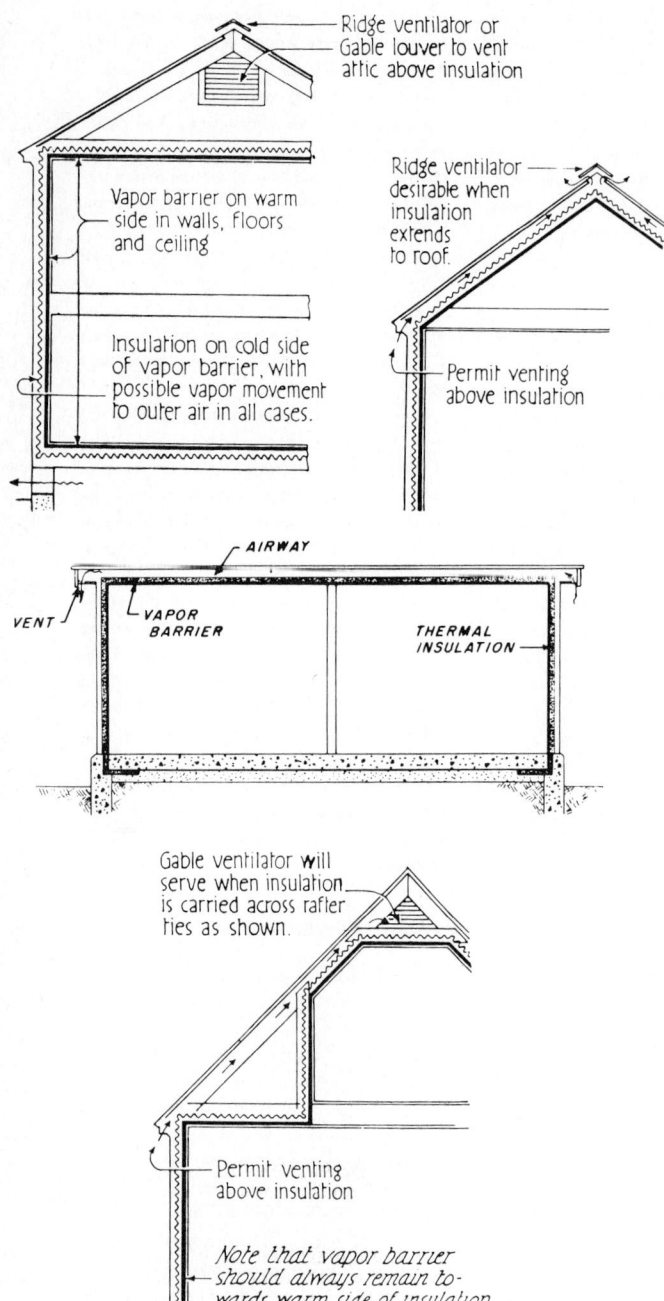

Fig. 4. Methods of ventilating roofs

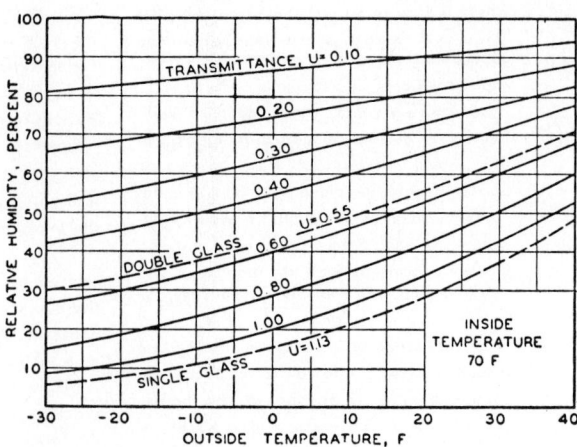

Fig. 5 Relative humidity at which visible condensation will appear on inside surface

Courtesy ASHRAE Handbook of Fundamentals, *1977*

effective technique for such control has, however, not been developed. Usually, subsurface dwellings designed for occupancy should be dehumidified.

A similar situation is seen in dwellings with concrete floor slabs laid on the ground, where such slabs are not a part of the heating system. In a northern climate where high dew-point temperatures occur in summer, condensation or very high relative humidity may damage rugs, which are themselves contributors to the trouble since they reduce the rise of floor slab temperature.

Faster warming is accomplished by the removal of the rugs and abundant ventilation at proper times. Suitable insulation below the slab, especially well-drained gravel, will help somewhat. A top surface cover of insulating value that is unaffected by water on its lower side would be desirable in the less favorable northern climates.

Condensation in cooled building: When the interior of a building is cooled, the vapor barrier should theoretically be located near the outer (warm) side of the structure. In the case of air-conditioned buildings, this is not necessary since the interior temperature is very rarely below the dew point of the outside air. In the case of cold storage buildings, however, the conditions are severe and a vapor barrier with a permeance of not more than 0.1 perm should be installed near the outside surface.

HUD REQUIREMENTS*

Vapor barriers: Test data indicating vapor transmission rate determined in accordance with ASTM dry-cup method may be required.

Walls: Vapor transmission rate not exceeding 1 perm; locate near warm side; required when *U*-value of wall is less than 0.25 or when siding, paper, and sheathing, or other materials or combination of materials on the cold side of the wall, have a combined vapor transmission rate of less than 5 perms.

Ceilings: Vapor transmission rate not exceeding 1 perm; locate near warm side.

Roof decks (no ceiling): Permeance not more than ½ perm; locate near warm side; seal at sides and ends; required where the outside design temperature is 10° or less.

Floors: Comply with ASTM E154 and E96; maximum permeance under concrete slabs ½ perm; maximum permeance for ground cover in crawl spaces 1 perm.

Sheathing paper: Comply with Federal Specification UUB-790 Grade D or ASTM D 226; permeance not less than 5 perms.

* *Minimum Property Standards for One and Two Family Dwellings, U.S. Department of Housing and Urban Development, 1973, Revised 1978.*

VENTILATION

Crawl spaces: Provide at least 4 vents, one near each corner, having an aggregate net area of not less than $\frac{1}{150}$ of the ground area, or install vapor barrier ground cover as specified above and provide 2 vents having an aggregate net area of $\frac{1}{1500}$ of the ground area. When used as a *plenum,* vapor barrier and insulation must have a flame spread rating of less than 200, and 2 vents with tight closures operated from outside must be provided.

Attics and spaces between ceiling and roof: Provide cross ventilation for each space, protected against entrance of rain and snow; total net area of vents should be not less than $\frac{1}{150}$th of ceiling area, except that it may be $\frac{1}{300}$th if a vapor barrier is provided in the ceiling or if 50 per cent of the required vent area is located 3 ft or more above eave vents which make up the remainder of the required vent area.

Screening: All required vents should be covered with $\frac{1}{8}$-in. mesh screen fabric: metallic screening must comply with Commercial Standard CS138; plastic-coated fibrous glass screening must comply with Federal Specification L-S-137.

HEATING AND COOLING OF HOUSES—1

System selection

By WILLIAM J. McGUINNESS, *McGuinness and Duncan, Consulting Engineers*
REVISED 1979 by August L. Hesselschwerdt, Jr., *Professor of Mechanical Engineering, Massachusetts Institute of Technology*

The heating of houses can be accomplished by systems using

1. Air
2. Water
3. Electricity

If cooling is desired, there is no choice and an air system must be used because only an air system can provide the simultaneous control over temperature, humidity, air motion, and air purity.

Air systems

Air systems usually consist of a heating unit (combustion equipment, heat exchanger, fan, and filter), supply and return ductwork, supply and return grilles. If cooling is desired, a direct expansion evaporator is placed in the airstream and is connected to a condensing unit. The latter may, if desired, be remotely located. When humidity control is desired, a humidifier can be installed in the return duct before the heat exchanger.

While air has the lowest carrying capacity in Btu per cubic foot circulated of all the fluids available, it does have the advantages of possible cooling and dehumidification, humidification, controlled ventilation, air cleaning, and the use of outdoor air.

Water systems

Water has the highest carrying capacity in Btu per cubic foot air circulated, and this results in minimal pipe sizes for the system. The minimal pipe sizes and quietness, together with uniformity of temperature in forced water systems, are the primary advantages of this system. The only variable which can be controlled by this system is temperature; and if summer cooling is desired, either window units or a separate system must be installed.

Past practice has been to use hot water from the heater in a heat transfer operation to produce domestic hot water. As long as the cost of fuel was low, this inefficient method (during summer operation) of producing domestic hot water was acceptable. Now, as an energy conservation measure, this type of operation is being abandoned in favor of the more efficient and economical methods of producing domestic hot water.

Electric systems

Perhaps the greatest advantage of electric resistance heating (baseboards, etc.) is the low cost of its installation. Well-designed warm-air and hot-water heating systems are often comparable to each other in installation cost, but both are more expensive to install than electric resistance designs. Another asset of electric heating is that every room can be a separately controlled zone; a thermostat at each wall switch can be set to control the temperature in that room.

Like hot-water heating, electric resistance units are not suitable for controlling air circulation, humidity, cleanliness, or freshness, and cooling must be provided separately.

CHOICE AND COST OF FUELS

There are six basic energy sources that can power a heating system:

1. Wood
2. Coal
3. Gas
4. Oil
5. Electricity
6. Solar

The selection of a particular energy source involves the evaluation of many variables, some of which involve direct dollar cost and others which have intangible values, such as the dollar value of space. The first step in making a selection would be to compare two energy sources, or fuels, on a cost per British thermal unit. For example, comparing fuel oil and electricity:

Oil @ 60¢/gallon—combustion
efficiency @ 65%—137,000 Btu per gallon

$$\text{Btu/penny} = \frac{137,000 \times 0.65}{60} = 1484$$

Power @ 6¢/kWh—100% efficiency—
3413 Btu/kW

$$\text{Btu/penny} = \frac{3413 \times 1}{6} = 569$$

This simple exercise demonstrates how easy it is to make a comparison between two or more energy sources and in this case it shows that oil delivers almost three times as much energy per penny as electricity, when the latter is used in resistance heating. No matter what the fuel, or application, the value for Btu/penny can always be established.

Wood

The past few years have seen a remarkable resurgence in the use of wood for house heating and many of the new house designs are incorporating wood-burning equipment as a supplement to the normal heating equipment. Wood has the disadvantages of being dirty and requiring a large storage area and, in urban areas, it is exorbitantly expensive. In addition, seasoned hardwoods must be burned if any semblance of efficiency is to be experienced.

Coal

Coal is another fuel which, under the right circumstances, could show a definite increase in favor. Automatic coal-burning equipment is available for the residential application and installations using this equipment perform well. A high Btu/penny does

much to negate the disadvantages of storage requirements, dirt, and refuse problems. An almost inexhaustible supply of coal exists, and the main problem holding back the resurgence of coal concerns the distribution and delivery of the coal.

Gas

Gas, after its Btu/penny has been established, has some decided intangible advantages. It requires no storage space thereby releasing about 40 ft² of floor area upon which it is difficult to place a dollar value. Gas burns more quietly than oil; but when a complete gas-fired, warm-air system is compared to an oil-fired, warm-air system, there is little difference in the noise level. Gas is definitely cleaner than other fuels, but the dollar value of this advantage is hard to establish.

Oil

Oil, in many areas of the United States, is the preferred fuel and this preference is based almost entirely on cost. Oil, as previously noted, has a high Btu/penny, but the value quoted is much less than before the oil embargo. At that time, the value was 5565 Btu/penny and this high figure overcame the disadvantages of storage space requirements, delivery problems, dirt, and maintenance problems.

Electricity

Electric resistance heating has formidable advantages and equally formidable disadvantages. It is the quietest and cleanest of all the systems and presents no storage problems. This system eliminates the need for a heating unit (boiler or furnace), a chimney, and massive ducts or pipes. The elimination of these items results in a great reduction in installation cost, and when one thermostat is used per room the system presents the ultimate in control and possible economy of operation.

The major disadvantage of electric resistance heating is operating cost. Except in areas of what might be called government subsidy, the cost per Btu, of useful heating, does not justify the installation of such a system. In addition, all of the disadvantages of a non-air system are applicable to resistance heating. It should be noted that the use of electric power in a heat-pump system is an entirely different situation.

Solar

The use of solar energy for space heating has been proved to be perfectly feasible, but in most cases cannot be economically justified even at the present fuel oil prices which have seen a 300 percent rise in 5 years. Its use as an energy source for domestic hot water has been relatively successful.

A solar energy system consists of a collector, storage system, energy transport system from collector to storage, an energy disseminator, an energy transport system from storage to disseminator, and all the necessary controls to operate the entire system. In addition, an auxiliary heating system must be available to cover periods of low collection when the energy in the storage system is at too low a thermal level to be of value. Figure 1 shows, in diagrammatic form, a simple solar heating system.

There is much controversy as to what constitutes the most desirable storage medium, the size of the storage system, the optimum energy transport systems, and the proper size of the auxiliary heating system.

From the foregoing, it can be seen that the use of solar energy for space heating involves extreme complications and should not be attempted without adequate engineering assistance.

SYSTEM DESIGN

Following a decision about system category and fuel preference, there are options within each category. In the use of air, the type and location of the furnace are of prime importance. The distribution system can be one of many types, including a fully ducted installation, sub-slab perimeter duct, a trunk duct system in slab, etc. Several choices are offered in hot-water heating. Piping of the series-loop type or one-pipe circuits with special diverting fittings are possibilities. Terminal heating units can be convectors in cabinets or baseboard heaters. Electric resistance heating can utilize recessed wall units, electric baseboards, or radiant ceilings.

In the design of residential installations, the services of a consulting engineer are not always available. Designs can be made by the architect or sometimes by the contractor who will make the installation. It is obviously impossible, in this brief treatment of the subject, to acquaint the designer with every possible choice of heating/cooling method or to supply full design data and an inventory of components. Rather, the essence of system selections is suggested and a few design examples are given, together with some of the usual supporting data. The types chosen are those most common in modern practice.

HEATING/COOLING BY AIR

Heating plant

Furnace types are shown in Fig. 2. Oil and gas firing are indicated at random because any of the models shown is obtainable adapted to either selected fuel. Electric central elements in the furnace may also supplant either fossil fuel for the heating phase of all-electric heating/cooling. The lowboy, Fig. 2(b), is a traditional model that developed when basement headroom was limited and ductwork bulky. Now the up-flow, type (a), is often preferred. Its use if shown in Example 1. For subslab perimeter heating, the down-flow model, (c), sits on the opening of the subfloor masonry plenum or raised on top of the evaporator (cooling)

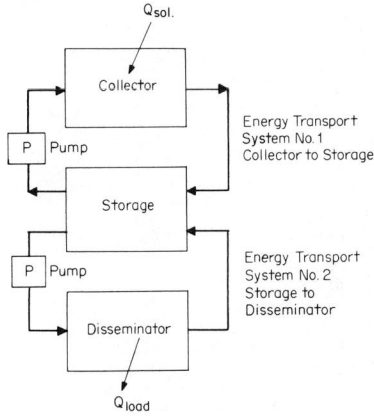

Fig. 1. Diagram of solar heating system

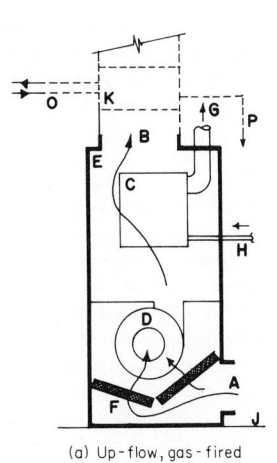

(a) Up-flow, gas-fired

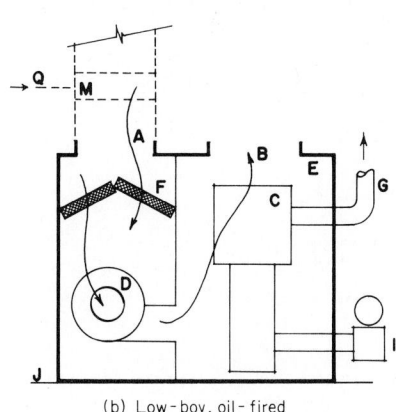

(b) Low-boy, oil-fired

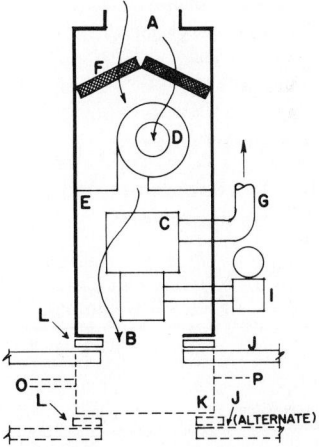

(c) Down flow, oil-fired

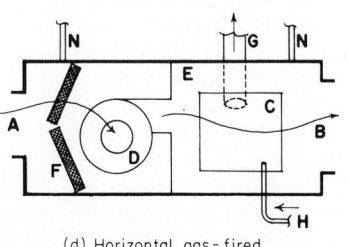

(d) Horizontal, gas-fired

A	Return air	
B	Supply air	
C	Heat exchanger	
D	Blower	
E	Bonnet	
F	Filter	
G	Flue	
H	Gas supply	
I	Oil burner	

J	Floor
K	Cooling unit, if used
L	Insulation pad
M	Humidifier, if used
N	Hangers
O	Refrigerant lines
P	Condensate drain
Q	Water connection

Fig. 2. Functional diagrams, typical warm air furnaces

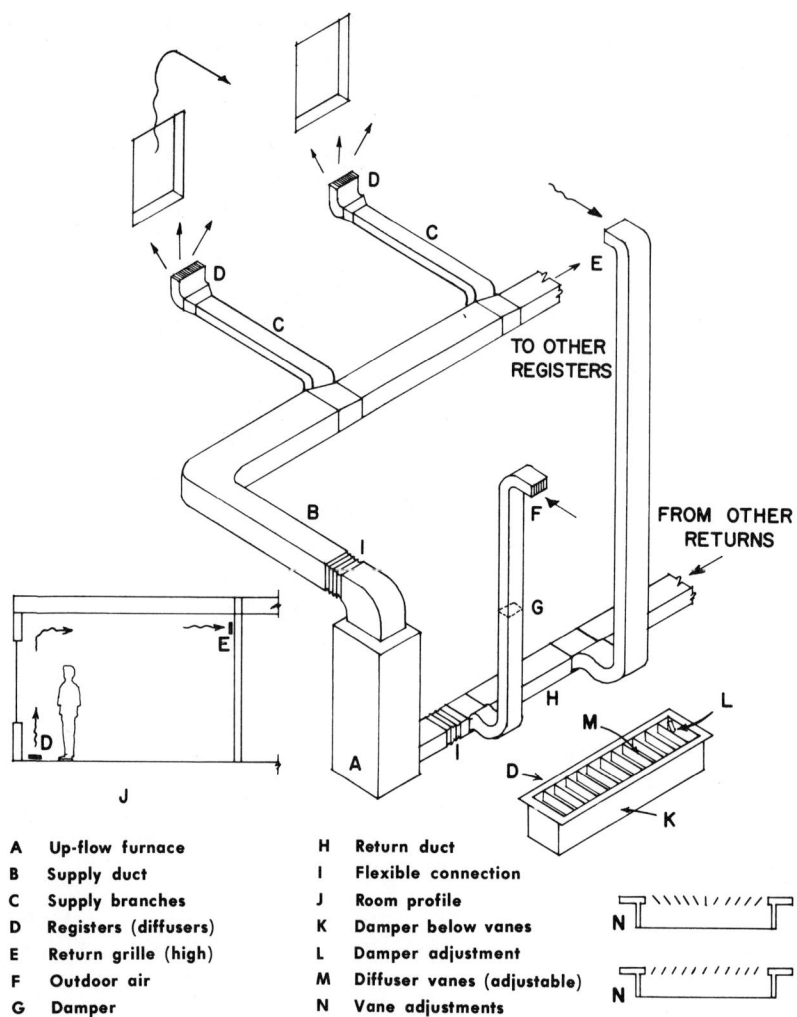

Fig. 3. Ducted system

A	Up-flow furnace	H	Return duct
B	Supply duct	I	Flexible connection
C	Supply branches	J	Room profile
D	Registers (diffusers)	K	Damper below vanes
E	Return grille (high)	L	Damper adjustment
F	Outdoor air	M	Diffuser vanes (adjustable)
G	Damper	N	Vane adjustments

Table 1.   Recommended thickness for duct materials*

Copyright by the American Society of Heating, Refrigerating and Air Conditioning Engineers, Inc. Reprinted by permission from ASHRAE Guide and Data Book, Systems, 1970.

Diameter, in.	Minimum thickness		Minimum weight of tin plate
	Galv. iron, U.S. gage	Aluminum, B&S gage	
Round ducts			
Less than 14	30	26	IX (135 lb)
14 or more	28	24	IX (135 lb)
Rectangular ducts enclosed in partitions			
14 or less	30	26	IX (135 lb)
Over 14	28	24	IX (135 lb)
Rectangular ducts not enclosed in partitions			
Less than 14	28	24	—
14 or more	26	23	—

The table is in accordance with Standard 90B of the National Board of Fire Underwriters. Industry practice is to use heavier gage metals where maximum duct widths exceed 24 in. (See also NBFU No. 90A).

coils which fit between it and the plenum. The horizontal "stowaway," type *(d)*, can down-feed from attic, up-feed from crawl space, or be tucked away in an accessible furred space.

Central plant components

The old "warm air" furnace has grown into a linear series of elements that begin to comprise an assembly that resembles the central station unit in large buildings. For full heating/cooling service, the return air (plus an addition of outdoor fresh air) will pass through:

1. Flexible return duct connection
2. Humidifier
3. Filters
4. Blower
5. Heat exchanger
6. Cooling coil
7. Flexible supply duct connection

Manufacturers are supplying prefabricated adjunct cabinets to house some of the optional components among the foregoing. Connections to the assembly can include:

1. Gas or oil feed
2. Electricity for central electric heat (if chosen)
3. Electricity for blower and for condensing unit
4. Refrigerant tubing
5. Water to the humidifier
6. Condensate drip, cooling coils to open drain

Access to all parts is highly essential. Periodic cleaning or replacement of filters is important not only for cleanliness but to restore air flow that has been partially impeded by dust.

Cooling plant

The most common method of cooling is to install a split system of refrigeration in which the noisy motor-driven compressor and fan-cooled condenser unit are placed outdoors on a concrete pad. The power of this heat-disposal unit also overcomes friction in the refrigerant tubing. This is often a factor that limits the distance from compressor to cooling coil to about 60 ft.

Ducts

These can be galvanized iron, aluminum, or fiber glass. If metal is used, suitable gages may be chosen from Table 1. Ducts may be round, square, or rectangular. Excessive width-to-depth ratios should be avoided. They cause increased friction. Turns should be of generous radius to minimize friction. Joints must be tight and metal surfaces rigid to prevent rattling. Metal ducts passing through unconditioned space should be covered with 1 to 2 in. of insulation. If such ducts carry cool air through uncooled space, a vapor barrier must be used on the exterior surface. Metal ducts in the vicinity of blowers are sometimes lined with acoustic material to reduce transmission of fan noise. The design size sets the dimensions of the *inside* of the lining. Fiber-glass ducts are effective for both thermal insulation and sound reduction. They are growing in popularity.

Registers and grilles

All supply diffusers should have vanes adjustable by wrench to give the air a preferred direction. Adjustable dampers housed in the diffuser body are also essential, though dampers in branch ducts are still used. Return grilles need no directional air control. When more than one return air pickup position is called for, some designers feel that dampers at the grilles or in the branch ducts are an aid in system balancing.

Air flow in conditioned space

For unusual circumstances the reader is referred to the many studies of air motion as affected by register and grille placement. For the average heating/cooling installation, the register and grille placement of Fig. 3 is quiet satisfactory and very often chosen. Criteria that apply to this or any other successful arrangement are as follows:

1. Delivered air must not blow on *people*.

2. Continuous air circulation has minimized many of the earlier considerations of stratification and the effects of gravity.

3. During the heating cycle, the high return is preferable to a low return that would cause discomfort to occupants sitting in the path of cool return air.

Duct routing

This phase of the design is a subject for mutual agreement between the architect, the engineer, and the installing contractor. The 3x14-in. supply risers that were commonly used in stud spaces are no longer very practical. Now that supply registers are located at the perimeter, furring of some vertical and horizontal ducts will usually be required. The old flat riser is distinctly unsuitable in an exterior wall that needs to provide *all* its 3½ in. space for insulation. One solution for second-story perimeter registers in the floor is to run branches out between the second-floor joists, with an elbow up to the register. This is only one of the many space situations that must be dealt with.

Controls

Continuous air circulation at all times and in all seasons is now much favored. During this air flow, the heating cuts in when demanded by the thermostat, as does the operation of the cooling plant. A control in

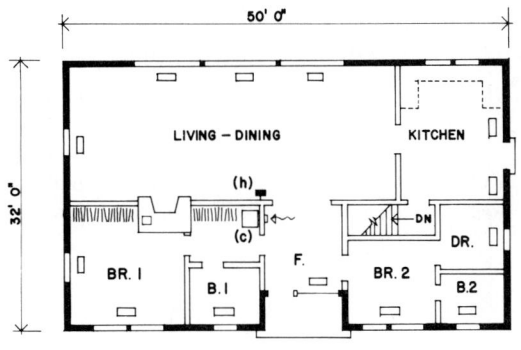

FIRST FLOOR

	Heat loss, MBh*	Total Heat gain, MBh* †
Liv/Din.	12.0	9.5
K.	7.0	5.5
B.R. 1	6.3	5.0
B.R. 2	4.9	3.8
Foyer	6.0	4.7
Dress.	2.4	1.9
B. 1	2.7	2.1
B. 2	2.9	2.3
Basement	3.0	2.4
	45.2	37.2

*MBh = 1,000 Btuh
†Total heat gain includes both sensible and latent gain.

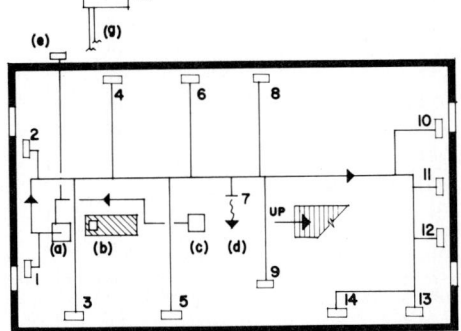

BASEMENT

(a) **Up-flow furnace with cooling coil**
(b) **Chimney**
(c) **Return duct from high register**
(d) **Air to basement**
(e) **Fresh (outside) air**
(f) **Outdoor remote compressor/condenser**
(g) **Refrigerant lines**
(h) **Thermostat**

Fig. 4. Example 1. Ducted warm air system with central cooling in a region of low daily temperature range

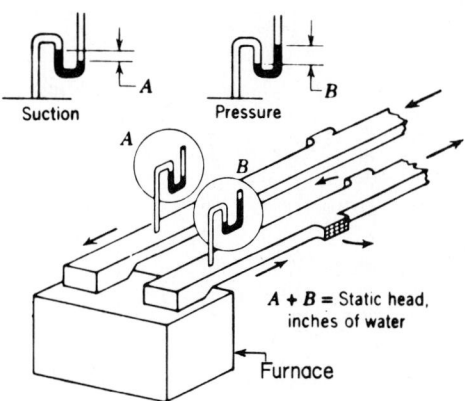

A + B = Static head, inches of water

Fig. 5. The static head is the pressure in inches of water available to overcome friction in the entire system

Reprinted with permission from McGuinness and Stein, Mechanical and Electrical Equipment for Buildings, 5th ed. *Copyright 1970 by John Wiley & Sons, Inc.*

the bonnet of the furnace assures delivery of warm air at temperatures suitable for the rooms. They will be a little lower at the register than at the bonnet, which is usually about 140°F. Recent improvements in furnace design afford two rates of air flow, one for heating and a higher one for cooling. By means of a relay and the utilization of two selected positions of the four provided in modern furnaces, the two speeds are achieved. The switch from heating air rate to cooling air rate is triggered by the thermostat when it is changed to a setting for cooling.

Table 2. Example 1: cfm for cooling—free area of diffusers and diffuser selection for 600 ft per min air speed at face of diffuser

1	2	3	4	5	6	7
Diffuser, no.	Duct length, bonnet to diffuser, ft	cfm per MBh	MBh†	cfm per run	Diffuser free area, sq in.	Diffuser choice, in.
1	10	26	2.5	65	16	2¼ × 10
2	10	26	2.4	62	15	2¼ × 10
3	30	28	2.4	68	16	2¼ × 10
4	26	28	2.4	68	16	2¼ × 10
5	40	29	2.1	61	15	2¼ × 10
6	34	29	2.4	70	17	2¼ × 10
7	32	28	2.4	67	16	2¼ × 10
8	42	29	2.4	70	17	2¼ × 10
9	46	30	4.7	140	34	4 × 10
10	54	31	2.7	84	20	2¼ × 12
11	55	31	2.8	87	21	2¼ × 12
12	63	32	1.9	59	14	2¼ × 10
13	66	32	2.3	71	17	2¼ × 10
14	73	34	3.8	130	31	4 × 10
Totals			37.2	1,102		
Refer to: Fig. 3	Fig. 3	Table 3, low range*	Fig. 3	Col 3 × col 4	cfm × 144 / 600	Table 4

*Indicates a small variation between day and night outdoor temperatures.
†Indicates thousands of Btu per hr.

Table 3. CFM per 1,000 Btuh (MBh) for total heat gain*

Copyright by the American Society of Heating, Refrigerating and Air Conditioning Engineers, Inc. Reprinted by permission from ASHRAE Guide and Data Book, Systems, 1970.

Duct length, bonnet to reg.	Daily temperature range†		
	Low	Medium	High
0	25	30	35
5	25	30	36
10	26	31	36
15	27	32	37
20	27	32	38
25	28	33	39
30	28	34	39
35	29	34	40
40	29	35	41
45	30	36	42
50	31	36	43
55	31	37	43
60	32	38	44
65	32	39	45
70	33	40	46
75	34	40	47
80	34	41	48
85	35	42	49
90	36	43	50
95	37	44	51
100	37	45	52

Calculated from Chapter 28 of the 1967 Handbook of Fundamentals. The values in this table are based on total heat gain. If the distribution system is to be based on sensible load only, multiply these values by 1.3.
†Based on: Low = 300 CFM per ton
  Medium = 360 CFM per ton
  High = 420 CFM per ton

Table 4. Approximate free area per diffuser*

Nominal face dimensions of diffuser, in.	Free area, sq in.
2¼ × 10	19
2¼ × 12	21
2¼ × 14	24
4 × 10	32
4 × 12	39
4 × 14	46
6 × 10	52

Consult manufacturer for available units and dimensions.

Example 1: Design a ducted heating/cooling system for the house in Fig. 4 based on schematic method of Fig. 3.

1. *Establish heat losses and gains:* These have already been calculated, based on data in other sections of this book, and are listed in Fig. 4.

2. *Select furnace:* For heating, the bonnet capacity can be a little larger than the design demand of the house. An up-flow furnace is chosen with an input of 82,000 Btuh and a bonnet output of 65,600 Btuh, which provides a margin above the 45,200 demand. The air flow (furnace blower rating) will be about 600 cfm for heating and a greater flow (to be calculated) for cooling. The furnace is adaptable to receive cooling coils and can develop a static pressure of 0.30 in. of water (see Fig. 5) external to the furnace with its filter in place. Bonnet temperature will be about 140°F.

3. *Select cooling unit:* Cooling units for *residential* use should be slightly undersized. Together with continuous circulation of air, the undersized unit, operating nearly continuously, will produce radiantly cool room surfaces and prevent the buildup of humidity. A 3-ton (36,000 Btuh) unit is chosen as adequate for the calculated 37,200 Btuh.

4. *Location of supply and return outlets:* The words "supply outlet," "register," and "diffuser" are usually considered to have the same connotation. Similarly, "return outlet" and "grille" are synonymous. It is usual to allow a minimum of one supply outlet for each 8,000 Btu of heat loss, but there must be at least one under each window. Thus 45,200/8,000-6, but 14 are preferred because of the window distribution. For cooling, a maximum of one for each 4,000 Btu is suggested unless the relation to windows predominates, which it does in this case (14 preferred to 9).

5. *Duct system layout:* Figure 4 (basement) shows the layout chosen. The supply

duct includes a branch to serve the basement, and a fresh-air branch joins the return just ahead of the furnace. This branch is dampered to control the addition of outdoor air. A single high return is used. In large houses, a return duct system with a return outlet in each room is preferred; but for this small home, a single central grille suffices provided the room doors are undercut by one or more inches at the bottom.

6. *Cubic feet per minute per run for cooling and calculation of register face areas (register selection, Table 2):* Since the total cfm for cooling usually exceeds that required for heating, it is calculated for use in the design of ducts and for the selection of registers. When, in winter, the thermostat switches the blower power to a lower rate, the air speed in ducts is lower, as is also the speed at faces of registers. Even when cooling is not contemplated, most warm-air heating systems have ducts and registers that are large enough to accommodate the possible later addition of cooling.

Duct length from bonnet to register together with data in Tables 3 and 4 are used to establish the cfm per run, the total cfm, the free area of register based on an air speed of 600 ft/min, and the register selection.

7. *Heating cfm:* When the ducts and registers are sized for cooling, in this case 1,102 cfm, the duct speed and register speed will be lower in winter based on the winter flow rate of 600 cfm. The register speed will be about 600 ft per min $\times$ 600/1,102 = 327 ft. per min. The speed of 600 or more is essential for cooling but not for heating as long as the registers are placed below windows. So the winter speed of 327 is acceptable, as is any speed above the minimum of 250 cfm.

8. *Pressure drop in the duct system:* The furnace selected can develop a static pressure of 0.30 in. of water (see Fig. 5) outside the furnace and its filters. This available pressure is reduced by the resistance in the cooling coil and at the register. The resistance of these items is about 0.15 and 0.03, respectively, for these conditions, a total of 0.18 in Example 1. The balance, 0.30 − 0.18 = 0.12 in., is finally the value that overcomes friction in the supply and return ducts and branches. It is the basis of duct design.

9. *Unit pressure drop and duct sizing:* By judgment, the pressure drop in the supply duct is about three-quarters of the total drop in both supply and return. The total drop in the supply duct would be 0.12 $\times$ 0.75 = 0.09 in. With this total drop and the total equivalent length (TEL) of the longest run, one can enter Table 5 to find the unit drop per 100 ft of duct. Diffuser 14 is 73 ft from the bonnet. The equivalent length due to fittings is 100 ft from bonnet to diffuser. The TEL is 173 ft.

From Table 5 one finds that for 173 ft total equivalent run and a total drop of 0.09 in. the *unit* pressure drop is 0.05 in. per 100 ft. This value is to be used in the sizing of all ducts—supply, return and branches.

Warm-air perimeter heating (Fig. 6)

For relatively small houses with no basements and with one living story on a concrete slab, a perimeter warm-air heating system is very effective. Partially radiant in its output through ducts that warm the slab, it has nevertheless a fast response when heat is called for. As in other air systems, this method most often employs the principle of continuous air circulation— the thermostat operating the fire but not the blower, which is always running. The radial feeder ducts and the perimeter (loop) duct must all be imbedded in dense

Table 5. Loss per 100 ft of duct length

Copyright by the American Society of Heating, Refrigerating and Air Conditioning Engineers, Inc. Reprinted by permission from ASHRAE Guide and Data Book, Systems, 1970.

Equivalent Length of Duct (Ft)	Total Pressure Drop in Duct (In. of Water)																
	0.04	0.05	0.06	0.07	0.08	0.09	0.10	0.11	0.12	0.13	0.14	0.15	0.16	0.17	0.18	0.19	0.20
35–44	0.10	0.13	0.15	0.18	0.20	0.23	0.25	0.28	0.30	0.33	0.35	0.38	0.40	0.43	0.45	0.48	0.50
45–54	0.08	0.10	0.12	0.14	0.16	0.18	0.20	0.22	0.24	0.26	0.28	0.30	0.32	0.34	0.36	0.38	0.40
55–64	0.07	0.08	0.10	0.12	0.13	0.15	0.17	0.18	0.20	0.22	0.23	0.25	0.27	0.28	0.30	0.32	0.33
65–74	0.06	0.07	0.09	0.10	0.11	0.13	0.14	0.16	0.17	0.19	0.20	0.21	0.23	0.24	0.26	0.28	0.29
75–84	0.05	0.06	0.08	0.09	0.10	0.11	0.13	0.14	0.15	0.16	0.18	0.19	0.20	0.21	0.23	0.24	0.25
85–94	0.05	0.06	0.07	0.08	0.09	0.10	0.11	0.12	0.13	0.14	0.16	0.17	0.18	0.19	0.20	0.21	0.22
95–104	0.04	0.05	0.06	0.07	0.08	0.09	0.10	0.11	0.12	0.13	0.14	0.15	0.16	0.17	0.18	0.19	0.20
105–114	0.04	0.05	0.05	0.06	0.07	0.08	0.09	0.10	0.11	0.12	0.13	0.14	0.15	0.15	0.16	0.17	0.18
115–129	0.03	0.04	0.05	0.06	0.07	0.08	0.08	0.09	0.10	0.11	0.12	0.12	0.13	0.14	0.15	0.16	0.17
130–149	0.03	0.04	0.04	0.05	0.06	0.07	0.07	0.08	0.09	0.09	0.10	0.11	0.11	0.12	0.13	0.14	0.14
150–169	0.03	0.03	0.04	0.04	0.05	0.06	0.06	0.07	0.08	0.08	0.09	0.09	0.10	0.11	0.11	0.12	0.13
170–189	0.02	0.03	0.03	0.04	0.04	0.05	0.06	0.06	0.07	0.07	0.08	0.08	0.09	0.09	0.10	0.11	0.11
190–214	0.02	0.03	0.03	0.04	0.04	0.05	0.05	0.06	0.06	0.07	0.07	0.08	0.08	0.09	0.09	0.10	0.10
215–239	0.02	0.02	0.03	0.03	0.04	0.04	0.05	0.05	0.05	0.06	0.06	0.07	0.07	0.08	0.08	0.09	0.09
240–264	0.02	0.02	0.02	0.03	0.03	0.04	0.04	0.04	0.05	0.05	0.06	0.06	0.06	0.07	0.07	0.08	0.08
265–289	0.01	0.02	0.02	0.03	0.03	0.03	0.04	0.04	0.04	0.05	0.05	0.05	0.06	0.06	0.07	0.07	0.07
290–324	0.01	0.02	0.02	0.03	0.03	0.03	0.03	0.04	0.04	0.04	0.05	0.05	0.05	0.06	0.06	0.06	0.07
325–374	0.01	0.02	0.02	0.02	0.02	0.03	0.03	0.03	0.03	0.04	0.04	0.04	0.05	0.05	0.05	0.05	0.06
375–424	0.01	0.01	0.02	0.02	0.02	0.02	0.03	0.03	0.03	0.03	0.04	0.04	0.04	0.04	0.05	0.05	0.05
425–474	0.01	0.01	0.01	0.02	0.02	0.02	0.02	0.03	0.03	0.03	0.03	0.03	0.04	0.04	0.04	0.04	0.05
475–524	0.01	0.01	0.01	0.02	0.02	0.02	0.02	0.02	0.02	0.03	0.03	0.03	0.03	0.03	0.04	0.04	0.04
525–574	0.01	0.01	0.01	0.01	0.02	0.02	0.02	0.02	0.02	0.02	0.03	0.03	0.03	0.03	0.03	0.03	0.04
575–625	0.01	0.01	0.01	0.01	0.01	0.02	0.02	0.02	0.02	0.02	0.02	0.03	0.03	0.03	0.03	0.03	0.03

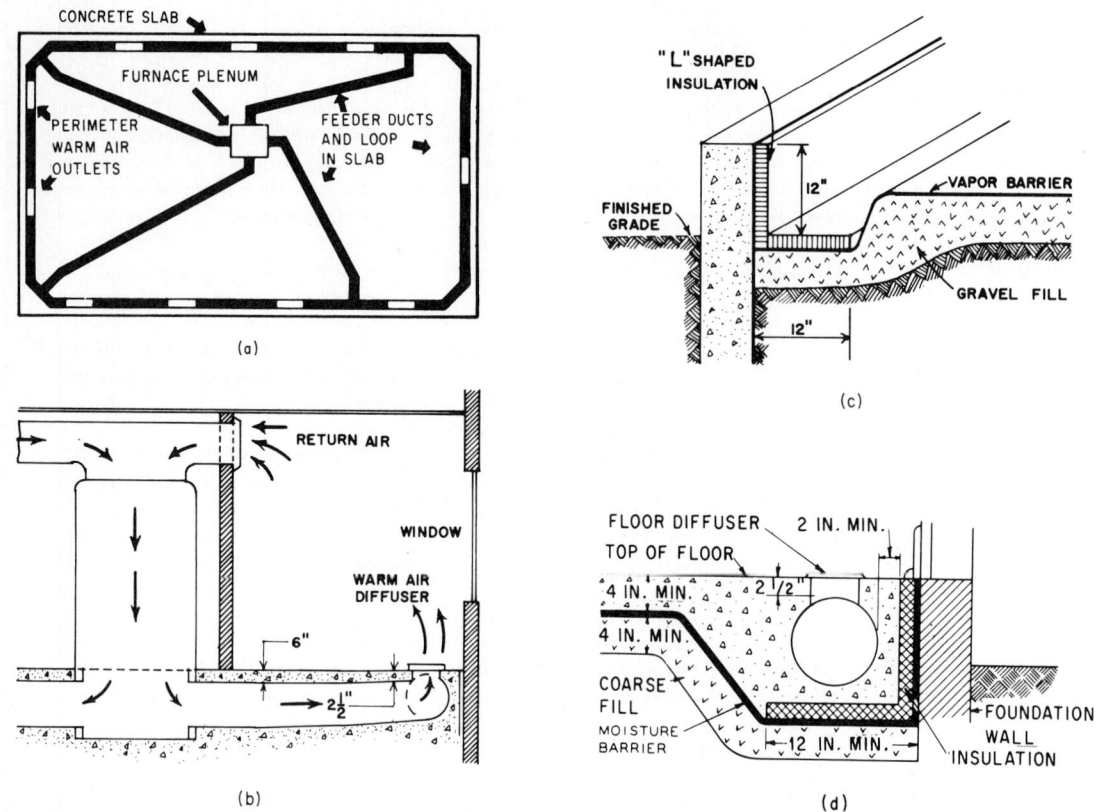

Fig. 6. Perimeter warm air heating with ducts and feeders imbedded in concrete slab

(a) *Schematic plan view showing the principle of the method**

(b) *Schematic cross-section of the system indicating circulation*

(c) *Construction phase showing trough ready to receive perimeter duct and concrete that will surround it*

(d) *Cross-section through complete installation of perimeter duct. Continuous mesh reinforcing not less than 6 x 6-10 gage, 18 in. wide, should be placed in the concrete centered over the duct.**

Copyright by the American Society of Heating, Refrigerating and Air Conditioning Engineers, Inc. Reprinted by permission from ASHRAE Guide and Data Book, Systems, *1970*

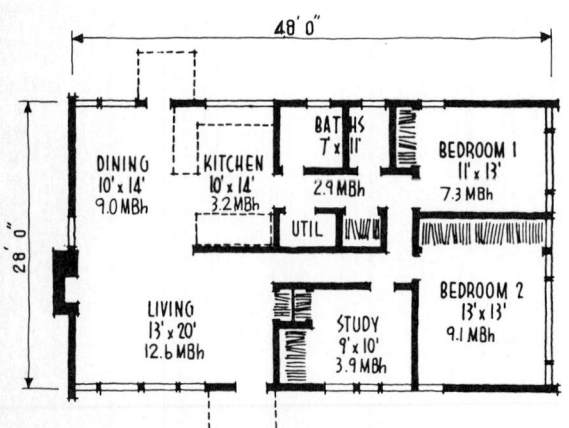

Fig. 7. Example 2. Room use, size, and hourly heat loss

Heat loss, Btuh	
Living	12,600
Dining	9,000
Kitchen	3,200
Baths	2,900
Study	3,900
Bedroom 1	7,300
Bedroom 2	9,100
Total	48,000
	(48 MBh)

Table 6. Diameter of feeders (in inches)

Copyright by the American Society of Heating, Refrigerating and Air Conditioning Engineers, Inc. Reprinted by permission from ASHRAE Guide and Data Book, Systems, *1970.*

	Length of feeder, ft	
Btuh per feeder	0–15	16–30
Up to 7,999	6	6
8,000 to 8,999	6	7
9,000 to 10,999	7	7
11,000 to 11,999	7	8
12,000 to 12,999	7	8
13,000 to 17,000	8	8

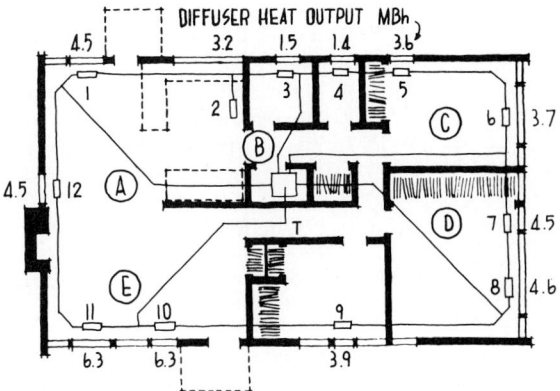

Fig. 8. Example 2. Diffuser and duct layout. For reference, feeders are lettered and diffusers numbered. T = thermostat.

Heat carried by feeders, Mbh

A		B		C		D		E	
No.	MBh	No.	MBh	No.	MBh	No.	MBh	No.	MBh
12	4.5	2	3.2	6	3.7	8	4.6	10	6.3
1	4.5	3	1.5	7	4.5	9	3.9	11	6.3
		4	1.4						
		5	3.6						
	9.0		9.7		8.2		8.5		12.6

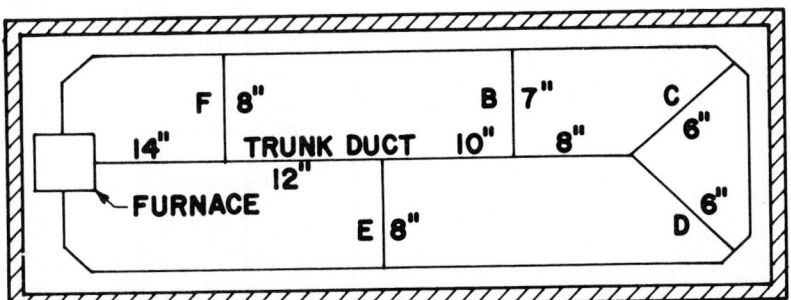

Fig. 9. Round trunk duct system. When the perimeter duct is fed by feeder ducts and a trunk duct, reference is made to design procedures in ASHRAE Guide and Data Book.

Copyright by the American Society of Heating, Refrigerating and Air Conditioning Engineers, Inc. Reprinted by permission from ASHRAE Guide and Data Book, Systems, *1970*

concrete to promote fast heat transmission and also to isolate the duct material from contact with the earth. A vapor barrier and dry, well-drained earth are both important lest the heat be lost downward through fast-conducting wet soil or wet building components. Equally mandatory is a 2-in. thickness of moisture- and vermin-resistant insulation placed as shown in Figs. 6(b) and c. Ducts can be of galvanized steel with

bituminous coating. The slab should have 6 x 6-in. 10 gage welded wire mesh reinforcement.

Perimeter diffusers set below the windows are of the type shown in Fig. 3(d). They are dropped into vertical outlets extending up from the perimeter duct. They are equipped with deflecting vanes for

"spread" and with dampers for air flow regulation.

Limitations for this type of heating system are as follows:

1. Upper limit of heat loss is 100,000 Btuh. For houses with greater loss, two furnaces are recommended. The system then would comprise two zones.

2. The perimeter supplied by one furnace must not exceed 210 ft.

3. The maximum length of any uninsulated feeder duct may not exceed 30 ft.

4. If a trunk duct is required by item 3 above, a different system of design is used. See Fig. 9.

Example 2: Design a perimeter heating system for the house-on-grade shown in Fig. 7.

1. *Calculate heat losses:* As in Example 1, these have already been calculated. They are listed in Fig. 7.

2. *Select furnace:* A down-flow furnace of 82,000 Btuh input and 65,600 Btuh output at the bonnet is chosen. Bonnet temperature is 140°F and a static pressure of 0.20 in. is provided.

3. *Locate perimeter duct, diffusers, and grille (Fig. 8):* The diffusers are placed below glass, about one to each 8,000 Btuh loss (thus not less than six). It is found that twelve are required by the disposition of the glass and the usual need for two diffusers in each of the corner rooms. The re-

Table 7. Example 2: Feeder diameters*

Feeder	Heat delivery Mbh, see Fig. I	Feeder length, ft	Feeder diam, in. (see Table 8)
A	9.0	26	7
B	9.7	11	7
C	8.2	23	7
D	8.5	25	7
E	12.6	23	8

Perimeter duct diameter: 8 in. (always the same as the largest feeder).

Table 8. Example 2: Diffuser free area and selection

Room	Heat output, Mbh (Fig. 7)	Length feeder under room plus ½ length perimeter duct under room, ft	Length of nearest feeder ft	Section in Table 9	Diffusers, free area, sq in.	Diffuser selection, see Table 4	Free area, sq in.
Living room	12.6	14 + 17 = 31	23	C	89	2 @ 4 × 14	92
Dining room	9.0	18 + 12 = 30	26	C	60	2 @ 4 × 10	64
Kitchen	3.0	8 + 7 = 15	11	B	18	1 @ 2¼ × 1	19
Baths	2.9	7 + 6 = 13	11	B	18	2 @ 2¼ × 10	38*
Bedroom 1	7.3	13 + 12 = 25	23	C	45	2 @ 2¼ × 14	48
Bedroom 2	9.1	16 + 13 = 29	25	C	60	2 @ 4 × 10	64
Study	3.9	0 + 5 = 5	25	C	27	1 @ 4 × 10	32

* The smallest available. Area can be reduced by partially closing dampers.

Table 9. Minimum diffuser free area required

Copyright by the American Society of Heating, Refrigerating and Air Conditioning Engineers, Inc. Reprinted by permission from ASHRAE Guide and Data Book, Systems, *1970.*

A.—Use this table if length of feeder which delivers major portion of warm air to room is from 2 to 10 ft.

Heat Loss of Room, Btuh	Lgt. of feeder duct under rm. plus ½ lgt. of perimeter duct under rm., ft						
	0–9	10–19	20–29	30–39	40–49	50–59	60–69
	Total Diffuser Free Area Required for Room, Sq In.						
0 to 3,999	20						
4,000 to 5,999	32	27	23	18			
6,000 to 7,999	43	39	34	29	25	20	
8,000 to 9,999	55	50	45	41	36	32	27
10,000 to 11,999	66	61	57	52	48	43	38
12,000 to 13,999	77	72	68	63	59	54	50
14,000 to 15,999	88	84	79	75	70	66	61
16,000 to 17,999	100	95	91	86	82	77	72
18,000 to 19,999	111	106	102	97	93	88	84
20,000 to 21,999	122	118	113	109	104	100	95
22,000 to 23,999	134	129	125	120	116	111	106
24,000 to 25,999	145	140	136	131	127	122	118

B.—Use this table if length of feeder which delivers major portion of warm air to room is from 10 to 20 ft.

Heat Loss of Room, Btuh	Lgt. of feeder duct under rm. plus ½ lgt. of perimeter duct under rm., ft						
	0–9	10–19	20–29	30–39	40–49	50–59	60–69
	Total Diffuser Free Area Required for Room, Sq In.						
0 to 3,999	23	18	18				
4,000 to 5,999	36	31	26	21	16	16	
6,000 to 7,999	49	44	39	34	29	24	19
8,000 to 9,999	61	56	51	46	41	36	31
10,000 to 11,999	73	68	63	58	53	48	43
12,000 to 13,999	86	81	76	71	66	61	56
14,000 to 15,999	99	94	89	84	79	74	69
16,000 to 17,999	111	106	101	96	91	86	81
18,000 to 19,999	123	118	113	108	103	98	93
20,000 to 21,999	135	130	125	120	115	110	105
22,000 to 23,999	148	143	138	133	128	123	118
24,000 to 25,999	161	156	151	146	141	136	131

C.—Use this table if length of feeder which delivers major portion of warm air to room is from 20 to 30 ft.

Heat Loss of Room, Btuh	Lgt. of feeder duct under rm. plus ½ lgt. of perimeter duct under rm., ft						
	0–9	10–19	20–29	30–39	40–49	50–59	60–69
	Total Diffuser Free Area Required for Room, Sq In.						
0 to 3,999	27	21	21				
4,000 to 5,999	42	36	30	24	18		
6,000 to 7,999	57	51	45	39	33	27	21
8,000 to 9,999	72	66	60	54	48	42	36
10,000 to 11,999	86	80	74	68	62	56	50
12,000 to 13,999	101	95	89	83	77	71	65
14,000 to 15,999	116	110	104	98	92	86	80
16,000 to 17,999	131	125	119	113	107	101	95
18,000 to 19,999	145	139	133	127	121	115	109
20,000 to 21,999	160	154	148	142	136	130	124
22,000 to 23,999	175	169	163	157	151	145	139
24,000 to 25,999	190	184	178	172	166	160	154

turn grille will be in a high position on the hall side of the wall of the utility room.

4. *Locate feeder ducts (Fig. 8):* Divide the total heat loss by 15,000 Btuh, which is the approximate capacity of one feeder. Our heat loss of 48,000 Btuh would suggest four, but one more is added due to some of the following considerations:
   a. Distance between the points where feeders connect to the loop should not exceed 35 ft.
   b. The number of diffusers between adjacent feeder connections to the loop should not exceed three.
   c. Connect all feeders to the loop at an angle of 90 deg. and not closer than 18 in. to any diffuser.
   d. Distance of any diffuser from any feeder should not exceed 15 ft.
   e. If the distance between two adjacent diffusers on the same run of loop exceeds 20 ft, provide another feeder between them.
   f. No diffuser should be located on a feeder duct.
5. *Size feeder and loop ducts (Fig. 8):* The following is a guide to this design:
   a. Identify diffusers by number and feeders by letter.
   b. Assign the heat to be delivered through each diffuser (Fig. 8).
   c. Find the heat supplied through each feeder, assuming that each diffuser is served by the nearest feeder.
   d. Measure and list the length of each feeder.
   e. With the feeder length and its Btuh capacity, select its size from Table 6. The sizes for Example 2 are summarized in Table 7.
   f. The loop (perimeter) duct diameter will be the same as that of the largest feeder. In this example, it is 8 in.
6. *Free area and selection—of diffusers:* In order to use Table 8 add the length of feeder duct under each room and half the length of the perimeter duct under that room. This aggregate length and the Btuh capacity of the feeder are used to enter an appropriate section of Table 9 for the purpose of finding the correct "diffuser free area" for that room. Sections A, B, and C of the table refer to feeders, the total lengths of which do not exceed 10, 20, and 30 ft respectively. This *total* length of the feeder nearest to the subject room determines the section to be used. Table 9 summarizes the diffuser design and selection for Example 2.

HEATING BY HOT WATER

Characteristics

Heating by hot water is frequently an appropriate method in houses. Pipes are small and require little or no pitch. Heating elements, either convectors or baseboard, can be placed below windows or glass or along exterior walls. Adjustments of heat output in each room is always possible, either by dampering the convected air flow at the heating unit or valving off the water flow, depending on the type of installation. Chosen with some extra capacity, the boiler can double as a thermal source for heating domestic hot water, precluding the need for a separate water heater.

Boiler, tubing, and heating units are always completely water-filled. Air must be vented out, especially where it can accumulate at high points. Drains must permit emptying the system at all low points. Temperatures at or above 200° F are possible; the water will not boil when exceeding 212° F because the system is under pressure. By means of an aquastat which has a sensing element in the boiler-water, the fire—gas or oil—goes on whenever necessary to maintain the boiler at maximum design temperature at all times. Thus when the house thermostat calls for heat and turns on the circulating pump, there is minimal waiting time for heat in the rooms.

Heating plant and accessories (Figs. 10 and 11)

In this closed system scheme there is very little loss of water. When, however, it is necessary to add some, it is done automatically whenever the pressure in the system drops below 12 psi. The street pressure in the cold-water main, often about 50 psi, will cause flow into the system. A stabilized air chamber above the water in the compression tank cushions the expansion of the system water with rises in temperature. The dip tube at the boiler keeps air from passing into the tubing and directs it to the tank. Excess air in the tank is exhausted through the tube and out the bottom of the air control fitting. Circulation through the heating system is controlled by the circulating pump and the flow control valve, which closes against gravity flow when the pump stops. Gravity circulation does, however, serve to keep hot water in the domestic hot-water heater, which encloses a coil in which water from the cold-water pipe is heated for use at lavatory and sink hot-water faucets. The pressure relief valve, which operates only in an emergency, must always sense system pressure. There must be no valve between it and the boiler.

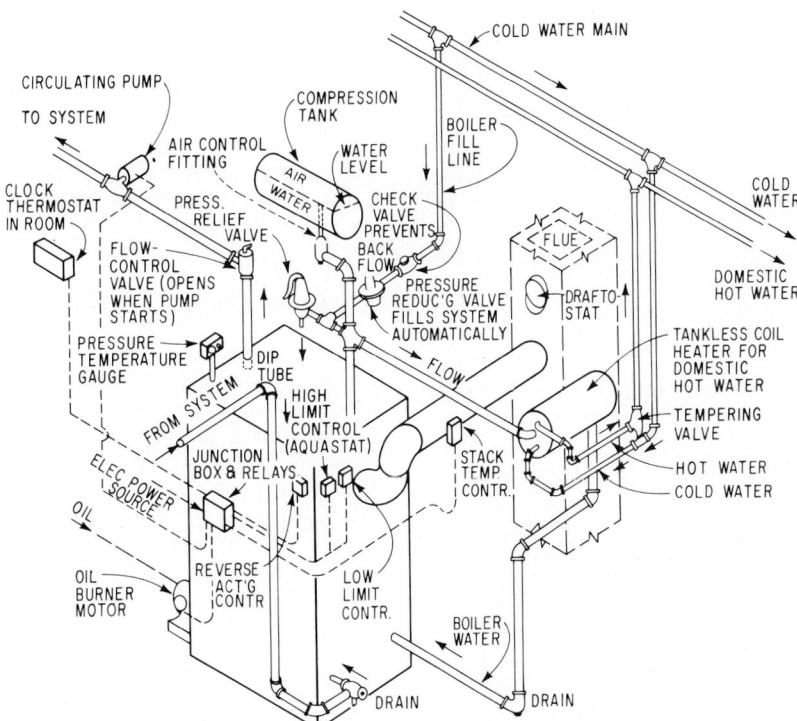

Fig. 10. Typical oil-fired boiler and equipment for one- or two-pipe water systems

Operation

1. When room thermostat calls for heat, oil burner and pump turn on simultaneously
2. If water drops below limiting temperature (160°), reverse-acting control turns off pump until oil burner has missed water temperature
3. Low-limit control turns on oil burner whenever water falls below 160°
4. High-limit control turns off oil burner when water temperature exceeds a high limit (often 200°), thus stabilizing water temperature during capacity operation
5. When room thermostat is satisfied, pump and oil burner turn off
6. Stack temperature control, an emergency control, shuts down burner if it does not ignite promptly
7. Pressure relief valve, an emergency control, opens to relieve any pressure in excess of a set value (often 30 lb. per sq. in.). This valve should be set above boiler, otherwise if it failed it would drain boiler, subjecting boiler to cracking

NOTE: Function of the high limit control and the reverse-acting control are often combined in an "aquastat."

Selection of a piping system (Figs. 12 and 13)

One-pipe systems have become almost universal in residences. When used with convectors (Fig. 11g), runouts are usually employed utilizing special tees (Fig. 11i), to assure flow through the convector. Such an installation is seen in Fig. 12(a). Larger or zoned systems using the same principle are seen in Fig. 12(b) and (c). When *two* special tees are used for upfeed to second floor or downfeed to basement as shown in Fig. 12(c), one should consult manufacturer's recommendations because the venturi element, Fig. 11(i) is positioned differently. When runouts are used for convectors or indeed for baseboard (Fig. 12(d)), there is the advantage of a valve at each heating element. With the advent of baseboard, however, the *series loop* has become very popular (Fig. 12(e) and (f)). It is very satisfactory and saves pipe. Control at the baseboard is by damper *only*, since no valve can be used in this *series* hookup.

A two-pipe system (Fig. 13) has an advantage: Water at a temperature close to that of the boiler is supplied to each heating element directly without the cooling effect that occurs toward the end of a one-pipe circuit where return water from the first-in-line elements lowers the effective temperature of the water. This advantage, how-

Hot water heating

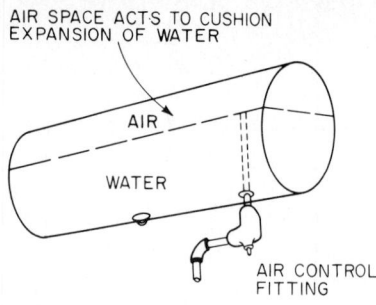

a. COMPRESSION TANK WITH AIR CONTROL FITTING

Minimum size 15 gals. Selected size dependent upon volume of water in system. Consult mfrs. literature. Air fitting exhausts excess air to stabilize air/water ratio in tank.

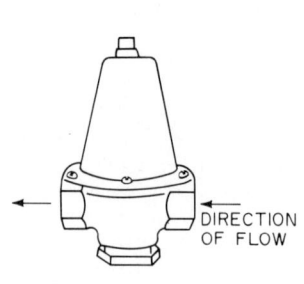

b. PRESSURE REDUCING VALVE

Fill line to boiler; adds water when pressure drops below 12 lb. per sq. in.
Other side connected to city water pressure (40 to 50 lb. per sq. in.; too high for system). Full system is needed; it's easy to forget to add water to boiler. This valve adds it automatically.

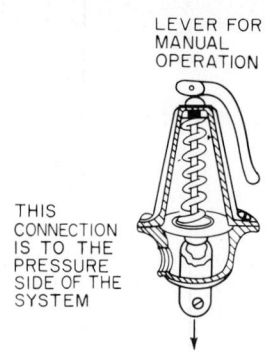

c. PRESSURE RELIEF VALVE

Spring-loaded diaphragm rises when system pressure exceeds 30 lb. per sq. in., permitting water flow through center tube. *Drip.* Valve seldom opens under proper operation. Drip must empty into dry well or sink, *not* sewer. This valve operates to relieve system and prevent bursting of parts.

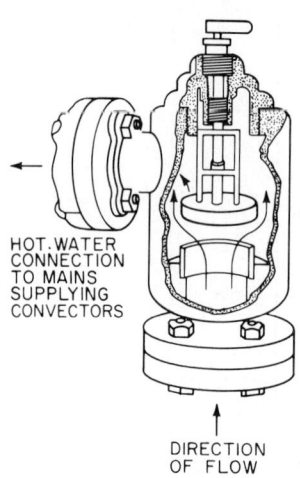

d. FLOW CONTROL VALVE

When circulating pump starts, water flow raises the valve seat. When the pump is not operating, it closes against circulation. This is important in summer when hot water must be retained in boiler (for domestic hot water) but must not flow through convectors.

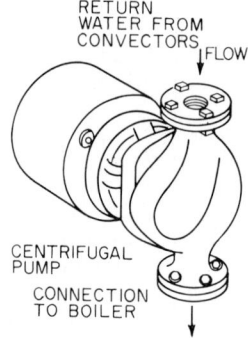

e. CIRCULATING PUMP

Electric motor turns on, forcing water through system, when heat is called for and if water is hot enough (160°). Select pump as directed on following pages.

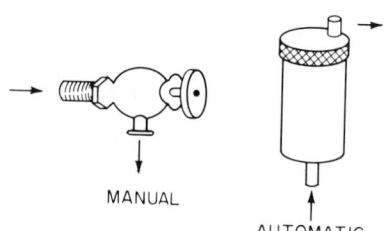

f. AIR VENTS

When manual vent is opened, pressure forces air out. When water starts to flow this vent must be closed. Automatic vents are available at slightly higher cost.

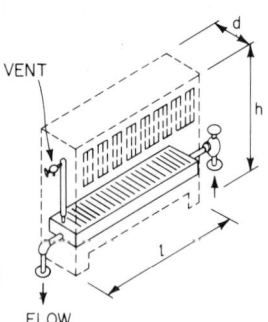

g. CONVECTOR

Air vent must be extended high above convectors to keep air out of the water passages. Dimensions d, h, and t, together with water temperature, fix output ratings. Consult mfr's literature.

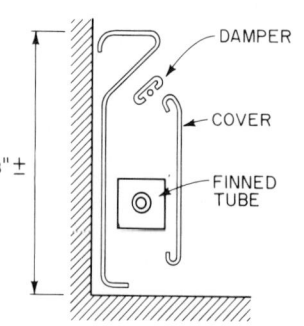

h. BASEBOARD (SECTION)

Damper most essential for heat adjustment in series loop systems

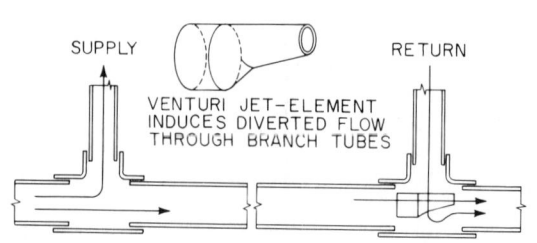

i. SPECIAL RETURN TEE FITTING

Venturi jet-element induces diverted flow through branch tubes

The author and editor wish to acknowledge with thanks the assistance of several manufacturers of heating equipment, and of the Institute of Boiler and Radiator Manufacturers.

Fig. 11. Boiler accessories and system components.

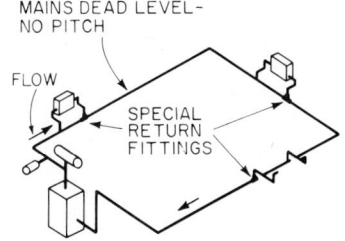

a. ONE-CIRCUIT ONE-PIPE SYSTEM

For larger installations multicircuit systems are preferred (see B)

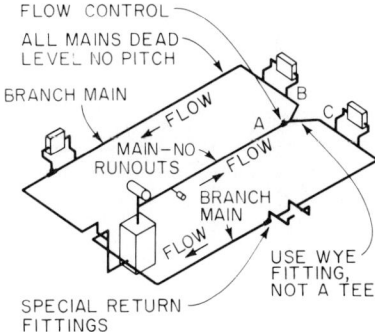

b. MULTI-CIRCUIT ONE-PIPE SYSTEM

Main A is sized to serve entire system; mains B and C are sized to serve respective circuits; same size held through to boiler. This type of system, with sufficient circuits, can serve the largest residence

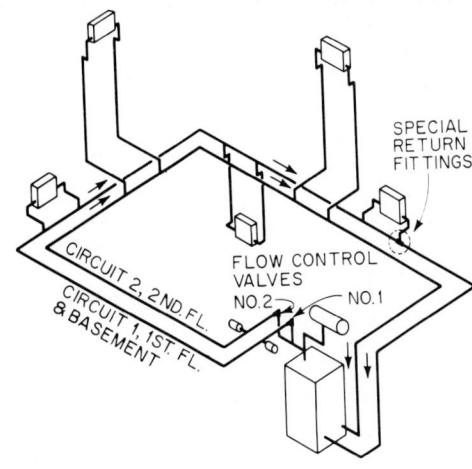

c. ZONED ONE-PIPE SYSTEM

Zoning

An advantage of hot water heating is its adaptability to zoning. When Zone 1 calls for heat, pump No. 1 starts; flow control valve No. 1 opens, permitting flow in circuit 1. Flow control valve No. 2 remains shut preventing circulation in circuit 2. If instead, Zone 2 called for heat, pump and valve No. 2 would operate with flow in circuit 2 and not in circuit 1. Simultaneous action is possible. Separate thermostats operate pumps 1 & 2. Joint use is made of one boiler whose water is kept hot by water temperature controls (aquastat).

Basement and Second Floor Heating

Aside from zoning, sketch also illustrates several uses of special return tees

1. *For 1st floor convectors,* **use of one special return fitting is common & riser size is found in Table 11, Section E. Two fittings are possible, in which case riser size is found in Table 11, Section A, and is smaller for same capacity**

2. *For 2nd & 3rd floor convectors,* **use of two special fittings is common & riser is found in Table 11, Sections B & C. If one fitting is used, larger riser is chosen from Table 11, Sections F & G**

3. *For downfeed risers to basement,* **use of two special fittings is necessary; size of riser is shown in Table 11, Section D**

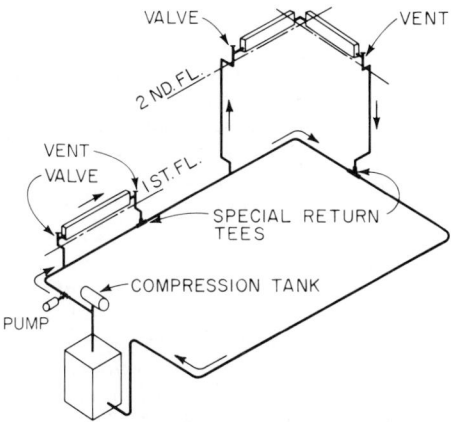

d. ONE PIPE, ONE ZONE, TWO STORY SYSTEM

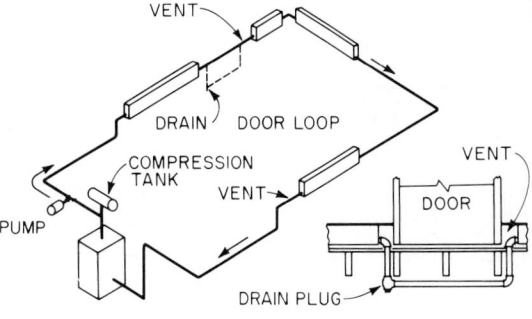

e. SERIES LOOP

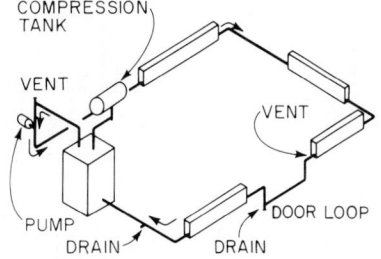

f. SERIES LOOP, DOWN-FEED (NO BASE-MENT)

Fig. 12. One-pipe systems

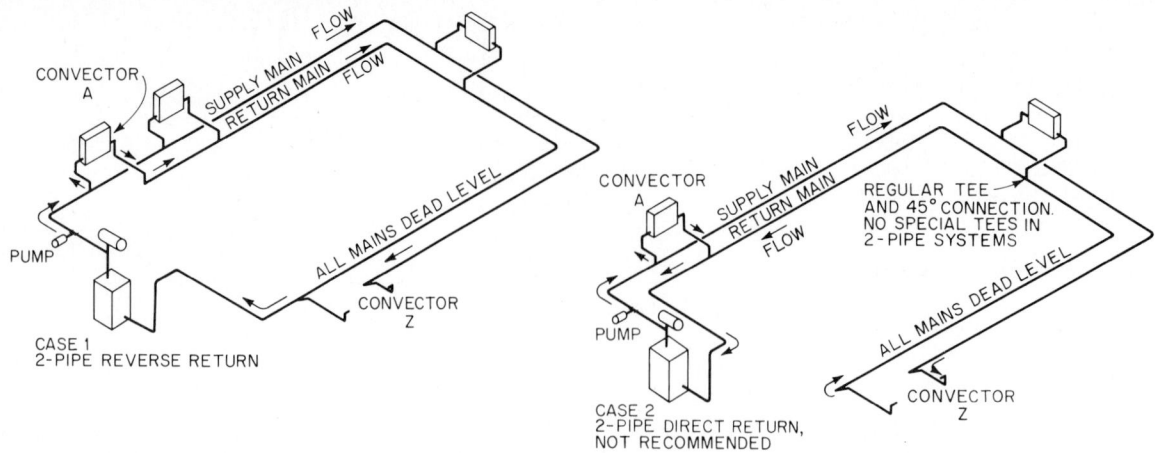

Fig. 13. Two-pipe systems

Of these two systems, the two-pipe reverse return is preferable and is usually chosen. Note (Case 1) that the length of circuit supply and return to A is identical with that to Z, giving equal heating. In Case 2 note how much convector A is favored by comparison with the long travel to and from Z. On a straightaway circuit the piping needed for Case 1 is somewhat greater. It is chosen, however, for its equal circuits through every convector.

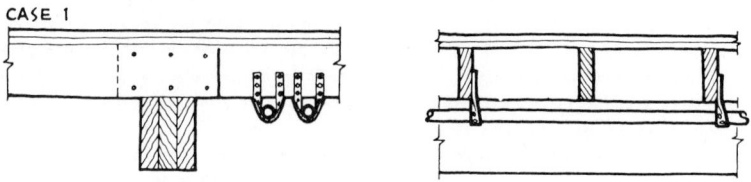

Mains not passing through girders can be supported dead level directly below joists but with slight clearance to prevent noise caused by expansion

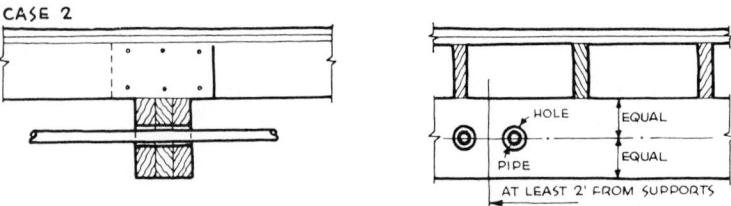

In average installations having mains of about 1" diameter, holes slightly oversize for clearance will provide convenient passage for the pipes without weakening girder, if holes are kept at mid-height and away from supports

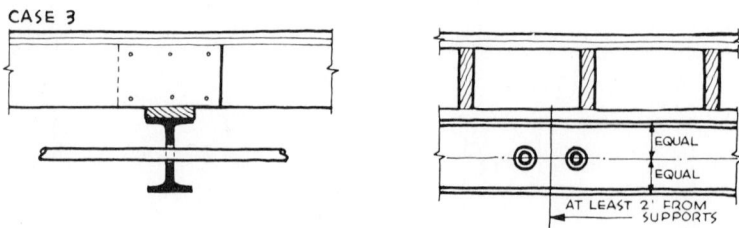

Similar arrangement with steel girder. In Cases 2 and 3 pipes should be supported on hangers, should not rest on bottom of girder-hole, which would result in noise during expansion. All mains and returns in forced systems can be level

Fig. 14. Structural details

ever, is of minimal value in residential systems. It is sometimes employed in large buildings. Prior to the use of pumps for forced circulation, it was employed in the older gravity systems in which temperature drops were great. In modern installations, the drop is not over 20 degrees and, in one-pipe systems, remote convectors or baseboards are essentially as well served as are those adjacent to the boiler.

Piping and construction details (Fig. 14)

Copper tubing and "sweat fittings" have almost entirely replaced the formerly used steel or wrought iron pipe. Slope, once important to enhance gravity flow, is now unnecessary. A slight gradient for drainage may sometimes be used, but actually systems are seldom drained since houses are not often left unoccupied during freezing weather. Small amounts of residual water in level tubing can be "blown" out. Pipe insulation is not necessary on copper tubing because copper has a very low emissivity. The very small heat emission from the tubing when the system is running contributes to warming the house. Expansion, however, can be a problem. Since copper expands considerably more than steel under the same temperature change, expansion fittings or loops are necessary on long straight runs. Copper tubing can be imbedded in concrete when necessary. The stresses set up by the restrained expansion can be taken by tubing and fittings.

Convectors and baseboards (Fig. 11(g) and (h), Tables 12, and 13)

These heating elements of copper tubing with fins of copper or aluminum have entirely replaced cast iron radiators in newly installed systems. In extending old systems that used cast iron, that material should be

Table 10. Pipe sizing table for mains

One- and two-pipe forced circulation hot water systems with special return fittings
Tables 10 and 11 courtesy of Bell & Gossett ITT

SECTION A

BOOSTER HEAD PRESSURES	TOTAL EQUIVALENT LENGTH OF PIPE IN FEET								
2′	40	48	60	68	80	96	120	160	240
2½′	50	60	75	86	100	120	150	200	300
3′	60	72	90	103	120	144	180	240	360
3½′	70	84	105	120	140	168	210	280	420
4′	80	96	120	137	160	192	240	320	480
4½′	90	108	135	154	180	216	270	360	540
5′	100	120	150	171	200	240	300	400	600
5½′	110	132	165	188	220	264	330	440	660
6′	120	144	180	206	240	288	360	480	720
6½′	130	156	195	223	260	312	390	520	780
7′	140	168	210	240	280	336	420	560	840
7½′	150	180	225	257	300	360	450	600	900
8′	160	192	240	274	320	384	480	640	960
8½′	170	204	255	291	340	408	510	680	1020
9′	180	216	270	308	360	432	540	710	1080
9½′	190	228	285	325	380	456	570	760	1140
10′	200	240	300	342	400	480	600	800	1200
10½′	210	252	315	360	420	504	630	840	1260
11′	220	264	330	377	440	528	660	880	1320
11½′	230	276	345	394	460	552	690	920	1380
12′	240	288	360	411	480	576	720	960	1440

SECTION B (Based on 20° Temperature Drop)

PIPE SIZE	MAIN CAPACITIES FOR ONE- AND TWO-PIPE SYSTEMS, AND BRANCHES FOR TWO-PIPE SYSTEMS†								
	MILINCHES								
	600	500	400	350	300	250	200	150	100
½″	19.1	18.2	16.3	15.1	13	12.5	10.8	9.2	7
¾″	41	37.7	33	30.5	28	26.7	23.5	20	15
1″	80	71	64	59	53	48	42	37	31
1¼″	170	160	140	130	118	102	90	78	63
1½″	260	240	210	185	175	156	140	121	94
2″	500	450	410	360	322	294	261	227	182
2½″	810	750	670	610	551	523	460	385	310
3″	1600	1400	1300	1150	1000	900	800	680	550
*3½″	2300	2100	1850	1650	1500	1350	1190	1020	825
*4″	3200	2900	2600	2300	2100	1950	1700	1350	1140

NOTE—*The figures shown in these tables apply to both steel pipe and Type L copper tubing, as capacity differences are not sufficient to cause design errors.*
* Trunk main capacities only. Fittings are not made larger than 3".
† MBh (thousands of Btu per hr).

used again in the form of radiators or cast iron convectors or baseboard. The latter two items are obtainable for this purpose. Finned tube and the slower cast iron should never be used in the same system, new or old. The speed of thermal response is too different. Outputs in Btuh for both convectors and baseboards are dependent on the average temperature of the water in the heating circuit. They also depend on the element chosen. With regard to convectors, Fig. 11(g), the length width, and height of the convector and its cabinet also affect the output. There is a wide choice of size combinations

in convectors. Obviously the manufacturers' literature and ratings must be consulted. Baseboards are rated in Btuh per linear ft for a given temperature (Table 13), and residential types do not vary greatly. Table 13 is representative of most available units, but again, the manufacturers' standards must be studied. When runouts (branches) and their valves are not used, the dampers supplied with both convectors and baseboards usually suffice to modulate or balance the heat supplied in the various rooms. When glass extends to floor, details in Fig. 19 are appropriate.

Tests and maintenance

All piped systems containing fluids need to be tested. Hot-water heating systems are no exception. They should be put under a pressure in excess of contemplated operating pressure but well within the ultimate rating of the tube for a period of 24 hr or more. Aside from attention to the burner, whether gas or oil (an obligation toward any system burning fossil fuels), hot-water systems need very little maintenance. It is important *not* to drain and refill the system periodically. After a short time the water, continuously circulated in the tubing, be-

Hot water heating

Table 11. Pipe sizing table for risers

One-pipe forced circulation hot water systems with special return fittings

(Based on 20° Temperature Drop)

CAPACITY OF RISERS WITH TWO FITTINGS (In Thousands of BTU)

	PIPE SIZE	600	500	400	350	300	250	200	150	100
					MILINCHES					
					Upfeed Risers—First Floor (See Note 1)					
A	½″	23	22	19	18	17	16	14	12	10
	¾″	43	41	37	33	30	28	26	22	20
	1″	80	73	64	60	55	50	45	39	32
	1¼″	180	140	120	110	100	93	80	74	62
					Upfeed Risers—Second Floor (See Note 2)					
B	½″	16	15	14	13	11	10	10	8	7
	¾″	31	28	25	24	22	21	18	15	13
	1″	58	52	45	43	37	33	32	28	25
	1¼″	122	108	92	90	79	72	68	59	50
					Upfeed Risers—Third Floor (See Note 2)					
C	½″	14	12	11	10	9	8	8	7	6
	¾″	26	24	23	21	19	18	16	14	12
	1″	47	43	38	36	34	31	29	28	25
	1¼″	99	91	81	77	70	66	59	56	46
					Downfeed Risers (See Note 3)					
D	½″	16	15	14	12	11	9	8	FOR LESS THAN 200 MILINCH RESISTANCE. BASE CALCULATIONS ON PUMP WITH HIGHER HEAD PRESSURE.	
	¾″	33	30	26	24	20	18	14		
	1″	58	52	43	41	34	29	25		
	1¼″	117	106	86	83	69	59	49		

NOTE — The figures shown in these tables apply to both steel pipe and Type L copper tubing, as capacity differences are not sufficient to cause design errors.

CAPACITY OF RISERS WITH ONE FITTING (In Thousands of BTU)

	PIPE SIZE	600	500	400	350	300	250	200	150	100
					MILINCHES					
					Upfeed Risers—First Floor					
E	½″	16.5	15	13	12	11	10.6	10	9.2	8
	¾″	29	27	25	24	21	19	18	17	15
	1″	50	48	44	41	37	35	33	31	28
	1¼″	95	88	78	76	69	62	55.6	48	40
					Upfeed Risers—Second Floor					
F	½″	11	10	9	8	7	7	6	6	4
	¾″	20	19	17	16	14	13	12	11	11
	1″	34	32	29	28	25	24	22	21	18
	1¼″	70	68	59	57	51	49	45	43	36
					Upfeed Risers—Third Floor					
G	½″	9	8	7	7	6	6	6	5	4
	¾″	18	16	14	14	12	12	11	10	9
	1″	31	29	28	27	24	22	21	20	18
	1¼″	63	60	56	52	48	45	43	41	36

READ THESE NOTES CAREFULLY BEFORE SIZING RISERS

NOTE 1. 1st FLOOR UPFEED RISERS—Capacities shown in the table are based upon horizontal branches not more than 3 feet long, with stubs 18″ long, or a total of 9 feet of pipe. 6 elbows, one valve and one union ell, and one C.I. radiator are added for the equivalent length.

For each additional 10 equivalent feet of pipe, move 2 milinch columns to the right.

NOTE 2. 2nd and 3rd FLOOR UPFEED RISERS—Capacities shown are based upon horizontal branches not more than 3 feet long, with risers 10 feet high and 20 feet high respectively. 8 elbows, one valve and one union ell, and C.I. radiator are added for the equivalent length.

For each additional 10 equivalent feet of pipe, move 2 milinch columns to the right.

NOTE 3. DOWNFEED RISERS—Capacities shown are based on a drop of seven feet to the center of the radiator, with not over 3 feet total in horizontal branches, 6 elbows, one valve and one union ell and one C.I. radiator. For every additional 2 feet of vertical drop, move one column to the right in milinch table.

On downfeed jobs the main MUST be pitched up and a vent installed on end of main.

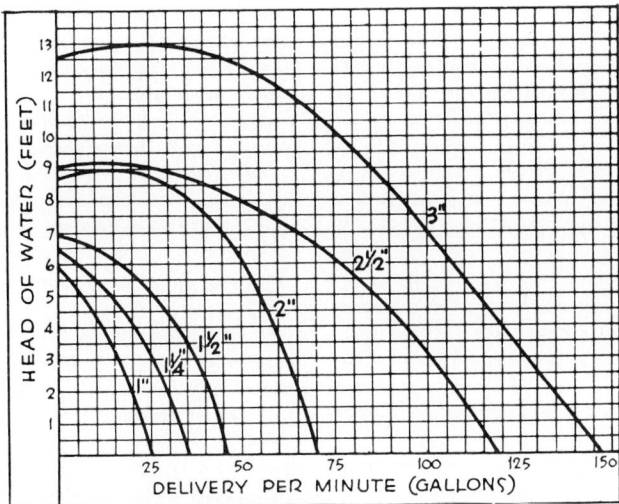

Fig. 15. Typical performance characteristics of circulating pumps (boosters)

For performance of specific equipment, consult manufacturers.

Table 12. Output MBh, of a typical convector cabinet 4 in. deep and 24 in. high (see Fig. 11(g))*

Convector length, in.	Output, MBh, at water temperature		
	180° F	190° F	200° F
20	1.8	2.1	2.3
24	2.2	2.5	2.8
28	2.7	3.0	3.4
32	3.1	3.5	4.0
36	3.5	4.0	4.5
40	3.9	4.5	5.0
44	4.4	5.0	5.6
48	4.8	5.5	6.1
56	5.6	6.4	7.2
64	6.5	7.4	8.3

* This table is a limited excerpt from a table with a wide range of choices such as:
Depths, in.—4 to 10
Heights, in.—24, 32, 38
Output, MBh—1.6 to 30.5
Consult manufacturers.

Table 13. Output of residential finned tube baseboard (see Fig. 11(h))*

Average water temp., °F	Btuh per linear ft of finned length
150	450
160	520
170	600
180	680
190	760
200	830
210	910
220	980

* Values are approximate for typically obtainable products.
Baseboard covers may extend beyond finned length for architectural effect.

comes inert chemically and will not corrode any metal. Added water always contains entrained air and corrosive compounds. The air that is thus brought in could also cause air binding in the vicinity of an unexpectedly clogged air vent.

Design methods (Fig. 15, Tables 10, 11, 12, 13)

It has often been said that there are, properly, as many design methods as there are designers. Knowledge of the principles involved and the materials available together with careful analysis of the problem will lead to successful conclusions. Yet it is possible to set up a framework against which a scheme may be developed. Eight steps might be considered.

1. *Hourly heat loss and system dimensions:* Heat loss rate, in Btuh, may be calculated from data in other sections of this book. Geometry of the piping system as related to the house is the basis for later calculations concerning pipe friction.

2. *Temperature and temperature drop of the water:* Higher temperatures permit smaller heating elements and so contribute to economy of installation. Lower temperatures may be chosen if milder, more continuous operation is preferred. The resulting more powerful heating units will permit pushing the system to greater outputs than the Btuh loss demands. The temperature *drop* is important because its value, together with the gallons per minute (gpm) circulated, are a measure of the rate of delivering heat to the house. A drop of 20° F is the value usually chosen for systems in houses. Neither the average temperature in the system nor the temperature drop affect the operating (fuel) cost of the installation.

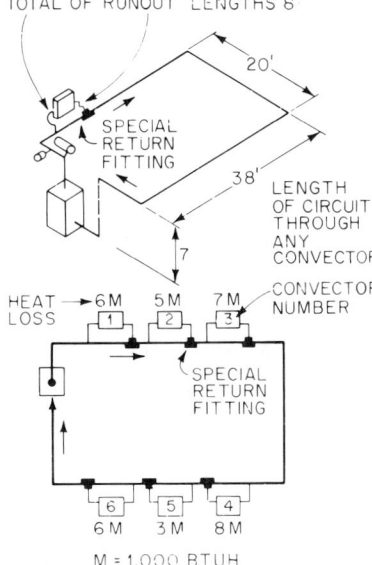

Fig. 16. Example 3

3. *Flow rate:* The heat equation by which the water flow rate is established is:

Btuh = gpm × water density lb/gal(8) × min/hr(60) × specific heat of water(1) × temp.drop(20)

or Btuh = gpm × 8 × 60 × 1 × 20
= gpm × 9,600

This figure, 9,600, becomes a "design constant," and thus

$$gpm = \frac{Btuh}{9,600}$$

where Btuh is the hourly heat loss of the house (step 1 above).

4. *Length of tubing:* The developed length (DL) and the total equivalent length (TEL) must be established. The developed length is the path of the water through the longest circuit when the system is "folded out" and can be had from the dimensions in step 1. The total equivalent length is the length of plain tube that would interpose the same friction as the actual (developed) tube length plus the effect of the fittings—ells, tees, etc. For our purpose, this can be approximated by adding 50 per cent to the developed length. Thus TEL = DL × 1.50.

5. *Select pump and establish the "head":* Using the flow rate established in step 3,

Hot water heating

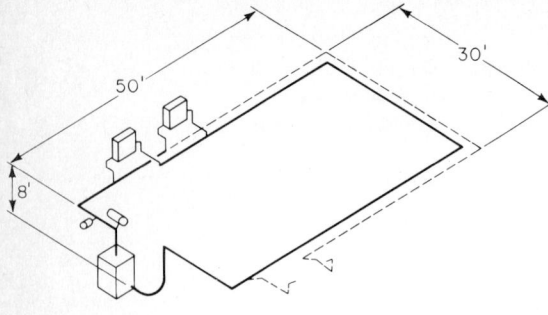

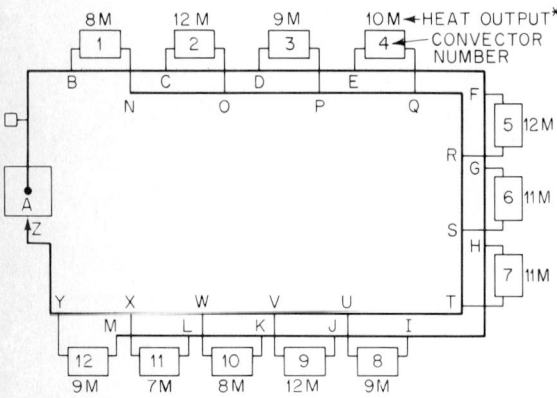

Fig. 17. Example 4
(*M = 1,000 Btuh)

consult Fig. 15, select a pump, and find the head against which it will deliver this flow rate. Enter Table 10 with the head at the left-hand column and go to the right until the total equivalent length of tubing is reached. This establishes the unit pressure drop in milinches per ft of TEL.

"Head" may be explained as follows: If, for instance, a pump will deliver a certain flow rate against 6 ft of head, it means that the friction in the system offers the same resistance to pumping as would the task of lifting the same rate of water (gpm) through 6 ft of height against gravity in an open pumping system. A milinch is 1/1,000 in. So 6 ft, for example, contains 72,000 milinches. Now, applied to the closed heating circuit with 6 ft of head, if the TEL is 200 ft, then the unit pressure drop due to friction is 72,000/200 = 360 milinches per ft.

6. *Select the tube size:* Staying in the milinch column established in step 5, go down to Section B at the bottom of the table and find the house heat loss expressed in Mbh (thousands of Btuh). To the left will be found the appropriate size of tube to be used —one in which the total head will be that which the selected pump will deliver. This assures the proper flow rate.

7. *Sizing the runouts:* In systems other than series loop, runouts are used. Enter Table 11 with information about number of special fittings and the story to be served by the specific convector. Staying in the established milinch column, find the number that corresponds to (or exceeds) the Mbh demand for the convector. To the left will be found the size of the runout.

8. *Boiler, compression tank, and heating elements:* The net rating of the boiler should be sufficient to carry the Mbh loss of the house plus the thermal demand of the domestic hot water. Compression tank must be large enough to cushion the expansion of the water in the system. This applies not only to water in the system tubing but also to the boiler water as well as that of all other components. See manufacturers' standards. The size of convectors must be chosen from catalogs, but if baseboards are used, their length can be approximated from Table 13.

Example 3 (Fig. 16): Design a one-pipe system using special return tees and convectors

1. *Hourly heat loss and dimensions:* Hourly heat loss and dimensions are as shown in Fig. 16.

2. *Water temperatures:* An average system temperature of 200° F is chosen, together with a 20 deg. drop. Water will leave the boiler at 210° F and return at 190° F.

3. *Rate of circulation:* Flow rate = 35,000/9,600 = 3.65 gpm.

4. *System length:* Developed length is as follows:

Length	38
	38
Width	20
	20
Height	7
	7
Runouts	8
	138

Allowing 50 per cent for the effect of fittings, total equivalent length = 138 × 1.50 = 207 ft.

5. *Pump:* A 1¼-in. pump is selected. Figure 15 shows that this pump will deliver the required 3.65 gpm if the head in the system is 6.2 ft.

6. *Tube size:* Table 10 shows that a head of 6 ft and a TEL of 207 ft establishes a position in the 350 milinch column. Going down the page in this column to section B, it is found that a 1-in. tube will deliver 59 Mbh, which is more than adequate.

7. *Runouts:* The largest convector requires an output of 6 Mbh. The 350-milinch column of Table 11 shows that, with supply upfeed to the first floor and one special fitting, a ½-in. runout (riser) will deliver 12 Mbh, which is more than adequate.

8. *Boiler, tank, and convectors:* See foregoing notes regarding boiler and compression tank. In selecting the convectors, the determining factors are required output of the convector and the average water temperature, namely, 200° F. Its style, height, depth, and length will fix its output and should be selected to conform to the architectural requirements. For instance, a convector to suit the output of 6 Mbh can be chosen from Table 12. It would be 4 in. deep, 24 in. high, and 48 in. long. It is selected from the column for 200°F average water temperature. Convectors are most effective below windows.

Example 4 (Fig. 17): Design a two-pipe reverse-return system using convectors

Special fittings are not necessary in this system type. The supply main is on the pressure side of the pump and the return main is on the suction side. The convectors are therefore under a pressure differential which causes flow.

1. *Heat loss and dimensions:* Btuh in the system totals 118,000. Dimensions are as shown in Fig. 17.

2. *Water temperatures:* Average temperature in the convectors is 200° F. Temperature drop in the system is 20° F. Water leaves boiler at 210° F and returns at 190° F.

3. *Rate of circulation:* 118,000/9600 = 12.2 gpm.

4. *System length:* Developed length is as follows:

Width	30
	30
Length	50
	50
Height	8
	8
Runouts, 1 convector	8
	184 ft.

Total equivalent length = 184 × 1.50 = 276 ft.

5. *Pump:* A 1½-in. pump is selected. Fig. 15 shows that it will deliver 12.2 gpm against a head of 6.4 ft.

6. *Size of mains:* Pressure loss in the system expressed in milinches is 6.4 ft × 12,000 = 76,800. The pressure loss per foot of TEL should be 76,800/276 = 278 milinches per foot. We will use the 300-milinch column in Table 10, Section B. Section AB of the supply main carries 118,000 Btuh, but after it has supplied convector no. 1 it carries, through section BC, 118,000 − 8,000 = 110,000. Mains will thus reduce in size. Return mains will correspondingly increase in size as more convectors are picked up. The results from Table 10, Section B indicate the following:

Main	*Capacity, M Btu/hr*	*Pipe size to be used, in.*
AB	118	1¼
BC	110	1¼
CD	98	1¼
DE	89	1¼
EF	79	1¼
FG	67	1¼
GH	56	1¼
HI	45	1
IJ	36	1
JK	24	¾
KL	16	¾
LM	9	½

In reverse order the return mains would be sized in similar manner.

Return	Capacity, M Btu/hr	Pipe size to be used, in.
NO	8	½
OP	20	¾
PQ	29	1
QR	39	1
RS	51	1
ST	62	1¼
TU	73	1¼
UV	82	1¼
UW	94	1¼
WX	102	1¼
XY	109	1¼
YZ	118	1¼

7. *Runouts:* The size of all convector branches, both supply and return, will be ½ in., selected also from Section B of Table 10 on the same basis. There it is seen that a ½-in. tube carries 13,000 Btuh at this unit pressure drop, which is more than is required by any convector.

8. *Boiler, tank, convectors:* See notes, Example 3.

Example 5 (Fig. 18): Design a series loop baseboard system

1. *Heat loss and dimensions:* Btuh totals 45,000. For dimensions, see Fig. 18.

2. *Water temperatures:* Average temperature in the baseboards will be 180°F and the drop 20°F. Water will leave the boiler at 190°F and return at 170°F.

3. *Rate of circulation:* 45,000/9,600 = 4.7 gpm.

4. *System length:*

Length	37
	37
Width	22
	22
Height	7
	7
	132 ft developed length

TEL = 132 × 1.5 = 197, say 200 ft.

5. *Pump:* A 1-in. pump will deliver 4.7 gpm against a head of 5.5 ft.

6. *Tube size:* From Table 10, Section A, the 350-milinch column is indicated for a head of 5.5 and a TEL of 200 ft. Section B of that table indicates that a 1-in. tube is satisfactory since it can deliver 59 Mbh, which is in excess of our demand of 45,000.

7. *Runouts:* None required.

8. *Boiler, tank, baseboards:* See note, Example 3, regarding boiler and tank. Table 13 shows the output of baseboards at 180°F water temperature to be 680 Btu per linear foot. The number of linear feet required in each room is obtained by dividing the room's hourly heat loss by 680. The lengths are here summarized and the layout is shown.

Baseboard covers may extend past the finned element ends to fill the room dimension.

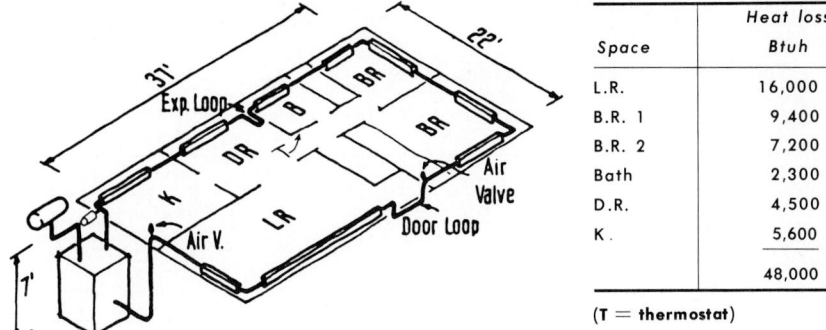

Space	Heat loss Btuh
L.R.	16,000
B.R. 1	9,400
B.R. 2	7,200
Bath	2,300
D.R.	4,500
K.	5,600
	48,000

(T = thermostat)

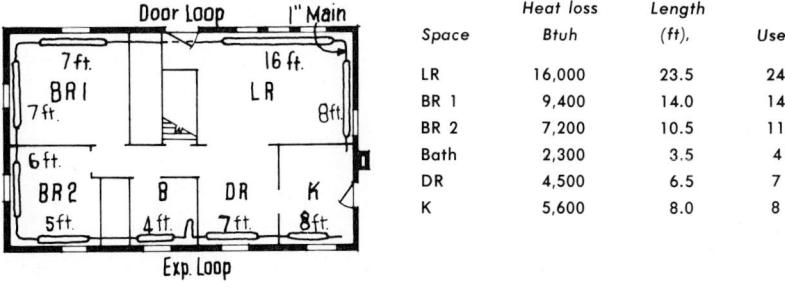

Space	Heat loss Btuh	Length (ft),	Use
LR	16,000	23.5	24
BR 1	9,400	14.0	14
BR 2	7,200	10.5	11
Bath	2,300	3.5	4
DR	4,500	6.5	7
K	5,600	8.0	8

Fig. 18. Example 5

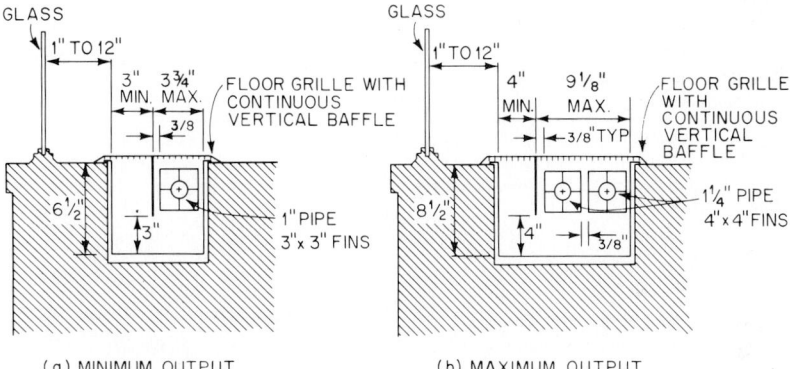

(a) MINIMUM OUTPUT   (b) MAXIMUM OUTPUT

Fig. 19. Underfloor convectors for hot water systems.

Essential when glass extends to the floor. Ratings shown below are based on 0°F outdoor temperature and 70°F. room temperature and only for glass walls, not conventional walls. Average temperature of downdraft, 47°F. Average air velocity, 60 ft per min, inside glass temperature 25°F. Sections (a) and (b) are for specific selected outputs. Consult manufacturer for all controlling conditions and intermediate ratings.

Output rating at a (reasonable) selected water temperature of 210°F
(a) Minimum 930 Btuh per lin ft
(b) Maximum 2430 Btuh per lin ft
NOTE: Architectural treatment of hatched area must conform to structure and provide insulation.

Note: The selection of pump sizes may seem arbitrary. Larger pumps can use smaller tubes and vice versa. Pressure drops will increase with smaller tubes and decrease with larger ones, with water velocities to correspond. High water velocities cause noise and low velocities result in sluggish flow. It is suggested that unit pressure drops of middle value be used (between about 200 and 400 milinches per foot).

HEATING BY ELECTRICITY

(This discussion applies to electric heating systems other than those using electrically powered furnaces or boilers. These obviously would be part of applications using warm air or hot water.)

Characteristics

For installations that do not need to in-

Table 14. Suggested insulation values

From Electric Comfort Heating, *no. HE-1-1966: The National Electric Manufacturers Association.*

Building section	Types of wall construction		
	Normal frame with nominal 4-in. studs and with siding, shingle, or masonry veneer exterior	Prefab frame with nominal 2-in. studs and with siding, shingle, or masonry veneer exterior	Masonry, 8-in. lightweight block, or brick cavity
Ceilings			
U value of section	0.05	0.04	0.04
Insulation R value*	R 19	R 24	R 24
Opaque walls			
U value of section	0.07	0.11	0.14
Insulation R value*	R 11	R 6	R 4
Floor over vented crawl spaces			
U value of section	0.07	0.05	0.05
Insulation R value*	R 13	R 19	R 19
Floor over unheated basements			
U value of section	0.09	0.07	0.07
Insulation R value*	R 9	R 13	R 13
or	or	or	or
Basement walls			
U value of section	0.08	0.08	0.08
Insulation R value*	R 7	R 7	R 7
Concrete slabs on grade			
Insulation R value*	R 7	R 7	R 7

* The insulation R *values shown refer to the installed resistance of the insulation when applied according to the manufacturer's instructions in the building section described. The total section resistance (*R_T *value) is the* R *value plus the resistance of the section construction materials.*

Table 15. Maximum winter heat loss limits for electrically heated houses

When based on an infiltration rate of three-quarters air change per hour, the total calculated heat loss shall not exceed the values shown below. These values are expressed in watts (or Btuh) per square foot of floor area of the space to be heated, measured to the outside of exterior walls.

Adapted from the All Weather Comfort Standard, *1971; published by the Electric Heating Association, Inc.*

Degree days	Maximum heat loss values	
	Watts/sq ft	Btuh/sq ft
Over 8,000	10.0	34
7,001 to 8,000	9.4	32
6,001 to 7,000	8.8	30
4,501 to 6,000	8.2	28
3,001 to 4,500	7.6	26
2,000 to 3,000	7.0	24

clude cooling as an integral part of the comfort conditioning equipment of a house, electric heating is often a suitable choice. Advantages include elimination of boiler, chimney, fuel storage space, and the distributing media of ducts or tubing. Cleanliness due to the absence of combustion is an asset, as is also the easy thermostatic control of the temperature in each separate room. Fast response of the heating elements to a signal for the beginning or discontinuance of heat supply is an inherent quality. The variation of this response by the several electric heating methods is very slight but might be listed in order of speed in three common devices as:

1. Fan-equipped wall units (fastest)
2. Baseboards
3. Ceiling radiant panels

Economy

Four important considerations are:
1. Cost of installation
2. Annual cost of energy
3. Maintenance and repair charges
4. Amortization of the cost of replacing the system at the end of its useful life

Regarding item 1, electric heating almost always wins. The credit item of the omission of a central heating plant and its appurtenances is not significantly offset by the debit charge of a somewhat larger electrical service installation and the cost of additional insulation.

Concerning the annual cost of energy compared to the cost of oil or gas, the former is usually higher but there is a sharp variation regionally. The seasonal power load of the local utility company will determine whether it can offer large blocks of energy in winter to keep its output steady throughout the year. Changes in nearby industrial demand can affect these offers within the relatively short period of a few years.

The annual maintenance cost of electrical systems is likely to be lower than that of systems which include boilers, furnaces, chimneys, filters, valves, and fans or pumps.

The amortization cost of systems that cost little to install will obviously be low for a corresponding span of useful life. Little is known about the "period of usefulness" of electric heating systems since the method is relatively new.

Favorable decisions on many of the above items may account for the recent rapid increase in electric heating installations.

Thermal planning

During the period when electric heating was struggling to be competitive with other

A. Baseboard
Below windows and on exterior walls. See Example 6 and, for output ratings, Table 16. Approximate output per linear foot 200 ± watts. Maximum per unit 2500 w±.

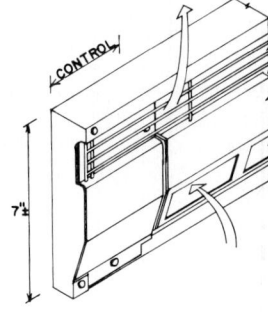

D. Wall units
Surface mounted or recessed; fan or gravity circulation. See Examples 6 and 7. Available units vary in output from about 750 to 4,000 watts.

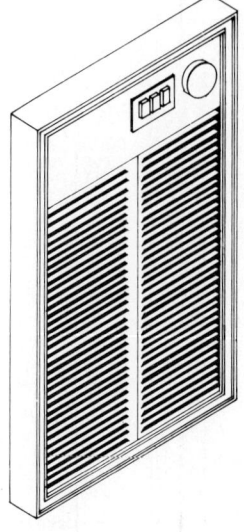

B. Drop-in floor insert for glass-to-glass locations. Output range 350 to 2,000 watts.

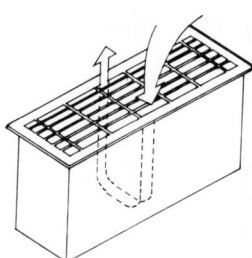

E. Prefabricated radiant ceiling panels

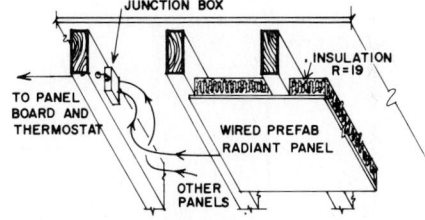

C. Heating cable
Fastened to "drywall" gypsum board and covered with plaster or plaster board. (Radiant)

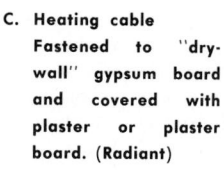
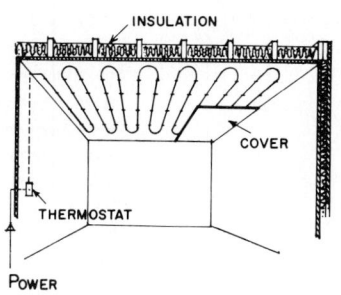

See Example 7 and, for output ratings, Table 17. Approximate unit output per sq ft of panel is 15 watts.

Fig. 20. Five types of equipment most suitable for residential electric heating

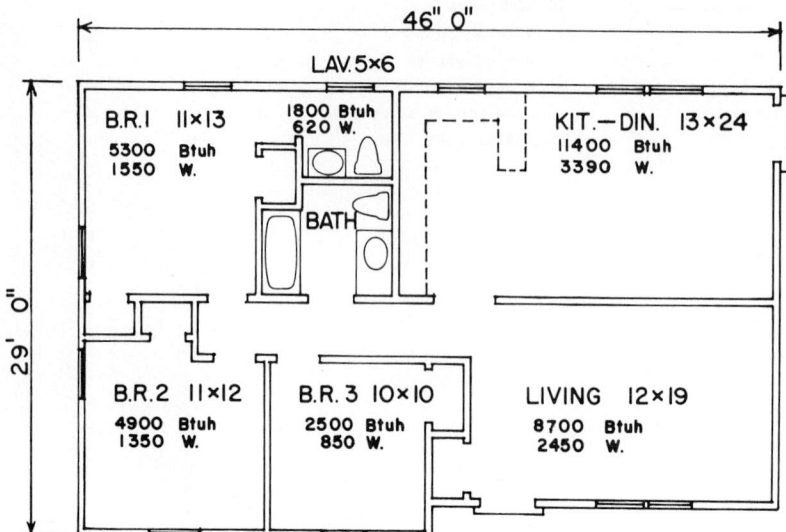

Fig. 21. Examples 6 and 7, typical frame house

Heat loss summary

Space	Btuh	Watts $\frac{Btuh}{3.41}$
Living	8,700	2,450
Kit/Din	11,400	3,390
B.R. 1	5,300	1,550
B.R. 2	4,900	1,350
B.R. 3	2,500	850
Bath*	Negligible	
Lav.	1,800	620
Total	34,600	10,210

Criteria

Indoors	75°
Outdoors	0°
R roof	19†
R walls	11†
R slab on grade (edge)	7†
Air change ¾ of the room vol. per hr	
Double glazing	
Degree days,	5,000
Wind	15 mph

Heating design efficiency watts/sq ft of house 10,210/1,300 = 7.9 OK, less than 8.2.
*Interior room, see Table 17.
†See Table 16.

Table 16. Electric heaters*†

Baseboard			
Unit	Length, in.	Watts	Volts
a	36	650	120
b	52	1000	120
c	68	1300	120
d	100	2000	120

Bathroom heaters, wall (fan) units			
Unit	Size (approx), in.	Watts	Volts
f	16 × 13 × 3½	1250	120
g	16 × 13 × 3½	750	120

*All the above are obtainable with built-in thermostat.
†This is a limited selection of equipment from a wide variety of products available. Consult manufacturers.

methods, there was a very constructive movement to plan homes for minimal heat loss. The planning thus established should be observed not only for electric heating but for any method of heating. Some of the recommendations appear in Table 14. For instance, insulation resistance of 19 for roofs (or ceilings) and of 11 for walls suggests 6 and 4 in. of effective batt insulation respectively. These assumptions should be checked carefully and the house provided with double glazing and with weatherstripping that will limit the infiltration to three-quarters air change per hour.

When this controlled hourly heat loss has been established, its effectiveness may be checked against Table 15, which lists desirable maximums for unit hourly heat losses per square foot of the floor area in the warmed section of the house.

Heating devices

Figure 20 illustrates the most commonly employed methods of electrical residential heating.

1. *Baseboard:* Unlike baseboards in hot-water systems where the covers over the limited length of finned elements can be extended wall to wall, electrical baseboards are generally of fixed lengths dependent upon their outputs. A thermostat at the end of each baseboard or on a selected baseboard in a group can control the heat in each room.

2. *Floor insert boxes:* Because so many modern designs feature glass walls or sliding glass doors through which, when open, one can walk outdoors, the drop-in insert heater has been developed. Usually adaptable on ground-level stories where they can project below slabs or into crawl spaces or basements, they are sometimes unsuitable, because of depth, to adapt to upper-story floor construction.

3. *Ceiling heating cables:* This very effective scheme is somewhat more expensive to install than other systems. Heating cables come in numerous fixed lengths with nonheating "leads" at their ends for connection to a power source and controls. These cables involve individual designs as to output, spacing, and clearance around ceiling light fixtures. This method may be considered a custom design. It has been used to some extent in high-rental apartments.

4. *Wall units:* These are seldom used for entire systems in houses. The main reason for this is that it is not usually convenient to locate them below windows. In bathrooms, however, they are very suitable. There, at a higher position on the wall, their controls are accessible for the con-

venience and personal preference of occupants.

5. *Prefabricated ceiling panels:* These provide a less expensive method than that afforded by heating cables of attaining effective radiant heat from ceilings. Nonheating "pigtail" leads from several panels terminate at a junction box. There, a circuit conductor supplies power from the house panelboard or a separate *heating* panelboard. The ceiling surfacing can be completed by conventional gypsum panels adjacent to the electric panels and the whole surface finished in "dry wall" techniques. It is evident that *nailing* of the electric panels must not occur close to wires. In this and other practices it is essential to follow the manufacturer's instructions.

Voltages and circuiting

Most units are obtainable for voltages of 120, 208, and 240. Less common are those for 277 volts. Example 6 is based upon 120 volts to suggest that in some cases higher voltages are not available. Whenever possible, higher voltages are usually selected and, of course, these make possible lighter wiring since the amperages are reduced by about half. The size and cost of the heating baseboard and wall panels are not materially affected by voltage.

All circuiting must conform to standards of the National Electrical Code, the National Building Code, and local codes. A group of circuits is usually assigned to the heating system only and not tapped for other casual electric use.

Power demand

It is not usually possible to merely "add" the heating system to a given residential electric installation. Note that in Examples 6 and 7 the watts per square foot of floor area for heating is 7.9 (Fig. 21). Very often the other uses in the house are satisfied by 3 to 5 watts per sq ft. It is seen that heating may more than double the demand.

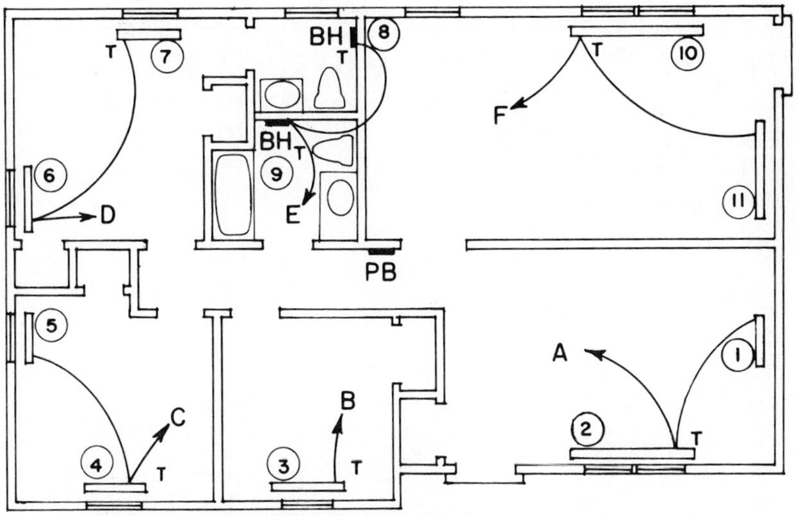

Fig. 22. Example 6, Electric Baseboard (and wall units)

Design Summary. (BH, bathroom heater; PB, panel board; T, thermostat in heating unit controls room temperature.) See Fig. 21 for heat losses and dimensions.

	Unit				
Circuit	*No. (above)*	*Style, Table 18*	*Watts*	*Circuit Watts*	*Circuit amps @ 120 volts*
A	1	a	650		
	2	d	2,000	2,650	21
B	3	b	1,000	1,000	8
C	4	a	650		
	5	a	650	1,300	11
D	6	b	1,000		
	7	a	650	1,650	14
E	8	g	750		
	9	g	750	1,500	13
F	10	d	2,000		
	11	c	1,300	3,300	28

Table 17. Examples 6 and 7: Design wattages and installed power

Space	*Fig. 21 design, watts*	*Fig. 22, Ex. 6, baseboard, watts*	*Fig. 23, Ex. 7, radiant, watts*
Living room	2,450	2,650	2,405
Kitchen/dining	3,390	3,300	3,355
Bedroom 1	1,550	1,650	1,675
Bedroom 2	1,350	1,300	1,340
Bedroom 3	850	1,000	930
Bath*	–	750	750
Lavatory*	620	750	750
Totals	10,210	11,400	11,205

* *In both solutions, bathroom and lavatory are served by fan-equipped wall-insert bathroom heaters.*

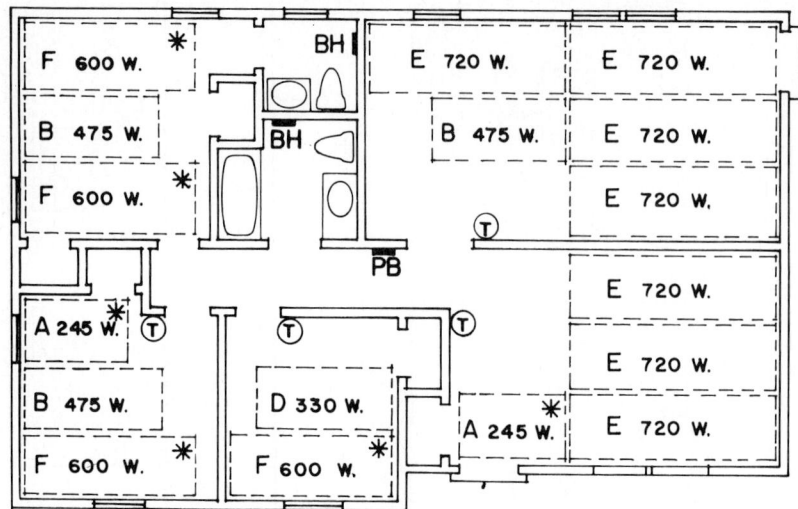

Fig. 23. Example 7, Electric radiant heating by ceiling gypsum panels with integral resistance wiring.

(PB, panel board—electric control center; BH, bathroom heater—wall type; T, thermostat controls heat in each room.) Design summary. Each panel is identified by letters that relate to Table 18. See Fig. 21 for heat losses and dimensions.
* Panel trimmed to fit, see Table 18.

Table 18. Gypsum ceiling panels with electric wires imbedded for radiant heating (typical sizes and ratings)

Type	Manufactured sizes	Trimming permitted in nonelectric area	Watts	Volts
A	4 × 6	24″ one end	245	240
B	4 × 8	None	475	240
C	4 × 8	32″ one end	330	240
D	4 × 8	15″ one side	330	240
E	4 × 12	None	720	240
F	4 × 12	30″ one end	600	240
G	4 × 12	15″ one side	450	240

VISUAL CHART OF ABOVE TABLE

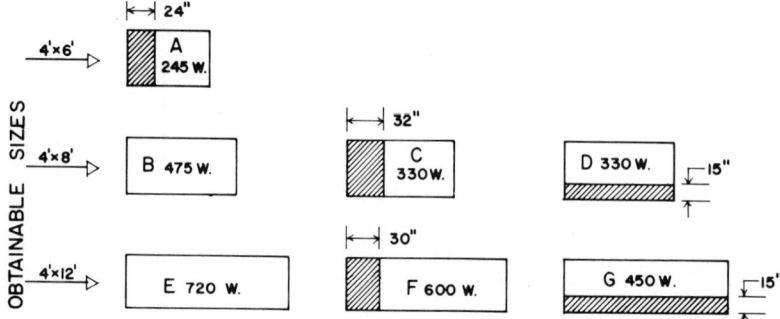

Note: *Hatched areas denote nonwired areas at specified and indicated positions on panels. They may be trimmed or cut away without affecting fixed output of remainder. Consult manufacturers for output, installation, wiring, and all other data pertaining to this method of radiant heating.*

Design Fig. 21)

Examples are given of two systems only, based in both cases upon the same house and its fixed heat loss.

Example 6: Baseboard (Figs. 21 and 22)

1. *Establish thermal specifications:* Design the house for minimal heat loss by observing the requirements of Table 14, column 1, and setting up the criteria (Fig. 21) for the design.

2. *Calculate hourly heat loss:* Using the data of step 1 above, calculate the hourly heat loss under design conditions by methods described in other sections of this book.

Divide Btuh by 3.41 to establish the required wattage for each room and for the entire house. One watt is the equivalent in power rate of 3.41 Btuh.

3. *Check thermal design efficiency:* Divide the hourly heat loss in watts by the gross area of the house. It is found that the result, 7.9 watts per sq ft, is less than the 8.2 maximum allowed in Table 15 for a 5000 degree-day region and a house with air change limited to three-quarters per hour. The design is efficient.

4. *Select baseboards:* These are chosen from the list in Table 16 and summarized in Fig. 22, where circuiting is also indicated. Bathroom and lavatory are equipped with fan-type wall units which are considered to be more convenient with controls at waist-high position.

5. *Summarize installed output:* See Table 17.

Example 7: Gypsum board ceiling panels (Figs. 21, 23)

Steps 1, 2 and 3 are identical to those in the foregoing example 6 since the same house is used.

4. *Select electric panels:* These are selected from Table 18. Their position and output are shown in Fig. 23. Bathroom heaters of the wall type are used.

5. *Summarize installed output:* See Table 17.

REFERENCES

ASHRAE Guide and Data Book, Systems (1970). The American Society of Heating, Refrigerating and Air Conditioning Engineers, Inc., New York.

Manual 4, Installation Techniques for Perimeter Heating and Cooling, 9th ed. (1964). National Environmental Systems Contractors Association, Chicago.

Installation Guide for Residential Hydronic Heating Systems, no. 200 (May, 1969). The Institute of Boiler and Radiator Manufacturers, New York.

Electric Heating and Cooling Handbook, secs. 1–4 (1965, as amended). Edison Electric Institute, New York.

The following information is based in part on the National Fuel Gas Code, ANSI Z223.1-1974 (NFPA No. 54), sponsored by The American Gas Association, the American Society of Mechanical Engineers, and the National Fire Protection Association. In applying these standards, reference should also be made to the manufacturer's instructions, serving gas supplier regulations, and local building, heating, plumbing, or other codes in effect in the area in which the installation is made.

PIPING PLAN

It is recommended that before proceeding with the installation of a gas piping system, a piping sketch or plan be prepared showing the proposed location of the piping as well as the size of different branches. Adequate consideration should be given to future demands and provisions made for added gas service.

Gas consumption

The quantity of gas to be provided at each outlet shall be determined, whenever possible, directly from the manufacturer's Btu rating of the appliance which will be installed. In case the ratings of the appliances to be installed are not known, Table 1 is given to show the approximate consumption of average appliances of certain types in Btu per hour.

Piping size

Size of gas piping required can be determined from Tables 2A, 2B, 2C, 4A, and 4B using the length from the meter to the most remote outlet. The tables include an allowance for an average number of fittings. For gas having a specific gravity greater than 0.70, multiply the capacities found in Tables 2A, 2B, or 2C by the factors listed in Table 3.

The diversity factor (ratio of maximum probable demand to maximum possible demand) is important for determining gas piping size in multifamily dwellings. Consult gas supplier for the diversity factor to be used.

Piping material:

Pipe: Gas pipe shall be steel or wrought-iron pipe complying with the American National Standard for Wrought-Steel and Wrought-Iron Pipe, ANSI B36.10-1970. Threaded copper, brass, or aluminum alloy pipe in iron pipe sizes may be used with gases not corrosive to such material. Aluminum alloy pipe shall be factory coated to protect against external corrosion where it is in contact with masonry, plaster, or insulation, or is subject to repeated wettings by such liquids as water (except rain water), detergents or sewage. Aluminum alloy pipe

Table 1. Approximate gas input for some common appliances

Appliance	Input Btu per hr (Approx.)
Range, Free Standing, Domestic	65,000
Built-In Oven or Broiler Unit, Domestic	25,000
Built-In Top Unit, Domestic	40,000
Water Heater, Automatic Storage 30 to 40 gal Tank	45,000
Water Heater, Automatic Storage 50 gal Tank	55,000
Water Heater, Automatic Instantaneous (2 gal per minute	142,800
Capacity (4 gal per minute	285,000
(6 gal per minute	428,400
Water Heater, Domestic, Circulating or Side-Arm	35,000
Refrigerator	3,000
Clothes Dryer, Type 1 (Domestic)	35,000
Gas Light	2,500
Incinerator, Domestic	35,000

For specific appliances or appliances not shown above, the input should be determined from the manufacturer's rating.

shall not be used in exterior locations or underground. Aluminum alloy pipe shall comply with American National Standard Specification for Aluminum-Alloy Seamless Pipe and Seamless Extruded Tube, ANSI H38.7-1972 (ASTM B241-71b)[1] (except that the use of alloy 5456 is prohibited), and shall be suitably marked at each end of each length indicating compliance with the Specification.

Metallic tubing: When acceptable to the serving gas supplier, seamless copper, aluminum alloy or steel tubing may be used with gases not corrosive to such material. Copper tubing shall comply with standard Type K or L, of *American National Standard Specification for Seamless Copper Water Tube*[1] H23.1-1970 (ASTM B88-69)[2] or *American National Standard Specification for Seamless Copper Tube for Air Conditioning and Refrigeration Field Service,* H23.5-1967 (ASTM B280-66a).[1] Steel tubing shall comply with the *Specification for Electric-Resistance-Welded Coiled Steel Tubing for Gas and Fuel Oil Lines,* ASTM A539-73,[2] or *American National Standard Specification for Copper Brazed Steel Tubing,* B36.35-1966 (ASTM A254-64).[1] Aluminum alloy tubing shall be of standard Type A or B, or equivalent, complying with *American National Standard Specification for Aluminum-Alloy Drawn Seamless Tubes,* H38.3-1972 (ASTM B210-71),[1] or Type A or equivalent

---

[1] *Available from the American National Standards Institute, Inc., 1430 Broadway, New York, New York 10018, or the American Society for Testing and Materials, 1916 Race Street, Philadelphia, Pennsylvania 19103.*

[2] *Available from the American Society for Testing and Materials, 1916 Race Street, Philadelphia, Pennsylvania 19103.*

complying with *American National Standard Specification for Aluminum-Alloy Seamless Pipe and Seamless Extruded Tube,* H38.7-1972 (ASTM B241-7 lb).[1] Aluminum-alloy tubing shall be factory coated to protect against external corrosion where it is in contact with masonry, plaster, or insulation or is subject to repeated wettings by such liquids as water (except rain water), detergents or sewage. Aluminum-alloy tubing shall not be used in exterior locations or underground.

Plastic pipe, tubing: When acceptable to the serving gas supplier, plastic pipe or tubing conforming with specification ASTM D2513-73, *Specification for Thermoplastic Gas Pressure Pipe, Tubing, and Fittings,*[2] or specification ASTM D2517-73, *Specification for Reinforced Thermosetting Plastic Gas Pressure Pipe and Fittings,*[2] and compatible fittings may be used for outside piping underground only. The installation shall be such as to avoid excessive stresses due to thermal contraction.

CONCEALED PIPING

Concealed piping shall not be located in solid partitions. In solid floors such as concrete, piping should be laid in channels in the floor and be suitably covered to permit access. Underground metallic piping must not be laid in contact with cinders. Where piping passes through the foundation it should be protected by a sleeve and sealed tight. Where piping passes under a building it should be run in a watertight, vented conduit.

INSTALLATION OF PIPING

All gas piping shall be pitched not less than ¼ in. in 15 ft. Provide drips at the low points for the collection of condensate and dirt. Piping should be supported by metal hangers spaced not more than shown in Table 5.

Electrical bonding and grounding

A gas piping system within a building shall be electrically continuous and bonded to any grounding electrode, as defined by the National Electrical Code, ANSI C1-1975.

Test methods for piping systems

Before appliances are connected, piping systems shall stand a pressure of at least 6 in. mercury or 3 lb gage for a period of not less than ten minutes without showing any drop in pressure.

Systems for undiluted liquefied petroleum gases shall stand the pressure test in accordance with the above or, when appliances are connected to the piping system, shall stand a pressure of not less than 10 in. water column for a period of not less than ten minutes without showing any drop in pressure.

APPLIANCE INSTALLATION

Gas appliances, accessories, and equipment shall be "Approved." "Approved" shall mean "acceptable to the authority having jurisdiction."

Note: In determining acceptability, the authority having jurisdiction would normally base acceptance on compliance with NFPA, ANSI or other appropriate standards. In the absence of such standards, said authority would normally require evidence of proper installation, procedure, or use. The authority having jurisdiction may also refer to the listings or labeling practices of nationally recognized testing laboratories, such as the Underwriters' Laboratories, Inc., the Factory Mutual Engineering Division, the American Gas Association Laboratories, the Underwriters' Laboratories of Canada, the Canadian Standards Association Testing Laboratories, and the Canadian Gas Association Approvals Division.

The National Fire Protection Association and the American National Standards Institute, Inc., do not approve, inspect, or certify any installations, procedures, equipment, or materials, nor do they approve or evaluate testing laboratories.

DRAFT HOODS

Every vented appliance, except incinerators, dual oven-type combination ranges, direct-vent appliances, and units designed for power burners or for forced venting, shall

Table 2A. Maximum capacity of pipe in cubic feet of gas per hour for gas pressures of 0.5 psig or less and a pressure drop of 0.3 in. water column

(Based on a 0.60 specific gravity gas)

Nominal iron pipe size, in.	Internal diameter, in.	Length of pipe, feet													
		10	20	30	40	50	60	70	80	90	100	125	150	175	200
¼	.364	32	22	18	15	14	12	11	11	10	9	8	8	7	6
⅜	.493	72	49	40	34	30	27	25	23	22	21	18	17	15	14
½	.622	132	92	73	63	56	50	46	43	40	38	34	31	28	26
¾	.824	278	190	152	130	115	105	96	90	84	79	72	64	59	55
1	1.049	520	350	285	245	215	195	180	170	160	150	130	120	110	100
1¼	1.380	1,050	730	590	500	440	400	370	350	320	305	275	250	225	210
1½	1.610	1,600	1,100	890	760	670	610	560	530	490	460	410	380	350	320
2	2.067	3,050	2,100	1,650	1,450	1,270	1,150	1,050	990	930	870	780	710	650	610
2½	2.469	4,800	3,300	2,700	2,300	2,000	1,850	1,700	1,600	1,500	1,400	1,250	1,130	1,050	980
3	3.068	8,500	5,900	4,700	4,100	3,600	3,250	3,000	2,800	2,600	2,500	2,200	2,000	1,850	1,700
4	4.026	17,500	12,000	9,700	8,300	7,400	6,800	6,200	5,800	5,400	5,100	4,500	4,100	3,800	3,500

Table 2B. Maximum capacity of pipe in cubic feet of gas per hour for gas pressures of 0.5 psig or less and a pressure drop of 0.5 in. water column

(Based on a 0.60 specific gravity gas)

Nominal iron pipe size, inches	Internal diameter, inches	Length of pipe, feet													
		10	20	30	40	50	60	70	80	90	100	125	150	175	200
¼	.364	43	29	24	20	18	16	15	14	13	12	11	10	9	8
⅜	.493	95	65	52	45	40	36	33	31	29	27	24	22	20	19
½	.622	175	120	97	82	73	66	61	57	53	50	44	40	37	35
¾	.824	360	250	200	170	151	138	125	118	110	103	93	84	77	72
1	1.049	680	465	375	320	285	260	240	220	205	195	175	160	145	135
1¼	1.380	1,400	950	770	660	580	530	490	460	430	400	360	325	300	280
1½	1.610	2,100	1,460	1,180	990	900	810	750	690	650	620	550	500	460	430
2	2.067	3,950	2,750	2,200	1,900	1,680	1,520	1,400	1,300	1,220	1,150	1,020	950	850	800
2½	2.469	6,300	4,350	3,520	3,000	2,650	2,400	2,250	2,050	1,950	1,850	1,650	1,500	1,370	1,280
3	3.068	11,000	7,700	6,250	5,300	4,750	4,300	3,900	3,700	3,450	3,250	2,950	2,650	2,450	2,280
4	4.026	23,000	15,800	12,800	10,900	9,700	8,800	8,100	7,500	7,200	6,700	6,000	5,500	5,000	4,600

Table 2C. **Maximum capacity of semirigid tubing in cubic feet of gas per hour for gas pressures of 0.5 psig or less and a pressure drop of 0.3 in. water column**

(Based on a 0.60 specific gravity gas)

Outside diameter, in.	Length of tubing, feet													
	10	20	30	40	50	60	70	80	90	100	125	150	175	200
3/8	20	14	11	10	9	8	7	7	6	6	5	5	4	4
1/2	42	29	23	20	18	16	15	14	13	12	11	10	9	8
5/8	86	59	47	40	36	33	30	28	26	25	22	20	18	17
3/4	150	103	83	71	63	57	52	49	46	43	38	35	32	30
7/8	212	146	117	100	89	81	74	69	65	61	54	49	45	42

Table 2D. **Maximum capacity of semirigid tubing in cubic feet of gas per hour for gas pressures of 0.5 psig or less and a pressure drop of 0.5 in. water column**

(Based on a 0.60 specific gravity gas)

Outside diameter, in.	Length of tubing, feet													
	10	20	30	40	50	60	70	80	90	100	125	150	175	200
3/8	27	18	15	13	11	10	9	9	8	8	7	6	6	5
1/2	56	38	31	26	23	21	19	18	17	16	14	13	12	11
5/8	113	78	62	53	47	43	39	37	34	33	29	26	24	22
3/4	197	136	109	93	83	75	69	64	60	57	50	46	42	39
7/8	280	193	155	132	117	106	98	91	85	81	71	65	60	55

Table 3. **Multipliers to be used only with Tables 2A, B, C, and D when applying the gravity factor**

Specific Gravity	Multiplier	Specific Gravity	Multiplier
.35	1.31	1.00	.78
.40	1.23	1.10	.74
.45	1.16	1.20	.71
.50	1.10	1.30	.68
.55	1.04	1.40	.66
.60	1.00	1.50	.63
.65	.96	1.60	.61
.70	.93	1.70	.59
.75	.90	1.80	.58
.80	.87	1.90	.56
.85	.84	2.00	.55
.90	.82	2.10	.54

Table 4A. **Maximum capacity of pipe in thousands of Btu per hour of undiluted liquefied petroleum gases**

Based on a pressure drop of 0.5 in. water column.

Nominal iron pipe size, in.	Length of pipe, ft											
	10	20	30	40	50	60	70	80	90	100	125	150
1/2	275	189	152	129	114	103	96	89	83	78	60	63
3/4	567	393	315	267	237	217	196	185	172	162	146	132
1	1,071	732	590	504	448	409	378	346	322	307	275	252
1 1/4	2,205	1,496	1,212	1,039	913	834	771	724	677	630	567	511
1 1/2	3,307	2,299	1,858	1,559	1,417	1,275	1,181	1,086	1,023	976	866	787
2	6,221	4,331	3,465	2,992	2,646	2,394	2,205	2,047	1,921	1,811	1,606	1,496

Table 4B. Maximum capacity of semirigid tubing in thousands of Btu per hour of undiluted liquefied petroleum gases

Based on a pressure drop of 0.5 in. water column.

Outside diameter, in.	Length of tubing, ft									
	10	20	30	40	50	60	70	80	90	100
⅜	39	26	21	19	—	—	—	—	—	—
½	92	62	50	41	37	35	31	29	27	26
⅝	199	131	107	90	79	72	67	62	59	55
¾	329	216	181	145	131	121	112	104	95	90
⅞	501	346	277	233	198	187	164	155	146	138

Table 5. Minimum spacing of supports for gas piping

Size of pipe (Inches)	(Feet)	Size of tubing (Inch O.D.)	(Feet)
½	6	½	4
¾ or 1	8	⅝ or ¾	6
1¼ or larger (horizontal)	10	⅞ or 1	8
1¼ or larger (vertical)	every floor level		

be installed with a draft hood. The draft hood supplied with or forming a part of listed vented appliances shall be installed without alteration, exactly as furnished and specified by the appliance manufacturer. If a draft hood is not supplied by the appliance manufacturer when one is required, it shall be supplied by the installing agency and be of a listed or approved type, and in the absence of other instructions shall be the same size as the appliance flue collar.

The draft hood shall be in the same room as the combustion air opening of the appliance. In no case shall a draft hood be installed in a false ceiling, in a different room, or in any manner that will permit a difference in pressure between the draft hood relief opening and the combustion air supply.

Accessibility for service

Every gas appliance shall be located with respect to building construction and other equipment so as to permit access to the appliance. Sufficient clearance shall be maintained to permit the cleaning of heating surfaces; the replacement of filters, blowers, motors, burners, controls, and vent connections; the lubrication of moving parts where required; and the adjustment and cleaning of burners and pilots. For attic installation the passageway and servicing area adjacent to the appliance shall be floored.

Permissible temperatures on combustible materials

All gas appliances and their vent connectors shall be installed so that continued or intermittent operation will not create a hazard to persons or property. They shall not, during operation, raise the temperature of unprotected combustible walls, partitions, floors, or ceilings more than 90°F above normal room temperature.

AIR FOR COMBUSTION AND VENTILATION

Appliances shall be installed in a location in which the facilities for ventilation permit satisfactory combustion of gas, proper venting, and the maintenance of ambient temperature at safe limits under normal conditions of use. Appliances shall be located in such a manner as not to interfere with proper circulation of air within the confined space. In unconfined spaces in buildings of conventional construction, infiltration normally is adequate to provide air for combustion, ventilation, and draft hood dilution. When buildings are so tight that normal infiltration does not meet air requirements, outside air shall be introduced.

Air for combustion, ventilation, and draft hood dilution for gas appliances vented by natural draft normally may be obtained by application of one of the methods covered in Figs. 1–5.

Louvers and grilles

In calculating free area, consideration shall be given to the blocking effect of louvers, grilles or screens protecting openings. Screens used shall not be smaller than ¼ in. mesh. If the free area through a design of louver or grille is known, it should be used in calculating the size opening required to provide the free area specified. If the design and free area are not known, it may be assumed that wood louvers will have 20–25 per cent free area and metal louvers and grilles will have 60–75 per cent free area.

CLEARANCES

Domestic ranges

Clearance from combustible material: Listed domestic ranges when installed on combustible floors shall be set on their own bases or legs and shall be installed with clearances of not less than shown on the marking plate and the manufacturer's instructions. In the absence of clearance information on the marking plate, the range shall be installed with clearances not less than shown in Table 6. In no case shall the clearance be such as to interfere with requirements for combustion air, accessibility for operation, and servicing.

Unlisted domestic ranges shall be installed with at least a 6-in. clearance from back and sides. Combustible floors under unlisted appliances shall be protected in an approved manner.[1]

Vertical clearance above cooking top

Domestic ranges shall have a vertical clearance above the cooking top of not

[1] *For details of protection refer to Code for the Installation of Heat Producing Appliances, available from the American Insurance Association, 85 John St., New York, N.Y. 10038.*

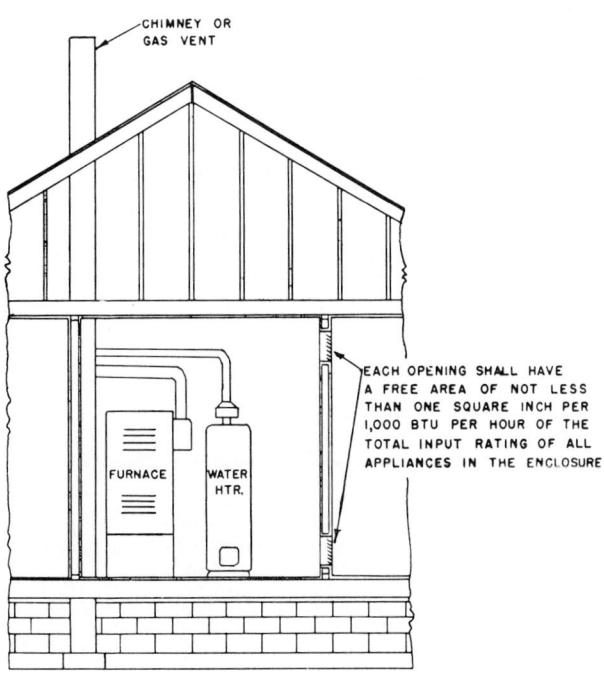

Fig. 1. Appliances located in confined spaces

All air from inside the building.

EACH OPENING SHALL HAVE A FREE AREA OF NOT LESS THAN ONE SQUARE INCH PER 1,000 BTU PER HOUR OF THE TOTAL INPUT RATING OF ALL APPLIANCES IN THE ENCLOSURE

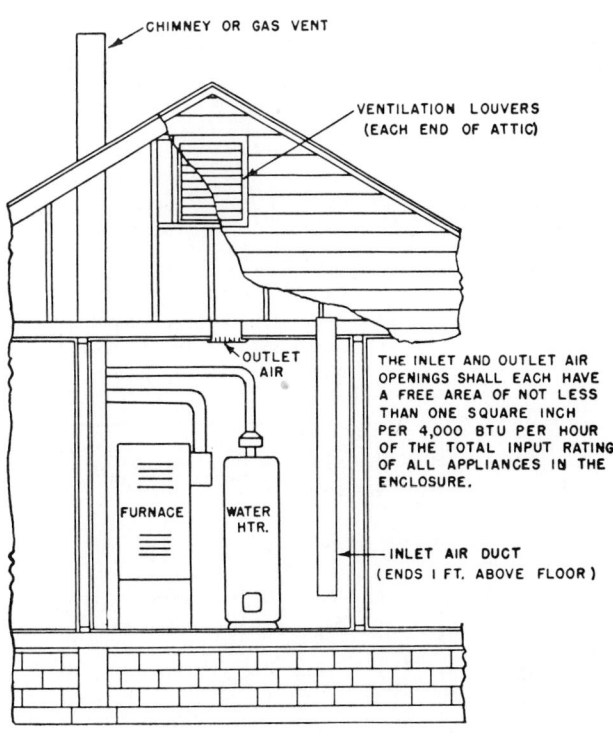

Fig. 3. Appliances located in confined spaces

All air from outdoors through ventilated attic.

CHIMNEY OR GAS VENT

VENTILATION LOUVERS (EACH END OF ATTIC)

OUTLET AIR

THE INLET AND OUTLET AIR OPENINGS SHALL EACH HAVE A FREE AREA OF NOT LESS THAN ONE SQUARE INCH PER 4,000 BTU PER HOUR OF THE TOTAL INPUT RATING OF ALL APPLIANCES IN THE ENCLOSURE.

INLET AIR DUCT (ENDS 1 FT. ABOVE FLOOR)

OUTLET AIR DUCT

EACH AIR DUCT OPENING SHALL HAVE A FREE AREA OF NOT LESS THAN ONE SQUARE INCH PER 2,000 BTU PER HOUR OF THE TOTAL INPUT RATING OF ALL APPLIANCES IN THE ENCLOSURE.*

INLET AIR DUCT

*IF THE APPLIANCE ROOM IS LOCATED AGAINST AN OUTSIDE WALL AND THE AIR OPENINGS COMMUNICATE DIRECTLY WITH THE OUTDOORS, EACH OPENING SHALL HAVE A FREE AREA OF NOT LESS THAN ONE SQUARE INCH PER 4,000 BTU PER HOUR OF THE TOTAL INPUT RATING OF ALL APPLIANCES IN THE ENCLOSURE.

Fig. 2. Appliances located in confined spaces

All air from outdoors.

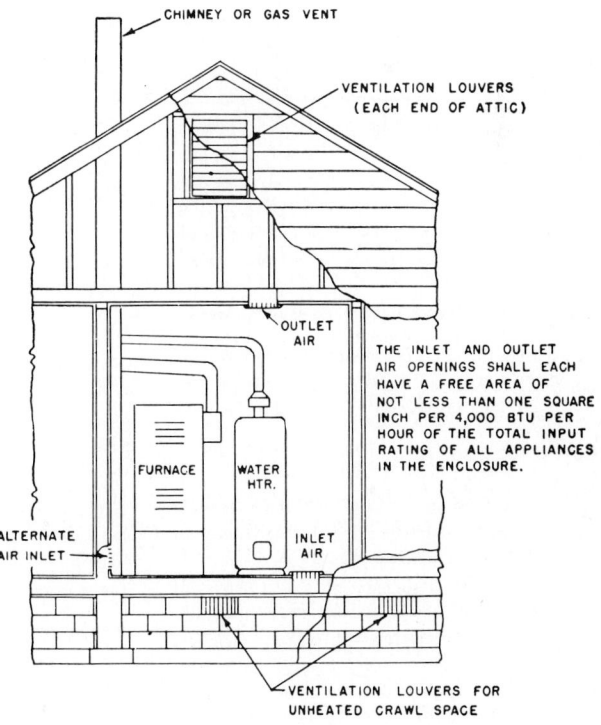

CHIMNEY OR GAS VENT

VENTILATION LOUVERS (EACH END OF ATTIC)

OUTLET AIR

THE INLET AND OUTLET AIR OPENINGS SHALL EACH HAVE A FREE AREA OF NOT LESS THAN ONE SQUARE INCH PER 4,000 BTU PER HOUR OF THE TOTAL INPUT RATING OF ALL APPLIANCES IN THE ENCLOSURE.

ALTERNATE AIR INLET

INLET AIR

VENTILATION LOUVERS FOR UNHEATED CRAWL SPACE

Fig. 4. Appliances located in confined spaces

All air from outdoors—inlet air from ventilated crawl space and outlet air to ventilated attic.

Table 6. Minimum clearances (unless otherwise marked) for listed domestic ranges

| | | Distance from combustile material, in. | | | |
| | | Sides | | Rear | |
Type of range	Spacing of center line of top burners from side of range	Wall not extending above cooking top	Wall extending above cooking top	Body of range	Projecting flue box
Insulated	Less than 10 in.	½	4½	1	1
Insulated	10 in. or more	½	½	1	1
Flush to wall	Less than 10 in.	Flush	4½	Flush	—
Flush to wall	10 in. or more	Flush	Flush	Flush	—

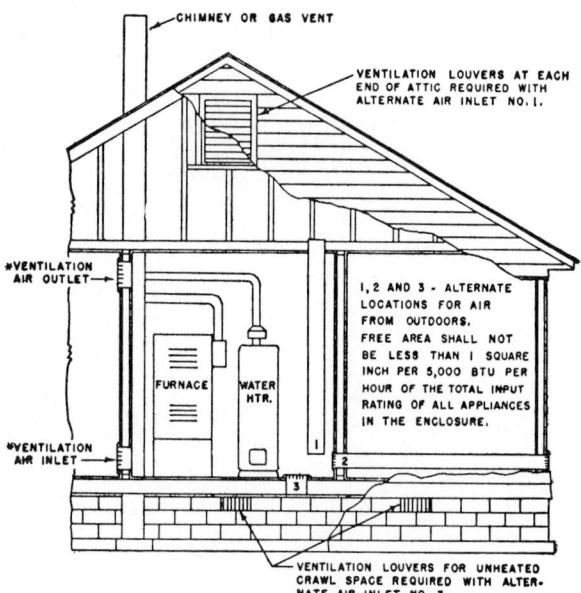

DUCTS USED FOR MAKE-UP AIR MAY BE CONNECTED TO THE COLD AIR RETURN OF THE HEATING SYSTEM ONLY IF THEY CONNECT DIRECTLY TO OUTDOOR AIR.

CHIMNEY OR GAS VENT

VENTILATION LOUVERS AT EACH END OF ATTIC REQUIRED WITH ALTERNATE AIR INLET NO. I.

*VENTILATION AIR OUTLET

1, 2 AND 3 - ALTERNATE LOCATIONS FOR AIR FROM OUTDOORS. FREE AREA SHALL NOT BE LESS THAN I SQUARE INCH PER 5,000 BTU PER HOUR OF THE TOTAL INPUT RATING OF ALL APPLIANCES IN THE ENCLOSURE.

FURNACE

WATER HTR.

*VENTILATION AIR INLET

VENTILATION LOUVERS FOR UNHEATED CRAWL SPACE REQUIRED WITH ALTERNATE AIR INLET NO. 3.

*EACH VENTILATION AIR OPENING FROM INSIDE THE BUILDING SHALL HAVE A FREE AREA OF NOT LESS THAN I SQUARE INCH PER 1,000 BTU PER HOUR OF THE TOTAL INPUT RATING OF ALL APPLIANCES IN THE ENCLOSURE.

Fig. 5. Appliances located in confined spaces

Ventilation air from inside building—combustion and draft hood dilution air from outside, ventilated attic or ventilated crawl space.

Table 7. Minimum clearances for listed water heaters

| Type of Heater* | Distance from Combustible Material Inches | |
	Nearest Part of Jacket	Flat Side
Type A	6	- - -
Type B	2	- - -
Type C	- - -	Flush
Counter Type Unit	In accordance with manufacturer's instructions.	

* Type A—Miscellaneous (including circulating tank, instantaneous, uninsulated, underfired).
Type B—Underfired, insulated automatic storage heaters.
Type C—Type B units with one or more flat sides and tested for installation flush to wall.
Counter Type—Type B units specifically designed for installation in or beneath a counter.

Table 8. Minimum clearances for listed room heaters

| Types of Appliance | Distance from Combustible Material, Inches | |
	Jacket, Sides and Rear	Projecting Flue Box or Draft Hood
Warm Air Circulators	6	2
Radiant Heaters	6	2
Wall Heaters	Flush	. . .

less than 30 in. to combustible material or metal cabinets. The clearance may be reduced to not less than 24 in. when

1. The underside of the combustible material or metal cabinet above the cooking top is protected with asbestos millboard at least ¼-inch thick, covered with sheet metal not lighter than no. 28 manufacturer's standard gage, or

2. A metal ventilating hood of not lighter than no. 28 manufacturer's standard gage sheet metal is installed above the cooking top with a clearance of not less than ¼ inch between the hood and the underside of the combustible material or metal cabinet and the hood is at least as wide as the range is and is centered over the range.

Built-in domestic cooking units

Listed built-in domestic cooking units shall be installed in accordance with their listing and the manufacturer's instructions. Listed built-in domestic cooking units may be installed in combustible material unless otherwise marked.

The installation shall not interfere with the requirements for combustion air and accessibility for operation and servicing.

Unlisted built-in domestic cooking units shall not be installed in, or adjacent to, combustible material.

Water heaters

Water heaters, with the exception of those having direct-vent systems, shall not be installed in bathrooms, bedrooms, or any occupied rooms normally kept closed.

Water heaters shall be located as close as practicable to the chimney or gas vent.

They should be located so as to provide short runs of piping to fixtures.

Listed water heaters shall be installed in accordance with their listing and the manufacturer's instructions. In no case shall the clearances be such as to interfere with the requirements for combustion air, draft hood clearance and relief, and accessibility for servicing (see Table 7).

Unlisted water heaters shall be installed with a clearance of 12 in. on all sides and rear. Combustible floors under unlisted water heaters shall be protected in an approved manner.[1]

Room heaters

Room heaters installed in sleeping quarters for use of transients, as in hotels and motels, shall be of the vented type and shall be connected to an effective chimney or gas vent and equipped with a safety shut off device.

Listed room heaters shall be installed with clearances not less than specified in Table 8. Unlisted room heaters shall be installed with clearances from combustible material not less than the following: circulating type with outer jacket, 12 in. at sides and rear; radiating type, 18 in. at sides and rear. Combustible floors under unlisted heaters shall be protected in an approved manner.[1]

Furnaces and boilers

Central heating boilers and furnaces installed in rooms which are large in comparison with the size of the appliance, shall be installed with clearances not less than specified in Table 9.

Central heating furnaces and boilers listed for installation at lesser clearances than specified in Table 9 may be installed in accordance with their listing and the manufacturers instructions.

Central heating furnaces and boilers installed in unconfined spaces may be installed with reduced clearances to combustible material provided the combustible material or the appliance is protected as described in Table 10.

Central heating furnaces and boilers installed in confined spaces shall be installed in accordance with their listing, and when such units are installed in spaces such as alcoves and closets, they shall be specifically listed for such installation. The installation clearances for furnaces and boilers in confined spaces shall not be reduced by the protection methods described in Table 10.

APPLIANCES REQUIRED TO BE VENTED

Appliances of the following types shall be vent connected or provided with other

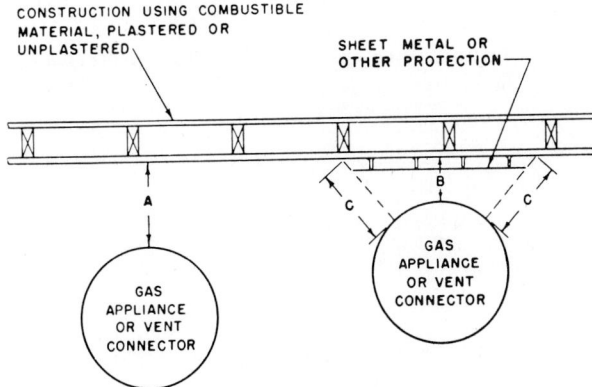

A equals the required clearance with no protection specified in Tables 9 and 11 and in the sections applying to various types of appliances.

B equals the reduced clearance permitted in accordance with Table 10. The protection applied to the construction using combustible material shall extend far enough in each direction to make C equal to A.

Fig. 6. Extent of protection required to reduce clearances from gas appliances or vent connectors

Table 9. Clearances to combustible material for furnaces and boilers installed in rooms which are large in comparison with size of appliance [i]

	Minimum clearance, in.				
	Above and sides of bonnet or plenum	Jacket sides and rear	Front[a]	Projecting flue box or Draft hood	Vent connector[b]
Listed automatically fired, forced air, or gravity system, with 250° F temperature limit control.	2[c,d]	6	18	6	6
Unlisted automatically fired, forced air, or gravity system, equipped with temperature limit control which cannot be set higher than 250° F.	6[e]	6	18	18[f]	18[f]
Listed automatically fired heating boilers—steam boilers operating at not over 15 psi gage pressure and hot water boilers operating at not in excess of 250° F.	6[g]	6	18	6	6
Unlisted automatically fired heating boilers—steam boilers operating at not over 15 psi gage pressure and hot water boilers operating at not in excess of 250° F.	6[g]	6	18	18[f]	18[f]
Central heating boilers and furnaces other than above.	18[h]	18	18	18[f]	18[f]

[a] *Front clearance shall be sufficient for servicing the burner and furnace or boiler.*
[b] *The vent connector clearance does not apply to listed Type B gas vents.*
[c] *This clearance may be reduced to 1 in. for a listed forced air or gravity furnace equipped with:*
  1. A limit control that cannot be set higher than 200° F or
  2. A marking to indicate that the outlet air temperature cannot exceed 200° F
[d] *Clearance from supply ducts within 3 ft of the plenum shall not be less than that specified from the bonnet or plenum. No clearance is required beyond this distance.*
[e] *Clearance from supply ducts within 6 ft of the plenum shall not be less than 6 in. No clearance is required beyond this distance.*
[f] *For unlisted gas appliances equipped with an approved draft hood, this clearance may be reduced to 9 in.*
[g] *This clearance is above top of boiler.*
[h] *Clearance from supply ducts shall not be less than 18 in. out to 3 ft from the bonnet or plenum, not less than 6 in. from 3 ft to 6 ft, and not less than 1 in. beyond 6 ft.*
[i] *Rooms which are large in comparison with the size of the appliance are rooms having a volume equal to at least 12 times the total volume of a furnace and at least 16 times the total volume of a boiler. Total volume of furnace or boiler is determined from exterior dimensions and is to include fan compartments and burner vestibules when used. When the actual ceiling height of a room is greater than 8 ft, the volume of a room shall be figured on the basis of a ceiling height of 8 ft.*

Table 10. Clearances, in inches, with specified forms of protection*

Type of Protection Applied to the combustible material unless otherwise specified and covering all surfaces within the distance specified as the required clearance with no protection. (See Fig. 11). Thicknesses are minimum.	36 inches Above	36 inches Sides & Rear	36 inches Vent Connector	18 inches Above	18 inches Sides & Rear	18 inches Vent Connector	12 inches Above	12 inches Sides & Rear	9 inches Vent Connector	6 inches Above	6 inches Sides & Rear	6 inches Vent Connector
(a) ¼ in. asbestos millboard spaced out 1 in. v	30	18	30	15	9	12	9	6	6	3	2	3
(b) 28 gage sheet metal on ¼ in. asbestos millboard	24	18	24	12	9	12	9	6	4	3	2	2
(c) 28 gage sheet metal spaced out 1 in. v	18	12	18	9	6	9	6	4	4	2	2	2
(d) 28 gage sheet metal on ⅛ in. asbestos millboard spaced out 1 in. v	18	12	18	9	6	9	6	4	4	2	2	2
(e) 1½ in. asbestos cement covering on heating appliance	18	12	36	9	6	18	6	4	9	2	1	6
(f) ¼ in. asbestos millboard on 1 in. mineral fiber bats reinforced with wire mesh or equivalent	18	12	18	6	6	6	4	4	4	2	2	2
(g) 22 gage sheet metal on 1 in. mineral fiber bats reinforced with wire or equivalent	18	12	12	4	3	3	2	2	2	2	2	2
(h) ¼ in. asbestos cement board or ¼ in. asbestos millboard	36	36	36	18	18	18	12	12	9	4	4	4
(i) ¼ in. cellular asbestos	36	36	36	18	18	18	12	12	9	3	3	3

* Except for the protection described in (e), all clearances shall be measured from the outer surface of the appliance to the combustible material disregarding any intervening protection applied to the combustible material.

v Spacers shall be of noncombustible material.

Table 11. Clearances for vent connectors

Appliance	Minimum Distance from Combustible Material — Listed Type B Gas Vent Material	Listed Type L Venting System Material	Connectors of Other than Type B or Type L Material
Listed appliances with draft hoods and appliances listed for use with Type B Gas Vents	as listed	as listed	6 in.
Boilers and furnaces with listed gas conversion burner and with draft hood	6 in.	6 in.	9 in.
Appliances listed for use with Type L venting systems	not permitted	as listed	9 in.
Residential incinerators	not permitted	9 in.	18 in.
Unlisted appliances with draft hood	not permitted	6 in.	9 in.
Appliances other than those above	not permitted	9 in.	18 in.

means for removing the flue gases to the outside atmosphere.

1. Steam and hot water boilers, warm air furnaces, floor furnaces, and wall furnaces.
2. Unit heaters and duct furnaces
3. Incinerators
4. Water heaters with inputs over 5,000 Btu per hour
5. Built-in domestic cooking units listed and marked as vented units only
6. Room heaters listed for vented use only
7. Type 2 clothes dryers
8. Appliances equipped with gas conversion burners
9. Other listed appliances which have draft hoods supplied by the appliance manufacturer
10. Unlisted appliances.

When unvented appliances are installed so that the aggregate input rating exceeds 30 Btu per hr per cu ft of room or space in which they are installed, one or more of them shall be vent connected or provided with an approved means for removing the vent gases to the outside atmosphere so that the aggregate input rating of the remaining unvented appliances does not exceed the 30 Btu per hr cu ft figure. When the room or space in which they are installed is directly connected to another room or space by a doorway, archway, or other opening of comparable size, which cannot be closed, the volume of such adjacent room or space may be included in the calculations.

METHODS OF VENTING

Chimneys shall be used for venting the following types of appliances:

1. Incinerators
2. Appliances which may be converted to the use of solid or liquid fuels

Chimneys may be listed, factory-built chimneys, installed in accordance with their listing and the manufacturer's instructions, or masonry or metal chimneys built and installed in accordance with nationally recognized building codes or standards.[2]

Appliances not required to be connected to chimneys may be vented by gas vents of Type B, B-W, or L or by single-wall metal pipe. Types B, B-W, and L are listed, factory-made products. Type B-W is for venting listed recessed wall heaters only. Single-wall metal pipe gas vent is constructed of sheet copper not less than No. 24 B&S gage or galvanized iron of not less than No. 20 Galvanized Sheet gage, or other approved noncombustible corrosion-resistant material.

Single-wall metal pipe shall be used only for runs directly from the space in which the appliance is located through the roof or exterior wall to the outer air. Such gas vents shall not originate in any unoccupied attic or concealed space, and shall not pass through any attic, inside wall, concealed space, nor through any floor.

When a single-wall metal pipe gas vent passes through an exterior wall or roof constructed of combustible material, it shall be guarded at the point of passage by a noncombustible thimble not less than 4 in. larger in diameter than the vent pipe.

SIZE OF GAS VENT OR CHIMNEY

The gas vent or chimney when connected to a single appliance shall be not less than the size of the draft hood outlet.

[2] Article X of the National Building Code of the American Insurance Association, 85 John St., New York 10038 or the American National Standard for Chimneys, Fireplaces, and Venting Systems, (ANSI A52.1-1971) (NFPA No. 211-1977), available from American National Standards Institute, 1430 Broadway, New York, N.Y. 10018, or National Fire Protection Association, 470 Atlantic Ave., Boston 02110, are such nationally recognized codes and standards.

When more than one appliance is connected to a gas vent or chimney, the area of the passageway shall be not less than the area of the largest vent connector plus 50 per cent of the areas of additional vent connectors.

Gas vents shall extend at least two feet above the highest point where they pass through a roof of a building and at least two feet higher than any portion of a building within ten feet. Chimneys shall extend at least three feet above the highest point where they pass through the roof of a building and at least two feet higher than any portion of the building within ten feet.

Gas vents or chimneys shall not terminate less than 5 ft in vertical height above the highest connected appliance draft hood outlet or flue collar.

Top of vent or chimney shall be of a design to prevent rain and debris from entering.

VENT CONNECTORS

That portion of the vent system which connects the gas appliance to the gas vent or chimney is called a vent connector.

Vent connectors used for gas appliances having draft hoods shall be constructed of materials having resistance to corrosion and heat not less than that of No. 28 Galvanized Sheet gage steel, or No. 26 B&S gage copper or No. 24 B&S gage aluminum.

Vent connectors serving listed gas appliances with draft hoods and other appliances listed for use with Type B vents may be constructed of Type B gas vent material.

Vent connectors made of Type L venting system material may be used with gas or combination gas-oil fuel-burning residential appliances including residential type incinerators.

Vent connectors shall not be smaller than the size of the flue collar or the draft hood outlet.

When two or more vent connectors enter a common vertical gas vent or chimney, the smaller connector should enter at the highest level consistent with available headroom or clearance to combustible material.

Two or more gas appliances may be vented through a common vent connector or manifold located at the highest level consistent with available headroom or clearance to combustible material.

The manifold, all junction fittings, and the common vent connector shall be of a size adequate for the combined volume of the vent gases.

The horizontal run of the vent connector shall be as short and direct as possible and the appliance shall be located as near the gas vent or chimney as practicable. The maximum length of horizontal run of single-wall vent connector shall not exceed 75 per cent of the height of the gas vent or chimney.

Minimum clearances of vent connectors to combustible material shall be in accordance with Table 11. The clearances from vent connectors to combustible materials may be reduced when the combustible material is protected as specified in Table 10.

By ALFRED GREENBERG, *P.E., Environmental and Energy Consultant*

INTRODUCTION

The purpose of this section is to present information that will be helpful to the reader in understanding and evaluating the heating, ventilating, and air conditioning (HVAC) design, operating and energy requirements for any building. Although it may be possible to design some complete, simple systems from the data given here, that is not the intent of this section. Except for the simplest

Table 1. Infiltration through windows and doors

Specification	Material	Type or class	Air leakage†
ANSI A134.1	Alumi-num	A-B1 (Awning)	0.75 cfm/ft crack
		A-A2 (Awning)	0.50 cfm/ft crack
		C-B1 (Casement)	0.50 cfm/ft crack
		C-A2 (Casement)	0.50 cfm/ft crack
		C-A3 (Casement)	0.50 cfm/ft crack
		DH-B1 (Hung)	0.75 cfm/ft crack
		DH-A2 (Hung)	0.50 cfm/ft crack
		DH-A3 (Hung)	0.50 cfm/ft crack
		DH-A4 (Hung)	0.50 cfm/ft crack
		HS-B1 (Sliding)	0.75 cfm/ft crack
		HS-B2 (Sliding)	0.75 cfm/ft crack
		HS-A2 (Sliding)	0.75 cfm/ft crack
		HS-A3 (Sliding)	0.50 cfm/ft crack
		J-B1 (Jalousie)	1.50 cfm/ft²
		JA-B1 (Jal-Awning)	0.75 cfm/ft crack
		P-B1 (Projected)	0.50 cfm/ft crack
		P-A2 (Projected)	0.50 cfm/ft crack
		P-A2.50 (Projected)	0.375 cfm/ft crack
		P-A3 (Projected)	0.50 cfm/ft crack‡
		TH-A2 (Inswinging)	0.375 cfm/ft crack
		TH-A3 (Inswinging)	0.50 cfm/ft crack‡
		VP-A2 (Pivoted)	0.375 cfm/ft crack
		VP-A3 (Pivoted)	0.50 cfm/ft crack‡
		VS-B1 (Vert. Sliding)	0.75 cfm/ft crack
ANSI A134.2	Alumi-num	SGD-B1 (Sliding Glass Door)	1.0 cfm/ft²
		SGD-B2 (Sliding Glass Door)	0.50 cfm/ft²
		SGD-A2 (Sliding Glass Door)	0.50 cfm/ft²
		SGD-A3 (Sliding Glass Door)	0.50 cfm/ft²‡
ANSI A200.1	Wood	All Types Windows Class A	0.50 cfm/ft linear ft
		Class B	0.50 cfm/ft linear ft
ANSI A200.2	Wood	All Types Sliding Glass Doors	0.50 cfm/ft²
Fed. MHC & SS*			
280.403	All	Windows (All Types) Sliding Glass Doors	0.50 cfm/ft²
Fed. MHC & SS*			
280.405	All	Vertical Entrance	1.20 cfm/ft² (1976)
			1.0 cfm/ft² (1977)

* Federal Mobile Home Construction and Safety Standard.
† At 1.56 psf (75 Pa) equivalent to 25 mph (11.2 m/s) wind velocity pressure.
‡ At 6.24 psf (300 Pa) equivalent to 50 mph (22.3 m/s) wind velocity pressure.
cfm/ft = 1.548 L/s/m; cfm/ft² = 5.080 L/s/m².

Table 2A. Infiltration through double-hung wood windows

Expressed in cubic feet per (hour) (foot of crack)[d]

		Pressure difference (inches of water)				
Type of window		0.10	0.20	0.30	0.40	0.50
A. Wood Double-Hung Window (Locked) (Leakage expressed as cubic feet per hour per foot of sash crack; only leakage around sash and through frame given)		25	50	25	100	125
1. Nonweatherstripped, loose fit[a]		77	122	150	194	225
2. Nonweatherstripped, average fit[b]		27	43	57	69	80
3. Weatherstripped, loose fit		28	44	58	70	81
4. Weatherstripped, average fit		14	23	30	36	42
B. Frame-Wall Leakage[c] (Leakage is that passing between the frame of a wood double-hung window and the wall)						
1. Around frame in masonry wall, not caulked		17	26	34	41	48
2. Around frame in masonry wall, caulked		3	5	6	7	8
3. Around frame in wood frame wall		13	21	29	35	42

[a] *A 0.094-in. crack and clearance represent a poorly fitted window, much poorer than average.*
[b] *The fit of the average double-hung wood window was determined as 0.0625-in. crack and 0.047-in. clearance.*
[c] *The values given for frame leakage are per foot of sash perimeter.*
[d] *Multiply by 0.0258 for L/s per meter of crack.*

Table 2B. Infiltration through walls

Expressed in cubic feet per (hour) (square foot)[e]

Type of wall		Pressure difference (inches of water)[f]				
		0.05	0.10	0.20	0.30	0.40
Brick Wall[a]		12	25	50	75	100
8.5 in.	Plain	5	9	16	24	28
	Plastered[b]	0.05	0.08	0.14	0.20	0.27
13 in.	Plain	5	8	14[e]	20	24
	Plastered[b]	0.01	0.04	0.05	0.09	0.11
	Plastered[c]	0.03	0.24	0.46	0.66	0.84
Frame Wall	Lath and Plaster[d]	0.09	0.15	0.22	0.29	0.32

[a] *Constructed of porous brick and lime mortar—workmanship poor.*
[b] *Two coats prepared gypsum plaster on brick.*
[c] *Furring, lath, and two coats prepared gypsum plaster on brick.*
[d] *Wall construction: bevel siding painted or cedar shingles, sheathing, building paper, wood lath, and three coats gypsum plaster.*
[e] *Multiply by 0.0258 for 1/s per meter of crack.*
[f] *1 inch of water = 249.082 pascals.*

Table 3. Coefficients of transmission (U) for slab doors

Btu per (hr ft²°F)

Thickness[a]	Winter			Summer
	Solid wood, No storm door	Storm door[b]		No storm door
		Wood	Metal	
1 in.	0.64	0.30	0.39	0.61
1.25 in.	0.55	0.28	0.34	0.53
1.5 in.	0.49	0.27	0.33	0.47
2 in.	0.43	0.24	0.29	0.42
Steel door				
1.75 in.				
A[c]	0.59	—	—	0.58
B[d]	0.19	—	—	0.18
C[e]	0.47	—	—	0.46

[a] Nominal thickness.
[b] Values for wood storm doors are for approximately 50% glass; for metal storm door values apply for any percent of glass.
[c] A = Mineral fiber core (2 lb/ft³).
[d] B = Solid urethane foam core with thermal break.
[e] C = Solid polystyrene core with thermal break.

buildings, all HVAC systems should be designed by a qualified environmental engineer, who should be consulted at the earliest design or planning stage. This is especially true when energy and operating costs must also be considered.

The first part of this section deals with the technical aspects of the subject—calculation of loads and design of systems—and in the second part the application to various building types is discussed.

Some of the data on the calculation of heating and cooling loads have been taken, with permission, from the *ASHRAE Handbook 1977 Fundamentals* published by the American Society of Heating, Refrigerating, and Air Conditioning Engineers. For further information, these publications (hereafter referred to as ASHRAE Handbook) should be consulted.

DEFINITION OF AIR CONDITIONING
(from ASHRAE Handbook)

"The process of treating air so as to control simultaneously its temperature, humidity, cleanliness and distribution to meet the requirements of the conditioned space."

PURPOSE

The reader should be generally acquainted with the tools and procedures used by engineers in arriving at heating and cooling loads and energy balances. The methods used and information given in the following pages are based upon sound present-day practices and should produce reasonably accurate results.

Table 4. Coefficients of transmission (U) of windows, skylights, and light transmitting partitions

These values are for heat transfer from air to air, Btu/(hr ft²°F)

PART A—VERTICAL PANELS (EXTERIOR WINDOWS, SLIDING PATIO DOORS, AND PARTITIONS)— FLAT GLASS, GLASS BLOCK, AND PLASTIC SHEET

Description	Exterior[a]		Interior
	Winter	Summer	
Flat Glass			
single glass	1.10	1.04	0.73
insulating glass—double			
0.1875-in. air space[b]	0.62	0.65	0.51
0.25-in. air space[b]	0.58	0.61	0.49
0.5-in. air space[c]	0.49	0.56	0.46
0.5-in. air space, low emittance coating[d]			
e = 0.20	0.32	0.38	0.32
e = 0.40	0.38	0.45	0.38
e = 0.60	0.43	0.51	0.42
insulating glass—triple			
0.25-in. air space[b]	0.39	0.44	0.38
0.5-in. air space[e]	0.31	0.39	0.30
storm windows			
1-in. to 4-in. air space[b]	0.50	0.50	0.44
Plastic Sheet			
single glazed			
0.125-in. thick	1.06	0.98	—
0.25-in. thick	0.96	0.89	—
0.5-in. thick	0.81	0.76	—
insulating unit—double			
0.25-in. air space[b]	0.55	0.56	—
0.5-in. air space[c]	0.43	0.45	—
Glass Block[f]			
6 x 6 x 4 in. thick	0.60	0.57	0.46
8 x 8 x 4 in. thick	0.56	0.54	0.44
—with cavity divider	0.48	0.46	0.38
12 x 12 x 4 in. thick	0.52	0.50	0.41
—with cavity divider	0.44	0.42	0.36
12 x 12 x 2 in. thick	0.60	0.57	0.46

[a] See Part C for adjustment for various window and sliding patio door types.
[b] 0.125-in. glass.
[c] 0.25-in. glass.
[d] Coating on either glass surface facing air space; all other glass surfaces uncoated.
[e] Window design: 0.25-in. glass—0.125-in. glass—0.25-in. glass.
[f] Dimensions are nominal.
[g] Based on area of opening, not total surface area.
[h] Values will be less than these when metal sash and frame incorporate thermal breaks. In some thermal break designs, U-values will be equal to or less than those for the glass. Window manufacturers should be consulted for specific data.

CALCULATION OF HEATING LOADS

The following information is required for determining heating and winter air-conditioning loads:

1. *Volume*, in cubic feet, of spaces.
2. *Areas* in square feet of all walls, floor, ceiling, roof, partitions, glass and doors between areas having different temperatures. These measurements may be taken room-by-room or zone-by-zone depending upon whether detailed loads or general information are desired.

3. *Infiltration* of air through windows and walls. See Tables 1 and 2. For infiltration through swinging and revolving doors, refer

Table 4 (cont.). Coefficients of transmission (U) of windows, skylights, and light transmitting partitions

These values are for heat transfer from air to air, Btu/(hr ft²°F)

PART B—HORIZONTAL PANELS (SKYLIGHTS)— FLAT GLASS, GLASS BLOCK, AND PLASTIC DOMES

Description	Winter[i]	Exterior[a] Summer[j]	Interior[f]
Flat Glass[c]			
single glass	1.23	0.83	0.96
insulating glass—double			
0.1875-in. air space[b]	0.70	0.57	0.62
0.25-in. air space[b]	0.65	0.54	0.59
0.5-in. air space[c]	0.59	0.49	0.56
0.5-in. air space, low emittance coating[d]			
e = 0.20	0.48	0.36	0.39
e = 0.40	0.52	0.42	0.45
e = 0.60	0.56	0.46	0.50
Glass Block[f]			
11 x 11 x 3 in. thick with cavity divider	0.53	0.35	0.44
12 x 12 x 4 in. thick with cavity divider	0.51	0.34	0.42
Plastic Domes[g]			
single-walled	1.15	0.80	—
double-walled	0.70	0.46	—

For footnotes see Table 4, Part A, on page 4-107.

Table 4 (cont.). Coefficients of transmission (U) of windows, skylights, and light transmitting partitions

These values are for heat transfer from air to air, Btu/(hr ft²°F)

PART C—ADJUSTMENT FACTORS FOR VARIOUS WINDOW AND SLIDING PATIO DOOR TYPES (MULTIPLY U-VALUES IN PARTS A AND B BY THESE FACTORS)

Description	Single glass	Double or triple glass	Storm windows
Windows			
All Glass	1.00	1.00	1.00
Wood Sash—80% Glass	0.90	0.95	0.90
Wood Sash—60% Glass	0.80	0.85	0.80
Metal Sash—80% Glass	1.00	1.20[h]	1.20[h]
Sliding Patio Doors			
Wood Frame	0.95	1.00	—
Metal Frame	1.00	1.10[h]	—

For footnotes see Table 4, Part A, on page 4-107.

Table 5A. Determination of U-value resulting from addition of insulation to the total area of any given building section

Given building section property*		Added R						
		R = 4	R = 6	R = 8	R = 12	R = 16	R = 20	R = 24
U	R	U	U	U	U	U	U	U
1.00	1.00	0.20	0.14	0.11	0.08	0.06	0.05	0.04
0.90	1.11	0.20	0.14	0.11	0.08	0.06	0.05	0.04
0.80	1.25	0.19	0.14	0.11	0.08	0.06	0.05	0.04
0.70	1.43	0.18	0.13	0.11	0.07	0.06	0.05	0.04
0.60	1.67	0.18	0.13	0.10	0.07	0.06	0.05	0.04
0.50	2.00	0.17	0.13	0.10	0.07	0.06	0.05	0.04
0.40	2.50	0.15	0.12	0.10	0.07	0.05	0.04	0.04
0.30	3.33	0.14	0.11	0.09	0.07	0.05	0.04	0.04
0.20	5.00	0.11	0.09	0.08	0.06	0.05	0.04	0.03
0.10	10.00	0.07	0.06	0.06	0.05	0.04	0.03	0.03
0.08	12.50	0.06	0.05	0.05	0.04	0.04	0.03	0.03

* For U- or R-values not shown in the table, interpolate as necessary.

Table 5B. Determination of U-value resulting from addition of insulation to uninsulated roof deck

U-value of roof without roof-deck insulation*	Conductance C of roof-deck insulation					
	0.12	0.15	0.19	0.24	0.36	0.72
	U	U	U	U	U	U
0.10	0.05	0.06	0.07	0.07	0.08	0.09
0.15	0.07	0.08	0.08	0.09	0.11	0.12
0.20	0.08	0.09	0.10	0.11	0.13	0.16
0.25	0.08	0.09	0.11	0.12	0.15	0.19
0.30	0.09	0.10	0.12	0.13	0.16	0.21
0.35	0.09	0.11	0.12	0.14	0.18	0.24
0.40	0.09	0.11	0.13	0.15	0.19	0.26
0.50	0.10	0.12	0.14	0.16	0.21	0.30
0.60	0.10	0.12	0.14	0.17	0.23	0.33
0.70	0.10	0.12	0.15	0.18	0.24	0.35

* Interpolation or mild extrapolation may be used.

to ASHRAE *Handbook of Fundamentals*.

4. *Coefficient of thermal transmission (U)* of each type of wall, floor, ceiling or roof, partition, glass and door construction. These may be found here and more fully in the ASHRAE *Handbook*. Tables 3 and 4 give *U*-factors for wood doors and for glass. *U*-factors for all other types of construction are given in the section on Insulation.

Table 5 gives information on the effects of adding various amounts of insulation to noninsulated walls and roofs. It can be clearly visualized how the addition of insulation substantially reduces the heat losses and gains.

WORK SHEETS

All calculations should be clearly recorded and properly filed for reference and checking. Many calculations required for determining heating loads are also needed for cooling-load calculations. Any form of record may be used, but Table 7 is recommended as a guide.

In using the work sheet, a separate line should be used for each area having a different *U*-value. It is usually advisable to calculate the glass area first. Fill in columns I, II, III, IV, V, VI, VII, VIII. Enter in column XII the product of columns V, VII, and VIII.

If air is used to heat or ventilate the room and more air is supplied than is exhausted (space is pressurized), then the infiltration can usually be neutralized and thus need not be considered in the heat-loss calculations. If infiltration is to be considered, then use the next line on the work sheet and fill in columns VII, IX, X, and XI. In column VII enter the factor 1.08.* In column XII en-
(Continued on p. 4-122.)

* *1.08 is a factor calculated from the specific heat of air, 0.24 Btu/(lb) (hr) (°F), and the density of air, 0.075 lb/per cu ft, and 60 min/per hr at 70°F, 29.92 in. Hg atmospheric pressure.*

Table 6. Suggested winter indoor dry-bulb temperatures

Type of building	°F	Type of building	°F	Type of building	°F
Schools:		Private rooms (surgical)	70–76	Dining rooms	70
Classrooms	68–70	Operating roons	70–95	Kitchens and laundries	60–66
Assembly rooms	68–72	Wards	70–74	Ballrooms	68–72
Gymnasiums	55–65	Kitchens and laundries	60–66	Toilets and service rooms	68
Toilets	68	Toilets	68		
Baths	76	Bathrooms	76–80	Homes	68–72
Wardrobe and locker rooms	65–68			Stores	65–68
Kitchens	66			Public buildings	68–70
Dining and lunch rooms	65–70	Theaters:		Warm air baths	120
Playrooms	60–65	Seatng space	68–72	Steam baths	110
Natatoriums	75	Lounge rooms	68–72	Factories and machine shops	60–65
		Toilets	68	Foundries and boiler shops	50–60
		Hotels:		Paint shops	72
Hospitals:		Bedrooms	70		
Private rooms	72–74				

NOTE: *The most comfortable dry-bulb temperature to be maintained depends on the relative humidity and air motion. These factors considered together constitute what is termed the* effective temperature. *(See ASHRAE Handbook). When relative humidity is not controlled separately, optimum dry-bulb temperature for comfort will be slightly higher than shown in this table. Suggested temperatures include concern for energy conservaton.*

Table 7. Heating calculations

Project No. _____ Designed by _____ Date _____ Checked by _____ Date _____

Project Name _____ Location _____

Outside Design Conditions: DB _____F   RH _____%   *Inside Design Conditions: DB _____°F   RH _____%

Outside Wind Velocity: _____MPH   Direction _____   Elevation _____

* Except where otherwise indicated.

I	II	III	IV	V	VI	VII	VIII	IX	X	XI	XII	XIII
								Crackage				
Room Name or No.	Item	Expo-sure	Dimen-sions	Net area sq. ft.	Volume cu. ft.	Temp. diff.	U or factor	Lineal Ft.	CFM/Lin. Ft.	Tot. CFM	Btu/ hr.	Remarks
A												
B												
C												
D												
E												
F												

Table 8. Climatic conditions for the United States and Canada—abstract

		Winter		Summer							
Col. 1	Col. 2	Col. 3		Col. 4			Col. 5		Col. 6		
	Annual heating degree-days	Design dry-bulb		Design dry-bulb and mean coincident wet-bulb			Mean daily range		Design wet-bulb		
State and station		99%	97.5%	1%	2.5%	5%		1%	2.5%	5%
ALABAMA											
Auburn		18	22	96/77	93/76	91/76	21	79	78	78
Birmingham	2551	17	21	96/74	94/75	92/74	21	78	77	76
Huntsville	3070	11	16	95/75	93/74	91/74	23	78	77	76
Mobile	1560	25	29	95/77	93/77	91/76	18	80	79	78
Montgomery	2291	22	25	96/76	95/76	93/76	21	79	79	78
Tuscaloosa		20	23	98/75	96/76	94/76	22	79	78	77
ALASKA											
Anchorage	10864	−23	−18	71/59	68/58	66/56	15	60	59	57
Barrow		−45	−41	57/53	53/50	49/47	12	54	50	47
Fairbanks	14279	−51	−47	82/62	78/60	75/59	24	64	62	60
Juneau	9075	−4	1	74/60	70/58	67/57	15	61	59	58
Kodiak		10	13	69/58	65/56	62/55	10	60	58	56
Nome	14171	−31	−27	66/57	62/55	59/54	10	58	56	55
ARIZONA											
Douglas		27	31	98/63	95/63	93/63	31	70	69	68
Flagstaff	7152	−2	4	84/55	82/55	80/54	31	61	60	59
Fort Huachuca		24	28	95/62	92/62	90/62	27	69	68	67
Kingman		18	25	103/65	100/64	97/64	30	70	69	69
Phoenix	1765	31	34	109/71	107/71	105/71	27	76	75	75
Prescott		4	9	96/61	94/60	92/60	30	66	65	64
Tuscon	1800	28	32	104/66	102/66	100/66	26	72	71	71
Winslow	4782	5	10	97/61	95/60	93/60	32	66	65	64
Yuma	974	36	39	111/72	109/72	107/71	27	79	78	77
ARKANSAS											
Blytheville AFB		10	15	96/78	94/77	91/76	21	81	80	78
Fayetteville		7	12	97/72	94/73	92/73	23	77	76	75
Fort Smith	3292	12	17	101/75	98/76	95/76	24	80	79	78
Hot Springs		17	23	101/77	97/77	94/77	22	80	79	78
Jonesboro		10	15	96/78	94/77	91/76	21	81	80	78
Little Rock	3219	15	20	99/76	96/77	94/77	22	80	79	78
Pine Bluff		16	22	100/78	97/77	95/78	22	81	80	80
Texarkana	2533	18	23	98/76	96/77	93/76	21	80	79	78
CALIFORNIA											
Bakersfield	2122	30	32	104/70	101/69	98/68	32	73	71	70
Bishop	4275	26	29	106/68	104/68	102/67	37	73	71	70
Burbank	1648	37	39	95/68	91/68	88/67	25	71	70	69
Fresno	2611	28	30	102/70	100/69	97/68	34	72	71	70
Hamilton AFB		30	32	89/68	84/66	80/65	28	72	69	62
Laguna Beach		41	43	83/68	80/68	77/67	18	70	69	68
Long Beach	1803	41	43	83/68	80/68	77/67	22	70	69	68
Los Angeles AP	2061	41	43	83/68	80/68	77/67	15	70	69	68
Los Angeles CO	1349	37	40	93/70	89/70	86/69	20	72	71	70
Oakland	2870	34	36	85/64	80/63	75/62	19	66	64	63
Palm Springs		33	35	112/71	110/70	108/70	35	76	74	73
Pasadena		32	35	98/69	95/68	92/67	29	73	71	70
Redding		29	31	105/68	102/67	100/66	32	71	69	68
Sacramento	2502	30	32	101/70	98/70	94/69	36	72	71	70
San Diego	1458	42	44	83/69	80/69	78/68	12	71	70	68
San Francisco CO	3001	38	40	74/63	71/62	69/61	14	64	62	61
San Jose		34	36	85/66	81/65	77/64	26	68	67	65
San Luis Obispo		33	35	92/69	88/70	84/69	26	73	71	70
Santa Cruz		35	38	75/63	71/61	68/61	28	64	62	61
Stockton		28	30	100/69	97/68	94/67	37	71	70	68
Yreka		13	17	95/65	92/64	89/63	38	67	65	64
COLORADO											
Alamosa	8529	−11	−6	84/57	82/57	80/57	35	62	61	60
Boulder		−6	0	93/59	91/59	89/59	27	64	63	62
Colorado Springs	6423	−3	2	91/58	88/57	86/57	30	63	62	61

		Winter		Summer						
		Col. 3		Col. 4			Col. 5	Col. 6		
Col. 1	Col. 2									
	Annual heating degree-days	Design dry-bulb		Design dry-bulb and mean coincident wet-bulb			Mean daily range	Design wet-bulb		
State and station		99%	97.5%	1%	2.5%	5%		1%	2.5%	5%
Denver	6283	−5	1	93/59	91/59	89/59	28	64	63	62
Grand Junction	5641	2	7	96/59	94/59	92/59	29	64	63	62
Leadville		−18	−14	84/52	81/51	78/50	30	56	55	54
Pueblo	5462	−7	0	97/61	95/61	92/61	31	67	66	65
CONNECTICUT										
Bridgeport	5617	6	9	86/73	84/71	81/70	18	75	74	73
Hartford	6235	3	7	91/74	88/73	85/72	22	77	75	74
New Haven	5897	3	7	88/75	84/73	82/72	17	76	75	74
New London		5	9	88/73	85/72	83/71	16	76	75	74
Waterbury		−4	2	88/73	85/71	82/70	21	75	74	72
DELAWARE										
Wilmington	4930	10	14	92/74	89/74	87/73	20	77	76	75
DISTRICT OF COLUMBIA										
Washington	4224	14	17	93/75	91/74	89/74	18	78	77	76
FLORIDA										
Daytona Beach	879	32	35	92/78	90/77	88/77	15	80	79	78
Jacksonville	1239	29	32	96/77	94/77	92/76	19	79	79	78
Key West	108	55	57	90/78	90/78	89/78	9	80	79	79
Lakeland	661	39	41	93/76	91/76	89/76	17	79	78	78
Miami	214	44	47	91/77	90/77	89/77	15	79	79	78
Orlando	766	35	38	94/76	93/76	91/76	17	79	78	78
Pensacola	1463	25	29	94/77	93/77	91/77	14	80	79	79
Tallahassee	1485	27	30	94/77	92/76	90/76	19	79	78	78
Tampa	683	36	40	92/77	91/77	90/76	17	79	79	78
West Palm Beach	253	41	45	92/78	91/78	90/78	16	80	79	79
GEORGIA										
Athens	2929	18	22	94/74	92/74	90/74	21	78	77	76
Atlanta	2961	17	22	94/74	92/74	90/73	19	77	76	75
Augusta	2397	20	23	97/77	95/76	93/76	19	80	79	78
Columbus, Lawson AFB	2383	21	24	95/76	93/76	91/75	21	79	78	77
Macon	2136	21	25	96/77	93/76	91/75	22	79	78	77
Rome	3326	17	22	94/76	93/76	91/76	23	79	78	77
Savannah	1819	24	27	96/77	93/77	91/77	20	80	79	79
HAWAII										
Hilo		61	62	84/73	83/72	82/72	15	75	74	74
Honolulu		62	63	87/73	86/73	85/72	12	76	75	74
IDAHO										
Boise	5809	3	10	96/65	94/64	91/64	31	68	66	65
Coeur d'Alene		−8	−1	89/62	86/61	83/60	31	64	63	61
Idaho Falls		−11	−6	89/61	87/61	84/59	38	65	63	61
Lewiston	5542	−1	6	96/65	93/64	90/63	32	67	66	64
Pocatello	7033	−8	−1	94/61	91/60	89/59	35	64	63	61
ILLINOIS										
Champaign/Urbana		−3	2	95/75	92/74	90/73		78	77	75
Chicago, Midway AP	6155	−5	0	94/74	91/73	88/72	20	77	75	74
Chicago, O'Hare AP	6639	−8	−4	91/74	89/74	86/72	20	77	76	74
Chicago, CO	5882	−3	2	94/75	91/74	88/73	15	79	77	75
Decatur		−3	2	94/75	91/74	88/73	21	78	77	75
Joliet		−5	0	93/75	90/74	88/73	20	78	77	75
Moline	6408	−9	−4	93/75	91/75	88/74	23	78	77	75
Peoria	6025	−8	−4	91/75	89/74	87/73	22	78	76	75
Rockford	6830	−9	−4	91/74	89/73	87/72	24	77	76	74
Springfield	5429	−3	2	94/75	92/74	89/74	21	79	77	76
INDIANA										
Bloomington		0	5	95/76	92/75	89/74	22	79	78	76
Crawfordsville		−2	3	94/75	91/74	88/73	22	79	77	76
Evansville	4435	4	9	95/76	93/75	91/75	22	79	78	77
Fort Wayne	6205	−4	1	92/73	89/72	87/72	24	77	75	74
Indianapolis	5699	−2	2	92/74	90/74	87/73	22	78	76	75

4-111

Climatic conditions

Table 8 (cont.). Climatic conditions for the United States and Canada—abstract

Col. 1	Col. 2	Col. 3 Winter		Col. 4 Summer			Col. 5	Col. 6		
	Annual heating degree-days	Design dry-bulb		Design dry-bulb and mean coincident wet-bulb			Mean daily range	Design wet-bulb		
State and station		99%	97.5%	1%	2.5%	5%		1%	2.5%	5%
Lafayette		−3	3	94/74	91/73	88/73	22	78	76	75
Peru, Bunker Hill AFB		−6	−1	90/74	88/73	86/73	22	77	75	74
South Bend	6439	−3	1	91/73	89/73	86/72	22	77	75	74
Terre Haute		−2	4	95/75	92/74	89/73	22	79	77	76
IOWA										
Burlington	6114	−7	−3	94/74	91/75	88/73	22	78	77	75
Des Moines	6588	−10	−5	94/75	91/74	88/73	23	78	77	75
Dubuque	7376	−12	−7	90/74	88/73	86/72	22	77	75	74
Sioux City	6951	−11	−7	95/74	92/74	89/73	24	78	77	75
Waterloo	7320	−15	−10	91/76	89/75	86/74	23	78	77	75
KANSAS										
Dodge City	4986	0	5	100/69	97/69	95/69	25	74	73	71
Salina		0	5	103/74	100/74	97/73	26	78	77	75
Topeka	5182	0	4	99/75	96/75	93/74	24	79	78	76
Wichita	4620	3	7	101/72	98/73	96/73	23	77	76	75
KENTUCKY										
Covington	5265	1	6	92/73	90/72	88/72	22	77	75	74
Lexington	4683	3	8	93/73	91/73	88/72	22	77	76	75
Louisville	4460	5	10	95/74	93/74	90/74	23	79	77	76
Paducah		7	12	98/76	95/75	92/75	20	79	78	77
LOUISIANA										
Alexandria	1921	23	27	95/77	94/77	92/77	20	80	79	78
Baton Rouge	1560	25	29	95/77	93/77	92/77	19	80	80	79
Lake Charles	1459	27	31	95/77	93/77	92/77	17	80	79	79
New Orleans	1385	29	33	93/78	92/78	90/77	16	81	80	79
Shreveport	2184	20	25	99/77	96/76	94/76	20	79	79	78
MAINE										
Augusta		−7	−3	88/73	85/70	82/68	22	74	72	70
Bangor, Dow AFB		−11	−6	86/70	83/68	80/67	22	73	71	69
Caribou	9767	−18	−13	84/69	81/67	78/66	21	71	69	67
Portland	7571	−6	−1	87/72	84/71	81/69	22	74	72	70
MARYLAND										
Baltimore AP	4654	10	13	94/75	91/75	89/74	21	78	77	76
Baltimore CO	4111	14	17	92/77	89/76	87/75	17	80	78	76
Frederick	5087	8	12	94/76	91/75	88/74	22	78	77	76
MASSACHUSETTS										
Boston	5334	6	9	91/73	88/71	85/70	16	75	74	72
Gloucester		2	5	89/73	86/71	83/70	15	75	74	72
Pittsfield	7578	−8	−3	87/71	84/70	81/68	23	73	72	70
Springfield, Westover AFB		−5	0	90/72	87/71	84/69	19	75	73	72
Worcester	6969	0	4	87/71	84/70	81/68	18	73	72	70
MICHIGAN										
Alpena	8506	−11	−6	89/70	85/70	83/69	27	73	72	70
Detroit	6232	3	6	91/73	88/72	86/71	20	76	74	73
Escanaba	8481	−11	−7	87/70	83/69	80/68	17	73	71	69
Flint	7377	−4	1	90/73	87/72	85/71	25	76	74	72
Grand Rapids	6894	1	5	91/72	88/72	85/70	24	75	74	72
Lansing	6909	−3	1	90/73	87/72	84/70	24	75	74	72
Marquette	8393	−12	−8	84/70	81/69	77/66	18	72	70	68
Muskegon	6696	2	6	86/72	84/70	82/70	21	75	73	72
Sault Ste. Marie	9048	−12	−8	84/70	81/69	77/66	23	72	70	68
MINNESOTA										
Duluth	10000	−21	−16	85/70	82/68	79/66	22	72	70	68
International Falls		−29	−25	85/68	83/68	80/66	26	71	70	68
Minneapolis/St Paul	8382	−16	−12	92/75	89/73	86/71	22	77	75	73
Rochester	8285	−17	−12	90/74	87/72	84/71	24	77	75	73
MISSISSIPPI										
Columbus AFB		15	20	95/77	93/77	91/76	22	80	79	78

		Winter		Summer							
Col. 1	Col. 2	Col. 3		Col. 4			Col. 5		Col. 6		
State and station	Annual heating degree-days	Design dry-bulb		Design dry-bulb and mean coincident wet-bulb			Mean daily range	Design wet-bulb				
		99%	97.5%	1%	2.5%	5%		1%	2.5%	5%	
Greenville AFB		15	20	95/77	93/77	91/76	21	80	79	78	
Jackson	2239	21	25	97/76	95/76	93/76	21	79	78	78	
Meridian	2289	19	23	97/77	95/76	93/76	22	80	79	78	
Natchez		23	27	96/78	94/78	92/77	21	81	80	79	
Vicksburg	2041	22	26	97/78	95/78	93/77	21	81	80	79	
MISSOURI											
Columbia	5048	−1	4	97/74	94/74	91/73	22	78	77	76	
Joplin		6	10	100/73	97/73	94/73	24	78	77	76	
Kansas City	4711	2	6	99/75	96/74	93/74	20	78	77	76	
Rolla		3	9	94/77	91/75	89/74	22	81	79	77	
St Joseph	5484	−3	2	96/77	93/76	91/76	23	81	79	77	
St Louis AP	4900	2	6	97/75	94/75	91/74	21	78	77	76	
St Louis CO	4484	3	8	98/75	94/75	91/74	18	78	77	76	
Springfield	4900	3	9	96/73	93/74	91/74	23	78	77	75	
MONTANA											
Billings	7049	−15	−10	94/64	91/64	88/63	31	67	66	64	
Bozeman		−20	−14	90/61	87/60	84/59	32	63	62	60	
Glasgow	8996	−22	−18	92/64	89/63	85/62	29	68	66	64	
Great Falls	7750	−21	−15	91/60	88/60	85/59	28	64	62	60	
Havre	8700	−18	−11	94/65	90/64	87/63	33	68	66	65	
Helena	8129	−21	−16	91/60	88/60	85/59	32	64	62	61	
Kalispell	8191	−14	−7	91/62	87/61	84/60	34	65	63	62	
Miles City	7723	−20	−15	98/66	95/66	92/65	30	70	68	67	
Missoula	8125	−13	−6	92/62	88/61	85/60	36	65	63	62	
NEBRASKA											
Grand Island	6530	−8	−3	97/72	94/71	91/71	28	75	74	74	
Lincoln	5884	−5	−2	99/75	95/74	92/74	24	78	77	76	
Norfolk	6979	−8	−4	97/74	93/74	90/73	30	78	77	75	
North Platte	6684	−8	−4	97/69	94/69	90/69	28	74	72	71	
Omaha	6612	−8	−3	94/76	91/75	88/74	22	78	77	75	
Scottsbluff	6673	−8	−3	95/65	92/65	90/64	31	70	68	67	
NEVADA											
Elko	7433	−8	−2	94/59	92/59	90/58	42	63	62	60	
Ely	7733	−10	−4	89/57	87/56	85/55	39	60	59	58	
Las Vegas	2709	25	28	108/66	106/65	104/65	30	71	70	69	
Reno	6332	5	10	95/61	92/60	90/59	45	64	62	61	
Winnemucca	6761	−1	3	96/60	94/60	92/60	42	64	62	61	
NEW HAMPSHIRE											
Concord	7383	−8	−3	90/72	87/70	84/69	26	74	73	71	
Keene		−12	−7	90/72	87/70	83/69	24	74	73	71	
Portsmouth, Pease AFB		−2	2	89/73	85/71	83/70	22	75	74	72	
NEW JERSEY											
Atlantic City	4812	10	13	92/74	89/74	86/72	18	78	77	75	
Newark	4589	10	14	94/74	91/73	88/72	20	77	76	75	
New Brunswick		6	10	92/74	89/73	86/72	19	77	76	75	
Paterson		6	10	94/74	91/73	88/72	21	77	76	75	
Phillipsburg		1	6	92/73	89/72	86/71	21	76	75	74	
Trenton	4980	11	14	91/75	88/74	85/73	19	78	76	75	
NEW MEXICO											
Albuquerque	4348	12	16	96/61	94/61	92/61	27	66	65	64	
Carlsbad		13	19	103/67	100/67	97/67	28	72	71	70	
Gallup		0	5	90/59	89/58	86/58	32	64	62	61	
Los Alamos		5	9	89/60	87/60	85/60	32	62	61	60	
Raton	6228	−4	1	91/60	89/60	87/60	34	65	64	63	
Roswell, Walker AFB	3793	13	18	100/66	98/66	96/66	33	71	70	69	
Santa Fe		6	10	90/61	88/61	86/61	28	63	62	61	
Silver City	3705	5	10	95/61	94/60	91/60	30	66	64	61	
Tucumcari		8	13	99/66	97/66	95/65	28	70	69	68	

Table 8 (cont.). Climatic conditions for the United States and Canada—abstract

State and station	Annual heating degree-days	Winter Col. 3 Design dry-bulb 99%	Winter Col. 3 Design dry-bulb 97.5%	Summer Col. 4 Design dry-bulb and mean coincident wet-bulb 1%	Summer Col. 4 Design dry-bulb and mean coincident wet-bulb 2.5%	Summer Col. 4 Design dry-bulb and mean coincident wet-bulb 5%	Summer Col. 5 Mean daily range	Summer Col. 6 Design wet-bulb 1%	Summer Col. 6 Design wet-bulb 2.5%	Summer Col. 6 Design wet-bulb 5%
NEW YORK										
Albany	6875	−6	−1	91/73	88/72	85/70	23	75	74	72
Binghamton	7286	−2	1	86/71	83/69	81/68	20	73	72	70
Buffalo	7062	2	6	88/71	85/70	83/69	21	74	73	72
Cortland		−5	0	88/71	85/71	82/70	23	74	73	71
Glen Falls		−11	−5	88/72	85/71	82/69	23	74	73	71
Ithaca		−5	0	88/71	85/71	82/70	24	74	73	71
Jamestown		−1	3	88/70	86/70	83/69	20	74	72	71
Massena		−13	−8	86/70	83/69	80/68	20	73	72	70
Newburg-Stewart AFB		−1	4	90/73	88/72	85/70	21	76	74	73
NYC-Central Park	4871	11	15	92/74	89/73	87/72	17	76	75	74
NYC-Kennedy AP	5219	12	15	90/73	87/72	84/71	16	76	75	74
Oneonta		−7	−4	86/71	83/69	80/68	24	73	72	70
Plattsburgh AFB		−13	−8	86/70	83/69	80/68	22	73	72	70
Poughkeepsie		0	6	92/74	89/74	86/72	21	77	75	74
Rochester	6748	1	5	91/73	88/71	85/70	22	75	73	72
Rome-Griffiss AFB		−11	−5	88/71	85/70	83/69	22	75	73	71
Suffolk County AFB		7	10	86/72	83/71	80/70	16	76	74	73
Syracuse	6756	−3	2	90/73	87/71	84/70	20	75	73	72
Utica		−12	−6	88/73	85/71	82/70	22	75	73	71
NORTH CAROLINA										
Ashville	4042	10	14	89/73	87/72	85/71	21	75	74	72
Charlotte	3191	18	22	95/74	93/74	91/74	20	77	76	76
Fayetteville, Pope AFB		17	20	95/76	92/76	90/75	20	79	78	77
Greensboro	3805	14	18	93/74	91/73	89/73	21	77	76	75
Raleigh/Durham	3393	16	20	94/75	92/75	90/75	20	78	77	76
Wilmington	2347	23	26	93/79	91/78	89/77	18	81	80	79
Winston-Salem	3595	16	20	94/74	91/73	89/73	20	76	75	74
NORTH DAKOTA										
Bismarck	8851	−23	−19	95/68	91/68	88/67	27	73	71	70
Devil's Lake	9901	−25	−21	91/69	88/68	85/66	25	73	71	69
Fargo	9226	−22	−18	92/73	89/71	85/69	25	76	74	72
Williston	9243	−25	−21	91/68	88/67	85/65	25	72	70	68
OHIO										
Akron-Canton	6037	1	6	89/72	86/71	84/70	21	75	73	72
Athens		0	6	95/75	92/74	90/73	22	78	76	74
Cincinnati	4410	1	6	92/73	90/72	88/72	21	77	75	74
Cleveland	6351	1	5	91/73	88/72	86/71	22	76	74	73
Columbus	5660	0	5	92/73	90/73	87/72	24	77	75	74
Dayton	5622	−1	4	91/73	89/72	86/71	20	76	75	73
Mansfield	6403	0	5	90/73	87/72	85/72	22	76	74	73
Sandusky	5796	1	6	93/73	91/72	88/71	21	76	74	73
Toledo	6494	−3	1	90/73	88/73	85/71	25	76	75	73
Youngstown	6417	−1	4	88/71	86/71	84/70	23	74	73	71
OKLAHOMA										
Bartlesville		6	10	101/73	98/74	95/74	23	77	77	76
Muskogee		10	15	101/74	98/75	95/75	23	79	78	77
Oklahoma City	3725	9	13	100/74	97/74	95/73	23	78	77	76
Tulsa	3860	8	13	101/74	98/75	95/75	22	79	78	77
OREGON										
Astoria	5186	25	29	75/65	71/62	68/61	16	65	63	62
Eugene	4726	17	22	92/67	89/66	86/65	31	69	67	66
Grants Pass		20	24	99/69	96/68	93/67	33	71	69	68
Klamath Falls		4	9	90/61	87/60	84/59	36	63	61	60
Medford	5008	19	23	98/68	94/67	91/66	35	70	68	67
Pendleton	5127	−2	5	97/65	93/64	90/62	29	66	65	63
Portland	4635	17	23	89/68	85/67	81/65	23	69	67	66
Roseburg	4491	18	23	93/67	90/66	87/65	30	69	67	66

Col. 1	Col. 2	Winter		Summer						
		Col. 3		Col. 4			Col. 5	Col. 6		
	Annual heating degree-days	Design dry-bulb		Design dry-bulb and mean coincident wet-bulb			Mean daily range	Design wet-bulb		
State and station		99%	97.5%	1%	2.5%	5%		1%	2.5%	5%
PENNSYLVANIA										
Allentown AP	5810	4	9	92/73	88/72	86/72	22	76	75	73
Erie	6451	4	9	88/73	85/72	83/71	18	75	74	72
Harrisburg	5251	7	11	94/75	91/74	88/73	21	77	76	75
Lancaster		4	8	93/75	90/74	87/73	22	77	76	75
Philadelphia	5144	10	14	93/75	90/74	87/72	21	77	76	75
Pittsburg AP	5987	1	5	89/72	86/71	84/70	22	74	73	72
Pittsburg CO	5053	3	7	91/72	88/71	86/70	19	74	73	72
Reading	4945	9	13	92/73	89/72	86/72	19	76	75	73
Scranton/Wilkes-Barre	6254	1	5	90/72	87/71	84/70	19	74	73	72
Williamsport	5934	2	7	92/73	89/72	86/70	23	75	74	73
York		8	12	94/75	91/74	88/73	22	77	76	75
RHODE ISLAND										
Providence	5954	5	9	89/73	86/72	83/70	19	75	74	73
SOUTH CAROLINA										
Charleston	1794	25	28	94/78	92/78	90/77	13	81	80	79
Columbia	2484	20	24	97/76	95/75	93/75	22	79	78	77
Greenville	2980	18	22	93/74	91/74	89/74	21	77	76	75
Spartanburg	2980	18	22	93/74	91/74	89/74	20	77	76	75
SOUTH DAKOTA										
Huron	8223	−18	−14	96/73	93/72	90/71	28	77	75	73
Pierre		−15	−10	99/71	95/71	92/69	29	75	74	72
Rapid City	7345	−11	−7	95/66	92/65	89/65	28	71	69	67
Sioux Falls	7539	−15	−11	94/73	91/72	88/71	24	76	75	73
TENNESSEE										
Bristol-Tri City	4143	9	14	91/72	89/72	87/71	22	75	75	73
Chattanooga	3254	13	18	96/75	93/74	91/74	22	78	77	76
Knoxville	3494	13	19	94/74	92/73	90/73	21	77	76	75
Memphis	3232	13	18	98/77	95/76	93/76	21	80	79	78
Nashville	3578	9	14	97/75	94/74	91/74	21	78	77	76
TEXAS										
Abilene	2624	15	20	101/71	99/71	97/71	22	75	74	74
Amarillo	3985	6	11	98/67	95/67	93/67	26	71	70	70
Austin	1711	24	28	100/74	98/74	97/74	22	78	77	77
Beaumont		27	31	95/79	93/78	91/78	19	81	80	80
Brownsville	600	35	39	94/77	93/77	92/77	18	80	79	79
Corpus Christi	914	31	35	95/78	94/78	92/78	19	80	80	76
Dallas	2363	18	22	102/75	100/75	97/75	20	78	78	77
El Paso	2700	20	24	100/64	98/64	96/64	27	69	68	68
Fort Worth	2405	17	22	101/74	99/74	97/74	22	78	77	76
Galveston	1274	31	36	90/79	89/79	88/78	10	81	80	80
Houston	1396	27	32	96/77	94/77	92/77	18	80	79	79
Laredo AFB	797	32	36	102/73	101/73	99/74	23	78	78	72
Lubbock	3578	10	15	98/69	96/69	94/69	26	73	72	71
Midland	2591	16	21	100/69	98/69	96/69	26	73	72	71
Port Arthur	1447	27	31	95/79	93/78	91/78	19	81	80	80
San Angelo, Good-fellow AFB	2255	18	22	101/71	99/71	97/70	24	75	74	73
San Antonio	1546	25	30	99/72	97/73	96/73	19	77	76	76
Victoria	1173	29	32	98/78	96/77	94/77	18	82	81	79
Waco	2030	21	26	101/75	99/75	97/75	22	78	78	77
Wichita Falls	2832	14	18	103/73	101/73	98/73	24	77	76	75
UTAH										
Logan		−3	2	93/62	91/61	88/60	33	65	64	63
Moab		6	11	100/60	98/60	96/60	30	65	64	63
Ogden		1	5	93/63	91/61	88/61	33	66	65	64
Provo		1	6	98/62	96/62	94/61	32	66	65	64

Table 8 (cont.). Climatic conditions for the United States and Canada—abstract

State/province and station	Annual heating degree-days	Winter Design dry-bulb 99%	Winter Design dry-bulb 97.5%	Summer Design dry-bulb and mean coincident wet-bulb 1%	2.5%	5%	Mean daily range	Design wet-bulb 1%	2.5%	5%
		Col. 3		Col. 4			Col. 5	Col. 6		
Salt Lake City	6052	3	8	97/62	95/62	92/61	32	66	65	64
VERMONT										
Burlington	8269	−12	−7	88/72	85/70	82/69	23	74	72	71
VIRGINIA										
Fredericksburg		10	14	96/76	93/75	90/74	21	78	77	76
Lynchburg	4166	12	16	93/74	90/74	88/73	21	77	76	75
Norfolk	3421	20	22	93/77	91/76	89/76	18	79	78	77
Richmond	3865	14	17	95/76	92/76	90/75	21	79	78	77
Roanoke	4150	12	16	93/72	91/72	88/71	23	75	74	73
Winchester		6	10	93/75	90/74	88/74	21	77	76	75
WASHINGTON										
Aberdeen		25	28	80/65	77/62	73/61	16	65	63	62
Bellingham		10	15	81/67	77/65	74/63	19	68	65	63
Bremerton		21	25	82/65	78/64	75/62	20	66	64	63
Ellensburg		2	6	94/65	91/64	87/62	34	66	65	63
Kennewick		5	11	99/68	96/67	92/66	30	70	68	67
Moses Lake, Larson AFB		1	7	97/66	94/65	90/63	32	67	66	64
Olympia	5236	16	22	87/66	83/65	79/64	32	67	66	64
Port Angeles		24	27	72/62	69/61	67/60	18	64	62	61
Seattle CO	4424	22	27	85/68	82/66	78/65	19	69	67	65
Seattle-Tacoma AP	5145	21	26	84/65	80/64	76/62	22	66	64	63
Spokane	6655	−6	2	93/64	90/63	87/62	28	65	64	62
Tacoma-McChord AFB		19	24	86/66	82/65	79/63	22	68	66	64
Walla Walla	4805	0	7	97/67	94/66	90/65	27	69	67	66
Yakima	5941	−2	5	96/65	93/65	89/63	36	68	66	65
WEST VIRGINIA										
Bluefield		−2	4	83/71	81/69	79/69	22	73	71	70
Charleston	4476	7	11	92/74	90/73	87/72	20	76	75	74
Elkins	5675	1	6	86/72	84/70	82/70	22	74	72	71
Huntington	4446	5	10	94/76	91/74	89/73	22	78	77	75
Morgantown		4	8	90/74	87/73	85/73	22	76	75	74
Parkersburg	4754	7	11	93/75	90/74	88/73	21	77	76	75
Wheeling		1	5	89/72	86/71	84/70	21	74	73	72
WISCONSIN										
Ashland		−21	−16	85/70	82/68	79/66	23	72	70	68
Beloit		−7	−3	92/75	90/75	88/74	24	78	77	75
Eau Claire		−15	−11	92/75	89/73	86/71	23	77	75	73
Green Bay	8029	−13	−9	88/74	85/72	83/71	23	76	74	72
La Crosse	7589	−13	−9	91/75	88/73	85/72	22	77	75	74
Madison	7863	−11	−7	91/74	88/73	85/71	22	77	75	73
Milwaukee	7635	−8	−4	90/74	87/73	84/71	21	76	74	73
Racine		−6	−2	91/75	88/73	85/72	21	77	75	74
WYOMING										
Casper	7410	−11	−5	92/58	90/57	87/57	31	63	61	60
Cheyenne	7381	−9	−1	89/58	86/58	84/57	30	63	62	60
Cody		−19	−13	89/60	86/60	83/59	32	64	63	61
Lander	7870	−16	−11	91/61	88/61	85/60	32	64	63	61
Laramie		−14	−6	84/56	81/56	79/55	28	61	60	59
ALBERTA										
Banff	10551									
Calgary	9703	−27	−23	84/63	81/61	79/60	25	65	63	62
Edmonton	10268	−29	−25	85/66	82/65	79/63	23	68	66	65
Grande Prairie		−39	−33	83/64	80/63	78/61	23	66	64	62
McMurray		−41	−38	86/67	82/65	79/64	26	69	67	65
Medicine Hat		−29	−24	93/66	90/65	87/64	28	70	68	66
BRITISH COLUMBIA										
Fort Nelson		−43	−40	84/64	81/63	78/62	23	67	65	64
Kamloops	6799	−21	−15	94/66	91/65	88/64	29	68	66	65

		Winter		Summer						
		Col. 3		Col. 4			Col. 5	Col. 6		
Col. 1	Col. 2	Design dry-bulb		Design dry-bulb and mean coincident wet-bulb			Mean daily range	Design wet-bulb		
Province and station	Annual heating degree-days	99%	97.5%	1%	2.5%	5%		1%	2.5%	5%
New Westminster		14	18	84/68	81/67	78/66	19	69	68	66
Prince George	9755	−33	−28	84/64	80/62	77/61	26	66	64	62
Prince Rupert	7029	−2	2	64/59	63/57	61/56	12	60	58	57
Vancouver	5575	15	19	79/67	77/66	74/65	17	68	67	66
Victoria	5579	20	23	77/64	73/62	70/60	16	64	62	60
MANITOBA										
Brandon	11036	−30	−27	89/72	86/70	83/68	25	74	72	70
Churchill	16728	−41	−39	81/66	77/64	74/62	18	67	65	63
The Pas	12281	−37	−33	85/68	82/67	79/66	20	71	69	68
Winnipeg	10679	−30	−27	89/73	86/71	84/70	22	75	73	71
NEW BRUNSWICK										
Fredericton	8671	−16	−11	89/71	85/69	82/68	23	73	71	70
Moncton	8727	−12	−8	85/70	82/69	79/67	23	72	71	69
Saint John	8219	−12	−8	80/67	77/65	75/64	19	70	68	66
NEWFOUNDLAND										
Corner Brook	8978	−5	0	76/64	73/63	71/62	17	67	66	65
Gander	9254	−5	−1	82/66	79/65	77/64	19	69	67	66
Goose Bay	11887	−27	−24	85/66	81/64	77/63	19	68	66	64
Saint John's	8991	3	7	77/66	75/65	73/64	18	69	67	66
NORTHWEST TERR.										
Forth Smith		−49	−45	85/66	81/64	78/63	24	68	66	65
Frobisher		−43	−41	66/53	63/51	59/50	14	54	52	51
Inuvik		−56	−53	79/62	77/60	75/59	21	64	62	61
Resolute	16021	−50	−47	57/48	54/46	51/45	10	50	48	46
NOVA SCOTIA										
Amherst		−11	−6	84/69	81/68	79/67	21	72	70	68
Halifax	7361	1	5	79/66	76/65	74/64	16	69	67	66
New Glasgow		−9	−5	81/69	79/68	77/67	20	72	70	69
Sydney	8049	−1	3	82/69	80/68	77/66	19	71	70	68
Yarmouth	7340	5	9	74/65	72/64	70/63	15	68	66	65
ONTARIO										
Kapuskasing	11572	−31	−28	86/70	83/69	80/67	23	72	70	69
Kitchener	7566	−6	−2	88/73	85/72	83/71	23	75	74	72
London	7349	−4	0	87/74	85/73	83/72	21	76	74	73
North Bay	9219	−22	−18	84/68	81/67	79/66	20	71	70	68
Ottawa	8735	−17	−13	90/72	87/71	84/70	21	75	73	72
Saint Catharines		−1	3	87/73	85/72	83/71	20	76	74	73
Sault Sainte Marie		−17	−13	85/71	82/69	79/68	22	73	71	70
Timmins		−33	−29	87/69	84/68	81/66	25	72	70	68
Toronto	6827	−5	−1	90/73	87/72	85/71	20	75	74	73
Windsor		0	4	90/74	88/73	86/72	20	77	75	74
PRINCE EDWARD ISLAND										
Charlottetown	8164	−7	−4	80/69	78/68	76/67	16	71	70	68
Summerside	8488	−8	−4	81/69	79/68	77/67	16	72	70	68
QUEBEC										
Bagotville		−28	−23	87/70	83/68	80/67	21	72	70	68
Drummondville		−18	−14	88/72	85/71	82/69	21	75	73	71
Montréal	7899	−16	−10	88/73	85/72	83/71	17	75	74	72
Québec	9372	−19	−14	87/72	84/70	81/68	20	74	72	70
Sept-Iles		−26	−21	76/63	73/61	70/60	17	67	65	63
Val d'Or		−32	−27	85/70	83/68	80/67	22	72	70	68
SASKATCHEWAN										
Moose Jaw		−29	−25	93/69	89/67	86/66	27	71	69	68
Prince Albert	11630	−42	−35	87/67	84/66	81/65	25	70	68	67
Regina	10806	−33	−29	91/69	88/68	84/67	26	72	70	68
Saskatoon	12870	−35	−31	89/68	86/66	83/65	26	70	68	67
YUKON TERRITORY										
Whitehorse	15000	−46	−43	80/59	77/58	74/56	22	61	59	58

Climatic conditions

Table 8A. Hourly weather occurrences

(Number of hours per year at various temperatures)

Location	72	67	62	57	52	47	42	37	32	27	22	17	12	7	2	−3	−8	−13	−18
Albany, NY	588	733	740	708	652	625	647	769	793	574	404	278	184	110	63	32	10	5	4
Albuquerque, NM	767	831	719	651	687	734	741	689	552	346	154	66	21	4	1	1			
Atlanta, GA	1185	926	823	784	735	676	598	468	271	112	44	19	8	2					
Bakersfield, CA	831	898	966	977	908	746	541	247	77	7									
Birmingham, AL	1138	908	805	742	668	614	528	433	292	143	69	17	6	3					
Bismarck, ND	454	566	614	606	563	520	518	604	653	550	474	371	338	292	278	208	131	77	80
Boise, ID	492	575	643	702	786	798	878	829	522	307	148	53	26	14	6	2			
Boston, MA	676	819	804	781	766	757	828	848	674	429	256	151	74	35	4	9	1		
Buffalo, NY	646	772	760	700	666	624	647	756	849	602	426	267	170	81	5	24	2		
Burlington, VT	573	670	703	694	655	603	637	716	752	561	491	336	272	216	135	81	39	17	8
Casper, WY	423	532	592	642	606	670	782	831	806	683	495	324	200	116	73	45	30	15	5
Charleston, SC	1267	1090	889	787	651	576	434	321	192	79	27	5							
Charleston, WV	912	949	767	689	661	667	607	633	630	356	252	135	73	22	7	1			
Charlotte, NC	1115	908	839	752	730	684	634	515	360	166	64	23	5	2					
Chattanooga, TN	1021	895	775	722	731	679	642	553	414	228	113	45	4	4	2				
Chicago, IL	762	769	653	592	569	543	591	800	822	551	335	196	117	85	59	25	12	3	
Cincinnati, OH	879	843	726	639	611	599	627	698	711	460	249	131	68	44	18	8	2		
Cleveland, OH	763	831	732	641	638	607	620	754	806	578	355	201	111	47	22	11	2		
Columbus, OH	774	820	720	648	622	603	658	730	722	502	280	169	94	40	20	10	4	1	
Corpus Christi, TX	1175	1041	748	551	444	302	180	83	27	9	3								
Dallas, TX	831	795	693	656	629	576	504	371	231	91	34	17	4	1					
Denver, CO	549	684	783	731	678	704	692	717	721	553	359	216	119	78	36	22	6	1	1
Des Moines, IA	707	751	681	600	585	512	510	627	747	557	405	281	211	152	104	59	23	8	1
Detroit, MI	721	783	695	633	592	566	595	808	884	618	377	248	131	61	17	4	1		
El Paso, TX	933	839	749	760	687	611	494	369	233	104	34	10	2						
Ft. Wayne, IN	728	777	699	608	569	552	601	725	905	596	381	205	124	69	40	19	6	1	
Fresno, CA	709	803	921	1006	1036	952	673	426	168	34									
Grand Rapids, MI	634	739	712	647	571	565	554	742	938	690	469	293	172	78	31	10	1	1	
Great Falls, MT	407	520	636	754	822	830	832	813	698	533	355	218	167	136	118	101	68	51	62
Harrisburg, PA	807	824	737	692	635	659	722	888	749	427	222	125	52	18	4	1			
Hartford, CT	617	755	751	752	649	575	683	807	825	552	370	233	153	77	33	11	3	2	
Houston, TX	1172	980	722	681	570	452	291	141	64	18	4	2							
Indianapolis, IN	821	815	722	585	586	579	605	712	791	551	293	152	97	60	35	13	3	2	
Jackson, MS	1169	922	790	677	618	605	484	367	224	103	41	6	2	2	1				
Jacksonville, FL	1334	975	879	692	530	355	288	154	83	24	2								
Kansas City, MO	761	723	601	572	553	562	628	625	591	407	265	175	99	51	21	4			
Knoxville, TN	1056	889	746	675	672	689	648	590	456	217	101	41	21	7	2				
Las Vegas, NV	651	644	699	786	769	716	591	396	194	44	7	1							
Little Rock, AR	940	803	725	672	638	669	605	509	363	172	50	25	5	1					
Los Angeles, CA	881	1654	2193	1904	1054	428	107	10											
Louisville, KY	869	758	693	654	619	634	649	703	631	332	169	97	45	25	8	3	1		
Lubbock, TX	833	829	688	700	642	618	620	546	490	346	180	86	33	7	5	1			
Memphis, TN	977	798	715	690	618	633	614	532	374	196	74	25	10	4					
Miami, FL	1705	810	452	277	147	71	26	4											
Milwaukee, WI	597	753	749	634	585	591	611	774	913	659	421	285	176	116	83	47	18	4	3
Minneapolis, MN	621	690	695	602	588	482	500	560	632	609	514	383	311	246	186	119	62	31	16
Mobile, AL	1411	1038	882	698	609	506	377	214	109	49	7	3							
Nashville, TN	933	838	738	697	637	619	627	565	463	263	132	67	28	9	3	1	1		
New Orleans, LA	1189	987	850	692	621	449	282	128	47	9	2								
New York, NY	926	877	754	745	722	796	838	858	603	330	188	2	26	10	1				
Oklahoma City, OK	881	769	717	643	645	611	641	570	468	287	173	77	36	12	3	1			
Omaha, NB	726	721	606	558	539	543	543	655	663	511	390	287	189	135	93	40	15	1	
Philadelphia, PA	863	809	735	710	663	701	758	818	654	335	189	100	32	9					
Phoenix, AZ	762	776	767	769	659	540	391	182	57	8									
Pittsburgh, PA	722	910	799	678	637	587	631	688	774	569	360	233	159	60	30	7	1		

Table 8A (cont.). Hourly weather occurrences

Location	Outdoor temperature, °F																		
	72	67	62	57	52	47	42	37	32	27	22	17	12	7	2	−3	−8	−13	−18
Portland, ME	407	627	780	808	760	748	772	839	820	599	408	293	190	109	60	29	15	5	1
Portland, OR	373	581	1001	1316	1274	1271	1238	772	343	123	40	10	4	1					
Raleigh, NC	1087	937	848	762	707	672	638	527	410	236	103	38	11	1					
Reno, NV	418	477	572	690	845	909	890	829	733	530	387	227	101	37	15	4	1		
Richmond, VA	953	850	784	745	690	673	699	632	478	285	138	67	19	2	1				
Sacramento, CA	630	773	1071	1329	1298	1049	701	355	93	8									
Salt Lake City, UT	569	615	614	635	682	685	755	831	798	564	328	158	80	41	16	2			
San Antonio, TX	1086	943	789	669	569	445	387	190	94	31	11	4	1	1					
San Francisco, CA	285	665	1264	2341	2341	1153	449	99	10										
Seattle, WA	258	0448	750	1272	1462	1445	1408	914	427	104	39	20	3						
Shreveport, LA	1063	886	772	679	619	609	516	361	200	72	23	6	2						
Sioux Falls, SD	566	684	669	605	522	498	501	625	712	585	520	448	293	208	152	102	59	45	18
St. Louis, MO	823	728	646	575	585	578	620	671	650	411	219	134	77	40	15	7	1		
Syracuse, NY	627	735	723	717	656	641	651	720	830	547	392	282	190	102	55	23	5	2	2
Tampa, FL	1387	1187	877	570	345	216	137	48	10	1									
Waco, TX	909	830	701	622	651	558	501	354	216	84	24	3	1						
Washington, DC	960	766	740	673	690	684	790	744	542	254	138	54	17	2					
Wichita, KS	758	709	641	603	589	592	611	584	607	426	273	161	85	45	14	3	1		

Table 9. Outdoor air ventilation requirements for occupants

	Estimated persons/ 1000 ft² floor area	Required ventilation air, per human occupant			
		Minimum		Recommended	
		cfm	L/s	cfm	L/s
RESIDENTIAL					
Single-Unit Dwellings					
General Living Areas, Bedrooms, Utility Rooms	5	5	2.5	7–10	3.5–5
Kitchens, Baths, Toilet Rooms	—	20	10	30–50	15–25
Multiple-Unit Dwellings and Mobile Homes					
General Living Areas, Bedrooms, Utility Rooms	7	5	2.5	7–10	3.5–5
Kitchens, Baths, Toilet Rooms	—	20	10	30–50	15–25
Garages	—	1.5	7.5	2–3	10–15
COMMERCIAL					
Public Rest Rooms	100	15	7.5	20–25	10–12.5
General Requirements—Merchandising (Apply to all forms unless specially noted)					
Sales Floors (Basement and Ground Floors)	30	7	3.5	10–15	5–7.5
Sales Floor (Upper Floors)	20	7	3.5	10–15	5–7.5
Storage Areas (Serving Sales Areas and Storerooms)	5	5	2.5	7–10	3.5–5
Dressing Rooms	—	7	3.5	10–15	5–7.5
Malls and Arcades	40	7	3.5	10–15	5–7.5
Shipping and Receiving Areas	10	15	7.5	15–20	7.5–10
Warehouses	5	7	3.5	10–15	5–7.5
Elevators	—	7	3.5	10–15	5–7.5
Meat Processing Rooms	10	5	2.5	5	2.5
Pharmacists' Workrooms	10	20	10	25–30	12.5–15
Pet Shops	—	1.0	5	1.5–2	7.5–10
Florists	10	5	2.5	7	3.5
Greenhouses	1	5	2.5	7–10	3.5–5

Table 9 (cont.). Outdoor air ventilation requirements for occupants

	Estimated persons/ 1000 ft² floor area	Required ventilation air, per human occupant			
		Minimum		Recommended	
		cfm	L/s	cfm	L/s
Bank Vaults	—	5	2.5	5	2.5
Dining Rooms	70	10	5	15–20	7.5–10
Kitchens	20	30	15	35	17.5
Cafeterias, Short Order; Drive-Ins, Seating Areas	100	30	15	35	17.5
Bars (Predominantly Stand-Up)	150	30	15	40–50	20–25
Cocktail Lounges	100	30	15	35–40	17.5–20
Hotels, Motels, Resorts					
Bedrooms	5	7	3.5	10–15	5–7.5
Living Rooms (Suites)	20	10	5	15–20	7.5–10
Baths, Toilets (attached to bedrooms)	—	20	10	30–50	15–25
Corridors	5	5	2.5	7–10	3.5–5
Lobbies	30	7	3.5	10–15	5–7.5
Conference Rooms (Small)	70	20	10	25–30	12.5–15
Assembly Rooms (Large)	140	15	7.5	20–25	10–12.5
Cottages (treat as single-unit dwellings)					
Dry Cleaners and Laundries					
Commercial	10	20	10	25–30	12.5–15
Storage/Pickup Areas	30	7	3.5	10–15	5–7.5
Coin-Operated	20	15	7.5	15–20	7.5–10
Barber, Beauty, and Health Services					
Beauty Shops (Hairdressers)	50	25	12.5	30–35	15–17.5
Reducing Salons (Exercise Rooms)	20	25	12.5	30–35	15–17.5
Sauna Baths and Steam Rooms	—	5	2.5	5	2.5
Barber Shops	25	7	3.5	10–15	5–7.5
Photo Studios					
Camera Rooms, Stages	10	5	2.5	7–10	3.5–5
Darkrooms	10	10	5	15–20	7.5–10
COMMERCIAL					
Shoe Repair Shops (Combined Workrooms/Trade Areas)	10	10	5	15–20	7.5–10
Garages, Auto Repair Shops, Service Stations					
Parking Garages (enclosed), Repair Workrooms	—	1.5	7.5	2–3	10–15
Service Station Offices	20	7	3.5	10–15	5–7.5
Theaters, Houses of Worship					
Ticket Booths	—	5	2.5	7–10	3.5–5
Lobbies (Foyers and Lounges)	150	20	10	25–30	12.5–15
Auditoriums (No Smoking)	150	5	2.5	5–10	2.5–5
Auditoriums (Smoking Permitted)	150	10	5	10–20	5–10
Stages (with Proscenium and Curtains)	70	10	5	12–15	6–7.5
Workrooms	20	10	5	12–15	6–7.5
Ballrooms (Public)	100	15	7.5	20–25	10–12.5
Bowling Alleys (Seating Area)	70	15	7.5	20–25	10–12.5
Gymnasiums and Arenas					
Playing Floors-Minimal or No Seating	70	20	10	25–30	12.5–15
Locker Rooms	20	30	15	40–50	20–25
Spectator Areas	150	20	10	25–30	12.5–15
Ramps, Foyers, and Lobbies	150	10	5	15–20	7.5–10
Amusement Parlors and Pool Rooms	25	20	10	25–30	12.5–15
Tennis, Squash, Handball Courts	—	20	10	25–30	12.5–15
Swimming Pools	25	15	7.5	20–25	10–12.5
Ice-Skating, Curling, and Roller Rinks	70	10	5	15–20	7.5–10

	Estimated persons/ 1000 ft² floor area	Required ventilation air, per human occupant			
		Minimum		Recommended	
		cfm	L/s	cfm	L/s
Transportation					
Waiting Rooms, Corridors, Ticket, Baggage, and Gate Areas	50	15	7.5	20–25	10–12.5
Control Towers	50	25	12.5	30–35	15–17.5
Hangars	2	10	5	15–20	7.5–10
Platform, Concourses	150	10	5	15–20	7.5–10
Repair Shops	—	10	5	15–20	7.5–10
Offices					
General Office Space	10	15	7.5	15–25	7.5–12.5
Conference Rooms	60	25	12.5	30–40	15–20
Drafting Rooms, Art Rooms	20	7	3.5	10–15	5–7.5
Doctors' Consultation Rooms	—	10	5	10–15	7.5–10
Waiting Rooms	30	10	5	15–20	7.5–10
Lithographing and Diazo Printing Rooms	20	7	3.5	10–15	5–7.5
Computer Rooms	20	5	2.5	7–10	3.5–5
Keypunching Rooms	30	7	3.5	10–15	5–7.5
Communication					
Broadcasting Booths, Studios, Stages	20	30	15	35–40	17.5–20
Pressrooms	100	15	7.5	20–25	10–12.5
Composing Rooms, Engraving Shops	30	7	3.5	10–15	5–7.5
Telephone Switchboard Rooms (Manual)	50	7	3.5	10–15	5–7.5
Telephone Switchgear Rooms (Automatic)	—	7	3.5	10–15	5–7.5
Teletypewriter/Facsimile Rooms	—	5	2.5	7–10	3.5–5

INDUSTRIAL (including agricultural processing)

(Occupational safety laws in the various states usually regulate the ventilation requirements, which are almost always far in excess of the ventilation requirements for the occupants.) ASHRAE Standard 62–73 lists requirements for occupants only. In general, 25 cfm (12.5 L/s) per occupant is recommended except for mining or metalworking, where 40 cfm (20 L/s) is recommended.

INSTITUTIONAL

	Estimated persons/ 1000 ft² floor area	Minimum cfm	Minimum L/s	Recommended cfm	Recommended L/s
Schools					
Classrooms	50	10	5	10–15	5–7.5
Multiple Use Rooms	70	10	5	10–15	5–7.5
Craft and Vocational Training Shops, Laboratories	30	10	5	10–15	5–7.5
Music, Rehearsal Rooms	70	10	5	15–20	7.5–10
Auditoriums	150	5	2.5	5–7.5	2.5–3.8
Gymnasiums	70	20	10	25–30	12.5–15
Libraries	20	7	3.5	10–12	5–6
Common Rooms, Lounges	70	10	5	10–15	5–7.5
Offices	10	7	3.5	10–15	5–7.5
Lavatories	100	15	7.5	20–25	10–12.5
Locker Rooms	20	30	15	40–50	20–25
Lunchrooms, Dining Halls	100	10	5	15–20	7.5–10
Corridors	50	15	7.5	20–25	10–12.5
Utility Rooms	3	5	2.5	7–10	3.5–5
Dormitory Bedrooms	20	7	3.5	10–15	5–7.5
Hospitals, Nursing and Convalescent Homes					
Foyers; Hallways	50	20	10	25–30	12.5–15
Single, Dual Bedrooms	15	10	5	15–20	7.5–10
Wards	20	10	5	15–20	7.5–10
Food Service Centers	20	35	17.5	35	17.5
Operating Rooms, Delivery Rooms	—	20	10	—	—
Amphitheatres	100	10	5	15–20	7.5–10
Physical Theapy Areas	20	15	7.5	20–25	10–12.5
Autopsy Rooms	10	30	15	40–50	20–25
Incinerator Service Areas	—	5	2.5	7–10	3.5–5
Ready Rooms, Recovery Rooms	—	15	7.5	—	—

Table 9 (cont.).   Outdoor air ventilation requirements for occupants

| | Estimated persons/ 1000 ft² floor area | Required ventilation air, per human occupant | | | |
| | | Minimum | | Recommended | |
		cfm	L/s	cfm	L/s
Research Institutes					
Laboratories, Machine Shops	50	15	7.5	20–25	10–12.5
Darkrooms, Spectroscopy Rooms	50	10	5	15–20	7.5–10
Animal Rooms	20	40	20	45–50	22.5–25
Military and Naval Installations					
Barracks	20	7	3.5	10–15	5–7.5
Toilets/Washrooms	100	15	7.5	20–25	10–12.5
Shower Rooms	100	10	5	15–20	7.5–10
Drill Halls	70	15	7.5	20–25	10–12.5
Ready Rooms, MP Station	40	7	3.5	10–15	5–7.5
Indoor Target Ranges	70	20	10	25–30	12.5–15
Museums					
Exhibit Halls	70	7	3.5	10–15	5–7.5
Workrooms	10	10	5	15–10	7.5–10
Warehouses	5	5	2.5	7–10	3.5–5
Correctional Facilities, Police and Fire Stations					
Cell Blocks	20	7	3.5	10–15	5–7.5
Eating Halls	70	15	7.5	20–25	10–12.5
Guard Stations	40	7	3.5	10–15	5–7.5
Veterinary Hospitals					
Kennels, Stalls, Operating Rooms	20	25	12.5	30–35	15–17.5
Reception Rooms	30	10	5	15–20	7.5–10
ORGANIZATIONAL					
Legislative Halls					
Committee Rooms and Conference Rooms, Chambers	70	20	10	25–30	12.5–15
Foyers, Corridors	50	20	10	25–30	12.5–15
Offices	10	10	5	15–20	7.5–10
Press/Radio/TV Booths; Lounges	20	20	10	25–30	12.5–15
Public Rest Rooms	20	15	7.5	20–25	10–12.5
Private Rest Rooms	—	20	10	30–50	15–25

NOTE: For special requirements see the ASHRAE Handbook and ASHRAE Standards 62–73 and 90–75R.

Table 10.   Design room conditions usually specified for summer average peak load in comfort air conditioning

Type of installation	Dry-bulb temp.	Wet-bulb temp.	Relative humidity, %	Moisture, grains per lb
Excess capacity	72–76	60–63.3	50	58–67.2
Normal application	78	65	50	72.7
Occupancy up to 40 minutes max	80	67	51	78.5

ter the product of columns VII, VIII, and XI.

If the particular exposure contains windows of different sizes, list each size on a different line. When all the glass has been accounted for, on the next line enter the wall. List the over-all dimensions of the wall in column IV and in column V enter the gross area of the wall less the glass area.

On succeeding lines follow the same procedure for other walls, roof, floor, ceiling or partitions. When all heat-loss items in a room have been tabulated, a room total may be obtained. Skip a line and proceed to the details of the next room.

Most engineers add a safety factor of about 15 per cent to allow for aging of the equipment and building, piping and start-up losses and extreme weather conditions. However, the engineer should also consider the heat given off by lights, people, and appliances and the heat-storage capacity of the room.

COOLING LOADS

Information required for calculating summer cooling loads is as follows:

1. Type, usage, and hours of occupancy of the building

2. Orientation of the building

3. Items I through VI and VIII from heating-load work sheet (Table 7)

4. Indoor design conditions

5. Outdoor design conditions

6. Type of glass and shades to be used

7. Ventilation requirements

8. Number of occupants and type of activity

9. Amount and type of artificial lighting and hours of use

10. Number and type of heat-producing appliances and equipment and extent of use

Work sheet suggested for use in calculating cooling loads is shown in Table 11. Lines

Table 11. Work sheet for calculating cooling loads

1	PROJECT_____				SHEET NO._____OF_____				
2	NOTE: FOR DETERMINATION OF FACTORS USED				CALC. BY_____DATE_____				
3	SEE SHEETS NOS._____DATE_____				CHECKED BY_____DATE_____				

	HEAT GAIN ITEM		$\triangle T$	FACTOR	AREA OR NO.	BTU/HR	AREA OR NO.	BTU/HR	AREA OR NO.	BTU/HR	AREA OR NO.	BTU/HR
4	ROOM NAME OR NUMBER											
5	DIMENSIONS & AREA											
6	VOLUME | CFM/AIR CHANGE				I		I		I		I	
7	HRS. OF OCCUPANCY—(SUNTIME)											
8	AIR CHANGES REQUIREMENTS—(PER HR.)											
9	COOLING DATA				DB WB %RH gr/lb		DB WB %RH gr/lb		DB WB %RH gr/lb		DB WB %RH gr/lb	
10	O. A. TEMP. AT PEAK ROOM LOAD											
11	ROOM DESIGN CONDITIONS											
12	DIFFERENCE				— —		— —		— —		— —	
14	SOLAR	N, NW GLASS	—									
15		E, NE "	—									
16		S, SE "	—									
17		W, SW "	—									
18	TRANSMISSION	N, NW GLASS										
19		E, NE "										
20		S, SE "										
21		W, SW "										
22		N, NW WALL										
23		E, NE "										
24		S, SE "										
25		W, SW "										
26		ROOF										
27		SKYLIGHT										
28		DOORS										
29	TOT. OUTSIDE LOAD		—	—	—		—		—		—	
30	INT. SENSIBLE	PEOPLE	—									
31		LIGHTS	—	3.41								
32		APPLIANCES										
33		MOTORS hp.	—	3000								
34		FLOOR, CLG.										
35		PARTITION										
36		INFILTRATION*		1.08								
37		FAN HORSEPOWER										
38	TOT. ROOM SENS.		—	—	—		—		—		—	
39	(A) = RSH = 1.1***TOT. RM. SENS.		—	—	—		—		—		—	
40	INT. LAT.	PEOPLE	—									
41		APPLIANCES										
42		INFILTRATION*	gr/lb	0.67								
43												
44	TOT. RM. LATENT		—	—	—		—		—		—	
45	(B) = RLH = 1.05**TOT. RM. LAT.		—	—	—		—		—		—	
46	(A+B) = ROOM TOTAL HEAT											
47	(C) = O. A. SENS = 1.08 × __ × $\triangle t$ × CFM											
48	(D) = O. A. LAT. = 0.67 × __ gr/lb × CFM											
49	(A+B+C+D) = GRAND TOT. HEAT											
50	SHF = (A) ÷ (A+B)											
51	CFM = (A) ÷ (1.08 × __ $\triangle t$)											
52	AIR CHANGES = 60 × CFM ÷ RM. VOL.											
53	REMARKS:											
	1. * USE WHEN NOT PRESSURIZED											
	** TYPICAL VALUES ONLY											
	2. COIL BY-PASS FACTORS NOT CONSIDERED											

2 and 3 of the work sheet refer to any calculations which may have been done on separate sheets. In line 6 "Cfm/Air Change" is the room volume divided by 60. In line 7 note that sun time, not daylight saving time, should be used. For line 8 see Table 9. For line 10 see Table 8. For line 11 see Table 10 or other criteria.

For lines 14 through 17 see Table 12. In lines 18 through 21 enter the appropriate figures from Tables 8 and 4. In lines 22 through 26 obtain the correct $\triangle t$ from Table 14 and U-factors from the section on *Insulation*. For line 27, see Table 4, and for line 28, see Table 3.

In lines 30 and 40 enter the number of people, if known; otherwise use Table 16 as a guide; sensible and latent heat for various degrees of activity may be found in Table 13. In line 31 enter the total lighting wattage, if known; otherwise refer to section on "Lighting" for recommended illumination levels and estimate the wattage on the basis of 1 watt per sq ft for 5 ft-c (foot-candles) of incandescent lighting and 15 ft-c of fluorescent lighting. In lines 32 and 41 enter the total sensible and latent data or tables in the ASHRAE Handbook. On line 33 list the total horsepower of all motors, including electric typewriters and business machines and apply a diversity factor which may range from 0.20 to 0.75.

(Continued on page 4-135.)

Cooling loads

Table 12A.   Maximum solar heat gain factors Btu/(h·ft²)

	\(0°N\) Latitude							\(8°N\) Latitude				
	N	NE/NW	E/W	SE/SW	S	HOR	N	NE/NW	E/W	SE/SW	S	HOR
Jan.	34	88	234	235	118	296	32	71	224	242	162	273
Feb.	36	132	245	210	67	306	34	114	239	219	110	294
Mar.	38	170	242	170	38	303	37	156	241	184	55	300
Apr.	71	193	221	118	37	284	44	184	225	134	39	289
May	113	203	201	80	37	265	74	198	209	97	38	277
June	129	206	190	65	37	255	90	200	200	82	39	269
July	115	201	195	77	38	260	77	195	204	93	39	272
Aug.	75	187	212	112	38	276	47	179	216	128	41	282
Sep.	40	163	231	163	40	293	38	149	230	176	56	290
Oct.	37	129	236	202	66	299	35	112	231	211	108	288
Nov.	35	88	230	230	117	293	33	71	220	238	160	273
Dec.	34	71	226	241	138	288	31	54	215	247	180	264

	\(16°N\) Latitude							\(24°N\) Latitude				
	N	NE/NW	E/W	SE/SW	S	HOR	N	NE/NW	E/W	SE/SW	S	HOR
Jan.	30	55	210	251	199	248	27	41	190	253	227	214
Feb.	33	96	231	233	154	275	30	80	220	243	192	249
Mar.	35	140	239	197	93	291	34	124	234	214	137	275
Apr.	39	172	227	150	45	289	37	159	228	169	75	283
May	52	189	215	115	41	282	43	178	218	132	46	282
June	66	194	207	99	41	277	56	184	212	117	43	279
July	55	187	210	111	42	277	45	176	213	129	46	278
Aug.	41	168	219	143	46	282	38	156	220	162	72	277
Sep.	36	134	227	191	93	282	35	119	222	206	134	266
Oct.	33	95	223	225	150	270	31	79	211	235	187	244
Nov.	30	55	206	247	196	246	27	42	187	249	224	213
Dec.	29	41	198	254	213	234	25	29	179	252	237	199

	\(32°N\) Latitude							\(40°N\) Latitude				
	N	NE/NW	E/W	SE/SW	S	HOR	N	NE/NW	E/W	SE/SW	S	HOR
Jan.	24	29	175	249	246	176	20	20	154	241	254	133
Feb.	27	65	205	248	221	217	24	50	186	246	241	180
Mar.	32	107	227	227	176	252	29	93	218	236	206	223
Apr.	36	146	227	187	115	271	34	140	224	203	154	252
May	38	170	220	155	74	277	37	165	220	175	113	265
June	47	176	214	139	60	276	48	172	215	161	95	268
July	40	167	215	150	72	273	38	163	216	170	109	262
Aug.	37	141	219	181	111	265	35	135	216	196	149	247
Sep.	33	103	215	218	171	244	30	87	205	226	200	215
Oct.	28	63	195	239	215	213	25	49	180	238	234	177
Nov.	24	29	173	245	243	175	18	20	151	237	250	132
Dec.	22	22	162	246	252	158	18	18	135	232	253	112

	\(48°N\) Latitude							\(56°N\) Latitude				
	N	NE/NW	E/W	SE/SW	S	HOR	N	NE/NW	E/W	SE/SW	S	HOR
Jan.	15	15	118	216	245	85	10	10	74	169	205	40
Feb.	20	36	168	242	250	138	16	21	139	223	244	91
Mar.	26	80	204	239	228	188	22	65	185	238	241	149
Apr.	31	132	219	215	186	226	28	123	211	223	210	195
May	35	158	218	192	150	247	36	149	215	206	181	222
June	47	165	215	180	134	252	53	161	213	195	167	231
July	37	156	214	187	146	244	37	147	211	201	177	221
Aug.	33	128	211	208	180	223	30	119	203	215	203	193
Sep.	27	72	191	228	220	182	23	58	171	227	231	144
Oct.	21	35	161	233	242	136	16	20	132	213	234	91
Nov.	15	15	115	212	240	85	10	10	72	165	200	40
Dec.	13	13	91	195	233	64	7	7	46	135	170	23

	\(64°N\) Latitude					
	N	NE/NW	E/W	SE/SW	S	HOR
Jan.	3	3	15	67	96	8
Feb.	11	11	89	177	210	45
Mar.	18	47	159	226	239	105
Apr.	25	113	201	225	224	160
May	48	150	211	215	204	192
June	62	162	213	208	193	203
July	49	148	207	211	200	192
Aug.	27	109	193	217	217	159
Sep.	19	43	148	213	227	101
Oct.	11	11	83	167	199	46
Nov.	4	4	15	66	93	8
Dec.	0	0	1	10	14	1

Table 12B. Solar intensity and solar heat gain factors for 0 deg North latitude

Date	Solar time am	Direct normal Btuh/ft²	N	NE	E	Solar heat Gain Factors, Btuh/ft² SE	S	SW	W	NW	HOR	Solar time pm
Jan 21	7	218	10	78	193	188	65	10	10	10	40	5
	8	288	19	88	234	235	91	19	19	19	121	4
	9	315	25	67	212	227	104	25	25	25	194	3
	10	328	30	40	158	195	112	31	30	30	250	2
	11	334	33	34	82	143	117	40	33	33	284	1
	12	335	34	34	36	83	118	83	36	34	296	12
HALF DAY TOTALS			135	329	909	1045	551	162	135	135	1037	
Feb 21	7	219	11	112	203	171	31	10	10	10	43	5
	8	287	20	132	245	210	47	19	19	19	128	4
	9	313	27	110	222	199	56	26	26	26	203	3
	10	325	32	70	166	162	62	31	31	31	260	2
	11	331	35	38	87	107	66	36	34	34	295	1
	12	333	36	36	37	53	67	53	37	36	306	12
HALF DAY TOTALS			142	488	954	891	297	146	140	140	1081	
Mar 21	7	206	12	138	197	138	12	11	11	11	43	5
	8	275	22	170	242	170	22	20	20	20	128	4
	9	302	29	156	221	156	29	27	27	27	202	3
	10	314	34	116	167	116	34	32	32	32	259	2
	11	320	37	65	86	65	37	36	35	36	293	1
	12	322	38	38	38	38	38	38	38	38	303	12
HALF DAY TOTALS			153	672	944	672	153	145	144	145	1075	
Apr 21	7	177	31	147	171	94	11	11	11	11	40	5
	8	249	49	193	221	118	21	21	21	21	118	4
	9	278	59	188	206	102	28	28	28	28	188	3
	10	291	66	156	157	67	33	33	33	33	241	2
	11	298	70	106	85	40	36	36	36	38	274	1
	12	300	71	57	39	38	37	38	39	56	284	12
HALF DAY TOTALS			311	826	864	442	147	147	148	155	1002	
May 21	7	156	53	145	149	63	12	12	12	12	37	5
	8	231	83	202	201	80	21	21	21	21	109	4
	9	261	97	203	190	65	28	28	28	28	174	3
	10	275	106	178	146	43	33	33	33	35	224	2
	11	282	111	134	81	38	36	36	36	43	255	1
	12	284	113	82	40	37	37	37	40	82	265	12
HALF DAY TOTALS			507	909	789	310	149	149	150	176	931	
Jun 21	7	146	60	141	137	51	12	12	12	12	35	5
	8	221	95	202	191	66	21	21	21	21	104	4
	9	252	112	206	182	53	28	28	28	29	167	3
	10	267	122	184	140	38	33	33	33	36	215	2
	11	274	127	143	79	38	36	36	36	50	245	1
	12	276	129	93	40	37	37	37	40	92	255	12
HALF DAY TOTALS			580	927	750	265	149	149	151	189	892	
Jul 21	7	146	53	139	141	59	12	12	12	12	36	5
	8	221	84	198	195	77	22	22	22	22	107	4
	9	252	99	201	186	63	29	29	29	29	171	3
	10	266	108	177	144	43	34	34	34	36	219	2
	11	274	113	135	81	39	37	37	37	45	250	1
	12	276	115	84	41	38	38	38	41	84	260	12
HALF DAY TOTALS			516	896	769	300	152	152	153	182	912	
Aug 21	7	159	32	136	157	85	12	12	12	12	39	5
	8	233	52	187	212	112	22	22	22	22	115	4
	9	262	63	185	200	98	29	29	29	29	182	3
	10	277	70	156	154	65	34	34	34	35	234	2
	11	284	74	109	85	41	37	37	37	40	266	1
	12	286	75	60	41	39	38	39	41	60	276	12
HALF DAY TOTALS			329	809	830	422	154	154	155	163	973	
Sep 21	7	184	13	127	181	127	13	11	11	11	42	5
	8	256	23	163	231	163	23	21	21	21	123	4
	9	284	30	152	214	152	30	28	28	28	195	3
	10	298	35	114	163	114	35	33	33	33	250	2
	11	304	39	66	88	66	39	37	36	37	283	1
	12	306	40	40	40	40	40	40	40	40	293	12
HALF DAY TOTALS			160	646	902	646	160	150	150	150	1039	
Oct 21	7	202	11	106	190	160	30	11	11	11	42	5
	8	273	20	129	236	202	45	20	20	20	125	4
	9	300	27	110	217	194	55	27	27	27	198	3
	10	313	33	71	164	158	61	32	32	32	254	2
	11	319	36	40	87	105	65	37	35	35	288	1
	12	321	37	37	38	53	66	53	38	37	299	12
HALF DAY TOTALS			146	481	921	856	290	149	144	143	1056	
Nov 21	7	210	10	77	187	182	62	10	10	10	39	5
	8	282	19	88	230	230	89	19	19	19	120	4
	9	309	25	67	210	224	102	25	25	25	192	3
	10	322	30	40	157	192	111	31	30	30	247	2
	11	328	34	35	82	142	115	40	34	34	282	1
	12	330	35	35	36	82	117	82	36	35	293	12
HALF DAY TOTALS			136	329	895	1025	540	162	137	136	1027	
Dec 21	7	215	10	64	186	190	77	10	10	10	38	5
	8	287	18	71	226	240	108	18	18	18	117	4
	9	314	25	52	206	235	123	25	25	25	189	3
	10	327	29	33	153	204	132	31	29	29	243	2
	11	333	33	33	79	155	137	46	33	33	277	1
	12	335	34	34	35	96	138	95	35	34	288	12
HALF DAY TOTALS			131	274	879	1089	648	172	132	131	1008	
			N	NW	W	SW	S	SE	E	NE	HOR	PM

Cooling loads

Table 12B (cont.).   Solar intensity and solar heat gain factors for 8 deg North latitude

Date	Solar time am	Direct normal Btuh/ft²	N	NE	E	SE	S	SW	W	NW	HOR	Solar time pm
Jan 21	7	187	8	62	165	165	61	8	8	8	26	5
	8	278	17	71	224	237	105	17	17	17	102	4
	9	309	23	47	207	242	131	24	23	23	174	3
	10	323	28	30	155	217	149	30	28	28	229	2
	11	330	31	32	80	172	159	55	31	31	264	1
	12	332	32	32	34	112	162	112	34	32	275	12
HALF DAY TOTALS			123	255	839	1084	683	183	124	123	931	
Feb 21	7	203	9	99	189	164	35	9	9	9	34	5
	8	282	18	114	239	219	63	18	18	18	116	4
	9	310	25	86	219	218	83	25	25	25	191	3
	10	323	30	47	164	188	98	31	30	30	247	2
	11	329	33	35	65	139	107	37	33	33	283	1
	12	331	34	34	36	78	110	78	36	34	294	12
HALF DAY TOTALS			133	397	914	971	440	155	133	133	1018	
Mar 21	7	205	12	132	196	143	13	11	11	11	42	5
	8	274	21	156	241	184	25	20	20	20	126	4
	9	301	28	133	220	178	37	27	27	27	199	3
	10	313	33	87	166	145	47	32	32	32	256	2
	11	319	36	44	88	94	53	36	35	35	290	1
	12	321	37	37	38	47	55	47	38	37	300	12
HALF DAY TOTALS			148	577	940	776	203	146	143	143	1062	
Apr 21	6	1	0	0	1	0	0	0	0	0	0	6
	7	189	28	152	183	106	13	12	12	12	47	5
	8	253	36	184	225	134	23	22	22	22	126	4
	9	280	39	169	208	125	30	28	28	28	195	3
	10	293	42	130	158	92	35	33	33	33	248	2
	11	299	43	78	86	54	38	36	36	38	279	1
	12	301	44	42	40	39	39	39	40	42	289	12
HALF DAY TOTALS			213	749	897	540	159	153	153	154	1041	
May 21	6	6	2	5	6	2	0	0	0	0	1	6
	7	177	54	160	170	78	14	14	14	14	50	5
	8	239	68	198	209	97	23	23	23	23	124	4
	9	265	72	189	194	86	30	30	30	30	188	3
	10	278	73	155	149	60	34	34	34	35	237	2
	11	285	74	107	82	41	37	37	37	40	267	1
	12	286	74	59	41	40	38	39	41	59	277	12
HALF DAY TOTALS			385	862	846	392	158	159	160	168	1005	
Jun 21	6	9	3	8	8	3	1	1	1	1	1	6
	7	170	64	161	162	66	14	14	14	14	50	5
	8	231	82	200	200	82	23	23	23	23	121	4
	9	257	88	194	187	72	30	30	30	30	183	3
	10	270	90	164	144	50	35	35	35	36	230	2
	11	277	90	117	81	40	38	38	38	41	260	1
	12	279	90	69	42	39	39	39	42	69	269	12
HALF DAY TOTALS			468	896	816	337	161	161	162	178	980	
Jul 21	6	5	2	5	5	2	0	0	0	0	1	6
	7	168	54	155	163	74	14	14	14	14	49	5
	8	230	70	195	204	93	24	24	24	24	122	4
	9	256	75	187	191	83	30	30	30	30	184	3
	10	270	76	156	147	59	35	35	35	36	233	2
	11	276	77	108	82	41	38	38	38	41	262	1
	12	278	77	61	42	40	39	40	42	61	272	12
HALF DAY TOTALS			398	853	827	380	162	162	163	173	988	
Aug 21	7	171	30	143	170	98	14	13	13	13	47	5
	8	237	39	179	216	128	24	23	23	23	123	4
	9	265	43	168	202	120	31	30	30	30	190	3
	10	278	45	131	155	90	37	35	35	35	241	2
	11	285	47	81	86	54	40	38	38	39	272	1
	12	287	47	45	42	41	41	41	42	45	282	12
HALF DAY TOTALS			230	737	864	516	167	160	160	162	1014	
Sep 21	7	183	13	122	179	131	14	11	11	11	41	5
	8	255	22	149	230	176	27	21	21	21	121	4
	9	283	29	129	213	172	38	28	28	28	193	3
	10	297	34	86	162	142	48	33	33	33	247	2
	11	303	37	46	87	93	54	38	36	36	280	1
	12	305	38	39	39	48	56	48	39	39	290	12
HALF DAY TOTALS			154	555	897	745	208	152	149	148	1027	
Oct 21	7	187	10	93	176	152	33	10	10	10	34	5
	8	267	19	112	231	210	60	19	19	19	113	4
	9	297	26	86	214	211	80	26	26	26	186	3
	10	311	31	49	161	184	95	32	31	31	242	2
	11	317	34	36	85	136	105	38	34	34	277	1
	12	319	35	35	37	77	108	77	37	35	288	12
HALF DAY TOTALS			136	392	803	935	426	157	137	136	995	
Nov 21	7	180	8	61	160	159	59	8	8	8	26	5
	8	271	17	71	220	233	103	17	17	17	101	4
	9	303	24	48	205	238	129	24	24	24	173	3
	10	318	29	31	154	214	146	30	29	29	227	2
	11	325	32	32	80	170	157	54	32	32	261	1
	12	327	33	33	34	111	160	111	34	33	273	12
HALF DAY TOTALS			125	256	827	1065	670	183	125	125	923	
Dec 21	7	177	7	48	152	160	68	7	7	7	22	5
	8	274	16	55	215	240	120	16	16	16	94	4
	9	307	22	36	200	247	147	23	22	22	166	3
	10	322	27	29	149	224	165	30	27	27	219	2
	11	329	30	31	77	182	176	65	30	30	253	1
	12	331	31	31	33	124	179	124	33	31	265	12
HALF DAY TOTALS			118	209	799	1109	762	198	119	118	886	
			N	NW	W	SW	S	SE	E	NE	HOR	PM

Table 12B (cont.). Solar intensity and solar heat gain factors for 16 deg North latitude

Date	Solar time am	Direct normal Btuh/ft²	N	NE	E	SE	S	SW	W	NW	HOR	Solar time pm
Jan 21	7	141	5	44	124	126	49	5	5	5	14	5
	8	262	14	55	210	233	114	14	14	14	79	4
	9	300	21	32	200	251	152	22	21	21	150	3
	10	317	26	27	150	233	178	31	26	26	203	2
	11	325	29	29	77	195	194	75	29	29	236	1
	12	327	30	30	32	139	199	138	32	30	248	12
HALF DAY TOTALS			110	196	760	1096	781	211	111	110	805	
Feb 21	7	182	8	84	169	150	36	8	8	8	25	5
	8	273	17	96	231	224	77	17	17	17	101	4
	9	305	23	64	214	233	110	23	23	23	174	3
	10	319	28	33	161	211	134	30	28	28	229	2
	11	326	32	32	83	167	149	49	32	32	263	1
	12	328	33	33	34	107	154	106	34	33	275	12
HALF DAY TOTALS			124	321	865	1034	582	174	124	124	930	
Mar 21	7	201	11	124	192	145	15	10	10	10	40	5
	8	272	20	140	239	195	35	19	19	19	120	4
	9	299	26	109	218	197	57	26	26	26	192	3
	10	312	31	61	165	172	76	32	31	31	247	2
	11	318	34	36	87	125	89	36	34	34	280	1
	12	320	35	36	37	69	93	68	37	36	291	12
HALF DAY TOTALS			141	494	928	879	319	153	139	139	1025	
Apr 21	6	14	2	12	14	8	1	1	1	1	1	6
	7	197	24	153	191	117	14	13	13	13	53	5
	8	256	27	172	227	150	24	22	22	22	131	4
	9	280	31	149	208	147	31	29	29	29	197	3
	10	293	35	102	158	120	37	33	33	33	249	2
	11	299	38	54	86	78	43	38	36	36	279	1
	12	301	39	39	40	43	45	43	40	39	289	12
HALF DAY TOTALS			179	674	922	653	174	157	155	155	1057	
May 21	6	44	14	41	43	19	3	3	3	3	5	6
	7	193	50	168	185	92	16	16	16	16	62	5
	8	244	52	189	215	115	25	24	24	24	135	4
	9	268	49	171	197	109	32	30	30	30	197	3
	10	280	47	130	150	84	37	35	35	35	245	2
	11	286	47	79	83	52	40	38	38	39	273	1
	12	288	46	44	42	41	41	41	42	444	282	12
HALF DAY TOTALS			283	804	897	493	172	167	167	169	1058	
Jun 21	6	53	20	52	51	20	4	4	4	4	7	6
	7	188	62	172	179	80	16	16	16	16	64	5
	8	238	66	194	207	99	25	25	25	25	135	4
	9	261	63	178	190	93	31	31	31	31	194	3
	10	273	59	140	145	70	37	36	36	36	241	2
	11	279	57	90	82	46	40	39	39	41	268	1
	12	281	57	50	43	41	41	41	42	50	277	12
HALF DAY TOTALS			356	850	876	430	174	171	172	176	1049	
Jul 21	6	41	14	39	40	18	3	3	3	3	6	6
	7	184	51	164	179	88	16	16	16	16	62	5
	8	236	55	187	210	111	25	25	25	25	133	4
	9	259	52	170	193	106	32	31	31	31	194	3
	10	272	50	131	148	81	38	36	36	36	241	2
	11	278	49	81	83	52	41	39	39	40	269	1
	12	279	49	46	43	42	42	42	43	46	277	12
HALF DAY TOTALS			296	799	878	478	176	171	171	173	1043	
Aug 21	6	11	2	10	12	6	1	1	1	1	1	6
	7	180	26	145	180	109	15	14	14	14	53	5
	8	240	30	168	219	143	25	23	23	23	128	4
	9	266	33	148	203	142	33	30	30	30	193	3
	10	279	37	104	155	117	39	35	35	35	243	2
	11	285	40	57	86	76	44	39	38	38	273	1
	12	287	41	41	42	44	46	44	42	41	282	12
HALF DAY TOTALS			191	666	891	624	180	165	163	163	1033	
Sep 21	7	179	12	114	176	133	15	11	11	11	39	5
	8	253	21	134	227	186	36	20	20	20	116	4
	9	281	28	106	211	191	57	27	27	27	185	3
	10	295	32	61	161	168	76	33	32	32	238	2
	11	302	35	37	86	123	88	38	35	35	271	1
	12	304	36	37	39	69	93	69	39	37	282	12
HALF DAY TOTALS			146	475	885	842	319	159	145	144	991	
Oct 21	7	166	8	79	156	139	33	8	8	8	25	5
	8	259	17	95	223	215	74	17	17	17	99	4
	9	292	24	65	209	225	106	24	24	24	170	3
	10	307	29	34	158	205	130	31	29	29	224	2
	11	314	32	33	83	163	145	49	32	32	258	1
	12	316	33	33	35	105	150	104	35	33	270	12
HALF DAY TOTALS			127	318	836	996	563	175	128	127	911	
Nov 21	7	134	5	43	119	120	47	5	5	5	14	5
	8	255	15	55	206	228	111	15	15	15	78	4
	9	295	21	33	197	247	150	22	21	21	149	3
	10	312	26	28	147	230	176	31	26	26	201	2
	11	320	29	29	77	192	191	74	29	29	234	1
	12	322	30	30	32	137	196	137	32	30	246	12
HALF DAY TOTALS			112	197	749	1077	767	210	112	112	799	
Dec 21	7	118	4	30	101	107	48	4	4	4	10	5
	8	255	13	41	198	231	124	13	13	13	69	4
	9	297	20	25	191	254	165	21	20	20	138	3
	10	315	25	26	144	239	192	35	25	25	191	2
	11	323	28	28	73	202	207	86	28	28	223	1
	12	325	29	29	30	149	212	149	30	29	234	12
HALF DAY TOTALS			104	159	710	1099	836	228	105	104	748	
			N	NW	W	SW	S	SE	E	NE	HOR	PM

Cooling loads

Table 12B (cont.).   Solar intensity and solar heat gain factors for 24 deg North latitude

Date	Solar time am	Direct normal Btuh/ft²	N	NE	E	SE	S	SW	W	NW	HOR	Solar time pm
Jan 21	7	71	2	21	62	63	25	2	2	2	5	5
	8	239	12	41	190	218	114	12	12	12	55	4
	9	288	18	23	190	253	166	19	18	18	121	3
	10	308	23	24	144	245	200	38	23	23	172	2
	11	317	26	26	73	211	220	95	26	26	204	1
	12	320	27	27	29	160	227	160	29	27	214	12
HALF DAY TOTALS			95	148	671	1076	840	241	96	95	664	
Feb 21	7	153	6	67	141	128	33	6	6	6	17	5
	8	262	15	80	220	224	89	15	15	15	83	4
	9	297	21	46	208	243	133	22	21	21	153	3
	10	314	26	28	157	228	165	28	26	26	205	2
	11	331	29	29	80	191	185	68	29	29	238	1
	12	323	30	30	32	134	192	133	32	30	249	12
HALF DAY TOTALS			113	257	806	1072	699	200	113	113	820	
Mar 21	7	194	11	115	186	145	17	10	10	10	36	5
	8	267	18	124	234	204	48	18	18	18	112	4
	9	295	25	85	215	214	82	25	25	25	180	3
	10	309	30	41	162	195	112	31	30	30	232	2
	11	315	33	34	85	154	139	43	33	33	264	1
	12	317	34	34	35	96	137	95	35	34	275	12
HALF DAY TOTALS			133	422	906	970	458	169	133	133	962	
Apr 21	6	40	6	33	39	22	2	2	2	2	4	6
	7	203	20	151	197	127	15	14	14	14	58	5
	8	256	24	159	228	164	24	22	22	22	132	4
	9	280	30	126	208	169	39	28	28	28	195	3
	10	292	34	75	157	148	56	33	33	33	244	2
	11	298	36	40	85	106	70	38	36	36	274	1
	12	299	37	38	39	59	75	58	39	38	283	12
HALF DAY TOTALS			168	607	940	773	244	163	155	154	1048	
May 21	6	86	25	79	84	38	6	6	6	6	13	6
	7	203	43	171	196	105	17	17	17	17	73	5
	8	248	38	178	218	132	26	25	25	25	142	4
	9	269	35	150	198	132	33	31	31	31	201	3
	10	280	38	103	150	111	39	35	35	35	247	2
	11	286	40	55	83	75	44	39	38	38	274	1
	12	288	41	41	42	44	46	44	42	41	282	12
HALF DAY TOTALS			238	749	943	614	187	174	172	172	1089	
Jun 21	6	97	36	93	94	39	7	7	7	7	17	6
	7	201	55	177	192	94	18	18	18	18	77	5
	8	242	50	184	212	117	27	26	26	26	145	4
	9	263	43	158	192	116	34	32	32	32	201	3
	10	274	41	113	146	96	39	36	36	36	245	2
	11	279	42	65	82	64	42	40	39	40	271	1
	12	281	43	43	43	43	43	43	43	43	279	12
HALF DAY TOTALS			284	802	932	544	187	180	179	180	1096	
Jul 21	6	81	26	76	80	36	6	6	6	6	13	6
	7	195	45	168	190	101	18	18	18	18	73	5
	8	239	41	176	213	128	27	26	26	26	141	4
	9	261	37	150	195	129	34	32	32	32	198	3
	10	272	39	104	149	108	39	36	36	36	243	2
	11	278	41	58	83	73	44	40	39	39	270	1
	12	280	42	42	43	45	46	45	43	42	278	12
HALF DAY TOTALS			247	746	925	595	191	178	177	177	1076	
Aug 21	6	35	6	30	35	19	2	2	2	2	4	6
	7	186	22	144	186	119	16	15	15	15	58	5
	8	241	26	156	220	157	26	24	24	24	130	4
	9	265	32	126	202	162	39	30	30	30	191	3
	10	278	36	78	155	143	55	35	35	35	239	2
	11	284	38	42	85	104	68	40	37	37	268	1
	12	286	38	40	41	58	72	58	41	40	277	12
HALF DAY TOTALS			179	601	910	740	243	171	164	163	1028	
Sep 21	8	248	19	119	222	194	48	19	19	19	108	4
	9	278	26	84	207	206	81	26	26	26	174	3
	10	292	31	42	158	190	110	32	31	31	224	2
	11	299	34	35	84	151	128	44	34	34	256	1
	12	301	35	35	37	95	134	94	37	35	266	12
HALF DAY TOTALS			139	406	863	927	451	174	139	138	930	
Oct 21	7	138	6	62	129	117	31	6	6	6	17	5
	8	247	16	79	211	214	85	16	16	16	82	4
	9	284	22	47	202	235	128	23	22	22	150	3
	10	301	27	29	154	222	160	29	27	27	201	2
	11	309	30	30	80	186	180	67	30	30	233	1
	12	311	31	31	33	131	187	130	33	31	244	12
HALF DAY TOTALS			116	255	778	1032	675	200	117	116	804	
Nov 21	7	67	2	20	59	60	24	2	2	2	5	5
	8	232	12	42	186	213	111	12	12	12	55	4
	9	282	19	23	187	249	163	20	19	19	120	3
	10	303	23	24	143	241	197	37	23	23	171	2
	11	312	26	26	73	209	217	93	26	26	202	1
	12	315	27	27	29	158	224	158	29	27	213	12
HALF DAY TOTALS			97	149	661	1056	825	239	98	97	659	
Dec 21	7	30	1	7	25	27	12	1	1	1	2	5
	8	225	10	29	174	209	118	11	10	10	44	4
	9	281	17	19	180	252	174	18	17	17	107	3
	10	304	22	22	137	247	209	44	22	22	157	2
	11	314	25	25	69	216	230	104	25	25	188	1
	12	317	26	26	27	167	237	167	27	26	199	12
HALF DAY TOTALS			88	118	611	1054	868	257	89	88	598	
			N	NW	W	SW	S	SE	E	NE	HOR	PM

Table 12B (cont.).   Solar intensity and solar heat gain factors for 32 deg North latitude

Date	Solar time am	Direct normal Btuh/ft²	N	NE	E	SE	S	SW	W	NW	HOR	Solar time pm
Jan 21	7	1	0	0	1	1	0	0	0	0	0	5
	8	203	9	29	160	189	103	9	9	9	32	4
	9	269	15	17	175	246	169	17	15	15	88	3
	10	295	20	20	135	249	212	46	20	20	136	2
	11	306	23	23	68	221	238	110	23	23	166	1
	12	310	24	24	25	174	246	174	25	24	176	12
HALF DAY TOTALS			79	107	570	1015	853	264	80	79	512	
Feb 21	7	112	4	47	102	95	26	4	4	4	9	5
	8	245	13	65	205	216	95	13	13	13	64	4
	9	287	19	32	199	248	149	20	19	19	127	3
	10	305	24	25	151	241	189	31	24	24	176	2
	11	314	26	26	76	208	212	87	26	26	207	1
	12	316	27	27	29	155	221	155	29	27	217	12
HALF DAY TOTALS			100	201	735	1080	780	228	100	100	691	
Mar 21	7	185	10	105	176	142	20	9	9	9	32	5
	8	260	17	107	227	209	62	17	17	17	100	4
	9	290	23	64	210	227	107	23	23	23	164	3
	10	304	28	30	158	215	144	29	28	28	211	2
	11	311	31	31	82	179	168	59	31	31	242	1
	12	313	32	32	33	122	176	122	33	32	252	12
HALF DAY TOTALS			124	359	875	1041	589	193	125	124	874	
Apr 21	6	66	9	54	66	38	4	3	3	3	7	6
	7	206	17	146	200	136	16	14	14	14	61	5
	8	255	23	144	227	177	30	22	22	22	129	4
	9	278	28	103	206	187	58	28	28	28	188	3
	10	290	32	52	155	172	87	33	32	32	233	2
	11	295	35	36	83	135	108	40	35	35	262	1
	12	297	36	36	38	82	115	82	38	36	271	12
HALF DAY TOTALS			161	550	952	889	360	177	153	152	1015	
May 21	6	119	33	108	116	56	8	8	8	8	21	6
	7	211	36	170	204	118	19	18	18	18	81	5
	8	250	29	165	220	149	27	25	25	25	146	4
	9	269	33	128	198	155	37	31	31	31	201	3
	10	280	36	76	150	138	54	35	35	35	243	2
	11	285	38	42	83	102	68	40	37	37	269	1
	12	286	38	40	41	59	74	59	41	40	277	12
HALF DAY TOTALS			222	702	985	747	250	183	175	174	1098	
Jun 21	6	131	44	123	127	55	10	10	10	10	28	6
	7	210	47	176	201	108	20	20	20	20	88	5
	8	245	36	171	214	135	28	27	27	27	151	4
	9	264	35	137	193	139	35	32	32	32	204	3
	10	274	38	86	146	123	45	36	36	36	244	2
	11	279	40	47	82	89	56	41	39	39	269	1
	12	280	41	41	42	52	60	52	42	41	276	12
HALF DAY TOTALS			261	762	985	678	225	189	184	183	1122	
Jul 21	6	113	34	105	113	53	9	9	9	9	22	6
	7	203	38	167	198	114	20	19	19	19	81	5
	8	241	31	163	215	145	28	26	26	26	145	4
	9	261	34	129	195	150	37	32	32	32	198	3
	10	271	37	78	148	134	53	36	36	36	240	2
	11	277	39	43	83	99	66	41	38	38	265	1
	12	279	40	41	42	58	72	58	42	41	273	12
HALF DAY TOTALS			231	701	967	726	248	187	180	179	1088	
Aug 21	6	59	10	50	60	34	4	4	4	4	8	6
	7	190	19	141	190	128	17	15	15	15	61	5
	8	240	25	141	219	170	31	23	23	23	128	4
	9	263	30	104	200	181	57	29	29	29	185	3
	10	276	34	55	153	167	84	35	34	34	229	2
	11	282	36	39	84	131	104	41	36	36	256	1
	12	284	37	37	40	81	111	81	40	37	265	12
HALF DAY TOTALS			171	546	922	854	352	184	162	160	999	
Sep 21	7	163	10	96	159	128	20	10	10	10	31	5
	8	240	18	103	215	198	60	18	18	18	96	4
	9	272	24	64	202	218	105	24	24	24	158	3
	10	287	29	32	154	208	141	31	29	29	204	2
	11	294	32	32	81	174	163	59	32	32	234	1
	12	296	33	33	35	120	171	120	35	33	244	12
HALF DAY TOTALS			130	345	831	993	574	197	130	129	845	
Oct 21	7	99	4	43	92	85	24	4	4	4	10	5
	8	229	13	63	195	206	90	13	13	13	63	4
	9	273	20	33	193	239	144	21	20	20	125	3
	10	293	24	26	147	234	183	32	24	24	173	2
	11	302	27	27	76	203	207	85	27	27	203	1
	12	304	28	28	30	151	215	151	30	28	213	12
HALF DAY TOTALS			103	200	708	1038	753	226	104	103	679	
Nov 21	7	2	0	0	1	1	1	0	0	0	0	5
	8	196	9	29	156	184	100	9	9	9	32	4
	9	263	16	17	173	241	166	17	16	16	88	3
	10	289	20	21	134	245	209	45	20	20	136	2
	11	301	23	23	67	218	234	109	23	23	165	1
	12	304	24	24	25	171	243	171	25	24	175	12
HALF DAY TOTALS			80	108	561	996	838	261	81	80	509	
Dec 21	8	176	7	19	135	166	97	7	7	7	22	4
	9	257	14	15	162	238	171	15	14	14	72	3
	10	288	18	18	127	246	216	52	18	18	119	2
	11	301	21	21	63	222	243	116	21	21	148	1
	12	304	22	22	23	177	252	177	23	22	158	12
HALF DAY TOTALS			71	84	500	965	852	275	71	71	440	
			N	NW	W	SW	S	SE	E	NE	HOR	PM

Cooling loads

Table 12B (cont.). Solar intensity and solar heat gain factors for 40 deg North latitude

Date	Solar time am	Direct normal Btuh/ft²	N	NE	E	SE	S	SW	W	NW	HOR	Solar time pm
						Solar heat Gain Factors, Btuh/ft²						
Jan 21	8	142	5	17	111	133	75	6	5	5	14	4
	9	239	12	13	154	224	160	13	12	12	55	3
	10	274	16	16	124	241	213	51	16	16	96	2
	11	289	19	19	61	222	244	118	19	19	124	1
	12	294	20	20	21	179	254	179	21	20	133	12
HALF DAY TOTALS			61	73	452	904	813	273	62	61	354	
Feb 21	7	55	2	23	51	47	14	2	2	2	4	5
	8	219	10	50	183	199	94	10	10	10	43	4
	9	271	16	22	186	245	157	17	16	16	98	3
	10	294	21	21	143	246	203	38	21	21	143	2
	11	304	23	23	71	219	231	103	23	23	171	1
	12	307	24	24	25	170	241	170	25	24	180	12
HALF DAY TOTALS			84	152	648	1049	821	250	85	84	548	
Mar 21	7	171	9	93	163	135	22	8	8	8	26	5
	8	250	16	91	218	211	74	16	16	16	85	4
	9	282	21	47	203	236	128	22	21	21	143	3
	10	297	25	27	153	229	171	29	25	25	186	2
	11	305	28	28	78	198	197	77	28	28	213	1
	12	307	29	29	31	145	206	145	31	29	223	12
HALF DAY TOTALS			114	302	832	1087	694	220	114	113	764	
Apr 21	6	89	11	72	88	52	5	5	5	5	11	6
	7	206	16	140	201	143	16	14	14	14	61	5
	8	252	22	128	224	188	41	21	21	21	123	4
	9	274	27	80	202	203	83	27	27	27	177	3
	10	286	31	37	152	193	121	32	31	31	217	2
	11	292	33	34	81	160	146	52	33	33	243	1
	12	293	34	34	36	108	154	108	36	34	252	12
HALF DAY TOTALS			154	501	957	994	488	199	148	147	957	
May 21	5	1	0	1	1	0	0	0	0	0	0	7
	6	144	36	128	141	71	10	10	10	10	31	6
	7	216	28	165	209	131	20	19	19	19	87	5
	8	250	27	149	220	164	29	25	25	25	146	4
	9	267	31	105	197	175	53	30	30	30	195	3
	10	277	34	54	148	163	83	35	34	34	234	2
	11	283	36	38	81	130	105	42	36	36	257	1
	12	284	37	37	40	82	113	82	40	37	265	12
HALF DAY TOTALS			215	666	1024	881	358	200	176	174	1083	
Jun 21	5	22	10	21	20	6	1	1	1	1	3	7
	6	155	48	143	151	70	13	13	13	13	40	6
	7	216	37	172	207	122	22	21	21	21	97	5
	8	246	30	156	216	152	29	27	27	27	153	4
	9	263	33	114	192	161	45	32	32	32	201	3
	10	272	35	63	145	148	69	36	35	35	238	2
	11	277	38	40	81	116	88	41	38	38	260	1
	12	279	38	38	41	72	95	72	41	38	267	12
HALF DAY TOTALS			253	734	1038	818	315	204	188	186	1126	
Jul 21	5	2	1	2	2	1	0	0	0	0	0	7
	6	138	37	125	137	68	11	11	11	11	32	6
	7	208	30	163	204	127	21	20	20	20	88	5
	8	241	28	148	216	160	30	26	26	26	145	4
	9	259	32	106	193	170	52	31	31	31	194	3
	10	269	35	56	146	159	81	36	35	35	231	2
	11	275	37	40	81	127	102	43	37	37	254	1
	12	276	38	38	41	80	109	80	41	38	262	12
HALF DAY TOTALS			223	666	1008	858	352	204	181	180	1076	
Aug 21	6	81	12	68	82	48	6	5	5	5	12	6
	7	191	17	135	191	135	17	16	16	16	62	5
	8	237	24	126	216	180	41	23	23	23	122	4
	9	260	28	82	197	196	80	28	28	28	174	3
	10	272	32	40	150	187	116	34	32	32	214	2
	11	278	35	36	81	156	141	52	35	35	239	1
	12	280	35	35	38	106	149	106	38	35	247	12
HALF DAY TOTALS			164	498	928	956	474	205	157	156	946	
Sep 21	7	149	9	84	146	121	21	9	9	9	25	5
	8	230	17	87	205	199	71	17	17	17	82	4
	9	263	22	47	194	226	124	23	22	22	138	3
	10	280	27	28	148	221	165	30	27	27	180	2
	11	287	29	29	78	192	191	77	29	29	206	1
	12	290	30	30	32	142	200	142	32	30	215	12
HALF DAY TOTALS			119	291	787	1033	672	222	119	118	738	
Oct 21	7	48	2	20	45	42	12	2	2	2	4	5
	8	204	11	49	173	188	89	11	11	11	43	4
	9	257	17	23	180	235	151	18	17	17	97	3
	10	280	21	22	139	238	196	38	21	21	140	2
	11	291	24	24	71	212	224	101	24	24	168	1
	12	294	25	25	27	165	234	165	27	25	177	12
HALF DAY TOTALS			88	152	623	1006	791	247	89	88	540	
Nov 21	8	136	5	18	108	129	72	6	5	5	14	4
	9	232	12	13	151	219	156	13	12	12	55	3
	10	268	16	16	122	237	209	50	16	16	96	2
	11	283	19	19	61	218	240	116	19	19	123	1
	12	288	20	20	21	176	250	176	21	20	132	12
HALF DAY TOTALS			63	75	445	887	798	269	63	63	354	
Dec 21	8	89	3	8	67	84	50	3	3	3	6	4
	9	217	10	11	135	205	151	13	10	10	39	3
	10	261	14	14	113	232	146	55	14	14	77	2
	11	280	17	17	56	217	242	120	17	17	104	1
	12	285	18	18	19	178	253	178	19	18	113	12
HALF DAY TOTALS			52	56	374	822	775	276	53	52	282	
			N	NW	W	SW	S	SE	E	NE	HOR	PM

Table 12B (cont.). Solar intensity and solar heat gain factors for 48 deg North latitude

Date	Solar time am	Direct normal Btuh/ft²	N	NE	E	SE	S	SW	W	NW	HOR	Solar time pm
Jan 21	8	37	1	4	29	35	20	1	1	1	2	4
	9	185	8	8	118	176	129	10	8	8	25	3
	10	239	12	12	106	216	195	50	12	12	55	2
	11	261	14	14	53	208	233	116	14	14	77	1
	12	267	15	15	16	171	245	171	16	15	85	12
HALF DAY TOTALS			43	46	316	729	701	259	43	43	203	
Feb 21	7	4	0	1	3	3	1	0	0	0	0	5
	8	180	8	36	149	166	82	8	8	8	25	4
	9	247	13	16	168	230	155	14	13	13	66	3
	10	275	17	17	131	242	207	44	17	17	105	2
	11	288	19	19	65	221	239	113	19	19	130	1
	12	292	20	20	22	176	250	176	22	20	138	12
HALF DAY TOTALS			68	107	541	968	813	261	68	68	395	
Mar 21	7	153	7	80	145	123	23	7	7	7	20	5
	8	236	14	76	204	206	82	14	14	14	68	4
	9	270	19	3	193	239	142	20	19	19	118	3
	10	287	23	24	146	237	189	33	23	23	156	2
	11	295	25	25	74	210	218	94	25	25	180	1
	12	298	26	26	27	161	228	161	27	26	188	12
HALF DAY TOTALS			100	250	775	1100	767	244	101	100	636	
Apr 21	6	108	12	86	107	64	6	6	6	6	15	6
	7	205	15	132	199	148	18	14	14	14	60	5
	8	247	20	111	219	196	55	20	20	20	114	4
	9	268	25	60	197	215	106	25	25	25	161	3
	10	280	28	31	148	209	150	31	28	28	196	2
	11	286	31	31	78	181	177	69	31	31	218	1
	12	288	31	31	34	131	186	131	34	31	226	12
HALF DAY TOTALS			162	482	982	1144	698	296	158	155	990	
May 21	5	41	17	40	39	14	3	3	3	3	5	7
	6	162	35	141	160	85	12	12	12	12	40	6
	7	219	23	158	212	142	21	19	19	19	91	5
	8	248	26	132	218	178	38	25	25	25	142	4
	9	264	29	82	194	192	77	29	29	29	185	3
	10	274	33	39	145	184	116	35	33	33	219	2
	11	279	35	36	79	155	142	54	35	35	240	1
	12	280	35	35	38	107	150	107	38	35	247	12
HALF DAY TOTALS			215	645	1065	1007	483	225	174	173	1045	
Jun 21	5	77	35	76	72	24	5	5	5	5	12	7
	6	172	46	155	169	84	14	14	14	14	51	6
	7	220	29	165	211	135	23	21	21	21	103	5
	8	246	29	139	215	168	34	27	27	27	152	4
	9	261	31	91	190	180	66	31	31	31	193	3
	10	269	34	45	143	171	101	36	34	34	225	2
	11	274	36	38	79	142	126	49	36	36	246	1
	12	275	37	37	40	96	134	96	40	37	252	12
HALF DAY TOTALS			257	722	1095	955	436	228	189	188	1108	
Jul 21	5	43	18	42	41	15	3	3	3	3	6	7
	6	156	37	138	156	82	13	13	13	13	41	6
	7	211	25	156	207	138	22	20	20	20	92	5
	8	240	27	132	214	174	38	26	26	26	142	4
	9	256	30	83	191	187	75	30	30	30	184	3
	10	266	34	41	143	180	113	36	34	34	217	2
	11	271	36	37	79	151	138	54	36	36	237	1
	12	272	36	36	39	104	146	104	39	36	244	12
HALF DAY TOTALS			223	646	1050	983	474	229	181	179	1042	
Aug 21	6	99	13	81	100	60	7	7	7	7	16	6
	7	190	17	128	190	141	19	15	15	15	61	5
	8	232	22	110	211	188	53	22	22	22	114	4
	9	154	27	63	192	108	102	27	27	27	159	3
	10	266	30	33	145	203	144	33	30	30	193	2
	11	272	32	32	78	175	171	68	32	32	215	1
	12	274	33	33	36	128	189	128	36	33	223	12
HALF DAY TOTALS			157	459	929	1040	587	231	151	149	869	
Sep 21	7	131	8	71	128	108	21	7	7	7	20	5
	8	215	15	72	191	193	77	15	15	15	65	4
	9	251	20	34	184	227	136	21	20	20	114	3
	10	269	24	25	141	228	182	34	24	24	151	2
	11	278	26	26	73	203	210	92	26	26	174	1
	12	280	27	27	29	156	220	156	29	27	182	12
HALF DAY TOTALS			105	240	729	1040	737	243	106	105	614	
Oct 21	7	4	0	2	4	3	1	0	0	0	0	5
	8	165	8	35	139	155	77	8	8	8	25	4
	9	233	14	16	161	220	148	15	14	14	66	3
	10	262	18	18	128	233	199	43	18	18	104	2
	11	274	20	20	64	213	231	109	20	20	128	1
	12	278	21	21	23	171	242	171	23	21	136	12
HALF DAY TOTALS			71	108	519	925	779	256	72	71	391	
Nov 21	8	36	1	4	29	35	20	1	1	1	2	4
	9	179	8	9	115	171	125	10	8	8	26	3
	10	233	12	12	104	212	191	49	12	12	55	2
	11	255	15	15	52	204	228	114	15	15	77	1
	12	261	15	15	17	168	240	168	17	15	85	12
HALF DAY TOTALS			44	47	310	713	686	255	44	44	204	
Dec 21	9	140	5	6	86	133	100	8	5	5	13	3
	10	214	10	10	91	194	179	49	10	10	38	2
	11	242	12	12	46	195	220	111	12	12	57	1
	12	250	13	13	14	163	233	168	14	13	65	12
HALF DAY TOTALS			33	34	233	610	616	247	34	33	141	
			N	NW	W	SW	S	SE	E	NE	HOR	PM

Cooling loads

Table 12B (cont.).   Solar intensity and solar heat gain factors for 56 deg North latitude

Date	Solar time am	Direct normal Btuh/ft²	N	NE	E	SE	S	SW	W	NW	HOR	Solar time pm
Jan 21	9	78	3	3	49	74	55	4	3	3	5	3
	10	170	7	7	74	156	143	38	7	7	21	2
	11	207	9	9	40	169	190	96	9	9	34	1
	12	217	10	10	11	144	205	144	11	10	40	12
HALF DAY TOTALS			23	24	163	468	487	206	24	23	80	
Feb 21	8	115	4	21	95	107	55	4	4	4	10	4
	9	203	10	11	139	197	136	10	10	10	36	3
	10	246	13	13	115	223	196	45	13	13	65	2
	11	262	15	15	57	210	232	112	15	15	84	1
	12	267	16	16	17	171	244	171	17	16	91	12
HALF DAY TOTALS			49	66	409	821	737	253	50	49	241	
Mar 21	7	128	6	65	121	105	21	6	6	6	14	5
	8	215	12	61	185	194	84	12	12	12	49	4
	9	253	16	23	179	233	148	17	16	16	89	3
	10	272	19	20	136	238	198	39	19	19	122	2
	11	282	21	21	68	215	230	106	21	21	142	1
	12	284	22	22	24	170	241	170	24	22	149	12
HALF DAY TOTALS			85	200	699	1071	800	258	86	85	491	
Apr 21	6	122	13	95	121	75	7	7	7	7	18	6
	7	201	15	123	195	152	21	14	14	14	56	5
	8	239	19	95	211	201	68	19	19	19	101	4
	9	260	23	44	190	223	126	24	23	23	140	3
	10	272	26	27	142	220	171	33	26	26	170	2
	11	278	28	28	74	195	200	86	28	28	189	1
	12	280	28	28	31	149	210	149	31	28	195	12
HALF DAY TOTALS			139	430	951	1147	699	252	132	131	772	
May 21	5	93	36	89	88	33	6	6	6	6	14	7
	6	175	33	148	173	97	14	14	14	14	48	6
	7	219	21	149	212	152	22	19	19	19	92	5
	8	244	25	115	215	189	52	24	24	24	135	4
	9	259	28	62	189	206	102	28	28	28	171	3
	10	268	31	33	141	200	145	33	31	31	199	2
	11	273	32	32	76	174	172	71	32	32	216	1
	12	275	33	33	36	129	181	129	36	33	222	12
HALF DAY TOTALS			222	644	1112	1120	604	256	172	170	986	
Jun 21	4	21	13	22	18	3	1	1	1	2	3	8
	5	122	53	119	115	40	9	9	9	9	25	7
	6	185	42	160	182	97	16	16	16	16	62	6
	7	222	25	156	213	147	24	22	22	22	105	5
	8	243	27	122	213	181	46	26	26	26	146	4
	9	257	30	69	187	196	91	30	30	30	181	3
	10	265	33	36	139	190	132	35	33	33	208	2
	11	269	34	35	76	164	159	65	34	34	225	1
	12	271	35	35	38	119	168	119	38	35	231	12
HALF DAY TOTALS			275	738	1162	1082	562	160	190	189	1070	
Jul 21	5	91	37	89	88	33	7	7	7	7	16	7
	6	169	34	145	170	95	15	14	14	14	50	6
	7	212	23	147	208	148	23	20	20	20	93	5
	8	237	26	115	211	185	51	25	25	25	135	4
	9	252	29	63	186	201	99	29	29	29	171	3
	10	261	32	34	139	196	142	35	32	32	198	2
	11	265	33	33	76	171	168	70	33	33	215	1
	12	267	34	34	37	126	177	126	37	34	221	12
HALF DAY TOTALS			231	646	1097	1096	593	259	179	177	987	
Aug 21	5	1	0	1	1	0	0	0	0	0	0	7
	6	112	14	91	114	71	8	8	8	8	20	6
	7	187	16	119	186	144	22	15	15	15	58	5
	8	225	20	94	203	192	66	20	20	20	101	4
	9	246	25	46	184	215	121	26	25	25	140	3
	10	258	28	30	139	213	165	34	28	28	169	2
	11	264	30	30	74	189	193	84	30	30	187	1
	12	266	30	30	30	145	203	145	33	30	198	12
HALF DAY TOTALS			149	429	923	1104	678	256	142	140	771	
Sep 21	7	107	6	56	104	90	19	6	6	6	14	5
	8	194	12	58	171	179	78	12	12	12	48	4
	9	233	17	24	170	220	140	18	17	17	86	3
	10	253	20	21	131	227	189	39	20	20	118	2
	11	263	22	22	67	206	220	103	22	22	137	1
	12	266	23	23	25	163	231	163	25	23	144	12
HALF DAY TOTALS			89	191	652	1004	761	255	90	89	474	
Oct 21	8	104	4	20	87	98	50	4	4	4	10	4
	9	193	10	11	132	186	129	11	10	10	37	3
	10	231	14	14	111	213	186	44	14	14	64	2
	11	248	16	16	56	202	222	108	16	16	84	1
	12	253	16	16	18	164	234	164	18	16	91	12
HALF DAY TOTALS			52	68	390	779	702	246	53	52	240	
Nov 21	9	76	3	3	48	72	54	4	3	3	6	3
	10	165	7	7	72	152	139	37	7	7	21	2
	11	201	9	9	39	165	186	94	9	9	35	1
	12	211	10	10	11	140	200	140	11	10	40	12
HALF DAY TOTALS			24	24	161	457	475	202	24	24	81	
Dec 21	9	5	0	0	3	5	4	0	0	0	0	3
	10	113	4	4	47	103	96	27	4	4	9	2
	11	166	6	6	30	135	154	78	6	6	19	1
	12	180	7	7	8	120	171	120	8	7	23	12
HALF DAY TOTALS			14	14	88	311	343	163	15	14	40	
			N	NW	W	SW	S	SE	E	NE	HOR	PM

Table 12B (cont.). Solar intensity and solar heat gain factors for 64 deg North latitude

Date	Solar time am	Direct normal Btuh/ft²	N	NE	E	SE	S	SW	W	NW	HOR	Solar time pm
Jan 21	10	22	1	1	9	20	19	5	1	1	1	2
	11	81	3	3	15	67	75	38	3	3	6	1
	12	100	3	3	4	67	96	67	4	3	8	12
HALF DAY TOTALS			5	5	25	121	141	75	5	5	11	
Feb 21	8	18	1	3	15	17	9	1	1	1	1	4
	9	134	5	6	89	128	90	6	5	5	13	3
	10	190	8	8	87	176	157	38	8	8	28	2
	11	215	10	10	44	177	197	97	10	10	41	1
	12	222	11	11	12	147	210	147	12	11	45	12
HALF DAY TOTALS			29	33	244	578	560	212	30	29	106	
Mar 21	7	95	4	47	90	79	17	4	4	4	9	5
	8	185	9	46	158	170	78	9	9	9	32	4
	9	227	13	16	159	215	143	14	13	13	59	3
	10	249	16	16	122	226	194	42	16	16	84	2
	11	260	17	17	60	209	228	109	17	17	99	1
	12	263	18	18	19	168	239	168	19	18	105	12
HALF DAY TOTALS			68	150	596	984	779	257	68	68	335	
Apr 21	5	27	8	24	26	12	1	1	1	1	2	7
	6	133	12	102	132	84	8	8	8	8	21	6
	7	194	14	113	189	153	25	13	13	13	51	5
	8	228	17	79	201	201	79	17	17	17	85	4
	9	248	21	32	180	225	138	22	21	21	116	3
	10	260	23	24	134	225	185	38	23	23	140	2
	11	266	24	24	68	202	214	99	24	24	155	1
	12	268	25	25	27	159	224	159	27	25	160	12
HALF DAY TOTALS			131	410	943	1186	763	273	121	120	651	
May 21	4	51	30	51	43	8	3	3	3	3	6	8
	5	132	48	125	125	50	9	9	9	9	26	7
	6	185	28	150	183	109	15	15	15	15	55	6
	7	218	21	138	211	161	24	19	19	19	90	5
	8	239	23	97	209	198	68	23	23	23	124	4
	9	252	26	45	183	215	123	27	26	26	152	3
	10	261	28	30	135	212	167	36	28	28	174	2
	11	265	30	30	72	188	195	87	30	30	188	1
	12	267	30	30	33	146	204	146	33	30	192	12
HALF DAY TOTALS			247	680	1177	1218	708	288	169	168	911	
Jun 21	4	93	53	96	78	14	7	7	7	7	16	8
	5	154	62	148	145	55	12	12	12	12	39	7
	6	194	36	162	192	110	18	17	17	17	71	6
	7	221	24	145	213	158	25	22	22	22	105	5
	8	239	25	104	208	192	62	25	25	25	137	4
	9	251	28	51	181	208	115	29	28	28	165	3
	10	258	30	32	134	204	157	36	30	30	186	2
	11	262	32	32	72	180	184	82	32	32	199	1
	12	263	32	32	35	138	193	138	35	32	203	12
HALF DAY TOTALS			322	801	1253	1195	679	296	192	191	1021	
Jul 21	4	53	32	55	46	9	4	4	4	4	8	8
	5	128	49	123	124	50	10	10	10	10	28	7
	6	179	30	148	180	106	16	15	15	15	57	6
	7	211	22	137	207	157	25	20	20	20	92	5
	8	231	24	97	205	193	67	24	24	24	124	4
	9	245	27	47	180	211	120	28	27	27	152	3
	10	253	29	31	134	208	164	37	29	29	174	2
	11	257	31	31	72	185	191	86	31	31	187	1
	12	259	31	31	34	143	200	143	34	31	192	12
HALF DAY TOTALS			258	684	1163	1193	697	292	177	175	918	
Aug 21	5	29	9	27	28	13	2	2	2	2	3	7
	6	123	13	97	125	80	9	9	9	9	23	6
	7	181	15	109	180	145	26	14	14	14	53	5
	8	214	19	78	193	192	76	19	19	19	87	4
	9	234	22	34	174	217	133	23	22	22	117	3
	10	246	25	26	131	217	178	39	25	25	140	2
	11	252	26	26	69	196	207	97	26	26	154	1
	12	254	27	27	29	155	217	155	29	27	159	12
HALF DAY TOTALS			142	410	914	1141	740	275	131	130	656	
Sep 21	7	77	4	39	74	65	15	4	4	4	8	5
	8	163	10	43	143	154	71	10	10	10	31	4
	9	206	14	17	148	200	133	15	14	14	57	3
	10	229	16	17	116	213	183	41	16	16	81	2
	11	240	18	18	59	198	216	104	18	18	96	1
	12	244	19	19	21	160	227	160	21	19	101	12
HALF DAY TOTALS			71	142	547	910	731	249	72	71	324	
Oct 21	8	17	1	3	14	16	8	1	1	1	1	4
	9	122	5	6	82	118	83	6	5	5	13	3
	10	176	9	9	83	165	147	36	9	9	29	2
	11	201	11	11	43	167	186	92	11	11	41	1
	12	208	11	11	13	140	199	140	13	11	46	12
HALF DAY TOTALS			31	34	231	542	527	202	32	31	108	
Nov 21	10	23	1	1	10	21	20	5	1	1	1	2
	11	79	3	3	15	65	74	37	3	3	6	1
	12	97	4	4	4	66	93	66	4	4	8	12
HALF DAY TOTALS			5	5	26	120	140	74	6	5	11	
Dec 21	11	4	0	0	1	3	4	2	0	0	0	1
	12	16	0	0	1	11	15	11	1	0	1	12
HALF DAY TOTALS			0	0	1	9	11	7	0	0	1	
			N	NW	W	SW	S	SE	E	NE	HOR	PM

Cooling loads

Table 13. Rates of heat gain from occupants of conditioned spaces[a]

Degree of activity	Typical Application	Total heat adults, male	Total heat adjusted[b]	Sensible heat	Latent heat
		Btuh	Btuh	Btuh	Btuh
Seated at rest	Theater, movie	400	350	210	140
Seated, very light work writing	Offices, hotels, apts	480	420	230	190
Seated, eating	Restaurant[c]	520	580[c]	255	325
Seated, light work, typing	Offices, hotels, apts	640	510	255	255
Standing, light work or walking slowly	Retail Store, bank	800	640	315	325
Light bench work	Factory	880	780	345	435
Walking, 3 mph, light machine work	Factory	1040	1040	345	695
Bowling[d]	Bowling alley	1200	960	345	615
Moderate dancing	Dance hall	1360	1280	405	875
Heavy work, heavy machine work, lifting	Factory	1600	1600	565	1035
Heavy work, athletics	Gymnasium	2000	1800	635	1165

[a] *Note: Tabulated values are based on 78°F room dry-bulb temperature. For 80°F room dry-bulb, the total heat remains the same, but the sensible heat value should be decreased by approximately 8% and the latent heat values increased accordingly.*

[b] *Adjusted total heat gain is based on normal percentage of men, women, and children for the application listed, with the postulate that the gain from an adult female is 85% of that for an adult male, and that the gain from a child is 75% of that for an adult male.*

[c] *Adjusted total heat value for eating in a restaurant, includes 60 Btuh for food per individual (30 Btu sensible and 30 Btu latent).*

[d] *For bowling figure one person per alley actually bowling, and all others as sitting (400 Btuh) or standing and walking slowly (790 Btuh).*

To convert to watts, divide Btuh by 3.413.
To convert to kcal/hr, divide Btuh by 4.

Table 14. Design equivalent temperature differences

Design temperature, °F	85		90			95			100		105	110
Daily temperature range[a]	L	M	L	M	H	L	M	H	M	H	H	H
WALLS AND DOORS												
1. Frame and veneer-on-frame	17.6	13.6	22.6	18.6	13.6	27.6	23.6	18.6	28.6	23.6	28.6	33.6
2. Masonry walls, 8-in. block or brick	10.3	6.3	15.3	11.3	6.3	20.3	16.3	11.3	21.3	16.3	21.3	26.3
3. Partitions, frame	9.0	5.0	14.0	10.0	5.0	19.0	15.0	10.0	20.0	15.0	20.0	25.0
masonry	2.5	0	7.5	3.5	0	12.5	8.5	3.5	13.5	8.5	13.5	18.5
4. Wood doors	17.6	13.6	22.6	18.6	13.6	27.6	23.6	18.6	28.6	23.6	28.6	33.6
CEILINGS AND ROOFS[b]												
1. Ceilings under naturally vented attic or vented flat roof—dark	38.0	34.0	43.0	39.0	34.0	48.0	44.0	39.0	49.0	44.0	49.0	54.0
—light	30.0	26.0	35.0	31.0	26.0	40.0	36.0	31.0	41.0	36.0	41.0	46.0
2. Built-up roof, no ceiling—dark	38.0	24.0	43.0	39.0	34.0	48.0	44.0	39.0	49.0	44.0	49.0	54.0
—light	30.0	26.0	35.0	31.0	26.0	40.0	36.0	31.0	41.0	36.0	41.0	46.0
3. Ceilings under unconditioned rooms	9.0	5.0	14.0	10.0	5.0	19.0	15.0	10.0	20.0	15.0	20.0	25.0
FLOORS												
1. Over unconditioned rooms	9.0	5.0	14.0	10.0	5.0	19.0	15.0	10.0	20.0	15.0	20.0	25.0
2. Over basement, enclosed crawl space or concrete slab on ground	0	0	0	0	0	0	0	0	0	0	0	0
3. Over open crawl space	9.0	5.0	14.0	10.0	5.0	19.0	15.0	10.0	20.0	15.0	20.0	25.0

[a] *Daily Temperature Range*
L (Low) Calculation Value: 12 deg F.   M (Medium) Calculation Value: 20 deg F.   H (High) Calculation Value: 30 deg F.
Applicable Range: Less than 15 deg F.   Applicable Range: 15 to 25 deg F.   Applicable Range: More than 25 deg F.

[b] *Ceilings and Roofs: For roofs in shade, 18-hr average = 11 deg temperature differential. At 90 F design and medium daily range, equivalent temperature differential for light-colored roof equals 11 + (0.71)(39 − 11) = 31 deg F.*

Table 15. Design transmitted and absorbed solar energy and air-to-air temperature difference, Btu/(h · ft²)

Outdoor	Regular single glass						Regular double glass						Heat absorbing double glass					
Design temp.	85	90	95	100	105	110	85	90	95	100	105	110	85	90	95	100	105	110
No Awnings or inside Shading																		
North	23	27	31	35	38	44	19	21	24	26	28	30	12	14	17	19	21	23
NE and NW	56	60	64	68	71	77	46	48	51	53	55	57	27	29	32	34	36	38
East and West	81	85	89	93	96	102	68	70	73	75	77	79	42	44	47	49	51	53
SE and SW	70	74	78	82	85	91	59	61	64	66	68	70	35	37	40	42	44	46
South	40	44	48	52	55	61	33	35	38	40	42	44	19	21	24	26	28	30
Draperies or Venetian Blinds																		
North	15	19	23	27	30	36	12	14	17	19	21	23	9	11	14	16	18	20
NE and NW	32	36	40	44	47	53	27	29	32	34	36	38	20	22	25	27	29	31
East and West	48	52	56	60	63	69	42	44	47	49	51	53	30	32	35	37	39	41
SE and SW	40	44	48	52	55	61	35	37	40	42	44	46	24	26	29	31	33	35
South	23	27	31	35	38	44	20	22	25	27	29	31	15	17	20	22	24	26
Roller Shades Half-Drawn																		
North	18	22	26	30	33	39	15	17	20	22	24	26	10	12	15	17	19	21
NE and NW	40	44	48	52	55	61	38	40	43	45	47	49	24	26	29	31	33	35
East and West	61	65	69	73	76	82	54	56	59	61	63	65	35	37	40	42	44	46
SE and SW	52	56	60	64	67	73	46	48	51	53	55	57	30	32	35	37	39	41
South	29	33	37	41	44	50	27	29	32	34	36	38	18	20	23	25	27	29
Awnings																		
North	20	24	28	32	35	41	13	15	18	20	22	24	10	12	15	17	19	21
NE and NW	21	25	29	33	36	42	14	16	19	21	23	25	11	13	16	18	20	22
East and West	22	26	30	34	37	43	14	16	19	21	23	25	12	14	17	19	21	23
SE and SW	21	25	29	33	36	42	14	16	19	21	23	25	11	13	16	18	20	22
South	21	24	28	32	35	41	13	15	18	20	22	24	11	13	16	18	20	22

Table 16. Average occupancy of various building types

Type of building space	Sq ft/person	Type of building space	Sq ft/person
Apartments	100–325	Libraries—Book stacks	100–200
Department and variety stores—1st & bsmt.	16–44	Reading areas	40–100
Rest	20–73	Museums	40–80
Eating places—quick service	13–17	Office buildings—General offices	80–130
Hotels—public spaces	10–78	Small suites	50–130
Hospitals—patients' rooms	80–100	Banks	40–80
Industrial buildings—general	100–300	Places of assembly	6–10
Laboratories	100–200	Schools	10–20

In lines 36 and 42 enter in the Area column the product of the linear feet of crack and the appropriate cfm of infiltration as determined from Table 1. In lines 39 and 45 add safety factors of 10 and 5 per cent, respectively. Lines 47 and 48 are used only if through-the-wall cooling units are to be employed; they are calculated in the same manner as for infiltration air.

Building tonnage: The tons of refrigeration required for cooling the room can be found by dividing the total heat (line 49) by 12,000. But the sum of the room tonnages should not be used for the building tonnage because it will be 20 to 50 per cent higher than necessary. To obtain the building tonnage, calculate the total instantaneous heat load for the building as a whole, divide it by 12,000, then multiply by 0.4 to 0.6.

Building cfm: Total air requirements for the building may be obtained by adding the cfm requirements for each room, for constant volume systems. It is more complex for variable volume systems.

SOLAR LOADS

Sun shining through glass produces high heat gains. The incident solar load received by a vertical surface often exceeds 200 Btu/(hr)(sq ft) (see Table 12). For single glass most of this heat is transmitted instanta-neously to the building interior. For every 100 sq ft of unshaded, unfavorably oriented glass in air-conditioned buildings in most parts of the country, an additional ton of cooling capacity must be provided at a cost of $600 to $1,800 (see Table 17). The annual operating cost of air conditioning directly attributable to each square foot of glass may be several dollars.

Solar loads may vary with latitude, orientation, ratio of glass to solid wall, type of glass, and degree of shading. Except for the first, all these factors are normally controllable by the architect.

Orientation: Glass facing north receives the least solar radiation, and glass facing

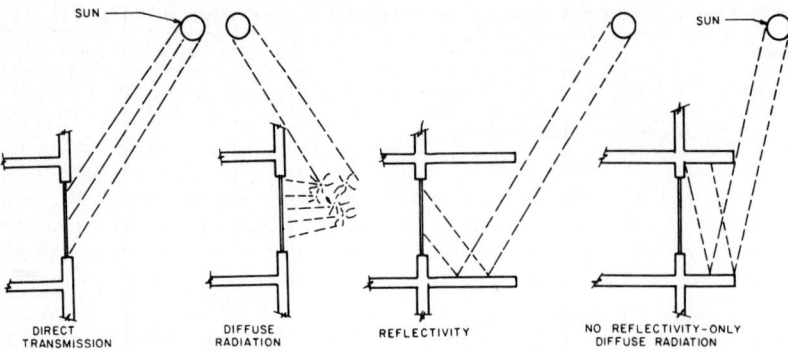

Fig. 1. Types of solar radiation

Table 17. Types of commercial glass and their effect on solar load

Type	Approximate installed cost, $/sq ft	Shading coefficient	U
Single clear plate, ¼ -in.	2.50	.93	1.13
Double clear plate, ½-in. air space	5.00–5.50	.82	.5
Single heat absorbent—tinted	3.00	.7	.13
Double, 1 clear plate, 1 heat absorbent, ½ -in. air space	5.50–6.00	.5	.5
Single, metallic coated	4.00–5.50	.25–.4	1.13
Double, coated glass	7.00–10.00	.15–.4	.5
Double, clear plate with venetian blind in air space	10.00	.3	.5
Metallized plastic film on existing single clear glass	$1.50 (Film only)	.6	1.09

south receives next least during the summer. Therefore, if a building can be oriented so that most of its glass faces north and south, it will have a much lower solar load than if the principal glass areas face east and west (see Table 25).

Glass ratio: Since the solar load is directly proportional to the glass area, it is obvious that the load can be reduced by the use of smaller windows.

Special glass: Various special types of glass may be used to reduce the solar load (Table 18). The extra cost of the glass must

be compared with the saving it produces by reduction in the cooling load. Sometimes used is "glare-reducing" or coated glass, which reduces the transmission of visible light as well as heat (see section on "Glass").

Shading: Large areas of glass may be used without significantly increasing the solar load if they are completely shaded from the direct rays of the sun. The effects of various common types of glass and shading are shown in Tables 18 through 24. As shown in the tables, the most effective type

of shading is external, since the reflected and absorbed heat can then be carried off by the ambient air. An effective external shading device is one which cuts off all direct sun during the cooling season only, and admits sun at other seasons. The shading device should be acceptable in architectural appearance, moderate in cost, durable in all kinds of weather, low in maintenance requirements; it should admit as much natural light as possible, and obscure the view outward as little as possible. New exterior shade materials are available which are sun

Table 18. Overall coefficients of heat transmission (U-factor) of windows and skylights, Btuh/(ft²) (°F)

		Part A.	Exterior vertical panels	
Description	Winter	Summer	Winter	Summer
	No Shade	No Shade	Indoor Shade	Indoor Shade
Flat Glass				
Single Glass	1.10	1.04	0.83	0.81
Insulating Glass; Double				
³⁄₁₆-in. air space	0.62	0.65	0.52	0.58
¼-in. air space	0.58	0.61	0.48	0.55
½-in. air space	0.49	0.56	0.42	0.52
½-in. air space, low emittance coating				
$e = 0.20$	0.32	0.38	0.30	0.37
$e = 0.40$	0.38	0.45	0.36	0.44
$e = 0.60$	0.43	0.51	0.38	0.48
Insulating Glass; Triple				
¼-in. air space	0.39	0.44	0.31	0.40
½-in. air space	0.31	0.39	0.26	0.36
Storm Windows				
1-in. to 4-in. air spaces	0.50	0.50	0.42	0.48

Part B. Exterior horizontal panels (skylights)

Description	Winter	Summer
Flat Glass		
Single Glass	1.23	0.83
Insulating Glass; Double		
³⁄₁₆-in. air space	0.70	0.57
¼-in. air space	0.65	0.54
½-in. air space	0.59	0.49
½-in. air space, low emittance coating		
$e = 0.20$	0.48	0.36
$e = 0.40$	0.52	0.42
$e = 0.60$	0.56	0.46
Plastic Domes		
Single Walled	1.15	0.80
Double Walled	0.70	0.46

Part C. Adjustment factors for various window and sliding patio door types; (multiply U-values in Parts A and B by these factors)

Description	Single glass	Double or triple glass	Storm windows
Windows			
All Glass	1.00	1.00	1.00
Wood Sash; 80% Glass	0.90	0.95	0.90
Wood Sash; 60% Glass	0.80	0.85	0.80
Metal Sash; 80% Glass	1.00	1.20	1.20
Sliding Patio Doors			
Wood Frame	0.95	1.00	—
Metal Frame	1.00	1.10	—

Note: For more detailed information see the ASHRAE Handbook.

and weather resistant. These have been combined into total assemblies which can be automatically raised and lowered, based on solar and wind conditions. Examples of various shading devices are shown in Figs. 10–12.

Solar radiation, both light and heat, consists of direct, diffused, and reflected radiation (Fig. 1). Direct radiation usually makes up the largest single component of the peak solar load. In clear weather the diffuse factor is usually about 7 to 15 per cent of the direct radiation. Reflected radiation is

the most difficult to calculate because it is determined not only by the location of the sun and the configuration of the shading device but also by the reflective characteristics of the surfaces off which the heat bounces. The reflectivity of various building and landscaping materials is given in the section on "Daylighting." Under ordinary conditions, for preliminary estimates, reflected radiation may be taken at twice the diffused factor at peak solar loads.

The solar load through glass is usually the most difficult portion of the cooling load

to establish accurately. This is especially true where overhangs or other types of external shading devices are used. The accurate calculation of solar loads through glass is somewhat complicated (see the Fundamental ASHRAE Guide). However, for estimating purposes, the curves in Fig. 3 may be used. The combined effect on the cooling load of glass ratio, type of glass, and degree of shading are shown in the charts on the page after next.

Table 19. Shading coefficients for single glass and insulating glass[a]

			Shading coefficient	
A. Single glass				
Type of glass	Nominal thickness[b]	Solar trans.[b]	$h_0 = 4.0$	$h_0 = 3.0$
Clear	⅛ in.	0.84	1.00	1.00
	¼ in.	0.78	0.94	0.95
	⅜ in.	0.72	0.90	0.92
	½ in.	0.67	0.87	0.88
Heat absorbing	⅛ in.	0.64	0.83	0.85
	¼ in.	0.46	0.69	0.73
	⅜ in.	0.33	0.60	0.64
	½ in.	0.24	0.53	0.58
B. Insulating glass				
Clear out, clear in	⅛ in.[c]	0.71[e]	0.88	0.88
Clear out, clear in	¼ in.	0.61	0.81	0.82
Heat absorbing[d] out, clear in	¼ in.	0.36	0.55	0.58

[a] Refers to factory-fabricated units with ³/₁₆, ¼, or ½-in. air space or to prime windows plus storm sash.
[b] Refer to manufacturer's literature for values.
[c] Thickness of each pane of glass, not thickness of assembled unit.
[d] Refers to gray, bronze, and green tinted heat-absorbing float glass.
[e] Combined transmittance for assembled unit.

Table 20. Solar optical properties and shading coefficients of transparent plastic sheeting

	Transmittance		
Type of plastic	Visible	Solar	SC
Acrylic			
Clear	0.92	0.85	0.98
Gray tint	0.16	0.27	0.52
"	0.33	0.41	0.63
"	0.45	0.55	0.74
"	0.59	0.62	0.80
"	0.76	0.74	0.89
Bronze tint	0.10	0.20	0.46
"	0.27	0.35	0.58
"	0.49	0.56	0.75
"	0.61	0.62	0.80
"	0.75	0.75	0.90
Reflective*	0.14	0.12	0.21
Polycarbonate			
Clear (⅛ -in.)	0.88	0.82	0.98
Gray (⅛ -in.)	0.50	0.57	0.74
Bronze (⅛ -in.)	0.50	0.57	0.74

* Aluminum metallized polyester film on plastic.

Table 21. Shading coefficients for single glass with indoor shading by venetian blinds or roller shades

			Type of shading				
			Venetian blinds		Roller shade		Translucent
					Opaque		
	Nominal thickness[a]	Solar trans.[b]	Medium	Light	Dark	White	Light
Clear	³/₃₂ to ¼	0.87 to 0.80					
Clear	¼ to ½	0.80 to 0.71					
Clear pattern	⅛ to ½	0.87 to 0.79	0.64	0.55	0.59	0.25	0.39
Heat-absorbing pattern	⅛	—					
Tinted	³/₁₆, ⁷/₃₂	0.74, 0.71					
Heat-absorbing[d]	³/₁₆, ¼	0.46					
Heat-absorbing pattern	³/₁₆, ¼	—	0.57	0.53	0.45	0.30	0.36
Tinted	⅛ , ⁷/₃₂	0.59, 0.45					
Heat-absorbing or pattern	—	0.44 to 0.30	0.54	0.52	0.40	0.28	0.32
Heat-absorbing[d]	⅜	0.34					
Heat-absorbing or pattern	—	0.29 to 0.15 / 0.24	0.42	0.40	0.36	0.28	0.31
Reflective-coated glass							
S.C.[c] = 0.30			0.25	0.23			
0.40			0.33	0.29			
0.50			0.42	0.38			
0.60			0.50	0.44			

[a] Refer to manufacturer's literature for values.
[b] For vertical blinds with opaque white and beige louvers in the tightly closed position, SC is 0.25 and 0.29 when used with glass of 0.71 to 0.80 transmittance.
[c] SC for glass with no shading device.
[d] Refers to gray, bronze, and green tinted heat-absorbing glass.

Table 22. Shading coefficients for insulating glass[a] with indoor shading by venetian blinds or roller shades

Type of glass	Nominal thickness in., each light	Solar trans.[b]		Type of shading				
				Venetian blinds[c]		Roller shade		
						Opaque		Translucent
		Outer pane	Inner pane	Medium	Light	Dark	White	Light
Clear out	3/32, 1/8	0.87	0.87					
Clear in				0.57	0.51	0.60	0.25	0.37
Clear out								
Clear in	1/4	0.80	0.80					
Heat-absorbing[d] out	1/4	0.46	0.80	0.39	0.36	0.40	0.22	0.30
Clear in								
Reflective-coated glass								
SC[e] = 0.20				0.19	0.18			
0.30				0.27	0.26			
0.40				0.34	0.33			

[a] *Refers to factory-fabricated units with 3/16, 1/4, or 1/2-in. air space, or to prime windows plus storm windows.*
[b] *Refer to manufacturer's literature for exact values.*
[c] *For vertical blinds with opaque white or beige louvers, tightly closed, SC is approximately the same as for opaque white roller shades.*
[d] *Refers to bronze, or green tinted, heat-absorbing glass.*

Table 23. Shading coefficients for double glazing with between-glass shading

| Type of glass | Nominal each pane, in. | Solar trans.[a] | | Description of air space | Type of shading | | |
| | | | | | Venetian blinds | | Louvered sun screen |
		Outer pane	Inner pane		Light	Medium	
Clear out	3/32, 1/8	0.87	0.87	Shade in contact with glass or shade separated from glass by air space.	0.33	0.36	0.43
Clear in							
Clear out	1/4	0.80	0.80	Shade in contact with glass-voids filled with plastic.	—	—	0.49
Clear in							
Heat-abs.[b] out				Shade in contact with glass or shade separated from glass by air space.	0.28	0.30	0.37
Clear in	1/4	0.46	0.80	Shade in contact with glass-voids filled with plastic.	—	—	0.41

[a] *Refer to manufacturer's literature for exact values.*
[b] *Refers to gray, bronze, and green tinted heat-absorbing glass.*
NOTE: Shading coefficient for glass with exterior draperies having moderate light transparency characteristics will vary from 0.12 to 0.22.

Table 24. Shading coefficients for single and insulating glass with draperies

Glazing	Glass Trans.	Glass SC*	A	B	C	D	E	F	G	H	I	J
Single glass												
1/4 in. clear	0.80	0.95	0.80	0.75	0.70	0.65	0.60	0.55	0.50	0.45	0.40	0.35
1/2 in. clear	0.71	0.88	0.74	0.70	0.66	0.61	0.56	0.52	0.48	0.43	0.39	0.35
1/4 in. heat abs.	0.46	0.67	0.57	0.54	0.52	0.49	0.46	0.44	0.41	0.38	0.36	0.33
1/2 in. heat abs.	0.24	0.50	0.43	0.42	0.40	0.39	0.38	0.36	0.34	0.33	0.32	0.30
Reflective coated	—	0.60	0.57	0.54	0.51	0.49	0.46	0.43	0.41	0.38	0.36	0.33
(See manufacturers' literature	—	0.50	0.46	0.44	0.42	0.41	0.39	0.38	0.36	0.34	0.33	0.31
for exact values)	—	0.40	0.36	0.35	0.34	0.33	0.32	0.30	0.29	0.28	0.27	0.26
	—	0.30	0.25	0.24	0.24	0.23	0.23	0.23	0.22	0.21	0.21	0.20
Insulating glass (1/2 in. Air Space)												
Clear out and clear in	0.64	0.83	0.66	0.62	0.58	0.56	0.52	0.48	0.45	0.42	0.37	0.35
Heat abs. out and clear in	0.37	0.56	0.49	0.47	0.45	0.43	0.41	0.39	0.37	0.35	0.33	0.32
Reflective coated	—	0.40	0.38	0.37	0.37	0.36	0.34	0.32	0.31	0.29	0.28	0.28
(see manufacturers' literature	—	0.30	0.29	0.28	0.27	0.27	0.26	0.26	0.25	0.25	0.24	0.24
for exact values)	—	0.20	0.19	0.19	0.18	0.18	0.17	0.17	0.16	0.16	0.15	0.15

* For glass alone, with no drapery.

** Shading Coefficient values for the SC lines in Fig. 2 for representative glazings. Substitute for SC index letters in Fig. 2 values on the line of the glazing selected.

SHADING COEFFICIENT
INDEX LETTER

GLAZING INDICATED IN TABLE 24

DRAPERIES ADD 100% FULLNESS
(Fabric width two times draped width)

Notes:

1. Shading Coefficients are for draped fabrics.
2. Other properties are for fabrics in flat orientation
3. Use Fabric Reflectance and Transmittance to obtain accurate Shading Coefficients.
4. Use Openness and Yarn Reflectance or Openness and Fabric Reflectance to obtain the Various Environmental Characteristics, or to obtain Approximate Shading Coefficients.

CLASSIFICATION OF FABRICS

- I = Open Weave
- II = Semi-open Weave
- III = Closed Weave
- D = Dark Color
- M = Medium Color
- L = Light Color

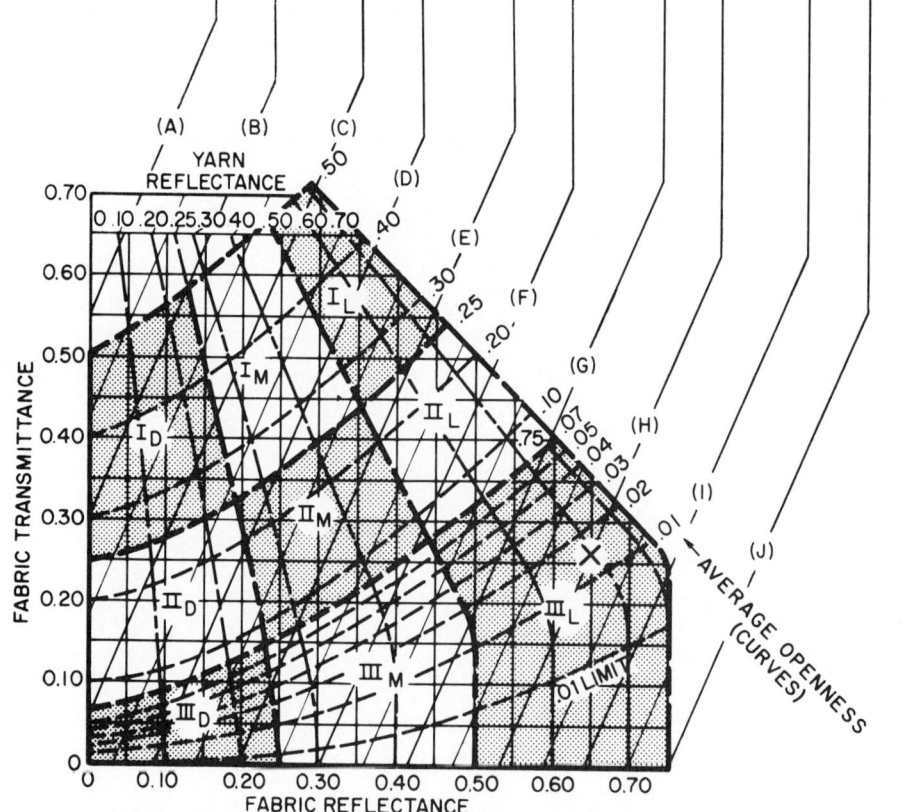

To Obtain Fabric Designator (III_L, I_M, etc): Using coordinates (1) Fabric Transmittance and Fabric Reflectance, or (2) Openness and Yarn Reflectance, find point on chart and note designator for that area. If properties are not known, classification may be approximated by eye.

To Obtain Shading Coefficient (SC): (1) Locate drapery fabric as a point using its known properties, or approximate using its fabric classification designator. For greatest accuracy use Fabric Transmittance and Fabric Reflectance. (2) Follow diagonal SC lines to lettered columns in Table 24. (3) Find SC on line with the glazing used. Example: SC of point "X" is 0.45 with 0.25 in. Clear Single Glass (Column H).

Note: SC are for 45 deg incident angle. For 30 deg or less, add 5% to number found in Table 24.

Fig. 2. Indoor shading properties of drapery fabrics

COOLING LOADS DUE TO GLASS AND ORIENTATION

A number of interrelated design factors influence the heat transfer through walls of buildings:

1. Building orientation
2. Proportion of transparent and opaque wall surfaces
3. Extent of sun control in the transparent areas of the wall, either by use of heat-resistant glass or by shading
4. Insulation of opaque areas

To deal with cooling loads on a generalized basis, the comparisons in the graphs are based on typical summer design temperatures. These may be used for preliminary design estimating purposes throughout the United States. Correction for latitude and energy optimization are necessary when the final design is developed.

The heat gains through several types of fenestration systems are shown in Fig. 3.

Building orientation

The direction a wall faces makes a considerable difference in the heat impact it receives. To illustrate these differences, a long narrow building with bilateral glazing may be assumed, and comparison is made in Table 26 of the cooling tonnage which will be required for east-west or north-south orientation of its length.

The amount of solar heat gain on the east, west and north walls differs little throughout the United States, but the impact on south-facing walls varies considerably.

Data shown for the 100 per cent shaded condition might indicate that orientation has little significance when glass is completely shaded. Provision of total fixed shading on east and west walls, however, is a relatively complex and expensive procedure. Automatically operated internal and external shading systems are available which eliminate many of the problems of fixed shading systems.

Cooling tonnage

The required cooling tonnage per square foot of wall surface, to counteract the solar heat impact, depends upon:

a. the cooling loads imposed due to the heat conductivity characteristics of the opaque and transparent materials.

b. the ratio of areas of these opaque and transparent materials.

Charts that follow indicate the cooling tonnages required to offset the heat gains imposed by the summer design temperatures on walls facing each of the four orientations. For each wall, values are indicated for a variety of transparent areas and a range of transparency ratios.

The ratio of transparent surface area to

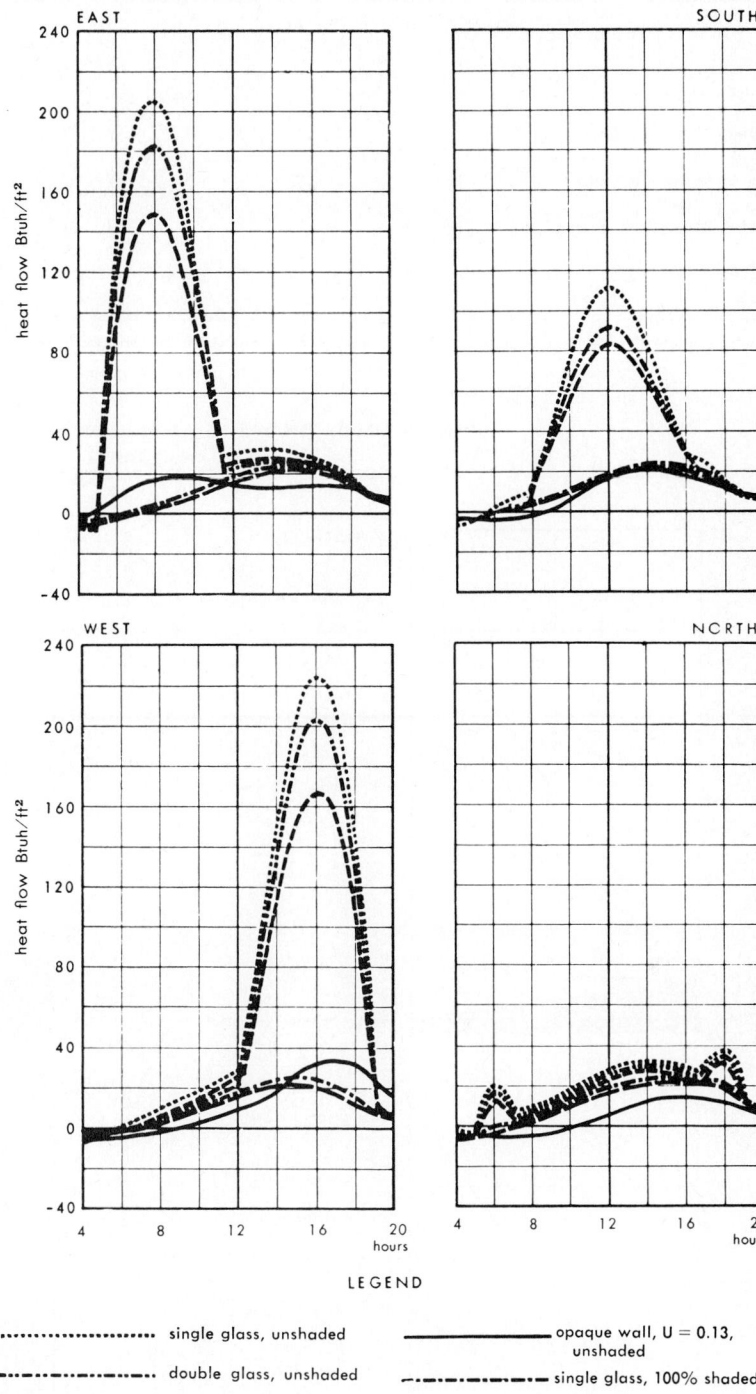

HEAT TRANSMISSION THROUGH MATERIALS AT SUMMER PEAK CONDITIONS

Fig. 3. Heat transmission through materials at summer peak conditions

By Victor and Aladar Olgyay

total wall area is seen as a highly significant factor in cooling costs, with almost a linear relationship indicated. In general, with any type of unshaded glass, or with shading of any amount up to 50 per cent, a tripling of the transparent area approximately doubles the cooling load.

The cooling load contributed by the opaque surface is shown by the trapezoidal shaded area in each of the charts.

Table 25. Effect of building orientation on cooling load (tons of refrigeration for 100 ft² of wall)

	I			II			III
	Long walls facing North-South			Long walls facing East-West			Preference ratio of I to II
Clear Glass Unshaded	N .15	S .45		W .87	E .76		2.7 to 1
Heat-Absorbing Glass	N .14	S .37		W .67	E .56		2.4 to 1
Clear Glass 50% Shaded	N .14	S .30		W .54	E .45		2.3 to 1
Clear Glass 100% Shaded	N .13	S .17		W .21	E .15		1.2 to 1

Note: Walls with glazing, 50% transparent, 50% opaque. Heat impact on solid end walls neglected

COOLING LOADS ON WALLS AT SUMMER PEAK CONDITIONS
per 100 ft² of surface

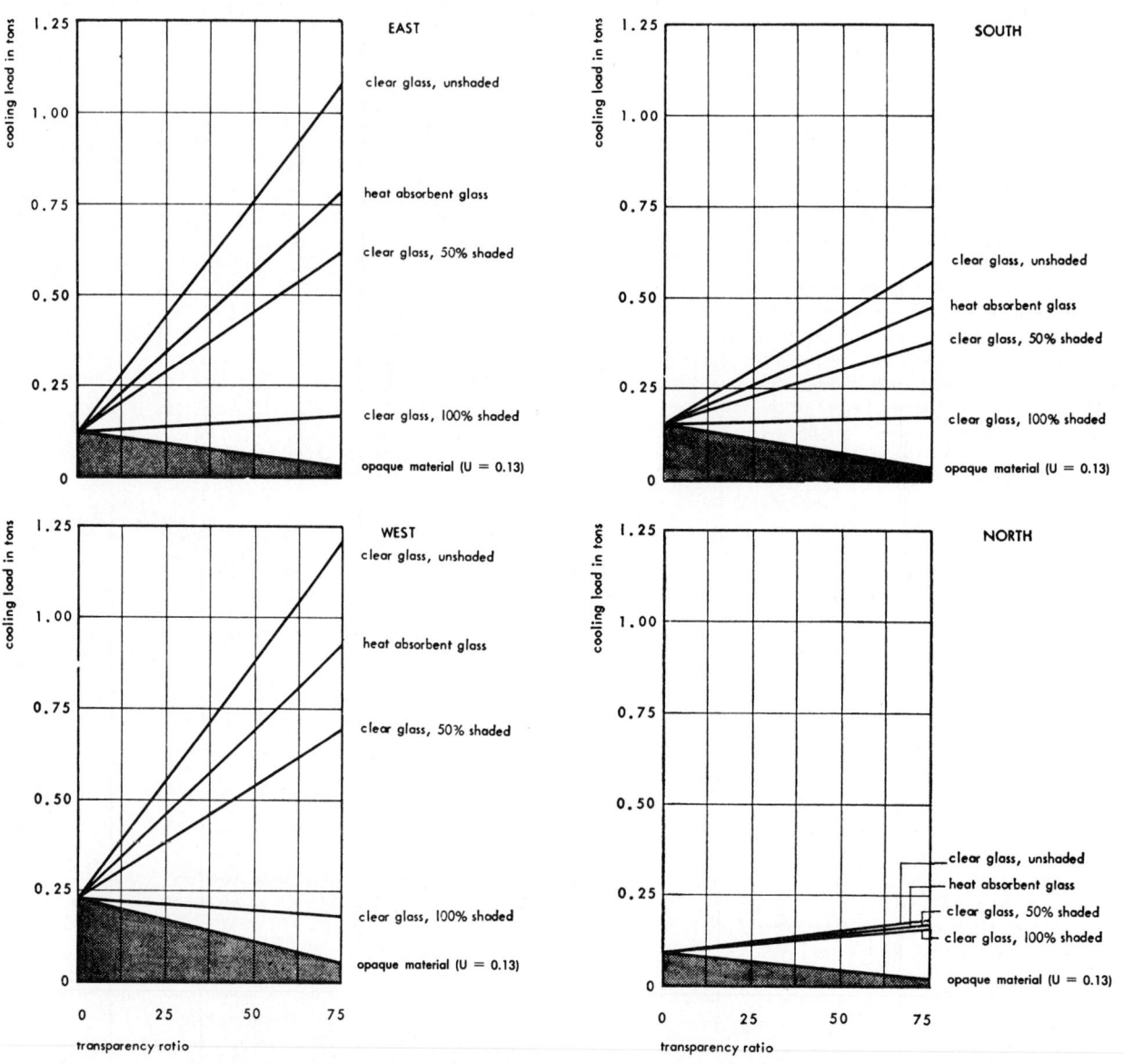

Fig 4. Cooling loads on walls at summer peak conditions

DESIGN OF SOLAR SHADING
By VICTOR *and* ALADAR OLGYAY

SUN PATHS

Location of the sun for any time of day can be found by use of the "sun path diagram," (Fig. 5) which shows the sky-vault (Fig. 6) projected onto the horizon plane. The horizon line appears as a circle at the outside edge, with the sun paths as curved lines. Only paths during the solstices and the equinox are drawn in this case. Connecting lines indicate the hours where the sun is at the given time. Thus the sun's position can be determined at any time by its bearing angle from the south point (on the perimeter of the diagram) and its altitude angle by means of an equally graduated scale measured from the center point.

The sun's paths will change according to the latitude of the location in question. Therefore a series of such diagrams will be required for various latitude ranges.

SHADING MASKS

Shading devices can be plotted in the same manner as sun paths to show during what time sun is excluded (Fig. 7–9). Shading masks are projections of the surface covered on the sky vault, as seen from an observation point at the center of the diagram. These projections also represent those parts of the sky vault from which no sunlight will come; if the sun passes through such an area, the observation point will be shaded.

Any building element will define a characteristic form in these projection diagrams. Masks of horizontal shading devices (overhangs) will show a segmental character; those of vertical fins produce a radial pattern; and masks of eggcrate types, are basically a combination of these forms. A shading mask can be drawn for any shading device, even for very complex ones, by simple geometrical methods. Since they are geometrical projections, they are independent of latitude and orientation, and may be used in any location.

By overlaying a shading mask in the proper orientation on the sun-path diagram, one can read off immediately the times when the sun's rays will be intercepted.

For design purposes, the process can be reversed. One can determine the needed shading mask and then find the proper shading device for it.

General rules can be deduced for the types of shading to be used for different orientations. Southerly orientations call for shading devices with segmental mask characteristics, and horizontal devices work in these directions efficiently. For easterly and westerly orientations vertical devices serve well, having radial shading masks.

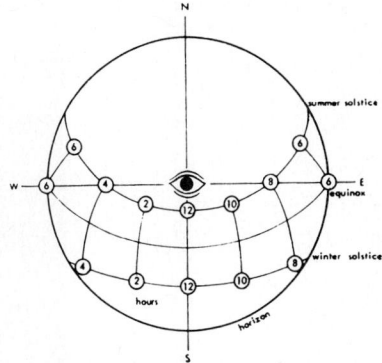

Projected diagram of the sky vault called "sun path diagram"

Fig. 5. Sun path diagram

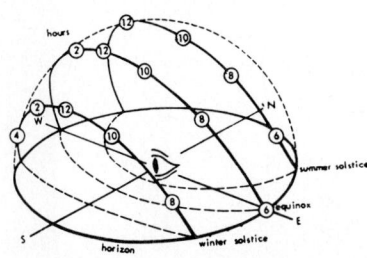

Half-sphere of the imaginary sky vault with sun paths. The projections of the sun paths are shown in dashed lines on the horizontal plane

Fig. 6. Sky vault with sun paths

TYPES OF DEVICES

HORIZONTAL

VERTICAL

EGGCRATE

DEVICES OBSTRUCTING AREAS OF SKY VAULT

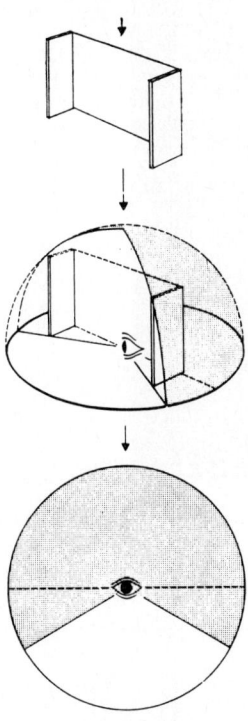

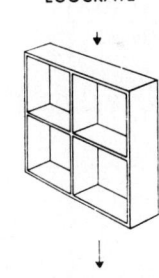

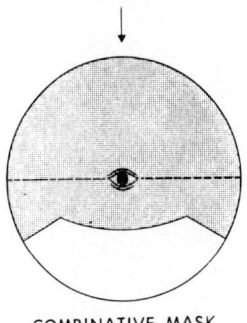

Obstructions of horizontal devices will show a segmental character; those of vertical fins will have a radial pattern, and eggcrate types will show a combination of these forms

SHADING MASK: The projection of the obstructed area of the sky vault

SEGMENTAL MASK

RADIAL MASK

COMBINATIVE MASK

Fig. 7. Horizontal obstruction

Fig. 8. Vertical obstruction

Fig. 9. Eggcrate obstruction

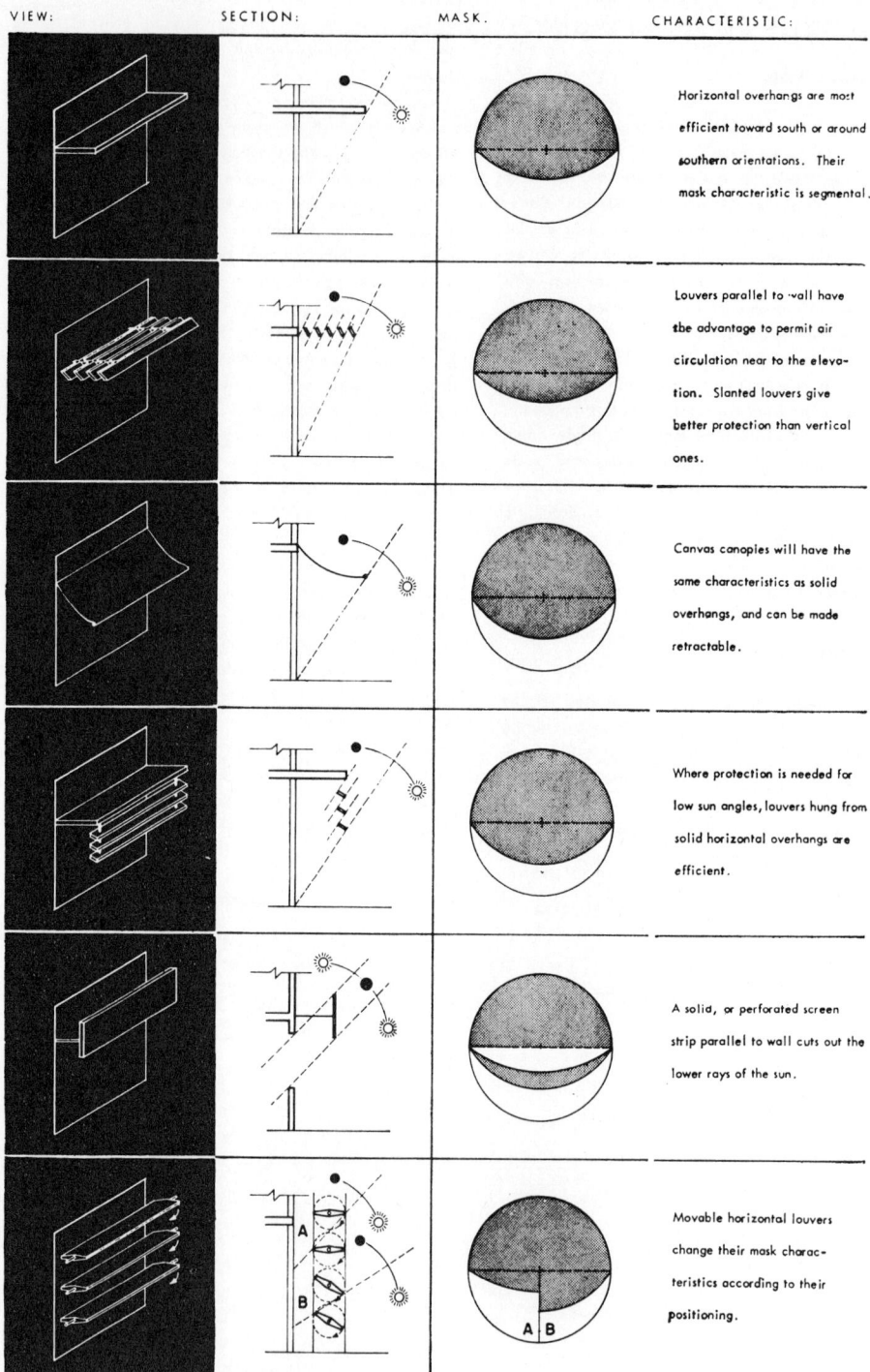

Fig. 10. Types of shading devices—horizontal

VIEW:	SECTION:	MASK.	CHARACTERISTIC:
			Horizontal overhangs are most efficient toward south or around southern orientations. Their mask characteristic is segmental.
			Louvers parallel to wall have the advantage to permit air circulation near to the elevation. Slanted louvers give better protection than vertical ones.
			Canvas canopies will have the same characteristics as solid overhangs, and can be made retractable.
			Where protection is needed for low sun angles, louvers hung from solid horizontal overhangs are efficient.
			A solid, or perforated screen strip parallel to wall cuts out the lower rays of the sun.
			Movable horizontal louvers change their mask characteristics according to their positioning.

If slanted, they should incline toward the north, to give more protection from the southern positions of the sun. The eggcrate type of shading works well on walls facing southeast, and is particularly effective for southwest orientation. Because of this type's high shading ratio and low winter heat admission, its best use is in hot climate regions. For north walls, fixed vertical devices are recommended but their use is needed only in hot regions. In the very low latitudes (under 23°) horizontal devices work well also for this orientation.

Whether the shading devices be fixed or movable, the same recommendations apply in respect to the different orientations.

The movable types can be most efficiently utilized where the sun's altitude and bearing change rapidly: on the east, southeast, and especially, because of the afternoon heat, on the southwest and west.

The illustrations on this and the previous page show a number of basic types of devices, classified as horizontal, vertical, and eggcrate types.

The dash lines shown on the section diagram in each case indicate the sun angle at the time of 100 per cent shading.

The shading mask for each device is also shown, the extent of 100 per cent shading being indicated by the gray area.

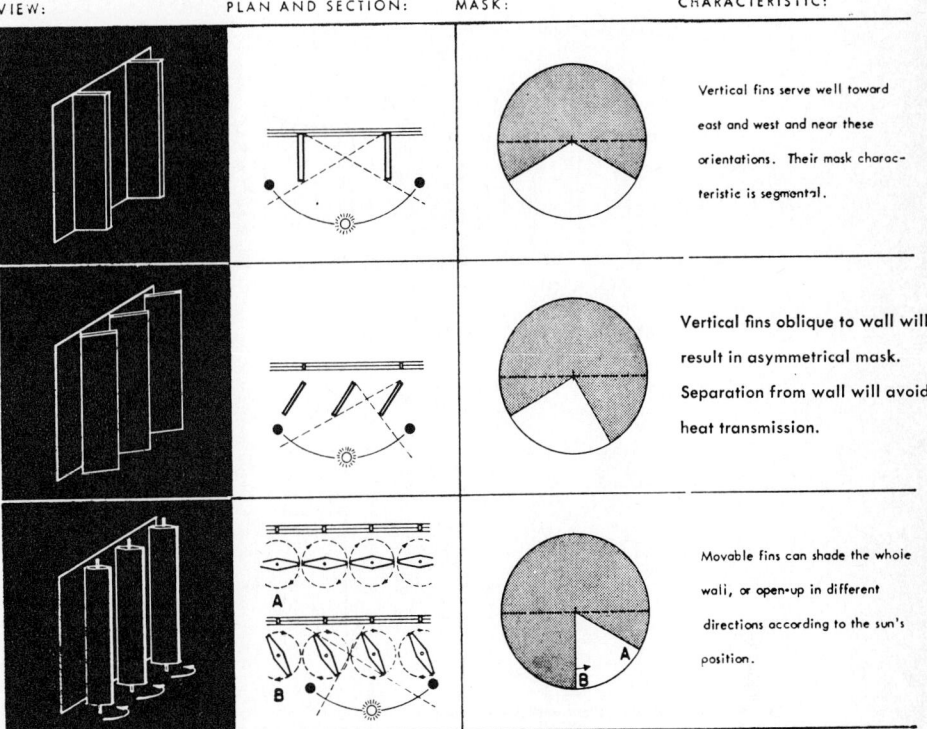

VIEW:	PLAN AND SECTION:	MASK:	CHARACTERISTIC:

Vertical fins serve well toward east and west and near these orientations. Their mask characteristic is segmental.

Vertical fins oblique to wall will result in asymmetrical mask. Separation from wall will avoid heat transmission.

Movable fins can shade the whole wall, or open-up in different directions according to the sun's position.

Fig. 11. Types of shading devices—vertical

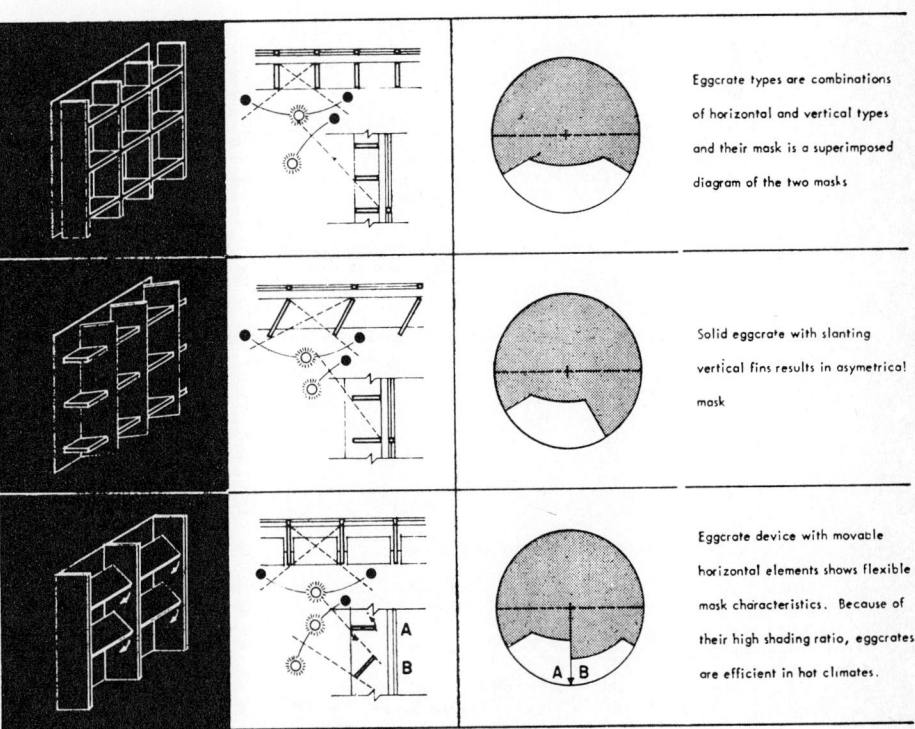

Eggcrate types are combinations of horizontal and vertical types and their mask is a superimposed diagram of the two masks

Solid eggcrate with slanting vertical fins results in asymetrical mask

Eggcrate device with movable horizontal elements shows flexible mask characteristics. Because of their high shading ratio, eggcrates are efficient in hot climates.

Fig. 12.   Types of shading devices—eggcrate

By ALFRED GREENBERG, *P.E., Environmental and Energy Consultant*

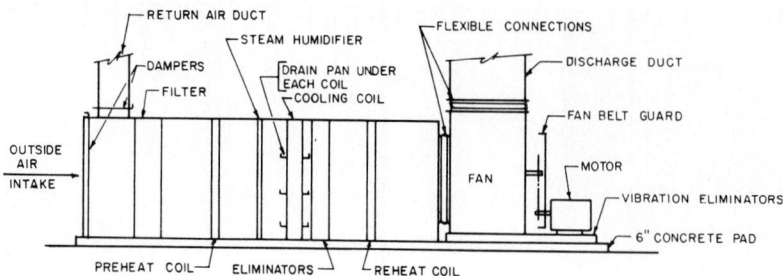

Fig. 13. Components of typical air-distribution system

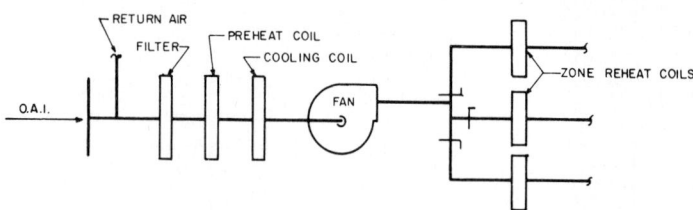

Fig. 14. Single-duct system with zoned reheat

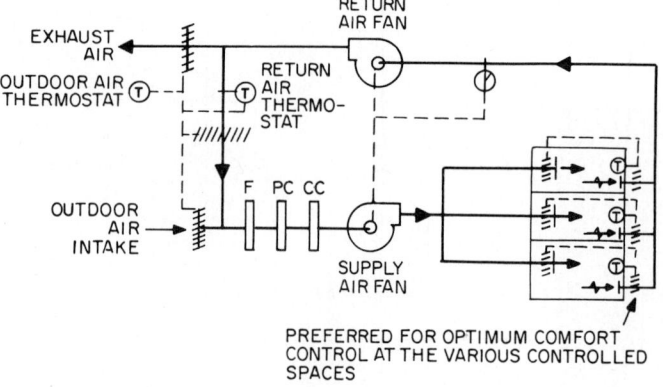

PREFERRED FOR OPTIMUM COMFORT CONTROL AT THE VARIOUS CONTROLLED SPACES

Fig. 15(a). Supply and return air outlets to zones have VAV dampers

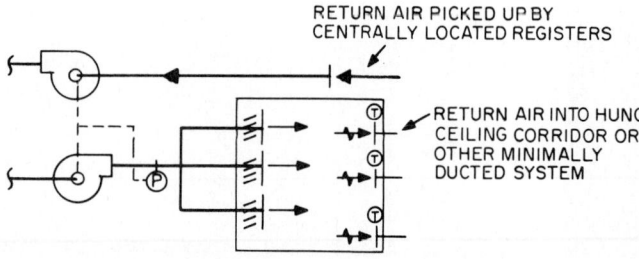

Fig. 15(b). Only supply air to zones have VAV dampers

TYPES OF SYSTEMS

Air-distribution systems include the following types:

1. Low velocity, single duct (conventional)
2. Low velocity with zone control
3. Air-water induction
4. Fan-coil units
5. High velocity, single duct (with and without reheat)
6. High velocity, dual duct
7. Self-contained and modular units, including heat pumps
8. Rooftop units

Components for each of the above systems are similar (Fig. 13). Many variations in arrangement and location of components are possible. Below about 20,000 cfm, factory-built units are generally used; above 20,000 cfm, field-built units are preferred by most engineers because their design characteristics can be more precisely established, although factory-built units are available in excess of 40,000 cfm.

1. *Low-velocity, single-duct* systems are the most commonly used because of their simplicity and low first cost. Two special types of low-velocity air-distribution systems are available which utilize the floor or ceiling plenum to provide heating or cooling partially by radiant means. The air eventually enters the room to furnish some thermal effect and satisfy ventilation requirements. The underfloor scheme consists of metal, clay, or concrete forms which, in effect, create a hollow floor through which conditioned air passes before it enters the space through registers at the walls.

2. *Low velocity with zone control.* For areas having widely differing heat loads, at a given time, it may be expedient to zone the low-velocity, single-duct system and place a heating (or cooling) coil in each branch to take care of peak loads (see Fig. 14). Where the building is comparatively small and only a few zones are required, the use of secondary coils is reasonably economical. On the other hand, using recooling coils involves a more costly initial investment with an elaborate automatic control setup. A third type of zone control (see Fig. 15) involves the automatic adjustment of the amount of air entering and/or leaving the zone as the heat load varies. This is called a variable air volume (VAV) system and several variations are available. VAV systems are potentially more energy efficient than other types of air handling systems. In the system shown in Fig. 15(a) fan air quantity is reset by the pressure controller in the return air duct which throttles the inlet vane dampers in both the supply and return fan

inlets to match loads. The controls can then readjust the exhaust, return, and outdoor air dampers for proper air balance requirements. Independently, the exhaust, return, and outdoor air dampers may adjust the quantity of outdoor air furnished and the amount of air exhausted and returned. This may be done by comparing outdoor to return air temperature (economizer control) or comparing the total heat available from the outdoor air to that in the return air and making a decision to use that which will require the least energy input and still provide comfort. Figure 15(b) shows a simpler, less costly system with reduced comfort capability. It is the most commonly used variation.

3. *Air-water induction* system is mostly used for perimeter applications. The air comes from a central source for each zone and furnishes the humidity control and outside air requirements for the room as well as taking care of the room's fixed heat load. This air, called the primary air, goes through nozzles and induces about 4 to 8 times as much room air along with it through the water coil and out into the room (see Fig. 16).

The water flow to each unit or group of units is controlled by an automatic control valve to take care of the variable portions of the room load and all the outside transmission and solar load. Each control valve will serve from 1 to 6 units and each thermostat from 1 to 4 control valves. The air ducts and the water piping are often run vertically at the perimeter of the building. Several common schemes are shown in Fig. 17. The ductwork is generally run at high velocity (2,500 to 4,500 fpm) especially when run at the perimeter, in order to conserve space although velocities should be as low as possible in order to conserve energy. Induction units serve a perimeter area which generally extends 14 to 18 ft from

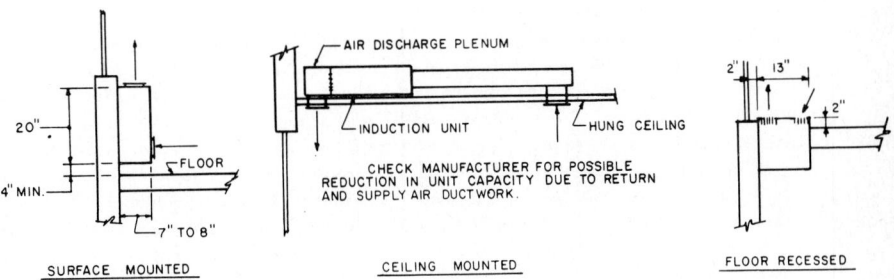

Fig. 16. Air-water induction units

Length of induction units varies from 20 to 64 in.

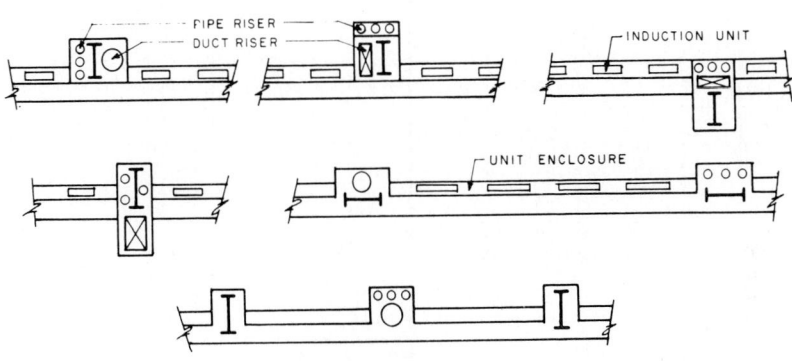

Fig. 17. Various arrangements of perimeter risers

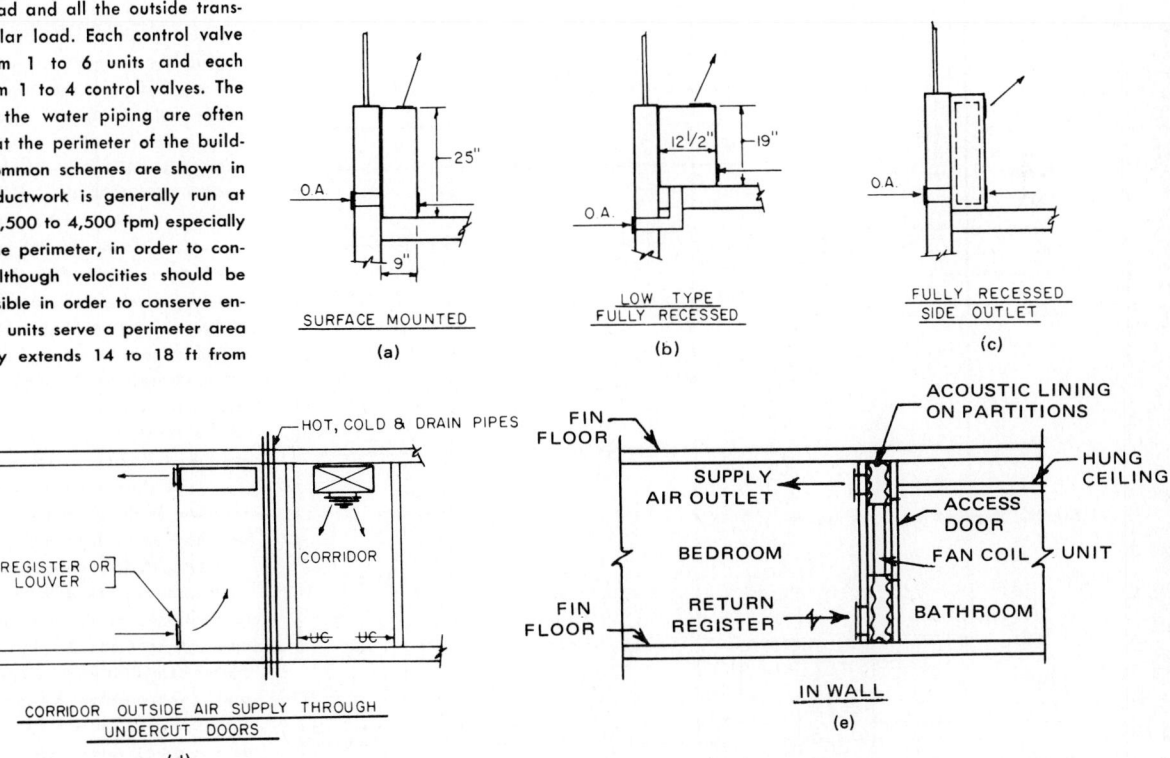

Fig. 18. Fan-coil units

Outside air openings can be any shape. The smaller the opening, the less the problem with stack effect, wind, and rain, but the less outside air can be brought in. Outside air grille can be located remotely by using ductwork to the unit, but this may reduce unit capacity because of higher static pressure.
For maximum coil protection, provide automatic outdoor air damper. Length of fan-coil units varies from about 16 to 60 in.

the exterior of the building. They find their greatest use in new multi-story buildings.

4. *Fan-coil units,* as the name implies, contain a fan and a coil and also filters and a condensate pan, if required. In most cases, these units are furnished for perimeter wall use and get their air from openings in the outside wall. See Fig. 18(a, b, and c). A central outside air supply may be furnished, especially when the fan-coil units are located in the interior of the room, generally at the ceiling, in a closet, or over the corri-

dor or door (Fig. 18(d)). The piping system is centralized, and a control system similar to that used for the induction system can be used for the water cycle. The standard fan-coil unit is not designed to handle outside air quantities in excess of about 40 per cent. However, for greater outside air quantities, the classroom-type unit ventilator (Fig. 19), which is a larger version of the fan-coil unit, can be used.

The fan-coil units serve an area up to 25 ft from the exterior wall. They are slightly

nosier than the induction system and do not maintain environmental conditions as closely, but are satisfactory for many applications. The fan-coil system has a lower first cost than the induction system but will probably require more maintenance as the years go by.

Three- or four-pipe systems: A refinement in temperature control of both air-water induction and fan-coil units is provided by furnishing a 3- or 4-pipe water system to each unit. Each has a hot and cold water pipe, and a common and separate return water line respectively. A special valve is used to meter just the proper amount of either hot or cold water to each unit thus maintaining correct room temperature all year round (see Fig. 20). It eliminates the problem of changeover temperature conditions since hot and cold water are always available to take care of all heat-load situations.

Changeover temperature is that outside temperature at which the air-conditioning system is switched from summer to winter use, i.e., from chilled water to hot water. This temperature is a function of many factors such as building construction, system operation, location of building, etc. The changeover temperature is generally different for each exposure. Therefore, on most large buildings, each exposure should be, but seldom is, zoned so that it can be individually changed from summer to winter operation or vice versa. In the intermediate seasons, it is possible to require changeover several times a day for a given zone.

5. *High-velocity, single-duct.* Where a single-duct air-distribution system is desired and zone control is sufficient for the areas served but conventionally sized ducts will not fit the space allotted, then a high-velocity single-duct system may be used. In all air systems, the lowest possible air velocities should be used to save energy and minimize noise transmission. The major difference besides the fact that it has smaller ducts is that a terminal box may be required for reducing the velocity and noise level of the air before discharging it into the room. A variation of this system is to use air-pressure-reducing valves in the ducts and acoustical lining before discharging the air into the space. A single-duct zone system with terminal boxes may be used where each box has a reheat coil (Fig. 21). If loads vary, volume control at each unit plus fan volume control will probably be more economical.

6. *Dual-duct,* all-air systems furnish a high degree of individual room flexibility. They furnish quantities of properly mixed hot and cold air to satisfy all load conditions (Fig. 22). They also require the largest amount of shaft and ceiling space and are generally the most expensive to install. Low-velocity

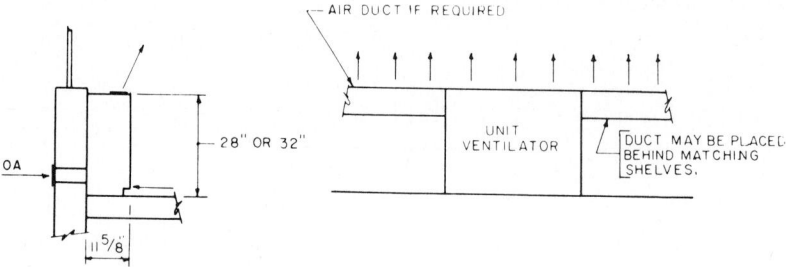

Fig. 19.   Classroom-type unit ventilator

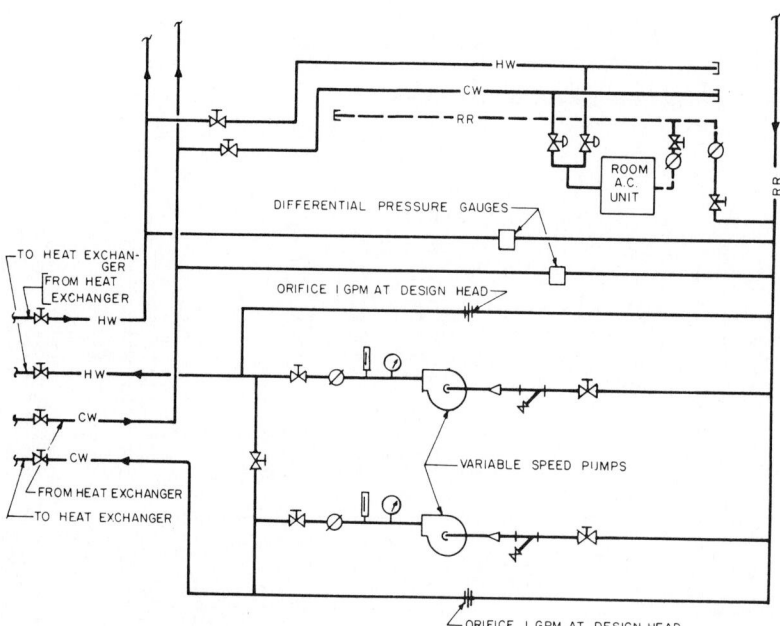

Fig. 20.   Unzoned three-pipe system

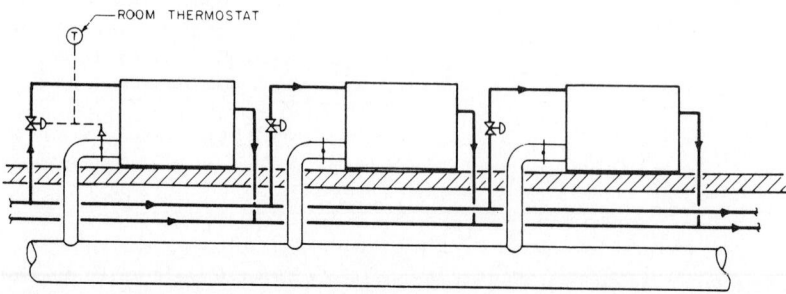

Fig. 21.   High-velocity single-duct system with reheat coils

dual-duct systems are seldom used because of space limitations.

There are several ways of controlling dual-duct systems. One method uses volume control for each unit; this is applicable for private offices and other comparatively small areas requiring individual control conditions. Another uses duct static pressure control; this is suitable for open offices, general manufacturing, stock, and other such areas. The duct static pressure controls must be properly located in order for the system to function properly. See Fig. 22. The energy efficiency of dual-duct systems can be improved by incorporating reheat coil or variable air volume designs.

7. *Self-contained air-conditioning units* furnish relief from the summer heat but most of them have poor air-distribution patterns, are comparatively noisy, and have no humidity control. However, they are the cheapest type of air-conditioning system available, are easy to install, have a high degree of portability, often furnish purge (100 per cent exhaust) air control, and can relieve building management of all operating and maintenance expenses. Operating and maintenance costs for these units are generally higher per ton of refrigeration than for any other system. Their greatest use is in existing buildings due to ease of installation.

There is a marked trend toward improving the characteristics and capabilities of unitary air conditioning equipment to make them more suitable for use in quality installations. Several approaches toward improving these systems are as follows:

1. Include heating elements within the units to provide integrated heating and/or cooling.

2. Design for central water-cooled condensing service to eliminate the large exterior wall grilles, to provide a degree of intermediate season reheat, and to obtain a quieter unit operation.

3. Provide a unitary heat pump system with a central condenser water system which transfers heat from one area to another, as available. A central outside air system is required with this system. This system must have substantial areas requiring heat removal, like interior spaces in order to be energy conservative.

DUCT DESIGN

Sizing within the pressure, temperature, and velocity ranges at which most commercial and many industrial air systems operate, reasonably accurate results can be obtained with a minimum of theoretical design considerations. The equation used for cal-

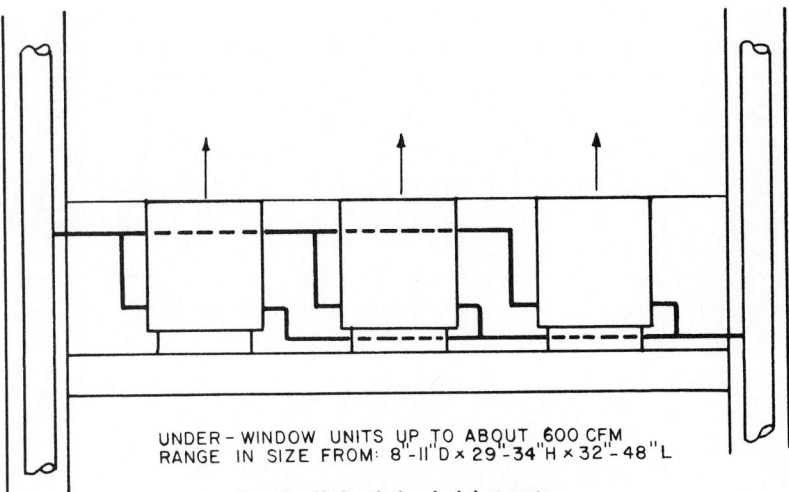

UNDER – WINDOW UNITS UP TO ABOUT 600 CFM RANGE IN SIZE FROM: 8"-11"D × 29"-34"H × 32"-48"L

Fig. 22. High-velocity dual-duct system

Approximate dual-duct box sizes

Cfm	D	W	L
Up to 300	8	24	30
301 to 600	10	30	36
601 to 1,000	12–14	42	48
1,001 to 4,000	25	30	54

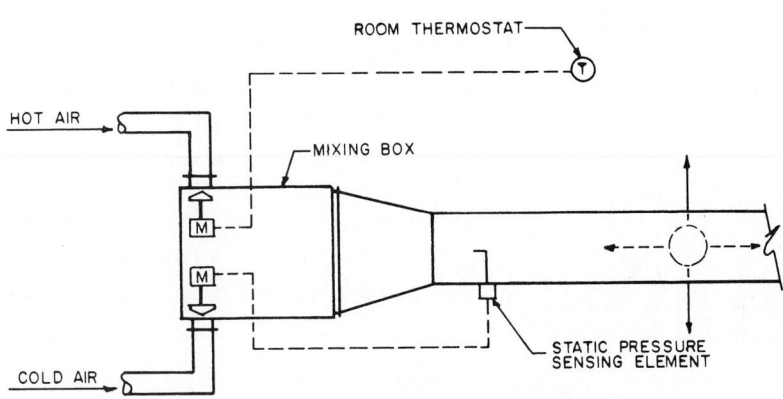

Fig. 23. Static pressure control for dual-duct system

culating air quantities is:

$$cfm = \frac{SH}{1.08 \times t_r - t_a}$$

where cfm = cu ft of air per min at 70°F and 29.92 in. Hg

SH = sensible heat load, Btu/hr of area for which air quantity is desired

t_r = room or area temperature, °F

t_a = temperature of air in duct entering room, °F

The sizing of all ductwork is generally based upon the ASHRAE criteria. Figures 24 and 25 show a convenient method of calculating duct sizes. Table 27 converts round duct sizes to equivalent rectangular ducts.

The duct-sizing charts are based on galvanized iron ducts. Where materials with rougher or smoother surfaces are used, correction factors should be applied as indicated in the ASHRAE Guide. Correction factors for friction loss of ducts internally lined for acoustic attenuation are shown in Table 29.

Regardless of which air-distribution system is used, it is imperative that the balance between supply and return and exhaust air for each area and the building as a whole be reasonably close to avoid drafts and improper system functioning.

In many instances a small percentage of positive or negative air pressure is desirable. Bathrooms and kitchens, for instance, are often kept under a 10 to 15 per cent negative pressure, and typical rooms with operable sash are usually kept under positive pressure, in order to prevent infiltration. (Continued on page 4-153.)

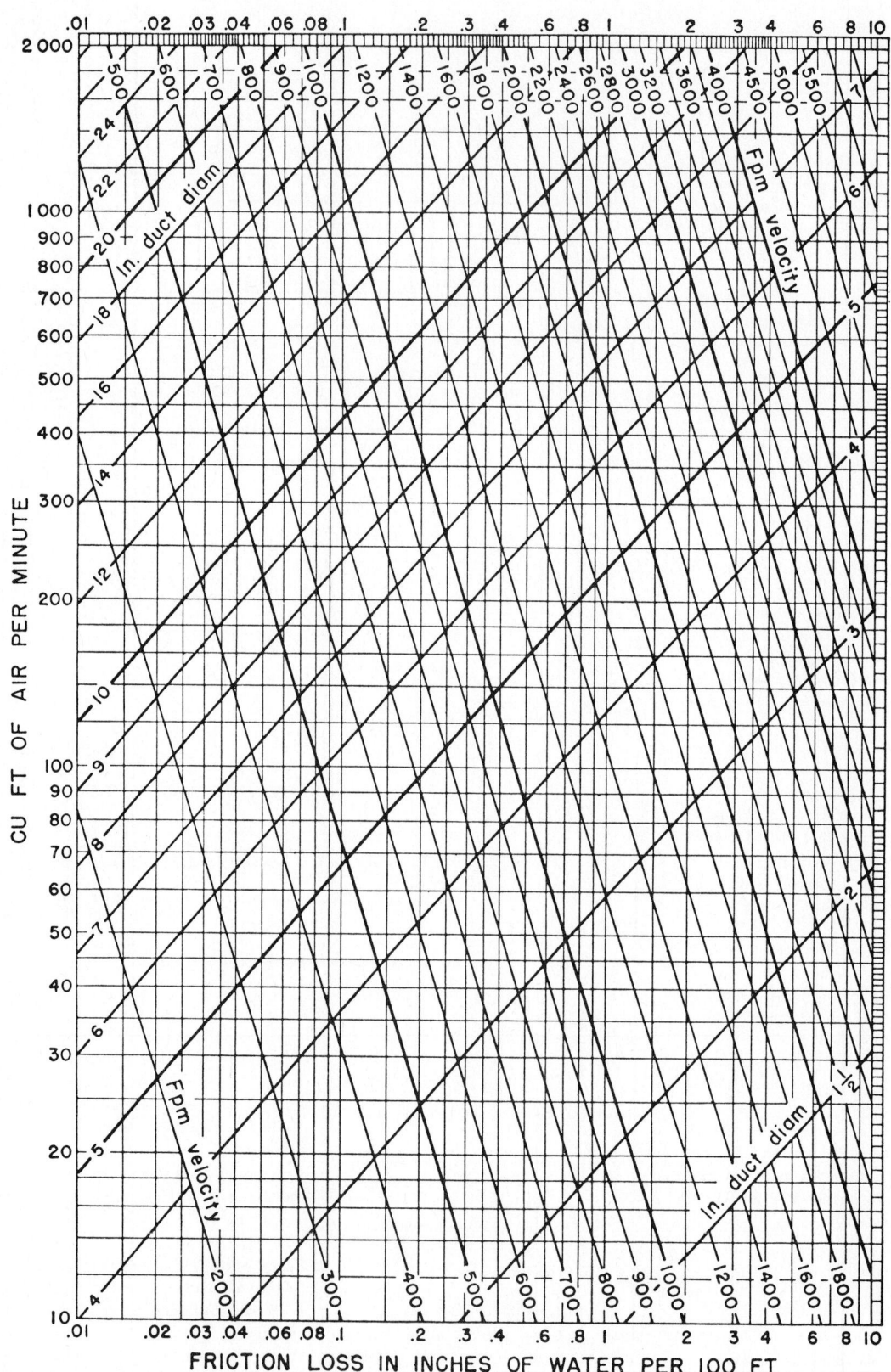

(Based on Standard Air of 0.075 lb per cu ft density flowing through average, clean, round, galvanized metal ducts having approximately 40 joints per 100 ft.) Caution: Do not extrapolate below chart.

Fig. 24. Friction of air in straight ducts for volumes of 10 to 2,000 cfm

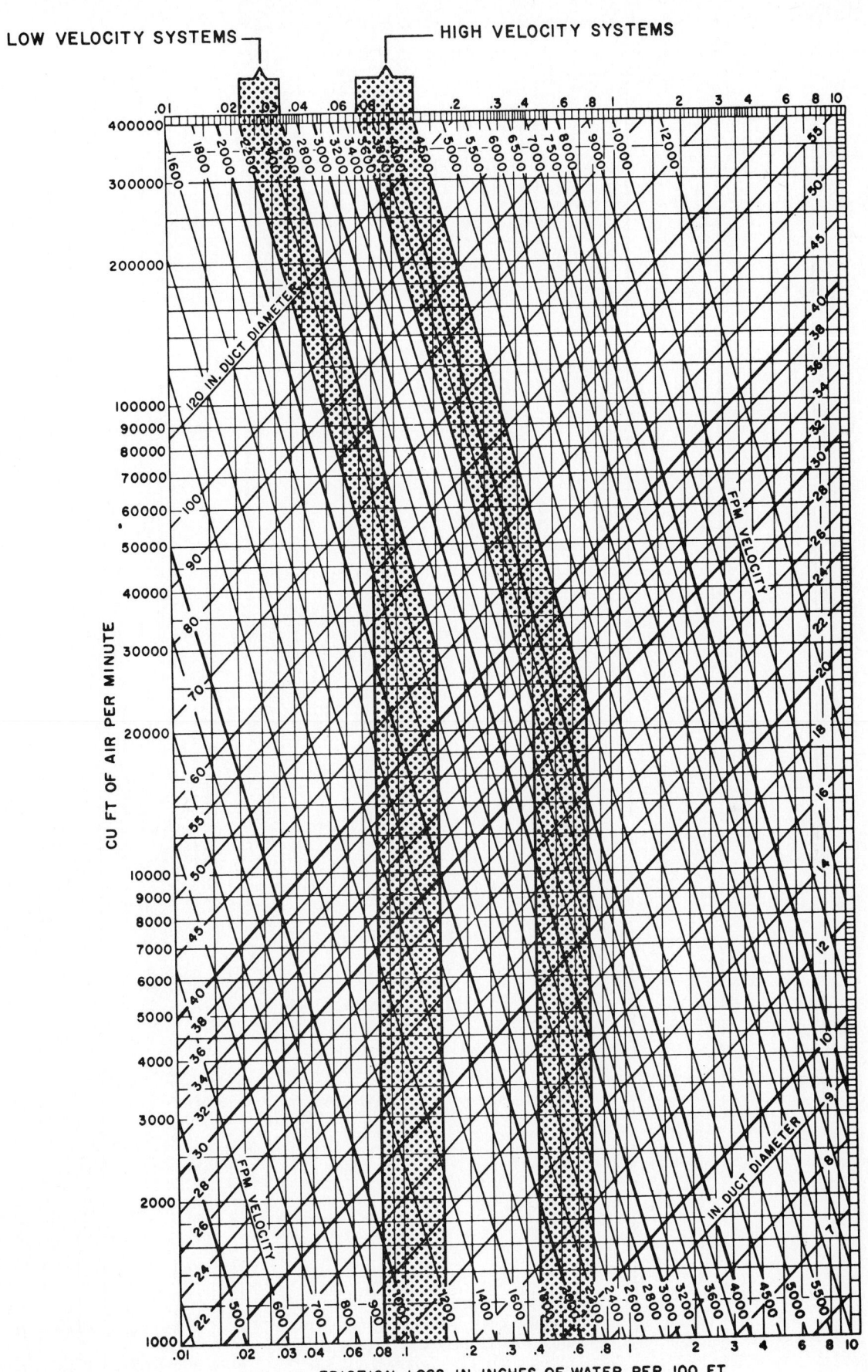

Figure 25. Suggested velocity and friction rate design limits

SOURCE: ASHRAE Handbook of Fundamentals, *1977.*

Air distribution

Table 26. Circular equivalents of rectangular ducts for equal friction and capacity

Dimensions in inches. (Reprinted by permission from ASHRAE Handbook of Fundamentals, 1977)

Side Rectangular Duct	4.0	4.5	5.0	5.5	6.0	6.5	7.0	7.5	8.0	9.0	10.0	11.0	12.0	13.0	14.0	15.0	16.0
3.0	3.8	4.0	4.2	4.4	4.6	4.8	4.9	5.1	5.2	5.5	5.7	6.0	6.2	6.4	6.6	6.8	7.0
3.5	4.1	4.3	4.6	4.8	5.0	5.2	5.3	5.5	5.7	6.0	6.3	6.5	6.8	7.0	7.2	7.4	7.6
4.0	4.4	4.6	4.9	5.1	5.3	5.5	5.7	5.9	6.1	6.4	6.8	7.1	7.3	7.6	7.8	8.1	8.3
4.5	4.6	4.9	5.2	5.4	5.6	5.9	6.1	6.3	6.5	6.9	7.2	7.5	7.8	8.1	8.4	8.6	8.9
5.0	4.9	5.2	5.5	5.7	6.0	6.2	6.4	6.7	6.9	7.3	7.6	8.0	8.3	8.6	8.9	9.1	9.4
5.5	5.1	5.4	5.7	6.0	6.3	6.5	6.8	7.0	7.2	7.6	8.0	8.4	8.7	9.0	9.4	9.6	9.8

Side Rectangular Duct	6	7	8	9	10	11	12	13	14	15	16	17	18	19	20	22	24	26	28	30	Side Rectangular Duct
6	6.6																				6
7	7.1	7.7																			7
8	7.5	8.2	8.8																		8
9	8.0	8.6	9.3	9.9																	9
10	8.4	9.1	9.8	10.4	10.9																10
11	8.8	9.5	10.2	10.8	11.4	12.0															11
12	9.1	9.9	10.7	11.3	11.9	12.5	13.1														12
13	9.5	10.3	11.1	11.8	12.4	13.0	13.6	14.2													13
14	9.8	10.7	11.5	12.2	12.9	13.5	14.2	14.7	15.3												14
15	10.1	11.0	11.8	12.6	13.3	14.0	14.6	15.3	15.8	16.4											15
16	10.4	11.4	12.2	13.0	13.7	14.4	15.1	15.7	16.3	16.9	17.5										16
17	10.7	11.7	12.5	13.4	14.1	14.9	15.5	16.1	16.8	17.4	18.0	18.6									17
18	11.0	11.9	12.9	13.7	14.5	15.3	16.0	16.6	17.3	17.9	18.5	19.1	19.7								18
19	11.2	12.2	13.2	14.1	14.9	15.6	16.4	17.1	17.8	18.4	19.0	19.6	20.2	20.8							19
20	11.5	12.5	13.5	14.4	15.2	15.9	16.8	17.5	18.2	18.8	19.5	20.1	20.7	21.3	21.9						20
22	12.0	13.1	14.1	15.0	15.9	16.7	17.6	18.3	19.1	19.7	20.4	21.0	21.7	22.3	22.9	24.1					22
24	12.4	13.6	14.6	15.6	16.6	17.5	18.3	19.1	19.8	20.6	21.3	21.9	22.6	23.2	23.9	25.1	26.2				24
26	12.8	14.1	15.2	16.2	17.2	18.1	19.0	19.8	20.6	21.4	22.1	22.8	23.5	24.1	24.8	26.1	27.2	28.4			26
28	13.2	14.5	15.6	16.7	17.7	18.7	19.6	20.5	21.3	22.1	22.9	23.6	24.4	25.0	25.7	27.1	28.2	29.5	30.6		28
30	13.6	14.9	16.1	17.2	18.3	19.3	20.2	21.1	22.0	22.9	23.7	24.4	25.2	25.9	26.7	28.0	29.3	30.5	31.6	32.8	30
32	14.0	15.3	16.5	17.7	18.8	19.8	20.8	21.8	22.7	23.6	24.4	25.2	26.0	26.7	27.5	28.9	30.1	31.4	32.6	33.8	32
34	14.4	15.7	17.0	18.2	19.3	20.4	21.4	22.4	23.3	24.2	25.1	25.9	26.7	27.5	28.3	29.7	31.0	32.3	33.6	34.8	34
36	14.7	16.1	17.4	18.6	19.8	20.9	21.9	23.0	23.9	24.8	25.8	26.6	27.4	28.3	29.0	30.5	32.0	33.0	34.6	35.8	36
38	15.0	16.4	17.8	19.0	20.3	21.4	22.5	23.5	24.5	25.4	26.4	27.3	28.1	29.0	29.8	31.4	32.8	34.2	35.5	36.7	38
40	15.3	16.8	18.2	19.4	20.7	21.9	23.0	24.0	25.1	26.0	27.0	27.9	28.8	29.7	30.5	32.1	33.6	35.1	36.4	37.6	40
42	15.6	17.1	18.5	19.8	21.1	22.3	23.4	24.5	25.6	26.6	27.6	28.5	29.4	30.4	31.2	32.8	34.4	35.9	37.3	38.6	42
44	15.9	17.5	18.9	20.2	21.5	22.7	23.9	25.0	26.1	27.2	28.2	29.1	30.0	31.0	31.9	33.5	35.2	36.7	38.1	39.5	44
46	16.2	17.8	19.2	20.6	21.9	23.2	24.3	25.5	26.7	27.7	28.7	29.7	30.6	31.6	32.5	34.2	35.9	37.4	38.9	40.3	46
48	16.5	18.1	19.6	20.9	22.3	23.6	24.8	26.0	27.2	28.2	29.2	30.2	31.2	32.2	33.1	34.9	36.6	38.2	39.7	41.2	48
50	16.8	18.4	19.9	21.3	22.7	24.0	25.2	26.4	27.6	28.7	29.8	30.8	31.8	32.8	33.7	35.5	37.3	38.9	40.4	42.0	50
52	17.0	18.7	20.2	21.6	23.1	24.4	25.6	26.8	28.1	29.2	30.3	31.4	32.4	33.4	34.3	36.2	38.0	39.6	41.2	42.8	52
54	17.3	19.0	20.5	22.0	23.4	24.8	26.1	27.3	28.5	29.7	30.8	31.9	32.9	33.9	34.9	36.8	38.7	40.3	42.0	43.6	54
56	17.6	19.3	20.9	22.4	23.8	25.2	26.5	27.7	28.9	30.1	31.2	32.4	33.4	34.5	35.5	37.4	39.3	41.0	42.7	44.3	56
58	17.8	19.5	21.1	22.7	24.2	25.5	26.9	28.2	29.3	30.5	31.7	32.9	33.9	35.0	36.0	38.0	39.8	41.7	43.4	45.0	58
60	18.1	19.8	21.4	23.0	24.5	25.8	27.3	28.7	29.8	31.0	32.2	33.4	34.5	35.5	36.5	38.6	40.4	42.3	44.0	45.8	60
62	18.3	20.1	21.7	23.3	24.8	26.2	27.6	29.0	30.2	31.4	32.6	33.8	35.0	36.0	37.1	39.2	41.0	42.9	44.7	46.5	62
64	18.6	20.3	22.0	23.6	25.2	26.5	27.9	29.3	30.6	31.8	33.1	34.2	35.5	36.5	37.6	39.7	41.6	43.5	45.4	47.2	64
66	18.8	20.6	22.3	23.9	25.5	26.9	28.3	29.7	31.0	32.2	33.5	34.7	35.9	37.0	38.1	40.2	42.2	44.1	46.0	47.8	66
68	19.0	20.8	22.5	24.2	25.8	27.3	28.7	30.1	31.4	32.6	33.9	35.1	36.3	37.5	38.6	40.7	42.8	44.7	46.6	48.4	68
70	19.2	21.	22.8	24.5	26.1	27.6	29.1	30.4	31.8	33.1	34.3	35.6	36.8	37.9	39.1	41.3	43.3	45.3	47.2	49.0	70
72															39.6	41.8	43.8	45.9	47.8	49.7	72
74															40.0	42.3	44.4	46.4	48.4	50.3	74
76															40.5	42.8	44.9	47.0	49.0	50.8	76
78															40.9	43.3	45.5	47.5	49.5	51.5	78
80															41.3	43.8	46.0	48.0	50.1	52.0	80
82															41.8	44.2	46.4	48.6	50.6	52.6	82
84															42.2	44.6	46.9	49.2	51.1	53.2	84
86															42.6	45.0	47.4	49.6	51.6	53.7	86
88															43.0	45.4	47.9	50.1	52.2	54.3	88
90															43.4	45.9	48.3	50.6	52.8	54.8	90
92															43.8	46.3	48.7	51.1	53.4	55.4	92
96															44.6	47.2	49.5	52.0	54.4	56.3	96

Equation for Circular Equivalent of a Rectangular Duct:[5]

$$d_c = 1.30 \frac{(ab)^{0.625}}{(a+b)^{0.250}} = 1.30 \sqrt[8]{\frac{(ab)^5}{(a+b)^2}}$$

where
a = length of one side of rectangular duct, inches.
b = length of adjacent side of rectangular duct, inches.
d_c = circular equivalent of a rectangular duct for equal friction and capacity, inches.

Table 26 (cont.). Circular equivalents of rectangular ducts for equal friction and capacity

Dimensions in inches. (Reprinted by permission from ASHRAE Handbook of Fundamentals, 1977)

Side Rectangular Duct	32	34	36	38	40	42	44	46	48	50	52	56	60	64	68	72	76	80	84	88	Side Rectangular Duct
32	35.0																				32
34	36.0	37.2																			34
36	37.0	38.2	39.4																		36
38	38.0	39.2	40.4	41.6																	38
40	39.0	40.2	41.4	42.6	43.8																40
42	39.9	41.1	42.4	43.6	44.8	45.9															42
44	40.8	42.0	43.4	44.6	45.8	46.9	48.1														44
46	41.7	43.0	44.3	45.6	46.8	47.9	49.1	50.3													46
48	42.6	43.9	45.2	46.5	47.8	48.9	50.2	51.3	52.6												48
50	43.5	44.8	46.1	47.4	48.8	49.8	51.2	52.3	53.6	54.7											50
52	44.3	45.7	47.1	48.3	49.7	50.8	52.2	53.3	54.6	55.8	56.9										52
54	45.0	46.5	48.0	49.2	50.6	51.8	53.2	54.3	55.6	56.8	57.9										54
56	45.8	47.3	48.8	50.1	51.5	52.7	54.1	55.3	56.5	57.8	58.9	61.3									56
58	46.6	48.1	49.6	51.0	52.4	53.7	55.0	56.2	57.5	58.8	60.0	62.3									58
60	47.3	48.9	50.4	51.8	53.3	54.6	55.9	57.1	58.5	59.8	61.0	63.3	65.7								60
62	48.0	49.7	51.2	52.6	54.2	55.5	56.8	58.0	59.4	60.7	62.0	64.3	66.7								62
64	48.7	50.4	52.0	53.4	55.0	56.4	57.7	59.0	60.3	61.6	62.9	65.3	67.7	70.0							64
66	49.5	51.1	52.8	54.2	55.8	57.2	58.6	59.9	61.2	62.5	63.9	66.3	68.7	71.1							66
68	50.2	51.8	53.5	55.0	56.6	58.0	59.5	60.8	62.1	63.4	64.8	67.3	69.7	72.1	74.4						68
70	50.9	52.5	54.2	55.8	57.3	58.8	60.3	61.7	63.0	64.3	65.7	68.3	70.7	73.1	75.4						70
72	51.5	53.2	54.9	56.5	58.0	59.6	61.1	62.6	63.9	65.2	66.6	69.2	71.7	74.1	76.4	78.8					72
74	52.1	53.9	55.6	57.2	58.8	60.4	61.9	63.3	64.8	66.1	67.5	70.1	72.7	75.1	77.4	79.9					74
76	52.7	54.6	56.3	57.9	59.5	61.2	62.7	64.1	65.6	67.0	68.4	71.0	73.6	76.1	78.4	80.9	83.2				76
78	53.3	55.2	57.0	58.6	60.3	62.0	63.4	64.9	66.4	67.9	69.3	71.8	74.5	77.1	79.4	81.8	84.2				78
80	53.9	55.8	57.6	59.3	61.0	62.7	64.1	65.7	67.2	68.7	70.1	72.7	75.4	78.1	80.4	82.8	85.2	87.5			80
82	54.5	56.4	58.2	60.0	61.7	63.4	64.9	66.5	68.0	69.5	71.0	73.6	76.3	79.0	81.4	83.8	86.2	88.6			82
84	55.1	57.0	58.9	60.7	62.4	64.1	65.7	67.3	68.8	70.3	71.8	74.5	77.2	79.9	82.4	84.8	87.2	89.6	91.9		84
86	55.7	57.6	59.5	61.3	63.0	64.8	66.4	68.0	69.5	71.1	72.6	75.4	78.1	80.8	83.3	85.8	88.2	90.6	92.9		86
88	56.3	58.2	60.1	62.0	63.7	65.4	67.0	68.7	70.3	71.8	73.4	76.3	79.0	81.6	84.2	86.8	89.2	91.6	93.9	96.3	88
90	56.9	58.8	60.7	62.6	64.4	66.0	67.8	69.4	71.1	72.6	74.2	77.1	79.9	82.5	85.1	87.8	90.2	92.6	94.9	97.3	90
92	57.4	59.4	61.3	63.2	65.0	66.8	68.5	70.1	71.8	73.3	74.9	77.9	80.8	83.4	86.0	88.7	91.2	93.6	95.9	98.3	92
94	57.9	60.0	61.9	63.8	65.6	67.5	69.2	70.8	72.5	74.1	75.6	78.7	81.7	84.3	86.9	89.6	92.1	94.6	96.9	99.3	94
96	58.4	60.5	62.4	64.4	66.2	68.2	69.8	71.5	73.2	74.3	76.3	79.4	82.6	85.2	87.8	90.5	93.0	95.6	97.9	100.3	96

Table 27. Correction factors for friction loss of ducts acoustically lined

Air velocity	Correction factor	Air velocity	Correction factor
500	1.25	1,800	1.41
600	1.28	2,000	1.42
700	1.30	2,500	1.45
800	1.31	3,000	1.47
900	1.32	3,500	1.49
1,000	1.33	4,000	1.50
1,200	1.36	4,500	1.52
1,400	1.38	5,000	1.54
1,600	1.40	5,500	1.55
		6,000	1.56

Static pressure: In commercial applications, the following criteria are widely used for sizing ductwork:

Type	Max static pressure/100 equiv. ft	Max vel.
Conventional low velocity supply	0.10	1,500
Exhaust	0.08	1,500
Medium velocity	0.50	2,500
High velocity	1.0	3,500

Table 28. Static pressure drop for louver assemblies

Net velocity through free area of louver	Static pressure, in. water
722	0.11
967*	0.198
1,220	0.308
1,360	0.397
1,522	0.501

Normal Design Standard.

It will be noted from the duct-sizing charts that for the larger air quantities, the static pressure will drop off in order not to exceed the maximum velocities. For best results and ease of balancing the systems, terminal unit static pressure should be relatively high compared to duct static pressure.

When system static pressures are calculated to determine fan horsepower requirements, the ASHRAE Handbook should be consulted to determine static pressure losses for ductwork fittings. Table 28 gives field-obtained values of static pressure for louver assemblies consisting of fixed architectural louvers, bird screens, and automatic louver dampers.

Air velocities: There are many types of supply and return air outlets and inlets available. Most air-outlet manufacturers give sufficiently reliable data to enable determination of the correct sizes for given applications and their operating characteristics.

Table 29 gives a guide for recommended and maximum duct and system component velocities for conventional systems.

Recommended return-intake face velocities are given in Table 30.

Air-handling equipment: The fan and motor should be set on an integral vibration eliminator base and the inlet and discharge connections should be made with flexible connections to minimize vibration transmission through the ducts.

Figure 13 shows typical air-handling components. Face velocity across components in the casing is generally kept at 500 fpm, although this may vary widely for different components. Air velocities across the cooling coils seldom exceed 500 fpm because of the possibility of water carryover due to condensation on the coil. When heating coils are located on the discharge side of fans, they are often sized at from 800 to

Table 29. Typical design velocities for duct components

Duct element	Actual face velocity, (ft/min)
Louvers	
A. Intake:	400
B. Exhaust:	500
Filters	
A. Fibrous Media Unit Filters:	
1. Viscous Impingement	250 to 700
2. Dry Type	Up to 750
3. HEPA	250
B. Renewable Media Filters:	
1. Moving-Curtain Viscous Impingement	500
2. Moving-Curtain Dry-Media	200
C. Electronic Air Cleaners:	
1. Ionizing Plate-Type	300 to 500
Heating coils	
A. Steam and Hot Water	500 to 600 (Most common) 200 min., 1500 max.
B. Electric:	
1. Open Wire	Refer to Mfg. Data
2. Finned Tubular	Refer to Mfg. Data
Dehumidifying coils	
A. Without Eliminators	500 to 600
B. With Eliminators	700 and greater
Air washers	
A. Spray-Type	300 to 700
B. Cell-Type	Refer to Mfg. Data
C. High Velocity Spray-Type	Refer to Mfg. Data

Table 30. Recommended return intake velocities

Intake location	Velocity over gross area, fpm
Above occupied zone	800 and up, depending on height
Within occupied zone, not near seats	600–800
Within occupied zone, near seats	400–600
Door or wall louvers	200–300
Undercutting of doors, through undercut area	200–300
Under seat mushrooms	100–200
Gravity part of mechanical supply—gravity exhaust or reverse	100–250

Table 31. Static pressure of filters (in inches of water)

Clean filter	Dirty filter (should be changed)
Up to 0.10	0.40–0.50
0.11–0.25	0.60–1.0
0.26–0.60	1.0–1.5
0.61 up	1.5 up

1,000 fpm face velocity to conserve space. When these higher velocities are used, discharge transitions must be carefully designed to minimize pressure losses (Fig. 26). Filters are generally not sized for face velocities exceeding 550 fpm because the static pressures increase rapidly above that figure. When calculating system static pressure, the value used for the filter should be that at which it should be replaced (Table 31). In systems using more than one filter it is customary to apply a diversity factor of 50 to 70 per cent.

FILTERS

Filtration is necessary to purify the air. Outside air is seldom clean enough to be used directly. Even though it may be satisfactory for breathing, the air deposits particles on equipment and occupied spaces with the result that extensive maintenance is required. Return air also has to be filtered because of the particles and odors which are entrained in it. Filtering of the return air can materially reduce the amount of outside air required, thus permitting reductions in refrigerating plant capacity and operating costs.

Determination of the type of filter to be used for a given application is based upon many factors, among which are the following:

1. Outside air characteristics for the various seasons of the year.
2. Inside air characteristics desired for the various functions of the building.
3. Type of maintenance expected for the building.
4. Space requirements for filters and spares.
5. Cost of filters.
6. Life expectancy of filters.

All of the above except the first and sixth can be ascertained with reasonable accuracy. Air pollution studies now make it possible to determine the first item for certain areas of the country.

There are four standard methods for testing filter efficiency, based on weight, discoloration, count, and radioactivity. Since, on the average, 10 per cent of the particles account for 90 per cent of the weight, the test based on weight is not suitable for use with atmospheric air. Radioactivity tests are too new and too expensive. For most applications, filter efficiency should be based upon the NBS discoloration test (ASHRAE std. 52–76), using atmospheric air, conducted at the locale where the filters are to be used. For more accurate results, the count test may be used.

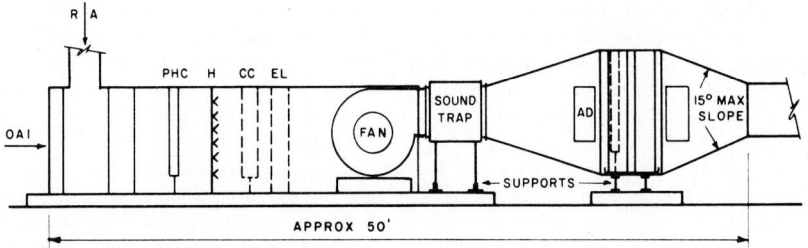

Fig. 26. Air-handling unit with heating coils on discharge side of fan

See Fig. 13 for explanation of terms.

Types of filters

All efficiencies are given in terms of the NBS Dust Spot Atmospheric Air Test.

1. *Electrostatic filters* in which ionized plates attract and hold particles. Efficiency 85 to 95 per cent. Prefilters are required only where linty atmospheres are anticipated, but after-filters are usually needed to catch large particles which may flake off from the plates, especially during starting and stopping of the fan. Automatic cleaning of the plates can be provided. First cost and maintenance cost are high. Not recommended for operating rooms, white rooms, and other critical areas unless very high efficiency after-filters are used.

2. *Replaceable cartridge filters:* Efficiency 30 to 99.9 per cent. These come in either rigid frame construction or expandable element type, in which the air flow keeps the filter element extended. Sizes are generally

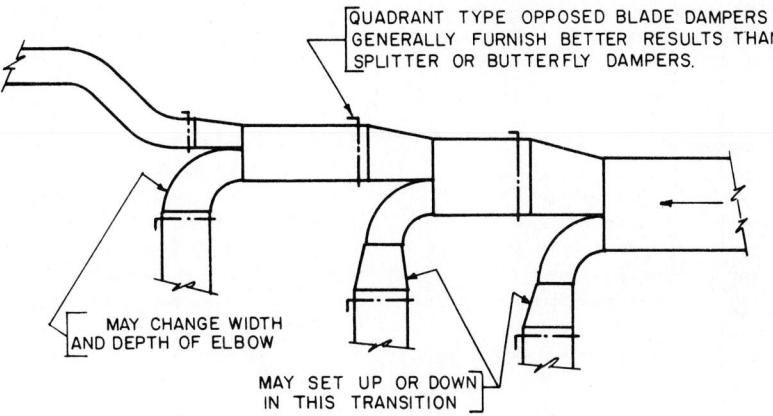

GOOD, BUT REQUIRES MOST CEILING SPACE

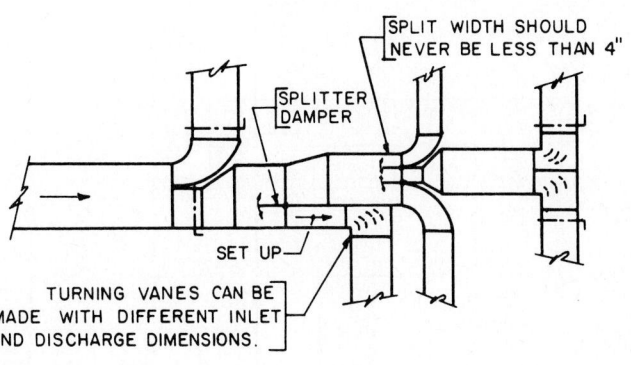

SATISFACTORY, MORE ECONOMICAL OF SPACE

Fig. 27. Ductwork details

24 by 24 in., with operating depths from 12 to 36 in. The high efficiency types compete with electrostatic filters and are often preferred in critical applications because of their positive action. The lower efficiency types are used for prefiltering and for main filters where economy is required and a high degree of cleanliness is not essential.

3. *Cleanable or renewable media filters:* Efficiency 20 to 95 per cent. These types offer certain maintenance economies where a staff is available for cleaning the filters and space exists for the cleaning equipment. The renewable media type is cut to size and wound through a multi-V-shaped frame. These have efficiencies in the higher ranges. The cleanable type consists of metal mesh frames which are cleaned with water and re-oiled.

4. *Roll-type disposable media filters:* Efficiency up to 30 per cent. This type is an economical prefilter.

5. *Throwaway filters:* Efficiency 3 to 10 per cent. These usually consist of ½ to 4-in. thickness of glass fiber or similar material in a cardboard or light metal frame. Their principal use is for unitary air conditioners and fan-coil units. In large systems this type is used only for prefiltering.

DUCTWORK

Ductwork: The layout of the ductwork should be carefully designed to provide smooth air flow, minimize motor power losses, keep fan and system noises to a minimum, and keep space headroom as high as possible. Figures 27 and 28 show some typical details of recommended practices.

Flush seam construction is more costly than the other types and should be used only where space conditions make it mandatory. Attempts should be made to keep volume dampers, air valves, and dual duct-mixing boxes out of finished spaces because they require ceiling access. Sometimes, access may be provided through ceiling lights or air outlets. It should be borne in mind that duct sizes given on drawings are almost always clear inside dimensions, and 2 or more inches must be added to these dimensions for total space requirements.

All ductwork should be constructed with no air leakage permitted in order to assure optimum results with minimum energy use.

Noise reduction: Transmission of noise through ductwork is not usually a problem in low-velocity, conventional systems. However, in high-velocity systems, fan noise is greater and ductwork, dampers, mixing boxes, induction units, and all other items must be carefully designed and selected to produce maximum attenuation and minimum noise regeneration from air-mixing boxes. In all systems, the outlet devices must be properly selected so that the sound-power level developed is less than the maximum noise criteria for the room. Noise criteria for various occupancies are given in the section on "Acoustics."

Low-velocity systems seldom require sound traps, although for low-sound-level spaces duct lining may be required. Generally, 25 ft of 1-in. duct lining is less expensive to install than an equivalent sound trap, but the trap does a better job, especially at the low frequencies. On high-velocity systems sound traps are usually required. Where special precautions are required to prevent noise transmission from one room

to another, special care in ductwork design will be less expensive than furnishing individual room sound traps (see Fig. 29).

Space requirements: Where perimeter air-distribution systems are employed, they generally take from 7 to 18 in. of space from the inside of the exterior wall and 11 to 30 in. of vertical height. Interior shaft space is also required to take care of return and exhaust air, interior supply air, chilled and condenser water piping, steam and return piping, electric closets, telephone closets, plumbing piping, and possibly pneumatic tubes. The combined shaft space requirements generally range from 2 to 5 per cent of gross floor area with the heating and air conditioning requiring about 70 per cent of the space requirements and plumbing and electrical each needing 15 per cent. These are rough averages but should be helpful in the development of core areas. In general, with duct shafts having a width-to-length ratio of 2:1 to 4:1, rectangular shapes are easier to develop than large square shafts.

Fan rooms require from 35 to 60 sq ft of floor space per 1,000 cfm of supply air furnished. The lower limit is applicable to simple air-handling systems in rooms with few columns and no interference from elevator machine rooms, electrical rooms, etc. Fan rooms usually require 13 to 18 ft clear height, depending upon the size of the ducts and the amount of crossovers necessary between ductwork, electrical conduits, and piping.

Shafts: From the foregoing, general shaft space requirements can be determined. Shafts should be centrally located so that each shaft serves all areas within 50 to 100 ft. Preliminary shaft sizes may be estimated on the basis of preliminary air quantity calculations (cfm) divided by 1,000. Multiply this figure by 1.3 to obtain total shaft requirements for all mechanical trades.

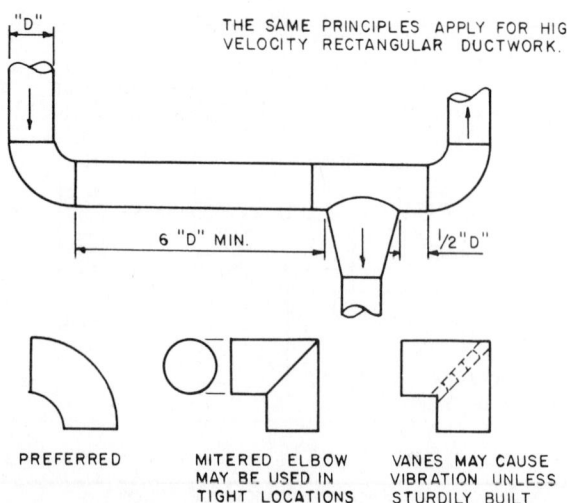

Fig. 28. High-velocity ductwork details

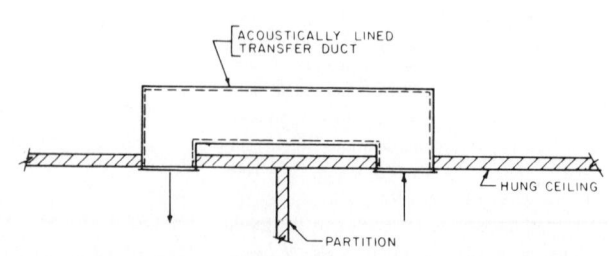

Fig. 29. Acoustically lined transfer duct

REFRIGERATING PLANT

Refrigeration and boiler-plant equipment space requirements are given later on in this section.

Tons: The unit by which refrigeration capacity is measured is the *ton*, which equals 12,000 Btu/hr. It derives from the fact that it requires 288,000 Btu to melt 1 ton of ice to water at 32°F. If this is assumed to take place in one day, the hourly rate would be 288,000 divided by 24 or 12,000 Btu/hr.

Systems: The most commonly used systems for air conditioning are as follows:

1. Air to refrigerant to air (Fig. 30). In this system, room air is cooled by contact with cool refrigerant, which then becomes warm. The warm refrigerant is then cooled by contact with outside air. This is the manner in which self-contained window units and most other packaged units operate.

2. Air to refrigerant to water to air (Fig. 31). If air-cooled condensers are not feasible and cheap water is not available, then a cooling tower must be used. This will take the water that has removed the heat from the hot refrigerant and allow it to give up its heat to the outdoor air. This type of system is practical for commercial installations up to about 150 tons.

3. Air to water to refrigerant to water to air (Fig. 32). Although five complete heat-transfer operations are required, this cycle has produced the most economical and practicable results for large systems to date.

Compressors: The types of refrigeration compressors are:

1. Reciprocating   3. Absorption
2. Centrifugal   4. Screw

For units up to 100 tons of refrigerant capacity, reciprocating (Fig. 33) or absorption units are used because centrifugal compressors are not manufactured in these sizes. In the tonnages from 100 to about 1,000, centrifugal, screw, and absorption machines are generally used. For units over 1,000 tons, centrifugal machines are usually used.

All types of compressors are available in open (Fig. 34) or hermetically sealed models. In general, hermetic units are used in the lower tonnages unless the building has an experienced operating staff which can maintain the machines themselves.

Hermetic machines are generally electrically driven, but open-type compressors can be driven by electric motors, steam turbines, gas engines, or any other motor or engine drive. Open-type machines are made in capacities of over 6,000 tons, whereas hermetics stop at about 1,700 tons.

Starters: Electric motors require starting devices which take up wall and floor space. A reduced-voltage autotransformer starter for a 250-hp machine will require approximately 14 sq ft of floor space and 7½ ft of height. Where a refrigeration plant has a number of motors, they may be combined in a motor control center, for centralized operation and maintenance.

Steam: With steam turbines, steam condensers are used to cool and condense the exhaust steam from the turbines (Fig. 35). This type of refrigeration plant takes up more floor space than any of the others discussed here, but where economic analysis shows steam to be the most economical fuel, space must be provided. Steam turbines are available for almost all steam pressures. The lower the steam pressure available, the larger will be the turbine for a given tonnage requirement.

Absorption machines (Fig. 36) are simpler to operate than steam turbines and take up less floor space, but they are limited in capacity to about 1,000 tons. They can use high-temperature hot water or steam up to 12 psi. Recent developments have made available high pressure steam and direct gas fired absorption machines in the intermediate and high tonnage ranges for absorption machines. In some areas licensed refrigeration operators are not required for absorption machines, which may give an economic advantage to this type of compressor. They are also quieter than reciprocating compressors and produce less vibration, but produce refrigeration less efficiently than other types of machines.

Well water: Where an assured, reasonably economical source of clean, pure well or river water is available for cooling the hot refrigerant, it may be used. The well water, if cold enough, may even be able to furnish part or all of the refrigeration effect (which would eliminate the need for a compressor). Adding a heat pump system increases the utility of a well water system. Provision must be made for disposing of the well water after it has been heated, in such a manner that it does not mix with the cool well water.

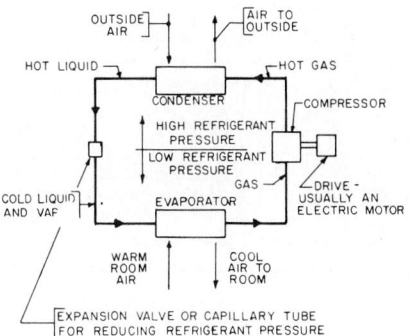

Fig. 30. Air to refrigerant to air system

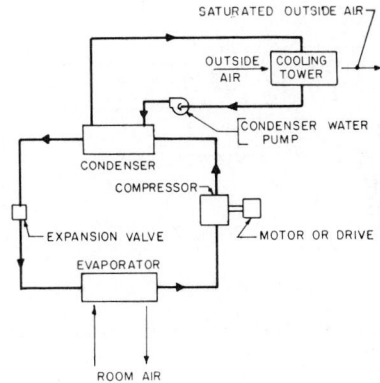

Fig. 31. Air to refrigerant to water to air system

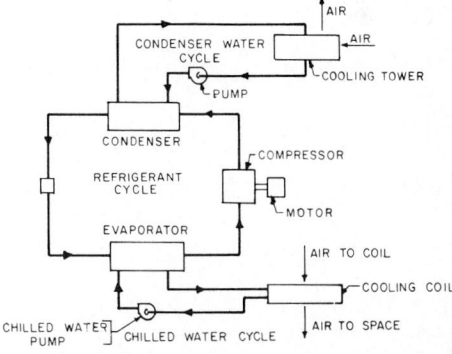

Fig. 32. Air to water to refrigerant to water to air system

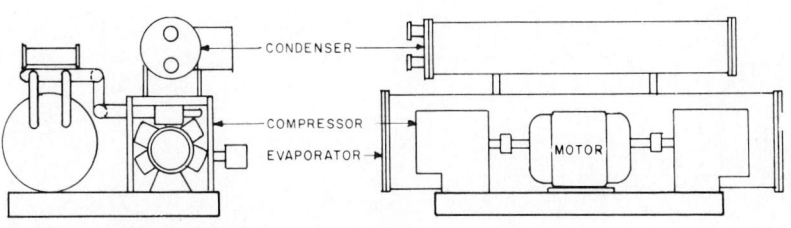

Fig. 33. Reciprocating compressor, 100 to 150 tons

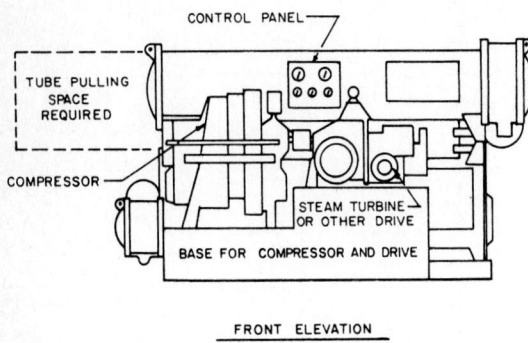

FRONT ELEVATION

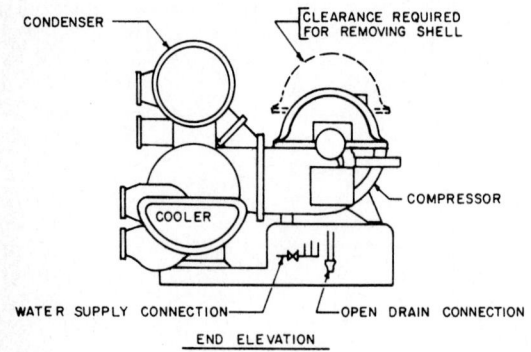

END ELEVATION

Fig. 34. Open-type centrifugal compressor

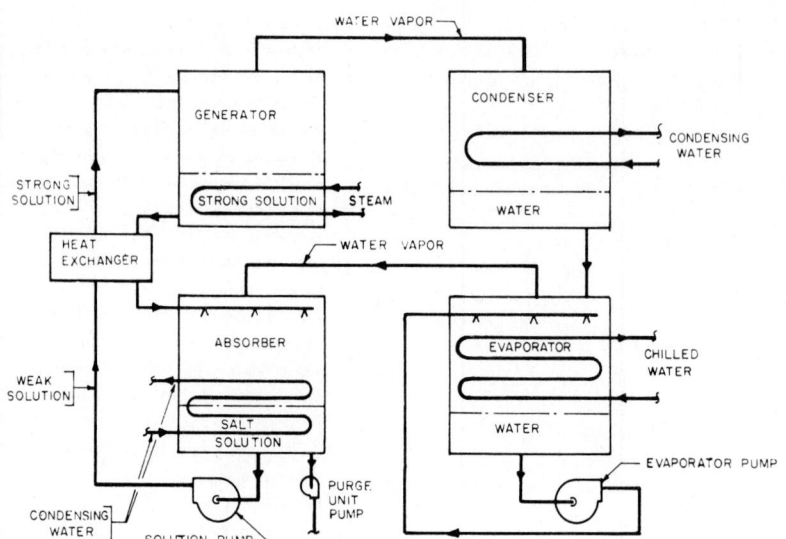

Fig. 36. Absorption refrigeration cycle using lithium bromide

(Reprinted by permission from ASHRAE Handbook)

Approximate sizes of absorption machines

Tons	L	W	H
50	11'6"	4'8"	8'0"
200	18'8"	4'10"	8'6"
500	19'6"	7'7"	12'2"
750	25'6"	7'7"	12'2"
1,000	34'6"	7'7"	14'0"

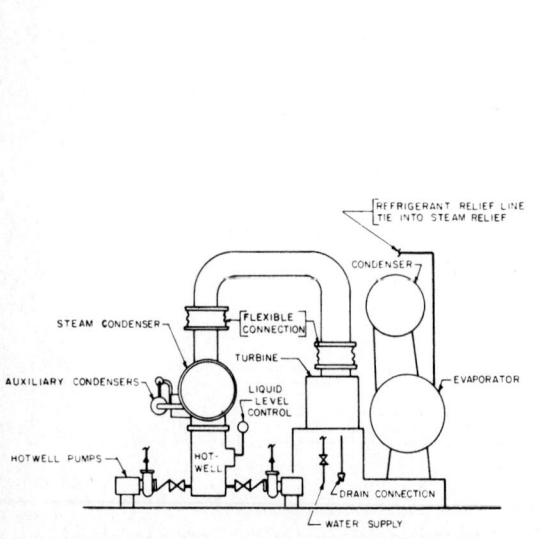

Fig. 35. Steam turbine compressor with steam condenser

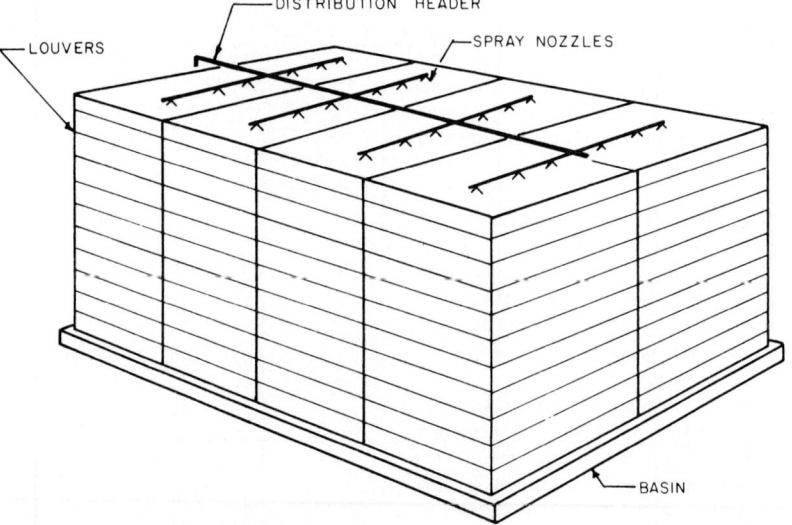

Fig. 37. Spray-filled atmospheric cooling tower

Cooling tower: In most instances a motor-driven induced- or forced-draft cooling tower is the most economical method for cooling and saving the water which removes the heat from the refrigerant (Fig. 37). Since the heat picked up inside the building has to be eliminated somewhere and since the air is the most convenient and cheapest place to get rid of it, cooling towers are the most effective device for transferring this heat to the air. For preliminary design purposes, a cooling tower for an electric-drive refrigeration compressor will require about 0.75 sq ft area per ton; for a steam-drive compressor, 1.0 sq ft per ton. Since cooling towers weigh from 120 to 200 psf when operating, their load must be considered in the design of the building structure. Another item is the noise and vibration from cooling towers. Airborne noise is generally a source of concern to areas within 100 ft of the cooling tower. To eliminate vibration, the fan platform, consisting of fan gearbox and motor, should be set on an isolation base consisting of either rubber-in-shear or springs, and the base of the tower should be set on ribbed neoprene pads.

For reasons of appearance the cooling tower is often enclosed in a louvered wall which must have sufficient free area so that enough air is drawn through the tower to remove the heat of the condenser water. As a general rule, a cooling tower needs about 320 cfm of air per ton of electric-drive refrigeration and 540 cfm per ton of steam-drive refrigeration, and the air velocity through the free area should not exceed 1,000 fpm. Also, in most cases, the cooling tower basin has to be set at least 4 ft above the roof in order to install the discharge piping and for maintenance purposes.

Double bundle condensers are sometimes used to reclaim refrigeration heat for other required uses, such as preheating domestic hot water.

Mechanical equipment room: In the refrigeration plant room there is generally other equipment, such as chilled-water pumps, condenser-water pumps, and an air-ventilation system. In larger buildings a refrigerant receiver tank and a pump-down compressor may be required. In some instances, air-handling, plumbing, and electrical equipment may be installed in the same room. For these reasons it is difficult to give space requirements for refrigeration rooms. A typical layout for a mechanical equipment room is shown in Fig. 38. In larger plants, a monorail system for moving equipment may be advantageous. Provision should be made for replacing equipment without interfering with the oper-

ation of the building, through areaways, etc.

Pumps are of three general classifications, all centrifugal: the close-coupled vertically split-casing type, used for smaller capacities (up to about 300 gal per min); and the horizontally split-casing type, used for larger applications. These two types overlap considerably in their range of operation. The vertically split pumps are generally cheaper, but the horizontally split pumps are more rugged and easier to maintain and service. The third type, in-line pumps, are connected directly into pipes up to 4 in. diameter. They are used mostly for small heating installations, domestic hot water recirculation, and freeze protection around coils.

Piping losses should be kept to a minimum in order to keep electric operating costs down. Piping should generally be sized to maintain a pressure drop of 3 to

6 ft of water pressure head loss per 100 equivalent lineal feet of pipe. Water velocities should be no more than 4 fps for pipes under 2 in. and less than 10 fps for pipes 6 in. and over to prevent water noise transmission.

Noise and vibration control: The pump should be set on an inertia block equal to one to two times the operating weight of the pump plus all piping to the first hangers. This block will minimize the transfer of vibrations from the pump to the piping. The inertia block should be set on some type of vibration isolation base, depending upon the degree of transmission desired (Fig. 39). Flexible connections may be used between pump and piping, and the latter should be supported by vibration-eliminating-type hangers (Fig. 40).

Vents: All systems except the absorption

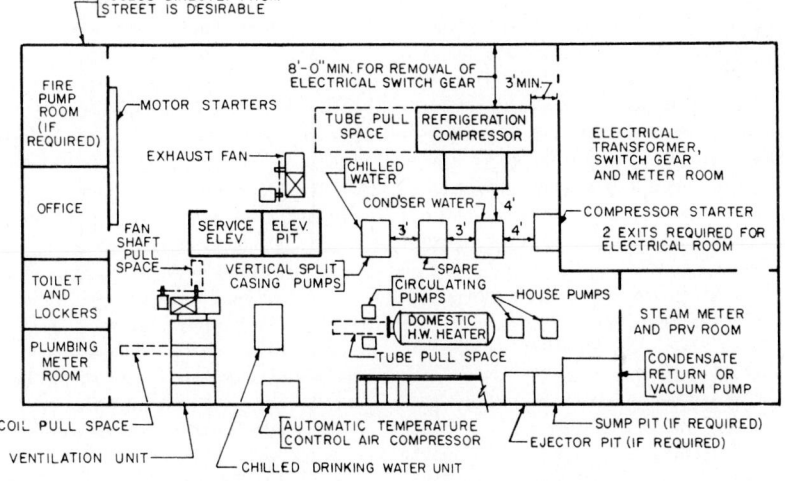

Fig. 38. Typical mechanical equipment room layout showing heating, ventilating, air-conditioning, electrical, and plumbing requirements

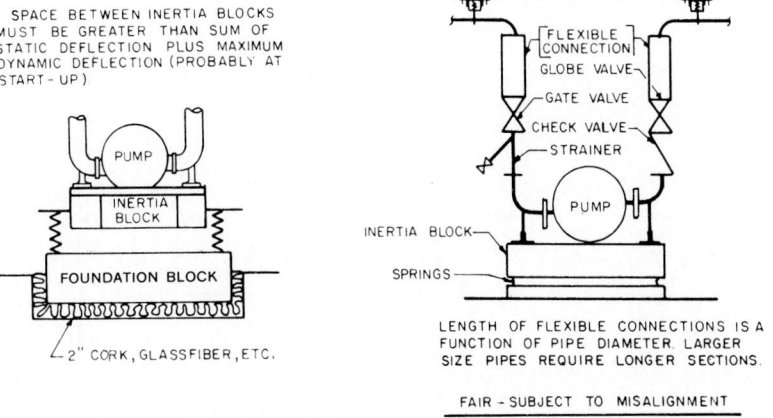

SPACE BETWEEN INERTIA BLOCKS MUST BE GREATER THAN SUM OF STATIC DEFLECTION PLUS MAXIMUM DYNAMIC DEFLECTION (PROBABLY AT START-UP)

FOR CRITICAL VIBRATION APPLICATIONS

Fig. 39. Vibration isolation of pump

LENGTH OF FLEXIBLE CONNECTIONS IS A FUNCTION OF PIPE DIAMETER. LARGER SIZE PIPES REQUIRE LONGER SECTIONS.

FAIR – SUBJECT TO MISALIGNMENT

Fig. 40. Flexible connections and vibration-reducing pipe hangers

system require a refrigerant relief-vent pipe to the atmosphere. The steam condensers on the steam turbine system require a steam pressure-relief pipe. The chilled-water system requires an expansion tank, which is usually of the open type.

Heat pump is the name given to any type of refrigeration compressor which is designed so that its evaporator and condenser sections can be interchanged to provide either cooling or heating, as required (Fig. 41). **The typical heat pump is the air-to-air system, which gives off excess heat to the outside air in the summer and takes in heat from the air in the winter to heat the building.** Well or river water or the ground can be used instead of outside air to carry off excess heat in the summer and to supply heat in the winter. The air-to-air system is the most commonly used, even though its horsepower requirements are greater, because water is usually not available and use of the ground presents operating and maintenance difficulties.

In the warmer climates where the temperatures do not get below 20°F, a single stage of refrigerant gas compression is usually sufficient to provide winter heating requirements. Below 20°F, either supplementary electric resistance heating must be used or two stages of refrigerant compression are required to furnish sufficient heating capacity.

A heat-pump system is generally considerably more costly to design and to install than an equivalent refrigeration system which performs summer cooling only. Air-to-air heat pumps should have the compressors reasonably close to the evaporative air condensers in order to keep the refrigerant lines as short as possible. Therefore, on taller buildings (over 50 or 60 ft high) the compressors should be located on the roof, and care must be taken to isolate their noise and vibration from the rest of the building.

Heat pumps often eliminate the need for a fossil fuel boiler plant. They can work on any source of available heat. They require more maintenance than standard refrigeration machines but less than that required if a fossil fuel plant is also needed.

Only under certain conditions is the heat pump the best choice; careful analysis of each case is required. Conditions that favor the use of the heat pump are:

1. Low electric power rates

2. Large interior area with high lighting load

3. Building with small amount of perimeter glass, with or without large interior area

4. Low outside air requirements

5. Ratio of design heating load to design cooling load of 0.6 or less. Simultaneous heating and cooling required in different parts of the building.

Central refrigeration plant: Where a number of air-conditioned buildings are contemplated in a given area, serious consideration should be given to the construction of a centralized refrigeration plant, similar to a central steam plant. Total investment costs will in most instances be less, maintenance and operating costs will be lower, and more space will be available **in the buildings for other uses. However, this must be balanced against the minimum and maximum air conditioning needs and the control capability of the central plant. Distribution system energy losses must be evaluated to assure energy optimization.**

To optimize results, terminal bleed versus interchanger, flow versus pressure controls, and individual versus central plant for independent operation must be analyzed.

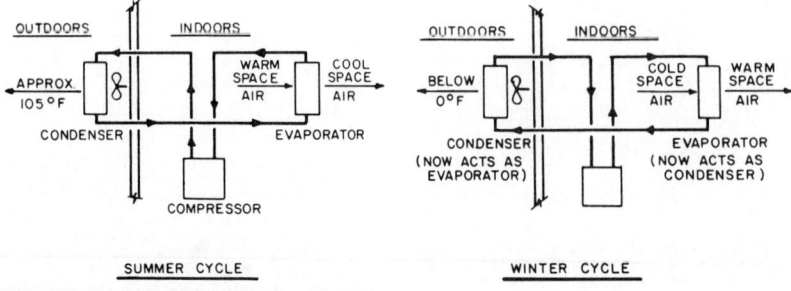

SUMMER CYCLE   WINTER CYCLE

Fig. 41.   Basic heat-pump cycle

By ALFRED GREENBERG, P.E., Environmental and Energy Consultant

HEATING PLANT

Most heating systems, other than residential, are based on the use of steam or hot water. However, a few other types of heating are occasionally used. These are outlined below.

1. *Space heaters* come in many sizes and shapes for floor, wall, or ceiling mounting (Fig. 42). They are often called "unit heaters," and they are discussed under this name in a later section of this book. They are usually gas- or oil-fired and are used in factories, warehouses, garages, markets, etc. Space heaters are relatively inexpensive and simple to operate and maintain; they can be relocated with a minimum of alteration.

2. *Electric* heating requires no maintenance, takes up the least space, provides individual control, and can produce uniform temperature conditions. It comes in a variety of forms: radiant element, infrared lamps, low-temperature radiant panel, fan-coil units, and baseboard convectors. Electric heating requires low electric rates and well-insulated buildings in order to be economical.

3. *Forced-warm-air* systems are often used in stores, small office buildings, etc., especially if summer cooling is to be provided. This is essentially a residential system, as discussed in an earlier section of this book.

4. *Heat pump,* as discussed previously.

Boiler plants: Most commercial and industrial buildings require boiler plants to furnish their heating and processing requirements. In some of the larger cities, steam is available for purchase from the local utility company. However, in the majority of cases, a boiler plant must be provided as part of the project.

Total heat load: To determine the total heat load the boiler must furnish, consider the following categories:

1. Direct heating-convectors, unit heaters, radiators, etc.
2. Tempering—heating of ventilation air
3. Domestic hot-water requirements
4. Kitchen requirements
5. Process requirements—laboratory hoods, sterilizers, cleaning, manufacturing, laundry, refrigeration plant, etc.

These items should be given in Btu's per hour or pounds of steam per hour. The loads should be tabulated on the basis of separate summer and winter requirements. Steam pressure requirements must also be known.

Boilers: They should always be designed for the lowest steam pressure or water temperature required for the service. Small loads having higher thermal requirements

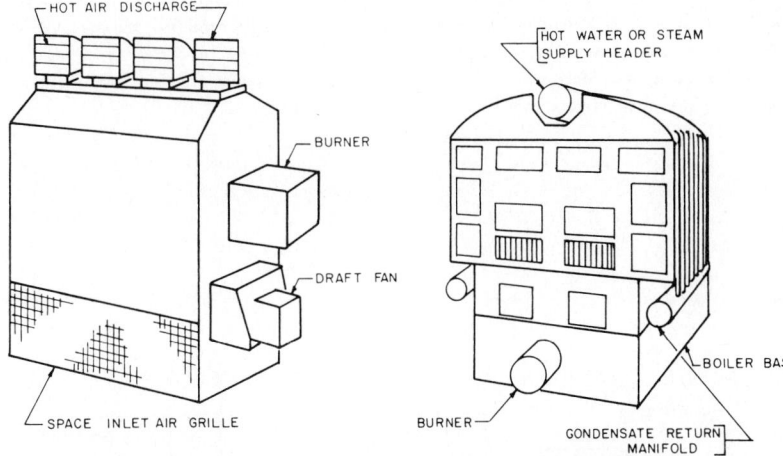

Fig. 42. **Direct-fired space heater**

Fig. 43. **Cast-iron sectional boiler**

Sizes range from approximately 3 to 8 ft wide, 6 to 9 ft high, and 3 to 16 ft long. Larger sizes are also available.

can usually be more economically served by separate units. The following types of boilers are in common use:

1. *Cast-iron sectional boilers* are used for capacities up to about 8,000 lb of steam per hour. They require less space than fire-tube types, and additional capacity can be obtained by adding more sections. These boilers have long life and low maintenance (see Fig. 43). Special units can be made in sizes up to about 25,000 lb per hour.

2. *Fire-tube boilers* may be furnished as complete packages with burner and controls or as a separate unit for mounting on a firebrick chamber. Capacities range to about 22,000 lb per hour and sizes from 10 to 27 ft long, 4 to 10 ft wide, and 6 to 12 ft high. Space must be provided in front of boiler for tube pulling (see Fig. 44).

3. *Packaged water-tube boilers* can be obtained in capacities from 8,000 to about 100,000 lb of steam per hour. Sizes vary greatly among manufacturers. These boilers are somewhat more costly than fire-tube boilers but are usually more efficient and long-lasting (see Fig. 45).

4. *Modular boilers* are unitary boiler-burner units with controls set to turn units on or off to meet load requirements. They usually use natural gas or No. 2 oil.

Where a project requires heating for comfort conditions and domestic hot water only, a hot-water boiler plant may be sufficient for its needs, as long as the water-pumping costs are not too high. On long, low buildings, it may be advantageous to use a hot-water heating system in order to save on the trenching costs that may be

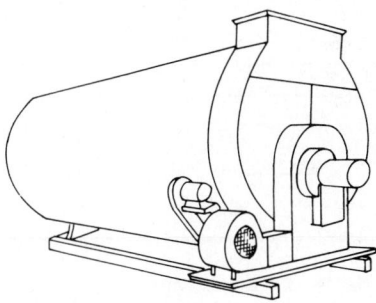

Fig. 44. **Fire-tube boiler**

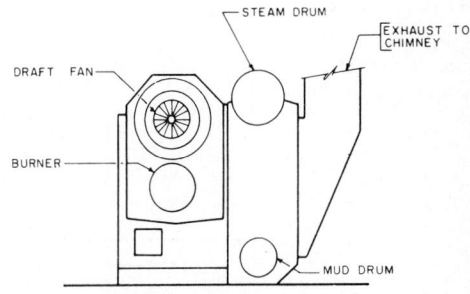

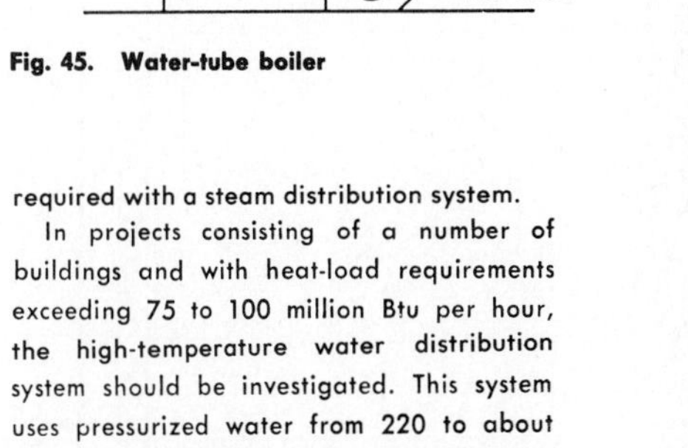

Fig. 45. **Water-tube boiler**

required with a steam distribution system.

In projects consisting of a number of buildings and with heat-load requirements exceeding 75 to 100 million Btu per hour, the high-temperature water distribution system should be investigated. This system uses pressurized water from 220 to about 450°F for furnishing heat and process requirements. For equivalent volumes, it does not hold more heat than steam but does not require pitched lines, and often saves on first, maintenance, and operating costs.

Location of boiler plant: In most projects which involve only one building, the boiler plant is generally located in the basement, which produces the least structural load and keeps the plant remote from the building's functional areas. Also, it allows the maximum height for the chimney, which may be sufficient to allow use of natural draft for boiler operation, thus saving on operating costs.

Undesirable rock excavation or soil conditions (high water table) or economic value of basement areas may make it necessary to locate the boiler plant elsewhere, such as in a separate structure on the site, or on the roof of the building. Where the plant is remote from the building, a piping distribution system is required. Steam return piping must usually be buried or placed in trenches or tunnels. Hot-water piping may be concealed in covered walkways, eliminating excavation problems.

Type of chimney: If the building is tall enough, the chimney need go no higher than 4 to 6 ft beyond the high point of the building. However, for most low buildings where appearance is an important consideration, mechanical-draft fans are used in order to keep the height of the chimney to a minimum, that is, just above the roof line. In industrial buildings, where low operating costs are more important than appearance, natural-draft chimneys are generally preferred. For many applications, these can be obtained in prefabricated metal sections.

Chimney sizing when taken in conjunction with pollution control requirements can be complex. Refer to the ASHRAE Handbook for further information.

Type of fuel: Most packaged fire-tube boilers are limited to either gas or oil as fuel. Water-tube boilers are available for use with any type of fuel. (See the ASHRAE Handbook for diagrams of typical coal-firing arrangements.)

Where gas is available, all that is usually required is a gas meter and possibly a pressure-reducing and/or pressure-regulating station. These do not take up much space. Where oil is to be used as the fuel, storage tanks are required. The capacity of these tanks usually ranges from 1 to 4 weeks' supply for the coldest month. A 2-week supply is average. Where tank size requirements exceed 20,000 to 30,000 gal (8 to 10 ft diameter by 30 to 40 ft long), multiple tanks are often installed. Most often the tanks are buried in the ground (Fig. 46), although sometimes they are placed in vaults which have to be explosion-proof and ventilated, if they are within the building. The tanks are generally secured to concrete foundations to prevent settling and floating. The tanks should have a cover of at least 3 ft and should be as close to the boiler plant as practicable in order to keep oil-pumping costs low (Fig. 47). Fill boxes for the oil tanks should be located so that the fuel trucks have ready access to them. Tank vent lines can usually be located inconspicuously alongside the building.

If coal is used for fuel, storage space (indoors, if possible) should be provided

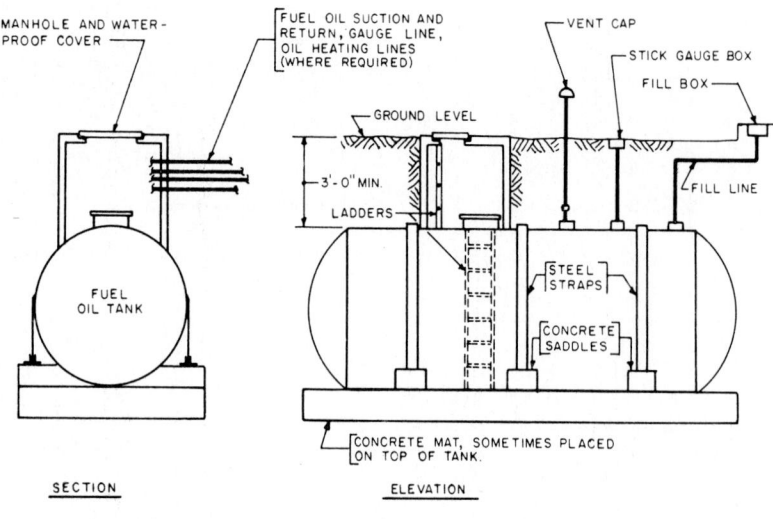

SECTION   ELEVATION

NOTE:
PIPING TO MANHOLE SHOULD GENERALLY BE PROTECTED BY SPLIT-TILE ENCLOSURE, TRENCH OR OTHER WATER-PROOF PROTECTION

Fig. 46. Oil storage tank

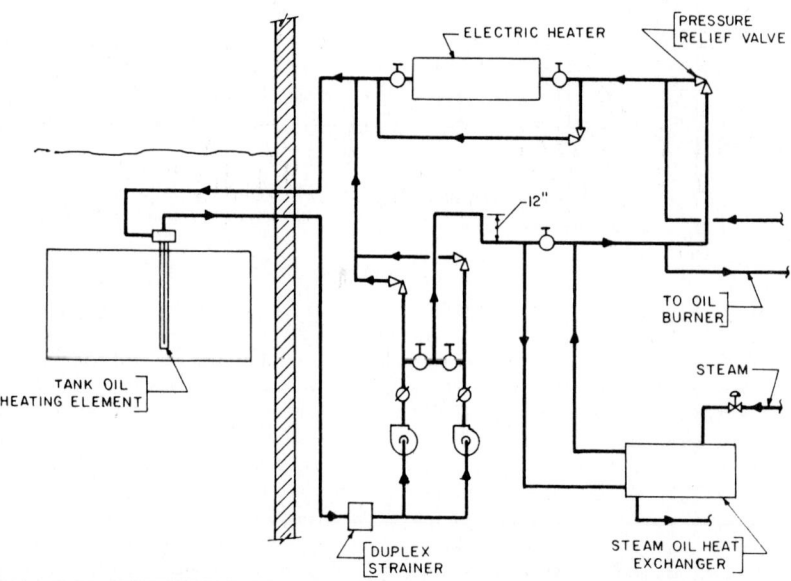

Fig. 47. Schematic piping diagram for heavy fuel oil

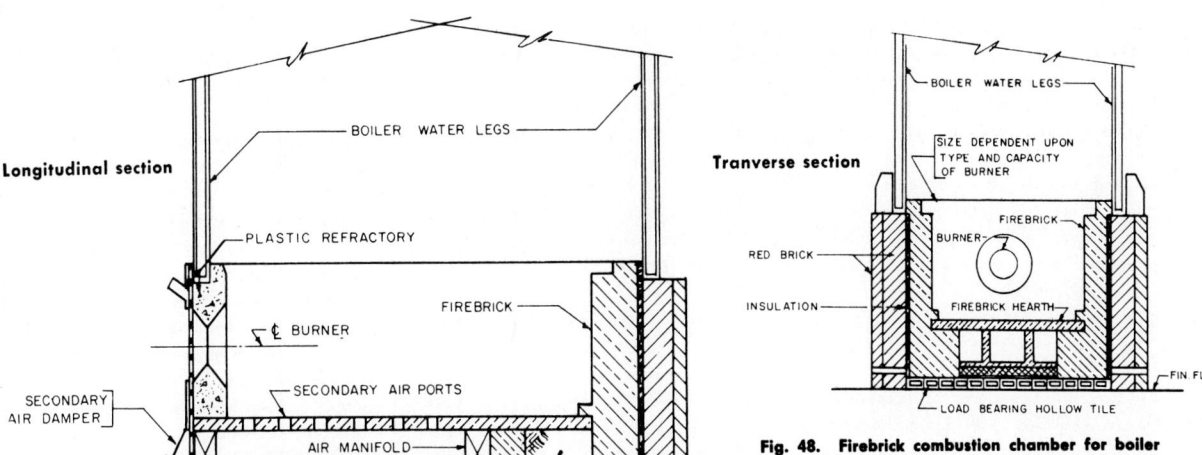

Longitudinal section

BOILER WATER LEGS

PLASTIC REFRACTORY

FIREBRICK

₵ BURNER

SECONDARY AIR PORTS

SECONDARY AIR DAMPER

AIR MANIFOLD

ASBESTOS MILLBOARD

RUBBLE FILL

Tranverse section

BOILER WATER LEGS

SIZE DEPENDENT UPON TYPE AND CAPACITY OF BURNER

FIREBRICK

RED BRICK

BURNER

INSULATION

FIREBRICK HEARTH

FIN. FL.

LOAD BEARING HOLLOW TILE

Fig. 48. Firebrick combustion chamber for boiler

Size of combustion chamber is dependent upon type and capacity of burner.

for a 45-day supply. One ton of coal requires 40 cu ft of space. In addition, handling equipment must be furnished to get the coal to the boilers and provisions taken for preventing spontaneous combustion.

The plant may be designed so that it can operate on either gas, oil or any other fuel, depending on costs and availability.

Firebrick combustion chambers: Boilers set on firebrick combustion chambers (see Fig. 48) have in the past provided the most reliable service and will probably outlast factory-assembled boiler packages and boiler-burner sets. They are somewhat more costly to install due to the brickwork, and if they are not properly installed, operated, and maintained, relining of the brick is an expensive item. For most applications, packages, and sets are expected to perform satisfactorily for at least ten years.

Water treatment: One item of continued maintenance on boilers is the feedwater treatment. A boiler that does not have its water treated will seldom last more than a few years before corrosion and leaks force it out of service. On the smaller installations, the chemicals are intermittently and manually fed to the boilers, whereas on larger systems, pumps and chemical feed systems are employed. Oxygen in the water is the most dangerous element tending to produce corrosion. Larger systems and deluxe smaller ones employ deaerator feedwater heaters to remove the oxygen. This piece of equipment can add many years to the life of a boiler plant and can pay for itself and the extra space required many times over.

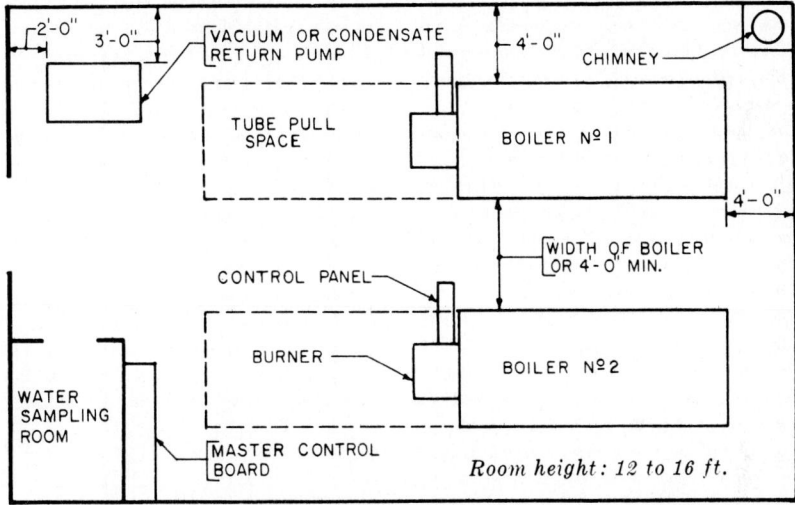

VACUUM OR CONDENSATE RETURN PUMP

CHIMNEY

TUBE PULL SPACE

BOILER NO 1

WIDTH OF BOILER OR 4'-0" MIN.

CONTROL PANEL

BURNER

BOILER NO 2

WATER SAMPLING ROOM

MASTER CONTROL BOARD

Room height: 12 to 16 ft.

Fig. 49. Layout of simple boiler room utilizing packaged fire-tube boiler-burner set

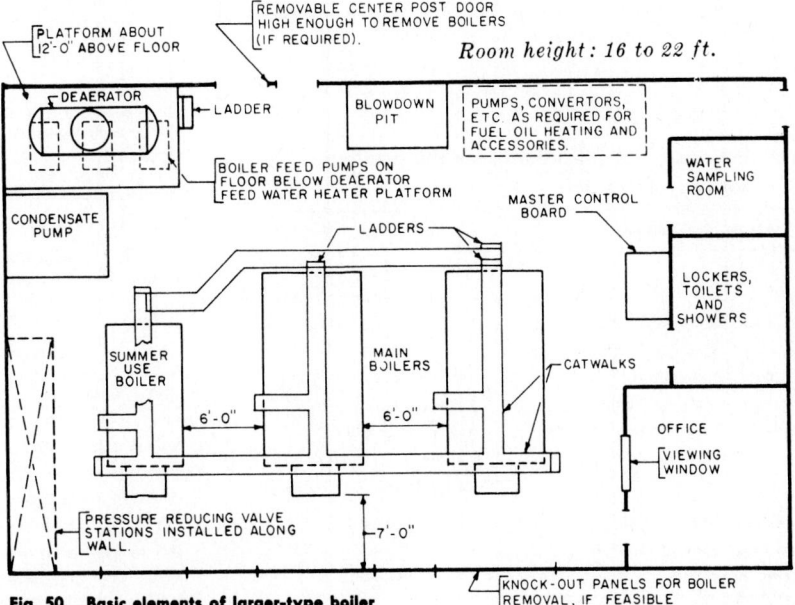

REMOVABLE CENTER POST DOOR HIGH ENOUGH TO REMOVE BOILERS (IF REQUIRED).

Room height: 16 to 22 ft.

PLATFORM ABOUT 12'-0" ABOVE FLOOR

DEAERATOR

LADDER

BLOWDOWN PIT

PUMPS, CONVERTORS, ETC AS REQUIRED FOR FUEL OIL HEATING AND ACCESSORIES.

WATER SAMPLING ROOM

CONDENSATE PUMP

BOILER FEED PUMPS ON FLOOR BELOW DEAERATOR FEED WATER HEATER PLATFORM

MASTER CONTROL BOARD

LADDERS

SUMMER USE BOILER

MAIN BOILERS

CATWALKS

LOCKERS, TOILETS AND SHOWERS

OFFICE VIEWING WINDOW

PRESSURE REDUCING VALVE STATIONS INSTALLED ALONG WALL.

KNOCK-OUT PANELS FOR BOILER REMOVAL, IF FEASIBLE

6'-0"   6'-0"   7'-0"

Fig. 50. Basic elements of larger-type boiler plant with water-tube boilers

Pressure-reducing stations: Where steam at various pressures is required, the steam boiler has to operate at the highest pressure. If the high-pressure quantities are comparatively small, then the main boiler may be operated at a lower pressure and a small high-pressure steam boiler can be provided. Where the steam pressure has to be reduced, pressure-reducing valve (PRV) stations are required. A sufficient number of stations must be provided to give the proper steam pressures and flexibility in operation. Because they emit large quantities of heat, pressure-reducing valve stations are often enclosed in separate rooms and provided with a mechanical exhaust ventilation system.

Steam-meter room: Where metering of the steam is required, a steam-meter room should be located as close to the source of the steam service as possible. The size of the service will determine the size room required. This room generally also contains the pressure reducing valve stations. Where the building has its own boiler plant, it may be advantageous to record the steam quantity produced by each boiler.

Ventilation: The boiler room and steam-meter room should also be ventilated to prevent heat buildup. The boiler room requires sufficient air for proper combustion. For preliminary size purposes only, the outdoor air requirements may be safely figured as ½ cfm per lb of steam capacity per hr. The boiler room exhaust ventilation system should be carefully designed so that the fan does not pull too much air out of the room and thus starve the boilers.

Safety relief valves are required on all boilers. Provision should be made to have the steam go to an isolated areaway or the roof.

Condensate return systems are of three general types. The high-temperature condensate pump system eliminates the need for flash tanks and has widespread use in the process industries, laundries, hospitals, etc. Low-pressure condensate return pump and vacuum return pump systems are most commonly used in commercial applications. Vacuum pumps are generally used on large direct-heating systems with long pipe runs. The advantages of this system are that it continuously removes the air entrapped in the piping, thus improving heat transfer, and uses smaller pipe sizes. Since the system operates under a vacuum (pressure less than atmospheric), if the condensate reaches the pump at too high a temperature, flashing into steam will occur, which will adversely affect pump operation. Where such conditions exist, condensate pumps should be used. When the building uses steam at pressures in excess of 5 to 10 psig, the condensate return should be emptied into a flash tank which will remove the excess heat and then return the condensate to the condensate pump. The excess heat in the flash tank will form some low-pressure steam and must be vented to the atmosphere or the low-pressure steam line.

Boiler rooms: Schematic layouts of typical boiler rooms are shown in Figs. 49 and 50. Boiler, PRV, and meter rooms located within a building must be well insulated thermally from the rest of the building. It may be desirable to provide a ventilated hung ceiling to reduce the heat transferred to the floor above. There are noise and vibration problems in connection with boiler plants and PRV rooms, and acoustical isolation may be required.

ESTIMATION OF ENERGY CONSUMPTION

The degree-day method has been generally used as the basis for estimating heating energy consumption. It was set up on a base of 65°F. However, improved insulation practices and the substantial increase in internal heat gains have tended to reduce the accuracy of the degree-day method by indicating higher heating consumption than is actually realized. More accurate estimating methods are in the process of being developed. A modified degree-day procedure has been developed:

$$E = \left(\frac{H_L \times D \times 24}{\Delta t \times \eta \times V}\right)(C_D)(C_F)$$

where E = fuel or energy consumption for the estimate period

H_L = design heat loss, including infiltration, Btuh

D = number of degree-days for the estimate period

η = rated full load efficiency, decimal

V = heating value of fuel, consistent with H_L and E

C_D = interim correction factor for heating effect vs. degree days

C_F = interim part-load correction factor for fueled systems only; equals 1.0 for electric resistance heating

Table for C_D

Outdoor design temp, °F	−20	−10	0	+10	+20
Factor C_D	0.57	0.64	0.71	0.79	0.89

Table for C_F

Per cent oversizing	0	20	40	60	80
Factor C_F	1.36	1.56	1.79	2.04	2.32

Table 32. Efficiency of utilization over the heating season—Estimated

Type of fuel-burning unit	Efficiency, %
Gas	50–60
Oil	40–60
Bituminous coal, hand-fired with controls	35–50
Bituminous coal, hand-fired without controls	30–45
Bituminous coal, stoker-fired	40–55
Anthracite, hand-fired with controls	About 5–10% Higher than Bituminous
Anthracite, hand-fired without controls	
Anthracite, stoker-fired	
Coke, hand-fired with controls	50–60
Coke, hand-fired without controls	30–45
Direct electric heating	90–100

Table 33. Approximate power inputs

System	Compressor Kw/design ton	Auxiliaries Kw/design ton
Window units	1.46	0.32
Through-wall units	1.64	0.30
Dwelling unit, central air-cooled	1.49	0.14
Central, group, or bldg. cooling plants		
(3 to 25 tons) air-cooled	1.20	0.20
(25 to 100 tons) air-cooled	1.18	0.21
(25 to 100 tons) water-cooled	0.94	0.17
(Over 100 tons) water-cooled	0.79	0.20

Table 32 gives average annual efficiency of utilization for various fuels. Degree-days may be found in Table 8. A period of 2 to 4 weeks is selected during the coldest month to determine peak fuel needs and thus, in the case of oil and coal, the storage capacity required.

For estimating cooling system energy consumption, Tables 33 and 34 may be used in conjunction with Table 8A which shows weather data for various locations in bin format. This simplifies the calculations and permits a rough estimate to be obtained.

PIPING

Piping is necessary to convey steam, condensate return, hot water, chilled water, condenser water, drain piping, and air (in pneumatic control systems). Problems encountered in the design of piping that require special attention are:

1. Expansion and contraction
2. Methods of supporting larger sizes due to heavy weights involved, especially where liquids are carried
3. Corrosion
4. Leakage
5. Relative inflexibility of piping in maneuvering through tight spaces
6. Pitching

Expansion: The ASHRAE Handbook suggests a formula which will satisfactorily solve many expansion problems:

$$L = 6.16 \sqrt{D\Delta}$$

where L = length of pipe, ft
D = outside diameter of pipe, in.
Δ = deformation, in. (based on a fiber stress less than or equal to 16,000 psi)

It is recommended that expansion loops (Fig. 51) be installed wherever practicable since they require almost no maintenance. Where space does not permit, expansion joints as made by various manufacturers may be used. In general, steam, condensate return, and hot-water systems will require expansion loops about every 150 to 200 lineal ft of straight pipe. To control the movement of the piping system, the piping is rigidly anchored to the structure midway between the loops. Changes in direction of the piping provide some protection against expansion and in some instances may be sufficient to take care of all expansion requirements.

Chilled-water systems may require an expansion loop every 300 to 400 ft of continuous linear pipe with an anchor in between. Condenser water pipes seldom need expansion loops; anchoring them is usually sufficient to minimize pipe stresses.

Table 34. Estimated equivalent rated full-load hours of operation for properly sized equipment during normal cooling season

Location	Hours	Location	Hours
Albuquerque, NM	800–2200	Indianapolis, IN	600–1600
Atlantic City, NJ	500–800	Little Rock, AR	1400–2400
Birmingham, AL	1200–2200	Minneapolis, MN	400–800
Boston, MA	400–1200	New Orleans, LA	1400–2800
Burlington, VT	200–600	New York, NY	500–1000
Charlotte, NC	700–1100	Newark, NJ	400–900
Chicago, IL	500–1000	Oklahoma City, OK	1100–2000
Cleveland, OH	400–800	Pittsburgh, PA	900–1200
Cincinnati, OH	1000–1500	Rapid City, SD	800–1000
Columbia, SC	1200–1400	St. Joseph, MO	1000–1600
Corpus Christi, TX	2000–2500	St. Petersburg, FL	1500–2700
Dallas, TX	1200–1600	San Diego, CA	800–1700
Denver, CO	400–800	Savannah, GA	1200–1400
Des Moines, IA	600–1000	Seattle, WA	400–1200
Detroit, MI	700–1000	Syracuse, NY	200–1000
Duluth, MN	300–500	Trenton, NJ	800–1000
El Paso, TX	1000–1400	Tulsa, OK	1500–2200
Honolulu, HI	1500–3500	Washington, DC	700–1200

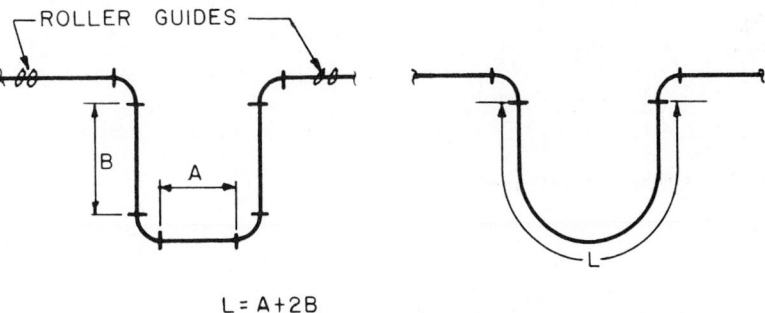

$$L = A + 2B$$

Fig. 51.   Expansion loops

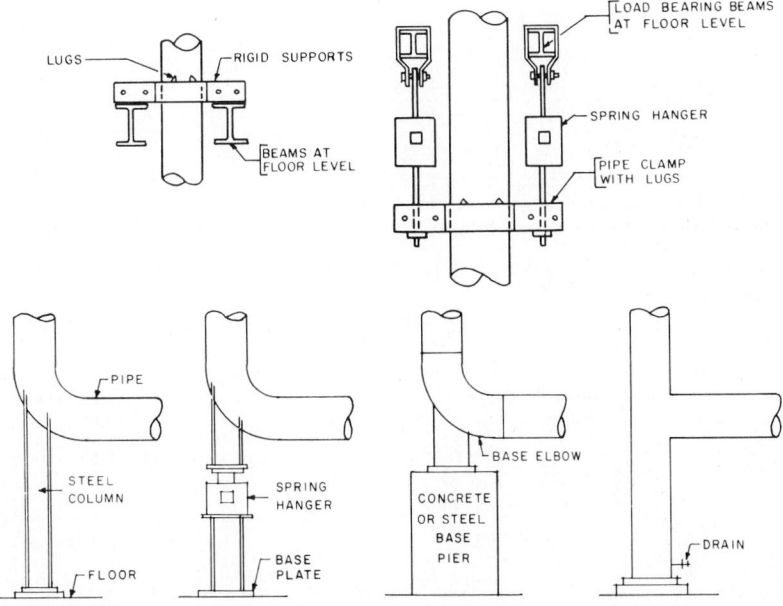

Fig. 52.   Methods of supporting vertical piping

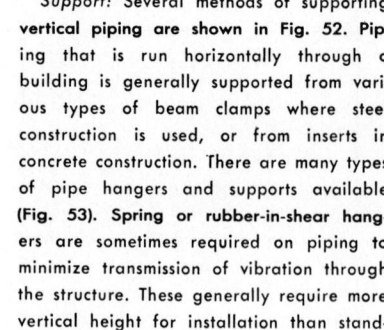

Support: Several methods of supporting **vertical piping are shown in Fig. 52.** Piping that is run horizontally through a building is generally supported from various types of beam clamps where steel construction is used, or from inserts in concrete construction. There are many types of pipe hangers and supports available **(Fig. 53).** Spring or rubber-in-shear hangers are sometimes required on piping to minimize transmission of vibration through the structure. These generally require more vertical height for installation than standard hangers.

Corrosion and leakage are problems that are best solved by proper specifications, installation, and maintenance.

Inflexibility: Piping, especially in hung ceilings, must be carefully coordinated with ductwork and recessed lighting as well as with the structure of the building. Where piping has to be diverted around an obstacle, Fig. 54 shows approved methods for doing it. Low-pressure condensate return and drain pipes should never be set up if possible. Where there is insufficient space for a pipe to pass below a beam, it may be possible to run it through the web **of the beam (Fig. 55);** it may be necessary to increase the size of the beam in order to do this.

Pitch: The difficulties of running piping through tight spaces are complicated by the necessity for pitching the pipes. Steam, drain, and condensate return pipes should pitch downward in the direction of flow, while pipes full of water should pitch upward in the direction of flow.

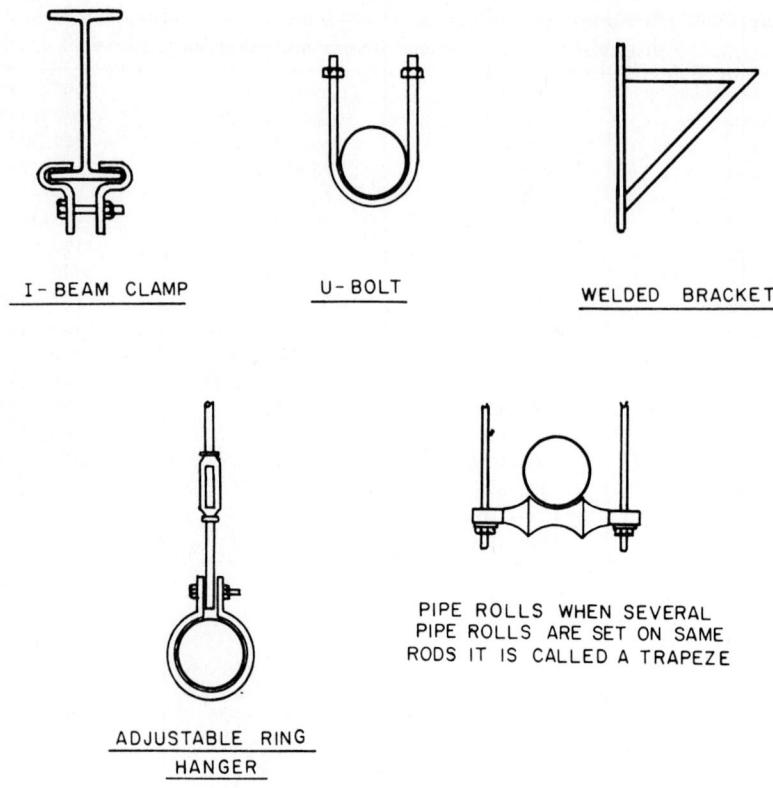

I-BEAM CLAMP   U-BOLT   WELDED BRACKET

PIPE ROLLS WHEN SEVERAL
PIPE ROLLS ARE SET ON SAME
RODS IT IS CALLED A TRAPEZE

ADJUSTABLE RING
HANGER

Fig. 53. Methods of supporting horizontal piping

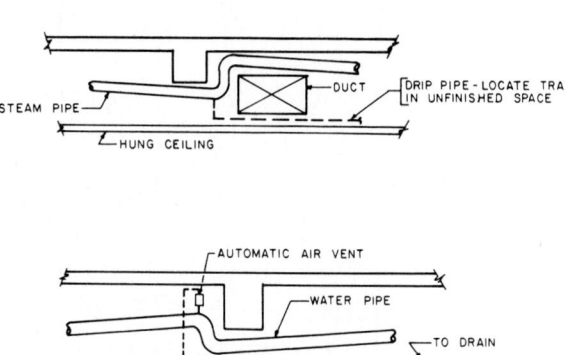

STEAM PIPE — DUCT — DRIP PIPE-LOCATE TRAP IN UNFINISHED SPACE
— HUNG CEILING

— AUTOMATIC AIR VENT
— WATER PIPE
— TO DRAIN

Fig. 54. Piping diverted around obstacles

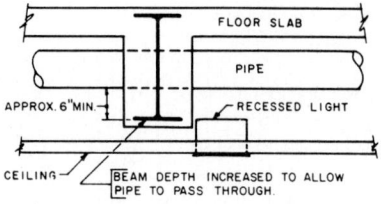

FLOOR SLAB
PIPE
APPROX. 6"MIN.— — RECESSED LIGHT
CEILING — BEAM DEPTH INCREASED TO ALLOW PIPE TO PASS THROUGH.

Fig. 55. Piping run through web of beam

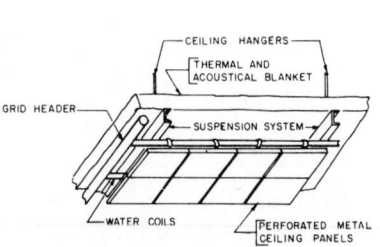

CEILING HANGERS
THERMAL AND ACOUSTICAL BLANKET
GRID HEADER — SUSPENSION SYSTEM
WATER COILS   PERFORATED METAL CEILING PANELS

Fig. 56. Integral radiant piping and ceiling

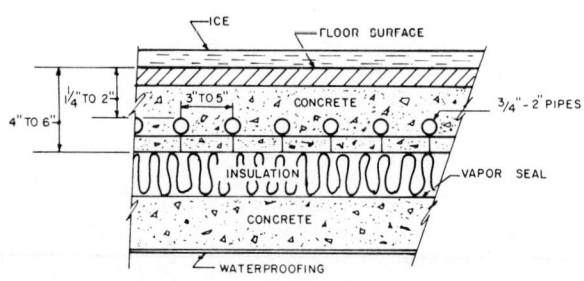

ICE — FLOOR SURFACE
1/4" TO 2"   3" TO 5"   CONCRETE   3/4"-2" PIPES
4" TO 6"   INSULATION   VAPOR SEAL
CONCRETE
WATERPROOFING

Fig. 57. Section through ice-rink floor

Table 35. Pressure drops in common use for sizing steam supply and condensate return pipes

(*Reprinted by permission from* ASHRAE Handbook of Fundamentals, *1977*)

Initial steam pressure, psig	Pressure drop per 100 ft, psi	Total pressure drop in steam supply piping, psi
Subatmos, or vacuum return	2–4 oz	1–2 psi
0	½ oz	1 oz
1	2 oz	1–4 oz
2	2 oz	8 oz
5	4 oz	1½ psi
10	8 oz	3 psi
15	1 psi	4 psi
30	2 psi	5–10 psi
50	2–5 psi	10–15 psi
100	2–5 psi	15–25 psi
150	2–10 psi	25–30 psi

Pressure drop per 100 ft, psi	Pressure in return line (Psig)	
	30 psi system	150 psi system
⅛	½	1¼
¼	1	2½
½	2	5
¾	3	7½
1	4	10
2	—	20

Table 36. Length in feet of pipe to be added to actual length of run—owing to fittings—to obtain equivalent length

	Length in feet to be added to run				
Size of pipe inches	Standard elbow	Side outlet tee	Gate valve	Globe valve	Angle valve
½	1.3	3	0.3	14	7
¾	1.8	4	0.4	18	10
1	2.2	5	0.5	23	12
1¼	3.0	6	0.6	29	15
1½	3.5	7	0.8	34	18
2	4.3	8	1.0	46	22
2½	5.0	11	1.1	54	27
3	6.5	13	1.4	66	34
3½	8	15	1.6	80	40
4	9	18	1.9	92	45
5	11	22	2.2	112	56
6	13	27	2.8	136	67
8	17	35	3.7	180	92
10	21	45	4.6	230	112
12	27	53	5.5	270	132
14	30	63	6.4	310	152

Table 37. Comparative capacity of steam lines at various pitches for steam and condensate flowing in opposite directions

(*Pitch of pipe in inches per 10 ft, velocity in ft per sec*)

Pitch of pipe	¼ in.		½ in.		1 in.		1½ in.		2 in.		3 in.		4 in.		5 in.	
Pipe size inches	Capacity	Max. Vel.	Capacity	Max. Vel.	Capacity	Max. Vel.	Capacity	Max. Vel.	Capacity	Max. Vel.	Capacity	Max. Vel.	Capacity	Max. Vel.	Capacity	Max. Vel.
					Capacity expressed in pounds per hour											
¾	3.2	8	4.1	11	5.7	13	6.4	14	7.1	16	8.3	17	9.9	22	10.5	22
1	6.8	9	9.0	12	11.7	15	12.8	17	14.8	19	17.3	22	19.2	24	20.5	25
1¼	11.8	11	15.9	14	19.9	17	24.6	20	27.0	22	31.3	25	33.4	26	38.1	31
1½	19.8	12	25.9	16	33.0	19	37.4	22	42.0	24	46.8	26	50.8	28	59.2	33
2	42.9	15	54.0	18	68.8	24	83.3	27	92.9	30	99.6	32	102.4	32	115.0	33

Reverse return: In the design of all but the simplest piping systems, it is desirable to set up a reverse return system. This simplifies the balancing of the system initially, and changes in flow to units on the system do not tend to upset this balance to any appreciable degree.

Sizing: Table 35 gives the pressure drops in common use for the sizing of steam piping. Low-pressure steam-piping systems (2 to 10 psig) are normally sized for pressure drops from ⅛ to ½ psi per 100 equivalent ft of pipe. The sizing must be such as to assure that all parts of the system have sufficient pressure to operate properly. Piping for higher-pressure systems may be sized at larger pressure drops, depending on operating pressures required at equipment. The pipe sizes should be such that the steam velocity does not exceed 6,000 to 10,000 fpm, depending on pipe size, since higher velocities will create noise.

Tables 35 through 39 and Figs. 58 and 59 provide some information to enable sizing low pressure steam and water systems for prelimanery purposes. See the ASHRAE Handbook for more detailed information.

Water-distribution systems, as previously noted, are generally sized on the basis of 3 to 6 ft of water head per 100 equivalent

Table 38. Steam pipe capacities for low-pressure systems

(For use on one-pipe systems or two-pipe systems in which condensate flows against the steam flow)

Nominal pipe size, inches	Capacity in pounds per hour				
	Two-pipe systems		One-pipe systems		
	Condensate flowing against steam		Supply risers up-feed	Radiator values and vertical connections	Radiator and riser runouts
	Vertical	Horizontal			
A	B[a]	C[c]	D[b]	E	F[c]
¾	8	7	6	—	7
1	14	14	11	7	7
1¼	31	27	20	16	16
1½	48	42	38	23	16
2	97	93	72	42	23
2½	159	132	116	—	42
3	282	200	200	—	65
3½	387	288	286	—	119
4	511	425	380	—	186
5	1,050	788	—	—	278
6	1,800	1,400	—	—	545
8	3,750	3,000	—	—	—
10	7,000	5,700	—	—	—
12	11,500	9,500	—	—	—
16	22,000	19,000	—	—	—

Note: Steam at an average pressure of 1 psig is used as a basis of calculating capacities.

[a] Do not use Column B for pressure drops of less than 1/16 psi per 100 ft of equivalent run.

[b] Do not use Column D for pressure drops of less than 1/24 psi per 100 ft of equivalent run except on sizes 3 in. and over.

[c] Pitch of horizontal runouts to risers and radiators should be not less than ½ in. per ft. Where this pitch cannot be obtained, runouts over 8 ft in length should be one pipe size larger than called for in this table.

Table 39. Return main and riser capacities for low-pressure systems—pounds per hour

Pipe size inches	1/32 psi or ½ oz drop per 100 ft			1/24 psi or ⅔ oz drop per 100 ft			1/16 psi or 1 oz drop per 100 ft			1/8 psi or 2 oz drop per 100 ft			¼ psi or 4 oz drop per 100 ft			½ psi or 8 oz drop per 100 ft		
	Wet	Dry	Vac.	Wet	Dry	Vac.	Wet	Dry	Vac.	Wet	Dry	Vac.	Wet	Dry	Vac.	Wet	Dry	Vac.
¾						42			100			142			200			283
1	125	62		145	71	143	175	80	175	250	103	249	350	115	350			494
1¼	213	130		248	149	244	300	168	300	425	217	426	600	241	600			848
1½	338	206		393	236	388	475	265	475	675	340	674	950	378	950			1,340
2	700	470		810	535	815	1,000	575	1,000	1,400	740	1,420	2,000	825	2,000			2,830
2½	1,180	760		1,580	868	1,360	1,680	950	1,680	2,350	1,230	2,380	3,350	1,360	3,350			4,730
3	1,880	1,460		2,130	1,560	2,180	2,680	1,750	2,680	3,750	2,250	3,800	5,350	2,500	5,350			7,560
3½	2,750	1,970		3,300	2,200	3,250	4,000	2,500	4,000	5,500	3,230	5,680	8,000	3,580	8,000			11,300
4	3,880	2,930		4,580	3,350	4,500	5,500	3,750	5,500	7,750	4,830	7,810	11,000	5,380	11,000			15,500
5						7,880			9,680			13,700			19,400			27,300
6						12,600			15,500			22,000			31,000			43,800
¾		48			48	143		48	175		48	249		48	350			494
1		113			113	244		113	300		113	426		113	600			848
1¼		248			248	388		248	475		248	674		248	950			1,340
1½		375			375	815		375	1,000		375	1,420		375	2,000			2,830
2		750			750	1,360		750	1,680		750	2,380		750	3,350			4,730
2½						2,180			2,680			3,800			5,350			7,560
3						3,250			4,000			5,680			8,000			11,300
3½						4,480			5,500			7,810			11,000			15,500
4						7,880			9,680			13,700			19,400			27,300
5						12,600			15,500			22,000			31,000			43,800

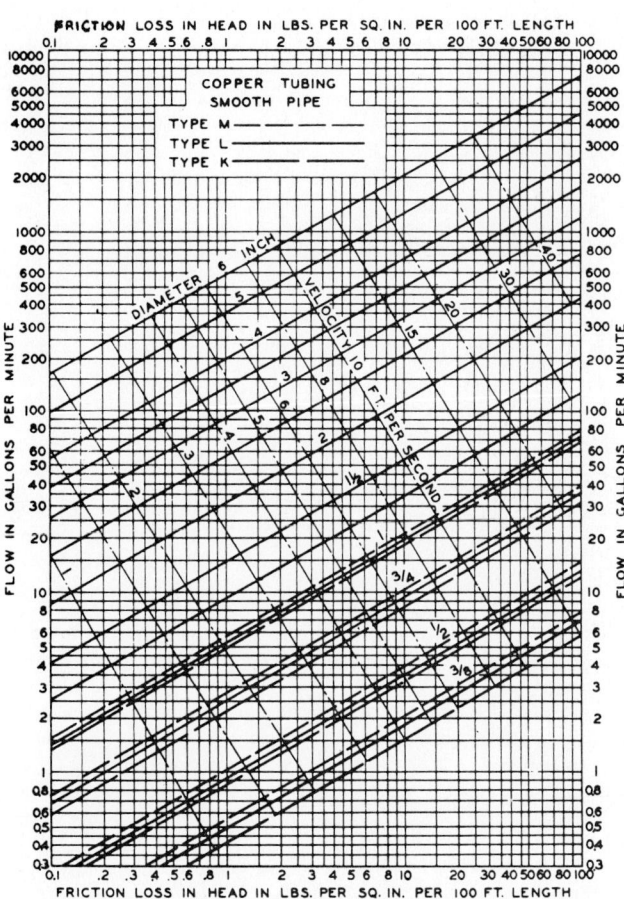

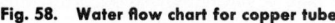

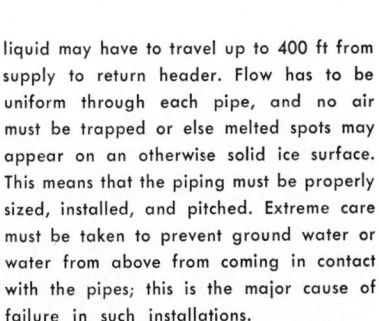

[a] Another type of copper tubing, known as Type TP, now is being used extensively. Type TP tubing has the same outside diameter as standard brass pipe sizes. It can be interchanged with brass pipe or connected to brass pipe, using silver solder. Type B tubing, made to U.S. Navy specifications, may be similarly used. For friction loss in Type TP or Type B tubing, the designer should adjust values for the actual inside diameter of the tubing.

Fig. 58. Water flow chart for copper tube

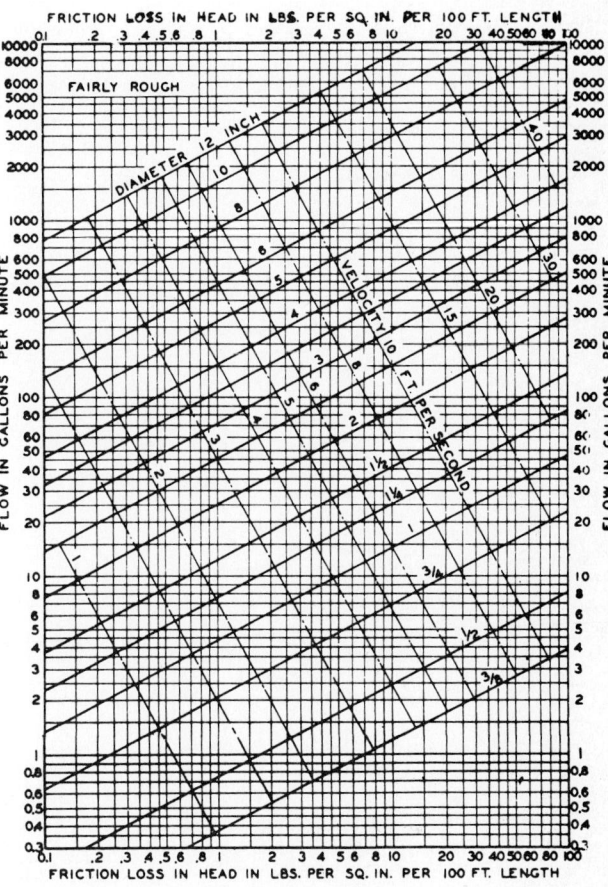

Fig. 59. Water flow chart for fairly rough pipe[7]

ft of pipe with a maximum water flow velocity of 4 fps for pipes under 2 in. and 10 fps for pipes over 6 in.

All piping systems should be carefully designed to minimize the possibility of water hammer and noise.

Radiant panels: Piping systems for radiant heating and/or cooling systems require special consideration since they generally form a part of the ceiling, wall, or floor. Details of typical radiant heating installations are shown in the section on *Residential Heating.* Another type of radiant heating and cooling ceiling panel is shown in Fig. 58. In this system the piping supports a perforated-metal-pan acoustical ceiling, in which lighting fixtures, air diffusers, and partitions are integrated.

One of the most critical examples of a radiant panel installation is an ice-skating or hockey rink (Fig. 57). The pipe lengths may be up to 200 ft long, and the

liquid may have to travel up to 400 ft from supply to return header. Flow has to be uniform through each pipe, and no air must be trapped or else melted spots may appear on an otherwise solid ice surface. This means that the piping must be properly sized, installed, and pitched. Extreme care must be taken to prevent ground water or water from above from coming in contact with the pipes; this is the major cause of failure in such installations.

Mechanical equipment rooms must be carefully laid out so that all piping that requires frequent operation or maintenance is easily accessible. It is customary to locate steam, chilled, hot, and condenser piping overhead at the lowest level above 8-ft headroom. Condensate return piping is usually run low along the walls. Above the piping are the various air ducts, and above these the plumbing lines, and at the highest level the electrical conduits. Of

course, clear access must be assured for plumbing piping cleanouts and valves and electrical junction and pull boxes.

AUTOMATIC CONTROLS

The automatic control system represents the nervous system of the heating, ventilating, and air-conditioning installation. It transmits environmental information from the outdoors and the controlled areas to central locations where adjustments are made to produce the required results. As buildings have increased in complexity, so have the automatic control requirements.

Many modern buildings feel the effect of weather changes much faster than older buildings because of more glass and less weight in the exterior walls. Further, there is the distinction between varying conditions at the exterior and the relatively stable thermal conditions in the interior of a building—all of which must be sensed and reacted to by the control system.

Because of solar and electrical loads, it is not uncommon for the refrigeration plant to operate throughout the winter months, making necessary another complex set of automatic devices to enable the cooling tower to operate in the heart of winter without the danger of freezing.

Automatic controls can save between 10 and 30 per cent of the annual operating costs for a given system. With controls costing about 10 per cent of the total for the heating and air-conditioning installation, this cost could be amortized in a reasonable period of time.

Automatic controls contribute to the following ends:

1. Human comfort.
2. Fuel economy (energy conservation)
3. Industrial process conditions. (This is where air conditioning began.)
4. Safety. (For example, shutdown of fans in case of fire, stopping a refrigeration condensing unit if there is no water in the system, or preventing steam coils from freezing.)
5. Preservation of building contents.
6. Improved energy, building and safety management.

DEFINITION OF AUTOMATIC CONTROLS

Automatic controls include three basic types of devices:

1. A sensing or pilot device
2. An actuating or motor device
3. A recording or indicator device

Sensing devices may be responsive to air or water temperature, humidity, steam pressure, or air velocity, and include such instruments as thermostats, aquastats, static pressure regulators, and similar devices. These are the "eyes and ears" of any control system. The sensing devices for any system may be electric, pneumatic, electronic, or combinations of any two or all three.

The second group, the actuating and operating devices, are essentially motor-controlled dampers or valves, corresponding to the fingers and muscles of the systems (Fig. 60). The "motors" may be hydraulic or pneumatic cylinders, air diaphragms, or electric motors, frequently with reversible and adjustable speeds.

The third type of equipment, the instrumentation of the system, in addition to thermometers and gages, include such refinements as clockwork mechanisms to start and stop motors, radiant thermometers, hygrostats, draft gages, two- and three-pen recording controllers, etc. (Fig. 61). These are now being made in "miniature" sizes, with dials approximately 3 in. in diameter.

All-electric controls are the usual choice for smaller systems. As the number of control devices and control points increases, a break-even point is reached after which pneumatic controls are less expensive. Packaged air-conditioning equipment up to about 50 tons usually falls within the range where electric controls afford optimum economy. Central systems with several zones, from roughly 30 tons or over, are usually controlled most effectively by pneumatic equipment. Above 50 tons, the economic advantage is generally with pneumatic systems.

More and more frequently, electric and

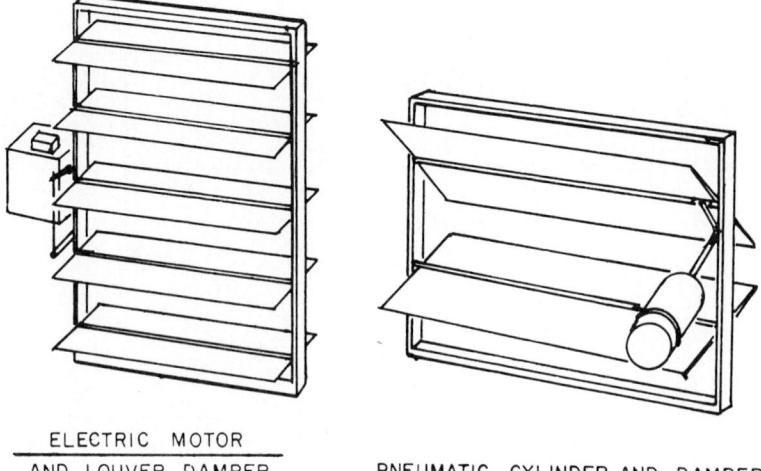

ELECTRIC MOTOR AND LOUVER DAMPER

PNEUMATIC CYLINDER AND DAMPER

Fig. 60. Motor-operated dampers

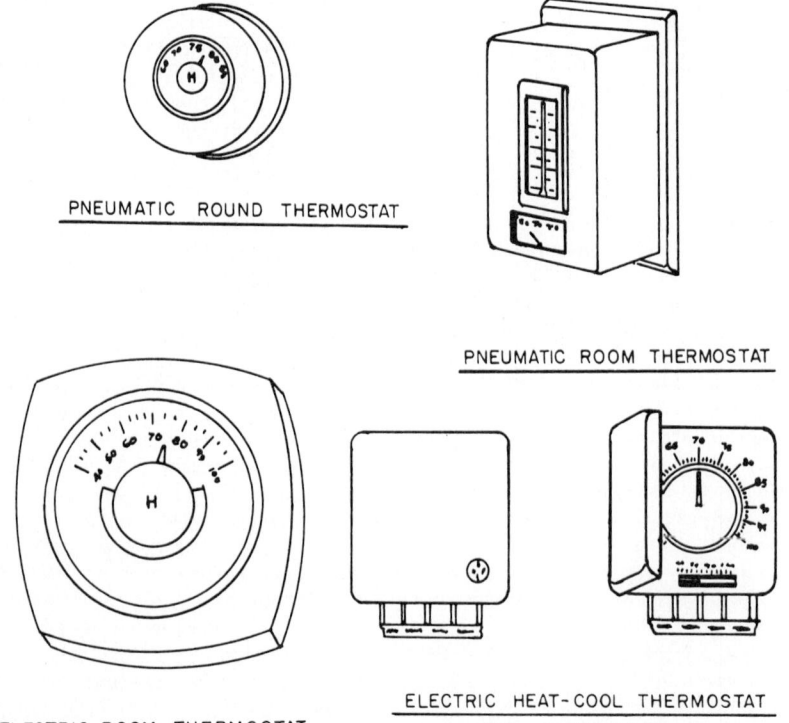

PNEUMATIC ROUND THERMOSTAT

PNEUMATIC ROOM THERMOSTAT

ELECTRIC ROOM THERMOSTAT

ELECTRIC HEAT-COOL THERMOSTAT

FAN CONTROLLER

Fig. 61. Thermostats

electronic devices are integrated with pneumatic systems. However, if the system has a central air compressor and runs of pneumatic (air) tubing, it is usually classed as pneumatic.

The difference between electric and electronic systems lies in a somewhat esoteric refinement in equipment. In an electric control system, the thermostat sends its signal directly to the damper or valve motor. In an electronic control system, the thermostat sends a minute signal to an electronic relay, where the signal is measured and amplified. The relay in turn effects the control over the damper or valve, or over supplementary control circuits. The electronic control equipment may be used to activate any type of electric or pneumatic device, in any of numerous modes or cycles of operation. Electronic controls are more economical when there are long control runs with local pneumatic controls at the terminal points.

REMOTE MOTOR CONTROLS

In a large plant or office bulding, centralized starting and stopping of small- and medium-sized motors for the air-conditioning equipment have distinct advantages. This applies to motors up to approximately 50 to 75 hp. Larger motors are preferably started locally, with the motor in full sight of the operator. It is now possible to have remote starting and stopping of electric motors without interconnecting control wiring. This system transmits a high-frequency signal through the house wiring from a central control panel. At some remote point, a crystal receiver acts as a relay to actuate a motor control circuit.

REMOTE READING GAGES

Electrically operated remote-reading temperature devices now offer the additional refinement of remote reset or remote adjustment of temperatures.

Plasticized or semirigid polyvinyl chloride or polyethylene tubing can now be used for pneumatic control piping, instead of steel or copper tubing. The plastic tubing is installed in multiple, with many color-keyed tubes grouped together inside a single protective jacket to protect against rodents.

PREWIRED PACKAGED CONTROL ASSEMBLIES

Complete preengineered control assemblies applied to small low-pressure steam

boilers and small air-conditioning plants are now generally available. The only wiring required in the field is that between the terminal strip and the actuating and operating devices.

Location of thermostats

The thermostat must be located where it can sense the needs of the space to be controlled. Care must be taken in locating the thermostat so that it is not exposed to conditions which are not representative of the space, such as direct sunlight or proximity to a heating or cooling unit.

If, for esthetic reasons, concealment of the thermostat is necessary, consider the following possibilities:

1. Eliminate the thermostat from the room by locating it in the return duct.

2. Install the thermostat in a recess behind a flush decorative wall plate, which permits convection of room air over the thermostat.

3. Aspirate room air with a small fan through a sampling tube which permits the thermostat to be located remotely, in a closet, behind a coat rack, or in any convenient location.

4. Use an electric-resistance-type thermostat which consists of wire electrically sensitive to changes in air temperature. The wire may be wrapped inconspicuously around a picture, sculpture, molding, chandelier, etc. Positive aspiration is essential.

CONTROL CENTERS

A touch of glamor as well as increased utility for heating and air conditioning resulted from the development of data-control centers, where over-all control readings can be taken and adjustments made in the settings of operating devices, thermostats, etc., located at remote points in the building (Fig. 62). Centralized indication and/or reset is available in many forms for almost every job. Newer energy management control systems are often modular and may contain typewriter control consoles, cathode-ray-tube screens, teletypewriters, etc. Such systems may also control fire and security systems.

CHECKLIST FOR PRELIMINARY HVAC PLANNING

1. Plot plan, including utility survey
2. Local code requirements for heating, ventilating, and air-conditioning requirements; addresses where codes can be obtained
3. Availability and rates of oil, gas, coal,

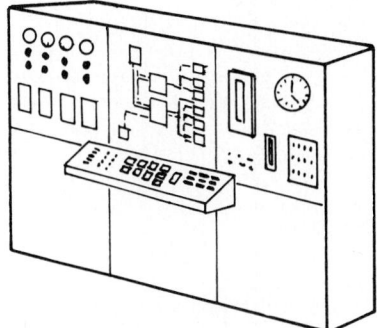

Fig. 62. Data-control center

Typical supervisory data center with visual portrayal of system selected for observation shown on screen. Approximate size of unit shown is 8 ft long by 6 ft 4 in. high by 26 in. wide with desk extending out an additional 10 in.

electricity, steam, hot water, river or well water, etc., for heating or air-conditioning requirements; addresses of utility and fuel companies

4. Orientation of building to true North
5. Necessity for heating plant and types considered
6. Heating, ventilating, and air-conditioning requirements for the various areas of the proposed building
7. Special heating, ventilating, and air-conditioning requirements
8. Hours of occupancy and usage of the various portions of the building
9. Location and sizes of boiler room and chimney, refrigeration plant, and other mechanical equipment rooms; determination of whether equipment should be located in roof penthouse or basement or elsewhere
10. Perimeter construction details and structural scheme for building, including insulation.
11. Adequacy of space above hung ceiling, including allowances for other trades
12. Location and sizes of duct and pipe shafts
13. Location and sizes of outside air-intake and exhaust-air louvers
14. Manner in which equipment can be brought into or taken from the mechanical equipment rooms
15. Snow melting requirements; details of construction to be thoroughly analyzed and coordinated
16. Location of cooling tower, if required
17. Requirements for incinerators and waste removal
18. Requirements for kitchen-range hood exhaust, laboratory hoods, etc.

By ALFRED GREENBERG, *P.E., Environmental and Energy Consultant*

BUILDING TYPES

To understand properly how a specific building will function it is necessary to know all the activities that will occur and to develop load or use versus time profiles to determine what per cent of full usage is occurring at any given time. If this is done sufficiently accurately for all energy using equipment, it will be possible to establish accurate energy utilization profiles which can be used for closely monitoring the building's energy usage and improving its energy utilization characteristics. Typical profiles for some energy using functions in a number of building types are included here as a guide for better understanding of when energy is used and how much.

OCCUPANCY

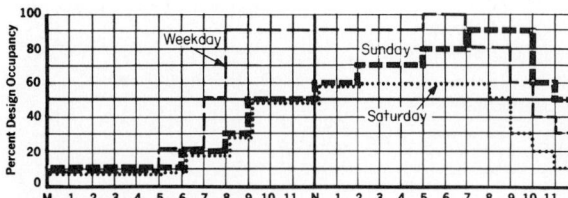

Fig. 63. Airlines terminal—weekday

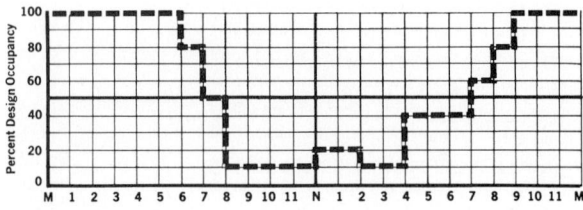

Fig. 68. Dormitory

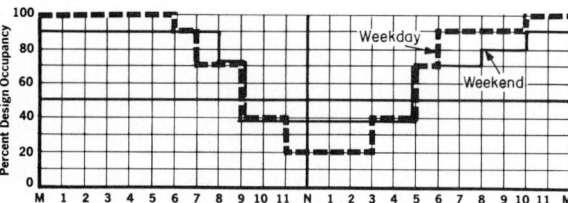

Fig. 64. Apartment house

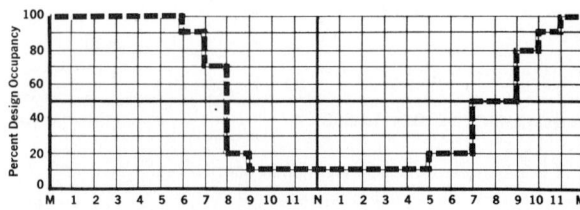

Fig. 69. Hotel/motel guest rooms
(Includes allowance for normal per cent occupancies)

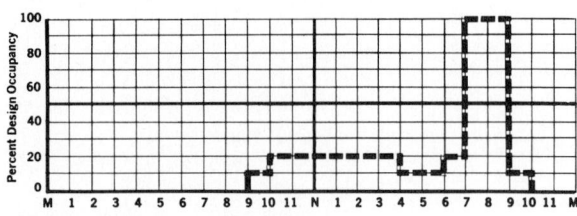

Fig. 65 Automobile and equipment sales

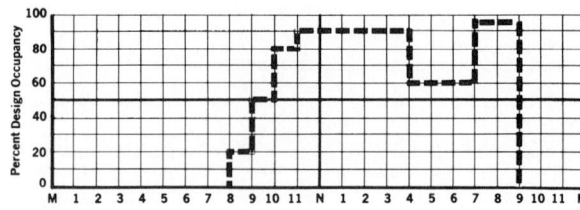

Fig. 70. Library or museum

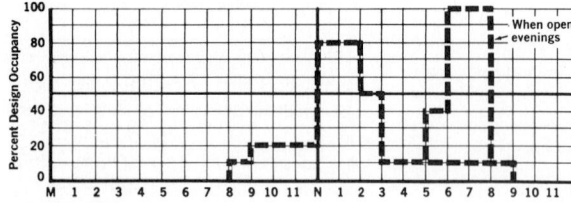

Fig. 66. Bank

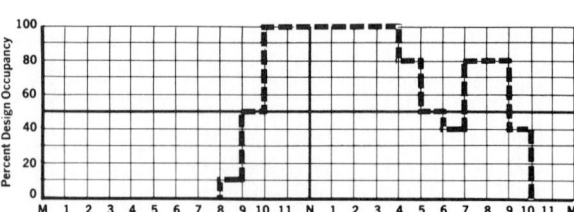

Fig. 71. Medical center/professional building

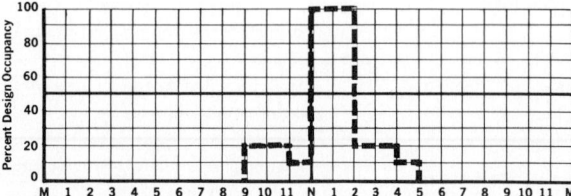

Fig. 67. Cafeteria

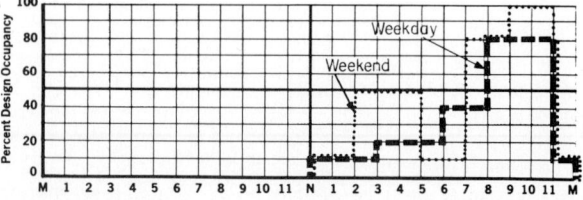

Fig. 72. Movie theater

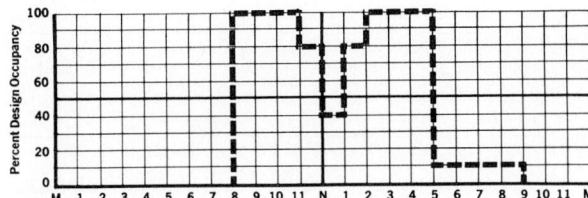

Fig. 73. Office building

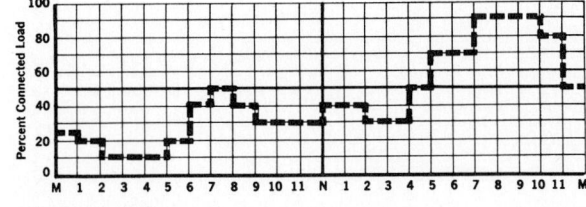

Fig. 79. Dormitory

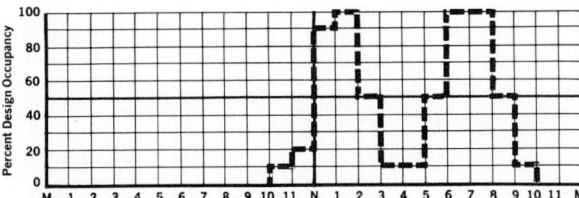

Fig. 74. Restaurant

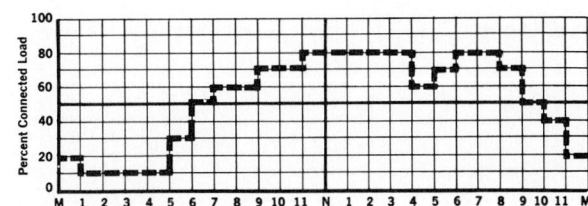

Fig. 80. Hospital

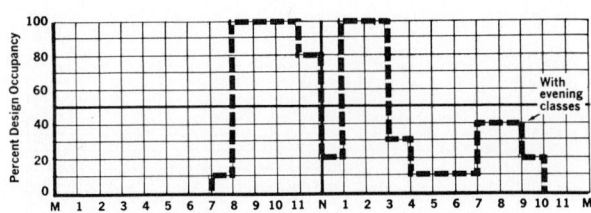

Fig. 75. School/classrooms

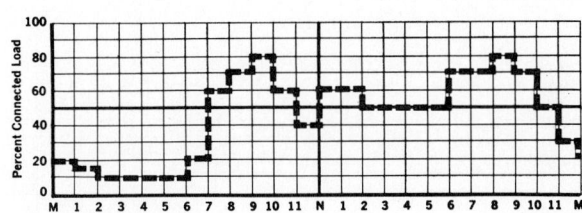

Fig. 81. Hotel/motel

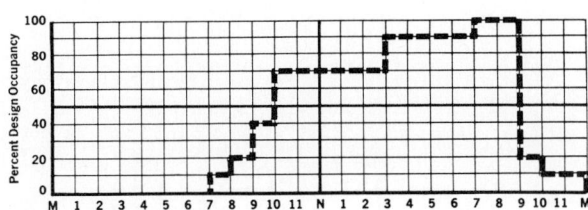

Fig. 76. Shopping center

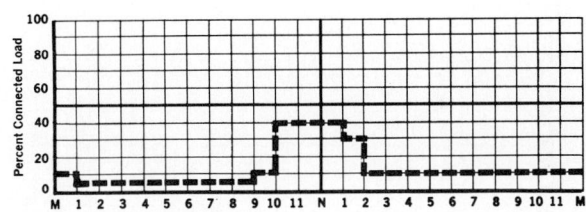

Fig. 82. Movie theater

LIGHTING

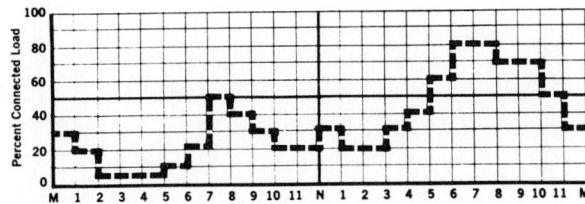

Fig. 77. Apartment house

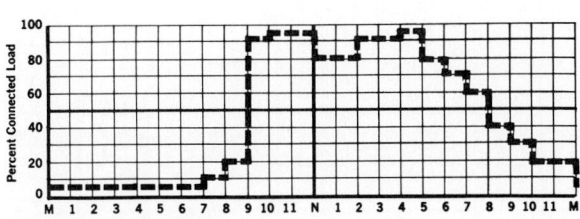

Fig. 83. Office building

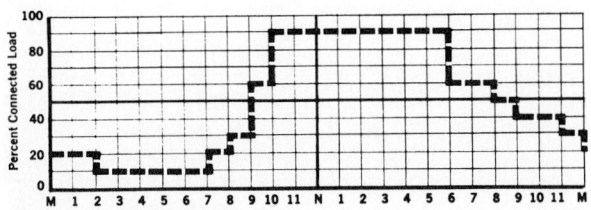

Fig. 78. Department store

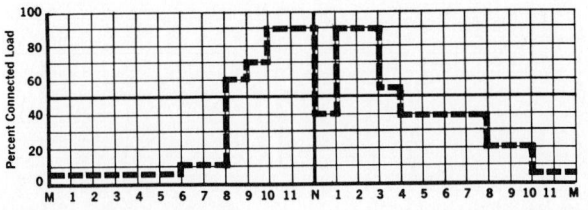

Fig. 84. Elementary school

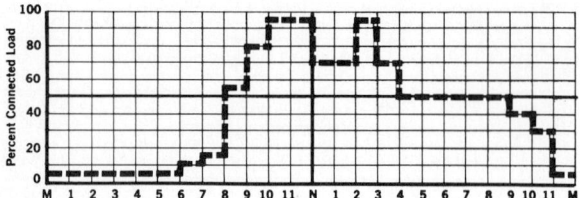

Fig. 85.   High school

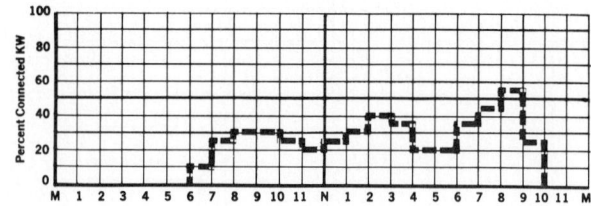

Fig. 91.   Medical center/professional building

ELEVATORS

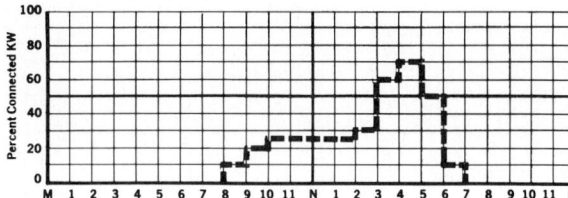

Fig. 86.   Apartment house

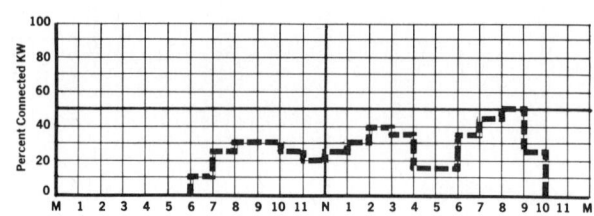

Fig. 92.   Nursing home

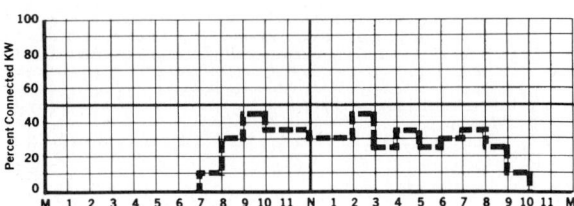

Fig. 87.   Department store

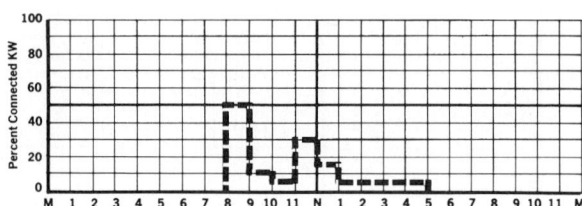

Fig. 93.   Office building

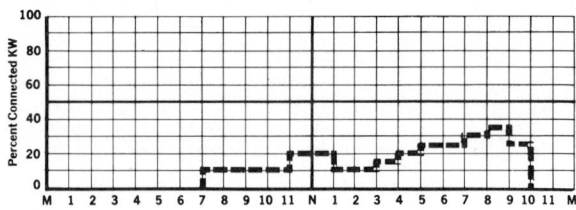

Fig. 88.   Dormitory

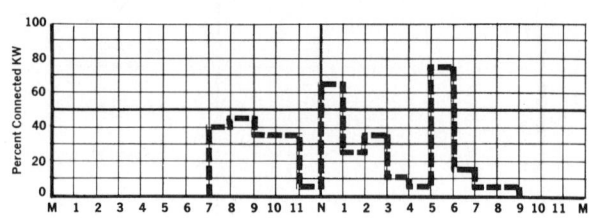

Fig. 94.   School

HOT WATER

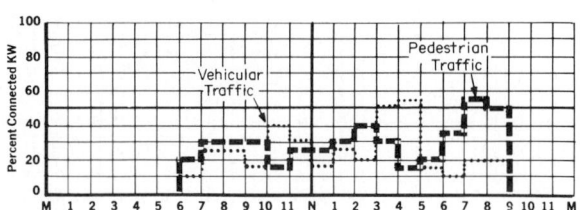

Fig. 89.   Hospital

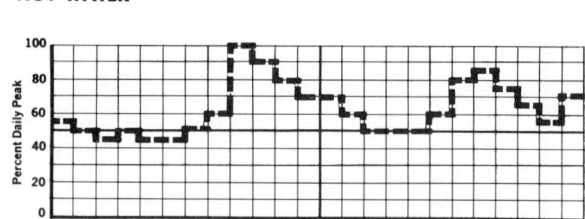

Fig. 95.   Apartments—Daily net peak of 2000 Btuh/apt.

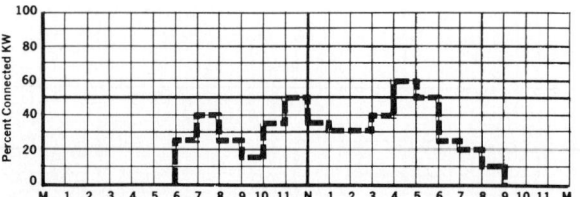

Fig. 90.   Hotel/motel

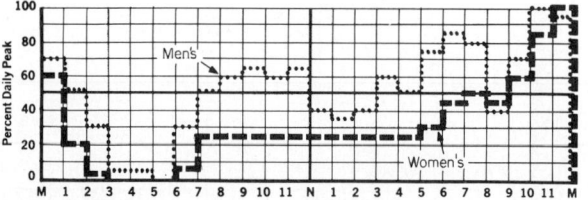

Fig. 96.   Dormitories—Daily net peak Btuh/student (2700 for women 1200 for men)

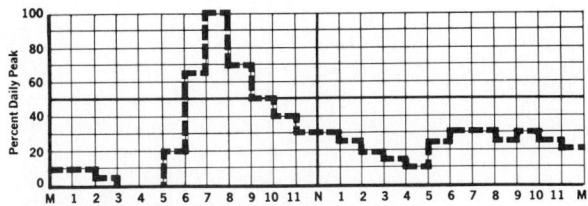

Fig. 97. Hotel/motel guest rooms

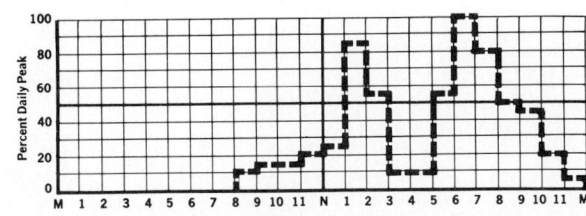

Fig. 101. Restaurants and cafeterias—Daily net peak of 850 Btuh/avg. meal

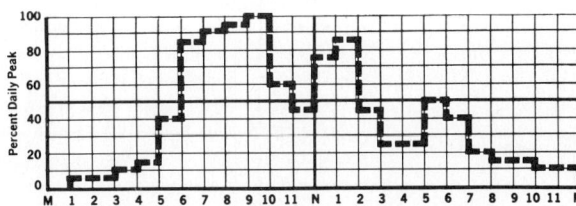

Fig. 98. Nursing home—Daily net peak of 1350 Btuh/resident

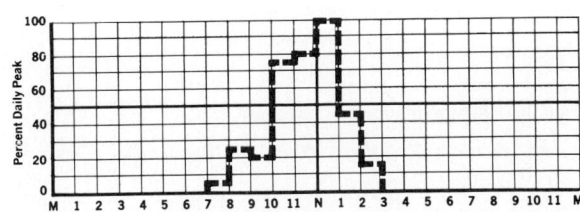

Fig. 102. School classroom areas—Daily net peak of 150 Btuh/student

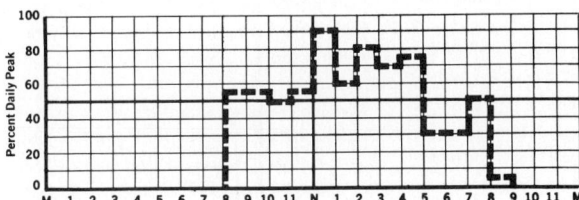

Fig. 99. Office building—Daily net peak of 100 Btuh/person

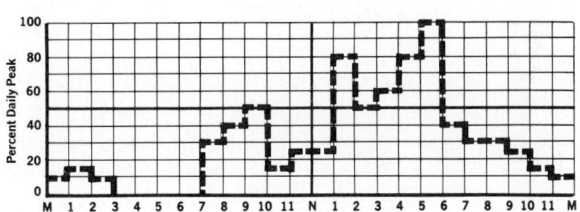

Fig. 103. School gymnasium and locker areas—Daily net peak of 160 Btuh/student

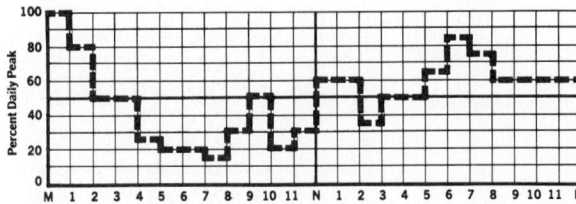

Fig. 100. Fast food restaurant—Daily net peak of 270 Btuh/avg. meals/day

19. Location of fuel-oil tanks or coal bins, and recommended size of same, depending upon availability of fuel

20. Operating weight of all major pieces of equipment

21. Sound and vibration isolation criteria

22. Pollution criteria

APARTMENT BUILDINGS

Air conditioning in apartment houses has the following characteristics:

1. 7-days-per-week, 24-hours-per-day requirements.

2. Low loads due to people and lights.

3. Heavy appliance load in kitchen all day.

4. Nonoccupancy of bedrooms during day except for preschool children, children using rooms as playrooms, sick and old people, etc.

5. Possible heavy people load in dining and living rooms during the day.

6. Interior kitchens and toilets must have exhaust ventilation. Exterior kitchens should also have exhaust ventilation.

7. Occasional heavy concentrated loads due to parties or meetings indicate the desirability of providing large amounts of outside air to eliminate odors with means of rapidly exhausting this vitiated air.

The above indicates a variable and shifting load that would require a complex system to maintain accurate conditions at all times in each room. Few systems will accomplish all the above results.

General practice today in non-air-conditioned buildings is to provide central-heating facilities serving all apartments. This is usually provided by gas, oil, or coal-fired boilers. Most of the taller existing buildings use a steam-distribution system to convectors. The newer ones have pumped hot water heating. Garden-type apartments and smaller tenements usually have hot-water systems.

Most new apartment houses built with air conditioning include through-the-wall self-contained units or sleeves for tenant-furnished units, sometimes with an integral heating coil for winter heating. The popularity of this system is due to its low first cost. Maintenance and operating costs are generally higher than for a central system. This type of system is usually the noisiest and produces the least uniform environmental conditions. One advantage it

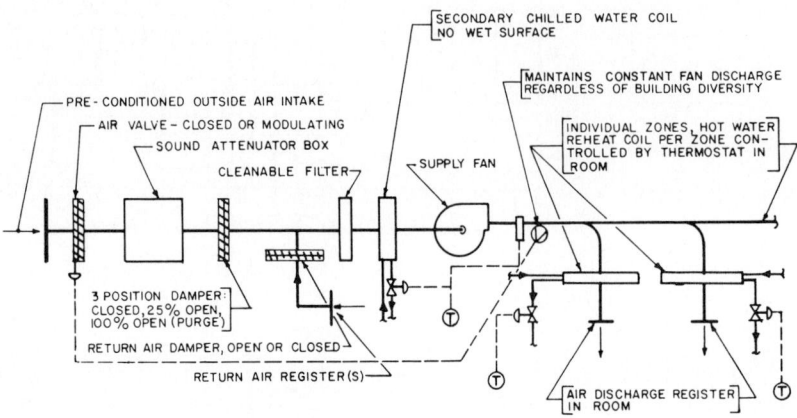

Fig. 104. Apartment air-conditioning unit

* Variable air volume dampers and controls may be substituted for the reheat coil system.

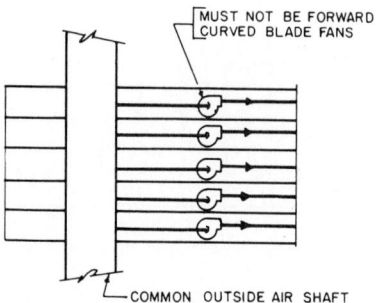

Fig. 105. Outside air from central shaft. Similar for exhaust air system central shaft.

does have is that many units include an exhaust fan setting for purging the room of odors and smoke. A central condenser water unitary-type system is sometimes used to eliminate or reduce the size of the wall air conditioning sleeve.

Of the central air-conditioning systems, the dual-duct and the 3 and 4-pipe induction systems have the potential of providing the most satisfactory results but they will use more energy annually. The ductwork required for the first takes up more space than any of the other systems, and it is the most expensive to install. With this system, the air is usually fed from the ceilings, or under the windows.

Induction systems, which use a combination of air and water to furnish both cooling and heating, have been used for some central air-conditioning systems for apartment house application. Next to the dual-duct system, induction systems require the most space and are the most costly to install. They furnish a high degree of tempera-

ture and humidity control, are quiet, and therefore are used in some deluxe applications. The 3- or 4-pipe system furnishes a more accurate degree of control, greater economy of operation, and elimination of changeover temperature problems.

Through-the-wall fan-coil units with perimeter vertical-pipe distribution are commonly used. This system is less costly than the induction system and furnishes a higher degree of control than is available with most self-contained units. Fan-coil units are also generally quieter than self-contained units but also provide poor air filtering efficiency and humidification control. In most cases, fan-coil motors are connected to the apartment's electric meter, if the apartment is separately metered.

All piping and ductwork is generally run vertically along the perimeter of the building so as not to cut down on interior closet and room space. Horizontal ductwork or piping, except over corridor ceilings, is generally avoided in apartment buildings.

One of the biggest drawbacks of all perimeter air-conditioning systems is that the air flow conflicts with window drapes and curtains and causes undesirable movement; this may affect the air distribution in an adverse manner. Also, the purging of odorous and smoky air is not possible in most cases.

As apartment buildings get taller, above 20 stories, through-the-wall units become increasingly more risky due to the effects of wind, rain, and stack effect. Because of this, through-the-wall units are not recommended for apartment houses over 20 stories high.

Stack effect also manifests itself in the interior toilet and corridor ducts of tall buildings. It is for this reason that the

New York City Code requires that no toilet exhaust duct be over 250 ft from the first to the last outlet. This increases the duct-shaft requirements but minimizes the possibility of drafts. The same criteria should apply to supply duct systems.

For the ultimate in flexibility and control of internal environment, as well as freedom from curtain rustle, a perimeter radiation system plus a central air-handling system for each apartment is required (Fig. 109). The proportion of outside air can be varied from 0 to 100 per cent and may come from exterior wall louvers or a central outside air shaft (Fig. 105). For tall buildings, care must be taken to guard against stack effect. Chilled water is furnished from a central system. The ductwork should be zoned with central hot-water or electric reheat coils or dampers to maintain temperatures or air flow as desired. Return ductwork to the unit is usually required.

This system requires a separate mechanical equipment room in the apartment, or the equipment may be placed in a furred soffit or above a hung ceiling over a corridor or closet. Access to the unit should be through the service corridor or entrance. This system is identical to that which might be installed in a deluxe single-family residence.

Interior corridors and lobbies must have ventilation, preferably designed so as not to draw apartment odors into the corridors.

In individual apartment buildings, heating and air-conditioning equipment is generally located in the basement with the cooling tower on the roof. Special care must be taken to prevent objectionable noise transmission of equipment to the apartments. In multiple-building projects, consideration should be given to a centralized air-conditioning and heating system for all the buildings in the project.

As a guide for establishing the shaft-space requirements for interior toilet and kitchen exhaust-duct systems, the following guidelines are offered:

1. Figure 50 cfm of exhaust air per toilet.
2. Figure 150 cfm of exhaust air per kitchen.
3. Calculate duct sizes using Figures 24 and 25, with a friction loss and air velocity not to exceed 0.08 in. and 1,500 fpm respectively.
4. Do not use masonry shafts for air flow. The walls crack with time and control of air flow becomes practically impossible. Use sheet-metal ducts and make the shafts a couple of inches larger to allow for proper duct construction and assure the proper interior duct area for the air quantity calculated.
5. If duct boots are used in order to eliminate the need for fire dampers, make sure the ducts are designed to assure adequate

free area to prevent excessive air velocities and static pressures.

6. Among the largest energy consumers are the interior kitchen and toilet exhaust fans which run 16–24 hours a day, often because of code requirements. The only times these fans really have to be on are when the toilets and kitchens are being used in a manner requiring exhaust ventilation. The amount of ventilation required at any time is a function of the number of rooms being used at that time. Therefore kitchen and toilet exhaust systems requiring mechanical ventilation should be designed so that only those rooms in use are exhausted and the fan capacities should match only the exhaust requirements at any given time. In effect, the fans or systems are a variable air volume system. There are a number of ways for achieving these results, ranging from individual exhaust fans in each kitchen and toilet actuated by local switches and discharging into common kitchen or toilet vent shafts, to a central pressure-controlled exhaust fan with individual space-actuated dampers when the rooms are in use. The prime energy wasted is not from motor operation but from the removal of heated air and the increase in infiltrated air which must be heated.

When laying out kitchen equipment, the refrigerators should be located remotely from ovens, ranges and windows to minimize their energy consumption and improve operation.

HOTELS AND MOTELS

Each guest room must have the ability to provide its own thermal environment as dictated by the occupant at all times. This limits the type of system to the following:

- Self-contained air cooling or heat pump units
- Single-duct, reheat, variable air volume, or recool-coil per room
- Dual-duct, VAV
- Fan-coil units
- Induction system

The first usually has the lowest initial cost and space requirements, but a separate heating system may be required for air cooling units.

The single-duct reheat-coil system and the dual-duct system are rarely used because of their high cost and large space requirements.

The dual-duct and VAV systems may be used in the dining- and meeting-room areas of hotels where the size of rooms is flexible and the load is highly variable.

The fan-coil-unit system is most commonly used in motels and hotels because it requires the least amount of additional equipment and is the least costly to install next to packaged window units. A 3 or 4-pipe fan-coil system should produce even greater comfort. Fan-coil units have a high ventilation rate for rapidly heating or cooling the room. The unit can be shut off when the room is not occupied. Fan-coil units are fairly quiet in operation and produce reasonably good environmental conditions.

Some new hotels use the induction system; motels can seldom justify the use of this system because of the comparatively small number of rooms served. This system furnishes a closer degree of control than fan-coil units, is slightly quieter, and produces better results in intermediate seasons when the outdoor temperature is between 40 and 50°F.

In tropical climates where humidity control and mildew are serious problems, a single duct system using a recool coil for each room may be economical and effective.

Whichever type of air-conditioning system is used, a source of hot water or steam must be available for heating the building. In motels, it is generally desirable to place the refrigeration and boiler units in a central location to minimize the piping. In milder climates, the central heating plant may be replaced by small gas-fired or electric heaters in each room.

Hotels usually locate the refrigeration and boiler plants in the basement, with some of the air-handling equipment and the cooling tower on the roof. In motels the cooling tower is usually located on the ground far enough away from the rooms so as not to be heard.

In both motels and hotels, the management office area and lobby are generally air conditioned. In most cases, a separate system is used for this area.

OFFICE BUILDINGS

Office buildings can vary from a structure no larger than a single-family residence to huge skyscrapers. This discussion will be limited to the multistory structures since they involve certain problems which are not present in low buildings.

The type of occupancy may have an important bearing on the type of air-distribution system to be used. If there is one owner or lessee for the entire building, his operations may be clearly enough defined so that a high degree of flexibility is not required. Where different tenants may occupy different floors or even parts of the same floor, the degree of complexity increases. This problem is more acute where tenants may have seasonal and varying overtime schedules.

Entrances and lobbies, stores, restaurants, club facilities, observation decks, etc., should generally be treated as separate entities with their own systems. Where a tenant has a large enough organization to warrant a separate medical department, this may be complex enough to be treated as a small hospital, with separate systems and controls.

One of the largest sources of concentrated heat load in an office area is the computing and tabulating machinery which is increasingly used in office operations. As accurate an appraisal as possible should be attempted of the amount, size, and type of computer equipment anticipated for the life of the building in order to size the refrigeration and air-handling equipment and to make provision for the future installation of added equipment.

Most new office buildings use some form of combination heating and cooling unit for the perimeter of the building. Most have combined air and water induction units or fan-coil units; but some use all-air perimeter induction units, and others use wall-type packaged air conditioners with integral heating coils. Ductwork and piping as required for any of these systems may be run either vertically at the perimeter of the building or vertically in the interior of the building with horizontal distribution at the ceiling for each floor. The latter is usually more costly, but the choice is dependent upon the architectural design of the building. The coordination and detailing of the relationship between perimeter unit location, perimeter wall glass, spandrel beams, piping, and ductwork are often critical and should be carefully examined in the early design stages to establish the most feasible and economical layout.

Interior spaces 15–20 feet from exterior glazed walls seldom need heating since they have continuous light and people heat load and possibly heat-producing equipment, too. Since their heat load is relatively constant, a conventional single-duct, low-velocity system, zoned to meet special conditions such as conference rooms, private interior offices, etc., is generally satisfactory. Where maximum flexibility or comfort is required for interior areas, such as on executive floors or where there may be multiple tenants on the floor, a dual-duct system is desirable. A common compromise is to provide both hot and cold ducts in the shafts, thus making it possible to provide either single- or dual-duct distribution systems on any floor (Fig. 106). If space conditions are very tight, the air can be run at high velocities and reduced near the outlets by means of air-reducing valves. The only justification for resorting to high-velocity air distribution is lack of

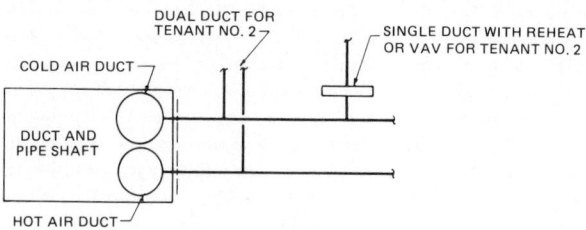

Fig. 106. Dual-duct risers provide flexibility in distribution systems

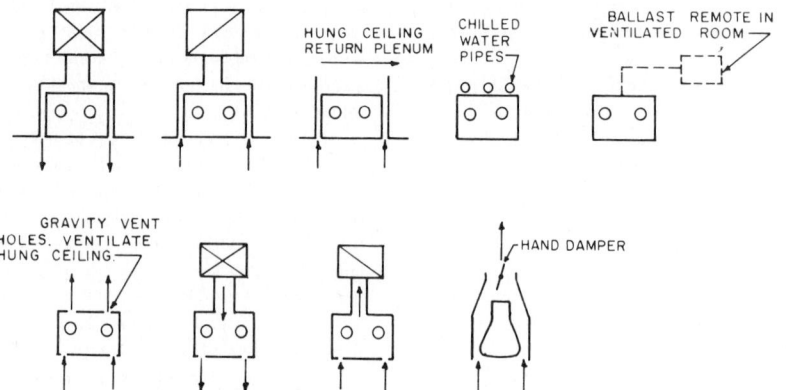

Fig. 107. Methods of drawing off heat from lighting fixtures

space, since first cost and operating cost are almost always greater.

The total mechanical space requirements for heating and air-conditioning equipment for office buildings range from 5 to 10 per cent of the gross area. The clear height required for fan rooms varies from about 13 to 18 ft, depending upon the complexity of the distribution system and the equipment involved. On typical office floors, the perimeter units take up 1 to 3 per cent of the gross floor area, and interior shafts require about 2 per cent more. Therefore, on each floor, ducts, pipes, and equipment require 3 to 5 per cent of the gross floor area. Electrical and plumbing space requirements per floor average up to 1 per cent of gross area.

The shaft space requirements vary, depending upon the number of fan rooms provided. One mechanical equipment room (MER) usually furnishes the air requirements for from eight to twenty floors, with about twelve being the average. The more floors served, the larger the duct shafts and the equipment in the MER's, with resultant higher fan room heights, greater equipment weight, and higher operating costs

due to increased motor horsepower. If fewer floors are served by a mechanical equipment room, then more are required to serve the building. This allows equipment to be smaller and lighter, and mechanical equipment rooms can often be the same height as typical floors. However, initial installation costs will probably be higher. In any case, mechanical equipment rooms must be thermally and acoustically isolated from office floors above or below them.

Cooling towers are the largest single piece of equipment required for the air-conditioning systems. Roughly speaking, the cooling tower requires about 1 sq ft of roof area per 400 sq ft of total building area, and is from 13 to 40 ft high. The building structure must be capable of carrying the cooling tower plus its full load of water (120 to 200 psf) and must also prevent transmission of vibration from the tower to the structure and wind-load stresses.

Where the building contains kitchens, low-temperature chimneys are usually required for range hoods. See Fig. 115. They must go up to the roof of the building, at least 100 ft away from any outside air or cooling tower intakes.

Since the lighting load in an office building makes up a large part of the total heat load (25 to 40 per cent), an effort should be made to withdraw the heat at the source by means of supply or exhaust air or water tubing (Fig. 107). By this means, 30 to 60 per cent of the total heat output of the lights can be withdrawn. To connect a duct to each fixture is expensive, so the hung ceiling is often used as a return air plenum and the air drawn into the space above the hung ceiling around the lights. This must be done carefully, with sufficient duct distribution to assure proper heat removal and return air distribution and noise control.

Areas in office buildings which require special ventilation are elevator machine rooms, electric and telephone closets, electrical switchgear, plumbing rooms, refrigeration rooms, and mechanical equipment rooms. The heat loads in some of these rooms may be so high as to require the installation of air-conditioning units for spot cooling or heat reclamation may be possible for other uses.

DEPARTMENT AND VARIETY STORES

Small stores seldom require more than a packaged air-conditioning unit with no ductwork. Occupancy in the store is for relatively short periods of time, and air distribution, even though uneven, need not be objectionable.

In department stores the diversity of operations is such that zone control becomes a necessity due to the variation in heat loads and customer location. The areas requiring the greatest attention are as follows:

Lunch counter—see the following pages.

Live-pet department—air distribution should be even and draftless especially where birds are concerned. Exhaust is important, too.

Lighting display counter—this area generally develops a large amount of heat which must be drawn off at the source. Air should be transferred from other areas, where possible, in order to cut down on the air-conditioning load.

Meat, vegetable, and fish counters should have local exhaust to prevent the spread of odors. The same is true for baked goods and candy counters, except that some odor carryover may be desirable to attract customers.

The main floor in multistory stores generally has a higher population density than the other floors. This is usually about 50 sq ft per person, with half as many people on the other floors.

In clothing and carpeting areas it may

be desirable to provide humidity control to minimize the effects of static electricity.

Other areas that might require special consideration are beauty parlors and tailor-shop areas. These areas have high-heat-producing equipment which must be properly exhausted. In addition, beauty parlors have odors that should be eliminated.

Dressing-room areas should have draftless air distribution. The store should be kept slightly pressurized to prevent outside air from coming in through the entrances. If possible, the food areas should be kept at a slightly negative air pressure.

In order to display their wares to advantage, department and variety stores generally have a high lighting intensity concentrated around display groupings. Since displays are frequently changed and moved, and the lighting with it, it is desirable to set up the air-distribution system on a modular basis. This is seldom done because of the added ductwork expense

and return air is generally taken back at only two or three points on a floor. This increases the cost of system operation since the conditioned air has to enter the space at a lower temperature than would be required if the lighting heat were drawn off directly. Commonly used systems of air distribution are shown in Fig. 108.

Perimeter solar load is seldom an important factor in this type of building because most of the wall space is used for storage. Where show windows are used, they must be properly ventilated to prevent heat buildup. Where the store is spread out over a large area, the roof heat load may become an appreciable factor. Several inches of roof insulation or roof sprays will materially reduce this load.

Care should be taken in designing the entrances and exits in order not to create drafts at the sales areas nearby. Revolving doors and/or vestibules will minimize this problem. Consideration should be given to

the use of an air curtain as an entrance and exit. If properly designed, it can keep outside and inside conditions separate and can prevent the wind from breaking through (Fig. 109).

In existing stores it is often convenient to put in a number of large self-contained packaged units and distribute the ductwork as required (Fig. 110). This involves a minimum of capital expenditure and usually space can be allocated without too much difficulty. Outside air must be furnished to the space, so some of the units are generally placed against exterior walls where openings can be cut through. A cooling tower will most likely be required, and provision must be made for running the condenser water piping to the tower. This type of system has a high degree of flexibility but will probably require higher maintenance costs than a central plant. These units can be obtained in sizes up to 50 to 60 tons each.

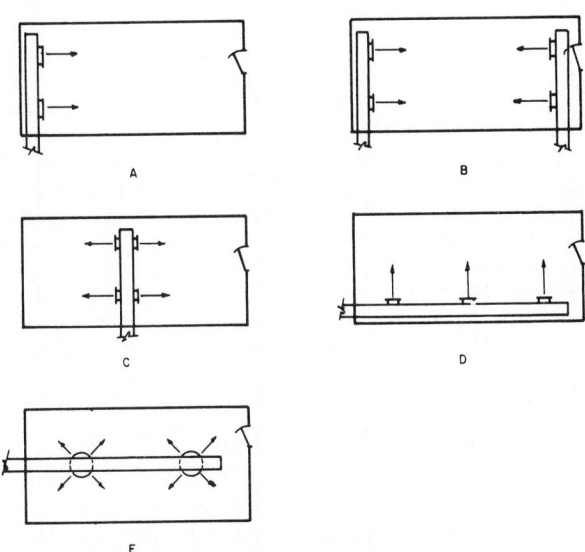

Fig. 108. Air distribution system for stores

A. *High outlet velocity; satisfactory for certain applications, if properly designed. Excessive air motion and drafts may result if outlets are too low or throw is too long.*
B. *Moderate air movement; air from outlets should not collide so as to cause down drafts in the center.*
C. *Good air movement; no collision of air streams; good results.*
D. *Good air movement; blow toward exposed wall; good results.*
E. *Generally gives best results, especially for low ceiling heights.*

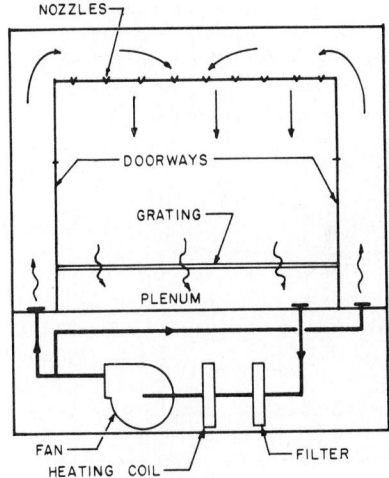

Fig. 109. Air curtain doorway

Nozzles should be adjustable.

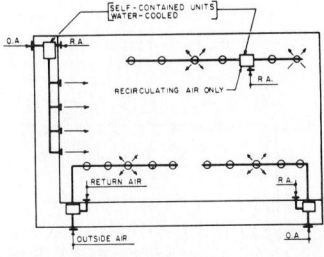

Fig. 110. Air conditioning for an existing store, using self-contained units with water-cooled condensers and central cooling tower.

RESTAURANTS, CAFETERIAS, LUNCHEONETTES, BARS, AND NIGHT CLUBS

Restaurant occupancy may vary from zero to maximum within less than one hour, and this may happen two or three times a day. This results in a great fluctuation in heating and cooling demands. Some form of modulating control is therefore desirable.

Heating and air-conditioning systems should be designed so that all areas, including private rooms, semiprivate accommodations such as booths or alcoves, table locations along windows, behind interior columns, and in general open areas, are equally comfortable. "Cold pockets" or drafts could result in loss of revenue. In restaurants the air conditioning should be neither felt nor heard (Fig. 111).

Cafeterias and luncheonettes generally have some or all of the food preparation in the same room as the diners. These eating places are usually noisier than restaurants, so noise from the air-conditioning equipment is not as critical a factor. Since the diners do not remain as long, they seldom require the degree of comfort that would be mandatory in restaurants. The air-distribution system must be designed so that the spread of food smells from the serving counters to the areas where patrons are eating is minimized (Fig. 112). This will

usually necessitate heavy exhaust-air requirements at the serving counters with the air coming from the eating areas. Exhaust air must also remove the heat from hot trays, coffee urns, ovens, etc., in order to minimize discomfort to patrons and employees. These factors will often create greater air-conditioning loads for cafeterias and luncheonettes than for restaurants, with correspondingly greater air quantities required in the eating areas.

Bars serving alcoholic beverages produce pungent vapors that must be drawn off in order not to build up strong odors. Therefore, the area of the bar should have a positive exhaust.

Night clubs where the patrons dine and dance require considerably greater air quantity and larger air-conditioning units than those which have only a floor show. Night clubs and bars generally have heavier smoking loads than other types of dining establishments, and therefore exhaust and outside air requirements are greater. Hence, special care must be taken with the air distribution to prevent discomfort to patrons from drafts.

In any type of dining establishment, the entrances and exits must be completely shielded from the diners so that they are not seated near drafts. Vestibules provide a measure of protection, but in practice both vestibule doors are often open simultaneously. To offset this disadvantage, re-

volving doors may be used and local means may be provided for heating or cooling the inflowing air.

Employee comfort is difficult to maintain at a uniform level, partly because of the difference in temperature between kitchen and dining room, partly because employees are constantly in motion while patrons are seated. However, maintenance of satisfactory temperature and atmospheric conditions for customers goes far toward alleviating employee discomfort.

The location of outside air-intake and kitchen exhaust louvers must be such that exhaust air is not drawn back into the system, nor should the exhaust air cause discomfort to outside passers-by. Also, louvers to kitchen must be designed so that kitchen noise is not heard in the eating areas.

Private dining rooms present such varied load conditions that individual control for each unit is generally a necessity. Depending upon the size of the areas to be partitioned, it may be expedient to use a dual-duct, single-duct reheat, variable air volume system (VAV), for a separate air-conditioning unit for each area (Fig. 113).

The kitchen has the greatest concentration of heat load and odors, and ventilation is the chief means of removing them. The most common method in small restaurants is the ordinary exhaust fan. Another method, applicable to larger establishments, employs a simple kitchen vent and requires the building up of a positive air pressure within dining areas. Under these conditions air flow is always from the dining room to the kitchen in a practically continuous current which carries smoke and odors along with it. In designing a system of this kind it is necessary to provide slightly more exhaust capacity than the supply of recirculated and fresh air. It is of course imperative than no air exhausted from kitchens, locker rooms, toilets, etc., be recirculated. Supplementary ventilation air may be required for the kitchen. Systems

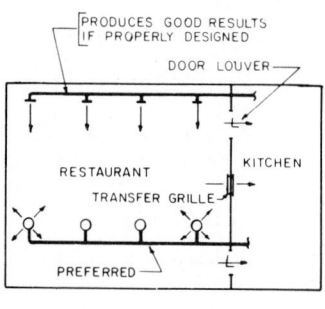

Fig. 111. Air-distribution system for restaurant

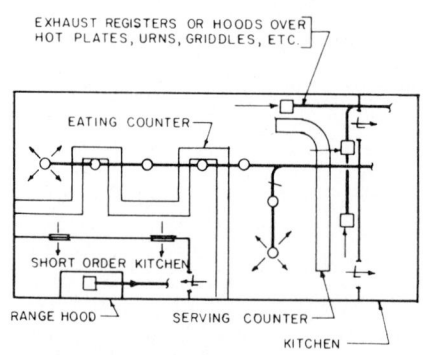

Fig. 112. Air-distribution systems for luncheonette and cafeteria

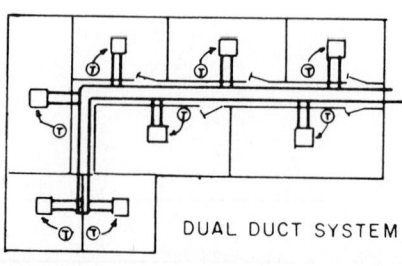

DUAL DUCT SYSTEM

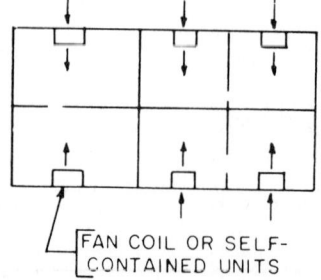

FAN COIL OR SELF-CONTAINED UNITS

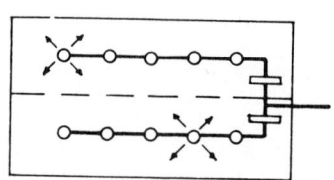

SINGLE DUCT SYSTEM WITH ZONE REHEAT OR VAV

Fig. 113. Air-conditioning systems for private dining rooms

are available for reclaiming some of the kitchen's heated air.

The air quantity required for kitchen ventilation is a function of the equipment in the kitchen. More efficient hoods (Fig. 114) generally cost more, but the resultant ventilation savings justify the extra cost. The provision of some air cooling for kitchens is becoming more commonly accepted.

Since fires at hoods over ranges are a serious problem, a steam water or CO_2 quenching system should be installed. The range-hood exhaust duct must be considered as a low-temperature chimney which has to go above the roof (Fig. 115).

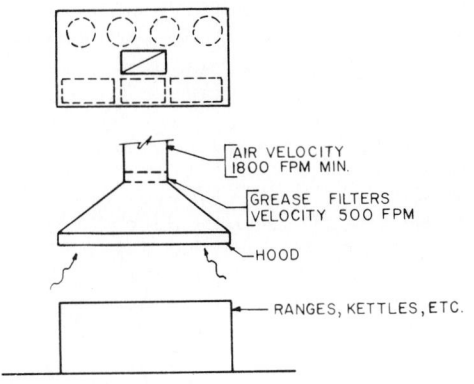

Fig. 114. Range hood

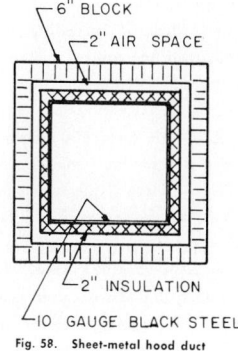

Fig. 58.   Sheet-metal hood duct

Fig. 115.   Sheet-metal hood duct

THEATERS, AUDITORIUMS, SPORTS ARENAS, HOUSES OF WORSHIP

The common denominator of these buildings is that large numbers of people are assembled in an enclosed space for appreciable periods of time. Although the purposes for congregation may differ, many of the problems and solutions are similar.

The primary problem is to furnish sufficient fresh air and to distribute it properly. Second, heating or cooling is required as environmental conditions dictate.

The seating areas' ventilation requirements are usually set by codes. See Table 9. In most cases this will give from five to eight air changes per hour, which is sufficient for good air circulation. The supply air has to be furnished from the ceiling, the side walls, and in some cases from the edges of balconies (Fig. 116). Uniform air distribution is difficult to attain in the center seating areas unless return air inlets are located there. This is usually done by means of mushrooms under the seats. In small balconies, side-wall supply distribution emptying into the central area is satisfactory, but deeper balconies require some ceiling supply air and possibly under-the-seat returns. Air outlet and inlet velocities must be low enough not to be noticeable. Concert halls have the most critical noise requirements, with opera houses and theaters next. Some exhaust air should be taken from the ceiling of the seating area to prevent pockets of hot air which can produce a radiant effect.

Because of the relatively high latent heat load due to the people, the seating area

system should be designed for proper dehumidification as well as humidification control. Thermostat and humidistat location in the seating areas usually is impractical, so they are best located in return air ducts.

The theater stage presents a more complex problem. The lighting load is very heavy, but 40 to 60 per cent of it can be negated by exhausting air around the lights (Fig. 117). Conditioned air should be introduced from the side stage and backstage and returned or exhausted around the lights. The air distribution is complicated by the fact that some pieces of scenery consist of light materials that flutter in the slightest air current. Therefore, low air-movement velocities are required. This demands that the air be distributed over a wide area with many supply and return registers. Special treatment should be provided for the stage manager and the control board area. Proper air distribution and balancing can minimize the billowing of the curtain when down.

The location of the mechanical and electrical equipment rooms can greatly affect the degree of sound attenuation treatment required to isolate the sound from the seating areas. If possible, mechanical equipment rooms should be located in an area which is separated from the main seating or stage area by a buffer such as lobbies, service areas, etc. Generally, at least one mechanical equipment room should be furnished somewhere on the roof to house the toilet, general exhaust, kitchen, and emergency stage exhaust fans. On the stage, cognizance must be taken of local code requirements for emergency exhaust ductwork requirements which are often sizable and should be incorporated in the earliest designs. See also section on "Skylights."

One of the most flexible of all building types is the combination sports arena and civic auditorium. It can be used for events as diverse as ice hockey, political rallies, rodeos, benefit luncheons, boxing and wrestling matches, basketball, etc. With the stage in the center of the arena for most events and with no possibility of

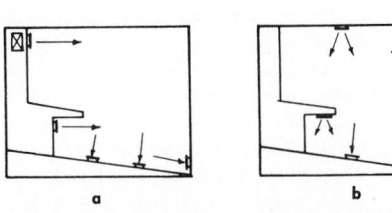
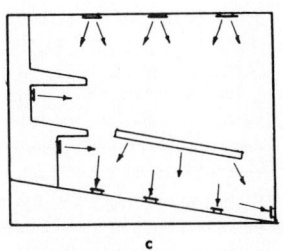

Fig. 116.   Air distribution in typical places of assembly

vertical ductwork, flexibility must be obtained through versatility in the design. Multispeed motors or auxiliary air systems are two common means of providing variation in air quantity for different events. Since all air generally originates from the ceiling, the air must come down at velocities sufficient to reach the arena floor area. Return or exhaust is generally from the lower seating areas, either at the side of the aisles or under the seats. The possibility of odors and smoking is greater than in other buildings of mass occupancy. Therefore, positive measures such as activated charcoal filters or electronic ionizers should be used to dissipate odors, whether gaseous or particulate.

When an ice-skating rink is designed into the structure, the problems of ground water conditions, site drainage, structural foundations, insulation, and waterproofing enter into the picture. Ice-melting pits of sufficient size must be furnished. If the arena is to be air conditioned, the possibility of combining the air-conditioning system with the ice-rink system should be considered. The radiant effect of the ice on

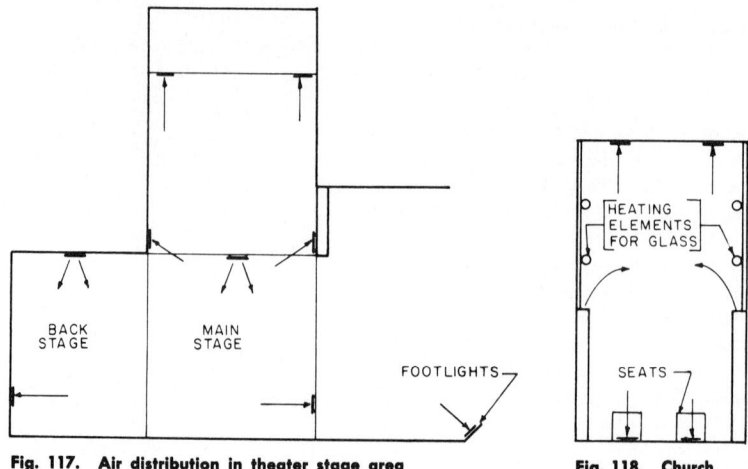

Fig. 117. Air distribution in theater stage area

Fig. 118. Church

Skylight or mechanical exhaust fan in accordance with applicable code requirements.

the people and of the roof heat on the ice must be considered in the design and operation of the system.

For churches where ceilings are often quite high, only the lower 12 to 15 ft need

be fully cooled because this is where the people are. The ceiling temperature may tend to get high and should be exhausted to minimize convective and radiation effects. See Fig. 118.

SCHOOLS

The simplest and usually the cheapest type of school heating and ventilating system consists of perimeter radiation (steam, hot water, or electric) with ventilation coming in through the windows. A mechanical exhaust system, with grilles on the interior or corridor wall, draws the air across the room. Gravity exhaust ventilation systems are not recommended for outside design temperatures below 30°F.

If mechanical exhaust systems are used in conjunction with window supply and the windows are closed, then the air will be drawn from corridors. This may produce sufficiently negative pressures in the building to produce poor operating conditions for hooded equipment, boilers, incinerators, etc. Therefore, rooms for such equipment must have adequate air supplies with airtight doors.

A variation of the above system has mechanical supply ventilation, properly filtered and tempered, admitted through registers on the interior wall or through ceiling diffusers.

The perimeter radiation system need be sized to handle only transmission losses if the room is positively pressurized by exhausting less than the supply air quantity. If mechanical supply air is furnished, gravity exhaust may produce satisfactory results.

The mechanical supply air system may be designed to take care of interior heat losses

and the radiation operated only when the outside temperature becomes low enough to cause window drafts. This combined system is not very satisfactory in operation since classroom heating requirements are satisfied at relatively low outside temperatures due to the heat load of the students and lights. Therefore, proper ventilation is required to remove this internal heat and allow the radiation to perform satisfactorily.

Panel heating is often used for kindergarten classrooms where students spend much time on the floor. Its biggest drawback is the storage effect which prevents it from following changing load conditions quickly enough. This often results in overheating, an effect which is minimized if a ventilation system is used in conjunction with the panel heating system. Floor-heating panels are relatively ineffective in preventing downdrafts from windows, although wall panels located under the windows have produced satisfactory results.

In general, the most satisfactory environmental conditions can be obtained by means of all-air or combination systems. Any of the air-distribution systems discussed earlier in this section may be adapted for schoolroom use, except the induction system which may not furnish sufficient ventilation to meet local code regulations. If air is not supplied from under the windows, then in order to counteract downdrafts, re-

turn grilles should be located on the window sills. If the returns are below the sills, they will lose most of their effectiveness.

In most instances, if a building is summer air conditioned, it may be possible to reduce the ventilation requirements, which may effect an appreciable saving in first costs. In fact, if a school building is designed for air conditioning, it is possible for total owning and operating costs to be less than for a non-air-conditioned building.

One of the most commonly employed all-air systems in use is the forced-warm-air heating system (see section on "Residential Heating and Air Conditioning"). It is essentially a low-velocity, single-duct, zoned system supplying filtered and heated and, if desired, cooled air.

Unit ventilators also find wide application in schools. They furnish individual room control for heating and provide ventilation usually from through-the-wall openings. They can also be adapted for air conditioning with a minimum amount of alteration and addition of equipment. They should be selected for quiet operation. Unit ventilators may be combined with extended air ducts or finned pipe radiation to combat downdrafts in adjacent windows. **Unitary packaged combination heating and cooling units are also widely used.**

LIBRARIES AND MUSEUMS

The primary purpose of libraries and museums is to house objects it is desired to exhibit, store, and preserve. For both types of buildings, rapid changes in temperature and humidity are more harmful than the maintenance of reasonable limits at all times. In general, if the atmospheric environment is kept from 70 to 78°F dry bulb temperature and 40 to 50 per cent relative humidity for most applications, then no harm will be done to the books, works of art, or exhibits. This range of temperature and humidity is the same as required for human comfort, which greatly simplifies the problems of design.

Libraries and museums are difficult to clean, by the very nature of items they contain. Therefore, the efficiency of the air-cleaning apparatus should be at least 85 per cent based on the National Bureau of Standards (NBS) atmospheric air discoloration test (ASHRAE Sta 52–76).

LIBRARIES

There are various types of libraries, but in general they consist of stack areas, working and office areas, reading rooms, rare-book vaults, and small study rooms.

The stack areas (usually interior spaces) have a relatively low lighting intensity and a low ratio of people to floor area, so the air-conditioning load is not heavy. However, sufficient air must be circulated to maintain uniform temperature conditions throughout the stacks. Generally, four to six air changes per hour are required. If the supply and return pattern is as shown in Fig. 119, then the lower limit may apply; otherwise, six air changes should be used. Where the ceiling is used as a return plenum or has return registers, the air circulation at the lower part of the stacks is not as positive. If the book stacks are adjacent to an exterior wall, then a perimeter air-conditioning system should be designed to act as a buffer, in order to maintain constant stack environmental conditions. Do not use air-conditioning systems that contain steam or water piping in areas where leakage can cause damage.

Office areas are treated in the same manner as those in office buildings. The work areas, however, may use special binding glues and other materials that require a separate exhaust system to eliminate odors.

Reading rooms have a fluctuating people load, which may be high; lighting intensities are high, and these rooms are gen-erally at the perimeter of the building. Therefore, the air-conditioning load is variable, and individual room or zone control is desirable. The reading rooms will generally require from eight to twelve air changes per hour for proper conditioning. Air movement should be below 50 fpm to prevent drafts on people reading at tables for long periods of time. The noise level should be maintained at NC-30 to -35; a level less than NC-30 will tend to accentuate background noises such as page rustling, foot shuffling, chair moving, etc.

Small study rooms (50 to 100 sq ft) are usually located at the exterior walls of the building. The lighting and people loads are relatively low and can be considered constant. When the rooms are located above

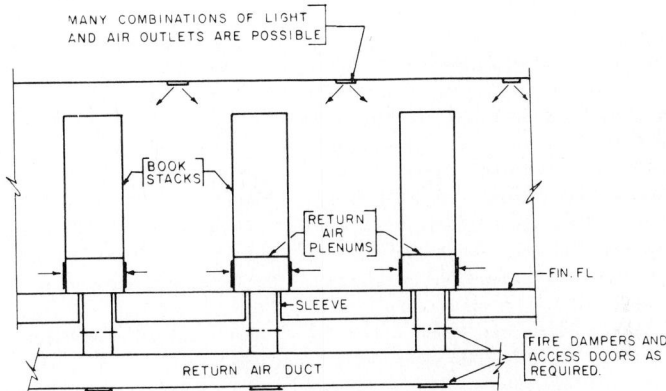

Fig. 119. Air-distribution system recommended for book stack areas

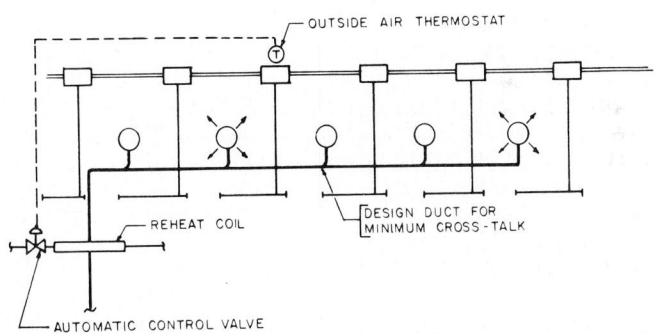

Fig. 120. Air-conditioning system for outside study rooms

Design ductwork for minimum crosstalk.

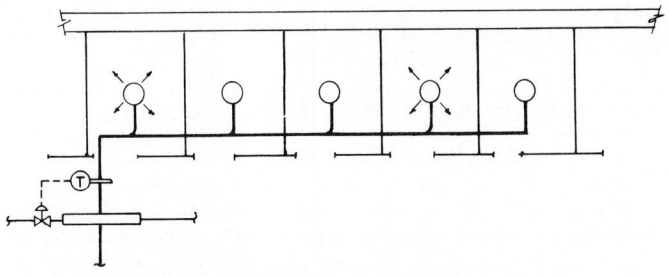

Fig. 121. Air conditioning for interior study rooms

grade and the exterior wall has glass, the glass presents the largest load. It is variable but the same for each room on that wall. Therefore, a simple design expedient is to put all the rooms on each facade on one zone and control the air conditions from an outdoor thermostat (Fig. 120). If the rooms are below grade or contain no exterior glass, the air conditions may be controlled from a preset, adjustable thermostat located on the zone discharge duct (Fig. 121).

Many libraries, especially college libraries, operate up to 16 hours a day and may run the air-conditioning equipment about 5,000 hours a year. Such constant usage requires the selection of heavy-duty, long-life equipment needing little maintenance. All book areas and especially the perimeter and roof areas should be on night thermostat and humidistat control to maintain reasonably constant environmental conditions at all times. Library vaults often require closer temperature and humidity control than the general book areas. Hence it is desirable to furnish a separate refrigeration compressor and air-handling system for the vaults. This system should be capable of operating 24 hours a day and should have alarms which indicate any

failure to maintain the required environmental conditions.

The location of the mechanical equipment rooms should be as remote as possible from the reading areas in order to minimize noise and vibration.

MUSEUMS

Museums generally have exhibit areas, work areas, offices, and storage areas.

The work areas in art museums consist of restoration rooms, picture framing, sculpture mounting, shipping, and repair rooms, etc. Paints, chemicals, plaster of paris, and other materials are used which may require special temperature, humidity, and air-circulating conditions. A greater variety of functions may be performed in the work areas of natural history museums. Odors and chemicals used may require larger exhaust air quantities. Individual room or area zone control will generally be necessary.

The storage areas in most museums contain large numbers of items for which exhibit space is not available. Most of the time, these storage areas must be kept within fairly close environmental conditions to preserve the stored items. For example,

art storage areas are often maintained at 65 to 72°F ± 1°F and 50 per cent RH ± 2 per cent. Stuffed fur-bearing animals should be stored at about 40 to 50°F and 50 per cent RH for maximum preservation, whereas fossils and old bones will keep better at higher humidities.

The exhibit areas are usually maintained at standard comfort conditions of 70 to 75°F, 50 per cent RH. Lighting loads for art museums are likely to run from 6 to 15 watts per sq ft. At the upper limit, this causes a substantial increase in the size of the air-conditioning equipment. Natural history museums range from 2 to 6 watts per sq ft. People loads vary widely depending on the popularity of the exhibit, the time of day, the weather, etc. All this seems to indicate that individually controlled zones are required to maintain optimum air conditions.

The most difficult problem encountered in designing the air-conditioning system for a museum is that the partitioned areas may be radically changed from one exhibit to another. The air-distribution system, and lighting system as well, must be set up in the most flexible manner possible so as to provide a minimum of obstacles to the setting up of any exhibit.

HOSPITALS

The general criteria for a comfortable atmospheric environment for healthy people are satisfactory for hospital patients, except that more attention must be given to the quietness of the system, the air distribution and pressurization, relative humidity (RH), and the degree of air filtration and freedom from bacteria. Typical design recommendations for the principal areas of a hospital are as follows:

Table 40. Recommended design criteria for hospitals

Area	Summer		Winter	
	°F, D.B.	%RH	°F, D.B.	%RH
Operating suite	68–85	55	68–85	55
Recovery suite	75–80	50–55	75–80	50–55
Patients' areas	74–78	40–50	72	40–50
Peripheral vascular	72–76	40	72–76	40
Maternity suite	74–80	40–50	74–80	40–50
Incubator and nursery	85–90	35–45	85–90	35–45
All other air-conditioned areas	74–78	40–50	72	40–50

D.B. = Dry Bulb Temperature
RH = Relative Humidity

Exercise, physical therapy, X-ray, and locker rooms and bathrooms should be maintained at 75°F minimum during the heating season. Patients' baths, swimming pools, sitz baths, etc., should be kept at 80°F. Many of the service areas such as kitchens, storage and repair spaces, etc., may be kept at 60°F in the winter.

Patients' bedrooms: The metabolic rate of bed patients is reduced, making them more sensitive to drafts. Hence air distribution should be uniform and air velocity at patients' level no more than 30 to 40 fpm. The air-distribution system must be designed for very quiet operation (NC-30 curve*). The exhaust air from patients' rooms should be exhausted from within the room or its associated bathroom. General patients' quarters and associated nurses' working areas should have their own air-distribution system because they require 24-hr operation.

Areas for patients having infectious diseases or allergies must have 100 per cent outside air, and each room must have sepa-

* Noise criteria curve defining maximum permissible sound level for various frequencies: see ASHRAE Handbook and section on "Acoustics."

rate exhaust air connections so that none of the air contaminates other areas. If room air is transferred into toilets adjacent to the room, it should be carried as a separate toilet exhaust system with its own fan.

Rooms for seriously disturbed mental patients should have heating and air outlets of such design that they are completely tamper-proof so that the patients will not be able to harm themselves or others.

Outpatient clinics and treatment rooms are usually open about 12 hr per day.

Administrative area is treated in much the same manner as an office-building area. Since its operation is usually 10 to 12 hr per day, it can be combined with the outpatient clinic area into one air-distribution system, if it is architecturally or mechanically feasible.

Operating rooms require a wider range of temperature and humidity control than most other areas. The temperature range is to provide optimum comfort conditions for both medical staff and patients and is controlled by the staff. The high level of RH is to minimize the possibility of electrostatic discharges, which may cause explosions. Also, certain types of operations may require a high RH.

The operating room may not require 100 per cent outside air, but should have no more than 80 per cent positive room exhaust, and individual room temperature and humidity control. Temperature control can be obtained by means of a reheat coil on a single-duct system or by a dual-duct system. Humidity control by means of evaporative or steam sprays is recommended rather than pan-type humidifiers because of the possibility of algae formation on the coils and pan (Fig. 122).

Since the heating loads for operating rooms are often substantial, 15 to 24 air changes per hour are normal. This makes good air distribution, preferably by means of perforated ceiling panels, a necessity in order to maintain no more than 50-fpm air velocity around the operating table (Fig. 123). For a good ceiling supply distribution system, low exhaust registers are recommended with a small ceiling outlet to remove operating light heat. A high degree of filtration is required. Much research must still be performed on methods for eliminating bacteria from the air simply and economically.

Maternity and incubator areas require a separate system operating 24 hr a day, with 100 per cent outside and exhaust air. Incubator rooms, delivery rooms, labor rooms, nurseries, and all auxiliary areas require individual temperature and humidity controls. Delivery rooms are treated as operating rooms. Air distribution should maintain about 30-fpm air velocity at infant or mother level.

X-ray and radiology suite operates about 12 hr per day with standard comfort conditions maintained. Ductwork is often lined with lead to minimize the dangers of the spread of radioactivity.

Laboratory and research areas will often require 100 per cent exhaust air, depending upon the nature of the work. The requirements for laboratories given in this section generally apply. All hood exhausts should be discharged above the highest roof level. These areas operate about 12 hr per day, but certain experiments may require that the air-conditioning system operate around the clock.

Animal areas require air conditioning 24 hr per day often with 100 per cent supply and exhaust air. Individual room control of temperature and humidity may be necessary.

Morgue contains a special refrigerated box and an open area for preparation of corpses. It should be served by its own air-handling system, and exhausted above the highest roof level. Exhaust should be 10 to 20 per cent greater than the supply air which should consist of 100 per cent outside air.

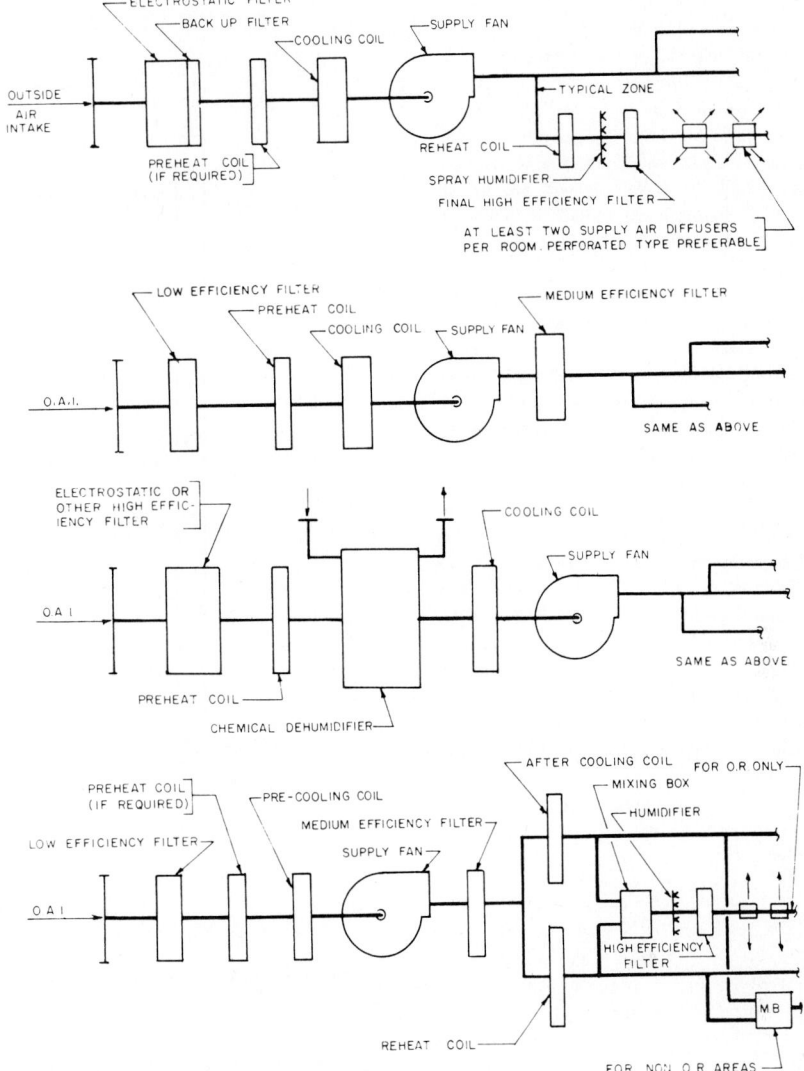

Fig. 122. Air-conditioning systems for operating rooms

Electrostatic filter system: Adequate if maintenance of cooling coils and drain pan is good. Requires least space.

Dry filter system: Less expensive than electrostatic system, but requires more space. Does not eliminate algae growth in cooling coil and drain pan if maintenance is inadequate.

Chemical dehumidification system: High first cost but in some cases may be the most economical. Keeps cooling coil clean since chemical dehumidifier does total dehumidification. Requires more space than previous systems, plus added ducts and louvers. May help to reduce micro-organisms. Relatively high operating costs.

Dual duct system: Excellent control at high operating cost. Each room can be custom designed for specific environmental requirements. Largest mechanical room space required.

Note: On any of the systems shown, prehumidifier may be used before cooling unit.

Central pharmaceutical and sterilizing area requires 100 per cent exhaust to minimize chemical odors and dissipate the heat from the sterilizers. A large portion of the air to this area may be transferred from other uncontaminated areas if it is feasible to do so. Exhaust registers should be placed over sterilizers, work benches, etc.

Soiled-linen rooms should have, where possible, a separate exhaust system discharging above the highest roof.

Mechanical equipment rooms should be located as far from patients' quarters as practicable in order to minimize noise and fumes. Similarly, the cooling tower should be located and designed so that it does not transmit noise to patients' areas, or cover the windows with mist.

The refrigeration and boiler plant should have sufficient flexibility so that if any piece of equipment is not able to function, the entire plant capacity will not be affected. Therefore, as a rule, hospitals require more mechanical space than most other types of buildings.

Boiler plants must provide steam requirements for kitchens (5 to 50 psig), sterilizers and warmers of all types (10 to 70 psig), and laundries (up to 125 psig). It is usually most economical to provide separate high-pressure boilers sized to handle only the medium and high-pressure loads.

Provision should be made to eliminate the possibility of an electrical service interruption by maintaining an emergency generator to cut in automatically if the electrical power fails. The emergency generator should be located sufficiently far away from patient and critical areas so that noise, vibration, and fumes are not a problem.

It is critical that the air distribution system be designed to maintain the proper air pressure relationships between hospital spaces to assure proper aseptic conditions insofar as these are affected by air movement.

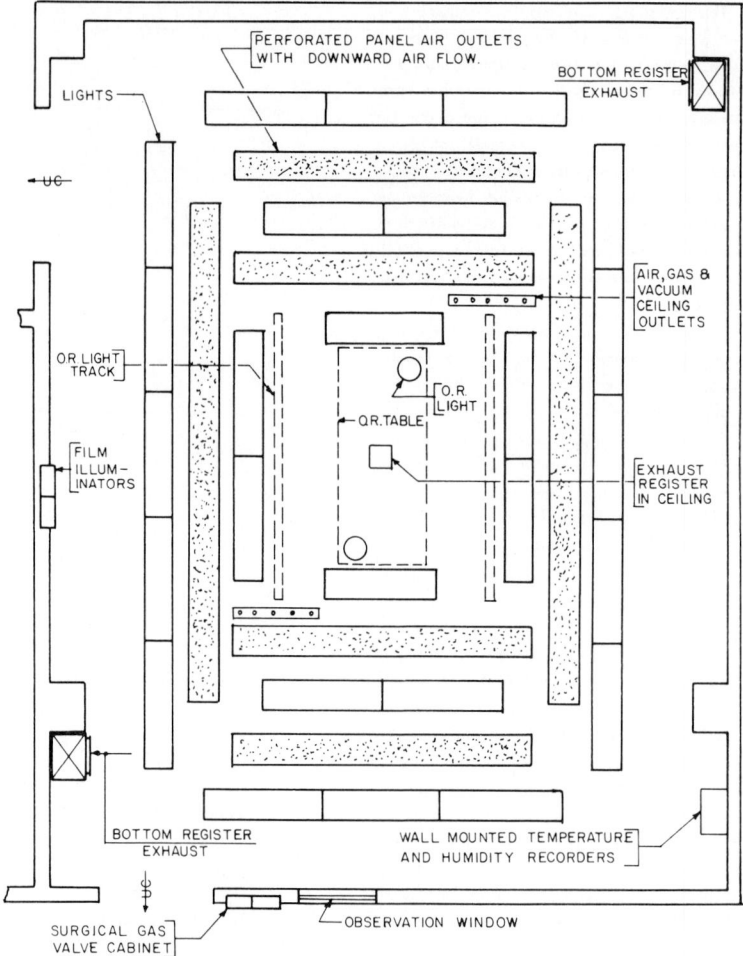

Fig. 123. Reflected ceiling plan of an operating room

Using fluorescent lights, perforated panel air outlets, and 100 per cent outside air; exhaust 80 per cent through bottom register, 15 per cent through doors, 5 per cent through ceiling register.

INDUSTRIAL BUILDINGS

Industrial heating, ventilating, and air conditioning involves several aspects, namely:

1. Product and/or process requirements
2. Personnel comfort requirements
3. Industrial ventilation and exhaust requirements

Product and process requirements are so varied and numerous that a detailed treatment is not possible here. This section will deal with personnel comfort and industrial exhaust requirements, including some data on the determination of exhaust hood requirements.

In plants where close machining tolerances are required, it is usually not the temperature itself that is critical but the variation in temperature. Therefore, conditions are usually maintained in the comfort range with close limits on the range.

Where static electricity is a problem, it is generally minimized by maintaining the relative humidity of the air at 55 per cent minimum, if it does not harm the product or process.

There are two basic kinds of heat release that will affect the comfort of personnel. One is a hot-dry heat which allows some relief by means of evaporation of body sweat. The other type is warm-moist heat which prevents evaporation of sweat. The latter presents the greater hazard to worker health and comfort. The introduction of outside air with low relative humidities will contribute greatly to personnel comfort in the warm-moist areas.

There are several general methods available for minimizing the effects of heat exposure. One is to control the heat at the source by proper insulation, location of machine or process in cool environment or out of doors, furnishing water or air jacketing for removal of the heat, or enclosing **the entire machine, process, or personnel in a hood and drawing off the heat. The latter is the extreme case of the use of hoods for removing air from a localized area. Hoods of all types, sizes, shapes, and materials are used in industrial applications to remove heat, dust, fumes, vapors, odors, etc.**

Most types of hoods are of an open-construction type and require 100 per cent of their air requirements from the space. For enclosing hoods where it is more expensive or undesirable to obtain the air from the space than from an auxiliary ventilation system, hoods may be designed to take a portion, usually half, of their air requirements from the space and the **rest from the auxiliary air system (Fig. 124).**

Hoods are applicable for exhaust of localized areas having comparatively acute heat, fume, vapor, odor, or dust conditions. In many large industrial areas it is unnecessary and impractical to have hoods over each piece of equipment. Furnishing supply air to the whole area (dilution ventilation) in sufficient quantity to reduce the level of most of the heat or other contaminant will usually be satisfactory. The determination of the air quantity is obtained from the formula:

$$Cfm = \frac{Btu/hr \ heat \ load}{1.08 \ (t \ space -- t \ outside)}$$

The temperature differential varies with the amount of heat to be removed, the type of work being done, the height of the roof (if gravity ventilation is used), and the cost of supplying and exhausting the air. The supply air should be introduced where the personnel are located in order to achieve maximum benefit. Gravity exhaust may produce satisfactory results if the roof is high, the temperature differential is sufficient for a large stack effect, and the wind conditions are favorable. However, for best and most uniform results mechanical exhaust should be used. In some areas, such as warehouses, which have relatively low heat loads spread over large areas, the cost of mechanical exhaust would not be practical unless the nature of the materials stored was such as to require it.

Where ovens, furnaces, foundries, etc., are located, the major portion of the heat load is in the form of radiant heat. Ventilation is ineffective in reducing the effects of radiant heat. Three methods commonly used to minimize the spread of the radiant heat energy are:

1. Insulation
2. Water-cooled surfaces
3. Radiation shields

Insulation reduces the rate at which the heat is emitted from the machine, whereas water cooling reduces the surface temperature. In both cases, since the surface temperature is lower, the radiant heat effect is reduced. Both methods are comparatively efficient.

Where it is not practicable to do either of the above, radiation shields are used. A shield is a sheet of material, opaque to infrared rays, which is placed as close as possible around the equipment emitting the radiant heat, short of touching it. There should be an air space between the equipment and the shield so that the shield is not heated by conduction.

Sheets of reflective metal, aluminum foil-faced curtains, transparent shields of heat-reflective tempered glass, reflective garments including asbestos suits with atomized aluminum exteriors, gauntlets, and face shields are effective radiation shields. There are many variations, depending upon the particular application involved.

In the design of the local ventilation or spot cooling system, care must be taken that the air velocity at the workers' level does not exceed 200 fpm for continuous exposure. For light-duty work, 50 fpm should be maintained. Air conditioning does increase the first cost but requires less air to do the same job and does it more effectively. In most instances, worker efficiency has gone up, and this has justified its use economically.

Where spot cooling is used, as stated before, the outlets should be close to the work level (about 7 ft high) to be most effective. Outlet velocities will normally be between 1,000 and 2,000 fpm, or higher if the outlets are located more remotely. Control of air direction is often essential from both the worker's and the product's viewpoint, so directional outlets are necessary. Various types are shown in Fig. 125.

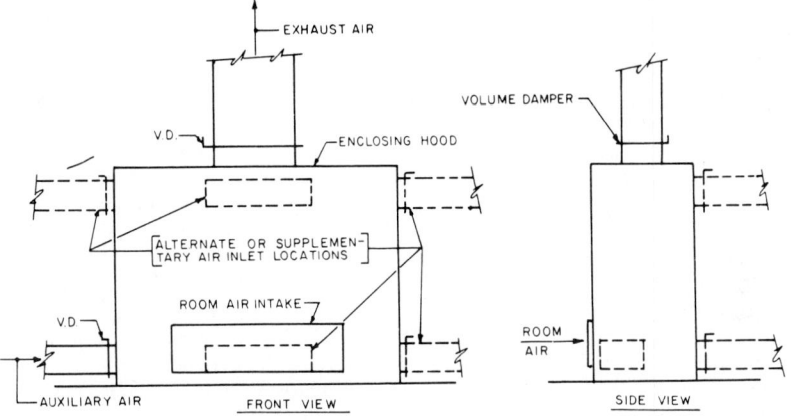

Fig. 124. Completely enclosing hood

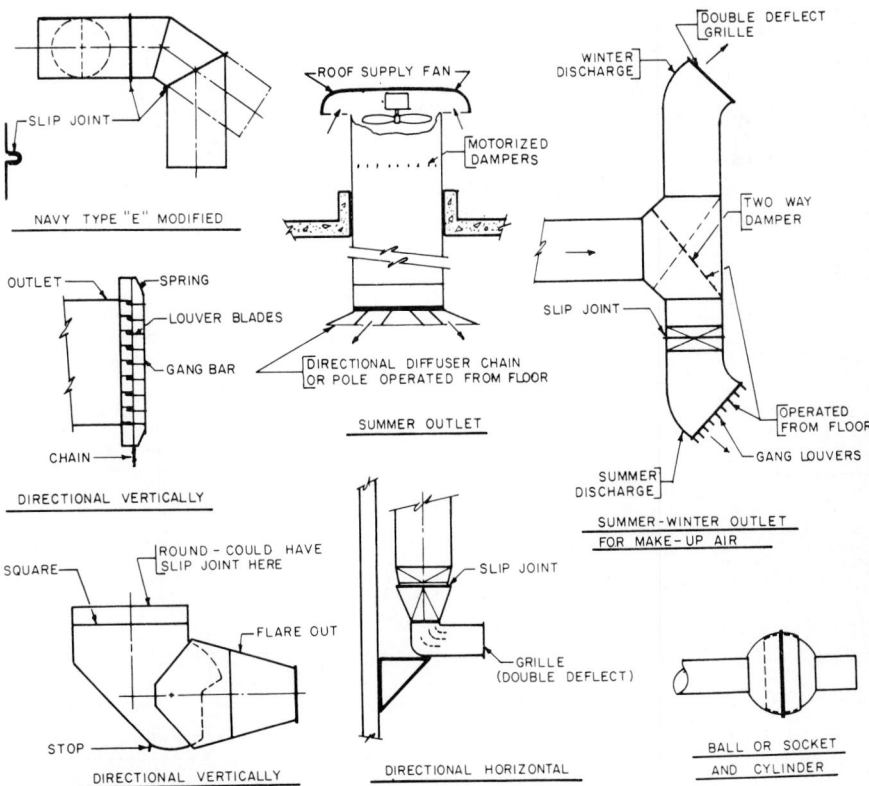

Fig. 125. Directional outlets for spot cooling

Reprinted from ASHRAE Handbook.

LABORATORIES

A laboratory is a place devoted to experimental study in any science, or to the testing and analysis of materials. It may be used for education, research, or product control. It may consist of a single room with very limited equipment in a building primarily used for other purposes, or it may be a large building with several floors, designed and constructed to provide a number of rooms with special equipment, or it may be some intermediate arrangement between these extremes.

The one item of equipment that differentiates laboratories from most other types of buildings is the necessity for partial or complete enclosure fume hoods. Even those laboratories that have no hoods often have special exhaust air requirements due to the nature of their operations. They may require large quantities of air which are in excess of room air-conditioning requirements, which means that additional sources of air must be obtained. In most cases, it is generally desirable to exhaust more air than is supplied.

There are several types of laboratory hoods available:

The conventional hood (Fig. 126) is the cheapest and simplest. When the hood door is closed, no air flows through the hood, and auxiliary means for exhausting room air must be furnished. When the hood is in use, auxiliary exhaust must be shut off to ensure hoods getting sufficient air. This involves a damper control arrangement which in a building wtih many hoods could become complex.

The modified hood (Fig. 127) is a simple variation intended to overcome this problem. An open slot is provided above or below the door so that it can never be completely closed and exhaust air goes through the hood at all times.

In air-conditioned laboratories the use of large quantities of conditioned air to satisfy the hood air requirements may be too expensive. Therefore, a third type of system has evolved (Fig. 127) which takes only 50 per cent of its total air requirements from the room, whether the hood door is open or closed. The rest of the air is furnished by an auxiliary air supply system consisting of outside air, tempered and filtered. This requires an additional fan and ductwork system and more expensive hoods, which may offset the savings in reduced room air quantities.

Secondary air hoods: With conventional or modified hoods it is difficult to maintain fixed air conditions in the laboratory room. To meet this objection the secondary air hood was developed. In this type auxiliary air is furnished to the hood at all times and practically no room air is used. It has the further advantage of reducing the minimum air speed across the face of the hood from 50 to 75 fpm to about half that amount.

In general, the following velocities across the face of the hood with a full front opening are considered advisable:

50 to 60 fpm for high schools.
60 to 80 fpm for colleges and hospitals.
80 to 100 fpm for industrial laboratories.
100 to 150 fpm for radioactive and virus laboratories.
Downdraft table-type hoods should have a capacity of about 150 cfm.

Room air-conditioning systems: Most laboratories are designed for dual-duct, single-duct with zone or individual reheat, or unit ventilators adapted for use with high outside air quantities. The first two systems require large ceiling spaces for distribution and are generally more costly than the unit ventilator system, but provide closer temperature and humidity control. The unit ventilator system generally uses through-the-wall air openings, although this is not essential.

Variable volume systems have been used for some laboratories but this requires careful, continuous checking of the air flows to assure proper air balancing and movement.

Space requirements: The amount of mechanical equipment room and shaft requirements for some laboratories may be as much as 25 to 50 per cent greater than for office buildings or other types of commercial buildings. This is due to hood and laboratory equipment duct and piping needs as well as the requirement for special systems to handle special functions such as animal quarters or radioactive materials.

Administrative areas should be air conditioned in a manner similar to office buildings. The main difference is that the supply air from these areas will probably have to be transferred to laboratory areas in order to make up the air requirements needed.

There are many different types of laboratories and processes requiring hoods or special ventilation. Specific criteria for each application can be obtained from many sources.

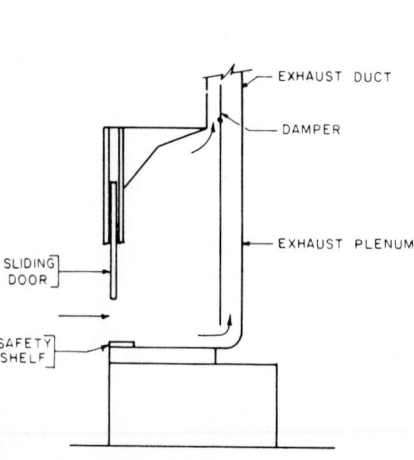

Fig. 126. Conventional hood

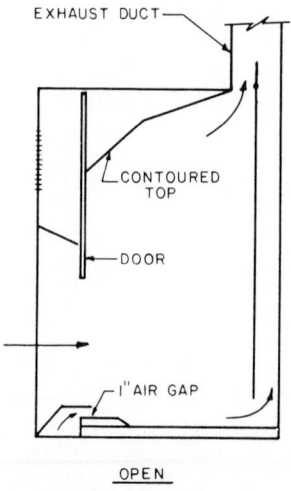

Fig. 127. Modified hood

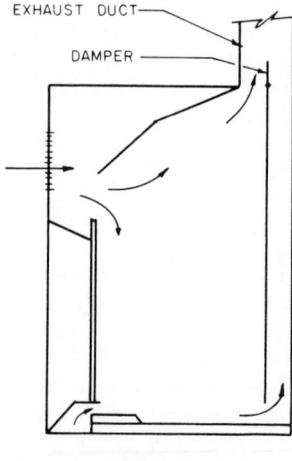

AIR FLOW

In order to reduce to a minimum the possibility of any flow of air from rooms where fumes, odors, or excess heat are generated to other parts of the building, such rooms should be maintained under negative pressure while in use, and other rooms should be kept under a positive pressure.

Canopy hoods over sinks for the disposal of fuming liquids, steam tables, etching tanks, and grinding operations should be larger than the area of the working surface below, and while it is desirable to keep hoods as low as possible, proper headroom for equipment and for access must be provided. As these canopy hoods are frequently open on all sides, cross drafts will carry the fumes and vapors outside the area of the canopy unless high inlet velocities at the hoods are maintained. The use of double hoods with a narrow slot around the periphery makes it possible to maintain high velocities around the perimeter of the hood without exhausting excessive quantities of air.

INDIVIDUAL VS. CENTRAL EXHAUST SYSTEMS

Individual exhaust systems offer these advantages:

1. A hood with a separate exhaust fan may be used if necessary when the full laboratory is not in use.

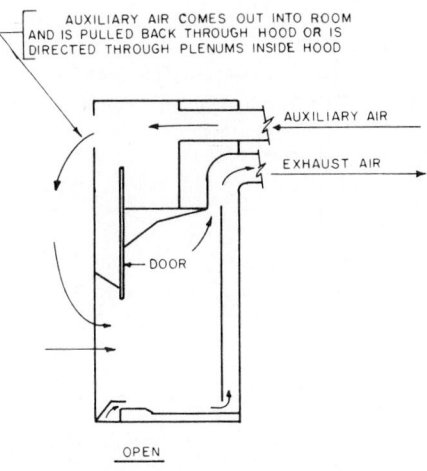

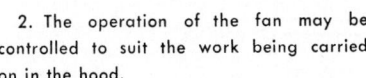

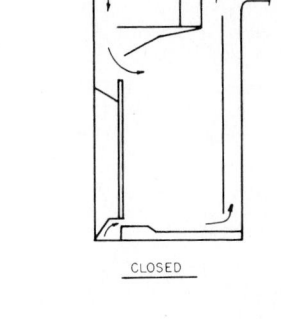

AUXILIARY AIR COMES OUT INTO ROOM AND IS PULLED BACK THROUGH HOOD OR IS DIRECTED THROUGH PLENUMS INSIDE HOOD

AUXILIARY AIR

EXHAUST AIR

DOOR

OPEN

CLOSED

Fig. 128. Auxiliary-air type laboratory hood

2. The operation of the fan may be controlled to suit the work being carried on in the hood.

3. Fans and ductwork which must be built of expensive materials to resist the corrosive effect of fumes may be kept small, thus reducing the cost.

4. The possibility of leakage of noxious or hazardous fumes between rooms through ductwork is reduced.

5. Small vertical discharge ducts from individual fans may be concealed in furred spaces and carried up through the roof.

Central exhaust systems have the following advantages:

1. Fans and motors may be easily serviced.

2. None of the ductwork conveying noxious or hazardous fumes will be under a positive pressure, thus reducing the possibility of leakage of fumes.

3. There is less chance that a room which is supposed to be operating under a negative pressure will actually be operating under a positive pressure due to the exhaust fans being shut down.

GARAGES

Of the various types of parking facilities, the only one that presents a serious problem to the health and safety of human beings is the underground or windowless garage. In this category should be included very large garages having interior areas which are more than 50 ft from the exterior.

The problem is threefold. The first and most serious is the carbon monoxide (CO) gas emitted by automobiles. This is a colorless, odorless gas which, in sufficient concentration, can cause death or serious illness. The second is the oil and gasoline fumes which can cause nausea in many people. The third involves the lack of movement of the air and the resultant stale atmosphere that develops due to the increase in the carbon dioxide (CO_2) content.

Minimum ventilation requirements, as set up by the National Bureau of Standards,

ASHRAE, and others, are primarily concerned with preventing the buildup of a noxious concentration of carbon monoxide. These are predicated on the basis that the CO concentration should never be higher than 2 pp (parts per) 10,000 air (1 pp/10,000 = 0.01 per cent concentration) for a continued occupancy of 8 hours or 175,000 cu ft per hr of air per car based on the production of 35 cu ft per hr of CO per car (see Fig. 129). Once it is determined how many cars will be in operation at any one time, it is a relatively easy matter to calculate the cfm requirements. Determining how many cars will probably be in operation at any given time is more difficult. An underground garage serving an apartment house would be expected to have a lower instantaneous traffic rate than one serving a sports stadium, for instance.

The third aspect affecting the buildup of CO is the length of time that the people are in the garage or that cars in operation will remain in the garage. This is a function of garage design and size. In general, this time will run from 1 to 10 min with 5 min as an average.

However, keeping the CO level within safe limits is no guarantee that patrons or employees in the garage will experience no discomfort. The air furnished will probably be sufficient to eliminate any staleness in the atmosphere, but the greatest discomfort is caused by oil and gasoline fumes. These fumes are especially noticeable in areas having poor air circulation and at poorly ventilated ramps. Present design standards for air circulation range from 4 to 25 air changes per hour. The former is for apartment house garages, the latter for large garages with short, concentrated peak usage periods. For comparison, most underground tunnels are designed for 20 to 30 air changes per hour.

The types of systems applicable to

garage use with their advantages and disadvantages are as follows:

1. *Mechanical supply and exhaust* (Fig. 130)
   a. Most positive means of air movement.
   b. Requires fewer air changes per hour.
   c. Requires less shaft space for ducts.
   d. Requires largest mechanical equipment space.
   e. Highest initial and operating costs.

2. *Gravity supply and mechanical exhaust*
   a. More air changes required.
   b. Larger supply airshafts and larger air intake louvers required.
   c. Less mechanical equipment space required.
   d. Lower initial and operating costs.
   e. Space is positively exhausted, preventing buildup of pockets of contaminated air.

3. *Mechanical supply and gravity exhaust*
   a, b, c, d, are same as No. 2 above except change supply to return.
   e. Since exhaust air is forced out of exhaust air louvers by means of positive pressure within the space, air movement is more sluggish than with the other two schemes, and pockets of contaminated air may form to cause local areas of discomfort.

Under any of the schemes, supply air may be brought in high or low, but air should be exhausted from both high and low levels. At the ramps, low exhaust registers are preferable (Fig. 131).

Ducts or shafts for mechanical systems should be sized for air velocities of from 1,500 to 2,000 fpm, depending on the size of the system. Gravity ducts should be sized for an air velocity no greater than 250 fpm in order to assure adequate free-air motion.

If possible, the supply and exhaust air should be distributed uniformly along opposite walls of the garage so that all areas get uniform air motion.

The areas that generally develop the greatest CO and oil and gas fumes are the ramps to the outside. These should be given from ten to twenty air changes per hour of exhaust ventilation.

Unless local codes require it, underground garages will generally not require any heat. Special areas such as toilets, offices, employee operating booths, and patrons' waiting rooms should have heat provided. Toilets will in most instances require a separate exhaust system.

If the garage has interior gasoline-dispensing pumps, a separate explosion-proof duct, fan, and motor system should be furnished. The exhaust register should be located right at the pumps, and the controls should operate so that when the fan is not running, the pumps cannot dispense gasoline. Furnish a minimum of 2,000 cfm per dispensing pump. If a vault is used to contain the gasoline tanks, it must have a continuously operating explosion-proof exhaust system with a constant source of supply air furnishing from fifteen to thirty air changes per hour.

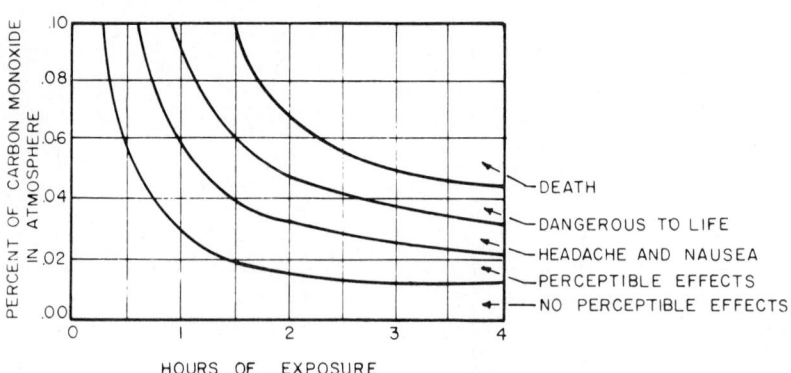

EFFECTS OF CARBON MONOXIDE
FOR A GIVEN TIME ON HUMAN BEINGS

DEATH
DANGEROUS TO LIFE
HEADACHE AND NAUSEA
PERCEPTIBLE EFFECTS
NO PERCEPTIBLE EFFECTS

HOURS OF EXPOSURE

DATA FROM NATIONAL BUREAU OF STANDARDS
TECHNICAL PAPER 212

Fig. 129. Effect of carbon monoxide on human beings

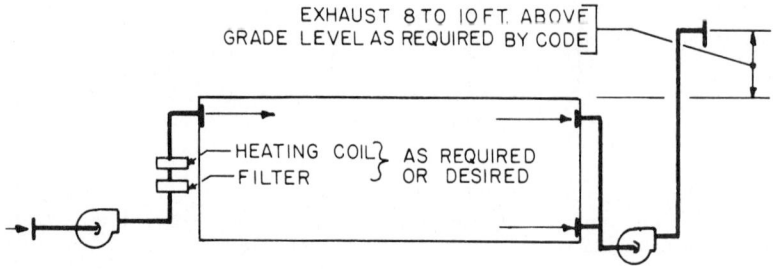

EXHAUST 8 TO 10 FT. ABOVE
GRADE LEVEL AS REQUIRED BY CODE

HEATING COIL } AS REQUIRED
FILTER } OR DESIRED

Fig. 130. Mechanical supply and exhaust system

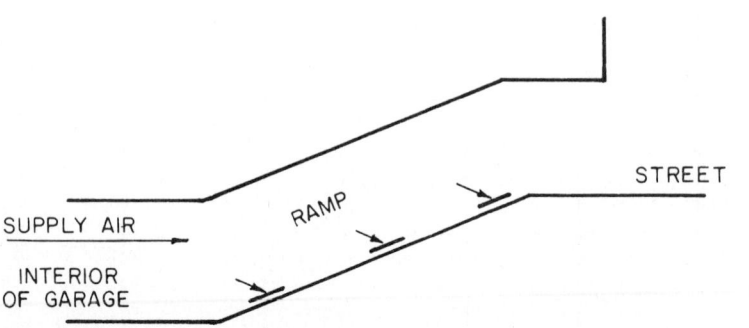

STREET
RAMP
SUPPLY AIR
INTERIOR OF GARAGE

Fig. 131. Low exhaust outlets on ramps

By ALFRED GREENBERG, P.E., Environmental and Energy Consultant

NONDEPLETABLE ENERGY RESOURCES

This term refers to sources of energy which are essentially omnipresent and available at all times or at least renewable on a cyclical basis. Typical nondepletable sources are:

1. Solar energy
2. Wind power
3. Hydropower and tidal motion
4. Wave movement
5. Rapid-growth biomass
6. Geothermal temperature differentials
7. Ocean-level thermal differentials

All of these sources have to be collected, converted, and distributed to the points of use.

SOLAR HEATING AND COOLING

The large scale use technology for most nondepletable sources is in the developmental stages for both thermal and electric production. However, the small-scale use of solar energy for domestic hot-water and space heating has been available and operational for half a century in many parts of the world, including the United States. The installation of solar energy systems, at least for domestic hot water, in all existing and new buildings would reduce total U.S. energy consumption by about 5 per cent. All new buildings should be designed to permit at least the future inclusion of solar energy for heating.

Governmental confusion and business diffidence toward the immediate implementation of solar energy systems must be countered by architect, engineer, contractor, and owner acceptance and use. The payback period will generally be in the 5- to 10-year range. All solar panels should be warranted to last at least 10 years, and preferably 20 years. All solar system components should last as long as any quality boiler or refrigeration system equipment. Reliable design information for solar energy systems is available from ASHRAE, U.S. Department of Energy, International Solar Engineers Society (ISES), and reputable manufacturers and consultants.

The heart of the solar energy system is the collector panel. There are many types available but they must all be able to withstand the cyclical high and extreme temperatures which can develop. A flat plate collector consists of the following general components (see Fig. 132):

1. Glazing may be one or more sheets of glass or other radiation transmitting material.
2. Distribution system for conducting or directing the heat-transfer fluid from inlet to outlet.

3. Absorber plate in various configurations and often with heat-absorbing coating to improve the transmission and absorption from the plate to the tubes or fins.
4. Headers or manifolds to admit and discharge the fluid.
5. Insulation which minimizes heat loss from the back and sides of the collector.
6. Container or casing which surrounds the foregoing components and keeps them free from dust, moisture, etc.

Flat-plate collectors have been built in a wide variety of designs from many different materials (see Fig. 133). They have been used to heat fluids such as water, water

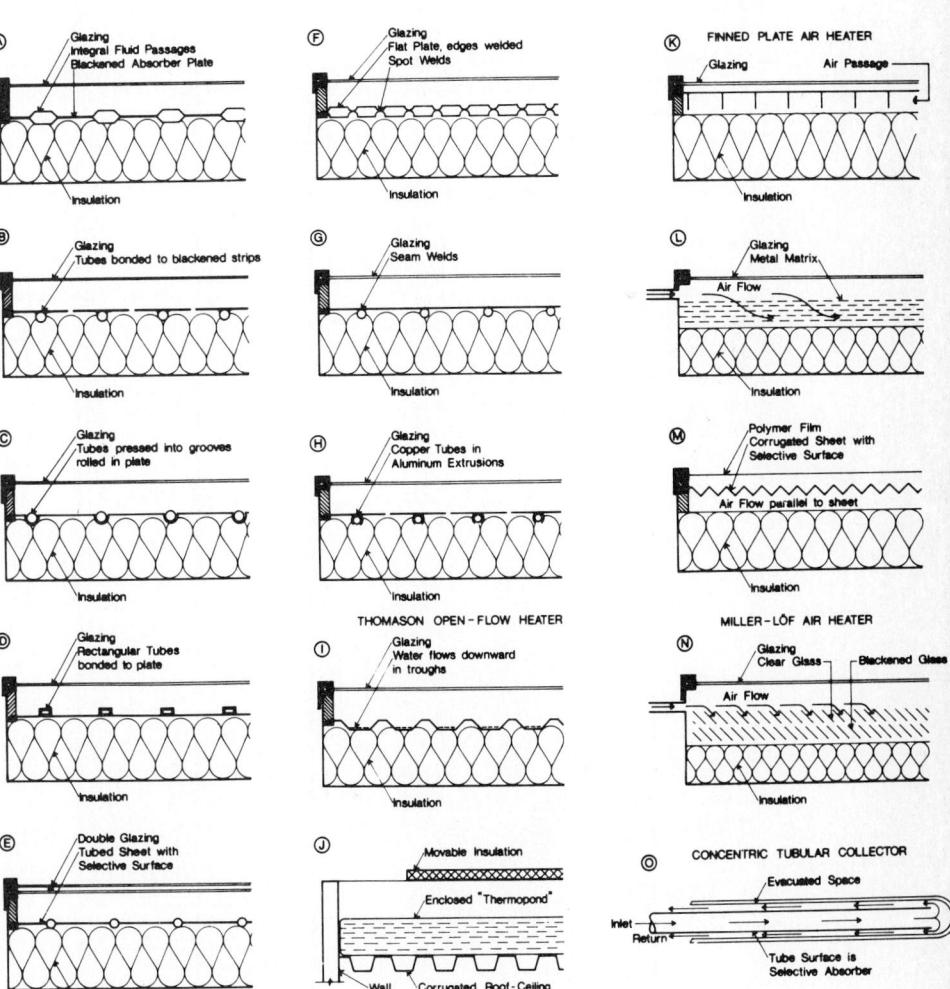

1. GLAZING – TWO COVER GLASSES SHOWN
2. FLUID TUBE
3. PLATE
4. INSULATION
5. CASING

Fig. 132. Exploded cross section through double-glazed solar water heater

Fig. 133. Variations of solar water and air heaters

plus an antifreeze additive, or gases such as air. The major objective has been to collect as much solar energy as possible at the lowest possible total cost. The collector should also have a long effective life, despite the adverse effects of: the sun's ultraviolet radiation; corrosion or clogging due to acidity, alkalinity, or hardness of the heat-transfer fluid; freezing or air-binding in the case of water, or deposition of dust or moisture in the case of air; breakage of the glazing due to thermal expansion, hail, vandalism, or other causes. (These problems can be minimized by the use of tempered glass.)

A simple form of solar heating system used for domestic hot water production is the thermosiphon solar water heater. Figure 134 shows the water flow. The warmed water flows slowly upward into the storage tank, and this process continues as long as the sun's radiation is strong enough to keep the collector plate hot.

By the end of a typical sunny day, the storage tank is full of hot water at temperatures ranging from 120°F (48.9°C) in winter to 165°F (73.9°C) in summer. For single-family residences, an absorber area of 16 to 20 ft² (1.5 to 1.9 m²) and a storage tank capacity of 40 to 60 gal (0.15 to 0.23 m³) have been found to give satisfactory results in Israel and in Australia. Both absorber and storage tank would have to be larger in the U.S.

Precautions are necessary in the use of the thermosiphon water heater. Reverse flow from the tank into the heater can occur on cold nights unless the tank is mounted above the top of the collector. Collectors with a single glass cover are susceptible to freezing in cold climates, and steps must be taken to prevent this. Where air temperatures

rarely fall far below 30°F (1.1°C), double glazing is generally adequate. For very cold climates, an indirect system must be used with an antifreeze-water solution circulating through the heater and a heat exchanger in the hot water tank.

Early collectors in the U.S. and Israel used continuous tubes in sinusoidal patterns. These tend to heat a relatively small amount of water to a temperature that is high enough to cause deposition of minerals and clogging in the upper part of the collector. The grid system has many advantages, including accessibility of the headers for cleaning, better coverage of the plate surface, and relative insensitivity. Experience has shown that tubes smaller than 0.5 in. (12.7 mm) standard size should not be used.

Forced-circulation water heaters

In many applications, the capacity of a thermosiphon system with one or two collector panels is inadequate to meet hot-water demands. There are other situations where architectural or other considerations require the storage tank to be below or at a considerable distance from the collectors. In these cases, forced-circulation systems are employed with flow rates on the order of 1 to 2 gph/ft² (11.3 to 22.6 mL/s per m²) of absorber surface. Centrifugal hot-water pumps have proved to be satisfactory at these relatively low flow rates and low

heads. See Fig. 135 for a typical system.

When a number of collector units are to be operated simultaneously, series-parallel arrangements are superior to operation with all of the collectors in parallel. Australian authorities with much experience in this field report that up to 24 tubes may be operated in parallel; for larger numbers, downcomers or multiple parallel systems may be installed. Use of vents to avoid air-binding is essential.

In Fig. 135, the differential thermostat controls the operation of the circulating pump and no further antifreeze protection is required. The heat exchanger is a jacket which surrounds the storage tank. Many other types of exchanger may be used, including pipe coils in the tank, tubing wrapped tightly around the tank, etc. Many building and plumbing codes require double-walled heat exchangers to give absolute protection against the possibility of introducing the antifreeze liquid into the potable supply; in this case, a more complex subsystem than that shown must be employed. Local authorities should always be consulted before a solar-water-heating system is selected.

Forced-circulation air heaters

There are many applications where air is a more suitable heat-transport fluid than water. Air cannot freeze and air leakage is

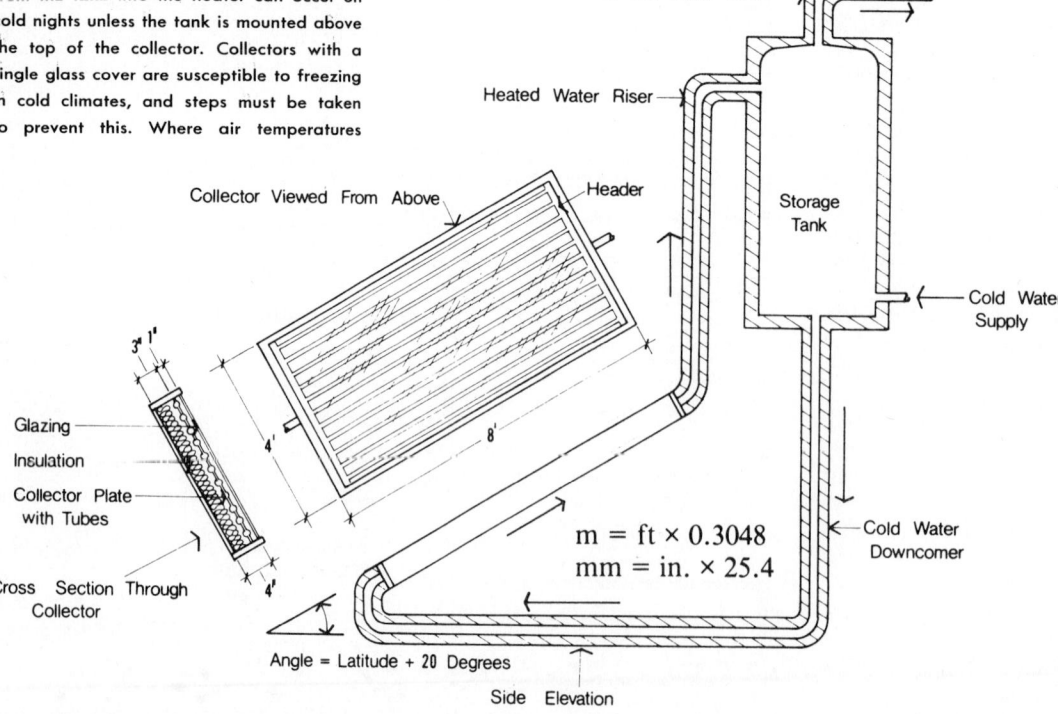

$$m = ft \times 0.3048$$
$$mm = in. \times 25.4$$

Fig. 134. Thermosiphon solar water heater

annoying but not as serious in its consequences as are water leaks. Because the specific heat of air is only ¼ that of water and its density is only about ⅟₈₀₀ that of water, the ducts needed to convey air to and from a solar collector must be far larger than the pipes used to carry water. However, most air-conditioning systems rely upon air to do the actual heating and cooling.

Forced-circulation air heaters have other applications than space heating, since they are now used with heat exchangers to provide service hot water. Some applications have been made of the evacuated tube collectors shown in Fig. 133(o) to heat air to temperatures above those normally used in HVAC applications, but most air heaters operate at the temperatures encountered in space heating. Agricultural and industrial drying processes represent another application where air heaters and blowers are successfully used.

Space heat and service hot water

One of the many systems for providing both service hot water and space heating is shown in Fig. 136. In this case, a large, atmospheric-pressure storage tank is used from which water is pumped up to the collectors by pump P1 in response to a signal from the differential thermostat T1. It is assumed that the drain-down system would be used here to prevent freezing since the amount of antifreeze required in such a system would be prohibitively expensive. Service hot water is obtained by a heat-exchanger coil in the tank near the top, where, if stratification is encouraged, the hottest water will be found.

An electric auxiliary hot-water heater is provided to boost the temperature of the sun-heated water when this is required. The space heating is accomplished in response to signals from thermostat T2 which senses the indoor temperature and starts P2 when warmth is needed. If the water in the storage tank becomes too cool to provide enough heat to the fan-coil units in the duct work, the second contact on the thermostat calls for heat from the electric auxiliary heater. Fuel-fired heaters may be used where an assured source of a suitable fuel is available, but it is highly probable that electricity will be the principal stand-by fuel in most solar installations.

The problem of providing standby heat becomes increasingly serious as latitude and elevation combine to give large heating requirements. The usual method of evaluating heating loads in terms of degree days [below 65°F (18.3°C) average temperature] gives the first input towards the solution of this problem. The winter availability of solar radiation provides the second input, while

the cost and availability of the auxiliary energy supply constitute the third input. It is very rarely cost-effective to try to do the entire heating job for either space or service hot water by using the solar heat collection and storage system alone.

The least expensive method of providing auxiliary heat, considering only first cost and without regard for energy conservation, is electric resistance heating. If the energy consumption becomes high because the auxiliary heater must be used frequently, however, the operating cost may offset the low first cost. The use of a water-to-air heat pump with warm or even cool sun-heated water from the storage tank as the evaporator energy source becomes an attractive alternative, because the coefficient of performance of the heat pump will generally be high enough to yield 10,000 to 14,000 Btu (10 550 to 14 770 kJ) of heat from the condenser for each kWh supplied to the compressor. When summer cooling is needed as well as winter heating, the heat pump becomes a logical solution, particularly in large systems where a cooling tower is used to dissipate the heat withdrawn from the system.

A simplified proprietary solar heating system known as Solaris (Fig. 137), has been in use in an increasing number of installations since 1958. It uses an open flow collector, similar to that shown in Fig. 133(i), mounted on a steeply tilted south-facing roof, with a combination water tank and rock-bed storage subsystem in the basement of the building. When the sun is shining, water is pumped from the bottom of the tank to a perforated pipe located at the top of the corrugated metal collector and the water is heated as it flows downward through the open troughs to the collector channel at the bottom of the collector. When the pump stops in response to a signal from the collector thermostat T1, the water automatically drains back to the storage tank. The rocks in contact with the tank are warmed by the sun-heated water in the tank and heat is spread throughout the rock bed by radiation, conduction, and convection.

The warmed rocks become the transfer surface to heat the air which is circulated through the storage subsystem when the house thermostat T2 calls for heat and starts the fan which draws air from return registers in the floor of the house. By combining 1600 gal (6064 L) of water with 50 tons (51 Mg) of rocks, a specific heat storage capacity of about 33,000 Btu/lb · °F (kJ/kg · °C) is created, and so the system does not have to operate at high temperatures to create overnight storage for a well-insulated house. The total heat-transfer area provided by the rocks is in excess of 20,000 ft² (1858 m²) and so only a very small temperature differ-

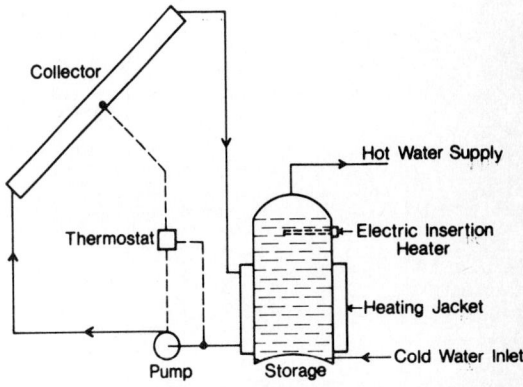

Fig. 135. Typical forced circulation domestic hot water system

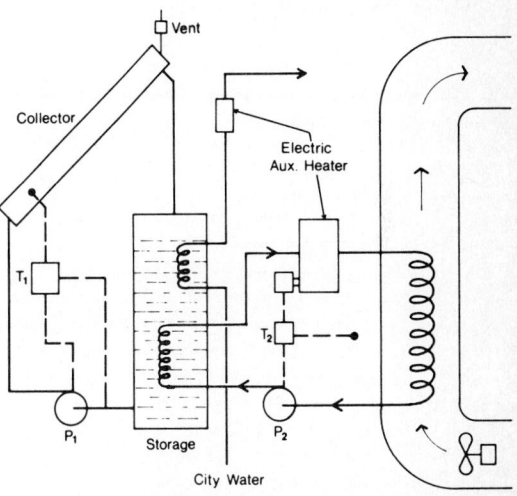

Fig. 136. Solar collection, storage, and distribution system for domestic hot water and space heating

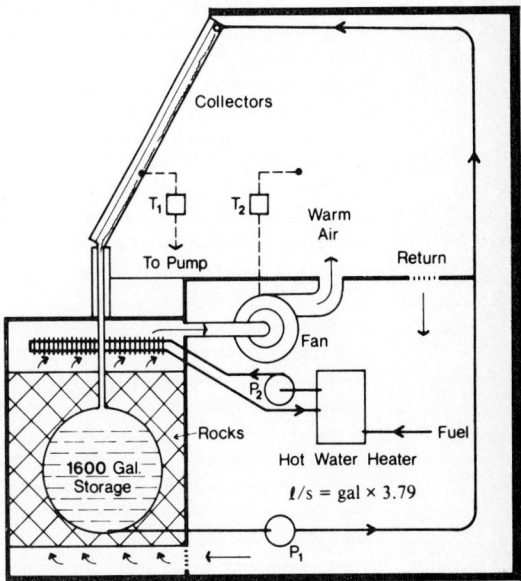

Fig. 137. Solaris solar heating system using open-flow water heater, rock-bed plus water tank storage, and warm air heat distribution

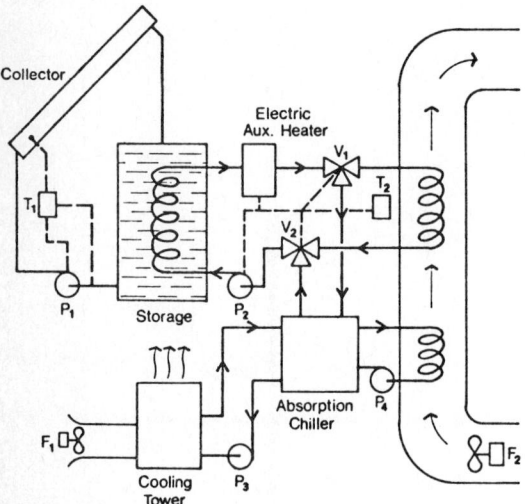

Fig. 138. Space heating and cooling system using lithium bromide-water absorption chiller

ence is needed to transfer the required heat from the rocks to the air.

Cooling can be provided by a small compression refrigeration subsystem which chills the water in the storage tank by running at night when the air-cooled condenser temperature is at its minimum and off-peak power rates should prevail. In the most recent models of Solaris homes, auxiliary heat is provided by hot water from the fuel-burning service water system.

Solar cooling with absorption refrigeration

When solar energy is to be used for cooling as well as heating, the absorption system shown in Fig. 138, or one of its many modifications, may be used. The collector and storage subsystems must be able to operate at temperatures approaching 200°F (93.3°C) on hot summer days when the water from the cooling tower exceeds 80°F (26.7°C); but considerably lower operating water temperatures may be used when cooler water is available from the tower.

Passive solar features

There are a number of design elements which can be incorporated or added onto building designs to improve their ability to utilize or dissipate the solar heat. Control, in most passive systems, is accomplished by moving a component which regulates the amount of solar radiation that is admitted into the structure. Window shades or venetian blinds, manually manipulated, are the most widely used and simplest controls, but these can be automated if the user so chooses vend can afford it.

There are a growing number of so-called passive systems being offered on the market. Some of them fill wall or roof containers with water at various times to store or release heat. One blows plastic beads into the air space of double glazing to control heat movement through the glass. Other systems use dampered wall openings to control convection air flow. The literature is replete with many successful examples of passive devices and systems. The following design considerations will help to optimize passive solar energy features:

1. Orientation of building
2. Shape of building
3. Percentage and type of glass
4. Types of solar shading
5. Amount of insulation in walls and roof
6. Types and locations of plantings
7. Colors of building envelope
8. Natural ventilation features
9. Relation of building to site

The sun's heat and light are always available. Their utilization now will help to preserve our limited and dwindling fuel supplies.

THERMAL STORAGE

Since the sun does not shine all the time, it is necessary to furnish some means for storing the sun's heat for use when it is needed. The two systems available for storing heat are specific heat storage, using water or rocks, and heat-of-fusion storage, which uses various salts. Water storage tanks are the most common, with rock beds often used where air-type solar systems are employed. These storage media require substantially more space than heat-of-fusion systems, but the latter's problems of longevity, recycling, cost, and containment have not yet been fully resolved.

Thermal storage systems need not necessarily be limited to use with solar heating systems. The large storage capacity of both heating and cooling media makes it practical to consider using smaller boiler and refrigeration plants. There are several installations which have sufficient storage capacity to permit cutting the size of their heating and cooling plants in half, with substantial savings in both first and operating costs.

ENERGY CONSERVATION

It is often noted that 80 to 85 per cent of the buildings which will be in use in the year 2010 are already in existence. Most of these buildings have been built with little consideration for energy-use optimization.

Since buildings use over 40 per cent of all energy used in the United States, there is a vast potential for energy conservation that has yet to be tapped. There are many items which purport to be able to save energy in buildings. Without professional analysis, confusion exists as to which items are best for a given building and which should be implemented first for optimum results and shortest payback period. The most effective way to initiate an energy management program is to conduct a detailed energy survey and audit of the building. This will involve the following steps:

1. Examine and catalog building systems, equipment, uses, hours of operation, operating and maintenance procedures and logs, as-built drawings, etc.
2. Examine records of energy usage for the past several years.
3. Develop actual or simulated profiles of energy utilization characteristics of all major systems, equipment, and building uses.
4. Analyze all reasonable energy conservation measures and determine initial costs, energy benefits, and payback periods.
5. Set up a prioritized energy master plan for implementation when and as conditions dictate.
6. During implementation, monitor the design and construction phases to ensure that the anticipated energy benefits are realized.
7. After implementation, audit the new energy usage. If the expected benefits are not realized, the causes should be sought and remedial measures taken.

As a general rule, the major areas in which problems are most likely to come to light are:

1. Air distribution system
2. Building air infiltration
3. Automatic control systems
4. Operating pattern of building systems
5. Heating and air conditioning equipment
6. Lighting

Most buildings have had changes in usage, operating characteristics, equipment, etc., since they were built. They often have insufficient instrumentation to establish what the building's operating characteristics are at present. It is therefore prudent to obtain current system performance characteristics and to improve instrumentation so that the operating staff will be better able to monitor and operate the building, and it will be easier to evaluate all energy conservation measures implemented.

DEFINITION

Unit heaters are defined by ASHRAE as consisting of a heating element and a fan or blower within a common enclosure which is placed within or adjacent to the space to be heated. In general no ducts are employed, although many applications may require equipping the heater with directional outlets, baffles, diffusers, or adjustable louvres.

TYPES

There are two major types of unit heaters: The centrifugal housed fan type, Fig. 1 (commonly called a "Blower"); and the propeller fan type with the fan mounted directly behind the heating element and blowing air through it as in Fig. 2, or with the fan mounted directly in front of the heating element and drawing air through it as in Fig. 3. When arranged in the latter manner the unit is commonly called a projection heater. Heat may be supplied by steam, gas, hot water, or electricity.

Centrifugal fan type heaters deliver heated air at velocities ranging from 1,300 to 3,000 ft. per minute, have rated capacities of 135,000 to 1,300,000 Btu, and may have lengths of throw up to approximately 200 ft.

Propeller fan type heaters have outlet velocities from 400 to 1,200 ft. per minute, rated capacities of 18,000 to 340,000 Btu., and maximum throws of almost 80 ft. The vertical delivery type or projection unit heaters may be mounted up to heights of approximately 50 ft.

OPERATING CHARACTERISTICS

In general, centrifugal fan type or blower units discharge heated air at high velocities and are, therefore, indicated where long horizontal distances of throw are necessary or where heat must be concentrated to overcome heavy loads due to infiltration, such as at frequently opened doors. This type is also effective for operation against resistance where duct work is used. Slow speed blower type units are indicated when quiet operation is a prerequisite because of the inherent quietness of the blower type fan.

Horizontal delivery propeller type heaters are best used in those applications where blower type units would be eliminated through economic reasons or where a positive directional throw toward or along an exposed surface is necessary to exert a mixing effect with cool air. Vertical delivery or projection type unit heaters are used to advantage in those applications where exceptionally high ceilings are encountered and

where ceiling construction is such that reservoirs of waste heat gather at the ceiling. They are to be recommended wherever conditions call for a more directly downward delivery of air than is provided by horizontal delivery units.

Unit heater systems properly installed should:

1. Provide quick heat where it is needed.
2. Reduce temperature differentials between floor and ceiling.
3. Provide rapid circulation of air without objectionable draft.
4. Direct heated air so that uniform temperature distribution will prevail in the space heated.
5. Eliminate cold air stratum usually at floor level.
6. Reduce piping because of fewer heating elements required.
7. Save valuable floor space due to flexibility of mounting on floor, wall or ceiling.

LOCATION

Location with respect to height above the floor and direction and length or spread of throw is an important factor in the application of unit heaters. Most manufacturers give the recommended maximum mounting height and maximum and minimum length of throw for each unit model and for each fan speed. In most cases the distances given, particularly those referring to the length of throw, are approximate only and must be regarded as representative for the average.

Centrifugal fan or blower type units in general may be floor, wall, or ceiling mounted. Floor mounted types draw cold air from the floor and discharge heated air immediately above the head level. They are particularly adapted to closely occupied quarters.

Horizontal delivery propeller fan type heaters are most effective in spaces with ceiling heights of 20 ft. or less. Suspended, they should be located as close to the working zone as possible without directly discharging heated air on room occupants. This and the blower types should be arranged to blow toward or along exposed surfaces, preferably striking the wall at a slight angle so the heated air will mix with cool air along the wall. They should also be arranged so that the resulting air circulation will be rotational, reinforcing one another rather than resisting.

Vertical delivery or projection type units should be installed as close to the ceiling as practical in order to overcome stratification of air at high points. If units are not near exposed walls, they may be placed as evenly as practical to produce only slight

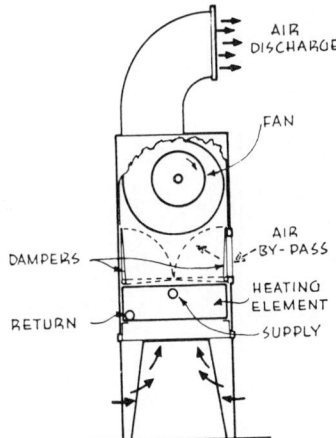

Fig. 1. Floor-mounted centrifugal fan (blower) type

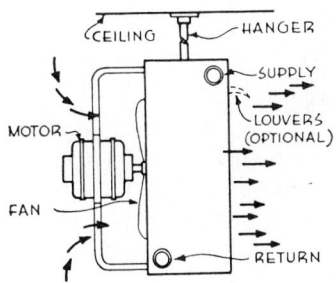

Fig. 2. Suspended propeller type

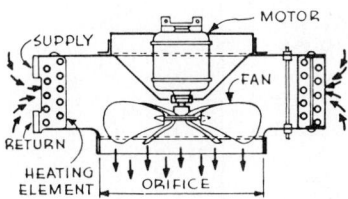

Fig. 3. Suspended projection type

overlapping of heat circles based on manufacturers' ratings of heat spread over floor areas.

SELECTION DATA

The performance of unit heaters is greatly affected by the care used in their selection and application. Of first importance is the unit heater capacity in Btu., which must be in all cases at least equivalent to the total heat load.

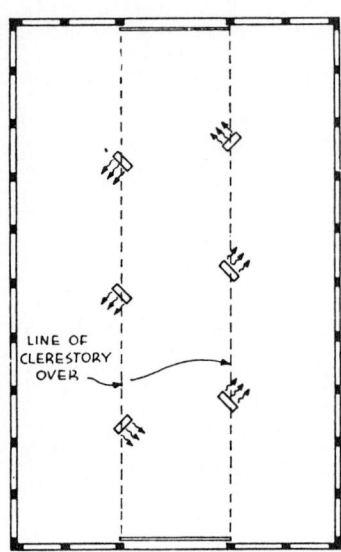

Fig. 4.   Horizontal delivery

Line installation arranged to direct the heated air at an angle to the wall, to blanket doors, and to reinforce general one-way circulation.

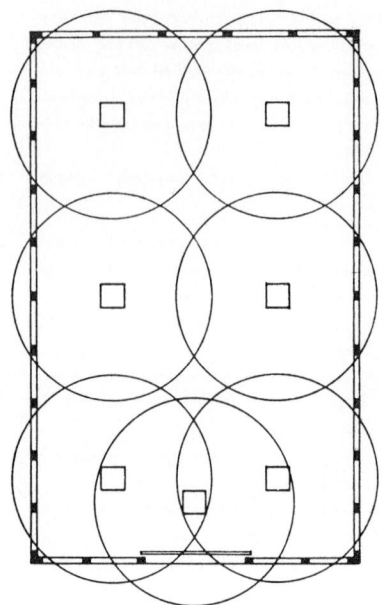

Fig. 5.   Vertical delivery

Projection type unit installation showing approximate floor and wall surface spread.

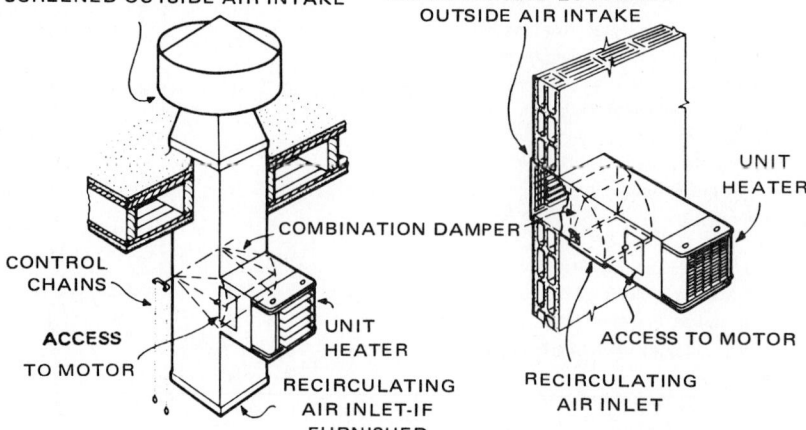

Fig. 6.   Ventilating details; outside connections

Entering-air temperatures will be higher for suspended type units than for floor mounted units, and this difference should be taken into account in determining the effective capacity of the units. Common practice allows 1½° increase in entering-air temperature per foot of height the unit suspended above the 5-ft. level.

Other factors upon which selection should be based are air quantity and distribution and final temperature. Good practice is to circulate the air at a rate not less than three air changes per hour based on room volume, and to avoid final temperatures in excess of 135°.

CONTROLS AND WIRING

Most manufacturers supply a range of manual, magnetic, and thermostatic temperature controls to meet any condition. Wiring diagrams are usually furnished with each unit and should be followed carefully to avoid blown fuses or damaged motors. Motors and all controls are of standard manufacture in almost all cases.

FRESH AIR CONNECTIONS

Although unit heaters are designed primarily to handle all recirculated air, they may be installed to handle either partial or total outdoor air. In such cases there will

be some reduction in the volume of air handled and in the Btu. capacity of the unit due to resistance of the ductwork. Fig. 6 shows details of outside ventilating connections. The proportion of fresh air to recirculated air can be regulated to suit almost any condition by simple damper control.

Where ventilators admit air at temperatures below freezing, as sometimes occurs in northern climates, a minimum steam pressure of 5 lbs. must be maintained on the heating surfaces to prevent freezing of condensate in the tubes.

PIPING

Piping for unit heaters must conform to the system requirements, at the same time allowing the units to serve as intended. Especially during heating-up periods rapid condensation of steam is characteristic of this type of equipment. Piping should be planned to accommodate this sudden condensation; at the same time be ample in supply to carry adequate steam to the surfaces to replace that condensed. Sufficient pipe size is, therefore, essential to all heating surfaces over which air is forced to flow. This is especially important where the fan operates under start-and-stop control and where air handled may consist either wholly or partly of cold air from outside. Condensation rate may vary rapidly in such installations and the need for ample pipe capacity may be acute.

PIPING CONNECTIONS

Heated air to do an effective job must be directed.

Practically all types of unit heaters employ some means to direct the air as it leaves the unit. These outlet air directional devices range from the simple louver type to the three-way multiple deflectors on triple nozzle blower units. Between these extremes is found variety of standard and special purpose outlet controls illustrated here.

Piping connections for proper operation of unit heaters should be installed per manufacturer's recommendations or as shown in the ASHRAE *Handbook*.

From Manual of Individual Water Supply Systems, Division of Environmental Engineering, Public Health Service, U.S. Department of Health, Education, and Welfare

Sources of water supply

When precipitation occurs, part of it may evaporate and return immediately to the atmosphere, part of it may infiltrate the soil, and part of it may flow across the surface of the ground.

Groundwater: Some of the moisture that penetrates into the soil replenishes the soil moisture or is used by growing plants and returned to the atmosphere by transpiration. Water that drains down below the root zone finally reaches a level at which all of the voids in the earth are filled with water. This is known as the zone of saturation, and the water in this zone is called groundwater. The upper surface of the zone of saturation, if not confined by impermeable material, is called the water table.

When an overlying impermeable formation confines the groundwater under a pressure greater than atmospheric, the water is said to be under artesian pressure. An underground layer of permeable rock or soil which permits the passage of water is called an aquifer. Seasonal variations in the supply of water to the underground reservoir may cause considerable changes to the elevation of the water table and the artesian pressure level. Wells which penetrate the water table and pump water out will lower the water table near the well. If the water is pumped out faster than it can be replaced, the results may be more serious than just depletion; salt-water encroachment or other undesirable pollution may occur. Where the water table intersects the ground surface, a spring is produced and the groundwater becomes surface water.

Surface water: Water which flows or is impounded on the surface of the earth is called surface water. Precipitation that does not enter the ground by infiltration or is not returned to the atmosphere by evaporation but flows over the ground surface is called direct runoff and is the principal source of surface water. Some surface water comes from groundwater reservoirs; examples are the springs mentioned above and the dry-weather flow of streams.

Table 1. Average daily water consumption for various buildings and other facilities

Types of establishments	Gallons per day
Airports (per passenger)	3–5
Apartments, multiple family (per resident)	60
Bath houses (per bather)	10
Camps:	
Construction, semipermanent (per worker)	50
Day with no meals served (per camper)	15
Luxury (per camper)	100–150
Resorts, day and night, with limited plumbing (per camper)	50
Tourist with central bath and toilet facilities (per person)	35
Cottages with seasonal occupancy (per resident)	50
Courts, tourist with individual bath units (per person)	50
Clubs:	
Country (per resident member)	100
Country (per nonresident member present)	25
Dwellings:	
Boarding houses (per boarder)	50
Additional kitchen requirements for nonresident boarders	10
Luxury (per person)	100–150
Multiple family apartments (per resident)	40
Rooming houses (per resident)	60
Single family (per resident)	50–75
Estates (per resident)	100–150
Factories (gallons per person per shift)	15–35
Hotels with private baths (two persons per room)	60
Hotels without private baths (per person)	50
Institutions other than hospitals (per person)	75–125
Hospitals (per bed)	250–400
Laundries, self-serviced (gallons per washing, i.e., per customer)	50
Livestock: (per animal):	
Cattle (drinking)	12
Dairy (drinking and servicing)	35
Goat (drinking)	2
Hog (drinking)	4
Horse (drinking)	12
Mule (drinking)	12
Sheep (drinking)	2
Steer (drinking)	12
Motels with bath, toilet and kitchen facilities (per bed space)	50
With bed and toilet (per bed space)	40
Parks:	
Overnight with flush toilets (per camper)	25
Trailers with individual bath units (per camper)	50
Picnic:	
With bath houses, showers, and flush toilets (per picnicker)	20
With toilet facilities only (gal. per picnicker)	10

Table 1 (cont.). Average daily water consumption for various buildings and other facilities

Types of establishments	Gallons per day
Poultry:	
Chickens (per 100)	5–10
Turkeys (per 100)	10–18
Restaurants with toilet facilities (per patron)	7–10
Without toilet facilities (per patron)	2½–3
With bar and cocktail lounge (additional quantity per patron)	2
Schools:	
Boarding (per pupil)	75–100
Day with cafeteria, gymnasiums, and showers (per pupil)	25
Day with cafeteria but no gymnasiums or showers (per pupil)	20
Day without cafeteria, gymnasiums, or showers (per pupil)	15
Service Stations (per vehicle)	10
Stores (per toilet room)	400
Swimming pools (per swimmer)	10
Theaters:	
Drive-in (per car space)	5
Movie (per auditorium seat)	5
Workers:	
Construction (per person per shift)	50
Day (school or offices per person per shift)	15

Table 2. Rates of flow for certain plumbing, household, and farm features

Location	Flow pressure,* psi	Flow rate, gpm
Ordinary basin faucet	8	2.0
Self-closing basin faucet	8	2.5
Sink faucet, ⅜ in.	8	4.5
Sink faucet, ½ in.	8	4.5
Bathtub faucet	8	6.0
Laundry tub faucet, ½ in.	8	5.0
Shower	8	5.0
Ball-cock for closet	8	3.0
Flush valve for closet	15	15–40†
Flushometer valve for urinal	15	15.0
Garden hose (50 ft, ¾-in. sill cock)	30	5.0
Garden hose (50 ft, ⅝-in. outlet)	15	3.33
Drinking fountains	15	0.75
Fire hose 1½ in., ½-in. nozzle	30	40.0

Flow pressure is the pressure in the supply near the faucet or water outlet while the faucet or water outlets is wide open and flowing.
† Wide range due to variation in design and type of closet flush valves.

Quality of water

Precipitation in the form of rain, snow, hail, or sleet contains very few impurities. Once it reaches the earth's surface, however, there are many opportunities for the introduction of mineral or organic pollution. Variations in the quality of water may be classified under four major headings:

1. *Physical* characteristics are such things as appearance, color, turbidity, temperature, taste, and odor.

2. *Chemical* differences between waters are sometimes evidenced by their observed reactions, such as the comparative performance of hard and soft waters in laundering.

3. *Biological* agents are very important in their relation to public health and may also be significant in modifying the physical and chemical characteristics of water.

4. *Radiological* factors must be considered in areas where there is a possibility that the water may have come in contact with radioactive substances.

Bacteriological quality: Water for drinking and cooking purposes must be free from disease-producing organisms such as bacteria, protozoa, virus, and helminths (worms). Unfortunately they are not easily identified; the techniques for comprehensive bacteriological examination are complex and time-consuming. It has been necessary to develop tests which indicate the relative degree of contamination in terms of an easily defined quantity. The most widely used test involves estimation of the number of bacteria of the coliform group, which are always present in fecal wastes. The recommended standards for drinking water permit not more than one organism per 100 milliliters (about half a cup) of water. A sample showing a higher concentration of coliforms is a good indication that the source has been contaminated. On the other hand, a negative result cannot be considered assurance of a continuously safe supply unless the results of a thorough sanitary survey of the surrounding area, together with subsequent negative samples, support this position.

Quantity of water

One of the first steps in the selection of a suitable water supply source is determining the demand which will be placed on it. The essential elements of water demand include the average daily water consumption and the peak rate of demand. Tables 1 and 2 will be helpful in preparing estimates of demand. When possible, the water system should have a minimum capacity of 500 to 600 gal per hr (8 to 10 gpm). This quantity of water will be adequate for normal household needs, including an average amount of lawn sprinkling, and is the smallest amount that can be really effective in firefighting.

Sanitary quality of groundwater

When water seeps downward through the underlying material to the water table, the particles held in suspension, including microorganisms, are usually filtered out and

Table 3. Minimum recommended distances between water supplies and various sources of contamination

Contamination sources	Well or suction line (distance in feet)
Building sewer	50
Septic tank	50
Disposal field	100
Seepage pit	100
Dry well	50
Cesspool	150

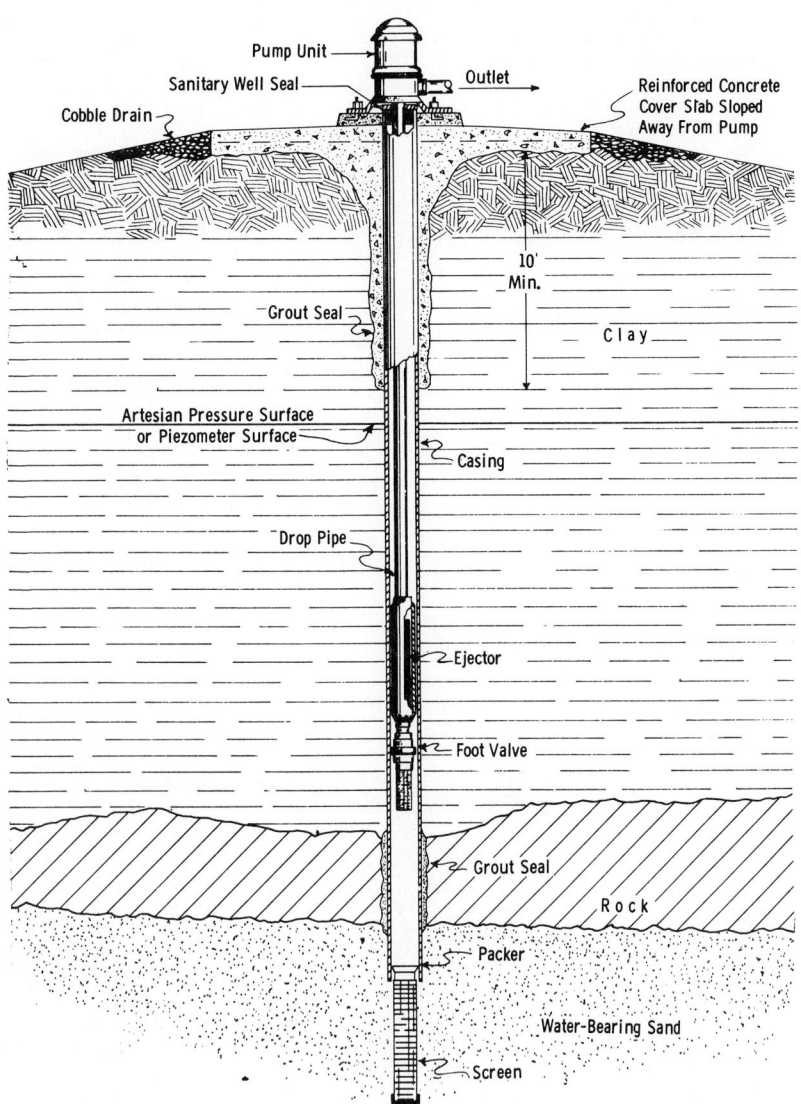

Fig. 1. Drilled Well

the length of time and storage conditions in the aquifer are usually unfavorable to bacterial multiplication or survival. On the other hand, since the water table may rise during periods of heavy precipitation, the upper part of the groundwater near the water table may easily be contaminated. Good protection is achieved through the construction of a deep well with a watertight casing, surrounded by cement grout extending a minimum of 10 ft below the ground surface. Wells should be located as far from sources of contamination as conditions will permit. Table 3 lists *minimum* recommended distances.

Wells

When a well is pumped, the level of the water table in the vicinity of the well will be lowered; this is known as drawdown. A common way to describe the yield of a well is to express its discharge capacity in relation to its drawdown. This relationship is called the specific capacity of the well and is expressed in gallons per minute (gpm) per foot of drawdown.

Wells may be *dug* by hand, *driven* by maul or pile-driver, *bored* by earth auger, *jetted* by water jet, or *drilled* by percussion or rotary drill. Only the drilled well can carry a casing of adequate size (6 in. or more in diameter) to a depth of several hundred feet, as is sometimes required. A typical drilled well is shown in Fig. 1. Note that in order to protect against contamination by surface water the casing should be surrounded at ground level by a 4-in. concrete slab extending at least 2 ft in each di-

rection and sloped away from the well; the surrounding finished grade should also be sloped away from the well. These precautions are in addition to the watertight casing surrounded by cement grout mentioned earlier. A sanitary well seal should be installed at the top of the well casing.

All newly constructed or repaired wells should be disinfected promptly, as soon as the work is complete. This can be done by using calcium hypochlorite (70 per cent free chlorine), available from swimming pool supply outlets and some hardware stores; 1 oz of dry chemical mixed with 2 quarts of water provides a stock solution which will treat 100 gal of water. It is usually more convenient to use readily available household bleach (soldium hypochlorite, 5.25 per cent available chlorine); this can be diluted

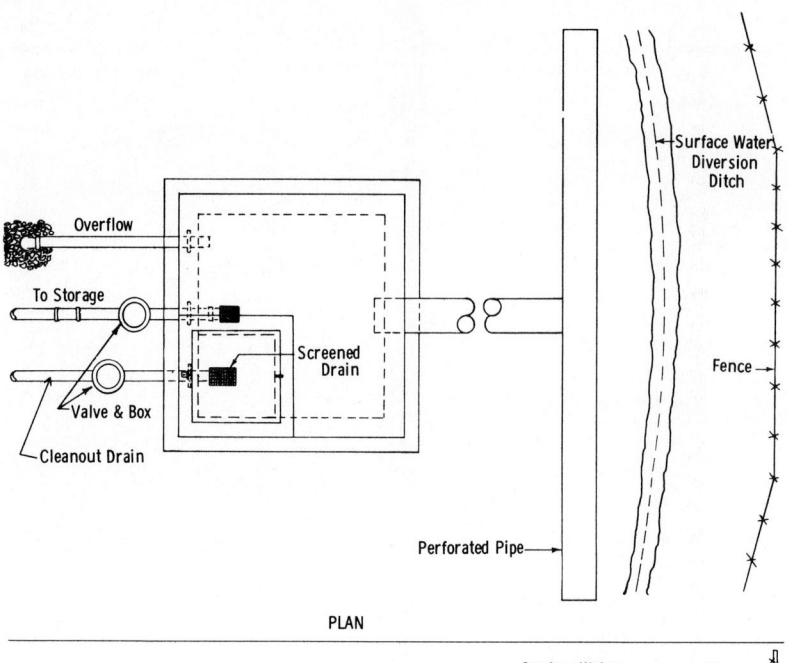

PLAN

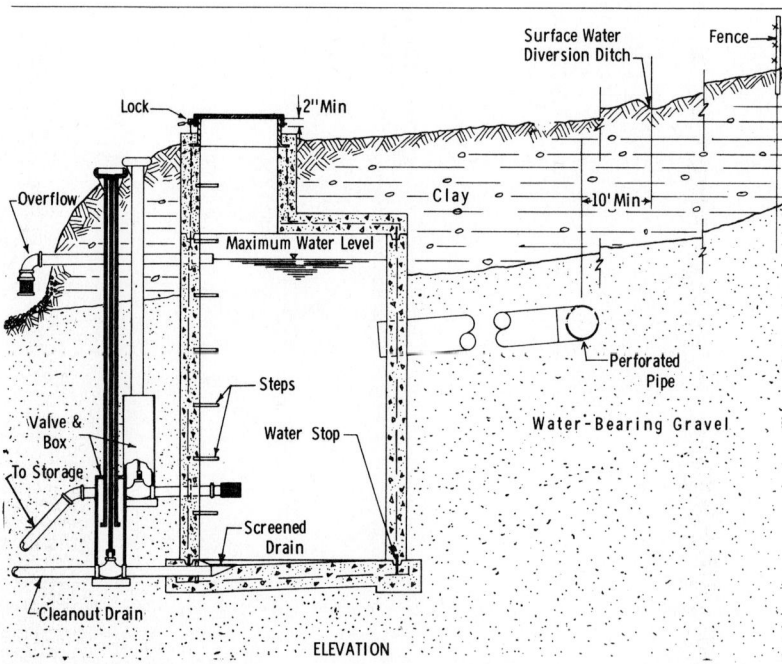

ELEVATION

Fig. 2. Spring protection

with two parts of water to form the stock solution for treating 100 gal of water.

Springs

Springs are sometimes used as sources of domestic water when investigation indicates that they have adequate capacity to meet the estimated needs throughout the year and seem to be reasonably safe from contamination. Recommended procedures for developing a spring for domestic water supply are shown in Fig. 2.

Surface water

Where groundwater sources are limited or nonexistent, it may be necessary to utilize surface water. This is best done by the use of controlled catchments and cisterns, augmented if necessary by filtration and disinfection facilities. The catchment may be a roof or a paved ground area. From it the water drains into the cistern, a covered storage tank, usually built under ground. If the catchment is on the ground it should have a curb all around to keep out unde-

sirable surface drainage and a fence to keep out animals. The size of the cistern and the area of the catchment will depend upon the size of the family and the length of time between periods of heavy rainfall. For example, for a family of four and a period of 150 days between heavy rains, the volume of the cistern required will be 15,000 gallons ($4 \times 25 \times 150$). The cistern could be 10 ft deep by 15 ft square. If the annual rainfall is 50 in. and we design for $\frac{2}{3}$ of that amount to allow for droughts, then the

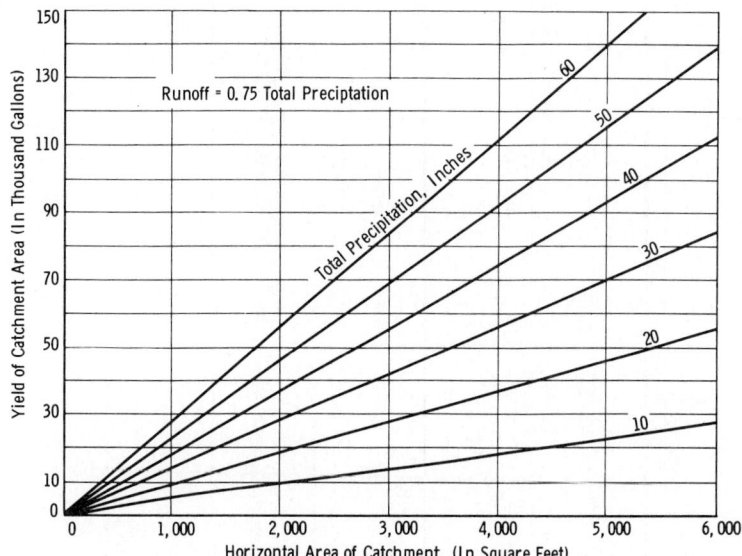

Fig. 3. Yield of impervious catchment areas

total design rainfall is 13.7 in. (50 $\times$ $^2/_3$ $\times$ $^{150}/_{365}$). Referring to Fig. 3, the required catchment area is found to be 2,600 sq ft. Recommended construction details for a cistern are shown in Fig. 4.

PUMPS

Pumps are of three generic types: positive displacement, centrifugal, and jet. One type of positive displacement pump is the reciprocating pump, in which a piston is moved back and forth in a tightly fitted cylinder. Another type is the helical or spiral rotor, consisting of a helical shaft which rotates in a rubber sleeve. Another is the regenerative turbine type in which a wheel with blades or "buckets" on its outer edge rotates in a fixed casing. Centrifugal pumps also contain a rotating impeller with blades which do not actually displace the water but impart a high velocity to it. If necessary,

the process can be repeated, resulting in a multistage pump. The vertical-shaft turbine and the submersible pump are types of centrifugal pumps often used for deep wells. In the submersible pump, not only is the pumping mechanism submerged, as it is in most pumps, but the motor is also submerged. The jet pump is actually a combined centrifugal and ejector pump; the deeper the well, the less efficient it is.

The size of the pump (rate of water delivery) depends on the time of pump operation and the total water consumption between periods of pumping. If the well yield will permit, a pump with a minimum capacity of 600 gph should be used for the average home water system. When the well yield is low in comparison with peak demand, an increase in the storage capacity is required. The life of a motor is reduced by excessive stopping and starting; therefore the system should be designed in such a way that the interval between starting and stopping is as long as practicable. Pumps that deliver water to pressure tanks of limited capacity should be capable of delivering at least 120 per cent of the peak demand. When storage for more than one day is provided, the pump should be capable of delivering three times the maximum daily rate of water consumption. Pumps delivering water to storage reservoirs with a capacity of more than one week's demand should have a capacity of 150 per cent of the maximum daily consumption.

The pump must be installed in such a manner as to prevent pollution of the water

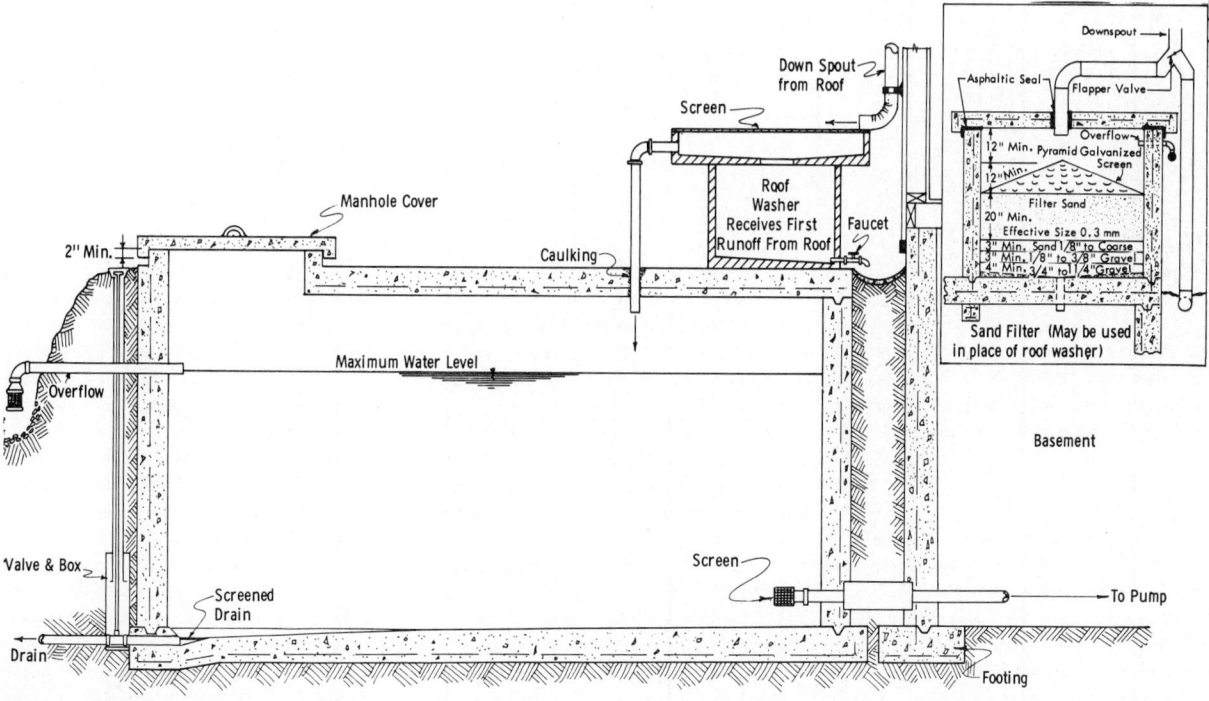

Fig. 4. Cistern

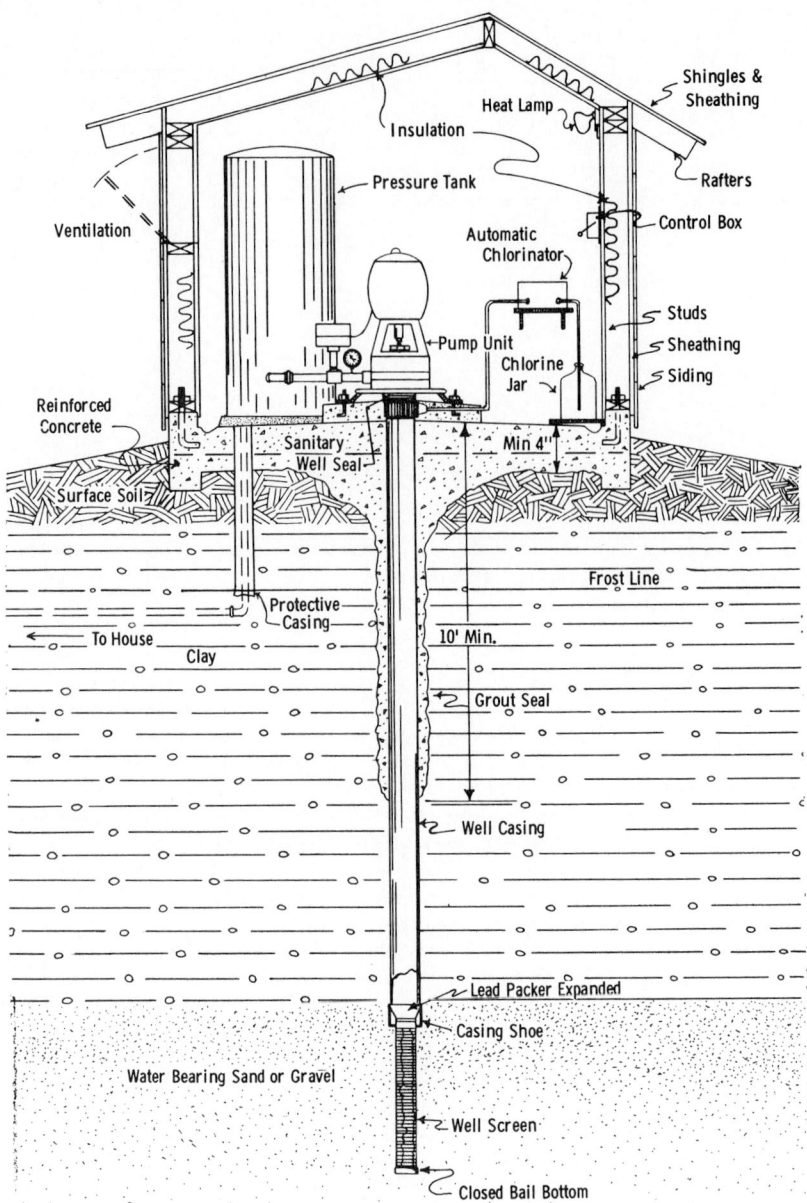

Fig. 5. Pump house

by lubricants or other maintenance materials as well as by dust, insects, and rodents. The most common type of installation is the over-the-well type. The pump should be placed on a concrete base rising at least 4 in. above the floor of the pumphouse. The top of the base should slope away from the well. Well casings should extend at least 6 in. above the pump house floor.

Pressure tanks

Water is pumped directly from the well into the pressure tank, thereby compressing the entrapped air in the tank. The compressed air supplies the pressure that sends the water through the distribution system. The air pressure and thus the water pressure in the tank can be controlled between

desired limits by means of pressure switches which stop the pump at the maximum setting and start it at the minimum setting. The capacity of pressure tanks is usually small when compared to the total daily water consumption; they should not be thought of as storage reservoirs. Generally, the pressure tank should be about ten times the pump capacity in gallons per minute. Pressure tanks for individual home installations should have a capacity of at least 42 gal or about 10 to 15 gal per person.

Pump houses

A pump house (Fig. 5) installed above the surface of the ground should be used. The pumproom floor should be of watertight construction, preferably concrete, and

should slope uniformly away in all directions from the well casing. The building should be well insulated so that by the use of a small heat source such as a light bulb or heating cable, freezing can be prevented. In areas where power failures may occur, the provision of an emergency gasoline-driven generator or pump should be considered. If the pumping rate lowers the water level in the well 10 ft or more, the use of a well vent is recommended. The upper end of the vent pipe, protected with proper screening, should be turned downward. It is desirable to provide a water sampling tap on the discharge line of the pump. Because of the pollution hazards involved, a well pit to house the pumping equipment or to permit access to the top of the well is *not* recommended.

By GEORGE R. JERUS, *P.E.*
Vice President—Meyer, Strong and Jones, P.C., Mechanical and Electrical Engineers

OUTLINE OF PIPING MATERIALS

Hot and cold water piping

a. Brass pipe with cast-brass fittings.

b. Copper tubing (Type K, or L) with cast- or wrought-copper fittings and 95–5 tin-antimony solder.

c. Type TP or B copper tubing with cast-brass fittings and silver solder.

d. Galvanized pipe with galvanized malleable fittings and/or cast iron fittings.

e. Plastic pipe and fittings.

f. Cast-iron waterworks pipe and fittings (for underground piping).

g. Galvanized pipe with victaulic fittings.

Gas

a. Black steel pipe with galvanized or black malleable iron fittings.

b. Black steel pipe with welded fittings.

Oxygen and nitrous oxide piping

a. Copper tubing (Type K or L) with wrought- or cast-copper fittings with 95–5 antimony solder.

Vacuum piping

a. Copper tubing with copper fittings and 95–5 tin-antimony solder.

Compressed air

a. Copper tubing with copper fittings and 95–5 tin-antimony solder.

b. Black steel pipe with galvanized malleable fittings.

Drainage piping including leaders

a. Cast-iron soil pipe and fittings.

b. Galvanized wrought-iron pipe with recessed black cast-iron fittings.

c. Galvanized steel pipe with black cast-iron recessed fittings.

d. Copper drainage tubing (Type K, L, or M) with cast- or wrought-copper fittings.

e. Cast iron no-hub pipe and fittings.

Acid drainage

a. Silicon iron pipe and fittings with cast-iron or tellurium lead traps; special oakum and lead caulking.

b. Glass pipe with glass fittings.

c. Plastic pipe with plastic fittings. (Type of discharge from fixture must be known in order to select proper plastic.)

d. Knightware pipe and fittings with poured-mastic joints.

Vent piping

a. Cast-iron pipe and fittings.

b. Galvanized-steel or wrought-iron pipe with black cast-iron or malleable cast-iron fittings.

c. Copper tubing and fittings.

d. Cast iron no-hub pipe and fittings.

Sewers (Outside building, more than 5 ft from foundation wall)

a. Extra-heavy cast-iron pipe with cast-iron fittings.

b. Vitreous tile pipe and fittings with hot-poured-mastic joints, factory-applied slip-seal joints, or cement joints.

c. Concrete pipe with hot-poured-mastic joints, ribbed neoprene gaskets or cement joints.

d. Asbestos-cement pipe and fittings with ribbed neoprene gaskets.

e. Asphalt-wrapped pipe (Orangeburg) with tapered joints and fittings.

Subsoil drainage

a. Agricultural tile with open joints.

b. Porous-wall cement pipe.

c. Perforated asbestos-cement pipe.

d. Perforated asphalt-wrapped pipe.

e. Corrugated-steel pipe for culverts.

WATER DISTRIBUTION SYSTEMS

The diagrams in Fig. 1 show typical good practice in the design of hot and cold water distribution systems for residences. These diagrams are based on the essentials of distribution under various sets of practical conditions, but should not be interpreted as a complete solution to any specific residential problem. The pipe sizes and arrangements shown, however, are generally adaptable without substantial change to most small houses, being adequate for dwellings that contain two bathrooms in addition to a first-floor lavatory and toilet and the usual kitchen and laundry fixtures.

Pipes for both hot and cold water are sized for permanently clean bores. It is assumed that the water supply will be comparatively soft, so that no precipitated coating will form on pipe walls, reduce inside diameters, and prevent free flow of water. In localities where the water contains a concentration of hardness (expressed as calcium carbonate) sufficient to cause even a slight precipitation in cold water lines, it may be necessary either to increase pipe sizes in both hot and cold lines or to install a water softener.

COLD WATER LINES

Tap from the street water main can be 5/8 in. for very small houses, and 3/4 in. for houses containing a number of fixtures equivalent to three bathrooms in addition to kitchen and laundry fixtures.

Service pipe, or house main, can be 3/4 in. for small houses, but must be at least 1 in. for larger houses as defined above.

Pressure-reducing valve **is unnecessary if the street pressure is 80 psi or less. Street pressures above 80 psi should be reduced through a valve located** in the house main on the street side of the meter.

Drips should be installed in the lower portions of basement lines so that the entire system can be completely drained.

Shut-off valves are necessary in the basement on the street side of fittings in the supply main, adjacent to the air chamber, on the line supplying the

hot water heater, and at the bases of all supply risers. Fixtures should be individually valved.

Air chambers **or shock absorbers will prevent water hammer throughout the piping system, and can be located in any convenient part of the main on the house side of the meter. The air chamber should be fitted with shut-offs and pet cocks, for it will require draining when the air within it is absorbed by the water. Instead of an air chamber, a commercially stocked shock absorber may be installed.**

Water softeners are available in various sizes and types, all of which require a salt tank for regeneration. Regeneration can be accomplished manually or automatically; automatic regeneration is usually controlled by a meter on the softened-water line. A floor drain for disposal of filter wash water is essential if a water-softening device is to be used.

Insulation of cold water pipes is desirable throughout the building, to prevent damage from condensation drip, to maintain proper water temperatures, and to muffle flow noises. Wrappings of 1/2-in. glass fiber (or similar material) with vapor-barrier jacket are satisfactory.

HOT WATER LINES

A simple form of circulation can be accomplished by connecting the hot water house supply to the hot water return circulation in a simple loop at the basement ceiling. Such a loop can be tapped by supply risers to serve all fixtures. Circulation serves to conserve energy by reducing or eliminating dead ends.

The type of circulating hot water distribution shown is adaptable to most residences. A more elaborate type would require individual supply and return risers to serve each bathroom or group of superimposed fixtures.

The hot water heating layout indicates an arrangement of pipes that will give unusually quick hot water service from fixtures in a noncirculating system and nearly instantaneous service in a circulating system. This service is ac-

With Non-circulating Hot Water

With Circulating Hot Water

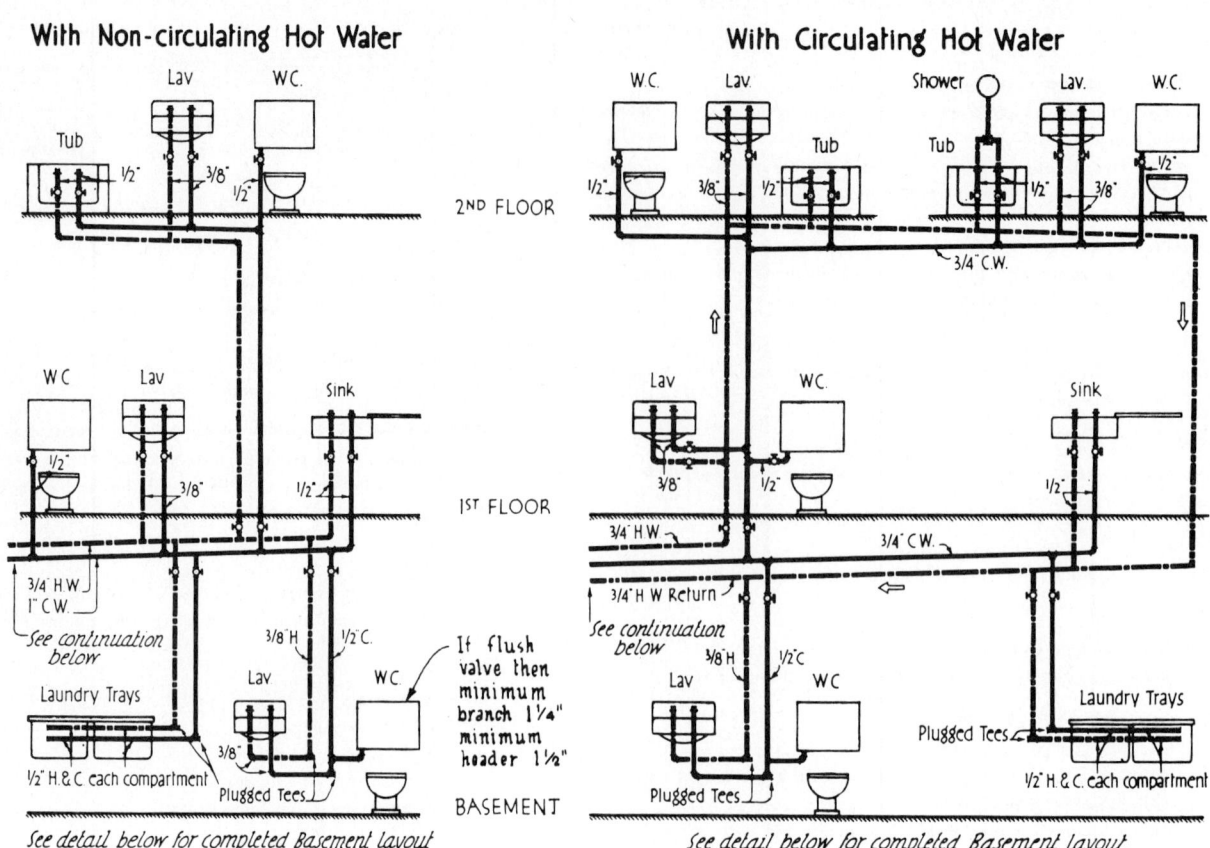

NOTE! *These sections are diagrammatic and drawn to no scale.*

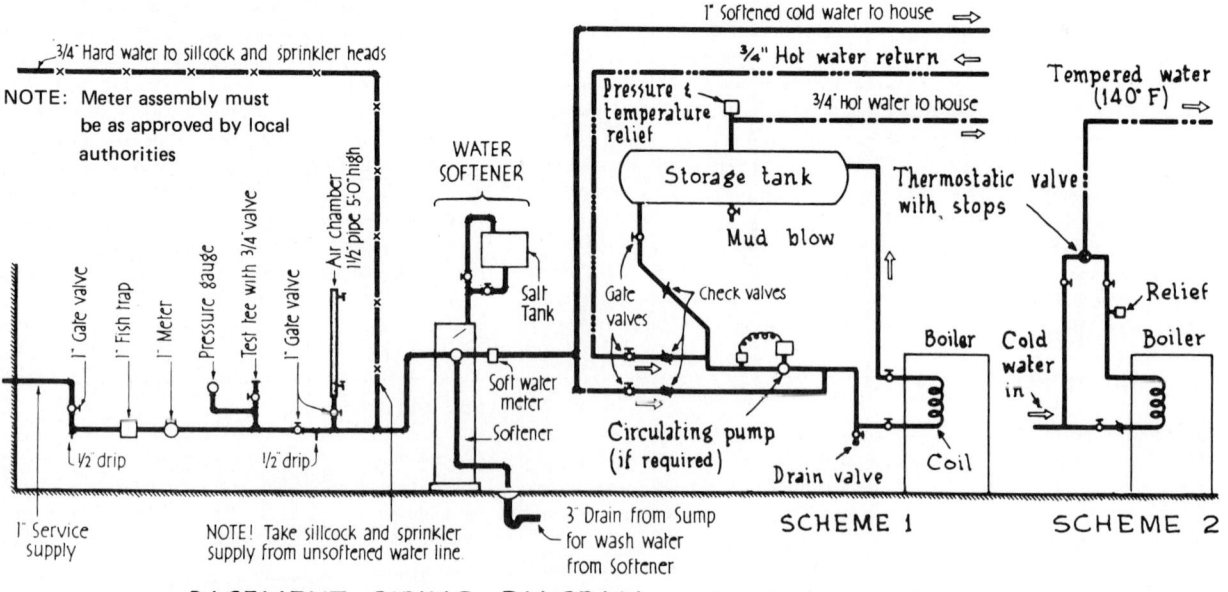

BASEMENT PIPING DIAGRAM *(see Sections above for continuations)*

Fig. 1. Basement piping diagram

complished by connecting the hot water supply line (from the heater) directly to the house supply instead of to the tank. When a faucet is opened, water is drawn first from the supply line from the heater, thus stimulating circulation in the returns from the tank. Check valves prevent cold water from being drawn into the house hot water supply pipe.

Insulation of hot water lines throughout the building conserves energy by ensuring quick service at faucets. Coverings of ½ to 1-in. glass fiber are satisfactory.

Drips should be sufficient in number to drain all hot water pipes, and should be installed approximately as shown in relation to water heating and storage equipment.

HOUSE TANKS

If the height of a building requires water pressure in excess of that in the city mains, a house tank must be provided. A tank would also be required if the peak draw would reduce the pressure on the highest usable floor to less than 10 psi—the minimum pressure required for satisfactory operation of fixtures, particularly those with flush valves. To provide sufficient pressure, the bottom of the tank must be elevated about 31 ft above the highest fixture, an elevation ensuring a static pressure of 13.5 psi. If water is required above the highest fixture (as, for example, in air conditioning), a booster pump or separate pressure tank may be needed.

More than one tank may have to be installed to provide pressure breaks within a very tall building; the supply from a tank in the penthouse might produce excessive pressures at the lower floors, and thus cause excessive wear on washers, valves, and other moving parts.

Basement shut-off valves are necessary to close the hot water return circulation line and to close individual risers in case of repairs or other emergencies. All fixtures should be individually valved.

Check valves should be installed on the heater return from the tank, on the cold water supply to the heater, and on the hot water return circulation line.

Relief valve should be installed on the hot water storage tank. A combination pressure and temperature relief valve should be used. An energy cut-off should also be provided.

Tanks usually serve a dual purpose: domestic water supply and a reserve for fire protection.

Materials for house tanks

Tanks may be constructed of either wood or steel. Wood tanks are circular and require ample ventilation to prevent dry rot. Table 1 gives the dimensions, weight, and capacity of wood tanks. Steel tanks may be built to any shape, and may include a dividing partition to permit cleaning of one compartment without interrupting water service to the building. Table 2 gives the dimensions and capacity of various steel tanks.

Capacities of tanks

The required capacity of a tank varies with the capacity and running time of the house or fill pumps. A half-hour supply of domestic water is generally sufficient if pump capacity is equal to the hourly load. Table 3 gives water-consumption figures that can be used to determine tank and pump capacities.

For example, assume that a commercial office building has an occupancy of 4500 persons:

$$4500 \times 3.8 \text{ gal per hr per person} = 17{,}100 \text{ gal per hr}$$
$$\text{Tank should have } \tfrac{1}{2}\text{-hr supply} = 8{,}550 \text{ gal}$$
$$\text{Pump should have 1-hr supply} = 17{,}100 \text{ gal per hr}$$
$$= 285 \text{ gpm}$$

Two pumps should be installed to provide breakdown service. The pump size would have to be modified to accommodate an air-conditioning load, which would be divided between the pumps. Make-up requirements for air conditioning are dependent upon the method of refrigeration, and therefore the design engineer should be consulted.

Table 1. Weight and capacity of wood tanks

| Weight per Ft Depth, Tons | Weight Tons | 1.68 | 2.12 | 2.61 | 3.16 | 3.75 | 4.39 | 5.07 | 5.81 | 6.60 | 7.43 | 8.32 | 9.25 | 10.23 | Special (dia. x H) | Weight Tons | Cap. Gal. |
Gal per Ft Depth → Cap. Gal		376.01	475.89	587.52	710.9	846.03	992.91	1151.5	1321.9	1504.1	1697.9	1903.6	2120.9	2350.1	(Inside Diameter / Depth of Tank, Feet)		
2,444	11.2	8						14								73.2	16,524
3,093	14.0		8				12									78.7	17,828
3,196	14.5				20											81.6	18,369
3,819	17.3			8			16									74.0	16,697
3,948	17.8	12					14									83.0	18,801
4,045	18.3			10			16									85.0	19,168
4,700	21.2	14						12								88.0	19,988
4,994	22.5			10											15'-3½" dia. x 16'-0" H	88.0	20,000
4,997	22.5		12			18										84.1	19,000
5,452	24.5	16						14								93.5	21,224
5,949	26.8		14					16								96.2	21,809
6,043	27.2			10		18										96.4	21,811
6,169	27.8		12						12							98.0	22,269
6,900	31.0	16			20											94.3	21,303
7,191	32.2				10			14								104.6	23,795
7,344	33.0		14			20										108.0	24,455
7,464	33.5			12				16								108.4	24,620
8,440	37.7				10		18									109.4	24,818
8,519	38.2					16									17'-0½" dia. x 16'-0" H	110.3	25,000
8,883	39.7				12				14							116.3	26,511
8,886	39.8			14				16								121.2	27,602
9,788	43.6					10	20									122.6	27,826
10,308	46.1			16				18								123.2	28,015
10,426	46.5					12				14						128.5	29,376
10,575	47.2				14										17'-6½" dia. x 18'-0" H	130.2	30,000
11,236	50.0						10		16							134.8	30,753
11,730	52.4		18					18								137.9	31,409
12,091	54.0					12		20								138.1	31,411
12,267	55.0				16					16						149.0	34,076
12,441	55.2						14		18							154.3	34,995
12,785	56.7						10	20								155.3	35,217
13,152	58.7				20					18						169.6	38,777
13,880	61.5					12				20						171.8	39,237
13,960	63.0				18										19'-1½" dia. x 20'-0" H	175.2	40,000
14,394	64.0						14							20		189.9	43,477
14,397	64.0						16							22		210.5	48,177
15,000	66.5	14'-2½" dia. x 14'-0"													21'-6½" dia. x 20'-0" H	220.6	50,000
15,652	70.0						20								23'-6½" dia. x 20'-0" H	260.4	60,000
15,793	69.8									12					23'-10½" dia. x 24'-0" H	325.0	75,000
16,383	73.0						18								28'-6" dia. x 24'-0" H	450.0	100,000

Table 2. Capacity of steel tanks

| Tank Area, Sq Ft | Height of Tank, Feet, Allowing 1 Ft for Floats and Overflow | | | | | | |
| | 4.0 | 4.5 | 5.0 | 5.5 | 6.0 | 7.0 | 8.0 |
	Capacity of Tanks, Gallons						
60	1350	1580	1800	2030	2250	2700	3150
80	1800	2100	2400	2700	3000	3600	4200
100	2250	2620	3000	3370	3750	4500	5250
120	2700	3150	3600	4050	4500	5400	6300
140	3150	3670	4200	4730	5250	6300	7350
160	3600	4190	4800	5400	6000	7200	8400
180	4050	4720	5400	6080	6750	8100	9450
200	4500	5230	6000	6730	7500	9000	10500
220	4950	5750	6600	7400	8250	9900	11600
240	5400	6300	7200	8100	9000	10800	12600
260	5850	6810	7800	8800	9750	11700	13600
280	6300	7350	8400	9450	10500	12600	14700
300	6750	7890	9000	10500	11250	13500	15800

Table 3. Water consumption in office buildings

Building Type	Consumption Gal per Hr per Person
Commercial, no air conditioning	3.8
Commerical, with air conditioning	7.3–9.2
Owner-occupied, with kitchen and laundry, no air conditioning	7.3
Owner-occupied, with kitchen, laundry, and air conditioning	9.0

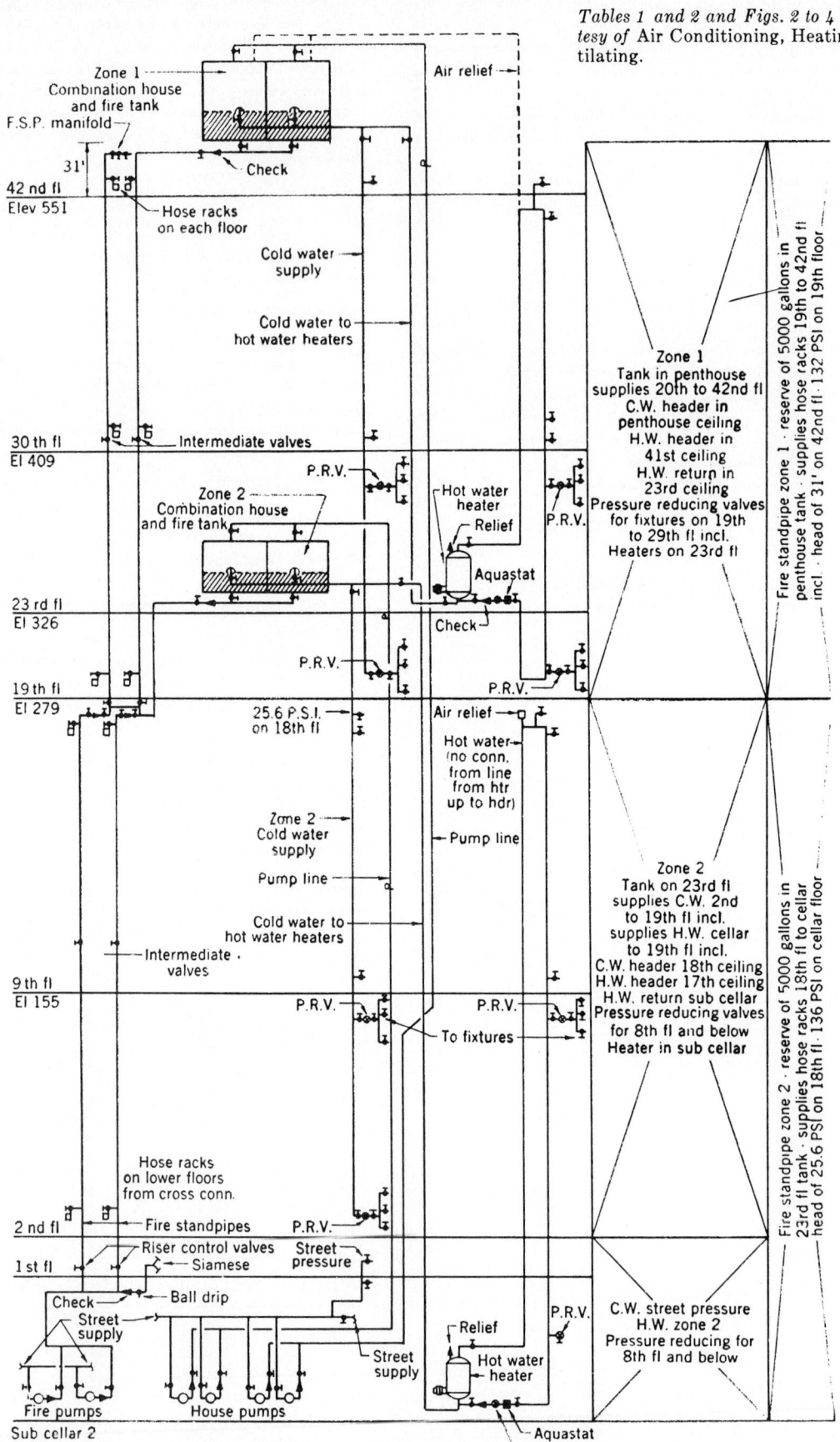

Tables 1 and 2 and Figs. 2 to 4 are by courtesy of Air Conditioning, Heating and Ventilating.

Fig. 2.   Gravity water supply system with pressure-reducing valves, serving two zones

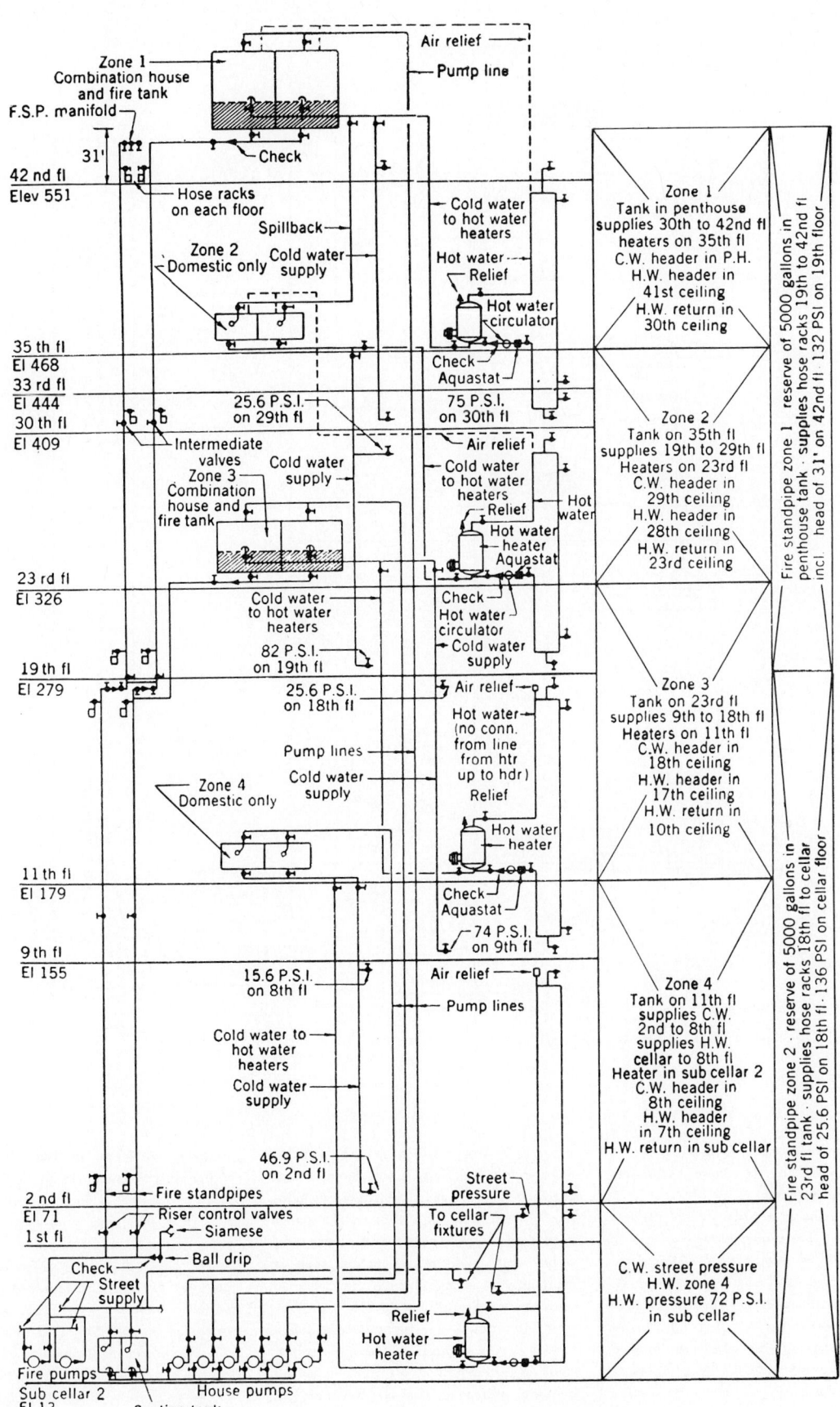

Fig. 3. Gravity water supply system without pressure-reducing valves, serving four zones

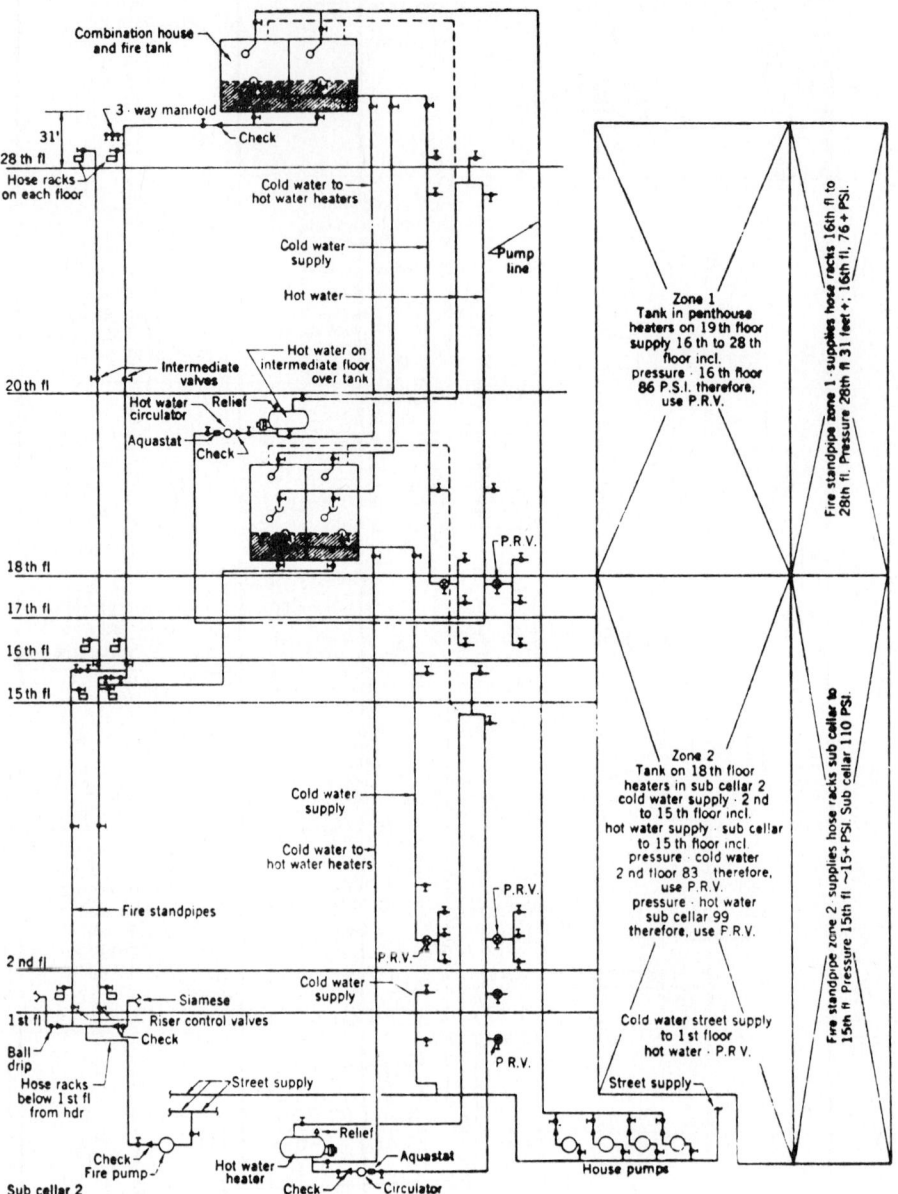

Fig. 4. Gravity tanks—spillback system

The riser diagrams in Fig. 2, 3, and 4 show typical methods of zoning the services for high-rise buildings.

Figure 2 shows a gravity water supply system with pressure-reducing valves. In this system, the pumps take suction from the city mains, and must therefore be selected with a nonoverload characteristic for varying street pressures. The number of zones is reduced, but pressure-reducing valves are required on the lower floors of each zone. These valves may require high maintenance and must be installed in accessible locations.

Figure 3 shows an ideal arrangement for a very tall building, since maintenance problems are cut to a minimum. Installation of a suction tank enables the pump head to be kept constant and a very efficient pump selected. A suction tank is mandatory in many localities in order to prevent excessive pressure drops in the city main. The equipment for supplying each zone, however, requires considerable space, which is usually at a premium in a tall building. Moreover, this system would be more expensive initially than the modified version shown in Fig. 2.

Figure 4 shows a "spillback" system. All of the water is pumped up to the highest tank, and some is then allowed to spill back into the tank supplying the lower zone. A system of this type is employed if the capacity of the high-zone pump is too small for the head required and pump efficiency is very low; the pumping of all water for the building into one tank enables a more efficient pump to be selected. The spillback line must be sized to provide for the peak draw in the lower zone.

A certain amount of calculation is necessary before equipment can be selected for heating, storing, and distributing domestic hot water. The calculation of precise requirements often involves many technicalities that call for specialized engineering knowledge. In any event, the architect's attention is required to solve planning problems that arise prior to the installation of any sort of mechanical equipment.

As a basis for the preliminary selection of domestic hot water equipment, and as an aid in planning its proper installation, rule-of-thumb approximations can be made that will allow the architect to determine with reasonable accuracy the required capacity and dimensions.

Determining domestic hot water requirements involves, first, the capacity of the heating plant and, second, the capacity of one or more hot water storage tanks, unless an instantaneous or tankless hot water heater is to be installed. Heating plant and tank capacities must be mutually adjusted to solve the particular problem at hand. For example, if space for hot water storage is at a premium, the capacity of the heating plant should be increased to deliver the amount of hot water required during periods of greatest demand. If, on the other hand, tanks are to be used, it is good practice to size the heater capacity to deliver hot water sufficient for average hourly demands and provide a storage tank of sufficient capacity to supply additional demands during peak periods.

SOLAR ENERGY

The use of solar energy for the production of domestic hot water has long been a familiar practice in subtropical regions. With the growing scarcity of other sources of energy more attention is now being given to the use of solar energy in temperate climates. Although many installations have been made in recent years, there are as yet no uniform standards in this field. In March 1979, the U.S. Department of Energy and the Department of Housing and Urban Development began a joint study aimed at developing such a standard.

COLD WATER CONSUMPTION

Domestic hot water requirements depend largely upon the type of building and its use. Since the types, characteristics, and activities of building occupants vary widely, a liberal estimate of water consumption should be made. Thus it is customary to estimate hot water requirements on the basis of cold water consumption per person.

It has been found that the average cold water consumption per person in a house of average size and equipment is close to 50 gal per day. On this basis, consumption allowances have been developed for other types of buildings.

For large residences, allow 100 gal per person per day. This figure includes supply for all normal requirements and wastage.

For low-rent apartments, allow 75 gal per person per day. This figure is a minimum based upon minimum plumbing fixture requirements.

For high-class apartments, allow 100 gal per person per day. A rough estimate of water consumption in apartments can be made by multiplying the number of bedrooms by 200.

For hotels, allow 100 gal per person per day. Approximate total water consumption in hotels is commonly figured on the basis of 60 per cent oc-cupancy. Thus, 60 per cent of the number of bedrooms, multiplied by 100, would give a reasonably safe average figure. That figure, however, would not include requirements for kitchen, laundry, or cold-storage equipment, or any other type of mechanical unit.

For office buildings, allow 25 gal per person per day. To estimate building occupancy, allow 125 sq ft of floor space per person, exclusive of elevator space, corridors, or service areas.

Probable maximum peak loads for cold water are relatively unimportant in apartments, hotels, and office buildings that use cold water storage tanks. Such tanks are required in most high-rise buildings (see House Tanks).

HOT WATER REQUIREMENTS

Consumption of domestic hot water is usually estimated as one-third the amount of the cold water consumption.

Heater capacities and storage tank sizes are based upon the maximum probable hourly demand for hot water—the hourly peak load. Instantaneous heaters, which have no storage tanks, are sized to satisfy a peak gallon-per-minute draw. If, for example, average hourly consumption in actual use was 60 gal per hr, all of which was used in 10 minutes, then the instantaneous heater would have to supply 60 gal within that 10 minutes. Thus, unless an unlimited quantity of heat is available, instantaneous heaters should not be used.

The heating load on a boiler or heater required for a desired supply of domestic hot water is based primarily upon the average hourly demand for hot water.

Rule 1. To determine total daily consumption of cold water, multiply the number of building occupants by the number of gallons per person per day as listed in Table 4.

Rule 2. To determine total daily consumption of hot water, divide the result of Rule 1 by 3.

Rule 3. To determine the maximum probable hourly demand for hot water, divide the total daily hot water consumption (from Rule 2) by 10.

Rule 4. To determine the average hourly demand for hot water, divide the total daily consumption of hot water (from Rule 2) by 24.

In lieu of the above calculations, Table 8 gives hot water consumption figures obtained from surveys of actual buildings.

HEATER CAPACITY

Domestic hot water is commonly considered as cold water whose temperature has been raised 100°F. The average temperature difference is between 40° and 140°F. Heater ratings are based on the number of square feet of steam or hot water radiation required to raise the temperature of 1 gal of water 100°F (see Table 5).

Steam boiler rating: One sq ft of steam radiation is equal to 240 Btu, and 833 Btu are required to raise the temperature of 1 gal of water 100°F. Therefore 833/240 (or 3.5) sq ft of equivalent direct steam radiation (EDR) would be required to accomplish that result.

Hot water boiler rating: One sq ft of hot water radiation is equal to 150 Btu (833 Btu are required to raise the temperature of 1 gal of water 100°F). Therefore 833/150 (5.6) sq ft of hot water radiation would be required to accomplish that result.

Table 4.   Cold water consumption

Type of Building	Gals. per person per day
Residence, Average	50
" Large	100
Apartments, Low-rent	75
" High-class	100
Hotels	100
Office Buildings	25

Rule 5. To find required capacity of hot water heater in terms of equivalent direct radiation (EDR) per hour:

For a steam boiler, multiply the average hourly demand for hot water (Rule 4) by 3.5. This gives a one-hour rating. For a two-hour rating, multiply by 1.75.

For a hot water heater, multiply the average hourly demand for hot water (Rule 4) by 5.6. This, also, is a one-hour rating. (For a two-hour rating, multiply by 2.8.)

STORAGE TANK CAPACITY

With the hourly demand for hot water determined, storage requirements can be quickly estimated. To ensure hot water at all faucets, it is customary to assume that only 75 per cent of the tank capacity will be available as hot water. Thus tanks should be oversized by 25 per cent of the calculated storage requirements.

Rule 6. To determine hourly storage requirements for hot water, subtract the average hourly demand (supplied by heater) from the probable maximum hourly demand (Rule 3 minus Rule 4). Then divide by 0.75.

If using hourly consumptions (Table 8), provide 1/3 storage and 2/3 heating.

Summary example

Suppose that an apartment building contains 50 bedrooms and is to be heated with a steam boiler plant. What will be the required size of the hot water storage tank, and what additional capacity must the boiler have to meet requirements for domestic hot water?

Total cold water consumption

$$50 \times 200 = 10{,}000 \text{ gal}$$
$$\text{For peak} \quad +50\% = 5{,}000$$
$$\text{Total} \qquad\qquad = 15{,}000 \text{ gal}$$

Total hot water consumption
$$15{,}000 \div 3 = 5{,}000 \text{ gal}$$

Maximum probable hourly demand
$$5{,}000 \div 10 = 500 \text{ gal}$$

Average hourly demand
$$5{,}000 \div 24 = 208 \text{ gal}$$

Required tank capacity on an hourly rating
$$\frac{500 - 208}{0.75} = 389 \text{ gal}$$

Additional boiler capacity required
$$208 \times 3.5 = 728 \text{ sq ft EDR}$$

In selecting a standard-sized tank to meet calculated storage requirements, choose one that slightly exceeds those figures rather than one that falls just short (see Table 7).

Table 5.   Equivalent direct radiation loads for heating domestic hot water

HOT WATER	REQUIRED HEATING CAPACITY	
Max. Probable Hourly Demand in Gallons	Sq. Ft. Radiation Required— Steam	Sq. Ft. Radiation Required— Hot Water
10	35	56
20	70	112
30	105	168
40	140	224
50	175	280
60	210	324
70	245	392
80	280	448
90	315	504
100	350	560
150	525	840
200	700	1120
250	875	1400
300	1050	1680
350	1225	1960
400	1400	2240
450	1575	2520
500	1750	2800
550	1925	3080
600	2100	3240
650	2275	3520
700	2450	3920
750	2625	4200
800	2800	4480
850	2975	4760
900	3150	5040
950	3325	5320
1000	3500	5600

Table 6. Range boilers

Capacity in gals.	Diameter	Length
18	1'-0"	3'-0"
24	1'-0"	4'-0"
30	1'-0"	5'-0"
32	1'-2"	4'-0"
40	1'-0"	5'-0"
42	1'-4"	4'-0"
52	1'-4"	5'-0"
66	1'-6"	5'-0"
82	1'-8"	5'-0"
100	1'-10"	5'-0"
120	2'-0"	5'-0"
144	2'-0"	6'-0"
192	2'-0"	8'-0"

Tanks are vertical.

Standard pressure is 85 lbs. per sq. in.

Extra-heavy pressure is 150 lbs. per sq. in.

Table 8. Hot water consumption in apartment buildings*

	Public housing, gal	Apt.-hotel, gal
Average daily		
per apartment	79	59
per person	28	41
per room	22	36
Maximum daily		
per apartment	92	69
per person	33	48
per room	26	43
Maximum hourly		
per apartment	8.9	7.6
per person	3.2	5.3
per room	2.5	4.9
Average of 4 peak hours		
per apartment	7.1	7.8
per person	2.5	5.0
per room	2.0	3.0

Allow 0.4 gal per hr per person for hot water consumption in office buildings and 1.0 gal per hr per meal in cafeterias.

Table 7. Hot water storage tanks

Average capacity, gal	48	60	72	84	96	108	120	132	144	156	168	180	192	Average weight, lb
				Diameter, in.										
89	24													1,514
112		24												1,830
136			24											2,154
159				24										2,470
179	30													2,510
210		30												2,918
252			30											3,442
289				30										3,924
298		36												3,948
326					30									4,362
351			36											4,563
362						30								4,800
402		42												5,037
404				36										5,178
457					36									5,793
474			42											5,834
510						36								6,408
545				42										6,623
562							36							7,023
614			48											7,801
615								36						7,630
617					42									7,421
690						42								8,727
708					48									8,866
762							42							9,025
802						48								9,851
833								42						9,325
889				54										10,175
896							48							10,837
905									42					9,625
977										42				9,925
990								48						11,862
1,005					54									11,325
1,049											42			10,225
1,084									48					12,917
1,120												42		10,525
1,124						54								13,279
1,178									48					13,942
1,234					60									14,500
1,243							54							14,530
1,272											48			14,958
1,362								54						15,755
1,366												48		15,983
1,381							60							16,312
1,460													48	17,018
1,481									54					17,022
1,528								60						17,912
1,600										54				18,280
1,675									60					19,502

Average capacity, gal	120	132	144	156	168	180	192	Average weight, lb
1,720						54		20,780
1,822		60						21,102
1,839							54	21,764
1,958	72							22,000
1,969					60			22,743
2,116					60			24,343
2,170		72						25,000
2,263						60		25,900
2,381			72					26,500
2,593				72				30,000
2,804					72			32,500
3,016						72		35,000
3,203			84					36,500
3,227							72	36,800
3,491				84				37,000
3,778					84			41,900
4,066						84		46,000
4,134			96					48,000
4,354							84	49,500
4,510				96				50,500
4,886					96			51,500
5,262						96		55,900
5,638							96	60,200

The trend in modern hospitals and laboratories is toward central systems to supply oxygen, vacuum, nitrous oxide, and compressed air. With the use of the tables on the following pages, central systems for these special services can be properly designed.

OXYGEN

Oxygen contained in a cylinder is in liquid form; when released to atmospheric pressure, it becomes a gas. Although the gas is nonflammable, it is dangerous to handle because it supports combustion vigorously and can cause the slightest glow to erupt into an inferno. (For methods of installing oxygen systems, consult the National Fire Protection Association, Pamphlet No. 56F.)

The oxygen system may be supplied from either a bulk supply or a cylinder manifold. Each should include both a normal service supply and an adequate reserve supply, which would become available automatically when the service supply was exhausted. Gas suppliers should be consulted on the type of storage most economical for a particular installation, considering the volume of gas to be used and the location of the installation. A bulk storage should not be located within 50 ft of any structure.

A low-pressure alarm should be installed where the supply line from the bulk storage or cylinder manifold enters the building. This alarm, signaling a loss of pressure in the supply line (that is, a leak), should be both visual and audible.

From that point, a copper tubing header-Type K or L with wrought or cast copper fittings-should supply all oxygen risers and outlets. Solder should have a melting point of 1000°F or more.

Each floor to be equipped for oxygen therapy should be served by more than one riser, so that if the supply to one riser is shut off, the entire floor will not be deprived of oxygen, and the patients can be moved to other rooms on the same floor for continuation of their oxygen therapy.

The size of the piping is usually determined by the length of piping required from the supply to the farthest outlet. It should be noted, however, that the piping for a particular outlet closer to the supply could be sized on the basis of its own length, although generally this would not substantially reduce the over-all cost of the system.

Having determined the over-all distance, and assuming a pressure drop of 2 psi, we can refer to Table 9 for a direct reading of the number of liters of oxygen that a given pipe can deliver per minute.

Operating rooms, recovery rooms, and delivery rooms should all be supplied directly from the main, with a shut-off valve outside each room. The supplies for patients' rooms must be zoned by valves, which should be located in boxes with break-glass fronts, in order to eliminate the possibility of their being shut off by unauthorized persons. Valves can be either the ball valve type or the packless diaphragm type.

Riser control valves and valves 1 in. or more in diameter must be specially packed for oxygen service and must be free of oil. All piping in the system must be washed with a solution of trisodium phosphate to remove all grease before oxygen is admitted to the system.

NITROUS OXIDE

All the statements made in reference to oxygen apply to a nitrous oxide installation with the exception of the bulk storage. Because of the small quantities of gas involved, the system manifold can be located within the building in a fireproof room. Table 10 can be used for sizing nitrous oxide piping.

COMPRESSED AIR SYSTEMS

Compressed air for use in laboratories and for patient resuscitation must be oil-free and cooled. The pumps for this system may be either rotary or reciprocating. If a reciprocating pump is used, an aftercooler is required to reduce the temperature of the compressed gas. The units should be lubricated by carbon rings in order to eliminate oil particles in the compressed gas.

A receiver is also required in a compressed air installation, and the supply header from the receiver must be provided with an air filter and regulator. (See Table 11 for pipe sizes and capacities.)

VACUUM

A high vacuum is rarely required, since even a 15-in. (mercury column) vacuum can damage skin tissue. It is the quantity, not the pressure, that is most important.

In this system also, sizing is determined by the pressure drop required and the length of the longest run (see Table 12). The vacuum pumps are sized for the peak draw; duplex pumps should be used to ensure a continuous source of supply. If the units required become too large for one pump, then two-thirds of the total capacity should be placed in each of two pumps. The pumps evacuate a receiving tank to which the vacuum header is connected. The exhaust from the pumps should discharge to the outside air, and should be provided with a silencer and a filter.

Pumps may be either rotary vane or reciprocating. Care must be taken in the location and installation of reciprocating pumps, however, because they are noisy and require a large foundation to prevent vibration and movement. The receiving tank should be hot-dipped galvanized steel, because condensation will form and collect in it.

Pressure switches for the motor starters should be mounted directly on the receiver, with only a wire running from the pressure switch to the starter, to ensure a continuous vacuum supply.

EXAMPLES

Oxygen: Assume that a line is to supply 60 oxygen outlets, with a developed length of 250 ft from the source to the farthest outlet. The piping being used is Type K copper tubing, and the allowable pressure drop is 2 psi. The required capacity can be expressed as follows: 60 outlets times 10 liters per min per outlet times 40 per cent diversity, or 240 liters per min.

In Table 9 we look opposite 277 ft under the column for ¾-in. K and find 212 liters per min, which is too small; under 1-in. K we find 450, which is ample even after deducting the percentage for fittings. Hence, the line should be 1 in. in size. If screw pipe were to be used, we would select the appropriate column marked "P," and if Type TP copper tubing were to be used, we would select a column marked "B".

Compressed Air: Assume that there is an outlet pressure of 40 psi, 1,000 ft of pipe, and an allowable pressure loss of 22 psi. In Table 11, in the column for 40 psi, we read down to 22, and then across, to find that a 1-in. black steel pipe of this length can supply 59 cfm, a 3-in. pipe can supply 1,020 cfm, and so on. Knowing the quantity required, we can easily select the proper pipe size.

Table 9. Capacity of oxygen piping

Quantities listed are for pressure drops of 1 in. and 55.36 in. (or 2 psi) of water (at specific gravity 1.105). Assume 10 liters per minute per outlet. Deduct 10 per cent from listed quantities for friction loss due to valves and fittings. Diversity factor (percentage of simultaneous use) is 40 to 100 (see Table 11). Key: P = IPS threaded brass pipe; B = Type TP (threadless pipe) copper tubing; K = Type K or Type L copper tubing.

Pipe size, in. — Capacity, liters per minute

Length of pipe, ft	Pressure drop, in. H_2O	3/8			1/2			3/4			1			1 1/4			1 1/2			2			2 1/2			3			4		
55.36	1	P	B	K	P	B	K	P	B	K	P	B	K	P	B	K	P	B	K	P	B	K	P	B	K	P	B	K	P	B	K
50	0.9	177	230	105	310	445	205	640	840	505	1210	1580	1050	2300	3120	1750	3350	4200	2800	6400	7820	5700	10500	13000	9800	11200	14400	10000			
55	1.0	165	212	100	290	420	193	610	800	480	1160	1490	980	2150	2850	1650	3200	3950	2650	6000	7400	5400	9800	12500	9100	9000	11800	8300			
111	2.0	118	155	70	210	300	138	435	580	335	820	1050	700	1520	2080	1200	2250	2820	1900	4300	5400	3800	6900	8800	6500	7900	10000	7200			
166	3.0	98	125	58	170	245	112	352	470	276	670	870	580	1250	1700	980	1850	2350	1530	3500	4250	3100	5700	7200	5200	7000	9100	6400			
221	4.0	84	110	50	148	212	98	310	400	240	580	760	500	1100	1480	850	1600	2010	1320	3050	3720	2700	5000	6300	4650	6400	8100	5900			
277	5.0	75	98	45	133	192	89	275	360	212	515	680	450	980	1300	760	1440	1800	1180	2720	3350	2410	4200	5500	4125	6000	7600	5450			
332	6.0	68	89	41	122	172	80	252	330	196	490	620	405	900	1200	700	1320	1650	1100	2500	3050	2200	4050	5050	3750	5500	7100	5100			
388	7.0	63	83	38	112	160	75	235	305	182	440	580	375	840	1110	640	1220	1530	1010	2320	2820	2080	3710	4650	3500	5200	6700	4800			
443	8.0	60	78	35	103	150	70	220	285	170	415	540	350	780	1050	610	1140	1450	960	2150	2650	1920	3500	4400	3250						
498	9.0	56	74	33	98	142	65	205	265	161	382	500	330	730	990	566	1080	1350	900	2030	2500	1850	3300	4080	3050						
554	10	53	69	32	94	135	62	196	255	153	375	480	316	700	930	540	1020	1280	860	1910	2350	1725	3150	3900	2900	5000	6400	4600	9900	11800	9300
1107	20	38	50	28	68	96	44	138	182	108	265	340	225	500	670	380	740	920	605	1360	1650	1210	2220	2800	2100	3520	4500	3200	6950	8300	6500
1661	30	31	40	18	55	77	36	113	148	89	218	280	185	400	550	316	595	730	490	1120	1380	1000	1850	2300	1720	2900	3720	2650	5800	6800	5400

Table 10. Capacity of nitrous oxide piping

Quantities listed are for pressure drops of 1 in. and 55.36 in. (or 2 psi) of water (at specific gravity 1.522). Assume 10 liters per minute per outlet. Deduct 10 per cent from listed quantities for friction loss due to valves and fittings. Diversity factor (percentage of simultaneous use) is 100. Key: P = IPS threaded brass pipe; B = Type TP copper tubing; K = Type K copper tubing.

Pipe size, in. — Capacity, liters per minute

Length of pipe, ft	Pressure drop, in. H_2O	3/8			1/2			3/4			1			1 1/4			1 1/2			2			2 1/2			3			4		
55.36	1	P	B	K	P	B	K	P	B	K	P	B	K	P	B	K	P	B	K	P	B	K	P	B	K	P	B	K	P	B	K
22	0.4	242	308	145	435	580	285	870	1150	680	1620	2180	1400	3050	4150	2420	4600	5900	3710	8200	10600	7600									
28	0.5	212	275	128	380	520	251	770	1020	600	1480	1920	1250	2720	3720	2120	4080	5300	3340	7400	9500	6700									
33	0.6	197	252	118	355	490	230	700	930	545	1320	1725	1140	2510	3400	1950	3710	4850	3050	6700	8600	6200									
39	0.7	182	230	108	327	445	210	650	850	500	1230	1600	1050	2320	3160	1820	3450	4500	2820	6210	8000	5600	10500	13000	9700						
44	0.8	170	218	100	302	417	200	608	810	470	1150	1520	970	2120	2920	1700	3260	4150	2650	5800	7400	5300	9800	12200	9100						
50	0.9	161	202	96	285	390	188	562	760	442	1090	1420	930	2050	2750	1600	3050	3900	2450	5420	7000	5000	9300	11400	8500						
55	1.0	151	195	91	270	375	176	550	725	420	1020	1350	883	1910	2600	1510	2860	3720	2320	5100	6700	4700	8800	10800	8000						
111	2.0	108	138	64	192	262	123	383	510	298	722	960	620	1350	1820	1060	2050	2600	1630	3620	4800	3320	6200	7800	5600	10100	12500	9100			
166	3.0	87	112	51	158	215	101	312	417	242	590	780	501	1120	1520	870	1630	2110	1350	2950	3800	2700	5000	6300	4650	8300	10200	7300			
221	4.0	75	97	45	135	185	89	271	355	210	510	662	435	960	1290	745	1450	1820	1160	2550	3300	2320	4320	5500	4000	7200	8800	6350			
277	5.0	68	87	40	122	165	79	243	318	188	450	600	388	860	1150	680	1280	1650	1050	2260	2950	2100	3850	4850	3520	6500	7900	5500			
332	6.0	61	79	37	110	151	77	220	290	171	418	550	355	780	1050	620	1160	1520	950	2100	2700	1900	3520	4450	3250	5900	7200	5200	11300	13500	10400
388	7.0	56	72	34	102	140	66	203	270	158	383	510	328	720	960	562	1070	1380	890	1910	2500	1760	3250	4100	3000	5420	6700	4800	10500	12500	9600

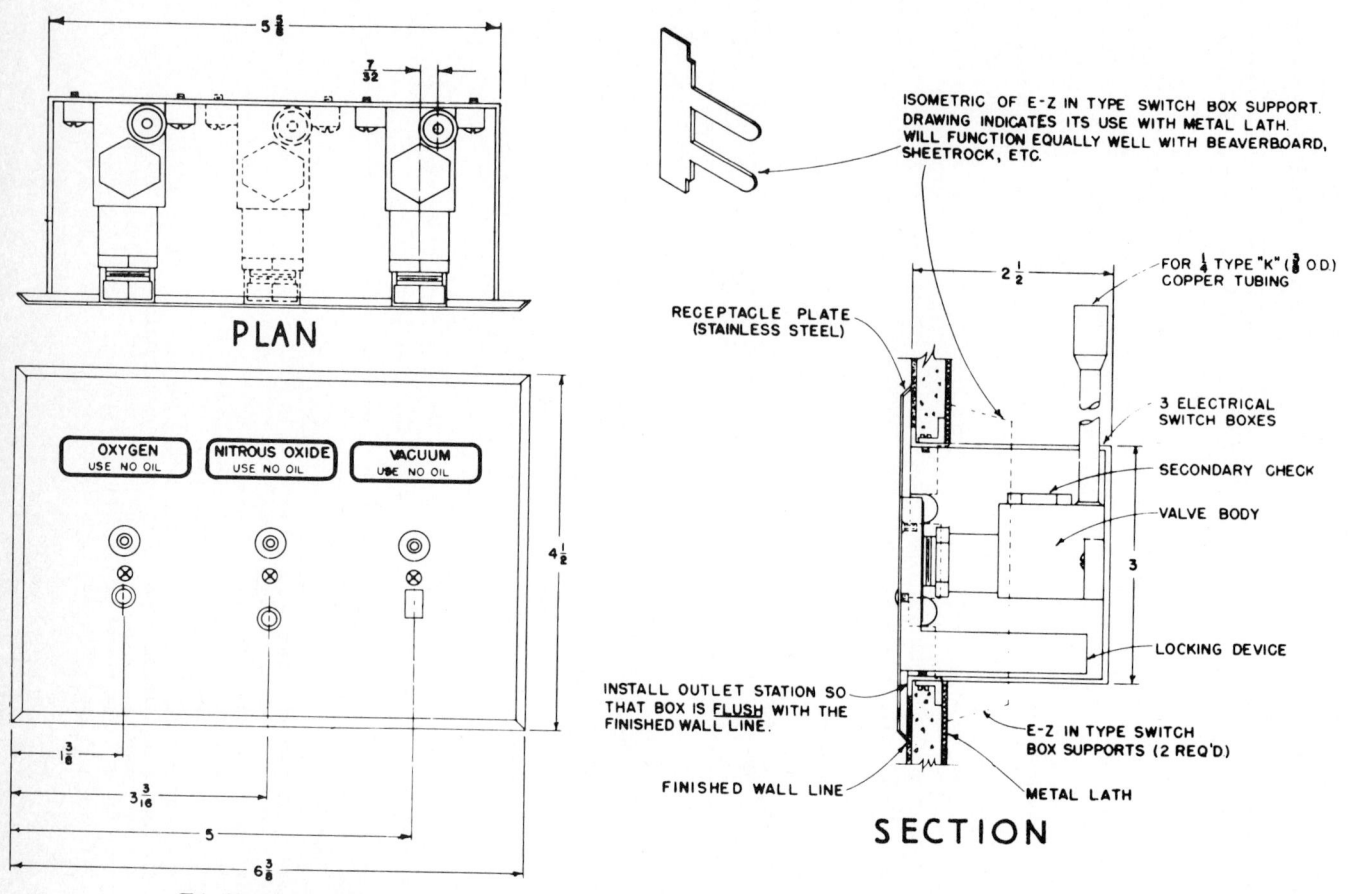

Fig. 5. Typical triple outlet for special services

Table 11.   Capacity of compressed air piping
Quantities are based on IPS steel pipe.

Outlet gauge pressure, psi															Pipe size, in.											
175	150	125	100	90	80	70	60	50	40	35	30	25	20	15	⅜	½	¾	1	1¼	1½	2	2½	3	4	5	6
															Factor for Type K copper tubing in per cent of IPS steel pipe											
				Pressure loss, psi per 1000 ft of pipe											60	64	76	84	77	81	93	93	89	90	90	90
															Capacity, cfm											
0.4	0.5	0.6	0.7	0.7	0.8	0.9	1	1.2	1.4	1.6	1.8	2.2	2.6	3.4	1.8	3.2	8.2	15	32	48	92	150	265	540	980	1600
0.8	1.0	1.1	1.4	1.5	1.6	1.8	2	2.4	2.9	3.2	3.6	4.3	5.2	6.7	2.5	4.5	11.5	21.5	45	67	130	210	375	770	1380	2300
1.2	1.4	1.7	2.0	2.2	2.4	2.7	3	3.6	4.3	4.8	5.5	6.5	7.8	10	3.1	5.5	14.0	26.5	55	82	160	260	460	940	1700	2800
1.6	1.9	2.2	2.7	2.9	3.2	3.5	4	4.8	5.7	6.4	7.3	8.6	10.4	13.4	3.5	6.3	16.0	30.5	64	95	185	300	530	1090	1950	3200
2.0	2.3	2.7	3.3	3.6	4.0	4.4	5	5.9	7.2	8	9.1	10.8	13	16.8	3.9	8.0	18.0	34	71	108	208	330	600	1200	2160	3600
4.0	4.6	5.4	6.6	7.1	7.9	8.8	10	11.8	14.3	16	18.2	21.5	26	34	5.5	10	25.5	48	100	150	290	470	840	1700	3100	5100
6.0	6.9	8.1	10	11	12	14	15	18	22	24	28	33	41	50	6.7	12	31	59	122	185	360	570	1020	2100	3700	6200
8	9.2	11	14	15	16	18	20	24	29	32	37	43	52	67	7.7	14	36	68	142	215	410	660	1180	2450	4300	7200
10	12	14	17	18	20	22	25	26	36	40	46	54	65	84	8.6	15.8	40	76	158	240	460	720	1320	2730	4420	8000
12	14	17	20	22	24	27	30	36	43	48	55	65	78	100	9.4	17.2	44	84	172	262	500	800	1450	3000	5300	8800
14	17	19	24	25	28	31	35	42	50	56	64	76	91	118	10	18.6	48	90	186	285	545	870	1570	3250	5700	9600
16	19	22	27	29	32	35	40	48	58	64	73	86	104	134	10.8	20	51	96	200	300	580	940	1700	3400	6100	10200
20	23	27	33	36	40	44	50	59	72	80	91	108	130	168	12	22	57	108	220	340	650	1050	1880	3850	6800	11500
24	28	33	40	43	48	53	60	71	86	96	110	129	156	201	13	24	62	118	245	375	720	1150	2050	4200	7500	12600
28	33	38	47	50	56	62	70	83	100	112	128	151	182	235	14	26	67	128	260	400	770	1230	2200	4500	8000	13600
32	37	44	53	57	64	71	80	95	115	128	146	175	208	268	15	28	72	137	280	430	820	1320	2350	4900	8600	14500
36	42	49	60	64	72	80	90	107	128	144	164	194	234	302	16	30	76	145	300	460	870	1400	2500	5200	9100	15500
40	46	54	66	71	79	88	100	118	144	160	182	215	260	340	17	31	80	150	310	480	910	1480	2600	5400	9600	16200

Table 12. Capacity of vacuum piping

Quantities listed are for pressure drops of 1 and 2 in. of mercury (at specific gravity 1.00). Deduct 10 per cent from listed quantities for friction loss due to valves and fittings. Key: P = IPS threaded brass pipe; B = Type TP (threadless) copper tubing; K = Type K or Type L copper tubing.

Capacity, cfm — Pipe size, in.

Length of pipe, ft (drop 2 in. Hg)	Length of pipe, ft (drop 1 in. Hg)	3/8 P	3/8 B	3/8 K	1/2 P	1/2 B	1/2 K	3/4 P	3/4 B	3/4 K	1 P	1 B	1 K	1¼ P	1¼ B	1¼ K	1½ P	1½ B	1½ K	2 P	2 B	2 K	2½ P	2½ B	2½ K	3 P	3 B	3 K	4 P	4 B	4 K
40	20	8.6	11.2	5.3	15.8	22.0	10.3	31.6	42.3	24.6	60.8	80.0	51.6	113	153	88.3	166	216	140	308	391	283	516	641	483						
60	30	7.2	9.2	4.3	13.0	18.0	8.3	25.8	34.5	20.0	49.1	65.0	41.6	91.6	125	71.6	138	175	113	250	320	233	416	525	391						
80	40	6.2	7.8	3.7	11.3	15.3	7.2	22.0	30.0	17.5	44.1	55.8	36.3	80.0	108	61.6	118	153	98.3	216	278	200	366	450	338	600	733	533			
100	50	5.6	7.0	3.3	10.0	13.6	6.4	20.0	26.6	15.5	38.3	50.0	32.5	70.0	96.6	55.0	106	136	88.3	191	246	176	323	400	300	533	666	475			
120	60	5.0	6.6	3.0	9.2	12.6	5.8	18.3	24.1	14.1	35.0	45.8	29.1	65.0	88.3	50.8	96.6	123	80.0	176	225	161	291	366	276	491	608	433			
140	70	4.7	5.9	2.8	8.5	11.6	5.4	16.6	22.5	13.0	32.0	42.5	27.1	60.0	81.6	46.6	90.0	115	73.3	165	208	150	273	341	256	450	566	400			
160	80	4.3	5.5	2.6	7.8	10.8	5.1	15.6	21.0	12.1	30.0	39.1	25.3	55.8	76.6	43.3	83.3	108	68.3	153	191	140	255	316	236	425	525	375			
180	90	4.1	5.2	2.5	7.5	10.1	4.7	14.8	19.5	11.5	28.3	36.6	24.1	52.5	71.5	41.1	78.3	101	65.0	143	181	131	241	300	225	396	500	350			
200	100	3.8	4.9	2.3	7.0	9.6	4.5	14.0	18.6	10.8	26.6	35.0	22.8	50.0	68.3	39.1	75.0	95.0	61.6	136	173	125	228	283	213	376	475	333			
250	125	3.4	4.4	2.1	6.3	8.6	4.1	12.6	16.6	9.8	24.1	30.8	20.1	44.1	60.0	35.0	66.6	85.0	55.0	121	153	111	203	253	188	333	425	300			
300	150	3.2	4.0	1.9	5.7	7.9	3.6	11.5	15.1	8.8	21.1	28.3	18.5	40.8	55.0	31.6	60.8	78.3	50.0	111	140	103	186	233	173	308	383	271	608	716	550
350	175	2.9	3.8	1.7	5.3	7.3	3.4	10.6	14.0	8.1	20.1	26.3	17.1	37.5	50.8	29.1	55.8	71.6	46.6	103	130	95.0	171	213	160	285	355	250	558	650	508
400	200	2.7	3.5	1.6	5.0	6.8	3.2	10.0	13.1	7.6	19.0	24.6	16.0	35.0	47.5	27.5	52.5	66.6	43.3	96.6	121	88.3	161	200	150	266	333	233	525	616	475
500	250	2.4	3.2	1.5	4.5	6.1	2.9	8.8	11.8	6.8	17.0	22.0	14.3	31.6	42.5	24.5	46.6	60.0	39.1	85.0	108	78.3	143	180	133	238	300	208	466	550	430
600	300	2.2	2.8	1.3	4.0	5.6	2.6	8.1	10.8	6.2	15.3	20.0	13.0	28.3	38.6	22.5	43.3	55.0	35.1	78.3	98.3	71.6	130	163	121	216	271	191	425	500	390
700	350	2.0	2.6	1.2	3.7	5.1	2.4	7.5	9.9	5.7	14.1	18.5	12.0	26.3	35.8	20.8	40.0	50.8	32.8	73.3	91.6	66.6	120	150	113	200	250	178	391	458	363
800	400	1.9	2.4	1.1	3.5	4.8	2.2	7.0	9.3	5.4	13.3	17.3	11.3	24.6	33.3	19.5	36.5	47.5	30.6	68.3	85.0	61.6	113	140	106	188	233	165	366	433	333
1000	500	1.7	2.2	1.0	3.1	4.3	2.0	6.2	8.3	4.8	11.8	15.5	10.0	22.1	30.0	17.1	33.0	44.1	27.0	60.8	76.6	55.0	100	125	93.3	166	208	148	330	383	300
1200	600	1.6	2.0	0.9	2.8	4.1	1.8	5.7	7.5	4.4	10.8	14.1	9.1	20.0	27.3	15.6	30.0	38.8	25.0	55.0	70.0	50.8	91.6	115	86.6	151	190	135	300	350	273

Table 12a. Required capacity of vacuum piping in hospital rooms

Type of room	Capacity, cfm	Per cent of simultaneous use
Laboratories, cystoscopic, and pharmacies	1.0	40
Dental operating rooms	0.5	40
Major operating rooms	2.0	100
Single rooms and wards	1.0	40
Surgical, acute medical, and single rooms for decompression (Tuberculosis hospital)	2.0	100
Surgical recovery and anesthesia rooms	1.0	40
Eye, ear, nose, and throat operating rooms	0.5	40
Broncography (Tuberculosis hospital)	1.0	100

Table 12b. Frequency of simultaneous use per number of vacuum outlets in hospitals

Number of outlets	Per cent
1–2	100
3	90
4–5	80
6	70
7–8	60
9	50
10 or more	40

By HOWARD P. VERMILYA, AIA

The design of sprinkler systems requires the services of an engineer with a specialized knowledge of such systems for several reasons. First, a system must be developed which will meet the requirements of local authorities and the insurance companies. Second, there is the tricky problem of integrating the sprinkler system with the structure, the mechanical and electrical services and the lighting equipment. While a complete design procedure is much beyond the scope of this article, it does give an orientation to the major features and design criteria of sprinkler systems so that their needs can be anticipated in the early planning of a building.

Sprinklers are recommended for all occupancies having combustible contents or flammable liquids. In non-combustible buildings the installations may be limited to specific areas, but in structures with combustible floors or roofs, it is advisable that sprinklers be provided throughout. Sprinklers are recommended also for all concealed spaces involving combustible construction which are not otherwise protected from fire.

A sprinkler system consists of (1) an adequate water supply, (2) a distribution system consisting of pumps, gages, valves, main, riser, feed and branch line piping, (3) sprinkler heads automatically activated by heat and (4) an alarm system. All equipment used must be listed as "approved." Both the Engineering Division of the Associated Factory Mutual Fire Insurance Companies and the Underwriters Laboratories, Inc. maintain testing facilities for the listing of "approved" equipment.

The building authorities and the insurance companies will require complete working drawings of the system for their approval. Sprinkler drawings should show the building construction, equipment, lighting, and storage facilities. The submission of preliminary sketches of proposed systems also is usually required. The system must be thoroughly tested and inspected before acceptance.

In multi-story buildings of fire-resistant construction, it is advisable, where possible, to locate the storage areas in the lower stories, preferably the basement, to facilitate the sprinkler installation and cost.

WATER SUPPLY

Small Properties (good construction):
Single source of water with adequate volume and pressure is required. Public water works connections to two streets is preferable.
Large or Valuable Properties:
Two independent sources are required—primary, which is instantly available, and secondary, which may or may not be automatic.

Primary supply should generally exceed 500 gal/min at a pressure of 15 psi at highest main roof level where cross mains connect to risers or feed mains. Additional volume and pressure are often required depending upon the hazard of occupancy or construction.

Sources
Public Water—one or more connections to reliable public water system of good pressure and capacity are preferable as a primary source.
Elevated Gravity Tanks—Acceptable as a primary source when public water is not available. Capacity is dependent upon height, construction and occupancy of building or buildings and the need to supply hose connections in addition to sprinklers. Tanks may supply secondary source for small property with a limited public supply.
Fire Pumps—A well located fire pump with ample suction supply, capable of maintaining high pressures over long periods is a most satisfactory secondary supply. (Suction supply may consist of tanks, reservoirs or public water mains of low pressure.)
Pressure Tanks—Ordinarily located on or above roof; sometimes an adequate single source.
Fire Department Pumper Connections—An auxiliary supply which utilizes a low pressure source for sprinklers and standpipes.

YARD SYSTEM

This is the portion of the sprinkler system which distributes water from the water supply source to the automatic sprinkler risers. For larger fire protection systems it also distributes water to standpipes and hose connections. All piping is underground (protected from freezing) and outside the building area. Valves are accessible in pits and by use of indicator posts. Manufacturing or domestic water service connections should be separated from fire service systems.

TYPES OF SYSTEMS

1. *Wet Pipe Automatic Systems.* Piping contains water under pressure for immediate release when valve of sprinkler head is activated. Most general type, used in heated areas or areas not subject to freezing.
2. *Dry Pipe Automatic Systems.* Piping contains air under pressure which, when released by activated sprinkler head, permits water to enter pipes automatically by action of dry pipe valve and flow through sprinklers. Generally used when not feasible to heat area which is subject to freezing weather. Small dry pipe systems may be used in conjunction with wet pipe systems for special areas.
3. *Deluge Systems.* A system of open sprinklers, or a combination of open and closed sprinklers controlled by a quick opening mechanical or hydraulic valve (deluge valve), the latter operating either by automatic heat-responsive devices, or by manual control or otherwise. A deluge system is designed to wet down an entire area in which fire may originate. It is designed for special hazards involving possible flash fires and for structures with high ceilings where heat may be dissipated in early stages of fire before it reaches ceiling. Water demands of deluge systems are usually great.
4. *Pre-Action Systems.* A normally closed, automatic dry sprinkler system in which water is admitted by deluge or hy-

draulic valve operated by a heat-responsive device before sprinklers operate. Designed to protect properties where there is danger of serious water damage.

5. *Limited Water Supply Pressure Tank System.* Uses water in tank usually located in basement, under air pressure of 100-110 psi, for light-hazard occupancies involving small areas where not more than 5 to 10 sprinklers will operate in any one fire. Designed for conditions where adequate water supply is not available for occupancies such as schools, small hotels, country clubs etc.

6. *"Junior Systems."* A wet pipe system with small orifice sprinkler heads, usually ⅜ in., which uses copper tubing and is connected to the service water supply where there is sufficient pressure and volume. Designed for basements of dwellings and similar occupancies where not more than 3 or 4 sprinklers are liable to operate.

7. *Special Systems.* Sprinkler systems employing limited water supplies, reduced pipe sizes and other departures from the requirements for standard systems are not classified by the National Board of Fire Underwriters as standard sprinkler systems. Systems of this type may include those pressurized with air or nitrogen. The authority having

jurisdiction may recognize the degree of protection afforded by special types of sprinkler systems.

Sprinkler installations are also classified by hazard of occupancy:

a. "Light-hazard"—residential, business, school, institutional.
b. "Ordinary-hazard"—storage, industrial, theatres, restaurants.
c. "Extra-hazard"—storage and processing of cotton and flammable liquids, dusty areas of woodworking plants.

PIPE SIZES

The number of sprinklers on any one floor undivided by a fire wall and supplied through given sizes of pipe should not exceed that given in Table 13 below, for ordinary hazard occupancy.

Where the piping arrangement provides long risers or feed mains an increase in pipe sizes may be needed to offset friction losses.

Risers
Each system riser should be of sufficient size to supply all sprinklers on the riser of any one floor of one fire section as determined by the schedule of pipe sizes. There should be one or more risers in each building and in each section of building divided by fire walls. Where conditions warrant, the sprinklers in ad-

joining buildings or sections cut off by fire walls may be fed from a system riser in another section or building.

Riser Location
"Center-central" or "side-central" feed to sprinklers is recommended. (See Fig. 6.)

Cross Main and Branch Line Sizes
Branch lines should ordinarily be limited to 8 sprinklers. Not more than 14 branch lines should be allowed on either side of cross main, riser or feed main.

Hangers
Only "approved" pipe hangers installed according to the standards are acceptable.

SPRINKLERS

Automatic Sprinkler Heads
Only "approved" and tested makes and types are acceptable. A ½ in. discharge orifice is standard for all systems other than the "Junior." Automatic sprinklers are designed to discharge water in spray form upon release of valve held on its seat by a mechanism employing some heat-responsive element. Older type deflectors discharged the spray in all directions, wetting the ceiling. The standard spray type deflector directs the spray downward. Side wall sprinkler head deflector directs the water in one direction.

Table 13. Pipe size vs. number of sprinklers

(a) When both the distance between sprinklers on branch lines and the distance between branch lines is 12 ft or less.				(b) When either the distance between sprinklers on branch lines or the distance between branch lines exceeds 12 ft.			
Size Pipe, In.	Max. No. Spklrs	Size Pipe, In.	Max. No. Spklrs	Size Pipe, In.	Max. No. Spklrs	Size Pipe, In.	Max. No. Spklrs
1	2	3	40	1	2	3	30
1¼	3	3½	65	1¼	3	3½	60
1½	5	4	100	1½	5	4	100
2	10	5	160	2	10	5	160
2½	20	6	275	2½	15	6	275
		8	400			8	400

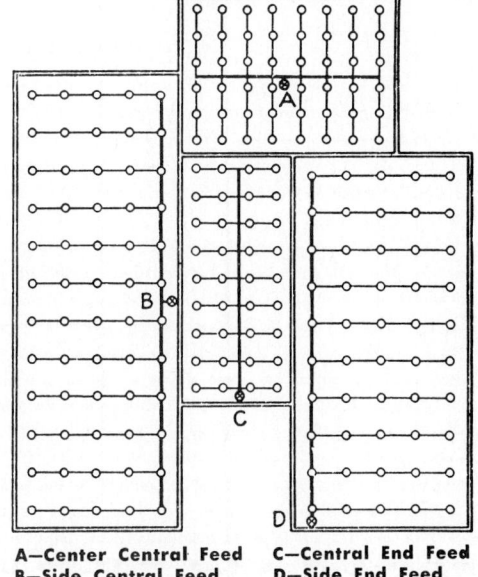

A—Center Central Feed   C—Central End Feed
B—Side Central Feed   D—Side End Feed

Fig. 6. Location of cross mains and risers

By GEORGE R. JERUS, *P.E.*
Vice President—Meyer, Strong and Jones, *P.C., Mechanical and Electrical Engineers*

Necessary data for the design of a plumbing drainage system in any building include discharge ratings of individual fixtures as a basis for estimating the probable load that the system must carry. Equally essential is a knowledge of safe limits for the carrying capacities of stacks and vents, gutters and leaders, house drains and horizontal branches.

The discharge ratings for the most commonly used plumbing fixtures are given in Table 1. On the following page are listed the limiting carrying capacities of soil and waste stacks (Table 2); the sizes and maximum lengths of vents in relation to safe carrying capacities of soil and waste pipes (Table 3); and the sizes of gutters in relation to the areas to be drained (Table 4). Data on the capacities of storm, sanitary, and combined house drains, and also house sewers, are given on subsequent pages. (All tables have been extracted from the New York City Building Code. The National Plumbing Code, ANSI A40.8–1955, is in the process of being revised.) The values in the tables do not always agree with all current building codes. Where differences exist, local requirements should of course govern. The data can be used, however, to establish limiting requirements applicable generally as a basis for drainage system design.

FIXTURE UNIT RATINGS (TABLE 1)

Carrying capacities of drainage pipes are listed in units of fixture discharge that indicate the rate of flow in cubic feet per minute. The unit of discharge flow is called a "fixture unit," and is equivalent to a flow of 1 cfm—the rate of discharge of an ordinary washbasin having a nominal $1\frac{1}{4}$-in. outlet, trap, and waste.

STACK CAPACITIES (TABLE 2)

The type of fitting used to connect fixtures or horizontal branches to waste and soil stacks has an important influence on the practical capacity of the stack. A stack will take the capacity discharge of two branches of the same diameter as the stack if the fitting is a double 45° Y or a combination Y-and-$\frac{1}{8}$ bend. Stack capacities are decreased, however, by "sanitary T" fittings.

Limitations of discharge within an 8-ft section of stack—a branch interval —are rarely significant in residential work, but constitute a desirable margin of safety in more extensive installations. In such installations, it is recommended that the discharge through a 45° Y or combination Y-and-$\frac{1}{8}$ bend never exceed, within any branch interval, $2\frac{1}{2}$ times the number of fixture units permissible on any one branch of the same diameter as the stack, pitched $\frac{1}{4}$ in. to the foot. Comparable limits for sanitary T fittings in a branch interval are $1\frac{1}{2}$ times the number of fixture units on a branch of similar size and pitch.

Base fittings that connect the lower ends of soil stacks to the house drain may be a size larger than the stack itself, in order to reduce the possibility of back pressure that exists even in small installations. In larger systems, if the house drain is more than one size larger than the stacks, fittings of intermediate size are advisable. For example: in a small system with a 3-in. stack and 4-in. house drain, a 4-in. fitting should be used.

Table 1. Sanitary drainage fixture unit values

Fixture or group	Fixture unit value	Trap size
Automatic clothes washer (2 in. standpipe)	3	
Bathroom group consisting of a lavatory, bathtub or shower stall, and a water closet (direct flushometer valve)	8	
Bathroom group consisting of a lavatory, bathtub or shower stall, and a water closet (flush tank)	6	
Bathtub with or without overhead shower	2	$1\frac{1}{2}$
Combination sink and wash tray	3	2
Dental unit or cuspidor	1	$1\frac{1}{2}$
Dental lavatory	1	$1\frac{1}{2}$
Drinking fountain	$\frac{1}{2}$	$1\frac{1}{2}$
Dishwasher, domestic type	2	$1\frac{1}{2}$
Floor drain	2	3
Kitchen sink, domestic type	2	2
Lavatory	1	$1\frac{1}{2}$
Lavatory (barber shop, beauty parlor or surgeon's)	2	$1\frac{1}{2}$
Lavatory, multiple type (wash fountain or wash sink), per each equivalent lavatory unit or set of faucets	2	$1\frac{1}{2}$
Laboratory cup sink	1	$1\frac{1}{2}$
Laboratory sink	2	2
Laundry tray (1 or 2 compartment)	2	$1\frac{1}{2}$
Shower stall	2	2
Showers (group) per head	2	3
Sink (surgeon's)	3	$1\frac{1}{2}$
Sink (flushing rim type, direct flush valve)	6	3
Sink (service type with trap standard)	3	3
Sink (service type with P trap)	2	2
Sink (pot, scullery, or similar type)	4	2
Urinal (1 in. flush valve) pedestal	6	3
Urinal (¾ in. flush valve) stall or wall hung	4	2
Urinal (flush tank)	4	2
Water closet (direct flush valve)	6	3
Water closet (flush tank)	4	3
Unlisted fixture, $1\frac{1}{4}$ in. fixture drain and $1\frac{1}{2}$ in. trap size	1	
Unlisted fixture, $1\frac{1}{2}$ in. fixture drain or trap size	2	
Unlisted fixture, 2 in. fixture drain or trap size	3	
Unlisted fixture, $2\frac{1}{2}$ in. fixture drain or trap size	4	
Unlisted fixture, 3 in. fixture drain or trap size	5	
Unlisted fixture, 4 in. fixture drain or trap size	6	

Notes—For computing unit values for devices with continuous or semicontinuous flows, 1 GPM = 1 F.U.

A shower head over a bathtub does not increase the fixture unit value.

Base fittings may be long-sweep ¼ bends with reducing hubs, two Y fittings, or a combination Y-and-⅛ bend. Sanitary T fittings should not be used as base fittings.

In going from a horizontal to a vertical line, a short-turn fitting may be used; but in going from a vertical flow to a horizontal flow, a long-turn fitting must be used. In buildings of any significant height, fixtures should not be connected to the horizontal piping from the base of the stack within 40 pipe diameters from the stack, to prevent back-up of fixtures on the lower floor from back pressure caused by a hydraulic jump in the stack base.

Suds pressure zones exist in the piping as shown in Fig. 1, and fixture connections in these areas should be avoided.

VENT REQUIREMENTS (TABLE 3)

The size and length of vent pipes are directly dependent upon the volume of discharge for which the soil or waste pipes were designed. Unless adequate venting is assured, the flow of fixture discharges through soil and waste stacks can produce pressure variations in branches that may damage the seals of fixture traps—"blowing" them because of positive or back pressure in lower parts of the system, and siphoning them because of negative pressure in upper parts.

Table 3 lists permissible sizes and lengths for the vent stacks and branch vents necessary to ensure the proper functioning of a drainage system.

Table 2. Maximum permissible loads for sanitary drainage piping (in terms of fixture units)

Pipe diameter (in.)	Any horizontal fixture branch or at one story of stack	Total for stack	House building drain, and building branches from stacks slope (in. per ft)			
			1/16	1/8	1/4	1/2
1½ [a]	3	4	np	np	np	np
2 [a]	6	8	np	np	21	26
2½ [a]	12	30	np	np	24	31
3	20[b]	97[b]	np	20[b]	27[b]	36[b]
4	160	507	np	180	216	250
5	360	1445	np	390	480	575
6		2918	np	700	840	1000
8		6992	1440	1600	1920	2300
10			2500	2900	3500	4200
12			3900	4600	5600	6700

[a] *No water closets permitted.*
[b] *Not over two water closets permitted.*
np = not permitted.

Table 3. Size of vent stacks and branch vents

Fixture units connected	Diameter of vent required (in.)								
	1½	2	2½	3	4	5	6	8	10
	Maximum developed length of vent (ft.)**								
4	100	†							
8	30	170	†						
30	15	70	175	†					
97	6	24	89	250	†				
507	*	*	11	78	310	†			
1445	*	*	*	16	110	380	†		
2918	*	*	*	*	34	143	380	†	
6992	*	*	*	*	*	14	73	340	†
...	*	*	*	*	*	*	*	*	†

* Not permitted.
** A 1½ in. vent may be used for 6 or less fixture units for a developed length of 15 ft. from the fixture to header regardless of developed length limiting the header size.
† Unlimited.

Table 4. Size of roof gutters [a]

Diameter of gutter [a] (in.)	Maximum projected roof area for gutters of various slopes			
	1/16 in. slope (sq. ft.)	1/8 in. slope (sq. ft.)	1/4 in. slope (sq. ft.)	1/2 in. slope (sq. ft.)
3	144	192	272	385
4	288	409	575	815
5	500	705	1,000	1,420
6	770	1,090	1,540	2,220
7	1,150	1,560	2,220	3,120
8	1,590	2,250	3,180	4,490
10	3,600	4,080	5,780	8,000

[a] *Gutters other than semicircular may be used provided they have the same cross-sectional area.*

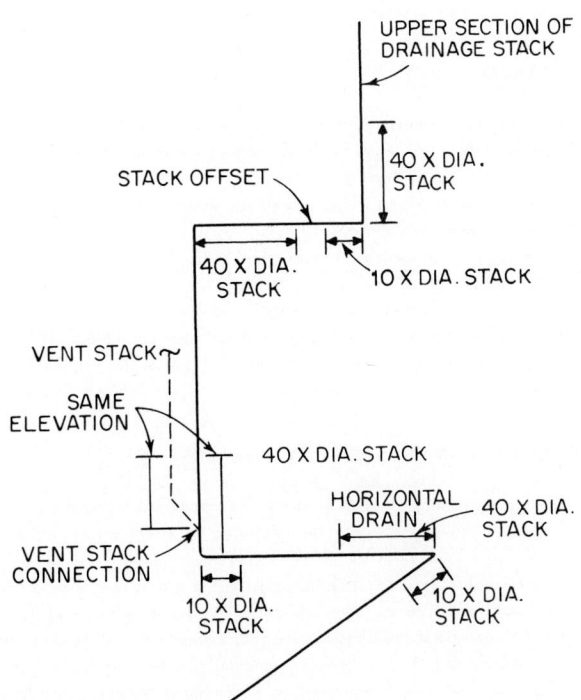

Fig. 1. Suds pressure zones

Note: Suds pressure zones shall be considered to exist at the indicated locations in sanitary drainage and vent systems when the piping serves fixtures on two or more floors that receive waste containing bubble bath or sudsy detergents.

Table 5. Size of vertical leaders

Diameter of leader or conductor (in.)	Maximum projected roof area	
	gpm	ft²
2	22.6	433
2½	39.6	779
3	66.6	1,278
4	143	2,745
5	261	4,992
6	423	8,121
8	911	17,491
10	1,652	31,718

Table 6. Size of horizontal storm drains

Diameter of drain (in.)	Maximum projected roof area for various slopes of drains		
	⅛ in. slope square feet	¼ in. slope square feet	½ in. slope square feet
2	250	350	500
2½	357	505	714
3	690	930	1,320
4	1,500	2,120	3,000
5	2,700	3,800	5,320
6	4,300	6,100	8,700
8	9,300	13,000	18,400
10	16,600	23,500	33,000
12	26,700	37,500	53,000
15	47,600	67,000	95,000

Table 7. "Fixture unit-drainage square footage" equivalent

Drainage area (ft²)	Fixture unit equivalent
180	6
260	10
400	20
490	30
1,000	105
2,000	271
3,000	437
4,000	604
5,000	771
7,500	1,188
10,000	1,500
15,000	2,500
20,000	3,500
28,000	5,500
each additional 3 ft²	1 fixture unit

Note: 1GPM = 19 ft²

Tabular data on this and the following page list limiting capacities for sanitary house drains, and storm drains, for slopes of ⅛ in., ¼ in., and ½ in. per ft. Figure 2 gives limiting capacities for combined sanitary and storm house drains and house sewers in terms of the sanitary load in fixture units and the drainage area in square feet. Although most communities prohibit combined systems the figure does give useful conversion data.

As previously noted, this material may not conform to some detailed provisions of various local building codes. it is generally applicable, however, as a basis for preliminary estimation in establishing safe limitations for drainage system design.

Capacities of house drains

Pipe capacities have been taken into account in determining the allowable maximum drainage loads. These loads have been expressed in fixture units, to allow for the probability of coincident and overlapping discharges of plumbing fixtures, and are based on mathematical calculation applied to documented experience.

SANITARY HOUSE DRAINS

The required size of a sanitary house drain for a given drainage load can be read directly from Table 2.

Rule 1. Determine total drainage requirements in fixture units (total discharge in cubic feet per minute) from values in Table 1.

Rule 2. Establish pitch of drain. Minimum pitch is ⅛ in. per ft, particularly in small installations; a lesser pitch would increase the possibility of fouling. Generally a ½-in. pitch is preferred.

Rule 3. Select the required pipe diameter from Table 2. The proper sizes for both a sanitary house sewer and a branch of the sanitary house drain not receiving discharge from fixtures on its own floor or level can be similarly determined from Table 2.

Table 2 is based on gravity flow in drains one-half full, since full practical capacity is reached at approximately that point because of trapped air.

STORM DRAINS

Tables 5 and 6 for leaders and storm drains are based upon gravity flow in a full pipe and a maximum rate of rainfall of 5 in. per hr. Required sizes can be read directly from the tables.

Rule 1. Determine drainage requirements in square feet of the horizontal projection of the area to be drained.

Rule 2. Select size of vertical leaders from Table 5.

Rule 3. Establish pitch of drain.

Rule 4. Determine required pipe diameter from Table 6.

Rule 5. To modify table if necessary to meet local conditions of rainfall, multiply each given drained area by $5/X$, with X, the prevailing rate of rainfall in inches per hour.

COMBINED HOUSE DRAINS OR HOUSE SEWERS

By reference to Table 7 fixture units can be converted to square feet and vice versa. After conversion either the drainage or storm water tables may be used.

Wherever sewage is treated, in either a private disposal system or a central plant, storm water must be excluded; hence, combined sewers cannot be used. Due to the Environmental Protection Agency's requirements to eliminate pollution, most communities do not permit combined systems within a building, even though they are to be connected to a combined public sewer. Then, if separate public sewers are installed at some future date, the new connections can be made with a minimum of expense and inconvenience to the occupants of the building.

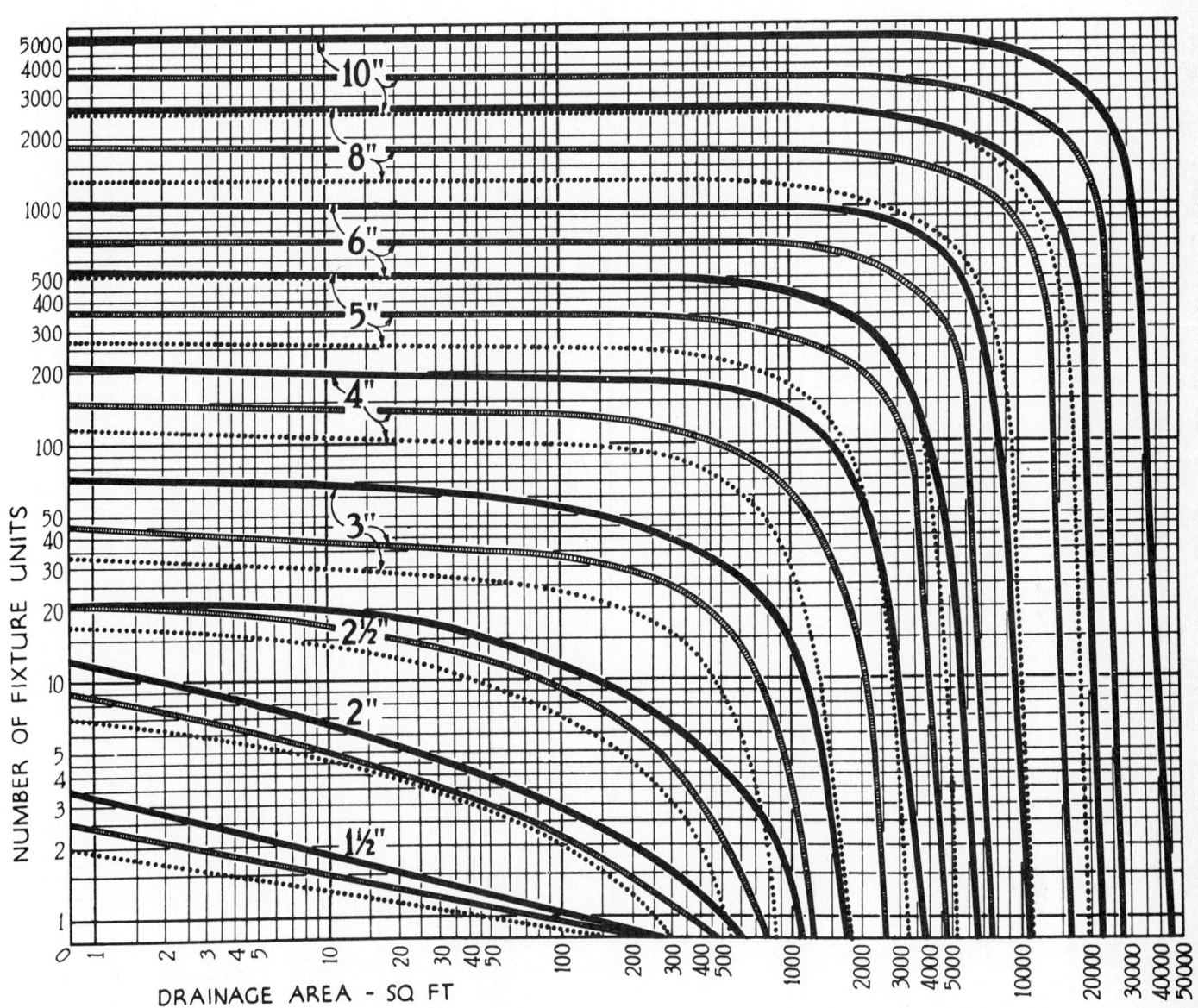

Fig. 2. Combined sanitary and storm house drains and house sewers

Diagrams on this sheet illustrate various types of plumbing details applicable to both residential and commercial buildings. Because of the wide variance in plumbing regulations throughout the country, some of these diagrammatic details may be prohibited in certain localities; other details may indicate methods far in excess of mandatory requirements in other localities. All of them, however, reflect solutions to typical drainage problems by methods that generally constitute good plumbing practice.

RESIDENTIAL DRAINAGE SYSTEMS

The pipe sizes shown in Fig. 3 will meet every requirement usually encountered in residential work. A 3-in. main soil stack is adequate for residential use in the opinion of many authorities; a 4-in. main soil stack is mandatory, however, in some localities. Main house drains should never be less than 4 in. If house sewers are connected to the septic tank of a private sewage disposal system, no house trap or fresh air inlet is necessary. In many communities individual venting may be eliminated and a system of wet venting or combined waste and vent system can be utilized.

COMMERCIAL DRAINAGE SYSTEMS

Figure 4 shows a composite of drainage problems encountered in a wide range of commercial and industrial work; the installations are not typical for any specific kind of building. As in the house sections, soil and waste lines are shown solid; vent lines are broken.

Group A: Bathroom unit is rated at 6 fixture units, individually vented and connected by preferred methods to main soil and vent stacks.

Group B: Bathroom unit is rated at 7 fixture units, individually vented and connected by the preferred method to a horizontal soil branch.

Loop vent, A, and *circuit vent, B,* are both types of venting in which the branch drain is a "double-duty" pipe carrying both air and discharge. The use of this pipe constitutes "wet-venting," prohibited by some codes. It is generally not a desirable method of venting. If used, circuit or loop vents should not be connected to a group of more than 8 fixtures in series. In a loop vent, a continuation of the branch runs up and over the fixtures to connect with the vent stack adjacent to the main soil. In a circuit vent, the connection is to a main vent stack opposite the main soil stack.

Yoke vent, C, connects the main soil and waste stacks, with the soil at the lower end of the yoke. The connection of fixtures as at C adds greatly to the safe capacity of soil stacks. This type of connection can be made to bathroom units in residential as well as commercial work.

Bow vent, D, can be used for light discharge loads to avoid installation of an additional vent stack.

Stacks 1 and 2 indicate the need for separate venting of the sewage ejector and the oil separator from garage drains. The vent from a pneumatic sewage ejector should not be joined to any other pipe; sewage pumps do not require any special considerations.

Stack 3 is the vent from an indirect waste line discharging into a cast-iron sink. Its fixtures must be trapped. If an indirect waste line is over 100 ft in developed length, it should be extended through the roof.

Stacks 4, 5, and 6: The vents should be connected into these stacks at their lower ends, so that discharge will scour the connection and thus prevent fouling. Such a connection is specifically required for cast iron because of scaling.

Stack 9 applies to a special-purpose type of installation. Corrosive wastes require acid-proof pipe for waste, soil, and vent lines, for fittings, and for the house drain up to the base fitting of the next main soil stack.

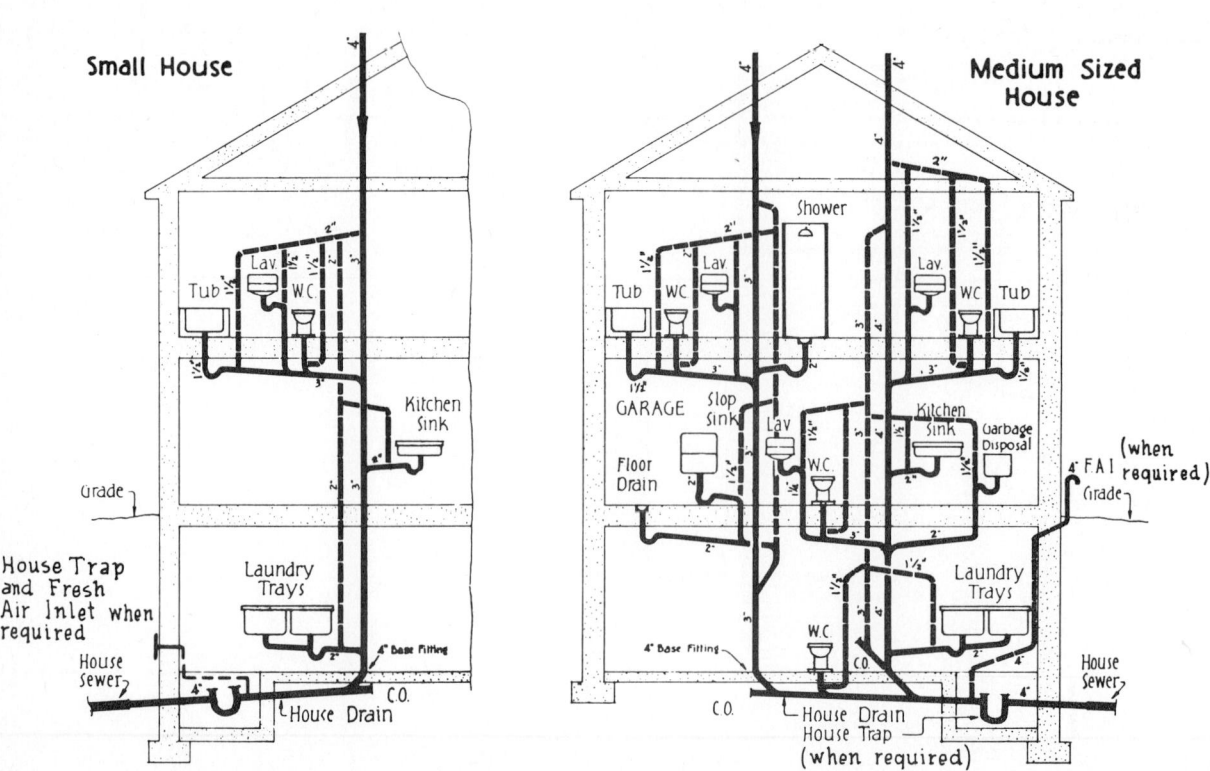

Fig. 3. Residential drainage systems

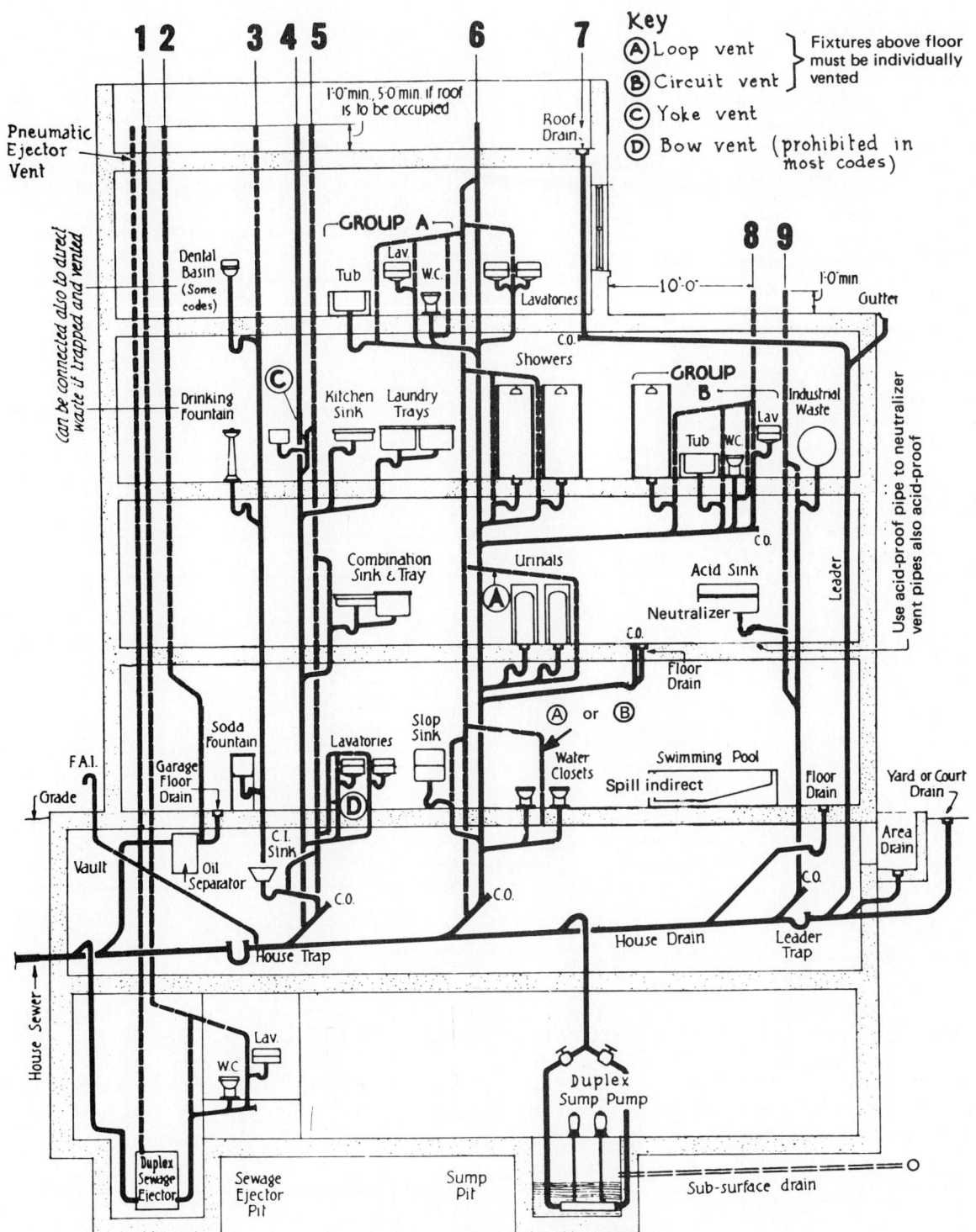

Fig. 4.   Drainage systems for commercial buildings

Cast-iron fittings

PURPOSE

Data on this and the following pages indicate limiting dimensions of cast-iron or malleable-iron fittings most commonly employed in building drainage systems.[1] Clearances necessary for concealed cast-iron fittings often determine the depth of floors, walls, or furred spaces in which they are housed. Therefore, these dimensions are safe maxima when space for pipe installations is a factor governing design.

Hub and spigot fittings are used with cast-iron or wrought-iron pipe and require a lead-caulked joint. Recessed-threaded fittings should be used preferably with wrought-iron or steel pipe, although threaded cast iron is available for verticle soil and vent lines.

Copper is also available for drainage piping, but, because of the wide variety of fittings, the manufacturers' catalogs should be consulted.

The proper weight classifications are designated in the tables by 'XH' (extra heavy) and 'SV' (service weight). Unless otherwise noted, dimension X in the tables indicates the laying length.

[1] *See "American National Standard Specifications for Cast Iron Soil Pipe and Fittings," ANSI/ASTM A74-72.*

⅛ bend offset (Tables 8–12)

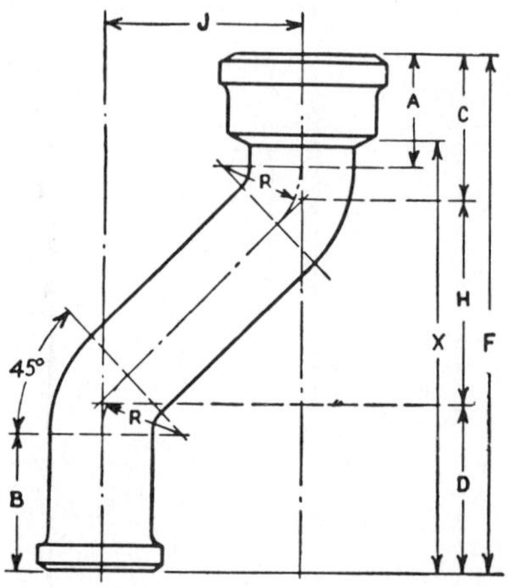

Table 8. ⅛ bend offset, 2-inch

Size (inches)	Dimensions in inches									Weight (pounds)	
	A	B	C	D	F	H	J	R	X	'XH'	'SV'
2 by 2	2¾	3½	3½	4¼	9¾	2	2	2	7¼	5	4½
2 by 4	2¾	3½	3½	4¼	11¾	4	4	2	9¼	6	5
2 by 6	2¾	3½	3½	4¼	13¾	6	6	2	11¼	8	6½
2 by 8	2¾	3½	3½	4¼	15¾	8	8	2	13¼	9	7¼
2 by 10	2¾	3½	3½	4¼	17¾	10	10	2	15¼	10	8
2 by 12	2¾	3½	3½	4¼	19¾	12	12	2	17¼	11	9
2 by 14	2¾	3½	3½	4¼	21¾	14	14	2	19¼	12	9¾
2 by 16	2¾	3½	3½	4¼	23¾	16	16	2	21¼	13	10½
2 by 18	2¾	3½	3½	4¼	25¾	18	18	2	23¼	14	11
2 by 20	2¾	3½	3½	4¼	27¾	20	20	2	25¼	15	12
2 by 22	2¾	3½	3½	4¼	29¾	22	22	2	27¼	16	13
2 by 24	2¾	3½	3½	4¼	31¾	24	24	2	29¼	17	13½

Table 9. ⅛ bend offset, 3-inch

Size (inches)	Dimensions in inches									Weight (pounds)	
	A	B	C	D	F	H	J	R	X	'XH'	'SV'
3 by 2	3¼	4	4¼	5	11¼	2	2	2½	8½	10	7
3 by 4	3¼	4	4¼	5	13¼	4	4	2½	10½	12	8
3 by 6	3¼	4	4¼	5	15¼	6	6	2½	12½	14	9½
3 by 8	3¼	4	4¼	5	17¼	8	8	2½	14½	16	11
3 by 10	3¼	4	4¼	5	19¼	10	10	2½	16½	18	12
3 by 12	3¼	4	4¼	5	21¼	12	12	2½	18½	20	13½
3 by 14	3¼	4	4¼	5	23¼	14	14	2½	20½	22	15
3 by 16	3¼	4	4¼	5	25¼	16	16	2½	22½	24	16
3 by 18	3¼	4	4¼	5	27¼	18	18	2½	24½	26	17½
3 by 20	3¼	4	4¼	5	29¼	20	20	2½	26½	27	18
3 by 22	3¼	4	4¼	5	31¼	22	22	2½	28½	29	19½
3 by 24	3¼	4	4¼	5	33¼	24	24	2½	30½	31	21

Table 10. ⅛ bend offset, 4-inch

Size (inches)	Dimensions in inches									Weight (pounds)	
	A	B	C	D	F	H	J	R	X	'XH'	'SV'
4 by 2	3½	4	4¾	5¼	12	2	2	3	9	14	10
4 by 4	3½	4	4¾	5¼	14	4	4	3	11	16	11
4 by 6	3½	4	4¾	5¼	16	6	6	3	13	19	13
4 by 8	3½	4	4¾	5¼	18	8	8	3	15	21	14
4 by 10	3½	4	4¾	5¼	20	10	10	3	17	24	16
4 by 12	3½	4	4¾	5¼	22	12	12	3	19	26	18
4 by 14	3½	4	4¾	5¼	24	14	14	3	21	29	20
4 by 16	3½	4	4¾	5¼	26	16	16	3	23	31	21
4 by 18	3½	4	4¾	5¼	28	18	18	3	25	34	23
4 by 20	3½	4	4¾	5¼	30	20	20	3	27	36	24
4 by 22	3½	4	4¾	5¼	32	22	22	3	29	39	26
4 by 24	3½	4	4¾	5¼	34	24	24	3	31	41	28

Table 11. ⅛ bend offset, 5-inch

Size (inches)	Dimensions in inches									Weight (pounds)	
	A	B	C	D	F	H	J	R	X	'XH'	'SV'
5 by 2	3½	4⅛	4 15/16	5 9/16	12½	2	2	3½	9½	17	12
5 by 4	3½	4⅛	4 15/16	5 9/16	14½	4	4	3½	11½	21	15
5 by 6	3½	4⅛	4 15/16	5 9/16	16½	6	6	3½	13½	24	17
5 by 8	3½	4⅛	4 15/16	5 9/16	18½	8	8	3½	15½	27	19
5 by 10	3½	4⅛	4 15/16	5 9/16	20½	10	10	3½	17½	30	21
5 by 12	3½	4⅛	4 15/16	5 9/16	22½	12	12	3½	19½	33	23
5 by 14	3½	4⅛	4 15/16	5 9/16	24½	14	14	3½	21½	36	25
5 by 16	3½	4⅛	4 15/16	5 9/16	26½	16	16	3½	23½	39	27
5 by 18	3½	4⅛	4 15/16	5 9/16	28½	18	18	3½	25½	42	29
5 by 20	3½	4⅛	4 15/16	5 9/16	30½	20	20	3½	27½	45	31
5 by 22	3½	4⅛	4 15/16	5 9/16	32½	22	22	3½	29½	48	33
5 by 24	3½	4⅛	4 15/16	5 9/16	34½	24	24	3½	31½	51	35

Table 12. ⅛ bend offset, 6-inch

Size (inches)	Dimensions in inches									Weight (pounds)	
	A	B	C	D	F	H	J	R	X	'XH'	'SV'
6 by 2	3½	4⅛	5	5⅝	13	2⅜	2	4	10	21	15
6 by 4	3½	4⅛	5 3/16	5 13/16	15	4	4	4	12	25	18
6 by 6	3½	4⅛	5 3/16	5 13/16	17	6	6	4	14	28	20
6 by 8	3½	4⅛	5 3/16	5 13/16	19	8	8	4	16	32	22½
6 by 10	3½	4⅛	5 3/16	5 13/16	21	10	10	4	18	36	25
6 by 12	3½	4⅛	5 3/16	5 13/16	23	12	12	4	20	39	27
6 by 14	3½	4⅛	5 3/16	5 13/16	25	14	14	4	22	43	30
6 by 16	3½	4⅛	5 3/16	5 13/16	27	16	16	4	24	46	32
6 by 18	3½	4⅛	5 3/16	5 13/16	29	18	18	4	26	50	35
6 by 20	3½	4⅛	5 3/16	5 13/16	31	20	20	4	28	54	37
6 by 22	3½	4⅛	5 3/16	5 13/16	33	22	22	4	30	57	40
6 by 24	3½	4⅛	5 3/16	5 13/16	35	24	24	4	32	61	42

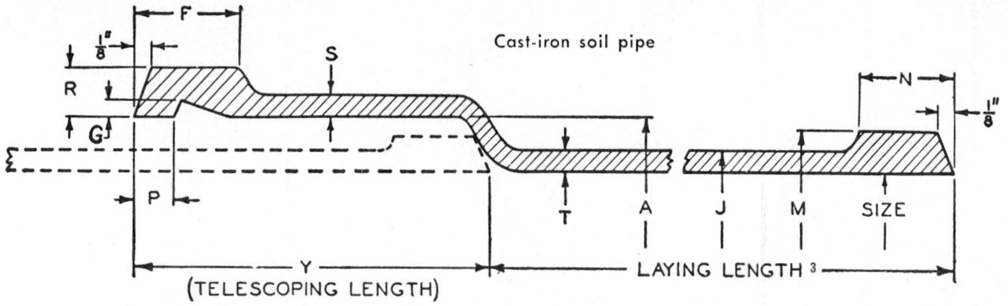

F
1"/8
S
Cast-iron soil pipe
R
G
N
1"/8
P
T
A
J
M
SIZE
Y
(TELESCOPING LENGTH)
LAYING LENGTH 3

Table 13. Hubs and spigots for extra-heavy soil pipe and fittings (dimensions in inches)

Size	Inside diameter of hub	Outside diameter of spigot	Outside diameter of barrel	Telescoping length	Thickness of barrel	
	A	M	J	Y	T (nominal)	T (min.)
inches	*inches*	*inches*	*inches*	*inches*	*inch*	*inch*
2	3.06	2.75	2.38	2.50	0.19	0.12
3	4.19	3.88	3.50	2.75	.25	.18
4	5.19	4.88	4.50	3.00	.25	.18
5	6.19	5.88	5.50	3.00	.25	.18
6	7.19	6.88	6.50	3.00	.25	.18
8	9.50	9.00	8.62	3.50	.31	.25
10	11.62	11.13	10.75	3.50	.37	.31
12	13.75	13.13	12.75	4.25	.37	.31
15	17.00	16.25	15.88	4.25	.44	.37

¼ bend

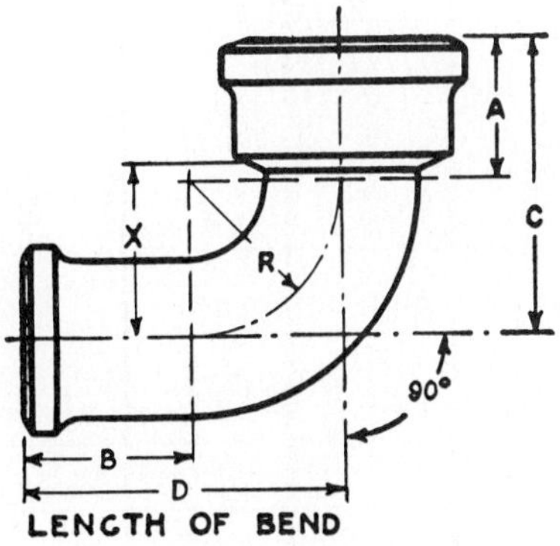

A
C
X
R
90°
B
D
LENGTH OF BEND

Table 14. ¼ bend

Size (inches)	Dimensions in inches						Weight (pounds)	
	A	B	C	D	R	X	'XH'	'SV'
2	2¾	3	5¾	6	3	3¼	5	4
3	3¼	3½	6¾	7	3½	4	10	7
4	3½	4	7½	8	4	4½	15	10½
5	3½	4	8	8½	4½	5	19	13
6	3½	4	8½	9	5	5½	24	17
8	4⅛	5½	10⅛	11½	6	6⅝	51	34
10	4⅛	5½	11⅛	12½	7	7⅝	78	55
12	5	7	13	15	8	8¾	111	80
15	5	7	14½	16½	9½	10¼	169	118

Short and long sweeps (Tables 15 and 16)

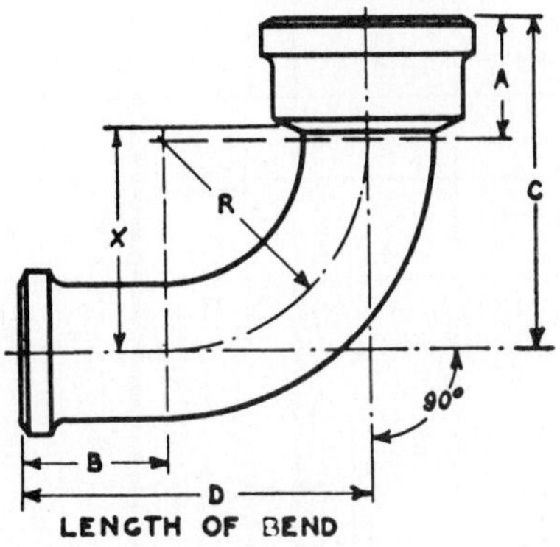

A
C
R
X
90°
B
D
LENGTH OF BEND

Table 15. Short sweep

Size (inches)	Dimensions in inches						Weight (pounds)	
	A	B	C	D	R	X	'XH'	'SV'
2	2¾	3	7¾	8	5	5¼	6	5
3	3¼	3½	8¾	9	5½	6	13	9
4	3½	4	9½	10	6	6½	18	12½
5	3½	4	10	10½	6½	7	23	16
6	3½	4	10½	11	7	7½	28	20
8	4⅛	5½	12⅛	13½	8	8⅝	57	38
10	4⅛	5½	13⅛	14½	9	9⅝	88	62
12	5	7	15	17	10	10¾	123	89
15	5	7	16½	18½	11½	12¼	187	130

Table 16. Long sweep

Size (inches)	Dimensions in inches						Weight (pounds)	
	A	B	C	D	R	X	'XH'	'SV'
2	2¾	3	10¾	11	8	8¼	8	6½
3	3¼	3½	11¾	12	8½	9	16	11
4	3½	4	12½	13	9	9½	22	15
5	3½	4	13	13½	9½	10	28	19½
6	3½	4	13½	14	10	10½	34	24
8	4⅛	5½	15⅛	16½	11	11⅝	67	45
10	4⅛	5½	16⅛	17½	12	12⅝	103	72
12	5	7	18	20	13	13¾	141	101
15	5	7	19½	21½	14½	15¼	212	147

Cast-iron fittings

Single and double Y branches

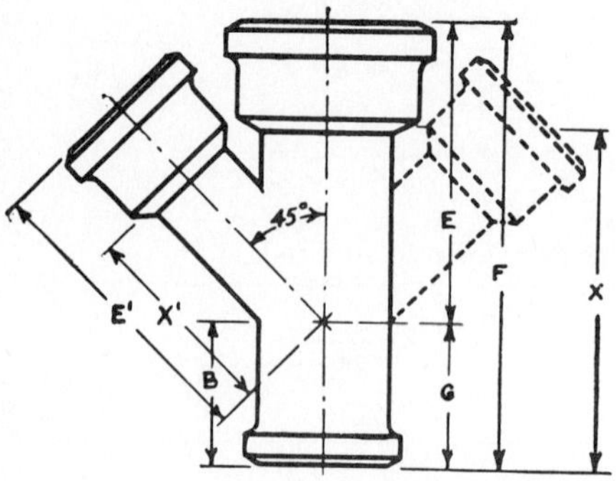

Table 17. Single and double Y branches

Size (inches)	Dimensions in inches							Weight, single (pounds)		Weight, double (pounds)	
	B (min.)	E	E′	F	G	X	X′	'XH'	'SV'	'XH'	'SV'
2	3½	6½	6½	10½	4	8	4	8	6½	11	9
3	4	8¼	8¼	13¼	5	10½	5½	17	12½	23	16
4	4	9¾	9¾	15	5¼	12	6¾	24	17	32	23
5	4	11	11	16½	5½	13½	8	32	22	41	28
6	4	12¼	12¼	18	5¾	15	9¼	40	28	51	36
8	5½	15 5/16	15 5/16	23	7 11/16	19½	11 13/16	82	55	107	73
10	5½	18	18	26	8	22½	14½	133	94	168	120
12	7	21⅛	21⅛	31¼	10⅛	27	16⅞	186	135	236	173
15	7	25	25	35¾	10¾	31½	20¾	290	204	368	262
3 by 2	4	7 9/16	7½	11¾	4 3/16	9	5	14	10	18	13
4 by 2	4	8⅜	8¼	12	3⅝	9	5¾	17	12	21	15
4 by 3	4	9 1/16	9	13½	4 7/16	10½	6¼	20	14	26	19
5 by 2	4	8⅞	9	12	3⅛	9	6½	20	14	24	17
5 by 3	4	9⅝	9¾	13½	3⅞	10½	7	24	16½	30	21
5 by 4	4	10 5/16	10½	15	4 11/16	12	7½	27	19	35	24
6 by 2	4	9 7/16	9¾	12	2 9/16	9	7¼	23	16½	27	20
6 by 3	4	10⅛	10½	13½	3⅜	10½	7¾	27	19	33	23
6 by 4	4	10 13/16	11¼	15	4 3/16	12	8¼	31	22	39	28
6 by 5	4	11 9/16	11¾	16½	4 15/16	13½	8¾	35	24	45	31
8 by 2	5½	10⅞	11	14	3⅛	10½	8½	42	29	46	32
8 by 3	5½	11 9/16	11¾	15½	3 15/16	12	9	47	32	53	37
8 by 4	5½	12¼	12½	17	4¾	13½	9½	52	36	60	42
8 by 5	5½	13	13	18½	5½	15	10	57	39	66	45
8 by 6	5½	13 11/16	13½	20	6 5/16	16½	10½	63	44	73	51
10 by 4	5½	13 7/16	14⅛	17	3 9/16	13½	11⅛	74	53	82	59
10 by 5	5½	14 3/16	14⅝	18½	4 5/16	15	11⅝	80	57	89	63
10 by 6	5½	14⅞	15⅛	20	5⅛	16½	12⅛	86	61	97	70
10 by 8	5½	16½	16 15/16	23	6½	19½	13 7/16	110	77	135	94
12 by 4	7	15⅛	15 7/16	19¼	4⅛	15	12 7/16	97	70	105	76
12 by 5	7	15⅞	15 15/16	20¾	4⅞	16½	12 15/16	104	74	113	81
12 by 6	7	16 9/16	16 7/16	22¼	5 11/16	18	13 7/16	111	80	122	88
12 by 8	7	18 3/16	18¼	25¼	7 1/16	21	14¾	136	96	161	113
12 by 10	7	19 11/16	19 5/16	28¼	8 9/16	24	15 13/16	160	115	195	142
15 by 6	7	18¼	18¾	22¼	4	18	15¾	152	109	163	117
15 by 8	7	19⅞	20 9/16	25¼	5⅜	21	17 1/16	182	127	207	146
15 by 10	7	21⅜	21⅝	28¼	6⅞	24	18⅛	213	152	248	176
15 by 12	7	22 13/16	23 7/16	31¼	8 7/16	27	19 3/16	242	170	292	210

View A showing cleanout plug on main

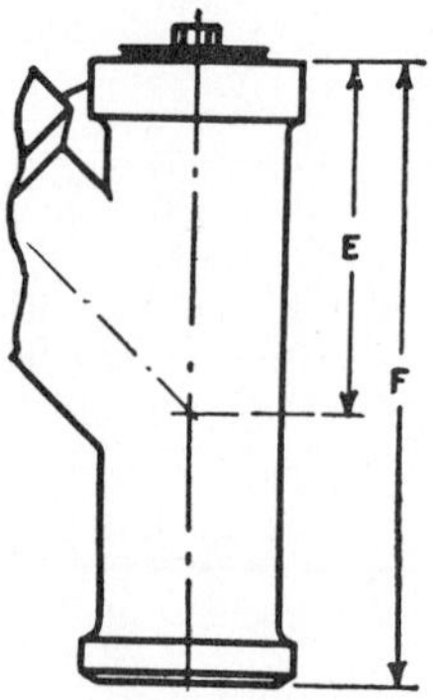

Table 18. Y branch cleanout with screw plug on main

Size (inches)	Dimensions in inches					Minimum I.P.S. tapping		Weight without plug (pounds)	
	E	E′	F	G	X′	'XH'	'SV'	'XH'	'SV'
2	5¼	6½	9¼	4	4	1½	1½	9	7¼
3	6⅝	8¼	11⅝	5	5½	2½	2½	15	10½
4	7⅞	9¾	13⅛	5¼	6¾	3½	3½	21	14½
5	9⅛	11	14⅝	5½	8	4	4	28	19
6	10⅜	12¼	16⅛	5¾	9¼	5	5	37	26

View B showing cleanout plug on branch

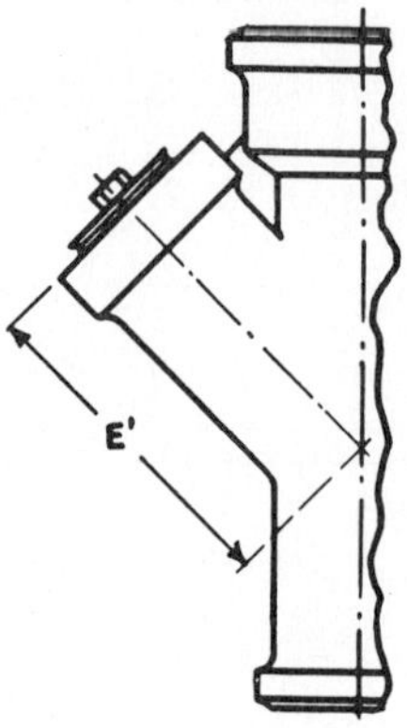

Table 19. Y branch cleanout with screw plug on branch

Size (inches)	Dimensions in inches					Minimum I.P.S. tapping		Weight without plug (pounds)	
	E	E′	F	G	X	'XH'	'SV'	'XH'	'SV'
2	6½	5¼	10½	4	8	1½	1½	9	7¼
3	8¼	6⅝	13¼	5	10½	2½	2½	15	10½
4	9¾	7⅞	15	5¼	12	3½	3½	21	14½
5	11	9⅛	16½	5½	13½	4	4	28	19
6	12¼	10⅜	18	5¾	15	5	5	37	26

Upright Y branch

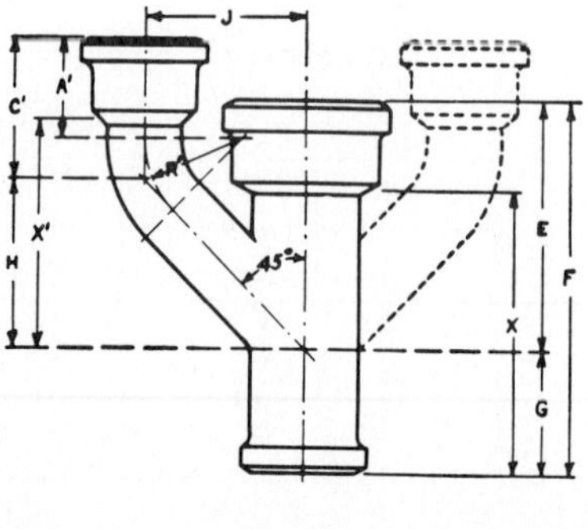

Table 20. Single and double upright Y branches

Size (inches)	Dimensions in inches										Weight, single (pounds)		Weight, double (pounds)	
	A′	C′	E	F	G	H	J	R′	X	X′	'XH'	'SV'	'XH'	'SV'
2	2¾	4	6½	10½	4	4½	4½	3	8	6	10	8	15	12
3	3¼	4 11/16	8¼	13¼	5	5½	5½	3½	10½	7 7/16	20	13½	30	20½
4	3½	5 3/16	9¾	15	5¼	6½	6½	4	12	8 11/16	28	19½	42	29
5	3½	5⅜	11	16½	5½	7½	7½	4½	13½	9⅞	37	25	56	38
6	3½	5 9/16	12¼	18	5¾	8½	8½	5	15	11 1/16	47	33	70	49
3 by 2	3	4¼	7 9/16	11¾	4 3/16	5	5	3	9	6¾	16	11¼	20	14
4 by 2	3	4¼	8 5/16	12	3 11/16	5½	5½	3	9	7¼	19	13½	24	17
4 by 3	3¼	4 11/16	9	13½	4½	6	6	3½	10½	7 15/16	23	16	34	23½
5 by 2	3	4¼	8⅝	12	3⅜	6	6	3	9	7¾	22	15	27	19
5 by 3	3¼	4 11/16	9½	13½	4	6½	6½	3½	10½	8 7/16	27	18½	38	26
5 by 4	3½	5 3/16	10¼	15	4¾	7	7	4	12	9 3/16	32	22	46	31
6 by 2	3	4¼	9 5/16	12	2 11/16	6½	6½	3	9	8¼	25	18	30	21½
6 by 3	3¼	4 11/16	10	13½	3½	7	7	3½	10½	8 15/16	30	21	41	28½
6 by 4	3½	5 3/16	10¾	15	4¼	7½	7½	4	12	9 11/16	35	24½	49	34
6 by 5	3½	5⅜	11 7/16	16½	5 1/16	8	8	4½	13½	10⅜	40	28	60	41

Table 21. Single and double combination Y-and-⅛ bend

Size (inches)	Dimensions in inches											Weight single (pounds)		Weight double (pounds)	
	A′	B min.	C′	E	E′	F	G	H	R′	X	X′	'XH'	'SV'	'XH'	'SV'
2	2¾	3½	4	6½	7⅜	10½	4	3⅜	3	8	4⅞	10	8	15	12
3	3¼	4	4 11/16	8¼	9¾	13¼	5	5 1/16	3½	10½	7	20	14	29	20
4	3½	4	5 3/16	9¾	12	15	5¼	6 13/16	4	12	9	29	20	43	30
5	3½	4	5⅜	11	14	16½	5½	8⅝	4½	13½	11	38	26	56	38
6	3½	4	5 9/16	12¼	15⅞	18	5¾	10 5/16	5	15	12⅞	50	35	75	53
3 by 2	3	4	4¼	7 9/16	8¼	11¾	4 3/16	4	3	9	5¾	15	10½	20	14
4 by 2	3	4	4¼	8 5/16	8¾	12	3 11/16	4½	3	9	6¼	18	13	23	16½
4 by 3	3¼	4	4 11/16	9	10¼	13½	4½	5 9/16	3½	10½	7½	24	17	33	23
5 by 2	3	4	4¼	8⅝	9¼	12	3⅜	5	3	9	6¾	21	14½	26	18
5 by 3	3¼	4	4 11/16	9½	10¾	13½	4	6 1/16	3½	10½	8	27	18½	36	25
5 by 4	3½	4	5 3/16	10¼	12½	15	4¾	7 5/16	4	12	9½	33	23	47	32
6 by 2	3	4	4¼	9 5/16	9¾	12	2 11/16	5½	3	9	7¼	24	17	29	21
6 by 3	3¼	4	4 11/16	10	11¼	13½	3½	6 9/16	3½	10½	8½	30	21	39	27
6 by 4	3½	4	5 3/16	10¾	13	15	4¼	7 13/16	4	12	10	36	25	50	35
6 by 5	3½	4	5⅜	11 7/16	14½	16½	5 1/16	9⅛	4½	13½	11½	42	29	60	41

Combination Y-and-⅛ bend

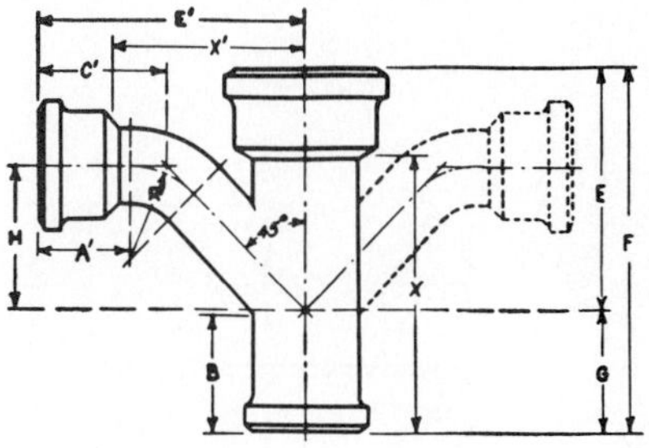

Table 22. Combination Y-and-⅛ bend cleanout with screw plug on main

Size (inches)	Dimensions in inches [1]		Min. I.P.S. tapping [2]	Weight without plug (pounds)		Size (inches)	Dimensions in inches [1]		Min. I.P.S. tapping [2]	Weight without plug (pounds)	
	E	F		'XH'	'SV'		E	F		'XH'	'SV'
2	5¼	9¼	1½	9	7¼	5	9⅛	14⅝	4	34	23½
3	6⅝	11⅝	2½	17	11½	6	10⅜	16⅛	5	47	33
4	7⅞	13⅛	3½	26	17½						

View A showing cleanout plug on main

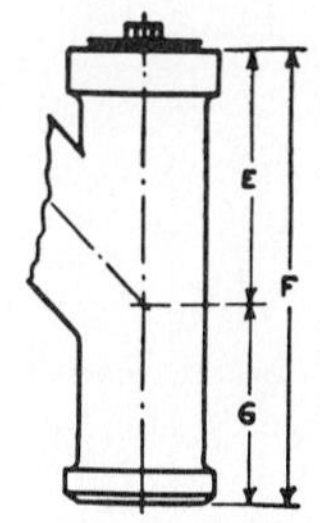

Table 23. Single and double inverted Y branches

Size (inches)	Dimensions in inches						Weight single (pounds)		Weight double (pounds)	
	E	F′	F	G	X	X′	'XH'	'SV'	'XH'	'SV'
2	3¼	5⅞	12	8¾	9½	3⅜	9	7¼	12	9¾
3	4	7⅜	15¼	11¼	12½	4⅝	18	12½	23	16
4	4½	8⅞	17	12½	14	5⅞	25	17½	32	22½
5	4¾	10⅛	18½	13¾	15½	7⅛	33	23	42	29
6	5	11⅜	20	15	17	8⅜	41	29	51	37
3 by 2	3¼	6⅝	13¾	10½	11	4⅛	15	11	18	13
4 by 2	3 1/16	7⅜	14	10 15/16	11	4⅞	18	13	21	15
4 by 3	3¾	8⅛	15½	11¾	12½	5⅜	22	15½	27	19
5 by 2	2⅝	8 1/16	14	11⅜	11	5 9/16	22	15	25	17½
5 by 3	3 5/16	8 13/16	15½	12 3/16	12½	6 1/16	25	17	31	21
5 by 4	4	9 9/16	17	13	14	6 9/16	29	20	37	26
6 by 2	2 3/16	8¾	14	11 13/16	11	6¼	25	18	29	21
6 by 3	2⅞	9½	15½	12⅝	12½	6¾	29	20	34	24
6 by 4	3 9/16	10¼	17	13 7/16	14	7¼	33	23	40	28
6 by 5	4¼	10¾	18½	14¼	15½	7¾	37	26	46	32

Inverted Y Branch

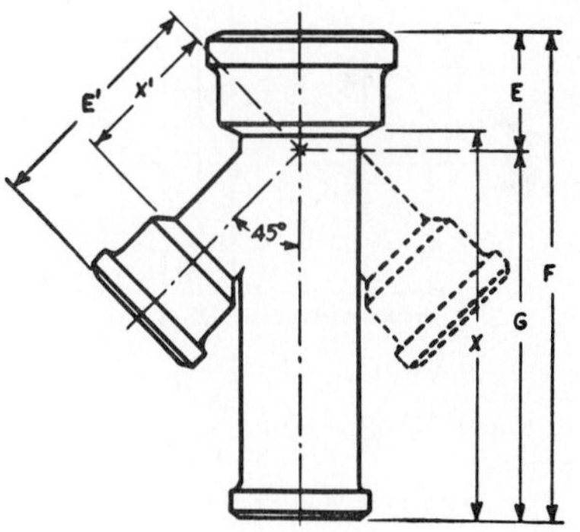

Table 24. Single and double vent branches

Size (inches)	Dimensions in inches							Weight single (pounds)		Weight double (pounds)	
	B	E	F	G	J	R′	X	'XH'	'SV'	'XH'	'SV'
2	3¼	4¼	10½	6¼	4½	3	8	9	7¼	12	9½
3	4	5¼	12¾	7½	5½	3½	10	18	12	23	15½
4	4	6	14	8	6½	4	11	25	17	32	22
5	4	6½	15	8½	7½	4½	12	32	22	41	28
6	4	7	16	9	8½	5	13	41	29	51	35
3 by 2	4	4¾	11¾	7	5	3	9	14	9½	17	11½
4 by 2	4	5	12	7	5½	3	9	18	12½	21	14½
4 by 3	4	5½	13	7½	6	3½	10	21	14½	26	18
5 by 2	4	5	12	7	6	3	9	21	14	24	16
5 by 3	4	5½	13	7½	6½	3½	10	24	16	29	17
5 by 4	4	6	14	8	7	4	11	28	19	35	24
6 by 2	4	5	12	7	6½	3	9	22	15½	25	17½
6 by 3	4	5½	13	7½	7	3½	10	27	19	32	22
6 by 4	4	6	14	8	7½	4	11	31	22	38	26
6 by 5	4	6½	15	8½	8	4½	12	36	25	45	31

Vent branch

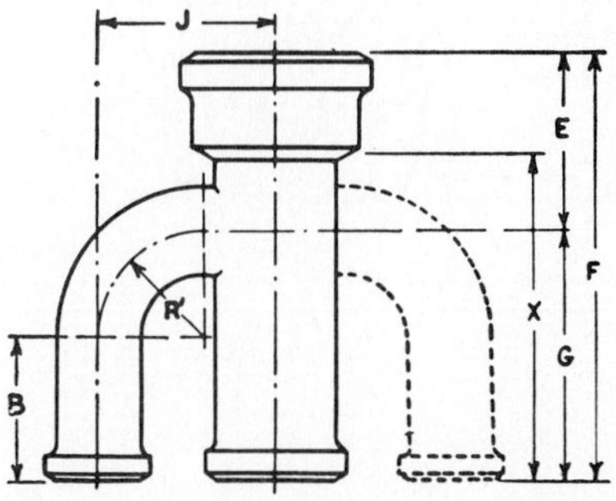

Cast-iron fittings

Sanitary T branch

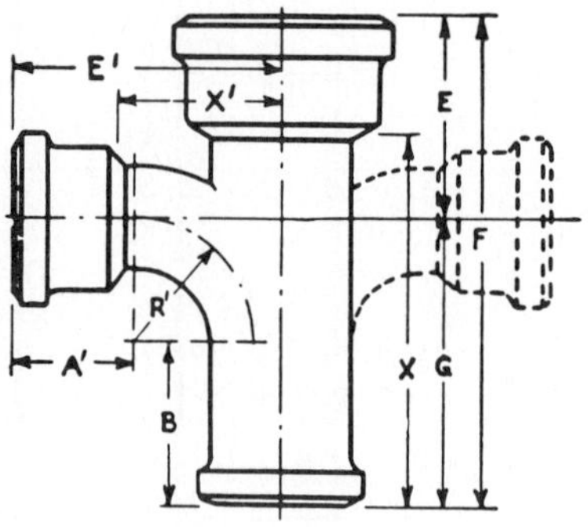

Table 25. Single and double sanitary T branches

Size (inches)	Dimensions in inches									Weight, single (pounds)		Weight, double (pounds)	
	A′	B	E	E′	F	G	R′	X	X′	'XH'	'SV'	'XH'	'SV'
2	2¾	3¾	4¼	5¼	10½	6¼	2½	8	2¾	8	6½	11	8¾
3	3¼	4	5¼	6¾	12¾	7½	3½	10	4	16	12	21	14½
4	3½	4	6	7½	14	8	4	11	4½	22	15½	29	20
5	3½	4	6½	8	15	8½	4½	12	5	28	19	36	25
6	3½	4	7	8½	16	9	5	13	5½	34	24½	44	32
8	4⅛	5¾	8¾	10⅛	20½	11¾	6	17	6⅝	72	49	92	63
10	4⅛	5¾	9¾	11⅛	22½	12¾	7	19	7⅝	108	78	132	97
12	5	7	11¾	13	26¾	15	8	22½	8¾	153	113	187	140
15	5	7	13¼	14½	29¾	16½	9½	25½	10¼	229	164	272	185
3 by 2	3	4	4¾	6½	11¾	7	3	9	4	14	10	18	13
4 by 2	3	4	5	7	12	7	3	9	4½	17	12	21	15
4 by 3	3¼	4	5½	7¼	13	7½	3½	10	4½	20	14	25	17½
5 by 2	3	4	5	7½	12	7	3	9	5	20	14	24	17
5 by 3	3¼	4	5½	7¾	13	7½	3½	10	5	23	16	28	19
5 by 4	3½	4	6	8	14	8	4	11	5	26	18	33	23
6 by 2	3	4	5	8	12	7	3	9	5½	23	16½	27	19
6 by 3	3¼	4	5½	8¼	13	7½	3½	10	5½	26	18½	31	22
6 by 4	3½	4	6	8½	14	8	4	11	5½	29	21	36	26
6 by 5	3½	4	6½	8½	15	8½	4½	12	5½	32	22	40	28
8 by 2	3	5¾	5¾	9	14½	8¾	3	11	6½	43	30	47	33
8 by 3	3¼	5¾	6¼	9¼	15½	9¼	3½	12	6½	47	32	52	36
8 by 4	3½	5¾	6¾	9½	16½	9¾	4	13	6½	51	35	58	40
8 by 5	3½	5¾	7¼	9½	17½	10¼	4½	14	6½	55	38	63	43
8 by 6	3½	5¾	7¾	9½	18½	10¾	5	15	6½	57	40	67	47
10 by 4	3½	5¾	6¾	10½	16½	9¾	4	13	7½	70	50	77	55
10 by 5	3½	5¾	7¼	10½	17½	10¼	4½	14	7½	73	52	81	58
10 by 6	3½	5¾	7¾	10½	18½	10¾	5	15	7½	76	55	85	62
10 by 8	4⅛	5¾	8¾	11⅛	20½	11¾	6	17	7⅝	96	68	115	81
12 by 4	3½	7	7¾	11½	18¾	11	4	14½	8½	95	69	102	74
12 by 5	3½	7	8¼	11½	19¾	11½	4½	15½	8½	99	71	107	76
12 by 6	3½	7	8¾	11½	20¾	12	5	16½	8½	103	74	113	82
12 by 8	4⅛	7	9¾	12⅛	22¾	13	6	18½	8⅝	120	85	140	99
12 by 10	4⅛	7	10¾	12⅛	24¾	14	7	20½	8⅝	134	97	155	114
15 by 6	3½	7	8¾	13	20¾	12	5	16½	10	142	102	150	108
15 by 8	4⅛	7	9¾	13⅝	22¾	13	6	18½	10⅛	162	115	180	128
15 by 10	4⅛	7	10¾	13⅝	24¾	14	7	20½	10⅛	180	130	200	145
15 by 12	5	7	11¾	14½	26¾	15	8	22½	10¼	198	143	230	168

T branch cleanout with screw plug

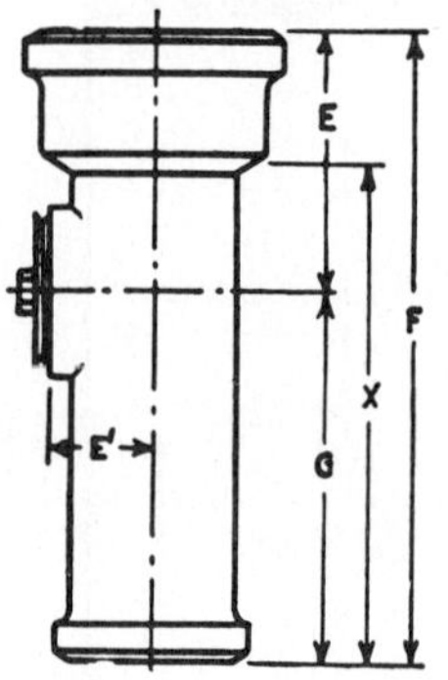

Table 26. T branch cleanout with screw plug

Size (inches)	Dimensions in inches					I.P.S. Tapping	Weight Without Plug (pounds)	
	E	E′	F	G	X		'XH'	'SV'
2	4¼	2	10½	6¼	8	1½	7	5¾
3	5¼	2½	12¾	7½	10	2½	13	8
4	6	3	14	8	11	3½	17	10½
5	6½	3½	15	8½	12	4	22	15
6	7	4	16	9	13	4	28	20

½-S trap with or without vent and cleanout

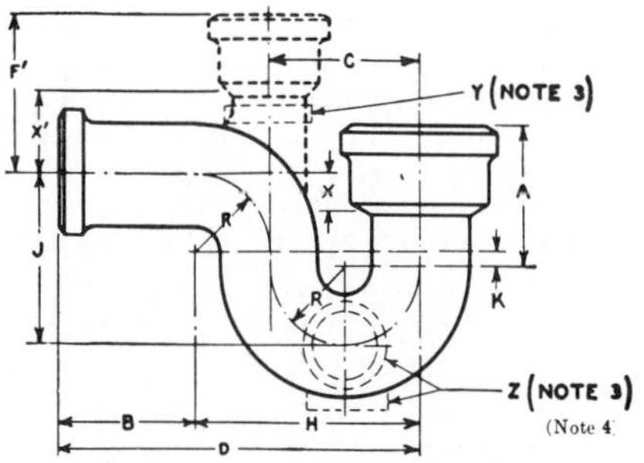

Table 27. ½-S traps with or without vent and cleanout

Size (inches)	Dimensions in inches (Notes 1 and 2)											Weight without hub vent (pounds)		Weight with hub vent (pounds)	
	A	B	C	D	F′	H	J	K	R	X	X′	'XH'	'SV'	'XH'	'SV'
2 by 2	3	3½	4	9½	4½	6	4	-----	2	1½	2	8	6½	11	9
3 by 2	4½	4½	5	12	5	7½	5½	½	2½	1¼	2½	17	11½	20	14
3 by 3	4½	4½	5	12	5¼	7½	5½	½	2½	1¼	2½	17	11½	21	14½
4 by 2	5½	5	6	14	5½	9	6½	½	3	1	3	25	17	28	19
4 by 3	5½	5	6	14	5¾	9	6½	½	3	1	3	25	17	29	20
4 by 4	5½	5	6	14	6	9	6½	½	3	1	3	25	17	31	21
5 by 4	6½	5	7	15½	6½	10½	7½	½	3½	½	3½	34	23	40	27
5 by 5	6½	5	7	15½	6½	10½	7½	½	3½	½	3½	34	23	41	28
6 by 4	7½	5	8	17	7	12	8½	½	4	-------	4	45	31	51	35
6 by 6	7½	5	8	17	7	12	8½	½	4	-------	4	45	31	54	38
8 by 4	10	7	10	22	8¼	15	11	1	5	½	5¼	97	65	103	70
8 by 6	10	7	10	22	8¼	15	11	1	5	½	5¼	97	65	107	73
10 by 6	12	7	12	25	9¼	18	13	1	6	1½	6¼	166	113	175	121
12 by 6	13½	8	15	30½	10¼	22½	15	-----	7½	1¾	7¼	242	171	251	173
12 by 8	13½	8	15	30½	10¾	22½	15	-----	7½	1¾	7¼	242	171	264	182
15 by 8	16¾	8	18½	35¾	12¼	27¾	18½	-----	9¼	3¼	8¾	398	270	425	292

NOTE 1.—A minimum water seal of 2 inches is provided for the 2-inch size; of 2½ inches for sizes 3 to 6 inches, inclusive; of 3 inches for sizes 8 to 12 inches, inclusive; and of 3½ inches for the 15-inch size.

NOTE 2.—Dimensions D, X, and X′ are laying lengths. Dimension X is measured below the horizontal center line on sizes 5 by 5 inches and smaller, and above the horizontal center line on sizes 8 by 4 inches and larger.

NOTE 3.—Traps with tapped vent and cleanout shall have tappings of sizes indicated below.

NOTE 4.—Tape at position Z shall be specified as right side, left side, or bottom.

Table 28. Running traps with or without single or double vents and cleanout

Size (inches)	Dimensions in inches (Notes 1 and 2)											Weight (pounds)					
												W_1		W_2		W_3	
	A	B	C	F	F'	H	J	K	R	X	X'	'XH'	'SV'	'XH'	'SV'	'XH'	'SV'
2 by 2	3	3½	4	14½	4½	8	4	---	2	12	2	9	7¼	12	9½	15	12
3 by 2	3¼	4½	5	17¾	5	10	5½	½	2½	15	2½	19	13	22	15	25	17½
3 by 3	3¼	4½	5	17¾	5¼	10	5½	½	2½	15	2½	19	13	23	16	27	19
4 by 2	3½	5	6	20½	5½	12	6½	½	3	17½	3	28	19	31	22	34	24
4 by 3	3½	5	6	20½	5¾	12	6½	½	3	17½	3	28	19	32	22	36	25
4 by 4	3½	5	6	20½	6	12	6½	½	3	17½	3	28	19	34	23	40	28
5 by 4	3½	5	7	22½	6½	14	7½	½	3½	19½	3½	37	26	43	29	49	34
5 by 5	3½	5	7	22½	6½	14	7½	½	3½	19½	3½	37	26	45	31	51	35
6 by 4	3½	5	8	24½	7	16	8½	½	4	21½	4	48	33	54	37	60	42
6 by 6	3½	5	8	24½	7	16	8½	½	4	21½	4	48	33	57	40	66	47
8 by 4	4⅛	7	10	31⅛	8¼	20	11	1	5	27⅝	5¼	103	70	109	74	115	78
8 by 6	4⅛	7	10	31⅛	8¼	20	11	1	5	27⅝	5¼	103	70	112	76	121	83
10 by 6	4⅛	7	12	35⅛	9¼	24	13	1	6	31⅝	6¼	175	120	184	127	193	134
12 by 6	5	8	15	43	10¼	30	15	---	7½	38¾	7¼	256	176	265	183	274	190
12 by 8	5	8	15	43	10¾	30	15	---	7½	38¾	7¼	256	176	278	191	300	206
15 by 8	5	8	18½	50	12¼	37	18½	---	9¼	45¾	8¾	414	284	436	299	463	317

Weights are given as follows: W_1, without hub vent; W_2, with single hub vent; W_3, with double hub vent.

NOTE 1.—A minimum water seal of 2 inches is provided for the 2-inch size; of 2½ inches for sizes 3 to 6 inches, inclusive; of 3 inches for sizes 8 to 12 inches inclusive; and of 3½ inches for the 15-inch size.
NOTE 2.—Dimensions X and X' are laying lengths.
NOTE 3.—For traps with tapping at Y and Z, see table 50, note 3.
NOTE 4.—Tap at position Z shall be specified as right side, left side, or bottom.

Running trap with or without single or double vents and cleanout

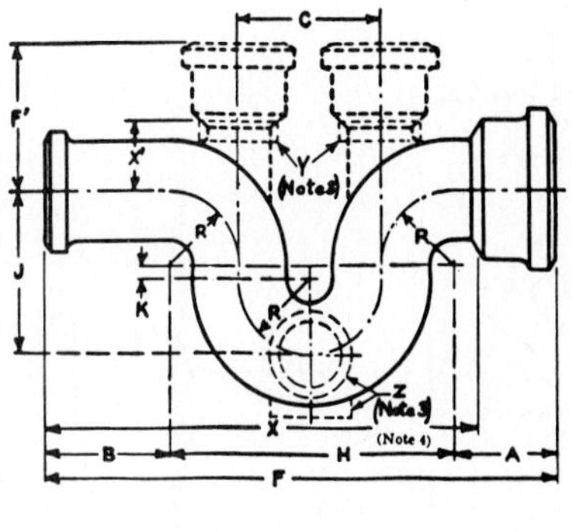

Table 29. Double hub

Size (inches)	F	X	Weight (pounds)		Size (inches)	F	X	Weight (pounds)	
			'XH'	'SV'				'XH'	'SV'
	Inches	*Inch*				*Inches*	*Inches*		
2	6	1	5	4	8	8¾	1¼	35	24
3	6½	1	8	6	10	8¾	1¼	50	40
4	7	1	11	8	12	10	1½	67	54
5	7	1	13	9	15	10	1½	91	73
6	7	1	15	11					

Double hub

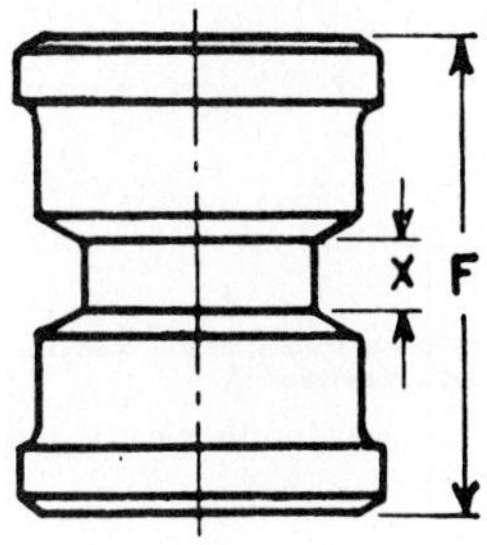

Table 30. Reducers

Size (inches)	B	F	X	Weight (pounds)		Size [1] (inches)	B	F	X	Weight (pounds)	
				'XH'	'SV'					'XH'	'SV'
	Inches	*Inches*	*Inches*				*Inches*	*Inches*	*Inches*		
3 by 2	3¾	7¼	4¾	6	4½	8 by 6	4½	9	6	21	15
4 by 2	4	7½	5	7	5	10 by 4	4½	9	6	25	17
4 by 3	4	7¾	5	9	6½	10 by 5	4½	9	6	26	17½
5 by 2	4	7½	5	8	6	10 by 6	4½	9	6	27	19
5 by 3	4	7¾	5	10	7	10 by 8	4½	9½	6	35	24
5 by 4	4	8	5	11	8	12 by 4	5¼	9½	6½	33	22
6 by 2	4	7½	5	9	6½	12 by 5	5¼	9½	6½	34	23
6 by 3	4	7¾	5	11	7½	12 by 6	5¼	9½	6½	35	24
6 by 4	4	8	5	12	8½	12 by 8	5¼	10	6½	45	31
6 by 5	4	8	5	13	9	12 by 10	5¼	10	6½	51	37
8 by 2	4½	8½	6	17	12	15 by 6	5¼	9½	6½	44	30
8 by 3	4½	8¾	6	18	12½	15 by 8	5¼	10	6½	55	38
8 by 4	4½	9	6	19	13	15 by 10	5¼	10	6½	60	43
8 by 5	4½	9	6	20	13½	15 by 12	5¼	10¾	6½	67	50

Reducer

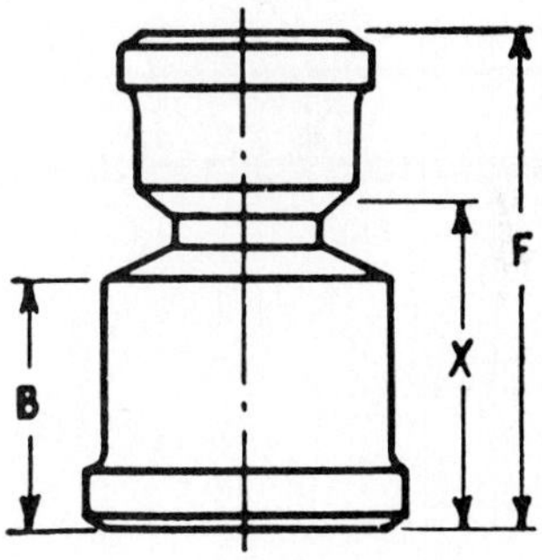

Table 31. Spigot and tapped long increasers

Sizes (inches) (Note 1)	A	B	C (Note 2)	L (Note 3)	D		Weight, spigot (pounds)		Weight, tapped (pounds)	
					'XH'	'SV'	'XH'	'SV'	'XH'	'SV'
	in.	*in.*	*in.*	*in.*	*in.*	*in.*				
2 by 4 by 24	8½	4	4½	24	4½	4¼	19	12½	19	13
2 by 4 by 30	8½	4	4½	30	4½	4¼	23	15½	24	16
2 by 4 by 36	8½	4	4½	36	4½	4¼	27	18	29	19
2 by 4 by 48	8½	4	4½	48	4½	4¼	39	26	40	27
3 by 4 by 24	8½	4	4½	24	4½	4¼	20	13½	20	13½
3 by 4 by 30	8½	4	4½	30	4½	4¼	25	17	26	17½
3 by 4 by 36	8½	4	4½	36	4½	4¼	30	20	31	21
3 by 4 by 48	8½	4	4½	48	4½	4¼	41	27	42	28
4 by 5 by 24	8½	4	4½	24	5½	5¼	25	17	26	17
4 by 5 by 30	8½	4	4½	30	5½	5¼	31	21	33	22
4 by 5 by 36	8½	4	4½	36	5½	5¼	38	25	39	26
4 by 5 by 48	8½	4	4½	48	5½	5¼	51	34	52	35
4 by 6 by 24	8½	4	4½	24	6½	6¼	29	19	30	20
4 by 6 by 30	8½	4	4½	30	6½	6¼	36	24	38	25
4 by 6 by 36	8½	4	4½	36	6½	6¼	44	29	45	30
4 by 6 by 48	8½	4	4½	48	6½	6¼	59	40	61	41

NOTE 1.—First size given for long increasers is spigot size.
First size given for long increasers, tapped, is tapping size.
NOTE 2.—All markings shall be on small end and in space indicated by dimension C.
NOTE 3.—Dimension L is the laying length.

Spigot and tapped long increaser

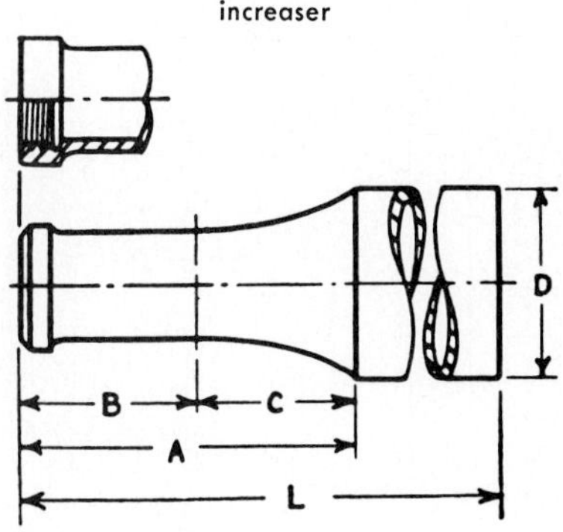

Cast-iron fittings

Tapped increaser

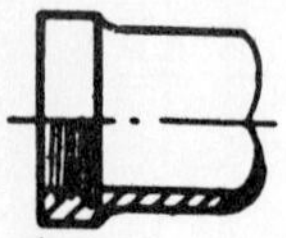

Increaser

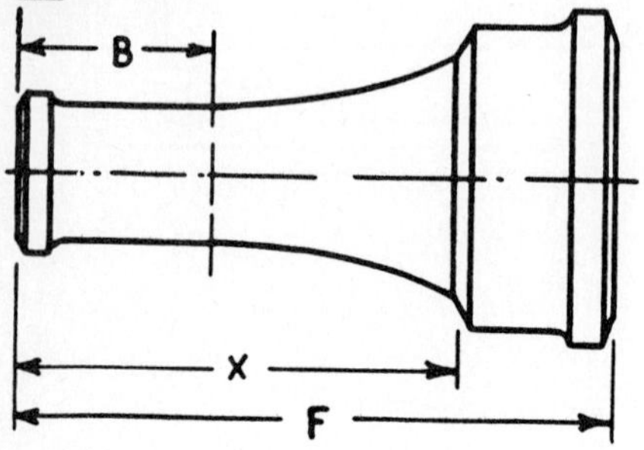

Table 32. Increasers

Size (inches)	B	F	X	Weight (pounds)		Size (inches)	B	F	X	Weight (pounds)	
				'XH'	'SV'					'XH'	'SV'
	Inches	*Inches*	*Inches*				*Inches*	*Inches*	*Inches*		
2 by 3	4	11¾	9	9	6½	5 by 8	4	15½	12	34	24
2 by 4	4	12	9	10	7	5 by 10	4	15½	12	44	33
2 by 5	4	12	9	12	8½	6 by 8	4	15½	12	35	24
2 by 6	4	12	9	13	9½	6 by 10	4	15½	12	45	33
3 by 4	4	12	9	12	9	6 by 12	4	16¼	12	58	44
3 by 5	4	12	9	14	9½	8 by 10	5½	15½	12	55	40
3 by 6	4	12	9	15	11	8 by 12	5½	16¼	12	64	48
4 by 5	4	12	9	15	10½	8 by 15	5½	16¼	12	82	61
4 by 6	4	12	9	16	11½	10 by 12	5½	16¼	12	73	54
4 by 8	4	15½	12	32	22	10 by 15	5½	16¼	12	88	65
5 by 6	4	12	9	18	13	12 by 15	7	16¼	12	97	71

Table 33. Tapped increasers

Size (inches) (note 1)	B	F	X	Weight (pounds)	
				'XH'	'SV'
	Inches	*Inches*	*Inches*		
1½ by 2	4	10½	8	7	5
2 by 3	4	11¾	9	9	6½
2 by 4	4	12	9	11	8
2 by 5	4	12	9	12	8½
2 by 6	4	12	9	14	10

NOTE 1.—Tapping boss may be tapped for 1¼-, 1½-, or 2-inch pipe, except size 1½ by 2 inches, which may be tapped 1¼ or 1½ inches only.

Plug for hub

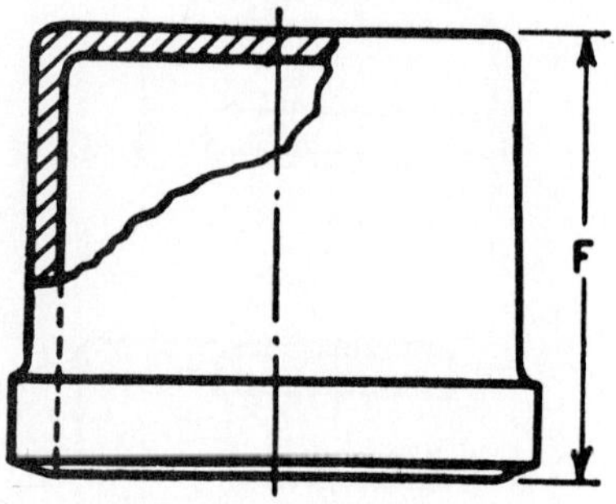

Table 34. Plugs for hub

Size (inches)	F	Weight (pounds)		Size (inches)	F	Weight (pounds)	
		'XH'	'SV'			'XH'	'SV'
	Inches				*Inches*		
2	3½	1¾	1¼	8	4½	15	11¼
3	3¾	3	2¼	10	4½	23	17¼
4	4	4½	3¼	12	5¼	33	24¾
5	4	6	4½	15	5¼	50	37½
6	4	8	6				

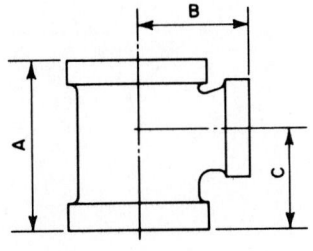

Reducing Y
(short TY)

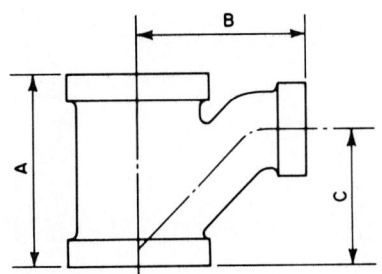

Reducing Y
(long TY)

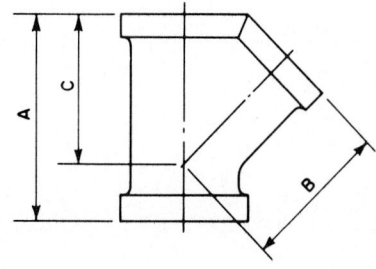

Reducing Y
(45° Y)

Table 35. Reducing Y branches

Size, in.	Dimensions in inches								
	Reducing short TY			Reducing long TY			Reducing 45° Y		
	A	B	C	A	B	C	A	B	C
1½x1¼	4⅜	2¾	2¾	5⁷/₁₆	4³/₁₆	3⅞	5¼	3⁷/₁₆	3⁷/₁₆
2x1¼x1½							5⅛	3⅝	3⅝
2x1½x1¼							5⅛	3⅝	3⅝
2x1½x1½	4½	2½	2¾				5⅛	3⅝	3⅝
2x1½x2							5⅞	3¹⁵/₁₆	4
2 x1¼	4⁷/₁₆	2¹³/₁₆	2¹¹/₁₆	5¹³/₁₆	4½	4½	5¹⁵/₁₆	4¼	4¼
2 x1½	4¹⁵/₁₆	3	2⅞	5¹³/₁₆	4½	4½	5¹⁵/₁₆	4¼	4¼
2½x1¼	5⅛	3¼	3						
2½x1½	5⅛	3¼	3	5¾	4½	4¼	6⅜	4¾	4⅝
2½x2	5½	3¹¹/₁₆	3⅛	8¼	6³/₁₆	6¹/₁₆	6⅜	4¾	4⅝
3 x1½	5¹/₁₆	3⁵/₁₆	2¹⁵/₁₆	5⅞	5¼	4⁹/₁₆	6⅝	5¹/₁₆	4¹¹/₁₆
3 x2	5¾	3⅝	3¼	6⅝	5½	4½	6¾	5¼	5⅛
3 x2½							8⅜	6	6
4 x1½	5¹³/₁₆	4¹/₁₆	3⅜	7	6⅜	5⅛	7⅝	5⅝	5⁷/₁₆
4 x2	5¹³/₁₆	4¹/₁₆	3⅜	7	6⅜	5⅛	6⅝	5⅞	5⅝
4 x2½	7⅜	4¾	4⁵/₁₆	9¼	7¾	6½	7¼	5⅞	5¾
4 x3	7⅜	4¾	4⁵/₁₆	9¼	7¾	6½	8½	6⅝	6⅜
5 x1½	5⁹/₁₆	4⅜	3³/₁₆	7⅜	6¹¹/₁₆	5⅝			
5 x2	6⅛	4½	3¹¹/₁₆	7⅜	6¹¹/₁₆	5⅝	7⅛	6¾	6
5 x3	7¾	5³/₁₆	4½	9½	8⁷/₁₆	7	8¾	7½	7⅛
5 x4	9¼	5¹³/₁₆	5¼	11⅛	9⁷/₁₆	7¹⁵/₁₆	10⁵/₁₆	8	7⅞
6 x2	6⁵/₁₆	5³/₁₆	3¹¹/₁₆	6½	6¾	4⁷/₁₆	7	7½	6⅝
6 x3	9¼	5¹⁵/₁₆	5⁷/₁₆	8⅞	7¼	6¼	8¹³/₁₆	8¼	7½
6 x4	9¼	5¹⁵/₁₆	5⁷/₁₆	11¼	9¹³/₁₆	8¼	10½	9	8⅞
6 x5	10⅜	5¹⁵/₁₆	5¹⁵/₁₆	13	10¹¹/₁₆	9⁷/₁₆	11½	9⅛	9
7 x4				10¼	9⅝	7	10¼	10½	9⅝
8 x3	11⅝	7⅝	7½	8¾	9¼	5⅞	10⅜	10	8⅞
8 x4	11⅝	7⅝	7½	10⅝	10	7¼	10⅜	10	8⅞
8 x5	12¾	8¹/₁₆	8⅜	14¼	10¾	8¾	11⅜	10⅝	9¾
8 x6	12¾	8¹/₁₆	8⅜	14¼	10¾	8¾	14	12	11½
10 x4	13⅜	9¹⁵/₁₆	8⅜	16⅛	14⅛	11⅝	11⅞	12⅝	11⅝
10 x5	13⅜	9¹⁵/₁₆	8⅜				13⅞	13⅝	13
10 x6	13⅜	9¹⁵/₁₆	8⅜	16⅛	14⅛	11⅝	13⅞	13⅝	13
10 x8	19½	12¼	12¼	17⅜	11¼	11⅛	20¼	15¼	15¼
12 x4							15	13⅜	11⅜

Cast-iron fittings

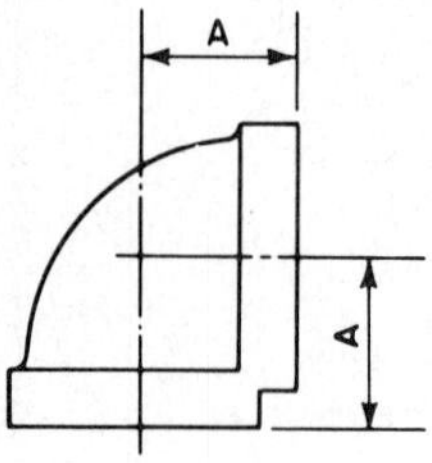

90° elbow
(short turn)

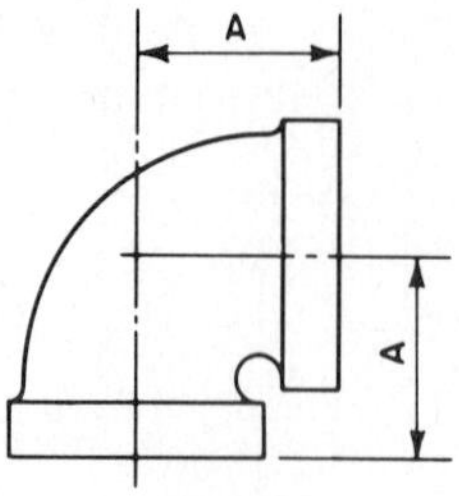

90° elbow
(long turn)

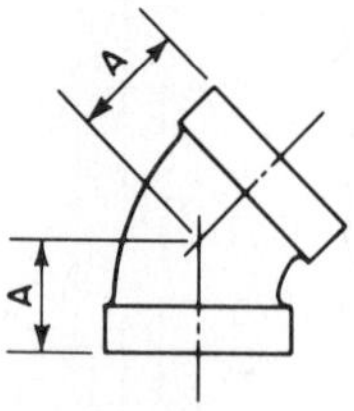

45° elbow
(short turn)

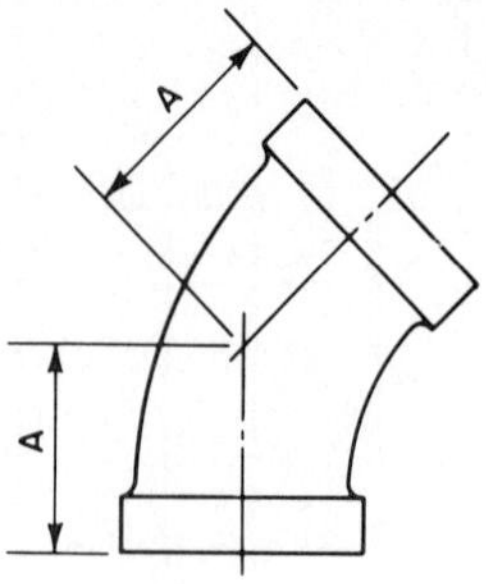

45° elbow
(long turn)

Table 36. Short- and long-turn elbows

Size, in.	Dimension A, in.			
	90° elbow		45° elbow	
	Short turn	Long turn	Short turn	Long turn
1 1/4	1 7/8	2 3/8	1 5/16	1 3/4
1 1/2	2	2 1/2	1 1/2	1 7/8
1 1/2x1 1/4	2			
2	2 1/4	3 1/16	1 5/8	2 1/4
2 1/2x1 1/2	2 1/8			
2 1/2	2 13/16	3 11/16	1 11/16	3
3	3 3/8	5 7/8	2 3/8	4 5/8
4	3 15/16	6 3/4	2 7/16	4 5/8
5	4 5/8	6 1/8	3 1/16	5 7/16
6	5 11/32	7 1/8	3	6
7	5 11/16	9 1/2	3 3/8	
8	6 1/2	11 7/8	3 1/2	6 3/4
10	7 7/8	12 1/4	4 7/16	7 1/2
12	9	13	5 1/2	8 1/4

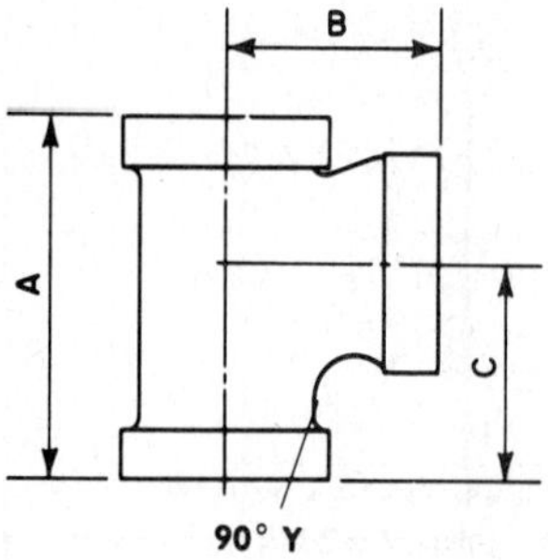

90° Y
(short TY)

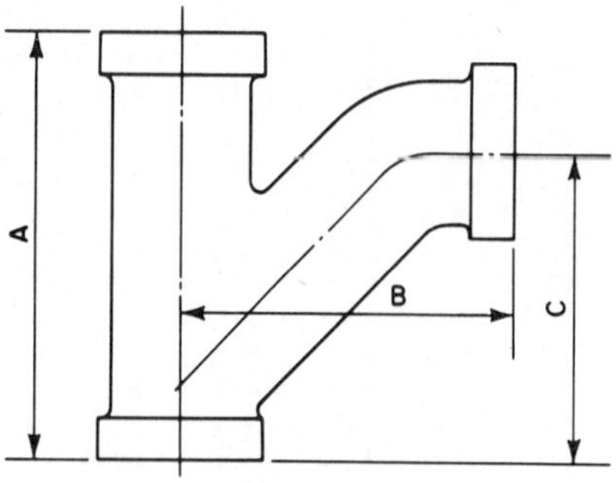

90° Y
(long TY)

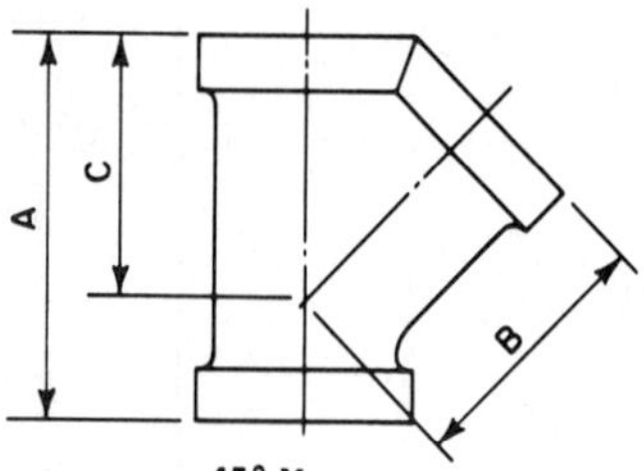

45° Y

Table 37. Y branches

Size, in.	Dimensions in inches								
	Short TY			Long TY			45° Y		
	A	B	C	A	B	C	A	B	C
1							4	2 11/16	2 11/16
1 1/4	3 13/16	2 3/16	2 3/16	4 3/4	3 5/8	3 1/16	5 3/16	3 7/16	3 7/16
1 1/2	4 5/16	2 1/2	2 7/16	5 7/16	4 3/16	3 7/8	5 1/4	3 7/16	3 7/16
2	5 3/4	3 3/16	3 3/16	6 1/2	5 1/8	4 5/8	6 1/4	4 1/8	4 1/8
2 1/2	6 5/8	3 7/8	3 3/4	8 1/4	6 3/16	6 1/16	8	5 1/4	5 1/4
3	7 1/4	4 3/16	4 3/16	9	7	6 1/2	8	6	6
4	8 3/4	5 3/16	5 3/16	10 3/4	8 3/8	7 5/8	10 7/8	7 11/16	7 11/16
5	10 1/4	6 3/16	6 3/16	13	10 3/16	9 5/16	11 3/8	8 3/8	8 3/8
6	12	7 1/8	7 1/8	14 1/4	10 3/4	10 1/4	13 1/4	10	10
7	13 3/4	8 5/8	8 1/2	16	12 1/8	11 1/4	15 1/4	11 1/4	11 1/4
8	15 1/4	9 1/8	9 5/16	17 7/16	13 1/4	11 5/8	16 1/2	12 3/8	12 3/8
10	19 1/2	12 1/4	12 1/4	22 3/4	16 7/16	15 3/8	20 1/4	15 1/4	15 1/4
12				26 5/8	19	20	24 1/4	19 5/8	19 5/8

By GEORGE R. JERUS, *P.E.*
Vice President Meyer, Strong and Jones, P.C., Mechanical and Electrical Engineers

PLANNING

On this and the following pages are presented data useful in the design of public toilets.

Park toilets

Park toilet installations are of two general types: (1) Small parks, small recreation areas, and city squares; (2) Municipal picnic grounds, bathing beaches, and large recreation areas. Both types should be accessible to, but not directly on, routes of main circulation; and should be provided with tamper-proof fixtures, door hinges, paper holders, hooks, and the like. Type 1 is purely utilitarian, with a minimum number of fixtures and space. Type 2 may be expanded to include pay toilets for both men and women or a women's lounge room equipped with settees or easy chairs, or may be planned in conjunction with locker or dressing rooms used in recreational areas.

Control is very important, because of uncertainty as to the type of patronage. Slop sinks and supply lockers (and attendant's office, if provided) should be located near the entrance. *Number of fixtures* is indeterminate, varying from 2 or 3 water closets per toilet for Type 1, to approximately 1 water closet per 1,500 persons for large municipal bathing beaches. *Access corridors* should be provided, with *wall-hung water closets* and *stall urinals* mounted so that plumbing is serviced through the access corridor.

Construction should be of impervious material throughout. Concrete and tile, with slate on the fixture wall, are often used; when cost will permit, however, denser materials (such as terrazzo for floors or flush metal partitions) are preferable.

Artificial ventilation is preferable, with a recommended minimum of 1 air change per 6 minutes (consult local codes). Access corridors may also serve as exhaust plenum chambers. If toilets are underground, exhaust vents should be carried up in sidewalk posts to a point more than 6 ft above the sidewalk.

Subway toilets are similar to park toilets, Type 1. New York City municipal subways employ as a toilet unit: 2 water closets, 2 urinals, and 1 lavatory (for men); 2 water closets and 1 lavatory (for women). One unit is provided per outlying local station; two per outlying express station; three per central local station; four per central express station.

Railroad-terminal toilets

Railroad-terminal toilets are likewise divided into two groups: (1) Terminals in highly developed urban centers; (2) Terminals in city outskirts. The distinction lies principally in the fixture and use ratios (see Table 1). Type 2 is used by large numbers of nonpassengers (ratio to passengers, approximately 5 to 1); Type 1 principally by passengers.

Location should be convenient for passengers but not too accessible to the man on the street. Space assigned to public toilets should be the least valuable. If several toilet rooms are provided, the largest should adjoin waiting rooms. *Size* should be determined by station capacity, which in turn is determined by track capacity; however, plans should permit additions to existing facilities to accommodate future increases.

Facilities should include showers, dressing rooms, men's smoking rooms, and women's restrooms, in addition to free and pay toilets, lavatories, and urinals. The modern tendency is to include as many pay toilets as possible within the required number. These need constant supervision, necessitating provision of a porter's closet, preferably opening off a common corridor serving all pay toilets. Storage space should be provided for towels, soap, combs, and the like, sold or rented by porters.

Plan: A lobby should give access to all parts of each toilet group; it may serve as a men's smoking room or women's lounge, and may also contain bootblack stands and the like. Use of separate corridors for free toilets, pay toilets, urinals, lavatories, showers, and dressing rooms provides an efficient and desirable means of segregating fixtures by types. Artificial ventilation is preferable, with 1 air change per 6 minutes.

Table 1. Fixtures and use ratios

TYPE OF TOILET	FIXTURE RATIO	USE RATIO
PARK (and Subway)	3 men to 2 women; allow 1 urinal & 1 lav. per 2 w.c. for men; 1 lav. per 2 w.c. for women	Indeterminate, depending on location
R. R. TERMINAL (City center)	3 men to 1 woman; allow 1 urinal & 1 lav. per 2 w.c. for men; 1 lav. per 2 w.c. for women	1 water closet per 1500 persons (passengers + transient)
R. R. TERMINAL (Outskirts)	2 men to 1 woman; allow 1 urinal & 1 lav. per 2 w.c. for men; 1 lav. per 2 w.c. for women	1 water closet per 500 persons (passengers + transient)
HOTEL (Restaurant, Bar, Lobby)	1 man to 1 woman; allow 2 urinals & 1 lav. per 2 w.c. for men; 1 lav. per 2 w.c. for women	1 water closet per 15 persons in restaurants; per 50 in public rooms
HOTEL (Ballroom)	2 men to 1 woman; allow 2 urinals & 1 lav. per 1 w.c. for men; 1 lav. per 2 w.c. for women	1 water closet per 50 persons
THEATER (Continuous)	7 men to 3 women	men { 1 w.c. per 75 persons; 1 urinal per 100; 1 lav. per 250 } women { 1 w.c. per 75 persons; 1 lav. per 250 }
THEATER (Legitimate)	7 men to 3 women	Increase no. fixtures given for continuous theaters by 20%
OFFICE BLDG.	See Table 2	

Theater toilets

Theater toilets serve two types of houses: "continuous" and "legitimate." In the former, audiences are constantly changing; in the latter, audiences change at stated intervals and consequently must have adequate facilities for peak loads. Continuous-show theaters are divided into three groups: *class A* (large theaters in metropolitan centers) with separate toilets on each floor; *class B* (neighborhood theaters) with only one group of toilets, usually on the mezzanine; and *class C* (intimate theaters, inexpensive theaters) with one group of toilets in the basement. In legitimate theaters, toilets are in the basement or on the mezzanine. Appearance of toilets is important in attracting patronage, especially for women. Fixtures, fittings, and interior finish should be of high quality. Artificial ventilation should be used, with 1 air change per 6 minutes.

Control is not important. In large installations, however, some supervision is generally provided, especially in women's rooms. Slop sinks and lockers should always be provided.

Hotel toilets

Hotel toilets should be convenient to guests, but not easily accessible from the street. They may be divided into two types: (1) Those serving restaurants and public rooms; (2) Those serving ballrooms and banquet floors. The location of both types should be in the least valuable areas—preferably on low-

Table 2. Minimum number of plumbing fixtures required[a]

Extracted from New York City Building Code. (The National Plumbing Code, ANSI A40.8-1955, is in process of revision.)

These are minimum requirements. Facilities should be increased if the type of occupancy calls for it and the budget permits.

In applying this schedule of facilities, the designer must consider the accessibility of the fixtures. Conformity purely on a numerical basis might not result in an installation suited to the needs of the individual establishment. Schools, for example, should be provided with toilet facilities on each classroom floor.

Facilities for temporary workmen: 1 water closet and 1 urinal for each 30 men. A 24-in. urinal trough can be considered equivalent to 1 urinal; a 36-in. trough, 2 urinals; a 48-in. trough, 2 urinals; a 60-in. trough, 3 urinals; a 72-in. trough, 4 urinals.

Type of building occupancy	Type of fixture					
	Water closets	Urinals	Lavatories	Bathtubs or showers	Drinking fountains	Other fixtures
Assembly—places of worship[b]	No. of Persons / No. of Fixtures 150 Women — 1 300 Men — 1	No. of Persons / No. of Fixtures 300 Men[c] — 1	1			
Assembly—other than places of worship (auditoriums, theaters, convention halls)	No. of Persons / No. of Fixtures 1-100 — 1 101-200 — 2 201-400 — 3 Over 400, add 1 fixture for ea. additional 500 men and 1 for ea. 300 women	No. of Persons / No. of Fixtures 1-200 — 1 201-400 — 2 401-600 — 3 Over 600, add 1 fixture for ea. 300 men[c]	No. of Persons / No. of Fixtures 1-200 — 1 201-400 — 2 401-750 — 3 Over 750, add 1 fixture for ea. 500 persons		1 for ea. 1,000 persons except that there shall be at least 1 fixture at each assembly floor level or tier	Where motion picture projection booths contain more than 2 projectors, at least 1 water closet and 1 lavatory shall be provided on the same level and within 20 ft of the booth
Dormitories—school or labor, also institutional	Men: 1 for ea. 10 persons Women: 1 for ea. 8 persons	1 for ea. 25 men; over 150, add 1 fixture for ea. 50 men[c]	1 for ea. 12 persons	1 for ea. 8 persons; for women's dormitories, 1 bathtub shall be substituted for 1 shower at the ratio of 1 for ea. 30 women		Laundry trays—1 for ea. 50 persons
Single room occupancies for sleeping accommodations only	1 for ea. 6 persons		1 for ea. 6 persons	1 for ea. 6 persons		
Dwellings—one- and two-family	1 for each dwelling unit		1 for each dwelling unit	1 for each dwelling unit		Kitchen sink—1 for each dwelling unit
Public buildings, offices, business mercantile, storage; warehouses, factories and institutional employees[d]	No. of Persons each sex / No. of Fixtures 1-15 — 1 16-35 — 2 36-55 — 3 56-80 — 4 81-110 — 5 115-150 — 6 1 fixture for ea. additional 40 persons	Urinals may be provided in men's[d] toilet rooms in lieu of water closets but for not more than ½ of the required number of water c 's when more than 35 persons	No. of Persons / No. of Fixtures 1-20 — 1 21-40 — 2 41-60 — 3 61-90 — 4 91-125 — 5 1 fixture for ea. additional 45 persons		1 for ea. 75 persons	

Table 2. Minimum number of plumbing fixtures required[a] (cont.)

Type of building occupancy	Type of fixture						
	Water Closets		Urinals	Lavatories	Bathtubs or Showers	Drinking Fountains	Other Fixtures
Public bathing	Men 1/60	Women 1/40	1/60	1/60	1/40		
Schools: Elementary Secondary	Boys 1/90 1/90	Girls 1/35 1/35	1/30 boys 1/30 boys	1/50 pupils 1/50 pupils Over 300 pupils 1/100 pupils	In gym or pool shower rooms, ⅓ pupils of a largest class using pool at any one time	1/50 persons but at least 1 per floor	
Workmen temporary facilities	1/30 workmen		1/30 workmen			At least 1 per floor equivalent for ea. 100 workmen	
Industrial— foundries only	No. of Persons 1-10 11-25 26-50 51-80 81-125 1 additional fixture for each additional 45 persons	No. of Fixtures 1 2	Where more than 10 men are employed: No. of Men[d] 11-29 30-79 1 additional fixture for each additional 80 males	No. of Persons 1-8 9-16 17-30 31-45 46-65 1 additional fixture for each additional 25 persons / No. of Fixtures 1 2 3 4 5 / No. of Urinals 1 2	1 shower for each 15 persons exposed to excessive heat or occupational hazard from poisonous, infectious, or irritating material	1 for ea. 75 persons	

Type of building occupancy	Water Closets	Urinals	Lavatories	Bathtubs or Showers	Other fixtures	
Kitchens for public or employees dining			1 lavatory for the personal use of kitchen employees		One machine or a 3-compartment sink for the effective washing and sanitizing of all cutlery, dishes and glasses before re-use.	
Dwellings—multiple or apartment	1 for each dwelling unit or apartment		1 for each dwelling unit or apartment	1 for each dwelling unit or apartment	Kitchen sink—1 for each dwelling unit or apartment. Within each dwelling unit, not designed for use by transients, one laundry tray or automatic laundry washing machine; or in a readily accessible location within a general laundry room. 1 two-compartment tray for each 10 dwelling units or 1 automatic laundry washing machine for each 20 dwelling units.	

Notes:
 a *The population used in determining the number of fixtures required shall be based on the number of people to occupy the space but in no case shall the population be less than that determined by allowing 125 ft², of net floor area per person.*
 b *Such facilities may be in adjacent buildings under the same ownership or control, and shall be accessible during periods when the assembly space is occupied.*
 c *Where urinals are provided for women, the same number of fixtures shall be provided as for men.*
 d *Facilities for employees in a storage building or warehouse may be located in an adjacent building, under the same ownership, where the maximum distance of travel from the working space to the toilet facilities does not exceed 500 ft horizontally.*

Table 3. Recommended aisle widths

TYPE OF W.C. DOOR		W.C. Doors Open IN	W.C. Doors (2'-2") Open OUT
CLEARANCE BETWEEN WALL AND FIXTURE ROW	Aisle lengths up to 16'-0"	3'-6" to 4'-0"	4'-6"
	Longer aisles	4'-0" to 6'-0"	4'-6" to 6'-6"
CLEARANCE BETWEEN TWO ROWS OF FIXTURES	Aisle lengths up to 16'-0"	5'-6" to 6'-0"	6'-6"
	Longer aisles	6'-0" to 8'-0"	7'-0" to 9'-0"

ceilinged mezzanines below ballroom floors, convenient to checkrooms. Restaurant and first-floor toilets may be located in the basement.

Type 1: Restaurants and first floors may have common toilet rooms, unless the floor area served is excessively large. In such cases, provide separate toilets for bars and grilles, since these will receive the heaviest use. Other facilities may be distributed as desired, preferably near coatrooms.

Type 2: Women's toilets should have adjoining lounge or powder rooms. Closets and lockers for porters and matrons must also be provided for slop sinks, equipment, and matron's accessories. Dressing rooms should be provided in the ratio of 1 dressing room per 2 water closets, and should contain, in addition to a water closet and lavatory, a pier glass, a small stool or chair, and a dressing table. Men's toilets should contain an attendant's locker and porter's slop sink.

Use and fixture ratios for Type 2 should be carefully followed to accommodate peak loads. Constant control of both types by a matron or attendant is usually provided.

Office-building toilets

Office-building toilets are restricted to the use of tenants; they are often kept locked, and keys distributed to tenants. Location is determined by the value of floor space and the position of plumbing stacks and other services. Rentable space is the building's only commodity; hence toilets should occupy the least valuable space, usually near the center of the building in windowless areas. Control is unnecessary.

The corridor plan is ordinarily used, with a battery of water closets on one side and urinals and lavatories on the other. Ventilation need only comply with minimum code requirements. Doors should open inward. Whenever possible, vestibules should be provided. If that is not possible, toilet doors should open so as to shield the interior. Wall-hung toilets and urinals and ceiling-hung partitions are generally used.

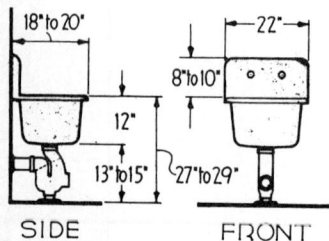

18" to 20" —22"— 8" to 10" 12" 13" to 15" 27" to 29"

SIDE   FRONT

Type shown is commonly used in Office Buildings, Hotels, R.R. Stations, etc.

For Parks or Subways, size usually is 22"x24" with cold water only

Sinks may be mounted at or close to floor line if traps can be concealed

Fig. 1. Slop sinks

FIXTURES

Lavatories may be leg, counter-set, or wall-hung. Wall-hung types are easiest to clean, but must be supported on suitable chair carriers in order to avoid unsightly cracks between wall and fixture. Color is preferably white or light shades, although other colors are in common use in hotels, theaters, and office buildings. Typical sizes are given in Fig. 2. Center-to-center spacing is normally between 1 ft 10 in. and 2 ft 2 in., but may be increased for greater comfort in theaters, hotels, and the like.

Urinals are of three types: stall, wall-hung, and pedestal. Wall-hung are recommended. Partitions or fins are usually installed between pedestal or wall-hung urinals, rarely between stall types. Many wall-hung urinals, however, have integral shields, which serve as partitions. Color is usually white. Dimensions are shown in the drawings. Center-to-center spacing ordinarily varies from 2 ft to 2 ft 4 in., but may be increased as suggested for lavatories. If the space between stall urinals will be too small for easy cleaning, pockets should be filled flush with materials having an impervious surface. Floor drains are generally not recommended in toilet rooms.

Water closets are of two types: wall-hung and floor (or pedestal). Floor types are most difficult to clean and consequently are recommended only for toilets whose use will be restricted. Wall-hung types are generally recommended. Seats should be unbreakable, with open fronts, and impervious surfaces—preferably white in color. Color recommendations are the same as for lavatories. Flushometers are recommended for all types. Floor treads or seat-operated valves are also used.

Water closet compartments may be of masonry, opaque glass, or metal. Doors are usually metal, and may be single or double. Compartment dimensions vary as shown in the drawings with inswinging or outswinging doors. Larger compartments are preferred where space permits, particularly in hotel or theater toilets.

Preferred compartments are those having flush surfaces. Doors are omitted on some park and subway compartments, and occasionally on other types as well. Partitions should be stopped approximately 1 ft above the floor.

Various kinds of metal partitions are manufactured, including post-and-panel assemblies with or without overhead bracing, and flush panels with integral posts, floor-supported or ceiling-hung.

Fittings, including lavatory, urinal, and water-closet fittings, should be tamper-proof and simple to operate. Clothes hooks should be provided in compartments and dressing rooms. Pay-toilet coinboxes should be easy to operate, and should clearly indicate when the compartment is in use.

Additional equipment may include scales, automatic hand driers, soap and towel dispensers, and mirrors. Smoking rooms or lounges should contain easy chairs, couches, and smoking stands; in railroad terminals, they should include bootblack and hat-cleaning stands as well.

FIXTURE ARRANGEMENT

For convenience, lavatories are usually nearest the door, urinals next, and water closets and dressing rooms farthest. Where space is at a premium (as in office buildings) in the narrow corridor plan commonly used, urinals are placed nearest the door to allow a wider aisle. Aisle dimensions are shown in Table 3.

Fixtures are arranged in batteries. Stall urinals have a trap beneath the floor level; if the floor-slab thickness will not accommodate the indicated average dimension of the trap, urinals may be placed on a platform 4 in. high by approximately 2 ft wide, with its surface pitched to the fixtures.

Dressing rooms are called for in men's and women's railroad-terminal and women's banquet-room or ballroom toilets. Those in terminals in outlying districts are usually of the smallest type shown, and contain only a lavatory and water closet; the largest type, containing showers, lavatories, and toilets, are ordinarily used only in large midcity terminals. Types used in hotel toilets should be generous in size to accommodate women in evening dress, but need not contain showers. Enclosures may be of any impervious material—

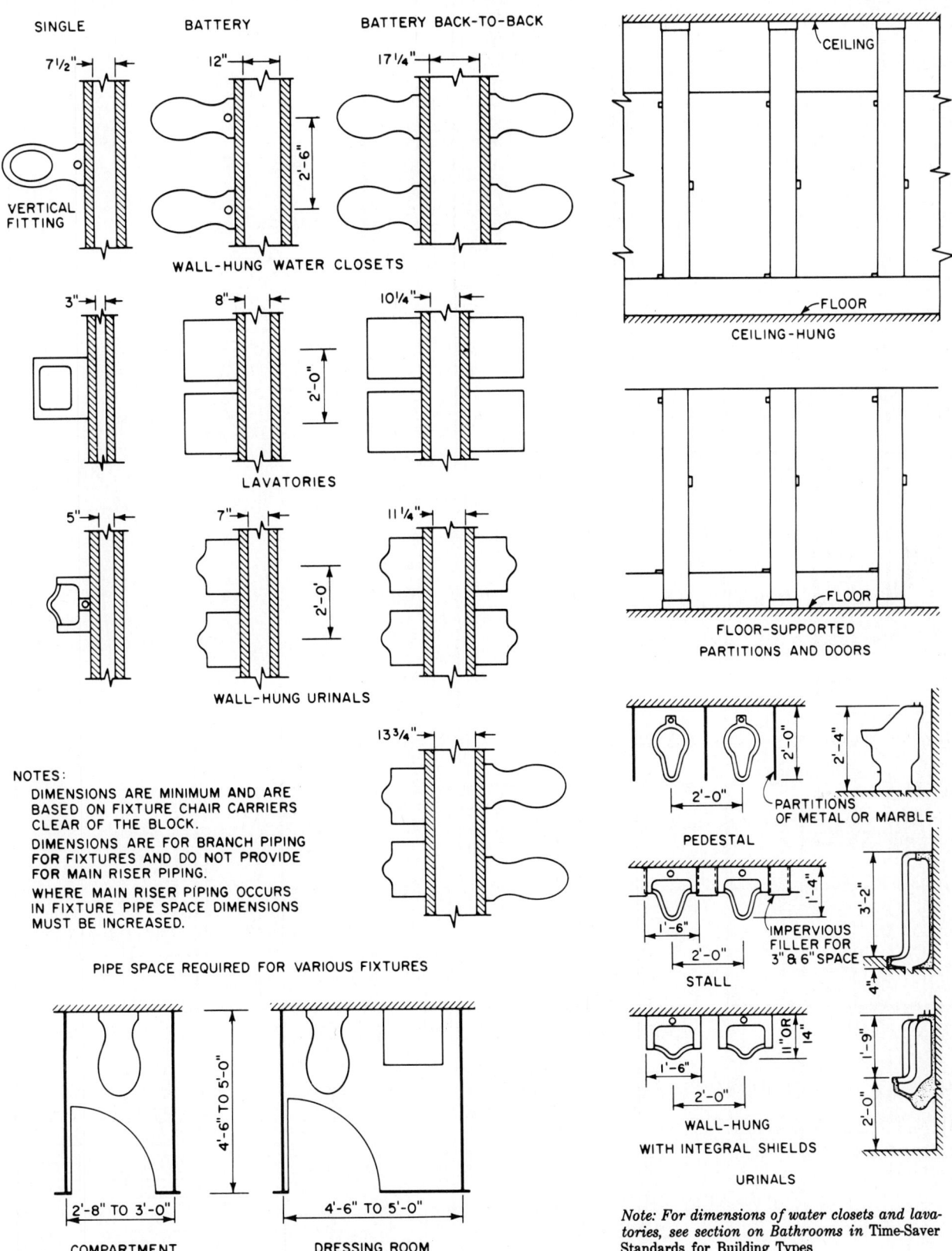

DETAILS OF FIXTURES AND PARTITIONS FOR PUBLIC TOILETS

SCALE: ¼" = 1'-0"

Fig. 2. Details of fixtures and partitions for public toilets

(See also section on Design for the Handicapped)

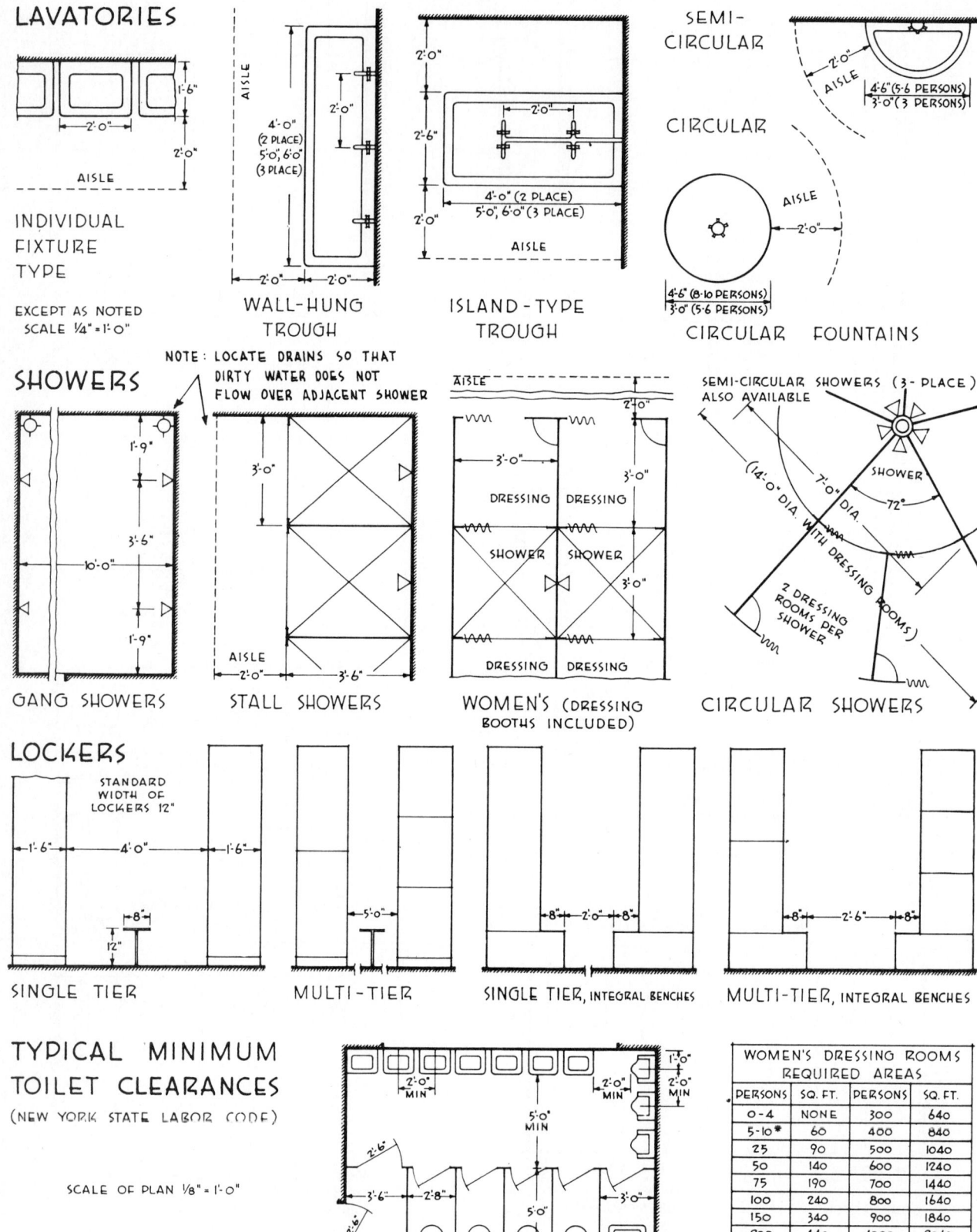

LAVATORIES

INDIVIDUAL FIXTURE TYPE

EXCEPT AS NOTED
SCALE ¼" = 1'-0"

WALL-HUNG TROUGH

ISLAND-TYPE TROUGH

SEMI-CIRCULAR

4'-6" (5-6 PERSONS)
3'-0" (3 PERSONS)

CIRCULAR

4'-6" (8-10 PERSONS)
3'-0" (5-6 PERSONS)

CIRCULAR FOUNTAINS

SHOWERS

NOTE: LOCATE DRAINS SO THAT DIRTY WATER DOES NOT FLOW OVER ADJACENT SHOWER

GANG SHOWERS

STALL SHOWERS

WOMEN'S (DRESSING BOOTHS INCLUDED)

SEMI-CIRCULAR SHOWERS (3-PLACE) ALSO AVAILABLE

2 DRESSING ROOMS PER SHOWER

CIRCULAR SHOWERS

LOCKERS

STANDARD WIDTH OF LOCKERS 12"

SINGLE TIER

MULTI-TIER

SINGLE TIER, INTEGRAL BENCHES

MULTI-TIER, INTEGRAL BENCHES

TYPICAL MINIMUM TOILET CLEARANCES

(NEW YORK STATE LABOR CODE)

SCALE OF PLAN ⅛" = 1'-0"

WOMEN'S DRESSING ROOMS REQUIRED AREAS			
PERSONS	SQ. FT.	PERSONS	SQ. FT.
0-4	NONE	300	640
5-10*	60	400	840
25	90	500	1040
50	140	600	1240
75	190	700	1440
100	240	800	1640
150	340	900	1840
200	440	1000	2040

*BASED ON 2 SQ. FT. ADDITIONAL PER EACH ADDITIONAL PERSON OVER TEN (NEW YORK STATE LABOR CODE)

Fig. 3. Typical minimum toilet clearances

Clearances shown are those specified by New York State Labor Code.

masonry, opaque glass, tile finish, or metal (either prefabricated or job-fitted).

Clearances between fixtures in batteries are covered in the center-to-center spacings given in Fig. 2. For water-closet and prefabricated dressing-room partitions, allow 1 in. per partition. Clearances between rows of fixtures or between fixtures and walls are shown in Table 3.

Slop-sink closets are ordinarily located close to the toilet rooms, generally with separate doors. Typical sinks are shown in Fig. 1.

The following data offer means of determining numbers of fixtures, clearances, and areas for factory toilets and locker rooms. Information was prepared, in part, by Jule Robert von Sternberg, Architect.

Factory sanitary facilities are of several general types. Most important is the "change" room (hereafter called "locker room"). This area may consist of a locker room proper, containing lavatories, lockers, and showers, plus a separate toilet room. Showers are sometimes located in a separate room.

Requirements vary, however, from industry to industry and from factory to factory. In a compact, single-building plant, one pair of locker rooms is ordinarily provided close to the employees' entrance. In plants that occupy several buildings, locker rooms are usually provided in each main unit. They are sometimes located in a separate building, or in an adjoining "tower" building, or on a mezzanine above the working floor. Whatever the general location, locker rooms should be as close to the job as possible, yet must not interfere with plant operation.

Architectural finish: Walls, floor, and ceiling have to resist penetration of water and water-borne dirt; ceilings are often acoustically treated; floors have to stand up under heavy traffic, soap and water, acid and alkali; every piece of equipment has to withstand punishment.

Ventilation: Windows are optional. Artificial light and forced ventilation are often substituted—usually to advantage, for they permit close control of light and air. The number of air changes varies from 10 to 20 per hr.

Lighting: Illumination should be bright enough to promote cleanliness and employee comfort. In general, 6 to 8 lumens per sq ft are adequate. Lights are placed to give direct illumination to lockers, lavatories, and occasionally showers. Lighting in toilets is placed to discourage reading.

Size varies with industry requirements. In general, the dirtier and hotter the work, the greater the demand for showers and lavatories.

Least standardized are lockers. The type usually recommended is the individual locker 12 in. wide, 18 in. deep, and 72 in. high, with a built-in lock. Smaller sized lockers are often used, however. Some manufacturers (of jewelry, for example) do not install lockers for fear employees will secrete company property in them. Instead, all clothing is hung in the open where it can be watched.

Arrangement: The locker room should be arranged to facilitate the flow of traffic. Toilets, lockers, showers, and lavatories have to be selected and arranged so that the entire working force can use them in the shortest time. Thus consideration must be given to the relative usefulness of each type of equipment, numbers of shifts and of men per shift, work habits of men, and the relationship of factory work areas and parking areas to the locker room. Because no modern factory is designed to remain fixed in form and function for its lifetime, locker rooms, whenever possible, should have provision for expansion.

Table 4. Minimum fixture requirements

Fixture requirements indicated are those specified by New York State Labor Code. Requirements of New York City Building Code (see Table 2) are somewhat higher, especially for lavatories.

No. of MEN	Water Closets	Urinals	No. of WOMEN	Water Closets	No. MEN or WOMEN	Wash Basins
1–9	1	0	1–15	1	1–20	1
10–15	1	1	16–35	2	21–40	2
16–40	2	1	36–55	3	41–60	3
41–55	2	2	56–80	4	61–80	4
56–80	3	2	81–110	5	81–100	5
81–100	4	2	111–150	6	101–125	6
101–150	4	3	151–190	7	126–150	7
151–160	5	3	191–240	8	151–175	8
161–190	5	4	241–270	9	176–200	9
191–220	6	4	271–300	10	201–225	10
221–270	6	5	301–330	11	226–250	11
271–280	7	5	331–360	12	251–275	12
281–300	7	6	361–390	13	276–300	13
301–340	8	6	391–420	14	301–325	14
341–360	8	7	421–450	15	326–350	15
361–390	9	7	451–480	16	351–375	16
391–400	10	7	481–510	17	376–400	17
401–450	10	8	511–540	18	401–425	18
451–460	11	8	541–570	19	426–450	19
461–480	11	9	571–600	20	451–475	20
481–520	12	9	601–630	21	476–500	21
521–540	12	10	631–660	22	501–525	22
541–570	13	10	661–690	23	526–550	23
571–580	14	10	691–720	24	551–575	24
581–630	14	11	721–750	25	576–600	25
631–640	15	11	751–780	26	601–625	26
641–660	15	12	781–810	27	626–650	27
661–700	16	12	811–840	28	651–675	28
701–720	16	13	841–870	29	676–700	29
721–750	17	13	871–900	30	701–725	30
751–760	18	13	901–930	31	726–750	31
761–810	18	14	931–960	32	751–775	32
811–820	19	14	961–990	33	776–800	33
821–840	19	15	991–1020	34	801–825	34
841–880	20	15			826–850	35
881–900	20	16			851–875	36
901–930	21	16			876–900	37
931–940	22	16			901–925	38
941–990	22	17			926–950	39
991–1000	23	17			951–975	40
					976–1000	41

Table 5. Wash fountains required

Number of Fixtures	Persons Accommodated By:			
	54" CIRCULAR (8 each)	54" SEMI-CIRCULAR (4 each)	36" CIRCULAR (5 each)	36" SEMI-CIRCULAR (3 each)
1	1–175	1–80	1–100	1–60
2	176–375	81–175	101–225	61–125
3	376–575	176–275	226–350	126–200
4	576–775	276–375	351–475	201–275
5	776–975	376–475	476–600	276–350
6	976–1175	476–575	601–725	351–425
7		576–675	726–850	426–500
8		676–775	851–975	501–575
9		776–875	976–1100	576–650
10		876–975		651–725
11		976–1075		726–800
12				801–875
13				876–950
14				951–1025

Other types of toilets: Secondary toilets, containing water closets, urinals, and lavatories, must be provided at convenient intervals. The average worker should not have to walk farther than 100 to 125 ft to a toilet. In areas where very few men work, that distance may be increased to a maximum of 200 ft.

A separately housed toilet may be provided in the yard if enough men work there. If not, yard workers can use boiler-house or plant toilets.

Toilets are also provided for office workers and visitors in the administration building. Such provisions are similar to those in office buildings.

Women's restrooms adjoin women's toilets. These restrooms must conform to local codes, and usually contain space for a couch and reclining chairs. It is also customary to provide women's showers with private dressing booths.

By GEORGE R. JERUS, P.E.
Vice President—Meyer, Strong and Jones, P.C., Mechanical and Electrical Engineers

The following data on sewage disposal enable the architect to design private (or self-contained) sewage disposal systems for residences, camps, summer cottages, schools, factories, hospitals, institutions, and the like, for any number of occupants up to the equivalent of fifty persons in residences. For larger systems, a sanitary engineer should be consulted. In some areas the EPA may require that all sewage disposal systems be designed by a professional engineer.

Past experience, engineering practice, and bacteriological research have proven that the old-time sewage cesspool is both a menace to health and a nuisance. Sanitary engineers agree that all sewage disposal systems must include a septic tank, in which sewage is decomposed by anaerobic bacteria into gases and an effluent liquid, which is then rendered harmless by earth leaching, in which aerobic bacteria oxidize all obnoxious components. This article has been prepared from data supplied by Ralph Eberlin, C.E., Harold R. Sleeper, AIA, and the U.S. Dept. of Health, Education and Welfare.

DESIGN

A complete sewage disposal system, with all essential and optional elements, is presented on the next page. The final design of a specific installation is influenced by (1) the amount of sewage to be handled and (2) the character of the soil, as expressed by its "relative absorption." Both of these factors can be determined for any project by the methods described below.

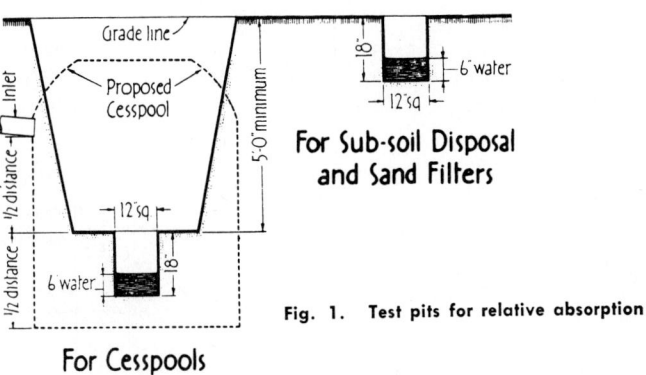

For Sub-soil Disposal and Sand Filters

For Cesspools

Fig. 1.   Test pits for relative absorption

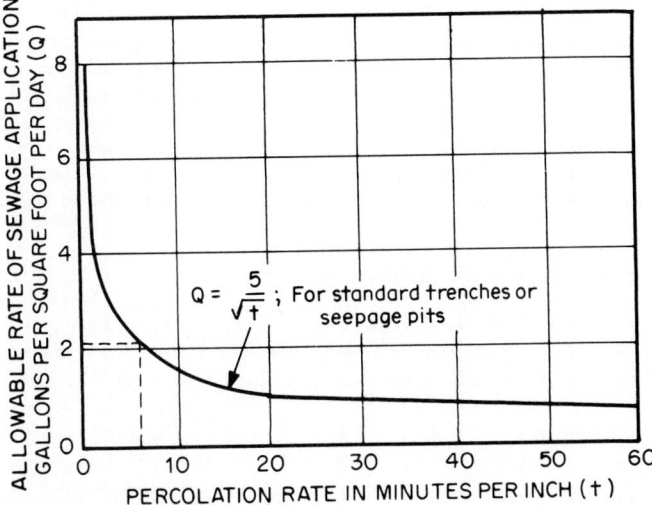

Fig. 2. Graph showing relation between percolation rate and allowable rate of sewage application

$$Q = \frac{5}{\sqrt{t}} \text{ ; For standard trenches or seepage pits}$$

Quantity of sewage

The amount of sewage that will be handled is related to the type of building and its occupancy, as shown in Table 1.

Relative absorption

The porosity or absorption of the soil is a vital factor in design. A simple field method of determining the characteristics of any soil in relation to effluent disposal, consists of digging a pit of fixed dimensions and measuring the outflow rate of water from the pit.

The depth below grade to which the test pit should be dug, varies according to the unit under consideration. The size of the pit is always 12 in. square and 18 in. deep, as illustrated in Fig. 1. The pit should first be filled with water, which is allowed to seep into the ground. Then, while the bottom is still wet, pour in water to a depth of 6 in. (about 3¾ gal). Note the time required for the water to disappear, and take 1/6 of that time as the average time required for the water level to fall 1 in. This average time is

Table 1.   Quantities of sewage flow

Type of establishment	Gallons per person per day
Small dwellings and cottages with seasonal occupancy	50
Single-family dwellings	75
Multiple-family dwellings (apartments)	60
Rooming houses	40
Boarding houses	50
Additional kitchen wastes for non-resident boarders	10
Hotels without private baths	50
Hotels with private baths (2 persons per room)	60
Restaurants (toilet and kitchen wastes per patron)	7–10
Restaurants (kitchen wastes per meal served)	2½–3
Additional for bars and cocktail lounges	2
Tourist camps or trailer parks with central bathhouse	35
Tourist courts or mobile home parks with individual bath units	50
Resort camps (night and day) with limited plumbing	50
Luxury camps	100–150
Work or construction camps (semipermanent)	50
Day camps (no meals served)	15
Day schools without cafeterias, gymnasiums, or showers	15
Day schools with cafeterias, but no gymnasiums or showers	20
Day schools with cafeterias, gyms, and showers	25
Boarding schools	75–100
Day workers at schools and offices (per shift)	15
Hospitals	150–250+
Institutions other than hospitals	75–125
Factories (gallons per person per shift, exclusive of industrial wastes)	15–35
Picnic parks (toilet wastes only), (gallons per picnicker)	5
Picnic parks with bathhouses, showers, and flush toilets	10
Swimming pools and bathhouses	10
Luxury residences and estates	100–150
Country clubs (per resident member)	100
Country clubs (per non-resident member present)	25
Motels (per bed space)	40
Motels with bath, toilet, and kitchen wastes	50
Drive-in theaters (per car space)	5
Movie theaters (per auditorium seat)	5
Airports (per passenger)	3–5
Self-service laundries (gallons per wash, i.e., per customer)	50
Stores (per toilet room)	400
Service stations (per vehicle served)	10

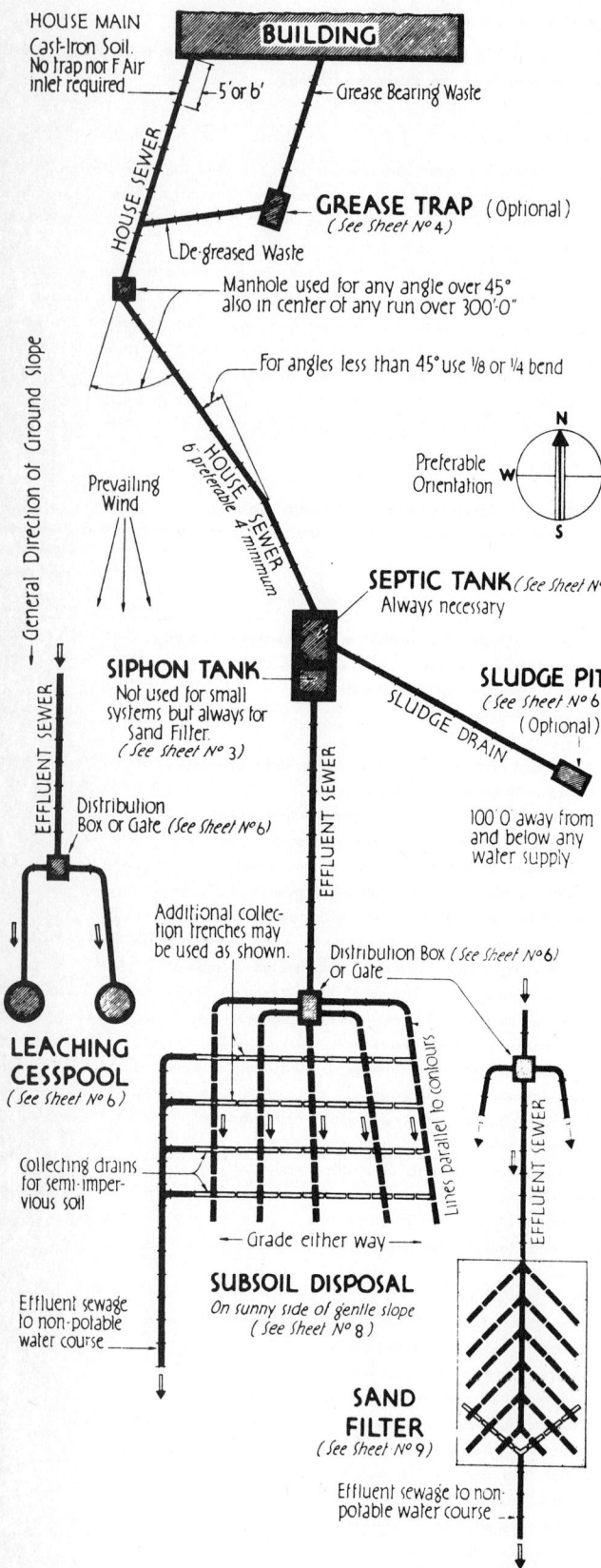

Fig. 3. Key diagram of sewage disposal system

4-242

HOUSE MAIN
Cast-Iron Soil.
No trap nor F Air
inlet required

5' or 6'

Grease Bearing Waste

GREASE TRAP (Optional)
(See Sheet N° 4)

De-greased Waste

Manhole used for any angle over 45°
also in center of any run over 300'-0"

For angles less than 45° use 1/8 or 1/4 bend

HOUSE SEWER

HOUSE SEWER
6' preferable
4' minimum

Prevailing
Wind

General Direction of Ground slope

Preferable
Orientation

N
W   E
S

SEPTIC TANK (See Sheet N° 3)
Always necessary

SIPHON TANK
Not used for small
systems but always for
Sand Filter.
(See Sheet N° 3)

SLUDGE PIT
(See Sheet N° 6)
(Optional)

SLUDGE DRAIN

EFFLUENT SEWER

Distribution
Box or Gate (See Sheet N° 6)

100'-0 away from
and below any
water supply

Additional collec-
tion trenches may
be used as shown.

Distribution Box (See Sheet N° 6)
or Gate

Lines parallel to contours

EFFLUENT SEWER

LEACHING
CESSPOOL
(See Sheet N° 6)

Collecting drains
for semi-imper-
vious soil

Grade either way

SUBSOIL DISPOSAL
On sunny side of gentle slope
(See Sheet N° 8)

EFFLUENT SEWER

Effluent sewage
to non-potable
water course

SAND
FILTER
(See Sheet N° 9)

Effluent sewage to non-
potable water course

Table 2. Relative absorption

Time—1" drop in minutes	Relative Absorption
0— 3	Rapid
3— 5	Medium
5—30	Slow
30—60	Semi-impervious
60—up	Impervious

For LEACHING CESSPOOLS see Sheet 4
SUB-SOIL DISPOSAL 5
SAND FILTERS 6

Table 3. Selection of effluent sewage disposal system

CONDITIONS	TYPE OF DISPOSAL SYSTEM		
	Leaching cesspool	Sub-soil drainage	Sand filter
RELATIVE ABSORPTION: Rapid	YES	YES	NO
Medium	YES	YES	NO
Slow	YES	YES	NO
Semi-impervious	NO	YES	NO
Impervious	NO	NO	YES
AVAILABLE AREA:			
Large	YES	YES	YES
Moderate	YES	YES	YES
Small	YES	NO	NO
GROUND WATER:			
Below Grade	8'0" minimum	2'0" minimum Only required	4'0" minimum
FINAL DISPOSAL OF EFFLUENT	Not Necessary	for semi-impervious soils	Always Necessary
RELATIVE INITIAL COST	LOW	MEDIUM	HIGH

the relative absorption factor for the soil; it is commonly expressed as rapid, medium, slow, semi-impervious, or impervious, as indicated in Table 2.

Design procedure

A tentative layout of the proposed sewage disposal system, similar to the diagrammatic plan in Fig. 3, should be made over a topographic plot plan of the property. Test pits should be dug at the sites of any proposed leaching cesspools or other effluent disposal areas, and the relative absorption of the soil determined.

With the tentative layout, quantity of sewage to be handled, relative absorption factor and absorption area required, reference can then be made to Table 3 to select the type of effluent disposal system best suited to project conditions.

ELEMENTS OF SEWAGE DISPOSAL SYSTEMS

House sewer: The house sewer extends from the "house main" to the septic tank. The house main is a continuation of the cast-iron soil line to a minimum of 5 ft beyond the foundation; no trap or fresh-air inlet is required in it.

The house sewer may be vitreous clay tile, cement bell and spigot pipe, or (preferably) cast-iron pipe, laid with poured joints. Always use cast-iron pipe within 100 ft of any potable water supply or near trees. Never connect surface drainage lines to a sewage disposal system.

Requirements: Size: 6 in. preferable; 4 in. minimum. Pitch: 1 in. in 8 ft for 6-in. pipe; 1 in. in 4 ft for 4-in. pipe. Grade: for northern latitudes, 1 ft 6 in. minimum below surface; for southern latitudes, sufficient depth to cover.

Grease-bearing waste and trap are optional elements, used to separate grease and oil from waste. If installed, grease-bearing waste is carried from the building to the trap, and degreased waste on to the house sewer.

Septic tank: The septic tank is the essential element of a sanitary disposal system. It should be located as far to leeward of the building as possible. Its function is to retain the raw sewage out of contact with air until anaerobic bacteria can break down the solids into gases (which escape through vents) and an effluent liquid (which is subsequently purified by oxidation). (In addition, some solids settle as sludge.) Construction and operating details are given on the following page.

A siphon tank is required in large installations or if a sand filter is used; it is desirable but not essential for small septic tanks. It collects effluent from the septic tank and periodically discharges it in the effluent disposal system.

Sludge drain and pit are optional; if used, they draw sludge from the septic tank without interrupting its operation for cleaning. The drain is similar in construction to a house sewer.

Effluent disposal: There are three principal types of effluent disposal systems—leaching cesspool, subsoil drainage, and sand filter—the choice of which is governed by soil conditions and topography. All are designed to permit the effluent to come in contact with air and soil, where it may be oxidized and rendered harmless by aerobic bacteria.

An effluent sewer is an element common to all systems. It is a closed sewerage line, similar in construction and size to the house sewer, which extends from the septic or siphon tank through a distribution box or gate to the chosen type of effluent disposal element. Minimum pitch is 1 in. in 16 ft.

The distribution box or gate is a device that distributes the effluent to one part or another of the disposal system in order to "rest" the part not in use.

The choice of a particular effluent disposal system is governed by factors determined from Tables 1 and 2 and Figure 2. Selection may be made from Table 3.

SEPTIC AND SIPHON TANKS

The septic and siphon tanks discussed here are of reinforced concrete construction, and can be constructed by any competent contractor without requiring the use of any patented or manufactured element other than the automatic siphon that is an essential part of every siphon tank. Septic tanks are also made as commercial units, however—of steel, precast concrete, and other materials—and are available in all parts of the country. If commercial septic and siphon tanks are used, the detailed design given here will not be needed; the data given, however, will still aid in the selection of a commercial unit of the proper size.

Operation

Raw sewage from the house sewer enters the septic tank, where, by means of a submerged intake, it reaches the liquid in the tank below the overflow level. The mixture quickly forms three distinct layers or strata: Solid matter or sludge settles to the bottom, effluent sewage forms the main, liquid content in the middle, and the upper stratum is composed of a scum that keeps air out of contact with the effluent sewage and permits anaerobic bacterial action (or septicization) to take place. Most of the suspended solid matter is changed by this action into gases that escape through vents provided for that purpose and effluent sewage that overflows either directly or through the siphon tank into the effluent sewer and then to the effluent disposal system.

The sludge that forms at the bottom of the septic tank must be periodically removed, to avoid filling the tank with solid matter. In large installations, where interruption of septic-tank operation for cleaning is undesirable, a sludge drain and sludge pit should be provided to permit removal of sludge while the tank is in continuous operation. Layout of sludge drain and pit is shown in Fig. 3, and the design of these elements is discussed on the following pages.

If an effluent disposal system of sand-filter type is used, whenever the system is designed for 1000 gal or more daily capacity (and also, preferably, in all residences), the septic tank should be equipped with a small siphon tank. The small tank, however, is not necessarily required in small installations using leaching cesspools or subsoil disposal beds.

The siphon tank collects overflow from the septic tank and discharges it periodically through the action of the automatic siphon into the effluent sewer and the disposal system, thus permitting the disposal units to absorb the effluent intermittently and preventing saturation of the disposal beds.

Design

The size of a septic tank—and thus the size of its companion siphon tank—is governed wholly by the number of gallons of sewage to be treated per 24 hours. This amount can be determined from the data given in Table 1.

Rule 1. To find the dimensions and construction details for any reinforced concrete septic tank and siphon tank detailed on the accompanying drawings, refer to Table 4. Find in the first column the sewage load nearest that calculated for the project, and read horizontally for all dimensions not given directly on the drawings.

Rule 2. To find the capacity of any commercial septic tank, find in Table 4 the capacity in gallons (second column) that corresponds to the sewage load calculated for the project (first column), and select a unit guaranteed by the manufacturer to treat that quantity of sewage per 24 hours. The siphon tank best adapted to the commercial tank will be indicated by the manufacturer's own data.

Table 4. Septic and siphon tanks—selection and design

Gallson of sewage per person per day	SEPTIC TANK					SIPHON TANK			SIPHON		CONCRETE THICKNESS		
	Cap. in gals.	Length A	Width B	Air space C	Liquid depth D	Length E	Width F	Depth G	Size L	Drawing depth M	Walls J	Top I	Bottom K
50–200	*325	5'-0"	2'-6"	1'-0"	3'-6"	**							
250–450	450	6'-0"	2'-6"	1'-0"	4'-0"	**3'-0"	**2'-6"	**3'-0"	3"	1'-6"	6"	4"	6"
500–700	720	7'-0"	3'-6"	1'-0"	4'-0"	**3'-6"	**3'-6"	**3'-0"	3"	1'-6"	6"	4"	6"
750–1000	1000	8'-0"	4'-0"	1'-0"	4'-0"	4'-0"	4'-0"	3'-0"	4"	1'-8"	6"	4"	6"
1050–1250	1250	9'-0"	4'-6"	1'-0"	4'-3"	4'-6"	4'-6"	3'-0"	4"	1'-8"	7"	5"	6"
1300–1500	1480	9'-6"	4'-8"	1'-3"	4'-6"	4'-8"	4'-8"	3'-6"	4"	2'-2"	8"	5"	6"
1550–1750	1720	10'-0"	5'-6"	1'-3"	4'-8"	5'-0"	5'-0"	3'-6"	4"	2'-2"	8"	5"	6"
1800–2000	1950	10'-6"	5'-3"	1'-3"	4'-9"	5'-3"	5'-3"	3'-6"	4"	2'-2"	9"	5"	6"
2050–2250	2175	11'-0"	5'-6"	1'-3"	4'-10"	5'-6"	5'-6"	3'-6"	5"	2'-2"	9"	5"	6"
2300–2500	2400	11'-6"	5'-9"	1'-3"	5'-0"	5'-9"	5'-9"	3'-6"	5"	2'-2"	9"	5"	6"

Capacity of tanks based on 50 gallons per Equivalent Occupancy per 24 hours.
* Smallest size recommended.
** Siphon Tank not essential for Septic Tanks under 1000 gallons capacity.

Location

If a septic tank is equipped with a sludge drain and pit, it can be buried, and its manhole cover identified merely by the position of the protruding vent or vents. The manhole for access to the sludge-drain gate valve, however, should be carried near enough to the surface so that it can be exposed conveniently in order to operate the valve. If no sludge drain and pit are provided, on the other hand, the septic tank should be so located that the covering earth can be periodically removed without disfiguring the property. The same precautions pertain to the manhole cover for the siphon tank.

Maintenance data

The owner of a septic tank should be provided by the designer with a written memorandum containing the following:

1. A plan indicating the exact location of the septic- and siphon-tank manholes (and sludge-drain gate valve manhole if used).

2. Advised inspection of the septic tank each spring and fall by removing the vent caps and testing the depth of the sludge with a rod or plumb-bob; also, the periodical examination of the vents during severe weather, to see that excess interior flow has not obstructed their operation.

3. Provision that whenever the sludge level appears to reach the low end of the intake or discharge pipes, or there are any signs of flooding, the septic tank should be cleaned out immediately (or the sludge drawn off to the sludge pit).

4. Provision that whenever the septic tank requires cleaning, it will be advisable to remove the manhole cover of the siphon tank as well, and inspect and clean the automatic siphon.

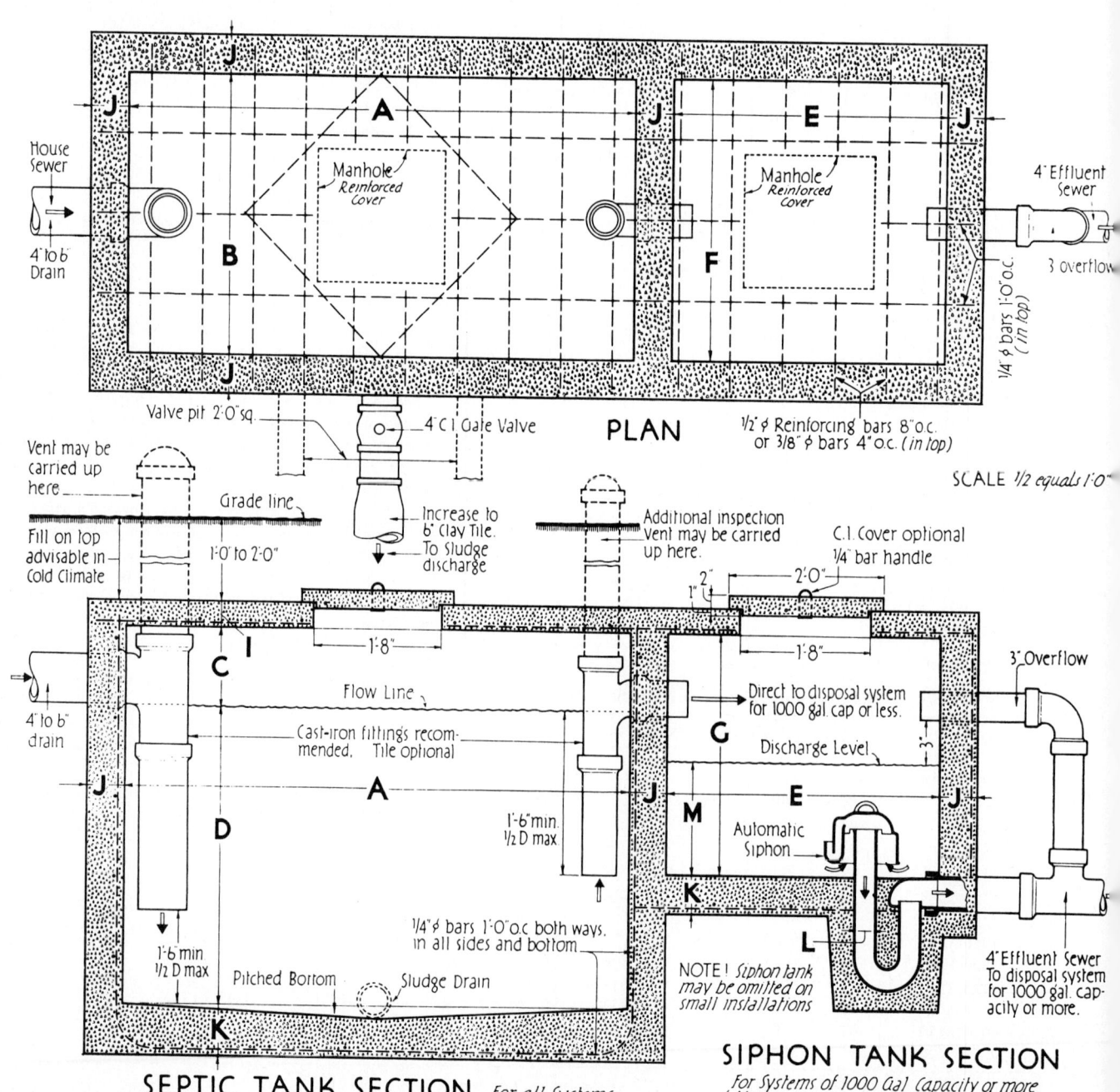

Fig. 4. Septic tanks and siphon tanks—construction details

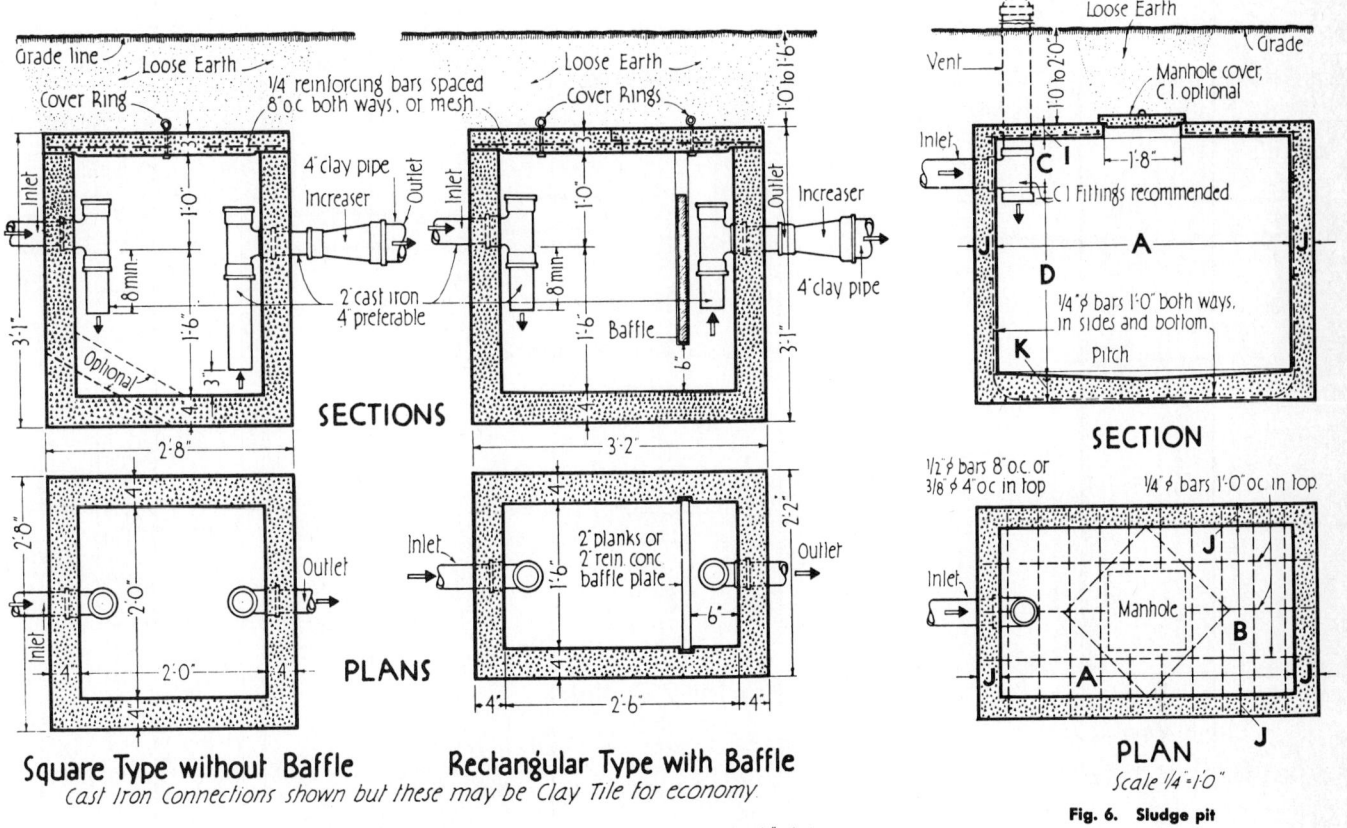

Fig. 5. Grease traps

Square Type without Baffle   Rectangular Type with Baffle

Cast Iron Connections shown but these may be Clay Tile for economy.

Scale ½"=1'0"

Fig. 6. Sludge pit

GREASE TRAPS

The function of a grease trap is to separate grease and oil from kitchen, laundry, and other specialized wastes, and thus prevent it from entering the sewage disposal system. Grease and oil may interfere with the formation of a proper scum in the septic tank, and may also clog or reduce the porosity of leaching cesspools, subsoil disposal beds, or sand filters. The use of a grease trap is therefore recommended in the majority of installations, but is not a mandatory requirement in small installations where no great quantity of grease or oil occurs.

The grease traps detailed in Fig. 5 are of concrete construction for use outside the house. Such a unit is not required where a metal grease trap is installed indoors in waste lines carrying grease or oil. Indoor traps offer greater convenience for cleaning, and may be used in small or medium-sized projects, if the odor that arises during their cleaning operation is not a serious objection.

Complete design data are contained in the accompanying drawings. The size of the grease trap does not vary materially with the size of the building it serves; if the quantity of waste causes rapid flow, however, it is advisable to use a rectangular trap with a baffle.

Owners should be advised to clean grease traps frequently; therefore, the trap should be located at a point where the loose earth over the cover may be removed and replaced without impairing the appearance of the property. The grease trap should be located as far as possible (within reason) from the building, and to the leeward, to minimize objections to the odor that always follows a grease-trap cleaning operation.

SLUDGE PITS

As previously indicated, the use of a sludge pit depends upon the need for cleaning septic tanks without interrupting their operation. The location of the sludge pit is shown in Fig. 5.

Since a sludge pit must have a capacity equivalent to the septic tank it serves, refer to preceding pages for methods of determining the size required, and to Table 5 for all dimensions not shown directly in Fig. 6.

DISTRIBUTION BOXES

The location and general use of distribution boxes are indicated in the **general design (Fig. 3), and also in the following pages concerning effluent disposal methods.**

Distribution boxes control and direct the flow of effluent sewage from the effluent sewage main to various parts of the effluent disposal system, permitting part of that system to recover while another part (or parts) is functioning.

The type of distribution box varies according to the number of outlets and the manner in which the flow must be controlled. It should be noted that in every installation the distribution box should be designed to provide one or more outlets in addition to those contemplated in the initial installation, to facilitate the extension, removal, or relocation of effluent disposal units. Complete design data for concrete distribution boxes are contained in Fig. 7.

LEACHING CESSPOOLS

The following page gives complete design data on leaching cesspools, which constitute one of the three types of effluent disposal methods from which the designer may choose. The choice is governed largely by soil conditions and the amount of land area available, as defined in detail on the first page of this series.

Advantages and limitations

Advantages of the leaching cesspool: It requires a minimum of land area, and can be used on a site of any slope. Its initial cost is low, and it seldom

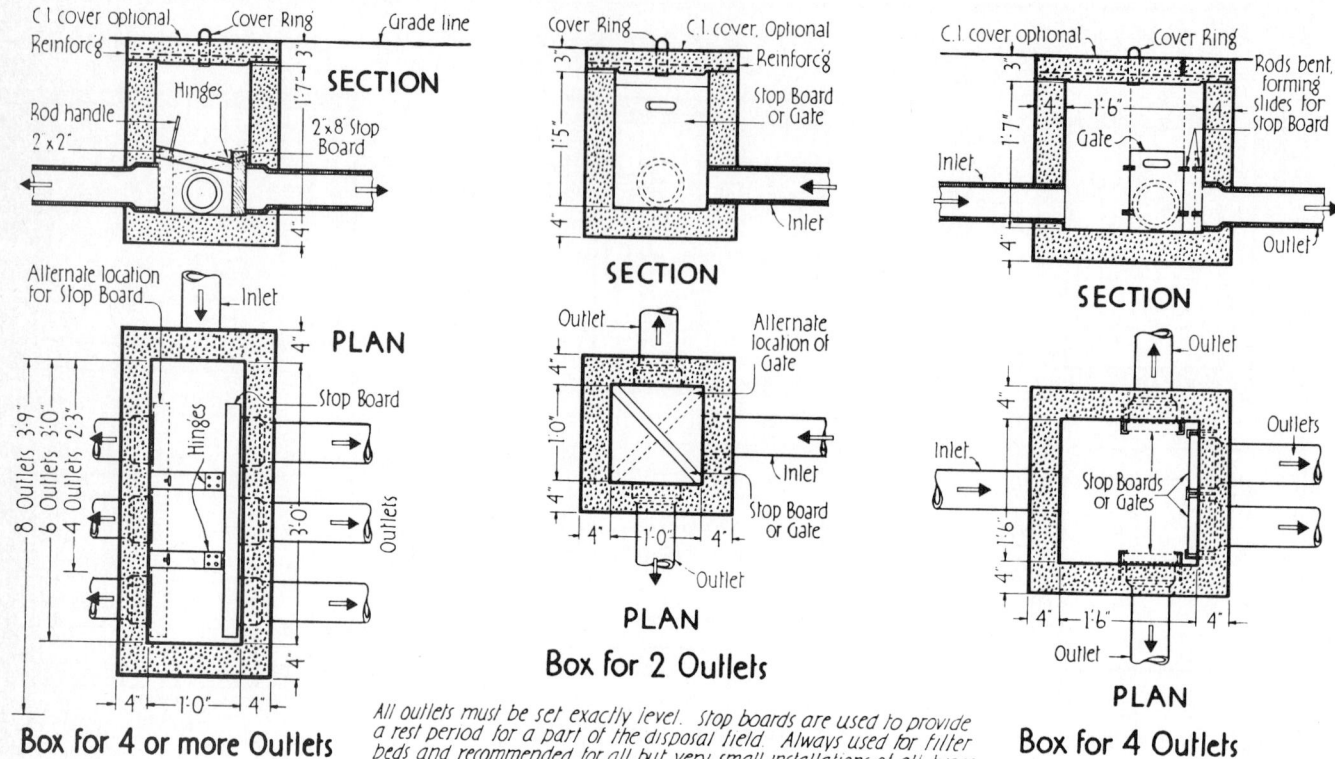

Fig. 7. Distribution boxes

All outlets must be set exactly level. Stop boards are used to provide a rest period for a part of the disposal field. Always used for filter beds and recommended for all but very small installations of all types

Scale 1/2"=1'0"

Table 5. Sludge pit dimensions

Gallons of sewage per person per day	Cap. in gallons	Length A	Width B	Air space C	Liquid depth D
50–200	325	5'-0"	2'-6"	1'-0"	3'-6"
250–450	450	6'-0"	2'-6"	1'-0"	4'-0"
500–700	720	7'-0"	3'-6"	1'-0"	4'-0"
750–1000	1000	8'-0"	4'-0"	1'-0"	4'-0"
1050–1250	1250	9'-0"	4'-6"	1'-0"	4'-3"
1300–1500	1480	9'-6"	4'-8"	1'-3"	4'-6"
1550–1750	1720	10'-0"	5'-0"	1'-3"	4'-8"
1800–2000	1950	10'-6"	5'-3"	1'-3"	4'-9"
2050–2250	2175	11'-0"	5'-6"	1'-3"	4'-10"
2300–2500	2400	11'-6"	5'-9"	1'-3"	5'-0"

Sludge pits should be of the same capacity as the septic tanks they serve.

requires cleaning at more frequent intervals than two years. It can be used in all reasonably absorptive soils.

Limitations of the leaching cesspool: It can never be used in a soil rated as semi-impervious or impervious. It requires a location where the normal ground water level is at least 8 ft below grade or 2 ft below the bottom of the cesspool. It should never be located within 100 ft of a potable water supply, nor within 15 ft of the building it serves.

Leaching cesspools are limited in capacity; thus several units may be required to handle the effluent from large septic tanks. The spacing (and thus the total land area) required for multiple leaching cesspools is indicated in **Fig. 8.** It is recommended that if two or more cesspools are used, at least the first pair be connected through a distribution box for alternate operation rather than installed in tandem.

Operation

Leaching cesspools receive the effluent sewage from the septic or siphon tank. The walls of the pool are laid below the inlet with open seepage joints, to allow the liquor to pass through to a surrounding layer of broken stone and thence into the earth. The bottom of the pool, also, is a porous surface. All masonry above the inlet, however, should be laid with tight mortar joints, to minimize the entrance of surface water as well as add structural strength. Precast units are also available. The cesspool should be set on spread footings to minimize settlement.

Design

To determine the size and number of leaching cesspools required by any project, it is first necessary to determine the amount of effluent to be treated and the relative absorption of the soil (which influences the capacity of the individual units). Methods of determining these two factors are given on the first page of this series.

To find the dimensions of any cesspool and the number of cesspools required for a given sewage load and relative absorption, refer to Table 6 and Fig. 7. Note that the table is divided into three parts, according to the type of soil; in each part, the first column indicates the number of cesspools required. Cesspools can be of other dimensions, but must provide the same surface area.

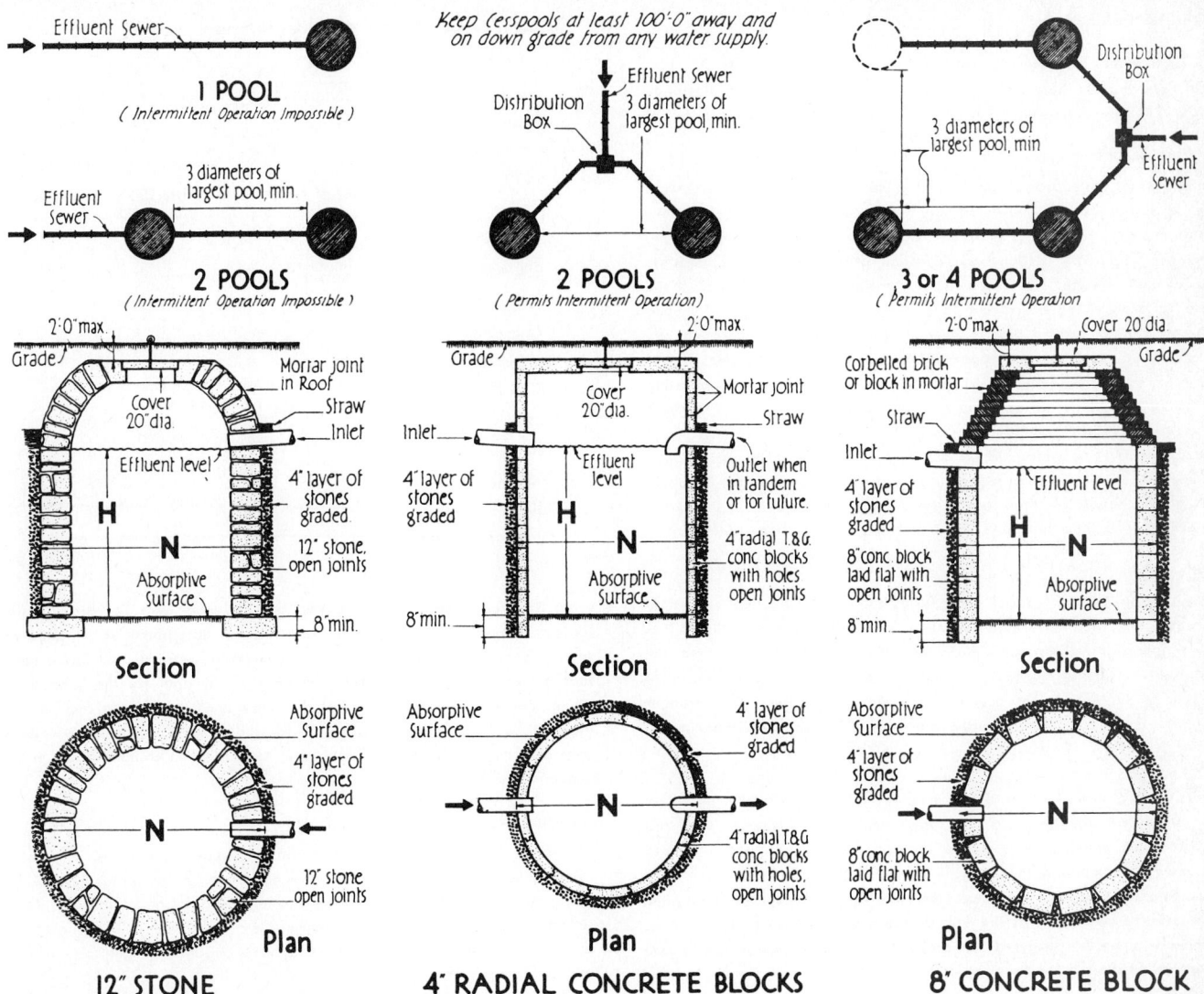

Fig. 8. Leaching cesspools—construction details

Table 6. Leaching cesspools—selection and design

Gallons of Sewage per Person per Day	RELATIVE ABSORPTION											
	RAPID ABSORPTION COARSE SAND OR GRAVEL				MEDIUM ABSORPTION FINE SAND OR SANDY LOAM				SLOW ABSORPTION CLAY WITH SAND OR LOAM			
	No. of Cess-pools	Dia. N	Depth H	Absorptive Area per Person (Sq Ft)	No. of Cess-pools	Dia. N	Depth H	Absorptive Area per Person (Sq Ft)	No. of Cess-pools	Dia. N	Depth H	Absorptive Area per Person (Sq Ft)
50–200	1	5'	5'	24.5	1	6'	6'	35.0	2	5'	5'	49.0
250–450	1	6'	6'	15.7	2	6'	6'	31.3	2	8'	7'	48.0
500–700	1	8'	6'	14.4	2	8'	6'	28.7	2	10'	8'	46.7
750–1000	2	6'	6'	14.1	2	9'	7'	26.14	3	10'	8'	49.5
1050–1250	2	7'	6'	13.6	2	10'	8'	27.1	4	9'	8'	46.4
1300–1500	2	8'	6'	13.4	3	9'	7'	26.14	4	10'	8'	43.6
1550–1750	{ 1 { 1	8' 9'	7' } 7' }	13.6	{ 1 { 2	9' 10'	7' } 8' }	26.1	5	10'	8'	46.7
1800–2000	{ 1 { 1	9' 9'	7' } 8' }	13.7	4	9'	7'	26.1	4	12'	10'	48.9
2050–2250	3	8'	6'	13.4	4	9'	8'	25.7	5	12'	10'	54.3
2300–2500	2	10'	8'	13.0	4	10'	8'	26.1	5	12'	10'	48.9

SUBSOIL DISPOSAL BEDS

This page covers the design of subsoil disposal beds—one of three methods for disposing of liquid effluent after it leaves the septic tank or siphon tank.

Advantages and limitations

Advantages of the subsoil disposal bed: It may be used in any soil except that rated as impervious. If used in soils rated as rapid, medium, or slow, distribution drains only are required; if used in soils rated as semi-impervious, however, both distribution and collection drains are needed, and the filtered effluent sewage from the collection drains must be either disposed to more absorptive soil or carried to a nonpotable watercourse. The bed may be located on ground that is level or slightly sloping, or occasionally on relatively steep slopes by proper arrangement of drainage lines. It requires little or no cleaning if the septic tank is kept in good operating condition. If possible, the disposal bed should be placed on a southern slope.

Limitations: Ground water should be more than 2 ft below grade. The initial cost of subsoil disposal beds is usually greater than the cost of leaching cesspools, though less than that of sand filters. The amount of land area required is greater than that required for either cesspools or sand filters.

Operation

Subsoil disposal beds consist of a series of drain lines laid with tight joints where the slopes are relatively steep, with continuations of these lines laid with open joints through which the effluent sewage filters into the surrounding soil. The open-lines are laid at slopes ranging from 1 in. in 24 ft. to 1 in. in 32 ft; thus they usually follow the contour lines. The arrangement of lines shown in the accompanying drawings is purely diagrammatic.

Design

Capacity of a subsoil disposal bed is governed by the number of lineal feet of 4-in. drainage line laid with open joints. The drainage lines laid with tight joints, which provide proper separation of the seepage lines, are not counted in computing the capacity of the bed. Capacity, of course, is related to both the quantity of sewage upon which the entire system is designed and the relative absorption of the soil. (Methods of determining these factors are covered in the first page of this section.) Porous wall pipe or perforated pipe can be substituted for the open-joint tile.

Table 7. Length of subsoil drainage lines

Gallons of Sewage per Person per Day	RELATIVE ABSORPTION		
	RAPID Coarse Sand or Gravel	MEDIUM Fine Sand or Sandy Loam	SLOW or SEMI-IMPERVIOUS Clay with Sand or Loam
	Lineal Feet of 4" Open Joint Tile Drain Required		
50–200	100	150	250
250–450	200	350	700
500–700	340	500	1000
750–1000	475	650	1250
1050–1250	600	800	1500
1300–1500	725	1025	1800
1550–1750	850	1150	2100
1800–2000	975	1300	2400
2050–2250	1100	1450	2700
2300–2500	1200	1600	3000

To find the number of lineal feet of 4-in. open-joint tile drain required for any quantity of sewage and any relative absorption (up to impervious soil), refer to Table 7. Find in the first column the sewage load figure nearest that determined for the project, and read to the right for the lineal feet in the proper soil column. Note that the same number of lineal feet of tile is used for soil of slow absorption as for that rated as semi-impervious; the only difference between the systems is the use of collection drains in semi-impervious soil.

Method of laying tile

Complete data on the layout of subsoil disposal drains are contained in Fig. 9 and 10, which also show accepted methods for protecting the open joints between tiles. It is suggested that stakes and boards be used for accurately aligning the slope of drainage lines. The choice of a particular type of drainage line is governed largely by local availability and cost, and ease of laying under project conditions.

  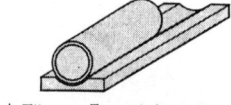 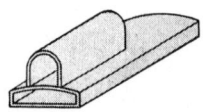 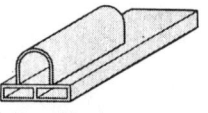 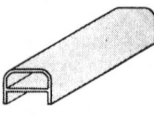

Round   Hexagon   Round Tile on Foundation Block   U-Tile on Hollow Foundation Blocks   Horse Shoe

TYPES OF DRAINAGE TILES

X—X (For Semi-Impervious Soil)

Distribution drain
Collection drain
Earth
Distribution drain parallel or at right angles to Collection drain.
Joint Covering
Trenches 10' to 12' o.c.
2'-0" to 2'-6" Medium Sand
Pitch 3" to 4" per 100'
Granulated Gravel
4'-0"
Stakes 1'-0" o.c.
1'-8"

COLLECTION TRENCH

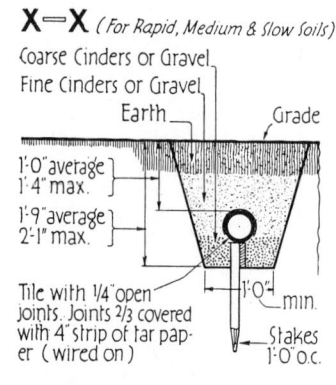
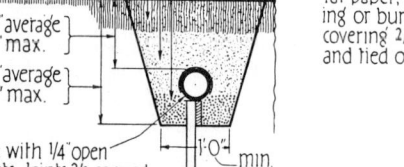

X—X (For Rapid, Medium & Slow Soils)

Coarse Cinders or Gravel
Fine Cinders or Gravel
Earth
Grade
1'-0" average 1'-4" max.
1'-9" average 2'-1" max.
Tile with 1/4" open joints. Joints 2/3 covered with 4" strip of tar paper (wired on)
1'-0" min.
Stakes 1'-0" o.c.

DRAIN TILE TRENCH

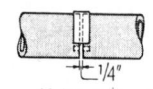 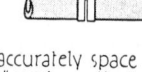

4"
1/4"
1/4"
Tar paper, screening or burlap, covering 2/3 tile and tied on.
Metal Collars accurately space and hold tile 1/4" apart...... Used instead of bldg paper or burlap.

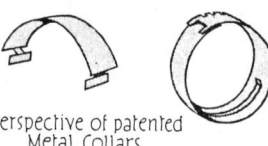

Perspective of patented Metal Collars

DRAIN TILE CONNECTORS

Fig. 9. Subsoil disposal beds—construction details

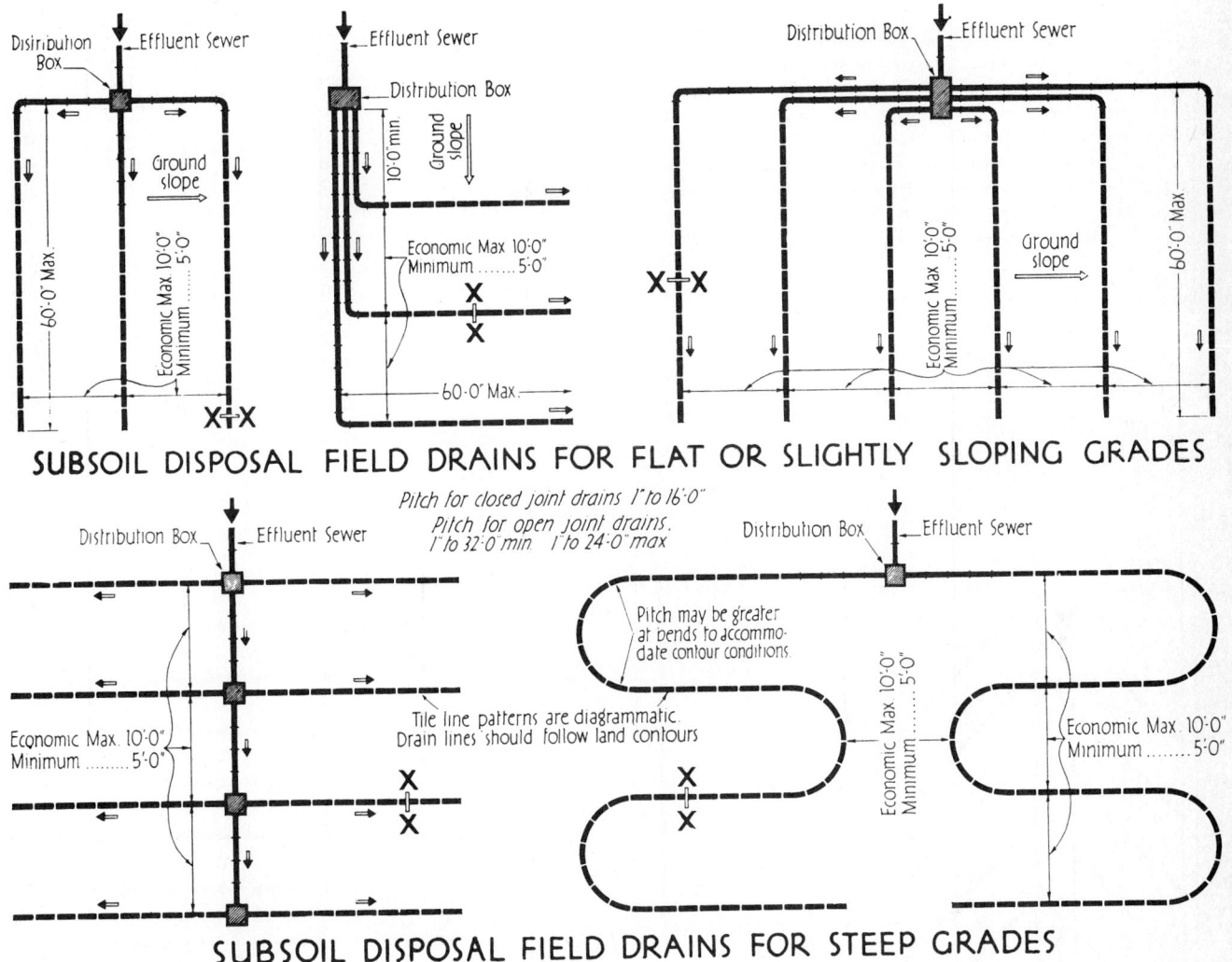

SUBSOIL DISPOSAL FIELD DRAINS FOR FLAT OR SLIGHTLY SLOPING GRADES

SUBSOIL DISPOSAL FIELD DRAINS FOR STEEP GRADES

Fig. 10. Subsoil disposal beds—layout

SAND FILTERS

The following page gives complete design data on sand filters, which constitute the last of the three types of effluent disposal methods from which the designer may choose. The choice, as indicated on the first page of this section, is largely governed by soil conditions. This type of system is the only effluent disposal method adaptable to soils rated as impervious; the other two methods, being less expensive, would normally be chosen for other soil conditions.

Advantages and limitations

The sole advantage of sand filters lies in their adaptability to impervious soils. Their limitations and disadvantages are that collection drains must be used, and the collected effluent carried either to a nonpotable watercourse or to leaching cesspools or subsoil disposal beds in more absorptive soil. The cost is relatively high, because the entire area of the filter bed must be ex-

cavated and refilled with suitable filtering material—usually clean, coarse sand. The total area, however, is considerably less than that required for subsoil disposal beds.

There are two types of sand filters: closed and open. The closed type carries both distribution and collection drains underground in the filter bed, with the upper layer of drains covered with earth. These closed sand filters may be laid out in approximately rectangular or round patterns as indicated in Fig. 11; or, if circumstances of both site and capacity permit, in the form of a long filter bed, having a single pair of distribution and collection drains.

The open type is usually far less desirable, because it exposes the effluent sewage and requires a filter bed free of any covering over the sand. In some instances, however, it is less expensive to construct, and may be adapted to institutions or large estates where the filter bed can be placed far from the building. The effluent sewage is conveyed in closed-joint drainage lines above the surface of the bed, with outlets discharging into wood troughs that serve as splash boards, which are laid out in the same manner as the lateral branches of a drain tile system.

Design

The capacity of a sand filter bed is expressed as its surface area in square feet, and is related, of course, to the sewage load of the building it serves. This system is normally used only in soil rated as impervious by tests for relative absorption. Methods of determining sewage load and relative absorption are discussed in the first page of this section.

To find the surface area of sand filter bed required for a project, find in the first column of Table 8 the sewage load nearest that computed for the project, and read to the right for the area in square feet of earth.

The detailed design for sand filters is shown in Fig. 11.

Table 8. Area of filter beds

Gallons of sewage per person per day	Area in Square Feet	
	Closed type	Open type
50–200	200	100
250–450	900	450
500–700	1400	700
750–1000	2000	1000
1050–1250	2500	1250
1300–1500	3000	1500
1550–1750	3500	1750
1800–2000	4000	2000
2050–2250	4500	2250
2300–2500	5000	2500

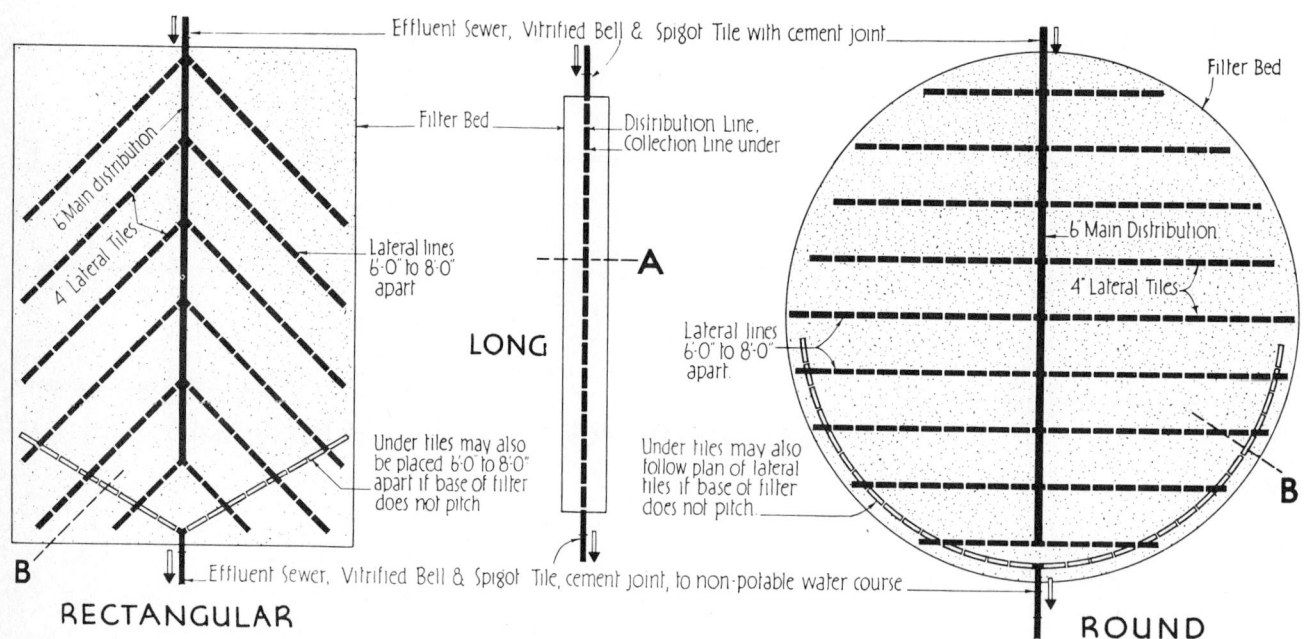

RECTANGULAR   LONG   ROUND

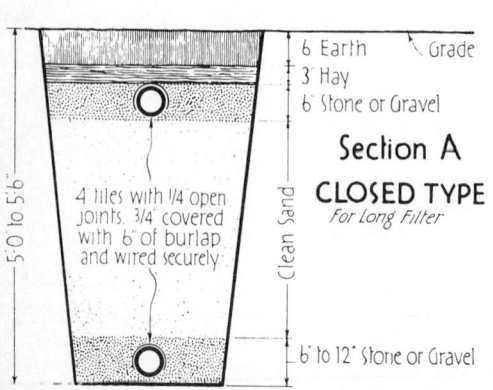

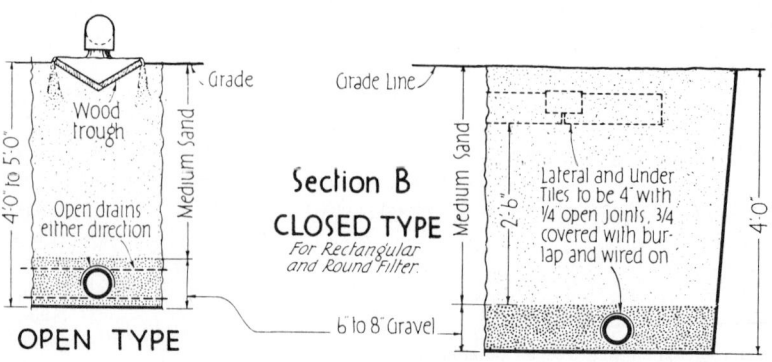

Pitch for closed joint drains 1" to 16'0"
Pitch for open joint drains 1" to 32'0" min 1" to 24'0" max
Bottom of Filter Beds to pitch 1" to 8'0"

Fig. 11. Sand filter beds—layout and construction

By SYSKA AND HENNESSY, INC., *Consulting Engineers*

NOTES

1. Consult local codes and NFPA standards for application to gravity chutes.
2. Twenty-four-inch diameter shown in minimum allowed.
3. The following items and conditions are recommended.
   a. Review details of chutes available in building locality
   b. Chute-washing device of proven effectiveness
   c. Washing and drain facilities in charging and collection rooms
   d. Wall and floor surfaces in charging and collection rooms suitable for frequent washing
   e. Stainless steel, aluminized steel, or galvanized steel used for chute and exposed metal parts
   f. Charging doors interlocked to allow only one to be open at any time
4. Soiled-linen chute would be similar except charging doors are usually side-hinged.

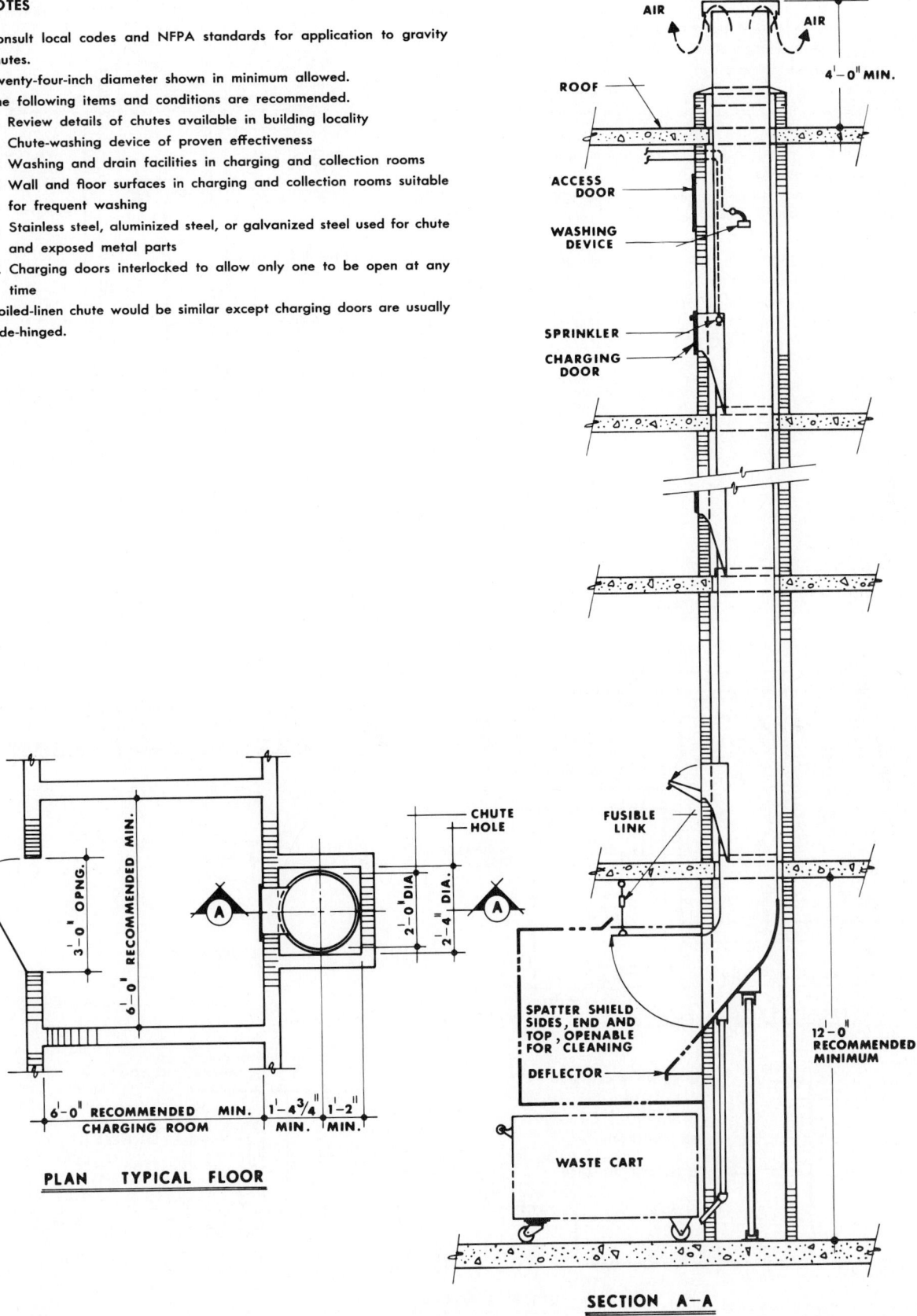

PLAN TYPICAL FLOOR

SECTION A—A

NOTES

1. Consult local codes and NFPA standards for application to pneumatic chutes.
2. Temperature within chute enclosure may fall below freezing when outside temperature is below freezing.
3. Physical size and weight of exhauster, silencer, filter, and collector and air volume will vary with specific system details.
4. The following items and conditions are recommended:
   a. Review details of pneumatic chute systems available in building locality.
   b. Minimum recommended chute diameter is 16 in.; allow for 18-in. diameter air line.
   c. Washing and drain facilities in charging and collector rooms.
   d. Wall and floor surfaces in charging and collector rooms suitable for frequent washing.
   e. Stainless, aluminized steel or galvanized steel used for chute or exposed metal parts.
5. Soiled-linen chute would be similar.

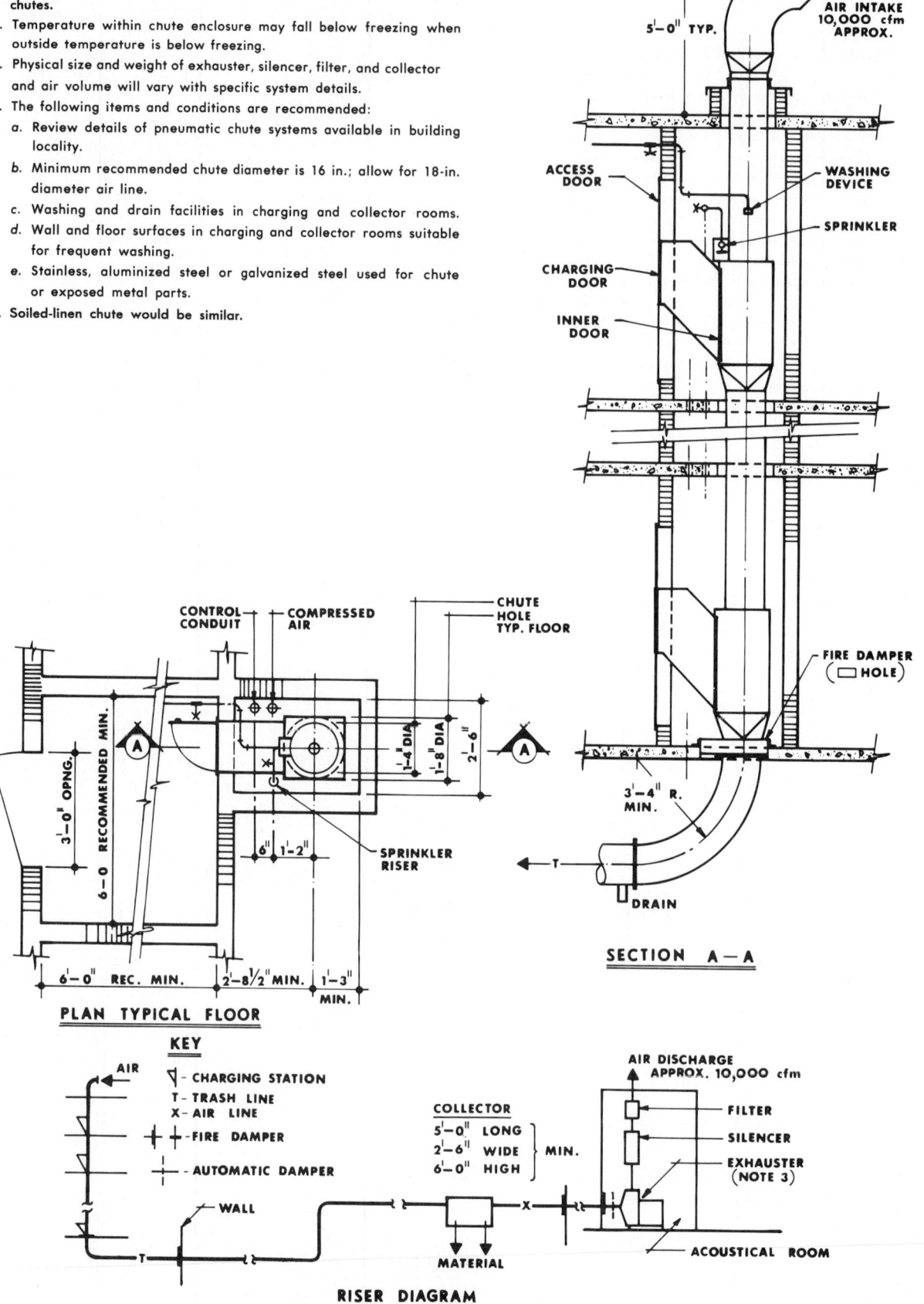

SECTION A—A

PLAN TYPICAL FLOOR

KEY

◁ – CHARGING STATION
T – TRASH LINE
X – AIR LINE
┿ – FIRE DAMPER
┼ – AUTOMATIC DAMPER
WALL

COLLECTOR
5'-0" LONG
2'-6" WIDE } MIN.
6'-0" HIGH

AIR DISCHARGE APPROX. 10,000 cfm
FILTER
SILENCER
EXHAUSTER (NOTE 3)
ACOUSTICAL ROOM

MATERIAL

RISER DIAGRAM

NOTES

1. Consult local codes and NFPA standards for application to gravity (vertical) and pneumatic (horizontal) chutes.
2. Details above the discharge valve are same as for gravity chute. Air flow is *in* at top of gravity-pneumatic chute.
3. Storage section is required where shown. Volume will govern discharge frequency. Minimum volume recommended: 1 cu yd.
4. Air supply:
   a. From outside of building, 15,000 cfm, plus 2,000 cfm. From within valve room, minimum.
   b. At top of chute, 500 cfm, minimum.
   c. Volumes will vary with specific system details.
5. Small exhauster will operate at all times. Large exhauster only for transport of waste.
6. Physical size and weight of filters, exhausters, silencers, and collector will vary with specific system details.
7. Temperature within chute enclosure may fall below freezing when outside temperature is below freezing.
8. Note 3 for gravity chutes applies.
9. Soiled-linen chute would be similar.

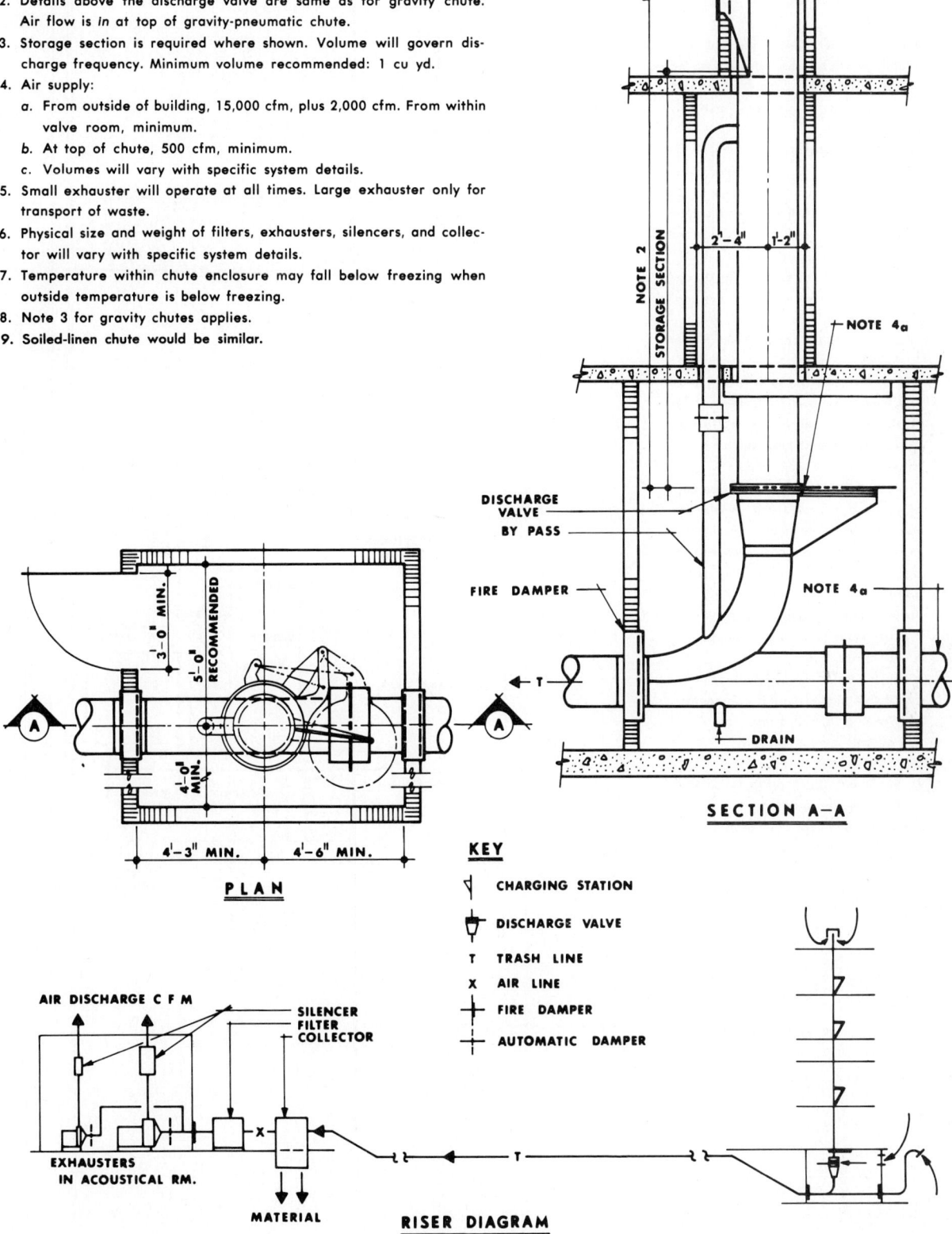

KEY

⊽	CHARGING STATION
	DISCHARGE VALVE
T	TRASH LINE
X	AIR LINE
	FIRE DAMPER
	AUTOMATIC DAMPER

PLAN

SECTION A—A

RISER DIAGRAM

NOTES

1. Local codes and NFPA standards should be consulted for application to compactors and rooms in which they are located.

2. There are several basic types of compactors available. Most types can be accommodated in space shown. Most can be chute and/or manually charged.

3. Types of compactors include:
   a. Extrusion, through a tapered tube, into cans, single or "sausage" bags
   b. Compaction within the machine and ejection of the compacted mass into bags or cans
   c. Compaction directly into a disposable container (bag or box)
   d. Compaction into a container compatible with front or rear loader trucks

4. The illustration shows a machine of the type described in paragraph 3b. It should not be interpreted as endorsement of that type machine over other types.

5. Engineer should determine amount of waste anticipated and should survey machines available in building locality. He should adjust room configuration and chute location as required.

6. The following items and conditions are recommended in the room:
   a. Room sprinkler
   b. Sprinkler within compactor
   c. Washing facility within compactor
   d. Washing facilities for room and reusable containers
   e. Floor drain
   f. Wall and floor surfaces suitable for frequent washing
   g. Automated odor-control device
   h. Positive ventilation

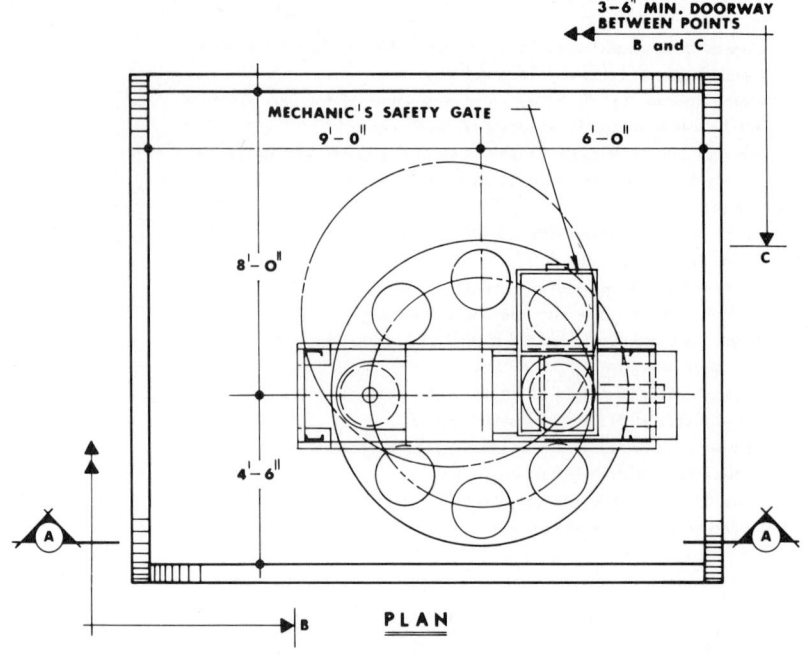

PLAN

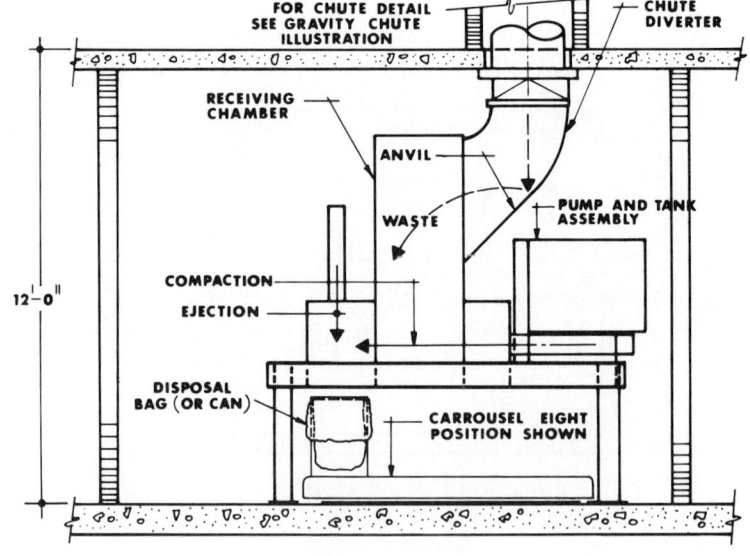

SECTION A—A

NOTES

1. Consult local codes and NFPA standards for application to loading dock, waste storage areas, compaction areas and compactors.
2. Compactor dimensions shown will accommodate most compactors with up to 3 cu yd hopper volume.
3. Some compactors incorporate oil reservoir, pump, and controls within main frame. Others are external, allow 2 ft 6 in. wide x 4 ft 6 in. long x 3 ft high space plus access space for external power unit.
4. Container dimensions shown will provide approximately 35 cu yd interior volume. Larger containers, to about 40 cu yd, are higher.
5. Heights shown will accommodate most combinations of containers and carting vehicles. Some combinations may be higher, some lower.
6. Space for vehicles to maneuver must be provided.
7. The following items and conditions are recommended:
   a. Floors should be smooth, waterproofed, pitched for drainage to adequate floor drain.
   b. Hot and cold water for washing or high-pressure washing equipment.
   c. Adequate lighting.
   d. If area is enclosed, adequate ventilation and/or cooling.
   e. Deodorizing substance metering device on compactor.
   f. Manually controlled sprinkler above charging hopper in addition to normal sprinkler system.

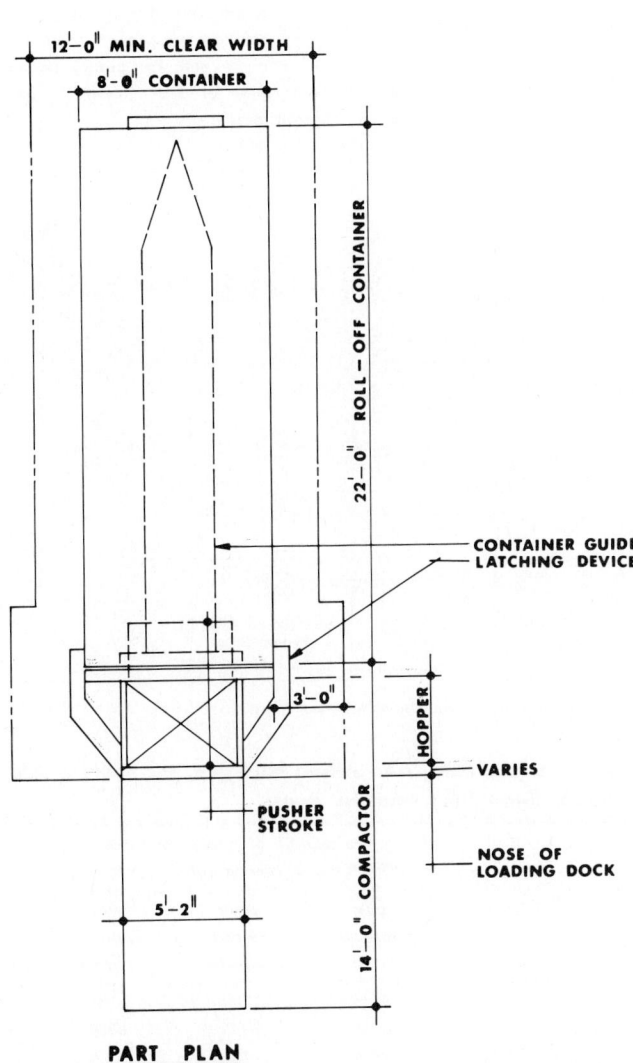

PART PLAN

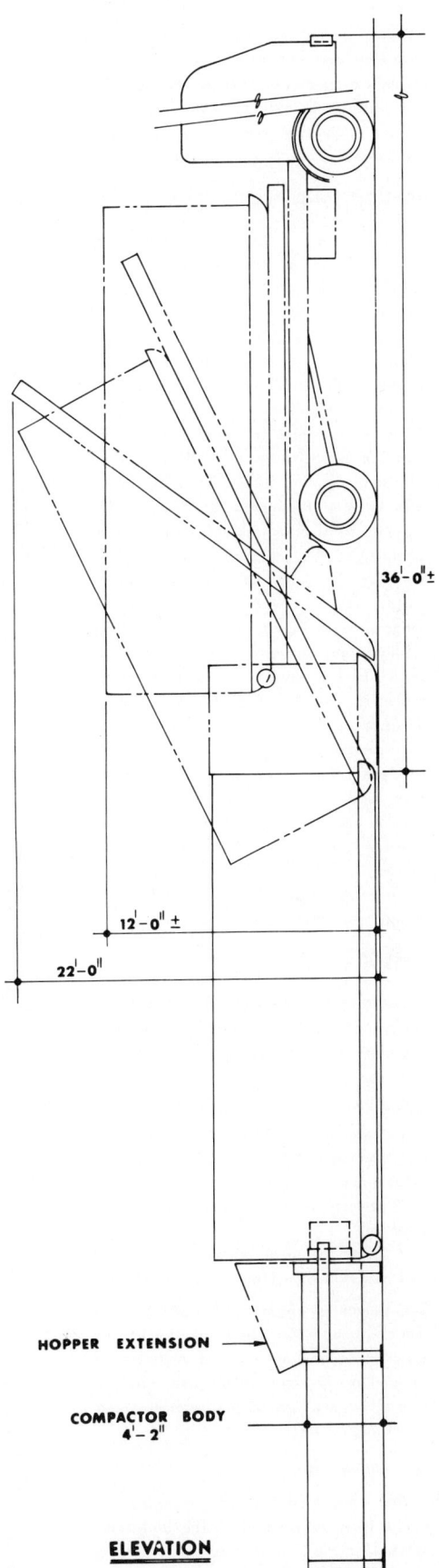

ELEVATION

Data on this and the following pages have been derived from *Recommended Practice of Daylighting* by Illuminating Engineering Society (1962); revisions from *IES Lighting Handbook* (1972). Updating and metrication by R. M. Harrold (1981).

DAYLIGHT AND ARCHITECTURE

Daylight is an integral part of the architectural design of the vast majority of modern buildings. It determines, in large part, the utilitarian as well as the esthetic environment provided by the designer. Consequently, it calls for the most careful planning and the highest skill of the architect and his engineers.

The requirements for good lighting design can be achieved by skillful application of daylighting techniques. These differ from the design methods for electric lighting because of the variations in the amount of daylight, the changing position of the sun, and the deep-seated desire of many persons for a view of the outdoors. The window, and/or other means for admitting daylight into an interior, can be treated much like any other light source, and effective correlation can readily be achieved between daylighting and electric lighting. The variations in the amount, the direction and the color of incident daylight, however, add an interest to the daylighted interior which no static lighting system can possibly produce. Daylight, skillfully employed, provides the architect with one of his most effective modes of esthetic architectural expression.

DESIGNING FOR DAYLIGHT

In order to use daylight to advantage, various design factors must be taken into account. These include the following:

1. Variations in the amount and direction of the incident daylight
2. Luminance (photometric brightness) and luminance distribution of clear, partly cloudy, and overcast skies
3. Variations in sunlight intensity and direction
4. Effect of local terrain, landscaping, and nearby buildings on the available light

The incident daylight which enters and is made available for use inside the lighted space depends upon (1) the architectural design of the fenestration and daylight control systems, and (2) the decoration and furnishings of the interior.

Daylight variability

The amount of daylight available for use is continually variable. The daily and seasonal motions of the sun with respect to a particular building surface, for the latitude at which the building is located, produce a regular and predictable pattern of gradual variation in the amount and direction of the available light. Superimposed, however, is another variable pattern caused by the less regular changes of the weather, particularly the degree of cloudiness. Finally, there are rapid changes often occurring in a matter of seconds, resulting from cloud movements and other local conditions which affect the amount, color, direction and character of the daylight received at the building.

This variability may seem the most difficult factor with which the daylighting designer must cope. However, it is precisely this variation which adds so much interest to the daylighted interior. Moreover, the seasonal variation in day length can be determined readily, and data on the number of clear and cloudy days, and the number of annual and daily sunshine hours have been collected for many years (see Fig. 1). These data, compiled for various points in the continental United States by the U.S. Weather Bureau, have been reviewed by various investigators and found to provide a statistically reliable guide to the daylight which can be anticipated in any area.

Table 1 shows the results of a continuous record for an entire year of the daylight illuminance received during the working day on exterior surfaces at Ann Arbor, Michigan. This study, conducted in one of the cloudier regions of the U.S., indicates that the daylight available during normal working hours is an important light source.

The sky as a light source

The primary source of light for daylighting is the sun. Light from the sun is scattered in its passage through the earth's atmosphere by dust and by the gaseous molecules of the air itself. As a result, the sky appears more or less bright during the daylight hours, and is a major source of daylight illuminance on exterior surfaces.

As compared with the sun, the sky has a large visual area and a relatively low brightness. The relative amounts of daylight received from the sky and the sun depend on the atmospheric conditions and position of the sun. For design evaluation, one or more of three conditions are usually considered:

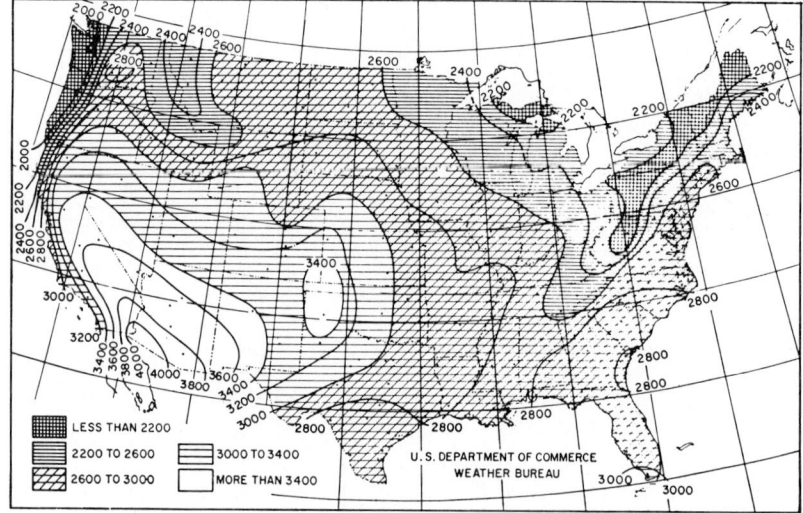

Fig. 1. Average annual amount of sunshine in hours

Table 1. Daylight availability, Ann Arbor, Michigan, for hours 8 AM to 5 PM, inclusive, throughout calendar year

Incident exterior illumination, footcandles (Lux)	Percentage of total time incident illumination exceeded value in left column				
	North vertical surface	East vertical surface	South vertical surface	West vertical surface	Horizontal surface
500 (5000)	83%	85%	86%	85%	92%
1000 (10,000)	58%	65%	74%	63%	82%
1500 (15,000)	35%	48%	66%	47%	74%
2000 (20,000)	20%	38%	59%	36%	67%

1. Incident light from overcast sky
2. Incident light from clear sky only
3. Incident light from clear sky plus direct sunlight

The amount of light received from an overcast sky, and the directions from which this light reaches the windows of a building, depend on the cloud pattern of the sky; the cloud pattern defining the luminous distribution. The luminance and luminous distribution of an overcast sky vary with the location, time, density, and uniformity of the overcast. A "uniformly" overcast sky is normally 2½ to 3 times as bright overhead as near the horizon. As a simplifying assumption, however, a single value representing equivalent uniform sky luminance may be employed for design purposes (Table 2). The sky luminance on clear days varies with the position of the sun and the amount of atmospheric dust or haze. Except in the immediate vicinity of the sun, the clear sky is normally brighter near the horizon than overhead. The concept of equivalent sky luminance may also be used for clear skies (Table 3).

The sun as a light source

Only about half the solar energy which reaches the earth's surface is visible. When absorbed, virtually all of the radiant energy from the sun, visible and invisible, is converted into heat. Thus sunlight and solar heat are merely different names for radiant solar energy. The proportion of visible light in the solar spectrum varies with the depth of atmosphere the light traverses. It depends upon both the elevation of the sun above the horizon and the variable atmospheric factors such as dust and moisture.

The position of the sun with respect to any reference point on the earth's surface at any instant is usually expressed in terms of two angles. One of these is the solar altitude, which is the vertical angle of the sun above the horizon. The second is the

Table 2. Equivalent sky luminance for average overcast day

Latitude	8 AM 4 PM fL	8 AM 4 PM cd/m²	9 AM 3 PM fL	9 AM 3 PM cd/m²	10 AM 2 PM fL	10 AM 2 PM cd/m²	11 AM 1 PM fL	11 AM 1 PM cd/m²	Noon fL	Noon cd/m²
					December 21					
30°N	420	1440	740	2540	1020	3490	1210	4150	1270	4350
32	350	1200	700	2400	960	3290	1150	3940	1200	4110
34	320	1100	650	2230	910	3120	1100	3770	1140	3910
36	260	890	600	2060	840	2880	1020	3490	1070	3670
38	230	790	550	1880	790	2710	940	3220	1000	3430
40	190	650	500	1710	740	2540	900	3080	930	3190
42	150	510	450	1540	660	2260	820	2810	860	2950
44	100	340	380	1300	600	2060	760	2600	790	2710
46	60	210	340	1160	550	1880	680	2330	730	2500
48	40	140	290	990	470	1610	630	2160	650	2230
50	0	0	240	820	420	1440	560	1920	580	1990
					March 21 or September 12					
30°N	910	3120	1320	4520	1710	5860	2010	6890	2140	7330
32	880	3010	1290	4420	1650	5650	1940	6650	2070	7096
34	860	2950	1250	4280	1600	5480	1870	6410	1980	6780
36	840	2880	1220	4180	1560	5340	1800	6170	1900	6510
38	800	2740	1200	4110	1500	5140	1740	5960	1840	6300
40	790	2710	1140	3910	1460	5000	1670	5720	1760	6030
42	760	2600	1120	3840	1410	4830	1600	5480	1690	5790
44	740	2540	1080	3700	1340	4590	1540	5280	1620	5550
46	710	2430	1030	3530	1229	4420	1470	5040	1550	5310
48	690	2360	990	3390	1240	4250	1410	4830	1480	5070
50	650	2230	940	3220	1180	4040	1330	4560	1400	4800
					June 21					
30°N	1270	4350	1730	5930	2250	7710				
32	1280	4390	1730	5930	2240	7670				
34	1290	4420	1730	5930	2220	7610				
36	1290	4420	1730	5930	2200	7540	2960	10140		
38	1290	4420	1720	5890	2160	7400	2840	9730		
40	1290	4420	1700	5820	2120	7260	2650	9080	3060	10480
42	1300	4450	1690	5790	2080	7130	2540	8700	2860	9800
44	1290	4420	1670	5720	2050	7020	2430	8330	2660	9110
46	1290	4420	1640	5620	2010	6890	2330	7980	2520	8630
48	1290	4420	1620	5550	1960	6710	2250	7710	2400	8220
50	1260	4320	1590	5450	1900	6510	2160	7400	2280	7810

Table 3. Equivalent sky luminance in footlamberts (candelas per square meter) for clear days*

Latitude	December 21					March and September 21					June 21				
	8 AM	10 AM	Noon	2 PM	4 PM	8 AM	10 AM	Noon	2 PM	4 PM	8 AM	10 AM	Noon	2 PM	4 PM
North															
30°N	450	600	600	600	450	700	1000	1050	1000	700	1550	1400	1000	1400	1550
	(1540)	(2060)	(2060)	(2060)	(1540)	(2400)	(3430)	(3600)	(3430)	(2400)	(5310)	(4800)	(3430)	(4800)	(5310)
34°	350	550	550	550	350	800	800	900	800	800	1350	1400	950	1400	1350
	(1200)	(1880)	(1880)	(1880)	(1200)	(2740)	(2740)	(2080)	(2740)	(2740)	(4630)	(4800)	(3250)	(4800)	(4630)
38°	300	550	550	550	300	750	800	900	800	750	1350	1300	950	1300	1350
	(1030)	(1880)	(1880)	(1880)	(1030)	(2570)	(2740)	(3080)	(2740)	(2570)	(4630)	(4450)	(3250)	(4450)	(4630)
42°	250	500	500	500	250	700	750	800	750	700	1300	1300	950	1300	1350
	(860)	(1710)	(1710)	(1710)	(860)	(2400)	(2570)	(2740)	(2570)	(2400)	(4450)	(4450)	(3250)	(4450)	(4630)
46°	150	450	500	450	150	700	750	750	750	700	1300	1250	950	1250	1300
	(510)	(1540)	(1710)	(1540)	(510)	(2400)	(2570)	(2570)	(2570)	(2400)	(4450)	(4280)	(3250)	(4280)	(4450)
South															
30°N	1100	1950	2250	1950	1100	1700	2300	2800	2300	1700	1200	1600	2400	1600	1200
	(3770)	(6680)	(7710)	(6680)	(3770)	(5820)	(7880)	(9590)	(7880)	(5820)	(4110)	(5480)	(8220)	(5480)	(4110)
34°	1100	1900	2200	1900	1100	1700	2650	2900	2650	1700	1350	1650	2300	1650	1350
	(3700)	(6510)	(7540)	(6510)	(3770)	(5820)	(9080)	(9940)	(9080)	(5820)	(4630)	(5650)	(7880)	(5650)	(4630)
38°	900	2300	2200	2300	900	1700	2700	2950	2700	1700	1350	1650	2300	1650	1350
	(3080)	(7190)	(7540)	(7880)	(3080)	(5820)	(9250)	(10100)	(9250)	(5820)	(4630)	(5650)	(7880)	(5650)	(4630)
42°	600	2100	2150	2100	600	1700	2700	2450	2700	1700	1350	2000	2500	2000	1350
	(2060)	(7190)	(7370)	(7190)	(2060)	(5820)	(9250)	(8390)	(9250)	(5820)	(4630)	(6850)	(8570)	(6850)	(4630)
46°	400	1900	2100	1900	400	1700	2700	2900	2710	1700	1350	2150	2700	2100	1350
	(1370)	(6510)	(7190)	(6510)	(1370)	(5820)	(9250)	(9940)	(9280)	(5820)	(4630)	(7190)	(9250)	(7190)	(4630)
East															
30°N	1550	1500	1000	700	400	2000	2500	1500	900	700	2800	2650	1400	1000	700
	(5310)	(5140)	(2400)	(2400)	(1370)	(6850)	(8570)	(5140)	(3080)	(2400)	(9590)	(9080)	(4800)	(3430)	(2400)
34°	1350	1400	950	700	400	2400	2600	1600	950	650	2800	2700	1450	1000	700
	(4630)	(4800)	(3250)	(2400)	(1370)	(8220)	(8910)	(5480)	(3250)	(2230)	(9590)	(9250)	(4970)	(3430)	(2400)
38°	1200	1300	950	600	350	2500	2600	1500	900	600	2800	2700	1400	1050	700
	(4110)	(4450)	(3080)	(2230)	(1200)	(8570)	(8910)	(5140)	(3080)	(2060)	(9590)	(9250)	(4800)	(3600)	(2400)
42°	750	1200	850	600	250	2400	2400	1450	800	600	2900	2600	1400	1000	700
	(2570)	(4110)	(2910)	(2060)	(860)	(8220)	(8220)	(4970)	(2740)	(2060)	(9940)	(8910)	(4800)	(3430)	(2400)
46°	500	1100	800	500	150	2300	2100	1400	700	600	2850	2600	1400	1000	700
	(1710)	(3770)	(2740)	(1710)	(510)	(7880)	(7190)	(4800)	(2400)	(2060)	(9760)	(8910)	(4800)	(3430)	(2400)
West															
30°N	400	700	1000	1500	1550	700	900	1500	2500	2000	700	1000	1440	2650	2800
	(1370)	(2400)	(3430)	(5140)	(5310)	(2400)	(3080)	(5140)	(8570)	(6850)	(2400)	(3430)	(4930)	(9080)	(9590)
34°	400	700	950	1400	1350	650	900	1600	2600	2400	700	1000	1400	2700	2800
	(1370)	(2400)	(3250)	(4800)	(4630)	(2230)	(3080)	(5480)	(8910)	(8220)	(2400)	(3430)	(4800)	(9250)	(9590)
38°	350	650	900	1300	1200	600	900	1500	2600	2500	700	1050	1400	2700	2800
	(1200)	(2230)	(3080)	(4450)	(4110)	(2060)	(3080)	(5140)	(8910)	(8570)	(2400)	(3600)	(4800)	(9250)	(9590)
42°	250	600	850	1200	750	600	800	1450	2400	2400	700	1000	1400	2600	2900
	(860)	(2060)	(2910)	(4110)	(2570)	(2060)	(2740)	(4970)	(8220)	(8220)	(2400)	(3430)	(4800)	(8910)	(9940)
46°	150	500	800	1100	500	600	700	1400	2100	2300	700	1000	1400	2600	2850
	(510)	(1710)	(2740)	(3770)	(1710)	(2060)	(2400)	(4800)	(7190)	(7880)	(2400)	(3430)	(4800)	(8910)	(9760)

Average values, direct sunlight excluded.

solar azimuth, which is usually taken as the horizontal angle of the sun from the due south line.

The illuminance produced on an exterior surface by the sun is influenced by the altitude angle of the sun, the angle between the incident sunlight and the surface on which the sunlight falls, and the amount of dust and haze in the atmosphere. Data on solar azimuth and altitude for various latitudes may be found in the section on "Solar Angles." Solar illuminance on exterior surfaces at selected seasons and hours is given in Table 4.

The ground as a light source

Light reflected from the ground, or from other exterior surfaces, is important in daylighting design. As with other light sources, it may require brightness control.

The light reflected from the ground on sunny elevations commonly represents 10 to 15 per cent of the total daylight reaching a window area. It frequently exceeds this proportion if reflected from light, sandy soils, light vegetation, or snow cover. On non-sun exposures, the light reflected from the ground may account for more than half the total light reaching the windows.

The direction from which the ground light is received is such that it can be utilized most effectively in the interior of the space, particularly at points well removed from the window area. Furthermore, ground light is under the control of the architect or engineer to a considerable extent. By use of light-colored ground-surfacing materials near the building, the daylight incident on the window areas and reaching

the inner portions of the rooms can be increased significantly. Reflectances of various ground-surfacing materials are shown in Table 5.

ARCHITECTURAL DESIGN

Because it influences building structure, daylighting design is a major concern of the architect. It must be incorporated into the building design in such a way that the building and its occupied spaces provide satisfactory visual and thermal environments. Daylight affects the architect's choice of the basic building section, the building arrangement on its site, and the architectural elements to be incorporated into the design for daylight control. Consequently, it affects profoundly the esthetic as well as the utilitarian aspects of the design—

Table 4. Average solar illuminance as a function of altitude

Latitude	Plane	Illuminance in footcandles (kilolux)								
		December 21			March, September 21			June 21		
		8 AM 4 PM	10 AM 2 PM	Noon	8 AM 4 PM	10 AM 2 PM	Noon	8 AM 4 PM	10 AM 2 PM	Noon
30°N	Perp.*	4200 (42)	7000 (70)	7700 (77)	6400 (64)	8300 (83)	8600 (86)	7700 (77)	8600 (86)	8900 (89)
	Horiz.	700 (7)	3400 (34)	4400 (44)	2600 (26)	5900 (55)	7000 (70)	4400 (44)	7200 (72)	8500 (85)
34°N	Perp.*	3100 (31)	6500 (65)	7100 (71)	6300 (63)	8100 (81)	8400 (84)	7600 (76)	8600 (86)	8900 (89)
	Horiz.	400 (4)	2700 (27)	3700 (37)	2400 (24)	5600 (56)	6700 (67)	4700 (47)	7100 (71)	8400 (84)
38°N	Perp.*	2500 (25)	6000 (60)	6900 (69)	6100 (61)	6000 (60)	8300 (83)	7600 (76)	8500 (85)	8900 (89)
	Horiz.	100 (1)	2000 (20)	3000 (30)	2100 (21)	5400 (54)	6200 (62)	4400 (44)	7000 (70)	8300 (83)
42°N	Perp.*	2000 (20)	5500 (55)	6400 (64)	6000 (60)	7800 (78)	8200 (82)	7600 (76)	8400 (84)	8800 (88)
	Horiz.	100 (1)	1600 (16)	2700 (27)	2000 (20)	4800 (48)	5800 (58)	4700 (47)	6800 (68)	7900 (79)
46°N	Perp.*	500 (5)	4500 (45)	5800 (58)	5800 (58)	7600 (76)	8100 (81)	7600 (76)	8100 (81)	8800 (88)
	Horiz.	——	1000 (10)	1800 (18)	1800 (18)	4400 (44)	5500 (55)	4400 (44)	6700 (67)	7400 (74)

Perpendicular to sun's rays.

the exterior appearance, as well as the interior atmosphere.

Building sections

Most of the "classic" building sections derive directly from daylighting considerations; virtually all are affected by them. From the daylighting standpoint, the items to be considered in selection of a particular building section are that it should admit enough light to all parts of the interior space, and that it should allow for adequate control of brightness to meet the visual requirements of the intended occupants.

Sidelighting: The placement of windows in the sidewall of the daylighted space has both advantages and disadvantages. In addition to admitting the daylight, the window area can provide for natural ventilation and can afford the room occupants a view of the outdoors, which is desirable. However, the distance from window to farthest work area is a design limitation, and the window, which is the light source for the room, is prominent in the field of view. Its brightness may be troublesome unless controlled.

Toplighting: Toplighting arrangements have the advantage that they can be used without limitation on the width of the lighted space. The daylight openings afford only a view of the sky, however, and even this is usually obstructed by diffusing or shielding elements. Consequently, buildings of this design are usually provided with some side-wall fenestration, to provide a view of the outdoors. Toplighting can be effectively controlled, so that illuminance can be distributed throughout the lighted space, and brightness can be held within desirable limits. In addition, the electric lighting design can be correlated readily with toplighting designs.

Unilateral section: The unilateral sidelighting design is shown, in section, in Fig. 2a. It is the simplest of the architectural sections, and the most common. The design lends itself to continuous fenestration and to curtain wall construction. In contemporary design, window heads are usually placed close to the ceiling line. In order to achieve recommended brightness ratios the effective width of the room should be limited to the range 2 to 2½ times the height from floor to window head.

Bilateral section: The bilateral daylighting design doubles the feasible room width. For a given ceiling height, it is possible to design a wider room by adding

Table 5. Reflectances of building materials and outside surfaces

Material	Reflectance, per cent	Material	Reflectance per cent
Bluestone, sandstone	18	Glass (cont.)	
Brick		Reflective	20–30
Light buff	48	Tinted	7
Dark buff	40	Asphalt (free from dirt)	7
Dark red glazed	30	Earth (moist cultivated)	7
Cement	27	Granolite pavement	17
Concrete	55	Grass (dark green)	6
Granite	40	Gravel	13
Marble (white)	45	Macadam	18
Paint (white)		Slate (dark gray)	8
New	75	Snow	
Old	55	New	74
Glass		Old	64
Clear	7	Vegetation (mean)	25

a window in the wall opposite the main window wall. This second window often occupies only the upper part of its wall, as shown in Fig. 2b. The two sets of windows afford a path for natural cross ventilation if both can be opened. The use of a reflecting roof under the secondary windows contributes materially to the total light entering the room. Since at least one set of windows in the bilateral design faces a sun exposure, sun controls are required with this design. It is also necessary to provide effective brightness controls, since persons in the room will face a window more often than in the unilateral design. Sloping ceilings sometimes employed with this design have little effect on either quantity or distribution of illuminance.

Roof monitor section: The building section employing a roof monitor as shown in Fig. 2c is usually an industrial building section. It is particularly advantageous for designs where a center high-bay area is needed between two low-bay areas. The roof monitor usually has windows only on opposite sides, but in some cases is provided with windows in all four sides. Consequently, sun controls are necessary on some of the window areas, and brightness controls are often more important. The roof surfaces below the monitor window should be treated as reflecting surfaces for maximum efficiency of the design.

Clerestory section: A clerestory window facing in the same direction as the main window is sometimes employed to overcome the room width limitations of the simple unilateral section. The clerestory window is used in a roof monitor in some designs, and with a sloping roof in others, as shown in Fig. 2d. Sun controls must be employed on sun exposures, but brightness control is not so prominent a problem as with the bilateral design. The roof under the clerestory window should be treated as a reflector. A more detailed consideration of clerestory lighting may be found in the following pages.

Sawtooth section: The sawtooth section shown in Fig. 2e is used principally for industrial building construction. It is suitable for low-roofed structures extending over a considerable area. The sawtooth windows usually are faced to the north in northern latitudes, so that sun controls are not required. The windows are sometimes slanted, which increases the admission of skylight. However, such slanting results in increased dust collection, adding to the maintenance problem.

Skylight section: Modern skylights assume many forms (Fig. 2f) and are widely used in contemporary architecture. Several recent developments in the field of toplighting design have added to the archi-

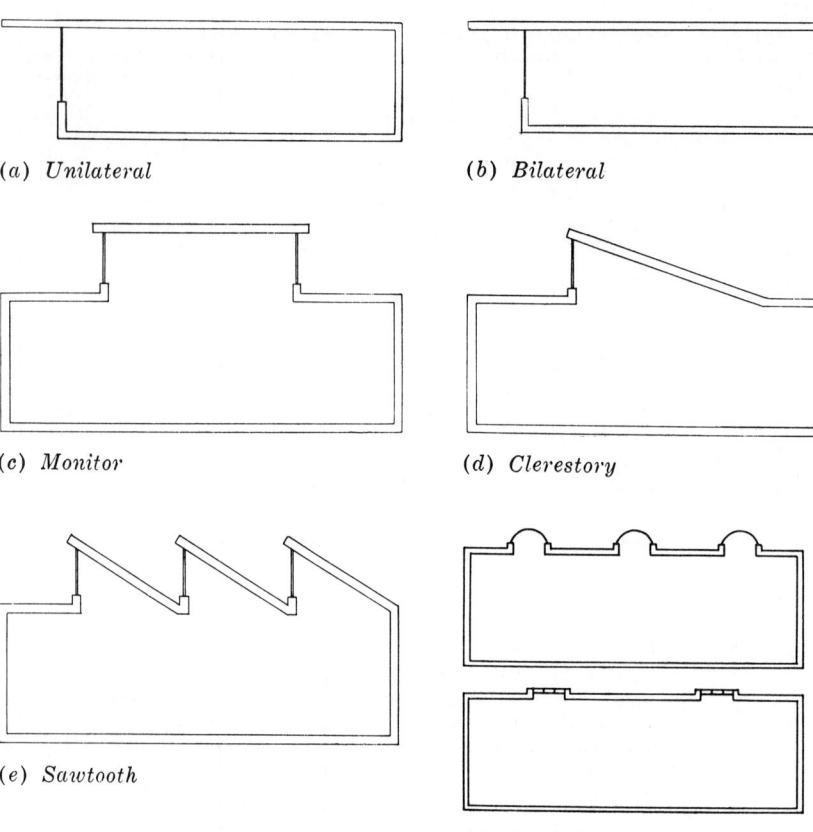

(a) *Unilateral*

(b) *Bilateral*

(c) *Monitor*

(d) *Clerestory*

(e) *Sawtooth*

(f) *Skylights*

Fig. 2. Typical building sections for daylighting

tect's range of choice. Among these are the plastic "sky dome," the roof panel of glass block with integral sun and brightness control, and the roof panel of glass-fiber reinforced plastic. Toplighting by means of skylights is an efficient method of admitting daylight to an interior.

Building arrangement

Orientation: In northern latitudes of the United States and Canada, consideration should be given to orientation of the windows in a southerly direction. Assuming suitable sun controls, this orientation affords the maximum daylight, particularly in the winter months, and permits the effective utilization of solar energy as an aid to heating. In southern latitudes of the United States, northerly exposures should be considered to limit the solar heating.

As a general rule, east-west orientations present the most difficult problems of daylight control, and complicate heating and air-conditioning designs.

Single-story construction: This type of construction greatly increases freedom of

daylighting design. Almost any version of sidewall lighting or toplighting, or combinations of the two, can be used.

Multiple story construction: In modern multistory buildings with large expanses of glass daylighting designs obviously are the sidewall type.

Where light courts are employed in the design, or tall buildings are located in close proximity, high-reflectance exterior walls and setbacks increase the daylight received at the lower floors.

Materials and control elements

Materials and control elements are selected for their ability to transmit, diffuse, refract, absorb, or reflect light.

Transmitting materials: (see Table 6).

Transparent materials: The transparent high-transmittance materials include sheet **glass, float glass and wire glass,** acrylic plastic sheet and formed panels, and clear glass block.

Low-transmittance glasses and plastics offer a measure of brightness control which increases as their transmittance is de-

Table 6. Transmittance data for glass and plastic materials

Material	Transmittance, per cent
Polished plate/float window glass	80–90
Sheet window glass	85–91
Heat-absorbing plate glass	70–80
Heat-absorbing sheet glass	70–85
Tinted polished plate glass	40–50
Reflective glass	5–60
Figured glass	70–90
Corrugated glass	80–85
Glass block	60–80
Clear plastic sheet	80–92
Tinted plastic sheet	42–90
Colorless patterned plastic	80–90
White translucent plastic	10–80
Glass fiber reinforced plastics	5–80
Double glazed—2 lights clear glass	77
Double glazed—tinted plus clear	37–45

creased. With such materials, view *out* is not noticeably affected during the day but view *in* is materially reduced. The reverse is true at night. Reduction in radiant solar heat transmittance accompanies the reduction in visible light transmittance. If these materials are neutral in the visible region, color distortion is avoided. The reduction in daylight which accompanies the use of low-transmittance materials must be allowed for in over-all lighting design.

Diffusing materials: Included in this category are the diffusing glasses such as opal and surface-treated glasses, diffusing and patterned plastics and sheet glass, corrugated glass and plastics, and diffusing glass block. All are characterized by a predominantly nonselective diffusion of the transmitted light, and by the fact that they prevent clear vision through the medium.

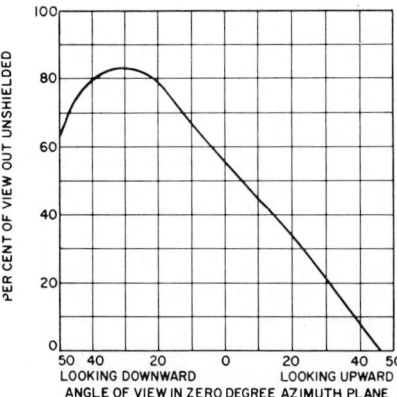

Fig. 3. Shielding of exterior view by use of darkened metal screening with minute horizontal louvers

As a rule, transmittance and brightness decrease as diffusion increases. Some types may become excessively bright on sun exposures, hence require brightness control.

Directional transmitting materials: These materials produce a definite, controlled change in the direction of the transmitted light by refraction. They include prismatic sheet glass and plastics, but the most widely used types are the light-directing glass blocks. They are also designed to restrict the brightness seen from normal viewing angles.

Selective transmitting materials: There are two types of selective transmitting materials used in daylighting: those which are directionally selective and those which are spectrally selective.

The directionally selective transmitting materials include two types of prismatic glass block; one for sidelighting, the other for toplighting installations. The materials are designed to reject most of the light from the directions along which the strongest sunlight arrives at the panel, admitting a greater proportion of the more diffuse light from the rest of the luminous exterior. Certain louvered materials and toplight closures described in later sections can also be considered as directionally selective transmitting materials.

The spectrally selective transmitting materials include the various colored and heat-absorbing transmitting materials. The heat-absorbing glasses are designed to pass the visible light but absorb the infrared radiations. Considerable research effort has been expended on most daylight-transmitting materials, so that they will not be color-selective in the visible part of the spectrum, both initially and after exposure

to sunlight and the weather. However, in some of the glass and plastic materials employed in daylighting, colors are incorporated deliberately. The esthetic effect of stained glass windows is a major attribute of the daylighting design in some of the finest church architecture.

Shielding elements and materials: The shielding elements and materials employed in daylighting practice include the various opaque structures, shades, and draperies which intercept light. They include building overhangs, vertical fins and similar building elements, as well as opaque and translucent screens, shades or curtains, and landscaping elements including trees. (See section on "Heating, Ventilating, and Air-Conditioning: Design of solar shading.")

Properly designed overhangs shade the windows from direct sunlight, and reduce the brightness of the upper part of the windows. They do this, however, at a sacrifice in the amount of light reaching the window. Overhangs of practical length do not provide complete shading at all times. In multiple-story buildings, a balcony can serve as overhang for the window of the story below.

Vertical elements have been employed effectively on east and west walls as sun controls. Combinations of vertical and horizontal elements have been used in some designs. They have been most common in tropical applications.

Shielding materials also include opaque shades and draperies used when it is desired to exclude daylight from a room.

Landscaping: Trees are effective shading devices when properly located with respect to the building and its fenestration. Deciduous trees and vines provide shade and protect against sky glare during the warm months but allow the sun to reach the building during the winter. The use of vegetation as a seasonal daylight control has not been exploited as imaginatively as it might be.

Louvers: Louvers are widely used as shielding elements in daylighting design. Practical louvers commonly embody slats which are reflecting elements as well as shielding elements. Some use slats which are made of diffuse transmitting materials. Louvers are found in many forms, located inside or outside the lighted space or serving as the weather closure itself. Slat widths range from minute dimensions to major dimensions as great as several feet. Slats can be either horizontal or vertical.

The adjustable horizontal louver is found as the interior venetian blind, the jalousie, and the exterior adjustable blind. It can be adjusted as needed for the varying solar altitude to prevent entry of direct sunlight, while reflecting a high proportion of sun and sky light into the interior. It permits entry of light reflected from the ground with minor obstruction. It also permits the passage of natural ventilation in warm weather periods.

The fixed horizontal louver is frequently employed as an exterior sun control and as a shield for high sky brightness. It is found with slats of all sizes, and it can be a very effective heat control as well as light control device. It permits the entry of ground light and light reflected from the top of the slats as well as natural ventilation. One type of horizontal louver employs minute louver slats, spaced so closely that they blend unobtrusively into the view, minimizing the psychological barrier presented by many other daylight controls (see Fig. 3).

Overhangs meant primarily for sun control are sometimes made of louver elements, so that more of the sky light can reach the windows than would be the case with a solid overhang (see Fig. 4). Louvers are also employed both above or below the skylight or other toplighting arrangement.

Light-reflecting materials and elements: All materials encountered in lighting practice reflect some light. Those which are employed specifically for their reflecting qualities are largely diffusely reflecting. Shiny surfaces which produce specular or mirror reflections are apt to cause disturbing brightness in the field of view and should be avoided where good visual conditions are desired.

Reflecting elements can often be incorporated effectively into the over-all architectural design. Reflecting pavements and similar treatment of the terrain surrounding the building can be particularly effective at distances from one-half to twice the height from the ground to the top of the windows. Reflecting materials or finishes on roofs and similar projections below window areas and vision strips can also add to the total daylight entering the space.

The interior reflecting surfaces of the building should be controlled by the architect. The use of white or near-white ceilings contribute to the effective utilization of ground light in the room. Wall finishes of 50 to 60 per cent reflectance make for effective daylight utilization and for good brightness control in the surroundings of visual tasks. Light finishes on the floors and on the interior furnishings are also recommended.

DAYLIGHTING COMPUTATIONS

Various computation methods have been developed for the design and evaluation of daylighting systems. Such a procedure in-

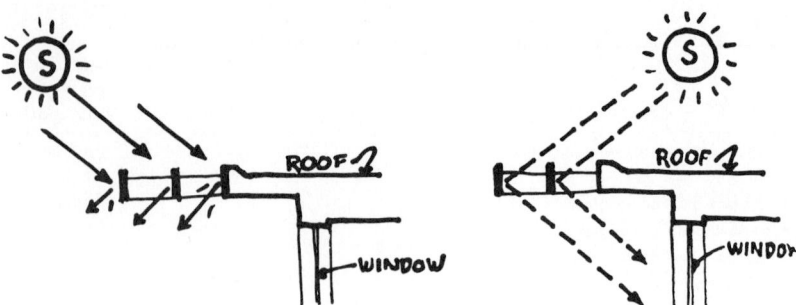

Fig 4. Louvered overhangs may be used to prevent entry of direct sunlight or to provide indirect sunlight

volves: (1) determination of the daylight incident on the windows, (2) the light flux actually entering the lighted space, (3) the distribution of the light flux within the room, and (4) the illumination produced on the surfaces of interest.

Determination of incident daylight

The daylight incident on the fenestration of a building consists of light received directly from the sky, directly from the sun, and by reflection from the ground or other surfaces visible from the windows. The actual amount is influenced by the location, the orientation of the windows, the date and time of day, the weather conditions and the local terrain. Consequently, tabular data for a geographic area should always be modified as necessary in order to account for the local conditions.

Sky light: The daylight received in the plane of the fenestration directly from the sky can be obtained from Tables 2 and 3. For purposes of comparative evaluation, it is sometimes assumed that the sky produces some arbitrary value of illumination at the windows. One such basis is that of a sky having a theoretically uniform brightness of 1,000 fL (3,430 cd/m²), such a sky would produce an illumination of 1,000 fc (10,000 lux) on a horizontal skylight and 500 fc (5,000 lux) on a vertical window. Some publications have used as an alternate basis an overcast sky which provides 1,000 fc (10,000 lux) on vertical windows, and 2½ times this value, or 2,500 fc (25,000 lux), on toplighting panels.

Sunlight: The direct sunlight incident on the fenestration can be obtained from Table 4. Given the exact angle of incidence, the illumination on a plane perpendicular to the sun's rays (Table 4) multiplied by the cosine of the angle of incidence, will give the illumination produced by the direct sunlight on the plane of the fenestration.

Ground light: The illuminance produced at the plane of a window by reflection from the ground is influenced by several factors. These include the illuminance produced on

the ground by the sky and the sun, the reflectance of the ground (Table 5), and the slope or tilt of the fenestration. There is, of course, no ground light reflected onto a horizontal window or skylight.

A vertical window, however, receives illuminance from a uniformly bright ground equal in footcandles (lux) to one-half the ground brightness in footlamberts (cd/m²). For example, a uniformly bright sky of 1,000 fL (10,000 lux), which produced 500 fc (5,000 lux) directly on the window, would also produce 1,000 fc (10,000 lux) on the ground. With a diffuse ground reflectance of 20 per cent, the ground brightness would be 200 fL (685 cd/m²). The illuminance produced on a vertical window by the ground brightness would be 100 fc (1,000 lux) which is one-fifth as much as was directed to the window from the sky alone.

With higher ground reflectance values, as for reflecting roofs under clerestory windows, or for cases where there is sun on the ground but not on the windows, the proportion of ground light to sky light may be much higher.

Determination of light flux entering room

Only a portion of the light flux incident on the fenestration area actually enters the lighted space. The gross fenestration area is reduced by the mechanical supports of the glazing material, such as mullions, window members, or mortar joints. The reduction in transmission area is a matter of simple geometry and can be readily determined.

There is also a transmission loss in the glazing material itself. Data on transmittance of glazing materials are included in Table 6. There is a further loss attributable to dirt collection on the glazing material (Table 7), which should be included in computations as a light loss factor. Finally, there is absorption or reflection by daylight controls, such as shades, louvers, prismatic devices, overhangs, or by the light wells of toplighting arrangements.

It should be emphasized that daylight is generally abundant, and that simple

Table 7. Typical light loss factors for daylighting design

Location	Glazing position		
	Vertical	Sloped	Horizontal
Clean areas	0.9	0.8	0.7
Industrial areas	0.8	0.7	0.6
Very dirty areas	0.7	0.6	0.5

efficiency of transmission into the room can and must often be compromised with other factors such as control of sunlight, heat gain, or glare, in the over-all daylighting design.

Toplighting illuminance

For toplighting systems of daylight design, employing lighting elements or areas mounted horizontally or in the plane of a nearly level roof, determination of the average illuminance produced in the lighted space can be made by much the same principles as are used for electric lighting practice. The basic relationship is

$$E_{tl} = \frac{E_h \times A_{tl} \times K_u \times K_m}{A_r}$$

where E_{tl} = average illuminance produced on the work plane by the top-lighting system, lumens per sq ft (fc) or lumens per m² (lux)

E_h = incident illuminance on exterior of toplighting element, lumens per sq ft or lumens per m²

A_{tl} = gross area of toplighting element

K_u = utilization coefficient, dependent on room geometry, reflectances, design of toplighting element (from Tables 8 and 9)

K_m = light loss factor (from Table 7)

A_r = room area

Toplight transmission: The net transmittance of a toplight can be obtained from the manufacturers of prefabricated units (see Table 10).

Light well effect: A toplight panel is usually located at the roof level, with a

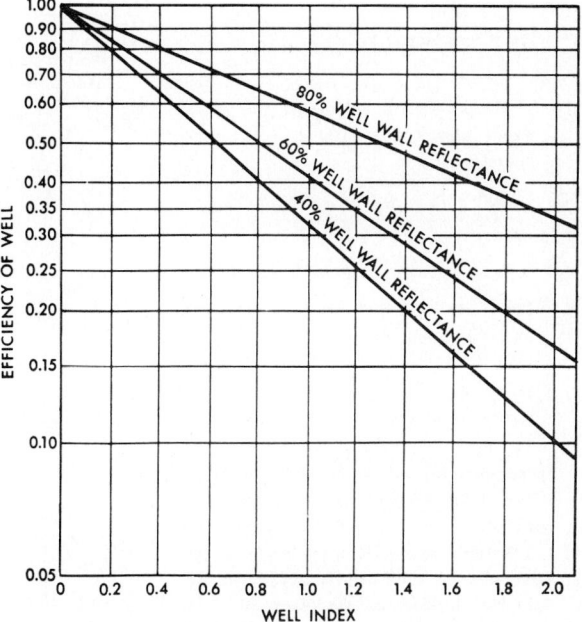

Fig. 5. Efficiency factors for various depths of light wells based on well interflectance values where:

$$\text{Well index} = \frac{\text{depth (length + width)}}{2 \times \text{length} \times \text{width}}$$

light well below it extending down to the ceiling level of the room. This depth may be in a range from a few inches to several feet, depending upon the depth of the roof trusses and other factors. The interflections of the light in this well result in a decrease in the net transmission of the total assembly. The magnitude of the light-well effect is shown in Fig. 5.

Uniformity: The formula above permits the calculation of the average illuminance produced on the work plane for the assumed exterior lighting conditions but gives no information concerning the uniformity of the lighting distribution over the work area. Uniformity of multiple toplighting will usually be adequate if the spacing between centers of adjacent toplighting elements does not exceed twice the height of the ceiling above the work plane for large area sources and one times the ceiling height for small area sources.

Toplighting example: As an example of the procedure, determine the average illuminance for a toplighting design based on the following assumed conditions:

Room 20 x 30 ft (6.6 x 9.8 m) with 12-ft (3.9-m) ceiling height

Reflectances: walls, 50 per cent; ceiling, 75 per cent; floor, 30 per cent

Overcast sky, producing 1,500 fc (15,000 lux) horizontal surface illuminance

Toplighting panels: six, each 3 x 5 ft, (0.98 x 1.6 m), of hammered heat-absorbing wire glass, with shallow light wells and egg-crate louvers

Table 8. Room ratios: toplighting

Room length in feet (meters)	Room width in feet (meters)	Ceiling height above floor in feet (meters)					
		8 (2.6)	10 (3.3)	12 (3.9)	15 (4.9)	19 (6.2)	23 (7.5)
12 (3.9)	12 (3.9)	1.1	0.8	0.6	0.5		
	16 (5.1)	1.3	0.9	0.7	0.6		
	20 (6.6)	1.4	1.0	0.8	0.6	0.5	
	24 (7.9)	1.5	1.1	0.8	0.7	0.5	
	30 (9.8)	1.6	1.1	0.9	0.7	0.5	
	40 (13.1)	1.7	1.2	1.0	0.7	0.6	0.5
20 (6.6)	20 (6.6)	1.8	1.3	1.1	0.8	0.6	0.5
	24 (7.9)	2.0	1.5	1.2	0.9	0.7	0.5
	30 (9.8)	2.2	1.6	1.3	1.0	0.7	0.6
	40 (13.1)	2.4	1.8	1.4	1.1	0.8	0.7
	60 (19.7)	2.7	2.0	1.6	1.2	0.9	0.7
	80 (26.2)	2.9	2.1	1.7	1.3	1.0	0.8
30 (9.8)	30 (9.8)	2.7	2.0	1.6	1.2	0.9	0.7
	40 (13.1)	3.1	2.3	1.8	1.4	1.0	0.8
	60 (19.7)	3.6	2.7	2.1	1.6	1.2	1.0
	80 (26.2)	4.0	2.9	2.3	1.7	1.3	1.1
	100 (32.8)	4.2	3.1	2.4	1.9	1.4	1.1
	120 (39.3)	4.4	3.2	2.5	1.9	1.5	1.2
40 (13.1)	40 (13.1)	3.6	2.7	2.1	1.6	1.2	1.0
	60 (19.7)	4.4	3.2	2.5	1.9	1.5	1.2
	80 (26.2)	4.9	3.6	2.8	2.1	1.6	1.3
	100 (32.8)	5+	3.8	3.0	2.3	1.7	1.4
	120 (39.3)	5+	4.0	3.2	2.4	1.8	1.5
	140 (45.9)	5+	4.1	3.3	2.5	1.9	1.5

Net transmittance: 40 per cent of incident light

Light loss factor: 0.7

Computation:

From Table 8, room ratio = 1.3
From Table 9, K_u = 0.30
Therefore, E_{tl} =

$$\frac{1500 \times (3 \times 5) \times 6 \times 0.30 \times 0.7}{(20 \times 30)}$$

= 47 fc (470/lux) average

Sidelighting illuminance

The calculation of illuminance produced by sidelighting is somewhat more complex than for toplighting. First, the light source is located asymmetrically with respect to the work plane. Second, light reaching the fenestration from above the horizontal is affected differently than light from below the horizontal in most daylighting systems.

The basic approach is the same as for toplighting. A coefficient is applied to the light flux incident on the fenestration, to determine the illuminance on the work plane in the room. Since the work-plane illuminance varies with the distance from the window, coefficients are determined for three points on the work plane in a line at right angles to the middle of the window. Five feet (1.6 m) from the window gives a value E_{max}. The midpoint of the room gives a value E_{mid}. Five feet (1.6 m) from the inner wall gives a value E_{min}. For each point, separate computations must be made for sky light and ground light, and the results added to obtain the total work-plane illuminance at the point.

The basic relationship for illumination produced by sidelighting is

$$E_p = E_i \times A_w \times K_u \times K_m$$

where E_p = work-plane illuminance at point P, lumens per sq ft or lumens per sq m

E_i = illuminance from sky or ground incident on vertical windows, lumens per sq ft or lumens per sq m

A_w = gross area of fenestration, sq ft or sq m

K_m = light loss coeffleicnt

K_u = utilization coefficient, which includes the effect of fenestration design, daylight controls, interior reflectances, and room geometry

Utilization coefficient tables: Values of the utilization coefficients $K_{u\ max}$, $K_{u\ mid}$, and $K_{u\ min}$ are given for several conditions in Table 11.

Combination designs: Daylighting designs which have side-wall fenestration in more than one wall or combined with toplighting, may be treated by superposition. That is, the values obtained by the several calculations may simply be added.

Table 9. Coefficients of utilization for toplighting

Net Toplight Transmittance (Including Light Well Effect, Controls, Etc.)	Room Ratio	Ceiling Reflectance			
		75 Per cent		50 Per cent	
		Wall Reflectance			
		50 Per cent	30 Per cent	50 Per cent	30 Per cent
70%	0.6 (J)	.37	.34	.36	.34
	0.8 (I)	.45	.42	.44	.41
	1.0 (H)	.49	.46	.48	.45
	1.25 (G)	.52	.50	.51	.49
	1.5 (F)	.55	.53	.53	.51
	2.0 (E)	.58	.56	.57	.55
	2.5 (D)	.61	.59	.60	.58
	3.0 (C)	.63	.61	.62	.60
	4.0 (B)	.65	.62	.63	.61
50%	0.6 (J)	.26	.24	.26	.24
	0.8 (I)	.32	.30	.31	.29
	1.0 (H)	.35	.33	.34	.32
	1.25 (G)	.37	.36	.36	.35
	1.5 (F)	.39	.38	.38	.36
	2.0 (E)	.41	.40	.41	.39
	2.5 (D)	.44	.42	.43	.41
	3.0 (C)	.45	.44	.44	.43
	4.0 (B)	.46	.44	.45	.44
30%	0.6 (J)	.16	.15	.16	.15
	0.8 (I)	.19	.18	.19	.18
	1.0 (H)	.21	.20	.21	.19
	1.25 (G)	.22	.21	.22	.21
	1.5 (F)	.24	.23	.23	.22
	2.0 (E)	.25	.24	.24	.24
	2.5 (D)	.26	.25	.26	.25
	3.0 (C)	.27	.26	.27	.26
	4.0 (B)	.28	.27	.27	.26
10%	0.6 (J)	.05	.05	.05	.05
	0.8 (I)	.06	.06	.06	.06
	1.0 (H)	.07	.07	.07	.06
	1.25 (G)	.07	.07	.07	.07
	1.5 (F)	.08	.08	.08	.07
	2.0 (E)	.08	.08	.08	.08
	2.5 (D)	.09	.08	.09	.08
	3.0 (C)	.09	.09	.09	.09
	4.0 (B)	.09	.09	.09	.09

Table 10. Net transmittance of white translucent plastic dome skylights, wells, and ceiling diffusers expressed as fractions of equivalent overcast sky luminance (well walls and axes of domes vertical)

Well Characteristics		Skylight Dome Transmittance											
		.30	.50	.70	.30			.50			.70		
Surface Reflectance	Well Index				Ceiling Diffuser Transmittance								
					.40	.60	.80	.40	.60	.80	.40	.60	.80
.80	0.1	.28	.47	.65	.16	.22	.25	.24	.33	.40	.30	.44	.55
	0.2	.25	.43	.60	.14	.19	.23	.21	.30	.38	.28	.40	.51
	0.3	.23	.40	.55	.13	.17	.21	.20	.28	.35	.26	.37	.47
	0.4	.22	.37	.51	.12	.16	.19	.18	.26	.32	.24	.34	.44
	0.5	.20	.35	.48	.11	.15	.18	.16	.24	.30	.22	.32	.41
	1.0	.14	.24	.34	....	.10	.12	.11	.17	.21	.15	.22	.29
	1.5	.10	.17	.25	....	....	.09	....	.12	.15	.11	.15	.20
.50	0.1	.26	.44	.63	.14	.21	.24	.22	.31	.38	.28	.41	.52
	0.2	.23	.38	.57	.11	.17	.21	.18	.26	.33	.24	.35	.46
	0.3	.20	.33	.51	.10	.15	.18	.16	.22	.28	.21	.31	.40
	0.4	.17	.30	.46	....	.12	.16	.13	.19	.25	.18	.27	.36
	0.5	.15	.27	.41	....	.10	.14	.12	.17	.22	.16	.24	.32
	1.0	.09	.15	.24	....	....	.08	....	.09	.12	.10	.14	.19
	1.5	....	.09	.14	....	....	....	....	....	.07	....	.08	.11

LUMINANCE

The methods for computing luminance in a lighted space are not too well advanced, particularly for daylighting designs. However, certain luminance values can be determined for almost any design.

Task luminance

Task luminance in footlamberts (cd/m²) can be computed by multiplying the work-plane illuminance in footcandles (lux) by the diffuse reflectance of the task. For paper work or printed matter, a diffuse reflectance of 70 per cent is a reasonable average value in common use. If work plane illuminance is 100 fc (1000 lux), a task of this sort has a luminance of 70 fL (240 cd/m²).

Surround luminance

The surround luminance is usually somewhat more difficult to determine. Where the immediate surround is in the work plane, such as a desk or table top, its luminance will be the work-plane illuminance multiplied by the diffuse reflectance of the desk surface. Reflectance of dark woods, and dark green or gray linoleums ranges from 10 to 20 per cent. Lighter woods and compositions range from 20 to 40 per cent reflectance. For a work-plane illuminance of 100 fc (1000 lux), a light gray desk top will have a luminance of 30 fL (103 cd/m²) if it has a reflectance of 30 per cent. For the two preceding examples, the luminance ratio of the visual task to its near surround will be 70/30, or 2.33/1, which is considered close to ideal (see section on "Lighting").

Luminances of floors, walls, or ceilings are more difficult to compute. However, considerable data showing room luminances have been published during recent years, and intelligent approximations can be made by those engineers who are familiar with these investigations.

Source luminance

Luminance of fenestration areas can be approximated in one of several ways. For clear glazing, luminance of the sky visible through the windows can be taken as the sky luminance assumed for the illuminance computation, multiplied by the transmittance of the glazing material. Thus a sky luminance of 1,500 fL (5140 cd/m²), viewed through a glass having a transmittance of 80 per cent, will have an apparent luminance of 1,200 fL (4110 cd/m²). For a low-transmittance glass of 30 per cent transmittance, the apparent luminance would be 450 fL (1542 cd/m²).

Luminance through minute louvers: The dark-colored, minute-louvered materials produce a reduction in apparent luminance of an exterior view by interposing the unobtrusive dark slats of the louver material

Table 11. Coefficients of utilization for sidelighting for rooms with a ceiling reflectance of 75 per cent and a floor reflectance of 30 per cent

0.8 ratio of net transmission area to gross window area—80 per cent transmittance of clear glazing medium—no other daylight control

K_u	Room length in feet (meters)	Room width in feet (meters)	Light from clear sky 10 (3.3) w70	w30	14 (4.6) w70	w30	Overcast sky 10 (3.3) w70	w30	14 (4.6) w70	w30	Uniform ground 10 (3.3) w70	w30	14 (4.6) w70	w30
Max.	20 (6.6)	20 (6.6)	.00191	.00165	.00149	.00123	.00240	.00223	.00197	.00176	.00147	.00109	.00096	.00070
		30 (9.8)	183	163	139	126	239	216	185	173	142	116	94	71
		40 (13.1)	194	162	139	120	254	223	189	172	138	115	92	71
	30 (9.8)	20 (6.6)	.00133	.00118	.00104	.00087	.00167	.00154	.00137	.00122	.00103	.00086	.00067	.00054
		30 (9.8)	123	113	93	87	165	150	128	121	98	90	65	55
		40 (13.1)	127	115	91	85	171	155	127	121	94	78	63	59
	40 (13.1)	20 (6.6)	.00102	.00094	.00080	.00070	.00125	.00121	.00102	.00095	.00082	.00062	.00053	.00044
		30 (9.8)	87	86	67	67	120	114	93	91	78	72	50	44
		40 (13.1)	93	88	66	65	126	118	94	92	73	70	49	43
Mid.	20 (6.6)	20 (6.6)	.00128	.00094	.00113	.00081	.00122	.00097	.00120	.00102	.00112	.00084	.00092	.00062
		30 (9.8)	65	50	66	47	39	41	51	48	64	46	66	31
		40 (13.1)	46	27	47	28	34	20	38	24	40	28	47	31
	30 (9.8)	20 (6.6)	.00084	.00072	.00074	.00062	.00078	.00071	.00077	.00076	.00083	.00066	.00068	.00048
		30 (9.8)	50	40	50	37	37	33	47	39	48	38	50	36
		40 (13.1)	35	24	36	24	27	18	37	22	32	26	38	28
	40 (13.1)	20 (6.6)	.00070	.00060	.00062	.00052	.00062	.00059	.00062	.00066	.00065	.00056	.00053	.00041
		30 (9.8)	36	34	37	31	23	27	30	32	38	33	39	31
		40 (13.1)	26	20	26	21	20	15	22	18	23	20	27	23
Min.	20 (6.6)	20 (6.6)	.00085	.00056	.00084	.00050	.00059	.00043	.00073	.00051	.00083	.00058	.00082	.00054
		30 (9.8)	42	25	42	25	23	16	29	18	36	19	45	22
		40 (13.1)	29	12	26	12	18	07	19	08	20	13	26	17
	30 (9.8)	20 (6.6)	.00064	.00045	.00063	.00041	.00044	.00035	.00054	.00042	.00065	.00045	.00063	.00041
		30 (9.8)	36	21	36	21	21	14	26	15	29	18	36	19
		40 (13.1)	25	11	23	11	14	07	15	08	18	09	23	12
	40 (13.1)	20 (6.6)	.00054	.00040	.00053	.00036	.00034	.00030	.00042	.00035	.00053	.00037	.00051	.00034
		30 (9.8)	25	19	25	19	15	12	18	13	24	16	29	18
		40 (13.1)	19	10	18	10	11	06	12	07	15	08	20	10

into the field of view. The luminance of the exterior viewed through such a material can be closely approximated by multiplying the luminance of the unshielded view by the proportion of the view unimpeded by the louver slats from Fig. 3. A sky having a luminance of 1,500 fL (5140 cd/m²) viewed at an angle where only 20 per cent of the view is visible through the slats, will have an apparent brightness of only 300 fL (1028 cd/m²).

OVERHANGS

The amount of window shaded from a long horizontal overhang mounted above the window (Fig. 6) can be calculated from the formula:

$$h = D_n \sec (\Psi_z - \Psi_N) \tan \theta$$

where
h = height of shadow below overhang
D_n = depth of overhang from the window surface
Ψ_z = solar azimuth
Ψ_N = angle between a line drawn (outward) normal to the window and true south
θ = solar altitude above the horizon

The amount of shading from a vertical projection mounted at the side of a window can be obtained from the formula:

$$W = D_v \tan (\Psi_z - \Psi_N)$$

where W = width of the shadow from the side projection
D_v = depth of vertical projection

In planning fixed horizontal and vertical projections for sunlight control, it is advisable to calculate the window shading for several different months and times.

See also Sheets 2 and 3 in section on "Solar Angles" and Sheets 38—40 in section on "Heating, Ventilating, and Air-conditioning."

GLOSSARY OF TERMS

Altitude: Angular distance of the sun measured up from the horizon of the great circle that passes perpendicular to the plane of the horizon through the sun and through the zenith.

Azimuth: Angular distance between the vertical plane containing the sun and the plane of the meridian.

Clear sky: Sky having less than 30 per cent cloud cover.

Clerestory: Part of a building rising clear of the roofs and whose walls contain windows for lighting the interior.

Daylighting factor: Ratio of the daylight illuminance on a plane to the exterior illuminance on a horizontal plane from the whole of an unobstructed sky of assumed or known luminance.

Fenestration: Any opening or arrangement of openings (normally filled with media for control) for the admission of daylight.

Orientation: Position of a building with respect to compass directions.

Overcast sky: One that has 100 per cent cloud cover; the sun is not visible.

Partly cloudy sky: One that has 30 to 70 per cent cloud cover.

Sky factor: Ratio of the illuminance on a horizontal plane inside a building due to light from the sky to the illuminance due to an unobstructed hemisphere of sky.

Sky light: Visible radiation from the sun redirected by the atmosphere.

Solar constant: Irradiance from the sun at its mean distance from the earth, before modificaton by the earth's atmosphere.

Sun bearing: Angle measured in the plane of the horizon between a vertical plane perpendicular to the window wall and the position of the plane after it has been rotated to contain the sun.

Sunlight: Direct visible radiation from the sun.

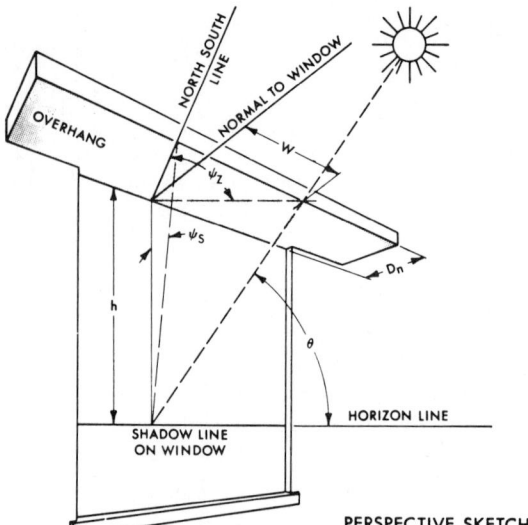

PERSPECTIVE SKETCH

DRAWINGS SHOW CASE WHERE Ψ_N IS GREATER THAN ZERO. WHEN Ψ_N = ZERO, Ψ_S IS SUNLIGHT PENETRATION ANGLE, TAN Ψ_S = D_n/h.

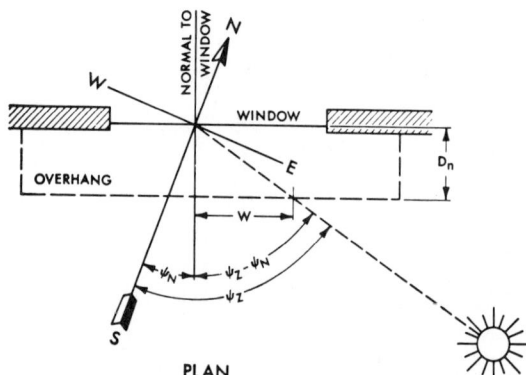

PLAN

Fig. 6. Sunlight shading from a horizontal overhang. Drawings show case where $\Psi_N > 0$. When $\Psi_N = 0$, Ψ_S is sunlight penetration angle, tan $\Psi_S = D_n/h$.

REFERENCES

Recommended Practice of Daylighting. Illuminating Engineering Society, New York, 1962. Includes a very comprehensive bibliography.

Walsh, J. W. T. *The Science of Daylight.* Pitman Publishing Co., New York, 1961.

Turner, D. P. (ed.). *Windows and Environment.* Pilkington Bros. Ltd., Newton-le-Willows, 1969.

Daylight—International Recommendations for the Calculation of Natural Daylight, CIE Publication No. 16, Commission Internationale de l'Eclairage, 1970.

Henderson, S. T. *Daylight and its Spectrum.* American Elsevier Publishing Co., New York, 1970.

By BERNARD F. GREENE, *Lighting Consultant, New York*

DESIGNING FOR DAYLIGHT WITH CLERESTORY WINDOWS

Natural lighting is an important part of the design of a building. For good lighting the type, area, and dimensions of the window openings must be carefully planned to obtain adequate, well-distributed illuminance which is free from glare. To meet this challenge the science of daylighting is steadily being developed. Daylighting designs based on intuition and fancy are gradually being replaced by products of sound engineering methods.

Designing for daylight can be accomplished today by the same rules used in artificial lighting systems. However, because of the many more factors involved in daylighting design, it is important to follow a systematic approach in which each phase of the problem is considered separately. The purpose of this section is to describe one phase of daylighting—the clerestory window. Other problems such as sunlight control, window spacing, skylight and monitor design, etc., are discussed separately.

The design of clerestory windows lends itself to engineering analysis; by the application of mathematical methods, clerestory window arrangements can be designed which are applicable to schools, offices, factories, or homes.

APPROACH TO DAYLIGHTING DESIGN

In the design of a system of lighting utilizing daylight, certain criteria must be established in order to ensure that there is enough light at different times and for different locations and weather conditions. One criterion, which is easy to use and which yields accurate results, is the assumption that the sky is a uniform source of light with a known luminance value. This can be taken as equal to that obtained in the late afternoon on an overcast day in December. If we assume this value to be 600 fL, (2056 cd/m²) then

the sky would be brighter than this value approximately 85 per cent of the daylight hours in the vicinity of 42° north latitude. Values of twice this brightness would be obtained 50 per cent of the daylight hours and values of three times this brightness 15 per cent of the daylight hours.

The assumed value of 600 fL (2056 cd/m²) is the basis for design. Recommended levels of light throughout a room can be obtained for this condition, and when the sky is brighter the illuminance levels are proportionately higher. When the sky luminance is less, however, an artificial lighting system should be used to maintain the desired illuminance.

Once the problem of daylighting has been reduced to that of calculating the light distribution from a source of uniform brightness, light distribution from different window arrangements can be obtained by the use of mathematical formulas. Following this procedure, the direct component light distribution from side-wall and clerestory arrangements was calculated, and the results were compiled to yield the recommended design principles for clerestory windows which are described below.

THE CLERESTORY ARRANGEMENT

A clerestory arrangement usually consists of a side-wall window and a clerestory window mounted overhead (Fig. 7). The problem is then to find the proper relationship between the side-wall and clerestory window, and to determine the clerestory setback, the height of the clerestory window, the room depth, the window positions, etc., in order to obtain the desired illuminance value and nearly uniform light distribution. Once these are obtained, it will be found that for the condition of an overcast sky, the luminance contrasts through the room for almost all daylighting designs will be less than those usually encountered in artificial lighting-system designs.

LIGHT DISTRIBUTION FROM SIDE-WALL WINDOWS

First let us consider the case of the side-wall window. The daylight distribution from such a window is at a maximum near the window sill, and drops off as the distance from the window increases (Figs. 8, 9). The amount and distribution of this daylight for any particular time varies with respect to the window height and width and the material in the window opening. The window widths given are for small windows (where the window width is approximately equal to the height) and for wide windows (where the window width is greater than four times the height).

The type of material in the window opening has little effect on the daylight distribution for overcast sky conditions. The light-distribution curves in Figs. 8 and 9 are based on clear or diffusing flat glass or acrylic plastic in the window opening.

LIGHT DISTRIBUTION FROM OVERHEAD WINDOWS

Now let us take the case of overhead or clerestory windows. By the use of the mathematical formulas by which light distribution from side-wall windows was calcu-

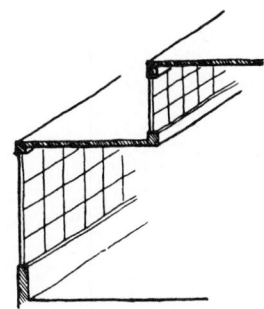

Fig. 7. Clerestory, side-wall window arrangement

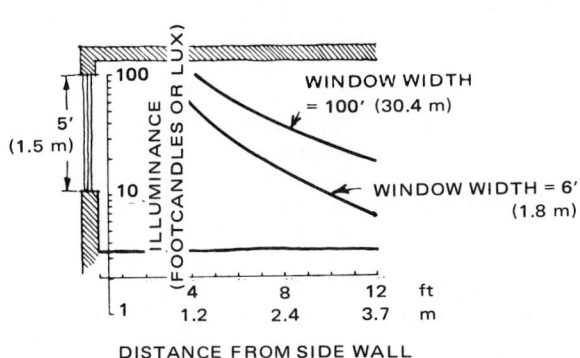

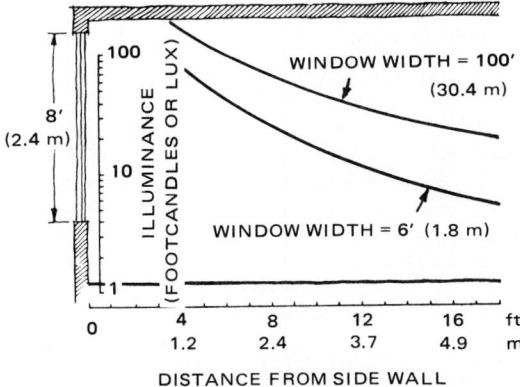

Figs. 8, 9. Daylight from side-wall windows is maximum near the window sill and decreases as the distance increases. Amount and distribution of light varies with window height, width as shown here

Note: curves are based on illumination at working plane; combination curves show total illumination from side-wall and clerestory windows.

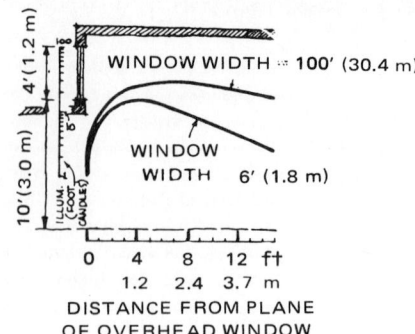

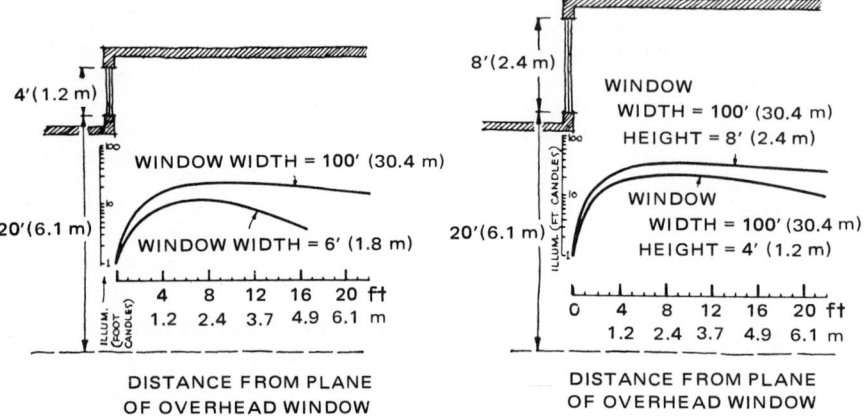

Figs. 10–12. Daylight directly below clerestory window is zero when window is mounted vertically. Both mounting height and window height affect the distribution of daylight

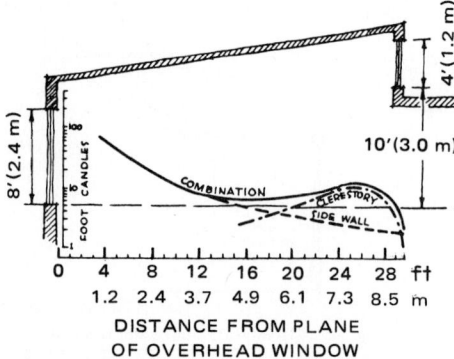

Fig. 13. Improper clerestory arrangement
When clerestory faces opposite direction from side-wall window, illumination is high near wall and very low near clerestory.

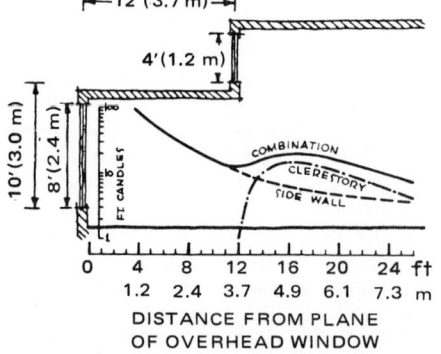

Fig. 14. Correct clerestory arrangement
Light from clerestory complements that from the sidewall window to get more even distribution. Window widths were taken as 6 ft for Figs. 13, 14. Curves for wide windows are similar (see Fig. 16).

lated, the illuminance from overhead windows can be similarly obtained. The results of these calculations for different arrangements of overhead windows are shown in Figs. 10–12.

From these diagrams it will be noted that the illuminance directly below the overhead windows is zero when the window is mounted on a vertical plane, and that it increases to a maximum value before tapering off. The position of the maximum varies with the mounting height of the window sill

above the working plane (Figs. 10 and 11). Increasing the height of the window itself (distance from sill to top of window) also has some effect on the distribution of illuminance (Fig. 12).

COMBINATION OF SIDE-WALL AND OVERHEAD WINDOW ARRANGEMENTS

The illuminance obtained from the combination of a side-wall window and an overhead or clerestory window can be calculated

by adding the values of illuminance for each window. Following this procedure, let us consider what is the most desirable plane for mounting the two windows. The combination of a side-wall window on one side of a room with the clerestory window mounted on the opposite wall results in an illuminance which is at a minimum at the rear of the room and which is nonuniform throughout (Fig. 13). Now by mounting the clerestory window on the opposite wall, or on the same side as the window wall, but set back from it, a more uniform light distribution can be obtained (Fig. 14).

It will be noted from Fig. 14 that the illumination from the clerestory window complements the illuminance from the side-wall window so that a more uniform illuminance is obtained. For our first rule, therefore, we can say that *for typical clerestory and side-wall window arrangements, the clerestory window should be mounted on the same side as the side-wall window.*

SETBACK OF CLERESTORY FROM SIDE WALL

The next step in clerestory window design is to determine the required setback between the window wall and the plane of the clerestory. The spacing between the planes of the clerestory and side-wall window wall are related to the window heights and widths. Figures 15–17 show the effects of different clerestory setbacks and window widths.

From these diagrams it will be noted that there is an optimum relation between the side-wall window height and the setback for near-uniform illuminance. *For narrow windows, the recommended setbacks are of the order of one and one-half times the side-wall window height. For wide windows these setbacks should be about twice the window height* (Fig. 16).

DISTANCE TO BACK WALL

Another factor in the design of clerestory windows is the effective room width measured from the plane of the overhead window to the opposite wall. From inspection of the light-distribution curves from overhead windows (Figs. 10–12) it will be noted that this effective width (flatter curves give better light distribution) depends upon the clerestory window mounting height. *For typical clerestory arrangements utilizing narrow windows, recommended depth from the plane of a clerestory window to the opposite wall should be approximately equal to the mounting height of the clerestory window above the working plane. For wide clerestory windows, the room depth from the plane of the clerestory window should be approximately one and one-half times the clerestory mounting height.* When the area near the back wall is not to be used for critical seeing, these values can be exceeded.

HEIGHT OF OVERHEAD WINDOW

It will be noted that the mounting height of the clerestory window has a pronounced effect on the light distribution (Figs. 10 and 11), while the height of the clerestory win-

dow for a given mounting height above the working plane has a greater effect on the amount of light (Fig. 12). In order to obtain a uniform and adequate level of light, *the height of the clerestory window should be approximately equal to one-half the side-wall window height, where the sill height of the clerestory window above the working plane is no greater than one and one-half times the side-wall window height. Where*

the sill height of the clerestory window is of the order of three times the side-wall window height, the clerestory window should be equal in height to the side-wall window.

SLOPING OVERHEAD WINDOWS

Changing the slope of the clerestory window also affects the light distribution. In

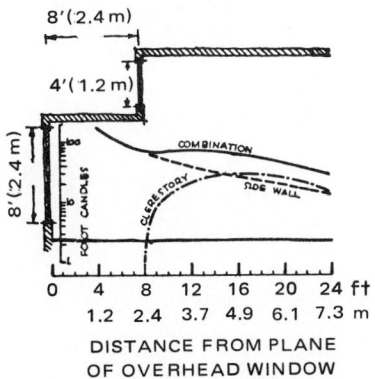

Fig. 15. When clerestory setback equals the side-wall window height, illuminance is high near wall and clerestory, but distance to the opposite wall is limited—illuminance at 24 (23 m) ft is about 15 fc (150/x).

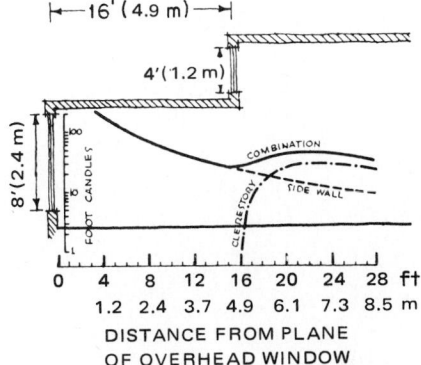

Fig. 16. When setback is twice side-wall window height, illuminance is well distributed and wall-to-wall distance can be greater than in Fig. 15. Illuminance at 28 ft (8.5m) is about 35 fc (350/x).

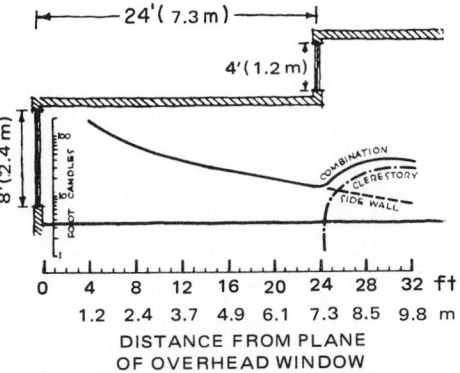

Fig. 17. When setback is too great, illuminance is not well distributed. At lowest point, illuminance is about 15 fc (150/x).

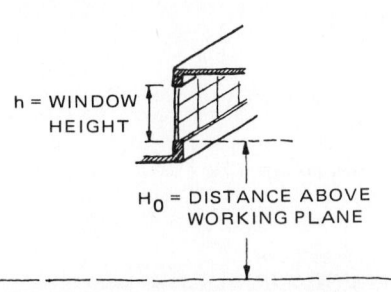

Fig. 18. Mounting height of the clerestory window affects light distribution, while height of the window, for a specific mounting height above the working plane, has greater effect on the amount of daylight

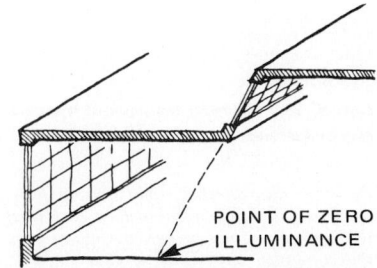

Fig. 19. Light from sloping clerestory window is zero at the point of intersection of the window plane and the working plane

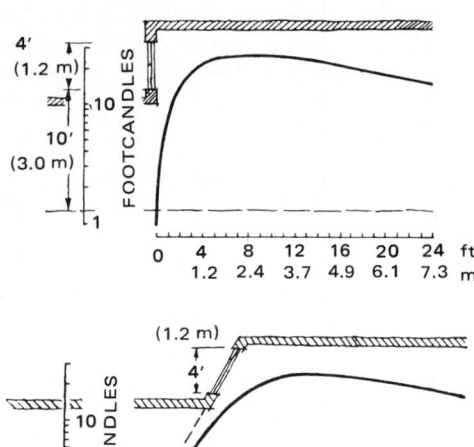

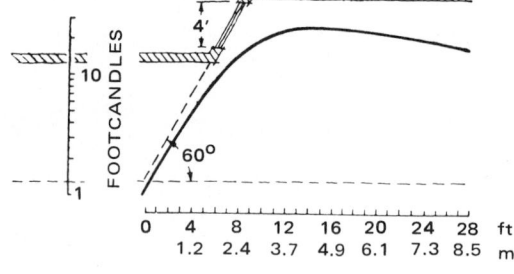

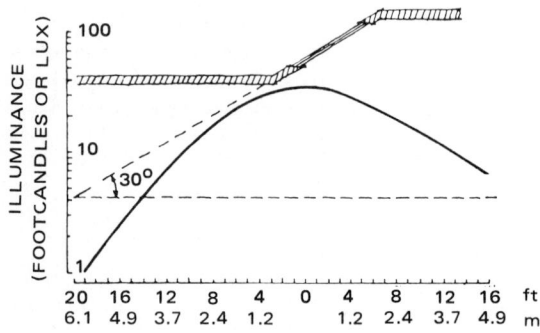

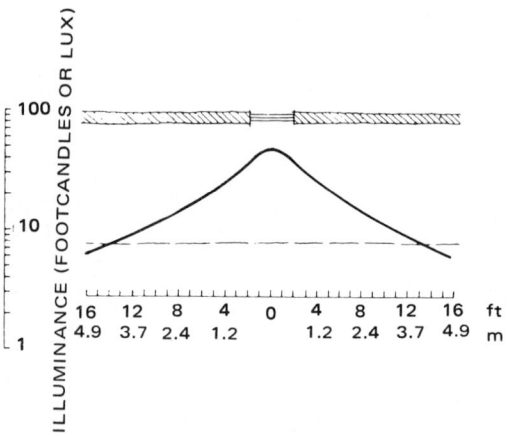

Figs. 20–23. Changing the slope of the clerestory affects the light distribution from the clerestory window

For obtaining the best light distribution from side-wall and clerestory windows combined, a clerestory slope of 30° from the vertical is best. When the clerestory window is vertical, the combined illumination curve has a dip in it (see Fig. 16) because the maximum point of the clerestory curve is almost directly above the minimum point. When the maximum point shifts to the right (this occurs with a 30° slope) the combination curve becomes flatter (see Fig. 24).

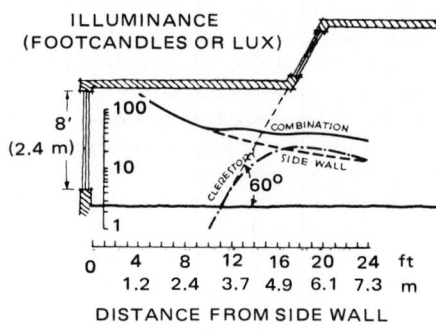

DISTANCE FROM SIDE WALL

Fig. 24. Best slope for a clerestory window is 30°, giving even light distribution

the case of sloping overhead windows, the point of zero illuminance is located at the point of intersection of the working plane and the plane of the sloping window (Fig. 19). Changing the slope of the window changes the point of zero illuminance as well as the light distribution. Distribution from clerestory windows arranged at slopes of 0°, 30°, 60°, and 90° are shown in Figs. 20–23.

The combination of sloping clerestory windows with vertical side-wall windows permits greater variation in room sizes. *By the use of a sloping clerestory window arrangement at an angle of 30° from the vertical, the distance from the side-wall window to the clerestory window can be increased to twice the side-wall window height when narrow windows are used, and two and one-half times the side-wall window height when wide windows are used* (Fig. 24).

CONCLUSIONS

The design principles for clerestory lighting described above illustrate how a rigid theoretical approach can be applied to yield simple and useful rules of thumb for daylighting designs. These principles can be applied in the design of clerestory windows for all types of buildings. Engineered daylighting designs make it both practical and economical to achieve buildings well lighted throughout most of the daylight hours.

Unless otherwise indicated, all data in this section have been abstracted, with permission, from the *IES Lighting Handbook*, 5th ed., published by the Illuminating Engineering Society in 1972, and from other publications of the Society, as noted.

GLOSSARY OF LIGHTING TERMS

Note: Many of these terms may be found in the *American National Standard Nomenclature and Definitions for Illuminating Engineering, ANSI/IES RP16-1967*. Others have appeared in more recent publications. Definitions of electrical terms common to lighting and to other fields are available in *American National Standard Definitions of Electrical and Electronics Terms, ANSI/IEEE Std 100–1972*.

For additional and more detailed definitions, see *IES Lighting Handbooks, 1981*.

Absorptance: Ratio of the flux absorbed by a medium to the incident flux.

Absorption: General term for the process by which incident flux is dissipated. (Note: All the incident flux is accounted for by the processes of reflection, transmission, and absorption.)

Accent lighting: Directional lighting to emphasize a particular object or draw attention to a part of the field of view.

Baffle: A single opaque or translucent element to shield a source from direct view at certain angles or to absorb unwanted light.

Ballast: Device used with electric discharge lamp to obtain the necessary circuit conditions for starting and operating.

"Black light": Popular term for ultraviolet energy near the visible spectrum.

Brightness: See *luminance*.

Candela (cd): The unit of luminous intensity (see Fig. 1).

Candlepower: Luminous intensity expressed in candelas (see Fig. 1).

Ceiling area lighting: General lighting system in which the entire ceiling is, in effect, one large luminaire, as in louvered ceilings and luminous ceilings.

Ceiling cavity: Cavity formed by the ceiling, the plane of the luminaires, and the wall surfaces between these two planes.

Channel: Enclosure containing the ballast, starter, lamp holders, and wiring for a fluorescent lamp.

Coefficient of utilization: Ratio of the luminous flux (lumens) from a luminaire received on the work plane to the lumens emitted by the luminaire's lamps alone.

Cold-cathode lamp: Electric discharge lamp of the glow discharge type.

Cornice lighting: Lighting by means of light sources shielded by a panel parallel to the wall and attached to the ceiling that distribute light over the wall.

Cove lighting: Lighting by means of sources shielded by a ledge or horizontal recess that distribute light over the ceiling and upper wall.

Cutoff angle (of a luminaire): The angle, measured up from the nadir, between the vertical axis and the first line of sight at which the bare source is not visible.

Diffuse reflectance: Ratio of the flux leaving a surface or medium by diffuse reflection to the incident flux.

Diffuse reflection: Process by which the incident flux is redirected over a range of angles.

Diffuse transmission: Process by which the incident flux passing through a surface or medium is scattered.

Diffuse transmittance: Ratio of the diffusely transmitted flux leaving a surface or medium to the incident flux.

Diffuse lighting: Light that is not predominantly incident from any particular direction.

Diffuser: Device to redirect or scatter the light from a source, primarily by the process of diffuse transmission.

Direct-indirect lighting: Variant of general diffuse lighting in which the luminaires emit little or no light at angles near the horizontal.

Direct lighting: Lighting by luminaires distributing 90 to 100 per cent of the emitted light in the direction (usually downward) of the surface to be illuminated.

Disability glare: Glare resulting in reduced visual performance and visibility.

Discomfort glare: Glare producing discomfort but not necessarily impairing visual performance or visibility.

Downlight: Small direct lighting unit that can be recessed, surface-mounted, or suspended.

Electric discharge lamp: Lamp in which light is produced by the passage of an electric current through a vapor or a gas, as in fluorescent, cold-cathode, and mercury lamps.

Filter: Device for changing, by transmission, the magnitude and/or the spectral composition of the flux incident upon it.

Floodlight: Projector designed for lighting a scene or object to a luminance considerably greater than its surroundings.

Floor cavity: Cavity formed by the work plane, the floor, and the wall surfaces between these two planes.

Fluorescent lamp: Low-pressure mercury electric discharge lamp in which a fluorescing coating (phosphor) transforms some of the ultraviolet energy generated by the discharge into light.

Flush-mounted or recessed: Luminaire

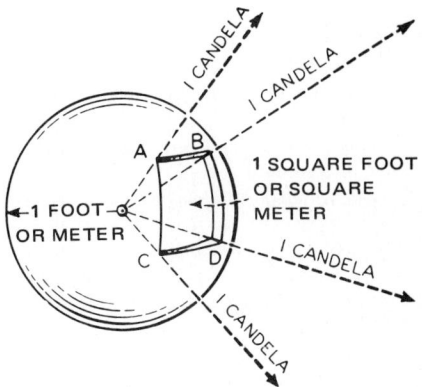

Fig. 1. Lumens

Relationship between candelas, lumens, and footcandles (lux). A uniform point source (luminous intensity or candlepower = 1 candela) is shown at the center of a sphere of 1 ft (1 m) radius. It is assumed that the sphere is perfectly transparent (i.e., has 0 reflectance). The illuminance at any point on the sphere is 1 fc (1 lm/ft²) when the radius is 1 ft, or 1 lx (1 lm/ m²) when the radius is 1 m. The solid angle subtended by the area A, B, C, D is 1 steradian (sr). The flux density is therefore, 1 lm/sr, which corresponds to a luminous intensity of 1 cd, as originally assumed. The sphere has a total area of 12.57 (4π) ft² or m², and there is a luminous flux of 1 lm falling on each square foot or square meter. Thus the source provides a total of 12.57 lm.

mounted above the ceiling with the opening of the luminaire flush with the surface of the ceiling.

Footcandle (fc): The unit of illumination; the illumination on a surface 1 sq ft in area on which there is a uniformly distributed flux of 1 lumen (see Fig. 1).

Footlambert (fL): Unit of luminance; the luminance of a perfectly diffusing surface emitting or reflecting light at the rate of 1 lumen per sq ft. (Note: The luminance in footlamberts of any reflecting surface is the product of the illumination in footcandles and the luminous reflectance of the surface.)

Gaseous discharge: Emission of light from gas atoms excited by an electric current.

General diffuse lighting: Lighting by luminaires distributing 40 to 60 per cent of the emitted light downward and the balance upward and horizontally.

Glare: Sensation produced by luminance within the visual field sufficiently greater than the luminance to which the eyes are adapted to cause annoyance, discomfort, or loss in visual performance and visibility.

Illuminance: The density of the luminous flux incident on a surface.

Indirect lighting: Lighting by luminaires distributing 90 to 100 per cent of the emitted light upward.

Infrared radiation: Radiant energy within the wavelength range 770 to 10^6 nanometers.

Instant start fluorescent lamp: One designed to start by high voltage without preheating of the electrodes.

Lamp: Generic term for a man-made source of light.

Laser: Acronym for Light Amplifcation by Stimulated Emission of Radiation. Highly monochromatic and coherent beam with a steady oscillation.

Light loss factor (LLF): Factor used in calculating level of illumination after a period of time. It takes into account temperature and voltage variations, dirt accumulation, lamp depreciation, etc.

Louver: Series of baffles used to shield a source from view at certain angles.

Louver shielding angle: Angle between the horizontal plane of baffles or louver grid and the plane at which the louver conceals all objects above.

Lumen (lm): The unit of luminous flux (see Fig. 1).

Luminaire: Complete lighting unit consisting of a lamp or lamps together with the parts designed to distribute the light, to position and protect the lamps, and to connect the lamps to the power supply.

Luminaire efficiency: Ratio of luminous flux emitted by a luminaire to that emitted by the lamp or lamps used therein.

Luminance (photometric brightness): The luminous intensity of a surface in a given direction per unit of projected area of the surface as viewed from that direction.

Luminous ceiling: Ceiling area lighting system comprising a continuous surface of diffuse transmitting material with light sources mounted above it.

Luminous density: Quantity of light per unit volume.

Luminous efficacy of a source of light: Quotient of the total luminous flux emitted by the total lamp power input expressed in lumens per watt.

Luminous flux: The time rate of flow of light (see Fig. 1).

Lux (lx): The SI unit of illuminance. One lux is one lumen per square meter (lm/m²).

Maintenance factor: See light loss factor.

Mercury lamp: Electric discharge lamp in which the major portion of the radiation is produced by excitation of mercury atoms.

Mounting height above the work plane: Distance from the work plane to the light center of the luminaire or to the plane of the ceiling for recessed equipment.

Polarization: Process by which the transverse vibrations of light waves are oriented in a specific plane.

Preheat (switch start) fluorescent lamp: One designed for operation in a circuit requiring a starting switch to preheat the electrodes in order to start the arc.

Rapid-start fluorescent lamp: One designed for operation with a ballast that provides for preheating the electrodes and initiating the arc without a starting switch or the application of high voltage.

Recessed: See flush-mounted.

Reflectance of a surface or medium: Ratio of the reflected flux to the incident flux.

Reflected glare: Glare resulting from specular reflections of high luminances in polished or glossy surfaces in the field of view, especially within or in close proximity to the visual task.

Reflection: Process by which the incident flux leaves a surface or medium from the incident side.

Reflector: Device used to redirect the luminous flux from a source by the process of reflection.

Refraction: Process by which the direction of a ray of light changes as it passes obliquely from one medium to another in which its speed is different.

Regressed luminaire: One mounted above the ceiling with the opening of the luminaire above the ceiling line.

Room cavity: Cavity formed by the plane of the luminaires, the work plane, and the wall surfaces between these two planes.

Semidirect lighting: Lighting by luminaires distributing 60 to 90 per cent of their emitted light downward and the balance upward.

Semi-indirect lighting: Lighting by luminaires distributing 60 to 90 per cent of their emitted light upward and the balance downward.

Shade: Screen made of opaque or diffusing material designed to prevent a light source from being directly visible at normal angles of view.

Shielding angle (of a luminaire): Angle between horizontal line through the light center and the line of sight at which the bare source first becomes visible.

Specular surface: One from which the reflection is predominantly regular (specular).

Starter: Device used in conjunction with a ballast for the purpose of starting an electric discharge lamp.

Surface-mounted luminaire: One mounted directly on the ceiling.

Suspended (pendent) luminaire: One hung from a ceiling by supports.

Transmission: Process by which the incident flux leaves a surface or medium on other than the incident side.

Transmittance: Ratio of the transmitted flux to the incident flux.

Troffer: Recessed lighting unit, usually long and installed with the opening flush with the ceiling.

Ultraviolet radiation: Radiant energy within the wavelength range 10 to 380 nanometers, often divided into the following bands:

Ozone-producing	180–220
Bactericidal	
(germicidal)	220–300
Erythemal	280–320
"Black light"	320–400

Valance: Longitudinal shielding member mounted across the top of a window or high on a wall to conceal light sources distributing light both upward and downward.

Veiling luminance: Luminance brightness superimposed on the retinal image which reduces its contrast and results in decreased visual performance and visibility.

Veiling reflection: Regular (specular) reflections superimposed upon diffuse reflections, partially or totally obscuring the details of the task by reducing the

Work plane: The plane at which work is usually done. Unless otherwise indicated, it is assumed to be a horizontal plane 30 in. (760 mm) above the floor.

LIGHT AND THE ENERGY SPECTRUM

Light (visible radiation) is only a small part of the entire radiant energy spectrum, as can be seen in Fig. 2.

VISUAL ENVIRONMENT

Physically, the visual environment is a three-dimensional pattern of brightness and colors visible to a person within the environment. It also includes emotional and esthetic values that are less easily measured but nonetheless important to the design.

The visual field

When a person with a normal seeing apparatus looks at an object with both eyes at the same time, the visual fields of the two eyes intermesh, as illustrated in Fig. 3. The areas seen by the two eyes are not coextensive because a portion of the field of each eye is blocked off by the nose, eyebrow, and cheek. Thus the visual field for both eyes includes more space than the field of either eye. The binocular field is that seen by both eyes simultaneously and is approximately 60 deg in radius.

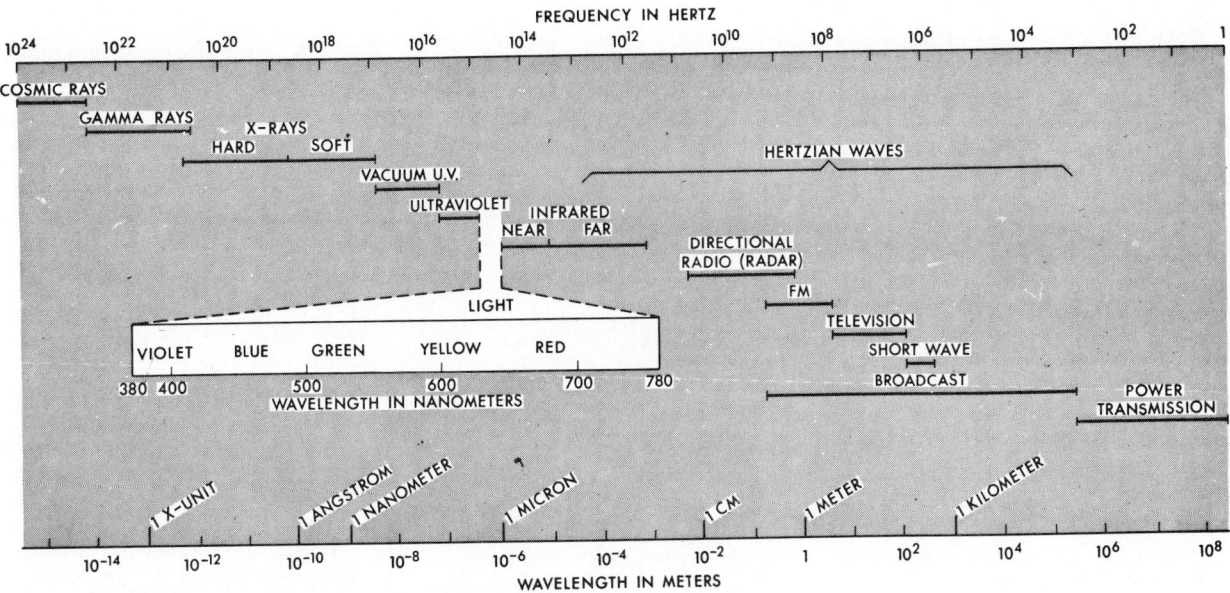

Fig. 2.   The radiant energy (electromagnetic) spectrum

That portion of a person's visual environment which can be detected by his eyes when they are directed along some particular line of sight is referred to as the visual field. Because of the nature and distribution of the photoreceptors in the eye, this visual field divides logically into two concentric regions, the central field and the surround (see Fig. 4).

The central field: The central field is that region of the visual space which extends roughly 1 deg outward from the line of sight, in all directions. Within this region lie the eye's greatest abilities to distinguish fine detail and perceive color. The eyes, the head, and the body of a person attempting to recognize some visual detail are adjusted by both conscious and subconscious adjusting mechanisms to bring the desired visual task into this portion of the visual field.

The surround: The surround is that portion of the visual field which extends outward from the central field to the spatial limits of visual sensation. The abilities to distinguish detail or to perceive color decrease rapidly as the angle with the line of sight increases and are virtually absent beyond 30 deg from the line of sight.

LIGHTING AND VISION

Light is needed for seeing and the amount required for good seeing is greater than that required for mere discernment. The luminance resulting from the amount of light on a task can be controlled more readily and extensively than can the other factors of seeing— contrast, size, and time of viewing. Luminance is therefore used to compensate for deficiencies in the other factors.

FACTORS AFFECTING VISUAL RECOGNITION

Most of the studies of light and vision conducted in the past have dealt with the ability to distinguish detail in the central field on or very near the line of sight. It has been found that the ability to recognize detail in this part of the visual field varies with respect to four physical factors:

1. Contrast between the details of a task and its immediate background
2. Luminance of the task
3. Size of the task
4. Time of viewing

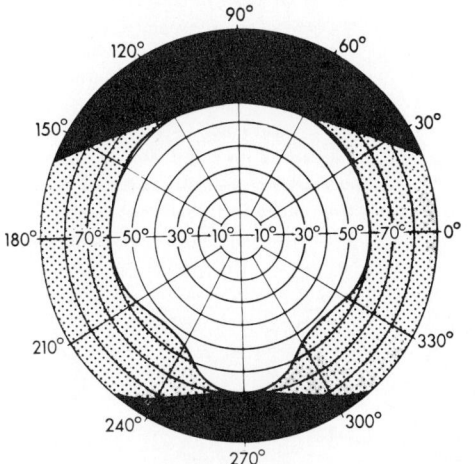

Fig. 3.   The normal field of view of a pair of human eyes. The white central portion represents the region seen by both eyes. The gray portions, right and left, represent the regions seen by the respective eyes alone. The cutoff by the eyebrows, cheeks, and nose is shown by the dark areas

Each factor is sufficiently dependent upon the magnitude of the others that a deficiency in one, within limits, may be compensated by augmenting one or more of the others. Only the factors of contrast, size, and, in certain instances, that of time, are inherent in the task itself.

Contrast: Each critical detail of a seeing task must differ in luminance or color from the surrounding background in order to be seen. Visibility is at a maximum when the luminance contrast (and color contrast if present) of details with the background is greatest. Task contrasts vary widely. For instance, examples of tasks with high con-

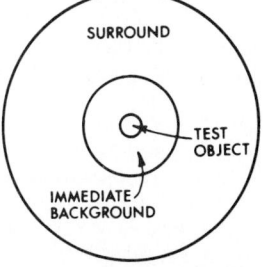

Fig. 4.   A simplified representation of a task, its immediate background, and the surround

Table 1. Recommended luminance ratios*

	Offices	Schools	Industrial Buildings	Homes
1. Between task and adjacent surroundings	1 to 1/3	1 to 1/3	1 to 1/3	1 to 1/10**
2. Between task and more remote darker surfaces	1 to 1/5	1 to 1/3	1 to 1/10	1 to 1/10
3. Between task and more remote lighter surfaces	1 to 5	1 to 5	1 to 10	1 to 10
4. Between fenestration (or luminaires) and adjacent surfaces	20 to 1	....	20 to 1	....
5. Anywhere within the normal field of view	40 to 1	....	40 to 1	....

These ratios are recommended maxima; reductions are generally beneficial.
**For special considerations (tasks of long duration and/or relatively high in luminance) no more than task and not less than 1/3 task.*

Table 2. Recommended reflectance values in per cent

Ceiling	80–90
Walls	40–60
Furniture and equipment	25–45
Floor	20–40

trast are: in schools, black type on white paper; in offices, typed originals with good ribbon; in stores, price tags in ink; and in industry, light stitiching on blue serge cloth. Examples of tasks of poor contrast in similar locations are: spirit-duplicated materials; typed carbon, 5th copy; price tags in pencil; and gray stitching on gray silk.

Size: Within a given range, the larger the task detail, the more easily or accurately seeing is done. It has been found that up to a certain point if the contrast and time

available for seeing are kept constant, the smallest detail which can be detected becomes progressively smaller as the luminance of the visual task is increased.

Time of viewing: Tests have shown that the time required to recognize an object of a given size and background with complete certainty is reduced as the luminance of the background is increased.

Luminance: The luminance of a seeing task is a product of the task reflectance and the quantity of illuminance incident on the task.

QUALITY OF ILLUMINATION

Luminance: Luminance relationships of the various surfaces in the visual area must be kept within recommended limits (Table 1). If there is much difference between task luminance and field luminance, visual acuity is reduced and discomfort is experienced. Under optimum conditions for visual comfort and efficiency, the luminance of the task should be equal to or slightly greater than the luminance of the entire visual environment. The luminance of surfaces immediately adjacent to the visual task is more critical than that of more remote surfaces in the visual surround. Surfaces immediately adjacent to the task should not exceed the luminance of the task and should not be less than one-third the luminance of the task. Daylighting and artificial lighting systems

should conform to the same luminance principles and should be coordinated in design to assure the effective contribution of both.

Glare: If anywhere within the visual field there are brightness conditions that reduce visibility or cause visual discomfort, they are categorically described as glare. Those which are directly associated with the source of lighting and its immediate surroundings are classified as causing *direct glare.* Those directly associated with the visual tasks and their immediate surroundings are considered as contributing to *reflected glare* (Fig. 5).

Direct glare: Unshaded windows are a frequent cause of *direct glare.* They often permit direct view of the sun, bright portions of the sky, and the luminance of adjacent buildings. These often constitute large areas of very high luminance in the usual fields of view. The condition may be controlled by employing shade, blind, louver or baffle systems on windows. (See section on "Daylighting.")

Luminaires which are too bright for the environment in which they are located produce direct glare. The eyes are quite susceptible to glare in the zone from the line of sight, which seldom is higher than horizontal, to about 45 deg above. The shading of luminaires visible below the 45-deg angle is therefore recommended (Fig. 6).

Visual performance: The term "visual performance" is a shorthand phrase to describe the visual components of total human performance of tasks having significant visual components. The visual performance criterion used in the IES method for prescribing illumination is measured by task visibility, since knowledge of this aspect of visual performance is most complete. Physical characteristics of the luminous environment which will influence task visibility may be listed as follows:

1. Level of illuminance, which will interact with task background luminance factors to determine task background luminance

2. Spatial pattern of illuminance reaching the task, plus the plane of polarization and the spectral composition of the illuminance, which will interact with task luminance factors and spectrophotometric characteristics to determine luminance and chromatic con-

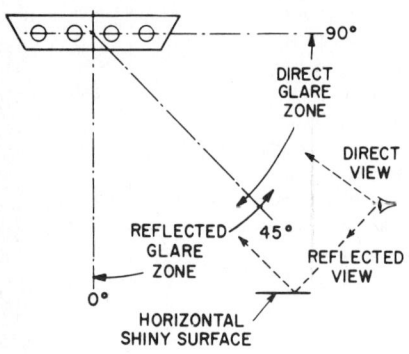

Fig. 5 The direct and reflected glare zones are generally defined as shown by the above diagram

It should be noted that there is no sharp line of demarcation between these zones at 45 deg.

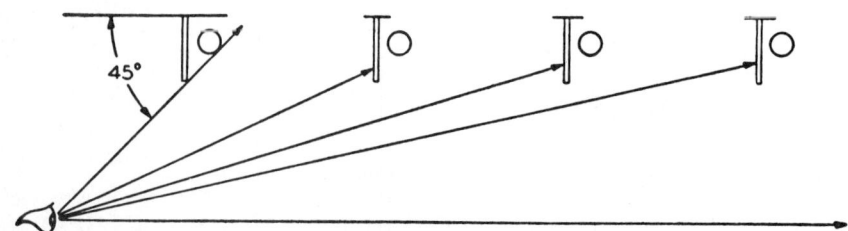

Fig. 6. To protect the eyes in the potential direct glare zone, luminaires should be shielded to about 45 deg, as illustrated

trast of the task detail with respect to the task background

3. Spatial pattern of luminances within the environment relative to task background luminance, which will determine the disability glare and transient adaptation effects

In assessing visual performance potential, the IES method takes quantitative account of task background luminance, the luminance contrast of the task, and the disability glare effect.

Allowance for veiling reflections: The spatial pattern and the plane of polarization of illumination striking the task affect task visibility due to the veiling reflection effect. The effect comes about from light rays which are reflected from the surface of tasks rather than absorbed and reradiated diffusely in the direction of the observer's eye. The result is a reflected luminance veil which reduces task contrast and visibility.

Basis for evaluating visual comfort: The visual comfort of a lighting system depends upon many factors: room size and shape; room surface reflectances; illuminance value; luminaire type, size, and light distribution; number and location of luminaires; luminance of entire field of view; observer location and line of sight; and differences in individual glare sensitivity. Extensive investigations and analyses have resulted in a comprehensive standard discomfort glare evaluation procedure which takes these factors into account. The final product of the evaluation procedure is a visual comfort probability (VCP) rating of the lighting system expressed as a per cent of people who, if seated in the most undesirable location, will be expected to find it acceptable.

Direct glare is reduced and seeing is improved by:

1. *Decreasing the luminance* of the light sources and lighting equipment

2. *Diminishing the area* of potentially glaring high luminances

3. *Increasing the angle* between the glare source and the line of sight

4. *Brightening the surroundings* against which the glare source is seen, but not increasing the surround luminance excessively to a point where the surround becomes a glare source (e.g., an overly bright ceiling with an indirect lighting installation)

Reflected glare: Reflected glare may occur within the visual task itself or in the area immediately surrounding the task. It occurs when shiny surfaces reflect images of bright sources of illumination toward the eye (Figs. 7 and 8). Such reflections in the task itself veil the detail and reduce visibility. Source reflections in shiny surfaces immediately adjacent to the task can be distracting, uncomfortable, and can reduce the ability to see.

A subtle form of reflected glare is some-

times called "veiling reflectance"; here the bright area is indistinct but nevertheless interferes with clear vision and causes real discomfort.

The effects of glare on both visual acuity and comfort are cumulative. Slight glare that may not be noticeable at first will result after continuous exposure in a reduction in visual acuity and an increase in discomfort.

The main controlling factors related to reflected glare are:

1. Degree of specularity (shininess) of task and surround

2. Reflectances of task and surround

3. Direction of light reflected from the task and adjacent area

4. Amount of illuminance contributed by the glare source as compared with the total illuminance on the task and adjacent area

5. Luminance and size of light source

All these factors should be controlled insofar as is practicable to provide the best seeing conditions at the task. To this end the following recommendations should be observed:

1. The task and its background should be matte (nonglossy).

2. The task and its background should have high reflectance, but the reflectance of the background should not exceed that of the task.

3. Locate work surfaces with respect to the fenestration and electric light sources so that the image of the source is reflected away from the observer's eyes.

4. Light sources should be so located that the illuminance on the task comes from several different directions.

5. When it is not possible or practicable to observe any of the above recommendations, special precautions as to fenestration

and luminaire luminance should be observed. Luminaires and fenestration having *maximum* luminances (brightest square inch), in the order of 350 fL (1199 cd/m²) and less, have generally proved satisfactory.

Lighting materials with reference to horizontal tasks may be compared as follows:

Diffusing: At small viewing angles (looking nearly straight down at the task), this

Fig. 7. Reflected glare

A lighting unit positioned at A is an inherent source of reflected glare in the desk top, whereas at B there is little likelihood of its causing this complaint.

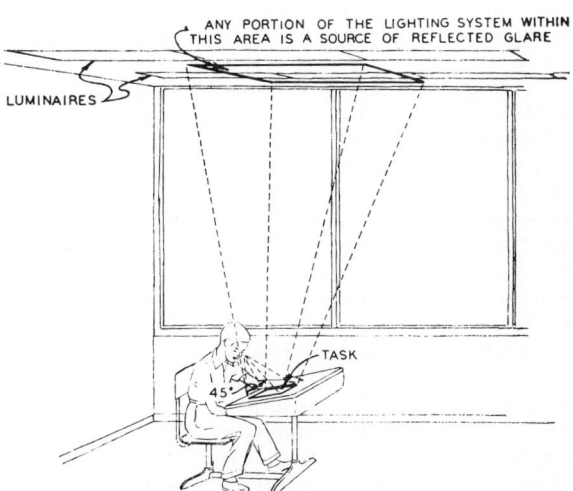

Fig. 8. A method for determining the zone in which potential reflected-glare sources may be located

Quality of illumination; quantity of illuminance; lighting systems

material has the minimum luminance exposed to be reflected in the task. At large viewing angles, it tends to have the highest luminance. This helps reduce veiling reflections but tends to reduce visual comfort per unit area.

Prismatic: A wide range of materials comes under this category, but generally they tend to expose greater flux toward the work for small viewing angles. Many of them have good light control at large viewing angles. Prismatic materials have been designed to produce special flux distributions referred to below.

Louvers: These materials expose the maximum luminance to the work at small viewing angles. They generally have lower luminance at large viewing angles. Translucent louvers have the least control, opaque louvers next, and specular parabolic wedge louvers have the maximum.

Polarizing: Available materials of the flake or layer type have a degree of diffusion that exposes less luminance to the work than prismatic or louver materials. They have less luminance at large angles than diffusing, about the same as prismatic and more than opaque louvers.

Polarization can reduce veiling reflections. The effect is greatest at large viewing angles and least at small viewing angles. For any single ray of light, polarization in a plane perpendicular to the task always tends to reduce veiling reflections.

UNIFORMITY OF ILLUMINANCE

In many places it is energy-inefficient to design a uniform lighting system, but if desirable, uniformity of illuminance is considered satisfactory if the minimum value (between luminaires) is two-thirds or more of the maximum value (under the luminaires). If the minimum value is half of or less than the maximum, perceptible differences in illuminance exist. Most manufacturers publish maximum spacing-to-mounting (or ceiling)-height ratios which should not be exceeded for their luminaires, and data are also available for predicting the daylight distribution from various types of fenestration. In most instances, the distance between luminaires and the wall should not exceed one-half the distance between luminaires; and where desks are along the wall, the distance between luminaires and walls should preferably be 2½ ft (0.69 m) and in no case should exceed one-third the spacing between luminaires. The ends of continuous rows of fluorescent luminaires should preferably be within 6 in. to 1 ft (153 to 305 mm) of the wall and in no case more than 2 ft (0.6 m) from the wall (see Fig. 15).

Shadows: Shadows cast *on the visual task* reduce the luminance of the task and hence impair effective seeing. When sharply defined at or near the task, shadows are annoying.

Shadows will be softened if the light comes from many directions. High-reflectance matte finishes on room surfaces become effective secondary light sources and materially reduce shadows by reflecting a significant amount of diffused light into shadowed areas.

QUANTITY OF ILLUMINANCE

Illumination as a quantity (illuminance) is expressed in footcandles (lux) and is a measure of the light incident on a surface. The light reflected from the surface (i.e., the luminance), the light by which we actually see, is expressed in footlamberts (candelas per square meter). The luminance in footlamberts (cd/m²) of common nonglossy tasks is equal to the illuminance in footcandles (lux) on the surface multiplied by the reflectance of the surface.

The lighting recommendations in the following pages are based on conservative interpretations of presently available data. They are graded according to the difficulty of the visual tasks encountered. These recommendations represent levels that are practical from the standpoints of techniques and economics.

The illuminance values given are target values which should be provided on the visual task, regardless of its location in the room, or other conditions which would reduce the illuminance level. An allowance should be made for such conditions as glare (since no lighting system is completely glare-free) and loss in illuminance through depreciation of luminaires, lamps, and painted surfaces. Even under conditions of good maintenance an average lighting level of from 25 to 35 per cent less than the initial value may be expected under normal operating conditions. With poor maintenance the lighting level may well average less than 50 per cent of the initial value.

In a sharp departure from its previous practice the Illuminating Engineering Society in its 1981 Handbook no longer gives illuminance recommendations in single-number values but rather in ranges of values. These ranges follow those in the 1975 CIE Publication No. 29 by the Commission Internationale d'Eclairage. The ranges are quite wide (e.g., 10–20, 20–50, 50–100) and they generally extend downward from the single-value recommendations previously published by IES which are listed in the later pages of this section. It should be noted that the tables of recommended illuminance values state that the values apply to the task only.

Nothing is said about the means by which the illuminance is provided, whether by general or local lighting.

Another new element in the 1981 IES Handbook is the emphasis on "task-ambient" lighting. The concept of providing a pleasant low level of general lighting along with local task lights (portable lamps) is not new, but because of the need to conserve energy it has been rediscovered and given a new name. Most visual task areas are quite small; in offices the task area is considerably less than the area of the desk top. Task-ambient lighting is most efficient (i.e., most energy-saving) when visual task areas are widely separated. An office, for example, having several task areas, each provided with 50–100 fc (500–1000 lx) might have nonuniform general lighting averaging 20 fc (200 lx). If properly designed, the result can be very pleasant and the visual environment can be excellent for productivity. Task-ambient lighting may not always be the best solution. A school classroom, for example, with perhaps 30 task areas, often movable, would be most simply and efficiently lighted by a uniform general lighting system providing, say 50 fc (500 lx).

ELECTRIC LIGHTING SYSTEMS

Lighting systems can be divided into five classifications: (1) Indirect; (2) Semiindirect; (3) General diffuse (or Direct-indirect); (4) Semidirect; and (5) Direct. They differ principally in the proportion of the light directed upward or downward, as shown in Table 3.

Indirect lighting systems are characterized by relatively low source luminances, good diffusion, freedom from shadows, and low to moderate utilization. On the other hand, utilization is generally good with direct lighting, but the quality of the lighting may be poor unless special precautions are taken. Intermediate systems combine the characteristics of direct and indirect lighting in varying degrees depending upon the predominant component. Indirect lighting systems require matte high-reflectance ceilings

Table 3. Types of lighting systems

Classification	Approximate distribution of light emitted by luminaire	
	Upward	Downward
Indirect	90–100%	10– 0%
Semi-Indirect	60– 90	40–10
General Diffuse	40– 60	60–40
Semi-Direct	10– 40	90–60
Direct	0– 10	100–90

Table 4. Reflecting and transmitting materials

Material	Reflectance or Transmittance (per cent)	Characteristics
Reflecting		
Specular		Provide directional control of light and brightness at specific viewing angles. Effective as efficient reflectors and for special decorative lighting effects.
Mirrored glass	80 to 99	
Metallized plastic	75 to 97	
Processed aluminum	75 to 95	
Polished aluminum	60 to 70	
Chromium	60 to 65	
Stainless steel	55 to 65	
Black structural glass	5	
Spread		General diffuse reflection with a high specular surface reflection of from 5 to 10 per cent of the light.
Processed aluminum (diffuse)	70 to 80	
Etched aluminum	70 to 85	
Satin chromium	50 to 55	
Brushed aluminum	55 to 58	
Aluminum paint	60 to 70	
Diffuse		Diffuse reflection results in uniform surface brightness at all viewing angles. Materials of this type are good reflecting backgrounds for coves and luminous forms.
White plaster	90 to 92	
White paint (matte)	75 to 90	
Porcelain enamel	65 to 90	
White terra-cotta	65 to 80	
White structural glass	75 to 80	
Limestone	35 to 65	
Transmitting		
Glass		
Clear	80 to 90	Low absorption; no diffusion; high concentrated transmission. Used as protective cover plates for concealed light sources.
Configurated, obscure, etched, ground, sandblasted, and frosted	70 to 85	Low absorption; high transmission; poor diffusion. Used only when backed by good diffusing glass or when light sources are placed at edges of panel to light the background.
Opalescent and alabaster	55 to 80	Lower transmission than above glasses; fair diffusion. Used for favorable appearance when indirectly lighted.
Flashed (cased) opal	30 to 65	Low absorption; excellent diffusion. Used for panels of uniform brightness with good efficiency.
Solid opal glass	15 to 40	Higher absorption than flashed opal glass; excellent diffusion. Used in place of flashed opal where a whiter appearance is required.
Plastics		
Clear prismatic lens	70 to 92	Low absorption; no diffusion; high concentrated transmission. Used as shielding for fluorescent luminaires, outdoor signs and luminaires.
White	30 to 70	High absorption; excellent diffusion. Used to diffuse lamp images and provide even appearance in fluorescent luminaires.
Colors	0 to 90	Available in any color for special color rendering lighting requirements or esthetic reasons.
Marble (impregnated)	5 to 30	High absorption; excellent diffusion; used for panels of low brightness. Seldom used in producing general illumination because of the low efficiency.
Alabaster	20 to 50	High absorption; good diffusion. Used for favorable appearance when directly lighted.

that are well maintained. With high values of illuminance the ceiling may become so bright as to be a source of glare. The shadowless light may be unsatisfactory for three-dimensional work. Direct light, on the other hand, may produce disturbing shadows and reflected glare unless the units are of large area or are closely spaced. The use of high-reflectance room and furniture surfaces is essential. Ceiling area lighting, extending essentially from wall to wall, is another form of direct lighting which greatly reduces reflected glare. Light from sources in a large cavity is directed downward, through cellular louvers or translucent diffusing material. Although this system is often used to obtain higher illuminance values, the luminance of the shielding or transmitting medium should be limited to acceptable value.

No one system can be recommended to the exclusion of all others. Each has qualities which may match the requirements for a given situation. Selection should be based on the performance, architectural, and budget requirements of the particular job.

MAINTENANCE OF ILLUMINANCE

In any system the illuminance value will fall below the initial value due to depreciation of lamps luminaires, and other light control elements and room surfaces. In the design stage, as a minimum level, one should select the lowest value which will be tolerated in the final installation. The initial value should be based on this minimum level and maintenance conditions.

The illuminance values depreciate in two ways: first, through the aging of the lamps themselves, and, second, through the collection of dirt, dust, and foreign matter on the luminaires and the reflecting surfaces of the room. The efficiency of some lighting systems is more affected by dirt than others, but all systems will require regular cleaning to ensure efficiency. The reflecting surfaces in a room will also require regular cleaning, especially when these surfaces are expected to supply a large amount of reflected light.

To help reduce the amount of dirt which collects on reflecting and transmitting surfaces, the ventilation system should be considered. With window ventilation dirt is carried about by convection currents and is deposited on reflecting surfaces and luminaires. If the ventilation system is mechanical, involving filtering or cleaning, less dirt will be present to lower the efficiency of the lighting system.

Some reflecting materials have texture characteristics which make them easy to clean. When designing a building, the architect should consider the type of material chosen with respect to the way in which it will be cleaned. For cleaning electric and daylight sources in special rooms such as gymnasiums and auditoriums, installations of catwalks or the use of luminaires having disconnecting hangers may be considered.

LIGHT SOURCES

The most commonly used electric light sources are incandescent, fluorescent, and high-intensity discharge.

Incandescent

Incandescent lamps are available in a wide variety of sizes, shapes, and colors. Some of the commoner types are illustrated in Fig. 9. Bulbs are designated by a letter referring to the shape and a number which is the maximum diameter in eighths of an inch. Thus, R-40 designates a bulb of the R shape which is 4⅝ in. or 5 in. in diameter. Wattages range from 10 to 1,500. The standard ("medium") base is used for lamps of up to 300 watts, and the large ("mogul") base for those of higher wattages; 300-watt lamps are available in both types of base. Incandescent lamps produce from 8 to 22 lumens per watt and have a life of 750 to 4,000 hours. Surface temperatures of the bulbs range from 106 to 588°F (74 to 327°C). Most incandescent bulbs are now inside-frosted, which makes the surface of the bulb the light source, instead of the much smaller and brighter filament.

Some standard-shape bulbs are available with a partial coating of silver for the purpose of concentrating the light in one direction only. More efficient for this purpose, though, are the special inside-silvered reflector lamps, available in spot (concentrated-beam) and flood (wide-beam) types, in sizes from 25 to 300 watts and in several colors. Projector lamps are similar but are of special construction that permits them to be used outdoors, exposed to the weather; they are available in spot or flood types, in sizes from 75 to 150 watts. ER (ellipsoidal reflector) lamps in 50, 75, and 120 watts improve energy utilization in deep, well-shielded downlights.

Another special incandescent lamp is the "three-lite" bulb, available in wattages of 30–70–100, 50–100–150, 50–200–250, and 100–200–300 (mogul base). Another special shape is the tubular lamp, known as "lumiline;" it is 1 in. in diameter and has a disk-type base at each end. Lumiline lamps are available in 30, 40, and 60-watt sizes in various colors.

Fluorescent

The fluorescent lamp is an electric discharge source in which light is produced predominantly by fluorescent powders activated by ultraviolet energy generated by a mercury arc. The lamp, usually in the form of a long tubular bulb with an electrode sealed into each end, contains mercury vapor at low pressure with a small amount of inert gas, principally argon, for starting. The inner walls of the bulb are coated with fluorescent powders commonly called phosphors. When the proper voltage is applied, an "arc" is produced by current flowing between the electrodes through the mercury vapor. This discharge generates some visible radiation, or light, but

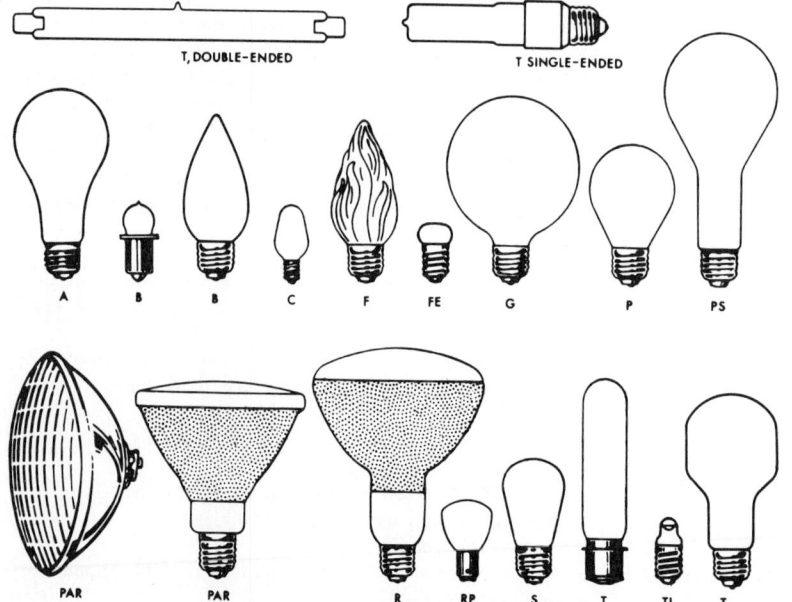

Fig. 9. Typical incandescent bulb shapes and designations (not to scale)

mostly invisible ultraviolet radiation is produced. The ultraviolet in turn excites the phosphors to emit light.

Like most electric discharge lamps, fluorescent lamps must be operated in series with a current limiting device. This auxiliary, commonly called a *ballast*, limits the current to the value for which each lamp is designed. It also provides the required starting and operating lamp voltages.

Fluorescent lamps are tubular light sources which are characterized by higher light efficiencies, cooler operating temperatures, and longer life than incandescent lamps giving the same quanity of illumination. They range in size from 4 watts, 6 in. (150 mm) to 215 watts, 96 in. (2.6 m), and from diameters of ⅜ in. (16 mm) T-5 to 2⅛ in. (54 mm) T-17.

Fluorescent lamps convert 21 per cent of the input energy into light, compared to 8 to 12 per cent for incandescent. Efficacy ranges up to 79 lumens per watt for cool white color. (The most efficient fluorescent lamp is the 96-in. T-12 in cool white.) Rated life ranges from 7,000 to 20,000 hours, based on 3 hours of operation per start. Fewer starts result in longer life; continuous operation almost doubles the life of the lamps.

The ballast is enclosed in a metal box and is usually part of the luminaire.

There are several methods of fluorescent-tube operation in common use:

Preheat: These require starters and take several seconds to light. The starter is a small metal can inserted into the fixture body or channel and is a replaceable part.

Rapid-start: No starter required, but rapid-start tubes and ballasts are needed; they light within one to two seconds.

Preheat-rapid-start: A new universal tube which replaces the former preheat and rapid-start types. This new tube will operate equally well in either preheat or rapid-start fixtures, but with a time delay in fixtures with starters.

Instant start: The "slimline" lamp which requires no starter and lights instantly. Slimline tubes vary in length from 42 to 96 in., have single-pin bases, and come in three diameters: ¾, 1, and 1½ in. They require bulky sockets and larger and heavier ballasts than do the preheat and rapid-start tubes.

Fluorescent tubes are also available in circular shape ("circline") in three sizes: 22 watts, 8¼-in. outside diameter; 32 watts, 12-in. diameter; and 40 watts, 16-in. diameter.

Fluorescent lamps are available in a number of colors and in no less than 14 "whites," ranging from a very cool blue-white to a warm pinkish-white. Listed below are seven of the "whites" with a description of the color characteristics of each.

Improved-color-rendition warm white: Creates a warm atmosphere and blends well with incandescent bulbs. Enhances complexions, foods, and warm tones in furniture, fabrics, and paint.

Improved-color-rendition cool white: Flatters all colors and creates a cool atmosphere. This type gives the most accurate color rendition[1] of all fluorescent tubes, but its cool light is quite different in appearance from the mellow, yellowish light from incandescent bulbs.

Warm white: Blends well with incandescent lighting but somewhat adversely affects both warm and cool colors.

Cool white: Produces a cool atmosphere, but dulls warm colors and intensifies cool colors.

White: Compromise between warm white and cool white; slightly dulls the appearance of warm colors.

Daylight: Very blue-white light, grays complexions, dulls warm colors, and creates a very cold atmosphere.

Soft white: Pinkish-white light that emphasizes reds and pinks but has a tendency to gray cool colors.

Prime color types: There are other white lamps available which radiate energy in several discrete wavelength bands; e.g., blue-violet, green, and red-orange. These provide excellent color rendition and their designs are based on a concept that the human visual system responds to particular color regions.

A variety of fluorescent lamps is also available for specific application purposes such as plant growth, medical therapy, sun tanning, and merchandise enhancement.

Current passing through a ballast produces a low humming sound. Generally this faint sound is not noticeable with even less than average noise levels. Ballast manufacturers publish sound ratings for their different models, but there is no industry standard to compare different brands. Once in a while there is an exceptional case where the room noise level is very low because of isolated surroundings or more than average insulation. In these unusual cases, if the lighting method requires a number of ballasts, it is recommended that they be placed in ventilated metal boxes in a remote location—attic, basement, or closet. Ballasts should be located where they will be easily accessible and where no obstruction of any kind can prevent ventilation or circulation of air around the metal box.

---

[1] *To produce the improved color rendition achieved, about 25 per cent of the light output is sacrificed. Improved-color-rendition tubes should be used only where color appearance is of importance.*

Fluorescent tubes may produce interference (noise) in radio reception, although television reception is not affected. Locating the radio and its aerial at a distance of about 9 ft from fluorescent tubes or installing proper radio interference filters will reduce direct radiation from the tubes.

Energy-saving fluorescent lamps: A line of retrofit lamps is available to operate on standard ballasts in an existing system. Wattage reduction is 10–20 per cent.

Other energy-saving types of lamps include those with a reactive impedance built into the end of the lamps. If used to replace one lamp in a two-lamp series rapid-start circuit, wattage and output of the total system is reduced 33 or 50 per cent depending on the lamp type chosen.

A third option is to use a non-light-producing device to replace one of the two lamps in series circuits. System wattage is then reduced 65 per cent and output 70 per cent.

High-intensity discharge

High-Intensity Discharge Lamps (HID) include the groups of lamps commonly known as mercury, metal halide, and high-pressure sodium lamps. They resemble incandescent lamps in that they provide a point source of light, but they are more closely related to fluorescent lamps since they are electric discharge lamps; ballasts are required and starting requires several minutes.

Mercury lamps: In mercury lamps, light is produced by the passage of an electric current through mercury vapor. Since mercury has a low vapor pressure at room temperature and an even lower one at cold temperatures, a small amount of more readily ionized argon gas is introduced to facilitate starting.

Most mercury lamps are constructed with two envelopes, an inner envelope (arc tube) which contains the arc and an outer envelope which (1) shields the arc tube from outside drafts and changes in temperature, (2) usually contains an inert gas (generally nitrogen) which prevents oxidation of internal parts and also maintains a relatively high breakdown voltage across the outer bulb parts, (3) provides an inner surface for coating of phosphors, and (4) in some cases acts as a filter to remove certain wavelengths of arc radiation. Typical construction details are shown in Fig. 10.

Clear mercury lamps emit greenish-blue light at efficacies of 30 to 65 lumens per watt. While the light source itself appears to be bluish-white, there is an absence of red radiation, especially in the low- and medium-pressure lamps, and most colored objects appear distorted in color rendition. Blue, green, and yellow colors in objects are

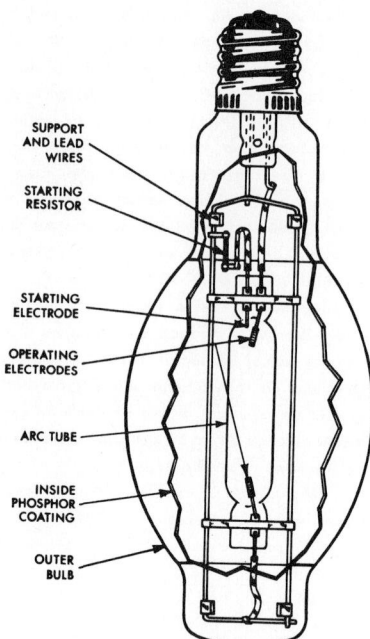

Fig. 10. A 400-watt phosphor-coated mercury lamp. Lamps of other sizes are constructed similarly

Labels: SUPPORT AND LEAD WIRES; STARTING RESISTOR; STARTING ELECTRODE; OPERATING ELECTRODES; ARC TUBE; INSIDE PHOSPHOR COATING; OUTER BULB

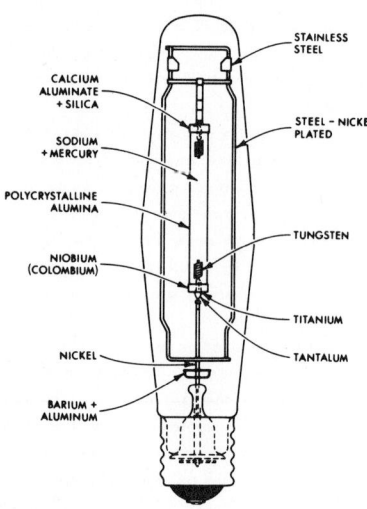

Fig. 11. Construction of a typical high-pressure sodium lamp

Labels: STAINLESS STEEL; CALCIUM ALUMINATE + SILICA; STEEL – NICKEL PLATED; SODIUM + MERCURY; POLYCRYSTALLINE ALUMINA; TUNGSTEN; NIOBIUM (COLOMBIUM); TITANIUM; NICKEL; TANTALUM; BARIUM + ALUMINUM

emphasized; orange and red appear brownish.

Phosphor-coated lamps: A significant portion of the energy radiated by the mercury arc is in the ultraviolet region. Through the use of phosphor coatings on the inside of the outer envelope, some of this ultraviolet energy is converted to visible light by the same mechanism employed in fluorescent lamps. One group of mercury lamps employs a fluorogermanate phosphor which emits most of its energy in the red region. As a result, color rendering is greatly improved over clear mercury types. Through the use of an orthophosphate phosphor, lamp efficacy can be increased above clear lamp values. Although color rendering is improved with this type of lamp as compared with clear mercury lamps, its color rendering properties are not as good as those of the previously mentioned lamp. A third phosphor emitting orange-red radiation, vanadate, improves efficacy and color rendition, rendering skin tones reasonably well.

Mercury lamps have very long-rated lives (16,000 to 24,000 hr) and excellent lumen maintenance.

Metal halide lamps: Metal halide lamps are very similar in construction to the mercury lamp, the major difference being that the arc tube contains various metal halides in addition to mercury.

Compared with mercury lamps, the efficacy of metal halide lamps is greatly superior. Commercially available metal halide lamps have efficacies 1.5 to almost 2 times that of mercury lamps. Almost all varieties of available "white"-light metal halide lamps produce color rendering which is equal to or superior to the presently available phosphor-coated mercury lamps. In addition, metal halide lamps are usually smaller than mercury lamps of similar voltage.

High-pressure sodium lamps: In the high-pressure sodium lamp, light is produced by electricity passing through sodium vapor. This lamp is constructed with two envelopes, the inner being polycrystalline alumina, which has the properties of resistance to sodium attack at high temperature as well as a high melting point and good light transmission (more than 90 per cent) even though this material is translucent. The construction of a typical high-pressure sodium lamp is shown in Fig. 11.

High-pressure sodium lamps radiate energy across the visible spectrum. This is in contrast to the low-pressure sodium lamp, which radiates principally the lines of sodium. The light produced by this lamp is consequently golden-white in color with all visible frequencies present. These lamps have efficacies of about 110 lumens per watt and 24,000 hours of life.

Improved-color high-pressure sodium: By increasing sodium pressure the percentage of red radiation is increased and color rendition improved, making the high-pressure sodium lamp suitable for additional applications both indoors and outdoors. Improved-color lamps do however, have reduced life and efficacy compared to standard sodium.

COMPARISON OF LIGHT SOURCES

The principal characteristics of the commonest types of light source are summarized below and in Table 5.

Incandescent bulbs

1. Provide a point source of light that can be focused or directed over a limited area if desired.

2. Most household bulbs have the same size base, thus lighting from fixtures or lamps can be increased or decreased within certain limits by a change to bulbs of a different wattage.

3. Most types are less expensive to buy than fluorescent tubes. Incandescent luminaires are also generally less expensive; they require no ballast or starter.

Fluorescent tubes

1. Provide a line of light, thus in work areas the light coming from several angles tends to wipe out the shadows. These "lines" of light can also be used over mirrors, kitchen work surfaces, and in window valances, cornices, and coves or other architectural features to provide both useful and decorative illumination.

2. Provide three to four times as much light per watt of electricity as incandescent bulbs, with less heat produced.

3. Will operate about seven to ten times longer than incandescent bulbs before replacement is required.

High-intensity discharge lamps

1. Provide a point source of light of very high intensity.

2. With long-rated lives (especially mercury), excellent lumen maintenance, and high efficacies (especially sodium), high-intensity discharge lamps are often the most economical light source.

LIGHTING DESIGN

The design procedure consists of 18 steps divided into four major groups, as shown in Table 6.

Of the 18 steps, the first three have already been discussed. Item 4 refers to dirt in the atmosphere; five categories have been established, from "very clean" to "very dirty." Step 5 calls for a complete description of the area to be lighted—room dimensions, reflectances, location of work plane, hours of operation, etc. Step 6, selection of luminaire, is based upon steps 1 to 5 and takes into consideration all other factors, including appearance and cost.

Item 7 concerns the ambient temperature

Table 5. Comparison of light sources (Compiled by R. M. Harrold)

Properties/ specifications	Incandescent including tungsten halogen	Fluorescent	High-intensity discharge			Low-pressure sodium
			Mercury-vapor (self-ballasted)	Metal halide	High-pressure sodium (improved color)	
Wattages (lamp only)	15–1,500	15–219	40–1,000	175–1,000	70–1,000	60–180
Life (hours)	750–12,000	7,500–24,000	16,000–24,000	1500–15,000	24,000 (7500)	16,000
Efficacy, lumens per watt (lamp only)	15–25	55–100	50–60 (20–25)	80–100	75–140 (67–112)	Up to 180
Lumen maintenance	Fair to excellent	Fair to excellent	Very good (good)	Good	Excellent	Excellent
Color rendition	Excellent	Good to excellent	Poor to excellent	Very good	Fair (very good)	Poor
Light direction control	Very good to excellent	Fair	Very good	Very good	Very good	Fair
Source size	Compact	Extended	Compact	Compact	Compact	Extended
Relight time	Immediate	Immediate	3–10 minutes	10–20 minutes	Less than 1 minute	Immediate
Comparative fixture cost	Low—simple fixtures	Moderate	Higher than incandescent and fluorescent	Generally higher than mercury	High	High
Comparative operating cost	High—short life and low efficacy	Lower than incandescent	Lower than incandescent	Lower than mercury	Lowest of HID types	Low
Auxiliary equipment needed	Not needed	Needed— medium cost	Needed— high cost	Needed— high cost	Needed— high cost	Needed— high cost

Table 6. Steps in calculating maintained illumination and luminance

A. Objectives and specifications	B. Light loss factors not to be recovered*	C. Light loss factors to be recovered* (Controlled by maintenance procedures)	D. Calculations
1. Seeing task	7. Luminaire ambient temperature	11. Room surface dirt depreciation	15. Total light loss factor
2. Quality required	8. Voltage to luminaire	12. Burnouts	16. Calculations
3. Quantity required	9. Ballast factor	13. Lamp lumen depreciation	17. Layout
4. Area atmosphere	10. Luminaire surface depreciation	14. Luminaire dirt depreciation	18. Review compliance with objectives†
5. Area description and use			
6. Selection of luminaire			

* If losses are too great, reselect luminaire for smaller losses.
† If neither the design objectives nor the budget requirements have been met, the design process should begin again.

within which the luminaires will operate. Variations in temperature, above or below those normally encountered in interiors, have little effect on the light output of incandescent and high-intensity discharge lamps but have considerable effect on the light output of fluorescent luminaires. To variations in voltage (item 8), incandescent lamps are more sensitive than fluorescent, each 1 per cent change in voltage resulting in a 3 per cent change in lumen output.

Fluorescent output changes 1 per cent for each 2½ per cent change in voltage. If the ballast (item 9) is not the correct one for the luminaire, the light output will be affected.

Item 10—Luminaire surface depreciation: Luminaire surface depreciation results from adverse changes in metal, paint, and plastic components which result in reduced light output. Surfaces of glass, porcelain, or processed aluminum have negligible depre-

ciation and can be restored to original reflectance. Baked enamel and other painted surfaces have a permanent depreciation due to all paints being porous to some degree. For plastics, acrylic is least susceptible to change, but its transmittance may be reduced by usage over a period of 15 to 20 years in certain atmospheres. For the same usage, polystyrene will have lower transmittance than acrylic and will depreciate faster.

Item 11—Room surface dirt depreciation: The accumulation of dirt on room surfaces reduces the amount of luminous flux reflected and interreflected to the work plane. To take this into account, Table 7 has been developed to provide room surface dirt depreciation (RSDD) factors for use in calculating maintained average illuminance values. These factors are determined as follows:

1. Find the expected dirt depreciation using the area atmosphere (step 4), the time between cleaning, and the curves in Table 7. For example, if the atmosphere is dirty and room surfaces are cleaned every 24 months, the expected dirt depreciation would be approximately 30 per cent.

2. Knowing the expected dirt depreciation the type of luminaire distribution (step 6), and the room cavity ratio (see Sheet 13), determine the RSDD factor from Table 7. For example, for a dirt depreciation of 30 per cent, a direct luminaire, and a room cavity ratio (RCR) of 4, the RSDD would be 0.92.

Item 12—Burnouts: Lamp burnouts contribute to loss of light. If lamps are not replaced promptly after burnout, the average illuminance value will be decreased proportionately. In some instances, more than just the faulty lamp may be lost. For example, when series sequence fluorescent ballasts are used and one lamp fails, both lamps go out. The lamp burnouts (LBO) factor is the ratio of the lamps remaining lighted to the total for the maximum number of burnouts permitted.

Item 13—Lamp lumen depreciation: Information about lamp lumen depreciation

is available from manufacturers' tables and graphs for lumen depreciation and mortality of the chosen lamp. Rated average life should be determined for the specific hours per start; it should be known when burnouts will begin in the lamp life cycle. From these facts, a practical relamping cycle will be established. Seventy per cent of average rated life is the minimum reached in an installation where burnouts are promptly replaced.

Item 14—Luminaire dirt depreciation: The accumulation of dirt on luminaires results in a loss in light output and therefore a loss on the work plane. This loss is known as the luminaire dirt depreciation (LDD) factor and is determined as follows:

1. The luminaire maintenance category is selected from manufacturers' data or by using Table 9.

2. The atmosphere (one of five degrees of dirt conditions) in which the luminaire will operate is found from step 4.

3. From the appropriate luminaire maintenance category curve of Fig. 12, the applicable dirt condition curve and the proper elapsed time in months of the planned cleaning cycle, the LDD factor is found. For example, if the category is I, the atmosphere dirty, and cleaning every 20 months, LDD is 0.80.

Item 15—Total light loss factor: The total light loss factor is simply the product of multiplying all the contributing factors described above: LLF = Items 7 × 8 × 9 × 10 × 11 × 12 × 13 × 14. Where factors are not known or applicable, they are assumed to be unity. At this point, if it

is found that the total light loss factor is excessive, it may be desirable to reselect the luminaire.

Item 16—Calculations: The lumen method is used in calculating the illuminance that represents the average of all points on the work plane in an interior. It is based on the definition of illuminance as luminous flux per unit area, or:

$$\text{Illuminance} = \frac{\text{luminous flux}}{\text{area}}$$

where luminous flux is expressed in lumens. If the area is in square feet, the illuminance is in footcandles (lumens per square foot). If the area is in square meters, the illuminance is in lux (lumens per square meter).

Because not all the lamp lumens will reach the work plane due to losses in the luminaire and at the room surfaces, they must be multiplied by a coefficient of utilization which represents the portion that reaches the work plane. Thus:

$$\text{Initial illuminance} = \frac{\text{lamp lumens} \times \text{coefficient of utilization}}{\text{area}}$$

Since the design objective is usually the minimum maintained illuminance, factors must be applied to account for the estimated depreciation in lamp lumens, the estimated losses from dirt collection on the luminaire surfaces (including lamps), etc.

The formula thus becomes:

$$\text{Maintained illuminance} = \frac{\text{lamp lumens} \times CU \times LLF}{\text{area}}$$

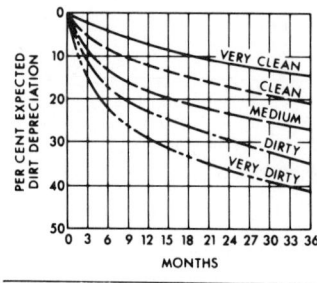

Table 7. Room surface dirt depreciation factors

	Luminaire Distribution Type																			
	Direct				Semi-Direct				Direct-Indirect				Semi-Indirect				Indirect			
Per Cent Expected Dirt Depreciation	10	20	30	40	10	20	30	40	10	20	30	40	10	20	30	40	10	20	30	40
Room Cavity Ratio																				
1	.98	.96	.94	.92	.97	.92	.89	.84	.94	.87	.80	.76	.94	.87	.80	.73	.90	.80	.70	.60
2	.98	.96	.94	.92	.96	.92	.88	.83	.94	.87	.80	.75	.94	.87	.79	.72	.90	.80	.69	.59
3	.98	.95	.93	.90	.96	.91	.87	.82	.94	.86	.79	.74	.94	.86	.78	.71	.90	.79	.68	.58
4	.97	.95	.92	.90	.95	.90	.85	.80	.94	.86	.79	.73	.94	.86	.78	.70	.89	.78	.67	.56
5	.97	.94	.91	.89	.94	.90	.84	.79	.93	.86	.78	.72	.93	.86	.77	.69	.89	.78	.66	.55
6	.97	.94	.91	.88	.94	.89	.83	.78	.93	.85	.78	.71	.93	.85	.76	.68	.89	.77	.66	.54
7	.97	.94	.90	.87	.93	.88	.82	.77	.93	.84	.77	.70	.93	.84	.76	.68	.89	.76	.65	.53
8	.96	.93	.89	.86	.93	.87	.81	.75	.93	.84	.76	.69	.93	.84	.76	.68	.88	.76	.64	.52
9	.96	.92	.88	.85	.93	.87	.80	.74	.93	.84	.76	.68	.93	.84	.75	.67	.88	.75	.63	.51
10	.96	.92	.87	.83	.93	.86	.79	.72	.93	.84	.75	.67	.92	.83	.75	.67	.88	.75	.62	.50

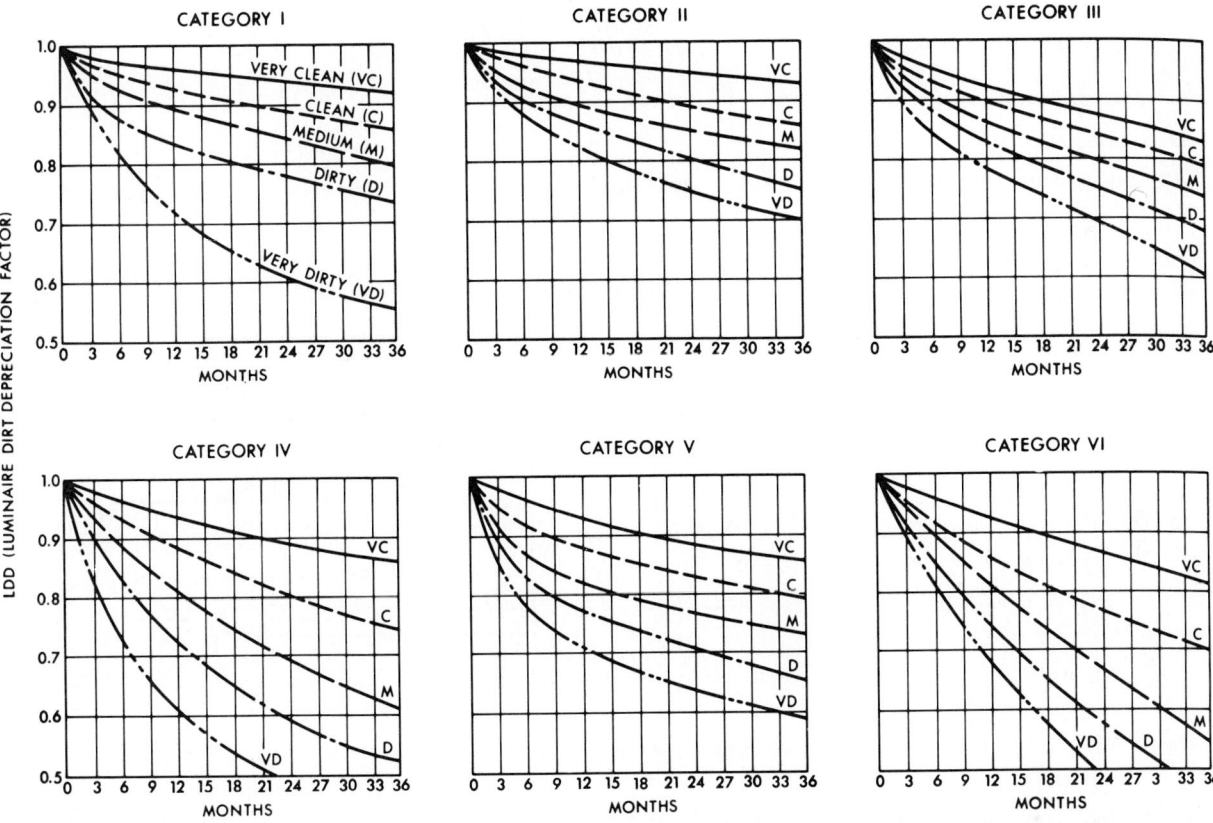

Fig. 12. Luminaire dirt depreciation factors (LDD) for six luminaire categories (I to VI) and for five degrees of dirtiness as determined from step 4

where CU = coefficient of utilization

LLF = light loss factor

The lamp lumens in the formula are most conveniently taken as the total rated lamp lumens in the luminaire, and the area then becomes the area per luminaire. Thus:

$$\text{Maintained illuminance} = \frac{\text{lamp lumens per luminaire} \times \text{CU} \times \text{LLF}}{\text{area per luminaire}}$$

or, if the desired illuminance is known, the area per luminaire (and hence the spacing between luminaires) to produce this illumination may be obtained by:

$$\text{Area per luminaire} = \frac{\text{lamp lumens per luminaire} \times \text{CU} \times \text{LLF}}{\text{maintained illuminance}}$$

A lighting system can be designed with spacings between units to approximate this area, but if the total number of luminaires is also desired, then:

$$\frac{\text{Total number of luminaires}}{} = \frac{\text{total room area}}{\text{area per luminaire}}$$

For a typical form for calculating illuminance, see Fig. 14.

Cavity ratios: in the zonal-cavity method, the effects of room proportions, luminaire suspension length, and work-plane height upon the coefficient of utilization are respec-

tively accounted for by the *room cavity ratio, ceiling cavity ratio,* and *floor cavity ratio.* These ratios are determined by dividing the room into three cavities as shown by Fig. 13 and substituting dimensions (in feet or meters) in the following formula:

$$\text{Cavity ratio} = \frac{5h\,(\text{room length} + \text{room width})}{(\text{room length}) \times (\text{room width})}$$

where h = height of cavity

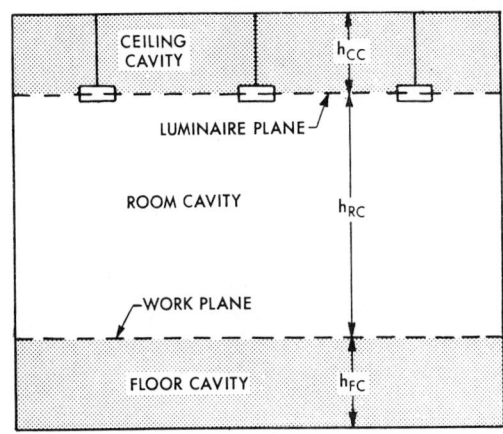

Fig. 13. The three cavities used in the zonal-cavity method

Luminaire coefficients of utilization: Absorption of light in a luminaire is accounted for in the computation of coefficients of utilization (CU) for that particular luminaire. Table 8 is a tabulation of coefficients of utilization calculated by the zonal-cavity method for representative luminaire types. These coefficients are for an effective floor cavity reflectance of 20 per cent. (continued on p. 4-285.)

GENERAL INFORMATION

Project identification:_____

(Give name of area and/or building and room number)

Average maintained illuminance for design:___footcandles   Lamp data:

Luminaire data:

    Type and color:_____

  Manufacturer:_____

    Number per luminaire:_____

  Catalog number:_____

    Total lumens per luminaire:_____

SELECTION OF COEFFICIENT OF UTILIZATION

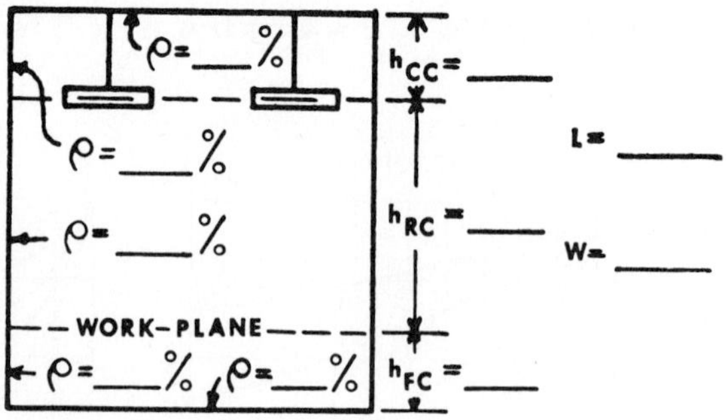

Step 1: Fill in sketch at right.

Step 2: Determine Cavity Ratios by use of formula.

    Room Cavity Ratio, RCR = _____

    Ceiling Cavity Ratio, CCR = _____

    Floor Cavity Ratio,   FCR = _____

Step 3: Obtain Effective Ceiling Cavity Reflectance (ρ_{CC}) from **Table 8**.

ρ_{CC} = _____

Step 4: Obtain Effective Floor Cavity Reflectance (ρ_{FC}) from **Table 8**.

ρ_{FC} = _____

Step 5: Obtain Coefficient of Utilization (CU) from Manufacturer's Data **or** from Table 9.

CU = _____

SELECTION OF LIGHT LOSS FACTORS

Unrecoverable		Recoverable	
Luminaire ambient temperature		Room surface dirt depreciation RSDD	_____
	_____		
Voltage to luminaire		Lamp lumen depreciation LLD	_____
	_____		
Ballast factor		Lamp burnouts factor LBO	_____
	_____		
Luminaire surface depreciation		Luminaire dirt depreciation LDD	_____
	_____		

Total light loss factor, LLF (product of individual factors above): ___

CALCULATIONS

(Average Maintained Illuminance)

$$\text{Number of Luminaires} = \frac{(\text{Illuminance}) \times (\text{Area})}{(\text{Lumens per Luminaire}) \times (\text{CU}) \times (\text{LLF})}$$

$$= \frac{\rule{4cm}{0.4pt}}{\rule{4cm}{0.4pt}} =$$

$$\text{Footcandles (lux)} = \frac{(\text{Number of Luminaires}) \times (\text{Lumens per Luminaire}) \times (\text{CU}) \times (\text{LLF})}{(\text{Area})}$$

$$= \frac{\rule{4cm}{0.4pt}}{\rule{4cm}{0.4pt}} =$$

Calculated by:_____ Date:_____

Fig. 14. Average illuminance calculation sheet

Since the light loss factor includes the effect of dirt depositing on wall surfaces, the selection of the proper column of wall reflectances, ρ_W, should be based upon the initial values expected. The wall reflectance should also represent the weighted average of the painted areas, glass fenestration or daylight controls, chalkboards, shelves, etc., in the area to be lighted. The weighting should be based on the relative areas of each type of surface.

Effective cavity reflectances: **Table 9** provides a means of converting the combination of wall and ceiling or wall and floor reflectances into a single *effective ceiling cavity reflectance*, ρ_{CC}, and a single effective floor cavity reflectance, ρ_{FC}. In calculations, ceiling, wall, and floor reflectances should be initial values. The RSDD factor compensates for the decrease of reflectance with time. Note that of surface-mounted and recessed luminaires, CCR = 0, and the ceiling reflectance may be used as ρ_{CC}.

Luminance

Average luminance of walls or ceilings can be calculated by using the luminance coefficients given in the *IES Lighting Handbook* in the following equation:

Average initial wall (or ceiling cavity) luminance in footlamberts (cd/m²)

$$= \frac{\substack{\text{total bare lamp lumens} \\ \times \text{ wall (or ceiling cavity)} \\ \text{luminance coefficient}}}{\text{floor area}}$$

Item 17—Luminaire layout: In making a luminaire layout, the task, quality requirements, the area, the type and distribution of the luminaire, the requirements for uniformity of illuminance, and appearance have to be considered. In most instances, the visual task is likely to be located (or relocated) at any point in the room being lighted. It follows, therefore, that the illuminance at any point should not differ materially from the calculated average. Illuminance uniformity is generally not feasible, but uniformity is considered acceptable if the maximum and minimum values in the room are not more than one-sixth above and below the average.

To achieve acceptable uniformity, luminaires should not be spaced too far apart or too far from the walls. Spacing limitations between luminaires are related to the intensity distribution of the luminaires, placement of the luminaires within the room, and the reflectances of the room surfaces. The principal factor for direct, semi-direct, and general diffuse luminaires is the mounting height above the work plane; for semi-indirect and indirect luminaires, it is the ceiling height above the workplane.

A guide for the maximum spacing-to-mounting height (S/MH) ratio of 25 generic types of luminaire is given in Table 9. The maximum S/MH ratio often quoted for luminaires is based on the comparison of a point directly under one luminaire with a point halfway between adjacent luminaires, considering only the effect of the two adjacent luminaires.

Since desks and benches are frequently located along the walls, a distance of 2½ ft (760 mm) from the wall to the center of the luminaire should be employed to avoid excessive drop-off in illumination. This will locate the luminaires over the edge of desks facing the wall or over the center of desks that are perpendicular to the wall (see Fig. 15b). To further improve illumination uniformity across the room, it is often desirable to use somewhat closer spacings between outer rows of luminaires than between central rows, taking care to be sure that no spacing exceeds the maximum permissible spacing.

To prevent excessive reduction in illuminance at the ends of the room, the ends of fluorescent luminaire rows should preferably be 6 to 12 in. (150-300 mm) from the walls, or in no case more than 2 ft (610 mm) from the walls. The arrangement shown in Fig. 15c is much more satisfactory. This technique not only improves uniformity but also eliminates scallops of light on the end walls and provides a uniform wash of light on all four walls.

Another excellent method of compensating for the normal reduction in illuminance that may be expected at the ends of rows is to use a greater number of lamps in the end units. Still another technique is to provide additional units between the rows at each end. The units could be either parallel or at right angles to the rows.

1. For individually mounted luminaires, the wall-to-luminaire spacing should be:

Wall-to-luminaire spacing

$$= \frac{\text{luminaire-to-luminaire spacing}}{3}$$

2. For individual units or crosswise spacing of continuous rows:

Minimum number of rows

$$= \frac{\text{room width}}{\substack{\text{maximum spacing} \\ \text{allowed}}}$$

3. For lengthwise spacing in continuous rows:

Maximum number of units per row

$$= \frac{\text{room length} - 1}{\text{luminaire length}}$$

(allows ½ ft (150 mm) end spacing)

Minimum number of units per row

$$= \frac{\text{room length} - 4}{\text{luminaire length}}$$

[allows 2 ft (610 mm) end spacing]

Item 18—Review for compliance with objectives: The final step in the design procedure is to review the solution to determine that the objectives for quantity and quality of illuminance have been met and that the solution meets the budget requirements. If not, the design process should begin again.

It should be recognized that if the completed lighting installation is not maintained (cleaned, relamped, etc.) in accordance with the assumptions used in arriving at the light loss factors, the illuminance value will not be as calculated. It is therefore important that the designer inform the user of the facts used in the design.

Quantity of light

Target values of illuminance are given on the following pages. While for convenience of use this table sometimes lists locations rather than tasks, the recommended footcandle (lux) values have been arrived at for specific visual tasks. The tasks selected for this purpose have been the more difficult ones which commonly occur in the various areas.

In order to assure these values at all times, higher initial levels should be provided as required by the maintenance conditions.

Illuminances shown in the table are intended to be minimum on the task irrespective of the plane in which it is located. Some visual tasks are on slanting or vertical surfaces where illumination is only one-half to one-third of that on a horizontal plane. Compensation should be made for such tasks and for work locations at the sides of a room where illumination is usually less than in the center.

Supplementary luminaires may be used in combination with general lighting to achieve these levels. The general lighting should be not less than 20 footcandles (200 lux) and should contribute at least one-tenth the total illuminance value.

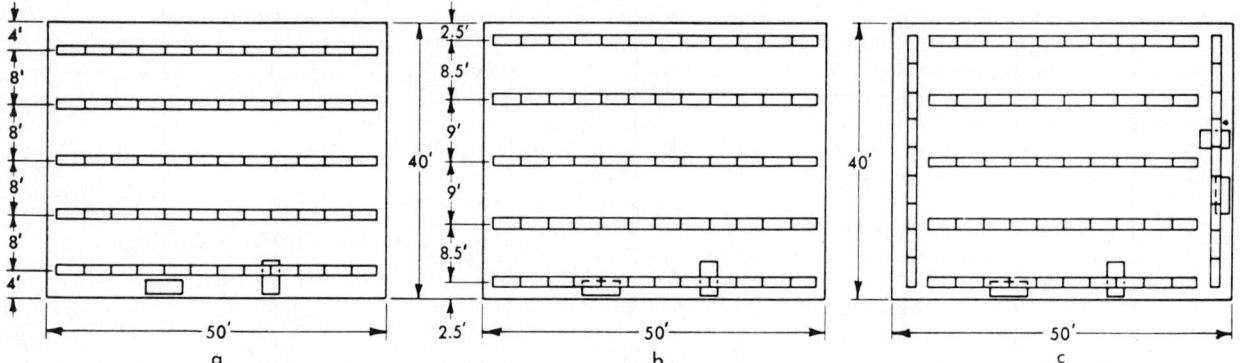

Fig. 15. (a) Lighting layout using equal spacing between continuous rows of luminaires. (b) Layout is changed to provide more illumination near side walls. (c) By adding four more 4-ft (1220 mm) units on each end, layout (b) can be modified to provide 80 per cent more light near the end walls and prevent possible scallop effects

Table 8. Coefficients of utilization and other data for typical luminaires

Typical Luminaire	Typical Distribution and Per Cent Lamp Lumens		ρcc →	80			70			50			30			10			0
			ρw →	50	30	10	50	30	10	50	30	10	50	30	10	50	30	10	0
	Maint. Cat.	Maximum S/MH Guide	RCR ↓	Coefficients of Utilization for 20 Per Cent Effective Floor Cavity Reflectance (ρFC = 20)															
Pendant diffusing sphere with incandescent lamp (V, 35½% ↑, 45% ↓)	V	1.5	0	.87	.87	.87	.81	.81	.81	.69	.69	.69	.59	.59	.59	.49	.49	.49	.44
			1	.71	.67	.63	.66	.62	.59	.56	.53	.50	.47	.45	.43	.39	.37	.35	.31
			2	.61	.54	.49	.56	.50	.46	.47	.43	.39	.39	.36	.33	.32	.29	.27	.23
			3	.52	.45	.39	.48	.42	.37	.41	.36	.31	.34	.30	.26	.27	.24	.22	.18
			4	.46	.38	.33	.42	.36	.30	.36	.30	.26	.30	.26	.22	.24	.21	.18	.15
			5	.40	.33	.27	.37	.30	.25	.32	.26	.22	.26	.22	.19	.21	.18	.15	.12
			6	.36	.28	.23	.33	.26	.21	.28	.23	.19	.23	.19	.16	.19	.15	.13	.10
			7	.32	.25	.20	.29	.23	.18	.25	.20	.16	.21	.16	.13	.17	.13	.11	.09
			8	.29	.22	.17	.27	.20	.16	.23	.17	.14	.19	.15	.12	.15	.12	.09	.07
			9	.26	.19	.15	.24	.18	.14	.20	.15	.12	.17	.13	.10	.14	.11	.08	.06
			10	.23	.17	.13	.22	.16	.12	.19	.14	.10	.16	.12	.09	.13	.09	.07	.05
Concentric-ring unit with incandescent silvered-bowl lamp (II, 83% ↑, 3½% ↓)	II	1.5	0	.83	.83	.83	.71	.71	.71	.49	.49	.49	.30	.30	.30	.12	.12	.12	.03
			1	.72	.69	.66	.62	.60	.57	.43	.42	.40	.26	.25	.25	.10	.10	.10	.03
			2	.63	.58	.54	.54	.50	.47	.38	.36	.33	.23	.22	.21	.09	.09	.08	.02
			3	.55	.49	.45	.48	.43	.39	.33	.30	.28	.20	.19	.17	.08	.08	.07	.02
			4	.48	.42	.37	.42	.37	.33	.29	.26	.24	.18	.16	.15	.07	.07	.06	.02
			5	.43	.36	.32	.37	.32	.28	.26	.23	.20	.16	.14	.13	.06	.06	.05	.01
			6	.38	.32	.27	.33	.28	.24	.23	.20	.17	.14	.12	.11	.06	.05	.04	.01
			7	.34	.28	.23	.30	.24	.21	.21	.17	.15	.13	.11	.09	.05	.04	.04	.01
			8	.31	.25	.20	.27	.21	.18	.19	.15	.13	.12	.10	.08	.05	.04	.03	.01
			9	.28	.22	.18	.24	.19	.16	.17	.14	.11	.10	.09	.07	.04	.03	.03	.01
			10	.25	.20	.16	.22	.17	.14	.16	.12	.10	.10	.08	.06	.04	.03	.03	.01
Porcelain-enameled ventilated standard dome with incandescent lamp (IV, 0% ↑, 83½% ↓)	IV	1.3	0	.99	.99	.99	.97	.97	.97	.92	.92	.92	.88	.88	.88	.85	.85	.85	.83
			1	.88	.85	.82	.86	.83	.81	.83	.80	.78	.79	.78	.76	.77	.75	.73	.72
			2	.78	.73	.68	.76	.72	.67	.73	.69	.66	.71	.67	.64	.68	.65	.63	.61
			3	.69	.62	.57	.67	.61	.57	.65	.60	.56	.63	.58	.55	.61	.57	.54	.52
			4	.61	.54	.49	.60	.53	.48	.58	.52	.48	.56	.51	.47	.54	.50	.46	.45
			5	.54	.47	.41	.53	.46	.41	.51	.45	.41	.50	.44	.40	.48	.43	.40	.38
			6	.48	.41	.35	.47	.40	.35	.46	.39	.35	.44	.39	.34	.43	.38	.34	.32
			7	.43	.35	.30	.42	.35	.30	.41	.34	.30	.39	.34	.30	.38	.33	.29	.28
			8	.38	.31	.26	.38	.31	.26	.37	.30	.26	.36	.30	.26	.35	.30	.26	.24
			9	.35	.28	.23	.34	.27	.23	.33	.27	.23	.32	.27	.23	.31	.26	.22	.21
			10	.31	.25	.20	.31	.24	.20	.30	.24	.20	.29	.24	.20	.29	.23	.20	.18
Prismatic square surface drum (V, 18½% ↑, 60½% ↓)	V	1.3	0	.89	.89	.89	.85	.85	.85	.77	.77	.77	.70	.70	.70	.63	.63	.63	.60
			1	.78	.75	.72	.74	.72	.69	.68	.66	.64	.62	.60	.58	.56	.55	.54	.51
			2	.69	.65	.61	.66	.62	.58	.61	.57	.54	.56	.53	.50	.51	.49	.47	.44
			3	.62	.57	.52	.60	.55	.50	.55	.51	.47	.50	.47	.44	.46	.44	.41	.39
			4	.56	.50	.46	.54	.49	.44	.50	.45	.42	.46	.42	.39	.42	.39	.37	.35
			5	.51	.45	.40	.49	.43	.39	.45	.41	.37	.42	.38	.35	.39	.36	.33	.31
			6	.46	.40	.36	.45	.39	.35	.42	.37	.33	.39	.35	.31	.36	.32	.30	.28
			7	.42	.36	.32	.41	.35	.31	.38	.33	.29	.35	.31	.28	.33	.29	.27	.25
			8	.39	.32	.28	.37	.32	.28	.35	.30	.26	.32	.28	.25	.30	.27	.24	.22
			9	.35	.29	.25	.34	.29	.25	.32	.27	.24	.30	.26	.23	.28	.24	.22	.20
			10	.32	.27	.23	.31	.26	.22	.29	.25	.21	.27	.23	.20	.26	.22	.20	.18
R-40 flood without shielding (IV, 0% ↑, 100% ↓)	IV	0.8	0	1.18	1.18	1.18	1.16	1.16	1.16	1.11	1.11	1.11	1.06	1.06	1.06	1.01	1.01	1.01	.99
			1	1.09	1.07	1.04	1.07	1.05	1.02	1.03	1.01	.99	.99	.98	.96	.96	.95	.94	.92
			2	1.01	.97	.93	.99	.95	.92	.96	.93	.90	.93	.90	.88	.90	.88	.86	.84
			3	.93	.88	.84	.92	.87	.83	.89	.85	.81	.87	.83	.80	.84	.82	.79	.77
			4	.87	.81	.76	.85	.80	.75	.83	.78	.75	.81	.77	.74	.79	.76	.73	.71
			5	.80	.74	.69	.79	.73	.69	.77	.72	.68	.76	.71	.67	.74	.70	.67	.65
			6	.74	.68	.63	.73	.67	.63	.72	.66	.62	.70	.66	.62	.69	.65	.61	.60
			7	.69	.62	.57	.68	.62	.57	.67	.61	.57	.65	.60	.56	.64	.60	.56	.55
			8	.64	.57	.53	.63	.57	.52	.62	.56	.52	.61	.56	.52	.60	.55	.52	.50
			9	.59	.52	.48	.59	.52	.48	.58	.52	.48	.57	.51	.48	.56	.51	.47	.46
			10	.55	.49	.44	.55	.48	.44	.54	.48	.44	.53	.48	.44	.52	.47	.44	.42

ª ρcc = per cent effective ceiling cavity reflectance.
b ρw = per cent wall reflectance.
c RCR = Room Cavity Ratio.
d Maximum *S/MH* guide—ratio of maximum luminaire spacing to mounting or ceiling height above work-plane.

Table 8 (cont.). Coefficients of utilization and other data for typical luminaires

Typical Luminaire	Maint. Cat.	Maximum S/MH Guide[d]	Dist. & % Lamp Lumens	RCR[c]	ρcc→ 80 ρw 50	30	10	70 50	30	10	50 50	30	10	30 50	30	10	10 50	30	10	0
R-40 flood with specular anodized reflector skirt; 45° cutoff	IV	0.7	0%↑ 85%↓	0	1.00	1.00	1.00	.98	.98	.98	.94	.94	.94	.90	.90	.90	.86	.86	.86	.84
				1	.96	.94	.92	.94	.92	.91	.90	.89	.88	.87	.86	.85	.84	.84	.83	.82
				2	.91	.88	.86	.90	.87	.85	.87	.85	.83	.84	.83	.82	.82	.81	.80	.79
				3	.87	.84	.81	.86	.83	.81	.84	.81	.79	.82	.80	.78	.80	.78	.77	.76
				4	.83	.80	.77	.82	.79	.77	.81	.78	.76	.79	.77	.75	.78	.76	.74	.73
				5	.79	.76	.73	.79	.75	.73	.77	.74	.72	.76	.73	.71	.75	.73	.71	.70
				6	.76	.73	.70	.76	.72	.70	.75	.72	.69	.74	.71	.69	.73	.70	.68	.67
				7	.73	.69	.66	.73	.69	.66	.72	.68	.66	.71	.68	.66	.70	.67	.65	.64
				8	.70	.66	.63	.70	.66	.63	.69	.65	.63	.68	.65	.63	.67	.65	.63	.62
				9	.67	.63	.60	.67	.63	.60	.66	.62	.60	.65	.62	.60	.65	.62	.60	.59
				10	.64	.60	.58	.64	.60	.58	.63	.60	.58	.63	.60	.57	.62	.59	.57	.56
Reflector downlight with baffles and inside frosted lamp	IV	0.7	0%↑ 44½%↓	0	.53	.53	.53	.52	.52	.52	.49	.49	.49	.47	.47	.47	.45	.45	.45	.44
				1	.51	.50	.49	.50	.49	.48	.48	.47	.47	.46	.46	.45	.45	.44	.44	.43
				2	.48	.47	.46	.48	.46	.45	.46	.45	.44	.45	.44	.44	.44	.43	.43	.42
				3	.47	.45	.44	.46	.45	.43	.45	.44	.43	.44	.43	.42	.43	.42	.41	.41
				4	.45	.43	.42	.44	.43	.42	.43	.42	.41	.43	.41	.41	.42	.41	.40	.40
				5	.43	.41	.40	.43	.41	.40	.42	.40	.39	.41	.40	.39	.41	.40	.39	.38
				6	.42	.40	.39	.41	.40	.38	.41	.39	.38	.40	.39	.38	.40	.39	.38	.37
				7	.40	.38	.37	.40	.38	.37	.39	.38	.37	.39	.38	.37	.38	.37	.36	.36
				8	.39	.37	.36	.38	.37	.36	.38	.37	.35	.38	.36	.35	.37	.36	.35	.35
				9	.37	.36	.34	.37	.35	.34	.37	.35	.34	.36	.35	.34	.36	.35	.34	.33
				10	.36	.34	.33	.36	.34	.33	.36	.34	.33	.35	.34	.33	.35	.34	.33	.32
Wide-distribution unit with lens plate and inside frost lamp	V	1.4	0%↑ 53½%↓	0	.63	.63	.63	.62	.62	.62	.59	.59	.59	.56	.56	.56	.54	.54	.54	.53
				1	.58	.56	.54	.57	.55	.54	.54	.53	.52	.52	.51	.50	.50	.50	.49	.48
				2	.53	.50	.48	.52	.49	.47	.50	.48	.46	.48	.47	.45	.47	.45	.44	.43
				3	.48	.45	.42	.47	.44	.42	.46	.43	.41	.44	.42	.40	.43	.41	.40	.39
				4	.44	.40	.37	.43	.40	.37	.42	.39	.37	.41	.38	.36	.40	.38	.36	.35
				5	.40	.36	.33	.39	.36	.33	.38	.35	.33	.37	.35	.32	.36	.34	.32	.31
				6	.36	.32	.30	.36	.32	.29	.35	.32	.29	.34	.31	.29	.33	.31	.29	.28
				7	.33	.29	.26	.33	.29	.26	.32	.28	.26	.31	.28	.26	.30	.28	.26	.25
				8	.30	.26	.23	.30	.26	.23	.29	.26	.23	.28	.25	.23	.28	.25	.23	.22
				9	.27	.23	.21	.27	.23	.21	.26	.23	.21	.26	.23	.20	.25	.22	.20	.19
				10	.25	.21	.18	.25	.21	.18	.24	.21	.18	.24	.20	.18	.23	.20	.18	.17
Recessed unit with dropped diffusing glass	V	1.3	1½%↑ 50½%↓	0	.61	.61	.61	.60	.60	.60	.57	.57	.57	.54	.54	.54	.51	.51	.51	.50
				1	.53	.51	.48	.52	.50	.47	.49	.47	.46	.47	.45	.44	.45	.44	.42	.41
				2	.46	.42	.39	.45	.42	.39	.43	.40	.38	.41	.39	.37	.39	.37	.35	.34
				3	.40	.36	.33	.40	.35	.32	.38	.34	.31	.36	.33	.31	.35	.32	.30	.29
				4	.36	.31	.28	.35	.31	.28	.34	.30	.27	.32	.29	.26	.31	.28	.26	.25
				5	.32	.27	.24	.31	.27	.24	.30	.26	.23	.29	.25	.23	.28	.25	.22	.21
				6	.29	.24	.20	.28	.24	.20	.27	.23	.20	.26	.22	.20	.25	.22	.19	.18
				7	.26	.21	.18	.25	.21	.18	.24	.20	.17	.23	.20	.17	.22	.19	.17	.16
				8	.23	.19	.16	.23	.18	.15	.22	.18	.15	.21	.18	.15	.20	.17	.15	.14
				9	.21	.17	.14	.21	.16	.14	.20	.16	.13	.19	.16	.13	.19	.15	.13	.12
				10	.19	.15	.12	.19	.15	.12	.18	.14	.12	.18	.14	.12	.17	.14	.12	.11
Intermediate-distribution ventilated reflector with clear HID lamp	III	1.0	1%↑ 76%↓	0	.91	.91	.91	.89	.89	.89	.84	.84	.84	.81	.81	.81	.77	.77	.77	.75
				1	.84	.81	.79	.82	.80	.78	.79	.77	.76	.76	.74	.73	.73	.72	.71	.69
				2	.77	.73	.70	.76	.72	.70	.73	.70	.68	.70	.68	.66	.68	.66	.65	.63
				3	.71	.66	.63	.69	.65	.62	.67	.64	.61	.65	.62	.60	.63	.61	.59	.57
				4	.65	.60	.56	.64	.59	.56	.62	.58	.55	.60	.57	.54	.59	.56	.54	.52
				5	.59	.54	.50	.59	.54	.50	.57	.53	.50	.56	.52	.49	.54	.51	.48	.47
				6	.54	.49	.45	.54	.49	.45	.52	.48	.45	.51	.47	.44	.50	.47	.44	.42
				7	.50	.44	.40	.49	.44	.40	.48	.43	.40	.47	.43	.39	.46	.42	.39	.38
				8	.45	.40	.36	.45	.40	.36	.44	.39	.36	.43	.39	.35	.42	.38	.35	.34
				9	.41	.36	.32	.41	.36	.32	.40	.35	.32	.39	.35	.32	.38	.35	.32	.30
				10	.38	.33	.29	.37	.32	.29	.37	.32	.29	.36	.32	.29	.35	.31	.28	.27

Coefficients of Utilization for 20 Per Cent Effective Floor Cavity Reflectance (ρFC = 20)

[a] ρcc = per cent effective ceiling cavity reflectance.
[b] ρw = per cent wall reflectance.
[c] RCR = Room Cavity Ratio.
[d] Maximum S/MH guide—ratio of maximum luminaire spacing to mounting or ceiling height above work-plane.

Table 8 (cont.). Coefficients of utilization and other data for typical luminaires

Typical Luminaire	Maint. Cat.	Maximum S/MH Guide[d]	RCR[c] ↓	ρcc→ 80			70			50			30			10			0
				ρw→ 50	30	10	50	30	10	50	30	10	50	30	10	50	30	10	0
				Coefficients of Utilization for 20 Per Cent Effective Floor Cavity Reflectance (ρFC = 20)															
Intermediate-distribution ventilated reflector with phosphor-coated (HID) lamp (6½% ↑, 75½% ↓)	III	1.0	0	.96	.96	.96	.93	.93	.93	.87	.87	.87	.82	.82	.82	.77	.77	.77	.75
			1	.89	.87	.84	.86	.84	.83	.82	.80	.79	.78	.76	.75	.74	.73	.72	.70
			2	.82	.79	.76	.80	.77	.74	.76	.74	.72	.73	.71	.69	.70	.68	.67	.65
			3	.76	.72	.68	.74	.70	.67	.71	.68	.65	.68	.66	.63	.66	.63	.61	.60
			4	.70	.66	.62	.69	.65	.61	.66	.63	.60	.64	.61	.58	.62	.59	.57	.55
			5	.65	.60	.56	.64	.59	.56	.62	.58	.54	.60	.56	.53	.58	.55	.52	.51
			6	.60	.55	.51	.59	.55	.51	.57	.53	.50	.56	.52	.49	.54	.51	.48	.47
			7	.56	.51	.47	.55	.50	.46	.53	.49	.46	.52	.48	.45	.50	.47	.44	.43
			8	.52	.47	.43	.51	.46	.43	.50	.45	.42	.48	.44	.41	.47	.43	.41	.40
			9	.48	.43	.39	.47	.42	.39	.46	.42	.39	.45	.41	.38	.44	.40	.38	.36
			10	.45	.40	.36	.44	.39	.36	.43	.39	.36	.42	.38	.35	.41	.37	.35	.34
Porcelain-enameled reflector with 35°CW shielding (22½% ↑, 65% ↓)	II	1.3	0	.99	.99	.99	.94	.94	.94	.84	.84	.84	.76	.76	.76	.68	.68	.68	.65
			1	.88	.85	.82	.84	.81	.78	.76	.74	.72	.69	.67	.66	.62	.61	.60	.57
			2	.78	.73	.68	.74	.70	.66	.68	.64	.61	.62	.59	.56	.56	.54	.52	.49
			3	.69	.63	.58	.66	.61	.56	.61	.56	.53	.56	.52	.49	.51	.48	.46	.43
			4	.62	.55	.50	.60	.53	.49	.55	.50	.46	.50	.46	.43	.46	.43	.40	.37
			5	.55	.48	.43	.53	.47	.42	.49	.44	.39	.45	.41	.37	.41	.38	.35	.32
			6	.50	.43	.38	.48	.41	.37	.44	.39	.35	.41	.36	.33	.37	.34	.31	.29
			7	.45	.38	.33	.43	.37	.32	.40	.34	.30	.37	.32	.29	.34	.30	.27	.25
			8	.40	.34	.29	.39	.32	.28	.36	.30	.27	.33	.28	.25	.31	.27	.24	.22
			9	.36	.30	.25	.35	.29	.24	.32	.27	.23	.30	.25	.22	.28	.24	.21	.19
			10	.33	.27	.22	.32	.26	.22	.29	.24	.20	.27	.23	.19	.25	.21	.18	.17
Diffuse aluminum reflector with 35°CW x 35°LW shielding (17% ↑, 56½% ↓)	II	1.5/1.1	0	.83	.83	.83	.79	.79	.79	.71	.71	.71	.65	.65	.65	.59	.59	.59	.56
			1	.75	.72	.70	.72	.69	.68	.65	.64	.62	.60	.59	.58	.55	.54	.53	.50
			2	.67	.63	.60	.65	.61	.58	.59	.57	.54	.55	.53	.51	.50	.49	.47	.45
			3	.61	.56	.52	.58	.54	.51	.54	.50	.48	.50	.47	.45	.46	.44	.42	.40
			4	.55	.49	.45	.53	.48	.44	.49	.45	.42	.45	.42	.40	.42	.39	.37	.36
			5	.49	.44	.40	.47	.42	.39	.44	.40	.37	.41	.38	.35	.38	.35	.33	.31
			6	.45	.39	.35	.43	.38	.34	.40	.36	.33	.37	.34	.31	.35	.32	.30	.28
			7	.40	.35	.31	.39	.34	.30	.36	.32	.29	.34	.30	.27	.32	.29	.26	.25
			8	.36	.31	.27	.35	.30	.26	.33	.28	.25	.31	.27	.24	.29	.25	.23	.21
			9	.33	.27	.23	.32	.26	.23	.29	.25	.22	.28	.24	.21	.26	.22	.20	.19
			10	.30	.24	.21	.29	.24	.20	.27	.22	.19	.25	.21	.19	.23	.20	.18	.16
1-ft (300 mm)-wide aluminum troffer with 40°CW x 45°LW shielding and single extra-high-output lamp (0% ↑, 42½% ↓)	IV	1.1/0.8	0	.50	.50	.50	.49	.49	.49	.47	.47	.47	.45	.45	.45	.43	.43	.43	.42
			1	.46	.45	.44	.45	.44	.43	.44	.43	.42	.42	.41	.41	.41	.40	.40	.39
			2	.43	.41	.39	.42	.40	.38	.40	.39	.38	.39	.38	.37	.38	.37	.36	.35
			3	.39	.37	.35	.39	.36	.34	.37	.35	.34	.36	.35	.33	.35	.34	.33	.32
			4	.36	.33	.31	.35	.33	.31	.35	.32	.31	.34	.32	.30	.33	.31	.30	.29
			5	.33	.30	.28	.33	.30	.28	.32	.29	.28	.31	.29	.27	.30	.29	.27	.26
			6	.31	.28	.26	.30	.28	.26	.30	.27	.25	.29	.27	.25	.28	.26	.25	.24
			7	.28	.25	.23	.28	.25	.23	.27	.25	.23	.27	.25	.23	.26	.24	.23	.22
			8	.26	.23	.21	.26	.23	.21	.25	.23	.21	.25	.23	.21	.24	.22	.21	.20
			9	.24	.21	.19	.24	.21	.19	.23	.21	.19	.23	.20	.19	.22	.20	.19	.18
			10	.22	.19	.17	.22	.19	.17	.21	.19	.17	.21	.19	.17	.21	.19	.17	.16
Prismatic bottom and sides, open top, 4 lamp suspended unit—multiply by 1.05 for 2 lamps (33% ↑, 50% ↓)	VI	1.4/1.2	0	.90	.90	.90	.84	.84	.84	.73	.73	.73	.63	.63	.63	.54	.54	.54	.49
			1	.80	.77	.74	.75	.73	.70	.66	.64	.62	.57	.56	.54	.49	.48	.47	.43
			2	.71	.66	.62	.67	.63	.59	.59	.56	.53	.51	.49	.47	.44	.43	.41	.38
			3	.63	.58	.53	.60	.55	.50	.53	.49	.45	.46	.43	.41	.40	.38	.36	.33
			4	.57	.50	.46	.53	.48	.43	.47	.43	.39	.41	.38	.35	.36	.34	.32	.29
			5	.50	.44	.39	.48	.42	.37	.42	.38	.34	.37	.34	.31	.33	.30	.28	.25
			6	.45	.39	.34	.43	.37	.33	.38	.33	.30	.34	.30	.27	.30	.27	.24	.22
			7	.41	.34	.30	.39	.33	.28	.34	.30	.26	.30	.27	.24	.27	.24	.21	.19
			8	.37	.30	.26	.35	.29	.25	.31	.26	.23	.27	.24	.21	.24	.21	.19	.17
			9	.33	.27	.22	.31	.26	.22	.28	.23	.20	.25	.21	.18	.22	.19	.16	.15
			10	.30	.24	.20	.28	.23	.19	.25	.21	.18	.23	.19	.16	.20	.17	.14	.13

[a] ρcc = per cent effective ceiling cavity reflectance.
[b] ρw = per cent wall reflectance.
[c] RCR = Room Cavity Ratio.
[d] Maximum S/MH guide--ratio of maximum luminaire spacing to mounting or ceiling height above work-plane.

Table 8 (cont.). Coefficients of utilization and other data for typical luminaires

Typical Luminaire	Maint. Cat.	Maximum S/MH Guide[d]	RCR[e] ↓	ρcc 80 / ρw 50	80 / 30	80 / 10	70 / 50	70 / 30	70 / 10	50 / 50	50 / 30	50 / 10	30 / 50	30 / 30	30 / 10	10 / 50	10 / 30	10 / 10	0 / 0
				Coefficients of Utilization for 20 Per Cent Effective Floor Cavity Reflectance ($\rho_{FC} = 20$)															
2-lamp prismatic wraparound —multiply by 0.95 for 4 lamps (11½% ↑, 58½% ↓)	V	1.5/1.2	0	.80	.80	.80	.77	.77	.77	.71	.71	.71	.66	.66	.66	.60	.60	.60	.58
			1	.71	.69	.66	.69	.66	.64	.64	.62	.60	.59	.58	.56	.55	.54	.53	.50
			2	.64	.59	.56	.61	.58	.54	.57	.54	.51	.53	.51	.49	.49	.48	.46	.44
			3	.57	.52	.48	.55	.50	.47	.51	.48	.45	.48	.45	.42	.45	.42	.40	.38
			4	.51	.46	.41	.49	.44	.40	.46	.42	.39	.43	.40	.37	.41	.38	.35	.34
			5	.46	.40	.36	.44	.39	.35	.41	.37	.34	.39	.35	.32	.37	.33	.31	.29
			6	.41	.35	.31	.40	.35	.31	.38	.33	.30	.35	.31	.28	.33	.30	.27	.26
			7	.37	.31	.27	.36	.31	.27	.34	.29	.26	.32	.28	.25	.30	.27	.24	.23
			8	.33	.28	.24	.32	.27	.23	.30	.26	.22	.29	.25	.22	.27	.24	.21	.19
			9	.30	.24	.20	.29	.24	.20	.27	.23	.19	.26	.22	.19	.24	.21	.18	.17
			10	.27	.22	.18	.26	.21	.18	.25	.20	.17	.23	.19	.16	.22	.18	.16	.15
2-lamp white diffuse wraparound—multiply by 0.90 for 4 lamps (8% ↑, 37½% ↓)	V	1.3	0	.52	.52	.52	.50	.50	.50	.46	.46	.46	.42	.42	.42	.39	.39	.39	.37
			1	.45	.43	.41	.43	.41	.39	.40	.38	.37	.36	.35	.34	.34	.33	.32	.30
			2	.39	.35	.33	.37	.34	.32	.34	.32	.30	.32	.30	.28	.29	.28	.26	.25
			3	.34	.30	.27	.33	.29	.26	.30	.27	.25	.28	.25	.23	.26	.24	.22	.21
			4	.30	.26	.23	.29	.25	.22	.27	.24	.21	.25	.22	.20	.23	.21	.19	.18
			5	.26	.22	.19	.25	.21	.19	.23	.20	.18	.22	.19	.17	.20	.18	.16	.15
			6	.23	.19	.16	.23	.19	.16	.21	.18	.15	.19	.17	.14	.18	.16	.14	.13
			7	.21	.17	.14	.20	.16	.14	.19	.16	.13	.17	.15	.13	.16	.14	.12	.11
			8	.19	.15	.12	.18	.14	.12	.17	.14	.11	.16	.13	.11	.15	.12	.10	.09
			9	.17	.13	.10	.16	.13	.10	.15	.12	.10	.14	.11	.09	.13	.11	.09	.08
			10	.15	.12	.09	.15	.11	.09	.14	.11	.09	.13	.10	.08	.12	.10	.08	.07
2-lamp, 1′ (300 mm)-wide troffer with 45° plastic louver—multiply by 0.90 for 3 lamps (0% ↑, 46% ↓)	IV	1.0	0	.54	.54	.54	.53	.53	.53	.51	.51	.51	.48	.48	.48	.46	.46	.46	.45
			1	.49	.48	.46	.48	.47	.46	.46	.45	.44	.45	.44	.43	.43	.42	.42	.41
			2	.44	.42	.40	.43	.41	.39	.42	.40	.38	.40	.39	.37	.39	.38	.37	.36
			3	.40	.37	.34	.39	.36	.34	.38	.36	.34	.37	.35	.33	.36	.34	.33	.32
			4	.36	.33	.30	.36	.32	.30	.35	.32	.30	.34	.31	.29	.33	.31	.29	.28
			5	.33	.29	.26	.32	.29	.26	.31	.28	.26	.30	.28	.26	.30	.27	.26	.25
			6	.30	.26	.24	.29	.26	.24	.29	.26	.23	.28	.25	.23	.27	.25	.23	.22
			7	.27	.24	.21	.27	.23	.21	.26	.23	.21	.26	.23	.21	.25	.22	.21	.20
			8	.25	.21	.19	.24	.21	.19	.24	.21	.19	.23	.21	.18	.23	.20	.18	.18
			9	.22	.19	.17	.22	.19	.17	.22	.19	.17	.21	.18	.16	.21	.18	.16	.16
			10	.21	.17	.15	.20	.17	.15	.20	.17	.15	.20	.17	.15	.19	.17	.15	.14
4-lamp, 2′ (610 mm)-wide troffer with 45° plastic louver—multiply by 1.05 for 2 lamps and 0.95 for 6 lamps (0% ↑, 50% ↓)	IV	1.0	0	.59	.59	.59	.58	.58	.58	.55	.55	.55	.53	.53	.53	.51	.51	.51	.50
			1	.54	.52	.50	.52	.51	.49	.50	.49	.48	.48	.47	.46	.47	.46	.45	.44
			2	.48	.45	.43	.47	.44	.42	.45	.43	.41	.44	.42	.40	.42	.41	.39	.39
			3	.43	.40	.37	.42	.39	.37	.41	.38	.36	.40	.37	.36	.39	.37	.35	.34
			4	.39	.35	.32	.38	.35	.32	.37	.34	.32	.36	.33	.31	.35	.33	.31	.30
			5	.35	.31	.28	.35	.31	.28	.34	.30	.28	.33	.30	.28	.32	.29	.27	.26
			6	.32	.28	.25	.32	.28	.25	.31	.27	.25	.30	.27	.25	.29	.26	.24	.23
			7	.29	.25	.22	.29	.25	.22	.28	.25	.22	.27	.24	.22	.27	.24	.22	.21
			8	.26	.22	.20	.26	.22	.20	.25	.22	.20	.25	.22	.19	.24	.21	.19	.18
			9	.24	.20	.17	.24	.20	.17	.23	.20	.17	.23	.19	.17	.22	.19	.17	.16
			10	.22	.18	.16	.22	.18	.16	.21	.18	.16	.21	.18	.15	.20	.17	.15	.15
Fluorescent unit with dropped white diffuser, 4-lamp 2′ (610 mm)-wide—multiply by 1.10 for 2 lamps and 0.90 for 6 lamps (1% ↑, 60½% ↓)	V	1.2	0	.72	.72	.72	.70	.70	.70	.67	.67	.67	.64	.64	.64	.61	.61	.61	.60
			1	.64	.61	.59	.62	.60	.58	.60	.58	.56	.57	.56	.54	.55	.54	.52	.51
			2	.56	.52	.49	.55	.51	.48	.52	.49	.47	.50	.48	.46	.48	.46	.44	.43
			3	.50	.45	.41	.49	.44	.41	.47	.43	.40	.45	.42	.39	.43	.41	.38	.37
			4	.44	.39	.35	.43	.38	.35	.42	.37	.34	.40	.36	.33	.39	.36	.33	.32
			5	.39	.34	.30	.38	.33	.29	.37	.32	.29	.36	.32	.29	.34	.31	.28	.27
			6	.35	.30	.26	.34	.29	.25	.33	.29	.25	.32	.28	.25	.31	.27	.25	.23
			7	.31	.26	.22	.31	.26	.22	.30	.25	.22	.29	.25	.22	.28	.24	.22	.20
			8	.28	.23	.19	.28	.23	.19	.27	.22	.19	.26	.22	.19	.25	.22	.19	.18
			9	.25	.20	.17	.25	.20	.17	.24	.20	.17	.23	.19	.16	.23	.19	.16	.15
			10	.23	.18	.15	.23	.18	.15	.22	.18	.15	.21	.17	.15	.21	.17	.14	.13

[a] ρ_{CC} = per cent effective ceiling cavity reflectance.
[b] ρ_w = per cent wall reflectance.
[c] RCR = Room Cavity Ratio.
[d] Maximum S/MH guide—ratio of maximum luminaire spacing to mounting or ceiling height above work-plane.

Table 8 (cont.). Coefficients of utilization and other data for typical luminaires

	ρ_{CC}[a] →	80			70			50			30			10			0
Typical Luminaire / Typical Distribution and Per Cent Lamp Lumens	ρ_W[b] →	50	30	10	50	30	10	50	30	10	50	30	10	50	30	10	0
Maint. Cat. / Maximum S/MH Guide[d]	RCR[c] ↓	Coefficients of Utilization for 20 Per Cent Effective Floor Cavity Reflectance (ρ_{FC} = 20)															

Fluorescent unit with flat prismatic lens, 4 lamp 2′ (610 mm)-wide—multiply by 1.10 for 2 lamp. Maint. Cat. V, Maximum S/MH Guide 1.4/1.2. 0%↑ 62%↓ 60°

RCR	50	30	10	50	30	10	50	30	10	50	30	10	50	30	10	0
0	.73	.73	.73	.72	.72	.72	.68	.68	.68	.66	.66	.66	.63	.63	.63	.62
1	.66	.64	.62	.65	.63	.61	.62	.60	.59	.60	.58	.57	.57	.56	.55	.54
2	.59	.55	.52	.58	.54	.52	.56	.53	.50	.54	.51	.49	.52	.50	.48	.47
3	.53	.48	.45	.52	.48	.44	.50	.46	.44	.48	.45	.43	.47	.44	.42	.41
4	.47	.42	.39	.46	.42	.38	.45	.41	.38	.43	.40	.37	.42	.39	.37	.36
5	.42	.37	.33	.41	.37	.33	.40	.36	.33	.39	.35	.32	.38	.35	.32	.31
6	.38	.33	.29	.37	.32	.29	.36	.32	.29	.35	.31	.28	.34	.31	.28	.27
7	.34	.29	.25	.33	.29	.25	.33	.28	.25	.32	.28	.25	.31	.27	.25	.23
8	.30	.25	.22	.30	.25	.22	.29	.25	.22	.28	.24	.21	.28	.24	.21	.20
9	.27	.22	.19	.27	.22	.19	.26	.22	.19	.25	.21	.19	.25	.21	.18	.17
10	.25	.20	.17	.24	.20	.16	.24	.19	.16	.23	.19	.16	.23	.19	.16	.15

Single-row fluorescent lamp cove without reflector, mult. by 0.93 for 2 rows and by 0.85 for 3 rows.

RCR	50	30	10	50	30	10	50	30	10	30/10/0
1	.42	.40	.39	.36	.35	.33	.25	.24	.23	Coves are not recommended for lighting areas having low reflectances.
2	.37	.34	.32	.32	.29	.27	.22	.20	.19	
3	.32	.29	.26	.28	.25	.23	.19	.17	.16	
4	.29	.25	.22	.25	.22	.19	.17	.15	.13	
5	.25	.21	.18	.22	.19	.16	.15	.13	.11	
6	.23	.19	.16	.20	.16	.14	.14	.12	.10	
7	.20	.17	.14	.17	.14	.12	.12	.10	.09	
8	.18	.15	.12	.16	.13	.10	.11	.09	.08	
9	.17	.13	.10	.15	.11	.09	.10	.08	.07	
10	.15	.12	.09	.13	.10	.08	.09	.07	.06	

Diffusing plastic or glass. ρ_{CC} from below ~65%.
(1) Ceiling efficiency ~60%; diffuser transmittance ~50%; diffuser reflectance ~40%. Cavity with minimum obstructions and painted with 80% reflectance paint—use ρ_c = 70.
(2) For lower reflectance paint or obstructions—use ρ_c = 50.

RCR	70: 50	30	10	50: 50	30	10
1	.60	.58	.56	.58	.56	.54
2	.53	.49	.45	.51	.47	.43
3	.47	.42	.37	.45	.41	.36
4	.41	.36	.32	.39	.35	.31
5	.37	.31	.27	.35	.30	.26
6	.33	.27	.23	.31	.26	.23
7	.29	.24	.20	.28	.23	.20
8	.26	.21	.18	.25	.20	.17
9	.23	.19	.15	.23	.18	.15
10	.21	.17	.13	.21	.16	.13

Prismatic plastic or glass. ρ_{CC} from below ~60%.
1) Ceiling efficiency ~67%; prismatic transmittance ~72%; prismatic reflectance ~18%. Cavity with minimum obstructions and painted with 80% reflectance paint—use ρ_c = 70.
2) For lower reflectance paint or obstructions—use ρ_c = 50.

RCR	70: 50	30	10	50: 50	30	10	30: 50	30	10
1	.71	.68	.66	.67	.66	.65	.65	.64	.62
2	.63	.60	.57	.61	.58	.55	.59	.56	.54
3	.57	.53	.49	.55	.52	.48	.54	.50	.47
4	.52	.47	.43	.50	.45	.42	.48	.44	.42
5	.46	.41	.37	.44	.40	.37	.43	.40	.36
6	.42	.37	.33	.41	.36	.32	.40	.35	.32
7	.38	.32	.29	.37	.31	.28	.36	.31	.28
8	.34	.28	.25	.33	.28	.25	.32	.28	.25
9	.30	.25	.22	.30	.25	.21	.29	.25	.21
10	.27	.23	.19	.27	.22	.19	.26	.22	.19

Louvered ceiling. ρ_{CC} from below ~45%. Ceiling efficiency ~50%; 45° shielding opaque louvers of 80% reflectance. Cavity with minimum obstructions and painted with 80% reflectance paint—use ρ_c = 50.

RCR	50: 50	30	10	10: 50	30	10
1	.51	.49	.48	.47	.46	.45
2	.46	.44	.42	.43	.42	.40
3	.42	.39	.37	.39	.38	.36
4	.38	.35	.33	.36	.34	.32
5	.35	.32	.29	.33	.31	.29
6	.32	.29	.26	.30	.28	.26
7	.29	.26	.23	.28	.25	.23
8	.27	.23	.21	.26	.23	.21
9	.24	.21	.19	.24	.21	.19
10	.22	.19	.17	.22	.19	.17

[a] ρ_{CC} = per cent effective ceiling cavity reflectance.
[b] ρ_W = per cent wall reflectance.
[c] RCR = Room Cavity Ratio.
[d] Maximum S/MH guide—ratio of maximum luminaire spacing to mounting or ceiling height above work-plane.

Table 9. Effective ceiling or floor cavity reflectances for various reflectance combinations

Per Cent Base* Reflectance	80								70								60								30								20								10							
Per Cent Wall Reflectance → Cavity Ratio ↓	80	70	60	50	40	30	20	10	80	70	60	50	40	30	20	10	80	70	60	50	40	30	20	10	80	70	60	50	40	30	20	10	80	70	60	50	40	30	20	10	80	70	60	50	40	30	20	10
0.2	78	78	77	77	76	76	75	74	69	68	68	67	67	66	66	65	59	59	58	57	57	56	56	55	31	30	30	29	29	29	28	28	20	20	20	20	20	19	19	19	11	11	11	10	10	10	09	09
0.4	77	76	75	74	73	72	71	70	68	67	66	65	64	63	62	61	59	59	58	57	55	54	53	52	31	30	30	29	29	28	27	26	21	20	20	20	19	19	18	18	11	11	11	11	10	10	09	09
0.6	76	75	73	71	70	68	66	65	67	65	64	63	61	59	58	57	58	57	56	55	53	51	51	50	31	30	29	28	27	26	26	25	21	21	20	19	19	18	18	17	12	12	11	11	10	10	09	09
0.8	75	73	71	69	67	65	63	61	66	64	62	60	58	56	55	53	57	56	55	54	51	48	47	46	31	30	29	28	26	25	25	23	22	21	21	20	19	18	17	16	13	12	12	11	11	10	09	08
1.0	74	72	69	67	65	62	60	57	65	62	60	58	55	53	52	50	57	55	53	51	48	45	44	43	32	30	29	27	25	24	23	22	23	22	20	19	18	17	16	15	14	13	12	11	11	10	09	08
1.2	73	70	67	64	61	58	55	53	64	61	59	57	54	50	48	46	56	54	51	49	46	44	42	40	32	30	28	27	25	23	22	21	23	22	20	19	17	16	14	14	15	14	13	12	11	10	09	07
1.4	72	68	65	62	59	55	53	50	63	60	58	55	51	47	45	41	56	53	49	47	44	41	39	38	32	30	28	26	24	22	20	19	24	22	20	18	17	16	15	13	16	14	13	12	11	10	09	07
1.6	71	67	63	60	57	53	50	47	62	59	56	53	47	45	43	41	55	52	48	45	42	39	37	35	33	29	27	25	23	22	20	18	24	22	20	18	16	15	13	13	17	15	14	12	11	09	08	07
1.8	70	66	62	58	54	50	47	44	61	58	54	51	46	42	40	38	55	51	47	44	40	37	35	33	33	29	27	25	23	21	19	17	25	23	20	18	16	14	12	11	17	15	14	13	11	09	08	07
2.0	69	64	60	56	52	48	45	41	60	56	52	49	45	40	38	36	54	50	46	43	39	35	33	31	33	29	26	24	22	20	18	16	25	23	20	18	15	13	12	11	18	16	14	13	11	09	08	06
2.2	68	63	58	54	49	45	42	38	60	55	51	48	43	38	36	34	53	49	45	42	37	34	31	29	32	29	26	24	22	19	17	15	26	23	20	18	16	14	12	10	19	16	14	13	11	09	07	06
2.4	67	61	56	52	47	43	40	36	60	54	50	46	41	37	35	32	53	48	44	41	36	32	30	27	32	29	26	24	22	19	16	14	26	23	20	18	16	14	12	10	19	17	15	13	11	09	07	06
2.6	66	60	55	50	45	41	38	34	59	54	49	45	40	35	33	30	53	48	43	39	35	31	28	26	32	29	25	23	21	18	16	14	26	23	20	18	16	14	11	09	20	17	15	13	11	09	07	06
2.8	65	59	53	48	43	39	36	32	59	53	48	43	38	33	30	28	53	47	43	38	34	29	27	24	33	29	25	23	21	17	15	13	27	23	20	18	15	13	11	09	20	18	15	13	11	09	07	05
3.0	65	58	52	47	42	37	34	30	58	52	47	42	37	32	29	27	52	46	42	37	32	28	25	23	33	29	25	22	20	17	15	12	27	23	20	17	15	13	11	09	21	18	16	13	11	09	07	05
3.2	65	57	51	45	40	35	33	28	58	51	46	40	36	31	28	25	51	45	41	36	31	27	23	22	33	28	24	22	19	16	14	12	27	23	20	17	15	12	11	09	21	18	16	13	11	09	07	05
3.4	64	56	49	44	39	34	32	27	57	50	45	39	35	29	27	24	51	45	40	35	30	26	23	20	33	28	24	21	19	16	14	11	27	24	20	17	14	11	09	07	22	18	16	13	11	09	07	05
3.6	63	54	48	43	38	32	30	25	56	49	44	38	33	28	25	22	50	44	39	34	29	25	22	19	33	28	24	21	18	15	13	10	28	24	20	17	14	11	09	07	22	19	16	13	11	09	06	04
3.8	62	53	47	41	36	31	28	24	56	49	43	37	32	27	24	21	50	43	38	33	28	24	21	18	33	28	24	21	18	15	13	10	29	24	20	17	14	11	08	06	23	19	17	14	11	09	06	04
4.0	61	53	46	40	35	30	26	22	55	48	42	36	31	26	23	20	49	42	37	32	28	23	20	18	33	28	24	21	18	14	12	09	29	24	20	17	14	11	08	06	23	20	17	14	11	09	06	04
4.2	60	52	45	39	34	29	25	21	55	47	41	35	30	25	22	19	49	42	37	32	27	22	19	17	33	28	24	20	17	14	12	09	28	23	20	17	14	11	09	07	24	20	17	14	11	09	06	04
4.4	60	51	44	38	33	28	24	20	54	46	40	34	29	24	21	18	49	42	36	31	27	22	19	16	33	28	24	20	17	13	10	08	28	24	20	17	14	11	09	07	24	20	17	14	11	08	06	04
4.6	59	50	43	37	32	27	23	19	53	45	39	33	28	24	21	17	49	41	35	30	26	21	18	16	33	28	23	20	17	13	10	08	29	24	20	17	13	10	08	06	25	20	17	14	11	08	06	04
4.8	58	49	42	36	31	26	22	18	53	45	38	32	27	23	20	16	48	41	34	29	25	21	18	15	33	28	23	20	17	13	10	08	29	24	20	16	13	10	08	06	25	20	17	14	11	08	06	04
5.0	58	48	41	35	30	25	21	18	52	44	36	31	26	22	19	16	48	40	34	28	24	20	17	14	33	28	24	19	16	13	10	08	29	24	20	16	13	10	08	06	25	20	17	14	11	08	06	04
6.0	55	44	38	31	27	22	19	15	51	41	35	28	24	19	16	13	45	37	31	25	21	17	14	11	33	27	23	18	15	11	09	06	30	24	20	16	13	10	08	05	26	21	18	14	11	08	06	03
7.0	53	41	35	28	24	19	16	12	48	38	32	26	22	17	14	11	43	35	30	24	20	15	12	09	33	26	22	17	14	10	08	05	30	24	20	15	12	09	07	04	27	21	17	13	11	08	06	03
8.0	50	38	32	25	21	17	14	11	46	35	29	23	19	15	13	10	42	33	28	22	18	14	11	08	33	26	21	16	13	09	07	04	30	23	19	15	12	08	06	03	27	21	17	13	10	07	05	03
9.0	49	36	30	23	19	15	13	10	45	33	27	21	18	14	12	09	40	31	26	20	16	12	10	07	33	25	20	15	12	09	07	04	29	23	19	14	11	08	06	03	28	21	17	13	10	07	05	02
10.0	46	33	27	21	18	14	11	08	43	31	25	19	16	12	10	08	39	29	24	18	15	11	09	07	32	24	19	14	11	08	06	03	29	22	18	13	10	07	05	03	28	21	17	12	10	07	05	02

* Ceiling, floor, or floor of cavity.

By R. M. HARROLD, *Director Lighting Design, Westinghouse Electric Corporation*

LIGHTING

For new buildings there is a need to limit the amount of power available for lighting, while still enabling the designer to provide a lighting system suitable for the needs of the client and occupants. Calculation procedures for establishing a lighting power limit have been developed in the Illuminating Engineering Society EMS-6 document* and are contained in many of the state codes.

Power reduction is only one aspect to be considered in an energy management program, since energy equals power times time. A savings in energy can be achieved by reducing either the amount of power consumed, or reducing the time the power is used. If both power and time are reduced, the energy-saving potential is further increased.

In an existing building lighting must first comply with the same power limits as in a new facility and then a program must be developed to reduce energy. There are many opportunities in existing buildings to improve not only the operating efficiency of the building to save energy, but at the same time to improve the quality of the lighting. In order to make a power comparison to find out if the lighting system in an existing building complies with a calculated limit, and therefore, if power reduction is required, the building must be surveyed. In a survey the actual connected wattages in all spaces are recorded, totaled, and compared to the calculated power limit. Along with lamp wattages, ballast and transformer losses need to be noted.

For example, for incandescent types the lamp wattage as found on the bulb is the number to be recorded, but if a transformer is used for low- and high-voltage operation, then the transformer wattage losses must be added; for fluorescent and HID light sources, ballast losses must be taken into account.

Comparison of connected versus calculated power limit

If the connected wattage for the building exceeds the calculated power limit, then an evaluation should be made of the differences for each space in the building and those areas with the greatest deviation selected as the basis for instituting a program to modify the existing lighting system. By repeating the process for one or more spaces, the connected wattage may be reduced to the power limit.

This procedure provides a "yardstick" for

---

determining in which areas power and energy may be saved. In an attempt to reduce power, care should be exercised to maintain good lighting practice, considering such factors as lighting needs for productivity, safety, and aesthetics. Seeing tasks and their locations should be identified so that recommended illumination can be provided. There may be an opportunity to reduce power, for example, in an existing space which is uniformly lighted to a level higher than the present tasks require, by modifying the system so that it relates to task lighting requirements with less illuminance in the surrounding noncritical areas.

In many existing buildings, power and energy savings may be achieved by an evaluation of the building maintenance and operating procedures. Improving a lighting maintenance program, or instituting a program where none exists, may allow some reductions in lighting energy and will certainly ensure the increase of lamp lumens closer to initial levels.

Energy management considerations

The following ideas are not only applicable to existing buildings, but should be reviewed for their impact on the design of a new building. Some modifications may be accomplished easily and at little or no cost, while others may involve replacing lighting systems and larger capital expenditures. Not all suggestions are applicable to all building types, and the owner must establish his or her own priorities for selecting and timing feasibility.

In developing a management program, not only should the electric lighting be considered, but also the value of the contribution of daylighting, controls, operating schedules, and maintenance procedures.

It should be noted that lighting contributes useful heat in wintertime, but does impose additional summer loads on cooling systems. In other words, lighting has thermal as well as visual implications and significant changes to the lighting system may affect these other systems. If lighting energy is reduced, the resulting savings do not represent a 100 per cent net savings in energy, because while there is a plus for the air conditioning, there is a subtraction from the heating system which must be made up elsewhere.

In addition, before undertaking any modifications to the lighting, it should be recognized that we are dealing with a *system*—a set of interrelated components and elements, as interrelated to one another as the lighting is to other systems in the building. For example, while energy can be saved by removing lamps or disconnecting luminaires, such measures should only be taken after a careful analysis of the entire system.

Evaluation points

1. *Lighting Needs.* The emphasis here is on the identification of the tasks performed in any area of the building so that the location of the lighting equipment, orientation of the tasks, and illuminance requirements can be coordinated. The intent is to provide task related illuminance and avoid unnecessarily high levels of uniform lighting which may have been installed without consideration for the task activities and locations.

If changes in placement of lighting equipment are not feasible, it may be possible to group similar tasks or work areas with the same illuminance requirements, closing off unused space with minimum heating, cooling, and lighting.

2. *Lighting Equipment.* One of the greatest opportunities for energy savings is in the selection of more efficient light sources for relighting an area. By using higher efficacy lamps (lumens per input watts), it is possible to obtain more light from the same number of sources, or the same amount of light using fewer lamps.

In the incandescent family, where possible and suitable to the application, fewer higher wattage lamps may be used to replace those of a low wattage and the efficiency of the system thereby improved (higher lumens). Similarly, R, PAR, and ER lamps may provide the required light with lower watts than A-type lamps.

Using reduced-wattage fluorescent lamps in existing luminaires and substituting interchangeable-types of metal halide or high-pressure sodium lamps in mercury systems on compatible ballasts will result in power reduction and increased light output.

Luminaire or component replacement is also suggested when these kinds of modifications or replacements will improve the efficiency of the lighting and/or reduce the energy consumed.

3. *Daylighting.* If daylighting can be effectively used, it should be considered either to replace some of the electric lighting, which can then be turned off for certain hours of the day, or as a supplementary source of lighting so that electric lighting in the immediate area can be reduced by switching or dimming.

4. *Controls and Distribution Systems.* Just as many buildings were uniformly lighted with "wall-to-wall" footcandles (lux); a common practice, for purposes of switching economy, has been to also control a large number of luminaires from one switch.

Switches and dimmer controls installed for selective control of luminaires provide flexibility of space use as well as energy savings, enabling lights to be turned off when areas are unoccupied during different working or cleaning hours. Photocell and time clocks afford additional means of control, particularly of exterior areas.

IES Procedure for Calculating Lighting Power Limits for New and Existing Buildings (Unit Power Density Procedure) EMS-6, Illuminating Engineering Society, New York, July 1980.

5. *Lighting Maintenance Procedures.* A regular maintenance schedule for cleaning luminaires and replacing lamps will ensure maintained efficiency of the system according to original design specifications. Some time spent with the maintenance personnel in checking, and, if necessary, revising the program already in existence may result in some immediate solutions for energy and financial savings in the facility. While only a few words are devoted here to this subject, this is one of the most important procedures for consideration, and in most cases one for which modifications can be immediately implemented.

6. *Operating Schedules.* An analysis of operating hours in the building may reveal the necessity for educating workers to turn off lighting when it is not required. Usage patterns should be identified during the building survey and modifications should be based on those results. Define the nature and duration of occupancy for each space and determine the lighting requirements consistent with the task and safety and security.

Adjusting cleaning schedules offers one solution. Other ideas include turning lights off during lunch hours except in circulation spaces; operating building facade lighting for fewer hours each night; restricting parking for employes to specific areas and reducing lighting in unused parking lots.

The possibilities are numerous and depend on an understanding of the present usage patterns, and spending time to evaluate possible profile changes.

Cost

In all segments of a management program, consideration must be given to the cost effectiveness of the modification as well as to the energy effectiveness of various methods of achieving savings. Contained within this section is an analysis form which can be used for recording changes in connected power and changes in controls and usage patterns and their effects on the annual energy used for lighting. The results will indicate savings to be obtained if the lighting alone is modified, because the operations schedule cannot be changed; or, if operations can be altered, but the lighting is already energy efficient and is not to be modified. The initial cost of modification should be balanced on an annual basis against the annual cost savings for operation and maintenance.

Energy management programs for lighting offer not only the means of achieving energy savings, but can result in improved lighting systems that benefit employes and their working environment.

LIGHTING ENERGY MANAGEMENT FORM

Space Descrip.	Description / Proposed Modifications	Cond.	Power-Load (W)			Operating Hours							Hours Per Week	Weeks Per Year	Hours Per Year	Annual Energy Consumption (kWh)		Cost of Mod.
	Existing Installation		Connect	Budget	Modified	M	T	W	T	F	S	S				Exist.	Mod.	
		Exist.																
		Mod.																
		Exist.																
		Mod.																
		Exist.																
		Mod.																
		Exist.																
		Mod.																
		Exist.																
		Mod.																
		Exist.																
		Mod.																
		Exist.																
		Mod.																
		Exist.																
		Mod.																
		Exist.																
		Mod.																
		Exist.																
		Mod.																
		Exist.																
		Mod.																
		Exist																
		Mod.																
TOTALS →																		

Data from American National Standard Practice for Office Lighting, (ANSI A 132,1–1973), sponsored and published by the Illuminating Engineering Society of North America.

LIGHTING QUANTITY

Recommended illuminance values for offices are shown in Table 10.

LIGHTING QUALITY

Room finishes

Ceilings, walls, and floors are important factors in determining the brightness ratios between the lighting equipment and its surrounding. They act as secondary light sources of large areas and, if finished in accordance with Table 2, will increase light utilization and reduce shadows.

However, under certain conditions either higher or lower reflectances may be satisfactory or even desirable. The ceiling finish may, for example, be carried down the walls to the level of pendant luminaires having a high upward component; utilization may be increased as much as 10 per cent by doing this. Conversely, a darker dado is sometimes employed on lower walls to minimize maintenance. Dadoes should have a reflectance of at least 25 per cent, however; darker dadoes are undesirable from the standpoint of visual comfort since the lower wall occupies an important part of the visual field. Small sections of walls may have reflectances higher or lower than the extremes permitted by the range given in Table 2. If these areas are thought of as accents and restricted to about 10 per cent of the total wall area in the room, little harm will be done to the efficiency of the lighting system or to the significant environmental brightness ratios, while the environment can be made to look considerably more pleasant and interesting.

Because it is human nature to desire at least occasional change, architects and lighting designers will be wise to specify the reflectances for all surfaces in an interior and plan the lighting so the colors can be changed without destroying the planned effect. If this information is included in the specifications and marked on all blueprints anyone can not only do the original color for the room but any replacement color plan as long as the lighting system is in use.

When window shielding media act as walls, they should have approximately the same reflectance as that recommended for the walls.

Office equipment finishes

Furniture: No surface in the office is more important visually than the desk top. For a person working at a desk, the top occupies most of the visual field. The task is usually of high reflectance, and desk tops having the reflectance recommended in Table 2 are necessary to prevent the luminance ratio between the task and its surround from exceeding the one to one-third ratio that is considered desirable and practical. Matte finishes are, of course, essential to minimize reflected glare.

All office furniture should have a light finish that harmonizes with the environment and promotes seeing comfort by minimizing luminance ratios between the various surfaces within the visual field. It is particularly important that the vertical surfaces of desks and file cabinets have finishes of the recommended reflectance, for they occupy a significant portion of the visual field. Since these surfaces receive less illuminance than adjacent horizontal surfaces, light finishes are necessary to make them even moderately bright.

Machines: Business machines rank with desk tops in visual importance. In use they occupy a central and dominating part of the visual field even when operated by the touch system. Finishes having the recommended reflectances are essential for seeing comfort; shiny surfaces and dial covers should be completely eliminated, for even a small amount of specular trim can be distracting and annoying even though it may not be viewed directly.

LIGHTING AND SEEING IN SPECIFIC AREAS

Private offices

Private offices are usually of moderate or small size. Either direct or indirect lighting can be applied satisfactorily since much of the lighting equipment on the ceiling itself is generally not within the visual field. The arrangement of furniture in the private office is often fixed and permits the placing of direct lighting equipment to minimize both direct and reflected glare.

Not only is it necessary to provide satisfactory illuminance for the occupant at the point of work, but sufficient luminance on walls, floors, and other areas is necessary to avoid high luminance ratios with the work. The use of dark-paneled walls, desks, and floor coverings is not conducive to comfortable seeing, and higher-reflectance ma-

Table 10. Recommended office illuminance value*

Area(s)	Footcandles (fc)	Lux (lx)†
Drafting rooms		
Detailed drafting and designing, cartography	200	2000
Rough layout drafting	150	1500
Accounting offices		
Auditing, tabulating, bookkeeping, business machine operation, computer operation	150	1500
General offices		
Reading poor reproductions, business machine operation, computer operation	150	1500
Reading handwriting in hard pencil or on poor paper, reading fair reproductions, active filing, mail sorting	100	1000
Reading handwriting in ink or medium pencil on good quality paper, intermittent filing	70	700
Private offices		
Reading poor reproductions, business machine operation	150	1500
Reading handwriting in hard pencil or on poor paper, reading fair reproductions	100	1000
Reading handwriting in ink or medium pencil on good quality paper	70	700
Reading high contrast or well printed materials	30	300
Conferring and interviewing	30	300
Conference rooms		
Critical seeing tasks	100	1000
Conferring	30	300
Note-taking during projection, (controllable) (dimmer)	30	300
Elevators, escalators, stairwells	20	200‡
Corridors	20	200
Washrooms	30	300

Minimum on the task at any time.
†*Lux is an SI unit equal to 0.0929 fc.*
‡*But no less than 20 percent of illuminance in adjacent areas.*

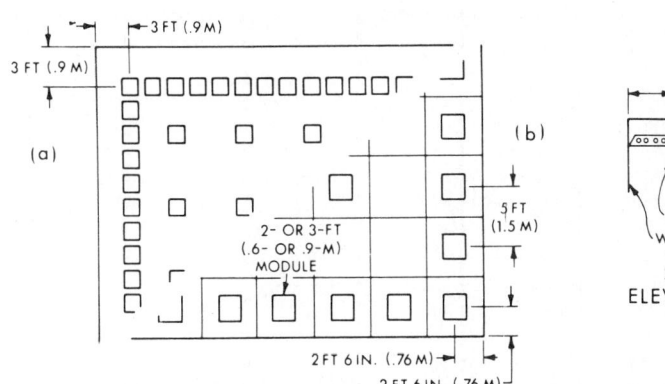
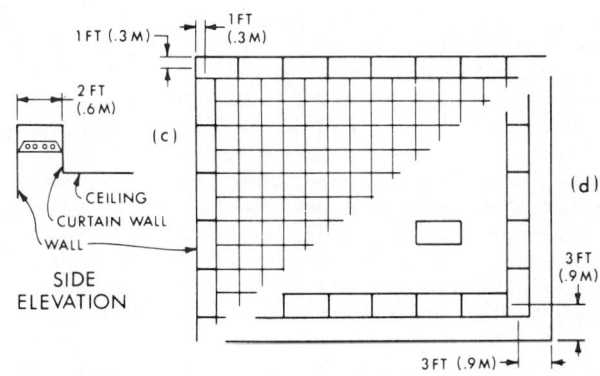

Fig. 16. Planned perimeter lighting can result in increased usable work area in the space. Typical perimeter lighting modular designs are: *(a)* **2- by 2-ft (0.6- by 0.6-m) luminaires and** *(b)* **5- by 5-ft (1.5- by 1.5-m) modules or 2-ft (0.6-m) or 3-ft (0.9-m) square luminaires. Other perimeter lighting methods include** *(c)* **luminaires mounted adjacent to wall areas with curtain wall shielding and** *(d)* **2-by 4-ft (0.6- by 1.2-m) modules or luminaires.**

terials with equal decorative character are now available.

The illuminance required in private offices varies from that necessary for casual seeing during interviews to high values for prolonged study of reports, financial statements, plans, and specifications. Where possible, the lighting system should be flexible to provide the order of illuminance the varying tasks require. The higher values should be employed only when adequate provision is made for reduced luminance ratios between the lighting system and the environment, between the work and the environment, and among the environmental areas themselves.

General offices

Most general offices are moderate- to large-sized areas in which there may be many luminaires located directly in the field of view. In these areas, it is particularly important that luminaire luminance limitations be observed. At the same time, it is in the general office that seeing is most frequently difficult and most nearly continuous and, for this reason, quality and seeing comfort should never be compromised. The minimum quantity of light in use should be in keeping with recommendations in Table 10. Finishes, color, and other environmental factors should be selected to assure full benefit from the lighting and to supplement all the advantages that can be realized in the tasks themselves.

Since many office operations require more than one orientation of personnel, lighting and seeing should be comfortable for all directions of view. Changes in routine or personnel frequently require rearrangement of desk locations and partitions. General lighting installations originally designed to be comfortable from all directions need not

be modified with changes in office procedure or organization.

Coordinated components and modules: It has become increasingly critical that electrical and mechanical components be compatible with other elements in the same building system so that the resulting assembly is an efficient and economical operating unit and an architecturally coordinated design. In this regard, an increasing number of luminaire types have been developed to supply both light and air to a space. This equipment offers the initial advantage of a simplified ceiling appearance due to the elimination of overlapping (and sometimes conflicting) mechanical and electrical ceiling patterns. These units may also offer considerable flexibility in space planning where the "mechanically coordinated module" is employed. Within each standard dimensional module, there should be (1) lighting, (2) air supply, (3) air return, and (4) sound absorption. Where this can be achieved, it means that modular floor and partition systems can be used (initially or in future modifications) to set off any module or any combination of modules as a separate room. Each room, then, would automatically include all the basic elements of the mechanical-electrical environment.

Care should be taken to provide the recommended quantity of illuminance on the actual work surfaces. Most are horizontal, but some are vertical or sloping. Extra precautions should also be taken to ensure proper distribution of light along the sides and ends of offices. Desks are frequently placed along walls where the amount of light is inherently less if provisions have not been made to offset this reduction. This is generally accomplished by the use of "perimeter lighting," with luminaires spaced

more closely along the walls of an office area as recommended in Fig. 15 (p. 4-286). Additional suggested layouts of perimeter lighting are shown in Fig. 16. For desks in such positions, use wall reflectances in the upper part of the range in Table 3 (p. 4-276).

Drafting rooms

Drafting makes very serious demands upon the eyes and requires a high level of high-quality illuminance. Drafting involves accurate discrimination of fine details, frequently over long periods of time. The contrast between the work detail and its background may be very poor, as, for example, when tracing a faint blueprint or worn pencil drawing. Specular drawing surfaces, polished T-squares, plastic triangles, and scales are potential sources of reflected glare. Shadows along the drawing edge of the T-square or a triangle may materially reduce visibility; or strong, multiple shadows from the drawing instruments or the drafter's hands may prove annoying.

Reflections: On nearly horizontal boards, any ceiling or luminaire luminance may be reflected by the work to the eyes of the drafter. Such reflections may sometimes be eliminated by proper positioning of the source or control of the direction of light flux with respect to the specular surfaces so that reflections will be directed away from the eye. It is usually more practical to minimize the effect of these reflections by controlling the brightness of the luminous area that is reflected to a low and fairly uniform value. This may be accomplished by employing lighting systems in which the lamps are completely concealed from the work. With the board in a nearly vertical position, specular reflections cause little if any trouble since they will be reflected toward the floor (see Fig. 17). Furthermore, the nearly vertical board may be high enough to shield the eyes of the draftsman from luminaire luminance otherwise in the field of view.

Shadows: Where boards are near horizontal, edges of T-squares or triangles parallel to line sources having strong direct components may cast sharp line shadows. The use of indirect, semi-indirect, or other forms of over-all ceiling lighting will minimize such shadows. Where this type of lighting is not applicable or feasible, the frequency of occurrence of such shadows may be minimized by orienting either the luminaires or the drafting tables to create an angle of 15 to 20 deg between the long axes of the luminaires and any of the major straight-edge positions. The use of vertical drafting boards also virtually eliminates shadows on the task.

Transillumination: A drafting table with a diffusing surface panel lighted from behind provides an efficient means of improving the visibility of tracing tasks. General room lighting should be used while tracing drawings since it also contributes to visibility and helps visual comfort by raising the surround brightness and reducing luminance ratios in the field of view.

For tracing original drawings which have a relatively high transmittance (40 to 50 per cent) a luminous surface having a brightness of about 200 fL (685 cd/m²) provides excellent visibility. For tracing reproductions which are usually on heavier paper of lower transmittance (such as blueprints) 300 to 400 fL (1028 to 1370 cd/m²) is desirable. To avoid direct glare, the drafter should use opaque paper to cover the portion of the glass which is not concealed by the drawing.

The varying requirements for luminance suggest that the lamps be dimmer-controlled to permit selection of the optimum value for a specific task. In addition, it is desirable to keep the temperature of the tracing table as low as possible. Therefore, fluorescent lamps having a high luminous efficacy should be used. Simple ballasts and variable auto-transformers are available for dimming 40-watt [48 in (1220 mm) long] and 30-watt [36 in (910 mm) long] rapid-start fluorescent lamps.

Files

Files present the particular problem of work surfaces that are vertical, inclined and horizontal, and frequently stacked one against the other. In order to provide the recommended values of illuminance *on work surfaces other than horizontal,* it is generally true that considerably higher values will need to be developed on horizontal positions. In *active filing* areas, the work is likely to be of protracted nature and the visual task is of more than average severity. Where the room is primarily devoted to files, consideration should be given to luminaires designed and located to provide the recommended illuminance value on vertical surfaces.

Cabinet finishes of recommended reflectance will provide comfortable luminance ratios within the environmental areas of file rooms and will improve the seeing conditions at the point of work. Lighter finishes will reflect more light down between filed items which frequently are read without removal from the files.

Mail rooms and stockrooms

Rapid sorting and routing of incoming mail involves rather difficult seeing, requiring the illuminance level recommended in Table 10.

Conference and board rooms

Effective coordination of good seeing conditions with the architectural and decorative designs of these rooms will result in comfortable and attractive areas. As in private offices, the use of these rooms varies considerably, but critical and prolonged seeing is encountered at times in most of them and the lighting level should be adequate for the most difficult, commonly occurring task. The illuminance should be *designed to minimize* shadows on the faces of persons seated around the table. Undesirable reflections should be avoided. Moderately high reflectance matte finishes are recommended. Special attention to lighting of vertical surfaces is important if charts, displays or illustrations are frequently studied. Supplementary lighting is recommended for this purpose. Flexibility in providing light suited to varying use can be provided through suitable switching or dimming.

Reception rooms

Lighting for casual seeing fulfills the requirements of the usual reception room. Glare should be avoided to make the room pleasant in general appearance and to provide comfortable seeing for those visitors who choose to read while waiting. The choice of higher reflectance values for room surfaces and furnishings will assist in making the room comfortable and seemingly more spacious.

If a receptionist occupies the room, this person should be provided with lighting in keeping with the tasks assigned. Frequently, general office work is part of the assignment and the seeing requirements are more exacting than those for the casual occupant. Luminance ratios in the receptionist's visual field should be limited to low values and either a uniform amount of light should be provided throughout the room or more light provided at the work area, commensurate with

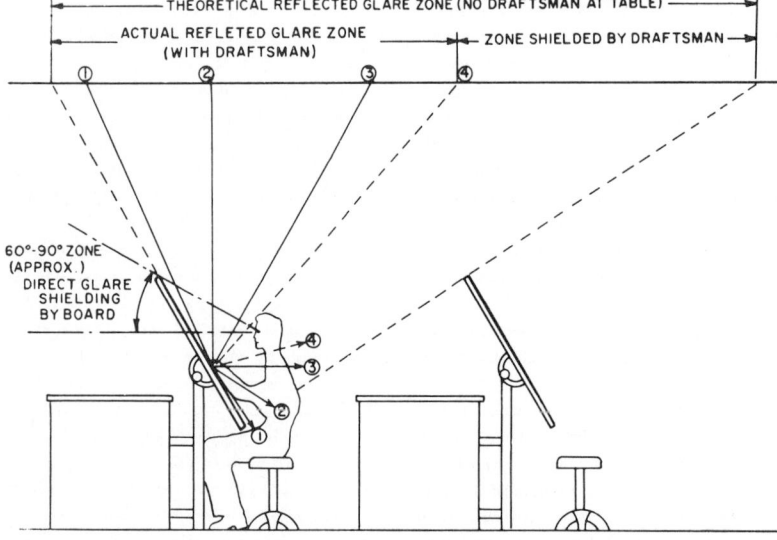

Fig. 17. Specular reflections

With drafting boards tilted in a nearly vertical position, as shown in drawing above, the specular reflections are reflected down toward the floor. The drafting boards may be high enough to shield the draftsmen's eyes from the luminaire brightness which, otherwise, would be in the field of view.

the severity of the work assignments. The latter requires particular attention to brightness patterns on walls, floors, and desk tops.

If a telephone switchboard with signal light indicators is present, it is important that the general lighting not "wash out" the signal lights (particularly if they are located on a horizontal plane). Care should also be taken to prevent reflections of bright light sources in the signal light caps.

Stairways, elevators, and escalators

The need for good lighting at these points is paramount in the interest of safety. Installations should be so designed that failure of one lamp will not leave an area inadequately lighted. Floor, wall, and overhead finishes should be of high reflectance to gain the maximum utilization of the light and to reduce shadows.

Stairways: Stairway lighting equipment should be so located and shielded that persons neither cast shadows on the stairs nor encounter glare at eye level. A unit should be located at least on every landing and closer if necessary.

Special treatment may be necessary to call attention to changes in elevation in corridors where one or two steps are necessary. This may be accomplished by placement of small, shielded lighting units recessed near the floor or by distinctive painting of the edges of the steps.

Elevators: Good lighting of the threshold should be provided to call attention to any difference in level between the landing and the car. It is recommended that the car interior be of as light a finish as is consistent with reasonable ease of maintenance.

Escalators: Good lighting should be provided on the tread, using shielded supplementary luminaires in the balustrade if necessary. Finishes should be of a light non-specular type.

Corridors and hallways

The primary considerations in lighting corridors and hallways are safety, general appearance, and luminance difference with adjacent offices. The spacing of lighting equipment from center to center should not exceed one and one-half times the mounting height. Hallway illuminance values that are at least one-fifth of the values in adjacent offices have been found to be preferable from the standpoint of relieving luminance differences between hallways and offices. The illuminance values recommended for hallways should be provided at floor level. Reflectances for ceilings, walls, and floors should equal or exceed those recommended for the offices. If dark finishes must be

Table 11. Approximate energy distribution (two 40-watt fluorescent lamps and ballast)

Light* (per cent)	Infrared energy † (per cent)	Conduction and convection (per cent)	Ballast (per cent)
19	31	36	14

* All radiant energy, including both visible and infrared, is converted to heat when absorbed by an object.
† Principally far infrared (wavelengths beyond 5000 nm.)

used from the maintenance standpoint, they should be limited to the dado.

Personal service

Sanitary maintenance of restrooms and washrooms is considerably improved by sufficient illuminance in the area of the urinals, stalls, and washbasins.

When lounges are incorporated as part of washrooms, casual reading will require an illuminance value in accordance with such tasks (see Table 10). This may be provided by supplementary lighting if desired. Mirror lighting and similar residential treatments improve the appearance and usefulness of these rooms.

Conservation of light heat energy

The control and removal of lighting heat can reduce heat gain in the occupied space, reduce air changes and fan horsepower, lower temperature differentials, and reduce luminaire and ceiling temperature, thereby minimizing radiant effects. It can also, if fluorescent lamps are used, result in more efficient lamp performance and longer ballast life.

The most efficient incandescent lamp utilizes less than 10 per cent of its input energy to produce light; the balance of the energy is heat. The fluorescent lamp is more than three times as efficient as the incandescent lamp in producing light, but it utilizes only one-fifth of the total energy input (Table 11). Every watt of energy supplied for lighting introduces 3.41 Btuh of heat into the space. Thus, 5 watts per unit area would produce over 17 Btuh of heat for the same unit area. This would total 6800 Btuh (2 kilowatts) in a 20- by 20-ft (6.1- by 6.1-m) office. One-half ton of refrigeration (12,000 Btuh = 1 ton) is necessary to take care of the heat from this lighting alone. This would be true whether the luminaires were suspended, surface mounted, or recessed.

Part of the heat from the lighting can be prevented from entering the occupied space by using recessed luminaires in a plenum with air return. More of the heat can

be picked up by returning the room air through the lamp compartment of the luminaire (Fig. 18). Theoretically about 85 per cent of the lighting heat can be picked up by this method. However, since the ceiling is not completely air tight and supply ducts carrying cool air pass through the plenum, the result is that 50 to 60 per cent of the heat remains in the plenum and 40 to 50 per cent enters the office space.

Since water is a better heat-transfer medium than air, circulating water through the housing of the luminaire (Fig. 19) will pick up heat more readily than the air system previously described. It has the further advantage that the heat picked up can be rejected from the building through evaporative cooling, thus reducing the refrigeration requirement required.

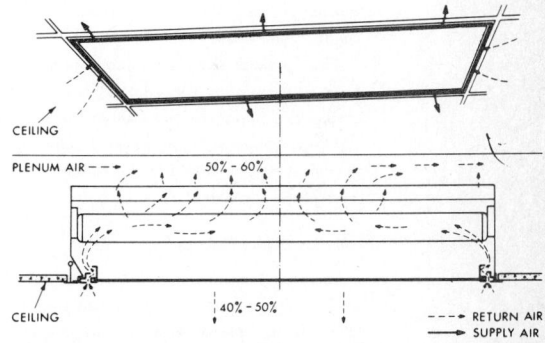

Fig. 18. Typical air-handling heat-transfer troffer. Return air, through slots at each end, passes over lamps and ballast cover and out through slots in top of luminaire; supply air to space passes through slots along side panel of troffer.

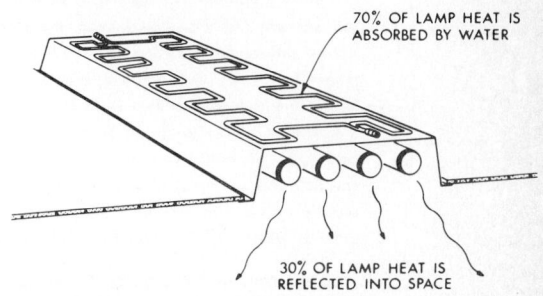

Fig. 19. Example of a water-cooled luminaire.

Data from American National Standard Practice for Industrial Lighting (ANSI A11.1-1973)

LIGHTING METHODS FOR INDUSTRIAL AREAS

Lighting must not only serve as a production tool and as a safety factor, but should also contribute to the over-all environmental conditions of the work space. The lighting system should be a part of the planned environment.

1. Quantity of illuminance must be sufficient for all visual tasks.

2. Quality of lighting must be in accordance with the recommendations given earlier in this section.

3. Lighting systems, painting of interior surfaces, machines, etc., should help provide a proper environment for the working interior.

The proper method of lighting a specific area is also dependent upon the size and proportions of the room.

General lighting

Modern industrial lighting practice requires the establishment of a base or minimum quantity of light throughout the room. This is termed general lighting. The quantity may vary depending upon the purpose for which the space is to be used. If visual tasks are particularly severe, higher illuminance over restricted areas can be added to this base. This additional light, known as supplementary lighting, is usually provided by luminaires placed relatively close to the area being illuminated.*

The general lighting system usually consists of luminaires placed ten feet or more above the floor. The purpose of the general lighting system is to provide sufficient light for most seeing tasks and promote safety and plant protection.

Localized general lighting

Many industrial plants have machinery of such a nature and so located that a uniform intensity of illuminance is not necessary throughout the area. Luminaires may be mounted above the visual task, supplying adequate illuminance values at the particular work points and at the same time providing sufficient illuminance for adjacent areas.

Where supplementary lighting is necessary the general lighting should keep the luminance difference between the well-lighted immediate work area and the surroundings within the ranges specified in Table 12.

Low-bay areas: In rooms relatively wide and long in proportion to the height, a spread type of direct lighting equipment is usually applicable. (Rooms of this category have a width greater than three times the

* See Recommended Practice for Supplementary Lighting by *Illuminating Engineering Society.*

height.) Here good quality illuminance is provided by fluorescent luminaires mounted in continuous rows, spaced to give the proper quantity and distribution of light.

The use of continuous rows of fluorescent units run at right angles, forming a grid or checkerboard pattern, provides higher illuminance values, reduces shadows, and assures more even luminance of machine dials, regardless of the angle at which these dials may be placed.

High-bay narrow interior: In areas where the width is equal to or less than the height, direct lighting equipment which concentrates the light is usually used in order to provide efficiently the necessary illuminance at the working plane. Usually incandescent or HID lamps are used for this application either alone or in combination.

HID lamps have the advantage of longer life and higher efficiency. When the two types of sources are used together the filament lamps supply an excess of red light to offset the deficiency in red of some HID types, the result being a synthetic "white" widely employed for industrial areas. Also the use of combination systems alleviates the problem created by temporary power interruptions since the HID lamps do not immediately restart.

High-bay wide interior: Some of the newer manufacturing areas, notably airplane assembly plants, are enormous in both length and width, while at the same time the ceiling height is 30 or 40 ft (9.1 or 12.2 m) or more. Concentrating types of direct lighting equipment can be used, mounted on appropriate spacings to provide the quantity of illumination required.

However, because of the extreme width and length, spread types of direct lighting

equipment can be used to good advantage with a large number of luminaires each contributing a small amount of light to any given point. This reduces shadows to a minimum and gives higher vertical surface illuminance. With fluorescent units the effect approaches that of indirect lighting. These fluorescent luminaires are preferably mounted in continuous rows, which simplifies installation and wiring.

Nonproductive and service areas: In areas such as warehouses, boiler and pump rooms, freight elevators, washrooms, lockers, corridors, etc., the lighting requirement is usually one of providing reasonable diffusion, comfort, and appearance with a minimum of cost. For these areas the requirements can be met with incandescent lamps in direct (spread) equipment or in semidirect units. Where better appearance is a factor or where a higher level of illumination is necessary, it is desirable to use direct or semidirect fluorescent equipment.

Special requirements: Some types of work require precise color discrimination, and for these areas special care in light source selection should be exercised. Where third-dimension perception is important, care should be taken to provide sufficient shadow for the modeling of solid forms. A wide variety of special types of lighting is used in connection with inspection processes. Among these are low-angle, silhouette, transillumination, magnification, projection, fluorescence, polarized, and stroboscopic lighting.

QUANTITY OF ILLUMINATION

Recommended illuminance values for several hundred specific industrial tasks are given in the Standard.

Table 12. Recommended maximum luminance ratios

	Environmental classification		
	A	B	C
1. Between tasks and adjacent darker surroundings	3 to 1	3 to 1	5 to 1
2. Between tasks and adjacent lighter surroundings	1 to 3	1 to 3	1 to 5
3. Between tasks and more remote darker surfaces	10 to 1	20 to 1	*
4. Between tasks and more remote lighter surfaces	1 to 10	1 to 20	*
5. Between luminaires (or windows, skylights, etc.) and surfaces adjacent to them	20 to 1	*	*
6. Anywhere within normal field of view	40 to 1	*	*

* *Luminance ratio control not practical.*
A—*Interior areas where reflectances of entire space can be controlled in line with recommendations for optimum seeing conditions.*
B—*Areas where reflectances of immediate work area can be controlled, but control of remote surround is limited.*
C—*Areas (indoor and outdoor) where it is completely impractical to control reflectances and difficult to alter environmental conditions.*

Data from American National Standard Guide for School Lighting (ANSI/IES RP-3, 1977)

CHANGING NEEDS IN SCHOOL LIGHTING

The goal of educational facility lighting is to provide an optimum environment for both student and instructor. The occupants of the space need to see their visual tasks accurately, quickly, and comfortably. Uniformity of lighting systems throughout the facility does not assure optimum visual performance because of the variety of visual tasks found in any school situation. The tasks are increasingly varied as the pupil moves upwards from elementary through high school to college.

Visual tasks in schools: The visual tasks occurring in the various school grades are numerous. Between the simplest and the most complex, there are hundreds varying in size, direction and viewing distance from the eye, brightness difference, and so on.

Within the total visual environment there are small area tasks, such as reading and writing, which commonly require prolonged and close attention. There may be close-to-the-eye tasks or distant tasks; small print or large print; tasks on matte or glossy paper. Pupils may be required to change from reading manuscript writing at the desk to reading cursive writing on the chalkboard; from looking almost straight down, to looking along and above the horizontal; from cutting and pasting, to viewing projected pictures.

Illuminance

Recommended illuminance value for various school tasks and spaces are listed in Table 13. To ensure the quality of the illuminance, luminance ratios should not exceed those shown in Fig. 20, and reflectances should not be less than those recommended in Fig. 21. Particular care should be taken to prevent glare, both direct and indirect, as discussed in detail in the section on "Light and vision."

Special tasks require special lighting

It would be impractical to light a classroom by providing only the amount needed for one given task. In a classroom, individual students may be performing different tasks at the same time. Also, the whole working area, as potential teaching space, must be provided with a satisfactory minimum illuminance value. The general lighting level will be designed for a commonly found, most difficult task.

Certain classrooms are used for special purposes. In these it is desirable, indeed necessary, to light for the specific task. Where physical disabilities play a part, special illuminance values will be required. In school shops, sewing rooms and art classrooms, lighting should be planned on a specific vi-

Table 13. Illuminance values* recommended for performing visual tasks in schools

Area	Foot-candles (fc)	Lux (lx)†
Tasks		
Reading printed material	30	300
Reading pencil writing	70	700
Spirit duplicated material		
Good	30	300
Poor	100	1000
Drafting, benchwork	100	1000
Lip reading, chalkboards, sewing	150	1500
Classrooms		
Art rooms	70	700
Drafting rooms	100	1000
Home economics rooms		
Sewing	150	1500
Cooking	50	500
Ironing	50	500
Sink activities	70	700
Notetaking areas	70	700
Laboratories	100	1000
Lecture rooms		
Audience area	70	700
Demonstration area	150	1500
Music rooms		
Simple scores	30	300
Advanced scores	70	700
Shops	100	1000
Sight-saving rooms	150	1500
Study halls	70	700
Typing	70	700
Corridors and stairways	20	200
Dormitories		
General	10	100
Reading books, magazines, newspapers	30	300
Study desk	70	700

* *Minimum on the task at any time for young adults with normal and better than 20/30 corrected vision.*
† *Lux is an SI unit equal to 0.0929 footcandle.*

sual task basis. In some cases, supplementary lighting may be used to provide sufficient illuminance for specific areas (e.g., the lighting of a chalkboard).

Chalkboards should meet two brightness standards. They should be light enough to blend well with the background, and dark enough to provide sufficient contrast to chalk writing. A chalkboard should be measured for reflectance under "in use" conditions, with a typical amount of chalk film on its surface. Colored boards should not exceed 20 per cent reflectance under these conditions. Black chalkboards in use are not usually black, but dark gray, with 5 to 10 per cent reflectance.

For viewing motion picture and slide projector screens or TV in the classroom the comfortable visual environment should be much the same as for any other visual work. The area immediately surrounding these screens should be slightly less bright than the screen itself, and the entire visual surroundings should be kept as light as possible without causing the image on the screen to lose contrast.

SPECIAL APPLICATIONS

Illuminance values recommended for various specific areas in schools are listed in Table 13. Some of these areas are discussed in the following paragraphs.

Art rooms: As the appearance of colors in an art room is a paramount consideration, the light source used should render the colors as accurately as possible. High color rendering light sources should be selected rather than the standard cool white.

Supplementary lighting from spot lamps

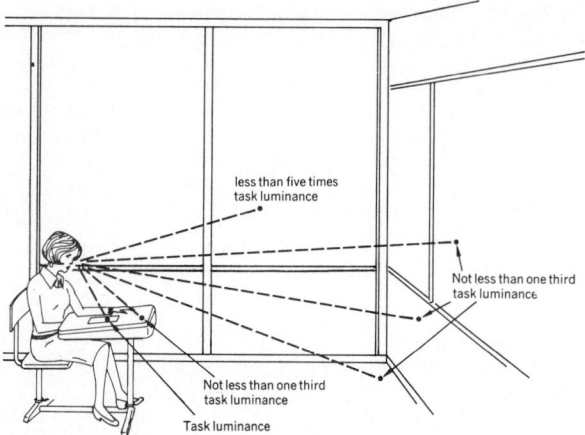

Fig. 20. Recommended maximum luminance ratios for school classrooms. Control media are used at the windows to reduce exterior luminances so that they are in balance with interior luminances.

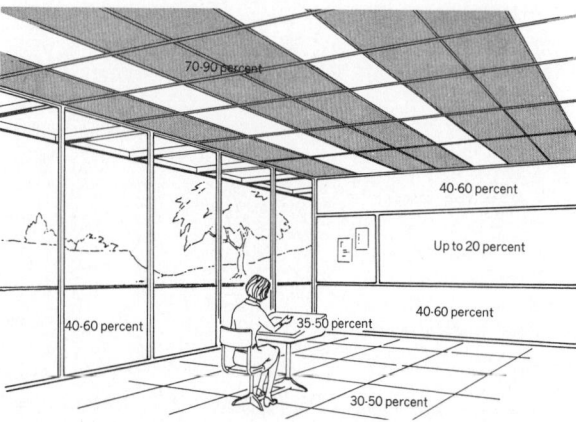

Fig. 21. Recommended reflectances for surfaces and furnishings in the classroom. Control media at windows should have reflectances similar to those of walls.

is useful on displays and models for improved visibility at a distance and for modeling purposes. Such lighting creates the desired highlights and shadows on art arrangements being painted or drawn. Supplementary lighting, such as that from adjustable desk lamps which can provide a definite directional light, is frequently desirable when students work on or study surfaces involving glaze or texture.

Auditoriums: The auditorium is made up of a seating area (house), and a stage area. It may serve as an assembly and lecture hall, study room, theater, concert hall, audiovisual aid room (including television), and for many other activities. Many schools today are developing speech and drama programs, not only among students, but also among adult groups. The auditorium serves so many purposes it must be well planned and properly equipped to satisfy them all.

For general auditorium use, there is need for atmosphere lighting which can be incorporated into the architecture as ceiling or wall coves, luminous ceiling treatments or decorative suspended indirect luminaires. Facilities to provide more than one level of illuminance are desirable since this area may serve several purposes.

The basic lighting for the seating area should be planned for audience assembly purposes, and at dramatic presentations for such intermission tasks as reading programs. It should be dimmer-controlled, preferably from several stations (stage lighting board, stage manager's station, rear of main floor seating area, projection booth) which will allow for gradual transitions and for lower levels to be used in showing slides and motion pictures. If windows are used, means should be provided to darken them during projection.

Supplementary illuminance is required if the seating area is used for study or testing purposes. Several circuits of this supplementary system, well distributed over the seating area and providing additional illuminance for penciled handwriting and reading, can be set up for independent switching. Special care should be taken to avoid specular reflection from any direct downlighting.

Aisle and exit lights, with a low level of nondistracting illuminance, should be provided. The aisle lights should not be visible to any of the seated audience. Because of the high luminance ratios in a semidarkened room, they may prove irritating despite low surface brightness. If there are steps in the aisles, small and well-shielded step lights offer a safety aid. These should be located in the side of the step, not in the riser, to prevent light spilling on the stage or into eyes of people going up the steps.

Particular attention should be given to local building codes regarding exit lights, panic controls, and so on. It is desirable that an emergency lighting system be installed which would be automatically operated and connected to a separate power supply from that of the main lighting system.

Proper lighting facilities for the stage must include more than sufficient illuminance. Stage lighting is an art embracing a knowledge of color, shading and three-dimensional composition. During a production all these factors are brought into account and may be changed continually from one scene to the next. The layout of lighting equipment and a lighting control system may range from a simple plan with a minimum of equipment to a complex plan with elaborate equipment, as might be required in a school with a strong dramatics program. The layout will be affected by the amount the stage may be used, the budget, and future plans for the auditorium. Detailed layout for a small school stage will be found at the end of this section.

Adequate provision must be made in the house area for spotlights to cover the downstage (close to the audience) area. These lights should be located at a sufficiently low angle with the horizontal to avoid unpleasant shadows from a strong downward beam of light. These spotlights should be mounted so that they may be adjusted vertically and horizontally and the focus changed by a person having a full view of the stage. In choosing a spotlight, first consideration should be given to the ease with which the shape and definition of the light beam can be controlled, since this is of prime importance in preventing light spill on the curtains and walls around the stage.

Spotlights are also required over the whole stage to light the various acting areas. Borderlights and footlights of the individual reflector or compartment type provide a convenient source of general lighting and add an over-all blending to the lighting picture. Auxiliary striplights, floodlights and spotlights may be required to light various areas and backings. The upstage (away from the audience) area will require as much attention as the downstage area, if the general effect of the whole stage lighting is to be uniform. In addition to circuits necessary for overhead lighting, groups of stage-type receptacles are required on or near the stage floor around the acting area for additional lighting units which may be plugged in from time to time. Separate work-lights are also necessary for the stage.

With the possible exception of border-lights and footlights, no lighting unit should be permanently wired to a branch lighting circuit. All other special lighting units should be wired to make them readily portable.

It is desirable that all stage lighting branch circuits be brought into a central interconnecting panel. The panel provides a switching or interplugging system whereby any stage branch circuit can be connected to any dimming circuit.

The dimming components may be either of the manually operated or remotely operated type. Manually operated systems are less expensive; remotely operated systems offer ease of control and added versatility. Dimmer systems may be of the thyratron, magnetic amplifier, saturable reactor, silicon controlled rectifier, or autotransformer types.

The operator of the equipment should be able to see and hear the stage action and be readily accessible. The interconnecting panel is usually placed in a convenient back-stage location.

Cafeterias and kitchens: In eating areas the lighting should create a cheerful, comfortable area. Good lighting promotes cleanliness. Dining areas are frequently used as supplementary study halls and when so used the lighting should provide the illuminance values recommended for the task. Where the appearance of food is a prime consideration, as in the cafeteria, high color rendering lamps should be used. Additional lighting may also be used over the serving counter to give the food eye appeal and to speed up the selection of food at the serving counter. Good general diffuse lighting is needed in the kitchen, especially at ranges, work tables and sinks, to assure cleanliness, safety and good housekeeping.

Corridors: Corridors are transition areas from the high luminances of the out-of-doors to the lower luminances of the learning areas. They should be well-lighted, particularly where monitors are stationed, to promote safety and discipline and to assure good housekeeping in the lockers which frequently line corridors. When corridors are used as work-study areas they should meet lighting standards for learning areas.

Corridors also provide an opportunity to add visual interest to school environments and visual importance to displays, bulletin boards, posters, notices, etc. Selected highlighted areas can add considerably to the pleasantness and visual vitality of corridors.

Dormitory rooms: Dormitory rooms are commonly provided with two systems of illuminance, one of relatively low level for general illuminance, the other of higher value for study purposes. Such an installation is particularly desirable where a room is shared by two or more students in order that one may retire with comfort if the other wishes to continue studying. See section on "Lighting: Residential."

Every dormitory room should be provided with sufficient convenience outlets to afford a variety of furniture arrangement. Outlets should be provided for such supplementary lighting units as dressing table lamps and bed lamps.

Drafting rooms: See section on "Lighting, Offices."

General-purpose rooms: This designation applies to rooms used both for gymnasium and auditorium activities or cafeteria. Since the primary use will be for physical education, the lighting should be appropriate for gymnasium use. With higher ceilings, greater utilization can be effected by use of semi-direct lighting where most of the light is directed downward and some is directed upward to lighten the ceiling. However, such lighting is strictly utilitarian in feeling, while direct-indirect or semi-indirect will give a diffusion which is considered more in keeping with the refinement of an auditorium or restaurant. If the area is to be used as an auditorium, and as such as a study room, then special attention should be paid to minimizing veiling reflections in pencil work and printed material by using luminaires providing a special distribution of downward component.

Gymnasiums: The modern school gymnasium is a multipurpose as well as a multisport area which can serve a variety of needs of the student body during the daytime, and in many instances, the community at night. In addition to its varied athletic uses, the school gymnasium is often used for such activities as assemblies, dances, concerts, lectures, and community meetings. Because of the wide divergence of seeing tasks that can be encountered, a choice of lighting levels may be desirable. Such variations in the general illuminance are most often achieved by circuiting. The lighting system is designed for the highest illuminance value required. Then, by placing portions of the total system on separate circuits which can be operated independently or in combination with other circuits, a range of illuminance value can be obtained.

For special activities, such as dances, where the creation of a mood or an atmosphere is the primary lighting objective, and low illuminance is desired, the most satisfactory results can often be achieved through the use of portable or temporary supplementary lighting equipment, such as small floodlights, reflectorized lamps, and colored filters.

Caution must be exercised in positioning luminaires relative to critical surfaces, such as glass backboards, to avoid blinding reflections. Windows in a gymnasium are unsatisfactory in the amount of illuminance they provide, and can produce undesirable reflections or blinding glare if improperly located. Gymnasium floors should be finished with a nonglossy finish to avoid undesirable reflections and possible veiling glare.

To prevent breakage, it may be necessary to cover otherwise unprotected luminaires with a protective cover or wire grid. This will reduce their efficiency and should be compensated for in the initial system design by multiplying the luminaire efficiency by the average transmittance of the cover or grid.

Laboratories: These involve special laboratory tables or benches at which very detailed work is carried out in dissection, inspection of reactions, instrumentation and measurement. Good diffusion with some directional component and appropriate color quality is required.

Many times fluorescent lighting equipment is run continuously along the benches or tables just above head height. This gives localized general lighting with maximum illuminance where the work is being carried out. An upward component for lighting the ceiling is essential, as is adequate shielding. Where color reactions are to be observed, and to avoid distortion, it is extremely important to exercise care in selecting the most appropriate color rendering lamps for the application.

Laboratories commonly require special electrical provisions such as portable table reflectors to assist in microscope work and in reading precision instruments and meters. Numerous convenience outlets should be provided at work tables and at the sides of rooms to permit connection to electrical apparatus and to portable lighting equipment for experiments. For zoology and anatomy lecture rooms, and laboratories where dissection by the instructor is part of the class work, a large mirror at an angle of about 45 deg, suitably located and combined with high level concentrated illumi-

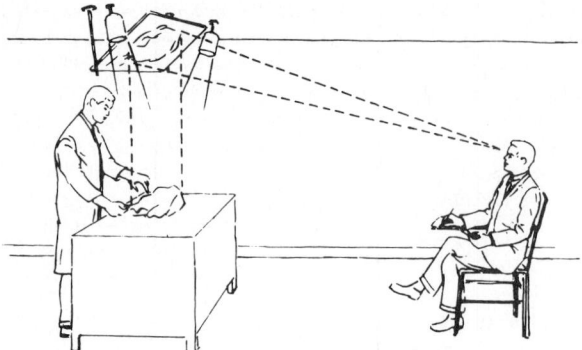

Fig. 22. Lighting and mirror arrangement for viewing laboratory lecture experiments

nance over the lecture table, will permit students to visualize experimental work in the top horizontal as well as the vertical plane (see Fig. 22).

Lecture rooms: The typical lecture room should be provided with a comfortable general lighting system which is flexible enough to provide a moderately high level for general use and a subdued level for use during projection or special demonstrations. Many times downlighting is used to avoid spilling light on the screen. However, all downlighting should be carefully designed to avoid loss of visibility due to veiling reflection in handwriting and printed materials. If a demonstration table is used, directional downlights should be aimed down on this table and the lecturer. These spotlights should be located within a 45 to 60-deg angle above horizontal as measured from the probable location of a speaker's head when he stands behind the table. This arrangement assures minimum glare and provides good lighting on the speaker's face. Special chalkboard lighting significantly improves visibility and attention power.

Libraries, reading rooms, and carrels: See section on Libraries.

Locker rooms: The lighting of locker rooms and dressing room areas is principally a matter of arranging the lighting equipment so that the interior of the lockers is illuminated and general lighting is supplied for safe movement about the room. This usually can be accomplished by means of continuous fluorescent luminaires located between rows of lockers.

Offices: These should be the same as classrooms but with higher illuminance to be commensurate with the greater difficulty of the tasks and longer time duration (see section on "Lighting: Offices").

Safety: Emergency lighting insures the safety of a school building's students when the normal lighting system fails. The illuminance provided by the emergency lighting system should permit an orderly accident-free exit from the building. If exiting is not required, the system should provide security and comfort to the remaining students until the general lighting can be restored.

The basic definitions are of three types as follows:

Type I must function when the normal lighting system fails, due to any fault in the building's power distribution system, due to the failure of the public utility, or any single manual act such as accidental opening of a switch.

Type II must function when a fault *within* the building's power distribution system causes the normal lighting to fail.

Type III must function when the public utility or other *outside* energy source fails.

The following two methods of electric emergency lighting systems are in present use:

1. A system of separate luminaires supplied by two independent power sources so arranged that on the failure of one, the other will operate automatically and immediately. The primary source of power is the public utility and the secondary source is a centrally located system of batteries automatically recharged and ready for further service when the primary source is again turned off. The secondary source can also be an on-the-premises auxiliary generator that can "kick-on" to provide the necessary illumination within ten seconds after the normal system fails.

2. Unit devices with individual batteries providing for the same functions as specified in item 1 above, for individual or groups of luminaires, except that the battery supplied luminaires may be operated on a separate circuit at any voltage, different from that used by the primary lighting system.

Exit lighting should provide the required illuminance on the floors of pathways to exits. This should include angles and intersections of corridors, passageways, stair landings and exit doors; and should also provide sufficient illuminance on the exit signs, either internal or external, to assure ready visibility without distracting glare, and in accordance with national and local safety codes.

Sewing rooms: In the high school the most difficult seeing tasks generally encountered by the girls are those involved in sewing. The process of seeing the fine stitching on cloth which matches the thread in color is inherently difficult and fatiguing. The stitching on a piece of fabric is seen in part by the reflected glint from the thread and by the variations in shades and shadows produced by the thread as it weaves in and out of the cloth. For this reason, equipment which provides a slight directional component to the lighting is desired. Supplementary lighting by spotlights, portable floor lamps and sewing machine attachment lamps is desirable for the same reason and is especially useful when the sewing is being done on dark cloth where the reflectance level is inherently low.

Shops: Students working with power tools are generally novices, inexperienced with the dangers of machine operation. The lighting of a school shop should follow the best industrial lighting practice (see section on "Lighting: Industrial") for the types of industrial activities practiced in the shop, with special emphasis to assist accuracy of manual operations and to make all elements of danger visually obvious. The painting of special backgrounds of the work points on the machinery is desirable to make them stand out; and special colors, following the American Standard Safety Color Code, Z53.1-1963, should be adopted for those machine controls, and for those machine parts that represent a hazard to the worker.

Luminaires similar to those used in the rest of the school and appropriate high-intensity discharge luminaires may be used, but consideration should be given to possible stroboscopic effect and temporary outages.

Stairs: The lighting installation for the corridor frequently does not adequately light the stair landings, in which case special lighting units must be installed for each landing. Care should be taken in locating stairway luminaires so that the edges of all steps are properly illuminated. These units should be out of the direct view of people using the stairs.

Special emergency lighting units powered by an emergency source should be considered for use in stairs, at least on every other landing, installed either on walls or ceiling.

Swimming pools: (see "Lighting, Sports")

Underwater pool lighting is an important safety provision and furnishes maximum satisfaction to the swimmers. The structural surfaces of the pool should always be finished in a light color.

Overhead general lighting luminaires in-stalled in swimming pool areas should be of a type which can withstand the high humidity which prevails in such areas. Continuously moist conditions are detrimental to the life of the units unless the internal portions are protected by sealing.

Care should be taken to avoid placing lighting units above the water where accessibility is difficult and breakage serious. Well-diffused illumination is desirable to avoid the reflection of light sources from the surface of the water.

By STANLEY McCANDLESS, *Professor of Lighting, Yale University; Research and Development, Century Lighting, Inc.*

Lighting the small school stage

These pages show a suggested layout and equipment for a small stage. Anything less should be considered a speaking platform and be treated as such. Equipment listed in the tables is a conservative minimum. A discussion of the lighting equipment and some special portable units follows:

Spotlights: Generally there should be acting area lights directed so that the actor is lighted from the front diagonals with a warm and a cool color. Ellipsoidal spotlights are used in front of the proscenium because they will not spill light on the audience; fresnel lens spots behind the proscenium blend the lighting of adjacent areas easily.

Border and background lights: There should be a borderlight behind each masking border to light the next cloth border or back curtain. Background lights are for lighting the backdrop or cyclorama (plastered back wall in this case), window backings, ground rows, and all parts of the scene visible to the audience but outside the acting area. These instruments are used primarily for exterior scenes. The back-drop or plastered back wall not over 75 ft away from the stage. As a measure of safety and reliability, all portable connections should be made by 20-A twistlocks.

Dimmers: Lighting equipment is useless without a certain number of dimmers to permit (1) color mixing and intensity balancing, (2) individual or group dimming or brightening at some course of action in the play. In theory each circuit should be dimmed sep-

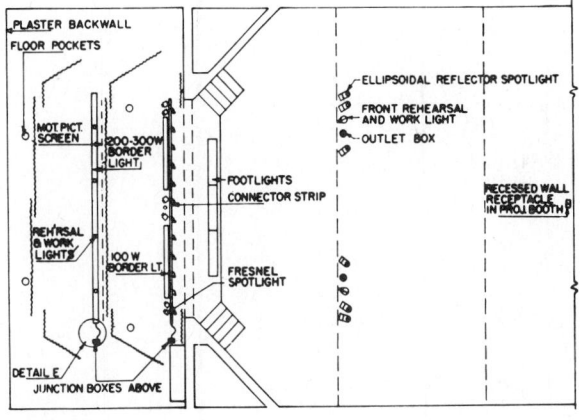

Lighting Layout

Switchboard Diagram

LIGHTS

UNIT	FUNCTION	QUANTITY
6-in. Ellipsoidal Reflector Spotlight, 250–750-w	Lighting front acting areas	6
Disappearing Footlight, 100-w, nine lamps	Toning of faces and set	3
6-in. Fresnel Spotlight, 250–750-w	Lighting rear acting areas	6
Borderlight, 100-w, 8-ft long, 16 lamps, four colors, one work light	Blending of acting areas	2
Borderlight, 200–300-w, 25 ft, 4 in., 36 lamps, three colors, four work lamps	Lighting background	1
Front Rehearsal and Work Lights, 500-w, R-40 lamps, adjustable sockets	As indicated by name	2

OUTLETS

UNIT	QUANTITY
Connector Strip, 24-ft long	1
Surface Mounted Outlet Box	2
Floor Pockets, 4-way	4
Recessed Wall Mounted Receptacle, 2-way, 50 amp	1

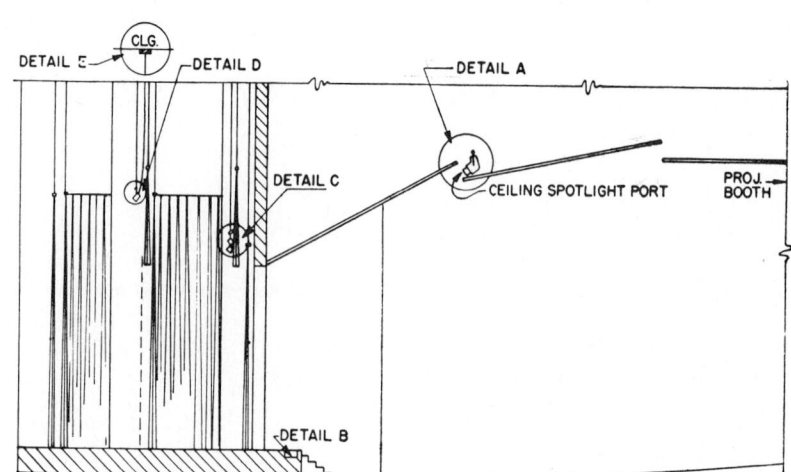

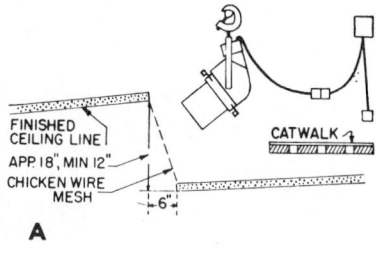

A

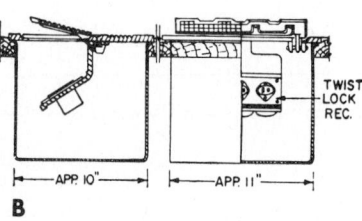

B

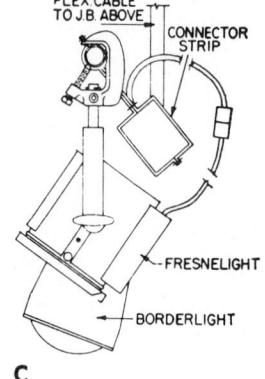

C

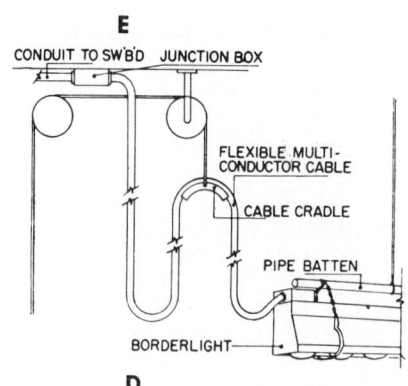

D

arately, but cost will probably necessitate a compromise. calls for considerable wattage. Strips placed close to the base at the foot of the backdrop can give effects of sunset, etc.

Special lights: (1) instruments used for emphasizing doorways and special pieces of furniture (generally spotlights); (2) high-powered units to simulate sunlight and moonlight (3) "effect machine" to project patterns or Linnebach Lantern for shadow patterns; (4) a 2000-W ellipsoidal reflector follow spot

for musicals, which should be mounted on a stand. A practical way for grouping several circuits is through use of an interplugging panel. With this panel any one or group of load circuits can be connected to any dimmer control. Autotransformer type dimmers are used because they will dim any load proportionally up to their rated capacity; this is not true of resistance dimmers. Note on the drawing of the switchboard that house light dimmers are separate. Large dimmers can serve as proportional masters

over the six smaller dimmers, or be used as individual large dimmers for controlling background lighting. In the patch panel, the 1000-W dimmer controls have two jack pockets and the 6000-W units have four jack pockets. Each load circuit representing outlets placed about the stage is protected by a circuit breaker, and the whole panel has a locked door to prevent tampering with the setup. As far as possible, switchboards should be placed so that the operator can see the stage.

Data from Recommended Practice of Library Lighting (IES RP-4 1974)

Library buildings are frequently important works of architecture. In such cases, as much care must be given to the proper lighting of the building as to the lighting of its library functions.

Reading is the visual task performed most often in a library. Reading tasks vary from children's books printed on 10- to 14-point type on good non-gloss paper, to newspapers printed in 7-point type on low contrast, off-white pulp paper, to law books with long paragraphs in condensed type, to old and rare books with unusual type faces printed on old paper which has darkened with age, to handwriting in pencil or pen. Other visual tasks include the study of maps, prints, slides, and microfilm viewers.

Recommended illumination levels for various areas are given in Table 14. Recommended luminance ratios are the same as those given for schools in Fig. 20. Recommended reflectances are given in Fig. 21.

The *main reading room* is usually furnished with tables and chairs and may also have lounge chairs. Lighting is generally uniform with supplementary lighting for some special tasks.

Individual study areas (carrels) may be located in many areas of the library—in the main reading room, the stack areas, or in special rooms. They may vary in type from compartments on a large table to almost fully enclosed rooms. They usually face in various directions. The principal lighting problems are shadows produced by the dividing partitions. It is desirable to provide lighting from as many directions as practicable so that shadows will be at a minimum. The ideal lighting system would be a luminous ceiling. The use of individual overhead luminaires produces the greatest number of shadows. Local lighting is recommended when feasible, preferably located at the side of the student. Carrels should be finished in light colors to reduce absorption losses and excessive luminance differences.

Shelving and stack areas occupy large portions of library buildings and present serious lighting and seeing problems. Open book shelves around the walls of reading rooms present no problem; they are usually adequately illuminated by the general lighting of the room. Freestanding book stacks are a problem. They are usually arranged in rows with aisles varying in width from 2 to 3 ft (0.61–0.92 m) and are usually about 7 ft, 6 in (2.3 m) high. The lowest shelf may be only 4 in (10 cm) above the floor and the top shelf could be 6 ft, 4 in (1.9 m) above the floor. When the width of the aisle is 3 ft the viewing angle will vary from 45 degrees above the horizontal to 60 degrees below (Fig. 23, left). Veiling reflections are likely to obscure the titles of books on the top shelf and the long viewing distance and the distortion caused by the extreme viewing angle make it very difficult to see the titles of the books on the bottom shelf. Continuous rows of fluorescent luminaires are usually located over the centers of the aisles, providing uniform illumination along the length of the stacks. Arranging the continuous rows at right angles to the rows provides higher illumination levels on the spines of books on the lower shelves (Fig. 23, right). Other advantages of this arrangement are that the rows may be spaced somewhat farther apart and the stack spacing may be changed without relocating the luminaires.

Card catalogs are usually located in the main reading rooms. The cards are almost always in a vertical position when in use; therefore, rows of luminaires should be located at right angles rather than parallel to the files. When located in this position, illumination comes from each side over the reader's shoulders and increased illumination on the vertical cards is provided.

Circulation desks are usually located near the entrance in the main reading room or near the entrance to the building. When located in the main reading room, the general overhead lighting system may provide sufficient illumination for the desk. When located in the lobby, a suspended group of lumi-

Table 14. Illuminance values[a] currently recommended for libraries (equivalent sphere illumination unless otherwise indicated[c])

Area	Illuminance fc	Illuminance lx[b]	Area	Illuminance fc	Illuminance lx[b]
Reading Areas			Audiovisual areas		
Reading printed material	30	300	Preparation rooms	70	700
Study and note taking	70	700	Viewing rooms (variable)	70	700
Conference areas	30	300	Television receiving room		
Seminar rooms	70	700	(shield viewing screen)	70	700
Book stacks (30 in [76 cm] above			Audio listening areas		
floor)			General	30	300
Active stacks	30[c]	300	For note taking	70	700
Inactive stacks	5[c]	50	Record inspection table	100	1000
Book repair and binding	70	700	Microform areas		
Cataloging	70	700	Files	70	700
Card files	100	1000	Viewing areas	30	300
Carrels, individual study areas	70	700	Office Areas		
Circulation desks	70	700	See Table 10		
Rare book rooms—archives	30	300	Corridors	20[e]	200
Storage areas	100	1000	Toilets and wash rooms	30	300
Reading areas					
Map, picture, and print rooms					
Storage areas	30	300			
Use areas	100	1000			

[a] *Minimum on the task at any time for young adults with normal and better than 20/30 corrected vision. (See section on Light and Vision.)*

[b] *Lux (lx) is an SI unit equal to 0.0929 footcandle.*

[c] *Vertical.*

[d] *Obtained with a combination of general lighting plus specialized supplementary lighting. Care should be taken to keep within the recommended luminance ratios.*

[e] *Or not less than 1/5 the level in adjacent areas.*

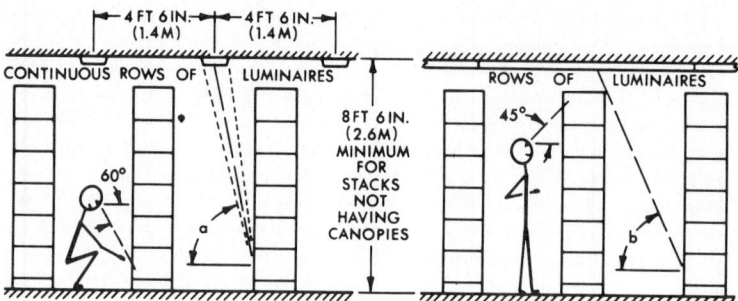

Fig. 23. (Left) Luminaires parallel with stacks. (Right) Luminaires at right angles to stacks provide better vertical illumination on lower-shelf books.

naires on long stems may be desirable as a floating luminous element over the desk.

Conference and seminar rooms are frequently provided in libraries. In addition to general overhead lighting, illumination should be provided for speakers and their materials at the lectern and at the seminar table. For example, the speaker can be lighted by adjustable recessed or ornamental exposed luminaires using reflector lamps. Two such spot lighting units should provide lighting at an angle of approximately 65 degrees above the horizontal and 35 degrees on each side of the speaker.

Display and exhibition areas are part of many libraries. When the displays are in glass covered horizontal cases, objectionable reflected glare and veiling reflections from the glass will reduce the ability to see objects. Where possible, overhead luminaires should be located above the front edge of the case so that the reflected image of the luminaire will be reflected away from the eyes (see Fig. 24).

Audio rooms are listening areas for lectures, music and other recorded material. These areas are either small rooms with indi-

vidual reproducing equipment, or large rooms where head receivers may be plugged into circuits at carrels. Lighting is similar to that required for other carrels.

Microfilm viewing areas: Most types of viewers are best used in an environment with a low level of general illumination. Because of this condition, viewers are usually grouped together in an area where the general illumination can be controlled or dimmed. Where viewers must be placed in reading areas or work areas with high levels of general illumination, the machines should be hooded and have screens which are treated to reduce reflections, or they can be viewed under normal conditions if they are of a television-type screen.

Viewing machines may be placed side by side on counter tops or in study carrels. The area containing the machines should be adjacent to the microform files, but the higher lighting levels of the file area should not be allowed to spill into the viewing area. A portable shaded luminaire may be provided at the side of each machine to illuminate a fixed shelf for note taking.

If flexibility and conversion of space is

Fig. 24. Lighting units should be mounted above the front side of the display so that the reflected image of the source will be directed away from the viewer's eyes.

planned for uses other than originally assigned, provisions in the wiring system should permit future installation of additional lighting units. In the areas which are assigned to microfilm viewing, the lighting level can be reduced by installing dimming control for general illumination, or by additional switching which would permit alternate groups of luminaires or pairs of lamps in the same luminaire to be turned off. For the machines themselves and for local lighting at each machine, it may be important to provide sufficient outlets in walls or floors of any spaces which might be assigned to microfilm viewing.

By NOYCE L. GRIFFIN, *Electrical Engineer, Architectural and Engineering Branch, Division of Hospital and Medical Facilities, U.S. Public Health Service. Revised 1972 by M. B. MANTOOTH, Chief Electrical Engineer, Office of Architecture and Engineering, U.S. Public Health Service*

Lighting in all areas of the hospital should be designed for comfortable seeing. Luminaires should be durable, a standard type, neat, attractively designed, easily cleaned and relamped.

WORK SPACES should be relatively free from shadows and have sufficient illumination on work areas to eliminate the need for portable units with extension cords on floor or work area.

GENERAL AREAS. The lighting of offices, corridors, assembly halls, shops, boiler and machine rooms, kitchens, and storage spaces can be treated as in other types of buildings. *The Illuminating Engineering Society Lighting Handbook,* 5th ed., 1972, should be consulted.

PATIENTS' ROOMS should have installed lighting for three distinct services: (1) general illumination for the room, (2) a reading light for each patient, and (3) a night light in the room. A fourth service, a doctor's examining light, may be an installed unit or a feature incorporated into the patient's reading light, or the light may be supplied by a portable lamp with an extension cord. This examining light should produce approximately 100 footcandles (1000 lux) over a limited area. A fixed ceiling-mounted examining light arranged to illuminate the entire bed area might be uncomfortably glaring for the patient, but it need not be left on longer than required for the examination. Such an arrangement is preferred to handheld or portable examining lights.

NIGHT LIGHTS can be included as an added feature to the reading light or other units, but the flush wall-mounted type is generally preferred. Wall-mounted night lights should be about 18 in. above the floor, located so that they are not likely to be covered by furniture or drapes. Night lights should be switched at the door.

RECOVERY ROOMS and intensive care rooms of Progressive Patient Care units should have about 30 footcandles (300 lux) of general illumination.

Patients frequently complain about the radiation of heat from a nearby reading light. A unit with an output intensity sufficient to permit adequate lighting when the unit is located a greater distance from the patient will reduce the objectionable heat. Where two or more beds are located in one room, the reading lights should be of a type that can be installed or adjusted so as not to shine in other patients' eyes. Each reading light should have a switch control accessible to the patient.

OPERATING AND DELIVERY ROOMS should have general illumination of about 100 footcandles (1000 lux) for the room area and special, separately controlled lights for the tables.

The major operating light should provide a multibeam of larger area for directing a minimum of 2500 footcandles (25,000 lux) in the center of a 10-in diameter circular area on the operating table, and tapering to not less than 500 footcandles (5000 lux) at the edge of that circle.

DELIVERY ROOMS require about the same general illumination as operating rooms. If the room is used for all deliveries, including Caesarean section and others which require extensive surgery, lighting at the table should be equal to that recommended for operating rooms. Where it is contemplated that the room will be used only for normal deliveries and for those which require only minor surgery, the light at the table may be somewhat less than that required for operating rooms.

MINOR SURGERY, EMERGENCY ROOMS, CYSTOSCOPIC ROOMS, AND AUTOPSY ROOMS should have about 100 footcandles (1000 lux) general illumination. These rooms should have supplemental lighting either by ceiling-mounted adjustable luminaires or portable units which will provide spot intensities of 2000 to 2500 footcandles, (20,000 to 25,000 lux).

FRACTURE ROOMS need about 90 footcandles (900 lux) general illumination with supplemental lighting for the table of about 200 fc (2000 lux).

LABORATORIES require about 50 to 100 footcandles (500 to 1000 lux) depending upon the seeing task. Currently recommended footcandles listed in the *IES Lighting Handbook,* should be consulted.

Where critical observation of color is required, as in surgery, laboratories, and autopsy rooms, color correction of the light may be necessary to provide a color effect as nearly as possible to that by which tests or specimens are ordinarily viewed. Daylight and incandescent filament lamp lighting have in the past been the most commonly accepted sources of illumination for critical seeing involving color determination.

EMERGENCY LIGHTING should be provided for safety of patients, staff, and protection of plant. As a minimum in any case, emergency lighting should be provided for operating and delivery rooms, exits, stairs, corridors, switchboard, and boiler rooms. Additional emergency lighting will be needed where hospitals may be without the normal service for days or weeks due to disasters and where care is to be provided for a large number of casualties.

Exit, stair, and corridor lighting should conform to local and State codes, or if such codes are not in effect, the Code for Safety to Life from Fire in Buildings and Structures, ANSI/NFPA No. 101-1973.

Illuminated signs may be required in areas where there is much visitor traffic, such as at the information desk, cashier's office, and outpatient department. Where such lighting is likely to be required, plug-in receptacles should be conveniently located.

An X-ray film illuminator is required in each operating room. It is also desirable that one be installed in the doctors' locker room of the obstetrical suite.

Recommended levels of illuminance for specific areas of hospitals are listed in Table 15.

Table 15. Illuminance values for specific areas in hospitals (minimum on the task at all times) in footcandles and lux*
(From IES 1977.)

Area	Illuminance		Area	Illuminance		Area	Illuminance	
Anesthetizing and preparation			Formula room (cont.)			Pediatric nursing unit (cont.)		
room	30	300	Preparation and filling	50	500	Treatment room, general	50	500
Autopsy and morgue			Fracture room			Treatment room, local	100	1000
Autopsy room	100	1000	General	50	500	Pharmacy		
Autopsy table	1000	10000	Fracture table	200	2000	Compounding and dispensing	100	1000
Morgue, general	20	200	Splint closet	50	500	Manufacturing	50	500
Museum	50	500	Plaster sink	50	500	Parenteral solution room	50	500
Central sterile supply			Intensive care nursing areas			Active storage	30	300
General, workroom	30	300	General	30	300	Alcohol vault	10	100
Work tables	50	500	Local	100	1000	Radioisotope facilities		
Glove room	50	500	Laboratories			Radiochemical laboratory,		
Syringe room	150	1500	General	50	500	general	30	300
Needle sharpening	150	1500	Close work areas	100	1000	Uptake or scanning room	20	200
Storage areas	30	300	Linens			Examining table	50	500
Issuing sterile supplies	50	500	Sorting soiled linen	30	300	Retiring room		
Corridor			Central (clean) linen room	30	300	General	10	100
General in nursing areas—			Sewing room, general	30	300	Local for reading	30	300
Daytime	20	200	Sewing room, work area	100	1000	Solarium		
Night (rest period)	3	30	Linen closet	10	100	General	20	200
Operating, delivery, recovery,			Lobby (or entrance foyer)			Local for reading	30	300
and laboratory suites and			During day	50	500	Stairways	20	200
service areas	30	300	During night	20	200	Surgical suite		
Cystoscopic room			Locker rooms	20	200	Instrument and sterile supply		
General	100	1000	Medical records room	100	1000	room	30	300
Cystoscopic table	2500	25000	Nurses' station			Clean-up room, instrument	100	1000
Dental suite			General—day	70	700	Scrub-up area (variable)	200	2000
Operatory, general	70	700	General—night	30	300	Operating room, general		
Instrument cabinet	150	1500	Desk for records and charting	70	700	(variable)	200	2000
Dental entrance to oral cavity	1000	10000	Table for doctors' making or			Operating table	2500	25000
Prosthetic laboratory bench	100	1000	viewing reports	70	700	Recovery room, general	30	300
Recovery room, general	5	50	Medicine counter	100	1000	Recovery room, local	100	1000
Recovery room, local for			Nurses gown room			Anesthesia storage	20	200
observation	70	700	General	30	300	Substerilizing room	30	300
(EEG) encepholographic suite			Mirror for grooming	50	500	Therapy physical		
Office (see section on			Nurseries, infant			General	20	200
"Offices")			General	30	300	Exercise room	30	300
Workroom, general	30	300	Examining, local at bassinet	100	1000	Treatment cubicles, local	30	300
Workroom, desk or table	100	1000	Examining and treatment			Whirlpool	20	200
Examining room	30	300	table	100	1000	Lip reading	150	1500
Preparation rooms, general	30	300	Nurses' station and work			Office (see section on "Offices")		
Preparation rooms, local	50	500	space (see Nurses Station)			Therapy, occupational		
Storage, records, charts	30	300	Obstetrical suite			Work area, general	30	300
Electromyographic suite			Labor room, general	20	200	Work tables or benches,		
Some as EEG but provisions			Labor room, local	100	1000	ordinary	50	500
for reducing level in			Scrub-up area	30	300	Work tables or benches,		
preparation area to 1			Delivery room, general	100	1000	fine work	100	1000
Emergency operating room			Substerilizing room	30	300	Toilets	30	300
General	100	1000	Delivery table	2500	25000	Utility room		
Local	2000	20000	Cleanup room	30	300	General	20	200
EKG, BMR, and specimen room			Recovery room, general	30	300	Work counter	50	500
General	30	300	Recovery room, local	100	1000	Waiting rooms, or areas		
Specimen table	50	500	Patients' rooms (private and			General	20	200
EKG machine	50	500	wards)			Local for reading	30	300
Examination and treatment room			General	20	200	X-ray suite		
General	50	500	Reading	30	300	Radiographic, general	10	100
Examining table	100	1000	Observation (by nurse)	2	20	Fluoroscopic, general		
Exits, at floor	5	50	Night light, maximum at			(variable)	0–50	0–500
Eye, ear, nose, and throat suite			floor (variable)	0.5	5	Deep and superficial therapy	10	100
Darkroom (variable)	0–10	0–100	Examining light	100	1000	Control room	10	100
Eye examination and			Toilets	30	300	Film viewing room	30	300
treatment	50	500	Pediatric nursing unit			Darkroom	10	100
Ear, nose, throat room	50	500	General, crib room	20	200	Light room	30	300
Flower room	10	100	General, bedroom	10	100	Filing room, developed films	30	300
Formula room			Reading	30	300	Storage, undeveloped films	10	100
Bottle washing	30	300	Playroom	30	300	Dressing rooms	10	100

* *Lux is an SI unit equal to 0.0929 footcandle.*

Data from Church Lighting, *Illuminating Engineering Society, 1962*

CHURCHES AND SYNAGOGUES

Lighting in architecture usually has a dual purpose. In addition to its utilitarian function of facilitating vision, it is also an important part of the architectural design. The spaces created by the architect can be seen, in the absence of daylight, only by means of the lighting he designs for them, and the lighting itself profoundly affects the appearance of the spaces. In no type of building is lighting so important a part of architectural expression as in the church or temple. Religious concepts vary widely from one religion to another, even from one congregation to another. But whatever concept the architect seeks to express, lighting is one of the tools he must use for this purpose.

In many cases church lighting is also designed to play an active part in the church service, creating different moods for the various parts of the service. It can also have a different character for different services or occasions—weddings and funerals, for example, or Easter and Christmas.

Illuminance values currently recommended for churches and synagogues are shown in Table 16.

LIGHTING FOR THE MAIN WORSHIP AREA

Pastor, Priest or Rabbi: In speaking to his congregation, a preacher wants his face to be seen. Part of the force of what he says comes from the earnestness of his facial expression. On the other hand, he does not wish to be annoyed by glare, nor should his face be distorted by lighting that creates black shadows around his eyes and harsh lines on his face. Many ministers prefer that general lighting in the pew area be decreased during the sermon so that the congregation may more easily keep its attention on the speaker.

The Congregation: People in the pews should not have to sit facing glaring light of any kind. Glare from the sky as well as from excessively bright panels of diffusing glass and exposed bulbs and fluorescent tubes are distressing.

Those in the congregation who are elderly must have ample light to be able to read fine print.

Lighting for the main body of the church usually consists of a combination of systems. For a high-ceilinged church where a feeling of mystery is sought, concealed downlights may furnish all the illumination. But in most cases downlights should be supplemented by cove lighting or luminaires which will light the walls and ceiling. Cove lighting or luminaires can supply up to 50 or 60 per cent of the total lighting, but the remainder should be downlighting. In most cases it is impossible to light a church satisfactorily by means of suspended luminaires only.

One lighting method is to cover the ceiling with light from a cove on each wall, and to provide downlights recessed in the ceiling. Each cove should have fluorescent tubes mounted end-to-end as follows:

For a meditation chapel 10 to 12 ft (3.0–3.7 m) wide—one line of 20- or 25-mm, 120-mA cold cathode tubing or equivalent low brightness hot cathode tubing.

For a church 12 to 18 ft (3.7 to 5.5 m) wide—one line of 40-watt T12 tubes.

For a church 25 to 35 ft (7.6 to 10.7 m) wide—two lines of 40-watt T12 tubes.

For a church 35 to 50 ft (10.7 to 15.2 m) wide—two lines of 800-mA* T12 tubes or one line of 1500-mA* tubes.

* Remote location of ballasts is suggested.

Table 16. Recommended illuminance values for churches and synagogues*
(From IES 1977.)

	Footcandles	Lux†
Altar, ark, reredos	100‡	1000
Choir§ and chancel	30‡	300
Classrooms	30	300
Pulpit, rostrum (supplementary illumination)	50‡	500
Main worship area§		
Light and medium interior finishes	15‡	150
For churches with special zeal	30	300
Art glass windows (test recommended)		
Light color	50	500
Medium color	100	1000
Dark color	500	5000
Especially dense windows	1000	10000

* Minimum on the task at any time.
† Lux is an SI unit equal to 0.0929 footcandle.
‡ Two-thirds this value if interior finishes are dark (less than 10 per cent reflectance) to avoid high luminance ratios, such as between hymnbook pages and the surround. Careful luminance planning is essential for good design.
§ Reduced or dimmed during sermon, prelude or meditation.

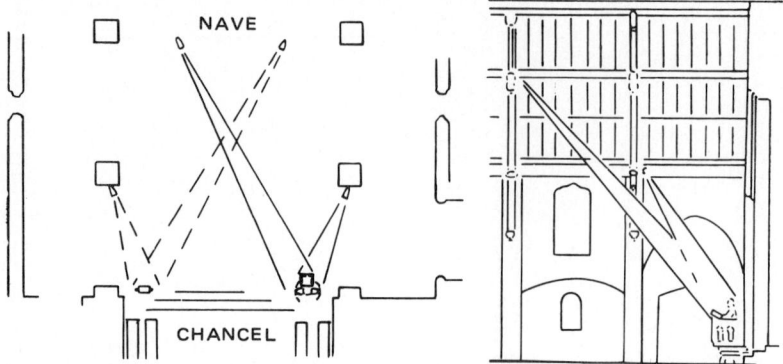

Fig. 25. Accent lighting should come from two or more locations well above the speaker's face

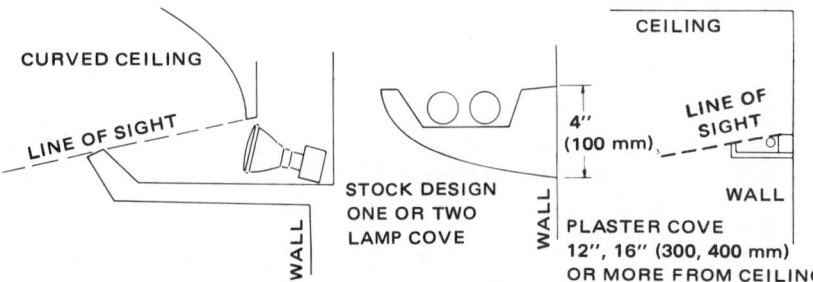

Fig. 26. Sections through several types of coves

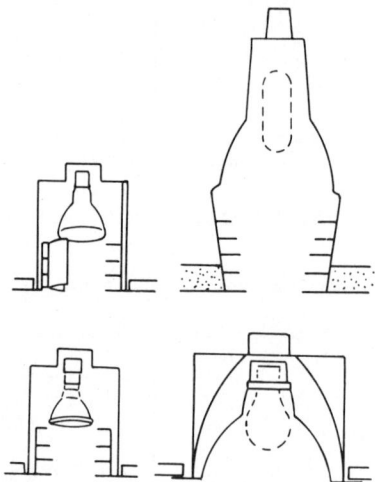

Fig. 27. Some types of fixed recessed downlights

Better light distribution on the ceiling is obtained from 75-watt louvered reflector spot lamps a foot apart in cove (Fig. 26). Also needed are 2 to 3 watts per sq ft (21.52 to 32.29 W/m²) of downlights or swiveled units behind beams. Where it is felt that the bright ceiling may offer psychological competition with the speaker, cove wattage may be cut in half, downlight wattage increased.

Another method for use in larger rooms, where some prefer the added interest of decorative lighting equipment, is the installation of appropriate luminaires (from 1 to 3 watts per sq ft) (10.76 to 32.29 W/m²) and recessed downlights (2 watts per sq ft, 21.52 W/m²) the latter for use on cloudy days and after dark.

The following specifications are for "lantern" (suspended luminaire) wattages used with the downlights: for light to be diffused out through the lantern sides—¼ to ½ watt per sq ft (2.69 to 5.38 W/m²), depending on lantern size; for light directed down and up—1 watt per sq ft (10.76 W/m²) to supplement the ceiling downlights.

The manufacturer's limits of spacing as related to mounting height should not be exceeded. Shielding should be greater than 45 deg.

Many authorities prefer a church lantern whose side panels or other means of control result in more light being directed toward the altar than toward the eyes of the congregation. These are called unsymmetric units.

Example of the use of swiveled units church 42 ft (12.8 m) wide with beams 16 ft (4.9 m) apart, use twelve 150-watt units behind each beam except the one nearest to the chancel, which should have 24 units; total wattage, 2.7 per sq ft (29 watts per

sq m), plus fluorescent cove lighting of 1.1 watts per sq ft (11.84 W/m²).

Stations of the cross should not be as bright as the main or side altars; a brightness one-third that of the main altar is suggested. Shielded light sources can be concealed in the ceiling or, in the case of churches with aisles, can be placed high on nearby columns.

Baptismal services should be lighted from several concealed sources so that sharp shadows are avoided. Lights should be shielded from the view of the audience.

Multipurpose auditoriums must provide lighting for a wide variety of functions. These are discussed further on in the section about parish halls.

Chancel lighting

In each form of worship, the relative importance of different features of the chancel's design and furnishing should be expressed in the relative luminance provided by the lighting. For example, in Roman Catholic churches, the high altar is brightest. In Ukrainian Catholic churches, the icon screen in front of the altar is brightest. In Quaker meeting houses, no part of the interior should be brighter than any other.

Light in the chancel should be largely directional, aimed from the front to the back. If the lighting comes from many sources, shadows will be softer. Multiplicity of sources also provides flexibility of control. Most chancel lights, whether incandescent or fluorescent, can be of the spot-flood type. Sometimes a controlled-beam spot, like a single pencil of light, is used for the cross or ark; an enclosed theatrical "box-spot" type of fixture is used for this purpose.

Light should arrive at the ark or altar from a direction that does not result in undesirable shadows. If the chancel is shallow, it may be necessary to have some of the spotlights out in the nave, partly or wholly concealed. When the priest or curate is reading with his back to the congregation, shadows should not prevent him from seeing his reading matter.

Both the ark and the Torah are a focus of interest and must have proper illuminance. The lighting within the ark is usually automatically turned on by the opening of the ark doors. The background behind the scrolls should have a lower reflectance than the scroll covers.

In general, the ark receives the most attention, the face of the speaker at the rostrum the next greatest amount of light, the cantor slightly less, and the whole chancel area a little less, but more than the seating space of the auditorium. Separately controlled floodlighting for bar mitzvah services in front of the ark has many advocates.

Wiring should be provided for the Eternal Light and the Menorahs. While the ordinary incandescent lamp is designed to operate efficiently for 750 or 1,000 hr, the life of any lamp can be extended indefinitely by reducing the voltage from the normal 115 or 120 volts to a lower figure. As a general guide, each time the voltage is reduced by 5 per cent, light output drops 15 per cent but life is doubled. Low-cost wall-box dimmers are available. Some congregations use a "fishtail" jet gas flame for the Eternal Light. The faint flicker is thought pleasant.

The choir is generally provided with more light than the pews but considerably less than the altar or ark. Supplementary lighting is often used for the organist and the choir to permit the reading of musical scores; it must be carefully shielded from the view of the worshippers, of course. Choir lighting should be reduced or dimmed during the sermon, prayer, and other nonmusical portions of the service.

Lighting on the face of the preacher in the pulpit or the reader at the lectern should come from well above the speaker's face and from several directions, in order to soften the shadows (Fig. 25). During the sermon, reading, or prayer, luminances in the chancel and nave should be reduced so that attention is focused on the speaker.

Lighting equipment

The following types of luminaires are used in church lighting: (1) Lanterns; (2) Wall brackets; (3) Wall urns; (4) Suspended bowls (indirect); (5) Coves; and (6) Downlights (several types, including recessed and swivel). Several of these are illustrated in Figs. 26–28. For additional data on the design of cove lighting, see the section on "Lighting: Residential;" for downlighting, see the section on "Lighting: Stores." Downlight shielding, however, should be greater than the 45 deg which is the usual standard in commercial lighting; 50 to 60 deg is recommended.

Controls can vary from simple load centers or panelboards with letter or color coding to complete theatrical-type switchboards with dimming and presetting features. Lighting plans of intermediate complexity can often achieve flexibility at low cost by the use of low-voltage controls. Motor-operated dimmer controls are preferred when funds are available. Even more convenient is the newer compact reactance or autotransformer. The slow lighting changes are scarcely noticed as one effect follows another without distracting from the service.

Lighting maintenance is likely to be poorer in churches than in other types of buildings.

Instead of the usual maintenance factor of 60 or 70 per cent, it is advisable to use a lower factor, in the order of 40 or 50 per cent.

Stained glass windows, which play such an important role in many types of church architecture, may be lighted from the outside for the benefit of worshippers attending evening services. If the church is surrounded by trees or other buildings, the outside lighting can be installed without injury to the exterior appearance of the building. The amount of light required may vary from more than 100 watts per sq ft (1076 W/m²) for thick glass in dark colors to 1 watt per sq ft (10.76 W/m²) for thin glass in light colors. An experimental installation is advisable to determine the exact amount of light required and the best location of the sources. Relative luminance of the window and the interior wall must be considered; to be fully effective the window must be considerably brighter than the interior wall. Windows may also be lighted from the inside on nonservice evenings, for the benefit of passers-by. Such installations are often clock-controlled.

Outdoor lighting

Floodlighting of the church may require as much as 1 watt per sq ft (10.76 W/m²) of wall surface to be lighted for a red brick church on a lighted city street, or as little as one-tenth that amount for a white-painted church on a dark country road. Light sources may be concealed in trees or behind planting, and for lighting the steeple they may, in some cases, be placed on the roof. In choosing locations for the lighting units, consideration must be given not only to the lighting effect created but also to the appearance of the units during the daytime and their accessibility for cleaning and relamping. An experimental installation, using portable units, is recommended. If only the front facade is to be lighted, some light should be allowed to fall on the sides in order to avoid the one-dimensional effect of a lighted billboard.

Outdoor services are best lighted, where conditions permit, by reflection from the leaves of trees overhead. For this purpose floodlights should be placed above eye level and aimed straight up. A light-colored wall of a building or a cliff may also be used as a source of reflected light, if the audience faces away from it. Otherwise, direct lighting must be used mounted on poles, preferably 20 ft (6.6 m) high, around the sides and rear of the seating area.

Lighting for other parts of the church

Narthex or vestibule should have sufficient light so that people can see each other's faces, read announcements, and make notes.

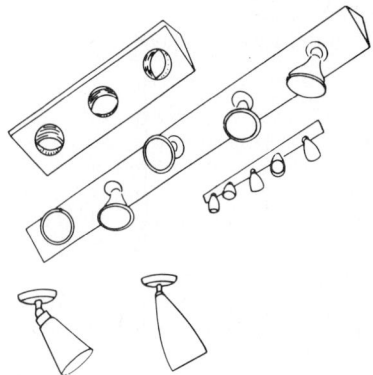

Fig. 28. Some types of swiveled accent units

Lighting should be sufficiently diffuse so that faces appear pleasantly lighted, without harsh shadows.

Many churches have a *parish hall* or *multipurpose room* used for various purposes other than worship. Each of these activities has its own lighting requirements. Recommended illuminance levels are as follows:

	Footcandles	(lux)
Fairs and exhibitions;		
study hall	30	(300)
Lectures; church dinners	15	(150)
Concerts	5	(50)
Plays, movies, slides	1/10	(1.0)
Plays, movies, slides,		
at intermission	5	(50)
Dances	1	(10)

In most cases supplementary lighting is also required, on the lecturer or orchestra, for example, and also for color and sparkle at dances. For stage lighting, see section on "Lighting: Schools." If the room is sometimes used for athletic activities, rugged equipment, suitably protected, should be specified. In such cases, spotlighting can be provided by the use of portable fixtures plugged into "fan receptacles"[1] on the walls or ceiling beams.

For information on *classroom* lighting, see section on "Lighting: Schools."

Clergyman's study is basically a workroom and should provide good seeing conditions for long hours of work. Most clergymen prefer a homelike atmosphere for the study, which may also be used for counseling. If the study is also used for board and committee meetings, appropriate lighting must be supplied.

[1]*The fan receptacle has a single receptacle and a screw post below it, so that a fan can be fastened by the post and plugged into the outlet. Thus a spotlight can be attached for a single performance.*

STORES

From IES Lighting Handbook, 1972.

Changes in store character

Radical changes in merchandising philosophy have resulted in the introduction of new techniques and patterns in store design. There has been an increasing emphasis on diversification, with many shops, such as drug, hardware, and food stores, expanding the types of merchandise carried.

Concurrent with these shifts in merchandising trends there have been changes in the methods of presenting and displaying the merchandise itself. Self-service and self-selection, both designed to reduce sales personnel, have become increasingly popular. Lighting can assist in presenting the merchandise to the customer in a manner which virtually makes the merchandise sell itself.

Circulation and merchandise

The lighting system often must be suitable for the display and appraisal of many different types of merchandise. Distinctive yet coordinated changes in the lighting may also serve as a means of identifying or setting off various departments.

The lighting pattern, together with supplementary accents, can be employed to attract customers into the store, influence the traffic flow of customers once there, and assist in emphasizing different types of merchandise.

Architectural changes

The use of large glass areas, the introduction of long-span bays, the increasing use of air conditioning, and the integration of store fixture design with the architectural structure all are important influences on the lighting design as an integral part of the structure.

Although the trend to large glass areas has provided the opportunity to utilize an effective and appealing interior to attract passers by, it has also created a visual problem by providing a surface for veiling reflections. To make the store interior and merchandise visible from the outside in the daytime, a sufficiently high level of lighting must be provided to overcome, as much as possible, the effect of these veiling reflections. It is particularly important that vertical surfaces in such stores be well illuminated.

Structural features of newer buildings, such as larger bays and clear spans, may give the lighting designer much more latitude in his layout pattern by producing clear ceiling areas. However, recessing space may be more restricted due to other mechanical equipment concealed in the plenum.

Interior design and the planning of store display and storage fixtures have become so closely related to store architecture that the lighting of these elements should be carefully integrated. Lighted valances, cornices, shadow boxes, illuminated countertops and other devices can contribute greatly to the over-all lighting effect. In addition, showcase and display lighting offer the designer a varied selection of equipment to give the store interior added sparkle and interest.

LIGHTING THE MERCHANDISE

Along with the consideration of the over-all architectural effect, it may be desirable to design the lighting specifically for the type of merchandise displayed. Color, pattern, texture, size, shape, and finish of the merchandise will influence the type of lighting in a given sales area. The directional quality of point sources, such as incandescent and high-intensity discharge sources, enhances some merchandise qualities that diffuse quality of a fluorescent linear source does not.

To show facets of jewelry, contours of silver, weave in fabrics, pile in rugs, or carving in furniture, directional light is needed. Diffuse light is suitable for hard goods and massed packaged merchandise. The emphasis will shift between point and linear depending on the merchandise and the type of store.

It is generally advisable to use high color rendering light sources for merchandise such as home furnishing, wearing apparel, jewelry, cosmetics, and meats, fresh fruits, and vegetables. It is also advisable to use a cool quality of light on furs, outdoor sporting goods, and garden supplies.

Table 17. Recommended illuminance values for merchandising areas. (From IES 1977.)

Areas or tasks	Description	Type of activity area*	Foot-candles	Lux†
Circulation	Area not used for display or appraisal of merchandise or for sales transactions	High	30	300
		Medium	20	200
		Low	10	100
Merchandise‡ (including showcases & wall displays)	That plane area, horizontal to vertical, where merchandise is displayed and readily accessible for customer examination	High	100	1000
		Medium	70	700
		Low	30	300
Feature displays‡	Single item or items requiring special highlighting to visually attract and set apart from the surround	High	500	5000
		Medium	300	3000
		Low	150	1500
Sales transactions area	The space needed for price verification and recording of transaction	High	70	700
		Medium	70	700
		Low	70	700

One store may encompass all three types within the building.
High activity area—Where merchandise displayed has readily recognizable usage. Evaluation and viewing time is rapid, and merchandise is shown to attract and stimulate the impulse buying decision.
Medium activity —Where merchandise is familiar in type or usage, but the customer may require time and/or help in evaluation of quality, usage, or for the decision to buy.
Low activity —Where merchandise is displayed that is purchased less frequently by the customer, who may be unfamiliar with the inherent quality, design, value or usage. Where assistance and time is necessary to reach a buying decision.
† Lux is an SI unit equal to 0.0929 footcandle.
‡ Lighting levels to be measured in the plane of the merchandise.

If used with great caution and taste, color tints are sometimes suitable. For example, straw tint may be used to dramatize beach and southern vacation equipment and apparel, or pale pinks can be used to glamorize lingerie and romantic evening wear.

Merchandise lighting should be both exciting and unobtrusive. Total finesse should be observed by the skilled designer to show the merchandise to best advantage, with no glare or other disquieting influence intruding on the consciousness of the customer. The totality of the interior then becomes a display and product information center.

To attract and retain customer attention, featured merchandise should be on the order of five times as bright as its surroundings. Compelling, brightly lighted displays strategically placed throughout the store can conduct shoppers on a buying tour. Even poorly located areas can be made sales productive.

LIGHTING TECHNIQUES

There are two basic approaches to lighting merchandising areas in stores. One is to design a specific lighting plan to conform to the layout of the merchandise fixtures, showcases, gondolas, etc., resulting in a luminaire layout which may not conform with the building architecture. The other technique is to employ a pattern of luminaires to provide uniform illuminance throughout the sales area. Both systems may be supplemented by various forms of accent lighting for merchandise emphasis.

Supplementary lighting

Supplementary lighting may be of many types; some of the principal ones are noted below.

Downlights: Usually recessed in the ceiling.

Valances, cornices, canopies, luminous soffits. Horizontal structures for the purpose of lighting vertical surfaces.

Bullet and hooded units: Pendent or wall-mounted.

Vertical reflectors: In shadow boxes or niches.

Individual shelf lighting: Opaque or translucent shelves.
Showcase lighting
Mirror lighting

SHOW WINDOW LIGHTING—DAYTIME EFFECTIVENESS

The selling force of a show window is very valuable during the daylight shopping hours, but the daylight often creates severe competition for the shopper's attention. This competition can be minimized with modern lighting equipment and latest techniques.

With windows on the shady side of the street, the glass tends to act as a mirror, reflecting an image of the sky, buildings across the street, etc. Measurements show that these objects, in direct sunlight, have a typical luminance of 1,000 fL (3430 cd/m²). The window reflects about 10 per cent of this luminance, or 100 fL (343 cd/m²). These reflected images are seen superimposed on the window display. Without adequate lighting they will completely veil the display itself.

In order to "see through" reflected images in the window glass, surfaces inside the window must be at least as bright as the reflected images; preferably several times as bright. Thus, when reflections have a luminance of 100 fL (343 cd/m²), vertical display surfaces should also have a luminance of at least 100 fL (343 cd/m²). With light-colored displays and background (averaging 50 per cent reflectance), 200 fc (2000 lux) of general illumination on vertical surfaces will produce this luminance, while for darker-colored displays or for greater effectiveness, higher levels are needed.

On the sunny side of the street, building and pavement surfaces adjacent to the windows are very bright. By comparison, inadequately lighted windows appear to be dark recesses in the store front. Therefore, it is necessary to light show windows on the sunny side to a higher illuminance value in the daytime than is needed at night. Window reflection can be partially controlled by an awning, marquee, or canopy. Dark paving of the sidewalk also helps reduce window reflections.

Table 18.   Recommended illuminance values for show windows

	Foot-candles	Lux*
Daytime lighting		
General	200	2000
Feature	1000	10000
Nightime lighting		
Main business districts—highly competitive		
General	200	2000
Feature	1000	10000
Secondary business districts or small towns		
General	100	1000
Feature	500	5000
Open-front stores (see display lighting under Store interiors)		

* Lux is an SI unit equal to 0.0929 footcandle.

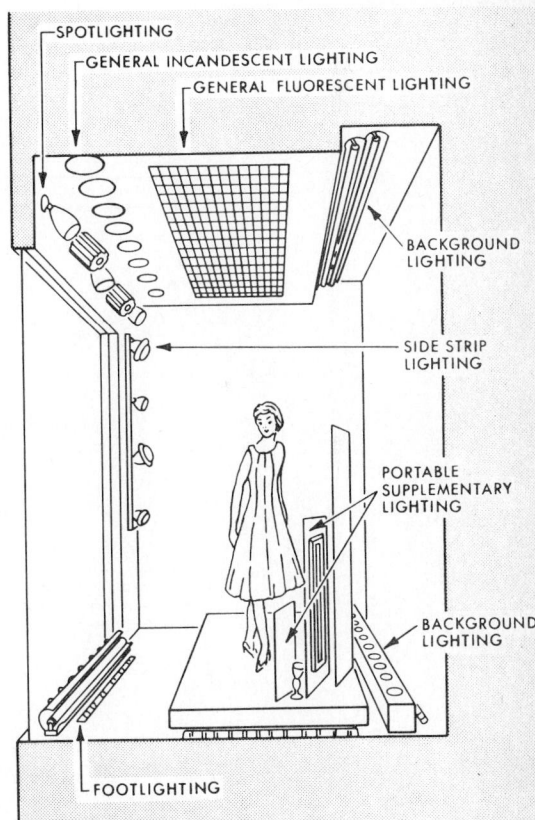

SPOTLIGHTING
GENERAL INCANDESCENT LIGHTING
GENERAL FLUORESCENT LIGHTING
BACKGROUND LIGHTING
SIDE STRIP LIGHTING
PORTABLE SUPPLEMENTARY LIGHTING
BACKGROUND LIGHTING
FOOTLIGHTING

Fig. 29.   Components of show-window lighting

By DANIEL SCHWARTZMAN, FAIA, Architect

GENERAL LIGHTING

1. Evenly Distributed Lighting Fixtures. Light source brightness reduced by use of recessed surfaces, louvers, lenses, diffusing glass or plastic.

   4- by 4-ft fixture recessed, surface mounted or suspended with six or eight fluorescent lamps, shielded by metal or plastic eggcrate louvers on 12- to 14-ft centers. These may be supplemented by incandescent spotlights, floodlights or downlights to fill odd spaces in an irregularly shaped area.

WALL LIGHTING

1. Continuous fluorescent strip light coves or cornices, or closely spaced incandescent floodlights supplement the general store lighting, while also lighting the merchandise in the wall cases.

2. Glass enclosed wall cases (and show cases) require additional fluorescent light. Strip lighting may be used over open shelves in self selection fixtures.

3. Certain types of merchandise (jewelry, silverware) require additional direct, incandescent light from continuous rows of reflector lamps in the ceiling.

ORNAMENTAL LIGHTING

Chandeliers and other pendant lighting fixtures can be used in key locations and high style departments, but should be limited in number and relied on only for supplementary lighting.

DISPLAY LIGHTING

At least two lights are required on each subject of a feature display to avoid deep shadows and to bring out the soft reflected light which emphasizes the form and texture of the merchandise on display.

SPECIAL REQUIREMENTS

The following selling departments have special electrical requirements:
1. Restaurant and Kitchen
2. Beauty Salon
3. Lamp department and Home Lighting
4. Radio, T.V. and Records (Master Antenna systems)
5. Appliances
6. Snack Bar
7. Refrigerated cases at delicacies, candy and bakery.

OUTLETS

All interior columns should have one duplex convenience outlet about 14 in (356 mm) above the floor; one duplex convenience outlet about 12 in (305 mm) below ceiling; and one telephone receptacle. All exterior columns should have one duplex outlet about 14 in (356 mm) above floor.

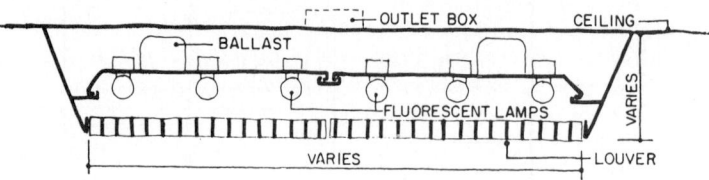

Surface Mounted Fluorescent with Metal or Plastic Louver

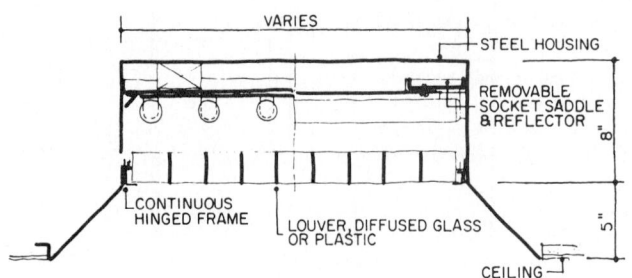

Recessed Fluorescent

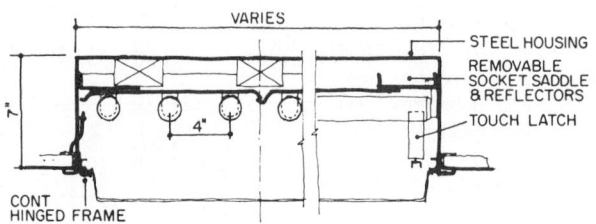

Flush Recessed Fluorescent with Plastic Shield

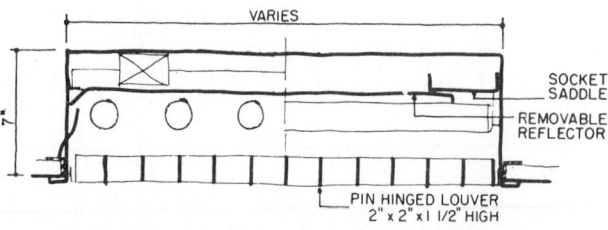

Flush Recessed Fluorescent with Metal Louver

Outlet Locations:

1. Cashier's Room for Calculating and adding machines
2. Cloth winder measurograph machines
3. Pilot lights for all machines, executive office equipment
4. Luggage stamping machines
5. Alteration Room for: Steam irons, sewing machines, steam generating unit boiler, pants pressing machine
6. Stationery department pen stamping machine
7. Drinking fountains and dispensing machines
8. Hospital sterilizer and stove
9. Pharmacy sterilizer and stove
10. Carpentry shop power equipment
11. Ticketing machines in marking areas
12. Store time-card clocks
13. Burglar protection
14. Sprinkler wiring system
15. Local fire alarm system
16. Store clock system and dismissal bell
17. High and low water alarm
18. Automatic time control system of exterior signs
19. Ventilating smoke and heat detection
20. Annunciator System
21. Automatic time control for show window lighting
22. Telephone system
23. Pneumatic tube blower system
24. Service bell at receiving platform
25. Night bell at store entrance
26. Cash register outlets on electric circuit separate from lighting circuits.

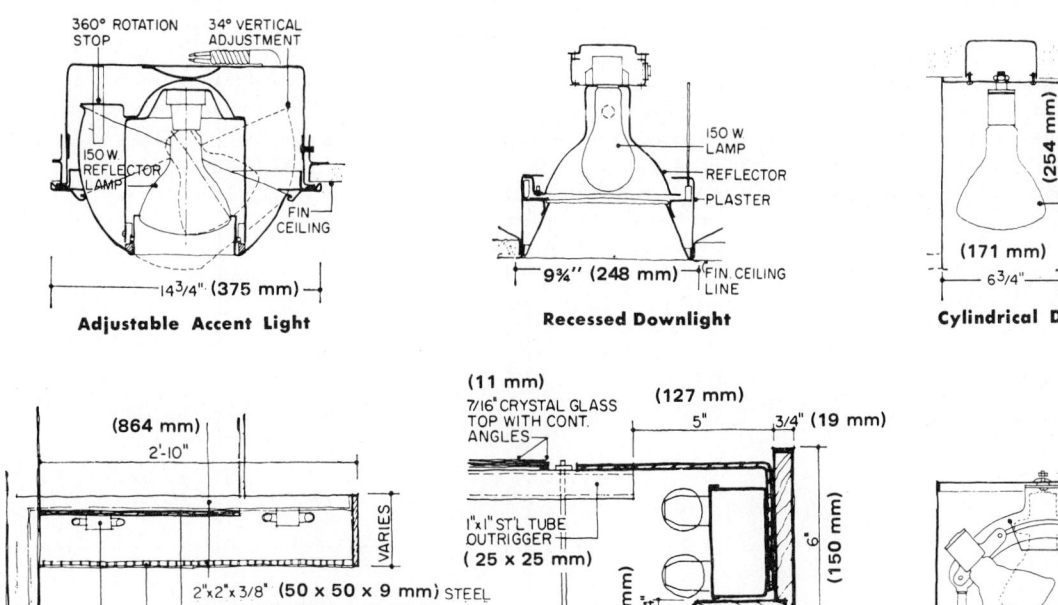

Adjustable Accent Light

Recessed Downlight

Cylindrical Downlight

Lighted Soffit at Back Wall

Typical Light Cornice

Recessed Adjustable Accent Light

By Henry L. Logan, Vice President in charge of Research, Holophane Company, Inc.

ESTIMATING LIGHTING REQUIREMENTS

Screen luminances have increased in recent years from a minimum of 9 footlamberts (fL (30.8 cd/m²) and a maximum of 14 fL (47.9 cd/m²) at the center of a blank lighted screen to 10 to 20 fL (34 to 69 cd/m²). The average screen luminance with film running, and the proper illuminance of the theater interior, can be related to these values.

Black and white film averages 8 per cent of blank screen luminance, and colored film averages 15 per cent, or from 0.8 to 3 fL (2.7 to 10.3 cd/m²). The general luminance of the auditorium from the viewpoint of spectators facing the screen can therefore be in this range while film is running, provided that the luminance of the same auditorium as viewed from the stage is as low as possible. Thus the auditorium must be designed and illuminated so that it has a luminance compatible with the screen luminance, as seen from the seats, but looks dark when viewed from the stage. One method is to construct the walls and ceiling with V-shaped ridges, as shown in the accompanying figure. The surface of each ridge that faces the spectators should be set at such an angle that no light from it can diffuse back towards the screen. This

surface can be of any color consistent with a reflection factor of about 50 per cent. The surface of each ridge that faces the screen should be a dark grey, with a reflection factor of no more than 10 per cent.

These ridges can be as small, or as large, as the designer wishes; they can be small on one area and large on another—an infinite variety of combinations can be worked out to produce original and pleasing architectural patterns. Most important is the accuracy of the angles of the surfaces in relation to the screen; that is, the high light-reflecting surfaces should be so angled as to be louvered from the screen.

A lighting layout that would give a total of 5 fc (50 lx) over the auditorium floor area is shown in plan and section below. The lighting system should be connected to dimmers so that the low level of light necessary during a performance can be determined by experiment and then pre-set. For the best reception of screen images, the surround should have about the same luminance as the screen itself with film running. Because of the variable luminance of film subjects, however, this is not practical, although it could be accomplished by a quick-

acting photo-cell circuit set to respond to screen luminances. Generally the most satisfactory compromise will be to preset the lighting at the level that is satisfactory for black and white subjects.

In a typical individual component of the most economical lighting system, the lights should be recessed above ceiling level to prevent stray light from reaching the screen. The two rows of lights nearest the screen would be out during a performance.

The reflection factors of auditorium surfaces, compatible with continuous film running, are as follows:

	Per cent
Floor	10
Seat coverings, except backs	20
Seat backs	40
Side walls and ceiling:	
Surface toward screen	10
Surface toward spectators	50
Surfaces parallel to screen, such as front balcony face and rear wall	20

The foyer illuminance should be about the same as the auditorium with all house lights on full, or 5 fc (50 lx).

For additional information, see section on "Movie theaters" in *Time-Saver Standards for Building Types.*

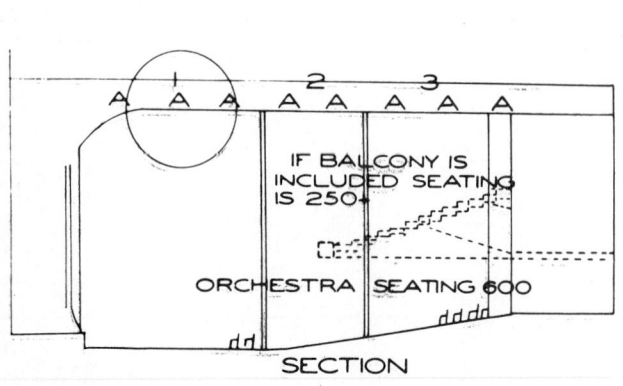

DETAIL OF SECTION OF WALL OR CEILING SHOWING CRITICAL ANGLE OF SURFACE OF WALL OR CEILING THAT FACES TOWARD AUDIENCE.

IF BALCONY IS INCLUDED SEATING IS 250

ORCHESTRA SEATING 600

SECTION

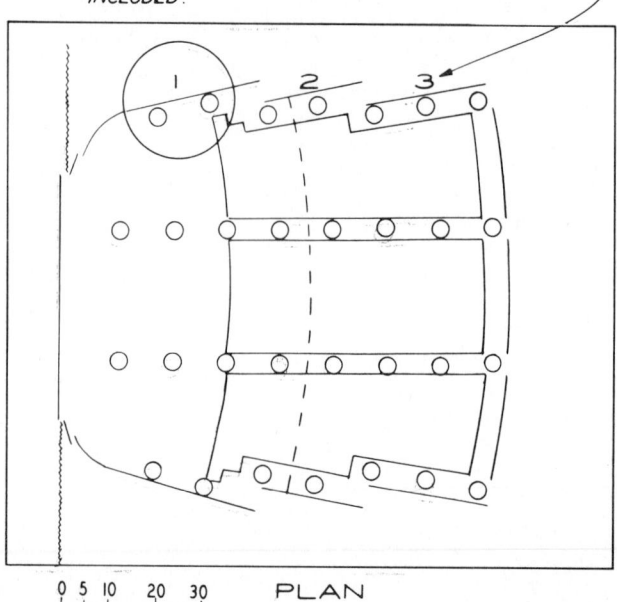

10° FOR WALL AND CEILING PANEL NO.1
25° FOR WALL AND CEILING PANEL NO.2
35° FOR WALL AND CEILING PANEL NO.3

○ LOCATIONS OF LIGHTING UNITS IN MAIN CEILING AND IN SOFFIT OF BALCONY WHEN BALCONY IS INCLUDED.

0 5 10   20   30

PLAN

Data from Lighting for Hotels, *Illuminating Engineering Society, 1958, and IES Handbook, 1972*

Illuminance values currently recommended for hotels are shown in Table 19. Additional comments on certain areas are given below.

Entrance foyer should have a high level of illuminance in order to create a smooth and comfortable transition between the brightly lighted marquee or bright daylight and the lobby.

Lobby should have a pleasant level of general illuminance with higher-level lighting in special locations such as the desk, news-stand, telephones, bulletin boards, displays, shops, etc. Lighting methods usually combine direct and indirect lighting. Totally indirect lighting may result in overly bright ceilings and insufficient shadows for perception of the third dimension; downlighting used ex-clusively may produce sharp shadows and unpleasantly dark ceilings.

Lounge lighting calls for a softer treat-ment, and the general illuminance value can be somewhat lower. Local lighting, often in the form of portable lamps, should be pro-vided for reading. Properly located outlets are required if portable lamps are to be used.

Corridors: Adequate corridor lighting cre-ates a pleasant atmosphere and makes it easier to read room numbers and find door keyholes. Well-designed ceiling fixtures spaced at intervals of twice the ceiling height usually give adequately uniform illu-minance. If possible, corridor switches should be placed near guest room doors. Building codes require emergency lighting for hotel corridors which will operate in the event of failure of the normal source of electricity.

Guest room lighting should provide for the following:

General room illumination
Writing at a desk
Reading in bed
Reading in an easy chair
Grooming at the dresser or dressing table
Lighting in clothes closets.

General illuminance should be controlled by a wall switch at the door, as a safety factor. Both general and local lighting may be sup-plied by ceiling or wall fixtures or by porta-ble lamps, or by a combination of the two see (section on "Lighting: Residential").

Table 19. Illuminance values for hotels. *(From IES recommended illuminance values, 1977.)*

Areas	Illuminance Foot-candles	Lux†	Areas	Illuminance Foot-candles	Lux†
Auditoriums			Laundry		
Assembly only	15	150	Washing	30	300
Exhibitions	30	300	Flat work ironing, weighing, listing, marking	50	500
Social activities	5	50	Machine and press finishing, sorting	70	700
Bars and cocktail lounges*			Fine hand ironing	100	1,000
Bathrooms			Linen room		
Mirror	30	300	Sewing	100	1,000
General	10	100	General	20	200
Bedrooms			Lobby		
Reading (books, magazines, newspapers)	30	300	General lighting	10	100
Inkwriting	30	300	Reading and working areas	30	300
Make-up	30	300	Machine shop		
General	10	100	Rough bench and machine work	50	500
Corridors, elevators, stairs	20	200	Medium bench and machine work	100	1,000
Dining areas			Fine bench and machine work	500	500
Cashier	50	500	Extra fine bench and machine work	1,000	10,000
Intimate type			Marquee		
Light environment	10	100	Dark surroundings	30	300
Subdued environment	3	30	Bright surroundings	50	500
For cleaning	20	200	Offices		
Leisure type			Accounting	150	1,500
Light environment	30	300	General	100	1,000
Subdued environment	15	150	Power plants		
Quick service type			Boiler rooms	10	100
Bright surroundings†	100	100	Equipment rooms	20	200
Normal surroundings‡	50	500	Store interiors		
Food displays	50	500	Circulation areas	30	300
Entrance foyer	30	300	General merchandise	100	1,000
Front office	50	500	Showcases	200	2,000
Kitchen			Feature displays	500	5,000
Inspecting, checking, preparation and pricing	70	700	Stock rooms	30	300
			Storerooms	10	100

* See Dining Areas—Intimate.
† Lux is an SI unit equal to 0.0929 footcandle.
‡ Including street and nearby establishments.

Guest bathrooms: see section on "Lighting: Residential."

Dining rooms and bar may be dimly lighted for effect, but the illuminance should be sufficient so that guests can read the menu without straining. Small dining rooms and cocktail lounges can often be effectively illuminated by means of brightly lighted mural decorations. If fluorescent lighting is used, care must be taken to specify colors that are flattering to food as well as to complexions (see section on "Lighting: General").

Kitchens: In the application of light to modern kitchens there is one very serious problem which probably cannot be completely overcome, i.e., the problem of reflections from highly polished surfaces such as stainless steel. Large lighting units with low brightness should be used; for example, fluorescent or large-area incandescent sources.

If fluorescent lamps are used, they should be of the improved-color-rendition type. Several areas in the kitchen require special lighting: at the bandsaw used in the meat department, at food choppers and mixers, in the hoods over the ranges, at the tables where clean silver and glassware are inspected, and at the checker's stand. Attention should be given to the form of the lighting unit, avoiding horizontal surfaces on which dust and dirt may collect. For more detailed information see *Lighting for Commercial Kitchens,* by the Illuminating Engineering Society, 1956.

Service areas should be lighted in accordance with the visual tasks. In areas where the seeing task is not critical, sufficient illuminance should be provided for safety and easy maintenance. Stairs, elevators, and moving machinery should be well lighted for safety. Pilot lights are recommended for rooms that are rarely entered. Telephone switchboard rooms should be lighted to not more than 15 ft-c so that switchboard signal lights will be readily visible.

RESIDENCES

Data from Lighting Keyed to Today's Homes, *Illuminating Engineering Society, 1960, and* IES Lighting Handbook, *1972*

Architectural lighting, planned as an integral part of the structural design of an interior, may be purely decorative or may be designed to provide functional lighting in a decorative manner. It may be applied to any type of architecture and to almost any room in the house.

Window and wall lighting

Window areas, the daytime source of light, may also be utilized to provide functional and decorative illuminance after the sun sets. In contemporary architecture particularly, with its large areas of glass, it seems appropriate to retain the concept of light emanating from those areas. The only other suitable treatment is to leave the glass uncovered and provide lighting outside in the garden or patio.

The simplest form of window or wall lighting is to conceal tubular light sources behind a valance or cornice board. A *valance* is a horizontal strip mounted on the wall across the top of the drapery treatment (see Fig. 30). A valance usually directs light up to the ceiling as well as down over the drapery. A cornice is a horizontal member similar to a valance but attached to the ceiling; thus all of the light is directed downward (see Figs. 35 and 36).

The faceboard of a valance may be tilted outward at the top to send more light across the ceiling, or it may be double tilted for added interest. In either case, the degree of tilt from vertical may be 15 to 20 deg. If the board is tilted outward at the bottom some form of shielding (diffusing glass, plastic or louvers) may be necessary to prevent a direct view of the light sources (see Fig. 31). Other variations of valance lighting are shown in Figs. 32–34.

For effective window or wall lighting the fabric or wall surface should be light in color. Nonglossy wall finishes of medium reflectance, generally between 35 and 55 per cent, are desirable.

Valance faceboard depth should be a minimum of 6 in (150 mm) for a length of not more than 8 ft (2.4 m). For longer lengths and/or greater ceiling heights the depth should be increased to 8 or 10 in (200–250 mm). In general, the depth of the valance or cornice faceboard in inches should be about the same as the height of the valance above the floor in feet.

Light leaks between the cornice faceboard and the ceiling can be prevented by the application of a molding or by attaching a piece of white felt to the top of the faceboard before it is installed.

Valance-type fixtures may also be used for local lighting. They should be installed at the correct height for their intended use and shielded when necessary (Fig. 37).

Dimensions of standard wiring channels and tubular light sources are shown in Fig. 38. In all cases of valance or cornice lighting there must be sufficient illumination from other sources so that the faceboards do not appear as silhouetted forms.

Incandescent lamps may also be used for wall or window lighting. Units may be of the reflector or lens type and may be suspended, surface-mounted, or recessed in the ceiling. They may be installed to give a uniform wash of light on the wall or, if preferred, a scalloped effect.

Tall, narrow windows with deep reveals, usually found in old houses, may often be effectively lighted by means of tubular sources at each side behind the draperies but in front of the shades (Fig. 39).

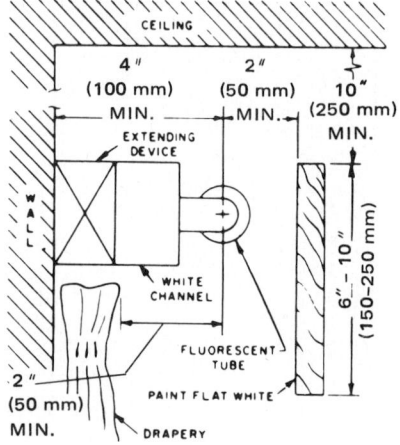

Fig. 30. Minimum dimensions for valance lighting installation

If draperies are bulky or heavily lined or if both glass curtains and overdrapes are used, distance of lamp from wall should be increased to 6 in (150 mm). If ceiling reflectance is less than 65 per cent, distance to top of faceboard should be increased to 12 in (300 mm).

Cove lighting

Cove lighting is a fully indirect system in which the ceiling is lighted from continuous sources concealed in a cove on one or more walls somewhat below the ceiling. It produces a feeling of height and spaciousness, but, if used alone, tends to be flat and monotonous. Direct lighting from downlights or portable lamps should be used with cove lighting to add shadows, highlights, and sparkle.

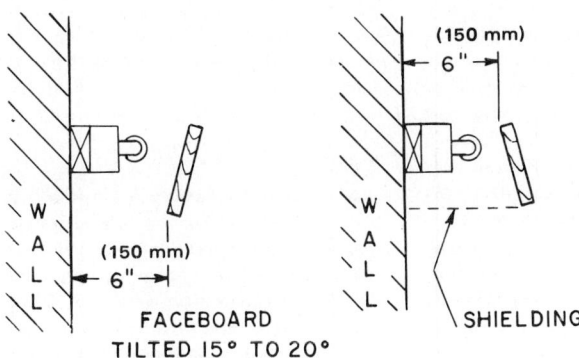

Fig. 31. Valance faceboard may be tilted

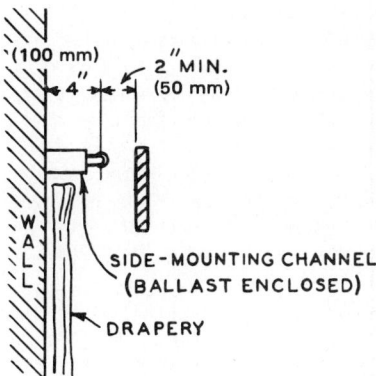

Fig. 32. With side-mounting channels, no extender is necessary

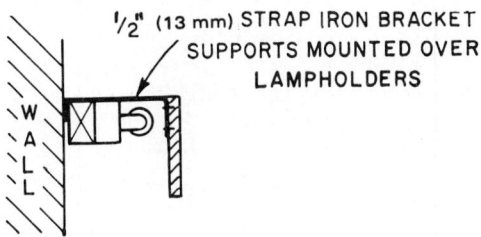

Fig. 33. Intermediate brackets are required to support long faceboards

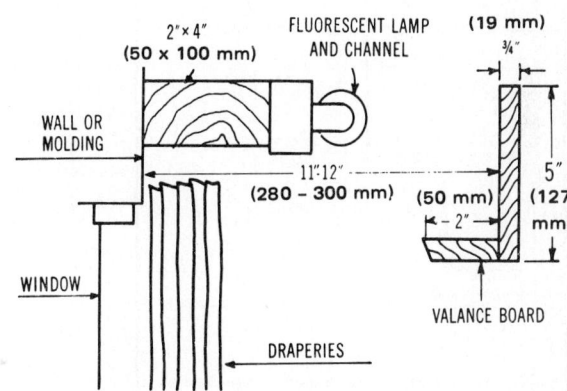

Fig. 34. Variation of valance lighting

If distance between wall and lamp is increased, light will be distributed more evenly, but shielding may be required at the bottom of the faceboard.

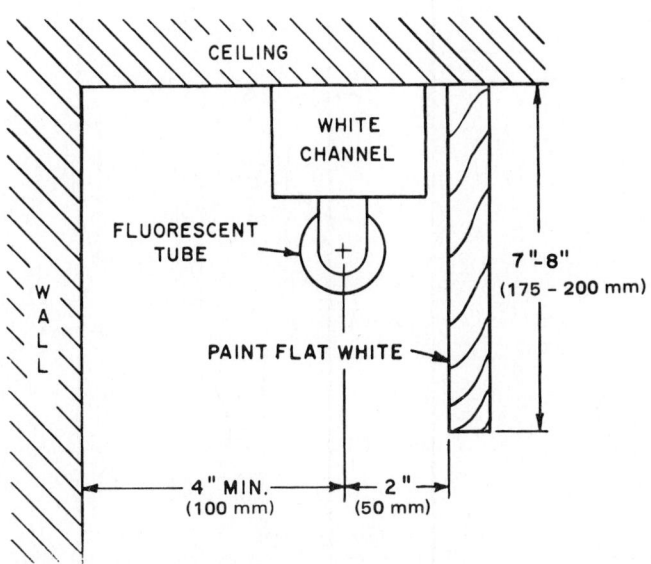

Fig. 35. Minimum dimensions for cornice lighting installation

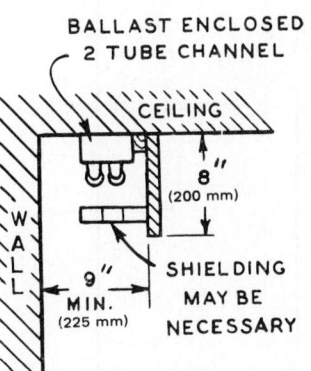

Fig. 36. Cornice lighting with two tubes may require shielding

Critical dimensions for the design of cove lighting are shown in Figs. 40 and 41 and must be carefully observed for a successful installation. Combinations of cove lighting and valance-type or downlighting are shown in Figs. 42 and 43.

The principle of cove lighting can also be used on walls (Fig. 44). Because walls are directly in the line of sight, luminance should be kept lower than for ceilings.

Downlighting

The term downlighting usually refers to relatively small units using incandescent lamps as light sources. They may be suspended or surface-mounted, but more often they are recessed in the ceiling. The recessed type consists of a square or round metal box with shielding of metal fins or louvers, or diffusing glass or a glass lens (Fig. 45). The box may contain a reflector for use with regular bulbs, or it may be designed for the use of reflector bulbs. Where more accurate control of the beam is required, special-purpose units may be specified. One of these is the "pinhole" spot (Fig. 46). Some of these are equipped with an optical system of light control and adjustable shutters, making it possible to shape the beam precisely—square, round, or rectangular—to the object to be lighted. Another useful fixture is the "eyeball" (Fig. 47). This semirecessed unit can be rotated and swiveled within its housing in order to direct the light where desired.

Downlighting is often called accent lighting because that is its principal use. It is not well suited to general lighting and should always be used with other types of lighting which will throw some light on the ceiling.

Luminous panel lighting

Luminous panel lighting is downlighting that is larger in area and often lower in luminance than accent lighting. The light sources are usually fluorescent tubes, and the shielding may be metal or plastic eggcrates but is more often a diffusing plastic sheet. In the smaller sizes (2 to 12 sq ft, 0.186 to 1.11 sq in) luminous panels may be used as local lighting (Fig. 48) and in the larger sizes they may serve as general lighting. In either case, other types of light-

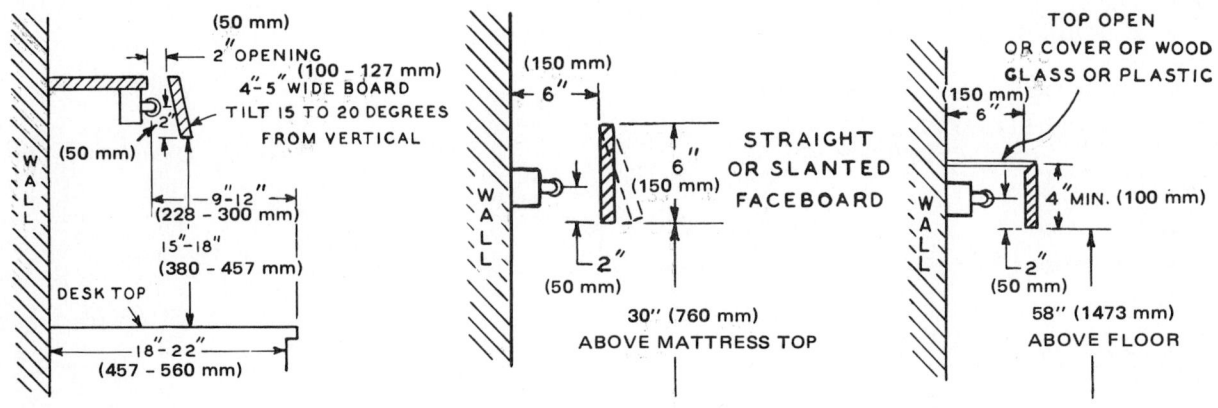

Fig. 37. Valance-type wall units for local lighting

(a) Desk, (b) bed, (c) range. Type b, installed 65 in. above the floor, can be used for lighting lounge furniture, dining tables, etc.

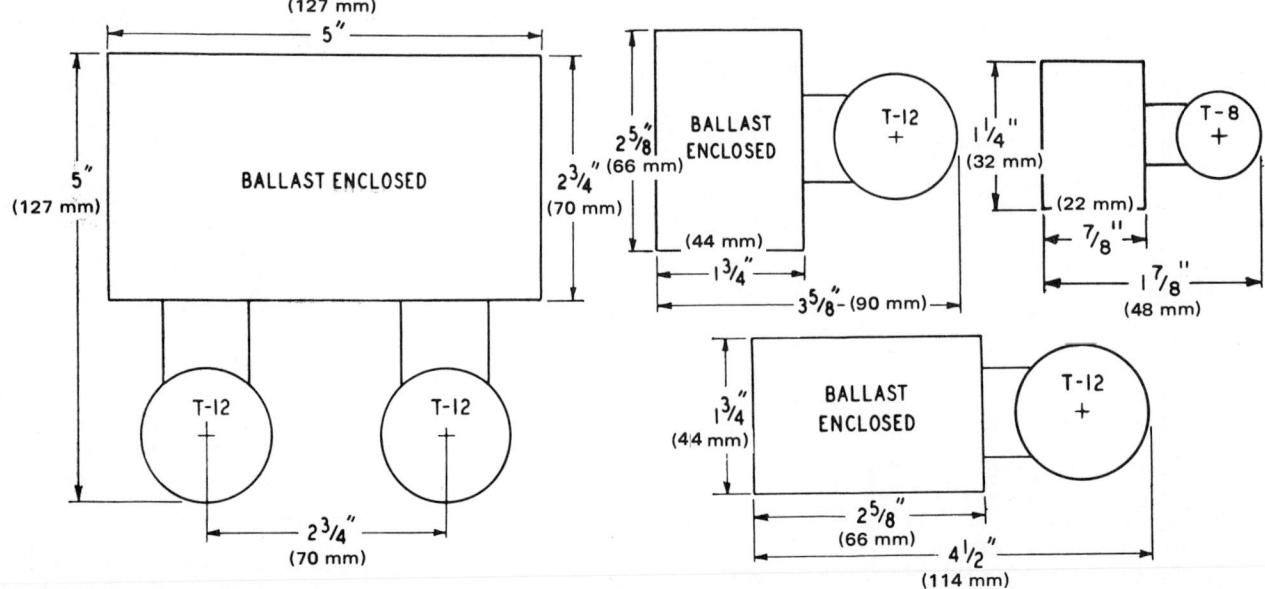

Fig. 38. Dimensions of standard metal wiring channels for fluorescent and lumiline tubes

ing should be employed to light the ceiling. If fluorescent and incandescent lamps are to be used in the same room, care must be exercised to select a fluorescent color which combines well with the yellowish light of incandescent lamps (see section on "Light and vision").

When a luminous panel fills the entire ceiling, it is known as a luminous ceiling. This gives an entirely different architectural character to the room, and of course eliminates the problem of the dark ceiling. When unlighted, the luminous ceiling has the appearance of a structural ceiling; when lighted, it has much the effect of a skylight. Luminous ceilings may be designed for high or low illuminance; dimmer control is advantageous for use in living and dining rooms.

The basic relationship for the design of luminous panels is shown in Fig. 49. An example of a luminous ceiling design is shown in Fig. 50.

Luminous walls may be designed in the same manner as luminous ceilings. When lighted, a luminous wall can give the effect of a sheer-curtained window wall.

Dimmers

Moderately priced and compact dimmers of sizes suitable for residential use are available for both incandescent and fluorescent lamps. They are of two types: the autotransformer type which reduces power consumption proportionally to illuminance, and the resistance type which consumes an appreciable amount of electricity even when the illuminance is at a low level. Fluorescent lights require special dimmer ballasts. Separate dimmers are required for fluorescent and incandescent lights. A compromise "dimmer" for incandescent lights is the high-low switch; the low setting gives approximately 30 per cent of the full light output. It should be noted that the light from incandescent bulbs becomes yellower as they are dimmed.

Outdoor lighting

There are four types of outdoor lighting:

1. To provide safe passage into and out of the house and between house and garage, patio, and garden

2. To discourage trespassers and disclose prowlers

3. To provide comfortable seeing for outdoor family activities

4. To enhance the beauty of garden and grounds. See section on "Landscaping" in *Time-Saver Standards for Building Types*, 1st ed.

A great variety of weatherproof lighting units is available for these applications. Light sources should always be concealed.

Illuminance

Illuminance values recommended for residences are shown in Table 20.

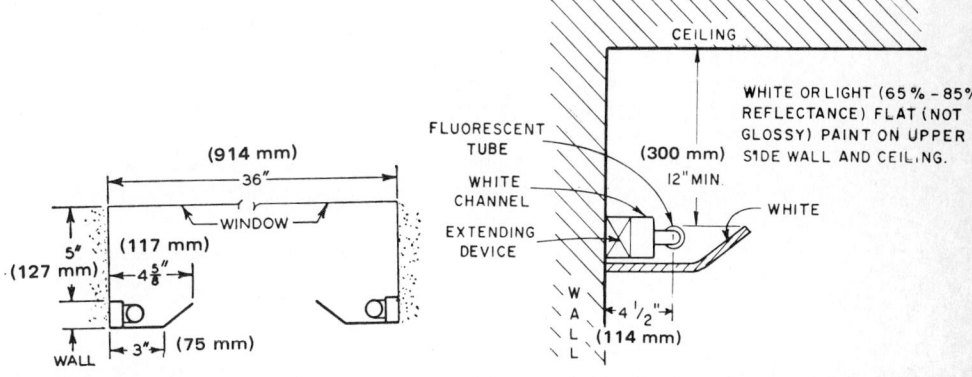

Fig. 39. The effect of sunshine coming in the windows is created by two 30-watt fluorescent tubes set end-to-end vertically behind metal shields in front of the venetian blinds but behind the draperies

Fig. 40. Critical dimensions for cove lighting installation

Lampholders should be butted back-to-back or overlapped, if space permits, to assure continuous light on walls and ceiling without dark spaces between tubes.

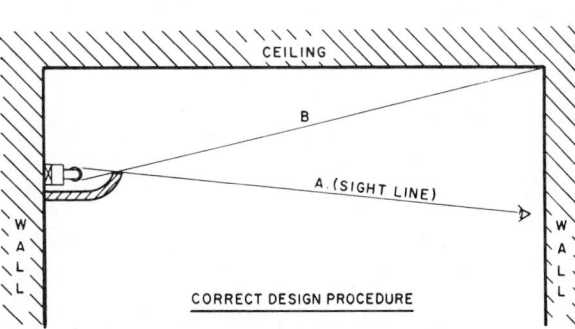

Fig. 41. Method of determining location of upper edge of cove so that light source is not visible and entire ceiling is lighted

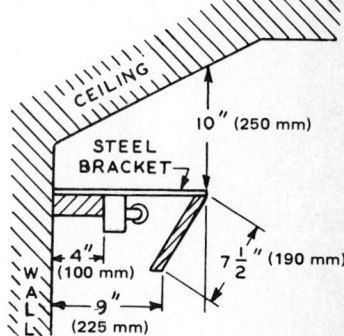

Fig. 42. Combination of cove and valance lighting

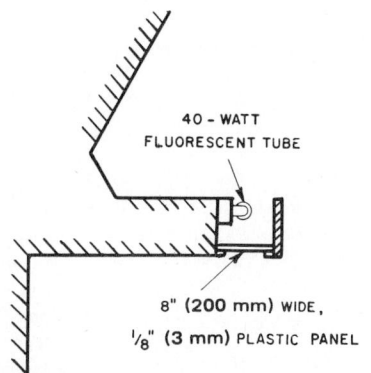

Fig. 43. Combination of cove and luminous panel downlighting

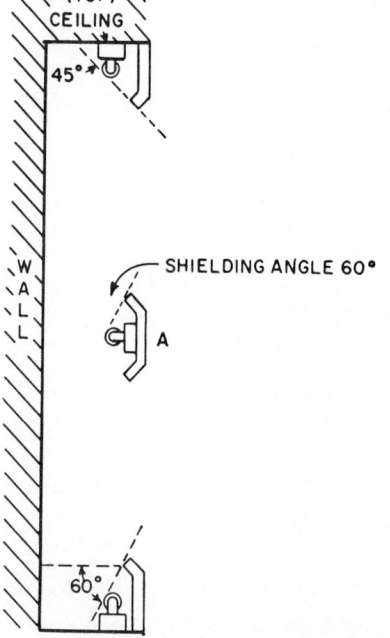

Fig. 44. Cove lighting used for walls

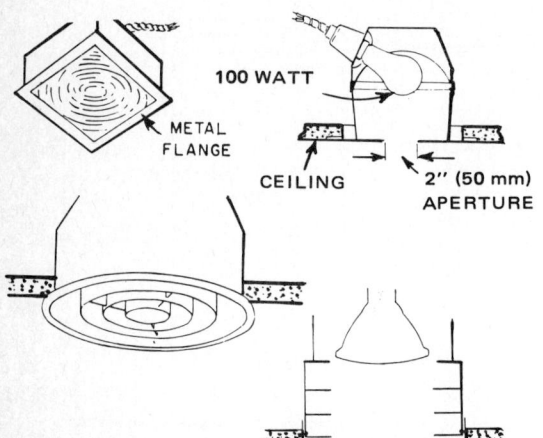

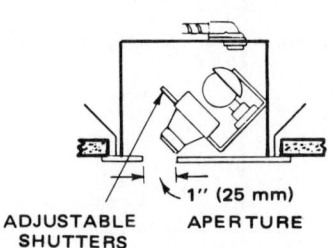

Fig. 46. Pinhole spot, a recessed downlight with adjustable shutters to shape beam pattern

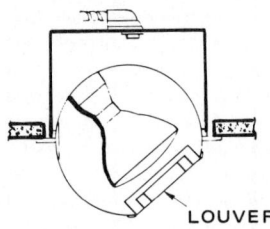

Fig. 47. "Eyeball" semirecessed fully adjustable downlight

Fig. 45. Common types of downlights

For other types see Store Lighting and Church Lighting.

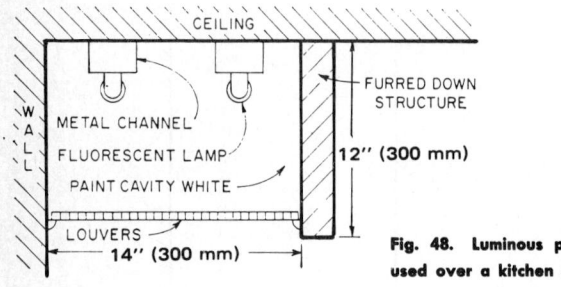

Fig. 48. Luminous panel or soffit lighting, used over a kitchen or bathroom counter

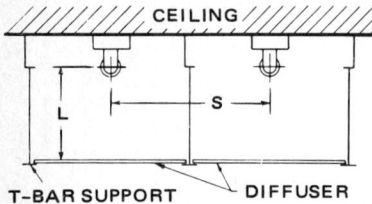

Fig. 49. Critical dimensions for luminous panel and luminous ceiling lighting

S should not exceed 1½ to 2 times L.

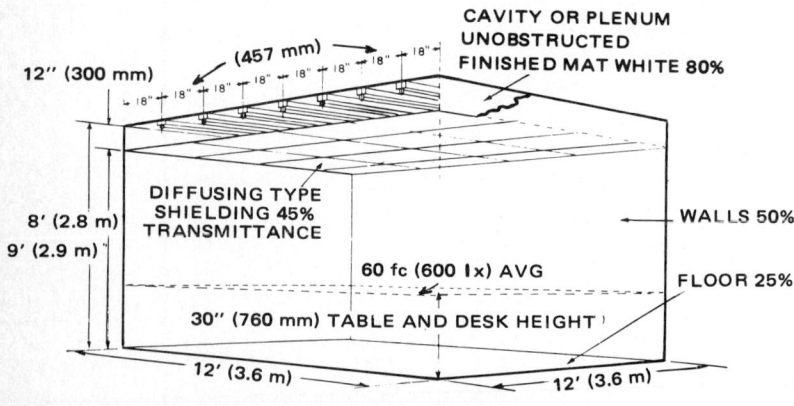

Fig. 50. Basic relationship for the design of luminous panels

A light level of 60 fc (600 lx) is produced by seven rows of three 40-watt fluorescent tubes on 18-in. (457 mm) centers. Light distribution and surface luminance are approximately uniform.

Table 20. Illuminance values for residences.*
(From IES recommended levels 1977.)

	Illuminance	
Specific visual tasks	Foot-candles	Lux†
Dining	15	150
Grooming, shaving, makeup	50	500
Handcraft		
Ordinary seeing tasks	70	700
Difficult seeing tasks	100	1000
Very difficult seeing tasks	150	1500
Critical seeing tasks	200	2000
Ironing (hand and machine)	50	500
Kitchen duties		
Food preparation and cleaning	150	1500
Serving and other noncritical tasks	50	500
Laundry		
Preparation, sorting, inspection	50	500
Tub area—soaking, tinting	50	500
Washer and dryer areas	30	300
Reading and writing		
Handwriting, reproductions, and poor copies	70	700
Books, magazines, newspapers	30	300
Reading piano or organ scores		
Advanced (substandard size)	150	1500
Advanced	70	700
Simple	30	300
Sewing (hand and machine)		
Dark fabrics	200	2000
Medium fabrics	100	1000
Light fabrics	50	500
Occasional—high contrast	30	300
Study	70	700
Table games	30	300
General lighting		
Conversation, relaxation, entertainment	10	100
Passage areas, for safety	10	100
Areas other than kitchen involving visual tasks	30	300
Kitchen	50	500

* *Minimum on the task at all times.*
† *Lux is an SI unit equal to 0.0929 footcandle.*

Table 21. Illuminance for various building types—minimum footcandles (lux)[a] on the task at all times. *(From IES recommended illuminances, 1977.)*

Building type	Illuminance		Building type	Illuminance	
	Fc	Lx		Fc	Lx
Aircraft hangars			Jail cells and interrogation rooms	30	300
Repair service only	100	1000	Fire		
Armories			Dormitory	20	200
Drill	20	200	Recreation room	30	300
Exhibitions	30	300	Wagon room	30	300
Art galleries			Museums (see Art galleries)		
General	30	300	Nursing homes		
On paintings (supplementary)[b]	30	300	Corridors and interior ramps	20	200
On statuary and other displays[c]	100	1000	Stairways other than exits	30	300
Auditoriums (see section on "Schools" and "Hotels")			Exit stairways and landings, on floor	5	50
Banks			Doorways	10	100
Lobby			Administrative and lobby areas, day	50	500
General	50	500	Administrative and lobby areas, night	20	200
Writing areas	70	700	Chapel or quiet area, general	5	50
Tellers' stations	150	1500	Chapel or quiet area, local for reading	30	300
Posting and keypunch	150	1500	Physical therapy	20	200
Barbershops and beauty parlors	100	1000	Occupational therapy	30	300
Courtrooms			Worktable, coarse work	100	1000
Seating area	30	300	Worktable, fine work	200	2000
Court activity area	70	700	Recreation area	50	500
Dance halls	5	50	Dining area	30	300
Depots, terminals, and stations			Patient care room, general	20	200
Waiting room	30	300	Patient care room, reading	30	300
Ticket offices	100	1000	Nurse's station, general		
Rest rooms and smoking room	30	300	Day	50	500
Baggage checking	50	500	Night	20	200
Concourse	10	100	Nurse's desk for charts and records	70	700
Platforms	20	200	Nurse's medicine cabinet	100	1000
Toilets and washrooms	30	300	Utility room, general	20	200
Building exteriors			Utility room, work counter	50	500
Entrances			Pharmacy area, general	30	300
Active (pedestrian and/or conveyance)	5	50	Pharmacy, compounding, and dispensing area	100	1000
Inactive (normally locked, infrequently used)	1	10	Janitor's closet	15	150
Vital locations or structures	5	50	Toilet and bathing facilities	30	300
Building surrounds	1	10	Barber and beautician areas	50	500
Buildings and monuments, floodlighted[d]			Post offices		
Bright surroundings			Lobby, on tables	30	300
Light surfaces	15	150	Sorting, mailing, etc.	100	1000
Medium light surfaces	20	200	Professional offices (see sections on "Hospitals" and		
Medium dark surfaces	30	300	"Offices")		
Dark surfaces	50	500	Restaurants (see section on "Hotels")		
Dark surroundings			Service stations		
Light surfaces	5	50	Service bays	30	300
Medium light surfaces	10	100	Sales room	50	500
Medium dark surfaces	15	150	Shelving and displays	100	1000
Dark surfaces	20	200	Rest rooms	15	150
Drafting rooms (see section on "Offices")			Storage	5	50
Elevators, freight and passenger	20	200	Service stations—exterior lighting		
Garages, automobile and truck			Dark surroundings		
Service garages			Approach	1.5	10.5
Repairs	100	1000	Driveway	1.5	10.5
Active traffic areas	20	200	Pump island area	20	200
Parking garages			Building faces (exclusive of glass)	10	100
Entrance	50	500	Service areas	3	30
Traffic lanes	10	100	Landscape highlights	2	20
Storage	5	50	Light surroundings		
Kitchens (see section on "Hotels")			Approach	3	30
Laundries (see section on "Hotels")			Driveway	5	50
Libraries (see section on "Libraries")			Pump island area	30	300
Locker rooms	20	200	Building faces (exclusive of glass)[d]	30	300
Machine shops (see section on "Hotels")			Service areas	7	70
Municipal buildings			Landscape highlights	5	50
Police					
Identification records	150	1500			

[a] *Lux is an SI unit equal to 0.0929 footcandle.*
[b] *Dark paintings with fine detail should have 2 to 3 times higher illuminance.*
[c] *In some cases much more illuminance is necessary to enhance the statuary.*
[d] *Vertical.*

SPORTS

Data from Current Recommended Practice for Sports Lighting, *Illuminating Engineering Society, 1961, and* IES Lighting Handbook, *1972*

The goal of sports lighting is to enable the players to perform their visual task and the spectators to follow the course of the play. The illuminance values recommended in Table 22 are currently considered minimum values of good practice, taking into account both players and spectators. Unless otherwise noted, the values in this table are footcandles (lux) on the horizontal playing surface or, for "aerial" sports, on a horizontal plane (36 in (914 mm) above the ground or floor.

As important as the quantity of light is the quality of the light. The principal factors affecting the quality of the lighting are glare, uniformity, and direction.

Glare control: A floodlight is inherently a glare source; therefore, one of the pri-

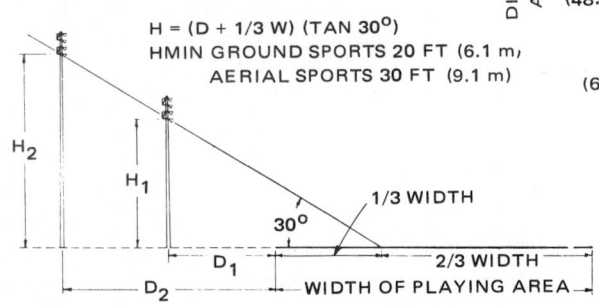

$$H = (D + 1/3\ W)\ (TAN\ 30°)$$
HMIN GROUND SPORTS 20 FT (6.1 m,
AERIAL SPORTS 30 FT (9.1 m)

Fig. 51. Formula for determination of minimum mounting height

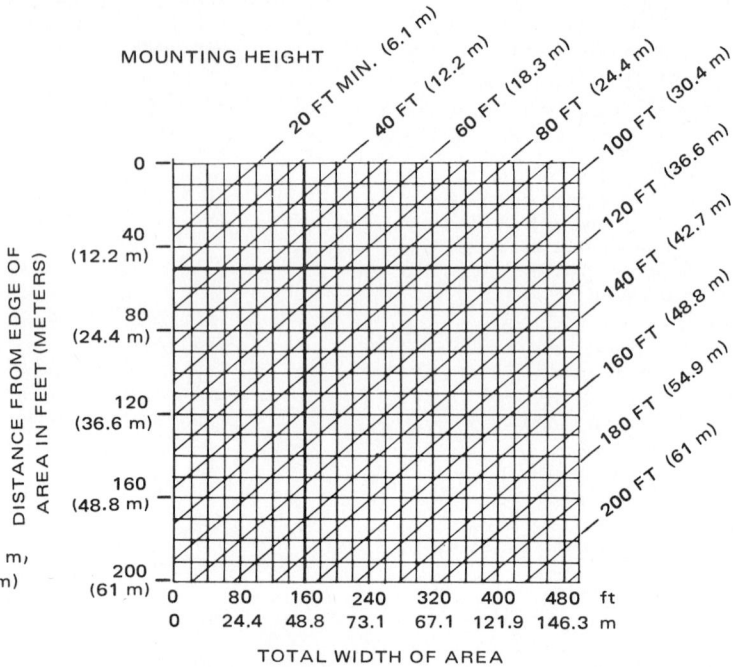

Fig. 52. Mounting height chart for all sports areas—minimum height to bottom floodlight crossarm

Read mounting height along diagonal at intersection of appropriate horizontal and vertical lines. For example, where area width = 160 ft (52.5 m) and pole setback = 50 ft (16.4 m), minimum height of 60 ft (19.6 m) is indicated by diagonal at intersection of 50 and 160 ft (16.4 and 52.5 m).

Table 22. Illuminance for sports—average footcandles (lux*) on horizontal playing surface *(From IES recommended levels of illuminance 1977.)*

Sport	Illuminance Fc	Lx	Sport	Illuminance Fc	Lx	Sport	Illuminance Fc	Lx
Archery (indoor)						Bathing beaches		
Target, tournament	50†	500	Outfield	30	300	On land	1	10
Target, recreational	30†	300	C and D league			150 feet from shore	3†	30
Shooting line, tournament	20	200	Infield	30	300	Billiards (on table)		
Shooting line, recreational	10	100	Outfield	20	200	Tournament	50	500
Archery (outdoor)			Semipro and municipal league			Recreational	30	300
Target, tournament	10†	100	Infield	20	200	Bowling‡		
Target, recreational	5†	50	Outfield	15	150	Tournament		
Shooting line, tournament	10	100	Recreational			Approaches	10	100
Shooting line, recreational	5	50	Infield	15	150	Lanes	20	200
Badminton			Outfield	10	100	Pins	50†	500
Tournament	30	300	Junior league (Class I and			Recreational		
Club	20	200	Class II)			Approaches	10	100
Recreational	10	100	Infield	30	300	Lanes	10	100
Baseball			Outfield	20	200	Pins	30†	300
Major league			On seats during game	2	20	Bowling on the green		
Infield	150	1500	On seats before and after			Tournament	10	100
Outfield	100	1000	game	5	50	Recreational	5	50
AA and AAA league			Basketball			Boxing or wrestling (ring)		
Infield	70	700	College and professional	50	500	Championship	500	5000
Outfield	50	500	College intramural and high			Professional	200	2000
A and B league			school	30	300	Amateur	100	1000
Infield	50	500	Recreational (outdoor)	10	100	Seats during bout	2	20

Table 22 (cont.). Illuminance values for sports

Sport	Fc	Lx
Seats before and after bout	5	50
Casting—bait, dry-fly, wet-fly		
Pier or dock	10	100
Target (at 80 feet for bait casting and 50 feet for wet or dry-fly casting)	5†	50
Croquet or Roque		
Tournament	10	100
Recreational	5	50
Curling		
Tournament		
Tees	50	500
Rink	30	300
Recreational		
Tees	20	200
Rink	10	100
Fencing		
Exhibitions	50	500
Recreational	30	300
Football		
Distance from nearest sideline to the farthest row of spectators		
Over 100 ft (over 30,000 spectators)	100	1000
50 feet to 100 ft (10,000–30,000)	50	500
30 feet to 50 ft (5,000–10,000)	30	300
Under 30 ft (under 5,000)	20	200
No fixed seating facilities	10	100
Football, six-man		
High school or college	20	200
Jr. high and recreational	10	100
Golf		
Tee	5	50
Fairway	3†	30
Green	5	50
Driving range		
At 200 yards	5*	50
Over tee area	10	100
Miniature	10	100
Practice putting green	10	100
Gymnasiums (see section on "Schools")		
Handball		
Tournament	50	500
Club		
Indoor—four-wall or squash	30	300
Outdoor—two-court	20	200
Recreational		
Indoor—four-wall or squash	20	200
Outdoor—two-court	10	100

Sport	Fc	Lx
Hockey, field	20	200
Hockey, ice (indoor)		
College or professional	100	1000
Amateur	50	500
Recreational	20	200
Hockey, ice (outdoor)		
College or professional	50	500
Amateur	20	200
Recreational	10	100
Horseshoes		
Tournament	10	100
Recreational	5	50
Horse shows	20	200
Jai-alai		
Professional	100	1000
Amateur	70	700
Lacrosse	20	200
Playgrounds	5	50
Quoits	5	50
Racing (outdoor)		
Auto	20	200
Bicycle		
Tournament	30	300
Competitive	20	200
Recreational	10	100
Dog	30	300
Dragstrip		
Staging area	10	100
Acceleration, 1320 ft	20	200
Deceleration, first 660 ft	15	150
Deceleration, second 660 ft	10	100
Shutdown, 820 ft	5	50
Horse	20	200
Motor (midget or motorcycle)	20	200
Rifle (50 yd—outdoor)		
On targets	50†	500
Firing point	10	100
Range	5	50
Rifle and pistol range (indoor)		
On targets	100†	1000
Firing point	20	200
Range	10	100
Rodeo		
Arena		
Professional	50	500
Amateur	30	300
Recreational	10	100
Pens and chutes	5	50
Roque (see Croquet)		
Shuffleboard (indoor)		
Tournament	30	300
Recreational	20	200
Shuffleboard (outdoor)		
Tournament	10	100

Sport	Fc	Lx
Recreational	5	50
Skating		
Roller rink	10	100
Ice rink, indoor	10	100
Ice rink, outdoor	5	50
Lagoon, pond, or flooded area	1	10
Skeet and trap		
Targets (at 100 ft for trap, 60 ft for skeet)	30†	300
Firing points	5	50
Ski slope	1	10
Soccer (see Football)		
Softball		
Professional and championship		
Infield	50	500
Outfield	30	300
Semiprofessional		
Infield	30	300
Outfield	20	200
Industrial league		
Infield	20	200
Outfield	15	150
Recreational (6-pole)		
Infield	10	100
Outfield	7	70
Squash (see Handball)		
Swimming (indoor)		
Exhibitions	50	500
Recreational	30	300
Underwater—100 lamp lumens per square foot of surface area		
Swimming (outdoor)		
Exhibitions	20	200
Recreational	10	100
Underwater—60 lamp lumens per square foot of surface area		
Tennis, lawn (indoor)		
Tournament	50	500
Club	30	300
Recreational	20	200
Tennis, lawn (outdoor)		
Tournament	30	300
Club	20	200
Recreational	10	100
Tennis, table		
Tournament	50	500
Club	30	300
Recreational	20	200
Volleyball		
Tournament	20	200
Recreational	10	100

* Lux is an SI unit equal to 0.0929 footcandle.
† On vertical surface.
‡ Values shown are based on visual considerations. Otherwise, for public attraction and increased business considerations, practice is as follows:

Class	Approaches		Lanes		Pins	
	Fc	Lx	Fc	Lx	Fc	Lx
Tournament	70	700	100	1000	200	2000 vertical
Recreation	50	500	70	700	150	1500 vertical

mary tasks of the illuminance designer should be to reduce the objectionable effects of glare to a minimum. The basic means by which the designer may accomplish this task are proper beam spread, adequate mounting heights, proper luminaire locations, and proper floodlight aiming.

Beam spread: As the distance from the floodlight to the area to be lighted increases, the beam spread of the floodlight used should be decreased. Beam spreads vary from a minimum of 10 to more than 100 deg.

Mounting height: Recommended minimum mounting heights are shown in Figs. 51 and 52.

Luminaire location: Every effort should be made to locate light sources so that they are not in the normal line of sight of either players or spectators. Glare shields and special louvers can be designed to reduce the luminance of spill light which may cause discomfort to spectators or sometimes even to the inhabitants of the surrounding area.

Uniformity: Acceptable uniformity occurs when the ratio of maximum to minimum luminance does not exceed 3 to 1.

Direction of light: Except for unidirectional sports such as archery, bowling, and golf driving, lighting should come from several directions in order to avoid excessive shadow contrast.

Floodlights: These are classified as heavy duty, general purpose, and open type. *Standards Publication for Floodlights* by the National Electrical Manufacturers Association specifies the minimum beam efficiency that each type should provide. Recommended maintenance factors are 75 per cent for the covered type and 65 per cent for the open type.

Layouts and tables showing the number, type, and location of the floodlights for 56 specific sports are given in *Current Recommended Practice for Sports Lighting* by the Illuminating Engineering Society, 1969.

PARKING AREAS

Data from Recommended Practice for Outdoor Parking Area Lighting, *Illuminating Engineering Society, 1960.*

The basic requirement in lighting an outdoor parking area is to provide good visibility with a minimum of glare. The most severe problem in such applications is to provide a measure of illuminance in the many small, narrow "corridors" formed by adjacent parked cars. In order to get some light into these "corridors" it is recommended that any point in the entire parking area be provided with illuminance from at least two, and preferably four, lighting (pole) locations with equipment mounted as high as possible, at a minimum of 20 ft (6.6 m).

Basic illuminance requirements: The minimum recommended illumination levels for the barest seeing essentials on the parking lot proper are as follows:

Type of parking area	Average maintained horizontal footcandles	lux
Self-parking area	1.0	10
Attendant parking area	2.0*	20*

* Higher illuminances are required for attendant parking lots than for self-parking lots because, with the former, closer parking, greater movement, and speed and accuracy of handling vehicles are important for greater monetary returns and avoidance of damage claims.

Where additional lighting is desired for business attraction or customer convenience, values of 5 fc (50 lx) and upward are often used.

Uniform illuminance is desirable, and the lowest foot-candle value at any point on the pavement should not be less than one-fourth the recommended average.

Entrances and exits: The illuminance levels of entrances, exits, loading zones, and collector lanes of parking areas should not be less than twice the illuminance of the adjacent parking area or the adjoining street, whichever is greater.

Light sources: Light sources used for the illuminance of outdoor parking areas can be incandescent, mercury, fluorescent or any combination of the three.

Types of lighting equipment: A number of different types of luminaires are available for parking area lighting although floodlights or street lighting units are most commonly employed.

Street lighting luminaires are available to accommodate incandescent, fluorescent, and mercury lamps (Fig. 53*a*), and are designed to produce both symmetric and asymmetric light control. Narrow and wide patterns of light are available.

Floodlights are available in a wide range of light distributions from concentrating (for lighting areas at a distance) to wide spread (for lighting close-up areas), in symmetric, asymmetric, and rectangular beam patterns to fit a large number of different requirements. Floodlights are available for use with many sizes of incandescent, mercury, fluorescent, and reflectorized lamps (Fig. 53*b*).

Isolux charts: As a design aid in determining illuminances and coverage, isolux diagrams, curves showing illuminance at various distances from the source, are often used. They may be obtained from manufacturers of lighting equipment. By superimposing these diagrams on a proposed layout of a parking area drawn to the same scale, the approximate illuminance at a specific point may be determined. This is useful also in studying the uniformity of illuminance that a particular lighting unit will provide in a particular arrangement.

Luminaire spacing: The ratio of the luminaire (or pole, in the event of multiple-mounted luminaires) spacing to the mounting height should be kept to a minimum. For both floodlights and street lights a maximum spacing-to-mounting height ratio of 4 to 1 represents current good practice.

Pole locations: Lighting poles should be located generally along the parking barriers and outside boundaries. Where poles are located near automobiles, the use of wheel barriers will save both cars and poles.

Aiming: Special care should be taken to avoid objectionable spill light and glare on adjacent property.

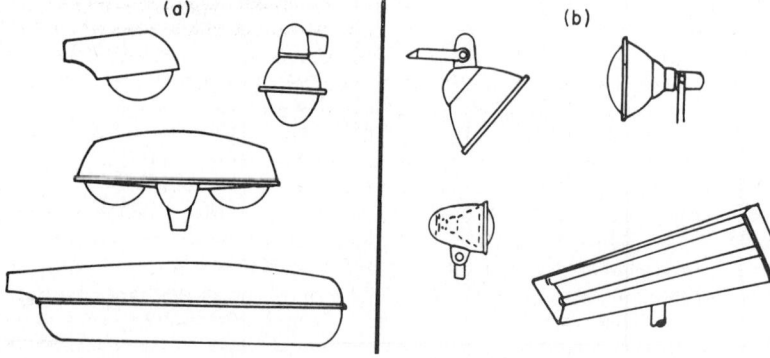

Fig. 53. Typical outdoor area lighting luminaires

(*a*) *Street lights;* (*b*) *floodlights.*

By LOUIS A. BELLO, *Vice President, Syska and Hennessy, Inc., Consulting Engineers*

ELECTRICAL LOADS IN LARGE BUILDINGS

In recent years the trend toward awareness of energy usage has helped to stabilize the spiraling increase in electrical usage in large buildings. Many of the energy-consuming devices have been re-engineered in such a manner as to make them produce the same results as before while using less electricity.

To assist the designer of electrical systems for large buildings, this section presents descriptions and tabulations of major loads for typical buildings.

TYPES OF ELECTRICAL LOADS

1. Lighting
2. Convenience outlets (floor power)
3. Heating, ventilating, and air conditioning (HVAC)
4. Sanitary equipment
5. Elevators, moving stairways, and materials handling equipment
6. Kitchen equipment
7. Data processing equipment
8. Laboratory equipment

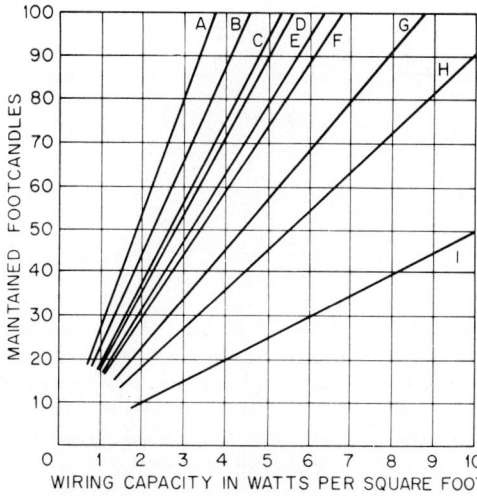

Fig. 1. Approximate wiring capacity to provide a given maintained level of illumination in a room of 2.5 room cavity ratio by means of the following: A, direct or semidirect industrial fluorescent; B, general diffuse fluorescent; C, direct fluorescent troffer; D, direct or semidirect mercury industrial; E, semi-indirect fluorescent; F, direct fluorescent luminous or louvered ceiling; G, indirect fluorescent; H, direct or semidirect incandescent; I, indirect incandescent.

(IES Lighting Handbook, 5th ed., 1972.)

Note: Recent improvements in light distribution devices such as lenses and louvers permit design of lighting with lower than usual energy usage while maintaining adequate illumination levels.

9. Shop equipment
10. X-ray equipment
11. Snow melting and pipe heating cable

Lighting

Lighting is generally the largest electrical load in most buildings, and a good understanding of it is essential before final building loads can be established. Various electrical codes have established minimum requirements for feeder capacities [see Article 220 in the National Electrical Code (NEC) and Article 20, N.Y.C. Electrical Code], but initial connected loads rarely reach these requirements. Once the minimum footcandle level and type of lighting system has been selected, preliminary load estimates can be determined on a watts per square foot basis (see Fig. 1).

Many states are in the process of defining energy codes which include, in most instances, a lighting energy budget indicating maximum energy usage in watts per square foot in various areas of buildings. Some codes are also applicable to renovations of existing buildings. These codes must be reviewed carefully before selecting lighting for new or remodeled projects.

Convenience outlets (floor power)

In general, about ½ to 1½ watts per sq ft are allowed for convenience outlets for preliminary load estimates. Connected loads are determined by code requirements for ratings, i.e. NEC rating of 180 watts per duplex receptacle.

Underfloor duct and cellular raceway systems are sometimes designed into office buildings to provide maximum flexibility. Allowances in circuiting are made for one convenience receptacle per 125 sq ft or approximately 1½ watts per sq ft.

Loads actually associated with floor power are office and business machines such as typewriters and adding machines.

Heating, ventilating, and air conditioning

Table 1 indicates a decrease or minimal change in electrical load for HVAC equipment over the last 10 years. This is a prime example of increased design and equipment efficiency. New methods of load calculation and new system developments have brought this about.

The following types of heating and ventilating equipment may be encountered:
1. Fans
2. Pumps (vacuum, condensate)
3. Electric heaters (unit, space, in-duct)
4. Unit ventilators
5. Fuel combustion motors
6. Fan coil units

Air conditioning equipment usually consists of:
1. Fans
2. Pumps
3. Refrigeration compressors—motor, engine, or turbine driven.

Sanitary equipment

This type of load makes a small contribution to the total building load. Major contributing equipment may be:

1. Sump pumps
2. Circulating pumps
3. Sewage ejectors
4. Drinking fountain systems
5. Compressors
6. Fire pumps
7. House pumps

Elevators, moving stairways, and materials handling equipment

These are formidable loads in tall buildings and hospitals and may consist of:
1. Elevators
2. Moving stairways
3. Dumbwaiters
4. Conveyors
5. Pneumatic tubes
6. Hoists and lifts
7. Linen and ash chutes

Major factors affecting the capacities of the above equipment are speed of travel and weight being handled.

Kitchen equipment

Cooking appliances can generally be classified into two categories:
1. All-electric
2. Gas and/or steam with or without electric auxiliaries.

The number of persons to be served, the type of service, and equipment used determine actual electrical load. Table 1 indicates kitchen loads of actual installations. The commercial-type dishwasher may require electric booster heaters to raise the temperature of the normal building hot water supply. Loads up to 50 kw for such purposes are not uncommon.

Data processing equipment

This specialized equipment has taken on a great deal of importance in the business world today. Almost all major buildings of every classification have at least one data processing center. These areas are specially designed, for maximum flexibility of space and wiring requirements, in the form of raised floors or troughs. Uninterrupted power supplies are sometimes required for these areas.

Table 1. Connected loads for various buildings per 1,000 sq ft of floor area

High and low values are unique for specific load. Values do not necessarily relate to building with high or low floor area.

		Floor area sq ft	Level of illumination, fc	Light and receptacles, kva	HVAC, hp	Plumbing, hp	Elevator, kva	Kitchen kva	Fire pump, hp	Laboratory kva	X-ray, kva	Emergency generator, kva	Electric heating and cooling, kva
Office buildings													
Early 1960s (10 buildings in eastern U.S.)	Avg	852,000	56	5.1		0.21	0.93	0.40	0.20				
Early 1970s (4 buildings in N.Y.C.)	Avg	2,300,000	75	5.7	3.1	0.18	1.9	0.34	0.16			0.38	
	High	2,450,000	75	6.9	4.2	0.25	2.5	0.72	0.20			0.52	3.25*
	Low	2,100,000	75	5.1	2.1	0.12	1.7	0.10	0.10			0.3	
Hospitals													
Early 1960s (4 general hospitals & 3 additions)	Avg	347,400		5.3	4.5	0.32	0.95	0.96		0.63	0.64	3.5	
Early 1970s (2 buildings)	1.	280,000	50	4.6	4.5	0.35	0.57	0.84		0.36	1.8	2.2	
	2.	148,000	80	6.1	5.0	0.45	1.1	0.58		0.34	2.0	4.1	
Schools													
Early 1960s (9 schools in N.Y.C.)	Avg	136,600	33	4.2	1.2	0.08	0.12	0.66					
Early 1970s (5 schools in N.Y.C.)	Avg	336,000	52	3.2	1.1	0.05	0.17	0.46		0.63		†	
	High	410,000	60‡	3.5	1.6§	0.09	0.36	0.74		0.73		0.61	0.74‡
	Low	180,000	50	2.9	0.60	0.02	0.01	0.37		0.48		0.15	0.16‡
Laboratories													
Early 1960s (6 laboratory buildings)	Avg	89,500	47		5.6	1.5	1.1	1.1		6.9			
Early 1970s (2 buildings)	1.¶	1,000,000	100		7.4	0.85	0.95			2.0#	3.5	3.6	
	2.	87,000	100		10.1	0.58	1.4			21.5	0.44	6.6	

*Motor-driven refrigeration compressor.
†Emergency generator provided in three schools.
‡All electric school.
§ This school provided with air conditioning.
¶ This building contains offices, operating suites and outpatient clinics.
#40 kw/1,000 sq ft in laboratories.

Laboratory equipment

Detailed electrical load data for this type of equipment are highly unpredictable due to the nature of use in each individual situation. The National Institute of Health (NIH) recommends that connected loads for branch circuit and panel design be estimated at 40 watts per sq ft for each laboratory. Special equipment, such as environmental rooms, is evaluated directly from nameplate values.

Shop equipment

This is usually a minor load for the commercial building. However, it may be heavy for concentrated areas in schools.

X-ray equipment

Although usually associated with hospitals, such equipment may also be found in office buildings and laboratories on a smaller scale. It is important to note that these loads tax a distribution system for only a few seconds, and they are usually well diversified with other x-ray equipment.

Snow melting and pipe heating cable

This type of equipment is being used with much greater frequency for keeping sidewalks and truck ramps clear and protecting piping from freeze-ups. Loads are dependent upon anticipated outdoor temperatures in the building area. In New York City, snow melting may be designed for approximately 40 watts per sq ft.

SUMMARY

The load values discussed have been for connected load only. When final demand and diversity factors are applied, feeders and building service will be sized for a much lower load requirement than a pure summation of all connected loads. Sample demand factors for building service are approximately as follows:

Floor power	50%
HVAC and sanitary loads	80%
Elevators	50%
Laboratory equipment	25%
X-ray equipment	10%

Diversity factors may range from 60 to 80 per cent depending on the type of building and equipment installed.

Table 2 shows typical load values, which can be useful for both preliminary estimates and final checking.

Table 2. Electrical capacities of building equipment

Cooking appliances

Appliance	Electrical capacity	Appliance	Electrical capacity
1. Range (4-burner)	12 kva	9. Food warmer	1.65 kva
2. All-purpose oven (1 section—60 lb of beef per hr)	6 kva	10. Steam table (8 wells)	12. kva
3. Bake ovens		11. Warming cabinet (dishes, utensils, etc., 300 to 400 watts per ft of length)	0.5–10 kva
1 section—40 lb of bread	7.5 kva	12. Coffee urn (500 watts per gal)	1.5–10 kva
1 section—60 lb of bread	11 kva	13. Compression steam cooker	12 kva
4. Broiler (1 section—100 lb per hr)	12 kva	14. Dishwasher	0.6–50 kva
5. Fry kettles		15. Glass washer	0.5 kva
40 lb potatoes per hr	12 kva	16. Food chopper	1/4–10 hp
90 lb potatoes per hr	18 kva	17. Food cutter	1/3–3/4 hp
6. Griddles		18. Food mixer	1/6–1/3 hp
16 hamburgers	3 kva	19. Slicer	1/8–1/3 hp
32 hamburgers	6 kva	20. Tenderizer	1/3 hp
48 hamburgers	12 kva	21. Peeler	1/3–1/2 hp
7. Hot plate (2 plates)	2.5 kva	22. Waste disposal	1 1/2 hp
8. Roll warmer (48 buns)	1.65 kva		

Shop equipment

Item	Electrical capacity	Size
1. Drill press	1/2 hp	15-in. diam stock
2. Grinder	1/3 hp	6-in. diam wheel
3. Grinder	1/2 hp	7-in. diam wheel
4. Grinder	3/4 hp	8-in. diam wheel
5. Grinder	1 hp	10-in. diam wheel
6. Jointer	3/4 hp	6-in. table width
7. Jointer	1 1/2 hp	8-in. table width
8. Kiln	4.5 kva	14 x 14 x 14 in. cabinet 2000° F
9. Kiln	6.0 kva	16 x 16 x 18 in. cabinet 2000° F
10. Lathe (variable speed)	1 hp	12-in. diam
11. Milling machine	1/3 hp	9-in. travel
12. Milling machine	1 hp	14-in. travel
13. Milling machine	2 hp	17-in. travel
14. Mortiser	3/4 hp	6 x 30 in. table
15. Oven	1 kva	28 x 24 x 20 in. cabinet
16. Oven	2 kva	
17. Planer	2 hp	4 x 12 in.
18. Potter's wheel	1/4 hp	19 x 30 in. table
19. Router	1 1/4 hp	
20. Sander, belt, and disk (floor mtd)	1/2 hp	10-in. diam, 6-in. belt
21. Sander, comb, belt and disk	1/2 hp	4-in. diam, 10-in. belt
22. Sander, spindle (floor mtd)	1 hp	20 x 24 in. table
23. Saw, arbor	2 hp	10-in. diam
24. Saw, band	1/2 hp	14-in. diam
25. Saw, band	1 1/2 hp	20-in. diam
26. Saw, circular	3 hp	10-in. diam
27. Saw, jig	1/3 hp	24-in. throat
28. Saw, radial	3/4 hp	9-in. diam
29. Saw, scroll	1/3 hp	26-in. throat
30. Surfacer	5 hp	6 x 18 in.
31. Surfacer	7 1/2 hp	8 x 24 in.
32. Surfacer	10 hp	8 x 30 in.
33. Welder, arc	7.5 kva	
34. Welder, spot	1.5 kva	1/8-in. metal thickness
35. Welder, spot	2.5 kva	3/16-in. metal thickness

Table 2 (cont.). Electrical capacities of building equipment

Residential appliances

Item	Watts	Item	Watts	Item	Watts
1. Air conditioners (room)		19. Power tools	up to 1,000	40. Sandwich grill	960
½ ton	880	20. Projector	300	41. Sewing machine	75
¾ ton	1,225	21. Radio	30	42. Serving tray	600
1 ton	1,540	22. Range	up to 23,000	43. Shaver	11
2. Aquarium aerator	50	23. Recorder	95	44. Steam iron	1,040
3. Aquarium aerator	250	24. Record player	50	45. Sun lamp	275
4. Blanket	175	25. Dehumidifier	185	46. Tea kettle	550
5. Blender	275	26. Door chime	15	47. Toaster	1,130
6. Bottle warmer	440	27. Dishwasher	1,325	48. Trivet	50
7. Broiler	1,400	28. Dry iron	1.025	49. TV receiver	
8. Casserole	510	29. Egg cooker	440	Black and white	275
9. Clock	2	30. Fans		Color	500
10. Clothes dryer	4,760	Floor circulator	120	50. Vacuum cleaners	
11. Coffee maker	up to 1,000	Attic	345	Bag type	340
12. Corn popper	440	Kitchen exhaust	75	Canister type	725
13. Heating equipment		Portable	50	Tank type	555
warm air furnace		31. Floor polisher	475	Hand type	310
fan	320	32. Food freezer	up to 460	51. Heat lamp	250
Oil burner	230	33. Food warmer	310	52. Heating pad	60
Humidifier	185	34. Fry kettle	1,300	53. Heater	up to 1,650
14. Ice cream freezer	115	35. Frying pan	1,085	54. Vaporizer	385
15. Iron	1.455	36. Food mixer	130	55. Waffle baker	960
16. Knife sharpener	50	37. Hair dryer	415	56. Washers	
17. Odorizer	11	38. Refrigerator	230	Automatic	400
18. Pressure cooker	1,400	39. Roaster	1,320	Nonautomatic	380

X-ray equipment

Use	kva
1. Simple radiography and fluoroscopy	66
2. Advanced radiography and fluoroscopy	150
3. Operating room radiography	75
4. Cystoscopic room radiography	125
5. Emergency (and/or admission) room radiography	150
6. Special procedures radiography and fluoroscopy	150
7. Cardiology radiology and fluoroscopy	135
8. Portable equipment	25

Data processing equipment

Item	Electrical capacity, kva* (not including air-conditioning requirements)
Processing unit	5–10
Printer	0.8–1.5
Reader	2–4
Control unit	3–5
Memory	1–2

Based on IBM 360

By RICHARD DiMONDA, *American Hospital Association*
and ROBERT PAUL, *Director of Engineering, Baylor University Medical Center*

INTRODUCTION

A modern medical center cannot function without electric power even for a short period of time. Almost every device utilized in every single department throughout the Medical Center relies on electrical power for operation. It is essential that the designer understand this total dependence upon electrical power before the electrical design is begun.

MAIN ELECTRIC SERVICE

The main incoming service into a hospital should be fed from two different sources, if at all possible, with an automatic transfer switch between the two feeders. The feed is best if it can be from two different generating stations, but even coming from two different substations helps increase reliability. It is preferable to bring the power in through an underground service if possible because of the danger of ice or other overhead disturbances.

Many smaller hospitals can be fed with a three-phase, 4-wire, 208Y, 120-volt(V) line directly from the power company. This is generally preferable to three-phase, 4-wire delta. This design would eliminate the necessity of providing a ground fault circuit interrupter, a device that has created problems for some installations with nuisance tripping.

TRANSFORMERS

Careful attention must be given to the installation of transformers serving a medical center. If primary transformers are supplied by the hospital and are located outdoors, it is essential that protection be provided by installing them on a concrete pad with adequate surrounding clearance. They must be enclosed with a heavy wire fence. Generally, the nonflammable, nonsludging, insulating, liquid-filled types offers high impulse strength and low maintenance. Sealed dry types can be installed outdoors but they have a lower impulse strength than the liquid-filled units and require less space. Open dry types can be used only indoors. Any transformers installed indoors should have good ventilation and be located so that leaks from pipes or other sources cannot cause them to become wet.

CIRCUIT BREAKERS

It is preferable for the primary switch gear to be of the draw-out design because that provides a higher degree of reliability, protection, and ease of maintenance. The molded case breakers are less expensive, but downtime for servicing is longer and the service life may be shorter in some instances.

DISTRIBUTION

The design of the electric service of a hospital must be carefully thought out with a proper balance established between space requirements, service continuity, flexibility, regulation, efficiency, maintenance and operations cost, and initial investment. A looped primary radial, conventional radial, double-ended with tie breakers, or some other of a dozen systems may be best in the overall picture for a particular hospital. It is important that all factors be considered, not only initial cost.

The three-phase, 4-wire, 208Y/120-V distribution system has many advantages for the average hospital, primarily because 120-V power is obtainable at any 208-V, three-phase, 4-wire panel. For larger systems, 480/277-V distribution systems may afford some economies, even though 120-V transformers and separate 120-V lines must be provided all over the building. Maintenance is somewhat simplified with the 208/120-V systems. A combination of the two tends to create more problems because of inventory of ballast, other parts, and the training of new people.

ENERGY CONSERVATION

It is imperative to design in as many energy conservation measures as possible and still have an attractive workable plan. High-pressure sodium exterior lighting and energy-saving fluorescent lamps and ballasts should be specified, and lighting levels held to the new standards developed by IEEE. Emphasis should be placed on task lighting rather than general illumination.

EMERGENCY POWER

A reliable source of emergency power for lighting and for operation of essential equipment is necessary. The three sources of power which have been used are storage batteries, second utility lines, and generators. In today's hospitals a generator on the hospital site has become a necessity. For primary power, storage batteries or a second utility line are not practical options for the following reasons: (1) storage batteries have a limited capacity and the direct current must be converted to alternating current for services such as operation of motorized equipment or fluorescent lighting; (2) a second utility line is usually subject to the same factors contributing to power interruption as those of the main utility service; most codes will not allow the use of a second utility

line as the only source of emergency power except for electric heating.

Batteries are commonly used to serve surgical lighting during a power failure. A major advantage is that transfer of power is nearly immediate without the usual delay of 10 seconds or more required of motor-driven generators.

When a second utility line is used as a source of emergency power, it should be from a generating plant separate from the source of main power and should be routed and connected so that any fault on the main feeder would not be transmitted to, or likely to cause an outage of, the emergency feeder.

Generators on a hospital site may be driven by any suitable prime mover such as gasoline, natural gas, or diesel oil internal combustion engines or steam turbines. The selection of the type of generating unit is usually influenced by the dependability of the fuel supply and whether the emergency power will be used frequently to carry a part of the load during normal operation. Single generator sets are permitted to be used to operate the essential electric system of the hospital for (1) peak demand control, (2) internal voltage control, or (3) load relief for the external utility, provided this use will not decrease the mean period between service overhauls to less than 3 years. Generally, the internal combustion engine generating units are intended as a standby service only, while the steam turbine units are sometimes operated during periods of maximum demands daily, and where such operation may result in a more favorable power rate from the utility company.

A switchover gas and gasoline fuel supply for small- and medium-sized internal combustion engines offers greater flexibility of operation in case of scarcity or depletion of either fuel. Starting gasoline engines on bottled gas and then switching to gasoline has been suggested as a more positive assurance of avoiding failure of automatic starting.

Emergency generators may be served by natural gas provided the facility is located in a geographical area where low probability of simultaneous failure of both the off-site fuel delivery system and power from the outside electrical utility company can be documented.

An arrangement of feeders so that a planned selection of loads may be connected or dropped from the emergency service is desirable, to more fully utilize the available capacity of the emergency service and also to prevent overloading to the point of trip-out of the entire service. Such a design is a particularly important convenience when adding fixed or mobile emergency capacity to an existing system and also for minimizing a trip-out of service to a highly important area. The switching of emergency power for critical areas, such as means of egress or patient care and protection, should be automatic. Pickup or dropout of other circuits should be selective and may be either manual or automatic.

The essential electric system for hospitals is normally divided into two systems: the *emergency system* and the *equipment system*. The emergency system is limited to circuits essential to life safety and critical-patient care. The equipment system supplies the major electric support equipment necessary for patient care and hospital operation such as heating, supply and exhaust ventilation, elevators, etc. Detailed requirements for these systems are specified in National Fire Protection Standard No. 76A *Essential Electrical Systems for Health Care Facilities*.

TELEPHONE SERVICE

Telephone service should be brought into a building underground, where practicable, and should be kept well-separated from electric power service. Telephone cables should be routed to avoid locations where they would be subject to mechanical injury, excessive heat, or chemical erosion. Telephone systems are extensively used for data transmission, and efforts to locate services well away from generators and high-voltage systems are recommended. Locating new computer-controlled telephone systems, for example, near elevator motors could erase the telephone switching system's memory.

PANELBOARDS AND SWITCHBOARDS

All panelboards and switchboards should be metal-enclosed with hinged doors and good latches. If locks are provided, all should be keyed alike.

Suitable working space should be provided and maintained around switchboards and panelboards. Specifications should call for permanent labels attached to the exteriors of the panels along with a connection schedule under a transparent protective cover. All labeling should meet OSHA and all other regulatory agency requirements. Switchboards should be located in well-ventilated, dry areas. Panelboards should be located on the floors they serve and should be spaced so as to limit branch circuit runs to 100 feet or less.

Automatic circuit breakers should be used for all power and lighting feeders and receptacle branch feeders. The breakers should be so designed that when one is tripped anyone can easily see which breaker is tripped without having to try each one. It is important to properly label each breaker so that most people can readily determine

which area each breaker controls. Each panel should be marked so as to indicate where the panel is fed from. All breaker panels should be designed with at least 25 per cent spare capacity for future expansion. The breakers feeding the receptacles in patient rooms and special-care areas should follow the design codes of NFPA, *NEC*®, Section 517.*

Local and wall switches should be of the high-quality, silent type in all patient areas to reduce noise.† Switches located in flammable storage areas should be designed for Class 1, Group C hazardous atmospheres. Many designers install switches outside the alcohol, acetone, and other flammable storage rooms to avoid the cost of these special switches. Some areas may use magnetic contactors to control lighting in parking lots, auditoriums, and other large areas.

The use of timers for parking areas is not as efficient as the use of photoelectric cells because photoelectric cells work summer, winter, cloudy, or bright, and take into consideration Daylight Saving Time, etc. Even astronomical timers have to be reset from time to time due to Daylight Saving Time and must come on a little earlier than photoelectric cells to ensure proper lighting, thus using more energy.

WIRE

Generally the use of copper wire is preferred for hospital use because the unfamiliarity with the use and maintenance of aluminum wire of hospital personnel as well as of some contractors has created problems in some hospitals. Proper wire size with proper insulation as needed for the particular job should be as specified in NFPA *NEC*, 70-1981. Methods of splicing, connecting to motors, motor control centers should be carefully and correctly done so as to minimize loose connections. Special attention must be given to exterior wiring where moisture and corrosive conditions exist. Some areas may have high ambient temperatures and this must be taken into consideration. (i.e., over oven's, boilers, etc.)

CONDUIT

As a general rule, all hospital wiring should be in conduit. However, there are some exceptions to this, particularly in residential and custodial homes. The *National Electrical Code*®* (1981) should be consulted for any special conduit requirements and to determine where nonmetallic and EMT can

be utilized. It is always advisable to add a few extra conduits when passing through poured walls, under floor slabs, or wherever expansion might take place at a later date. The use of pull boxes and junction boxes at fairly close intervals facilitates changes of call systems.

RECEPTACLES AND BRANCH CIRCUIT WIRING

With the advent of straight-blade, three-pronged, grounding-type, hospital-grade single and duplex receptacles, the need for the specialized twist-lock-type receptacles previously seen in hospital operating and intensive-care areas have been virtually eliminated. Twist-lock receptacles evolved from code requirements for explosion-proof attachment plugs. Research has now indicated that their design features were unnecessary because if mounted on the wall they were never in a position to be surrounded with a concentration of a flammable inhalation anesthetizing agent.

In operating and delivery rooms, which have been classified by the hospital to administer only nonflammable anesthetizing agents, straight-blade, hospital-grade duplex receptacles are now permitted to be installed. In locations where flammable anesthetizing agents are used, these receptacles are also permitted provided they are installed 5 feet above the floor. The new edition of National Fire Protection Association Standard No. 56A, *Safe Use of Inhalation-Anesthetics* contains these and other important provisions.

Patients' bedrooms should have at least three duplex outlets for single-patient rooms, with two outlets near the head of the bed. Rooms for more than one patient should have two duplex outlets at the head of each bed, or at least three outlets on the head wall for each two beds side by-side.

Each bed in recovery rooms and in intensive-care nursing rooms should have two duplex receptacles near the head of the bed. Intensive-care nursing rooms should have a minimum of three duplex receptacles and have provision for connection of mobile x-ray units with branch circuits and receptacles designed for the load, unless battery-operated or capacitive-discharge x-ray units are used.

Each patient-bed location needs to be supplied by two branch circuits, at least one of which originates from a normal system panelboard to prevent all circuits serving a bed from being connected to the emergency system. In patient areas not served by the emergency system it is advisable to provide emergency power capability to selected corridor receptacles. Corridors should have outlets installed every 50 feet for use of cleaning machines.

---

* *See footnote, page 4-338.*
† *All major manufacturers of hospital electric equipment supply "hospital grade" switches and receptacles specifically to meet NFPA codes. These units cost more than ordinary ones.*

GROUNDING AND ISOLATED POWER SYSTEMS

In all areas used for patient care, receptacles and fixed electric equipment should be grounded by an insulated copper conductor installed with the branch circuit conductors. Over the past 10 years considerable emphasis had been made in national codes and standards, such as the *NEC* Article 517 and NFPA 56A (1973) to install a variety of redundant grounding systems beyond that which has been specified above. Attempts by code-making panels to create "equipotential" environments to protect catheterized patients from a potential hazard termed "microshock" have finally been turned around. Research with grounding systems in existing hospitals has demonstrated that systems were already equipotential and that redundant grounding by installation of "green" bonding wires did not significantly improve the grounding performance. Consequently, requirements for such specialized systems have been largely removed from operating rooms and critical-care areas. Performance specifications capable of being met by standard construction methods have been included in the national standards. Local and state codes should be reviewed to determine compliance.

Isolated power systems, or ungrounded electric systems, are not required by any national code or standard in critical care areas. In these environments, their installation does not significantly improve reliable grounding safety and often results in maintenance, electric interference, and false-alarm problems for the hospital staff.

HAZARDOUS ANESTHETIZING LOCATIONS

Anesthetic storage rooms within the surgical suites, where flammable agents are kept, are considered hazardous throughout. Rooms for bulk storage of unopened containers of flammable anesthetic agents in a relatively remote area are generally not considered hazardous locations.

The extent of the hazardous location of an anesthetizing location for administering flammable anesthetics such as operating rooms and delivery rooms is considered to include the entire floor area of the room and to a height of 5 feet above the floor. All hazardous locations require special attention to construction, equipment, and operation as precautions against ignition of these agents. All equipment used in these areas should be approved for use in Class 1, Group C hazardous atmospheres. For specific requirements see NFPA No. 56A.

All hazardous locations require conductive floors for electrically intercoupling all people

and equipment in the room to prevent electrostatic sparks which might ignite flammable gases or vapors.

When equipment, such as receptacles, is installed lower than 5 feet above the floor, special attention is required to minimize the potential for this equipment to generate sparks and thereby cause an explosion in the presence of a flammable concentration of an anesthetizing agent. Serious overemphasis of this *actual* hazardous area led to a plethora of costly and unnecessary measures most of which have been corrected in newer codes and standards addressing the subject. Research has shown that the actual hazardous area is not 5 feet but only 2–3 inches (5 to 7 cm) away from the anesthetic mask. Beyond this zone (commonly referred to as the "zone of risk") the delivered gas has diluted to a nonflammable level.

The most important measures to be taken in minimizing risks of explosions in these locations is to eliminate the possibility of electrostatic sparks by providing conductive flooring. Staff use of conductive booties, use of conductive anesthetic and suction tubing, controlled humidity of about 50 per cent, and furniture and mobile equipment mounted on conductive carts with conductive covers are all proper practice.

Equipment used below the 5-foot level is still required to be explosion-proof (Class 1, Group C) by codes and standards. Most equipment available, both lighting and medical, is adequately enclosed to guard against the possibility of sparks or hot particles from falling into the zone of risk.

Operating and delivery rooms also require isolated power systems (an ungrounded electric distribution system) for all wiring, except for fixed nonsurgical lighting fixtures located more than 8 feet above the floor. The initial purpose of this requirement was to minimize line-to-ground spaces generated by the equipment. A line isolation monitor, formerly a ground detector system, is required for the purpose of warning of accidental or fault ground on the ungrounded system. Wiring and equipment installed above hazardous location, more than 5 feet above the floor, should be enclosed or guarded to prevent sparks or hot particles from falling into the hazardous location.

With the widespread use and acceptance of nonflammable agents, many of these provisions have been removed by the standards. Currently, the need for isolated power systems anywhere in the hospital is widely challenged. If a facility is classified by policy as nonflammable, conductive flooring is not required, nor is 50% relative humidity or the use of conductive furniture or tubing. Considerable savings in design and use can result if areas can be classified to prohibit the use of flammable anesthetic agents.

COMMUNICATION SYSTEMS

Nurses' call systems

Call systems for nursing service vary in complexity from the simplest type of a signal system to two-way voice communication with staff locator boards. An important feature common to all systems is that the switch provided for patients' use will register the call at the nurses' station. Sometimes cord-operated switches are preferable for isolation or contagious areas because these cords are inexpensive and may be removed and incinerated. A new cord can then be installed for each new patient.

Registration of calls should include a signal light in the corridor over the door of the room where the call originates. A selection of lights, buzzers, bells, chimes, and annunciators is available for registering calls at the nurses' station, floor pantries, utility rooms, or other duty stations.

Emergency calls, actuating distinctive signals, are usually installed in patients' toilets and sometimes incorporated into the regular call station at the patient's bed for use by the nurse when she needs assistance. Call stations should be provided for nurses' use in nurseries, children's wards, operating, and delivery rooms.

Some hospitals have call buttons labeled "Cardiac Arrest" in patients' head walls, these route an alert signal to nursing stations, central telephone room, and nursing offices. Codes in some states require such "Code Blue" alarms to be wired to the telephone room for each nursing station.

Two-way voice communication is a feature which may be added to the signal system described, although most systems installed today already have such features. Where it is planned for economy reasons to first install a signal system and later add the voice feature, conduits large enough to accommodate the wiring of the final installation should be included in the original installation.

Doctors' in-and-out register/paging systems

Most of the doctors' in-and-out registers utilize a telephone microprocessor system whereby a doctor can pick up any phone upon entering a building and, by dialing the proper access number, enter his or her name into the system. The doctor can receive any of a number of stored messages and, when leaving, can call up and take his or her name out of the storage. Other systems utilize pocket pagers, coded magnetic cards (some of which are activated at the parking lot zone), and a few still use the in-and-out toggle-switch panelboard containing all the doctors' names with switches that the doctor activates to indicate status.

Paging systems for doctors and staff may

be wired, radio-type, or telephone accessed. The wired paging systems, usually include a microphone and/or a sending station for calling or signaling to one or a combination of the following: loudspeakers, coded chimes, illuminated numerals, bell taps, or annunciator drops. Zone paging is highly preferred to minimize ambient noise for patients. Such a system can be directed only to nursing stations and administrative offices as opposed to corridors. Special equipment is available for areas, such as cafeterias, where ambient noise levels vary throughout the day to automatically increase paging sound levels in an area to overcome high ambient noise levels.

Call-back system

Call-back systems provide a relatively inexpensive means of "wake-up" or calling service for interns and nurses. Calls originating in the office or at the switchboard in older systems actuate a bell or buzzer in the quarters. An answer switch is provided for acknowledgement that the call has been received.

Today the telephone system is commonly used with programs available to enable users to program their own phones, thereby eliminating the need for operator assistance. Automatic call-back features are available for inside or outside calls.

Telephones

An internal access system should be provided to enable dial access between staff and departments within a facility without the assistance of an operator.

Telephones should be installed at all private and semi-private beds since new systems can allow the central telephone console to program the phones in or out of service, thereby eliminating the need for portable phones. Modular-type jacks are advisable since these can permit access for data transmission.

Conduit should be provided for all telephone wiring. Installation and connection of wiring is usually done by the telephone company. Consideration should be given to installing separate conduit systems for computerized hospital information systems depending upon whether use of the telephone system is planned. Provision should be made for public telephones at convenient locations for visitors and others requiring the use of pay stations. Recent regulations to make hospitals and other public facilities more accessible to the handicapped require installation of telephones at recommended heights and installation of special equipment for the hard of hearing.

Operating room (O.R.) systems

In addition to the usual intercom, some hospitals have installed specialized systems to indicate the progress of surgical procedures back to the O.R. supervisor central location. A central panel containing a series of lights for each O.R. is installed to report on surgical progress. The lights are consecutively activated by toggle switches by members of the surgical staff team. The system has been reported to improve scheduling possibilities and increase the number of operations that can be performed each day.

Environmental monitoring systems

Consideration should be given to the economies which can result through the use of automated systems which can monitor, control and supervise HVAC energy demands, fire alarms, sprinkler systems, and security systems. In urban areas, security systems to monitor the condition of exit/entrance doors can be important in minimizing thefts and crime in drug storage and cash areas.

Intercommunication systems

Telautograph transcribers or facsimile units are used to transmit written messages from one department to another. These systems leave a written record of the message at the sending and receiving stations. Where installation of this equipment is contemplated, conduit should be installed for the necessary wiring. This equipment may be obtained on a rental or purchase agreement.

Audible speaker systems are frequently used for communication between departments and within specific branches. These systems may be arranged for individual as well as collective announcements. This system is commonly interconnected with the telephone system.

Loudspeaker systems, often referred to as sound reinforcement systems, include microphones, amplifiers, and loudspeakers and are often required for extending the voice range in auditoriums, outdoor assembly areas, parking lots, or for issuing general instructions as in the case of fire or any other type of emergency. Such systems are often placed in cafeterias to permit their use as auxiliary meeting rooms.

Radio/TV systems

In the modern medical facility a number of antenna systems are required to serve communications needs. These include (1) UHF reception for emergency medicine, (2) VHF high band for hospital-to-hospital and hospital-to-ambulance communication, (3) security/engineering two-way radio, (4) radio paging, (5) special TV reception from satellite-generated hospital educational programs or government programs, and (6) reception of Civil Defense and National Weather Service Alerts.

Master antenna (MATV) and cable TV (CATV) systems have been used for a multi-tude of purposes including: staff and patient educational programming, security, and patient entertainment. Some systems facilitate central control of patient viewing capability to minimize need for installing or turning on of TV sets in rooms where patients request TV entertainment.

Carrier tube systems

Pneumatic tube systems are extremely useful for carrying records, prescriptions, or orders from one department to another. The carriers of these systems are propelled by electrically operated vacuum systems or vacuum-pressure combinations. Non-powered gravity drops with hand-operated lifts are sometimes useful between one floor and another directly above or below.

Elevators

Elevators in hospitals vary from simple hydraulic to complex high-speed gearless machines (see section on Elevators). Some large complexes will have applications for hydraulic units in storerooms, kitchens, or laundries, where there is a need for moving primarily bulky materials one to two floors and where floor-to-floor times are not critical. The normal speed of the hydraulic is 100–150 feet per minute. Other areas of one to five floors can often utilize a geared electric-drive type capable of traveling 300–400 feet per minute. This type is less costly than the gearless traction elevators. Where buildings are higher than six floors, it may be advisable to install the high-speed gearless machine that travels from 400–600 feet per minute or more.

The Joint Commission on Accreditation of Hospitals (JCAH) Functional Safety and Sanitation Standard requires that one elevator in each bank be equipped for use by firemen. Also, it is advisable to design in an emergency key control so that anyone with a key can bypass car and floor calls to take patients in emergencies from one level to another, nonstop if necessary. Generally, it is advisable to arrange the emergency power to a bank of elevators so that each car can be lowered to the ground floor in sequence to remove passengers from the car in case of power failure. Following this procedure, one car can be kept in service on emergency power.

Newer designs of elevator control systems are utilizing solid state controllers that eliminate the larger motor-generator sets and take up far less room.

FIRE ALARMS

Fire alarms are required in every hospital. Standards as required by the Life Safety Code apply except where they may be modified by additional requirements of local or state codes.

Devices used in the alarm system should be listed by Underwriters Laboratories, Inc., or Factory Mutual Laboratories or certified to comply with the requirements of the listed devices. In all cases, the system should be electrically supervised, should preferably be the code signal type and should comply with NFPA No. 72D, *Proprietary Signaling Systems.* Recent regulations for the handicapped require fire-alarm annunciators to have visible signals for the deaf.

CLOCKS

An electric clock system, rather than individual clocks, should be provided with clocks in all offices, nurses' stations, waiting rooms, kitchens, dining rooms, operating rooms, and delivery rooms as well as the main lobby, telephone switchboard, laundry, and boiler room. The clocks should be of the recessed type, preferably with a narrow frame. Clocks in operating and delivery rooms should have sweep second hands. The need for elapsed-time indicators in operating and delivery rooms is controversial.

Two types of clock systems are available: wired and electronic. The wired system requires wiring from the individual clocks to the master control clock. The electronic system requires no wiring connection between the individual clocks and the master clock. Control is by means of electrical impulses sent out by the master control clock and picked up by a radio-type receiver in each clock. The individual clock receivers are operated from any convenience outlet.

X-RAY

Voltage supplied to the x-ray unit should be nearly constant so that images and pictures will be uniform. An independent feeder with capacity sufficient to prevent a voltage drop greater than 3 per cent is recommended. A separate transformer for the x-ray feeder is desirable and is a requirement for most installations.

REFERENCES

1. National Fire Protection Association, *National Electrical Code®*, ANSI/NFPA 70, Quincy, Mass. (1981).
2. Illuminating Engineering Society, *IES Lighting Handbook,* 5th ed., New York (1972).
3. National Fire Protection Association, *Code for Safety to Life from Fire in Buildings and Structures,* ANSI/NFPA 101, National Fire Protection Association, Quincy, Mass. (1976).
4. National Fire Protection Association, *Safe Use of Inhalation Anesthetics,* NFPA No. 56A, National Fire Protection Association, Quincy, Mass. (1979).
5. *American National Safety Code for Elevators, Dumbwaiters, Escalators, and Moving Walks,* ANSI A17.1-1978, The American National Standards Institute, New York (1978).
6. Underwriters Laboratories, Inc., 207 East Ohio Street, Chicago.
7. Factory Mutual Laboratories, 1151 Boston–Providence Turnpike, Norwood, Mass.
8. National Fire Protection Association, *Proprietary, Auxiliary, Remote Station and Local Protective Signaling Systems,* NFPA No. 72D, National Fire Protection Association, Quincy, Mass. (1969).
9. *American National Standard, Voltage Rating for Electric Power Systems and Equipment.* ANSI C84.1 (EEI R-6; NEMA 117), American National Standards Institute, New York (1970).
10. Kusters, N. L., "The Ground Detector Problem in Hospital Operating Rooms," *Transactions,* vol. 2, no. 1, Engineering Institute of Canada, Ottawa (1958).
11. diMonda, Richard J. and Sprague, Joseph G., "Hospitals Have Say In Code-Making Process," *Hospitals, J.A.H.A.,* September 16, 1977 Vol. 51 pg. 154 (addresses new National Medical Code requirements).
12. *Lighting For Health Care Facilities,* Illuminating Engineering Society, 345 East 47th Street, New York, NY 10017 (1978).
13. *Hospital Engineering,* Newsletter of the American Society for Hospital Engineering of the American Hospital Association, contains timely articles on codes and standards updates.
14. Drue, Roger, "System Links Nurse Call/Locator, Intercom, Emergency Call," *Hospitals, J.A.H.A.* Vol. 50 Sept. 1, 1976.

Revised 1979 by LOUIS A. BELLO, *Vice President, Syska and Hennessy, Consulting Engineers*

SERVICE ENTRANCES

For the calculation of service entrance sizes, requirements of the *National Electrical Code®** or local codes govern. Unless unusual circumstances occur (such as exceptionally heavy lighting installations) the *Code* requirements will result in safe, conservative design. A sample calculation, based on the *National Electrical Code®* and on the ratings given in the load and circuit table (Table 4, opposite), is shown below.

First the loads are figured for the branch circuits, which are divided into three categories:

1. *General-purpose circuits:* They serve lights throughout the house and convenience outlets everywhere except in kitchen, laundry, dining area, and utility room. Generally, circuit capacity can be figured on the basis of 3 watts per ft² (W/ft²).

$$3 \text{ W/ft}^2 \times 1500 \text{ ft}^2 = 4500 \text{ W}$$

2. *Small-appliance circuits.* They serve convenience outlets in the kitchen (including the refrigerator), pantry, dining room, breakfast room, and family room. At least two small-appliance circuits must be included. If there is a laundry room, a third small-appliance circuit is required. A load of 1500 W for each appliance circuit must be included.

$$3 \text{ circuits} \times 1500 \text{ W} = 4500 \text{ Watts}$$

However, it can be assumed that not all of the load on these two types of branch circuits will be used at any one time. So, in order to determine the service require-

* *National Electrical Code® is a registered trademark of the National Fire Protection Association, Inc., Quincy, MA for a triennial electrical publication. The term National Electrical Code, as used herein, means the triennial publication constituting the National Electrical Code and is used with the permission of the National Fire Protection Association, Inc.*

ments for them, the code assumes that the first 3000 W will be operated at 100 per cent capacity and the remainder at only 35 per cent.

$$3000 \text{ W} \times 100 \text{ per cent} = 3000 \text{ W}$$
$$6000 \text{ W} \times 35 \text{ per cent} = 2100 \text{ W}$$

Total service requirements of general-purpose and small-appliance circuits = 5100 W

3. *Fixed appliance circuits:* They serve the heavy-duty appliances, each of which requires a separate circuit.

A demand factor of 0.75 may be applied to all fixed appliance circuits, except electric ranges, electric clothes dryers, space heating and air conditioning equipment. The range is calculated at 8 kW even though its rating may be up to 12 kW, since all its elements are not expected to operate fully at one time. The electric clothes dryer is assumed to be 5000 W or its actual rating, whichever is larger, and up to four units are assumed to have a demand factor of 100 per cent.

Calculations for fixed appliances are then as follows:

Dishwasher	1,500 W
Clothes washer	1,200
Water heater	3,000
Workshop	1,500
	7,200

$$7,200 \text{ W} \times 0.75 = 5,400 \text{ W}$$

Range	8,000
Clothes dryer	5,000
	18,400 W

In calculating the heating-cooling load, the higher value of the two systems is used, since it is assumed that they will not be operating at the same time. It is recommended that the architect consult the local utility for information about central air-con-

ditioning systems. However, for purposes of this calculation a value of 5000 W is assumed. Since this is higher than the total of 600 W for the heating plant and 1500 W for the bathroom heater, this will be the value used.

Central air conditioning .... 5000 W
Total capacity of fixed appliance circuits = 23,400 W
Total watts of service capacity = 5100 + 23,400 = 28,500 W

Thus, the required current-carrying capacity of the service entrance conductors for a 120/240-V, 3-wire, single-phase service is

$$I = \frac{P}{V} = \frac{28,500}{240} = 119 \text{ A}$$

Knowing the current requirements for the service entrance, the proper combination of switches, control center units and wire sizes can be determined easily, as in the typical service entrance schedule shown below.

RECEPTACLE AND LIGHTING OUTLETS

From *National Electrical Code®*†

(a) *General Provisions.* In every kitchen, family room, dining room, living room, parlor, library, den, sun room, bedroom, recreation room, or similar rooms, receptacle outlets shall be installed so that no point along the floor line in any wall space is more than 6 feet (1.83 m), measured horizontally, from an outlet in that space, includ-

† *Reprinted by permission from NFPA 70-1981, National Electrical Code®. Copyright © 1980, National Fire Protection Association, Quincy, MA. This reprinted material is not the complete and official position of the NFPA on the referenced subject which is represented only by the standard in its entirety.*

Table 3.   Typical service entrance schedules for various levels of utilization (120/240 volts, 3-wire, single-phase)

Nominal Rating, Amperes	Maximum Capacity, Watts	Main Switch	Main Control Center Units	Size of Service Wire	Size of Conduit	Utilization Circuits
100	24,000	100A Sw. or 100A Cir. Bkr.	2-50A 1-20A (Water heater)	2 #2 1 #4	1¼"	General Purpose Electric Cooking Electric Laundry Water Heater Air Conditioning
150	36,000	200A Sw. (150A Fuses) or 150A Cir. Bkr.	3-50A 1-20A (Water heater)	2 #2/0 2 #2	2"	Same as for 100 amp plus electric heating for small homes
200	48,000	200A Sw. (200A Fuses) or 200A Cir. Bkr.	4-50A 1-20A (Water heater)	2 #4/0 1 #2/0	2"	Same as for 150 amp in temperate climates

From Live Better . . . Electrically.

Table 4. Load and circuit chart

	Typical Connected Watts	Preferred Circuit	Volts	Wires	Circuit Breaker or Fuse	Outlets on Circuit	Type of Outlet	Notes
Kitchen								
Range	12000	10 kw	120/240	3 #6	50A	1	Special Purpose	Use of more than one outlet is not recommended.
Oven (built-in)	4500	6 kw	120/240	3 #10	30A	1	Special Purpose	
Range Top	6000	6 kw	120/240	3 #10	30A	1	Special Purpose	May be direct-connected.
Range Top	3300	4 kw	120/240	3 #12	20A	1	Special Purpose	
Dishwasher	1200	2 kw	120	2 #12	20A	1	Parallel Grounding	These appliances may be direct-connected on a single circuit.
Waste Disposer	300	2 kw	120	2 #12	20A	1	Parallel Grounding	Grounded receptacles required, otherwise.
Broiler	1500	2 kw	120	2 #12	20A	1 or more	Parallel Grounding or Parallel	
Fryer	1300	2 kw	120	2 #12	20A	1 or more	Parallel Grounding or Parallel	Heavy-duty appliances regularly used at one location should have a separate circuit. Only one such unit should be attached to a single circuit at one time.
Coffeemaker	1000	2 kw	120	2 #12	20A	1 or more	Parallel Grounding or Parallel	
Refrigerator	300	2 kw	120	2 #12	20A	1 or more	Parallel Grounding or Parallel	Separate circuit serving only refrigerator and freezer is recommended.
Freezer	350	2 kw	120	2 #12	20A	1 or more	Parallel Grounding or Parallel	
Laundry								
Washing Machine	1200	2 kw	120	2 #12	20A	1 or more	Parallel Grounding	Grounding type receptacle required. Separate circuit is recommended.
Dryer	5000	6 kw	120/240	3 #10	30A	1	Special Purpose	Appliance may be direct-connected —must be grounded.
Ironer	1650	2 kw	120	2 #12	20A	1 or more	Parallel Grounding	
Hand Iron	1000	2 kw	120	2 #12	20A	1 or more	Parallel	Consider possible use in other locations.
Water Heater	3000						Special Purpose	Consult utility company for load requirements.
Living Areas								
Workshop	1500	2 kw	120	2 #12	20A	1 or more	Parallel Grounding	Separate circuit recommended.
Portable Heater	1300	2 kw	120	2 #12	20A	1	Parallel	Should not be connected to circuit serving other heavy duty loads.
Television	300	2 kw	120	2 #12	20A	1 or more	Parallel	Should not be connected to circuit serving appliances.
Portable Lighting	1200	2 kw	120	2 #12	20A	1 or more	Parallel	Provide one circuit for each 500 sq ft. Divided receptacle may be switch-controlled.
Fixed Utilities								
Fixed Lighting	1200	2 kw	120	2 #12	20A	1 or more		Provide at least one circuit for each 1200 watts of fixed lighting.
Air Conditioner (¾ hp)	1200	2 kw	120	2 #12	20A	1	Parallel Grounding	Consider 4-kw 3-wire circuits to all window or console type air conditioners. Outlets may then be adapted to individual 120- or 240-volt machines. Connection to general purpose or appliance circuits is not recommended.
Air Conditioner (1½ hp)	2400	4 kw	120/240	3 #12	20A	1	Tandem Grounding	
Central Air Conditioner	5000	6 kw	120/240				Special Purpose	Consult manufacturer for recommended connections.
Sump Pump	300	2 kw	120	2 #12	20A	1 or more	Parallel Grounding	May be direct-connected.
Heating Plant	600	2 kw	120	2 #12	20A	1		Direct-connected. Individual circuit is recommended.
Fixed Bathroom Heater	1500	2 kw	120	2 #12	20A	1		Direct-connected.
Attic Fan	300	2 kw	120	2 #12	20A	1 or more	Parallel Grounding	May be direct-connected. Individual circuit is recommended.

Table 5. Wires and cables

Type	Description	Applications
R	Single conductor with rubber insulation and braided cotton covering.	General wiring where moisture is not present. Temperature rating 60 C.
RH	Similar to Type R except rubber insulation has higher resistivity to heat.	General wiring where moisture is not present; has higher current carrying capacity than Type R. Temperature rating 75 C.
RW	Similar to Type R except with moisture-resistant rubber insulation.	In all areas including damp conditions. Temperature rating and current-carrying capacity same as Type R.
RH-RW	Rubber insulation has heat- and moisture-resistant properties of Types RH and RW.	For damp locations, the temperature rating and current-carrying capacity of Type RW are used; otherwise the higher ratings of Type RH apply.
RHW	Similar to Type RH-RW.	Similar to Type RH-RW except ratings of Type RH apply for all installations.
TW	Thermoplastic insulation is highly resistant to moisture, heat and corrosion. Rated at 60 C. Current capacity of Type R.	General use and use in damp areas. While allowable conduit occupancy is the same as Type R in new installations, the smaller dimensions of Type TW are used in calculating the number of conductors allowed in existing conduit or rewiring; this permits substantially higher capacities than other types of wire.
THW	Similar to Type TW in construction and to Type RHW in applications.	
THWN	Similar to Type THW except for nylon insulation and smaller outside diameter (O.D.)	
NM (non metallic sheathed cable)	Rubber or thermoplastic-insulated conductors, with or without separate grounding conductor, covered by heavy paper wrapping and a strong braid.	Interior wiring—exposed or concealed in dry locations. Not allowed where exposed to corrosive fumes or vapors, nor embedded in masonry, concrete, fill or plaster. Use non-metallic boxes or surface devices unless grounding wire is in NM cable.
NMC (moisture- and corrosion-resistant)	Same as NM except with corrosion-resistant outer covering of impregnated braid or other material.	Same as NM except may be embedded in plaster or run in chase provided protection is afforded from nails by 1/16-in. steel plate. Neither NM or NMC may be embedded in concrete or used for service entrances.
UF (underground feeder)	Thermoplastic-insulated and jacketed conductors in single or multiple conductor styles.	Single conductor for direct burial feeders (all legs in one trench). Multi-conductor UF may be used as NMC.
AC and ACT (called armored cable)	Rubber (AC)- or thermoplastic (ACT)-insulated conductors enclosed in wound and interlocked steel armor; bonding strip under armor.	All interior wiring except in moist areas embedded in masonry, or in block walls below grade.
ACL	Same as Type AC except with lead sheath.	Moist areas, underground and embedded in concrete.
SE Style U (un-armored)	2 rubber-insulated conductors and bare neutral strands (usually spiraled around insulated conductors) covered by protective layers of rubber tape and impregnated braid. Also available with insulated neutral.	For service entrances; interior wiring of range, dryer or water heater providing heater is not fed by uninsulated conductor. With insulated neutral, use is governed by code provisions on NMC.
SE Style A (armored)	Same as Style U except with bonded steel tape under outer layer of rubber tape. Interlocked armor (not bonded) sometimes used in place of steel tape.	Same as Style U except interior applications governed by code provisions on armored cable. For interior use, tape or armor must be grounded.
SD (service drop)	Similar to SE Style U.	Primarily for drop from pole to service mast.
USE Style RR	Rubber-insulated conductors encased in neoprene jacket single or multiple conductor. (All RR conductors are not UL-approved for USE applications.)	Underground service entrances and runs in conduit or direct burial. Also used for aerial runs.
MI (mineral insulated—metal sheathed)	Conductors insulated by highly compressed refractory mineral material and enclosed in a liquid- and gas-tight flexible metallic tube.	All normal residential applications including underground, embedded in concrete and service entrance. Approved connectors required.

ing any wall space 2 feet (610 mm) or more in width and the wall space occupied by sliding panels in exterior walls. The wall space afforded by fixed room dividers, such as free-standing bar-type counters, shall be included in the 6-foot (1.83 m) measurement.

As used in this section a "wall space" shall be considered a wall unbroken along the floor line by doorways, fireplaces, and similar openings. Each wall space 2 or more feet (610 mm or more) wide shall be treated individually and separately from other wall spaces within the room. A wall space shall be permitted to include two or more walls of a room (around corners) where unbroken at the floor line.

The purpose of this requirement is to minimize the use of cords across doorways, fireplaces, and similar openings.

Receptacle outlets shall, insofar as practicable, be spaced equal distances apart. Receptacle outlets in floors shall not be counted as part of the required number of receptacle outlets unless located close to the wall.

The receptacle outlets required by this section shall be in addition to any receptacle that is part of any lighting fixture or appliance, located within cabinets or cupboards, or located over 5½ (1.68 m) feet above the floor.

Exception: Permanently installed electric baseboard heaters equipped with factory installed receptacle outlets, or outlets provided as a separate assembly by the manufacturer, shall be permitted as the required outlet or outlets for the wall space utilized by such

permanently installed heaters. Such receptacle outlets shall not be connected to the heater circuits.

(b) *Countertops.* In kitchen and dining areas of dwelling units a receptacle outlet shall be installed at each counter space wider than 12 inches (305 mm). Counter top spaces separated by range tops, refrigerators, or sinks shall be considered as separate counter top spaces. Receptacles rendered inaccessible by appliances fastened in place or appliances occupying dedicated space shall not be considered as these required outlets.

(c) *Bathrooms.* In dwelling units, at least one wall receptacle outlet shall be installed in the bathroom adjacent to the basin location.

(d) *Outdoor Outlets.* For one- and two-family dwellings at least one receptacle outlet shall be installed outdoors.

(e) *Laundry Areas.* In dwelling units at least one receptacle outlet shall be installed for the laundry.

Exception No. 1: In a dwelling unit that is an apartment or living area in a multi-family building where laundry facilities are provided on the premises that are available to all building occupants, a laundry receptacle shall not be required.

Exception No. 2: In other than one-family dwellings where laundry facilities are not to be installed or permitted, a laundry receptacle shall not be required.

(f) *Basements and Garages.* For a one-family dwelling at least one receptacle outlet in addition to any provided for laundry

equipment shall be installed in each basement and in each attached garage.

Guest Rooms. Guest rooms in hotels, motels, and similar occupancies shall have receptacle outlets installed in accordance with the above requirements.

Exception: In rooms of hotels and motels, receptacle outlets may be located convenient for the permanent furniture layout.

Lighting outlets required. Lighting outlets shall be installed where specified in (a) and (b) below.

(a) *Dwelling unit(s):* At least one wall switch-controlled lighting outlet shall be installed in every habitable room; in bathrooms, hallways, stairways, and attached garages; and at outdoor entrances.

A vehicle door in an attached garage is not considered as an outdoor entrance.

At least one lighting outlet shall be installed in an attic, underfloor space, utility room and basement only where these spaces are used for storage or containing equipment requiring servicing.

Exception No. 1: In habitable rooms, other than kitchens, one or more receptacles controlled by a wall switch shall be permitted in lieu of lighting outlets.

Exception No. 2: In hallways, stairways, and at outdoor entrances remote, central, or automatic control of lighting shall be permitted.

(b) *Guest Rooms.* At least one wall switch-controlled lighting outlet or wall switch-controlled receptacle shall be installed in guest rooms in hotels, motels, or similar occupancies.

CONDUITS

Data from *Aspects of Electrical Conduit Installations in Houses* by Jefferson D. Brooks. Technical Bulletin No. 12, Housing and Home Finance Agency.

Revised 1979 by LOUIS A. BELLO, *Syska and Hennessy, Inc., Consulting Engineers*

Types and Uses

1. *Rigid conduit* is an older, heavier type, softer than water pipe for easy bending, but sized for same tools. Internal diameter is a bit larger than nominal size. Galvanized or other rust-resistant finish is required if exposed to dampness. Enameled iron conduits may be used only indoors, with no severe corrosive influences. Materials especially suited to such conditions must be used; avoid dissimilar materials. Place conduit at least 18 in. under cinder fill subject to permanent moisture, or encase in 2 in. of non-cinder concrete. In wet locations, system must be water tight; leave at least ¼ in. air space between conduit or boxes and wall.

2. *Thin wall conduit or EMT* (electrical metallic tubing) is a lighter type, usually galvanized or similarly finished. It is used for exposed or concealed work where not subject to severe mechanical injury. Use is re-

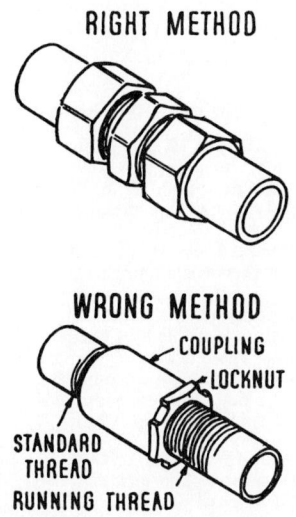

Fig. 2. Conduit connections

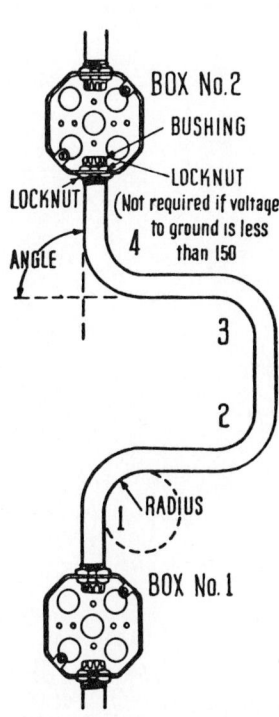

Fig. 3. Bends in circuit

Note: Tables 10 through 15 are from National Electrical Code®

stricted in hazardous locations. Otherwise it is used as rigid conduit.

3. *Aluminum conduit* is available and, in sizes of 1½ in. or larger, is more economical than steel. It should not be buried in concrete.

4. *Flexible conduit* is strong flexible tubing of spirally wound, interlocked steel strip, usually galvanized. Use in dry locations unless lead-covered or type RW (moisture resistant) wiring is employed. Do not use in hazardous locations. Conduits less than ½ in. size are used only for under-plaster extensions, fixtures, motor leads. Occasionally

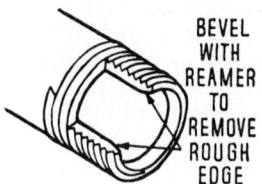

Fig. 4.   Reamed end of conduit

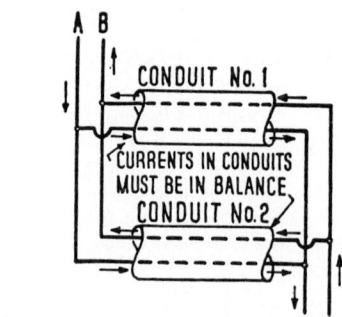

Fig. 5.   Conductors in multiple

⅜ in. size is permitted up to 48 in. (or longer) where larger size is not practicable.

Fittings

1. Running threads must not be used on rigid conduit for connections at couplings; unions must be used. Threads are finer than for standard pipe; threadless connectors are often used. The latter must be watertight

TABLE 6. Radius of conduit bends in inches

Conduit (trade size) (inches)	Ordinary conductors	Lead-covered conductors
½	3.7	6.2
¾	4.9	8.3
1	6.3	10.5
1¼	8.3	13.8
1½	9.6	16.1
2	12.4	20.6
2½	14.8	24.6
3	18.4	30.6
3½	21.3	35.5
4	24.1	40.2
4½	27.0	45.0
5	30.3	50.4
6	36.4	60.6

TABLE 8. Max No. of Wires To Be Installed in Multiple

No. of wires:	Size
3	No. 0
4	No. 00
5	No. 000 to 500 MCM

if buried in masonry, concrete, fill, or used in wet places

2. Bushings must be used on ends of conduit unless box or fitting affords equal protection. A bushing may replace box where more than 4 conductors leave conduit at control apparatus, if wires are bunched, taped and painted; bushings must be of insulated type, except for lead-covered wires

TABLE 7. Max Support Intervals For Conductors in Vertical Conduits

	Feet
No. 0 and smaller	100
No. 00 to No. 000	80
250 to 350 MCM	60
400 to 500 MCM	50
600 to 750 MCM	40
800 MCM and larger	35

TABLE 9. Temp Reduction Factors (percentages)

Max Temp (°F)	Type of insulation			
	R, RW, RU, T, and TW	RH	V and AVB	AVA and AVL
104	82	88	90	94
113	71	82	85	90
122	58	75	80	87
131	41	67	74	83
140		58	67	79
158		35	52	71
167			43	66
176			30	61
194				50

Table 10.   Percent of cross section of conduit and tubing for conductors*
(See Table 11 for Fixture Wires)

Number of Conductors	1	2	3	4	Over 4
All conductor types except lead-covered (new or rewiring)	53	31	40	40	40
Lead-covered conductors	55	30	40	38	35

Note 1. See Tables 3A, 3B, and 3C for number of conductors all of the same size in trade sizes of conduit ½ inch through 6 inch.

Note 2. For conductors larger than 750 MCM or for combinations of conductors of different sizes, use Tables 4 through 8, Chapter 9, for dimensions of conductors, conduit and tubing.

Note 3. Where the calculated number of conductors, all of the same size, includes a decimal fraction, the next higher whole number shall be used where this decimal is 0.8 or larger.

Note 4. When bare conductors are permitted by other sections of this Code, the dimensions for bare conductors in Table 8 of Chapter 9 shall be permitted.

Note 5. A multiconductor cable of two or more conductors shall be treated as a single conductor cable for calculating percentage conduit fill area. For cables that have elliptical cross section, the cross-sectional area calculation shall be based on using the major diameter of the ellipse as a circle diameter.

3. All ends of conduit must be reamed to remove rough edges

Bends must not injure conduit or effectively reduce internal diameter. Radius of the inner edge of any bend not made by manufacturer must not be less than shown in Table 6. Conduit between 2 outlets, fittings, or combination, must not have more than equivalent of 4 quarter bends (Fig. 3)

Supports

Conductors in vertical conduits must be supported by clamps, wedges or insulators at intervals not greater than shown in Table 7. All conduits must be securely fastened in place. Runs must be continuous from box to box with no splices.

Miscellaneous Requirements

Wires must not be inserted in conduits until rough mechanical work on house is completed. Pull wires are inserted after making up conduit connections. Graphite, talc or approved compound are used as wire lubricant; cleaning agents must not be used.

Conductors of signal or radio systems must not occupy same conduit with those of light or power systems, except for elevators, sound recording and remote control. Conduits must not pass through dust or vapor removal ducts. Rigid conduit, or flexible conduit with lead covered conductors, may pass through air-conditioning ducts only where necessary, and must not obstruct fire dampers. Switch enclosures must not be used as junction boxes to make taps or feed through.

Secondary wiring to cold cathode lamps of 1000 volts or less may occupy same conduit as branch circuit conductors. Light and power circuits of 600 volts or less may occupy same conduit, whether a-c or d-c. Circuits over 600 volts must be separated from those under 600 volts. Prevent air circulation from warmer to colder areas through conduit.

Vertical conductors No. 1 or larger require the following gutter widths if deflected where they leave cabinet:

No. 1 . . . . 3 in.
No. 0 to 200 MCM . . . . 4 in.
250 to 900 MCM . . . . 6 in.

Where ungrounded conductors of No. 4 or larger are deflected more than 30 deg at ends of conduit run, an insulating bushing is required.

Conductors in Multiple

Where circuit capacity makes it impracticable to run all conductors in one conduit, additional conduits may be used if conductors in any one conduit are balanced in size and include one from each phase. Current in one direction must substantially equal current in the opposite direction (Fig. 5). In the case of circuits supplying cold cathode tubes, x-ray apparatus, and underplaster extensions, currents are so small that a single conductor may be placed in a conduit without trouble from induction. Conductors in sizes No. 0 to 500 MCM may be run in multiple if they are same length and have same area and type of insulation. Terminate both ends in manner to insure equal division of current. Except by special permission, not more than number of wires shown in Table 8 may be installed in multiple.

Table 11. Maximum number of fixture wires in trade sizes of conduit or tubing*
(40 Percent Fill Based on Individual Diameters)

Conduit Trade Size (Inches)	½					¾					1					1¼					1½					2				
Wire Types	18	16	14	12	10	18	16	14	12	10	18	16	14	12	10	18	16	14	12	10	18	16	14	12	10	18	16	14	12	10
PTF, PTFF, PGFF, PGF, PFF, PF, PAF, PAFF, ZF, ZFF	23	18	14			40	31	24			65	50	39			115	90	70			157	122	95			257	200	156		
TFFN, TFN	19	15				34	26				55	43				97	76				132	104				216	169			
SF-1	16					29					47					83					114					186				
SFF-1, FFH-1	15					26					43					76					104					169				
CF	13	10	8	4	3	23	18	14	7	6	38	30	23	12	9	66	53	40	21	16	91	72	55	29	22	149	118	90	48	37
TF	11	10				20	18				32	30				57	53				79	72				129	118			
RFH-1	11					20					32					57					79					129				
TFF	11	10				20	17				32	27				56	49				77	66				126	109			
AF	11	9	7	4	3	19	16	12	7	5	31	26	20	11	8	55	46	36	19	15	75	63	49	27	20	123	104	81	44	34
SFF-2	9	7	6			16	12	10			27	20	17			47	36	30			65	49	42			106	81	68		
SF-2	9	8	6			16	14	11			27	23	18			47	40	32			65	55	43			106	90	71		
FFH-2	9	7				15	12				25	19				44	34				60	46				99	75			
RFH-2	7	5				12	10				20	16				36	28				49	38				80	62			
KF-1, KFF-1, KF-2, KFF-2	36	32	22	14	9	64	55	39	25	17	103	89	63	41	28	182	158	111	73	49	248	216	152	100	67	406	353	248	163	110

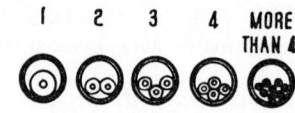

Fig. 6. Cross-sectional area of conduit which conductors may occupy

Wire Carrying Capacity

Standard tabulated carrying capacities of wires are based upon 3 or less wires in a conduit, and a surrounding temperature of not more than 86 F. Capacity must be reduced to 80 per cent of that listed for 4, 5 or 6 wires in a conduit; to 70 per cent for 7, 8 or 9 wires. A neutral conductor used with balanced circuits is not counted in applying percentages. If one of the system wires is missing from circuit (as in a 3-wire circuit from a 4-wire system) the neutral conductor must be counted, for it carries the unbalanced current which would have been carried by the missing wire. All current-carrying capacity must be separately reduced for high surrounding temperatures by percentages given in Table 9. If room temp is within 18 deg of a maximum allowable temp, use insulation with next higher maximum.

Conduit Size Selection

Due to bunching effect of wires in conduit, all space inside conduit cannot be filled with wire (Fig. 6). Percentages of allowable fill are calculated in sq in. of net cross-sectional area for standard size conduits, for various numbers of wires, in Table 13 for non-lead-covered wires and for lead-covered wires.

Where conduits cannot be replaced without damage to house, it is satisfactory to rewire conduits, for increased capacity, with more or larger wires which occupy more space than permitted for original installations. Consult local code.

Cross-sectional areas of the various types of wires, in sq in., are given in Tables 14 and 15. Values are added together for any combination of wires to be installed in a single conduit. This total permits ready selection of a conduit size, filled to a given percentage, from Table 10. Portion of conduit available for wires must be not less than shown for number and kinds of wires involved.

Where all wires are of one size, non-lead-covered, and for new installations, use Table 12 to select conduit size.

In general, one conduit must not contain more than 9 wires. Table 12 shows conduit capacity for a greater no. of wires, where specially permitted.

Table 12. Maximum number of conductors in trade sizes of conduit or tubing

(Based on Table 10)

Type Letters	Conductor Size AWG, MCM	½	¾	1	1¼	1½	2	2½	3	3½	4	4½	5	6
TW, T, RUH, RUW, XHHW (14 thru 8)	14	9	15	25	44	60	99	142						
	12	7	12	19	35	47	78	111	171					
	10	5	9	15	26	36	60	85	131	176				
	8	2	4	7	12	17	28	40	62	84	108			
RHW and RHH (without outer covering), THW	14	6	10	16	29	40	65	93	143	192				
	12	4	8	13	24	32	53	76	117	157				
	10	4	6	11	19	26	43	61	95	127	163			
	8	1	3	5	10	13	22	32	49	66	85	106	133	
TW, T, THW, RUH (6 thru 2), RUW (6 thru 2), FEPB (6 thru 2), RHW and RHH (without outer covering)	6	1	2	4	7	10	16	23	36	48	62	78	97	141
	4	1	1	3	5	7	12	17	27	36	47	58	73	106
	3	1	1	2	4	6	10	15	23	31	40	50	63	91
	2	1	1	2	4	5	9	13	20	27	34	43	54	78
	1		1	1	3	4	6	9	14	19	25	31	39	57
	0		1	1	2	3	5	8	12	16	21	27	33	49
	00		1	1	1	3	5	7	10	14	18	23	29	41
	000		1	1	1	2	4	6	9	12	15	19	24	35
	0000			1	1	1	3	5	7	10	13	16	20	29
	250			1	1	1	2	4	6	8	10	13	16	23
	300			1	1	1	2	3	5	7	9	11	14	20
	350				1	1	1	3	4	6	8	10	12	18
	400				1	1	1	2	4	5	7	9	11	16
	500					1	1	1	3	4	6	7	9	14
	600					1	1	1	3	4	5	6	7	11
	700					1	1	1	2	3	4	5	7	10
	750					1	1	1	2	3	4	5	6	9

Table 12 (Cont.). Maximum number of conductors in trade sizes of conduit or tubing

Type Letters	Conductor Size AWG, MCM	½	¾	1	1¼	1½	2	2½	3	3½	4	4½	5	6
THWN,	14	13	24	39	69	94	154							
	12	10	18	29	51	70	114	164						
	10	6	11	18	32	44	73	104	160					
	8	3	5	9	16	22	36	51	79	106	136			
THHN, FEP (14 thru 2), FEPB (14 thru 8), PFA (14 thru 4/0), PFAH (14 thru 4/0), Z (14 thru 4/0) XHHW (4 thru 500MCM)	6	1	4	6	11	15	26	37	57	76	98	125	154	
	4	1	2	4	7	9	16	22	35	47	60	75	94	137
	3	1	1	3	6	8	13	19	29	39	51	64	80	116
	2	1	1	3	5	7	11	16	25	33	43	54	67	97
	1		1	1	3	5	8	12	18	25	32	40	50	72
	0		1	1	3	4	7	10	15	21	27	33	42	61
	00		1	1	2	3	6	8	13	17	22	28	35	51
	000		1	1	1	3	5	7	11	14	18	23	29	42
	0000		1	1	1	2	4	6	9	12	15	19	24	35
	250			1	1	1	3	4	7	10	12	16	20	28
	300			1	1	1	3	4	6	8	11	13	17	24
	350			1	1	1	2	3	5	7	9	12	15	21
	400				1	1	1	3	5	6	8	10	13	19
	500				1	1	1	2	4	5	7	9	11	16
	600				1	1	1	1	3	4	5	7	9	13
	700					1	1	1	3	4	5	6	8	11
	750					1	1	1	2	3	4	6	7	11
XHHW	6	1	3	5	9	13	21	30	47	63	81	102	128	185
	600				1	1	1	1	3	4	5	7	9	13
	700				1	1	1	1	3	4	5	6	7	11
	750					1	1	1	2	3	4	6	7	10
RHW,	14	3	6	10	18	25	41	58	90	121	155			
	12	3	5	9	15	21	35	50	77	103	132			
	10	2	4	7	13	18	29	41	64	86	110	138		
	8	1	2	4	7	9	16	22	35	47	60	75	94	137
RHH (with outer covering)	6	1	1	2	5	6	11	15	24	32	41	51	64	93
	4	1	1	1	3	5	8	12	18	24	31	39	50	72
	3	1	1	1	3	4	7	10	16	22	28	35	44	63
	2	1	1	1	3	4	6	9	14	19	24	31	38	56
	1		1	1	1	3	5	7	11	14	18	23	29	42
	0		1	1	1	2	4	6	9	12	16	20	25	37
	00			1	1	1	3	5	8	11	14	18	22	32
	000			1	1	1	3	4	7	9	12	15	19	28
	0000			1	1	1	2	4	6	8	10	13	16	24
	250				1	1	1	3	5	6	8	11	13	19
	300				1	1	1	3	4	5	7	9	11	17
	350				1	1	1	2	4	5	6	8	10	15
	400				1	1	1	1	3	4	6	7	9	14
	500				1	1	1	1	3	4	5	6	8	11
	600					1	1	1	2	3	4	5	6	9
	700					1	1	1	1	3	3	4	5	8
	750						1	1	1	3	3	4	5	8

Tables 13 through 15 give the nominal size of conductors and conduit or tubing for use in computing size of conduit or tubing for various combinations of conductors. The dimensions represent average conditions only, and variations will be found in dimensions of conductors and conduits of different manufacture.

Table 13. Dimensions and percent area of conduit and of tubing*

Areas of Conduit or Tubing for the Combinations of Wires Permitted in Table 10.

Trade Size	Internal Diameter Inches	Area — Square Inches								
			Not Lead Covered			Lead Covered				
		Total 100%	2 Cond. 31%	Over 2 Cond. 40%	1 Cond. 53%	1 Cond. 55%	2 Cond. 30%	3 Cond. 40%	4 Cond. 38%	Over 4 Cond. 35%
½	.622	.30	.09	.12	.16	.17	.09	.12	.11	.11
¾	.824	.53	.16	.21	.28	.29	.16	.21	.20	.19
1	1.049	.86	.27	.34	.46	.47	.26	.34	.33	.30
1¼	1.380	1.50	.47	.60	.80	.83	.45	.60	.57	.53
1½	1.610	2.04	.63	.82	1.08	1.12	.61	.82	.78	.71
2	2.067	3.36	1.04	1.34	1.78	1.85	1.01	1.34	1.28	1.18
2½	2.469	4.79	1.48	1.92	2.54	2.63	1.44	1.92	1.82	1.68
3	3.068	7.38	2.29	2.95	3.91	4.06	2.21	2.95	2.80	2.58
3½	3.548	9.90	3.07	3.96	5.25	5.44	2.97	3.96	3.76	3.47
4	4.026	12.72	3.94	5.09	6.74	7.00	3.82	5.09	4.83	4.45
4½	4.506	15.94	4.94	6.38	8.45	8.77	4.78	6.38	6.06	5.56
5	5.047	20.00	6.20	8.00	10.60	11.00	6.00	8.00	7.60	7.00
6	6.065	28.89	8.96	11.56	15.31	15.89	8.67	11.56	10.98	10.11

Table 14. Dimensions of rubber-covered and thermoplastic-covered conductors*

Size AWG MCM	Types RFH-2, RH, RHH,*** RHW,*** SF-2				Types TF, T, THW,† TW, RUH,** RUW**		Types TFN, THHN, THWN		Types**** FEP, FEPB, FEPW, TFE, PF, PFA, PFAH, PGF, PTF, Z, ZF, ZFF				Type XHHW, ZW††		Types KF-1, KF-2, KFF-1, KFF-2	
	Approx. Diam. Inches		Approx. Area Sq. In.		Approx. Diam. Inches	Approx. Area Sq. In.	Approx. Diam. Inches	Approx. Area Sq. In.	Approx. Diam. Inches		Approx. Area Sq. Inches		Approx. Diam. Inches	Approx. Area Sq. In.	Approx. Diam. Sq. In.	Approx. Area Sq. In.
	Col. 2		Col. 3		Col. 4	Col. 5	Col. 6	Col. 7	Col. 8		Col. 9		Col. 10	Col. 11	Col. 12	Col. 13
18	.146		.0167		.106	.0088	.089	.0064	.081		.0052		. . .	. . . .	.065	.0033
16	.158		.0196		.118	.0109	.100	.0079	.092		.0066		. . .	. . . .	.070	.0038
14	30 mils	.171	.0230		.131	.0135	.105	.0087	.105	.105	.0087	.0087	. . .	. . . .	.083	.0054
14	45 mils	.204*	.0327*		. . .	. . .	. . .	. . .	. . .	. . .	. . .	. . .	. . .	. . . .	. . .	. . . .
14	. . . . . .		. . . .		.162†	.0206†	. . .	. . .	. . .	. . .	. . .	. . .	.129	.0131	. . .	. . . .
12	30 mils	.188	.0278		.148	.0172	.122	.0117	.121	.121	.0115	.0115	. . .	. . . .	.102	.0082
12	45 mils	.221*	.0384*		. . .	. . .	. . .	. . .	. . .	. . .	. . .	. . .	. . .	. . . .	. . .	. . . .
12	. . . . . .		. . . .		.179†	.0251†	. . .	. . .	. . .	. . .	. . .	. . .	.146	.0167	. . .	. . . .
10	. . . . . .		.242		.168	.0224	.153	.0184	.142	.142	.0159	.0159	. . .	. . . .	.124	.0121
10	. . . . . .		.0460		.199†	.0311†	. . .	. . .	. . .	. . .	. . .	. . .	.166	.0216	. . .	. . . .
8	. . . . . .		.328		.245	.0471	.218	.0373	.206	.186	.0333	.0272	. . .	. . . .	. . .	. . . .
8	. . . . . .		. . . .		.276†	.0598†	. . .	. . .	. . .	. . .	. . .	. . .	.241	.0456	. . .	. . . .
6	.397		.1238		.323	.0819	.257	.0519	.244	.302	.0467	.0716	.282	.0625	. . .	. . . .
4	.452		.1605		.372	.1087	.328	.0845	.292	.350	.0669	.0962	.328	.0845	. . .	. . . .
3	.481		.1817		.401	.1263	.356	.0995	.320	.378	.0803	.1122	.356	.0995	. . .	. . . .
2	.513		.2067		.433	.1473	.388	.1182	.352	.410	.0973	.1316	.388	.1182	. . .	. . . .
1	.588		.2715		.508	.2027	.450	.1590	.420	. . .	.1385	. . . .	.450	.1590	. . .	. . . .
0	.629		.3107		.549	.2367	.491	.1893	.462	. . .	.1676	. . . .	.491	.1893	. . .	. . . .
00	.675		.3578		.595	.2781	.537	.2265	.498	. . .	.1974	. . . .	.537	.2265	. . .	. . . .
000	.727		.4151		.647	.3288	.588	.2715	.560	. . .	.2463	. . . .	.588	.2715	. . .	. . . .
0000	.785		.4840		.705	.3904	.646	.3278	.618	. . .	.2999	. . . .	.646	.3278	. . .	. . . .

Reprinted by permission from NFPA 70-1981, National Electrical Code®, Copyright © 1980, National Fire Protection Association, Quincy, MA. This reprinted material is not the complete and official position of the NFPA on the referenced subject which is represented only by the standard in its entirety.

Table 14 (Continued)*

Size AWG MCM	Types RFH-2, RH, RHH,*** RHW,*** SF-2		Types TF, T, THW,† TW, RUH,** RUW**		Types TFN, THHN, THWN		Types**** FEP, FEPB, FEPW, TFE, PF, PFA, PFAH, PGF, PTF, Z, ZF, ZFF		Type XHHW, ZW††	
	Approx. Diam. Inches	Approx. Area Sq. In.	Approx. Diam. Inches	Approx. Area Sq. In.	Approx. Diam. Inches	Approx. Area Sq. In.	Approx. Diam. Inches	Approx. Area Sq. Inches	Approx. Diam. Inches	Approx. Area Sq. In.
Col. 1	Col. 2	Col. 3	Col. 4	Col. 5	Col. 6	Col. 7	Col. 8	Col. 9	Col. 10	Col. 11
250	.868	.5917	.788	.4877	.716	.4026	. . .	. . . .	.716	.4026
300	.933	.6837	.843	.5581	.771	.4669	. . .	. . . .	.771	.4669
350	.985	.7620	.895	.6291	.822	.5307	. . .	. . . .	.822	.5307
400	1.032	.8365	.942	.6969	.869	.5931	. . .	. . . .	.869	.5931
500	1.119	.9834	1.029	.8316	.955	.7163	. . .	. . . .	.955	.7163
600	1.233	1.1940	1.143	1.0261	1.058	.8792	. . .	. . . .	1.073	.9043
700	1.304	1.3355	1.214	1.1575	1.129	1.0011	. . .	. . . .	1.145	1.0297
750	1.339	1.4082	1.249	1.2252	1.163	1.0623	. . .	. . . .	1.180	1.0936
800	1.372	1.4784	1.282	1.2908	1.196	1.1234	. . .	. . . .	1.210	1.1499
900	1.435	1.6173	1.345	1.4208	1.259	1.2449	. . .	. . . .	1.270	1.2668
1000	1.494	1.7531	1.404	1.5482	1.317	1.3623	. . .	. . . .	1.330	1.3893
1250	1.676	2.2062	1.577	1.9532	. . .	. . . .	. . .	. . . .	1.500	1.7672
1500	1.801	2.5475	1.702	2.2748	. . .	. . . .	. . .	. . . .	1.620	2.0612
1750	1.916	2.8895	1.817	2.5930	. . .	. . . .	. . .	. . . .	1.740	2.3779
2000	2.021	3.2079	1.922	2.9013	. . .	. . . .	. . .	. . . .	1.840	2.6590

* The dimensions of Types RHH and RHW.

** No. 14 to No. 2.

† Dimensions of THW in sizes No. 14 to No. 8. No. 6 THW and larger is the same dimension as T.

*** Dimensions of RHH and RHW without outer covering are the same as THW No. 18 to No. 10, solid; No. 8 and larger, stranded.

**** In Columns 8 and 9 the values shown for sizes No. 1 thru 0000 are for TFE and Z only. The right-hand values in Columns 8 and 9 are for FEPB, Z, ZF, and ZFF only.

†† No. 14 to No. 2.

Table 15. Dimensions of lead-covered conductors*

Types RL, RHL, and RUL

Size AWG-MCM	Single Conductor		Two Conductor		Three Conductor	
	Diam. Inches	Area Sq. In.	Diam. Inches	Area Sq. In.	Diam. Inches	Area Sq. In.
14	.28	.062	.28 × .47	.115	.59	.273
12	.29	.066	.31 × .54	.146	.62	.301
10	.35	.096	.35 × .59	.180	.68	.363
8 sol.	.41	.132	.41 × .71	.255	.82	.528
8 str.	.43	.145	.43 × .75	.282	.86	.581
6	.49	.188	.49 × .86	.369	.97	.738
4	.55	.237	.54 × .96	.457	1.08	.916
2	.60	.283	.61 × 1.08	.578	1.21	1.146
1	.67	.352	.70 × 1.23	.756	1.38	1.49
0	.71	.396	.74 × 1.32	.859	1.47	1.70
00	.76	.454	.79 × 1.41	.980	1.57	1.94
000	.81	.515	.84 × 1.52	1.123	1.69	2.24
0000	.87	.593	.90 × 1.64	1.302	1.85	2.68
250	.98	.754	. . . .	. . . . .	2.02	3.20
300	1.04	.85	. . . .	. . . . .	2.15	3.62
350	1.10	.95	. . . .	. . . . .	2.26	4.02
400	1.14	1.02	. . . .	. . . . .	2.40	4.52
500	1.23	1.18	. . . .	. . . . .	2.59	5.28

The above cables are limited to straight runs or with nominal offsets equivalent to not more than two quarter bends.

Note — No. 14 to No. 10, solid conductors; No. 8, solid or stranded conductors; No. 6 and larger, stranded conductors.

* Reprinted by permission from NFPA 70-1981, National Electrical Code®, Copyright © 1980, National Fire Protection Association, Quincy, MA. This reprinted material is not the complete and official position of the NFPA on the referenced subject which is represented only by the standard in its entirety.

By SYSKA AND HENNESSY, INC., *Consulting Engineers*

Electric traction elevator
Passenger service
Geared machine
Capacity: 2,000 to 4,000 lbs
Speed: 200 to 350 fpm

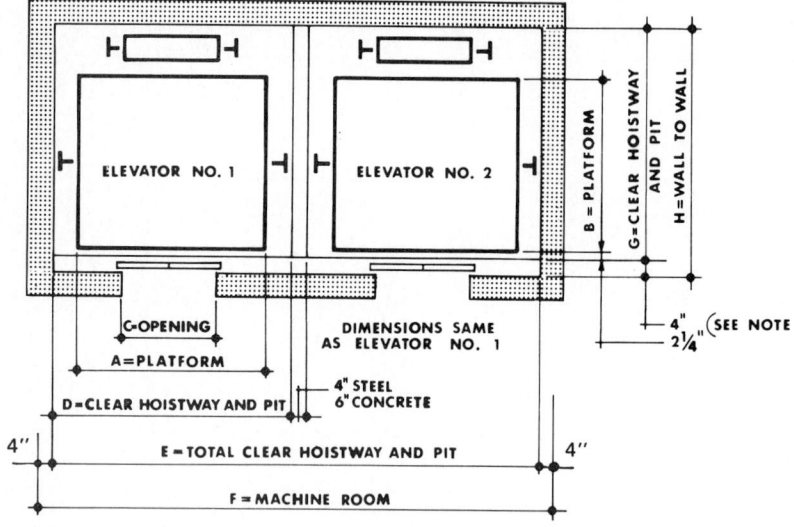

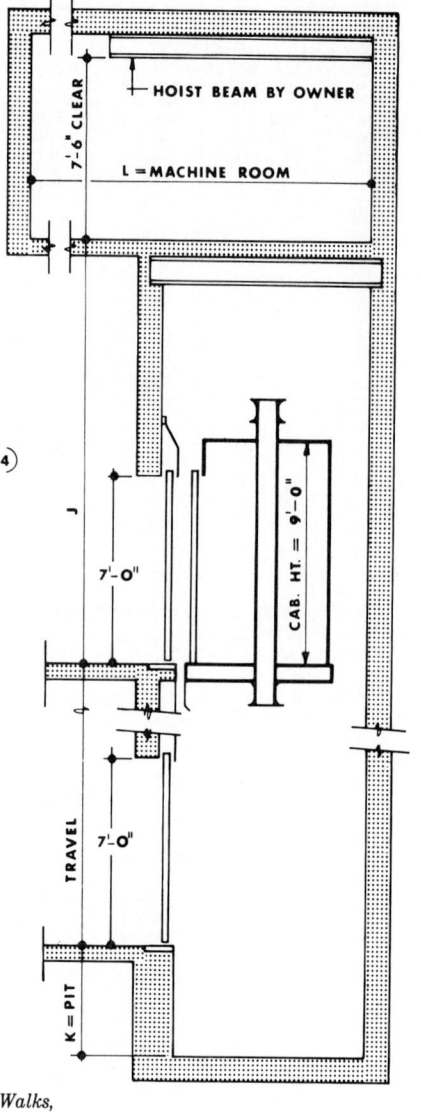

Notes:

1. *American National Safety Code for Elevators** and local codes govern elevator installations.

2. When total cab height exceeds 9', add excess to J.

3. When there is occupied space below elevator pit, increase G and H by 3" to allow for counterweight safeties.

4. When flush transoms are desired, increase 4" to 5½"; increase H by 1½".

5. When 6" divider beam is used, add 2" to E. Where seismic protection is required, allow 8" or more.

6. Alternate platform dimensions.

7. Provide machine room with access and ventilation as required by code.

8. For poured concrete structures, additional clearances are recommended.

American National Safety Code for Elevators, Dumbwaiters, Escalators, and Moving Walks, ANSI A17.1-1978

Capacity, lb	Speed, fpm	Dimensions										
		A	B	C	D	E	F	G	H	J	K	L
2,000	200	6'-4"	4'-5"	3'-0"	7'-8"	15'-8"	16'-4"	5'-9"	6'-1"	16'-0"	5'-0"	12'-6"
	300									17'-0"	5'-6"	12'-6"
	350									17'-0"	6'-0"	12'-6"
2,500	200	7'-0"	5'-0"	3'-6"	8'-4"	17'-0"	17'-8"	6'-4"	6'-8"	16'-0"	5'-0"	12'-6"
	300									17'-0"	5'-6"	12'-6"
	350									17'-6"	6'-0"	12'-6"
3,000	200	7'-0"	5'-6"	3'-6"	8'-4"	17'-0"	17'-8"	6'-10"	7'-2"	16'-0"	5'-0"	12'-6"
	300									17'-0"	6'-8"	12'-6"
	350									17'-6"	7'-6"	13'-0"
3,500 (Note 6)	200	7'-0"	6'-2"	3'-6"	8'-4"	17'-0"	17'-8"	7'-6"	7'-10"	16'-6"	5'-0"	12'-6"
	300									17'-0"	6'-9"	13'-0"
	350									17'-6"	7'-6"	14'-0"
3,500	200	8'-0"	5'-6"	4'-0"	9'-4"	19'-0"	19'-8"	6'-10"	7'-2"	16'-6"	5'-0"	13'-6"
	300									17'-0"	6'-9"	13'-0"
	350									17'-6"	7'-6"	14'-0"
4,000	200	8'-0"	6'-2"	4'-0"	9'-4"	19'-0"	19'-8"	7'-6"	7'-10"	16'-9"	5'-2"	13'-6"
	300									18'-0"	6'-9"	13'-6"
	350									18'-6"	7'-6"	14'-0"

Electric traction elevator
Passenger service
Gearless machine
Capacity: 2,500 to 4,000 lbs
Speed: 500 fpm

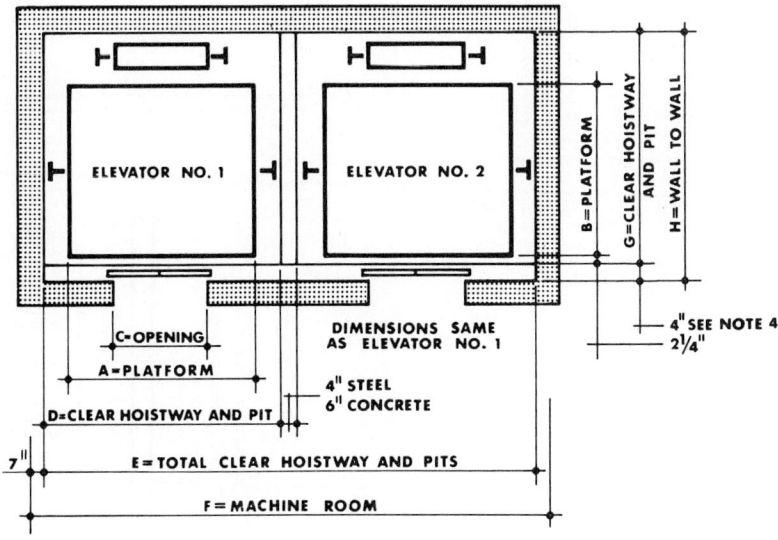

Notes:

1. *American National Safety Code for Elevators* and local codes govern elevator installation.

2. When total cab height exceeds 9', add excess to J.

3. When there is occupied space below elevator pit, increase G and H by 3" to allow for counterweight safeties.

4. When flush transoms are desired, increase 4" to 5½"; increase H by 1½".

5. When 6" divider beam is used, add 2" to E. Where seismic protection is required, allow 8" or more.

6. Alternate platform dimensions.

7. Provide machine room with access and ventilation as required by code.

8. For poured concrete structures, additional clearances are recommended.

Capacity, lb	Speed, fpm	Dimensions										
		A	B	C	D	E	F	G	H	J	K	L
2,500	500	7'-0"	5'-0"	3'-6"	8'-5"	17'-4"	18'-0"	6'-4"	6'-8"	24'-8"	10'-0"	20'-6"
3,000	500	7'-0"	5'-6"	3'-6"	8'-5"	17'-4"	18'-0"	6'-10"	7'-2"	24'-8"	10'-0"	20'-6"
3,500 (Note 6)	500	7'-0"	6'-2"	3'-6"	8'-5"	17'-4"	18'-0"	7'-6"	7'-10"	24'-8"	10'-0"	20'-6"
3,500	500	8'-0"	5'-6"	4'-0"	9'-5"	19'-4"	20'-0"	6'-10"	7'-2"	25'-0"	10'-0"	20'-6"
4,000	500	8'-0"	6'-2"	4'-0"	9'-5"	19'-4"	20'-0"	7'-6"	7'-10"	25'-0"	10'-0"	20'-6"

Electric traction elevator
Passenger service
Gearless machine
Capacity: 2,500 to 4,000 lbs
Speed: 700 to 1,200 fpm

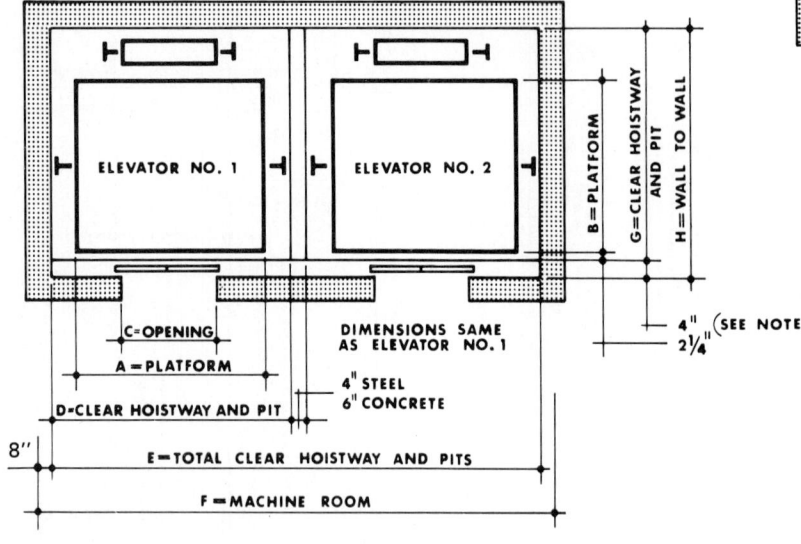

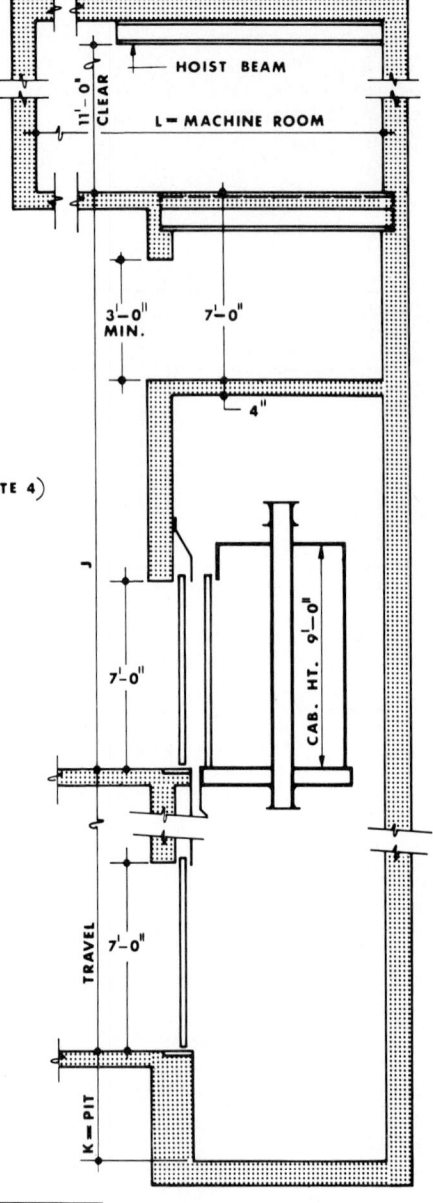

Notes:

1. *American National Safety Code for Elevators* and local codes govern elevator installation.

2. When total cab height exceeds 9', add excess to J.

3. When there is occupied space below elevator pit, increase G and H by 3" to allow for counterweight safeties.

4. When flush transoms are desired, increase 4" to 5½"; increase H by 1½".

5. When 6" divider beam is used, add 2" to E. Where seismic protection is required, allow 8" or more.

6. Alternate platform dimensions.

7. Provide machine room with access and ventilation as required by code.

8. For poured concrete structures, additional clearances are recommended.

Capacity, lb	Speed, fpm	Dimensions										
		A	B	C	D	E	F	G	H	J	K	L
2,500	700	7'-0"	5'-0"	3'-6"	8'-6"	17'-6"	22'-6"	6'-5½"	6'-9½"	26'-6"	12'-6"	
	800									29'-0"	14'-0"	23'-0"
3,000	700	7'-0"	5'-6"	3'-6"	8'-6"	17'-6"	22'-6"	6'-11½"	7'-3½"	26'-6"	12'-6"	
	800									29'-0"	14'-0"	23'-0"
	1,000									30'-9"	18'-0"	
3,500 (Note 6)	800	7'-0"	6'-2"	3'-6"	8'-6"	17'-6"	22'-6"	7'-7½"	7'-11½"	29'-0"	14'-0"	
	1,000									30'-9"	18'-0"	24'-0"
	1,200									31'-6"	19'-6"	
3,500	800	8'-0"	5'-6"	4'-0"	9'-6"	19'-6"	24'-0"	6'-11½"	7'-3½"	29'-0"	14'-0"	
	1,000									30'-9"	18'-0"	24'-0"
	1,200									31'-6"	19'-6"	
4,000	800	8'-0"	6'-2"	4'-0"	9'-6"	19'-6"	24'-0"	7'-7½"	7'-11½"	29'-0"	14'-0"	
	1,000									30'-9"	18'-0"	24'-0"
	1,200									31'-6"	19'-6"	

Electric traction elevator
Hospital service
Geared and gearless machines
Capacity: 4,000 to 5,000 lbs
Speed: 200 to 800 fpm

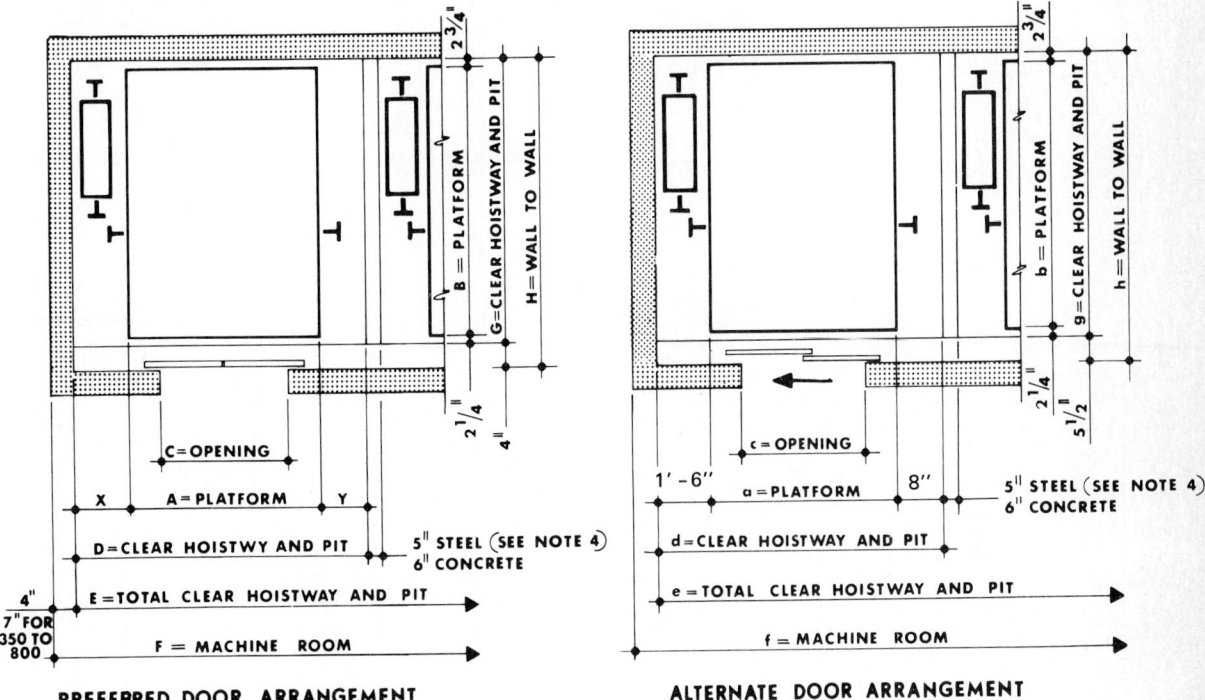

PREFERRED DOOR ARRANGEMENT   **ALTERNATE DOOR ARRANGEMENT**

Notes:

1. *American National Safety Code for Elevators* and local codes govern elevator installation.

2. For vertical dimensions, see sectional view of passenger elevators of the same speed.

3. When total cab height exceeds 9', add excess to J.

4. When 6" divider beam is used, add 1" to E. Where seismic protection is required, allow 8" or more.

5. Provide machine room with access and ventilation as required by code.

6. For poured concrete structures, additional clearances are recommended.

Capacity, lb	Speed, fpm	Preferred arrangement A	B	C	D	E	F	G	H	J	K	L	X	Y	Alternate arrangement a	b	c	d	e	f	g	h	i	k	l
4,000	200 300 350 500 800	5'-8"	8'-8"	4'-0"	18'-10"	18'-2"	25'-9"	9'-1"	9'-5"	16'-9" 17'-6" 18'-0" 25'-0" 29'-0"	5'-0" 6'-9" 7'-8" 10'-0"	13'-6" 13'-6" 14'-0"	1'-7"	1'-7"	5'-8"	8'-8"	4'-0"	7'-10"	16'-2"	23'-9"	9'-1"	9'-6½"	16'-9" 17'-6" 18'-0" 25'-0" 29'-0"	5'-0" 6'-9" 7'-8" 10'-0"	13'-6" 13'-6" 14'-0"
4,500	200 300 350 500 800	6'-0"	8'-11"	4'-0"	18'-10"	18'-2"	25'-9"	9'-4"	9'-8"	16'-9" 17'-6" 18'-0" 25'-0" 29'-0"	5'-0" 6'-9" 7'-8" 10'-0"	13'-6" 13'-6" 14'-0"	1'-5"	1'-5"	6'-0"	9'-0"	4'-3"	8'-2"	16'-10"	23'-9"	9'-5"	9'-10½"	16'-9" 17'-6" 18'-0" 25'-0" 29'-0"	5'-0" 6'-9" 7'-8" 10'-0"	13'-6" 13'-6" 14'-0"
5,000	200 300 350 500 800	6'-0"	9'-6"	4'-0"	18'-10"	18'-2"	25'-9"	9'-11"	10'-3"	16'-9" 18'-0" 18'-6" 25'-6" 29'-6"	5'-2" 6'-9" 7'-8" 10'-3"	13'-6" 13'-6" 14'-0"	1'-5"	1'-5"	6'-0"	9'-7"	4'-8"	8'-2"	16'-10"	23'-9"	10'-0"	10'-5½"	16'-9" 18'-0" 18'-6" 25'-6" 29'-6"	5'-2" 6'-9" 7'-8" 10'-3"	13'-6" 13'-6" 14'-0"

Electric traction elevator
Freight service
Geared machine
Capacity: 4,000 to 10,000 lbs
Speed: 75 to 200 fpm

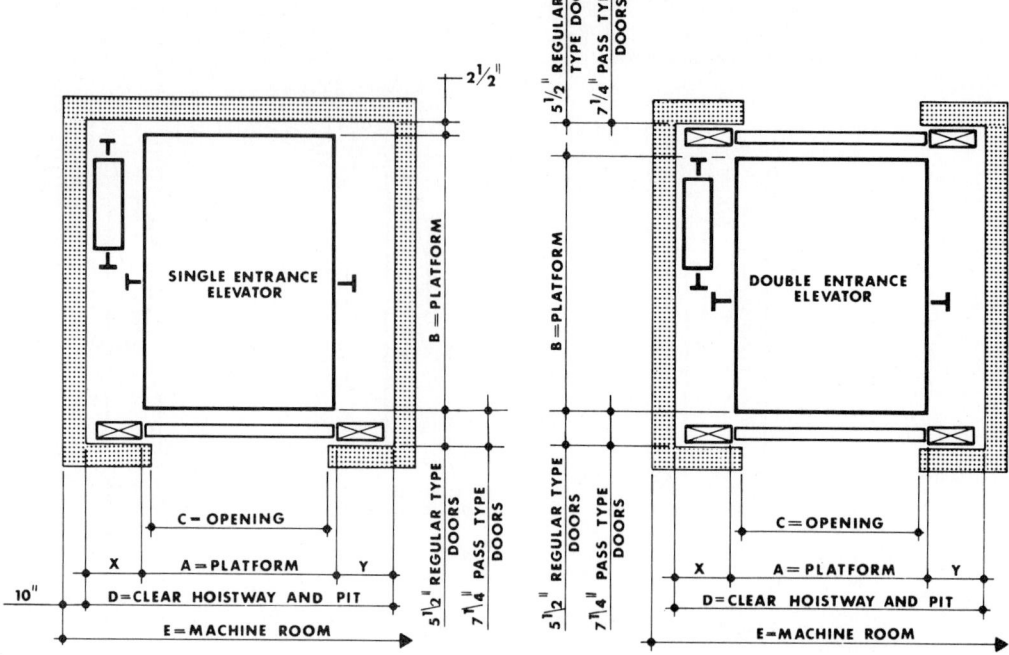

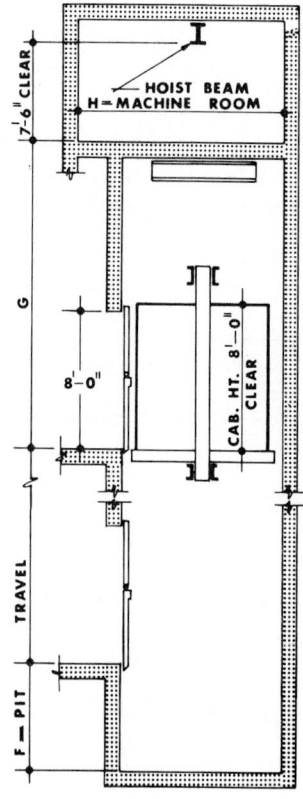

Notes:

1. *American National Safety Code for Elevators* and local codes govern elevator installation.

2. Dimensions provided are based on class A loading. For power truck loading and/or other special loadings, (classes B, C1, C2, C3) see code requirements.

3. Provide machine room with access and ventilation as required by code.

4. See door detail sheet for vertical biparting door requirements.

5. When door height exceeds 8', add excess to G.

6. For poured concrete structures, additional clearances are recommended.

Capacity, lb	Speed, fpm	Dimensions										
		A	B		C	D	E	F	G	H	X	Y
			Single entrance	Double entrance								
4,000	75	6'-4"	7'-6"	7'-7"	6'-0"	8'-7"	11'-6"	5'-0"	16'-6"	13'-9"	1'-4"	11"
	100						12'-8"	5'-0"	16'-6"	13'-9"		
	200						14'-0"	5'-6"	17'-6"	15'-4"		
5,000	75	7'-4"	8'-0"	8'-1"	7'-0"	9'-7"	11'-6"	5'-0"	16'-6"	13'-9"	1'-4"	11"
	100						12'-8"	5'-0"	16'-6"	13'-9"		
	200						14'-0"	5'-6"	17'-6"	15'-4"		
6,000	75	8'-4"	8'-0"	8'-1"	8'-0"	10'-9"	11'-6"	5'-0"	16'-6"	13'-9"	1'-6"	11"
	100						12'-8"	5'-0"	16'-6"	13'-9"		
	200						14'-0"	5'-6"	17'-6"	15'-4"		
8,000	75	8'-4"	10'-6"	10'-7"	8'-0"	10'-11"	12'-0"	5'-6"	17'-0"	13'-9"	1'-8"	11"
	100						13'-0"	5'-6"	17'-0"	13'-9"		
	200						14'-6"	5'-6"	18'-0"	15'-4"		
10,000	75	8'-4"	12'-6"	12'-7"	8'-0"	10'-11"	12'-0"	5'-6"	17'-0"	15'-4"	1'-8"	11"
	100						13'-0"	5'-6"	17'-0"	15'-4"		
	200						14'-6"	6'-0"	18'-0"	15'-10"		

Hydraulic elevator
Passenger and hospital service
Capacity: 2,000 to 4,000 lbs (passenger)
4,000 to 5,000 lbs (hospital)
Speed: 50 to 150 fpm

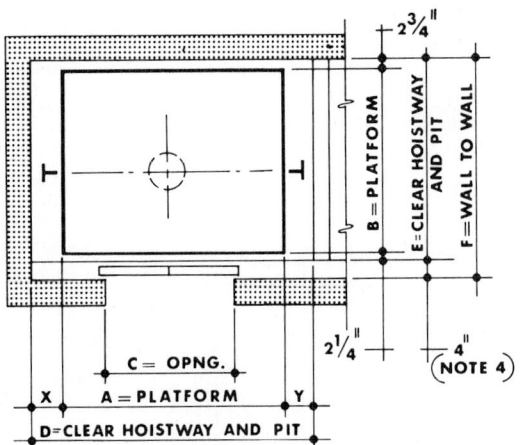

PASSENGER ELEVATOR

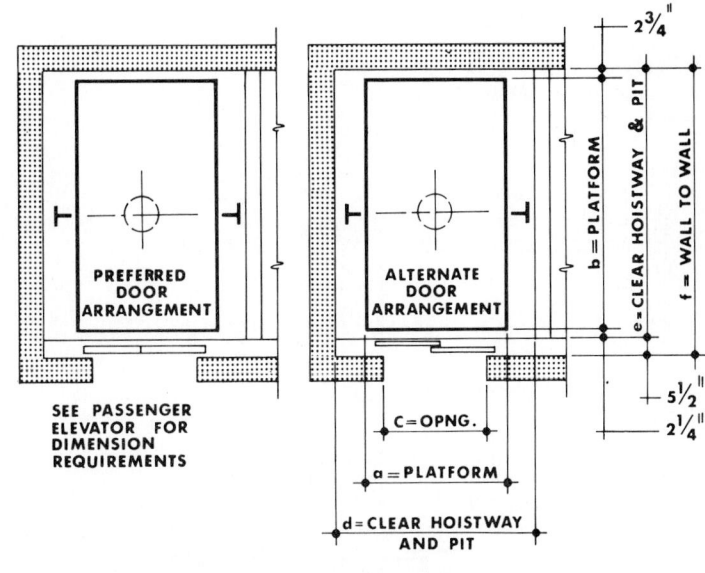

PREFERRED DOOR ARRANGEMENT

SEE PASSENGER ELEVATOR FOR DIMENSION REQUIREMENTS

ALTERNATE DOOR ARRANGEMENT

HOSPITAL TYPE ELEVATOR

Notes:

1. *American National Safety Code for Elevators* and local codes govern elevator installation.

2. For vertical dimensions, see sectional view of hydraulic freight service elevator, sheet 7.

3. When total cab height exceeds 9', add excess to H.

4. When flush transoms are desired, increase 4" to 5½"; increase F by 1½".

5. Alternate platform dimensions.

6. Provide machine room with access and ventilation as required by code.

7. Where seismic protection is required, allow 8" or more for divider beam.

Passenger elevator dimensions

Capacity, lb	A	B	C	D	E	F	X	Y	G	H	J
2,000	6'-4"	4'-5"	3'-0"	7'-8"	4'-10"	5'-2"					
2,500	7'-0"	5'-0"	3'-6"	8'-4"	5'-5"	5'-9"					
3,000	7'-0"	5'-6"	3'-6"	8'-4"	5'-11"	6'-3"	8"	8"	7'-0"	13'-0"	4'-6"
3,500											
Note 5	7'-0"	6'-2"	3'-6"	8'-4"	6'-7"	6'-11"					
3,500	8'-0"	5'-6"	4'-0"	9'-4"	5'-11"	6'-3"					
4,000	8'-0"	6'-2"	4'-0"	9'-4"	6'-7"	6'-11"					

Hospital type elevator dimensions, preferred door arrangement

Capacity lb	A	B	C	D	E	F	X	Y	G	H	J
4,000	5'-8"	8'-8"	4'-0"	8'-10"	9'-1"	9'-5"	1'-7"	1'-7"			4'-6"
4,500	6'-0"	9'-0"	4'-0"	8'-10"	9'-5"	9'-9"	1'-5"	1'-5"	7'-0"	13'-0"	4'-6"
5,000	6'-0"	9'-6"	4'-0"	8'-10"	9'-5"	9'-9"	1'-2"	1'-2"			5'-0"

Hospital type elevator dimensions, alternate door arrangement

Capacity lb	a	b	c	d	e	f	x	y	g	h	i
4,000	5'-8"	8'-8"	4'-0"	7'-7"	9'-1"	9'-6½"	1'-3"				4'-6"
4,500	6'-0"	9'-0"	4'-0"	7'-4"	9'-5"	9'-10½"	8"	8"	7'-0"	13'-0"	4'-6"
5,000	6'-0"	9'-6"	4'-3"	7'-10"	9'-5"	10'-4½"	8"				5'-0"

Hydraulic elevator
Freight service
Capacity: 2,000 to 10,000 lbs
Speed: 50 to 150 fpm

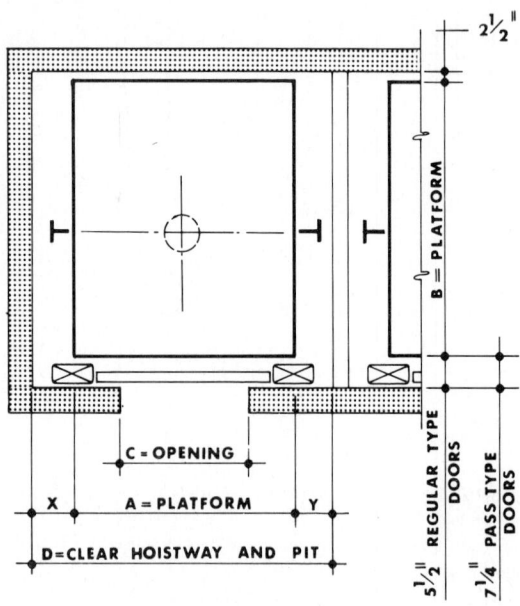

FREIGHT ELEVATOR

Notes:

1. *American National Safety Code for Elevators and* local codes govern elevator installation.

2. Dimensions provided are based on class A loading for power truck loading and/or other special loadings (Classes B, C-1, C-2, C-3) see code requirements.

3. Provide a machine room of approx. 9 x 11 x 7 ft high for a single elevator. Larger area is required when two or more power units are used or for two (2) elevators with a common machine room. Machine room can be located remote from shaft, preferably on the lowest level served. Provide machine room with access and ventilation as required by code.

4. When door height exceeds 8 ft, add excess to H.

5. See door detail sheet for vertical biparting door requirements.

6. A waterproof outer casing is recommended. It is required when water condition is known to exist.

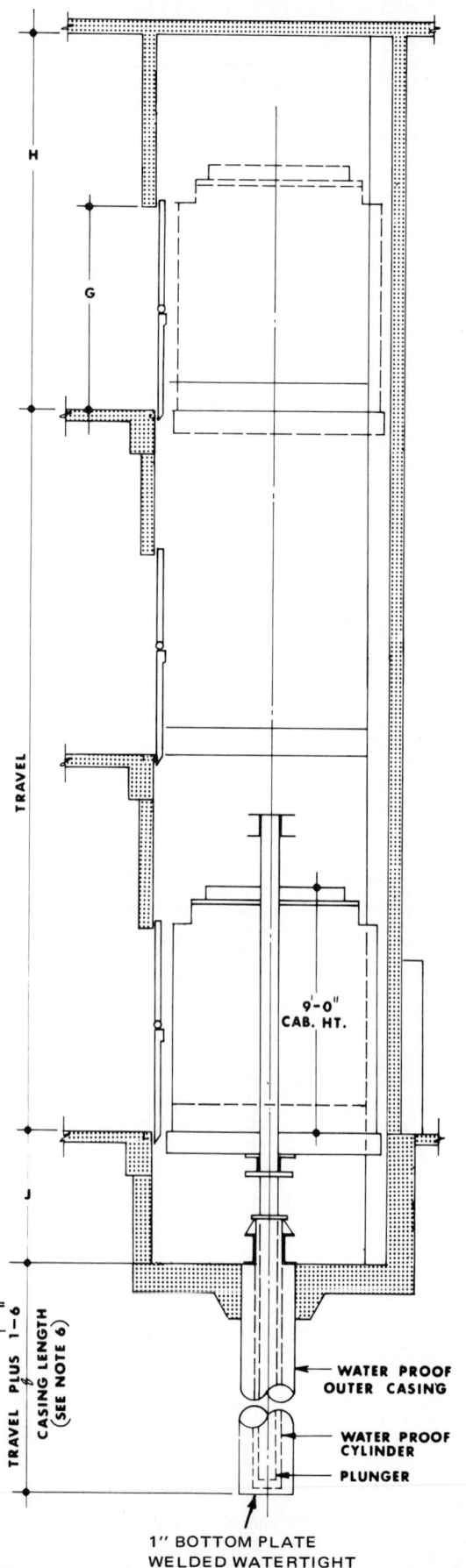

9'-0" CAB. HT.

WATER PROOF OUTER CASING

WATER PROOF CYLINDER

PLUNGER

1" BOTTOM PLATE WELDED WATERTIGHT

	Dimensions								
Capacity, lb	A	B	C	D	X	Y	G	H	J
2,000	4'-4"	5'-6"	4'-0"	6'-2"					
3,000	5'-4"	6'-6"	5'-0"	7'-2"					4'-6"
4,000	6'-4"	7'-6"	6'-0"	8'-2"					
5,000	7'-4"	8'-0"	7'-0"	9'-2"	11"	11"	8'-0"	15'-0"	
6,000	8'-4"	8'-0"	8'-0"	10'-2"					5'-0"
8,000	8'-4"	10'-6"	8'-0"	10'-2"					
10,000	8'-4"	12'-6"	8'-0"	10'-2"					5'-6"

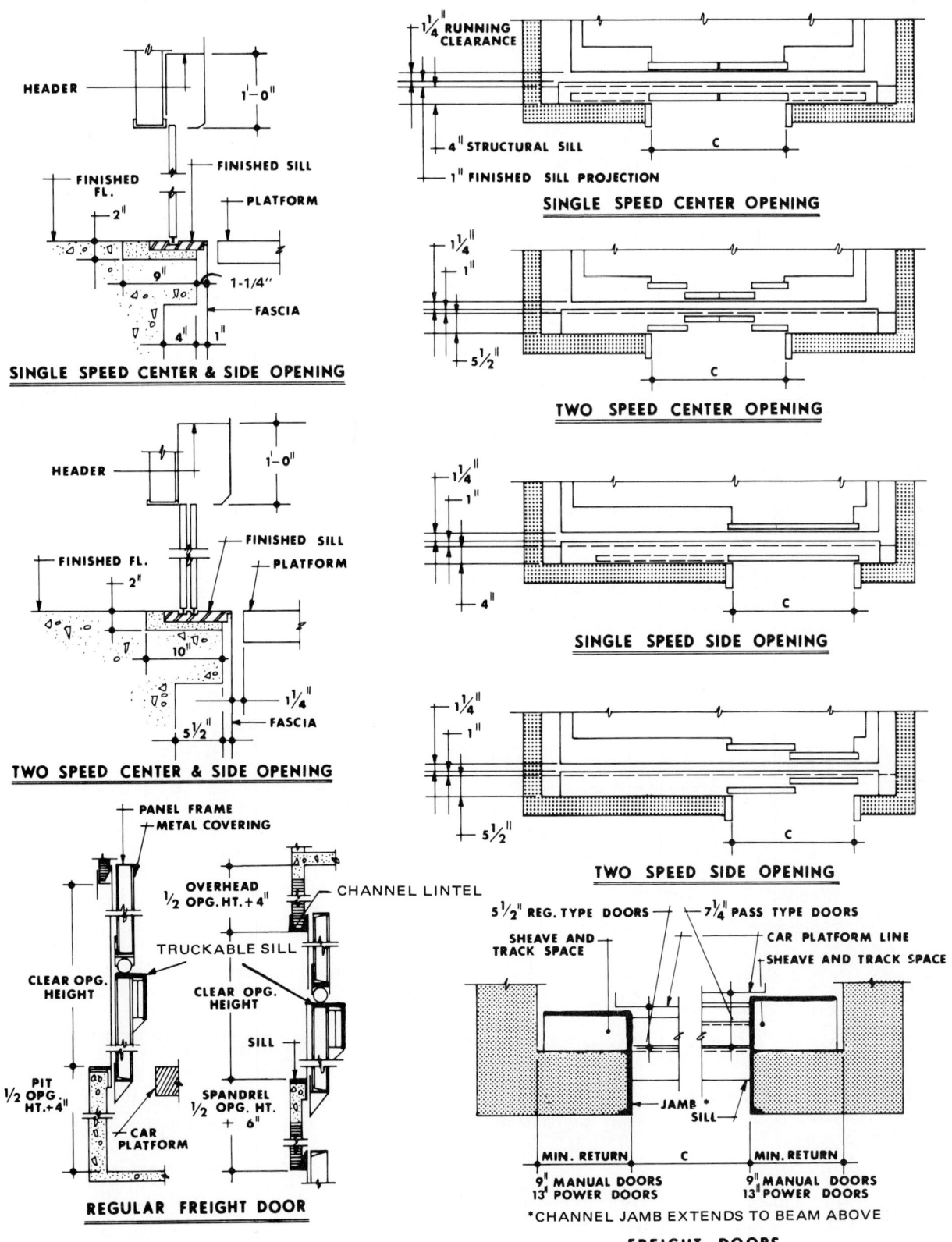

SINGLE SPEED CENTER & SIDE OPENING

TWO SPEED CENTER & SIDE OPENING

REGULAR FREIGHT DOOR

SINGLE SPEED CENTER OPENING

TWO SPEED CENTER OPENING

SINGLE SPEED SIDE OPENING

TWO SPEED SIDE OPENING

FREIGHT DOORS

*CHANNEL JAMB EXTENDS TO BEAM ABOVE

NOTE: FRONT WALLS SHOULD BE LEFT OUT UNTIL ENTRANCES ARE SET IN PLACE, OR MINIMUM ROUGH OPENING PROVIDED 12" WIDER AND 6" HIGHER THAN DOORWAY SIZE.

By SYSKA AND HENNESSY, INC., *Consulting Engineers*

See American National Safety Code for Elevators, Dumbwaiters, Escalators, Moving Walks, ANSI A17.1-1978.

Electric stairway
Angle of incline: 30 deg
Speed: 90 or 120 fpm
Width: 32 or 48 in.

Stair width		Contractors variable dimensions		
		X	Y	Z
32"	J	4'-4"	4'-3 7/16"	4'-4"
	K	2'-8"	2'-8 1/16"	2'-8"
	L	2'-0"	1'-11 5/16"	2'-0"
	M	4'-4"	4'-3 7/16"	4'-4"
48"	J	5'-8"	5'-8"	5'-8"
	K	4'-0"	4'-1 3/16"	4'-0"
	L	3'-4"	3'-3 7/8"	3'-4"
	M	5'-8"	5'-8"	5'-8"

	Contractors variable dimensions		
	X	Y	Z
A	5'-8"	4'-9"	6'-6"
B	9'-2"	10'-1"	8'-4"
C	4'-7 7/8"	3'-8 15/16"	5'-2 9/16"
D	5'-5 1/8"	6'-7"	5'-4 1/16"
E	3'-4 3/4"	3'-6 3/8"	3'-2 7/16"
F	3'-4 1/2"	3'-7"	3'-8 1/2"
G	3'-11"	3'-11"	4'-2"
H	Moving stair rise		
I	12'-10"	12'-4"	13'-3"

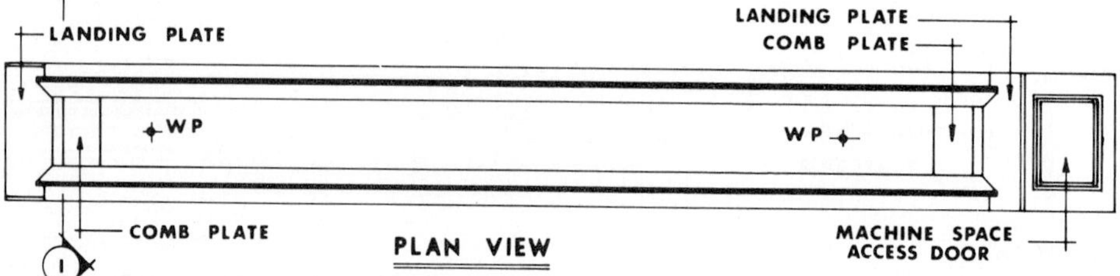

SECTION
1—1

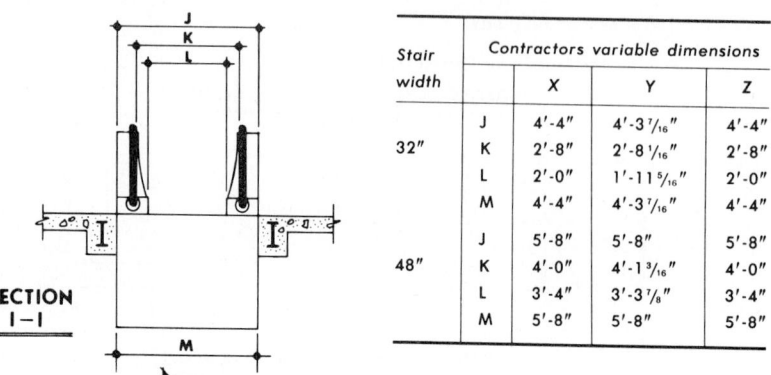

LANDING PLATE

LANDING PLATE
COMB PLATE

+ W P

W P +

COMB PLATE

PLAN VIEW

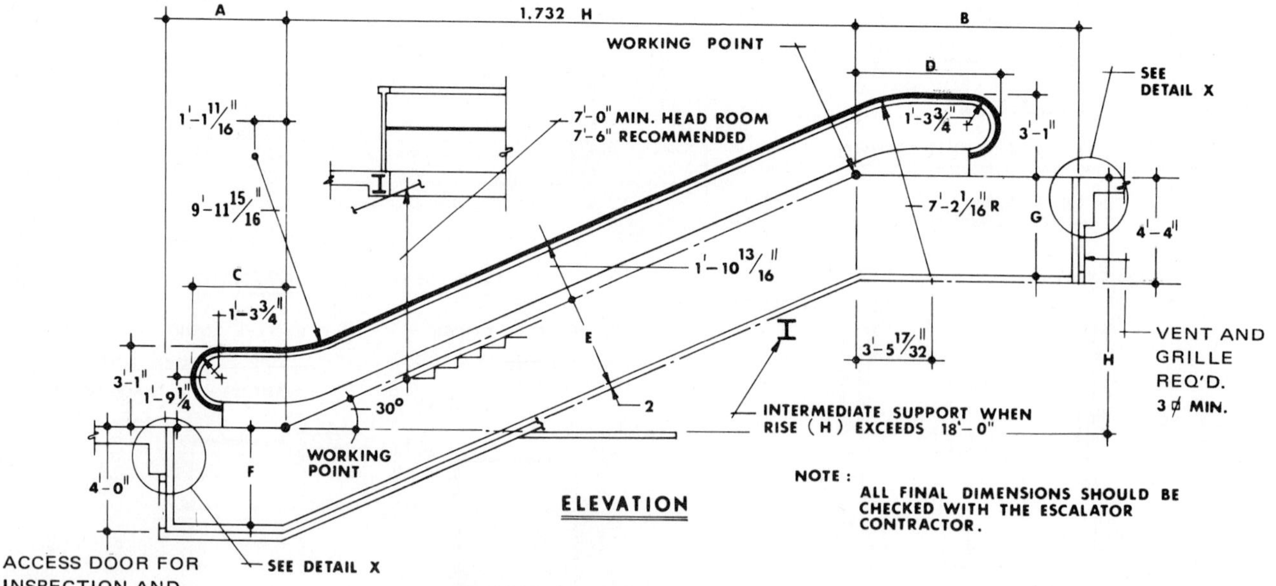

MACHINE SPACE
ACCESS DOOR

1.732 H

WORKING POINT

SEE DETAIL X

7'-0" MIN. HEAD ROOM
7'-6" RECOMMENDED

1'-1 11/16"

1'-3 3/4"

3'-1"

9'-11 15/16"

7'-2 1/16" R

G

4'-4"

C

1'-3 3/4"

1'-10 13/16"

VENT AND GRILLE REQ'D. 3∅ MIN.

3'-1"
1'-9 1/4"

3'-5 17/32"

30°

E

2

H

4'-0"

WORKING POINT

INTERMEDIATE SUPPORT WHEN RISE (H) EXCEEDS 18'-0"

ELEVATION

NOTE:
ALL FINAL DIMENSIONS SHOULD BE CHECKED WITH THE ESCALATOR CONTRACTOR.

ACCESS DOOR FOR INSPECTION AND MAINT. REQ'D.

SEE DETAIL X

ACCESS DOOR

3'-0"

2"

4'-0"

WP

LADDER

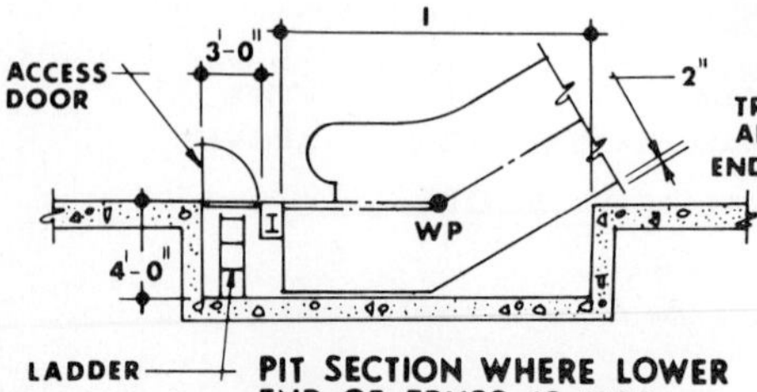

PIT SECTION WHERE LOWER END OF TRUSS IS NOT ACCESSIBLE FROM BELOW

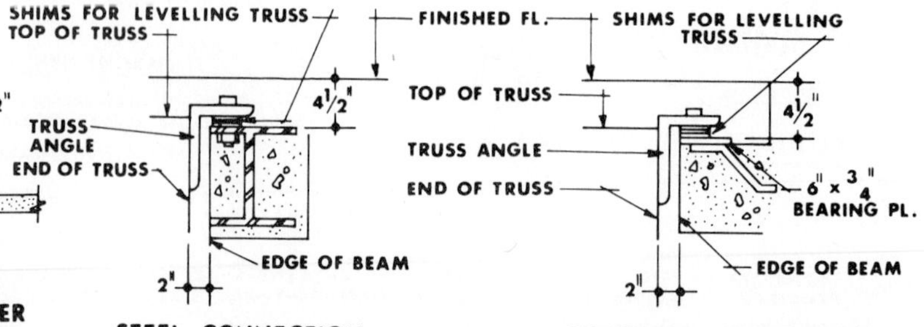

SHIMS FOR LEVELLING TRUSS TOP OF TRUSS

FINISHED FL.

SHIMS FOR LEVELLING TRUSS

4 1/2"

TRUSS ANGLE
END OF TRUSS

TOP OF TRUSS

TRUSS ANGLE

4 1/2"

END OF TRUSS

6" x 3/4" BEARING PL.

2"

EDGE OF BEAM

2"

EDGE OF BEAM

STEEL CONNECTION

CONCRETE CONNECTION

DETAIL X

Data from the Bell Telephone System

Recent improvements and expansion of telephone service, such as direct in and out dialing, teletypewriters, telephone-connected data-processing machines, cordless switchboards, loud-speaker telephones, automatic answering telephones, etc., require more wiring and switching equipment than the earlier and simpler systems. Adequate space must be provided for this purpose.

In recent years, major advances have been made in determining the most effective and economical allowances for telephone equipment installation. These average allowances are presented here with a word of caution. With telephone technology ever changing, these equipment-to-floor area ratios should be used only as a guide or starting point for planning. The local telephone company consultant should be called in to review the specific requirements for any building.

Underfloor layouts

For the two general types of underfloor distribution systems—duct-type and cellular steel—minimum telephone requirements for the modern building are as follows.

Duct-type underflooring: Parallel runs should be spaced approximately every 4½ ft. Cross runs and junction boxes should be located every 40 ft or less, depending on floor layout.

Cellular steel: The system must have sufficient header ducts connecting to telephone equipment closets. These headers should be connected to the cell area at intervals of not more than 50 ft.

It is desirable to have telephone raceways separate from electrical conduit systems. The standard space allocation: one desk per 100 sq ft floor space. Allow one telephone per desk.

Raceway capacity should be provided accordingly: 1 sq in. of raceway for every 100 sq ft of floor area served.

Zones

Large floor areas should be divided into smaller areas called "zones" with an equipment closet for each. Maximum zone size, limited by the resistance of the cable, is 10,000 sq ft. Recommended zone size for economy is 4,000 to 6,000 sq ft.

Zone equipment closets

Preferred practice is to locate switching equipment for all telephones in one zone in a special closet provided for that purpose. This eliminates noise, improves overall office appearance, and permits telephone personnel to work without seriously disturbing the tenants. The total effect is more efficient use of building space than if separate equipment were mounted near each of the telephone set locations.

Planning data for the zone equipment closet are shown in the following table:

	Walk-in closet	Shallow closet
Depth (feet)		
Minimum	3	1½
Maximum	None	2½
Width (feet)		
Minimum	5	3 ft
Maximum	None	None
Floor area (sq ft/ 1,000 sq ft floor)	6	None
Length of walls (ft/ 1,000 sq ft floor)	2½	2½
Minimum height doors	6 ft 8 in.	6 ft 8 in.*
Minimum width doors	3 ft	3 ft †

When shallow closets are used, the center post between double doors should be eliminated, where possible.

†*Minimum for single door: 2½ ft for double doors.*

In addition, all closets should have the following:

Walls lined with ¾-in. thick 8-ft high plyboard

At least one ceiling light controlled by a wall switch

One separately fused 20-ampere 3-wire circuit run to at least two 110-volt duplex receptacles or an electrical plug-in strip

Terminal rooms and equipment rooms

Main terminal rooms and equipment rooms (where needed) should be centrally located and adequately sized. They must be properly lighted, well ventilated, provided with power outlets, as dustproof as possible, and located in areas not subject to dampness or flooding. They must be readily accessible to telephone service personnel at all times. Equipment loads may be heavy and special structural provisions may be required. It is imperative that the telephone company be consulted in the design of these rooms.

Separate equipment rooms are required in most large installations, especially where switchboards or PBX systems are used. Where direct in and out dialing is used, equipment rooms may not be required.

Risers: Riser cables from the main terminal room to the various floors of the building may be brought up through conduits or shafts, depending upon the type and size of the building. For maximum efficiency they should be centrally located. **Large buildings may require more than one riser shaft.**

Entrance: Telephone service is brought to the building by the telephone company by either underground or aerial cable, depending upon the type of service available in the area. Where the local service is overhead, the entrance to the building may be by underground cable through a conduit provided by the owner according to the specifications of the telephone company.

By L. T. CHANDLER

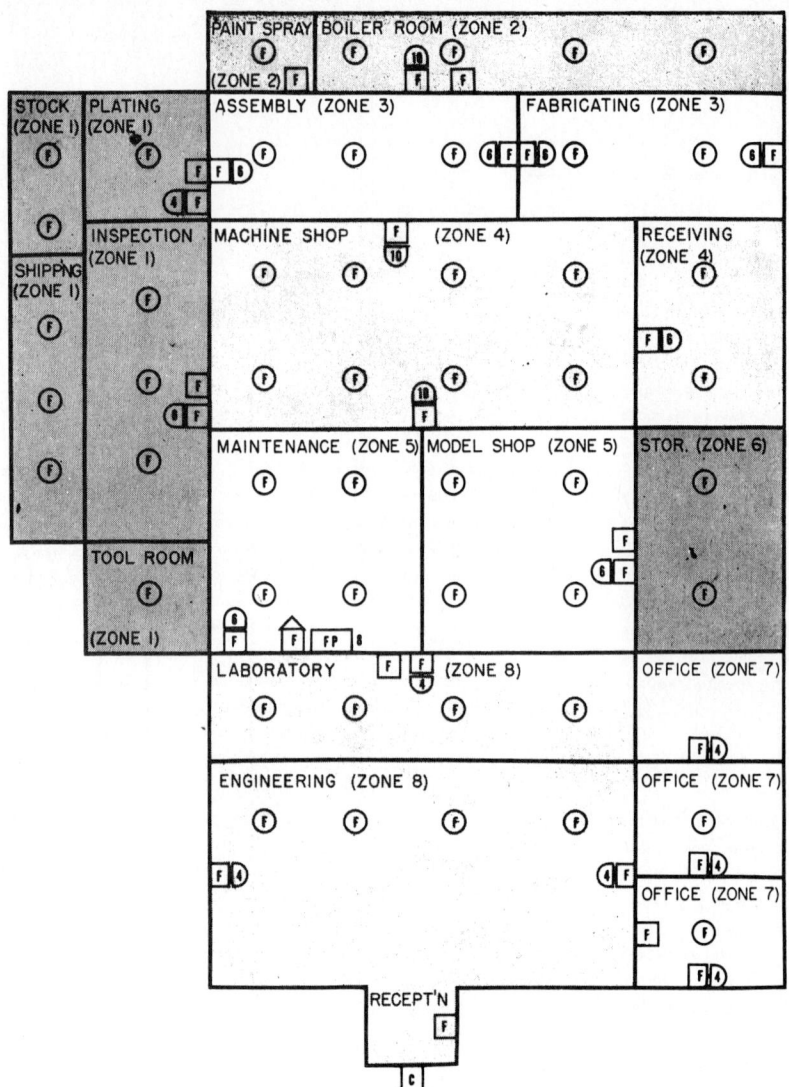

TYPICAL ALARM SYSTEM FOR AN INDUSTRIAL BUILDING

LEGEND

F MANUAL STATION. IN CASE OF CODED SYSTEM, THESE
   STATIONS ARE CODED

F FIRE DETECTOR

F BELL. NUMERAL INDICATES DIAMETER OF BELL
   IN INCHES

F HORN

FP CONTROL PANEL. NUMERAL, IF INCLUDED, INDICATES
    NUMBER OF ZONES

F PRESIGNAL CHIME

F TROUBLE SIGNAL

T EXTENSION TROUBLE SIGNAL

FA ANNUNCIATOR

R PUNCH REGISTER AND TIME STAMP

C CITY FIRE ALARM BOX ON PREMISES

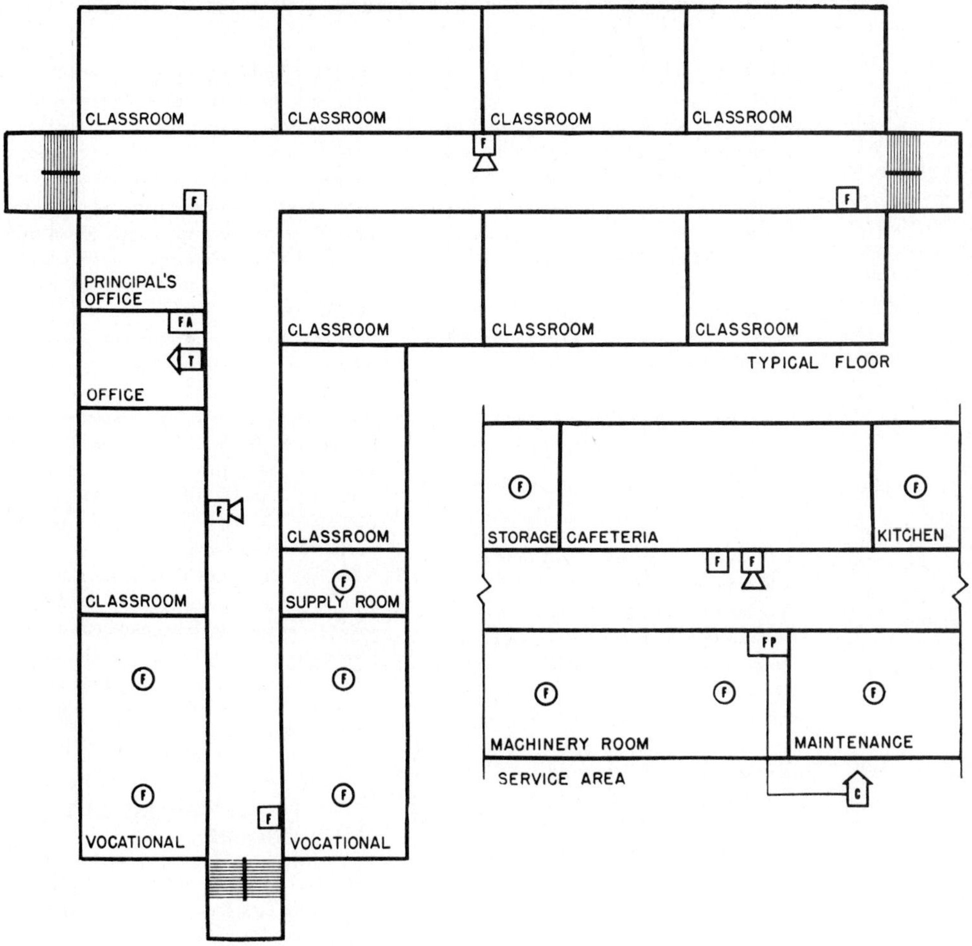

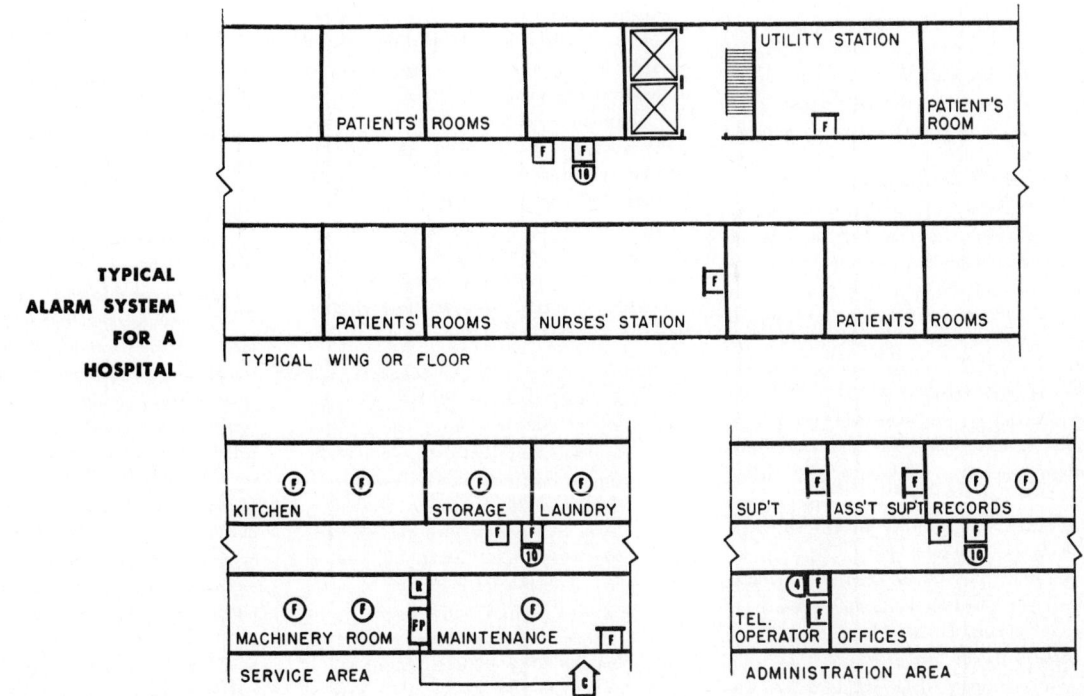

TYPICAL
ALARM SYSTEM
FOR AN
AVERAGE SCHOOL

TYPICAL
ALARM SYSTEM
FOR A
HOSPITAL

SOUND SYSTEMS – 1

Objectives; design considerations

By MELVIN C. SPRINKLE, P. E., Sprinkle & Associates, Consulting Audio-Acoustical Engineers, Kensington, Maryland

SOUND SYSTEM DESIGN PURPOSE AND SCOPE

This section is intended to give the architect or engineer who is charged with the design of a building requiring a sound reinforcement or distribution system an insight into the several considerations which go into an engineered system design. It is not intended to make the reader an "instant expert," but rather it is intended to give enough information so that he or she may talk intelligently on the subject with an audio consultant, acoustical consultant, or other engineer charged with the design of a sound system.

The spectacular growth of FM broadcasting, long-playing phonograph records, magnetic tape recording, and high-fidelity sound equipment have made a large part of the public aware of high-quality reproduction and, hence, more critical of reproduced sound quality. This sophisticated public will no longer tolerate the cheap and inadequate systems that have been prevalent in the past.

WHEN IS A SOUND SYSTEM NECESSARY?

A sound system is required whenever the acoustic power of a talker is unable to create adequate sound levels. A good rule is that a sound system is required when an outdoor talker and audience are separated by 25 ft or more. Indoors, a sound system is generally required in a church or auditorium whose cubic volume is 50,000 ft³ (1416 m³) or more.

THE ACOUSTICAL ENVIRONMENT

It must be kept in mind that a sound amplification or distribution system is *not* a cure for a hostile acoustical environment. A sound system is really an information transferral device, whereby information from a source (talker) is transferred to an audience who hear(s) the message. It is of vital importance, therefore, that the system be designed and constructed so that this mission is fulfilled; not only that the words of the source be heard by the listeners, but also that the listeners be able to understand the message transmitted. The performance of a sound system, even with the best of electronic components can fail if the acoustical environment is unfavorable or if the designer failed to understand the problems associated with poor acoustical properties and designed accordingly.

Recently, two Dutch acousticians, Peutz and Klein, discovered that the comprehension of speech in any language could be measured by the loss of consonants—for it is the consonants which enable one to discern between such phrases as "ma," "pa," "ba," "la," "da," etc. They developed means by which the loss of consonants could be measured and found that if the loss was 15 per cent then comprehension was adequate for the average listener, and that as the per cent loss decreased, the comprehension improved rapidly. Thus they established that a 15 per cent loss of consonants in reproduced speech represents a limiting value, and thereby, is a design requirement in speech reproduction systems.

Peutz and Klein also established the requirements for the acoustical environment in rooms with sound systems. These are:

1. The loss of consonants is affected by the room's reverberation time and by the residual ambient acoustical noise in the room. These factors are interrelated for possible trade-offs.

2. An acoustic signal-to-noise ratio of at least 25 dB is essential for a maximum consonant loss of 15 per cent in rooms whose reverberation time does not exceed 1.6 second(s). Higher noise levels (lower signal-to-noise ratios) may be tolerated if the room's reverberation time is reduced.

3. The reverberation time in any room should not exceed 1.6 s measured in the octave bands centered at 1,000 and 2,000 Hz. A longer reverberation time may be tolerated, provided that the distance from source to listener (or loudspeaker to listener) is correspondingly shortened.

PERFORMANCE OBJECTIVES IN A SOUND SYSTEM

The preceding section has established some of the *acoustical* performance objectives for a sound system. It must be realized that the electrical performance of a sound system means very little except to supply electric energy to the acoustical transducers or loudspeakers, and it is the type, location, and number of loudspeakers which governs sound system performance and success or failure. This fact often creates an unfortunate situation because most sound system designers, especially contractors, are far more familiar with electronics than with acoustics. We can, however, state the performance objectives as follows:

1. The sound must be of adequate loudness. Generally, levels of 75 dBA or a maximum of 80 dBA are satisfactory, since conversational speech between two individuals 2 ft apart is carried on with sound levels at the listener of 70 to 75 dBA. (For music, sound levels of 100–106 dBA are required.)

2. The sound level must be uniform throughout the audience area. This is generally measured with a noise signal in the sound system, and the tolerance is ±3.0 dBA from the 75 to 80-dBA objective.

3. The reproduced speech must have a favorable ratio of direct to reverberant sound—in the same manner as conversation at 2- to 4-ft separation.

4. The reproduced sound must have a natural quality—having approximately the same spectrum shape as the voice of the original source. Thus the sound system *must* contain low frequency reproducers capable of reproducing components of male speech at 100 Hz.

5. The system must have low acoustical distortion. The maximum permissible electrical distortion at rated power should be 2 per cent and this must be maintained over a bandwidth of from 50 to 10,000 Hz inclusive. The loudspeakers must be provided with electric power well within their ratings and must use this power to generate the necessary sound levels.

6. The system must have an adequate electrical signal-to-noise ratio. When no sound is emanating from the loudspeakers, there must be dead silence—no hum or hiss, or crackles. Electric noise should be at least 60 dB below the desired signal at any point in the audio system.

SOUND SYSTEM PLANNING AND DESIGN CONSIDERATIONS

In planning the facilities of a sound system, the following checklist may be of value:

1. The system must have enough microphones, with individual premixing amplifiers and individual gain controls for each. Parallel operation of two or more microphones into a single amplifier input is very poor practice.

2. In the case of conference rooms or churches where several microphones may be in use simultaneously, it is prudent to use an "automatic mixer." Such mixers are now available from at least two manufacturers and are considered later in this section.

3. If a phonograph record player is required, there must be an operator nearby to change records. Disco installations require special considerations and are considered as a separate topic later in this section.

4. Is there a requirement for a magnetic tape recorder-reproducer? Reel-type machines are probably best for overall quality, while cassette machines are preferred for making recordings of conferences, for historical archives, or for transcription to written form. In athletic arenas a cartridge machine of the broadcast type is necessary for reproducing the "charge" bugle call to incite the home team to strive to win the game. Such machines are also useful for reproducing the national anthem at the beginning of a game.

5. Is there a requirement for a radio tuner? If so, it must be equipped with its own antenna to ensure noise-free reception

of the desired stations. The tuner must cover both the AM and FM broadcast bands.

6. Avoid over-complex remote control and/or switching requirements. These are expensive to design and construct and have a tendency to malfunction unless properly designed and carefully made.

7. Is a mixing console needed? All systems with several microphones require some sort of mixing facility. If an operator is required, then the mixing and control are best done in a mixing console of professional-broadcasting-station type. These consoles are well worth their cost.

8. If the system requires an operator at a mixing console, then this operator *must* be located in the same room as the audience, preferably in the rear. It is impossible to operate a sound system from a monitor loudspeaker, especially the 8-in. or smaller variety. Even so, every system should have a monitor loudspeaker in the equipment rack.

9. All equipment must be of professional grade and completely solid-state. Avoid the use of home music equipment or loudspeakers. In general, these units are not suited for sound-system usage.

10. All equipment using 120-V electric power should carry Underwriters Laboratories approval or label and the entire installation must comply with the requirements of the *National Electrical Code* and all local codes.

11. Equipment should be installed in standard 19-in. rack cabinets. Both wall-hung and floor-standing types are available.

12. For systems installed in theaters and auditoriums, do not overlook the installation of a telephone-type intercommunication system. Stations should be provided for the sound operator, the lighting director, the lighting control operator, the stage manager, the prompter's desk, etc.

13. All wiring outside the equipment rack must be housed in ferrous conduit. In general, three independent conduit systems are required:

    a. A conduit system for low-level wiring such as microphone lines. If several microphone wall outlets are used, *separate* microphone wires must be used, one for each individual outlet. It is *not* good practice to parallel microphone wall outlets.

    b. A separate conduit system for "line level" circuits. This is wiring carrying audio signals having power levels from about −15 dBm to +15 dBm.*

    c. A conduit system for loudspeaker lines, either at voice coil impedance

(4, 8, or 16 ohms) or at 25- or 70.7-V distribution. It should be noted that some local electrical codes permit Class II wiring for loudspeaker systems, while others require conduit. Your local code must govern. Naturally, conduit or surface molding must be used where there is a possibility of mechanical abrasion or damage.

14. The mixing system must be equipped with volume unit or VU* meters.

15. Some installations in auditoriums or churches require a special feed for hearing-aid headphones. This should not be overlooked. The headphones should be of a type designed for hearing-aid service. Hi-fi headphones are, in general, unsatisfactory for this service.

16. Will the system require music from a local tape installation or a commercial music service? If so, provision for feeds and switching must be considered.

17. The system should be equipped with a series of telephone-type, "normal through," jacks. These permit instant access to signal paths for emergency equipment substitution or signal sampling, injection, or measurement without disturbing wiring and interconnections.

18. Time delay must be considered. If the system, for example, contains a number of ceiling loudspeakers under a balcony to supplement coverage from a front cluster, then the underbalcony loudspeakers should be fed through a time-delay device so that they receive signals *after* the cluster. In this way, although the audience under the balcony hears sound from their ceiling speakers, it appears to come from the front.

19. The system designer *must* know the acoustical properties of the room in which the system will be installed. In the optimum case, the sound system will be designed by the acoustician who designed the acoustical properties of the room. If the room is in existence, then a competent designer will measure the room's acoustical properties using laboratory-grade acoustical instrumentation. Designs by persons who do not take these factors into account almost always end up with an unsatisfactory system and a dissatisfied owner.

20. The system must be properly specified. An ideal specification will include performance requirements for each major piece of equipment as well as an overall system performance objective. Specifications prepared by contractors almost invariably describe in minute detail the very brand of equipment that they sell; these "purchase order" specifications are almost always based upon merchandising considerations rather than engineering. It is essential that proper equipment be specified, that inferior, cheaper substitutes be prohibited, and that

the job be done at the least cost. This latter condition is assured by specifications which ensure competitive bidding. An often neglected portion of the bidding process is the omission of a system block diagram or drawing, and a conduit riser diagram. These are the minimal requirements.

21. Subsequent to installation, the system should undergo a series of proof-of-performance measurements using professional laboratory-grade electrical and acoustical instrumentation. These measurements may be made by the installing contractor but should be witnessed by a knowledgeable person representing the interests of the architect and owner.

22. Proper *as built* documentation of the system must be provided to the owner by the installing contractor. This consists of drawings, instruction manuals, and proof-of-performance measurements, which are bound into a booklet and given to the owner.

TYPES OF SOUND SYSTEMS

Sound systems can generally be classified according to the following general types:

1. A sound reinforcement system where the objective is to permit the audience to hear well and create the illusion that the sound emanates directly from the talker. This type of system is installed in auditoriums and churches.

2. An announcing system where the objective is to reproduce the voice with clarity and a high degree of comprehension and where the illusion of source location is nonexistent or unimportant. Systems of this type are commonly found in airports, racetracks, sports arenas, etc.

3. A conference room system where there may be many microphones around a conference table and several talkers. In this case the objective is to enable all present in the room to hear and perhaps to make a magnetic tape recording of the proceedings.

4. A music-reproduction system. Such a system would be installed at an outdoor music pavilion or concert shell. It would also be used in radio-TV stations and recording studios as a monitor. Background music systems in offices, hotels, restaurants, etc., are other examples. Some of these systems may be, and often are, stereophonic.

ACOUSTIC GAIN

The acoustic gain of a sound reinforcement system is the improvement in loudness which is achieved by having a sound system. Specifically, it is defined as the ratio of sound level at a listener's ears with the sound system operating to the sound level

---

For explanation of dBm and VU see "Terminology" farther on in this section.

at the same location *without* any amplification.

The maximum acoustic gain which may be achieved in a given installation is controlled by natural laws which engineers call the Nyquist criteria for oscillation. A sound system will go into sing, or acoustic howling, when the reproduced level of sound from the loudspeaker at the microphone location is equal to the sound level from the talker, also at the microphone location. When this condition is attained, the system is said to have unity gain because, at the microphone location, the sound levels from the talker and loudspeaker are equal. The trick in achieving adequate acoustic gain in a sound system is to achieve unity gain at the microphone and more than unity in the audience.

LOUDSPEAKER LOCATIONS

There are two and only two types of loudspeaker locations which have been found to be satisfactory and which are recommended for system design. These are (1) a central cluster of loudspeakers located in the center and at the upper portion of the front of an auditorium, and (2) a distributed system consisting of numerous loudspeakers located in the ceiling of a room and firing sound vertically downward. These two types of installation are also considered in the acoustics subsection in this section. Several common types of loudspeaker locations must be avoided as they never work well and can cause problems with acoustic response and sound quality. These are:

1. *Never* place a loudspeaker on each side of a wide stage. Such installations produce an area of confusion in the middle of the room while listeners on the sides have a very ragged acoustical response due to wave cancellation and addition.

2. *Never* place loudspeakers on both sidewalls of a room with each loudspeaker firing into the center of the room. A system of this type can be made to operate well if the loudspeakers face the rear of the room (instead of firing into the center) and *provided* that the system is equipped with a time-delay mechanism so that sound appears to originate at the front.

3. *Never* place loudspeakers at the corners of a room or on the rear wall firing forward.

TYPES OF LOUDSPEAKERS

In a church or auditorium, the central loudspeaker cluster mentioned above is always composed of one or more direct throw horns of either the multicellular or sectoral type. Folded or re-entrant horns are never used in a quality installation of this type. Re-entrant horns are used in outdoor installations where cost and weatherproofing are considerations. The loudspeaker cluster must be carefully designed for proper coverage and adequate power, remembering that the sound pattern from a downward-angled horn is "keystoned" just as the light pattern from a slide projector would be similarly "keystoned."* The rules of descriptive geometry are used in layout. Highly directive, narrow-beam horns are used for the *long throw* into the rear of the room, with the centerline or axis directed at the rear row of seats. Wider-angled horns with horizontal angles of 60 and 90 deg are used for the *short throw* coverage of the front of the room.

A properly designed loudspeaker cluster always contains low-frequency (LF) or *woofer* loudspeakers. These are usually of the 15-in.-diameter paper-cone type housed in a bass reflex resonant cabinet or in a short exponential horn cabinet. Because these mechanisms are far less efficient than the multicell horns, more electric power must be supplied to them. A good rule is to make the acoustical output power equal to the acoustical power delivered by the high-frequency (HF) units, provided that the woofer power ratings for continuous duty are adequate. Never forget that in a 2% efficient loudspeaker, for 100 W of electric input power, the output consists of 2 W acoustical power and 98 W of heat which appears in the voice coil. Thus in most cluster designs several woofers are used.

Until recently, it was customary for the HF and LF loudspeakers in a cluster to be fed through a dividing or crossover network. This consists of a network of inductors and capacitors which separates the program material into frequencies above and below the crossover frequency and directs them to the proper loudspeaker. For central clusters, the preferred crossover is 500 Hz but where space is a problem and the sound throw is moderate and a less directive HF horn may be used, a crossover frequency of 800 Hz may be used.

In recent years the principle of biamplification has been resurrected from the home-music phonographs of the mid-1930s. In this system, the HF and LF loudspeakers are fed from separate power amplifiers, with the crossover or dividing network ahead of the power amplifiers. Biamplification has much to recommend it and is, wherever possible, the preferred system. Loudspeaker systems with 3-way or 4-way crossovers, which are touted for home-music systems, are never used in professional sound reinforcement.

In the distributed loudspeaker systems, the best practice is to place the loudspeakers in the room's ceiling, firing vertically downward. Loudspeakers for this service are almost always of 8-in. nominal diameter, circular in configuration, and housed in a metal enclosure with perforated decorative grille. Such loudspeakers are suitable in rooms with ceiling heights up to about 20 ft from the floor, or a throw length of 14 to 16 ft depending upon whether the listeners are standing (as at an airport) or seated (as in a night club). For higher ceilings, 12-in.-or even 15-in.-diameter loudspeakers should be considered because they have higher power ratings; the saving being in that fewer units are needed in rooms with higher ceilings. Furthermore, in a high-ceilinged room with a distributed system, the acoustical properties of the room become increasingly important. Consider the fact that only one or perhaps two loudspeakers give direct sound to a listener, while the others in the room excite the reverberant field and thereby tend to degrade the direct-to-reverberant sound ratio. For proper comprehension, a high ratio of direct to reverberant sound is essential.

Recently, several manufacturers have introduced a high-quality, professional grade 4-in.-diameter loudspeaker. Such units have the advantage of a wider coverage angle and are recommended for distributed systems in low-ceilinged rooms where the throw is short and power requirements per loudspeaker are modest.

In the layout of distributed loudspeaker systems, the most common deficiency is the tendency to use too few units. Proper layout is considered later in this section.

Sound column–type loudspeakers are often touted as a panacea for loudspeaker problems. These consist of a series of cone loudspeakers stacked vertically to form a column; the loudspeaker mechanisms are usually of the 4- to 8-in. size. The advantage of the column configuration is that the vertical coverage angle is decreased, while the horizontal coverage is increased. Column loudspeakers have their place and are used in situations where voice-only reinforcement is needed, where the room is quite dead (low reverberation), and where a human source can be heard but needs a little "helping horsepower." The proper location for a sound column is in the center of the front of the room, elevated to be near the ceiling. Only one is used, as two or more cause the same problems as mentioned previously with loudspeakers widely spaced. One disadvantage with sound columns is that when a listener is off the vertical axis by some 40 to 60 deg, a large midrange "bump" occurs in the acoustic frequency response;

---

* The image projected on a plane which is not perpendicular to the axis of the beam will be distorted from rectangular to keystone shape.

this is due to wave addition of sound from the several loudspeakers; it may or may not be objectionable.

TERMINOLOGY

The most common and confusing term encountered by the nonprofessional in audio and acoustical work is the "decibel," commonly abbreviated to dB. This is a dimensionless logarithmic unit expressing a ratio between two powers which may be electric or acoustical. The basic definition of the dB is *always* based upon *power,* although it may be used (often incorrectly) to express ratios of voltage, current, sound pressure, or intensity. (The decibel is further discussed in the *Acoustics* section of this book.) It should be noted that a power ratio of 2:1 (either doubling or halving) is 3 dB; that a power ratio of 4:1 is 6 dB and that a power ratio of 10:1 is 10 dB.

The term dBA refers to decibels read on a standard sound meter with a frequency-rating network which attenuates the low frequencies, much as the human ear does in hearing. Other frequency-rating networks are designed B and C.

Closely allied with the decibel is the term "dBm." This is an *absolute* value of power, expressed in decibel form with reference to 1 milliwatt (mW, 0.001 W). Thus we have the following: 0 dBm is 1 mW; 2 mW is +3 dBm, 1 W (1000 mW) is +30 dBm, 50 W is +47 dBm, 100 W is +50 dBm, etc.; dBm is *identical* to watts except that it is expressed in logarithmic form.

Another unit used in audio work is VU. This is a unit used to measure the level or power of program material in electrical form. The VU is a logarithmic unit with reference to 1 mW (like dBm) except that a special volume-unit meter is used, called the VU (pronounced Vee-You) meter.

A common error is the notion that 0 dBm occurs only in termination resistors of 600 ohms when the voltage is 0.775 V across the resistor. It should be emphasized that dBm is an *absolute* value of power which may be dissipated in resistors of *any value* with the voltage and current being determined by Ohm's law.

BEHAVIOR OF SOUND IN ROOMS

As we are well aware, when a listener walks away from a source (or loudspeaker) the sound level or loudness decreases for a while and then remains fairly constant. When the listener and source are near each other, the listener hears a predominance of direct sound or sound which proceeds directly from the source to the listener. Under these conditions, the listener is said to be in the *direct* sound field. With increased sep-

aration, the sound level dropoff follows the inverse-square law; which is that each time the separation distance is doubled, the sound pressure drops by 6 dB. When the separation is such that the sound pressure dropoff nearly ceases or becomes constant, the listener is said to be in the room's reverberant field. This field is random in the direction of sound arrival and is produced by the innumerable reflections of the sound wave from the source by the walls, ceiling, floor, and the objects in the room. The line of demarcation separating these two fields, is called the *critical distance.* Closely associated with the critical distance is another distance called the *limiting distance.*

This behavior of sound in a room may be determined physically or mathematically through a formula from which a graphic plot is made. The latter course is used when computers or programmable calculators are used in system design.

The critical distance is of extreme importance in sound system design. Any reader who has ever been in a very reverberant room, such as a large church with stone walls, is familiar with the fact that two persons may converse at a normal voice level and with perfect comprehension at a separation of 2 ft. If, however, the separation between the talker and listener is increased to say, 100 ft, then speech is virtually impossible to understand even if the talker shouts to overcome the separation loss. The reason for this effect is that at 2-ft separation, the listener heard almost entirely the direct sound component of the speech, while at the greater distance, the amount of the reverberant component has increased. If the separation is greater than the critical distance, then the listener hears almost entirely the reverberant component. The critical distance is defined as the distance from the sound source at which the sound levels of the direct field and reverberant fields are equal. The limiting distance, mentioned above, is the greatest distance from the source where comprehension is possible; this distance is considered to be 3.16 times the critical distance. At the critical distance, the direct and reverberant sound fields are equal; at the limiting distance the direct field is 10 dB *below* the reverberant field's sound level.

In the layout of a sound reinforcement system in an auditorium, the distance between the microphone near the source and the loudspeaker should be at least equal to the critical distance but not exceeding about 50 ft. The critical distance is within 3 dB of the maximum possible acoustical separation between the two; while the 50 ft represents a distance beyond which the time of transit of sound from the loudspeaker to the microphone will be sufficient

to cause hesitation or impairment of speech fluency in the average talker unless he or she is a skilled orator.

The parameters cited above may be calculated from the formula given below, which originated in a paper by Hopkins and Stryker of the Bell Telephone Laboratories and was later used by Beranek in his text on acoustics:

$$RSPL = 10 \log [(Q/4 \, pl \, r^2) + (4/R)] + 0.5 \text{ dB} \quad (1)$$

where $RSPL$ = relative sound pressure level
Q = directivity factor of sound source
r = distance, ft from sound source to point of consideration
R = room constant, ft^2

The room constant may be calculated from the formula:

$$R = Sa/(1 - a) \quad (2)$$

where S = surface area of room, ft^2
a = average absorption coefficient for room

Example of calculation

Suppose we have an auditorium in the form of a rectangular solid whose dimensions are:

Height	35 ft
Width	55 ft
Length	90 ft
Surface area	20,050 ft^2
Volume	173,250 ft^3

Let us assume two conditions for this room: (1) the walls are concrete and the average absorption is 0.05, and (2) the room has been acoustically treated and the average absorption coefficient is now 0.25.

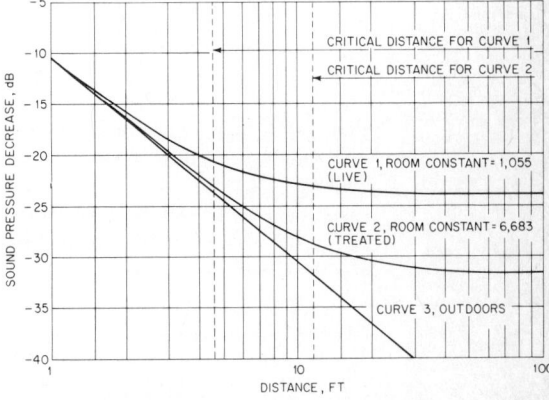

Fig. 1 Loss in sound pressure level from an omnidirectional sound source ($Q = 1$) in example room.

Using Eq. (2) above and the Norris-Eyring reverberation time formula, we have

a	Reverb time, s	Room constant, ft²
0.05	8.25	1,055
0.25	1.47	6,683

Using Eq. (1) above, we have plotted the relative sound loss versus distance for the example room. This is presented in Fig. 1. The three curves represent the decrease in sound for three conditions: (1) room constant, 1,055 (very live room), (2) room constant 6,683 (treated room), (3) outdoors (room constant infinite). It will be seen that for the third case (outdoors) the sound loss follows an inverse-square law in which the loss increases by 6 dB for each doubling of distance. For the other cases, it will be seen that the sound loss departs from the inverse-square low curve and becomes asymptotic to a value which is $10 \log_{10}(4/R)$.

Sound which is transmitted *directly* from a source to a listener follows the inverse-square law relationship. Sound which has been reflected one or more times from room boundaries is called "reverberant sound" and the sound level in the reverberant field is given by the asymptotic value of $4/R$.

If one extends the reverberant field level ($4/R$ line) to the left until it intersects the inverse-square low line, then the distance on the abscissa will be called the critical distance because here the direct field and reverberant field are equal. Dotted abscissas have been drawn at these points. It will be seen that the solid line which represents the actual sound field is 3 dB above the intersection. This follows from the laws of decibel "addition." The decibel is a logarithmic measure and, therefore, the sum of two equal quantities expressed in decibels is 3 dB higher than either.

The critical distance may also be calculated from the following formula:

$$D_c = 0.141 \sqrt{QR} \qquad (3)$$

where Q = directivity factor of sound source
R = room constant, in ft²

In Fig. 1 we assumed a nondirectional sound source for which case $Q = 1$. Using Eq. (3), the critical distance is calculated as Case 1 where $R = 1,055$.

$$D_c = 0.141 \sqrt{1 \times 1,055}$$
$$= 0.141 \times 32.48 = 4.48 \text{ ft}$$

Case 2

$$D_c = 0.141 \sqrt{1 \times 6,683}$$
$$= 0.141 \times 81.75 = 11.53 \text{ ft}$$

Table 1. Directivity (Q) factors for various sound sources

Type of sound source	Approximate Q at 500 Hz
Person talking (no sound system)	2
Typical 8-in. cone loudspeaker (direct radiator) in flat baffle	2
Cone-type "woofer" in short horn	5
Two-way "packaged" system with horn and woofer	8
Theatre system, two-way with multicell and woofer	8
Coaxial two-way system in infinite baffle	5
Multicellular horn	5 to 15 depending upon coverage angle (above 500 Hz)
Sectoral horn	5 to 15 depending upon coverage angle (above 500 Hz)
Sound column	5

Note: *The directivity factors varies with frequency.*

DIRECTIVITY FACTOR

The directivity factor is a dimensionless number which expresses the ratio of sound intensity in a given direction to that at the same point if the same sound source were radiating in all directions (omnidirectional).

An omnidirectional sound source (isotropic source) would radiate sound in a spherical pattern. The directivity factor is 1. If we take such a source and place it on a flat surface (such as the ground), then the same energy is now radiated into a hemisphere so that in the direction of radiation there would be twice the energy, or a directivity factor of 2. If the sound source is placed at the junction of a floor and a vertical wall, the radiation solid angle is 90° in one direction and 180° the other or one-quarter of a sphere. The directivity factor is now 4.

Directivity factors may be obtained for practical sound sources by measurement of the vertical and horizontal radiation patterns and using mathematical formulas to determine the directivity factor from the data.

Since the directivity factor influences the critical distance as much as the room constant, as can be seen from an inspection of Eq. (3), it is important that the Q of a loudspeaker be known. The major manufacturers of sound system loudspeakers have measured the Q factor of their several models and the designer can obtain this information from the manufacturer's engineering department.

For *estimation purposes only* the values of Q in Table 1 may be used.

IMPORTANCE OF ROOM REVERBERATION TIME

The important work of Peutz and Klein in establishing the basic requirements for good hearing and comprehension of speech have been mentioned above. These workers have shown that for a maximum articulation of consonants loss of 15 per cent (which is the maximum value they permitted) it is essential that the farthest listener be no more than about 3.16 times the critical distance. They have also shown that for proper comprehension, the reverberation time of the room be no greater than about 1.75 s for a listener *at this limiting distance.* If, for example, the reverberation time of a sports arena is, say, 5 s, then the distance of the farthest listener must be no greater than about 0.5 times the limiting distance.

Peutz and Klein* found that the per cent articulation loss of consonants could be calculated from the following formula:

$$AL = \frac{200 \times D^2 \times T^2}{V}$$

where: AL = articulation loss in per cent
D = distance of listener from source in meters
T = reverberation time in seconds
V = room volume in cubic meters

Davis† has combined this relationship with the limiting distance ($D_L = 3.16 D_c$) for various values of reverberation time in the form of a ratio between a listener's distance from the source and the limiting distance. The formula is:

$$AL = \left(\frac{D}{D_L}\right)^2 \times 9 \times T$$

where: AL = articulation loss in per cent
D = source-listener distance, any unit
D_L = limiting distance in same units
T = reverberation time in seconds
This equation holds until $D/D_L = 1$ ($D = D_L$) then the per cent loss is simply

* Journal Audio Eng. Soc., *Vol. 19, No. 11, Dec. 1971.*
† *Don Davis, SYN-AUD-CON Lecture Notes.*

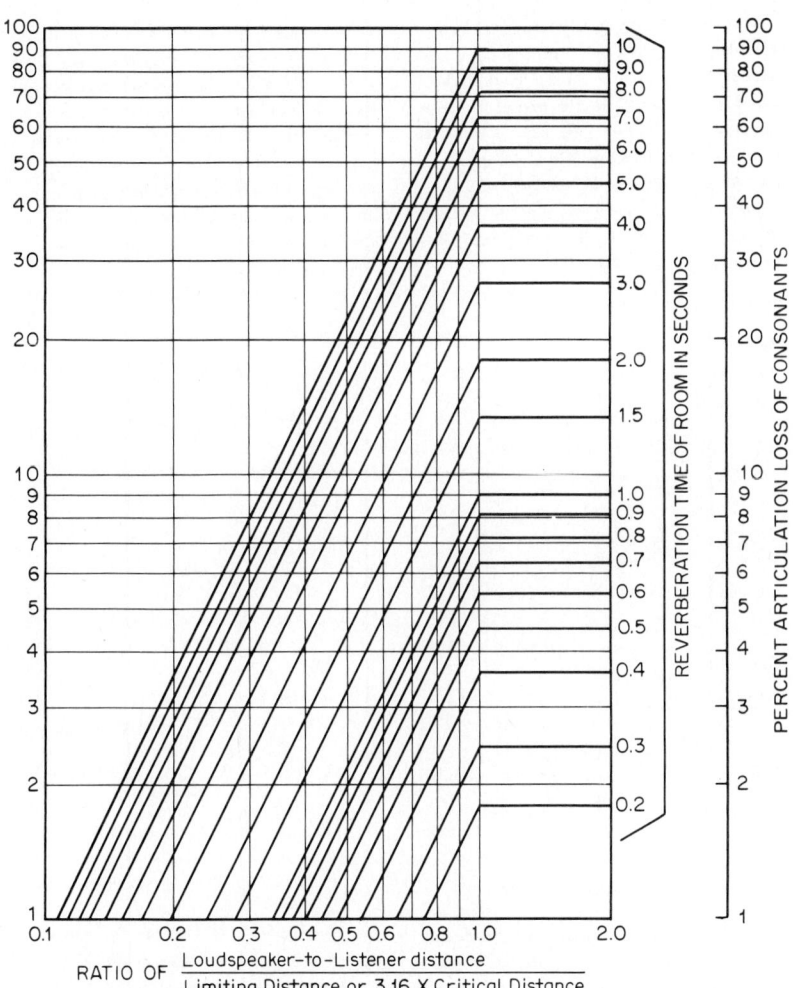

Fig. 2. Articulation loss of consonants as function of source-to-listener distance for several values of reverberation time of room.

(After Davis, Peutz and Klein)

9*T*. The relationship is graphically presented in Fig. 2.

LOUDSPEAKER CONSIDERATIONS

The secret of a sound reinforcement system with good comprehension and uniform sound level over the audience lies in the selection of the type and location of the loudspeakers. As has previously been mentioned, there are *only* two types of locations which are considered as good engineering practice: the central cluster and the ceiling distributed system.

Central-cluster loudspeaker systems either in the front of an auditorium or in the center of a sports arena are always of the two-way type, being composed of one or more straight horns of the multicellular, or sectoral, type supplemented by a number of low-frequency or woofer loudspeakers.

There is no such thing as a voice-only loudspeaker system consisting of horns only *without* complementary low-frequency loudspeakers. Fundamental research into the frequency content of speech reported by Knudsen and Harris from work by Dunn and White, indicate that 50 per cent of speech power lies below 400 Hz, 20 per cent below 250 Hz, and about 2 per cent below 100 Hz. Thus to reproduce speech with naturalness, it is *essential* that the system response be maintained down to 100 Hz.

The low-frequency or woofer loudspeakers are always of the large-diameter (15-in.) paper-cone type and capable of handling high values of electric power (50–100 W). They may be housed in enclosures that employ a short, rapidly tapered horn, or in a properly designed bass reflex enclosure, or in a so-called infinite baffle which is a closed box with a volume of 6 to 10 ft³. In the

latter case, several may be housed in the same enclosure with beneficial results arising from mutual loading effects. The design of low-frequency enclosures is beyond the scope of this article, and best results will be obtained by using the manufacturer's recommended enclosure or bass reflex cabinet. Low-frequency enclosures of the infinite type are usually lined with absorptive fiberglass material, 1 to 2 in. thick.

In selecting horns for a cluster, it should always be remembered that, in general, horns with high Q values are desirable because the Q factor increases the D_c and D_L, desirable conditions for coverage and comprehension.

Loudspeakers for distributed systems commonly employ cone-type direct radiator mechanisms. The most popular size is 8 in., and the usual faults are that an inadequate number are used and that they are housed in baffles or containers which are too small. An adequate baffle for an 8-in. loudspeaker is of the order of 2 ft³ minimum. The commonly specified metal "can" ceiling enclosures have a volume of the order of 500 in.³ which is about ⅛ of an adequate amount.

Eight-inch loudspeakers may be used in ceilings up to about 20 ft in height from the listener's ears. Higher ceilings require 12- or 15-in. loudspeakers in appropriately larger baffle boxes.

Since horns are almost always angled downward, the methods of descriptive geometry must be used to determine the actual floor coverage areas. The coverage problem is especially "sticky" in stadiums with curved seating areas. It is absolutely essential that a plan and elevation drawing of the room be used for loudspeaker layout. Every member of the audience to be covered must be able to "look" directly into the HF horn loudspeaker.

A loudspeaker cluster has considerable weight, and it is essential that the supporting structure be designed by a structural engineer. Provision should be made in the support method for field adjustment of the vertical and horizontal orientation of the horns.

Auditoriums of any size usually require one or more "long-throw" horns with narrow coverage angles (and high Q factor) to cover the rear portion of the room. The front portion of the room is then covered with one or more horns with larger coverage angles, usually of the sectoral type. The long-throw and short-throw territories should slightly overlap.

Should higher Q factors be required, horns may be stacked and aimed to cover the same area. This increases the Q (directivity) factor and also the sound pressure level.

The layout of a distributed system is based upon the coverage pattern of a cone loudspeaker, firing vertically downward from the ceiling. The pattern is a cone with the loudspeaker at the apex. The area of sound coverage is the area of the bottom of the cone, which is circular and whose radius is the tangent of half the cone's apex angle multiplied by the cone's altitude. The apex angle of a cone loudspeaker of the type used in distributed systems should be considered 60° maximum for a high-quality music system and 90° for a typical paging system.

The spacing rule is based upon the fact that one of the objectives in a sound system is uniformity of coverage in the listening area and since the coverage area is a function of the height of the ceiling, this is the parameter which governs the spacing. If the audience is standing, as would be the case at an airport, then the loudspeaker spacing for a 90° coverage angle is

$$D = 2(H - 6) \quad \text{feet} \quad (4)$$

If the audience is seated, as would be the case in an under-the-balcony installation in a church or auditorium, we have

$$D = 2(H - 4) \quad \text{feet} \quad (5)$$

For the highest quality and uniformity, the 60° coverage angle should be used and the speaker spacing becomes

$$D = 1.15(H - 6) \quad \text{feet} \\ \text{for standing audience} \quad (6)$$

$$D = 1.15(H - 4) \quad \text{feet} \\ \text{for seated audience} \quad (7)$$

In all these formulas, H is the floor-to-ceiling height in feet. They are based upon circles touching at either a 4- or 6-ft height above the floor.

In laying out a loudspeaker system, the arrangement may be considerably improved by staggering the rows of speakers. In this arrangement the loudspeaker spacing is in the form of a series of equilateral triangles rather than squares.

The geometry of distributed loudspeaker layout is shown in Figs. 3 and 4. Tables 2 and 3 give values of coverage radius and area for various ceiling heights. The number of loudspeakers may be estimated by dividing the audience area by the coverage area of one loudspeaker.

WARNING ON DISTRIBUTED SPEAKER SYSTEMS

In designing a distributed loudspeaker system, there are several pitfalls in which the unwary may be snared with disastrous results.

Distributed systems work best in rooms or areas with fairly low ceilings. The loud-speakers employed are invariably of the paper-cone type and the usual size is the nominal 8-in. diameter. These loudspeakers have a fairly low Q factor as can be seen from Table 1. Thus, if the ceiling is 20 ft or more in height there is the danger that, with the low Q, the listener, especially if seated, may be at or beyond the limiting distance, D_L. One should check this point carefully.

The second pitfall is that distributed systems never work well in rooms with "live" acoustical properties (long reverberation time). It must be remembered that *only* the loudspeaker directly above the listener is useful in communicating information; the remaining loudspeakers simply dump energy into the reverberant field and increase the ambient noise which in turn impairs information transmittal.

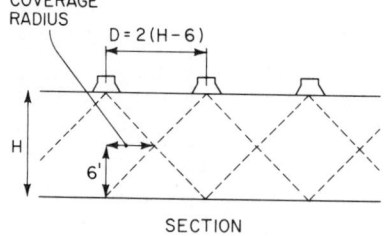

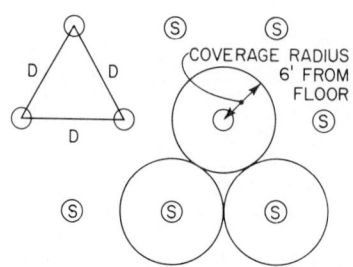

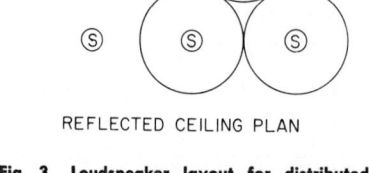

Fig. 3. Loudspeaker layout for distributed system with 90° average angle, voice-only system, standing audience.

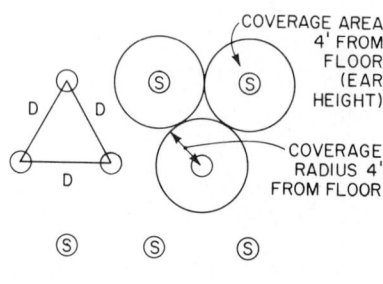

Fig. 4. Loudspeaker layout for distributed system with 60° coverage angle, music and voice, seated audience.

Table 2. Loudspeaker spacing, coverage radius and coverage area for ceiling heights as indicated based upon 90° central angle. Suitable for voice or paging distributed system

Ceiling height, ft	Standing Audience			Seated Audience		
	Spacing, ft	Coverage radius, ft	Coverage area, ft^2	Spacing, ft	Coverage radius, ft	Coverage area, ft^2
9	6	3	28.3	10	5.0	78.5
10	8	4.0	50.3	12	6.0	113.1
11	10	5.0	78.5	14	7.0	153.9
12	12	6.0	113.1	16	8.0	201.1
13	14	7.0	153.9	18	9.0	254.5
14	16	8.0	201.1	20	10.0	314.2
15	18	9.0	254.5	22	11.0	380.1
16	20	10.0	314.2	24	12.0	452.4
17	22	11.0	380.1	26	13.0	530.9
18	24	12.0	452.4	28	14.0	615.8
19	26	13.0	530.9	30	15.0	706.9
20	28	14.0	615.8	32	16.0	804.2
22	32	16.0	804.2	36	18.0	1017.9
24	36	18.0	1017.9	40	20.0	1256.6
26	40	20.0	1256.6	44	22.0	1520.5
28	44	22.0	1520.5	48	24.0	1809.6
30	48	24.0	1809.6	52	26.0	2123.7

Table 3. Loudspeaker spacing, coverage radius and coverage area for ceiling heights as indicated based upon 60° central angle. Suitable for high quality paging or music distributed system

	Standing audience			Seated audience		
	Spacing, ft	Coverage radius, ft	Coverage area, ft²	Spacing, ft	Coverage radius, ft	Coverage area, ft²
9	3.5	1.7	9.4	5.8	2.9	26.2
10	4.6	2.3	16.8	6.9	3.5	37.7
11	5.8	2.9	26.2	8.1	4.0	51.3
12	6.9	3.5	37.9	9.2	4.6	67.0
13	8.1	4.0	51.3	10.4	5.2	84.8
14	9.2	4.6	67.0	11.5	5.8	104.7
15	10.4	5.2	84.8	12.7	6.4	126.7
16	11.5	5.8	104.7	13.8	6.9	150.8
17	12.7	6.4	126.7	15.0	7.5	177.0
18	13.8	6.9	150.8	16.1	8.1	205.3
19	15.0	7.5	177.0	17.3	8.7	235.6
20	16.1	8.1	205.3	18.4	9.2	268.1
22	18.4	9.2	268.1	20.7	10.4	339.3
24	20.7	10.4	339.3	23.0	11.5	418.9
26	23.0	11.5	418.9	25.3	12.7	506.8
28	25.3	12.7	506.8	27.6	13.9	603.2
30	27.6	13.9	603.2	29.9	15.0	707.9

In large rooms such as hotel ballrooms, distributed systems may be improved by the use of time-delay devices. These create the illusion that the sound emanates from the source's location rather than the sky!

As has been mentioned, in rooms with high ceilings, the usual 8-in. loudspeaker simply does not have enough power to generate proper sound levels, and serious consideration must be given to using 12- or 15-in. loudspeakers with more watts per unit and larger enclosures.

ELECTRIC AUDIO POWER REQUIREMENTS

In general, especially until recent years, most sound systems have been underpowered. The reason is that most system designers never realized that the sound generated by loudspeakers follows a decibel law—not a watt law. Thus, doubling the electric audio power into a loudspeaker results in an increase of sound level of 3 dB, and to create a sound level "twice as loud," one must increase the electric power into a loudspeaker by 10 dB which increases the power by a factor of 10.

The electric power ratings of loudspeakers must be carefully observed. The average small-cone loudspeaker used in ceilings has an efficiency of perhaps 2 per cent so that if one feeds it 10 W of sine-wave power, one obtains 0.2 W of acoustical power to generate sound and the remaining 9.8 W of energy appears as heat in the voice coil.

The sound system should be designed using loudspeakers with transducer efficiencies and power-handling capabilities so that the following sound-level objectives are met:

1. For voice announcing systems in airports, or sound reinforcement in auditoriums where the ambient acoustical noise is not over 55 dBA [re 20 micropascals (μPa)], the sound system should lay down an average sound level of 80 dBA (re 20 μPa) and have an available headroom of 10 to 15 dB above this value.

2. For music reproduction systems, especially those used for discos or for rock music, the system should be capable of generating undistorted sound levels of 100 to 106 dB with 10 dB headroom. Such requirements require some amplifiers and loudspeakers of heroic size.

The loudspeaker system *must* be capable of operating at the electric power levels necessary to meet these acoustic objectives on a *continuous* basis, 24 hours per day, 7 days per week.

In certain environments, such as some airports, the ambient acoustical noise levels may be higher than the ideal maximum value of 55 dBA and the sound system must be capable of sound levels 10 dB higher than the ambient noise. Sound-system levels greater than 90 dB are not practicable except in extraordinary circumstances since the ambient acoustical noise is approaching ear-damaging values. A better system is to use one of the several expansion systems made by several manufacturers. These sample the ambient noise and adjust the sound system's level accordingly. A far better system, where practical, is to reduce the ambient acoustical noise.

The sound pressure produced by a given loudspeaker follows a decibel law. The manufacturer will give a sound-level rating for its loudspeaker as producing so many dB sound level at a specified distance from so many electrical watts. To get a 3-dB increase in sound level, the electric *power* fed into the loudspeaker must be increased 3 dB (doubled). For a sound to be judged "twice as loud" the sound level must be increased by 10 dB and the electric level increased by 10 dB (tenfold increase in power). All audio systems must be designed to operate with an average power level 10 dB *below* sine-wave capability or rating. This provides the necessary "headroom" to prevent clipping the peaks and introducing distortion.

These principles are demonstrated in Fig. 5 which is based on an actual loudspeaker performance chart. The manufacturer's data sheet says that a sound level of 97 dB is produced at 4 ft from 1 W electric on axis. On a sheet of two-cycle semi-log paper locate the sound with a dot. Then double the distance to 8 ft and decrease the ordinate by 6 dB and locate another point. Then halve the distance (2 ft) and increase the ordinate by 6 dB. These three points are then connected by a straight line extrapolated to the paper's edge. This line is labeled "1 W + 30 dBm." From this line we can proceed to draw a family of straight lines parallel to the original. We count up the 4-ft ordinate 10 dB and draw another line, labeling it "10 W + 40 dBm."

We can now use this graph sheet for system design. Suppose we have a 12-ft ceiling in an airport corridor and we want to be able to lay down 100-dB sound level to a standing audience. Our throw is 12 − 6 = 6 ft. On the 6-ft abscissa we find that 1 W produces about 94-dB sound level, so to get 100 dB at 6 ft we require a power of 6 dB more than 1 W or a power of 4 W per loudspeaker.

The actual dropoff of sound with distance in a room follows the Hopkins–Stryker curves of Fig. 1, while the above method gives the pure inverse-square loss. Since intelligibility is directly related to direct sound (inverse-square), the method is valid up to the critical distance at which point the loss becomes an asymptote.

The method is valid for horns, giving the on-axis sound. Sound levels off-axis can be determined from the manufacturer's polar plot data.

In the case of low-frequency woofers, the recommended procedure is to supply enough electrical power to overcome their lower efficiency and generate the same *acoustical power in watts* as the far more efficient horns. In this way, a balanced sound quality will be attained. The methods for this calculation are somewhat esoteric and beyond the scope of this article; hence they are best done by an acoustical consultant. In most cases where biamplification is *not* used, the full amplifier power is applied to one or more woofers via the crossover network, and a resistive attenuator is used to pad down the HF horns to compensate for their greater efficiency.

NOISE

All sound systems have an inherent background noise which may or may not be audible but which can be detected and measured. If an adequate signal-to-noise ratio is maintained, then the noise will be inaudible to the listener or so low in sound level as to be unobjectionable. The objectionable noise level occurs not with full signal but with no signal or when the system is silent.

A realistic signal-to-noise ratio value is 60 dB and the minimum acceptable under "economy" conditions is 50 dB. These are measured as the difference between average signal in the output of the power amplifier and the residual hum and noise under no signal conditions.

MICROPHONES

Microphones come in several types, but on a practical basis, there are only two basic types that are used in sound systems. These are: (1) dynamic and (2) condenser or, the preferable term, capacitor microphones. Both the dynamic and capacitor microphones come in two types: (1) omnidirectional and (2) cardioid or directional. The omnidirectional microphone has no real directional pattern and picks up sound equally well from any direction. The cardioid microphone on the other hand is most sensitive to sounds arriving on an axis perpendicular to the diaphragm and least sensitive to sound arriving from the back.

Generally, an omnidirectional microphone has a much smoother frequency response than a cardioid. This is especially true of miniature capacitor mikes which have very smooth response. A smooth response with absence of peaks makes for more gain before sing.

The advantage of the cardioid is that it can be used with care to discriminate against room noises provided that the noise-to-microphone distance is such that the microphone is *not* in the reverberant field.

When a microphone is mounted on a lectern, it is important that only *one* microphone be used. If a lecturer has to move about, or moves consciously or unconsciously, or if he or she moves to a chart or screen to illustrate a point, it is far better to equip him or her with a lavalier microphone. These are light, unobtrusive, and give good voice pickup.

With low impedance microphones and balanced lines, microphone signals may be run for around 100 ft or so without too many problems.

TIME-DELAY CONSIDERATIONS

In many sound-reinforcement situations, it is essential that time delay be considered and perhaps included in the system. Sound travels at "people comfort" temperatures at 1130 ft/s or 0.885 ms/ft. If sound reaches a listener by two *different* paths, and the difference in path length is greater than about 50 ft, then the sound over the longer path will be delayed by 50 × 0.885 = 44 ms.

Two acoustical scientists, Lochner and Berger, found that if two sounds reach a listener within 30 ms, they will combine to reinforce each other and contribute to intelligibility. On the other hand if the time difference between the two signals is 50 ms or more, then there will be garbling and reduction of intelligibility.

Thus in a sound reinforcement system, if there is a low overhanging balcony which blocks a direct throw from a central cluster over center stage, then one should install distributed loudspeakers under the balcony and feed them through a time-delay device. The proper delay time may be calculated by multiplying the difference in path length times the speed of sound as above. In these cases it is also essential that the calculated time delay be *increased* by 20 ms. This is done to take advantage of the Haas or precedence effect in which a listener's hearing is fooled into establishing the origin of a sound as the direction if first arrival. Thus with the extra delay, the sound heard by listeners under the balcony seems to come from the stage, even though they are hearing the ceiling loudspeakers.

Where distributed systems are installed in large rooms such as a hotel ballroom, or where there is a pew-back system in a church, a time-delay system with several zones at intervals of 15 to 20 ms establishes sound origin at the front of the room.

Time delay is an often overlooked essential part of some sound systems and one which can straighten out otherwise garbled locations.

EQUALIZATION

All sound systems employing either two-way loudspeaker clusters or distributed systems with 8-in. or larger loudspeakers should be equalized. The process consists of inserting an equalizing device into the electrical system just ahead of the dividing network in biamplified systems or ahead of the power amplifier in conventional systems. The equalizing device may be either active or completely passive, and consists of a series of loss filters centered on the ISO standard third-octave frequencies. Each filter is individually adjustable with loss varying from 0 to 14 dB. The filters *must* be of the minimum-phase type so that their attenuations combine in additive fashion. Filters with boost characteristics are *not* suitable for sound system equalization.

The objective in system equalization is to make the system response, measured acoustically, flat within say ±2 dB from 100 to 1600 Hz. For systems employing multicell or sectoral horns a rolloff of higher frequencies of about 1 dB per third octave is recommended for a euphonious sound. Monitoring loudspeakers should be made flat to 5000 Hz before allowing a rolloff. Low frequencies below 80 Hz should be rapidly attenuated in sound-reinforcement systems to prevent amplification of unwanted noises such as air-conditioning noise, footfalls, hand thumps on lecterns, ect. Music and monitoring systems should reproduce flat to 50 Hz or so, provided that the loudspeaker is capable of reproducing these low frequencies.

Equalization has two main effects: (1) It makes the system more pleasant to hear; (2) It makes possible a dramatic increase

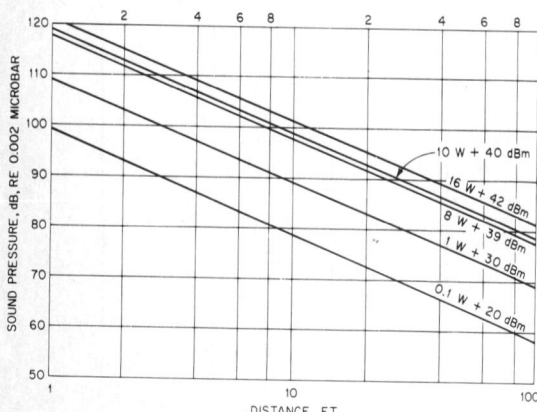

Fig. 5. Loudspeaker performance curves for Altec Lansing 409B, Dukane 5A401, and Jensen K-950.

in acoustic gain which can approach the theoretical value.

It must be thoroughly understood that equalization requires expensive and very specialized instrumentation as well as personnel trained and experienced in the technique. It is folly to attempt equalization otherwise.

It should also be realized that equalization is *not* a panacea for such problems as nonuniform coverage, shoddy or inferior equipment, inadequate power, failure to match the loudspeakers to the room's acoustical properties, etc. Indeed, it has just the opposite effect of emphasizing system deficiencies. It is equally futile to attempt equalization with re-entrant type horns or some types of column loudspeakers.

INSTALLATION

Every sound system, should be installed in a rack-cabinet. These are an adaptation of telephone practice where the rack was found to be the best method of installing equipment.

Commercial racks are standardized for 19-in. width panels; the overall width is 22 in. or so. They come in various heights with the largest practical size providing 77-in. panel space. Usual depth is 18 in.

Small racks which hang on the wall are available. They are double-hinged for access to the rear. Free-standing rack-cabinets must be located so as to give access to both the front and rear.

One conduit system is required for microphone wiring; a separate system for "line level," i.e., power levels from say —10 dBm to +20 dBm; and a third for loudspeaker wiring. All conduits should be of the ferrous type for magnetic shielding (not plastic).

HEAT LOAD

In large systems it is essential that the contractor prepare a thermal budget, which is the amount of heat in Btu per hour generated by the electronic equipment. A conservative method is to add the power consumption of all equipment in watts and then convert to Btuh by the formula:

$$1 \text{ W} = 0.0568 \text{ Btu/min or } 3.414 \text{ Btuh}$$

The heat budget should be discussed with the mechanical engineer so that adequate heat dissipation may be provided in the sound room.

PROOF OF PERFORMANCE

Every sound system should have its performance tested by a series of objective measurements using professional, laboratory-grade, electronic and acoustical equipment. The measurements encompass physical, electrical, and acoustical tests. The test program should include:

1. A visual examination of the installation for neatness, workmanship, appearance, cleanliness, safety, professional practices, and specification compliance.

2. An operational test to determine if the system operates as planned, specified, and desired by the owner, and if all the operational features, facilities, and conveniences specified have been included.

3. A series of electrical tests on the main electronic equipments. These should include (a resistive dummy load is used for these in place of the loudspeakers):
   a. Amplitude-frequency response from microphone input to power amplifier output. An artificial microphone is used to feed signals into the system.
   b. System power output, harmonic distortion and headroom
   c. Freedom from spurious signal pickup and self-oscillation
   d. Overall system signal-to-noise ratio

4. The electric impedance of loudspeaker lines is measured. This is especially important in large distributed systems. The impedance may be measured with a bridge or comparison circuit and should be within ±10 per cent of the calculated value.

5. A series of acoustical measurements using a pink-type random noise signal and the loudspeakers connected. These include:
   a. Additive phase conditions on two-way systems at crossover.
   b. In distributed systems, all loudspeakers should have:
      (1) For identical wattage taps, equal sound level within ±2 dB from each loudspeaker
      (2) All loudspeakers in phase
   c. Uniformity of room coverage within ±3.0 dB using an octave band filter centered at 4000 Hz
   d. All system microphones in additive phase when tested per EIA Standard RS-221
   e. Overall acoustic loudness when system is operating at "normal" levels with pink noise test signal
   f. Overall amplitude-frequency response, measured acoustically subsequent to equalization. Real-time equipment may be used for adjustment of equalization, but a graphic level pen recorder with connected third-octave filter analyzer should be used for a documentary record
   g. System acoustic gain, using a single microphone, then all microphones normally used open simultaneously

TECHNICAL DOCUMENTATION

Every sound system should have a technical documentation package. This consists of a record of the system's design, installation, and test. It is prepared by the contractor in conjunction with the engineer or designer.

An adequate documentation package will contain as a minimum:

1. A copy of the as-built system block diagram, with normal signal levels indicated thereon. Signal levels at jacks or test points are very important for troubleshooting.

2. A rack elevation drawing.

3. Contractor's shop drawings showing the type and location (including aiming information) of loudspeakers.

4. Wiring sheets or drawings showing all equipment interconnections within the rack-cabinet. All wiring in the rack should be identified by a number attached to the wire or cable.

5. Wiring sheets or drawings identifying all system wiring outside the rack-cabinet (microphone lines, speaker lines, etc.).

6. A copy of the proof-of-performance measurement data.

7. Instruction manuals as furnished by the manufacturer for all amplifiers and for any other equipment having such manuals.

8. Specification sheets on equipment such as loudspeakers which would not normally have a full instruction pamphlet.

9. Drawing with patch-panel-jack layout and identification keyed to the system block diagram and with terminal block connection identification.

10. Copies of contractor's shop drawings.

This section presents essential data for preliminary planning of proper space for a pipe organ. Any organ, because it is a wind-driven instrument, must have space to breathe. Its musical value may easily be lost if crowded into inadequate space.

Usually the smallest pipe organ that should be considered for any church should have at least five stops (a "stop" being one complete set of pipes). Such an organ could be used in a church seating up to three hundred people, but its limited variety of tone would be more in keeping with a chapel seating up to one hundred people.

In Table 1, below, church auditoriums have been listed by size together with what normally can be accepted as a minimum and fair size pipe organ. This table is based upon no scientific or musical law and will therefore be a rough guide in early stages of planning. It provides an indication of the minimum number of stops that should be included in the pipe organ for a church of known seating capacity.

Table 2 is a specification for a typical pipe organ installation having eleven stops and one independent pedal stop (a large, deep-toned set of pipes played by foot pedals), and perhaps a set of chimes. The names of the stops in the specifications are given in the picturesque technical nomenclature of the art. The architect will naturally confer with a qualified organist and organ manufacturers and the budget committee before final decisions regarding the specifications are made.

The recommended height for the organ loft is sixteen feet which includes space for pipes and wind chest. However, it is possible to "squeeze" the organ into a twelve-foot height by mitering some of the pipes. The wind chest will determine the length and width of the organ loft. The average length of each chest is 8 ft. 6 in. There will probably be three or more chests, one for each division of the organ ("great," "swell,"

"choir," etc.). The chest width varies with the number of stops that must be mounted on it, allowing not less than nine inches for each stop. In addition to the width of the chest itself there should run parallel to it a walkboard not less than fifteen inches wide, for servicing. See Fig. 1. On three sides of the chest it would be well to add one foot for the installation of the bass pipes, which may not be installed on the wind chest because of their large size.

The required space for each division of the organ can be estimated as follows: (See Fig. 1)

1. Height = 12' to 16'
2. Length = 8'-6" (Length of wind chest) + 2'-0" (1' on each end for bass pipes), a total of 10'-6".
3. Width = (number of stops) times 9" + 15" (walkboard) + 1' 0" (for base pipes).

TABLE 1
Number of Manual Stops

No. of Seats	Min.	Fair	No. of Manuals
100 or less	5	8 to 10	2
250	6	12 to 15	2
400	8	15 to 20	2-3
600	10	20 to 30	2-3
800	12	25 to 35	2-3-4
1000	15	35 to 40	2-3-4
1500	20	40 to 45	3-4
2000	30	50 to 75	3-4

TABLE 2

Stop Name	No. of Pipes
Great Organ	
8' Diapason	73 Pipes
8' Clarabella	73 Pipes
4' Octave	73 Pipes
8' Tromba	73 Pipes
8' Stopped Flute ⎫	From
4' Flute d'Amour ⎬	
8' Aeoline ⎭	Swell
Chimes	20 Tubes
Swell Organ	
8' Diapason	73 Pipes
16' Bourdon ⎫	
8' Stopped Flute ⎪	97 Pipes
4' Flute d'Amour ⎬	Unit Stop
2' Flageolet ⎭	
8' Viole d'Orchestre	73 Pipes
8' Viole Celeste	73 Pipes
8' Aeoline	73 Pipes
8' Oboe	73 Pipes
8' Vox Humana	73 Pipes
Pedal Organ	
16' Bourdon	44 Pipes
8' Flute	From Bourdon
16' Gedeckt ⎫	From
8' Stopped Flute ⎭	Swell

TABLE 3

	Pipes	Length	Width	Height
1. Bourdon	16'	44	13'6"	3'6"	10'6"
2. Open Diapason	16'	44	12'0"	2'6"	19'0"
3. Trombone	16'	44	10'4"	1'4"	12'0"*
4. Violone	16'	44	10'4"	1'5"	19'4½"
5. Diapason	32'	12	18'9"	3'8"	34'9"
6. Bombarde	32'	12	10'3"	2'4"	23'0"*
7. Second Bourdon	16'	44	Same as No. 1 approx.		
8. Metal Diapason	16'	44	8'9"	2'9"	21'0"
9. Bourdon	32'	12	15'3"	2'0"	18'0"

*—Average mitered length.

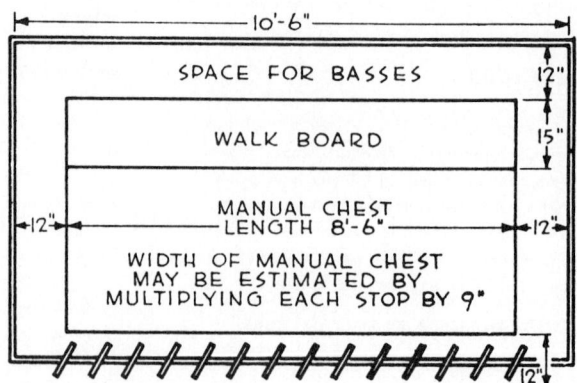

Fig. 1. Above plan is one section of total organ shown below

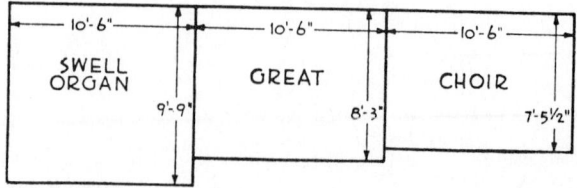

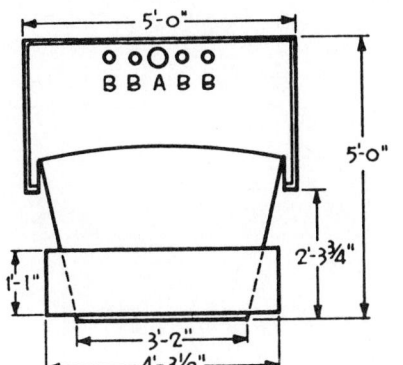

A 2"-3" CONDUIT, LOW VOLTAGE, CONSOLE TO ORGAN MECHANISM.

B ONE EACH OF FOLLOWING: 1"-1½" CONDUIT TO LOW VOLTAGE FEED LINES AT GENERATOR. ¾"-1" CONDUIT, MOTOR STARTING LINES FROM CONSOLE TO BLOWER MOTOR. CONDUIT, LIGHTS TO CONSOLE. CONDUIT TO CHIME OR CARILLON.

Fig. 2. Plan of organ console

The average organ console is about 4 ft 3 in. high. An organ having more than three manuals requires 3 in. additional height for each manual added.

These figures would hold good for a pipe organ having up to twelve stops; over that it would be well to allow two feet on three sides of the chest for bass and other large parts that may require extra room.

There still remains for consideration the space that will be required by the pedal organ. Recalling that there should be at least one pedal stop for every six or seven manual stops, it will be necessary to know which stops are most likely to be installed first. Table 3 gives the name and size of the pedal stops in the usual order. To determine which will be used and the size of the pipes, determine how many pedal stops

the manual stops require on the basis of one to six or seven, and then take the required number of pedal stops in order, starting at the top of the list.

In order to supply air to the organ an electrically driven blower, similar to that shown in Fig. 3, will probably be used. From the chart and this diagram it is possible to determine the size of the room required for housing the blower, the weight of the equipment, and the size of the air duct. The horsepower required for the blower will have to be determined by the organ manufacturer. The room housing the blower, usually located below the organ, should allow

standing height and a clearance of at least 15 in. on all sides.

Electronic organs are being increasingly used, especially in the smaller churches. They cost considerably less than pipe organs and require much less space. The console is usually somewhat smaller than for a pipe organ, and the only additional space required is for one or more speakers. Electronic organs may also provide carillon effects.

Carillons require an average space of 11 ft. square by 7 ft. high. They are usually electrically operated from a small keyboard about 18 in. long by 12 in. deep. The carillon speaker is usually located in the tower.

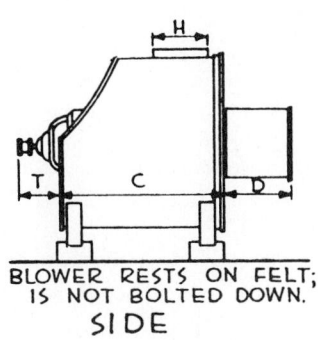

BLOWER RESTS ON FELT; IS NOT BOLTED DOWN.
SIDE

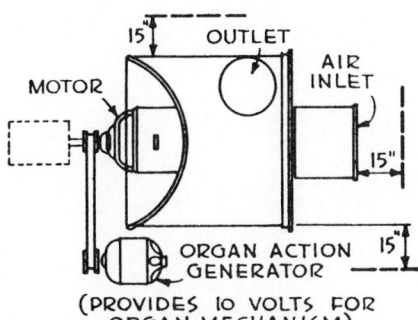

(PROVIDES 10 VOLTS FOR ORGAN MECHANISM) (MAY BE IN DOTTED POSITION AT LEFT)
PLAN

FRONT

DIMENSIONS IN INCHES

HORSE POWER	½ *	¾	1	2	3	5	7½
B	27	33½	33½	40	40	46	46
C	22	25	28½	31	36	38	38
D	12	15	15	15	15	15	15
F	34	40	40	46	46	53	53
H	8	10	12	12	15	15	15
T	5	5	7	7	9	10	10

WEIGHT IN POUNDS

WEIGHT (LBS)	400	650	700	950	1025	1150	1300

* SPEED: 1750 R.P.M.   ALL OTHER MOTORS: 1150 R.P.M.

Fig. 3. Plans and chart below may be used to determine the space required for blower room

By ALBERT R. RIENSTRA

Church Design for Music

Reverberation Times

Figure 4 gives reverberation times for church auditoriums from 10,000 to 1,000,000 cu ft in size. These values are higher than generally used for other types of auditoriums because with them organ music is enchanced a great deal and choral music somewhat. While the reverberation times for churches may fall within the range indicated by the gray band, it is recommended that the upper limit be used if possible.

The values in Fig. 4 are absolute reverberation times for the frequency range from 300 to 5,000 cps. Fig. 5, then, gives correction factors to be applied to Fig. 4 for frequencies outside this range.

Organ Space Requirements

Fig. 6 can be used as a guide for the allotment of pipe organ space. Fig. 6A gives dimensions of the pipe space required for organs installed in one section. Solid lines apply when pedal pipes are at the sides and dotted lines when they are in the rear of this section. In large churches it becomes necessary to install the pipes in two or three sections and these situations are covered in Fig. 6B. The depth curves here have a saw-tooth shape, a tooth occurring at every place where the width increases a step. The height of organ space has only two values; 13 ft and 20 ft. If there are no 16-ft open pipes, at least 13 ft height is required for the open, 8-ft pipes. For 16-ft open pipes, at least 20-ft height is required. The height then remains constant until 32 ft pipes come into the picture. For this size, it is not possible to give estimates of space as this falls into the four manual (keyboard) and cathedral classes, and each installation becomes a special one. In the region just below this, after the depth has increased to the second maximum (Fig. 6B) three-keyboard organs are specified. For this size, a third section of width may be added, the choir-pipe division, which is placed on one side of the chancel with the swell division on the other.

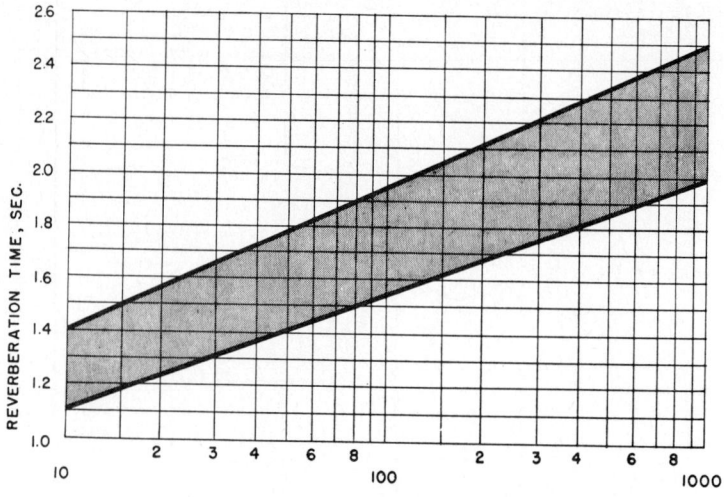

Fig. 4

ROOM VOLUME - THOUSANDS OF CUBIC FEET

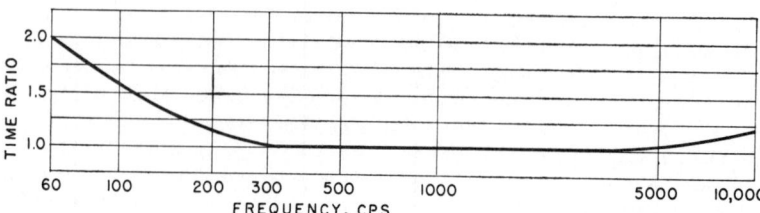

Fig. 5

FREQUENCY, CPS

Modified from Beranek

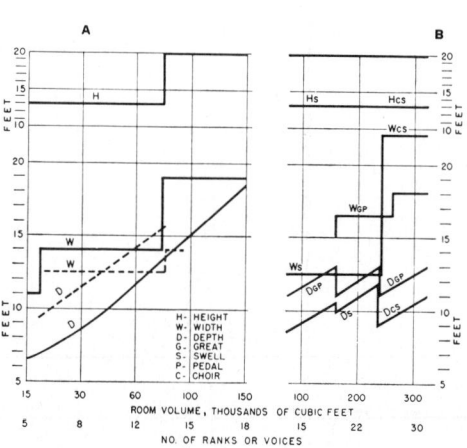

Fig. 6

H- HEIGHT
W- WIDTH
D- DEPTH
G- GREAT
S- SWELL
P- PEDAL
C- CHOIR

ROOM VOLUME, THOUSANDS OF CUBIC FEET

NO. OF RANKS OR VOICES

5

Metric Units in Building

Metric Units in Building

The following standard is reprinted with the permission of the copyright owner, the American Society for Testing and Materials, 1916 Race Street, Philadelphia, Pennsylvania 19103. It is complete except for four minor excisions made to save space. The spelling of *metre* and *litre* used by ASTM differs from the alternate spelling (*meter* and *liter*) normally used as McGraw-Hill's editorial standard. Both spellings are accepted by ANSI.

ANSI/ASTM E 621-78
Standard Practice for the Use of
METRIC (SI) UNITS IN BUILDING DESIGN
AND CONSTRUCTION
(COMMITTEE E-6 SUPPLEMENT TO E 380)

This Standard is under the fixed designation E 621; the number immediately following the designation indicates the year of original adoption or, in the case of revision, the year of last revision. A number in parentheses indicates the year of last reapproval.

This practice has been approved for use by agencies of the Department of Defense and for listing in the DoD Index of Specifications and Standards.

INTRODUCTION

The International System of Units (SI) was developed by the General Conference on Weights and Measures (CGPM), which is an international treaty organization. The abbreviation SI, derived from the French "Système International d'Unités," is used in all languages.

SI is a rational, coherent, international, and preferred measurement system which is derived from earlier decimal metric systems but supersedes all of them.

The use of the metric system in the United States was legalized by an Act of Congress in 1866, but was not made obligatory.

On December 23, 1975, Public Law 94-168, "The Metric Conversion Act of 1975," was signed by President Ford, committing the United States to a coordinated voluntary conversion to the metric system of measurement. The Act specifically defines the "metric system of measurement" as "the International System of Units as established by the General Conference on Weights and Measures in 1960, and as interpreted or modified for the United States by the Secretary of Commerce."

There have been refinements of the system since 1960, and the United States has a special opportunity to change from the outdated customary system to the most up-to-date international system in one single step.

In the building design and construction community the application of SI units, together with preferred numerical values, will simplify and speed up calculations and facilitate all measurement intensive activity.

This document has been prepared to provide a single, comprehensive, and authoritative standard for SI units to be used in building design, product manufacture, and construction applications.

List of Tables

Appendixes

1. Scope

1.1 This standard outlines a selection of SI units, with multiples and submultiples, for general use in building design and construction.

1.2 In addition, rules and recommendations are given for the presentation of SI units and symbols, and for numerical values shown in conjunction with SI.

1.3 A selection of conversion factors appropriate for use within the construction community is given in Appendix X1.

1.4 The SI units included in this document comply with and augment the ASTM Standard for Metric Practice E 380 – 76 (also identified as American National Standard Z210.1 – 1976 or IEEE Std 268 – 1976), and are generally consistent with ISO 1000 – 1973 (E), SI Units and Recommendations for the Use of Their Multiples and Certain Other Units.

2. Definitions

2.1 *SI* – The International System of Units (abbreviation for "le Système International d'Unités) as defined by the General Conference on Weights and Measures (CGPM) – based upon seven base units, two supplementary units, and derived units, which together form a coherent system.

2.2 *quantity* – measurable attribute of a physical phenomenon. There are base units for seven quantities and supplementary units for two quantities upon which units for *all* other quantities are founded.

2.3 *unit* – reference value of a given quantity as defined by CGPM Resolution or ISO Standards. There is *only one* unit for each quantity in SI.

2.4 *coherent unit system* – system in which relations between units contain as numerical factor only the number "one" or "unity," because all derived units have a unity relationship to the constituent base and supplementary units.

2.5 *numerical value of a quantity* – magnitude of a quantity expressed by the product of a number and the unit in which the quantity is measured.

3. The Concept of SI

3.1 The International System of Units (SI) was developed to provide a universal, coherent, and preferred system of measurement for world-wide use and appropriate to the needs of modern science and technology.

3.2 The principal features of SI are:

3.2.1 There is only one recognized unit for each physical quantity.

3.2.2 The system is fully coherent; this means that all units in the system relate to each other on a unity (one-to-one) basis.

3.2.3 A set of internationally agreed prefixes can be attached to units to form preferred multiples and submultiples of 10 raised to a power that is a multiple of 3. This provides for convenient numerical values when the magnitude of a quantity is stated.

3.2.4 Units and their prefixes are represented by a set of standardized and internationally recognized symbols.

3.3 Because of their practical significance, the use of additional non-SI units in conjunction with SI is permitted for some quantities.

3.4 SI units, permissible non-SI units, and prefixes are discussed in Sections 4, 5, and 6.

4. SI Units

4.1 The International System of Units (SI) has three classes of units:

4.1.1 Base units for independent quantities,

4.1.2 Supplementary units for plane angle and solid angle, and

4.1.3 Derived units.

4.2 The seven base units and two supplementary units are unique units which, except for the kilogram (Note 1), are defined in terms of reproducible phenomena.

NOTE 1 – The primary standard for mass is the international prototype kilogram maintained under specified conditions at the International Bureau of Weights and Measures (BIPM) near Paris in France.

4.3 Derived units can all be defined in terms of their derivation from base and supplementary units. They are listed in two categories:

4.3.1 Derived units with *special* names and symbols, and

4.3.2 Derived units with *generic* or complex names.

4.5 Table 1 contains base, supplementary, and derived units of significance in design and construction, listing:

4.5.1 Quantity,

4.5.2 Unit name,

4.5.3 Unit symbol,

4.5.4 Unit formula,

4.5.5 Unit derivation (in terms of base and supplementary units), and

4.5.6 Remarks.

5. Non-SI Units for Use with SI

5.1 There is an additional group of acceptable, but non-coherent traditional units retained in association with SI, because of their practical significance in general applications.

5.2 Non-SI units of significance to design and construction are shown in Table 2, under two categories:

5.2.1 Units for general use, and

5.2.2 Units for limited application only.

5.3 Appendix X2 shows a group of superseded metric units not recommended for use with SI in design and construction applications.

6. SI Unit Prefixes

6.1 SI is based on the decimal system of multiples and submultiples, and therefore the use of common fractions is minimized. Multiples are formed by attaching standard prefixes to SI units.

6.2 Preferred multiples range in geometric steps of 1000 (10^3) up to 10^{18}; submultiples range in geometric steps of 1/1000 (10^{-3}) down to 10^{-18}.

6.3 *Preferred Multiples and Submultiples* – The preferred prefixes shown in Table 3 are relevant in design and construction. Prefixes outside the range 10^{-6} (micro) to 10^6 (mega) will occur only in rare instances.

6.4 *Other Multiples for Limited Application* – SI includes a number of additional historically used multiples and submultiples, shown in Table 4, but these should be avoided as far as possible.

7. Rules and Recommendations for the Use of SI

7.1 Two tables of rules and recommendations have been prepared to facilitate the correct application of SI units and symbols and the correct presentation of units, symbols, and numerical values shown in conjunction with units and symbols.

7.2 Table 5 gives "Rules and Recommendations for the Presentation of SI Units and Symbols."

7.3 Table 6 gives guidance on "Presentation of Numerical Values with SI."

7.4 The tables provide a convenient reference guide for the editorial checking of metric documents to ensure that the presentation of data is in line with accepted practice.

8. SI Units for Use in Design and Construction

8.1 Correct selection of units for use in building design calculations and in documentation is essential to minimize errors and to optimize the coordination between the various sectors and groups within the construction community.

8.2 Tables 7 to 12 list SI units, and other units acceptable with SI as recommended, for use in building design and construction related activities. Where appropriate, working ranges are indicated for selected units, and typical examples of their field(s) of application provided. In addition, explanatory remarks are provided to briefly deal with special considerations.

8.3 The following subdivision, similar to that used for ISO 1000, has been adopted:

Table 7	Space and Time: Geometry, Kinematics, and Periodic Phenomena
Table 8	Mechanics: Statics and Dynamics
Table 9	Heat, Thermal Effects, Heat Transfer
Table 10	Electricity and Magnetism
Table 11	Lighting
Table 12	Acoustics

8.4 *Preferred Range of Values* – The use of an appropriate unit or multiple of a unit depends upon the context in which it is used.

8.4.1 In printed or typed material it is preferable to use numbers between 1 and 1000, wherever possible, by selecting an appropriate prefix. For example: 725 m is preferred to 0.725 km or 725 000 mm.

8.4.2 If the numerical quantity is part of a group of numbers in a different range, select the prefix that most adequately covers the range, without unduly large or small numbers. For example: If 725 m is part of a group of numbers shown in kilometres, show it as 0.725 km.

8.4.3 Although physical data generally should be presented in the most condensed form possible, by using appropriate prefixes, it will be advantageous in calculations to use exponential notation, instead of prefixes, for example: 900 mm^2 = 0.9 × 10^{-3} m^2; 36 MPa = 36 × 10^6 Pa = 36 × 10^6 N/m^2.

8.4.4 In drawings it will be of advantage to show one measurement unit throughout, so that numerical values can be represented by numbers only, and the unit symbol can be deleted. For example, in a drawing on which all dimensions are shown in millimetres, 5-digit numbers (indicating millimetres) are quite acceptable.

9. Special Considerations in the Use of SI Units in Building Design and Construction

9.1 *Linear Measurement (Length):*

9.1.1 The preferred units for measurement of length in building design, construction, and production are the millimetre (mm) and the metre (m).

9.1.2 In special applications, the kilometre (km) is used for the measurement of long distances, and the micrometre (μm) is used for precision measurements.

9.1.3 The centimetre (cm) is to be avoided in all building design and construction applications.

9.1.4 The reasons for the deletion of the centimetre are:

9.1.4.1 The centimetre is not consistent with the preferred use of multiples that represent ternary powers of 10.

9.1.4.2 The order of magnitude between millimetre and centimetre is only 10, and the use of both units would lead to confusion.

9.1.4.3 The millimetre (mm) provides integers within appropriate tolerances for all building dimensions and nearly all building product dimensions, so that decimal fractions are almost entirely eliminated from documents. In contrast, acceptance of the centimetre would inevitably lead to extensive use of decimal fractions, which is undesirable.

9.1.5 On drawings, unit symbols may be deleted if the following rules are applied:

9.1.5.1 The drawing is designated "all dimensions shown in millimetres unless otherwise noted" or "all dimensions shown in metres unless otherwise noted."

9.1.5.2 Whole numbers always indicate millimetres, for example, 3600; 300; 25.

(*1*) Any length up to 328 ft can be shown by a simple 5-digit number, for example, 327 ft 10¹¹/₁₆ in. = 99 941 mm.

(*2*) Similarly, any length up to 32 ft 9 in. can be shown by a 4-digit number; any length up to 3 ft 3⁵/₁₆ in. can be shown by a 3-digit number.

(*3*) Decimalized expressions taken to three places always indicate metres, for example, 3.600; 0.300; 0.025.

9.1.6 The use of millimetres and metres, as recommended, saves both space and time in drawing, typing, and computer applications, and it also improves clarity in drawings with a lot of dimensions.

9.1.7 *Survey Measurement* — The change to SI units will also eliminate the discrepancies between "international" foot and "U.S. survey" foot, "international" mile and "U.S. survey" mile (the survey mile is approximately 3 mm longer), and corresponding derived units for area measurement.

NOTE 2 — Since 1893, the U. S. basis of length measurement has been derived from metric standards. In 1959, the definition of the length of the "foot" was changed from 1200/3937 to 0.3048 m exactly, which resulted in the new value being shorter by two parts in a million.
At the same time it was decided that any data derived from and published as a result of geodetic surveys within the United States would remain with the old standard.

Thus all land measurements in U. S. customary units are based upon the "U. S. survey foot" which relates to the metre by the old standard (1200/3937 = 0.304 800 6 m).

9.2 *Area:*

9.2.1 The preferred unit for area measurement is the square metre (m²). Very large areas can be expressed in square kilometres km²), and small areas will be expressed in square millimetres (mm²), or in square metres using exponential notation (for example, 10⁻⁶ m²).

9.2.2 The hectare (ha) is used for land and water measurement *only*. (1 ha = (100 m)² = 10 000 m² = 10⁴ m² = 10⁻² km²).

9.2.3 The square centimetre (cm²) is to be avoided to minimize confusion. Any measurement given in square centimetres should be converted to square millimetres or square metres. (1 cm² = 100 mm² = 10⁻⁴ m²)

9.2.4 At times, it will be more appropriate to indicate the surface or cross-sectional area of building products by linear dimensions, for example, 40 by 90 mm; 300 by 600. It is preferred practice to indicate the width dimension first and height second.

9.3 *Volume and Fluid Capacity:*

9.3.1 The preferred unit for measurement of volume in construction and for large storage tank capacities is the cubic metre (m³).

9.3.2 The preferred units for measurement of fluid capacity (liquid volume) are the litre (L) and the millilitre (mL).

9.3.3 By international definition, in 1964, the litre is equal to one thousandth of a cubic metre or one cubic decimetre (dm³). (1 L = 10⁻³ m³); (1 L = 1 dm³); (1 m³ = 1000 L)

9.3.4 Because the cubic metre contains one billion (10⁹) cubic millimetres, the cubic decimetre (dm³) and the cubic centimetre (cm³) may find limited application, particularly as they represent preferred steps of 1000 in volume measurement. It is suggested that any such cases be converted to preferred units for volume measurement as shown in Table 13.

9.4 *Geometrical Cross-Sectional Properties:*

9.4.1 The expression of geometrical cross-sectional properties of structural sections involves raising the unit of length to the third, fourth, or sixth power. Values can be shown either in mm³, mm⁴, or mm⁶ with exponential notation, or in m³, m⁴, or m⁶, with exponential notation.

9.4.2 The following are appropriate measurement units:

9.4.2.1 Modulus of section:
$$\text{mm}^3 \text{ or m}^3 \ (1 \text{ mm}^3 = 10^{-9} \text{ m}^3);$$

9.4.2.2 Second moment of area or torsional constant:
$$\text{mm}^4 \text{ or m}^4 \ (1 \text{ mm}^4 = 10^{-12} \text{ m}^4);$$

9.4.2.3 Warping constant:
$$\text{mm}^6 \text{ or m}^6 \ (1 \text{ mm}^6 = 10^{-18} \text{ m}^6).$$

9.4.3 The cross-sectional properties of a wide-flange beam, 460 mm deep with 82 kg/m mass per unit length, could be expressed as follows:

9.4.3.1 Plastic modulus, Z_x
= 1.835×10^6 mm³ or 1.835×10^{-3} m³;

9.4.3.2 Second moment of area, I_{x-x}
= 0.371×10^9 mm⁴ or 0.371×10^{-3} m⁴;

9.4.3.3 Torsional constant, J
= 0.691×10^6 mm⁴ or 0.691×10^{-6} m⁴;

9.4.3.4 Warping constant, C_w
= 0.924×10^{12} mm⁶ or 0.924×10^{-6} m⁶.

9.5 *Plane Angle:*

9.5.1 While the SI unit for plane angle, the radian (rad), should be used in calculations for reasons of its coherence, the customary units of angular measure, degree (°), minute ('), and second (") of arc are likely to continue to be used in many applications in cartography and surveying.

9.5.2 The degree (°). with parts denoted by decimals (as in 27.25°). is likely to be utilized in engineering and in construction.

9.6 *Time Interval:*

9.6.1 In general applications, the day (d), hour (h), and minute (min) are permitted non-SI alternatives to the SI base unit for time, the second.

9.6.2 It is recommended that the minute (min) be avoided as far as possible to minimize the variety of units in which time is a dimension.

9.6.3 For instance, *flow rates* should be expressed in cubic metres per second, litres per second, or cubic metres or litres per hour, rather than in cubic metres per minute or litres per minute. For example:

1 m³/s = 1000 L/s	(DO NOT USE 60 m³/min)
1 L/s = 3.6 m³/h	(DO NOT USE 60 L/min)
1 m³/h = 1000 L/h	(DO NOT USE 16.67 L/min)

9.6.4 Because of its variability, the month should not be used to indicate a time dimension, unless a specific calendar month is referred to.

9.6.5 Where the calendar year (symbol "a") is used as a measurement for time interval, it represents 365 days or 31 536 000 s.

9.7 *Temperature and Temperature Interval:*

9.7.1 The SI base unit of (thermodynamic) temperature is the kelvin (K), and this unit is used for expressing both thermodynamic temperature and temperature interval.

9.7.2 Wide use is also made of the degree Celsius (°C) for the expression of ambient temperature levels in Celsius temperature and temperature intervals.

9.7.3 The temperature interval of one degree Celsius equals exactly one kelvin. For this reason, the degree Celsius (°C) may be used instead of the kelvin in calculations involving temperature interval.

9.7.4 A temperature expressed in degrees Celsius is equal to the temperature expressed in kelvins less 273.15. There are no negative (minus) temperature values in the kelvin scale.

9.8 *Mass, Weight, and Force:*

9.8.1 A significant feature of SI is the use of explicit and distinctly separate units for "mass" and for "force."

9.8.2 The SI base unit *kilogram* (kg) denotes the *base unit of mass* (the unit quantity of matter of an object which is constant and independent of gravitational attraction).

9.8.3 The derived SI unit *newton* (N) denotes the *absolute derived unit of force* (mass times acceleration: kg · m/s²).

9.8.4 The general use of the term "weight" should be avoided in technical practice for the following reasons:

9.8.4.1 Considerable confusion exists because the term "weight" has been used to mean either "mass" or "force of gravity."

9.8.4.2 In commercial and everyday use, the term "weight" has nearly always meant mass.

9.8.4.3 In technical use, the term "weight" has often been applied to mean "force of gravity," a *particular force*, related solely to gravitational acceleration, which varies on the surface of the earth.

9.8.4.4 Where quantities are shown as "weight" it is important to establish whether "mass" or "force" is intended, and to use the appropriate SI units, that is, kilogram for "mass" and newton for "force."

9.8.5 As serviceable as customary gravitational systems may seem in the area of "statics," the absolute and more universally useful concepts of the clear SI distinction between "mass" and "force" will become increasingly significant as engineering and construction become more and more involved in "dynamic" considerations.

9.8.6 In dynamic calculations, the value of a mass in kilograms (kg) is used directly with the appropriate acceleration to determine force, the applicable equation being $F = ma$. The frequently used equation $W = mg$, in which W is considered to equal "weight" should be superseded (see 9.8.4) by $F_g = mg$, in which F_g is the force of gravity.

9.8.7 For engineering design purposes, in United States locations the recommended value to be used for acceleration of gravity is: $g = 9.8$ m/s². (The standard international value is 9.806 65.)

9.8.8 The use of the factor 9.8 (m/s²) is recommended for g because:

9.8.8.1 It provides adequate accuracy in nearly all instances,

9.8.8.2 It gives fewer decimal places than the use of 9.81 or 9.806 65 which was advocated in Britain, and

9.8.8.3 It provides a different number in the product than would be obtained with the use of a factor of 10 (advocated by some), which can be easily overlooked and cause errors, as well as introducing overdesign by 2 %.

9.8.9 The newton extends through to derived quantities for pressure and stress, energy, work and quantity of heat, power, and many of the electrical units.

9.8.10 The unit kilogram-force (kgf) is inconsistent with SI, and is in the process of being dropped and replaced by the newton in traditionally metric countries. The kilogram-force (kgf) should *not* be used in the United States.

9.9 *Pressure, Stress, and Elastic Modulus:*

9.9.1 The SI unit for both pressure and stress (force per unit area) is the pascal (Pa). It replaces a large number of customary units and also supersedes a few traditional but non-SI metric units.

9.9.2 While it may be useful in some applications to read out test results in N/mm² (which is identical with MN/m²), or in kN/m², it is preferable and recommended always to show calculations and results in MPa or kPa.

9.9.3 The non-SI units, the "bar" (which equals 100 kPa or 0.1 MPa) and the "millibar" (which equals 100 Pa or 0.1 kPa) should *not* be used.

9.10 *Energy, Work, and Quantity of Heat:*

9.10.1 The SI unit of energy, work, and quantity of heat is the joule (J), which is equal to a newton meter (N·m) and a watt second (W·s).

9.10.2 The joule provides one coherent unit to supersede a large number of traditional units: Btu, therm, calorie, kilocalorie, foot pound-force, etc.

9.10.3 For many years, and since long before the joule was named, the kilowatthour (kWh) (Note 3) has been used extensively as the unit of energy in electrical energy consumption. Most existing electricity meters show kWh, and recalibration in megajoules (MJ) would be needlessly costly. For this reason, the kWh will be permitted as an alternative unit in electrical applications, but should not be introduced in new areas.

Note 3 – The accepted symbol in the United States is "kWh," but the correct SI symbol would be kW·h.

9.10.4 The joule should *never* be used for torque for which the widely designated unit is newton metre (N·m).

9.10.5 For dimensional consistency in rotational dynamics, torque should be expressed as newton metre per radian (N·m/rad), and moment of inertia as kilogram square metre per radian squared (kg·m²/rad²).

9.11 *Power and Heat Flow Rate:*

9.11.1 The SI unit for power and heat flow rate is the watt (W), which is already in worldwide use as the general unit for electrical power.

9.11.2 The watt, and its multiples, will now replace a number of traditional units of power and heat flow rate:

9.11.2.1 For general power: the horsepower (electric, boiler) and the foot pound-force per hour (or minute or second)

9.11.2.2 For heat flow rate: the Btu per hour and the calorie (or kilocalorie) per minute (or second); the ton of refrigeration

9.12 *Electrical Units:*

9.12.1 There are no changes in units used in electrical engineering, except

9.12.1.1 The renaming of the unit of conductance to siemens (S) from "mho."

9.12.1.2 The use of the SI unit for frequency, hertz (Hz), instead of cycles per second (cps).

9.13 *Lighting Units:*

9.13.1 The SI unit for luminous intensity, candela (cd), and for luminous flux, lumen (lm), are already in common use.

9.13.2 The candela (cd) directly replaces the former units "candle" and "candlepower."

9.13.3 Illuminance will be expressed in the SI unit lux (lx), which is equal to the lumen per square metre (lm/m²), and replaces lumen per square foot and footcandle.

9.13.4 Luminance will be expressed in candela per square metre (cd/m²), which replaces candela per square foot, footlambert, and lambert.

9.14 *Dimensionless Quantitites* – Dimensionless quantities, or ratios, such as relative humidity, specific gravity, decibel (dB), pH, parts per million, etc., remain unchanged when converting to SI.

9.15 *Constants for Use in Building Design Calculations* – Table 14 shows a selection of internationally agreed values and empirical constants for use in design calculations, taken to no more than six significant figures.

Table 1. Units in the international system-SI

Unit Group Quantity	Unit Name	Symbol	Formula	Unit Derivation	Remarks
Base Units:					
Length	metre	m			
Mass	kilogram	kg			
Time	second	s			Already in common use
Electric current	ampere	A			Already in common use
Thermodynamic temperature	kelvin	K			The customary unit for temperature is the degree Celsius (°C).
Amount of substance	mole	mol			The "mol" has no application in construction.
Luminous intensity	candela	cd			Already in common use
Supplementary Units:					
Plane angle	radian	rad			Already in common use
Solid angle	steradian	sr			Already in common use
Derived Units with Special Names:					
Frequency (of a periodic phenomenon)	hertz	Hz	l/s	s^{-1}	The hertz replaces "cycle per second."
Force	newton	N	$kg \cdot m/s^2$	$m \cdot kg \cdot s^{-2}$	
Pressure, stress, elastic modulus	pascal	Pa	N/m^2	$m^{-1} \cdot kg \cdot s^{-2}$	
Energy, work, quantity of heat	joule	J	$N \cdot m$	$m^2 \cdot kg \cdot s^{-2}$	
Power, radiant flux	watt	W	J/s	$m^2 \cdot kg \cdot s^{-3}$	Already in common use
Quantity of electricity, electric charge	coulomb	C	$A \cdot s$	$s \cdot A$	Already in common use
Electric potential, potential difference, electromotive force	volt	V	J/C or W/A	$m^2 \cdot kg \cdot s^{-3} \cdot A^{-1}$	Already in common use
Electric capacitance	farad	F	C/V	$m^{-2} \cdot kg^{-1} \cdot s^4 \cdot A^2$	Already in common use
Electric resistance	ohm	Ω	V/A	$m^2 \cdot kg \cdot s^{-3} \cdot A^{-2}$	Already in common use
Electric conductance	siemens	S	A/V or l/Ω	$m^{-2} \cdot kg^{-1} \cdot s^3 \cdot A^2$	The 'siemens' was formerly referred to as "mho."
Magnetic flux	weber	Wb	$V \cdot s$	$m^2 \cdot kg \cdot s^{-2} \cdot A^{-1}$	Already in common use
Magnetic flux density	tesla	T	Wb/m^2	$kg \cdot s^{-2} \cdot A^{-1}$	Already in common use
Electric inductance	henry	H	Wb/A	$m^2 \cdot kg \cdot s^{-2} \cdot A^{-2}$	Already in common use
Luminous flux	lumen	lm	$cd \cdot sr$	$cd \cdot sr$	Already in common use
Illuminance	lux	lx	lm/m^2	$m^{-2} \cdot cd \cdot sr$	
Activity (of a radionuclide)	becquerel	Bq	l/s	s^{-1}	No application in construction.
Absorbed dose	gray	Gy	J/kg	$m^2 \cdot s^{-2}$ (*)	(*) kg is canceled out. No application in construction.
Derived Units with Generic Names:					
a. Units Expressed in Terms of One Base Unit:					
Area	square metre	m^2		m^2	
Volume, capacity	cubic metre	m^3		m^3	(1 m³ = 1000 L)
Section modulus	metre to third power		m^3	m^3	
Second moment of area	metre to fourth power		m^4	m^4	
Curvature	reciprocal (of) metre		l/m	m^{-1}	
Rotational frequency	reciprocal (of) second		l/s	s^{-1}	Revolution per second (r/s) is used in specifications for rotating machinery.
Coefficient of linear thermal expansion	reciprocal (of) kelvin		l/K	K^{-1}	
b. Units Expressed in Terms of Two or More Base Units:					
Linear velocity	metre per second		m/s	$m \cdot s^{-1}$	
Linear acceleration	metre per second squared		m/s^2	$m \cdot s^{-2}$	
Kinematic viscosity	square metre per second		m^2/s	$m^2 \cdot s^{-1}$	
Volume rate of flow	cubic metre per second		m^3/s	$m^3 \cdot s^{-1}$	
Specific volume	cubic metre per kilogram		m^3/kg	$m^3 \cdot kg^{-1}$	
Mass per unit length	kilogram per metre		kg/m	$m^{-1} \cdot kg$	
Mass per unit area	kilogram per square metre		kg/m^2	$m^{-2} \cdot kg$	
Density (mass per unit volume)	kilogram per cubic metre		kg/m^3	$m^{-3} \cdot kg$	In this SI form, mass density is conveniently 1000 times specific gravity.
Moment of inertia	kilogram metre squared		$kg \cdot m^2$	$m^2 \cdot kg$	
Mass flow rate	kilogram per second		kg/s	$kg \cdot s^{-1}$	
Momentum	kilogram metre per second		$kg \cdot m/s$	$m \cdot kg \cdot s^{-1}$	
Angular momentum	kilogram metre squared per second		$kg \cdot m^2/s$	$m^2 \cdot kg \cdot s^{-1}$	
Magnetic field strength	ampere per metre		A/m	$m^{-1} \cdot A$	
Current density	ampere per square metre		A/m^2	$m^{-2} \cdot A$	
Luminance	candela per square metre		cd/m^2	$m^{-2} \cdot cd$	
c. Units Expressed in Terms of Base Units and/or Derived Units with Special Names:					
Moment of force, torque	newton metre		$N \cdot m$	$m^2 \cdot kg \cdot s^{-2}$	
Flexural rigidity	newton square metre		$N \cdot m^2$	$m^3 \cdot kg \cdot s^{-2}$	
Force per unit length, surface tension	newton per metre		N/m	$kg \cdot s^{-2}$ (1)	(1) m is canceled out

Table 1 (cont.). Units in the international system-SI

Unit Group	Quantity	Unit Name	Symbol	Formula	Unit Derivation	Remarks
	c. *Units Expressed in Terms of Base Units and/or Derived Units with Special Names:* (continued)					
	Dynamic viscosity	pascal second	Pa·s	$m^{-1}·kg·s^{-1}$		
	Impact ductility	joule per square metre	J/m²	$kg·s^{-2}$ (2)		(2) m² is canceled out
	Combustion heat (per unit volume)	joule per cubic metre	J/m³	$m^{-1}·kg·s^{-2}$		
	Combustion heat (per unit mass), specific energy, specific latent heat	joule per kilogram	J/kg	$m^2·s^{-2}$ (3)		(3) kg is canceled out
	Heat capacity, entropy	joule per kelvin	J/K	$m^2·kg·s^{-2}·K^{-1}$		
	Specific heat capacity, specific entropy	joule per kilogram kelvin	J/(kg·K)	$m^2·s^{-2}·K^{-1}$ (4)		(4) kg is canceled out
	Heat flux density, irradiance, sound intensity	watt per square metre	W/m²	$kg·s^{-3}$ (5)		(5) m² is canceled out
	Thermal conductivity	watt per metre kelvin	W/(m·K)	$m·kg·s^{-3}·K^{-1}$		
	Coefficient of heat transfer	watt per square metre kelvin	W/(m²·K)	$kg·s^{-3}·K^{-1}$ (6)		(6) m² is canceled out
	Thermal resistance, thermal insulance	square metre kelvin per watt	m²·K/W	$kg^{-1}·s^3·K$ (7)		(7) m² is canceled out
	Electric field strength	volt per metre	V/m	$m·kg·s^{-3}·A^{-1}$		
	Electric flux density	coulomb per square metre	C/m²	$m^{-2}·s·A$		
	Electric charge density	coulomb per cubic metre	C/m³	$m^{-3}·s·A$		
	Electric permittivity	farad per metre	F/m	$m^{-3}·kg^{-1}·s^4·A^2$		
	Electric permeability	henry per metre	H/m	$m·kg·s^{-2}·A^{-2}$		
	Electric resistivity	ohm metre	Ω·m	$m^3·kg·s^{-3};·A^{-2}$		
	Electric conductivity	siemens per metre	S/m	$m^{-3}·kg^{-1}·s^3·A^2$		
	Light exposure	lux second	lx·s	$m^{-2}·s·cd·sr$		
	Luminous efficacy	lumen per watt	lm/W	$m^{-2}·kg^{-1}·s^3·cd·sr$		
	d. *Units Expressed in Terms of Supplementary Units and Base and/or Derived Units:*					
	Angular velocity	radian per second	rad/s	$s^{-1}·rad$		
	Angular acceleration	radian per second squared	rad/s²	$m^{-2}·rad$		
	Radiant intensity	watt per steradian	W/sr	$m^2·kg·s^{-3}·sr^{-1}$		
	Radiance	watt per square metre steradian	W/(m²·sr)	$kg·s^{-3}·sr^{-1}$ (8)		(8) m² is canceled out

Table 2. Other units whose use is permitted with SI

Quantity	Unit Name	Symbol	Relationship to SI Unit	Remarks
Units for General Use:				
Volume	litre[A]	L	$1 L = 0.001 m^3 = 10^6 mm^3$	The litre may only be used with the SI prefix "milli."
Mass	metric ton[B]	t	$1 t = 1000 kg = (1 Mg)$	
Time	minute	min	$1 min = 60 s$	See also Section 9.6.
	hour	h	$1 h = 3600 s = (60 min)$	
	day (mean solar)	d	$1 d = 86\ 400 s = (24 h)$	
	year (calendar)	a	$1 a = 31\ 536\ 000 s = (365 d)$	
Temperature interval	degree Celsius	°C	$1°C = 1 K$	The Celsius temperature 0°C corresponds to 273.15 K exactly · ($t_C = T_K - 273.15$)
Plane angle	degree (of arc)	°	$1° = 0.017\ 453 rad = 17.453 mrad$	$1° = (\pi/180) rad$
Velocity	kilometre per hour	km/h	$1 km/h = 0.278 m/s$	$1 m/s = 3.6 km/h$
Units Accepted for Limited Application Only:				
Area	hectare	ha	$1 ha = 10\ 000 m^2$	For use in land measurement.
Energy	kilowatthour	kWh	$1 kWh = 3.6 MJ$	For measurement of electrical energy consumption only.
Speed of rotation	revolution per minute	r/min	$1 r/min = \frac{1}{60} r/s = \frac{2\pi}{60} rad/s$	To measure rotational speed in slow-moving equipment only.

[A] The international symbol for "litre" is the lowercase "l", which can be easily confused with the numeral "1." Several English-speaking countries have adopted the script "ℓ" as symbol for "litre" in order to avoid any misinterpretation. The symbol "L" (capital ell) is recommended for United States use to prevent confusion.
[B] The international name for "metric ton" is "tonne." The metric ton is equal to the "megagram" (Mg).

Table 3. Preferred multiples and submultiples

Multiplication Factor		Prefix		Pronunciation
		Name	Symbol	
10^{12} or	1 000 000 000 000	tera	T	as in *terrace*
10^9 or	1 000 000 000	giga	G	jig'a
10^6 or	1 000 000	mega	M	as in *mega*phone
10^3 or	1 000	kilo	k	kill'oh
10^{-3} or	0.001	milli	m	as in *mili*tary
10^{-6} or	0.000 001	micro	μ	as in *micro*phone
10^{-9} or	0.000 000 001	nano	n	nan'oh
10^{-12} or	0.000 000 000 001	pico	p	peek'oh

Table 4. Other multiples for limited application

Multiplication Factor	Prefix Name	Prefix Symbol	Pronunciation
10^2 or 100	hecto	h	heck'toe
10^1 or 10	deka	da	deck'a
10^{-1} or 0.1	deci	d	as in *deci*mal
10^{-2} or 0.01	centi	c	as in *senti*ment

Table 5. Rules and recommendations for the presentation of SI units and symbols

Rule	Typical Examples	Remarks
A. General		
1. All unit names should either be denoted by correct symbols or be written in full. In the interest of simplification and to reduce the amount of writing, use unit symbols rather than fully written forms.	USE: J/kg or joule per kilogram	NOT: joule per kg NOT: J/kilogram
2. DO NOT USE mixtures of names and symbols.		
B. Symbols for Unit Quantities and Prefixes		
1. SI symbols are internationally agreed and there is only one symbol for each unit. Multiples and submultiples are formed by using the unit symbol and attaching a prefix symbol in front of it.	m, kg, s, A, cd, L	See also B.5–B.7
2. All unit symbols are shown in upright letters, and can be produced by a normal typewriter keyboard with the exceptions of the symbols for the SI unit "ohm" and the prefix "micro" which are represented by Greek letters "Ω" and "μ" respectively.		EXCEPTIONS: Ω, μ
3. Unit symbols are NEVER followed by a period (full stop), except at the end of a sentence.	60 kg/m	NOT: 60 kg./m.
4. Unit symbols are normally written in lowercase, except for unit names derived from a proper name, in which case the initial is capitalized. Some units have symbols consisting of two letters from a proper name, of which only the first letter is capitalized. (The symbol for the unit name "ohm" is the capital Greek letter Ω.)	m, kg, s, mol, cd, etc. A, K, N, J, W, V, etc. Pa, Hz, Wb, etc.	EXCEPTION: L
5. Prefixes for magnitudes from 10^6 to 10^{18} have capital upright letter symbols.	M, G, T, etc.	See also C.1
6. Prefixes for magnitudes from 10^{-18} through to 10^3 have lowercase upright letter symbols. (The symbol for 10^{-6} or micro is the lowercase Greek letter μ.)	p, n, μ, m, k, etc.	See also C.1
7. Prefix symbols are directly attached to the unit symbol, without a space between them.	mm, kW, MN, etc.	NOT: m m, k W, M N
8. DO NOT USE compound prefixes to form a multiple or submultiple of a unit (for example, USE nanometre. DO NOT USE micromillimetre or millimicrometre).	nm	NOT: μmm or mμm
9. In the case of the base unit kilogram, prefixes are attached to the "gram" (for example, milligram, NOT microkilogram).	mg	NOT: μkg
10. USE ONLY ONE PREFIX when forming a multiple or a submultiple of a compound unit.	km/s; mV/m	NOT: mm/μs; μV/mm EXCEPTION: MJ/kg NOT kJ/g
11. Any prefix should appear only in the numerator and never in the denominator with the exception of the base unit kg.	MN/m	NOT: kN/mm
C. Areas of Possible Confusion Requiring Special Care		
1. The symbols for SI units and the conventions that govern their use shall be followed. A number of prefix and unit symbols use the same letter, but in different form. EXERCISE CARE to present the correct symbol for each unit and prefix.	g (gram); G (giga) k (kilo); K (kelvin) m (milli); M (mega) m (metre) n (nano); N (newton)	OTHERS: c (centi); C (coulomb) °C (degree Celsius) s (second); S (siemens) t (metric ton); T (tera) T (tesla)
2. All prefix and unit symbols retain their prescribed form regardless of the surrounding typography. In printouts from limited character sets (telex, computer printers) special considerations apply to symbols for mega, micro, ohm, and siemens. Where confusion is likely to arise, WRITE UNITS IN FULL.	metre, newton, etc.	NOT: Metre, Newton EXCEPTION: degree Celsius
D. Unit Names Written Out in Full		
1. Unit names, including prefixes, are treated as common names and are *not capitalized*, except at the beginning of sentences or in titles. (The only exception is "Celsius" in "degree Celsius," where degree is considered as the unit name and is shown in lowercase, while Celsius represents an adjective and is capitalized.)	millimetre; kilowatt	NOT: milli-metre NOT: kilo watt
2. Where a prefix is attached to an SI unit to form a multiple or submultiple, the combination is written as one word. (There are three cases where the final vowel of the prefix is omitted in the combination: megohm, kilohm, and hectare.)		
3. Where a compound unit is formed by multiplication of two units, the use of a space between units is preferred, but a hyphen is acceptable and in some situations more appropriate, to avoid any risk of misinterpretation.	newton metre or newton-metre	NOT: newtonmetre
4. Where a compound unit is formed by division of two units, this is expressed by inserting "per" between the numerator and the denominator.	metre per second joule per kelvin	NOT: metre/second NOT: joule/kelvin
5. Where the numerical value of a unit is written in full, the unit should also be written in full.	seven metres	NOT: seven m
E. Plurals		
1. Units written in full are subject to the normal rules of grammar. For any unit with a numerical value greater than one (1), an "s" is added to the written unit to denote the plural.	1.2 metres; 2.3 newtons; 33.2 kilograms	BUT: 0.8 metre
2. The following units have the same plural as singular when written out in full: hertz, lux, siemens.	350 kilohertz 12.5 lux	
3. Symbols NEVER change in the plural.	2.3 N; 33.2 kg	NOT: 2.3 Ns; 33.2 kgs
F. Compound Unit Symbols – Products and Quotients		
1. The product of two units is indicated by a dot placed at mid-height between the unit symbols.	kN·m; Pa·s	NOT: kNm; Pas NOT: kN m; Pa s
2. To express a derived unit formed by division, any one of the following methods may be used: a. a solidus (slash, /) b. a horizontal line between numerator and denominator c. a negative index (or negative power)	kg/m²; W/(m·K) $\dfrac{kg}{m^3 \cdot K}$ kg·m⁻³; W·m⁻¹·K⁻¹	See also F.3 and F.5
3. *Only one solidus* may be used in any combination.	m/s²; m·kg/(s³·A)	NOT: m/s/s NOT: m·kg/s³/A
4. DO NOT USE the abbreviation "p" for "per" in the expression of a division.	km/h	NOT: kph or k.p.h.
5. Where the denominator is a product, this should be shown in parentheses.	W/(m²·K)	

Table 6. Presentation of numerical values with SI

	Typical Examples	Remarks
A. Decimal Marker		
1. Whereas most European countries use the comma on the line as the decimal marker and this practice is advocated by ISO, a special exception is made for documents in the English language which have traditionally used the point (dot) on the line, or period, as decimal marker.		See also under G.
2. The recommended decimal marker for use in the United States is the point on the line (period), and the comma should not be used.	9.9; 15.375	NOT: 9,9; 15,375
3. Always show a zero before the decimal point for all numbers smaller than 1.0 (one).	0.1; 0.725	NOT: .1; .725
B. Spacing		
1. Always leave a gap between the numerical value associated with a symbol and the symbol, of at least half a space in width.	900 MHz; 200 mg; 10^6 mm² or 10^6 mm²	NOT: 900MHz; 200mg; NOT: 10^6mm²
2. In the case of the symbol for the "degree Celsius" this space is optional, but the degree symbol must always be attached to C.	20°C or 20 °C	NOT: 20° C
3. In non-SI expressions of plane angle (°, '), DO NOT LEAVE A SPACE between the numerical value and the symbol.	27°30' (of arc)	NOT: 27° 30'
4. Always leave a space on each side of signs for multiplication, division, addition, and subtraction.	100 mm × 100 mm; 36 MPa + 8 MPa	NOT: 100 mm×100 mm; NOT: 36 MPa+ 8 MPa
C. Fractions		
1. Avoid common fractions in connection with SI units.	WRITE: 0.5 kPa	NOT: $\frac{1}{2}$ kPa
2. Always use decimal notation to express fractions of any number larger than 1.0 (one).	1.5; 16.375	NOT: $1\text{-}\frac{1}{2}$; $16\text{-}\frac{3}{8}$
3. While the most common fractions such as half, third, quarter, and fifth will remain in speech, always show decimal notation in written, typed, or printed material.	0.5; 0.33; 0.25; 0.2	NOT: $\frac{1}{2}$; $\frac{1}{3}$; $\frac{1}{4}$; $\frac{1}{5}$
D. Powers of Units and Exponential Notation		
1. When writing unit names with a modifier "squared" or "cubed," the following rules should be applied: a. In the case of area and volume, the modifier is written before the unit name as "square" and "cubic."	cubic metre; square millimetre	NOT: metre cubed; millimetre squared
b. In all other cases, the modifier is shown after the unit name as "squared," "cubed," "to the fourth power," etc.	metre per second squared	NOT: metre per square second; (or "metre per second per second")
c. The abbreviations "sq." for "square," and "cu." for "cubic" should not be used.		NOT: sq. millimetre NOT: cu. metre
2. For unit symbols with modifiers (such as square, cubic, fourth power, etc.) always show the superscript immediately after the symbol.	m²; mm³; s⁴	NOT: m²; mm³; s⁴
3. Show the superscript as a reduced size numeral raised half a line space. Where a typewriter without superscript numerals is used, the full size numeral should be raised half a line space, provided that this does not encroach on print in the line above.	mm³, m/s²	PERMITTED: mm³, m/s²
4. Where an exponent is attached to a prefixed symbol, it indicates that that multiple (or submultiple) is raised to the power expressed by the exponent.	$1\ \text{mm}^3 = (10^{-3}\ \text{m})^3 = 10^{-9}\ \text{m}^3$ $1\ \text{km}^2 = (10^3\ \text{m})^2 = 10^6\ \text{m}^2$	NOT: $1\ \text{mm}^3 = 10^{-3}\ \text{m}^3$
E. Ratios		
1. Do not mix units in expressing a ratio of like unit quantities.	0.01 m/m 0.03 m²/m²	NOT: 10 mm/m NOT: 30 000 mm²/m²
2. Wherever possible, use a non-quantitative expression (ratio or percentage) to indicate measurement of slopes, deflections, etc.		PREFERRED: 1:100; 0.01; 1 % 1:33; 0.03; 3 %
F. Range		
1. The choice of the appropriate prefix to indicate a multiple or submultiple of an SI unit is governed by convenience to obtain numerical values within a practical range and to eliminate nonsignificant digits.		
2. In preference, use prefixes representing ternary powers of 10 (10 raised to a power which is a multiple of 3).	milli, kilo, mega	AVOID: centi, deci, deka, hecto
3. Select prefixes so that the numerical value or values occur in a common range between 0.1 and 1000.	120 kN 3.94 mm 14.5 MPa	INSTEAD OF: 120 000 N 0.003 94 m 14 500 kPa
4. Compatibility with the general range must be a consideration; for example, if all dimensions on a drawing are shown in millimetres (mm), a range from 1 to 99 999 (a maximum of five numerals) would be acceptable to avoid mixing of units.		NOTE: Drawings should show "All dimensions shown in millimetres unless otherwise noted".

TABLE 6 *Continued*

	Typical Examples	Remarks
G. *Presentation and Tabulation of Numbers*		
1. In numbers with many digits it has been common practice in the United State to separate digits into groups of three by means of commas. This practice must *not* be used with SI, to avoid confusion. It is recommended international practice to arrange digits in long numbers in groups of three from the decimal marker, with a gap of not less than half a space, and not more than a full space, separating each group.	54 375.260 55 54 375.260 55	NOT: 54,375.260.55 NOT: 54375.26055
2. For individual numbers with four digits before (or after) the decimal marker this space is not necessary.	4500; 0.0355	
3. In all tabulations of numbers with five or more digits before or after the decimal marker or both, group digits into groups of three: For example, 12.5255; 5735; 98 300; 0.425 75	12.525 5 5 735 98 300 0.425 75 104 047.951 25	
H. *Use of Unprefixed Units in Calculations*		
Errors in calculations involving compound units can be minimized if all prefixed units are reverted back to coherent base or derived units, with numerical values expressed in powers-of-ten notation.	PREFERRED: 136 kJ = 136 × 10³ J 20 MPa = 20 × 10⁶ Pa 1.5 t (Mg) = 1.5 × 10³ kg	ALSO ACCEPTABLE: (or 1.36 × 10⁵ J) (or 2 × 10⁷ Pa)

Table 7. Space and time: geometry, kinematics, and periodic phenomena

Quantity (and SI Unit Symbol)	Preferred Units (Symbols)	Other Acceptable Units	Unit Name	Typical Applications	Remarks
Length (m)	m		metre	*Architecture and General Engineering:* Levels, overall dimensions, spans, column heights, etc., in engineering computations. *Estimating and Specification:* Trenches, curbs, fences, lumber lengths, pipes and conduits; lengths of building materials generally. *Land Surveying:* Boundary and cadastral surveys; survey plans; heights, geodetic surveys, contours. *Hydraulic Engineering:* Pipe and channel lengths, depth of storage tanks or reservoirs, height of potentiometric head, hydraulic head, piezometric head	Use metres on all drawings with scale ratios between 1:200 and 1:2000. Where required for purposes of accuracy, show dimensions to three decimal places.
	mm		millimetre	*Architecture and General Engineering:* Spans, dimensions in buildings, dimensions of buildings products; depth and width of sections; displacement, settlement, deflection, elongation; slump of concrete, size of aggregate; radius of gyration, eccentricity; detailed dimensions generally; rainfall. *Estimating and Specification:* Lumber cross sections; thicknesses, diameters, sheet metal gages, fasteners; all other building product dimensions. *Hydraulic Engineering:* Pipe diameters; radii of ground water wells; height of capillary rise; precipitation, evaporation	Use millimetres on drawings with scale ratios between 1:1 and 1:200. Avoid the use of centimetres (cm). Where "cm" is shown in documents, such as for snow depth, body dimensions, or carpet sizes, etc., convert to "mm" or "m".
	km		kilometre	Distances for transportation purposes geographical or statistical applications in surveying; long pipes and channels	
	µm		micrometre	Thickness of coatings (paint, galvanizing etc.), thin sheet materials, size of fine aggregate	
Area (m²)	m²		square metre	*General Applications:* Small land areas; area of cross section of earthworks, channels and larger pipes; surface area of tanks and small reservoirs; areas in general	(1 m² = 10⁶ mm²)
				Estimating and Specification: Site clearing; floor areas; paving, masonry construction, roofing, wall and floor finishes, plastering, paintwork, glass areas, membranes, lining materials, insulation, reinforcing mesh, formwork; areas of all building components	Replaces sq. ft.; sq. yd., and square. Specify masonry construction by wall area × wall thickness.
	mm²		square millimetre	Area of cross section for structural and other sections, bars, pipes, rolled and pressed shapes, etc.	Avoid the use of cm² (square centimetre) by conversion to mm². (1 cm² = 10² mm² = 100 mm²)
	km²		square kilometre	Large catchment areas or land areas	
		ha	hectare	Land areas; irrigation areas; areas on boundary and other survey plans	(1 ha = (10² m)² = 10⁴ m² = 10 000 m²)
Volume, Capacity (m³)	m³		cubic metre	*General Applications:* Volume, capacity (large quantities); volume of earthworks, excavation, filling, waste removal; concrete, sand, all bulk materials supplied by volume and large quantities of timber. *Hydraulic Engineering:* Water distribution, irrigation, diversions, sewage, storage capacity, underground basins	1 m³ = 1000 L As far as possible, use the cubic metre as the preferred unit of volume for engineering purposes.
	mm³		cubic millimetre	Volume, capacity (small quantities)	
		L	litre	Volume of fluids and containers for fluids; liquid materials, domestic water supply, consumption; volume/capacity of full tanks	The litre and its multiples or submultiples may be used for domestic and industrial supplies of liquids 1 L = 1 dm³ See Section 9.3
		mL	millilitre	Volume of fluids and containers for fluids (limited application only)	
Modulus of Section (m³)	mm³		millimetre to third power	Geometric properties of structural sections, such as plastic section modulus, elastic section modulus, etc.	See Section 9.4
	m³		metre to third power		

Table 7 (cont.).   Space and time: geometry, kinematics, and periodic phenomena

Quantity (and SI Unit Symbol)	Preferred Units (Symbols)	Other Acceptable Units	Unit Name	Typical Applications	Remarks
Second Moment of Area (m⁴)	mm⁴		millimetre to fourth power	Geometric properties of structural sections: moment of inertia of a section, torsional constant of cross section	See Section 9.4
	m⁴		metre to fourth power		
Plane Angle (rad)	rad mrad		radian milliradian	Generally used in calculations only to preserve coherence *General Applications:*	Slopes and gradients may be expressed as a ratio or as a percentage: 26.57° = 1:2 = 50% = 0.4637 rad
		(_°)	degree (of arc)	Angular measurement in construction generally; angle of rotation, torsion, shear resistance, friction, internal friction, etc. (decimalized degrees) *Land Surveying:*	
				Bearings shown on boundary and cadastral survey plans; geodetic surveying	(1 rad = 57.2958°) See Section 9.5
Time, Time Interval (s)	s		second	Time used in test methods; all calculations involving derived units with a time component, in order to preserve coherence	Avoid the use of minute (min) as far as possible
		h d a	hour day year (annum)	Time used in test methods; all calculations involving labor time, plant hire, maintenance periods, etc.	(1 h = 3600 s) (1 d = 86 400 s) = 86.4 ks)
Frequency (Hz)	Hz			Frequence of sound, vibration, shock; frequency of electromagnetic waves	(1 Hz = 1/s = s⁻¹) Replaces cycle per second (c/s or cps)
	kHz MHz		kilohertz megahertz		
Rotational Frequency, Speed of Rotation (s⁻¹)		r/s	revolution per second	Widely used in the specification of rotational speed of machinery Use r/min *only* for slow-moving equipment.	(1 r/s = 2π rad/s)
Velocity, Speed (m/s)	m/s		metre per second	Calculations involving rectilinear motion, velocity and speed in general; wind velocity; velocity of fluids; pipe flow velocity	(1 m/s = 3.6 km/h)
		km/h	kilometre per hour	Wind speed; speed used in transportation; speed limits	
		mm/h	millimetre per hour	Rainfall intensity	
Angular Velocity (rad/s)	rad/s		radian per second	Calculation involving rotational motion	
Linear Acceleration (m/s²)	m/s²		metre per second squared	Kinematics and calculation of dynamic forces	Recommended value of acceleration of gravity for use in U.S.: g_{us} = 9.8 m/s²
Volume Rate of Flow (m³/s)	(m³/s)		cubic metre per second	Volumetric flow in general; flow in pipes, ducts, channels, rivers, irrigation spray demand	(1 m³/s = 1000 L/s)
		m³/d L/s L/d	cubic metre per day litre per second litre per day	Volumetric flow of fluids only	

Table 8. Mechanics: statics and dynamics

Quantity (and SI Unit Symbol)	Preferred Units (Symbols)	Other Acceptable Units	Unit Name	Typical Applications	Remarks
Mass (kg)	kg		kilogram	Mass of materials in general, mass of structural elements and machinery	USE kilograms (kg) in calculations and specifications
	g		gram	Mass of samples of material for testing	Masses greater than 10^4 kg (10 000 kg) may be conveniently expressed in metric tons (t):
		t	metric ton	Mass of large quantities of materials, such as structural steel, reinforcement, aggregates, concrete, etc.; ratings of lifting equipment	1 t $= 10^3$ kg $= 1$ Mg $= 1000$ kg
Mass per Unit Length (kg/m)	kg/m		kilogram per metre	Mass per unit length of sections, bars, and similar items of uniform cross section	Also known as "linear density"
		g/m	gram per metre	Mass per unit length of wire and similar material of uniform cross section	
Mass per Unit Area (kg/m²)	kg/m²		kilogram per square metre	Mass per unit area of slabs, plates, and similar items of uniform thickness or depth; rating for load-carrying capacities on floors (display on notices only)*	*DO NOT USE in stress calculations
		g/m²	gram per square metre	Mass per unit area of thin sheet materials, coatings, etc.	
Mass Density, Concentration (kg/m³)	kg/m³		kilogram per cubic metre	Density of materials in general; mass per unit volume of materials in a concrete mix; evaluation of masses of structures and materials	Also known as "mass per unit volume"
		g/m³	gram per cubic metre	Mass per unit volume (concentration) in pollution control	
		µg/m³	microgram per cubic metre		
Momentum (kg·m/s)	kg·m/s		kilogram metre per second	Used in applied mechanics; evaluation of impact and dynamic forces	
Moment of Inertia (kg·m²)	kg·m²		kilogram square metre	Rotational dynamics. Evaluation of the restraining forces required for propellers, windmills, etc.	See also Section 9.10.5
Mass per Unit Time (kg/s)	kg/s		kilogram per second	Rate of transport of material on conveyors and other materials handling equipment	1 kg/s = 3.6 t/h
		t/h	metric ton per hour		
Force (N)	N		newton	Unit of force for use in calculations	1 N $= 1$ kg·m/s²
	kN		kilonewton	Forces in structural elements, such as columns, piles, ties, pre-stressing tendons, etc.; concentrated forces; axial forces; reactions; shear force; gravitational force	See also Section 9.8
Force per Unit Length (N/m)	N/m		newton per metre	Unit for use in calculations	
	kN/m		kilonewton per metre	Transverse force per unit length on a beam, column, etc.; force distribution in a linear direction	
Moment of Force, Torsional or Bending Moment, Torque (N·m)	N·m kN·m MN·m		newton metre kilonewton metre meganewton metre	Bending moments (in structural sections), torsional moment; overturning moment; tightening tension for high-strength bolts; torque in engine drive shafts, axles, etc.	See also Sections 9.10.4 and 9.10.5
Pressure, Stress, Modulus of Elasticity (Pa)	Pa		pascal	Unit for use in calculations; low differential pressure in fluids	(1 Pa = 1 N/m²)
	kPa		kilopascal	Uniformly distributed pressure (loads) on floors; soil bearing pressure; wind pressure (loads), snow loads, dead and live loads; pressure in fluids; differential pressure (for example, in ventilating systems)	Where wind pressure, snow loads, dead and live loads are shown in kN/m², CHANGE units to kPa
	MPa		megapascal	Modulus of elasticity; stress (ultimate, proof, yield, permissible, calculated, etc.) in structural materials; concrete and steel strength grades	1 MPa = 1 MN/m² = 1 N/mm²
	GPa µPa		gigapascal micropascal	Modulus of elasticity in high-strength materials Sound pressure (20 µPa is the reference quantity for sound pressure level)	
Compressibility (Pa⁻¹)	1/Pa		reciprocal (of) pascal	Settlement analysis, coefficient of compressibility, bulk compressibility	(1/Pa = 1 m²/N)
	1/kPa		reciprocal (of) kilopascal		
Dynamic Viscosity (Pa·s)	Pa·s mPa·s		pascal second millipascal second	Shear stresses in fluids	(1 Pa·s = 1 N·s/m²) The centipoise (cP) = 10^{-3} Pa·s WILL NOT BE USED

Table 8 (cont.). Mechanics: statics and dynamics

Quantity (and SI Unit Symbol)	Preferred Units (Symbols)	Other Acceptable Units	Unit Name	Typical Applications	Remarks
Kinematic Viscosity (m^2/s)	m^2/s		square metre per second		The centistokes (cSt) $= 10^{-6}$ m^2/s WILL NOT BE USED
	mm^2/s		square millimetre per second	Computation of Reynold's number, settlement analysis (coefficient of consolidation)	1 cSt $= 1$ mm^2/s
Work, Energy (J)	J kJ MJ		joule kilojoule megajoule	Energy absorbed in impact testing of materials; energy in general; calculations involving mechanical and electrical energy	
		kWh	kilowatthour	Electrical energy applications only	1 kWh $= 3.6$ MJ
Impact Strength (J/m^2)	J/m^2		joule per square metre	Impact strength; impact ductility	
	kJ/m^2		kilojoule per square metre		
Power (W)	W kW		watt kilowatt	Power in general (mechanical, electrical, thermal); input/output rating, etc., of motors, engines, heating and ventilating plant, and other equipment in general	
	MW		megawatt	Power input/output rating, etc., of heavy power plant	
	pW		picowatt	Sound power level (1 pW is the reference quantity for sound power level)	

Table 9. Heat, thermal effects, heat transfer

Quantity (and SI Unit Symbol)	Preferred Units (Symbols)	Other Acceptable Units	Unit Name	Typical Applications	Remarks
Temperature Value (K)	K		kelvin	Expression of thermodynamic temperature; calculations involving units of temperature	($t_C = T_K - 273.15$)
		°C	degree Celsius	Common temperature scale for use in meteorology and general applications; ambient temperature values	Temperature values will normally be measured in °C (degrees Celsius)
Temperature Interval (K)	K		kelvin	Heat transfer calculations; temperature intervals in test methods, etc.	(1 K $= 1$°C) The use of K (kelvin) in compound units is recommended
		°C	degree Celsius		
Coefficient of Linear Thermal Expansion (1/K)	1/K		reciprocal (of) kelvin	Expansion of materials subject to a change in temperature (generally expressed as a ratio per kelvin or degree Celsius)	
		1/°C	reciprocal (of) degree Celsius		
Heat, Quantity of Heat (J)	J		joule	Thermal energy calculations. Enthalpy, latent heat, sensible heat	
	kJ MJ		kilojoule megajoule		
Specific Energy. Specific Latent Heat; Combustion Heat (mass basis) (J/kg)	J/kg kJ/kg MJ/kg		joule per kilogram kilojoule per kilogram megajoule per kilogram	Heat of transition; heat and energy contained in materials; combustion heat per unit mass; calorific value of fuels (mass basis); specific sensible heat. specific latent heat in psychrometric calculations	
Energy Density. Combustion Heat (volume basis) (J/m^3)	J/m^3 kJ/m^3		joule per cubic metre kilojoule per cubic metre	Combustion heat per unit volume	(1 $kJ/m^3 = 1$ J/L)
	MJ/m^3		megajoule per cubic metre	Calorific value of fuels (volume basis)	(1 $MJ/m^3 = 1$ kJ/L)
Heat Capacity. Entropy (J/K)	J/K		joule per kelvin	Thermal behavior of materials. heat transmission calculations. entropy	
	kJ/K		kilojoule per kelvin		
Specific Heat Capacity, Specific Entropy ($J/(kg \cdot K)$)	$J/(kg \cdot K)$		joule per kilogram kelvin	Thermal behavior of materials. heat transmission calculations	
	$kJ/(kg \cdot K)$		kilojoule per kilogram kelvin		
Heat Flow Rate (W)	W		watt	Heat flow through walls, windows, etc.; heat demand	(1 W $= 1$ J/s)
	kW		kilowatt		

Table 9 (cont.). Heat, thermal effects, heat transfer

Quantity (and SI Unit Symbol)	Preferred Units (Symbols)	Other Acceptable Units	Unit Name	Typical Applications	Remarks
Power Density, Heat Flux, Density, Irradiance (W/m²)	W/m² kW/m²		watt per square metre kilowatt per square metre	Density of power or heat flow through building walls and other heat transfer surfaces; heat transmission calculations	
Heat Release Rate (W/m³)	W/m³ kW/m³		watt per cubic metre kilowatt per cubic metre	Rate of heat release per unit volume over time (for gases and liquids)	1 W/m³ = 1 J/(m³·s)
Thermal Conductivity (W/(m·K))	W/(m·K)		watt per metre kelvin	Estimation of thermal behavior of materials and systems; heat transmission calculations Thermal conductivity of structural and building materials in fire-resistance testing, insulation, etc.	1 W/(m·K) = 1 W/(m·°C) ("k" value)
Coefficient of Heat Transfer (Thermal Conductance) (W/(m²·K))	W/(m²·K) kW/(m²·K)		watt per square metre kelvin kilowatt per square metre kelvin	Heat transfer calculations for buildings, building components, and equipment. Transmittance of construction elements	("U" value)
Thermal Resistivity ((m·K)/W)	(m·K)/W		metre kelvin per watt	Heat transmission calculations (reciprocal of thermal conductivity)	
Thermal Insulance (Thermal-Resistance) ((m²·K)/W)	(m²·K)/W		square metre kelvin per watt	Heat transmission calculations (reciprocal of thermal conductance)	("R" value)

Table 10. Electricity and magnetism

Quantity (and SI Unit Symbol)	Preferred Units (Symbols)	Other Acceptable Units	Unit Name	Typical Applications	Remarks
Electric Current (A)	A kA mA μA		ampere kiloampere milliampere microampere	Maintenance rating of an electrical installation. Leakage current	
Magnetomotive Force, Magnetic Potential Difference (A)				Used in the calculations involved in magnetic circuits	
Magnetic Field Strength, Magnetization (A/m)	A/m kA/m		ampere per metre kiloampere per metre	Magnetic field strength is used in calculation of magnetic circuitry such as transformers, magnetic amplifiers, and general cores.	(1 kA/m = 1 A/mm)
Current Density (A/m²)	A/m² kA/m²	A/mm²	ampere per square metre kiloampere per square metre ampere per square millimetre	Design of cross-sectional area of electrical conductor	(1 A/mm² = 1 MA/m²)
Electric Charge, Quantity of Electricity (C)	C kC μC nC pC		coulomb kilocoulomb microcoulomb nanocoulomb picocoulomb	The voltage on a unit with capacitive-type characteristics may be related to the amount of charge present (for example, electrostatic precipitators). Storage battery capacities	1 C = 1 A·s DO NOT USE ampere hour: 1 A·h = 3.6 kC
Electric Potential, Potential Difference, Electromotive Force (V)	V MV kV mV μV		volt megavolt kilovolt millivolt microvolt		1 V = 1 W/A
Electric Field Strength (V/m)	V/m MV/m kV/m mV/m μV/m		volt per metre megavolt per metre kilovolt per metre millivolt per metre microvolt per metre	The electric field strength gives the potential gradient at points in space. This may be used to calculate or test electrical parameters such as dielectric strength.	
Active Power (W)	W GW MW kW mW μW		watt gigawatt megawatt kilowatt milliwatt microwatt	The useful power of an electrical circuit is expressed in watts (W). (The apparent power in an electrical circuit is expressed in volt-amperes (V·A).)	1 W = 1 V·A
Capacitance (F)	F mF μF nF pF		farad millifarad microfarad nanofarad picofarad	Electronic components. Electrical design and performance calculators	1 F = 1 C/V

Table 10 (cont.). Electricity and magnetism

Quantity (and SI Unit Symbol)	Preferred Units (Symbols)	Other Acceptable Units	Unit Name	Typical Applications	Remarks
Resistance (Ω)	Ω $G\Omega$ $M\Omega$ $k\Omega$ $m\Omega$		ohm gigaohm megohm kilohm milliohm	The design of electrical devices with resistance, such as motors, generators, heaters, electrical distribution systems, etc.	$1\ \Omega = 1\ V/A$
Conductance, Admittance, Susceptance (S)	S MS kS mS μS		siemens megasiemens kilosiemens millisiemens microsiemens		The siemens (S) was formerly known as "mho"
Resistivity ($\Omega \cdot m$)	$\Omega \cdot m$ $G\Omega \cdot m$ $M\Omega \cdot m$ $k\Omega \cdot m$ $m\Omega \cdot m$ $\mu\Omega \cdot m$ $n\Omega \cdot m$		ohm metre gigaohm metre megohm metre kilohm metre milliohm metre microohm metre nanoohm metre		
(Electrical) Conductivity (S/m)	S/m MS/m kS/m μS/m		siemens per metre megasiemens per metre kilosiemens per metre microsiemens per metre	A parameter for measuring water quality	
Magnetic Flux, Flux of Magnetic Induction (Wb)	mWb		milliweber	Used in the calculations involved in magnetic circuits	$1\ Wb = 1\ V \cdot s$
Magnetic Flux Density, Magnetic Induction (T)	T mT μT nT		tesla millitesla microtesla nanotesla	Used in the calculations involved in magnetic circuits	$1\ T = 1\ Wb/m^2$
Magnetic Vector Potential (Wb/m²)	kWb/m²		kiloweber per square metre	Used in the calculations involved in magnetic circuits	
Self-Inductance, Mutual Inductance, Permeance (H)	H mH μH nH pH		henry millihenry microhenry nanohenry picohenry	Used in analysis and calculations involving transformers	$1\ H = 1\ Wb/A$
Reluctance (1/H)	1/H		reciprocal of henry	Design of motors and generators	
Permeability (H/m)	H/m μH/m nH/m		henry per metre microhenry per metre nanohenry per metre	Permeability gives the relationship between the magnetic flux density and the magnetic fluid strength.	

Table 11. Lighting

Quantity (and SI Unit Symbol)	Preferred Units (Symbols)	Other Acceptable Units	Unit Name	Typical Applications	Remarks
Luminous Intensity (cd)	cd		candela		
Solid Angle (sr)	sr		steradian		
Luminous Flux (lm)	lm klm		lumen kilolumen	Luminous flux of light sources, lamps and light bulbs	$1\ lm = 1\ cd \cdot sr$ Already in general use
Quantity of Light (lm·s)	lm·s	lm·h	lumen second lumen hour		$1\ lm \cdot h = 3600\ lm/s$
Luminance (cd/m²)	cd/m² kcd/m²	cd/mm²	candela per square metre kilocandela per square metre candela per square millimetre	Assessment of surface brightness; luminance of light sources, lamps and light bulbs; calculation of glare in lighting layouts	Replaces stilb ($1\ sb = 10^4\ cd/m^2$) and apostilb ($1\ apostilb = cd/\pi m^2$)
Illuminance (lx)	lx klx		lux kilolux	Luminous flux per unit area is used in determination of illumination levels and design/evaluation of interior lighting layouts. (Outdoor daylight illumination on a horizontal plane ranges up to 100 klx.)	a) Formerly referred to as illumination $1\ lx = 1\ lm/m^2$ b) Replaces phot ($1\ ph = 10^4\ lx$) c) Luminous exitance is described in lm/m^2
Light Exposure (lx·s)	lx·s klx·s		lux second kilolux second		
Luminous Efficacy (lm/W)	lm/W		lumen per watt	Rating of luminous efficacy of artificial light sources	

Table 12. Acoustics

Quantity (and SI Unit Symbol)	Preferred Units (Symbols)	Other Acceptable Units	Unit Name	Typical Applications	Remarks
Wavelength (m)	m		metre	Definition of sound wave pitch	
	mm		millimetre		
Area of Absorptive Surface (m²)	m²		square metre	Calculations of room absorption	
Period, Periodic Time (s)	s		second	Measurement of time and reverberation time	
	ms		millisecond		
Frequency (Hz)	Hz		hertz	Frequency ranges in sound absorption calculations and sound pressure measurement	1 Hz = 1 cycle per second (cps)
	kHz		kilohertz		
(Instantaneous) Sound Pressure (Pa)	Pa		pascal	Measurement of sound pressure; reference level for sound pressure is 20 μPa, but sound pressure is shown in decibels (dB) based upon a logarithmic scale.	Do NOT USE dyne (1 dyn = 10 μPa)
	mPa		millipascal		
		μPa	micropascal	Sound pressure level $L_p = $ $20 \log_{10} \dfrac{\text{actual pressure (Pa)}}{20 \times 10^{-6} \text{ (Pa)}}$	
Sound Power, Sound Energy Flux (W)	W		watt	Measurement of sound power; reference level for sound power is 1 pW.	
	mW		milliwatt		
	μW		microwatt		
		pW	picowatt	Sound power level, $L = $ $10 \log_{10} \dfrac{\text{actual power (W)}}{10^{-12} \text{ (W)}}$	
Sound Intensity (W/m²)	W/m²		watt per square metre	Measurement of sound intensity; reference level for sound intensity is 1 pW/m².	
		pW/m²	picowatt per square metre	Sound intensity level $L_I = $ $10 \log_{10} \dfrac{\text{actual intensity (W/m²)}}{10^{-12} \text{ (W/m²)}} \text{ dB}$	
Specific Acoustic Impedance (Pa·s/m)	Pa·s/m		pascal second per metre	Sound impedance measurement	(1 Pa·s/m = 1 N·s/m³)
Acoustic Impedance, Resistance (Pa·s/m³)	Pa·s/m³		pascal second per cubic metre	Sound impedance measurement	

Table 13. Units for volume and fluid capacity and their relationships

Preferred Units		Limited Application	Relationships
All Volumes	**Fluid Volume Only**		
m³			1 m³ = 1000 L = 1000 dm³
	L	dm³	1 L = 1 dm³ = $\dfrac{10^{-3} \text{ m}^3}{10^6 \text{ mm}^3}$ = 1000 mL
	mL	cm³	1 mL = 1 cm³ = $\dfrac{10^{-6} \text{ m}^3}{10^3 \text{ mm}^3}$
mm³			1 mm³ = 10^{-9} m³

Table 14. Constants for use in building design calculations

Name	Symbol	Value	Unit
Standard atmosphere pressure (international value)	P_o	101.325	kPa
Absolute (zero) temperature	T	0.0	K
		(−273.15)	(°C)
Velocity of sound in air (P_o, 20°C, 50 % relative humidity)	M	344	m/s
Specific volume of perfect gas at STP	V_o	22.414	m³/kmol
			(L/mol)
Characteristic gas constant for air	R_a	287.045	J/(kg·K)
Characteristic gas constant for water vapor	R_r	461.52	J/(kg·K)

APPENDIXES

X1. Conversion factors for the most common units used in building design and construction

X1.1 Where appropriate, conversion factors are taken to six significant figures. Underlined values denote exact conversions.

Metric to Customary			Customary to Metric		

LENGTH

1 km	= 0.621 371	mile (international)	1 mile (international)	= 1.609 344	km
	= 49.7096	chain	1 chain (survey unit)	= 20.1168	m
1 m	= 1.093 61	yd	1 yd	= 0.9144	m
	= 3.280 84	ft	1 ft	= 0.3048	m
1 mm	= 0.039 370 1	in		= 304.8	mm
			1 in	= 25.4	mm
			(1 U.S. survey foot	= 0.304 800 6	m)*

* Section 9.1.7 deals with U.S. survey measurement.

AREA

1 km²	= 0.386 101	mile² (U.S. survey)	1 mile² (U.S. survey)	= 2.590 00	km²
1 ha	= 2.471 04	acre (U.S. survey)	1 acre (U.S. survey)	≈ 0.404 687	ha
1 m²	= 1.195 99	yd²		= 4046.87	m²
	= 10.7639	ft²	1 yd²	= 0.836 127	m²
1 mm²	= 0.001 550	in²	1 ft²	= 0.092 903	m²
			1 in²	= 645.16	mm²

VOLUME, MODULUS OF SECTION

1 m³	= 0.810 708 × 10⁻³	acre feet (U.S. survey)	1 acre ft (U.S. survey)	= 1233.49	m³
	= 1.307 95	yd³	1 yd³	= 0.764 555	m³
	= 35.3147	ft³	100 board ft	= 0.235 974	m³
	= 423.776	board ft	1 ft³	= 0.028 316 8	m³
1 mm³	= 61.0237 × 10⁻⁶	in³		= 28.3168	L (dm³)
			1 in³	= 16 387.1	mm³
				=16.3871	mL (cm³)

(FLUID) CAPACITY

1 L	= 0.035 314 7	ft³	1 gal (U.S. liquid)**	= 3.785 41	L
	= 0.264 172	gal (U.S.)	1 qt (U.S. liquid)	= 946.353	mL
	= 1.056 69	qt (U.S.)	1 pt (U.S. liquid)	= 473.177	mL
1 mL	= 0.061 023 7	in³	1 fl oz (U.S.)	= 29.5735	mL
	0.033 814	fl oz (U.S.)			

** 1 gal(U.K.) approx. 1.2 gal(U.S.)

SECOND MOMENT OF AREA

1 mm⁴	= 2.402 51 × 10⁻⁶	in⁴	1 in⁴	= 416 231	mm⁴
				= 0.416 231 × 10⁻⁶	m⁴

PLANE ANGLE

1 rad	= 57° 17′ 45″	(degree)	1° (degree)	= 0.017 453 3	rad
	= 57.2958°	(degree)		= 17.4533	mrad
	= 3437.75′	(minute)	1′ (minute)	= 290.888	μrad
	= 206 265″	(second)	1″ (second)	= 4.848 14	μrad

VELOCITY, SPEED

1 m/s	= 3.280 84	ft/s	1 ft/s	= 0.3048	m/s
	= 2.236 94	mile/h	1 mile/h	= 1.609 344	km/h
1 km/h	= 0.621 371	mile/h		= 0.447 04	m/s

ACCELERATION

1 m/s²	= 3.280 84	ft/s²	1 ft/s²	= 0.3048	m/s²

VOLUME RATE OF FLOW

1 m³/s	= 35.3147	ft³/s	1 ft³/s	= 0.028 316 8	m³/s
	= 22.8245	million gal/d	1 ft³/min	= 0.471 947	L/s
	= 0.810 709 × 10⁻³	acre ft/s	1 gal/min	= 0.063 090 2	L/s
1 L/s	= 2.118 88	ft³/min	1 gal/h	= 1.051 50	mL/s
	= 15.8503	gal/min	1 million gal/d	= 43.8126	L/s
	= 951.022	gal/h	1 acre ft/s	=1233.49	m³/s

TEMPERATURE INTERVAL

1°C	= 1 K = 1.8°F		1°F	= 0.555 556	°C or K
				= 5/9°C = 5/9 K	

EQUIVALENT TEMPERATURE VALUE ($t_C = T_K - 273.15$)

t_C	= 5/9 (t_F − 32)		t_F	= 9/5 t_C + 32	

MASS

1 kg	= 2.204 62	lb (avoirdupois)	1 ton (short)***	= 0.907 185	metric ton
	= 35.2740	oz (avoirdupois)		= 907.185	kg
1 metric ton	= 1.102 31	ton (short, 2000 lb)	1 lb	= 0.453 592	kg
	= 2204.62	lb	1 oz	= 28.3495	g
1 g	= 0.035 274	oz	1 pennyweight	= 1.555 17	g
	= 0.643 015	pennyweight	*** (1 long ton (2240 lb)	= 1016.05	kg)

MASS PER UNIT LENGTH

1 kg/m	= 0.671 969	lb/ft	1 lb/ft	= 1.488 16	kg/m
1 g/m	= 3.547 99	lb/mile	1 lb/mile	= 0.281 849	g/m

MASS PER UNIT AREA

1 kg/m²	= 0.204 816	lb/ft²	1 lb/ft²	= 4.882 43	kg/m²
1 g/m²	= 0.029 494	oz/yd²	1 oz/yd²	= 33.9057	g/m²
	= 3.277 06 × 10⁻³	oz/ft²	1 oz/ft²	= 305.152	g/m²

DENSITY (MASS PER UNIT VOLUME)

1 kg/m³	= 0.062 428	lb/ft³	1 lb/ft³	= 16.0185	kg/m³
	= 1.685 56	lb/yd³	1 lb/yd³	= 0.593 276	kg/m³
1 t/m³	= 0.842 778	ton/yd³	1 ton/yd³	= 1.186 55	t/m³

MOMENT OF INERTIA

1 kg·m²	= 23.7304	lb·ft²	1 lb·ft²	= 0.042 140 1	kg·m²
	= 3417.17	lb·in²	1 lb·in²	= 292.640	kg·mm²

Appendix X1 (cont.). Conversion factors for the most common units used in building design and construction

Metric to Customary			Customary to Metric		
MASS PER UNIT TIME					
1 kg/s	= 2.204 62	lb/s	1 lb/s	= 0.453 592	kg/s
1 t/h	= 0.984 207	ton/h	1 ton/h	= 1.016 05	t/h
FORCE					
1 MN	= 112.404	tonf (ton-force)	1 tonf (ton-force)	= 8.896 44	kN
1 kN	= 0.112 404	tonf	1 kip (1000 lbf)	= 4.448 22	kN
	= 224.809	lbf (pound-force)	1 lbf (pound-force)	= 4.448 22	N
1 N	= 0.224 809	lbf			
MOMENT OF FORCE, TORQUE					
1 N·m	= 0.737 562	lbf·ft	1 lbf·ft	= 1.355 82	N·m
	= 8.850 75	lbf·in	1 lbf·in	= 0.112 985	N·m
1 kN·m	= 0.368 781	tonf·ft	1 tonf·ft	= 2.711 64	kN·m
	= 0.737 562	kip·ft	1 kip·ft	= 1.355 82	kN·m
FORCE PER UNIT LENGTH					
1 N/m	= 0.068 521 8	lbf/ft	1 lbf/ft	= 14.5939	N/m
1 kN/m	= 0.034 260 9	tonf/ft	1 lbf/in	= 175.127	N/m
			1 tonf/ft	= 29.1878	kN/m
PRESSURE, STRESS, MODULUS OF ELASTICITY (FORCE PER UNIT AREA)					
(1 Pa = 1 N/m²)					
1 MPa	= 0.072 518 8	tonf/in²	1 tonf/in²	= 13.7895	MPa
	= 10.4427	tonf/ft²	1 tonf/ft²	= 95.7605	kPa
	= 145.038	lbf/in²	1 kip/in²	= 6.894 76	MPa
1 kPa	= 20.8854	lbf/ft²	1 lbf/in²	= 6.894 76	kPa
			1 lbf/ft²	= 47.8803	Pa
WORK, ENERGY, HEAT (1 J = 1 N·m = 1 W·s)					
1 MJ	= 0.277 778	kWh	1 kWh	= 3.6	MJ
1 kJ	= 0.947 817	Btu	1 Btu (Int. Table)	= 1.055 06	kJ
1 J	= 0.737 562	ft·lbf	1 ft·lbf		
				= 1.355 82	J
POWER, HEAT FLOW RATE					
1 kW	= 1.341 02	hp (horsepower)	1 hp (550 ft·lbf/s)	= 0.745 700	kW
1 W	= 3.412 14	Btu/h		= 745.700	W
	= 0.737 562	ft·lbf/s	1 Btu/h	= 0.293 071	W
			1 ft·lbf/s	= 1.355 82	W
HEAT FLUX DENSITY					
1 W/m²	= 0.316 998	Btu/(ft²·h)	1 Btu/(ft²·h)	= 3.154 59	W/m²
COEFFICIENT OF HEAT TRANSFER					
1 W/(m²·K)	= 0.176 110	Btu/(ft²·h·°F)	1 Btu/(ft²·h·°F)	= 5.678 26	W/(m²·K)
THERMAL CONDUCTIVITY					
1 W/(m·K)	= 0.577 789	Btu/(ft·h·°F)	1 Btu/(ft·h·°F)	= 1.730 73	W/(m·K)
CALORIFIC VALUE (MASS AND VOLUME BASIS)					
1 kJ/kg					
(1 J/g)	= 0.429 923	Btu/lb	1 Btu/lb	= 2.326	kJ/kg (J/g)
1 kJ/m³	= 0.026 839 2	Btu/ft³	1 Btu/ft³	= 37.2589	kJ/m³
THERMAL CAPACITY (MASS AND VOLUME BASIS)					
1 kJ/(kg·K)	= 0.238 846	Btu/(lb·°F)	1 Btu/(lb·°F)	= 4.1868	kJ/(kg·K)
1 kJ/(m³·K)	= 0.014 910 7	Btu/(ft³·°F)	1 Btu/(ft³·°F)	= 67.0661	kJ/(m³·K)
ILLUMINANCE					
1 lx (lux)	= 0.092 903	lm/ft² (footcandle)	1 lm/ft² (footcandle)	= 10.7639	lx (lux)
LUMINANCE					
1 cd/m²	= 0.092 903	cd/ft²	1 cd/ft²	= 10.7639	cd/m²
	= 0.291 864	footlambert	1 footlambert	= 3.426 26	cd/m²
1 kcd/m²	= 0.314 159	lambert	1 lambert	= 3.183 01	kcd/m²

X2. Superseded metric units not recommended for use with SI

X2.1 It is strongly recommended that the traditional and "cgs" metric (non-SI) units listed below be *avoided* in building design or construction applications. Any data showing these units should be converted to the appropriate SI units that supersede them.

Unit Name	Symbol	Value in SI Units	
dyne	dyn	10^{-5} N	(or 10 μN)
bar	bar	10^5 Pa	(or 100 kPa)
erg	erg	10^{-7} J	(or 100 nJ)
poise	P	10^{-1} Pa·s	(or 100 mPa·s)
stokes	St	10^{-4} m²/s	(or 100 mm²/s)
gauss	Gs,(G)	10^{-4} T	(or 100 μT)
maxwell	Mx	10^{-8} Wb	(or 10 nWb)
stilb	sb	10^4 cd/m²	(or 10 kcd/m²)
phot	ph	10^4 lx	(or 10 klx)
kilogram-force	kgf	9.806 65 N	
calorie (int.)	cal	4.1868 J	
kilocalorie (int.)	kcal	4.1868 kJ	
torr	torr	133.322 Pa	
oersted	Oe	79.5775 A/m	

REFERENCES

(1) American National Standard for Metric Practice ASTM E 380 76/ANSI Z210.1-1976/IEEE Std 268-1976
Available from:
—(ASTM E 380)—American Society for Testing and Materials, 1916 Race St., Philadelphia, Pa. 19013
—(ANSI Z210.1)—American National Standards Institute, 1430 Broadway, New York, N.Y. 10018
—(IEEE Std 268)—Institute of Electrical and Electronics Engineers, 345 East 47th St., New York, N.Y. 10017

(2) ANMC *Metric Editorial Guide*, 3rd Edition, 1978
Available from American National Metric Council, 1625 Massachusetts Ave., N.W., Washington, D.C. 20036.

(3) U.S. Department of Commerce/National Bureau of Standards NBS Special Publication 330, *The International System of Units (SI)* (1977 Revised Edition)
Available from U.S. Government Printing Office, Washington, D.C., 20402

(4) U.S. Federal Register—The National Archives of the United States, Vol 41, No. 239, pp. 54018 and 54019, *The Metric System of Measurement* (Interpretation and Modification of the International System of Units for the United States) (Issued Dec. 10, 1976)
Available from the Office of Technical Publications, National Bureau of Standards, Washington, D.C. 20234.

(5) Public Law 94-168, *Metric Conversion Act of 1975* (Dec. 23, 1975)
Available from U.S. Government Printing Office, Washington, D.C. 20402
Available from the Office of Technical Publications, National Bureau of Standards, Washington, D.C. 20234.

(6) International Standard ISO 1000-1973 (E) *SI Units and Recommendations for the Use of Their Multiples and Certain Other Units* (1973 Edition)
Available from American National Standards Institute, 1430 Broadway, New York, N.Y. 10018

(7) International Standard ISO 31/0-1974 (E) General Introduction to ISO 31-*General Principles Concerning Quantities, Units, and Symbols*
Available from American National Standards Institute, 1430 Broadway, New York, N.Y. 10018

CONVERSION FACTORS – 1

Alphabetical list

CONVERSION FROM U.S. CUSTOMARY UNITS TO SI METRIC UNITS

By HANS J. MILTON, FRAIA *Center for Building Technology, National Bureau of Standards*

Table 1. Alphabetical list of conversion factors for units used in building design and construction

This list of conversion factors is based on units and values given in *ASTM E380-79, Standard for Metric Practice (Appendix X.3)*, modified to show powers of 10 rather than an alpha-numerical representation. An additional column gives expressions in working units, such as prefixed SI-units and, in the case of the liter (L), a non-SI unit permitted for use with SI.

In general, the names of non-SI units are spelled out, although some compound units for heat use the abbreviation Btu for British thermal unit. All SI units are spelled out, and symbols are given in parentheses.

While conversion factors are shown with seven significant digits (six places of decimals), the use of factors with fewer digits will sometimes be appropriate to avoid the appearance of excessive precision. Where exact conversion factors result in fewer than seven digits, they are shown to the last significant digit, followed by an asterisk (*) to indicate that all additional digits would be zeros.

Footnotes have been added where it is desirable to provide additional explanatory information.

To convert from	to	Multiply by	Expression in Working Units
acre [U.S. survey] (ac) [1]	square meter (m²)	4.046 873 x 10³	4046.873 m² [2]
acre foot (ac·ft)	cubic meter (m³)	1.233 489 x 10³	1233.489 m³
ampere hour (A·h)	coulomb (C)	3.6* x 10³	3.6 kC
atmosphere [standard] (atm)	pascal (Pa)	1.013 25* x 10⁵	101.325 kPa
board foot (bf) [3]	cubic meter (m³)	2.359 737 x 10⁻³	0.002 360 m³
British thermal unit [Int. Table] (Btu) [4]	joule (J)	1.055 056 x 10³	1.055 056 kJ
Btu foot per hour square foot degree Fahrenheit [Btu·ft/(h·ft²·°F)]	watt per meter kelvin [W/(m·K)] [5]	1.730 735	1.730 735 W/(m·K)
Btu inch per hour square foot degree Fahrenheit [Btu·in/(h·ft²·°F)]	watt per meter kelvin [W/(m·K)]	1.442 279 x 10⁻¹	0.144 228 W/(m·K)
Btu per cubic foot (Btu/ft³)	joule per cubic meter (J/m³)	3.725 895 x 10⁴	37.258 95 kJ/m³
Btu per cubic foot degree Fahrenheit [Btu/(ft³·°F)]	joule per cubic meter kelvin [J/(m³·K)]	6.706 610 x 10⁴	67.0661 kJ/(m³·K)
Btu per hour (Btu/h)	watt (W)	2.930 711 x 10⁻¹	0.293 071 W
Btu per hour foot degree Fahrenheit [Btu/(h·ft·°F)]	watt per meter kelvin [W/(m·K)]	1.730 735	1.730 735 W/(m·K)
Btu per hour square foot degree Fahrenheit [Btu/(h·ft²·°F)]	watt per square meter kelvin [W/(m²·K)]	5.678 263	5.678 263 W/(m²·K)
Btu per pound (Btu/lb)	joule per kilogram (J/kg)	2.326* x 10³	2.326 kJ/kg
Btu per pound degree Fahrenheit [Btu/(lb·°F)]	joule per kilogram kelvin [J/(kg·K)]	4.186 8* x 10³	4.1868 kJ/(kg·K)
Btu per second (Btu/s)	watt (W)	1.055 056 x 10³	1.055 056 kW
Btu per second square foot degree Fahrenheit [Btu/(s·ft²·°F)]	watt per square meter kelvin [W/(m²·K)]	2.044 175 x 10⁴	20.441 75 kW/(m²·K)
Btu per square foot (Btu/ft²)	joule per square meter (J/m²)	1.135 653 x 10⁴	11.356 53 kJ/m²
Btu per square foot hour [Btu/(ft²·h)]	watt per square meter (W/m²)	3.154 591	3.154 591 W/m²
Btu per square foot second [Btu/(ft²·s)]	watt per square meter (W/m²)	1.135 653 x 10⁴	11.356 53 kW/m²
calorie [International Table] (cal)	joule (J)	4.186 8*	4.1868 J
candela per square foot (cd/ft²)	candela per square meter (cd/m²)	1.076 391 x 10¹	10.763 91 cd/m²
candela per square inch (cd/in²)	candela per square meter (cd/m²)	1.550 003 x 10³	1.550 003 kcd/m²
centipoise (cP)	pascal second (Pa·s)	1.0* x 10⁻³	1.0 mPa·s
centistokes (cSt)	square meter per second (m²/s)	1.0* x 10⁻⁶	1.0 mm²/s
chain [survey chain] [6]	meter (m)	2.011 684 x 10¹	20.116 84 m
circular mil	square meter (m²)	5.067 075 x 10⁻¹⁰	506.7075 µm²
cubic foot (ft³)	cubic meter (m³)	2.831 685 x 10⁻²	0.028 316 85 m³
cubic foot per hour (ft³/h)	cubic meter per second (m³/s)	7.865 791 x 10⁻⁶	7865.791 mm³/s
cubic foot per minute (ft³/min, cfm)	cubic meter per second (m³/s)	4.719 474 x 10⁻⁴	0.000 471 95 m³/s
cubic foot per second (ft³/s)	cubic meter per second (m³/s)	2.831 685 x 10⁻²	0.028 317 m³/s
cubic inch (in³)	cubic meter (m³)	1.638 706 x 10⁻⁵	16 387.06 mm³
cubic inch per minute (in³/min)	cubic meter per second (m³/s)	2.731 177 x 10⁻⁷	273.1177 mm³/s
cubic yard (yd³)	cubic meter (m³)	7.645 549 x 10⁻¹	0.764 555 m³
cubic yard per hour (yd³/h)	cubic meter per second (m³/s)	2.123 763 x 10⁻⁴	0.028 316 85 m³/s
cubic yard per minute (yd³/min)	cubic meter per second (m³/s)	1.274 258 x 10⁻²	0.012 742 58 m³/s
degree [angle] (°)	radian (rad)	1.745 329 x 10⁻²	17.453 29 mrad
degree Fahrenheit (°F) *(Temperature Interval)*	degree Celsius (°C) [5]	5.555 556 x 10⁻¹	0.555 556 °C
degree Fahrenheit (°F) *(Temperature Interval)*	kelvin (K) [5]	5.555 556 x 10⁻¹	0.555 556 K
degree Fahrenheit (°F) *(Temperature Value)*	degree Celsius (°C) [5]	$t_{°C} = (t_{°F} - 32)/1.8$	
degree Fahrenheit (°F) *(Temperature Value)*	kelvin (K) [5]	$T_K = (t_{°F} + 459.67)/1.8$	
degree Fahrenheit hour square foot per Btu (°F·h·ft²/Btu) [4]	kelvin square meter per watt (K·m²/W)	1.761 102 x 10⁻¹	0.176 110 K·m²/W
degree Fahrenheit hour square foot per Btu inch [°F·h·ft²/(Btu·in)]	kelvin meter per watt (K·m/W)	6.933 471	6.933 471 K·m/W
fathom	meter (m)	1.828 804	1.828 804 m
fluid ounce [U.S.] (fl oz)	cubic meter (m³)	2.957 353 x 10⁻⁵	29.573 53 mL [7]
foot (ft, ')	meter (m)	3.048* x 10⁻¹	0.3048 m; 304.8 mm
foot [U.S. survey] [1] [6]	meter (m)	3.048 006 x 10⁻¹	0.304 800 6 m
footcandle (fc)	lux (lx)	1.076 391 x 10¹	10.763 91 lx
footlambert (fL)	candela per square meter (cd/m²)	3.426 259	3.426 259 cd/m²

Table 1 (cont.). Alphabetical list of conversion factors for units used in building design and construction

To convert from	to	Multiply by	Expression in Working Units
foot per hour (ft/h)	meter per second (m/s)	$8.466\ 667 \times 10^{-5}$	$84.666\ 67\ \mu m/s$
foot per minute (ft/min, fpm)	meter per second (m/s)	$5.08^* \times 10^{-3}$	$5.08\ mm/s$
foot per second (ft/s)	meter per second (m/s)	$3.048^* \times 10^{-1}$	$0.3048\ m/s$
foot per second squared (ft/s²)	meter per second squared (m/s²)	$3.048^* \times 10^{-1}$	$0.3048\ m/s^2$
foot pound-force (ft·lbf)	joule (J)	$1.355\ 818$	$1.355\ 818\ J$
foot pound-force per hour (ft·lbf/h)	watt (W)	$3.766\ 161 \times 10^{-4}$	$0.376\ 616\ mW$
foot pound-force per minute (ft·lbf/min)	watt (W)	$2.259\ 697 \times 10^{-2}$	$22.596\ 97\ mW$
foot pound-force per second (ft·lbf/s)	watt (W)	$1.355\ 818$	$1.355\ 818\ W$
foot of water [39.2°F – 4°C] (ft H₂O)	pascal (Pa)	$2.988\ 98 \times 10^3$	$2.988\ 98\ kPa$
free fall [standard] (g)	meter per second squared (m/s²)	$9.806\ 65^*$	$9.806\ 65\ m/s^2$
gallon [U.S. liquid] (gal)	cubic meter (m³)	$3.785\ 412 \times 10^{-3}$	$3.785\ 412\ L^{(7)}$
gallon per day (gal/d)	cubic meter per second (m³/s)	$4.381\ 264 \times 10^{-8}$	$43.812\ 64\ \mu L/s\ (mm^3/s)$
gallon per minute (gal/min, gpm)	cubic meter per second (m³/s)	$6.309\ 020 \times 10^{-5}$	$63.0902\ mL/s$
grain (gr)	kilogram (kg)	$6.479\ 891^* \times 10^{-5}$	$64.798\ 91\ mg$
horsepower [550 ft·lbf/s] (hp)	watt (W)	$7.456\ 999 \times 10^2$	$745.6999\ W$
horsepower [boiler]	watt (W)	$9.809\ 50 \times 10^3$	$9.809\ 50\ kW$
horsepower [electric]	watt (W)	$7.46^* \times 10^2$	$746\ W$
hundredweight [100 lb] (cwt)	kilogram (kg)	$4.535\ 924 \times 10^1$	$45.359\ 24\ kg$
inch (in, ")	meter (m)	$2.54^* \times 10^{-2}$	$25.4\ mm;\ 0.0254\ m$
inch per second (in/s)	meter per second (m/s)	$2.54^* \times 10^{-2}$	$25.4\ mm/s$
inch per second squared (in/s²)	meter per second squared (m/s²)	$2.54^* \times 10^{-2}$	$25.4\ mm/s^2$
inch to the fourth power (in⁴)	meter to the fourth power (m⁴)	$4.162\ 314 \times 10^{-7}$	$416\ 231\ mm^4$
inch of mercury [32°F – 0°C] (in Hg)	pascal (Pa)	$3.386\ 38 \times 10^3$	$3.386\ 38\ kPa$
inch of mercury [60°F] (in Hg)	pascal (Pa)	$3.376\ 85 \times 10^3$	$3.376\ 85\ kPa$
inch of water [39.2°F – 4°C] (in H₂O)	pascal (Pa)	$2.490\ 82 \times 10^2$	$249.082\ Pa$
inch of water [60°F] (in H₂O)	pascal (Pa)	$2.488\ 4 \times 10^2$	$248.84\ Pa$
kilowatthour (kW·h, kWh)	joule (J)	$3.6^* \times 10^6$	$3.6\ MJ$
kip [1000 lbf]	newton (N)	$4.448\ 222 \times 10^3$	$4.448\ 222\ kN$
kip foot (kip·ft)	newton meter (N·m)	$1.355\ 818 \times 10^3$	$1.355\ 818\ kN·m$
kip per foot (kip/ft)	newton per meter (N/m)	$1.459\ 390 \times 10^4$	$14.5939\ kN/m$
kip per square inch (kip/in², ksi)	pascal (Pa)	$6.894\ 757 \times 10^6$	$6.894\ 757\ MPa$
lambert (L)	candela per square meter (cd/m²)	$3.183\ 099 \times 10^3$	$3.1831\ kcd/m^2$
langley (ly)	joule per square meter (J/m²)	$4.184^* \times 10^4$	$41.84\ kJ/m^2$
lumen per square foot (lm/ft² = fc)	lux (lx)	$1.076\ 391 \times 10^1$	$10.763\ 91\ lx$
microinch	meter (m)	$2.54^* \times 10^{-8}$	$25.4\ nm$
mil [0.001"]	meter (m)	$2.54^* \times 10^{-5}$	$25.4\ \mu m$
mile [international] (mi)	meter (m)	$1.609\ 344^* \times 10^3$	$1.609\ 344\ km$
mile [U.S. statute] (6)	meter (m)	$1.609\ 347 \times 10^3$	$1.609\ 347\ km$
mile per hour (mi/h, mph)	meter per second (m/s)	$4.470\ 4^* \times 10^{-1}$	$0.447\ 04\ m/s$
minute [angle] (')	radian (rad)	$2.908\ 882 \times 10^{-4}$	$0.290\ 888\ mrad$
nautical mile (nmi)	meter (m)	$1.852^* \times 10^3$	$1.852\ km$
ounce [avoirdupois] (oz)	kilogram (kg)	$2.834\ 952 \times 10^{-2}$	$28.349\ 52\ g$
ounce per gallon (oz/gal)	kilogram per cubic meter (kg/m³)	$7.489\ 152$	$7.489\ 152\ kg/m^3$
ounce per square foot (oz/ft²)	kilogram per square meter (kg/m²)	$3.051\ 517 \times 10^{-1}$	$305.1517\ g/m^2$
ounce per square yard (oz/yd²)	kilogram per square meter (kg/m²)	$3.390\ 575 \times 10^{-2}$	$33.905\ 75\ g/m^2$
pennyweight (dwt)	kilogram (kg)	$1.555\ 174 \times 10^{-3}$	$1.555\ 174\ g$
perm [0°C]	kilogram per pascal second square meter [kg/(Pa·s·m²)]	$5.721\ 35 \times 10^{-11}$	$57.2135\ ng/(Pa·s·m^2)$
perm [23°C]	kilogram per pascal second square meter [kg/(Pa·s·m²)]	$5.745\ 25 \times 10^{-11}$	$57.4525\ ng/(Pa·s·m^2)$
perm-inch [0°C] (perm·in)	kilogram per pascal second meter [kg/(Pa·s·m)]	$1.453\ 22 \times 10^{-12}$	$1.453\ 22\ ng/(Pa·s·m)$
perm-inch [23°C] (perm·in)	kilogram per pascal second meter [kg/(Pa·s·m)]	$1.459\ 29 \times 10^{-12}$	$1.459\ 29\ ng/(Pa·s·m)$
pint [U.S. liquid] (pt)	cubic meter (m³)	$4.731\ 765 \times 10^{-4}$	$473.1765\ mL^{(7)}$
pound [avoirdupois] (lb)	kilogram (kg)	$4.535\ 924 \times 10^{-1}$	$0.453\ 592\ 4\ kg$
poundal (pdl)	newton (N)	$1.382\ 550 \times 10^{-1}$	$0.138\ 255\ N$
poundal per square foot (pdl/ft²)	pascal (Pa)	$1.488\ 164$	$1.488\ 164\ Pa$
poundal second per square foot (pdl·s/ft²)	pascal second (Pa·s)	$1.488\ 164$	$1.488\ 164\ Pa·s$
pound-force (lbf)	newton (N)	$4.448\ 222$	$4.448\ 222\ N$
pound-force foot (lbf·ft)	newton meter (N·m)	$1.355\ 818$	$1.355\ 818\ N·m$
pound-force inch (lbf·in)	newton meter (N·m)	$1.129\ 848 \times 10^{-1}$	$0.112\ 985\ N·m$
pound-force per foot (lbf/ft)	newton per meter (N/m)	$1.459\ 390 \times 10^1$	$14.5939\ N/m$
pound-force per inch (lbf/in)	newton per meter (N/m)	$1.751\ 268 \times 10^2$	$175.1268\ N/m$
pound-force per square foot (lbf/ft², psf)	pascal (Pa)	$4.788\ 026 \times 10^1$	$47.880\ 26\ Pa$
pound-force per square inch (lbf/in², psi)	pascal (Pa)	$6.894\ 757 \times 10^3$	$6.894\ 757\ kPa$
pound per cubic foot (lb/ft³)	kilogram per cubic meter (kg/m³)	$1.601\ 846 \times 10^1$	$16.018\ 46\ kg/m^3$
pound per cubic inch (lb/in³)	kilogram per cubic meter (kg/m³)	$2.767\ 990 \times 10^4$	$27\ 679.9\ kg/m^3$
pound per cubic yard (lb/yd³)	kilogram per cubic meter (kg/m³)	$5.932\ 764 \times 10^{-1}$	$0.593\ 276\ kg/m^3$

Table 1 (cont.). Alphabetical list of conversion factors for units used in building design and construction

To convert from	to	Multiply by	Expression in Working Units
pound per foot (lb/ft)	kilogram per meter (kg/m)	1.488 164	1.488 164 kg/m
pound per gallon (lb/gal)	kilogram per cubic meter (kg/m^3)	1.198 264 x 10^2	119.8264 kg/m^3
pound per mile (lb/mi)	kilogram per meter (kg/m)	2.818 492 x 10^{-4}	0.281 849 g/m
pound per second (lb/s)	kilogram per second (kg/s)	4.535 924 x 10^{-1}	0.453 592 kg/s
pound per square foot (lb/ft^2)	kilogram per square meter (kg/m^2)	4.882 428	4.882 428 kg/m^2
quart [U.S. liquid] (qt)	cubic meter (m^3)	9.463 529 x 10^{-4}	0.946 353 L [7]
rod [pole, perch] [6]	meter (m)	5.029 210	5.029 21 m
second [angle]	radian (rad)	4.848 137 x 10^{-6}	4.848 137 μrad
slug	kilogram (kg)	1.459 390 x 10^1	14.5939 kg
square foot (ft^2)	square meter (m^2)	9.290 304* x 10^{-2}	0.092 903 m^2
square foot per hour (ft^2/h)	square meter per second (m^2/s)	2.580 64* x 10^{-5}	25.8064 mm^2/s
square foot per second (ft^2/s)	square meter per second (m^2/s)	9.290 304 x 10^{-2}	0.092 903 m^2/s
square inch (in^2)	square meter (m^2)	6.451 6* x 10^{-4}	645.16 mm^2
square mile [U.S. statute] [1]	square meter (m^2)	2.589 998 x 10^6	2.589 998 km^2
square mile [international] (mi^2)	square meter (m^2)	2.589 988 x 10^6	2.589 988 km^2
square yard (yd^2)	square meter (m^2)	8.361 274 x 10^{-1}	0.836 127 m^2
therm [100 000 Btu]	joule (J)	1.055 056 x 10^8	105.5056 MJ
ton [long, 2240 lb]	kilogram (kg)	1.016 047 x 10^3	1016.047 kg
ton [short, 2000 lb] (ton)	kilogram (kg)	9.071 847 x 10^2	907.1847 kg
ton (of refrigeration)	watt (W)	3.516 800 x 10^3	3.5168 kW
ton-force [2000 lbf] (tonf)	newton (N)	8.896 444 x 10^3	8.896 444 kN
ton-force foot (tonf·ft)	newton meter (N·m)	2.711 636 x 10^3	2.711 636 kN·m
ton-force per foot (tonf/ft)	newton per meter (N/m)	2.918 781 x 10^4	29.1878 kN/m
ton-force per square foot (tonf/ft^2)	pascal (Pa)	9.576 052 x 10^4	95.7605 kPa
ton-force per square inch (tonf/in^2)	pascal (Pa)	1.378 951 x 10^7	13.789 51 MPa
ton per cubic yard (ton/yd^3)	kilogram per cubic meter (kg/m^3)	1.186 553 x 10^3	1186.553 kg/m^3
ton per hour (ton/h)	kilogram per second (kg/s)	2.519 958 x 10^{-1}	0.251 996 kg/s
watt-hour (W·h)	joule (J)	3.6* x 10^3	3.6 kJ
watt per square foot (W/ft^2)	watt per square meter (W/m^2)	1.076 391 x 10^1	10.763 91 W/m^2
watt per square inch (W/in^2)	watt per square meter (W/m^2)	1.550 003 x 10^3	1.550 003 kW/m^2
yard (yd)	meter (m)	9.144* x 10^{-1}	0.9144 m

NOTES:

(1) *Conversion factors for the acre (ac) and the square mile (U.S. statute) are based on the U.S. survey foot (0.304 800 6 m), which is two parts in a million longer than the international foot (0.3048 m). This discrepancy results in a difference of approximately 56 square feet between the square mile (U.S. statute) and the square mile (international).*

(2) *Measurement of land areas and water surfaces in metric units may also be expressed in the non-SI unit hectare (ha), which equals 10 000 m^2 (exactly). Therefore, 1 acre is equal to 0.404 697 3 ha.*

(3) *The "board foot" measures a theoretical volume of 12" x 12" x 1" for wood products.*

(4) *All conversion factors in this list showing Btu or derived units that include Btu, are based on the British Thermal Unit (International Table), which was defined in 1956 as 1.055 055 852 62 x 10^3 J (exactly).*

(5) *The "degree Celsius" (°C) has been approved by the International Committee for Weights and Measures (CIPM) as a derived unit with special name for Celsius temperature, but has not yet been adopted by the General Conference on Weights and Measures (CGPM). Compound units, with a temperature component, are shown in terms of the SI base unit "kelvin (K)," which has an identical temperature interval to the degree Celsius but has its origin at absolute zero temperature and, therefore, no negative values. (Equivalent temperature value: 0 K = -273.15 °C; 273.15 K = 0 °C).*

(6) *The U.S. Metric Law of 1866 gave the relationship, 1 meter (m) equals 39.37 inches. Since 1893, the U.S. yard has been derived from the meter. In 1959, a refinement was made in the definition of the yard to bring it into agreement with the yard used in other countries, and it was changed from 3600/3937 m to 0.9144 m (exactly). At the same time, it was decided that all data published as a result of geodetic surveys within the U.S. would remain with the old standard, and the foot (1200/3937) was named the U.S. survey foot (0.304 800 6 m). The following units are based on the U.S. survey foot: chain, fathom, rod (pole, or perch), and U.S. statute mile.*

(7) *The "liter" (symbol: L) is a special name adopted for the cubic decimeter (dm^3), and equals 0.001 m^3 (exactly). It is used for liquid and dry measurement of volume (capacity), and may also be used with the prefixes milli and micro (1 mL = 1000 mm^3; 1 μL = 1 mm^3).*

Table 2. Classified list of conversion factors for units used in building design and construction

This list of conversion factors is based on units and values given in _ASTM E380-79, Standard for Metric Practice (Appendix X.3)_, modified to show powers of 10 rather than an alpha-numerical representation. An additional column gives expressions in working units, such as prefixed SI-units and, in the case of the liter (L), a non-SI unit permitted for use with SI. The conversion factors have been grouped by physical quantity.

In general, the names of non-SI units are spelled out, although some compound units for heat use the abbreviation Btu for British thermal unit. All SI units are spelled out, and symbols are given in parentheses.

While conversion factors are shown with seven significant digits (six places of decimals), the use of factors with fewer digits will sometimes be appropriate to avoid the appearance of excessive precision. Where <u>exact</u> conversion factors result in fewer than seven digits, they are shown to the last significant digit, followed by an asterisk (*) to indicate that all additional digits would be zeros.

Footnotes have been added, where appropriate, at the end of each physical quantity segment.

To convert from	to	Multiply by	Expression in Working Units
ACCELERATION			
foot [feet] per second squared (ft/s²)	meter per second squared (m/s²)	3.048* x 10⁻¹	0.3048 m/s²
free fall, standard (g)	meter per second squared (m/s²)	9.806 65*	9.806 65 m/s²
ANGLE			
degree [angle] (°)	radian (rad)	1.745 329 x 10⁻²	17.453 29 mrad
minute [angle] (')	radian (rad)	2.908 882 x 10⁻⁴	0.290 888 mrad
second [angle] (")	radian (rad)	4.848 137 x 10⁻⁶	4.848 137 μrad
AREA			
acre [U.S. survey] (ac) (1)	square meter (m²)	4.046 873 x 10³	4046.873 m² (2)
circular mil	square meter (m²)	5.067 075 x 10⁻¹⁰	506.7075 μm²
square foot (ft²)	square meter (m²)	9.290 304*x 10⁻²	0.092 903 m²
square inch (in²)	square meter (m²)	6.451 6* x 10⁻⁴	645.16 mm²
square mile [U.S. statute] (mi²) (1)	square meter (m²)	2.589 998 x 10⁶	2.589 998 km²
square mile [international] (mi²)	square meter (m²)	2.589 988 x 10⁶	2.589 988 km²
square yard (yd²)	square meter (m²)	8.361 274 x 10⁻¹	0.836 127 m²

NOTES: (1) _Conversion factors for the acre (ac) and the square mile (U.S. statute) are based on the U.S. survey foot (0.304 800 6 m), which is two parts in a million longer than the international foot (0.3048 m). This discrepancy results in a difference of approximately 56 square feet between the square mile (U.S. statute) and the square mile (international)._

(2) _Measurement of land areas and water surfaces in metric units may also be expressed in the non-SI unit hectare (ha), which equals 10 000 m² (exactly). Therefore, 1 acre is equal to 0.404 697 3 ha._

To convert from	to	Multiply by	Expression in Working Units
BENDING MOMENT or TORQUE			
kip foot (kip·ft)	newton meter (N·m)	1.355 818 x 10³	1.355 818 kN·m
pound-force foot (lbf·ft)	newton meter (N·m)	1.355 818	1.355 818 N·m
pound-force inch (lbf·in)	newton meter (N·m)	1.129 848 x 10⁻¹	0.112 985 N·m
BENDING MOMENT or TORQUE PER UNIT LENGTH			
pound-force foot per inch (lbf·ft/in)	newton meter per meter (N·m/m)	5.337 866 x 10¹	53.378 66 N·m/m
pound-force inch per inch (lbf·in/in)	newton meter per meter (N·m/m)	4.448 222	4.448 222 N·m/m
CAPACITY (See VOLUME)			
DENSITY (See MASS PER UNIT VOLUME)			
ENERGY (Includes WORK, QUANTITY OF HEAT)			
British thermal unit [Int. Table] (Btu)	joule (J)	1.055 056 x 10³	1.055 056 kJ
calorie [Int. Table] (cal)	joule (J)	4.186 8*	4.1868 J
foot pound-force (ft·lbf)	joule (J)	1.355 818	1.355 818 J
kilowatt-hour (kW·h, kWh)	joule (J)	3.6* x 10⁶	3.6 MJ
therm [100 000 Btu]	joule (J)	1.055 056 x 10⁸	105.5056 MJ
watt-hour	joule (J)	3.6* x 10³	3.6 kJ

NOTE: _All conversion factors in this list are based on the British thermal unit (International Table), which was defined in 1956 as 1.055 055 852 62 x 10³ J (exactly)._

To convert from	to	Multiply by	Expression in Working Units
FLOW (See MASS PER UNIT TIME or VOLUME PER UNIT TIME)			
FORCE			
kip [1000 lbf]	newton (N)	4.448 222 x 10³	4.448 222 kN
pound-force (lbf)	newton (N)	4.448 222	4.448 222 N
ton-force [2000 lbf] (tonf)	newton (N)	8.896 444 x 10³	8.896 444 kN

Table 2 (cont.).   Classified list of conversion factors for units used in building design and construction

To convert from	to	Multiply by	Expression in Working Units
FORCE PER UNIT AREA *(See PRESSURE AND STRESS)*			
FORCE PER UNIT LENGTH			
kip per foot (kip/ft)	newton per meter (N/m)	$1.459\ 390 \times 10^4$	14.5939 kN/m
pound-force per foot (lbf/ft)	newton per meter (N/m)	$1.459\ 390 \times 10^1$	14.5939 N/m
pound-force per inch (lbf/in)	newton per meter (N/m)	$1.751\ 268 \times 10^2$	175.1268 N/m
ton-force per foot (tonf/ft)	newton per meter (N/m)	$2.918\ 781 \times 10^4$	29.1878 kN/m
HEAT, THERMAL PROPERTIES			
Btu foot per hour square foot degree Fahrenheit [Btu·ft/(h·ft²·°F)]	watt per meter kelvin [W/(m·K)]	1.730 735	1.730 735 W/(m·K)
Btu inch per hour square foot degree Fahrenheit [Btu·in/(h·ft²·°F)]	watt per meter kelvin [W/(m·K)]	$1.442\ 279 \times 10^{-1}$	0.144 228 W/(m·K)
Btu per cubic foot (Btu/ft³)	joule per cubic meter (J/m³)	$3.725\ 895 \times 10^4$	37.258 95 kJ/m³
Btu per cubic foot degree Fahrenheit [Btu/(ft³·°F)]	joule per cubic meter kelvin [J/(m³·K)]	$6.706\ 610 \times 10^4$	67.0661 kJ/(m³·K)
Btu per hour (Btu/h)	watt (W)	$2.930\ 711 \times 10^{-1}$	0.293 071 W
Btu per hour foot degree Fahrenheit [Btu/(h·ft·°F)]	watt per meter kelvin [W/(m·K)]	1.730 735	1.730 735 W/(m·K)
Btu per hour square foot degree Fahrenheit [Btu/(h·ft²·°F)]	watt per square meter kelvin [W/(m²·K)]	5.678 263	5.678 263 W/(m²·K)
Btu per pound (Btu/lb)	joule per kilogram (J/kg)	$2.326* \times 10^3$	2.326 kJ/kg
Btu per pound degree Fahrenheit [Btu/(lb·°F)]	joule per kilogram kelvin [J/(kg·K)]	$4.186\ 8* \times 10^3$	4.1868 kJ/(kg·K)]
Btu per second (Btu/s)	watt (W)	$1.055\ 056 \times 10^3$	1.055 056 kW
Btu per second square foot degree Fahrenheit [Btu/(s·ft²·°F)]	watt per square meter kelvin [W/(m²·K)]	$2.044\ 175 \times 10^4$	20.441 75 kW/(m²·K)
Btu per square foot (Btu/ft²)	joule per square meter (J/m²)	$1.135\ 653 \times 10^4$	11.356 53 kJ/m²
Btu per square foot hour [Btu/(ft²·h)]	watt per square meter (W/m²)	3.154 591	3.154 591 W/m²
Btu per square foot second (Btu/(ft²·s)]	watt per square meter (W/m²)	$1.135\ 653 \times 10^4$	11.356 53 kW/m²
degree Fahrenheit hour square foot per Btu (°F·h·ft²/Btu) *(R-value)*	kelvin square meter per watt (K·m²/W)	$1.761\ 102 \times 10^{-1}$	0.176 110 K·m²/W
degree Fahrenheit hour square foot per Btu inch [°F·h·ft²/(Btu·in)]	kelvin meter per watt (K·m/W)	6.933 471	6.933 471 K·m/W
LENGTH			
chain	meter (m)	$2.011\ 684 \times 10^1$	20.1168 m
fathom	meter (m)	1.828 804	1.828 804 m
foot (ft, ')	meter (m)	$3.048* \times 10^{-1}$	0.3048 m; 304.8 mm
foot [U.S. survey]	meter (m)	$3.048\ 006 \times 10^{-1}$	0.304 800 6 m
inch (in, ")	meter (m)	$2.54* \times 10^{-2}$	0.0254 m; 25.4 mm
microinch	meter (m)	$2.54* \times 10^{-8}$	25.4 nm
mil [0.001"]	meter (m)	$2.54* \times 10^{-5}$	25.4 µm
mile [international] (mi)	meter (m)	$1.609\ 344* \times 10^3$	1.609 344 km
mile [U.S. statute]	meter (m)	$1.609\ 347 \times 10^3$	1.609 347 km
nautical mile (nmi)	meter (m)	$1.852* \times 10^3$	1.852 m
rod [pole, perch]	meter (m)	5.029 210	5.029 21 m
yard (yd)	meter (m)	$9.144* \times 10^{-1}$	0.9144 m; 914.4 mm

NOTE: *The U.S. Metric Law of 1866 gave the relationship, 1 meter (m) equals 39.37 inches. Since 1893, the U.S. yard has been derived from the meter.   In 1959, a refinement was made in the definition of the yard to bring it into agreement with the yard used in other countries, and it was changed from 3600/3937 m to 0.9144 m (exactly). At the same time, it was decided that all data published as a result of geodetic surveys within the U.S. would remain with the old standard, and the foot (1200/3937) was named the U.S. survey foot (0.304 800 6 m). The following units are based on the U.S. survey foot: chain, fathom, rod (also known as pole or perch), and U.S. statute mile.*

LIGHT and LUMINOUS QUANTITIES			
candela per square foot (cd/ft²)	candela per square meter (cd/m²)	$1.076\ 391 \times 10^1$	10.763 91 cd/m²
candela per square inch (cd/in²)	candela per square meter (cd/m²)	$1.550\ 003 \times 10^3$	1.550 003 kcd/m²
footcandle (fc)	lux (lx)	$1.076\ 391 \times 10^1$	10.763 91 lx
footlambert (fL)	candela per square meter (cd/m²)	3.426 259	3.426 259 cd/m²
lambert	candela per square meter (cd/m²)	$3.183\ 099 \times 10^3$	3.1831 kcd/m²
lumen per square foot (lm/ft²)	lux (lx)	$1.076\ 391 \times 10^1$	10.763 91 lx
MASS			
grain (gr)	kilogram (kg)	$6.479\ 891* \times 10^{-5}$	64.798 91 mg
hundredweight [100 lb] (cwt)	kilogram (kg)	$4.535\ 924 \times 10^1$	45.359 24 kg
ounce [avoirdupois] (oz)	kilogram (kg)	$2.834\ 952 \times 10^{-2}$	28.349 52 g
pennyweight	kilogram (kg)	$1.555\ 174 \times 10^{-3}$	1.555 174 g
pound [avoirdupois] (lb)	kilogram (kg)	$4.535\ 924 \times 10^{-1}$	0.453 592 kg
slug	kilogram (kg)	$1.459\ 390 \times 10^1$	14.5939 kg
ton [long, 2240 lb]	kilogram (kg)	$1.016\ 047 \times 10^3$	1016.047 kg
ton [short, 2000 lb] (ton)	kilogram (kg)	$9.071\ 847 \times 10^2$	907.1847 kg

Table 2 (cont.). Classified list of conversion factors for units used in building design and construction

To convert from	to	Multiply by	Expression in Working Units
MASS PER UNIT AREA			
ounce per square foot (oz/ft²)	kilogram per square meter (kg/m²)	$3.051\ 517 \times 10^{-1}$	305.1517 g/m²
ounce per square yard (oz/yd²)	kilogram per square meter (kg/m²)	$3.390\ 575 \times 10^{-2}$	$33.905\ 75$ g/m²
pound per square foot (lb/ft²)	kilogram per square meter (kg/m²)	$4.882\ 428$	$4.882\ 428$ kg/m²
MASS PER UNIT LENGTH			
pound per foot (lb/ft)	kilogram per meter (kg/m)	$1.488\ 164$	$1.488\ 164$ kg/m
pound per mile (lb/mi)	kilogram per meter (kg/m)	$2.818\ 492 \times 10^{-4}$	$0.281\ 849$ g/m
MASS PER UNIT TIME (Includes FLOW)			
pound per second (lb/s)	kilogram per second (kg/s)	$4.535\ 924 \times 10^{-1}$	$0.453\ 592$ kg/s
ton per hour (ton/h)	kilogram per second (kg/s)	$2.519\ 958 \times 10^{-1}$	$0.251\ 996$ kg/s
perm [0°C]	kilogram per pascal second square meter [kg/(Pa·s·m²)]	$5.721\ 35 \times 10^{-11}$	57.2135 ng/(Pa·s·m²)
perm [23°C]	kilogram per pascal second square meter [kg/(Pa·s·m²)]	$5.745\ 25 \times 10^{-11}$	57.4525 ng/(Pa·s·m²)
perm-inch [0°C]	kilogram per pascal second meter [kg/(Pa·s·m)]	$1.453\ 22 \times 10^{-12}$	$1.453\ 22$ ng/(Pa·s·m)
perm-inch [23°C]	kilogram per pascal second meter [kg/(Pa·s·m)]	$1.459\ 29 \times 10^{-12}$	$1.459\ 29$ ng/(Pa·s·m)
MASS PER UNIT VOLUME (Includes DENSITY and MASS CAPACITY)			
ounce per gallon (oz/gal)	kilogram per cubic meter (kg/m³)	$7.489\ 152$	$7.489\ 152$ kg/m³
pound per cubic foot (lb/ft³)	kilogram per cubic meter (kg/m³)	$1.601\ 846 \times 10^{1}$	$16.018\ 46$ kg/m³
pound per cubic inch (lb/in³)	kilogram per cubic meter (kg/m³)	$2.767\ 990 \times 10^{4}$	$27\ 679.9$ kg/m³
pound per cubic yard (lb/yd³)	kilogram per cubic meter (kg/m³)	$5.932\ 764 \times 10^{-1}$	$0.593\ 276$ kg/m³
pound per gallon (lb/gal)	kilogram per cubic meter (kg/m³)	$1.198\ 264 \times 10^{2}$	119.8264 kg/m³
ton per cubic yard (ton/yd³)	kilogram per cubic meter (kg/m³)	$1.186\ 553 \times 10^{3}$	1186.553 kg/m³

NOTE: 1 kg/m³ = 1 g/L; therefore, 1 lb/gal = 119.8264 g/L, or 0.119 826 kg/L; and, 1 oz/gal = 7.489 152 g/L.

To convert from	to	Multiply by	Expression in Working Units
POWER, ENERGY PER UNIT TIME			
Btu per hour (Btu/h)	watt (W)	$2.930\ 711 \times 10^{-1}$	$0.293\ 071$ W
Btu per second (Btu/s)	watt (W)	$1.055\ 056 \times 10^{3}$	$1.055\ 056$ kW
foot pound-force per hour (ft·lbf/h)	watt (W)	$3.766\ 161 \times 10^{-4}$	$0.376\ 616$ mW
foot pound-force per minute (ft·lbf/min)	watt (W)	$2.259\ 697 \times 10^{-2}$	$22.\ 596\ 97$ mW
foot pound-force per second (ft·lbf/s)	watt (W)	$1.355\ 818$	$1.355\ 818$ W
horsepower [550 ft·lbf/s] (hp)	watt (W)	$7.456\ 999 \times 10^{2}$	745.6999 W
horsepower [boiler]	watt (W)	$9.809\ 50 \times 10^{3}$	$9.809\ 50$ kW
horsepower [electric]	watt (W)	$7.46* \times 10^{2}$	746 W
ton (of refrigeration)	watt (W)	$3.516\ 800 \times 10^{3}$	3.5168 kW
PRESSURE OR STRESS (FORCE PER UNIT AREA)			
atmosphere [standard] (atm)	pascal (Pa)	$1.013\ 25* \times 10^{5}$	101.325 kPa
foot of water [39.2°F - 4°C] (ft H₂O)	pascal (Pa)	$2.988\ 98 \times 10^{3}$	$2.988\ 98$ kPa
inch of mercury [32°F - 0°C] (in Hg)	pascal (Pa)	$3.386\ 38 \times 10^{3}$	$3.386\ 38$ kPa
inch of mercury [60°F] (in Hg)	pascal (Pa)	$3.376\ 85 \times 10^{3}$	$3.376\ 85$ kPa
inch of water [39.2°F - 4°C] (in H₂O)	pascal (Pa)	$2.490\ 82 \times 10^{2}$	249.082 Pa
inch of water [60°F] (in H₂O)	pascal (Pa)	$2.488\ 4 \times 10^{2}$	248.84 Pa
kip per square inch (kip/in², ksi)	pascal (Pa)	$6.894\ 757 \times 10^{6}$	$6.894\ 757$ MPa
poundal per square foot (pdl/ft²)	pascal (Pa)	$1.488\ 164$	$1.488\ 164$ Pa
pound-force per square foot (lbf/ft², psf)	pascal (Pa)	$4.788\ 026 \times 10^{1}$	$47.880\ 26$ Pa
pound-force per square inch (lbf/in², psi)	pascal (Pa)	$6.894\ 757 \times 10^{3}$	$6.894\ 757$ kPa
ton-force per square foot (tonf/ft²)	pascal (Pa)	$9.576\ 052 \times 10^{4}$	95.7605 kPa
ton-force per square inch (tonf/in²)	pascal (Pa)	$1.378\ 951 \times 10^{7}$	$13.789\ 51$ MPa
SPEED (See VELOCITY)			
STRESS (See PRESSURE)			
TEMPERATURE			
degree Fahrenheit (°F) (Temperature Interval)	degree Celsius (°C)	$5.555\ 556 \times 10^{-1}$	$0.555\ 556$ °C
degree Fahrenheit (°F) (Temperature Interval)	kelvin (K)	$5.555\ 556 \times 10^{-1}$	$0.555\ 556$ K
degree Fahrenheit (°F) (Temperature Value)	degree Celsius (°C)		$t_{°C} = (t_{°F} - 32)/1.8$
degree Fahrenheit (°F) (Temperature Value)	kelvin (K)		$T_K = (t_{°F} + 459.67)/1.8$

NOTE: The "degree Celsius (°C)" has been approved by the International Committee for Weights and Measures (CIPM) as a derived SI unit with special name for Celsius temperature, but has not yet been adopted by the General Conference on Weights and Measures (CGPM). Compound units, with a temperature component, are shown in terms of the SI base unit kelvin (K), which has an identical temperature interval to the degree Celsius but has its origin at absolute zero temperature and, therefore, no negative values. (Equivalent temperature value: 0 K = -273.15 °C; 273.15 K = 0 °C).

Table 2 (cont.). Classified list of conversion factors for units used in building design and construction

To convert from	to	Multiply by	Expression in Working Units
TORQUE (See BENDING MOMENT)			
VELOCITY (Includes SPEED)			
foot per hour (ft/h)	meter per second (m/s)	8.466 667 x 10^{-5}	84.666 67 µm/s
foot per minute (ft/min)	meter per second (m/s)	5.08* x 10^{-3}	5.08 mm/s
foot per second (ft/s)	meter per second (m/s)	0.304 8* x 10^{-1}	0.3048 m/s
inch per second (in/s)	meter per second (m/s)	2.54* x 10^{-2}	25.4 mm/s
mile per hour (mi/h, mph)	meter per second (m/s)	4.470 4* x 10^{-1}	0.447 04 m/s
mile per hour (mi/h, mph)	kilometer per hour (km/h)*	1.609 344*	1.609 344 km/h

NOTE: Although speedometers will be graduated in km/h, the SI unit is m/s.

VISCOSITY (DYNAMIC AND KINEMATIC)			
centipoise (cP)	pascal second (Pa·s)	1.0* x 10^{-3}	1.0 mPa·s
poundal second per square foot (pdl·s/ft^2)	pascal second (Pa·s)	1.488 164	1.488 164 Pa·s
pound-force second per square foot (lbf·s/ft^2)	pascal second (Pa·s)	4.788 026 x 10^1	47.880 26 Pa·s
pound-force second per square inch (lbf·s/in^2)	pascal second (Pa·s)	6.894 757 x 10^3	6.894 757 kPa·s
pound per foot second [lb/(ft·s)]	pascal second (Pa·s)	1.488 164	1.488 164 Pa·s
centistokes (cSt)	square meter per second (m^2/s)	1.0* x 10^{-6}	1.0 mm^2/s
square foot per second (ft^2/s)	square meter per second (m^2/s)	9.290 304*x 10^{-2}	0.092 903 m^2/s

VOLUME (Includes CAPACITY)			
acre-foot (ac·ft)	cubic meter (m^3)	1.233 489 x 10^3	1233.489 m^3
board foot (bf) [1]	cubic meter (m^3)	2.359 737 x 10^{-3}	0.002 360 m^3
cubic foot (ft^3)	cubic meter (m^3)	2.831 685 x 10^{-2}	0.028 317 m^3
cubic inch (in^3)	cubic meter (m^3)	1.638 706 x 10^{-5}	16 387.06 mm^3
cubic yard (yd^3)	cubic meter (m^3)	7.645 549 x 10^{-1}	0.764 555 m^3
fluid ounce [U.S.] (fl oz)	cubic meter (m^3)	2.957 353 x 10^{-5}	29 573.53 mm^3
fluid ounce [U.S.] (fl oz)	liter (L) [2]	2.957 353 x 10^{-2}	29.573 53 mL
gallon [U.S.] (gal)	cubic meter (m^3)	3.785 412 x 10^{-3}	0.003 785 412 m^3
gallon [U.S.] (gal)	liter (L)	3.785 412	3.785 412 L
pint [U.S.] (pt)	cubic meter (m^3)	4.731 765 x 10^{-4}	473 176.5 mm^3
pint [U.S.] (pt)	liter (L)	4.731 765 x 10^{-1}	0.473 176 5 L
quart [U.S.] (qt)	cubic meter (m^3)	9.463 529 x 10^{-4}	946 352.9 mm^3
quart [U.S.] (qt)	liter (L)	9.463 529 x 10^{-1}	0.946 353 L

NOTES: (1) The "board foot" measures a theoretical volume of 12" x 12" x 1" for wood products.

(2) The "liter" (symbol: L) is a special name adopted for the cubic decimeter (dm^3), and equals 0.001 m^3 (exactly). It is used for liquid and dry measurement of volume (capacity), and may also be used with the prefixes milli and micro (1 mL = 1000 mm^3; 1 uL = 1 mm^3).

VOLUME PER UNIT TIME (Includes FLOW)			
cubic foot per hour (ft^3/h)	cubic meter per second (m^3/s)	7.865 791 x 10^{-6}	7865.791 mm^3/s
cubic foot per minute (ft^3/min)	cubic meter per second (m^3/s)	4.719 474 x 10^{-4}	0.000 471 95 m^3/s
cubic foot per second (ft^3/s)	cubic meter per second (m^3/s)	2.831 685 x 10^{-2}	0.028 316 85 m^3/s
cubic inch per minute (in^3/min)	cubic meter per second (m^3/s)	2.731 177 x 10^{-7}	273.1177 mm^3/s
cubic yard per hour (yd^3/h)	cubic meter per second (m^3/s)	2.123 763 x 10^{-4}	0.000 212 38 m^3/s
cubic yard per minute (yd^3/min)	cubic meter per second (m^3/s)	1.274 258 x 10^{-2}	0.012 742 58 m^3/s
gallon per day (gal/d)	cubic meter per second (m^3/s)	4.381 264 x 10^{-8}	43.812 64 mm^3/s
gallon per minute (gal/min, gpm)	cubic meter per second (m^3/s)	6.309 020 x 10^{-5}	63 090.2 mm^3/s
gallon per minute (gal/min, gpm)	liter per second (L/s)	6.309 020 x 10^{-2}	63.0902 mL/s
gallon per second (gal/s)	cubic meter per second (m^3/s)	3.785 412 x 10^{-3}	0.003 785 41 m^3/s
gallon per second (gal/s)	liter per second (L/s)	3.785 412	3.785 412 L/s
million gallons per day	cubic meter per second (m^3/s)	4.381 264 x 10^{-2}	0.043 812 64 m^3/s

CONVERSION FROM U.S. CUSTOMARY UNITS TO SI METRIC UNITS

By HANS J. MILTON, FRAIA *Center for Building Technology, National Bureau of Standards*

Table 1. Inches and fractions (multiples of ⅟₃₂″) up to 12 inches to millimeters (mm)

Conversion Factor: 1 in. = 25.4 mm (exactly)

Rounding: To nearest 0.1 mm*

Inches	0	1	2	3	4	5	6	7	8	9	10	11
					millimeters (mm)							
0	–	25.4	50.8	76.2	101.6	127.0	152.4	177.8	203.2	228.6	254.0	279.4
1/32	0.8	26.2	51.6	77.0	102.4	127.8	153.2	178.6	204.0	229.4	254.8	280.2
1/16	1.6	27.0	52.4	77.8	103.2	128.6	154.0	179.4	204.8	230.2	255.6	281.0
3/32	2.4	27.8	53.2	78.6	104.0	129.4	154.8	180.2	205.6	231.0	256.4	281.8
1/8	3.2	28.6	54.0	79.4	104.8	130.2	155.6	181.0	206.4	231.8	257.2	282.6
5/32	4.0	29.4	54.8	80.2	105.6	131.0	156.4	181.8	207.2	232.6	258.0	283.4
3/16	4.8	30.2	55.6	81.0	106.4	131.8	157.2	182.6	208.0	233.4	258.8	284.2
7/32	5.6	31.0	56.4	81.8	107.2	132.6	158.0	183.4	208.8	234.2	259.6	285.0
1/4*	6.4	31.8	57.2	82.6	108.0	133.4	158.8	184.2	209.6	235.0	260.4	285.8
9/32	7.1	32.5	57.9	83.3	108.7	134.1	159.5	184.9	210.3	235.7	261.1	286.5
5/16	7.9	33.3	58.7	84.1	109.5	134.9	160.3	185.7	211.1	236.5	261.9	287.3
11/32	8.7	34.1	59.5	84.9	110.3	135.7	161.1	186.5	211.9	237.3	262.7	288.1
3/8	9.5	34.9	60.3	85.7	111.1	136.5	161.9	187.3	212.7	238.1	263.5	288.9
13/32	10.3	35.7	61.1	86.5	111.9	137.3	162.7	188.1	213.5	238.9	264.3	289.7
7/16	11.1	36.5	61.9	87.3	112.7	138.1	163.5	188.9	214.3	239.7	265.1	290.5
15/32	11.9	37.3	62.7	88.1	113.5	138.9	164.3	189.7	215.1	240.5	265.9	291.3
1/2	12.7	38.1	63.5	88.9	114.3	139.7	165.1	190.5	215.9	241.3	266.7	292.1
17/32	13.5	38.9	64.3	89.7	115.1	140.5	165.9	191.3	216.7	242.1	267.5	292.9
9/16	14.3	39.7	65.1	90.5	115.9	141.3	166.7	192.1	217.5	242.9	268.3	293.7
19/32	15.1	40.5	65.9	91.3	116.7	142.1	167.5	192.9	218.3	243.7	269.1	294.5
5/8	15.9	41.3	66.7	92.1	117.5	142.9	168.3	193.7	219.1	244.5	269.9	295.3
21/32	16.7	42.1	67.5	92.9	118.3	143.7	169.1	194.5	219.9	245.3	270.7	296.1
11/16	17.5	42.9	68.3	93.7	119.1	144.5	169.9	195.3	220.7	246.1	271.5	296.9
23/32	18.3	43.7	69.1	94.5	119.9	145.3	170.7	196.1	221.5	246.9	272.3	297.7
3/4*	19.0	44.4	69.8	95.2	120.6	146.0	171.4	196.8	222.2	247.6	273.0	298.4
25/32	19.8	45.2	70.6	96.0	121.4	146.8	172.2	197.6	223.0	248.4	273.8	299.2
13/16	20.6	46.0	71.4	96.8	122.2	147.6	173.0	198.4	223.8	249.2	274.6	300.0
27/32	21.4	46.8	72.2	97.6	123.0	148.4	173.8	199.2	224.6	250.0	275.4	300.8
7/8	22.2	47.6	73.0	98.4	123.8	149.2	174.6	200.0	225.4	250.8	276.2	301.6
29/32	23.0	48.4	73.8	99.2	124.6	150.0	175.4	200.8	226.2	251.6	277.0	302.4
15/16	23.8	49.2	74.6	100.0	125.4	150.8	176.2	201.6	227.0	252.4	277.8	303.2
31/32	24.6	50.0	75.4	100.8	126.2	151.6	177.0	202.4	227.8	253.2	278.6	304.0

* Where greater precision is required, use the exact conversion factor and round to two places of decimals.

CONVERSION TABLES – 2

Linear measurement

Table 2.   Feet, inches, and fractions (multiples of ⅛ in.), up to 100 ft, to nearest whole millimeter (mm)

Conversion Factors: 1 inch = 25.4 mm;   1 foot = 304.8 mm   (exactly)
Rounding: To nearest millimeter.
Exact values are underlined.

Feet and Inches		0	1/8"	1/4"	3/8"	1/2"	5/8"	3/4"	7/8"
		millimeters (mm)							
0"		–	3	6	10	13	16	19	22
1"		25	29	32	35	38	41	44	48
2"		51	54	57	60	64	67	70	73
3"		76	79	83	86	89	92	95	98
4"		102	105	108	111	114	117	121	124
5"		**127**	130	133	137	140	143	146	149
6"		152	156	159	162	165	168	171	175
7"		178	181	184	187	190	194	197	200
8"		203	206	210	213	216	219	222	225
9"		229	232	235	238	241	244	248	251
10"		**254**	257	260	264	267	270	273	276
11"		279	283	286	289	292	295	298	302
(12")	1'-0"	305	308	311	314	318	321	324	327
(13")	1'-1"	330	333	337	340	343	346	349	352
(14")	1'-2"	356	359	362	365	368	371	375	378
(15")	1'-3"	**381**	384	387	391	394	397	400	403
(16")	1'-4"	406	410	413	416	419	422	425	429
(17")	1'-5"	432	435	438	441	444	448	451	454
(18")	1'-6"	457	460	464	467	470	473	476	479
(19")	1'-7"	483	486	489	492	495	498	502	505
(20")	1'-8"	**508**	511	514	518	521	524	527	530
(21")	1'-9"	533	537	540	543	546	549	552	556
(22")	1'-10"	559	562	565	568	572	575	578	581
(23")	1'-11"	584	587	591	594	597	600	603	606
(24")	2'-0"	610	613	616	619	622	625	629	632
(25")	2'-1"	**635**	638	641	645	648	651	654	657
(26")	2'-2"	660	664	667	670	673	676	679	683
(27")	2'-3"	686	689	692	695	698	702	705	708
(28")	2'-4"	711	714	718	721	**724**	727	730	733
(29")	2'-5"	737	740	743	746	749	752	756	759
(30")	2'-6"	**762**	765	768	772	775	778	781	784
(31")	2'-7"	787	791	794	797	800	803	806	810
(32")	2'-8"	813	816	819	822	826	829	832	835
(33")	2'-9"	838	841	845	848	851	854	857	860
(34")	2'-10"	864	867	870	873	876	879	883	886
(35")	2'-11"	**889**	892	895	899	902	905	908	911

Feet and Inches	0	1/8"	1/4"	3/8"	1/2"	5/8"	3/4"	7/8"
	millimeters (mm)							
3'-0" (36")	914	918	921	924	927	930	933	937
3'-1" (37")	940	943	946	949	952	956	959	962
3'-2" (38")	965	968	972	975	978	981	984	987
3'-3" (39")	991	994	997	1000	1003	1006	1010	1013
3'-4" (40")	**1016**	1019	1022	1026	1029	1032	1035	1038
3'-5" (41")	1041	1045	1048	1051	1054	1057	1060	1064
3'-6" (42")	1067	1070	1073	1076	1079	1083	1086	1089
3'-7" (43")	1092	1095	1099	1102	1105	1108	1111	1114
3'-8" (44")	1118	1121	1124	1127	1130	1133	1137	1140
3'-9" (45")	**1143**	1146	1149	1153	1156	1159	1162	1165
3'-10" (46")	1168	1172	1175	1178	1181	1184	1187	1191
3'-11" (47")	1194	1197	1200	1203	1206	1210	1213	1216
4'-0" (48")	1219	1222	1226	1229	1232	1235	1238	1241
4'-1" (49")	1245	1248	1251	1254	1257	1260	1264	1267
4'-2" (50")	**1270**	1273	1276	1280	1283	1286	1289	1292
4'-3" (51")	1295	1299	1302	1305	1308	1311	1314	1318
4'-4" (52")	1321	1324	1327	1330	1333	1337	1340	1343
4'-5" (53")	1346	1349	1353	1356	1359	1362	1365	1368
4'-6" (54")	1372	1375	1378	1381	1384	1387	1391	1394
4'-7" (55")	**1397**	1400	1403	1407	1410	1413	1416	1419
4'-8" (56")	1422	1426	1429	1432	1435	1438	1441	1445
4'-9" (57")	1448	1451	1454	1457	1460	1464	1467	1470
4'-10" (58")	1473	1476	1480	1483	1486	1489	1492	1495
4'-11" (59")	1499	1502	1505	1508	1511	1514	1518	1521
5'-0" (60")	**1524**	1527	1530	1534	1537	1540	1543	1546
5'-1" (61")	1549	1553	1556	1559	1562	1565	1568	1572
5'-2" (62")	1575	1578	1581	1584	1587	1591	1594	1597
5'-3" (63")	1600	1603	1607	1610	1613	1616	1619	1622
5'-4" (64")	1626	1629	1632	1635	1638	1641	1645	1648
5'-5" (65")	**1651**	1654	1657	1661	1664	1667	1670	1673
5'-6" (66")	1676	1680	1683	1686	1689	1692	1695	1699
5'-7" (67")	1702	1705	1708	1711	1714	1718	1721	1724
5'-8" (68")	1727	1730	1734	1737	1740	1743	1746	1749
5'-9" (69")	1753	1756	**1759**	1762	1765	1768	1772	1775
5'-10" (70")	**1778**	1781	1784	1788	1791	1794	1797	1800
5'-11" (71")	1803	1807	1810	1813	1816	1819	1822	1826
6'-0" (72")	1829	1832	1835	1838	1841	1845	1848	1851
6'-1" (73")	1854	1857	1861	1864	1867	1870	1873	1876
6'-2" (74")	1880	1883	1886	1889	1892	1895	1899	1902
6'-3" (75")	**1905**	1908	1911	1915	1918	1921	1924	1927
6'-4" (76")	1930	1934	1937	1940	1943	1946	1949	1953
6'-5" (77")	1956	1959	1962	1965	1968	1972	1975	1978
6'-6" (78")	1981	1984	1988	1991	1994	1997	2000	

Table 2 (cont.). Feet, inches, and fractions (multiples of ⅛ in.), up to 100 ft, to nearest whole millimeter (mm)

Feet and Inches		0	1/8"	1/4"	3/8	1/2"	5/8"	3/4"	7/8"
		millimeters (mm)							
6'-6"	(78")	1981	1984	1988	1991	1994	1997	2000	2003
6'-7"	(79")	2007	2010	2013	2016	2019	2022	2026	2029
6'-8"	(80")	2032	2035	2038	2042	2045	2048	2051	2054
6'-9"	(81")	2057	2061	2064	2067	2070	2073	2076	2080
6'-10"	(82")	2083	2086	2089	2092	2095	2099	2102	2105
6'-11"	(83")	2108	2111	2115	2118	2121	2124	2127	2130
7'-0"	(84")	2134	2137	2140	2143	2146	2149	2153	2156
7'-1"	(85")	2159	2162	2165	2169	2172	2175	2178	2181
7'-2"	(86")	2184	2188	2191	2194	2197	2200	2203	2207
7'-3"	(87")	2210	2213	2216	2219	2222	2226	2229	2232
7'-4"	(88")	2235	2238	2242	2245	2248	2251	2254	2257
7'-5"	(89")	2261	2264	2267	2270	2273	2276	2280	2283
7'-6"	(90")	2286	2289	2292	2296	2299	2302	2305	2308
7'-7"	(91")	2311	2315	2318	2321	2324	2327	2330	2334
7'-8"	(92")	2337	2340	2343	2346	2349	2353	2356	2359
7'-9"	(93")	2362	2365	2369	2372	2375	2378	2381	2384
7'-10"	(94")	2388	2391	2394	2397	2400	2403	2407	2410
7'-11"	(95")	2413	2416	2419	2423	2426	2429	2432	2435
8'-0"	(96")	2438	2442	2445	2448	2451	2454	2457	2461
8'-1"	(97")	2464	2467	2470	2473	2476	2480	2483	2486
8'-2"	(98")	2489	2492	2496	2499	2502	2505	2508	2511
8'-3"	(99")	2515	2518	2521	2524	2527	2530	2534	2537
8'-4"	(100")	2540	2543	2546	2550	2553	2556	2559	2562
8'-5"	(101")	2565	2569	2572	2575	2578	2581	2584	2588
8'-6"	(102")	2591	2594	2597	2600	2603	2607	2610	2613
8'-7"	(103")	2616	2619	2623	2626	2629	2632	2635	2638
8'-8"	(104")	2642	2645	2648	2651	2654	2657	2661	2664
8'-9"	(105")	2667	2670	2673	2677	2680	2683	2686	2689
8'-10"	(106")	2692	2696	2699	2702	2705	2708	2711	2715
8'-11"	(107")	2718	2721	2724	2727	2730	2734	2737	2740
9'-0"	(108")	2743	2746	2750	2753	2756	2759	2762	2765
9'-1"	(109")	2769	2772	2775	2778	2781	2784	2788	2791
9'-2"	(110")	2794	2797	2800	2804	2807	2810	2813	2816
9'-3"	(111")	2819	2823	2826	2829	2832	2835	2838	2842
9'-4"	(112")	2845	2848	2851	2854	2857	2861	2864	2867
9'-5"	(113")	2870	2873	2877	2880	2883	2886	2889	2892
9'-6"	(114")	2896	2899	2902	2905	2908	2911	2915	2918
9'-7"	(115")	2921	2924	2927	2931	2934	2937	2940	2943
9'-8"	(116")	2946	2950	2953	2956	2959	2962	2965	2969
9'-9"	(117")	2972	2975	2978	2981	2984	2988	2991	2994
9'-10"	(118")	2997	3000	3004	3007	3010	3013	3016	3019
9'-11"	(119")	3023	3026	3029	3032	3035	3038	3042	3045

Feet and Inches		0	1/8"	1/4"	3/8"	1/2"	5/8"	3/4"	7/8"
		millimeters (mm)							
10'-0"	(120")	3048	3051	3054	3058	3061	3064	3067	3070
10'-1"	(121")	3073	3077	3080	3083	3086	3089	3092	3096
10'-2"	(122")	3099	3102	3105	3108	3111	3115	3118	3121
10'-3"	(123")	3124	3127	3131	3134	3137	3140	3143	3146
10'-4"	(124")	3150	3153	3156	3159	3162	3165	3169	3172
10'-5"	(125")	3175	3178	3181	3185	3188	3191	3194	3197
10'-6"	(126")	3200	3204	3207	3210	3213	3216	3219	3223
10'-7"	(127")	3226	3229	3232	3235	3238	3242	3245	3248
10'-8"	(128")	3251	3254	3258	3261	3264	3267	3270	3273
10'-9"	(129")	3277	3280	3283	3286	3289	3292	3296	3299
10'-10"	(130")	3302	3305	3308	3312	3315	3318	3321	3324
10'-11"	(131")	3327	3331	3334	3337	3340	3343	3346	3350
11'-0"	(132")	3353	3356	3359	3362	3365	3369	3372	3375
11'-1"	(133")	3378	3381	3385	3388	3391	3394	3397	3400
11'-2"	(134")	3404	3407	3410	3413	3416	3419	3423	3426
11'-3"	(135")	3429	3432	3435	3439	3442	3445	3448	3451
11'-4"	(136")	3454	3458	3461	3464	3467	3470	3473	3477
11'-5"	(137")	3480	3483	3486	3489	3492	3496	3499	3502
11'-6"	(138")	3505	3508	3512	3515	3518	3521	3524	3527
11'-7"	(139")	3531	3534	3537	3540	3543	3546	3550	3553
11'-8"	(140")	3556	3559	3562	3566	3569	3572	3575	3578
11'-9"	(141")	3581	3585	3588	3591	3594	3597	3600	3604
11'-10"	(142")	3607	3610	3613	3616	3619	3623	3626	3629
11'-11"	(143")	3632	3635	3639	3642	3645	3648	3651	3654
12'-0"	(144")	3658	3661	3664	3667	3670	3673	3677	3680
12'-1"	(145")	3683	3686	3689	3693	3696	3699	3702	3705
12'-2"	(146")	3708	3712	3715	3718	3721	3724	3727	3731
12'-3"	(147")	3734	3737	3740	3743	3746	3750	3753	3756
12'-4"	(148")	3759	3762	3766	3769	3772	3775	3778	3781
12'-5"	(149")	3785	3788	3791	3794	3797	3800	3804	3807
12'-6"	(150")	3810	3813	3816	3820	3823	3826	3829	3832
12'-7"	(151")	3835	3839	3842	3845	3848	3851	3854	3858
12'-8"	(152")	3861	3864	3867	3870	3873	3877	3880	3883
12'-9"	(153")	3886	3889	3893	3896	3899	3902	3905	3908
12'-10"	(154")	3912	3915	3918	3921	3924	3927	3931	3934
12'-11"	(155")	3937	3940	3943	3947	3950	3953	3956	3959
13'-0"	(156")	3962	3966	3969	3972	3975	3978	3981	3985
13'-1"	(157")	3988	3991	3994	3997	4000	4004	4007	4010
13'-2"	(158")	4013	4016	4020	4023	4026	4029	4032	4035
13'-3"	(159")	4039	4042	4045	4048	4051	4054	4058	4061
13'-4"	(160")	4064	4067	4070	4074	4077	4080	4083	4086
13'-5"	(161")	4089	4093	4096	4099	4102	4105	4108	4112

Table 2 (cont.). Feet, inches, and fractions (multiples of ⅛ in.), up to 100 ft, to nearest whole millimeter (mm)

Feet and Inches		0	1/8"	1/4"	3/8"	1/2"	5/8"	3/4"	7/8"
					millimeters (mm)				
17'-0"	(204")	5182	5185	5188	5191	5194	5197	5201	5204
17'-1"	(205")	5207	5210	5213	5217	5220	5223	5226	5229
17'-2"	(206")	5232	5236	5239	5242	5245	5248	5251	5255
17'-3"	(207")	5258	5261	5264	5267	5270	5274	5277	5280
17'-4"	(208")	5283	5286	5290	5293	5296	5299	5302	5305
17'-5"	(209")	5309	5312	5315	5318	5321	5324	5328	5331
17'-6"	(210")	5334	5337	5340	5344	5347	5350	5353	5356
17'-7"	(211")	5359	5363	5366	5369	5372	5375	5378	5382
17'-8"	(212")	5385	5388	5391	5394	5397	5401	5404	5407
17'-9"	(213")	5410	5413	5417	5420	5423	5426	5429	5432
17'-10"	(214")	5436	5439	5442	5445	5448	5451	5455	5458
17'-11"	(215")	5461	5464	5467	5471	5474	5477	5480	5483
18'-0"	(216")	5486	5490	5493	5496	5499	5502	5505	5509
18'-1"	(217")	5511	5515	5518	5521	5524	5528	5531	5534
18'-2"	(218")	5537	5540	5544	5547	5550	5553	5556	5559
18'-3"	(219")	5563	5566	5569	5572	5575	5578	5582	5585
18'-4"	(220")	5588	5591	5594	5598	5601	5604	5607	5610
18'-5"	(221")	5613	5617	5620	5623	5626	5629	5632	5636
18'-6"	(222")	5639	5642	5645	5648	5651	5655	5658	5661
18'-7"	(223")	5664	5667	5671	5674	5677	5680	5683	5686
18'-8"	(224")	5690	5693	5696	5699	5702	5705	5709	5712
18'-9"	(225")	5715	5718	5721	5725	5728	5731	5734	5737
18'-10"	(226")	5740	5744	5747	5750	5753	5756	5759	5763
18'-11"	(227")	5766	5769	5772	5775	5778	5782	5785	5788
19'-0"	(228")	5791	5794	5798	5801	5804	5807	5810	5813
19'-1"	(229")	5817	5820	5823	5826	5829	5832	5836	5839
19'-2"	(230")	5842	5845	5848	5852	5855	5858	5861	5864
19'-3"	(231")	5867	5871	5874	5877	5880	5883	5886	5890
19'-4"	(232")	5893	5896	5899	5902	5905	5909	5912	5915
19'-5"	(233")	5918	5921	5925	5928	5931	5934	5937	5940
19'-6"	(234")	5944	5947	5950	5953	5956	5959	5963	5966
19'-7"	(235")	5969	5972	5975	5979	5982	5985	5988	5991
19'-8"	(236")	5994	5998	6001	6004	6007	6010	6013	6017
19'-9"	(237")	6020	6023	6026	6029	6032	6036	6039	6042
19'-10"	(238")	6045	6048	6052	6055	6058	6061	6064	6067
19'-11"	(239")	6071	6074	6077	6080	6083	6086	6090	6093
20'-0"	(240")	6096	6099	6102	6106	6109	6112	6115	6118
20'-1"	(241")	6121	6125	6128	6131	6134	6137	6140	6144
20'-2"	(242")	6147	6150	6153	6156	6159	6163	6166	6169
20'-3"	(243")	6172	6175	6179	6182	6185	6188	6191	6194
20'-4"	(244")	6198	6201	6204	6207	6210	6213	6217	6220
20'-5"	(245")	6223	6226	6229	6233	6236	6239	6242	6245

Feet and Inches		0	1/8"	1/4"	3/8"	1/2"	5/8"	3/4"	7/8"
					millimeters (mm)				
13'-6"	(162")	4115	4118	4121	4124	4127	4131	4134	4137
13'-7"	(163")	4140	4143	4147	4150	4153	4156	4159	4162
13'-8"	(164")	4166	4169	4172	4175	4178	4181	4185	4188
13'-9"	(165")	4191	4194	4197	4201	4204	4207	4210	4213
13'-10"	(166")	4216	4220	4223	4226	4229	4232	4235	4239
13'-11"	(167")	4242	4245	4248	4251	4254	4258	4261	4264
14'-0"	(168")	4267	4270	4274	4277	4280	4283	4286	4289
14'-1"	(169")	4293	4296	4299	4302	4305	4308	4312	4315
14'-2"	(170")	4318	4321	4324	4328	4331	4334	4337	4340
14'-3"	(171")	4343	4347	4350	4353	4356	4359	4362	4366
14'-4"	(172")	4369	4372	4375	4378	4381	4385	4388	4391
14'-5"	(173")	4394	4397	4401	4404	4407	4410	4413	4416
14'-6"	(174")	4420	4423	4426	4429	4432	4435	4439	4442
14'-7"	(175")	4445	4448	4451	4455	4458	4461	4464	4467
14'-8"	(176")	4470	4474	4477	4480	4483	4486	4489	4493
14'-9"	(177")	4496	4499	4502	4505	4508	4512	4515	4518
14'-10"	(178")	4521	4524	4528	4531	4534	4537	4540	4543
14'-11"	(179")	4547	4550	4553	4556	4559	4562	4566	4569
15'-0"	(180")	4572	4575	4578	4582	4585	4588	4591	4594
15'-1"	(181")	4597	4601	4604	4607	4610	4613	4616	4620
15'-2"	(182")	4623	4626	4629	4632	4635	4639	4642	4645
15'-3"	(183")	4648	4651	4655	4658	4661	4664	4667	4670
15'-4"	(184")	4674	4677	4680	4683	4686	4689	4693	4696
15'-5"	(185")	4699	4702	4705	4709	4712	4715	4718	4721
15'-6"	(186")	4724	4728	4731	4734	4737	4740	4743	4747
15'-7"	(187")	4750	4753	4756	4759	4762	4766	4769	4772
15'-8"	(188")	4775	4778	4782	4785	4788	4791	4794	4797
15'-9"	(189")	4801	4804	4807	4810	4813	4816	4820	4823
15'-10"	(190")	4826	4829	4832	4836	4839	4842	4845	4848
15'-11"	(191")	4851	4855	4858	4861	4864	4867	4870	4874
16'-0"	(192")	4877	4880	4883	4886	4889	4893	4896	4899
16'-1"	(193")	4902	4905	4909	4912	4915	4918	4921	4924
16'-2"	(194")	4928	4931	4934	4937	4940	4943	4947	4950
16'-3"	(195")	4953	4956	4959	4963	4966	4969	4972	4975
16'-4"	(196")	4978	4982	4985	4988	4991	4994	4997	5001
16'-5"	(197")	5004	5007	5010	5013	5016	5020	5023	5026
16'-6"	(198")	5029	5032	5036	5039	5042	5045	5048	5051
16'-7"	(199")	5055	5058	5061	5064	5067	5070	5074	5077
16'-8"	(200")	5080	5083	5086	5090	5093	5096	5099	5102
16'-9"	(201")	5105	5109	5112	5115	5118	5121	5124	5128
16'-10"	(202")	5131	5134	5137	5140	5143	5147	5150	5153
16'-11"	(203")	5156	5159	5163	5166	5169	5172	5175	5178

Table 2 (cont.). Feet, inches, and fractions (multiples of ⅛ in.), up to 100 ft, to nearest whole millimeter (mm)

Feet and Inches		0	1/8"	1/4"	3/8"	1/2"	5/8"	3/4"	7/8"
		millimeters (mm)							
20'-6"	(246")	6248	6252	6255	6258	6261	6264	6267	6271
20'-7"	(247")	6274	6277	6280	6283	6286	6290	6293	6296
20'-8"	(248")	6299	6302	6306	6309	6312	6315	6318	6321
20'-9"	(249")	6325	6328	6331	6334	6337	6340	6344	6347
20'-10"	(250")	6350	6353	6356	6360	6363	6366	6369	6372
20'-11"	(251")	6375	6379	6382	6385	6388	6391	6394	6398
21'-0"	(252")	6401	6404	6407	6410	6413	6417	6420	6423
21'-1"	(253")	6426	6429	6433	6436	6439	6442	6445	6448
21'-2"	(254")	6452	6455	6458	6461	6464	6467	6471	6474
21'-3"	(255")	6477	6480	6483	6487	6490	6493	6496	6499
21'-4"	(256")	6502	6506	6509	6512	6515	6518	6521	6525
21'-5"	(257")	6528	6531	6534	6537	6540	6544	6547	6550
21'-6"	(258")	6553	6556	6560	6563	6566	6569	6572	6575
21'-7"	(259")	6579	6582	6585	6588	6591	6594	6598	6601
21'-8"	(260")	6604	6607	6610	6614	6617	6620	6623	6626
21'-9"	(261")	6629	6633	6636	6639	6642	6645	6648	6652
21'-10"	(262")	6655	6658	6661	6664	6667	6671	6674	6677
21'-11"	(263")	6680	6683	6687	6690	6693	6696	6699	6702
22'-0"	(264")	6706	6709	6712	6715	6718	6721	6725	6728
22'-1"	(265")	6731	6734	6737	6741	6744	6747	6750	6753
22'-2"	(266")	6756	6760	6763	6766	6769	6772	6775	6779
22'-3"	(267")	6782	6785	6788	6791	6794	6798	6801	6804
22'-4"	(268")	6807	6810	6814	6817	6820	6823	6826	6829
22'-5"	(269")	6833	6836	6839	6842	6845	6848	6852	6855
22'-6"	(270")	6858	6861	6864	6868	6871	6874	6877	6880
22'-7"	(271")	6883	6887	6890	6893	6896	6899	6902	6906
22'-8"	(272")	6909	6912	6915	6918	6921	6925	6928	6931
22'-9"	(273")	6934	6937	6941	6944	6947	6950	6953	6956
22'-10"	(274")	6960	6963	6966	6969	6972	6975	6979	6982
22'-11"	(275")	6985	6988	6991	6995	6998	7001	7004	7007
23'-0"	(276")	7010	7014	7017	7020	7023	7026	7029	7033
23'-1"	(277")	7036	7039	7042	7045	7048	7052	7055	7058
23'-2"	(278")	7061	7064	7068	7071	7074	7077	7080	7083
23'-3"	(279")	7087	7090	7093	7096	7099	7102	7106	7109
23'-4"	(280")	7112	7115	7118	7122	7125	7128	7131	7134
23'-5"	(281")	7137	7141	7144	7147	7150	7153	7156	7160
23'-6"	(282")	7163	7166	7169	7172	7175	7179	7182	7185
23'-7"	(283")	7188	7191	7195	7198	7201	7204	7207	7210
23'-8"	(284")	7214	7217	7220	7223	7226	7229	7233	7236
23'-9"	(285")	7239	7242	7245	7249	7252	7255	7258	7261
23'-10"	(286")	7264	7268	7271	7274	7277	7280	7283	7287
23'-11"	(287")	7290	7293	7296	7299	7302	7306	7309	7312

Feet and Inches		0	1/8"	1/4"	3/8"	1/2"	5/8"	3/4"	7/8"
		millimeters (mm)							
24'-0"	(288")	7315	7318	7322	7325	7328	7331	7334	7337
24'-1"	(289")	7341	7344	7347	7350	7353	7356	7360	7363
24'-2"	(290")	7366	7369	7372	7376	7379	7382	7385	7388
24'-3"	(291")	7391	7395	7398	7401	7404	7407	7410	7414
24'-4"	(292")	7417	7420	7423	7426	7429	7433	7436	7439
24'-5"	(293")	7442	7445	7449	7452	7455	7458	7461	7464
24'-6"	(294")	7468	7471	7474	7477	7480	7483	7487	7490
24'-7"	(295")	7493	7496	7499	7503	7506	7509	7512	7515
24'-8"	(296")	7518	7522	7525	7528	7531	7534	7537	7541
24'-9"	(297")	7544	7547	7550	7553	7556	7560	7563	7566
24'-10"	(298")	7569	7572	7576	7579	7582	7585	7588	7591
24'-11"	(299")	7595	7598	7601	7604	7607	7610	7614	7617
25'-0"	(300")	7620	7623	7626	7630	7633	7636	7639	7642
25'-1"	(301")	7645	7649	7652	7655	7658	7661	7664	7668
25'-2"	(302")	7671	7674	7677	7680	7683	7687	7690	7693
25'-3"	(303")	7696	7699	7703	7706	7709	7712	7715	7718
25'-4"	(304")	7722	7725	7728	7731	7734	7737	7741	7744
25'-5"	(305")	7747	7750	7753	7757	7760	7763	7766	7769
25'-6"	(306")	7772	7776	7779	7782	7785	7788	7791	7795
25'-7"	(307")	7798	7801	7804	7807	7810	7814	7817	7820
25'-8"	(308")	7823	7826	7830	7833	7836	7839	7842	7845
25'-9"	(309")	7849	7852	7855	7858	7861	7864	7868	7871
25'-10"	(310")	7874	7877	7880	7884	7887	7890	7893	7896
25'-11"	(311")	7899	7903	7906	7909	7912	7915	7918	7922
26'-0"	(312")	7925	7928	7931	7934	7937	7941	7944	7947
26'-1"	(313")	7950	7953	7957	7960	7963	7966	7969	7972
26'-2"	(314")	7976	7979	7982	7985	7988	7991	7995	7998
26'-3"	(315")	8001	8004	8007	8011	8014	8017	8020	8023
26'-4"	(316")	8026	8030	8033	8036	8039	8042	8045	8049
26'-5"	(317")	8052	8055	8058	8061	8064	8068	8071	8074
26'-6"	(318")	8077	8080	8084	8087	8090	8093	8096	8099
26'-7"	(319")	8103	8106	8109	8112	8115	8118	8122	8125
26'-8"	(320")	8128	8131	8134	8138	8141	8144	8147	8150
26'-9"	(321")	8153	8157	8160	8163	8166	8169	8172	8176
26'-10"	(322")	8179	8182	8185	8188	8191	8195	8198	8201
26'-11"	(323")	8204	8207	8211	8214	8217	8220	8223	8226
27'-0"	(324")	8230	8233	8236	8239	8242	8245	8249	8252
27'-1"	(325")	8255	8258	8261	8265	8268	8271	8274	8277
27'-2"	(326")	8280	8284	8287	8290	8293	8296	8299	8303
27'-3"	(327")	8306	8309	8312	8315	8318	8322	8325	8328
27'-4"	(328")	8331	8334	8338	8341	8344	8347	8350	8353
27'-5"	(329")	8357	8360	8363	8366	8369	8372	8376	8379

Table 2 (cont.). Feet, inches, and fractions (multiples of ⅛ in.), up to 100 ft, to nearest whole millimeter (mm)

Feet and Inches		0	1/8"	1/4"	3/8"	1/2"	5/8"	3/4"	7/8"
					millimeters (mm)				
31'-0"	(372")	9449	9452	9455	9458	9461	9465	9468	9471
31'-1"	(373")	9474	9477	9481	9484	9487	9490	9493	9496
31'-2"	(374")	9500	9503	9506	9509	9512	9515	9519	9522
31'-3"	(375")	9525	9528	9531	9535	9538	9541	9544	9547
31'-4"	(376")	9550	9554	9557	9560	9563	9566	9569	9573
31'-5"	(377")	9576	9579	9582	9585	9588	9592	9595	9598
31'-6"	(378")	9601	9604	9608	9611	9614	9617	9620	9623
31'-7"	(379")	9627	9630	9633	9636	9639	9642	9646	9649
31'-8"	(380")	9652	9655	9658	9662	9665	9668	9671	9674
31'-9"	(381")	9677	9681	9684	9687	9690	9693	9696	9700
31'-10"	(382")	9703	9706	9709	9712	9715	9719	9722	9725
31'-11"	(383")	9728	9731	9735	9738	9741	9744	9747	9750
32'-0"	(384")	9754	9757	9760	9763	9766	9769	9773	9776
32'-1"	(385")	9779	9782	9785	9789	9792	9795	9798	9801
32'-2"	(386")	9804	9808	9811	9814	9817	9820	9823	9827
32'-3"	(387")	9830	9833	9836	9839	9842	9846	9849	9852
32'-4"	(388")	9855	9858	9862	9865	9868	9871	9874	9877
32'-5"	(389")	9881	9884	9887	9890	9893	9896	9900	9903
32'-6"	(390")	9906	9909	9912	9916	9919	9922	9925	9928
32'-7"	(391")	9931	9935	9938	9941	9944	9947	9950	9954
32'-8"	(392")	9957	9960	9963	9966	9969	9973	9976	9979
32'-9"	(393")	9982	9985	9989	9992	9995	9998	10001	10004
32'-10"	(394")	10008	10011	10014	10017	10020	10023	10027	10030
32'-11"	(395")	10033	10036	10039	10043	10046	10049	10052	10055
33'-0"	(396")	10058	10062	10065	10068	10071	10074	10077	10081
33'-1"	(397")	10084	10087	10090	10093	10096	10100	10103	10106
33'-2"	(398")	10109	10112	10116	10119	10122	10125	10128	10131
33'-3"	(399")	10135	10138	10141	10144	10147	10150	10154	10157
33'-4"	(400")	10160	10163	10166	10170	10173	10176	10179	10182
33'-5"		10185	10189	10192	10195	10198	10201	10204	10208
33'-6"		10211	10214	10217	10220	10223	10227	10230	10233
33'-7"		10236	10239	10243	10246	10249	10252	10255	10258
33'-8"		10262	10265	10268	10271	10274	10277	10281	10284
33'-9"		10287	10290	10293	10297	10300	10303	10306	10309
33'-10"		10312	10316	10319	10322	10325	10328	10331	10335
33'-11"		10338	10341	10344	10347	10350	10354	10357	10360
34'-0"		10363	10366	10370	10373	10376	10379	10382	10385
34'-1"		10389	10392	10395	10398	10401	10404	10408	10411
34'-2"		10414	10417	10420	10424	10427	10430	10433	10436
34'-3"		10439	10443	10446	10449	10452	10455	10458	10462
34'-4"		10465	10468	10471	10474	10477	10481	10484	10487
34'-5"		10490	10493	10497	10500	10503	10506	10509	10512

Feet and Inches		0	1/8"	1/4"	3/8"	1/2"	5/8"	3/4"	7/8"
					millimeters (mm)				
27'-6"	(330")	8382	8385	8388	8392	8395	8398	8401	8404
27'-7"	(331")	8407	8411	8414	8417	8420	8423	8426	8430
27'-8"	(332")	8433	8436	8439	8442	8445	8449	8452	8455
27'-9"	(333")	8458	8461	8465	8468	8471	8474	8477	8480
27'-10"	(334")	8484	8487	8490	8493	8496	8499	8503	8506
27'-11"	(335")	8509	8512	8515	8519	8522	8525	8528	8531
28'-0"	(336")	8534	8538	8541	8544	8547	8550	8553	8557
28'-1"	(337")	8560	8563	8566	8569	8572	8576	8579	8582
28'-2"	(338")	8585	8588	8592	8595	8598	8601	8604	8607
28'-3"	(339")	8611	8614	8617	8620	8623	8626	8630	8633
28'-4"	(340")	8636	8639	8642	8646	8649	8652	8655	8658
28'-5"	(341")	8661	8665	8668	8671	8674	8677	8680	8684
28'-6"	(342")	8687	8690	8693	8696	8699	8703	8706	8709
28'-7"	(343")	8712	8715	8719	8722	8725	8728	8731	8734
28'-8"	(344")	8738	8741	8744	8747	8750	8753	8757	8760
28'-9"	(345")	8763	8766	8769	8773	8776	8779	8782	8785
28'-10"	(346")	8788	8792	8795	8798	8801	8804	8807	8811
28'-11"	(347")	8814	8817	8820	8823	8826	8830	8833	8836
29'-0"	(348")	8839	8842	8846	8849	8852	8855	8858	8861
29'-1"	(349")	8865	8868	8871	8874	8877	8880	8884	8887
29'-2"	(350")	8890	8893	8896	8900	8903	8906	8909	8912
29'-3"	(351")	8915	8919	8922	8925	8928	8931	8934	8938
29'-4"	(352")	8941	8944	8947	8950	8953	8957	8960	8963
29'-5"	(353")	8966	8969	8973	8976	8979	8982	8985	8988
29'-6"	(354")	8992	8995	8998	9001	9004	9007	9011	9014
29'-7"	(355")	9017	9020	9023	9027	9030	9033	9036	9039
29'-8"	(356")	9042	9046	9049	9052	9055	9058	9061	9065
29'-9"	(357")	9068	9071	9074	9077	9080	9084	9087	9090
29'-10"	(358")	9093	9096	9100	9103	9106	9109	9112	9115
29'-11"	(359")	9119	9122	9125	9128	9131	9134	9138	9141
30'-0"	(360")	9144	9147	9150	9154	9157	9160	9163	9166
30'-1"	(361")	9169	9173	9176	9179	9182	9185	9188	9192
30'-2"	(362")	9195	9198	9201	9204	9207	9211	9214	9217
30'-3"	(363")	9220	9223	9227	9230	9233	9236	9239	9242
30'-4"	(364")	9246	9249	9252	9255	9258	9261	9265	9268
30'-5"	(365")	9271	9274	9277	9281	9284	9287	9290	9293
30'-6"	(366")	9296	9300	9303	9306	9309	9312	9315	9319
30'-7"	(367")	9322	9325	9328	9331	9334	9338	9341	9344
30'-8"	(368")	9347	9350	9354	9357	9360	9363	9366	9369
30'-9"	(369")	9373	9376	9379	9382	9385	9388	9392	9395
30'-10"	(370")	9398	9401	9404	9408	9411	9414	9417	9420
30'-11"	(371")	9423	9427	9430	9433	9436	9439	9442	9446

Table 2 (cont.). Feet, inches, and fractions (multiples of ⅛ in.), up to 100 ft, to nearest whole millimeter (mm)

Feet and Inches	0	1/8"	1/4"	3/8"	1/2"	5/8"	3/4"	7/8"
				millimeters (mm)				
34'-6"	10 516	10 519	10 522	10 525	10 528	10 531	10 535	10 538
34'-7"	10 541	10 544	10 547	10 551	10 554	10 557	10 560	10 563
34'-8"	10 566	10 570	10 573	10 576	10 579	10 582	10 585	10 589
34'-9"	10 592	10 595	10 598	10 601	10 604	10 608	10 611	10 614
34'-10"	10 617	10 620	10 623	10 627	10 630	10 633	10 636	10 639
34'-11"	10 643	10 646	10 649	10 652	10 655	10 658	10 662	10 665
35'-0"	10 668	10 671	10 674	10 678	10 681	10 684	10 687	10 690
35'-1"	10 693	10 697	10 700	10 703	10 706	10 709	10 712	10 716
35'-2"	10 719	10 722	10 725	10 728	10 731	10 735	10 738	10 741
35'-3"	10 744	10 747	10 751	10 754	10 757	10 760	10 763	10 766
35'-4"	10 770	10 773	10 776	10 779	10 782	10 785	10 789	10 792
35'-5"	10 795	10 798	10 801	10 805	10 808	10 811	10 814	10 817
35'-6"	10 820	10 824	10 827	10 830	10 833	10 836	10 839	10 843
35'-7"	10 846	10 849	10 852	10 855	10 858	10 862	10 865	10 868
35'-8"	10 871	10 874	10 878	10 881	10 884	10 887	10 890	10 893
35'-9"	10 897	10 900	10 903	10 906	10 909	10 912	10 916	10 919
35'-10"	10 922	10 925	10 928	10 932	10 935	10 938	10 941	10 944
35'-11"	10 947	10 951	10 954	10 957	10 960	10 963	10 966	10 970
36'-0"	10 973	10 976	10 979	10 982	10 985	10 989	10 992	10 995
36'-1"	10 998	11 001	11 005	11 008	11 011	11 014	11 017	11 020
36'-2"	11 024	11 027	11 030	11 033	11 036	11 039	11 043	11 046
36'-3"	11 049	11 052	11 055	11 059	11 062	11 065	11 068	11 071
36'-4"	11 074	11 078	11 081	11 084	11 087	11 090	11 093	11 097
36'-5"	11 100	11 103	11 106	11 109	11 112	11 116	11 119	11 122
36'-6"	11 125	11 128	11 132	11 135	11 138	11 141	11 144	11 147
36'-7"	11 151	11 154	11 157	11 160	11 163	11 166	11 170	11 173
36'-8"	11 176	11 179	11 182	11 186	11 189	11 192	11 195	11 198
36'-9"	11 201	11 205	11 208	11 211	11 214	11 217	11 220	11 224
36'-10"	11 227	11 230	11 233	11 236	11 239	11 243	11 246	11 249
36'-11"	11 252	11 255	11 259	11 262	11 265	11 268	11 271	11 274
37'-0"	11 278	11 281	11 284	11 287	11 290	11 293	11 297	11 300
37'-1"	11 303	11 306	11 309	11 313	11 316	11 319	11 322	11 325
37'-2"	11 328	11 332	11 335	11 338	11 341	11 344	11 347	11 351
37'-3"	11 354	11 357	11 360	11 363	11 366	11 370	11 373	11 376
37'-4"	11 379	11 382	11 386	11 389	11 392	11 395	11 398	11 401
37'-5"	11 405	11 408	11 411	11 414	11 417	11 420	11 424	11 427
37'-6"	11 430	11 433	11 436	11 440	11 443	11 446	11 449	11 452
37'-7"	11 455	11 459	11 462	11 465	11 468	11 471	11 474	11 478
37'-8"	11 481	11 484	11 487	11 490	11 493	11 497	11 500	11 503
37'-9"	11 506	11 509	11 513	11 516	11 519	11 522	11 525	11 528
37'-10"	11 532	11 535	11 538	11 541	11 544	11 547	11 551	11 554
37'-11"	11 557	11 560	11 563	11 567	11 570	11 573	11 576	11 579

Feet and Inches	0	1/8"	1/4"	3/8"	1/2"	5/8"	3/4"	7/8"
				millimeters (mm)				
38'-0"	11 582	11 586	11 589	11 592	11 595	11 598	11 601	11 605
38'-1"	11 608	11 611	11 614	11 617	11 620	11 624	11 627	11 630
38'-2"	11 633	11 636	11 640	11 643	11 646	11 649	11 652	11 655
38'-3"	11 659	11 662	11 665	11 668	11 671	11 674	11 678	11 681
38'-4"	11 684	11 687	11 690	11 694	11 697	11 700	11 703	11 706
38'-5"	11 709	11 713	11 716	11 719	11 722	11 725	11 728	11 732
38'-6"	11 735	11 738	11 741	11 744	11 747	11 751	11 754	11 757
38'-7"	11 760	11 763	11 767	11 770	11 773	11 776	11 779	11 782
38'-8"	11 786	11 789	11 792	11 795	11 798	11 801	11 805	11 808
38'-9"	11 811	11 814	11 817	11 821	11 824	11 827	11 830	11 833
38'-10"	11 836	11 840	11 843	11 846	11 849	11 852	11 855	11 859
38'-11"	11 862	11 865	11 868	11 871	11 874	11 878	11 881	11 884
39'-0"	11 887	11 890	11 894	11 897	11 900	11 903	11 906	11 909
39'-1"	11 913	11 916	11 919	11 922	11 925	11 928	11 932	11 935
39'-2"	11 938	11 941	11 944	11 948	11 951	11 954	11 957	11 960
39'-3"	11 963	11 967	11 970	11 973	11 976	11 979	11 982	11 986
39'-4"	11 989	11 992	11 995	11 998	12 001	12 005	12 008	12 011
39'-5"	12 014	12 017	12 021	12 024	12 027	12 030	12 033	12 036
39'-6"	12 040	12 043	12 046	12 049	12 052	12 055	12 059	12 062
39'-7"	12 065	12 068	12 071	12 075	12 078	12 081	12 084	12 087
39'-8"	12 090	12 094	12 097	12 100	12 103	12 106	12 109	12 113
39'-9"	12 116	12 119	12 122	12 125	12 128	12 132	12 135	12 138
39'-10"	12 141	12 144	12 148	12 151	12 154	12 157	12 160	12 163
39'-11"	12 167	12 170	12 173	12 176	12 179	12 182	12 186	12 189
40'-0"	12 192	12 195	12 198	12 202	12 205	12 208	12 211	12 214
40'-1"	12 217	12 221	12 224	12 227	12 230	12 233	12 236	12 240
40'-2"	12 243	12 246	12 249	12 252	12 255	12 259	12 262	12 265
40'-3"	12 268	12 271	12 275	12 278	12 281	12 284	12 287	12 290
40'-4"	12 294	12 297	12 300	12 303	12 306	12 309	12 313	12 316
40'-5"	12 319	12 322	12 325	12 329	12 332	12 335	12 338	12 341
40'-6"	12 344	12 348	12 351	12 354	12 357	12 360	12 363	12 367
40'-7"	12 370	12 373	12 376	12 379	12 382	12 386	12 389	12 392
40'-8"	12 395	12 398	12 402	12 405	12 408	12 411	12 414	12 417
40'-9"	12 421	12 424	12 427	12 430	12 433	12 436	12 440	12 443
40'-10"	12 446	12 449	12 452	12 456	12 459	12 462	12 465	12 468
40'-11"	12 471	12 475	12 478	12 481	12 484	12 487	12 490	12 494
41'-0"	12 497	12 500	12 503	12 506	12 509	12 513	12 516	12 519
41'-1"	12 522	12 525	12 529	12 532	12 535	12 538	12 541	12 544
41'-2"	12 548	12 551	12 554	12 557	12 560	12 563	12 567	12 570
41'-3"	12 573	12 576	12 579	12 583	12 586	12 589	12 592	12 595
41'-4"	12 598	12 602	12 605	12 608	12 611	12 614	12 617	12 621
41'-5"	12 624	12 627	12 630	12 633	12 636	12 640	12 643	12 646

Linear measurement

Table 2 (cont.). Feet, inches, and fractions (multiples of ⅛ in.), up to 100 ft, to nearest whole millimeter (mm)

Feet and Inches	0	1/8"	1/4"	3/8"	1/2"	5/8"	3/4"	7/8"
				millimeters (mm)				
45'-0"	13 716	13 719	13 722	13 726	13 729	13 732	13 735	13 738
45'-1"	13 741	13 745	13 748	13 751	13 754	13 757	13 760	13 764
45'-2"	13 767	13 770	13 773	13 776	13 779	13 783	13 786	13 789
45'-3"	13 792	13 795	13 799	13 802	13 805	13 808	13 811	13 814
45'-4"	13 818	13 821	13 824	13 827	13 830	13 833	13 837	13 840
45'-5"	13 843	13 846	13 849	13 853	13 856	13 859	13 862	13 865
45'-6"	13 868	13 872	13 875	13 878	13 881	13 884	13 887	13 891
45'-7"	13 894	13 897	13 900	13 903	13 906	13 910	13 913	13 916
45'-8"	13 919	13 922	13 926	13 929	13 932	13 935	13 938	13 941
45'-9"	13 945	13 948	13 951	13 954	13 957	13 960	13 964	13 967
45'-10"	13 970	13 973	13 976	13 980	13 983	13 986	13 989	13 992
45'-11"	13 995	13 999	14 002	14 005	14 008	14 011	14 014	14 018
46'-0"	14 021	14 024	14 027	14 030	14 033	14 037	14 040	14 043
46'-1"	14 046	14 049	14 053	14 056	14 059	14 062	14 065	14 068
46'-2"	14 072	14 075	14 078	14 081	14 084	14 087	14 091	14 094
46'-3"	14 097	14 100	14 103	14 107	14 110	14 113	14 116	14 119
46'-4"	14 122	14 126	14 129	14 132	14 135	14 138	14 141	14 145
46'-5"	14 148	14 151	14 154	14 157	14 160	14 164	14 167	14 170
46'-6"	14 173	14 176	14 180	14 183	14 186	14 189	14 192	14 195
46'-7"	14 199	14 202	14 205	14 208	14 211	14 214	14 218	14 221
46'-8"	14 224	14 227	14 230	14 234	14 237	14 240	14 243	14 246
46'-9"	14 249	14 253	14 256	14 259	14 262	14 265	14 268	14 272
46'-10"	14 275	14 278	14 281	14 284	14 287	14 291	14 294	14 297
46'-11"	14 300	14 303	14 307	14 310	14 313	14 316	14 319	14 322
47'-0"	14 326	14 329	14 332	14 335	14 338	14 341	14 345	14 348
47'-1"	14 351	14 354	14 357	14 361	14 364	14 367	14 370	14 373
47'-2"	14 376	14 380	14 383	14 386	14 389	14 392	14 395	14 399
47'-3"	14 402	14 405	14 408	14 411	14 414	14 418	14 421	14 424
47'-4"	14 427	14 430	14 434	14 437	14 440	14 443	14 446	14 449
47'-5"	14 453	14 456	14 459	14 462	14 465	14 468	14 472	14 475
47'-6"	14 478	14 481	14 484	14 488	14 491	14 494	14 497	14 500
47'-7"	14 503	14 507	14 510	14 513	14 516	14 519	14 522	14 526
47'-8"	14 529	14 532	14 535	14 538	14 541	14 545	14 548	14 551
47'-9"	14 554	14 557	14 561	14 564	14 567	14 570	14 573	14 576
47'-10"	14 580	14 583	14 586	14 589	14 592	14 595	14 599	14 602
47'-11"	14 605	14 608	14 611	14 615	14 618	14 621	14 624	14 627
48'-0"	14 630	14 634	14 637	14 640	14 643	14 646	14 649	14 653
48'-1"	14 656	14 659	14 662	14 665	14 668	14 672	14 675	14 678
48'-2"	14 681	14 684	14 687	14 691	14 694	14 697	14 700	14 703
48'-3"	14 707	14 710	14 713	14 716	14 719	14 722	14 726	14 729
48'-4"	14 732	14 735	14 738	14 742	14 745	14 748	14 751	14 754
48'-5"	14 757	14 761	14 764	14 767	14 770	14 773	14 776	14 780

Feet and Inches	0	1/8"	1/4"	3/8"	1/2"	5/8"	3/4"	7/8"
				millimeters (mm)				
41'-6"	12 649	12 652	12 656	12 659	12 662	12 665	12 668	12 671
41'-7"	12 675	12 678	12 681	12 684	12 687	12 690	12 694	12 697
41'-8"	12 700	12 703	12 706	12 710	12 713	12 716	12 719	12 722
41'-9"	12 725	12 729	12 732	12 735	12 738	12 741	12 744	12 748
41'-10"	12 751	12 754	12 757	12 760	12 763	12 767	12 770	12 773
41'-11"	12 776	12 779	12 783	12 786	12 789	12 792	12 795	12 798
42'-0"	12 802	12 805	12 808	12 811	12 814	12 817	12 821	12 824
42'-1"	12 827	12 830	12 833	12 837	12 840	12 843	12 846	12 849
42'-2"	12 852	12 856	12 859	12 862	12 865	12 868	12 871	12 875
42'-3"	12 878	12 881	12 884	12 887	12 890	12 894	12 897	12 900
42'-4"	12 903	12 906	12 910	12 913	12 916	12 919	12 922	12 925
42'-5"	12 929	12 932	12 935	12 938	12 941	12 944	12 948	12 951
42'-6"	12 954	12 957	12 960	12 964	12 967	12 970	12 973	12 976
42'-7"	12 979	12 983	12 986	12 989	12 992	12 995	12 998	13 002
42'-8"	13 005	13 008	13 011	13 014	13 017	13 021	13 024	13 027
42'-9"	13 030	13 033	13 037	13 040	13 043	13 046	13 049	13 052
42'-10"	13 056	13 059	13 062	13 065	13 068	13 071	13 075	13 078
42'-11"	13 081	13 084	13 087	13 091	13 094	13 097	13 100	13 103
43'-0"	13 106	13 110	13 113	13 116	13 119	13 122	13 125	13 129
43'-1"	13 132	13 135	13 138	13 141	13 144	13 148	13 151	13 154
43'-2"	13 157	13 160	13 164	13 167	13 170	13 173	13 176	13 179
43'-3"	13 183	13 186	13 189	13 192	13 195	13 198	13 202	13 205
43'-4"	13 208	13 211	13 214	13 218	13 221	13 224	13 227	13 230
43'-5"	13 233	13 237	13 240	13 243	13 246	13 249	13 252	13 256
43'-6"	13 259	13 262	13 265	13 268	13 271	13 275	13 278	13 281
43'-7"	13 284	13 287	13 291	13 294	13 297	13 300	13 303	13 306
43'-8"	13 310	13 313	13 316	13 319	13 322	13 325	13 329	13 332
43'-9"	13 335	13 338	13 341	13 345	13 348	13 351	13 354	13 357
43'-10"	13 360	13 364	13 367	13 370	13 373	13 376	13 379	13 383
43'-11"	13 386	13 389	13 392	13 395	13 398	13 402	13 405	13 408
44'-0"	13 411	13 414	13 418	13 421	13 424	13 427	13 430	13 433
44'-1"	13 437	13 440	13 443	13 446	13 449	13 452	13 456	13 459
44'-2"	13 462	13 465	13 468	13 472	13 475	13 478	13 481	13 484
44'-3"	13 487	13 491	13 494	13 497	13 500	13 503	13 506	13 510
44'-4"	13 513	13 516	13 519	13 522	13 525	13 529	13 532	13 535
44'-5"	13 538	13 541	13 545	13 548	13 551	13 554	13 557	13 560
44'-6"	13 564	13 567	13 570	13 573	13 576	13 579	13 583	13 586
44'-7"	13 589	13 592	13 595	13 599	13 602	13 605	13 608	13 611
44'-8"	13 614	13 618	13 621	13 624	13 627	13 630	13 633	13 637
44'-9"	13 640	13 643	13 646	13 649	13 652	13 656	13 659	13 662
44'-10"	13 665	13 668	13 672	13 675	13 678	13 681	13 684	13 687
44'-11"	13 691	13 694	13 697	13 700	13 703	13 706	13 710	13 713

Table 2 (cont.). Feet, inches, and fractions (multiples of ⅛ in.), up to 100 ft, to nearest whole millimeter (mm)

Feet and Inches	0	1/8"	1/4"	3/8"	1/2"	5/8"	3/4"	7/8"
	millimeters (mm)							
48'-6"	14 783	14 786	14 789	14 792	14 795	14 799	14 802	14 805
48'-7"	14 808	14 811	14 815	14 818	14 821	14 824	14 827	14 830
48'-8"	14 834	14 837	14 840	14 843	14 846	14 849	14 853	14 856
48'-9"	14 859	14 862	14 865	14 869	14 872	14 875	14 878	14 881
48'-10"	14 884	14 888	14 891	14 894	14 897	14 900	14 903	14 907
48'-11"	14 910	14 913	14 916	14 919	14 922	14 926	14 929	14 932
49'-0"	14 935	14 938	14 942	14 945	14 948	14 951	14 954	14 957
49'-1"	14 961	14 964	14 967	14 970	14 973	14 976	14 980	14 983
49'-2"	14 986	14 989	14 992	14 996	14 999	15 002	15 005	15 008
49'-3"	15 011	15 015	15 018	15 021	15 024	15 027	15 030	15 034
49'-4"	15 037	15 040	15 043	15 046	15 049	15 053	15 056	15 059
49'-5"	15 062	15 065	15 069	15 072	15 075	15 078	15 081	15 084
49'-6"	15 088	15 091	15 094	15 097	15 100	15 103	15 107	15 110
49'-7"	15 113	15 116	15 119	15 123	15 126	15 129	15 132	15 135
49'-8"	15 138	15 142	15 145	15 148	15 151	15 154	15 157	15 161
49'-9"	15 164	15 167	15 170	15 173	15 176	15 180	15 183	15 186
49'-10"	15 189	15 192	15 196	15 199	15 202	15 205	15 208	15 211
49'-11"	15 215	15 218	15 221	15 224	15 227	15 230	15 234	15 237
50'-0"	15 240	15 243	15 246	15 250	15 253	15 256	15 259	15 262
50'-1"	15 265	15 269	15 272	15 275	15 278	15 281	15 284	15 288
50'-2"	15 291	15 294	15 297	15 300	15 303	15 307	15 310	15 313
50'-3"	15 316	15 319	15 323	15 326	15 329	15 332	15 335	15 338
50'-4"	15 342	15 345	15 348	15 351	15 354	15 357	15 361	15 364
50'-5"	15 367	15 370	15 373	15 377	15 380	15 383	15 386	15 389
50'-6"	15 392	15 396	15 399	15 402	15 405	15 408	15 411	15 415
50'-7"	15 418	15 421	15 424	15 427	15 430	15 434	15 437	15 440
50'-8"	15 443	15 446	15 450	15 453	15 456	15 459	15 462	15 465
50'-9"	15 469	15 472	15 475	15 478	15 481	15 484	15 488	15 491
50'-10"	15 494	15 497	15 500	15 504	15 507	15 510	15 513	15 516
50'-11"	15 519	15 523	15 526	15 529	15 532	15 535	15 538	15 542
51'-0"	15 545	15 548	15 551	15 554	15 557	15 561	15 564	15 567
51'-1"	15 570	15 573	15 577	15 580	15 583	15 586	15 589	15 592
51'-2"	15 596	15 599	15 602	15 605	15 608	15 611	15 615	15 618
51'-3"	15 621	15 624	15 627	15 631	15 634	15 637	15 640	15 643
51'-4"	15 646	15 650	15 653	15 656	15 659	15 662	15 665	15 669
51'-5"	15 672	15 675	15 678	15 681	15 684	15 688	15 691	15 694
51'-6"	15 697	15 700	15 704	15 707	15 710	15 713	15 716	15 719
51'-7"	15 723	15 726	15 729	15 732	15 735	15 738	15 742	15 745
51'-8"	15 748	15 751	15 754	15 758	15 761	15 764	15 767	15 770
51'-9"	15 773	15 777	15 780	15 783	15 786	15 789	15 792	15 796
51'-10"	15 799	15 802	15 805	15 808	15 811	15 815	15 818	15 821
51'-11"	15 824	15 827	15 831	15 834	15 837	15 840	15 843	15 846

Feet and Inches	0	1/8"	1/4"	3/8"	1/2"	5/8"	3/4"	7/8"
	millimeters (mm)							
52'-0"	15 850	15 853	15 856	15 859	15 862	15 865	15 869	15 872
52'-1"	15 875	15 878	15 881	15 885	15 888	15 891	15 894	15 897
52'-2"	15 900	15 904	15 907	15 910	15 913	15 916	15 919	15 923
52'-3"	15 926	15 929	15 932	15 935	15 938	15 942	15 945	15 948
52'-4"	15 951	15 954	15 958	15 961	15 964	15 967	15 970	15 973
52'-5"	15 977	15 980	15 983	15 986	15 989	15 992	15 996	15 999
52'-6"	16 002	16 005	16 008	16 012	16 015	16 018	16 021	16 024
52'-7"	16 027	16 031	16 034	16 037	16 040	16 043	16 046	16 050
52'-8"	16 053	16 056	16 059	16 062	16 065	16 069	16 072	16 075
52'-9"	16 078	16 081	16 085	16 088	16 091	16 094	16 097	16 100
52'-10"	16 104	16 107	16 110	16 113	16 116	16 119	16 123	16 126
52'-11"	16 129	16 132	16 135	16 139	16 142	16 145	16 148	16 151
53'-0"	16 154	16 158	16 161	16 164	16 167	16 170	16 173	16 177
53'-1"	16 180	16 183	16 186	16 189	16 192	16 196	16 199	16 202
53'-2"	16 205	16 208	16 212	16 215	16 218	16 221	16 224	16 227
53'-3"	16 231	16 234	16 237	16 240	16 243	16 246	16 250	16 253
53'-4"	16 256	16 259	16 262	16 266	16 269	16 272	16 275	16 278
53'-5"	16 281	16 285	16 288	16 291	16 294	16 297	16 300	16 304
53'-6"	16 307	16 310	16 313	16 316	16 319	16 323	16 326	16 329
53'-7"	16 332	16 335	16 339	16 342	16 345	16 348	16 351	16 354
53'-8"	16 358	16 361	16 364	16 367	16 370	16 373	16 377	16 380
53'-9"	16 383	16 386	16 389	16 393	16 396	16 399	16 402	16 405
53'-10"	16 408	16 412	16 415	16 418	16 421	16 424	16 427	16 431
53'-11"	16 434	16 437	16 440	16 443	16 446	16 450	16 453	16 456
54'-0"	16 459	16 462	16 466	16 469	16 472	16 475	16 478	16 481
54'-1"	16 485	16 488	16 491	16 494	16 497	16 500	16 504	16 507
54'-2"	16 510	16 513	16 516	16 520	16 523	16 526	16 529	16 532
54'-3"	16 535	16 539	16 542	16 545	16 548	16 551	16 554	16 558
54'-4"	16 561	16 564	16 567	16 570	16 573	16 577	16 580	16 583
54'-5"	16 586	16 589	16 593	16 596	16 599	16 602	16 605	16 608
54'-6"	16 612	16 615	16 618	16 621	16 624	16 627	16 631	16 634
54'-7"	16 637	16 640	16 643	16 647	16 650	16 653	16 656	16 659
54'-8"	16 662	16 666	16 669	16 672	16 675	16 678	16 681	16 685
54'-9"	16 688	16 691	16 694	16 697	16 700	16 704	16 707	16 710
54'-10"	16 713	16 716	16 720	16 723	16 726	16 729	16 732	16 735
54'-11"	16 739	16 742	16 745	16 748	16 751	16 754	16 758	16 761
55'-0"	16 764	16 767	16 770	16 774	16 777	16 780	16 783	16 786
55'-1"	16 789	16 793	16 796	16 799	16 802	16 805	16 808	16 812
55'-2"	16 815	16 818	16 821	16 824	16 827	16 831	16 834	16 837
55'-3"	16 840	16 843	16 847	16 850	16 853	16 856	16 859	16 862
55'-4"	16 866	16 869	16 872	16 875	16 878	16 881	16 885	16 888
55'-5"	16 891	16 894	16 897	16 901	16 904	16 907	16 910	16 913

Linear measurement

Table 2 (cont.). Feet, inches, and fractions (multiples of ⅛ in.), up to 100 ft, to nearest whole millimeter (mm)

Feet and Inches	0	1/8"	1/4"	3/8"	1/2"	5/8"	3/4"	7/8"
				millimeters (mm)				
55'-6"	16 916	16 920	16 923	16 926	16 929	16 932	16 935	16 939
55'-7"	16 942	16 945	16 948	16 951	16 954	16 958	16 961	16 964
55'-8"	16 967	16 970	16 974	16 977	16 980	16 983	16 986	16 989
55'-9"	16 993	16 996	16 999	17 002	17 005	17 008	17 012	17 015
55'-10"	17 018	17 021	17 024	17 028	17 031	17 034	17 037	17 040
55'-11"	17 043	17 047	17 050	17 053	17 056	17 059	17 062	17 066
56'-0"	17 069	17 072	17 075	17 078	17 081	17 085	17 088	17 091
56'-1"	17 094	17 097	17 101	17 104	17 107	17 110	17 113	17 116
56'-2"	17 120	17 123	17 126	17 129	17 132	17 135	17 139	17 142
56'-3"	17 145	17 148	17 151	17 155	17 158	17 161	17 164	17 167
56'-4"	17 170	17 174	17 177	17 180	17 183	17 186	17 189	17 193
56'-5"	17 196	17 199	17 202	17 205	17 208	17 212	17 215	17 218
56'-6"	17 221	17 224	17 228	17 231	17 234	17 237	17 240	17 243
56'-7"	17 247	17 250	17 253	17 256	17 259	17 262	17 266	17 269
56'-8"	17 272	17 275	17 278	17 282	17 285	17 288	17 291	17 294
56'-9"	17 297	17 301	17 304	17 307	17 310	17 313	17 316	17 320
56'-10"	17 323	17 326	17 329	17 332	17 335	17 339	17 342	17 345
56'-11"	17 348	17 351	17 355	17 358	17 361	17 364	17 367	17 370
57'-0"	17 374	17 377	17 380	17 383	17 386	17 389	17 393	17 396
57'-1"	17 399	17 402	17 405	17 409	17 412	17 415	17 418	17 421
57'-2"	17 424	17 428	17 431	17 434	17 437	17 440	17 443	17 447
57'-3"	17 450	17 453	17 456	17 459	17 462	17 466	17 469	17 472
57'-4"	17 475	17 478	17 482	17 485	17 488	17 491	17 494	17 497
57'-5"	17 501	17 504	17 507	17 510	17 513	17 516	17 520	17 523
57'-6"	17 526	17 529	17 532	17 536	17 539	17 542	17 545	17 548
57'-7"	17 551	17 555	17 558	17 561	17 564	17 567	17 570	17 574
57'-8"	17 577	17 580	17 583	17 586	17 589	17 593	17 596	17 599
57'-9"	17 602	17 605	17 609	17 612	17 615	17 618	17 621	17 624
57'-10"	17 628	17 631	17 634	17 637	17 640	17 643	17 647	17 650
57'-11"	17 653	17 656	17 659	17 663	17 666	17 669	17 672	17 675
58'-0"	17 678	17 682	17 685	17 688	17 691	17 694	17 697	17 701
58'-1"	17 704	17 707	17 710	17 713	17 716	17 720	17 723	17 726
58'-2"	17 729	17 732	17 736	17 739	17 742	17 745	17 748	17 751
58'-3"	17 755	17 758	17 761	17 764	17 767	17 770	17 774	17 777
58'-4"	17 780	17 783	17 786	17 790	17 793	17 796	17 799	17 802
58'-5"	17 805	17 809	17 812	17 815	17 818	17 821	17 824	17 828
58'-6"	17 831	17 834	17 837	17 840	17 843	17 847	17 850	17 853
58'-7"	17 856	17 859	17 863	17 866	17 869	17 872	17 875	17 878
58'-8"	17 882	17 885	17 888	17 891	17 894	17 897	17 901	17 904
58'-9"	17 907	17 910	17 913	17 917	17 920	17 923	17 926	17 929
58'-10"	17 932	17 936	17 939	17 942	17 945	17 948	17 951	17 955
58'-11"	17 958	17 961	17 964	17 967	17 970	17 974	17 977	17 980

Feet and Inches	0	1/8"	1/4"	3/8"	1/2"	5/8"	3/4"	7/8"
				millimeters (mm)				
59'-0"	17 983	17 986	17 990	17 993	17 996	17 999	18 002	18 005
59'-1"	18 009	18 012	18 015	18 018	18 021	18 024	18 028	18 031
59'-2"	18 034	18 037	18 040	18 044	18 047	18 050	18 053	18 056
59'-3"	18 059	18 063	18 066	18 069	18 072	18 075	18 078	18 082
59'-4"	18 085	18 088	18 091	18 094	18 097	18 101	18 104	18 107
59'-5"	18 110	18 113	18 117	18 120	18 123	18 126	18 129	18 132
59'-6"	18 136	18 139	18 142	18 145	18 148	18 151	18 155	18 158
59'-7"	18 161	18 164	18 167	18 171	18 174	18 177	18 180	18 183
59'-8"	18 186	18 190	18 193	18 196	18 199	18 202	18 205	18 209
59'-9"	18 212	18 215	18 218	18 221	18 224	18 228	18 231	18 234
59'-10"	18 237	18 240	18 244	18 247	18 250	18 253	18 256	18 259
59'-11"	18 263	18 266	18 269	18 272	18 275	18 278	18 282	18 285
60'-0"	18 288	18 291	18 294	18 298	18 301	18 304	18 307	18 310
60'-1"	18 313	18 317	18 320	18 323	18 326	18 329	18 332	18 336
60'-2"	18 339	18 342	18 345	18 348	18 351	18 355	18 358	18 361
60'-3"	18 364	18 367	18 371	18 374	18 377	18 380	18 383	18 386
60'-4"	18 390	18 393	18 396	18 399	18 402	18 405	18 409	18 412
60'-5"	18 415	18 418	18 421	18 425	18 428	18 431	18 434	18 437
60'-6"	18 440	18 444	18 447	18 450	18 453	18 456	18 459	18 463
60'-7"	18 466	18 469	18 472	18 475	18 478	18 482	18 485	18 488
60'-8"	18 491	18 494	18 498	18 501	18 504	18 507	18 510	18 513
60'-9"	18 517	18 520	18 523	18 526	18 529	18 532	18 536	18 539
60'-10"	18 542	18 545	18 548	18 552	18 555	18 558	18 561	18 564
60'-11"	18 567	18 571	18 574	18 577	18 580	18 583	18 586	18 590
61'-0"	18 593	18 596	18 599	18 602	18 605	18 609	18 612	18 615
61'-1"	18 618	18 621	18 625	18 628	18 631	18 634	18 637	18 640
61'-2"	18 644	18 647	18 650	18 653	18 656	18 659	18 663	18 666
61'-3"	18 669	18 672	18 675	18 679	18 682	18 685	18 688	18 691
61'-4"	18 694	18 698	18 701	18 704	18 707	18 710	18 713	18 717
61'-5"	18 720	18 723	18 726	18 729	18 732	18 736	18 739	18 742
61'-6"	18 745	18 748	18 752	18 755	18 758	18 761	18 764	18 767
61'-7"	18 771	18 774	18 777	18 780	18 783	18 786	18 790	18 793
61'-8"	18 796	18 799	18 802	18 806	18 809	18 812	18 815	18 818
61'-9"	18 821	18 825	18 828	18 831	18 834	18 837	18 840	18 844
61'-10"	18 847	18 850	18 853	18 856	18 859	18 863	18 866	18 869
61'-11"	18 872	18 875	18 879	18 882	18 885	18 888	18 891	18 894
62'-0"	18 898	18 901	18 904	18 907	18 910	18 913	18 917	18 920
62'-1"	18 923	18 926	18 929	18 933	18 936	18 939	18 942	18 945
62'-2"	18 948	18 952	18 955	18 958	18 961	18 964	18 967	18 971
62'-3"	18 974	18 977	18 980	18 983	18 986	18 990	18 993	18 996
62'-4"	18 999	19 002	19 006	19 009	19 012	19 015	19 018	19 021
62'-5"	19 025	19 028	19 031	19 034	19 037	19 040	19 044	19 047

Table 2 (cont.). Feet, inches, and fractions (multiples of ⅛ in.), up to 100 ft, to nearest whole millimeter (mm)

Feet and Inches	millimeters (mm)							
	0	1/8"	1/4"	3/8"	1/2"	5/8"	3/4"	7/8"
62'-6"	19 050	19 053	19 056	19 060	19 063	19 066	19 069	19 072
62'-7"	19 075	19 079	19 082	19 085	19 088	19 091	19 094	19 098
62'-8"	19 101	19 104	19 107	19 110	19 113	19 117	19 120	19 123
62'-9"	19 126	19 129	19 133	19 136	19 139	19 142	19 145	19 148
62'-10"	19 152	19 155	19 158	19 161	19 164	19 167	19 171	19 174
62'-11"	19 177	19 180	19 183	19 187	19 190	19 193	19 196	19 199
63'-0"	19 202	19 206	19 209	19 212	19 215	19 218	19 221	19 225
63'-1"	19 228	19 231	19 234	19 237	19 240	19 244	19 247	19 250
63'-2"	19 253	19 256	19 260	19 263	19 266	19 269	19 272	19 275
63'-3"	19 279	19 282	19 285	19 288	19 291	19 294	19 298	19 301
63'-4"	19 304	19 307	19 310	19 314	19 317	19 320	19 323	19 326
63'-5"	19 329	19 333	19 336	19 339	19 342	19 345	19 348	19 352
63'-6"	19 355	19 358	19 361	19 364	19 367	19 371	19 374	19 377
63'-7"	19 380	19 383	19 387	19 390	19 393	19 396	19 399	19 402
63'-8"	19 406	19 409	19 412	19 415	19 418	19 421	19 425	19 428
63'-9"	19 431	19 434	19 437	19 441	19 444	19 447	19 450	19 453
63'-10"	19 456	19 460	19 463	19 466	19 469	19 472	19 475	19 479
63'-11"	19 482	19 485	19 488	19 491	19 494	19 498	19 501	19 504
64'-0"	19 507	19 510	19 514	19 517	19 520	19 523	19 526	19 529
64'-1"	19 533	19 536	19 539	19 542	19 545	19 548	19 552	19 555
64'-2"	19 558	19 561	19 564	19 568	19 571	19 574	19 577	19 580
64'-3"	19 583	19 587	19 590	19 593	19 596	19 599	19 602	19 606
64'-4"	19 609	19 612	19 615	19 618	19 621	19 625	19 628	19 631
64'-5"	19 634	19 637	19 641	19 644	19 647	19 650	19 653	19 656
64'-6"	19 660	19 663	19 666	19 669	19 672	19 675	19 679	19 682
64'-7"	19 685	19 688	19 691	19 695	19 698	19 701	19 704	19 707
64'-8"	19 710	19 714	19 717	19 720	19 723	19 726	19 729	19 733
64'-9"	19 736	19 739	19 742	19 745	19 748	19 752	19 755	19 758
64'-10"	19 761	19 764	19 768	19 771	19 774	19 777	19 780	19 783
64'-11"	19 787	19 790	19 793	19 796	19 799	19 802	19 806	19 809
65'-0"	19 812	19 815	19 818	19 822	19 825	19 828	19 831	19 834
65'-1"	19 837	19 841	19 844	19 847	19 850	19 853	19 856	19 860
65'-2"	19 863	19 866	19 869	19 872	19 875	19 879	19 882	19 885
65'-3"	19 888	19 891	19 895	19 898	19 901	19 904	19 907	19 910
65'-4"	19 914	19 917	19 920	19 923	19 926	19 929	19 933	19 936
65'-5"	19 939	19 942	19 945	19 949	19 952	19 955	19 958	19 961
65'-6"	19 964	19 968	19 971	19 974	19 977	19 980	19 983	19 987
65'-7"	19 990	19 993	19 996	19 999	20 002	20 006	20 009	20 012
65'-8"	20 015	20 018	20 022	20 025	20 028	20 031	20 034	20 037
65'-9"	20 041	20 044	20 047	20 050	20 053	20 056	20 060	20 063
65'-10"	20 066	20 069	20 072	20 076	20 079	20 082	20 085	20 088
65'-11"	20 091	20 095	20 098	20 101	20 104	20 107	20 110	20 114

Feet and Inches	millimeters (mm)							
	0	1/8"	1/4"	3/8"	1/2"	5/8"	3/4"	7/8"
66'-0"	20 117	20 120	20 123	20 126	20 129	20 133	20 136	20 139
66'-1"	20 142	20 145	20 149	20 152	20 155	20 158	20 161	20 164
66'-2"	20 168	20 171	20 174	20 177	20 180	20 183	20 187	20 190
66'-3"	20 193	20 196	20 199	20 203	20 206	20 209	20 212	20 215
66'-4"	20 218	20 222	20 225	20 228	20 231	20 234	20 237	20 241
66'-5"	20 244	20 247	20 250	20 253	20 256	20 260	20 263	20 266
66'-6"	20 269	20 272	20 276	20 279	20 282	20 285	20 288	20 291
66'-7"	20 295	20 298	20 301	20 304	20 307	20 310	20 314	20 317
66'-8"	20 320	20 323	20 326	20 330	20 333	20 336	20 339	20 342
66'-9"	20 345	20 349	20 352	20 355	20 358	20 361	20 364	20 368
66'-10"	20 371	20 374	20 377	20 380	20 383	20 387	20 390	20 393
66'-11"	20 396	20 399	20 403	20 406	20 409	20 412	20 415	20 418
67'-0"	20 422	20 425	20 428	20 431	20 434	20 437	20 441	20 444
67'-1"	20 447	20 450	20 453	20 457	20 460	20 463	20 466	20 469
67'-2"	20 472	20 476	20 479	20 482	20 485	20 488	20 491	20 495
67'-3"	20 498	20 501	20 504	20 507	20 510	20 513	20 517	20 520
67'-4"	20 523	20 526	20 530	20 533	20 536	20 539	20 542	20 545
67'-5"	20 549	20 552	20 555	20 558	20 561	20 564	20 568	20 571
67'-6"	20 574	20 577	20 580	20 584	20 587	20 590	20 593	20 596
67'-7"	20 599	20 603	20 606	20 609	20 612	20 615	20 618	20 622
67'-8"	20 625	20 628	20 631	20 634	20 637	20 641	20 644	20 647
67'-9"	20 650	20 653	20 657	20 660	20 663	20 666	20 669	20 672
67'-10"	20 676	20 679	20 682	20 685	20 688	20 691	20 695	20 698
67'-11"	20 701	20 704	20 707	20 711	20 714	20 717	20 720	20 723
68'-0"	20 726	20 730	20 733	20 736	20 739	20 742	20 745	20 749
68'-1"	20 752	20 755	20 758	20 761	20 764	20 768	20 771	20 774
68'-2"	20 777	20 780	20 784	20 787	20 790	20 793	20 796	20 799
68'-3"	20 803	20 806	20 809	20 812	20 815	20 818	20 822	20 825
68'-4"	20 828	20 831	20 834	20 838	20 841	20 844	20 847	20 850
68'-5"	20 853	20 857	20 860	20 863	20 866	20 869	20 872	20 876
68'-6"	20 879	20 882	20 885	20 888	20 891	20 895	20 898	20 901
68'-7"	20 904	20 907	20 911	20 914	20 917	20 920	20 923	20 926
68'-8"	20 930	20 933	20 936	20 939	20 942	20 945	20 949	20 952
68'-9"	20 955	20 958	20 961	20 965	20 968	20 971	20 974	20 977
68'-10"	20 980	20 984	20 987	20 990	20 993	20 996	20 999	21 003
68'-11"	21 006	21 009	21 012	21 015	21 018	21 022	21 025	21 028
69'-0"	21 031	21 034	21 038	21 041	21 044	21 047	21 050	21 053
69'-1"	21 057	21 060	21 063	21 066	21 069	21 072	21 076	21 079
69'-2"	21 082	21 085	21 088	21 092	21 095	21 098	21 101	21 104
69'-3"	21 107	21 111	21 114	21 117	21 120	21 123	21 126	21 130
69'-4"	21 133	21 136	21 139	21 142	21 145	21 149	21 152	21 155
69'-5"	21 158	21 161	21 165	21 168	21 171	21 174	21 177	21 180

Table 2 (cont.). Feet, inches, and fractions (multiples of ⅛ in.), up to 100 ft, to nearest whole millimeter (mm)

Feet and Inches	0	1/8"	1/4"	3/8"	1/2"	5/8"	3/4"	7/8"
				millimeters (mm)				
69'-6"	21 184	21 187	21 190	21 193	21 196	21 199	21 203	21 206
69'-7"	21 209	21 212	21 215	21 219	21 222	21 225	21 228	21 231
69'-8"	21 234	21 238	21 241	21 244	21 247	21 250	21 253	21 257
69'-9"	21 260	21 263	21 266	21 269	21 272	21 276	21 279	21 282
69'-10"	21 285	21 288	21 292	21 295	21 298	21 301	21 304	21 307
69'-11"	21 311	21 314	21 317	21 320	21 323	21 326	21 330	21 333
70'-0"	21 336	21 339	21 342	21 346	21 349	21 352	21 355	21 358
70'-1"	21 361	21 365	21 368	21 371	21 374	21 377	21 380	21 384
70'-2"	21 387	21 390	21 393	21 396	21 399	21 403	21 406	21 409
70'-3"	21 412	21 415	21 419	21 422	21 425	21 428	21 431	21 434
70'-4"	21 438	21 441	21 444	21 447	21 450	21 453	21 457	21 460
70'-5"	21 463	21 466	21 469	21 473	21 476	21 479	21 482	21 485
70'-6"	21 488	21 492	21 495	21 498	21 501	21 504	21 507	21 511
70'-7"	21 514	21 517	21 520	21 523	21 526	21 530	21 533	21 536
70'-8"	21 539	21 542	21 546	21 549	21 552	21 555	21 558	21 561
70'-9"	21 565	21 568	21 571	21 574	21 577	21 580	21 584	21 587
70'-10"	21 590	21 593	21 596	21 600	21 603	21 606	21 609	21 612
70'-11"	21 615	21 619	21 622	21 625	21 628	21 631	21 634	21 638
71'-0"	21 641	21 644	21 647	21 650	21 653	21 657	21 660	21 663
71'-1"	21 666	21 669	21 673	21 676	21 679	21 682	21 685	21 688
71'-2"	21 692	21 695	21 698	21 701	21 704	21 707	21 711	21 714
71'-3"	21 717	21 720	21 723	21 727	21 730	21 733	21 736	21 739
71'-4"	21 742	21 746	21 749	21 752	21 755	21 758	21 761	21 765
71'-5"	21 768	21 771	21 774	21 777	21 780	21 784	21 787	21 790
71'-6"	21 793	21 796	21 800	21 803	21 806	21 809	21 812	21 815
71'-7"	21 819	21 822	21 825	21 828	21 831	21 834	21 838	21 841
71'-8"	21 844	21 847	21 850	21 854	21 857	21 860	21 863	21 866
71'-9"	21 869	21 873	21 876	21 879	21 882	21 885	21 888	21 892
71'-10"	21 895	21 898	21 901	21 904	21 907	21 911	21 914	21 917
71'-11"	21 920	21 923	21 927	21 930	21 933	21 936	21 939	21 942
72'-0"	21 946	21 949	21 952	21 955	21 958	21 961	21 965	21 968
72'-1"	21 971	21 974	21 977	21 981	21 984	21 987	21 990	21 993
72'-2"	21 996	22 000	22 003	22 006	22 009	22 012	22 015	22 019
72'-3"	22 022	22 025	22 028	22 031	22 034	22 038	22 041	22 044
72'-4"	22 047	22 050	22 054	22 057	22 060	22 063	22 066	22 069
72'-5"	22 073	22 076	22 079	22 082	22 085	22 088	22 092	22 095
72'-6"	22 098	22 101	22 104	22 108	22 111	22 114	22 117	22 120
72'-7"	22 123	22 127	22 130	22 133	22 136	22 139	22 142	22 146
72'-8"	22 149	22 152	22 155	22 158	22 161	22 165	22 168	22 171
72'-9"	22 174	22 177	22 181	22 184	22 187	22 190	22 193	22 196
72'-10"	22 200	22 203	22 206	22 209	22 212	22 215	22 219	22 222
72'-11"	22 225	22 228	22 231	22 235	22 238	22 241	22 244	22 247

Feet and Inches	0	1/8"	1/4"	3/8"	1/2"	5/8"	3/4"	7/8"
				millimeters (mm)				
73'-0"	22 250	22 254	22 257	22 260	22 263	22 266	22 269	22 273
73'-1"	22 276	22 279	22 282	22 285	22 288	22 292	22 295	22 298
73'-2"	22 301	22 304	22 308	22 311	22 314	22 317	22 320	22 323
73'-3"	22 327	22 330	22 333	22 336	22 339	22 342	22 346	22 349
73'-4"	22 352	22 355	22 358	22 362	22 365	22 368	22 371	22 374
73'-5"	22 377	22 381	22 384	22 387	22 390	22 393	22 396	22 400
73'-6"	22 403	22 406	22 409	22 412	22 415	22 419	22 422	22 425
73'-7"	22 428	22 431	22 435	22 438	22 441	22 444	22 447	22 450
73'-8"	22 454	22 457	22 460	22 463	22 466	22 469	22 473	22 476
73'-9"	22 479	22 482	22 485	22 489	22 492	22 495	22 498	22 501
73'-10"	22 504	22 508	22 511	22 514	22 517	22 520	22 523	22 527
73'-11"	22 530	22 533	22 536	22 539	22 542	22 546	22 549	22 552
74'-0"	22 555	22 558	22 562	22 565	22 568	22 571	22 574	22 577
74'-1"	22 581	22 584	22 587	22 590	22 593	22 596	22 600	22 603
74'-2"	22 606	22 609	22 612	22 616	22 619	22 622	22 625	22 628
74'-3"	22 631	22 635	22 638	22 641	22 644	22 647	22 650	22 654
74'-4"	22 657	22 660	22 663	22 666	22 669	22 673	22 676	22 679
74'-5"	22 682	22 685	22 689	22 692	22 695	22 698	22 701	22 704
74'-6"	22 708	22 712	22 714	22 717	22 720	22 723	22 727	22 730
74'-7"	22 733	22 736	22 739	22 743	22 746	22 749	22 752	22 755
74'-8"	22 758	22 762	22 765	22 768	22 771	22 774	22 777	22 781
74'-9"	22 784	22 787	22 790	22 793	22 796	22 800	22 803	22 806
74'-10"	22 809	22 812	22 816	22 819	22 822	22 825	22 828	22 831
74'-11"	22 835	22 838	22 841	22 844	22 847	22 850	22 854	22 857
75'-0"	22 860	22 863	22 866	22 870	22 873	22 876	22 879	22 882
75'-1"	22 885	22 889	22 892	22 895	22 898	22 901	22 904	22 908
75'-2"	22 911	22 914	22 917	22 920	22 923	22 927	22 930	22 933
75'-3"	22 936	22 939	22 943	22 946	22 949	22 952	22 955	22 958
75'-4"	22 962	22 965	22 968	22 971	22 974	22 977	22 981	22 984
75'-5"	22 987	22 990	22 993	22 997	23 000	23 003	23 006	23 009
75'-6"	23 012	23 016	23 019	23 022	23 025	23 028	23 031	23 035
75'-7"	23 038	23 041	23 044	23 047	23 050	23 054	23 057	23 060
75'-8"	23 063	23 066	23 070	23 073	23 076	23 079	23 082	23 085
75'-9"	23 089	23 092	23 095	23 098	23 101	23 104	23 108	23 111
75'-10"	23 114	23 117	23 120	23 124	23 127	23 130	23 133	23 136
75'-11"	23 139	23 143	23 146	23 149	23 152	23 155	23 158	23 162
76'-0"	23 165	23 168	23 171	23 174	23 177	23 181	23 184	23 187
76'-1"	23 190	23 193	23 197	23 200	23 203	23 206	23 209	23 212
76'-2"	23 216	23 219	23 222	23 225	23 228	23 231	23 235	23 238
76'-3"	23 241	23 244	23 247	23 251	23 254	23 257	23 260	23 263
76'-4"	23 266	23 270	23 273	23 276	23 279	23 282	23 285	23 289
76'-5"	23 292	23 295	23 298	23 301	23 304	23 308	23 311	23 314

Table 2 (cont.). Feet, inches, and fractions (multiples of ⅛ in.), up to 100 ft, to nearest whole millimeter (mm)

Feet and Inches	0	1/8"	1/4"	3/8"	1/2"	5/8"	3/4"	7/8"
				millimeters (mm)				
80'-0"	24 384	24 387	24 390	24 394	24 397	24 400	24 403	24 406
80'-1"	24 409	24 413	24 416	24 419	24 422	24 425	24 428	24 432
80'-2"	24 435	24 438	24 441	24 444	24 447	24 451	24 454	24 457
80'-3"	24 460	24 463	24 467	24 470	24 473	24 476	24 479	24 482
80'-4"	24 486	24 489	24 492	24 495	24 498	24 501	24 505	24 508
80'-5"	24 511	24 514	24 517	24 521	24 524	24 527	24 530	24 533
80'-6"	24 536	24 540	24 543	24 546	24 549	24 552	24 555	24 559
80'-7"	24 562	24 565	24 568	24 571	24 574	24 578	24 581	24 584
80'-8"	24 587	24 590	24 594	24 597	24 600	24 603	24 606	24 609
80'-9"	24 613	24 616	24 619	24 622	24 625	24 628	24 632	24 635
80'-10"	24 638	24 641	24 644	24 648	24 651	24 654	24 657	24 660
80'-11"	24 663	24 667	24 670	24 673	24 676	24 679	24 682	24 686
81'-0"	24 689	24 692	24 695	24 698	24 701	24 705	24 708	24 711
81'-1"	24 714	24 717	24 721	24 724	24 727	24 730	24 733	24 736
81'-2"	24 740	24 743	24 746	24 749	24 752	24 755	24 759	24 762
81'-3"	24 765	24 768	24 771	24 775	24 778	24 781	24 784	24 787
81'-4"	24 790	24 794	24 797	24 800	24 803	24 806	24 809	24 813
81'-5"	24 816	24 819	24 822	24 825	24 828	24 832	24 835	24 838
81'-6"	24 841	24 844	24 848	24 851	24 854	24 857	24 860	24 863
81'-7"	24 867	24 870	24 873	24 876	24 879	24 882	24 886	24 889
81'-8"	24 892	24 895	24 898	24 902	24 905	24 908	24 911	24 914
81'-9"	24 917	24 921	24 924	24 927	24 930	24 933	24 936	24 940
81'-10"	24 943	24 946	24 949	24 952	24 955	24 959	24 962	24 965
81'-11"	24 968	24 971	24 975	24 978	24 981	24 984	24 987	24 990
82'-0"	24 994	24 997	25 000	25 003	25 006	25 009	25 013	25 016
82'-1"	25 019	25 022	25 025	25 029	25 032	25 035	25 038	25 041
82'-2"	25 044	25 048	25 051	25 054	25 057	25 060	25 063	25 067
82'-3"	25 070	25 073	25 076	25 079	25 082	25 086	25 089	25 092
82'-4"	25 095	25 098	25 102	25 105	25 108	25 111	25 114	25 117
82'-5"	25 121	25 124	25 127	25 130	25 133	25 136	25 140	25 143
82'-6"	25 146	25 149	25 152	25 156	25 159	25 162	25 165	25 168
82'-7"	25 171	25 175	25 178	25 181	25 184	25 187	25 190	25 194
82'-8"	25 197	25 200	25 203	25 206	25 209	25 213	25 216	25 219
82'-9"	25 222	25 225	25 229	25 232	25 235	25 238	25 241	25 244
82'-10"	25 248	25 251	25 254	25 257	25 260	25 263	25 267	25 270
82'-11"	25 273	25 276	25 279	25 283	25 286	25 289	25 292	25 295
83'-0"	25 298	25 302	25 305	25 308	25 311	25 314	25 317	25 321
83'-1"	25 324	25 327	25 330	25 333	25 336	25 340	25 343	25 346
83'-2"	25 349	25 352	25 356	25 359	25 362	25 365	25 368	25 371
83'-3"	25 375	25 378	25 381	25 384	25 387	25 390	25 394	25 397
83'-4"	25 400	25 403	25 406	25 410	25 413	25 416	25 419	25 422
83'-5"	25 425	25 429	25 432	25 435	25 438	25 441	25 444	25 448

Feet and Inches	0	1/8"	1/4"	3/8"	1/2"	5/8"	3/4"	7/8"
				millimeters (mm)				
76'-6"	23 317	23 320	23 324	23 327	23 330	23 333	23 336	23 339
76'-7"	23 343	23 346	23 349	23 352	23 355	23 358	23 362	23 365
76'-8"	23 368	23 371	23 374	23 378	23 381	23 384	23 387	23 390
76'-9"	23 393	23 397	23 400	23 403	23 406	23 409	23 412	23 416
76'-10"	23 419	23 422	23 425	23 428	23 431	23 435	23 438	23 441
76'-11"	23 444	23 447	23 451	23 454	23 457	23 460	23 463	23 466
77'-0"	23 470	23 473	23 476	23 479	23 482	23 485	23 489	23 492
77'-1"	23 495	23 498	23 501	23 505	23 508	23 511	23 514	23 517
77'-2"	23 520	23 524	23 527	23 530	23 533	23 536	23 539	23 543
77'-3"	23 546	23 549	23 552	23 555	23 558	23 562	23 565	23 568
77'-4"	23 571	23 574	23 578	23 581	23 584	23 587	23 590	23 593
77'-5"	23 597	23 600	23 603	23 606	23 609	23 612	23 616	23 619
77'-6"	23 622	23 625	23 628	23 632	23 635	23 638	23 641	23 644
77'-7"	23 647	23 651	23 654	23 657	23 660	23 663	23 666	23 670
77'-8"	23 673	23 676	23 679	23 682	23 685	23 689	23 692	23 695
77'-9"	23 698	23 701	23 705	23 708	23 711	23 714	23 717	23 720
77'-10"	23 724	23 727	23 730	23 733	23 736	23 739	23 743	23 746
77'-11"	23 749	23 752	23 755	23 759	23 762	23 765	23 768	23 771
78'-0"	23 774	23 778	23 781	23 784	23 787	23 790	23 793	23 797
78'-1"	23 800	23 803	23 806	23 809	23 812	23 816	23 819	23 822
78'-2"	23 825	23 828	23 832	23 835	23 838	23 841	23 844	23 847
78'-3"	23 851	23 854	23 857	23 860	23 863	23 866	23 870	23 873
78'-4"	23 876	23 879	23 882	23 886	23 889	23 892	23 895	23 898
78'-5"	23 901	23 905	23 908	23 911	23 914	23 917	23 920	23 924
78'-6"	23 927	23 930	23 933	23 936	23 939	23 943	23 946	23 949
78'-7"	23 952	23 955	23 959	23 962	23 965	23 968	23 971	23 974
78'-8"	23 978	23 981	23 984	23 987	23 990	23 993	23 997	24 000
78'-9"	24 003	24 006	24 009	24 013	24 016	24 019	24 022	24 025
78'-10"	24 028	24 032	24 035	24 038	24 041	24 044	24 047	24 051
78'-11"	24 054	24 057	24 060	24 063	24 066	24 070	24 073	24 076
79'-0"	24 079	24 082	24 086	24 089	24 092	24 095	24 098	24 101
79'-1"	24 105	24 108	24 111	24 114	24 117	24 120	24 124	24 127
79'-2"	24 130	24 133	24 136	24 140	24 143	24 146	24 149	24 152
79'-3"	24 155	24 159	24 162	24 165	24 168	24 171	24 174	24 178
79'-4"	24 181	24 184	24 187	24 190	24 193	24 197	24 200	24 203
79'-5"	24 206	24 209	24 213	24 216	24 219	24 222	24 225	24 228
79'-6"	24 232	24 235	24 238	24 241	24 244	24 247	24 251	24 254
79'-7"	24 257	24 260	24 263	24 267	24 270	24 273	24 276	24 279
79'-8"	24 282	24 286	24 289	24 292	24 295	24 298	24 301	24 305
79'-9"	24 308	24 311	24 314	24 317	24 320	24 324	24 327	24 330
79'-10"	24 333	24 336	24 340	24 343	24 346	24 349	24 352	24 355
79'-11"	24 359	24 362	24 365	24 368	24 371	24 374	24 378	24 381

Linear measurement

Table 2 (cont.). Feet, inches, and fractions (multiples of ⅛ in.), up to 100 ft, to nearest whole millimeter (mm)

Feet and Inches	0	1/8"	1/4"	3/8"	1/2"	5/8"	3/4"	7/8"
				millimeters (mm)				
87'-0"	26 518	26 521	26 524	26 527	26 530	26 533	26 537	26 540
87'-1"	26 543	26 546	26 549	26 553	26 556	26 559	26 562	26 565
87'-2"	26 568	26 572	26 575	26 578	26 581	26 584	26 587	26 591
87'-3"	26 594	26 597	26 600	26 603	26 606	26 610	26 613	26 616
87'-4"	26 619	26 622	26 626	26 629	26 632	26 635	26 638	26 641
87'-5"	26 645	26 648	26 651	26 654	26 657	26 660	26 664	26 667
87'-6"	26 670	26 673	26 676	26 680	26 683	26 686	26 689	26 692
87'-7"	26 695	26 699	26 702	26 705	26 708	26 711	26 714	26 718
87'-8"	26 721	26 724	26 727	26 730	26 733	26 737	26 740	26 743
87'-9"	26 746	26 749	26 753	26 756	26 759	26 762	26 765	26 768
87'-10"	26 772	26 775	26 778	26 781	26 784	26 787	26 791	26 794
87'-11"	26 797	26 800	26 803	26 807	26 810	26 813	26 816	26 819
88'-0"	26 822	26 826	26 829	26 832	26 835	26 838	26 841	26 845
88'-1"	26 848	26 851	26 854	26 857	26 860	26 864	26 867	26 870
88'-2"	26 873	26 876	26 880	26 883	26 886	26 889	26 892	26 895
88'-3"	26 899	26 902	26 905	26 908	26 911	26 914	26 918	26 921
88'-4"	26 924	26 927	26 930	26 934	26 937	26 940	26 943	26 946
88'-5"	26 949	26 953	26 956	26 959	26 962	26 965	26 968	26 972
88'-6"	26 975	26 978	26 981	26 984	26 987	26 991	26 994	26 997
88'-7"	27 000	27 003	27 007	27 010	27 013	27 016	27 019	27 022
88'-8"	27 026	27 029	27 032	27 035	27 038	27 041	27 045	27 048
88'-9"	27 051	27 054	27 057	27 061	27 064	27 067	27 070	27 073
88'-10"	27 076	27 080	27 083	27 086	27 089	27 092	27 095	27 099
88'-11"	27 102	27 105	27 108	27 111	27 114	27 118	27 121	27 124
89'-0"	27 127	27 130	27 134	27 137	27 140	27 143	27 146	27 149
89'-1"	27 153	27 156	27 159	27 162	27 165	27 168	27 172	27 175
89'-2"	27 178	27 181	27 184	27 188	27 191	27 194	27 197	27 200
89'-3"	27 203	27 207	27 210	27 213	27 216	27 219	27 222	27 226
89'-4"	27 229	27 232	27 235	27 238	27 241	27 245	27 248	27 251
89'-5"	27 254	27 257	27 261	27 264	27 267	27 270	27 273	27 276
89'-6"	27 280	27 283	27 286	27 289	27 292	27 295	27 299	27 302
89'-7"	27 305	27 308	27 311	27 315	27 318	27 321	27 324	27 327
89'-8"	27 330	27 334	27 337	27 340	27 343	27 346	27 349	27 353
89'-9"	27 356	27 359	27 362	27 365	27 368	27 372	27 375	27 378
89'-10"	27 381	27 384	27 388	27 391	27 394	27 397	27 400	27 403
89'-11"	27 407	27 410	27 413	27 416	27 419	27 422	27 426	27 429
90'-0"	27 432	27 435	27 438	27 442	27 445	27 448	27 451	27 454
90'-1"	27 457	27 461	27 464	27 467	27 470	27 473	27 476	27 480
90'-2"	27 483	27 486	27 489	27 492	27 495	27 499	27 502	27 505
90'-3"	27 508	27 511	27 515	27 518	27 521	27 524	27 527	27 530
90'-4"	27 534	27 537	27 540	27 543	27 546	27 549	27 553	27 556
90'-5"	27 559	27 562	27 565	27 569	27 572	27 575	27 578	27 581

Feet and Inches	0	1/8"	1/4"	3/8"	1/2"	5/8"	3/4"	7/8"
				millimeters (mm)				
83'-6"	25 451	25 454	25 457	25 460	25 463	25 467	25 470	25 473
83'-7"	25 476	25 479	25 483	25 486	25 489	25 492	25 495	25 498
83'-8"	25 502	25 505	25 508	25 511	25 514	25 517	25 521	25 524
83'-9"	25 527	25 530	25 533	25 537	25 540	25 543	25 546	25 549
83'-10"	25 552	25 556	25 559	25 562	25 565	25 568	25 571	25 575
83'-11"	25 578	25 581	25 584	25 587	25 590	25 594	25 597	25 600
84'-0"	25 603	25 606	25 610	25 613	25 616	25 619	25 622	25 625
84'-1"	25 629	25 632	25 635	25 638	25 641	25 644	25 648	25 651
84'-2"	25 654	25 657	25 660	25 664	25 667	25 670	25 673	25 676
84'-3"	25 679	25 683	25 686	25 689	25 692	25 695	25 698	25 702
84'-4"	25 705	25 708	25 711	25 714	25 717	25 721	25 724	25 727
84'-5"	25 730	25 733	25 737	25 740	25 743	25 746	25 749	25 752
84'-6"	25 756	25 759	25 762	25 765	25 768	25 771	25 775	25 778
84'-7"	25 781	25 784	25 787	25 791	25 794	25 797	25 800	25 803
84'-8"	25 806	25 810	25 813	25 816	25 819	25 822	25 825	25 829
84'-9"	25 832	25 835	25 838	25 841	25 844	25 848	25 851	25 854
84'-10"	25 857	25 860	25 864	25 867	25 870	25 873	25 876	25 879
84'-11"	25 883	25 886	25 889	25 892	25 895	25 898	25 902	25 905
85'-0"	25 908	25 911	25 914	25 918	25 921	25 924	25 927	25 930
85'-1"	25 933	25 937	25 940	25 943	25 946	25 949	25 952	25 956
85'-2"	25 959	25 962	25 965	25 968	25 971	25 975	25 978	25 981
85'-3"	25 984	25 987	25 991	25 994	25 997	26 000	26 003	26 006
85'-4"	26 010	26 013	26 016	26 019	26 022	26 025	26 029	26 032
85'-5"	26 035	26 038	26 041	26 045	26 048	26 051	26 054	26 057
85'-6"	26 060	26 064	26 067	26 070	26 073	26 076	26 079	26 083
85'-7"	26 086	26 089	26 092	26 095	26 098	26 102	26 105	26 108
85'-8"	26 111	26 114	26 118	26 121	26 124	26 127	26 130	26 133
85'-9"	26 137	26 140	26 143	26 146	26 149	26 152	26 156	26 159
85'-10"	26 162	26 165	26 168	26 172	26 175	26 178	26 181	26 184
85'-11"	26 187	26 191	26 194	26 197	26 200	26 203	26 206	26 210
86'-0"	26 213	26 216	26 219	26 222	26 225	26 229	26 232	26 235
86'-1"	26 238	26 241	26 245	26 248	26 251	26 254	26 257	26 260
86'-2"	26 264	26 267	26 270	26 273	26 276	26 279	26 283	26 286
86'-3"	26 289	26 292	26 295	26 299	26 302	26 305	26 308	26 311
86'-4"	26 314	26 318	26 321	26 324	26 327	26 330	26 333	26 337
86'-5"	26 340	26 343	26 346	26 349	26 352	26 356	26 359	26 362
86'-6"	26 365	26 368	26 372	26 375	26 378	26 381	26 384	26 387
86'-7"	26 391	26 394	26 397	26 400	26 403	26 406	26 410	26 413
86'-8"	26 416	26 419	26 422	26 426	26 429	26 432	26 435	26 438
86'-9"	26 441	26 445	26 448	26 451	26 454	26 457	26 460	26 464
86'-10"	26 467	26 470	26 473	26 476	26 479	26 483	26 486	26 489
86'-11"	26 492	26 495	26 499	26 502	26 505	26 508	26 511	26 514

Table 2 (cont.). Feet, inches, and fractions (multiples of ⅛ in.), up to 100 ft, to nearest whole millimeter (mm)

Feet and Inches	0	1/8"	1/4"	3/8"	1/2"	5/8"	3/4"	7/8"
				millimeters (mm)				
94'-0"	28 651	28 654	28 658	28 661	28 664	28 667	28 670	28 673
94'-1"	28 677	28 680	28 683	28 686	28 689	28 692	28 696	28 699
94'-2"	28 702	28 705	28 708	28 712	28 715	28 718	28 721	28 724
94'-3"	28 727	28 731	28 734	28 737	28 740	28 743	28 746	28 750
94'-4"	28 753	28 756	28 759	28 762	28 765	28 769	28 772	28 775
94'-5"	28 778	28 781	28 785	28 788	28 791	28 794	28 797	28 800
94'-6"	28 804	28 807	28 810	28 813	28 816	28 819	28 823	28 826
94'-7"	28 829	28 832	28 835	28 839	28 842	28 845	28 848	28 851
94'-8"	28 854	28 858	28 861	28 864	28 867	28 870	28 873	28 877
94'-9"	28 880	28 883	28 886	28 889	28 892	28 896	28 899	28 902
94'-10"	28 905	28 908	28 912	28 915	28 918	28 921	28 924	28 927
94'-11"	28 931	28 934	28 937	28 940	28 943	28 946	28 950	28 953
95'-0"	28 956	28 959	28 962	28 966	28 969	28 972	28 975	28 978
95'-1"	28 981	28 985	28 988	28 991	28 994	28 997	29 000	29 004
95'-2"	29 007	29 010	29 013	29 016	29 019	29 023	29 026	29 029
95'-3"	29 032	29 035	29 039	29 042	29 045	29 048	29 051	29 054
95'-4"	29 058	29 061	29 064	29 067	29 070	29 073	29 077	29 080
95'-5"	29 083	29 086	29 089	29 093	29 096	29 099	29 102	29 105
95'-6"	29 108	29 112	29 115	29 118	29 121	29 124	29 127	29 131
95'-7"	29 134	29 137	29 140	29 143	29 146	29 150	29 153	29 156
95'-8"	29 159	29 162	29 166	29 169	29 172	29 175	29 178	29 181
95'-9"	29 185	29 188	29 191	29 194	29 197	29 200	29 204	29 207
95'-10"	29 210	29 213	29 216	29 220	29 223	29 226	29 229	29 232
95'-11"	29 235	29 239	29 242	29 245	29 248	29 251	29 254	29 258
96'-0"	29 261	29 264	29 267	29 270	29 273	29 277	29 280	29 283
96'-1"	29 286	29 289	29 293	29 296	29 299	29 302	29 305	29 308
96'-2"	29 312	29 315	29 318	29 321	29 324	29 327	29 331	29 334
96'-3"	29 337	29 340	29 343	29 347	29 350	29 353	29 356	29 359
96'-4"	29 362	29 366	29 369	29 372	29 375	29 378	29 381	29 385
96'-5"	29 388	29 391	29 394	29 397	29 400	29 404	29 407	29 410
96'-6"	29 413	29 416	29 420	29 423	29 426	29 429	29 432	29 435
96'-7"	29 439	29 442	29 445	29 448	29 451	29 454	29 458	29 461
96'-8"	29 464	29 467	29 470	29 474	29 477	29 480	29 483	29 486
96'-9"	29 489	29 493	29 496	29 499	29 502	29 505	29 508	29 512
96'-10"	29 515	29 518	29 521	29 524	29 527	29 531	29 534	29 537
96'-11"	29 540	29 543	29 547	29 550	29 553	29 556	29 559	29 562
97'-0"	29 566	29 569	29 572	29 575	29 578	29 581	29 585	29 588
97'-1"	29 591	29 594	29 597	29 601	29 604	29 607	29 610	29 613
97'-2"	29 616	29 620	29 623	29 626	29 629	29 632	29 635	29 639
97'-3"	29 642	29 645	29 648	29 651	29 654	29 658	29 661	29 664
97'-4"	29 667	29 670	29 674	29 677	29 680	29 683	29 686	29 689
97'-5"	29 693	29 696	29 699	29 702	29 705	29 708	29 712	29 715

Feet and Inches	0	1/8"	1/4"	3/8"	1/2"	5/8"	3/4"	7/8"
				millimeters (mm)				
90'-6"	27 584	27 588	27 591	27 594	27 597	27 600	27 603	27 607
90'-7"	27 610	27 613	27 616	27 619	27 622	27 626	27 629	27 632
90'-8"	27 635	27 638	27 642	27 645	27 648	27 651	27 654	27 657
90'-9"	27 661	27 664	27 667	27 670	27 673	27 676	27 680	27 683
90'-10"	27 686	27 689	27 692	27 696	27 699	27 702	27 705	27 708
90'-11"	27 711	27 715	27 718	27 721	27 724	27 727	27 730	27 734
91'-0"	27 737	27 740	27 743	27 746	27 749	27 753	27 756	27 759
91'-1"	27 762	27 765	27 769	27 772	27 775	27 778	27 781	27 784
91'-2"	27 788	27 791	27 794	27 797	27 800	27 803	27 807	27 810
91'-3"	27 813	27 816	27 819	27 823	27 826	27 829	27 832	27 835
91'-4"	27 838	27 842	27 845	27 848	27 851	27 854	27 857	27 861
91'-5"	27 864	27 867	27 870	27 873	27 876	27 880	27 883	27 886
91'-6"	27 889	27 892	27 896	27 899	27 902	27 905	27 908	27 911
91'-7"	27 915	27 918	27 921	27 924	27 927	27 930	27 934	27 937
91'-8"	27 940	27 943	27 946	27 950	27 953	27 956	27 959	27 962
91'-9"	27 965	27 969	27 972	27 975	27 978	27 981	27 984	27 988
91'-10"	27 991	27 994	27 997	28 000	28 003	28 007	28 010	28 013
91'-11"	28 016	28 019	28 023	28 026	28 029	28 032	28 035	28 038
92'-0"	28 042	28 045	28 048	28 051	28 054	28 057	28 061	28 064
92'-1"	28 067	28 070	28 073	28 077	28 080	28 083	28 086	28 089
92'-2"	28 092	28 096	28 099	28 102	28 105	28 108	28 111	28 115
92'-3"	28 118	28 121	28 124	28 127	28 130	28 134	28 137	28 140
92'-4"	28 143	28 146	28 150	28 153	28 156	28 159	28 162	28 165
92'-5"	28 169	28 172	28 175	28 178	28 181	28 184	28 188	28 191
92'-6"	28 194	28 197	28 200	28 204	28 207	28 210	28 213	28 216
92'-7"	28 219	28 223	28 226	28 229	28 232	28 235	28 238	28 242
92'-8"	28 245	28 248	28 251	28 254	28 257	28 261	28 264	28 267
92'-9"	28 270	28 273	28 277	28 280	28 283	28 286	28 289	28 292
92'-10"	28 296	28 299	28 302	28 305	28 308	28 311	28 315	28 318
92'-11"	28 321	28 324	28 327	28 331	28 334	28 337	28 340	28 343
93'-0"	28 346	28 350	28 353	28 356	28 359	28 362	28 365	28 369
93'-1"	28 372	28 375	28 378	28 381	28 384	28 388	28 391	28 394
93'-2"	28 397	28 400	28 404	28 407	28 410	28 413	28 416	28 419
93'-3"	28 423	28 426	28 429	28 432	28 435	28 438	28 442	28 445
93'-4"	28 448	28 451	28 454	28 458	28 461	28 464	28 467	28 470
93'-5"	28 473	28 477	28 480	28 483	28 486	28 489	28 492	28 496
93'-6"	28 499	28 502	28 505	28 508	28 511	28 515	28 518	28 521
93'-7"	28 524	28 527	28 531	28 534	28 537	28 540	28 543	28 546
93'-8"	28 550	28 553	28 556	28 559	28 562	28 565	28 569	28 572
93'-9"	28 575	28 578	28 581	28 585	28 588	28 591	28 594	28 597
93'-10"	28 600	28 604	28 607	28 610	28 613	28 616	28 619	28 623
93'-11"	28 626	28 629	28 632	28 635	28 638	28 642	28 645	28 648

Table 2 (cont.).   Feet, inches, and fractions (multiples of ⅛ in.), up to 100 ft, to nearest whole millimeter (mm)

Feet and Inches	0	1/8"	1/4"	3/8"	1/2"	5/8"	3/4"	7/8"
				millimeters (mm)				
97'-6"	29 718	29 721	29 724	29 728	29 731	29 734	29 737	29 740
97'-7"	29 743	29 747	29 750	29 753	29 756	29 759	29 762	29 766
97'-8"	29 769	29 772	29 775	29 778	29 781	29 785	29 788	29 791
97'-9"	29 794	29 797	29 801	29 804	29 807	29 810	29 813	29 816
97'-10"	29 820	29 823	29 826	29 829	29 832	29 835	29 839	29 842
97'-11"	29 845	29 848	29 851	29 855	29 858	29 861	29 864	29 867
98'-0"	29 870	29 874	29 877	29 880	29 883	29 886	29 889	29 893
98'-1"	29 896	29 899	29 902	29 905	29 908	29 912	29 915	29 918
98'-2"	29 921	29 924	29 928	29 931	29 934	29 937	29 940	29 943
98'-3"	29 947	29 950	29 953	29 956	29 959	29 962	29 966	29 969
98'-4"	29 972	29 975	29 978	29 982	29 985	29 988	29 991	29 994
98'-5"	29 997	30 001	30 004	30 007	30 010	30 013	30 016	30 020
98'-6"	30 023	30 026	30 029	30 032	30 035	30 039	30 042	30 045
98'-7"	30 048	30 051	30 055	30 058	30 061	30 064	30 067	30 070
98'-8"	30 074	30 077	30 080	30 083	30 086	30 089	30 093	30 096
98'-9"	30 099	30 102	30 105	30 109	30 112	30 115	30 118	30 121
98'-10"	30 124	30 128	30 131	30 134	30 137	30 140	30 143	30 147
98'-11"	30 150	30 153	30 156	30 159	30 162	30 166	30 169	30 172
99'-0"	30 175	30 178	30 182	30 185	30 188	30 191	30 194	30 197
99'-1"	30 201	30 204	30 207	30 210	30 213	30 216	30 220	30 223
99'-2"	30 226	30 229	30 232	30 236	30 239	30 242	30 245	30 248
99'-3"	30 251	30 255	30 258	30 261	30 264	30 267	30 270	30 274
99'-4"	30 277	30 280	30 283	30 286	30 289	30 293	30 296	30 299
99'-5"	30 302	30 305	30 309	30 312	30 315	30 318	30 321	30 324
99'-6"	30 328	30 331	30 334	30 337	30 340	30 343	30 347	30 350
99'-7"	30 353	30 356	30 359	30 363	30 366	30 369	30 372	30 375
99'-8"	30 378	30 382	30 385	30 388	30 391	30 394	30 397	30 401
99'-9"	30 404	30 407	30 410	30 413	30 416	30 420	30 423	30 426
99'-10"	30 429	30 432	30 436	30 439	30 442	30 445	30 448	30 451
99'-11"	30 455	30 458	30 461	30 464	30 467	30 470	30 474	30 477
100'-0"	30 480							

Table 3. Feet to meters (m), in increments of 1 ft to 1000 ft, with an auxiliary table in increments of 0.01 ft to 0.99 ft

Conversion Factor: 1 ft = 0.3048 m [exactly]. Rounding: To nearest 0.001 m (or 1 mm)

Decimal Feet (ft)	0	0.01	0.02	0.03	0.04	0.05	0.06	0.07	0.08	0.09
					meters (m)					
0	–	0.003	0.006	0.009	0.012	0.015	0.018	0.021	0.024	0.027
0.10	0.030	0.034	0.037	0.040	0.043	0.046	0.049	0.052	0.055	0.058
0.20	0.061	0.064	0.067	0.070	0.073	0.076	0.079	0.082	0.085	0.088
0.30	0.091	0.094	0.098	0.101	0.104	0.107	0.110	0.113	0.116	0.119
0.40	0.122	0.125	0.128	0.131	0.134	0.137	0.140	0.143	0.146	0.149
0.50	0.152	0.155	0.158	0.162	0.165	0.168	0.171	0.174	0.177	0.180
0.60	0.183	0.186	0.189	0.192	0.195	0.198	0.201	0.204	0.207	0.210
0.70	0.213	0.216	0.219	0.223	0.226	0.229	0.232	0.235	0.238	0.241
0.80	0.244	0.247	0.250	0.253	0.256	0.259	0.262	0.265	0.268	0.271
0.90	0.274	0.277	0.280	0.283	0.287	0.290	0.293	0.296	0.299	0.302

Feet (ft)	0	1	2	3	4	5	6	7	8	9
					meters (m)					
0	0	0.305	0.610	0.914	1.219	1.524	1.829	2.134	2.438	2.743
10	3.048	3.353	3.658	3.962	4.267	4.572	4.877	5.182	5.486	5.791
20	6.096	6.401	6.706	7.010	7.315	7.620	7.925	8.230	8.534	8.839
30	9.144	9.449	9.754	10.058	10.363	10.668	10.973	11.278	11.582	11.887
40	12.192	12.497	12.802	13.106	13.411	13.716	14.021	14.326	14.630	14.935
50	15.240	15.545	15.850	16.154	16.459	16.764	17.069	17.374	17.678	17.983
60	18.288	18.593	18.898	19.202	19.507	19.812	20.117	20.422	20.726	21.031
70	21.336	21.641	21.946	22.250	22.555	22.860	23.165	23.470	23.774	24.079
80	24.384	24.689	24.994	25.298	25.603	25.908	26.213	26.518	26.822	27.127
90	27.432	27.737	28.042	28.346	28.651	28.956	29.261	29.566	29.870	30.175
100	30.480	30.785	31.090	31.394	31.699	32.004	32.309	32.614	32.918	33.223
110	33.528	33.833	34.138	34.442	34.747	35.052	35.357	35.662	35.966	36.271
120	36.576	36.881	37.186	37.490	37.795	38.100	38.405	38.710	39.014	39.319
130	39.624	39.929	40.234	40.538	40.843	41.148	41.453	41.758	42.062	42.367
140	42.672	42.977	43.282	43.586	43.891	44.196	44.501	44.806	45.110	45.415
150	45.720	46.025	46.330	46.634	46.939	47.244	47.549	47.854	48.158	48.463
160	48.768	49.073	49.378	49.682	49.987	50.292	50.597	50.902	51.206	51.511
170	51.816	52.121	52.426	52.730	53.035	53.340	53.645	53.940	54.254	54.559
180	54.864	55.169	55.474	55.778	56.083	56.388	56.693	56.998	57.302	57.607
190	57.912	58.217	58.522	58.826	59.131	59.436	59.741	60.046	60.350	60.655
200	60.960	61.265	61.570	61.874	62.179	62.484	62.789	63.094	63.398	63.703
210	64.008	64.313	64.618	64.922	65.227	65.532	65.837	66.142	66.446	66.751
220	67.056	67.361	67.666	67.970	68.275	68.580	68.885	69.190	69.494	69.799
230	70.104	70.409	70.714	71.018	71.323	71.628	71.933	72.238	72.542	72.847
240	73.152	73.457	73.762	74.066	74.371	74.676	74.981	75.286	75.590	75.895
250	76.200	76.505	76.810	77.114	77.419	77.724	78.029	78.334	78.638	78.943
260	79.248	79.553	79.858	80.162	80.467	80.772	81.077	81.382	81.686	81.991
270	82.296	82.601	82.906	83.210	83.515	83.820	84.125	84.430	84.734	85.039
280	85.344	85.649	85.954	86.258	86.563	86.868	87.173	87.478	87.782	88.087
290	88.392	88.697	89.002	89.306	89.611	89.916	90.221	90.526	90.830	91.135
300	91.440	91.745	92.050	92.354	92.659	92.964	93.269	93.574	93.878	94.183
310	94.488	94.793	95.098	95.402	95.707	96.012	96.317	96.622	96.926	97.231
320	97.536	97.841	98.146	98.450	98.755	99.060	99.365	99.670	99.974	100.279
330	100.584	100.889	101.194	101.498	101.803	102.108	102.413	102.718	103.022	103.327
340	103.632	103.937	104.242	104.546	104.851	105.156	105.461	105.766	106.070	106.375
350	106.680	106.985	107.290	107.594	107.899	108.204	108.509	108.814	109.118	109.423
360	109.728	110.033	110.338	110.642	110.947	111.252	111.557	111.862	112.166	112.471
370	112.776	113.081	113.386	113.690	113.995	114.300	114.605	114.910	115.214	115.519
380	115.824	116.129	116.434	116.738	117.043	117.348	117.653	117.958	118.262	118.567
390	118.872	119.177	119.482	119.786	120.091	120.396	120.701	121.006	121.310	121.615
400	121.920									

Table 3 (cont.). Feet to meters (m), in increments of 1 ft to 1000 ft, with an auxiliary table in increments of 0.01 ft to 0.99 ft

Feet (ft)	. 0 .	1 .	2 .	3 .	4 .	5 .	6 .	7 .	8 .	9 .
					meters (m)					
400	121.920	122.225	122.530	122.834	123.139	123.444	123.749	124.054	124.358	124.663
410	124.968	125.273	125.578	125.882	126.187	126.492	126.797	127.102	127.406	127.711
420	128.016	128.321	128.626	128.930	129.235	129.540	129.845	130.150	130.454	130.759
430	131.064	131.369	131.674	131.978	132.283	132.588	132.893	133.198	133.502	133.807
440	134.112	134.417	134.722	135.026	135.331	135.636	135.941	136.246	136.550	136.855
450	137.160	137.465	137.770	138.074	138.379	138.684	138.989	139.294	139.598	139.903
460	140.208	140.513	140.818	141.122	141.427	141.732	142.037	142.342	142.646	142.951
470	143.256	143.561	143.866	144.170	144.475	144.780	145.085	145.390	145.694	145.999
480	146.304	146.609	146.914	147.218	147.523	147.828	148.133	148.438	148.742	149.047
490	149.352	149.657	149.962	150.266	150.571	150.876	151.181	151.486	151.790	152.095
500	152.400	152.705	153.010	153.314	153.619	153.924	154.229	154.534	154.838	155.143
510	155.448	155.753	156.058	156.362	156.667	156.972	157.277	157.582	157.886	158.191
520	158.496	158.801	159.106	159.410	159.715	160.020	160.325	160.630	160.934	161.239
530	161.544	161.849	162.154	162.458	162.763	163.068	163.373	163.678	163.982	164.287
540	164.592	164.897	165.202	165.506	165.811	166.116	166.421	166.726	167.030	167.335
550	167.640	167.945	168.250	168.554	168.858	169.164	169.469	169.774	170.078	170.383
560	170.688	170.993	171.298	171.602	171.907	172.212	172.517	172.822	173.126	173.431
570	173.736	174.041	174.346	174.650	174.955	175.260	175.565	175.870	176.174	176.479
580	176.784	177.089	177.394	177.698	178.003	178.308	178.613	178.918	179.222	179.527
590	179.832	180.137	180.442	180.746	181.051	181.356	181.661	181.966	182.270	182.575
600	182.880	183.185	183.490	183.794	184.099	184.404	184.709	185.014	185.318	185.623
610	185.928	186.233	186.538	186.842	187.141	187.452	187.757	188.062	188.366	188.671
620	188.976	189.281	189.586	189.890	190.195	190.500	190.805	191.110	191.414	191.719
630	192.024	192.329	192.634	192.938	193.243	193.548	193.853	194.158	194.462	194.767
640	195.072	195.277	195.682	195.986	196.291	196.596	196.901	197.206	197.510	197.815
650	198.120	198.425	198.730	199.034	199.339	199.644	199.949	200.254	200.558	200.863
660	201.168	201.473	201.778	202.082	202.387	202.692	202.997	203.302	203.606	203.911
670	204.216	204.521	204.826	205.130	205.435	205.740	206.045	206.350	206.654	206.959
680	207.264	207.569	207.874	208.178	208.483	208.788	209.093	209.398	209.702	210.007
690	210.312	210.617	210.922	211.226	211.531	211.836	212.141	212.446	212.750	213.055
700	213.360	213.665	213.970	214.274	214.579	214.884	215.189	215.494	215.798	216.103
710	216.408	216.713	217.018	217.322	217.627	217.932	218.237	218.542	218.846	219.151
720	219.456	219.761	220.066	220.370	220.675	220.980	221.285	221.590	221.894	222.199
730	222.504	222.809	223.114	223.418	223.723	224.028	224.333	224.638	224.942	225.247
740	225.552	225.857	226.162	226.466	226.771	227.076	227.381	227.686	227.990	228.295
750	228.600	228.905	229.210	229.514	229.819	230.124	230.429	230.734	231.038	231.343
760	231.648	231.953	232.258	232.562	232.867	233.172	233.477	233.782	234.086	234.391
770	234.696	235.001	235.306	235.610	235.915	236.220	236.525	236.830	237.134	237.439
780	237.744	238.049	238.354	238.658	238.963	239.268	239.573	239.878	240.182	240.487
790	240.792	241.097	241.402	241.706	242.011	242.316	242.621	242.926	243.230	243.535
800	243.840	244.145	244.450	244.754	245.059	245.364	245.669	245.974	246.278	246.583
810	246.888	247.193	247.498	247.802	248.107	248.412	248.717	249.022	249.326	249.631
820	249.936	250.241	250.546	250.850	251.155	251.460	251.765	252.070	252.374	252.679
830	252.984	253.289	253.594	253.898	254.203	254.508	254.813	255.118	255.422	255.727
840	256.032	256.337	256.642	256.946	257.251	257.556	257.861	258.166	258.470	258.775
850	259.080	259.385	259.690	259.994	260.299	260.604	260.909	261.214	261.518	261.823
860	262.128	262.433	262.738	263.042	263.347	263.652	263.957	264.262	264.566	264.871
870	265.176	265.481	265.786	266.090	266.395	266.700	267.005	267.310	267.614	267.919
880	268.224	268.529	268.834	269.138	269.443	269.748	270.053	270.358	270.662	270.967
890	271.272	271.577	271.882	272.186	272.491	272.796	273.101	273.406	273.710	274.015
900	274.320	274.625	274.930	275.234	275.539	275.844	276.149	276.454	276.758	277.063
910	277.368	277.673	277.978	278.282	278.587	278.892	279.197	279.502	279.806	280.111
920	280.416	280.721	281.026	281.330	281.635	281.940	282.245	282.550	282.854	283.159
930	283.464	283.769	284.074	284.378	284.683	284.988	285.293	285.598	285.902	286.207
940	286.512	286.817	287.122	287.426	287.731	288.036	288.341	288.646	288.950	289.255
950	289.560	289.865	290.170	290.474	290.779	291.084	291.389	291.694	291.998	292.303
960	292.608	292.913	293.218	293.522	293.827	294.132	294.437	294.742	295.046	295.351
970	295.656	295.961	296.266	296.570	296.875	297.180	297.485	297.790	298.094	298.399
980	298.704	299.009	299.314	299.618	299.923	300.228	300.533	300.838	301.142	301.447
990	301.752	302.057	302.362	302.666	302.971	303.276	303.581	303.886	304.190	304.495
1000	304.800									

Table 4. Miles to kilometers (km), in increments of 1 mile up to 100 miles, and increments of 10 miles from 100 miles to 1000 miles

Conversion Factor: 1 mile = 1.609 344 km (exactly) = 1609.344 m

Rounding: To nearest 0.001 km [or 1 m] up to 100 miles, and to nearest 0.01 km above

Miles	0	1	2	3	4	5	6	7	8	9
				kilometers (km)						
0	-	1.609	3.219	4.828	6.437	8.047	9.656	11.265	12.875	14.484
10	16.093	17.703	19.312	20.921	22.531	24.140	25.750	27.359	28.968	30.578
20	32.187	33.796	35.406	37.015	38.624	40.234	41.843	43.452	45.062	46.671
30	48.280	49.890	51.499	53.108	54.718	56.327	57.936	59.546	61.155	62.764
40	64.374	65.983	67.592	69.202	70.811	72.420	74.030	75.639	77.249	78.858
50	80.467	82.077	83.686	85.295	86.905	88.514	90.123	91.733	93.342	94.951
60	96.561	98.170	99.779	101.389	102.998	104.607	106.217	107.826	109.435	111.045
70	112.654	114.263	115.873	117.482	119.091	120.701	122.310	123.919	125.529	127.138
80	128.748	130.357	131.966	133.576	135.185	136.794	138.404	140.013	141.622	143.232
90	144.841	146.450	148.060	149.669	151.278	152.888	154.497	156.106	157.716	159.325

Miles	0	10	20	30	40	50	60	70	80	90
100	160.93	177.03	193.12	209.21	225.31	241.40	257.50	273.59	289.68	305.78
200	321.87	337.96	354.06	370.15	386.24	402.34	418.43	434.52	450.62	466.71
300	482.80	498.90	514.99	531.08	547.18	563.27	579.36	595.46	611.55	627.64
400	643.74	659.83	675.92	692.02	708.11	724.20	740.30	756.39	772.49	788.58
500	804.67	820.77	836.86	852.95	869.05	885.14	901.23	917.33	933.42	949.51
600	965.61	981.70	997.79	1013.89	1029.98	1046.07	1062.17	1078.26	1094.35	1110.45
700	1126.54	1142.63	1158.73	1174.82	1190.91	1207.01	1223.10	1239.19	1255.29	1271.38
800	1287.48	1303.57	1319.66	1335.76	1351.85	1367.94	1384.04	1400.13	1416.22	1432.32
900	1448.41	1464.50	1480.60	1496.69	1512.78	1528.88	1544.97	1561.06	1577.16	1593.25
1000	1609.34									

Table 5. Square inches to square millimeters (mm²), up to 1 square foot (144 in²)

Conversion Factor: 1 sq. in. = 645.16 mm² (exactly)

Rounding: To nearest square millimeter. Exact values are underlined.

Square Inches	0	1	2	3	4	5	6	7	8	9
				square millimeters (mm²)						
0	-	645	1 290	1 935	2 581	3 226	3 871	4 516	5 161	5 806
10	6 452	7 097	7 742	8 387	9 032	9 677	10 323	10 968	11 613	12 258
20	12 903	13 548	14 194	14 839	15 484	_16 129_	16 774	17 419	18 064	18 710
30	19 355	20 000	20 645	21 290	21 935	_22 581_	23 226	23 871	24 516	25 161
40	25 806	26 452	27 097	27 742	28 387	29 032	29 677	30 323	30 968	31 613
50	_32 258_	32 903	33 548	34 193	34 839	35 484	36 129	36 774	37 419	38 064
60	_38 710_	39 355	40 000	40 645	41 290	41 935	42 581	43 226	43 871	44 516
70	45 161	45 806	46 452	47 097	47 742	_48 387_	49 032	49 677	50 322	50 968
80	51 613	52 258	52 903	53 548	54 193	_54 839_	55 484	56 129	56 774	57 419
90	58 064	58 710	59 355	60 000	60 645	61 290	61 935	62 581	63 226	63 871
100	_64 516_	65 161	65 806	66 451	67 097	67 742	68 387	69 032	69 677	70 322
110	_70 968_	71 613	72 258	72 903	73 548	74 193	74 839	75 484	76 129	76 774
120	77 419	78 064	78 710	79 355	80 000	_80 645_	81 290	81 935	82 580	83 226
130	83 871	84 516	85 161	85 806	86 451	_87 097_	87 742	88 387	89 032	89 677
140	90 322	90 968	91 613	92 258	92 903					

Table 6. Square feet to square meters (m²), in increments of 1 ft² to 100 ft², and increments of 10 ft² between 100 and 1000 ft²

Conversion Factor: 1 square foot = 0.092 903 m²

Rounding: To nearest 0.001 m² up to 100 ft², and to nearest 0.01 m² above.

Square Feet	. 0 .	1 .	2 .	3 .	4 .	5 .	6 .	7 .	8 .	9 .
					square meters (m²)					
0	–	0.093	0.186	0.279	0.372	0.465	0.557	0.650	0.743	0.836
10	0.929	1.022	1.115	1.208	1.301	1.394	1.486	1.579	1.672	1.765
20	1.858	1.951	2.044	2.137	2.230	2.323	2.415	2.508	2.601	2.694
30	2.787	2.880	2.973	3.066	3.159	3.252	3.345	3.437	3.530	3.623
40	3.716	3.809	3.902	3.995	4.088	4.181	4.274	4.366	4.459	4.552
50	4.645	4.738	4.831	4.924	5.017	5.110	5.203	5.295	5.388	5.481
60	5.574	5.667	5.760	5.853	5.946	6.039	6.132	6.225	6.317	6.410
70	6.503	6.596	6.689	6.782	6.875	6.968	7.061	7.154	7.246	7.339
80	7.432	7.525	7.618	7.711	7.804	7.897	7.990	8.083	8.175	8.268
90	8.361	8.454	8.547	8.640	8.733	8.826	8.919	9.012	9.104	9.197
	0	10	20	30	40	50	60	70	80	90
100	9.29	10.22	11.15	12.08	13.01	13.94	14.86	15.79	16.72	17.65
200	18.58	19.51	20.44	21.37	22.30	23.23	24.15	25.08	26.01	26.94
300	27.87	28.80	29.73	30.66	31.59	32.52	33.45	34.37	35.30	36.23
400	37.16	38.09	39.02	39.95	40.88	41.81	42.74	43.66	44.59	45.52
500	46.45	47.38	48.31	49.24	50.17	51.10	52.03	52.95	53.88	54.81
600	55.74	56.67	57.60	58.53	59.46	60.39	61.32	62.25	63.17	64.10
700	65.03	65.96	66.89	67.82	68.75	69.68	70.61	71.54	72.46	73.39
800	74.32	75.25	76.18	77.11	78.04	78.97	79.90	80.83	81.75	82.68
900	83.61	84.54	85.47	86.40	87.33	88.26	89.19	90.12	91.04	91.97
1000	92.90									

Table 7. Square feet to square meters (m²), in increments of 100 ft² between 1000 and 10 000 ft², and increments of 1000 ft² between 10 000 and 100 000 ft²

Conversion Factor: 1 square foot = 0.092 903 m²

Rounding: To nearest 0.1 m² up to 10 000 ft², and to nearest whole m² above.

Square Feet	0 .	100 .	200 .	300 .	400 .	500 .	600 .	700 .	800 .	900 .
					square meters (m²)					
1000	92.9	102.2	111.5	120.8	130.1	139.4	148.6	157.9	167.2	176.5
2000	185.8	195.1	204.4	213.7	223.0	232.3	241.5	250.8	260.1	269.4
3000	278.7	288.0	297.3	306.6	315.9	325.2	334.5	343.7	353.0	362.3
4000	371.6	380.9	390.2	399.5	408.8	418.1	427.4	436.6	445.9	455.2
5000	464.5	473.8	483.1	492.4	501.7	511.0	520.3	529.5	538.8	548.1
6000	557.4	566.7	576.0	585.3	594.6	603.9	613.2	622.5	631.7	641.0
7000	650.3	659.6	668.9	678.2	687.5	696.8	706.1	715.4	724.6	733.9
8000	743.2	752.5	761.8	771.1	780.4	789.7	799.0	808.3	817.5	826.8
9000	836.1	845.4	854.7	864.0	873.3	882.6	891.9	901.2	910.4	919.7
	0	1000	2000	3000	4000	5000	6000	7000	8000	9000
10 000	929	1022	1115	1208	1301	1394	1486	1579	1672	1765
20 000	1858	1951	2044	2137	2230	2323	2415	2508	2601	2694
30 000	2787	2880	2973	3066	3159	3252	3345	3437	3530	3623
40 000	3716	3809	3902	3995	4088	4181	4274	4366	4459	4552
50 000	4645	4738	4831	4924	5017	5110	5203	5295	5388	5481
60 000	5574	5667	5760	5853	5946	6039	6132	6225	6317	6410
70 000	6503	6596	6689	6782	6875	6968	7061	7154	7246	7339
80 000	7432	7525	7618	7711	7804	7897	7990	8083	8175	8268
90 000	8361	8454	8547	8640	8733	8826	8919	9012	9104	9197
100 000	9290									

Table 8. Square yards to square meters (m²), in increments of 0.1 yd² to 10 yd², and increments of 1 yd² to 100 yd²

Conversion factor: 1 yd² = 0.836 127 m²

Rounding: To nearest 0.001 m² up to 10 yd² and to nearest 0.01 m² above 10 yd²

Square Yards (yd²)	0	0.1	0.2	0.3	0.4	0.5	0.6	0.7	0.8	0.9
					square meters (m²)					
0	–	0.084	0.167	0.251	0.334	0.418	0.502	0.585	0.669	0.753
1	0.836	0.920	1.003	1.087	1.171	1.254	1.338	1.421	1.505	1.589
2	1.672	1.756	1.839	1.923	2.007	2.090	2.174	2.258	2.341	2.425
3	2.508	2.592	2.676	2.759	2.843	2.926	3.010	3.094	3.177	3.261
4	3.345	3.428	3.512	3.595	3.679	3.763	3.846	3.930	4.013	4.097
5	4.181	4.264	4.348	4.431	4.515	4.599	4.682	4.766	4.850	4.933
6	5.017	5.100	5.184	5.268	5.351	5.435	5.518	5.602	5.686	5.769
7	5.853	5.937	6.020	6.104	6.187	6.271	6.355	6.438	6.522	6.605
8	6.689	6.773	6.856	6.940	7.023	7.107	7.191	7.274	7.358	7.442
9	7.525	7.609	7.692	7.776	7.860	7.943	8.027	8.110	8.194	8.278
	0	1	2	3	4	5	6	7	8	9
10	8.36	9.20	10.03	10.87	11.71	12.54	13.38	14.21	15.05	15.89
20	16.72	17.56	18.39	19.23	20.07	20.90	21.74	22.58	23.41	24.25
30	25.08	25.92	26.76	27.59	28.43	29.26	30.10	30.94	31.77	32.61
40	33.45	34.28	35.12	35.95	36.79	37.63	38.46	39.30	40.13	40.97
50	41.81	42.64	43.48	44.31	45.15	45.99	46.82	47.66	49.50	49.33
60	50.17	51.00	51.84	52.68	53.51	54.35	55.18	56.02	56.86	57.69
70	58.53	59.37	60.20	61.04	61.87	62.71	63.55	64.38	65.22	66.05
80	66.89	67.73	68.56	69.40	70.23	71.07	71.91	72.74	73.58	74.42
90	75.25	76.09	76.92	77.76	78.60	79.43	80.27	81.10	81.94	82.78
100	83.61									

Table 9. Acres to hectares (ha), in increments of 0.1 acre to 10 acres, and increments of 1 acre between 10 and 100 acres

Conversion Factor: 1 acre*[43 560 ft²] = 0.404 687 ha = 4046.873 m²

Rounding: To nearest 0.0001 ha (or 1 m²) up to 10 acres, and nearest 0.001 ha above.

Acres	0	0.1	0.2	0.3	0.4	0.5	0.6	0.7	0.8	0.9
						hectares (ha)				
0	–	0.0405	0.0809	0.1214	0.1619	0.2023	0.2428	0.2833	0.3237	0.3642
1	0.4047	0.4452	0.4856	0.5261	0.5666	0.6070	0.6475	0.6880	0.7284	0.7689
2	0.8094	0.8498	0.8903	0.9308	0.9712	1.0117	1.0522	1.0927	1.1331	1.1736
3	1.2141	1.2545	1.2950	1.3355	1.3759	1.4164	1.4569	1.4973	1.5378	1.5783
4	1.6187	1.6592	1.6997	1.7401	1.7806	1.8211	1.8616	1.9020	1.9425	1.9830
5	2.0234	2.0639	2.1044	2.1448	2.1853	2.2258	2.2662	2.3067	2.3472	2.3876
6	2.4281	2.4686	2.5091	2.5495	2.5900	2.6305	2.6709	2.7114	2.7519	2.7923
7	2.8328	2.8733	2.9137	2.9542	2.9947	3.0351	3.0756	3.1161	3.1565	3.1970
8	3.2375	3.2780	3.3184	3.3589	3.3994	3.4398	3.4803	3.5208	3.5612	3.6017
9	3.6422	3.6826	3.7231	3.7636	3.8040	3.8445	3.8850	3.9255	3.9659	4.0064
	0	1	2	3	4	5	6	7	8	9
10	4.047	4.452	4.856	5.261	5.666	6.070	6.475	6.880	7.284	7.689
20	8.094	8.498	8.903	9.308	9.712	10.117	10.522	10.927	11.331	11.736
30	12.141	12.545	12.950	13.355	13.759	14.164	14.569	14.973	15.378	15.783
40	16.187	16.592	16.997	17.401	17.806	18.211	18.616	19.020	19.425	19.830
50	20.234	20.639	21.044	21.448	21.853	22.258	22.662	23.067	23.472	23.876
60	24.281	24.686	25.091	25.495	25.900	26.305	26.709	27.114	27.519	27.923
70	28.328	28.733	29.137	29.542	29.947	30.351	30.756	31.161	31.565	31.970
80	32.375	32.780	33.184	33.589	33.994	34.398	34.803	35.208	35.612	36.017
90	36.422	36.826	37.231	37.636	38.040	38.445	38.850	39.255	39.659	40.064
100	40.469									

*Note: The acre is based on the U.S. survey foot, which equals 0.304 800 6 m.

Table 10. Cubic feet to cubic meters (m^3), in increments of 1 ft³ up to 100 ft³, and increments of 10ft³ from 100 ft³ to 1000 ft³

Conversion Factor: 1 cubic foot = 0.028 317 m^3 = [28.317 L]

Rounding: To nearest 0.001 m^3 (or liter).

Cubic Feet	0	1	2	3	4	5	6	7	8	9
	cubic meters (m^3)									
0	–	0.028	0.057	0.085	0.113	0.142	0.170	0.198	0.227	0.255
10	0.283	0.311	0.340	0.368	0.396	0.425	0.453	0.481	0.510	0.538
20	0.566	0.595	0.623	0.651	0.680	0.708	0.736	0.765	0.793	0.821
30	0.850	0.878	0.906	0.934	0.963	0.991	1.019	1.048	1.076	1.104
40	1.133	1.161	1.189	1.218	1.246	1.274	1.303	1.331	1.359	1.386
50	1.416	1.444	1.472	1.501	1.529	1.557	1.586	1.614	1.642	1.671
60	1.699	1.727	1.756	1.784	1.812	1.841	1.869	1.897	1.926	1.954
70	1.982	2.010	2.034	2.067	2.095	2.124	2.152	2.180	2.209	2.237
80	2.265	2.294	2.322	2.350	2.379	2.407	2.435	2.464	2.492	2.520
90	2.549	2.577	2.605	2.633	2.662	2.690	2.718	2.747	2.775	2.803
	0	10	20	30	40	50	60	70	80	90
100	2.832	3.115	3.398	3.681	3.964	4.248	4.531	4.814	5.097	5.380
200	5.663	5.947	6.230	6.513	6.796	7.079	7.362	7.646	7.929	8.212
300	8.495	8.778	9.061	9.345	9.628	9.911	10.194	10.477	10.760	11.044
400	11.327	11.610	11.893	12.176	12.459	12.743	13.026	13.309	13.592	13.875
500	14.158	14.442	14.725	15.008	15.291	15.574	15.857	16.141	16.424	16.707
600	16.990	17.273	17.556	17.840	18.123	18.406	18.689	18.972	19.255	19.539
700	19.822	20.105	20.388	20.671	20.954	21.238	21.521	21.804	22.087	22.370
800	22.653	22.937	23.220	23.503	23.786	24.069	24.352	24.636	24.919	25.202
900	25.485	25.768	26.051	26.335	26.618	26.901	27.184	27.467	27.751	28.034
1000	28.317									

Note: If decimal point is deleted, the conversions show _liters_ (1 m^3 = 1000 L)

Table 11. Cubic yards to cubic meters (m^3), in increments of 0.1 yd³ to 10 yd³, and increments of 1 yd³ between 10 yd³ and 100 yd³

Conversion Factor: 1 yd³ = 0.836 127 m^3. Rounding: To nearest 0.001 m^3.

Cubic Yards (yd³)	0	0.1	0.2	0.3	0.4	0.5	0.6	0.7	0.8	0.9
	cubic meters (m^3)									
0	–	0.084	0.167	0.251	0.334	0.418	0.502	0.585	0.669	0.753
1	0.836	0.920	1.003	1.087	1.171	1.254	1.338	1.421	1.505	1.589
2	1.672	1.756	1.839	1.923	2.007	2.090	2.174	2.258	2.341	2.425
3	2.508	2.592	2.676	2.759	2.843	2.926	3.010	3.094	3.177	3.261
4	3.345	3.428	3.512	3.595	3.679	3.763	3.846	3.930	4.013	4.097
5	4.181	4.264	4.348	4.431	4.515	4.599	4.682	4.766	4.850	4.933
6	5.017	5.100	5.184	5.268	5.351	5.435	5.518	5.602	5.686	5.769
7	5.853	5.937	6.020	6.104	6.187	6.271	6.355	6.438	6.522	6.605
8	6.689	6.773	6.856	6.940	7.023	7.107	7.191	7.274	7.358	7.442
9	7.525	7.609	7.692	7.776	7.860	7.943	8.027	8.110	8.194	8.278
	0	1	2	3	4	5	6	7	8	9
10	8.361	9.197	10.034	10.870	11.706	12.542	13.378	14.214	15.050	15.886
20	16.723	17.559	18.395	19.231	20.067	20.903	21.739	22.575	23.412	24.248
30	25.084	25.920	26.756	27.592	28.428	29.264	30.101	30.937	31.773	32.609
40	33.445	34.281	35.117	35.953	36.790	37.626	38.462	39.298	40.134	40.970
50	41.806	42.642	43.479	44.315	45.151	45.987	46.823	47.659	48.495	49.332
60	50.168	51.004	51.840	52.676	53.512	54.348	55.184	56.021	56.857	57.693
70	58.529	59.365	60.201	61.037	61.873	62.710	63.546	64.382	65.218	66.054
80	66.890	67.726	68.562	69.399	70.235	71.071	71.907	72.743	73.579	74.415
90	75.251	76.088	76.924	77.760	78.596	79.432	80.268	81.104	81.940	82.777
100	83.613									

Capacity (liquid volume)

Table 12. U.S. gallons to liters (L), in increments of 1 gal up to 100 gal, and increments of 10 gal from 100 gal to 1000 gal

Conversion Factor: 1 U.S. Gallon = 3.785 412 L = 0.003 785 412 m^3
Rounding: To nearest 0.01 L up to 100 gallons, and to nearest 0.1 L above.

U.S. Gallons	0	1	2	3	4	5	6	7	8	9
					liters (L)					
0	–	3.79	7.57	11.36	15.14	18.93	22.71	26.50	30.28	34.07
10	37.85	41.64	45.42	49.21	53.00	56.78	60.57	64.35	68.14	71.92
20	75.71	79.49	83.28	87.06	90.85	94.64	98.42	102.21	105.99	109.78
30	113.56	117.35	121.13	124.92	128.70	132.49	136.27	140.06	143.85	147.63
40	151.42	155.20	158.99	162.77	166.56	170.34	174.13	177.91	181.70	185.49
50	189.27	193.06	196.84	200.63	204.41	208.20	211.98	215.77	219.55	223.34
60	227.12	230.91	234.70	238.48	242.27	246.05	249.84	253.62	257.41	261.19
70	264.98	268.76	272.55	276.34	280.12	283.91	287.69	291.48	295.26	299.05
80	302.83	306.62	310.40	314.19	317.97	321.76	325.55	329.33	333.12	336.90
90	340.69	344.47	348.26	352.04	355.83	359.61	363.40	367.18	370.97	374.76
	0	10	20	30	40	50	60	70	80	90
100	378.5	416.4	454.2	492.1	530.0	567.8	605.7	643.5	681.4	719.2
200	757.1	794.9	832.8	870.6	908.5	946.4	984.2	1022.1	1059.9	1097.8
300	1135.6	1173.5	1211.3	1249.2	1287.0	1324.9	1362.7	1400.6	1438.5	1476.3
400	1514.2	1552.0	1589.9	1627.7	1665.6	1703.4	1741.3	1779.1	1817.0	1854.9
500	1892.7	1930.6	1968.4	2006.3	2044.1	2082.0	2119.8	2157.7	2195.5	2233.4
600	2271.2	2309.1	2347.0	2384.8	2422.7	2460.5	2498.4	2536.2	2574.1	2611.9
700	2649.8	2687.6	2725.5	2763.4	2801.2	2839.1	2876.9	2914.8	2952.6	2990.5
800	3028.3	3066.2	3104.0	3141.9	3179.7	3217.6	3255.5	3293.3	3331.2	3369.0
900	3406.9	3444.7	3482.6	3520.4	3558.3	3596.1	3634.0	3671.8	3709.7	3747.6
1000	3785.4									

Note: 1000 L = 1 m^3 exactly.

Table 13. U.S. gallons to cubic meters (m^3), in increments of 100 gal up to 10 000 gal, and increments of 1000 gal between 10 000 gal and 100 000 gal

Conversion Factor: 1 U.S. Gallon = 0.003 785 412 m^3 = 3.785 412 L
Rounding: To nearest 0.001 m^3 up to 10 000 gallons, and nearest 0.01 m^3 above.

U.S. Gallons	0	100	200	300	400	500	600	700	800	900
					cubic meters (m^3)					
0	–	0.379	0.757	1.136	1.514	1.893	2.271	2.650	3.028	3.407
1000	3.785	4.164	4.542	4.921	5.300	5.678	6.057	6.435	6.814	7.192
2000	7.571	7.949	8.328	8.706	9.085	9.464	9.842	10.221	10.599	10.978
3000	11.356	11.735	12.113	12.492	12.870	13.249	13.627	14.006	14.385	14.763
4000	15.142	15.520	15.899	16.277	16.656	17.034	17.413	17.791	18.170	18.549
5000	18.927	19.306	19.684	20.063	20.441	20.820	21.198	21.577	21.955	22.334
6000	22.712	23.091	23.470	23.848	24.227	24.605	24.984	25.362	25.741	26.119
7000	26.498	26.876	27.255	27.634	28.012	28.391	28.769	29.148	29.526	29.905
8000	30.283	30.662	31.040	31.419	31.797	32.176	32.555	32.933	33.312	33.690
9000	34.069	34.447	34.826	35.204	35.583	35.961	36.340	36.718	37.097	37.476
	0	1000	2000	3000	4000	5000	6000	7000	8000	9000
10 000	37.85	41.64	45.42	49.21	53.00	56.78	60.57	64.35	68.14	71.92
20 000	75.71	79.49	83.28	87.06	90.85	94.64	98.42	102.21	105.99	109.78
30 000	113.56	117.35	121.13	124.92	128.70	132.49	136.27	140.06	143.85	147.63
40 000	151.42	155.20	158.99	162.77	166.56	170.34	174.13	177.91	181.70	185.49
50 000	189.27	193.06	196.84	200.63	204.41	208.20	211.98	215.77	219.55	223.34
60 000	227.12	230.91	234.70	238.48	242.27	246.05	249.84	253.62	257.41	261.19
70 000	264.98	268.76	272.55	276.34	280.12	283.91	287.69	291.48	295.26	299.05
80 000	302.83	306.62	310.40	314.19	317.97	321.76	325.55	329.33	333.12	336.90
90 000	340.69	344.47	348.26	352.04	355.83	359.61	363.40	367.18	370.97	374.76
100 000	378.54									

Note: 1 m^3 = 1000 L exactly.

Table 14. Pounds and ounces (lb and oz) to kilograms (kg), in increments of 1 oz to 9 lb 15 oz

Conversion Factor: 1 lb = 0.453 592 kg [453.592 g]; 1 oz = 0.028 350 kg [28.350 g]

Rounding: To nearest 0.001 kg (or nearest g)

Pounds (lb) and Ounces (oz)	0	1	2	3	4	5	6	7	8	9
					kilograms (kg)					
0	–	0.454	0.907	1.361	1.814	2.268	2.722	3.175	3.629	4.082
1	0.028	0.482	0.936	1.389	1.843	2.296	2.750	3.203	3.657	4.111
2	0.057	0.510	0.964	1.417	1.871	2.325	2.778	3.232	3.685	4.139
3	0.085	0.539	0.992	1.446	1.899	2.353	2.807	3.260	3.714	4.167
4 ($^1/_4$ lb)	0.113	0.567	1.021	1.474	1.928	2.381	2.835	3.289	3.742	4.196
5	0.142	0.595	1.049	1.503	1.956	2.410	2.863	3.317	3.770	4.224
6	0.170	0.624	1.077	1.531	1.984	2.438	2.892	3.345	3.799	4.252
7	0.198	0.652	1.106	1.559	2.013	2.466	2.920	3.374	3.827	4.281
8 ($^1/_2$ lb)	0.227	0.680	1.134	1.588	2.041	2.495	2.948	3.402	3.856	4.309
9	0.255	0.709	1.162	1.616	2.070	2.523	2.977	3.430	3.884	4.337
10	0.283	0.737	1.191	1.644	2.098	2.551	3.005	3.459	3.912	4.366
11	0.312	0.765	1.219	1.673	2.126	2.580	3.033	3.487	3.941	4.394
12 ($^3/_4$ lb)	0.340	0.794	1.247	1.701	2.155	2.608	3.062	3.515	3.969	4.423
13	0.369	0.822	1.276	1.729	2.183	2.637	3.090	3.544	3.997	4.451
14	0.397	0.850	1.304	1.758	2.211	2.665	3.118	3.572	4.026	4.479
15	0.425	0.879	1.332	1.786	2.240	2.693	3.147	3.600	4.054	4.508

Table 15. Pounds (lb) to kilograms (kg), in increments of 1 lb to 100 lb, and in increments of 10 lb between 100 lb and 1000 lb

Conversion Factor: 1 lb = 0.453 592 kg

Rounding: To nearest 0.001 kg (or 1 g) up to 100 lb, and to nearest 0.01 kg (10 g) above

Pounds (lb)	0	1	2	3	4	5	6	7	8	9
					kilograms (kg)					
0	–	0.454	0.907	1.361	1.814	2.268	2.722	3.175	3.629	4.082
10	4.536	4.990	5.443	5.897	6.350	6.804	7.257	7.711	8.165	8.618
20	9.072	9.525	9.979	10.433	10.886	11.340	11.793	12.247	12.701	13.154
30	13.608	14.061	14.515	14.969	15.422	15.876	16.329	16.783	17.237	17.690
40	18.144	18.597	19.051	19.504	19.956	20.412	20.865	21.319	21.772	22.226
50	22.680	23.133	23.587	24.040	24.494	24.948	25.401	25.855	26.308	26.762
60	27.216	27.669	28.123	28.576	29.030	29.484	29.937	30.391	30.844	31.298
70	31.751	32.205	32.659	33.112	33.566	34.019	34.473	34.927	35.380	35.834
80	36.287	36.741	37.195	37.648	38.102	38.555	39.009	39.463	39.916	40.370
90	40.823	41.277	41.730	42.184	42.638	43.091	43.545	43.998	44.452	44.906

Pounds (lb)	0	10	20	30	40	50	60	70	80	90
100	45.36	49.90	54.43	58.97	63.50	68.04	72.57	77.11	81.65	86.18
200	90.72	95.25	99.79	104.33	108.86	113.40	117.93	122.47	127.01	131.54
300	136.08	140.61	145.15	149.69	154.22	158.76	163.29	167.83	172.37	176.90
400	181.44	185.97	190.51	195.04	199.58	204.12	208.65	213.19	217.72	222.26
500	226.80	231.33	235.87	240.40	244.94	249.48	254.01	258.55	263.08	267.62
600	272.16	276.69	281.23	285.76	290.30	294.84	299.37	303.91	308.44	312.98
700	317.51	322.05	326.59	331.12	335.66	340.19	344.73	349.27	353.80	358.34
800	362.87	367.41	371.95	376.48	381.02	385.55	390.09	394.63	399.16	403.70
900	408.23	412.77	417.30	421.84	426.38	430.91	435.45	439.98	444.52	449.06
1000	453.59									

Table 16. U.S. tons (2000 lb) to metric tons (1000 kg), in increments of 0.1 ton to 10 tons, and increments of 1 ton between 10 tons and 100 tons

Conversion Factor: 1 U.S. (Short) Ton [2000 lb] = 0.907 185 metric ton (t) [1000 kg]

Rounding: To nearest 0.001 metric ton (t) [or nearest 1 kg]

U.S. Short Ton	0	0.1	0.2	0.3	0.4	0.5	0.6	0.7	0.8	0.9
					metric tons (t)					
0	-	0.091	0.181	0.272	0.363	0.454	0.544	0.635	0.726	0.816
1	0.907	0.998	1.089	1.179	1.270	1.361	1.451	1.542	1.633	1.724
2	1.814	1.905	1.996	2.087	2.177	2.268	2.359	2.449	2.540	2.631
3	2.722	2.812	2.903	2.994	3.084	3.175	3.266	3.357	3.447	3.538
4	3.629	3.719	3.810	3.901	3.992	4.082	4.173	4.264	4.354	4.445
5	4.536	4.627	4.717	4.808	4.899	4.990	5.080	5.171	5.262	5.352
6	5.443	5.534	5.625	5.715	5.806	5.897	5.987	6.078	6.169	6.260
7	6.350	6.441	6.532	6.622	6.713	6.804	6.895	6.985	7.076	7.167
8	7.257	7.348	7.439	7.530	7.620	7.711	7.802	7.893	7.983	8.074
9	8.165	8.255	8.346	8.437	8.528	8.618	8.709	8.800	8.890	8.981
	0	1	2	3	4	5	6	7	8	9
10	9.072	9.979	10.886	11.793	12.701	13.608	14.515	15.422	16.329	17.237
20	18.144	19.051	19.958	20.865	21.772	22.680	23.587	24.494	25.401	26.308
30	27.216	28.123	29.030	29.937	30.844	31.751	32.659	33.566	34.473	35.380
40	36.287	37.195	38.102	39.009	39.916	40.823	41.730	42.638	43.545	44.452
50	45.359	46.266	47.174	48.081	48.988	49.895	50.802	51.710	52.617	53.524
60	54.431	55.338	56.245	57.153	58.060	58.967	59.874	60.781	61.689	62.596
70	63.503	64.410	65.317	66.224	67.132	68.030	68.946	69.853	70.760	71.668
80	72.575	73.482	74.389	75.296	76.204	77.111	78.018	78.925	79.832	80.739
90	81.647	82.554	83.461	84.368	85.275	86.183	87.090	87.997	88.904	89.811
100	90.718									

Table 17. Pounds per lineal foot (lb/ft) to kilograms per meter (kg/m), in increments of 0.1 lb/ft to 10 lb/ft, and increments of 1 lb/ft from 10 lb/ft to 100 lb/ft

Conversion Factor: 1 lb/ft [plf] = 1.488 164 kg/m

Rounding: To nearest 0.001 kg/m (or 1 g/m) up to 10 lb/ft, and to nearest 0.01 kg/m above.

Pounds per Foot (lb/ft)	0	0.1	0.2	0.3	0.4	0.5	0.6	0.7	0.8	0.9
					kilograms per meter (kg/m)					
0	-	0.149	0.298	0.446	0.595	0.744	0.893	1.042	1.191	1.339
1	1.488	1.637	1.786	1.935	2.083	2.232	2.381	2.530	2.679	2.828
2	2.976	3.125	3.274	3.423	3.572	3.720	3.869	4.018	4.167	4.316
3	4.464	4.613	4.762	4.911	5.060	5.209	5.357	5.506	5.655	5.804
4	5.953	6.101	6.250	6.399	6.548	6.697	6.846	6.994	7.143	7.292
5	7.441	7.590	7.738	7.887	8.036	8.185	8.334	8.483	8.631	8.780
6	8.929	9.078	9.227	9.375	9.524	9.673	9.822	9.971	10.120	10.268
7	10.417	10.566	10.715	10.864	11.012	11.161	11.310	11.459	11.608	11.756
8	11.905	12.054	12.203	12.352	12.501	12.649	12.798	12.947	13.096	13.245
9	13.393	13.542	13.691	13.840	13.989	14.138	14.286	14.435	14.584	14.733
	0	1	2	3	4	5	6	7	8	9
10	14.88	16.37	17.86	19.35	20.83	22.32	23.81	25.30	26.79	28.28
20	29.76	31.25	32.74	34.23	35.72	37.20	38.69	40.18	41.67	43.16
30	44.64	46.13	47.62	49.11	50.60	52.09	53.57	55.06	56.55	58.04
40	59.53	61.01	62.50	63.99	65.48	66.97	68.46	69.94	71.43	72.92
50	74.41	75.90	77.38	78.87	80.36	81.85	83.34	84.83	86.31	87.80
60	89.29	90.78	92.27	93.75	95.24	96.73	98.22	99.71	101.20	102.68
70	104.17	105.66	107.15	108.64	110.12	111.61	113.10	114.59	116.08	117.56
80	119.05	120.54	122.03	123.52	125.01	126.49	127.98	129.47	130.96	132.45
90	133.93	135.42	136.91	138.40	139.89	141.38	142.86	144.35	145.84	147.33
100	148.82									

MASS PER UNIT AREA

Table 18. Pounds per square foot (lb/ft²) to kilograms per square meter (kg/m²), in increments of 0.1 lb/ft² to 10 lb/ft², and increments of 1 lb/ft² from 10 lb/ft² to 100 lb/ft²

Conversion Factor: 1 lb/ft² = 4.882 428 kg/m²

Rounding: To nearest 0.001 kg/m² (or 1 g/m²) up to 10 lb/ft², and to nearest 0.01 kg/m² above.

Pounds per Square Foot (lb/ft²)	0	.0.1	.0.2	.0.3	.0.4	.0.5	.0.6	.0.7	.0.8	.0.9 .
					kilograms per square meter (kg/m²)					
0	-	0.488	0.976	1.465	1.953	2.441	2.929	3.418	3.906	4.394
1	4.882	5.371	5.859	6.347	6.835	7.324	7.812	8.300	8.788	9.277
2	9.765	10.253	10.741	11.230	11.718	12.206	12.694	13.183	13.671	14.159
3	14.647	15.136	15.624	16.112	16.600	17.088	17.577	18.065	18.553	19.041
4	19.530	20.018	20.506	20.994	21.483	21.971	22.459	22.947	23.436	23.924
5	24.412	24.900	25.389	25.877	26.365	26.875	27.342	27.830	28.318	28.806
6	29.295	29.783	30.271	30.759	31.248	31.736	32.224	32.712	33.201	33.689
7	34.177	34.665	35.153	35.642	36.130	36.618	37.106	37.595	38.083	38.571
8	39.059	39.548	40.036	40.524	41.012	41.501	41.989	42.477	42.965	43.454
9	43.942	44.430	44.918	45.407	45.895	46.383	46.871	47.360	47.848	48.336
	0	1	2	3	4	5	6	7	8	9
10	48.82	53.71	58.59	63.47	68.35	73.24	78.12	83.00	87.88	92.77
20	97.65	102.53	107.41	112.30	117.18	122.06	126.94	131.83	136.71	141.59
30	146.47	151.36	156.24	161.12	166.00	170.88	175.77	180.65	185.53	190.41
40	195.30	200.18	205.06	209.94	214.83	219.71	224.59	229.47	234.36	239.24
50	244.12	249.00	253.89	258.77	263.65	268.53	273.42	278.30	283.18	288.06
60	292.95	297.83	302.71	307.59	312.48	317.36	322.24	327.12	332.01	336.89
70	341.77	346.65	351.53	356.42	361.30	366.18	371.06	375.95	380.83	385.71
80	390.59	395.48	400.36	405.24	410.12	415.01	419.89	424.77	429.65	434.54
90	439.42	444.30	449.18	454.07	458.95	463.83	468.71	473.60	478.48	483.36
100	488.24									

MASS PER UNIT VOLUME (MASS DENSITY)

Table 19. Pounds per cubic foot (lb/ft³) to kilograms per cubic meter (kg/m³), in increments of 1 lb/ft³ to 200 lb/ft³, with auxiliary increments of 0.1 lb/ft³ to 1 lb/ft³

Conversion factor: 1 lb/ft³ = 16.0185 kg/m³   Rounding: To nearest 0.1 kg/m³

Pounds per cubic foot (lb/ft³)	0	0.1	0.2	0.3	0.4	0.5	0.6	0.7	0.8	0.9
					kilograms per cubic meter (kg/m³)					
	-	1.6	3.2	4.8	6.4	8.0	9.6	11.2	12.8	14.4
	0	1	2	3	4	5	6	7	8	9
0	--	16.0	32.0	48.1	64.1	80.1	96.1	112.1	128.1	144.2
10	160.2	176.2	192.2	208.2	224.3	240.3	256.3	272.3	288.3	304.4
20	320.4	336.4	352.4	368.4	384.4	400.5	416.5	432.5	448.5	464.5
30	480.6	496.6	512.6	528.6	544.6	560.6	576.7	592.7	608.7	624.7
40	640.7	656.8	672.6	688.8	704.8	720.8	736.8	752.9	768.9	784.9
50	800.9	816.9	833.0	849.0	865.0	881.0	897.0	913.1	929.1	945.1
60	961.1	977.1	993.1	1009.2	1025.2	1041.2	1057.2	1073.2	1089.3	1105.3
70	1121.3	1137.3	1153.3	1169.3	1185.4	1201.4	1217.4	1233.4	1249.4	1265.5
80	1281.5	1297.5	1313.5	1329.5	1345.6	1361.6	1377.6	1393.6	1409.6	1425.6
90	1441.7	1457.7	1473.7	1489.7	1505.7	1521.8	1537.8	1553.8	1569.8	1585.8
100	1601.8	1617.9	1633.9	1649.9	1665.9	1681.9	1698.0	1714.0	1730.0	1746.0
110	1762.0	1778.0	1794.1	1810.1	1826.1	1842.1	1858.1	1874.2	1890.2	1906.2
120	1922.2	1938.2	1954.2	1970.3	1986.3	2002.3	2018.3	2034.3	2050.4	2066.4
130	2082.4	2098.4	2114.4	2130.5	2146.5	2162.5	2178.5	2194.5	2210.5	2226.6
140	2242.6	2258.6	2274.6	2290.6	2306.7	2322.7	2338.7	2354.7	2370.7	2386.8
150	2402.8	2418.8	2434.8	2450.8	2466.8	2482.9	2498.9	2514.9	2530.9	2546.9
160	2563.0	2579.0	2595.0	2611.0	2627.0	2643.0	2659.1	2675.1	2691.1	2707.1
170	2723.1	2739.2	2755.2	2771.2	2787.2	2803.2	2819.2	2835.3	2851.3	2867.3
180	2883.3	2899.3	2915.4	2931.4	2947.4	2963.4	2979.4	2995.5	3011.5	3027.5
190	3043.5	3059.5	3075.5	3091.6	3107.6	3123.6	3139.6	3155.6	3171.7	3187.7
200	3203.7									

Table 20. Feet per minute (ft/min, fpm) to meters per second (m/s), in increments of 1 ft/ min to 100 ft/min, and increments of 10ft/min to 1000 ft/min

Conversion Factor: 1 ft/min (fpm) = 0.005 08 m/s = 5.08 mm/s

Rounding: To nearest 0.0001 m/s up to 100 ft/min, and nearest 0.001 m/s above.

Feet per Minute (ft/min)	0	.1	.2	.3	.4	.5	.6	.7	.8	.9
					meter per second (m/s)					
0	–	0.0051	0.0102	0.0152	0.0203	0.0254	0.0305	0.0356	0.0406	0.0457
10	0.0508	0.0559	0.0610	0.0660	0.0711	0.0762	0.0813	0.0864	0.0914	0.0965
20	0.1016	0.1067	0.1118	0.1168	0.1219	0.1270	0.1321	0.1372	0.1422	0.1473
30	0.1524	0.1575	0.1626	0.1676	0.1727	0.1778	0.1829	0.1880	0.1930	0.1981
40	0.2032	0.2083	0.2134	0.2184	0.2235	0.2286	0.2337	0.2388	0.2438	0.2489
50	0.2540	0.2591	0.2642	0.2692	0.2743	0.2794	0.2845	0.2896	0.2946	0.2997
60	0.3048	0.3099	0.3150	0.3200	0.3251	0.3302	0.3353	0.3404	0.3454	0.3505
70	0.3556	0.3607	0.3658	0.3708	0.3759	0.3810	0.3861	0.3912	0.3962	0.4013
80	0.4064	0.4115	0.4166	0.4216	0.4267	0.4318	0.4369	0.4420	0.4470	0.4521
90	0.4572	0.4623	0.4674	0.4724	0.4775	0.4826	0.4877	0.4928	0.4978	0.5029

Feet per Minute (ft/min)	0	10	20	30	40	50	60	70	80	90
100	0.508	0.559	0.610	0.660	0.711	0.762	0.813	0.864	0.914	0.965
200	1.016	1.067	1.118	1.168	1.219	1.270	1.321	1.372	1.422	1.473
300	1.524	1.575	1.626	1.676	1.727	1.778	1.829	1.880	1.930	1.981
400	2.032	2.083	2.134	2.184	2.235	2.286	2.337	2.388	2.438	2.489
500	2.540	2.591	2.642	2.692	2.743	2.794	2.845	2.896	2.946	2.997
600	3.048	3.099	3.150	3.200	3.251	3.302	3.353	3.404	3.454	3.505
700	3.556	3.607	3.658	3.708	3.759	3.810	3.861	3.912	3.962	4.013
800	4.064	4.115	4.166	4.216	4.267	4.318	4.369	4.420	4.470	4.521
900	4.572	4.623	4.674	4.724	4.775	4.826	4.877	4.928	4.978	5.029
1000	5.080									

Table 21. Feet per minute (ft/min, fpm) to meters per second (m/s), in increments of 100 ft/min from 1000 ft/min to 15 000 ft/min

Conversion Factor: 100 ft/min = 0.508 m/s [exactly]

Rounding: To nearest 0.001 m/s (or 1 mm/s)

Feet per Minute (ft/min)	0	100	200	300	400	500	600	700	800	900
					meter per second (m/s)					
0	–	0.508	1.016	1.524	2.032	2.540	3.048	3.556	4.064	4.572
1000	5.080	5.588	6.096	6.604	7.112	7.620	8.128	8.636	9.144	9.652
2000	10.160	10.668	11.176	11.684	12.192	12.700	13.208	13.716	14.224	14.732
3000	15.240	15.748	16.256	16.764	17.272	17.780	18.288	18.796	19.308	19.812
4000	20.320	20.828	21.336	21.844	22.352	22.860	23.368	23.876	24.384	24.892
5000	25.400	25.908	26.416	26.924	27.432	27.940	28.448	28.956	29.464	29.972
6000	30.480	30.988	31.496	32.004	32.512	33.020	33.528	34.036	34.544	35.052
7000	35.560	36.068	36.576	37.084	37.592	38.100	38.608	39.116	39.624	40.132
8000	40.640	41.148	41.656	42.164	42.672	43.180	43.688	44.196	44.704	45.212
9000	45.720	46.228	46.736	47.244	47.752	48.260	48.768	49.276	49.784	50.292
10 000	50.800	51.308	51.816	52.324	52.832	53.340	53.848	54.356	54.864	55.372
11 000	55.880	56.388	56.896	57.404	57.912	58.420	58.928	59.436	59.944	60.452
12 000	60.960	61.468	61.976	62.484	62.992	63.500	64.008	64.516	65.024	65.532
13 000	66.040	66.548	67.056	67.564	68.072	68.580	69.088	69.596	70.104	70.612
14 000	71.120	71.628	72.136	72.644	73.152	73.660	74.168	74.676	75.184	75.692
15 000	76.200									

Note: All conversions given are exact.

Table 22. Pound-force (lbf) to newtons (N), in increments of 1 lb to 100 lbf, and increments of 10 lbf to 1000 lbf

Conversion Factor: 1 lbf = 4.448 222 N

Rounding: To nearest 0.1 N up to 100 lbf, and to nearest 1 N from 100 to 1000 lbf.

Pound-force (lbf)	0	1	2	3	4	5	6	7	8	9
					newtons (N)					
0	–	4.4	8.9	13.3	17.8	22.2	26.7	31.1	35.6	40.0
10	44.5	48.9	53.4	57.8	62.3	66.7	71.2	75.6	80.1	84.5
20	89.0	93.4	97.9	102.3	106.8	111.2	115.7	120.1	124.6	129.0
30	133.4	137.9	142.3	146.8	151.2	155.7	160.1	164.6	169.0	173.5
40	177.9	182.4	186.8	191.3	195.7	200.2	204.6	209.1	213.5	218.0
50	222.4	226.9	231.3	235.8	240.2	244.7	249.1	253.5	258.0	262.4
60	266.9	271.3	275.8	280.2	284.7	289.1	293.6	298.0	302.5	306.9
70	311.4	315.8	320.3	324.7	329.2	333.6	338.1	342.5	347.0	351.4
80	355.9	360.3	364.8	369.2	373.7	378.1	382.5	387.0	391.4	395.9
90	400.3	404.8	409.2	413.7	418.1	422.6	427.0	431.5	435.9	440.4

Pound-force (lbf)	0	10	20	30	40	50	60	70	80	90
100	445	489	534	578	623	667	712	756	801	845
200	890	934	979	1023	1068	1112	1157	1201	1246	1290
300	1334	1379	1423	1468	1512	1557	1601	1646	1690	1735
400	1779	1824	1868	1913	1957	2002	2046	2091	2135	2180
500	2224	2269	2313	2358	2402	2447	2491	2535	2580	2624
600	2669	2713	2758	2802	2847	2891	2936	2980	3025	3069
700	3114	3158	3203	3247	3292	3336	3381	3425	3470	3514
800	3559	3603	3648	3692	3737	3781	3825	3870	3914	3959
900	4003	4048	4092	4137	4181	4226	4270	4315	4359	4404
1000	4448									

Note: 1000 N = 1 kN (kilonewton); e.g. 4448 N = 4.448 kN.

PRESSURE AND STRESS

Table 23. Pound-force per square foot (lbf/ft², psf) to pascals (Pa) and kilopascals (kPa), in increments of 1 psf up to 100 psf, and increments of 10 psf from 100 to 1000 psf

Conversion Factor: 1 lbf/ft² (psf) = 47.880 26 Pa = 0.047 880 kPa

Rounding: To nearest 0.1 Pa up to 100 psf, and to nearest 0.001 kPa (or 1 Pa) above.

Pound-force per Square Foot (psf)	0	1	2	3	4	5	6	7	8	9
					pascals (Pa)					
0	–	47.9	95.8	143.6	191.5	239.4	287.3	335.2	383.0	430.9
10	478.8	526.7	574.6	622.4	670.3	718.2	766.1	814.0	861.8	909.7
20	957.6	1005.5	1053.4	1101.2	1149.1	1197.0	1244.9	1292.8	1340.6	1388.5
30	1436.4	1484.3	1532.2	1580.0	1627.9	1675.8	1723.7	1771.6	1819.4	1867.3
40	1915.2	1963.1	2011.0	2058.9	2106.7	2154.6	2202.5	2250.4	2298.3	2346.1
50	2394.0	2441.9	2489.8	2537.7	2585.5	2633.4	2681.3	2729.2	2777.1	2824.9
60	2872.8	2920.7	2968.6	3016.5	3064.3	3112.2	3160.1	3208.0	3255.9	3303.7
70	3351.6	3399.5	3447.4	3495.3	3543.1	3591.0	3638.9	3686.8	3734.7	3782.5
80	3830.4	3878.3	3926.2	3974.1	4021.9	4069.8	4117.7	4165.6	4213.5	4261.3
90	4309.2	4357.1	4405.0	4452.9	4500.7	4548.6	4596.5	4644.4	4692.3	4740.1

Pound-force per Square Foot (psf)	0	10	20	30	40	50	60	70	80	90
					kilopascals (kPa)					
100	4.788	5.267	5.746	6.224	6.703	7.182	7.661	8.140	8.618	9.097
200	9.576	10.055	10.534	11.012	11.491	11.970	12.449	12.928	13.406	13.885
300	14.364	14.843	15.322	15.800	16.279	16.758	17.237	17.716	18.194	18.673
400	19.152	19.631	20.110	20.589	21.067	21.546	22.025	22.504	22.983	23.461
500	23.940	24.419	24.898	25.377	25.855	26.334	26.813	27.292	27.771	28.249
600	28.728	29.207	29.686	30.165	30.643	31.122	31.601	32.080	32.559	33.037
700	33.516	33.995	34.474	34.953	35.431	35.910	36.389	36.868	37.347	37.825
800	38.304	38.783	39.262	39.741	40.219	40.698	41.177	41.656	42.135	42.613
900	43.092	43.571	44.050	44.529	45.007	45.486	45.965	46.444	46.923	47.401
1000	47.880									

Table 24. Pound-force per square inch (lbf/in², psi) to kilopascals (kPa), in increments of 0.1 lbf/in² to 10 lbf/in², and increments of 1 lbf/in² from 10 to 100 lbf/in²

Conversion Factor: 1 lbf/in² = 6.894 757 kPa

Rounding: To nearest 0.001 kPa up to 10 lbf/in², and to nearest 0.01 kPa above.

Pound-force per Square. Inch (psi)	0	.0.1	.0.2	.0.3	.0.4	.0.5	.0.6	.0.7	.0.8	.0.9
					kilopascals (kPa)					
0	-	0.689	1.379	2.068	2.758	3.447	4.137	4.826	5.516	6.205
1	6.895	7.584	8.274	8.963	9.653	10.342	11.032	11.721	12.411	13.100
2	13.790	14.479	15.168	15.858	16.547	17.237	17.926	18.616	19.305	19.995
3	20.684	21.374	22.063	22.753	23.442	24.132	24.821	25.511	26.200	26.890
4	27.579	28.269	28.958	29.647	30.337	31.026	31.716	32.405	33.095	33.784
5	34.474	35.163	35.853	36.542	37.232	37.921	38.611	39.300	39.990	40.679
6	41.369	42.058	42.747	43.437	44.126	44.816	45.505	46.195	46.884	47.574
7	48.263	48.953	49.642	50.332	51.021	51.711	52.400	53.090	53.779	54.469
8	55.158	55.848	56.537	57.226	57.916	58.605	59.295	59.984	60.674	61.363
9	62.053	62.742	63.432	64.121	64.811	65.500	66.190	66.879	67.569	68.258
	0	1	2	3	4	5	6	7	8	9
10	68.95	75.84	82.74	89.63	96.53	103.42	110.32	117.21	124.11	131.00
20	137.90	144.79	151.68	158.58	165.47	172.37	179.26	186.16	193.05	199.95
30	206.84	213.74	220.63	227.53	234.42	241.32	248.21	255.11	262.00	268.90
40	275.79	282.69	289.58	296.47	303.37	310.26	317.16	324.05	330.95	337.84
50	344.74	351.63	358.53	365.42	372.32	379.21	386.11	393.00	399.90	406.79
60	413.69	420.58	427.47	434.37	441.26	448.16	455.05	461.95	468.84	475.74
70	482.63	489.53	496.42	503.32	510.21	517.11	524.00	530.90	537.79	544.69
80	551.58	558.48	565.37	572.26	579.16	586.05	592.95	599.84	606.74	613.63
90	620.53	627.42	634.32	641.21	648.11	655.00	661.90	668.79	675.69	682.58
100	689.48									

Table 25. Pound-force per square inch (lbf/in², psi) to megapascals (MPa), in increments of 10 lbf/in² to 100 lbf/in², and increments of 100 lbf/in² from 1000 to 10 000 lbf/in²

Conversion Factor: 1 lbf/in² = 0.006 895 MPa; 1000 lbf/in² [1 kip/in²] = 6.894 757 MPa

Rounding: To nearest 0.001 MPa

Pound-force per Square Inch (psi)	0	.10	.20	.30	.40	.50	.60	.70	.80	.90
					megapascals (MPa)					
0	-	0.069	0.138	0.207	0.276	0.345	0.414	0.483	0.552	0.621
100	0.689	0.758	0.827	0.896	0.965	1.034	1.103	1.172	1.241	1.310
200	1.379	1.448	1.517	1.586	1.655	1.724	1.793	1.862	1.931	1.999
300	2.068	2.137	2.206	2.275	2.344	2.413	2.482	2.551	2.620	2.689
400	2.758	2.827	2.896	2.965	3.034	3.103	3.172	3.241	3.309	3.378
500	3.447	3.516	3.585	3.654	3.723	3.792	3.861	3.930	3.999	4.068
600	4.137	4.206	4.275	4.344	4.413	4.482	4.551	4.619	4.688	4.757
700	4.826	4.895	4.964	5.033	5.102	5.171	5.240	5.309	5.378	5.447
800	5.516	5.585	5.654	5.723	5.792	5.861	5.929	5.998	6.067	6.136
900	6.205	6.274	6.343	6.412	6.481	6.550	6.619	6.688	6.757	6.826
	0	.100	.200	.300	.400	.500	.600	.700	.800	.900
1000	6.895	7.584	8.274	8.963	9.653	10.342	11.032	11.721	12.411	13.100
2000	13.790	14.479	15.168	15.858	16.547	17.237	17.926	18.616	19.305	19.995
3000	20.684	21.374	22.063	22.753	23.442	24.132	24.821	25.511	26.200	26.890
4000	27.579	28.269	28.958	29.647	30.337	31.026	31.716	32.405	33.095	33.784
5000	34.474	35.163	35.853	36.542	37.232	37.921	38.611	39.300	39.990	40.679
6000	41.369	42.058	42.747	43.437	44.126	44.816	45.505	46.195	46.884	47.574
7000	48.263	48.953	49.642	50.332	51.021	51.711	52.400	53.090	53.779	54.469
8000	55.158	55.848	56.537	57.226	57.916	58.605	59.295	59.984	60.674	61.363
9000	62.053	62.742	63.432	64.121	64.811	65.500	66.190	66.879	67.569	68.258
10 000	68.948									

Work; energy

Table 26. Foot pound-force (ft·lbf) to joules (J), in increments of 1 ft·lbf to 100 ft·lbf, and increments of 10 ft·lbf from 100 ft·lbf to 1000 ft·lbf

Conversion Factor: 1 ft·lbf = 1.355 818 J [1 J = 1 N·m = 1 W·s]

Rounding: To nearest 0.01 J up to 100 ft·lbf, and nearest 0.1 J above.

FOOT POUND-FORCE	0	1	2	3	4	5	6	7	8	9
					joules (J)					
0	-	1.36	2.71	4.07	5.42	6.78	8.13	9.49	10.85	12.20
10	13.56	14.91	16.27	17.63	18.98	20.34	21.69	23.05	24.40	25.76
20	27.12	28.47	29.83	31.18	32.54	33.90	35.25	36.61	37.96	39.32
30	40.67	42.03	43.39	44.74	46.10	47.45	48.81	50.17	51.52	52.88
40	54.23	55.59	56.94	58.30	59.66	61.01	62.37	63.72	65.08	66.44
50	67.78	69.15	70.50	71.86	73.21	74.57	75.93	77.28	78.64	79.99
60	81.35	82.70	84.06	85.42	86.77	88.13	89.48	90.84	92.20	93.55
70	94.91	96.26	97.62	98.97	100.33	101.69	103.04	104.40	105.75	107.11
80	108.47	109.82	111.18	112.53	113.89	115.24	116.60	117.96	119.31	120.67
90	122.02	123.38	124.74	126.09	127.45	128.80	130.16	131.51	132.87	134.23
	0	10	20	30	40	50	60	70	80	90
100	135.6	149.1	162.7	176.3	189.8	203.4	216.9	230.5	244.0	257.6
200	271.2	284.7	298.3	311.8	325.4	339.0	352.5	366.1	379.6	393.2
300	406.7	420.3	433.9	447.4	461.0	474.5	488.1	501.7	515.2	528.8
400	542.3	555.9	569.4	583.0	596.6	610.1	623.7	637.2	650.8	664.4
500	677.9	691.5	705.0	718.6	732.1	745.7	759.3	772.8	786.4	799.9
600	813.5	827.0	840.6	854.2	867.7	881.3	894.8	908.4	922.0	935.5
700	949.1	962.6	976.2	989.7	1003.3	1016.9	1030.4	1044.0	1057.5	1071.1
800	1084.7	1098.2	1111.8	1125.3	1138.9	1152.4	1166.0	1179.6	1193.1	1206.7
900	1220.2	1233.8	1247.4	1260.9	1274.5	1288.0	1301.6	1315.1	1328.7	1342.3
1000	1355.8									

ENERGY, QUANTITY OF HEAT

Table 27. British thermal units (Btu) to kilojoules (kJ), in increments of 1 Btu to 100 Btu, and increments of 10 Btu between 100 and 1000 Btu

Conversion Factor: 1 Btu (Int. Table) = 1.055 056 kJ [= 1055.056 J]

Rounding: To nearest 0.01 kJ (10 J) up to 100 Btu, and nearest 0.1 kJ (100 J) above.

British Thermal Units (Btu)	0	1	2	3	4	5	6	7	8	9
					kilojoules (kJ)					
0	-	1.055	2.110	3.165	4.220	5.275	6.330	7.385	8.440	9.496
10	10.551	11.606	12.661	13.716	14.771	15.826	16.881	17.936	18.991	20.046
20	21.101	22.156	23.211	24.266	25.321	26.376	27.431	28.487	29.542	30.597
30	31.652	32.707	33.762	34.817	35.872	36.927	37.982	39.037	40.092	41.147
40	42.202	43.257	44.312	45.367	46.422	47.478	48.533	49.588	50.643	51.698
50	52.753	53.808	54.863	55.918	56.973	58.028	59.083	60.138	61.193	62.248
60	63.303	64.358	65.413	66.469	67.524	68.579	69.634	70.689	71.744	72.799
70	73.854	74.909	75.964	77.019	78.074	79.129	80.184	81.239	82.294	83.349
80	84.404	85.460	86.515	87.570	88.625	89.680	90.735	91.790	92.845	93.900
90	94.955	96.010	97.065	98.120	99.175	100.230	101.285	102.340	103.395	104.451
	0	10	20	30	40	50	60	70	80	90
100	105.51	116.06	126.61	137.16	147.71	158.26	168.81	179.36	189.91	200.46
200	211.01	221.56	232.11	242.66	253.21	263.76	274.31	284.87	295.42	305.97
300	316.52	327.07	337.62	348.17	358.72	369.27	379.82	390.37	400.92	411.47
400	422.02	432.57	443.12	453.67	464.22	474.78	485.33	495.88	506.43	516.98
500	527.53	538.08	548.63	559.18	569.73	580.28	590.83	601.38	611.93	622.48
600	633.03	643.58	654.13	664.69	675.24	685.79	696.34	706.89	717.44	727.99
700	738.54	749.09	759.64	770.19	780.74	791.29	801.84	812.39	822.94	833.49
800	844.04	854.60	865.15	875.70	886.25	896.80	907.35	917.90	928.45	939.00
900	949.55	960.10	970.65	981.20	991.75	1002.30	1012.85	1023.40	1033.95	1044.51
1000	1055.06									

HEAT FLOW RATE (HEAT GAIN, HEAT LOSS)

Table 28. British thermal unit per hour (Btu/h) to watt (W), in increments of 1 Btu/h to 100 Btu/h, and increments of 10 Btu/h from 100 Btu/h to 1000 Btu/h

Conversion Factor: 1 Btu/h = 0.293 071 1 W

Rounding: To nearest 0.001 W up to 100 Btu/h, and 0.01 W above.

Btu per hour (Btu/h)	0	1	2	3	4	5	6	7	8	9
					watts (W)					
0	–	0.293	0.586	0.879	1.172	1.465	1.758	2.051	2.345	2.638
10	2.931	3.224	3.517	3.810	4.103	4.396	4.689	4.982	5.275	5.568
20	5.861	6.154	6.448	6.741	7.034	7.327	7.620	7.913	8.206	8.499
30	8.792	9.085	9.378	9.671	9.964	10.257	10.551	10.844	11.137	11.430
40	11.723	12.016	12.309	12.602	12.895	13.188	13.481	13.774	14.067	14.360
50	14.654	14.947	15.240	15.533	15.826	16.119	16.412	16.705	16.998	17.291
60	17.584	17.877	18.170	18.463	18.757	19.050	19.343	19.636	19.929	20.222
70	20.515	20.808	21.101	21.394	21.687	21.980	22.273	22.566	22.860	23.153
80	23.446	23.739	24.032	24.325	24.618	24.911	25.204	25.497	25.790	26.083
90	26.376	26.669	26.963	27.256	27.549	27.842	28.135	28.428	28.721	29.014

	0	10	20	30	40	50	60	70	80	90
100	29.31	32.24	35.17	38.10	41.03	43.96	46.89	49.82	52.75	55.68
200	58.61	61.54	64.48	67.41	70.34	73.27	76.20	79.13	82.06	84.99
300	87.92	90.85	93.78	96.71	99.64	102.57	105.51	108.44	111.37	114.30
400	117.23	120.16	123.09	126.02	128.95	131.88	134.81	137.74	140.67	143.60
500	146.54	149.47	152.40	155.33	158.26	161.19	164.12	167.05	169.98	172.91
600	175.84	178.77	181.70	184.63	187.57	190.50	193.43	196.36	199.29	202.22
700	205.15	208.08	211.01	213.94	216.87	219.80	222.73	225.66	228.60	231.53
800	234.46	237.39	240.32	243.25	246.18	249.11	252.04	254.97	257.90	260.83
900	263.76	266.69	269.63	272.56	275.49	278.42	281.35	284.28	287.21	290.14
1000	293.07									

THERMAL CONDUCTIVITY (k)

Table 29. Btu/(ft·h·°F) to watt per meter kelvin [W/(m·K)], in increments of 0.01 Btu/(ft·h·°F) to 2.00 Btu/(ft·h·°F)

Conversion Factor: 1 Btu/(ft·h·°F) [= 1 Btu·ft/(ft²·h·°F)] = 1.730 735 W/(m·K)

Rounding: To nearest 0.001 W/(m·K)

Btu/(ft·h·°F)	0	0.01	0.02	0.03	0.04	0.05	0.06	0.07	0.08	0.09
				watt per meter kelvin (W/(m·K))						
0	–	0.017	0.035	0.052	0.069	0.087	0.104	0.121	0.138	0.156
0.1	0.173	0.190	0.208	0.225	0.242	0.260	0.277	0.294	0.312	0.329
0.2	0.346	0.363	0.381	0.398	0.415	0.433	0.450	0.467	0.485	0.502
0.3	0.519	0.537	0.554	0.571	0.588	0.606	0.623	0.640	0.658	0.675
0.4	0.692	0.710	0.727	0.744	0.762	0.779	0.796	0.813	0.831	0.848
0.5	0.865	0.883	0.900	0.917	0.935	0.952	0.969	0.987	1.004	1.021
0.6	1.038	1.056	1.073	1.090	1.108	1.125	1.142	1.160	1.177	1.194
0.7	1.212	1.229	1.246	1.263	1.281	1.298	1.315	1.333	1.350	1.367
0.8	1.385	1.402	1.419	1.437	1.454	1.471	1.488	1.506	1.523	1.540
0.9	1.558	1.575	1.592	1.610	1.627	1.644	1.662	1.679	1.696	1.713
1.0	1.731	1.748	1.765	1.783	1.800	1.817	1.835	1.852	1.869	1.887
1.1	1.904	1.921	1.938	1.956	1.973	1.990	2.008	2.025	2.042	2.060
1.2	2.077	2.094	2.111	2.129	2.146	2.163	2.181	2.198	2.215	2.233
1.3	2.250	2.267	2.285	2.302	2.319	2.336	2.354	2.371	2.388	2.406
1.4	2.423	2.440	2.458	2.475	2.492	2.510	2.527	2.544	2.561	2.579
1.5	2.596	2.613	2.631	2.648	2.667	2.683	2.700	2.717	2.735	2.752
1.6	2.769	2.786	2.804	2.821	2.838	2.856	2.873	2.890	2.908	2.925
1.7	2.942	2.960	2.977	2.994	3.011	3.029	3.046	3.063	3.081	3.098
1.8	3.115	3.133	3.150	3.167	3.185	3.202	3.219	3.236	3.254	3.271
1.9	3.288	3.306	3.323	3.340	3.358	3.375	3.392	3.410	3.427	3.444
2.0	3.461									

LUMINANCE

Table 30. Footlamberts (fL) to candelas per square meter (cd/m²), in increments of 1 fL to 100 fL, and increments of 10 fL from 100 fL to 1000 fL

Conversion Factor: 1 footlambert (fL) = 3.426 259 cd/m²

Rounding: To nearest 0.01 fL to 100 fL, and nearest 0.1 fL above.

Footlambert	0	1	2	3	4	5	6	7	8	9
				candelas per square meter (cd/m²)						
0	-	3.43	6.85	10.28	13.71	17.13	20.56	23.98	27.41	30.84
10	34.26	37.69	41.12	44.54	47.97	51.39	54.82	58.25	61.67	65.10
20	68.53	71.95	75.38	78.80	82.23	85.66	89.08	92.51	95.94	99.36
30	102.79	106.21	109.64	113.07	116.49	119.92	123.35	126.77	130.20	133.62
40	137.05	140.48	143.90	147.33	150.76	154.18	157.61	161.03	164.46	167.89
50	171.31	174.74	178.17	181.59	185.02	188.44	191.87	195.30	198.72	202.15
60	205.58	209.00	212.43	215.85	219.28	222.71	226.13	229.56	232.99	236.41
70	239.84	243.26	246.69	250.12	253.54	256.97	260.40	263.82	267.25	270.67
80	274.10	277.53	280.95	284.38	287.81	291.23	294.66	298.08	301.51	304.94
90	308.36	311.79	315.22	318.64	322.07	325.49	328.92	332.35	335.77	339.20
	0	10	20	30	40	50	60	70	80	90
100	342.6	376.9	411.2	445.4	479.7	513.9	548.2	582.5	616.7	651.0
200	685.3	719.5	753.8	788.0	822.3	856.6	890.8	925.1	959.4	993.6
300	1027.9	1062.1	1096.4	1130.7	1164.9	1199.2	1233.5	1267.7	1302.0	1336.2
400	1370.5	1404.8	1439.0	1473.3	1507.6	1541.8	1576.1	1610.3	1644.6	1678.9
500	1713.1	1747.4	1781.7	1815.9	1850.2	1884.4	1918.7	1953.0	1987.2	2021.5
600	2055.8	2090.0	2124.3	2158.5	2192.8	2227.1	2261.3	2295.6	2329.9	2364.1
700	2398.4	2432.6	2466.9	2501.2	2535.4	2569.7	2604.0	2638.2	2672.5	2706.7
800	2741.0	2775.3	2809.5	2843.8	2878.1	2912.3	2946.6	2980.8	3015.1	3049.4
900	3083.6	3117.9	3152.2	3186.4	3220.7	3254.9	3289.2	3323.5	3357.7	3392.0
1000	3426.3									

ILLUMINANCE

Table 31. Lumens per square foot (lm/ft²) to lux (lx) and kilolux (klx), in increments of 1 lm/ft² up to 100 lm/ft², and increments of 10 lm/ft² from 100 lm/ft² to 1000 lm/ft²

Conversion factor: 1 lm/ft² = 10.7639 lx [1m/m²]

Rounding: To nearest 0.1 lx up to 100 lm/ft², and to nearest 0.001 klx (or 1 lx) above.

Lumens per Square Foot (lm/ft²)	0	1	2	3	4	5	6	7	8	9
					lux (lx) [= 1m/m²]					
0	-	10.8	21.5	32.3	43.1	53.8	64.6	75.3	86.1	96.9
10	107.6	118.4	129.2	139.9	150.7	161.5	172.2	183.0	193.8	204.5
20	215.3	226.0	236.8	247.6	258.3	269.1	279.9	290.6	301.4	312.2
30	322.9	333.7	344.4	355.2	366.0	376.7	387.5	398.3	409.0	419.8
40	430.6	441.3	452.1	462.8	473.6	484.4	495.1	505.9	516.7	527.4
50	538.2	549.0	559.7	570.5	581.3	592.0	602.8	613.5	624.3	635.1
60	645.8	656.6	667.4	678.1	688.9	699.7	710.4	721.2	731.9	742.7
70	753.5	764.2	775.0	785.8	796.5	807.3	818.1	828.8	839.6	850.3
80	861.1	871.9	882.6	893.4	904.2	914.9	925.7	936.5	947.2	958.0
90	968.8	979.5	990.3	1001.0	1011.8	1022.6	1033.3	1044.1	1054.9	1065.6
	0	10	20	30	40	50	60	70	80	90
					kilolux (klx) [= 1000 lx]					
100	1.076	1.184	1.292	1.399	1.507	1.615	1.722	1.830	1.938	2.045
200	2.153	2.260	2.368	2.476	2.583	2.691	2.799	2.906	3.014	3.122
300	3.229	3.337	3.444	3.552	3.660	3.767	3.875	3.983	4.090	4.198
400	4.306	4.413	4.521	4.628	4.736	4.844	4.951	5.059	5.167	5.274
500	5.382	5.490	5.597	5.705	5.813	5.920	6.028	6.135	6.243	6.351
600	6.458	6.566	6.674	6.781	6.889	6.997	7.104	7.212	7.319	7.427
700	7.535	7.642	7.750	7.858	7.965	8.073	8.181	8.288	8.396	8.503
800	8.611	8.719	8.826	8.934	9.042	9.149	9.257	9.365	9.472	9.580
900	9.688	9.795	9.903	10.010	10.118	10.226	10.333	10.441	10.549	10.656
1000	10.764									

Table 32. Degrees Fahrenheit (°F) to degrees Celsius (°C), from −100°F to 1000°F in increments of 1°F

Conversion Factor: (°F − 32)/1.8 = °C

Rounding: To nearest 0.1°C; exact values are underlined

Degrees Fahrenheit (°F)	0	-1	-2	-3	-4	-5	-6	-7	-8	-9
					degrees Celsius (°C)					
-100	−73.3	−73.9	−74.4	−75.0						
-90	−67.8	−68.3	−68.9	−69.4	−70.0	−70.6	−71.1	−71.7	−72.2	−72.8
-80	−62.2	−62.8	−63.3	−63.9	−64.4	−65.0	−65.6	−66.1	−66.7	−67.2
-70	−56.7	−57.2	−57.8	−58.3	−58.9	−59.4	−60.0	−60.6	−61.1	−61.7
-60	−51.1	−51.7	−52.2	−52.8	−53.3	−53.9	−54.4	−55.0	−55.6	−56.1
-50	−45.6	−46.1	−46.7	−47.2	−47.8	−48.3	−48.9	−49.4	−50.0	−50.6
-40	−40.0	−40.6	−41.1	−41.7	−42.2	−42.8	−43.3	−43.9	−44.4	−45.0
-30	−34.4	−35.0	−35.6	−36.1	−36.7	−37.2	−37.8	−38.3	−38.9	−39.4
-20	−28.9	−29.4	−30.0	−30.6	−31.1	−31.7	−32.2	−32.8	−33.3	−33.9
-10	−23.3	−23.9	−24.4	−25.0	−25.6	−26.1	−26.7	−27.2	−27.8	−28.3
0	−17.8	−18.3	−18.9	−19.4	−20.0	−20.6	−21.1	−21,7	−22.2	−22.8

Degrees Fahrenheit (°F)	0	1	2	3	4	5	6	7	8	9
0	−17.8	−17.2	−16.7	−16.1	−15.6	−15.0	−14.4	−13.9	−13.3	−12.8
10	−12.2	−11.7	−11.1	−10.6	−10.0	−9.4	−8.9	−8.3	−7.8	−7.2
20	−6.7	−6.1	−5.6	−5.0	−4.4	−3.9	−3.3	−2.8	−2.2	−1.7
30	−1.1	−0.6	0	0.6	1.1	1.7	2.2	2.8	3.3	3.9
40	4.4	5.0	5.6	6.1	6.7	7.2	7.8	8.3	8.9	9.4
50	10.0	10.6	11.1	11.7	12.2	12.8	13,3	13.9	14.4	15.0
60	15.6	16.1	16.7	17.2	17.8	18.3	18.9	19.4	20.0	20.6
70	21.1	21.7	22.2	22.8	23.3	23.9	24.4	25.0	25.6	26.1
80	26.7	27.2	27.8	28.3	28.9	29.4	30.0	30.6	31.1	31.7
90	32.2	32.8	33.3	33.9	34.4	35.0	35.6	36.1	36.7	37.2
100	37.8	38.3	38.9	39.4	40.0	40.6	41.1	41.7	42.2	42.8
110	43.3	43.9	44.4	45.0	45.6	46.1	46.7	47.2	47.8	48.3
120	48.9	49.4	50.0	50.6	51.1	51.7	52.2	52.8	53.3	53.9
130	54.4	55.0	55.6	56.1	56.7	57.2	57.8	58.3	58.9	59.4
140	60.0	60.6	61.1	61.7	62.2	62.8	63.3	63.9	64.4	65.0
150	65.6	66.1	66.7	67.2	67.8	68.3	68.9	69.4	70.0	70.6
160	71.1	71.7	72.2	72.8	73.3	73.9	74.4	75.0	75.6	76.1
170	76.7	77.2	77.8	78.3	78.9	79.4	80.0	80.6	81.1	81.7
180	82.2	82.8	83.3	83.9	84.4	85.0	85.6	86.1	86.7	87.2
190	87.8	88.3	88.9	89.4	90.0	90.6	91.1	91.7	92.2	92.8
200	93.3	93.9	94.4	95.0	95.6	96.1	96.7	97.2	97.8	98.3
210	98.9	99.4	100.0	100.6	101.1	101.7	102.2	102.8	103.3	103.9
220	104.4	105.0	105.6	106.1	106.7	107.2	107.8	108.3	108.9	109.4
230	110.0	110.6	111.1	111.7	112.2	112.8	113.3	113.9	114.4	115.0
240	115.6	116.1	116.7	117.2	117.7	118.3	118.9	119.4	120.0	120.6
250	121.1	121.7	122.2	122.8	123.3	123.9	124.4	125.0	125.6	126.1
260	126.7	127.2	127.8	128.3	128.9	129.4	130.0	130.6	131.1	131.7
270	132.2	132.8	133.3	133.9	134.4	135.0	135.6	136.1	136.7	137.2
280	137.8	138.3	138.9	139.4	140.0	140.6	141.1	141.7	142.2	142.8
290	143.3	143.9	144.4	145.0	145.6	146.1	146.7	147.2	147.8	148.3
300	148.9	149.4	150.0	150.6	151.1	151.7	152.2	152.8	153.3	153.9
310	154.4	155.0	155.6	156.1	156.7	157.2	157.8	158.3	158.9	159.4
320	160.0	160.6	161.1	161.7	162.2	162.8	163.3	163.9	164.4	165.0
330	165.6	166.1	166.7	167.2	167.8	168.3	168.9	169.4	170.0	170.6
340	171.1	171.7	172.2	172.8	173.3	173.9	174.4	175.0	175.6	176.1
350	176.7	177.2	177.8	178.3	178.9	179.4	180.0	180.6	181.1	181.7
360	182.2	182.8	183.3	183.9	184.4	185.0	185.6	186.1	186.7	187.2
370	187.8	188.3	188.9	189.4	190.0	190.6	191.1	191.7	192.2	192.8
380	193.3	193.9	194.4	195.0	195.6	196.1	196.7	197.2	197.8	198.3
390	198.9	199.4	200.0	200.6	201.1	201.7	202.2	202.8	203.3	203.9

Table 32 (cont.). Degrees Fahrenheit (°F) to degrees Celsius (°C), from −100°F to 1000°F in increments of 1°F

Degrees Fahrenheit (°F)	0	1	2	3	4	5	6	7	8	9
				degrees Celsius (°C)						
400	204.4	205.0	205.6	206.1	206.7	207.2	207.8	208.3	208.9	209.4
410	210.0	210.6	211.1	211.7	212.2	212.8	213.3	213.9	214.4	215.0
420	215.6	216.1	216.7	217.2	217.8	218.3	218.9	219.4	220.0	220.6
430	221.1	221.7	222.2	222.8	223.3	223.9	224.4	225.0	225.6	226.1
440	226.7	227.2	227.8	228.3	228.9	229.4	230.0	230.6	231.1	231.7
450	232.2	232.8	233.3	233.9	234.4	235.0	235.6	236.1	236.7	237.2
460	237.8	238.3	238.9	239.4	240.0	240.6	241.1	241.7	242.2	242.8
470	243.3	243.9	244.4	245.0	245.6	246.1	246.7	247.2	247.8	248.3
480	24 .9	249.4	250.0	250.6	251.1	251.7	252.2	252.8	253.3	253.9
490	254.4	255.0	255.6	256.1	256.7	257.2	257.8	258.3	258.9	259.4
500	260.0	260.6	261.1	261.7	262.2	262.8	263.3	263.9	264.4	265.0
510	265.6	266.1	266.7	267.2	268.3	268.9	269.4	270.0	270.6
510	265.6	266.1	266.7	267.2	268.3	268.9	269.4	270.0	270.6
520	271.1	271.7	272.2	272.8	273.3	273.9	274.4	275.0	275.6	276.1
530	276.7	277.2	277.8	278.3	278.9	279.4	280.0	280.6	281.1	281.7
540	282.2	282.8	283.3	283.9	284.4	285.0	285.6	286.1	286.7	287.2
550	287.8	288.3	288.9	289.4	290.0	290.6	291.1	291.7	292.2	292.8
560	293.3	293.9	294.4	295.0	295.6	296.1	296.7	297.2	297.8	298.3
570	298.9	299.4	300.0	300.6	301.1	301.7	302.2	302.8	303.3	303.9
580	304.4	305.0	305.6	306.1	306.7	307.2	307.8	308.3	308.9	309.4
590	310.0	310.6	311.1	311.7	312.2	312.8	313.3	313.9	314.4	315.0
600	315.6	316.1	316.7	317.2	317.8	318.3	318.9	319.4	320.0	320.6
610	321.1	321.7	322.2	322.8	323.3	323.9	324.4	325.0	325.6	326.1
620	326.7	327.2	327.8	328.3	328.9	329.4	330.0	330.6	331.1	331.7
630	332.2	332.8	333.3	333.9	334.4	335.0	335.6	336.1	336.7	337.2
640	337.8	338.3	338.9	339.4	340.0	340.6	341.1	341.7	342.2	342.8
650	343.3	343.9	344.4	345.0	345.6	346.1	346.7	347.2	347.8	348.3
660	348.9	349.4	350.0	350.6	351.1	351.7	352.2	352.8	353.3	353.9
670	354.4	355.0	355.6	356.1	356.7	357.2	357.8	358.3	358.9	359.4
680	360.0	360.6	361.1	361.7	362.2	362.8	363.3	363.9	364.4	365.0
690	365.6	366.1	366.7	367.2	367.8	368.3	368.9	369.4	370.0	370.6
700	371.1	371.7	372.2	372.8	373.3	373.9	374.4	375.0	375.6	376.1
710	376.7	377.2	377.8	378.3	378.9	379.4	380.0	380.6	381.1	381.7
720	382.2	382.8	383.3	383.9	384.4	385.0	385.6	386.1	386.7	387.2
730	387.8	388.3	388.9	389.4	390.0	390.6	391.1	391.7	392.2	392.8
740	393.3	393.9	394.4	395.0	395.6	396.1	396.7	397.2	397.8	398.3
750	398.9	399.4	400.0	400.6	401.1	401.7	402.2	402.8	403.3	403.9
760	404.4	405.0	405.6	406.1	406.7	407.2	407.8	408.3	408.9	409.4
770	410.0	410.6	411.1	411.7	412.2	412.8	413.3	413.9	414.4	415.0
780	415.6	416.1	416.7	417.2	417.8	418.3	418.9	419.4	420.0	420.6
790	421.1	421.7	422.2	422.8	423.3	423.9	424.4	425.0	425.6	426.1
800	426.7	427.2	427.8	428.3	428.9	429.4	430.0	430.6	431.1	431.7
810	432.2	432.8	433.3	433.9	434.4	435.0	435.6	436.1	436.7	437.2
820	437.8	438.3	438.9	439.4	440.0	440.6	441.1	441.7	442.2	442.8
830	443.3	443.9	444.4	445.0	445.6	446.1	446.7	447.2	447.8	448.3
840	448.9	449.4	450.0	450.6	451.1	451.7	452.2	452.8	453.3	453.9
850	454.4	455.0	455.6	456.1	456.7	457.2	457.8	458.3	458.9	459.4
860	460.0	460.6	461.1	46 .7	462.2	462.8	463.3	463.9	464.4	465.0
870	465.6	4 6.1	466.7	467.2	467.8	468.3	468.9	469.4	470.0	470.6
880	471.1	471.7	472.2	472.8	473.3	473.9	474.4	475.0	475.6	476.1
890	476.7	477.2	477.8	478.3	478.9	479.4	480.0	480.6	481.1	481.7
900	482.2	482.8	483.3	483.9	484.4	485.0	485.6	486.1	486.7	487.2
910	487.8	488.3	488.9	489.4	490.0	490.6	491.1	491.7	492.2	492.8
920	493.3	493.9	494.4	495.0	495.6	496.1	496.7	497.2	497.8	498.3
930	498.9	499.4	500.0	500.6	501.1	501.7	502.2	502.8	503.3	503.9
940	504.4	505.0	505.6	506.1	506.7	507.2	507.8	508.3	508.9	509.4
950	510.0	510.6	511.1	511.7	512.2	512.8	513.3	513.9	514.4	515.0
960	515.6	516.1	516.7	517.2	517.8	518.3	518.9	519.4	520.0	520.6
970	521.1	521.7	522.2	522.8	523.3	523.9	524.4	525.0	525.6	526.1
980	526.7	527.2	527.8	528.3	528.9	529.4	530.0	530.6	531.1	531.7
990	532.2	532.8	533.3	533.9	534.4	535.0	535.6	536.1	536.7	537.2

Table 33. Degrees (°) and minutes (') to radians (rad), in increments of 5 minutes to 90 degrees

Conversion Factor: 1 degree (1°) = π/180 rad = 0.017 453 rad = 17.453 293 mrad

Rounding: To nearest 0.0001 rad [or 0.1 mrad]

Degrees (°)	Minutes (')											
	. 0	. 5	. 10	. 15	. 20	. 25	30	. 35	. 40	. 45	. 50	. 55 .
	radians (rad)										
0	—	0.0015	0.0029	0.0044	0.0058	0.0073	0.0087	0.0102	0.0116	0.0131	0.0145	0.0160
1	0.0175	0.0189	0.0204	0.0218	0.0233	0.0247	0.0262	0.0276	0.0291	0.0305	0.0320	0.0335
2	0.0349	0.0364	0.0378	0.0393	0.0407	0.0422	0.0436	0.0451	0.0465	0.0480	0.0495	0.0509
3	0.0524	0.0538	0.0553	0.0567	0.0582	0.0596	0.0611	0.0625	0.0640	0.0654	0.0669	0.0684
4	0.0698	0.0713	0.0727	0.0742	0.0756	0.0771	0.0785	0.0800	0.0814	0.0829	0.0844	0.0858
5	0.0873	0.0887	0.0902	0.0916	0.0931	0.0945	0.0960	0.0974	0.0989	0.1004	0.1018	0.1033
6	0.1047	0.1062	0.1076	0.1091	0.1105	0.1120	0.1134	0.1149	0.1164	0.1178	0.1193	0.1207
7	0.1222	0.1236	0.1251	0.1265	0.1280	0.1294	0.1309	0.1324	0.1338	0.1353	0.1367	0.1382
8	0.1396	0.1411	0.1425	0.1440	0.1454	0.1469	0.1484	0.1498	0.1513	0.1527	0.1542	0.1556
9	0.1571	0.1585	0.1600	0.1614	0.1629	0.1644	0.1658	0.1673	0.1687	0.1702	0.1716	0.1731
10	0.1745	0.1760	0.1774	0.1789	0.1804	0.1818	0.1833	0.1847	0.1862	0.1876	0.1891	0.1905
11	0.1920	0.1934	0.1949	0.1963	0.1978	0.1993	0.2007	0.2022	0.2036	0.2051	0.2065	0.2080
12	0.2094	0.2109	0.2123	0.2138	0.2153	0.2167	0.2182	0.2196	0.2211	0.2225	0.2240	0.2254
13	0.2269	0.2283	0.2298	0.2313	0.2327	0.2342	0.2356	0.2371	0.2385	0.2400	0.2414	0.2429
14	0.2443	0.2458	0.2473	0.2487	0.2502	0.2516	0.2531	0.2545	0.2560	0.2574	0.2589	0.2603
15	0.2618	0.2633	0.2647	0.2662	0.2676	0.2691	0.2705	0.2720	0.2734	0.2749	0.2763	0.2778
16	0.2793	0.2807	0.2822	0.2836	0.2851	0.2865	0.2880	0.2894	0.2909	0.2923	0.2938	0.2953
17	0.2967	0.2982	0.2996	0.3011	0.3025	0.3040	0.3054	0.3069	0.3083	0.3098	0.3113	0.3127
18	0.3142	0.3156	0.3171	0.3185	0.3200	0.3214	0.3229	0.3243	0.3258	0.3272	0.3287	0.3302
19	0.3316	0.3331	0.3345	0.3360	0.3374	0.3389	0.3403	0.3418	0.3432	0.3447	0.3462	0.3476
20	0.3491	0.3505	0.3520	0.3534	0.3549	0.3563	0.3578	0.3592	0.3607	0.3622	0.3636	0.3651
21	0.3665	0.3680	0.3694	0.3709	0.3723	0.3738	0.3752	0.3767	0.3782	0.3796	0.3811	0.3825
22	0.3840	0.3854	0.3869	0.3883	0.3898	0.3912	0.3927	0.3942	0.3956	0.3971	0.3985	0.4000
23	0.4014	0.4029	0.4043	0.4058	0.4072	0.4087	0.4102	0.4116	0.4131	0.4145	0.4160	0.4174
24	0.4189	0.4203	0.4218	0.4232	0.4247	0.4262	0.4276	0.4291	0.4305	0.4320	0.4334	0.4349
25	0.4363	0.4378	0.4392	0.4407	0.4422	0.4436	0.4451	0.4465	0.4480	0.4494	0.4509	0.4523
26	0.4538	0.4552	0.4567	0.4581	0.4596	0.4611	0.4625	0.4640	0.4654	0.4669	0.4683	0.4698
27	0.4712	0.4727	0.4741	0.4756	0.4771	0.4785	0.4800	0.4814	0.4829	0.4843	0.4858	0.4872
28	0.4887	0.4901	0.4916	0.4931	0.4945	0.4960	0.4974	0.4989	0.5003	0.5018	0.5032	0.5047
29	0.5061	0.5076	0.5091	0.5105	0.5120	0.5134	0.5149	0.5163	0.5178	0.5192	0.5207	0.5221
30	0.5236	0.5251	0.5265	0.5280	0.5294	0.5309	0.5323	0.5338	0.5352	0.5367	0.5381	0.5396
31	0.5411	0.5425	0.5440	0.5454	0.5469	0.5483	0.5498	0.5512	0.5527	0.5541	0.5556	0.5571
32	0.5585	0.5600	0.5614	0.5629	0.5643	0.5658	0.5672	0.5687	0.5701	0.5716	0.5730	0.5745
33	0.5760	0.5774	0.5789	0.5803	0.5818	0.5832	0.5847	0.5861	0.5876	0.5890	0.5905	0.5920
34	0.5934	0.5949	0.5963	0.5978	0.5992	0.6007	0.6021	0.6036	0.6050	0.6065	0.6080	0.6094
35	0.6109	0.6123	0.6138	0.6152	0.6167	0.6181	0.6196	0.6210	0.6225	0.6240	0.6254	0.6269
36	0.6283	0.6298	0.6312	0.6327	0.6341	0.6356	0.6370	0.6385	0.6400	0.6414	0.6429	0.6443
37	0.6458	0.6472	0.6487	0.6501	0.6516	0.6530	0.6545	0.6560	0.6574	0.6589	0.6603	0.6618
38	0.6632	0.6647	0.6661	0.6676	0.6690	0.6705	0.6720	0.6734	0.6749	0.6763	0.6778	0.6792
39	0.6807	0.6821	0.6836	0.6850	0.6865	0.6880	0.6894	0.6909	0.6923	0.6938	0.6952	0.6967
40	0.6981	0.6996	0.7010	0.7025	0.7039	0.7054	0.7069	0.7083	0.7098	0.7112	0.7127	0.7141
41	0.7156	0.7170	0.7185	0.7199	0.7214	0.7229	0.7243	0.7258	0.7272	0.7287	0.7301	0.7316
42	0.7330	0.7345	0.7359	0.7374	0.7389	0.7403	0.7418	0.7432	0.7447	0.7461	0.7476	0.7490
43	0.7505	0.7519	0.7534	0.7549	0.7563	0.7578	0.7592	0.7607	0.7621	0.7636	0.7650	0.7665
44	0.7679	0.7694	0.7709	0.7723	0.7738	0.7752	0.7767	0.7781	0.7796	0.7810	0.7825	0.7839
45	0.7854	0.7869	0.7883	0.7898	0.7912	0.7927	0.7941	0.7956	0.7970	0.7985	0.7999	0.8014
46	0.8029	0.8043	0.8058	0.8072	0.8087	0.8101	0.8116	0.8130	0.8145	0.8159	0.8174	0.8189
47	0.8203	0.8218	0.8232	0.8247	0.8261	0.8276	0.8290	0.8305	0.8319	0.8334	0.8348	0.8363
48	0.8378	0.8392	0.8407	0.8421	0.8436	0.8450	0.8465	0.8479	0.8494	0.8508	0.8523	0.8538
49	0.8552	0.8567	0.8581	0.8596	0.8610	0.8625	0.8639	0.8654	0.8668	0.8683	0.8698	0.8712
50	0.8727	0.8741	0.8756	0.8770	0.8785	0.8799	0.8814	0.8828	0.8843	0.8858	0.8872	0.8887
51	0.8901	0.8916	0.8930	0.8945	0.8959	0.8974	0.8988	0.9003	0.9018	0.9032	0.9047	0.9061
52	0.9076	0.9090	0.9105	0.9119	0.9134	0.9148	0.9163	0.9178	0.9192	0.9207	0.9221	0.9236
53	0.9250	0.9265	0.9279	0.9294	0.9308	0.9323	0.9338	0.9352	0.9367	0.9381	0.9396	0.9410
54	0.9425	0.9439	0.9454	0.9468	0.9483	0.9498	0.9512	0.9527	0.9541	0.9556	0.9570	0.9585

Table 33 (cont.). Degrees (°) and minutes (') to radians (rad), in increments of 5 minutes to 90 degrees

Degrees (°)	Minutes (')											
	. 0	. 5	. 10	. 15	. 20	. 25	30	. 35	. 40	. 45	. 50	. 55 .
						radians (rad)						
55	0.9599	0.9614	0.9628	0.9643	0.9657	0.9672	0.9687	0.9701	0.9716	0.9730	0.9745	0.9759
56	0.9774	0.9788	0.9803	0.9817	0.9832	0.9847	0.9861	0.9876	0.9890	0.9905	0.9919	0.9934
57	0.9948	0.9963	0.9977	0.9992	1.0007	1.0021	1.0036	1.0050	1.0065	1.0079	1.0094	1.0108
58	1.0123	1.0137	1.0152	1.0167	1.0181	1.0196	1.0210	1.0225	1.0239	1.0254	1.0268	1.0283
59	1.0297	1.0312	1.0327	1.0341	1.0356	1.0370	1.0385	1.0399	1.0414	1.0428	1.0443	1.0457
60	1.0472	1.0487	1.0501	1.0516	1.0530	1.0545	1.0559	1.0574	1.0588	1.0603	1.0617	1.0632
61	1.0647	1.0661	1.0676	1.0690	1.0705	1.0719	1.0734	1.0748	1.0763	1.0777	1.0792	1.0806
62	1.0821	1.0835	1.0850	1.0865	1.0879	1.0894	1.0908	1.0923	1.0937	1.0952	1.0966	1.0981
63	1.0995	1.1010	1.1025	1.1039	1.1054	1.1068	1.1083	1.1097	1.1112	1.1126	1.1141	1.1155
64	1.1170	1.1185	1.1199	1.1214	1.1228	1.1243	1.1257	1.1272	1.1286	1.1301	1.1315	1.1330
65	1.1344	1.1359	1.1374	1.1388	1.1403	1.1417	1.1432	1.1446	1.1461	1.1475	1.1490	1.1504
66	1.1519	1.1534	1.1548	1.1563	1.1577	1.1592	1.1606	1.1621	1.1635	1.1650	1.1664	1.1679
67	1.1694	1.1708	1.1723	1.1737	1.1752	1.1766	1.1781	1.1795	1.1810	1.1824	1.1839	1.1854
68	1.1868	1.1883	1.1897	1.1912	1.1926	1.1941	1.1955	1.1970	1.1984	1.1999	1.2014	1.2028
69	1.2043	1.2057	1.2072	1.2086	1.2101	1.2115	1.2130	1.2144	1.2159	1.2174	1.2188	1.2203
70	1.2217	1.2232	1.2246	1.2261	1.2275	1.2290	1.2305	1.2319	1.2334	1.2348	1.2363	1.2377
71	1.2392	1.2406	1.2421	1.2436	1.2450	1.2465	1.2479	1.2494	1.2508	1.2523	1.2537	1.2552
72	1.2566	1.2581	1.2596	1.2610	1.2625	1.2639	1.2654	1.2668	1.2683	1.2697	1.2712	1.2726
73	1.2741	1.2756	1.2770	1.2785	1.2799	1.2814	1.2828	1.2843	1.2857	1.2872	1.2886	1.2901
74	1.2915	1.2930	1.2945	1.2959	1.2974	1.2988	1.3003	1.3017	1.3032	1.3046	1.3061	1.3075
75	1.3090	1.3105	1.3119	1.3134	1.3148	1.3163	1.3177	1.3192	1.3206	1.3221	1.3235	1.3250
76	1.3265	1.3279	1.3294	1.3308	1.3323	1.3337	1.3352	1.3366	1.3381	1.3395	1.3410	1.3425
77	1.3439	1.3454	1.3468	1.3483	1.3497	1.3512	1.3526	1.3541	1.3555	1.3570	1.3585	1.3599
78	1.3614	1.3628	1.3643	1.3657	1.3672	1.3686	1.3701	1.3715	1.3730	1.3745	1.3759	1.3774
79	1.3788	1.3803	1.3817	1.3832	1.3846	1.3861	1.3875	1.3890	1.3905	1.3919	1.3934	1.3948
80	1.3963	1.3977	1.3992	1.4006	1.4021	1.4035	1.4050	1.4065	1.4079	1.4094	1.4108	1.4123
81	1.4137	1.4152	1.4166	1.4181	1.4195	1.4210	1.4224	1.4239	1.4254	1.4268	1.4283	1.4297
82	1.43 2	1.4326	1.4341	1.4355	1.4370	1.4384	1.4399	1.4414	1.4428	1.4443	1.4457	1.4472
83	1.4486	1.4501	1.4515	1.4530	1.4544	1.4559	1.4574	1.4588	1.4603	1.4617	1.4632	1.4646
84	1.4661	1.4675	1.4690	1.4704	1.4719	1.4734	1.4748	1.4763	1.4777	1.4792	1.4806	1.4821
85	1.4835	1.4850	1.4864	1.4879	1.4894	1.4908	1.4923	1.4937	1.4952	1.4966	1.4981	1.4995
86	1.5010	1.5024	1.5039	1.5054	1.5068	1.5083	1.5097	1.5112	1.5126	1.5141	1.5155	1.5170
87	1.5184	1.5199	1.5213	1.5228	1.5243	1.5257	1.5272	1.5286	1.5301	1.5315	1.5330	1.5344
88	1.5359	1.5373	1.5388	1.5403	1.5417	1.5432	1.5446	1.5461	1.5475	1.5490	1.5504	1.5519
89	1.5533	1.5548	1.5563	1.5577	1.5592	1.5606	1.5621	1.5635	1.5650	1.5664	1.5679	1.5693
90	1.5708											

Table 34. Degrees (°) to radians (rad), in increments of 1 degree (1°) from 90° to 360°

Conversion Factor: 1 degree (1°) = 0.017 453 rad.   Rounding: To nearest 0.0001 rad.

Degrees (°)	0	1	2	3	4	5	6	7	8	9
					radians (rad)					
90	1.5708	1.5882	1.6057	1.6232	1.6406	1.6581	1.6755	1.6930	1.7104	1.7279
100	1.7453	1.7628	1.7802	1.7977	1.8151	1.8326	1.8500	1.8675	1.8850	1.9024
110	1.9199	1.9373	1.9548	1.9722	1.9897	2.0071	2.0246	2.0420	2.0595	2.0769
120	2.0944	2.1118	2.1293	2.1468	2.1642	2.1817	2.1991	2.2166	2.2340	2.2515
130	2.2689	2.2864	2.3038	2.3213	2.3387	2.3562	2.3736	2.3911	2.4086	2.4260
140	2.4435	2.4609	2.4784	2.4958	2.5133	2.5307	2.5482	2.5656	2.5831	2.6005
150	2.6180	2.6354	2.6529	2.6704	2.6878	2.7053	2.7227	2.7402	2.7576	2.7751
160	2.7925	2.8100	2.8274	2.8449	2.8623	2.8798	2.8972	2.9147	2.9322	2.9496
170	2.9671	2.9845	3.0020	3.0194	3.0369	3.0543	3.0718	3.0892	3.1067	3.1241
180	3.1416	3.1590	3.1765	3.1940	3.2114	3.2289	3.2463	3.2638	3.2812	3.2987
190	3.3161	3.3336	3.3510	3.3685	3.3859	3.4034	3.4208	3.4383	3.4558	3.4732
200	3.4907	3.5081	3.5256	3.5430	3.5605	3.5779	3.5954	3.6128	3.6303	3.6477
210	3.6652	3.6826	3.7001	3.7176	3.7350	3.7525	3.7699	3.7874	3.8048	3.8223
220	3.8397	3.8572	3.8746	3.8921	3.9095	3.9270	3.9444	3.9619	3.9794	3.9968
230	4.0143	4.0317	4.0492	4.0666	4.0841	4.1015	4.1190	4.1364	4.1539	4.1713
240	4.1888	4.2062	4.2237	4.2412	4.2586	4.2761	4.2935	4.3110	4.3284	4.3459
250	4.3633	4.3808	4.3982	4.4157	4.4331	4.4506	4.4680	4.4855	4.5029	4.5204
260	4.5379	4.5553	4.5728	4.5902	4.6077	4.6251	4.6426	4.6600	4.6775	4.6949
270	4.7124	4.7298	4.7473	4.7647	4.7822	4.7997	4.8171	4.8346	4.8520	4.8695
280	4.8869	4.9044	4.9218	4.9393	4.9567	4.9742	4.9916	5.0091	5.0265	5.0440
290	5.0615	5.0789	5.0964	5.1138	5.1313	5.1487	5.1662	5.1836	5.2011	5.2185
300	5.2360	5.2534	5.2709	5.2883	5.3058	5.3233	5.3407	5.3582	5.3756	5.3931
310	5.4105	5.4280	5.4454	5.4629	5.4803	5.4978	5.5152	5.5327	5.5501	5.5676
320	5.5851	5.6025	5.6200	5.6374	5.6549	5.6723	5.6898	5.7072	5.7247	5.7421
330	5.7596	5.7770	5.7945	5.8119	5.8294	5.8469	5.8643	5.8818	5.8992	5.9167
340	5.9341	5.9516	5.9690	5.9865	6.0039	6.0214	6.0388	6.0563	6.0737	6.0912
350	6.1087	6.1261	6.1436	6.1610	6.1785	6.1959	6.2134	6.2308	6.2483	6.2657
360	6.2832									

Index

Index

Index

Index

Index

Index

ABOUT THE EDITOR-IN-CHIEF

JOHN HANCOCK CALLENDER, a well-known author and editor, was for many years professor of architecture at Pratt Institute, Brooklyn, New York. He has been involved in research on new materials and methods of construction since 1932, including such subjects as industrialized construction, curtain wall construction, arctic shelters, low-cost housing, and school construction. In addition to Pratt Institute he has taught at Columbia University and directed research work at Princeton University. His private practice has been mostly in the residential field.

Professor Callender is the co-editor (with Joseph DeChiara) of *Time-Saver Standards for Building Types*, now in its Second Edition, and the author of *Before You Buy a House*. He has also written extensively for professional journals and has lectured on the theory of architecture, both here and abroad.